*The*
# AMERICAN HERITAGE®
# CROSSWORD
# PUZZLE
# DICTIONARY

names of poets 602
" " song writers & lyrists = 743
" " Litery Characters
METALIC Symbols page 493
461 " "
Names of Capital Cities - page 119

# HOUGHTON MIFFLIN
BOSTON · NEW YORK

Based on the *Chambers Concise Crossword Dictionary*
© Chambers Harrap Publishers Ltd. 2002

Adapted and Published by arrangement with Chambers Harrap Publishers Ltd.

Visit our website: www.houghtonmifflinbooks.com

*Library of Congress Cataloging-in-Publication Data*

The American Heritage crossword puzzle dictionary.
   p. cm.
   ISBN 0-618-28053-7
   1. Crossword puzzles–Glossaries, vocabularies, etc. I. Houghton Mifflin Company.

GV1507.C7A49 2003
793.73'2–dc21

2003050849

Designed and typeset by Chambers Harrap Publishers Ltd.

Manufactured in the United States of America

QWM 10 9 8 7 6 5 4 3 2 1

# Staff

**Vice President, Publisher of Dictionaries**
Margery S. Berube

**Vice President, Executive Editor**
Joseph P. Pickett

**Vice President, Managing Editor**
Christopher Leonesio

**Editorial Project Director**
David R. Pritchard

**Consulting Editor**
John Wright

**Editor**
Vali Tamm

**Associate Editors**
Kirsten Patey
Matthew Heidenry

**Assistant Editor (project coordinator)**
Uchenna Ikonné

**Administrative Coordinator**
Kevin McCarthy

# Preface

*The American Heritage Crossword Puzzle Dictionary* is for lovers of crosswords of all kinds. It contains an enormous number of words and phrases that provide the user with over 230,000 possible solutions to crossword clues. As well as including synonyms for thousands of words, it includes wide-ranging reference lists that group together words usually found only in encyclopedias. The user will find, for example, lists of people (such as actors, US presidents, Nobel prize winners, and poets), geographical lists (such as rivers, cities, mountains, and lakes), lists of technical terms (such as printing terms, musical terms, and scientific terms), lists from natural history (such as flowers and trees), lists from art and culture (such as singers, novels, operas, paintings), lists from belief and religion (such as Biblical characters, gods and goddesses) and lists from sports (such as baseball players, boxers, and races). All of the words in this dictionary have been carefully categorized by topic or meaning to be presented in over 15,000 one-stop entries that combine both synonym lists and reference lists.

*The American Heritage Crossword Puzzle Dictionary* can be used on its own, or alongside a standard dictionary, and is an ideal companion to *The American Heritage Dictionary of the English Language*. We hope that it contributes to our users' enjoyment of crossword puzzles, that it helps them find solutions that are evading them, and that it helps them meet the intellectual challenges set by the cruciverbalists in our daily and Sunday newspapers.

# Introduction

## Word length

The words and phrases given in this dictionary contain 15 letters or fewer, reflecting the most commonly used crossword grids. However, the additional information given in many lists (see below) means that the dictionary will also be of use to people attempting crosswords that have longer answers. Also, where a list represents a closed set, that is, where a list is clearly defined and limited, then all relevant terms have been included regardless of length. For example, all of the Canadian provinces have been included even though some of these are longer than 15 letters in length:

> ▶ *Names of Canadian*
> *provinces and territories*:
> 05  Yukon
> 06  Quebec
> 07  Alberta, Nunavut, Ontario
> 08  Labrador, Manitoba
> 10  Nova Scotia
> 12  New Brunswick,
>       Newfoundland,
>       Saskatchewan
> 14  Yukon Territory
> 15  British Columbia
> 18  Prince Edward Island
> 20  Northwest Territories
> 23  Newfoundland and
>       Labrador

## Organization of entries

1. Within the dictionary, words have been sorted into over 15,000 one-stop alphabetical entries by meaning or subject category. Thus, entries present a range of words that are relevant to the headword; in many cases these words have been broadly grouped into two types of list:

- Synonym lists, which present words with similar meanings to the headword
- Reference lists, which present a diverse variety of words and names such as personal names and place names.

   Thus the entry for **fuel** presents both synonyms and a list of the different types of fuel:

   **fuel**
   03  fan
   04  feed, fire
   05  stoke
   07  inflame, nourish, stoke up

09 encourage, incentive
10 ammunition, propellant
11 combustible, provocation
13 encouragement

---

► *Types of fuel*:
03 gas, log, oil
04 coal, coke, peat, wood
06 butane, diesel, Sterno
07 briquet, methane, propane
08 charcoal, firewood, gasoline,
    kerosense, kindling, paraffin
09 briquette, petroleum
10 fossil fuel
11 electricity
12 nuclear power
14 liquid hydrogen

2. Within entries, words are grouped first by length, that is, by the total number of letters in each word or phrase, and then ordered alphabetically within these word-length groupings:

**abate**
04 ease, fade, sink, slow, wane
05 allay, let up, quell, remit
06 lessen, pacify, reduce,
    soothe, weaken
07 decline, dwindle, subside
08 decrease, diminish, mitigate,
    moderate, taper off
09 alleviate, attenuate

3. The synonym lists are not constrained by conventional dictionary or thesaurus rules. Thus no distinctions are made between parts of speech, or between homonyms (words spelled the same but with different meanings), as crossword editors often play on multiple meanings and possible ambiguity in their clues. For example, the entry for **frequent** lists synonyms for both the verb (meaning "visit") and the adjective (meaning "regular" or "recurring"):

**frequent**
05 haunt, usual, visit
06 attend, common, normal
08 everyday, familiar, habitual,
    numerous, repeated
09 countless, customary, hang
    out at, patronize, prevalent,
    recurring
11 commonplace
13 go to regularly
14 go to frequently, happening
    often

4. We have also included synonym lists for idioms and phrasal verbs derived from many of the headwords. Sections for idioms and phrasal verbs are marked by ❑ :

---

**behest**

❏ **at the behest of**

12  at the order of

13  on the wishes of

14  at the bidding of, at the command of, at the request of

# Reference lists

1.  Material in the reference lists is extremely wide-ranging, and includes, for example, the names of people from a variety of professions (including the arts, science, politics and history); literary, fictional, Biblical and mythological characters; place names; scientific terms; and works of art, music and literature. These reference lists are entered in the dictionary at the appropriate headword to make information easy to find. Thus users will find the names of actors and actresses at the entry for **actor, actress**; a list of parts of the brain at **brain**; lists of ancient cities, capital cities and other major towns and cities at **city**; a list of collective nouns at **collective**; names of novelists, and a list of novels and fictional works, at the entry for **novel**.

2.  The reference lists include both historical and current information. For example, in the list of novelists users will find not only Jane Austen and John Steinbeck, but also contemporary writers such as Elmore Leonard and Toni Morrison. And in the list of films, classics such as *Casablanca* can be found alongside modern blockbusters such as *Titanic*.

3.  The reference lists are not intended to be all-inclusive, but to focus on terms that are reasonably common and that are likely to occur in crossword solutions.

## Organization of reference material

Words and phrases have sometimes been categorized to make finding information easier. For example, there is not one list of scientists, but separate lists of, for example, *anthropologists*, *astronomers*, *physicists*, *chemists* and *computer scientists*.

## Additional information

Many of the reference lists contain additional information in parentheses following core information. For example, first names or nicknames are given in parentheses following a surname. In such lists, the core term (the term outside the parentheses) is presented in bold type to make these lists easier to browse through:

➤ *Names of astronauts*:

04  **Bean** (Alan), **Ride** (Sally)

05  **Foale** (Michael), **Glenn** (John), **Titov** (Gherman), **White** (Edward)

06  **Aldrin** (Edwin Eugene "Buzz"), **Borman** (Frank), **Conrad** (Charles "Pete"), **Cooper** (Gordon), **Lovell** (James "Jim")

07  **Chaffee** (Roger), **Collins**

(Michael), **Gagarin** (Yuri),
**Grissom** (Virgil "Gus"),
**Sharman**
(Helen), **Shepard** (Alan)
09 **Armstrong** (Neil),
**Carpenter** (Scott)
10 **Tereshkova** (Valentina)

Additional information may appear in parentheses but is not included in the word-length count, although it may form part of the solution to some crossword clues.

## Generic terms

Common generic terms have been omitted from many of the names and terms presented in some lists, to avoid unwieldy and unnecessary repetition. For example, the word *disease* has not been included in names in the list of diseases at **disease**, and the word *saint* has been omitted from the list of saints at **saint**. Users should be aware that terms such as these may form part of the solution to crossword clues, and key instances of this have been clearly marked. For example, at the entry for **mountain** the following note precedes the list of clues:

> ➤ *Names of mountains and mountain ranges. We have omitted the words* **mount**, **mountain** *and* **mountains** *from names given in the following list but you may need to include one of these words as part of the solution to some crossword clues.*

## Cross-references

A number of entries contain groups of cross-references listing all of the reference entries by subject or category. For example, at the entry for **music** there is a cross-reference listing all of the other entries in the dictionary which include reference lists that fall within the broad category of *music*:

> ➤ See also COMPOSER;
> CONDUCTOR; INSTRUMENT;
> JAZZ; LIBRETTO; MUSICAL;
> MUSICIAN; OPERA;
> ORATORIO; SINGER; SONG;
> SONGWRITER

At each of the headwords listed in the cross-reference at **music**, users will find a cross-reference back to the entry for **music**. Thus if a user does not find the solution needed at the entry for **singer**, he or she is directed back to **music** for alternative lists to search:

**singer**
> ➤ See also MUSIC

## abandon
04 drop, dump, jilt, junk, quit
05 abort, cease, chuck, ditch, leave, scrap, waive, yield
06 desert, escape, forego, get out, give up, maroon, resign, strand, vacate
07 bail out, forsake, yield to
08 abdicate, evacuate, forswear, leave off, renounce, run out on, wildness
09 walk out on
10 break loose, depart from, relinquish
11 discontinue, impetuosity, leave behind, unrestraint
12 carelessness, recklessness
15 leave high and dry, leave in the lurch, thoughtlessness

## abandoned
03 mad
04 axed, wild
05 crazy, empty
06 unused, vacant, wanton, wicked
07 corrupt, forlorn, immoral
08 derelict, deserted, forsaken
09 debauched, dissolute, neglected, reprobate
10 profligate, unoccupied
11 uninhibited

## abandonment
07 cession, jilting, leaving, neglect, waiving
08 ditching, dropping, giving-up, stopping
09 cessation, desertion, forsaking, marooning, scrapping, stranding
10 abdication, decampment
11 dereliction, resignation
12 renunciation, running out on

## abase
06 debase, demean, humble, malign
07 mortify
08 belittle
09 disparage, humiliate

## abashed
07 ashamed, floored, humbled
08 confused
09 affronted, mortified

10 bewildered, confounded, humiliated, shamefaced
11 discomfited, discomposed, embarrassed
12 disconcerted
15 discountenanced

## abate
04 ease, fade, sink, slow, wane
05 allay, let up, quell, remit
06 lessen, pacify, reduce, soothe, weaken
07 decline, dwindle, subside
08 decrease, diminish, mitigate, moderate, taper off
09 alleviate, attenuate

## abatement
04 wane
06 easing, relief
07 decline
08 decrease, lowering
09 dwindling, lessening, reduction, remission
10 diminution, mitigation, moderation, palliation, slackening, subsidence
11 alleviation, assuagement, attenuation

## abbey
06 friary, priory
07 convent, minster, nunnery
08 cloister, seminary
09 cathedral, monastery

## abbreviate
03 cut
04 clip, trim
06 digest, précis
07 abridge, curtail, shorten
08 condense, contract, truncate
09 constrict, summarize

## abbreviation
06 digest, précis, résumé
07 acronym, summary
08 abstract, clipping, synopsis
09 reduction, short form
10 abridgment, shortening, truncation
11 compression, contraction, curtailment
13 summarization

## abdicate
04 cede, quit

06 abjure, forego, give up, resign, retire
07 abandon
08 abnegate, renounce
09 repudiate, stand down

## abdication
07 refusal
08 giving-up
10 abjuration, abnegation, retirement
11 abandonment, repudiation, resignation
12 renunciation
14 relinquishment

## abdomen
03 gut, tum
04 guts
05 belly, tummy
06 paunch, venter
07 midriff, stomach
08 pot belly
11 breadbasket, corporation

## abdominal
05 colic
06 celiac
07 gastric, ventral
08 visceral
10 intestinal
11 ventricular

## abduct
05 seize
06 kidnap, seduce, snatch
08 carry off, shanghai
11 appropriate, make off with
12 hold to ransom

## aberrant
03 odd
05 rogue
06 quirky
07 corrupt, deviant
08 abnormal, atypical
09 anomalous, different, divergent, irregular
11 incongruous

## aberration
05 lapse
06 oddity
07 anomaly, mistake
08 delusion, straying
09 deviation, oversight, variation, wandering
10 divergence

11 abnormality, peculiarity
12 eccentricity, irregularity

**abet**
03 aid
04 back, help, spur
05 egg on
06 assist, succor
07 condone, endorse, promote, support
09 encourage

**abeyance**
❑**in abeyance**
05 on ice
06 tabled
07 dormant, pending, shelved
09 suspended

**abhor**
04 hate, shun
05 spurn
06 detest, loathe
07 despise
08 execrate
09 abominate

**abhorrence**
04 hate
05 odium
06 enmity, hatred, malice
07 disgust
08 aversion, contempt, distaste, loathing
09 animosity, revulsion
10 execration, repugnance
11 abomination, detestation

**abhorrent**
05 hated
06 horrid, odious
07 hateful, heinous
08 horrible
09 execrable, loathsome, obnoxious, offensive, repellent, repugnant, repulsive, revolting
10 abominable, detestable, disgusting, nauseating

**abide**
04 bear, last, take
05 brook, stand
06 accept, endure, remain
07 persist, stomach
08 continue, tolerate

❑**abide by**
04 obey
06 accept, follow, hold to, keep to, uphold
07 agree to, fulfill, observe, respect
08 adhere to
09 conform to, discharge
10 comply with, toe the line

**abiding**
04 firm
07 eternal, lasting
08 constant, enduring, immortal, lifelong, long-term, unending
09 continual, immutable, permanent
10 continuous, persistent, unchanging
11 everlasting, long-lasting, long-running

**ability**
04 gift
05 flair, forte, knack, power, savvy, skill, touch
06 genius, powers, talent
07 caliber, faculty, know-how, prowess, the hang
08 aptitude, capacity, deftness, facility, strength, the knack
09 adeptness, expertise
10 adroitness, capability
11 proficiency, savoir-faire
13 qualification

**abject**
03 low
04 base, mean, vile
06 sordid
07 debased, forlorn, ignoble, outcast, servile
08 degraded, hopeless, pathetic, wretched
09 groveling, miserable, worthless
10 degenerate, submissive
11 humiliating, ignominious
12 contemptible

**abjure**
04 deny
06 disown, eschew, reject
07 abandon, disavow, retract
08 abnegate, forswear, renege on, renounce

**ablaze**
05 afire, aglow, angry
06 aflame, alight, ardent, fuming, on fire, raging
07 aroused, burning, excited, fervent, flaming, furious, glowing, lighted, radiant
08 flashing, frenzied, gleaming
10 passionate, stimulated

**able**
03 fit
05 adept
06 adroit, clever, expert, fitted, gifted, strong, up to it
07 capable, skilled
08 skillful

09 competent, dexterous, effective, efficient, practiced, qualified
10 proficient
11 experienced, intelligent
12 accomplished

**able-bodied**
03 fit
04 fine, hale
05 hardy, lusty, sound
06 hearty, robust, rugged, strong, sturdy
07 healthy, staunch
08 powerful, stalwart, vigorous
09 strapping
12 in good health
13 hale and hearty

**abnegation**
08 eschewal, giving-up
09 surrender
10 abjuration, abstinence, self-denial, temperance
12 renunciation
13 self-sacrifice
14 relinquishment

**abnormal**
03 odd
05 outré, queer, weird
07 deviant, erratic, oddball, strange, uncanny, unusual
08 aberrant, atypical, peculiar, singular, uncommon
09 anomalous, different, divergent, eccentric, irregular, unnatural
10 paranormal, unexpected
11 exceptional
13 extraordinary, preternatural

**abnormality**
04 flaw
06 oddity
07 anomaly
09 deformity, deviation
10 aberration, difference, divergence
11 peculiarity, singularity, strangeness, unusualness
12 eccentricity, irregularity, malformation
13 unnaturalness

**abode**
03 pad
04 home
07 habitat
08 domicile, dwelling, lodgings
09 residence
10 habitation
13 dwelling-place

**abolish**
02 ax
03 ban, end

**abolition**
04 stop
05 annul, erase, quash
06 cancel, repeal, revoke
07 blot out, destroy, expunge, nullify, rescind, subvert, vitiate, wipe out
08 abrogate, overturn, stamp out, suppress
09 eliminate, eradicate, overthrow, terminate
10 annihilate, do away with, obliterate, put an end to

**abolition**
06 ending, repeal
09 annulment, overthrow
10 abrogation, extinction, rescission, revocation
11 destruction, dissolution, elimination, eradication, extirpation, rescindment
12 annihilation, obliteration
13 nullification

**abominable**
04 base, foul, vile
06 cursed, horrid, odious
07 hateful, heinous
08 damnable, horrible, wretched
09 abhorrent, appalling, atrocious, execrable, loathsome, obnoxious, offensive, repellent, repugnant, repulsive, revolting
10 despicable, detestable, disgusting, nauseating
12 contemptible

**abominate**
04 hate
05 abhor
06 detest, loathe
07 condemn, despise
08 execrate

**abomination**
04 evil, hate
05 curse, odium
06 hatred, horror, plague
07 offense, outrage, torment
08 anathema, atrocity, aversion, disgrace, distaste, loathing
09 hostility, revulsion
10 abhorrence, execration, repugnance
11 detestation

**aboriginal**
05 first, local
06 native, primal
07 ancient
08 earliest, original, primeval
09 primitive
10 indigenous
13 autochthonous

**abort**
02 ax
03 end
04 fail, halt, stop
05 check
06 thwart
07 call off, nullify, suspend
08 cut short, miscarry
09 frustrate, terminate
13 pull the plug on

**abortion**
04 idle, vain
06 barren, failed, futile
07 sterile, useless
08 abortive
10 unavailing
11 ineffective, ineffectual
12 unproductive, unsuccessful

**abound**
04 teem
05 crowd, swarm, swell
06 be full, thrive
08 brim over, flourish, overflow
09 exuberate, luxuriate
11 be plentiful, proliferate

**about**
02 on, re
04 near
05 circa, round
06 almost, around, beside, nearby, nearly
07 roughly
09 apropos of, regarding
10 adjacent to, concerning, encircling, more or less, relating to, throughout
11 referring to, surrounding
12 encompassing, here and there, with regard to
13 approximately, in the region of, with respect to

❑**about to**
06 all but, soon to
07 going to, ready to
12 on the point of, on the verge of

**about-face**
05 U-turn
08 reversal
09 turnabout, volte-face

**above**
04 atop, over
05 aloft, prior
06 before, beyond, high up, higher, on high
07 earlier, on top of
08 overhead, senior to
09 aforesaid, exceeding, foregoing, preceding
10 superior to, surpassing
14 aforementioned

**aboveboard**
04 open, true
05 frank
06 candid, honest, square
07 upright
08 straight, truthful
09 reputable, veracious
10 legitimate, on the level
11 trustworthy
13 fair and square

**abrade**
03 rub
05 chafe, erode, grate, graze, grind, scour
06 scrape
07 scratch
08 wear away, wear down

**abrasion**
03 cut
05 chafe, graze
06 scrape
07 chafing, erosion, grating, rubbing, scratch
08 abrading, friction, grinding, scouring, scraping
10 scratching

**abrasive**
05 harsh, nasty, rough, sharp
06 biting
07 brusque, caustic, chafing, erodent, erosive, grating, hurtful
08 annoying, scraping
09 corrosive
10 frictional, irritating, scratching, unpleasant

**abreast**
04 up on
05 level
06 au fait
07 in touch
08 familiar, informed, up to date
09 au courant, on the ball
10 acquainted, side by side
12 in the picture

**abridge**
03 cut, lop
04 clip
05 prune
06 digest, lessen, précis, reduce
07 curtail, cut down, shorten
08 abstract, compress, condense, contract
09 summarize, synopsize
10 abbreviate

**abridgment**
06 abrégé, digest, précis, résumé
07 cutting, epitome, outline, summary
08 abstract, synopsis

**abroad**
09 reduction
10 conspectus, diminution, shortening, truncation
11 contraction

**abroad**
05 about
06 around, widely
07 at large, current
08 overseas, publicly
10 far and wide
14 in foreign parts, to foreign parts

**abrogate**
02 ax
03 end
05 annul, scrap
06 cancel, repeal, revoke
07 abolish, rescind, retract
08 disenact, dissolve
09 repudiate
10 do away with, invalidate
11 countermand

**abrupt**
04 curt, rude
05 blunt, brisk, gruff, hasty, quick, rapid, sharp, sheer, short, steep, swift, terse
06 direct, snappy, sudden
07 brusque, hurried, instant, offhand, uncivil
08 dramatic, impolite, snappish
10 surprising, unexpected

**abscond**
03 fly
04 bolt, flee, quit
05 scram, split
06 beat it, decamp, escape, run off, vanish
07 make off, run away, vamoose
09 disappear, skedaddle
12 absquatulate
15 take French leave

**absence**
04 lack, need, want
06 dearth
07 default, paucity, truancy, vacancy, vacuity
08 omission, scarcity
09 privation
10 deficiency

**absent**
03 off, out
04 away, gone
05 blank
06 dreamy, truant, vacant
07 faraway, lacking, missing
09 elsewhere, oblivious
10 distracted, in absentia
11 daydreaming, inattentive, preoccupied

**absent-minded**
06 dreamy, musing
07 faraway, pensive, unaware
08 absorbed, distrait, dreaming, heedless
09 distraite, engrossed, forgetful, miles away, oblivious, unheeding
10 abstracted, distracted, unthinking
11 inattentive, not all there, preoccupied
13 wool-gathering
14 scatterbrained

**absolute**
04 full, pure, rank, sure
05 final, sheer, total, utter
06 entire
07 certain, decided, genuine, plenary, supreme
08 almighty, complete, decisive, definite, despotic, outright, positive, thorough
09 downright, out-and-out
10 autocratic, conclusive, consummate, definitive, exhaustive, omnipotent
11 autarchical, dictatorial, indubitable, unequivocal, unmitigated, unqualified
12 totalitarian, unrestrained, unrestricted
13 authoritarian, unadulterated, unconditional
14 unquestionable

**absolutely**
04 dead
05 fully, truly
06 purely, surely, wholly
07 exactly, finally, totally, utterly
08 entirely
09 certainly, decidedly, genuinely, perfectly, precisely, supremely
10 completely, decisively, definitely, infallibly, positively, thoroughly
12 conclusively, exhaustively
13 categorically, unequivocally
14 unquestionably, wholeheartedly
15 unconditionally

**absolution**
05 mercy
06 pardon, shrift
07 amnesty, freedom, release
09 acquittal, discharge, purgation, remission
10 liberation, redemption
11 deliverance, exculpation, exoneration, forgiveness, vindication

12 emancipation

**absolve**
04 free
05 clear, loose, remit
06 acquit, excuse, let off, pardon
07 deliver, forgive, justify, release, set free
08 liberate
09 discharge, exculpate, exonerate, vindicate
10 emancipate

**absorb**
04 fill, hold
06 devour, digest, draw in, engage, engulf, fill up, imbibe, ingest, occupy, retain, soak up, take in
07 consume, drink in, engross, involve, receive
08 enthrall
09 captivate, fascinate, integrate, preoccupy, swallow up
10 assimilate, understand
11 incorporate

**absorbed**
07 riveted
08 involved, occupied
09 engrossed
10 captivated, enthralled, fascinated, interested
11 preoccupied, taken up with

**absorbent**
06 porous
07 soaking
08 blotting, pervious
09 permeable, receptive, resorbent, retentive
10 absorptive
12 assimilative

**absorbing**
07 amusing
08 gripping, riveting
09 diverting, enjoyable
10 compelling, compulsive, engrossing, intriguing
11 captivating, enthralling, fascinating, interesting
12 entertaining, spellbinding
13 unputdownable

**absorption**
07 holding, osmosis
08 monopoly, riveting
09 devouring, drawing-in, ingestion, soaking-up
10 engagement, engrossing, intentness, occupation
11 captivating, consumption, involvement
13 concentration, preoccupation

## abstain
04 shun, stop
05 avoid
06 desist, eschew, forego, give up, refuse, reject, resist
07 decline, forbear, refrain
08 keep from, renounce, teetotal
09 do without, go without

## abstemious
05 sober
06 frugal
07 ascetic, austere, sparing
08 moderate, teetotal
09 abstinent, temperate
11 disciplined, self-denying

## abstention
09 not voting
13 refusal to vote

## abstinence
07 refusal
08 eschewal, sobriety
09 avoidance, frugality, restraint
10 asceticism, continence, declension, desistance, moderation, temperance
11 forbearance, self-control, teetotalism
12 going-without, renunciation
14 abstemiousness

## abstract
03 cut
04 deep
06 arcane, detach, digest, précis, remove, résumé
07 abridge, complex, cut down, epitome, extract, general, isolate, outline, shorten, summary, take out
08 abstruse, compress, condense, notional, separate, synopsis, take away, withdraw
09 contrived, recondite, summarize
10 abbreviate, abridgment, conceptual, conspectus, indefinite
11 compression, theoretical
12 hypothetical, intellectual, metaphysical
14 recapitulation

## abstracted
06 absent, dreamy, musing
07 bemused, pensive, unaware
08 absorbed, dreaming
09 engrossed, forgetful, oblivious, unheeding
10 distracted, unthinking
11 inattentive, preoccupied
12 absent-minded

13 wool-gathering
14 scatterbrained

## abstraction
04 idea
05 dream
06 notion, theory
07 concept, theorem, thought
10 absorption, conception, dreaminess, extraction, hypothesis, separation
11 inattention, pensiveness
13 preoccupation
14 generalization

## abstruse
04 deep
06 arcane
07 complex, cryptic, obscure
08 esoteric, profound, puzzling
09 enigmatic, recondite
10 mysterious, perplexing
11 inscrutable
12 unfathomable

## absurd
04 daft
05 crazy, funny, inane, silly
06 stupid
07 asinine, comical, foolish, idiotic, risible
08 derisory, farcical, humorous
09 fantastic, illogical, laughable, ludicrous, senseless, untenable
10 irrational, ridiculous
11 harebrained, implausible, nonsensical, paradoxical
12 preposterous, unreasonable

## absurdity
04 joke
05 farce, folly, humor
06 drivel, idiocy
07 charade, inanity, paradox, rubbish, twaddle
08 claptrap, daftness, nonsense, travesty
09 craziness, gibberish, silliness, stupidity
10 balderdash
11 incongruity

## abundance
04 bags, glut, lots
05 heaps, loads, piles, scads
06 bounty, excess, masses, oodles, plenty, riches, stacks, wealth
07 bonanza, fortune
08 fullness, opulence, overflow, plethora, richness
09 affluence, amplitude, plenitude, profusion
10 exuberance, generosity

11 copiousness, great supply, munificence, prodigality

## abundant
04 full, rich
05 ample
06 filled, galore, lavish
07 copious, opulent, profuse
08 affluent, generous, in plenty
09 bounteous, bountiful, exuberant, plentiful
11 overflowing
14 more than enough

## abuse
03 hit
04 beat, harm, hurt, rail
05 bully, curse, libel, scold, slate, smear, wrong
06 batter, damage, defame, injure, injury, insult, malign, misuse, molest, oppugn, pick on, revile, tirade
07 affront, beating, calumny, censure, cruelty, cursing, exploit, insults, offense, oppress, slander, swear at, torture, upbraid, vitriol
08 derision, diatribe, ill-treat, maltreat, reproach, scolding, swearing
09 castigate, contumely, denigrate, disparage, invective, victimize
10 calumniate, defamation, oppression, upbraiding
11 castigation, denigration, malediction, molestation
12 calumniation, exploitation, ill-treatment, maltreatment, mistreatment, vilification, vituperation

## abusive
04 rude
05 cruel
06 brutal
07 harmful, hurtful, railing
08 libelous, reviling, scathing, scolding
09 injurious, insulting, maligning, vilifying
10 censorious, defamatory, derogatory, pejorative, slanderous, upbraiding
11 castigating, denigrating, destructive, disparaging, opprobrious, reproachful
12 calumniating, contumelious, vituperative

## abut
04 join
05 touch
06 adjoin, border

## abysmal
05 awful, utter
06 dismal
08 complete, dreadful, shocking
09 appalling
11 disgraceful

## abyss
03 pit
04 gulf, void
05 chasm, depth, gorge
06 canyon, crater, depths
07 fissure
08 crevasse
09 barathrum

## academic
05 smart, tutor
06 brainy, fellow, pedant
07 bookish, erudite, learned, scholar
08 educated, highbrow, lecturer, literary, notional, pedantic, well-read
09 professor, scholarly
10 irrelevant, ivory-tower, scholastic
11 conjectural, educational, impractical, pedagogical, speculative, theoretical
12 hypothetical, intellectual

## accede
05 admit, bow to
06 accept, assume, attain, come to, concur, give in
07 agree to, inherit, succeed
08 assent to, back down
09 acquiesce, consent to, succeed to

## accelerate
05 hurry, speed
06 hasten, step up
07 advance, forward, further, promote, quicken, speed up
08 expedite, go faster, step on it
09 stimulate
10 facilitate
11 gather speed, pick up speed, precipitate
15 put your foot down

## acceleration
08 momentum
09 hastening, promotion
10 expedition, forwarding, speeding-up, stepping-up
11 advancement, furtherance

## accent
04 beat, tone
05 drawl, force, pitch, pulse, twang
06 brogue, rhythm, stress
07 cadence, diction
08 emphasis, priority

09 intensity, pulsation
10 inflection, intonation, modulation, prominence
11 enunciation, underlining
12 accentuation, articulation, highlighting
13 pronunciation

## accentuate
06 accent, show up, stress
08 heighten
09 emphasize, highlight, intensify, underline
10 strengthen, underscore

## accept
03 buy, get
04 bear, gain, take
05 abide, admit, adopt, allow, bow to, stand, trust
06 endure, give in, obtain, secure, take on, take up
07 abide by, agree to, believe, embrace, receive, stomach, swallow
08 accede to, tolerate
09 believe in, consent to, put up with, undertake
10 comply with, concur with
11 acknowledge, go along with, take on board
12 be resigned to
13 make the best of
15 come to terms with

## acceptable
02 OK
04 okay, so-so
08 adequate, moderate, passable
09 agreeable, allowable, desirable, tolerable
10 admissible, delightful, gratifying, reasonable
11 appropriate, permissible
12 satisfactory, the done thing

## acceptance
02 OK
04 okay
05 faith, trust
06 assent, belief, taking
07 bearing, consent, gaining, getting, receipt
08 adoption, approval
09 accepting, accession, acquiring, admission, agreement, embracing, endurance, obtaining, receiving, tolerance
10 assumption, facing up to
11 affirmation, concurrence, endorsement, undertaking
12 acquiescence, ratification
14 acknowledgment

## accepted
05 usual
06 agreed, common, normal
07 correct, regular
08 admitted, approved, orthodox, ratified, received, standard
09 customary, universal
10 authorized, recognized, sanctioned
11 appropriate, established, time-honored, traditional
12 acknowledged, conventional

## access
03 key
04 door, path, road
05 drive, entry, way in
06 course, entrée
07 gateway, ingress, passage
08 approach, driveway, entering, entrance
09 admission
10 admittance

## accessible
04 near
05 handy, ready
06 nearby, on hand
09 available, reachable
10 attainable, convenient, obtainable, procurable
12 intelligible, user-friendly
14 understandable

## accession
04 gift
08 addition, increase, purchase
10 assumption, possession, succession
11 acquisition, inheritance

## accessory
03 aid, hat
04 belt, help
05 extra, frill, shoes
06 gloves, helper
07 abettor, adjunct, fitting, handbag, jewelry, partner
08 addition, conniver, ornament, trimming
09 ancillary, appendage, assistant, associate, auxiliary, colleague, component, secondary
10 accomplice, additional, attachment, complement, decoration, incidental, subsidiary, supplement
11 confederate, subordinate
12 contributory, supplemental
13 embellishment

## accident
04 blow, fate, luck
05 crash, fluke, shunt, wreck

**accidental**

06 chance, hazard, mishap, pileup
07 fortune, smashup, tragedy
08 calamity, casualty, disaster, fatality, fortuity, good luck
09 collision, mischance
10 misfortune
11 coincidence, contretemps, good fortune, serendipity
12 fender bender, happenstance, misadventure

**accidental**

05 fluky
06 casual, chance, random
08 aleatory
09 haphazard, uncertain, unplanned, unwitting
10 fortuitous, incidental, unexpected
11 inadvertent, unlooked-for
12 adventitious, uncalculated
13 serendipitous, unintentional

**accidentally**

08 bechance, by chance, randomly
09 by mistake
11 haphazardly, unwittingly
12 fortuitously, incidentally, unexpectedly
13 inadvertently
14 adventitiously
15 serendipitously, unintentionally

**acclaim**

04 clap, hail, laud
05 cheer, exalt, extol, honor, toast
06 cheers, eulogy, homage, praise, salute
07 applaud, commend, fanfare, ovation, tribute, welcome
08 applause, approval, eulogize, plaudits
09 extolment, laudation
10 exaltation
11 acclamation, approbation, celebration
12 commendation

**acclamation**

05 honor, paean
06 bravos, eulogy, homage, praise
07 ovation, tribute, welcome
08 applause, approval, cheering, clapping, shouting
09 panegyric
10 enthusiasm, exaltation
11 approbation, celebration
12 commendation
13 felicitations
15 congratulations

**acclimate**

05 adapt, inure
06 adjust, attune
08 accustom
09 get used to, habituate
10 naturalize
11 acclimatize, accommodate, acculturate, familiarize
12 find your feet
15 get your bearings

**accolade**

05 award, honor, kudos
06 praise
07 tribute

**accommodate**

03 aid, fit
04 help, hold, take
05 adapt, board, house, lodge, put up, serve
06 adjust, assist, billet, modify, oblige, settle, supply, take in
07 cater to, provide, shelter
08 accustom, domicile
09 acclimate, harmonize, reconcile
11 acclimatize, be helpful to, give a hand to, have room for, lend a hand to
12 have space for

**accommodating**

04 kind
07 helpful, pliable, willing
08 friendly, obliging
09 agreeable, unselfish
10 hospitable
11 complaisant, considerate, cooperative, sympathetic

**accommodation**

05 board
07 harmony, housing, lodging, quarter, shelter
08 quarters
09 agreement
10 compromise, settlement
11 negotiation
12 negotiations
14 reconciliation

► *Types of accommodation:*
03 inn, pad
04 digs
05 B and B, hotel, motel, rooms, squat, villa
06 billet, hostel
07 lodging, shelter
08 dwelling, quarters, lodgings
09 apartment, flophouse, residence, timeshare
10 guesthouse
11 youth hostel
12 room and board, lodging house, rooming house

13 boardinghouse
15 bed and breakfast
➢ See also HOUSE

**accompaniment**

04 vamp
06 backup
07 adjunct, backing, support
08 addition
09 accessory, obbligato
10 background, complement, supplement
11 coexistence, concomitant

**accompany**

05 usher
06 attend, convoy, escort, follow, go with, squire
07 coexist, consort, partner
08 chaperon, come with, play with
09 chaperone
10 complement, supplement
13 associate with
14 hang around with

**accomplice**

04 aide, ally, mate
06 flunky, helper, stooge
07 abettor, partner
08 henchman, sidekick
09 accessory, assistant, associate, colleague
11 confederate, conspirator
12 collaborator

**accomplish**

02 do
06 attain, effect, finish
07 achieve, execute, fulfill, perform, produce, realize
08 bring off, carry out, complete
09 discharge, pull it off
10 bring about, effectuate
15 deliver the goods

**accomplished**

05 adept
06 adroit, expert, gifted
07 skilled
08 masterly, polished, skillful, talented
09 practiced
10 consummate, proficient
11 experienced
12 professional

**accomplishment**

03 art
04 deed, feat, gift
05 forte, skill
06 stroke, talent
07 ability, faculty, triumph
08 aptitude, fruition
09 execution, finishing
10 attainment, completion, conclusion, production

**accord**
11 achievement, fulfillment, performance, proficiency, realization
12 consummation

**accord**
04 give, suit
05 agree, allow, endow, grant, match, unity
06 assent, bestow, concur, confer, tender
07 concert, conform
08 sympathy
09 agreement, congruity, harmonize, unanimity, vouchsafe
10 accordance, conformity, congruence, correspond
11 concurrence
14 correspondence

❑ **of your own accord**
06 freely
09 willingly
11 voluntarily

❑ **with one accord**
09 of one mind
11 unanimously

**accordance**

❑ **in accordance with**
05 after
10 in line with, obedient to
12 in relation to, in the light of
13 in concert with

**according**

❑ **according to**
05 after, as per
10 in line with, obedient to
11 as claimed by, depending on
12 in relation to, in the light of
13 in keeping with
14 in proportion to

**accordingly**
02 so
04 ergo, thus
05 hence
08 properly, suitably
09 as a result, therefore
12 consequently, consistently

**accost**
04 halt, stop
06 attack, detain, molest, waylay
07 solicit
08 approach, confront
09 importune
10 buttonhole

**account**
03 tab
04 bill, deem, hold, tale
05 story

06 detail, esteem, import, ledger, memoir, record, regard, report, sketch
07 adjudge, details, history, invoice, version, write-up
08 appraise, consider
09 chronicle, inventory, narration, narrative, portrayal, statement
10 commentary, communiqué, importance
11 consequence, description, distinction, explanation

❑ **account for**
06 make up, supply
07 clear up, explain, justify, provide
09 answer for, elucidate, represent, vindicate
10 constitute, illuminate
11 rationalize

**accountability**
09 liability
10 obligation
13 answerability
14 responsibility

**accountable**
05 bound
06 liable
07 obliged
09 obligated
10 answerable, chargeable
11 responsible

**accouterments**
03 kit
04 gear
06 outfit
08 fittings, fixtures
09 caparison, equipment, trappings, trimmings
10 adornments
11 decorations, furnishings, odds and ends
13 appurtenances, bits and pieces, paraphernalia

**accredited**
08 approved, endorsed, licensed, official
09 appointed, certified, qualified
10 authorized, recognized
12 certificated, commissioned

**accrue**
05 amass, mount
07 augment, build up, collect
08 increase
10 accumulate

**accumulate**
04 gain, grow
05 amass, hoard, stash, store

06 accrue, gather, pile up
07 acquire, augment, collect
08 assemble, increase, multiply, snowball
09 aggregate, stockpile

**accumulation**
04 gain, mass, pile
05 hoard, stack, stock, store
06 growth
07 accrual, build-up, reserve
08 assembly, increase
09 aggregate, gathering, stockpile
10 collection, cumulation
11 acquisition
12 augmentation
14 conglomeration

**accuracy**
05 truth
06 verity
08 fidelity, veracity
09 closeness, exactness, precision
10 exactitude
11 carefulness, correctness
12 authenticity, faithfulness, scrupulosity, truthfulness, veridicality

**accurate**
04 fair, true
05 exact, right, sound, valid
06 strict
07 correct, perfect, precise
08 faithful, rigorous, truthful, unerring
09 authentic, veracious, veridical, well-aimed
10 meticulous
11 on the button, word-for-word, word-perfect

**accursed**
06 damned, doomed
07 hateful
08 wretched
09 bedeviled, bewitched, execrable
10 abominable, despicable

**accusation**
05 blame
06 charge
08 citation, delation, gravamen
09 complaint
10 allegation, imputation, indictment
11 arraignment, crimination, impeachment, inculpation
12 denunciation
13 incrimination, recrimination

**accuse**
04 book, cite
05 blame, frame

**accustom** *(continued)*
06 allege, impugn, impute, indict
07 arraign, censure, impeach
08 confront, denounce
09 attribute, criminate, implicate, prosecute
11 incriminate, recriminate
12 bring charges, press charges

**accustom**
05 adapt, inure
06 adjust, attune
07 conform
09 get used to, habituate
11 accommodate, familiarize

**accustomed**
04 used, wont
05 fixed, given, usual
06 at home, inured, normal, wonted
07 general, regular, routine
08 everyday, familiar, habitual, ordinary
09 customary
10 acquainted, habituated, prevailing
11 established, traditional
12 acclimatized, conventional
14 consuetudinary

**ace**
03 one
04 whiz
05 great
06 expert, genius, master, superb, winner
07 hotshot, maestro, perfect
08 champion, virtuoso
09 brilliant, excellent
10 first-class
11 outstanding

**acerbic**
05 harsh, sharp
06 biting
07 caustic, mordant
08 abrasive, stinging
09 rancorous, trenchant, vitriolic
10 astringent
11 acrimonious

**ache**
04 hurt, itch, kill, long, pain, pang, pine
05 agony, crave, pound, smart, sting, throb, yearn
06 desire, hanker, hunger, suffer, thirst, twinge
07 craving, longing
08 pounding, smarting, soreness, stinging, yearning
09 hankering, suffering, throbbing

**achieve**
02 do
03 get, win

04 earn, gain
05 reach
06 attain, effect, finish, manage, obtain
07 acquire, execute, fulfill, perform, realize, succeed
08 carry out, complete
10 accomplish, bring about, consummate, effectuate

**achievement**
03 act
04 deed, feat
06 action, effort
07 exploit, success
08 activity, fruition
09 execution
10 attainment, completion
11 acquirement, fulfillment, performance, procurement, realization
12 consummation
14 accomplishment

**achiever**
04 doer
08 go-getter
09 highflier, performer
12 success story
14 mover and shaker

**acid**
04 sour, tart
05 harsh, sharp
06 acetic, acidic, biting, bitter, morose, unkind
07 acerbic, acetous, caustic, cutting, hurtful, mordant
08 critical, incisive, stinging, vinegary
09 acidulous, corrosive, sarcastic, trenchant, vitriolic
10 astringent

► *Types of acid. We have omitted the word* **acid** *from names given in the following list but you may need to include this word as part of the solution to some crossword clues.*
03 DNA, RNA
04 uric
05 amino, boric, folic
06 acetic, citric, formic, lactic, nitric, oxalic, phenol, tannic
07 benzoic, boracic, chloric, nitrous, nucleic, prussic, pyruvic, silicic
08 ascorbic, carbolic, carbonic, lysergic, sulfonic, sulfuric, tartaric
09 salicylic, sulfurous
10 aqua fortis, barbituric, carboxylic, phosphoric
11 hydrocyanic, ribonucleic

12 hydrochloric, hydrofluoric
➤ See also AMINO ACID

**acknowledge**
04 avow, hail
05 admit, allow, grant, greet, thank
06 accede, accept, answer, avouch, notice, salute
07 address, agree to, concede, confess, confirm, declare, own up to, react to, reply to
09 acquiesce, recognize, respond to, write back

**acknowledged**
06 avowed
08 accepted, approved, attested, declared
09 confirmed, professed
10 accredited, recognized

**acknowledgment**
03 nod
04 wave
05 reply, smile
06 answer, credit, notice
07 tribute
08 greeting, reaction, response
09 admission
10 acceptance, confession, profession, salutation
11 affirmation, recognition

**acme**
04 apex, peak
05 crown
06 apogee, climax, height, summit, zenith
08 pinnacle
09 high point
11 culmination

**acolyte**
06 helper
08 adherent, follower
09 assistant, attendant

**acoustic**
05 aural, sound
06 audile
07 hearing
08 auditory

**acquaint**
04 tell
05 brief
06 advise, inform, notify, reveal
07 apprise, divulge, let know
08 accustom, announce, disclose
09 enlighten, introduce
11 familiarize

**acquaintance**
06 friend
07 contact

08 confrère, intimacy
09 associate, colleague,
    companion, knowledge
10 cognizance, fellowship
11 association, familiarity
12 relationship
13 companionship

**acquainted**
05 aware
06 au fait
07 abreast
08 apprised, familiar, friendly
09 cognizant, in the know
10 conversant, well-versed
12 well-informed
13 knowledgeable

**acquiesce**
05 agree, allow, defer
06 accede, accept, concur, give
    in, submit
07 approve, consent

**acquiescence**
06 assent
07 consent
08 approval, yielding
09 agreement, deference
10 acceptance, compliance
11 concurrence

**acquiescent**
07 servile
08 acceding, agreeing,
    amenable, obedient,
    yielding
09 accepting, agreeable,
    approving, compliant
10 concurrent, consenting
11 complaisant, deferential

**acquire**
03 bag, buy, cop, get, net, win
04 earn, gain
05 amass
06 attain, come by, gather,
    obtain, secure
07 achieve, collect, procure,
    realize, receive
08 purchase
10 accumulate

**acquisition**
04 gain
08 property, purchase,
    securing, takeover
09 accession, obtaining
10 attainment, possession
11 achievement, procurement

**acquisitive**
04 avid
06 greedy
08 covetous, grasping
09 predatory, rapacious,
    voracious

10 avaricious

**acquisitiveness**
05 greed
07 avarice, avidity
08 rapacity, voracity
12 covetousness, graspingness

**acquit**
03 act
04 bear, free
05 clear, repay
06 behave, excuse, let off, settle
07 absolve, comport, conduct,
    deliver, dismiss, perform,
    release, relieve, satisfy
08 liberate, reprieve
09 discharge, exculpate,
    exonerate, vindicate
13 let off the hook

**acquittal**
06 relief
07 freeing, release
08 excusing, reprieve
09 discharge, dismissal
10 absolution, liberation
11 deliverance, exculpation,
    exoneration, vindication
12 compurgation

**acrid**
04 acid, sour, tart
05 harsh, nasty, sharp
06 biting, bitter
07 acerbic, burning, caustic,
    cutting, mordant, pungent
08 incisive, sardonic, stinging,
    venomous, virulent
09 malicious, sarcastic,
    trenchant, vitriolic
10 astringent
11 acrimonious

**acrimonious**
05 sharp
06 biting, bitter, severe
07 abusive, acerbic, caustic,
    crabbed, cutting, waspish
08 petulant, spiteful, venomous,
    virulent
09 irascible, rancorous,
    splenetic, trenchant, vitriolic
10 astringent, censorious
11 ill-tempered

**acrimony**
04 gall
05 spite, venom
06 rancor, spleen
07 sarcasm, vitriol
08 acerbity, acridity, asperity,
    mordancy
09 harshness, ill temper,
    petulance, virulence
10 bitterness, causticity,
    resentment, trenchancy

11 astringency
12 irascibility

**acrobat**
07 gymnast, tumbler
09 aerialist
11 equilibrist, funambulist
12 somersaulter
13 contortionist, trapeze artist

**act**
02 be, do
03 gig, law
04 bill, deed, fake, feat, item,
    mime, move, play, sham,
    show, skit, step, turn, work
05 edict, enact, feign, front,
    mimic, put on, react, serve
06 affect, assume, behave,
    decree, ruling, sketch, stroke
07 exploit, imitate, measure,
    operate, perform, portray,
    pretend, routine, statute
08 function, pretense
09 execution, ordinance,
    represent, take steps
10 enterprise, take effect
11 achievement, affectation,
    counterfeit, dissimulate,
    impersonate, make-believe,
    performance, undertaking
12 characterize, dissemblance

❏ **act on**
04 heed, obey, take
05 alter
06 affect, change, follow
07 fulfill
08 carry out
09 influence, transform
10 comply with

❏ **act up**
05 cut up
09 misbehave
11 malfunction
12 cause trouble

**acting**
05 drama
06 deputy, pro tem, relief,
    supply
07 interim, reserve, stand-by,
    stand-in, stopgap, theater
08 artistry, covering
09 dramatics, imitating,
    portrayal, temporary
10 footlights, performing, play-
    acting, stagecraft, substitute
11 histrionics, performance,
    provisional, theatricals
13 impersonation
14 performing arts

**action**
04 case, deed, feat, fray, move,
    step, suit, work

05 clash, fight, force, power
06 affray, battle, combat, effect, effort, energy, motion
07 exploit, lawsuit, measure, process, warfare
08 activity, conflict, exercise, exertion, movement, practice, skirmish, vitality
09 encounter, influence, mechanism, operation
10 engagement, enterprise, get-up-and-go, litigation, liveliness, proceeding
11 achievement, performance, prosecution, undertaking
14 accomplishment

**activate**
04 fire, move, stir, trip
05 impel, put on, rouse, spark, start
06 arouse, bestir, excite, prompt, propel, turn on
07 actuate, animate, trigger
08 energize, initiate, mobilize, motivate, switch on
09 galvanize, stimulate
10 trigger off
11 set in motion

**active**
04 busy, spry
05 agile, alert, astir, manic, quick, vital
06 lively, nimble
07 devoted, engaged, in force, on the go, vibrant, working
08 animated, forceful, frenetic, involved, militant, occupied, spirited, vigorous
09 committed, energetic, sprightly
11 functioning, hard-working, industrious, light-footed
12 contributing, enterprising, enthusiastic
13 indefatigable

**activity**
03 job
04 deed, life, task, work
05 hobby, labor
06 bustle, motion
07 pastime, project, pursuit, venture
08 business, endeavor, exercise, exertion, industry, interest, movement
09 avocation, commotion, diversion
10 enterprise, hurly-burly, liveliness, occupation
11 distraction, undertaking
14 to-ing and fro-ing

**actor, actress**
03 ham
04 mime
05 extra
06 artist, mummer, player, walk-on
07 stand-in, trouper
08 film star, thespian
09 bit player, movie star, performer, tragedian
10 leading man, understudy
11 leading lady
12 impersonator
14 character actor
15 supporting actor
16 background artist
➤ See also COMEDIAN

► *Names of actors:*
03 **Fox** (Michael J.), **Lee** (Christopher)
04 **Cage** (Nicolas), **Chan** (Jackie), **Cobb** (Lee J.), **Dean** (James), **Depp** (Johnny), **Ford** (Glenn), **Ford** (Harrison), **Gere** (Richard), **Hope** (Bob), **Hurt** (John), **Kaye** (Danny), **Ladd** (Alan), **Peck** (Gregory), **Penn** (Sean), **Pitt** (Brad), **Reed** (Oliver)
05 **Autry** (Gene), **Bacon** (Kevin), **Bates** (Alan), **Caine** (Michael), **Clift** (Montgomery), **Crowe** (Russell), **Damon** (Matt), **Flynn** (Errol), **Fonda** (Henry), **Fonda** (Peter), **Gable** (Clark), **Grant** (Cary), **Grant** (Hugh), **Hanks** (Tom), **Irons** (Jeremy), **Jones** (James Earl), **Jones** (Tommy Lee), **Kelly** (Gene), **Lanza** (Mario), **Lorre** (Peter), **Mason** (James), **Mills** (John), **Moore** (Dudley), **Moore** (Roger), **Nimoy** (Leonard), **Niven** (David), **Nolte** (Nick), **Power** (Tyrone), **Price** (Vincent), **Reeve** (Christopher), **Scott** (George C.), **Sheen** (Charlie), **Sheen** (Martin), **Smith** (Will), **Tracy** (Spencer), **Wayne** (John)
06 **Beatty** (Warren), **Bogart** (Humphrey), **Brando** (Marlon), **Burton** (Richard), **Cagney** (James), **Chaney** (Lon), **Coburn** (James), **Cooper** (Gary), **Cruise** (Tom), **Culkin** (Macaulay),

**Curtis** (Tony), **De Niro** (Robert), **DeVito** (Danny), **Dillon** (Matt), **Duvall** (Robert), **Finney** (Albert), **Gibson** (Mel), **Heston** (Charlton), **Holden** (William), **Hopper** (Dennis), **Hudson** (Rock), **Kilmer** (Val), **Lemmon** (Jack), **Lugosi** (Bela), **Marvin** (Lee), **Neeson** (Liam), **Newman** (Paul), **O'Toole** (Peter), **Pacino** (Al), **Quayle** (Anthony), **Reeves** (Keanu), **Rogers** (Roy), **Rooney** (Mickey), **Sharif** (Omar), **Snipes** (Wesley), **Spacey** Kevin, **Swayze** (Patrick), **Welles** (Orson), **Wilder** (Gene), **Willis** (Bruce)
07 **Bogarde** (Dirk), **Branagh** (Kenneth), **Bridges** (Jeff), **Bridges** (Lloyd), **Bronson** (Charles), **Brosnan** (Pierce), **Brynner** (Yul), **Clooney** (George), **Connery** (Sean), **Costner** (Kevin), **Douglas** (Kirk), **Douglas** (Michael), **Fiennes** (Ralph), **Freeman** (Morgan), **Gielgud** (John), **Hackman** (Gene), **Hoffman** (Dustin), **Hopkins** (Anthony), **Karloff** (Boris), **Marceau** (Marcel), **Matthau** (Walter), **McQueen** (Steve), **Mitchum** (Robert), **Olivier** (Laurence), **Perkins** (Anthony), **Phoenix** (River), **Poitier** (Sidney), **Redford** (Robert), **Robeson** (Paul), **Roscius**, **Russell** (Kurt), **Savalas** (Telly), **Shatner** (William), **Steiger** (Rod), **Stewart** (James), **Ustinov** (Peter)
08 **Day-Lewis** (Daniel), **Dreyfuss** (Richard), **Eastwood** (Clint), **Garfield** (John), **Guinness** (Alec), **Harrison** (Rex), **Kingsley** (Ben), **Laughton** (Charles), **McGregor** (Ewan), **Redgrave** (Michael), **Reynolds** (Burt), **Robinson** (Edward G.), **Scofield** (Paul), **Stallone** (Sylvester), **Travolta** (John), **Van Cleef** (Lee), **Van Damme** (Jean-Claude), **Williams** (Robin)
09 **Barrymore** (Lionel), **Chevalier** (Maurice),

Depardieu (Gérard),
Fairbanks (Douglas),
Lancaster (Burt),
Nicholson (Jack), **Strasberg**
(Lee), **Valentino** (Rudolph)
10 **Richardson** (Ralph),
**Sutherland** (Donald),
**Sutherland** (Kiefer),
**Washington** (Denzel)
11 **Mastroianni** (Marcello)
12 **Attenborough** (Richard),
**Stanislavsky**
14 **Schwarzenegger** (Arnold)

► *Names of actresses:*
03 **Bow** (Clara)
04 **Ball** (Lucille), **Bara**
(Theda), **Dern** (Laura), **Gish**
(Lillian), **Hawn** (Goldie),
**Hunt** (Helen), **Judd**
(Ashley), **Rigg** (Diana),
**Ryan** (Meg), **West** (Mae),
**Wood** (Natalie)
05 **Close** (Glenn), **Davis**
(Bette), **Dench** (Judi), **Evans**
(Edith), **Field** (Sally), **Fonda**
(Jane), **Gabor** (Zsa Zsa),
**Garbo** (Greta), **Lange**
(Jessica), **Leigh** (Janet),
**Leigh** (Vivien), **Loren**
(Sophia), **Moore** (Demi),
**Ryder** (Winona), **Smith**
(Maggie), **Stone** (Sharon),
**Welch** (Raquel)
06 **Bacall** (Lauren), **Bardot**
(Brigitte), **Bisset**
(Jacqueline), **Curtis** (Jamie
Lee), **Driver** (Minnie),
**Farrow** (Mia), **Foster**
(Jodie), **Grable** (Betty),
**Keaton** (Diane), **Kidman**
(Nicole), **Mirren** (Helen),
**Monroe** (Marilyn), **Moreau**
(Jeanne), **Streep** (Meryl),
**Taylor** (Elizabeth), **Temple**
(Shirley), **Turner** (Lana),
**Weaver** (Sigourney)
07 **Andress** (Ursula), **Andrews**
(Julie), **Aniston** (Jennifer),
**Bergman** (Ingrid), **Bullock**
(Sandra), **Colbert**
(Claudette), **Deneuve**
(Catherine), **Gardner** (Ava),
**Hepburn** (Audrey),
**Hepburn** (Katharine),
**Jackson** (Glenda), **Langtry**
(Lillie), **Paltrow** (Gwyneth),
**Roberts** (Julia), **Russell**
(Jane), **Seymour** (Jane),
**Shearer** (Norma), **Shields**
(Brooke), **Swanson** (Gloria),
**Thurman** (Uma), **Ullmann**
(Liv), **Winslet** (Kate)

08 **Bancroft** (Anne), **Bankhead**
(Tallulah), **Basinger** (Kim),
**Crawford** (Joan), **Dietrich**
(Marlene), **Goldberg**
(Whoopi), **Griffith**
(Melanie), **Hayworth** (Rita),
**MacLaine** (Shirley),
**Minnelli** (Liza), **Pickford**
(Mary), **Redgrave**
(Vanessa), **Thompson**
(Emma)
09 **Barrymore** (Drew),
**Bernhardt** (Sarah),
**MacDowell** (Andie),
**Mansfield** (Jayne),
**Streisand** (Barbra),
**Thorndike** (Sybil)
12 **Bonham-Carter** (Helena),
**Lollobrigida** (Gina)

**actual**
04 real, true
07 certain, de facto, genuine
08 absolute, bona fide,
concrete, definite, material,
physical, positive, tangible,
truthful, verified
09 authentic, realistic
10 legitimate

**actuality**
04 fact
05 truth
07 reality
09 substance
10 factuality
11 historicity, materiality

**actually**
04 even
05 truly
06 in fact, indeed, really
07 de facto, in truth
09 in reality
10 absolutely

**actuate**
04 move, stir
05 rouse, start
06 arouse, prompt, set off
07 trigger
08 activate, motivate
09 instigate, stimulate
10 trigger off
11 set in motion

**acumen**
03 wit
05 sense
06 wisdom
07 insight
08 gumption, judgment,
keenness, sagacity, sapience
09 ingenuity, intuition
10 astuteness, cleverness,
perception, shrewdness

11 discernment, penetration,
percipience, perspicuity
12 intelligence, perspicacity
13 judiciousness

**acute**
04 keen
05 grave, sharp, smart, vital
06 astute, clever, severe,
shrewd, urgent
07 crucial, extreme, intense,
sapient, serious, violent
08 critical, decisive, incisive
09 dangerous, judicious,
observant, sensitive
10 discerning, insightful,
perceptive, percipient
11 distressing, penetrating
13 perspicacious

**acutely**
06 keenly
07 gravely, sharply
08 strongly
09 extremely, intensely

**adage**
03 saw
05 axiom, maxim
06 byword, saying
07 precept, proverb
08 aphorism, apothegm

**adamant**
03 set
04 firm, hard
05 fixed, rigid, stiff, tough
08 obdurate, resolute, stubborn
09 immovable, insistent,
unbending
10 determined, inflexible,
unshakable, unyielding
12 intransigent

**adapt**
03 fit
04 suit
05 alter, match, shape
06 adjust, change, comply,
modify, tailor
07 conform, convert, prepare,
qualify, remodel
09 customize, harmonize

**adaptable**
07 plastic
08 amenable, flexible, variable
09 alterable, compliant,
easygoing, malleable,
versatile
10 adjustable, changeable
11 conformable, convertible

**adaptation**
05 shift
06 change
07 fitting, shaping

## add
08 matching, revision
09 refitting, reshaping, reworking, variation
10 adjustment, alteration, conversion, remodeling
11 acclimation, habituation
12 modification, refashioning
13 accommodation
15 acclimatization

## add
05 affix, annex, count, put in, put on, total
06 adjoin, append, attach, tack on
07 augment, build on, combine, count up, include
08 increase
10 supplement

## ❏add up
03 add, fit
04 jibe, mean
05 count, spell, tally, total
06 amount, come to, reckon
07 compute, include, signify
08 indicate, ring true
09 calculate, make sense
10 constitute
11 add together
12 hang together
13 stand to reason

## added
03 new
04 more
05 extra, fresh, spare
07 adjunct, another, further
10 additional
13 supplementary

## addendum
07 adjunct, allonge, codicil
08 addition, appendix
09 appendage
10 attachment, postscript, supplement
11 endorsement
12 augmentation

## addict
03 fan
04 buff, head, user
05 fiend, freak
06 junkie
07 devotee, hophead, tripper
08 adherent, follower
09 dope fiend, drug taker, mainliner
10 enthusiast

## addicted
04 fond
06 hooked
07 devoted
08 obsessed
09 dependent

## addiction
05 habit, mania
06 monkey
07 craving
09 obsession
10 dependence

## addition
04 gain
05 annex, extra, rider
06 adding
07 adjunct
08 addendum, additive, appendix, increase, totaling
09 accession, accretion, appendage, extension, increment, reckoning
10 annexation, attachment, increasing, postscript, supplement
11 computation, enlargement
12 afterthought, appurtenance

## ❏in addition
03 too
04 also
06 as well
07 besides, further
08 moreover
11 furthermore
12 not to mention, over and above
14 into the bargain

## additional
03 new
04 more
05 extra, fresh, other, spare
07 another, further
09 increased
10 excrescent
12 adscititious, adventitious, supervenient
13 supplementary

## additionally
03 too
04 also
06 as well
07 besides, further
08 moreover
10 in addition
11 furthermore
12 over and above
14 for good measure, into the bargain

## additive
05 extra
10 supplement
12 preservative

## addled
07 mixed-up, muddled
08 confused
09 befuddled, flustered, perplexed

10 bewildered

## address
04 call, home, send, talk
05 abode, house, orate
06 sermon, speech
07 lecture, lodging, oration, speak to, welcome, write to
08 deal with, diatribe, greeting, location
09 apartment, discourse, monologue, philippic, sermonize, situation, soliloquy
10 apostrophe, directions, invocation, salutation
11 communicate
12 disquisition, dissertation
15 general delivery

## ❏address (yourself) to
07 focus on
08 deal with, engage in
09 undertake
10 take care of
13 concentrate on

## adduce
04 cite
07 mention, present, proffer, refer to
08 allude to, evidence, point out
10 put forward

## adept
04 able, deft, good, whiz
05 handy, sharp
06 adroit, clever, expert, nimble, versed, wizard
07 capable, maestro, skilled
08 hot stuff, masterly, polished
09 competent, practiced
10 proficient
11 experienced, nobody's fool
12 accomplished

## adequacy
07 ability, fitness
08 fairness
10 capability, competence, mediocrity
11 passability, sufficiency, suitability
12 tolerability
13 acceptability

## adequate
02 OK
03 fit
04 okay
06 enough, patchy, will do
07 average, capable
08 all right, passable, suitable
09 competent, tolerable
10 acceptable, reasonable, sufficient

## adhere
12 commensurate, run of the mill, satisfactory
13 unexceptional

## adhere
03 fix
04 glue, grip, heed, hold, join, keep, link, obey
05 cling, paste, stick
06 attach, cement, cohere, defend, fasten, follow
07 abide by, espouse, fulfill, observe, respect, stand by, support
08 cleave to, coalesce
10 comply with

## adherent
03 fan, nut
04 buff
05 freak
06 votary
07 admirer, devotee, sectary
08 advocate, disciple, follower, hanger-on, partisan
09 satellite, supporter
10 aficionado, enthusiast

## adhesion
04 bond, grip
08 cohesion
10 attachment

## adhesive
03 gum
04 glue, tape
05 gluey, gummy, paste, tacky
06 cement, gummed, sticky
07 holding
08 clinging, cohesive, fixative, mucilage, sticking
09 attaching, glutinous, super glue
10 Elmer's glue, Scotch tape
12 mucilaginous

## adieu
06 bye-bye, so long
07 goodbye
08 au revoir, farewell
11 leave-taking, valediction, valedictory

## adjacent
04 near, next, nigh
05 close
06 beside, nearby
07 closest, nearest, vicinal
08 abutting, next-door
09 adjoining, alongside, bordering, proximate
10 contiguous, juxtaposed
11 neighboring
12 conterminous

## adjoin
03 add

04 abut, join, link, meet
05 annex, unite, verge
06 append, attach, border
07 combine, connect
08 neighbor
09 juxtapose
12 interconnect

## adjoining
04 near, next
07 joining, linking, uniting, verging, vicinal
08 abutting, adjacent, next-door
09 bordering, combining, impinging, proximate
10 conjoining, connecting, contiguous, juxtaposed
11 neighboring

## adjourn
04 stay
05 defer, delay, pause
06 put off, repair, retire
07 suspend
08 break off, postpone, prorogue, withdraw
09 interrupt
11 discontinue

## adjournment
04 stay
05 break, delay, pause
06 recess
08 deferral, interval
09 deferment
10 putting-off, suspension
11 dissolution, prorogation
12 intermission, interruption, postponement
15 discontinuation

## adjudicate
05 judge
06 decide, settle, umpire
07 adjudge, referee
09 arbitrate

## adjust
03 fit, fix, set
04 suit, tune
05 adapt, align, alter, amend, shape, tweak
06 change, modify, repair, revise, settle, square, temper
07 arrange, compose, convert, rectify, remodel, reshape
08 fine-tune, regulate
09 harmonize, refashion
11 accommodate

## adjustable
07 movable
08 flexible
09 adaptable
11 convertible

## adjustment
06 change, fixing, tuning
07 fitting, setting, shaping
08 ordering, revision
09 amendment, arranging
10 adaptation, alteration, conversion, regulation, remodeling
11 acclimation, arrangement, habituation, orientation, rearranging
12 modification
13 accommodation, rearrangement
15 acclimatization

## ad-lib
06 invent, made-up, make up
09 extempore, impromptu, improvise
10 improvised, off the cuff, unprepared
11 extemporize, unrehearsed

## administer
03 run
04 give, head, lead, rule
05 apply
06 direct, govern, impose, manage, supply
07 conduct, control, dole out, execute, give out, mete out, oversee, provide
08 disburse, dispense, organize, regulate
09 officiate, supervise
10 distribute, measure out
11 preside over, superintend

## administration
06 regime, ruling
07 control, red tape, running
08 ministry
09 direction, execution, executive, governing, paperwork
10 government, leadership, management, overseeing
11 supervision
12 term of office
13 governing body
15 superintendence

## administrative
09 executive
10 management, managerial, regulatory
11 directorial, legislative, supervisory
12 governmental
13 authoritative, gubernatorial
14 organizational

► *Types of administrative area*:
04 area, city, town, ward

**administrator** (cont.)
05 state
06 county, parish, region, sector
07 borough, enclave, village
08 district, division, precinct, province
09 territory
12 constituency

**administrator**
04 boss, head
05 chief, ruler
06 leader
07 manager, trustee
08 chairman, director, governor, guardian, overseer
09 custodian, executive, organizer, president
10 controller, supervisor
14 chief executive, superintendent

**admirable**
04 fine, rare
06 choice, worthy
08 laudable, masterly, superior
09 deserving, estimable, excellent, exquisite
10 creditable
11 commendable, meritorious
12 praiseworthy

**admiration**
03 yen
05 kudos
06 esteem, praise, regard, wonder
07 delight, idolism, respect, worship
08 approval, pleasure, surprise
09 adulation, affection, amazement, reverence
10 veneration
11 approbation
12 appreciation, astonishment

**admire**
04 laud, like
05 adore, prize, value
06 esteem, praise, revere
07 applaud, approve, iconize, idolize, respect, worship
08 look up to, venerate
09 approve of
11 hero-worship
14 put on a pedestal
15 think the world of

**admirer**
03 fan
04 beau, buff
05 fiend, freak, lover, wooer
06 suitor
07 devotee, gallant
08 adherent, disciple, follower, idolater, idolizer
09 boyfriend, supporter

10 aficionado, enthusiast, girlfriend, sweetheart

**admissible**
05 licit
06 lawful
07 allowed
08 passable
09 allowable, permitted, tolerable, tolerated
10 acceptable, legitimate
11 justifiable, permissible

**admission**
06 access, avowal, exposé
07 ingress, peccavi
08 entrance, mea culpa
09 allowance
10 acceptance, concession, confession, disclosure, divulgence, revelation
11 affirmation, declaration, entrance fee, recognition
14 acknowledgment

**admit**
05 agree, allow, grant, let in, own up
06 accept, affirm, reveal, take in
07 concede, confess, declare, divulge, profess, receive
08 disclose, initiate, intromit
09 come clean, recognize
11 acknowledge

**admittance**
05 entry
06 access
07 ingress
08 entrance
09 letting in, reception
10 acceptance, initiation
12 introduction, right of entry
13 right of access

**admixture**
03 mix
05 alloy, blend
06 fusion
07 amalgam
08 compound, tincture
11 combination
12 amalgamation

**admonish**
04 warn
05 chide, scold
06 berate, exhort, rebuke
07 censure, correct, counsel, reprove, tell off, upbraid
09 reprimand
10 discipline

**admonition**
06 rebuke
07 censure, counsel, reproof, warning

08 berating, scolding
09 reprimand
10 correction, telling-off
11 exhortation
12 reprehension

**adolescence**
05 teens, youth
07 boyhood, puberty
08 girlhood, minority
10 boyishness, immaturity, juvenility, pubescence
11 development, girlishness
12 juvenescence, teenage years, youthfulness

**adolescent**
05 minor, young, youth
06 boyish
07 girlish, puerile, teenage
08 childish, immature, juvenile, teenager, youthful
09 pubescent
10 developing, young adult
11 juvenescent, young person

**adopt**
04 back
06 accept, assume, choose, follow, foster, ratify, select, take in, take on, take up
07 approve, embrace, endorse, espouse, support
08 maintain, nominate

**adoption**
06 choice
07 backing, support
08 approval, espousal, taking-in, taking-on, taking-up
09 embracing, fostering
10 acceptance
11 approbation, embracement, endorsement
12 ratification

**adorable**
04 dear
05 sweet
07 darling, lovable, winsome
08 charming, fetching, pleasing, precious
09 appealing, wonderful
10 attractive, bewitching, delightful, enchanting
11 captivating

**adoration**
04 love
06 esteem, homage, praise, regard
07 worship
08 devotion, doting on
09 reverence
10 admiration, exaltation, idolizaton, veneration
13 glorification, magnification

## adore
04 love
05 honor
06 admire, dote on, esteem, relish, revere
07 cherish, worship
08 hold dear, venerate
11 be devoted to, be partial to
15 think the world of

## adorn
04 deck, gild, trim
05 array, crown, grace
06 bedeck, doll up, tart up
07 apparel, bejewel, dress up, enhance, festoon, furbish, garnish
08 beautify, decorate, emblazon, ornament, prettify
09 embellish

## adornment
05 frill
06 fallal, finery, ruffle
07 flounce, garnish, gilding, jewelry
08 frippery, furbelow, ornament
09 accessory, fallalery, trappings, trimmings
10 decoration, enrichment
11 enhancement
13 embellishment, ornamentation

## adrift
05 at sea
07 aimless
08 goalless, insecure
09 off course, unsettled
10 anchorless
13 directionless

## adroit
04 able, deft
05 adept
06 clever, expert
08 skillful
09 dexterous, masterful
10 proficient

## adroitness
05 skill
07 ability, finesse, mastery
08 deftness, facility
09 adeptness, dexterity, expertise
10 cleverness, competence
11 proficiency
12 skillfulness

## adulation
06 praise
07 fawning
08 flattery
10 sycophancy
11 hero worship, idolization

12 blandishment

## adulatory
07 fawning, fulsome, servile
08 praising, unctuous
10 flattering, obsequious
11 blandishing, bootlicking, brown-nosing, sycophantic

## adult
04 ripe
05 of age
06 mature
07 ephebic, grown-up, obscene, ripened
09 developed, full-grown
12 pornographic

## adulterate
05 taint
06 debase, defile, dilute, weaken
07 corrupt, degrade, devalue, pollute, vitiate
09 attenuate, water down
10 bastardize, make impure
11 contaminate, deteriorate

## adultery
06 affair
08 cheating
10 hanky-panky, infidelity, unchastity
13 playing around
14 unfaithfulness
15 playing the field

## advance
03 pay
04 cite, give, grow, help, lend, loan, step
05 offer, speed
06 adduce, allege, assist, credit, foster, growth, hasten, move on, submit, supply
07 benefit, deposit, forward, furnish, further, go ahead, headway, present, proceed, proffer, promote, provide, suggest, support, upgrade
08 expedite, increase, progress
10 accelerate, betterment, facilitate, prepayment
11 advancement, development, down payment, furtherance, improvement, progression
12 amelioration, breakthrough, early payment, make progress

## ◻ in advance
05 ahead, early
06 sooner
07 earlier, up front
09 in the lead
10 beforehand, previously

## advanced
05 ahead
06 hi-tech, higher
07 complex, forward, leading
08 foremost, high-tech, up-to-date
10 avant-garde, precocious
11 progressive, ultramodern
13 sophisticated, state-of-the-art
15 ahead of the times

## advancement
04 gain
05 raise
06 growth
07 advance, headway
08 progress
09 promotion
10 betterment, preferment
11 development, furtherance, improvement

## advances
05 moves
09 addresses, overtures
10 approaches, attentions
11 proposition

## advantage
03 aid, pro, use
04 boon, edge, gain, good, help, lead, plus, sway
05 asset, avail, fruit
06 beauty, payoff, profit, virtue
07 benefit, service
08 blessing, interest, leverage
09 dominance, head start, upper hand
10 assistance, precedence
11 convenience, preeminence, superiority

## advantageous
06 useful
07 gainful, helpful
08 valuable
09 favorable, of service, opportune, rewarding
10 beneficial, convenient, profitable, propitious, worthwhile
11 furthersome
12 of assistance, remunerative

## advent
04 dawn
05 birth, onset
06 coming
07 arrival
08 approach, entrance
09 beginning, inception
10 appearance, occurrence
12 introduction

## adventure
04 risk

**adventurer**
05 peril
06 chance, danger, hazard
07 exploit, romance, venture
08 incident
10 enterprise, excitement, experience, occurrence
11 speculation, undertaking

**adventurer**
04 hero
07 heroine, voyager
08 explorer, traveler, venturer, wanderer

**adventurous**
04 bold, rash
05 gutsy, risky
06 daring, spunky
08 exciting, intrepid, perilous, reckless, romantic
09 audacious, dangerous, hazardous, impetuous
10 headstrong
11 venturesome

**adversary**
03 foe
05 enemy, rival
07 opposer
08 attacker, opponent
09 assailant
10 antagonist, competitor

**adverse**
07 counter, harmful, hostile, hurtful, unlucky
08 contrary, negative, opposing, untoward
09 injurious
10 unfriendly
11 conflicting, detrimental, inexpedient, inopportune, uncongenial, unfavorable, unfortunate
12 antagonistic, inauspicious, unpropitious
15 disadvantageous

**adversity**
03 woe
05 trial
06 misery, sorrow
07 bad luck, ill luck, trouble
08 calamity, disaster, distress, hardship
09 hard times, suffering
10 affliction, misfortune
11 catastrophe, tribulation
12 wretchedness

**advertise**
04 hype, plug, push, sell, tout
06 inform, market, notify, praise
07 display, promote, publish
08 announce, proclaim
09 broadcast, make known, publicize

10 make public, promulgate
11 merchandise

**advertisement**
02 ad
04 bill, hype, plug
05 blurb
06 jingle, notice, poster
07 display, handout, leaflet, placard, trailer
08 circular, handbill
09 marketing, promotion, publicity
10 commercial, propaganda

**advice**
03 tip
04 help, view, word
06 notice, wisdom
07 caution, counsel, warning
08 guidance
09 direction
10 counseling, injunction, suggestion
11 dos and don'ts, information, instruction
14 recommendation

**advisability**
06 wisdom
07 aptness
08 prudence
09 soundness
10 expediency
11 suitability
12 desirability
13 judiciousness
15 appropriateness

**advisable**
03 apt, fit
04 best, wise
05 sound
06 proper, wisest
07 correct, fitting, politic, prudent
08 sensible, suitable
09 desirable, judicious
10 beneficial, profitable
11 appropriate, recommended

**advise**
04 tell, urge, warn
05 guide, teach, tutor
06 enjoin, inform, notify, report
07 apprise, caution, commend, counsel, suggest
08 acquaint, forewarn, instruct
09 make known, recommend

**adviser**
04 aide, guru
05 coach, guide, tutor
06 helper, lawyer, mentor
07 counsel, teacher
09 authority, confidant, counselor

10 confidante, consultant, instructor

**advisory**
07 helping, warning
08 advising
10 consulting, counseling
12 recommending

**advocacy**
07 backing, defense, support
08 adoption, espousal, proposal
09 patronage, promotion, upholding
11 advancement, campaigning, championing, propagation
12 promulgation
13 encouragement, justification
14 recommendation

**advocate**
04 back, urge
05 adopt, be pro, favor, lobby
06 advise, back up, defend, lawyer, uphold
07 counsel, endorse, espouse, justify, pleader, promote, propose, speaker, support
08 argue for, attorney, be behind, champion, defender, exponent, plead for, promoter, upholder
09 believe in, encourage, proponent, recommend, solicitor, supporter
10 campaigner, vindicator
11 countenance
12 spokesperson

**aegis**
04 wing
05 favor
07 backing, support
08 advocacy, auspices
09 patronage
11 sponsorship
12 championship, guardianship

**affability**
06 warmth
08 courtesy, mildness
09 benignity, geniality, good humor
10 amiability, cordiality, kindliness
11 amicability, benevolence, sociability
12 congeniality, friendliness, obligingness, pleasantness
15 approachability

**affable**
04 mild, open, warm
06 genial, kindly
07 amiable, cordial
08 amicable, friendly, gracious, obliging, pleasant, sociable

**affair**

09 agreeable, congenial
10 benevolent
11 good-humored
12 approachable

**affair**

05 amour, event, fling, topic
06 matter
07 concern, episode, liaison, project, romance, subject
08 activity, business, incident, interest, intrigue, question
09 happening, operation
11 transaction, undertaking
12 circumstance, relationship
14 responsibility

**affect**

04 fake, move, sham, sway
05 act on, adopt, alter, feign, put on, touch, upset
06 assume, attack, change, impact, modify, strike
07 concern, disturb, imitate, involve, perturb, pretend, profess, trouble
08 bear upon, interest, overcome, relate to, simulate
09 influence, transform
11 counterfeit, impinge upon

**affectation**

03 act
04 airs, pose, sham, show
06 façade
08 pretense
09 imitation, mannerism
10 appearance, simulation
11 insincerity, theatricism
13 artificiality
15 pretentiousness

**affected**

04 fake, sham
05 moved, phony, put-on, stiff
06 la-di-da
07 assumed, feigned, pompous, studied
08 mannered, precious, spurious
09 concerned, contrived, insincere, simulated, unnatural
10 artificial
11 counterfeit, pretentious

**affecting**

03 sad
06 moving
07 piteous, pitiful
08 pathetic, pitiable, poignant, stirring, touching

**affection**

04 care, love
05 amity, favor
06 desire, warmth

07 feeling, passion
08 devotion, fondness, kindness, penchant
10 attachment, partiality, proclivity, propensity, tenderness
11 inclination
12 friendliness, predilection
14 predisposition

**affectionate**

04 fond, kind, warm
06 caring, loving, tender
07 amiable, cordial, devoted
08 attached, friendly
11 warm-hearted

**affiliate**

04 ally, join
05 annex, merge, unite
07 combine, conjoin, connect
09 associate, syndicate
10 amalgamate
11 confederate, incorporate

**affiliation**

03 tie
04 bond, link
05 union
06 league, merger
07 joining
08 alliance
09 coalition
10 connection, federation, membership
11 association, combination
12 amalgamation, relationship

**affinity**

04 bond
06 liking
07 analogy, rapport
08 fondness, likeness
09 chemistry, good terms
10 attraction, partiality, propensity, similarity
11 resemblance
13 comparability, compatibility

**affirm**

04 aver, avow
05 state, swear
06 assert, attest, avouch, ratify
07 certify, confirm, declare, endorse, testify, witness
10 asseverate
11 corroborate

**affirmation**

04 oath
06 avowal
07 witness
08 averment
09 assertion, statement, testimony
10 affirmance, avouchment, deposition

11 attestation, declaration, endorsement
12 asseveration, confirmation, ratification
13 certification, corroboration

**affirmative**

08 agreeing, emphatic, positive
09 approving, assenting
10 concurring, confirming
13 corroborative

**affix**

03 add, tag
04 bind, glue, join, tack
05 annex, paste, pin on, stick
06 append, attach, fasten
07 connect

**afflict**

03 try
04 harm, hurt, pain
05 beset, smite, visit, wound
06 burden, grieve, harass, plague, strike
07 oppress, torment, trouble
08 distress

**affliction**

03 woe
04 pain
05 cross, curse, grief, trial
06 ordeal, plague, sorrow
07 disease, illness, trouble
08 calamity, disaster, distress, hardship, sickness
09 adversity, suffering
10 depression, misfortune
11 tribulation

**affluence**

06 plenty, riches, wealth
07 fortune, tidy sum
08 opulence, property
09 abundance, profusion
10 easy street, prosperity

**affluent**

04 rich
05 flush
06 loaded
07 moneyed, opulent, wealthy, well-off
08 well-to-do
10 in the money, prosperous, well-heeled
11 comfortable, rolling in it

**afford**

04 bear, give
05 allow, grant, offer, spare
06 impart, manage, pay for
07 furnish, produce, provide

**affray**

05 brawl, brush, fight, melee, scrap, set-to
06 fracas, tussle

**affront**
07 quarrel, scuffle, wrangle
08 skirmish, squabble
09 fistfight
10 fisticuffs, free-for-all

**affront**
03 vex
04 slur, snub
05 anger, annoy, pique, wrong
06 injury, insult, offend, slight
07 incense, outrage, provoke
08 irritate, rudeness, vexation
09 aspersion, indignity
10 disrespect
11 discourtesy, provocation
13 slap in the face
14 kick in the teeth

**afoot**
05 about, astir
06 abroad, around
07 brewing, current
08 in the air
13 in the pipeline

**afraid**
05 sorry
06 aghast, scared, yellow
09 concerned, regretful, tremulous
10 frightened

**afresh**
04 anew
05 again, newly

**after**
07 owing to
09 because of, following, in honor of
11 as a result of

**aftermath**
04 wake
06 upshot
07 effects, outcome, results
12 aftereffects, consequences
13 repercussions

**afterward**
04 next, then
05 later
12 subsequently

**again**
04 anew
06 afresh, encore
08 once more
11 one more time

❑**again and again**
10 constantly, repeatedly
11 continually
12 time and again

**against**
02 on
04 anti
06 facing, versus

**age**
03 day, eon, era
04 date, days, span, time
05 epoch, ripen, years
06 dotage, grow up, mature, mellow, old age, period, season, wither
07 decline, grow old
08 duration, maturity, senility
09 seniority
10 generation, senescence
11 decrepitude, elderliness

**aged**
03 old
04 gray
05 aging, hoary
06 past it
07 ancient, doddery, elderly
08 advanced
09 geriatric, senescent
11 over the hill, patriarchal
13 superannuated
15 no spring chicken

**agency**
04 firm, work
05 force, means, power
06 action, bureau, effect, medium, office
07 company
08 activity, business, workings
09 influence, operation
12 intervention, organization

**agenda**
04 list, menu, plan
05 diary
07 program
08 calendar, schedule
09 timetable

**agent**
03 rep, spy
04 doer, mole
05 cause, envoy, force, means, mover, proxy
06 agency, broker, deputy, factor, worker
07 channel, trustee, vehicle
08 assignee, delegate, emissary, minister, operator
09 go-between, middleman, operative, performer
10 instrument, negotiator
12 intermediary
14 representative

**agglomeration**
05 store
07 buildup

**aggression**
06 attack, injury, strike
07 assault, offense
08 invasion
09 hostility, incursion, intrusion, militancy, offensive, onslaught, pugnacity
10 antagonism
11 bellicosity, provocation
12 belligerence
13 combativeness

**aggressive**
04 bold
05 pushy
06 brutal, savage
07 go-ahead, hostile, zealous
08 forceful, vigorous
09 assertive, cutthroat, ferocious, offensive
10 in-your-face, pugnacious
11 belligerent, provocative, quarrelsome
13 argumentative

08 abutting, fronting, opposing, touching
09 close up to, hostile to, opposed to, resisting
10 adjacent to, opposite to

08 increase
09 aggregate, gathering
11 aggregation
12 accumulation

**aggrandize**
05 exalt, widen
06 enrich
07 amplify, elevate, enhance, enlarge, ennoble, glorify, inflate, magnify, promote
09 glamorize
10 exaggerate, make richer

**aggravate**
03 irk, try, vex
05 annoy, tease
06 harass, needle, pester, worsen
07 inflame, magnify, provoke
08 compound, heighten, increase, irritate
09 intensify, make worse
10 exacerbate, exasperate

**aggravation**
06 hassle
08 vexation
09 annoyance
10 irritation
11 irksomeness, provocation
15 thorn in the flesh

**aggregate**
03 sum
05 total, whole
08 entirety, sum total, totality
10 collection, grand total
11 combination
12 accumulation

**aggressor**
07 invader
08 attacker, intruder, offender
09 assailant, assaulter

**aggrieved**
04 hurt
05 upset
06 bitter, pained
07 ill-used, unhappy, wronged
08 offended, saddened
09 resentful
10 distressed, maltreated

**aghast**
06 amazed
07 shocked, stunned
08 appalled, dismayed, startled
09 astounded, stupefied
10 astonished, confounded

**agile**
04 spry
05 acute, alert, brisk, fleet, lithe, quick, sharp, swift
06 active, astute, clever, limber, lisson, mobile, nimble
07 lissome
08 athletic, flexible
09 sprightly

**agility**
08 mobility
09 alertness, quickness, sharpness, swiftness
10 astuteness, nimbleness
11 flexibility

**agitate**
04 beat, rock, stir, toss
05 argue, churn, fight, rouse, shake, upset, whisk, worry
06 arouse, excite, flurry, incite, rattle, ruffle, stir up, work up
07 disturb, ferment, fluster, perturb, trouble, unnerve
08 campaign, disquiet, unsettle
10 discompose, disconcert

**agitated**
05 upset
07 anxious, nervous, worried
08 troubled, unnerved
09 disturbed, flustered, in a lather, unsettled
10 distraught
12 disconcerted

**agitator**
07 inciter, stirrer
08 activist, fomenter
09 firebrand
10 instigator, subversive
12 rabble-rouser, troublemaker

**agnostic**
07 doubter, skeptic
10 unbeliever

**ago**
04 gone, past
05 since
07 earlier
10 previously

**agog**
04 avid, keen
05 eager
07 curious, excited
09 impatient
10 enthralled, in suspense
13 on tenterhooks

**agonize**
05 labor, worry
06 strain, strive
07 trouble, wrestle
08 struggle

**agonizing**
07 painful, racking
08 worrying
09 harrowing, torturous
10 tormenting
11 distressing
12 excruciating

**agony**
03 woe
04 hurt, pain
05 spasm
06 misery, throes
07 anguish, torment, torture
08 distress
09 suffering
10 affliction

**agree**
04 suit
05 admit, allow, get on, grant, match, tally, yield
06 accede, accept, accord, assent, comply, concur, go with, permit, settle
07 be at one, concede, conform, consent
08 say yes to
10 compromise, correspond
11 be of one mind, go along with, rubber-stamp, see eye to eye

**agreeable**
04 fine, nice
07 likable, willing
08 amenable, amicable, charming, friendly, pleasant
09 compliant, congenial, enjoyable
10 acceptable, attractive
11 good-natured, sympathetic

**agreement**
04 deal, deed, pact
05 tally, union
06 accord, assent, treaty
07 bargain, compact, concord, fitting, harmony
08 affinity, contract, covenant, matching, sympathy
09 concordat, consensus, indenture, unanimity
10 conformity, consonance, settlement, similarity
11 arrangement, concurrence, consistency
12 complaisance
13 compatibility, understanding
➤ See also TREATY

**agricultural**
05 rural
07 bucolic, farming, georgic
08 agrarian, pastoral

➤ *Types of agricultural equipment*:
02 ax
03 ATV, hoe, saw
04 fork, plow, rake
05 baler, drill, mower, spade
06 harrow, scythe, shovel, sickle, weeder
07 hayfork, tractor
08 chainsaw, thresher
09 harvester, pitchfork, Rotovator, seed drill, whetstone
10 cultivator, grain drill
11 reaping hook, wheelbarrow
12 slurry tanker
13 forklift truck
14 manure spreader, milking machine

**agriculture**
07 farming, tillage
08 agronomy
09 husbandry
10 agronomics

➤ *Names of agriculturists*:
04 **Coke** (Thomas William), **Tull** (Jethro)
05 **Lawes** (John Bennet)
06 **Carver** (George Washington), **Taylor** (John)
07 **Burbank** (Luther), **Johnson** (Samuel)

**aground**
05 stuck
06 ashore
07 beached, wrecked
08 grounded, stranded
09 foundered
10 high and dry, on the rocks

**ahead**
06 before, onward
07 forward, in front, leading
08 advanced, superior

**aid**
09 earlier on, in advance, in the lead, to the fore

**aid**
04 ease, gift, hand, help, prop
05 boost, grant, serve
06 a leg up, assist, backup, oblige, relief, second, succor
07 benefit, funding, promote, service, speed up, subsidy, support, sustain
08 donation, expedite
09 encourage, patronage, subsidize
10 assistance, facilitate, subvention
11 accommodate, helping hand, rally around, sponsorship
12 contribution
13 a shot in the arm

**aide**
07 adviser, attaché
08 adjutant, advocate
09 assistant, confidant
12 right-hand man

**ail**
04 fail, pain
05 upset, worry
06 bother, sicken, weaken
07 afflict, trouble
08 distress, irritate

**ailing**
03 ill
04 sick, weak
05 frail, unfit
06 feeble, infirm, poorly, sickly, unwell
07 failing, invalid, unsound
08 off-color
09 suffering
10 indisposed, out of sorts
15 under the weather

**ailment**
06 malady
07 disease, illness
08 disorder, sickness, weakness
09 complaint, infirmity
10 affliction, disability
13 indisposition

**aim**
03 end, try
04 goal, hope, mark, mean, plan, seek, want, wish
05 level, point, sight, train
06 aspire, course, design, desire, direct, intend, motive, strive, target
07 attempt, mission, propose, purpose, resolve, shoot at
08 ambition, endeavor, zero in on

09 direction, intention, objective
10 aspiration

**aimless**
05 stray
06 chance, futile, random
07 erratic, wayward
08 drifting, goalless, rambling
09 haphazard, pointless, unsettled, wandering
10 irresolute, undirected
11 purposeless, unmotivated
13 directionless, unpredictable

**air**
03 sky
04 aura, look, waft, wind
05 blast, draft, ether, state, utter, voice
06 aerate, aerial, breath, breeze, effect, manner, oxygen, zephyr
07 bearing, declare, express, freshen, heavens
08 ambience, carriage, demeanor
09 make known, publicize, ventilate
10 appearance, atmosphere, impression, make public
11 communicate, disseminate

**aircraft**

► *Types of aircraft*:
03 jet, MIG
04 kite, STOL, VTOL, Zero
05 AWACS, blimp, drone, jumbo, plane
06 Airbus, Boeing, bomber, bomber, Fokker, glider
07 airship, balloon, biplane, Chinook, chopper, fighter, jump-jet, Mustang, Phantom, stealth, Tornado
08 airliner, airplane, Concorde, Enola Gay, Hercules, jumbo jet, Sabrejet, seaplane, Spitfire, Spitfire, spy plane, warplane, zeppelin
09 delta-wing, dirigible, Hurricane, Lancaster, monoplane
10 dive bomber, hang glider, helicopter, Thunderjet, ultralight
12 Flying Boxcar, Sopwith Camel
13 hot-air balloon, Messerschmitt
14 Stratofortress
➤ See also VEHICLE

► *Parts of an aircraft include*:
04 wing
06 canopy, rudder
07 aileron, airfoil, ammeter, cockpit, tail fin
08 elevator, fuselage
09 altimeter, propeller, stablizer, tailplane
11 landing flap, landing gear, landing gear, vertical fin
12 control stick, radio compass, rudder pedals
13 control column
15 magnetic compass

**airing**
07 voicing
08 aeration, exposure, uttering
09 broadcast, statement
10 disclosure, divulgence, expression, freshening
11 circulation, declaration, publication, ventilation

**airless**
05 close, heavy, muggy
06 stuffy, sultry
08 stifling
10 oppressive
11 suffocating

**airport**

► *Names of international airports*:
03 JFK, Zia
05 Logan, McCoy, O'Hare
06 Changi, Dulles, Midway
07 Ataturk, Bradley, Entebbe, Gatwick, Hopkins, Lincoln, Lubbock, Roberts, Schipol
08 Ciampino, El Dorado, G. Marconi, Heathrow, Jan Smuts, McCarran, Sangster
09 Ben Gurion, Charleroi, Fiumicino, J. F. Kennedy, Jose Marti, Lindbergh, Marco Polo
10 George Bush, Golden Rock, Hartsfield, Hellenikon, King Khaled, Louis Botha, Sky Harbour
11 Capodichino, Jorge Chavez, Las Americas, Ninoy Aquino, Pointe Noire, Tito Menniti
12 Benito Juarez, Berline-Tegel, Hancock Field, Indira Gandhi, Jomo Kenyatta, Norman Manley, Queen Beatrix, Simon Bolivar
13 Château Bougon, Chiang Kai Shek
14 Lambert-St. Louis
15 Charles de Gaulle, Galilieo

Galilei, Leonardo da Vinci

**airs**
05 swank
06 posing
07 hauteur
09 arrogance, pomposity
11 affectation, pretensions
12 affectedness

**airtight**
06 closed, sealed
11 impermeable
12 impenetrable, tight-fitting

**airy**
04 open
05 blowy, gusty, happy, roomy, windy
06 breezy, casual, drafty, jaunty, lively
07 offhand
08 cheerful, spacious
10 nonchalant
12 high-spirited, light-hearted
14 well-ventilated

**aisle**
04 lane, path
07 gangway, passage, walkway
08 alleyway, corridor
10 passageway

**alarm**
04 bell, fear
05 alert, daunt, panic, scare, shock, siren
06 dismay, fright, horror, rattle, terror, tocsin
07 agitate, anxiety, perturb, startle, terrify, unnerve, warning
08 affright, distress, frighten
09 alarm bell
10 make afraid, uneasiness
11 nervousness, trepidation
12 apprehension, perturbation
13 consternation
14 distress signal

**alarming**
05 scary
07 ominous
08 daunting, dreadful, shocking, worrying
09 dismaying, startling, unnerving
10 disturbing, perturbing, terrifying
11 distressing, frightening, threatening

**alarmist**
09 doomsayer, pessimist
11 scaremonger

**alcohol**
05 booze, drink

06 liquor
07 spirits
09 firewater, hard stuff, the bottle
10 intoxicant, stiff drink
12 Dutch courage
➤ See also DRINK

**alcoholic**
04 alky, hard, lush, soak, wino
05 dipso, drunk, toper
06 ardent, boozer, strong
07 drinker, tippler
08 drunkard
09 distilled, inebriate
11 dipsomaniac, inebriating
12 heavy drinker, intoxicating

**alcove**
03 bay
04 nook
05 booth, niche
06 carrel, corner, recess
07 cubicle
09 cubbyhole

**alert**
04 warn, wary
05 agile, alarm, awake, brisk, quick, ready
06 active, inform, lively, nimble, notify, signal, tip off
07 careful, heedful, qui vive
08 forewarn, prepared, spirited, vigilant, watchful
09 attentive, observant, on the ball, wide-awake
10 on your toes, perceptive
11 circumspect, sharp-witted
12 on the lookout

**algae**

➤ *Types of algae and lichen:*
04 kelp
05 dulse, fucus, laver, wrack
06 desmid, diatom, nostoc
07 oakmoss, oarweed, redware, sea lace, seaware, seaweed
08 bull kelp, conferva, gulfweed, lecanora, rockweed, sea wrack
09 Irish moss, rock tripe, sargassum, sea tangle, spirogyra, stonewort
10 Ceylon moss, sea lettuce
12 bladder wrack
18 carrageen chlorella
➤ See also PLANT

**alias**
03 a k a
06 anonym
07 allonym, pen name
08 formerly, nickname
09 pseudonym, sobriquet

10 also called, nom de plume
11 also known as, assumed name, nom de guerre

**alibi**
05 story
06 excuse, reason
07 coverup, defense, pretext
11 explanation
13 justification

**alien**
06 exotic, remote
07 foreign, opposed, strange
08 newcomer, outsider, stranger
09 foreigner, immigrant
10 outlandish, unfamiliar
11 conflicting, incongruous

**alienate**
08 estrange, separate, turn away
09 disaffect
10 antagonize, set against

**alienation**
08 disunion
09 isolation, severance
10 remoteness, separation
11 turning away
12 disaffection, estrangement

**alight**
03 lit
04 land
05 alive, fiery, lit up, perch
06 ablaze, bright, debark, get off, lively, on fire, settle
07 blazing, burning, descend, flaming, get down, ignited, lighted, radiant, shining
08 come down, dismount
09 disembark, touch down
10 come to rest
11 illuminated

**align**
04 ally, even, join, side
05 agree, order, range, unite
06 adjust, even up, line up
07 arrange, combine
08 regulate
09 affiliate, associate
10 coordinate, join forces, regularize, straighten

**alignment**
04 line
05 order
06 siding
07 ranging
08 alliance, lining up, sympathy
09 agreement
11 affiliation, arrangement, association, cooperation

**alike**
04 akin, even
05 equal

**alive**
07 cognate, equally, similar, the same, uniform
08 in common, parallel
09 analogous, duplicate, identical, similarly
10 comparable, equivalent, resembling
11 analogously, much the same

**alive**
05 alert, awake, brisk, vital
06 active, extant, lively, living
07 alert to, animate, aware of, vibrant, zestful
08 animated, spirited, vigorous
09 breathing, energetic, heedful of, vivacious
10 full of life, having life
11 abounding in, going strong, in existence, teeming with
12 crawling with
15 overflowing with

**all**
03 sum
04 each, full
05 every, fully, total, utter, whole
06 entire, the lot, utmost, wholly
07 perfect, totally, utterly
08 complete, entirely, entirety, everyone, greatest, outright
09 aggregate, everybody
10 altogether, completely, every bit of, everything
12 each and every, universality
13 in its entirety

**allay**
04 calm, ease
05 blunt, check, quell, quiet
06 lessen, pacify, reduce, smooth, soften, soothe
07 compose, mollify, relieve
08 diminish, moderate
09 alleviate

**allegation**
05 claim
06 avowal, charge
09 assertion, statement, testimony
10 accusation, deposition
11 affirmation, declaration
12 asseveration

**allege**
04 hold
05 claim, state
06 affirm, assert, attest, insist
07 contend, declare, profess
08 maintain
10 put forward

**alleged**
06 stated
07 claimed, reputed, suspect

08 declared, doubtful, inferred, putative, so-called, supposed
09 described, professed
10 designated, ostensible

**allegiance**
04 duty
06 fealty
07 loyalty, support
08 devotion, fidelity
09 adherence, constancy, obedience
10 friendship, solidarity
12 faithfulness

**allegorical**
08 symbolic
09 parabolic
10 emblematic, figurative
11 significant, symbolizing
12 metaphorical
13 significative
14 representative

**allegory**
04 myth, tale
05 fable, story
06 emblem, legend, symbol
07 analogy, parable
08 metaphor
09 symbolism

**allergic**
06 averse
07 hostile, opposed
08 affected
09 sensitive
11 dyspathetic, susceptible
12 antagonistic
14 hypersensitive

**allergy**
08 aversion
09 antipathy, hostility
10 antagonism, opposition
11 sensitivity
14 susceptibility

**alleviate**
04 dull, ease
05 abate, allay, check
06 deaden, lessen, reduce, soften, soothe, subdue, temper
07 assuage, mollify, relieve
08 diminish, mitigate, moderate, palliate

**alleviation**
06 easing, relief
07 dulling
08 soothing
09 abatement, deadening, lessening, reduction
10 diminution, mitigation, moderation, palliation

11 assuagement
13 mollification

**alley**
04 gate, lane, road, walk
06 street
07 passage, pathway, walkway
10 back street, passageway

**alliance**
04 bloc, bond, pact
05 guild, union
06 cartel, league, treaty
07 compact
08 marriage
09 agreement, coalition, syndicate
10 connection, consortium, federation
11 affiliation, association, combination, partnership
12 conglomerate
13 confederation

**allied**
03 wed
05 bound, joint
06 joined, linked, united
07 coupled, kindred, married, related, unified
08 combined, in league
09 connected, in cahoots
10 affiliated, associated, hand in hand
11 amalgamated, hand in glove

**allocate**
04 mete
05 allot, allow
06 assign, budget, divide, ration
07 earmark, mete out
08 dispense, set aside, share out
09 admeasure, apportion, designate, parcel out
10 distribute

**allocation**
03 cut, lot
05 grant, quota, share, stint
06 budget, ration
07 measure, portion
09 allotment, allowance
12 distribution
13 apportionment
14 slice of the cake

**allot**
04 mete
05 allow, grant
06 assign, budget, divide, ration
07 dole out, earmark
08 allocate, dispense, set aside, share out
09 admeasure, apportion, designate
10 distribute

**allotment**
03 cut
05 grant, quota, share, stint
06 ration
07 measure, portion
08 division
09 allowance, partition
10 allocation, percentage
13 apportionment

**all-out**
04 full
05 total
06 utmost
07 maximum
08 complete, powerful, resolute, thorough, vigorous
09 full-scale, intensive, undivided, wholesale
10 determined, exhaustive
12 wholehearted
13 comprehensive, no-holds-barred, thoroughgoing

**allow**
02 OK
03 let, own
04 give, okay
05 admit, agree, allot, grant
06 afford, assign, enable, endure, permit, suffer
07 agree to, approve, concede, consent, provide, warrant
08 allocate, sanction, say yes to, tolerate
09 apportion, authorize, consent to, put up with
11 acknowledge
14 give the go-ahead

❑**allow for**
07 foresee, include
08 consider
10 bear in mind
15 take into account

**allowable**
05 legal, legit, licit
06 lawful
08 all right, approved
10 acceptable, admissible, legitimate
11 justifiable, permissible
12 sanctionable

**allowance**
03 lot
05 grant, quota, share
06 amount, income, ration, rebate
07 annuity, benefit, payment, pension, portion, stipend
08 discount, expenses
09 deduction, reduction, weighting
10 allocation, concession, remittance
11 maintenance
12 contribution

❑**make allowances**
06 excuse, pardon
07 forgive
08 consider
10 bear in mind, keep in mind

**alloy**
05 blend
06 fusion
07 amalgam, mixture
08 compound
09 admixture, composite
11 coalescence, combination

**all right**
02 OK
04 fair, okay, safe, well
05 sound, whole
06 secure, unhurt
07 average, healthy
08 adequate, passable, passably, suitably, unharmed
09 allowable, uninjured
10 acceptable, acceptably, adequately, reasonable, reasonably, unimpaired
12 satisfactory
13 appropriately
14 satisfactorily

**allude**
04 hint
05 imply, refer
06 remark
07 mention, speak of, suggest
08 intimate
09 adumbrate, insinuate, touch upon

**allure**
04 coax, lure
05 charm, tempt
06 appeal, cajole, disarm, entice, glamor, lead on, seduce
07 attract, beguile, enchant, win over
08 entrance, interest, persuade
09 captivate, fascinate, magnetism, seduction
10 attraction, temptation
11 captivation, enchantment, fascination

**alluring**
04 sexy
07 winning
08 arousing, engaging, enticing, fetching, sensuous, tempting
09 beguiling, desirable, seductive

10 attractive, bewitching, come-hither, enchanting
11 captivating

**allusion**
04 hint
06 remark
07 mention
08 citation
09 quotation, reference
10 intimation, suggestion
11 implication, insinuation

**ally**
04 join, link, side
05 marry, unify, unite
06 friend, helper, team up
07 combine, connect, partner
08 co-worker, sidekick
09 affiliate, associate, colleague, supporter
10 accomplice, amalgamate, fraternize, join forces
11 collaborate, confederate
12 band together, collaborator

**almanac**
06 annual
08 calendar, register, yearbook

**almighty**
05 awful, great
06 severe
07 intense, supreme
08 absolute, enormous, terrible
09 desperate
10 invincible, omnipotent
11 all-powerful, plenipotent

**almost**
05 about, quasi-
06 all but, nearly
07 close on, close to, nearing
08 as good as, well-nigh
09 just about, virtually
10 more or less, not far from, pretty much, pretty well
11 approaching, practically
13 approximately

**alone**
04 only, sole, solo
05 apart
06 lonely, single, unique
07 forlorn, unaided
08 deserted, detached, forsaken, isolated, separate, singular, solitary, unpaired
09 abandoned, on your own
12 single-handed
13 unaccompanied

**aloof**
04 cold, cool
06 chilly, formal, offish, remote
07 distant, haughty
08 detached, reserved

10 antisocial, forbidding, unfriendly, unsociable
11 indifferent, standoffish
12 inaccessible, supercilious, uninterested, unresponsive

**aloud**
07 audibly, clearly, noisily
10 distinctly, sonorously
12 intelligibly, resoundingly

**alphabet**

➤ *Names of alphabets:*
03 IPA, ita
04 kana
05 Greek, kanji, Kufic, ogham, Roman, runic
06 Arabic, Hebrew, Nagari, Naskhi, Romaji
07 futhark
08 Cyrillic, Georgian, hiragana, katakana
09 Byzantine, cuneiform
10 Devanagari, pictograph
11 hieroglyphs
13 hieroglyphics

➤ *Letters of the Arabic alphabet:*
02 ba, fa, ha, ra, ta, ya, za
03 ayn, dad, dai, jim, kaf, kha, lam, mim, nun, qaf, sad, sin, tha, waw, zay
04 alif, dhai, shin
05 ghayn

➤ *Letters of the Greek alphabet:*
02 mu, nu, pi, xi
03 chi, eta, phi, psi, rho, tau
04 beta, iota, zeta
05 alpha, delta, gamma, kappa, omega, sigma, theta
06 lambda
07 epsilon, omicron, upsilon

➤ *Letters of the Hebrew alphabet:*
02 he, pe
03 mem, nun, sin, tav, taw, vaw, waw, yod
04 alef, ayin, heth, kaph, koph, qoph, resh, sade, shin, teth, yodh
05 aleph, gimel, sadhe, zayin
06 daleth, lamedh, samekh

➤ *Letters of the U.S. military phonetic alphabet:*
04 Echo, Golf, Kilo, Lima, Mike, Papa, X-ray, Zulu
05 Alpha, Bravo, Delta, Hotel, India, Oscar, Romeo, Tango
06 Juliet, Quebec, Sierra, Victor, Whisky, Yankee
07 Charlie, Foxtrot, Uniform
08 November

**already**
06 so soon
07 even now, just now
08 even then, hitherto
09 before now
10 beforehand, previously

**also**
03 and, too
04 plus
06 as well
07 besides, further
08 as well as, moreover
09 along with, including
10 in addition
11 furthermore

**alter**
04 turn, vary
05 adapt, amend, emend, shift
06 adjust, change, modify, recast, reform, revise
07 convert, remodel, reshape
09 diversify, transform, transmute, transpose
12 metamorphose
13 make different

**alteration**
05 shift
06 change
08 revision, variance
09 amendment, reshaping, variation
10 adaptation, adjustment, conversion, difference, remodeling
11 reformation, vicissitude
12 modification
13 metamorphosis, transmutation, transposition
14 transformation

**altercation**
03 row
05 clash
06 fracas
07 dispute, quarrel, wrangle
08 argument, squabble
09 logomachy
10 dissension
12 disagreement

**alternate**
04 vary
05 alter
06 change, rotate
08 rotating
09 fluctuate, oscillate, take turns
10 every other, substitute
11 consecutive, every second, intersperse, reciprocate
13 take it in turns

**alternative**
05 other
06 backup, choice, fringe, option, second
09 different, selection
10 substitute, unorthodox
14 unconventional

**although**
03 yet
05 while
06 albeit, even if
09 in spite of
11 granted that
15 notwithstanding

**altitude**
06 height
07 stature
09 elevation, loftiness

**altogether**
05 fully, in all, quite
06 in toto, wholly
07 all told, in total, totally, utterly
08 all in all, entirely
09 perfectly
10 absolutely, thoroughly

**altruistic**
06 humane
08 generous, selfless
09 unselfish
10 benevolent, charitable
11 considerate
12 humanitarian
13 disinterested, philanthropic
14 public-spirited

**always**
07 forever
08 evermore
09 endlessly, eternally
10 all the time, constantly, habitually, invariably, repeatedly
11 continually, in perpetuum, perpetually, unceasingly
12 consistently
13 again and again

**amalgam**
05 alloy, blend, union
06 fusion
07 mixture
08 compound
09 admixture, aggregate, synthesis
10 commixture
11 coalescence, combination

**amalgamate**
04 ally, fuse
05 alloy, blend, merge, unite
06 mingle
07 combine
08 coalesce, intermix

**amalgamation**
09 commingle, integrate
10 homogenize, synthesize
11 incorporate

**amalgamation**
05 blend, union, unity
06 fusion, merger
07 joining
08 alliance, compound
09 admixture, synthesis
11 coalescence, combination, commingling, integration
13 incorporation
14 homogenization

**amass**
04 gain, heap, pile
05 hoard, store
06 accrue, garner, gather, heap up, pile up
07 acquire, collect, store up
08 assemble
09 aggregate
10 accumulate, foregather

**amateur**
03 ham
04 buff
06 layman
07 dabbler, fancier
09 lay person
10 dilettante, enthusiast
15 nonprofessional

**amateurish**
03 lay
05 crude, inept
06 clumsy, unpaid
08 inexpert
09 untrained
10 unskillful
11 unqualified
14 unprofessional
15 nonprofessional

**amaze**
03 wow
04 daze, stun
05 floor, shock
06 dismay
07 astound, perplex, stagger, stupefy
08 astonish, bowl over, confound, surprise
09 dumbfound, electrify
10 disconcert, strike dumb
11 flabbergast
12 blow your mind

**amazement**
05 shock
06 dismay, marvel, wonder
08 surprise
09 confusion
10 wonderment
12 astonishment, stupefaction

**ambassador**
05 agent, envoy
06 consul, deputy, legate
08 delegate, diplomat, emissary, minister
14 representative
15 plenipotentiary

**ambience**
03 air
04 aura, feel, mood, tone
05 tenor, vibes
06 milieu, spirit
07 feeling, setting
09 character
10 atmosphere, vibrations

**ambiguity**
05 doubt
06 enigma, puzzle
07 dubiety, paradox
08 polysemy
09 confusion, vagueness
10 woolliness
11 ambivalence, uncertainty
12 equivocality, equivocation
13 double meaning
14 double entendre

**ambiguous**
05 vague
06 woolly
07 cryptic, dubious, unclear
08 confused, doubtful, puzzling, two-edged
09 confusing, enigmatic, equivocal, uncertain
10 backhanded, indefinite
11 double-edged, paradoxical

**ambit**
05 range, scope
06 bounds, extent
07 circuit, compass
08 confines

**ambition**
03 aim
04 goal, hope, push, wish, zeal
05 dream, drive, ideal
06 design, desire, hunger, intent, object, target, thrust
07 craving, longing, purpose
08 striving, yearning
09 eagerness, objective
10 aspiration, get-up-and-go

**ambitious**
04 bold, hard, keen
05 eager, pushy
06 ardent, gung-ho
07 driving, go-ahead, hopeful, zealous
08 aspiring, exacting, full of go
09 demanding, difficult, elaborate
10 formidable, purposeful

11 power-hungry
**ambivalence**
05 clash, doubt
08 conflict, wavering
09 confusion
10 hesitation, opposition
11 fluctuation, uncertainty, vacillation
13 contradiction, inconsistency
14 irresoluteness

**ambivalent**
05 mixed
06 unsure
07 opposed, warring
08 clashing, confused, doubtful, hesitant, wavering
09 debatable, uncertain, undecided, unsettled
10 irresolute, unresolved
11 conflicting, fluctuating, vacillating
12 inconclusive, inconsistent
13 contradictory

**amble**
04 walk
05 drift
06 dawdle, ramble, stroll, toddle, wander
07 meander, saunter
09 promenade
10 mosey along
11 perambulate

**ambush**
04 jump, trap
05 snare
06 attack, turn on, waylay
07 ensnare
08 pounce on, surprise
09 ambuscade, bushwhack, lie in wait, waylaying

**ameliorate**
04 ease, mend
05 amend
06 better, remedy
07 benefit, elevate, enhance, improve, promote, relieve
08 mitigate
09 alleviate

**amenable**
04 open
07 willing
08 flexible
09 agreeable, compliant, tractable
10 responsive, submissive
11 acquiescent, complaisant, persuadable
13 accommodating

**amend**
03 fix

**amendment**

05 alter, emend
06 adjust, better, change, modify, reform, revise
07 correct, enhance, improve, qualify, rectify, redress
08 emendate
10 ameliorate

**amendment**

06 change, reform, remedy
07 adjunct, proviso
08 addendum, revision
10 adjustment, alteration, correction, emendation
11 enhancement
12 modification
13 qualification, rectification

**amends**

07 redress
08 requital
09 atonement, expiation, indemnity
10 recompense, reparation
11 restitution, restoration
12 compensation, satisfaction

**amenity**

07 service, utility
08 facility, resource
09 advantage
11 convenience

**American**

➤ *Names of American Indian peoples*:

03 Fox, Ute
04 Cree, Crow, Hopi, Zuni
05 Creek, Huron, Sioux
06 Apache, Cayuga, Dakota, Lakota, Mohawk, Navaho, Navajo, Nootka, Ojibwa, Ottawa, Pawnee, Pueblo, Quapaw, Seneca
07 Arapaho, Chinook, Choctaw, Mohican, Natchez, Shawnee, Tlingit
08 Cherokee, Cheyenne, Comanche, Iroquois, Seminole, Shoshone
09 Algonkian, Blackfoot, Chickasaw, Tuscarora
10 Algonquian, Athabascan, Athabaskan, Athapascan

➤ *Names of some American Indians*:

07 Cochise, Osceola, Pontiac, Sequoya
08 Geronimo, Hiawatha, Powhatan, Tecumseh
09 Massasoit, Sacajawea
10 Crazy Horse, Little Crow, Pocahontas
11 Chief Joseph, Sitting Bull

**amiable**

04 kind, warm
06 genial
07 affable, likable
08 friendly, obliging, pleasant, sociable
09 agreeable, congenial
11 good-natured

**amicable**

05 civil
07 cordial
08 friendly, peaceful
09 civilized
10 harmonious
11 good-natured

**amid**

05 among, midst
06 amidst
07 amongst
12 in the midst of, in the thick of

**amino acid**

➤ *Types of amino acid*:

04 dopa
06 lysine, serine, valine
07 alanine, cystine, glycine, leucine, proline
08 cysteine, tyrosine
09 glutamine, histidine
10 tryptophan
12 aspartic acid
13 phenylalanine
➤ See also ACID

**amiss**

04 awry
05 false, wrong
06 faulty, flawed
08 improper, untoward
09 defective, imperfect
10 inaccurate, out of order
11 out of kilter

**amity**

05 peace
06 accord, comity
07 concord, harmony
08 goodwill, kindness
10 cordiality, fellowship, fraternity, friendship
12 friendliness, peacefulness
13 brotherliness, understanding

**ammunition**

04 mine, shot
05 bombs, slugs
06 shells
07 bullets, rockets
08 grenades, missiles
09 gunpowder
10 cartridges
12 hand grenades

**amnesty**

05 mercy
06 pardon
08 immunity, lenience, reprieve
09 remission
10 absolution, indulgence
11 forgiveness
12 dispensation

**amok**

05 crazy, madly
06 wildly
07 berserk
08 frenzied, insanely

**among**

04 amid, with
05 midst
06 amidst
07 amongst, between
12 in the midst of, in the thick of, surrounded by
13 in the middle of

**amorous**

06 erotic, in love, loving, tender
07 amatory, lustful
08 lovesick
10 passionate
11 impassioned

**amorphous**

05 vague
08 formless, inchoate, nebulous
09 irregular, shapeless, undefined
10 indistinct
11 featureless

**amount**

03 lot, sum
04 bulk, mass
05 quota, total, whole
06 extent, number, volume
07 expanse, measure
08 entirety, quantity, sum total
09 aggregate, magnitude

❑**amount to**

04 make, mean
05 equal, total
07 add up to
09 aggregate
10 boil down to, come down to
12 correspond to

**amphibian**

➤ *Types of amphibian*:

03 eft, olm
04 frog, newt, toad
07 axolotl, tadpole
08 bullfrog, polliwog, tree frog, tree toad
09 caecilian, conger eel
10 hellbender, horned toad, natterjack, salamander

## ample
11 Surinam toad
➤ See also ANIMAL

## ample
03 big
04 full, wide
05 broad, great, large
06 enough, plenty
07 copious, profuse
08 abundant, generous
09 expansive, extensive, plentiful
10 commodious, sufficient
11 substantial
12 considerable, unrestricted
14 more than enough

## amplify
05 add to, boost, raise, widen
06 deepen, expand, extend
07 augment, broaden, bulk out, develop, enhance, fill out
08 flesh out, heighten, increase
09 enlarge on, intensify
10 make louder, strengthen
13 go into details

## amplitude
04 bulk, mass
05 width
06 extent, volume
07 expanse
08 capacity, fullness, vastness
09 greatness, magnitude, plenitude, profusion

## amputate
03 lop
04 dock
05 sever
06 cut off, remove
07 chop off, curtail
08 dissever, separate, truncate

## amulet
04 juju
05 charm
06 fetish
07 periapt
08 gris-gris, pentacle, talisman
10 lucky charm, phylactery

## amuse
05 charm, cheer, crack, relax
06 divert, occupy, please, regale, tickle
07 cheer up, delight, disport, engross, gladden
08 distract, enthrall, interest, recreate
09 entertain, make laugh

## amusement
03 fun
04 game
05 hobby, mirth, sport
07 delight, pastime

08 hilarity, interest, pleasure
09 diversion, merriment
10 recreation
11 distraction
13 entertainment

## amusing
05 droll, funny, jolly, witty
07 comical, jocular, waggish
08 charming, humorous
09 enjoyable, facetious, hilarious, laughable
12 entertaining

## analogous
04 akin, like
07 kindred, similar
08 agreeing, matching, parallel
10 comparable, equivalent
11 correlative
13 corresponding

## analogy
06 simile
08 likeness, metaphor, parallel
09 agreement, semblance
10 comparison, similarity
11 correlation, equivalence, resemblance
14 correspondence

## analyze
04 sift, test
05 assay, judge, study
06 divide, reduce, review
07 dissect, examine, inquire
08 consider, evaluate, separate
09 anatomize, interpret
10 scrutinize
11 investigate

## analysis
04 test
05 assay, check, study
06 review
07 inquiry, opinion, sifting
08 division, judgment, scrutiny
09 breakdown, reasoning, reduction
10 dissection, evaluation, exposition, inspection, resolution, separation
11 examination, explanation, explication
13 anatomization, investigation
14 interpretation

## analytical
07 in-depth, logical
08 critical, detailed, rational
09 inquiring, searching
10 diagnostic, dissecting, methodical, systematic
11 explanatory, inquisitive, questioning
13 investigative
14 interpretative

## anarchic
07 chaotic, lawless, riotous
08 confused, mutinous, nihilist
10 anarchical, disordered, ungoverned
11 anarchistic, libertarian
12 disorganized
13 revolutionary

## anarchist
05 rebel
08 nihilist
09 insurgent, terrorist
11 libertarian
13 revolutionary

## anarchy
04 riot
05 chaos
06 mutiny, unrule
07 misrule
08 disorder
09 confusion, rebellion
10 revolution
11 lawlessness, pandemonium
12 insurrection

## anathema
04 bane
05 curse, taboo
07 bugbear
08 aversion
09 bête noire
10 abhorrence
11 abomination
12 proscription

## anatomy
05 build, frame
06 makeup
07 zootomy
09 framework, structure

▶ *Anatomical terms*:
04 bone, hock, womb
05 aural, elbow, groin, helix, nasal, pedal, renal, spine, uvula, vulva
06 biceps, dental, dorsal, gullet, larynx, lumbar, muscle, neural, ocular, tendon, uterus
07 cardiac, gastric, jugular, mammary, optical, triceps
08 cerebral, duodenal, foreskin, ligament, pectoral, voice box, windpipe
09 cartilage, diaphragm, epidermis, esophagus, funny bone, hamstring, pulmonary
10 epiglottis
14 Fallopian tubes

▶ *Names of anatomists*:
04 **Baer** (Karl Ernst von), **Bell** (Charles)
05 **Monro** (Alexander)

06 **Adrian** (Edgar Douglas),
   **Cuvier** (Georges, **Harvey**
   (William), **Stubbs** (George),
   **Warren** (John), **Wistar**
   (Caspar)
07 **Galvani** (Luigi)
08 **Alcmaeon, Malpighi**
   (Marcello), **Vesalius**
   (Andreas)
09 **Bartholin** (Caspar),
   **Fallopius** (Gabriel)
10 **Herophilus**
➢ See also SCIENTIST

**ancestor**
08 forebear
09 precursor
10 antecedent, forefather,
   forerunner, progenitor
11 predecessor
12 primogenitor

**ancestral**
06 lineal
07 genetic
08 familial, parental
10 hereditary
12 genealogical

**ancestry**
04 line, race
05 blood, roots, stock
06 family, origin
07 descent, lineage
08 heredity, heritage, pedigree
09 ancestors, forebears,
   genealogy, parentage
10 extraction, family tree
11 forefathers, progenitors

**anchor**
03 fix
04 moor
05 affix, berth, tie up
06 attach, fasten
08 make fast

▶ *Types of anchor:*
03 car, sea
04 navy
05 kedge
06 drogue
07 grapnel, killick
08 mushroom

**ancient**
03 old
04 aged
05 early, olden, passé
06 age-old
07 antique, archaic
08 outmoded, primeval,
   pristine, time-worn
09 atavistic, out-of-date
10 antiquated, fossilized,
   primordial

11 prehistoric
12 antediluvian, old-fashioned
13 superannuated
15 as old as the hills

**ancillary**
05 extra
07 helping
08 adjuvant
09 auxiliary, secondary
10 subsidiary, supporting
11 subordinate

**and**
03 too
04 also, plus, then
06 as well
07 besides
08 as well as, moreover
09 including, what's more
10 in addition
11 furthermore

**anecdote**
04 tale, yarn
05 story
06 sketch
12 reminiscence

**anemic**
03 wan
04 pale, weak
05 ashen, frail, livid, pasty
06 pallid, sallow, sickly
07 insipid
09 bloodless, wheyfaced

**anesthetic**
06 opiate
07 anodyne
08 epidural, narcotic, sedative
09 analgesic, soporific
10 painkiller, palliative

**anesthetize**
04 dope, drug, dull, numb
06 deaden
07 stupefy
11 desensitize

**anew**
05 again
06 afresh
08 once more
09 once again

**angel**
03 gem
05 ideal, power, saint
07 darling, paragon
08 treasure
12 principality
13 heavenly being
15 divine messenger

▶ *Orders of angel:*
05 angel, power
06 cherub, seraph, throne,

   virtue
08 dominion
09 archangel
10 domination
12 principality
➢ See also RELIGION

**angelic**
04 holy, pure
05 pious
06 divine, lovely
07 saintly
08 cherubic, empyreal,
   empyrean, ethereal,
   heavenly, innocent, seraphic
09 beautiful, celestial

**anger**
03 ire, irk, vex
04 fume, fury, gall, miff, rage,
   rant, rile
05 annoy, pique, wrath
06 enrage, madden, needle,
   nettle, offend, rancor, ruffle,
   temper
07 chagrin, dudgeon, incense,
   outrage, provoke
08 irritate, paroxysm, vexation
09 aggravate, infuriate
10 antagonism, antagonize,
   bitterness, conniption,
   exasperate, resentment
11 displeasure, indignation
12 exasperation, irritability

**angle**
04 bend, edge, face, hook,
   knee, nook, side, turn
05 elbow, facet, point, slant
06 aspect, corner, direct
07 flexure, outlook
08 approach, gradient, position
09 direction, viewpoint
10 projection, standpoint
11 perspective, point of view
12 intersection

❏ **angle for**
03 aim
04 seek
11 make a bid for

**angry**
03 hot, mad
05 cross, irate, livid
06 bitter, heated, raging
07 annoyed, enraged, furious,
   peevish
08 choleric, incensed, outraged,
   seething, up in arms,
   wrathful
09 indignant, irritated,
   rancorous, resentful, seeing
   red, splenetic
10 aggravated, displeased,
   hopping mad, infuriated

11 disgruntled, exasperated
12 on the warpath

**anguish**
03 woe
04 pain, pang, rack
05 agony, dolor, grief
06 misery, sorrow
07 anxiety, torment, torture
08 distress
09 heartache, suffering
10 desolation, heartbreak

**anguished**
08 dolorous, stricken, tortured
09 afflicted, miserable,
    suffering, tormented
10 distressed

**angular**
04 bony, lank, lean, thin
05 gaunt, gawky, lanky, spare
06 skinny
07 scrawny
08 rawboned

**animal**
04 wild
05 beast, brute, swine
06 bodily, carnal, savage
07 bestial, brutish, fleshly,
    inhuman, monster, sensual
08 creature, physical
➤ See also AMPHIBIAN; APE;
    BEETLE; BIRD; BUTTERFLY;
    CAT; CATTLE; CHICKEN;
    CRUSTACEAN; DINOSAUR;
    DOG; DUCK; FISH; INSECT;
    INVERTEBRATE; LIZARD;
    MAMMAL; MARSUPIAL;
    MOLLUSK; MONKEY; MOTH;
    PIG; REPTILE; RODENT;
    SHARK; SHEEP; SNAKE;
    SPIDER; WHALE; WORM

➤ *Female animals*:
03 cow, dam, doe, ewe, hen,
    pen, sow
04 duck, hind, mare
05 bitch, goose, jenny, nanny,
    queen, vixen
06 peahen
07 lioness, tigress
10 leopardess

➤ *Male animals*:
03 cob, dog, ram, tom
04 boar, buck, bull, cock, hart,
    jack, stag
05 billy, drake
06 gander
07 bullock, peacock, rooster
08 stallion

➤ *Young animals*:
03 cub, fry, kid, kit, pup

04 brit, calf, colt, eyas, fawn,
    foal, joey, lamb, parr
05 bunny, chick, elver, owlet,
    poult, puppy, smolt, squab,
    whelp
06 cygnet, eaglet, grilse, heifer,
    kitten, lionet, piglet
07 gosling, leveret, tadpole
08 duckling, nestling
09 fledgling

**animate**
04 fire, goad, live, move, spur,
    stir, urge
05 alive, impel, rouse, spark
06 arouse, excite, incite, kindle,
    living, revive, vivify
07 enliven, inspire, quicken
08 activate, embolden,
    energize, inspirit, vitalize
09 breathing, conscious,
    instigate, stimulate
10 invigorate, reactivate

**animated**
05 alive, eager, quick, vital
06 active, ardent, lively
07 buoyant, excited, fervent,
    glowing, radiant, vibrant
08 spirited, spritely, vehement
09 ebullient, sprightly
10 passionate
11 full of beans, impassioned
12 enthusiastic

**animation**
03 pep
04 life, zeal, zest, zing
05 verve, vigor
06 action, energy, fervor,
    spirit
07 passion, sparkle
08 activity, vibrancy, vitality
10 ebullience, enthusiasm,
    excitement, liveliness
11 high spirits

**animosity**
04 feud, hate
05 odium, spite
06 animus, enmity, malice,
    rancor
07 ill will
08 acrimony, loathing
09 hostility, malignity
10 antagonism, bitterness, ill
    feeling, resentment

**annals**
07 history, memoirs, records
08 archives, journals
09 registers
10 chronicles

**annex**
03 add
04 join, wing

05 affix, seize, unite, usurp
06 adjoin, append, attach,
    fasten, occupy
07 acquire, connect, conquer
08 arrogate, take over,
    addition
09 expansion, extension
10 attachment, supplement
11 appropriate, incorporate

**annexation**
07 seizure
08 conquest, takeover,
    usurping
10 arrogation, occupation
11 acquisition
13 appropriation

**annihilate**
04 raze, rout, slay
05 erase
06 defeat, murder, rub out
07 abolish, conquer, destroy,
    trounce, wipe out
09 eliminate, eradicate
10 extinguish, obliterate
11 assassinate, exterminate

**annihilation**
06 defeat, murder
07 erasure
09 abolition
10 extinction
11 destruction, elimination,
    eradication
12 obliteration
13 assassination, extermination

**anniversary**

➤ *Names of wedding
anniversaries*:
03 tin
04 gold, iron, jade, lace, ruby,
    silk, wood, wool
05 china, coral, glass, ivory,
    linen, paper, pearl, steel
06 bronze, copper, cotton,
    silver
07 crystal, diamond, emerald,
    leather, pottery
08 aluminum, platinum,
    sapphire

**annotate**
04 note
05 gloss
07 comment, explain
09 elucidate, explicate, interpret

**annotation**
04 note
05 gloss
07 comment
08 exegesis, footnote
10 commentary

**announce**
11 elucidation, explanation, explication

**announce**
05 state
06 blazon, notify, report, reveal
07 declare, divulge, publish
08 disclose, proclaim, propound
09 advertise, broadcast, make known, preconize, publicize
10 make public, promulgate

**announcement**
06 report
07 message
08 bulletin, dispatch
09 broadcast, publicity, reporting, statement
10 communiqué, disclosure, divulgence, revelation
11 declaration, publication
12 notification, proclamation

**announcer**
02 MC
04 host
05 emcee
06 herald
07 compère
09 anchorman, messenger, town crier
10 newscaster
11 anchorwoman, broadcaster, commentator

**annoy**
03 bug, irk, nag, vex
04 gall, rile
05 anger, grate, tease
06 badger, bother, harass, hassle, madden, molest, pester, plague, ruffle
07 bedevil, disturb, hack off, provoke, trouble
08 irritate
09 aggravate, displease, drive nuts
10 drive crazy, exasperate
11 drive insane, get your goat
13 get your back up, put your back up
14 drive up the wall, rub the wrong way
15 get on your nerves

**annoyance**
04 bind, bore, drag, pain, pest
05 anger, tease
06 bother
07 trouble
08 headache, irritant, nuisance, vexation
10 harassment, irritation
11 aggravation
13 pain in the neck

**annoyed**
05 angry, cross, upset, vexed
06 bugged, miffed, peeved, piqued
07 hassled, in a huff
08 harassed, provoked
09 disturbed, hacked off, indignant, irritated
11 exasperated

**annoying**
05 pesky
06 trying
07 galling, irksome, teasing
08 tiresome
09 harassing, intrusive, maddening, provoking, unwelcome, vexatious
10 bothersome, irritating
11 aggravating, troublesome
12 exasperating

**annual**
06 yearly
07 almanac
08 calendar, register, yearbook

**annul**
04 void
06 cancel, negate, recall, repeal, revoke
07 abolish, nullify, rescind, retract, reverse, suspend
08 abrogate
10 invalidate
11 countermand

**annulment**
06 recall, repeal
07 reverse, voiding
08 negation, quashing
09 abolition
10 abrogation, rescission, revocation, suspension
11 countermand, rescindment
12 cancellation, invalidation
13 nullification

**anodyne**
05 bland
07 neutral
09 deadening
11 inoffensive

**anoint**
03 oil, rub
04 daub
05 bless, smear
06 grease, ordain
08 apply oil, dedicate, sanctify
09 embrocate, lubricate
10 consecrate

**anomalous**
03 odd
04 rare
05 freak
07 deviant, unusual
08 abnormal, atypical, freakish, peculiar, singular
09 eccentric, irregular
11 exceptional, incongruous
12 inconsistent

**anomaly**
05 freak
06 misfit, oddity, rarity
09 deviation, exception
10 aberration, divergence
11 abnormality, incongruity, peculiarity
12 eccentricity, irregularity
13 inconsistency

**anonymous**
07 unknown, unnamed
08 faceless, nameless, unsigned
09 incognito
10 impersonal, innominate
11 nondescript, unspecified
12 unidentified

**another**
04 more
05 added, extra, other, spare
06 second
07 further, variant
09 different
10 additional, not the same
11 alternative

**answer**
03 fit, key
04 fill, meet, pass, suit
05 agree, react, reply, serve
06 refute, result, retort
07 fulfill, respond, riposte, satisfy
08 comeback, reaction, rebuttal, response, solution
09 get back to, rejoinder, retaliate, write back
10 come back to, resolution
11 acknowledge, explanation, retaliation
14 acknowledgment

❏**answer back**
04 sass
05 argue, rebut
06 retort
07 dispute, riposte
08 disagree, talk back
09 retaliate
10 be cheeky to, contradict

**answerable**
06 liable
07 to blame
10 chargeable
11 accountable, blameworthy, responsible

**antagonism**
06 enmity
07 discord, ill will, rivalry
08 conflict, friction
09 animosity, antipathy, hostility
10 contention, dissension, ill feeling, opposition

**antagonist**
03 foe
05 enemy, rival
08 opponent
09 adversary, contender
10 competitor, contestant

**antagonistic**
06 averse
07 adverse, hostile, opposed
10 at variance, unfriendly
11 belligerent, conflicting, contentious, ill-disposed
12 incompatible

**antagonize**
05 anger, annoy, repel
06 insult, offend
07 incense, provoke
08 alienate, embitter, estrange
09 disaffect

**antecedent**
09 ancestors, forebears, precedent, precursor
10 extraction, forerunner
11 forefathers

**anthem**
04 hymn, song
05 chant, paean, psalm
07 chorale
08 canticle
12 song of praise

**anthology**
06 digest
08 treasury
09 selection
10 collection, compendium, miscellany
11 compilation

**anthropologist**

► *Names of anthropologists:*
04 **Buck** (Peter Henry), **Mead** (Margaret)
05 **Tylor** (Edward Burnett)
06 **Frazer** (James George)
07 **Chapple** (Eliot)
09 **Heyerdahl** (Thor)
10 **Malinowski** (Bronislaw)
11 **Lévi-Strauss** (Claude)
➤ See also SCIENTIST

**anticipate**
05 await
06 bank on, expect

07 count on, foresee, hope for, obviate, predict, preempt
08 figure on, forecast, preclude, reckon on
09 forestall, intercept, visualize
10 prepare for

**anticipation**
04 hope
10 excitement, expectancy, prediction
11 bated breath, expectation

**anticlimax**
06 bathos, bummer, fiasco
07 letdown
08 comedown, nonevent
14 disappointment

**antics**
06 capers, pranks, stunts
07 foolery, frolics
08 clowning, mischief
09 horseplay, silliness
10 skylarking, tomfoolery
12 monkeyshines

**antidote**
04 cure
05 serum
06 remedy
07 theriac
09 antitoxin, antivenin
10 corrective, mithridate
12 counter-agent

**antipathy**
04 hate
05 odium
06 animus, enmity, hatred
07 disgust, dislike, ill will
08 aversion, bad blood, distaste, loathing
09 animosity, hostility, repulsion
10 abhorrence, antagonism
15 incompatibility

**antiquated**
05 dated, passé
06 bygone, démodé, old hat
07 ancient, archaic, outworn
08 obsolete, outdated, outmoded
09 out-of-date
12 antediluvian, old-fashioned
13 anachronistic

**antique**
03 old
05 curio, relic
06 bygone, quaint, rarity
07 ancient, archaic, veteran, vintage
08 heirloom, outdated
09 antiquity, curiosity
11 museum piece, period piece
12 old-fashioned

**antiquity**
03 age
06 old age
07· oldness
08 agedness
09 olden days
11 distant past
12 ancient times
14 time immemorial

**antiseptic**
04 pure
05 clean
07 aseptic, sterile
08 cleanser, germ-free, hygienic, purifier, sanitary
09 germicide, sanitized
10 sterilized, unpolluted
12 disinfectant
14 uncontaminated

**antisocial**
07 asocial, hostile, lawless
08 anarchic, reserved, retiring
09 alienated, withdrawn
10 disorderly, disruptive, rebellious, unfriendly
11 belligerent
12 antagonistic, misanthropic

**antithesis**
07 reverse
08 contrast, converse, opposite, reversal
12 other extreme
13 contradiction
15 opposite extreme

**anxiety**
04 care
05 dread, worry
06 strain, stress
07 anguish, concern, tension
08 disquiet, distress, suspense
09 misgiving, worriment
10 foreboding, uneasiness
11 disquietude, fretfulness, nervousness
12 apprehension, restlessness

**anxious**
04 keen, taut
05 eager, tense
06 afraid, uneasy
07 fearful, fretful, in a stew, longing, nervous, worried
08 restless, troubled
09 concerned, disturbed, expectant, impatient
10 distressed, solicitous
11 overwrought
12 apprehensive, enthusiastic
13 on tenterhooks

**apace**
04 fast
07 quickly, rapidly, swiftly

**apart**

08 speedily
10 at top speed, double-time
11 at full speed, double-quick

**apart**
04 afar, away
05 alone, aloof, aside
06 cut off, in bits, singly, to bits
07 distant
08 distinct, divorced, excluded, in pieces, isolated, separate
09 on your own, privately, separated, to one side
10 by yourself, separately

□**apart from**
06 but for, except
08 excepted
09 except for, excluding
11 not counting

**apathetic**
04 cold, cool, numb
05 blasé
07 passive, unmoved
08 listless, lukewarm
09 impassive, lethargic, unfeeling
10 uninvolved
11 emotionless, halfhearted, indifferent, unambitious, unconcerned, unemotional
12 uninterested, unresponsive

**apathy**
06 acedia, torpor
07 accidie, inertia, languor
08 coldness, coolness, lethargy
09 passivity, unconcern
11 impassivity
12 indifference, listlessness, sluggishness

**ape**
04 copy, echo, mock
05 mimic
06 affect, mirror, monkey, parody, parrot, simian
07 imitate, take off
10 caricature

► *Types of apes*:
06 gibbon
07 gorilla
09 orangutan
10 chimpanzee
11 orangoutang
➤ See also ANIMAL

**aperture**
03 eye, gap
04 hole, rent, slit, slot, vent
05 chink, cleft, mouth, space
06 breach
07 fissure, foramen, opening, orifice, passage
10 interstice

**apex**
03 tip, top
04 acme, peak
05 crest, crown, point
06 apogee, climax, height, summit, vertex, zenith
08 pinnacle
09 fastigium, high point
11 culmination
13 crowning point

**aphorism**
03 saw
05 adage, axiom, gnome, maxim
06 dictum, saying
07 epigram, precept, proverb
08 apothegm
09 witticism

**aphrodisiac**
06 erotic
07 amative, amatory
08 venerous
09 erogenous, stimulant
10 love potion
11 erotogenous

**aplomb**
05 poise
07 balance
08 audacity, calmness, coolness
09 assurance, composure, sang-froid
10 confidence, equanimity
11 savoir-faire
13 self-assurance
14 self-confidence

**apocryphal**
08 doubtful, mythical, spurious
09 concocted, equivocal, imaginary, legendary
10 fabricated, fictitious, unverified
11 unsupported
12 questionable

**apologetic**
05 sorry
06 rueful
08 contrite, penitent
09 regretful, repentant
10 remorseful

**apologize**
05 plead
06 regret
07 confess, explain, justify
08 say sorry
09 ask pardon
11 acknowledge
12 eat humble pie, eat your words
14 ask forgiveness

**apology**
04 plea
06 excuse
07 defense, regrets
10 confession, palliation
11 explanation, vindication
13 justification
14 acknowledgment

**apostasy**
06 heresy
07 perfidy
09 defection, desertion, falseness, recreance, recreancy, treachery
10 disloyalty, recidivism, renegation
12 renunciation

**apostate**
07 heretic, traitor
08 defector, deserter, recreant, renegade, turncoat
10 recidivist
13 tergiversator

**apostle**
07 pioneer
08 advocate, champion, crusader, disciple, reformer
09 proponent, supporter
10 evangelist, missionary
12 proselytizer

**appall**
05 alarm, daunt, scare, shock
06 dismay
07 disgust, horrify, outrage, terrify, unnerve
08 frighten
10 disconcert, intimidate

**appalling**
04 dire, grim
05 awful
06 horrid
07 ghastly, hideous
08 alarming, daunting, dreadful, horrible, horrific, shocking, terrible
09 atrocious, frightful, harrowing, loathsome
10 disgusting, horrifying, outrageous, terrifying
11 frightening, nightmarish
12 intimidating

**apparatus**
04 gear
05 means, setup, tools
06 device, gadget, outfit, system, tackle
07 machine, network
09 appliance, equipment, machinery, materials
10 implements
11 contraption

**apparel**
04 garb
05 dress
06 outfit
07 clothes, costume
08 clothing, garments, wardrobe

**apparent**
04 open
05 clear, plain
06 marked, patent
07 evident, obvious, outward, seeming, visible
08 declared, distinct, manifest
10 noticeable, ostensible
11 conspicuous, perceptible, superficial

**apparently**
07 clearly, plainly
08 patently
09 obviously, outwardly, reputedly, seemingly
10 manifestly, ostensibly
13 on the face of it, superficially

**apparition**
05 ghost, spook
06 spirit, vision
07 chimera, phantom, specter
08 presence, visitant
13 manifestation
15 materialization

**appeal**
03 ask, beg, sue
04 draw, lure, plea, pray, suit
05 apply, charm, claim, plead
06 allure, beauty, engage, entice, invite, invoke, orison, please, prayer
07 beseech, entreat, implore, request, retrial, solicit
08 call upon, charisma, entreaty, interest, petition
09 fascinate, magnetism
10 adjuration, attraction, invocation, supplicate
11 application, enchantment, fascination
12 solicitation, supplication

**appear**
03 act
04 look, loom, play, seem, show
05 arise, enter, occur, pop up
06 arrive, attend, crop up, emerge, show up, turn up
07 come out, develop, perform, surface, turn out
10 be a guest in
11 come to light, materialize, show signs of
12 come into view

**appearance**
03 air
04 face, form, look, mien, show
05 début, front, guise, image
06 advent, aspect, façade, figure, manner, visage
07 arrival, bearing
08 demeanor, illusion, presence, pretense
09 semblance
10 attendance, complexion, expression, impression

**appease**
06 pacify
07 placate, satisfy
08 mitigate
09 reconcile
10 conciliate, propitiate
13 make peace with

**appellation**
04 name
05 title
07 epithet
09 sobriquet
11 description, designation

**append**
03 add
04 join
05 affix, annex
06 adjoin, attach, fasten
07 conjoin, subjoin

**appendage**
04 tail
07 adjunct
08 addendum, addition, appendix
09 tailpiece
10 supplement

**appendix**
05 rider
07 adjunct, codicil
08 addendum, addition, epilogue
09 appendage
10 postscript, supplement

**appetite**
04 lust, zeal, zest
06 desire, hunger, relish, thirst
07 longing, passion, stomach
09 eagerness
11 inclination

**appetizing**
05 tasty
06 savory
07 piquant
08 inviting, tempting
09 appealing, delicious, palatable, succulent
11 scrumptious
13 mouthwatering

**applaud**
04 clap, laud
05 cheer
06 extoll, praise
07 acclaim, approve, commend
08 eulogize
12 congratulate
14 give a big hand to

**applause**
06 bravos, cheers, praise
07 acclaim, ovation
08 a big hand, accolade, cheering, clapping
11 acclamation
12 commendation
14 congratulation
15 standing ovation

**appliance**
04 tool
06 device, gadget
07 machine
09 apparatus, implement
10 instrument
11 contraption, contrivance

**applicable**
03 apt, fit
06 proper, suited, useful
07 fitting
08 apposite, relevant, suitable
09 pertinent
10 legitimate
11 appropriate

**applicant**
06 suitor
08 aspirant, claimant, inquirer
09 candidate, postulant
10 petitioner
11 interviewee

**application**
03 use
04 suit
05 claim, value
06 appeal, demand, effort
07 aptness, bearing, inquiry, purpose, request
08 function, hard work, industry, keenness, petition
09 assiduity, diligence, relevance
10 commitment, dedication, pertinence
11 germaneness
12 perseverance, sedulousness, significance

**apply**
03 fit, ply, rub, sue, use
04 give, suit
05 claim, exert, lay on, paint, put on, refer, smear, study

**appoint**
06 anoint, appeal, ask for, devote, direct, draw on, employ, engage, relate
07 address, execute, harness, inquire, pertain, request, solicit, utilize
08 dedicate, exercise, petition, practice, put in for, resort to, spread on, work hard
09 appertain, implement, persevere
10 administer, be relevant, buckle down, settle down
11 bring to bear, concentrate, requisition, write off for

**appoint**
03 fix, set
04 hire, name, pick
05 allot, co-opt, elect
06 assign, choose, decide, direct, employ, engage, ordain, select, settle, take on
07 arrange, command, destine, install, recruit
08 delegate, nominate
09 designate, establish
10 commission

**appointed**
03 set
05 fixed
06 chosen
07 decided, decreed, settled
08 allotted, arranged, assigned, destined, ordained
10 designated, determined
11 established, preordained

**appointment**
03 job
04 date, post
05 place, tryst
06 choice, naming, office
07 meeting
08 choosing, election, position
10 delegation, engagement, nomination, rendezvous
11 arrangement, assignation
12 consultation
13 commissioning

**apportion**
04 deal, mete
05 allot, grant, share
06 assign, divide, ration
07 deal out, dole out, hand out, mete out
08 allocate, dispense, share out
09 admeasure, ration out
10 distribute, measure out

**apportionment**
05 grant, share
06 ration
07 dealing, handout

08 division
09 allotment, rationing
10 allocation, assignment
12 dispensation, distribution

**apposite**
03 apt
06 suited
07 apropos, germane
08 relevant, suitable
09 befitting, pertinent
10 applicable, to the point
11 appropriate

**appraisal**
05 assay
06 rating, review, survey
07 opinion
08 estimate, once-over
09 going-over, reckoning, valuation
10 assessment, estimation, evaluation, inspection
11 examination

**appraise**
04 rate
05 assay, judge, sum up, value
06 assess, size up, survey
07 examine, inspect
08 estimate, evaluate

**appreciable**
08 definite
10 noticeable
11 discernible, perceptible, significant, substantial
12 considerable, recognizable

**appreciate**
03 see
04 go up, grow, know, like, rise
05 enjoy, grasp, savor, thank, value
06 admire, esteem, regard, relish
07 cherish, enhance, improve, inflate, realize
08 increase, perceive, treasure
09 be aware of, recognize
10 comprehend, understand

**appreciation**
04 gain, rise
06 esteem, growth, liking, praise, regard, relish
07 respect, valuing
08 analysis, critique, increase, judgment
09 awareness, enjoyment, gratitude, inflation, knowledge, valuation
10 admiration, assessment, cognizance, escalation, evaluation

11 enhancement, improvement, realization, recognition, sensitivity
12 gratefulness, indebtedness, thankfulness

**appreciative**
07 mindful, obliged, pleased
08 admiring, beholden, grateful, indebted, thankful
09 conscious, sensitive
10 perceptive, respectful, responsive
11 encouraging
12 enthusiastic
13 knowledgeable

**apprehend**
03 nab, see
04 bust, grab, twig
05 catch, grasp, run in, seize
06 arrest, collar, detain
07 capture, realize
08 conceive, perceive
09 recognize, visualize
10 comprehend, understand

**apprehension**
04 fear
05 alarm, doubt, dread, qualm, worry
06 arrest, taking
07 anxiety, capture, seizure
08 disquiet, mistrust
09 misgiving, suspicion
10 foreboding, perception, the jitters, the willies, uneasiness
11 butterflies, nervousness, realization, trepidation
12 perturbation

**apprehensive**
06 afraid, uneasy
07 alarmed, anxious, fearful, nervous, worried
08 bothered, doubtful
09 concerned
10 suspicious
11 distrustful, mistrustful

**apprentice**
04 tiro, tyro
05 pupil
06 novice, rookie
07 learner, recruit, starter, student, trainee
08 beginner, newcomer
11 probationer

**apprise**
04 tell, warn
05 brief
06 advise, inform, notify, tip off
08 acquaint, intimate
09 enlighten

## approach
04 meet, near, plea, road
05 begin, drive, greet, means, reach, style, treat
06 accost, arrive, avenue, broach, invite, manner, method, system, tackle
07 address, advance, arrival, catch up, contact, mention, request, speak to, tactics
08 commence, deal with, draw near, driveway, entrance, overture, proposal, sound out, strategy
09 overtures, procedure, technique, threshold
10 come closer, come near to, come nearer, move toward
11 application, approximate, come close to, get closer to, proposition
13 modus operandi
14 course of action

## approachable
04 open, warm
07 affable
08 friendly, informal, sociable
09 agreeable, congenial, getatable, reachable
10 accessible, attainable

## appropriate
03 apt, fit
04 meet, take
05 filch, pinch, right, seize, steal, swipe, usurp
06 pilfer, pocket, proper, seemly, thieve, timely
07 apropos, correct, fitting, germane, impound, purloin
08 accepted, arrogate, becoming, embezzle, peculate, relevant, suitable
09 befitting, opportune, pertinent, well-timed
10 applicable, commandeer, confiscate, felicitous
11 appurtenant, expropriate, make off with, requisition

## approval
02 OK
03 nod
04 okay, wink
05 favor, honor, leave
06 assent, esteem, liking, praise, regard
07 consent, go-ahead, license, mandate, respect, support
08 applause, blessing, sanction, thumbs up
09 agreement
10 green light, imprimatur, permission, validation

## approve
02 OK
03 buy
04 back, like, okay, pass
05 adopt, allow, bless, carry, favor
06 accept, admire, concur, esteem, permit, praise, ratify, second
07 acclaim, agree to, applaud, commend, confirm, endorse, mandate, support
08 sanction, validate
09 authorize, consent to
10 appreciate
11 countenance, rubber-stamp, think well of
12 give the nod to

## approved
06 proper
07 correct
08 accepted, official, orthodox
09 permitted, preferred
10 authorized, recognized, sanctioned
11 permissible, recommended

## approximate
04 like, near
05 close, loose, rough
07 guessed, inexact, similar, verge on
08 approach, ballpark, border on, relative, resemble
09 estimated

## approximately
05 about, circa
06 around, nearly
07 close to, loosely, roughly
09 just about, not far off
10 give or take, more or less, round about
11 approaching, around about
13 in the region of, or thereabouts, something like
15 in the vicinity of

## approximation
05 guess
08 estimate, likeness
09 rough idea, semblance
10 conjecture
11 guesstimate, resemblance
14 ballpark figure

## apropos
02 re
03 apt
05 right
06 proper, seemly, timely

11 concurrence, endorsement, good opinion, rubber stamp
12 confirmation, ratification
13 authorization, certification

07 correct, fitting
08 accepted, becoming, relevant, suitable
09 befitting, opportune, pertinent, regarding
10 applicable, felicitous, respecting, seasonable, to the point, well-chosen
11 in respect of
12 in relation to, with regard to

## apt
03 fit
05 given, prone, ready
06 liable, likely, proper, seemly, timely
07 correct, fitting, germane
08 apposite, disposed, inclined, relevant, suitable
09 pertinent
10 applicable, seasonable
11 appropriate

## aptitude
04 bent, gift
05 flair, skill
06 talent
07 ability, faculty, leaning
08 capacity, facility, tendency
10 capability, cleverness
11 disposition, proficiency
14 natural ability

## aquatic
03 sea
05 fluid, river, water
06 liquid, marine, watery
07 fluvial
08 maritime, nautical

## arable
06 fecund
07 fertile
08 fruitful, plowable, tillable
10 productive

## arachnid see SPIDER

## arbiter
05 judge
06 expert, master, umpire
07 referee
09 authority
10 controller
11 adjudicator

## arbitrary
06 chance, random
08 despotic, dogmatic
09 illogical, whimsical
10 autocratic, capricious, high-handed, irrational, subjective, unreasoned
11 dictatorial, domineering, instinctive, overbearing
12 inconsistent, unreasonable
13 discretionary

## arbitrate
05 judge
06 decide, settle, umpire
07 mediate, referee
09 determine
10 adjudicate
13 sit in judgment

## arbitration
08 decision, judgment
09 mediation
10 settlement
11 arbitrament, negotiation
12 adjudication, intervention
13 determination

## arbitrator
05 judge
06 umpire
07 arbiter, referee
08 mediator
09 go-between, moderator
10 negotiator
11 adjudicator
12 intermediary

## arc
03 bow
04 arch, bend
05 curve
09 curvature

## arcade
04 mall, stoa
06 loggia, piazza
07 gallery, portico, veranda
08 cloister, precinct
09 colonnade, peristyle

## arcane
06 hidden, occult, secret
07 cryptic, obscure
08 abstruse, esoteric, mystical
09 concealed, enigmatic, recondite
10 mysterious

## arch
03 arc, bow, sly
04 bend, dome, span
05 curve, vault
06 bridge, camber
07 archway, concave, cunning
09 curvature

► *Types of arch*:
04 keel, ogee, skew
05 round, Tudor
06 convex, corbel, Gothic, lancet, Norman, tented
07 trefoil
09 horseshoe, parabolic
10 shouldered
12 basket-handle

## archaeology

► *Archaeological terms*:
03 cup, jar, jug, urn
04 bowl, cist, tell
05 blade, burin, cairn, flask, flint, henge, hoard, mound, mummy, stele, whorl
06 barrow, beaker, bogman, dolmen, eolith, hand ax, mosaic
07 amphora, cave art, neolith, obelisk, papyrus, rock art, tumulus
08 artefact, cromlech, hill fort, ley lines, megalith
09 cartouche, earthwork, hypocaust, microlith
10 hieroglyph
11 rock shelter, stone circle
12 amphitheater
13 hieroglyphics

► *Names of archaeologists*:
05 **Evans** (Arthur), **Guthe** (Carl)
06 **Anning** (Mary), **Breuil** (Henri), **Carter** (Howard), **Daniel** (Glyn), **Layard** (Austen Henry), **Leakey** (Louis Seymour Bazett), **Leakey** (Mary Douglas), **McKern** (Will), **Morris** (Earl), **Petrie** (Flinders)
07 **Thomsen** (Christian), **Wheeler** (Mortimer), **Woolley** (Leonard)
08 **Koldewey** (Robert), **Mariette** (Auguste)
10 **Schliemann** (Heinrich)
11 **Champollion** (Jean François)
➤ See also SCIENTIST

## archaic
05 passé
06 old hat
08 outmoded
10 antiquated
11 out of the ark
12 old-fashioned

## archbishop

► *Names of archbishops*:
03 **Law** (Bernard)
04 **Egan** (Edward), **Hume** (Basil), **Laud** (William), **Tutu** (Desmond Mpilo)
05 **Carey** (George), **Maida** (Adam)
06 **Becket** (Thomas à), **Coggan** (Donald), **Fisher** (Geoffrey), **George** (Francis), **Hickey** (James), **Keeler** (William),

**Mahony** (Roger), **Ramsay** (Michael), **Runcie** (Robert), **Wolsey** (Thomas)
07 **Arundel** (Thomas), **Cranmer** (Thomas), **Dunstan** (St)
08 **Adalbert, Ambrozic** Aloysius), **Makarios, Williams** (Rowan)
09 **Augustine** (St), **McCarrick** (Theodore)
10 **Bevilacqua** (Anthony)
➤ See also RELIGION

## archetypal
05 ideal, model, stock
07 classic, typical
08 original, standard
09 exemplary
14 characteristic, representative

## archetype
04 form, type
05 ideal, model
07 classic, epitome, pattern
08 exemplar, original, paradigm, standard
09 precursor, prototype
10 stereotype

## architect
05 maker
06 author, shaper
07 creator, founder, planner
08 designer, engineer, inventor
09 draftsman
10 instigator, mastermind, originator, prime mover
11 constructor
13 master builder

► *Names of architects*:
03 **Pei** (Ieoh Ming)
04 **Adam** (Robert), **Hood** (Raymond), **Loos** (Adolf), **Nash** (John), **Wren** (Christopher)
05 **Aalto** (Alvar), **Gaudí** (Antonio), **Gehry** (Frank), **Hoban** (James), **Jones** (Inigo), **Meier** (Richard), **Nervi** (Pier Luigi), **Piano** (Renzo), **Pugin** (Augustus), **Scott** (George Gilbert), **Speer** (Albert)
06 **Foster** (Sir Norman), **Fuller** (R. Buckminster), **Paxton** (Joseph), **Pisano** (Giovanni), **Rogers** (Richard), **Semper** (Gottfried), **Serlio** (Sebastiano), **Wright** (Frank Lloyd)
07 **Alberti** (Leon Battista), **Asplund** (Erik Gunnar),

**architecture**

Behrens (Peter), **Bernini**
(Gian Lorenzo), **Gropius**
(Walter), **Ictinus**, **Imhotep**,
Lutyens (Edwin), **Olmsted**
(Frederick Law), **Sotsass**
(Ettore)
08 **Bramante** (Donato),
**Harrison** (Wallace),
Jacobsen (Arne), **Palladio**
(Andrea), **Piranesi**
(Giambattista), **Yamasaki**
(Minoru)
09 **Belluschi** (Pietro),
**Borromini** (Francesco),
**Vitruvius**
11 **Le Corbusier**
12 **Brunelleschi** (Filippo)

**architecture**
05 style
06 design, makeup
08 building, planning
09 designing, framework,
structure
11 arrangement, composition
12 construction

➤ *Architectural and building*
*terms*:
04 cove, dado, dome, jamb, roof
05 annex, Doric, eaves, groin,
Ionic, ridge, Tudor
06 alcove, coving, façade,
fascia, finial, frieze, Gothic,
lintel, Norman, pagoda,
plinth, rococo, scroll, soffit,
stucco, Tuscan
07 baroque, cornice, festoon,
fluting, mullion, pantile,
parapet, rafters, Regency,
rotunda
08 baluster, capstone, gargoyle,
Georgian, pinnacle, wainscot
09 bas relief, copestone,
Edwardian, elevation,
gatehouse, Queen-Anne
10 architrave, bargeboard,
Corinthian, drawbridge,
flamboyant, ground plan,
Romanesque
11 cornerstone, Elizabethan,
Flemish bond
12 Early English, half-timbered

**archives**
05 deeds
06 annals, papers
07 ledgers, records
09 documents, registers
10 chronicles
11 memorabilia

**arctic**
05 polar
06 boreal, frozen

07 glacial, subzero
08 far north, freezing
11 hyperborean

**ardent**
03 hot
04 avid, keen, warm
05 eager, fiery
06 fervid, fierce, strong
07 devoted, fervent, zealous
08 spirited, vehement
09 dedicated
10 passionate
11 impassioned
12 enthusiastic

**ardor**
04 fire, heat, lust, zeal, zest
06 fervor, spirit, warmth
07 avidity, passion
08 devotion, keenness
09 animation, eagerness,
intensity, vehemence
10 dedication, enthusiasm
12 empressement

**arduous**
04 hard
05 harsh, heavy, tough
06 severe, taxing, tiring, uphill
07 onerous
08 daunting, grueling, wearying
09 difficult, laborious,
punishing, strenuous
11 burdensome, formidable
12 backbreaking

**area**
04 part, size, zone
05 field, patch, range, realm,
scope, tract, width, world
06 branch, domain, extent,
parish, region, sector, sphere
07 enclave, expanse, portion,
quarter, section, terrain
08 district, environs, locality,
precinct, province
09 territory
10 department
12 neighborhood

**arena**
04 area, bowl, ring, rink
05 field, realm, scene, world
06 domain, ground, sphere
07 stadium
08 coliseum, province
10 department, hippodrome
11 battlefield
12 amphitheater, battleground

**arguable**
04 moot
09 debatable, undecided
10 disputable
11 contentious
12 questionable

14 controvertible, open to
question
**argue**
03 row
04 feud, hold, show
05 claim, fight, imply, plead
06 assert, bicker, debate,
denote, haggle, reason
07 contend, discuss, dispute,
exhibit, fall out, quarrel,
suggest, wrangle
08 disagree, have a row,
maintain, persuade,
question, squabble
09 altercate, have it out, have
words, take issue
11 cross swords, demonstrate,
expostulate, remonstrate
13 have it out with
15 be at loggerheads, have a
bone to pick

**argument**
03 row
04 case, feud, fuss, plot, spat, tiff
05 clash, fight, logic, set-to
06 debate, dustup, reason,
ruckus, rumpus
07 defense, dispute, outline,
quarrel, summary, wrangle
08 conflict, ding-dong, rebuttal,
squabble
09 assertion, rationale,
reasoning
10 contention, discussion
11 altercation, controversy
12 disagreement
13 expostulation, running battle,
shouting match

**argumentative**
08 captious, contrary, perverse
09 litigious, polemical
11 belligerent, contentious,
dissentious, quarrelsome
12 cantankerous, disputatious

**arid**
03 dry
04 drab, dull
05 baked, vapid, waste
06 barren, boring, desert,
dreary, jejune, torrid
07 parched, sterile, tedious
08 lifeless
09 colorless, infertile, torrefied,
waterless
10 dehydrated, desiccated
12 moistureless, unproductive

**aright**
05 aptly, fitly, truly
07 exactly, rightly
08 properly, suitably
09 correctly

**arise**
04 go up, lift, soar, stem
05 begin, climb, ensue, get up, issue, occur, start, tower
06 appear, ascend, come up, crop up, emerge, follow, result, rise up, spring
07 proceed, stand up
08 commence
11 come to light

**aristocracy**
05 elite
06 gentry
07 peerage
08 nobility
09 gentility, top drawer
10 haute monde, patricians, patriciate, upper class, upper crust
11 high society, ruling class

**aristocrat**
04 lady, lord, peer
05 dandy, noble
07 grandee, peeress
08 eupatrid, nobleman
09 patrician
10 noblewoman

**aristocratic**
05 elite, noble
06 lordly, titled
07 courtly, elegant, refined
08 highborn, well-born
09 dignified, patrician
10 upper-class, upper-crust
11 blue-blooded

**arm**
03 bay, rig
04 cove, gird, limb, wing
05 array, brace, equip, firth, inlet, issue, prime, steel
06 branch, outfit, supply
07 channel, estuary, forearm, fortify, furnish, prepare, protect, provide, section
08 accouter, accoutre, brachium, division, offshoot
09 appendage, extension, reinforce, upper limb
10 department, detachment, projection, strengthen

**armada**
04 navy
05 fleet
08 flotilla, squadron
10 naval force

**armaments**
04 arms, guns
06 cannon
07 weapons
08 ordnance, weaponry
09 artillery, munitions

10 ammunition

**armistice**
05 peace, truce
09 ceasefire
11 peace treaty

**armor**
04 mail
07 panoply
09 chain mail
12 ironcladding

**armored**
08 ironclad
09 bombproof, protected
10 reinforced
11 armor-plated, bulletproof, steel-plated

**armory**
05 depot, stock
07 arsenal
08 magazine
09 arms depot, garderobe, stockpile
10 repository
13 ordnance depot
14 ammunition dump

**arms**
04 guns
05 crest
06 shield
07 weapons
08 blazonry, firearms, heraldry, insignia, ordnance, weaponry
09 armaments, artillery, munitions
10 ammunition, coat of arms, escutcheon

**army**
03 mob
04 host, pack
05 crowd, horde, swarm
06 throng, troops
07 cohorts, legions, militia
08 infantry, military, soldiers
09 multitude

**aroma**
04 odor
05 scent, smell
07 bouquet, perfume
09 fragrance, redolence

**aromatic**
05 balmy, fresh, spicy
06 savory
07 pungent, scented
08 fragrant, perfumed, redolent
11 odoriferous
13 sweet-smelling

**around**
04 near

05 about, circa, close, round
06 at hand, nearby, nearly
07 all over, roughly
08 framed by, to and fro
09 enclosing
10 encircling, everywhere, more or less, on all sides
11 surrounding
12 circumjacent, encompassing
13 approximately, circumambient
15 in all directions

**arouse**
04 goad, spur, whet
05 cause, evoke, incur, rouse, spark, waken
06 awaken, excite, incite, induce, kindle, prompt, stir up, turn on, wake up
07 agitate, animate, inflame, provoke, quicken
09 instigate, stimulate

**arraign**
06 accuse, charge, impugn, indict
07 impeach
09 prosecute
11 incriminate
13 call to account

**arrange**
03 fix, set
04 file, list, plan, sift, sort, tidy
05 align, array, class, fix up, grade, group, order, set up
06 adjust, codify, decide, design, devise, lay out, line up, set out, settle
07 dispose, marshal, prepare, project, sort out
08 classify, organize, pencil in, position, regulate, settle on
09 catalogue, determine
10 categorize, coordinate
11 orchestrate, systematize

**arrangement**
04 plan
05 array, order, plans, score, setup, terms
06 design, detail, format, layout, lineup, method, scheme, system
07 details, display, setting
08 contract, grouping, planning, schedule
09 agreement, structure
10 adaptation, compromise, groundwork, settlement
11 disposition, preparation
12 modus vivendi, organization, preparations
13 orchestration

14 classification, interpretation

**arrant**
04 rank, vile
05 gross, utter
06 brazen
07 blatant, extreme
08 absolute, complete, flagrant, outright, thorough
09 barefaced, downright, egregious, out-and-out
11 unmitigated
12 incorrigible

**array**
04 deck, robe, show
05 adorn, align, dress, group, order, range
06 attire, clothe, draw up, line up, lineup, muster, parade
07 apparel, arrange, bedizen, display, exhibit, marshal
08 accouter, accoutre, assemble, decorate, position
09 formation
10 assemblage, assortment, collection, exhibition, exposition, habilitate, marshaling
11 arrangement, disposition

**arrears**
04 debt
05 debts
07 balance, deficit
11 liabilities
12 indebtedness

◻**in arrears**
04 late
05 owing
06 behind, in debt
07 overdue
10 behindhand
11 outstanding

**arrest**
02 do
03 nab
04 book, bust, grab, grip, halt, nail, slow, stem, stop
05 block, catch, check, delay, rivet, run in, seize, stall
06 collar, detain, hinder, impede, pick up, retard
07 attract, capture, engross, inhibit, seizure
08 restrain, slow down
09 apprehend, interrupt
11 nip in the bud
15 take into custody

◻**under arrest**
09 in custody
11 in captivity

**arresting**
07 amazing, notable
08 engaging, striking, stunning
10 impressive, noteworthy, remarkable, surprising
11 conspicuous, outstanding
13 extraordinary

**arrival**
05 entry, guest
06 advent, coming
07 fresher, visitor
08 approach, débutant, entrance, freshman, newcomer, visitant
09 débutante, emergence
10 appearance, occurrence

**arrive**
04 come, dock, land, show
05 enter, get in, get to, occur, reach
06 appear, blow in, come in, drop in, happen, make it, roll up, show up, turn up
07 check in, clock in
08 get there
09 be present, touch down
14 come on the scene

**arrogance**
05 nerve, pride, scorn
06 hubris, vanity
07 conceit, disdain, hauteur
08 boasting, contempt
09 contumely, insolence, lordiness, pomposity
11 haughtiness, presumption
12 snobbishness
13 condescension, imperiousness
14 high-handedness, self-importance

**arrogant**
05 cocky, proud
06 lordly, snooty, uppity
07 haughty, stuck-up
08 assuming, boastful, insolent, scornful, snobbish, superior
09 bigheaded, conceited, egotistic, hubristic, imperious
10 disdainful, high-handed, hoity-toity
11 overbearing, patronizing
12 contemptuous, presumptuous, supercilious
13 condescending, high and mighty, self-important
14 full of yourself

**arrogate**
05 seize, usurp
06 assume
07 presume

10 commandeer
11 appropriate

**arrow**
04 bolt, dart
05 shaft
06 marker
07 pointer
08 sagittal
09 indicator

**arsenal**
05 depot, stock
06 armory
08 magazine
09 arms depot, stockpile
10 repository, storehouse
13 ordnance depot
14 ammunition dump

**arson**
09 pyromania
12 incendiarism

**arsonist**
07 firebug
10 incendiary, pyromaniac

**art**
04 gift
05 craft, flair, guile, knack, skill
06 design, method, talent
07 cunning, drawing, finesse, mastery, slyness
08 aptitude, artistry, facility, painting, trickery, wiliness
09 dexterity, expertise, ingenuity, sculpture
10 adroitness, astuteness, craftiness, profession, shrewdness, virtuosity
➤ See also ARTIST; PAINT; PAINTER; PAINTING; PHOTOGRAPH; PICTURE; SCULPTURE

▶ *Schools of art include:*
05 op art
06 Cubism, Gothic, pop art, Purism, Rococo
07 Art Deco, Baroque, Dadaism, folk art, Realism
08 abstract, Barbizon, Bohemian, Futurism
09 Byzantine, Modernism, Symbolism, Vorticism
10 Art Nouveau, classicism, Minimal Art, Minimalism, Naturalism, Romanesque, Surrealism
11 Hellenistic, renaissance, Romanticism, Suprematism
12 Aestheticism
13 Expressionism, Impressionism, Neoclassicism,

Postmodernism
14 action painting,
Constructivism

➤ *Arts and crafts:*
04 film
05 batik, video
06 fresco, mosaic
07 collage, crochet, etching, jewelry, origami, pottery, weaving
08 ceramics, graphics, knitting, modeling, painting, spinning, tapestry
09 enameling, engraving, marquetry, metalwork, sculpture, sketching
10 caricature, embroidery, needlework, watercolor
11 calligraphy, lithography, oil painting, photography, portraiture, woodcarving
12 architecture, illustration, stained glass
14 motion pictures

**artful**
03 sly
04 foxy, wily
05 sharp, smart
06 clever, crafty, shrewd, subtle
07 cunning, devious, vulpine
08 masterly, scheming
09 deceitful, ingenious
11 resourceful

**article**
04 item, part, unit
05 essay, paper, piece, point, story, thing
06 object, report, review
07 account, feature, portion, section, writeup
08 artefact, offprint
09 commodity, monograph, paragraph, thingummy
11 composition, constituent, thingamabob, thingamajig

**articulate**
03 say
04 talk
05 clear, lucid, speak, state, utter, vocal, voice
06 fluent
07 breathe, express
08 coherent, distinct, eloquent, vocalize
09 enunciate, pronounce, verbalize
10 expressive, meaningful
12 intelligible
14 comprehensible, understandable

**articulated**
04 said
05 joint
06 hinged, joined, linked, stated
07 coupled
08 attached, fastened
09 connected, expressed
11 interlocked

**articulation**
06 saying
07 diction, talking, voicing
08 delivery, speaking
09 utterance
10 expression
11 enunciation
12 vocalization
13 pronunciation, verbalization

**artifact**
04 item, tool
05 thing
06 object

**artifice**
04 ruse, wile
05 craft, dodge, guile, trick
06 deceit, scheme, tactic
07 cunning, slyness
08 strategy, subtlety, trickery
09 chicanery, stratagem
10 artfulness, cleverness, craftiness, subterfuge
11 contrivance

**artificial**
04 fake, mock, sham
05 bogus, false, phony, pseud
06 made-up, pseudo
07 assumed, feigned, man-made, plastic, studied
08 affected, mannered, specious, spurious
09 contrived, imitation, insincere, synthetic
10 nonnatural
11 counterfeit
12 manufactured

**artisan**
06 expert
08 mechanic
09 artificer, craftsman, operative
10 journeyman, technician
11 craftswoman
13 skilled worker

**artist**

➤ *Types of artist:*
06 master, potter
07 painter
08 designer, engraver, sculptor
09 architect, craftsman, draftsman, goldsmith
10 cartoonist
11 craftswoman, illustrator,

silversmith
12 photographer
13 draughtswoman
15 graphic designer
➤ See also ART

**artiste**
05 actor, comic
06 dancer, player, singer
07 actress, trouper
08 comedian, musician
09 performer
10 comedienne
11 entertainer
12 vaudevillian

**artistic**
06 gifted
07 elegant, skilled, stylish
08 creative, cultured, talented
09 aesthetic, beautiful, exquisite, sensitive
10 attractive, decorative, harmonious, ornamental
11 imaginative

**artistry**
05 craft, flair, skill, style, touch
06 genius, talent
07 ability, finesse, mastery
08 deftness
09 expertise
10 brilliance, creativity
11 proficiency, sensitivity, workmanship
13 craftsmanship
14 accomplishment

**artless**
04 open, pure, true
05 frank, naïve, plain
06 candid, direct, honest, simple, unwary
07 genuine, natural, sincere
08 innocent, trusting
09 guileless, ingenuous

**as**
04 like, when
05 being, since, while
07 because, owing to, through
10 for example, seeing that
13 at the same time
14 simultaneously

❏**as for**
12 in relation to, with regard to
13 with respect to
14 on the subject of
15 with reference to

❏**as it were**
06 in a way
07 so to say
09 in some way, so to speak

**ascend**
04 go up, rise, soar

**ascendancy**

05 arise, climb, fly up, mount, scale, tower
06 move up
07 float up, lift off, take off

**ascendancy**

04 edge, sway
05 power
07 command, control, mastery
08 dominion, hegemony
09 authority, dominance, supremacy, upper hand
10 domination, prevalence
11 preeminence, superiority

**ascent**

04 hill, ramp, rise
05 climb, slope
07 advance, incline, scaling
08 climbing, gradient, mounting, progress
09 acclivity, ascending, ascension, elevation
10 escalation

**ascertain**

03 fix
05 learn
06 detect, locate, settle, verify
07 confirm, find out, pin down
08 discover, identify
09 determine, establish
11 make certain

**ascetic**

03 nun
04 monk, yogi
05 fakir, harsh, plain, stern
06 hermit, severe, strict
07 austere, dervish, puritan, recluse, Spartan
08 celibate, rigorous, solitary
09 abstainer, abstinent, anchorite
10 abstemious
11 puritanical, self-denying

**ascribe**

06 assign, credit, impute
07 put down
08 accredit
09 attribute

**ashamed**

05 sorry
06 guilty, modest
07 abashed, bashful, humbled
08 blushing, contrite, hesitant, red-faced, sheepish
09 mortified, reluctant
10 apologetic, distressed, humiliated, remorseful
11 crestfallen, discomfited, discomposed, embarrassed
13 self-conscious

**ashen**

03 wan
04 gray, pale
05 livid, pasty, white
06 anemic, leaden, pallid
07 ghastly
08 blanched, bleached
09 colorless

**aside**

05 alone, apart
07 whisper
08 secretly
09 alongside, departure, monologue, on one side, privately, soliloquy
10 digression, separately
11 parenthesis
12 stage whisper

**asinine**

04 daft
05 inane, nutty, silly
06 absurd, stupid
07 fatuous, idiotic, moronic
08 mindless
09 imbecilic, senseless
10 half-witted
11 nonsensical

**ask**

03 beg, bid, sue
04 pray, pump, quiz, seek
05 crave, grill, order, plead, posit, press, query
06 clamor, demand, invite, summon
07 beseech, canvass, entreat, implore, inquire, propose, request, require, solicit, suggest
08 petition, question
09 interview, postulate
10 put forward, supplicate
11 interrogate, requisition
12 cross-examine

**askance**

08 sideways
09 dubiously, obliquely
10 doubtfully, indirectly
11 skeptically
12 disdainfully, suspiciously
13 distrustfully, mistrustfully
14 disapprovingly

**askew**

04 awry, skew
07 crooked, oblique
08 lopsided, sideways
09 crookedly

**asleep**

04 numb
05 inert
06 dozing
07 dormant, napping, resting

08 comatose, inactive, sleeping, snoozing
09 flaked out
11 unconscious
13 out like a light
14 dead to the world

**aspect**

03 air
04 face, look, side, view
05 angle, facet, light, point
06 factor, manner
07 bearing, feature, outlook
08 position
09 dimension, direction
10 appearance, expression, standpoint
11 countenance, point of view

**asperity**

08 acerbity, acrimony, severity, sourness
09 crossness, harshness, roughness, sharpness
10 bitterness, causticity
11 astringency, crabbedness, peevishness
12 churlishness, irascibility, irritability

**aspersion**

▫**cast aspersions on**

04 slur
05 smear
06 defame, vilify
07 censure, slander
08 reproach
09 criticize, denigrate, deprecate, disparage
10 sling mud at, throw mud at

**asphyxiate**

05 choke
06 stifle
07 smother
08 strangle, throttle
09 suffocate
11 strangulate

**aspiration**

03 aim
04 goal, hope, wish
05 dream, ideal
06 desire, intent, object
07 craving, longing, purpose
08 ambition, endeavor, yearning
09 objective

**aspire**

03 aim
04 hope, long, seek, wish
05 crave, dream, yearn
06 desire, hanker, pursue

**aspiring**

04 keen
05 eager

07 budding, hopeful, longing, wishful, would-be
08 aspirant, striving
09 ambitious
10 optimistic
11 endeavoring
12 enterprising

**ass**
04 fool, jerk, mule, nerd, pony, twit
05 burro, hinny, idiot, ninny, twerp
06 dimwit, donkey, nitwit
07 jackass
08 dipstick, imbecile, numskull
09 blockhead, numbskull, simpleton
10 nincompoop

**assail**
05 beset, worry
06 attack, invade, malign, plague, strike
07 bedevil, bombard, perplex, set upon, torment, trouble
08 maltreat, set about, tear into
09 criticize

**assailant**
05 enemy
06 abuser, mugger
07 invader, reviler
08 assailer, attacker, opponent
09 adversary, aggressor

**assassin**
06 gunman, hitman, killer
08 murderer
09 cutthroat, terrorist
10 hatchet man, liquidator
11 contract man, executioner

**assassinate**
03 hit
04 do in, kill, slay
06 murder, rub out
07 bump off
08 dispatch
09 eliminate, liquidate

**assault**
03 hit, mug
04 bomb, raid, rape
05 abuse, blitz, go for, pound, storm
06 attack, beat up, charge, fall on, invade, strike
07 battery, bombard, lay into, mugging, set upon
08 invasion, storming
09 incursion, offensive, onslaught
11 molestation

**assemblage**
04 mass

05 crowd, flock, group, rally
06 throng
09 gathering, multitude
10 collection
12 accumulation

**assemble**
04 join, make, mass, meet
05 amass, build, flock, group, rally, set up
06 gather, join up, muster
07 collate, collect, compose, connect, convene, marshal, round up, summons
08 mobilize
09 construct, fabricate
10 accumulate, congregate
11 manufacture, put together

**assembly**
04 body
05 agora, crowd, flock, group, rally, synod
06 caucus, muster, powwow, throng, troupe
07 cluster, company, council, meeting
08 building, congress
09 gathering, multitude
10 assemblage, collection, conference, convention
11 convocation
12 congregation

**assent**
05 agree, allow, grant, yield
06 accede, accept, accord, comply, concur, permit
07 approve, concede, consent
08 approval, sanction
09 acquiesce, agreement
10 acceptance, compliance, concession, permission
11 approbation, concurrence
12 acquiescence, capitulation

**assert**
05 argue, claim, state, swear
06 affirm, attest, defend, stress
07 confirm, contend, declare, profess, protest
08 insist on, maintain
09 establish, pronounce, testify to, vindicate

**assertion**
05 claim
06 avowal
09 statement
10 allegation, contention, insistence, profession
11 affirmation, attestation, declaration, predication, vindication
13 pronouncement

**assertive**
04 bold, firm
05 pushy
07 decided, forward
08 dominant, emphatic, forceful, positive
09 confident, insistent
10 aggressive
11 self-assured
12 strong-willed
13 self-confident

**assess**
03 fix, tax
04 levy, rate
05 gauge, judge, value, weigh
06 impose, review, size up
07 compute
08 appraise, check out, consider, estimate, evaluate
09 calculate, determine

**assessment**
04 levy, rate, toll
06 demand, review, tariff
07 opinion, testing
09 appraisal, valuation
10 estimation, evaluation
11 computation
14 reconnaissance

**asset**
03 aid
04 boon, help, plus
05 bonds, funds, goods, money
06 estate, stocks, virtue, wealth
07 benefit, capital, savings
08 blessing, holdings, property, reserves, resource, strength
09 advantage, liability, plus point, resources, valuables
10 securities
11 possessions, strong point

**assiduous**
06 steady
07 devoted
08 constant, diligent, sedulous, studious, untiring
09 attentive, dedicated
10 persistent, unflagging
11 hard-working, industrious
13 conscientious, indefatigable

**assign**
03 fix, set
04 give, name
05 allot, grant
06 detail, impute, select
07 appoint, ascribe, consign, install, put down, specify
08 accredit, allocate, delegate, dispense, nominate
09 apportion, attribute, chalk up to, designate, determine
10 commission, distribute

## assignation
04 date
05 tryst
10 engagement, rendezvous
11 appointment, arrangement

## assignment
03 job
04 duty, post, task
06 charge, errand
07 project
08 position
10 allocation, commission, delegation, nomination
11 appointment, designation
12 distribution
14 responsibility

## assimilate
03 mix
05 adapt, blend, learn, unite
06 absorb, mingle, take in
08 accustom
09 acclimate, integrate
11 acclimatize, incorporate

## assist
03 aid
04 abet, back, help
05 serve
06 back up, enable, second, succor
07 benefit, further, relieve, support, sustain
08 expedite
09 cooperate, do your bit, encourage, give a hand, lend a hand, reinforce
10 facilitate, give a leg up
11 collaborate, rally around

## assistance
03 aid
04 help
05 boost
06 a leg up, relief, succor
07 backing, benefit, service, support
11 cooperation, furtherance
12 a helping hand
13 reinforcement

## assistant
04 aide, ally
06 backer, deputy, helper, second
07 abettor, partner
09 accessory, ancillary, associate, auxiliary, colleague, supporter
10 accomplice
11 confederate, subordinate
12 collaborator, driving force, right-hand man
15 second in command

## associate
03 mix
04 ally, join, link, mate, pair, peer, yoke
05 crony, unite
06 attach, fellow, friend, hobnob, mingle, relate
07 combine, comrade, connect, consort, hang out, partner
08 co-worker, identify, sidekick
09 affiliate, assistant, colleague, companion, correlate, socialize, syndicate
10 amalgamate, fraternize
11 confederate, keep company
12 collaborator, go hand in hand, rub shoulders

## association
03 tie
04 band, bond, club, link
05 group, guild, union
06 cartel, clique, league
07 company, society
08 alliance, relation, sodality, sorority
09 coalition, syndicate
10 connection, consortium, federation, fellowship, fraternity, friendship
11 affiliation, confederacy, corporation, correlation, involvement, partnership
12 organization, relationship

## assorted
05 mixed
06 motley, sundry, varied
07 diverse, several, various
08 manifold
09 different, differing
10 variegated
12 multifarious
13 heterogeneous, miscellaneous

## assortment
03 lot, mix
05 bunch, group
06 choice, jumble, medley
07 farrago, mixture, variety
08 grouping
09 potpourri, selection
10 collection, miscellany, salmagundi
11 arrangement, olla-podrida

## assuage
04 calm, ease, lull
05 allay, lower, slake
06 lessen, pacify, quench, reduce, soften, soothe
07 appease, lighten, mollify, relieve, satisfy
08 mitigate, moderate, palliate

## assume
05 adopt, fancy, feign, guess, infer, put on, think, usurp
06 accept, affect, deduce, expect, take on
07 imagine, presume, suppose, surmise
08 arrogate, simulate, take over
09 postulate, undertake
10 commandeer, presuppose, take as read, understand
11 appropriate, counterfeit
14 take for granted

## assumed
04 fake, sham
05 bogus, false, phony
06 made-up
07 feigned
08 affected, invented, putative
09 pretended, simulated
10 fictitious
11 counterfeit

## assumption
04 idea
05 fancy, guess
06 belief, notion, theory
07 premise, seizure, surmise
08 adoption, takeover
09 inference, postulate
10 arrogation, conjecture, hypothesis
11 expectation, postulation, presumption, supposition
13 appropriation, commandeering
14 presupposition

## assurance
03 vow
04 oath, word
05 nerve
06 aplomb, pledge
07 courage, promise
08 audacity, boldness, security
09 certainty, guarantee
10 confidence, conviction
11 affirmation, assuredness, declaration, undertaking

## assure
03 vow
04 seal
05 swear
06 affirm, attest, insure, pledge, secure, soothe
07 certify, comfort, confirm, hearten, promise, warrant
08 convince, persuade
09 encourage, guarantee

## assured
04 bold, sure
05 fixed

09 alleviate

06 secure
07 certain, ensured, settled
08 definite, positive, promised
09 assertive, audacious, confident, confirmed
10 guaranteed
11 cut and dried, irrefutable
12 indisputable

**astonish**
03 wow
04 daze, stun
05 amaze, floor, shock
07 astound, stagger, startle, stupefy
08 bewilder, confound, dumfound, surprise
09 dumbfound, take aback
11 flabbergast

**astonished**
05 dazed
06 amazed
07 shocked, stunned
08 startled
09 astounded, staggered, surprised
10 bewildered, bowled over, confounded, dumfounded, taken aback
11 dumbfounded
13 flabbergasted

**astonishing**
07 amazing
08 shocking, striking, stunning
09 startling
10 astounding, impressive, staggering, surprising
11 bewildering
12 breathtaking, mind-boggling

**astonishment**
05 shock
06 dismay, wonder
08 surprise
09 amazement, confusion, disbelief
12 bewilderment, stupefaction
13 consternation

**astound**
04 stun
05 amaze, shock
07 startle, stupefy
08 astonish, bewilder, bowl over, surprise
09 overwhelm
11 flabbergast

**astounding**
07 amazing
08 shocking, stunning
09 startling
10 staggering, stupefying, surprising
11 astonishing, bewildering

12 breathtaking, overwhelming

**astray**
04 awry, lost, miss
05 amiss, wrong
06 adrift
07 missing
09 off course

**astringent**
04 acid, hard
05 harsh, stern
06 biting, severe
07 acerbic, caustic, mordant, styptic
08 scathing
09 trenchant

**astronaut**
08 spaceman
09 cosmonaut
10 spacewoman
13 space traveler

➤ *Names of astronauts:*
04 **Bean** (Alan), **Ride** (Sally)
05 **Foale** (Michael), **Glenn** (John), **Titov** (Gherman), **White** (Edward)
06 **Aldrin** (Edwin Eugene "Buzz"), **Borman** (Frank), **Conrad** (Charles "Pete"), **Cooper** (Gordon), **Lovell** (James "Jim")
07 **Chaffee** (Roger), **Collins** (Michael), **Gagarin** (Yuri), **Grissom** (Virgil "Gus"), **Sharman** (Helen), **Shepard** (Alan)
09 **Armstrong** (Neil), **Carpenter** (Scott)
10 **Tereshkova** (Valentina)

**astronomer and astro-physicist**

➤ *Names of astronomers and astrophysicists:*
03 **See** (Thomas Jefferson)
04 **Airy** (George Biddell), **Biot** (Jean-Baptiste), **Bopp** (Thomas), **Gold** (Thomas), **Hale** (Alan), **Hale** (George Ellery), **Oort** (Jan Hendrik)
05 **Adams** (Walter Sydney), **Baade** (Walter), **Brahe** (Tycho), **Gauss** (Carl Friedrich), **Hoyle** ( Fred), **Sagan** (Carl), **Vogel** (Hermann Carl)
06 **Halley** (Edmond), **Hewish** (Antony), **Hubble** (Edwin Powell), **Jansky** (Karl Guthe), **Kepler** (Johannes), **Kuiper** (Gerard Peter), **Lovell** ( Bernard), **Lowell**

(Percival), **Olbers** (Heinrich Wilhelm Matthäus),
**Laplace** (Pierre Simon)
07 **Babcock** (Harold Delos), **Barnard** (Edward Emerson), **Cassini** (Giovanni Domenico), **Celsius** (Anders), **Galileo**, **Hawking** (Stephen William), **Langley** (Samuel), **Newcomb** (Simon), **Penrose** (Roger), **Penzias** (Arno Allan), **Ptolemy**, **Seyfert** (Carl Keenan), **Shapley** (Harlow), **Whipple** (Fred Lawrence)
08 **Herschel** (William), **Korolyov** (Sergei), **Tombaugh** (Clyde William)
09 **Eddington** (Arthur Stanley), **Fabricius** (David), **Pickering** (Edward), **Sosigenes**
10 **Copernicus** (Nicolaus), **Hipparchos**
11 **Schlesinger** (Frank), **Tsiolkovsky** (Konstantin)
12 **Schiaparelli** (Giovanni Virginio)
13 **Chandrasekhar** (Subrahmanyan)
➤ See also SCIENTIST

**astute**
03 sly
04 keen, wily, wise
05 canny, sharp
06 clever, crafty, shrewd, subtle
07 cunning, knowing, prudent
09 sagacious
10 discerning, perceptive
11 intelligent, penetrating
13 perspicacious

**asylum**
05 haven
06 refuge
07 retreat, shelter
08 loony bin, madhouse
09 funny farm, sanctuary
11 institution
12 port in a storm

**asymmetrical**
04 awry
06 uneven
07 crooked, unequal
08 lopsided
09 distorted, irregular
10 unbalanced
13 unsymmetrical

**asymmetry**
09 imbalance

**atheism**
10 distortion, inequality, unevenness
11 crookedness
12 irregularity, lopsidedness

**atheism**
07 impiety
08 nihilism, paganism, unbelief
09 disbelief, nonbelief
10 heathenism, infidelity, irreligion, skepticism
11 godlessness, rationalism

**atheist**
05 pagan
07 heathen, heretic, infidel, skeptic
08 humanist, nihilist
10 unbeliever
11 freethinker, nonbeliever, nullifidian, rationalist

**athlete**
03 pro
04 jock
05 boxer, cager, racer
06 golfer, jumper, player, runner
07 gymnast
09 contender, letterman, sportsman
10 competitor, contestant
11 all-American, sportswoman
14 baseball player, football player
➤ See also SPORTS

**athletic**
03 fit
04 wiry
06 active, sinewy, sporty, strong, sturdy
08 muscular, powerful, vigorous, well-knit
09 energetic, gymnastic
➤ See also SPORTS

**athletics**
05 games
06 sports
08 exercise
10 gymnastics, recreation
13 callisthenics

**atmosphere**
03 air, sky
04 aura, feel, mood, tone
05 ether, tenor
06 flavor, milieu, spirit
07 climate, feeling, heavens, quality, setting
08 ambience
09 character
10 background
11 environment
12 surroundings

➤ *Names of layers of the atmosphere:*
09 exosphere
10 ionosphere, mesosphere
11 troposphere
12 stratosphere, thermosphere

**atom**
03 bit, jot
04 hint, iota, mite, spot, whit
05 crumb, grain, scrap, shred, speck, trace
06 morsel
08 fragment, molecule, particle
09 scintilla

➤ *Types of subatomic particle:*
04 kaon, muon, pion
06 photon, proton
07 neutron
08 electron, neutrino, positron
10 antiproton
11 antineutron, psi particle
12 antineutrino

**atone**
06 offset, pay for, redeem, remedy, repent
07 appease, expiate, redress
08 make good
09 indemnify, make right, make up for, reconcile
10 compensate, make amends, propitiate, recompense

**atonement**
06 amends
07 payment, penance, redress
08 requital
09 expiation, indemnity, repayment
10 recompense, reparation
11 appeasement, eye for an eye, restitution, restoration
12 compensation, propitiation
13 reimbursement

**atrocious**
05 cruel
06 brutal, savage, wicked
07 ghastly, heinous, hideous
08 dreadful, fiendish, grievous, horrible, shocking, terrible
09 appalling, merciless, monstrous, nefarious
10 abominable, horrendous

**atrocity**
04 evil
06 horror
07 cruelty, outrage
08 savagery, vileness, villainy
09 barbarity, brutality, violation
10 wickedness
11 abomination, monstrosity

**atrophy**
04 fade
05 decay, waste
06 shrink, wither
07 decline, shrivel, wasting
08 diminish, emaciate, marasmus
09 waste away, withering
10 degenerate, diminution, emaciation, shriveling
11 deteriorate, wasting away
12 degeneration
13 deterioration

**attach**
03 add, fix, pin, put, tie
04 ally, bind, join, link, nail, weld
05 affix, annex, stick, unite
06 adhere, assign, couple, fasten, impute, secure
07 ascribe, connect
09 affiliate, associate, attribute, latch onto

**attached**
04 fond
06 liking, loving
07 devoted, engaged, married
08 appended, friendly
09 spoken for
11 going steady

**attachment**
03 tie
04 bond, link, love
07 adjunct, codicil, fitting, fixture, loyalty
08 affinity, devotion, fondness
09 accessory, affection, appendage, extension
10 attraction, friendship, partiality, tenderness
12 accoutrement, appurtenance

**attack**
03 fit, mug, pan
04 bomb, bout, raid, rush, slam
05 abuse, begin, blitz, decry, foray, go for, knock, sally, slate, spasm, start, storm
06 access, ambush, assail, beat up, berate, charge, do over, fall on, impugn, malign, revile, sortie, strike, stroke, tackle, vilify
07 assault, battery, besiege, censure, lay into, seizure, set upon, slander, slating
08 commence, deal with, denounce, embark on, invasion, knocking, paroxysm, pounce on, set about, slamming, storming

09 criticism, criticize, have a go at, incursion, invective, irruption, offensive, onslaught, undertake
10 calumniate, convulsion, impugnment, revilement
11 bombardment, pick holes in
12 pull to pieces, tear to pieces, tear to shreds, vilification

**attacker**
06 abuser, critic, mugger, raider
07 invader, reviler
09 aggressor, assailant, detractor
10 persecutor

**attain**
03 get, hit, net, win
04 earn, find, gain
05 grasp, reach, touch
06 effect, obtain, secure
07 achieve, acquire, fulfill, realize
08 arrive at, complete
10 accomplish

**attainable**
06 at hand, doable, viable
08 feasible, possible, probable
09 potential, reachable, realistic
10 accessible, achievable, manageable, obtainable
11 conceivable, within reach

**attainment**
04 feat, gift
05 skill
06 talent
07 ability, mastery, success
08 aptitude, facility
10 capability, competence, completion
11 achievement, acquirement, fulfillment, proficiency, realization
12 consummation
14 accomplishment

**attempt**
02 go
03 aim, bid, try
04 bash, push, seek, shot, stab
05 crack, trial
06 effort, set out, strive, tackle
07 have a go, venture
08 endeavor
09 have a go at, undertake
10 experiment, have a crack
11 try your hand, undertaking
12 give it a whirl, have a crack at
13 try your hand at
15 do your level best

**attend**
04 go to, hear, heed, help, mark, mind, note, show, tend

05 nurse, serve, visit, watch
06 escort, follow, listen, notice, show up, turn up
07 care for, go along, observe
08 take note, wait upon
09 accompany, be present, chaperone, look after
10 minister to, take notice
12 pay attention

❑**attend to**
04 heed
06 direct, handle, manage
07 control, oversee, process
08 deal with, follow up
09 look after, supervise

**attendance**
04 gate
05 crowd, house
07 showing, turnout
08 audience, presence
10 appearance

**attendant**
04 aide, page
05 guard, guide, usher
06 escort, server, waiter
07 marshal, related, servant, steward
08 attached, follower, retainer
09 companion, custodian, resultant
10 associated, consequent, incidental, subsequent
11 concomitant
12 accompanying

**attention**
04 care, heed, help, mind
06 notice, regard
07 service, therapy, thought
08 courtesy
09 alertness, limelight, treatment, vigilance
11 compliments, observation, recognition
13 concentration, consideration

❑**pay attention to**
07 focus on
10 take notice
13 concentrate on
14 watch carefully
15 listen carefully

**attentive**
04 kind
05 alert, awake, aware, civil
07 all ears, careful, devoted, gallant, heedful, mindful
08 gracious, noticing, obliging, vigilant, watchful, watching
09 courteous, listening, observant
10 chivalrous, on the alert, thoughtful

11 considerate
12 on the qui vive
13 accommodating, conscientious

**attest**
04 aver, show
05 prove, swear
06 adjure, affirm, evince, verify
07 certify, confirm, declare, display, endorse
08 evidence, vouch for
10 asseverate
11 corroborate, demonstrate
13 bear witness to

**attic**
04 loft
06 garret
07 mansard

**attire**
04 duds, garb, gear, togs, wear
05 dress, habit
06 finery, outfit
07 apparel, clothes, costume, raiment
08 clothing, garments
11 habiliments
13 accouterments

**attired**
07 adorned, arrayed, clothed, dressed
09 decked out, dressed up, rigged out, turned out
11 habilitated

**attitude**
04 mood, pose, view
05 stand
06 aspect, manner, stance
07 bearing, feeling, mindset, opinion, outlook, posture
08 approach, carriage, position
09 mentality, worldview
10 deportment
11 disposition, perspective, point of view
13 way of thinking
14 Weltanschauung

**attract**
04 draw, lure, pull
05 charm, tempt
06 allure, engage, entice, excite, invite, pull in, seduce
07 bewitch, bring in, enchant
08 appeal to, interest
09 captivate, fascinate

**attraction**
04 bait, draw, lure, pull
05 charm, sight
06 allure, appeal
07 feature
08 affinity, interest

09 magnetism, seduction
10 enticement, inducement, invitation, temptation
11 captivation, fascination
13 entertainment

**attractive**
04 cute, fair, sexy
05 bonny
06 bonnie, comely, lovely, pretty
07 dashing, winning, winsome
08 engaging, enticing, fetching, gorgeous, handsome, inviting, magnetic, pleasing, striking, stunning, tempting
09 appealing, beautiful, desirable, seductive
11 captivating, fascinating, good-looking, picturesque
12 irresistible
13 prepossessing

**attribute**
04 mark, note, side, sign
05 facet, quirk, refer, trait
06 aspect, assign, charge, credit, impute, streak, symbol, virtue
07 ascribe, feature, quality
08 accredit, property
11 peculiarity
12 idiosyncrasy
14 characteristic

**attrition**
07 chafing, erosion, rubbing
08 abrasion, friction, grinding
09 detrition
10 harassment
11 attenuation, wearing away

**attuned**
03 set
07 adapted
08 adjusted
09 regulated
10 acclimated, accustomed, harmonized
11 assimilated, coordinated
12 acclimatized, familiarized

**atypical**
07 deviant, unusual
08 aberrant, abnormal, freakish
09 anomalous, divergent, eccentric, untypical
11 exceptional
13 extraordinary

**auburn**
04 rust
05 henna, tawny
06 copper, russet, titian
08 chestnut

**audacious**
04 bold, pert, rash, rude

05 brave, risky
06 brazen, cheeky, daring
07 assured, forward, valiant
08 fearless, impudent, insolent, intrepid, reckless
09 dauntless, shameless, unabashed
10 courageous
11 adventurous, impertinent, venturesome
12 enterprising, presumptuous

**audacity**
04 risk
05 cheek, pluck, valor
06 daring
07 bravery, courage
08 boldness, defiance, pertness, rashness, rudeness
09 impudence, insolence
10 brazenness, effrontery, enterprise
11 forwardness, intrepidity, presumption
12 fearlessness, impertinence
13 shamelessness

**audible**
05 clear, heard
08 distinct, hearable
10 detectable
11 appreciable, discernible, perceptible

**audience**
04 fans
05 crowd, house
06 public
07 hearing, meeting, turnout, viewers
08 assembly, audition, devotees, regulars
09 following, gathering, interview, listeners
10 spectators
12 congregation, consultation

**audit**
05 check
06 go over, review, verify
07 balance, examine, inspect
08 analysis, scrutiny
09 go through, statement
10 inspection, scrutinize
11 examination, investigate

**augment**
04 grow
05 add to, boost, raise, swell
06 expand, extend
07 amplify, build up, enhance, enlarge, inflate, magnify
08 heighten, increase, multiply
09 intensify, reinforce
10 strengthen

**augur**
04 bode
06 herald
07 betoken, portend, predict, presage, promise, signify
08 forebode, foretell, prophesy
09 be a sign of, harbinger

**augury**
04 omen, sign
05 token
06 herald
07 portent, promise, warning
08 prodrome, prophecy
09 harbinger, haruspicy
10 foreboding, prediction
11 forewarning
13 haruspication
15 prognostication

**august**
05 grand, lofty, noble
06 solemn
07 exalted, stately
08 glorious, imposing, majestic
09 dignified
10 impressive
11 magnificent
12 awe-inspiring

**aura**
03 air
04 feel, hint, mood
05 vibes
06 nimbus
07 feeling, quality
08 ambience
09 emanation
10 atmosphere, vibrations

**auspices**
☐ **under the auspices of**
11 in the care of
13 in the charge of
15 under the aegis of

**auspicious**
04 rosy
05 happy, lucky
06 bright, timely
07 hopeful
08 cheerful
09 favorable, fortunate, promising
10 felicitous, optimistic, propitious
11 encouraging

**austere**
04 cold, grim, hard
05 bleak, grave, harsh, plain, rigid, sober, stark, stern
06 chaste, frugal, severe, solemn, somber, strict
07 ascetic, serious, spartan
08 exacting, rigorous

## austerity

09 stringent, unadorned
10 abstemious, economical, forbidding, inflexible
11 puritanical, self-denying

## austerity

07 economy
08 coldness, hardness, severity
09 harshness, plainness
10 abstinence, asceticism, puritanism, self-denial
13 inflexibility

## authentic

04 real, true
05 legal, valid
06 honest, kosher, lawful
07 certain, factual, genuine
08 accurate, bona fide, credible, faithful, reliable
10 dependable, legitimate
12 the real McCoy

## authenticate

05 prove
06 attest, ratify, verify
07 certify, confirm, endorse
08 accredit, validate, vouch for
09 authorize, guarantee
11 corroborate
12 substantiate

## authenticity

05 truth
07 honesty
08 accuracy, fidelity, legality, validity, veracity
09 certainty
10 legitimacy
11 correctness, credibility, genuineness, reliability

## author

03 pen
04 poet
05 maker, mover
06 parent, writer
07 creator, founder, planner
08 composer, essayist, lyricist, novelist, reporter
09 dramatist, initiator
10 biographer, journalist, librettist, originator, playwright, songwriter
11 ghostwriter
12 screenwriter

## authoritarian

05 harsh, rigid, tough
06 severe, strict
08 despotic, dogmatic
09 imperious
10 autocratic, oppressive, tyrannical, unyielding
11 dictatorial, doctrinaire, domineering
12 totalitarian

14 disciplinarian

## authoritative

04 bold, true
05 sound, valid
07 factual, learned
08 accepted, accurate, approved, decisive, faithful, official, reliable, truthful
09 authentic, confident, masterful, scholarly
10 authorized, definitive, legitimate, sanctioned
11 self-assured, trustworthy

## authority

04 buff, rule, sage, sway, they
05 clout, power, right, state
06 expert, master, muscle, permit, pundit
07 command, control, council, license, scholar, warrant
08 dominion, sanction
09 influence, supremacy
10 government, management, permission, specialist
11 bureaucracy, connoisseur, credentials, officialdom
12 carte blanche, jurisdiction
13 authorization, establishment
14 administration
15 the powers that be

## authorization

02 OK
04 okay
05 leave
06 permit
07 consent, go-ahead, license, mandate
08 approval, sanction, warranty
10 green light, permission
11 credentials, entitlement
12 confirmation, ratification
13 accreditation

## authorize

02 OK
03 let
04 okay
05 allow
06 enable, permit, ratify
07 approve, confirm, empower, entitle, license, warrant
08 legalize, sanction, validate
09 consent to, make legal
10 commission
14 give the go-ahead

## autobiography

05 diary
07 journal, memoirs
09 life story

## autocracy

07 fascism, tyranny
09 despotism

10 absolutism
12 dictatorship
15 totalitarianism

## autocrat

06 despot, Hitler, tyrant
07 fascist
08 dictator
10 absolutist, panjandrum
12 little Hitler, totalitarian
13 authoritarian

## autocratic

08 absolute, despotic
09 imperious
10 tyrannical
11 all-powerful, dictatorial, domineering, overbearing
12 totalitarian
13 authoritarian

## autograph

04 mark, name, sign
07 endorse, initial
08 initials
09 signature

## automatic

06 reflex
07 natural, robotic, routine
08 knee-jerk, unmanned
09 automated, necessary
10 inevitable, mechanical, mechanized, programmed
11 inescapable, instinctive, involuntary, spontaneous
12 computerized

## automobile

03 car
07 vehicle
12 motor vehicle

► *Types of car (mostly trademarks)*:

02 MG, VW
03 BMW, cab
04 Audi, auto, Fiat, Ford, Jeep, jeep, Lada, limo, Merc, Mini, Nash, Olds, Opel, Polo, taxi
05 Astra, buggy, Buick, coupé, Dodge, Edsel, racer, Rolls, sport, stock, T-Bird, Volvo
06 banger, Beetle, DeSoto, hearse, Jaguar, jalopy, Morris, patrol, Roller, saloon, sports, Toyota, wheels
07 Bentley, classic, Daimler, DeLoren, Ferrari, flivver, hardtop, Lagonda, Packard, Pontiac, Porsche, Rambler, Triumph, veteran, vintage
08 Cadillac, Chrysler, Corvette, dragster, Maserati, Plymouth, roadster, runabout
09 cabriolet, hatchback, Land

Rover, limousine
10 Oldsmobile, Range Rover, Rolls-Royce, Studebaker, Volkswagen
11 convertible, Silver Ghost, Thunderbird
12 Mercedes-Benz, station wagon
14 four-wheel drive

➤ *Parts of an automobile*:
03 fan, tag
04 axle, body, cowl, gear, hood, horn, tire, vent
05 brake, choke, gauge, grill, motor, trunk, wheel
06 airbag, bumper, clutch, engine, fender, hubcap, window
07 battery, blinker, chassis, chassis, exhaust, gas tank, gearbox, muffler, starter, sunroof
08 brake pad, ignition, radiator, seat belt
09 brake drum, brake shoe, crankcase, dashboard, gearshift, generator, hand brake, headlight, rear light, spare tire, taillight
10 alternator, carburetor, power brake, side mirror, stick shift, suspension, windshield
11 antiroll bar, distributor, exhaust pipe, speedometer
12 license plate, parking light, transmission
13 cruise control, power steering, rack and pinion, shock absorber, steering wheel
14 rearview mirror
15 instrument panel, windshield wiper
➤ See also MOTOR; VEHICLE

**auto racing**
04 CART
06 NASCAR
09 SportsCar
10 drag racing, Formula One, Indy racing
12 hot rod racing
14 stock car racing

➤ *Names of auto racing drivers*:
04 **Foyt** (A.J., Jr.), **Hill** (Damon), **Hill** (Graham), **Moss** (Sterling)
05 **Brack** (Kenny), **Mears** (Rick), **Petty** (Richard), **Prost** (Alain), **Senna** (Ayrton), **Unser** (Al), **Unser**

(Bobby)
06 **Fangio** (Juan), **Gordon** (Jeff), **Lazier** (Buddy)
07 **Allison** (Bobby), **Cheever** (Eddie), **Emerson** (Fittipaldi), **Jarrett** (Dale), **Labonte** (Terry), **Montoya** (Juan), **Pearson** (David), **Stewart** (Jackie), **Waltrip** (Darrell)
08 **Andretti** (Mario), **Hakkinen** (Mika), **Luyendyk** (Arie)
09 **Earnhardt** (Dale)
10 **Schumacher** (Michael), **Villeneuve** (Jacques), **Yarborough** (Cale)
11 **Castroneves** (Helio)

**autonomy**
07 autarky, freedom
08 free will, home rule, self-rule
11 sovereignty
12 independence
14 self-government
15 self-sufficiency

**auxiliary**
05 extra, spare
06 helper, second
07 helping, partner, reserve
09 ancillary, assistant, assisting, secondary, supporter
10 subsidiary, supporting
11 subordinate
12 right-hand man
13 supplementary
15 second-in-command

**available**
04 free
05 handy, on tap, ready
06 at hand, on hand, to hand, usable, vacant
07 untaken
10 accessible, convenient, disposable, obtainable, unoccupied, up for grabs
11 forthcoming, within reach
12 up your sleeve
14 at your disposal

**avalanche**
04 wave
05 flood
06 deluge
07 barrage, cascade, torrent
08 landslip
09 landslide
10 inundation

**avant-garde**
06 far-out, modern, way-out
07 go-ahead
08 advanced, original
09 inventive

10 futuristic, innovative, innovatory, pioneering
11 progressive
12 contemporary, experimental
14 unconventional

**avarice**
05 greed
08 meanness
10 greediness
11 materialism, selfishness
12 covetousness
15 acquisitiveness

**avaricious**
04 mean
06 greedy
07 miserly
08 covetous, grasping
09 mercenary, rapacious
11 acquisitive

**avenge**
05 repay
06 punish
07 pay back, redress, requite
09 get back at, retaliate
11 get even with
14 take revenge for

**average**
03 par, run
04 mean, mode, norm, so-so
05 usual
06 common, medial, median, medium, middle, normal
07 regular, routine, typical
08 everyday, mediocre, middling, ordinary
09 tolerable
11 indifferent, not up to much
12 intermediate, run-of-the-mill, satisfactory
13 no great shakes, unexceptional
14 fair to middling, nothing special

**averse**
05 loath
07 hostile, opposed
09 reluctant, unwilling
11 disinclined, ill-disposed
12 antagonistic, antipathetic

**aversion**
04 hate
06 hatred, horror, phobia
07 disgust, dislike
08 distaste, loathing
09 hostility, repulsion, revulsion
10 abhorrence, antagonism, reluctance, repugnance
11 abomination, detestation
13 unwillingness
14 disinclination

## avert
04 stop
05 avoid, evade, parry
07 deflect, fend off, head off, obviate, prevent, ward off
08 preclude, stave off, turn away
09 forestall, frustrate, turn aside

## aviation
06 flight, flying
11 aeronautics

## aviator

➤ *Names of aviators*:
04 **Byrd** (Richard Evelyn), **Post** (Wiley), **Udet** (Ernst), Baron von)
05 **Brown** (Arthur Whitten)
06 **Alcock** (John William), **Harris** (Arthur Travers "Bomber"), **Hughes** (Howard), **Wright** (Orville), **Wright** (Wilbur), **Yeager** (Charles Elwood "Chuck")
07 **Blériot** (Louis), **Branson** (Richard), **Dornier** (Claudius), **Douglas** (Donald Wills), **Earhart** (Amelia), **Fossett** (Steve), **Goering** (Hermann Wilhelm), **Johnson** (Amy), **Piccard** (Auguste Antoine), **Sopwith** (Thomas Octave Murdoch)
08 **Zeppelin** (Count Ferdinand von)
09 **Doolittle** (James "Jimmy"), **Lindbergh** (Charles Augustus)
10 **Lindstrand** (Per), **Richthofen** (Manfred)
11 **Montgolfier** (Jacques Étienne), **Montgolfier** (Joseph Michel)
12 **Rickenbacker** (Eddie)
13 **Messerschmidt** (Willy)
➤ See also MILITARY

## avid
03 mad
04 keen
05 crazy, eager, great
06 ardent, greedy, hungry
07 devoted, earnest, fervent, intense, thirsty, zealous
08 covetous, grasping
09 dedicated, fanatical
10 insatiable, passionate
12 enthusiastic

## avoid
04 balk, duck, shun, snub
05 avert, dodge, elude, evade, hedge, shirk
06 bypass, escape, eschew

07 forbear, prevent
08 sidestep
09 get around
10 circumvent
11 abstain from, shy away from
12 steer clear of

## avoidable
08 eludible
09 avertible, escapable
11 preventable

## avowed
04 open
05 overt, sworn
08 admitted, declared
09 confessed, professed
12 acknowledged
13 self-confessed
14 self-proclaimed

## await
06 expect
07 hope for, look for

## awake
04 stir, wake
05 alert, alive, aware, rouse
06 arouse, wake up
07 aroused, wakeful
08 stirring, vigilant, watchful
09 attentive, conscious, observant, sensitive

## awakening
05 birth
06 waking
07 arousal, revival, rousing
09 animating
10 activation, enlivening
11 stimulation
12 vivification

## award
04 gift, give, gong
05 grant, medal, order, prize
06 bestow, confer, trophy
07 adjudge, present
08 allocate, bestowal, citation
09 allotment, allowance, apportion, endowment
10 decoration, distribute
11 certificate
12 commendation, dispensation, presentation

➤ *Theater, television and film awards (mostly trademarks)*:
04 Emmy, Tony
05 Bafta, Oscar
06 Grammy
07 Olivier
08 Palme d'Or
10 Golden Bear, Golden Lion, Golden Palm, Golden Rose
11 Golden Globe
12 Academy Award

## aware
05 alert, sharp
06 shrewd
07 heedful, knowing, mindful
08 apprised, familiar, informed, sensible, sentient, vigilant
09 attentive, au courant, cognizant, conscious, in the know, on the ball, sensitive
10 acquainted, conversant
11 enlightened
12 appreciative
13 knowledgeable

## awe
04 fear
05 dread, honor
06 terror, wonder
07 respect
09 amazement, reverence
10 admiration, veneration
12 apprehension

## awe-inspiring
06 moving, solemn
07 amazing, exalted, sublime
08 daunting, majestic, numinous, striking, stunning
09 wonderful
10 formidable, impressive
11 magnificent, spectacular
12 breathtaking, overwhelming

## awful
04 dire, ugly
05 nasty
06 horrid
07 abysmal, fearful, ghastly, heinous, hideous
08 alarming, dreadful, gruesome, horrible, horrific, shocking, terrible
09 appalling, atrocious, frightful
10 disgusting, horrifying
11 distressing

## awkward
03 shy
05 inept
06 clumsy, fiddly, gauche
07 prickly
08 annoying, delicate, inexpert, lubberly, stubborn, ungainly, unwieldy
09 all thumbs, difficult, graceless, ham-fisted, ill at ease, inelegant, irritable, maladroit, obstinate
10 cumbersome, perplexing, ungraceful, unpleasant
11 problematic, troublesome
12 embarrassing, inconvenient
13 uncomfortable

## awry
05 amiss, askew, wrong

06 askant, uneven
07 crooked, oblique, twisted
08 cockeyed
09 off-center
10 misaligned

**ax**
03 adz, cut, hew
04 adze, chop, fell, fire, sack
06 cancel, cleave, remove
07 chopper, cleaver, cut down, dismiss, hatchet
08 battle-ax, get rid of, tomahawk
09 discharge, eliminate, terminate

11 discontinue

❑ **get the ax**
10 get the boot, get the chop

**axiom**
05 adage, maxim, truth
06 byword, dictum, truism
07 precept
08 aphorism

**axiomatic**
05 given
06 gnomic
07 assumed, certain, granted
08 accepted, manifest

10 aphoristic, proverbial, understood
11 indubitable, self-evident
12 apothegmatic, unquestioned
14 apophthegmatic

**axis**
05 hinge, pivot
08 vertical
10 centerline, horizontal

**axle**
03 pin, rod
05 pivot, shaft
07 spindle

**babble**
04 blab
05 babel, prate
06 burble, clamor, gibber, gurgle, hubbub, jabber
07 blabber, chatter
09 gibberish

**babe**
04 baby
05 child
06 infant

**babel**
03 din
05 chaos
06 babble, bedlam, clamor, hubbub, tumult, uproar
07 turmoil
09 commotion, confusion
10 hullabaloo
11 pandemonium

**baby**
03 tot, wee
04 babe, mini, tiny
05 bairn, child, small
06 coddle, dote on, infant, little, minute, pamper
09 miniature
10 diminutive, small-scale

**babyish**
05 naïve, silly, sissy, young
07 foolish, puerile
08 childish, immature, juvenile
09 infantile

**back**
03 aid, end
04 abet, help, hind, rear, tail
05 boost, other, spine, stern
06 assist, behind, dorsum, former, recede, recoil, retire, second, tergum
07 bolster, confirm, earlier, endorse, finance, promote, regress, retreat, reverse, sponsor, support, sustain
08 advocate, backbone, backside, backward, champion, hindmost, outdated, previous, sanction, side with, withdraw
09 backtrack, backwards, encourage, subsidize
10 underwrite

11 countenance
12 hindquarters

❑**back away**
06 recede, recoil
07 retreat
08 draw back, fall back, move back, step back, withdraw
10 give ground

❑**back down**
05 yield
06 give in, submit
07 concede, retreat
08 withdraw
09 backpedal, backtrack, climb down, surrender

❑**back out**
06 cancel, give up, recant, resign
08 go back on, withdraw
10 chicken out
11 get cold feet

❑**back up**
03 aid
06 assist, second
07 bear out, bolster, confirm, endorse, support
09 reinforce
11 corroborate

❑**behind your back**
05 slyly
08 covertly, secretly, sneakily
09 furtively
15 surreptitiously

**backbiting**
05 abuse, libel, spite
06 gossip, malice
07 calumny, slander
09 cattiness, criticism
10 bitchiness, defamation
11 denigration, mudslinging
12 depreciation, spitefulness, vilification
13 disparagement

**backbone**
04 core, grit, guts
05 basis, nerve, pluck, ridge, spine
06 mettle
07 courage, support
08 firmness, mainstay, strength
09 character, toughness, vertebrae, willpower
12 spinal column

13 determination
15 vertebral column

**backbreaking**
04 hard
07 arduous, killing
08 grueling
09 laborious, punishing, strenuous
10 exhausting

**backer**
06 patron, second
07 sponsor
08 promoter, seconder
09 supporter
10 benefactor, well-wisher
11 underwriter

**backfire**
04 fail, flop
06 recoil
07 explode, rebound
08 detonate, miscarry, ricochet
09 boomerang

**background**
05 scene
06 family, milieu, record, status
07 context, culture, factors, origins, setting
08 backdrop, breeding
09 backcloth, framework, grounding, tradition
10 experience, upbringing
11 credentials, environment, preparation
13 circumstances
14 social standing

**backhanded**
06 ironic
07 dubious, oblique
08 indirect, two-edged
09 ambiguous, equivocal
11 double-edged, duplicitous

**backing**
03 aid
04 help
05 funds, grant
07 finance, helpers, subsidy, support
08 advocacy, approval
09 patronage, promotion, seconding
10 assistance

**backlash**
11  championing, endorsement, sponsorship
12  moral support
13  accompaniment, encouragement

**backlash**
06  recoil
08  backfire, kickback, reaction, reprisal, response
09  boomerang
11  retaliation
12  repercussion

**backlog**
05  hoard, stock
06  excess, supply
07  reserve
08  mountain, reserves
09  resources
12  accumulation

**backpedal**
05  U-turn, yield
06  give in, submit
07  concede, retract, retreat
08  take back, withdraw
09  backtrack, climb down, surrender
12  tergiversate
14  change your mind

**backslide**
03  sin
04  slip
05  lapse, stray
06  defect, desert, go back, renege, revert
07  default, regress, relapse
10  apostatize
12  tergiversate, turn your back

**backslider**
07  reneger
08  apostate, defector, deserter, recreant, renegade, turncoat
09  defaulter
10  recidivist
13  tergiversator

**backsliding**
05  lapse
07  relapse
08  apostasy
09  defection, desertion
10  defaulting, regression
14  tergiversation

**bacteriologist**

► *Names of bacteriologists*:
04  **Cohn** (Ferdinand Julius), **Gram** (Hans Christian Joachim), **Koch** (Robert), **Roux** (Émile)
05  **Avery** (Oswald Theodore), **Smith** (Theobald)

06  **Enders** (John Franklin)
07  **Behring** (Emil von), **Buchner** (Hans), **Ehrlich** (Paul), **Fleming** ( Alexander), **Noguchi** (Hideyo), **Theiler** (Max)
➤  See also SCIENTIST

**backup**
03  aid
04  help
07  support
09  equipment, resources
10  assistance
11  endorsement
12  confirmation
13  encouragement, reinforcement

**backward**
03  shy
04  slow
05  timid
07  bashful, reverse
08  hesitant, immature, rearward, rearward, retarded, retiring
09  backwards, shrinking, subnormal, to the back
10  regressive, retrograde
11  undeveloped
12  regressively
13  retrogressive
14  underdeveloped

**backwash**
04  flow, path, wake, wash
05  swell, waves
06  result
09  aftermath
11  aftereffect, consequence
13  repercussions

**backwoods**
04  bush
06  sticks
07  boonies
09  boondocks
15  middle of nowhere

**bacteria**
04  bugs
05  germs
07  bacilli, viruses
08  microbes
14  microorganisms

**bad**
03  ill
04  evil, high, poor, sour, vile
05  acute, awful, grave, harsh, lousy, moldy, nasty, unfit
06  aching, crappy, crummy, faulty, gloomy, poorly, putrid, rancid, rotten, severe, sinful, unruly, unwell, wicked

07  adverse, botched, corrupt, decayed, harmful, hurtful, immoral, intense, naughty, painful, serious, spoiled, tainted, useless, wayward
08  criminal, critical, damaging, diseased, dreadful, hopeless, inferior, mediocre, pathetic, shameful, terrible
09  appalling, atrocious, dangerous, defective, deficient, dishonest, imperfect, obnoxious, offensive, reprobate, third-rate
10  degenerate, deplorable, ill-behaved, inadequate, indisposed, mismanaged, outrageous, putrescent, refractory, second-rate, unpleasant, unsuitable
11  deleterious, destructive, detrimental, disobedient, distressing, incompetent, ineffective, ineffectual, mischievous, substandard, unfavorable, unwholesome
12  badly behaved, contaminated, disagreeable, inauspicious, inconvenient, putrefactive, unacceptable
13  inappropriate, reprehensible
14  unsatisfactory

❑**not bad**
02  OK
04  fair, okay, so-so
07  average
08  adequate, all right, passable
09  quite good, tolerable
10  reasonable
12  satisfactory

**badge**
04  logo, mark, sign
05  brand, crest, stamp, token
06  emblem, ensign, symbol
08  insignia
09  indicator, trademark
10  escutcheon, indication

**badger**
03  nag
04  bait, goad
05  bully, harry, hound
06  harass, hassle, pester, plague
09  importune

**badinage**
05  chaff, humor
06  banter
07  ribbing, teasing, waggery
08  drollery, raillery, repartee, wordplay
10  jocularity, persiflage

**badly**
06 deeply, evilly, poorly
07 acutely, awfully, gravely, greatly, wrongly
08 bitterly, faultily, severely, sinfully, terribly, unfairly, very much, wickedly
09 adversely, immorally, intensely, painfully, seriously, unhappily
10 carelessly, criminally, critically, enormously, improperly, shamefully
11 desperately, dishonestly, exceedingly, imperfectly, incorrectly, negligently, unfavorably
12 inadequately, tremendously, unacceptably
13 incompetently, ineffectually

**bad-tempered**
05 cross, gruff, ratty, sulky
06 crabby, cranky, grumpy
07 crabbed, grouchy, waspish
08 choleric, petulant
09 crotchety, fractious, impatient, irritable
10 ill-humored, in a bad mood
12 cantankerous
13 quick-tempered

**baffle**
04 daze, foil
05 block, check, stump, upset
06 bemuse, defeat, hinder, puzzle, thwart
07 flummox, mystify, perplex
08 bewilder, confound
09 bamboozle, frustrate

**baffling**
08 bemusing, puzzling
09 confusing
10 astounding, mysterious, perplexing, stupefying, surprising
11 bewildering
12 unfathomable

**bag**
03 get
04 grab, kill, land, sack, take, trap
05 catch, shoot
07 acquire, capture, handbag, reserve
09 container
10 commandeer, receptacle
11 appropriate

**baggage**
04 bags, gear
06 things
07 effects, luggage
09 equipment, suitcases

10 belongings
11 impedimenta
13 paraphernalia

**baggy**
05 loose, roomy, slack
06 droopy, floppy
07 bulging, sagging
08 oversize
09 billowing, shapeless
10 ballooning, ill-fitting
12 loose-fitting

**bail**
04 bond
06 pledge, surety
08 security, warranty
09 guarantee

❑ **bail out**
03 aid
04 help, quit
06 assist, escape, rescue
07 back out, finance, retreat
08 withdraw

**bait**
04 goad, lure
05 annoy, bribe, harry, hound, snare, tease
06 badger, harass, hassle, needle, plague
07 provoke, torment
08 irritate
09 incentive, persecute
10 attraction, enticement, inducement, temptation

**balance**
04 rest
05 level, match, poise, weigh
06 adjust, equate, equity, excess, juggle, parity, square
07 compare, residue, surplus
08 calmness, consider, equality, equalize, evenness, symmetry
09 composure, equipoise, remainder, sangfroid, stability
10 counteract, difference, equanimity, steadiness
11 equilibrium, equivalence
12 counterweigh
13 compensate for
14 correspondence, counterbalance, self-possession

**balanced**
04 calm, fair
07 assured, healthy
08 sensible, unbiased
09 equitable, impartial, objective
10 coolheaded, evenhanded
12 unprejudiced

13 self-possessed

❑ **on balance**
08 all in all
13 all considered

**balcony**
04 gods
06 loggia
07 gallery, terrace
09 mezzanine
13 peanut gallery

**bald**
04 bare
05 blunt, naked, plain, stark
06 barren, direct, severe, simple, smooth
07 denuded, exposed
08 glabrate, glabrous, hairless, outright, straight, treeless
09 depilated, outspoken, unadorned, uncovered
11 bald as a coot, unsheltered
15 straightforward

**balderdash**
03 rot
04 bunk
05 bilge, trash, tripe
06 bunkum, drivel, hot air, piffle
07 palaver, rubbish, twaddle
08 claptrap, nonsense, tommyrot
09 gibberish, poppycock

**balding**
08 receding
09 thin on top
14 losing your hair

**baldness**
08 alopecia, bareness, psilosis
09 calvities, starkness
12 glabrousness, hairlessness

**bale**
03 woe
04 pack
06 bundle, parcel, sorrow
07 package

**baleful**
04 evil
06 deadly
07 harmful, hurtful, noxious, ominous, ruinous
08 menacing, sinister
09 injurious, malignant
10 malevolent, pernicious
11 destructive, threatening

**balk, baulk**
03 bar, jib
04 foil
05 check, dodge, evade, stall

**ball**
06 baffle, defeat, eschew, flinch, hinder, impede, recoil, refuse, shrink, thwart
08 hesitate, obstruct
09 forestall, frustrate

**ball**
03 orb, wad
04 drop, pill, shot, slug
05 dance, globe, party
06 bullet, masque, pellet, sphere
07 globule
09 cotillion
11 dinner dance

❑**play ball**
07 go along, respond
09 cooperate, play along
11 collaborate, reciprocate

**ballad**
04 poem, song
05 ditty
08 folk song, love song

**ballet**
05 dance
07 dancing
➤ See also CHOREOGRAPHER; DANCE; DANCER

▬ *Terms used in ballet*:
04 jeté, plié, tutu
05 barre, battu
06 ballon, chassé, écarté, splits
07 à pointe, bourrée, ciseaux, company, fouetté, leotard, pointes
08 attitude, batterie, capriole, coryphée, fish dive, glissade, stulchak
09 arabesque, ballerina, battement, entrechat, élevation, pas de deux, pas de seul, pirouette, point shoe, régisseur
10 ballet shoe, grande jeté, répétiteur
11 ports de bras
12 choreography
13 corps de ballet, five positions, sur les pointes
14 divertissement, prima ballerina

▬ *Names of ballets*:
05 Rodeo
06 Apollo, Boléro, Façade, Ondine, Onegin, Parade
07 Giselle, Orpheus, Requiem
08 Coppélia, Les Noces, Swan Lake
09 Fancy Free, Mayerling, Petrushka, The Sylphs
10 Cinderella, Don Quixote,

Pulcinella
11 Billy the Kid, Las Hermanas, The Firebird
12 Les Sylphides
13 Pineapple Poll, The Nutcracker
14 Daphnis et Chloé, Romeo and Juliet, The Prodigal Son
15 The Rite of Spring
16 Frankie and Johnny

**balloon**
03 bag
05 belly, bulge, swell
06 billow, blow up, dilate
07 distend, inflate, puff out

**ballot**
04 poll, vote
08 election
10 plebiscite, referendum

**ballyhoo**
04 fuss, hype, to-do
05 noise
06 clamor, hubbub, racket, tumult
07 buildup
09 commotion, hue and cry, promotion, publicity
10 excitement, hullabaloo
11 advertising, disturbance

**balm**
05 cream, salve
06 balsam, lotion
07 anodyne, bromide, comfort
08 curative, lenitive, ointment
09 calmative, emollient
10 palliative
11 consolation, embrocation

**balmy**
04 mild, soft, warm
06 gentle
07 clement, summery
08 pleasant, soothing

**bamboozle**
03 con
04 daze, dupe, fool, gull
05 cheat, trick, upset
06 bemuse, puzzle
07 confuse, deceive, mystify, perplex, swindle
08 bewilder, confound, hoodwink
10 disconcert
11 hornswoggle

**ban**
03 bar
04 veto
05 curse, taboo
06 banish, censor, forbid, outlaw
07 boycott, embargo, exclude
08 prohibit, restrict, stoppage

09 proscribe, sanctions
10 disqualify, injunction
11 prohibition, restriction
12 interdiction, proscription

**banal**
04 dull
05 bland, corny, empty, inane, stale, stock, tired, trite, vapid
06 boring
07 clichéd, humdrum, mundane, trivial
08 everyday, ordinary, overused
09 hackneyed
11 commonplace, stereotyped
13 unimaginative

**banality**
06 cliché, truism
07 bromide, fatuity
08 dullness, vapidity
09 emptiness, inaneness, platitude, tiredness, triteness
11 commonplace
12 ordinariness

**band**
03 tie
04 belt, body, bond, club, cord, crew, gang, join, tape
05 crowd, group, horde, party, strap, strip, troop, unite
06 clique, fetter, gather, ribbon
07 binding, manacle, shackle
08 ensemble, ligature, pop group
09 affiliate, gathering, orchestra
10 amalgamate, connection, contingent, join forces
12 musical group, pull together
13 stand together

**bandage**
04 bind
05 cover, dress, gauze
06 bind up, swathe
07 Band-aid, swaddle
08 compress, dressing, ligature
10 tourniquet

**bandit**
05 crook, thief
06 badman, gunman, outlaw, pirate, robber
07 brigand
08 criminal, gangster, hijacker, marauder
09 buccaneer, desperado
10 highwayman

**bandy**
04 bent, pass, swap, toss
05 bowed, throw, trade
06 curved
07 crooked
08 exchange
09 bowlegged, misshapen

11 interchange, reciprocate

**bane**
03 woe
04 evil, pest, ruin
05 curse, trial
06 blight, misery, plague
07 scourge, torment, trouble
08 distress, nuisance, vexation
09 adversity, annoyance, bête
noire
10 affliction, irritation,
misfortune, pestilence
11 destruction

**bang**
03 hit, pop, rap
04 bash, blow, boom, bump,
clap, drum, shot, slam, thud
05 burst, clang, crash, knock,
noise, pound, punch, right,
smack, stamp, thump, whack
06 hammer, report, thrill, wallop
07 collide, exactly, explode,
thunder
08 directly, headlong, straight,
suddenly
09 enjoyment, explosion,
precisely
10 absolutely, detonation,
excitement

**banish**
03 ban, bar
04 oust
05 debar, evict, exile, expel
06 deport, dispel, outlaw
07 cast out, dismiss, exclude
08 get rid of, send away
09 drive away, eliminate,
eradicate, ostracize,
rusticate, transport
13 excommunicate

**banishment**
05 exile
08 eviction, outlawry
09 exclusion, expulsion,
ostracism
11 deportation, extradition
12 expatriation
14 transportation
15 excommunication

**banister, bannister**
04 rail
08 handrail
10 balustrade

**bank**
03 row, tip
04 heap, keep, pile, pool, rank,
rise, save, side, tier, tilt
05 array, bench, cache, drift,
hoard, knoll, levee, mound,
pitch, ridge, shore, slant,
slope, stack, stock, store

06 margin, save up, series
07 deposit, hillock, incline,
parados, reserve, savings
08 riparian, treasury
09 earthwork, stockpile
10 accumulate, depository,
embankment, repository
11 credit union, savings bank
12 finance house
14 finance company, investment
bank

□**bank on**
05 bet on, trust
06 rely on
07 count on
08 depend on
14 pin your hopes on

**bank note**
04 bill, note
14 promissory note

**bankrupt**
04 bust, ruin
05 broke, spent
06 beggar, busted, debtor,
failed, folded, pauper, ruined
07 belly up
08 in the red
09 destitute, gone under,
insolvent, penurious
10 on the rocks
11 impecunious
12 impoverished
13 gone to the wall, in
liquidation

**bankruptcy**
04 lack, ruin
06 penury
07 beggary, failure
09 ruination
10 beggarhood, exhaustion,
insolvency
11 liquidation
12 indebtedness
13 financial ruin

**banner**
04 flag, sign
06 burgee, colors, ensign,
pennon
07 labarum, pennant, placard
08 banderol, gonfalon, standard
09 banderole

**banquet**
04 meal
05 feast, party, treat
06 dinner, spread

**banter**
03 kid, rag, rib
04 jest, joke, mock
05 chaff
06 deride, joking

07 jesting, kidding, ribbing
08 badinage, chaffing, raillery,
repartee, word play
10 persiflage, pleasantry
15 pull someone's leg

**baptism**
05 début
06 launch, naming
08 affusion
09 beginning, immersion
10 dedication, initiation,
sprinkling
11 christening
12 inauguration, introduction

**baptize**
04 call, name, term
07 cleanse, immerse
08 christen, initiate, sprinkle

**bar**
03 ban, inn, pub, rod
04 bolt, cake, lock, lump, pole,
rail, save, slab, stop
05 block, chunk, court, debar,
grill, ingot, stick, table
06 batten, boozer, but for,
except, fasten, forbid,
lounge, nugget, paling,
saloon, secure, tavern
07 barrier, counsel, counter,
exclude, lawyers, prevent,
railing, suspend, taproom
08 alehouse, blockade, hostelry,
obstacle, obstruct, omitting,
prohibit, restrain, tribunal
09 apart from, barricade,
brasserie, excepting,
excluding, honky-tonk,
lounge bar
10 crosspiece, disqualify,
impediment
11 obstruction
12 watering hole

**barb**
03 dig
04 gibe
05 arrow, fluke, point, scorn,
sneer, spike, thorn
06 insult, needle, rebuff
07 bristle, prickle, sarcasm

**barbarian**
03 oaf
04 boor, lout, wild
05 brute, crude, rough
06 coarse, savage, vulgar
07 brutish, ruffian, uncouth
08 hooligan
09 ignoramus
10 philistine, uncultured
11 uncivilized
12 uncultivated
15 unsophisticated

**barbaric**
04 rude, wild
05 crude, cruel
06 brutal, coarse, fierce, savage
07 bestial, brutish, inhuman, uncouth, vicious
08 ruthless
09 barbarous, ferocious, murderous, primitive
11 uncivilized

**barbarism**
07 cruelty
08 ferocity, savagery, wildness
09 brutality, crudeness
10 bestiality, fierceness
11 brutishness, inhumanness, uncouthness, viciousness
12 ruthlessness
13 murderousness

**barbarity**
07 cruelty, outrage
08 atrocity, enormity, ferocity, savagery, wildness
09 brutality
10 inhumanity
11 brutishness, viciousness
12 ruthlessness
13 barbarousness

**barbarous**
04 rude, wild
05 crude, cruel, rough
06 brutal, fierce, savage, vulgar
07 bestial, inhuman, vicious
08 barbaric, ignorant, ruthless
09 barbarian, ferocious, heartless, murderous, primitive, unrefined
11 uncivilized
15 unsophisticated

**barbed**
04 acid
05 nasty, snide, spiny
06 hooked, jagged, spiked, thorny, unkind
07 caustic, cutting, hostile, hurtful, pointed, prickly, pronged, toothed

**bare**
04 bald, cold, hard, mere, nude
05 basic, bleak, empty, naked, plain, sheer, stark
06 barren, simple, vacant
07 denuded, exposed
08 absolute, desolate, in the raw, stripped, treeless
09 essential, in the nude, unadorned, unclothed, uncovered, undressed
10 defoliated, unforested
11 unfurnished, unsheltered
15 straightforward

**barefaced**
04 bald, bold, open
05 brash, naked
06 arrant, brazen, patent
07 blatant, glaring, obvious
08 flagrant, insolent, manifest
09 audacious, shameless, unabashed
11 undisguised

**barefooted**
06 unshod
08 barefoot, shoeless
09 discalced

**barely**
04 just
06 almost, hardly
08 no sooner, only just, scarcely
12 be a near thing
13 be a close thing

**bargain**
04 deal, pact, sell
05 steal, trade
06 barter, dicker, haggle, treaty
07 good buy, promise, traffic
08 beat down, covenant, discount, giveaway
09 agreement, concordat, negotiate, reduction
11 arrangement, negotiation, transaction
12 special offer
13 understanding

❏**bargain for**
06 expect
07 foresee, imagine, include, look for, plan for
08 consider, reckon on
10 anticipate
13 be prepared for
15 take into account

❏**into the bargain**
06 as well
07 besides
12 additionally

**bargaining**
08 dealings, haggling
09 bartering
11 negotiation, trafficking
12 horse-trading

**barge**
03 hit
04 bump, plow, push, rush, scow
05 elbow, press, shove, smash
06 jostle, push in
07 collide, lighter
08 flatboat
09 canalboat, houseboat

❏**barge in**
05 cut in
06 butt in
07 break in, burst in, intrude
09 gatecrash, interrupt

**bark**
03 bay, cry, yap
04 hide, howl, husk, peel, rind, skin, snap, woof, yell, yelp
05 crust, shell, shout, snarl
06 casing, cortex
08 covering

**baroque**
05 showy
06 florid, ornate, rococo
08 fanciful, vigorous
09 decorated, elaborate, exuberant, grotesque
10 convoluted, flamboyant
11 embellished, extravagant
13 overdecorated

**barracks**
06 billet, casern
07 caserne, lodging
08 garrison, quarters
13 accommodation

**barrage**
04 hail, mass, rain
05 burst, flood, salvo, storm
06 attack, deluge, shower
07 assault, battery, gunfire
08 shelling
09 abundance, broadside, cannonade, onslaught
11 bombardment

**barrel**
03 keg, tun, vat
04 butt, cask, rush
05 speed
06 tierce

**barren**
03 dry
04 arid, dull, flat
05 empty, vapid, waste
06 desert
07 sterile, useless
08 desolate, infecund
09 childless, fruitless, infertile, pointless, valueless
10 profitless, unfruitful
12 uncultivable, unproductive
13 uninformative

**barricade**
03 bar
04 shut
05 block, close, fence
06 defend
07 barrier, bulwark, defense, fortify, protect, shut off
08 blockade, obstacle, obstruct, palisade, stockade
10 protection, strengthen

**barrier**
03 bar
04 boom, gate, wall
05 check, ditch, fence
06 hurdle
07 railing, rampart
08 blockade, handicap, stockade
09 barricade, hindrance, restraint, roadblock
10 difficulty, impediment
11 obstruction, restriction
13 fortification
14 stumbling block

**barring**
06 except, unless
09 except for

**bartender**
07 barkeep
09 barkeeper
10 mixologist

**barter**
04 deal, sell, swap
05 trade
06 haggle
07 bargain, dealing, trading
08 exchange, haggling, swapping
10 bargaining

**base**
03 bed, key, low
04 camp, core, evil, foot, home, mean, poor, post, prop, rest, root, site, stay, vile
05 basis, build, stand
06 abject, bottom, center, depend, derive, fundus, ground, origin, plinth, sordid, source, vulgar, wicked
07 corrupt, essence, immoral, install, pitiful, station, support
08 depraved, keystone, pedestal, shameful, wretched
09 essential, establish, low-minded, miserable, principal, reprobate, valueless, worthless
10 despicable, foundation, groundwork, underneath
11 disgraceful, fundamental, ignominious
12 contemptible, disreputable, headquarters, unprincipled
15 foundation stone

**baseball**

➤ *Names of baseball players:*
03 **Ott** (Mel)
04 **Cobb** (Ty), **Dean** (Jay "Dizzy"), **Mack** (Connie),

**Mays** (Willie), **Rose** (Pete), **Ruth** (George Herman "Babe"), **Ryan** (Nolan), **Sosa** (Sammy)
05 **Aaron** (Hank), **Aaron** (Henry "Hank"), **Bench** (Johnny Lee), **Banks** (Ernie), **Berra** (Yogi), **Boggs** (Wade), **Bonds** (Barry), **Carew** (Rod), **Lemon** (Bob), **Maris** (Roger), **Paige** (Satchel), **Spahn** (Warren), **Young** (Cy)
06 **Feller** (Bob), **Gehrig** (Lou), **Gibson** (Josh), **Gibson** (Robert), **Gooden** (Dwight), **Koufax** (Sandford "Sandy"), **Mantle** (Mickey), **Musial** (Stan), **Ripken** (Cal), **Wagner** (Honus)
07 **Griffey** (Ken), **Hornsby** (Rogers), **Jackson** (Reggie), **McGwire** (Mark), **Stengel** (Casey)
08 **Clemente** (Roberto Walker), **DiMaggio** (Joe), **Durocher** (Leo), **Robinson** (Brooks), **Robinson** (Jackie), **Williams** (Ted)
09 **Alexander** (Grover Cleveland), **Killebrew** (Harmon), **Mathewson** (Christy)
10 **Campanella** (Roy)
➤ See also SPORT

**baseless**
09 unfounded
10 gratuitous, groundless
11 unconfirmed, unjustified
15 unsubstantiated

**basement**
05 crypt, vault
06 cellar

**bash**
02 go
03 hit, try
04 belt, shot, slug, sock, stab
05 break, crack, crash, knock, party, punch, smack, smash, whack, whirl
06 strike, wallop
08 wingding

**bashful**
03 coy, shy
05 timid
07 abashed, nervous
08 backward, blushing, hesitant, reserved, reticent, retiring, sheepish, timorous
09 diffident, inhibited, shrinking
10 shamefaced

11 embarrassed
12 self-effacing
13 self-conscious

**bashfulness**
07 blushes, coyness, modesty, reserve, shyness
08 timidity
09 hesitancy, reticence
10 diffidence, inhibition
11 nervousness
12 sheepishness
13 embarrassment
14 self-effacement

**basic**
03 key
04 core, root
05 crude, first, plain, stark, vital
06 simple, staple
07 austere, central, minimum, primary, radical, spartan
08 inherent, standard, starting
09 essential, important, intrinsic, necessary, primitive, unadorned
10 elementary, underlying
11 fundamental, preparatory
13 garden-variety, indispensable
15 meat-and-potatoes

**basically**
07 at heart
09 in essence, in the main, primarily, radically
10 inherently
11 essentially, principally
13 fundamentally, intrinsically

**basics**
05 facts
07 bedrock
09 realities, rudiments
10 brass tacks, essentials, principles, rock bottom
11 necessaries, nitty-gritty
12 fundamentals, introduction, nuts and bolts
15 meat and potatoes

**basin**
04 bowl, dish, sink
06 cavity, crater, hollow
10 depression

**basis**
04 base, core
05 heart, terms
06 bottom, ground, reason
07 bedrock, essence, footing, grounds, keynote, premise
08 approach
09 condition, essential, principle, rationale
10 conditions, essentials, foundation, groundwork

11 arrangement, cornerstone
12 fundamentals, quintessence
13 starting point
15 first principles

**bask**
03 lie
04 laze, loll
05 enjoy, lap up, relax, revel, savor
06 relish, wallow
08 sunbathe
09 delight in, luxuriate

**basket**
04 skep
06 gabion, hamper
07 pannier
08 bassinet

**basketball**

► *Names of basketball players:*
04 **Bird** (Larry), **West** (Jerry)
05 **Cousy** (Bob), **Hayes** (Elvin), **O'Neal** (Shaquille)
06 **Baylor** (Elgin), **Erving** (Julius), **Jordan** (Michael), **Malone** (Karl), **Malone** (Moses), **Pettit** (Bob), **Walton** (Bill)
07 **Barkley** (Charles), **Bradley** (Bill), **Iverson** (Allen), **Johnson** (Earvin "Magic"), **Russell** (Bill)
08 **Alcindor** (Lew), **Havlicek** (John), **Maravich** (Pete)
09 **Robertson** (Oscar)
11 **Abdul-Jabbar** (Kareem), **Chamberlain** (Wilt)

**bass**
03 low
04 deep, rich
09 deep-toned
10 low-pitched

**bastard**
09 love child
12 illegitimate, natural child

**bastardize**
06 debase, defile, demean
07 cheapen, corrupt, degrade, devalue, distort, pervert
10 adulterate, depreciate
11 contaminate

**bastion**
04 prop, rock
06 pillar
07 bulwark, citadel, defense
08 fortress, mainstay
10 protection, stronghold

**batch**
03 lot, set
04 mass, pack
06 amount, parcel
07 cluster
08 quantity
10 collection, contingent
11 consignment

**bath**
03 dip, spa, tub
04 soak
05 sauna
06 douche, shower
07 thermae
08 ablution
09 steam bath, steam room
10 bubble bath, Jacuzzi
11 Turkish bath
13 whirlpool bath

**bathe**
03 dip, wet
04 soak, wash
05 cover, flood, rinse, steep
06 shower
07 cleanse, immerse, moisten, suffuse
08 take a dip

**bathos**
07 letdown
08 comedown
10 anticlimax

**baton**
03 rod
05 billy, staff, stick
08 bily club
09 truncheon
10 nightstick

**battalion**
04 herd, host, mass, unit
05 force, horde
06 legion, throng, troops
07 section
08 garrison
09 multitude
11 ground force

**batten**
03 bar, fix
05 board, strip
06 fasten, secure
07 board up, tighten
08 nail down
09 barricade, clamp down

**batter**
03 hit
04 bash, beat, club, dash, lash
05 abuse, pound, smash, whack
06 bruise, buffet, pummel, strike, thrash, wallop
07 assault, wear out
10 knock about

□**batter down**
05 smash, wreck
07 destroy
08 demolish
09 break down

**battered**
06 abused, beaten, shabby
07 bruised, crushed, damaged
10 ill-treated, tumbledown
11 dilapidated
13 weather-beaten

**battery**
03 set
04 cell, guns
06 attack, cannon, series
07 beating, mugging
08 striking, violence
09 artillery, thrashing
10 succession
12 emplacements

**battle**
03 row, war
04 feud, fray, race
05 argue, brawl, clash, fight
06 action, attack, combat, debate, fracas, strife, strive
07 contest, crusade, dispute, quarrel, warfare
08 campaign, conflict, disagree, skirmish, struggle
09 encounter
10 Armageddon, engagement
11 altercation, competition, controversy, hostilities
12 disagreement
13 armed conflict

► *Names of battles. We have omitted the words* **battle of** *and* **battle of the** *from names given in the following list but you may need to include these words as part of the solution to some crossword clues.*
03 Kop
04 Guam, Jena, Neva, Nile, Troy (Siege of), Zama
05 Alamo, Anzio, Boyne, Bulge, Crécy, Issus, Marne, Mylae, Pavia, Rhine, Sedan, Somme, Spion, Spurs, Varna, Ypres
06 Actium, Amiens, Arnhem, Cannae, Kosovo, Midway, Mycale, Naseby, Pinkie, Shiloh, Tobruk, Verdun, Wagram
07 Antwerp, Atlanta, Britain, Bull Run, Cambrai, Corunna, Cowpens, Dresden, Flodden, Iwo Jima, Jutland, Lepanto, Marengo, Orléans (Siege of), Plassey, Salamis, Salerno,

Thapsus
08 Antietam, Atlantic, Blenheim, Culloden, Hastings, Manassas, Marathon, Omdurman, Philippi, Poitiers, Pyramids, Saratoga, Waterloo
09 Agincourt, Balaclava, Balaklava, Bay of Pigs, Chaeronea, El Alamein, Five Forks, Lexington, Nashville, Pharsalus, Princeton, Ramillies, Sedgemoor, Seven Days, Singapore, Solferino, Trafalgar, Vicksburg (Siege of)
10 Aboukir Bay, Adrianople, Austerlitz, Brandywine, Bunker Hill, Cold Harbor, Copenhagen, Germantown, Gettysburg, Long Island, Malplaquet, Oudenaarde, River Plate, Sevastopol (Siege of), Seven Pines, Stalingrad, Tannenberg, Tel-El-Kebir
11 Bannockburn, Chattanooga, Chickamauga, Guadalcanal, Marston Moor, Navarino Bay, Pearl Harbor, Prestonpans, Stones River, Wounded Knee
12 First Bull Run, Hampton Roads, Monte Cassino, Spotsylvania, Tet Offensive
13 Bosworth Field, Killiecrankie, Little Bighorn, Passchendaele, Second Bull Run
14 Fredericksburg
15 Glencoe Massacre

**battle-ax**
06 dragon, tartar, virago
08 harridan, martinet
09 termagant

**battle cry**
06 slogan, war cry
07 war song
09 rebel yell
11 rallying cry
12 rallying call

**battlefield**
05 arena, front
07 war zone
09 front line
10 combat zone
12 battleground

**batty**
03 mad, odd
04 bats, daft, nuts
05 crazy, dippy, dotty, loony, loopy, nutty, silly
06 insane, screwy

07 bonkers, cracked, foolish, idiotic
08 peculiar
09 eccentric
10 out to lunch
13 off your rocker, out of your head, out of your mind

**bauble**
03 toy
05 curio
06 gewgaw, tinsel, trifle
07 bibelot, chachka, trinket
08 gimcrack, kickshaw, ornament
09 tchotchke
10 knickknack

**baulk** see BALK

**bawd**
04 pimp
05 madam
09 panderess, procuress
13 brothel-keeper

**bawdy**
04 blue, lewd, rude
05 dirty, gross
06 coarse, erotic, ribald, risqué, smutty, vulgar
07 lustful, obscene
08 improper, indecent, prurient
09 lecherous, salacious
10 lascivious, suggestive

**bawl**
03 cry, sob
04 call, howl, roar, wail, weep, yell
05 shout
06 bellow, snivel, squall

▫ **bawl out**
05 scold
06 rebuke, yell at
07 chew out, tell off
09 reprimand

**bay**
03 arm, cry
04 bark, cove, gulf, howl, roar
05 bight, inlet, niche, sound
06 alcove, bellow, lagoon, recess

▸ *Names of bays. We have omitted the words* **bay** *and* **bay of** *from names given in the following list but you may need to include these words as part of the solution to some crossword clues.*
03 Tor
04 Acre, Bull, Daya, Kiel, Long, Pigs, Tees
05 Algoa, Fundy, Green, Hawke,

Morro, Tampa
06 Baffin, Bantry, Bengal, Biscay, Boston, Botany, Drake's, Dublin, Galway, Hudson, Mobile, Naples, Plenty, Tasman, Walvis
07 Aboukir, Cape Cod, Donegal, Dundalk, Glacier, Halifax, Hudson's, Jamaica, Montego, New York, Saginaw, Thunder, Trinity
08 Biscayne, Cardigan, Delaware, Monterey, Plymouth, Portland, San Diego, Sarasota, Weymouth
09 Admiralty, Apalachee, Frobisher, Galveston, Hermitage, Mackenzie, Morecombe, Pensacola
10 Carmarthen, Chesapeake, Conception, Heligoland, Robin Hood's
11 Atchafalaya, Port Jackson, Santa Monica
12 Narragansett, Saint George's, San Francisco
13 Massachusetts

**bayonet**
04 pike, stab
05 blade, knife, spear, stick
06 dagger, impale, pierce
07 poniard

**bazaar**
04 fair, fête, mart, sale, souk
06 market
08 exchange

**be**
03 lie
04 form, last, live, make, stay
05 abide, exist, occur, stand
06 endure, happen, remain
07 add up to, breathe, develop, persist, prevail, survive
08 amount to, continue
09 be located, come about, take place, transpire
10 come to pass, constitute

**beach**
04 sand
05 coast, sands, shore
06 strand
07 seaside, shingle
08 littoral, seaboard, seashore
10 water's edge

**beachcomber**
07 forager
09 scavenger, scrounger

**beacon**
04 beam, fire, sign
05 flare, light
06 Pharos, rocket, signal

**bead**

07 bonfire
10 lighthouse, watchtower

**bead**

04 ball, blob, drip, drop, glob
05 jewel, pearl
06 bubble, pellet
07 droplet, globule

**beak**

03 nib
04 bill, nose
07 rostrum
09 mandibles, proboscis

**beaker**

03 cup, jar, mug
05 glass
07 tankard, tumbler

**beam**

03 aim, bar, ray
04 boom, glow, grin, send, spar
05 glare, joist, plank, relay, shaft, shine, smile
06 direct, girder, lintel, rafter, stream, timber
07 radiate, support, transom
08 stringer, transmit
09 broadcast, scantling, stanchion
10 cantilever

**bean**

09 fabaceous
10 leguminous

► *Varieties of bean and pulse. We have omitted the word* **bean** *from names given in the following list but you may need to include this word as part of the solution to some crossword clues.*

03 dal, pea, pea, red, soy, wax
04 fava, lima, mung, okra, snap
05 broad, carob, green, pinto
06 adzuki, butter, chilli, cow pea, French, kidney, legume, lentil, locust, runner, string
07 alfalfa, haricot
08 chickpea, garbanzo, navy bean, split pea
09 marrow pea, marrowfat, red kidney
10 beansprout
12 black-eyed pea
➤ See also FOOD

**bear**

03 pay
04 have, hold, hump, like, move, show, take, tote, turn, veer
05 abide, admit, allow, beget, breed, bring, carry, curve, drive, fetch, stand, yield

06 accept, convey, endure, give up, harbor, permit, suffer, uphold
07 develop, deviate, display, diverge, produce, stomach, support, sustain
08 engender, generate, live with, shoulder, tolerate
09 put up with, transport
10 bring forth
11 give birth to

❑**bear in mind**

04 note
08 consider, remember
11 be mindful of
15 take into account

❑**bear out**

05 prove
06 back up, ratify, uphold, verify
07 confirm, endorse, support
11 corroborate, demonstrate

❑**bear up**

04 cope
06 endure, suffer
07 carry on, survive
09 soldier on, withstand

❑**bear with**

08 tolerate
09 put up with
13 be patient with

**bearable**

08 passable
09 endurable, tolerable
10 acceptable, manageable
11 supportable, sustainable

**beard**

04 dare, defy, face, tuft
06 beaver, goatee, oppose
07 bristle, stubble, Vandyke
08 confront, imperial, whiskers
09 burnsides, challenge, sideburns
10 facial hair
11 muttonchops
14 stand up against

**bearded**

05 bushy, hairy
06 shaggy, tufted
07 bristly, hirsute, stubbly
08 unshaven
09 whiskered
11 bewhiskered

**bearer**

05 payee
06 holder, porter, runner
07 carrier, courier
08 conveyor
09 consignee, messenger, possessor

**bearing**

04 gait, mien
05 poise, track
06 aspect, course, manner
07 concern, posture, stature
08 behavior, carriage, demeanor, location, position
09 direction, influence, reference, relevance
10 deportment, pertinence
11 comportment, orientation
12 significance

**beast**

03 pig
05 brute, devil, fiend, swine
06 animal, savage
07 monster
08 creature

**beastly**

04 foul
05 awful, cruel, nasty
06 brutal, horrid, rotten
08 horrible, terrible
09 repulsive
10 unpleasant

**beat**

03 box, hit, mix, tan, way
04 bang, bash, belt, best, biff, blow, cane, club, dash, drub, flap, flay, flog, lash, lick, path, pelt, rout, slap, stir, time, walk, welt, wham, whip
05 birch, clout, forge, knock, knout, meter, outdo, paste, pound, pulse, punch, round, route, shake, smack, stamp, strap, swing, swipe, tempo, throb, thump, tired, whack, whisk
06 batter, bruise, buffet, cudgel, defeat, fill in, hammer, outrun, outwit, pummel, quiver, rhythm, rounds, strike, stroke, subdue, thrash, thwack, wallop, zonked
07 circuit, clobber, combine, conquer, contuse, flutter, lambast, lay into, measure, outplay, pulsate, shellac, surpass, tremble, trounce, vibrate, wearied, worn out
08 fatigued, malleate, outsmart, outstrip, overcome, vanquish
09 exhausted, overpower, overwhelm, palpitate, subjugate, territory, transcend, vibration, zonked out
10 annihilate

❑**beat up**

03 mug

**beaten**
06 attack, batter
07 assault, rough up
10 knock about
11 knock around

**beaten**
05 foamy, mixed
06 forged, formed, frothy
07 blended, stamped, trodden, whipped, whisked, wrought
08 hammered, trampled, well-used, well-worn
11 well-trodden

**beatific**
06 divine, joyful
07 angelic, blessed, exalted, sublime
08 blissful, ecstatic, heavenly
09 rapturous

**beatify**
05 bless, exalt
06 hallow
08 sanctify

**beating**
04 rout, ruin
06 caning, defeat
07 hitting, lashing, the cane
08 bruising, clubbing, conquest, drubbing, flogging, punching, slapping, the birch, the strap, thumping, whipping
09 battering, hammering, slaughter, thrashing, trouncing, walloping
11 outsmarting, vanquishing
12 overwhelming

**beau**
05 lover
06 escort, fiancé, steady, suitor
07 admirer
09 boyfriend
10 sweetheart

**beautician**
07 friseur
11 cosmetician, hairdresser, hairstylist

**beautiful**
04 fair, fine
05 bonny
06 comely, lovely, pretty, seemly
07 radiant
08 becoming, gorgeous, graceful, handsome, smashing, striking, stunning
09 exquisite, ravishing
10 voluptuous
11 good-looking, magnificent
15 pulchritudinous

**beautify**
04 deck, gild

05 adorn, array, grace
06 bedeck, doll up
07 enhance, improve, smarten
08 decorate, ornament, spruce up, titivate
09 embellish, glamorize

**beauty**
04 doll
05 belle, bonus, glory, grace, merit, peach, siren, Venus
06 allure, appeal, corker, virtue
07 benefit, charmer, dazzler, stunner
08 dividend, knockout, radiance, symmetry
09 advantage, good looks, good point, plus point
10 attraction, excellence, good-looker, loveliness, prettiness, seemliness
11 femme fatale, pulchritude
12 gorgeousness, gracefulness, handsomeness
13 exquisiteness

**beaver**

❑**beaver away**
06 work at
07 persist
08 plug away, work hard
09 persevere, slave away

**becalmed**
05 still, stuck
08 marooned, stranded
10 motionless
13 at a standstill

**because**
02 as
03 for
05 due to, since
07 owing to, through
08 seeing as, thanks to
10 by reason of, by virtue of
11 as a result of, on account of

**beckon**
04 call, coax, draw, lure, pull
05 tempt
06 allure, entice, induce, invite
07 attract, gesture
11 gesticulate

**become**
03 get, wax
04 grow, suit, turn
05 befit, grace
06 set off
07 enhance, flatter
08 grow into, ornament
09 embellish, harmonize
10 change into, look good on
11 develop into, turn out to be
13 be changed into

**becoming**
06 comely, pretty
07 elegant, fitting
08 charming, fetching, graceful
10 attractive, compatible, consistent, flattering
11 appropriate

**bed**
03 cot, fix, hay, row
04 base, bunk, bury, plot, rack, sack
05 couch, divan, embed, floor, futon, layer, patch, plant, strip
06 border, bottom, garden, ground, insert, matrix, settle
07 channel, implant, stratum
09 Murphy bed
10 foundation, substratum
11 watercourse

❑**bed down**
05 sleep
06 turn in
07 go to bed
09 hit the hay
10 hit the sack, settle down

❑**go to bed with**
09 sleep with
10 make love to
11 have sex with

**bedclothes**
06 covers, sheets
07 bedding
08 bed linen, blankets
10 comforters
11 pillowcases

**bedeck**
04 deck, trim
05 adorn, array
07 festoon, garnish
08 beautify, decorate, ornament, trick out

**bedevil**
03 irk, vex
04 fret
05 annoy, tease, worry
06 harass, pester, plague
07 afflict, besiege, torment, torture, trouble
08 confound, distress, irritate
09 frustrate

**bedlam**
05 babel, chaos, furor, noise
06 clamor, tumult, uproar
07 anarchy, turmoil
08 madhouse
09 commotion, confusion
10 hullabaloo
11 pandemonium

**bedraggled**
03 wet

05 dirty, messy, muddy
06 soaked, soiled, untidy
07 scruffy, soaking, unkempt
08 drenched, dripping
10 disheveled, disordered, soaking wet

**bedridden**
06 laid up
13 confined to bed, incapacitated
14 flat on your back

**bedrock**
04 base
05 basis, heart
06 basics, bottom, reason
07 premise, reasons, support
09 rationale
10 essentials, foundation
12 fundamentals
15 first principles

**beef**
04 moan
05 gripe
06 grouse, object
07 dispute, grumble
08 complain, disagree

❑**beef up**
07 build up, toughen
09 establish, reinforce
10 invigorate, strengthen
11 consolidate
12 substantiate

**beefy**
03 fat
05 bulky, burly, heavy, hefty
06 brawny, stocky, sturdy
07 hulking
08 muscular, stalwart
09 corpulent

**beer**

▶ *Types of beer*:
03 ale, keg
04 kvas, lite, Pils
05 draft, kvass, lager, light, plain, stout
06 bitter, porter
07 bottled, Pilsner
08 brown ale, homebrew, light ale, Pilsener
09 weiss beer, wheat beer
➢ See also DRINK

**beetle**

▶ *Beetles include*:
03 dor, oil
04 bark, dorr, dung, musk, rose, rove, stag
05 click, water
06 chafer, ground, scarab, weevil

07 blister, burying, cadelle, carabid, firefly, ladybug
08 Colorado, glowworm, ladybird, woodworm
09 goldsmith, longicorn, tumblebug, whirligig
10 bombardier, cockchafer, deathwatch, long-horned, rhinoceros, rose chafer
12 lightning bug
➢ See also ANIMAL

**beetle, beetling**
03 jut
07 jutting, pendent, project
08 overhang, protrude, stick out
10 projecting, protruding
11 overhanging, sticking out

**befall**
05 ensue, occur
06 arrive, betide, chance, follow, happen, result
09 supervene, take place

**befitting**
03 apt, fit
04 meet
05 right
06 decent, proper, seemly
07 correct, fitting
08 becoming, suitable
11 appropriate

**before**
07 ahead of, already, earlier, in front, prior to
08 formerly
09 in advance, in front of
10 on the eve of, previous to, previously, sooner than
15 in the presence of

**beforehand**
06 before, sooner
07 already, earlier
09 in advance
10 previously

**befriend**
03 aid
04 back, help
05 favor
06 assist, defend, succor, uphold
07 benefit, comfort, protect, stand by, support, sustain, welcome
09 encourage, get to know
10 fall in with, stick up for
11 keep an eye on

**befuddle**
04 daze
06 baffle, muddle, puzzle
07 confuse, stupefy
08 bewilder

09 disorient

**beg**
04 pray
05 cadge, crave, mooch, plead
06 appeal, ask for, sponge
07 beseech, entreat, implore
08 petition, scrounge
09 importune
10 supplicate

**beget**
04 sire
05 breed, cause, spawn
06 create, effect, father
07 produce
08 engender, generate
09 procreate, propagate
10 bring about, give rise to

**beggar**
03 bum
04 defy
05 tramp
06 cadger, exceed, pauper
07 bludger, moocher, sponger, surpass, vagrant
09 mendicant, schnorrer, scrounger, transcend
10 down-and-out, freeloader, panhandler, supplicant
12 down-and-outer

**beggarly**
03 low
04 mean
06 abject, meager, paltry, stingy
07 miserly, pitiful
08 pathetic, wretched
10 despicable, inadequate

**begin**
04 open
05 arise, found, start
06 appear, crop up, embark, emerge, launch, set off, spring
07 actuate, do first, kick off
08 activate, commence, initiate, set about
09 instigate, institute, introduce, originate
11 get cracking, set in motion

**beginner**
03 cub
04 tiro, tyro
06 novice, rookie
07 learner, recruit, starter, student, trainee
08 freshman, initiate, neophyte
09 fledgling, greenhorn
10 apprentice, raw recruit, tenderfoot
11 abecedarian, probationer

## beginning

04 dawn, rise, root, seed
05 birth, intro, onset, start
06 day one, launch, origin, outset, source
07 genesis, kickoff, opening
09 first base, first part, inception, square one, the word go
10 conception, first stage, fresh start, inchoation, incipience, initiation
11 institution, pastures new
12 commencement, fountainhead, inauguration, starting gate
13 establishment, starting point

## begrudge

04 envy, mind
05 covet, stint
06 grudge, resent
11 be jealous of

## beguile

04 dupe, fool
05 amuse, charm, cheat, cozen, trick
06 delude, divert, seduce
07 attract, bewitch, deceive, delight, enchant, mislead
08 distract, hoodwink
09 captivate, entertain

## beguiling

08 alluring, charming, enticing
09 appealing, seductive
10 bewitching, delightful, enchanting, intriguing
11 captivating, interesting

## behalf

❏ **on behalf of**
07 in aid of
09 acting for
11 in the name of, speaking for
12 for the sake of, representing
13 to the profit of

## behave

03 act
04 work
05 react
06 be good
07 operate, perform, respond
08 function
10 act your age
15 comport yourself, conduct yourself, mind your manners, mind your p's and q's

## behavior

04 ways
06 action, habits, manner
07 conduct, manners

08 dealings, demeanor, reaction, response
09 attitudes
10 deportment
11 comportment, performance

## behead

07 execute
10 decapitate, guillotine

## behest

❏ **at the behest of**
12 at the order of
13 on the wishes of
14 at the bidding of, at the command of, at the request of

## behind

03 bum, for
04 butt, late, next, slow
05 after
06 bottom, in debt
07 backing, causing, overdue
08 backside, buttocks
09 at the back, endorsing, following, in arrears, in the rear, later than, posterior
10 behindhand, explaining, initiating, supporting
11 instigating, running late
12 giving rise to, subsequently
13 at the bottom of
14 responsible for
15 slower than usual

## behindhand

04 late, slow
05 tardy
07 delayed
08 backward, dilatory

## behold

02 lo
03 see
04 ecce, look, mark, note, view
05 voici, voila, watch
06 gaze at, look at, regard
07 discern, observe, witness
08 consider, perceive

## beholden

05 bound, owing
07 obliged
08 grateful, indebted, thankful
09 obligated

## behoove

05 befit
08 be proper, be seemly
11 be essential, be necessary

## beige

03 tan
04 buff, ecru, fawn
05 camel, khaki, sandy
06 coffee, greige

07 neutral, oatmeal
08 mushroom

## being

03 man
04 esse, life, soul
05 beast, human, thing, woman
06 animal, entity, mortal, nature, person, spirit
08 creature
09 actuality, existence, haecceity, substance
10 human being, individual

## belabor

03 hit
04 beat, belt, flay, flog, whip
05 scold
06 attack, thrash

## belated

04 late
05 tardy
07 delayed, overdue

## belch

04 burp, emit, spew, vent
05 eject, eruct
06 hiccup
07 give off, give out
08 disgorge, eructate
09 discharge
11 bring up wind

## beleaguered

05 beset, vexed
07 plagued, worried
08 badgered, besieged, bothered, harassed, pestered
09 blockaded
10 surrounded, under siege

## belie

04 deny
06 negate, refute
07 conceal, confute, deceive, falsify, gainsay, mislead
08 disguise, disprove
10 contradict

## belief

03 ism
04 view
05 creed, dogma, faith, tenet, trust
06 credit, notion, theory
07 feeling, opinion
08 doctrine, ideology, sureness
09 assurance, certainty, principle, viewpoint
10 confidence, conviction, impression, persuasion
11 point of view, presumption

## believable

06 likely
08 credible, possible, probable
09 plausible

**believe**
10 acceptable, imaginable
11 conceivable, trustworthy

**believe**
03 buy
04 deem, hold, wear
05 guess, opine, think, trust
06 accept, assume, reckon
07 imagine, suppose, swallow
08 consider, maintain
10 understand
11 be certain of, take on board

❑ **believe in**
05 favor, trust
06 rely on
07 swear by
08 depend on
09 approve of, recommend
11 value highly
13 be convinced of, be
    persuaded by

**believer**
06 zealot
07 convert, devotee
08 adherent, disciple, follower
09 proselyte, supporter

**belittle**
05 decry, scorn
06 demean, deride, lessen
07 dismiss, run down
08 diminish, minimize, play
    down, ridicule
09 deprecate, disparage
10 understate, undervalue
11 detract from

**bellicose**
07 violent, warlike, warring
08 bullying, militant
09 combative
10 aggressive, pugnacious
11 contentious, quarrelsome
12 antagonistic

**belligerence**
03 war
08 bullying, violence
09 militancy, pugnacity
10 aggression, antagonism
12 warmongering
13 saber rattling

**belligerent**
07 violent, warlike, warring
08 bullying, militant
09 combative, truculent
10 aggressive, pugnacious
11 contentious, provocative
12 antagonistic, disputatious,
    warmongering
13 argumentative, saber rattling

**bellow**
03 cry
04 bawl, howl, roar, yell

05 shout
06 holler, scream, shriek
14 raise your voice

**belly**
03 gut
04 guts
05 tummy
06 paunch, venter
07 abdomen, insides, stomach
08 potbelly
10 intestines
11 breadbasket, corporation

**belong**
05 fit in
06 go with
07 be yours
08 attach to, be part of
09 be owned by, tie up with
10 be included, link up with
11 be a member of
13 have as its home
14 be affiliated to, be an
    adherent of, have as its place
15 be the property of

**belonging**
05 links
07 kinship, loyalty, rapport
08 affinity
09 closeness
10 acceptance, fellowship
11 association
13 compatibility, fellow-feeling

**belongings**
04 gear
05 goods, stuff
06 things
07 effects
08 chattels, property
11 possessions
13 accouterments,
    appurtenances,
    paraphernalia

**beloved**
04 dear, love, wife
05 flame, honey, loved, lover,
    sweet
06 adored, fiancé, spouse
07 darling, dearest, fiancée,
    husband, partner, revered
08 favorite, precious
09 betrothed, boyfriend,
    cherished, inamorata,
    inamorato, much loved,
    treasured
10 girlfriend, sweetheart

**below**
03 sub
04 down
05 later, lower, under
07 beneath
09 further on, subject to

10 inferior to, lesser than,
    underneath
13 subordinate to

**belt**
03 box, fly, hit, tan, zip
04 area, bang, bash, biff, cane,
    dash, flay, flog, gulp, lash,
    pelt, rush, sash, slap, tear,
    whip, zone
05 birch, clout, knock, punch,
    smack, speed, strap, strip,
    swipe, thump, tract, whack
06 bruise, career, cestus, girdle,
    region, strike, swathe,
    thwack, wallop
07 baldric, bashing, stretch
08 cincture, cingulum, district
09 waistband
10 cummerbund

❑ **belt up**
05 can it
06 shut up
07 be quiet
08 cut it out, pipe down
10 knock it off
12 shut your face
13 shut your mouth

**bemoan**
03 rue
05 mourn
06 bewail, lament, regret
07 deplore, sigh for, weep for
09 grieve for
10 sorrow over

**bemuse**
07 confuse, perplex, stupefy
08 befuddle, bewilder

**bemused**
05 dazed
07 muddled, puzzled
08 confused
09 astounded, befuddled,
    perplexed, stupefied
10 astonished, bewildered

**bench**
03 pew
04 form, seat
05 board, judge, ledge, table
06 settle
07 counter
08 tribunal
09 judiciary, workbench,
    worktable
10 judicature, magistrate
11 substitutes

**benchmark**
04 norm
05 level, model, scale
08 standard

## bend

09 criterion, guideline, reference, yardstick
10 guidelines, touchstone

**bend**
03 arc, bow
04 arch, flex, hook, kink, lean, loop, sway, turn, veer, warp
05 angle, crook, curve, elbow, kneel, shape, stoop, twist, yield
06 affect, buckle, corner, crouch, dogleg, swerve
07 contort, deviate, diverge, flexure, hairpin, incline, meander
08 persuade
09 curvature, influence
10 deflection, divergence
11 hairpin turn, incurvation
12 hairpin curve

**beneath**
05 below, lower, under
10 underneath, unworthy of
11 unbefitting

**benediction**
05 favor, grace
06 prayer
07 benison
08 blessing
10 invocation

**benefactor**
05 angel, donor, giver
06 backer, friend, helper, patron
07 sponsor
08 promoter, provider
09 supporter
10 subsidizer, well-wisher
11 contributor
14 philanthropist

**beneficent**
04 kind
06 benign
07 helpful, liberal
08 generous
09 bountiful, unselfish
10 altruistic, benevolent, charitable, munificent

**beneficial**
06 useful
07 helpful
08 edifying, salutary, valuable
09 favorable, improving, promising, rewarding, wholesome
10 profitable
12 advantageous

**beneficiary**
04 heir
05 payee
07 heiress, legatee

08 receiver
09 inheritor, recipient

**benefit**
03 aid, use
04 boon, dole, gain, good, help
05 asset, avail, bonus, favor, serve
06 assist, better, credit, income, payoff, profit
07 advance, enhance, further, improve, payment, pension, promote, service, sick pay, support, welfare
08 dividend, do good to, Medicaid, Medicare
09 advantage, allowance
10 assistance
12 sick benefits
13 be of service to, fringe benefit, retirement pay
14 social security

**benevolence**
04 care, pity
05 grace, mercy
08 altruism, goodwill, kindness
10 compassion, generosity
11 magnanimity, munificence
12 friendliness, philanthropy
14 charitableness
15 humanitarianism, kindheartedness

**benevolent**
04 kind
06 benign, caring, kindly
08 friendly, generous, merciful
10 altruistic, charitable, munificent
11 considerate, kindhearted, magnanimous, softhearted
13 compassionate, philanthropic

**benighted**
08 backward, ignorant
09 unknowing
10 illiterate, uncultured, uneducated, unschooled
11 unfortunate
13 unenlightened

**benign**
04 good, kind, mild, warm
06 genial, gentle
07 affable, amiable, cordial, curable, healthy, liberal
08 friendly, gracious, harmless
09 agreeable, favorable, temperate, treatable
10 auspicious, beneficial, benevolent, charitable, propitious
11 restorative, sympathetic
12 nonmalignant, providential

**bent**
04 gift, wont
05 bowed, flair, forte, knack
06 angled, arched, curved, desire, folded, talent, warped
07 ability, crooked, faculty, hunched, leaning, stooped, twisted
08 aptitude, facility, fondness, penchant, tendency
09 contorted
10 preference, proclivity, propensity
11 curvilinear, disposition, inclination, predilecton
14 predisposition

❑**bent on**
05 set on
07 fixed on
08 intent on
10 resolved to
11 insistent on
12 determined to

**bequeath**
04 give, will
05 endow, grant, leave
06 assign, bestow, commit, impart, pass on
07 consign, entrust
08 hand down, make over

**bequest**
04 gift
05 trust
06 estate, legacy
07 devisal
08 bestowal, donation, heritage
09 endowment
10 bequeathal, settlement
11 inheritance

**berate**
05 blast, chide, scold, slate
06 rail at, rebuke, revile
07 censure, chew out, reprove, tell off, upbraid
08 chastise, give hell, reproach, tear into
09 castigate, criticize, dress down, fulminate, reprimand
10 tongue-lash, vituperate

**bereaved**
06 robbed
07 widowed
08 deprived, orphaned
12 dispossessed

**bereavement**
04 loss
05 death, grief
06 sorrow
07 passing, sadness
11 deprivation, passing-away
13 dispossession

## bereft

**❏ bereft of**
05 minus
07 lacking, wanting
08 devoid of, robbed of
10 cut off from, deprived of, parted from, stripped of

## berserk
03 mad
04 wild
05 crazy, manic, rabid
06 crazed, insane, raging, raving
07 frantic, furious, violent
08 demented, deranged, frenzied, maniacal
10 hysterical
14 uncontrollable

## berth
03 bed
04 bunk, dock, land, moor
05 tie up
06 anchor, billet
07 hammock, mooring
09 anchorage
10 cast anchor, drop anchor

## beseech
03 ask, beg, sue
04 pray
05 crave, plead
06 adjure, desire, exhort
07 entreat, implore, solicit
08 appeal to, petition
09 importune
10 supplicate

## beset
05 hem in, worry
06 assail, attack, harass, hassle, pester, plague
07 bedevil, torment
08 entangle, surround

## besetting
08 constant, habitual
09 harassing, recurring
10 inveterate, persistent
11 troublesome
12 irresistible
14 uncontrollable

## beside
02 by
04 near
06 next to
07 close to
08 abutting, adjacent
09 abreast of, alongside
10 next door to
11 neighboring

**❏ beside the point**
09 pointless, unrelated
10 extraneous, immaterial, incidental, irrelevant

**❏ beside yourself**
03 mad
05 crazy
06 crazed, insane
07 berserk, frantic
08 demented, deranged, frenetic, frenzied, unhinged
09 delirious
10 distraught, unbalanced

## besides
03 too
04 also
06 as well
07 further
08 as well as, moreover
09 apart from, aside from, excluding, other than, what's more
10 in addition
11 furthermore
12 additionally, in addition to, over and above

## besiege
03 nag
05 beset, hem in, hound, worry
06 assail, badger, bother, harass, pester, plague, shut in
07 confine, trouble
08 blockade, encircle, surround
09 beleaguer, encompass, importune

## besmirch
04 soil
05 dirty, smear, stain, sully
06 damage, defame, defile
07 blacken, slander, tarnish
08 dishonor

## besotted
06 doting
07 smitten
08 obsessed
09 bewitched, stupefied
10 infatuated, spellbound

## bespeak
04 show
05 imply
06 attest, denote, evince, reveal
07 display, exhibit, signify, suggest
08 evidence, indicate, proclaim
11 demonstrate

## best
03 ace, top
04 most, pick, rout, star, tops
05 cream, elite, first, ideal, prime
06 choice, finest, outwit, subdue, thrash, utmost
07 clobber, conquer, hardest, highest, largest, leading,
optimal, optimum, perfect, supreme, the tops, trounce
08 favorite, foremost, greatest, peerless, ultimate
09 damnedest, excellent, extremely, first-rate, matchless, nonpareil, number one, unequaled, unrivaled, worthiest
10 first-class, preeminent
11 excellently, outstanding, superlative, unsurpassed
12 second to none
13 have the edge on, superlatively, unsurpassedly
14 record-breaking

## bestial
04 vile
05 cruel, feral, gross
06 animal, brutal, carnal, savage, sordid
07 beastly, brutish, inhuman
08 barbaric, depraved
09 barbarous

## bestir
05 exert
06 arouse, awaken, incite
07 actuate, animate
08 activate, energize, motivate
09 galvanize, stimulate

## bestow
04 give
05 allot, award, endow, grant
06 accord, commit, confer, donate, impart, lavish
07 entrust, present
08 bequeath, transmit
09 apportion

## bestride
08 dominate, straddle
10 overshadow, sit astride

## bet
03 bid, lay, put
04 ante, back, risk, view
05 place, stake, wager
06 be sure, chance, choice, expect, gamble, hazard, option, parlay, pledge, theory
07 lottery, venture
09 be certain, intuition, speculate, viewpoint
10 conviction, sweepstake
11 be convinced, speculation

► *Types of bet and betting system*:
03 win
04 tote
05 place
06 exacta, tierce, triple

07 each way
08 perfecta, quinella, quiniela, trifecta, win-place
09 martingal, on the nose, quadrella
10 martingale, parimutuel
11 daily double, totalizator
13 running double

**bête noire**
04 bane
05 curse
07 bugbear, pet hate
08 anathema, aversion
11 abomination, pet aversion

**betide**
05 ensue, occur
06 befall, chance, happen
08 overtake

**betoken**
04 bode, mark
05 augur
06 denote, signal
07 bespeak, portend, presage, promise, signify, suggest
08 evidence, forebode, indicate, manifest
09 represent

**betray**
04 dupe, sell, show, tell
06 delude, desert, expose, reveal, tell on, turn in, unmask
07 deceive, divulge, forsake, let slip, mislead, sell out
08 disclose, give away, inform on, manifest, squeal on
11 double-cross, turn traitor
12 be disloyal to, bring to light
13 stab in the back
14 be unfaithful to, break faith with

**betrayal**
07 perfidy, sellout, treason
08 trickery
09 deception, duplicity, falseness, treachery
10 disloyalty
13 double-dealing
14 double-crossing

**betrayer**
05 Judas
06 snitch
07 stoolie, traitor
08 apostate, informer, renegade
13 double-crosser, whistle-blower
14 Benedict Arnold

**betrothal**
04 vows
05 troth

07 promise
08 espousal
10 engagement

**betrothed**
07 engaged
08 espoused, promised
09 affianced

**better**
03 cap, top
04 beat, mend, well
05 cured, finer, outdo, raise
06 bigger, enrich, exceed, fitter, healed, larger, longer, reform
07 correct, enhance, improve, promote, rectify, surpass
08 outstrip, overtake, restored, stronger, superior, worthier
09 a cut above, healthier, on the mend, recovered
10 ameliorate, preferable
11 more fitting, progressing
14 fully recovered

**betterment**
10 enrichment
11 advancement, edification, enhancement, furtherance, improvement, melioration
12 amelioration

**between**
03 mid
04 amid
05 among
06 amidst
07 amongst, halfway
11 in the middle

**bevel**
04 bias, cant, tilt
05 angle, bezel, slant, slope
07 chamfer, oblique

**beverage**
05 draft, drink
06 liquid, liquor
07 potable
08 potation
11 refreshment

**bevy**
04 band, pack
05 bunch, crowd, flock, group
06 gaggle, throng, troupe
07 company
08 assembly
09 gathering

**bewail**
03 rue
04 keen, moan, sigh
05 mourn
06 bemoan, lament, regret
07 cry over, deplore
08 wail over
10 grieve over, sorrow over

**beware**
04 heed, mind, shun
05 avoid
06 be wary
07 look out
08 take heed, watch out
09 be careful
10 be cautious
12 guard against, steer clear of
13 be on your guard

**bewilder**
05 mix up, stump
06 baffle, bemuse, muddle, puzzle
07 confuse, mystify, perplex, stupefy
08 befuddle, confound
09 bamboozle, disorient
10 disconcert

**bewildered**
05 at sea
07 baffled, bemused, muddled, puzzled, stunned
08 confused
09 befuddled, mystified, perplexed
10 bamboozled, nonplussed
11 disoriented

**bewilderment**
03 awe
09 confusion
10 perplexity, puzzlement
12 stupefaction
13 disconcertion, mystification
14 disorientation

**bewitch**
05 charm
06 allure, obsess, seduce
07 beguile, delight, enchant, possess
08 enthrall, entrance, intrigue, transfix
09 captivate, enrapture, fascinate, hypnotize, mesmerize, spellbind

**beyond**
04 over, past
05 above, after, ultra
08 away from, upward of
09 later than
10 remote from
11 further than, greater than
12 out of range of, out of reach of
14 on the far side of

**bias**
04 bent, load, sway, warp
05 angle, cross, slant, twist
06 earwig, weight
07 bigotry, distort, leaning
08 diagonal, jaundice, tendency

09 influence, prejudice
10 distortion, favoritism, partiality, predispose, proclivity, propensity, unfairness
11 inclination, intolerance, load the dice
12 one-sidedness, predilection

**biased**
06 angled, loaded, swayed, unfair, warped
07 bigoted, partial, slanted
08 one-sided, partisan, weighted
09 distorted, jaundiced
10 influenced, prejudiced
11 predisposed, tendentious

**Bible**
03 law
05 canon
06 manual, primer
07 Gospels, letters, lexicon
08 epistles, good book, handbook, holy writ, prophets, textbook, writings
09 Apocrypha, authority, guidebook, Holy Bible
10 revelation, Scriptures
12 New Testament, Old Testament
13 reference book
➢ See also RELIGION

▶ *Names of biblical characters*:
03 Dan, Eve, Gad, Ham, Job, Lot
04 Abel, Adam, Ahab, Amos, Baal, Cain, Esau, Ezra, Joel, John, Leah, Levi, Luke, Mark, Mary, Noah, Paul, Ruth, Saul, Shem
05 Aaron, Asher, David, Herod (the Great), Hosea, Isaac, Jacob, James, Jesus, Jonah, Judah, Judas, Micah, Moses, Nahum, Peter, Sarah, Sheba (Queen of), Simon, Titus, Tobit
06 Andrew, Baruch, Christ, Daniel, Elijah, Elisha, Esther, Gideon, Isaiah, Joseph, Joshua, Judith, Philip, Pilate, Rachel, Reuben, Salome, Samson, Samuel, Simeon, Thomas
07 Abraham, Absalom, Delilah, Ezekiel, Gabriel, Goliath, Ishmael, Japheth, Jezebel, Lazarus, Malachi, Matthew, Michael, Rebecca, Rebekah, Solomon, Susanna, Timothy, Zebulun

08 Barabbas, Benjamin, Caiaphas, Habbakuk, Hezekiah, Issachar, Jeremiah, Jonathan, Manasseh, Naphtali, Nehemiah, Thaddeus, Zedekiah
09 Bathsheba, Beelzebub, Nicodemus, Zechariah, Zephaniah
10 Adam and Eve, Belshazzar, Methuselah, Simon Magus
11 Bartholomew, Gog and Magog, Jesus Christ
12 Herod Agrippa, Herod Antipas
13 Judas Iscariot, Mary Magdalene, Pontius Pilate
14 Nebuchadnezzar, Simon the Zealot

▶ *Books of the Bible*:
03 **Job** (Book of)
04 **Amos** (Book of), **Ezra** (Book of), **Joel** (Book of), **John** (Gospel according to), **John** (Letters of), **Jude** (Letter of), **Luke** (Gospel according to), **Mark** (Gospel according to), **Ruth** (Book of)
05 **Hosea** (Book of), **James** (Letter of), **Jonah** (Book of), **Kings** (Books of), **Micah** (Book of), **Nahum** (Book of), **Peter** (Letters of), **Titus** (Letter of Paul to), **Tobit** (Book of)
06 **Baruch** (Book of), **Daniel** (Book of), **Esdras** (Books of), **Esther** (Book of), **Exodus** (Book of), **Haggai** (Book of), **Isaiah** (Book of), **Joshua** (Book of), **Judges** (Book of), **Judith** (Book of), **Psalms** (Book of), **Romans** (Letter of Paul to the), **Samuel** (Books of), **Sirach** (Book of)
07 **Ezekiel** (Book of), **Genesis** (Book of), **Gospels**, **Hebrews** (Letter of Paul to the), **Malachi** (Book of), **Matthew** (Gospel according to), **Numbers** (Book of), **Obadiah** (Book of), **Susanna** (History of), **Timothy** (Letters of Paul to)
08 **Habakkuk** (Book of), **Jeremiah** (Book of), **Jeremiah** (Letter of), **Nehemiah** (Book of), **Philemon** (Letter of Paul to), **Proverbs** (Book of)

09 **Apocrypha**, **Ephesians** (Letter of Paul to the), **Galatians** (Letter of Paul to the), **Hexateuch**, **Leviticus** (Book of), **Maccabees**, **Zechariah** (Book of), **Zephaniah** (Book of)
10 **Apocalypse**, **Chronicles** (Books of), **Colossians** (Letter of Paul to the), **Heptateuch**, **Pentateuch**, **Revelation**
11 **Corinthians** (Letters of Paul to the), **Deuteronomy** (Book of), **Philippians** (Letter of Paul to the)
12 **Ecclesiastes** (Book of), **Lamentations**, **New Testament**, **Old Testament**
13 **Song of Solomon**, **Thessalonians** (Letters of Paul to the)
14 **Ecclesiasticus** (Book of), **Pauline Letters**
15 **Bel and the Dragon**, **Pastoral Letters**, **Prayer of Azariah**, **Wisdom of Solomon**
16 **Prayer of Manasseh**, **Revelation of John**
17 **Acts of the Apostles**
22 **Song of the Three Young Men**

**bibliography**
07 catalog
08 book list

**bicker**
03 row
04 spar
05 argue, clash, fight, scrap
07 fall out, quarrel, wrangle
08 disagree, squabble
09 altercate

**bicycle**
04 bike
05 cycle, racer

▶ *Types of bicycle*:
03 BMX
05 hobby, racer
06 safety, tandem
08 mountain, ten-speed, tricycle, unicycle
09 free-style
10 fixed-wheel, two-wheeler, velocipede
14 all-terrain bike
➢ See also VEHICLE

**bid**
02 go
03 ask, say, sum, try
04 call, tell, wave, wish

05 greet, offer, order, price
06 amount, demand, desire,
   direct, effort, enjoin, invite,
   submit, summon, tender
07 advance, attempt, command,
   proffer, propose, request
08 instruct, proposal
10 put forward, submission

**bidding**
04 call
05 order
06 behest, charge, desire
07 command, request,
   summons
11 instruction, requirement

**big**
03 fat
04 huge, main, mega, tall, vast
05 adult, beefy, bulky, burly,
   giant, great, hefty, jumbo,
   large, major, obese, older
06 brawny, bumper, famous
07 eminent, grown-up, leading,
   serious, sizable, weighty
08 critical, generous, gracious,
   muscular, spacious
09 cavernous, corpulent,
   extensive, important,
   momentous, principal,
   prominent, unselfish, well-
   known
10 extra large, voluminous
11 fundamental, kind-hearted,
   magnanimous, substantial

**bigot**
03 MCP
06 racist, sexist, zealot
09 dogmatist, racialist, sectarian
10 chauvinist

**bigoted**
06 biased, closed, narrow,
   swayed, warped
07 partial, twisted
08 dogmatic
09 blinkered, obstinate
10 intolerant, prejudiced
11 opinionated
12 narrow-minded

**bigotry**
04 bias
06 racism, sexism
08 jingoism
09 dogmatism, injustice,
   prejudice, racialism
10 chauvinism, partiality
11 intolerance
12 sectarianism

**bigwig**
03 VIP
05 mogul
06 big gun, fat cat

07 big shot, notable
08 big noise, somebody
09 big cheese, dignitary
10 panjandrum
11 heavyweight
13 high muck-a-muck

**bile**
04 gall
05 anger
06 choler, rancor, spleen
08 ill humor
09 bad temper
10 bitterness
12 irascibility, irritability

**bilge**
03 rot
05 trash, tripe
06 drivel, hot air, piffle
07 hogwash, rubbish, twaddle
08 claptrap, nonsense,
   tommyrot
09 gibberish, poppycock

**bilious**
04 edgy, sick
05 cross, testy
06 crabby, queasy, sickly
07 grouchy, peevish
08 choleric
09 crotchety, irritable
10 disgusting, nauseating, out of
   sorts
11 ill-tempered

**bilk**
02 do
03 con
05 cheat, sting, trick
06 diddle, fleece
07 deceive, defraud, swindle

**bill**
02 ad
03 act, nib, tab
04 beak, post
05 check, debit, flyer, money,
   tally
06 charge, notice, poster
07 account, handout, invoice,
   leaflet, placard, program,
   statute
08 bank note, bulletin, circular,
   handbill, mandible, playbill,
   proposal
09 advertise, reckoning,
   statement
11 legislation
13 advertisement

**billet**
03 job
04 post
05 berth, lodge
07 housing, lodging, quarter
08 barracks, position, quarters

10 employment, occupation
11 accommodate
13 accommodation

**billow**
04 mass, rise, roll, rush, wave
05 bulge, cloud, surge, swell
07 balloon, breaker, puff out

**billowy**
07 heaving, rolling, surging,
   tossing
08 rippling, swelling, swirling
10 undulating

**bin**
03 box
06 basket
09 container
10 receptacle

**bind**
03 tie
04 bond, bore, drag, join, lash,
   rope, spot, tape, wrap, yoke
05 chain, clamp, cover, stick,
   strap, truss, unify, unite
06 attach, fasten, fetter, hamper,
   oblige, secure, tether
07 bandage, confine, dilemma,
   impasse, require, shackle
08 nuisance, restrain, restrict
09 constrain, tight spot
10 difficulty, irritation
11 necessitate, predicament
12 pull together
13 inconvenience

**binding**
04 tape
05 cover, tight, valid
06 border, edging, strict
07 bandage
08 covering, rigorous, trimming,
   wrapping
09 mandatory, necessary,
   permanent, requisite
10 compulsory, conclusive,
   obligatory
11 irrevocable, unalterable,
   unbreakable
12 indissoluble

**binge**
03 jag
04 bout, lark, orgy
05 blast, fling, spree
06 bender, guzzle

**biochemist**

► *Names of biochemists:*
04 **Abel** (John Jacob), **Duve**
   (Christian René de)
05 **Chain** (Ernst Boris), **Doisy**
   (Edward Adelbert), **Krebs**
   (Hans Adolf), **Monod**

(Jacques Lucien), **Moore**
(Stanford)
06 **Oparin** (Alexandr), **Perutz**
(Max Ferdinand), **Porter**
(Rodney Robert), **Sanger**
(Frederick)
07 **Edelman** (Gerald Maurice),
**Hopkins** (Frederick
Gowland), **Waksman**
(Selman Abraham),
**Warburg** (Otto Heinrich)
08 **Anfinsen** (Christian
Boehmer), **Chargaff**
(Erwin), **Kornberg** (Arthur),
**Meyerhof** (Otto Fritz),
**Northrop** (John Howard)
09 **Bergström** (Sune),
**Butenandt** (Adolf Friedrich
Johann)
➢ See also SCIENTIST

**biography**
02 CV
04 life
06 biopic, record
07 account, history, profile
09 life story
13 autobiography

► *Names of biographers*:
05 **Weems** (Mason Locke)
06 **Wilson** (Andrew Norman)
07 **Ackroyd** (Peter), **Bedford**
(Sybille), **Boswell** (James),
**Ellmann** (Richard),
**Holroyd** (Michael), **Pearson**
(Hesketh), **Sitwell**
(Sacheverell)
08 **Plutarch**, **Sandburg** (Carl),
**Strachey** (Lytton), **Van
Doren** (Carl)
09 **Aldington** (Richard),
**Kingsmill** (Hugh),
**Suetonius**
11 **Schlesinger** (Arthur)
➢ See also WRITER

**biology**

► *Biological terms include*:
03 DNA, RNA
04 cell, gene
05 class, virus
06 enzyme, fossil
07 meiosis, microbe, mitosis,
nucleus, osmosis, protein
08 bacillus, bacteria, genetics,
membrane, molecule,
mutation, organism,
ribosome
09 corpuscle, cytoplasm,
ecosystem, ectoplasm,
evolution, food chain,
symbiosis
10 chromosome, extinction,

metabolism, parasitism,
protoplasm
11 homeostasis, respiration
12 conservation, reproduction
13 flora and fauna,
microorganism
14 photosynthesis
15 nuclear membrane,
ribonucleic acid

► *Names of biologists and
naturalists*:
03 **His** (Wilhelm)
04 **Berg** (Paul), **Cohn**
(Ferdinand Julius), **Gram**
(Hans Christian Joachim),
**Hess** (Walter Rudolf), **Katz**
(Bernard), **Roux** (Emile)
05 **Avery** (Oswald Theodore),
**Bacon** (Francis), **Beebe**
(Charles William), **Crick**
(Francis Harry Compton),
**Golgi** (Camillo), **Gould**
(Stephen Jay), **Scott** (Peter),
**Selby** (Prideaux John),
**White** (Gilbert)
06 **Anning** (Mary), **Bordet**
(Jules), **Buffon** (George-
Louis Leclerc), **Cannon**
(Walter Bradford), **Carson**
(Rachel Louise), **Claude**
(Albert), **Darwin** (Charles
Robert), **Huxley** (Julian
Sorell), **Huxley** (Thomas
Henry), **Lartet** (Edouard
Arman Isidore Hippolyte),
**Leakey** (Louis Seymour
Bazett), **Leakey** (Mary
Douglas), **Leakey**
(Richard), **Morgan**
(Thomas Hunt), **Sloane**
(Hans), **Sperry** (Roger),
**Watson** (James Dewey),
**Wilson** (Edward Osborne)
07 **Adamson** (Joy), **Andrews**
(Roy Chapman), **Banting**
(Frederick Grant), **Behring**
(Emil von), **Burbank**
(Luther), **Dawkins**
(Richard), **Haeckel** (Ernst
Heinrich Philipp August),
**Hershey** (Alfred Day),
**Jackson** (Barbara),
**Lamarck** (Jean), **Mantell**
(Gideon Algernon),
**Pasteur** (Louis), **Wallace**
(Alfred Russel)
08 **Cousteau** (Jacques Yves),
**Delbrück** (Max), **Franklin**
(Rosalind Elsie), **Johanson**
(Donald Carl), **Linnaeus**
(Carl), **Weismann** (August
Friedrich Leopold)

09 **Helmholtz** (Hermann von),
**Lederberg** (Joshua)
10 **Darlington** (Cyril Dean)
11 **Leeuwenhoek** (Antoni van),
**Spallanzani** (Lazaro)
12 **Attenborough** (David)
➢ See also SCIENTIST

**bird**
05 avian, avine
09 ornithoid, volucrine

► *Birds include*:
03 ani, auk, emu, hen, jay, kea,
moa, owl, roc, tit
04 aves, chat, coly, coot, crow,
dodo, dove, duck, erne, fowl,
guan, gull, hawk, ibis, kagu,
kite, kiwi, lark, loon, lory,
myna, rail, rhea, rook, ruff,
shag, skua, swan, teal, tern,
tody, wren
05 avian, booby, capon, chick,
crane, diver, eagle, egret,
eider, finch, flier, galah,
goose, grebe, heron, hobby,
macaw, mynah, ousel, ouzel,
pewit, piper, pipit, potoo,
quail, raven, robin, ruffe,
snipe, squab, stilt, stork,
swift, vireo, wader
06 avocet, avoset, bantam,
barbet, budgie, bulbul,
canary, chough, condor,
cuckoo, curlew, darter,
dipper, drongo, dunlin,
falcon, fulmar, gannet,
godwit, grouse, hoopoe,
Houdan, jabiru, jacana,
kakapo, linnet, magpie,
martin, merlin, motmot,
oriole, osprey, parrot,
peahen, peewit, petrel,
pigeon, plover, puffin, pullet,
raptor, roller, shrike, siskin,
thrush, tomtit, toucan,
trogon, turaco, turkey
07 apteryx, babbler, barn owl,
bittern, blue jay, bluetit,
bunting, bustard, buzzard,
catbird, chicken, cotinga,
cowbird, creeper, dottrel,
fantail, flicker, goshawk,
grackle, halcyon, harrier,
jacamar, jackdaw, kestrel,
lapwing, leghorn, mallard,
manakin, moorhen, mudlark,
ostrich, peacock, pelican,
penguin, phoenix, pintail,
poultry, quetzal, redbird,
redpoll, redwing, rooster,
seagull, skylark, sparrow,
sunbird, swallow, tanager,
tiercel, tinamou, titlark,

touraco, vulture, wagtail, warbler, waxbill, waxwing, wryneck

08 accentor, adjutant, bee eater, blackcap, bluebird, bobolink, bobwhite, cardinal, cockatoo, dabchick, dotterel, fish hawk, flamingo, great tit, grosbeak, hornbill, land rail, leafbird, lorikeet, lovebird, lyrebird, megapode, myna bird, night owl, nightjar, nuthatch, oxpecker, palm chat, parakeet, pheasant, redshank, redstart, ringtail, sea eagle, shoebill, starling, thrasher, titmouse, water hen, whimbrel, white-eye, woodcock, woodlark

09 aepyornis, albatross, bald eagle, blackbird, blackhead, bowerbird, broadbill, bullfinch, cassowary, chaffinch, chickadee, cockatiel, cormorant, corncrake, crossbill, eider duck, fairy tern, fieldfare, gerfalcon, goldfinch, goosander, guillemot, gyrfalcon, jacksnipe, little owl, merganser, mousebird, mynah bird, nighthawk, partridge, peregrine, ptarmigan, razorbill, red grouse, sandpiper, scrub-bird, sheldrake, snakebird, stonechat, trumpeter, turnstone

10 budgerigar, chiffchaff, fledgeling, flycatcher, goatsucker, greenfinch, greenshank, guinea fowl, harpy eagle, honeyeater, honeyguide, kingfisher, kookaburra, nutcracker, sanderling, sandgrouse, shearwater, woodpecker

11 butcherbird, frigatebird, golden eagle, hummingbird, mockingbird, nightingale, reed warbler, sparrowhawk, stone curlew, storm petrel, thunderbird, tree creeper, waterthrust

12 adjutant bird, cedar waxwing, whippoorwill, yellowhammer

13 barnacle goose, oystercatcher, secretary bird, trumpeter swan

14 bird of paradise, scarlet tanager

15 passenger pigeon, peregrine falcon
➤ See also ANIMAL; CHICKEN; DUCK

**birth**
04 dawn, line, race, rise, root
05 blood, issue, labor, start, stock
06 advent, family, origin, source, strain
07 arrival, descent, genesis, lineage, origins
08 ancestry, breeding, delivery, nativity, pedigree
09 beginning, parentage
10 appearance, extraction
11 confinement, parturition
12 blessed event

**birthday**
10 genethliac
11 anniversary, date of birth

**birthmark**
04 mole
05 nevus
06 nevoid
07 blemish

**birthplace**
04 home, root
06 cradle, source
08 hometown
10 fatherland
12 place of birth
13 mother country, native country, place of origin

**birthright**
06 legacy
09 privilege
11 inheritance, prerogative

**biscuit**

➤ *Biscuits include*:
03 bun
04 drop, roll, rusk, snap, tack
06 cookie, bisque
07 cracker, pretzel
08 hardtack, zwieback
09 sourdough
10 buttermilk
11 ship biscuit
➤ See also FOOD

**bisect**
04 fork
05 cross, halve, split
06 divide
09 bifurcate, cut in half

**bisexual**
02 bi
05 AC/DC
07 epicene
11 androgynous, monoclinous

13 hermaphrodite
15 gynandromorphic

**bishop**
07 pontiff, prelate, primate
08 diocesan
09 patriarch, suffragan
10 archbishop
15 episcopal bishop

**bit**
03 jot
04 atom, chip, dash, drop, hint, iota, lump, mite, part, whit
05 chunk, crumb, flake, grain, piece, scrap, shred, slice, speck, touch, trace
06 morsel, sliver, tittle
07 portion, segment, soupçon
08 fragment, mouthful, particle
09 scintilla

❑**a bit**
05 jiffy
06 a while, minute, moment, rather
07 a little, not much, not very
08 slightly

❑**bit by bit**
06 slowly
08 in stages
09 gradually, piecemeal
10 step by step
14 little by little

**bitch**
03 cat
04 moan
05 gripe, harpy, scold, shrew, vixen, whine
06 virago
07 grumble, tigress
08 bad-mouth, complain
09 criticize, female dog
13 find fault with

**bitchy**
04 mean
05 catty, cruel, nasty, snide
07 cutting, vicious
08 shrewish, spiteful, venomous, vixenish
09 malicious, rancorous
10 backbiting, vindictive

**bite**
03 bit, eat, nip
04 chew, gnaw, grip, hold, kick, peck, rend, snap, tear, work
05 champ, crush, munch, piece, pinch, prick, punch, seize, smart, snack, sting, taste
06 crunch, lesion, morsel, nibble, pierce, tingle
08 mouthful, piquancy
09 spiciness

**biting**
10 take effect

**biting**
03 raw
04 cold, tart
05 harsh, sharp
06 bitter, severe
07 caustic, cutting, hurtful
08 incisive, piercing, scathing
09 trenchant

**bitter**
03 raw, sad
04 acid, sour, tart
05 acrid, angry, harsh, sharp
06 arctic, biting, fierce, severe
07 acerbic, caustic, cynical,
   hostile, pungent
08 freezing, piercing, scathing,
   spiteful, stinging, venomous
09 aggrieved, jaundiced,
   rancorous, resentful
10 astringent, embittered,
   vindictive
11 acrimonious, unsweetened
12 freezing cold, vituperative
13 heartbreaking

**bitterness**
04 bite, pain
05 anger, spite, venom
06 grudge, rancor
07 acidity, rawness
08 acrimony, cynicism, jaundice,
   pungency, severity, sourness,
   tartness
09 hostility, sharpness, virulence
10 acerbity, resentment

**bizarre**
03 odd
05 queer, wacky, weird
06 way-out
07 comical, curious, oddball,
   offbeat, strange, unusual
08 abnormal, freakish, peculiar
09 eccentric, fantastic,
   grotesque, ludicrous
13 extraordinary
14 unconventional

**blab**
04 leak, tell
06 gossip, reveal, squeal, tattle
07 divulge, let slip
08 blurt out, disclose

**black**
03 ban, bar, dim, hit, jet, sad
04 dark, inky
05 angry, awful, bleak, dingy,
   dirty, ebony, grimy, muddy,
   Negro, raven, sooty
06 bruise, dismal, filthy, gloomy,
   grubby, soiled, somber
07 blacken, boycott, Stygian,
   swarthy, unclean

08 funereal, hopeless, jet-black,
   menacing, moonless, starless
09 blacklist, Cimmerian, coal-
   black, depressed, miserable
10 depressing, fuliginous,
   melanistic, pitch-black
11 dark-skinned, threatening
13 unilluminated
15 African-American

❑ **black out**
05 faint
06 censor, darken
07 conceal, cover up, pass out
08 collapse, flake out, suppress

❑ **blackout**
04 coma
05 faint, swoon
07 coverup, secrecy, syncope
08 oblivion, power cut
10 censorship, flaking-out
11 concealment, suppression
12 power failure
15 unconsciousness

❑ **in the black**
07 solvent
08 in credit
11 without debt

**blackball**
03 ban, bar
04 oust, snub, veto
05 expel
06 reject
07 drum out, exclude, shut out
08 throw out
09 blacklist, ostracize

**blacken**
04 soil
05 cloud, decry, dirty, libel,
   smear, stain, sully, taint
06 darken, defame, defile,
   malign, revile, vilify
07 run down, slander, tarnish
08 besmirch, dishonor
09 discredit
10 calumniate

**blackguard**
03 cad
04 heel
05 devil, knave, rogue, swine
06 rascal, wretch
07 bounder, stinker, villain
09 miscreant, reprobate,
   scoundrel

**blacklist**
03 ban, bar
04 snub, veto
05 debar, expel, taboo
06 outlaw, reject
07 boycott, exclude, shut out
09 ostracize, proscribe

**blackmail**
05 bleed, exact, force
06 coerce, extort, lean on
07 bribery, squeeze
08 exaction, threaten
09 extortion, hush money
12 hold to ransom, intimidation

**blackmailer**
07 vampire
11 bloodsucker, extortioner
12 extortionist

**blade**
04 edge, vane
05 knife, razor, sword
06 dagger
07 scalpel
11 cutting edge

**blame**
03 rap, tax
04 onus
05 chide, fault, guilt, stick
06 accuse, berate, charge
07 censure, condemn, reprove
08 reproach, tear into
09 criticism, criticize, liability
10 accusation, find guilty
11 culpability
12 condemnation
14 accountability, responsibility
15 hold responsible

**blameless**
05 clear
07 perfect, sinless, upright
08 innocent, virtuous
09 faultless, guiltless, stainless
11 unblemished
12 without fault
13 unimpeachable
14 irreproachable

**blameworthy**
06 guilty
07 at fault
08 culpable, shameful
10 flagitious
11 inexcusable
12 indefensible, reproachable
13 discreditable, reprehensible

**blanch**
04 boil
05 scald
06 whiten
07 go white
08 grow pale, turn pale

**bland**
04 dull, flat, mild, weak
06 boring
07 humdrum, insipid
08 ordinary
09 tasteless

10 flavorless, monotonous,
   unexciting
11 inoffensive, nondescript,
   uninspiring
13 characterless, uninteresting

**blandishments**
07 blarney, coaxing, fawning
08 cajolery, flattery, soft soap
09 sweet talk, wheedling
10 sycophancy
11 compliments, enticements
12 ingratiation, inveiglement

**blank**
03 gap
04 bare, void
05 clean, clear, empty, space
06 glazed, vacant, vacuum
07 deadpan, vacuity, vacuous
08 lifeless, unfilled, unmarked
09 apathetic, impassive
10 empty space, poker-faced
11 emotionless, indifferent,
   inscrutable, nothingness
14 expressionless
15 uncomprehending

**blanket**
04 coat, film, hide, mask
05 cloak, cloud, cover, layer,
   sheet, total
06 deaden, global, mantle
07 coating, conceal, overlay
08 bedcover, covering, coverlet,
   envelope, surround,
   sweeping
09 bedspread, inclusive
11 wide-ranging
12 all-embracing, all-inclusive
13 comprehensive
14 across-the-board

**blare**
04 boom, hoot, roar, toot
05 blast, clang
07 boom out, trumpet
08 blast out
11 sound loudly

**blarney**
05 spiel
08 cajolery, flattery, soft soap
09 sweet talk, wheedling
13 blandishments
14 persuasiveness

**blasé**
04 cool
05 bored, jaded, weary
07 offhand, unmoved
09 apathetic, unexcited
10 nonchalant, phlegmatic
11 indifferent, unimpressed
12 uninterested

**blaspheme**
04 cuss, damn
05 abuse, curse, swear
06 revile
07 profane
09 desecrate, imprecate
10 utter oaths

**blasphemous**
07 godless, impious, profane
10 irreverent
11 imprecatory, irreligious
12 sacrilegious

**blasphemy**
05 curse, oaths
08 swearing
09 expletive, profanity,
   sacrilege, violation
11 desecration, imprecation,
   irreverence, profaneness

**blast**
04 bang, blow, boom, clap, gale,
   gust, honk, hoot, roar
05 blare, burst, crash, draft,
   sound
06 attack, bellow, blow up,
   clamor, volley
07 boom out, destroy, explode,
   thunder
08 blare out, demolish, outburst
09 discharge, explosion
10 detonation
12 blow to pieces

❏ **blast off**
07 lift off, take off
10 be launched

**blatant**
04 open
05 overt, sheer
06 arrant, brazen, patent
07 glaring, obvious
08 flagrant, manifest, outright
09 bald-faced, barefaced,
   obtrusive, out and out,
   prominent
11 undisguised, unmitigated

**blaze**
04 beam, burn, fire, glow, rage
05 blast, burst, erupt, flare, flash,
   glare, light, shine
06 flames, see red, seethe
07 bonfire, explode, flare-up,
   glitter, inferno
09 catch fire, explosion
10 brilliance
13 conflagration
15 burst into flames

**blazon**
05 vaunt
06 flaunt
07 trumpet

08 announce, proclaim
09 broadcast, celebrate, make
   known, publicize

**bleach**
04 fade, pale
06 blanch, whiten
07 lighten
08 etiolate, peroxide

**bleak**
03 raw
04 bare, cold, dark, drab, dull,
   grim, open
05 empty, windy
06 barren, chilly, dismal, dreary
07 exposed, joyless
08 desolate, hopeless
09 cheerless, desperate,
   miserable, windswept
10 depressing
11 comfortless, unpromising
12 discouraging
13 disheartening

**bleary**
03 dim
05 tired
06 blurry, cloudy, rheumy
07 blurred

**bleat**
03 baa, cry, maa
04 blat, call, moan
05 whine
08 complain

**bleed**
03 run, sap
04 flow, gush, milk, ooze, seep,
   weep
05 drain, exude, spurt
06 extort, reduce
07 extract, suck dry, trickle
09 lose blood, shed blood
10 hemorrhage
11 extravasate
12 exsanguinate, phlebotomize

**blemish**
03 mar
04 blot, flaw, mark, spot
05 fault, speck, spoil, stain, sully
06 blotch, damage, defect
09 deformity, disfigure
12 imperfection
13 discoloration, disfigurement

► _Types of blemish_:
03 zit
04 acne, boil, bump, corn, mole,
   scab, scar, spot, wart
05 nevus
06 bunion, callus, pimple
07 blister, freckle, pustule,
   verruca
08 pockmark

**blench**
09 birthmark, blackhead, carbuncle, chilblain, whitehead
14 strawberry mark

**blench**
03 shy
05 cower, quail, quake, wince
06 falter, flinch, recoil, shrink
07 shudder
08 hesitate

**blend**
03 fit, mix
04 beat, fuse, stir, suit
05 admix, alloy, match, merge, union, unite, whisk
06 fusion, mingle
07 amalgam, combine, merging, mixture, uniting
08 coalesce, compound
09 composite, synthesis
10 amalgamate, commixture, concoction, go together, homogenize, synthesize
11 combination
12 amalgamation

**bless**
04 laud
05 exalt, thank
06 anoint, extoll, hallow, ordain, praise
08 dedicate, sanctify
10 consecrate

**blessed**
04 glad, holy
05 happy, lucky
06 divine, graced, sacred
07 endowed, favored, revered
08 hallowed
09 contented, fortunate
10 prosperous, sanctified

**blessing**
04 gain, gift, help
05 favor, grace, leave
06 bounty, profit
07 backing, benefit, benison, consent, darshan, godsend, kiddush, service, support
08 approval, sanction, windfall
09 advantage, agreement
10 dedication, permission
11 approbation, benediction, concurrence, good fortune
12 commendation, consecration

**blight**
03 mar, rot, woe
04 bane, dash, evil, kill, ruin
05 blast, curse, spoil, wreck
06 cancer, canker, damage, fungus, mildew, wither

07 destroy, disease, scourge, shatter, shrivel, trouble
09 frustrate, pollution
10 affliction, misfortune
11 infestation
13 contamination

**blind**
03 mad
04 mask, rash, slow, trap, wild
05 cover, drunk, front, shade, trick
06 closed, dazzle, façade, hidden, screen
07 eyeless, shutter, unaware
08 careless, ignorant, mindless, reckless, unseeing
09 concealed, oblivious, sightless, unsighted
10 obstructed, out of sight, uncritical, unthinking
11 distraction, insensitive, intoxicated, smokescreen, unconscious, unobservant, window shade
12 imperceptive
13 inconsiderate, make sightless, Venetian blind
14 indiscriminate

**blindly**
05 madly
06 rashly, wildly
10 mindlessly, unseeingly
11 senselessly, sightlessly
12 uncritically, unthinkingly, without sight
13 thoughtlessly, without vision

**blink**
04 wink
05 flash, gleam, shine
07 flicker, nictate, twinkle
09 nictitate

**bliss**
03 joy
06 heaven, utopia
07 ecstasy, elation, nirvana, rapture
08 euphoria, gladness, paradise
09 happiness
11 blessedness
13 seventh heaven

**blissful**
05 happy
06 elated, joyful, joyous
07 idyllic
08 ecstatic, euphoric
09 enchanted, rapturous

**blister**
03 wen
04 boil, cyst, sore
05 bulla, ulcer

06 canker, papula, papule, pimple
07 abscess, pustule, vesicle
08 furuncle, swelling
09 carbuncle

**blistering**
03 hot
05 cruel
06 fierce, savage
07 caustic, extreme, intense, vicious
08 scathing
09 scorching, withering

**blithe**
06 casual, cheery
08 carefree, careless, cheerful, heedless, uncaring
10 unthinking, untroubled
11 thoughtless, unconcerned
12 light-hearted

**blitz**
04 raid, rush
06 attack, effort, strike
07 attempt
09 offensive, onslaught
10 blitzkrieg
11 bombardment
12 all-out effort

**blizzard**
05 storm
06 squall
07 tempest
09 snowstorm

**bloated**
04 full
05 puffy
07 blown up, stuffed, swollen
08 enlarged, expanded, inflated
09 distended

**blob**
03 dab, gob
04 ball, drop, glob, lump, spot
05 pearl
07 droplet, globule

**bloc**
04 axis, ring
05 cabal, group, union
06 cartel, clique, league
07 entente, faction
08 alliance
09 coalition, syndicate
10 federation

**block**
03 bar, jam
04 bloc, cake, clog, cube, halt, lump, mass, plug, seal, slab, stop
05 brick, choke, chunk, close, dam up, delay, piece, wedge

06 bung up, scotch, series, square, stop up, thwart
07 barrier, cluster, section
08 blockage, obstruct, quantity, stoppage
09 frustrate, hindrance, stonewall
10 be in the way, city square, impediment
11 development, obstruction
14 stumbling block

**blockade**
04 stop
05 block, check, siege
07 barrier, besiege, closure
08 encircle, obstacle, obstruct, surround
09 barricade
11 obstruction, restriction
12 encirclement, prevent using

**blockage**
03 jam
04 clot
06 logjam
09 hindrance, occlusion
10 congestion, impediment
11 obstruction

**blockhead**
04 dork, fool, geek, jerk, nerd, twit
05 dunce, idiot, ninny, twerp
06 dimwit, nitwit
08 dipstick, imbecile, numskull
10 nincompoop

**blond, blonde**
04 fair
06 flaxen, golden
08 bleached
09 towheaded
10 fair-haired
12 golden-haired, light-colored

**blood**
04 gore
05 birth, hemal, hemic
06 family
07 descent, hematal, hematic, kinship, lineage
08 ancestry
09 lifeblood, relations
10 extraction, vital fluid

**bloodcurdling**
05 scary
07 fearful
08 chilling, dreadful, horrible
10 horrendous, horrifying, terrifying
11 frightening, hair-raising
13 spine-chilling

**bloodless**
03 wan

04 cold, pale
05 ashen, pasty
06 anemic, chalky, pallid, sallow
07 drained, insipid
08 lifeless, listless, peaceful
09 colorless, nonviolet
11 passionless, unemotional

**bloodshed**
04 gore
06 murder, pogrom
07 carnage, killing, slaying
08 butchery, massacre
09 blood bath, slaughter
12 bloodletting

**bloodsucker**
05 leech
07 sponger
08 parasite
11 blackmailer, extortioner

**bloodthirsty**
05 cruel
06 brutal, savage
07 inhuman, vicious, warlike
08 barbaric, ruthless
09 barbarous, ferocious
10 sanguinary

**bloody**
04 gory
05 cruel
06 brutal, fierce, savage
08 bleeding, sanguine
10 sanguinary
11 sanguineous
12 bloodstained, bloodthirsty, sanguinolent

**bloom**
03 bud
04 glow, grow, open
05 blush, flush, prime
06 beauty, flower, health, luster, sprout, thrive
07 blossom, develop, prosper
08 flourish, radiance, rosiness
11 florescence
13 efflorescence

**blooming**
04 rosy
05 bonny, ruddy
07 healthy
09 flowering
10 blossoming, florescent

**blossom**
03 bud
05 bloom
06 flower, mature, thrive
07 burgeon, prosper, succeed
08 flourish
11 florescence
13 efflorescence

**blot**
03 dry, mar
04 blur, flaw, mark, soak, spot
05 dry up, fault, smear, speck, spoil, stain, sully, taint
06 absorb, blotch, defect
08 disgrace
12 imperfection

❏**blot out**
04 hide
06 cancel, darken, delete, efface, screen, shadow
07 conceal, expunge, obscure
10 obliterate

**blotch**
04 blot, mark, spot
05 patch, stain
06 smudge, splash

**blotchy**
06 smeary, spotty, uneven
08 inflamed, reddened
09 blemished

**blow**
03 box, fan, hit, rap
04 bang, bash, belt, biff, clip, cuff, gale, gust, hook, jolt, pant, pipe, play, puff, rush, slap, sock, toot, waft, wind
05 blare, blast, clout, draft, knock, punch, shock, smack, sound, spoil, swipe, thump, upset, waste, whack, whirl, wreck
06 buffet, exhale, flurry, squall, stream, stroke, wallop
07 breathe, flutter, puff out, reverse, screw up, setback, tempest, trumpet
08 comedown, misspend
09 bombshell, dissipate
10 affliction, breathe out
11 fritter away, make a mess of
14 disappointment
15 bolt from the blue

❏**blow out**
07 smother
08 snuff out
10 extinguish

❏**blow over**
03 end
04 pass
05 cease
06 finish, vanish
07 die down, subside
09 dissipate, fizzle out
11 be forgotten

❏**blow up**
04 bomb, fill, flip, go up
05 blast, bloat, burst, erupt, go ape, go mad, go off, swell

**blowout** *continued*
06 expand, lose it, puff up, pump up
07 balloon, distend, enlarge, explode, inflate, magnify
08 detonate, dynamite
09 overstate
10 exaggerate, hit the roof
11 become angry, blow your top, flip your lid, go ballistic
14 lose your temper
15 fly off the handle

**blowout**
04 bash, flat
05 binge, feast, party
06 shindy
07 shindig
08 flat tire, puncture
11 celebration

**blowy**
05 fresh, gusty, windy
06 breezy, stormy
07 squally
08 blustery

**blowzy, blowsy**
05 dowdy, messy, ruddy
06 sloppy, untidy
07 tousled, unkempt
08 slipshod, slovenly
10 disheveled

**blubber**
03 cry, fat, sob
04 weep
06 snivel
07 sniffle, whimper

**bludgeon**
03 hit
04 beat, club, cosh
05 baton, bully, force
06 batter, coerce, cudgel, harass, hector, strike
08 browbeat, bulldoze
09 terrorize, truncheon
10 intimidate, pressurize

**blue**
03 low, sad
04 cyan, glum, lewd, navy
05 adult, azure, dirty, fed up
06 coarse, cobalt, erotic, gloomy, indigo, risqué, smutty, steamy, vulgar
07 obscene, raunchy, sky-blue, unhappy
08 cerulean, dejected, downcast, indecent, navy blue, sapphire
09 depressed, miserable, royal blue, turquoise
10 aquamarine, despondent, dispirited, melancholy
11 downhearted, ultramarine
12 pornographic

14 down in the dumps

**blueprint**
03 map
04 plan
05 draft, guide, model, pilot
06 design, scheme, sketch
07 outline, pattern, project
08 game plan
09 archetype, prototype

**blues**
05 dumps, gloom
08 doldrums, miseries
09 dejection, moodiness
10 depression, gloominess, melancholy
11 despondency

**bluff**
03 lie
04 bank, brow, crag, fake, fool, open, peak, sham, show
05 blind, blunt, cliff, feign, frank, fraud, ridge, scarp, trick
06 candid, deceit, direct, escarp, genial, hearty, height
07 affable, deceive, pretend
08 headland, pretense
09 deception, downright, outspoken, precipice
10 escarpment, promontory
11 good-natured, plain-spoken
15 straightforward

**blunder**
03 err
04 goof, slip
05 boner, botch, error, fault, fluff, gaffe
06 boo-boo, bungle, howler, slip-up
07 blooper, faux pas, go wrong, mistake, screw up, stumble
08 get wrong, solecism
09 mismanage, oversight
10 inaccuracy
12 indiscretion, make a mistake

**blunt**
04 curt, dull, numb, rude, worn
05 abate, allay, frank, stark
06 abrupt, candid, dampen, direct, honest, weaken
07 brusque, rounded, uncivil
08 edgeless, explicit, hebetate, impolite, not sharp, tactless
09 alleviate, downright, outspoken, pointless
10 forthright
11 unsharpened
13 unceremonious
14 take the edge off
15 straightforward

**blur**
03 dim, fog

04 haze, mask, mist, spot, veil
05 befog, cloud, smear, stain
06 darken, muddle, smudge
07 becloud, dimness, obscure
09 confusion, fuzziness
10 cloudiness
14 indistinctness

**blurb**
02 ad
04 copy, hype, plug, puff
05 spiel
13 advertisement

**blurred**
03 dim
04 hazy
05 foggy, fuzzy, misty, vague
06 bleary, cloudy
07 clouded, obscure, unclear
08 confused
10 indistinct, out of focus

**blurt**
▫**blurt out**
04 blab, gush, leak, tell
05 spout, utter
06 cry out, let out, reveal
07 divulge, exclaim, let slip
08 disclose
09 ejaculate
11 come out with
13 spill the beans

**blush**
04 glow
05 color, flush, go red
06 blanch, redden
08 rosiness
09 reddening, ruddiness

**blushing**
03 red
04 rosy
06 modest
07 ashamed, flushed, glowing
11 embarrassed, erubescence

**bluster**
04 brag, crow, rant, roar
05 bluff, boast, bully, storm
06 hector
07 bravado, crowing, show off, swagger, talk big
08 boasting, harangue
11 braggadocio, domineering

**blustery**
04 wild
05 gusty, windy
06 stormy
07 squally, violent
11 tempestuous

**board**
04 food, grub, slab, slat

05 embus, enter, get in, get on,
meals, panel, plank, sheet
06 embark, timber
07 council, emplane, entrain,
get into, rations
08 advisers, trustees, victuals
09 committee, directors,
governors
10 commission, management,
provisions, sustenance
11 directorate

❑**board up**
04 seal, shut
06 shut up
07 close up, cover up

**boast**
04 brag, crow
05 claim, enjoy, prate, pride,
strut, swank, vaunt
06 hot air
07 bluster, crowing, show off,
swagger, talk big, trumpet
08 treasure
09 gasconade, loudmouth
10 blustering, jactiation, self-
praise
11 fanfaronade, rodomontade
15 blow your own horn

**boastful**
04 vain
05 cocky, proud
06 swanky
07 crowing
08 arrogant, bragging
09 big-headed, conceited
10 swaggering
11 egotistical, swellheaded
12 vainglorious

**boat**

► *Types of boat or ship*:
02 PT
03 ark, cog, gig, hoy, LST, tub,
tug
04 bark, brig, dhow, dory, junk,
keel, prau, proa, prow, punt,
scow, yawl
05 barge, canoe, ferry, kayak,
ketch, liner, razee, scull, skiff,
sloop, smack, U-boat, xebec,
yacht
06 barque, bateau, caique,
coaler, convoy, cutter, dinghy,
dogger, dugout, galiot,
galley, launch, lugger, packet,
sampan, tanker, wherry
07 bum-boat, caravel, catboat,
clipper, coaster, collier,
coracle, corsair, cruiser,
dredger, felucca, frigate,
galleon, galliot, gondola,
gunboat, lighter, pinnace,

rowboat, steamer, trawler,
trireme, tugboat, warship
08 corvette, faltboat, foldboat,
ironclad, lifeboat, longboat,
longship, mackinaw, man-of-
war, schooner, showboat, tall
ship, trimaran
09 catamaran, destroyer,
freighter, houseboat,
hydrofoil, jolly boat,
lightship, motorboat,
outrigger, riverboat,
speedboat, steamboat,
steamship, submarine,
transport, troopship,
vaporetto
10 battleship, brigantine, cargo
liner, hovercraft, icebreaker,
quadrireme, tea clipper,
windjammer
11 dreadnought, merchantman,
minesweeper, quinquereme,
torpedo boat
12 cabin cruiser, square-rigger
13 container ship, paddle
steamer
14 blockade-runner
15 aircraft carrier
➤ See also SAIL; SHIP; VEHICLE

**boatman**
05 rower
06 sailor
07 oarsman
08 bargeman, ferryman,
waterman
09 gondolier, oarswoman,
yachtsman
11 yachtswoman

**bob**
03 bow, hop, nod
04 jerk, jolt, jump, leap, skip
06 bounce, curtsy
09 oscillate
13 move up and down

❑**bob up**
04 rise
05 arise, pop up
06 appear, arrive, show up
07 surface
08 spring up
11 materialize

**bode**
04 warn
05 augur
06 herald
07 betoken, portend, predict,
presage, purport, signify
08 forebode, foreshow, foretell,
forewarn, indicate, intimate,
prophesy, threaten

**bodily**
04 real
06 actual, carnal, in toto, wholly
07 en masse, fleshly, totally
08 as a whole, concrete,
material, physical, tangible
09 corporeal
11 substantial

**body**
03 mob
04 band, bloc, bulk, form, mass
05 build, crowd, frame, group,
stiff, torso, trunk
06 cartel, corpse, figure, throng
07 cadaver, carcass, council,
density, essence, phalanx
08 dead body, firmness, fullness,
main part, physique,
richness, skeleton, solidity
09 substance, syndicate
11 association, central part,
consistency, largest part
12 organization

**bodyguard**
05 guard
06 escort
08 defender, guardian
09 protector

**bog**
03 fen
04 mire, quag
05 marsh, swamp
06 morass, slough
08 quagmire, wetlands
09 marshland, swampland

❑**bog down**
04 halt, mire, sink
05 delay, stall, stick
06 hold up, impede, slow up
08 encumber, slow down
09 overwhelm

**boggle**
05 alarm, amaze
07 astound, confuse, stagger
08 bowl over, surprise
09 overwhelm
11 flabbergast

**boggy**
04 miry, oozy, soft
05 fenny, muddy
06 marshy, spongy, swampy
07 morassy, paludal
11 waterlogged

**bogus**
04 fake, sham
05 dummy, false, phony
06 forged, pseudo
08 spurious
09 imitation
10 artificial, fraudulent

11 counterfeit, make-believe

**bohemian**
04 arty
07 beatnik, bizarre, dropout
08 artistic, original
09 eccentric
10 avant-garde, unorthodox
13 nonconformist
14 unconventional

**boil**
04 brew, cook, fizz, foam, fume, heat, rage, rave, stew
05 erupt, froth, steam, ulcer
06 bubble, seethe, simmer
07 abscess, blister, pustule
09 carbuncle, fulminate
10 effervesce, hit the roof
11 blow your top
12 fly into a rage, inflammation
15 go off the deep end

❏**boil down**
06 amount, reduce
07 distill
08 abstract, condense
09 summarize
11 concentrate

**boiling**
03 hot
05 angry
06 baking, fuming, torrid
07 enraged, flaming, furious
08 broiling, bubbling, incensed, roasting, scalding, steaming
09 indignant, scorching
10 blistering, sweltering

**boisterous**
04 loud, wild
05 noisy, rough, rowdy
06 active, bouncy, lively, unruly
07 riotous, romping
08 spirited
09 energetic, exuberant
10 disorderly, rollicking

**bold**
04 loud, pert
05 brash, brave, showy, vivid
06 brassy, brazen, bright, daring, heroic, plucky
07 forward, gallant, valiant
08 definite, distinct, fearless, insolent, intrepid, outgoing, spirited, striking, valorous
09 audacious, barefaced, confident, dauntless, prominent, shameless, unabashed, undaunted
10 courageous, pronounced
11 adventurous, bold as a lion, bold as brass, eye-catching

**bolster**
03 aid
04 help, prop, stay
05 boost, brace
06 buoy up, firm up, pillow
07 augment, cushion, shore up, stiffen, support
09 reinforce
10 strengthen, supplement

**bolt**
03 bar, fly, peg, pin, rod, run
04 dash, flee, gulp, lock, wolf
05 catch, gorge, latch, rivet, screw, shaft, stuff
06 devour, escape, fasten, gobble, guzzle, hurtle, run off, secure, sprint
07 abscond, run away

**bomb**
03 dud
04 flop, mine
05 shell
06 attack, blow up, rocket
07 bombard, car bomb, failure, grenade, missile, torpedo
08 atom bomb, firebomb, time bomb
09 bombshell, explosive, stink bomb
10 atomic bomb, letter bomb, projectile
11 blockbuster, depth charge, hand grenade, neutron bomb, nuclear bomb
12 hydrogen bomb
14 incendiary bomb
15 Molotov cocktail

**bombard**
04 bomb, pelt, raid
05 blast, pound, shell, stone
06 assail, attack, pester, strafe
07 besiege, torpedo
10 carpet-bomb

**bombardment**
04 fire, flak
05 blitz, salvo
06 attack
07 air raid, assault, barrage, bombing
08 hounding, shelling
09 besieging, cannonade, fusillade, onslaught

**bombastic**
05 windy, wordy
06 turgid
07 fustian, pompous, verbose
08 affected, inflated
09 grandiose, high-flown
10 euphuistic, portentous
11 pretentious
13 grandiloquent

**bona fide**
04 real, true
05 legal, valid
06 actual, honest, kosher
07 genuine
08 rightful
09 authentic
10 legitimate
12 the real McCoy

**bonanza**
04 boon, mine
07 godsend
08 blessing, gold mine, windfall
12 stroke of luck

**bond**
03 gum, tie, vow
04 bail, band, bind, cord, fuse, glue, join, link, pact, weld, word
05 chain, stick, union, unite
06 attach, fasten, fetter, pledge
07 binding, connect, manacle, promise, rapport, shackle
08 affinity, contract, covenant
09 agreement, chemistry
10 attachment, connection
12 relationship

**bondage**
04 yoke
07 serfdom, slavery
08 thraldom
09 captivity, restraint, servitude, vassalage
10 subjection
11 enslavement, subjugation
12 imprisonment, subservience
13 incarceration

**bone**
04 bony
06 osteal
07 osseous

➤ *Human bones. We have omitted the word* **bone** *from names given in the following list but you may need to include this word as part of the solution to some crossword clues.*

02 os
03 jaw, rib
04 coxa, shin, ulna
05 ankle, anvil, costa, femur, funny, hyoid, ilium, incus, jugal, pubis, skull, spine, talus, thigh, tibia, vomer
06 coccyx, fibula, hammer, pecten, pelvis, radius, sacrum, stapes, tarsus
07 cranium, ethmoid, hipbone, humerus, ischium, kneecap, malleus, ossicle, patella, phalanx, scapula, sternum,

stirrup
08 backbone, clavicle,
    mandible, parietal, scaphoid,
    vertebra
09 calcaneum, calcaneus,
    cheekbone, navicular,
    occipital, trapezium,
    zygomatic
10 breastbone, collarbone,
    metacarpal, metatarsal
12 pelvic girdle
13 shoulder blade

**bonny**
04 fair, fine
06 cheery, joyful, lovely, pretty
08 blooming, bouncing
09 beautiful
10 attractive

**bonus**
03 tip
04 gain, gift, perk, plus
05 extra, prize
06 reward
07 benefit, handout, premium
08 dividend, gratuity
09 advantage, lagniappe
10 honorarium, perquisite

**bony**
04 lean, thin
05 drawn, gaunt, gawky, lanky
06 skinny
07 angular, scraggy, scrawny
08 gangling, skeletal
09 emaciated

**book**
04 tome, work
05 blame, novel, order, tract
06 charge, engage, volume
07 arrange, booklet, reserve
08 organize, schedule
09 reference
11 publication

▶ *Terms used in*
*bookbinding*:
03 aeg
04 case, head, limp, tail, yapp
05 bolts, hinge, spine
06 boards, gather, jacket, lining
07 binding, buckram, flyleaf,
    morocco
08 backbone, endpaper,
    hardback, headband,
    tailband
09 backboard, book block, dust
    cover, embossing, loose-leaf,
    millboard, paperback,
    softcover
10 dust jacket, pasteboard
11 dust wrapper, ring binding
12 quarter-bound
14 circuit binding, library

binding, quarter binding
15 divinity circuit

❏ **book in**
06 enroll
07 check in
08 register

**bookish**
07 donnish, erudite, learned
08 academic, highbrow,
    lettered, literary, pedantic,
    studious, well-read
09 scholarly
10 scholastic
12 bluestocking, intellectual

**books**
07 ledgers, records
08 accounts
12 balance sheet

**boom**
04 bang, clap, grow, roar, roll
05 blare, blast, boost, burst,
    crash, spurt, surge, swell
06 bellow, do well, expand,
    growth, rumble, thrive
07 explode, prosper, resound,
    success, thunder, upswing
08 escalate, flourish, increase
09 expansion, explosion
10 escalation, strengthen
11 improvement, reverberate
13 reverberation

**boomerang**
06 recoil
07 rebound
08 backfire, ricochet
10 bounce back, spring back

**boon**
04 gift, help, plus
05 bonus, favor, grant
07 benefit, godsend, present
08 blessing, kindness, windfall
09 advantage

**boor**
03 oaf
04 clod, lout
05 yahoo, yokel
06 rustic
07 peasant
09 barbarian, vulgarian
10 clodhopper, philistine

**boorish**
04 rude
05 crude, gruff, rough
06 coarse, oafish, rustic, vulgar
07 ill-bred, loutish, uncouth
08 ignorant, impolite
09 unrefined
10 uneducated
11 ill-mannered, uncivilized

**boost**
03 aid
04 help, hype, lift, plug, rise
05 put up, raise
06 assist, expand, fillip, uplift
07 advance, amplify, augment,
    bolster, develop, ego trip,
    enhance, enlarge, further,
    improve, inspire, promote
08 addition, heighten, increase,
    maximize, stimulus
09 advertise, encourage,
    expansion, promotion,
    publicity, publicize
10 assistance, supplement
11 enhancement, enlargement,
    furtherance, improvement
12 augmentation, shot in the
    arm
13 amplification,
    encouragement

**boot**
04 kick
05 shove, wader
06 bootee, brogan, buskin,
    galosh
07 galoshe
08 overshoe
10 cowboy boot, riding boot,
    Wellington
11 walking boot
12 climbing boot

❏ **boot out**
02 ax
04 fire, sack, shed
05 eject, expel
07 dismiss, kick out, suspend
12 give the heave
13 make redundant

❏ **to boot**
06 as well
10 in addition
14 into the bargain

**booth**
03 box, hut
05 kiosk, stall, stand
06 carrel
07 cubicle
09 newsstand
11 compartment

**bootless**
04 vain
06 barren, futile
07 sterile, useless
09 fruitless, pointless, worthless
10 profitless, unavailing
11 ineffective
12 unproductive, unsuccessful

**booty**
04 haul, loot, swag
05 gains, prize, spoil

**border**
06 spoils
07 pillage, plunder, profits
08 pickings, winnings

**border**
03 bed, hem, rim
04 abut, brim, edge, join, trim
05 bound, frill, skirt, verge
06 adjoin, bounds, frieze, fringe, margin
07 impinge, marches, valance
08 be next to, boundary, confines, frontier, surround
09 perimeter, state line
10 borderline, county line, marchlands
12 be adjacent to, circumscribe

❏**border on**
07 verge on
08 approach, be almost, be nearly, resemble
13 approximate to

**borderline**
04 iffy
08 doubtful, marginal
09 uncertain
10 ambivalent, indecisive
13 indeterminate

**bore**
03 dig, irk, sap, tap, vex
04 drag, gape, gawk, mine, sink, tire, wave
05 annoy, drill, weary, worry
06 burrow, dig out, hollow, pall on, pierce, tunnel
07 exhaust, fatigue, trouble, turn off, turnoff, wear out
08 irritate, nuisance
09 hollow out, penetrate, perforate, undermine
11 be tedious to, send to sleep
13 pain in the neck
15 bore the pants off

**bored**
05 fed up, tired
06 ennuyé, in a rut
07 ennuied, wearied, worn out
09 turned off, unexcited
10 bored stiff
12 bored to death, sick and tired, uninterested

**boredom**
05 ennui
06 acedia, apathy, tedium
07 humdrum, malaise
08 dullness, monotony, sameness
11 frustration, tediousness
12 listlessness
14 world-weariness

**boring**
03 dry
04 dull, flat
05 samey, stale, trite
06 dreary, jejune, tiring
07 humdrum, insipid, prosaic, routine, tedious
08 tiresome, unvaried
10 long-winded, monotonous, uneventful, unexciting, uninspired
11 repetitious, stultifying
13 unimaginative, uninteresting
14 soul-destroying

**borough**
04 burg, town
07 village
08 township
➤ See also COUNTY; PROVINCE; STATE

▬ *Names of New York boroughs:*
06 Queens
08 Brooklyn, The Bronx
09 Manhattan
12 Staten Island

**borrow**
04 draw, hire, rent, take
05 adopt, cadge, lease
06 derive, obtain, sponge
07 acquire, charter
08 scrounge, take over
10 have on loan, take on loan
11 appropriate
12 take out a loan
14 use temporarily

**borrowing**
03 use
04 hire, loan
06 calque, rental
07 charter, leasing
08 adoption, loanword
11 acquisition
12 temporary use
15 loan-translation

**bosom**
04 bust, dear, soul
05 chest, close, heart
06 breast, loving
07 breasts
08 faithful, intimate

**boss**
04 head
05 bully, chief, owner
06 leader, master
07 captain, foreman, headman, manager, supremo
08 browbeat, bulldoze, director, dominate, domineer,

employer, governor, overseer, superior
09 executive, tyrannize
10 push around, supervisor
11 order around
12 give orders to
13 lay down the law

**bossy**
09 assertive, imperious
10 autocratic, dominating, high-handed, tyrannical
11 dictatorial, domineering, overbearing
13 authoritarian

**botanist**

▬ *Names of botanists:*
03 **Mee** (Margaret Ursula), **Ray** (John)
04 **Bary** (Heinrich Anton de), **Bose** (Jagadis Chandra), **Cohn** (Ferdinand Julius), **Gray** (Asa)
05 **Banks** (Joseph), **Sachs** (Julius von)
06 **Carver** (George Washington), **Haller** (Albrecht von), **Hooker** (Joseph Dalton), **Mendel** (Gregor Johann), **Nägeli** (Karl Wilhelm von)
07 **Bartram** (John), **Bellamy** (David), **Bentham** (George), **Burnank** (Luther), **De Vries** (Hugo Marie), **Vavilov** (Nikolai)
08 **Candolle** (Augustin Pyrame de)
09 **Schleiden** (Matthias Jakob)
10 **Camerarius** (Rudolph Jacob), **Pringsheim** (Nathaniel)
➤ See also SCIENTIST

**botch**
03 mar
04 flub, goof, hash, mess, muff, ruin
05 farce, fluff, patch, spoil
06 bobble, bungle, foul up, fumble, mess up, muddle
07 blunder, failure, louse up, screw up
09 mismanage
11 make a hash of, make a mess of, miscarriage

**both**
04 each
06 the two
07 the pair

**bother**
03 bug, nag, vex

04 fuss, pest
05 annoy, pains, upset, worry
06 bustle, dismay, effort, flurry, harass, hassle, molest, pester, plague, put out, strain
07 concern, disturb, problem, trouble
08 distress, exertion, irritate, nuisance, vexation
09 annoyance, incommode
10 difficulty, irritation
11 aggravation
12 make an effort, troublemaker
13 inconvenience, make the effort, pain in the neck
15 concern yourself

**bothersome**
06 boring, vexing
07 irksome, tedious
08 annoying, tiresome
09 vexatious, wearisome
10 irritating
11 aggravating, distressing, infuriating, troublesome
12 exasperating, inconvenient

**bottle**
04 curb, hide
06 shut in
07 contain, enclose, inhibit
08 bottle up, hold back, keep back, restrain, restrict, suppress
11 keep in check

**bottleneck**
04 snag
05 block, snarl
08 blockage, clogging, slowdown
09 narrowing
10 congestion, traffic jam
11 obstruction, restriction
12 constriction

**bottom**
03 bed, end
04 base, butt, foot, rear, rump, seat, sole, tail
05 floor, lower, nadir
06 behind, depths, far end, ground, lowest, plinth
07 support
08 backside, buttocks, pedestal
09 posterior, underside
10 foundation, underneath

**bottomless**
04 deep
08 infinite, profound
09 limitless, unlimited
10 fathomless, unfathomed
12 immeasurable
13 inexhaustible

**bough**
04 limb
06 branch

**boulder**
04 rock
05 stone

**boulevard**
04 mall, road
05 drive
06 avenue, median, parade, street
08 prospect
09 promenade
12 thoroughfare

**bounce**
02 go
03 bob, zip
04 give, jump, leap
05 bound, throw, vigor
06 energy, recoil, spring
07 dribble, rebound
08 ricochet, vitality, vivacity
09 animation
10 ebullience, exuberance, get-up-and-go, liveliness, resilience, spring back
11 springiness
12 spiritedness

❏**bounce back**
07 improve, recover
09 get better
15 get back to normal

**bouncing**
05 bonny
06 lively, robust, strong
07 healthy

**bound**
03 bob, hop, off
04 curb, edge, held, jump, leap, line, skip, sure, tied
05 brink, caper, check, dance, fated, fixed, flank, frisk, going, limit, off to, roped, skirt, vault, verge
06 bounce, coming, doomed, forced, frolic, gambol, headed, lashed, liable, prance, spring, tied up
07 certain, chained, clamped, confine, contain, enclose, heading, obliged, outline, pledged, secured, trussed
08 attached, bandaged, beholden, destined, fastened, fettered, required, restrain, shackled, strapped, surround, tethered
09 committed, compelled, duty-bound, extremity, perimeter, restraint, traveling

10 limitation, proceeding, restricted
11 constrained, on your way to, restriction, termination
12 circumscribe

❏**bound up with**
09 related to
10 linked with, tied up with
11 dependent on
13 connected with
14 associated with, hand in hand with

❏**out of bounds**
05 taboo
06 banned, barred
09 forbidden, off-limits, out of play
10 disallowed, prohibited

**boundary**
04 edge, line
05 brink, verge
06 border, bounds, fringe, limits, margin
07 barrier, Rubicon
08 confines, frontier
09 extremity, perimeter
10 borderline, perimetric

**bounded**
05 edged
07 defined, limited
08 bordered, confined, enclosed, hemmed in
09 delimited, encircled
10 controlled, demarcated, restrained, surrounded
11 encompassed
13 circumscribed

**bounder**
03 cad, cur, pig, rat
05 cheat, knave, rogue, swine
08 dirty dog
09 miscreant, scoundrel
10 blackguard

**boundless**
04 vast
06 untold
07 endless, immense
08 infinite, unending
09 countless, limitless, unbounded, unlimited
10 numberless, unflagging
11 everlasting, illimitable, innumerable, never-ending
12 immeasurable, incalculable, interminable
13 indefatigable, inexhaustible

**bounds**
05 edges, scope
06 limits
07 borders, fringes, margins

08 confines
09 perimeter, periphery
10 boundaries, parameters
12 demarcations, restrictions
13 circumference

❑ **out of bounds**
09 forbidden, off limits, out of play
10 not allowed, prohibited

**bountiful**
05 ample
07 copious, liberal, profuse
08 abundant, generous, princely, prolific
09 boundless, bounteous, plenteous, plentiful
10 munificent, openhanded
11 magnanimous, overflowing

**bounty**
04 gift
05 bonus, grant
06 reward
07 charity, premium, present
08 donation, gratuity, kindness, largesse
10 almsgiving, generosity, liberality, recompense
11 beneficence, munificence
12 philanthropy

**bouquet**
04 nose, posy
05 aroma, scent, smell, spice, spray
06 wreath
07 corsage, nosegay, perfume
09 fragrance, redolence
15 odoriferousness

**bourgeois**
04 dull
07 humdrum
08 ordinary
09 hidebound
10 conformist, uncultured, uninspired, unoriginal
11 middle-class, traditional
12 conservative, conventional
13 materialistic, unimaginative
15 money-orientated

**bout**
02 go
03 fit, run
04 heat, term, time, turn
05 fight, match, round, set-to, spell, spree, stint, touch
07 contest, session, stretch
08 struggle
09 encounter
11 competition

**bovine**
04 dull, dumb, slow

06 stupid
07 cowlike, doltish
09 dimwitted
10 cattlelike, slow-witted

**bow**
03 arc, bob, nod
04 arch, bend, head, prow
05 crook, crush, curve, defer, front, stoop, yield
06 accede, accept, comply, crouch, curtsy, give in, humble, kowtow, salaam, subdue, submit
07 bending, concede, consent, incline, rostrum, succumb
09 acquiesce, genuflect, give way to, overpower, subjugate, surrender
10 capitulate, salutation
11 inclination
12 genuflection
13 make obeisance

❑ **bow out**
04 quit
05 leave
06 defect, desert, give up, resign, retire
07 abandon, back out, pull out
08 step down, withdraw

**bowdlerize**
03 cut
04 edit
05 purge
06 censor, excise, modify
07 clean up, expunge
09 expurgate
10 blue-pencil

**bowels**
03 gut
04 core, guts
05 belly, colon, heart
06 center, depths, inside, middle
07 innards, insides, viscera
08 entrails, interior
10 intestines

**bower**
03 bay
05 arbor
06 alcove, grotto, recess
07 retreat, shelter
09 sanctuary

**bowl**
04 dish, hurl, roll, sink, spin
05 arena, basin, pitch, throw, whirl
07 revolve, stadium
09 container
10 receptacle

❑ **bowl over**
04 fell, stun

05 amaze, floor
07 astound, stagger
08 astonish, push into, surprise
09 dumbfound, knock down
11 flabbergast
14 impress greatly

**box**
03 hit, pyx
04 case, cuff, pack, slap, slug, sock, spar, wrap
05 bijou, chest, clout, fight, punch, pyxis, thump, whack
06 batter, buffet, carton, casket, packet, strike, wallop
07 coffret, package, present
09 container
10 receptacle

❑ **box in**
04 cage, trap
05 hem in
06 coop up, corner, shut in
07 block in, confine, contain, enclose, fence in
08 imprison, restrict, surround
12 circumscribe

**boxer**
07 fighter
08 pugilist
12 prizefighter
15 sparring partner
➤ See also SPORT

━ *Weight divisions in professional boxing:*
09 flyweight
11 heavyweight, lightweight, strawweight
12 bantamweight, middleweight, welterweight
13 cruiserweight, featherweight
15 junior flyweight

━ *Names of boxers:*
03 **Ali** (Muhammad)
04 **Clay** (Cassius)
05 **Bruno** (Frank), **Hamad** ("Prince" Nasseem), **Lewis** (Lennox), **Louis** (Joe), **Tyson** (Mike)
06 **Holmes** (Larry), **Liston** (Sonny), **Spinks** (Leon), **Tunney** (Gene)
07 **Charles** (Ezzard), **Corbett** (Jim), **Dempsey** (Jack), **Foreman** (George), **Frazier** (Joe), **Johnson** (Jack), **Leonard** (Sugar Ray)
08 **Marciano** (Rocky), **Robinson** (Sugar Ray), **Sullivan** (John L.)
09 **Holyfield** (Evander), **Patterson** (Floyd)

11 **Fitzsimmons** (Bob)

**boxing**
08 pugilism, sparring
10 fisticuffs, pugilistic
13 prizefighting

**boy**
03 kid, lad, son
05 child, sonny, youth
06 fellow, junior, nipper
08 teenager, young man
09 schoolboy, stripling, youngster
10 adolescent
14 whippersnapper

**boycott**
05 avoid, black, spurn
06 eschew, ignore, outlaw, refuse, reject
07 embargo, exclude
09 blacklist, ostracize
12 cold shoulder

**boyfriend**
03 man
04 beau, date
05 lover
06 fiancé, steady, suitor
07 admirer, partner
08 paramour, young man
09 betrothed
10 sweetheart

**boyish**
05 green, young
06 tomboy
07 puerile
08 childish, immature, innocent, juvenile, youthful
09 childlike
10 adolescent, unfeminine

**brace**
03 duo, tie
04 bind, pair, prop, stay, vise
05 clamp, strap, strut, truss
06 couple, fasten, hold up, prop up, secure, splint, steady, uphold
07 bolster, fortify, shore up, shoring, support, twosome
08 buttress, fastener
09 reinforce, stanchion
10 strengthen
13 reinforcement

**bracelet**
04 band
06 bangle
07 circlet
09 handcuffs

**bracing**
05 brisk, crisp, fresh, tonic
07 rousing
08 reviving, vigorous

10 energizing, enlivening, fortifying, refreshing
11 stimulating
12 exhilarating, invigorating
13 strengthening

**brackish**
04 salt
05 briny, salty
06 bitter, saline

**brag**
04 crow
05 boast, vaunt
07 bluster, show off, talk big
12 lay it on thick
15 blow your own horn

**braggart**
06 gascon
07 bluffer, boaster, bragger, showoff
08 big mouth, fanfaron
09 blusterer, loudmouth
11 braggadocio

**bragging**
06 hot air
07 bluster, bravado
08 boasting
10 showing-off
12 boastfulness, exaggeration

**braid**
04 lace, wind
05 plait, twine, twist, weave
07 entwine
09 interlace
10 intertwine, interweave

**brain**
03 wit
04 head, mind, nous
05 savvy, sense
06 acumen, brains, genius, pundit, reason
07 egghead, prodigy, scholar
08 highbrow
09 intellect, sensorium
10 encephalon, gray matter, mastermind, shrewdness
11 common sense
12 intellectual, intelligence

► *Parts of the brain*:
04 pons
08 cerebrum, midbrain, thalamus
09 brainstem, forebrain, hindbrain
10 cerebellum, gray matter, spinal cord
11 frontal lobe
12 hypothalamus, temporal lobe
14 cerebral cortex, corpus callosum, pituitary gland

**brainless**
04 daft
05 crazy, inept, silly
06 stupid
07 foolish, idiotic
08 mindless
09 senseless

**brainteaser**
05 poser
06 puzzle, riddle
07 problem
09 conundrum

**brainwashing**
09 menticide
11 mind-control
12 conditioning, pressurizing
14 indoctrination

**brainy**
04 wise
05 smart
06 bright, clever, gifted
07 sapient
09 brilliant
11 intelligent
12 intellectual

**brake**
04 curb, drag, halt, slow, stop
05 check
06 pull up, retard
08 moderate
09 restraint
10 constraint, decelerate
11 reduce speed, restriction

**branch**
03 arm
04 limb, part, stem, wing
05 bough, prong, ramus, shoot
06 office
07 section
08 division, offshoot
10 department, discipline, subsection, subsidiary

❑**branch off**
04 fork
06 divide
07 diverge, furcate
08 separate
09 bifurcate

❑**branch out**
04 vary
06 expand, extend, ramify
07 develop, enlarge
09 diversify, subdivide
10 broaden out
11 proliferate

**brand**
03 tag
04 burn, kind, line, logo, make, mark, scar, sign, sort, type
05 label, stain, stamp, taint

**brandish**
06 burn in, emblem, symbol
07 censure, species, variety
08 denounce, hallmark, typecast
09 brand name, discredit, trademark, tradename
10 stigmatize
14 identification
15 identifying mark

**brandish**
04 wave
05 raise, shake, swing, wield
06 flaunt, parade
07 display, exhibit
08 flourish

**brash**
04 bold, rash, rude
05 cocky, hasty, pushy
06 brazen
08 impudent, insolent, reckless
09 audacious, foolhardy, impetuous, impulsive
10 incautious, indiscreet
11 impertinent, precipitate
13 self-confident

**brass**
04 gall
05 alloy, cheek, metal, nerve
08 audacity, chutzpah, rudeness, temerity
09 impudence, insolence
10 brazenness, effrontery
11 presumption
12 impertinence

**brassy**
04 bold, hard, loud
05 brash, harsh, noisy, pushy
06 brazen
07 blaring, forward, grating, jarring, raucous
08 insolent, piercing, strident
09 dissonant, shameless
11 loud-mouthed

**brat**
03 kid
05 puppy
06 nipper, rascal
10 jackanapes
11 guttersnipe
14 whippersnapper

**bravado**
04 show, talk
05 boast
07 bluster, bombast, swagger
08 boasting, bragging
10 showing-off
11 braggadocio, fanfaronade, rodomontade

**brave**
04 bear, bold, dare, defy, face

05 gutsy, hardy
06 daring, endure, gritty, heroic, plucky, spunky, suffer
07 gallant, valiant
08 confront, face up to, fearless, intrepid, unafraid, valorous
09 audacious, dauntless, stand up to, undaunted
10 courageous
11 indomitable, lion-hearted
12 face the music
14 keep your chin up

**bravery**
04 grit, guts
05 pluck, spunk, valor
06 daring, mettle, spirit
07 courage, heroism
08 audacity, boldness, valiance
09 fortitude, gallantry
11 intrepidity
12 fearlessness, stalwartness
13 dauntlessness

**brawl**
03 row
04 fray
05 broil, fight, melee, scrap
06 affray, dust-up, fracas, ruckus, rumpus
07 dispute, quarrel, scuffle, wrangle, wrestle
08 disorder, skirmish
10 donnybrook, fisticuffs, free-for-all

**brawn**
04 beef, bulk
05 might, power
06 muscle, sinews
08 strength
11 muscularity

**brawny**
05 beefy, bulky, burly, hardy, hefty, husky, solid
06 robust, strong, sturdy
07 hulking, massive
08 athletic, muscular, powerful
09 strapping, well-built

**bray**
05 blare, neigh
06 bellow, heehaw, whinny
07 screech, trumpet

**brazen**
04 bold, defy, pert
05 brash, pushy, saucy
06 brassy
07 blatant, defiant, forward
08 flagrant, immodest, impudent, insolent
09 audacious, barefaced, shameless, unabashed, unashamed

**breach**
03 gap
04 gulf, hole, rift
05 break, chasm, cleft, crack, lapse, space, split
07 crevice, fissure, opening, parting, quarrel, rupture
08 aperture, breaking, division, infringe, trespass, variance
09 break open, violation
10 contravene, difference, disruption, dissension, infraction, separation
12 burst through, disagreement, dissociation, estrangement, infringement
13 contravention, transgression

**bread**
04 cash, fare, food, loaf, roll
05 funds, manna, money, toast
07 biscuit
08 sandwich, victuals
09 eucharist
10 provisions, sustenance
11 nourishment

► *Types of bread*:
03 bun, rye
04 azym, pita, pone, rusk
05 azyme, bagel, matzo
06 baguet, matzoh, sliced
07 brioche, challah, chapati, wheaten
08 baguette, chapatti, corn pone, leavened, tortilla, zwieback
09 cornbread, hush puppy, sourdough
10 black bread, brown bread, unleavened, white bread, whole-wheat
11 French bread
12 pumpernickel
➤ See also FOOD

**breadth**
04 size, span
05 range, reach, scope, width
06 extent, spread
07 compass, expanse, measure
08 latitude, vastness, wideness
09 amplitude, broadness
13 extensiveness

**break**
03 gap
04 fail, gash, halt, hole, luck, lull, open, rend, rest, rift, snap, stop, tame, tear, tell
05 cleft, crack, crash, excel, flout, letup, outdo, pause, sever, smash, solve, split
06 breach, chance, change, cut off, cut out, divide, escape,

exceed, impart, inform, open up, reveal, schism, subdue, weaken, worsen
07 crevice, destroy, disobey, divulge, fissure, fortune, go kaput, holiday, opening, respite, rupture, shatter, surpass, time off, timeout, violate, work out
08 announce, breather, decipher, demolish, disclose, fracture, half time, interval, overcome, puncture, separate, splinter, vacation
09 advantage, figure out, interlude, interrupt, perforate
10 contravene, demoralize, separation, suspension
11 discontinue, opportunity
12 bring to an end, disintegrate, estrangement, go on the blink, intermission, interruption, stroke of luck

**□break away**
03 fly
04 flee, quit
05 leave, rebel, split
06 depart, escape, secede
07 run away
08 separate, split off
11 part company

**□break down**
04 fail, stop
06 detail
07 analyze, conk out, crack up, give way, itemize, seize up
08 collapse, separate
10 be overcome, go to pieces
11 fall through, lose control, stop working

**□break in**
05 cut in, train
06 burgle, butt in
07 impinge, intrude
09 condition, force open, get used to, interject, interpose, interrupt, intervene
14 enter illegally

**□break off**
03 end
04 halt, part, stop .
05 cease, pause, sever
06 detach, divide, finish
07 snap off, suspend
11 discontinue
12 bring to an end

**□break out**
04 bolt, flee
05 begin, erupt, occur, start
06 emerge, escape, happen
08 burst out, commence

09 come out in
13 begin suddenly

**□break through**
06 breach
07 succeed
08 overcome, progress
09 penetrate
11 make headway

**□break up**
04 part, stop
05 sever, split
06 divide, finish
07 adjourn, destroy, disband, divorce, split up, suspend
08 demolish, disperse, separate
09 dismantle, take apart
11 discontinue
12 disintegrate

**□break with**
04 drop, jilt
05 ditch
06 reject
08 part with, renounce
09 repudiate

**breakable**
05 frail
06 flimsy
07 brittle, fragile, friable
08 delicate
09 frangible

**breakaway**
05 rebel
08 apostate, renegade, seceding
09 heretical
10 dissenting, schismatic
12 secessionist

**breakdown**
07 failure
08 analysis, collapse, stoppage
11 itemization, malfunction
12 interruption
14 classification, disintegration

**breaker**
04 wave
06 billow, roller
08 whitecap
11 white horses

**break-in**
04 raid
07 larceny, robbery
08 burglary, invasion, trespass
09 intrusion
13 housebreaking

**breakthrough**
04 find, gain, leap, step
07 advance, finding, headway
08 progress
09 discovery, invention
10 innovation

11 development, leap forward, quantum leap, step forward

**breakup**
04 rift
05 split
06 finish
07 divorce, parting
09 crumbling, dispersal
10 separation
11 dissolution, splitting-up
12 estrangement
14 disintegration

**breakwater**
04 dock, mole, pier, quay, spur
05 groin
06 groyne

**breast**
04 bust
05 bosom, chest, front, heart
06 thorax
07 brisket

**breath**
03 air
04 gasp, gulp, gust, hint, odor, pant, puff, sigh, waft
05 aroma, smell, whiff
06 breeze, murmur, pneuma
07 whisper
09 breathing, suspicion
10 exhalation, inhalation, suggestion

**breathe**
04 gasp, pant, puff, sigh, tell
05 imbue, snore, utter, voice
06 exhale, expire, infuse, inhale, inject, murmur
07 inspire, instill, respire, whisper

**breather**
04 halt, rest, walk
05 break, pause
06 recess
07 respite
11 easy contest

**breathless**
04 agog
05 eager
06 puffed, winded
07 anxious, choking, excited, gasping, panting, puffing
08 feverish, wheezing
09 expectant, puffed out
10 in suspense
11 out of breath, short-winded

**breathtaking**
06 moving
07 amazing
08 exciting, stirring, stunning
09 thrilling
10 impressive

**breed**

11 astonishing, magnificent, spectacular
12 awe-inspiring

**breed**

04 kind, line, race, rear, type
05 cause, class, hatch, raise
06 arouse, create, family, foster, hybrid, strain
07 bring up, develop, lineage, nourish, nurture, produce, progeny, species, variety
08 engender, generate, multiply, occasion, pedigree
09 procreate, propagate, pullulate, reproduce
10 bring forth, give rise to

**breeding**

05 stock
07 culture, lineage, manners, nurture, raising, rearing
08 ancestry, training, urbanity
09 education, gentility
10 politeness, refinement, upbringing
11 development, good manners, procreation
12 reproduction

**breeding-ground**

04 nest
06 hotbed, school
07 nursery
14 training ground

**breeze**

03 air
04 flit, gust, puff, waft, wind
05 draft
06 breath, flurry, wander
08 pushover
11 easy contest

**breezy**

04 airy
05 fresh, gusty, light, windy
06 blithe, bright, casual, jaunty
07 blowing, buoyant, squally
08 blustery, carefree, cheerful
09 confident, easy-going

**brevity**

07 economy
08 curtness, laconism
09 briefness, concision, shortness, terseness
10 abruptness, transience
11 conciseness
12 incisiveness, succinctness

**brew**

04 cook, plan, plot, soak
05 blend, drink, hatch, steep
06 devise, foment, infuse, liquor, potion, scheme, seethe

07 build up, concoct, develop, ferment, mixture, prepare
08 beverage, contrive, infusion
10 concoction
11 preparation

**bribe**

03 fix
06 boodle, buy off, grease, pay off, payola, square, suborn
07 corrupt, douceur
08 kickback
09 hush money, incentive, slush fund, sweetener
10 allurement, enticement, inducement
13 grease the palm
15 protection money

**bribery**

05 graft
10 corruption, protection
12 palm-greasing

**bric-à-brac**

06 curios
07 baubles
08 antiques, trinkets, trumpery
09 ornaments
11 knickknacks

**brick**

03 nog
04 rock
05 adobe, block, stone
06 header
07 klinker
09 briquette, firebrick

**bridal**

07 marital, nuptial, wedding
08 conjugal, marriage
11 matrimonial

**bride**

04 wife
06 spouse
08 newlywed, war bride
11 honeymooner
15 marriage partner

**bridegroom**

05 groom
06 spouse
07 husband
08 newlywed
11 honeymooner
15 marriage partner

**bridge**

03 tie
04 arch, bind, bond, fill, join, link, span
05 cross, unite
07 connect
08 card game, causeway, traverse
10 connection

11 reach across

▶ *Types of bridge. We have omitted the word* **bridge** *from names given in the following list but you may need to include this word as part of the solution to some crossword clues.*

04 arch, rope, toll
05 swing
06 Bailey, flying
07 covered, pontoon, railway, trestle, viaduct
08 aqueduct, humpback, overpass, railroad
10 cantilever, drawbridge, footbridge, suspension

**bridle**

04 curb
05 check
06 halter, master, subdue
07 bristle, contain, control, repress
08 moderate, restrain
09 restraint

**brief**

04 case, curt, data
05 blunt, crisp, hasty, pithy, prime, quick, remit, sharp, short, surly, swift, terse
06 abrupt, advice, advise, direct, fill in, inform, orders
07 brusque, concise, cursory, defense, dossier, explain, mandate, outline, passing, prepare, summary
08 abridged, abstract, argument, briefing, fleeting, instruct, succinct
09 condensed, directive, fugacious, momentary, temporary, transient
10 aphoristic, directions, short-lived, transitory
12 instructions

**briefing**

03 gen
06 advice, orders, report
07 lowdown, meeting, priming, rundown
09 filling-in
10 conference, directions
11 information, preparation
12 instructions

**briefly**

07 in a word, in brief, quickly
09 concisely, cursorily, precisely, summarily
10 succinctly, to the point
11 in a few words, in a nutshell

**brigade**
04 band, body, crew, team, unit
05 corps, force, squad, troop
07 company
10 contingent
11 fire brigade

**brigand**
06 bandit, outlaw, pirate, robber
08 gangster, marauder
09 desperado, plunderer
10 freebooter, highwayman

**bright**
04 fine, glad, keen, rosy
05 acute, happy, jolly, quick, sharp, smart, sunny, vivid
06 astute, brainy, clever, lively
07 beaming, blazing, glaring, hopeful, intense, shining
08 blinding, cheerful, dazzling, flashing, gleaming, glorious, luminous, lustrous, splendid
09 brilliant, cloudless, effulgent, favorable, promising, refulgent, sparkling, unclouded
10 auspicious, glistening, glittering, optimistic, perceptive
11 encouraging, illuminated, intelligent, resplendent
12 incandescent

**brighten**
05 gleam, pep up, rub up, shine
06 buck up, perk up, polish
07 burnish, cheer up, enliven, gladden, hearten, light up, lighten, liven up
09 encourage
10 illuminate, make bright

**brilliance**
05 glory, gloss, sheen
06 dazzle, genius, glamor, luster, talent
07 glitter, sparkle
08 aptitude, radiance, splendor
09 greatness, intensity, vividness
10 brightness, cleverness, effulgence, excellence, refulgence, virtuosity
11 coruscation, distinction
12 magnificence, resplendence

**brilliant**
05 great, quick, showy, vivid
06 astute, brainy, bright, clever, expert, glossy, superb
07 blazing, erudite, fulgent, glaring, intense, shining
08 dazzling, glorious, masterly, splendid, talented
09 effulgent, fantastic, refulgent, sparkling

10 celebrated, glittering
11 exceptional, illustrious, intelligent, magnificent, outstanding, resplendent
13 scintillating

**brim**
03 lip, rim, top
04 edge
05 brink, limit, verge
09 perimeter
10 be full with
12 be filled with, overflow with

**bring**
04 bear, lead, take
05 carry, cause, fetch, force, guide, usher
06 convey, create, escort
07 deliver, produce, provoke
08 engender, result in
09 accompany, transport

❑**bring about**
05 cause
06 create, effect, manage
07 achieve, fulfill, produce, realize
08 generate, occasion

❑**bring down**
04 oust
05 lower
06 defeat, reduce, topple, unseat
07 destroy
08 vanquish
09 overthrow, shoot down
11 cause to drop, cause to fall

❑**bring forward**
07 advance
11 make earlier

❑**bring in**
03 net
04 earn
05 fetch, gross, set up, yield
06 accrue, import, return
07 realize, usher in
08 initiate
09 introduce, originate

❑**bring off**
03 win
07 achieve, execute, fulfill, pull off
09 discharge, succeed in
10 accomplish

❑**bring on**
05 cause
06 foster, induce, lead to
07 advance, improve, inspire, nurture, provoke
08 expedite, occasion
10 accelerate, give rise to
11 precipitate

❑**bring out**
05 issue, print
06 launch, stress
07 draw out, enhance, produce, publish
09 emphasize, highlight

❑**bring around, bring round**
04 coax
05 rouse
06 awaken, cajole, revive
07 bring to, convert, win over
08 convince, persuade
11 resuscitate

❑**bring up**
04 form, puke, rear, rear
05 raise, teach, train, vomit
06 broach, foster, submit
07 care for, educate, mention, nurture, propose, throw up
09 introduce
11 regurgitate

**brink**
03 lip, rim
04 bank, brim, edge
05 limit, verge
09 extremity, threshold

**brisk**
04 busy, cold, good
05 agile, crisp, fresh, quick
06 active, lively, nimble, snappy
07 bracing
08 bustling, spirited, vigorous
09 energetic
10 no-nonsense, refreshing
11 stimulating
12 businesslike, exhilarating

**bristle**
03 awn
04 barb, hair
05 quill, spine, thorn
06 seethe
07 prickle, stubble, whisker
08 bridle at, teem with
11 be thick with, horripilate
13 draw oneself up

**bristly**
05 hairy, rough, spiky, spiny
06 hispid, thorny
07 bearded, hirsute, stubbly
08 unshaven
09 whiskered
10 barbellate

**brittle**
04 curt, hard
05 crisp, frail, nervy, tense
07 crumbly, fragile, friable
08 delicate, shattery, unstable
09 breakable, crumbling, frangible, irritable

12 easily broken

**broach**
05 raise
06 hint at
07 mention, propose, suggest
09 introduce

**broad**
04 vast, wide
05 ample, large, plain, vague
07 general, obvious
08 catholic, spacious, sweeping
09 extensive, inclusive
10 widespread
11 far-reaching, wide-ranging
12 all-embracing,
     encyclopedic, latitudinous
13 comprehensive

**broadcast**
03 air
04 beam, show
05 cable, relay
06 report, spread
07 program, publish, scatter
08 announce, televise, transmit
09 advertise, circulate, publicize
10 promulgate
11 disseminate
12 transmission

**broaden**
05 widen
06 expand, extend, open up,
     spread
07 develop, enlarge, stretch ⸱
09 branch out, diversify

**broad-minded**
07 liberal
08 tolerant, unbiased
09 indulgent, receptive
10 forbearing, open-minded
11 enlightened, progressive
12 free-thinking, unprejudiced

**broadside**
05 blast, flyer, salvo, sheet
06 attack, folder, volley
07 assault, handout, leaflet
08 brickbat, circular, diatribe,
     handbill, harangue
09 battering, cannonade
10 broadsheet
11 bombardment, fulmination

**brochure**
07 booklet
08 pamphlet
10 prospectus

**broil**
03 fry
04 bake, cook, fray
05 grill, roast
06 braise
08 barbecue

10 donnybrook, free-for-all

**broiling**
06 baking
07 boiling
08 roasting, sizzling
09 scorching
10 blistering, sweltering

**broke**
04 bust, flat, poor
06 ruined
08 bankrupt, dirt poor, indigent,
     strapped
09 destitute, insolvent,
     penniless, penurious
10 cleaned out, stone-broke
11 gone belly up, impecunious
12 impoverished, on your
     uppers
14 on your beam ends
15 poverty-stricken, strapped
     for cash

**broken**
04 bust, down, weak
05 burst, kaput, tamed
06 beaten, faulty, feeble
07 crushed, damaged, erratic,
     halting, smashed, subdued
08 defeated, ruptured
09 defective, destroyed,
     fractured, gone wrong,
     separated, shattered,
     spasmodic
10 disjointed, hesitating, not
     working, on the blink, out of
     order, splintered,
     stammering
11 demoralized, fragmentary,
     inoperative, out of action
12 disconnected, intermittent
13 discontinuous
14 malfunctioning

**broken-down**
04 bust
05 kaput
06 faulty, ruined
07 damaged, decayed
08 decrepit
09 collapsed, defective
10 on the blink, out of order
11 dilapidated, in disrepair,
     inoperative

**broken-hearted**
03 sad
07 forlorn, unhappy
08 dejected, desolate,
     mournful, wretched
09 miserable, sorrowful
10 despairing, despondent,
     devastated, prostrated
11 crestfallen, heartbroken
12 disconsolate, inconsolable

13 grief-stricken

**broker**
05 agent
06 dealer, factor, jobber
07 handler
09 middleman
10 negotiator
11 arbitrageur, stockbroker,
     stockjobber
12 intermediary

**bromide**
06 cliché, truism
07 anodyne
08 banality
09 platitude
11 commonplace

**bronze**
03 tan
04 rust
06 auburn, copper, titian
08 chestnut
12 reddish-brown
13 copper-colored

**brooch**
03 pin
04 clip
05 badge, cameo, clasp

**brood**
03 set, sit
04 fret, mope, muse, sulk
05 hatch, issue, worry, young
06 chicks, clutch, family, go over,
     litter, ponder
07 agonize, dwell on, progeny
08 children, incubate, mull over,
     rehearse, ruminate
09 offspring

**brook**
04 bear, gill
05 allow, creek, inlet, stand
06 accept, endure, permit,
     runnel, stream
07 channel, rivulet, support
08 tolerate
09 put up with, withstand
11 countenance, watercourse

**brothel**
06 bagnio
08 bordello, cathouse, red light
10 bawdyhouse
13 sporting house
14 house of ill fame

**brother**
04 chum, mate, monk
05 friar
06 fellow, friend
07 comrade, partner, sibling
08 relation, relative
09 associate, colleague
12 blood brother

## brotherhood
04 club
05 guild, order, union
06 clique, league
07 society
08 alliance
09 community
10 fellowship, fraternity, friendship
11 association, comradeship

## brotherly
04 kind
05 loyal
06 caring, loving
08 amicable, friendly
09 fraternal
10 benevolent
11 sympathetic
12 affectionate
13 philanthropic

## brow
03 tip, top
04 peak
05 brink, cliff, ridge, verge
06 summit
07 temples
08 forehead

## browbeat
05 bully, force, hound
06 coerce
07 dragoon, oppress
08 bulldoze, threaten
09 tyrannize
10 intimidate

## brown
03 bay, fry, tan
04 cook, dark, fawn, rust, seal
05 beige, dusky, hazel, rusty, sepia, tawny, toast, umber
06 auburn, bronze, coffee, ginger, russet, tanned
07 bronzed, browned
08 brunette, chestnut, mahogany, sunburnt
09 chocolate, sunburned

## browned off
05 angry, fed up, weary
10 cheesed off, frustrated
11 discouraged, disgruntled
12 discontented, disheartened

## browse
03 eat
04 feed, scan, skim
05 graze
06 nibble, peruse, survey
07 dip into, pasture
11 leaf through

## bruise
04 hurt, mark
05 crush, spoil, upset, wound

06 damage, injure, injury, insult, offend, shiner
07 blacken, blemish
08 black eye, discolor
09 contusion
10 ecchymosis

## brunt
05 force, shock
06 burden, impact, strain, thrust, weight
09 main force
10 full weight

## brush
03 rub
04 bush, kiss
05 besom, broom, clash, clean, flick, graze, scrub, set-to, shine, sweep, touch, whisk
06 bushes, polish, scrape, shrubs, stroke
07 burnish, contact, sweeper
08 argument, conflict, skirmish
09 brushwood, encounter
11 ground cover, undergrowth
12 disagreement

## ❑ brush aside
05 flout
06 ignore
07 dismiss
08 override, pooh-pooh
09 disregard

## ❑ brush off
05 spurn
06 disown, ignore, rebuff, reject, slight
07 dismiss, repulse
09 disregard, repudiate
12 cold-shoulder

## ❑ brush up
04 cram, tidy
05 clean, study
06 read up, review, tidy up
07 improve, refresh, relearn
08 bone up on, polish up
09 freshen up
15 clean yourself up

## brushoff
04 snub
06 rebuff, slight
09 dismissal, rejection
11 repudiation
12 cold shoulder

## brusque
04 curt
05 blunt, sharp, short, terse
06 abrupt
07 uncivil
12 discourteous, undiplomatic

## brutal
05 cruel, harsh

06 animal, savage, severe
07 beastly, bestial, brutish, callous, inhuman, vicious
08 inhumane, pitiless, ruthless
09 ferocious, heartless, merciless, unfeeling
12 bloodthirsty

## brutality
07 cruelty
08 ferocity, savagery, violence
09 barbarism, barbarity
10 coarseness, inhumanity
11 brutishness, callousness, viciousness
12 ruthlessness

## brute
04 lout, ogre
05 beast, bully, devil, fiend
06 animal, sadist, savage
08 creature, depraved, mindless, physical
09 senseless
10 unthinking
11 instinctive

## brutish
05 crass, crude, cruel, feral, gross
06 brutal, coarse, ferine, savage, stupid, vulgar
07 bestial, loutish, uncouth
08 barbaric
09 barbarian, barbarous
11 uncivilized

## bubble
04 fizz, foam, head, suds
05 fraud, froth, spume
06 bounce, burble, gurgle, lather, seethe, trifle, vanity
07 blister, droplet, fantasy, globule, sparkle, vesicle
08 be elated, be filled, illusion
10 effervesce
13 effervescence

## bubbly
05 fizzy, happy, merry, sudsy
06 bouncy, elated, frothy, lively
07 excited, foaming
09 ebullient, sparkling
10 carbonated
12 effervescent

## buccaneer
06 pirate
07 corsair, sea wolf
09 plunderer, privateer, sea robber
10 filibuster, freebooter

## buck
## ❑ buck up
05 cheer, hurry, rally
06 hasten, perk up

**bucket**
07 brace up, enliven, hearten, hurry up
08 inspirit, step on it
09 encourage, stimulate
10 get a move on

**bucket**
03 can
04 bail, pail
07 pitcher, scuttle

**buckle**
04 bend, clip, hook, kink, warp
05 bulge, catch, clasp, twist
07 connect, crumple, distort
08 collapse, fastener

**bucolic**
04 hick
05 rural, yokel
06 rustic
07 country
08 agrarian, pastoral
09 hillbilly
11 countrified
12 agricultural

**bud**
04 germ, grow
05 knosp, shoot, sprig
06 embryo, sprout
09 pullulate

**budding**
07 growing, nascent
09 embryonic, fledgling, incipient, promising

**budge**
03 fur
04 give, move, push, roll, stir
05 shift, slide, yield
06 change, give in, remove
07 give way
08 dislodge, lambskin, persuade

**budget**
04 plan
05 allot, allow, funds, means
08 allocate, estimate, finances
09 allotment, allowance, apportion, resources
10 allocation

**buff**
03 fan, rub, tan
04 fawn
05 brush, fiend, freak, khaki, maven, sandy, shine, straw
06 addict, expert, polish
07 devotee
10 aficionado, enthusiast
11 connoisseur

**buffer**
03 pad
06 air bag, bumper, fender, pillow

07 bulwark, cushion
12 intermediary
13 shock absorber

**buffet**
03 box, hit, jar
04 bang, beat, blow, bump, café, cuff, jolt, push, slap
05 clout, knock, pound, thump
06 batter, pummel, strike
07 counter
08 cold meal, snackbar
09 cafeteria
11 self-service, smorgasbord

**buffoon**
04 fool
05 clown, comic, droll, joker
06 jester
08 comedian

**buffoonery**
07 jesting
08 clowning, nonsense
09 pantomime, silliness
10 tomfoolery

**bug**
03 fad, fly, irk, tap, vex
04 flaw, flea, germ, gnat
05 annoy, craze, error, fault, virus
06 bother, defect, harass, insect, needle
07 disease, disturb, failing, gremlin, microbe, wiretap
08 irritate, listen in, phonetap
09 bacterium, eavesdrop, infection, obsession
12 creepy-crawly, imperfection
13 microorganism
15 listening device

**bugbear**
04 bane
05 dread, fiend
06 horror
07 pet hate
08 anathema
09 bête noire, nightmare

**build**
04 body, form, make, size
05 erect, frame, put up, raise, shape
06 extend, figure
07 develop, enlarge, fashion
08 assemble, escalate, increase, physique
09 construct, fabricate, intensify, structure
11 put together

**◻build up**
04 hype, plug
05 boost
06 expand, extend

07 develop, enhance, enlarge, fortify, improve, promote
08 assemble, escalate, heighten, increase
09 intensify, reinforce
13 piece together

**building**
07 edifice
11 development, fabrication
12 architecture, construction

━━━━━━━━━━━━━━━━━━━━

► *Building materials*:
04 clay, sand, tile, wood
05 adobe, brick, glass, grout, slate, steel, stone
06 ashlar, ashler, cement, girder, gravel, gypsum, lintel, lumber, marble, mortar, Tarmac, thatch, timber
07 asphalt, bitumen, granite, lagging, plaster, plywood, shingle
08 aluminum, cast iron, concrete, roof tile
09 chipboard, flagstone, floor tile, hardboard, sandstone
10 fiberboard, insulation
12 plasterboard
13 wattle and daub
14 stainless steel

━━━━━━━━━━━━━━━━━━━━

► *Types of building*:
03 bar, gym, inn
04 barn, café, fort, mill, pier, shed, shop, silo
05 abbey, cabin, condo, hotel, house, store, villa
06 castle, chapel, church, garage, gazebo, mosque, museum, pagoda, palace, prison, school, stable, tavern, temple
07 chateau, cottage, factory, library, mansion, stadium, theater
08 barracks, bungalow, fortress, hospital, monument, outhouse, pavilion, windmill
09 boathouse, cathedral, clubhouse, farmhouse, gymnasium, mausoleum, monastery, synagogue, treehouse, warehouse
10 auditorium, beach house, lighthouse, opera house, ranch house, restaurant, skyscraper
11 condominium, observatory
14 apartment house

━━━━━━━━━━━━━━━━━━━━

► *Names of religious buildings*:
04 Kaba

05 Ka'aba
06 Kasbah
07 Abu Mena, al-Azhar
08 Pantheon
09 Acropolis, Borobudur, Eye
Temple, Parthenon,
Propylaea, Sacred Way, Sun
Temple
10 Blue Mosque, Cluny Abbey,
Erechtheum, Meaux Abbey,
Sacre Coeur
11 Erechtheion, Great Sphinx,
Hagia Sophia, Temple
Mount, Wailing Wall, York
Minster
12 Golden Temple, Great
Pyramid, Mormon Temple,
Temple of Hera, Tintern
Abbey
13 Dome of the Rock, Fontenay
Abbey, Muhammad's Tomb,
Rievaulx Abbey, Rila
Monastery
14 Belém Monastery, Fountains
Abbey, Golden Pavilion,
Kazan Cathedral, Reims
Cathedral, Sagrada Familia,
Temple of Amon-Ra, Temple
of Apollo, Temple of Athena
15 Pyramid of Cheops, Pyramid
of the Sun, Temple of
Artemis, Temple of Hathoor,
Temple of Solomon
➢ See also RELIGION

**buildup**
04 gain, heap, hype, load, mass
05 drift, stack, store
06 growth
08 increase
09 accretion, promotion,
publicity, stockpile
10 escalation
11 development, enlargement
12 accumulation

**built-in**
06 fitted
08 implicit, included, inherent,
integral
09 essential, intrinsic
11 fundamental, inseparable
12 incorporated

**bulb**

► *Plants grown from bulbs
and corms*:
04 iris, ixia, lily
05 tulip
06 allium, crocus, garlic, scilla
07 jonquil
08 amarylis, bluebell, cyclamen,
daffodil, hyacinth, snowdrop
09 buttercup, gladiolus,

narcissus
10 fritillary, ranunculus
12 autumn crocus
13 crown imperial, grape
hyacinth, winter aconite
➢ See also PLANT

**bulbous**
06 convex
07 bloated, bulging, rounded,
swollen
09 distended

**bulge**
03 sag
04 bump, hump, lump, rise
05 surge, swell
06 dilate, expand
07 distend, enlarge, project, puff
out, upsurge
08 increase, protrude, swelling
10 distension, projection
12 protuberance

**bulk**
04 body, mass, most, size
06 extent, volume, weight
07 bigness
08 majority
09 amplitude, immensity,
largeness, magnitude, nearly
all, substance
10 dimensions, lion's share
13 preponderance

**bulky**
03 big
04 huge
05 heavy, hefty, large
07 awkward, hulking, immense,
mammoth, massive, weighty
08 colossal, enormous,
unwieldy
10 cumbersome, voluminous
11 substantial

**bulldoze**
04 push, raze
05 bully, clear, force, level
06 coerce
07 flatten
08 browbeat
09 knock down, steamroll
10 intimidate
11 push through, steamroller

**bullet**
04 ball, shot, slug
06 pellet
07 missile
09 cartouche, cartridge
10 projectile, propellant

**bulletin**
06 report
07 leaflet, message
08 dispatch

09 newspaper, statement
10 communiqué, newsletter
12 announcement, notification

**bullish**
06 upbeat
07 buoyant, hopeful
08 cheerful, positive, sanguine
09 confident
10 optimistic

**bully**
04 thug
05 heavy, tough
06 coerce, pick on
07 oppress, ruffian, torment
08 browbeat, bulldoze, bully
boy, bullyrag, domineer
09 persecute, terrorize,
tyrannize, victimize
10 browbeater, intimidate,
persecutor, push around

**bulwark**
05 guard
06 buffer
07 bastion, defense, outwork,
rampart, redoubt, support
08 buttress, mainstay, security
10 embankment
13 fortification

**bumbling**
05 inept
06 clumsy
07 awkward, muddled
09 maladroit, stumbling
10 blundering
11 incompetent, inefficient

**bump**
03 hit, jar
04 bang, blow, hump, jerk, jolt,
knur, lump, slam, thud
05 bulge, crash, knock, prang,
shake, shock, smash, thump
06 impact, injury, strike
07 collide, papilla
08 swelling
09 collision

❏**bump into**
04 meet
07 run into
09 encounter, light upon
10 chance upon, come across,
happen upon

❏**bump off**
03 top
04 do in, kill
06 murder, remove, rub out
09 eliminate, liquidate
11 assassinate

**bumper**
05 great, large
07 massive

08 abundant, enormous

**bumpkin**
03 oaf
04 boor, clod, hick, rube
05 yokel
06 rustic
07 hayseed, peasant
09 hillbilly
12 country yokel

**bumptious**
05 cocky, pushy
07 forward, pompous
08 arrogant, boastful, impudent
09 conceited, officious
10 swaggering
13 self-important
14 full of yourself

**bumpy**
05 lumpy, rough
06 knobby, uneven
07 knobbly

**bunch**
03 lot, mob, wad
04 band, crew, gang, heap,
     mass, pack, pile, posy, tuft
05 batch, clump, crowd, group,
     party, sheaf, spray, stack
06 bundle, gather, huddle
07 bouquet, cluster, collect,
     corsage, nosegay
08 assemble, fascicle, quantity
09 fascicule, gathering
10 assortment, collection

**bundle**
03 bag, box, set, tie
04 bale, bind, heap, mass, pack,
     pile, roll, rush, wrap
05 batch, bunch, fagot, group,
     hurry, sheaf, shove, stack,
     truss
06 carton, fasten, gather,
     packet, parcel
07 cluster, package
08 fascicle, quantity
09 fascicule
11 consignment, push roughly

**bungle**
04 flub, muff, ruin
05 botch, fluff, spoil
06 foul up, fumble, mess up
07 blunder, louse up, screw up
09 mismanage
11 make a mess of

**bungler**
07 botcher
09 blunderer
11 incompetent
13 butterfingers

**bungling**
05 inept

06 clumsy
07 awkward
08 botching
09 ham-handed, maladroit
10 blundering
11 incompetent

**bunkum**
03 rot
04 bosh, bunk
05 bilge, hooey, trash, tripe
06 piffle
07 baloney, garbage, hogwash,
     rubbish, twaddle
08 nonsense, tommyrot
09 poppycock
10 balderdash

**buoy**
05 float
06 beacon, marker, signal

❏**buoy up**
04 lift
05 boost, cheer, raise
07 cheer up, hearten, support
09 encourage

**buoyant**
05 happy, light, peppy
06 afloat, bouncy, bright, lively
07 bullish
08 cheerful, floating
09 floatable, vivacious
10 optimistic, weightless
12 light-hearted

**burble**
03 lap
06 babble, gurgle, murmur

**burden**
04 care, duty, load, onus
05 cargo, crush, trial, worry
06 bother, sorrow, weight
07 anxiety, oppress, trouble
08 encumber, handicap,
     overload, pressure
09 millstone, weigh down
10 affliction, lie heavy on
11 encumbrance

**burdensome**
05 heavy
06 taxing, trying
07 irksome, onerous, weighty
09 difficult, wearisome
11 troublesome

**bureau**
04 desk
06 agency, branch, office
07 counter, dresser, highboy,
     service
11 writing desk
14 chest of drawers

**bureaucracy**
07 red tape
08 ministry
10 government
11 officialdom
12 civil service
14 administration, the
     authorities

**bureaucrat**
07 officer
08 mandarin, minister, official
11 apparatchik, functionary
12 civil servant, officeholder
13 administrator
15 committee member

**bureaucratic**
08 official
10 inflexible, procedural
14 administrative

**burglar**
05 thief
06 robber
10 cat burglar
12 housebreaker

**burglary**
05 heist, theft
07 break-in, larceny, robbery
13 housebreaking

**burial**
07 burying, funeral
08 exequies
09 interment, obsequies
10 entombment, inhumation

**burial place**
04 tomb
05 crypt, grave, vault
07 tumulus
08 catacomb, cemetery
09 graveyard, mausoleum,
     sepulcher
10 churchyard, necropolis

**burlesque**
03 ape
04 mock
05 comic, farce, spoof
06 comedy, parody, satire
07 mockery, mocking, takeoff
08 ridicule, travesty
10 caricature, vaudeville

**burly**
03 big
05 beefy, heavy, hefty
06 brawny, strong, sturdy
07 hulking
08 muscular, powerful, thickset
09 strapping, well-built

**burn**
04 bite, char, fume, glow, hurt,
     itch, long, sear

05 blaze, brand, flame, flare,
parch, scald, singe, smart,
smoke, sting, toast, yearn
06 desire, ignite, kindle, scorch
07 consume, corrode, cremate,
destroy, flare up, flicker,
smolder
08 be ablaze, be on fire, burn
down
09 catch fire, cauterize
10 be in flames, incinerate
11 catch ablaze, conflagrate, go
up in smoke, put a match to
15 burst into flames

**burning**
03 hot, lit
05 acrid, acute, afire, fiery
06 ablaze, aflame, alight,
ardent, biting, fervid, urgent
07 blazing, caustic, crucial,
earnest, fervent, flaming,
frantic, glowing, intense,
pungent, searing
08 frenzied, gleaming, piercing,
pressing, scalding, smarting,
stinging, tingling, vehement
09 consuming, essential,
important, prickling,
scorching
10 passionate, smoldering
11 illuminated

**burnish**
04 buff
05 glaze, shine
06 polish
08 brighten, polish up

**burp**
05 belch
08 eructate
11 bring up wind

**burrow**
03 den, dig, set
04 hole, lair, mine
05 delve, earth
06 search, tunnel, warren
08 excavate

**burst**
03 fit, run
04 dart, gush, race, rush, tear
05 barge, break, crack, erupt,
hurry, spate, split, surge
07 blow out, explode, rupture
08 fragment, outbreak,
outburst, puncture
09 break in on, break open
10 outpouring

❑**burst out**
03 cry
05 begin, start, utter
06 cry out
07 call out, exclaim

08 blurt out, commence

**bury**
04 hide, sink
05 cover, embed, inter, plant
06 engulf, entomb, inhume,
occupy, shroud
07 conceal, enclose, engross,
immerse, implant
08 enshroud, submerge
09 lay to rest, sepulcher
15 put six feet under

**bush**
05 brush, hedge, plant, scrub,
shrub, wilds
09 backwoods, scrubland

❑**not beat about the bush**
11 speak openly
12 speak plainly

**bushy**
05 fuzzy, rough, stiff, thick
06 fluffy, shaggy
07 bristly
09 luxuriant, spreading

**busily**
04 hard
07 briskly
08 actively, speedily
10 diligently
11 assiduously, strenuously
13 energetically, industriously

**business**
03 job
04 duty, firm, line, shop, task,
work
05 issue, store, topic, trade
06 affair, career, matter, métier
07 calling, company, concern,
subject, trading
08 commerce, dealings,
industry, vocation
09 operation, syndicate
10 bargaining, consortium,
employment, enterprise,
occupation, profession
11 corporation
12 conglomerate, organization,
transactions
13 establishment,
manufacturing, multinational
14 responsibility

**businesslike**
07 correct, orderly, precise
09 efficient, organized,
practical, pragmatic
10 impersonal, methodical,
systematic
11 painstaking, well-ordered
12 matter-of-fact, professional

**businessman, business-
woman**
06 trader, tycoon
07 magnate
08 employer, merchant
09 executive, financier
10 capitalist
12 entrepreneur
13 industrialist

▶ *Names of businesspeople:*
04 **Benz** (Karl Friedrich), **Case**
(Steve), **Cook** (Thomas),
**Ford** (Henry), **Jobs** (Steven),
**Kroc** (Ray), **Wang** (An)
05 **Astor** (John Jacob), **Gates**
(Bill), **Getty** (Jean Paul),
**Heinz** (Henry John), **Honda**
(Soichiro), **Klein** (Calvin),
**Krupp** (Friedrich), **Perot**
(H. Ross), **Rolls** (Charles
Stewart), **Royce** (Sir Henry),
**Trump** (Donald)
06 **Boeing** (William Edward),
**Cunard** (Sir Samuel), **Du
Pont** (Pierre Samuel),
**Dunlop** (John Boyd), **Eisner**
(Michael), **Forbes**
(Malcolm), **Hammer**
(Armand), **Hilton** (Conrad
Nicholson), **Hoover**
(William Henry), **Hughes**
(Howard), **Kaiser** (Henry J.),
**Lauder** (Estee), **Mellon**
(Andrew William), **Morgan**
(J. Pierpont), **Morgan** (John
Pierpont), **Turner** (Ted)
07 **Branson** (Richard), **Bugatti**
(Ettore), **Citroën** (André
Gustave), **Eastman**
(George), **Iacocca** (Lee),
**Kellogg** (Will), **Kennedy**
(Joseph Patrick), **Murdoch**
(Rupert), **Onassis**
(Aristotle), **Strauss** (Levi),
**Tiffany** (Charles Lewis)
08 **Birdseye** (Clarence),
**Carnegie** (Andrew),
**Helmsley** (Leona),
**Michelin** (André), **Olivetti**
(Adriano), **Pulitzer** (Joseph)
09 **Annenberg** (Walter),
**Firestone** (Harvey Samuel),
**Woolworth** (Frank
Winfield)
10 **Rothschild** (Meyer
Amschel), **Vanderbilt**
(Cornelius)
11 **Rockefeller** (John Davison)

**bust**
04 head, ruin
05 bosom, chest, torso
06 breast, demote, statue

**bustle**
07 breasts
08 bankrupt
09 sculpture

**bustle**
03 ado
04 belt, dash, fuss, rush, stir, tear
05 haste, hurry
06 bestir, flurry, hasten, pother, scurry, tumult
08 activity, rush hour, to and fro
09 agitation, commotion
10 excitement, hurly-burly
15 hustle and bustle

**bustling**
04 busy, full
05 astir
06 active, hectic, lively
07 buzzing, crowded, humming, rushing, teeming
08 restless, stirring, swarming

**busy**
04 at it
05 fussy
06 active, employ, hectic, lively, occupy, tied up, tiring
07 crowded, engaged, hopping, humming, involve, on the go, working
08 bustling, employed, hard at it, interest, involved, occupied
09 energetic, engrossed
10 busy as a bee, meddlesome
11 industrious, unavailable
14 having a lot to do

**busybody**
03 pry
06 gossip
07 meddler, snooper
08 intruder, quidnunc
10 interferer

**butcher**
04 kill, slay
05 cut up
06 killer, slayer
07 meatman
08 massacre, murderer, mutilate
09 liquidate, slaughter
10 meat-seller, meatcutter, meatpacker
11 assassinate, exterminate, slaughterer
12 mass murderer

**butchery**
06 murder
07 carnage, killing
08 massacre
09 bloodshed, slaughter
10 mass murder
12 bloodletting
15 mass destruction

**butt**
03 end, hit, jab, ram, tip
04 base, bump, foot, haft, mark, prod, push, stub
05 knock, shaft, shove, stock
06 bottom, buffet, fag end, handle, target
07 subject, tail end
08 buttocks
09 posterior, scapegoat
13 laughingstock

❏ **butt in**
05 cut in
07 intrude
09 interfere, interject, interpose, interrupt
12 put your oar in
15 stick your nose in

**butter**

❏ **butter up**
06 cajole, kowtow, praise
07 blarney, flatter, wheedle
08 pander to, soft-soap

**butterfly**
12 lepidopteran
14 papilionaceous

➤ *Types of butterfly*:
05 comma, satyr, zebra
07 admiral, buckeye, monarch, skipper, troilus, vanessa, viceroy
08 crescent, grayling
10 fritillary, hairstreak, red admiral
11 meadow-brown, painted lady, swallowtail
12 white admiral
➤ See also ANIMAL

**buttocks**
04 butt, rear, rump, seat
05 nates
06 behind, bottom, breech
07 gluteal, gluteus
08 derrière, haunches
09 posterior
12 hindquarters

**button**
04 disk, knob
06 switch
08 fastener
09 fastening

**buttonhole**
03 nab
04 grab
05 catch
06 accost, detain, waylay
09 importune, take aside

**buttress**
04 pier, prop, stay
05 brace, shore, strut

06 back up, hold up, prop up
07 shore up, support, sustain
08 mainstay, underpin
09 bolster up, reinforce, stanchion
10 strengthen

**buxom**
05 ample, busty, plump
06 bosomy, chesty, comely
10 voluptuous
11 well-endowed

**buy**
03 fix, get
05 bribe
06 buy off, obtain, pay for, pick up, snap up, suborn
07 acquire, bargain, procure
08 invest in, purchase
11 acquisition, splash out on

**buyer**
06 client, emptor, vendee
07 shopper
08 consumer, customer
09 purchaser

**buzz**
03 hum
04 call, high, kick, race, ring
05 kicks, pulse, rumor, throb, whirr
06 bustle, gossip, latest, murmur, thrill
07 buzzing, hearsay, scandal
08 susurrus, tinnitus
09 bombinate, phone call, susurrate
10 excitement
11 bombination, stimulation, susurration

**by**
02 at
03 via
04 away, near, over, past
05 along, aside, close, handy
06 at hand, before, beside, beyond, next to
07 close by, close to, through
09 alongside, by means of
11 according to, no later than
12 in relation to

**bygone**
04 lost, past
05 olden
06 former
07 ancient, onetime
08 departed, forepast, previous
09 erstwhile, forgotten

**bypass**
05 avoid, dodge, skirt
06 detour, ignore
07 beltway

08 sidestep
09 diversion
10 circumvent
14 find a way around

**byproduct**
06 result
07 fallout, spinoff
10 derivative, side effect

11 aftereffect, consequence
12 repercussion

**bystander**
07 watcher, witness
08 looker-on, observer,
    onlooker
09 spectator
10 eyewitness, rubberneck

12 rubbernecker

**byword**
05 adage, maxim, motto
06 dictum, saying, slogan
07 precept, proverb
08 aphorism, apothegm
09 catchword
10 apophthegm

**cab**
04 hack, taxi
07 hackney, taxicab
08 quarters
11 compartment

**cabal**
03 set
05 junta, junto, party
06 clique, league
07 coterie, faction
08 conclave, plotters
09 coalition

**cabaret**
04 show
06 comedy
07 dancing, singing
09 nightclub
13 entertainment
14 cocktail lounge

**cabin**
03 hut
04 room, shed
05 berth, lodge, shack
06 chalet, refuge, shanty
07 cottage, shelter
08 log cabin, quarters
09 stateroom
11 compartment

**cabinet**
04 case
05 chest, store
06 closet, locker
07 dresser
08 advisors, cupboard, ministry
09 executive, ministers
10 government, leadership
14 administration

**cable**
03 fax, guy
04 cord, lead, rope, wire
05 chain, radio
06 hawser
07 message
08 telegram
09 facsimile, telegraph

**cache**
04 fund
05 hoard, stash, stock, store
06 garner, supply
07 reserve
09 stockpile
10 collection, repository

13 treasure-store

**cachet**
05 favor
06 esteem
08 eminence, prestige
10 reputation, street cred

**cackle**
04 crow
06 giggle, guffaw, titter
07 chortle, chuckle, snigger

**cacophonous**
05 harsh
07 grating, jarring, raucous
08 strident
09 dissonant
10 discordant

**cacophony**
07 discord, jarring
09 harshness, stridency
10 disharmony, dissonance
12 caterwauling

**cad**
03 rat
04 heel
05 devil, knave, louse, rogue, swine
06 rascal, wretch
07 bounder, stinker, villain
08 deceiver
09 reprobate, scoundrel
10 blackguard

**cadaver**
04 body
05 stiff
06 corpse
07 carcass, remains

**cadaverous**
03 wan
04 pale, thin
05 ashen, gaunt
07 ghostly, haggard
08 skeletal
09 deathlike, emaciated

**cadence**
04 beat, lilt, rate
05 meter, pulse, swing, tempo
06 accent, rhythm, stress
07 measure, pattern
10 intonation, modulation

**cadge**
03 beg, bum

06 sponge
08 scrounge

**café**
05 diner
06 bistro, buffet
07 tearoom, wine bar
08 snack bar
09 brasserie, cafeteria, coffee bar, cybercafé
10 coffee shop, restaurant
11 coffeehouse

**cafeteria**
04 café
06 buffet
07 automat, canteen
10 restaurant

**cage**
03 pen
04 coop, jail
05 hutch, pound
06 aviary, corral, lock up
08 imprison
09 enclosure

**caged**
06 shut up
08 confined, cooped up, fenced in, locked up
09 impounded
10 imprisoned, restrained
12 incarcerated

**cagey**
04 wary, wily
05 chary
06 shrewd
07 careful, guarded
08 cautious, discreet
09 secretive
11 circumspect

**cajole**
04 coax, dupe, lure
05 tempt
06 entice, seduce
07 beguile, flatter, wheedle
08 inveigle, persuade, soft soap
09 sweet-talk

**cajolery**
06 duping
07 blarney, coaxing
08 flattery, soft soap
09 sweet talk, wheedling
10 enticement, inducement, inveigling, persuasion

11 beguilement, inducements
13 blandishments

**cake**
04 coat, lump, mass, slab
05 block, chunk, cover
06 harden, pastry
07 congeal, plaster, thicken
08 solidify
09 coagulate
11 consolidate

► *Types of cake and pudding*:
04 baba
05 bombe, crèpe, donut, scone, torte
06 cookie, Danish, gateau, muffin, trifle, waffle
07 baklava, brioche, brownie, crumpet, cupcake, pancake, stollen, strudel, teacake
08 doughnut, macaroon, seedcake, streusel, turnover
09 angel cake, apple cake, bundt cake, fruitcake, fudge cake, pecan cake, poundcake, shortcake, spice cake
10 Battenburg, carrot cake, cheesecake, coffeecake, marble cake, spongecake, walnut cake
11 baked Alaska, gingerbread, griddlecake
12 birthday cake, Danish pastry, wedding cake,
13 angel food cake, banana-nut cake, chocolate cake
14 applesauce cake, charlotte russe, devil's-food cake, upside-down cake
15 Black Forest cake, chocolate éclair
➤ See also FOOD

**calamitous**
04 dire
05 fatal
06 deadly, tragic, woeful
07 ghastly, ruinous
08 dreadful, grievous, wretched
10 disastrous
11 cataclysmic, devastating
12 catastrophic

**calamity**
04 ruin
05 trial
06 mishap
07 scourge, tragedy, trouble
08 disaster, distress, downfall
09 adversity, mischance
10 affliction, misfortune
11 catastrophe, tribulation
12 misadventure

**calculate**
04 make, plan, rate
05 count, gauge, judge, weigh
06 derive, design, figure, reckon
07 compute, measure, work out
08 consider, estimate, reckon up
09 determine, enumerate

**calculated**
07 planned, willful
08 intended, purposed
10 considered, deliberate, purposeful
11 intentional
12 premeditated

**calculating**
03 sly
05 sharp
06 crafty, shrewd
07 cunning, devious
08 scheming
09 designing
10 contriving
12 manipulative
13 Machiavellian

**calculation**
03 sum
06 answer, result
08 estimate, figuring, forecast, judgment
09 reckoning
10 estimation, working-out
11 computation

**caliber**
04 bore, size
05 gauge, gifts, merit, worth
06 talent
07 ability, measure, quality, stature
08 capacity, diameter, strength
09 character
10 competence, excellence
11 distinction

**call**
03 bid, cry, dub, run
04 bawl, bell, buzz, name, need, roar, term, yell
05 brand, label, phone, shout, style, title, visit
06 appeal, ask for, bellow, call in, come by, cry out, demand, drop in, invite, reason, signal, stop by, summon
07 baptize, command, convene, exclaim, grounds, phone up, send for, summons
08 assemble, christen, occasion
09 pay a visit, telephone
11 exclamation

❏**call for**
04 need
05 fetch, go for

06 demand, entail, pick up, summon
07 collect, involve, justify, push for, require, suggest, warrant
08 occasion, press for

❏**call off**
04 drop
05 scrub
06 cancel, revoke, shelve
07 abandon, rescind
08 break off, withdraw
11 discontinue

❏**call on**
03 ask, bid
04 urge
05 plead, visit
06 appeal, demand, summon
07 entreat, request
08 appeal to, go and see
10 supplicate

❏**on call**
05 ready
10 standing by

**call girl**
06 harlot, hooker
07 hustler
10 loose woman, prostitute
12 street-walker
14 lady of the night

**calling**
03 job
04 line, work
05 field, trade
06 career, métier
07 mission, pursuit
08 business, province, vocation
10 employment, line of work, occupation, profession
14 line of business

**callous**
04 cold
05 harsh, stony, tough
08 hardened, obdurate, uncaring
09 heartless, unfeeling
11 coldblooded, coldhearted, hardhearted, indifferent, insensitive
12 thick-skinned
13 unsympathetic

**callow**
03 raw
05 green, naïve
06 jejune
07 puerile, untried
08 immature, innocent, juvenile
09 guileless, unfledged
11 uninitiated
13 inexperienced

**calm**
04 cool, lull, mild
05 allay, peace, quiet, relax, still
06 pacify, placid, poised, repose, sedate, serene, settle, soothe, steady
07 appease, assuage, ataraxy, compose, mollify, placate, quieten, relaxed, restful
08 ataraxia, composed, laid back, peaceful, quietude, serenity, tranquil, waveless, windless
09 collected, impassive, placidity, sang-froid, stillness, unclouded, unexcited, unruffled
10 coolheaded, equanimity, untroubled
11 contentment, impassivity, restfulness, tranquility, undisturbed, unemotional, unexcitable, unflappable, unflustered
12 peacefulness, tranquillize
13 dispassionate, self-possessed
14 self-controlled, unapprehensive

**calumny**
05 abuse, libel, lying, smear
06 insult
07 obloquy, slander
09 aspersion
10 backbiting, defamation, derogation, revilement
11 denigration
12 vilification, vituperation
13 disparagement

**camaraderie**
07 rapport
08 affinity, intimacy
09 closeness
10 fellowship
11 brotherhood, comradeship
12 togetherness
13 companionship, esprit de corps

**camera**

▶ *Types of camera:*
02 TV
03 box, TLR
04 disk, film
05 movie, plate, still, video
06 reflex, Super 8
07 Brownie, compact, digital, pinhole
08 Kodak SLR, Polaroid, security
09 automatic, binocular, camcorder, miniature, throwaway

10 cinecamera, disposable
13 camera obscura, daguerreotype, point-and-shoot
14 twin-lens reflex

**camouflage**
04 hide, mask, veil
05 cloak, cover, front, guise
06 façade, screen
07 conceal, cover up, obscure
08 disguise

**camp**
04 side
05 crowd, group, party
06 clique, encamp
07 bivouac, faction, in-group, section
08 affected, mannered
10 artificial, effeminate, encampment, pitch tents, theatrical
12 ostentatious

**campaign**
03 war
04 push, work
05 drive, fight
06 attack, battle, strive
07 crusade, promote
08 advocate, movement, strategy, struggle
09 offensive, operation, promotion
10 expedition

**camp follower**
09 nonmember
10 prostitute
14 civilian vendor

**can**
03 jar, jug, may, tin
04 fire, jail, pail, stir
06 prison
07 dismiss
08 canister, jerry can
09 container

**canal**
05 ditch
07 channel, passage
08 waterway
11 watercourse

**cancel**
02 ax
04 drop, stop
05 annul, erase, scrap, scrub
06 delete, repeal, revoke, shelve
07 abandon, abolish, call off, nullify, rescind, vitiate
08 abrogate, break off, dissolve, override, postpone
09 eliminate
10 invalidate, obliterate

11 countermand, discontinue

❑**cancel out**
06 offset, redeem
07 balance, nullify
09 make up for
10 compensate, counteract, neutralize
14 counterbalance

**cancellation**
06 repeal
08 deletion, dropping, quashing, shelving, stopping
09 abolition, annulment, scrubbing
10 abandoning, calling-off, nullifying, revocation
11 abandonment, elimination
12 invalidation
14 neutralization

**cancer**
03 rot
04 evil
05 tumor
06 blight, canker, growth, plague
07 disease, scourge
08 sickness
09 carcinoma
10 corruption, malignancy, pestilence

**candelabrum**
07 menorah
11 candlestick

**candid**
04 open
05 blunt, clear, frank, plain
06 honest, simple
07 sincere
08 truthful
09 guileless, ingenuous
10 forthright
11 plain-spoken, unequivocal

**candidate**
06 runner, seeker
07 entrant, nominee
08 aspirant
09 applicant, contender
10 competitor, contestant
12 office-seeker

**candle**
05 taper
06 bougie
09 rushlight
10 rush candle

**candor**
07 honesty, naïvety
08 openness
09 bluntness, frankness, plainness, sincerity
10 directness, simplicity

## candy

11 artlessness, brusqueness
12 plain-dealing, truthfulness
13 guilelessness, ingenuousness, outspokenness

## candy

05 fudge, sweet, taffy
06 bonbon, nougat, sweets, toffee
08 lollipop, lollypop, marzipan
09 jelly bean
10 chocolates, jawbreaker
13 confectionery

## cane

03 rod
05 crook, staff, stick
06 crutch, ferule
10 alpenstock
12 walking stick

## canker

03 rot
04 bane, boil, evil, sore
05 ulcer
06 blight, cancer, lesion, plague
07 disease, scourge
08 sickness
09 corrosion, infection
10 corruption, pestilence

## cannabis

03 kef, pot, tea
04 bang, blow, dope, hash, hemp, leaf, weed
05 bhang, ganja, grass
06 ganjah
07 hashish
09 marijuana

## cannibal

08 man-eater
15 anthropophagite

## cannibalism

09 man-eating
13 anthropophagy

## cannon

03 gun
06 big gun, mortar
07 battery
08 field gun, howitzer, ordnance
09 artillery
10 fieldpiece

## cannonade

05 salvo
06 volley
07 barrage
08 pounding, shelling
09 broadside
11 bombardment

## canny

03 sly
04 wise

05 acute, sharp
06 artful, clever, shrewd, subtle
07 careful, knowing, prudent
08 cautious
09 judicious, sagacious
11 circumspect, worldly-wise
13 perspicacious

## canon

04 rule
05 vicar
06 priest
07 dictate, precept, statute
08 minister, reverend, standard
09 clergyman, criterion, principle, yardstick
10 prebendary, regulation

## canonical

07 regular
08 accepted, approved, orthodox
10 authorized, recognized, sanctioned
13 authoritative

## canonical hours

► *Names of canonical hours:*
04 sext
05 lauds, nones, prime, terce
06 matins, tierce
07 vespers
08 compline, evensong

## canopy

03 sky
04 tilt
05 cover, shade
06 awning, tester
07 shelter
08 pavilion, sunshade
09 baldachin
10 baldachino
11 baldacchino

## cant

05 argot, lingo, slang
06 jargon
09 hypocrisy
10 vernacular
11 insincerity

## cantankerous

05 cross, testy
06 crabby, crusty, grumpy
07 crabbed, grouchy, peevish
08 contrary, perverse
09 crotchety, difficult, irritable
10 ill-humored
11 bad-tempered, quarrelsome

## canter

03 jog, run
04 lope, trot
05 amble
06 gallop

07 jog trot

## canvass

04 poll, scan, sift
05 study
06 debate, survey
07 analyze, examine, explore
08 campaign, evaluate
10 scrutinize
11 electioneer, investigate
13 drum up support

## canyon

05 abyss, chasm, gorge, gully
06 ravine, valley

## cap

03 hat, lid, top
04 beat, bung, kepi, plug
05 beret, cover, crown, excel, limit, outdo
06 better, bonnet, calpac, kalpak
07 calpack, control, eclipse, surpass
08 balmoral, coonskin, outshine, outstrip, restrain, restrict, skullcap
09 forage cap, glengarry, peaked cap, transcend
11 baseball cap, mortarboard, tam-o'-shanter
15 glengarry bonnet

## capability

05 means, power, skill
06 talent
07 ability, faculty
08 aptitude, capacity, facility
09 potential
10 competence, efficiency
11 proficiency
12 skillfulness
13 qualification
14 accomplishment

## capable

04 able
05 adept, apt to, smart
06 clever, fitted, gifted, suited
07 needing
08 masterly, skillful, talented
09 competent, efficient, qualified
10 proficient
11 experienced, intelligent
12 accomplished, businesslike

## capacious

03 big
04 huge, vast, wide
05 ample, broad, large, roomy
07 liberal, sizable
08 generous, spacious
09 expansive, extensive
10 commodious, voluminous
11 comfortable, substantial

**capacity**
03 job
04 gift, post, role, room, size
05 power, range, scope, space
06 extent, talent, volume
07 ability, compass, faculty
08 aptitude, function, position
09 largeness, magnitude, potential, resources
10 capability, competence, dimensions
11 proficiency, proportions
12 intelligence

**cape**
04 coat, head, ness, robe, wrap
05 cloak, point, shawl
06 mantle, poncho, tongue
07 pelisse
08 headland, pelerine
09 peninsula
10 promontory

**caper**
03 hop
04 dido, jape, jest, jump, lark, leap, romp, skip
05 antic, bound, dance, frisk, prank, stunt
06 affair, bounce, cavort, frolic, gambol, spring
08 business, escapade
09 high jinks

**capital**
04 cash, main
05 chief, first, funds, major, means, money, prime, stock
06 assets, uncial, wealth
07 central, finance, leading, primary, savings, serious
08 cardinal, foremost, reserves
09 majuscule, principal, resources, uppercase
10 investment
11 investments, wherewithal
12 liquid assets

► *Names of state capitals*:
05 **Boise** (Idaho), **Dover** (Delaware), **Salem** (Oregon)
06 **Albany** (New York), **Austin** (Texas), **Boston** (Massachusetts), **Denver** (Colorado), **Helena** (Montana), **Juneau** (Alaska), **Pierre** (South Dakota), **St. Paul** (Minnesota), **Topeka** (Kansas)
07 **Atlanta** (Georgia), **Augusta** (Georgia), **Concord** (New Hampshire), **Jackson** (Mississippi), **Lansing** (Michigan), **Lincoln**

(Nebraska), **Madison** (Wisconsin), **Olympia** (Washington), **Phoenix** (Arizona), **Raleigh** (North Carolina), **Santa Fe** (New Mexico), **Trenton** (New Jersey)
08 **Bismarck** (North Dakota), **Cheyenne** (Wyoming), **Columbia** (South Carolina), **Columbus** (Ohio), **Hartford** (Connecticut), **Honolulu** (Hawaii), **Richmond** (Virginia)
09 **Annapolis** (Maryland), **Des Moines** (Iowa), **Frankfort** (Kentucky), **Nashville** (Tennessee)
10 **Baton Rouge** (Louisiana), **Carson City** (Nevada), **Charleston** (West Virginia), **Harrisburg** (Pennsylvania), **Little Rock** (Arkansas), **Montgomery** (Alabama), **Montpelier** (Vermont), **Providence** (Rhode Island), **Sacramento** (Calfornia)
11 **Springfield** (Illinois), **Tallahassee** (Florida)
12 **Indianapolis** (Indiana), **Oklahoma City** (Oklahoma), **Salt Lake City** (Utah)
13 **Jefferson City** (Missouri)

**capitalism**
12 laissez-faire
14 free enterprise

**capitalist**
05 mogul
06 banker, fat cat, tycoon
07 magnate
08 financier, investor, moneyman
09 financier, moneybags, plutocrat

**capitalize**
❑**capitalize on**
07 exploit
08 cash in on
10 profit from
13 make the most of
15 take advantage of

**capitulate**
05 yield
06 give in, relent, submit
07 succumb
08 back down
09 surrender
15 throw in the towel

**capitulation**
08 giving-in, yielding

09 relenting, surrender
10 submission, succumbing
11 backing-down

**caprice**
03 fad
04 whim
05 fancy, quirk
06 notion, vagary, whimsy
07 fantasy, impulse
10 fickleness, fitfulness
11 inconstancy

**capricious**
03 odd
05 queer
06 fickle, fitful, quirky
07 erratic, wayward
08 fanciful, freakish, variable
09 impulsive, mercurial, uncertain, whimsical
10 changeable, inconstant
13 unpredictable

**capsize**
05 upset
06 invert
07 tip over
08 keel over, overturn, turn over
10 turn turtle

**capsule**
03 pod
04 pill
05 craft, probe, shell
06 module, sheath, tablet
07 lozenge
09 condensed

**captain**
04 boss, head
05 chief, pilot
06 leader, master
07 officer, skipper
09 commander

**caption**
04 note
05 title
06 legend
07 cutline, heading, wording
08 headline
11 inscription

**captivate**
03 win
04 lure
05 charm
06 allure, dazzle, enamor, seduce
07 beguile, bewitch, delight, enchant
08 enthrall
09 enrapture, fascinate, hypnotize, mesmerize

**captivating**
07 winsome

08 alluring, charming, dazzling
09 beautiful, beguiling,
   seductive
10 attractive, bewitching,
   delightful, enchanting
11 enthralling, fascinating

**captive**
05 caged, slave
06 secure, shut-up
07 convict, hostage
08 confined, detained,
   detainee, enslaved, interned,
   internee, jailbird, locked up,
   prisoner
09 enchained, in bondage
10 imprisoned, locked away
12 incarcerated

**captivity**
06 duress
07 bondage, custody, slavery
09 detention, restraint,
   servitude
10 constraint, internment
11 confinement
12 imprisonment
13 incarceration

**capture**
03 nab, win
04 take, trap
05 catch, seize, snare
06 arrest, collar, entrap, pick up,
   record, secure
07 embrace, ensnare, seizure
08 hunt down, imprison
09 apprehend, represent
11 encapsulate

**car**
04 auto
05 buggy, motor
06 banger, wheels
07 vehicle
10 automobile
12 motor vehicle
➤ See also AUTOMOBILE;
   MOTOR; VEHICLE

**carafe**
03 jug
05 flask
06 bottle, flagon
07 pitcher
08 decanter

**carbuncle**
04 boil, sore
06 pimple
07 anthrax
12 inflammation

**carcass**
04 body, hulk
05 shell
06 corpse

07 cadaver, remains
08 dead body, skeleton
09 framework, structure

**card**
❏ **in the cards**
06 likely
08 possible, probable
11 looking as if, looking like
13 the chances are

**cardinal**
03 key
04 main
05 chief, first, prime
07 leading, primary
08 foremost, greatest
09 paramount, principal
10 preeminent
11 fundamental

───────────────

➤ *Names of cardinals. We
have omitted the word* **cardinal**
*from names given in the
following list but you may need
to include this word as part of
the solution to some crossword
clues.:*

04 **Hume** (Basil)
05 **Baum** (William), **Szoka**
   (Edmund)
06 **Borgia** (Rodrigo), **Fisher**
   (John), **Heenan** (John
   Carmel), **Medici** (Giovanni
   de'), **Newman** (John Henry),
   **Rovere** (Francesco della),
   **Wolsey** (Thomas)
07 **Mazarin** (Jules), **Mendoza**
   (Pedro Gonzalez de),
   **Wiseman** (Nicholas),
   **Ximenes** (Francisco)
09 **Richelieu** (Armand Jean
   Duplessis, Duc de),
   **Wyszynski** (Stefan)
10 **Bellarmine** (Robert),
   **Breakspear** (Nicolas)
➤ See also RELIGION

**care**
04 heed, keep, mind, tend
05 pains, worry
06 burden, charge, hang-up,
   regard, strain, stress
07 anxiety, caution, concern,
   control, custody, trouble
08 accuracy, distress, interest,
   pressure, tutelage, vexation
09 attention, vigilance
10 affliction, protection
11 forethought, safekeeping,
   supervision, tribulation
12 guardianship, watchfulness
13 consideration
14 responsibility

❏ **care for**
04 like, love, mind, tend, want
05 enjoy, nurse
06 attend, desire
07 cherish, protect
08 be fond of, maintain
09 look after, watch over
10 minister to, provide for

**career**
03 job, run
04 bolt, dash, race, rush, tear
05 shoot, speed, trade
06 gallop, hurtle, métier
07 calling, pursuit
08 lifework, vocation
10 employment, livelihood,
   occupation, profession

**carefree**
05 happy
06 blithe, breezy, cheery
08 cheerful, laid back
09 easygoing, unworried
10 insouciant, nonchalant
12 happy-go-lucky,
   lighthearted

**careful**
04 wary
05 alert, aware, chary
07 guarded, heedful, mindful,
   precise, prudent, tactful
08 accurate, cautious, detailed,
   diligent, discreet, rigorous,
   thorough, vigilant, watchful
09 assiduous, attentive
10 fastidious, methodical,
   meticulous, particular,
   scrupulous, thoughtful
11 circumspect, painstaking

**careless**
03 lax
05 hasty, messy, slack
06 breezy, casual, remiss,
   simple, sloppy, untidy
07 artless, cursory, offhand
08 carefree, cheerful, heedless,
   slapdash, slipshod, tactless
09 easygoing, forgetful,
   negligent, unguarded
10 disorderly, inaccurate,
   indiscreet, insouciant,
   nonchalant, unthinking
11 perfunctory, thoughtless
12 absent-minded,
   disorganized, happy-go-
   lucky, lighthearted
13 inconsiderate, irresponsible

**caress**
03 hug, pat, pet, rub
04 kiss
05 grope, touch
06 cuddle, fondle, nuzzle, stroke

**07** embrace, petting, snuggle
**08** canoodle

**caretaker**
**06** keeper, porter, regent, warden
**07** curator, janitor, ostiary, steward, trustee
**08** watchman
**09** concierge, custodian
**10** doorkeeper

**careworn**
**05** gaunt, tired, weary
**07** haggard, worn-out
**08** fatigued
**09** exhausted

**cargo**
**04** haul, load
**05** goods
**06** lading
**07** baggage, freight, payload, tonnage
**08** contents, shipment
**11** consignment, merchandise

**caricature**
**04** mock
**05** mimic
**06** parody, satire
**07** cartoon, distort, imitate, lampoon, mimicry, take off, takeoff
**08** ridicule, satirize, travesty
**09** burlesque, imitation

**carnage**
**06** murder
**07** killing
**08** butchery, genocide, massacre
**09** bloodbath, bloodshed, holocaust, slaughter
**10** mass murder

**carnal**
**04** lewd
**06** animal, bodily, erotic, impure, sexual, wanton
**07** fleshly, lustful, natural, sensual
**08** physical
**09** corporeal, lecherous
**10** lascivious, libidinous, licentious

**carnival**
**04** fair, fête, gala
**06** fiesta
**07** holiday, jubilee, revelry
**08** festival, jamboree
**09** Mardi Gras
**11** celebration, merrymaking

**carnivorous**
**10** meat-eating
**11** flesh-eating

**carol**
**04** hymn, noel, song
**06** chorus, strain
**07** wassail

**carouse**
**05** booze, drink, party, revel
**06** imbibe
**07** roister, wassail
**09** celebrate, make merry

**carousing**
**08** drinking, partying
**11** celebrating, merrymaking

**carp**
**03** nag
**05** knock
**07** censure, nit-pick, quibble
**08** complain, reproach
**09** criticize
**10** find faults

**carpenter**
**06** joiner
**10** woodworker
**12** cabinetmaker

**carpet**
**03** bed, mat, rug
**04** kali
**05** kilim, layer
**06** Wilton
**07** blanket, matting
**08** Aubusson, covering
**09** Axminster
**10** wall-to-wall
**13** Kidderminster

**carriage**
**03** air, cab, car, gig
**04** mien, trap
**05** buggy, guise, wagon
**06** hansom, landau, manner
**07** bearing, conduct, freight, hackney, postage, posture
**08** attitude, behavior, demeanor, presence, rockaway
**09** buckboard
**10** conveyance, deportment

**carrier**
**06** bearer, porter, runner, vector
**07** airline, vehicle
**08** conveyor
**09** messenger
**11** transmitter, transporter

**carry**
**03** lug
**04** bear, cart, haul, have, hold, mean, move, pass, pipe, sell, show, take, tote
**05** bring, drive, fetch, print, relay, shift, stand, stock
**06** accept, convey, entail, ratify, retail, uphold

**07** conduct, contain, deliver, display, support, sustain
**08** sanction, shoulder, transfer, transmit, underpin
**09** authorize, transport
**11** communicate, disseminate

❑**carry on**
**03** run
**04** go on, last
**06** endure, keep on, keep up, manage, play up, resume
**07** persist, proceed, restart
**08** continue, maintain, progress, return to
**09** misbehave, persevere
**10** administer, mess around

❑**carry out**
**02** do
**06** effect
**07** achieve, conduct, deliver, execute, fulfill, perform, realize
**08** bring off
**09** discharge, implement, undertake

**cart**
**03** lug
**04** bear, dray, haul, move, tote
**05** carry, shift, truck, wagon
**06** barrow, convey
**08** handcart, transfer
**11** wheelbarrow

**carton**
**03** box
**04** case, pack
**06** packet, parcel
**07** package
**09** container

**cartoon**
**06** parody, sketch
**07** balloon, drawing, lampoon, picture, takeoff
**09** animation, burlesque
**10** caricature, comic strip
**12** animated film

► *Names of cartoonists:*
**04** **Capp** (Al), **Gray** (Harold)
**05** **Avery** (Tex), **Davis** (Jim), **Gould** (Chester), **Hanna** (Bill), **Kelly** (Walt), **Lantz** (Walter)
**06** **Addams** (Charles), **Caniff** (Milton), **Disney** (Walt), **Larson** (Gary), **Schulz** (Charles), **Walker** (Mort)
**07** **Barbera** (Joe), **Ketcham** (Hank), **Mauldin** (Bill), **Trudeau** (Garry)
**08** **Goldberg** (Rube), **Herblock**, **Oliphant** (Pat)

## cartridge
04 case, tube
05 round, shell
06 charge
08 cassette, magazine

## carve
03 cut, hew
04 chip, chop, etch, form, hack, mold
05 cut up, shape, slice
06 chisel, incise, indent, sculpt
07 engrave, fashion, whittle
09 sculpture

## ❏carve up
05 share, split
06 divide
08 separate, share out
09 parcel out, partition
10 distribute

## carving
04 bust
05 cameo
06 bronze, statue
08 incision
09 sculpture, statuette

## cascade
04 fall, gush, pour, rush
05 chute, falls, flood, surge
06 deluge, shower, tumble
07 descend, torrent, trickle
08 cataract, fountain, overflow
09 avalanche, waterfall
10 outpouring

## case
03 bag, box
04 suit
05 chest, cover, crate, event, shell, trial, trunk
06 action, carton, casket, client, sheath, valise, victim
07 attaché, capsule, examine, example, handbag, holdall, invalid, lawsuit, patient, wrapper
08 argument, instance, occasion, specimen
09 cartridge, container, flight bag, portfolio, situation, travel bag
10 look around, occurrence, receptacle
11 contingency, hand-luggage, portmanteau
12 illustration, overnight bag

## cash
04 jack
05 bread, coins, dough, funds, money, notes
06 change
07 bullion, capital, realize, scratch
08 currency, exchange
09 banknotes, hard money
10 ready money
11 legal tender, wherewithal

## cashier
04 sack
05 break, clerk, expel
06 banker, bursar, purser, teller
07 discard, dismiss, unfrock
08 get rid of, throw out
09 discharge, treasurer
10 accountant, bank teller

## cask
03 keg, tub, tun, vat
04 butt
06 barrel, firkin
08 hogshead
09 kilderkin

## casket
03 box
04 case
05 chest, pyxis
06 coffer, coffin
08 jewel box
11 sarcophagus
13 jewel box

## cast
03 lob, put, see, shy
04 emit, form, hurl, look, mold, shed, toss, view, vote
05 drive, fling, found, heave, impel, model, pitch, place, shape, sling, throw
06 actors, direct, glance, launch, look at, record, spread, troupe
07 company, diffuse, fashion, give off, give out, glimpse, players, radiate, scatter
08 covering, register
10 characters, performers

## ❏cast down
05 crush
06 deject, sadden
07 depress
08 desolate
10 discourage, dishearten

## caste
04 race, rank
05 class, grade, group, order
06 degree, estate, status
07 lineage, station, stratum
08 position
10 background

## castigate
05 chide, scold
06 berate, punish, rebuke
07 censure, chasten, correct, reprove, upbraid
08 chastise

09 criticize, reprimand
10 discipline, tongue-lash

## castle
04 fort, keep
05 tower
06 casbah, kasbah, palace
07 château, citadel, schloss
08 fortress
10 stronghold

━ *Parts of a castle*:
04 keep, moat, ward
05 ditch, fosse, motte, mound, scarp, tower
06 bailey, chapel, corbel, crenel, donjon, merlon, turret
07 bastion, dungeon, parapet, postern, rampart
08 approach, barbican, buttress, stockade
09 courtyard, gatehouse, inner wall
10 drawbridge, portcullis, watchtower
11 battlements, crenelation, curtain wall
12 lookout tower

━ *Names of famous castles*:
04 York
05 Corfe, Doune, Leeds
06 Cawdor, Glamis, Kalmar, Ludlow
07 Alnwick, Arundel, Blarney, Caister, Dunster, Harlech, Kremlin, Peveril, Warwick, Windsor
08 Balmoral, Bamburgh, Bastille, Egremont, Elsinore, Gaillard, Stirling, Stokesay, Tintagel
09 Beaumaris, Dunsinane, Edinburgh, Tantallon
10 Caernarvon, Carmarthen, Rockingham, Sant'Angelo
11 Chillingham, Craigmillar, Fotheringay, Lindisfarne, Ravenscraig
12 Conisborough
14 Neuschwanstein

## castrate
04 geld
05 unman, unsex
06 neuter
07 evirate
10 emasculate

## casual
05 blasé
06 chance, random
07 cursory, offhand, relaxed
08 informal, laid back
09 apathetic, easy-going, short-term, temporary

10 accidental, incidental, insouciant, nonchalant
11 free-and-easy, indifferent, superficial, unconcerned
12 happy-go-lucky, intermittent
13 lackadaisical, serendipitous
15 couldn't-care-less

**casualty**
04 loss
05 death
06 injury, victim
07 injured, missing, wounded
08 fatality, sufferer

**casuistry**
07 sophism
09 chicanery, sophistry
12 equivocation, speciousness

**cat**
03 tom
04 puss
05 pussy, tabby
06 feline, kitten, mouser
09 grimalkin
➢ See also ANIMAL

━ *Breeds of cat*:
03 Rex
04 Manx
06 Birman, Bombay, Cymric
07 Burmese, Persian, Siamese, Tiffany
09 Singapura, Tonkinese
10 Abyssinian, Turkish Van
11 Egyptian Mau, Russian Blue
12 Scottish Fold
15 British longhair, Japanese Bobtail

━ *Famous cats include*:
03 Tom
04 Bast
05 Dinah, Felix
06 Top Cat
07 Simpkin
08 Garfield, Krazy Kat, Macavity
09 Sylvester, Tom Kitten
10 Heathcliff
11 Cat in the Hat, Cheshire Cat, Pink Panther, Puss in Boots
14 Bustopher Jones, Mr Mistoffelees, Old Deuteronomy

**cataclysm**
04 blow
07 debacle
08 calamity, disaster, upheaval
11 catastrophe, devastation

**catacomb**
04 tomb
05 crypt, vault

07 ossuary

**catalog**
04 file, list, roll
05 guide, index, table
06 record, roster
08 brochure, bulletin, calendar, classify, register, tabulate
09 catalogue, checklist, directory, inventory, make a list
10 prospectus

**catapult**
04 fire, hurl, toss
05 fling, pitch, shoot, sling, throw
06 hurtle, launch, propel

**cataract**
05 falls, force
06 deluge, rapids
07 cascade, torrent
08 downpour
09 waterfall

**catastrophe**
04 blow, ruin
06 fiasco
07 debacle, failure, tragedy
08 calamity, disaster, upheaval
09 adversity, cataclysm
10 affliction, misfortune
11 devastation

**catastrophic**
05 awful, fatal
06 tragic
08 dreadful, terrible
10 calamitous, disastrous
11 cataclysmic, devastating

**catcall**
03 boo
04 gibe, hiss, jeer, jibe
07 whistle
10 Bronx cheer

**catch**
03 get, nab, net
04 bolt, clip, find, grab, grip, hasp, hear, hold, hook, lock, nick, snag, take, trap
05 clasp, grasp, hitch, latch, seize, snare
06 arrest, collar, corner, entrap, expose, fathom, follow, pick up, snatch, take in
07 attract, develop, discern, ensnare, problem, round up, startle
08 contract, discover, drawback, fastener, perceive, surprise
09 apprehend, lay hold of
10 comprehend, difficulty, go down with, understand

12 disadvantage

❑**catch on**
05 grasp
06 fathom, follow, take in
10 comprehend, understand
13 become popular

❑**catch up**
06 gain on
08 overtake
09 draw level

**catch phrase**
05 motto
06 byword, jingle, saying, slogan
07 formula
08 password
09 catchword, watchword

**catching**
10 contagious, infectious
12 communicable
13 transmissible, transmittable

**catchy**
07 melodic, popular, tuneful
08 haunting
09 appealing, memorable
10 attractive
11 captivating
13 unforgettable

**catechize**
04 test
05 drill, grill
07 examine
08 instruct, question
11 interrogate
12 cross-examine

**categorical**
05 clear, total, utter
06 direct
07 express
08 absolute, definite, emphatic, explicit, positive
09 downright
10 conclusive, unreserved

**categorize**
04 list, rank, sort
05 class, grade, group, order
07 arrange
08 classify, tabulate
10 pigeonhole, stereotype

**category**
04 kind, list, rank, sort, type
05 class, genre, grade, group, order, title
06 rubric
07 chapter, heading, listing, section, variety
08 division, grouping

**cater**
05 serve

**caterwaul** (cont.)
06 pander, supply
07 furnish, provide, victual

**caterwaul**
03 cry
04 bawl, howl, meow, wail, yowl
06 scream, shriek, squall
07 screech

**catharsis**
07 purging, release
09 cleansing, epuration, purifying
10 abreaction, abstersion, lustration
12 purification

**cathartic**
07 lustral, purging, release
09 cleansing, purifying
10 abreactive, abstersive

**cathedral**
04 dome
05 duomo
06 church
07 minster

**catholic**
04 wide
05 broad
06 global, varied
07 diverse, general, liberal
08 eclectic, tolerant
09 inclusive, universal
10 broad-based, open-minded, widespread
11 broad-minded, wide-ranging
13 comprehensive

**cattle**
04 cows, oxen
05 bulls, stock
06 beasts, bovine
09 livestock

━━━━━━━━━━━━━━━━━━━

► *Breeds of cattle*:
05 Devon, Luing
06 Ankole, dexter, Durham, Jersey
07 Brahman, Red Poll
08 Ayrshire, Friesian, Galloway, Guernsey, Hereford, Highland, Holstein, Limousin, Longhorn
09 Charolais, Shorthorn, Teeswater
10 Africander
11 Chillingham
12 Simmenthaler
13 Aberdeen Angus
➤ See also ANIMAL

**catty**
04 mean
06 bitchy

07 vicious
08 spiteful, venomous
09 malicious, rancorous

**caucus**
03 set
06 clique, parley
07 meeting, session
08 assembly, conclave
09 gathering
10 convention

**causative**
04 root
07 causing, factive
09 factitive

**cause**
03 aim, end
04 make, root, suit
05 agent, basis, begin, breed, force, ideal, maker, mover
06 agency, compel, create, effect, factor, incite, induce, lead to, motive, origin, prompt, reason, source, spring
07 grounds, lawsuit, produce, provoke, purpose, trigger
08 generate, motivate, movement
09 beginning, incentive, originate, stimulate
10 bring about, conviction, enterprise, give rise to, motivation, prime mover, trigger off
11 explanation, precipitate, undertaking

**caustic**
04 acid, keen
05 snide
06 biting, bitter, severe
07 burning, cutting, mordant, pungent
08 scathing, stinging, virulent
09 corrosive, sarcastic
10 astringent
11 acrimonious, destructive

**cauterize**
04 burn, sear
05 singe
09 carbonize, disinfect, sterilize

**caution**
04 care, heed, urge, warn
05 alert, deter
06 advice, advise, caveat
07 counsel, warning
08 admonish, prudence, wariness
09 alertness, vigilance
10 admonition, discretion, injunction
11 carefulness, forethought

12 deliberation, watchfulness
14 circumspection

**cautious**
04 wary
05 alert, cagey, chary
06 shrewd
07 careful, guarded, heedful, prudent, tactful
08 discreet, gingerly, vigilant, watchful
09 judicious, tentative
11 circumspect

**cavalcade**
05 array, train, troop
06 parade
07 cortège, retinue
09 march-past
10 procession

**cavalier**
04 curt
05 lofty, spahi
06 casual, escort, knight, lordly, spahee
07 gallant, haughty, offhand
08 arrogant, chasseur, horseman, Ironside
09 chevalier, gentleman
10 cavalryman, swaggering
11 bashi-bazouk, free-and-easy, patronizing
12 horse soldier, supercilious
13 high-and-mighty

**cavalry**
07 hussars, lancers
08 dragoons, horsemen, troopers
13 horse soldiers

**cave**
04 hole
06 cavern, cavity, dugout, grotto, hollow, tunnel
07 pothole

❑**cave in**
04 fall, slip
05 yield
07 give way, subside
08 collapse

**caveat**
05 alarm
07 caution, warning
10 admonition

**cavern**
03 den
04 cave
05 vault
06 cavity, dugout, grotto, hollow, tunnel
07 pothole

**cavernous**
04 dark, deep, huge, vast
06 gaping, hollow, sunken
07 immense, yawning
08 resonant, spacious
10 bottomless
12 unfathomable

**cavil**
03 nag
04 carp
07 censure, nit-pick, quibble
08 complain, reproach
09 criticize, find fault

**cavity**
03 gap, pit
04 dent, hole, well
05 sinus
06 crater, hollow, lacuna
07 orifice, pothole
08 aperture
09 ventricle

**cavort**
04 romp, skip
05 caper, dance, frisk, sport
06 frolic, gambol, prance

**cease**
03 die, end
04 fail, halt, quit, stop
05 abate, leave, let up
06 desist, finish, pack in
07 refrain, suspend
08 break off, conclude, leave off, peter out
09 call a halt, fizzle out
11 come to a halt, come to an end, discontinue

**ceaseless**
07 endless, eternal, nonstop
08 constant, unending, untiring
09 continual, incessant, perpetual, unceasing
10 continuous, persistent
11 everlasting, never-ending, unremitting
12 interminable

**cede**
05 allow, grant, yield
06 convey, give up, resign
07 abandon, concede, deliver
08 abdicate, hand over, renounce, transfer, turn over
09 surrender
10 relinquish

**ceiling**
04 most, roof
05 beams, limit, vault
06 awning, canopy
07 maximum, plafond, rafters
10 upper limit
11 cutoff point

12 glass ceiling

**celebrate**
04 keep, mark, rave
05 binge, extol, honor, revel, toast
07 drink to, have fun, observe, perform, rejoice
08 live it up, remember
09 have a ball, whoop it up
11 commemorate, throw a party
14 go out on the town
15 paint the town red

**celebrated**
05 famed, great, noted
06 famous
07 eminent, notable, popular
08 glorious, renowned
09 acclaimed, legendary, prominent, well-known
11 illustrious, outstanding
13 distinguished

**celebration**
04 gala, rave
05 binge, party, spree
06 fiesta
07 banquet, jubilee, revelry
08 jamboree
09 festivity
11 merrymaking
13 jollification

---

► *Types of religious celebration and service:*
04 fête, Mass
05 feast
06 May Day
07 baptism, funeral, jubilee, tribute, wedding
08 evensong, festival, High Mass, marriage
09 communion, Eucharist, saint's day
10 bar mitzvah, bat mitzvah, dedication
11 christening, Lord's Supper, nuptial Mass, remembrance, Requiem Mass
12 confirmation, Midnight Mass, thanksgiving
13 Holy Communion, Holy Matrimony
14 evening service, morning prayers, morning service
15 harvest festival, memorial service
➤ See also RELIGION

**celebrity**
03 VIP
04 hero, idol, name, star
06 bigwig, legend, worthy
07 big name, big shot, notable

08 luminary
09 dignitary, superstar
11 personality
12 living legend
13 household name

**celerity**
05 haste, speed
08 dispatch, fastness, rapidity, velocity
09 fleetness, quickness, swiftness

**celestial**
04 holy
06 astral, divine, starry
07 angelic, elysian, eternal, godlike, sublime
08 empyrean, ethereal, heavenly, immortal, seraphic
09 spiritual

**celibacy**
06 purity
08 chastity
09 virginity
10 abnegation, abstinence, continence, self-denial
12 bachelorhood, spinsterhood
13 self-restraint

**celibate**
04 pure
06 chaste, single, virgin
08 bachelor, spinster
09 abstinent

**cell**
04 jail, room, unit
05 crowd, group, party, spore
06 caucus, clique, cytoid, gamete, lockup, matrix, prison, zygote
07 chamber, cubicle, dungeon, faction, nucleus, section
08 organism
09 cytoplasm, enclosure
10 protoplasm, protoplast
11 compartment

**cellar**
05 crypt, vault
08 basement
09 storeroom
10 wine cellar

**cement**
03 gum
04 bind, bond, glue, join, weld
05 affix, grout, paste, stick
06 attach, cohere, matrix, mortar, solder
07 bonding, combine, plaster
08 adhesive, concrete

**cemetery**
07 charnel
08 God's acre

09 graveyard
10 churchyard, necropolis
12 burial ground, charnel house

**censor**
03 ban, cut
04 edit
06 delete, editor
09 expurgate
10 blue-pencil, bowdlerize

**censorious**
06 severe
07 carping
08 captious, caviling, critical
11 disparaging
12 condemnatory, disapproving, faultfinding
13 hypercritical

**censure**
03 rap
05 blame, knock, scold
06 rebuke
07 condemn, obloquy, reproof, reprove, tell off, upbraid
08 admonish, denounce, reproach, scolding
09 castigate, criticism, criticize, reprehend, reprimand
10 admonition, upbraiding
11 castigation, disapproval
12 admonishment, condemnation, denunciation, vituperation
15 come down heavy on

**center**
03 hub
04 core, crux
05 arena, focus, heart, pivot
06 kernel, middle
07 nucleus, revolve
08 bull's-eye, midpoint
09 gravitate
10 focal point

**central**
03 key, mid
04 core, main
05 basic, chief, focal, inner, major, prime, vital
06 medial, median, middle
07 crucial, pivotal, primary
08 dominant, foremost, interior
09 essential, principal
11 fundamental, significant
13 most important

**centralize**
05 focus, unify
07 compact
08 condense, converge
10 amalgamate, streamline
11 concentrate, rationalize

**ceramics**
04 raku, ware
06 bisque
07 faience, pottery
09 ironstone, porcelain
11 earthenware

**cereal**
05 grain
06 farina
07 oatmeal
08 porridge
10 cornflakes

▶ *Types of cereal*:
03 oat, rye
04 corn, oats, ragi, rice, sago, teff
05 emmer, spelt, wheat
06 barley, bulgur, millet
07 cassava, sorghum, tapioca
08 semolina
09 buckwheat

**ceremonial**
04 rite
06 custom, formal, ritual
07 stately
08 official, protocol
09 dignified
11 ritualistic

**ceremonious**
05 civil, exact, grand, stiff
06 formal, polite, ritual, solemn
07 courtly, precise, stately
08 official
09 courteous, dignified

**ceremony**
04 form, pomp, rite, show
06 burial, custom, parade, ritual
07 decorum, liturgy, service, wedding
08 festival, function, protocol
09 etiquette, formality, pageantry, propriety, tradition, unveiling
10 bar mitzvah, dedication, graduation, observance
11 anniversary, investiture
12 inauguration
13 commemoration, ribbon-cutting

**certain**
04 some, sure, true
05 bound, fated, fixed, plain
07 assured, decided, evident, obvious, precise, settled
08 absolute, definite, destined, home free, in the bag, positive, specific
09 confident, convinced
10 conclusive, convincing, determined, individual,

inevitable, inexorable, particular
11 cut and dried, established, inescapable, irrefutable, open-and-shut, unavoidable
12 indisputable, no ifs and buts
13 bound to happen

**certainly**
06 surely
07 clearly, for sure, no doubt
08 of course
09 assuredly, naturally
10 absolutely, by all means, definitely, positively
11 doubtlessly, undoubtedly
13 without a doubt

**certainty**
04 fact
05 faith, trust, truth
06 shoo-in
07 reality, safe bet
08 sureness, validity
09 assurance, certitude, sure thing
10 confidence, conviction

**certificate**
03 IOU
04 pass
05 award
07 diploma, license, voucher
08 document
09 guarantee
11 credentials, endorsement, testimonial
13 authorization, qualification

**certify**
04 aver
05 vouch
06 assure, attest, ratify, verify
07 confirm, endorse, license, testify, warrant, witness
08 accredit, validate
09 authorize, guarantee, pronounce, recognize
11 corroborate
12 authenticate, substantiate
13 bear witness to

**certitude**
08 sureness
09 assurance, certainty
10 confidence, conviction
11 assuredness

**cessation**
03 end
04 halt, rest, stay
05 break, letup, pause
06 ending, hiatus, recess
07 ceasing, halting, respite
08 abeyance, interval, stoppage, stopping
09 remission

**chafe**

10 conclusion, desistance, standstill, suspension
11 termination
12 intermission, interruption
15 discontinuation

**chafe**

03 rub, vex
04 rasp, wear
05 anger, annoy, grate, peeve
06 abrade, enrage, scrape
07 inflame, provoke, scratch
08 irritate
09 excoriate
10 exasperate

**chaff**

03 kid, rib
04 pods, raze
05 cases, husks
06 banter, shells
07 teasing

**chagrin**

03 irk, vex
05 annoy, peeve, shame
07 mortify
08 disquiet, irritate, vexation
09 annoyance, displease, embarrass, humiliate
10 disappoint, dissatisfy, exasperate, irritation
11 displeasure, fretfulness, humiliation, indignation
12 discomfiture, discomposure, exasperation
13 embarrassment, mortification

**chain**

03 row, set, tie
04 bind, bond, firm, line, link
05 cuffs, group, hitch, train, union
06 fasten, fetter, secure, series, string, tether
07 company, confine, enslave, manacle, shackle, trammel
08 catenary, coupling, handcuff, restrain, sequence
13 concatenation

**chair**

02 MC
04 form, lead, seat
05 bench, emcee, stool
06 direct, rocker
07 convene, rocking, speaker
08 chairman, convener, director, recliner
09 president, supervise
10 chairwoman
11 chairperson, preside over, toastmaster

**chalk**

❏**chalk up**
04 gain
05 score, tally
06 attain, charge, credit, record
07 achieve, ascribe, put down
08 register

**chalky**

03 wan
04 pale
05 ashen, white
06 pallid
07 powdery
10 calcareous, cretaceous

**challenge**

03 tax, try
04 call, dare, defy, risk, test
05 brave, demur, query, trial
06 accost, hazard, hurdle, invite, summon
07 dispute, problem, provoke, stretch, summons
08 confront, defiance, object to, obstacle, question
09 objection, ultimatum
10 opposition
11 provocation
12 disagree with, disagreement
13 confrontation, interrogation

**challenging**

06 taxing
07 testing
08 exacting, exciting
09 demanding
10 stretching

**chamber**

04 hall, room
05 house, vault
06 cavity
07 bedroom, boudoir, council
08 assembly
09 ventricle
10 auditorium, parliament
11 compartment, legislature
12 assembly hall
13 reception room

**champion**

03 ace
04 back, hero
05 angel, champ
06 backer, defend, patron, uphold, victor, winner
07 espouse, promote, support
08 maintain, upholder
09 conqueror, protector
10 stand up for, vindicator
11 titleholder

**chance**

03 bet, try
04 fate, luck, odds, risk

05 break, fluke, occur, stake
06 casual, flukey, follow, gamble, happen, hazard, kismet, random, result
07 destiny, develop, fortune, opening, venture
08 accident, fortuity, prospect
09 arbitrary, haphazard, speculate
10 accidental, fortuitous, likelihood, providence, unexpected
11 bet your life, coincidence, opportunity, possibility, probability, serendipity, speculation
12 bet your boots, push your luck, your best shot
13 serendipitous

❏**chance on, chance upon**
04 meet
07 run into
08 bump into, discover
09 stumble on
10 come across

**chancy**

05 risky
06 tricky
07 fraught
09 hazardous, uncertain
11 speculative

**change**

04 cash, move, swap, turn, vary
05 adapt, alter, amend, coins, shift, trade, trend, U-turn
06 adjust, barter, become, evolve, modify, mutate, reform, revise, silver, switch
07 convert, develop, novelty, remodel, replace, shake-up, variety
08 exchange, mutation, revision, transfer, upheaval
09 about-face, amendment, customize, evolution, fluctuate, transform, transpose, turnabout, vacillate, variation, volte-face
10 adaptation, adjustment, difference, ebb and flow, innovation, remodeling, reorganize, revolution, substitute, transition
11 development, fluctuation, replacement, restructure, state of flux, transfigure, transmutate, vacillation, vicissitude
12 metamorphose, modification, substitution

13 metamorphosis,
restructuring, transmutation,
transposition
14 transformation

**changeable**
05 fluid
06 fickle, labile, mobile
07 erratic, mutable, protean,
varying
08 shifting, unstable, unsteady,
variable, volatile, wavering
09 irregular, mercurial,
uncertain, unsettled
10 capricious, inconstant
11 fluctuating, vacillating
13 unpredictable

**channel**
03 way
04 duct, main, neck, path, send
05 agent, canal, flume, guide,
gully, means, route, sound
06 agency, avenue, convey,
course, direct, furrow,
groove, gutter, medium,
strait, trough
07 conduct, conduit, passage
08 approach, spillway, waterway
11 concentrate, watercourse

**chant**
03 cry
04 sing, song
05 psalm, shout
06 chorus, intone, mantra,
recite, slogan, war cry
07 refrain
09 plainsong

**chaos**
04 mess, riot
05 snafu
06 bedlam, tumult, uproar
07 anarchy
08 disorder, madhouse,
shambles, tohubohu,
upheaval
09 confusion
11 lawlessness, pandemonium

**chaotic**
05 snafu
06 unruly
07 lawless, riotous
08 anarchic, confused,
deranged
09 disrupted, orderless,
shambolic
10 disordered, topsy-turvy,
tumultuous
12 disorganized, uncontrolled
13 all over the lot
15 all over the place

**chap**
03 boy, guy, jaw, lad, man

04 gent, sort, type
05 cheek, split
06 fellow, person
09 gentleman

**chaperone, chaperon**
04 mind
05 guard
06 attend, duenna, escort
07 protect
08 shepherd
09 accompany, companion,
safeguard, watch over

**chapped**
03 raw
04 sore
05 split
06 chafed
07 cracked

**chapter**
04 part, time
05 phase, stage, topic
06 clause, period
07 episode, portion, section
08 division

**char**
04 burn, sear
05 brown, singe
06 scorch
09 carbonize, cauterize

**character**
04 case, logo, mark, part, role,
rune, sign, sort, type
05 charm, ethos, image, stamp,
style, trait
06 appeal, cipher, device,
emblem, figure, letter,
makeup, nature, oddity,
person, psyche, status,
symbol
07 caliber, courage, essence,
feature, honesty, oddball,
persona, quality
08 identity, interest, original,
position, property, strength
09 eccentric, ideograph
10 attributes, hieroglyph, moral
fiber, reputation
11 disposition, peculiarity,
personality, specialness,
temperament, uprightness
13 determination, individuality

**characteristic**
04 mark
05 trait
06 factor
07 feature, quality, special,
symptom, typical
08 hallmark, peculiar, property,
specific, symbolic
09 attribute, mannerism
11 distinctive, peculiarity

12 idiosyncrasy
13 idiosyncratic

**characterize**
04 mark
05 brand, stamp
06 typify
07 portray, present, specify
08 describe, identify, indicate
09 designate, represent

**charade**
04 fake, sham
05 farce
06 parody
07 mockery
08 pretense, travesty
09 pantomime

**charge**
03 ask, fee, tax
04 bill, care, cost, dues, duty,
levy, rate, rent, rush, tear, toll,
ward
05 blame, debit, exact, price,
storm, trust
06 accuse, amount, ask for,
assail, attack, burden,
demand, indict, onrush,
outlay, rental, sortie
07 arraign, assault, custody,
expense, impeach, keeping,
payment
08 price tag, storming
09 fix a price, incursion,
onslaught, set a price
10 accusation, allegation,
imputation, indictment,
obligation, protection
11 arraignment, impeachment,
incriminate, safekeeping
12 guardianship

❏**in charge of**
08 managing
10 overseeing
11 controlling, supervising
12 looking after, taking care of
14 responsible for

**charitable**
04 kind
06 benign, kindly
07 lenient, liberal
08 generous, gracious, tolerant
09 bounteous, forgiving
10 beneficent, benevolent,
openhanded
11 considerate, magnanimous
12 eleemosynary, humanitarian
13 philanthropic

**charity**
03 aid
04 alms, fund, gift, love
05 trust
06 relief

07 caritas, funding, handout
08 altruism, clemency, goodwill, humanity, kindness, largesse
09 affection, tolerance
10 almsgiving, assistance, benignness, compassion, generosity
11 beneficence, benevolence
12 contribution, philanthropy

**charlatan**
04 fake, sham
05 cheat, fraud, phony, quack
06 con man
08 impostor, swindler
09 con artist, pretender, trickster
10 mountebank
13 confidence man

**charm**
03 hex, obi, win
04 draw, idol, juju
05 magic, spell
06 allure, amulet, appeal, cajole, enamor, fetish, mascot, please, seduce
07 attract, beguile, bewitch, delight, enchant, periapt, sorcery, trinket
08 gris gris, talisman
09 captivate, enrapture, fascinate, mesmerize
10 allurement, attraction
11 abracadabra
12 desirability

**charming**
04 cute
05 sweet
06 lovely
07 winning, winsome
08 alluring, engaging, fetching, pleasant, pleasing, tempting
09 appealing, seductive
10 attractive, delectable, delightful, enchanting

**chart**
03 map
04 list, mark, note, plan, plot
05 draft, graph, place, table
06 follow, map out, record, sketch, top ten
07 diagram, dope out, monitor, outline
08 document, nomogram, top forty
09 blueprint, delineate, flowchart, flowsheet, hit parade, nomograph, top twenty

**charter**
04 bond, deed, hire, rent
05 grant, lease, right
06 employ, engage, permit

07 license, warrant
08 contract, covenant, document, sanction
09 authority, authorize, franchise, indenture, privilege
10 commission, conveyance

**chary**
04 slow, wary
05 leery
06 uneasy
07 careful, guarded, heedful, prudent
08 cautious
09 reluctant, unwilling

**chase**
04 hunt, rush, tail
05 court, drive, expel, hound, hurry, track, trail
06 follow, pursue, shadow
07 hunting, pursuit
08 coursing, run after

**chasm**
03 gap
04 gulf, rift, void
05 abyss, cleft, crack, gorge, split
06 breach, canyon, cavity, crater, hollow, ravine
· 07 fissure, opening
08 crevasse
10 alienation, separation

**chassis**
05 frame
08 bodywork, fuselage, skeleton
09 framework, structure
13 undercarriage

**chaste**
04 pure
05 moral, plain
06 modest, simple, single
08 celibate, innocent, virginal, virtuous
09 abstinent, continent
10 immaculate, restrained

**chasten**
04 curb, tame
06 humble, punish, subdue
07 correct, repress, reprove
08 chastise, moderate, restrain
09 castigate, humiliate
10 discipline

**chastise**
04 beat, cane, flog, lash, whip
05 scold, smack, spank, strap
06 berate, punish, wallop
07 censure, correct, reprove, scourge, upbraid
08 admonish

09 castigate, dress down, reprimand
10 discipline, take to task

**chastity**
06 purity, virtue
07 modesty
08 celibacy
09 innocence, virginity
10 abstinence, continence, maidenhood, singleness
13 temperateness

**chat**
03 gas, jaw, yak
04 talk
06 babble, confab, gossip, jabber, yak-yak
07 chatter, chinwag, prattle
08 converse
09 small talk, tête-à-tête, yakety-yak
10 chew the fat, chew the rag
12 conversation, heart-to-heart, tittle-tattle

**chatter**
03 gab, gas, jaw, yak
04 chat, talk
06 babble, confab, gossip, jabber, tattle, yak-yak
07 chinwag, prattle
08 chitchat
09 tête-à-tête, yakety-yak
12 conversation, tittle-tattle

**chatterbox**
06 gabber, gasbag, gossip
07 babbler, blabber, tattler, windbag
08 bigmouth, jabberer
09 chatterer, gossipper
12 blabbermouth
13 tittle-tattler

**chatty**
04 glib
05 gabby
07 gossipy, gushing, verbose
08 effusive, friendly, informal
09 garrulous, talkative
10 colloquial, loquacious

**chauvinism**
04 bias
06 sexism
08 jingoism
09 prejudice
10 flag-waving
11 nationalism
12 partisanship

**chauvinist**
05 jingo
06 biased, sexist
08 jingoist
09 flag-waver

**cheap**

10 flag-waving, prejudiced
11 nationalist

**cheap**
03 low
04 mean, poor, sale
05 tacky
06 a steal, budget, paltry, shoddy, sleazy, sordid, tawdry, two-bit, vulgar
07 bargain, economy, low-cost, reduced, slashed
08 cut-price, giveaway, inferior, twopenny
09 knock-down, low-priced, worthless
10 affordable, despicable, discounted, economical, marked-down, reasonable, rock-bottom, second-rate
11 inexpensive
12 contemptible, reduced price

**cheapen**
05 lower
06 demean
07 degrade, devalue
08 belittle, derogate
09 denigrate, downgrade
10 depreciate

**cheat**
02 do
03 con, fix, gyp, rig
04 bilk, dupe, fake, fool, hoax
05 bluff, check, cozen, crook, fraud, rogue, shark, sting, trick, welsh
06 conman, diddle, dodger, fiddle, fleece, rip off, thwart
07 beguile, cozener, deceive, defraud, deprive, mislead, swindle, two-time
08 deceiver, hoodwink, impostor, swindler
09 bamboozle, charlatan, frustrate, trickster
11 double-cross, short-change
12 double-dealer, put one over on, take for a ride
13 double-crosser

**check**
03 bar, tab
04 bill, curb, damp, halt, scan, slow, stem, stop, test
05 audit, delay, limit, probe, study, tally
06 arrest, bridle, hinder, impede, police, rein in, screen, thwart, verify
07 analyze, compare, confirm, control, examine, inhibit, inquiry, inspect, invoice, monitor, repress

08 analysis, make sure, obstruct, once-over, research, restrain, scrutiny, slow down, validate
09 go through, take stock
10 inspection, scrutinize
11 corroborate, examination, inquire into, investigate, nip in the bud
15 give the once-over

❑**check in**
06 book in, enroll, report
08 register

❑**check out**
03 die
04 test
05 leave, study
07 examine
08 look into
11 investigate

❑**check up**
06 assess, verify
07 analyze, confirm, inspect
08 evaluate, make sure
09 ascertain
11 inquire into, investigate

**checkered**
05 mixed
06 varied
07 diverse
15 with ups and downs

**check-up**
05 audit, probe
07 inquiry, medical
08 analysis, physical, research
09 appraisal
10 evaluation, inspection
11 examination
13 investigation

**cheek**
03 lip
04 gall
05 mouth, nerve, sauce
07 chutzpa
08 audacity, chutzpah, temerity
09 impudence, insolence
10 brazenness, effrontery
12 impertinence

**cheeky**
04 pert
05 fresh, lippy, sassy, saucy
06 brazen
07 forward
08 impudent, insolent
09 audacious
11 impertinent
12 overfamiliar

**cheer**
03 rah
04 clap, hail, warm
05 bravo, elate, shout

06 buck up, buoy up, hurrah, hurray, perk up, salute, solace, uplift
07 acclaim, applaud, comfort, console, enliven, fanfare, gladden, hearten, ovation, revelry, root for, support
08 applause, brighten, clapping, gladness
09 celebrate, encourage, happiness, merriment
10 exhilarate, joyfulness
11 high spirits, merrymaking

❑**cheer up**
05 liven, rally
06 buck up, perk up
07 comfort, console, hearten
08 brighten
09 encourage, take heart

**cheerful**
03 gay
04 glad, warm
05 happy, jolly, merry, sunny
06 blithe, bright, chirpy, genial, hearty, jovial, joyful, joyous, lively
07 buoyant, smiling
08 animated, carefree, laughing, spirited, stirring
09 agreeable, contented, exuberant, sparkling
10 delightful, heartening, optimistic
12 happy-go-lucky
13 in good spirits

**cheerio**
03 bye
05 adieu
06 bye-bye, so long
07 goodbye
08 au revoir, farewell, toodle-oo
11 see you later

**cheerless**
03 sad
04 cold, dark, drab, dull, grim
05 bleak, dingy
06 barren, dismal, dreary, gloomy, lonely, somber
07 austere, forlorn, joyless, sunless, unhappy
08 dejected, desolate, dolorous, mournful, winterly
09 miserable, sorrowful
10 depressing, uninviting
11 comfortless

**cheery**
03 gay
04 glad
05 happy, jolly, merry
06 bright, chirpy, genial, hearty, jovial, joyful, lively

07 buoyant, smiling
08 animated, carefree
09 exuberant, sparkling
10 optimistic
12 enthusiastic, lighthearted
13 in good spirits

## cheese

▶ *Varieties of cheese*:
04 Brie, Edam, Feta
05 Caboc, Carré, Derby, Gouda, quark
06 Dunlop, Orkney
07 Boursin, Cheddar, Gruyère, Limburg, ricotta, Stilton
08 Bel Paese, Cheshire, Emmental, Huntsman, Longhorn, Parmesan, raclette
09 Amsterdam, Blue Vinny, Camembert, Jarlsberg, Killarney, Leicester, Limburger, Lymeswold, Port Salut, Roquefort
10 Caerphilly, curd cheese, Danish blue, Dolcelatte, Emmentaler, Gloucester, Gorgonzola, Lancashire, mascarpone, mozzarella, Neufchâtel, Red Windsor
11 cream cheese, Liederkranz, pasteurized, Wensleydale
12 Monterey Jack, Red Leicester
13 cottage cheese
➤ See also FOOD

## chef

▶ *Names of chefs*:
04 **Flay** (Bobby), **Kerr** (Graham)
05 **Beard** (James), **Brown** (L. Edwin), **Child** (Julia), **Davis** (Frank), **Folse** (John), **Gaebe** (Morris J.W.), **Pepin** (Jacques), **Pyles** (Stephan), **Woods** (Sylvia)
06 **Boulud** (Daniel), **Lawson** (Nigella), **Oliver** (Jamie), **Waters** (Alice)
07 **English** (Todd), **Guillas** (Bernard), **Lagasse** (Emeril), **Moulton** (Sara), **Stewart** (Martha), **Trotter** (Charlie)
08 **Harriott** (Ainsley), **Palladin** (Jean-Louis)
09 **Matsuhisa** (Nobu), **Prudhomme** (Paul), **Rautoreau** (Thierry)

## chemical

03 tin (Sn)
04 gold (Au), iron (Fe), lead (Pb), neon (Ne), zinc (Zn)
05 argon (Ar), boron (B), radon (Rn), xenon (Xe)
06 barium (Ba), carbon (C), cerium (Ce), cesium (Cs), cobalt (Co), copper (Cu), curium (Cm), erbium (Er), helium (He), indium (In), iodine (I), nickel (Ni), osmium (Os), oxygen (O), radium (Ra), silver (Ag), sodium (Na), sulfur (S)
07 arsenic (As), bismuth (Bi), bromine (Br), cadmium (Cd), calcium (Ca), fermium (Fm), gallium (Ga), hafnium (Hf), hahnium (Ha), holmium (Ho), iridium (Ir), krypton (Kr), lithium (Li), mercury (Hg), niobium (Nb), rhenium (Re), rhodium (Rh), silicon (Si), terbium (Tb), thorium (Th), thulium (Tm), uranium (U), yttrium (Y)
08 actinium (Ac), aluminum (Al), antimony (Sb), astatine (At), chlorine (Cl), chromium (Cr), europium (Eu), fluorine (F), francium (Fr), hydrogen (H), lutetium (Lu), nitrogen (N), nobelium (No), platinum (Pt), polonium (Po), rubidium (Rb), samarium (Sm), scandium (Sc), selenium (Se), tantalum (Ta), thallium (Tl), titanium (Ti), tungsten (W), vanadium (V)
09 americium (Am), berkelium (Bk), beryllium (Be), germanium (Ge), lanthanum (La), magnesium (Mg), manganese (Mn), neodymium (Nd), neptunium (Np), palladium (Pd), plutonium (Pu), potassium (K), ruthenium (Ru), strontium (Sr), tellurium (Te), ytterbium (Yb), zirconium (Zr)
10 dysprosium (Dy), gadolinium (Gd), lawrencium (Lr) (Lw), molybdenum (Mo), phosphorus (P), promethium (Pm), technetium (Tc)
11 californium (Cf), einsteinium (Es), mendelevium (Md)
12 praseodymium (Pr), protactinium (Pa)
13 rutherfordium (Rf)

## chemistry

▶ *Terms used in chemistry*:
02 pH
03 gas, ion
04 acid, atom, base, bond, mass, mole, salt
05 ester, lipid
06 alkali, isomer, liquid, matter, proton
07 crystal, formula, halogen, isotope, neutron, nucleus, organic, polymer, solvent, valence
08 analysis, catalyst, compound, electron, emulsion, inert gas, molecule, noble gas, reaction, solution
09 allotrope, catalysis, corrosion, diffusion, electrode, inorganic, ionic bond, oxidation, substance, synthesis, titration
10 combustion, hydrolysis, litmus test, suspension
11 free radical, litmus paper
12 atomic number, biochemistry, chemical bond, chlorination, covalent bond, distillation, electrolysis, fermentation, metallic bond
13 chain reaction, decomposition, periodic table, radioactivity
15 atomic structure, chemical element

▶ *Names of chemists*:
04 **Davy** (Humphry), **Hess** (Germain Henri), **Kohn** (Walter), **Kuhn** (Richard), **Mond** (Ludwig), **Urey** (Harold Clayton)
05 **Boyer** (Paul), **Boyle** (Robert), **Curie** (Marie), **Darby** (Abraham), **Dewar** (James), **Haber** (Fritz), **Libby** (Willard Frank), **Nobel** (Alfred), **Soddy** (Frederick)
06 **Baeyer** (Adolf von), **Bunsen** (Robert Wilhelm), **Dalton** (John), **Heeger** (Alan), **Hevesy** (George Charles von), **Liebig** (Justus von), **Miller** (Stanley Lloyd), **Ramsay** (William), **Remsen** (Ira), **Sumner** (James), **Zewail** (Ahmed)
07 **Bergius** (Friedrich), **Buchner** (Eduard), **Faraday** (Michael), **Fischer** (Emil Hermann), **Fischer** (Hans), **Hodgkin** (Dorothy Mary), **Onsager** (Lars), **Pasteur** (Louis), **Pauling** (Linus

Carl), **Scheele** (Carl
Wilhelm), **Seaborg** (Glen
Theodore), **Smalley**
(Richard), **Stanley**
(Wendell)
08 **Avogadro** (Amedeo),
**Chevreul** (Michel Eugène),
**Hoffmann** (Roald),
**Klaproth** (Martin
Heinrich), **Langmuir**
(Irving), **Lonsdale** (Dame
Kathleen), **Mulliken**
(Robert Sanderson),
**Regnault** (Henri Victor),
. **Richards** (Theodore),
**Sidgwick** (Nevil Vincent),
**Svedberg** (Theodor),
**Tiselius** (Arne Wilhelm
Kaurin), **Woodward**
(Robert)
09 **Arrhenius** (Svante August),
**Baekeland** (Leo Hendrik),
**Berzelius** (Jöns Jacob),
**Cavendish** (Henry),
**Lavoisier** (Antoine
Laurent), **Priestley**
(Joseph), **Prigogine** (Ilya)
10 **Mendeleyev** (Dmitri)
12 **Boussingault** (Jean Baptiste
Joseph)
➤ See also SCIENTIST

**cherish**
04 love
05 adore, nurse, prize, value
06 foster, harbor
07 care for, nurture, shelter,
support, sustain
08 hold dear, treasure
09 entertain, look after

**cherub**
05 angel
06 seraph

**cherubic**
04 cute
05 sweet
06 lovely
07 angelic, lovable
08 adorable, heavenly, innocent,
seraphic

**chess**

───────────────

➤ *Names of chess players*:
03 **Tal** (Mikhail)
04 **Euwe** (Max)
05 **Short** (Nigel)
06 **Karpov** (Anatoly), **Lasker**
(Emmanuel), **Polgar** (Judit),
**Polgar** (Zsuzsa), **Timman**
(Jan)
07 **Fischer** (Bobby), **Spassky**
(Boris)
08 **Alekhine** (Alexander),

**Deep Blue**, **Kasparov**
(Gary), **Korchnoi** (Viktor),
**Steinitz** (Wilhelm)
09 **Botvinnik** (Mikhail),
**Petrosian** (Tigran)
10 **Capablanca** (José)
➤ See also SPORT

**chest**
03 box
04 case
05 crate, trunk
06 breast, casket, coffer, thorax
07 sternum

**chew**
04 bite, gnaw
05 champ, chomp, munch
06 crunch
09 masticate

❑ **chew over**
06 muse on, ponder
07 weigh up
08 consider, mull over

**chic**
05 smart
06 dapper, modish, trendy
07 à la mode, elegant, stylish
11 fashionable
13 sophisticated

**chicanery**
04 hoax
05 dodge, fraud, guile, wiles
08 artifice, intrigue, trickery
09 deception, duplicity,
sophistry
10 dishonesty, subterfuge
11 deviousness, hoodwinking
13 deceitfulness, double-
dealing, sharp practice

**chicken**

───────────────

► *Breeds of chicken*:
06 Ancona, bantam, Cochin,
Houdan
07 Dorking, Leghorn, Minorca
09 Orpington, Wyandotte
10 Australorp, jungle fowl
12 Plymouth Rock
14 Rhode Island Red
➤ See also ANIMAL; BIRD

**chide**
05 blame, scold
06 berate, rebuke
07 censure, lecture, reprove, tell
off, upbraid
08 admonish, reproach
09 criticize, objurgate,
reprehend, reprimand

**chief**
03 key
04 arch, boss, head, lord, main

05 grand, major, prime, ruler
06 big gun, bigwig, honcho,
leader, master, top dog
07 captain, headman, leading,
premier, primary, supreme,
supremo
08 big noise, big wheel,
dominant, foremost,
governor, overlord, suzerain
09 big cheese, chieftain,
commander, number-one,
president, principal,
uppermost
10 prevailing, ringleader
11 controlling, outstanding,
predominant, supervising

**chiefly**
06 mainly, mostly
07 usually
09 generally, in the main
10 especially, on the whole
11 essentially, principally
13 predominantly
14 for the most part

**child**
03 boy, kid, son, tot
04 baby, brat, girl, tike
05 issue, minor, sprog, youth
06 infant
07 progeny, tiny tot, toddler
08 daughter, juvenile, young
one
09 offspring, youngster
10 adolescent, descendant

**childbirth**
05 labor
07 lying-in, travail
08 delivery
09 maternity, pregnancy
11 confinement, parturition
12 accouchement

**childhood**
05 youth
07 boyhood, infancy
08 babyhood, girlhood,
minority
10 immaturity, schooldays
11 adolescence

**childish**
05 silly
07 babyish, foolish, puerile
08 immature, juvenile
09 frivolous, infantile
13 irresponsible

**childlike**
05 naïve
06 simple
07 artless, natural
08 innocent, trustful, trusting
09 credulous, guileless,
ingenuous

**chill**
03 flu, ice, icy, nip, raw
04 bite, cold, cool, fear
05 bleak, dread, fever, nippy, scare, sharp, virus
06 biting, freeze, shiver, wintry
07 anxiety, depress, iciness, rawness, terrify
08 coldness, cool down, coolness, freezing, frighten
09 crispness, influenza
10 discourage, dishearten
11 refrigerate
12 apprehension

◻**chill out**
05 relax
07 cool out
08 calm down
10 take it easy

**chilly**
03 icy, raw
04 cold, cool
05 aloof, brisk, crisp, fresh, nippy, sharp, stony
06 biting, frigid, wintry
07 distant, hostile
08 freezing
10 unfriendly
11 unwelcoming

**chime**
04 boom, ding, dong, peal, ring, toll
05 clang, sound
06 jingle, strike, tinkle
07 resound
11 reverberate
14 tintinnulate

◻**chime in**
05 agree, blend, cut in, fit in
06 butt in, chip in
09 harmonize, interrupt
10 correspond

**chimera**
05 dream, fancy
07 fantasy, specter
08 delusion, illusion
09 idle fancy, pipe dream
12 will-o'-the-wisp
13 hallucination

**chimney**
04 flue, vent
05 shaft, stack
06 funnel
08 femerell
10 smokestack

**china**
06 dishes, plates
07 ceramic, pottery
08 crockery
09 porcelain, tableware
10 terracotta
11 earthenware

**Chinese calendar**

➤ *Animals which represent years in the Chinese calendar:*
03 dog, pig, rat
04 goat, hare
05 horse, sheep, snake, tiger
06 dragon, monkey, rabbit
07 buffalo, rooster

**chink**
03 cut, gap
04 rift, slit, slot
05 cleft, crack, space, split
06 cavity
07 crevice, fissure, opening
08 aperture

**chip**
04 dent, disk, flaw, gash, nick
05 break, crack, flake, notch, scrap, shard, shred, snick
06 chisel, damage, paring, sliver
07 counter, scratch, shaving
08 break off, fragment, splinter

◻**chip in**
03 pay
04 ante
05 cut in
06 ante up, butt in, donate
07 chime in
09 interpose, interrupt
10 contribute
12 club together
13 make a donation

**chirp**
04 peep, pipe, sing
05 cheep, trill, tweet
06 warble
07 chirrup, twitter, whistle

**chirpy**
03 gay
05 happy, merry, perky
06 blithe, bright, cheery, jaunty
08 cheerful, springly

**chitchat**
04 chat, talk
06 confab, gossip
07 chatter, chinwag
09 small talk, tête-à-tête
10 idle gossip
12 tittle-tattle

**chivalrous**
04 bold
05 brave, noble
06 heroic, polite
07 gallant, valiant
08 gracious
09 courteous, honorable
10 courageous

11 gentlemanly

**chivalry**
05 honor
07 bravery, courage
08 boldness, courtesy
09 gallantry, integrity
10 politeness
11 courtliness, good manners
12 graciousness, truthfulness
15 gentlemanliness

**chivy, chivvy**
03 nag
04 goad, prod, urge
05 annoy, hound, hurry
06 badger, harass, hassle, pester, plague
07 hurry up, torment

**choice**
04 best, fine, plum
05 prime, prize, range
06 option, select
07 picking, special, variety
08 decision, druthers, election, superior, valuable
09 excellent, exclusive, exquisite, first-rate, selection
10 first-class, preference

**choke**
03 bar, dam, gag
04 clog, plug, stop
05 block, close, cough, retch
06 stifle
07 congest, occlude, smother
08 strangle, suppress, throttle
09 constrict, suffocate
10 asphyxiate

◻**choke back**
04 curb
05 check
07 control, inhibit, repress
08 restrain, suppress
09 fight back

**choleric**
05 angry, fiery, testy
06 crabby, touchy
08 petulant
09 crotchety, irascible, irritable
11 bad-tempered

**choose**
04 pick, take, want, wish
05 adopt, elect, favor, fix on, go for
06 decide, desire, opt for, prefer, see fit, select
07 appoint, espouse, pick out
08 plump for, settle on
09 designate, single out

**choosy**
05 fussy, picky
07 finicky

08 exacting
09 selective
10 fastidious, particular
11 persnickety
14 discriminating

**chop**
02 ax
03 cut, hew, lop, saw
04 fell, hack
05 carve, sever, slash, slice, split
06 cleave, divide
07 dissect
08 truncate

▢**chop up**
03 cut
04 cube, dice
05 grate, mince, shred, slice
06 divide, hackle

**choppy**
04 wavy
05 rough
06 broken, stormy, uneven
07 ruffled, squally
08 blustery
09 turbulent
11 tempestuous

**chore**
03 job
04 duty, task
06 burden, errand

**choreographer**

▶ *Names of choreographers*:
04 **Page** (Ruth)
05 **Cohan** (Robert), **Dolin**
(Anton), **Fosse** (Bob), **Jooss**
(Kurt), **Laban** (Rudolf von),
**Lifar** (Serge), **Shawn** (Ted),
**Tharp** (Twyla)
06 **Ashton** (Frederick), **Cranko**
(John), **Davies** (Siobhan),
**Duncan** (Isadora), **Fokine**
(Michel), **Graham**
(Martha), **Morris** (Mark),
**Petipa** (Marius), **Wigman**
(Mary)
07 **de Mille** (Agnes George),
**Joffrey** (Robert), **Massine**
(Léonide), **Robbins**
(Jerome)
08 **Berkeley** (Busby),
**Champion** (Gower), **de
Valois** (Ninette), **Humphrey**
(Doris), **Nijinska**
(Bronislava), **Nikolais**
(Alwin)
09 **Macmillan** (Kenneth)
10 **Balanchine** (George)
11 **Baryshnikov** (Mikhail),
**Littlefield** (Catherine)
➤ See also BALLET; DANCE;

DANCER

**chortle**
04 crow
05 laugh, snort
06 cackle, guffaw
07 chuckle, snigger

**chorus**
05 choir, shout
06 unison
07 refrain, singers
08 ensemble, response
09 vocalists
10 choristers

**christen**
03 dub
04 call, name, term
05 style, title
07 baptize
09 designate
10 begin using, inaugurate

**Christmas**
04 Noel, Xmas, Yule
08 Nativity, Yuletide

**chronic**
05 awful
08 constant, dreadful, habitual,
long-term, terrible
09 appalling, atrocious,
confirmed, continual,
incessant, recurring
10 deep-rooted, deep-seated,
inveterate, persistent

**chronicle**
04 epic, list, saga, tell
05 diary, enter, story
06 annals, record, relate, report
07 account, history, journal,
narrate, recount, set down
08 archives, calendar, register
09 narrative, write down

**chronicler**
06 scribe
07 diarist
08 annalist, narrator, reporter
09 archivist, historian
11 chronologer
13 chronographer
15 historiographer

**chronological**
06 serial
07 in order, ordered
10 historical, sequential
11 consecutive, progressive

**chubby**
03 fat
04 full
05 plump, podgy, pudgy, round,
stout, tubby
06 flabby, fleshy, portly, rotund

07 paunchy
08 roly-poly

**chuck**
03 shy
04 dump, food, hurl, jilt, quit,
toss
05 fling, pitch, sling, throw
06 give up, pack in, reject
07 abandon, discard, forsake
08 get rid of, jettison
12 give the elbow
15 give the brushoff

**chuckle**
04 crow
05 laugh, snort
06 cackle, giggle, titter
07 chortle, snigger

**chum**
03 pal
04 mate
05 buddy, crony
06 friend
07 comrade
09 companion

**chummy**
04 cozy
05 close, thick
08 friendly, intimate, sociable
10 buddy-buddy

**chunk**
04 hunk, lump, mass, slab
05 block, piece, wedge
06 dollop
07 portion

**church**
04 cult, sect
05 abbey
06 bethel, chapel, shrine
07 chantry, minster
09 cathedral, tradition
10 house of God, tabernacle
12 congregation, meeting-
house
13 house of prayer
14 place of worship

▶ *Parts of a church or
cathedral*:
03 pew
04 apse, arch, font, loft, nave,
rood, slip
05 aisle, altar, choir, crypt,
porch, slype, spire, stall,
stoup, tower, vault
06 arcade, belfry, chapel, parvis,
portal, pulpit, sedile, shrine,
squint, vestry
07 almonry, chancel, frontal,
gallery, lectern, narthex,
piscina, reredos, steeple
08 cloister, credence, crossing,

keystone, pinnacle, predella, sacristy, transept
09 baptistry, bell tower, sanctuary, triforium
10 ambulatory, baptistery, bell screen, clerestory, fenestella, presbytery, rood screen
12 confessional
➤ See also RELIGION

**churlish**
04 rude
05 harsh, rough, surly
06 morose, oafish, sullen
07 boorish, brusque, crabbed, ill-bred, loutish, uncivil
08 impolite
10 unmannerly, unsociable
11 bad-tempered, ill-mannered, ill-tempered
12 discourteous

**churn**
04 beat, boil, foam, puke, toss, turn
05 froth, heave, retch, swirl
06 seethe
07 agitate

**chute**
04 ramp
05 shaft, slide, slope
06 funnel, gutter, runway, trough
07 channel, incline
09 waterfall

**cigarette**
03 cig, fag
04 butt, stub, weed
05 cigar, joint, smoke, whiff
06 fag end, low-tar, reefer, spliff
07 high-tar, menthol, regular
08 king-size
09 filter tip
10 coffin nail

**cinch**
04 snip
06 breeze, stroll
08 cakewalk, duck soup, kid stuff, pushover, walkover
10 child's play
11 piece of cake

**cinders**
04 coke, slag
05 ashes
06 embers
07 clinker
08 charcoal

**cinema**
05 films
06 flicks, movies
09 big screen, multiplex
11 picture show
12 movie theater, silver screen

**cipher**
03 zip
04 code, zero
05 aught, ought, zilch
06 naught, nobody, nought, yes man
08 goose egg
09 nonentity
10 cryptogram
11 cryptograph
12 coded message

**circle**
03 set
04 band, belt, club, coil, gang, gird, loop, obit, ring, turn, wind
05 crowd, group, pivot, whirl
06 clique, gyrate, rotate, swivel
07 company, coterie, enclose, envelop, revolve
08 assembly, encircle, surround
09 encompass
10 fellowship, fraternity, move around

---

► *Types of circles:*
03 lap, orb
04 ball, band, belt, coil, curl, disk, eddy, halo, hoop, loop, oval, ring, tire, turn
05 crown, cycle, globe, orbit, plate, round, wheel
06 cordon, corona, discus, girdle, saucer, sphere, spiral, vortex
07 annulus, circuit, compass, coronet, ellipse

**circuit**
03 lap
04 area, beat, oval, tour
05 ambit, limit, orbit, range, round, route, track
06 bounds, course, region
07 compass
08 boundary, district
09 racetrack
10 revolution
12 running track

**circuitous**
07 devious, oblique, winding
08 indirect, rambling, tortuous
10 meandering, roundabout
12 labyrinthine, periphrastic

**circular**
04 bill
05 flier, flyer, round
06 letter, notice
07 annular, leaflet
08 handbill, pamphlet
09 spherical
10 disk-shaped, ring-shaped
12 announcement

13 advertisement

**circulate**
04 flow
05 issue, swirl, whirl
06 gyrate, rotate, spread
07 diffuse, give out, publish, revolve
08 go around, transmit
09 broadcast, get around, propagate, publicize
10 distribute, move around, pass around, promulgate
11 disseminate

**circulation**
04 flow
06 motion, spread
08 circling, movement, rotation
09 blood flow, publicity
10 readership
11 propagation, publication
12 distribution, transmission
13 dissemination

**circumference**
03 rim
04 edge
05 girth, verge
06 border, bounds, fringe, limits, margin
07 circuit, outline
08 boundary, confines
09 extremity, perimeter, periphery

**circumlocution**
08 pleonasm
09 euphemism, prolixity, tautology, verbosity, wordiness
10 redundancy
11 convolution, diffuseness, periphrasis
12 indirectness

**circumlocutory**
05 wordy
06 prolix
07 diffuse, verbose
08 indirect
09 redundant
10 convoluted, discursive, pleonastic, roundabout
11 euphemistic
12 periphrastic, tautological

**circumscribe**
03 bar
05 bound, hem in, limit, pen in
06 define, hamper
07 confine, curtail, delimit, enclose
08 encircle, restrain, restrict, surround
09 delineate, demarcate, encompass

## circumspect
04 wary, wise
05 canny, chary
07 careful, guarded, prudent
08 cautious, discreet, watchful
09 attentive, judicious, observant, sagacious

## circumspection
04 care
07 caution
08 prudence, wariness
09 canniness, chariness, vigilance
10 discretion

## circumstance
03 lot
04 case, fact, fate, item
05 event, means, state, thing
06 detail, factor, plight, status
07 element, fortune, respect
08 position
09 condition, happening, lifestyle, resources, situation
10 background, occurrence
11 arrangement, environment

## circumstantial
07 deduced, hearsay
08 indirect, presumed
10 contingent, evidential, incidental
11 conjectural, inferential, presumptive, provisional

## circumvent
05 avoid, evade
06 bypass, outwit, thwart
07 get past
08 get out of, sidestep
09 get around
12 steer clear of

## cistern
03 sac, vat
04 sink, tank
05 basin
06 cavity
09 reservoir

## citadel
04 keep
05 tower
06 castle
07 bastion
08 fortress
09 acropolis
10 stronghold
13 fortification

## citation
05 award, honor, quote
06 notice, source
07 mention, passage, summons, tribute
09 quotation, reference

12 commendation, illustration

## cite
04 name
05 quote
06 adduce
07 advance, bring up, mention, refer to, specify
08 allude to, evidence
09 enumerate, exemplify

## citizen
05 local, towny, voter
06 towner
07 burgess, burgher, denizen, freeman, oppidan, subject
08 national, resident, taxpayer, townsman, urbanite
10 inhabitant, townswoman
11 city-dweller

## city
04 town
05 civic, urban
06 ghetto
08 downtown, precinct, suburbia
09 inner city, urban area
10 city center, cosmopolis, metropolis
11 conurbation, megalopolis, urban sprawl
12 municipality
14 concrete jungle

▶ *Names of ancient cities:*
02 Ur
04 Susa, Troy, Tula, Tyre, Uruk
05 Aksum, Bosra, Copán, Hatra, Huari, Mitla, Moche, Petra, Tikal, Uxmal
06 Byblos, Jamnia, Nippur, Sardis, Shiloh, Thebes, Ugarit
07 Babylon, Ephesus, Miletus, Mycenae, Nineveh, Pompeii, Samaria, Sybaris
08 Pergamon, Pergamum
09 Byzantium
10 Carchemish, Heliopolis, Hierapolis, Persepolis
13 Halicarnassus

▶ *Names of capital cities:*
04 Apia, Baku, Bern, Doha, Kiev, Lima, Lomé, Malé, Oslo, Riga, Rome, San'a, Suva
05 Abuja, Accra, Amman, Berne, Cairo, Dacca, Dakar, Dhaka, Hanoi, Kabul, Koror, La Paz, Minsk, Paris, Praia, Quito, Rabat, Seoul, Sofia, Sucre, Tokyo, Tunis, Vaduz
06 Akmola, Ankara, Asmara, Athens, Bamako, Bangui, Banjul, Beirut, Berlin, Bissau,

Bogotá, Dodoma, Dublin, Harare, Havana, Kigali, Lisbon, London, Luanda, Lusaka, Madrid, Majuro, Malabo, Manama, Manila, Maputo, Maseru, Moroni, Moscow, Muscat, Nassau, Niamey, Ottawa, Peking, Prague, Riyadh, Roseau, Skopje, Taipei, Tarawa, Tehran, Tirana, Vienna, Warsaw, Yangon, Zagreb
07 Abidjan, Algiers, Alma-Ata, Baghdad, Bangkok, Beijing, Belfast, Bishkek, Caracas, Cardiff, Cayenne, Colombo, Conakry, Godthab, Honiara, Jakarta, Kampala, Managua, Mbabane, Nairobi, Nicosia, Palikir, Papeete, Rangoon, San José, San Juan, St. John's, Tallinn, Tbilisi, Teheran, Thimphu, Tripoli, Valetta, Vilnius, Yaoundé, Yerevan
08 Abu Dhabi, Asunción, Belgrade, Belmopan, Brasília, Brussels, Budapest, Canberra, Cape Town, Castries, Chisinau, Damascus, Djibouti, Dushanbe, Freetown, Gaborone, Helsinki, Khartoum, Kingston, Kinshasa, Kishinev, Lilongwe, Monrovia, Ndjamena, New Delhi, Port-Vila, Pretoria, Santiago, Sarajevo, São Tomé, Tashkent, The Hague, Tórshavn, Victoria, Windhoek
09 Amsterdam, Ashkhabad, Bucharest, Bujumbura, Edinburgh, Fongafale, Islamabad, Jerusalem, Kathmandu, Kingstown, Ljubljana, Mogadishu, Nuku'alofa, Phnom Penh, Port Louis, Porto Novo, Pyongyang, Reykjavík, San Marino, Singapore, St. George's, Stockholm, Ulan Bator, Vientiane
10 Addis Ababa, Basseterre, Bratislava, Bridgetown, Copenhagen, Georgetown, Kuwait City, Libreville, Luxembourg, Mexico City, Montevideo, Nouakchott, Panama City, Paramaribo, Wellington, Willemstad
11 Brazzaville, Buenos Aires, Kuala Lumpur, Monaco-Ville, Ouagadougou, Port Moresby, Port of Spain, San

Salvador, Tegucigalpa, Vatican City

12 Antananarivo, Fort-de-France, Port-au-Prince, Santo Domingo, Washington DC, Yamoussoukro

13 Guatemala City

17 Bandar Seri Begawan

▶ *Names of towns and cities:*

02 Bo

03 Åbo, Ayr, Ely, Fès, Fez, Gao, Hué, Lae, Nis, Pau, Qom, Ufa, Ulm, Vac, Zug

04 Acre, Aden, Agra, Bari, Bath, Bonn, Brno, Bury, Caen, Cali, Cebu, Como, Cork, Deal, Edam, Elat, Eton, Faro, Gent, Gifu, Graz, Györ, Homs, Hove, Hull, Iasi, Icel, Ipoh, Jima, Jixi, Kano, Kiel, Kobe, Kota, Köln, León, Linz, Lódz, Lund, Lvov, Metz, Mold, Mons, Naha, Nara, Nice, Oban, Oita, Omsk, Oran, Pegu, Perm, Pécs, Pisa, Rand, Reno, Rhyl, Ruse, Ryde, Safi, Sian, Sion, Soul, Suez, Tema, Thun, Tula, Tyre, Vasa, Vigo, Waco, Wick, Wien, Wuhu, Wuxi, Xi'an, York, Zibo

05 Adana, Ahvaz, Al Ayn, Aosta, Aqaba, Argos, Arles, Arras, Aspen, Aswan, Ávila, Åland, Århus, Baden, Banff, Baoji, Basle, Basra, Beira, Belém, Benxi, Blyth, Boise, Bondi, Breda, Brest, Bursa, Busan, Cádiz, Chiba, Chita, Colón, Conwy, Cowes, Crewe, Cuzco, Davao, Davos, Delft, Delhi, Derby, Dijon, Dover, Duala, Dubai, Dukou, Eilat, Essen, Fiume, Frome, Fuxin, Genoa, Ghent, Gomel, Gorky, Gouda, Haifa, Halle, Hefei, Hohot, Honan, Iwaki, Izmir, Jaffa, Jedda, Jilin, Jinan, Kandy, Karaj, Kazan, Kelso, Kirov, Kitwe, Kochi, Konya, Kursk, Kyoto, Lagos, Leeds, Lewes, Lhasa, Liège, Lille, Luton, Luxor, Lyons, Mainz, Malmö, Masan, Mâcon, Mecca, Medan, Miami, Milan, Mopti, Mosul, Namur, Nancy, Natal, Ndola, Nîmes, Omagh, Omaha, Omiya, Oryol, Osaka, Otley, Oujda, Padua, Parma, Patna, Pavia, Penza, Perth, Poole, Poona, Pusan, Reims, Ripon, Rouen, Rugby, Sakai, Salem, Sidon,

Siena, Sochi, Split, Suita, Surat, Suwon, Taegu, Tampa, Thane, Tomsk, Tours, Trier, Troon, Truro, Tulsa, Turin, Turku, Ulsan, Urawa, Utica, Vaasa, Varna, Wells, Wigan, Worms, Wuhan, Ypres, Zarqa

06 Aachen, Aarhus, Agadir, Albany, Aleppo, Amiens, Annecy, Anshan, Arezzo, Armagh, Arnhem, Ashdod, Austin, Bangor, Baotou, Bengpu, Bergen, Bhopal, Bilbao, Biloxi, Bochum, Bolton, Bombay, Bootle, Boston, Brasov, Bremen, Bruges, Brugge, Burgos, Buxton, Cairns, Calais, Callao, Camden, Campos, Cannes, Canton, Carlow, Chonju, Cochin, Cracow, Crosby, Dalian, Dallas, Danzig, Daqing, Darwin, Datong, Dayton, Denver, Dieppe, Douala, Dudley, Duluth, Dundee, Durban, Durham, El Gîza, El Paso, Eugene, Evreux, Exeter, Fatima, Fresno, Fushun, Fuzhou, Galway, Gdansk, Geneva, Grozny, Guelph, Gujrat, Handan, Harbin, Harlem, Harlow, Hebron, Hegang, Himeji, Hobart, Howrah, Ibadan, Inchon, Indore, Jaffna, Jaipur, Jarrow, Jeddah, Jiddah, Juneau, Kaluga, Kanpur, Kassel, Kaunas, Kendal, Khulna, Kirkby, Kirkuk, Kosice, Kraków, Kurgan, Lahore, Lanark, Le Mans, Leiden, Leuven, Leyden, Lublin, Ludlow, Lugano, Lübeck, Málaga, Maceio, Madras, Malang, Manaus, Meknès, Meshed, Mobile, Mukden, Multan, Munich, Murcia, Mysore, Nablus, Nagano, Nagoya, Nagpur, Nantes, Napier, Naples, Narvik, Newark, Ningbo, Odessa, Oldham, Oporto, Osasco, Ostend, Oviedo, Oxford, Padang, Paphos, Phuket, Pierre, Pilsen, Potosí, Poznan, Puebla, Quebec, Raipur, Rajkat, Ranchi, Recife, Redcar, Reggio, Regina, Rennes, Rheims, Saigon, Santos, Sendai, Shiraz, Slough, Smyrna, Soweto, Sparta, St. Ives, St. John, St.

Malo, St. Paul, Stroud, Suzhou, Sydney, Szeged, Tabriz, Tacoma, Taejon, Tainan, Tamale, Tambov, Tarsus, Thurso, Tobruk, Toledo, Topeka, Torbay, Toulon, Toyama, Toyota, Tralee, Trento, Treves, Tubruq, Tucson, Urumqi, Vargas, Venice, Verona, Viborg, Weimar, Whitby, Widnes, Woking, Xining, Xuzhou, Yeovil, Yichun, Zurich

07 Aberfan, Airdrie, Aligarh, Alnwick, Antibes, Antioch, Antwerp, Atlanta, Augusta, Auxerre, Avignon, Baalbek, Badajoz, Banares, Banbury, Bandung, Bedford, Beeston, Benares, Bendigo, Bergamo, Bexhill, Blarney, Bologna, Boulder, Brescia, Bristol, Buffalo, Burnley, Calgary, Calicut, Catania, Cheadle, Cheddar, Chelsea, Cheng-tu, Chengdu, Chester, Chicago, Chungho, Coblenz, Coimbra, Cologne, Concord, Corinth, Corunna, Córdoba, Crawley, Detroit, Devizes, Donetsk, Douglas, Dresden, Dundalk, Dunedin, Dunkirk, Entebbe, Esfahan, Evesham, Exmouth, Falkirk, Fareham, Ferrara, Fukuoka, Glasgow, Goiânia, Gosport, Granada, Grimsby, Guiyang, Gwalior, Gwangju, Halifax, Hamburg, Hamhung, Hanover, Harwich, Houston, Huainan, Ipswich, Iquique, Iquitos, Irkutsk, Izhevsk, Jackson, Jericho, Jinzhou, Jodhpur, Kalinin, Karachi, Kayseri, Kenitra, Keswick, Kharkov, Kherson, Koblenz, Kunming, La Plata, Lanzhou, Larnaca, Latakia, Le Havre, Leghorn, Leipzig, Lerwick, Limoges, Lincoln, Liuzhou, Livorno, Louvain, Lucerne, Lucknow, Luoyang, Madison, Madurai, Malvern, Maracay, Marburg, Margate, Mashhad, Matlock, Matsudo, Memphis, Mendoza, Mogilev, Mombasa, Morpeth, Münster, Nanjing, Nanking, Nanning, New York, Newbury, Newport, Newquay, Norfolk, Norwich, Novi Sad, Oakland, Okayama, Okinawa,

Olympia, Orlando, Orleans,
Paisley, Palermo, Peebles,
Penrith, Perugia, Phoenix,
Piraeus, Pistoia, Plovdiv,
Poltava, Potsdam, Preston,
Prizren, Raleigh, Ravenna,
Reading, Redwood, Reigate,
Roanoke, Rosario, Rostock,
Runcorn, Salamis, Salerno,
Salford, Sandown, Santa Fe,
Sapporo, Saratov, Seattle,
Segovia, Seville, Shannon,
Songnam, Spokane, Spoleto,
St. Denis, St. Louis, Staines,
Stanley, Sudbury, Swansea,
Swindon, Taiyuan, Tangier,
Taunton, Tel Aviv, Telford,
Tianjin, Tijuana, Tilbury,
Toronto, Torquay, Tournai,
Trenton, Trieste, Uppsala,
Utrecht, Ventnor, Vicenza,
Vitebsk, Walsall, Warwick,
Watford, Wexford, Wichita,
Windsor, Wrexham,
Wroclaw, Yonkers, Zwickau

08 Aberdeen, Acapulco,
Adelaide, Alicante, Amarillo,
Amritsar, Arbroath,
Auckland, Augsburg,
Aviemore, Ayia Napa,
Bareilly, Barnsley, Bathurst,
Bayreuth, Beauvais,
Belgorod, Benghazi,
Benidorm, Besançon,
Biarritz, Bismarck, Blantyre,
Bordeaux, Boulogne,
Bradford, Braganza, Brighton,
Brindisi, Brisbane, Bulawayo,
Burgundy, Cagliari, Calcutta,
Carlisle, Changsha, Chartres,
Chemnitz, Chepstow,
Cheyenne, Clevedon,
Columbia, Columbus,
Coventry, Curitiba, Dartford,
Dearborn, Djakarta,
Dortmund, Drogheda,
Duisburg, Dumfries,
Dunleary, Ebbw Vale,
Edmonton, Elsinore,
Europort, Falmouth,
Florence, Flushing, Freeport,
Fribourg, Fukuyama,
Grantham, Grasmere,
Greenock, Grenoble,
Guernica, Haiphong,
Hamilton, Hangzhou,
Hannover, Hartford,
Hastings, Hereford, Hertford,
Holyhead, Holywell, Hong
Kong, Honolulu, Iowa City,
Istanbul, Jabalpur, Kandahar,
Karlsbad, Katowice,
Kawasaki, Kilkenny, Kirkwall,

Kismaayo, Klosters,
Konstanz, Las Vegas,
Lausanne, Legoland,
Limassol, Limerick, Longford,
Makassar, Mandalay,
Mannheim, Marbella,
Medellín, Mercedes,
Montreal, Montreux,
Montrose, Mulhouse,
Murmansk, Nagasaki,
Nanchang, Nazareth, New
Haven, Newhaven,
Novgorod, Nuneaton,
Nürnberg, Oak Ridge,
Omdurman, Oostende,
Oswestry, Pago Pago,
Pamplona, Pasadena,
Penzance, Peshawar,
Piacenza, Plymouth, Poitiers,
Port Said, Portland, Portrush,
Pristina, Ramsgate, Redditch,
Richmond, Rochdale,
Rockford, Roskilde, Rosslare,
Salonica, Salonika, Salvador,
Salzburg, San Diego, Santa
Ana, Savannah, São Luis,
Schwerin, Shanghai,
Shanklin, Shenyang,
Sholapur, Skegness,
Smolensk, Solihull,
Southend, Srinagar, St.
Albans, St. David's, St. Gallen,
St. Helens, St. Helier, St.
Moritz, St.-Tropez, Stafford,
Stamford, Stirling, Stockton,
Strabane, Surabaya, Swan
Hill, Syracuse, Taganrog,
Taichung, Tamworth,
Tangshan, Teesside, Teresina,
Thetford, Tiberias, Timbuktu,
Titograd, Toulouse, Trujillo,
Tübingen, Ullapool,
Vadodara, Valencia, Varanasi,
Veracruz, Vila Real, Vittoria,
Vladimir, Voronezh, Wallasey,
Wallsend, Weymouth,
Winnipeg, Worthing,
Würzburg, Yokohama,
Yorktown, Zakopane,
Zanzibar

09 Ahmadabad, Albufeira,
Aldershot, Algeciras,
Allahabad, Ambleside,
Anchorage, Annapolis,
Archangel, Astrakhan,
Audenarde, Aylesbury,
Baltimore, Bangalore,
Barcelona, Beersheba,
Bethlehem, Blackburn,
Blackpool, Botany Bay,
Brunswick, Cambridge,
Cartagena, Castlebar,
Changchun, Charleroi,

Charlotte, Cherbourg,
Chernobyl, Chiang Mai,
Chihuahua, Chongqing,
Chungking, Cleveland,
Colwyn Bay, Constance, Des
Moines, Doncaster,
Dordrecht, Dubrovnik,
Dumbarton, Dungannon,
Dunstable, Eastleigh,
Eindhoven, Esztergom,
Fairbanks, Famagusta,
Fishguard, Fleetwood, Fort
Worth, Frankfort, Frankfurt,
Fremantle, Galveston,
Gateshead, Gaziantep, Gold
Coast, Gravesend,
Greenwich, Groningen,
Guayaquil, Guildford,
Harrogate, Haslemere,
Heraklion, Hiroshima,
Humpty Doo, Hyderabad,
Immingham, Innsbruck,
Inverness, Ismailiya,
Jamestown, Johnstone,
Kamchatka, Karlsruhe,
Killarney, Kimberley, King's
Lynn, Kirkcaldy, Kisangani,
Kuybyshev, Lancaster,
Leicester, Lexington,
Lichfield, Liverpool,
Llangefni, Long Beach,
Lowestoft, Lymington,
Magdeburg, Maidstone,
Mansfield, Maracaibo,
Marrakesh, Melbourne,
Middleton, Milwaukee,
Monterrey, Morecambe,
Nashville, Neuchâtel,
Newcastle, Newmarket,
Nuremberg, Osnabrück,
Palembang, Perpignan,
Peterhead, Port Natal, Port
Sudan, Pressburg, Prestwick,
Princeton, Riverside,
Rochester, Rotherham,
Rotterdam, Salisbury,
Samarkand, San Miguel,
Santa Cruz, Santander,
Saragossa, Saskatoon, São
Paulo, Sheerness, Sheffield,
Sioux City, South Bend,
Southport, Southwark, St.
Andrews, St.-Étienne, St.-
Quentin, Stavanger,
Stavropol, Stevenage,
Stockport, Stornoway,
Stranraer, Stuttgart,
Tarragona, Timisoara,
Toamasina, Trondheim,
Tullamore, Vancouver,
Vicksburg, Volgograd,
Wakefield, Walvis Bay,
Waterford, Wiesbaden,

Wimbledon, Wolfsburg,
Worcester, Wuppertal,
Yaroslavl, Zhengzhou

10 Addis Ababa, Alexandria,
Baton Rouge, Belize City,
Birkenhead, Birmingham,
Bridgeport, Bridgwater,
Broken Hill, Caernarvon,
Caerphilly, Canterbury,
Carmarthen, Carnoustie,
Carson City, Casablanca,
Chandigarh, Charleston,
Chelmsford, Cheltenham,
Chichester, Chittagong,
Cincinnati, Colchester,
Concepción, Darjeeling,
Darlington, Dorchester,
Düsseldorf, Eastbourne,
Faisalabad, Felixstowe,
Folkestone, Fray Bentos,
Galashiels, George Town,
Gillingham, Glenrothes,
Gloucester, Goose Green,
Gothenburg, Haddington,
Harrisburg, Hartlepool,
Heidelberg, Hildesheim,
Huntingdon, Huntsville,
Kansas City, Kenilworth,
Kilmarnock, Kompong Som,
Lake Placid, Launceston,
Leeuwarden, Letchworth,
Linlithgow, Little Rock,
Livingston, Llangollen, Los
Angeles, Louisville,
Lubumbashi, Maastricht,
Maidenhead, Manchester,
Marseilles, Medjugorje,
Miami Beach, Monte Carlo,
Montego Bay, Montgomery,
Montpelier, Motherwell,
New Orleans, Nottingham,
Nova Iguacu, Oudenaarde,
Palmerston, Petersburg,
Pittsburgh, Pontefract,
Portishead, Portsmouth,
Providence, Quezon City,
Rawalpindi, Regensburg,
Sacramento, San Antonio,
San Ignacio, Scunthorpe,
Sebastopol, Shepparton,
Shreveport, Shrewsbury,
Sioux Falls, Strasbourg,
Sunderland, Sverdlovsk,
Tananarive, Thunder Bay,
Townsville, Trivandrum,
Trowbridge, Valladolid,
Valparaíso, Wagga Wagga,
Warrington, Washington,
Whitehorse, Wilmington,
Winchester, Windermere,
Winterthur, Wittenberg,
Wollongong, Workington,
Yogyakarta

11 Aberystwyth, Albuquerque,
Basingstoke, Bognor Regis,
Bournemouth, Brandenburg,
Bremerhaven, Bridlington,
Broadstairs, Brownsville,
Carcassonne, Charlestown,
Chattanooga, Cirencester,
Cleethorpes, Cockermouth,
Coney Island, Conisbrough,
Constantine, Cumbernauld,
Dar es Salaam, Downpatrick,
Dunfermline, Enniskillen,
Farnborough, Fort William,
Francistown, Fraserburgh,
Fredericton, Glastonbury,
Grangemouth, Guadalajara,
High Wycombe, Juan-les-
Pins, Kaliningrad,
Londonderry, Lossiemouth,
Medicine Hat, Minneapolis,
Montpellier, New York City,
Northampton, Novosibirsk,
Palm Springs, Pointe-Noire,
Port Augusta, Prestonpans,
Punta Arenas, Rockhampton,
Rostov-on-Don,
Scarborough, Southampton,
Spanish Town, Springfield,
Stourbridge, Tallahassee,
Trincomalee, Vladivostok,
Westminster, White Plains,
Yellowknife

12 Alice Springs, Atlantic City,
Barranquilla, Beverly Hills,
Bloemfontein, Chesterfield,
Christchurch, East Kilbride,
Great Malvern, Huddersfield,
Indianapolis, Jacksonville,
Johannesburg, Kota
Kinabalu, Loughborough,
Luang Prabang,
Macclesfield, Magnitogorsk,
Milton Keynes, New
Amsterdam, Oklahoma City,
Peterborough, Philadelphia,
Port Harcourt, Rio de Janeiro,
Salt Lake City, San Francisco,
Santa Barbara, Skelmersdale,
South Shields, St. Petersburg,
Stoke-on-Trent, Tel Aviv-Jaffa,
Tennant Creek, Thessaloníki,
Trichinopoly, West
Bromwich, Williamsburg,
Winston-Salem

13 Aix-en-Provence,
Charlottetown, Ellesmere
Port, Epsom and Ewell, Great
Yarmouth, Ho Chi Minh City,
Jefferson City, Kidderminster,
Kirkcudbright, Kirkintilloch,
Leamington Spa, Lytham St
Anne's, Middlesbrough, Port
Elizabeth, Semipalatinsk,

Sihanoukville, Virginia Beach,
Wolverhampton,
Yekaterinburg

14 Andorra-la-Vella,
Elisabethville, Hemel
Hempstead, Henley-on-
Thames, Santiago de Cuba,
Stockton-on-Tees, Tunbridge
Wells

15 Barrow-in-Furness, Burton-
upon-Trent, Charlottesville,
Chester-le-Street, Clermont-
Ferrand, Colorado Springs,
Frankfurt am Main, Nizhniy
Novgorod, Palma de
Mallorca, Sutton Coldfield,
Weston-super-Mare

## civic
04 city
05 local, urban
06 public
07 borough
08 communal, suburban
09 community, municipal
12 metropolitan

## civil
04 home
05 civic, local, state
06 polite, public, urbane
07 affable, courtly, refined,
secular
08 domestic, interior, internal,
mannerly, national, obliging,
polished, well-bred
09 courteous, municipal
10 cultivated, respectful
11 complaisant
12 well-mannered
13 accommodating

## civility
04 tact
06 comity
07 amenity, manners, respect
08 breeding, courtesy, urbanity
10 affability, politeness,
refinement
11 good manners
12 graciousness, pleasantness
13 courteousness

## civilization
07 culture, society
08 progress, urbanity
09 community, education
10 refinement
11 advancement, cultivation
13 enlightenment
14 sophistication

## civilize
04 tame
06 polish, refine
07 educate, improve, perfect

08 humanize, instruct
09 cultivate, enlighten, socialize
12 sophisticate

**civilized**
06 polite, urbane
07 refined
08 advanced, cultured, educated, sensible, sociable
09 developed
10 cultivated, reasonable
11 enlightened
13 sophisticated

**clad**
07 attired, clothed, covered, dressed, wearing
05 claim
03 ask
04 aver, avow, call, hold, kill, need, take
05 cause, exact, right, stake, state
06 allege, assert, assume, avowal, demand, insist
07 collect, contend, deserve, pretend, profess, purport, request, require
08 averment, maintain
09 assertion, postulate
10 allegation, contention, insistence, pretension
11 affirmation, application, declaration, entitlement, requirement, requisition

**claimant**
08 litigant
09 applicant, candidate, pretender, suppliant
10 petitioner, pretendant, supplicant

**clairvoyance**
03 ESP
09 telepathy
13 psychic powers
14 fortune-telling

**clairvoyant**
04 seer
05 augur
06 oracle
07 diviner, prophet, psychic
08 telepath
09 prophetic, visionary
10 prophetess, soothsayer
12 extrasensory
13 fortuneteller

**clamber**
04 claw, shin
05 climb, crawl, mount, scale
06 ascend, shinny
08 scrabble, scramble

**clammy**
04 damp, dank
05 close, moist, muggy, slimy
06 sticky, sweaty

**clamorous**
05 lusty, noisy
07 blaring, riotous
08 vehement
09 deafening, insistent
10 tumultuous, vociferous

**clamor**
03 din
04 urge
05 blare, noise
06 demand, hubbub, insist, outcry, racket, uproar
09 agitation, commotion
12 vociferation

**clamp**
03 fix
04 grip, hold, vice
05 brace, clasp, press
06 clench, clinch, fasten, secure
07 bracket, squeeze

❑**clamp down on**
04 stop
05 limit
07 confine, control
08 restrain, restrict, suppress
10 put a stop to
11 crack down on
14 come down hard on

**clan**
03 mob, set
04 band, folk, line, race, sect, sept
05 group, house, tribe
06 circle, clique, family
07 coterie, faction, society
10 fraternity
11 brotherhood

**clandestine**
03 sly
06 closet, covert, hidden, secret, sneaky
07 furtive, private
08 backroom, hush-hush, stealthy
09 concealed, underhand
10 fraudulent, undercover
11 underground
13 surreptitious, under-the-table
14 cloak-and-dagger
15 under-the-counter

**clang**
04 bong, peal, ring, toll
05 chime, clank, clash, clunk
06 jangle
07 clatter, resound

11 reverberate

**clank**
04 ring, toll
05 clang, clash, clunk
06 jangle
07 clatter, resound
11 reverberate

**clannish**
06 cliquy, narrow, select, tribal
07 cliquey, insular
08 cliquish
09 exclusive, parochial
10 unfriendly

**clap**
04 bang, slap
05 cheer, smack, whack
06 strike, wallop
07 acclaim, applaud

**claptrap**
03 rot
04 bull, bunk
05 bilge, hokum, trash, tripe
06 bunkum, drivel, hot air, humbug
07 baloney, blarney, rubbish, twaddle
08 nonsense, tommyrot
09 gibberish, poppycock
10 codswallop

**clarification**
05 gloss
10 definition, exposition
11 elucidation, explanation

**clarify**
05 clear, gloss
06 define, filter, purify, refine
07 clear up, explain, resolve
08 simplify, spell out
09 elucidate, make clear, make plain
10 illuminate
12 throw light on

**clarity**
08 lucidity
09 clearness, plainness, precision, sharpness
10 definition, simplicity
12 explicitness, transparency
15 intelligibility, unambiguousness

**clash**
03 jar, war
04 bang, feud
05 clank, crash, fight, noise
06 differ, jangle, rattle, strike
07 clatter, contend, grapple, quarrel, warring, wrangle
08 coincide, conflict, disagree, fighting, showdown
09 collision, not go with

**clasp**

12 disagreement
13 confrontation

**clasp**

03 hug, pin
04 clip, grip, hasp, hold, hook
05 catch, grasp, press
06 attach, brooch, buckle, clutch, cuddle, enfold, fasten
07 cling to, connect, embrace, grapple, squeeze
08 barrette, fastener

**class**

03 set
04 form, kind, rank, rate, sort, type, year
05 brand, caste, genre, genus, grade, group, order, style
06 course, lesson, period, phylum, sphere, status
07 arrange, lecture, quality, section, seminar, species
08 category, classify, division, elegance, grouping, standing, tutorial, workshop
09 designate
10 background, categorize, department, pigeonhole
11 distinction, social order, stylishness
12 denomination, social status
14 social standing, sophistication

**classic**

04 best, true
05 great, ideal, model, prime
06 finest
07 abiding, ageless, antique, lasting, regular, typical, undying
08 enduring, exemplar, immortal, masterly, standard, timeless
09 brilliant, exemplary, first-rate, prototype
10 archetypal, consummate, definitive, first-class
11 established, masterpiece, outstanding, traditional
12 paradigmatic
14 quintessential

**classical**

04 pure
05 Attic, Latin, plain
07 concert, elegant, Grecian, refined, serious
08 Hellenic
09 excellent, symphonic
10 harmonious, restrained
12 ancient Greek, ancient Roman

**classification**

07 grading, sorting
08 grouping, taxonomy
10 tabulation
11 arrangement, cataloguing
12 codification
14 categorization

**classify**

04 file, rank, sort, type
05 class, grade, group, order
06 codify
07 arrange, dispose
08 tabulate
09 catalogue
10 categorize, pigeonhole
11 systematize

**classy**

04 chic, fine, posh
05 grand, ritzy
06 select, swanky
07 elegant, stylish
08 superior, upmarket
09 exclusive, high-class
13 sophisticated

**clatter**

03 jar
04 bang
05 clang, clank, clunk, crash
06 jangle, rattle, strike

**clause**

04 item, part
05 point, rider
06 phrase
07 article, chapter, heading, passage, proviso, section
08 loophole
09 condition, provision
10 subsection

**claw**

03 rip
04 maul, nail, tear
05 chela, graze, talon
06 mangle, nipper, pincer, scrape, ungual, unguis
07 gripper, scratch
08 lacerate, scrabble

**clean**

04 fair, good, neat, pure, tidy
05 blank, fresh, fully, moral
06 chaste, decent, honest, proper, simple, smooth, unused, washed
07 aseptic, perfect, regular, sterile, totally, upright
08 flawless, hygienic, innocent, purified, sanitary, spotless, straight, unmarked, unsoiled, virtuous
09 faultless, guiltless, honorable, laundered, reputable,

righteous, speckless, unstained, unsullied
10 aboveboard, antiseptic, immaculate, sterilized, unpolluted, upstanding
11 respectable, unblemished, well-defined
12 spick-and-span

**cleaner**

04 maid
07 janitor, sweeper
08 cleanser
09 charwoman
13 window cleaner

**cleanse**

04 wash
05 bathe, clear, purge, rinse
06 purify
07 absolve, deterge
08 lustrate
09 disinfect, sterilize

**cleanser**

04 soap
06 bleach
07 cleaner, scourer, solvent
08 purifier
09 detergent
10 soap powder
12 disinfectant
14 scouring powder

**clear**

03 net, rid
04 earn, fair, fine, free, gain, jump, keen, make, move, open, pass, sure, tidy, wipe
05 allow, bring, clean, empty, erase, let go, light, lucid, plain, quick, sharp, shift, sunny, vault
06 acquit, bright, excuse, glassy, go over, limpid, pardon, patent, permit, refine, remove, unclog, unload, unstop, vacate
07 absolve, approve, audible, bring in, certain, cleanse, evident, logical, obvious, release, unblock
08 apparent, coherent, definite, distinct, evacuate, explicit, get rid of, innocent, jump over, liberate, luminous, manifest, pellucid, sanction, sensible, undimmed
09 authorize, blameless, cloudless, colorless, decongest, exculpate, exonerate, extricate, guiltless, unclouded, vindicate

10 diaphanous, perceptive, pronounced, see-through, unhindered
11 beyond doubt, conspicuous, crystalline, translucent, transparent, unequivocal, well-defined
12 intelligible, recognizable, unmistakable, unobstructed
14 beyond question, comprehensible, give the go-ahead, unquestionable

**clear out**
04 sort, tidy
05 empty, leave, scram
06 beat it, depart, tidy up
07 get lost, push off, skiddoo, sort out
08 clear off, shove off, throw out, withdraw
10 skeddaddle

**clear up**
04 sort, tidy
05 clear, crack, order, solve
06 answer, remove
07 clarify, dope out, explain, improve, iron out, resolve, unravel
08 brighten
09 elucidate, figure out, rearrange
10 brighten up, put in order
13 straighten out

**clearance**
02 OK
03 gap
04 okay, room
05 leave, say-so, space
06 leeway, margin, moving
07 bargain, consent, freeing, go-ahead
08 emptying, headroom, sanction, vacating
09 allowance, unloading
10 demolition, evacuation, green light, permission
11 endorsement
13 authorization

**clear-cut**
05 clear, plain
07 precise
08 definite, distinct, explicit
09 trenchant
11 cut and dried, unambiguous, unequivocal, well-defined
15 straightforward

**clearing**
03 gap
05 glade, space
07 opening

**clearly**
06 openly
07 plainly
08 markedly, patently
09 evidently, obviously
10 distinctly, manifestly, undeniably
11 undoubtedly
12 indisputably, unmistakably, without doubt
13 incontestably

**cleave**
03 cut, hew
04 chop, hold, open, part, rend
05 cling, crack, halve, sever, slice, split, stick, unite
06 adhere, attach, cohere, divide, remain, sunder
08 dissever, disunite, separate

**cleft**
03 gap
04 rent
05 chasm, chink, crack, split
06 breach, cranny
07 crevice, fissure, opening
08 fracture

**clemency**
04 pity
05 mercy
08 leniency, mildness, sympathy
10 compassion, generosity, indulgence, tenderness
11 forbearance, forgiveness, magnanimity

**clench**
04 grip, grit, hold, seal, shut
05 clasp, close, grasp
06 clutch, double, fasten

**clergy**
07 clerics
08 ministry, the cloth
09 churchmen, the church
10 holy orders, priesthood

**clergyman**
04 dean, imam
05 canon, mulla, padre, rabbi, vicar
06 cleric, curate, deacon, divine, father, mullah, parson, pastor, priest, rector
07 muezzin
08 chaplain, man of God, minister, reverend
09 churchman, presbyter
12 ecclesiastic
13 man of the cloth

**clerical**
06 filing, office, typing
08 official, pastoral, priestly
09 canonical, episcopal

10 pen-pushing
11 keyboarding, ministerial, secretarial, white-collar
14 administrative, ecclesiastical

**clerk**
05 steno
06 cleric, notary, scribe, typist, writer
07 copyist
08 official, recorder, salesman
09 assistant, pen-pusher, salesgirl, saleslady, secretary
10 accountant, bookkeeper, salesclerk
11 transcriber
12 notary public, receptionist, stenographer
13 administrator

**clever**
03 apt
04 able, keen
05 quick, sharp, smart, witty
06 adroit, brainy, bright, expert, gifted, shrewd
07 capable, cunning, knowing, sapient
08 rational, sensible, talented
09 brilliant, ingenious, inventive, sagacious
10 discerning, perceptive
11 intelligent, quick-witted, resourceful, sharp-witted
13 knowledgeable

**cliché**
06 truism
07 bromide
08 banality, chestnut
09 platitude
10 stereotype
11 commonplace, old chestnut

**clichéd, clichéed**
04 dull, worn
05 banal, corny, stale, stock, tired, trite
06 common
07 routine, worn-out
08 overused, timeworn
09 hackneyed
10 overworked, pedestrian, threadbare
11 commonplace, stereotyped, wearing thin
12 run-of-the-mill
13 platitudinous, stereotypical, unimaginative

**click**
04 beat, snap, snip, tick, twig
05 clack, clink, snick
06 pan out
07 come off, succeed
09 make sense

**client**

10 understand
13 fall into place

**client**

06 patron
07 patient, regular, shopper
08 consumer, customer
09 applicant, purchaser

**clientéle**

05 trade
06 market
07 clients, patrons
08 regulars, shoppers
09 clientage, consumers, customers, following, patronage

**cliff**

03 tor
04 crag, face, scar
05 bluff, scarp
08 overhang, rock face
09 precipice
10 escarpment, promontory

**climactic**

07 crucial
08 critical, decisive, exciting
09 paramount

**climate**

04 mood
05 trend
06 milieu, temper
07 feeling, setting, weather
08 ambience, tendency
10 atmosphere
11 disposition, environment, temperature

**climax**

03 top
04 acme, apex, head, peak
06 apogee, height, summit, zenith
08 pinnacle
09 high point, highlight

**climb**

03 top
04 go up, move, rise, soar, stir
05 mount, scale, shift
06 ascend, shin up
07 clamber, shoot up
08 increase, scramble, surmount

**❏climb down**

07 concede, descend, retract, retreat
08 back down
12 eat your words

**clinch**

03 hug
04 land, seal
05 close, grasp

06 decide, secure, settle, verify
07 confirm, embrace, grapple
08 conclude
09 determine

**cling**

03 hug
04 grip, hold
05 clasp, grasp, stick
06 adhere, cleave, clutch
07 embrace, stick to, support

**clinic**

04 ward
07 seminar
08 hospital
09 infirmary
10 dispensary
12 health center
13 medical center

**clinical**

04 cold
05 basic, plain, stark
06 simple
07 austere, medical, patient
08 analytic, detached, hospital
09 impassive, objective
10 impersonal, scientific
11 emotionless, unemotional
12 business-like
13 disinterested, dispassionate

**clip**

03 box, cut, fix, pin
04 crop, cuff, dock, hold, pare, poll, slap, snip, trim
05 clout, prune, punch, shear, thump, whack
06 attach, fasten, staple, wallop
07 curtail, cutting, excerpt, extract, passage, pollard, section, shorten, snippet
08 citation, cut short, truncate
09 quotation
10 abbreviate

**clipping**

07 cutting, excerpt, extract, passage, section, snippet
08 citation
09 quotation

**clique**

03 set
04 band, clan, gang, pack
05 bunch, crowd, group
06 circle
07 coterie, faction, in-crowd
08 sorority
10 fraternity

**cloak**

04 cape, coat, cope, hide, mask, robe, veil, wrap
05 blind, cover, front, shawl

06 mantle, poncho, screen, shroud
07 conceal, obscure, pretext
08 disguise
10 camouflage

**clock**

**❏clock up**

05 reach
06 attain, record
07 archive, chalk up, notch up
08 register

**clog**

03 dam, jam
05 block, choke, dam up
06 bung up, burden, hamper, hinder, impede, stop up
07 congest, occlude
08 encumber, obstruct

**cloister**

05 aisle
06 arcade
07 convent, portico, seclude, walkway
08 corridor, pavement
09 monastery, sequester
10 ambulatory

**cloistered**

07 secluse
08 confined, enclosed, hermitic, isolated, secluded
09 protected, reclusive, sheltered, withdrawn

**close**

03 bar, end
04 a hop, bolt, clog, cork, dear, fold, fuse, good, join, like, lock, near, plug, seal, shut, stop, true
05 block, bosom, cease, dense, exact, heavy, humid, muggy, place, tight
06 at hand, clinch, ending, fasten, finale, finish, go bust, lock up, loving, narrow, nearby, not far, secret, secure, sticky, stingy, stuffy, sultry, wind up
07 airless, careful, compact, confirm, cramped, crowded, devoted, miserly, occlude, padlock, private, similar
08 adjacent, attached, conclude, detailed, faithful, familiar, imminent, intimate, obstruct, shut down, stifling, taciturn
09 adjoining, cessation, condensed, determine, establish, impending, secretive, terminate

10 comparable, completion, conclusion, dénouement, hard-fought, oppressive, sweltering

11 culmination, draw to an end, go to the wall, inseparable, neck and neck, suffocating, well-matched

12 a stone's throw, bring to an end, concentrated, parsimonious, skip and a jump

13 corresponding, evenly matched, in the vicinity, penny-pinching

14 on your doorstep

◻ **close in**

08 approach, draw near, encircle, surround

10 come nearer

**closet**

06 covert, hidden, pantry, secret

07 furtive, private

08 cupboard, wardrobe

10 undercover, unrevealed

13 surreptitious

**closure**

03 end

07 failure, folding

08 shutdown

10 bankruptcy, bottleneck, stopping-up

**clot**

03 gel, set

04 glob, lump, mass

05 clump

06 curdle

07 congeal, thicken

08 coalesce, solidify, thrombus

09 coagulate

10 thrombosis

11 coagulation, obstruction

**cloth**

03 rag

05 towel

06 duster, fabric

07 textile

08 material

09 dishcloth, washcloth

10 tablecloth

**clothe**

03 rig

04 deck, robe, vest

05 cover, drape, dress, habit

06 attire, fit out, invest, outfit

07 apparel, deck out, dress up

08 accouter, accoutre

09 caparison

**clothes**

04 garb, gear, togs, wear

05 dress, get-up

06 attire, outfit

07 apparel, costume, raiment, vesture

08 garments, wardrobe

09 sartorial, vestments

10 habilatory, habiliments

11 hand-me-downs

16 castoffs clothing

▶ *Types of clothes*:

03 aba, bra, tie, tux

04 abba, belt, gown, kilt, sari, slip, sock, suit, sulu, toga, veil, vest

05 cloak, cords, dhoti, dress, frock, glove, jeans, Levis, lungi, pants, parka, scarf, shawl, shift, shirt, skirt, smock, stole, tails, teddy, thong, tunic

06 basque, bikini, blouse, bodice, bow tie, briefs, caftan, corset, cravat, denims, dhooti, dirndl, garter, girdle, jersey, jumper, kimono, mitten, poncho, sarong, shorts, slacks, T-shirt, tights, top hat, topper, trunks, tuxedo

07 cutaway, doublet, hosiery, leotard, muffler, necktie, nightie, pajamas, singlet, sweater, topcoat, twin set, yashmac, yashmak

08 bermudas, breeches, camisole, cardigan, culottes, earmuffs, flannels, hot pants, jodhpurs, jumpsuit, leggings, lingerie, negligee, overcoat, pantsuit, pinafore, pullover, sack coat, sneakers, swimsuit, tee shirt, trousers

09 bed jacket, brassière, corduroys, coveralls, dungarees, hair shirt, housecoat, maxiskirt, midiskirt, miniskirt, pants suit, pantyhose, petticoat, plus fours, polo shirt, sack dress, separates, stockings, string tie, tracksuit

10 cummerbund, dress shirt, leg warmers, nightdress, sport shirt, suspenders, sweat shirt, turtleneck, underpants, wraparound

11 bathing suit, bell-bottoms, boxer shorts, cutaway coat, riding habit, string shirt

12 body stocking, dressing gown, evening dress

13 Bermuda shorts, sports clothes

14 evening clothes, knickerbockers

**cloud**

03 dim, fog

04 blur, dull, mist, veil

05 cover, shade

06 darken, mantle, shroud

07 confuse, eclipse, obscure

09 obfuscate

10 overshadow

▶ *Types of cloud*:

06 cirrus, nimbus

07 cumulus, stratus

11 altocumulus, altostratus

12 cirrocumulus, cirrostratus, cumulonimbus, nimbostratus

13 fractocumulus, fractostratus, stratocumulus

**cloudy**

03 dim

04 dark, dull, gray, hazy

05 foggy, heavy, milky, misty, muddy, murky

06 blurry, gloomy, leaden

07 blurred, obscure, sunless

08 nebulous, overcast

10 indistinct

**clout**

03 box, hit

04 cuff, pull, slap, slug, sock

05 power, punch, smack, thump, whack

06 muscle, strike, wallop

09 authority, influence

**cloven**

05 cleft, split

07 divided

08 bisected

**clown**

04 dork, fool, geek, jerk, jest, joke, nerd, twit, zany

05 comic, idiot, joker, ninny, twerp

06 dimwit, jester, nitwit

07 buffoon, pierrot

08 comedian, dipstick, imbecile, numskull

09 harlequin

10 act the fool, fool around, mess around, nincompoop

11 play the fool

**cloying**

06 sickly

07 choking, fulsome

09 oversweet, sickening

10 disgusting, nauseating

## club

03 bat, hit, set
04 bash, beat, cosh, mace
05 billy, clout, group, guild, order, staff, stick, union
06 batter, circle, clique, cudgel, league, pummel, strike
07 clobber, company, society
08 bludgeon, sorority
09 civic club
10 federation, fraternity
11 association, brotherhood
12 organization

➤ *Names of clubs. We have omitted the word* **club** *from names given in the following list but you may need to include this word as part of the solution to some crossword clues.*

04 Boys, Elks, YMCA, YWCA
05 Girls, Lions
06 Eagles, Rotary, Sierra
07 Circle K, Kiwanis, Sertoma
10 Odd Fellows
12 Junior League

### ❑ club together
06 chip in
10 contribute
12 share the cost

## clue

03 tip
04 hint, idea, lead, sign
05 trace
06 notion, tip-off
07 inkling, pointer
08 evidence
09 suspicion
10 indication, suggestion

## clump

03 lot
04 mass, plod, thud, tuft
05 amass, bunch, clomp, group, stamp, stomp, thump, tramp
06 bundle, lumber, trudge
07 cluster, thicket
10 accumulate, collection
12 accumulation

## clumsy

05 bulky, crude, gawky, heavy, inept, rough
06 gauche, wooden
07 awkward, uncouth
08 bungling, tactless, ungainly, unwieldy
09 all thumbs, ham-handed, lumbering, maladroit
10 blundering, cumbersome, ungraceful
11 heavy-handed, insensitive
13 accident-prone

## cluster

04 band, knot, mass
05 batch, bunch, clump, crowd, flock, group, truss
06 gather, huddle, raceme
07 collect, panicle
08 assemble, assembly
09 gathering
10 assemblage, assortment, collection, congregate

## clustered

06 massed
07 bunched, grouped
08 gathered
09 assembled, glomerate

## clutch

04 grab, grip, hold, nest
05 brood, clasp, claws, grasp, group, lever, pedal, seize
06 clench, snatch
07 cling to, embrace, grapple, handbag, keeping, squeeze
09 get hold of

## clutter

04 fill, mess
05 chaos, cover, strew
06 jumble, litter, mess up, muddle
07 scatter
08 disarray, disorder, encumber
09 confusion, make a mess

## coach

03 bus, cab, car, gig
04 trap
05 drill, prime, teach, train, tutor, wagon
06 hansom, landau, mentor
07 hackney, teacher, trainer
08 brougham, carriage, educator, instruct
09 charabanc, Greyhound, Trailways
10 instructor

## coagulate

03 gel
04 clot, melt
06 curdle
07 congeal, thicken
08 solidify

## coalesce

03 mix
04 fuse, join
05 blend, merge, unite
06 cohere, commix
07 combine
09 affiliate, commingle, integrate
10 amalgamate
11 consolidate, incorporate
12 join together

## coalition

04 bloc
05 union
06 fusion, league, merger
07 compact, joining
08 alliance
10 federation
11 affiliation, association, confederacy
12 amalgamation
13 confederation

## coarse

04 blue, rank, rude
05 bawdy, crude, gross, hairy, lumpy, rough, scaly
06 earthy, ribald, rugged, smutty, uneven, vulgar
07 boorish, bristly, loutish, obscene, prickly, raunchy
08 immodest, impolite, improper, indecent
09 offensive, unrefined
10 indelicate, unpolished
11 foul-mouthed, ill-mannered, unprocessed

## coarsen

06 deaden, harden
07 roughen, thicken
08 indurate
11 desensitize

## coarseness

04 smut
07 crudity
08 ribaldry
09 bawdiness, crassness, indecency, obscenity, vulgarity
10 crassitude, earthiness, indelicacy, smuttiness
13 offensiveness

## coast

04 sail, taxi
05 beach, drift, glide, shore
06 cruise, strand
07 seaside
08 seaboard, seashore
09 foreshore, freewheel

## coat

03 fur
04 cake, daub, film, hair, hide, pave, pelt, skin, wool
05 apply, cover, glaze, layer, paint, put on, sheet, smear
06 finish, fleece, mantle, spread, veneer
07 blanket, encrust, varnish
08 cladding, covering, laminate, pellicle

## coating

04 film, skin, wash
05 crust, glaze, layer, sheet

06 enamel, finish, patina, veneer
07 blanket, dusting, varnish
08 covering, membrane

**coax**
05 tempt
06 allure, cajole, entice, induce
07 beguile, flatter, wheedle, win over
08 inveigle, persuade, soft-soap, talk into
09 get around, sweet-talk, win around

**cock**
03 tap
04 lift
05 capon, point, raise, slant
06 faucet
07 chicken, incline, rooster
08 cockerel
11 chanticleer

**cockeyed**
04 awry, daft
05 askew, crazy
06 absurd
07 crooked
08 lopsided
09 ludicrous
10 catawampus
11 cattywampus

**cocktail**

➤ *Names of cocktails*:
05 Bronx, zombi
06 gimlet, zombie
07 martini, Sazerac, sidecar, stinger
08 daiquiri, pink lady, salty dog, snowball
09 Manhattan, margarita, mint julip, rusty nail, white lady
10 Bloody Mary, margarita, Tom Collins
11 Black Velvet, screwdriver, whiskey sour
12 black Russian, Old-Fashioned
13 planter's punch
14 singapore sling
15 Brandy Alexander
➤ See also DRINK

**cocky**
04 vain
05 brash
08 arrogant, cocksure
09 bumptious, conceited, hubristic
10 swaggering
11 egotistical, self-assured, swell-headed
13 self-important

**cocoon**
04 wrap
05 cover
07 cushion, envelop, isolate, protect
08 cloister, insulate, preserve

**coddle**
03 pet
05 humor, spoil
06 cosset, pamper
07 indulge, protect
11 mollycoddle, overprotect

**code**
04 laws
05 rules, signs
06 cipher, custom, ethics, morals, system
07 bar code, conduct, manners
08 morality, postcode, practice
09 etiquette, Morse code
10 convention, cryptogram
11 cryptograph, regulations

**coerce**
05 bully, drive, force
06 compel, lean on
07 dragoon
08 bludgeon, browbeat, bulldoze, railroad, threaten
09 strong arm
10 intimidate, pressurize

**coercion**
05 force
06 duress
08 bullying, pressure
10 compulsion, constraint
11 browbeating

**coffer**
03 box
04 case, safe
05 chest, trunk
06 casket
08 moneybox, treasury
09 strongbox
10 repository

**cogent**
06 potent, strong, urgent
07 weighty
08 forceful, forcible, powerful
09 effective
10 compelling, persuasive
11 influential
12 irresistible, unanswerable

**cogitate**
04 muse
06 ponder
07 reflect
08 consider, mull over
10 deliberate
11 contemplate, think deeply

**cognate**
04 akin
05 alike
06 agnate, allied
07 kindred, related, similar
09 analogous, connected
10 affiliated, associated
13 corresponding

**cognition**
06 reason
07 insight
08 learning, thinking
09 awareness, knowledge, reasoning
10 perception
11 discernment, rationality
12 apprehension, intelligence
13 comprehension, understanding

**cognizance**
❏**take cognizance of**
06 accept, regard
09 recognize
11 acknowledge

**cognizant**
05 aware
06 versed
07 witting
08 familiar, informed
09 conscious
10 acquainted, conversant
13 knowledgeable

**cohabit**
07 shack up
08 live with
12 live together

**cohere**
04 bind, fuse, hold
05 agree, cling, stick, unite
06 adhere, square
07 combine
08 coalesce
09 harmonize, make sense
10 correspond
11 consolidate
12 hang together

**coherence**
05 sense, union, unity
07 harmony
09 agreement, congruity
10 connection, consonance
11 concordance, consistency

**coherent**
05 clear, lucid
07 logical, orderly
08 rational, reasoned, sensible
09 organized
10 articulate, consistent
12 intelligible
14 comprehensible

## cohesion
05 union, unity, whole
07 harmony
09 agreement, coherence
10 connection
11 consistency

## cohort
04 band, body, mate
05 buddy, squad, troop
06 column, legion
07 brigade, company, partner
08 division, follower, myrmidon, regiment, sidekick, squadron
09 companion, supporter

## coil
04 curl, loop, ring, roll, wind
05 helix, twine, twist, whorl
06 spiral, wreath, writhe
09 convolute, corkscrew

## coin
04 cash, mint
05 forge, money, piece
06 change, copper, create, devise, invent, make up, silver, specie
07 dream up, nummary, produce, think up
08 conceive
09 neologize, nummulary, originate
11 loose change, small change

► *Types of coin:*
02 at, xu
03 bit, bob, fen, hao, ore, pul, pya, rap, sen, sou
04 anna, cent, chon, dime, fils, jiao, joey, lwei, mite, obol, para, quid, real, sent
05 angel, butut, copec, crown, ducat, groat, kopek, louis, noble, pence, penny, pound
06 aureus, bezant, copeck, copper, dollar, florin, guinea, kopeck, nickel, obolus, satang, stater, talent, tanner, thaler
07 centavo, centime, centimo, guilder, ha'penny, moidore, Pfennig, piaster, quarter, solidus
08 australe, denarius, doubloon, ducatoon, farthing, Groschen, imperial, louis d'or, millième, napoleon, sesterce, shilling, sixpence, ten pence, two pence, two pound
09 centesimo, dandiprat, gold crown, half crown, half eagle, halfpenny, sovereign
10 half dollar, half florin, half

guinea, krugerrand, sestertius
11 double eagle, sixpenny bit, twenty pence, twopenny bit
12 silver dollar
13 brass farthing, half sovereign, threepenny bit
► See also CURRENCY; MONEY

## coincide
05 agree, clash, match, tally
06 accord, concur, square
09 be the same, harmonize
10 correspond
11 synchronize

## coincidence
04 luck
05 clash, fluke
06 chance
08 accident, clashing, fortuity
11 coexistence, concurrence, conjunction, correlation, eventuality, serendipity

## coincidental
05 lucky
06 casual, chance, flukey
09 unplanned
10 accidental, fortuitous
13 serendipitous, unintentional

## cold
03 ice, icy, raw
04 cool, rimy, snow
05 aloof, chill, fresh, frost, gelid, nippy, polar
06 arctic, biting, bitter, chilly, frigid, frosty, frozen, remote, winter, wintry
07 callous, chilled, distant, glacial, hostile
08 clinical, coolness, freezing, reserved, Siberian, uncaring
09 frigidity, heartless, unfeeling
10 phlegmatic, unfriendly
11 indifferent, insensitive, passionless, standoffish, unemotional, unexcitable
12 antagonistic, unresponsive

## coldblooded
05 cruel
06 brutal, savage
07 callous, inhuman
08 barbaric, pitiless, ruthless
09 barbarous, heartless, merciless, unfeeling

## coldhearted
04 cold
06 flinty, unkind
07 callous, inhuman
08 detached, uncaring
09 heartless, unfeeling
11 indifferent, insensitive

## collaborate
05 unite
06 betray, team up
07 collude
08 conspire
09 cooperate
10 fraternize, join forces
11 participate, turn traitor

## collaboration
05 union
08 alliance, teamwork
09 collusion
11 association, cooperation, joint effort, partnership
12 fraternizing

## collaborator
07 partner, traitor
08 betrayer, co-worker, colluder, quisling, renegade, teammate, turncoat
09 assistant, associate, colleague
10 accomplice
11 conspirator, fraternizer

## collapse
04 fail, flop, fold, ruin, sink
05 faint, slump, swoon
06 cave in, cave-in, fall in, finish
07 crumble, crumple, debacle, failure, founder, give way, pass out, sinking, subside
08 black out, blackout, downfall, fainting, flake out, keel over
10 foundering, subsidence
11 come to an end, fall through
12 disintegrate, fall to pieces
13 come to nothing

## collar
03 nab
04 grab, nick, ring, ruff, stop
05 catch, ruche, seize
06 arrest, Bertha, gorget, rabato, rebato
07 capture
08 neckband
09 apprehend, dog collar
14 clerical collar

## collate
04 sort
05 order
06 gather
07 arrange, collect, compose
08 organize
10 put in order

## collateral
05 bonds, funds
06 pledge, stocks, surety
07 deposit, related
08 security

**colleague**
09 assurance, guarantee, secondary

**colleague**
04 aide, ally
06 helper
07 comrade, partner
08 co-worker, confrère, teammate, workmate
09 assistant, associate, auxiliary, companion
11 confederate

**collect**
03 get
04 heap, mass, meet, save
05 amass, fetch, hoard, rally
06 gather, muster, pick up
07 acquire, call for, come for, compose, convene, prepare, solicit
08 assemble, converge
09 aggregate, stockpile
10 accumulate, congregate
14 gather together

**collected**
04 calm, cool
06 placid, poised, serene
08 composed, unshaken
09 unruffled
10 controlled
11 unperturbed
13 self-possessed

**collection**
03 set
04 gift, heap, mass, pile
05 gifts, group, hoard, store
06 job-lot
07 cluster
08 assembly, donation, offering
09 anthology, offertory, stockpile
10 assemblage, assortment
11 compilation
12 accumulation, contribution
14 collected works, conglomeration

**collective**
05 joint
06 common, moshav, shared, united
07 commune, kibbutz, kolkhoz
08 combined
09 aggregate, community, composite, unanimous
10 cumulative, democratic
11 cooperative
12 conglomerate
13 collaborative

▶ *Collective nouns*:
03 **gam** (of whales), **nye** (of pheasants), **pod** (of seals)

04 **army** (of frogs), **bask** (of crocodiles), **cete** (of badgers), **dole** (of doves), **herd** (of deer), **pack** (of dogs), **pack** (of hounds), **rout** (of wolves), **team** (of ducks), **zeal** (of zebras)
05 **brood** (of chickens), **brood** (of hens), **charm** (of finches), **covey** (of partridges), **crash** (of rhinoceros), **drove** (of cattle), **flock** (of sheep), **pride** (of lions), **shoal** (of fish), **skein** (of geese), **swarm** (of bees), **swarm** (of locusts), **tribe** (of goats), **troop** (of kangaroos), **troop** (of monkeys), **watch** (of nightingales)
06 **colony** (of rats), **gaggle** (of geese), **litter** (of pigs), **murder** (of crows), **muster** (of peacocks), **muster** (of penguins), **parade** (of elephants), **rafter** (of turkeys), **school** (of dolphins), **school** (of porpoises), **string** (of horses)
10 **exaltation** (of larks), **parliament** (of owls), **shrewdness** (of apes), **unkindness** (of ravens)

**collector**
___

▶ *Types of collectors and enthusiasts*:
07 gourmet
08 cineaste, zoophile
09 antiquary, cinephile
10 audiophile, discophile, gastronome, monarchist
11 bibliophile, etymologist, numismatist, philatelist
12 cartophilist, entomologist
13 arachnologist, campanologist, chirographist, lepidopterist, ornithologist
15 conservationist

**college**
06 school
07 academy
08 seminary
09 alma mater, institute
10 university
11 polytechnic
13 junior college
➤ See also UNIVERSITY

**collide**
03 hit, ram
04 bump, feud

05 clash, crash, smash
07 quarrel, run into
08 bump into, conflict, disagree, plow into
09 crash into, smash into
10 meet head on

**collision**
04 bump, feud
05 brush, clash, crash, fight, prang, smash, wreck
06 impact, pileup
07 quarrel, wrangle
08 accident, conflict, disaster, fighting, showdown

**colloquial**
06 casual, chatty
07 demotic, popular
08 everyday, familiar, informal
09 idiomatic
10 vernacular
14 conversational

**collude**
04 plot
06 scheme
08 conspire, intrigue
09 machinate
11 collaborate

**collusion**
04 plot
06 deceit, league, scheme
07 cahoots
08 artifice, intrigue, scheming
10 complicity, conspiracy
11 machination
13 collaboration

**colonist**
07 pioneer, settler
08 colonial, emigrant
09 immigrant

**colonize**
05 found
06 occupy, people, settle
07 pioneer
08 populate

**colonnade**
04 stoa
06 arcade
07 portico
09 cloisters, peristyle

**colony**
05 group
07 outpost
08 dominion, province
09 community, satellite
10 dependency, possession, settlement
12 protectorate

**colossal**
04 huge, vast

## color

- 05 great
- 07 immense, mammoth, massive
- 08 enormous, gigantic, whopping
- 09 herculean, monstrous
- 10 gargantuan, monumental
- 14 Brobdingnagian

## color

- 03 dye, hue
- 04 bias, flag, life, tint, tone
- 05 blush, flush, go red, paint, shade, slant, taint, tinge
- 06 affect, banner, crayon, emblem, ensign, redden
- 07 distort, pennant, pigment
- 08 insignia, standard, tincture
- 09 highlight, influence, overstate, prejudice
- 10 complexion, exaggerate, liveliness

► *Names of colors*:

- 03 jet, red, tan
- 04 anil, blue, ecru, fawn, gold, gray, jade, navy, pink, rose
- 05 amber, beige, black, brown, coral, cream, ebony, green, khaki, lilac, mauve, ocher, ochre, sepia, taupe, umber, white
- 06 auburn, canary, cerise, cobalt, copper, indigo, maroon, orange, purple, silver, violet, yellow
- 07 crimson, emerald, gentian, magenta, saffron, scarlet
- 08 burgundy, charcoal, chestnut, lavender, magnolia, sapphire
- 09 tangerine, turquoise
- 10 aquamarine, vermillion
- ➤ See also DYE; PIGMENT; RAINBOW

## colorful

- 04 deep, rich
- 05 gaudy, vivid
- 06 bright, garish, lively
- 07 graphic, intense, vibrant
- 08 animated, exciting
- 11 interesting, picturesque, stimulating

## colorless

- 03 wan
- 04 drab, dull, pale, tame
- 05 ashen, faded, plain
- 06 anemic, boring, dreary, sickly
- 07 insipid, neutral
- 08 bleached
- 09 washed out
- 10 lackluster, monochrome
- 11 transparent, unmemorable

- 13 characterless, uninteresting
- 15 in black and white

## column

- 03 row
- 04 asta, file, item, line, list, pier, post, rank
- 05 Atlas, piece, shaft, story
- 06 parade, pillar, string
- 07 article, feature, obelisk, support, telamon, upright
- 08 caryatid, pilaster
- 10 procession

## columnist

- 06 critic, editor, writer
- 08 reporter, reviewer
- 10 journalist
- 11 news analyst
- 13 correspondent

## coma

- 05 sopor
- 06 stupor, torpor, trance
- 08 hypnosis, lethargy, oblivion
- 09 catalepsy
- 10 drowsiness, somnolence

## comatose

- 05 dazed
- 06 drowsy, sleepy, torpid
- 07 in a coma, out cold, stunned
- 08 sluggish, soporose
- 09 lethargic, somnolent
- 10 cataleptic, insensible
- 11 unconscious

## comb

- 04 hunt, rake, sift, tidy
- 05 dress, groom, scour, sweep
- 06 neaten, screen, search
- 07 arrange, ransack, rummage

## combat

- 03 war
- 04 bout, defy, duel
- 05 clash, fight
- 06 action, battle, oppose, resist
- 07 contest, wage war, warfare
- 08 conflict, do battle, fighting, skirmish, struggle
- 09 encounter, withstand
- 10 engagement, take up arms
- 11 hostilities

## combatant

- 05 enemy
- 07 fighter, soldier, warrior
- 08 opponent
- 09 adversary, contender
- 10 antagonist

## combative

- 07 warlike
- 08 militant
- 09 bellicose, truculent
- 10 aggressive, pugnacious

- 11 belligerent, contentious, quarrelsome
- 12 antagonistic
- 13 argumentative

## combination

- 03 mix
- 05 blend, cross, group, union
- 06 fusion, merger
- 07 amalgam, mixture
- 08 alliance, compound
- 09 coalition, composite, syndicate, synthesis
- 10 collection, consortium
- 11 association, coalescence, confederacy, conjunction, integration, unification
- 12 amalgamation
- 13 confederation

## combine

- 03 mix
- 04 ally, bind, bond, fuse, join, link, pool, stir, weld
- 05 admix, alloy, blend, marry, merge, unify, unite
- 06 mingle, team up
- 08 compound
- 09 associate, integrate
- 10 amalgamate, homogenize, join forces, synthesize
- 11 incorporate, put together
- 13 bring together

## combustible

- 05 tense
- 06 stormy
- 07 charged
- 08 burnable, volatile
- 09 explosive, flammable, ignitable, sensitive
- 10 incendiary
- 11 inflammable

## combustion

- 06 firing
- 07 burning
- 08 igniting, ignition

## come

- 04 gain, hail, near, stem, turn
- 05 arise, issue, occur, reach
- 06 appear, arrive, attain, attend, become, dawn on, evolve, follow, happen, secure
- 07 achieve, advance, barge in, burst in, develop, get here, occur to, surface, think of
- 08 approach, draw near, pass into, remember
- 09 take place, transpire
- 10 evolve into, move toward, result from
- 11 be a native of, develop into, materialize, move forward

## come about
05 arise, occur
06 befall, happen, result
09 take place, transpire

## come across
04 find
07 run into
08 bump into, discover
09 encounter
10 chance upon, happen upon
13 stumble across

## come along
05 rally
07 advance, develop, improve, recover
08 progress
09 get better
10 recuperate
11 make headway
12 make progress

## come apart
04 tear
05 break, split
07 break up, crumble
08 collapse, separate
10 fall to bits
12 disintegrate, fall to pieces

## come between
04 part
06 divide
07 split up
08 alienate, estrange, separate

## come by
03 get
06 obtain, secure
07 acquire, procure
09 get hold of

## come clean
05 admit, own up
06 reveal
07 confess, tell all
13 spill the beans

## come down
06 reduce, worsen
07 decline, descend
08 decrease
10 degenerate
11 deteriorate

## come down on
05 blame, chide
06 berate, rebuke
07 reprove, upbraid
08 admonish, tear into
09 criticize, reprimand
13 find fault with

## come down to
04 mean
08 amount to
10 boil down to
12 correspond to

## come down with
03 get
05 catch
06 pick up
07 develop
08 contract
09 succumb to
10 go down with

## come forward
05 offer
09 volunteer

## come in
05 enter
06 arrive, finish, show up

## come in for
03 get
06 endure, suffer
07 receive, undergo
13 be subjected to

## come into
06 be left
07 acquire, inherit, receive

## come off
04 work
05 occur
06 go well, happen
07 succeed, work out
11 be effective
12 be successful

## come out
05 end up
06 appear, finish, result
10 be produced
11 be published, become known
15 become available

## come out with
03 say
05 state
06 affirm
07 declare, divulge, exclaim
08 blurt out, disclose

## come around
04 wake
05 agree, allow, awake, yield
06 accede, relent
07 concede, recover
09 be won over
11 be persuaded
14 change your mind

## come through
06 endure
07 achieve, prevail, succeed, survive, triumph
09 withstand

## come to
04 make, wake
05 awake, equal, run to, total
07 add up to, recover

08 amount to

## come up
04 rise
05 arise, occur
06 crop up, happen, turn up

## come up to
04 meet
05 reach
08 approach, live up to
09 match up to
11 measure up to
12 make the grade

## come up with
05 offer
06 submit
07 advance, dream up, present, propose, suggest, think of
08 conceive
10 put forward

## comeback
05 rally
06 return
07 revival
08 recovery
10 resurgence
12 reappearance

## comedian, comedienne
03 wag, wit
05 clown, comic, joker
07 gagster
08 humorist
11 entertainer

► *Famous comedians/comediennes*:

03 **Fry** (Stephen), **Sim** (Alastair)
04 **Ball** (Lucille), **Coca** (Imogene), **Hawn** (Goldie), **Hill** (Benny), **Hope** (Bob), **Idle** (Eric), **Kaye** (Danny), **Marx** (Chico), **Marx** (Groucho), **Marx** (Harpo), **Raye** (Martha), **Tati** (Jacques)
05 **Allen** (Woody), **Benny** (Jack), **Berle** (Milton), **Bruce** (Lenny), **Burns** (George), **Carey** (Drew), **Chase** (Chevy), **Cosby** (Bill), **Gobel** (George), **Hardy** (Oliver), **Lewis** (Jerry), **Lloyd** (Harold), **Moore** (Dudley), **Olsen** (Ole), **Palin** (Michael), **Pryor** (Richard)
06 **Abbott** (Bud), **Brooks** (Mel), **Caesar** (Sid), **Cantor** (Eddie), **Carrey** (Jim), **Cleese** (John), **DeVito** (Danny), **Diller** (Phyllis),

Fields (W. C.), **Keaton**
(Buster), **Lauder** (Harry),
**Laurel** (Stan), **Martin**
(Steve), **Murphy** (Eddie),
**Radner** (Gilda), **Rivers**
(Joan), **Ullman** (Tracey),
**Wilder** (Gene)
07 **Aykroyd** (Dan), **Burnett**
(Carol), **Buttons** (Red),
**Chaplin** (Charlie), **Crystal**
(Billy), **Gleason** (Jackie),
**Grammer** (Kelsey),
**Johnson** (Chic), **Matthau**
(Walter), **Roscius, Sandler**
(Adam), **Sellers** (Peter),
**Skelton** (Red)
08 **Arbuckle** (Roscoe "Fatty"),
**Atkinson** (Rowan),
**Connolly** (Billy), **Costello**
(Lou), **Goldberg** (Whoopi),
**Roseanne, Seinfeld** (Jerry),
**Williams** (Robin)
09 **Fernandel**
10 **Cantinflas**
11 **Dangerfield** (Rodney),
**Monty Python, Terry-
Thomas**
12 **Keystone Kops, Marx
Brothers, Three Stooges**
14 **Laurel and Hardy**
15 **Olsen and Johnson**
16 **Smothers Brothers**
➤ See also ACTOR, ACTRESS

**comedown**
04 blow
07 decline, descent, letdown
08 demotion, reversal
09 deflation
10 anticlimax
14 disappointment

**comedy**
03 wit
05 farce, humor
06 joking, satire, sitcom
07 jesting
08 clowning, drollery, hilarity
09 burlesque, funniness,
pantomime, slapstick
10 vaudeville

**comely**
04 fair
05 bonny, buxom
06 lovely, pretty
07 winsome
08 blooming, graceful, pleasing
10 attractive
11 good-looking

**come-on**
04 lure
05 shill
08 swindler

10 allurement, enticement,
inducement, temptation
13 encouragement

**comeuppance**
04 dues
05 merit
06 rebuke
07 deserts
08 requital
10 punishment, recompense
11 just deserts, retribution

**comfort**
03 aid
04 ease, help
05 cheer
06 luxury, relief, solace, soothe,
succor
07 assuage, console, enliven,
gladden, hearten, refresh,
relieve, support
08 opulence, reassure
09 alleviate, empathize,
encourage, well-being
10 condolence, invigorate,
relaxation, sympathize
11 alleviation, consolation,
contentment, reassurance
12 compensation, satisfaction
13 bring solace to

**comfortable**
04 cozy, easy, safe, snug
05 comfy, happy, roomy
06 at ease
07 opulent, relaxed, restful,
well-off
08 affluent, well-to-do
09 agreeable, confident,
contented, luxurious
10 convenient, prosperous

**comforting**
07 helpful
08 cheering, soothing
09 consoling
10 heartening, reassuring
11 consolatory, inspiriting
12 heartwarming

**comic**
03 wag, wit
04 rich, zany
05 clown, droll, funny, joker,
light, witty
06 absurd, joking
07 amusing, buffoon, gagster,
jocular
08 comedian, farcical, humorist,
humorous
09 hilarious, laughable,
ludicrous, priceless
10 comedienne
11 entertainer

**comic strip**

➤ *Names of comic strips*:
02 B.C.
04 Pogo, Shoe
05 Agnes, Cathy, Momma,
Nancy, Ziggy
06 Archie, Gordon, Herman,
Popeye, Tarzan
07 Blondie, Dilbert, Fat Cats,
Peanuts
08 Alley Oop, Andy Capp,
Garfield, Li'l Abner,
Superman, The Gumps
09 Betty Boop, Dick Tracy,
Doonsbury, Jungle Jim,
Marmaduke, Miss Peach,
That's Life, Yellow Kid
10 Broom Hilda, Buzz Sawyer,
Heathcliff, Joe Palooka, Rose
is Rose, The Far Side, The Sad
Sack, Wizard of Id
11 Buster Brown, Captain Easy,
Moon Mullins, Mutt and Jeff,
Steve Canyon
12 Barney Google, Beetle
Bailey, Little Iodine, Over the
Hedge, The Born Loser
13 Gasoline Alley, Happy
Hooligan, Prince Valiant
14 Calvin and Hobbs, Frank and
Ernest
15 Dennis the Menace
18 Flash Flo and Friends

**comical**
05 droll, funny, witty
06 absurd
07 amusing
08 farcical, humorous
09 diverting, hilarious,
laughable, ludicrous
10 ridiculous
12 entertaining

**coming**
03 due
04 dawn, near, next
05 birth
06 advent, future, rising
07 arrival, nearing
08 approach, aspiring,
imminent, upcoming
09 accession, advancing,
impending, promising
11 approaching

**command**
03 bid, get
04 gain, head, lead, rule, sway
05 edict, order, power, reign
06 adjure, behest, charge,
compel, decree, demand,
direct, govern, manage

07 bidding, control, dictate, mandate, mastery
08 dominion, instruct
09 authority, direction, directive, supervise
10 government, injunction, leadership, management
11 instruction, preside over, requirement, supervision
12 give orders to
15 superintendence

**commandeer**
05 seize, usurp
06 hijack
07 impound
08 arrogate
09 sequester
10 confiscate
11 appropriate, expropriate, requisition, sequestrate

**commander**
04 boss, head
05 chief
06 leader
07 admiral, captain, general, officer

**commanding**
05 lofty
06 strong
08 dominant, forceful, imposing, powerful, superior
09 assertive, confident
10 autocratic, dominating, impressive, peremptory
13 authoritative

**commemorate**
04 keep, mark
05 honor
06 salute
07 observe
08 remember
09 celebrate, recognize
11 immortalize, memorialize
12 pay tribute to

**commemoration**
05 honor
06 memory, salute
07 tribute
08 ceremony, honoring
11 celebration, remembrance

**commemorative**
07 marking
08 honoring, memorial, saluting
09 in honor of
10 dedicatory, in memoriam, in memory of
11 celebratory, remembering
12 as a tribute to
15 in remembrance of

**commence**
04 open
05 begin, start
06 launch
07 go ahead
08 embark on, initiate
10 inaugurate, make a start

**commend**
04 give, laud
05 extol, trust, yield
06 commit, praise
07 acclaim, applaud, approve, confide, consign, deliver, entrust, propose, suggest
08 advocate, hand over
13 speak highly of

**commendable**
05 noble
06 worthy
08 laudable
09 admirable, deserving, estimable, exemplary
10 creditable
11 meritorious
12 praiseworthy

**commendation**
06 credit, praise
07 acclaim
08 accolade, applause, approval, encomium
09 panegyric
11 acclamation, approbation, good opinion, recognition
13 encouragement
14 special mention

**commensurate**
03 due
07 fitting
08 adequate
10 acceptable, comparable, equivalent, sufficient
11 according to
13 appropriate to
14 compatible with, consistent with, in proportion to

**comment**
03 say
04 note, view
05 opine
06 remark
07 mention, observe, opinion
08 footnote, point out
09 criticism, elucidate, interject, interpret, statement
10 annotation, exposition
11 elucidation, explanation, observation
12 illustration, marginal note

**commentary**
05 notes
06 report, review
07 account
08 analysis, critique, exegesis, treatise
09 narration, voice-over
10 annotation, exposition
11 description, elucidation, explanation
14 interpretation

**commentator**
06 critic
07 exegete
08 narrator, reporter
09 annotator, columnist, commenter, expositor
11 broadcaster, interpreter

**commerce**
05 trade
07 dealing, traffic
08 business, dealings, exchange, industry
09 marketing, relations
13 merchandising

**commercial**
02 ad
04 bill, hype, plug
05 blurb, trade, venal
06 jingle, notice, poster
07 display, handout, leaflet, placard, popular, salable, trading
08 business, circular, handbill, monetary, sellable
09 marketing, mercenary, promotion, publicity
10 industrial, profitable
12 profit-making
13 advertisement, materialistic
15 entrepreneurial

**commiserate**
07 comfort, console
10 sympathize, understand
15 send condolences

**commiseration**
04 pity
06 solace
07 comfort
08 sympathy
10 compassion, condolence
11 consolation
13 consideration, understanding

**commission**
03 cut, fee, job
04 duty, send, task, work
05 board, order, share, trust
06 assign, charge, depute, employ, engage, errand
07 empower, mandate, rake-off, request, royalty, warrant
08 contract, function, nominate

**commit**
09 allowance, authority, authorize, committee
10 assignment, deputation, employment, percentage
11 appointment, piece of work
12 advisory body

**commit**
02 do
04 bind, give
05 enact, trust
06 assign, decide, effect, engage, pledge
07 commend, confide, consign, deliver, deposit, entrust, execute, get up to, perform, promise
08 carry out, covenant, hand over, obligate
10 perpetrate

**commitment**
03 tie, vow
04 duty, word
06 effort, pledge
07 loyalty, promise
08 covenant, devotion, hard work
09 adherence, assurance, guarantee, liability
10 allegiance, dedication, engagement, obligation
11 involvement, undertaking
14 responsibility

**committed**
05 loyal
06 active, engagé
07 devoted, fervent, zealous
08 diligent, involved, studious
09 dedicated
11 hard-working, industrious
12 card-carrying, enthusiastic

**commodious**
05 ample, large, roomy
08 spacious
09 capacious, expansive, extensive

**commodity**
04 item
05 goods, stock, thing, wares
07 article, produce, product
11 merchandise

**common**
03 low
05 crude, daily, joint, usual
06 coarse, mutual, public, shared, simple, vulgar
07 average, general, ill-bred, loutish, popular, regular, routine, uncouth
08 accepted, communal, everyday, familiar, frequent,

habitual, inferior, ordinary, plebeian, workaday
09 customary, prevalent, universal, unrefined
10 collective, widespread
11 a dime a dozen
12 conventional, run-of-the-mill

**commonly**
07 as a rule, usually
08 normally
09 generally, routinely, typically
14 for the most part

**commonplace**
05 banal, stale, stock, trite
06 boring
07 humdrum, mundane, obvious, routine, worn out
08 everyday, frequent, ordinary, timeworn
09 hackneyed
10 pedestrian, widespread

**common sense**
04 nous
05 savvy, sense
06 reason, sanity, wisdom
08 gumption, judgment, prudence
10 astuteness, experience, pragmatism, shrewdness
11 discernment
12 practicality, sensibleness
13 judiciousness
15 levelheadedness

**common-sense**
04 sane, wise
05 sound
06 astute, shrewd
07 prudent
08 sensible
09 judicious, practical, pragmatic, realistic
10 discerning, reasonable
11 down-to-earth
12 matter-of-fact

**commotion**
03 ado, row
04 fuss, riot, stir, to-do
05 furor
06 bustle, clamor, fracas, hubbub, racket, rumpus, tumult, uproar
07 ferment, turmoil
08 ballyhoo, brouhaha, disorder, disquiet, upheaval
10 excitement, hullabaloo

**communal**
05 joint
06 common, public, shared
07 general
10 collective

**commune**
04 talk
06 colony, confer
07 kibbutz
08 converse
10 collective, fellowship, get in touch, settlement
11 cooperative, make contact

**communicable**
08 catching
09 infective
10 contagious, conveyable, infectious, spreadable
12 transferable
13 transmissible, transmittable

**communicate**
04 talk
05 phone, relay, speak, write
06 convey, impart, inform, notify, pass on, report, reveal, spread, unfold
07 contact, declare, diffuse, divulge, express, publish
08 acquaint, announce, converse, disclose, intimate, proclaim, transmit
09 broadcast, make known
10 correspond, get in touch
11 disseminate

**communication**
07 contact
10 connection, disclosure
11 information
12 intelligence, transmission
13 dissemination

➤ *Methods of communication*:
02 IT, TV
03 fax, Web
04 drum, mail, memo, note, post, wire, word
05 cable, e-mail, media, press, radar, radio, telex
06 gossip, letter, medium, notice, poster, speech, the net
07 bleeper, Braille, handout, hotline, journal, leaflet, message, Telstar
08 aerogram, bulletin, bullhorn, circular, computer, dispatch, Intelsat, intercom, junk mail, magazine, PA system, pamphlet, postcard, telegram, teletext, wireless
09 facsimile, grapevine, mass media, megaphone, Morse code, newsflash, newspaper, satellite, semaphore, telephone
10 communiqué, dictaphone,

television, walky-talky
11 advertising, chain letter, smoke signal, teleprinter, the Internet
12 broadcasting, conversation, press release, sign language, walkie-talkie, World Wide Web
13 carrier pigeon, press briefing
14 electronic mail, teletypewriter
15 press conference

**communicative**
04 free, open
05 frank
06 candid, chatty
07 voluble
08 friendly, outgoing, sociable
09 expansive, extrovert, talkative
10 unreserved
11 forthcoming, informative

**communion**
04 Mass
05 unity
06 accord
07 concord, empathy, harmony
08 affinity, sympathy
09 Eucharist, Sacrament
10 fellowship
11 intercourse, Lord's Supper

**communiqué**
06 report
07 message
08 bulletin, dispatch
09 newsflash, statement
12 announcement
13 communication

**communism**
06 Maoism
07 Marxism, Titoism
08 Leninism
09 socialism, Stalinism
10 Bolshevism, Trotskyism
11 revisionism
12 collectivism
15 totalitarianism

**community**
05 group, state
06 colony, people, public
07 commune, kibbutz, society
08 district, locality, populace
09 residents
10 fellowship, population
12 neighborhood

**commute**
05 remit
06 adjust, reduce, soften
07 curtail, journey, lighten, shorten, shuttle
08 decrease, mitigate

12 travel to work

**commuter**
08 traveler
09 passenger
11 straphanger, suburbanite

**compact**
04 bond, cram, deal, firm, neat, pact, tamp
05 brief, close, dense, pithy, short, small, solid, terse
06 little, pocket, treaty
07 bargain, concise, entente, flatten, squeeze
08 alliance, compress, condense, contract, covenant, succinct
09 agreement, concordat, indenture, press down
10 compressed, settlement
11 consolidate, transaction

**companion**
03 pal
04 aide, ally, mate
05 buddy, crony
06 escort, fellow, friend
07 comrade, consort, partner
08 follower, intimate, sidekick
09 associate, attendant, colleague, confidant
10 accomplice, confidante
11 confederate

**companionable**
06 genial
07 affable, amiable
08 familiar, friendly, informal, outgoing, sociable
09 congenial, convivial
10 gregarious, neighborly
11 sympathetic
12 approachable

**companionship**
07 company, rapport, support
08 intimacy, sympathy
10 fellowship, friendship
11 association, camaraderie, comradeship, contubernal
12 conviviality, togetherness
13 esprit de corps

**company**
03 set
04 band, body, crew, firm, team
05 crowd, party, troop, trust
06 cartel, circle, guests, troupe
07 callers, concern, society
08 assembly, business, ensemble, visitors
09 gathering, syndicate
10 attendance, consortium, fellowship, subsidiary
11 association, comradeship, corporation, partnership

12 conglomerate, conviviality
13 establishment, multinational

**comparable**
04 akin, like
05 alike, equal
07 cognate, related, similar
08 parallel
09 analogous
10 equivalent, tantamount
12 commensurate, proportional
13 corresponding, proportionate

**comparative**
04 near
08 relative

**compare**
04 link
05 equal, liken, match, weigh
06 equate
07 balance, measure
08 contrast, parallel, resemble
09 analogize, correlate, juxtapose

**comparison**
07 analogy
08 contrast, likeness, parallel
10 similarity
11 correlation, differences, distinction, resemblance
12 relationship
13 comparability, juxtaposition
15 differentiation

**compartment**
03 bay
04 area, cell, part
05 berth, booth, niche, stall
06 alcove, carrel, locker
07 chamber, cubicle, section
08 carriage, category, division
09 cubbyhole, partition
10 pigeonhole

**compass**
04 area, zone
05 field, limit, range, reach, realm, scale, scope, space
06 bounds, circle, extent, limits, realms, sphere
07 circuit, stretch
08 boundary
09 enclosure
13 circumference
15 pair of compasses

**compassion**
04 care, pity
05 mercy
06 sorrow
07 concern
08 clemency, kindness, leniency, sympathy
10 condolence, tenderness

**compassionate**

11 benevolence
13 consideration, fellow-feeling, understanding

**compassionate**

06 caring, gentle, humane, kindly, tender
07 clement, lenient, pitying
08 merciful
10 benevolent, supportive
11 kindhearted, sympathetic, warmhearted
12 humanitarian
13 understanding

**compatible**

06 suited
07 similar
08 matching, suitable
09 consonant, in harmony
10 consistent, harmonious, like-minded, well-suited
11 conformable, sympathetic, well-matched

**compatriot**

09 associate, colleague
10 countryman
12 countrywoman
13 fellow citizen

**compel**

04 make, urge
05 bully, drive, force, impel
06 coerce, lean on, oblige
07 dragoon
08 browbeat, bulldoze, insist on, pressure
09 constrain, strong-arm
10 intimidate, pressurize
14 put the screws on

**compelling**

06 cogent, urgent
07 weighty
08 forceful, gripping, mesmeric, riveting
09 absorbing
10 compulsive, convincing, overriding, persuasive
11 enthralling, irrefutable
12 irresistible, spellbinding

**compendium**

06 digest, manual
07 summary
08 handbook, synopsis
09 companion, guidebook, vade mecum

**compensate**

05 atone, repay
06 cancel, offset, redeem, refund, reward
07 balance, nullify, redress, restore, satisfy
08 make good

09 indemnify, make up for, reimburse
10 counteract, make amends, recompense, remunerate
14 make reparation

**compensation**

06 amends, refund, reward
07 comfort, damages, payment, redress
08 requital
09 atonement, indemnity, repayment
10 recompense, reparation
11 restitution, restoration
12 remuneration, satisfaction
13 reimbursement
15 indemnification

**compete**

03 run, vie
04 race
05 enter, fight, rival
06 battle, jostle, oppose, strive
07 contend, contest, go in for
08 struggle, take part
09 challenge
11 participate, pit yourself

**competence**

05 skill
07 ability, fitness
08 aptitude, capacity, facility
09 expertise, technique
10 capability, experience
11 proficiency

**competent**

03 fit
04 able
05 adept, equal
06 expert
07 capable, skilled, trained
08 adequate, skillful, suitable
09 efficient, qualified
10 acceptable, proficient
11 appropriate, experienced
12 accomplished, satisfactory

**competition**

03 cup
04 bout, game, meet, quiz, race
05 event, field, match, vying
06 rivals, strife
07 contest, rivalry, tourney
08 conflict, struggle
09 challenge, opponents
10 contention, tournament
11 challengers, competitors
12 championship

**competitive**

04 keen
05 pushy
09 ambitious, combative, cutthroat, dog-eat-dog

**competitiveness**

07 rat race, rivalry
08 keenness
09 pugnacity, pushiness
10 aggression, antagonism
13 ambitiousness, combativeness

**competitor**

05 rival
06 player
07 entrant
08 emulator, opponent
09 adversary, candidate, contender
10 antagonist, challenger, contestant, opposition
11 competition, participant

**compilation**

04 opus, work
05 album
06 corpus
07 omnibus
08 treasury
09 amassment, anthology, collation, selection
10 assemblage, collection, compendium, miscellany

**compile**

04 edit
05 amass
06 garner, gather
07 arrange, collate, collect, compose, marshal
08 assemble, organize

**complacency**

05 pride
07 triumph
08 gloating, pleasure, smugness
11 contentment
12 satisfaction

**complacent**

04 smug
05 proud
07 conceit, pleased
08 gloating
09 contented, satisfied
10 triumphant
11 self-assured, unconcerned
13 self-righteous, self-satisfied

**complain**

03 nag
04 ache, beef, carp, fuss, moan
05 bleat, gripe, groan, whine
06 bemoan, bewail, grouse, repine, whinge
07 grumble, protest
08 be in pain, feel pain
09 bellyache, criticize
10 suffer from
11 kick up a fuss, remonstrate
15 have a bone to pick

**complainer**
06 moaner, whiner
07 grouser, niggler, whinger
08 grumbler
09 nit-picker
10 bellyacher, fussbudget

**complaint**
04 moan
05 gripe, upset
06 charge, grouse, malady
07 ailment, censure, disease, grumble, illness, malaise, protest, trouble
08 disorder, sickness
09 annoyance, condition, criticism, grievance, objection
10 accusation, affliction

**complaisant**
06 docile
07 amiable
08 amenable, biddable, obedient, obliging
09 agreeable, compliant, tractable
10 solicitous
11 conformable, deferential
12 conciliatory
13 accommodating

**complement**
03 sum
05 crown, match, quota, total
06 set off
08 complete, entirety, round off, totality
09 accessory, aggregate, allowance, companion
10 completion, go well with
11 counterpart
12 consummation
14 go well together

**complementary**
06 fellow
08 matching
09 companion, finishing
10 completing, perfecting, reciprocal
12 complemental
13 corresponding

**complete**
03 cap, end
04 done, full, over
05 close, crown, ended, total, uncut, utter, whole
06 answer, clinch, entire, fill in, finish, intact, wind up
07 achieve, execute, fill out, fulfill, perfect, perform, plenary, realize, settled
08 absolute, conclude, detailed, finalize, finished, outright,

round off, thorough, unbroken
09 concluded, discharge, downright, finalized, out-and-out, polish off, terminate, undivided
10 accomplish, consummate, exhaustive, unabridged
11 unmitigated
13 comprehensive

**completely**
05 fully, quite
06 in full, wholly
07 solidly, totally, utterly
08 entirely
09 every inch, perfectly
10 absolutely, altogether, thoroughly
12 heart and soul
13 bag and baggage, root and branch
14 in every respect

**completion**
03 end
05 close
06 finish
08 fruition
09 discharge, execution
10 conclusion, perfection, settlement
11 achievement, culmination, fulfillment, realization, termination
12 consummation, finalization

**complex**
05 mixed, thing
06 hang-up, phobia, scheme, system, varied
07 devious, diverse, network
08 compound, disorder, fixation, involved, multiple, neurosis, ramified, tortuous
09 Byzantine, composite, difficult, elaborate, institute, intricate, obsession, structure
10 circuitous, convoluted
11 development
12 organization
13 establishment, preoccupation

**complexion**
04 look, skin, tone, type
05 color, guise, light, stamp
06 aspect, nature
08 coloring
09 character
10 appearance
12 pigmentation

**complexity**
09 intricacy

11 convolution, deviousness, diverseness, elaboration, involvement
12 complication, entanglement, multiplicity, ramification, repercussion

**compliance**
06 assent
08 yielding
09 agreement, deference, obedience, passivity
10 submission
11 concurrence
12 acquiescence, complaisance
14 submissiveness

**compliant**
06 docile
07 passive, pliable
08 biddable, obedient, yielding
09 agreeable, tractable
10 submissive
11 acquiescent, complaisant, deferential, subservient
13 accommodating

**complicate**
05 mix up
06 jumble, muddle, tangle
07 confuse, involve
08 compound, entangle
09 elaborate

**complicated**
06 fiddly
07 complex, cryptic
08 involved, puzzling, tortuous
09 difficult, elaborate, intricate
10 convoluted, perplexing
11 problematic

**complication**
03 web
04 snag
06 tangle
07 mixture, problem
08 drawback, obstacle
09 confusion, intricacy
10 complexity, difficulty
11 convolution, elaboration
12 ramification, repercussion

**complicity**
08 abetment, approval
09 agreement, collusion, knowledge
10 connivance
11 concurrence, involvement

**compliment**
04 laud
05 extol, honor
06 admire, eulogy, homage, praise, salute
07 applaud, commend, devoirs, flatter, tribute

08 accolade, approval,
   encomium, eulogize, flattery,
   respects
09 greetings, laudation
10 admiration, best wishes,
   felicitate, salutation
11 speak well of
12 commendation,
   congratulate, felicitation
13 speak highly of
15 congratulations

**complimentary**
04 free
06 gratis
08 admiring, courtesy
09 approving, favorable
10 eulogistic, flattering, on the
   house
11 panegyrical
12 appreciative, commendatory

**comply**
04 meet, obey
05 agree, defer, yield
06 accede, accord, assent,
   follow, oblige, submit
07 abide by, conform, consent,
   fulfill, observe, perform,
   satisfy
09 acquiesce, discharge
11 accommodate

**component**
03 bit
04 item, part, unit
05 basic, piece
06 factor, module
07 element, section
08 inherent, integral
09 essential, intrinsic, spare part
10 ingredient

**comport**
03 act
04 bear
05 carry
06 acquit, behave, deport
07 conduct, perform

**compose**
04 calm, form, make
05 frame, quiet, still, write
06 create, devise, invent, make
   up, pacify, settle, soothe
07 arrange, assuage, collect,
   concoct, control, produce
08 assemble, calm down
10 constitute

**composed**
04 calm, cool
06 placid, sedate, serene
07 relaxed
08 tranquil
09 collected, confident,
   unruffled, unworried

10 calmed down, controlled
11 levelheaded, unflappable
13 imperturbable, quietened
   down, self-possessed
14 self-controlled
15 cool as a cucumber

**composer**
04 bard, poet
05 maker
06 author, writer
07 creator
08 arranger, musician, producer
09 songsmith, tunesmith
10 originator, songwriter

▶ *Names of composers*:
03 **Bax** (Arnold)
04 **Arne** (Thomas), **Bach**
   (Johann Sebastian), **Berg**
   (Alban), **Byrd** (William),
   **Cage** (John), **Ives** (Charles),
   **Orff** (Carl)
05 **Bizet** (Georges), **Bliss**
   (Arthur), **Dukas** (Paul),
   **Elgar** (Edward), **Falla**
   (Manuel de), **Fauré**
   (Gabriel), **Glass** (Philip),
   **Gluck** (Christoph), **Grieg**
   (Edvard), **Haydn** (Joseph),
   **Holst** (Gustav), **Jobim**
   (Antonio Carlos), **Liszt**
   (Franz), **Lully** (Jean
   Baptiste), **Parry** (Hubert),
   **Ravel** (Maurice), **Satie**
   (Erik), **Verdi** (Giuseppe),
   **Weber** (Carl Maria von)
06 **Barber** (Samuel), **Bartók**
   (Béla), **Boulez** (Pierre),
   **Brahms** (Johannes), **Casals**
   (Pablo), **Chopin** (Frédéric),
   **Coates** (Eric), **Delius**
   (Frederick), **Dvorák**
   (Antonín), **Franck** (César),
   **Glinka** (Mikhail), **Gounod**
   (Charles), **Handel** (George
   Frideric), **Hanson**
   (Howard), **Harris** (Roy),
   **Ligeti** (György), **Mahler**
   (Gustav), **Mozart**
   (Wolfgang Amadeus),
   **Powell** (Mel), **Rameau** (Jean
   Philippe), **Rubbra**
   (Edmund), **Varèse** (Edgard),
   **Wagner** (Richard), **Walton**
   (Sir William), **Webern**
   (Anton von)
07 **Albéniz** (Isaac), **Bellini**
   (Vincenzo), **Berlioz**
   (Hector), **Borodin**
   (Alexander), **Britten**
   (Benjamin), **Copland**
   (Aaron), **Corelli**
   (Arcangelo), **Debussy**

(Claude), **Delibes** (Léo),
**Dowland** (John), **Janácek**
(Leos), **Menotti** (Gian-
Carlo), **Nielsen** (Carl),
**Poulenc** (Francis), **Puccini**
(Giacomo), **Purcell**
(Henry), **Rossini**
(Gioacchino), **Salieri**
(Antonio), **Shankar** (Ravi),
**Smetana** (Bedrich), **Strauss**
(Johann), **Strauss**
(Richard), **Tavener** (John),
**Tippett** (Michael), **Vivaldi**
(Antonio)
08 **Berkeley** (Lennox),
**Bruckner** (Anton),
**Couperin** (François),
**Gershwin** (George),
**Grainger** (Percy),
**Hoffmann** (Ernst Theodor
Wilhelm), **Holliger** (Heinz),
**Honegger** (Arthur),
**Massenet** (Jules), **Messiaen**
(Olivier), **Respighi**
(Ottorino), **Schubert**
(Franz), **Schumann**
(Robert), **Scriabin**
(Aleksandr), **Sibelius** (Jean),
**Sullivan** (Arthur), **Williams**
(John)
09 **Beethoven** (Ludwig van),
**Bernstein** (Leonard),
**Boulanger** (Nadia),
**Buxtehude** (Diderik),
**Donizetti** (Gaetano),
**Hindemith** (Paul),
**Hovhaness** (Alan),
**Meyerbeer** (Giacomo),
**Offenbach** (Jacques),
**Pachelbel** (Johann),
**Prokofiev** (Sergei),
**Scarlatti** (Alessandro),
**Scarlatti** (Domenico),
**Tortelier** (Paul)
10 **Birtwistle** (Harrison),
**Ellington,** (Edward
Kennedy "Duke"),
**Monteverdi** (Claudio),
**Mussorgsky** (Modeste),
**Praetorius** (Michael),
**Rubinstein** (Anton), **Saint-
Saëns** (Camille),
**Schoenberg** (Arnold),
**Stravinsky** (Igor), **Villa-
Lobos** (Heitor)
11 **Humperdinck** (Engelbert),
**Leoncavallo** (Ruggiero),
**Mendelssohn** (Felix),
**Rachmaninov** (Sergei),
**Stockhausen** (Karlheinz),
**Tchaikovsky** (Piotr),
**Theodorakis** (Mikis)
12 **Shostakovich** (Dmitri)

## composite

13 **Khatchaturian** (Aram), **Maxwell Davies** (Sir Peter)
14 **Rimsky-Korsakov** (Nikolai)
15 **Vaughan Williams** (Ralph)
➤ See also MUSIC

## composite

05 alloy, blend, fused, mixed
06 fusion
07 amalgam, blended, complex, mixture
08 compound, pastiche
09 patchwork, synthesis
11 agglutinate, combination, synthesized
12 conglomerate

## composition

04 form, opus, poem, work
05 essay, novel, opera, paper, piece, story, theme
06 design, layout, makeup
07 balance, drawing, harmony, mixture, picture, writing
08 creation, devising, exercise, painting, symphony
09 arranging, character, formation, invention, structure, work of art
10 concoction, consonance, production, proportion
11 arrangement, combination, compilation, formulation
12 conformation, constitution, organization

## compost

04 peat
05 humus, mulch
06 manure
08 dressing
10 fertilizer

## composure

04 calm, ease
05 poise
06 aplomb
07 dignity
08 coolness, serenity
09 assurance, placidity
10 confidence, equanimity
11 impassivity, self-control, tranquility

## compound

03 mix, pen
04 fold, fuse, yard
05 add to, alloy, blend, court, fused, mixed, pound, unite
06 corral, fusion, hybrid, medley, mingle, worsen
07 amalgam, combine, complex, magnify, mixture, paddock

08 coalesce, heighten, increase, multiple, stockade
09 admixture, aggravate, composite, enclosure, intensify, intricate, synthesis
10 amalgamate, complicate, exacerbate, synthesize
11 combination, composition, intermingle, synthesized
12 amalgamation, conglomerate

## comprehend

03 get, see
04 know
05 cover, grasp
06 fathom, take in
07 contain, discern, embrace, include, involve, realize
08 comprise, perceive
09 encompass, penetrate
10 appreciate, understand

## comprehensible

05 clear, lucid, plain
06 simple
08 coherent, explicit
09 graspable
10 accessible
11 conceivable, discernible
12 intelligible
14 understandable
15 straightforward

## comprehension

03 ken
05 grasp, sense
07 insight
08 judgment
09 knowledge
10 conception, perception
11 discernment, realization
12 appreciation, intelligence
13 understanding

## comprehensive

04 full, wide
05 broad
07 blanket, general, overall
08 complete, thorough
09 all-around, extensive, inclusive
10 exhaustive, widespread
14 across-the-board

## compress

03 jam
04 cram, tamp
05 crush, press, stuff, wedge
06 impact, reduce, squash
07 abridge, astrict, compact, flatten, shorten, squeeze
08 condense, contract
09 coarctate, constrict, summarize, synopsize
10 abbreviate, pressurize

11 concentrate, consolidate

## comprise

06 embody, make up, take in
07 compose, contain, embrace, include, involve
09 consist of, encompass
10 comprehend, constitute
11 incorporate

## compromise

05 adapt, agree, shame
06 adjust, damage, expose, settle, weaken
07 balance, bargain, concede, imperil, involve
08 endanger, trade-off
09 agreement, arbitrate, discredit, implicate, mediation, negotiate, prejudice, undermine
10 concession, settlement
11 give and take, meet halfway, negotiation
13 accommodation, understanding

## compulsion

04 need, urge
05 drive, force
06 demand, desire, duress
07 impulse, longing
08 coercion, pressure
09 necessity, obsession
10 obligation, temptation

## compulsive

06 hooked, urgent
07 driving
08 addicted, gripping, habitual, hardened, hopeless, mesmeric, riveting
09 absorbing, dependent, incurable, obsessive
10 compelling
11 enthralling, fascinating
12 irresistible, overpowering, overwhelming, pathological, spellbinding

## compulsory

03 set
06 forced
07 binding
08 required
09 de rigueur, essential, mandatory, necessary, requisite
10 obligatory, stipulated

## compunction

05 guilt, qualm, shame
06 regret, sorrow, unease
07 remorse
09 misgiving, penitence
10 contrition, hesitation, repentance, uneasiness

## compute

03 sum
04 rate
05 add up, count, tally, total
06 assess, figure, reckon
07 count up, measure
08 estimate, evaluate
09 calculate, enumerate

## computer

► *Computer terms*:
02 PC, VR
03 bit, bug, CPU, DOS, DTP, FAQ, GUI, ISP, RAM, ROM, VDU, Web, WWW
04 boot, byte, chip, data, disk, down, game, GIGO, HTML, icon, ISDN, menu, PROM
05 ALGOL, ASCII, BASIC, CD-ROM, COBOL, crash, e-mail, input, macro, modem, mouse, PILOT, pixel, virus
06 analog, backup, buffer, cursor, DVD-ROM, format, laptop, memory, PASCAL, screen, server, SNOBOL, the Net, the Web, toggle, window
07 browser, digital, FORTRAN, hacking, monitor, network, printer, program, readout, toolbar, upgrade, Web page, Web site, WYSIWYG
08 bookmark, chat room, databank, database, diskette, emoticon, firewall, freeware, function, gigabyte, graphics, hard disk, hardware, home page, joystick, keyboard, kilobyte, megabyte, mouse pad, printout, software, template, terminal, user name
09 character, directory, disk drive, e-commerce, hypertext, interface, mainframe, newsgroup, processor, scrolling, shareware, video game
10 domain name, floppy disk, multimedia, netiquette, peripheral, programmer
11 cut and paste, motherboard, screen saver, silicon chip, the Internet, work station
12 laser printer, magnetic disk, search engine, spellchecker, World Wide Web
13 file extension, ink-jet printer, user interface, word processor
14 electronic mail, microprocessor, read only

memory, virtual reality, word processing
15 operating system

► *Names of computer scientists*:
04 **Cray** (Seymour), **Jobs** (Steven), **Zuse** (Konrad)
05 **Gates** (William Henry "Bill"), **Olsen** (Kenneth Harry), **Sugar** (Alan)
06 **Amdahl** (Gene Myron), **Backus** (John), **Eckert** (John Presper), **Michie** (Donald), **Turing** (Alan), **Wilkes** (Maurice Vincent)
07 **Babbage** (Charles), **Mauchly** (John William), **Shannon** (Claude Elwood), **Stibitz** (George Robert)
08 **Atansoff** (John Vincent), **Lovelace** (Ada), **Shockley** (William Bradford), **Sinclair** (Clive)
09 **Forrester** (Jay Wright), **Hollerith** (Herman)
10 **Von Neumann** (John)
➤ See also SCIENTIST

## comrade

03 pal
04 aide, ally, mate
05 buddy, crony
06 escort, fellow, friend
07 consort, partner
08 follower, intimate, sidekick
09 associate, colleague, companion, confidant
10 accomplice, confidante
11 confederate

## con

02 do
04 bilk, dupe, hoax, rook, scam
05 bluff, cheat, fraud, trick
06 fiddle, fleece, racket, rip off
07 deceive, defraud, swindle
08 hoodwink, inveigle
09 bamboozle
11 double-cross, hornswoggle

## concatenation

05 chain, nexus, trail, train
06 course, series, string, thread
07 linking
08 progress, sequence
10 connection, succession
11 progression
12 interlinking, interlocking

## concave

06 cupped, hollow, sunken
07 scooped
08 hollowed, indented
09 depressed, excavated, incurvate

## conceal

04 bury, hide, mask, veil
05 cloak, cover, stash
06 hush up, screen, shroud
07 cover up, obscure, secrete
08 disguise, keep dark, submerge, suppress
09 keep quiet, whitewash
10 camouflage, keep secret

## concealed

06 covert, hidden, latent, unseen
07 covered
08 screened
09 disguised

## concealment

04 mask, veil
05 cloak, cover
06 hiding, screen, shroud
07 coverup, hideout, secrecy
08 disguise, hideaway
09 secretion, whitewash
10 camouflage, protection
11 smokescreen, suppression

## concede

03 own
04 cede
05 admit, allow, grant, yield
06 accede, accept, give up
07 confess, forfeit
08 hand over
09 recognize, surrender
10 relinquish
11 acknowledge

## conceit

05 pride
06 vanity
07 egotism, swagger
08 self-love
09 arrogance, vainglory
10 narcissism
11 complacency, haughtiness
12 boastfulness
13 conceitedness
14 self-importance

## conceited

04 smug
05 cocky, proud
07 haughty, stuck-up
08 arrogant, boastful, immodest, puffed up
09 big-headed
10 complacent
11 egotistical
12 narcissistic, supercilious, vainglorious
13 self-important, self-satisfied
14 full of yourself
15 swellheaded vain

## conceivable

06 likely

**conceive**
07 tenable
08 credible, possible, probable
09 thinkable
10 believable, imaginable

**conceive**
05 fancy, grasp, think
06 create, design, devise, invent
07 believe, develop, imagine, picture, produce, realize
08 contrive, envisage, perceive
09 formulate, originate, reproduce, visualize
10 appreciate, come up with, comprehend, understand

**concentrate**
05 focus, rivet, think
06 attend, center, elixir, gather, reduce
07 cluster, collect, distill, essence, extract, thicken
08 boil down, compress, condense, converge
09 decoction, decocture, evaporate, intensify
10 centralize, congregate
12 distillation, pay attention
13 apply yourself
15 devote attention

**concentrated**
04 deep, hard, rich
05 dense
06 all-out, strong
07 intense, reduced
08 vigorous
09 condensed, intensive, thickened, undiluted
10 compressed, evaporated

**concentration**
04 heed, mind
05 crowd
07 cluster
08 focusing, grouping
09 alertness, attention, intensity, reduction, thickness
10 absorption, collection
11 application, boiling-down, compression, convergence, deep thought, evaporation
12 accumulation, distillation

**concept**
04 idea, plan, view
05 image
06 notion, theory
07 picture, thought
10 hypothesis, impression
13 visualization

**conception**
04 clue, idea, plan, view
05 birth, image
06 design, notion, origin, outset, theory

07 inkling, picture, thought
09 beginning, formation, invention, knowledge
10 hypothesis, impression, initiation, perception
11 fecundation, origination
12 impregnation, inauguration, insemination, reproduction
13 visualization

**concern**
03 job
04 busy, care, duty, heed, task
05 alarm, field, touch, worry
06 affair, affect, bear on, bother, charge, devote, matter, regard, strain, unease
07 anxiety, apply to, company, disturb, involve, perturb, problem, refer to, trouble
08 business, disquiet, distress, interest, relate to
09 attention, syndicate
10 enterprise
11 corporation, disturbance, involvement, make anxious, make worried, partnership
12 organization, perturbation

**concerned**
04 kind
05 upset
06 caring, uneasy
07 anxious, helpful, related, unhappy, worried
08 affected, bothered, gracious, involved, troubled
09 attentive, connected, disturbed, perturbed, sensitive, unselfish
10 altruistic, implicated, interested, thoughtful
11 considerate
12 apprehensive

**concerning**
02 re
04 as to
05 about
07 apropos
09 as regards, regarding
10 relating to, respecting
11 referring to
12 with regard to
13 in the matter of, with respect to

**concert**
03 gig
04 show
05 union
06 accord, soirée, unison
07 concord, harmony, recital
09 agreement, unanimity

10 appearance, consonance, engagement, jam session
11 concordance, performance

**concerted**
05 joint
06 shared, united
08 combined
10 collective
12 concentrated
13 collaborative

**concession**
03 cut, sop
05 favor, grant, right
06 ceding
08 decrease, giving-up, handover, yielding
09 admission, allowance, exception, franchise, privilege, reduction, sacrifice
10 adjustment, compromise
11 appeasement, recognition

**conciliate**
06 disarm, pacify, soothe
07 appease, mollify, placate, satisfy
09 reconcile

**conciliation**
09 placation
11 appeasement, peacemaking
12 pacification
13 mollification
14 reconciliation

**conciliator**
04 dove
08 mediator
10 negotiator, peacemaker, reconciler
12 intermediary

**conciliatory**
06 irenic
07 pacific
09 appeasing, peaceable, placatory
10 mollifying
11 peacemaking
12 pacificatory
14 reconciliatory

**concise**
05 brief, crisp, pithy, short, terse
07 compact, summary
08 abridged, succinct, synoptic
09 condensed
10 compressed, to the point
11 abbreviated, compendious
12 epigrammatic

**conclave**
05 cabal
06 parley, powwow
07 council, meeting
08 assembly

**conclude**
10 conference
13 confabulation

**conclude**
03 end
05 cease, close, infer, judge
06 assume, clinch, decide, deduce, effect, finish, gather, reason, reckon, settle, wind up, wrap up
07 arrange, pull off, resolve, suppose, surmise, work out
08 complete
09 culminate, determine, establish, negotiate, polish off, terminate
11 come to an end, discontinue, draw to an end
12 bring to an end

**conclusion**
03 end
05 close, issue
06 finale, finish, result, upshot
07 opinion, outcome, verdict
08 decision, judgment, settling, solution
09 deduction, inference
10 completion, conviction, pulling-off, resolution, settlement, working-out
11 arrangement, consequence, culmination, termination
12 consummation

**conclusive**
05 clear, final
08 decisive, definite, ultimate
10 convincing, definitive
11 irrefutable
12 indisputable, unanswerable

**concoct**
03 mix
04 brew, cook, make, plan, plot
05 blend, hatch
06 cook up, devise, invent
07 develop, prepare
08 contrive, rustle up
09 fabricate, formulate

**concoction**
04 brew
06 potion
07 mixture
08 compound, creation
11 combination, preparation

**concomitant**
09 attendant, secondary
10 coexistent, concurrent, incidental, side effect
11 associative, synchronous
12 accompanying, coincidental, conterminous, contributing, simultaneous
13 accompaniment

15 contemporaneous

**concord**
05 amity, peace
06 accord, treaty, unison
07 compact, entente, harmony
09 agreement, consensus, unanimity
10 consonance, friendship

**concourse**
04 hall
05 crowd, crush, foyer, lobby, plaza, press, swarm
06 lounge, piazza, throng
07 meeting
08 assembly, entrance
09 gathering, multitude

**concrete**
04 firm, real
05 solid
06 actual
07 factual, genuine, visible
08 definite, material, physical, positive, specific, tangible
11 perceptible, road surface, substantial

**concubine**
05 leman, lover
08 mistress, paramour
09 courtesan, kept woman

**concupiscence**
04 lust
06 desire, libido
07 lechery, passion
08 appetite, lewdness
09 lubricity
11 lustfulness
14 lasciviousness, libidinousness

**concupiscent**
04 lewd
05 horny
07 lustful, satyric
08 prurient
09 lecherous
10 lascivious, libidinous, lubricious

**concur**
05 agree
06 accord, assent, comply
07 approve, consent
09 acquiesce, cooperate, harmonize

**concurrence**
06 assent
08 approval
09 agreement, synchrony
10 acceptance
11 association, coexistence, coincidence, convergence

12 acquiescence, common ground, simultaneity

**concurrent**
10 coexistent, coexisting, coincident, coinciding
11 concomitant, synchronous
12 simultaneous
15 contemporaneous

**condemn**
03 ban, bar
04 damn, doom, slam
05 blame, force, judge
06 berate, punish, revile
07 censure, consign, convict, reprove, upbraid
08 demolish, denounce, reproach, sentence
09 castigate, criticize
12 declare unfit

**condemnation**
05 blame
07 censure, reproof
08 judgment, reproach, sentence
09 criticism, damnation
10 conviction, thumbs-down
11 castigation
12 denunciation

**condemnatory**
08 accusing, critical
09 damnatory
10 accusatory, censorious
11 deprecatory, reprobatory, unfavorable
12 denunciatory, discouraging, proscriptive
13 incriminating

**condensation**
06 digest, précis
08 synopsis
09 reduction
10 abridgment
11 boiling-down, compression, contraction, curtailment, evaporation
12 distillation, liquefaction
13 concentration

**condense**
03 cut
06 précis, reduce
07 abridge, compact, curtail, cut down, distil, shorten, thicken
08 boil down, compress
09 evaporate, summarize
10 abbreviate, deliquesce
11 concentrate, encapsulate

**condensed**
03 cut
06 strong

07 clotted, compact, concise, cut down, reduced
09 curtailed, shortened, thickened, undiluted
10 abstracted, coagulated, compressed, contracted, evaporated, summarized
12 concentrated

**condescend**
05 deign, stoop
06 see fit
09 patronize
10 talk down to
13 lower yourself

**condescending**
05 lofty
06 lordly, snooty
07 haughty, stuck-up
08 snobbish, superior
09 imperious
10 disdainful
11 patronizing
12 supercilious

**condescension**
04 airs
07 disdain
09 loftiness
10 lordliness
11 haughtiness, superiority
12 snobbishness

**condition**
04 form, mold, rule, tone, tune
05 equip, groom, limit, order, prime, rider, setup, shape, state, terms
06 adjust, demand, fettle, health, kilter, malady, milieu, plight, revive
07 ailment, climate, context, disease, factors, fitness, illness, prepare, problem, proviso, restore, setting
08 accustom, quandary, weakness
09 brainwash, complaint, essential, influence, necessity, provision, situation, way of life
10 atmosphere, background, limitation, obligation
11 environment, familiarize, predicament, requirement, restriction, stipulation
12 indoctrinate, prerequisite, surroundings, working order
13 state of health

**conditional**
04 tied
07 limited, subject
08 relative
09 dependent, qualified

10 contingent, restricted
11 provisional

**condolence**
04 pity
07 support
08 sympathy
10 compassion
11 consolation
13 commiseration

**condone**
05 allow, brook
06 excuse, ignore, pardon
07 forgive, let pass
08 overlook, tolerate
15 turn a blind eye to

**conducive**
06 useful
07 helpful, leading, tending
09 favorable, promoting
10 beneficial, productive
11 encouraging
12 advantageous

**conduct**
02 do
03 act, run
04 bear, lead, show, take, ways
05 bring, carry, chair, guide, pilot, steer, usher
06 acquit, behave, direct, escort, handle, manage
07 actions, bearing, comport, control, manners, perform
08 attitude, behavior, carry out, demeanor, guidance, organize
09 accompany, operation
10 administer, deportment, leadership, management
11 comportment, orchestrate, supervision

**conductor**
➤ *Names of conductors:*
04 **Böhm** (Karl), **Wood** (Henry)
05 **Boult** (Adrian), **Bülow** (Hans von), **Davis** (Colin), **Hallé** (Charles), **Kempe** (Rudolf), **Masur** (Kurt), **Ozawa** (Seiji), **Solti** (Georg), **Sousa** (John Philip)
06 **Abbado** (Claudio), **Previn** (André), **Rattle** (Simon), **Thomas** (Michael Tilson), **Walter** (Bruno)
07 **Beecham** (Thomas), **Haitink** (Bernard), **Karajan** (Herbert von), **Lambert** (Constant), **Richter** (Hans), **Salonen** (Esa-Pekka), **Sargent** (Malcolm)

08 **Goossens** (Eugene)
09 **Ashkenazy** (Vladimir), **Barenboim** (Daniel), **Bernstein** (Leonard), **Klemperer** (Otto), **Tortelier** (Paul), **Toscanini** (Arturo)
10 **Barbirolli** (John)
11 **Furtwängler** (Wilhelm)
12 **Rostropovich** (Mstislav)
➤ See also MUSIC

**conduit**
04 duct, main, pipe, tube
05 canal, chute, ditch, drain, flume
06 gutter, tunnel
07 channel, culvert, passage
08 waterway
10 passageway
11 watercourse

**confectionery**
04 rock
05 candy, fudge, sweet, taffy
06 bonbon, sweets, tablet, toffee
07 truffle
08 lollipop, lollypop
09 jelly bean
10 chocolates

**confederacy**
06 league
07 compact
08 alliance
09 coalition
10 federation
11 partnership

➤ *Names of Confederate states:*
05 Texas
07 Alabama, Florida, Georgia
08 Arkansas, Virginia
09 Louisiana, Tennessee
11 Mississippi
13 North Carolina, South Carolina

**confederate**
04 ally
05 rebel
06 allied, friend, united
07 abettor, federal, partner
08 combined, federate
09 accessory, associate, colleague, supporter
10 accomplice, associated

**confederation**
05 union
06 league
07 compact
08 alliance
09 coalition
10 federation

## confer

11 association, partnership
12 amalgamation

## confer

04 give, lend, talk
05 award, grant
06 accord, bestow, impart
07 consult, discuss, present
08 converse
10 deliberate

## conference

05 forum
06 debate, summit
07 meeting, seminar
08 congress, dialogue
09 symposium
10 colloquium, discussion
11 convocation

## confess

03 own
05 admit, grant, own up
06 assert, expose
07 concede, declare, divulge, profess, tell all, unbosom
08 disclose, unburden
09 come clean, make known
11 accept blame, acknowledge
13 spill the beans
15 get off your chest

## confession

08 exposure, owning-up
09 admission, assertion
10 disclosure, divulgence, profession, revelation
11 declaration, unburdening
14 acknowledgment

## confidant, confidante

03 pal
04 mate
05 crony
06 friend
08 intimate
09 companion
11 bosom friend, close friend

## confide

04 tell
05 admit
06 impart, reveal
07 confess, divulge
08 disclose, intimate, unburden
11 tell a secret
15 get off your chest

## confidence

05 faith, poise, trust
06 aplomb, belief, secret
07 courage
08 boldness, calmness, credence, intimacy, reliance
09 certainty, composure
10 conviction, dependence
12 self-reliance

13 self-assurance
14 self-possession

## ▢in confidence

08 in secret
09 entre nous, in privacy, in private, privately
15 between you and me

## confident

04 bold, calm, cool, sure
06 upbeat
07 assured, certain
08 composed, positive
09 dauntless, unabashed
10 courageous, optimistic
11 self-assured, self-reliant
12 unhesitating
13 self-possessed
14 sure of yourself

## confidential

05 privy
06 secret
07 private
08 hush-hush, intimate
09 sensitive, top secret
10 classified, restricted
12 off-the-record

## confidentially

08 in camera, in secret
09 entre nous, in privacy, in private, privately
10 on the quiet, personally
15 between you and me

## configuration

04 cast, form
05 shape
06 figure
07 contour, outline
11 arrangement, composition

## confine

04 bind, cage, edge, shut
05 bound, limit, scope
06 border, coop up, immure, intern, lock up, shut up
07 enclose, impound, inhibit, repress, shackle, trammel
08 boundary, frontier, imprison, lock away, restrain, restrict
09 constrain, parameter, perimeter
10 limitation
11 hold captive, incarcerate
12 circumscribe, hold prisoner

## confined

06 narrow, shut in
07 limited
08 enclosed
10 housebound, restricted
11 constrained
13 circumscribed

## confinement

05 birth, labor
07 custody
09 captivity, detention
10 childbirth, internment
11 house arrest, parturition
12 imprisonment
13 incarceration

## confirm

05 check, prove
06 affirm, assert, assure, clinch, harden, ratify, settle, verify
07 approve, endorse, fortify, promise, support, warrant
08 evidence, sanction, validate
09 authorize, establish, guarantee, reinforce
10 asseverate, strengthen
11 corroborate, demonstrate

## confirmation

05 proof
07 backing, support
08 approval, sanction
09 agreement, testimony
10 acceptance, validation
11 affirmation, endorsement
12 ratification, verification
13 accreditation, corroboration

## confirmed

03 set
05 fixed
06 inured, rooted
07 chronic
08 hardened, seasoned
09 incurable
10 entrenched, inveterate
11 established
12 incorrigible, long-standing
13 dyed-in-the-wool

## confiscate

05 seize
07 impound
08 arrogate, take away
09 sequester
10 commandeer
11 appropriate, expropriate

## confiscation

07 escheat, removal, seizure
09 distraint
10 forfeiture
12 distrainment
13 appropriation, expropriation, sequestration

## conflagration

04 fire
05 blaze
07 inferno
09 holocaust
12 deflagration

## conflict
03 row, war
04 feud
05 brawl, clash, fight, set-to
06 battle, combat, differ, fracas, oppose, strife, strive, unrest
07 contend, contest, dispute, ill-will, quarrel, warfare
08 be at odds, disagree, friction, skirmish, struggle, variance
09 antipathy, hostility
10 antagonism, contradict, dissension, opposition
12 disagreement
13 confrontation

## confluence
05 union
07 conflux, meeting
08 junction
11 concurrence, convergence
12 meeting point

## conform
04 obey
05 adapt, agree, match, tally
06 adjust, comply, follow
07 observe
09 be uniform, harmonize
10 correspond, toe the line
13 go with the flow
14 follow the crowd

## conformist
06 yes man
11 rubber stamp
13 stick-in-the-mud
14 traditionalist
15 conventionalist

## conformity
07 harmony
08 affinity, likeness
09 agreement, congruity, obedience, orthodoxy
10 compliance, consonance, observance, uniformity
11 resemblance
13 accommodation
14 correspondence

## confound
04 beat, ruin, stun
05 amaze, upset
06 baffle, defeat, puzzle, thwart
07 astound, confuse, destroy, flummox, mystify, nonplus, perplex, startle, stupefy
08 astonish, bewilder, demolish, surprise
09 bamboozle, discomfit, dumbfound, frustrate
11 flabbergast

## confront
04 defy, face, meet, show
05 brave

06 accost, attack, oppose, resist, tackle
07 address, assault, present
08 deal with, face up to
09 challenge, encounter, stand up to, withstand
10 meet head on, reckon with
12 face the music
14 get to grips with

## confrontation
05 clash, fight, set-to
06 battle
07 contest, quarrel
08 conflict, showdown
09 collision, encounter
10 engagement
12 disagreement

## confuse
05 floor, mix up, throw, upset
06 baffle, bemuse, mingle, muddle, puzzle, tangle
07 fluster, involve, mistake, mortify, mystify, perplex
08 bewilder, confound, disorder, entangle
09 disorient, elaborate
10 complicate, discompose, disconcert, tie in knots

## confused
05 at sea, dazed
06 addled
07 at a loss, baffled, bemused, chaotic, floored, jumbled, mixed-up, muddled, puzzled
09 flummoxed, flustered, mystified, perplexed
10 bewildered, confounded, nonplussed
11 disarranged
12 disconcerted, disorganized
13 disorientated

## confusing
07 cryptic, unclear
08 baffling, involved, muddling, puzzling, tortuous
09 ambiguous, difficult
10 misleading, perplexing
11 bewildering, complicated

## confusion
04 mess
05 chaos, mix-up
06 foul-up, jumble, muddle
07 clutter, turmoil
08 disarray, shambles, upheaval
09 commotion
10 bafflement, perplexity, puzzlement, untidiness
12 bewilderment
13 mystification

## congeal
03 gel, set

04 cake, clot, fuse
06 curdle, freeze, harden
07 stiffen, thicken
08 coalesce, solidify
09 coagulate

## congenial
06 genial, homely
08 friendly, pleasant, relaxing
09 agreeable, favorable
10 compatible, like-minded, well-suited
11 complaisant, sympathetic

## congenital
05 utter
06 inborn, inbred, innate
07 chronic, connate, natural
08 complete, habitual, hardened, inherent, seasoned, thorough
09 incurable, inherited
10 hereditary, inveterate

## congested
04 full
06 choked, jammed, packed
07 blocked, clogged, crammed, crowded, stuffed
11 overcrowded, overflowing

## congestion
03 jam
05 snarl
07 choking
08 blockage, blocking, clogging, gridlock
10 bottleneck, traffic jam
12 overcrowding

## conglomerate
04 firm
06 cartel, merger
07 company, concern
08 business
10 consortium
11 association, corporation, partnership
13 establishment, multinational

## conglomeration
04 mass
06 medley
09 composite
10 collection, hotchpotch
11 aggregation
12 accumulation
13 agglomeration

## congratulate
04 laud
06 praise
08 wish well
10 compliment, felicitate
12 pat on the back

## congratulations
09 greetings

**congregate**
10 best wishes, good wishes
11 compliments
12 pat on the back
13 felicitations

**congregate**
04 form, mass, meet
05 clump, crowd, flock, rally
06 gather, muster, throng
07 cluster, collect, convene
08 assemble, converge
10 accumulate, rendezvous

**congregation**
04 host, mass
05 crowd, flock, group, laity
06 parish, throng
07 meeting
08 assembly
09 multitude
10 fellowship
12 parishioners

**congress**
04 diet
05 forum, synod
07 council, meeting
08 assembly, conclave
09 gathering
10 convention, parliament
11 Capitol Hill, convocation,
   legislature

**congruence**
07 harmony
09 agreement
10 concinnity, similarity
11 coincidence, concurrence,
   consistency, parallelism
13 compatibility
14 correspondence

**conical**
07 pointed, tapered
08 tapering
09 pyramidal, turbinate
10 cone-shaped
12 funnel-shaped, infundibular
13 infundibulate

**conjectural**
07 assumed, posited
08 supposed, surmised
09 tentative
10 postulated
11 speculative, theoretical
12 hypothetical

**conjecture**
05 fancy, guess, infer
06 notion, reckon, theory
07 imagine, presume, suppose,
   surmise, suspect
08 estimate, theorize
09 guesswork, inference,
   speculate, suspicion

10 conclusion, hypothesis,
   projection
11 hypothesize, presumption,
   speculation, supposition
13 extrapolation

**conjugal**
06 bridal, wedded
07 marital, married, nuptial,
   spousal
08 hymeneal
09 connubial
11 epithalamic, matrimonial

**conjunction**
05 union
11 association, coexistence,
   combination, unification
12 amalgamation

**❑in conjunction with**
04 with
09 along with, alongside
12 together with

**conjure**
05 charm, evoke, raise, rouse
06 call up, invoke, summon
07 bewitch, do magic
08 do tricks
09 fascinate

**❑conjure up**
05 evoke
06 awaken, create, excite, recall
07 produce
09 recollect
10 call to mind
11 bring to mind

**conjurer**
06 wizard
08 magician, sorcerer
11 illusionist, thaumaturge
12 prestigiator
15 prestidigitator

**conk**

**❑conk out**
03 die
04 fail
08 pass away
09 break down, go haywire
10 fall asleep
12 go on the blink

**connect**
03 tie
04 ally, fuse, join, link
05 affix, clamp, unite
06 attach, bridge, couple, fasten,
   relate, secure
07 bracket, combine
08 identify, relate to
09 associate, correlate
11 concatenate

**connected**
04 akin, tied
06 allied, joined, linked, united
07 coupled, related, secured
08 combined, fastened
10 affiliated, associated

**connection**
03 tie
04 bond, link
05 clasp, joint
07 analogy, contact
08 alliance, coupling, junction,
   parallel, relation, relative
09 fastening, relevance
10 attachment
11 association, correlation
12 acquaintance, relationship

**connivance**
07 consent
08 abetment, abetting
09 collusion, condoning
10 complicity

**connive**
04 plot
05 allow, cabal, coact, let go
06 ignore, scheme, wink at
07 collude, condone, let pass
08 conspire, overlook, tolerate
09 disregard, gloss over
15 turn a blind eye to

**conniving**
05 nasty
07 corrupt, immoral
08 plotting, scheming
09 colluding
10 conspiring

**connoisseur**
04 buff
05 judge
06 expert, pundit
07 devotee, epicure, gourmet
08 aesthete, virtuoso
09 authority
10 aficionado, specialist
11 cognoscente

**connotation**
04 hint
06 nuance
08 allusion, coloring, overtone
09 undertone
10 intimation, suggestion
11 implication, insinuation

**connote**
05 imply
06 hint at, import
07 purport, signify, suggest
08 allude to, indicate, intimate
09 associate, insinuate

**conquer**
03 win

**conqueror**
04 beat, best, rout, take
05 annex, crush, quell, seize
06 defeat, humble, master, obtain, occupy, subdue
07 overrun, succeed, trounce
08 overcome, vanquish
09 overpower, overthrow, rise above, subjugate
11 triumph over
14 get the better of

**conqueror**
04 hero, lord
06 master, victor, winner
08 champion
10 subjugator, vanquisher
12 conquistador

**conquest**
03 win
04 coup, rout
05 catch, lover
06 defeat
07 capture, mastery, success, triumph, victory
08 crushing, invasion
09 overthrow
10 annexation, occupation
11 acquisition, subjugation
12 vanquishment
13 appropriation

**conscience**
06 ethics, morals, qualms
08 scruples
09 moral code, standards
10 moral sense, principles

**conscience-stricken**
05 sorry
06 guilty
07 ashamed
08 contrite, penitent, troubled
09 regretful, repentant
10 remorseful
11 guilt-ridden
12 compunctious

**conscientious**
06 honest
07 careful, dutiful, upright
08 diligent, faithful, thorough
09 assiduous, dedicated
10 methodical, meticulous, particular, scrupulous
11 hard-working, painstaking

**conscious**
05 alert, alive, awake, aware
07 heedful, knowing, studied, willful
08 rational, sensible, sentient
09 cognizant, reasoning
10 calculated, deliberate, responsive, volitional
11 intentional
12 premeditated

**consciousness**
04 mind
09 alertness, awareness, intuition, sentience
10 cognizance, perception
11 realization, recognition, sensibility, wakefulness

**conscript**
05 draft
06 call up, enlist, enroll, muster
07 draftee, recruit, round up
08 enlistee

**consecrate**
05 bless, exalt
06 anoint, devote, hallow, ordain, revere
08 dedicate, make holy, sanctify, venerate

**consecutive**
06 in turn, serial
07 running, seriate
08 straight, unbroken
09 following
10 back to back, continuous, sequential, successive

**consensus**
05 unity
07 concord, consent, harmony
09 agreement, unanimity
11 concurrence

**consent**
05 agree, allow, grant, yield
06 accede, accept, assent, comply, concur, permit
07 concede
08 approval, sanction
09 acquiesce, agreement, authorize, clearance
10 acceptance, compliance, concession, consensual, permission, the go-ahead
11 acquiescence, go along with
12 acquiescence
13 authorization, the green light
14 give the go-ahead
15 give the thumbs-up

**consequence**
03 end
05 issue, value
06 effect, import, moment, result, upshot, weight
07 concern, outcome
09 substance
10 importance, side effect
11 eventuality, implication
12 repercussion, significance
13 reverberation

**consequent**
07 ensuing
09 following, resultant

10 sequential, subsequent

**consequently**
04 ergo, then, thus
05 hence
09 as a result, therefore
11 accordingly, necessarily
12 subsequently

**conservation**
06 saving, upkeep
07 custody, economy, keeping
09 husbandry
10 protection
11 maintenance, safekeeping
12 preservation, safeguarding

**conservatism**
09 orthodoxy
14 traditionalism
15 conventionalism

**conservative**
04 Tory
05 sober
07 careful, die-hard, guarded
08 cautious, moderate, orthodox, rightest
09 hidebound, right-wing
10 inflexible
11 reactionary, right-winger, traditional
12 conventional
13 set in your ways, stick-in-the-mud, unprogressive
14 traditionalist

**conservatory**
06 school
07 academy, college
08 hothouse
10 greenhouse
11 music school
13 conservatoire

**conserve**
04 keep, save
05 guard, hoard
07 protect, store up
08 keep back, maintain
09 safeguard
10 take care of

**consider**
04 deem, feel, hold, muse, note, rate
05 count, judge, study, think, weigh
06 ponder
07 believe, examine, reflect, respect, toy with, weigh up
08 chew over, cogitate, meditate, mull over
10 bear in mind, deliberate
11 contemplate

**considerable**
03 big

**considerably**
04 tidy
05 ample, great, large
06 lavish, marked
07 sizable
08 abundant, generous
09 important, plentiful
10 noteworthy, reasonable
11 appreciable, perceptible, significant, substantial

**considerably**
04 much
07 greatly
08 markedly
10 noticeably, remarkably
11 appreciably
13 significantly, substantially

**considerate**
04 kind
06 caring
07 helpful, tactful
08 discreet, generous, gracious, obliging, selfless
09 attentive, concerned, sensitive, unselfish
10 altruistic, charitable, solicitous, thoughtful
11 sympathetic
13 compassionate

**consideration**
04 care, fact, heed, tact
05 issue, point
06 factor, notice, regard, review
07 concern, respect, thought
08 altruism, analysis, kindness, scrutiny, sympathy
09 attention, reckoning
10 cogitation, compassion, generosity, meditation, reflection, rumination
11 examination, sensitivity
12 circumstance, deliberation, graciousness, selflessness
13 contemplation
14 thoughtfulness

**considering**
08 all in all, in view of
12 in the light of
13 bearing in mind

**consign**
04 ship
06 assign, banish, convey
07 commend, deliver, entrust
08 give over, hand over, relegate, transfer, transmit

**consignment**
04 load
05 batch, cargo, goods
08 delivery, shipment

**consist**
03 lie

06 embody, inhere, reside
07 embrace, include, involve
08 amount to, comprise
11 be contained, incorporate

**consistency**
07 density, harmony
08 cohesion, evenness, firmness, identity, sameness
09 agreement, constancy, thickness, viscosity
10 accordance, consonance, regularity, uniformity
11 persistence, reliability
13 dependability, steadfastness
14 correspondence

**consistent**
04 same
06 stable, steady
07 logical, regular, uniform
08 constant, matching
09 accordant, congruous, consonant, unfailing
10 compatible, conforming, dependable, harmonious, unchanging
13 corresponding

**consolation**
04 ease, help
05 cheer
06 relief, solace, succor
07 comfort, support
08 soothing, sympathy
11 alleviation, reassurance
13 commiseration

**console**
04 calm, help
05 board, cheer, dials, panel
06 buck up, levers, solace, soothe, succor
07 buttons, comfort, condole, hearten, relieve, support
08 controls, keyboard, reassure
09 dashboard, encourage
11 commiserate, instruments
12 control panel

**consolidate**
04 fuse, join
05 merge, unify, unite
06 cement, secure
07 combine, fortify
09 reinforce, stabilize
10 amalgamate, strengthen

**consolidation**
06 fusion, merger
07 joining, uniting
08 alliance, securing
09 cementing
10 federation
11 affiliation, association, combination, unification
12 amalgamation

13 confederation, reinforcement, stabilization, strengthening

**consonance**
07 concord, harmony
09 agreement, congruity
10 accordance, conformity
11 consistency, suitability
14 correspondence

**consonant**
08 agreeing, suitable
09 accordant, according, congruous, in harmony
10 consistent, harmonious
12 in accordance
13 correspondent

**consort**
03 mix
04 wife
06 escort, mingle, spouse
07 husband, partner
09 associate, companion
10 fraternize

**consortium**
04 bloc, bond, pact
05 guild, union
06 cartel, league, treaty
07 compact, company
08 alliance, marriage
09 coalition, syndicate
10 federation
11 affiliation, association, corporation, partnership
12 conglomerate, organization
13 confederation

**conspicuous**
05 clear, showy
06 flashy, garish, marked, patent
07 blatant, evident, glaring, obvious, visible
08 flagrant, manifest, striking
09 prominent
10 noticeable, observable
11 discernible, perceptible
12 ostentatious, recognizable

**conspiracy**
04 plot
05 cabal
06 league, scheme
07 frame-up, treason
08 intrigue
09 collusion, stratagem
10 connivance
11 machination
13 collaboration

**conspirator**
07 plotter, schemer, traitor
08 colluder
09 conspirer, intriguer
12 collaborator

## conspire

04 ally, join, link, plot
06 scheme
07 collude, connect, connive
08 intrigue, maneuver
09 associate, cooperate, machinate
10 hatch a plot, join forces
11 act together, collaborate

## constancy

07 loyalty
08 devotion, fidelity, firmness
09 stability
10 permanence, resolution, steadiness, uniformity
12 faithfulness, perseverance
13 dependability, steadfastness
15 trustworthiness

## constant

04 even, firm, true
05 loyal
06 stable, steady
07 devoted, endless, eternal, nonstop, staunch, uniform
08 faithful, resolute, unbroken
09 ceaseless, continual, incessant, perpetual, steadfast, unvarying
10 changeless, continuous, dependable, persistent, unchanging, unwavering
11 everlasting, never-ending, trustworthy, unremitting
12 interminable
13 uninterrupted
14 without respite

## constantly

06 always
07 forever, nonstop
09 ad nauseam, endlessly
10 all the time, invariably
11 ceaselessly, continually, incessantly, perpetually
12 continuously, interminably, relentlessly

## constellation

➤ *Names of constellations:*

03 Ara, Fly, Fox, Leo, Net, Ram
04 Crab, Crow, Crux, Dove, Harp, Lion, Lynx, Lyra, Pavo, Swan, Vela, Wolf
05 Altar, Aries, Arrow, Cetus, Clock, Crane, Draco, Eagle, Hydra, Lepus, Libra, Lupus, Mensa, Musca, Norma, Orion, Pyxis, Sails, Table, Twins, Virgo, Whale
06 Antlia, Aquila, Archer, Auriga, Boötes, Cancer, Corvus, Crater, Cygnus, Dragon, Fishes, Gemini, Hydrus, Lizard, Octans, Octant, Pictor, Pisces, Scales, Taurus, Virgin
07 Centaur, Cepheus, Columba, Dolphin, Giraffe, Lacerta, Peacock, Pegasus, Perseus, Phoenix, Sagitta, Serpens, Serpent, Sextans, Sextant, Unicorn
08 Aquarius, Eridanus, Great Dog, Hercules, Herdsman, Leo Minor, Scorpion, Scorpius
09 Andromeda, Centaurus, Chameleon, Delphinus, Great Bear, Little Dog, Monoceros, Swordfish, Telescope, Ursa Major, Ursa Minor
10 Canis Major, Canis Minor, Cassiopeia, Chamaeleon, Charioteer, Little Bear, Little Lion, Microscope, Sea Serpent, Triangulum
11 Capricornus, Sagittarius, Telescopium, Water Bearer, Winged Horse
12 Microscopium
13 Northern Crown, River Eridanus, Southern Cross, Southern Crown
14 Camelopardalis, Corona Borealis
15 Corona Australis, Mariner's Compass

➤ See also STAR

## consternation

04 fear
05 alarm, dread, panic, shock
06 dismay, fright, horror, terror
07 anxiety
11 disquietude, trepidation
12 bewilderment, perturbation

## constituent

03 bit
04 part, unit
05 basic, voter
07 content, elector, element
08 inherent, integral
09 component, principle
10 ingredient
13 component part

## constitute

02 be
04 form, make, mean
05 found, set up
06 create, make up
07 add up to, appoint, charter, compose, empower
08 amount to, comprise
09 authorize, establish, institute, represent

10 commission

## constitution

04 code, laws
05 rules
06 health, makeup, nature
07 charter
08 physique, statutes
09 character, condition, formation, structure
11 codified law, composition, disposition, temperament
12 organization

## constitutional

04 turn, walk
05 amble, by law, legal
06 airing, lawful, stroll, vested
08 codified, official, ratified
09 promenade, statutory
10 authorized, legitimate
11 legislative
12 governmental

## constrain

04 bind, curb, urge
05 check, force, impel, limit
06 coerce, compel, oblige
07 confine
08 hold back, pressure, restrict
09 constrict
10 pressurize

## constrained

05 stiff
06 forced, uneasy
07 guarded
08 reserved, reticent
09 inhibited, unnatural

## constraint

04 curb
05 check, force
06 damper, demand, duress
08 coercion, pressure
09 necessity, restraint
10 compulsion, impediment, limitation, obligation
11 restriction

## constrict

04 bind, curb
05 check, cramp, limit, pinch
06 hamper, hinder, impede, narrow, shrink
07 confine, inhibit, squeeze, tighten
08 compress, contract, hold back, restrict, strangle
09 constrain

## constriction

04 curb
05 check, cramp
08 blockage, pressure, stenosis

**construct**
09 hindrance, narrowing, reduction, squeezing, stricture, tightness
10 constraint, impediment, limitation, tightening
11 compression, restriction

**construct**
04 form, make
05 build, erect, found, model, put up, raise, set up, shape
06 create, design, devise
07 compose, elevate, fashion
08 assemble, engineer
09 establish, fabricate
11 manufacture, put together

**construction**
04 form
05 model, shape
06 fabric, figure, making
07 edifice, meaning, reading
08 assembly, building, erection
09 elevation, framework, inference, structure
11 fabrication, manufacture
14 interpretation

**constructive**
06 useful
07 helpful
08 positive, valuable
09 practical
10 beneficial, productive

**construe**
04 read
05 infer, see as
06 deduce, render
07 analyze, explain, expound
08 regard as
09 interpret
10 take to mean, understand

**consult**
06 confer, look up, turn to
07 discuss, refer to
08 question
09 ask advice
10 deliberate, seek advice

**consultant**
06 expert
07 adviser, advisor
09 authority
10 specialist

**consultation**
04 talk
05 forum
07 hearing, meeting, session
08 dialogue
09 interview
10 conference, discussion
11 appointment, examination
12 deliberation

**consultative**
08 advising, advisory
10 counseling
12 recommending

**consume**
03 eat, gut, use
04 grip, take
05 drain, drink, eat up, spend, touch, use up, waste
06 absorb, devour, expend, gobble, guzzle, ingest, obsess, ravage, tuck in
07 deplete, destroy, drink up, engross, swallow, utilize
08 demolish, dominate, gobble up, lay waste, squander, tuck into
09 go through, overwhelm, polish off, preoccupy
10 annihilate, get through

**consumer**
04 user
05 buyer
06 client, patron
07 shopper
08 customer

**consuming**
08 gripping
09 absorbing, devouring, obsessive
10 compelling, dominating, engrossing, tormenting
12 overwhelming, preoccupying

**consummate**
03 cap, end
05 crown, total, utter
06 finish, gifted, superb
07 fulfill, perfect, perform, realize, skilled, supreme
08 absolute, complete, polished, ultimate
09 matchless, practiced, terminate
10 accomplish, proficient
12 accomplished, transcendent
13 distinguished

**consummation**
03 end
06 finish
07 capping
08 crowning
09 execution
10 completion, conclusion, perfection
11 achievement, culmination, fulfillment, realization, termination
13 actualization
14 accomplishment

**consumption**
02 TB
05 waste
06 eating
07 using-up
08 draining, drinking, guzzling, spending
09 devouring, expending, ingestion, tucking-in
10 exhaustion, swallowing
11 expenditure, utilization
12 tuberculosis

**contact**
03 fax
04 call, meet
05 e-mail, phone, reach, touch, union
06 friend, impact, notify
07 speak to, sponsor, write to
08 approach
09 get hold of, proximity, telephone
10 connection, contiguity
11 association
12 acquaintance
13 communication
14 get in touch with

**contagious**
08 catching, epidemic, pandemic
09 spreading
10 compelling, infectious
12 communicable, irresistible
13 transmissible, transmittable

**contain**
04 curb, hold, seat, stop, take
05 carry, check, limit
06 embody, stifle, take in
07 control, embrace, enclose, include, involve, repress
08 comprise, keep back, restrain, suppress
11 incorporate, keep in check

**container**
06 holder, vessel
10 receptacle, repository

**contaminate**
04 foul, harm, soil
05 decay, spoil, stain, sully, taint
06 debase, defile, infect
07 corrupt, pollute, tarnish
10 adulterate, make impure

**contamination**
05 decay, filth, stain, taint
07 soiling, tarnish
08 impurity, spoiling, sullying
09 infection, pollution, vitiation
10 corruption, debasement, defilement, rottenness
12 adulteration

**contemplate**
04 muse, plan, view
05 dwell, study, weigh
06 design, expect, intend, look at, ponder, regard, survey
07 examine, foresee, inspect, observe, propose, weigh up
08 cogitate, consider, envisage, meditate, mull over, ruminate
09 reflect on
10 deliberate, think about

**contemplation**
05 dwell, study
06 gazing, musing, regard
07 thought
08 scrutiny, weighing
09 pondering
10 cogitation, meditation, reflection, rumination
11 cerebration, mulling-over
12 deliberation
13 consideration

**contemplative**
06 intent, musing
07 pensive
08 cerebral
10 meditative, reflective, ruminative, thoughtful
13 deep in thought

**contemporary**
06 coeval, latest, modern, recent, trendy, with it
07 current, present, topical
08 up-to-date
10 avant-garde, coetaneous, futuristic, newfangled, present-day
11 fashionable, synchronous, ultramodern
13 up-to-the-minute

**contempt**
05 scorn
06 hatred
07 disdain, dislike, neglect
08 derision, dishonor, loathing, ridicule
09 disregard
10 disrespect
11 detestation

**contemptible**
03 low
04 base, mean, vile
06 abject, paltry
07 pitiful
08 shameful, wretched
09 loathsome, worthless
10 degenerate, despicable, detestable, lamentable
11 ignominious

**contemptuous**
07 cynical, jeering, mocking
08 arrogant, derisive, derisory, insolent, scornful, sneering
09 insulting, withering
10 disdainful
12 contumelious, supercilious
13 condescending, disrespectful

**contend**
03 vie, war
04 aver, cope, deal, hold
05 argue, brave, claim, clash, fight, state
06 affirm, allege, assert, battle, combat, oppose, reckon, strive, tackle, tussle
07 address, compete, contest, declare, dispute, grapple, profess, wrestle
08 face up to, maintain, struggle
09 challenge
10 asseverate, meet head on

**content**
04 cozy, ease, glad, load, size
05 happy, ideas, items, parts, peace, theme, topic
06 at ease, matter, pacify, please, volume
07 appease, comfort, delight, essence, gratify, meaning, placate, pleased, satisfy, section, subject, willing
08 capacity, cheerful, elements, gladness, material, pleasure
09 fulfilled, happiness, satisfied, substance, unworried
10 components
11 comfortable, ingredients

**contented**
04 glad
05 happy
07 pleased, relaxed
08 cheerful
09 fulfilled, satisfied, unworried
10 untroubled
11 comfortable

**contention**
04 view
05 claim, stand
06 belief, debate, enmity, notion, strife, theory, thesis
07 discord, dispute, feeling, feuding, opinion, rivalry
08 argument, judgment, position, struggle
09 assertion, hostility, intuition, viewpoint
10 conviction, dissension, impression, persuasion
11 controversy, point of view
12 disagreement

**contentious**
07 hostile
08 disputed, doubtful, perverse
09 debatable, polemical
10 disputable, pugnacious
11 quarrelsome
12 antagonistic, questionable
13 argumentative, controversial

**contentment**
04 ease
05 peace
07 comfort
08 gladness, pleasure, serenity
09 happiness
10 equanimity
11 complacency, fulfillment
12 cheerfulness, peacefulness, satisfaction

**contest**
03 vie
04 deny, game, race
05 doubt, event, fight, match, set-to, vying
06 battle, combat, debate, oppose, refute, strive, tussle
07 compete, contend, dispute, tourney
08 conflict, litigate, question, skirmish, struggle
09 challenge, encounter
10 tournament
11 competition, controversy
12 championship

**contestant**
05 rival
06 player
07 entrant
08 aspirant, opponent
09 adversary, contender
10 competitor

**context**
07 factors, setting
09 framework, situation
10 background, conditions
12 surroundings
13 circumstances

**contiguous**
04 near, next
05 close
06 beside
07 vicinal
08 abutting, adjacent, touching
09 adjoining, bordering
10 conjoining, tangential
11 neighboring
12 conterminous

**continent**

▶ *Names of continents:*
04 Asia
06 Africa, Europe

09 Australia
10 Antarctica
12 North America, South America

**contingency**
05 event
06 chance
08 accident, fortuity, incident
09 emergency, happening
10 randomness
11 chance event, eventuality, possibility, uncertainty

**contingent**
04 body
05 batch, group, party, quota
06 chance, likely
07 company, mission, section, subject
08 possible, probable
09 dependent
10 complement, delegation, deputation, detachment
11 conditional
15 representatives

**continual**
07 eternal, regular
08 constant, frequent, repeated, unending
09 incessant, perpetual, recurrent
10 continuous, persistent, repetitive
11 everlasting
12 interminable

**continually**
06 always
07 forever, nonstop
09 endlessly, eternally, regularly
10 all the time, constantly, habitually, repeatedly
11 ceaselessly, incessantly, perpetually, recurrently
12 continuously, interminably, persistently

**continuance**
04 term
06 period
08 duration
10 permanence
11 persistence, protraction
12 continuation

**continuation**
06 sequel
07 renewal
08 addition
09 extension
10 resumption, supplement
11 development, furtherance, lengthening, protraction
12 prolongation

**continue**
04 go on, last, rest, stay
05 abide, renew
06 endure, extend, keep on, pursue, remain, resume
07 carry on, hold out, persist, press on, proceed, prolong, survive, sustain
08 lengthen, maintain, progress
09 keep going, soldier on
10 keep on with, recommence, start again
11 persevere in

**continuity**
04 flow
07 linkage
08 cohesion, sequence
10 connection, succession
11 progression

**continuous**
05 solid
07 endless, lasting, nonstop
08 constant, extended, unbroken, unending
09 ceaseless, unceasing
11 consecutive, never-ending, unremitting, with no letup
12 interminable
13 uninterrupted

**contort**
04 knot, warp
05 gnarl, twist
06 deform, wrench, writhe
07 distort, wriggle
08 misshape
09 convolute, disfigure
14 bend out of shape

**contortionist**
07 acrobat
09 rubber man
12 escape artist

**contour**
04 form
05 curve, lines, shape
06 aspect, figure, relief
07 outline, profile
10 silhouette

**contraband**
03 hot
06 banned
07 bootleg, illegal
08 smuggled
10 bootlegged

**contract**
03 get
04 bond, deal, pact
05 agree, catch, tense
06 draw in, engage, lessen, narrow, pick up, pledge, reduce, settle, shrink, treaty

07 abridge, arrange, bargain, compact, curtail, develop, promise, shorten, shrivel, tighten, wrinkle
08 compress, condense, decrease, diminish
09 agreement, concordat, constrict, negotiate, stipulate, succumb to, undertake
10 abbreviate, agree terms, go down with, settlement
11 arrangement, transaction
12 come down with

**contraction**
07 tensing
09 drawing-in, lessening, narrowing, reduction, shrinkage
10 abridgment, shortening, shriveling, tightening
11 astringency, compression, curtailment
12 abbreviation, constriction
13 shortened form

**contradict**
04 deny
05 clash, rebut
06 impugn, negate, oppose, refute
07 confute, counter, gainsay
08 be at odds, conflict, contrast, disagree
09 disaffirm, go against
14 fly in the face of

**contradiction**
07 dispute, paradox
08 conflict, negation, rebuttal, variance
09 challenge
10 antithesis, refutation
11 confutation, incongruity
12 disagreement
13 disaffirmance, inconsistency
14 disaffirmation
15 counterargument

**contradictory**
08 clashing, contrary, opposing, opposite
11 conflicting, dissentient, incongruous, paradoxical
12 antagonistic, antithetical, incompatible, inconsistent

**contraption**
03 rig
06 device, gadget
07 machine
09 apparatus, mechanism
11 contrivance, thingamabob, thingamajig, thingumabob, thingumajig

## contrary

07 adverse, awkward, counter, hostile, opposed, reverse, wayward
08 clashing, converse, opposing, opposite, perverse, stubborn
09 difficult, obstinate
10 antithesis, headstrong
11 disobliging, intractable
12 antagonistic, cantankerous, incompatible, inconsistent
14 just the reverse

❑**on the contrary**
15 just the opposite, quite the reverse

## contrast

04 foil
06 differ, oppose, relief
07 compare
08 be at odds, conflict, disagree, opposite
09 disparity, go against
10 contradict, difference, divergence, opposition
11 distinction, distinguish

❑**in contrast to**
09 as against, opposed to
10 rather than

## contravene

04 defy
05 break, flout
06 breach
07 disobey, violate
08 infringe
10 transgress

## contretemps

05 hitch
06 mishap
08 accident
10 difficulty, misfortune
11 predicament
12 misadventure

## contribute

04 give, help, make
05 add to, cause, endow, grant
06 bestow, chip in, create, donate, lead to, supply
07 compile, compose, conduce, furnish, produce, promote, provide
08 generate, occasion, result in
09 originate, subscribe
10 bring about, give rise to
11 play a part in

## contribution

04 gift, item
05 grant, input, piece, story
06 column, report, review
07 article, feature, handout
08 addition, bestowal, donation, gratuity, offering
09 endowment
12 subscription

## contributor

05 donor, giver
06 author, backer, patron, writer
07 sponsor
08 compiler, reporter, reviewer
09 columnist, freelance
10 benefactor, freelancer, journalist, subscriber
13 correspondent

## contrite

05 sorry
06 humble
08 penitent
09 chastened, regretful, repentant
10 remorseful
11 guilt-ridden, penitential

## contrition

05 shame
06 regret, sorrow
07 remorse
09 penitence
10 repentance
11 compunction, humiliation

## contrivance

04 plan, plot, ploy, ruse, tool
05 dodge, trick
06 device, gadget, scheme
07 machine, project
08 artifice, intrigue
09 apparatus, appliance, implement, invention, mechanism, stratagem
11 contraption, machination

## contrive

04 plan, plot
06 design, devise, invent, manage, scheme, wangle
07 arrange, concoct, finagle, succeed
08 engineer, find a way, maneuver
09 construct
11 orchestrate, stage-manage

## contrived

05 false, set-up
06 forced
07 labored
08 mannered, overdone, strained
09 elaborate, unnatural
10 artificial

## control

03 run
04 curb, dial, head, keep, knob, lead, rule, sway, work
05 brake, check, lever, limit, power, reign, steer
06 direct, govern, manage, subdue, switch, verify
07 command, contain, mastery, monitor, oversee, repress
08 dominate, guidance, regulate, restrain, restrict
09 be the boss, constrain, dominance, hindrance, influence, restraint, supervise, supremacy
10 constraint, discipline, government, limitation, management, regulation, repression, run the show
11 call the tune, preside over, restriction, supervision
12 call the shots, jurisdiction, rule the roost, wear the pants
14 pull the strings

## controversial

07 at issue
08 disputed, doubtful
09 debatable, polemical
10 disputable
11 contentious

## controversy

06 debate, strife
07 discord, dispute, eristic, polemic, quarrel, wrangle
08 argument, friction, squabble
10 contention, discussion, dissension, war of words
11 altercation
12 disagreement

## contusion

04 bump, lump, mark
05 knock
06 bruise, injury
07 blemish
08 swelling
10 ecchymosis

## conundrum

05 poser
06 enigma, puzzle, riddle
07 anagram, problem
08 word game
11 brain-teaser
12 brain-twister
13 Chinese puzzle

## convalescence

08 recovery
11 improvement, restoration
12 recuperation
14 rehabilitation

## convene

04 call, meet
05 rally
06 gather, muster, summon
07 collect, convoke

**convenience**
08 assemble
10 congregate
12 call together

**convenience**
03 use
06 device, gadget, toilet
07 amenity, benefit, fitness, service, utility
08 facility, resource
09 advantage, appliance, ease of use, handiness
10 expediency, usefulness
11 propinquity, suitability
13 accessibility, opportuneness
14 propitiousness, serviceability

**convenient**
05 handy
06 at hand, fitted, nearby, suited, timely, useful
07 adapted, fitting, helpful
08 suitable
09 available, expedient, opportune, well-timed
10 accessible, near at hand
11 close at hand, labor-saving, within reach

**convention**
04 bond, code, deal, pact
05 synod, usage
06 custom, treaty
07 compact, council, meeting
08 assembly, conclave, practice, protocol
09 agreement, concordat, delegates, etiquette, formality, gathering, propriety, punctilio, tradition
10 conference, settlement
11 convocation, transaction

**conventional**
05 trite, usual
06 normal, proper, ritual
07 correct, regular, routine
08 accepted, expected, ordinary, orthodox, received, standard, straight
09 customary, prevalent
10 button-down, conformist, mainstream, pedestrian, unoriginal
11 commonplace, stereotyped
12 conservative, run-of-the-mill

**converge**
04 form, join, mass, meet
05 focus, merge, unite
07 close in, combine
08 approach, coincide
10 move toward
11 concentrate
12 come together

**convergence**
05 union
07 meeting, merging
08 blending, junction
10 confluence
11 coincidence, combination
12 intersection

**conversant**
□ **conversant with**
08 versed in
09 skilled in
10 apprised of, au fait with
11 practiced in
12 familiar with, proficient in
13 experienced in
14 acquainted with

**conversation**
04 chat, talk
06 confab, gossip
08 colloquy, cozy chat, dialogue, exchange
09 discourse, tête-à-tête
10 discussion
12 heart-to-heart

**conversational**
06 casual, chatty
07 relaxed
08 informal
10 colloquial
13 communicative

**converse**
04 chat, talk
06 confer, gossip
07 chatter, commune, counter, discuss, obverse, reverse
08 contrary, opposing, opposite, reversed
09 discourse
10 antithesis, transposed
11 communicate

**conversion**
06 change, switch
07 rebirth, turning
08 exchange, mutation
09 reshaping
10 adaptation, adjustment, alteration, persuasion, remodeling
11 reformation
12 modification, regeneration
13 metamorphosis, transmutation
14 reconstruction, transformation

**convert**
04 make, turn
05 adapt, alter
06 adjust, change, modify, mutate, reform, revise, switch

07 rebuild, remodel, reshape, restyle, win over
08 adherent, believer, disciple, exchange, go over to, neophyte, persuade, transfer
09 proselyte, refashion, transform, transmute
11 reconstruct
12 metamorphose
13 changed person

**convertible**
07 open car
09 adaptable
10 adjustable, modifiable, permutable, topless car
15 interchangeable

**convex**
07 bulging, gibbous, rounded
08 swelling
11 protuberant

**convey**
04 bear, move, pipe, send, tell
05 carry, drive, fetch, guide
06 impart, relate, reveal
07 conduct, deliver, express
08 disclose, transfer, transmit
09 make known, transport
11 communicate

**conveyance**
03 bus, cab, car, van
04 auto, cart, taxi
05 coach, truck, wagon
06 ceding
07 bicycle, vehicle
08 carriage, delivery, granting, movement, transfer
10 automobile, bequeathal, motorcycle
12 transporting
14 transportation

**convict**
03 lag
05 crook, felon, judge, thief
06 inmate, robber, termer
07 burglar, condemn, villain
08 criminal, imprison, jailbird, offender, prisoner, sentence
09 wrongdoer
10 find guilty, lawbreaker

**conviction**
05 creed, faith, tenet
06 belief, fervor
07 opinion
08 firmness, judgment, sentence
09 assurance, certainty, certitude
10 confidence, persuasion
12 condemnation, imprisonment

**convince**
04 sway
06 assure, prompt, sell on
07 prove to, win over
08 persuade, talk into
09 influence
11 bring around

**convincing**
06 cogent, likely
07 telling
08 credible, forceful, powerful
09 plausible
10 compelling, conclusive, impressive, persuasive

**convivial**
03 gay
05 jolly, merry
06 genial, hearty, jovial, lively
07 cordial, festive
08 cheerful, friendly, sociable
09 fun-loving

**conviviality**
05 cheer, mirth
06 gaiety
07 jollity
08 bonhomie
09 festivity, geniality, joviality
10 cordiality, liveliness
11 merrymaking, sociability

**convocation**
04 diet
05 synod
07 council, meeting, retreat
08 assembly, conclave, congress
10 assemblage, convention
12 congregation, forgathering

**convoluted**
07 complex, winding
08 involved, tortuous, twisting
11 complicated

**convolution**
04 coil, loop, turn
05 gyrus, helix, twist, whorl
06 spiral
07 coiling, winding
08 curlicue
09 intricacy, sinuosity
10 complexity
11 involvement
12 complication

**convoy**
04 line
05 fleet, group, guard, train
06 escort
07 caravan
10 attendance, protection

**convulse**
04 jerk
05 seize
07 disturb

08 unsettle

**convulsion**
03 fit, tic
05 cramp, furor, spasm
06 attack, tremor, tumult, unrest
07 seizure, turmoil
08 disorder, eruption, outburst, paroxysm, upheaval
09 agitation, commotion

**convulsive**
05 jerky
06 fitful
07 violent
08 sporadic
09 spasmodic
12 uncontrolled

**cook**
04 burn, heat, warm
07 prepare
08 rustle up

▶ *Cooking methods:*
03 fry
04 bake, boil, stew
05 broil, brown, grill, poach, roast, sauté, shirr, steam, toast
06 braise, coddle, simmer
07 deep-fry, parboil, stir-fry
08 barbecue, scramble
09 fricassee

❑**cook up**
04 brew, plan, plot
06 devise, invent, scheme
07 concoct, dream up, prepare

**cool**
03 fan, ice
04 calm, cold, iced
05 abate, allay, aloof, chill, crisp, fresh, great, nippy, poise
06 chilly, dampen, frigid, frosty, placid, poised, sedate, temper, trendy
07 assuage, bracing, chilled, control, distant, elegant, relaxed, stylish, unmoved
08 composed, diminish, laid back, moderate, reserved
09 apathetic, collected, composure, crispness, excellent, fantastic, freshness, impassive, unexcited, unruffled
10 refreshing, unfriendly, untroubled
11 fashionable, halfhearted, levelheaded, refrigerate, self-control, standoffish, unflappable, unwelcoming
12 uninterested

13 defervescence, defervescency

**cooling**
08 chilling, freezing
11 refrigerant, ventilation
13 defervescence, defervescency, refrigeration, refrigerative, refrigeratory

**coop**
03 box, pen
04 cage
05 hutch, pound
09 enclosure

❑**coop up**
03 pen
04 cage, shut
06 immure, keep in, lock up, shut up
07 enclose, impound
08 imprison, lock away
11 incarcerate

**cooperate**
03 aid
04 help, pool
05 share, unite
06 assist, team up
07 combine
08 conspire, play ball, side with
10 contribute, join forces
11 collaborate, participate
12 band together

**cooperation**
03 aid
04 help
05 unity
08 teamwork
10 assistance
11 give-and-take
13 collaboration, participation

**cooperative**
04 co-op
05 joint
06 shared, united
07 helpful, helping, willing
08 combined, obliging
09 assisting, co-op store, compliant
10 supportive
11 co-op society, coordinated
13 accommodating, collaborative

**coordinate**
04 mesh
05 match, order
07 arrange
08 organize, regulate, tabulate
09 cooperate, correlate, harmonize, integrate
11 collaborate, synchronize

## cope
05 get by
06 make do, manage
07 carry on, succeed, survive

### ❏ cope with
06 endure, handle, manage
07 weather
08 deal with
09 encounter
11 contend with, grapple with, wrestle with

## copious
04 full, huge, lush, rich
05 ample, great
06 bags of, lavish
07 liberal, profuse
08 abundant, generous
09 bounteous, bountiful, extensive, plentiful

## cop-out
05 alibi, dodge, fraud
06 renege
07 confess, evasion, pretext
08 back down, pretense, shirking
14 passing the buck

## copse
04 bush, wood
05 brush, grove
07 coppice, thicket

## copy
03 ape, fax
04 crib, echo, fake, scan
05 clone, ditto, forge, image, issue, mimic, model, print, trace, Xerox
06 borrow, mirror, parrot, pirate, repeat, sample
07 emulate, example, forgery, imitate, replica, tracing
08 likeness, simulate, specimen
09 duplicate, facsimile, imitation, photocopy, replicate, reproduce
10 carbon copy, plagiarism, plagiarize, transcribe
11 counterfeit, impersonate
12 Photostat, reproduction

## coquettish
06 flirty
07 flighty, teasing, vampish
08 dallying, inviting
10 come-hither
11 flirtatious

## cord
03 tie
04 bond, line, link, rope
05 cable, twine
06 string
07 funicle

09 funiculus

## cordial
04 warm
06 genial, hearty
07 affable, earnest, liqueur
08 amicable, cheerful, friendly, pleasant, sociable
09 agreeable, heartfelt, welcoming

## cordiality
06 warmth
07 earnest, welcome
09 affection, geniality, sincerity
10 affability, heartiness
11 sociability
12 cheerfulness, friendliness
13 agreeableness

## cordon
04 line, ring
05 chain, fence
07 barrier

### ❏ cordon off
07 enclose, isolate
08 close off, encircle, fence off, separate, surround

## core
03 nub
04 crux, gist
05 heart
06 center, kernel, middle
07 essence, nucleus
11 nitty-gritty
12 quintessence

## corn
05 grain
06 cereal
07 popcorn
09 sweet corn
11 corn whiskey

## corner
03 hog
04 bend, fork, hole, nook, trap
05 angle, catch, crook, curve, joint, niche
06 cavity, cranny, cut off, pickle, plight, recess
07 confine, control, crevice, retreat, straits, turning
08 hardship, hideaway, hunt down, junction, monopoly
09 situation, tight spot
10 monopolize, run to earth
11 predicament

## corny
04 dull
05 banal, stale, trite
06 feeble
07 clichéd, maudlin, mawkish
08 overused
09 hackneyed

11 commonplace, sentimental

## corollary
06 result, upshot
08 illation
09 deduction, inference
10 conclusion
11 consequence

## coronation
08 crowning
12 enthronement

## coronet
05 crown, tiara
06 diadem, wreath
07 circlet, garland

## corporal
03 NCO
06 bodily, carnal
07 fleshly, officer, somatic
08 material, physical, tangible
09 corporeal

## corporate
05 joint
06 allied, merged, pooled, shared, united
08 combined, communal
10 collective
13 collaborative

## corporation
04 firm
05 trust
06 cartel
07 company, concern, council
08 business, industry
09 authority, syndicate
10 consortium
11 association, partnership
12 conglomerate, organization
13 establishment, governing body, multinational
14 holding company

## corporeal
05 human
06 actual, bodily, mortal
07 fleshly
08 material, physical, tangible
11 substantial

## corps
04 band, body, crew, team, unit
06 branch
07 service
08 division, regiment
10 contingent, detachment
11 Marine Corps

## corpse
04 body
05 mummy, stiff
06 zombie
07 cadaver, carcass, remains
08 dead body, skeleton

## corpulent
03 fat
05 beefy, bulky, burly, large, obese, plump, podgy, pudgy, stout, tubby
06 fleshy, portly, rotund
07 adipose
10 overweight, potbellied

## corpus
04 body
05 whole
08 entirety
10 collection

## corral
03 pen, sty
04 coop, fold
05 kraal, pound, stall
06 shut in
07 close in, round up
08 stockade, surround
09 enclosure
10 take hold of

## correct
04 cure, just, real, true
05 amend, debug, emend, exact, right, scold
06 actual, adjust, proper, punish, rebuke, reform, remedy, revise, seemly
07 fitting, improve, precise, rectify, redress, reprove
08 accepted, accurate, admonish, put right, regulate, standard, suitable
09 faultless, reprimand
10 ameliorate, discipline
11 appropriate, put straight, word-perfect

## correction
06 rebuke
07 reproof
08 scolding
09 amendment, reprimand
10 alteration, discipline, emendation, punishment
11 improvement, reformation
12 amelioration, modification
13 rectification

## corrective
08 curative, punitive, remedial
09 medicinal
10 emendatory, palliative
11 reformatory, therapeutic
12 disciplinary

## correlate
04 link
05 agree, tie in
06 equate, relate
07 compare, connect
08 interact, parallel
10 coordinate, correspond

## correlation
04 link
10 connection
11 interaction, interchange, reciprocity
12 relationship
14 correspondence

## correspond
03 fit, pen
05 agree, match, tally, write
06 accord, answer, concur
07 conform, match up
08 coincide, dovetail
09 correlate, harmonize
11 communicate, fit together, keep in touch

## correspondence
04 mail
05 match
07 analogy, harmony, letters
08 relation
09 agreement, congruity
10 consonance, similarity
11 coincidence, concurrence, correlation, resemblance
13 communication

## correspondent
06 pen pal, writer
08 reporter
10 journalist
11 contributor

## corresponding
04 like
07 similar
08 matching, parallel
09 analogous, identical
10 reciprocal
13 complementary

## corridor
04 hall
05 aisle
07 hallway, passage
10 passageway

## corroborate
06 back up, ratify, uphold, verify
07 bear out, certify, confirm, endorse, support, sustain
08 document, evidence, underpin, validate
12 authenticate, substantiate

## corroborative
09 endorsing, verifying
10 confirming, supporting, supportive, validating
14 substantiating

## corrode
03 rot
04 rust
05 erode, waste
06 abrade, impair

07 consume, crumble, destroy, eat away, eat into, oxidize, tarnish, wear out
08 wear away
09 waste away
11 deteriorate
12 disintegrate

## corrosive
04 acid
07 caustic, cutting, erosive, wasting, wearing
08 abrasive
09 consuming, corroding
11 destructive

## corrugated
06 fluted, folded, ridged
07 creased, grooved, striate
08 crinkled, furrowed, wrinkled
09 channeled

## corrupt
03 buy, mar
04 bent, evil, lure, warp
05 bribe, shady, taint, venal
06 blight, buy off, debase, defile, infect, rotten, suborn
07 debauch, deprave, immoral, pervert, pollute, vitiate
08 bribable, depraved
09 dishonest, dissolute
10 adulterate, degenerate, fraudulent, lead astray
11 contaminate
12 contaminated

## corruption
04 evil, vice
05 fraud, graft
07 bribery
08 impurity, iniquity, villainy
09 depravity, extortion, pollution, shadiness
10 debauchery, dishonesty, distortion, immorality, perversion, rottenness, wickedness
11 criminality, crookedness, degradation, subornation
12 degeneration
13 contamination

## corset
05 stays
06 bodice, girdle
07 support
08 corselet
11 panty girdle

## cortége
05 suite, train
06 column, parade
07 retinue
09 cavalcade, entourage
10 procession

## cosmetic
05 minor
06 beauty, makeup, slight
07 shallow, surface, trivial
08 external
10 peripheral
11 beautifying, superficial

## cosmic
04 huge, vast
07 immense, in space
08 infinite
09 grandiose, limitless, universal, worldwide

## cosmonaut
08 spaceman
09 astronaut, rocketman
13 space traveler

## cosmopolitan
06 urbane
07 worldly
08 cultured
09 universal
11 broad-minded, multiracial
12 well-traveled
13 international, multicultural, sophisticated

## cosmos
05 world
06 galaxy, system, worlds
08 creation, universe

## cosset
03 pet
04 baby
05 spoil
06 coddle, fondle, pamper
07 cherish, indulge
11 mollycoddle

## cost
03 tab
04 harm, hurt, loss, rate
05 price, quote, value, worth
06 amount, budget, charge, come to, damage, figure, injure, injury, outlay, tariff
07 expense, payment, penalty
08 estimate, expenses, price tag
09 calculate, detriment, outgoings, overheads, quotation, sacrifice, valuation
11 asking price, expenditure
12 disbursement, selling price

## costly
04 dear, rich
05 pricy, steep
06 lavish, pricey
07 harmful, ruinous
08 precious, splendid, valuable
09 expensive, priceless

10 disastrous, exorbitant, high-priced, loss-making
11 destructive, detrimental

## costume
05 dress, get-up, habit, robes
06 attire, livery, outfit
07 apparel, clothes, uniform
08 clothing, ensemble, garments
09 vestments
10 fancy dress

## coterie
03 set
04 camp, club, gang
05 cabal, group
06 caucus, circle, clique
07 faction, in-group

## cottage
03 hut
05 cabin, lodge, shack
06 chalet
08 bungalow

## couch
03 bed, set
04 bear, sofa, word
05 divan, frame, utter
06 cradle, daybed, settee
07 express, ottoman, sofa bed
09 davenport
12 chaise longue, chesterfield

## cough
03 hem
04 bark, hack, hawk
06 tussis

## ❏ cough up
03 pay
04 give
06 pay out
07 fork out
08 shell out

## council
04 body
05 board, group, junta, panel, rally, synod
06 senate, throng
07 cabinet, company, meeting
08 advisers, assembly, congress, ministry, trustees
09 committee, gathering, governors, multitude
10 commission, convention, government, parliament
11 city council, convocation, directorate
12 advisory body
13 governing body
14 administration

## counsel
04 urge, warn
05 guide

06 advice, advise, direct, exhort, lawyer
07 caution, opinion, suggest
08 admonish, advocate, attorney, guidance, instruct
10 admonition, suggestion
11 exhortation, information
12 consultation
14 recommendation

## count
03 add, sum
04 deem, hold, list, poll, tell
05 add up, check, score, tally, think, total
06 census, esteem, matter, number, reckon, regard
07 compute, include
08 consider, look upon
09 calculate, enumerate, inventory, reckoning
10 cut some ice, full amount
11 calculation, computation, enumeration
15 make a difference

## ❏ count on
05 trust
06 bank on, expect, rely on
08 depend on, reckon on

## ❏ count out
04 omit
06 ignore
07 exclude
08 leave out, pass over
09 disregard, eliminate

## countenance
04 back, face, look, mien
05 agree, allow, brook
06 endure, visage
07 approve, condone, endorse
08 features, sanction, tolerate
09 put up with
10 appearance, expression
11 physiognomy

## counter
04 chip, coin, disk, meet
05 parry, piece, table, token
06 answer, combat, marker, offset, oppose, resist, return
07 adverse, against, dispute, opposed, respond, surface
08 contrary, opposing, opposite
09 hit back at, retaliate
10 contrary to, conversely
11 work surface

## counteract
04 foil, undo
05 annul, check
06 defeat, hinder, negate, offset, oppose, resist, thwart
09 frustrate
10 invalidate, neutralize

## counterbalance
04 undo
06 offset
08 equalize
09 make up for
10 counteract, neutralize
11 countervail
12 counterpoise
13 compensate for

## counterfeit
04 copy, fake, sham
05 bogus, faked, false, feign, forge, fraud, phony, pseud
06 forged, pirate
07 falsify, feigned, forgery, imitate, pretend
08 simulate, spurious
09 fabricate, imitation, reproduce, simulated
10 artificial, fraudulent
12 reproduction

## countermand
05 annul, quash
06 cancel, repeal, revoke
07 rescind, reverse
08 abrogate, override, overturn

## counterpart
04 copy, mate, twin
05 equal, match
06 fellow
07 obverse
08 likeness, parallel
09 duplicate
14 opposite number

## countless
06 myriad, untold
07 endless, teeming, umpteen
08 infinite
09 boundless, limitless
10 numberless, without end
11 innumerable, measureless
12 immeasurable, incalculable

## countrified
04 hick
05 rural
06 cloddy, rustic
07 bucolic, idyllic
08 agrarian, cloddish, pastoral
10 provincial
12 agricultural

## country
04 area, land
05 realm, rural, state
06 landed, nation, people, region, rustic, voters
07 bucolic, idyllic, kingdom, terrain, the bush
08 agrarian, citizens, electors, pastoral, republic, the wilds

09 backwater, backwoods, greenbelt, provinces, residents, territory, the sticks
10 population, provincial
12 agricultural, principality, the boondocks

► *Countries of the world*:
02 UK
03 USA
04 Chad, Cuba, Fiji, Iran, Iraq, Laos, Mali, Oman, Peru, Togo, USSR
05 Benin, Chile, China, Congo, Egypt, Gabon, Ghana, Haiti, India, Italy, Japan, Kenya, Libya, Malta, Nauru, Nepal, Niger, Palau, Qatar, Samoa, Spain, Syria, Tonga, Yemen
06 Angola, Belize, Bhutan, Brazil, Brunei, Canada, Cyprus, France, Greece, Guinea, Guyana, Israel, Jordan, Kuwait, Latvia, Malawi, Mexico, Monaco, Norway, Panama, Poland, Russia, Rwanda, Sweden, Taiwan, Turkey, Tuvalu, Uganda, Zambia
07 Albania, Algeria, Andorra, Armenia, Austria, Bahrain, Belarus, Belgium, Bolivia, Burundi, Comoros, Croatia, Denmark, Ecuador, Eritrea, Estonia, Finland, Georgia, Germany, Grenada, Holland, Hungary, Iceland, Ireland, Jamaica, Lebanon, Lesotho, Liberia, Moldova, Morocco, Myanmar, Namibia, Nigeria, Romania, Senegal, Somalia, St. Lucia, Tunisia, Ukraine, Uruguay, Vanuatu, Vietnam
08 Barbados, Botswana, Bulgaria, Cambodia, Cameroon, Colombia, Djibouti, Dominica, Ethiopia, Honduras, Kiribati, Malaysia, Maldives, Mongolia, Pakistan, Paraguay, Portugal, Rhodesia, Slovakia, Slovenia, Sri Lanka, Suriname, Tanzania, Thailand, The Sudan, Zimbabwe
09 Argentina, Australia, Cape Verde, Costa Rica, Guatemala, Indonesia, Lithuania, Macedonia, Mauritius, Nicaragua, San Marino, Singapore, Swaziland, The Gambia, Venezuela
10 Azerbaijan, Bangladesh, El

Salvador, Ivory Coast, Kazakhstan, Kyrgyzstan, Luxembourg, Madagascar, Mauritania, Micronesia, Mozambique, New Zealand, North Korea, Seychelles, South Korea, Tajikistan, The Bahamas, Uzbekistan
11 Afghanistan, Burkina Faso, Côte d'Ivoire, Philippines, Saudi Arabia, Sierra Leone, South Africa, Switzerland, Vatican City
12 Guinea-Bissau, Turkmenistan
13 Congo Republic, Czech Republic, Liechtenstein, United Kingdom
14 Papua New Guinea, Solomon Islands, The Netherlands
15 Marshall Islands, St. Kitts and Nevis
16 Equatorial Guinea
17 Antigua and Barbuda, Dominican Republic, Trinidad and Tobago
18 São Tomé and Príncipe, United Arab Emirates
19 Serbia and Montenegro
20 Bosnia and Herzegovina
21 United States of America
22 Central African Republic
25 St. Vincent and the Grenadines

## countryman, countrywoman
04 boor, clod, hick, hind, rube
05 yokel
06 farmer, rustic
07 bumpkin, hayseed, peasant
09 hillbilly
10 clodhopper, compatriot
11 bushwhacker
12 backwoodsman

## country music

► *Names of country singers*:
03 **Lee** (Brenda)
04 **Cash** (Johnny), **Ford** (Tennessee Ernie), **Gill** (Vince), **Hill** (Faith), **Lynn** (Loretta), **Snow** (Hank), **Tubb** (Ernest)
05 **Acuff** (Roy), **Autry** (Gene), **Cline** (Patsy), **Foley** (Red), **Gayle** (Crystal), **Jones** (George), **Owens** (Buck), **Pride** (Charley), **Smith** (Carl), **Twain** (Shania), **Wells** (Kitty), **Young** (Faron)
06 **Arnold** (Eddie), **Brooks** (Garth), **Carter** (June),

Harris (Emmylou),
McGraw (Tim), **Nelson**
(Willie), **Parton** (Dolly),
Rogers (Kenny), **Strait**
(George), **Tillia** (Pam), **Tillis**
(Mel), **Travis** (Randy),
**Tucker** (Tanya)
07 **Alabama, Jackson** (Alan),
**McBride** (Martina),
**Rodgers** (Roy), **Wynette**
(Tammy)
08 **Campbell** (Glen), **Jennings**
(Waylon), **Mandrell**
(Barbara), **McEntire**
(Reba), **Williams** (Hank),
**Yearwood** (Trisha)
09 **Carpenter** (Mary-Chapin)
10 **Montgomery** (John
Michael)
12 **Oak Ridge Boys**
14 **The Dixie Chicks**
15 **Statler Brothers, The**
   **Carter Family**

**countryside**
08 farmland
09 green belt, landscape

**county**
04 area, seat
05 shire
06 region
08 district
13 state division
➤ See also BOROUGH; STATE;
   PROVINCE

**coup**
04 blow, deed, feat
06 action, putsch, revolt, stroke
07 exploit
08 maneuver, takeover, uprising
09 coup d'état, overthrow,
   rebellion
10 revolution
12 masterstroke

**coup de grâce**
04 kill
06 kibosh
07 quietus
08 clincher
09 death blow

**coup d'état**
04 coup
06 putsch, revolt
08 takeover, uprising
09 overthrow, rebellion
10 revolution

**couple**
03 duo, wed
04 ally, bind, join, link, pair, yoke
05 brace, hitch, marry
06 attach, buckle, fasten, lovers
07 conjoin, connect, twosome

08 partners
09 associate, newlyweds
13 married couple

**coupon**
04 form, slip, stub
05 check, token
06 ticket
07 voucher
11 certificate

**courage**
04 grit, guts
05 nerve, pluck, spunk, valor
06 mettle, spirit
07 bravery, heroism
08 audacity, backbone
09 fortitude, gallantry

**courageous**
04 bold
05 brave, gutsy, hardy
06 daring, heroic, plucky,
   spunky
07 gallant, valiant
08 fearless, intrepid, valorous
09 audacious, dauntless
10 determined
11 indomitable, lionhearted

**courier**
05 envoy, guide
06 bearer, escort, herald, legate,
   nuncio, runner
07 carrier
08 emissary
09 estafette, messenger
10 pursuivant
13 dispatch rider

**course**
03 run, way
04 dish, flow, gush, hunt, lane,
   line, path, plan, pour, race,
   rise, road, tack, term, time
05 chase, lapse, march, orbit,
   order, route, spell, stage,
   surge, track, trail
06 afters, entrée, follow, ground,
   manner, period, policy,
   pursue, remove, series,
   stream, system
07 channel, circuit, dessert,
   passage, process, program,
   regimen, studies
08 approach, duration,
   progress, run after, schedule,
   sequence, syllabus
09 appetizer, direction,
   entremets, procedure,
   racetrack
10 curriculum, flight path,
   succession, trajectory
11 development, furtherance,
   progression
12 hors d'oeuvres

❏**in due course**
07 finally
10 eventually
13 sooner or later

❏**of course**
06 surely
07 no doubt
08 to be sure
09 certainly, naturally
10 by all means, definitely
11 doubtlessly, indubitably,
   undoubtedly
13 needless to say

**court**
03 bar, woo
04 date, quad, ring, seek, yard
05 arena, bench, green, motel,
   patio, plaza, train, trial
06 castle, incite, invite, palace,
   prompt, pursue, street
07 assizes, attract, cortège,
   flatter, provoke, retinue,
   session, solicit
08 cloister, go steady, law court,
   tribunal
09 courtyard, cultivate,
   enclosure, entourage,
   esplanade, household,
   judiciary
10 attendants, motor court,
   quadrangle
11 tennis court
14 royal residence

──────────────
➤ *Names of courts. We have*
*omitted the word* **court** *from*
*names given in the following list*
*but you may need to include this*
*word as part of the solution to*
*some crossword clues.:*
06 county, family
07 circuit, federal, Supreme
08 criminal, district, juvenile,
   kangaroo
09 appellate, municipal
➤ See also LEGAL

**courteous**
04 kind
05 civil
06 polite, urbane
07 courtly, gallant, refined
08 debonair, obliging, polished,
   well-bred
09 attentive
10 chivalrous, respectful
11 considerate, gentlemanly
12 well-mannered

**courtesy**
04 tact
05 favor
07 manners, respect

08 breeding, chivalry, civility, kindness, urbanity
09 deference, gallantry
10 politeness, refinement
11 good manners

## courtier
04 page
05 toady
07 steward
08 follower
09 attendant, flatterer, sycophant
13 lady-in-waiting

## courtly
05 civil
06 formal, lordly, polite
07 elegant, gallant, refined, stately
08 decorous, gracious, obliging, polished
09 dignified
10 chivalrous, flattering

## courtship
04 suit
06 affair, dating, wooing
07 chasing, pursuit, romance
08 courting, going out
11 going steady

## courtyard
04 area, quad, yard
05 court, patio, plaza
06 atrium, square
08 cloister
09 enclosure, esplanade
10 quadrangle

## cove
03 bay
05 bight, creek, fiord, firth, inlet
07 estuary

## covenant
04 bond, deed, pact
05 agree, trust
06 engage, pledge, treaty
07 compact, promise
08 contract
09 concordat, indenture, stipulate, undertake
10 commitment
11 arrangement, stipulation, undertaking

## cover
03 cup, lid, top
04 bury, cake, case, coat, daub, film, hide, skin, veil, wrap
05 cross, dress, duvet, front, guard, layer, treat
06 attire, canopy, carpet, clothe, encase, insure, jacket, mantle, screen, shield, shroud

07 binding, blanket, coating, conceal, envelop, hide-out, obscure, overlay, plaster, replace, shelter, stretch, swaddle, wrapper, wreathe
08 accouter, accoutre, blankets, clothing, deal with, describe, disguise, envelope, go across, pretense
09 assurance, bedspread, encompass, indemnify, indemnity, insurance, safe house, safeguard, whitewash
10 bedclothes, camouflage, conspiracy, provide for, recompense, stand in for, travel over
11 concealment, hiding place, incorporate, investigate, smoke screen
12 compensation
15 indemnification

## ❏cover up
06 hush up
07 conceal, repress
08 keep dark, suppress
09 dissemble, gloss over, whitewash
10 keep secret

## coverage
04 item
05 story
06 report
07 account, reports
08 analysis
09 insurance, reportage, reporting

## covering
03 top
04 case, coat, film, roof, skin
05 cover, crust, layer, shell
06 carpet, casing, jacket, veneer
07 blanket, coating, housing, overlay, roofing, shelter, wrapper
08 clothing, wrapping
10 protection
11 descriptive, explanatory

## covert
06 hidden, secret, veiled
07 private
08 sidelong, stealthy, ulterior
09 concealed, underhand
10 dissembled
11 clandestine, unsuspected
13 subreptitious, surreptitious

## coverup
05 front
06 façade, screen
09 whitewash
10 complicity, conspiracy

11 concealment, smoke screen

## covet
04 envy, want
05 crave, fancy
06 desire
07 long for
08 begrudge, yearn for
09 hanker for, hunger for, lust after, thirst for

## covetous
06 greedy
07 craving, envious, jealous, longing, wanting
08 desirous, grasping, yearning
09 hankering, hungering, rapacious, thirsting
10 avaricious, insatiable

## covey
04 bevy
05 brood, flock, group, skein
06 flight
07 cluster

## cow
05 bully, daunt, scare
06 bovine, dismay, rattle, subdue
07 overawe, unnerve
08 browbeat, domineer
10 dishearten, intimidate

## coward
04 wimp
05 sissy
06 craven
07 chicken, crybaby
08 deserter, poltroon, recreant
10 faintheart, scaredy-cat
11 lily-livered, yellow-belly

## cowardice
04 soft, weak
06 craven, scared, yellow
07 chicken, gutless, jittery
08 cowardly, timorous, unheroic
09 spineless, weak-kneed
11 lily-livered
12 faint-hearted
13 pusillanimous, yellow-bellied

## cowboy
05 waddy
06 drover, gaucho, herder
07 cowhand, cowpoke, rancher, vaquero
08 buckaroo, herdsman, ranchero, stockman, wrangler
09 cattleman
10 cowpuncher
12 broncobuster, cattle herder

**cower**
05 quail, quake, shake, skulk, wince
06 cringe, crouch, flinch, grovel, recoil, shiver, shrink
07 tremble

**coy**
03 shy
04 arch, prim
05 timid
06 demure, modest
07 bashful, evasive, prudish
08 backward, reserved, retiring, skittish
09 shrinking, withdrawn
10 coquettish
11 flirtatious

**cozy**
04 safe, snug, warm
05 comfy
06 homely, secure
08 intimate
09 congenial, sheltered
11 comfortable

**crabbed, crabby**
04 sour, tart
05 acrid, cross, surly, testy
06 cranky, morose, snappy
07 awkward, fretful, grouchy, iracund, prickly
08 captious, churlish, perverse, petulant, snappish
09 crotchety, difficult, irascible, irritable, splenetic
11 acrimonious, bad-tempered, ill-tempered
12 cantankerous, iracundulous

**crack**
02 go
03 dig, gag, gap, hit, pop, try
04 bump, chip, clap, flaw, gibe, joke, line, quip, rift, shot, slap, snap, stab
05 break, chink, cleft, smack, solve, split
06 breach, cavity, choice, cranny, expert, report
07 attempt, crevice, fissure, rupture, shatter, unravel
08 collapse, decipher, fracture, one-liner, splinter, superior, top-notch
09 break down, brilliant, excellent, explosion, figure out, first-rate, witticism
10 first-class, go to pieces, handpicked

❏**crack down on**
04 stop
05 check, crush, limit
07 confine, control, repress

08 restrict, suppress
10 act against, put a stop to
11 clamp down on

❏**crack up**
05 go mad
09 break down
10 go to pieces
11 lose control

**crackdown**
05 check
08 crushing
09 clampdown
10 repression
11 suppression

**cracked**
04 daft, nuts, torn
05 batty, crazy, loony, nutty, split
06 broken, crazed, faulty, flawed, insane
07 damaged, foolish, idiotic
08 crackpot, deranged, fissured
09 defective, imperfect
13 off your rocker

**cracker**
05 wafer
07 biscuit, saltine
08 hardtack
11 firecracker

**crackle**
04 snap, spit
06 rustle, sizzle
09 crepitate
11 crepitation, decrepitate
13 decrepitation

**crackpot**
03 nut
04 case, dork, fool
05 crank, freak, idiot, loony
06 weirdo
07 dingbat, oddball
09 screwball

**cradle**
03 bed, cot
04 crib, hold, lull, rock, tend
05 fount, nurse
06 nestle, origin, source, spring
07 carrier, hammock, nurture, shelter, support
08 bassinet
10 birthplace, wellspring

**craft**
03 art, job
04 boat, line, ship, work
05 flair, knack, skill, trade
06 talent, vessel
07 ability, calling, pursuit
08 aircraft, aptitude, artistry
09 dexterity, expertise, handiwork, spaceship, technique

10 employment, handicraft, occupation, spacecraft
11 workmanship
12 skillfulness

**craftsman, craftswoman**
05 maker, smith
06 artist, expert, master, wright
07 artisan
10 technician
13 skilled worker

**craftsmanship**
05 skill
07 mastery
08 artistry
09 dexterity, expertise, technique
11 workmanship

**crafty**
03 sly
04 foxy, wily
05 canny, sharp
06 artful, astute, shrewd, subtle
07 crooked, cunning, devious
08 scheming
09 conniving, designing
11 calculating, duplicitous

**crag**
03 tor
04 peak, rock
05 bluff, cliff, ridge, scarp
08 pinnacle
10 escarpment

**craggy**
05 rocky, rough, stony
06 jagged, rugged, uneven
07 cragged
11 precipitous

**cram**
03 jam, ram
04 fill, glut, pack
05 crowd, crush, force, gorge, grind, press, study, stuff
06 fill up, review
07 compact, squeeze
08 bone up on, compress

**cramp**
04 ache, pain, pang
05 check, crick, limit, spasm
06 arrest, bridle, hamper, hinder, impede, stitch, stymie, thwart, twinge
07 confine, inhibit, shackle
08 handicap, obstruct, restrict
09 frustrate
14 pins and needles

**cramped**
04 full, poky
05 small, tight
06 narrow, packed
07 crowded

**crane**
08 closed in, confined,
   squashed, squeezed
09 congested, jam-packed
11 overcrowded
13 uncomfortable

**crane**
05 davit, hoist, winch
06 tackle
07 derrick
14 block and tackle

**crank**
05 freak, idiot, loony
06 madman, weirdo
07 oddball
08 crackpot
09 character, eccentric

**cranky**
05 cross, surly, testy
06 crabby, snappy, tetchy,
   touchy
07 awkward, prickly
08 freakish, peculiar
09 crotchety, difficult, eccentric,
   irritable
11 bad-tempered, ill-tempered
12 cantankerous
13 idiosyncratic
14 unconventional

**cranny**
03 gap
04 hole, nook, rent
05 chink, cleft, crack
07 crevice, fissure, opening
10 interstice

**crash**
03 din, hit
04 bang, boom, bump, dash,
   fail, fall, fold, ruin, thud
05 clang, clank, clash, prang,
   rapid, smash, thump
06 batter, cut out, fold up, go
   bust, pileup, plunge, topple
07 clatter, collide, crackup,
   founder, go under, run into,
   shatter
08 accident, collapse, downfall
09 collision, drive into,
   explosion, go belly up
10 bankruptcy, depression
11 go to the wall, stop working
12 go on the blink
13 come uninvited

**crass**
04 rude
05 crude, dense
06 coarse, oafish, stupid
08 tactless, unsubtle
09 unrefined
10 blundering, indelicate
11 insensitive
15 unsophisticated

**crate**
03 box
04 case
06 jalopy
08 tea chest
09 container
11 packing case

**crater**
03 dip, pit
04 hole
05 abyss, chasm
06 cavity, hollow
10 depression

**crave**
04 need, want, wish
05 covet, fancy
06 desire
07 long for, pine for
08 yearn for
09 hunger for, lust after

**craven**
06 afraid, scared, yellow
07 chicken, fearful, gutless
08 cowardly, poltroon, recreant,
   timorous, unheroic
09 spineless, weak-kneed
11 lily-livered
12 faint-hearted, mean-spirited
13 pusillanimous, yellow-
   bellied

**craving**
04 lust, need, urge, wish
06 desire, hunger, pining, thirst
07 longing, panting, sighing
08 appetite, yearning
09 hankering

**crawl**
04 drag, edge, fawn, inch, teem
05 creep, swarm, toady
06 cringe, grovel, seethe,
   squirm, suck up, writhe
07 bristle, flatter, slither, wriggle
10 curry favor
12 bow and scrape

**craze**
03 fad
04 mode, rage, whim
05 mania, trend, vogue
06 frenzy
07 fashion, novelty, passion
09 obsession, the latest
14 the latest thing

**crazed**
03 mad
04 nuts, wild
05 crazy, goofy, loony
06 insane, screwy
07 berserk, lunatic
08 demented, deranged,
   unhinged

10 unbalanced
13 off your rocker, out of your
   mind

**crazy**
03 mad, odd
04 avid, keen, nuts, wild
05 batty, loony, loopy, nutty, silly
06 absurd, ardent, insane
07 bananas, berserk, bonkers,
   idiotic, lunatic, smitten,
   zealous
08 crackpot, demented,
   deranged, unhinged
09 disturbed, fanatical,
   foolhardy, half-baked,
   ludicrous
10 infatuated, out to lunch,
   ridiculous, unbalanced
11 harebrained, nonsensical,
   not all there, unrealistic
12 crackbrained
13 off your rocker, out of your
   mind

❏**go crazy**
04 flip
05 go ape, go mad
09 go bananas
11 flip your lid, go ballistic
15 lose your marbles

**creak**
04 rasp
05 grate, grind, groan
06 scrape, squeak, squeal
07 scratch, screech

**creaky**
05 rusty
07 grating, rasping, squeaky
08 grinding, groaning, scraping
09 squeaking, squealing
10 scratching, screeching

**cream**
04 best, pale, pick
05 elite, paste, prime, salve
06 flower, lotion
07 unguent
08 emulsion, liniment, off-white,
   ointment
09 emollient
10 choice part, select part
14 crème de la crème, pick of
   the bunch

**creamy**
04 oily, pale, rich
05 milky, pasty, thick
06 creamy, smooth
07 buttery, velvety
08 off-white

**crease**
04 fold, line, ruck, tuck
05 crimp, pleat, ridge

**create**
06 furrow, groove, pucker
07 crinkle, crumple, wrinkle
09 corrugate
11 corrugation

**create**
04 coin, form, make, mold
05 build, erect, found, frame, hatch, set up, shape
06 design, devise, father, invent, lead to, ordain
07 appoint, compose, concoct, develop, install, produce
08 engender, generate
09 construct, establish, fabricate, formulate, institute, originate, procreate
10 bring about, inaugurate
14 bring into being

**creation**
04 life, work
05 birth, world
06 cosmos, design, making, nature, origin
07 concept, genesis, product
08 universe
09 formation, invention
10 brainchild, conception, concoction, foundation, initiation, innovation
11 achievement, chef d'oeuvre, fabrication, institution, masterpiece, origination
12 constitution, construction
13 establishment

**creative**
06 clever, gifted
07 fertile
08 artistic, inspired, talented
09 ingenious, intuitive, inventive, visionary
10 productive
11 imaginative, resourceful

**creativity**
06 talent, vision
08 artistry
09 fertility, ingenuity
10 cleverness
11 imagination, inspiration
13 inventiveness

**creator**
03 God
05 maker
06 author, father, mother
07 builder, founder
08 composer, designer, inventor, producer
09 architect, initiator
10 originator, prime mover

**creature**
03 man
04 bird, body, fish, soul

05 beast, being, human
06 animal, insect, person
07 critter
11 living thing

**credence**
05 faith, trust
06 belief, credit
10 confidence, dependence

**credentials**
04 deed
05 title
06 papers, permit
07 diploma, license, warrant
09 documents, reference
11 certificate, testimonial
12 identity card
15 proof of identity

**credibility**
05 truth
09 integrity
10 likelihood, street cred
11 probability, reliability
12 plausibility

**credible**
06 honest, likely
07 sincere, tenable
08 possible, probable, reliable
09 plausible, thinkable
10 believable, convincing, persuasive, reasonable
11 conceivable, trustworthy

**credit**
04 fame
05 asset, glory, honor, pride, trust
06 accept, assign, belief, charge, esteem, impute, praise, thanks
07 acclaim, ascribe, believe, fall for, put down, tribute
08 approval, credence
09 attribute, laudation
10 confidence, estimation, in the black, reputation
11 distinction, pride and joy, recognition, subscribe to
14 acknowledgment

❏ **on credit**
09 on account
14 by installments

**creditable**
04 good
06 worthy
08 laudable
09 admirable, deserving, estimable, excellent, exemplary, honorable, reputable
11 commendable, respectable
12 praiseworthy

**creditor**
06 lender, usurer
09 loan shark

**credulity**
07 naïvety
09 silliness, stupidity
10 dupability, simplicity
11 gullibility

**credulous**
05 naïve
07 dupable
08 gullible, trusting, wide-eyed
12 overtrusting, unsuspecting

**creed**
05 canon, credo, dogma, faith
06 belief, tenets
08 articles, doctrine, teaching
09 catechism
10 persuasion, principles

**creek**
05 brook
06 rillet, rivlet, runlet, runnel, stream

**creep**
04 edge, inch, worm
05 crawl, skulk, slink, sneak, toady
06 cringe, fawner, grovel, tiptoe, writhe, yes man
07 slither, wriggle
09 pussyfoot, sycophant
10 bootlicker

**creeper**
03 ivy
04 vine
05 liana, liane, plant
06 runner
07 climber, crawler, rambler, skulker, trailer
13 climbing plant, trailing plant

**creepy**
05 eerie, scary, weird
06 spooky
07 macabre, ominous
08 gruesome, horrible, horrific, menacing, sinister
10 disturbing, horrifying, terrifying, unpleasant
11 frightening, hair-raising, nightmarish, threatening
13 bloodcurdling, spine-chilling

**crescent-shaped**
06 lunate
07 falcate, lunated, lunular
08 falcated
09 bow-shaped, falciform
12 sickle-shaped

## crest

- 03 top
- 04 apex, comb, mane, peak
- 05 badge, crown, plume, ridge
- 06 aigret, device, emblem, summit, symbol, tassel
- 07 panache, regalia
- 08 aigrette, caruncle, insignia, pinnacle
- 09 cockscomb
- 10 coat of arms

## crestfallen

- 03 sad
- 08 dejected, downcast
- 09 depressed
- 10 despondent, dispirited
- 11 discouraged, downhearted
- 12 disappointed, disheartened
- 13 in the doldrums
- 14 down in the dumps

## crevasse

- 05 abyss, chasm, cleft, crack
- 07 fissure
- 11 bergschrund

## crevice

- 03 gap
- 04 hole, rift, slit
- 05 chink, cleft, crack, split
- 06 cranny
- 07 fissure, opening
- 10 interstice

## crew

- 03 lot, mob, set
- 04 band, gang, pack, team, unit
- 05 bunch, corps, crowd, force, group, party, squad, troop
- 07 company
- 10 complement

## crib

- 03 bed, cot
- 04 copy, lift
- 05 cheat, steal
- 06 pirate
- 07 carrier, purloin
- 08 bassinet
- 10 plagiarize

## crick

- 05 cramp, spasm
- 06 twinge
- 10 convulsion

## cricket

➤ See also SPORT

▶ *Cricket terms include*:

- 03 bat
- 04 bail
- 05 stump
- 06 bowled, crease, googly, howzat, maiden, not out, run out, wicket, yorker
- 07 batsman, declare, infield
- 08 how's that
- 09 fieldsman
- 10 maiden over, spin-bowler
- 12 wicket-keeper
- 22 innings leg before wicket

## crier

- 06 herald, wailer
- 09 announcer, messenger
- 10 proclaimer

## crime

- 03 sin
- 04 vice
- 06 felony
- 07 misdeed, offense, outrage
- 08 atrocity, iniquity, villainy
- 09 violation
- 10 misconduct, wrongdoing
- 11 delinquency, lawbreaking, lawlessness, malfeasance, misdemeanor
- 13 transgression

▶ *Types of crime*:

- 04 rape
- 05 arson, fraud, theft
- 06 felony, murder, piracy
- 07 assault, battery, bribery, forgery, larceny, mugging, perjury, robbery, treason
- 08 burglary, homicide
- 09 blackmail, espionage, extortion, hijacking, joy riding, pilfering, terrorism, vandalism
- 10 corruption, kidnapping, laundering, tax evasion
- 11 hooliganism, misdemeanor
- 12 drunk-driving, embezzlement, manslaughter
- 13 drug-smuggling
- 14 counterfeiting

➤ See also LEGAL

## criminal

- 04 bent, evil, gang
- 05 felon, wrong
- 06 wicked
- 07 convict, corrupt, crooked, culprit, illegal, illicit, lawless, obscene, villain
- 08 culpable, offender, prisoner, unlawful
- 09 felonious, miscreant, nefarious, wrongdoer
- 10 delinquent, indictable, iniquitous, law-breaker, malefactor, scandalous, underworld, villainous
- 11 disgraceful, law-breaking
- 13 reprehensible

▶ *Types of criminal*:

- 04 hood, thug
- 05 crook, thief
- 06 bandit, forger, gunman, killer, mugger, outlaw, pirate, rapist, robber, vandal
- 07 brigand, burglar, hoodlum, mobster, poacher, rustler
- 08 arsonist, assassin, bigamist, car thief, gangster, hijacker, jailbird, joyrider, murderer, perjurer, smuggler, swindler
- 09 buccaneer, desperado, embezzler, kidnapper, larcenist, racketeer, terrorist
- 10 bootlegger, cat burglar, dope-pusher, highwayman, pickpocket, shoplifter, trespasser
- 11 armed robber, blackmailer, safecracker, war criminal
- 12 drug-smuggler, extortionist, housebreaker
- 13 counterfeiter

▶ *Names of criminals*:

- 03 **Ray** (James Earl)
- 04 **Aram** (Eugene), **Hood** (Robin), **Lobe** (Richard), **Todd** (Sweeney)
- 05 **Biggs** (Ronald), **Blood** (Thomas), **Booth** (John Wilkes), **Brady** (Ian), **Bundy** (Ted), **James** (Jesse), **Kelly** (Ned)
- 06 **Barrow** (Clyde), **Bonney** (William H.), **Borden** (Lizzie Andrew), **Capone** (Al), **Manson** (Charles), **Nelson** (Lester "Baby Face"), **Oswald** (Lee Harvey), **Parker** (Bonnie), **Rob Roy, Sirhan** (Sirhan), **Turpin** (Dick)
- 07 **Cassidy** (Butch), **Chapman** (Mark), **Crippen** (Hawley Harvey), **DeSalvo** (Albert), **Hindley** (Myra), **Leopole** (Nathan), **Luciano** (Charles "Lucky"), **Shipman** (Harold)
- 08 **Barabbas, Christie** (John Reginald Halliday)
- 09 **Berkowitz** (David), **Dillinger** (John), **Hauptmann** (Richard Bruno), **Sutcliffe** (Peter)
- 11 **Billy the Kid**
- 13 **Jack the Ripper**
- 15 **Boston Strangler, Yorkshire Ripper**

## crimp
04 fold, tuck
05 flute, pleat, ridge
06 crease, furrow, gather, groove, pucker, rumple
07 crinkle, crumple, wrinkle
09 corrugate

## cringe
03 bow, shy
04 bend, fawn
05 cower, crawl, creep, quail, start, stoop, toady, wince
06 blench, crouch, flinch, grovel, recoil, shrink
07 flatter, tremble
08 draw back

## crinkle
04 curl, fold, line, ruck, tuck, wave
05 crimp, pleat, ridge, twist
06 crease, furrow, groove, pucker, ruffle, rumple
07 crinkle, crumple, wrinkle
09 corrugate
11 corrugation

## crinkly
05 curly, kinky
06 fluted, frizzy, ridged, tucked
07 creased, crimped, grooved, pleated, rumpled, wrinkly
08 crumpled, furrowed, puckered, wrinkled
10 corrugated

## cripple
04 lame, maim, ruin
05 spoil
06 damage, hamper, impair, impede, injure, weaken
07 destroy, disable, vitiate
08 handicap, paralyze, sabotage
09 hamstring
10 debilitate
12 incapacitate

## crippled
04 lame
08 disabled
09 paralyzed
11 handicapped
13 incapacitated

## crisis
03 fix, jam
04 hole, mess
06 crunch, pickle, scrape
07 dilemma, problem, trouble
08 hot water, quandary
09 emergency, extremity

## crisp
04 cool, firm, hard
05 brisk, clear, fresh, short, terse
06 chilly, crispy, snappy

07 bracing, brittle, crumbly, crunchy, friable
08 incisive, succinct
10 refreshing

## criterion
04 norm, rule, test
05 canon, gauge, model, scale
07 measure
08 exemplar, standard
09 benchmark, yardstick
10 touchstone

## critic
05 judge
06 carper, censor, pundit
07 analyst, knocker
08 attacker, censurer, reviewer
09 backbiter, muckraker, nit-picker
11 commentator, faultfinder

## critical
05 grave, major, vital
06 urgent
07 carping, crucial, exigent, pivotal, probing, serious
08 captious, caviling, deciding, decisive, historic, niggling, perilous, pressing, scathing
09 essential, important, momentous, quibbling, vitriolic
10 analytical, censorious, derogatory, diagnostic, discerning, judgmental, nit-picking, precarious
11 disparaging, explanatory, penetrating
12 all-important, disapproving, faultfinding, vituperative

## criticism
04 flak
05 blame
06 niggle, review
07 censure, reproof
08 analysis, bad press, brickbat, critique, judgment, knocking
09 appraisal
10 assessment, commentary, evaluation, nit-picking
11 disapproval, explanation
12 condemnation, faultfinding

## criticize
03 nag, pan
04 carp, slam
05 blame, decry, judge, knock, roast, snipe
06 assess, attack, review
07 analyze, censure, condemn, explain, nit-pick, rubbish, run down
08 appraise, bad-mouth, denounce, evaluate

09 denigrate, disparage, excoriate, interpret
10 go to town on, vituperate
11 pick holes in
12 pull to pieces, tear to shreds
13 find fault with
15 do a hatchet job on

## critique
05 essay
06 review
07 write-up
08 analysis, judgment
09 appraisal
10 assessment, commentary, evaluation, exposition
11 explanation, explication
14 interpretation

## croak
03 caw, die
04 crow, gasp, rasp
06 squawk, wheeze

## crock
03 jar, pot
06 vessel

## crockery
04 jars, pots
05 china
06 dishes
07 pottery
08 ceramics
09 porcelain, tableware
11 earthenware

## crony
03 pal
04 ally, chum, mate
05 buddy
06 friend
07 comrade
08 follower, sidekick
09 associate, companion
10 accomplice

## crook
03 bow
04 bend, flex, hook, warp
05 cheat, curve, fraud, rogue, shark, thief, twist
06 con man, deform, robber
07 distort, villain
08 criminal, swindler
09 con artist
10 lawbreaker

## crooked
04 awry, bent
05 askew, bowed, shady
06 curved, hooked, shifty, uneven, warped, zigzag
07 corrupt, illegal, illicit, sinuous, twisted, winding
08 criminal, deformed, lopsided, slanting, unlawful

**croon**

09 contorted, deceitful, dishonest, distorted, irregular, misshapen, nefarious, off-center, underhand
10 asymmetric, catawampus, fraudulent
11 cattywampus

**croon**

03 hum
04 lilt, sing
06 warble

**crop**

03 cut, lop, lot, mow, set
04 clip, pare, snip, trim
05 batch, prune, shear, yield
06 fruits, growth, reduce
07 curtail, harvest, produce, shorten, vintage

❑**crop up**

05 arise, occur
06 appear, arrive, come up, emerge, happen, turn up
09 take place
10 come to pass

**cross**

03 mix, woe
04 foil, ford, join, lace, load, meet, pain, span
05 angry, blend, check, short, surly, trial, vexed, worry
06 bridge, burden, crabby, grumpy, hybrid, impede, oppose, peeved, put out, snappy, thwart
07 annoyed, grouchy, mixture, mongrel, prickly
08 converge, diagonal, obstruct, pass over, snappish, traverse
09 crotchety, difficult, fractious, hybridize, intersect, irascible, irritable, splenetic
10 affliction, crisscross, crossbreed, interbreed, interweave, transverse
11 bad-tempered, combination, ill-tempered, tribulation
12 cantankerous, disagreeable

► *Types of cross:*

03 tau
04 ankh, rood
05 Greek, Latin, papal
06 botoné, Celtic, fleury, fylfot, moline, potent, Y-cross
07 Calvary, capital, Cornish, Maltese, Russian, saltire
08 cardinal, crosslet, crucifix, Lorraine, quadrate, St. Peter's, swastika
09 encolpion, Jerusalem, St. Andrew's, St. George's

11 patriarchal
13 Constantinian

**cross-examine**

04 pump, quiz
05 grill
07 examine
08 question
11 interrogate

**crossing**

04 trip
06 voyage
07 fording, journey, passage
08 junction

**crosswise, crossways**

04 awry, over
06 across, aslant
07 athwart
08 sideways
09 obliquely
10 crisscross, diagonally

**crotchety**

05 cross, surly, testy
06 crabby, crusty, grumpy
07 awkward, crabbed, grouchy, iracund, peevish, prickly
08 contrary, petulant
09 difficult, fractious, irritable
11 bad-tempered
12 cantankerous, disagreeable, iracundulous, obstreperous

**crouch**

03 bow
04 bend, duck
05 cower, kneel, squat, stoop
06 cringe

**crow**

04 brag
05 boast, exult, gloat, vaunt
07 bluster, rejoice, show off
15 blow your own horn

**crowd**

03 jam, lot, mob, set
04 army, cram, gate, herd, host, mass, pack, pile, push
05 bunch, crush, drove, flock, group, horde, press, shove, stuff, surge, swarm
06 circle, clique, gather, huddle, jostle, masses, people, rabble, squash, throng
07 cluster, company, congest, squeeze, turnout, viewers
08 assembly, audience, overflow, populace, riffraff
09 listeners, multitude
10 congregate, fraternity, spectators

**crowded**

04 busy, full
06 filled, jammed, packed

07 crammed, cramped, crushed, teeming
08 overfull, swarming
09 chock-full, congested, jampacked
11 chockablock
14 full to bursting

**crown**

03 cap, tip, top
04 acme, apex, king, peak
05 adorn, crest, glory, honor, kudos, prize, queen, ruler, tiara
06 anoint, climax, diadem, height, invest, summit, top off, trophy, wreath
07 circlet, coronet, dignify, emperor, empress, festoon, garland, install, laurels, monarch, perfect, royalty
08 complete, enthrone, finalize, monarchy, pinnacle
09 sovereign

**crowning**

03 top
05 final
07 perfect, supreme
08 ultimate
09 climactic, paramount, sovereign, unmatched
10 consummate, coronation
11 culminating, investiture
12 enthronement

**crucial**

03 key
05 major, vital
06 trying, urgent
07 central, pivotal, testing
08 critical, decisive, historic
09 essential, important

**crucify**

06 punish
07 execute, torment, torture
08 ridicule
09 criticize, persecute

**crude**

03 hot, raw
04 blue, lewd, rude
05 basic, bawdy, dirty, rough
06 coarse, earthy, risqué, simple, smutty, vulgar
07 obscene, raunchy, uncouth
08 indecent
09 makeshift, offensive, primitive, unrefined

**cruel**

04 evil, grim, mean
05 nasty
06 bitter, brutal, fierce, flinty, savage, severe, unkind

07 callous, cutting, hellish, inhuman, painful, vicious
08 barbaric, fiendish, indurate, inhumane, pitiless, ruthless, sadistic, spiteful, vengeful
09 barbarous, heartless, merciless, unfeeling
10 malevolent
11 coldblooded, hardhearted, remorseless, unrelenting
12 bloodthirsty

**cruelty**
05 abuse, spite, venom
06 malice, sadism
07 tyranny
08 bullying, ferocity, meanness, savagery, severity, violence
09 barbarity, brutality, harshness
10 inhumanity
11 callousness, viciousness
12 ruthlessness
13 heartlessness

**cruise**
04 roam, sail, taxi, trip
05 coast, drift, glide, slide
06 travel, voyage, wander
07 journey
09 freewheel

**crumb**
03 bit, jot
04 atom, iota, mite
05 flake, grain, piece, scrap, shred, speck
06 morsel, sliver, titbit
07 snippet, soupçon
08 particle

**crumble**
03 rot
05 crush, decay, grind, pound
06 powder
07 break up
08 collapse, fragment
09 break down, decompose, fall apart, pulverize
12 disintegrate, fall to pieces

**crumbly**
05 short
07 brittle, friable, powdery
11 pulverulent

**crummy**
06 rotten, shabby, shoddy, trashy
07 useless
08 inferior, pathetic, rubbishy
09 half-baked, worthless

**crumple**
04 fall, fold
05 crush
06 crease, pucker, rumple
07 crinkle, wrinkle
08 collapse

**crunch**
04 bite, chew, crux, test
05 champ, chomp, crush, grind, munch, pinch, smash
06 crisis
09 emergency, masticate
13 moment of truth

**crusade**
04 push, work
05 cause, drive, fight, jihad
06 attack, battle, strive
07 holy war, promote
08 advocate, campaign, movement, struggle

**crusader**
06 zealot
07 fighter, pilgrim
08 champion, promoter
10 campaigner, enthusiast

**crush**
03 jam
04 mash, mill, pash, pulp
05 abash, break, crowd, grind, pound, press, quash, quell, shame, smash, upset
06 crunch, squash, subdue
07 conquer, crumble, passion, put down, screw up, shatter, squeeze, wrinkle
08 demolish, overcome, suppress, vanquish
09 devastate, humiliate, overpower, overwhelm, pulverize, triturate
11 infatuation

**crust**
04 coat, husk, rind, scab, skin
05 layer, shell
06 caking, casing, mantle
07 coating, surface, topping
08 covering, exterior

**crustacean**

➤ *Types of crustacean*:
04 crab
05 krill, prawn
06 shrimp
07 camaron, lobster
08 barnacle, crawfish, crayfish
09 centipede, langouste, millipede, water flea, woodlouse
10 hermit crab, sand hopper, spider crab
11 fiddler crab, langoustine
➤ See also ANIMAL

**crusty**
04 firm, hard
05 cross, gruff, surly, testy
06 crabby, grumpy, touchy

07 brusque, crabbed, crunchy, grouchy, peevish, prickly
08 contrary, petulant
09 breakable, difficult, fractious, irascible, irritable, splenetic, well-baked
11 bad-tempered
12 cantankerous, disagreeable, obstreperous

**crux**
03 nub
04 core
05 heart
06 center, kernel
07 essence, nucleus
13 the bottom line

**cry**
03 sob
04 bawl, call, howl, plea, roar, wail, weep, yell
05 shout, tears, whine
06 scream, shriek, snivel
07 blubber, call out, screech, sobbing, weeping, whimper

❑**cry off**
06 cancel
07 back out
08 withdraw
09 backpedal
14 change your mind, excuse yourself

❑**cry out for**
04 need, want
06 demand
07 call for, require
11 necessitate

**crypt**
04 tomb
05 vault
08 catacomb
09 mausoleum
10 undercroft
13 burial chamber

**cryptic**
04 dark
06 hidden, occult, secret
07 bizarre, obscure, strange
08 abstruse, esoteric, puzzling
09 ambiguous, enigmatic
10 mysterious, perplexing

**crystallize**
04 form
06 appear, emerge, harden
07 clarify
08 solidify

**cub**
03 pup
04 baby, tiro, tyro
05 puppy, whelp, youth
06 novice, rookie

**cubbyhole**
07 learner, recruit, starter, student, trainee
08 beginner, freshman, initiate, neophyte
09 fledgling, greenhorn, offspring, youngster
10 apprentice, raw recruit, tenderfoot

**cubbyhole**
03 den
04 hole, slot
05 niche
06 recess
08 hideaway

**cube**
03 die
04 chop, dice
05 block, solid
10 hexahedron

**cuddle**
03 hug, pet
04 hold, neck
05 clasp, nurse
06 caress, enfold, fondle, nestle, nuzzle, smooch
07 embrace, snuggle
08 canoodle

**cuddly**
04 cozy, soft, warm
05 plump
07 lovable
08 huggable

**cudgel**
03 bat, hit
04 bash, beat, club, cosh, mace
05 billy, clout, pound, stick
06 batter, strike, thwack
07 clobber
08 bludgeon
09 bastinado, truncheon
10 billystick, nightstick, shillelagh

**cue**
03 nod
04 hint, sign
06 prompt, signal
08 reminder, stimulus
10 indication, intimation, suggestion

**cuff**
03 box, hit
04 beat, belt, biff, clip, slap
05 clout, smack, thump, whack
06 buffet, strike
07 clobber

❏**off the cuff**
05 ad lib
09 extempore, impromptu
10 improvised, unprepared
11 unrehearsed

13 spontaneously

**cuisine**
07 cookery, cooking
10 cordon bleu
12 haute cuisine
15 nouvelle cuisine

**cul-de-sac**
06 pocket
07 dead end, impasse
10 blind alley

**cull**
04 kill, pick, sift, thin
05 amass, glean, pluck
06 choose, gather, select
07 destroy, pick out, thin out

**culminate**
03 end
05 close, end up
06 climax, finish, wind up
08 conclude

**culmination**
03 top
04 acme, apex, peak
05 crown
06 climax, finale, height, summit, zenith
08 pinnacle
09 high point
10 completion, conclusion

**culpable**
06 guilty, liable, sinful
07 at fault, peccant, to blame
09 offending
10 answerable, censurable
11 blameworthy, responsible

**culprit**
05 felon
07 convict, villain
08 criminal, offender
09 miscreant, wrongdoer
10 delinquent, lawbreaker
11 guilty party

**cult**
03 fad
04 sect
05 craze, faith, trend, vogue
06 belief, school
07 faction, fashion, in-thing
08 movement, religion
09 obsession

**cultivate**
03 aid, dig, sow, woo
04 farm, grow, help, plow, till, work
05 court, plant, raise, train
06 assist, foster, polish, pursue, refine, work on

07 develop, enhance, forward, further, harvest, improve, nurture, prepare, produce
09 encourage, enlighten

**cultivated**
06 urbane
07 genteel, refined
08 cultured, educated, polished, well-bred, well-read
09 civilized, scholarly
10 discerning
11 enlightened
13 sophisticated

**cultural**
04 folk
06 ethnic, tribal
07 liberal
08 artistic, communal, edifying, national, societal
09 aesthetic, educative, elevating, improving
10 broadening, civilizing, humanizing
11 educational, traditional

**culture**
05 mores, music
06 growth, habits
07 customs, society, the arts
08 behavior, heritage, learning, painting
09 lifestyle, way of life
10 humanities, literature, philosophy, traditions
12 civilization

**cultured**
04 arty
06 polite, urbane
07 erudite, genteel, learned, refined
08 artistic, educated, polished, tasteful, well-bred, well-bred, well-read
09 civilized, scholarly
10 cultivated
11 enlightened
12 intellectual, well-educated, well-informed
13 sophisticated

**culvert**
04 duct
05 drain, sewer
06 gutter
07 channel, conduit
11 watercourse

**cumbersome**
04 slow
05 bulky, heavy
06 clumsy
07 awkward, weighty
08 cumbrous, unwieldy
10 burdensome

11  complicated, inefficient

**cumulative**
07  growing
08  mounting
09  enlarging
10  collective, increasing
11  multiplying, snowballing

**cunning**
03  sly
04  deep, deft, foxy, wily
05  canny, sharp, skill, wiles
06  artful, astute, clever, crafty, shifty, shrewd, subtle, tricky
07  devious, slyness
08  deftness, fiendish, guileful, skillful, subtlety, trickery
09  deceitful, dexterous, ingenious
10  artfulness, astuteness, cleverness, craftiness

**cup**
03  mug
04  wine
05  award, medal, prize, punch
06  beaker, goblet, trophy
07  chalice, tankard

**cupboard**
06  closet, larder, pantry
07  armoire, highboy
08  wardrobe
10  closepress
12  Welsh dresser

**cupidity**
05  greed
06  hunger
07  avarice, avidity, longing
08  rapacity, voracity, yearning
09  eagerness, hankering
10  greediness
12  covetousness

**curative**
05  tonic
07  healing
08  remedial, salutary
09  healthful, medicinal, vulnerary
10  corrective, febrifugal
11  restorative, therapeutic
12  health-giving

**curator**
06  keeper
07  steward
08  guardian
09  attendant, caretaker, custodian

**curb**
04  rein
05  brake, check
06  bridle, damper, hinder, impede
07  control, inhibit, repress

08  hold back, moderate, restrain, restrict, suppress
09  constrain
10  constraint, impediment, limitation, repression

**curdle**
04  clot, sour, turn
07  congeal, ferment, thicken
08  solidify, turn sour
09  coagulate

**cure**
03  dry, fix
04  ease, heal, help, mend, salt
05  smoke, treat
06  elixir, kipper, pickle, remedy
07  correct, cure-all, healing, panacea, rectify, relieve, restore, therapy
08  antidote, make well, medicine, preserve
09  alleviate, treatment
11  restorative

**curio**
06  geegaw
07  antique, bibelot, trinket, whatnot
09  bric-a-brac, curiosity, objet d'art
10  knickknack

**curiosity**
05  curio, freak
06  marvel, oddity, rarity, wonder
07  antique, exotica, inquiry, novelty, trinket
08  interest, nosiness, snooping
09  objet d'art, spectacle
10  knickknack, phenomenon

**curious**
03  odd
04  nosy, rare
05  funny, novel, queer, weird
06  exotic, prying, quaint, unique
07  bizarre, strange, unusual
08  peculiar, puzzling, querying, snooping
09  inquiring, intrigued, searching
10  mysterious, remarkable, unorthodox
11  inquisitive, interfering, questioning
13  extraordinary
14  unconventional

**curl**
04  bend, coil, kink, loop, ring, turn, wave, wind
05  crimp, curve, frizz, helix, snake, swirl, twine, twirl, twist, whorl
06  ripple, scroll, spiral
07  crinkle, ringlet, wreathe

08  curlicue
09  corkscrew

**curly**
04  wavy
05  fuzzy, kinky
06  curled, frizzy, permed
07  coiling, crimped, curling, looping, turning, winding
08  spiraled, twirling, twisting
09  corkscrew, spiraling

**currency**
04  cash
05  bills, coins, dough, money, notes
07  coinage
10  acceptance, popularity, prevalence
11  circulation, legal tender
13  dissemination

► *Names of currencies*:
03  ecu, kip, lei, lek, leu, lev, som, sum, won, yen
04  baht, birr, cedi, dong, dram, euro, kina, kuna, kyat, lari, lats, lira, loti, mark, peso, pula, punt, rand, real, rial, riel, taka, tala, vatu, yuan
05  colon, dinar, dobra, franc, frank, krona, krone, kroon, kunar, leone, litas, manat, marka, naira, nakfa, pence, pound, riyal, ruble, rupee, sucre, tenge, tolar, zloty
06  balboa, dalasi, dirham, dollar, escudo, forint, gourde, gulden, hryvna, koruna, kwacha, kwanza, markka, new sol, pa'anga, pataca, peseta, rupiah, shekel, tugrik
07  Afghani, bolivar, cordoba, drachma, guarani, guilder, lempira, metical, ouguiya, quetzal, ringgit, rufiyaa
08  ngultrum, shilling, sterling, U.S. dollar
09  boliviano, lilangeni, schilling
10  Swiss franc
11  Deutschmark, French franc, karbovanets, Turkish lira
12  Belgian franc, Deutsche mark
14  Canadian dollar
➤ See also COIN; MONEY

**current**
02  in
03  ebb, jet
04  flow, mood, tide
05  draft, drift, swirl, tenor, trend
06  common, course, extant, modern, stream, trendy

**curriculum**
07 feeling, general, in vogue, ongoing, present
08 accepted, reigning, undertow, up-to-date
09 in fashion, prevalent
10 mainstream, present-day, prevailing, widespread
11 fashionable
12 contemporary

**curriculum**
07 courses
08 subjects, syllabus
13 course of study

**curse**
04 bane, cuss, damn, jinx, oath
05 beset, blast, spell, swear
06 blight, ordeal, plague
07 scourge, torment, trouble
08 anathema, calamity, cussword, denounce, disaster
09 blaspheme, expletive, imprecate, obscenity, profanity, swearword
10 affliction, execration
11 bad language, imprecation, malediction, tribulation
14 four-letter word

**cursed**
04 vile
06 damned, dashed, odious
07 blasted, hateful
08 fiendish, infernal
09 execrable, loathsome
10 abominable, confounded

**cursory**
05 brief, hasty, quick, rapid
06 casual, slight
07 offhand, passing, summary
08 careless, fleeting, slapdash
09 desultory
10 dismissive
11 perfunctory, superficial

**curt**
04 rude, tart
05 blunt, brief, gruff, pithy, sharp, short, terse
06 abrupt
07 brusque, concise, laconic, offhand, summary, uncivil
08 snappish, succinct
13 short and sweet

**curtail**
03 cut
04 pare, slim, trim
05 limit, prune
06 lessen, reduce, shrink
07 abridge, shorten
08 cut short, decrease, restrict, truncate

**curtailment**
03 cut
06 paring
07 cutback, docking, pruning
08 decrease
09 lessening, reduction
10 abridgment, shortening, truncation
11 contraction

**curtain**
05 blind, cover, drape
06 screen
07 drapery, hanging, shutter, tieback
08 backdrop, portiere, tapestry
13 window hanging

**curtsy**
03 bob, bow
06 kowtow, salaam
09 genuflect

**curvaceous**
05 buxom, curvy
06 bosomy, comely
07 shapely
10 voluptuous

**curve**
03 arc, bow
04 arch, bend, coil, hook, kink, loop, turn, wind
05 crook, helix, round, swell, twist
06 camber, circle, spiral
07 flexure, incurve, winding
08 crescent

**curved**
04 bent
05 bowed
06 arched, convex, cupped, humped, warped
07 arcuate, bending, concave, crooked, rounded, sinuous, twisted
08 sweeping, swelling
10 serpentine

**cushion**
03 mat, pad
05 squab
06 absorb, buffer, dampen, deaden, lessen, muffle, pillow, reduce, soften
07 beanbag, bolster, hassock, padding, protect, support
08 buttress, diminish, headrest, mitigate, suppress

**cushy**
04 cozy, easy, plum, soft
11 comfortable, undemanding

**custodian**
05 guard
06 keeper, warden, warder
07 curator
08 guardian, overseer, watchdog, watchman
09 caretaker, castellan, protector
11 conservator

**custody**
04 care
06 arrest, charge
07 keeping
08 guidance, wardship
09 captivity, detention
10 possession, protection
11 confinement, safekeeping
12 guardianship, imprisonment, preservation

**custom**
03 use, way
04 form, rite
05 habit, style, trade, usage
06 manner, policy, ritual
07 fashion, folkway, routine
08 business, practice
09 etiquette, patronage, procedure, tradition
10 convention, observance

**customarily**
07 as a rule, usually
08 commonly, normally
09 generally
10 habitually, ordinarily
13 traditionally
14 conventionally

**customary**
03 set
05 usual
06 common, normal
07 general, regular, routine
08 accepted, everyday, familiar, habitual, ordinary
11 established, traditional
12 conventional

**customer**
05 buyer
06 client, patron
07 regular, shopper
08 consumer
09 clientele, purchaser

**customize**
03 fit
04 suit
05 adapt, alter
06 adjust, modify, tailor
07 convert
08 fine-tune

**cut**
02 ax
03 bit, hew, lop, mow, row
04 chop, clip, crop, dice, dock, edit, form, gash, hack, nick,

omit, pare, slit, snip, snub, stab, trim
05 carve, grate, mince, notch, prune, quota, score, scorn, sever, share, shave, shear, shred, slash, slice, split, style, wound
06 chisel, chop up, cleave, divide, excise, ignore, incise, insult, pierce, ration, rebuff, reduce, slight
07 abridge, curtail, dissect, engrave, fashion, portion, section, shorten
08 decrease, diminish, incision, lacerate
09 expurgate, lessening, reduction, summarize
10 abbreviate, laceration
14 slice of the cake

❏**cut across**
08 go beyond, surmount
09 rise above, transcend

❏**cut and dried**
05 clear, fixed
06 sewn up
07 certain, settled
08 definite
13 predetermined

❏**cut back**
03 lop
04 crop, curb, trim
05 check, lower, prune, slash
06 lessen, reduce
07 curtail
08 decrease, downsize, retrench
09 economize, scale down

❏**cut down**
03 hew, lop, saw
04 curb, fell, raze
05 level, lower, prune
06 lessen, reduce
07 curtail
08 decrease, diminish

❏**cut in**
06 butt in
07 barge in, break in, intrude
09 interject, interpose, interrupt, intervene

❏**cut off**
03 end
04 halt, stop
05 block, sever
06 detach, remove, unhook
07 isolate, seclude, shelter
08 amputate, break off, separate
09 intercept, interrupt

❏**cut out**
04 drop, edit, fail, omit, stop
05 cease
06 delete, desist, excise, lay off, pack in, remove

07 conk out, exclude, extract
09 break down
11 discontinue, malfunction, stop working

❏**cut out for**
07 good for, made for
08 right for
09 suited for
11 suitable for
12 qualified for

❏**cut up**
04 chop, dice, romp
05 carve, clown, mince, slash, slice
06 cavort, chop up, divide
07 dissect, show off, slice up
09 dismember

**cutback**
06 saving
07 economy
08 decrease, lowering, slashing
09 lessening, reduction
11 curtailment
12 retrenchment

**cut-rate**
04 sale
05 cheap
07 bargain, reduced
08 discount
09 low-priced

**cutter**

► *Types of cutter*:
02 ax
03 saw
04 ship
05 blade, hewer, knife, mower, plane, razor, sword
06 chisel, jigsaw, lopper, scythe, shears, sickle, slicer
07 chopper, fret saw, hacksaw, machete, scalpel
08 billhook, chainsaw, clippers, penknife, scissors
09 lawnmower
10 bowie knife, guillotine
11 pocketknife, switchblade
13 pinking shears
14 Swiss army knife
➤ See also SAW; WEAPON

**cutthroat**
04 keen, thug
05 cruel
06 brutal, fierce
08 assassin, murderer, pitiless, ruthless
09 dog-eat-dog, merciless, murderous

**cutting**
03 raw
04 acid, keen

05 chill, piece, sharp, snide
06 bitchy, biting, bitter
07 caustic, excerpt, extract, hurtful, mordant, pointed
08 incisive, piercing, scathing, wounding
09 sarcastic, trenchant
11 penetrating

**cycle**
03 age, eon, era
04 bike, ride
05 epoch, order, phase, round, wheel
06 circle, course, period, rhythm, roster, series
07 circuit, pattern
08 rotation, sequence
09 biorhythm, body clock
10 revolution, succession
11 oscillation
15 biological clock

**cyclone**
05 storm
07 monsoon, tempest, tornado, twister, typhoon
09 hurricane, whirlwind
13 tropical storm

**cylinder**
04 drum, pipe, reel, tube
05 spool
06 barrel, bobbin, column
07 spindle

**cynic**
07 doubter, killjoy, knocker, scoffer, skeptic
09 defeatist, pessimist
10 spoilsport

**cynical**
07 mocking
08 critical, derisive, doubtful, doubting, negative, sardonic, scoffing, scornful, sneering
09 sarcastic, skeptical
10 suspicious
11 distrustful, pessimistic

**cynicism**
05 doubt, irony, scorn
07 mocking, sarcasm
08 contempt, distrust, scoffing, sneering
09 disbelief, pessimism, suspicion
10 skepticism
11 misanthropy

**cyst**
03 sac, wen
04 bleb
06 growth
07 bladder, blister, utricle, vesicle
08 atheroma

**dab**
03 bit, pat, tap
04 daub, spot, swab, wipe
05 press, smear, tinge, touch
06 dollop, expert, smudge, stroke

**dabble**
03 dip, toy, wet
04 play
05 dally
06 dampen, paddle, putter, splash, tinker, trifle
07 moisten
08 splatter, sprinkle

**dabbler**
07 amateur, dallier, trifler
09 lay person
10 dilettante

**daft**
03 mad, odd
04 avid, dumb, keen, loco, nuts
05 batty, crazy, dotty, inane, loony, loopy, nutty, potty, silly, sweet, wacky
06 absurd, crazed, insane, mental, psycho, stupid, unwise
07 berserk, bonkers, devoted, foolish, idiotic, lunatic, smitten, touched, zealous
08 crackpot, demented, deranged, enamored, peculiar
09 disturbed, fanatical, foolhardy, imprudent, senseless
10 infatuated, irrational, outrageous, passionate, ridiculous, unbalanced
11 harebrained, nonsensical
12 enthusiastic
13 off your rocker, out of your mind

**dagger**
04 dirk, kris
05 blade, knife, kukri, skean, skeen, skene
06 crease, creese
07 bayonet, jambiya, poniard
08 stiletto

**daily**
07 diurnal, per diem, regular, routine
08 day by day, every day, everyday, habitual, once a day, ordinary
09 circadian, quotidian
11 commonplace, day after day

**dainty**
04 fine, neat, trim
05 fancy, fussy, juicy, small, tasty
06 bonbon, choosy, little, petite, pretty, savory, tidbit, titbit
07 elegant, refined
08 delicacy, delicate
09 exquisite, squeamish, sweetmeat
10 fastidious, particular
11 bonne bouche, persnickety

**dais**
05 stage, stand
06 podium
07 rostrum
08 platform

**dale**
04 dell, glen, vale
06 dingle, strath, valley

**dally**
03 toy
04 play
05 delay, flirt, tarry
06 dawdle, linger, loiter, trifle
13 procrastinate

**dam**
04 stem, wall
05 block, check, levee
07 barrage, barrier, staunch
08 blockage, obstruct, restrict
09 barricade, hindrance
10 embankment
11 obstruction

► *Names of dams:*
04 Guri, Kiev, Oahe
05 Aswan, Nurek, Rogun
06 Bratsk, Hoover, Itaipu, Kariba
07 Boulder, Cochiti, San Luis
08 Akosombo, Fort Peck, Garrison, Gezhouba, Oroville
09 Aswan High, Owen Falls
13 Grande Dixence
14 Afsluitdijk Sea

**damage**
03 mar
04 fine, harm, hurt, loss, ruin
05 abuse, havoc, spoil, wreck
06 deface, impair, injure, injury
08 mischief, mutilate, sabotage
09 desecrate, detriment, vandalism, vandalize
10 defacement, impairment, mutilation, reparation
11 devastation, restitution
12 compensation, incapacitate
13 reimbursement

**damaging**
03 bad
07 harmful, hurtful, ruinous
09 injurious
11 deleterious, detrimental, prejudicial, unfavorable
15 disadvantageous

**dame**
03 gal
04 lady
05 broad, woman
06 female, matron
07 dowager
09 matriarch

**damn**
03 jot, pan
04 cuss, dash, doom, slam
05 blast, curse, decry, knock
06 swear,
07 accurse, censure, condemn, inveigh, monkey's, run down
08 denounce, execrate, maledict
09 blaspheme, castigate, criticize, denigrate, excoriate, fulminate, imprecate
10 come down on, denunciate

**damnable**
06 cursed, wicked
08 horrible, infernal
09 execrable, offensive
10 abominable, detestable

**damnation**
04 doom, hell
09 perdition
12 condemnation, denunciation

**damned**
04 lost, vile
06 cursed, darned, doomed

## damning

07 blasted, hateful
08 accursed, annoying, blooming, dratting, infernal
09 condemned
10 abominable, confounded

## damning

09 damnatory
10 condemning
11 implicating, inculpatory
12 accusatorial, condemnatory
13 incriminating

## damp

03 dew, fog, wet
04 calm, dank, dewy, dull, mist, rain
05 check, humid, misty, moist, muggy, vapor
06 clammy, deaden, lessen, reduce, rheumy
07 drizzle, drizzly, wetness
08 decrease, diminish, moderate, moisture, restrain, vaporous
10 clamminess

## dampen

03 wet
04 damp, dash, dull
05 check, deter, spray
06 deaden, dismay, lessen, muffle, reduce, stifle
07 inhibit, moisten, smother
08 damp down, decrease, diminish, moderate, restrain
12 put a damper on

## damper

□ **put a damper on**

04 dash, dull
05 check, deter
06 dismay, lessen, reduce
07 depress, inhibit, smother
08 damp down, decrease, diminish, moderate, restrain
10 discourage, dishearten

## dampness

03 dew, fog, wet
04 damp, mist, rain
05 vapor
07 drizzle, wetness
08 dankness, humidity, moisture
10 clamminess

## damsel

04 girl, lass
06 maiden
09 young lady
10 young woman

## dance

03 hop, jig
04 ball, play, rock, skip, sway
05 caper, flash, frisk, stomp, swing, twirl, waver, whirl

06 bounce, frolic, gambol, hoof it, prance, social
07 flicker, shindig
09 cut the rug, pirouette, shake a leg
➤ See also BALLET; CHOREOGRAPHER; DANCER

───────────────

▶ *Names of dances*:

03 bop, jig
04 jive, reel, swim
05 conga, limbo, mambo, polka, rumba, samba, skank, stomp, tango, twist, waltz
06 bolero, cancan, cha-cha, minuet, watusi
07 beguine, foxtrot, gavotte, hoedown, Lancers, mazurka, one-step, two-step
08 cakewalk, fandango, flamenco, galliard, hornpipe, soft-shoe
09 bossanova, clog dance, jitterbug, pasodoble, quadrille, quickstep, rock 'n' roll
10 belly dance, Charleston, hokeypokey, turkey trot
11 black bottom, morris dance, square dance
12 mashed potato
13 Highland fling

───────────────

▶ *Types of dancing*:

03 tap
04 folk
05 disco, Irish
06 ballet
07 country, old-time
08 ballroom, Highland, robotics
12 breakdancing
13 Latin-American

───────────────

▶ *Types of dance function*:

03 hop
04 ball, prom
05 dance, disco
06 social
09 barn dance

## dancer

07 danseur
08 coryphee, danseuse
09 ballerina, chorus boy, tap-dancer
10 chorus girl
11 belly dancer
12 ballet dancer

───────────────

▶ *Names of dancers*:

04 **Bull** (Deborah), **Edur** (Thomas), **Oaks** (Agnes), **Tune** (Tommy)
05 **Baker** (Josephine), **Cohan**

(Robert), **Dolin** (Anton), **Kelly** (Gene), **Laban** (Rudolf von), **Lifar** (Serge), **Tharp** (Twyla)
06 **Ashton** (Frederick), **Béjart** (Maurice), **Blasis** (Carlo), **Davies** (Siobhan), **Dowell** (Anthony), **Duncan** (Isadora), **Fokine** (Michel), **Graham** (Martha), **Petipa** (Marius), **Rogers** (Ginger), **Sibley** (Antoinette), **Wigman** (Mary)
07 **Astaire** (Fred), **Bussell** (Darcey), **Fonteyn** (Margot), **Gregory** (Cynthia), **Guillem** (Sylvie), **Markova** (Alicia), **Martins** (Peter), **Massine** (Léonide), **McBride** (Patricia), **Nureyev** (Rudolf), **Pavlova** (Anna), **Rambert** (Marie), **Seymour** (Lynn), **Tamiris** (Helen), **Ulanova** (Galina)
08 **Charisse** (Cyd), **Danilova** (Alexandra), **De Valois** (Ninette), **Helpmann** (Robert), **Humphrey** (Doris), **Kirkland** (Gelsey), **Nijinska** (Bronislava), **Nijinsky** (Vaslav), **Robinson** (Bill), **Villella** (Edward)
09 **Diaghilev** (Sergei), **Macmillan** (Kenneth), **Tallchief** (Maria)
10 **Balanchine** (George), **Cunningham** (Merce)
11 **Baryshnikov** (Mikhail), **Mistinguett**
12 **The Rockettes**

## dandy

03 fop
04 beau, dude, fine, toff
05 blade, great, swell
08 gay blade, popinjay, splendid
09 excellent, exquisite, first-rate
12 man about town

## danger

04 risk
05 peril
06 hazard, menace, threat
07 pitfall
08 jeopardy
13 vulnerability

## dangerous

05 dicey, grave, hairy, risky
06 chancy, severe, unsafe
07 exposed, ominous, serious
08 critical, high-risk, menacing, perilous, reckless
09 hazardous, minacious
10 precarious, vulnerable

11 threatening, treacherous

**dangle**
04 flap, hang, sway
05 droop, swing, trail
06 flaunt
07 suspend

**dank**
03 wet
04 damp, dewy
05 moist, slimy, soggy
06 clammy, sticky

**dapper**
04 chic, neat, spry, trim
05 brisk, natty, smart
06 dainty, nimble, spruce
07 stylish
11 well-dressed, well-groomed
13 well-turned-out

**dappled**
04 pied
06 dotted
07 flecked, mottled, spotted
08 freckled, speckled, stippled

**dare**
04 defy, face, goad, risk
05 brave, flout, stake, taunt
06 gamble, hazard, resist
09 adventure, challenge
12 be bold enough
13 be brave enough
14 have the courage

**daredevil**
04 bold, rash
05 brave
06 daring, madcap, plucky
08 fearless, intrepid, stuntman
09 audacious, dauntless,
 desperado, impetuous
10 adventurer
11 adventurous

**daring**
04 bold, gall, guts, rash, wild
05 brave, nerve, pluck, valor
06 plucky, spirit
07 bravery, courage, valiant
08 audacity, boldness, defiance,
 intrepid, reckless
09 audacious, dauntless
10 courageous
12 fearlessness

**dark**
03 dim, fog, sad
04 drab, dusk, grim, mist
05 awful, black, brown, dingy,
 dusky, foggy, gloom, murky,
 night, shade, shady, unlit
06 dismal, gloomy, hidden,
 morose, secret, somber

07 dimness, evening, mystery,
 obscure, ominous, secrecy,
 shadows, shadowy, sunless
08 abstruse, badly lit, brunette,
 darkness, dimly lit, hopeless,
 menacing, overcast, sinister,
 twilight
09 blackness, cheerless,
 enigmatic, half-light,
 ignorance, murkiness,
 nightfall, nighttime,
 obscurity, shadiness
10 cloudiness, dark-haired,
 forbidding, mysterious
13 unilluminated

**darken**
03 dim, fog
04 fade
05 cloud, frown, shade
06 deject, sadden, shadow
07 blacken, depress, eclipse
09 cloud over, grow angry
10 grow darker, make gloomy,
 obnubilate, overshadow

**darling**
03 pet
04 dear, love
05 angel, honey
06 adored
07 beloved, dearest
08 favorite, precious, treasure
09 cherished
10 sweetheart
11 blue-eyed boy, teacher's pet
13 fair-haired boy
14 apple of your eye

**darn**
03 sew
04 damn, mend
05 patch, sew up
06 cursed, cussed, repair, stitch
07 blasted, doggone

**dart**
03 fly, run
04 barb, bolt, dash, flit, hurl,
 leap, race, rush, send, tear
05 arrow, flash, shoot, throw
07 feather, project

**dash**
03 bit, fly, nip, pop, run
04 beat, bolt, dart, hurl, lash,
 race, ruin, rush, slam, tear
05 break, crash, crush, fling,
 hurry, pound, smash, speed,
 spoil, throw, touch, trace
06 blight, dampen, flavor, hurtle,
 little, sprint, strike
07 shatter, smidgen, soupçon
08 confound
10 disappoint, suggestion

◻**dash off**
06 scrawl
08 scribble

**dashing**
04 bold
05 showy, smart
06 daring, lively, plucky
07 elegant, gallant, stylish
08 debonair, spirited, vigorous
10 attractive, flamboyant
11 fashionable

**dastardly**
03 low
04 base, mean, vile
06 craven, wicked
08 cowardly
09 underhand
10 despicable
12 contemptible, fainthearted

**data**
05 facts, input
07 details, figures
08 material, research
10 statistics
11 information, particulars

**date**
03 age, day, era
04 time, week, year
05 court, go out, month
06 decade, escort, friend, go
 back, period, steady
07 meeting, partner, take out
08 come from, deadline, go
 steady
09 boyfriend, exist from, go out
 with, obsolesce, originate
10 be together, engagement,
 girlfriend, go out of use,
 millennium, rendezvous
11 appointment, assignation

◻**out of date**
05 dated, passé
06 old hat
07 archaic
08 obsolete, outdated,
 outmoded
10 antiquated, superseded
11 obsolescent
12 old-fashioned
13 unfashionable

◻**to date**
05 so far
07 up to now
08 until now
14 up to the present

◻**up to date**
06 modern, trendy
07 current
11 fashionable
12 contemporary

**dated**
13 up to the minute

**dated**
05 passé
06 old hat
07 archaic
08 obsolete, outdated, outmoded
09 out-of-date
10 antiquated, superseded
11 obsolescent
12 old-fashioned
13 unfashionable

**daub**
03 dab
04 blot, coat, spot
05 paint, smear, stain, sully
06 blotch, smudge, splash
07 plaster, splodge, splotch

**daughter**
04 girl, lass
05 child, fille
06 lassie
08 disciple
09 offspring
10 descendant, inhabitant

**daunt**
03 cow
05 alarm, deter, scare
06 dismay, put off
07 overawe, unnerve
08 dispirit, frighten
09 take aback
10 demoralize, disconcert, discourage, dishearten, intimidate

**dauntless**
04 bold
05 brave
06 daring, plucky
07 valiant
08 fearless, intrepid, resolute
09 undaunted
10 courageous

**dawdle**
03 lag
05 dally, delay, tarry, trail
06 linger, loiter, putter
09 hang about
10 dillydally
15 go at a snail's pace

**dawn**
04 open, rise
05 begin, birth, onset, start
06 advent, appear, be born
07 arrival, genesis, glimmer, lighten, morning, sunrise
08 brighten, commence, daybreak, daylight
09 beginning, originate
10 break of day, first light

12 commencement

□**dawn on**
03 hit
05 click
06 sink in, strike
07 occur to, realize

**day**
03 age, era
04 date, time
05 epoch
06 period
07 daytime, diurnal
08 daylight

□**call it a day**
06 retire
08 stop work
11 call it quits

□**day after day**
09 endlessly, regularly
11 continually, perpetually
12 monotonously, persistently

□**day by day**
08 steadily
09 gradually
13 progressively
15 slowly but surely

□**have had its day**
08 be past it
11 be out of date

**daybreak**
04 dawn
05 sunup
07 morning, sunrise
08 cockcrow, daylight
10 break of day, first light
11 crack of dawn

**daydream**
04 muse, wish
05 dream, fancy
06 musing, vision
07 fantasy, imagine, reverie
09 fantasize, pipe dream, switch off
14 stare into space
15 castles in the air

**daylight**
03 day
04 dawn
05 light
07 daytime, morning, sunrise
08 daybreak, sunlight
10 break of day, first light
11 crack of dawn
12 natural light

**daze**
04 numb, stun
05 amaze, blind, shock
06 baffle, dazzle, stupor, trance
07 confuse, perplex, stupefy

08 bewilder, numbness, paralyze, surprise
09 confusion, dumbfound, take aback
12 bewilderment

**dazed**
06 amazed, numbed
07 baffled, dazzled, shocked, stunned
08 confused, startled
09 paralyzed, perplexed, staggered, stupefied
10 astonished, bewildered, speechless, taken aback
11 dumbfounded, unconscious

**dazzle**
03 awe, wow
05 amaze, blind, glare, gleam
07 bewitch, confuse, impress, overawe, sparkle, stupefy
08 astonish, bedazzle, bowl over, knock out, splendor
09 dumbfound, fascinate, hypnotize
10 brightness, brilliance, razzmatazz
11 scintillate
12 magnificence, razzle-dazzle
13 scintillation

**dazzling**
05 grand
06 superb
07 glaring, radiant, shining
08 glorious, splendid, stunning
09 brilliant, ravishing, sparkling
11 sensational, spectacular
12 awe-inspiring, breathtaking
13 scintillating

**dead**
04 dull, gone, late, numb, very
05 dated, exact, inert, passé, quiet, quite, tired, total, utter
06 no more, old hat
07 defunct, exactly, extinct, humdrum, perfect, tedious, totally, utterly, worn out
08 absolute, complete, deceased, departed, entirely, lifeless, obsolete, perished, tired out
09 exanimate, exhausted, inanimate, insensate, out of date, out of play, paralyzed, precisely, stillborn
10 absolutely, completely, insentient, thoroughly
11 dead as a dodo, gone to sleep, ready to drop
12 discontinued, unresponsive
14 no longer spoken
15 dead as a doornail

## deaden
04 dull, hush, mute, numb
05 abate, allay, blunt, check
06 dampen, lessen, muffle, reduce, soothe, subdue
07 assuage, quieten, smother
08 diminish, mitigate, paralyze, suppress
09 alleviate
11 anesthetize
14 take the edge off

## deadlock
04 halt
07 dead end, impasse
08 stoppage
09 checkmate, stalemate
10 standstill

## deadly
04 dull, grim, sure, true
05 fatal, great, quite, toxic
06 boring, lethal, mortal
07 intense, noxious, precise, serious, totally, utterly
08 accurate, entirely, venomous
09 dangerous, malignant, murderous, perfectly
10 absolutely, completely, dreadfully, implacable, pernicious, thoroughly
11 destructive

## deadpan
05 blank, empty
09 impassive
10 poker-faced
11 inscrutable
12 inexpressive, unexpressive
13 dispassionate, straight-faced
14 expressionless

## deaf
07 unmoved
08 heedless
09 oblivious, stone-deaf
10 impervious
11 deaf as a post, indifferent, unconcerned
13 hard of hearing

## deafening
07 booming, ringing, roaring
08 piercing, very loud
09 very noisy
10 resounding, thunderous
12 ear-splitting, overwhelming

## deal
03 buy, lot
04 hand, load, mete, pact
05 allot, share, trade
06 assign, direct, divide, export, handle, market
07 bargain, deliver, dole out, give out, inflict, mete out, operate, traffic
08 contract, dispense, quantity
09 agreement, apportion
10 administer, buy and sell, distribute, do business
11 arrangement, transaction
12 distribution

## ❑deal with
05 cover, see to, treat
06 handle, manage, tackle
07 concern, process, sort out
08 attend to, cope with
10 take care of
14 get to grips with

## dealer
06 pusher, trader, vendor
08 marketer, merchant, retailer, salesman
10 saleswoman, trafficker, wholesaler
11 salesperson
12 merchandiser

## dealings
05 trade, truck
07 traffic
08 business, commerce
09 relations
10 operations
12 negotiations, transactions

## dear
03 pet
05 close, honey, loved, steep
06 adored, costly, pricey, valued
07 beloved, darling, favored
08 esteemed, favorite, high-cost, loved one, not cheap, precious, treasure
09 cherished, endearing, expensive, respected, treasured
10 exorbitant, high-priced, overpriced, sweetheart

## dearly
06 deeply, fondly
07 greatly
08 lovingly, tenderly, very much
09 adoringly, extremely, with favor
10 profoundly
12 at a great cost, at a high price
13 with great loss
14 affectionately

## dearth
04 lack, need, want
06 famine
07 absence, paucity, poverty
08 scarcity, shortage, sparsity
10 deficiency, scantiness
13 insufficiency

## death
03 end

04 loss, ruin
06 demise, finish, mortal
07 decease, passing, quietus
08 curtains, fatality, the grave
09 departure, perishing
10 expiration, extinction, loss of life
11 destruction, eradication, eternal rest, passing away, termination
12 annihilation, last farewell
13 extermination, the grim reaper

## ❑put to death
03 gas
04 hang, kill
05 shoot
06 behead, martyr
07 execute
10 guillotine
11 electrocute, exterminate

## deathless
07 eternal, undying
08 immortal, timeless
11 everlasting, never-ending

## deathly
04 grim, pale
05 ashen, fatal
06 deadly, mortal, pallid
07 extreme, ghastly, intense
09 colorless
10 cadaverous

## debacle
05 farce, havoc
06 defeat, fiasco
07 failure, turmoil
08 collapse, disaster, reversal
09 cataclysm, overthrow

## debar
03 ban, bar
04 deny, stop
05 eject, expel
06 forbid, hamper, hinder
07 exclude, keep out, prevent, shut out
08 obstruct, preclude, prohibit
09 blackball, proscribe

## debase
05 alloy, lower, shame, taint
06 defile, demean, humble
07 cheapen, corrupt, degrade, devalue, pollute, vitiate
08 disgrace, dishonor
09 discredit
10 adulterate
11 contaminate

## debased
03 low
04 base, vile
06 fallen, impure, shamed

**debasement**

07 corrupt, defiled, tainted
08 degraded, devalued, polluted
09 cheapened, disgraced
10 degenerate, humiliated
11 adulterated, discredited
12 contaminated

**debasement**

05 shame
08 disgrace, dishonor
09 abasement, pollution
10 cheapening, corruption, defilement, perversion
11 degradation, depravation, devaluation, humiliation
12 adulteration, degeneration
13 contamination

**debatable**

04 moot
06 unsure
08 arguable, doubtful
09 uncertain, undecided
10 disputable
11 contentious, contestable
12 questionable
13 controversial, problematical
14 open to question

**debate**

05 argue, forum, weigh
06 ponder, reason
07 contend, contest, discuss, dispute, polemic, wrangle
08 argument, consider
09 altercate, talk about
10 contention, discussion
11 altercation, controversy

**debauch**

04 ruin
06 ravish, seduce
07 corrupt, deprave, pervert, pollute, subvert, violate
10 lead astray

**debauched**

04 lewd
06 wanton
07 corrupt, debased, immoral
08 decadent, degraded, depraved
09 abandoned, carousing, corrupted, dissolute, excessive, perverted
10 degenerate, dissipated, licentious
11 intemperate, promiscuous
13 overindulgent

**debauchery**

04 lust, orgy, riot
06 excess
08 carousal, lewdness
09 decadence, depravity

10 corruption, degeneracy, immorality, wantonness
11 degradation, dissipation, libertinism
12 intemperance
13 dissoluteness
14 licentiousness, overindulgence

**debilitate**

06 impair, weaken
07 cripple, exhaust, wear out
08 enervate, enfeeble
09 undermine
10 devitalize
12 incapacitate

**debilitating**

06 tiring
09 crippling, fatiguing, impairing, weakening
10 enervating, enervative, enfeebling, exhausting
11 undermining
14 incapacitating

**debility**

05 atony
07 fatigue, frailty, malaise
08 asthenia, weakness
09 atonicity, faintness, infirmity
10 feebleness, incapacity
11 decrepitude
12 enfeeblement

**debonair**

05 suave
06 breezy, smooth, urbane
07 dashing, elegant, refined
08 charming, well-bred
12 light-hearted

**debris**

04 bits
05 ruins, trash, waste, wreck
06 litter, pieces, rubble
07 remains, rubbish
08 detritus, wreckage
09 fragments, sweepings

**debt**

03 due, IOU
04 bill, duty
05 claim, debit, score
06 the red
07 arrears
09 liability, overdraft
10 money owing

**debtor**

04 ower
08 bankrupt, borrower
09 defaulter, insolvent

**debunk**

06 expose, show up
07 deflate, explode, lampoon
08 disprove, puncture, ridicule

13 cut down to size

**debut**

06 maiden
08 entrance, première
09 beginning, coming-out, first time, launching
10 first night, initiation
12 inauguration, introduction
15 first appearance

**decadence**

09 depravity
10 debauchery, degeneracy, immorality, perversion
11 dissipation, dissolution
14 degenerateness, licentiousness, self-indulgence

**decadent**

07 corrupt, debased, immoral
08 degraded, depraved
09 debauched, dissolute
10 degenerate, dissipated, licentious
13 self-indulgent

**decamp**

04 bolt, flee, flit
06 desert, escape, vamose
07 abscond, make off, run away, skiddoo, take off, vamoose
09 skedaddle
10 hightail it

**decapitate**

06 behead, unhead
07 execute
10 guillotine

**decay**

03 rot
04 fail, rust, sink
05 go bad, spoil
06 fester, perish, wither
07 atrophy, corrode, crumble, decline, failing, putrefy, rotting, shrivel, wasting
08 collapse, going bad
09 decadence, decompose, putridity, waste away
10 degenerate
11 deteriorate, putrescence
12 degeneration, disintegrate, putrefaction
13 decomposition, deterioration
14 disintegration

**decayed**

03 bad, off
04 rank, sour
05 moldy, stale
06 addled, putrid, rotten, wasted
07 carious, carrion, spoiled
08 corroded, perished

09 putrefied
10 decomposed

**decease**
03 die
05 death, dying
06 demise
07 passing
08 pass away
09 departure
10 expiration
11 dissolution, passing away

**deceased**
04 dead, gone, late, lost
06 former
07 defunct, expired, extinct
08 departed, finished

**deceit**
04 fake, ruse, sham, wile
05 abuse, feint, fraud, guile
07 cunning, slyness, swindle
08 artifice, cheating, pretense, trickery, wiliness
09 chicanery, deception, duplicity, hypocrisy
10 subterfuge
11 fraudulence
13 double-dealing
15 underhandedness

**deceitful**
05 false, lying
06 crafty, sneaky, tricky
07 cunning, knavish
08 guileful, illusory, two-faced
09 deceiving, deceptive, designing, dishonest, insincere, underhand
10 fraudulent, mendacious, perfidious, untruthful
11 counterfeit, dissembling, duplicitous, treacherous
13 double-dealing

**deceive**
03 con, kid
04 dupe, fool, gull, hoax
05 abuse, bluff, cheat, trick
06 betray, delude, entrap, lead on, outwit, seduce
07 beguile, cheat on, ensnare, mislead, swindle, two-time
08 hoodwink, misguide
09 bamboozle, dissemble
11 double-cross, string along
12 put one over on, take for a ride
14 pull a fast one on
15 pull someone's leg

**deceiver**
05 cheat, crook, fraud, quack
06 abuser, con man, hoaxer
08 betrayer, impostor, swindler
09 charlatan, con artist, trickster

10 dissembler, mountebank
12 double-dealer
13 confidence man, double-crosser

**decelerate**
05 brake
08 slow down
11 reduce speed
14 put the brakes on

**decency**
07 decorum, fitness, modesty
08 civility, courtesy
09 etiquette, good taste, integrity, propriety
10 seemliness
11 helpfulness, uprightness
14 respectability

**decent**
02 OK
03 fit
04 kind, nice, okay, pure
06 chaste, modest, polite, proper, seemly, worthy
07 ethical, helpful, upright
08 adequate, becoming, decorous, generous, gracious, obliging, suitable, tasteful, virtuous
09 befitting, courteous
10 acceptable, thoughtful
11 presentable, respectable
12 satisfactory
13 accommodating

**decentralize**
07 devolve
08 delegate, localize
11 regionalize
13 deconcentrate, spread outward

**deception**
03 con, lie
04 hoax, ruse, sham, wile
05 bluff, cheat, fraud, guile, snare, trick
06 deceit, humbug
07 cunning, leg-pull, swindle
08 artifice, cheating, pretense, put-up job, trickery
09 chicanery, duplicity, imposture, treachery
10 craftiness, subterfuge
11 dissembling, fraudulence
13 double-dealing
15 underhandedness

**deceptive**
04 fake, mock, sham
05 bogus, false
06 crafty
07 crooked, cunning
08 cheating, illusive, illusory, specious, spurious

09 dishonest, underhand
10 fallacious, misleading
11 dissembling, duplicitous

**decide**
03 fix
04 pick, rule
05 go for, judge
06 choose, opt for, select, settle
07 resolve
08 conclude, plump for
09 arbitrate, determine
10 adjudicate
11 give a ruling
13 give a judgment, make a decision
14 make up your mind, reach a decision

**decided**
04 firm
05 clear
06 marked
07 certain, express, obvious
08 absolute, clear-cut, decisive, definite, positive, resolute
10 deliberate, determined, forthright, purposeful, unswerving, unwavering
11 categorical, unequivocal
12 unhesitating, unmistakable

**decidedly**
04 very
05 quite
07 clearly
09 certainly, downright
10 decisively, definitely, distinctly, positively
12 unmistakably
13 unequivocally
14 unquestionably

**decider**
08 clincher
10 determiner
11 coup de grâce

**deciding**
05 chief, final, prime
06 crunch
07 crucial, supreme
08 critical, decisive
10 conclusive
11 determining, significant

**decipher**
05 crack
06 decode
07 make out, unravel, work out
09 figure out, interpret, translate
10 understand, unscramble
13 transliterate

**decision**
06 decree, result, ruling

**decisive**
07 finding, opinion, outcome, purpose, resolve, verdict
08 firmness, judgment
10 conclusion, resolution
12 adjudication, decisiveness
13 determination

**decisive**
04 firm
05 final, prime
06 strong
07 crucial, decided, fateful
08 critical, deciding, definite, forceful, positive, resolute
10 conclusive, definitive, determined, forthright, unswerving, unwavering
11 determining, influential
12 strong-minded

**deck**
04 trim
05 adorn, array, grace
06 bedeck, enrich
07 festoon, garland, garnish
08 beautify, decorate, ornament, prettify, trick out
09 embellish

**declaim**
04 rant
05 orate, spiel, spout
07 lecture
08 harangue, proclaim
09 hold forth, sermonize

**declamation**
04 rant
06 sermon, speech, tirade
07 address, lecture, oration
08 harangue

**declamatory**
04 bold
07 fustian, orotund, pompous
08 dramatic, inflated
09 bombastic, grandiose, high-flown, overblown
10 oratorical, theatrical
12 magniloquent
13 grandiloquent

**declaration**
05 edict
06 avowal, decree
08 averment
09 affidavit, assertion, broadcast, manifesto, statement, testimony
10 confession, disclosure, profession, revelation
11 affirmation, attestation
12 announcement, confirmation, notification, proclamation, promulgation
13 pronouncement

**declare**
04 aver, avow, show
05 claim, state, swear
06 affirm, assert, attest, decree
07 certify, confess, profess, publish, testify, witness
08 announce, disclose, maintain, proclaim, validate
09 make known, pronounce
10 promulgate

**decline**
03 dip, ebb, rot
04 balk, deny, drop, fade, fall, flag, hill, sink, slip, wane
05 abate, decay, forgo, lapse, slant, slide, slope, slump
06 forego, go down, lessen, refuse, reject, waning, weaken, wither, worsen
07 descend, descent, dwindle, failing, failure, fall off, get less, incline, plummet, regress, say no to, subside
08 decrease, diminish, downturn, turn down
09 abatement, declivity, dwindling, lessening, recession, reduction, weakening, worsening
10 degenerate, diminution, divergence, falling-off
11 declination, deteriorate
12 degeneration
13 deterioration

**decode**
05 crack
07 make out, unravel, work out
08 construe, decipher
09 figure out, interpret, translate
10 understand, unscramble
13 transliterate

**decomposable**
10 degradable
12 destructible
13 biodegradable

**decompose**
03 rot
05 decay, spoil
06 fester
07 break up, crumble, putrefy
09 break down
12 disintegrate

**decomposition**
03 rot
05 decay
07 rotting
08 going bad
09 perishing, putridity
11 dissolution, putrescence
12 putrefaction
14 disintegration

**décor**
07 scenery
10 decoration
11 color scheme, furnishings

**decorate**
04 cite, deck, do up, trim
05 adorn, color, grace, honor, paint, paper
06 bedaub
07 bedizen, bemedal, festoon, garland, garnish, smarten
08 beautify, ornament, prettify, renovate, trick out
09 embellish, refurbish
12 give a honor to, give a medal to

**decoration**
04 star
05 award, badge, cross, crown, décor, frill, honor, medal, mural, order, title
06 bauble, colors, emblem, laurel, ribbon, scroll, wreath
07 bunting, garland, garnish, laurels, trinket
08 flourish, ornament, trimming
09 adornment
11 color scheme, elaboration, enhancement
13 embellishment, ornamentation
14 beautification

**decorative**
05 fancy
06 ornate, pretty, rococo
09 elaborate, enhancing
10 ornamental
13 nonfunctional

**decorous**
03 fit
05 staid
06 decent, modest, polite, proper, sedate, seemly
07 correct, courtly, refined
08 becoming, suitable
09 befitting, dignified
11 comme il faut, well-behaved

**decorum**
05 grace
07 decency, dignity, modesty
08 breeding, good form
09 etiquette, propriety
10 conformity, deportment, politeness, seemliness
11 good manners
14 respectability

**decoy**
04 bait, draw, lead, lure, trap
05 dummy, snare, tempt
06 allure, entice, entrap, seduce
07 attract, deceive, ensnare

09 diversion
10 allurement, attraction, temptation
11 ensnarement

**decrease**
03 ebb
04 drop, fall, loss, slim, wane
05 abate, let up, lower, slide
06 go down, lessen, plunge, reduce, shrink
07 cut back, cut down, cutback, decline, dwindle, fall off, plummet, slacken, subside
08 come down, contract, diminish, downturn, lowering, make less, slim down, step-down, taper off
09 abatement, dwindling, lessening, reduction, scale down, shrinkage
10 become less, diminution, falling-off, subsidence
11 contraction

**decree**
03 act, law
04 fiat, rule
05 edict, enact, irade, order
06 decide, direct, enjoin, firman, ordain, ruling
07 command, dictate, lay down, precept, statute
08 proclaim, psephism, rescript
09 determine, enactment, manifesto, ordinance, prescribe, pronounce
12 proclamation

**decrepit**
03 old
04 aged, weak
05 frail
06 feeble, flimsy, infirm, senile
07 elderly, run-down, worn-out
08 battered
09 crumbling, doddering, senescent, tottering
10 broken-down, in bad shape, ramshackle, tumbledown
11 dilapidated
12 falling apart
13 falling to bits

**decrepitude**
04 ruin
05 decay
06 dotage, old age
08 debility, senility, weakness
09 infirmity
10 disability, feebleness, incapacity, senescence
12 degeneration, dilapidation

**decry**
03 boo, pan

05 blame, knock, snipe
06 attack
07 censure, condemn, devalue, nit-pick, run down, traduce
08 belittle, denounce, derogate
09 criticize, denigrate, disparage, underrate
10 animadvert, come down on
12 pull to pieces, tear to shreds
13 find fault with
14 inveigh against
15 do a hatchet job on

**dedicate**
04 give, name
05 bless, offer
06 assign, commit, devote, hallow, pledge
07 address, present
08 inscribe, make holy, sanctify, set apart
10 consecrate, give over to

**dedicated**
07 bespoke, devoted, zealous
08 diligent
09 committed
10 customized, purposeful
11 custom-built, given over to, hard-working, industrious
12 enthusiastic, single-minded, wholehearted

**dedication**
04 zeal
07 address, loyalty
08 blessing, devotion
09 adherence, hallowing
10 allegiance, commitment
11 inscription
12 consecration, faithfulness
13 self-sacrifice

**deduce**
04 draw
05 glean, infer
06 derive, gather, reason
07 surmise
08 conclude
10 understand

**deduct**
06 remove
07 take off
08 knock off, reduce by, subtract, take away
10 decrease by

**deduction**
07 finding, removal
08 decrease, discount
09 abatement, allowance, corollary, inference, reasoning, reduction, surmising, taking off
10 assumption, conclusion, diminution, taking away

11 presumption, subtraction

**deed**
03 act
04 fact, feat
05 title, truth
06 action, record
07 exploit, reality
08 activity, contract, document

**deem**
04 hold
05 judge, think
06 esteem, reckon, regard
07 account, adjudge, believe, imagine, suppose
08 conceive, consider, estimate

**deep**
03 far, low, sea
04 bass, dark, rich, warm, wise
05 briny, grave, ocean, quiet
06 ardent, severe, strong
07 booming, earnest, extreme, fervent, glowing, intense, obscure, serious
08 abstruse, esoteric, high seas, immersed, profound, reserved
09 brilliant, cavernous, difficult, heartfelt, recondite, sagacious, unplumbed
10 bottomless, discerning, fathomless, low-pitched, mysterious, passionate, perceptive, unfathomed
13 perspicacious

**deepen**
04 grow
05 lower
06 dig out, extend, worsen
07 build up, magnify
08 excavate, get worse, heighten, increase
09 intensify, reinforce
10 strengthen
11 deteriorate

**deeply**
05 sadly
07 acutely, gravely
08 ardently, movingly, severely, strongly, very much
09 earnestly, extremely, fervently, intensely, seriously
10 completely, profoundly, thoroughly, to the quick
12 passionately

**deep-seated**
04 deep
05 fixed
07 settled
09 confirmed, ingrained
10 deep-rooted, entrenched

## deer
03 doe, elk, roe
04 buck, hart, hind, stag
05 moose
07 caribou, cervine
08 reindeer

## deface
03 mar
05 spoil, sully
06 damage, deform, injure
07 blemish, destroy, tarnish
08 mutilate
09 disfigure, vandalize

## de facto
04 real
06 actual, really
08 actually, existing, in effect

## defamation
04 slur
05 libel, smear
07 calumny, obloquy, scandal, slander
08 innuendo
09 aspersion
10 backbiting, opprobrium
11 denigration, malediction
12 vilification
13 smear campaign

## defamatory
08 libelous
09 insulting, vilifying
10 calumnious, derogatory, pejorative, slanderous
11 denigrating, disparaging, maledictory
12 contumelious

## defame
05 libel, smear
06 infame, malign, vilify
07 asperse, blacken, run down, slander, traduce
08 dishonor
09 denigrate, discredit, disparage
10 calumniate, sling mud at, stigmatize, vituperate
11 speak evil of
14 cast aspersions

## default
04 fail, lack, want
05 dodge, evade, fault, lapse, welsh
06 defect, renege
07 absence, defraud, failure, forfeit
08 omission
09 backslide
10 negligence, nonpayment

## defaulter
08 absentee, nonpayer, offender

## defeat
04 balk, beat, foil, lick, rout
05 block, crush, excel, quell, repel, skunk, smash, thump, worst
06 baffle, hammer, reject, subdue, thrash, thwart
07 beating, conquer, debacle, failure, setback, shellac, trounce
08 confound, conquest, downfall, overcome, vanquish, waterloo
09 checkmate, devastate, frustrate, overpower, overthrow, overwhelm, rejection, repulsion, slaughter, thrashing, thwarting, trouncing
12 vanquishment
14 get the better of
15 make mincemeat of

## defeatist
06 gloomy
07 quitter, yielder
08 helpless, hopeless, resigned
09 doomsayer, pessimist
10 despondent, fatalistic
11 pessimistic
13 prophet of doom

## defecate
05 egest, purge
06 purify, refine
07 clarify, excrete
08 evacuate

## defect
03 bug
04 flaw, lack, snag, spot, want
05 error, fault, rebel, taint
06 desert, renege, revolt
07 abandon, absence, blemish, failing, frailty, mistake
08 weak spot, weakness
09 deformity, shortfall
10 apostatize, break faith, deficiency, inadequacy
11 change sides, shortcoming, turn traitor
12 imperfection, tergiversate

## defection
06 mutiny, revolt
07 perfidy, treason
08 apostasy, betrayal
09 desertion, rebellion
11 abandonment, dereliction
14 tergiversation

## defective
04 bust
06 broken, faulty, flawed
09 deficient, imperfect
10 on the blink, out of order

14 malfunctioning

## defector
03 rat
05 Judas, rebel
07 traitor
08 apostate, betrayer, deserter, mutineer, quisling, recreant, renegade, turncoat
13 tergiversator

## defend
04 back
05 cover, deter, guard, plead
06 resist, screen, uphold
07 contest, explain, fortify, justify, protect, stand by
08 argue for, buttress, champion, garrison
09 barricade, exonerate, safeguard, vindicate
10 go to bat for, speak up for, stand up for, stick up for
12 keep from harm

## defendant
07 accused
08 litigant, offender, prisoner
09 appellant
10 respondent

## defender
05 guard
06 backer, keeper, patron
08 advocate, champion, endorser, guardian
09 apologist, bodyguard, protector, supporter

## defense
04 army, case, fort, keep, navy, plea
05 alibi, cover, guard
06 screen, shield, troops
07 bastion, bulwark, marines, outpost, rampart, shelter, weapons
08 air force, apologia, argument, buttress, fortress, garrison, immunity, military, pleading, security, soldiers
09 armaments, barricade, deterrent, safeguard
10 coast guard, deterrence, protection, resistance, stronghold
11 armed forces, explanation, explication, vindication
13 defensive team, fortification, justification

## defenseless
04 weak
07 exposed, unarmed
08 helpless, impotent
09 powerless, unguarded
10 undefended, vulnerable

11 unprotected
12 open to attack

**defensible**
07 tenable
08 arguable
09 plausible
10 pardonable, vindicable
11 justifiable, permissible

**defensive**
04 wary
08 cautious, watchful
09 defending
10 apologetic, protective
14 self-justifying

**defer**
03 bow
05 delay, table, waive, yield
06 accede, comply, give in, put off, shelve, submit
07 give way, put back, respect
08 hold over, postpone, prorogue, put on ice
09 acquiesce, surrender
10 capitulate

**deference**
05 honor
06 esteem, regard
07 respect
08 civility, courtesy, yielding
09 obedience, reverence
10 compliance, politeness
12 acquiescence
13 attentiveness, consideration

**deferential**
05 civil
06 polite
07 dutiful
08 obeisant, reverent
09 attentive, courteous
10 morigerous, obsequious, respectful, thoughtful
11 considerate, reverential
12 ingratiating

**deferment**
04 stay
05 delay
07 tabling, waiving
08 shelving
10 moratorium, suspension
11 adjournment, prorogation
12 postponement
15 procrastination

**defiance**
08 contempt
09 challenge, disregard
10 opposition, resistance
12 disobedience
13 confrontation, recalcitrance
14 rebelliousness
15 insubordination

**defiant**
04 bold
08 insolent, militant, scornful
09 obstinate, resistant
10 aggressive, rebellious
11 challenging, disobedient
12 antagonistic, contumacious, intransigent, recalcitrant
13 insubordinate

**deficiency**
04 flaw, lack, want
05 fault
06 dearth, defect
07 absence, deficit, failing
08 scarcity, shortage, weakness
10 inadequacy, scantiness
11 shortcoming
12 imperfection
13 insufficiency

**deficient**
04 weak
05 short
06 meager, scarce, skimpy
07 lacking, wanting
08 exiguous, inferior
10 inadequate, incomplete
12 insufficient
14 unsatisfactory

**deficit**
04 lack, loss
07 arrears, default
08 shortage
09 shortfall
10 deficiency

**defile**
04 pass, soil
05 dirty, gorge, gully, spoil, stain, sully, taint
06 debase, defame, infect, ravine, valley
07 blacken, corrupt, degrade, passage, pollute, profane, tarnish, violate, vitiate
08 disgrace, dishonor
09 denigrate, desecrate
10 make impure
11 contaminate, make unclean

**definable**
08 definite, specific
10 explicable
11 describable, perceptible
12 determinable, identifiable
13 ascertainable

**define**
03 fix
05 bound, limit
07 delimit, explain, mark out
08 describe, spell out
09 delineate, demarcate, establish, interpret
12 characterize, circumscribe

**definite**
04 firm, sure
05 clear, exact, fixed
06 marked
07 assured, certain, decided, obvious, precise, settled
08 clear-cut, explicit, positive
10 determined, guaranteed

**definitely**
06 easily, indeed, surely
07 clearly, plainly
09 certainly, doubtless, no denying, obviously
10 absolutely, positively
11 indubitably, undoubtedly
12 unmistakably, without doubt
13 categorically
14 unquestionably
15 without question

**definition**
05 focus, sense
07 clarity, meaning
08 contrast
09 clearness, precision, sharpness
11 description, explanation
12 distinctness, significance

**definitive**
05 exact, final
07 correct, perfect
08 absolute, complete, standard, ultimate
11 categorical
13 authoritative

**deflate**
04 dash, void
05 empty, lower
06 debunk, humble, lessen, reduce, shrink, squash
07 chasten, depress, devalue, exhaust, flatten, let down, mortify, put down, squeeze
08 collapse, contract, diminish, dispirit, puncture
09 humiliate
10 depreciate, disappoint

**deflect**
04 bend, turn, veer, wind
05 avert, drift, twist
07 deviate, diverge
08 ricochet
09 glance off, turn aside
12 change course

**deflection**
04 bend, veer
06 swerve
08 ricochet, twisting
09 deviation
10 divergence, refraction
11 glancing-off
12 sidetracking, turning aside

14 changing course

**deflower**
03 mar
04 harm, rape, ruin
05 force, spoil
06 defile, ravish, seduce
07 assault, despoil, violate
09 desecrate

**deform**
03 mar
04 maim, ruin, warp
05 spoil, twist
06 buckle, damage, deface
07 contort, distort, pervert
08 misshape, mutilate
09 disfigure

**deformation**
04 bend, warp
05 curve, twist
06 buckle
08 twisting
10 contortion, defacement, distortion, mutilation
12 diastrophism, malformation
13 misshapenness

**deformed**
04 bent
06 maimed, marred, warped
07 buckled, crooked, defaced, gnarled, mangled, twisted
08 crippled
09 contorted, distorted, malformed, misshapen, mutilated, perverted
10 disfigured

**deformity**
06 defect
08 ugliness, vileness
09 grossness
10 defacement, distortion
11 abnormality, crookedness
12 imperfection, malformation
13 disfigurement, misshapenness

**defraud**
02 do
03 con, gyp, rob
04 bilk, dupe, fool, hoax, rook
05 cheat, cozen, stick, sting, trick
06 delude, diddle, fiddle, fleece, outwit, rip off
07 deceive, mislead, swindle
08 embezzle, hoodwink
09 victimize

**defray**
03 pay
05 repay
06 refund, settle

**deft**
04 able, neat
05 adept, agile, handy, nifty
06 adroit, expert, nimble
08 skillful
09 dexterous

**defunct**
04 dead, gone
05 passé
06 bygone
07 expired, extinct, invalid
08 obsolete, outmoded
11 inoperative

**defy**
04 dare, face, foil
05 avoid, beard, brave, elude, flout, repel, scorn, spurn
06 baffle, defeat, slight, thwart
07 despise, disobey, provoke
08 confront
09 challenge, disregard, stand up to, withstand
12 rebel against

**degeneracy**
08 vileness
09 decadence
10 corruption, debasement, debauchery, immorality, sinfulness, wickedness
11 degradation, depravation
13 deterioration, dissoluteness

**degenerate**
03 low, rot
04 base, mean, sink, slip, vile
05 decay, lapse
06 effete, fallen, wicked, worsen
07 corrupt, debased, decline, fall off, go to pot, ignoble, immoral, regress
08 decadent, decrease, degraded, depraved
09 debauched, dissolute
10 go downhill, profligate
11 degenerated, deteriorate
13 go down the tube
14 go down the tubes

**degeneration**
04 drop, slip
05 decay, lapse, slide
07 atrophy, decline, sinking
08 decrease
09 worsening
10 debasement, regression
13 deterioration

**degradation**
05 shame
07 decline
08 demotion, disgrace, dishonor, ignominy, vileness
09 abasement

10 corruption, debasement, debauchery, degeneracy, fallenness, immorality, sinfulness, wickedness
11 downgrading, humiliation
12 degeneration
13 deterioration, dissoluteness

**degrade**
04 bump, bust
05 abase, lower, shame, sully
06 debase, defile, demean, demote, depose, humble, impair, unseat, weaken
07 cashier, cheapen, corrupt, deprive, devalue
08 belittle, disgrace, dishonor, relegate
09 discredit, downgrade, humiliate
10 adulterate
11 deteriorate, lower in rank
12 reduce in rank

**degrading**
04 base
07 ignoble
08 debasing, shameful
09 demeaning
10 belittling, cheapening
11 disgraceful, humiliating
12 dishonorable

**degree**
04 mark, rank, rung, step, unit
05 class, grade, level, limit, order, point, range, stage
06 amount, extent, status
07 measure
08 position, standing, strength
09 intensity
14 academic degree

**dehydrate**
03 dry
05 drain, dry up, parch
06 dry out
09 desiccate, lose water

**deification**
07 worship
09 elevation, extolling
10 apotheosis, exaltation
11 ennoblement, idolization
12 divinization, idealization
13 glorification
14 divinification
15 immortalization

**deify**
05 exalt, extol
07 elevate, ennoble, glorify, idolize, worship
08 idealize, venerate
11 immortalize

### deign
05 stoop
10 condescend
13 lower yourself
14 demean yourself

### deity
03 god
04 idol
05 power
06 spirit
07 eternal, goddess, godhead
08 divinity, immortal
11 divine being
12 supreme being

### dejected
03 low, sad
04 blue, down, glum
06 dismal, gloomy, morose
07 crushed, doleful
08 cast down, downcast, wretched
09 depressed, miserable
10 despondent, dispirited, melancholy, spiritless
11 crestfallen, demoralized, discouraged, downhearted
12 disconsolate, disheartened
14 down in the dumps

### dejection
05 blues, gloom
06 misery, sorrow
07 despair, sadness
08 the dumps
10 depression, gloominess, low spirits, melancholy
11 despondency, dolefulness
12 wretchedness
14 disconsolation, dispiritedness
15 downheartedness

### de jure
05 legal
07 legally
08 rightful
10 rightfully

### delay
03 lag
04 halt, keep, stay, wait
05 check, defer, stall, table, tarry
06 detain, dither, hinder, hold up, holdup, impede, linger, loiter, put off, shelve
07 adjourn, set back, suspend
08 dawdling, hold back, hold over, obstruct, postpone, put on ice, reprieve, restrain, stalling, stoppage
09 deferment, hindrance, lag behind, lingering, stonewall

10 cunctation, dilly-dally, filibuster, moratorium, putting-off, suspension
11 adjournment, holding-over
12 interruption, postponement
15 procrastination

### delectable
05 tasty, yummy
06 dainty, savory
08 adorable, charming, engaging, exciting, luscious
09 agreeable, delicious, palatable, succulent
10 appetizing, delightful, flavorsome
11 scrumptious
13 mouthwatering

### delectation
06 relish
07 comfort, delight
08 pleasure
09 amusement, diversion, enjoyment, happiness
12 satisfaction
13 entertainment, gratification

### delegate
04 give, name
05 agent, envoy, leave, proxy
06 assign, charge, commit, depute, deputy, pass on
07 appoint, consign, devolve, empower, entrust
08 emissary, nominate
09 authorize, designate, messenger, spokesman
10 ambassador, commission
11 spokeswoman
12 commissioner, spokesperson
14 representative

### delegation
06 naming
07 embassy, mission
08 legation
09 committal, passing on
10 commission, contingent, deputation, devolution
11 consignment, empowerment
15 representatives

### delete
03 cut
04 edit
05 erase
06 cancel, cut out, efface, excise, remove, rub out, strike
07 blot out, expunge, take out
08 cross out
09 strike out
10 blue-pencil, obliterate

### deleterious
03 bad
07 harmful, hurtful, noxious
08 damaging
09 injurious
10 pernicious
11 destructive, detrimental

### deliberate
04 muse, slow
05 think, weigh
06 debate, ponder, steady
07 careful, planned, prudent, reflect, studied, weigh up
08 cautious, consider, designed, measured, meditate, mull over, resolute, ruminate
09 conscious, think over
10 calculated, considered, methodical, preplanned
11 circumspect, intentional
12 premeditated

### deliberately
06 slowly
08 by design, steadily
09 carefully, knowingly, on purpose, pointedly, willfully
11 consciously, in cold blood
12 methodically, thoughtfully
13 intentionally

### deliberation
04 care
05 study
06 debate, musing
07 caution, mulling, thought
09 pondering
10 cogitation, discussion, meditation, reflection, rumination, weighing-up
11 calculation, forethought
13 consideration
14 circumspection, thoughtfulness

### delicacy
04 care, tact
05 taste, treat
06 dainty, luxury, relish, savory, tidbit, titbit
07 finesse
08 elegance, subtlety
09 diplomacy, fragility, specialty, sweetmeat
10 daintiness, discretion
11 sensitivity

### delicate
04 fine, mild, pale, soft, weak
05 bland, faint, frail, muted
06 ailing, dainty, flimsy, infirm, pastel, sickly, slight, subtle, touchy, tricky, unwell
07 awkward, brittle, fragile
08 critical, discreet, graceful

**delicious**
09 breakable, difficult, exquisite, sensitive
11 debilitated, problematic
12 easily broken, in poor health
13 controversial, easily damaged, insubstantial

**delicious**
04 good
05 juicy, tasty, yummy
06 choice, morish
09 ambrosial, palatable, succulent, toothsome
10 appetizing, delectable, enchanting, nectareous
11 captivating, scrumptious
13 mouthwatering

**delight**
03 joy
04 glee, like, love
05 amuse, bliss, charm, cheer, savor
06 excite, please, ravish, relish, thrill, tickle
07 ecstasy, elation, enchant, gladden, gratify, rapture
08 euphoria, gladness, pleasure, wallow in
09 amusement, captivate, enjoyment, enrapture, entertain, happiness
10 appreciate, tickle pink
13 entertainment, gratification
14 take pleasure in

**delighted**
04 glad
05 happy
06 elated, joyful, joyous
07 charmed, excited, gleeful
08 ecstatic, jubilant, thrilled
09 enchanted, entranced, gratified, overjoyed
10 captivated, enraptured
11 tickled pink
14 pleased as Punch

**delightful**
05 yummy
06 dreamy
07 amusing
08 charming, engaging, exciting, pleasant, pleasing
09 diverting, enjoyable, thrilling
10 delectable, enchanting
11 captivating, fascinating
12 entertaining

**delimit**
03 fix
04 mark
05 bound
06 define
09 demarcate, determine, establish

**delineate**
03 fix
04 draw, mark
05 bound, chart, trace
06 define, depict, design
07 outline, portray
08 describe, set forth
09 determine, establish, represent

**delinquency**
05 crime
07 misdeed, offense
10 misconduct, wrongdoing
11 criminality, lawbreaking, misbehavior

**delinquent**
06 guilty, remiss, vandal
07 culprit, lawless, overdue, ruffian
08 criminal, hooligan, offender
09 miscreant, negligent, offending
10 lawbreaker, neglectful
11 lawbreaking
13 young offender

**delirious**
03 mad
04 wild
05 crazy
06 elated, insane, raving
07 frantic
08 babbling, demented, deranged, ecstatic, euphoric, frenzied, jubilant, unhinged
09 overjoyed
10 incoherent, irrational
11 carried away, lightheaded
13 out of your mind
14 beside yourself

**delirium**
03 joy
05 fever
06 frenzy, lunacy, raving
07 ecstasy, elation, jimjams, jitters, madness, passion
08 euphoria, hysteria, wildness
10 excitement, jubilation
11 derangement, incoherence

**deliver**
02 do
04 give, make, save, send, take
05 bring, carry, grant, speak
06 commit, convey, direct, launch, ransom, redeem, rescue, strike, supply
07 entrust, give out, inflict, provide, release, set free
08 announce, carry out, dispatch, hand over, liberate
09 give birth, implement, pronounce

10 distribute, emancipate

**deliverance**
06 escape, ransom, rescue
07 freedom, release
09 salvation
10 liberation, redemption
11 extrication
12 articulation, emancipation

**delivery**
05 birth, labor
06 speech, supply
08 carriage, dispatch, shipment, transfer
09 elocution, transport
10 childbirth, conveyance
11 confinement, consignment, enunciation, parturition
12 articulation, distribution, transmission
14 transportation

**dell**
04 dean, vale
06 dingle, hollow, valley

**delude**
04 dupe, fool, hoax
05 cheat, trick
06 lead on, take in
07 beguile, deceive, mislead
08 hoodwink, misguide
09 bamboozle, misinform
12 take for a ride

**deluge**
04 rush, soak, wave
05 drown, flood, spate, swamp
06 drench, engulf
07 torrent
08 downpour, inundate
10 inundation

**delusion**
05 fancy
07 fallacy
08 illusion, tricking
09 deception, misbelief
11 false belief
13 hallucination, misconception
14 misinformation
15 false impression, misapprehension

**deluxe, de luxe**
04 fine, rich
05 grand, plush
06 choice, costly, lavish, luxury, select
07 elegant, opulent, quality, special
08 palatial, splendid, superior
09 exclusive, expensive, luxurious, sumptuous

**delve**
04 poke, root

05 probe
06 burrow, go into, hunt in, search
07 dig into, examine, explore, ransack, rummage
08 look into, research
11 hunt through, investigate

## demagogue, demagog
06 orator
08 agitator
09 firebrand, haranguer
10 tub-thumper
12 rabble-rouser

## demand
03 ask
04 call, need, take, tell, want
05 claim, exact, order
06 clamor
07 call for, dictate, inquire, inquiry, require
08 exigency, insist on, petition, press for, pressure, question
09 cry out for, stipulate
10 hold out for, insistence
11 interrogate, necessitate
13 interrogation

## ❏ in demand
03 big
06 trendy
07 popular
08 asked for
09 requested
11 fashionable, sought after

## demanding
04 hard
05 tough
06 taxing, trying, urgent
07 exigent, nagging, testing, wearing
09 difficult, harassing, insistent
11 challenging

## demarcate
04 mark
05 bound
06 define
07 delimit, mark out
09 determine, establish

## demarcation
04 line
05 bound, limit
08 boundary, division
09 enclosure
10 marking off, marking out
12 delimitation
13 determination, establishment

## demean
05 abase, lower, stoop
06 debase, demote, humble
07 degrade, descend

08 belittle
09 deprecate, humiliate

## demeanor
03 air
04 mien
06 manner
07 bearing, conduct
08 behavior
10 deportment
11 comportment

## demented
03 mad
04 loco, luny, nuts, wild
05 loony, loopy, nutty
06 crazed, insane
07 berserk, bonkers, lunatic
08 deranged, unhinged
10 unbalanced
13 around the bend, out of your mind

## demise
03 end
05 death
07 decease, failure, passing
08 collapse, downfall
10 expiration

## democracy
08 autonomy, republic
12 commonwealth
14 self-government

## democratic
07 popular
08 populist
10 autonomous, republican
11 egalitarian
13 self-governing

## demolish
04 beat, raze, rout, ruin, undo
05 crush, level, repel, wreck
06 hammer, subdue, thrash
07 break up, destroy, flatten
08 bulldoze, overturn, pull down, tear down
09 devastate, dismantle, knock down, pulverize, slaughter, subjugate
10 annihilate

## demolition
04 rout
06 razing
07 beating, licking
08 leveling
09 hammering, slaughter, thrashing
10 breaking-up, flattening
11 destruction, dismantling, pulling-down, tearing-down
12 knocking-down

## demon
03 ace, imp

05 afrit, beast, brute, devil, fiend, freak, ghoul, rogue
06 addict, afreet, daemon, wizard
07 fanatic, incubus, monster, vampire, villain
08 succubus
09 cacodemon
10 cacodaemon, evil spirit

## demonic
03 mad
05 manic
06 crazed
07 furious, hellish, satanic
08 devilish, fiendish, frenetic, frenzied, infernal, maniacal
10 diabolical

## demonstrable
05 clear
07 certain, evident, obvious
08 arguable, positive, provable
09 evincible
10 attestable, verifiable
11 self-evident

## demonstrate
04 show
05 march, prove, rally, sit in
06 betray, evince, parade, picket, verify
07 bespeak, betoken, display, exhibit, express, protest
08 indicate, manifest, validate
09 make clear, testify to
10 illustrate
12 substantiate
13 bear witness to

## demonstration
04 demo, test
05 march, proof, rally, sit-in, trial
06 parade, picket
07 display, protest
08 evidence
09 mass rally, testimony
10 evincement, exhibition, indication, validation
11 affirmation, explanation
12 confirmation, illustration, presentation, verification
13 manifestation
14 substantiation

## demonstrative
04 open, warm
06 loving
07 gushing
08 effusive
09 emotional, extrovert
10 expressive, unreserved
12 affectionate

## demoralize
05 crush, daunt, lower
06 debase, deject, weaken

**demote**

07 corrupt, deprave, depress, pervert
08 cast down, dispirit
09 undermine
10 discourage, dishearten

**demote**

04 bump, bust
06 humble
07 cashier, degrade
08 relegate
09 downgrade

**demotic**

06 vulgar
07 popular
08 enchoric
09 enchorial
10 colloquial, vernacular

**demur**

03 shy
04 balk
05 cavil, doubt, qualm
06 object, refuse
07 dissent, protest, scruple
08 demurral, disagree, hesitate
09 misgiving, objection
10 hesitation
11 compunction, reservation
12 disagreement
13 express doubts

**demure**

03 coy, shy
04 prim
05 grave, quiet, staid, timid
06 modest, prissy
07 prudish, serious
08 reserved, reticent, retiring
11 strait-laced
13 straight-laced

**den**

04 dive, hole, lair
05 haunt, joint, study
06 hollow
07 hangout, hideout, retreat, shelter
08 hideaway
09 sanctuary

**denial**

04 veto
06 rebuff
07 dissent, refusal
08 negation
09 disavowal, dismissal, disowning, rejection
10 abjuration, disclaimer
11 prohibition, repudiation
12 disagreement, renunciation
13 contradiction

**denigrate**

05 abuse, decry

**denizen**

06 assail, defame, impugn, malign, revile, vilify
07 run down, slander
08 belittle, besmirch, vilipend
09 criticize, deprecate, disparage
10 calumniate

**denizen**

07 citizen, dweller, habitué
08 habitant, occupant, resident
10 inhabitant

**denomination**

04 cult, kind, sect, sort, unit
05 class, creed, faith, grade, order, value, worth
09 communion, face value
10 persuasion

**denote**

04 mark, mean, show
05 imply
06 typify
07 betoken, express, refer to, signify, suggest
08 indicate, stand for
09 represent, symbolize

**dénouement**

05 close
06 climax, finale, finish, upshot
07 last act, outcome
08 solution
10 conclusion, resolution
13 clarification

**denounce**

05 decry
06 accuse, attack, betray, impugn, indict, revile, vilify
07 arraign, censure, condemn
09 castigate, criticize, fulminate, inculpate
13 inform against

**dense**

03 dim
04 dull, slow
05 close, heavy, solid, thick
06 opaque, packed, stupid
07 compact, crammed
09 close-knit, condensed, dimwitted
10 compressed, slow-witted
12 concentrated, impenetrable
13 tightly packed

**density**

04 body, bulk, mass
09 closeness, denseness, solidness, thickness, tightness
11 compactness, consistency

**dent**

03 dip, pit
04 dint

**denude**

06 crater, dimple, hollow, indent, push in
07 depress
09 concavity
10 depression
11 indentation

**denude**

04 bare
05 strip
06 divest, expose
07 uncover
08 deforest
09 defoliate

**denunciation**

06 attack
07 censure, decrial, obloquy
09 criticism, invective
10 accusation
11 castigation, fulmination
12 condemnation, denouncement

**deny**

04 veto
05 rebut
06 abjure, disown, forbid, negate, oppose, rebuff, recant, refuse, refute, reject
07 decline, disavow, dismiss, gainsay, nullify
08 disclaim, disprove, prohibit, renounce, turn down, withhold
09 disaffirm, repudiate

**deodorant**

10 deodorizer
12 air-freshener
14 antiperspirant

**deodorize**

06 aerate, purify
07 freshen, refresh, sweeten
09 ventilate

**depart**

02 go
03 die
04 exit, quit, scat, vary, veer
05 leave, scoot, scram, split
06 decamp, differ, escape, remove, retire, set off, set out, swerve, vamose, vanish
07 deviate, digress, diverge, make off, migrate, pull out, push off, retreat, skiddoo, skip out, take off, vamoose
08 clear off, get going, pass away, shove off, start out, up sticks
09 branch off, disappear, skedaddle
10 hit the road, make tracks
13 take your leave

15 make a break for it, take to your heels

**departed**
04 dead, gone, late
07 expired
08 deceased
10 passed away

**department**
04 area, line, unit, wing
05 field, realm
06 agency, branch, bureau, domain, office, region
07 concern, section, station
08 district, division, province
11 subdivision

**departure**
04 exit
05 going, shift
06 change, escape, exodus
07 leaving, removal, retreat
09 branching, deviation, going away, variation
10 difference, digression, divergence, innovation, retirement, setting-off, setting-out, withdrawal
11 leave-taking
14 leave of absence

**depend**
04 need
06 bank on, hang on, lean on, rely on, rest on, turn on
07 count on, hinge on, trust in
09 be based on, build upon
11 be decided by, be subject to
13 be dependent on, revolve around
14 be contingent on, be determined by

**dependable**
04 sure
06 honest, stable, steady, trusty
07 certain
08 faithful, reliable
09 steadfast, unfailing
11 responsible, trustworthy
13 conscientious
14 tried and tested

**dependence**
04 need
05 abuse, faith, trust
08 reliance
09 addiction
12 helplessness, subservience
13 subordination

**dependency**
05 abuse, habit

06 colony
07 support
08 province, reliance, weakness
09 addiction
10 attachment, immaturity
12 helplessness, protectorate
13 subordination

**dependent**
04 ward, weak
05 based, child, minor
06 charge, client, minion
07 decided, protégé, reliant, subject
08 hanger-on, helpless, immature, parasite, relative
09 supported, sustained
10 contingent, controlled, determined, influenced
11 conditional, subordinate

**depict**
04 draw, show
05 paint, trace
06 detail, record, render, sketch
07 outline, picture, portray
08 describe
09 delineate, represent
10 illustrate

**depiction**
05 image
07 drawing, outline, picture
08 likeness
09 portrayal, rendering
10 caricature
11 delineation, description
12 illustration
14 representation

**deplete**
05 drain, empty, spend, use up
06 lessen, reduce, weaken
07 eat into, exhaust, run down
08 decrease, diminish
09 attenuate
10 impoverish
11 whittle away

**depletion**
08 decrease, lowering
09 dwindling, lessening, reduction, shrinkage, weakening
10 diminution, exhaustion
11 attenuation, consumption

**deplorable**
04 dire
08 grievous, shameful, wretched
09 appalling, miserable

10 abominable, despicable, disastrous, lamentable, outrageous, scandalous
11 blameworthy, disgraceful, distressing, regrettable
12 dishonorable, disreputable
13 reprehensible

**deplore**
03 cry, rue
05 blame, mourn
06 bemoan, berate, bewail, lament, regret, revile
07 censure, condemn, reprove
08 denounce, reproach
09 castigate, criticize, deprecate, grieve for
12 disapprove of

**deploy**
03 use
07 arrange, station, utilize
08 position
09 spread out
10 distribute

**depopulate**
05 empty

**deport**
03 act
04 bear, hold, oust
05 carry, exile, expel
06 acquit, banish, behave
07 comport, conduct
09 extradite, transport
10 repatriate

**deportation**
05 exile
07 ousting
09 expulsion, ostracism
10 banishment
11 extradition
12 repatriation
14 transportation

**deportment**
03 air
04 mien, pose
06 aspect, manner, stance
07 bearing, conduct, posture
08 behavior, carriage, demeanor
09 etiquette
10 appearance
11 comportment

**depose**
04 fire, oust, sack
06 remove, topple, unseat
08 dethrone, displace
09 discharge, overthrow

**deposit**
03 lay, put, set, sit
04 bank, drop, dump, file, gage, lees, park, save, silt, stow

## deposition

05 dregs, hoard, lodge, place, plant, put by, stake, store
06 locate, pledge, settle
07 consign, entrust, put away, put down, set down
08 retainer, security, sediment
11 down payment

## deposition

07 ousting, removal
08 evidence, toppling
09 affidavit, statement, testimony, unseating
11 declaration, information
12 dethronement, displacement

## depository

05 depot, store
06 armory
07 arsenal
09 warehouse
10 repository, storehouse
15 bonded warehouse

## depot

05 cache, store
06 armory, garage
07 arsenal, station
08 terminal, terminus
09 warehouse
10 depository, repository, storehouse

## deprave

06 debase, defile, infect
07 corrupt, debauch, degrade, pervert, pollute, subvert
10 demoralize, lead astray
11 contaminate

## depraved

04 base, evil, vile
06 sinful, wicked
07 corrupt, debased, immoral
09 debauched, dissolute, perverted, reprobate, shameless
10 degenerate, licentious

## depravity

04 evil, vice
08 baseness, iniquity, vileness
09 reprobacy, turpitude
10 corruption, debasement, debauchery, degeneracy, immorality, perversion
13 dissoluteness

## deprecate

04 slam
05 blame, knock
06 berate, reject, revile
07 censure, condemn, deplore
08 denounce, reproach
09 castigate, criticize, disparage, reprehend

12 disapprove of

## deprecatory

09 regretful
10 apologetic, censorious, dismissive, protesting
11 reproachful
12 condemnatory, disapproving

## depreciate

06 defame, lessen, malign, reduce, revile, slight
07 decline, deflate, devalue, run down
08 belittle, mark down
09 denigrate, disparage, downgrade
11 make light of
13 go down in value

## depreciation

04 fall
05 slump
08 markdown
09 deflation
10 cheapening, depression
11 denigration, devaluation
12 belittlement
13 disparagement
15 underestimation

## depredation

05 theft
07 looting, pillage, plunder, raiding, robbery
08 harrying, ravaging
09 marauding
10 denudation, despoiling
11 destruction, devastation, laying waste

## depress

05 daunt, lower, press, weary
06 deject, lessen, reduce
07 devalue, get down, oppress
08 cast down, enervate
09 bring down, weigh down
10 discourage, dishearten

## depressant

06 downer
07 calmant
08 relaxant, sedative
09 calmative
13 tranquillizer

## depressed

03 low, sad
04 blue, down, glum, poor
05 fed up, moody, needy
06 dented, gloomy, hollow, morose, sunken
07 concave, unhappy
08 cast down, dejected, deprived, downcast, indented, pushed in

10 despondent, dispirited, distressed, melancholy
11 crestfallen, discouraged, downhearted, low-spirited
12 disheartened, low in spirits
13 disadvantaged
14 down in the dumps

## depressing

03 sad
04 gray
05 black, bleak, grave
06 dismal, dreary, gloomy
08 daunting, hopeless
09 cheerless, dejecting
10 melancholy
11 dispiriting, distressing
12 discouraging
13 disheartening

## depression

03 dip, pit
04 bowl, dent, dint, hole, sink
05 blues, dumps, gloom, slump
06 cavity, dimple, hollow, valley
07 decline, despair, sadness
08 doldrums, glumness
09 concavity, dejection, hard times, pessimism, recession
10 desolation, excavation, gloominess, impression, low spirits, melancholy
11 despondency, indentation, melancholia, unhappiness
12 hopelessness
14 discouragement
15 downheartedness

## deprivation

04 lack, need, want
06 denial, penury
07 poverty, removal
08 hardship
09 privation
10 withdrawal
11 destitution, withholding
12 disadvantage
13 dispossession

## deprive

03 rob
04 deny
05 strip
06 denude, divest, refuse
08 take away, withhold
10 confiscate, dispossess
11 expropriate

## deprived

04 poor
05 needy
06 bereft, in need
07 lacking
12 impoverished
13 disadvantaged
15 underprivileged

## depth
04 deep, drop, glow, gulf
05 abyss, floor, midst, scope
06 acumen, amount, bottom, extent, warmth, wisdom
07 measure, passion
08 darkness, deepness, richness, severity, strength
09 intensity, intuition
10 profundity, shrewdness
11 discernment, earnestness, penetration, seriousness
12 profoundness, remotest area, thoroughness
13 extensiveness

## ❑in depth
08 in detail
10 thoroughly
11 extensively
12 exhaustively
15 comprehensively

## deputation
07 embassy, mission
08 legation
09 committee
10 commission, delegation
15 representatives

## depute
06 charge
07 appoint, consign, empower, entrust, mandate
08 accredit, delegate, hand over
09 authorize, designate
10 commission

## deputize
05 cover
06 act for, double, sub for
07 relieve, replace
10 stand in for, substitute, understudy
14 take the place of

## deputy
04 vice-
05 agent, envoy, locum, proxy
06 depute, legate
07 stand-in
08 delegate
09 assistant, coadjutor, suffragan, surrogate
10 ambassador, substitute
11 subordinate
12 commissioner, vice-chairman
13 vice-president
14 representative, vice-chancellor
15 second-in-command

## deranged
03 mad
04 loco, luny, nuts
05 crazy, loony, loopy, nutty

06 insane, psycho
07 berserk, bonkers, lunatic
08 demented, unhinged
09 delirious, disturbed, non compos
10 distraught, irrational, out to lunch, unbalanced
13 of unsound mind, off your rocker, out of your mind
15 non compos mentis

## derangement
05 mania
06 frenzy, lunacy
07 madness
08 delirium, dementia, disorder, insanity
11 distraction, disturbance

## derelict
03 bum
04 hobo
05 tramp
06 beggar, dosser, wretch
07 drifter, outcast, run-down, vagrant
08 deserted, desolate, forsaken
09 abandoned, neglected
10 down-and-out, ramshackle, tumbledown
11 dilapidated, in disrepair
15 falling to pieces

## dereliction
04 ruin
05 ruins
07 evasion, failure, neglect
08 apostasy, betrayal
09 desertion, disrepair
10 abdication, renegation
11 abandonment
12 dilapidation, renunciation

## deride
03 rag
04 gibe, jeer, mock, razz
05 knock, scoff, scorn, sneer, taunt, tease
06 insult
08 belittle, pooh-pooh, ridicule, satirize
09 disparage, make fun of

## de rigueur
04 done
05 right
06 decent, proper
07 correct, fitting
08 decorous, required
09 necessary
12 conventional, the done thing

## derision
05 scorn
06 insult, satire
07 mockery, ragging, teasing

08 contempt, ridicule, scoffing, sneering, taunting
10 disrespect
13 disparagement

## derisive
07 jeering, mocking
08 scoffing, scornful, taunting
09 insulting
10 disdainful, irreverent
12 contemptuous
13 disrespectful

## derisory
04 tiny
06 absurd, paltry
07 risible
09 insulting, laughable, ludicrous
10 outrageous, ridiculous
12 contemptible, preposterous

## derivation
04 root
05 basis
06 origin, source
07 descent, lineage
08 ancestry
09 beginning, etymology, genealogy, inference
10 extraction, foundation

## derivative
06 branch, copied
07 cribbed, derived, spinoff
08 offshoot, rehashed
09 byproduct, imitative
10 derivation, descendant, secondhand, unoriginal

## derive
03 get
04 draw, flow, gain, stem
05 arise, issue
06 borrow, evolve, follow
07 descend, develop, emanate, proceed, procure, receive
09 originate
14 have its roots in
15 have as the source

## derogatory
08 critical
09 injurious, insulting, offensive, slighting, vilifying
10 defamatory, pejorative
11 denigratory, disparaging, unfavorable
12 depreciative, disapproving
15 uncomplimentary

## descend
03 dip
04 drop, fall, sink, stem
05 deign, slope, stoop, swoop
06 alight, arrive, go down, invade, plunge, tumble

## descendants

07 decline, emanate, incline, plummet, proceed, subside
08 dismount, move down
09 originate
10 degenerate, go downhill
11 deteriorate, go to the dogs
14 arrive suddenly

## descendants

04 line, seed
05 issue
06 scions
07 lineage, progeny
08 children
09 offspring, posterity
10 successors

## descent

03 dip
04 drop, fall, line
05 slant, slope, stock
06 origin, plunge
07 decline, incline, lineage
08 ancestry, heredity
09 decadence, declivity, genealogy, parentage, subsiding
10 debasement, degeneracy, extraction, family tree
11 degradation
13 deterioration

## describe

04 call, draw, hail, talk, tell
05 brand, label, style, think
06 depict, detail, relate, report
07 explain, mark out, narrate, portray, recount, specify
09 delineate, designate
12 characterize
13 give details of

## description

04 kind, make, sort, type
05 brand, breed, class, order
06 report, sketch
07 account, outline, profile
09 depiction, narration, portrayal
10 commentary, exposition
11 delineation, designation
14 representation

## descriptive

05 vivid
07 graphic
08 colorful, detailed, striking
09 pictorial
10 expressive

## descry

03 see
04 espy, mark, spot
06 detect, notice
07 discern, glimpse, observe
08 discover, perceive
09 recognize

11 distinguish
12 catch sight of

## desecrate

05 abuse
06 debase, defile, insult
07 pervert, pollute, profane, violate
09 blaspheme, vandalize

## desecration

06 insult
07 impiety
09 blasphemy, pollution, sacrilege, violation
10 debasement, defilement
11 profanation

## desert

03 dry, due, fly
04 arid, bare, flee, jilt, quit
05 empty, leave, merit, rat on, right, waste, wilds, worth
06 barren, betray, bolson, decamp, defect, give up, go AWOL, maroon, recant, reward
07 abandon, abscond, cast off, deserts, dried up, forsake, parched, payment, run away
08 desolate, renounce, run out on, solitary
09 infertile, walk out on
10 apostasize, recompense, relinquish, wilderness
11 change sides, comeuppance, retribution
12 moistureless, tergiversate, uncultivated
14 turn your back on, what you deserve
15 leave high and dry, leave in the lurch

► *Names of deserts:*
04 Gobi
05 Kavir, Namib, Ordos, Sturt
06 Indian, Mohave, Mojave, Nubian, Sahara
07 Arabian, Atacama, Kara Kum, Painted, Simpson, Sonoran
08 Kalahari, Kyzyl Kum
09 Dzungaria
10 Chihuahuan, Great Basin, Great Sandy, Patagonian, Syrian Thar
11 Death Valley
13 Great Victoria
14 Bolson de Mapimi

## deserted

04 left
05 empty
06 bereft, lonely, vacant
08 derelict, desolate, forsaken, isolated, solitary, stranded

09 abandoned, neglected
10 unoccupied
11 godforsaken, uninhabited

## deserter

03 rat
06 truant
07 escapee, runaway, traitor
08 apostate, betrayer, defector, fugitive, renegade, turncoat
09 absconder

## desertion

06 cop-out, denial, flight
07 jilting, leaving, truancy
08 apostasy, betrayal, giving-up, quitting
09 defection, forsaking
10 absconding, renegation
11 abandonment, dereliction
12 renunciation
14 tergiversation

## deserve

04 earn, rate
05 incur, merit
07 justify, warrant
10 be worthy of
12 be entitled to, have a right to

## deserved

03 apt, due
04 fair, just, meet
05 right
06 earned, proper
07 condign, fitting, merited
08 apposite, rightful, suitable
09 justified, warranted
10 legitimate, well-earned

## deserving

06 worthy
07 upright
08 laudable, virtuous
09 admirable
11 commendable, meritorious
12 praiseworthy

## desiccated

03 dry
05 dried
07 drained, parched, sterile
08 lifeless, powdered
10 dehydrated, exsiccated

## desiccation

07 aridity, dryness
08 parching
11 dehydration, exsiccation

## design

03 aim, end, map
04 draw, form, gear, goal, hope, logo, make, mean, plan, plot
05 draft, dream, guide, hatch, model, motif, shape, style
06 cipher, create, device, devise, draw up, emblem,

figure, format, intend, invent, makeup, object, scheme, sketch, tailor
07 develop, diagram, fashion, meaning, pattern, purpose
08 conceive, contrive, monogram
09 blueprint, construct, fabricate, intention, objective, originate, prototype, structure
11 arrangement, composition
12 construction, organization

**❏by design**
09 knowingly, on purpose, pointedly, willfully, wittingly
11 consciously
12 deliberately
13 calculatingly, intentionally

**designate**
03 dub
04 call, name, show, term
05 elect, style, title
06 assign, choose, select
07 appoint, earmark, specify
08 christen, describe, indicate, nominate, set aside
09 stipulate

**designation**
03 tag
04 name, term
05 label, style, title
07 epithet, marking, moniker
08 category, denoting, election, nickname
10 definition, nomination
11 appellation, appointment
14 classification

**designer**
05 maker
06 author
07 creator, planner, stylist
08 inventor, producer
09 architect, contriver

**designing**
03 sly
04 wily
06 artful, crafty, shrewd, tricky
07 cunning, devious
08 guileful, plotting, scheming
09 deceitful, underhand
10 conspiring, intriguing
11 calculating

**desirability**
05 merit, worth
06 allure, profit
07 benefit
08 sexiness
09 advantage
10 attraction, popularity, preference, usefulness

12 advisability
13 seductiveness
14 attractiveness

**desirable**
04 good, sexy
07 popular
08 alluring, fetching, in demand, sensible, tempting
09 advisable, agreeable, expedient, seductive
10 attractive, beneficial, preferable, profitable
11 appropriate, sought-after
12 advantageous

**desire**
03 yen
04 itch, lust, need, want, wish
05 ardor, covet, crave, fancy
06 hunger, libido, pining
07 craving, longing, passion, pine for
08 appetite, sex drive, yearning
09 hankering, sexuality
10 aspiration, preference, proclivity, sensuality
11 hanker after
12 have a crush on, predilection
13 concupiscence
14 lasciviousness, predisposition, set your heart on
15 give the world for

**desired**
05 exact, right
07 correct, fitting
08 accurate, expected, required
09 necessary
11 appropriate

**desirous**
04 avid, keen
05 eager, ready
06 hoping
07 anxious, burning, craving, hopeful, itching, longing, willing, wishing
08 aspiring, yearning
09 ambitious

**desist**
03 end
04 halt, stop
05 cease, pause, remit
06 give up
07 forbear, refrain, suspend
08 break off, leave off, peter out
11 discontinue

**desk**
04 ambo
06 bureau
07 lectern
09 davenport, secretary
10 escritoire, secretaire

11 reading desk, roll-top desk
12 writing table

**desolate**
03 sad
04 arid, bare
05 bleak, floor, upset, waste
06 barren, bereft, dismal, dreary, gloomy, lonely
07 forlorn, get down, nonplus, shatter, unhappy
08 dejected, deserted, downcast, forsaken, isolated, solitary, wretched
09 abandoned, depressed, devastate, miserable, overwhelm, take aback
10 depressing, despondent, distressed, unoccupied
11 godforsaken, heartbroken, uninhabited
13 broken-hearted

**desolation**
04 ruin
05 gloom, grief
06 misery, sorrow
07 anguish, despair, sadness
08 distress, solitude, wildness
09 bleakness, dejection, emptiness, isolation
10 depression, loneliness, melancholy, remoteness
11 despondency, devastation, laying waste, unhappiness
12 wretchedness

**despair**
05 gloom
06 give in, give up, misery
07 anguish
08 collapse, distress, lose hope
09 lose heart, surrender
10 depression, melancholy
11 desperation, despondency
12 hopelessness, wretchedness
13 hit rock bottom
15 throw in the towel

**despairing**
08 dejected, desolate, dismayed, downcast, hopeless, suicidal, wretched
09 anguished, depressed, desperate, miserable
10 despondent, distraught
11 heartbroken, pessimistic
12 disheartened, inconsolable

**despatch** see DISPATCH

**desperado**
04 thug
06 badman, bandit, gunman, outlaw
07 bandido, brigand, hoodlum, ruffian

**desperate**

08 criminal, gangster
09 cutthroat, terrorist
10 lawbreaker

**desperate**

04 bold, dire, rash, wild
05 acute, grave, great, risky
07 crucial, do-or-die, drastic, extreme, frantic, serious, violent
08 dejected, desolate, dismayed, frenzied, hopeless, reckless, suicidal, wretched
09 dangerous, miserable, sorrowful
10 compelling, despondent, determined, distraught
11 in great need
12 crying out for, inconsolable
15 needing very much, wanting very much

**desperately**

05 badly
07 acutely, gravely, greatly
08 severely, urgently
09 extremely, fearfully, seriously
10 critically, dreadfully, hopelessly
11 dangerously, frightfully

**desperation**

05 agony, gloom, worry
06 misery, sorrow
07 anguish, despair, trouble
11 despondency
12 hopelessness, wretchedness

**despicable**

04 mean, vile
07 caitiff
08 shameful, wretched
09 loathsome, reprobate
10 abominable, detestable
11 disgraceful
12 contemptible, disreputable
13 reprehensible

**despise**

04 hate, mock, shun
05 abhor, scorn, sneer, spurn
06 deride, detest, loathe, revile
07 condemn, deplore, disdain

**despite**

07 against, defying
09 in spite of
11 in the face of
12 regardless of, undeterred by
15 notwithstanding

**despoil**

03 rob
04 loot
05 rifle, strip, wreck
06 denude, maraud, ravage

07 deprive, destroy, pillage, plunder, ransack
08 spoliate
09 depredate, devastate, vandalize
10 dispossess

**despondency**

05 blues, gloom, grief
06 misery, sorrow
07 despair, sadness
08 distress, glumness
09 dejection, heartache
10 depression, melancholy
11 desperation, melancholia
12 hopelessness, wretchedness
14 discouragement, dispiritedness
15 downheartedness, inconsolability

**despondent**

03 low, sad
04 blue, down, glum
06 gloomy
07 doleful
08 dejected, downcast, mournful, wretched
09 depressed, miserable, sorrowful
10 despairing, distressed, melancholy
11 discouraged, heartbroken
12 disheartened, inconsolable
14 down in the dumps

**despot**

04 boss
06 tyrant
08 autocrat, dictator
09 oppressor
10 absolutist
13 absolute ruler

**despotic**

08 absolute, arrogant
09 arbitrary, imperious
10 autocratic, highhanded, oppressive, tyrannical
11 dictatorial, domineering
13 authoritarian

**despotism**

07 tyranny
09 autocracy
10 absolutism, oppression, repression
12 dictatorship
15 totalitarianism

**dessert**

05 sweet
06 sweets
10 last course

**destination**

03 aim, end

04 goal, stop
06 design, object, target
08 ambition, terminus
09 intention, objective
11 journey's end
12 end of the line
15 final port of call

**destined**

05 bound, fated, meant
06 doomed, headed, routed
07 certain, en route, heading
08 assigned, expected, intended, ordained, set apart
09 appointed, scheduled
10 inevitable
11 inescapable, unavoidable
13 predetermined

**destiny**

03 lot
04 doom, fate, luck
05 karma
06 future, kismet
07 fortune, portion
10 predestiny
14 predestination

**destitute**

04 poor
05 broke, needy
06 bereft, hard up
07 lacking, wanting
08 badly off, bankrupt, devoid of, dirt poor, indigent
09 flat broke, penniless, penurious
10 cleaned out, down and out, stone-broke
11 impecunious
12 impoverished
14 on the breadline
15 poverty-stricken

**destitution**

06 penury
07 beggary, poverty, straits
09 indigence, pauperism
10 bankruptcy, starvation
13 pennilessness
14 impoverishment, on the breadline
15 impecuniousness

**destroy**

03 gut, zap
04 kill, raze, ruin, slay, undo
05 break, crush, level, smash, spoil, waste, wreck
06 rub out
07 flatten, nullify, put down, shatter, unshape, vitiate
08 decimate, demolish, lay waste, sabotage, stamp out, tear down

09 devastate, eliminate, eradicate, extirpate, knock down, slaughter
10 annihilate, put to sleep

**destroyer**
06 locust, vandal
07 ravager, warship, wrecker
09 despoiler, ransacker
11 annihilator, kiss of death

**destruction**
03 end
04 ruin
05 havoc
06 defeat, murder, razing
07 killing, undoing, wastage
08 crushing, downfall, leveling, smashing, wreckage
09 ruination, slaughter, vandalism
10 demolition, desolation, extinction, ravagement
11 depredation, devastation, dismantling, elimination, eradication, liquidation
12 annihilation, knocking-down, obliteration
13 extermination, nullification

**destructive**
05 fatal
06 deadly, lethal
07 harmful, hostile, hurtful, noxious, ruinous, vicious
08 damaging, negative
09 injurious, malignant, murderous
10 disastrous, disruptive, nullifying, pernicious, subversive, unfriendly
11 deleterious, denigrating, detrimental, devastating, mischievous, undermining
12 catastrophic, slaughterous

**desultory**
05 loose
06 fitful, random
07 aimless, chaotic, erratic
09 haphazard, irregular
11 halfhearted
12 disconnected, inconsistent, unmethodical, unsystematic
13 uncoordinated

**detach**
04 free, undo
05 sever, split, unfix
06 cut off, divide, loosen, remove
07 disjoin, divorce, isolate, take off, tear off, unhitch
08 estrange, separate, uncouple, unfasten
09 disengage, segregate

10 disconnect, dissociate
11 disentangle

**detached**
04 cold, free
05 aloof, loose
06 remote, single
07 divided, neutral, severed
08 clinical, discrete, divorced, separate
09 impartial, objective
10 impersonal
11 dissociated, independent, indifferent, unconcerned, unemotional
12 disconnected
13 disinterested, dispassionate

**detachment**
04 unit
05 corps, force, squad
06 patrol
07 brigade, divorce, removal, undoing
08 coolness, disunion, fairness
09 aloofness, isolation, loosening, severance, task force, unconcern
10 neutrality, remoteness, separation, withdrawal
11 objectivity, unfastening
12 impartiality, indifference
13 disconnection, disengagement, disentangling

**detail**
04 fact, item, list
05 count, point
06 aspect, assign, charge, factor, nicety, set out
07 appoint, element, feature, itemize, recount, specify
08 allocate, delegate, describe, minutiae, point out, specific, spell out, tabulate
09 attribute, component, enumerate, intricacy
10 complexity, ins and outs, particular, refinement, small print, triviality
11 elaboration, nitty-gritty
12 complication, technicality
13 specification

◻**in detail**
05 fully
07 in depth
08 at length
09 carefully
10 item by item, thoroughly
12 exhaustively, point by point
15 comprehensively

**detailed**
04 full

05 exact
07 complex, in-depth, precise
08 itemized, specific, thorough
09 elaborate, intricate
10 blow-by-blow, convoluted, exhaustive, meticulous
13 comprehensive

**detain**
04 hold, keep, slow, stay, stop
05 check, delay
06 arrest, hinder, hold up, impede, intern, lock up
07 confine, inhibit
08 hold back, imprison, keep back, make late, restrain
11 incarcerate, put in prison
13 hold in custody

**detect**
04 find, note, spot
06 expose, notice, reveal, turn up, unmask
07 discern, make out, observe, uncover, unearth
08 disclose, discover, identify, perceive
09 ascertain, track down
12 bring to light

**detection**
06 exposé
08 exposure, noticing, sighting
09 discovery, unmasking
10 disclosure, perception, revelation, uncovering, unearthing
11 discernment, observation
12 ascertaining, tracking-down
14 distinguishing, identification

**detective**
04 dick, tail
06 shamus, sleuth
07 gumshoe
09 inspector
10 private eye
12 investigator
13 police officer

▶ *Names of famous detectives:*
04 **Chan** (Charlie), **Drew** (Nancy), **Moto** (Mr.)
05 **Brown** (Father), **Dupin** (C. Auguste), **Mason** (Perry), **Morse** (Inspector), **Queen** (Ellery), **Spade** (Sam)
06 **Carter** (Nick), **Hammer** (Mike), **Holmes** (Sherlock), **Marple** (Miss Jane), **Poirot** (Hercule), **Wimsey** (Peter)
07 **Cadfael** (Brother), **Charles** (Nick), **Charles** (Nora), **Columbo** (Lieutenant), **Maigret** (Inspector),

Marlowe (Philip)
08 **Bergerac** (Jim), **Clouseau**
(Inspector), **Lestrade**
(Inspector)
09 **Hardy Boys**

**detention**
05 delay
07 custody
09 captivity, hindrance,
restraint, slowing-up
10 constraint, detainment,
internment, punishment,
quarantine
11 confinement, holding-back
12 imprisonment
13 incarceration

**deter**
04 stop, warn
05 check, daunt
06 hinder, put off
07 inhibit, prevent, turn off
08 dissuade, frighten, restrain
09 talk out of
10 discourage, disincline

**detergent**
04 soap
07 cleaner
08 cleanser
10 abstergent, soap powder

**deteriorate**
03 rot
05 decay, go bad, lapse, slide
06 weaken, worsen
07 break up, decline, fall off, go
to pot, relapse
08 get worse, go to seed
09 decompose, fall apart
10 degenerate, depreciate, go
downhill, retrograde,
retrogress
12 disintegrate, fall to pieces

**deterioration**
05 decay, lapse, slide
06 waning
07 decline, failure, relapse
08 downturn, slipping
09 corrosion, worsening
10 debasement, pejoration
11 degradation
12 degeneration, exacerbation
13 retrogression

**determinate**
05 fixed
07 certain, decided, defined,
express, precise, settled
08 absolute, clear-cut, decisive,
definite, distinct, explicit
09 specified
10 conclusive, definitive,
quantified
11 established

**determination**
04 grit, guts, push, will
05 drive
07 purpose, resolve, stamina
08 backbone, decision,
firmness, tenacity
09 fortitude, willpower
10 conclusion, insistence, moral
fiber, resolution
11 persistence, self-control
12 perseverance, resoluteness
13 steadfastness

**determine**
05 fix on, guide, impel, learn
06 affect, choose, clinch,
decide, detect, direct,
govern, ordain, settle, verify
07 agree on, control, dictate,
find out, purpose, resolve
08 conclude, discover, identify
09 ascertain, influence
14 make up your mind

**determined**
03 out, set
04 bent, firm
05 fixed
06 dogged, intent, strong
07 dead set, decided
08 hellbent, resolute, resolved,
stubborn
09 convinced, insistent,
steadfast, tenacious
10 persistent, unwavering
11 persevering, unflinching
12 single-minded, strong-
minded, strong-willed
14 uncompromising

**deterrent**
03 bar
04 curb
05 block, check
07 barrier
08 obstacle
09 hindrance, repellent
12 disincentive
14 discouragement

**detest**
04 hate
05 abhor
06 loathe
07 deplore, despise, dislike
08 execrate
09 abominate, can't stand

**detestable**
04 vile
06 odious, sordid
07 hateful, heinous
08 accursed, shocking
09 abhorrent, execrable,
loathsome, obnoxious,

offensive, repellent,
repugnant, repulsive
10 abominable, despicable
12 contemptible

**detestation**
04 hate
05 odium
06 hatred
08 anathema, aversion, loathing
09 animosity, revulsion
10 abhorrence, execration,
repugnance
11 abomination

**dethrone**
04 oust
06 depose, topple, unseat
07 uncrown
08 unthrone

**detonate**
05 blast, go off
06 blow up, let off, set off
07 explode
08 spark off
09 discharge, fulminate

**detonation**
04 bang, boom
05 blast, burst
06 blowup, report
08 igniting, ignition
09 discharge, explosion
11 fulmination

**detour**
05 avoid, byway
06 bypass, bypath, byroad,
divert
09 deviation, diversion
10 digression
11 scenic route
13 indirect route

**detract**
03 mar
05 lower, spoil
06 lessen, reduce
08 belittle, diminish
09 devaluate, disparage
10 depreciate
12 take away from

**detractor**
07 defamer, reviler
08 traducer, vilifier
09 backbiter, belittler,
muckraker, slanderer
10 denigrator, disparager

**detriment**
03 ill
04 evil, harm, hurt, loss
05 wrong
06 damage, injury
08 mischief
09 prejudice

10 disservice, impairment
12 disadvantage

**detrimental**
07 adverse, harmful, hurtful
08 damaging, inimical
09 injurious
10 pernicious
11 destructive, prejudicial
15 disadvantageous

**detritus**
04 junk, scum
05 waste
06 debris, litter, rubble
07 garbage, remains, rubbish
08 wreckage
09 fragments

**devalue**
05 lower
06 reduce
07 deflate
08 decrease
09 devaluate

**devastate**
04 raze, ruin, sack
05 floor, level, waste, wreck
06 ravage
07 despoil, destroy, flatten,
   pillage, ransack, shatter
08 desolate, lay waste

**devastating**
07 harmful
08 incisive, stunning
09 effective
10 disastrous, shattering
11 destructive
12 catastrophic, overwhelming

**devastation**
04 ruin
05 havoc, ruins, waste
07 pillage, plunder, ravages
08 wreckage
10 desolation, spoliation
11 destruction
12 annihilation

**develop**
03 get
04 grow
05 arise, begin, catch, ensue
06 create, evolve, expand,
   happen, invent, mature, pick
   up, spread, unfold
07 acquire, advance, enhance,
   enlarge, improve, nurture,
   produce, prosper, work out
08 commence, contract,
   expand on, flourish,
   generate, progress
09 branch out, come about,
   elaborate, establish
10 go down with

**development**
06 center, change, estate,
   growth, result, spread
07 advance, complex, outcome
08 incident, increase, maturity,
   progress
09 evolution, expansion,
   extension, happening,
   promotion, unfolding
10 blossoming, refinement
11 elaboration, enlargement,
   flourishing, furtherance,
   improvement, progression
14 housing project

**deviant**
04 bent, geek, goof, kook
05 crank, freak, kinky
06 misfit, oddity, quirky, weirdo
07 bizarre, dropout, odd sort,
   oddball, pervert, twisted,
   variant, wayward
08 aberrant, abnormal, freakish,
   perverse
09 anomalous, disparity,
   divergent, eccentric,
   irregular, perverted

**deviate**
03 err, yaw
04 part, turn, vary, veer
05 drift, stray
06 change, depart, differ,
   swerve, wander
07 deflect, digress, diverge
08 go astray
09 turn aside

**deviation**
05 drift, freak, quirk, shift
06 change, detour
07 anomaly
08 variance
09 disparity, variation
10 aberration, deflection,
   digression, divergence
11 abnormality, fluctuation
12 eccentricity, irregularity
13 inconsistency

**device**
04 logo, plan, ploy, ruse, wile
05 gizmo, motif, trick
06 design, emblem, gadget,
   gambit, scheme, symbol
07 machine, utensil
08 artifice, insignia, strategy
09 apparatus, appliance,
   doohickey, implement,
   mechanism
10 coat of arms, instrument
11 contraption, contrivance

**devil**
03 imp
04 ogre

05 beast, brute, demon, fiend,
   rogue, Satan
06 rascal, savage, terror, wretch
07 Lucifer, Old Nick
08 diabolic, Mephisto, Old
   Harry
09 Beelzebub
10 evil spirit, Old Scratch, the
   Evil One
12 the archfiend
14 Mephistopheles

**devilish**
04 evil, vile
06 wicked
07 demonic, hellish, satanic
08 damnable, diabolic,
   dreadful, fiendish, infernal
09 execrable, nefarious
10 diabolical, outrageous

**devil-may-care**
04 rash
06 casual
08 careless, cavalier, flippant,
   heedless, reckless
09 easy-going, frivolous
10 insouciant, nonchalant
11 unconcerned
12 happy-go-lucky

**devious**
03 sly
04 wily
06 artful, crafty, tricky
07 crooked, cunning, erratic,
   evasive, winding
08 indirect, rambling,
   scheming, slippery, tortuous
09 deceitful, designing,
   deviating, insidious,
   insincere, wandering
10 circuitous, roundabout
11 calculating, treacherous
12 disingenuous, unscrupulous
13 double-dealing,
   surreptitious

**devise**
04 form, plan, plot
05 forge, frame, hatch, shape
06 cook up, create, design,
   invent, scheme
07 arrange, compose, concoct,
   dream up, imagine, project,
   think up, work out
08 conceive, contrive
09 construct, fabricate,
   formulate, originate
10 come up with
11 put together

**devoid**
04 bare, free, void
05 empty
06 barren, bereft, vacant

07 lacking, wanting, without

**devolution**
09 dispersal
12 distribution

**devolve**
06 convey, depute, fall to
07 consign, deliver, entrust
08 delegate, hand down, rest with, transfer

**devote**
04 give
05 allot, apply, offer, put in
06 assign, commit, pledge
08 dedicate, enshrine, set aside
09 sacrifice, surrender
10 consecrate

**devoted**
04 fond, true
05 loyal
06 caring, devout, loving
08 constant, faithful, tireless
09 attentive, committed, dedicated, steadfast
10 unswerving

**devotee**
03 fan
04 buff
05 fiend, freak, hound
06 addict, zealot
08 adherent, disciple, follower
09 supporter
10 aficionado, enthusiast

**devotion**
04 love, zeal
05 ardor, faith, piety
06 prayer, regard
07 loyalty, passion, worship
08 fidelity, trueness, warmness
09 adherence, adoration, affection, constancy
10 admiration, allegiance, attachment, commitment, dedication, devoutness
11 earnestness, staunchness
12 faithfulness, spirituality
13 steadfastness

**devotional**
04 holy
06 devout, sacred, solemn
09 pietistic, religious, spiritual
11 reverential

**devour**
03 eat
04 bolt, cram, gulp
05 eat up, gorge, stuff
06 gobble, guzzle, relish
07 consume, destroy, envelop, feast on, put away, swallow
08 tuck into, wolf down

09 finish off, knock back, polish off
10 appreciate, gormandize

**devout**
04 deep, holy
05 godly, pious
06 ardent
07 devoted, earnest, fervent, intense, saintly, serious, sincere, staunch, zealous
08 constant, faithful, orthodox, profound, reverent
09 committed, heartfelt, prayerful, religious, steadfast
10 passionate, practicing
12 wholehearted

**devoutly**
06 deeply
07 piously
08 ardently
09 earnestly, fervently, sincerely, staunchly, zealously
10 faithfully, reverently
11 prayerfully, steadfastly
12 passionately
14 wholeheartedly

**dewy**
04 damp
05 moist

❑**dewy-eyed**
08 innocent, youthful
10 starry-eyed

**dexterity**
03 art
05 knack, skill
07 ability, address, agility, finesse, mastery, sleight
08 aptitude, artistry, deftness
09 adeptness, expertise, handiness, ingenuity
10 adroitness, expertness, nimbleness
11 legerdemain, proficiency
12 skillfulness

**dexterous**
04 able, deft
05 adept, agile, handy, nifty
06 adroit, expert, nimble
08 skillful
10 neat-handed, proficient
12 accomplished
14 nimble-fingered

**diabolical**
04 evil, vile
05 nasty
06 sinful, wicked
07 demonic, hellish, satanic
08 damnable, devilish, fiendish, infernal
09 execrable, monstrous

**diadem**
05 crown, miter, round, tiara
07 circlet, coronet
08 headband

**diagnose**
06 detect
07 analyze, explain, isolate
08 identify, pinpoint
09 determine, recognize

**diagnosis**
06 answer
07 opinion, verdict
08 analysis, judgment, scrutiny
09 detection
10 conclusion
11 examination, recognition
13 investigation
14 identification, interpretation

**diagnostic**
10 analytical, indicative
14 distinguishing, interpretative

**diagonal**
05 cross
06 angled
07 crooked, oblique, sloping
08 crossing, slanting
09 crosswise

**diagonally**
06 aslant
09 at an angle, crossways, crosswise, obliquely, on the bias
10 on the cross, on the slant

**diagram**
04 plan
05 chart, draft, graph, table
06 figure, layout, schema
07 drawing, outline, picture
08 bar chart, bar graft, pie chart
09 flow chart
12 exploded view, illustration

**diagrammatic, dia-grammatical**
07 graphic, tabular
09 schematic

**dial**
04 call, disk, face, knob
05 phone
06 tune in
09 clock face, telephone

**dialect**
05 argot, idiom, lingo
06 jargon, patois, speech
07 diction, variety
08 language, localism
10 vernacular

**dialectic**
05 logic
06 debate

**dialogue**
07 logical
08 analysis, logistic, polemics
09 rationale, reasoning
10 analytical, dialectics
11 dialectical, disputation
13 argumentation, ratiocination, rationalistic

**dialogue, dialog**
04 chat, talk
06 debate, gossip, script
08 colloquy, converse
09 discourse, tête-à-tête
10 conference, discussion
11 interchange
12 conversation
13 interlocution

**diametrically**
07 utterly
08 directly
10 absolutely, completely

**diaphanous**
04 fine, thin
05 filmy, gauzy, light, sheer
08 delicate, gossamer, pellucid
10 see-through
11 translucent, transparent

**diaper**
04 didy
05 didie, towel
06 change, napkin
07 pattern

**diary**
03 log
07 daybook, journal, logbook
09 chronicle
10 Filofax
14 engagement book
15 appointment book

▶ *Names of diarists*:
03 **Nin** (Anais)
04 **Byrd** (William), **Gide** (André), **Hone** (Philip)
05 **Frank** (Anne), **James** (Alice), **Pepys** (Samuel), **Reyes** (Alfonso), **Scott** (Robert Falcon), **Torga** (Miguel)
06 **Burney** (Fanny), **Evelyn** (John)
08 **Chestnut** (Mary Boykin), **Greville** (Charles Cavendish Fulke), **Robinson** (Henry Crabb)
➤ See also WRITER

**diatribe**
05 abuse
06 attack, insult, rebuke, tirade
07 reproof
08 harangue, knocking

09 criticism, invective, onslaught, philippic
10 upbraiding
12 denunciation, vituperation

**dickey**
03 bib
04 seat
06 collar
08 back seat, pinafore
11 driver's seat

**dictate**
03 law, say
04 read, rule, word
05 edict, order, speak, utter
06 behest, charge, decree, demand, direct, govern, ruling
07 bidding, command, lay down, mandate, precept, read out, set down, statute
08 announce, instruct, transmit
09 direction, ordinance, prescribe, pronounce, read aloud, ultimatum
11 requirement

**dictator**
06 despot, tyrant
07 supremo
08 autocrat
09 oppressor
10 autarchist, Big Brother
13 absolute ruler

**dictatorial**
05 bossy
08 absolute, despotic
09 autarchic, imperious
10 autocratic, oppressive, repressive, tyrannical
11 all powerful, domineering
12 totalitarian, unrestricted
13 authoritarian

**dictatorship**
07 fascism, tyranny
09 autocracy, despotism
11 police state
12 absolute rule
13 reign of terror
15 totalitarianism

**diction**
06 speech
08 delivery, language, phrasing
09 elocution
10 expression, inflection, intonation
11 enunciation
12 articulation
13 pronunciation

**dictionary**
07 lexicon
08 glossary, wordbook

09 thesaurus
10 vocabulary
11 concordance
12 encyclopedia

**dictum**
04 fiat
05 axiom, edict, maxim, order
06 decree, ruling, saying
07 command, dictate, precept, proverb
08 aphorism
09 utterance
13 pronouncement

**didactic**
05 moral
08 pedantic
09 educative, pedagogic
10 moralizing
11 educational, instructive
12 prescriptive

**die**
03 ebb, end
04 fade, mold, pass, stop, wane, wilt
05 be mad, croak, decay, lapse, yearn
06 depart, desire, expire, finish, pass on, perish, pop off, vanish, wither
07 conk out, dwindle, kick off, long for, pine for, snuff it, subside
08 check out, decrease, dissolve, pass away, peter out
09 break down, go belly up, lose power
10 buy the farm
11 be desperate, bite the dust, come to an end
12 lose your life
13 kick the bucket, meet your maker, push up daisies
14 depart this life, give up the ghost
15 breathe your last, cash in your chips

❑**die away**
04 fade
09 disappear
10 become weak
11 become faint

❑**die down**
04 stop
07 decline, quieten, subside
08 decrease

❑**die out**
06 vanish
08 peter out
09 disappear
13 become extinct

**die-hard**
05 blimp
06 zealot
07 old fogy
08 rightist
09 hardliner
11 reactionary, right-winger
12 intransigent
13 stick-in-the-mud

**diet**
04 fare, fast, food, slim
06 reduce, viands
07 abstain, rations, regimen
08 victuals
09 nutrition
10 foodstuffs, lose weight,
   parliament, provisions,
   sustenance
11 comestibles, weight-watch

**differ**
04 vary
05 argue, clash
06 debate, oppose
07 deviate, diverge, quarrel
08 be unlike, contrast, disagree
12 be at odds with, be at
   variance, be dissimilar
14 not see eye to eye

**difference**
03 row
04 rest
05 clash, set-to
07 balance, dispute, quarrel
08 argument, conflict, contrast,
   variance
09 deviation, disparity, diversity,
   remainder, variation
10 divergence, unlikeness
11 altercation, controversy,
   discrepancy, disputation,
   distinction, singularity
12 disagreement, distinctness
13 dissimilarity, dissimilitude

**different**
03 odd
05 other
06 at odds, sundry, unique,
   unlike, varied
07 a far cry, another, diverse,
   opposed, several, special,
   strange, unusual, various
08 assorted, discrete, distinct,
   peculiar, separate
09 disparate, divergent
10 at variance, dissimilar,
   individual, poles apart
11 contrasting, distinctive,
   worlds apart
13 extraordinary, miscellaneous
14 unconventional

**differentiate**
07 mark off
08 contrast, separate
09 tell apart
11 distinguish
12 discriminate

**differentiation**
08 contrast
10 separation
11 demarcation, distinction
14 discrimination

**difficult**
04 dark, hard
05 tough
06 arcane, knotty, thorny, tiring,
   tricky, trying, uphill
07 arduous, awkward
08 abstruse, baffling, esoteric,
   exacting, grueling, perverse,
   puzzling, stubborn, tiresome
09 demanding, intricate,
   laborious, obstinate,
   recondite
10 exhausting, formidable,
   perplexing, refractory
11 intractable, troublesome
12 backbreaking, recalcitrant,
   unmanageable
13 problematical,
   uncooperative

**difficulty**
03 fix, jam
04 hole, mess, snag, spot
05 block, devil, trial
06 hiccup, hurdle, pickle, plight
07 barrier, Catch-22, dilemma,
   pitfall, problem, trouble
08 distress, exigency, hardship,
   obstacle, quandary
09 deep water, hindrance,
   objection
10 impediment, perplexity,
   pretty pass
11 arduousness, dire straits,
   predicament, tribulation
12 complication
13 embarrassment,
   strenuousness
14 stumbling block

☐**in difficulties**
06 in a fix, in a jam
07 in a hole, in a mess
09 in a pickle, in a scrape, in
   trouble
11 in deep water, up against it
12 in a tight spot
13 in dire straits
14 having problems, out of your
   depth

**diffidence**
07 modesty, reserve, shyness

08 humility, meekness, timidity
09 hesitancy, self-doubt
10 inhibition, reluctance
11 bashfulness
12 backwardness, self-distrust
14 self-effacement
15 unassertiveness

**diffident**
03 shy
04 meek
05 timid
06 modest, unsure
07 abashed, bashful, nervous
08 hesitant, insecure, reserved,
   sheepish
09 inhibited, reluctant,
   shrinking, tentative
11 unassertive
12 self-effacing
13 self-conscious

**diffuse**
05 vague, wordy
06 prolix, spread
07 profuse, scatter, verbose
08 diffused, dispense, disperse,
   rambling
09 dispersed, imprecise,
   propagate, scattered
10 discursive, distribute, long-
   winded, loquacious,
   promulgate
11 disseminate
12 disconnected, periphrastic
14 circumlocutory

**dig**
03 jab
04 gibe, jeer, mine, plow, till
05 delve, gouge, probe, scoop,
   spade
06 burrow, go into, harrow,
   hollow, insult, pierce, quarry,
   tunnel
08 excavate, research, turn over
09 cultivate, make a hole
11 insinuation, investigate

☐**dig up**
04 find
06 exhume, expose
07 root out, uncover, unearth
08 discover, disinter, retrieve
12 bring to light

**digest**
05 grasp, study
06 absorb, ponder, reduce, take
   in
07 process, shorten, summary
08 abstract, compress,
   condense, consider, dissolve,
   macerate, meditate, mull
   over
09 break down, reduction

10 abridgment, assimilate, compendium, comprehend, understand
11 compression, contemplate, incorporate

**digestion**
08 eupepsia
09 ingestion
10 absorption
12 assimilation, breaking-down

**dignified**
05 grand, grave, lofty, noble
06 august, formal, solemn
07 courtly, exalted, stately
08 imposing, majestic
11 ceremonious
13 distinguished

**dignify**
05 adorn, exalt, grace, honor, raise
07 advance, elevate, enhance, ennoble, glorify, promote
10 aggrandize
11 apotheosize, distinguish

**dignitary**
03 VIP
06 bigwig, worthy
07 big name, big shot, notable
08 luminary, somebody, top brass
09 personage
13 high muck-a-muck
15 high muckety-muck

**dignity**
05 honor, poise, pride
06 status
07 decorum, majesty
08 eminence, grandeur, nobility, standing
09 elevation, greatness, loftiness, solemnity
10 self-esteem
11 courtliness, self-respect
14 respectability

**digress**
05 drift, stray
06 depart, ramble, wander
07 deviate, diverge
09 turn aside
13 be sidetracked
15 go off at a tangent, go off the subject

**digression**
05 aside
08 excursus, footnote, straying
09 departure, deviation, diversion, wandering
10 apostrophe, divagation, divergence
11 parenthesis

12 obiter dictum

**dilapidated**
05 shaky
06 ruined, shabby
07 decayed, in ruins, rickety, run-down, worn-out
08 decaying, decrepit
09 crumbling, neglected
10 broken-down, ramshackle, tumbledown, uncared-for
12 falling apart

**dilapidation**
04 ruin
05 decay, waste
08 collapse
09 disrepair
13 deterioration
14 disintegration

**dilate**
05 bloat, swell, widen
06 expand, extend, spread
07 distend, enlarge, inflate
08 increase
09 spread out

**dilatory**
04 lazy, slow
05 slack, tardy
08 dawdling, delaying, sluggish, stalling, tarrying
09 lingering, snail-like
11 time-wasting
13 lackadaisical
15 procrastinating

**dilemma**
03 fix, jam
04 mess, spot
06 plight, puzzle
07 Catch-22, problem
08 conflict, quandary
09 conundrum
10 difficulty, perplexity
11 predicament, tight corner
12 tight squeeze
13 embarrassment

**dilettante**
07 amateur, dabbler, trifler
08 aesthete, putterer, sciolist

**diligence**
04 care
08 industry
09 assiduity, attention, constancy
10 dedication, intentness
11 application, earnestness
12 perseverance, sedulousness, thoroughness
13 assiduousness, attentiveness, laboriousness

**diligent**
04 busy

07 careful, earnest
08 constant, sedulous, studious, thorough, tireless
09 assiduous, attentive, dedicated
10 meticulous, persistent
11 hard-working, industrious, painstaking, persevering
13 conscientious

**dilly**
03 pip
05 beaut, dandy, peach
06 doozer
08 jim-dandy, knockout
09 humdinger
11 crackerjack

**dillydally**
05 dally, delay, hover, tarry
06 dawdle, dither, linger, putter
08 hesitate
09 vacillate
12 shilly-shally, take your time

**dilute**
04 thin
06 lessen, reduce, weaken
07 diffuse, thin out
08 decrease, diminish, mitigate, moderate, tone down
09 attenuate, water down
10 adulterate, make weaker
11 make thinner

**dim**
04 blur, dark, dull, dumb, fade, gray, hazy, pale, weak
05 cloud, dense, dingy, dusky, faint, foggy, fuzzy, misty, shade, thick, unlit, vague
06 cloudy, darken, feeble, gloomy, leaden, obtuse, somber, stupid
07 adverse, blurred, doltish, obscure, shadowy, tarnish
08 overcast
09 dimwitted, tenebrous
10 ill-defined, indistinct, lackluster, obfuscated, slow-witted, tenebrious
11 crepuscular, unpromising
13 become blurred

**dime novel**
07 chiller
08 dreadful
11 pulp fiction
13 penny dreadful

**dimension**
04 area, bulk, mass, side, size
05 depth, facet, range, scale, scope, width
06 aspect, extent, factor, height, length, volume

**diminish**
07 breadth, element, feature, measure
08 capacity
09 greatness, largeness, magnitude
11 measurement, proportions

**diminish**
03 cut, ebb
04 fade, sink, wane
05 abate, lower
06 defame, lessen, recede, reduce, shrink, weaken
07 decline, deflate, devalue, dwindle, slacken, subside
08 belittle, contract, decrease, derogate, grow less, peter out, retrench, taper off
09 denigrate, deprecate, disparage
10 become less, grow weaker

**diminution**
03 cut, ebb
05 decay
07 cutback, decline
08 decrease
09 abatement, lessening, reduction, shrinkage
10 shortening, subsidence
11 contraction, curtailment

**diminutive**
03 wee
04 mini, tiny
05 dinky, elfin, pygmy, small
06 little, midget, minute, petite, pocket
07 compact
08 dwarfish, pint-size
09 miniature, minuscule, pint-sized
10 homuncular, small-scale, teeny-weeny, undersized
11 Lilliputian, microscopic, pocket-sized
12 teensy-weensy

**dimple**
04 dint
05 fovea
06 hollow
09 concavity, umbilicus
10 depression

**dimwit**
04 dolt, fool, twit
05 dunce, idiot
06 nitwit
07 dullard
08 bonehead, numskull
09 blockhead, ignoramus, simpleton
10 dunderhead

**din**
03 row

05 clash, crash, noise, shout
06 babble, clamor, hubbub, outcry, racket, tumult, uproar
07 clangor, clatter, yelling
08 brouhaha
09 commotion, loud noise
10 hullabaloo

**dine**
03 eat, sup
04 feed
05 feast, lunch
07 banquet
10 have dinner

**dingy**
03 dim
04 dark, drab, dull, worn
05 dirty, dusky, faded, grimy, murky, seedy
06 dismal, dreary, gloomy, shabby, soiled, somber
07 run-down, squalid
09 cheerless
10 discolored

**dinky**
05 minor, small
06 petite
08 piddling
09 miniature
11 unimportant
13 insignificant

**dinner**
04 meal
05 feast
06 repast, spread, supper
07 banquet, blowout
08 main meal, prandial
09 refection
11 evening meal

**dinosaur**

► *Types of dinosaur*:
04 T-Rex
08 Sauropod, Theropod
09 Hadrosaur, Iguanodon
10 Allosaurus, Barosaurus, Diplodocus, Saurischia, Torosaurus
11 Apatosaurus, Coelophysis, Deinonychus, Dromaeosaur, Polacanthus, Stegosaurus, Triceratops
12 Ankylosaurus, Brontosaurus, Camptosaurus, Megalosaurus, Ornithischia, Ornithomimus, Plateosaurus, Velociraptor
13 Brachiosaurus, Compsognathus, Corythosaurus, Edmontosaurus, Ornitholestes,

Styracosaurus, Tyrannosaurus
15 Parasaurolophus
➤ See also ANIMAL

**dint**
04 blow, dent
06 hollow, stroke
09 concavity
10 depression, impression
11 indentation

❏**by dint of**
09 by means of
10 by virtue of

**dip**
04 dent, dive, drop, duck, dunk, fall, hole, sink, soak, swim
05 basin, bathe, douse, lower, sauce, slope, slump, souse
06 go down, hollow, plunge
07 descend, descent, ducking, immerse, soaking, subside
08 decrease, dressing, infusion, lowering, submerge
09 concavity, immersion
10 depression
11 indentation

❏**dip into**
04 skim
06 browse, draw on, look at
11 leaf through, look through
12 flick through, thumb through

**diplomacy**
04 tact
07 finesse
08 delicacy, politics, subtlety
10 discretion, statecraft
11 maneuvering, negotiation, savoir-faire, tactfulness
13 judiciousness, statesmanship

**diplomat**
05 envoy
06 consul, legate
07 attaché
08 emissary, mediator
09 moderator, statesman
10 ambassador, arbitrator, negotiator, politician
11 conciliator
15 chargé d'affaires, plenipotentiary

**diplomatic**
06 clever, subtle
07 politic, prudent, tactful
08 consular, discreet
13 ambassadorial

**dire**
05 awful, grave, vital
06 urgent
07 crucial, drastic, extreme

## direct

08 alarming, dreadful, horrible, pressing, shocking, terrible
09 appalling, atrocious, desperate, frightful
10 calamitous, disastrous
12 catastrophic

## direct

03 aim, run
04 lead, mean, open, show, turn
05 bluff, blunt, frank, guide, order, point, steer, usher
06 adjure, candid, escort, govern, handle, manage
07 command, conduct, control, nonstop, through, upfront
08 explicit, instruct, organize, personal, straight, unbroken
09 first-hand, immediate, outspoken, supervise
10 administer, face-to-face, forthright, give orders, show the way, unswerving
11 plainspoken, point the way, preside over, superintend, undeviating, unequivocal
12 be in charge of, call the shots
13 be in control of
15 straightforward

## direction

03 way
04 line, path, plan, road
05 brief, drift, route, track, trend
06 course, orders
07 bearing, control, running
08 briefing, guidance, handling, tendency
10 government, guidelines, indication, leadership, management, regulation
11 inclination, orientation, regulations, supervision
12 instructions
14 administration

## directive

04 fiat
05 edict, order
06 charge, decree, notice
07 bidding, command, dictate, mandate
09 ordinance
10 imperative, injunction
11 instruction

## directly

04 soon
05 right
06 at once, pronto
07 bluntly, clearly, exactly, frankly, plainly, quickly
08 candidly, honestly, promptly, speedily, straight

09 forthwith, instantly, presently, right away
10 explicitly
11 immediately
12 straightaway, without delay
13 unequivocally
15 instantaneously

## director

04 boss, head
05 chair, chief
06 leader, top dog
07 manager
08 chairman, governor
09 conductor, executive, organizer, president, principal, régisseur
10 chairwoman, controller
11 chairperson
13 administrator
14 chief executive

► *Names of film and theater directors*:

03 Lee (Spike), **Ray** (Satyajit)
04 **Coen** (Ethan), **Coen** (Joel), **Ford** (John), **Hall** (Peter), **Hare** (David), **Lang** (Fritz), **Lean** (David), **Nunn** (Trevor), **Reed** (Carol), **Roeg** (Nicolas), **Todd** (Mike), **Wong** Kar-Wai
05 **Allen** (Woody), **Brook** (Peter), **Capra** (Frank), **Carné** (Marcel), **Cukor** (George Dewey), **Dante** (Joe), **Hawks** (Howard), **Ivory** (James Francis), **Kazan** (Elia), **Korda** (Alexander), **Leigh** (Mike), **Lucas** (George), **Lynch** (David), **Malle** (Louis), **Mayer** (Louis B.), **Roach** (Hal), **Scott** (Ridley), **Stone** (Oliver), **Vadim** (Roger), **Wyler** (William)
06 **Altman** (Robert), **Artaud** (Antoni), **Besson** (Luc), **Brecht** (Bertolt), **Brooks** (Mel), **Buñuel** (Luis), **Burton** (Tim), **Corman** (Roger), **De Sica** (Vittorio), **Disney** (Walt), **Forbes** (Bryan), **Forman** (Milos), **Frears** (Stephen), **Fuller** (Samuel), **Godard** (Jean-Luc), **Herzog** (Werner), **Hughes** (Howard), **Huston** (John), **Jarman** (Derek), **Ophuls** (Max), **Parker** (Alan), **Powell** (Michael), **Renoir** (Jean), **Welles** (Orson), **Wilder** (Billy)
07 **Aldrich** (Robert), **Bergman**

(Ingmar), **Boorman** (John), **Chabrol** (Claude), **Coppola** (Francis Ford), **De Mille** (Cecil B.), **De Palma** (Brian), **Fellini** (Federico), **Gaumont** (Léon), **Gilliam** (Terry), **Kubrick** (Stanley), **Pollack** (Sydney), **Redford** (Robert), **Resnais** (Alain), **Russell** (Ken), **Sennett** (Mack), **Wenders** (Wim)
08 **Berkeley** (Busby), **Eastwood** (Clint), **Friedkin** (William), **Jarmusch** (Jim), **Kurosawa** (Akira), **Lubitsch** (Ernst), **Merchant** (Ismail), **Pasolini** (Pier Paulo), **Polanski** (Roman), **Scorsese** (Martin), **Truffaut** (François), **Visconti** (Luchino)
09 **Almodovar** (Pedro), **Antonioni** (Michelangelo), **Greenaway** (Peter), **Grotowski** (Jerzy), **Hitchcock** (Alfred), **Peckinpah** (Sam), **Preminger** (Otto), **Spielberg** (Steven), **Strasberg** (Lee), **Tarantino** (Quentin)
10 **Bertolucci** (Bernardo), **Cronenberg** (David), **Eisenstein** (Sergei), **Fassbinder** (Rainer Werner), **Kieslowski** (Krzystof), **Rossellini** (Roberto), **Zeffirelli** (Franco)
11 **Bogdanovich** (Peter), **Pressburger** (Emeric), **Riefenstahl** (Leni), **Schlesinger** (John)
12 **Stanislavsky** (Constantin)

## dirge

05 elegy
06 lament, monody
07 requiem
08 coronach, threnody
09 dead-march
11 funeral song

## dirt

03 mud
04 clay, crud, dust, gunk, loam, mire, muck, smut, soil, soot, yuck
05 earth, filth, grime
06 gossip, grunge, sleaze, sludge, smudge
07 garbage
08 impurity, lewdness

**dirty**

09  excrement, indecency, obscenity, pollution
11  pornography
13  salaciousness

**dirty**
04  blue, dull, foul, lewd, soil
05  bawdy, dusty, grimy, messy, mucky, muddy, slimy, sooty, spoil, stain, sully, yucky
06  coarse, cruddy, defile, filthy, greasy, grotty, grubby, mess up, ribald, risqué, sleazy, smudge, smutty, soiled, sordid, splash, vulgar
07  begrime, blacken, corrupt, defiled, obscene, pollute, squalid, stained, sullied, tarnish, unclean
08  besmirch, indecent, polluted, unwashed
09  salacious, tarnished
10  suggestive, unhygienic
11  contaminate
12  contaminated, pornographic

**disability**
06  defect, malady
07  ailment, illness
08  disorder, handicap, weakness
09  complaint, inability, infirmity, unfitness
10  affliction, impairment, incapacity

**disable**
04  lame, stop
06  damage, impair, weaken
07  cripple
08  enfeeble, handicap, paralyze
09  hamstring, make unfit
10  deactivate, debilitate, immobolize, invalidate
12  incapacitate
14  put out of action

**disabled**
04  lame, weak
05  unfit
06  bedrid, infirm, maimed
07  wrecked
08  crippled, impaired
09  bedridden, enfeebled, paralyzed
10  indisposed
11  debilitated, handicapped, immobilized, out of action
13  incapacitated

**disadvantage**
04  flaw, lack, loss, snag
06  damage, defect, injury
07  penalty, trouble
08  downside, drawback, handicap, weakness

09  detriment, hindrance, liability, prejudice, privation
10  impediment, limitation

**disadvantaged**
04  poor
06  in need, in want
08  deprived
10  in distress, struggling
11  handicapped
15  poverty stricken, underprivileged

**disadvantageous**
07  adverse, harmful, hurtful
08  damaging, ill-timed
09  injurious
11  deleterious, detrimental, inopportune, prejudicial, unfavorable
12  inconvenient

**disaffected**
07  hostile
08  disloyal, mutinous
09  alienated, estranged
10  rebellious, unfriendly
11  disgruntled
12  antagonistic, discontented, dissatisfied

**disaffection**
07  discord, dislike, ill will
08  aversion, coolness
09  animosity, hostility
10  alienation, antagonism, disloyalty, resentment
12  disagreement, estrangement
14  discontentment, unfriendliness

**disagree**
05  argue, clash, fight, upset
06  bicker, differ, object, oppose
07  contend, contest, dispute, dissent, diverge, fall out, quarrel, wrangle
09  be against, take issue
10  contradict, make unwell
11  beg to differ
12  argue against, be at odds with, cause illness
13  agree to differ, take issue with

**disagreeable**
04  rude, sour
05  cross, nasty, surly
06  snappy
07  brusque, grouchy, peevish
08  churlish, contrary, impolite, unsavory
09  difficult, irritable, obnoxious, offensive, repellent, repugnant, repulsive, unhelpful

10  disgusting, ill-humored, ill-natured, unfriendly, unpleasant
11  bad-tempered, disobliging
13  objectionable

**disagreement**
03  row
04  tiff
05  clash
06  strife
07  discord, dispute, dissent, quarrel, wrangle
08  argument, conflict, friction, squabble, variance
09  deviation, disparity, diversity
10  contention, difference, dissension, falling-out
11  altercation, discrepancy, disputation, incongruity
13  dissimilarity, inconsistency
15  incompatibility

**disallow**
03  ban
04  veto
05  debar
06  abjure, cancel, disown, forbid, rebuff, refuse, reject
07  exclude, say no to
08  disclaim, prohibit
09  proscribe, repudiate

**disappear**
02  go
03  ebb, end, fly
04  exit, fade, flee, hide, wane
05  cease
06  depart, go AWOL, perish, recede, vamose
07  die away, get lost, scarper, vamoose
08  dissolve, evanesce, melt away, withdraw
09  be missing, evaporate, go missing
12  go out of sight
13  become extinct, dematerialize

**disappearance**
03  end
04  exit, loss
06  expiry, fading, flight
07  passing
08  dying-out
09  desertion, vanishing
10  extinction, withdrawal
11  evanescence, evaporation

**disappoint**
04  fail, foil
06  dismay, hamper, hinder, sadden, thwart
07  deceive, depress, let down
08  dispirit

09 frustrate
10 disenchant, dishearten
11 disillusion

## disappointed
05 upset, vexed
06 miffed
07 let down
08 cast down, deflated, saddened, thwarted
09 depressed
10 despondent, frustrated
11 discouraged, downhearted
12 disenchanted, disheartened
13 disillusioned

## disappointing
03 sad
05 sorry
08 inferior, pathetic, unworthy
10 depressing, inadequate
12 discouraging, insufficient
13 anticlimactic, underwhelming
14 unsatisfactory

## disappointment
04 blow
07 chagrin, failure, letdown, sadness, setback, washout, wipeout
08 comedown, nonevent
09 damp squib
10 anticlimax, bitter pill
11 cold comfort, frustration
14 disenchantment
15 disillusionment

## disapprobation
05 blame
07 censure, dislike, reproof
08 reproach
09 criticism, objection
11 approbation, disapproval, displeasure
12 condemnation
13 disparagement
15 dissatisfaction

## disapproval
04 veto
05 blame
06 rebuke
07 censure, dislike, reproof
08 reproach
09 criticism, exception, objection, rejection
11 displeasure
12 condemnation, denunciation
13 disparagement, remonstration, the thumbs down
14 disapprobation
15 dissatisfaction

## disapprove
04 veto

05 blame, spurn
06 reject
07 censure, condemn, deplore, dislike, frown on
08 disallow, object to
09 deprecate, disparage
10 animadvert, look down on
11 not hold with
12 think badly of
14 discountenance, take a dim view of
15 take exception to

## disapproving
08 critical
10 censorious, derogatory, pejorative
11 deprecatory, disparaging, improbative, improbatory, reproachful
12 condemnatory
14 disapprobative, disapprobatory

## disarm
05 charm, unarm
07 appease, disable, disband, mollify, placate, win over
10 conciliate, deactivate, demobilize, immobilize
11 lay down arms
12 demilitarize
13 make powerless
14 put out of action

## disarmament
11 arms control
12 deactivation
13 arms reduction
14 arms limitation, demobilization

## disarming
07 winning
08 charming, likeable
12 conciliatory, irresistible

## disarrange
04 mess
06 jumble, untidy
07 confuse, disturb, shuffle
08 disorder, unsettle
11 disorganize

## disarray
04 mess
05 chaos, upset
06 jumble, muddle, tangle
07 clutter
08 disorder, shambles
09 confusion
10 unruliness, untidiness
12 dishevelment, indiscipline
15 disorganization

## disaster
04 blow, flop, ruin

06 fiasco, mishap, stroke
07 debacle, failure, reverse, tragedy, trouble, wash out
08 accident, act of God, calamity, reversal
09 adversity, cataclysm, mischance, ruination
10 misfortune
11 catastrophe

## disastrous
04 dire
05 fatal
06 tragic
07 adverse, ruinous, unlucky
08 dreadful, terrible
09 appalling, injurious
10 calamitous, ill-starred
11 cataclysmic, devastating
12 catastrophic

## disavowal
06 denial
07 dissent
09 rejection
10 abjuration
11 repudiation
12 renunciation
13 contradiction
14 disaffirmation

## disband
07 break up, dismiss, scatter
08 disperse, dissolve, separate
10 demobilize
11 part company
14 go separate ways

## disbelief
05 doubt
07 dubiety
08 distrust, mistrust, unbelief
09 discredit, suspicion
10 skepticism
11 incredulity, questioning

## disbelieve
05 doubt
06 reject
07 suspect
08 distrust, mistrust, question
09 discredit, repudiate
13 be unconvinced

## disbeliever
07 atheist, doubter, skeptic
08 agnostic
10 questioner, unbeliever
11 nullifidian
14 doubting Thomas

## disburse
05 allot, spend
06 expend, lay out, pay out
07 cough up, fork out
08 shell out

## disbursement

06 outlay
07 payment
08 disposal, spending
09 disbursal
11 expenditure

## discard

04 drop, dump, shed
05 ditch, scrap
06 reject, remove
07 abandon, forsake, toss out
08 chuck out, get rid of, jettison, throw out
09 cast aside, chuck away, dispose of, throw away
12 dispense with

## discern

03 see
05 judge
06 descry, detect, notice
07 make out, observe
08 discover, perceive
09 ascertain, recognize
11 distinguish
12 discriminate
13 differentiate

## discernible

05 clear, plain
06 patent
07 obvious, visible
08 apparent, distinct, manifest
10 detectable, noticeable, observable
11 appreciable, conspicuous, perceptible
15 distinguishable

## discerning

04 wise
05 acute, quick, sharp, sound
06 astute, clever, shrewd, subtle
07 prudent, sapient
08 critical, piercing
09 eagle-eyed, sensitive
10 perceptive, percipient
11 intelligent, penetrating
12 clearsighted
13 perspicacious
14 discriminating

## discernment

05 taste
07 insight
08 judgment, keenness, sagacity
09 acuteness, awareness, good taste, sharpness
10 perception, shrewdness
11 penetration, percipience
12 intelligence, perspicacity
13 understanding
14 discrimination, perceptiveness

## discharge

02 ax, do
03 pay, pus
04 emit, fire, flow, free, gush, leak, meet, ooze, oust, sack
05 clear, doing, eject, expel, exude, honor, let go, shoot
06 acquit, firing, let off, let out, pardon, remove, set off, settle
07 absolve, boot out, discard, dismiss, excrete, explode, fulfill, give off, kick out, perform, release, relieve, removal, sacking, set free, the boot, the gate, the sack
08 carry out, detonate, disgorge, dispense, emission, get rid of, liberate, pink slip
09 acquittal, dismissal, excretion, exculpate, execution, exonerate, expulsion, secretion
10 absolution, disembogue, liberation
11 exculpation, exoneration, fulfillment, performance, show the door, suppuration
13 walking papers

## disciple

05 pupil
06 votary
07 devotee, learner, student
08 adherent, believer, follower, upholder
09 proselyte, supporter

## disciplinarian

06 despot, tyrant
08 autocrat, martinet, stickler
10 taskmaster
13 authoritarian

## discipline

05 check, drill, inure, limit, train
06 branch, course, punish, rebuke
07 chasten, control, correct, educate, regimen, reprove, routine, subject
08 chastise, exercise, instruct, penalize, practice, regulate, restrain, restrict, training
09 castigate, inculcate, reprimand, restraint
10 correction, punishment, regulation, strictness
11 area of study, castigation, self-control
12 chastisement, field of study
13 self-restraint

## disclaim

04 deny
06 abjure, disown, refuse, reject

07 abandon, decline, disavow
08 renounce
09 repudiate
15 wash your hands of

## disclaimer

06 denial
09 disavowal, rejection
10 disownment, retraction
11 repudiation
12 renunciation
14 disaffirmation

## disclose

04 blab, leak, show, tell
06 expose, impart, relate, reveal, squeal, unveil
07 confess, divulge, lay bare, let slip, publish, uncover
08 blurt out, discover
09 broadcast, make known
10 make public
12 bring to light
13 spill the beans

## disclosure

04 leak
06 exposé
08 exposure
09 admission, broadcast
10 confession, divulgence, revelation, uncovering
11 declaration, publication
12 announcement

## discoloration

04 blot, mark, spot
05 patch, stain
06 blotch, streak
07 blemish, splotch
08 dyschroa
10 ecchymosis

## discolor

04 fade, mark, rust, soil
05 stain, tinge
06 streak
07 tarnish, weather

## discomfit

03 jar, vex
04 faze
05 upset
06 outwit, rattle, ruffle, thwart
07 confuse, fluster, perplex
08 confound, unsettle
09 embarrass, frustrate
10 discompose, disconcert

## discomfiture

06 unease
09 abashment, confusion
11 frustration, humiliation
12 discomposure
13 embarrassment

## discomfort

04 ache, hurt, pain, pang

06 bother, twinge, unease
07 malaise, trouble
08 disquiet, distress, nuisance, soreness, vexation
10 uneasiness
13 embarrassment

**discomposure**
05 upset
06 unease
07 anxiety, fluster
09 agitation, annoyance
10 inquietude, irritation, uneasiness
11 disquietude, disturbance
12 perturbation, restlessness

**disconcert**
03 vex
04 faze
05 alarm, shake, upset
06 dismay, put off, rattle, ruffle
07 confuse, disturb, fluster, perturb, startle, unnerve
08 bewilder, surprise, unsettle
09 embarrass, frustrate, take aback
14 discombobulate
15 throw off balance

**disconcerting**
07 awkward
08 alarming, baffling, daunting
09 confusing, unnerving
10 disturbing, perturbing
11 bewildering, distracting

**disconnect**
04 part, undo
05 sever, split
06 cut off, detach, divide, unhook, unplug
07 unhitch
08 separate, uncouple
09 disengage

**disconnected**
05 loose
07 garbled, jumbled, mixed-up
08 confused, staccato
09 illogical, wandering
10 disjointed, incoherent

**disconsolate**
03 low, sad
04 down
06 gloomy
07 crushed, forlorn, unhappy
08 dejected, desolate, downcast, hopeless, wretched
09 depressed, miserable
10 despondent, dispirited, melancholy
11 heartbroken, low-spirited
12 heavy-hearted
14 down in the dumps

**discontent**
06 misery, regret, unrest
08 disquiet, vexation
10 impatience, uneasiness
11 displeasure, fretfulness, unhappiness
12 disaffection, restlessness
15 dissatisfaction

**discontented**
05 fed up
07 unhappy
08 restless, wretched
09 miserable
10 browned off
11 complaining, disaffected, disgruntled, exasperated
12 dissatisfied

**discontinue**
03 end
04 drop, halt, quit, stop
05 cease, scrap
06 cancel, finish
07 abandon, abolish, refrain, suspend
08 break off
09 interrupt, terminate
11 come to an end

**discontinuity**
07 rupture
10 disruption
11 incoherence
12 interruption
13 disconnection
14 disjointedness

**discontinuous**
06 broken, fitful
08 periodic
09 irregular, spasmodic
11 interrupted
12 disconnected, intermittent

**discord**
03 row
05 split
06 jangle, strife
07 dispute, dissent, jarring
08 argument, clashing, conflict, disunity, division, friction
09 cacophony, wrangling
10 contention, difference, disharmony, dissension, dissonance, opposition
12 disagreement
15 incompatibility

**discordant**
04 flat
05 harsh, sharp
06 at odds, atonal
07 grating, hostile, jarring
08 clashing, jangling, strident
09 differing, dissonant
10 at variance, dissenting

11 cacophonous
12 incompatible, inconsistent

**discount**
03 cut
05 slash
06 deduct, ignore, reduce
07 take off
08 cut price, knock off, mark down, overlook
09 deduction, disregard, gloss over, reduction
10 concession, disbelieve

**discourage**
05 daunt, deter
06 dampen, dismay, put off
07 depress, prevent, unnerve
08 cast down, dispirit, dissuade
09 talk out of
10 demoralize, dishearten
12 put a damper on
13 advise against

**discouraged**
04 glum
06 dashed
07 daunted, let-down
08 deflated, dejected, dismayed, downcast
09 depressed
10 dispirited
11 crestfallen, demoralized, pessimistic
12 disheartened

**discouragement**
04 curb
05 gloom
06 damper, dismay, rebuff
07 barrier, despair, setback
09 deterrent, pessimism
10 depression, impediment
12 disincentive, hopelessness

**discouraging**
08 daunting
09 dampening
10 depressing, dissuasive, dissuasory
11 dehortatory, dispiriting, unfavorable
12 demoralizing, inauspicious, unpropitious
13 disheartening

**discourse**
04 chat, talk
05 essay, speak
06 confer, debate, dialog, homily, preach, sermon, speech
07 discuss, lecture, oration
08 converse, dialogue
10 discussion
12 conversation, dissertation
13 confabulation

## discourteous
04 curt, rude
05 gruff, short
07 boorish, brusque, ill-bred, offhand, uncivil, uncouth
08 impolite, impudent, insolent
10 ungracious, unmannerly
11 bad-mannered, ill-mannered, impertinent
13 disrespectful

## discourtesy
04 snub
06 insult, rebuff, slight
07 affront
08 curtness, rudeness
09 indecorum, insolence
10 bad manners, incivility
12 impertinence, impoliteness
14 ungraciousness, unmannerliness

## discover
03 see
04 find, spot
05 dig up, learn
06 detect, devise, fathom, invent, locate, notice, reveal, turn up
07 discern, get onto, light on, pioneer, realize, uncover, unearth, work out
08 disclose, perceive, tumble to
09 ascertain, determine, establish, fathom out, ferret out, get wind of, stumble on
10 come across, come to know
13 stumble across

## discoverer
06 author, finder
07 deviser, founder, pioneer
08 explorer, inventor
09 initiator
10 originator

## discovery
04 find
07 finding
08 devising, learning, research
09 detection, invention
10 disclosure, revelation
11 discernment, exploration, realization, recognition
12 breakthrough, introduction

## discredit
04 deny, slur
05 blame, doubt, shame, smear
06 damage, debunk, defame, infamy, stigma, vilify
07 censure, degrade, tarnish
08 belittle, disgrace, dishonor, distrust, ignominy, mistrust, reproach

09 aspersion, disparage, disrepute
10 disbelieve, invalidate, opprobrium
11 humiliation
14 put in a bad light, reflect badly on

## discreditable
08 improper, infamous, shameful
09 degrading
10 scandalous
11 blameworthy, disgraceful
12 dishonorable, disreputable
13 reprehensible

## discreet
04 wary, wise
07 careful, guarded, politic, prudent, tactful
08 cautious, delicate, reserved
10 diplomatic
11 circumspect, considerate

## discrepancy
08 conflict, variance
09 deviation, disparity, variation
10 difference, divergence
11 discordance, incongruity
12 disagreement
13 contradiction, inconsistency

## discrete
08 detached, distinct, separate
10 individual, unattached
12 disconnected
13 discontinuous

## discretion
04 care, tact, will, wish
06 choice, desire, wisdom
07 caution, freedom, reserve
08 judgment, prudence, volition, wariness
09 good sense
11 discernment, inclination
13 consideration, judiciousness
14 circumspection

## discretionary
04 open
08 elective, optional
09 voluntary

## discriminate
07 discern
08 be biased, separate
09 segregate, tell apart, victimize
11 distinguish
12 be intolerant, be prejudiced
13 differentiate

## discriminating
04 keen
06 astute, shrewd
08 critical, tasteful

09 selective, sensitive
10 discerning, fastidious, particular, perceptive

## discrimination
04 bias
05 agism, taste
06 ageism, racism, sexism
07 bigotry, insight
08 inequity, judgment, keenness, subtlety
09 prejudice, racialism
10 astuteness, favoritism, homophobia, perception, unfairness
11 discernment, intolerance, segregation
12 perspicacity
14 male chauvinism

## discriminatory
06 biased, loaded, unfair, unjust
07 partial
08 favoring, one-sided, partisan, weighted
10 prejudiced
11 inequitable, prejudicial
12 preferential

## discursive
05 wordy
06 prolix
07 diffuse, verbose
08 rambling
10 circuitous, digressing, long-winded, meandering

## discuss
05 argue, study
06 confer, debate, parley
07 analyze, consult, weigh up
08 consider, converse, talk over
09 discourse, talk about
10 deliberate, kick around, toss around
11 confabulate

## discussion
04 talk
05 forum, study, talks
06 debate, dialog, parley, powwow
07 seminar
08 analysis, argument, dialogue, exchange, scrutiny
09 discourse, symposium
10 colloquium, conference
11 examination
12 consultation, conversation, deliberation, negotiations

## disdain
04 snub
05 scorn, spurn
06 deride, rebuff, reject, slight
07 despise, dislike, sneer at

08 belittle, contempt, derision, pooh-pooh, sneering
09 arrogance, disregard
10 look down on, undervalue
11 deprecation, haughtiness
12 cold shoulder, snobbishness
13 disparagement

**disdainful**
05 aloof, proud
07 haughty, pompous
08 arrogant, derisive, insolent, scornful, sneering, superior
09 slighting
11 disparaging
12 contemptuous, supercilious

**disease**
03 bug
05 virus
06 malady
07 ailment, illness
08 disorder, epidemic, sickness
09 complaint, contagion, infection, infirmity
10 affliction, disability

► *Names of diseases. We have omitted the word* **disease** *from names given in the following list, but you may need to include this word as part of the solution to some crossword clues.*

02 ME, MS, TB
03 flu
04 acne, AIDS, mono
05 croup, mumps, polio, ulcer
06 anemia, angina, asthma, autism, cancer, chorea, dropsy, herpes, rabies, scurvy, thrush, typhus
07 anthrax, Bright's, bulimia, cholera, leprosy, lockjaw, malaria, Marburg, measles, pinkeye, rickets, rubella, scabies, tetanus, typhoid, vertigo
08 alopecia, anorexia, beriberi, botulism, diabetes, gangrene, glaucoma, Hodgkin's, impetigo, leukemia, ringworm, shingles, smallpox, syphilis, tapeworm, tinnitus
09 arthritis, bilharzia, black lung, cirrhosis, dysentery, emphysema, enteritis, gonorrhea, hepatitis, influenza, pneumonia, psoriasis, silicosis
10 Alzheimer's, asbestosis, Black Death, bronchitis, chickenpox, common cold, diphtheria, gingivitis,

hemophilia, laryngitis, Lassa fever, meningitis, Parkinson's, septicemia, thrombosis
11 brucellosis, consumption, dengue fever, green monkey, Huntington's, hydrophobia, peptic ulcer, peritonitis, psittacosis, tonsillitis, yellow fever
12 appendicitis, athlete's foot, encephalitis, foot-and-mouth, hoof-and-mouth, osteoporosis, scarlet fever, tuberculosis
13 bubonic plague, cerebral palsy, endometriosis, German measles, mononucleosis, osteomyelitis, poliomyelitis, schizophrenia, whooping cough
14 conjunctivitis, cystic fibrosis, glandular fever, rheumatic fever
15 anorexia nervosa, blackwater fever, gastroenteritis, schistosomiasis

**diseased**
03 ill
04 sick
08 blighted, infected
09 unhealthy
12 contaminated

**disembark**
04 land
05 leave
06 alight, arrive, debark, get off
07 deplane, detrain, step off

**disembodied**
07 ghostly, phantom
08 bodiless, spectral
09 spiritual
10 discarnate, intangible
11 incorporeal

**disembowel**
03 gut
04 draw
06 paunch
08 disbowel
10 eviscerate, exenterate

**disenchanted**
05 blasé, fed up
06 soured
07 cynical, let down
09 jaundiced
11 discouraged, indifferent
13 disillusioned

**disenchantment**
08 cynicism
11 disillusion

15 disillusionment

**disengage**
04 free, undo
05 untie
06 detach, loosen, unhook
07 release, unhitch
08 liberate, separate, uncouple, unfasten, withdraw
09 extricate
10 disconnect
11 disentangle

**disengaged**
04 free
05 freed, loose
08 detached, released
09 separated, unhitched
10 unattached
11 unconnected
12 disentangled

**disentangle**
04 free, undo
05 loose
06 detach, unknot, unwind
07 clarify, release, resolve, unravel, unsnarl, untwist
08 separate, simplify, untangle
09 disengage, extricate
11 distinguish

**disfavor**
07 dislike
08 distaste, ignominy
09 disregard, disrepute
10 low opinion, opprobrium
11 disapproval, displeasure
12 unpopularity
14 disapprobation

**disfigure**
03 mar
04 flaw, maim, ruin, scar
05 spoil
06 damage, deface, deform
07 blemish, distort
08 make ugly, mutilate

**disfigurement**
04 scar, spot
05 stain
06 blotch, defect, injury
07 blemish
09 deformity
10 defacement, distortion

**disgorge**
04 spew
05 belch, eject, empty, expel, spout, vomit
07 throw up
09 discharge, surrender
10 relinquish
11 regurgitate

**disgrace**
04 blot, slur

**disgraced**

- 05 abase, blame, shame, smear, stain, sully, taint
- 06 defame, infamy, stigma
- 07 degrade, obloquy, scandal
- 08 belittle, black eye, dishonor, ignominy, reproach
- 09 black mark, discredit, disparage, disrepute, humiliate
- 10 debasement, defamation, disrespect, opprobrium, put to shame, stigmatize
- 11 degradation, humiliation
- 12 bring shame on
- 15 cause to lose face

**disgraced**

- 06 shamed
- 07 branded
- 08 degraded
- 10 dishonored, humiliated
- 11 discredited, stigmatized
- 13 in the doghouse

**disgraceful**

- 05 awful
- 08 culpable, dreadful, shameful, shocking, terrible, unworthy
- 09 appalling
- 10 despicable, outrageous, scandalous
- 11 blameworthy, ignominious
- 12 contemptible, dishonorable, disreputable
- 13 reprehensible

**disgruntled**

- 05 cross, fed up, sulky, testy, vexed
- 06 grumpy, peeved, put out
- 07 annoyed, peevish
- 08 petulant
- 09 hacked off, irritated, resentful
- 10 browned off, displeased
- 12 discontented, dissatisfied

**disguise**

- 04 fake, hide, mask, veil
- 05 cloak, cover, feign, front
- 06 façade, screen, shroud
- 07 conceal, costume, cover up, dress up, falsify, pretend
- 08 pretense, suppress, travesty
- 09 deception, dissemble, gloss over, whitewash
- 10 camouflage, masquerade
- 12 be undercover

**disguised**

- 04 fake
- 05 false
- 06 covert, hidden, made up, masked, veiled
- 07 cloaked, feigned
- 09 incognito
- 10 undercover

- 11 camouflaged

**disgust**

- 05 repel
- 06 hatred, nausea, offend, put off, revolt, sicken
- 07 outrage, turn off
- 08 aversion, nauseate
- 09 repulsion, revulsion
- 10 abhorrence, repugnance
- 11 detestation
- 15 turn your stomach

**disgusted**

- 05 fed up
- 06 put off
- 08 appalled, offended, repelled, repulsed, revolted, sickened
- 12 sick and tired

**disgusting**

- 03 bad
- 04 foul, vile
- 05 gross, nasty, yucky
- 06 odious
- 07 obscene
- 08 nauseous, shocking
- 09 offensive, repellent, repugnant, repulsive, revolting, sickening
- 10 nauseating, outrageous, unpleasant
- 11 disgraceful, distasteful, rebarbative, unpalatable
- 13 objectionable

**dish**

- 04 bowl, fare, food
- 05 plate
- 06 course, recipe, tureen
- 07 platter
- 09 specialty

◻**dish out**

- 07 dole out, give out, hand out, inflict, mete out
- 08 allocate, share out
- 10 distribute, hand around, pass around

◻**dish up**

- 05 ladle, scoop, serve, spoon
- 07 present

**disharmony**

- 05 clash
- 07 discord
- 08 conflict, friction
- 09 disaccord
- 10 dissonance
- 11 discordance
- 15 incompatibility

**dishearten**

- 05 crush, daunt, deter
- 06 dampen, deject, dismay
- 07 depress
- 08 cast down, dispirit

- 09 weigh down
- 10 disappoint, discourage

**disheartened**

- 07 crushed, daunted
- 08 dejected, dismayed, downcast
- 09 depressed
- 10 dispirited
- 11 crestfallen, discouraged, downhearted

**disheveled**

- 05 messy
- 06 untidy
- 07 in a mess, ruffled, rumpled, tousled, unkempt
- 08 slovenly, uncombed
- 10 bedraggled, disordered
- 11 disarranged

**dishonest**

- 03 sly
- 04 iffy
- 05 false, fishy, lying, shady
- 06 crafty, shifty
- 07 corrupt, crooked, devious
- 08 cheating, two-faced
- 09 deceitful, deceptive
- 10 fraudulent, mendacious, perfidious, untruthful
- 11 duplicitous, treacherous
- 12 dishonorable
- 13 double-dealing, untrustworthy

**dishonesty**

- 05 fraud
- 06 deceit
- 07 falsity, perfidy
- 08 cheating, trickery
- 09 chicanery, duplicity, falsehood, improbity, shadiness, treachery
- 10 corruption, dirty trick
- 11 criminality, crookedness, fraudulence, insincerity
- 13 double-dealing, sharp practice
- 14 untruthfulness

**dishonor**

- 04 slur
- 05 abuse, shame, stain, sully
- 06 debase, defame, defile, demean, infamy, insult, offend, slight, stigma
- 07 degrade, outrage, scandal
- 08 disfavor, disgrace, ignominy
- 09 abasement, aspersion, discredit, disrepute, indignity
- 10 debasement, opprobrium
- 11 degradation, humiliation

**dishonorable**

- 05 shady
- 07 corrupt, ignoble

**disillusion**

08 shameful, unworthy
09 shameless, unethical
10 despicable, perfidious, scandalous
11 disgraceful, ignominious
12 disreputable, unscrupulous
13 discreditable, untrustworthy

**disillusion**
08 disabuse
10 disappoint, disenchant

**disillusioned**
07 let-down
09 disabused
10 undeceived
12 disappointed, disenchanted

**disincentive**
08 obstacle
09 determent, deterrent, hindrance, repellent
10 dissuasion, impediment
11 restriction
14 discouragement

**disinclination**
09 loathness, objection
10 averseness, hesitation, opposition, reluctance, repugnance, resistance
13 unwillingness

**disinclined**
05 loath
06 averse
07 opposed
08 hesitant
09 reluctant, resistant, unwilling
14 unenthusiastic

**disinfect**
05 clean, purge
06 purify
07 cleanse
08 fumigate, sanitize
09 sterilize
13 decontaminate

**disinfectant**
08 fumigant
09 germicide, sanitizer
10 antiseptic, sterilizer
11 bactericide
13 decontaminant

**disingenuous**
03 sly
04 foxy, wily
06 artful, crafty, shifty
07 cunning, devious, feigned
08 guileful, two-faced
09 designing, dishonest, insidious, insincere
11 duplicitous

**disinherit**
06 cut off, reject

08 renounce
09 repudiate
10 dispossess, impoverish
14 turn your back on

**disintegrate**
03 rot
05 decay, smash
06 molder
07 break up, crumble, shatter
08 separate, splinter
09 decompose, fall apart
10 break apart
12 fall to pieces

**disinterest**
08 fairness
10 detachment, neutrality
12 impartiality, unbiasedness

**disinterested**
04 fair, just
07 neutral
08 detached, unbiased
09 equitable, impartial, objective, unselfish
10 evenhanded, open-minded, uninvolved
12 unprejudiced
13 dispassionate

**disjointed**
05 loose, split
06 broken, fitful
07 muddled
08 confused, rambling
09 separated, spasmodic
10 dislocated, disordered, incoherent
11 unconnected
12 disconnected
14 disarticulated

**disk**
02 CD, LP
04 disc, ring
05 album, CD-ROM, plate
06 circle, record, saucer
07 counter
08 diskette, hard disk
10 floppy disk
11 compact disk

**dislike**
06 animus, detest, enmity
07 despise, disgust
08 aversion, disfavor, distaste, object to
09 animosity, antipathy, disesteem, disrelish
10 antagonism, disapprove, repugnance, resentment
11 disapproval, displeasure
14 disapprobation

**dislocate**
04 do in, pull

05 shift, twist
06 luxate, put out, sprain, strain
07 confuse, disrupt, disturb
08 disjoint, disorder, displace
09 disengage
10 disconnect
11 disorganize
13 put out of joint, put out of place

**dislocation**
08 disarray, disorder
10 disruption
11 disturbance
15 disorganization

**dislodge**
04 move, oust
05 eject, shift
06 remove, uproot
08 displace, force out
09 extricate

**disloyal**
05 false
06 untrue
08 apostate, two-faced
09 deceitful, faithless
10 perfidious, traitorous, unfaithful
11 treacherous, unpatriotic
13 double-dealing

**disloyalty**
06 deceit
07 falsity, perfidy, treason
08 adultery, apostasy, betrayal, sedition
09 falseness, treachery
10 infidelity
11 inconstancy
13 breach of trust, double-dealing
14 perfidiousness, unfaithfulness

**dismal**
04 dark, drab, dull
05 bleak, dingy
06 dreary, gloomy, somber
07 forlorn
08 desolate, hopeless
09 cheerless, long-faced, miserable, sorrowful
10 depressing, despondent, lugubrious, melancholy

**dismantle**
05 strip
08 demolish, separate
09 pull apart, strip down, take apart
11 disassemble
12 take to pieces

**dismay**
04 fear

**dismember**

05 alarm, daunt, dread, scare, shock, upset, worry
06 fright, horror, put off, terror
07 concern, depress, disturb, horrify, perturb, unnerve
08 cast down, dispirit, distress, frighten, unsettle
09 agitation, take aback
10 disappoint, disconcert, discourage, dishearten
11 disillusion, trepidation
13 consternation
14 disappointment, discouragement

**dismember**

06 divide
07 break up, dissect
08 amputate, mutilate, separate

**dismiss**

02 ax
04 drop, fire, free, sack
05 expel, let go, spurn
06 lay off, reject, remove
07 boot out, cashier, kick out, release
08 discount, dissolve, relegate, send away, set aside, throw out
09 discharge, disregard
10 demobilize, give notice
11 send packing
13 make redundant
15 pour cold water on

**dismissal**

04 boot, push, sack
06 firing, notice, papers
07 removal, sacking, the gate, the sack
09 discharge, expulsion, laying-off
10 redundancy
11 the pink slip
13 walking papers
14 marching orders

**dismissive**

07 offhand
08 scornful, sneering
10 disdainful, dismissory
12 contemptuous

**dismount**

06 alight, get off
07 descend, get down

**disobedience**

06 mutiny, revolt
08 defiance
09 contumacy, rebellion
10 infraction, unruliness
11 contumacity, waywardness, willfulness
12 contrariness, indiscipline
13 recalcitrance

15 insubordination

**disobedient**

06 unruly
07 defiant, froward, naughty, wayward, willful
08 contrary, recusant
10 rebellious, refractory
11 intractable, mischievous
12 contumacious, obstreperous, recalcitrant
13 insubordinate

**disobey**

04 defy
05 flout, rebel
07 violate
08 infringe, overstep
10 contravene, transgress
13 step out of line

**disobliging**

04 rude
07 awkward, uncivil
09 unhelpful, unwilling
12 disagreeable, discourteous
13 uncooperative

**disorder**

04 mess, riot, rout
05 brawl, chaos, fight, melee
06 clamor, fracas, hubbub, malady, muddle, tumult, unrest, uproar
07 ailment, clutter, disease, illness, quarrel
08 brouhaha, disarray, shambles, sickness
09 commotion, complaint, condition, confusion
10 affliction, disability, disruption, untidiness
11 disturbance

**disordered**

05 messy, upset
06 untidy
07 jumbled, muddled
08 confused, troubled
09 cluttered, disturbed
10 unbalanced, upside-down
11 maladjusted
12 disorganized

**disorderly**

04 wild
05 messy, rough, rowdy
06 unruly, untidy
07 chaotic, jumbled, lawless
08 confused
09 cluttered, irregular, turbulent
10 in disarray, rebellious, refractory, tumultuous
12 disorganized, obstreperous
13 undisciplined

**disorganization**

05 chaos
06 muddle
08 disarray, disorder, shambles
09 confusion
10 disruption, untidiness

**disorganize**

05 mix up, upset
06 jumble, mess up, muddle
07 confuse, disrupt, disturb
08 disorder, unsettle
10 disarrange, discompose
13 play havoc with

**disorganized**

07 chaotic, jumbled, muddled
08 careless, confused, unsorted
09 haphazard
10 disordered, topsy-turvy
12 unstructured, unsystematic

**disorient, disorientate**

04 faze
05 upset
06 muddle, puzzle
07 confuse, mislead, perplex

**disoriented, disorientated**

04 lost
05 at sea, upset
06 adrift, astray
07 mixed up, muddled, puzzled
08 confused
09 perplexed, unsettled
10 bewildered, unbalanced

**disown**

04 deny
06 reject
07 abandon, disavow, forsake
08 abnegate, disclaim, renounce
09 repudiate
14 turn your back on

**disparage**

05 decry, scorn
06 defame, malign, vilify
07 disdain, run down, slander
08 belittle, derogate, minimize, ridicule, vilipend
09 criticize, denigrate, deprecate, discredit
10 calumniate, undervalue

**disparagement**

05 scorn
07 decrial, disdain, slander
08 contempt, decrying
09 aspersion, contumely, criticism, discredit
10 debasement, derogation, detraction
11 degradation, deprecation
12 belittlement, denunciation, vilification

## disparaging
05 snide
07 mocking
08 critical, derisive, scornful
09 insulting
10 derogatory, dismissive
11 deprecatory

## disparate
06 unlike
07 diverse, unequal
08 contrary, distinct
09 different
10 discrepant, dissimilar

## disparity
03 gap
04 bias, gulf
08 contrast, inequity
09 imbalance
10 difference, inequality
11 discrepancy, distinction
13 dissimilarity, dissimilitude

## dispassionate
04 calm, cool, fair
07 neutral
08 detached, unbiased
09 equitable, impartial,
   objective, unexcited
10 impersonal
11 unemotional
12 unprejudiced
13 disinterested, self-possessed
14 self-controlled

## dispatch, despatch
04 do in, kill, mail, post, send
05 haste, piece, remit, speed
06 convey, finish, letter, report
07 account, article, bump off,
   consign, execute, express,
   forward, message, perform
08 alacrity, celerity, conclude,
   expedite, transmit
09 discharge, dispose of,
   slaughter, swiftness
10 accelerate, communiqué,
   expedition, promptness
11 assassinate, promptitude
13 communication

## dispel
03 rid
04 rout
05 allay, expel
06 banish
07 dismiss, scatter
08 disperse, get rid of
09 dissipate, eliminate
11 disseminate

## dispensable
07 useless
10 disposable, expendable
11 inessential, replaceable,
   superfluous, unnecessary

12 nonessential

## dispensation
04 plan
05 issue, order
06 relief, scheme, system
07 economy, license, release
08 immunity, reprieve
09 authority, direction,
   endowment, exception,
   exemption, remission
10 allocation, permission
12 distribution, organization
13 apportionment
14 administration

## dispense
05 allot, apply, share
06 assign, bestow, confer
07 deal out, dole out, execute,
   give out, hand out, mete out
08 allocate, carry out, share out
09 apportion, discharge, divide
   out, implement
10 administer, distribute

## ❏ dispense with
04 omit
05 waive
06 cancel, forego, revoke
07 abolish, discard, rescind
08 get rid of, renounce
09 dispose of, disregard, do
   without

## disperse
06 dispel, spread
07 break up, diffuse, disband,
   dismiss, scatter, thin out
08 dissolve, melt away, separate
09 dissipate
10 distribute
11 disseminate

## dispersion
08 diaspora
09 broadcast, diffusion,
   dispersal, spreading
10 scattering
11 circulation, dissipation
12 distribution
13 dissemination

## dispirit
04 damp, dash
06 dampen, deject, sadden
07 depress
10 discourage, dishearten
12 put a damper on

## dispirited
03 low, sad
04 down, glum
05 fed up
06 gloomy, morose
08 cast down, dejected,
   downcast

09 depressed
10 browned off, despondent
11 crestfallen, discouraged
12 disheartened
14 down in the dumps

## displace
04 move, oust
05 eject, evict, expel, shift
06 depose, remove
07 boot out, dismiss
08 crowd out, dislodge, force
   out
09 dislocate, supersede

## displacement
06 ectopy, moving
07 ectopia
08 shifting
10 dislodging
11 dislocation, disturbance,
   heterotaxis, heterotopia
14 disarrangement

## display
04 show
05 array, boast
06 blazon, evince, expose,
   flaunt, parade, reveal
07 exhibit, pageant, present,
   promote, show off
08 disclose, evidence, manifest
09 advertise, publicize, put on
   show, spectacle
10 exhibition, revelation
11 demonstrate
12 presentation
13 demonstration,
   manifestation

## displease
03 bug, irk, vex
05 anger, annoy, upset
06 offend, put out
07 incense, perturb, provoke
10 discompose, dissatisfy

## displeased
05 angry, upset
06 peeved, piqued, put out
07 annoyed, furious
08 offended
09 irritated
11 disgruntled, exasperated

## displeasure
03 ire
05 anger, pique, wrath
07 chagrin, disgust, offense
08 disfavor
09 annoyance
10 irritation, resentment
11 disapproval, indignation
14 disapprobation,
   discontentment
15 dissatisfaction

**disport**
04 play, romp
05 amuse, cheer, frisk, revel
06 cavort, divert, frolic, gambol
07 delight
09 entertain

**disposable**
09 throwaway
10 expendable
13 nonreturnable

**disposal**
07 command, control, removal
08 grouping, riddance
09 clearance, scrapping
10 discarding
11 arrangement, jettisoning
12 throwing-away

❑ **at someone's disposal**
05 on tap, ready
06 at hand, to hand
09 available
10 obtainable

**dispose**
03 put
04 do in, dump, kill, shed
05 align, group, order, place
06 decide, finish, handle, line
   up, murder, settle, tackle
07 arrange, bump off, destroy,
   discard, situate, sort out
08 attend to, clear out, deal with,
   get rid of, jettison, organize,
   position, throw out
09 determine, throw away
10 do away with, put to death

**disposed**
03 apt
05 eager, prone, ready
06 liable, likely, minded
07 subject, willing
08 inclined, prepared

**disposition**
04 bent, mood
05 habit, humor, order
06 lineup, makeup, nature,
   spirit, temper
07 leaning, pattern, placing
08 disposal, grouping,
   sequence, tendency
09 alignment, character
10 allocation, conveyance,
   proclivity, propensity
11 arrangement, inclination,
   positioning, temperament
12 constitution, distribution,
   predilection

**dispossess**
03 rob
04 oust
05 eject, evict, expel, strip

06 divest
07 deprive
08 dislodge, take away

**disproportion**
09 asymmetry, imbalance
10 inadequacy, inequality,
   unevenness
11 discrepancy
12 lopsidedness
13 insufficiency

**disproportionate**
06 uneven
07 unequal
09 excessive
10 unbalanced
12 unreasonable
14 incommensurate
15 out of proportion

**disprove**
04 deny
05 rebut
06 debunk, negate, refute
07 confute
09 discredit
10 contradict, controvert,
   invalidate, prove false
12 give the lie to

**disputable**
04 moot
07 dubious
08 arguable, doubtful
09 debatable, uncertain
12 questionable
13 controversial

**disputation**
06 debate
07 dispute
08 argument, polemics
10 dissension
11 controversy

**disputatious**
08 captious
09 litigious, polemical
10 pugnacious
11 contentious, quarrelsome
13 argumentative

**dispute**
03 row
05 argue, clash, doubt
06 bicker, debate, strife
07 contend, contest, discuss,
   quarrel, wrangle
08 argument, conflict, question,
   squabble
09 challenge
11 altercation, controversy
12 disagreement

**disqualified**
08 debarred
09 precluded, struck off

10 eliminated, ineligible

**disqualify**
05 debar
07 disable, rule out, suspend
08 handicap, preclude, prohibit
09 eliminate
10 immobilize, invalidate

**disquiet**
03 vex
04 fear, fret
05 alarm, shake, upset, worry
06 bother, harass, ruffle
07 anxiety, concern, disturb,
   perturb, trouble, unnerve
08 distress, unsettle
09 agitation, incommode
10 discompose, foreboding,
   uneasiness
11 disquietude, disturbance,
   nervousness

**disquisition**
05 essay, paper
06 sermon, thesis
08 treatise
09 discourse, monograph
10 exposition
11 explanation
12 dissertation

**disregard**
05 flout
06 ignore, insult, slight
07 disdain, disobey, neglect
08 brush off, contempt,
   discount, laugh off, overlook,
   set aside
09 denigrate, disparage
10 brush aside, negligence
11 denigration, make light of
12 carelessness, indifference
14 take no notice of
15 turn a blind eye to

**disrepair**
04 ruin
05 decay
10 shabbiness
11 rack and ruin
12 dilapidation
13 deterioration

**disreputable**
03 low
04 base, mean
05 seedy, shady
06 shabby, shifty, untidy
07 corrupt, dubious, scruffy
08 infamous, shameful, slovenly,
   unworthy
10 outrageous, scandalous
11 disgraceful, ignominious
12 dishonorable
13 unrespectable

## disrepute
05 shame
06 infamy
07 obloquy
08 disgrace, dishonor, ignominy
09 discredit

## disrespect
05 cheek, scorn
08 contempt, dishonor, rudeness
09 disregard, impudence, insolence
11 discourtesy, irreverence
12 impertinence, impoliteness

## disrespectful
04 rude
05 sassy
06 cheeky
08 impolite, impudent, insolent
09 insulting
10 irreverent, unmannerly
11 impertinent
12 contemptuous, discourteous

## disrobe
04 bare, shed
05 strip
06 denude, divest, remove
07 take off, uncover, undress
08 unclothe
10 disapparel

## disrupt
05 upset
07 break up, confuse, disturb
08 sabotage, unsettle
09 interrupt
10 disarrange
11 disorganize
13 interfere with

## disruption
05 upset
07 turmoil
08 disorder, stoppage, upheaval
09 confusion
11 disturbance
12 interference, interruption
14 disorderliness
15 disorganization

## disruptive
05 noisy
06 unruly
09 turbulent, upsetting
10 boisterous, disorderly, disturbing, unsettling
11 distracting, troublesome

## dissatisfaction
06 regret
07 chagrin, dislike
08 vexation
09 annoyance

10 discomfort, discontent, irritation, resentment
11 disapproval, displeasure, frustration, unhappiness
12 exasperation, restlessness
14 disappointment, disapprobation

## dissatisfied
05 angry, fed up, irked, vexed
07 annoyed, unhappy
09 irritated
10 displeased, frustrated
11 disgruntled, exasperated
12 disappointed, discontented, malcontented

## dissatisfy
03 vex
05 anger, annoy
06 put out
08 irritate
09 displease, frustrate
10 disappoint, discontent

## dissect
05 cut up, probe, study
07 analyze, examine, inspect
08 pore over, vivisect
09 anatomize, break down, dismember
10 scrutinize
11 investigate

## dissection
05 probe, study
07 autopsy
08 analysis, necropsy, scrutiny
09 breakdown, cutting up
10 inspection
11 examination, vivisection
13 dismemberment, investigation

## dissemble
04 fake, hide, mask, sham
05 cloak, feign
06 affect
07 conceal, falsify, pretend
08 disguise, simulate
10 camouflage, play possum
11 counterfeit, dissimulate

## dissembler
04 fake
05 fraud
07 feigner
08 deceiver, impostor
09 charlatan, pretender

## disseminate
03 sow
06 spread
07 diffuse, publish, scatter
08 disperse, proclaim
09 broadcast, circulate
10 distribute, promulgate

## dissemination
06 spread
09 diffusion
10 dispersion, publishing
11 circulation, propagation
12 broadcasting, distribution, promulgation

## dissension
06 strife
07 discord, dissent, quarrel
08 argument, conflict, friction
12 disagreement

## dissent
06 differ, object, refuse
07 discord, dispute, protest
08 disagree, friction
09 objection
10 difference, dissension, opposition, resistance
12 disagreement

## dissenter
05 rebel
07 heretic, sectary
08 objector, recusant
09 dissident, protester
10 protestant, schismatic
13 nonconformist, revolutionary

## dissentient
08 opposing, recusant
09 differing, dissident, heretical
10 dissenting, rebellious
11 conflicting, disagreeing

## dissertation
05 essay, paper
06 thesis
08 critique, treatise
09 discourse, monograph
10 exposition
12 disquisition, propaedeutic

## disservice
04 harm, hurt
05 wrong
06 injury
07 bad turn
08 disfavor
09 injustice
10 dirty trick, unkindness
14 kick in the teeth

## dissidence
04 feud
06 schism
07 dispute, dissent, rupture
08 variance
09 recusancy
11 discordance
12 disagreement

## dissident
05 rebel
07 heretic

**dissimilar**
08 agitator, objector, recusant
09 differing, dissenter, protester
10 discordant, dissenting, protesting, rebellious
11 conflicting, disagreeing
13 nonconformist, revolutionary

**dissimilar**
06 unlike
07 diverse, various, varying
08 distinct
09 different, disparate, divergent, unrelated
13 heterogeneous

**dissimilarity**
09 disparity, diversity
10 difference, unlikeness
11 discrepancy, distinction
13 dissimilitude, heterogeneity

**dissimulate**
03 lie
04 fake, hide, mask
05 cloak, feign
06 affect
07 conceal, cover up, pretend
08 disguise
09 dissemble

**dissipate**
05 drain, spend, use up, waste
06 burn up, dispel, vanish
07 break up, consume, deplete, diffuse, exhaust, scatter
08 disperse, dissolve, melt away, squander
09 disappear, evaporate
11 fritter away

**dissipated**
04 wild
06 rakish, wasted
08 depraved
09 debauched, dissolute
10 degenerate, licentious, profligate
11 intemperate

**dissipation**
06 excess
07 license
09 depletion, depravity, diffusion, dispersal
10 corruption, debauchery
11 consumption, evaporation, expenditure, prodigality, squandering
12 extravagance, intemperance
13 disappearance
14 licentiousness, self-indulgence

**dissociate**
04 part, quit
05 sever
06 cut off, detach, secede
07 break up, disband, disrupt, divorce, isolate
08 break off, distance, disunite, separate, withdraw
09 disengage, segregate
10 disconnect
12 disassociate

**dissociation**
05 break, split
07 divorce, parting
08 disunion, division, severing
09 isolation, severance
10 cutting-off, detachment, distancing, separation
11 dissevering, segregation
13 disconnection, disengagement

**dissolute**
04 lewd, wild
06 rakish, wanton
07 corrupt, immoral
08 depraved
09 abandoned, debauched
10 degenerate, dissipated, licentious, profligate
11 intemperate
13 self-indulgent

**dissolution**
06 ending
07 breakup, divorce
08 collapse, disposal, division
09 annulment, overthrow
10 conclusion, suspension
11 destruction, evaporation
13 decomposition
14 disintegration
15 discontinuation

**dissolve**
03 end
04 melt
05 begin, break, burst, start
06 finish, vanish, wind up
07 break up, disband, liquefy
08 collapse, disperse, evanesce, melt away
09 dissipate, evaporate
10 deliquesce
12 bring to an end, disintegrate

**dissonance**
05 clash
06 jangle
07 discord, grating, jarring
08 variance
09 cacophony, harshness
10 disharmony, dissension
11 discordance, incongruity
12 disagreement
13 inconsistency

**dissonant**
05 harsh
07 grating, jarring, raucous
08 clashing, jangling, tuneless
09 anomalous, unmusical
10 discordant
11 cacophonous, disagreeing
12 incompatible, inconsistent

**dissuade**
04 stop
05 deter
06 put off
09 talk out of
10 discourage, disincline

**dissuasion**
09 deterring
10 deterrence
12 remonstrance
13 expostulation, remonstration
14 discouragement

**distance**
03 gap
04 span
05 break, depth, range, reach, space, width
06 cut off, extent, height, length, remove, secede
07 breadth, reserve, stretch
08 coldness, coolness, separate
09 aloofness, formality, stiffness
10 dissociate, separation
14 unfriendliness

**distant**
03 far
04 cold, cool
05 aloof, stiff
06 far-off, formal, remote
07 faraway
08 detached, far-flung, not close, outlying, reserved
10 antisocial, unfriendly
11 out-of-the-way, stand-offish
12 unresponsive
14 unapproachable
15 uncommunicative

**distaste**
06 horror
07 disgust, dislike
08 aversion, loathing
09 antipathy, revulsion
10 abhorrence, repugnance
11 displeasure

**distasteful**
08 unsavory
09 loathsome, obnoxious, offensive, repellent, repugnant, repulsive, revolting
10 disgusting, unpleasant
11 displeasing, undesirable
12 disagreeable
13 objectionable

## distend
04 puff
05 bloat, bulge, swell, widen
06 dilate, expand
07 balloon, enlarge, fill out, inflate, stretch
09 intumesce

## distended
05 puffy
07 bloated, dilated, swollen
08 enlarged, expanded, inflated, varicose
09 puffed-out, stretched, tumescent

## distension
06 spread
08 bloating, dilation, swelling
09 expansion, extension
10 tumescence
11 enlargement
12 intumescence

## distill
04 brew, drip, flow, leak
06 derive, purify, refine
07 draw out, express, extract
08 condense, vaporize
09 evaporate, sublimate

## distillation
06 spirit
07 brewing, essence, extract
10 extraction
11 evaporation
12 condensation

## distinct
05 clear, plain, sharp
06 marked
07 defined, evident, obvious
08 apparent, clear-cut, definite, discrete, separate
09 different, disparate
10 dissimilar, noticeable
11 unambiguous, well-defined
12 recognizable, unmistakable

## distinction
04 fame, mark
05 merit, worth
06 credit, renown, repute
07 feature, quality
08 eminence, prestige
09 celebrity, greatness
10 difference, importance, reputation, separation
11 discernment, peculiarity
12 significance
13 dissimilarity, individuality
14 discrimination
15 differentiation

## distinctive
07 special, typical
08 original, peculiar, singular

09 different
10 individual, particular
13 extraordinary, idiosyncratic
14 characteristic, distinguishing

## distinctly
07 clearly, plainly
08 markedly
09 evidently, obviously
10 definitely, noticeably
12 unmistakably
13 unambiguously

## distinguish
03 see
04 mark
05 excel, stamp
06 descry, detect, notice
07 discern, make out, mark off, pick out
08 classify, identify, perceive
09 ascertain, determine, recognize, single out, tell apart
10 categorize
12 characterize, discriminate
13 differentiate

## distinguishable
07 evident, obvious
10 noticeable, observable
11 appreciable, conspicuous, discernible, perceptible
12 recognizable

## distinguished
05 famed, noble, noted
06 famous, marked
07 eminent, notable, refined
08 esteemed, renowned
09 acclaimed, well-known
10 celebrated
11 conspicuous, illustrious
13 extraordinary

## distinguishing
06 marked, unique
07 typical
08 peculiar, singular
09 different
10 individual
11 diacritical, distinctive
14 characteristic, discriminatory
15 differentiating

## distort
04 bend, bias, warp
05 color, slant, twist
06 buckle, deform
07 contort, falsify, pervert
08 misshape
09 disfigure
12 misrepresent

## distorted
03 wry
04 awry, bent, skew

06 biased, skewed, warped
07 twisted
08 deformed
09 misshapen, perverted
10 disfigured, out of shape

## distortion
04 bend, bias, skew, warp
05 slant, twist
06 buckle
08 coloring, garbling, twisting
09 deformity
10 contortion, perversion
11 crookedness

## distract
05 amuse
06 divert, put off, puzzle
07 confuse, deflect, disturb, engross, fluster, perplex
08 bewilder, confound, draw away, turn away
09 entertain, sidetrack
10 discompose, disconcert

## distracted
03 mad
04 wild
05 crazy, upset
06 raving
07 anxious, frantic
08 agitated, worked up
09 miles away, not with it
10 abstracted, distraught, distressed, hysterical
11 inattentive, overwrought, preoccupied
12 absent-minded
14 beside yourself

## distracting
08 annoying
09 confusing
10 disturbing, irritating, perturbing
13 disconcerting

## distraction
04 game
05 hobby, sport
07 pastime
09 amusement, diversion
10 recreation
11 derangement, disturbance
13 entertainment
14 divertissement

## ▫drive someone to distraction
05 anger, annoy, upset
06 madden
10 drive crazy, exasperate

## distraught
03 mad
04 wild
05 crazy, het up, upset

**distress**
06 raving
07 anxious, frantic
08 agitated, in a state, worked up
10 distracted, distressed, hysterical
11 overwrought
14 beside yourself

**distress**
03 vex, woe
04 hurt, need, pain
05 agony, trial, upset, worry
06 grieve, harrow, penury, sadden, sorrow, unease
07 afflict, agonize, anguish, anxiety, disturb, perturb, sadness, trouble
08 calamity, hardship
09 adversity, heartache, indigence, suffering
10 affliction, desolation
11 make anxious, tribulation
12 difficulties, perturbation

**distribute**
04 deal
05 allot, issue, share
06 divide, spread, supply
07 deal out, deliver, diffuse, dish out, dole out, give out, hand out, mete out, scatter
08 allocate, dispense, disperse
09 circulate
10 pass around
11 disseminate

**distribution**
06 supply
07 dealing, sharing
08 delivery, division, handling
09 dispersal, placement, spreading
10 allocation, conveyance, scattering
11 arrangement, circulation
13 dissemination

**district**
04 area, ward, zone
05 block, place
06 parish, region, sector
07 quarter
08 locality, precinct, vicinity
11 subdivision
12 constituency, neighborhood

**distrust**
05 doubt, qualm
07 suspect
08 mistrust, question, wariness
09 chariness, discredit, misgiving, suspicion
10 disbelieve, skepticism
11 questioning
12 doubtfulness

14 be suspicious of
15 have doubts about

**distrustful**
04 wary
05 chary
06 uneasy
07 cynical, dubious
08 doubtful, doubting
09 skeptical
10 suspicious, untrusting
12 disbelieving

**disturb**
04 stir
05 annoy, upset, worry
06 bother, dismay, pester, stir up
07 agitate, confuse, disrupt, fluster, perturb, trouble
08 distract, distress, unsettle
09 discomfit, interrupt
10 disarrange, disconcert
11 disorganize, make anxious

**disturbance**
03 row
04 fray, riot
05 brawl, upset
06 bother, fracas, hubbub, racket, rumpus, tumult, uproar
07 illness, trouble, turmoil
08 disorder, neurosis, upheaval
09 agitation, annoyance, commotion, intrusion
10 disruption, hullabaloo
11 distraction
12 interference, interruption

**disturbed**
05 upset
06 hung-up, uneasy
07 anxious, worried
08 bothered, confused, neurotic, paranoid, troubled
09 concerned, flustered, psychotic, screwed-up
10 unbalanced
11 discomposed, maladjusted

**disturbing**
08 alarming, worrying
09 agitating, confusing, dismaying, startling, troubling, upsetting
10 perturbing, unsettling
11 bewildering, disquieting, distressing, frightening
13 disconcerting

**disunited**
05 split
07 divided
08 divorced
09 alienated, disrupted, estranged, separated

**disunity**
05 split
06 breach, schism, strife
07 discord, dissent, rupture
08 conflict, division
10 alienation, dissension
12 disagreement, estrangement

**disuse**
07 neglect
09 desuetude
11 abandonment

**disused**
06 unused
09 abandoned, neglected

**ditch**
04 drop, dump, dyke, junk, moat
05 canal, drain, gully, scrap
06 furrow, gutter, trench
07 abandon, channel, discard
08 get rid of, jettison, throw out
09 dispose of, throw away
11 watercourse

**dither**
04 flap, fuss, stew
05 delay, panic, quake, shake, tizzy, waver
06 bother, pother
07 fluster, flutter
08 hang back, hesitate
09 confusion, vacillate
10 dillydally, indecision
12 be in two minds, shilly-shally, take your time

**divan**
04 café, sofa
05 couch
06 daybed, lounge, settee
07 chamber, lounger, ottoman
12 chaise longue, chesterfield

**dive**
03 bar, dip, fly
04 club, dart, dash, drop, fall, hole, rush, tear
05 hurry, joint, lunge, swoop
06 go down, plunge
07 descend, go under, plummet
08 nose dive, submerge
09 nightclub, roadhouse

**diverge**
04 fork, part, vary
05 clash, drift, split, stray
06 branch, depart, differ, divide, spread, wander
07 deviate, digress, radiate
08 disagree, divagate, separate
09 bifurcate, branch off
10 contradict
12 be at variance

**divergence**
05 clash

07 parting
08 conflict
09 departure, deviation
10 deflection, difference, digression, separation
12 branching-out

**divergent**
07 diverse, variant, varying
08 separate
09 deviating, different, differing
10 tangential

**divers**
04 many, some
07 several, various, varying
08 manifold, numerous

**diverse**
05 mixed
06 sundry, unlike, varied
07 several, various, varying
08 assorted, discrete, distinct
09 different, differing
10 all means of, dissimilar
13 heterogeneous, miscellaneous

**diversify**
04 vary
06 assort, change, expand, extend, modify
09 branch out, spread out, variegate

**diversion**
03 fun
04 game, play
05 hobby, sport
06 change
07 pastime
09 amusement, deviation
10 recreation
11 distraction, redirection
13 entertainment
14 divertissement

**diversionary**
09 divertive
11 distracting

**diversity**
05 range
06 medley
07 mixture, variety
10 assortment, difference
11 variegation
13 dissimilarity, dissimilitude, heterogeneity

**divert**
05 amuse, avert
06 absorb, occupy, switch
07 deflect, delight
08 distract, draw away, interest, intrigue, redirect, turn away
09 entertain, sidetrack

**diverting**
03 fun
05 funny, witty
07 amusing
08 humorous, pleasant
09 enjoyable
11 pleasurable
12 entertaining

**divest**
04 doff
05 strip
06 denude, remove
07 deprive, disrobe, undress
10 dispossess

**divide**
03 cut
04 fork, part, rank, sort
05 cut up, group, sever, split
06 bisect, branch, detach
07 arrange, break up, deal out, diverge, hand out, split up
08 alienate, classify, dispense, disunite, estrange, separate
09 break down, segregate
10 disconnect, distribute
11 come between

❑**divide up**
05 allot, share
07 dole out
08 allocate, share out
10 measure out

**dividend**
03 cut
04 gain, plus
05 bonus, extra, share
07 benefit, portion, surplus
08 interest

**divination**
05 -mancy
06 augury, mantic
07 presage
08 prophecy, taghairm
09 astrology
10 hydromancy, numerology, prediction
11 foretelling, rhabdomancy, second sight, soothsaying
12 clairvoyance
14 fortunetelling
15 prognostication

**divine**
04 holy
05 godly, guess, infer
06 cleric, deduce, intuit, lovely, parson, pastor, priest, sacred
07 angelic, exalted, godlike, prelate, saintly, suppose, supreme, surmise, suspect
08 heavenly, minister, mystical, perceive, reverend, seraphic

09 beautiful, celestial, churchman, clergyman, religious, spiritual
10 sanctified, understand
11 clergywoman, consecrated
12 ecclesiastic, supernatural, transcendent
13 prognosticate

**diviner**
04 seer
05 augur, sibyl
06 dowser, oracle
07 prophet
08 haruspex
09 divinator
10 astrologer, soothsayer

**divinity**
03 god
05 candy, deity
06 spirit
07 goddess, godhead
08 holiness, religion, sanctity, theology
09 godliness

**division**
03 arm
04 feud, part, rift, zone
05 class, group, split
06 border, branch, breach, divide, schism, sector
07 chapter, cutting, discord, parting, rupture, section, segment
08 boundary, category, conflict, disunion, dividing, frontier
09 allotment, cutting up, partition, severance
10 alienation, allocation, department, separation
11 compartment
12 disagreement, distribution, dividing line, estrangement

**divisive**
08 damaging
09 injurious
10 alienating, discordant, disruptive, estranging
11 troublesome
13 troublemaking

**divorce**
04 part
05 annul, sever, split
06 breach, detach, divide
07 break up, rupture, split up, split-up
08 dissolve, disunite, separate
09 annulment, partition, severance
10 disconnect, dissociate, separation

**divulge**
04 leak, tell
06 betray, impart, reveal, tattle
07 confess, declare, let slip,
   publish, uncover
08 disclose, proclaim
09 broadcast, make known
11 communicate
12 break the news
13 spill the beans

**dizzy**
05 dazed, ditsy, ditzy, faint,
   giddy, shaky, silly, woozy
07 foolish, muddled, reeling
08 confused
10 bewildered, off-balance
11 lightheaded, vertiginous
14 featherbrained,
   scatterbrained

**do**
03 act, end, fix
04 go at, have, make, read, take,
   work
05 cause, crack, get on, learn,
   offer, put on, reach, serve,
   study
06 affair, behave, come on,
   create, finish, manage,
   master, supply, tackle, work
   as, work at, work on
07 achieve, arrange, execute,
   fulfill, perform, prepare,
   present, proceed, produce,
   provide, satisfy, suffice
08 be enough, carry out,
   complete, conclude, deal
   with, get along, organize,
   progress
09 discharge, implement,
   undertake
10 accomplish, be adequate,
   effectuate, fit the bill
12 be sufficient, take for a ride
14 be satisfactory

❏**do away with**
04 do in, kill, slay
06 murder, remove
07 abolish, bump off, discard
08 get rid of, knock off
09 dispose of, eliminate
11 assassinate, discontinue,
   exterminate

❏**do in**
04 kill, slay
06 murder
07 bump off
08 knock off
09 slaughter
11 assassinate, exterminate

❏**do out of**
06 fleece

08 con out of
09 deprive of
10 cheat out of, trick out of
11 diddle out of
12 swindle out of

❏**dos and don'ts**
04 code
05 rules
07 customs
09 etiquette, standards
11 regulations
12 instructions

❏**do up**
03 tie
04 lace, pack
05 zip up
06 button, fasten, repair
07 restore
08 decorate, renovate
09 modernize
10 redecorate
11 recondition

❏**do without**
05 forgo
06 forego, give up
09 go without
10 relinquish
11 abstain from
12 deny yourself, dispense with
13 manage without

**docile**
08 amenable, obedient,
   obliging, yielding
09 compliant, tractable
10 controlled, manageable
11 cooperative
12 controllable

**docility**
07 pliancy
08 meekness
09 ductility, obedience
10 compliance, pliability
11 amenability
12 biddableness, complaisance,
   tractability
13 manageability
14 submissiveness

**dock**
03 cut
04 clip, crop, moor, pier, quay,
   slip
05 berth, jetty, tie up, wharf
06 anchor, deduct, harbor,
   lessen, marina, reduce,
   remove
07 curtail, shorten
08 boatyard, decrease, subtract,
   truncate, withhold
10 drop anchor, waterfront

**docket**
04 file, list
06 agenda
07 program
08 schedule
11 trial docket

**doctor**
03 doc, JSD, PhD
04 drug, lace, mend
05 bones, medic, quack, spike,
   treat
06 dilute, medico, repair, shrink,
   weaken
07 falsify, pervert
08 disguise, sawbones
09 clinician, physician
10 adulterate, consultant
11 contaminate
13 interfere with
14 medical officer
➤ See also MEDICAL

━ *Types of doctor*:
02 GP, MO
03 vet
06 intern
07 dentist, oculist, surgeon
08 resident
09 herbalist, osteopath,
   otologist
10 consultant, pediatrist,
   podiatrist, specialist
11 chiropodist, medicine man,
   neurologist, witch doctor
12 cardiologist, family doctor,
   gynecologist, obstetrician,
   orthodontist, pediatrician,
   psychiatrist, veterinarian
13 dermatologist
14 medical officer

━ *Names of doctors*:
04 **Bell** (Charles), **Koch**
   (Robert), **Lind** (James),
   **Mayo** (Charles), **Mayo**
   (William), **Reed** (Walter),
   **Ross** (Ronald), **Salk** (Jonas)
05 **Broca** (Paul Pierre), **Bruce**
   (David), **Galen, Paget**
   (James), **Spock** (Benjamin),
   **Steno** (Nicolaus)
06 **Bichat** (Marie François
   Xavier), **Bright** (Richard),
   **Carrel** (Alexis), **Celsus**
   (Aulus Cornelius), **Cooper**
   (Astley), **Garrod** (Archibald
   Edward), **Gorgas** (William),
   **Harvey** (William), **Hunter**
   (John), **Jenner** (Edward),
   **Lister** (Joseph), **Manson**
   (Patrick), **Mesmer** (Franz
   Anton)
07 **Addison** (Thomas),

Barnard (Christian Neethling), **Cushing** (Harvey Williams), **Gilbert** (William), **Winston** (Robert)
08 **Anderson** (Elizabeth Garrett), **Beaumont** (William), **Billroth** (Theodor), **Charnley** (John), **Duchenne** (Guillaume Benjamin Amand), **Tournier** (Paul)
09 **Bartholin** (Erasmus), **Dutrochet** (Henri), **Hahnemann** (Samuel), **Parkinson** (James)
10 **Paracelsus**, **Sanctorius**
11 **Hippocrates**
12 **Erasistratus**
➤ See also SURGEON

## doctrinaire
05 rigid
08 dogmatic, pedantic
09 fanatical, insistent
10 inflexible

## doctrine
05 canon, credo, creed, dogma, tenet
08 teaching
09 principle

## document
04 cite, deed, form, list
05 chart, paper, proof, prove
06 record, report, verify
07 charter, support
08 contract, evidence, register, validate
09 affidavit, chronicle
11 certificate, corroborate, put on record
12 give weight to, keep on record, substantiate

## documentary
07 charted, written
08 detailed, recorded
09 TV program
10 chronicled

## doddering
04 aged, weak
05 frail
06 feeble, infirm
08 decrepit
09 tottering

## doddery
04 aged, weak
05 shaky
06 feeble, infirm
07 tottery
08 unsteady
09 doddering, faltering

## dodge
04 duck, ploy, ruse, shun, wile
05 avoid, elude, evade, shift, shirk, trick
06 bypass, scheme, swerve
08 get out of, jump away, maneuver, side step
09 deception, get around
10 subterfuge
11 contrivance, machination

## dodger
06 evader
07 dreamer, shirker, slacker
08 circular, handbill, layabout, slyboots
09 goldbrick, lazybones, throwaway, trickster
10 corndodger

## doer
06 dynamo, worker
08 achiever, activist, executor
09 organizer
20 powerhouse workaholic

## doff
03 tip
04 lift, shed
05 raise, touch
06 remove
07 discard, take off

## dog
03 cur, pup
04 mutt, tail
05 bitch, harry, hound, pooch, puppy, track, trail, worry
06 canine, follow, plague, pursue, shadow, wretch
07 mongrel, trouble, villain
09 scoundrel
➤ See also ANIMAL

➤ *Breeds of dog*:
03 Pom, pug
04 chow, Peke
05 boxer, corgi, dingo, husky
06 basset, beagle, borzoi, collie, gun dog, poodle, saluki, setter, Westie, Yorkie
07 bulldog, griffon, lurcher, Maltese, mastiff, pit bull, pointer, Scottie, sheltie, shih tzu, spaniel, terrier, whippet
08 Airedale, Alsatian, Doberman, foxhound, Labrador, Pekinese, Sealyham, sheepdog
09 chihuahua, dachshund, Dalmatian, Great Dane, greyhound, Pekingese, retriever, Schnauzer, St. Bernard, wolfhound
10 bloodhound, fox terrier, Pomeranian, Rottweiler

11 Afghan hound, basset hound, bull mastiff, bull terrier, Jack Russell
12 Border collie, cairn terrier, Newfoundland
13 cocker spaniel
14 German Shepherd, Irish wolfhound, pit bull terrier
15 golden retriever, Scottish terrier, springer spaniel

➤ *Names of famous dogs*:
04 Asta, Nana, Odie, Shep, Toto
05 Argos, Butch, Daisy, Falla, Goofy, Laika, Pluto, Pongo, Spike
06 Droopy, Gromit, Hector, Lassie, Snoopy
07 Perdita
08 Bullseye, Cerberus, Checkers
09 Marmaduke, Old Yeller, Rin Tin Tin, Scooby Doo
10 Deputy Dawg, Fred Basset
15 Greyfriars Bobby

## dogged
06 intent, steady
08 obdurate, resolute, stubborn, tireless
09 obstinate, steadfast, tenacious
10 determined, persistent, relentless, unflagging, unshakable, unyielding
11 persevering, unfaltering
12 pertinacious, single-minded
13 indefatigable

## doggedness
08 firmness, tenacity
09 endurance, obstinacy
10 resolution, steadiness
11 persistence, pertinacity
12 perseverance, stubbornness
13 determination, steadfastness, tenaciousness
14 indomitability, relentlessness

## dogma
04 code
05 credo, creed, maxim, tenet
06 belief
07 article, opinion, precept
08 doctrine, teaching
09 principle
10 conviction
12 code of belief
14 article of faith

## dogmatic
08 arrogant, emphatic, positive
09 arbitrary, assertive, canonical, doctrinal, imperious, insistent
10 ex cathedra, pontifical

**dogmatism**
11 categorical, doctrinaire, domineering, opinionated
13 authoritarian, authoritative

**dogmatism**
07 bigotry
11 presumption
13 arbitrariness, assertiveness, imperiousness
14 peremptoriness

**doings**
04 acts
05 deeds, feats
06 events
07 actions, affairs
08 concerns, dealings, exploits
09 handiwork
10 activities, adventures
11 enterprises, proceedings
12 achievements, transactions

**doldrums**
05 blues, dumps, ennui, gloom
06 acedia, apathy, torpor
07 boredom, inertia, malaise
08 dullness
09 dejection, lassitude
10 depression, stagnation
12 listlessness, sluggishness

**dole**
06 credit, income, relief
07 benefit, payment, support
09 allowance
14 social security

❏**dole out**
04 deal
05 allot, issue, share
06 assign, divide, ration
07 deal out, dish out, give out, hand out, mete out
08 allocate, dispense, divide up, share out
09 apportion
10 administer, distribute

**doleful**
03 sad
04 blue
06 dismal, dreary, gloomy, rueful, somber, woeful
07 forlorn, painful, pitiful
08 dolorous, mournful, pathetic, wretched
09 cheerless, miserable, sorrowful, woebegone
10 depressing, lugubrious, melancholy
12 disconsolate
14 down in the dumps

**doll**
03 Ken, toy
04 babe, baby, dame
05 broad, chick, dolly, woman

06 Barbie, figure, Kewpie, puppet
08 figurine
09 paper doll, plaything
10 marionette, Raggedy Ann, voodoo doll
11 Raggedy Andy
12 action figure

❏**doll up**
05 preen, primp
07 deck out, dress up
08 titivate, trick out

**dollop**
03 gob
04 ball, blob, dash, dram, glob, lump, shot
06 jigger

**dolorous**
03 sad
06 rueful, somber, woeful
07 doleful, painful
08 grievous, mournful, wretched
09 anguished, harrowing, miserable, sorrowful, woebegone
10 lugubrious, melancholy
12 heart-rending

**dolor**
05 grief
06 misery, sorrow
07 anguish, sadness
08 distress, mourning
09 heartache, suffering
10 heartbreak
11 lamentation

**dolt**
03 ass
04 clod, dope, fool, nerd
05 chump, dunce, idiot, ninny, twerp
06 dimwit, nitwit
08 dipstick, dumbbell, imbecile, numskull
09 blockhead, simpleton
10 nincompoop

**domain**
04 area
05 field, lands, realm, world
06 empire, region, sphere
07 concern, kingdom, section
08 dominion, province
09 specialty, territory
10 discipline
12 jurisdiction

**dome**
04 roof
05 mound, vault
06 cupola
07 rotunda

10 hemisphere

**domestic**
03 pet
04 cook, home, maid, tame
06 au pair, family, native
07 private, servant
08 internal, personal
09 charwoman, household
10 home-loving, indigenous
11 domiciliary, housebroken

**domesticate**
04 tame
05 break, train
07 break in
09 acclimate, habituate
10 housebreak, naturalize
11 acclimatize, familiarize

**domesticated**
03 pet
04 tame
05 tamed
08 broken in, domestic
11 housebroken, housewifely, naturalized

**domesticity**
08 home life
10 family life, homemaking
12 housekeeping

**domicile**
04 home
05 abode, house
07 lodging, mansion
08 dwelling, lodgings, quarters
09 residence, residency
10 habitation, settlement
15 take up residence

**dominance**
04 rule, sway
05 power
07 command, control, mastery
08 hegemony
09 authority, supremacy
10 ascendancy, government
11 preeminence

**dominant**
03 key
04 main
05 chief, major, prime
06 ruling, strong
07 leading, primary, supreme
09 assertive, prevalent, principal, prominent
10 preeminent, prevailing
11 outstanding, predominant
13 authoritative

**dominate**
04 lead, rule
06 direct, govern, master
07 control, eclipse, prevail

**domination**
08 domineer, overbear, overlook, overrule
09 tower over, tyrannize
10 monopolize, overshadow
11 predominate

**domination**
04 rule, sway
05 power
07 command, control, tyranny
09 despotism, supremacy
10 ascendancy, oppression, repression, subjection
11 preeminence, superiority, suppression
12 dictatorship, predominance
13 subordination

**domineering**
05 bossy, pushy
08 arrogant, coercive, despotic, forceful
09 imperious, masterful
10 autocratic, highhanded, oppressive, tyrannical
11 dictatorial, overbearing
13 authoritarian

**dominion**
04 rule, sway
05 power, realm
06 colony, domain, empire
07 command, control, country, kingdom, mastery
08 lordship, province
09 authority, direction, supremacy, territory
11 sovereignty
12 jurisdiction

**don**
04 wear
05 put on
06 clothe, invest
07 dress in
08 slip into

**Don Juan**
04 rake
05 lover, Romeo
06 gigolo
08 Casanova
09 ladies' man, philander, womanizer
10 lady-killer
11 philanderer

**donate**
04 give
06 bestow, chip in, pledge
07 cough up, fork out, present
08 give away, shell out
09 make a gift, subscribe
10 contribute

**donation**
04 alms, gift

07 bequest, charity, largess, present
08 gratuity, largesse, offering
11 benefaction
12 contribution, presentation

**done**
02 OK
04 okay, over
05 baked, ended, ready, right
06 agreed, boiled, cooked, proper, seemly, stewed
07 decided, fitting, settled
08 accepted, arranged, complete, decorous, executed, finished, prepared, realized, suitable
09 completed, concluded, fulfilled
10 acceptable, terminated
11 appropriate, consummated
12 accomplished, conventional

❏**done for**
04 lost
05 kaput
06 broken, dashed, doomed, foiled, killed, ruined, undone
07 wrecked
08 defeated, finished
09 destroyed

❏**done in**
04 dead
05 all in, weary
06 bushed, pooped, zonked
08 dead beat, dog-tired, fatigued, tired out
09 exhausted, fagged out, shattered, zonked out
14 on your last legs

❏**have done with**
08 over with
12 finished with

**donkey**
03 ass
04 mule
05 burro, hinny, jenny
07 jackass

**donor**
05 angel, giver
06 backer
07 donator, grantor
10 benefactor
11 contributor
14 fairy godmother

**doom**
03 lot
04 damn, fate, ruin
05 death, judge
07 condemn, consign, destine, destiny, portion, verdict
08 judgment

09 ruination
11 destruction, rack and ruin

**doomed**
05 fated
06 cursed, damned, ruined
07 unlucky
08 destined, hopeless, ill-fated, luckless
09 bedeviled, condemned, ill-omened
11 star-crossed

**door**
04 exit, road
05 entry, hatch, route, way in
06 access, portal
07 doorway, gateway, opening
08 entrance, entryway, open door
11 entranceway

**doorkeeper**
06 porter
07 doorman, janitor, ostiary
09 concierge
10 gatekeeper
14 commissionaire

**dope**
01 E
03 LSD, pot
04 acid, clod, coke, dolt, drug, fool, hash, info, junk, weed
05 crack, drugs, dunce, facts, ganja, grass, idiot, ninny, speed
06 dimwit, doctor, heroin, inject, nitwit, opiate, sedate
07 cocaine, Ecstasy, half-wit, lowdown
08 cannabis, narcotic
09 blockhead, marijuana
10 nincompoop
11 amphetamine, anesthetize, barbiturate, information, particulars
12 hallucinogen

**dopey**
04 daft, dozy
05 daxed
06 drowsy, groggy, simple, sleepy, stupid, torpid
07 foolish, nodding
08 confused
09 lethargic, somnolent

**dormant**
05 inert
06 asleep, fallow, latent, torpid
07 resting
08 comatose, inactive, sleeping, sluggish
10 slumbering, unrealized
11 hibernating, undeveloped

**dose**
04 shot
05 draft
06 amount, dosage, potion
07 measure, portion
08 medicate, quantity

**dot**
03 dab, jot
04 atom, iota, mark, spot, stud
05 fleck, point, speck
06 period
07 scatter, speckle, stipple
08 particle, pinpoint, sprinkle
12 decimal point

**▢on the dot**
05 sharp
08 promptly
09 precisely
10 punctually
13 exactly on time

**dotage**
06 old age
08 senility, weakness
10 feebleness, imbecility
11 decrepitude
15 second childhood

**dote**
**▢dote on**
05 adore, spoil
06 admire, pamper
07 idolize, indulge, worship
08 hold dear, treasure

**doting**
04 fond, soft
06 loving, tender
07 adoring, devoted
09 indulgent
12 affectionate

**dotty**
04 daft
05 barmy, batty, crazy, goofy, potty, shaky, wacky
06 feeble
07 touched
08 peculiar
09 eccentric
12 feeble-minded

**double**
04 copy, dual, fold, twin
05 binal, clone, match, twice
06 binate, paired, repeat, ringer, two-ply
07 coupled, doubled, magnify, replica, stand in, twofold
09 bifarious, duplicate, facsimile, lookalike
10 dead ringer, substitute, understudy
11 counterpart, double-edged
12 doppelgänger

13 have a dual role, multiply by two, spitting image
14 be an understudy
15 have a second role

**▢at the double, on the double**
06 at once
07 quickly
09 right away
11 at full speed, immediately
12 in double time, straight away, without delay

**▢double back**
04 loop
06 circle, return
07 reverse
09 backtrack

**double-cross**
03 con
05 cheat, trick
06 betray
07 defraud, swindle, two-time
08 hoodwink
12 take for a ride
14 pull a fast one on

**double-dealing**
07 perfidy
08 betrayal, cheating, tricking
09 duplicity, mendacity, swindling, treachery, two-timing
10 defrauding, misleading
11 crookedness, hoodwinking
12 two-facedness

**double entendre**
03 pun
08 innuendo, wordplay
09 ambiguity
11 play on words
13 double meaning
14 suggestiveness

**doubly**
03 bis
05 again, extra, twice
07 twofold

**doubt**
04 fear
05 demur, qualm, query, waver
07 dilemma, problem, suspect
08 distrust, mistrust, question
09 ambiguity, be dubious, misgiving, suspicion
10 difficulty, disbelieve, hesitation, indecision, skepticism, uneasiness
11 be uncertain, be undecided, incredulity, reservation, uncertainty
12 apprehension, be suspicious, mixed feeling

15 have qualms about

**▢in doubt**
09 ambiguous, debatable, uncertain, undecided
10 in question, unreliable, unresolved, up in the air
12 questionable
14 open to question

**▢no doubt**
06 surely
08 of course, probably
09 certainly, doubtless
10 definitely, presumably
11 undoubtedly
12 without doubt
13 without a doubt
14 unquestionably

**doubter**
05 cynic
07 scoffer, skeptic
08 agnostic
10 questioner, unbeliever
11 disbeliever
14 doubting Thomas

**doubtful**
04 iffy
05 fishy, shady, vague
06 uneasy, unsure
07 dubious, in doubt, unclear
08 hesitant, unlikely, wavering
09 debatable, tentative, uncertain, undecided
10 improbable, in two minds, irresolute, suspicious
11 distrustful, vacillating
12 inconclusive, questionable

**doubtless**
05 truly
06 surely
07 clearly, no doubt
08 of course, probably
09 certainly, seemingly
10 most likely, presumably
11 undoubtedly
12 indisputably, without doubt
13 without a doubt
14 unquestionably

**dour**
04 grim, hard, sour
05 gruff, harsh, rigid, stern
06 dismal, dreary, gloomy, morose, severe, strict, sullen
07 austere
08 churlish, rigorous
09 obstinate, unsmiling
10 forbidding, inflexible

**douse**
03 dip, wet
04 duck, dunk, soak
05 flood, snuff, souse, steep

06 deluge, drench, plunge, put out, quench, splash
07 blow out, immerge, immerse, smother
08 saturate, submerge
10 extinguish

**dovetail**
04 join, link
05 agree, match, tally
08 coincide
09 harmonize, interlock
10 correspond
11 fit together

**dowdy**
04 drab
05 dingy, tacky
08 frumpish, slovenly
12 old-fashioned
13 unfashionable

**down**
03 low, nap, sad
04 blue, bust, fell, flue, fuzz, gulp, pile, shag, swig, wool
05 bloom, drink, floor, fluff
06 pappus
07 consume, crashed, floccus, put away, swallow, unhappy
08 dejected, wretched
09 depressed, knock back, miserable, prostrate
10 dispirited, melancholy, not working, out of order
11 inoperative, out of action
12 soft feathers
13 to a lower level
14 down in the dumps

❑**down with**
04 hobo
05 loser, tramp
06 dosser, ruined
07 vagrant
08 derelict, vagabond
09 destitute, penniless
10 down-and-out
12 impoverished, on your uppers

**down-at-heel**
04 drab, poor
05 dingy, seedy, tacky
06 frayed, ragged, shabby
08 slovenly, tattered

**downbeat**
03 low
04 calm
06 casual, gloomy
07 cynical, relaxed
08 informal, laid back
09 cheerless, depressed, unhurried, unworried
10 insouciant, nonchalant
11 pessimistic

**downcast**
03 low, sad
04 blue, down, glum
05 fed up
06 gloomy
07 daunted, unhappy
08 dejected, wretched
09 depressed, miserable
10 despondent, dispirited
11 crestfallen, discouraged
12 disappointed, disconsolate

**downfall**
04 fall, ruin
07 debacle, failure, undoing
08 collapse, disgrace
10 debasement
11 degradation, destruction

**downgrade**
06 demote, depose, humble
07 deflate, degrade, run down
08 belittle, minimize, relegate
09 denigrate, disparage
11 lower in rank, make light of

**downhearted**
03 sad
04 glum
06 gloomy
07 daunted, unhappy
08 dejected, downcast
09 depressed
10 despondent, dispirited
11 discouraged, low-spirited
12 disconsolate, disheartened

**downpour**
05 flood
06 deluge
07 torrent
09 rainstorm
10 cloudburst, inundation

**downright**
05 clear, plain, sheer, total, utter
07 clearly, plainly, totally, utterly
08 absolute, complete, outright, thorough
09 out-and-out, wholesale
10 absolutely, completely, thoroughly
11 categorical, unequivocal, unqualified
13 categorically

**down-to-earth**
04 sane
07 mundane
08 sensible
09 practical, realistic
10 hardheaded, no-nonsense
11 commonsense
12 matter-of-fact
13 unsentimental
14 commonsensical

**downtrodden**
06 abused
07 bullied
09 exploited, oppressed
10 subjugated, trampled on, tyrannized, victimized
11 subservient

**downward**
07 sliding
08 downhill, slipping
09 declining, going down
10 descending, moving down

**dowry**
04 gift
05 dower, share
06 legacy
07 faculty, portion
09 endowment, provision
11 inheritance
12 wedding dower
15 marriage portion

**doze**
03 nap
04 zizz
05 go off, sleep
06 catnap, drowse, nod off, siesta, snooze
07 drop off, shut-eye
08 drift off, take a nap
09 drowse off
10 forty winks

**drab**
04 dull, flat, gray
05 dingy
06 boring, dismal, dreary, gloomy, shabby, somber
08 lifeless
09 cheerless, colorless
10 lackluster

**draft**
04 draw, plan
05 check, drink, rough
06 draw up, potion, sketch
07 compose, current, drawing, outline, pulling
08 abstract, protocol
09 blueprint, formulate
10 money order
11 delineation
12 current of air
14 bill of exchange, letter of credit

**drag**
03 lag, lug, tow, tug
04 bind, bore, draw, haul, pain, pest, pull, race, yank
05 crawl, creep, trail
06 dawdle
08 go slowly, nuisance
09 annoyance, go on and on, lag behind

13  pain in the neck

**□drag out**

06  extend, hang on
07  draw out, prolong, spin out
08  lengthen, protract

**□drag up**

05  raise
06  rake up, remind, revive
07  bring up, mention

**dragoon**

05  bully, drive, force, impel
06  coerce, compel, harass
08  browbeat
09  constrain, strongarm
10  cavalryman, intimidate

**drain**

03  dry, sap, tap, tax
04  duct, leak, milk, pipe, void
05  bleed, ditch, empty, sewer
06  effuse, gutter, outlet, remove, strain, trench
07  channel, conduit, consume, culvert, deplete, draw off, drink up, exhaust, extract, flow out, pump off, seep out, swallow, trickle
10  exhaustion
11  consumption

**drama**

04  play, show
05  piece, scene
06  acting, crisis, thrill
07  program, tension, theater, tragedy
09  dramatics, sensation, TV program
10  excitement, stagecraft
11  histrionics

➤ *Names of TV drama series*:

02  ER
04  Fame, I Spy
05  Kojak, L.A. Law
06  Dallas, Lassie, Quincy, The FBI
07  Bonanza, Columbo, Dragnet, Omnibus, Rawhide
08  Ben Casey, Gunsmoke, Ironside, NYPD Blue, Star Trek
09  Burke's Law, Dr. Kildare, Miami Vice, Peter Gunn, Studio One, The X-Files
10  Perry Mason, The Waltons, Wagon Train
11  Chicago Hope, Hawaii Five-O, Law and Order, Marcus Welby, Mayberry RFD, My Three Sons, Playhouse 90, St. Elsewhere, The Fugitive, The Sopranos, The West Wing
12  Picket Fences, The Alcoa

Hour, The Goldbergs, The Virginian
13  Fantasy Island, I Remember Mama
14  Cagney and Lacey, Charlie's Angels
15  Armchair Theatre, Father Knows Best, Hill Street Blues, Philco Playhouse, The Twilight Zone, The Untouchables, thirtysomething, Zane Grey Theater
16  The Rockford Files

**dramatic**

05  stage, tense, vivid
06  abrupt, marked, sudden
07  graphic
08  distinct, exciting, stirring, striking, Thespian
09  effective, thrilling
10  expressive, flamboyant, histrionic, noticeable, theatrical, unexpected
11  sensational, spectacular
12  melodramatic

**dramatist**

08  comedian
09  tragedian
10  dramaturge, playwright
12  dramaturgist, screenwriter, scriptwriter

**dramatize**

03  act, ham
05  adapt, ham up, put on, stage
06  overdo
07  ham it up, playact
09  overstate
10  exaggerate
12  lay it on thick

**drape**

04  drop, fold, hang, veil, wrap
05  adorn, cloak, cover, droop
06  shroud
07  envelop, overlay, suspend
08  decorate

**drapery**

05  arras, blind, cloth
06  blinds
07  curtain, hanging, valance
08  backdrop, covering, curtains, hangings, tapestry

**drastic**

04  dire
05  harsh
06  severe, strong
07  extreme, radical
09  desperate, Draconian
11  far-reaching

**draw**

02  go
03  get, lug, tie, tug
04  bait, come, drag, haul, lure, move, pull
05  chart, paint, trace, trail
06  allure, appeal, come to, deduce, depict, design, doodle, elicit, entice, gather, inhale, map out, obtain, pencil, remove, sketch
07  advance, attract, bring in, extract, portray, produce, pull out, respire, take out
08  approach, bring out, conclude, dead heat, progress, scribble, withdraw
09  breathe in, delineate, magnetism, represent, stalemate
10  attraction, enticement

**□draw back**

05  wince
06  flinch, recoil, shrink
07  retract, retreat
08  take away, withdraw

**□draw on**

03  use
05  apply
07  exploit, utilize
08  put to use
09  make use of
14  have recourse to

**□draw out**

05  leave, start
06  extend
07  move out, prolong, pull out, spin out, stretch
08  continue, elongate, lengthen, protract

**□draw up**

04  halt, stop
06  pull up
07  compose, prepare
08  write out
09  formulate

**drawback**

04  flaw, snag
05  catch, fault, hitch
06  damper, defect, hurdle
07  barrier, problem, trouble
08  handicap, nuisance, obstacle, weak spot
10  deficiency, difficulty, impediment, limitation
12  disadvantage, imperfection
14  stumbling block

**drawing**

05  study
06  sketch

**drawl**
07 cartoon, diagram, graphic, outline, picture
08 portrait
09 depiction, portrayal
10 attracting
11 composition, delineation
12 illustration
14 representation

**drawl**
05 drone
10 slow speech
14 southern drawl,

**drawn**
04 taut, worn
05 gaunt, tense, tired
07 fraught, haggard, pinched
08 fatigued, strained, stressed
09 washed out

**dread**
04 dire, fear, funk
05 alarm, awful, quail, worry
06 dismay, feared, flinch, fright, grisly, horror, terror
07 ghastly, shudder, tremble
08 blue funk, disquiet, dreadful, gruesome, horrible, terrible
09 cold sweat, frightful
10 blind panic, shrink from, terrifying
11 fit of terror, trepidation
12 awe-inspiring
13 be terrified by

**dreadful**
04 dire, grim
05 awful, nasty
07 ghastly, heinous, hideous
08 alarming, grievous, horrible, horrific, shocking, terrible
09 appalling, frightful
10 horrendous, outrageous, terrifying, unpleasant
11 frightening

**dream**
03 aim, joy
04 goal, hope, muse, plan, wish
05 fancy, ideal, model, yearn
06 beauty, design, desire, superb, trance, vision
07 fantasy, imagine, reverie
08 ambition, daydream, delusion, envisage, illusion
09 fantasize, nightmare, pipe dream, switch off
10 aspiration
11 hallucinate, inattention
13 hallucination
14 phantasmagoria, stare into space
15 castles in the air

□**dream up**
04 spin

05 hatch
06 create, devise, invent
07 concoct, imagine, think up
08 conceive, contrive
09 conjure up, fabricate

□**not dream of**
08 not think
10 not imagine
11 not conceive, not consider

**dreamer**
07 Utopian
08 idealist, romancer, romantic
09 fantasist, stargazer, theorizer, visionary
10 daydreamer

**dreamlike**
06 unreal
07 phantom, surreal
08 ethereal, illusory
09 visionary
10 chimerical, trance-like
13 hallucinatory, insubstantial, unsubstantial
14 phantasmagoric

**dreamy**
03 dim
04 hazy, soft
05 faint, misty, vague
06 absent, gentle, groovy, lovely, peachy, unreal
07 calming, faraway, lulling, pensive, shadowy, unclear
08 ethereal, fanciful, relaxing, romantic, soothing
09 fantastic, imaginary, visionary
10 abstracted, idealistic, indistinct, thoughtful
11 fantasizing, preoccupied
12 absent-minded

**dreary**
03 sad
04 dark, drab, dull
05 bleak
06 boring, dismal, gloomy, somber
07 humdrum, routine, tedious
08 lifeless, mournful, overcast
09 cheerless, colorless, wearisome
10 depressing, monotonous, uneventful

**dredge**

□**dredge up**
05 dig up, raise
06 drag up, fish up, rake up
07 scoop up, uncover, unearth
08 discover

**dregs**
04 lees, scum

05 dross, trash, waste
06 rabble
07 deposit, grounds, residue
08 detritus, residuum, riffraff, sediment
09 settlings, sublimate

**drench**
03 wet
04 duck, soak
05 douse, drown, flood, imbue, souse, steep, swamp
08 inundate, permeate, saturate
13 soak to the skin

**dress**
02 do
03 don, fit, rig
04 comb, deck, garb, gear, gown, robe, tend, tidy, togs, trim, wear
05 adorn, array, clean, cover, drape, frock, get-up, groom, preen, primp, put on, treat
06 adjust, attire, bind up, clothe, fit out, outfit, swathe
07 apparel, bandage, clothes, costume, garment, garnish, prepare, throw on, turn out
08 accouter, accoutre, clothing, decorate, garments
13 put a bandage on

□**dress down**
05 chide, scold
06 berate, carpet, rebuke
07 reprove, tell off, upbraid
09 castigate, reprimand
15 call on the carpet

□**dress up**
04 deck, gild
05 adorn, tog up
06 doll up, tog out
07 improve
08 decorate, disguise, ornament

**dressing**
03 pad
04 lint
05 gauze, sauce, spica
07 Band-Aid, bandage, plaster
08 compress, ligature, poultice
10 tourniquet

**dressmaker**
06 tailor
07 modiste
09 couturier, tailoress
10 seamstress
11 needlewoman

**dressy**
04 chic
05 natty, ritzy, smart, swish
06 classy, formal, frilly, ornate
07 elegant, stylish

09 elaborate
**dribble**
03 run
04 drip, drop, leak, ooze, seep
05 drool, exude
06 drivel, slaver
07 seepage, slobber, trickle

**dried**
04 arid
07 drained, parched, wizened
08 withered
09 mummified, shriveled
10 dehydrated, desiccated, exsiccated

**drift**
04 bank, core, flow, gist, heap, mass, pile, roam, rove, waft
05 amass, coast, drive, float, mound, point, stray, sweep
06 course, gather, import, pile up, thrust, wander
07 current, essence, meaning
08 movement, tendency
09 direction, intention, substance, variation
10 accumulate, digression
12 accumulation, significance
13 go with the flow
14 be carried along
15 go with the stream

**drifter**
03 bum
04 hobo
05 nomad, rover, tramp
07 vagrant
08 vagabond, wanderer
09 itinerant
11 beachcomber
12 rolling stone

**drill**
03 awl, bit
04 bore
05 borer, coach, teach, train
06 gimlet, ground, school
07 routine, tuition
08 coaching, exercise, instruct, practice, rehearse, training
09 inculcate, procedure
10 discipline, repetition
11 inculcation, instruction

**drink**
03 sea, sip, sup
04 brew, down, gulp, lush, swig
05 booze, draft, ocean, quaff, swill, toast
06 absorb, guzzle, imbibe, liquid, liquor, salute, tipple
07 alcohol, carouse, indulge, spirits, swallow
08 beverage, infusion

09 hard stuff, knock back, partake of, polish off, soft drink, stiffener, the bottle
11 refreshment, strong drink
12 hit the bottle
13 knock back a few
14 be a hard drinker, drink like a fish, thirst-quencher
15 be a heavy drinker

► *Types of nonalcoholic drink*:
03 pop
04 coke, malt, milk, soda
05 cocoa, float, juice, julep, latte, mixer, Vichy
06 coffee, squash, tisane
07 cordial, limeade, mineral, ptisane, seltzer, soda pop
08 café noir, espresso, fruit tea, green tea, lemon tea, lemonade, root beer
09 cream soda, ginger ale, herbal tea, milk shake, soda water
10 apple juice, café au lait, café filtre, cappuccino, fruit juice, ginger beer, grape juice, rosehip tea, tonic water, Vichy water
11 camomile tea, orange juice
12 hot chocolate, ice-cream soda, mineral water, sarsaparilla
13 peppermint tea, Turkish coffee
15 lapsang souchong
➤ See also BEER; COCKTAIL; LIQUEUR; SPIRITS; WINE

**drinkable**
07 potable
10 fit to drink

**drinker**
03 sot
04 alky, lush, soak, wino
05 alkie, dipso, drunk, souse, toper
06 bibber, boozer, soaker
07 guzzler, imbiber, tippler, tosspot
08 drunkard
09 inebriate
11 dipsomaniac

**drip**
03 wet
04 bead, bore, drop, leak, ooze, pest, plop, tear, weep, wimp
05 creap
06 filter, splash
07 dribble, drizzle, trickle
09 percolate

**drive**
02 go
03 dig, ram, run, tax, vim, zip
04 come, dash, goad, herd, lead, move, need, prod, push, ride, road, send, sink, spin, spur, take, trip, urge, will
05 carry, fight, force, guide, impel, jaunt, knock, motor, power, press, steer, verve, vigor
06 action, appeal, avenue, coerce, compel, convey, direct, effort, energy, hammer, incite, manage, oblige, outing, plunge, propel, strike, thrust
07 actuate, control, crusade, dragoon, go by car, journey, operate, overtax, provoke, resolve, roadway, round up
08 ambition, campaign, instinct, motivate, overdo it, overwork, persuade, pressure, struggle, tenacity
09 chauffeur, come by car, excursion, transport
10 enterprise, fund-raiser, get-up-and-go, initiative, motivation, pressurize, propulsion
11 travel by car, work too hard
12 be at the wheel
13 determination
14 propeller shaft
15 be at the controls

❑**drive at**
04 hint, mean
05 aim at, get at, imply
06 intend
07 refer to, signify, suggest
08 allude to, indicate, intimate
09 insinuate
10 have in mind

**drivel**
03 rot
04 crap
05 tripe
06 bunkum, humbug, waffle
07 garbage, hogwash, rubbish, twaddle
08 claptrap, nonsense
09 gibberish, poppycock
10 balderdash, mumbo jumbo
12 gobbledygook

**driver**
05 cabby, rider
06 cabbie
07 cyclist, trucker
08 motorist, motorman, teamster
09 cabdriver, chauffeur

12 motorcyclist

**driving**
05 heavy
07 dynamic, violent
08 forceful, sweeping, vigorous
09 energetic
10 compelling, forthright

**drizzle**
04 mist, rain, spit, spot
06 mizzle, shower
09 light rain, misty rain

**droll**
03 odd
04 zany
05 comic, funny, queer, witty
07 amusing, comical, jocular
08 clownish, farcical, humorous, peculiar
09 diverting, eccentric, laughable, ludicrous
10 ridiculous
12 entertaining

**drone**
03 bee, hum
04 buzz, purr
05 chant, idler, leech, whirr
06 intone, loafer
07 bagpipe, slacker, sponger, vibrate
08 hanger-on, honeybee, layabout, parasite, whirring
09 bombinate, go on and on, murmuring, scrounger, vibration
10 lazy person

**drool**
04 dote, gush
06 drivel, slaver
07 dribble, enthuse, slobber
08 salivate
11 slobber over
15 water at the mouth

**droop**
03 bow, sag
04 bend, drop, flag, sink, wilt
05 faint, slump, stoop
06 dangle, falter, slouch, wither
08 fall down, hang down

**drop**
03 bit, dab, end, nip, sip, tad
04 bead, blob, dash, dive, drip, fall, fire, jilt, leak, omit, plop, quit, sack, sink, spot, stop, tear
05 abyss, chasm, chuck, ditch, droop, gutta, let go, lower, pinch, slope, slump, trace
06 bubble, disown, finish, forego, give up, goutte,

lessen, little, plunge, reject, splash, tumble, weaken
07 abandon, cut back, decline, descend, descent, dismiss, droplet, dwindle, exclude, fall off, forsake, globule, let fall, miss out, plummet, smidgen, trickle
08 decrease, downturn, globulet, leave out
09 declivity, precipice, reduction, terminate, throw over, walk out on
10 falling-off, relinquish, slacken off
11 devaluation, discontinue
12 depreciation, dispense with

❑**drop back**
03 lag
07 retreat
08 fall back
09 lag behind
10 fall behind

❑**drop in**
04 call
05 pop by, pop in, visit
06 call by, call on, come by
08 come over
09 pop around
10 call around, come around

❑**drop off**
04 doze, sink
06 catnap, hand in, lessen, nod off, snooze, unload
07 decline, deliver, deposit, dwindle, fall off, set down
08 decrease, drift off
10 fall asleep, slacken off
14 have forty winks

❑**drop out**
04 quit
05 leave
06 cry off, give up
07 abandon, back out, forsake
08 renounce, withdraw

❑**drop out of**
04 quit
05 leave
07 abandon, pull out
08 opt out of, renounce
09 back out of
10 cry off from
12 withdraw from

**dropout**
05 hippy, loner, rebel
06 hermit, hippie
07 quitter
08 bohemian
09 dissenter
11 nongraduate
13 nonconformist

**droppings**
04 dung
05 feces, guano
06 egesta, manure, ordure, stools
07 excreta
09 excrement

**dross**
05 dregs, trash, waste
06 debris, refuse, scoria
07 remains, rubbish

**drought**
04 want
07 aridity, dryness
08 shortage
11 dehydration, desiccation

**drove**
03 mob
04 herd, host, pack
05 crowd, flock, horde, swarm
06 throng
09 gathering, multitude

**drown**
04 sink
05 flood, swamp
06 deluge, drench, engulf
07 go under, immerse, wipe out
08 inundate, overcome, submerge
09 overpower, overwhelm

**drowsiness**
06 torpor
08 dopiness, doziness, lethargy
09 oscitancy, weariness
10 sleepiness, somnolence

**drowsy**
04 dozy
05 dopey, tired, weary
06 dreamy, sleepy, torpid
07 nodding, yawning
09 lethargic, somnolent
10 half-asleep

**drubbing**
06 defeat
07 beating, licking
08 flogging, whipping
09 hammering, thrashing, trouncing, walloping

**drudge**
04 hack, plod, slog, toil, work
05 grind, grunt, labor, slave
06 beaver, lackey, menial, skivvy, toiler, worker
07 laborer, servant
08 dogsbody, factotum

**drudgery**
04 slog, toil
05 chore, grind, labor, sweat
07 slavery

**drug**

08 taskwork
10 donkeywork, menial work
12 sweated labor

**drug**

04 cure, dope, dose, numb
06 potion, remedy, sedate
07 stupefy
08 knock out, medicine
10 medication
11 anesthetize, tranquilize

➤ *Types of drug*:
03 LSD
04 acid, dope, MDMA
05 crack, opium, smack, speed
06 downer, heroin, opiate, peyote, Valium, Viagra
07 aspirin, cocaine, codeine, Ecstasy, insulin, quinine, steroid
08 cannabis, diazepam, estrogen, laudanum, morphine, narcotic, sedative
09 analgesic, cortisone, digitalis, marijuana, stimulant
10 anesthetic, antibiotic, chloroform, penicillin
11 amphetamine, barbiturate, paracetamol
12 progesterone
13 antihistamine, tranquillizer
14 antidepressant, hallucinogenic
➤ See also MEDICINE

**drug addict**

04 head, user
05 freak
06 abuser, junkie
07 hophead, pothead, tripper
08 cokehead, snowbird
09 dope fiend, mainliner

**drugged**

04 high
05 doped
06 spaced, stoned, zonked
07 on a trip, sedated
08 hopped up, turned on
09 spaced-out, stupefied
10 knocked out, tripped out

**drum**

03 rap, tap
04 beat, skin
05 bongo, knock, throb, thrum
06 tattoo, tom-tom, tympan
07 pulsate
08 bass drum
09 snare drum

❑**drum into**

06 hammer, harp on
07 din into, instill
09 drive home, inculcate

❑**drum out**

05 expel
08 throw out
09 discharge

❑**drum up**

03 get
06 gather, obtain, summon
07 attract, canvass, collect, round up, solicit
08 petition

**drunk**

03 sot
04 alky, lush, soak, wino
05 alkie, dipso, happy, merry, tight, tipsy, toper, woozy
06 blotto, bombed, boozer, canned, loaded, soaker, soused, stewed, stoned, tiddly, wasted, zonked
07 bevvied, drinker, drunken, legless, pickled, sloshed, smashed, sozzled, squiffy, tippler, tosspot, wrecked
08 bibulous, drunkard, squiffed
09 alcoholic, paralytic, plastered, well-oiled
10 blind drunk, inebriated
11 dipsomaniac, hard drinker, have had a few, intoxicated
12 drunk as a lord, heavy drinker, roaring drunk
13 under the table

**drunkard**

03 sot
04 alky, lush, soak, wino
05 alkie, dipso, drunk, toper
06 boozer, soaker
07 drinker, guzzler, tippler, tosspot
09 alcoholic
10 inebriated
11 dipsomaniac, hard drinker
12 heavy drinker

**drunken**

05 boozy, drunk, merry, tipsy
07 riotous, sloshed
09 crapulent, debauched
11 intoxicated
12 bacchanalian

**drunkenness**

09 inebriety, tipsiness
10 alcoholism, crapulence, debauchery, insobriety
11 inebriation
12 bibulousness, intoxication

**dry**

04 arid, dull, flat, wilt
05 drain, droll, witty, xeric
06 barren, boring, dreary, ironic, subtle, wither
07 cutting, cynical, laconic, parched, shrivel, thirsty
08 rainless, scorched, withered
09 dehydrate, desiccate, dry as dust, sarcastic, shriveled, wearisome
10 dehydrated, desiccated, dry as a bone
12 moistureless

❑**dry up**

04 fade, fail, stop
06 die out, shrink, shut up, wither
09 disappear
11 come to an end, stop talking
15 forget your lines

**dryness**

06 thirst
07 aridity, drought
08 aridness
10 barrenness
11 dehydration, thirstiness

**dual**

04 twin
06 binary, double, paired
07 coupled, matched, twofold

**dub**

03 tag
04 call, name, term
05 label, style
06 bestow, confer
07 entitle
08 christen, nickname
09 designate

**dubiety**

05 doubt, qualm
08 mistrust
09 misgiving, suspicion
10 hesitation, indecision, skepticism
11 incertitude, uncertainty
12 doubtfulness

**dubious**

04 iffy
05 fishy, shady
06 shifty, unsure
07 obscure, suspect
09 ambiguous, debatable, skeptical, uncertain
10 suspicious, unreliable
12 questionable
13 untrustworthy

**duck**

03 bob, dip, wet
04 bend, dive, drop, dunk, shun
05 avoid, dodge, douse, elude, evade, lower, shirk, souse, squat, stoop
06 crouch, plunge
07 bow down, immerse

08 sidestep, submerge
12 steer clear of, wriggle out of

---

➤ *Breeds of duck*:
04 blue, musk, smew, teal
05 eider, Pekin, scaup
06 garrot, herald, runner, scoter, wigeon
07 gadwall, mallard, Muscovy, pintail, pochard, widgeon
08 baldpate, garganey, mandarin, old squaw, shelduck, shoveler, teal blue
09 Aylesbury, goldeneye, goosander, harlequin, merganser, sheldrake
10 bufflehead, canvasback
➤ See also ANIMAL; BIRD

**duct**
04 pipe, tube
05 canal
06 funnel, vessel
07 channel, conduit, passage

**ductile**
06 pliant
07 plastic, pliable
08 amenable, biddable, flexible, yielding
09 compliant, malleable, tractable
10 manageable, refractory

**dud**
04 bust, duff, flop
05 kaput
06 broken, failed
07 failure, washout
08 nugatory
09 valueless, worthless

**due**
03 fee
04 dead, levy, owed
05 ample, owing, right
06 charge, direct, enough, merits, proper, rights, unpaid
07 charges, correct, deserts, exactly, fitting, merited, payable
08 adequate, deserved, expected, plenty of, required, rightful, straight, suitable
09 in arrears, justified, privilege, requisite, scheduled
10 birthright, sufficient
11 anticipated, appropriate, comeuppance, just deserts, long-awaited, outstanding, prerogative
12 contribution, subscription
13 membership fee

**◻ due to**
07 owing to
08 caused by
09 because of
11 as a result of

**duel**
05 clash, fight
06 battle, combat
07 contest, rivalry
10 engagement
11 competition
13 affair of honor

**duffer**
03 oaf
04 clod, dolt, fool
05 idiot
06 dimwit
08 bonehead
09 blunderer, ignoramus

**dulcet**
04 soft
05 sweet
06 gentle, mellow
08 pleasant, soothing
09 agreeable, melodious
10 harmonious
11 mellifluous
13 sweet-sounding

**dull**
03 dim
04 dark, drab, drug, dumb, fade, flat, gray, idle, matt, mild, numb, slow, weak
05 allay, bland, blunt, dense, faint, heavy, inert, murky, muted, plain, thick
06 boring, cloudy, dampen, darken, deaden, dismal, dreary, feeble, gloomy, leaden, lessen, reduce, sadden, soften, somber, stupid, subdue, torpid
07 assuage, humdrum, insipid, muffled, obscure, relieve, stupefy, tedious, wash out
08 decrease, diminish, edgeless, inactive, lifeless, mitigate, moderate, overcast, tiresome, tone down
09 alleviate, lethargic, ponderous, wearisome
10 indistinct, lackluster, monotonous, pedestrian, uneventful, unexciting
11 stereotyped, stultifying, troublesome, unsharpened
13 unimaginative, uninteresting
15 slow on the uptake

**dullard**
03 oaf
04 clod, dolt, dope

05 chump, dunce, idiot, moron
06 dimwit, nitwit
08 bonehead, imbecile
09 blockhead, simpleton
10 dunderhead

**dullness**
06 tedium, torpor
07 dryness, vacuity
08 flatness, monotony, slowness, vapidity
10 dreariness
12 sluggishness

**duly**
05 fitly
08 properly, suitably
09 correctly, fittingly
10 decorously, deservedly, rightfully, sure enough
11 accordingly, befittingly
13 appropriately

**dumb**
03 mum
04 mute
05 dense, thick
06 silent, stupid
07 foolish
08 wordless
09 brainless, dimwitted
10 speechless, tongue-tied
12 inarticulate, lost for words
13 unintelligent, without speech

**dumbfounded**
04 dumb
06 amazed, thrown
07 baffled, floored, stunned
08 overcome, startled
09 astounded, paralyzed, staggered
10 astonished, bewildered, bowled over, confounded, nonplussed, speechless, taken aback
11 overwhelmed
12 lost for words
13 flabbergasted, thunderstruck

**dummy**
03 oaf
04 clod, copy, fake, fool, form, mock, sham
05 bogus, chump, dunce, false, idiot, model, trial
06 dimwit, figure, nitwit
08 numskull, practice
09 blockhead, imitation, lay figure, mannequin
10 artificial, substitute

**dump**
04 drop, mess, park, slum

05 chuck, ditch, hovel, joint, leave, place, plonk, plunk, scrap
06 pigpen, pigsty, tip out, unload
07 abandon, arsenal, deposit, discard, forsake, let fall, offload, pour out, put down
08 empty out, get rid of, jettison, junkyard, landfill, throw out
09 chuck away, discharge, dispose of, fling down, scrapyard, throw away
11 rubbish heap

## ◻down in the dumps
03 low, sad
04 blue
07 unhappy
08 dejected, downcast
09 depressed, miserable
10 dispirited, melancholy
11 downhearted

## dumpy
05 plump, podgy, pudgy, short, squab, squat, stout, tubby
06 chubby, chunky, stubby

## dun
04 dull
05 dingy, dusky
10 mud-colored
12 grayish-brown

## dunce
04 fool, nerd
05 idiot, ninny, twerp
06 dimwit, nitwit
08 bonehead, dipstick, imbecile, numskull
09 blockhead
10 nincompoop

## dung
05 feces
06 manure, ordure
09 droppings, excrement
11 animal waste

## dungeon
04 cage, cell, jail, keep
05 vault
06 donjon, lockup, prison
09 oubliette

## dupe
03 con
04 fool, gull, hoax, pawn
05 cheat, trick
06 delude, outwit, rip off, stooge, sucker, take in, victim
07 deceive, defraud, fall guy, swindle
08 hoodwink, pushover
09 bamboozle, simpleton

## duplicate
03 fax
04 copy, echo, mate, twin
05 clone, model, Xerox
06 carbon, double, paired, repeat, ringer
07 do again, forgery, matched, replica, twofold
08 matching
09 facsimile, identical, lookalike, photocopy, replicate, reproduce
10 carbon copy, dead ringer
12 reproduction
13 spitting image

## duplication
04 copy
05 clone
07 cloning, copying
08 doubling
09 photocopy
10 gemination, repetition
11 dittography, replication
12 photocopying, reproduction

## duplicity
05 fraud, guile
06 deceit
07 perfidy
08 artifice, betrayal
09 chicanery, deception, falsehood, hypocrisy, mendacity, treachery
10 dishonesty
13 dissimulation, double-dealing

## durability
08 strength
09 constancy, endurance, longevity, stability
10 permanence
11 durableness, lastingness
15 imperishability

## durable
04 fast, firm
05 fixed, solid, sound, tough
06 robust, stable, strong, sturdy
07 abiding, lasting
08 constant, enduring, reliable
09 heavy-duty, permanent
11 hard-wearing, long-lasting

## duration
04 span, time
05 spell
06 extent, length, period
07 stretch
08 fullness, time span
09 time scale
12 continuation, length of time

## duress
05 force
06 threat

08 coercion, exaction, pressure
10 compulsion, constraint
11 arm-twisting, enforcement

## during
02 in
10 throughout
11 all the while, at the time of
13 in the course of

## dusk
05 gloom, shade
06 sunset
07 evening, shadows, sundown
08 darkness, gloaming, twilight
09 nightfall

## dusky
03 dim
04 dark, hazy
05 black, brown, murky
06 cloudy, gloomy, twilit
07 shadowy, swarthy
09 tenebrous
10 fuliginous
11 crepuscular, dark-skinned

## dust
04 clay, dirt, grit, smut, soil, soot, wipe
05 clean, cover, earth, spray
06 defeat, ground, pollen, powder, spread
08 sprinkle
09 confusion, particles

## dust-up
05 brawl, brush, fight, run-in, scrap
06 fracas, tussle
07 quarrel, scuffle
08 argument, conflict, skirmish
09 commotion
11 disturbance

## dusty
05 dirty, grimy, sandy, sooty
06 chalky, filthy, grubby
07 crumbly, friable, powdery

## dutiful
06 filial
08 obedient
10 respectful, submissive
11 deferential, reverential
13 conscientious

## duty
03 job, tax
04 dues, levy, onus, part, role, task, toll, work
05 chore
06 charge, excise, tariff
07 calling, customs, loyalty, mission, respect, service
08 business, fidelity, function
10 allegiance, obligation
11 requirement

12 faithfulness
14 responsibility

**❑ off duty**
03 off
04 free
07 off work, resting
10 on vacation

**❑ on duty**
06 active, at work, on call
07 engaged, working

**dwarf**
04 baby, tiny
05 check, gnome, pygmy, small, stunt
06 bantam, goblin, midget, pocket
07 atrophy, stunted
08 dominate, Tom Thumb
09 miniature, tower over
10 diminutive, overshadow, undersized
11 Lilliputian

**dwell**
04 live, rest, stay
05 abide, lodge
06 reside, settle
07 hang out, inhabit

**❑ dwell on**
07 brood on
09 elaborate, emphasize, expatiate, reflect on
10 linger over, meditate on

**dweller**
07 denizen
08 occupant, occupier, resident
10 inhabitant

**dwelling**
03 hut
04 flat, home, tent
05 abode, condo, house, igloo, lodge, tepee
06 shanty, teepee, wigwam
07 cottage, lodging
08 domicile, quarters
09 apartment, residence

10 habitation
11 condominium
13 dwelling house, dwelling place, establishment

**dwindle**
03 ebb
04 fade, fall, wane
06 die out, lessen, shrink, vanish, weaken, wither
07 decline, subside, tail off
08 decrease, diminish, grow less, peter out, taper off
09 disappear, waste away

**dye**
03 hue
04 tint, wash
05 color, imbue, shade, stain, tinge
07 pigment

▶ *Names of dyes*:
04 anil, chay, weld, woad
05 eosin, henna, mauve
06 anatto, archil, cyanin, flavin, fustic, indigo, kamala, madder, orcein, orchil
07 alkanet, annatto, annatto, cudbear, flavine, gallein, magenta, saffron, thionin
08 amaranth, fuchsine, induline, orpiment, purpurin, safranin, thionine, turnsole
09 cochineal, nigrosine, safranine, Saxon blue, Turkey red, Tyrian red
10 Saxony blue, tartrazine
12 Tyrian purple
➤ See also COLOR; PIGMENT

**dyed-in-the-wool**
05 fixed
07 die-hard, settled
08 complete, hard-core, hardened, thorough
09 confirmed
10 deep-rooted, entrenched, inveterate, unshakable

12 card-carrying, long-standing, unchangeable

**dying**
05 final, going
06 ebbing, fading, mortal
07 failing, passing
08 deathbed, expiring, moribund
12 at death's door
14 on your last legs

**dynamic**
05 vital
06 active, lively, potent, strong
07 driving, go-ahead
08 forceful, magnetic, powerful, spirited, vigorous
09 energetic, go-getting
11 high-powered
12 full of energy

**dynamism**
02 go
03 pep, vim, zap, zip
04 push
05 drive, get up, vigor
06 energy
07 pizzazz
10 enterprise, get-up-and-go, initiative, liveliness
12 forcefulness

**dynasty**
04 line, rule
05 house
06 empire, regime
09 authority
10 government, succession
11 sovereignty

**dyspeptic**
05 testy
06 crabby, gloomy, touchy
07 crabbed, grouchy, peevish
08 snappish
09 crotchety
10 indigested
11 bad-tempered
13 short-tempered

# E e

**each**
05 every
06 apiece, singly
07 each one, per head
09 per capita, per person
12 individually, respectively
15 every individual

**eager**
04 avid, keen
06 ardent, hungry, intent
07 earnest, thirsty, zealous
08 diligent, yearning
09 impatient
12 enthusiastic, wholehearted

**eagerly**
06 avidly, keenly
08 ardently, greedily, intently
09 earnestly, zealously
11 impatiently
14 wholeheartedly

**eagerness**
04 zeal
05 ardor
06 fervor, hunger, thirst
07 avidity, longing
08 fervency, keenness, yearning
09 fervidity
10 enthusiasm, impatience
11 earnestness, impetuosity

**ear**
05 skill, taste
07 ability, hearing
10 perception
11 sensitivity
12 appreciation
14 discrimination

► *Parts of the ear*:
04 lobe
05 anvil, helix, incus, pinna
06 concha, hammer, stapes, tragus
07 auricle, cochlea, eardrum, malleus, stirrup
08 tympanum
09 labyrinth, vestibule
13 auditory canal, auditory nerve
14 eustachian tube

❑ **play it by ear**
05 ad lib
09 improvise
11 extemporize

**early**
05 first
06 at dawn
07 ancient, initial, opening
08 advanced, primeval
09 premature, primitive
10 beforehand, in good time, precocious, primordial
11 ahead of time, prematurely
13 autochthonous
15 ahead of schedule

**earmark**
03 tag
05 label
07 mark out, reserve
08 put aside, set aside
09 designate

**earn**
03 get, net, win
04 draw, gain, make, rate, reap
05 clear, gross, merit
06 attain, be paid, pocket
07 achieve, bring in, deserve, get paid, receive, warrant
08 take home

**earnest**
04 firm, keen
05 eager, grave, token, truth
06 intent, solemn, steady
07 deposit, devoted, fervent, intense, promise, serious, sincere, zealous
08 resolute, security
09 assurance, committed, dedicated, guarantee, heartfelt, sincerity
10 resolution, thoughtful
11 down payment, seriousness

❑ **in earnest**
07 genuine, serious, sincere
08 ardently, intently, steadily
09 not joking, seriously
10 resolutely
14 wholeheartedly
15 conscientiously

**earnestly**
06 firmly, keenly, warmly
07 eagerly
08 intently
09 seriously, sincerely, zealously
10 resolutely

**earnestness**
04 zeal
05 ardor
06 warmth
08 devotion, keenness
09 eagerness, sincerity
10 enthusiasm, resolution
11 seriousness

**earnings**
03 fee, pay
05 wages
06 income, reward, salary
07 profits, revenue, stipend
08 gross pay, proceeds, receipts
09 emolument
10 honorarium
12 remuneration

**earth**
03 orb, sod
04 clay, dirt, land, loam, soil, turf
05 globe, humus, world
06 ground, planet, sphere

**earthenware**
04 pots
07 pottery
08 ceramics, crockery
09 stoneware

**earthly**
05 human
06 likely, mortal
07 fleshly, sensual, worldly
08 feasible, material, physical, possible, telluric, temporal
10 imaginable
11 conceivable, terrestrial

**earthquake**
05 quake, seism, shake
06 tremor
07 seismal, seismic
10 aftershock
11 earth tremor, terremotive

**earthy**
04 blue, rude
05 bawdy, crude, rough
06 coarse, ribald, robust, vulgar
07 natural, raunchy
11 down-to-earth, uninhibited
15 unsophisticated

**ease**
04 edge, inch, rest
05 abate, allay, guide, peace, quiet, relax, salve, steer

**easily**
06 lessen, reduce, relent, repose, smooth, soothe
07 assuage, comfort, leisure, lighten, quieten, relieve
08 deftness, diminish, facility, grow less, mitigate
09 alleviate, happiness
10 adroitness, ameliorate, bed of roses, facilitate, prosperity, relaxation
11 contentment, lap of luxury, life of Riley, naturalness
14 effortlessness

**◻at ease**
04 calm
06 at home, secure
07 natural, relaxed
11 comfortable

**◻ease off**
04 wane
05 abate
06 relent
07 die down, slacken, subside
08 decrease, diminish
10 become less

**easily**
04 well
05 by far
06 simply, surely
07 clearly, readily
09 certainly
10 definitely, far and away
11 comfortably, undoubtedly
12 effortlessly, indisputably

**easy**
04 calm
05 cushy
06 a cinch, casual, simple
07 natural, relaxed
08 informal, laid-back
09 a cakewalk, a pushover, easy as ABC, foolproof, leisurely
10 child's play, effortless
11 comfortable, undemanding
12 a piece of cake
15 straightforward

**easy-going**
04 calm
06 placid, serene
07 lenient, relaxed
08 amenable, carefree, laid-back, tolerant
10 insouciant, nonchalant
12 happy-go-lucky

**eat**
04 chew, dine, feed
05 decay, erode, graze, lunch, munch, snack
06 devour, gobble, ingest
07 consume, corrode, swallow

08 bolt down, dissolve, wear away, wolf down
09 breakfast, partake of

**eatable**
04 good
06 edible
09 palatable, wholesome

**eavesdrop**
03 bug, spy, tap
05 snoop
08 listen in, overhear

**eavesdropper**
03 spy
05 snoop
07 monitor, snooper
08 listener

**ebb**
04 drop, fall, flag, sink, wane
05 abate, decay, go out
06 lessen, recede, weaken
07 decline, dwindle, low tide, retreat, slacken, subside
08 decrease, diminish, fade away, fall back, flow back, going out, low water
09 dwindling, lessening, retrocede, weakening
10 degenerate, slackening

**ebony**
03 jet
04 dark, wood
05 black, jetty, sable, sooty
08 jet-black

**ebullience**
04 zest
07 elation
08 buoyancy, vivacity
10 brightness, enthusiasm, excitement, exuberance
11 high spirits
12 effusiveness, exhilaration

**ebullient**
06 breezy, bright, chirpy, elated
07 buoyant, excited, zestful
09 exuberant, vivacious
11 exhilarated
12 effervescent, enthusiastic
13 irrepressible

**eccentric**
03 nut, odd
04 case, geek, kook
05 batty, crank, kooky, loony, loopy, nutty, queer, wacky, weird
06 oddity, quirky, way-out
07 bizarre, erratic, odd fish, oddball, offbeat, strange
08 aberrant, abnormal, freakish, peculiar, singular
09 character

13 idiosyncratic, nonconformist
14 unconventional

**eccentricity**
05 quirk
06 oddity
07 anomaly
09 weirdness
10 aberration
11 abnormality, peculiarity, singularity, strangeness
12 freakishness, idiosyncrasy
13 nonconformity

**ecclesiastic**
04 dean
05 canon, padre, vicar
06 cleric, curate, deacon, father, parson, pastor, priest, rector
08 chaplain, man of God, minister, preacher, reverend
09 churchman, clergyman, deaconess, presbyter
10 woman of God
11 churchwoman, clergywoman
13 man of the cloth
15 woman of the cloth

**ecclesiastical**
04 holy
06 church, divine
08 churchly, clerical, priestly
09 religious, spiritual
10 sacerdotal

**echelon**
04 rank, rung, tier
05 grade, level, place
06 degree, status
08 position

**echo**
04 copy, hint, ring
05 clone, image, mimic, trace
06 memory, parrot, repeat
07 imitate, reflect, resound
08 allusion, reminder, resemble
09 duplicate, evocation, reiterate, reproduce
10 reflection, repetition
11 reiteration, reverberate
12 reproduction

**éclat**
04 fame, show
05 glory
06 effect, luster, renown
07 acclaim, display, success
08 applause, approval, plaudits, splendor
09 celebrity
10 brilliance
11 acclamation, distinction

**eclectic**
05 broad

**eclipse**

06 varied
07 diverse, general, liberal
08 catholic
09 many-sided, selective
11 diversified, wide-ranging
12 all-embracing, multifarious
13 heterogeneous

**eclipse**

03 dim, ebb
04 fall, loss, veil
05 cloud, cover, dwarf, outdo
06 darken, exceed, shroud
07 blot out, conceal, decline, dimming, failure, obscure, shading, surpass, veiling
09 darkening, transcend
10 concealing, overshadow
11 blotting-out, obscuration
13 overshadowing
15 cast a shadow over, put into the shade

**economic**

05 trade
06 fiscal, viable
08 business, monetary
09 budgetary, financial
10 commercial, profitable
11 money-making
12 profit-making, remunerative
13 cost-effective

**economical**

05 cheap
06 budget, frugal, modest
07 low-cost, sparing, thrifty
08 skimping
09 efficient, low-budget, low-priced, scrimping
10 reasonable
11 inexpensive
13 cost-effective, penny-pinching

**economize**

04 save
05 skimp
06 budget, scrimp
07 cut back, use less
08 cut costs, retrench
10 buy cheaply, cut corners
13 scrimp and save
14 cut expenditure
15 tighten your belt

**economy**

04 care
06 saving, thrift
08 prudence, skimping
09 husbandry, parsimony, restraint, scrimping
10 providence
11 carefulness
15 financial system

➤ *Names of economists:*

04 **Ward** (Barbara), **Webb** (Sidney)
05 **Meade** (James Edward), **Smith** (Adam), **Solow** (Robert Merton), **Tobin** (James)
06 **Cobden** (Richard), **Cripps** (Stafford), **Debreu** (Gerard), **Erhard** (Ludwig), **Fisher** (Irving), **Frisch** (Ragnar), **George** (Henry), **Keynes** (John Maynard), **Myrdal** (Gunnar), **Tawney** (Richard Henry), **Veblen** (Thorstein)
07 **Bagehot** (Walter), **Commons** (John), **Kuznets** (Simon), **Malthus** (Thomas Robert), **Ricardo** (David), **Toynbee** (Arnold)
08 **Friedman** (Milton), **Laughlin** (James), **Mirrlees** (James), **Schiller** (Karl)
09 **Beveridge** (William), **Galbraith** (John Kenneth), **Tinbergen** (Jan)
10 **Schumpeter** (Joseph)
➤ See also SCIENTIST

**ecstasy**

01 E
03 joy
04 dope, drug
05 bliss
06 fervor
07 elation, rapture
08 euphoria, pleasure
10 exultation, jubilation

**ecstatic**

06 elated, joyful
07 fervent
08 blissful, euphoric, jubilant
09 delirious, overjoyed, rapturous, rhapsodic
10 enraptured
11 high as a kite, on cloud nine, tickled pink
13 jumping for joy
15 in seventh heaven

**eddy**

05 swirl, twist, whirl
06 vortex
08 swirling
09 maelstrom, whirlpool

**edge**

03 lip, rim
04 bite, brim, inch, line, side
05 brink, crawl, creep, elbow, limit, sidle, steal, sting, verge
06 border, fringe, margin
07 outline

08 acerbity, boundary, frontier, keenness, severity
09 advantage, dominance, extremity, perimeter, periphery, sharpness, threshold, upper hand
10 ascendancy, outer limit
11 pick your way, superiority

❑**on edge**

04 edgy
05 nervy, tense
06 touchy
07 keyed up, nervous, uptight
09 ill at ease, irritable
12 apprehensive

**edgy**

05 nervy, tense
06 on edge, touchy
07 anxious, keyed up, nervous, uptight
09 ill at ease, irritable

**edible**

04 good
07 eatable
08 fit to eat, harmless
10 comestible, digestible

**edict**

03 act, law
04 fiat, rule
05 order, ukase
06 decree, ruling
07 command, mandate, statute
10 injunction, regulation
12 proclamation
13 pronouncement

**edification**

08 guidance, teaching
09 education, uplifting
11 improvement, instruction
13 enlightenment

**edifice**

08 building, erection
09 structure
12 construction

**edify**

05 coach, guide, teach, tutor
06 inform, school, uplift
07 educate, improve, nurture
08 instruct
09 enlighten

**edit**

05 adapt, check, emend
06 modify, redact, revise, select
07 compile, correct, reorder
08 annotate, rephrase
09 rearrange
10 blue-pencil

**edition**

04 copy

05 issue
06 number, volume
07 version
08 printing
10 impression
11 publication

**educable**
09 teachable, trainable
12 instructible

**educate**
05 coach, drill, edify, prime, teach, train, tutor
06 inform, school
07 develop, improve, prepare
08 instruct
09 enlighten, inculcate
12 indoctrinate

**educated**
04 wise
06 brainy, taught
07 erudite, learned, refined, trained, tutored
08 cultured, informed, lettered, literate, schooled, well-read
10 cultivated, instructed
11 enlightened
13 knowledgeable

**education**
07 letters, nurture, tuition
08 coaching, drilling, guidance, teaching, training, tutoring
09 knowledge, schooling
10 catechesis, upbringing
11 development, edification, improvement, inculcation, instruction, scholarship
13 enlightenment
14 indoctrination

**educational**
08 academic, cultural, didactic, edifying, learning, teaching
09 educative, pedagogic
10 scholastic
11 informative, instructive, pedagogical
12 enlightening

**educative**
08 didactic, edifying
09 improving
10 catechetic
11 catechismal, catechistic, informative, instructive
12 catechetical, enlightening
13 catechistical

**educator**
05 coach, tutor
06 mentor
07 teacher, trainer
08 academic, lecturer
09 pedagogue, professor

10 instructor
12 schoolmaster
13 schoolteacher
14 schoolmistress, student teacher

**eerie**
05 scary, weird
06 creepy, spooky
07 ghostly, strange, uncanny
09 unearthly, unnatural
10 mysterious
11 frightening
13 spine-chilling

**efface**
05 erase
06 cancel, delete, excise, remove, rub out
07 blot out, expunge, wipe out
08 blank out, cross out
09 eradicate, extirpate
10 obliterate

**effect**
04 gear, make
05 cause, drift, force, fruit, issue, power
06 create, impact, import, result, upshot
07 achieve, execute, fulfill, outcome, perform, produce
08 carry out, complete, efficacy, generate, initiate, strength
09 aftermath, influence
10 accomplish, bring about, conclusion, give rise to, impression
11 consequence
12 significance

❑**in effect**
06 in fact, really
07 in truth
08 actually
09 in reality, virtually
10 in practice
11 effectively, essentially
12 in actual fact

❑**take effect**
04 work
05 begin
08 function
11 be effective, become valid
13 come into force
15 become operative

**effects**
05 goods, stuff
06 things
07 baggage, luggage
08 chattels, property
10 belongings
11 possessions
13 accoutrements, paraphernalia

14 accourterments

**effective**
05 valid
06 active, actual, potent
07 capable, current, in force
08 adequate, powerful, striking
09 efficient, operative
10 attractive, convincing, impressive, persuasive, productive, successful
11 efficacious, functioning

**effectiveness**
03 use
05 clout, force, power
07 cogency, potency, success
08 efficacy, strength, validity
09 influence
10 capability, efficiency

**effectual**
05 legal, sound, valid
06 lawful, useful
07 binding, capable
08 forcible, powerful
09 effective, operative
10 productive, successful

**effeminate**
05 sissy
07 unmanly, wimpish, womanly
08 delicate, feminine

**effervesce**
04 boil, fizz, foam
05 froth
06 bubble
07 ferment, sparkle
09 ebullient

**effervescence**
04 fizz, foam, zing
05 froth
07 bubbles, ferment, foaming
08 bubbling, buoyancy, frothing, vitality, vivacity
09 animation
10 ebullience, excitement, exuberance, liveliness
11 excitedness, high spirits
12 exhilaration, fermentation

**effervescent**
05 fizzy, vital
06 bubbly, frothy, lively
07 excited, fizzing, foaming
08 animated, bubbling
09 ebullient, exuberant, sparkling, vivacious
10 carbonated, fermenting

**effete**
04 weak
05 spent
06 barren, feeble, wasted
07 corrupt, debased, decayed, drained, sterile, worn out

**efficacious**
08 decadent, decrepit
09 enervated, enfeebled, exhausted, fruitless
10 degenerate, unfruitful
12 unproductive

**efficacious**
06 active, potent, strong, useful
07 capable
08 adequate, powerful
09 competent, effective, effectual, operative
10 productive, successful

**efficacy**
03 use
05 force, power
06 effect, energy, virtue
07 ability, potency, success
08 strength
09 influence
10 capability, usefulness
13 effectiveness

**efficiency**
05 skill
07 ability
09 expertise
10 capability, competence
11 proficiency
12 skillfulness
13 effectiveness

**efficient**
04 able
07 capable, well-run
08 powerful, skillful
09 competent, effective
10 productive, proficient
11 streamlined, well-ordered
12 businesslike, rationalized
13 well-organized

**effigy**
04 icon, idol
05 dummy, image
06 figure, statue
07 carving, picture, waxwork
08 likeness, portrait
14 representation

**effluent**
05 waste
06 efflux, sewage
07 outflow
08 emission
09 discharge, emanation, pollutant, pollution

**effort**
02 go
03 try
04 deed, feat, opus, shot, stab, toil, work
05 force, labor, power, sweat
06 energy, strain, stress
07 attempt, travail, trouble

08 creation, endeavor, exertion, hard work, striving, struggle
11 application, elbow grease, muscle power
15 sweat of your brow

**effortless**
04 easy
06 facile, simple, smooth
08 painless
11 undemanding

**effrontery**
03 lip
04 face, gall
05 brass, cheek, nerve
08 audacity, boldness, chutzpah, temerity
09 arrogance, brashness, impudence, insolence
10 brazenness, cheekiness
11 presumption
12 impertinence

**effulgent**
07 glowing, radiant, shining
09 brilliant, refulgent
11 resplendent
12 incandescent

**effusion**
04 gush
07 outflow
08 outburst, voidance
09 discharge, effluence
10 outpouring

**effusive**
05 gabby, gassy
07 fulsome, gushing, profuse
08 all mouth
09 expansive, exuberant, rhapsodic, talkative
10 big-mouthed, unreserved
11 extravagant, overflowing
12 enthusiastic, unrestrained
13 demonstrative

**egg**

◻**egg on**
04 coax, goad, push, spur, urge
06 exhort, incite, prompt
08 talk into
09 encourage, stimulate

**egghead**
05 brain
06 genius
07 scholar, thinker
08 academic, Einstein, highbrow
09 intellect, know-it-all
12 intellectual

**ego**
04 self
08 identity

09 self-image, self-worth
10 self-esteem
14 self-confidence, self-importance

**egoism**
07 egotism
08 egomania, self-love
10 narcissism, self-esteem, self-regard
11 amour-propre, selfishness
12 self-interest
13 egocentricity
14 self-absorption, self-importance
16 self-centeredness

**egoist**
07 egotist
09 egomaniac, swellhead
10 narcissist, self-seeker

**egoistic**
09 egotistic
10 egocentric, egoistical
11 egomaniacal, egotistical, self-seeking
12 narcissistic, self-absorbed, self-centered
13 self-important

**egotism**
05 pride, swank
06 egoism, vanity
08 egomania, self-love
10 narcissism, self-regard
11 braggadocio, selfishness
12 boastfulness
13 bigheadedness, conceitedness, egocentricity
14 self-admiration, self-importance
16 self-centeredness

**egotist**
06 egoist
07 bighead, boaster, showoff
08 big mouth, braggart
09 egomaniac, smart alec
10 smart aleck
11 braggadocio, self-admirer

**egotistic**
04 vain
05 proud
07 selfish
08 boasting, bragging, egoistic
09 bigheaded, conceited
10 egocentric
12 narcissistic, self-admiring, self-centered
13 self-important

**egregious**
04 rank
05 gross
06 arrant

**egress**
07 glaring, heinous
08 flagrant, infamous, shocking
09 monstrous, notorious
10 outrageous, scandalous
11 intolerable
12 insufferable

**egress**
04 exit, vent
06 escape, outlet, way out
07 leaving
09 departure, emergence

**ejaculate**
03 cry
04 call, emit, yell
05 blurt, eject, shout, utter
06 cry out, scream
07 call out, exclaim, release
08 blurt out, shout out
09 discharge

**ejaculation**
03 cry
04 call, yell
05 shout
08 ejection, emission
09 discharge, expulsion
11 exclamation

**eject**
04 emit, fire, oust, sack, spew
05 evict, expel, exude, spout
06 banish, deport, get out, propel, remove
07 boot out, discard, dismiss, excrete, kick out, release, turn out
08 chuck out, disgorge, drive out, get rid of, throw out
09 discharge, thrust out
10 dispossess

**ejection**
05 exile
06 firing
07 ousting, removal, sacking
08 eviction
09 discharge, expulsion
10 banishment
11 deportation

**eke**

□ **eke out**
04 cope
05 get by, skimp
06 manage, scrape, scrimp
07 scratch, spin out, stretch
13 scrimp and save

**elaborate**
05 exact, fancy, fussy, showy
06 ornate, refine, rococo
07 amplify, complex, develop, enhance, explain, improve, labored

08 detailed, expand on, flesh out, involved
09 decorated, enlarge on, expatiate, extensive, intricate, perfected
11 complicated, extravagant

**élan**
04 brio, dash, zest
05 flair, oomph, style, verve, vigor
06 esprit, pizazz, spirit
07 panache, pizzazz
08 flourish, vivacity
10 confidence, liveliness

**elapse**
04 go by, go on, pass
05 lapse
06 slip by

**elastic**
04 easy
05 fluid
06 bouncy, pliant, supple
07 buoyant, plastic, pliable, rubbery, springy
08 flexible, stretchy, yielding
09 adaptable, compliant
10 adjustable
13 accommodating

**elasticity**
04 give
06 bounce
07 stretch
09 tolerance
10 plasticity, pliability, resilience, suppleness
11 flexibility, springiness
12 adaptability, stretchiness
13 adjustability

**elated**
06 joyful, joyous
07 excited
08 blissful, ecstatic, euphoric, exultant, jubilant
09 delighted, overjoyed, rapturous, rhapsodic
11 exhilarated, on cloud nine

**elation**
03 joy
04 glee
05 bliss
07 delight, ecstasy, rapture
08 euphoria
10 exultation, joyfulness, joyousness, jubilation
11 high spirits
12 exhilaration

**elbow**
04 bump, push
05 ancon, barge, joint, knock, nudge, press, shove

09 funny bone

**elbowroom**
04 play, room
05 scope, space
06 leeway
07 freedom
08 latitude

**elder**
05 older
06 senior
08 old-timer
09 firstborn
13 senior citizen

**elderly**
03 old
04 aged
05 aging, hoary
06 past it, senile
09 graybeard, senescent
10 gray-haired, gray-headed, pensioners
11 older adults, over the hill
13 retired people
14 long in the tooth, senior citizens
15 older generation

**eldest**
05 first
06 oldest
09 firstborn

**elect**
04 pick, to be
05 adopt, elite
06 choice, choose, chosen, opt for, picked, prefer, select
07 appoint, vote for
08 decide on, plump for
09 cast a vote, designate
11 prospective

**election**
04 poll, vote
06 ballot, choice, voting
08 choosing, decision, hustings
09 selection
10 preference, referendum

**elector**
05 voter
10 electorate
11 constituent

**electric**
04 live
05 tense
07 charged, dynamic, powered, rousing
08 cordless, exciting, stirring
09 startling, thrilling
11 stimulating
12 electrifying

**electrify**
04 fire, jolt, stir
05 amaze, rouse, shock
06 charge, excite, thrill
07 animate, astound, stagger
08 astonish, energize
09 galvanize, stimulate
10 invigorate

**elegance**
04 chic
05 grace, poise, style, taste
06 beauty, luxury, polish
07 dignity
08 grandeur
09 gentility, propriety
10 politeness, refinement
11 discernment, distinction
12 gracefulness, tastefulness
14 sophistication
15 fashionableness

**elegant**
04 chic, fine, neat
05 smart
06 lovely, modish, smooth
07 genteel, refined, stylish
08 delicate, graceful,
   handsome, polished, tasteful
09 beautiful, exquisite
10 cultivated
11 fashionable
13 sophisticated

**elegiac**
03 sad
07 doleful, keening
08 funereal, mournful
09 lamenting, plaintive,
   threnodic
10 threnodial
11 melancholic

**elegy**
05 dirge
06 lament, plaint
07 requiem
08 threnode, threnody
09 epicedial, epicedian,
   epicedium
11 funeral poem, funeral song

**element**
04 hint, part
05 group, piece, touch, trace
06 basics, clique, factor,
   member, strand
07 faction, feature
09 component, rudiments,
   situation
10 essentials, individual,
   ingredient, principles
11 constituent, environment,
   foundations, individuals,
   small amount
12 fundamentals

15 chemical element

**elemental**
05 basic
07 immense, natural, radical
08 forceful, powerful
09 primitive
11 fundamental, rudimentary

**elementary**
04 easy
05 basic, clear
06 simple
07 primary
09 principal
11 fundamental, rudimentary
12 introductory
13 uncomplicated
15 straightforward

**elephantine**
04 huge, vast
05 bulky, heavy, large
06 clumsy
07 awkward, hulking, immense,
   massive, weighty
08 enormous
09 lumbering

**elevate**
04 lift
05 boost, exalt, hoist, raise
06 buoy up, hike up, uplift
07 advance, ennoble, gladden,
   magnify, promote, upgrade
08 brighten, heighten
10 aggrandize
15 move up the ladder

**elevated**
04 high
05 grand, great, lofty, noble
06 lifted, raised, rising
07 exalted, hoisted, sublime
08 advanced, lifted up, uplifted
09 dignified, important

**elevation**
04 hill, rise
05 leg up, mound, mount
06 height
08 altitude, eminence, grandeur,
   nobility, tallness
09 loftiness, promotion,
   sublimity, upgrading
10 exaltation, preferment
11 advancement
14 aggrandizement
15 step up the ladder

**elf**
03 imp
04 puck
05 elfin, elvan, fairy, gnome
06 elfish, elvish, goblin, sprite
07 banshee, brownie
09 hobgoblin

10 leprechaun

**elfin**
05 small
06 elfish, impish, petite
07 elflike, playful, puckish
08 charming, delicate
09 sprightly
11 mischievous

**elicit**
05 educe, evoke, exact, wrest
06 derive, extort, obtain
07 draw out, extract, worm out
08 bring out

**eligible**
03 fit
06 proper, worthy
07 fitting
08 suitable
09 desirable, qualified
11 appropriate

**eliminate**
04 beat, do in, drop, kill, omit
05 expel
06 cut out, defeat, delete,
   hammer, murder, reject,
   remove, rub out, thrash
07 exclude, take out, wipe out
08 get rid of, stamp out
09 dispose of, disregard,
   eradicate, liquidate
10 do away with, extinguish, put
   a stop to, put an end to
11 exterminate
12 dispense with

**elite**
04 best, pick
05 cream, elect, noble
06 choice, gentry, jet set
08 nobility, selected
09 exclusive
10 first-class, upper class
11 aristocracy, high society
12 aristocratic, upper classes
14 crème de la crème, pick of
   the bunch

**elixir**
05 syrup
06 potion, remedy
07 cure-all, essence, extract,
   mixture, nostrum, panacea
08 solution, tincture
12 quintessence

**elliptical**
04 oval
05 ovoid, terse
07 concise, cryptic, laconic,
   obscure, oviform, ovoidal
08 abstruse
09 ambiguous, condensed, egg-
   shaped, recondite

12 concentrated

**elocution**
06 speech
07 diction, oratory
08 delivery, phrasing, rhetoric
11 enunciation
12 articulation
13 pronunciation
15 voice production

**elongate**
06 extend
07 draw out, prolong, stretch
08 lengthen, protract
10 make longer

**elongated**
04 long
08 extended
09 prolonged, stretched
10 lengthened, protracted

**elope**
04 bolt, flee
06 decamp, escape, run off
07 abscond, make off, run away
08 slip away

**eloquence**
07 blarney, fluency, oratory
08 facility, rhetoric
09 gassiness
11 flow of words
12 forcefulness, gift of the gab
14 articulateness,
   expressiveness

**eloquent**
05 vivid, vocal
06 fluent, moving
07 voluble
08 forceful, graceful, stirring
09 effective, plausible
10 articulate, persuasive
13 well-expressed

**elsewhere**
06 abroad, absent
07 not here, removed
12 another place
13 somewhere else

**elucidate**
06 fill in, unfold
07 clarify, clear up, explain
08 simplify, spell out
09 exemplify, explicate,
   interpret, make clear
10 illuminate, illustrate
11 shed light on, state simply
12 throw light on
13 give an example

**elucidation**
05 gloss
08 footnote

10 annotation, commentary,
   exposition, marginalia
11 explanation, explication
12 illumination, illustration,
   marginal note
13 clarification
14 interpretation

**elude**
04 duck, flee, foil
05 avoid, dodge, evade, shirk
06 baffle, escape, thwart
08 confound, shake off
09 frustrate
10 circumvent
11 get away from

**elusive**
06 shifty, subtle, tricky
07 evasive
08 baffling, puzzling, slippery
09 deceptive, transient
10 intangible, transitory
11 hard to catch, indefinable
15 difficult to find

**emaciated**
04 lean, thin
05 drawn, gaunt
06 meager, skinny, wasted
07 haggard, pinched, scrawny
08 anorexic, skeletal
10 attenuated, cadaverous
11 thin as a rake
12 skin and bones
15 all skin and bones

**emaciation**
07 atrophy
08 leanness, thinness
09 gauntness
11 haggardness, scrawniness

**emanate**
04 come, emit, flow, stem
05 arise, issue
06 derive, emerge, spring
07 give off, give out, proceed,
   radiate, send out
09 discharge, originate

**emanation**
04 flow
06 efflux
08 effluent, effusion, emission
09 discharge, effluence,
   effluvium, radiation

**emancipate**
04 free
05 loose, untie
06 unyoke
07 deliver, manumit, release, set
   free, unchain
08 liberate, set loose, unfetter
09 discharge, unshackle

**emancipation**
07 freedom, liberty, release
10 liberation, unchaining
11 deliverance, manumission,
   setting free, unfettering
15 enfranchisement

**emasculate**
04 geld, spay
06 neuter, soften, weaken
07 cripple
08 castrate, enervate
10 debilitate, impoverish

**embalm**
05 store
06 lay out
07 cherish, mummify
08 conserve, enshrine,
   preserve, treasure

**embankment**
03 dam
04 dike
05 levee
07 rampart
09 earthwork

**embargo**
03 ban, bar
04 stop
05 block, check, seize
06 impede
07 barrier, seizure
08 blockage, obstruct, prohibit,
   restrain, restrict, stoppage
09 hindrance, restraint
10 impediment
11 prohibition, restriction

**embark**
04 sail
05 board
08 go aboard

◻**embark on**
05 begin, enter, start
07 enter on
08 commence, initiate, set
   about
09 undertake
10 launch into

**embarrass**
05 shame, upset
06 show up
07 confuse, fluster, mortify
08 distress
09 discomfit, humiliate
10 discompose, disconcert
14 discountenance

**embarrassed**
05 upset
06 guilty, shamed
07 abashed, ashamed,
   awkward, shown up
08 confused, sheepish

**embarrassing**
09 mortified
10 distressed, humiliated
11 discomfited
12 disconcerted
13 self-conscious, uncomfortable

**embarrassing**
06 touchy, tricky
07 awkward, painful, shaming
08 delicate, shameful
09 sensitive, upsetting
10 indelicate, mortifying
11 distressing, humiliating
12 compromising, discomfiting
13 disconcerting, uncomfortable

**embarrassment**
06 excess, pickle, plight, scrape
07 chagrin, dilemma, surplus
08 distress
09 confusion, profusion
10 constraint, difficulty
11 awkwardness, bashfulness, humiliation, predicament
12 discomfiture, discomposure
13 mortification
14 superabundance

**embassy**
07 mission
08 legation, ministry
09 consulate
10 delegation, deputation

**embed**
04 root, sink
05 drive, plant
06 hammer, insert
07 implant

**embellish**
04 deck, gild, trim
05 adorn, grace
06 bedeck, enrich
07 dress up, enhance, garnish
08 decorate, ornament
09 elaborate, embroider

**embellishment**
07 garnish, gilding
08 ornament, trimming
09 adornment
10 decoration, embroidery, enrichment
11 elaboration, enhancement
13 ornamentation

**embers**
05 ashes
07 cinders, residue

**embezzle**
05 filch, pinch, steal
06 pilfer, rip off
07 purloin, swindle
08 peculate

09 defalcate
11 appropriate
14 misappropriate

**embezzlement**
05 fraud, theft
08 filching, stealing
09 pilfering
11 defalcation
13 appropriation

**embezzler**
05 cheat, crook, fraud, thief
08 criminal
09 peculator
10 defalcator

**embittered**
04 sour
05 angry
06 bitter, piqued
09 resentful
11 disaffected, exasperated
12 disenchanted
13 disillusioned

**emblazon**
05 adorn, color, extol, paint
06 depict, extoll, praise
07 glorify, publish, trumpet
08 decorate, ornament
09 embellish, publicize

**emblem**
04 logo, mark, sign
05 badge, crest, image, token
06 device, figure, symbol
08 insignia

**emblematic**
08 symbolic
10 figurative, symbolical
14 representative

**embodiment**
05 model
07 epitome, example
10 expression
11 incarnation, realization
13 manifestation
15 exemplification, personification

**embody**
06 take in, typify
07 combine, contain, include
08 manifest, stand for
09 exemplify, personify, represent, symbolize
11 incorporate

**embolden**
05 cheer, nerve, rouse
07 hearten, inflame, inspire
08 make bold, reassure, vitalize
09 encourage, make brave
10 invigorate, strengthen
13 give courage to

**embrace**
03 hug
04 hold, neck, span
05 clasp, cover, grasp
06 accept, clinch, take in
07 contain, include, involve, necking, squeeze, welcome
09 encompass
11 incorporate, take on board

**embrocation**
05 cream, salve
06 lotion
07 epithem
08 ointment

**embroider**
03 sew
05 color
06 enrich, stitch
07 dress up, enhance, garnish
08 decorate
09 elaborate, embellish
10 exaggerate

**embroidery**
06 sewing
08 lacework, tapestry
10 needlework
11 needlepoint
13 embellishment

➤ *Types of embroidery stitch*:
04 moss, stem, tent
05 chain, cross, satin
07 blanket, chevron, feather, running
08 fishbone, straight
09 half cross, lazy daisy
10 backstitch, French knot, longstitch
11 herringbone
12 long-and-short

**embroil**
05 mix up
06 enmesh
07 involve
08 draw into, entangle
09 catch up in, implicate

**embryo**
04 germ, root
05 fetus
06 basics
11 unborn child

**embryonic**
05 early
08 germinal, inchoate
09 beginning, incipient
11 rudimentary, undeveloped

**emcee**
02 MC
06 direct
07 present

11 toastmaster

**emend**
04 edit
05 alter, amend
06 polish, redact, refine, revise
07 correct, improve, rectify

**emendation**
07 editing
08 revision
09 amendment, redaction
10 alteration, correction
13 rectification

**emerge**
05 arise, issue
06 appear, crop up, turn up
07 come out, develop, emanate, proceed, surface
09 come forth, transpire
11 come to light, materialize
12 come into view

**emergence**
06 advent, coming
07 arrival
09 unfolding
10 appearance, disclosure
11 development, springing-up

**emergency**
06 backup, crisis, danger, pickle, plight, scrape, strait
07 dilemma, reserve
08 accident, calamity, disaster, exigency, fallback, hot water, quandary
10 difficulty, substitute
11 alternative, catastrophe

**emergent**
06 coming, rising
07 budding
08 emerging
10 developing

**emetic**
07 emtical
08 vomitary, vomitive, vomitory

**emigrate**
07 migrate
08 relocate, resettle
10 move abroad

**emigration**
06 exodus
07 journey, removal
09 departure, migration
10 relocation
12 expatriation, moving abroad

**eminence**
04 fame, note, rank
06 esteem, renown
08 prestige
09 celebrity, greatness

10 importance, notability, prominence, reputation
11 distinction, preeminence

**eminent**
05 grand, great
06 famous
07 notable
08 elevated, esteemed, renowned, superior
09 important, prominent, respected, well-known
10 celebrated, noteworthy
11 conspicuous, high-ranking, illustrious, prestigious
13 distinguished

**eminently**
04 very, well
06 highly
07 greatly, notably
08 signally
09 extremely
10 remarkably, strikingly
11 exceedingly, prominently
13 exceptionally, outstandingly

**emissary**
03 spy
05 agent, envoy, scout
07 courier
08 delegate
09 go-between, messenger
10 ambassador
12 intermediary
14 representative

**emission**
05 issue
07 release
08 ejection
09 diffusion, discharge, emanation, exudation, giving-out, radiation

**emit**
04 leak, ooze, shed, vent
05 eject, exude, issue
06 let out
07 diffuse, emanate, excrete, express, give off, produce, radiate, release, send out
08 throw out
09 discharge, send forth

**emollient**
03 oil
04 balm
05 cream, salve
06 lotion
07 calming, unguent
08 balsamic, lenitive, liniment, ointment, poultice, soothing
09 appeasing, assuaging, placatory, softening
10 mitigative, mollifying
11 moisturizer

**emolument**
03 fee, pay
05 wages
06 profit, return, reward, salary
07 benefit, payment, stipend
08 earnings
10 honorarium, recompense
12 compensation, remuneration

**emotion**
03 joy
04 fear, hate
05 anger, ardor, dread, grief, sense
06 fervor, sorrow, warmth
07 despair, ecstasy, feeling, passion, sadness
09 happiness, sensation, sentiment, vehemence
10 excitement

**emotional**
04 warm
05 fiery, moved, soppy
06 ardent, heated, loving, moving, roused, tender
07 emotive, feeling, fervent
08 exciting, stirring, touching
09 excitable, thrilling
10 hotblooded, passionate
11 impassioned, sentimental, tear-jerking, tempestuous
12 enthusiastic, heartwarming, soul-stirring
13 demonstrative, temperamental

**emotionless**
03 icy
04 cold, cool
05 blank
06 frigid, remote
07 distant, glacial
08 clinical, detached
09 impassive, unfeeling
10 phlegmatic
11 coldblooded, indifferent, unemotional
15 undemonstrative

**emotive**
06 touchy
09 sensitive
12 inflammatory
13 controversial

**empathize**
05 share
07 comfort, feel for, support
10 understand
12 identify with

**emperor**
04 czar
05 ruler
06 kaiser, mikado, shogun

09 imperator, sovereign

► *Names of emperors. We have omitted the word* **emperor** *from names given in the following list but you may need to include this word as part of the solution to some crossword clues. The regnal numerals of individual emperors have also been omitted.*

03 Leo

04 John, Nero, Otho, Otto, Paul, Pu Yi

05 Akbar (the Great), Babur, Basil, Boris, Galba, Henry, Louis, Murad, Nerva, Pedro, Peter, Selim, Titus

06 Julian, Justin, Mehmet, Philip (the Arab), Trajan

07 Agustín (de Itúrbide), Akihito, Alamgir, Alexius, Charles (the Bald), Charles (the Fat), Gordian, Hadrian, Leopold, Lothair, Marcian, Severus

08 Augustus, Aurelius, Caligula, Claudius, Commodus, Constans, Domitian, Galerius, Hirohito, Honorius, Jahangir, Maximian, Napoleon, Nicholas, Suleiman, Tiberius, Valerian

09 Alexander, Antoninus, Aurangzeb, Caracalla, Carausius, Ferdinand, Frederick, Justinian, Kubla Khan, Maxentius, Montezuma, Sigismund, Vespasian, Vitellius

10 Andronicus, Diocletian, Elagabalus, Kublai Khan, Maximilian, Theodosius

11 Charlemagne, Constantine, Valentinian

12 Chandragupta, Heliogabalus

13 Antoninus Pius, Haile Selassie

14 Marcus Aurelius

► *Names of empresses. We have omitted the word* **empress** *from names given in the following list but you may need to include this word as part of the solution to some crossword clues. The regnal numerals of individual empresses have also been omitted.*

02 Lu, Wu

03 Zoë

04 Anna

05 Irene, Livia

06 Helena (Saint)

08 Faustina, Theodora, Victoria

09 Alexandra, Catherine (the Great), Elizabeth, Joséphine (de Beauharnais), Kunigunde (Saint), Messalina

11 Marie Louise

12 Maria Theresa

**emphasis**
04 mark
05 force, power
06 accent, stress, weight
07 urgency
08 priority, strength
09 attention, intensity
10 importance, insistence
12 accentuation, underscoring

**emphasize**
06 accent, play up, stress
08 heighten, insist on
09 highlight, press home, spotlight, underline
10 accentuate, strengthen

**emphatic**
06 direct, marked, strong
07 certain, decided, earnest
08 definite, forceful, positive, powerful, striking, vigorous
09 energetic, insistent
10 pronounced, punctuated
11 categorical, distinctive, significant, unequivocal

**empire**
04 rule, sway
05 power, realm
06 domain
07 command, control, kingdom
08 dominion, province
09 authority, supremacy
11 sovereignty
12 commonwealth, jurisdiction

**empirical**
08 observed
09 practical, pragmatic
12 experiential, experimental

**employ**
03 ply, use
04 fill, hire
05 apply, exert
06 draw on, engage, enlist, occupy, retain, sign up, take on, take up
07 appoint, exploit, utilize
08 exercise, put to use
09 make use of
10 apprentice, commission
11 bring to bear

**employed**
04 busy
05 hired

06 active, in work
07 earning, engaged, working
08 occupied, with a job
12 in employment

**employee**
04 hand
06 worker
07 artisan, laborer
09 assistant, hired hand, operative
10 wage earner, working man
11 staff member
12 office worker, working woman
13 member of staff, working person

**employer**
04 boss, firm, head, user
05 owner
07 company, manager, skipper
08 business, director
09 executive
10 management, proprietor
12 organization

**employment**
03 job
04 hire, line, work
05 craft, trade
06 employ, hiring, métier
07 calling, pursuit, service
08 business, vocation
09 signing-up, situation
10 line of work, occupation, profession

**emporium**
04 fair, mall, mart, shop
05 store
06 bazaar, market
11 marketplace

**empower**
05 equip
06 enable, permit
07 entitle, license, warrant
09 authorize
10 commission

**emptiness**
04 void
06 hiatus, hunger, vacuum
08 bareness, futility, voidness
10 desolation, hollowness
13 senselessness, worthlessness
15 meaninglessness, purposelessness

**empty**
03 gut
04 bare, free, idle, vain, void
05 blank, clear, drain, go out, inane, issue, leave, use up
06 barren, futile, hollow, unload, vacant, vacate

07 pour out, turn out, vacuous
08 deserted, desolate, evacuate, unfilled
09 discharge, fruitless, insincere, senseless, worthless
10 unoccupied
11 ineffective, ineffectual, meaningless, purposeless
14 expressionless
15 with nothing in it

**empty-headed**
04 daft
05 dopey, dotty, inane, silly
06 stupid
07 foolish
08 ignorant
09 brainless, frivolous
14 featherbrained

**emulate**
04 copy, echo
05 match, mimic, rival
06 follow
07 imitate, vie with
15 model yourself on

**emulation**
06 strife
07 copying, mimicry, rivalry
08 conflict, matching
09 challenge, following, imitation

**enable**
04 help
05 allow, endue, equip
06 permit
07 empower, entitle, license, prepare, qualify, warrant
08 accredit, sanction, validate
09 authorize
10 commission, facilitate
12 make possible

**enact**
04 pass, play, rule
06 act out, decree, depict
07 command, make law, perform, portray
09 establish, legislate

**enactment**
03 act, law
04 bill, play, rule
06 acting, decree
07 command, passing, playing, staging, statute
09 ordinance, portrayal
10 performing, regulation
11 legislation, performance
12 ratification
14 representation

**enamored**
07 charmed, smitten
09 entranced

10 captivated, enthralled, fascinated, in love with, infatuated

**encampment**
04 base, camp
05 tents
07 bivouac
08 campsite, quarters
13 camping ground

**encapsulate**
05 sum up
06 digest, précis, take in, typify
07 capture, contain, include
08 compress, condense
09 epitomize, exemplify, represent, summarize

**enchant**
05 charm
06 enamor
07 attract, beguile, bewitch, delight, enthral
08 enthrall, entrance
09 captivate, enrapture, fascinate, hypnotize, mesmerize, spellbind

**enchanter**
05 magus, witch
06 wizard
07 warlock
08 conjurer, magician, sorcerer
09 mesmerist, voodooist
11 necromancer, spellbinder

**enchanting**
06 lovely
08 alluring, charming, pleasant
09 appealing, endearing, ravishing, wonderful
10 attractive, bewitching, delightful, entrancing
11 captivating, fascinating, mesmerizing

**enchantment**
05 bliss, charm, magic, spell
06 glamor
07 delight, ecstasy, rapture, sorcery
08 wizardry
09 hypnotism, mesmerism
10 necromancy, witchcraft
11 fascination, incantation

**enchantress**
04 vamp
05 Circe, lamia, siren, witch
07 charmer
08 conjurer
09 sorceress
10 seductress
11 femme fatale, necromancer

**encircle**
04 gird, ring

05 crowd, hem in, orbit
06 circle, enfold, girdle
07 close in, compass, enclose, envelop
08 surround
09 encompass
12 circumscribe

**enclose**
03 pen
04 cage, hold, ring, wrap
05 bound, cover, fence, frame, hedge, hem in, pen in, put in
06 circle, cocoon, corral, encase, insert, shut in
07 confine, contain, embrace, envelop, include
08 encircle, send with, surround
09 encompass
12 circumscribe

**enclosure**
03 pen, run, sty
04 area, fold, ring, yard
05 arena, court, kraal, pound
06 corral
07 fencing, paddock
08 addition, cloister, compound, stockade
09 inclusion, insertion

**encompass**
04 gird, hold, ring, span
06 circle, shut in, take in
07 circle, confine, contain, embrace, enclose, envelop, include, involve
08 comprise, encircle, surround
11 incorporate
12 circumscribe

**encore**
06 recall, repeat
10 repetition

**encounter**
04 face, meet
05 brush, clash, run-in, set-to
06 action, battle, tussle
07 contact, meeting, run into
08 bump into, conflict, confront, happen on, skirmish
09 collision, run across
10 chance upon, come across, engagement, experience
11 be up against, grapple with
13 come up against, stumble across
15 cross swords with

**encourage**
04 back, help, spur, sway, urge
05 cheer, egg on, rally, rouse
06 exhort, foster, incite, prompt
07 comfort, console, hearten, inspire, promote, support

**encouragement**
08 advocate, embolden, motivate, reassure
09 influence, stimulate
10 strengthen
14 be supportive to

**encouragement**
05 boost, cheer
06 urging
07 backing, pep talk, support
08 stimulus
09 incentive, promotion
10 assistance, incitement, motivation, persuasion
11 consolation, exhortation, furtherance, inspiration, reassurance, stimulation
12 shot in the arm

**encouraging**
04 rosy
06 bright
07 hopeful
08 cheerful, cheering
09 inspiring, promising
10 auspicious, heartening
11 stimulating

**encroach**
05 usurp
06 invade
07 impinge, intrude, overrun
08 infringe, overstep, trespass
10 infiltrate, muscle in on
11 make inroads

**encroachment**
08 invasion
09 incursion, intrusion
11 trespassing
12 infiltration, infringement

**encumber**
06 burden, hamper, hinder, impede, retard, saddle
07 congest, oppress, prevent
08 handicap, overload, restrain, slow down
09 constrain, weigh down
13 inconvenience

**encumbrance**
04 load
06 burden, strain, stress, weight
08 handicap, obstacle
09 albatross, hindrance, millstone, restraint
10 constraint, difficulty, impediment, obligation
13 inconvenience

**encyclopedic**
04 vast
05 broad
08 complete, thorough
09 universal
10 exhaustive

11 compendious
12 all-embracing, all-inclusive
13 comprehensive
15 all-encompassing

**end**
03 aim, tip
04 area, butt, doom, edge, goal, part, ruin, side, stop, stub
05 cease, close, death, issue, limit, point, scrap
06 be over, demise, design, die out, ending, epilog, expire, finale, finish, intent, motive, object, reason, result, run out, upshot, wind up
07 abolish, outcome, purpose, remnant, section, vestige
08 break off, conclude, dissolve, downfall, epilogue, fade away, fragment, left-over, round off
09 cessation, culminate, extremity, intention, objective, terminate
10 annihilate, completion, conclusion, denouement, dénouement, extinction, extinguish
11 consequence, culmination, destruction, discontinue, dissolution, exterminate, termination
13 extermination

**□the end**
06 enough
07 too much
08 the limit, the worst
10 unbearable
11 intolerable, the greatest, unendurable
12 insufferable, the final blow, the last straw
15 beyond endurance

**endanger**
04 risk
06 expose, hazard
07 imperil
08 threaten
09 put at risk
10 compromise, jeopardize
11 put in danger
13 put in jeopardy

**endearing**
05 sweet
07 lovable, winsome
08 adorable, charming, engaging
09 appealing
10 attractive, delightful

**endearment**
04 love

07 pet name
08 fondness
09 affection
10 diminutive, hypocorism
12 sweet nothing

**endeavor**
02 go
03 aim, try
04 seek
05 labor
06 aspire, effort, strive
07 attempt, venture
08 striving, struggle
09 take a shot, take a stab, take pains, undertake
10 do your best, enterprise, take a crack
11 undertaking

**ending**
03 end
05 close
06 climax, epilog, finale, finish
08 epilogue
09 cessation
10 completion, conclusion, dénouement, resolution
11 culmination, termination
12 consummation

**endless**
06 boring, entire
07 eternal, undying
08 constant, infinite, unbroken, unending
09 boundless, ceaseless, continual, limitless, perpetual, unlimited
10 continuous, without end
11 everlasting, measureless
12 interminable
13 uninterrupted

**endorse**
04 back, sign
05 favor
06 affirm, ratify, uphold
07 approve, confirm, support, sustain, warrant
08 advocate, be behind, sanction, vouch for
09 authorize, get behind, recommend
11 countersign, subscribe to

**endorsement**
02 OK
04 okay
07 backing, support, warrant
08 advocacy, approval, sanction
09 signature
11 affirmation, testimonial
12 commendation, confirmation, ratification
13 authorization

14 recommendation, seal of approval

**endow**
04 fund, give, have, will
05 award, boast, grant, leave
06 bestow, confer, donate
07 furnish, present, provide
08 bequeath, make over

**endowment**
04 fund, gift
05 award, dowry, flair, grant
06 income, legacy, talent
07 ability, bequest, present, quality, revenue
08 aptitude, bestowal, donation
09 attribute, financing, provision
10 capability, settlement
11 benefaction
13 qualification

**endurable**
08 bearable
09 tolerable
10 manageable, sufferable
11 supportable, sustainable

**endurance**
07 stamina
08 patience, stoicism, tenacity
09 fortitude, stability
10 resolution, toleration
11 persistence, resignation
12 perseverance, staying power, stickability

**endure**
04 bear, face, hold, last, stay
05 abide, brave, stand, stick
06 permit, remain, suffer
07 persist, prevail, survive, sustain, undergo, weather
08 continue, tolerate
09 encounter, go through, put up with, withstand
10 experience

**enduring**
04 firm
06 stable, steady
07 abiding, chronic, durable, eternal, lasting
08 immortal
09 permanent, perpetual, remaining, steadfast, surviving
10 continuing, persistent, persisting, prevailing
11 long-lasting, unfaltering
12 imperishable, long-standing

**enemy**
03 foe
05 rival
08 opponent
09 adversary, other side

10 antagonist, competitor

**energetic**
05 brisk, zippy
06 active, lively, potent
07 dynamic, zestful
08 animated, forceful, powerful, spirited, vigorous
09 go-getting, strenuous
10 boisterous
11 full of beans, high-powered

**energize**
04 stir
05 liven, pep up
06 arouse, vivify
07 animate, enliven, quicken
08 activate, motivate, vitalize
09 electrify, galvanize, stimulate
10 invigorate

**energy**
03 vim, zip
04 brio, fire, life, push, zeal, zest
05 ardor, drive, force, get-up, power, verve, vigor
06 pizazz, spirit
07 pizzazz, sparkle, stamina
08 activity, dynamism, exertion, strength, vitality, vivacity
09 animation, intensity
10 efficiency, enthusiasm, get-up-and-go, liveliness
12 forcefulness
13 effectiveness, effervescence

**enervated**
04 limp, weak
05 spent, tired
06 done in, effete, sapped
07 run-down, worn out
08 fatigued, unmanned, unnerved, weakened
09 exhausted, washed-out
11 debilitated, devitalized
13 incapacitated

**enfeeble**
03 sap
04 geld
06 reduce, weaken
07 deplete, exhaust, fatigue, unhinge, unnerve, wear out
08 diminish, enervate
09 undermine
10 debilitate, devitalize

**enfold**
03 hug
04 fold, hold, wrap
05 clasp
06 shroud, swathe, wrap up
07 embrace, enclose, envelop
08 encircle
09 encompass

**enforce**
05 apply, force
06 coerce, compel, impose, oblige
07 execute, fulfill, require
08 carry out, insist on, pressure
09 discharge, implement, prosecute, reinforce
10 administer, pressurize
11 necessitate

**enforced**
06 forced
07 binding, imposed, obliged
09 compelled, necessary
10 compulsory, prescribed
11 involuntary, unavoidable

**enforcement**
08 coaction, coercion, pressure
09 discharge, execution
10 compulsion, imposition, insistence, obligation
11 prosecution, requirement
14 implementation

**enfranchise**
04 free
07 manumit, release
08 liberate
10 emancipate
13 give the vote to
14 give suffrage to

**enfranchisement**
07 freedom, freeing, release
08 suffrage
10 liberating, liberation
11 manumission
12 emancipation, voting rights

**engage**
03 win
04 busy, draw, fill, gain, grip, hire, hold, join, mesh
05 catch, charm, fight, tie up
06 allure, attach, attack, employ, enlist, enmesh, join in, occupy, sign up, take on, take up
07 appoint, involve, recruit
08 contract, embark on, interact, practice, take part
09 captivate, clash with, encounter, enter into, interlock, undertake
10 battle with, commission
11 fit together, participate
12 interconnect
15 put on the payroll

**engaged**
04 busy
05 in use, taken
06 active, tied up
07 pledged

08 employed, espoused, involved, occupied, plighted, promised
09 affianced, betrothed, committed, spoken for
11 preoccupied, unavailable

**engagement**
04 bond, date
05 clash, fight, troth
06 action, battle, pledge
07 contest, fixture, meeting
08 conflict, contract, struggle
09 agreement, assurance, betrothal, encounter, interview, offensive
10 commitment, rendezvous
11 appointment, assignation
13 confrontation

**engaging**
05 sweet
07 lovable, winning, winsome
08 adorable, charming, fetching, pleasant, pleasing
09 agreeable, appealing
10 attractive, delightful
11 captivating, fascinating

**engender**
05 beget, breed, cause
06 arouse, create, effect, excite, incite, induce, kindle, lead to
07 inspire, produce, provoke
08 generate, occasion
09 instigate, propagate
10 bring about, give rise to

**engine**
05 motor
06 device, dynamo
07 machine
09 appliance, generator, machinery, mechanism
10 instrument, locomotive

► *Engine parts*:
03 cam
05 choke, rotor
06 gasket, oil pan, piston, tappet
07 fan belt, oil pump, push-rod, starter
08 camshaft, flywheel, manifold, radiator, rotor arm
09 air filter, drive belt, oil filter, rocker arm, rockshaft, spark plug
10 alternator, carburetor, cooling fan, crankshaft, drive shaft, inlet valve, petrol pump, piston ring, timing belt
12 cylinder head, exhaust valve, fuel injector, ignition coil, turbocharger
13 connecting rod, cylinder block, inlet manifold

15 exhaust manifold

► *Types of engine*:
03 gas, jet
05 steam, turbo
06 diesel, donkey
07 turbine
08 turbojet
09 turboprop
13 fuel-injection

**engineer**
03 rig
04 plan, plot
05 cause
06 create, devise, direct, driver, effect, manage, scheme
07 arrange, builder, control, deviser, planner
08 contrive, designer, inventor, maneuver, mechanic, operator
10 bring about, manipulate, mastermind, technician
11 orchestrate, stage-manage

► *Names of engineers*:
04 **Bell** (Alexander Graham), **Benz** (Karl), **Bush** (Vannevar), **Eads** (James Buchanan), **Ford** (Henry), **Page** (Frederick Handley), **Watt** (James)
05 **Baird** (John Logie), **Braun** (Wernher), **Maxim** (Hiram Stevens), **Rolls** (Charles Stewart), **Royce** (Henry), **Tesla** (Nikola)
06 **Brunel** (Isambard Kingdom), **Brunel** (Marc Isambard), **Diesel** (Rudolf Christian Karl), **Eckert** (John Presper), **Edison** (Thomas Alva), **Eiffel** (Gustave), **Fokker** (Anthony Herman Gerard), **Fuller** (Buckminster), **Jansky** (Karl Guthe), **McAdam** (John Loudon), **Rennie** (John), **Savery** (Thomas), **Taylor** (Frederick Winslow), **Vauban** (Sebastien le Prestre de), **Wallis** (Barnes Neville), **Wankel** (Felix), **Wright** (Orville), **Wright** (Wilbur)
07 **Citroën** (André Gustave), **Daimler** (Gottlieb), **Dornier** (Claude), **Eastman** (George), **Fleming** (John Ambrose), **Goddard** (Robert Hutchings), **Lesseps** (Ferdinand Marie, **Mauchly** (John), **Nasmyth** (James), **Parsons** (Charles

Algernon), **Porsche** (Ferdinand), **Rankine** (William John Macquorn), **Siemens** (Werner von), **Siemens** (William), **Sopwith** (Thomas Octave Murdoch), **Telford** (Thomas), **Tupolev** (Andrei), **Whittle** (Frank)
08 **Bessemer** (Henry), **De Forest** (Lee), **Ericsson** (John), **Ferranti** (Sebastian Ziani de), **Goethals** (George), **Korolyov** (Sergei), **Poncelet** (Jean Victor), **Sikorsky** (Igor), **Sinclair** (Clive), **Zeppelin** (Ferdinand, von)
09 **Cockerell** (Christopher Sydney), **Issigonis** (Alec), **Trésaguet** (Pierre Marie Jerome), **Whitworth** (Joseph)
10 **Bazalgette** (Joseph William), **Farnsworth** (Philo), **Lilienthal** (Otto), **Stephenson** (George), **Stephenson** (Robert), **Trevithick** (Richard)
11 **De Havilland** (Geoffrey), **Montgolfier** (Joseph Michel)
12 **Westinghouse** (George)
13 **Messerschmitt** (Willy)
➤ See also SCIENTIST

**engrave**
03 cut, fix, set
04 etch, mark
05 brand, carve, chase, embed
06 chisel, incise
07 engrain, impress, imprint
08 inscribe

**engraving**
03 cut
04 mark
05 block, plate, print
07 carving, cutting, etching, imprint, woodcut
08 drypoint, intaglio
09 chiseling
10 impression
11 inscription

**engross**
04 grip, hold
05 rivet
06 absorb, engage, occupy
07 enthral, involve
08 enthrall, interest, intrigue
09 captivate, fascinate

**engrossed**
04 lost, rapt
06 intent

07 engaged, fixated, gripped, riveted, taken up, wrapped
08 absorbed, caught up, immersed, occupied
09 intrigued
10 captivated, enthralled, fascinated, mesmerized

**engrossing**
08 gripping, riveting
09 absorbing
10 compelling, intriguing
11 captivating, enthralling, fascinating, interesting
13 unputdownable

**engulf**
04 bury
05 drown, flood, swamp
06 absorb, devour, plunge
07 consume, engross, envelop, immerse, overrun
08 inundate, overtake, submerge
09 overwhelm, swallow up

**enhance**
04 lift
05 add to, boost, exalt, raise
06 enrich, stress
07 augment, improve, upgrade
08 heighten, increase
09 embellish, emphasize, intensify, reinforce
10 strengthen

**enhancement**
05 boost
06 stress
08 emphasis, increase
10 enrichment
11 heightening, improvement
12 augmentation
13 reinforcement
15 intensification

**enigma**
05 poser
06 puzzle, riddle
07 mystery, paradox, problem
09 conundrum
11 brain-teaser

**enigmatic**
06 arcane
07 cryptic, obscure, strange
08 baffling, esoteric, puzzling
09 recondite
10 mysterious, mystifying, perplexing
11 paradoxical
12 inexplicable, unfathomable

**enjoin**
04 urge
05 order

06 advise, charge, decree, demand, direct, ordain
07 command, require
08 disallow, instruct, prohibit
09 interdict, proscribe

**enjoy**
04 have, like, love
05 savor
06 relish
07 possess, revel in
08 be fond of
09 delight in, rejoice in
14 take pleasure in

◻**enjoy yourself**
07 have fun
08 live it up
09 make merry
13 have a good time
15 let your hair down

**enjoyable**
03 fun
04 fine, good, nice
06 lovely
07 amusing
08 pleasant, pleasing
09 agreeable, delicious
10 gratifying, satisfying
11 pleasurable
12 entertaining

**enjoyment**
03 fun, joy, use
04 zest
05 favor, gusto
06 relish
08 blessing, gladness, pleasure
09 amusement, diversion, happiness
10 indulgence, recreation
11 delectation
12 satisfaction
13 entertainment, gratification

**enlarge**
05 add to, swell, widen
06 blow up, dilate, expand, extend
07 amplify, augment, broaden, develop, distend, inflate, magnify, stretch
08 elongate, expand on, heighten, increase, lengthen
09 intumesce
10 make bigger, supplement
11 elaborate on, expatiate on
12 become bigger

**enlargement**
05 edema
06 blowup
08 dilation, increase, swelling
09 expansion, extension, inflation
10 distension, stretching

11 development
12 augmentation, intumescence
13 amplification, magnification

**enlighten**
05 edify, teach, tutor
06 advise, inform
07 apprise, counsel, educate
08 instruct
09 cultivate, make aware
10 illuminate

**enlightened**
04 wise
05 aware
07 erudite, learned, liberal
08 educated, informed
09 civilized
10 conversant, cultivated
13 knowledgeable

**enlightenment**
06 wisdom
07 insight
08 learning, teaching
09 awareness, education, erudition, knowledge
11 cultivation, edification, information, instruction
13 comprehension, understanding

**enlist**
04 hire, join
05 draft, enter
06 employ, engage, enroll, join up, muster, sign on, sign up, take on
07 procure, recruit
08 register
09 conscript, volunteer

**enliven**
05 cheer, liven, pep up, rouse
06 buoy up, excite, kindle, perk up, vivify, wake up
07 animate, cheer up, hearten, inspire, liven up, quicken
08 brighten
10 invigorate, revitalize
11 give a lift to

**en masse**
05 as one
06 en bloc
07 in a body
08 as a group, as a whole, ensemble, together
09 all at once, wholesale
11 all together

**enmity**
04 feud, hate
05 venom
06 hatred, malice, rancor, strife
07 discord, ill will

**ennoble**

08 acrimony, bad blood
09 animosity, antipathy, hostility
10 antagonism, bitterness
11 malevolence

**ennoble**

05 exalt, honor, raise
06 uplift
07 dignify, elevate, enhance, glorify, magnify
10 aggrandize, nobilitate

**ennui**

06 acedia, apathy, tedium
07 accidia, accidie, boredom, languor
09 lassitude, tiredness
12 listlessness
15 dissatisfaction

**enormity**

04 evil
06 horror
07 outrage
08 atrocity, iniquity, vastness, vileness
09 depravity, immensity, magnitude, violation
10 wickedness
11 abomination, monstrosity
13 atrociousness
14 outrageousness

**enormous**

04 huge, vast
05 gross, jumbo
07 immense, mammoth, massive
08 colossal, gigantic, great big
09 monstrous
10 astronomic, gargantuan, stupendous, tremendous

**enormously**

06 hugely
09 immensely, massively
11 exceedingly
12 tremendously
13 to a huge extent
15 extraordinarily

**enormousness**

07 expanse
08 hugeness, vastness
09 greatness, magnitude
11 immenseness, massiveness
13 extensiveness

**enough**

05 ample, amply
06 fairly, plenty
08 abundant, adequacy, adequate, passably
09 abundance, amplitude
10 adequately, moderately, reasonably, sufficient
11 ample supply, sufficiency

12 sufficiently
14 satisfactorily

**en passant**

08 by the way
09 cursorily, in passing
12 incidentally

**enquire, enquirer, enquiring, enquiry** see INQUIRE, INQUIRER, INQUIRING, INQUIRY

**enrage**

04 rile
05 anger, annoy
06 incite, madden
07 agitate, incense, inflame
09 infuriate, make angry
10 exasperate, push too far

**enraged**

03 mad
04 wild
05 angry, irate, livid
06 fuming, raging
07 angered, annoyed, furious
08 incensed, storming
10 aggravated, infuriated
11 exasperated

**enrapture**

05 charm
06 ravish, thrill
07 beguile, bewitch, delight, enchant, enthral
08 enthrall, entrance
09 captivate, fascinate, spellbind, transport

**enrich**

04 gild
05 add to, adorn, endow, grace
07 enhance, garnish, improve
08 decorate, ornament
09 cultivate, embellish
10 aggrandize, supplement

**enroll**

05 admit, enter
06 engage, enlist, induct, join up, record, sign on, sign up
07 go in for, put down, recruit
08 inscribe, register
15 put your name down

**enrollment**

09 admission, enlisting, joining up, signing on, signing up
10 acceptance, enlistment
11 recruitment
12 registration

**en route**

08 on the way
09 in transit, on the move, on the road

**ensconce**

05 lodge, place

06 nestle, screen, settle, shield
07 install, protect, shelter
08 entrench
09 establish

**ensemble**

03 set, sum
04 band, cast, suit
05 get-up, group, total, whole
06 chorus, outfit, troupe
07 company, costume
08 entirety
10 collection
11 coordinates

**enshrine**

05 exalt, guard
06 embalm, hallow, revere
07 cherish, idolize, protect
08 preserve, sanctify, treasure
10 consecrate
11 apotheosize, immortalize

**enshroud**

04 hide, pall, veil, wrap
05 cloak, cloud, cover
06 enfold, enwrap, shroud
07 enclose, envelop, obscure

**ensign**

04 flag, jack
05 badge, crest
06 banner, colors, shield
07 pennant
08 standard
10 coat of arms
12 naval officer

**enslave**

04 bind, trap, yoke
07 enchain, oppress, subject
09 subjugate

**enslavement**

07 bondage, serfdom, slavery
08 thraldom
09 captivity, servitude
10 oppression, repression, subjection
11 enthralment, subjugation
12 enthrallment

**ensnare**

03 net
04 trap
05 catch, snare
06 enmesh, entrap
07 capture, embroil
08 entangle

**ensue**

04 flow, stem
05 arise, issue, occur
06 befall, derive, follow, happen, result
07 proceed, succeed, turn out
08 come next
09 transpire

**ensure**
05 guard
06 effect, secure
07 certify, protect, warrant
08 make safe, make sure
09 guarantee, safeguard
11 make certain

**entail**
04 need
05 cause
06 demand, lead to
07 involve, produce, require
08 occasion, result in
10 bring about, give rise to
11 necessitate

**entangle**
05 mix up, ravel, snare, twist
06 enmesh, jumble, muddle
07 embroil, ensnare, involve
10 complicate, intertwine

**entanglement**
04 knot, mesh, mess, trap
05 mix-up, snare, snarl
06 affair, muddle, tangle
07 liaison
09 confusion
11 involvement, predicament
12 complication, love triangle
13 embarrassment

**entente**
04 deal, pact
06 treaty
07 compact
09 agreement
10 friendship
11 arrangement
13 understanding
15 entente cordiale

**enter**
03 log
04 go in, join, list, note
05 begin, board, get in, input, lodge, start
06 arrive, enlist, enroll, go into, insert, occupy, record, sign up, submit, take up
07 break in, burst in, get into, go in for, put down
08 engage in, inscribe, register, take down, take part
09 introduce, penetrate
10 embark upon, infiltrate
11 participate, put on record
15 become a member of

**enterprise**
04 firm, plan, push, task
05 drive, get-up, oomph
06 effort, energy, scheme, spirit
07 company, project, venture
08 boldness, business, endeavor, industry

09 operation
10 get-up-and-go, initiative
11 undertaking
13 establishment
15 adventurousness, resourcefulness

**enterprising**
04 bold, keen
05 eager, pushy
06 active, daring, gung-ho
07 go-ahead, zealous
08 aspiring, spirited, vigorous
09 ambitious, energetic
11 adventurous, imaginative, resourceful, self-reliant
15 entrepreneurial

**entertain**
04 host
05 amuse, charm, cheer
06 divert, engage, foster, harbor, occupy, please, regale
07 delight, engross, imagine, nurture, receive
08 consider, interest
09 captivate
10 have around, have guests, think about
11 contemplate, countenance

► *Types of entertainer*:
02 DJ
05 actor, clown, comic, mimic
06 busker, dancer, deejay, jester, player, singer
07 acrobat, actress, artiste, juggler
08 comedian, conjuror, magician, minstrel, musician, stripper
09 hypnotist, performer, presenter, trapezist
10 comedienne, disc jockey, mime artist, mind reader
12 escapologist, stand-up comic
13 impressionist, trapeze artist, ventriloquist
15 song-and-dance act, tightrope walker
➤ See also ACTOR, ACTRESS; COMEDIAN; MUSICIAN; SINGER

**entertaining**
03 fun
05 funny, witty
07 amusing, comical
08 humorous, pleasing
09 diverting, enjoyable
11 interesting, pleasurable

**entertainment**
03 fun
04 play, show

05 hobby, sport
07 leisure, pastime
08 activity, pleasure
09 amusement, diversion, enjoyment, spectacle
10 recreation
11 distraction, performance
12 extravaganza, presentation

► *Types of entertainment*:
03 zoo
04 fête, game
05 dance, disco, movie, opera, radio, revue, rodeo, sport, video
06 casino, circus
07 cabaret, concert, karaoke, musical, pageant, recital, show biz, theater
08 carnival, festival, gymkhana, waxworks
09 magic show, nightclub, pantomime
10 puppet show, television, vaudeville
11 discothèque, variety show
12 show business
➤ See also THEATRICAL

**enthrall, enthral**
04 grip
05 charm, rivet
06 absorb, thrill
07 beguile, bewitch, delight, enchant, engross
08 entrance, intrigue
09 captivate, fascinate, hypnotize, mesmerize

**enthralling**
08 charming, gripping, mesmeric, riveting
09 beguiling, thrilling
10 compelling, compulsive, enchanting, entrancing
11 captivating, fascinating, hypnotizing, mesmerizing
12 spellbinding

**enthuse**
04 fire, gush, rave
05 drool
06 excite, praise
07 inspire
08 motivate
10 bubble over, wax lyrical

**enthusiasm**
04 fire, rage, zeal, zest
05 ardor, craze, hobby, mania, thing
06 fervor, frenzy, relish, spirit
07 passion, pastime
08 devotion, interest, keenness
09 eagerness, vehemence
10 commitment, excitement

**enthusiast**
03 fan
04 buff
05 fiend, freak, lover
06 zealot
07 admirer, devotee, fanatic
09 supporter
10 aficionado

**enthusiastic**
03 mad
04 avid, daft, keen, nuts, wild
05 crazy, eager, potty
06 ardent
07 excited, fervent, zealous
08 spirited, vehement, vigorous
09 ebullient, fanatical
10 passionate
12 wholehearted

**entice**
04 coax, draw, lure
05 tempt
06 cajole, induce, lead on,
   seduce
07 attract, beguile
08 inveigle, persuade
09 sweet-talk

**enticement**
04 bait, lure
05 decoy
06 come-on
07 coaxing
08 cajolery
09 seduction, sweet-talk
10 allurement, attraction,
   inducement, temptation

**entire**
04 full
05 sound, total, whole
08 absolute, complete

**entirely**
04 only
05 fully
06 in toto, solely, wholly
07 totally, utterly
09 every inch, perfectly
10 absolutely, altogether,
   completely, thoroughly
11 exclusively
12 unreservedly

**entirety**
05 whole
08 fullness, totality
09 wholeness
12 completeness

**entitle**
03 dub
04 call, name, term
05 allow, label, style, title
06 enable, know as, permit
07 license, qualify, warrant

08 accredit, christen, sanction
09 authorize, designate

**entity**
04 body
05 being, thing
06 object
08 creature, organism
09 existence, substance

**entombment**
06 burial
09 interment, sepulture
10 inhumation

**entourage**
05 court, staff, suite, train
06 escort
07 company, cortège, retinue
09 followers, hangers-on,
   retainers
10 attendants, companions

**entrails**
04 guts
05 offal
06 bowels, tripes
07 giblets, innards, insides,
   numbles, viscera
10 intestines

**entrance**
04 door, gate, hall
05 charm, debut, drive, entry,
   foyer, lobby, porch, way in
06 access, atrium, entrée, ravish
07 arrival, beguile, bewitch,
   delight, doorway, enchant,
   enthral, gateway, ingress
08 approach, driveway, enthrall
09 admission, captivate,
   enrapture, fascinate,
   hypnotize, mesmerize,
   spellbind, threshold,
   transport, vestibule
10 admittance, appearance
12 introduction, right of entry

**entrant**
05 entry, pupil, rival
07 convert, learner, starter,
   student, trainee
08 beginner, freshman, initiate,
   newcomer, opponent
09 applicant, candidate,
   contender
10 competitor, contestant
11 participant, probationer

**entrap**
03 net
04 lure, trap
05 catch, snare, trick
06 allure, ambush, delude,
   enmesh, entice, seduce
07 beguile, capture, deceive,
   embroil, ensnare

08 entangle, inveigle

**entreat**
03 ask, beg
04 pray
07 beseech, implore, request
08 appeal to, petition
09 importune, plead with
10 supplicate

**entreaty**
03 cry
04 plea, suit
06 appeal, prayer
07 request
08 petition
10 invocation
12 solicitation, supplication

**entrench**
03 fix, set
04 root, seat
05 dig in, embed, lodge, plant
06 anchor, settle
07 ingrain, install
08 ensconce, stop a gap
09 establish
10 strengthen

**entrenched**
03 set
04 firm
05 fixed
06 inbred, rooted
07 die-hard
09 indelible, ingrained
10 deep-rooted, deep-seated,
   inflexible, unshakable
12 ineradicable, intransigent
13 dyed-in-the-wool
15 well-established

**entrepreneur**
05 agent
06 broker, dealer, tycoon
07 magnate, manager
08 promoter
09 financier, middleman
10 impresario, speculator
11 businessman
13 businesswoman, industrialist

**entrepreneurial**
08 business, economic
09 budgetary, financial
10 commercial, managerial

**entrust**
05 trust
06 charge, commit, invest
07 commend, confide, consign
08 delegate, hand over
09 authorize
11 put in charge

**entry**
04 door, gate, hall, item, note
05 foyer, lobby, porch, way in

**entwine**
06 access, minute, record
07 doorway, entrant, gateway, listing, opening, passage
08 approach, entrance
09 admission, applicant, candidate, statement, threshold, vestibule
10 admittance, appearance, competitor, contestant
12 introduction

**entwine**
04 knit, knot, wind
05 braid, plait, ravel, twine, twist, weave
07 embroil, intwine, wreathe
08 entangle
09 interlace, interlink
10 intertwine, interweave

**enumerate**
04 cite, list, name, tell
05 count, quote
06 detail, number, recite, reckon, relate
07 itemize, recount, specify
09 calculate

**enunciate**
03 say
05 sound, speak, state, voice
07 declare, express
08 announce, vocalize
09 pronounce
10 articulate, put forward

**envelop**
04 hide, veil, wrap
05 cloak, cover
06 encase, enfold, engulf, enwrap, shroud, swathe
07 conceal, enclose, obscure
08 encircle, surround
09 encompass

**envelope**
04 case, skin
05 cover, shell
06 casing, jacket, sheath
07 coating, wrapper
08 covering, wrapping

**enviable**
05 lucky
07 favored
09 desirable, fortunate
10 privileged
11 sought-after
12 advantageous

**envious**
05 green
07 jealous
08 covetous, grudging
09 green-eyed, jaundiced, resentful
10 begrudging

12 dissatisfied
13 green with envy

**environment**
06 locale, medium, milieu
07 climate, context, element, habitat, setting
08 ambience
09 situation, territory
10 atmosphere, background, conditions, influences
12 surroundings
13 circumstances

**environmentalist**
05 green
09 ecologist
15 conservationist, preservationist

**environs**
07 suburbs
08 locality, purlieus, vicinity
09 outskirts, precincts
12 neighborhood, surroundings

**envisage**
03 see
07 foresee, imagine, picture, predict, think of
09 see coming, visualize
10 anticipate, conceive of
11 contemplate, preconceive

**envoy**
05 agent
06 consul, deputy, legate, nuncio
07 attaché, courier
08 delegate, diplomat, emissary, mediator, minister
09 go-between, messenger
10 ambassador
12 intermediary
14 representative

**envy**
05 covet, crave, spite
06 grudge, malice, resent
08 begrudge, jealousy
10 resentment
12 covetousness
13 resentfulness

**ephemeral**
05 brief, short
07 fungous, passing
08 fleeting, flitting
09 fugacious, momentary, temporary, transient
10 evanescent, short-lived, transitory

**epic**
04 huge, long, myth, saga, vast
05 grand, great, large, lofty
06 heroic, legend
07 exalted, history, sublime

08 colossal, elevated, long poem, majestic
09 ambitious, long story
10 impressive, large-scale

**epicure**
07 glutton, gourmet
08 gourmand, hedonist, Sybarite
09 bon vivant, bon viveur, epicurean
10 gastronome, sensualist
11 connoisseur, gastronomer
12 gastronomist

**epicurean**
07 gourmet, sensual
08 luscious
09 libertine, luxurious, Sybaritic
10 gluttonous, hedonistic
11 gastronomic
12 unrestrained
13 gastronomical, gourmandizing

**epidemic**
04 rash, rife, rise, wave
05 spate
06 growth, plague, spread
07 rampant, scourge, upsurge
08 increase, pandemic
09 pervasive, prevalent
10 prevailing, widespread
11 wide-ranging

**epigram**
04 poem, quip
05 adage, gnome, maxim
06 bon mot, saying
07 proverb
08 aphorism
09 witticism
10 apophthegm

**epigrammatic**
05 pithy, sharp, short, witty
06 ironic
07 concise, laconic, piquant, pointed, pungent
08 incisive, succinct
10 aphoristic

**epilogue, epilog**
02 P.S.
04 coda
08 appendix, swan song
09 afterword
10 conclusion, postscript

**episode**
04 part
05 event, scene
06 affair, matter
07 chapter, passage, section
08 business, incident, occasion
09 adventure, happening
10 experience

11 installment

**episodic**
08 periodic, sporadic
09 anecdotal, irregular
10 occasional, picaresque
12 disconnected, intermittent

**epistle**
04 line, note
06 letter
07 message, missive
08 bulletin
13 communication
14 correspondence

**epitaph**
03 R.I.P.
08 here lies, hic jacet, obituary
11 inscription, rest in peace

**epithet**
03 tag
04 name
05 title
08 nickname
09 sobriquet
11 appellation, description

**epitome**
04 type
05 model
06 digest, précis, résumé
07 essence, example, summary
08 abstract, exemplar, synopsis
10 abridgment, embodiment
12 quintessence
14 representation
15 personification

**epitomize**
03 cut
05 sum up
06 embody, précis, typify
07 abridge, curtail, shorten
08 abstract, compress,
   condense, contract
09 exemplify, personify,
   represent, summarize
11 encapsulate

**epoch**
03 age, era
04 date, time
06 period

**equable**
04 calm, even
06 placid, serene, smooth,
   stable, steady
08 composed, constant, laid-
   back, moderate, tranquil
09 easy-going, temperate
10 consistent, unchanging
11 levelheaded, unflappable
12 even-tempered
13 imperturbable

**equal**
03 fit, tie
04 able, draw, even, fair, just,
   like, make, mate, peer, twin
05 alike, level, match, rival, total
07 add up to, balance, capable,
   matched, regular, the same
08 adequate, amount to,
   balanced, come up to,
   equalize, parallel, suitable
09 competent, identical, tally
   with
10 comparable, equate with,
   equivalent, fifty-fifty, square
   with, sufficient, unchanging
11 be level with, be the same as,
   counterpart, measure up to,
   neck and neck, nonpartisan,
   symmetrical
12 be on a par with, coincide
   with, commensurate,
   correspond to
13 corresponding, evenly
   matched

**equality**
03 par
06 parity
07 balance, justice
08 evenness, fairness, likeness,
   sameness, symmetry
10 similarity, uniformity
11 equal rights, equivalence
13 comparability
14 correspondence,
   egalitarianism

**equalize**
03 tie
04 draw
05 equal, level, match
06 equate, even up, square
07 balance, even out
08 keep pace, make even
09 draw level
10 compensate, regularize
11 standardize

**equanimity**
04 calm, ease, pose
06 aplomb
07 dignity
08 coolness, serenity
09 assurance, composure,
   placidity, sangfroid
10 confidence
11 impassivity, self-control,
   tranquility
13 self-assurance
14 self-possession,
   unflappability
15 levelheadedness

**equate**
06 offset

07 balance, be equal, liken to
08 equalize, pair with, parallel
09 agree with, tally with
10 correspond, square with
15 bracket together

**equation**
05 match
07 pairing
08 equality, identity, likeness,
   matching, parallel
09 agreement, balancing
10 comparison, similarity
11 equivalence
14 correspondence

**equestrian**
05 rider
06 cowboy, equine, herder,
   hussar, jockey, knight, riding
07 courier, cowgirl, mounted,
   rancher, trooper
08 cavalier, horseman
10 cavalryman, horsewoman
11 horse-riding

**equilibrium**
05 poise
06 aplomb, stasis
07 balance, dignity
08 calmness, coolness,
   evenness, symmetry
09 assurance, composure,
   sangfroid, stability
10 equanimity, steadiness
11 self-control
14 self-possession
15 levelheadedness

**equip**
03 arm, rig
05 array, dress, endow, fit up,
   issue, stake, stock
06 fit out, supply
07 furnish, prepare, provide
08 accouter, accoutre
09 grubstake

**equipment**
03 kit
04 gear
05 tools
06 outfit, tackle, things
08 material, rig stuff, supplies
09 apparatus, furniture
11 accessories, furnishings
13 accouterments,
   accoutrements,
   paraphernalia

**equipoise**
07 balance, ballast
08 evenness, symmetry
09 stability
11 equibalance, equilibrium
12 counterpoise
13 counterweight

14 counterbalance

**equitable**
03 due
04 fair, just
05 right
06 honest, proper, square
07 ethical
08 rightful, unbiased
09 impartial, objective
10 even-handed, reasonable
12 unprejudiced
13 disinterested, fair-and-
   square

**equity**
07 honesty, justice
08 fair play, fairness, justness
13 equitableness
14 even-handedness,
   reasonableness

**equivalence**
06 parity
08 equality, sameness
11 correlation
13 comparability
14 correspondence

**equivalent**
04 even, like, peer, same, twin
05 alike, equal, match
07 homolog
08 parallel
09 homologue, identical
10 comparable, tantamount
11 correlative, counterpart
12 commensurate
13 correspondent,
   corresponding
14 opposite number
15 interchangeable

**equivocal**
05 vague
07 evasive, oblique, obscure
09 ambiguous, uncertain
10 ambivalent, suspicious

**equivocate**
05 dodge, evade, fence, hedge
06 waffle
09 pussyfoot, vacillate
11 prevaricate
12 shilly-shally, tergiversate
13 hedge your bets

**equivocation**
07 evasion, hedging
10 double talk
11 weasel words
12 pussyfooting
13 prevarication
·14 tergiversation
15 dodging the issue

**era**
03 age, day, eon

04 date, days, time
05 cycle, epoch, stage, times
06 period, season
07 century
10 generation

**eradicate**
05 erase
06 efface, remove, uproot
07 abolish, destroy, expunge,
   root out, weed out, wipe out
08 get rid of, stamp out
09 eliminate, extirpate
10 annihilate, obliterate
11 crack down on, exterminate

**eradication**
07 removal
08 riddance
09 abolition
10 effacement, extinction
11 destruction, elimination
12 annihilation, obliteration
13 extermination

**erasable**
09 removable
10 effaceable, eradicable

**erase**
04 kill
06 cancel, delete, efface, excise,
   remove, rub out
07 blot out, expunge, wipe out
08 get rid of
09 eradicate
10 obliterate

**erasure**
07 removal
08 deletion
09 cleansing, erasement
11 elimination, eradication
12 cancellation, obliteration

**erect**
04 firm, form, hard, lift, rear
05 build, mount, pitch, put up,
   raise, rigid, set up, stiff
06 create, raised
07 elevate, upright
08 standing, straight, vertical
09 construct, establish, institute
10 upstanding

**erection**
04 pile
07 edifice, raising
08 assembly, building, rigidity
09 elevation, structure
12 construction
13 establishment

**ergo**
02 so
04 then, thus
05 hence
09 therefore

11 accordingly
12 consequently
13 for this reason

**erode**
05 spoil
06 abrade
07 consume, corrode, deplete,
   destroy, eat away, eat into
08 wear away, wear down
09 excoriate, grind down,
   undermine
11 deteriorate
12 disintegrate

**erosion**
04 wear
08 abrasion
10 denudation
11 destruction, excoriation,
   undermining, wearing away
13 deterioration
14 disintegration

**erotic**
04 blue, sexy
05 adult, dirty
06 carnal, steamy
07 lustful, raunchy, sensual
09 erogenous, seductive
10 lascivious, suggestive
11 stimulating, titillating
12 pornographic

**err**
03 sin
06 bungle, foul up, mess up,
   offend, slip up, trip up
07 be wrong, deviate, mistake,
   screw up
08 go astray, misjudge
09 make a slip, misbehave
10 transgress
11 be incorrect, misconstrue
12 miscalculate
13 fall from grace,
   misunderstand

**errand**
03 job
04 duty, task
06 charge
07 message, mission
10 assignment, commission
11 undertaking

**errant**
05 loose, stray, wrong
06 erring, roving, sinful
07 deviant, lawless, nomadic,
   roaming, sinning, wayward
08 aberrant, criminal, straying
09 itinerant, offending
10 journeying
11 disobedient, peripatetic

**erratic**
06 fitful
07 varying
08 sporadic, unstable, unsteady, variable, volatile
09 desultory, eccentric, irregular, unsettled
10 capricious, changeable, inconstant, unreliable
11 fluctuating
12 inconsistent, intermittent
13 unpredictable

**erring**
05 loose, stray, wrong
06 errant, guilty, sinful
07 deviant, lawless, peccant, sinning, wayward
08 criminal, straying

**erroneous**
05 false, wrong
06 faulty, flawed, untrue
07 inexact, invalid
08 mistaken, specious, spurious
09 incorrect, misguided, misplaced, unfounded
10 fallacious, inaccurate

**error**
04 flaw, slip
05 fault, gaffe, lapse, mix-up
06 boo-boo, howler, miscue, slip-up
07 blunder, literal, mistake
08 misprint, omission, solecism
09 oversight
10 aberration, inaccuracy
11 misjudgment
13 misconception
14 miscalculation
15 misapprehension, slip of the tongue, spelling mistake

**ersatz**
04 fake, sham
05 bogus, phony
07 man-made
09 imitation, synthetic
10 artificial, substitute
11 counterfeit

**erstwhile**
02 ex
03 old
04 late, once, past
06 bygone, former
07 one-time
08 previous, sometime

**erudite**
06 brainy
07 learned
08 academic, cultured, educated, highbrow, lettered, profound, well-read
09 scholarly

12 intellectual, well-educated
13 knowledgeable

**erudition**
05 facts
06 wisdom
07 culture, letters
08 learning
09 education, knowledge
10 profundity
11 learnedness, scholarship

**erupt**
04 emit, gush, spew, vent
05 belch, break, burst, eject, eruct, expel, spout, vomit
07 explode, flare up
08 break out, eructate
09 discharge, pour forth

**eruption**
04 rash
07 flare-up, venting
08 ejection, emission, outbreak, outburst
09 discharge, explosion
12 inflammation

**escalate**
04 grow, rise, soar
05 climb, mount, raise
06 ascend, extend, spiral
07 develop, enlarge, magnify
08 heighten, increase
09 intensify
10 accelerate, hit the roof

**escalator**
12 moving stairs
14 moving stairway
15 moving staircase

**escapable**
09 avertible, avoidable

**escapade**
04 lark, romp
05 caper, fling, prank, stunt
07 exploit
09 adventure
10 skylarking

**escape**
03 fly
04 bolt, duck, flee, flit, flow, gush, leak, ooze, pass, scat, seep, shun, skip, slip
05 avoid, dodge, drain, elude, evade, issue, scoot, scram
06 decamp, efflux, flight, forget
07 abscond, evasion, fantasy, getaway, leakage, run away, seepage, trickle
08 breakout, dreaming, emission, shake off, sidestep, slip away

09 avoidance, break free, discharge, diversion, emanation, jailbreak
10 break loose, decampment, recreation, relaxation
11 distraction, fantasizing
13 circumvention
14 make a bolt for it
15 make a break for it, not be remembered, take to your heels

**escapee**
06 truant
07 refugee, runaway
08 defector, deserter, fugitive
09 absconder
11 jailbreaker

**escapism**
07 fantasy, pastime
08 dreaming
09 diversion
10 recreation, relaxation
11 distraction, fantasizing
15 wishful thinking

**escapist**
07 dreamer, ostrich
10 daydreamer, fantasizer

**eschew**
04 shun
05 avoid, forgo, spurn
06 abjure, give up
07 abandon, disdain
08 forswear, renounce
09 repudiate
11 abstain from, keep clear of

**escort**
04 aide, beau, date, lead, take
05 bring, guard, train, usher
07 company, conduct, cortège, partner, protect, retinue
08 attend on, chaperon, come with, defender, shepherd
09 accompany, attendant, bodyguard, chaperone, companion, entourage
10 attendants

**esoteric**
06 arcane, hidden, inside, mystic, occult, secret
07 cryptic, obscure, private
08 abstruse, mystical
09 recondite
10 mysterious
11 inscrutable
12 confidential

**especial**
06 marked, signal, unique
07 express, notable, special
08 peculiar, singular, specific
09 exclusive

10 noteworthy, particular, preeminent, remarkable
11 exceptional, outstanding
13 extraordinary

**especially**
04 very
06 mainly
07 chiefly, notably
08 markedly, uniquely
09 expressly, primarily, supremely, unusually
10 remarkably, strikingly, uncommonly
11 exclusively, principally
12 particularly, preeminently
13 exceptionally, outstandingly
15 extraordinarily

**espionage**
06 spying
07 bugging, probing
08 snooping
11 fifth column, wiretapping
12 infiltration, intelligence, intercepting, surveillance
14 reconnaissance, undercover work

**espousal**
07 backing, defense, support
08 adoption, advocacy
09 embracing, promotion
11 championing, maintenance

**espouse**
04 back
05 adopt
06 defend, opt for, take up
07 embrace, support
08 advocate, champion
09 patronize
10 stand up for

**espy**
03 see, spy
04 spot
05 sight
06 behold, detect, notice
07 discern, glimpse, make out
08 discover, perceive
11 distinguish
12 catch sight of

**essay**
03 try
04 test
05 go for, paper, piece, tract
06 review, take on, thesis
07 article, attempt, have a go
08 critique, struggle, treatise
09 discourse, undertake
10 assignment, commentary
11 composition
12 disquisition, dissertation

► *Names of essayists:*
04 **Agee** (James), **Hunt** (Leigh), **Lamb** (Charles), **Will** (George)
05 **Bacon** (Francis), **Cooke** (Alistair), **Couch** (Arthur Quiller), **Gould** (Stephen Jay), **Pater** (Walter Horatio), **Smith** (Sydney), **White** (Elwyn Brooks)
06 **Borges** (Jorge Luis), **Holmes** (Oliver Wendell), **Orwell** (George), **Ruskin** (John), **Steele** (Richard)
07 **Addison** (Joseph), **Buckley** (William), **Calvino** (Italo), **Carlyle** (Thomas), **Emerson** (Ralph Waldo), **Hazlitt** (William), **Montagu** (Mary Wortley), **Thoreau** (Henry David)
08 **Beerbohm** (Max), **Benchley** (Robert), **Macaulay** (Thomas Babington)
09 **De Quincey** (Thomas), **Montaigne** (Michel Eyquem de)
10 **Chesterton** (Gilbert Keith)
19 **Mencken (Henry Louis)**
➤ See also WRITER

**essence**
04 core, crux, life, pith, soul
05 being, heart, point
06 center, entity, kernel, marrow, nature, spirit
07 extract, reality, spirits
09 character, substance
11 concentrate
12 distillation, quintessence
13 concentration

❏**in essence**
09 basically
11 essentially
13 fundamentally, substantially

❏**of the essence**
05 vital
06 needed
07 crucial
08 required
09 important, necessary, requisite
13 indispensable

**essential**
03 key
04 gist, main, must
05 basic, vital
06 innate, needed
07 central, crucial, typical
08 inherent, key point, required

09 important, intrinsic, necessary, necessity, principal, principle, requisite
10 definitive, sine qua non
11 fundamental, requirement
12 prerequisite
13 indispensable

**establish**
04 base, form, open, show
05 begin, found, lodge, plant, prove, set up, start
06 affirm, attest, create, ratify, secure, settle, verify
09 institute, introduce
11 corroborate, demonstrate
12 authenticate, substantiate
14 bring into being

**established**
05 fixed
06 proved, proven, secure
07 settled
10 entrenched
11 experienced, traditional
12 conventional
14 tried and tested

**establishment**
04 firm, shop
07 company, concern, forming
08 business, creation, founding
09 formation, inception, institute, the system
10 enterprise, foundation
11 corporation, institution
12 inauguration, installation
14 the authorities
15 the powers that be

**estate**
04 area, land, rank
05 goods, lands, manor, place
06 assets, center, region, status
07 effects
08 holdings, position, property
09 condition, situation
10 belongings, real estate
11 development, possessions

**esteem**
04 deem, hold, love, rate, view
05 count, honor, judge, think, value
06 admire, credit, reckon, regard, revere
07 adjudge, believe, respect
08 consider, judgment, treasure, venerate
09 reckoning
10 admiration, estimation
11 approbation, good opinion
12 appreciation, regard highly
13 consideration

**esteemed**
06 prized, valued, worthy

07 admired, honored, revered
09 admirable, excellent, honorable, reputable, respected, treasured, venerated
11 respectable
13 distinguished, well-respected, well-thought-of
14 highly regarded

**estimable**
04 good
06 valued, worthy
07 notable
08 esteemed, valuable
09 admirable, excellent, honorable, reputable, respected
10 creditable
11 commendable, meritorious
12 praiseworthy
13 distinguished

**estimate**
05 gauge, guess, value
06 assess, belief, reckon
07 opinion
08 evaluate, judgment, thinking
09 quotation, reckoning, valuation
10 assessment, estimation, evaluation, rough guess
11 computation, guesstimate
13 approximation
14 ballpark figure

**estimation**
05 guess
06 belief, credit, esteem, regard
07 feeling, opinion, respect
08 estimate, judgment, thinking
09 valuation
10 assessment, conclusion, evaluation, rough guess
11 calculation, computation
13 consideration

**estrange**
04 part
05 sever
06 divide
07 break up, divorce, split up
08 alienate, disunite, separate
09 disaffect
10 antagonize, drive apart
13 set at variance

**estranged**
07 divided
08 divorced, separate
09 alienated, separated
11 antagonized, disaffected

**estrangement**
05 split
06 breach
07 breakup, parting

08 disunity, division
09 antipathy, hostility
10 alienation, antagonism, separation
12 disaffection, dissociation
14 antagonization

**estuary**
03 arm, bay
05 delta, firth, fjord, inlet, mouth

**et cetera**
03 etc.
04 et al.
07 and so on
10 and so forth, and the like, and the rest, or whatever
11 and suchlike, and whatever
14 and what have you

**etch**
03 cut, dig
04 bite, burn
05 carve, stamp
06 furrow, groove, incise
07 corrode, engrave, impress, imprint, ingrain
08 inscribe

**etching**
03 cut
05 print
06 sketch
07 carving, imprint
09 engraving
10 impression
11 inscription

**eternal**
07 abiding, endless, lasting, nonstop, undying
08 constant, enduring, immortal, infinite, timeless, unending
09 ceaseless, deathless, limitless, perpetual
10 continuous, persistent, relentless, unchanging
11 everlasting, never-ending
12 imperishable, interminable
14 indestructible

**eternally**
06 always
07 forever
09 endlessly, lastingly
10 constantly
11 ceaselessly, perpetually
12 interminably
13 everlastingly

**eternity**
06 heaven
08 infinity, long time, paradise
09 afterlife, hereafter, next world
10 perpetuity

11 ages and ages, endlessness
12 immutability, timelessness
15 everlasting life, world without end

**ethereal**
04 fine
05 light
06 dainty, subtle
07 refined, tenuous
08 delicate, empyreal, empyrean, gossamer, heavenly, rarefied
09 celestial, exquisite, spiritual, unearthly, unworldly
10 diaphanous, intangible
13 insubstantial

**ethical**
04 fair, good, just
05 moral, noble, right
06 decent, honest, seemly
07 correct, fitting, upright
08 decorous, virtuous
09 honorable
10 principled

**ethics**
04 code
05 rules
06 equity, morals, values
07 beliefs
08 morality
09 moral code, standards
10 conscience, principles
11 moral values
14 moral standards
15 moral philosophy

**ethnic**
04 folk
06 native, racial, tribal
08 cultural, national
10 aboriginal, indigenous
11 traditional

**ethos**
04 code
05 tenor
06 ethics, flavor, spirit
07 beliefs, manners
08 attitude, morality
09 character, rationale
10 principles
11 disposition

**etiquette**
04 code, form
05 rules
07 customs, decency, decorum, manners
08 ceremony, civility, courtesy, good form, protocol
09 propriety, standards
10 politeness
11 conventions, correctness, formalities, good manners

12 unwritten law
13 code of conduct
14 code of behavior, code of
   practice

**etymology**
06 origin, source
08 word-lore
09 philology, semantics
10 derivation, lexicology
11 linguistics, word history,
   word origins

**eulogize**
04 hype, laud, plug
05 exalt, extol, honor
06 extoll, praise
07 acclaim, applaud, approve,
   commend, glorify, magnify
10 panegyrize, wax lyrical

**eulogy**
04 laud
05 paean
06 praise
07 acclaim, plaudit, tribute
08 accolade, encomium
09 laudation, panegyric
10 compliment, exaltation
11 acclamation
12 commendation
13 glorification

**euphemism**
07 evasion
09 softening
10 genteelism, polite term
12 substitution

**euphemistic**
05 vague
06 polite
07 evasive, genteel, neutral
08 indirect
11 understated

**euphonious**
04 soft
05 clear, sweet
06 dulcet, mellow
07 melodic, musical, silvery
09 consonant, melodious
10 harmonious, sweet-toned
11 dulcifluous, mellifluous
13 sweet-sounding

**euphoria**
03 joy
04 glee, high
05 bliss
07 ecstasy, elation, rapture
08 buoyancy
09 transport, well-being
10 exultation, jubilation
11 high spirits
12 cheerfulness, exhilaration,
   intoxication

**euphoric**
04 high
05 happy
06 elated, joyful, joyous
07 buoyant, exulted, gleeful
08 blissful, cheerful, ecstatic,
   exultant, jubilant
09 rapturous
11 exhilarated, intoxicated

**euthanasia**
07 quietus, release
12 happy release, mercy killing
15 merciful release

**evacuate**
04 quit, void
05 clear, eject, empty, expel,
   leave, purge
06 decamp, depart, desert,
   remove, vacate
07 abandon, excrete, forsake
08 clear out, defecate
09 discharge, eliminate, make
   empty, pull out of

**evacuation**
06 exodus, flight
07 leaving, purging, removal
08 ejection, emptying, vacating
09 clearance, departure,
   desertion, discharge,
   expulsion, forsaking
10 defecation, retirement
11 abandonment, elimination

**evade**
04 balk, duck, shun
05 avoid, dodge, elude, fudge,
   hedge, parry, shirk
06 cop out, escape
08 sidestep
09 get around
10 circumvent, equivocate, play
   truant
11 prevaricate
12 steer clear of

**evaluate**
04 rank, rate
05 gauge, judge, value, weigh
06 assess, reckon, size up
07 compute, measure
08 appraise, estimate
09 calculate, determine

**evaluation**
07 opinion
08 estimate, judgment
09 appraisal, reckoning,
   valuation
10 assessment, estimation
11 calculation, computation

**evanescent**
05 brief
06 fading

07 passing
08 fleeting, unstable
09 ephemeral, momentary,
   temporary, transient,
   vanishing
10 short-lived, transitory
12 disappearing
13 insubstantial

**evangelical**
07 zealous
08 biblical, orthodox
09 apostolic, crusading,
   reforming
10 missionary, scriptural
11 campaigning
12 Bible-bashing, evangelistic
13 Bible-punching, Bible-
   thumping, proselytizing
14 fundamentalist

**evangelist**
07 apostle
08 crusader, preacher
10 campaigner, missionary,
   revivalist
13 televangelist

► *Names of evangelists*:
04 **John, Luke, Mark**
06 **Bakker** (Jim), **Graham**
   (Billy), **Sunday** (Billy),
   **Wesley** (John)
07 **Falwell** (Jerry), **Matthew,**
   **Roberts** (Oral)
08 **Swaggart** (Jimmy)
09 **McPherson** (Aimee
   Semple), **Robertson** (Pat)

**evangelize**
06 preach
07 baptize, convert, crusade
08 campaign
09 proselyte
11 proselytize
13 spread the word

**evaporate**
03 dry
04 fade, melt
06 dispel, exhale, vanish
08 disperse, dissolve, evanesce,
   melt away, vaporize
09 dehydrate, dissipate

**evaporation**
06 drying, fading
07 melting
09 vanishing
11 dehydration, desiccation
12 condensation, distillation,
   vaporization

**evasion**
05 dodge
06 deceit, escape, excuse

**evasive**

07 dodging, ducking, fencing, fudging, hedging, quibble
08 shirking, shunning, trickery
09 avoidance, deception
12 equivocation
13 circumvention, prevarication
14 tergiversation
15 steering clear of

**evasive**

05 cagey, vague
06 shifty
07 cunning, devious, oblique
08 indirect, slippery
09 deceitful, secretive
12 equivocating
13 prevaricating

**eve**

04 dusk
06 sunset
07 evening, sundown
08 twilight
09 day before, threshold

**even**

03 too
04 also, calm, cool, fair, flat, just, like, more, same, true
05 at all, equal, flush, level, match, oddly, plane, still
06 as well, hardly, indeed, placid, serene, smooth, square, stable, steady
07 equable, flatten, regular
08 balanced, composed, constant, matching, parallel, scarcely, tranquil
09 equitable, impartial, make equal, stabilize, still more, unruffled, unvarying
10 all the more, consistent, fifty-fifty, straighten, unchanging, unwavering
11 neck and neck, nonpartisan, symmetrical, unexcitable, unflappable
12 even-tempered, surprisingly
13 fair and square, more precisely

❑ **even so**

03 but, yet
05 still
07 however
10 all the same
11 despite that, nonetheless
12 nevertheless
13 in spite of that

**evenhanded**

04 fair, just
06 square
07 neutral
08 balanced, unbiased
09 equitable, impartial

10 reasonable
12 unprejudiced
13 disinterested, dispassionate

**evening**

03 eve
04 dusk
06 sunset
07 sundown
08 eventide, twilight
09 nightfall
10 close of day

**event**

04 case, fact, game, item, race
05 issue, match, round
06 affair, matter, result, upshot
07 contest, episode, fixture, meeting, outcome
08 business, incident, occasion
09 adventure, aftermath, happening, milestone
10 experience, occurrence
11 competition, possibility
12 circumstance

**even-tempered**

04 calm, cool
06 placid, serene, stable, steady
07 equable, unfazed
08 composed, laid-back, peaceful, tranquil
09 peaceable
13 imperturbable

**eventful**

04 busy, full
06 active, lively
09 important, memorable
11 interesting, significant
12 action-packed

**eventual**

04 last
05 final, later
06 future
07 closing, ensuing, planned
08 ultimate
09 impending, projected, resulting
10 concluding, subsequent

**eventuality**

04 case
05 event
06 chance, crisis, mishap
07 outcome
09 emergency, happening
10 likelihood
11 contingency, possibility
12 circumstance

**eventually**

06 at last
07 finally
08 after all, at length, in the end
10 ultimately

12 in the long run
13 sooner or later

**ever**

05 at all
06 always
07 for ever
08 evermore
09 at any time, endlessly, eternally, in any case
10 at all times, constantly
11 continually, incessantly, permanently, perpetually
12 on any account
13 on any occasion

❑ **ever so**

04 very
06 really
08 very much
09 extremely

**everlasting**

07 endless, eternal, undying
08 constant, immortal, timeless
09 permanent, perpetual
10 continuous, persistent
11 never-ending, unremitting
12 imperishable, interminable
14 indestructible

**evermore**

04 ever
06 always
07 for ever
09 eternally, ever after, hereafter
10 henceforth
11 in perpetuum, unceasingly
14 for ever and a day, for ever and ever, to the end of time

**every**

03 all
04 each, full
11 all possible, every single
15 every individual

**everybody**

03 all
08 everyone
09 one and all
10 each person
11 every person
13 the whole world

**everyday**

05 basic, daily, plain, usual
06 common, normal, simple
07 average, regular, routine
08 day-to-day, familiar, frequent, habitual, ordinary, standard, workaday
11 commonplace
12 run-of-the-mill

**everyone**

03 all
07 each one

09 everybody, one and all
10 each person
11 every person
12 all and sundry, every man Jack
13 the whole world

**everything**
03 all
06 the lot, the sum
08 the total, the works
09 all things, each thing
11 the entirety, the whole lot
15 the whole shebang
17 the whole enchilada

**everywhere**
07 all over
09 all around
10 every place, far and near, far and wide, high and low, near and far, throughout
11 in all places, to all places
12 the world over
14 right and center

**evict**
04 oust
05 eject, expel
06 put out, remove
07 kick out, turn out
08 chuck out, dislodge, force out, throw out
10 dispossess
11 expropriate
12 force to leave

**eviction**
07 removal, the boot, the push
08 ejection, the elbow
09 clearance, expulsion
11 the bum's rush
12 dislodgement
13 dispossession, expropriation

**evidence**
04 data, hint, mark, show, sign
05 proof, prove, token, trace
07 exhibit, grounds, support, symptom, witness
09 affidavit, testimony
10 indication, suggestion
11 affirmation, declaration
12 confirmation, verification
13 corroboration, documentation
14 substantiation

**◻in evidence**
05 clear, plain
06 patent
07 obvious, visible
08 apparent, clear-cut
10 noticeable
11 conspicuous

**evident**
05 clear, plain
06 patent
07 obvious, visible
08 apparent, manifest, tangible
10 noticeable
11 conspicuous, discernible, perceptible
12 indisputable, unmistakable

**evidently**
07 clearly, plainly
08 patently
09 doubtless, obviously, outwardly, seemingly
10 apparently, manifestly, ostensibly
11 so it appears

**evil**
03 bad, ill, sin, woe
04 base, blow, dire, foul, harm, hurt, pain, ruin, vice, vile
05 black, cruel, curse, wrong
06 injury, misery, sinful, wicked
07 badness, corrupt, demonic, harmful, heinous, immoral, noxious, ruinous, vicious
08 baseness, depraved, devilish, diabolic, iniquity, mischief, sinister, vileness
09 adversity, depravity, malicious, malignant, malignity, nefarious
10 affliction, calamitous, corruption, immorality, iniquitous, malevolent, pernicious, sinfulness, wickedness
11 catastrophe, deleterious, heinousness, viciousness
12 catastrophic, devilishness

**evildoer**
05 crook, felon, rogue
06 sinner
07 villain
08 criminal, offender
09 miscreant, reprobate, scoundrel, wrongdoer
12 transgressor

**evince**
04 show
06 attest, reveal
07 bespeak, betoken, declare, display, exhibit, express
08 evidence, indicate, manifest
11 demonstrate

**eviscerate**
03 gut
04 draw
10 disembowel, exenterate

**evocation**
04 echo

08 inducing, kindling, stirring
10 activation, excitation, invocation, suggestion
11 elicitation, stimulation, summoning-up

**evocative**
05 vivid
07 graphic
08 redolent
09 memorable
10 expressive, indicative, suggestive
11 reminiscent

**evoke**
04 call, stir
05 cause, raise
06 arouse, awaken, call up, elicit, excite, induce, invoke, kindle, recall, summon
07 provoke
08 summon up
09 call forth, conjure up

**evolution**
06 growth
07 descent
08 increase, progress, ripening
09 unfolding, unrolling
10 derivation, opening-out
11 development, progression

**evolve**
04 grow
06 derive, emerge, expand, mature, result, unfold, unroll
07 descend, develop, unravel

**exacerbate**
03 vex
06 deepen, enrage, worsen
07 inflame, provoke, sharpen
08 heighten, increase, irritate
09 aggravate, infuriate, intensify, make worse
10 exaggerate, exasperate
15 make things worse

**exact**
04 just, milk, true
05 bleed, claim, close, force, right, wrest, wring
06 compel, demand, extort, impose
07 call for, careful, command, correct, extract, literal, on a dime, precise, require, squeeze
08 accurate, definite, detailed, explicit, faithful, flawless, insist on, specific, thorough
09 identical, on the nail
10 blow-by-blow, methodical, meticulous, scrupulous
11 on the button, painstaking, punctilious, word-perfect

**exacting**
04 firm, hard
05 harsh, stern, tough
06 severe, strict, taxing, tiring
07 arduous, onerous
08 rigorous
09 demanding, difficult, laborious, stringent
11 challenging, painstaking

**exactitude**
04 care
05 rigor
06 detail
08 accuracy
09 exactness, precision
10 strictness
11 carefulness, correctness, orderliness
14 meticulousness

**exactly**
04 dead, just, to a T, true
05 plumb, quite, right, truly
06 agreed, indeed, just so, spot on
07 on a dime
08 of course, on the dot, strictly, verbatim
09 correctly, expressly, literally, on the nail, precisely
10 absolutely, accurately, definitely, faithfully, unerringly
11 faultlessly, on the button, religiously, to the letter
12 particularly, scrupulously, specifically, to perfection, without error

**exactness**
08 accuracy
09 precision
10 exactitude, strictness
11 correctness, orderliness
12 rigorousness, thoroughness
14 meticulousness

**exaggerate**
05 color
06 overdo, stress
07 amplify, enlarge, magnify
08 overplay, oversell, pile it on
09 dramatize, embellish, embroider, overstate
10 aggrandize, caricature, shoot a line
12 lay it on thick
13 overdramatize, pile it on thick
15 stretch the truth

**exaggerated**
04 tall
08 inflated, overdone
09 amplified, excessive
10 hyperbolic, overstated
11 caricatured, embellished

**exaggeration**
06 excess, parody
09 burlesque, hyperbole
10 caricature
11 enlargement
12 extravagance, overemphasis
13 amplification, magnification, overstatement
14 overestimation

**exalt**
04 laud
05 adore, bless, extol, honor, raise
06 extoll, praise, prefer, revere
07 acclaim, applaud, elevate, glorify, magnify, promote, upgrade, worship
08 eulogize, venerate
09 reverence, transport

**exaltation**
03 joy
05 bliss, glory, honor
06 eulogy, praise
07 acclaim, ecstasy, elation, rapture, worship
08 adoration, reverence
10 jubilation, veneration
11 high spirits
12 exhilaration
13 glorification

**exalted**
04 high
05 grand, lofty, noble, regal
06 elated, joyful, lordly
07 eminent, stately
08 blissful, ecstatic, elevated
09 rapturous
13 in high spirits
15 in seventh heaven

**exam**
04 oral, quiz, test
05 final, paper
07 midterm, midyear
08 physical
09 practical, questions
11 examination

**examination**
04 exam, oral, scan, test
05 audit, check, final, paper, probe, study
06 review, search, survey
07 checkup, inquiry, midterm, midyear, perusal
08 analysis, critique, once-over, physical, research, scrutiny
09 appraisal
10 assessment, inspection, post-mortem
11 exploration, inquisition, observation, questioning
13 interrogation, investigation

**examine**
03 eye, vet
04 case, pump, quiz, scan, sift, test
05 assay, audit, check, grill, probe, study
06 assess, look at, peruse, ponder, review, survey
07 analyze, explore, inquire, inspect, observe, weigh up
08 appraise, check out, consider, look into, pore over, question, research
11 interrogate, investigate
12 cross-examine
13 cross-question

**examinee**
07 entrant
09 applicant, candidate
10 competitor, contestant
11 interviewee

**examiner**
05 judge
06 censor, critic, marker, tester
07 analyst, arbiter, auditor, coroner
08 assessor, reviewer
09 examinant, inspector
10 questioner
11 adjudicator, interviewer, scrutinizer
12 interlocutor

**example**
04 case, type
05 guide, ideal, model
06 lesson, sample
07 epitome, pattern, warning
08 exemplar, instance, paradigm, specimen
09 archetype, precedent, prototype, role model
11 case in point, typical case
12 illustration
15 exemplification

❑**for example**
02 e.g.
03 say
11 as an example, for instance
12 as an instance, to illustrate

**exasperate**
03 irk
04 gall, goad, rile
05 anger, annoy, get to, rouse
06 enrage, madden, rankle
07 incense, provoke
09 infuriate
14 drive up the wall

**exasperated**
05 angry, fed up, irked, riled
06 bugged, galled, goaded
07 angered, annoyed, needled

08 incensed, maddened
10 aggravated, infuriated

**exasperating**
09 maddening, provoking
10 bothersome, pernicious
11 aggravating, infuriating

**excavate**
03 cut, dig
04 mine
05 delve, dig up, gouge, scoop
06 burrow, dig out, exhume, hollow, quarry, reveal, tunnel
07 uncover, unearth
08 disinter

**excavation**
03 dig, pit
04 hole, mine
05 ditch, shaft
06 burrow, cavity, crater, dugout, hollow, quarry, trench, trough
08 colliery, diggings

**exceed**
03 cap, top
04 beat, pass
05 outdo
06 better, go over, outrun
07 eclipse, surpass
08 go beyond, outshine, outstrip, overstep
09 outnumber, transcend
10 be more than
12 be larger than
13 be greater than

**exceedingly**
04 very
06 highly, hugely, vastly
07 greatly
08 very much
09 amazingly, extremely, immensely, unusually
10 enormously, especially
11 excessively
12 inordinately, surpassingly
13 astonishingly, exceptionally
15 extraordinarily

**excel**
04 beat
05 outdo, shine
07 eclipse, outrank, surpass
08 outclass, outrival, stand out
10 outperform
11 be excellent, predominate
12 be better than
13 be outstanding

**excellence**
05 merit, skill, value, worth
06 purity, virtue
08 fineness, goodness
09 greatness, supremacy

10 perfection
11 distinction, preeminence
13 transcendence

**excellent**
03 A-OK, ace
04 cool, fine, good, mega, neat
05 great, noted, prime
06 groovy, select, superb, way-out, wicked, worthy
07 crucial, eminent, notable, perfect, radical
08 flawless, inspired, splendid, sterling, top-notch, very good
09 admirable, brilliant, exemplary, fantastic, faultless, first-rate, marvelous, matchless, unequaled, wonderful
10 first-class, noteworthy, preeminent, remarkable
11 commendable, exceptional, outstanding, superlative
12 praiseworthy, second to none, unparalleled
13 distinguished
14 out of this world

**except**
03 bar, but
04 less, omit, save
05 minus
06 but for, reject
07 barring, besides, rule out
08 leave out, omitting
09 apart from, aside from, except for, excepting, excluding, other than
10 leaving out
11 not counting

**exception**
05 freak, quirk
06 oddity, rarity
07 anomaly
11 abnormality, peculiarity, special case
12 irregularity
13 inconsistency

❑**with the exception of**
03 bar, but
04 less, save
05 minus
07 barring, besides
08 omitting
09 apart from, except for, excepting, excluding, other than
10 leaving out
11 not counting

**exceptionable**
09 abhorrent, offensive, repugnant

10 deplorable, disgusting, unpleasant
12 disagreeable, unacceptable
13 objectionable

**exceptional**
03 odd
04 rare
07 notable, special, unusual
08 aberrant, abnormal, atypical, peculiar, singular, superior, uncommon
09 anomalous, brilliant, excellent, irregular, marvelous, unequaled
10 noteworthy, phenomenal, prodigious, remarkable
11 outstanding
13 extraordinary

**exceptionally**
06 rarely
07 notably
09 extremely, unusually
10 abnormally, especially, remarkably, uncommonly
13 outstandingly
15 extraordinarily

**excerpt**
04 clip, part
05 piece, quote, scrap
07 extract, passage
08 citation, clipping, fragment
09 quotation, selection

**excess**
04 glut
05 extra, flood, spare
07 backlog, residue, surfeit, surplus, too much
08 bellyful, left-over, overflow, overkill, plethora, residual
09 leftovers, redundant, remainder, remaining
10 additional, debauchery
11 dissipation, prodigality, superfluity, superfluous
12 extravagance, intemperance
13 dissoluteness
14 more than enough, overindulgence, superabundance

**excessive**
05 steep, undue
07 extreme, too much
08 needless, overdone
10 exorbitant, immoderate, inordinate
11 extravagant, superfluous, uncalled-for, unnecessary
12 unreasonable
13 superabundant

**excessively**
06 overly, unduly

07 too much
08 overmuch, to a fault
09 extremely
10 needlessly
12 exorbitantly, immoderately, inordinately, unreasonably
13 extravagantly, intemperately, superfluously, unnecessarily

**exchange**
04 chat, swap
05 bandy, trade, truck
06 barter, change, switch
07 commute, convert, replace
08 argument, trade-off
09 transpose
11 give and take, interchange, reciprocate, reciprocity, replacement
12 conversation, substitution

**excise**
03 cut, tax
04 duty, levy, toll
05 erase
06 cut out, delete, impost, remove, tariff
07 customs, destroy, expunge, extract, rescind
09 eradicate, expurgate, extirpate, surcharge

**excision**
07 removal
08 deletion
11 destruction, eradication, expurgation, extirpation

**excitable**
05 fiery, hasty
07 nervous
08 choleric, volatile
09 emotional, hotheaded, irascible, mercurial, sensitive
11 hot-tempered, susceptible
12 highly strung
13 quick-tempered, temperamental

**excite**
04 fire, move, sway
05 evoke, rouse, touch, upset
06 arouse, awaken, ignite, incite, induce, kindle, stir up, thrill, turn on
07 agitate, animate, impress, inflame, inspire, provoke
08 engender, generate
09 stimulate, titillate

**excited**
04 high, wild
05 eager, hyper, moved
06 elated, roused
07 aroused, fired up, stirred
08 agitated, animated, frenzied, restless, turned on, worked up

10 stimulated
11 exhilarated, overwrought
12 enthusiastic
13 in high spirits
14 thrilled to bits

**excitement**
03 ado
04 fuss, kick, stir
05 fever, furor, kicks
06 action, thrill, tumult
07 elation, emotion, passion
09 adventure, agitation, animation, commotion
10 enthusiasm
11 stimulation
12 exhilaration, perturbation

**exciting**
04 sexy
06 moving
07 rousing
08 dramatic, stirring, striking
09 inspiring, thrilling
10 nail-biting
11 enthralling, provocative, sensational, stimulating
12 action-packed, breathtaking, cliff-hanging, electrifying, exhilarating

**exclaim**
03 cry
04 call, roar, yell
05 blurt, shout, utter
06 bellow, cry out, shriek
07 declare
08 blurt out, proclaim
09 ejaculate

**exclamation**
03 cry
04 call, roar, yell
05 shout
06 bellow, outcry, shriek
09 expletive, utterance
11 ejaculation
12 interjection

**exclude**
03 ban, bar
04 drop, omit, skip, veto
05 eject, evict, expel
06 banish, delete, disbar, forbid, ignore, put out, refuse, reject, remove
07 keep out, lock out, rule out
08 disallow, leave out, preclude, prohibit
09 blacklist, eliminate, ostracize
13 excommunicate

**exclusion**
03 ban, bar
04 veto
07 boycott, embargo, refusal
08 ejection, eviction, omission

09 exception, expulsion, interdict, ruling out
10 preclusion
11 elimination, prohibition
12 proscription

**exclusive**
04 chic, only, posh, sole
05 plush, ritzy, total, whole
06 choice, classy, cliquy, closed, select, single, unique
07 cliquey, limited, private, upscale
08 cliquish, complete, peculiar, snobbish, up-market
09 undivided
10 individual, restricted
11 fashionable, restrictive

❏**exclusive of**
06 except
07 barring
08 omitting
09 debarring, except for, excepting, ruling out
10 leaving out
11 not counting
12 not including

**excommunicate**
03 ban, bar
05 debar, eject, expel
06 banish, outlaw, remove
07 exclude
08 denounce, unchurch
09 blacklist, proscribe
12 anathematize

**excoriate**
05 blame, decry, knock
06 attack
07 censure, condemn, run down
08 denounce
09 denigrate, disparage
10 animadvert, vituperate

**excrement**
04 dirt, dung, muck, scat
05 feces, guano
06 egesta, manure, ordure, refuse
09 droppings, excretion
11 waste matter

**excrescence**
04 boil, bump, knob, lump, wart
05 tumor
06 cancer, growth, pimple
08 swelling
09 appendage, outgrowth
10 projection, prominence
12 intumescence, protuberance
13 disfigurement

**excrete**
04 pass, void
05 egest, eject, expel, exude

07 secrete
08 defecate, evacuate
09 discharge

**excretion**
04 dung
05 feces
06 ordure
07 excreta
09 discharge, droppings, excrement
10 defecation, evacuation
12 perspiration

**excruciating**
05 acute, sharp
06 bitter, savage, severe
07 intense, painful, racking
09 agonizing, atrocious
10 tormenting, unbearable
11 intolerable
12 insufferable

**exculpate**
05 clear
06 acquit, excuse, let off, pardon
07 absolve, forgive, release
09 exonerate, vindicate

**excursion**
04 ride, tour, trip, walk
05 drive, jaunt
06 detour, junket, outing, ramble
07 day trip, journey
08 side trip
09 departure, diversion
10 digression, expedition
12 pleasure trip

**excusable**
09 allowable
10 defensible, forgivable, pardonable
11 explainable, justifiable
14 understandable

**excuse**
04 free, plea
05 alibi, shift, spare
06 acquit, cop-out, exempt, let off, pardon, reason
07 absolve, coverup, defense, evasion, forgive, grounds, indulge, justify, release
08 mitigate, overlook, tolerate
09 discharge, exculpate, exonerate, vindicate, whitewash
11 explanation, vindication
13 justification

**execrable**
04 foul, vile
06 odious
07 hateful, heinous
08 accursed, damnable, horrible, shocking

09 abhorrent, appalling, atrocious, loathsome, obnoxious, offensive, repulsive, revolting
10 abominable, deplorable, despicable, disgusting

**execrate**
04 damn, hate
05 abhor, blast, curse
06 detest, loathe, revile, vilify
07 condemn, deplore, despise
08 denounce
09 abominate, excoriate, fulminate, imprecate

**execute**
02 do
04 hang, kill
05 enact, lynch, serve, shoot, stage
06 behead, effect, finish
07 achieve, crucify, deliver, enforce, fulfill, perform, realize
08 bring off, carry out, complete, dispatch, engineer, expedite, validate
09 discharge, liquidate
10 accomplish, decapitate, guillotine, put to death
11 electrocute
15 put into practice

**execution**
07 killing, staging
08 delivery, dispatch
09 discharge, operation, rendition, technique
10 completion
11 achievement, enforcement, fulfillment, performance, realization
12 death penalty
13 death sentence
14 accomplishment, implementation, putting to death

► *Methods of execution*:
07 burning, gassing, hanging, stoning
08 lynching, shooting
09 beheading, garroting
11 crucifixion, firing squad
12 decapitation, guillotining
13 electrocution
15 lethal injection

**executioner**
05 axman
06 hit man, killer
07 hangman
08 assassin, headsman, murderer
10 hatchet man
12 exterminator

**executive**
06 leader
07 guiding, leading, manager
08 director, governor, official
09 directing, governing, hierarchy, organizer, president
10 controller, government, leadership, management, managerial, organizing
11 controlling, directorial
12 presidential
13 administrator
14 administrative, decision-making, organizational

**exegesis**
10 exposition, expounding
11 explanation, explication
13 clarification
14 interpretation

**exemplar**
04 copy, type
05 ideal, model
07 epitome, example, paragon
08 instance, paradigm, specimen, standard
09 archetype, criterion, prototype, yardstick
10 embodiment
12 illustration
15 exemplification

**exemplary**
04 good
05 ideal, model
06 worthy
07 correct, perfect, warning
08 flawless, laudable
09 admirable, estimable, excellent, faultless, honorable
10 cautionary
11 commendable, meritorious
12 praiseworthy

**exemplify**
04 cite, show
06 depict, embody, typify
08 instance, manifest
09 epitomize, represent
10 illustrate
11 demonstrate
12 characterize
13 be an example of

**exempt**
05 clear, spare, waive
06 excuse, let off, spared
07 absolve, dismiss, exclude, excused, release, relieve
08 absolved, excluded, released
09 dismissed, exonerate, liberated, not liable
10 discharged, not subject

15 grant immunity to, make an
exception

**exemption**
07 freedom, release
08 immunity
09 discharge, exception,
exclusion, privilege
10 absolution, indulgence
11 exoneration
12 dispensation

**exercise**
02 PE, PT
03 try, use, vex
04 task, work
05 annoy, apply, drill, exert, train,
upset, wield, worry
06 burden, effort, employ,
lesson, sports, warm-up
07 afflict, disturb, exploit,
jogging, keep fit, keep-fit,
perturb, running, trouble,
utilize, work out, workout
08 activity, aerobics, distress,
exertion, movement,
practice, practice, training
09 implement, make use of,
operation, preoccupy
10 assignment, discipline,
employment, gymnastics,
isometrics
11 application, bring to bear,
eurhythmics, fulfillment,
piece of work
13 bring into play, callisthenics,
exert yourself
14 implementation

**exert**
03 use
05 apply, spend, wield
06 employ, expend
08 exercise
11 bring to bear

**❏ exert yourself**
04 toil, work
05 labor, sweat
06 strain, strive
07 try hard
08 endeavor, go all out, struggle
09 take pains
10 do your best
11 give your all
12 do your utmost
13 apply yourself
15 make every effort

**exertion**
03 use
04 toil, work
05 labor, pains, trial
06 effort, strain, stress
07 attempt, travail

08 endeavor, exercise, industry,
struggle
09 operation
11 application, elbow grease,
utilization

**exhale**
04 blow, emit
05 expel, issue, steam
06 expire
07 breathe, emanate, give off,
respire
10 breathe out

**exhaust**
03 dry, sap, tax
04 do in, tire
05 drain, empty, fumes, smoke,
spend, steam, use up, vapor,
waste
06 expend, finish, strain, weaken
07 consume, deplete, fatigue,
overtax, tire out, wear out
08 bankrupt, emission,
enervate, knock out,
overwork, squander
09 discharge, dissipate, tucker
out
10 exhalation, impoverish

**exhausted**
04 dead, done, void, weak
05 all in, jaded, spent
06 bushed, done in, pooped,
used up
07 drained, worn out
08 consumed, depleted, dog-
tired, fatigued, finished, tired
out
09 burned out, dead tired,
enervated
11 ready to drop, tuckered out

**exhausting**
04 hard
06 severe, taxing, tiring
07 arduous, testing, wearing
08 draining, grueling
09 laborious, punishing,
strenuous
10 enervating, formidable

**exhaustion**
07 fatigue
09 tiredness, weariness
10 enervation, feebleness

**exhaustive**
04 full
05 total
06 all-out
07 in-depth
08 complete, detailed, sweeping,
thorough, whole-hog
09 extensive, full-blown, full-
scale
10 definitive

11 far-reaching
12 all-embracing, all-inclusive
13 comprehensive

**exhibit**
03 air
04 show
05 array, model, offer
06 expose, flaunt, parade,
reveal, set out, unveil
07 display, express, present, trot
out
08 disclose, indicate, manifest
11 demonstrate
12 illustration, presentation
13 demonstration

**exhibition**
04 expo, fair, show
06 airing
07 display, exhibit, showing
09 spectacle
10 disclosure, exposition,
indication, revelation
12 presentation
13 demonstration

**exhibitionist**
05 poser
06 poseur
07 showoff
09 extrovert

**exhilarate**
04 lift
05 elate
06 excite, perk up, thrill
07 animate, cheer up, delight,
enliven, gladden
08 brighten, vitalize
10 invigorate, revitalize

**exhilarating**
05 heady
08 cheerful, cheering, exciting
09 thrilling
10 enlivening, gladdening
11 mind-blowing, stimulating
12 breathtaking, invigorating,
revitalizing

**exhilaration**
03 joy
04 dash, élan, glee, zeal
05 ardor
06 gaiety, thrill
07 delight, elation
08 gladness, hilarity, vivacity
09 animation, happiness
10 enthusiasm, excitement,
joyfulness, liveliness
11 high spirits, stimulation
12 cheerfulness, invigoration
14 revitalization

**exhort**
03 bid

**exhortation**
04 goad, spur, urge, warn
05 press
06 advise, enjoin, prompt
07 beseech, caution, counsel, entreat, implore, inspire
08 admonish, persuade
09 encourage, instigate

**exhortation**
06 advice, sermon, urging
07 bidding, caution, counsel, goading, lecture, warning
08 entreaty
09 enjoinder
10 admonition, beseeching, incitement, persuasion
13 encouragement

**exhume**
05 dig up
07 unearth
08 disinter, excavate
09 disentomb, resurrect

**exigency**
04 need
06 crisis, demand, plight, stress
07 urgency
08 distress, pressure, quandary
09 emergency, necessity
10 difficulty
11 predicament, requirement

**exigent**
06 urgent
07 crucial
08 critical, exacting, pressing
09 demanding, insistent, necessary, stringent

**exiguous**
04 bare, slim
05 scant
06 meager, scanty, slight
10 negligible
12 insufficient

**exile**
03 ban, bar
04 oust
05 eject, ex-pat, expel
06 banish, deport, émigré, outlaw, pariah, uproot
07 cast out, outcast, refugee
08 deportee, drive out
09 expulsion, extradite, ostracism, ostracize, transport
10 banishment, expatriate, repatriate, separation
11 deportation
12 expatriation
15 displaced person

**exist**
02 be
04 last, live
06 endure, happen, remain

07 breathe, subsist, survive
08 continue, have life
09 be present, have being
10 have breath

**existence**
04 fact, life
05 being, thing
06 breath, entity, living
07 reality
08 creation, creature, survival
09 actuality, endurance, lifestyle, way of life
11 continuance, subsistence

**existent**
04 real
05 alive
06 actual, around, extant, living
07 abiding, current, present
08 enduring, existing, standing
09 remaining, surviving
10 prevailing
12 contemporary

**exit**
02 go
04 door, gate, vent
05 going, issue, leave
06 depart, egress, exodus, flight, outlet, retire, way out
07 doorway, leaving, retreat
08 farewell, withdraw
09 departure
10 retirement, withdrawal
11 leave-taking
13 take your leave

**exodus**
04 exit
06 escape, flight, hegira
07 fleeing, leaving, retreat
09 departure, migration
10 evacuation, withdrawal

**exonerate**
04 free
05 clear, spare
06 acquit, excuse, exempt, let off, pardon
07 absolve, justify, release
09 exculpate, vindicate

**exoneration**
06 pardon, relief
07 amnesty, freeing, release
08 excusing, immunity
09 acquittal, dismissal, exemption, indemnity
10 absolution, liberation
11 exculpation, vindication

**exorbitant**
05 undue
07 a rip-off
09 excessive, monstrous
11 extravagant, unwarranted

12 extortionate, unreasonable
15 daylight robbery

**exorcism**
07 freeing
09 expulsion
10 adjuration, casting-out
11 deliverance
12 exsufflation, purification

**exorcize**
04 free
05 expel
06 adjure, purify
07 cast out
08 drive out
10 exsufflate

**exotic**
05 alien
07 bizarre, curious, foreign, strange, unusual
08 colorful, external, imported, peculiar, striking, tropical
09 different, glamorous, nonnative
10 impressive, introduced, outlandish, outrageous, remarkable, unfamiliar
11 extravagant, fascinating
13 extraordinary

**expand**
04 grow
05 swell, widen
06 blow up, dilate, extend, fatten, spread, unfold, unfurl
07 amplify, broaden, develop, distend, enlarge, fill out, inflate, magnify, open out, puff out, stretch, thicken
08 escalate, increase, lengthen
09 branch out, diversify, intensify, intumesce

❑**expand on**
09 embroider, enlarge on
11 elaborate on, expatiate on
13 go into details

**expanse**
04 area
05 field, plain, range, space, sweep, tract
06 extent, region
07 breadth, stretch
13 extensiveness

**expansion**
06 growth, spread
07 expanse
08 dilation, increase, swelling
09 diffusion, extension, inflation, unfolding
10 broadening, dilatation, distension, thickening

**expansive**
11 development, enlargement, lengthening
12 augmentation
13 amplification, magnification
14 multiplication
15 diversification

**expansive**
04 open, warm, wide
05 broad
06 genial
07 affable, growing
08 effusive, friendly, outgoing, sociable, thorough
09 enlarging, expanding, extensive, talkative
10 developing, increasing, loquacious, widespread
11 uninhibited, wide-ranging
12 all-embracing, diversifying
13 comprehensive

**expatiate**
06 dilate, expand
07 amplify, develop, dwell on, enlarge, expound
09 elaborate, embellish

**expatriate**
04 oust
05 ex-pat, exile, expel
06 banish, deport, émigré, exiled, uproot
07 outcast, refugee
08 banished, deported, drive out, emigrant, expelled
09 extradite, ostracize
15 displaced person

**expect**
04 want, wish
05 await, guess, think, trust
06 assume, bank on, demand, reckon, rely on
07 believe, call for, count on, foresee, hope for, imagine, look for, predict, presume, project, require, suppose
08 envisage, forecast, insist on
10 anticipate, bargain for
11 contemplate
13 look forward to

**expectancy**
04 hope
07 waiting
08 suspense
09 curiosity, eagerness
10 conjecture
11 expectation
12 anticipation

**expectant**
05 eager, ready
06 gravid
07 anxious, curious, hopeful
08 awaiting, enceinte, pregnant, watchful
09 expecting, with child
10 in suspense
12 anticipating, apprehensive
13 on tenterhooks
14 in the family way
15 with bated breath

**expectantly**
07 eagerly
09 hopefully
10 in suspense
14 apprehensively, in anticipation, optimistically

**expectation**
04 hope, want, wish
05 trust
06 belief, demand
07 outlook, promise, surmise
08 forecast, optimism, prospect, reliance, suspense
09 assurance, eagerness
10 assumption, confidence, conjecture, insistence, prediction, projection
11 calculation, possibility, presumption, probability, requirement, supposition
12 anticipation

**expecting**
06 gravid
08 enceinte, pregnant
09 expectant, with child
14 in the family way

**expedience**
07 aptness, benefit, fitness
09 advantage, propriety
10 expediency, pragmatism, properness, usefulness
11 convenience, suitability
12 desirability, practicality
13 effectiveness, profitability

**expedient**
04 plan, ploy
05 dodge, means, shift, trick
06 device, method, scheme, tactic, useful
07 fitting, politic, prudent
08 sensible, suitable, tactical
09 advisable, opportune, practical, pragmatic
10 convenient, profitable
11 appropriate, contrivance
12 advantageous

**expedite**
05 hurry, press
06 assist, hasten, step up
07 further, quicken, speed up
08 dispatch
09 discharge
10 accelerate, facilitate

11 precipitate
12 hurry through

**expedition**
04 crew, hike, raid, sail, team, tour, trek, trip
05 haste, party, quest, speed
06 outing, ramble, safari
07 crusade, journey, mission
08 alacrity, campaign, celerity
09 adventure, excursion
10 enterprise, pilgrimage
11 exploration, undertaking

**expeditious**
04 fast
05 alert, brisk, hasty, quick, rapid, ready, swift
06 active, prompt, speedy
08 diligent, meteoric
09 efficient, immediate

**expel**
03 ban, bar
04 oust, void
05 belch, eject, evict, exile
06 banish, outlaw, reject
07 boot out, cast out, dismiss, kick out, lock out, spew out
08 chuck out, drive out, evacuate, throw out
09 discharge, proscribe
10 expatriate

**expend**
03 buy, pay, sap, use
05 empty, spend, use up, waste
06 employ, lay out
07 consume, deplete, exhaust, fork out, fritter, utilize
08 shell out, squander
09 dissipate, go through, overspend, splash out

**expendable**
10 disposable
11 dispensable, inessential, replaceable, unnecessary
12 nonessential

**expenditure**
03 use
05 costs, waste
06 outlay, output
07 expense, payment
08 expenses, overhead, spending
09 outgoings
11 consumption, dissipation, squandering, utilization
12 disbursement

**expense**
03 fee
04 cost, harm, loss, rate
05 costs, price
06 charge, outlay
07 payment

**expensive**

08 overhead, spending
09 detriment, outgoings, paying-out, sacrifice, sumptuary
11 expenditure, incidentals
12 disadvantage, disbursement

**expensive**

04 dear
05 steep
06 costly, lavish
10 exorbitant, high-priced, overpriced
12 extortionate
15 costing the earth, daylight robbery

**experience**

03 try
04 case, face, feel, know, meet
06 affair, endure, ordeal, suffer
07 contact, episode, know-how, sustain, undergo
08 exposure, incident, learning, perceive, practice, training
09 adventure, encounter, go through, knowledge
11 familiarity, involvement, live through, observation
13 participate in, participation

**experienced**

04 wise
05 adept, tried
06 au fait, expert, mature
07 capable, skilled, trained, veteran
08 familiar, seasoned, skillful
09 au courant, competent, practiced, qualified
10 streetwise, well-versed
11 street-smart, worldly wise
12 accomplished, professional

**experiment**

03 try
04 test
05 proof, trial
06 dry run, try out, verify
07 attempt, examine, explore, observe, test out, testing, venture
08 analysis, research, trial run
10 pilot study
11 examination, investigate
13 carry out tests, investigation, trial and error
15 experimentation

**experimental**

04 test
05 pilot, trial
09 empirical
11 exploratory, preliminary, provisional, speculative
13 investigative, trial-and-error
15 at the trial stage

**expert**

03 ace, pro
04 able, buff, up on
05 adept, crack, maven, mavin
06 master, pundit
07 egghead, maestro, old hand, skilled, wise guy
08 masterly, skillful, top-notch, virtuoso, well up on
09 authority, brilliant, dexterous, excellent, first-rate, old master, practiced, qualified
10 proficient, specialist
11 connoisseur, experienced
12 accomplished, professional

**expertise**

05 knack, skill
07 ability, command, know-how, mastery
08 deftness, facility
09 dexterity, knowledge
10 cleverness, virtuosity
11 proficiency
12 skillfulness
15 professionalism

**expiate**

05 purge
06 pay for
07 redress
08 atone for
09 make up for
12 do penance for
13 make amends for

**expiation**

06 amends, ransom, shrift
07 penance, redress
09 atonement
10 recompense, reparation

**expire**

03 die, end
04 stop
05 cease, close, lapse
06 depart, finish, pass on, perish, pop off, run out
07 decease, snuff it
08 conclude, pass away
09 have had it, terminate
10 buy the farm
11 bite the dust, come to an end, discontinue
12 lose your life
13 kick the bucket, meet your maker
14 depart this life, give up the ghost
15 be no longer valid, breathe your last, cash in your chips

**expiry**

03 end
05 close, lapse
06 finish

09 cessation
10 conclusion, expiration
11 termination

**explain**

05 solve, teach
06 decode, defend, define, excuse, set out, unfold
07 clarify, expound, justify, resolve, unravel
08 decipher, describe, disclose, simplify, spell out, untangle
09 delineate, elaborate, elucidate, explicate, interpret, make clear, translate, vindicate
10 account for, illustrate
11 demonstrate, explain away, rationalize, shed light on
12 throw light on
14 give a reason for

**explanation**

05 alibi, gloss
06 answer, excuse, reason
07 account, comment, defense, meaning, warrant
08 apologia, decoding, exegesis, footnote
10 annotation, commentary, definition, expounding
11 deciphering, delineation, description, elucidation
13 demonstration, justification
14 interpretation
15 rationalization

**explanatory**

10 exegetical, justifying
11 elucidatory, explicative
12 illustrative, interpretive
13 demonstrative
14 interpretative

**expletive**

04 oath
05 curse
08 cussword
09 blasphemy, curse word, obscenity, profanity, swearword
10 execration
11 bad language, imprecation
14 four-letter word

**explicable**

08 solvable
10 resolvable
11 explainable, justifiable
12 determinable, intelligible
13 interpretable
14 understandable

**explicate**

06 define, unfold
07 clarify, explain, expound, unravel, work out

**explicit**
08 describe, spell out, untangle
09 elucidate, make clear
10 illustrate
11 demonstrate

**explicit**
04 open
05 clear, exact, frank, plain
06 candid, direct, stated
07 certain, express, precise
08 declared, definite, detailed, distinct, positive, specific
09 outspoken
10 forthright, unreserved
11 categorical, plain-spoken, unambiguous, unequivocal
15 straightforward

**explode**
04 boom, go up, leap
05 blast, burst, erupt, go off
06 blow up, debunk, go bang, refute, rocket, see red, set off
08 burst out, detonate, disprove, escalate, mushroom
09 blow a fuse, discharge, do your nut, go bananas, repudiate
10 hit the roof, invalidate
11 blow your top, go up the wall, lose your rag
12 fly into a rage, give the lie to, lose your cool
13 hit the ceiling
15 fly off the handle

**exploit**
03 act, tap, use
04 deed, feat, milk
05 abuse, apply, bleed, stunt
06 action, draw on, employ, fleece, misuse, rip off
07 oppress, utilize
08 activity, cash in on, ill-treat, impose on, profit by
09 adventure, profiteer
10 attainment, manipulate
11 achievement, walk all over
12 capitalize on, put to good use, take for a ride
13 take liberties
14 play off against
15 take advantage of

**exploration**
04 tour, trip
05 probe, quest, study
06 safari, search, survey, travel
08 analysis, research, scrutiny
10 expedition, inspection
11 examination, observation
13 investigation
14 reconnaissance

**exploratory**
05 pilot, trial

07 probing
08 analytic
09 searching, tentative
11 fact-finding
12 experimental
13 investigative

**explore**
05 probe, scout, study
06 review, search, survey, travel
07 analyze, examine, inspect
08 look into, research
11 inquire into, investigate, reconnoiter, see the world

**explorer**
05 scout
08 surveyor, traveler
09 navigator
10 discoverer, prospector
11 trailblazer
13 reconnoiterer

► *Names of explorers and pioneers:*
04 **Byrd** (Richard Evelyn), **Cano** (Juan Sebastian del), **Cody** (William "Buffalo Bill"), **Cook** (James), **Diaz** (Bartolomeu), **Gama** (Vasco da), **Polo** (Marco), **Ross** (James Clark)
05 **Barth** (Heinrich), **Boone** (Daniel), **Cabot** (John), **Clark** (William), **Drake** (Francis), **Hanno**, **Lewis** (Meriwether), **Oates** (Lawrence), **Peary** (Robert Edwin), **Scott** (Robert Falcon), **Smith** (John), **Young** (Brigham)
06 **Balboa** (Vasco Núñez de), **Burton** (Richard), **Carson** (Kit), **Cortez** (Hernando), **De Soto** (Hernando), **Nansen** (Fridtjof), **Tasman** (Abel Janszoon)
07 **Fiennes** (Ranulph Twistleton-Wykeham), **Fremont** (John Charles), **Pytheas**, **Raleigh** (Walter), **Stanley** (Henry Morton)
08 **Amundsen** (Roald), **Columbus** (Christopher), **Coronado** (Francisco Vasquez de), **Crockett** (Davy), **Linnaeus** (Carolus), **Magellan** (Ferdinand), **Standish** (Myles), **Vespucci** (Amerigo), **Winthrop** (John)
09 **Heyerdahl** (Thor), **Rasmussen** (Knud), **Vancouver** (George)
10 **Erik the Red, Shackleton**

(Ernest Henry)
11 **Livingstone** (David), **Ponce de Leon** (Juan)
12 **Leif Ericsson**
14 **Blashford-Snell** (Colonel John)

**explosion**
03 fit
04 bang, boom, clap, rage, roll
05 blast, burst, crack, surge
06 report, rumble
07 flare-up, tantrum, thunder
08 eruption, outbreak, outburst, paroxysm
09 discharge
10 detonation
14 dramatic growth, sudden increase

**explosive**
03 TNT
05 angry, fiery, nitro, rapid, tense
06 abrupt, Semtex, touchy
07 charged, cordite, fraught, violent
08 critical, dramatic, dynamite, unstable, volatile
09 gelignite, gunpowder, hazardous, sensitive
10 burgeoning, unexpected
11 mushrooming, overwrought
14 nitroglycerine

**exponent**
06 backer, expert, master
08 adherent, advocate, champion, defender, promoter, upholder
09 performer, proponent, spokesman, supporter
11 spokeswoman
12 practitioner, spokesperson

**export**
04 ship
05 trade
08 transfer
09 traffic in, transport
10 sell abroad
12 foreign trade, sell overseas

**expose**
04 risk, show
06 betray, detect, hazard, reveal, unmask, unveil
07 display, divulge, exhibit, imperil, lay bare, present, uncover, unearth
08 denounce, disclose, endanger, manifest, muckrake
09 lay open to, make known, put at risk, subject to
11 introduce to
12 acquaint with, bring to light
13 take the lid off

14 blow the whistle
**exposé**
07 account, article
08 exposure
10 disclosure, divulgence, revelation, uncovering
**exposed**
04 bare, open
06 on show, on view
08 laid bare, revealed
09 in the open, on display
10 vulnerable
11 susceptible, unprotected
**exposition**
04 expo, fair, show
05 paper, study
06 thesis
07 account, display
08 analysis, critique, exegesis
09 discourse, monograph
10 commentary, exhibition
11 description, elucidation, explanation, explication
12 illumination, presentation
13 clarification, demonstration
14 interpretation
**expository**
08 exegetic
11 declaratory, descriptive, elucidative, explanatory, explicatory, hermeneutic
12 illustrative, interpretive
13 hermeneutical
14 interpretative
**expostulate**
05 argue, plead
06 reason
07 protest
08 dissuade
11 remonstrate
**exposure**
04 hype, plug, risk
05 press
06 airing, danger, exposé
07 contact, display, showing
09 awareness, detection, discovery, publicity, unmasking, unveiling
10 disclosure, divulgence, exhibition, experience, revelation, uncovering
11 advertising, familiarity
12 denunciation, presentation
15 public attention
**expound**
06 preach, set out, unfold
07 analyze, clarify, dissect, explain, unravel
08 describe, set forth, spell out
09 elucidate, explicate

10 illuminate, illustrate
**express**
03 air, say
04 fast, show, sole, tell, vent
05 plain, quick, rapid, speak, state, swift, utter, voice
06 assert, convey, denote, reveal, speedy, stated
07 certain, declare, nonstop, precise, put over, signify
08 announce, clear-cut, definite, distinct, explicit, indicate, intimate, manifest, point out, specific, stand for
09 enunciate, high-speed, pronounce, put across, represent, symbolize
10 articulate, particular
11 categorical, communicate, give voice to, well-defined
12 put into words
**expression**
04 look, mien, show, sign, term, tone, word
05 frown, idiom, power, scowl, smile, style, vigor
06 aspect, phrase, saying, speech, symbol
07 diction, gesture, grimace, passion, voicing, wording
08 artistry, delivery, language, locution, phrasing
09 assertion, set phrase, statement, utterance
10 appearance, exhibition, indication, intimation, intonation, modulation
11 countenance, declaration, enunciation, imagination
12 announcement, articulation, illustration, turn of phrase
13 communication, demonstration, manifestation
14 representation
**expressionless**
05 blank, empty
06 glassy
07 deadpan, vacuous
09 impassive
10 poker-faced
11 emotionless, inscrutable
13 straight-faced
**expressive**
05 vivid
06 lively, moving
07 showing, telling
08 animated, eloquent, emphatic, forceful
09 evocative, revealing
10 articulate, meaningful, suggestive, thoughtful

11 significant, sympathetic
13 communicative, demonstrative
**expressly**
06 solely
07 clearly, exactly, plainly
09 decidedly, on purpose, pointedly, precisely, purposely, specially
10 definitely, distinctly, especially, explicitly
12 particularly, specifically
13 categorically, intentionally
**expropriate**
04 take
05 annex, seize, usurp
08 arrogate, disseise, disseize, take away
09 sequester
10 commandeer, confiscate
11 appropriate, requisition
**expulsion**
05 exile
07 removal, sacking, the boot, the sack, voiding
08 belching, ejection, eviction
09 discharge, exclusion, excretion, rejection
10 banishment, evacuation
**expunge**
05 annul, erase
06 cancel, delete, efface, remove, rub out
07 abolish, blot out, wipe out
08 cross out, get rid of
09 eradicate, extirpate
10 annihilate, obliterate
11 exterminate
**expurgate**
03 cut
05 emend, purge
06 censor, purify
07 clean up
08 sanitize
10 blue-pencil, bowdlerize
**exquisite**
04 fine, keen, rare
05 acute, sharp
06 choice, dainty, lovely, pretty
07 elegant, fragile, intense, perfect, refined
08 charming, cultured, delicate, flawless, piercing, precious
09 beautiful, excellent
10 delightful, impeccable
**extant**
05 alive
06 living
08 existent, existing
09 remaining, surviving

## extempore
10 subsistent, subsisting
11 in existence

## extempore
05 ad-lib
09 impromptu, unplanned
10 improvised, off the cuff, unprepared, unscripted
11 spontaneous, unrehearsed
13 spontaneously
14 extemporaneous

## extemporize
05 ad-lib
06 make up
09 improvise
11 play it by ear
15 think on your feet

## extend
03 run
04 give, last
05 grant, offer, reach, widen
06 bestow, come to, confer, expand, go up to, impart, spread, step up, unwind
07 amplify, augment, broaden, carry on, develop, drag out, draw out, enlarge, hold out, present, proffer, prolong, spin out, stretch
08 continue, elongate, go down to, increase, lengthen, protract, reach out
09 go as far as, intensify

## extended
04 long
07 lengthy
08 enlarged, expanded
09 developed, increased
10 lengthened

## extension
04 wing
05 add-on, annex, delay
07 adjunct
08 addendum, addition, appendix, increase
09 expansion
10 broadening, elongation, stretching, supplement
11 development, lengthening, protraction
12 continuation, postponement, prolongation

## extensive
04 huge, long, vast, wide
05 broad, large, roomy
07 general, lengthy
08 complete, extended, sizeable, spacious, thorough
09 boundless, capacious, universal, unlimited
10 commodious, widespread
11 far-reaching, wide-ranging

12 all-inclusive
13 comprehensive

## extent
04 area, bulk, size, term, time
05 level, limit, range, reach, scope, sweep, width
06 amount, bounds, degree, length, sphere, spread
07 breadth, compass, expanse, lengths, measure, stretch
08 coverage, duration, quantity
09 dimension, magnitude

## extenuate
06 excuse, lessen, soften
07 qualify
08 diminish, minimize, mitigate

## extenuating
08 excusing
09 lessening, softening
10 justifying, minimizing, mitigating, moderating, palliative, qualifying
11 diminishing, exculpatory, extenuative, extenuatory

## exterior
04 face, skin
05 outer, shell
06 façade, finish
07 coating, outside, surface
08 covering, external
09 extrinsic, outermost
10 appearance, peripheral
11 superficial, surrounding
12 outer surface
15 external surface

## exterminate
04 kill
07 abolish, destroy, wipe out
08 massacre
09 eliminate, eradicate, extirpate, slaughter
10 annihilate

## extermination
07 killing
08 genocide, massacre
11 destruction, elimination, eradication, extirpation
12 annihilation

## external
05 outer
07 outside, outward, surface
08 apparent, exterior, visiting
10 extramural, peripheral
11 independent, superficial

## extinct
04 dead, gone, lost
06 bygone
07 defunct, died out, expired
08 inactive, quenched, vanished, wiped out

09 burned out
11 nonexistent
12 exterminated, extinguished

## extinction
05 death
08 dying-out, excision
09 abolition, vanishing
11 destruction, eradication
12 annihilation, obliteration
13 extermination

## extinguish
04 kill
05 choke, douse, erase
06 put out, quench, stifle
07 abolish, blow out, destroy, expunge, smother, stub out
08 snuff out, suppress
09 eliminate, extirpate
10 annihilate, dampen down
11 exterminate

## extirpate
05 erase
06 cut out, remove, uproot
07 abolish, destroy, expunge, root out, wipe out
09 eliminate, eradicate
10 annihilate, deracinate, extinguish
11 exterminate

## extol, extoll
04 laud
05 exalt
06 praise
07 acclaim, applaud, commend, glorify, magnify
08 eulogize

## extort
04 milk
05 bleed, exact, wrest, wring
06 coerce
07 extract, squeeze
09 blackmail

## extortion
05 force
06 demand
07 milking
08 coercion, exaction
09 blackmail
12 racketeering

## extortionate
08 exacting, grasping
09 excessive, rapacious
10 exorbitant, immoderate, inordinate, outrageous
12 preposterous, unreasonable

## extra
03 new, too
04 also, more
05 added, bonus, fresh, spare

**extract**

06 as well, excess, unused, walk-on
07 adjunct, another, besides, further, reserve, surplus
08 addendum, addition, additive, left-over, let alone
09 accessory, along with, ancillary, appendage, auxiliary, extension, redundant, unusually
10 additional, attachment, especially, in addition, remarkably, supplement
11 superfluous, unnecessary
12 additionally, particularly, spear carrier, together with
13 exceptionally, not forgetting, supernumerary, supplementary
14 above and beyond
15 extraordinarily
16 background artist

**extract**

03 get
04 cite, clip, copy, cull, draw
05 exact, glean, juice, pluck, prize, quote, wrest, wring
06 choose, cut out, derive, elicit, gather, get out, obtain, remove, select, uproot, wrench
07 distill, draw out, essence, excerpt, pull out, spirits, take out
08 abstract, citation, clipping
09 quotation, selection
10 deracinate, distillate
11 concentrate
12 distillation

**extraction**

04 race
05 birth, blood, stock
06 family, origin
07 descent, drawing, lineage, pulling, removal
08 ancestry, pedigree
09 parentage, taking out
10 derivation, withdrawal

**extradite**

05 exile, expel
06 banish, deport
08 send back, send home
10 repatriate

**extradition**

05 exile
09 expulsion
10 banishment
11 deportation, sending back

**extraneous**

05 alien, extra, inapt
07 foreign, strange

08 exterior, needless, unneeded
09 extrinsic, redundant
10 additional, immaterial, incidental, irrelevant, peripheral, tangential
11 inessential, superfluous, unconnected, unnecessary
12 inapplicable, nonessential
13 inappropriate, supplementary

**extraordinary**

03 odd
04 rare
06 unique
07 amazing, bizarre, curious, notable, special, strange, unusual
08 peculiar, uncommon
09 fantastic, marvelous, wonderful
10 astounding, noteworthy, remarkable, surprising, unexpected
11 exceptional, outstanding
14 out of this world

**extravagance**

05 folly, waste
06 excess
08 wildness
10 lavishness, profligacy
11 prodigality, squandering
12 immoderation, improvidence, overspending, recklessness, wastefulness
14 thriftlessness

**extravagant**

04 dear, wild
06 costly, flashy, lavish, ornate
08 prodigal, reckless, wasteful
09 excessive, expensive, fantastic, imprudent
10 exorbitant, flamboyant, immoderate, outrageous, profligate
11 improvident, spendthrift
12 ostentatious, unrestrained

**extravaganza**

04 show
05 revue
07 display, pageant
09 spectacle
11 spectacular

**extreme**

03 end, top
04 acme, apex, dire, edge, last, line, mark, peak, pole
05 acute, depth, final, great, harsh, limit, rigid, stern
06 climax, excess, height, severe, utmost, zenith

07 distant, drastic, faraway, highest, intense, maximum, radical, supreme, zealous
08 farthest, greatest, pinnacle, remotest, terminal, ultimate
09 Draconian, excessive, extremist, extremity, fanatical, out-and-out, outermost, stringent, uttermost
10 immoderate, most remote
14 uncompromising

◻**in the extreme**

04 very
06 highly
07 greatly, utterly
09 intensely
10 remarkably, uncommonly
11 exceedingly, excessively
12 immoderately, inordinately
13 exceptionally
15 extraordinarily

**extremely**

04 very
06 highly, really
07 acutely, greatly, utterly
08 severely, terribly
09 decidedly, intensely
10 dreadfully, remarkably, thoroughly, uncommonly
11 exceedingly, excessively
12 immoderately, inordinately, terrifically, unreasonably
13 exceptionally
15 extraordinarily

**extremism**

04 zeal
08 zealotry
10 fanaticism, radicalism
13 excessiveness

**extremist**

05 rebel, ultra
06 zealot
07 die-hard, fanatic, radical
08 militant
09 hard-liner, terrorist
14 fundamentalist

**extremity**

03 arm, end, leg, tip, toe, top
04 acme, apex, edge, foot, hand, limb, peak, pole
05 brink, depth, limit, verge
06 apogee, border, crisis, danger, excess, finger, height, margin, plight, zenith
07 maximum, minimum
08 boundary, exigency, frontier, hardship, pinnacle, terminal, terminus, ultimate
09 adversity, emergency, indigence, periphery
11 termination

## extricate
04 free
05 clear
06 detach, get out, rescue
07 deliver, extract, release
08 let loose, liberate, withdraw
09 disengage
11 disentangle

## extrinsic
05 alien
06 exotic
07 foreign, outside
08 exterior, external, imported
10 extraneous

## extrovert
10 socializer
14 outgoing person, sociable person

## extroverted
06 hearty
07 amiable
08 amicable, friendly, outgoing, sociable
09 exuberant
13 demonstrative

## extrude
04 mold
05 eject, expel
08 force out, press out
10 squeeze out

## exuberance
03 vim
04 life, zest
05 vigor
06 energy, pizazz
07 elation, pizzazz
08 buoyancy, rankness, richness, vitality, vivacity
09 plenitude, profusion
10 ebullience, excitement, lavishness, liveliness
11 copiousness, fulsomeness, high spirits, prodigality
12 cheerfulness, effusiveness, exaggeration, exhilaration
13 effervescence

## exuberant
04 lush, rank, rich
06 elated, lavish, lively
07 buoyant, excited, fulsome, profuse, zestful
08 abundant, animated, cheerful, effusive, spirited, thriving, vigorous
09 ebullient, energetic, luxurious, plenteous, sparkling, vivacious
10 full of life
11 exaggerated, exhilarated
12 effervescent, enthusiastic, high-spirited, unrestrained

13 irrepressible

## exude
04 emit, leak, ooze, seep, weep
05 bleed, issue, sweat
07 display, emanate, excrete, exhibit, secrete, trickle
08 manifest, perspire

## exult
04 crow
05 gloat, glory, revel
06 relish
07 delight, rejoice, triumph
08 be joyful
09 celebrate

## exultant
06 elated, joyful, joyous
07 gleeful
08 exulting, jubilant
09 cock-a-hoop, delighted, overjoyed, rejoicing
10 enraptured, triumphant

## exultation
03 joy
04 glee
05 glory, paean
06 eulogy
07 crowing, elation, triumph
08 gloating, glorying, reveling
09 merriness, rejoicing, transport
10 joyfulness, joyousness, jubilation
11 celebration

## eye
04 scan, view
05 sight, study, taste, watch
06 assess, gaze at, look at, peruse, regard, survey
07 examine, inspect, observe, opinion, stare at
08 eyesight, glance at, judgment
09 awareness, viewpoint, vigilance
10 estimation, perception, scrutinize
11 contemplate, discernment, observation, point of view, recognition, sensitivity
12 appreciation, surveillance
13 look up and down
14 discrimination

◄ *Parts of the eye*:
03 rod
04 cone, iris, lens, uvea
05 fovea, pupil
06 cornea, retina, sclera
07 choroid, eyelash, papilla
09 blind spot
10 optic nerve
11 ciliary body, conjunctiva, lower eyelid, upper eyelid

12 aqueous humor, lacrimal duct, ocular muscle, vitreous body
13 vitreous humor
15 anterior chamber

## ❏ keep an eye on
04 mind
07 monitor
08 attend to
09 look after
10 keep tabs on, take care of
12 watch closely

## ❏ see eye to eye
05 agree
07 be at one
11 be of one mind, go along with

## ❏ set eyes on
03 see
04 meet
06 behold, notice
07 observe
09 encounter, lay eyes on
10 clap eyes on, come across

## eyeball

## ❏ up to your eyeballs
04 busy
06 tied up
08 involved, occupied
09 engrossed, inundated
11 overwhelmed, snowed under
14 fully stretched

## eye-catching
08 gorgeous, imposing, striking, stunning
09 arresting, prominent
10 attractive, impressive, noticeable
11 captivating, conspicuous, spectacular

## eyesight
04 view
05 sight
06 ocular, vision, visual
07 optical
11 observation
13 power of seeing
14 faculty of sight

## eyesore
04 blot, mess, scar
06 blight, horror
08 atrocity, disgrace, ugliness
10 defacement
11 monstrosity
13 disfigurement

## eyewitness
07 watcher, witness
08 looker-on, observer, onlooker, passer-by
09 bystander, spectator

## fable
03 lie
04 epic, myth, saga, tale, yarn
05 story
06 legend
07 fiction, parable, untruth
08 allegory, apologue
09 falsehood, invention, moral
 tale, tall story
11 fabrication
12 old wives' tale

---

➤ *Names of fable writers*:
03 **Fay** (András), **Gay** (John)
05 **Aesop, Torga** (Miguel)
06 **Dryden** (John), **Krylov**
 (Ivan), **Ramsay** (Allan)
07 **Babrius, Fénelon** (François
 de Salignac de la Mothe),
 **Kipling** (Rudyard)
08 **Phaedrus, Saltykov**
 (Michail)
10 **La Fontaine** (Jean de)
➤ See also WRITER

## fabled
05 famed
06 famous
08 renowned
09 legendary

## fabric
05 cloth, stuff
07 textile, texture
08 material
09 framework, structure
11 foundations
14 infrastructure

---

➤ *Types of fabric*:
03 kid, net, rep
04 cord, felt, jean, lamé, lawn,
 repp, silk, wool
05 camel, chino, crêpe, denim,
 gauze, linen, lisle, llama,
 loden, Lurex, Lycra, nylon,
 Orlon, piqué, rayon, satin,
 scrim, serge, suede, terry,
 toile, tulle, tweed, twill, voile
06 alpaca, angora, burlap,
 calico, canvas, chintz, cotton,
 Dacron, damask, duffel,
 duffle, fleece, jersey, merino,
 mohair, muslin, nankin,
 sateen, velour, velvet, vicuna
07 brocade, buckram, cambric,

chamois, chiffon, flannel,
 fustian, gingham, hessian,
 kidskin, leather, morocco,
 nankeen, organdy, organza,
 paisley, taffeta, ticking,
 veiling, velours, Viyella,
 webbing, worsted
08 barathea, buckskin,
 cashmere, chenille, corduroy,
 gossamer, moleskin, oilcloth,
 organdie, quilting, Terylene,
 waxcloth
09 astrakhan, bombasine,
 bombazeen, bombazine,
 flannelet, gaberdine,
 haircloth, horsehair,
 polyester, sackcloth,
 sailcloth, sharkskin,
 sheepskin, velveteen
10 candlewick, seersucker, terry
 cloth
11 cheesecloth, flannelette,
 Harris tweed
12 Brussels lace, cavalry twill,
 crêpe de Chine, Shetland
 wool
13 terry toweling

## fabricate
04 fake, form, make
05 erect, forge, frame, shape
06 cook up, create, devise,
 invent, make up
07 concoct, falsify, fashion,
 produce, trump up
08 assemble
09 construct
11 counterfeit, manufacture

## fabrication
04 fake, myth
05 fable, story
07 fiction, forgery, untruth
08 assembly, building, erection
09 falsehood, invention
10 assemblage, concoction,
 fairy story, production
11 manufacture
12 construction

## fabulous
04 cool
05 great, magic, super
06 fabled, made-up, superb,
 unreal, way-out
08 invented, mythical

09 fantastic, fictional, imaginary,
 legendary, marvelous
10 astounding, fictitious,
 incredible, phenomenal,
 remarkable
11 astonishing, spectacular
12 unbelievable, unimaginable
13 inconceivable
14 out of this world

## façade
04 face, mask, show, veil
05 cloak, cover, front, guise
06 veneer
08 disguise, exterior, frontage
09 semblance
10 appearance

## face
03 air, map, mug, pan
04 clad, coat, look, meet, name,
 phiz, puss, side
05 brave, clock, cover, dress,
 front, frown, honor, looks,
 scowl
06 aspect, facial, façade, kisser,
 oppose, polish, resist,
 smooth, tackle, veneer,
 visage
07 grimace, outside, surface
08 confront, cope with, deal
 with, exterior, face up to,
 features, frontage, overlook,
 prestige, standing
09 encounter, go against
10 appearance, be opposite,
 expression, reputation
11 countenance, physiognomy
12 be at variance, be in conflict
13 come up against

❑ **face to face**
06 facing
08 eye to eye, opposite
11 confronting
15 in confrontation

❑ **face up to**
06 accept
08 confront, cope with, deal
 with
09 recognize, stand up to
10 meet head-on
11 acknowledge
15 come to terms with

❑ **fly in the face of**
05 clash

**facelift**
06 oppose
08 be at odds, conflict, contrast, disagree
09 go against
10 contradict
12 be at variance, be in conflict

## on the face of it
09 obviously, outwardly, reputedly, seemingly
10 apparently, manifestly, ostensibly
12 on the surface
13 superficially

## make a face
04 lour, pout, sulk
05 frown
06 glower
07 grimace
13 knit your brows

**facelift**
10 renovation
11 restoration
14 plastic surgery
15 cosmetic surgery

**facet**
04 face, side
05 angle, plane, point, slant
06 aspect, factor
07 element, feature, surface
14 characteristic

**facetious**
05 comic, droll, funny, witty
06 jocose, joking
07 amusing, jesting, jocular
08 flippant, humorous
09 frivolous
12 lighthearted
13 tongue-in-cheek

**facile**
04 easy, glib
05 hasty, quick, ready, slick
06 fluent, simple, smooth
07 shallow
10 simplistic
11 superficial
13 uncomplicated

**facilitate**
04 ease, help
06 assist, smooth
07 advance, forward, further, promote, speed up
08 expedite
12 smooth the way

**facility**
04 ease, gift
05 knack, means, skill
06 talent
07 ability, amenity, fluency, service, utility
08 resource

09 appliance, dexterity, eloquence, equipment, quickness, readiness
11 convenience, opportunity, proficiency
12 skillfulness

**facing**
06 façade, lining, veneer
07 coating, overlay, surface
08 cladding, covering, trimming
09 revetment
10 false front
13 looking toward

**facsimile**
03 fax
04 copy
05 ditto, image, print, repro, Xerox
07 replica
09 duplicate, imitation, photocopy, Photostat
10 carbon copy, mimeograph, transcript
12 reproduction

**fact**
04 deed, info, item
05 datum, point, score, truth
06 detail, factor
07 feature, lowdown, reality
09 actuality, certainty, component, happening
11 information
12 circumstance, fait accompli

## in fact
05 truly
06 indeed, really
07 in truth
08 actually
09 in reality
10 in practice
12 in actual fact
13 in point of fact
15 as a matter of fact

**faction**
03 set
04 band, camp, ring, side
05 cabal, junta, lobby, party
06 caucus, clique, sector, strife
07 coterie, discord, section
08 argument, conflict, division, friction, minority, quarrels
10 contention, contingent, disharmony, infighting
12 disagreement
13 splinter group

**factious**
05 rival
06 at odds
07 warring
08 clashing, divisive, mutinous
09 seditious, turbulent

10 discordant, quarreling, rebellious, refractory, tumultuous
11 conflicting, contentious, quarrelsome
12 disputatious
13 at loggerheads

**factor**
04 fact, item, part
05 cause, facet, point
06 aspect, detail
07 element, feature
09 component, influence
10 ingredient
11 constituent, contingency
13 consideration
14 characteristic

**factory**
04 mill
05 plant, works
07 foundry
08 workshop
12 assembly line

**factotum**
07 servant
08 handyman
09 man Friday, odd jobber
10 girl Friday
15 jack-of-all-trades

**factual**
04 real, true
05 close, exact
06 actual, strict
07 correct, genuine, precise
08 accurate, detailed, faithful, truthful, unbiased
09 authentic, realistic
10 historical, true-to-life

**faculties**
04 wits
06 powers, reason, senses
07 ability
12 capabilities, intelligence

**faculty**
04 bent, gift
05 flair, knack, power, skill
06 talent
07 ability, section
08 aptitude, capacity, facility, teachers
10 capability, department, professors
11 proficiency

**fad**
04 mode, rage, whim
05 craze, fancy, mania, trend, vogue
07 fashion
10 enthusiasm
11 affectation

## fade

- 03 die, dim, ebb
- 04 fail, flag, melt, pale, wane
- 06 blanch, bleach, blench, perish, recede, vanish, weaken, whiten, wither
- 07 decline, die away, dwindle, ebb away, shrivel, wash out
- 08 diminish, discolor, dissolve, etiolate, evanesce, peter out
- 09 disappear, fizzle out, lose color, waste away
- 11 become paler
- 12 become weaker

## fag

- 03 cig
- 04 flag, tire
- 05 weary
- 09 cigarette
- 10 coffin nail
- 11 cancer stick

## fag end

- 04 butt, rump, stub
- 07 remnant
- 08 last part

## fagged

- 05 all in, jaded, weary
- 07 flagged, worn out
- 08 fatigued
- 09 exhausted
- 14 on your last legs

## fail

- 04 bomb, fade, flag, flop, fold, omit, sink, stop, wane
- 05 crash, droop, flunk, leave
- 06 blow it, cut out, forget, go bust, weaken
- 07 abandon, conk out, decline, forsake, founder, go kaput, go under, go wrong, let down, neglect, not work
- 08 diminish, fall flat, not start
- 09 break down, go belly up, not make it
- 10 disappoint, get nowhere, go bankrupt, not come off
- 11 bite the dust, come to grief, come unglued, come unstuck, fall through, go to the wall, malfunction
- 12 come a cropper
- 13 come to nothing
- 14 be unsuccessful
- 15 become insolvent, blow your chances

## ❑ without fail

- 08 reliably
- 09 regularly
- 10 constantly, dependably, faithfully, punctually
- 11 predictably, religiously, unfailingly
- 13 like clockwork

## failing

- 04 flaw
- 05 error, fault, lapse
- 06 defect, foible
- 07 blemish, lacking, without
- 08 drawback, weakness
- 10 deficiency
- 11 in default of, shortcoming
- 12 imperfection
- 14 in the absence of

## failure

- 03 dud
- 04 bomb, bust, flop, mess, miss, no go, ruin
- 05 crash, lemon, loser
- 06 defeat, fiasco, misfit, reject, slip-up, turkey, victim, waning
- 07 also-ran, decline, default, dropout, has-been, letdown, neglect, sinking, washout, wipeout
- 08 abortion, collapse, dead loss, disaster, downfall, omission, shutdown, stalling, stopping, write-off
- 09 born loser, breakdown, weakening
- 10 bankruptcy, conking-out, cutting-out, foundering, going under, insolvency, negligence, nonstarter
- 11 dereliction, miscarriage
- 12 going belly up
- 13 deterioration, lack of success
- 14 disappointment, going to the wall, malfunctioning
- 15 coming to nothing

## faint

- 03 dim, low
- 04 drop, dull, pale, soft, weak
- 05 dizzy, faded, giddy, light, muted, swoon, vague
- 06 feeble, hushed, slight
- 07 blurred, muffled, obscure, pass out, syncope, unclear
- 08 black out, collapse, flake out, keel over
- 10 indistinct
- 11 halfhearted, lightheaded
- 15 unconsciousness

## fainthearted

- 04 weak
- 05 timid
- 06 yellow
- 08 timorous
- 09 diffident
- 10 irresolute, spiritless

- 11 halfhearted, lily-livered

## faintly

- 04 a bit
- 06 feebly, softly, weakly
- 07 a little, vaguely
- 08 slightly

## fair

- 02 OK
- 03 dry
- 04 expo, fête, fine, gala, just, okay, pale, show, so-so
- 05 blond, clear, cream, legit, light, right, sunny
- 06 bazaar, blonde, bright, decent, honest, kosher, lawful, market, modest, not bad, proper, square, yellow
- 08 adequate, all right, carnival, detached, mediocre, middling, moderate, passable, sporting, unbiased
- 09 cloudless, equitable, impartial, objective, tolerable, unclouded
- 10 above board, acceptable, evenhanded, fair-haired, on the level, reasonable, straight up, sufficient
- 11 respectable, trustworthy
- 12 satisfactory, unprejudiced
- 13 disinterested, dispassionate
- 15 played by the book

## fairly

- 05 fully, quite
- 06 justly, pretty, rather, really
- 07 legally
- 08 honestly, lawfully, somewhat
- 09 equitably, tolerably, veritably
- 10 absolutely, adequately, moderately, positively, reasonably, unbiasedly
- 11 impartially, objectively

## fairness

- 06 equity
- 07 decency, justice
- 12 impartiality, unbiasedness
- 13 equitableness
- 14 evenhandedness

## fairy

- 03 elf, fay, hob, imp
- 04 peri, pixy, Puck
- 05 nymph, pixie
- 06 goblin, sprite
- 07 brownie
- 09 hobgoblin
- 10 leprechaun, Tinkerbell
- 15 Robin Goodfellow

## fairy tale

- 03 lie
- 04 myth
- 07 fantasy, fiction, untruth

08 folk tale
11 fabrication

**faith**
04 sect
05 creed, dogma, honor, trust
06 belief, church, fealty
07 honesty, loyalty
08 credence, devotion,
  doctrine, fidelity, reliance,
  religion, teaching
09 assurance, sincerity
10 allegiance, commitment,
  confidence, conviction,
  dedication, persuasion
12 denomination, truthfulness

**faithful**
04 true
05 close, exact, loyal
06 strict, trusty
07 devoted, precise, staunch
08 accurate, brethren, constant,
  obedient, reliable, truthful
09 adherents, believers,
  committed, dedicated,
  followers, steadfast
10 dependable, supporters
11 trustworthy
12 communicants,
  congregation

**faithfulness**
06 fealty
07 loyalty
08 accuracy, devotion, fidelity
09 closeness, constancy
10 allegiance, commitment,
  dedication, strictness
11 reliability, staunchness
13 dependability, steadfastness

**faithless**
05 false
06 fickle, untrue
08 disloyal, doubting
10 adulterous, inconstant,
  perfidious, traitorous,
  unfaithful, untruthful
11 treacherous, unbelieving
12 disbelieving, falsehearted

**faithlessness**
06 deceit
07 perfidy
08 adultery, apostasy, betrayal
09 treachery
10 disloyalty, infidelity
11 inconstancy

**fake**
04 copy, hoax, mock, sham
05 bogus, false, feign, forge,
  fraud, phony, pseud, put on,
  quack
06 affect, assume, forged,
  phoney, pirate, pseudo

07 forgery, pretend, replica
08 affected, impostor, simulate
09 charlatan, fabricate,
  imitation, simulated
10 artificial, fraudulent,
  mountebank, simulation
11 counterfeit
12 reproduction

**fall**
03 cut, die
04 dive, drop, grow, pass, ruin,
  sink, slip, trip, turn
05 crash, occur, pitch, slant,
  slide, slope, slump, yield
06 autumn, become, defeat,
  demise, give in, go down,
  happen, lessen, perish,
  plunge, recede, topple,
  tumble
07 be slain, be taken, capture,
  decline, descend, dwindle,
  failure, fall off, incline,
  plummet, stumble, subside
08 be killed, collapse, decrease,
  diminish, downfall, giving-in,
  grow into, keel over, yielding
09 come about, dwindling,
  lessening, overthrow,
  reduction, surrender
10 be defeated, plummeting
11 be conquered, destruction,
  keeling-over, resignation
12 be vanquished, capitulation,
  lose your life, pitch forward

❏**fall apart**
05 break, decay
07 break up, crack up, crumble,
  shatter
08 collapse, come away,
  dissolve, go to bits
09 decompose
10 fall to bits, go to pieces
12 come to pieces, disintegrate,
  fall to pieces
15 break into pieces

❏**fall back**
06 depart, recoil
07 retreat
08 draw back, pull back,
  withdraw
09 disengage

❏**fall back on**
06 call on, look to, turn to
08 resort to
09 make use of
12 call into play
14 have recourse to

❏**fall behind**
03 lag
05 trail
08 drop back

09 lag behind, not keep up

❏**fall for**
03 buy
05 fancy
06 accept, desire, take to
07 swallow
10 be fooled by
11 be taken in by
12 be attached to, be deceived
  by, have a crush on
14 fall in love with

❏**fall in**
04 sink
05 crash
06 cave in
07 give way, subside
08 assemble, collapse, come
  down

❏**fall in with**
06 accept
07 support
08 assent to
09 agree with
10 comply with
11 go along with
13 cooperate with

❏**fall off**
04 drop, slow
05 slump
06 lessen, worsen
07 decline, drop off, slacken
08 decrease
11 deteriorate

❏**fall on**
06 assail, attack, snatch
07 assault, lay into, set upon
08 pounce on
09 descend on

❏**fall out**
05 argue, clash, fight
06 bicker, differ
07 quarrel
08 disagree, squabble

❏**fall through**
04 fail
08 collapse, miscarry
11 come to grief
13 come to nothing

❏**fall to**
05 begin, set to, start
06 launch
08 set about
13 apply yourself

**fallacious**
05 false, wrong
06 untrue
08 illusory, mistaken, spurious
09 deceptive, erroneous,
  illogical, incorrect, sophistic
10 fictitious, inaccurate

11 casuistical, sophistical

**fallacy**
04 flaw, myth
07 mistake, sophism
08 delusion, illusion
09 casuistry, false idea, falsehood, sophistry
13 misconception
14 miscalculation
15 misapprehension

**fallen**
04 dead, died, lost
05 loose, slain
06 killed, shamed
07 immoral
08 perished
09 disgraced
10 degenerate
11 promiscuous, slaughtered

**fallible**
04 weak
05 frail, human
06 errant, erring, flawed, mortal
09 imperfect, uncertain

**fallow**
04 idle
06 barren, unsown, unused
07 dormant, resting
08 inactive
09 unplanted
10 unploughed
11 undeveloped
12 uncultivated, unproductive

**false**
04 fake, mock, sham
05 bogus, lying, phony, wrong
06 forged, untrue
07 assumed, feigned, pretend
08 disloyal, illusory, two-faced
09 deceitful, dishonest, erroneous, faithless, imitation, incorrect, insincere, pretended, simulated, synthetic
10 artificial, fabricated, fallacious, fictitious, fraudulent, inaccurate, misleading, perfidious, traitorous, unfaithful
11 counterfeit, treacherous
12 hypocritical
13 double-dealing, untrustworthy

**falsehood**
03 fib, lie
05 story
06 deceit
07 fiction, perfidy, untruth
09 deception, duplicity, hypocrisy, invention, tall story, treachery

10 dishonesty, fairy story
11 fabrication, insincerity
12 two-facedness
13 double-dealing
14 untruthfulness

**falsification**
06 change, deceit
07 forgery
10 alteration, perversion
12 adulteration
13 dissimulation

**falsify**
03 rig
04 fake
05 alter, forge, twist
06 doctor, fiddle
07 distort, massage, pervert
10 adulterate, tamper with
11 counterfeit
12 misrepresent

**falter**
04 fail, flag
05 delay, quail, shake, waver
06 flinch, totter
07 stammer, stumble, stutter
08 hesitate
10 be unsteady, dillydally
12 be in two minds, drag your feet, shilly-shally

**faltering**
04 weak
05 timid
06 broken
07 failing
08 flagging, hesitant, unsteady
09 tentative, uncertain
10 irresolute, stammering

**fame**
04 name, note
05 glory, honor
06 esteem, renown
07 stardom
08 eminence
09 celebrity, greatness
10 importance, notability, prominence, reputation
11 distinction

**famed**
05 noted
06 famous
08 esteemed, renowned
09 acclaimed, well-known
10 celebrated, recognized
11 widely known

**familiar**
04 bold, dear, easy, free, near
05 close, known, pally, usual
06 au fait, casual, chummy, common, smarmy, versed
07 natural, relaxed, routine

08 everyday, friendly, habitual, informal, intimate, ordinary
09 au courant, customary, household, well-known
10 accustomed, acquainted, conversant, unreserved
11 commonplace, free-and-easy, impertinent
12 over-friendly, presumptuous, recognizable, run-of-the-mill
13 disrespectful

**familiarity**
04 ease
07 liberty, mastery
08 boldness, intimacy, nearness, openness
09 closeness, impudence, knowledge, pushiness
10 casualness, chumminess, disrespect, experience
11 forwardness, informality, presumption, sociability
12 acquaintance, friendliness, impertinence

**familiarize**
05 brief, coach, prime, teach, train
08 accustom, instruct
09 habituate, make aware
11 acclimatize
14 make acquainted

**family**
03 kin
04 clan, folk, kids, line, race
05 birth, blood, class, genus, house, issue, stock, tribe
06 people, scions, stirps, strain
07 descent, dynasty, kindred, kinfolk, kinsmen, lineage, parents, progeny, species
08 ancestry, children, kinsfolk, pedigree
09 ancestors, forebears, household, next of kin, offspring, parentage, relations, relatives
11 descendants, you and yours

❑ **family tree**
04 line
07 lineage
08 ancestry, pedigree
09 genealogy
10 background, extraction

**famine**
04 lack, want
05 death
06 dearth, hunger
08 scarcity
10 starvation
11 deprivation, destitution

12 malnutrition
14 shortage of food

**famished**
06 hungry
07 starved
08 ravenous, starving
09 famishing, voracious

**famous**
05 famed, great, noted
07 eminent, honored, notable, popular
08 esteemed, infamous, renowned
09 acclaimed, legendary, notorious, prominent, venerable, well-known
10 celebrated, remarkable
11 illustrious
13 distinguished

**fan**
03 air, nut
04 blow, buff, cool, vane
05 fiend, freak, lover, rouse
06 addict, arouse, backer, blower, cooler, incite, kindle, stir up, whip up, work up
07 admirer, air-cool, devotee, freshen, provoke, refresh
08 adherent, follower, increase
09 air cooler, propeller, stimulate, supporter, ventilate
10 aficionado, enthusiast, ventilator
14 air conditioner

◻**fan out**
06 unfold, unfurl
07 move out, open out
09 spread out

**fanatic**
05 bigot, fiend, freak
06 addict, maniac, zealot
07 devotee, radical
08 activist, militant
09 extremist, visionary
10 enthusiast
14 fundamentalist

**fanatical**
03 mad
04 wild
05 rabid
07 bigoted, burning, extreme, fervent, radical, zealous
08 activist, frenzied, militant
09 extremist, obsessive
10 immoderate, passionate
12 narrow-minded, single-minded
14 fundamentalist

**fanaticism**
04 zeal
06 fervor, frenzy
07 bigotry, madness
08 activism, wildness
09 dogmatism, extremism, militancy, monomania
13 obsessiveness
14 fundamentalism

**fanciful**
04 wild
06 ornate, unreal
07 curious, flighty
08 creative, fabulous, illusory, mythical, romantic
09 decorated, elaborate, fairy-tale, fantastic, imaginary, legendary, whimsical
11 extravagant, imaginative, make-believe, unrealistic

**fancy**
03 yen
04 idea, itch, like, urge, want, whim, wish
05 dream, favor, guess, showy, think
06 desire, lavish, liking, notion, ornate, reckon, rococo, take to, vision
07 adorned, baroque, believe, caprice, dream of, elegant, fantasy, imagine, long for, not mind, opinion, picture, suppose, surmise, thought
08 conceive, delusion, fanciful, feel like, fondness, illusion, penchant, yearn for
09 decorated, elaborate, fantastic
10 be mad about, conjecture, creativity, far-fetched, have in mind, not say no to, ornamented, preference
11 embellished, extravagant, imagination, inclination
12 ostentatious
13 be attracted to
14 be interested in, find attractive

**fanfare**
04 pomp, show
06 tucket
08 flourish
11 trumpet call

**fang**
04 tusk
05 prong, tooth
10 venom tooth
11 canine tooth

**fantasize**
05 dream

06 invent
07 imagine, romance
08 daydream
11 hallucinate
12 live in a dream

**fantastic**
03 ace, odd
04 cool, neat, wild
05 great, magic, weird
06 exotic, superb, unreal
07 amazing, bizarre, strange
08 fabulous, fanciful, illusory, romantic, terrific
09 brilliant, eccentric, first-rate, imaginary, marvelous, visionary, wonderful
10 impressive, incredible, outlandish
11 extravagant, imaginative
12 unbelievable
14 out of this world

**fantasy**
04 myth
05 dream, fancy
06 mirage, vision
07 reverie
08 daydream, delusion, illusion
09 invention, nightmare, pipe dream, unreality
10 apparition, creativity
11 imagination, originality, pie in the sky, speculation
13 flight of fancy, hallucination

**far**
04 much
05 miles, other
06 far-off, remote
07 distant, faraway, further, greatly, removed
08 a good way, a long way, far-flung, markedly, opposite, outlying, secluded
09 decidedly, extremely
11 God-forsaken, nowhere near, out-of-the-way
12 considerably, immeasurably, in the boonies, inaccessible, incomparably
13 great distance
14 in the boondocks

◻**far and wide**
06 widely
07 broadly
08 all about
09 worldwide
10 far and near
11 extensively, in all places
13 from all places

◻**far out**
05 weird
06 exotic, way out

07 bizarre, extreme, strange
10 outlandish

◻**go far**
05 get on
08 go places
12 be successful
14 achieve success
15 get on in the world

◻**so far**
06 to date
07 thus far, till now, up to now
08 hitherto, until now
13 up to this point

**faraway**
06 absent, dreamy, remote
07 distant
08 far-flung, outlying
10 abstracted
11 preoccupied
12 absent-minded

**farce**
04 joke, sham
06 comedy, parody, satire
07 mockery
08 nonsense, travesty
09 absurdity, slapstick
10 buffoonery
14 ridiculousness

**farcical**
05 comic, silly
06 absurd, stupid
08 derisory
09 laughable, ludicrous
10 ridiculous
11 nonsensical
12 preposterous

**fare**
02 be, do, go
03 fee
04 cost, diet, eats, food, menu
05 get on, meals, price, table
06 charge, ticket, viands
07 make out, passage, prosper, rations, succeed, vittles
08 eatables, get along, progress, victuals
10 provisions, sustenance
11 nourishment

**far-fetched**
05 crazy
07 dubious
08 fanciful, unlikely
09 fantastic
10 improbable, incredible
11 implausible, unrealistic
12 preposterous, unbelievable

**farm**
04 land, plow, till
05 acres, croft, plant, ranch
06 grange

07 acreage, holding, station
08 farmland
09 cultivate, farmstead, homestead
11 cooperative, work the land

◻**farm out**
08 delegate
11 contract out, subcontract

**farmer**
07 granger, planter, rancher
08 ranchero, ranchman
10 agronomist
12 sharecropper
13 agriculturist

**farming**
07 tilling
08 agronomy
09 husbandry
11 agriculture, cultivation

**farrago**
04 hash, olio
06 jumble, medley
07 mélange, mixture
08 mishmash, mishmosh
09 potpourri
10 hodgepodge, hotchpotch, miscellany, salmagundi
11 gallimaufry

**far-reaching**
04 wide
05 broad
08 sweeping, thorough
09 extensive, important
10 widespread
11 significant, wide-ranging
13 comprehensive

**farsighted**
05 acute, canny
06 shrewd
07 politic, prudent
09 farseeing, judicious, prescient, provident
10 discerning
11 circumspect
14 forward-looking

**farther**
07 further, remoter
11 more distant, more extreme

**farthest**
08 furthest, remotest
11 most distant, most extreme

**fascinate**
04 draw, lure
05 charm, rivet
06 absorb, allure, entice
07 attract, beguile, delight, enchant, engross
08 enthrall, intrigue, transfix

09 captivate, hypnotize, mesmerize, spellbind

**fascinated**
06 hooked
07 charmed, curious, smitten
08 absorbed, beguiled
09 bewitched, engrossed, entranced, intrigued
10 captivated, enthralled, hypnotized, infatuated, mesmerized, spellbound

**fascinating**
08 alluring, charming, engaging, enticing, exciting, gripping, riveting, tempting
09 absorbing, seductive
10 bewitching, compelling, delightful, enchanting, engrossing, intriguing
11 captivating, interesting, mesmerizing, stimulating

**fascination**
04 draw, lure, pull
05 charm, magic, spell
06 allure, appeal
08 interest
09 magnetism
10 attraction, compulsion
11 captivation, enchantment

**fascism**
09 autocracy, Hitlerism
10 absolutism
12 dictatorship
15 totalitarianism

**fascist**
04 Nazi
08 autocrat
09 Falangist, Hitlerite
10 absolutist, autocratic, Blackshirt
12 totalitarian
13 authoritarian

**fashion**
03 cut, fad, fit, way
04 form, kind, line, look, make, mode, mold, rage, sort, suit, type
05 adapt, alter, craze, shape, style, trend, vogue
06 adjust, create, custom, design, latest, manner, method, system, tailor
07 clothes, couture, pattern
08 approach, rag trade
12 haute couture
15 clothes industry

▶ *Names of fashion designers:*
04 **Dior** (Christian), **Head** (Edith), **Muir** (Jean)

05  **Blass** (Bill), **Dache** (Lilly),
    **Ellis** (Perry), **Farhi** (Nicole),
    **Karan** (Donna), **Kenzo**
    (Takada), **Klein** (Anne),
    **Klein** (Calvin), **Pucci**
    (Emilio), **Quant** (Mary)
06  **Armani** (Giorgio), **Ashley**
    (Laura), **Cardin** (Pierre),
    **Chanel** (Coco), **Conran**
    (Jasper), **Lauren** (Ralph),
    **Mackie** (Bob), **Miyake**
    (Issey), **Ozbeck** (Rifat),
    **Rhodes** (Zandra)
07  **Galanos** (James), **Hamnett**
    (Katharine), **Lacroix**
    (Christian), **Laroche** (Guy),
    **Mizrahi** (Isaac), **Picasso**
    (Paloma), **Versace** (Gianni)
08  **Galliano** (John), **Gaultier**
    (Jean-Paul), **Givenchy**
    (Hubert James Marcel
    Taffin de), **Hilfiger**
    (Tommy), **Oldfield** (Bruce),
    **Westwood** (Vivienne),
    **Yamamoto** (Yohji)
09  **Claiborne** (Liz), **de la Renta**
    (Oscar), **Gernreich** (Rudi),
    **Lagerfeld** (Karl),
    **McCartney** (Stella),
    **Valentino**
12  **Saint Laurent** (Yves),
    **Schiaparelli** (Elsa)

□ **after a fashion, in a fashion**
11  not very well
12  to some extent

**fashionable**
02  in
03  hip
04  chic, cool, posh
05  funky, natty, ritzy, smart
06  latest, modern, modish,
    snazzy, trendy, with-it
07  à la mode, current, elegant,
    in vogue, popular, stylish
08  designer, up-to-date
10  all the rage, prevailing
12  contemporary
13  up-to-the-minute

**fast**
04  diet, firm, shut, slim
05  apace, brisk, fixed, fully,
    hasty, quick, rapid, sound,
    swift, tight
06  deeply, firmly, flying, presto,
    secure, speedy, starve
07  express, fixedly, flat-out,
    hastily, hurried, like mad,
    quickly, rapidly, refrain,
    swiftly, tightly
08  doggedly, go hungry, in a
    hurry, securely, speedily

09  breakneck, high-speed,
    hurriedly, immovable, like a
    shot
10  abstinence, like a flash,
    resolutely, starvation
11  lickety-spit, like the wind
13  like lightning
14  hell-for-leather

**fasten**
03  fix, pin, tie, zip
04  bind, bolt, clip, do up, grip,
    join, lace, link, lock, nail, seal,
    shut, tack
05  affix, chain, clamp, close,
    focus, hitch, rivet, zip up
06  anchor, attach, buckle,
    button, direct, secure, tether
07  connect

**fastener**
▶ *Types of fastener*:
03  peg, tie
04  bond, clip, frog, hasp, hook,
    knot, lace, link, lock, loop,
    nail, snap, stud, tack
05  catch, clamp, clasp, hinge,
    latch, rivet, screw
06  button, eyelet, holder, staple,
    stitch, toggle, Velcro, zipper
08  cuff link, shoelace
09  paperclip, thumbtack
10  hook-and-eye
12  collar button

**fastidious**
05  fussy, picky
06  choosy, dainty
07  choosey, finicky, precise
10  meticulous, particular
11  persnickety, punctilious
12  hard-to-please
13  hypercritical

**fat**
03  big, pot
04  bulk, flab, lard, suet, wide
05  broad, buxom, cream,
    dumpy, gross, heavy, lardy,
    large, obese, plump, podgy,
    pudgy, round, solid, sonsy,
    stout, thick, tubby
06  butter, cheese, chubby,
    flabby, fleshy, greasy, portly,
    rotund, tallow
07  adipose, blubber, fatness,
    obesity, paunchy, pinguid
08  potbelly, roly-poly, sizeable
09  corpulent, fat as a pig,
    margarine, plumpness,
    sebaceous, solidness,
    stoutness
10  chubbiness, corpulence,
    oleaginous, overweight,
    potbellied

12  considerable, steatopygous

**fatal**
05  final
06  deadly, lethal, mortal
07  killing
08  terminal
09  incurable, malignant
10  calamitous, disastrous
12  catastrophic

**fatalism**
08  stoicism
09  endurance, passivity
10  acceptance
11  resignation
13  preordination
14  predestination

**fatality**
04  dead, loss
05  death
08  casualty, disaster
09  lethality, mortality
10  deadliness

**fate**
03  end, lot
04  doom, luck, ruin
05  death, issue, karma, stars
06  chance, future, kismet
07  destiny, fortune, outcome
08  disaster, God's will
09  horoscope
10  providence
11  catastrophe, destruction

**fated**
04  sure
06  doomed
07  certain
08  destined
10  inevitable
11  ineluctable, inescapable,
    predestined, preordained

**fateful**
07  crucial, pivotal
08  critical, decisive
09  important, momentous

**father**
02  pa
03  dad, pop
04  abbé, curé, dada, papa, sire
05  beget, daddy, padre, pappy,
    pater, poppa
06  leader, old man, parent,
    parson, pastor, priest
07  creator, founder, produce
08  ancestor, begetter, engender,
    forebear, inventor, paternal
09  architect, clergyman,
    initiator, patriarch, procreate
10  forefather, give life to,
    originator, prime mover,
    procreator, progenitor

11 predecessor
13 paterfamilias

**fatherland**
04 home
08 homeland
10 motherland, native land, old country
11 home country
13 mother country, native country

**fatherly**
06 benign, kindly, tender
08 paternal
09 avuncular, indulgent
10 benevolent, forbearing, protective, supportive
11 patriarchal
12 affectionate

**fathom**
05 gauge, plumb, probe, sound
07 measure, work out
08 estimate, perceive
09 interpret, penetrate
10 comprehend, understand

**fatigue**
03 sap, tax
04 tire
05 drain, weary
06 weaken
07 exhaust, wear out
08 enervate, lethargy, weakness
09 lassitude, tiredness, weariness
10 debilitate, enervation, exhaustion
11 take it out of
12 listlessness

**fatigued**
04 beat
05 all in, jaded, tired, weary
06 bushed, done in, fagged, wasted, zonked
08 dead-beat, tired out
09 exhausted, fagged out, overtired

**fatness**
04 bulk, flab
07 obesity
09 bulkiness, grossness, largeness, plumpness, podginess, rotundity, stoutness, tubbiness
10 corpulence, overweight

**fatten**
04 cram, feed
05 bloat, stuff, swell, widen
06 expand, feed up, spread
07 broaden, build up, fill out, nourish, nurture, thicken

**fatty**
03 fat
04 oily, waxy
06 creamy, fleshy, greasy, lipoid
07 adipose, buttery, pinguid
08 unctuous
09 sebaceous
10 oleaginous

**fatuous**
05 dense, inane, silly
06 absurd, stupid
07 asinine, foolish, idiotic, lunatic, moronic, puerile, vacuous, witless
08 mindless
09 brainless, ludicrous
10 ridiculous, weak-minded

**fault**
03 bug, sin
04 flaw, slam, slip
05 blame, error, hitch, knock, lapse, wrong
06 boo-boo, defect, foible, glitch, impugn, slip-up
07 blemish, blooper, censure, failing, misdeed, mistake, offense
09 criticize, liability, weak point
10 deficiency, negligence, peccadillo, wrongdoing
11 culpability, misdemeanor, pick holes in
12 imperfection, indiscretion, pull to pieces
14 accountability, responsibility
15 blameworthiness

◻**at fault**
05 wrong
06 guilty
07 to blame
08 culpable
10 in the wrong
11 accountable, blameworthy, responsible

◻**to a fault**
06 unduly
07 too much
09 extremely
10 to extremes
11 excessively
12 immoderately, in the extreme, inordinately
13 unnecessarily

**fault-finding**
07 carping, nagging
08 captious, caviling, critical, niggling
09 criticism, querulous, quibbling
10 censorious, nit-picking
12 pettifogging

13 hair-splitting, hypercritical
14 finger-pointing

**faultless**
04 pure
07 correct, perfect
08 accurate, flawless, spotless
09 blameless, exemplary, unsullied
10 immaculate, impeccable
11 unblemished

**faulty**
04 bust, weak
05 kaput, wrong
06 broken, flawed
07 damaged, invalid
09 casuistic, defective, erroneous, illogical, imperfect, incorrect
10 inaccurate, not working, on the blink, out of order
11 inoperative, out of action
14 malfunctioning

**faux pas**
04 goof
05 boner, gaffe
06 boo-boo, howler, slip-up
07 blooper, blunder, mistake
08 screamer
12 indiscretion

**favor**
02 OK
04 back, help, like, okay, pick
06 assist, choose, esteem, opt for, prefer, select, succor
07 benefit, endorse, indulge, service, support
08 approval, champion, courtesy, good deed, good turn, kindness, sympathy
09 patronage, recommend
10 favoritism, partiality, preference
11 approbation

◻**in favor of**
03 for, pro
06 all for, behind
07 backing
10 supporting
11 on the side of

**favorable**
04 fair, good, kind
08 pleasing, positive, suitable
09 opportune, promising
10 auspicious, beneficial, convenient, heartening, propitious, reassuring
11 encouraging, sympathetic
12 advantageous, well-disposed
13 complimentary

**favorably**
04 well
09 agreeably, helpfully
10 positively, profitably
11 approvingly, opportunely
12 auspiciously, propitiously
14 advantageously
15 sympathetically

**favored**
05 elite
06 chosen
07 blessed
08 favorite, selected
09 preferred
10 advantaged, privileged
11 predilected, recommended

**favorite**
03 pet
04 idol, pick
06 choice, chosen
07 beloved, darling, dearest, favored
08 esteemed
09 best-loved, most-liked, number one, preferred
11 first choice, teacher's pet
13 fair-haired boy

**favoritism**
04 bias
08 inequity, nepotism
09 injustice, prejudice
10 inequality, partiality, preference, unfairness
12 one-sidedness, partisanship

**fawn**
03 dow
04 buck, buff, deer
05 beige, court, crawl, creep, khaki, sandy, smarm, toady
06 cringe, grovel, kowtow
07 flatter
08 bootlick, butter up, pay court, soft-soap, suck up to
10 curry favor
12 bow and scrape, have a crush on, ostentatious
13 be attracted to
14 yellowish-brown
15 dance attendance

**fawning**
06 abject
07 servile
08 crawling, cringing, toadying, toadyish, unctuous
09 groveling
10 flattering, obsequious
11 deferential, sycophantic
12 ingratiating

**fear**
03 awe
04 fear, funk, risk

05 alarm, angst, doubt, dread, honor, panic, scope, worry
06 chance, dismay, expect, fright, horror, phobia, qualms, revere, terror, unease, wonder
07 anxiety, concern, suspect
08 aversion, be afraid, disquiet, distress, prospect, venerate
09 agitation, bête noire, fear of God, nightmare, reverence, shudder at, suspicion
10 anticipate, be afraid of, be scared of, foreboding, misgivings, the jitters, tremble for, uneasiness, veneration
11 fearfulness, possibility, probability, trepidation
12 apprehension, stand in awe of, take fright at
13 be uneasy about, consternation, have a horror of, lose your nerve
14 be anxious about, be in a cold sweat
15 have qualms about

**fearful**
04 dire, grim
05 awful, nervy, tense, timid
06 afraid, scared, uneasy
07 alarmed, anxious, ghastly, hideous, in dread, nervous, panicky, shaking
08 agitated, dreadful, fearsome, hesitant, horrible, horrific, shocking, terrible
09 appalling, atrocious, frightful, harrowing, monstrous, petrified, spineless, trembling
10 frightened
12 apprehensive, faint-hearted

**fearfully**
07 awfully, timidly
08 terribly
09 anxiously, extremely, intensely, nervously
10 dreadfully, hesitantly
11 exceedingly, frightfully
14 apprehensively

**fearless**
04 bold, game
05 brave, gutsy
06 daring, gritty, heroic, plucky
07 doughty, gallant, valiant
08 intrepid, unafraid, valorous
09 confident, dauntless, unabashed, undaunted
10 courageous, unblinking
11 indomitable, lionhearted, unblenching, unflinching

**fearsome**
05 awful
07 awesome
08 alarming, daunting, horrible, horrific, menacing, terrible
09 frightful, unnerving
10 formidable, horrifying
11 frightening, hair-raising

**feasibility**
09 viability
11 possibility, workability
13 achievability
14 practicability

**feasible**
06 doable, likely, viable
08 possible, workable
09 practical, realistic
10 achievable, attainable, realizable, reasonable
11 practicable

**feast**
04 dine, fête, gala, luau
05 binge, gorge, treat
06 dinner, festal, junket, repast, revels, spread, wealth
07 banquet, holiday, holy day
08 feast day, festival
09 abundance, partake of, profusion, saint's day
10 cornucopia
11 celebration, eat your fill

**feat**
03 act
04 deed
06 action
07 exploit
10 attainment
11 achievement, performance
14 accomplishment

**feather**
04 down, tuft
05 crest, penna, pinna, plume, quill
06 aigret
07 plumlet, plumule
08 aigrette

**feathery**
04 soft
05 downy, light, plumy, wispy
06 fleecy, fluffy, plumed
07 plumate, plumose, plumous
09 feathered
10 pennaceous

**feature**
03 act, mug, pan
04 ears, eyes, face, item, mark, nose, phiz, show, side, star
05 motif, mouth, movie, point, story, trait

06 appear, aspect, factor, figure, play up, report, visage
07 article, imagine, perform, present, promote, quality
08 hallmark, property
09 attribute, emphasize, highlight, specialty, spotlight
10 accentuate, attraction, focal point, lineaments
11 countenance, participate, peculiarity, physiognomy
14 characteristic

**febrile**
03 hot
05 fiery
07 burning, febrile, fevered, flushed, pyretic
08 feverish, inflamed
09 delirious

**feces**
04 dung
06 ordure, stools
07 excreta
09 body waste, droppings, excrement
11 waste matter

**feckless**
04 weak
06 feeble, futile
07 aimless, useless
08 hopeless
09 worthless
11 incompetent, ineffectual
13 irresponsible

**fecund**
07 fertile, teeming
08 fruitful, prolific
09 feracious, fructuous
10 productive
12 fructiferous

**fecundity**
08 feracity
09 fertility
12 fruitfulness
14 productiveness

**fed up**
04 blue, down, glum
05 bored, tired, weary
06 dismal, gloomy
09 depressed, disgusted, hacked off
10 cheesed off
12 discontented, dissatisfied, sick and tired
13 have had enough

**federal**
06 allied, united
07 unified
08 combined, in league
10 associated, integrated

11 amalgamated
12 confederated

**federate**
05 unify, unite
07 combine
09 integrate, syndicate
10 amalgamate
11 confederate
12 join together

**federation**
05 union
06 league
08 alliance, federacy
09 coalition, syndicate
11 association, confederacy
12 amalgamation
13 confederation

**fee**
04 bill, cost, hire, rent, toll
05 price, terms
06 charge, reward
07 account, payment
08 retainer
09 emolument
10 honorarium, recompense
12 remuneration, subscription

**feeble**
03 wet
04 poor, puny, tame, thin, weak
05 faint, frail
06 ailing, effete, flimsy, futile, infirm, sickly, slight
07 failing, wimpish
08 decrepit, delicate, helpless
09 enervated, exhausted
11 debilitated, ineffectual
12 unconvincing, unsuccessful

**feebleminded**
05 dotty
06 simple, stupid
09 deficient, dimwitted
10 half-witted, slow-witted, weak-minded
13 soft in the head
15 slow on the uptake

**feed**
03 eat, put
04 crop, dine, food, fuel, slip
05 graze, slide
06 browse, dine on, fodder, forage, foster, silage, suckle
07 consume, gratify, nourish, nurture, pasture, provide
08 cater for, ruminate
09 encourage, partake of
10 provide for, strengthen

**feel**
02 be
03 air, paw, rub

04 aura, bear, deem, hold, know, look, mood, seem
05 enjoy, flair, grasp, grope, judge, knack, sense, skill, think, touch, vibes
06 appear, caress, clutch, endure, finger, finish, fondle, fumble, handle, notice, reckon, stroke, suffer, talent
07 ability, believe, contact, faculty, feeling, massage, observe, quality, realize, surface, texture, undergo
08 ambience, aptitude, consider, perceive
09 be aware of, go through
10 atmosphere, experience, impression, understand
11 consistency

❑**feel for**
04 pity
07 weep for
09 be moved by, grieve for
10 be sorry for, sympathize
11 commiserate
13 empathize with

❑**feel like**
04 want, wish
05 fancy
06 desire

**feeler**
04 horn, palp
05 probe
06 palpus
07 advance, antenna
08 approach, overture, tentacle
12 trial balloon

**feeling**
03 air, ego
04 aura, feel, idea, mood, pity
05 ardor, hunch, sense, vibes
06 fervor, notion, warmth
07 emotion, inkling, opinion, passion, quality
08 emotions, fondness, instinct, passions, sympathy
09 affection, intuition, sensation, suspicion
10 affections, atmosphere, compassion, impression, perception, self-esteem
11 sensibility, sensitivity
12 appreciation
13 sensitivities, understanding
14 sentimentality, susceptibility

**feign**
03 act
04 fake, sham
05 forge, put on
06 affect, assume, invent
07 imitate, pretend, put it on

08 simulate
09 dissemble, fabricate
11 counterfeit, dissimulate

**feint**
04 play, ruse, wile
05 blind, bluff, dodge, trick
06 gambit
08 artifice, maneuver, pretense
09 deception, expedient, stratagem
10 subterfuge
11 distraction, mock assault

**felicitous**
03 apt
05 happy
06 timely
07 apropos, fitting
08 apposite, inspired, suitable
09 fortunate, opportune
10 delightful, propitious
11 appropriate

**felicity**
03 joy
05 bliss
07 aptness, delight, ecstasy
09 eloquence, happiness
11 delectation, suitability
12 suitableness
13 applicability
15 appropriateness

**feline**
03 cat, tom
04 lion, puss
05 pussy, sleek, tiger
06 bobcat, slinky, smooth, tomcat
07 catlike, leonine, lioness, sinuous, tigress, wildcat
08 graceful, pussycat, stealthy
09 seductive

**fell**
03 hew
04 raze
05 floor, level
07 cut down, flatten
08 demolish
09 knock down, overthrow, shoot down
10 strike down

**fellow**
02 co-
03 boy, guy, lad, man, pal
04 beau, chap, like, male, mate, peer
05 buddy, crony, equal
06 double, friend, person, suitor
07 comrade, partner, related
08 co-worker, confrère
09 associate, character, colleague, companion
10 associated, individual

11 counterpart
12 contemporary

**fellow feeling**
07 empathy
08 sympathy
10 compassion
13 commiseration

**fellowship**
04 club
05 guild, order, union
06 league
07 society
08 intimacy
09 communion
10 affability, amiability, friendship, sisterhood
11 affiliation, association, brotherhood, camaraderie, comradeship, familiarity
13 companionship

**female**
03 she-
04 girl, lady
05 woman
07 girlish, womanly
08 feminine, ladylike

**feminine**
05 sissy
06 female, gentle, pretty, tender
07 girlish, unmanly, womanly
08 delicate, graceful, ladylike
10 effeminate

**femininity**
08 delicacy
09 sissiness, womanhood
10 effeminacy, gentleness, prettiness, tenderness
11 girlishness, womanliness
12 feminineness, gracefulness

**feminism**
09 women's lib
11 equal rights
12 women's rights
14 women's movement

**feminist**

➤ *Names of feminists:*

04 **Daly** (Mary), **Hite** (Shere), **Mott** (Lucretia), **Shaw** (Anna Howard), **Wolf** (Naomi)
05 **Abzug** (Bella), **Astor** (Nancy), **Greer** (Germaine)
06 **Faludi** (Susan), **Friday** (Nancy), **Gilman** (Charlotte Anna Perkins), **Rankin** (Jeannette), **Stopes** (Marie), **Weldon** (Fay)
07 **Anthony** (Susan Brownell), **Friedan** (Betty), **Goldman**

(Emma), **Ireland** (Patricia), **Millett** (Kate), **Steinem** (Gloria), **Tennant** (Emma)
08 **Beauvoir** (Simone de), **Brittain** (Vera)
09 **Blackwell** (Elizabeth), **Pankhurst** (Emmeline)
14 **Wollstonecraft** (Mary)

**femme fatale**
04 vamp
05 siren
07 charmer
09 temptress
10 seductress
11 enchantress

**fen**
03 bog
04 moss, quag
05 marsh, swamp

**fence**
03 pen
04 coop, rail, wall
05 bound, dodge, evade, guard, hedge, parry
06 paling, secure, shut in
07 barrier, confine, defense, enclose, fortify, protect, quibble, railing, rampart
08 encircle, palisade, restrict, stockade, surround
09 barricade, enclosure, pussyfoot, windbreak
10 equivocate

❑**sit on the fence**
06 dither
08 be unsure
09 vacillate
11 be uncertain, be undecided
12 be irresolute, shilly-shally
13 be uncommitted

**fencing**

➤ *Fencing terms:*

03 hit
04 épée, foil, pink, volt
05 feint, forte, lunge, parry, prime, saber, sabre, sixte, touch
06 attack, foible, octave, quarte, quinte, remise, thrust, tierce, touché
07 barrage, en garde, on guard, reprise, riposte, seconde, septime
08 plastron, tac-au-tac
09 disengage
12 counterparry
14 counterriposte

**fend**
05 avert, parry, repel

07 beat off, deflect, keep off, provide, repulse, shut out, support, sustain, ward off
08 maintain, stave off
09 hold at bay, turn aside

**feral**
04 wild
06 brutal, fierce, savage
07 bestial, untamed, vicious
08 unbroken
09 ferocious
14 undomesticated

**ferment**
04 boil, brew, foam, fuss, heat, rise, stew, stir, work
05 cause, fever, froth, furor, rouse
06 bubble, excite, fester, foment, frenzy, hubbub, incite, seethe, stir up, tumult, unrest, uproar
07 agitate, provoke, smolder, turmoil
08 brouhaha
09 agitation, commotion
10 disruption, effervesce, excitement, turbulence

**ferocious**
04 deep, wild
05 cruel, feral
06 bitter, brutal, fierce, savage, severe, strong
07 extreme, inhuman, intense, untamed, vicious, violent
08 barbaric, pitiless, vigorous
09 barbarous, murderous
12 bloodthirsty

**ferocity**
06 sadism
07 cruelty
08 savagery, violence, wildness
09 barbarity, brutality
10 fierceness, inhumanity
11 viciousness

**ferret**
04 hunt
05 rifle, scour
06 forage, search
07 rummage
09 go through

❑**ferret out**
04 find
05 dig up, trace
07 extract, root out, unearth
08 discover, hunt down
09 search out, track down

**ferry**
03 ply, run
04 boat, move, ship, take, taxi, tote

05 carry
06 convey, vessel
07 shuttle
08 car ferry
09 ferryboat, transport

**fertile**
04 rich
06 fecund, potent, virile
08 creative, fruitful, prolific
09 inventive, luxuriant
10 generative, productive
11 imaginative, resourceful

**fertility**
07 potency
08 richness, virility
09 abundance, fecundity
10 luxuriance
12 fruitfulness, prolificness
14 productiveness

**fertilization**
11 fecundation, pollination, procreation, propagation
12 implantation, impregnation, insemination

**fertilize**
04 dung, feed
05 dress, mulch
06 enrich, manure
08 fructify, top-dress
09 fecundate, pollinate
10 impregnate, inseminate
12 make fruitful, make pregnant

**fertilizer**
04 dung
05 humus, mulch
06 manure
07 compost
08 bone meal, dressing
11 top-dressing

**fervent**
04 warm
05 eager, fiery
06 ardent, devout
07 earnest, excited, intense, sincere, zealous
08 spirited, vehement, vigorous
09 emotional, heartfelt
10 passionate
11 full-blooded, impassioned
12 enthusiastic, wholehearted

**fervor**
04 fire, zeal
05 ardor, verve
06 energy, spirit, warmth
07 emotion, passion
09 eagerness, intensity, sincerity, vehemence
10 enthusiasm, excitement
11 earnestness

**fester**
03 irk, rot
05 anger, chafe, decay, go bad
06 gather, infect, perish, rankle
07 putrefy, smolder
08 maturate, ulcerate
09 decompose, suppurate

**festival**
04 fair, fête, gala
05 feast, party
06 fiesta
07 gala day, holiday, jubilee
08 carnival
11 anniversary, celebration
13 commemoration, entertainment

► *Names of religious festivals:*
04 Holi, Lent
05 Purim
06 Advent, Easter, Hanuka, Pesach, Sukkot
07 Hanukka, Ramadan, Sukkoth
08 All Souls, Epiphany, Hanukkah, Passover
09 All Saints, Ascension, Candlemas, Christmas, Easter Day, Mardi Gras, Pentecost, Yom Kippur
10 Assumption, Good Friday, Lupercalia, Michaelmas, Palm Sunday, Rosh Hasona, Whitsunday
11 All Souls Day, Rosh Hashana, Rosh Hashana, Saturnalia,
12 All Saints' Day, Annunciation, Ascension Day, Ash Wednesday, Christmas Day, Easter Sunday, Holy Saturday, Rosh Hashanah
13 Corpus Christi, Holy Innocents, Passion Sunday, Trinity Sunday
14 Day of Atonement, Easter Saturday
15 Transfiguration
➤ See also RELIGION

**festive**
05 happy, jolly, merry
06 cheery, joyful, joyous
07 cordial, holiday
08 carnival, cheerful, jubilant
09 convivial
11 celebratory
12 lighthearted

**festivity**
03 fun
05 party, revel, sport
07 jollity, revelry
08 carousal, feasting, festival

**festoon**
09 amusement, enjoyment, joviality, merriment
10 banqueting, jubilation
11 celebration, fun and games, merrymaking
12 cheerfulness, conviviality
13 entertainment

**festoon**
04 deck, hang, swag
05 adorn, array, drape
06 bedeck, swathe, wreath
07 garland, garnish, wreathe
08 decorate, ornament

**fetch**
03 get
05 bring, carry, go for, yield
06 convey, escort
07 bring in, collect, conduct, deliver, realize, sell for
08 go and get

**fetching**
04 cute
05 sweet
06 pretty
07 winsome
08 alluring, charming
10 attractive, enchanting
11 captivating, fascinating

**fête**
04 fair, gala
05 feast, honor, party
06 bazaar, regale
07 lionize, welcome
08 carnival, festival
09 entertain
13 entertainment

**fetid**
04 foul, rank
06 filthy, rancid, sickly, smelly
07 noisome, noxious, odorous, reeking
08 mephitic, stinking
10 malodorous, nauseating

**fetish**
04 idol, juju
05 charm, image, mania, thing
06 amulet
08 fixation, gris-gris, idée fixe, talisman
09 obsession

**fetter**
04 bind, curb
05 chain, tie up, truss
06 hamper, hinder, impede
07 confine, manacle, shackle
08 encumber, obstruct, restrain, restrict
09 constrain, hamstring

**fetters**
05 bonds, curbs, irons

06 chains, checks
07 bondage
08 manacles, shackles
09 bracelets, handcuffs
11 constraints, inhibitions

**feud**
03 row, war
05 argue, brawl, clash, fight
06 bicker, enmity, strife
07 contend, discord, dispute, ill will, quarrel, rivalry, wrangle
08 argument, bad blood, be at odds, conflict, vendetta
09 altercate, animosity, bickering, hostility
10 antagonism, bitterness

**fever**
04 ague, heat
06 frenzy, unrest
07 ecstasy, febrile, ferment, passion, pyrexia, turmoil
09 agitation, calenture
10 excitement
12 feverishness, restlessness
15 high temperature

**feverish**
03 hot, red
06 hectic, rushed
07 burning, excited, flushed, frantic, hurried, nervous
08 agitated, frenzied, in a tizzy, troubled, worked up
09 delirious, flustered
11 overwrought
14 hot and bothered

**few**
04 rare, some, thin
05 scant
06 meager, scanty, scarce
07 a couple, handful, not many
08 one or two, uncommon
09 a minority, hardly any
10 inadequate, infrequent, scattering, sprinkling
11 scarcely any
12 insufficient
15 thin on the ground

**fiancé, fiancée**
08 intended, wife-to-be
09 betrothed, bride-to-be
10 future wife
11 husband-to-be
13 future husband
14 bridegroom-to-be
15 prospective wife

**fiasco**
04 flop, mess, rout, ruin
06 turkey
07 debacle, failure, washout
08 calamity, collapse, disaster

**fiat**
02 OK
04 okay
05 edict, order
06 decree, dictum, diktat
07 command, dictate, mandate, precept, warrant
08 sanction
09 directive, ordinance
10 injunction, permission
12 proclamation
13 authorization

**fib**
03 lie
04 tale, yarn
05 evade, story
07 evasion, falsify, fantasy, fiction, untruth, whopper
08 sidestep, white lie
09 dissemble, falsehood
10 concoction

**fiber**
05 cloth, nerve, sinew, stuff
06 fibril, nature, strand, thread
07 caliber, courage, stamina
08 backbone, filament, firmness, material, strength
09 character, substance, toughness, willpower
11 disposition, temperament
12 resoluteness
13 determination

**fickle**
07 flighty
08 disloyal, unstable, unsteady, variable, volatile
09 faithless, mercurial
10 capricious, changeable, inconstant, irresolute, unfaithful, unreliable
13 unpredictable

**fickleness**
10 fitfulness, volatility
11 flightiness, inconstancy
13 changeability, faithlessness, unreliability
14 capriciousness, unfaithfulness

**fiction**
03 fib, lie
04 myth, tale, yarn
05 fable, story
06 legend, novels
07 fantasy, romance, untruth
09 falsehood, tall story
10 concoction
11 fabrication

► *Names of works of nonfiction*:
05 Roots

06 Cosmos, Walden
07 Capital
09 Kama Sutra, Leviathan, Mein Kampf
10 Das Kapital, The Gorgias, The Poetics
11 The Joy of Sex, The Republic
12 Angela's Ashes, Silent Spring, The City of God, The Second Sex, The Symposium
13 The Story of Art
14 Birds of America, Men Are from Mars, Modern Painters, Sartor Resartus, The Age of Reason, The Ascent of Man, The Golden Bough, The Life of Jesus, The Rights of Man, The Selfish Gene
15 Lives of the Poets, Roget's Thesaurus, The Female Eunuch
17 Death of a President, Profiles in Courage, Women Are from Venus
18 The Elements of Style, The New English Bible
19 All the President's Men
23 Iacocca: An Autobiography
24 The Guinness Book of Records
26 The Power of Positive Thinking
22 The Rise and Fall of the Third Reich
33 How to Win Friends and Influence People
46 A Brief History of Time: From the Big Bang to Black Holes

**fictional**
06 made-up, unreal
08 fabulous, invented, literary, mythical
09 imaginary, legendary
11 make-believe, nonexistent
12 mythological

► *Names of fictional places:*
02 Ix, Oz
04 Alph (River), Rhun, Tara
05 Arnor, Moria, Rohan
06 Baucis, Gondor, Icaria, Laputa, Lorien, Mordor, Narnia, Titipu, Utopia, Vulcan, Xanadu
07 Camelot, Camford, Erewhon, Midwich, Mole End, Prydain, Toyland
08 Blefuscu, Calormen, Earthsea, El Dorado, Kings Row, Llaregyb, Mirkwood, New Crete, Polyglot, Ragnarok, Stepford, Sylvania, Tartarus, The Shire, Toad Hall

09 Barataria, Concordia, Discworld, Freedonia, Manderley, Ringworld, Rivendell, River Alph, Ruritania, Shangri-La
10 Archenland, Moominland, Vanity Fair, Wonderland
11 Airstrip One, Brobdingnag, Gormenghast, Lake Wobegon, Middle-Earth, Orbitsville, Peyton Place, The Wild Wood, Tobacco Road
12 Alderley Edge, Celesteville, Cold Mountain, Jurassic Park, Sleepy Hollow
13 Christminster, Madison County, Watership Down
14 Doubting-Castle, Never-Never Land, Nightmare Abbey, Oroonoko Island, Raintree County, Treasure Island

**fictitious**
04 fake, sham
05 bogus, false
06 made-up, untrue
08 invented, spurious
09 concocted, imaginary
10 apocryphal, fabricated

**fiddle**
03 con, fix, toy
04 fuss, play
05 cheat, fraud, graft
06 diddle, fidget, juggle, meddle, racket, rip-off, tamper, tinker, trifle
07 falsify, swindle
08 maneuver
09 racketeer
10 fool around, mess around
13 sharp practice

**fiddling**
06 paltry
07 trivial
08 trifling
10 negligible
13 insignificant

**fidelity**
07 loyalty
08 accuracy, devotion
09 adherence, closeness, constancy, exactness
10 allegiance, strictness
11 devotedness, reliability
12 authenticity, faithfulness

**fidget**
03 toy
04 fret, fuss, jerk, jump
06 fiddle, jiggle, squirm, twitch
07 shuffle, twiddle, wriggle
10 play around

**fidgety**
05 jumpy
06 on edge, uneasy
07 jittery, nervous, twitchy
08 agitated, restless
09 impatient

**field**
03 lea
04 area, lawn, line, mead, stop, turf
05 catch, forte, green, pitch, range, scope, sward
06 answer, domain, ground, handle, meadow, pick up, regime, return, sphere
07 deflect, infield, paddock, pasture
08 cope with, deal with, entrants, gridiron, outfield, province
09 grassland, opponents, possibles, specialty, territory
10 applicants, candidates, contenders, discipline
11 competitors, contestants, field of play
12 participants, playing field

**fiend**
03 fan, nut
04 buff, ogre
05 beast, brute, demon, devil
06 addict, savage
07 devotee, fanatic, monster
10 aficionado, enthusiast

**fiendish**
06 brutal, clever, wicked
07 complex, cunning, inhuman
08 barbaric, devilish, infernal, involved, ruthless
09 difficult, ferocious, ingenious, intricate
10 aggressive, diabolical, horrendous, malevolent
11 challenging, complicated, imaginative, resourceful

**fierce**
03 hot
04 grim, keen, wild
05 cruel, grave, stern
06 brutal, raging, savage, severe, strong
07 intense, vicious, violent
08 menacing, powerful, ruthless, terrible
09 cutthroat, dangerous, ferocious, murderous
10 aggressive, passionate
11 frightening, threatening
12 bloodthirsty, uncontrolled

**fiercely**
06 keenly, wildly

07 cruelly, sternly
08 bitterly, brutally, savagely, severely, strongly, terribly
09 intensely, viciously, violently
10 implacably, menacingly, powerfully, ruthlessly
11 dangerously, fanatically, ferociously, murderously
12 aggressively, passionately, relentlessly, tooth and nail

**fiery**
03 hot
05 afire, aglow, sharp, spicy
06 ablaze, aflame, ardent, fierce, heated, red-hot, spiced, sultry, torrid
07 blazing, burning, fervent, flaming, flushed, glowing, piquant, pungent, violent
08 inflamed, seasoned
09 excitable, hotheaded, impetuous, impulsive
10 passionate

**fight**
03 box, hit, row, war
04 defy, duel, feud, fray, riot
05 argue, brawl, brush, clash, drive, fence, joust, melee, punch, scrap, set-to
06 action, attack, battle, bicker, combat, dust-up, engage, fracas, oppose, resist, ruckus, ruffle, shindy, spirit, strive, take on, tussle
07 be at war, contend, contest, crusade, dispute, fall out, grapple, lay into, make war, quarrel, scuffle, wage war, wrangle, wrestle
08 argument, campaign, champion, conflict, do battle, have a row, movement, object to, set about, skirmish, squabble, struggle, tenacity
09 altercate, encounter, stand up to, weigh into, willpower, withstand
10 aggression, dissension, donnybrook, engagement, free-for-all, will to live
11 altercation, come to blows, cross swords, hostilities
12 disagreement, resoluteness
13 confrontation, determination
15 campaign against

❑**fight back**
05 check, reply
06 resist, retort
07 contain, control, repress
08 hold back, restrain, suppress
09 force back, retaliate

11 put up a fight
13 counterattack
14 defend yourself

❑**fight off**
04 rout
05 repel
06 rebuff, resist
07 beat off, hold off, ward off
08 stave off
09 hold at bay, keep at bay

**fighter**
02 GI
03 pug
05 boxer, rival
07 soldier, trouper, warrior
08 opponent, pugilist, wrestler
09 adversary, contender, disputant, gladiator, mercenary, swordsman
10 antagonist, contestant

**figment**
❑**a figment of your imagination**
05 fable, fancy
08 delusion, illusion
09 falsehood, invention
11 fabrication

**figurative**
08 symbolic
09 parabolic, pictorial
11 allegorical, descriptive
12 metaphorical, naturalistic

**figure**
03 sum
04 body, form, sign
05 build, digit, guess, image, shape, think, torso, total
06 amount, appear, crop up, design, emblem, figure, leader, number, person, reckon, sketch, symbol
07 believe, compute, diagram, drawing, feature, imagery, integer, numeral, outline, picture
08 consider, estimate
09 celebrity, character, dignitary, personage
11 mathematics, personality
12 be included in, illustration
13 be mentioned in
14 representation

❑**figure out**
03 see
05 count
06 fathom, reason, reckon
07 compute, drop out, make out, work out
08 decipher, estimate
09 calculate, puzzle out

10 understand

**figurehead**
04 bust, name
05 dummy, image, token
06 figure, puppet
08 front man, straw man
10 man of straw, mouthpiece

**figure of speech**
05 image
06 figure
07 imagery
12 turn of phrase

**filament**
04 cord, hair, pile, wire
05 cable, fiber
06 strand, string, thread

**filch**
04 crib, lift, palm, take
05 steal, swipe
06 pilfer, rip off, snitch, thieve
07 purloin, snaffle
08 embezzle, knock off, peculate
14 misappropriate

**file**
03 box, row, rub
04 case, data, hone, line, make, note, rasp, sand, whet
05 enter, march, put in, shape, store, trail, train
06 abrade, binder, column, folder, papers, polish, record, scrape, smooth, stream, string, submit
07 catalog, details, dossier, rub down
08 classify, document
09 catalogue, portfolio
10 categorize, pigeonhole, procession, walk in line
11 information, particulars

**filial**
05 loyal
06 loving
07 devoted, dutiful
10 daughterly, respectful
12 affectionate

**filibuster**
06 hinder, impede, put off, speech
08 obstruct, perorate
09 hindrance, speechify
10 impediment, peroration
12 speechifying
13 procrastinate
15 procrastination

**filigree**
04 lace
07 lattice, tracery
08 fretwork, wirework

09 interlace
10 scrollwork

**fill**

04 bung, clog, cork, cram, hold, pack, plug, seal, soak, stop
05 ample, block, close, crowd, imbue, stock, stuff
06 charge, occupy, stop up, supply, take up
07 congest, fulfill, perform, pervade, provide, satisfy, suffuse
08 complete, saturate
09 abundance, replenish
10 all you want, impregnate
11 sufficiency
14 more than enough

**❑ fill in**

05 brief
06 act for, answer, inform
07 fill out, replace, stand in
08 complete, deputize
10 substitute, understudy
13 bring up to date

**❑ fill out**

06 answer, fill in
08 complete
10 gain weight, grow fatter
11 put on weight

**filling**

05 ample, heavy, large, solid
06 filler, inside, square, stodgy
07 padding, wadding
08 contents, generous, stuffing
10 nutritious, satisfying
11 substantial

**fillip**

03 tap
04 goad, prod, push, snap, spur
05 boost, shove
07 impetus, liven up
08 stimulus
09 incentive
13 encouragement

**film**

04 coat, mist, reel, skin, veil
05 cloud, cover, flick, glaze, layer, movie, sheet, shoot, short, spool, video
07 blanket, coating, dusting, footage, picture
08 cassette, covering, membrane, televise
09 cartridge, videotape
11 documentary, feature film
13 motion picture, videocassette

➢ See also DIRECTOR

---

► *Kinds of film*:

03 war
04 blue, cult, epic, road
05 adult, buddy, farce, indie, short, weepy
06 action, B-movie, biopic, comedy, Disney, family, horror, remake, silent, weepie
07 cartoon, classic, diorama, fantasy, musical, new wave, tragedy, western
08 animated, disaster, film noir, gangster, newsreel, romantic, thriller, travelog, whodunit
09 adventure, burlesque, flashback, Hitchcock, Hollywood, James Bond, love story, low-budget, melodrama, Spielberg
10 avant-garde, tear-jerker, travelogue
11 black comedy, blockbuster, cliffhanger, documentary, independent, kitchen sink, period drama, tragicomedy
12 cinéma-vérité, Ealing comedy, mockumentary, pornographic
13 murder mystery
14 Charlie Chaplin, rites of passage, romantic comedy, science-fiction
15 cowboy and Indian, screwball comedy

---

► *Names of films*:

02 ET, If
03 JFK, Kes, Now, Ran
04 Babe, Bird, Diva, Gigi, Jaws, Reds, Tess, X-Men
05 Alfie, Alien, Bambi, Crash, Dumbo, Ghost, Giant, Greed, Klute, Marty, Paris, Rocky, Shane, Shrek, Texas
06 Ben-Hur, Blow-Up, Brazil, Gandhi, Grease, Heimat, Mad Max, Patton, Psycho, The Fly, The Kid, Top Gun
07 Amadeus, Die Hard, Dracula, L'Age d'Or, Platoon, Rain Man, Rebecca, Robocop, The Boat, The Omen, The Robe, Titanic, Tootsie, Voyager
08 Born Free, Duck Soup, Fantasia, High Noon, Key Largo, King Kong, Star Wars, The Piano, The Sting, The Thing, Toy Story
09 Annie Hall, Betty Blue, Cat Ballou, Gladiator, GoldenEye, Home Alone, Local Hero, Manhattan, Ninotchka, Nosferatu, Notorious, Pinocchio, Spartacus
10 Bagdad Café, Blue Velvet, Braveheart, Casablanca, Dirty Harry, East of Eden, Goldfinger, GoodFellas, Grand Hotel, Jungle Book, Mrs. Miniver, Raging Bull, Rear Window, Safety Last, Taxi Driver, The Hustler, The Mission, The Servant, The Shining, The Wild One, Unforgiven, Wall Street, Way Out West
11 All About Eve, American Pie, Blade Runner, Citizen Kane, Deliverance, Forrest Gump, Heaven's Gate, Jungle Fever, La Dolce Vita, Mary Poppins, Modern Times, Notting Hill, Out of Africa, Pearl Harbor, Pretty Woman, Pulp Fiction, The Exorcist, The Graduate, The Lion King, The Music Man, The Third Man, Wayne's World
12 A View to a Kill, Delicatessen, Eyes Wide Shut, Frankenstein, Ghostbusters, Jurassic Park, The Apartment, The Go-Between, The Godfather, The Naked City
13 Apocalypse Now, Babette's Feast, Basic Instinct, Death in Venice, Doctor Zhivago, Educating Rita, Erin Brokovich, Live and Let Die, Reservoir Dogs, Scent of a Woman, Some Like It Hot, Sophie's Choice, The Deer Hunter, The Dirty Dozen, The Jazz Singer, The Longest Day, The Right Stuff, The Wizard of Oz, Trainspotting, West Side Story, Zorba the Greek
14 American Beauty, Animal Crackers, Black Narcissus, Bonnie and Clyde, Brief Encounter, Chariots of Fire, Cinema Paradiso, Enter the Dragon, Midnight Cowboy, Schindler's List, The Commitments, The Elephant Man, The King of Kings, The Ladykillers, The Last Emperor, The Music Lovers
15 Back to the Future, Company of Wolves, Crocodile Dundee, Do The Right Thing, Double Indemnity, Fantastic Voyage, Forbidden Planet, Full Metal Jacket, Gone With the Wind, Independence

Day, Midnight Express, On the Waterfront, Return of the Jedi, Sunset Boulevard, Tarzan the Ape Man, The African Queen, The Bicycle Thief, The King of Comedy, The Lady Vanishes, The Sound of Music, Thelma and Louise

**◻ film over**
05 glaze
08 mist over
09 cloud over
13 become blurred

**filmy**
04 fine, thin
05 gauzy, light, sheer
06 flimsy, floaty
08 delicate, gossamer
10 diaphanous, see-through, shimmering
11 translucent, transparent
13 insubstantial

**filter**
04 leak, mesh, ooze, seep, sift
05 drain, gauze, leach, sieve
06 purify, refine, screen, strain
07 dribble, netting, trickle
08 membrane, strainer
09 percolate

**filth**
04 crud, dirt, gunk, muck, porn, smut, yuck
05 grime, gunge, slime, trash
06 grunge, sleaze, sludge
07 garbage, rubbish, squalor
08 effluent, foulness, hard porn
09 blue films, excrement, indecency, obscenity, pollution, vulgarity
10 coarseness, defilement
11 pornography, putrescence, raunchiness, uncleanness
12 putrefaction
13 sexploitation

**filthy**
04 base, blue, foul, lewd, vile
05 adult, bawdy, black, dirty, fecal, grimy, gross, mucky, muddy, nasty, slimy, sooty, yucky
06 coarse, grubby, impure, putrid, rotten, smutty, soiled, sordid, vulgar
07 corrupt, obscene, squalid
08 decaying, depraved, indecent, polluted, unwashed
09 offensive, worthless
10 despicable, putrefying, suggestive

11 foulmouthed
12 contemptible, pornographic

**final**
03 end
04 exam, last
05 dying
07 closing, settled
08 decisive, definite, eventual, terminal, ultimate
09 finishing
10 concluding, conclusive, definitive, last-minute
11 examination, irrevocable, terminating

**finale**
03 end
05 close
06 climax, ending, epilog
08 epilogue, final act
10 conclusion, dénouement
11 culmination
13 crowning glory

**finality**
08 firmness, ultimacy
09 certitude
10 conviction, resolution
12 decisiveness, definiteness
14 conclusiveness, irrevocability, unavoidability
15 irreversibility

**finalize**
05 agree, close, sew up
06 clinch, decide, finish, settle, wrap up
07 resolve, work out
08 complete, conclude, round off

**finally**
06 at last, lastly
07 for good, forever
08 at length, in the end
10 decisively, eventually, to conclude, ultimately
11 irrevocably, permanently
12 in conclusion, irreversibly
13 once and for all

**finance**
04 back, cash, fund
05 float, funds, means, money
06 assets, pay for, wealth
07 affairs, banking, capital, funding, revenue, savings, sponsor, subsidy, support
08 accounts, commerce
09 economics, liquidity, resources, subsidize
10 investment, underwrite
11 sponsorship, wherewithal
15 money management

**financial**
05 money
06 fiscal
08 economic, monetary
09 budgetary, pecuniary
10 commercial
15 entrepreneurial

**financier**
06 banker
08 investor
10 moneymaker, speculator
11 stockbroker

**find**
03 get, win
04 boon, deem, earn, gain
05 catch, judge, think, trace
06 attain, come by, detect, dig out, locate, notice, obtain, regain, reveal, turn up
07 achieve, acquire, declare, get back, godsend, good buy, observe, procure, realize, recover, uncover, unearth
08 consider, discover, perceive
09 discovery, encounter, stumble on, track down
10 chance upon, come across, happen upon
12 bring to light
13 stumble across

**◻ find out**
05 get at, learn
06 detect, expose, reveal, rumble, show up, unmask
07 realize, uncover
08 disclose, discover, identify, perceive, pinpoint
09 ascertain, establish, get wind of
12 bring to light

**finding**
04 find
07 verdict
08 decision, judgment
09 discovery
10 conclusion, innovation
12 breakthrough
13 pronouncement

**fine**
02 OK
03 dry, fit
04 fair, nice, okay, slim, thin, well
05 clear, exact, gauzy, great, light, mulct, sheer, sunny
06 amerce, bright, choice, dainty, flimsy, ground, lovely, narrow, select, slight, strong
07 clement, crushed, damages, elegant, forfeit, fragile, healthy, penalty, powdery, precise, slender, stylish

08 accurate, all right, critical, delicate, gossamer, handsome, penalize, splendid, superior, vigorous
09 admirable, beautiful, brilliant, cloudless, excellent, expensive, exquisite
10 acceptable, amercement, attractive, forfeiture
11 exceptional, fashionable, fine-grained, magnificent
12 in good health, satisfactory

**finery**
07 jewelry, regalia
08 frippery, glad rags, splendor
09 ornaments, trappings
10 Sunday best
11 best clothes

**finesse**
05 bluff, evade, flair, skill, trick
06 polish
07 know-how
08 deftness, delicacy, elegance, neatness, subtlety
09 adeptness, diplomacy, expertise, quickness
10 adroitness, cleverness, manipulate, refinement
14 sophistication

**finger**
03 paw
04 feel
05 place, touch
06 caress, fondle, handle, locate, recall, stroke
07 hit upon, isolate, toy with
08 identify, indicate, pinpoint
10 fiddle with, manipulate
13 play about with

**□put your finger on**
06 locate, recall
07 hit upon, isolate, pin down
08 discover, identify, indicate, pinpoint, remember

**finicky**
05 faddy, fussy, picky
06 choosy, fiddly, tricky
09 difficult, finickety, intricate
10 fastidious, meticulous, nit-picking, particular, scrupulous
11 persnickety
13 hypercritical

**finish**
03 eat, end, use
04 rout, ruin, stop
05 cease, close, crush, drain, drink, empty, glaze, gloss, grain, sew up, shine, use up
06 attain, be over, defeat, devour, ending, expend,

finale, luster, pack in, polish, settle, veneer, wind up, windup, wrap up
07 achieve, coating, deplete, destroy, exhaust, fulfill, lacquer, surface, texture, wipe out
08 carry out, complete, conclude, curtains, deal with, get rid of, round off
09 be through, cessation, culminate, get shot of, overpower, overthrow, polish off, terminate
10 accomplish, annihilate, be done with, call it a day, completion, conclusion, perfection, smoothness
11 achievement, come to an end, culmination, destruction, discontinue, exterminate, termination
12 bring to an end

**finished**
04 done, over
05 empty, spent
06 doomed, expert, ruined, sewn up, undone, washed up
07 at an end, done for, drained, perfect, refined, through
08 complete, defeated, masterly, polished, unwanted, washed up
09 completed, concluded, dealt with, exhausted, played out, wrapped up
10 consummate, proficient
12 accomplished, professional
13 sophisticated
15 over and done with

**finite**
05 fixed
07 bounded, limited
08 numbered
09 countable, definable
10 calculable, measurable, restricted, terminable

**fire**
04 flak, heat, hurl, sack, stir, whet
05 ardor, blaze, eject, light, rouse, salvo, shoot, snipe, verve
06 arouse, attack, energy, excite, fervor, flames, heater, incite, kindle, launch, let off, set off, spirit, stir up
07 animate, bombing, bonfire, boot out, burning, dismiss, enliven, explode, gunfire, igneous, inferno, inflame,

inspire, passion, sniping, sparkle, trigger
08 detonate, get rid of, motivate, shelling, shooting, spark off
09 animation, convector, discharge, galvanize, holocaust, intensity, set ablaze, set alight, set fire to, set on fire, stimulate, terminate
10 combustion, creativity, enthusiasm, excitement, liveliness, trigger off
11 bombardment, put a match to
13 conflagration, inventiveness

**□on fire**
05 eager, fiery
06 ablaze, aflame, alight, ardent
07 blazing, burning, excited, flaming, ignited
08 creative, in flames, inspired
10 passionate

**firearm**
03 gun, rod
05 rifle
06 musket, pistol, weapon
07 handgun, shotgun
08 revolver
09 automatic

**fireworks**
04 rage, rows
06 sparks, temper, uproar
07 trouble
08 outburst
09 hysterics
10 explosions
12 pyrotechnics
13 illuminations

► *Types of firework*:
05 squib, wheel
06 banger, floral, rocket
07 cracker, spinner, volcano
08 black cat, fountain, pinwheel, sky flyer, sparkler, whiz-bang
09 girandola, girandole, parachute, skyrocket, smoke ball, whizz-bang
11 firecracker, jumping-jack, Roman candle, tourbillion
12 bottle rocket
14 Catherine wheel, indoor firework
15 whistling chaser

**firm**
03 set
04 fast, hard, sure, true
05 close, dense, fixed, rigid, solid, stiff, tight
06 dogged, secure, stable, steady, strict, strong, sturdy

**firmly**

07 adamant, compact, company, concern, decided, riveted, settled, staunch
08 anchored, business, constant, definite, embedded, fastened, hardened, obdurate, resolute, resolved, stubborn
09 committed, immovable, obstinate, steadfast, syndicate, tenacious
10 compressed, dependable, determined, enterprise, inflexible, solidified, unshakable, unswerving, unwavering, unyielding
11 corporation, established, institution, long-lasting, partnership, unalterable, unfaltering, unflinching
12 conglomerate, long-standing, organization
13 establishment

**firmly**

06 stably
07 tightly
08 robustly, securely, steadily, strictly, strongly, sturdily
09 immovably, staunchly
10 decisively, inflexibly, resolutely, unshakably
11 steadfastly, unalterably
12 unchangeably, unwaveringly

**firmness**

07 density, resolve, tension
08 hardness, obduracy, rigidity, solidity, strength, tautness
09 constancy, stability, stiffness
10 conviction, resolution, steadiness, strictness
11 compactness, reliability
12 immovability, inelasticity
13 dependability, determination, inflexibility, steadfastness
14 indomitability, strength of will

**first**

04 best, head, main
05 basic, chief, prime, prior
06 eldest, oldest, outset, senior
07 at first, earlier, highest, initial, leading, opening, origins, primary, supreme
08 earliest, foremost, greatest, original, première, primeval
09 beginning, inaugural, initially, paramount, primitive, principal, prototype, sovereign, square one, the word go, unveiling, uppermost
10 beforehand, elementary, first of all, originally, preeminent, primordial
11 at the outset, fundamental, predominant, preliminary, to begin with, to start with
12 in preference, introduction, introductory
15 in the first place

**firstborn**

04 aine, heir
05 eigne, elder, older
06 eldest, oldest, senior
12 primogenital
13 primogenitary

**firsthand**

06 direct
08 directly, on the job, personal
10 personally

**first name**

08 forename
09 given name
13 baptismal name, Christian name

**first-rate**

03 ace, top
04 A one, cool, fine, mega
05 crack, prime, super
07 leading, premier, supreme
08 peerless, superior, top-notch
09 admirable, excellent, matchless, top-flight
10 first-class
11 outstanding, superlative
12 second-to-none

**fiscal**

05 money
07 capital
08 economic, monetary
09 financial, pecuniary

**fish**

04 dupe, fool
05 angle, chump, delve, grope, trawl
09 go fishing

▶ *Names of and types of fish and shellfish*:

03 cod, dab, eel, ray
04 bass, carp, chub, clam, crab, dace, dory, hake, pike, sole, tuna
05 bream, brill, guppy, perch, prawn, roach, shark, skate, smelt, sprat, squid, tench, trout, whelk
06 angler, bonito, cockle, dorado, kipper, marlin, minnow, mullet, mussel, oyster, plaice, salmon, shrimp, turbot, wrasse
07 anchovy, bloater, catfish, crawdad, dogfish, dolphin, grouper, gurnard, haddock, halibut, herring, lobster, octopus, piranha, pompano, sardine, scallop, sea bass, sea carp, snapper, whiting
08 blowfish, brisling, crawfish, crayfish, flounder, goldfish, John Dory, mackerel, monkfish, Moray eel, pilchard, sea bream, seahorse, skipjack, stingray, sturgeon
09 angelfish, barracuda, conger eel, Dover sole, king prawn, lemon sole, red mullet, swordfish, whitebait
10 Bombay duck, cuttlefish, damselfish, flying fish, jellied eel, parrotfish
11 electric eel, stickleback, triggerfish
12 rainbow trout
13 flying gurnard
➤ See also ANIMAL; CRUSTACEAN

❏**fish out**

07 extract, haul out, produce, pull out, take out
08 dredge up, retrieve
10 come up with

**fisherman**

06 angler, fisher, whaler
07 trawler, troller
08 piscator

**fishing**

07 angling, seeking, whaling
08 trawling, trolling
09 piscatory
11 piscatorial

**fishy**

05 funny, queer, shady
07 dubious, piscine, suspect
08 doubtful, fishlike
09 irregular, piscatory
10 improbable, suspicious
11 implausible, piscatorial
12 questionable

**fission**

06 schism
07 parting, rending, rupture
08 breaking, cleavage, division
09 severance, splitting

**fissure**

03 gap
04 gash, hole, rent, rift, slit
05 break, chasm, chink, cleft, crack, fault, grike, split
06 breach, cranny, sulcus
07 crevice, opening, rupture

08 cleavage, crevasse, scissure
10 interstice

**fist**
04 hand, mitt, palm

**fit**
02 go
03 apt, arm, due, fix
04 able, bout, meet, suit, well
05 alter, equip, hardy, ictus, prime, put in, ready, right, spasm, spell, surge, tally
06 adjust, attach, attack, belong, change, in trim, insert, proper, robust, seemly, strong, sturdy, tailor
07 arrange, be right, capable, conform, connect, get into, healthy, in shape, install, qualify, seizure, tantrum
08 decorous, outbreak, outburst, paroxysm, position, prepared, suitable, vigorous
09 competent, explosion, harmonize, interlock
10 able-bodied, convulsion, correspond, in good form, put in place
11 accommodate, appropriate, flourishing, in good shape, put together
12 be consistent, in good health
13 fit like a glove, hale and hearty, put in position
15 in good condition

▢**fit in**
04 slot
05 agree, match
06 accord, belong, square
07 conform, squeeze

▢**fit out**
03 arm
05 equip
06 outfit, rig out, supply
07 furnish, prepare, provide
08 accouter, accoutre

▢**in fits and starts**
08 brokenly, fitfully, off and on
11 erratically, irregularly
12 occasionally, sporadically
14 intermittently

**fitful**
06 broken, uneven
07 erratic
08 sporadic
09 disturbed, haphazard, irregular, spasmodic
12 disconnected, intermittent

**fitness**
05 vigor

06 health
07 aptness
08 adequacy, strength
09 condition, readiness
10 competence, good health, pertinence, robustness
11 healthiness, suitability
12 preparedness
13 applicability

**fitted**
05 armed, fixed, right
06 cut out, suited
08 equipped, prepared, provided, suitable, tailored
09 permanent

**fitting**
03 apt, fit
04 meet, part, unit
06 extras, proper, seemly
07 correct, fitment, fixture
08 decorous, deserved, fitments, fixtures, suitable
09 accessory
10 attachment, connection
11 appropriate
13 accouterments, accoutrements, installations

**fix**
03 aim, hit, jam, pin, rig, set, tie
04 bind, cook, dose, glue, join, link, make, mend, nail, shot, slug, spot, tidy, turn
05 bribe, clamp, embed, focus, order, rivet, screw, see to, stick
06 adjust, anchor, attach, cement, decide, define, fasten, harden, muddle, pickle, plight, remedy, repair, secure, settle
07 agree on, arrange, connect, correct, dilemma, falsify, patch up, prepare, rectify, resolve, restore, situate, station, stiffen, the soup
08 arrive at, finalize, position, put right, quandary, solidify
09 determine, injection, stabilize, tight spot
10 difficulty, put in order, straighten, tamper with
11 predicament, put together

▢**fix up**
05 equip, lay on
06 settle, supply
07 agree on, arrange, furnish, produce, provide, sort out
08 organize

**fixation**
05 mania, thing
06 fetish, hang-up, phobia

07 complex
08 idée fixe
09 obsession
11 infatuation
13 preoccupation

**fixed**
03 set
04 fast, firm
06 rooted, secure, steady
07 decided, planned, settled
08 arranged, constant, definite
09 permanent
10 inflexible, set in stone
11 cast in stone, established

**fixity**
09 constancy, stability
10 permanence, steadiness
11 persistence
12 immutability

**fixture**
07 regular
09 equipment, furniture
11 furnishings
13 installations

**fizz**
04 foam, hiss
05 froth
06 bubble, fizzle
07 sparkle
10 effervesce

**fizzle**

▢**fizzle out**
04 fail, flop, fold, stop
07 die away, die down, subside
08 collapse, peter out, taper off
09 disappear, dissipate, evaporate
13 come to nothing

**fizzy**
05 gassy
06 bubbly, frothy
07 aerated, foaming
08 bubbling
09 sparkling
10 carbonated
12 effervescent

**flabbergasted**
06 amazed
07 stunned
09 astounded, staggered
10 astonished, bowled over, nonplussed, speechless
11 dumbfounded

**flabby**
03 fat, lax
04 limp, soft, weak
05 loose, plump, slack
06 feeble, fleshy, floppy
07 flaccid, hanging, sagging

**flaccid**
08 drooping, yielding

**flaccid**
04 limp, soft, weak
05 loose, slack
06 clammy, flabby, floppy
07 relaxed, sagging
08 drooping, toneless

**flag**
03 die, ebb, sag, tag
04 fade, fail, flop, hail, mark, sink, slow, tire, wane, wave
05 droop, faint, label, slump
06 falter, salute, signal, weaken
07 decline, dwindle, fall off
08 diminish, indicate, peter out, taper off, wave down
09 grow tired, vexillary
12 signal to stop

► *Types of flag*:
04 jack
06 banner, burgee, colors, ensign
07 bunting, pennant
08 banderol, gonfalon, standard, streamer, vexillum
09 banderole, oriflamme, pilot flag
10 signal flag
11 swallowtail

► *Names of flags*:
07 Saltire
08 Crescent, Old Glory, Tricolor
09 Blue Peter, Red Ensign, Rising Sun, Union Jack
10 Blue Ensign, Jolly Roger, Yellow Jack
11 Olympic Flag, White Ensign
12 Stars and Bars
15 Cross of St. George, Hammer and Sickle, Stars and Stripes

**flagellation**
07 flaying, lashing, whaling
08 flogging, whipping
09 scourging, thrashing
11 castigation, verberation

**flagging**
06 ebbing, fading, tiring
07 abating, failing, sagging, sinking, slowing, wilting
09 declining, dwindling, faltering, lessening, subsiding, weakening

**flagon**
03 jug
04 ewer
05 flask
06 bottle, carafe, vessel
07 pitcher

**flagrant**
04 bold, open, rank
06 arrant, brazen
07 blatant, glaring, heinous
08 dreadful, enormous
09 atrocious, audacious, barefaced, egregious, notorious, shameless
10 outrageous, scandalous
11 conspicuous, undisguised
12 ostentatious

**flail**
04 beat, whip
06 batter, strike, thrash, thresh

**flair**
04 bent, feel, gift
05 knack, skill, style, taste
06 acumen, genius, talent
07 ability, faculty, panache
08 aptitude, elegance, facility
11 discernment, stylishness

**flak, flack**
05 abuse, blame
06 ack-ack
07 gunfire
09 brickbats, criticism, invective
10 complaints, opposition
12 condemnation, fault-finding
14 disapprobation

**flake**
03 bit
04 chip, peel
06 furfur, paring, sliver
07 blister, peeling, shaving
11 exfoliation

❑**flake out**
05 faint
07 pass out
08 collapse, keel over
10 fall asleep

**flaky**
03 odd
05 batty, goofy, scaly
07 erradic, laminar, layered
08 scabrous
11 exfoliative

**flamboyance**
04 dash, élan
06 glamor, pizazz
07 panache, pizzazz
09 showiness
10 brilliance
12 extravagance
13 theatricality

**flamboyant**
05 gaudy, showy
06 bright, flashy, florid, ornate
08 colorful, dazzling, exciting, striking

09 brilliant, elaborate, glamorous
10 theatrical
11 extravagant

**flame**
04 beam, burn, fire, heat, zeal
05 blaze, flare, flash, glare, gleam, light, lover, shine
06 fervor
07 partner, passion, radiate, sparkle
08 fervency, keenness, radiance
09 boyfriend, catch fire, eagerness, intensity
10 enthusiasm, excitement, girlfriend, sweetheart

**flaming**
03 mad
05 angry, fiery, vivid
06 aflame, alight, bright, on fire, raging, red-hot
07 blazing, burning, enraged, furious, intense, violent
08 in flames, incensed
09 brilliant
10 infuriated

**flammable**
09 ignitable
11 combustible, inflammable

**flank**
04 edge, line, loin, side, wing
05 bound, skirt, thigh
06 border, haunch, screen
07 confine, quarter
10 pass around

**flap**
03 fly, lug, tab, tag, wag
04 beat, fold, fuss, tail, wave
05 apron, lapel, panic, skirt, state, swing, swish, tizzy
06 dither, lappet, thrash, waggle
07 agitate, aileron, airfoil, fluster, flutter, overlap, vibrate
08 covering, overhang
09 agitation, commotion

**flare**
04 beam, burn, glow
05 blaze, burst, erupt, flame, flash, glare, splay, widen
06 beacon, dazzle, rocket, signal, spread
07 broaden, explode, flicker
10 broadening
13 warning signal
14 distress signal

❑**flare up**
06 blow up
07 explode
08 break out, burst out
11 lose control

**flash**

12 lose your cool
14 lose your temper

**flash**

03 fly, ray
04 beam, bolt, dart, dash, race, rush, show, tear, zoom
05 blaze, bound, burst, dance, flare, gaudy, glare, gleam, glint, shaft, shine, shoot, showy, smart, spark, speed
06 career, flaunt, kitsch, streak
07 flicker, glimmer, glisten, glitter, light up, shimmer, show off, sparkle, twinkle
08 flourish, outbreak, outburst
09 coruscate, expensive, fulgurate, glamorous
11 fashionable, pretentious
12 ostentatious

**◻in a flash**

06 pronto
08 in a jiffy, in a trice, in no time
09 in a moment
11 in an instant
12 in a twinkling
13 in no time at all
14 in a split second

**flashy**

04 bold, loud
05 flash, gaudy, showy, tacky
06 garish, glitzy, kitsch, vulgar
09 glamorous, tasteless
10 flamboyant
11 pretentious
12 ostentatious

**flask**

06 bottle, carafe, flagon
07 matrass, thermos
08 decanter, lekythos

**flat**

04 dead, down, dull, even, firm, slow, weak
05 bland, broke, burst, empty, final, fixed, level, plain, plane, prone, rigid, rooms, slack, stale, suite, total, vapid
06 boring, busted, direct, smooth, supine, watery
07 exactly, insipid, leveled, not deep, not tall, plainly, planned, shallow, tedious, totally, uniform, utterly
08 blown-out, definite, deflated, dejected, directly, downcast, entirely, explicit, lifeless, not thick, outright, positive, ruptured, straight, unbroken
09 apartment, collapsed, depressed, downright, miserable, out and out,

penthouse, prostrate, punctured, reclining, recumbent
10 horizontal, monotonous, point-blank, spiritless, unexciting
11 categorical, discouraged, unequivocal, unqualified
13 categorically, uninteresting
14 flat as a pancake

**◻flat out**

06 all out
10 at top speed
11 at full speed

**flatly**

10 absolutely, completely, point-blank, positively
12 peremptorily
13 categorically
15 unconditionally

**flatness**

06 tedium
07 boredom, languor
08 dullness, evenness, monotony, vapidity
09 emptiness, staleness
10 insipidity, uniformity

**flatten**

04 fell, iron, raze, roll
05 crush, floor, level, press
06 smooth, squash, subdue
07 even out
08 compress, demolish, make even, make flat, tear down
09 knock down, overwhelm, prostrate

**flatter**

04 fawn, suit
05 befit, court, creep, toady
06 become, kowtow, praise
08 butter up, eulogize, inveigle, make up to, play up to, soft-soap, suck up to
09 embellish, sweet-talk
10 compliment, look good on
12 sycophantize

**flatterer**

05 toady
06 fawner, lackey
07 crawler, creeper
08 groveler
09 encomiast, eulogizer, sycophant
10 bootlicker

**flattering**

07 fawning, fulsome, honeyed
08 effusive, unctuous
09 adulatory, enhancing, favorable
10 obsequious

11 sycophantic
12 honey-tongued, ingratiating, smooth-spoken
13 complimentary

**flattery**

06 eulogy, praise
07 blarney, fawning
08 cajolery, soft soap, toadyism
09 servility, sweet talk
10 sycophancy
11 compliments, fulsomeness
13 blandishments

**flatulence**

03 gas
04 wind
06 flatus
09 gassiness, ventosity
10 eructation
11 borborygmus

**flatulent**

05 gassy, windy
07 pompous, ventose
11 pretentious

**flaunt**

03 air
05 boast, flash, sport, vaunt
06 dangle, parade
07 display, disport, show off
08 brandish, flourish

**flavor**

04 feel, hint, lace, odor, soul, tang, tone, zest, zing
05 aroma, imbue, smack, spice, style, taste, tinge, touch
06 aspect, infuse, nature, relish, season, spirit
07 essence, feeling, quality
08 ginger up, piquancy
10 atmosphere, suggestion

**flavoring**

04 tang, zest, zing
06 flavor
07 essence, extract
08 additive, piquancy
09 seasoning

**flaw**

04 chip, mark, rent, rift, slip
05 break, cleft, crack, error, fault, lapse, speck, split
06 defect, foible
07 blemish, crevice, failing, fallacy, fissure, mistake
08 weak spot, weakness
11 shortcoming
12 imperfection

**flawed**

06 broken, faulty, marked, marred
07 cracked, damaged, spoiled, unsound

**flawless**
09 blemished, defective, erroneous, imperfect
10 fallacious

**flawless**
05 sound, whole
07 perfect
08 spotless, unbroken
09 faultless, stainless, undamaged
10 immaculate, impeccable
11 unblemished

**flay**
04 flog, skin
07 lambast, scourge, upbraid
08 execrate
09 excoriate, skin alive
10 tongue-lash
12 pull to pieces
13 tear a strip off

**fleck**
03 dot
04 dust, mark, spot
05 point, speck
06 dapple, mottle, streak
07 freckle, spatter, speckle

**fledgling**
06 novice, rookie
07 learner, recruit, trainee
08 neophyte, newcomer
09 greenhorn, novitiate
10 apprentice, tenderfoot

**flee**
03 fly, lam
04 bolt, rush
05 leave, scoot, scram
06 decamp, escape, vamose, vanish
07 abscond, get away, make off, retreat, run away, take off, vamoose
08 clear off, withdraw
09 cut and run, disappear
10 take flight
15 take to your heels

**fleece**
03 con, rob
04 bilk, coat, down, gull, wool
05 bleed, cheat, steal, sting
06 diddle, fiddle, rip off
07 defraud, plunder, swindle
10 overcharge
12 pull a fast one, take for a ride
13 have someone on

**fleecy**
04 soft
05 downy, hairy, nappy
06 fluffy, pilose, shaggy, woolly
07 velvety
08 floccose

10 flocculent, lanuginose, lanuginous

**fleet**
04 fast, navy
05 quick, rapid, swift
06 armada, speedy, winged
08 flotilla, meteoric, squadron
09 mercurial, task force
10 naval force
11 expeditious, light-footed

**fleeting**
05 brief, quick, short
06 flying, rushed, sudden
07 passing
09 ephemeral, fugacious, momentary, temporary, transient
10 short-lived, transitory

**flesh**
03 fat, kin
04 body, meat, pith, pulp, skin
05 brawn, folks, stuff
06 family, matter, muscle, tissue, weight
08 relative, solidity
09 carnality, substance
11 human nature, physicality
12 carnal nature, corporeality, in actual life, significance

❑**flesh and blood**
03 kin
05 folks
06 family
08 relative
09 relations

❑**flesh out**
09 elaborate
10 add details
11 give details
12 make complete

❑**in the flesh**
08 in person
10 in real life
12 in actual life

**fleshly**
05 human
06 animal, bodily, carnal, earthy, erotic, sexual, wordly
07 bestial, brutish, earthly, lustful, sensual
08 corporal, material, physical
09 corporeal

**fleshy**
03 fat
05 ample, hefty, meaty, obese, plump, podgy, pudgy, stout, tubby
06 brawny, chubby, chunky, flabby, portly, rotund
09 corpulent

10 overweight, well-padded

**flex**
03 bow, ply
04 bend
05 angle, crook, curve
07 stretch, tighten
08 contract, double up

**flexibility**
04 give
06 spring
07 flexion, pliancy
10 elasticity, pliability, resilience, suppleness
11 amenability, springiness
12 adaptability, complaisance

**flexible**
05 agile, bendy, lithe
06 limber, pliant, supple
07 elastic, plastic, pliable
08 amenable, bendable, moldable, stretchy, variable, yielding
09 adaptable, malleable, open-ended
10 adjustable, manageable
13 accommodating

**flick**
03 dab, hit, rap, tap
04 film, flip, jerk, lash, snap, whip
05 click, movie, swish, touch
13 motion picture

❑**flick through**
04 scan, skim, skip
08 glance at
10 glance over
11 flip through, leaf through
12 thumb through
13 browse through

**flicker**
04 flit, iota, wink
05 blink, flare, flash, gleam, glint, spark, trace, waver
06 gutter, quiver
07 flutter, glimmer, glitter, shimmer, sparkle, twinkle
10 indication, woodpecker

**flight**
03 set
05 steps
06 escape, exodus, flying, stairs, voyage
07 fleeing, getaway, journey, retreat, shuttle
08 aviation, stairway
09 departure, staircase
10 absconding, running off
11 aeronautics, running away

❑**take flight**
03 fly

**flighty**
05 leave
06 depart, escape, vanish
07 abscond, get away, make off, retreat, run away, take off
09 cut and run, disappear

**flighty**
05 silly
06 fickle
08 skittish, unsteady, volatile
09 frivolous, impetuous, impulsive, mercurial
10 capricious, changeable, inconstant, unbalanced
11 birdbrained, harebrained, lightheaded, thoughtless
13 irresponsible, rattlebrained
14 scatterbrained

**flimsy**
04 fine, poor, thin, weak
05 filmy, light, shaky, sheer
06 feeble, meager, slight
07 fragile, rickety, shallow, trivial
08 delicate, ethereal, trifling
10 inadequate, jerry-built
11 implausible, lightweight
13 insubstantial

**flinch**
04 balk, duck, flee
05 avoid, baulk, cower, dodge, quail, quake, shirk, start, wince
06 blench, cringe, crouch, recoil, shiver, shrink
07 retreat, shy away, tremble
08 draw back, pull back

**fling**
02 go
03 lob, try
04 cast, hurl, send, shot, toss
05 chuck, crack, dance, heave, pitch, sling, spree, throw
06 gamble, let fly, propel
07 attempt, venture
08 catapult
10 indulgence, send flying

**flip**
04 cast, flap, spin, toss, turn
05 flick, pitch, throw

❑**flip through**
04 scan, skim, skip
10 glance over
11 leaf through
12 thumb through
13 browse through

**flippancy**
05 cheek
06 levity
08 glibness, pertness
09 frivolity, sauciness

10 cheekiness, disrespect, persiflage
11 irreverence, shallowness
12 impertinence
13 facetiousness

**flippant**
04 flip, glib, pert, rude
06 cheeky
07 offhand, shallow
09 facetious, frivolous
10 insouciant, irreverent
11 impertinent, superficial
12 lighthearted
13 disrespectful, irresponsible

**flirt**
04 ogle, vamp
05 dally, eye up, hussy, tease
06 chat up, chippy, coquet, lead on, trifle, wanton
08 coquette, make up to
09 philander
10 make eyes at
11 make a pass at, philanderer
12 heartbreaker

❑**flirt with**
03 try
07 toy with
08 dabble in, play with
09 entertain
10 trifle with

**flirtation**
05 amour, sport
06 affair, toying
08 coquetry, dallying, trifling
09 dalliance
10 chatting up
12 philandering

**flirtatious**
06 come-on, flirty, wanton
07 amorous, teasing
10 come-hither, coquettish
11 promiscuous, provocative

**flit**
03 bob, fly
04 dart, dash, pass, rush, skim
05 dance, flash, speed, whisk
07 flitter, flutter

**float**
03 bob
04 hang, sail, swim, waft
05 drift, glide, set up, slide
06 launch, submit, wander
07 present, promote, propose, suggest, suspend
08 get going, initiate
09 be buoyant, recommend

**floating**
06 afloat
07 bobbing, buoyant, movable, sailing, wafting

08 drifting, hovering, swimming, variable
09 migratory, unsettled
10 transitory, unattached
11 fluctuating, uncommitted

**flock**
04 fold, herd, host, mill, pack
05 bunch, crowd, drove, group, swarm, troop
06 gather, huddle, throng
07 cluster, collect
08 assemble, converge
09 gathering, multitude
10 collection, congregate
12 congregation

**flog**
04 beat, belt, cane, drub, flay, lash, whip
05 birch, strap, whack
06 punish, thrash, wallop
07 scourge
09 horsewhip
10 flagellate

**flogging**
06 caning, hiding
07 beating, flaying, lashing
08 birching, whipping
09 scourging, strapping, thrashing, walloping
12 flagellation
13 horsewhipping

**flood**
04 fill, flow, glut, gush, pour, rush, soak, tide
05 drown, spate, surge, swell
06 deluge, drench, engulf, excess, stream
07 immerse, torrent
08 brim over, downpour, inundate, overflow, plethora, saturate, submerge
09 abundance, overwhelm
10 inundation, outpouring

**floor**
04 base, beat, deck, fell, tier
05 basis, level, story, stump, throw
06 baffle, defeat, ground, puzzle
07 landing, nonplus, perplex
08 bewilder, confound, flooring
09 discomfit, dumbfound, frustrate, knock down, overwhelm, prostrate
10 disconcert, strike down

**flop**
04 bomb, drop, fail, fall, fold, hang, sink
05 crash, droop, slump, stiff
06 dangle, fiasco, go bust, pack up, slip-up, topple, tumble

**floppy**
07 debacle, failure, founder, misfire, washout
08 collapse, disaster, shambles
10 non-starter
11 go to the wall
12 go into the red

**floppy**
04 limp, soft
05 baggy, loose
06 droopy, flabby
07 hanging, sagging
08 dangling

**flora**
06 botany, plants
07 herbage
09 plant life
10 vegetation

**florid**
03 red
05 fussy, ruddy
06 ornate, purple, rococo
07 baroque, flowery, flushed, pompous, reddish, verbose
08 red-faced, rubicund
09 bombastic, elaborate
10 flamboyant, melismatic
11 embellished, extravagant

**flotsam**
04 junk
06 debris, jetsam
07 rubbish
08 detritus, wreckage
11 odds and ends

**flounce**
04 jerk, toss
05 fling, frill, stamp, storm, throw, twist
06 bounce, fringe, prance, ruffle, sashay, spring
07 falbala, valance
08 furbelow, trimming

**flounder**
06 dither, falter, fumble, wallow
07 blunder, go under, stumble
08 flatfish
10 be confused, flail about
11 thresh about

**flourish**
03 wag, wax
04 boom, élan, show, wave
05 bloom, get on, serif, shake, sweep, swing, swirl, swish, twirl, twist, vaunt, wield
06 do well, flaunt, flower, parade, pizazz, thrive
07 blossom, burgeon, develop, display, exhibit, fanfare, gesture, panache, pizzazz, prosper, show off, succeed

08 be strong, brandish, curlicue, increase, ornament, progress
10 decoration

**flourishing**
07 booming
08 blooming, thriving
10 prosperous, successful

**flout**
04 defy, mock
05 break, scorn, spurn
06 jeer at, reject
07 disdain, disobey, laugh at, scoff at, sneer at, violate
09 disregard
15 show contempt for

**flow**
03 jet, run
04 drip, flux, gush, pour, rush, spew, stem, teem, tide, well
05 flood, issue, spate, spill, spout, spurt, surge, swirl
06 babble, bubble, course, deluge, emerge, gurgle, ripple, spring, squirt, stream
07 cascade, current, emanate, proceed, trickle
08 effusion, overflow, plethora
09 circulate, originate
10 outpouring

**flower**
03 bud
04 best, grow, open, pick
05 bloom, cream, elite
06 choice, finest, floral, floret, mature, select, sprout, thrive
07 blossom, burgeon, come out, develop, prosper
08 flourish, floweret
11 florescence
13 efflorescence, inflorescence
➤ See also PLANT

▶ *Parts of a flower*:
05 calyx, ovary, ovule, petal, sepal, spike, stalk, style, torus, umbel
06 anther, carpel, corymb, pistil, spadix, stamen, stigma
07 corolla, nectary
08 filament, gynecium, thalamus
09 capitulum
10 receptacle

▶ *Names of flowers*:
03 mum
04 flag, glad, iris, lily, pink, rose
05 aster, daisy, pansy, phlox, poppy, stock, tulip, viola
06 azalea, crocus, dahlia, lupine, orchid, salvia, violet, zinnia

07 alyssum, anemone, begonia, cowslip, freesia, fuchsia, jonquil, lobelia, nemesia, petunia, primula, verbena
08 bluebell, camellia, cyclamen, daffodil, dianthus, foxglove, gardenia, geranium, gloxinia, hyacinth, larkspur, magnolia, marigold, primrose, snowdrop, sweet pea
09 aubrietia, calendula, candytuft, carnation, digitalis, gladiolus, hollyhock, hydrangea, impatiens, narcissus, nicotiana, sunflower
10 bluebonnet, cornflower, cranesbill, delphinium, nasturtium, poinsettia, polyanthus, snapdragon, wallflower
11 antirrhinum, forget-me-not, love-in-a-mist
12 sweet william
13 African violet, chrysanthemum
15 lily-of-the-valley

▶ *Names of wildflowers*:
05 clary, daisy, oxeye, poppy, sedum
06 clover, mallow, teasel, violet, yarrow
07 bistort, campion, comfrey, cowslip, goldcup, heather
08 bluebell, crowfoot, foxglove, harebell, lungwort, primrose, rockrose, selfheal, toadflax, wild iris
09 birthwort, broomrape, buttercup, celandine, columbine, dandelion, edelweiss, goldenrod, horsetail, stonecrop, waterlily, wild pansy
10 goatsbeard, heartsease, lady's-smock, pennyroyal, wild endive, wild orchid
11 lady-slipper, ragged robin, wild chicory, wood anemone
12 cuckooflower, lady's-slipper, solomon's seal, white campion
13 butter-and-eggs
14 black-eyed Susan, bladder campion, evening campion

**flowery**
05 fancy
06 florid, ornate, purple
07 baroque, pompous, verbose
09 elaborate, high-flown
10 euphuistic, rhetorical
13 grandiloquent

## flowing
04 easy
06 fluent, moving, smooth
07 falling, gushing, hanging, pouring, rolling, rushing, seeping, surging, welling
08 sweeping, unbroken
09 cascading, streaming
10 continuous, effortless
13 uninterrupted

## fluctuate
04 sway, vary
05 alter, shift, swing, waver
06 change, seesaw
08 hesitate, undulate
09 alternate, oscillate, vacillate
10 ebb and flow
11 go up and down, rise and fall

## fluctuation
05 shift, swing
06 change
10 fickleness
11 alternation, inconstancy, instability, oscillation, vacillation, variability
12 irresolution, unsteadiness

## flue
04 duct, pipe, vent
05 shaft
07 channel, chimney, passage

## fluency
04 ease
07 command, control
08 facility, glibness
09 assurance, eloquence, facundity, slickness
10 smoothness, volubility
14 articulateness

## fluent
04 easy, glib
05 fluid, ready, slick
06 smooth
07 elegant, flowing, natural
08 eloquent, graceful
10 articulate, effortless
11 mellifluous
13 silver-tongued

## fluff
03 nap
04 blow, down, dust, fuzz, lint, muff, pile
05 boner, botch, floss, spoil
06 bungle, foul up, fumble, goof up, mess up, muck up
07 blooper, do badly, louse up, screw up
11 make a mess of

## fluffy
04 soft
05 downy, furry, hairy, silky

06 fleecy, shaggy, woolly
08 feathery

## fluid
04 easy, open
05 juice, runny
06 liquid, liquor, melted, mobile, molten, smooth
07 aqueous, elegant, flowing, natural, protean, running
08 flexible, graceful, shifting, unstable, unsteady, variable
09 adaptable, unsettled
10 adjustable, changeable, effortless, inconstant

## fluke
05 break, freak, quirk
06 chance, stroke
08 accident, fortuity, windfall
10 lucky break
11 coincidence, serendipity
12 stroke of luck

## fluky
05 lucky
09 fortunate, uncertain
10 accidental, fortuitous
12 coincidental, incalculable
13 serendipitous

## flummox
03 fox
05 stump, stymy
06 baffle, puzzle, stymie
07 mystify, nonplus, perplex
08 bewilder, confound
09 bamboozle

## flummoxed
05 at sea, foxed
07 at a loss, baffled, puzzled, stumped, stymied
09 mystified, perplexed
10 confounded, nonplussed

## flunkey, flunky
05 slave, toady, valet
06 drudge, lackey, menial, minion, yes man
07 cringer, footman
08 hanger-on
09 assistant, underling
10 bootlicker, manservant

## flurry
04 bout, flap, fuss, gust, stir
05 blast, burst, hurry, spell, spurt, upset, whirl
06 bother, bustle, hassle, hubbub, hustle, rattle, ruffle, shower, squall, tumult
07 agitate, confuse, disturb, fluster, flutter, perturb
08 bewilder, outbreak, unsettle
09 agitation, commotion
10 disconcert, excitement

11 disturbance

## flush
04 burn, even, flat, full, glow, hose, rich, swab, true, wash
05 bloom, blush, clear, color, eject, empty, expel, go red, level, plane, rinse, rouse, start, vigor
06 lavish, redden, smooth, square
07 cleanse, crimson, moneyed, redness, suffuse, turn red, uncover, wealthy, well-off
08 discover, drive out, evacuate, force out, generous, rosiness, well-to-do
09 freshness, ruddiness
10 prosperous, well-heeled

## flushed
03 hot, red
04 rosy
05 aglow, ruddy
06 ablaze, aflame, elated
07 aroused, burning, crimson, excited, glowing, scarlet
08 animated, blushing, exultant, inspired, rubicund
11 embarrassed, intoxicated

## fluster
04 faze, flap, tizz
05 panic, state, tizzy, upset
06 bother, bustle, dither, flurry, put off, rattle, ruffle
07 agitate, confuse, disturb, perturb, turmoil, unnerve
08 confound, distract, unsettle
09 confusion, embarrass
10 discompose, disconcert
13 embarrassment

## fluted
06 ribbed, ridged
09 channeled
10 corrugated

## flutter
03 bat, bet
04 beat, flap, risk, toss, wave
05 dance, hover, wager, waver
06 gamble, quiver, ripple, ruffle, shiver, tremor, twitch
07 agitate, flicker, flitter, pulsate, shudder, tremble, vibrate
09 fluctuate, palpitate, vibration
11 palpitation, speculation

## flux
04 flow
06 change, motion, unrest
08 fluidity, movement
10 alteration, transition
11 development, instability
12 modification

**fly**
03 bug, jet
04 bolt, dart, dash, flit, race, rise, rush, show, soar, tear, wave, wing, zoom
05 glide, hover, hurry, pilot, shoot, speed
06 ascend, hasten, slip by, sprint
07 display, exhibit, flutter, fly ball, operate, present, take off
08 maneuver
09 go quickly
11 pass quickly

❏**fly at**
03 hit
05 go for
06 attack, charge, let fly, strike
07 lay into
08 fall upon
09 lash out at

**fly-by-night**
05 shady
07 dubious
09 ephemeral
10 short-lived, unreliable
12 disreputable, questionable
13 discreditable, untrustworthy

**flying**
04 fast
05 brief, hasty, rapid
06 rushed, speedy, winged
07 hurried, soaring, winging
08 airborne, flapping, fleeting, floating, hovering
09 wind-borne

**foam**
04 boil, fizz, head, suds
05 froth, spume
06 bubble, lather, seethe
07 bubbles
10 effervesce
13 effervescence

**foamy**
05 spumy, sudsy
06 bubbly, frothy
07 foaming, lathery, spumous
10 spumescent

**fob**
❏**fob off**
05 foist
06 impose, put off, unload
07 inflict, palm off, pass off
08 get rid of

**focus**
03 aim, fix, hub
04 axis, core, crux, join, meet
05 heart, hinge, pivot
06 center, direct, home in, kernel, zero in, zoom in

07 nucleus
08 converge, linchpin, pinpoint
09 spotlight
10 focal point
11 concentrate

❏**in focus**
05 clear, sharp
08 distinct
11 well-defined

❏**out of focus**
04 hazy
06 blurry
07 blurred
10 ill-defined, indistinct

**fodder**
04 feed, food
06 forage, silage
07 lucerne, pabulum, rations
09 foodstuff, provender
11 nourishment

**foe**
05 enemy, rival
08 opponent
09 adversary, combatant
10 antagonist

**fetus**
05 fetal
06 embryo
11 unborn child

**fog**
04 blur, daze, haze, mist, smog
05 cloud, gloom
06 baffle, darken, muddle
07 confuse, obscure, pea soup, steam up
08 bewilder, haziness
09 mistiness, murkiness, obfuscate, obscurity, vagueness
10 perplexity, puzzlement
12 bewilderment
14 disorientation

**foggy**
03 dim
04 dark, gray, hazy
05 misty, murky, vague
06 cloudy, gloomy, smoggy
07 clouded, obscure, unclear
10 indistinct

**foible**
05 fault, habit, quirk
06 defect, oddity
07 failing, oddness
08 weakness
11 peculiarity, shortcoming
12 eccentricity, imperfection

**foil**
04 balk, stop
05 baulk, block, check, elude

06 baffle, defeat, hamper, hinder, outwit, relief, thwart
07 counter, nullify, prevent, scupper, scuttle, setting
08 contrast, obstruct
09 frustrate
10 antithesis, circumvent

**foist**
05 force
06 fob off, impose, thrust, unload, wish on
07 palm off, pass off
08 get rid of

**fold**
03 hug, pen, ply
04 bend, fail, flop, line, ring, tuck, turn, wrap, yard
05 clasp, close, crash, crimp, flock, kraal, layer, pleat
06 crease, double, enfold, furrow, gather, go bust, pack up, pucker, wrap up
07 crinkle, crumple, embrace, enclose, envelop, overlap, paddock, squeeze, wrinkle
08 collapse, shut down, stockade, turn down
09 enclosure, gathering, go belly up, knife-edge, turn under
11 corrugation, go to the wall
12 congregation, parishioners
15 go out of business

**folder**
04 file
05 folio
06 binder, pocket, wallet
07 booklet, leaflet
08 envelope
09 portfolio

**foliage**
06 leaves
07 leafage, verdure
08 greenery
09 foliation, foliature, vernation
10 vegetation
12 frondescence

**folk**
03 kin
04 clan, race
05 tribe
06 ethnic, family, nation, native, people, public, tribal
07 kindred, parents, popular
08 national
09 ancestral, relations, relatives
10 indigenous, population
11 ethnic group, traditional

**folklore**
05 myths, tales
06 fables

07 beliefs, customs, legends, stories
09 mythology, tradition
13 superstitions

**follow**
03 dog
04 flow, heed, hunt, mind, note, obey, tail
05 arise, chase, ensue, hound, issue, stalk, track, trail
06 accept, escort, fathom, go with, pursue, result, shadow, take in
07 develop, emanate, go after, observe, proceed, replace, succeed, support, yield to
08 adhere to, be a fan of, carry out, come next, go behind, run after, supplant, tag after, tag along
09 accompany, conform to, give chase, supersede
10 appreciate, comply with, keep up with, understand
14 be a supporter of, be interested in

❏**follow through**
06 finish, pursue
07 fulfill
08 complete, conclude
09 implement
10 see through

❏**follow up**
06 pursue
08 check out, continue, look into, research
09 reinforce
11 consolidate, investigate

**follower**
03 fan
05 freak, pupil
06 backer, escort, helper
07 admirer, apostle, devotee
08 adherent, believer, disciple, emulator, hanger-on, imitator, retainer, sidekick
09 attendant, supporter
10 enthusiast

**following**
04 fans, next
05 later, suite
06 circle, public
07 backers, backing, coterie, ensuing, retinue, support
08 admirers, audience
09 adherents, clientèle, entourage, followers, patronage, resulting
10 consequent, subsequent, succeeding, successive

**folly**
04 whim
05 tower
06 gazebo, idiocy, lunacy
07 inanity, madness
08 insanity, monument, nonsense, rashness
09 absurdity, belvedere, craziness, silliness, stupidity
10 imbecility, imprudence
11 fatuousness, foolishness
12 indiscretion, recklessness
13 ludicrousness, senselessness

**foment**
04 brew, goad, spur
05 raise, rouse
06 arouse, foster, incite, kindle, prompt, stir up, whip up
07 agitate, promote, provoke
08 activate
09 encourage, instigate, stimulate

**fond**
04 vain, warm
05 naïve
06 absurd, caring, doting, keen on, liking, loving, tender
07 adoring, amorous, deluded, devoted, foolish
09 indulgent, partial to
10 addicted to, attached to, enamored of
11 impractical
12 affectionate

**fondle**
03 hug, pat, pet
06 caress, cuddle, stroke

**fondness**
04 love
05 fancy, taste
06 liking
08 devotion, kindness, penchant, soft spot
09 affection
10 attachment, enthusiasm, partiality, tenderness
12 predilection

**food**
04 chow, diet, dish, eats, fare, feed, grub, menu, nosh
05 board, meals, table
06 fodder, stores, viands
07 cooking, cuisine, rations
08 delicacy, eatables, junk food, victuals
09 nutriment, nutrition, specialty
10 foodstuffs, provisions, sustenance
11 comestibles, nourishment
12 refreshments

► *Types of food:*
03 BLT, cod, egg, poi
04 beef, hash, lamb, olio, pork, tuna
05 bread, brose, grits, gumbo, kebab, kebob, pilaf, pilau, pilaw, pizza, salmi, satay, sushi, trout
06 borsch, caviar, fondue, haggis, hotdog, hummus, kipper, mousse, omelet, paella, pilaff, quiche, ragout, salami, samosa, scampi, tamale, turkey, waffle
07 borscht, burrito, catfish, chicken, compote, fajitas, falafel, fritter, gnocchi, goulash, gravlax, lasagne, lobster, pancake, ramekin, rarebit, risotto, sashimi, soufflé, tempura, terrine, timbale, tostada
08 calamari, chop suey, chow mein, consommé, coq au vin, couscous, fish ball, fish cake, gazpacho, kedgeree, meatloaf, moussaka, porridge, pot roast, raclette, ramequin, souvlaki, tandoori, teriyaki, yakitori
09 cassoulet, corn bread, fricassee, galantine, guacamole, hamburger, hush puppy, jambalaya, meatballs, souvlakia, spaghetti, succotash
10 cannelloni, chef's salad, enchiladas, fish finger, minestrone, mixed grill, salmagundi, sauerkraut, shish kebab, stroganoff
11 clam chowder, cockaleekie, French fries, gefilte fish, ratatouille, smorgasbord, timbale case, vichyssoise
12 eggs Benedict, fish and chips, fried chicken, mulligatawny, shepherd's pie, taramasalata, Waldorf salad, Welsh rarebit
13 barbequed ribs, bouillabaisse, cottage cheese, salade niçoise
14 chilli con carne, macaroni cheese, shrimp cocktail
15 Wiener schnitzel
➤ See also BEAN; BISCUIT; BREAD; CAKE; CHEESE; FRUIT; HERBS AND SPICES; MEAT; MUSHROOM; NUT; PASTA; PASTRY; SAUCE; SAUSAGE; VEGETABLE

## fool

03 ass, con, kid
04 butt, clod, dope, dork, dupe, gull, hoax, jerk, jest, joke, sham
05 bluff, chump, clown, comic, dunce, idiot, moron, ninny, trick, twerp
06 cretin, delude, dimwit, jester, nitwit, stooge, take in
07 buffoon, deceive, fathead, half-wit, mislead, pretend, swindle
08 hoodwink, imbecile
09 bamboozle, birdbrain, blockhead, lark about, mess about, play about, simpleton
10 act the fool, mess around, nincompoop, play tricks
11 clown around, horse around, make believe, monkey about, string along
12 put one over on
13 laughingstock

### □play the fool

09 fool about, mess about
10 fool around, mess around
11 clown around
12 monkey around

## foolery

05 farce, folly, larks
06 antics, capers, pranks
07 fooling, waggery
08 clowning, drollery, nonsense
09 high jinks, horseplay, silliness
10 buffoonery, tomfoolery
11 carryings-on, shenanigans
12 childishness, monkey tricks
14 practical jokes

## foolhardy

04 bold, rash
08 reckless
09 daredevil, imprudent
10 ill-advised, incautious
13 irresponsible

## foolish

03 mad
04 daft, dumb
05 batty, crazy, dotty, inane, inept, nutty, silly
06 simple, stupid, unwise
07 fatuous, idiotic, moronic
08 ignorant
09 half-baked, ludicrous, pointless, senseless
10 half-witted, ill-advised
11 harebrained, injudicious
12 short-sighted, simple-minded, unreasonable
13 ill-considered

## foolishly

08 absurdly, stupidly, unwisely
09 fatuously
11 idiotically, imprudently
12 ill-advisedly, incautiously, indiscreetly, ridiculously
13 injudiciously

## foolishness

04 bunk
05 bilge, folly
06 bunkum, lunacy, piffle
07 baloney, foolery, hogwash, inanity, madness, rubbish
08 claptrap, daftness, nonsense, weakness
09 absurdity, craziness, incaution, poppycock, silliness, stupidity
10 imprudence, ineptitude
13 senselessness

## foolproof

04 safe, sure
07 certain
08 fail-safe, sure-fire
09 unfailing
10 dependable, guaranteed, idiot-proof, infallible

## foot

03 end, leg, pad, paw, pes, toe
04 heel, hoof, sole
05 pedal
06 bottom, tootsy
07 trotter
09 extremity

## football

05 rugby
06 soccer
11 pro football
13 touch football
15 college football
➤ See also SPORT

► *Names of football teams:*
04 **Jets** (New York), **Rams** (St. Louis)
05 **Bears** (Chicago), **Bills** (Buffalo), **Colts** (Indianapolis), **Lions** (Detroit)
06 **Browns** (Cleveland), **Chiefs** (Kansas City), **Eagles** (Philadelphia), **Giants** (New York), **Oilers** (Houston), **Ravens** (Baltimore), **Saints** (New Orleans), **Titans** (Tennessee)
07 **Bengals** (Cincinnati), **Broncos** (Denver), **Cowboys** (Dallas), **Falcons** (Atlanta), **Jaguars** (Jacksonville), **Packers** (Green Bay), **Raiders** (Los Angeles),

**Vikings** (Minnesota)
08 **Chargers** (San Diego), **Dolphins** (Miami), **Panthers** (Carolina), **Patriots** (New England), **Redskins** (Washington), **Seahawks** (Seattle), **Steelers** (Pittsburgh)
09 **Cardinals** (Arizona)
10 **Buccaneers** (Tampa Bay)
11 **Forty-Niners** (San Francisco)

► *Names of football players:*
04 **Lane** (Dick "Night Train"), **Monk** (Art), **Rice** (Jerry)
05 **Allen** (Marcus), **Baugh** (Sammy), **Brown** (Jim), **Ditka** (Mike), **Elway** (John), **Faulk** (Marshall), **Favre** (Brett), **Fouts** (Dan), **Green** (Joe), **Halas** (George), **Jones** (David "Deacon"), **Starr** (Bart)
06 **Blanda** (George), **Butkus** (Dick), **Csonka** (Larry), **Graham** (Otto), **Grange** (Red), **Hirsch** (Elroy "Crazylegs"), **Hutson** (Don), **Marino** (Dan), **Namath** (Joe Willie), **Payton** (Walter), **Sayers** (Gale), **Thorpe** (Jim), **Tittle** (Y.A.), **Unitas** (Johnny), **Warner** (Kurt)
07 **Dorsett** (Tony), **Gifford** (Frank), **Hornung** (Paul), **Montana** (Joe), **Simpson** (Orenthal James), **Stabler** (Ken)
08 **Bradshaw** (Terry), **Campbell** (Earl), **Lombardi** (Vince), **Nagurski** (Bronko), **Staubach** (Roger)
09 **Tarkenton** (Fran)

## footing

04 base, grip, rank
05 basis, grade, state, terms
07 balance, support
08 foothold, position, standing
10 conditions, foundation
12 relationship

## footling

05 minor, petty
06 paltry
07 trivial
08 piffling, trifling
10 irrelevant
13 insignificant

## footnotes

04 note
05 gloss

07 scholia
10 annotation, commentary, marginalia
12 marginal note

**footprint**
04 step
05 trace, track, trail, tread

**footstep**
04 plod, step
05 track, tramp, tread
08 footfall, footmark

**footwear**

► *Types of footwear:*
04 boot, clog, mule, pump, shoe
05 sabot, thong, wader
06 bootee, brogan, brogue, casual, galosh, lace-up, loafer, oxford, sandal, slip-on
07 galoshe, jodhpur, slipper, sneaker
08 flip-flop, moccasin, overshoe, platform, snowshoe
09 slingback
10 ballet shoe, clodhopper, espadrille, tennis shoe
11 walking boot
12 football shoe, stiletto-heel
13 ballet slipper
14 Wellington boot
16 riding boot rubber

**fop**
04 beau, dude
05 blade, dandy, swell
07 coxcomb, peacock
08 popinjay

**foppish**
04 vain
05 showy
06 dainty, dapper, la-di-da
08 affected, dandyish, preening
09 dandified
11 overdressed

**forage**
04 feed, food, hunt, loot, raid
06 fodder, ravage, search
07 assault, plunder, ransack, rummage, scratch
08 scavenge, scrounge
09 cast about, provender
10 foodstuffs

**foray**
04 raid
05 sally, swoop
06 attack, inroad, ravage, sortie
09 incursion, offensive
14 reconnaissance

**forbear**
04 hold, omit, stay, stop
05 avoid, cease, pause
06 desist, eschew
07 abstain, decline, refrain
08 hesitate, hold back

**forbearance**
08 clemency, leniency, mildness, patience
09 avoidance, endurance, restraint, tolerance
10 abstinence, moderation, refraining, sufferance, temperance, toleration
11 resignation, self-control
13 long-suffering

**forbearing**
04 easy, mild
07 clement, lenient, patient
08 merciful, moderate, tolerant
09 forgiving, indulgent
10 restrained
14 self-controlled

**forbid**
03 ban
04 deny, veto
05 block, debar
06 hinder, not let, outlaw, refuse
07 inhibit, prevent, rule out
08 disallow, not allow, preclude, prohibit
09 blacklist, interdict, proscribe

**forbidden**
05 taboo
06 banned, vetoed
07 illicit
08 debarred, excluded, outlawed
10 prohibited, proscribed
11 out of bounds

**forbidding**
04 grim
05 harsh, stern
06 severe
07 awesome, ominous
08 daunting, menacing, sinister
10 formidable, unfriendly, uninviting
11 frightening, threatening

**force**
03 pry
04 army, body, make, push, unit
05 blast, bully, corps, drive, impel, might, power, squad, troop, vigor, wrest, wring
06 coerce, compel, duress, dynamo, effort, energy, extort, impose, lean on, muscle, oblige, propel, stress, wrench

07 binding, current, essence, extract, impetus, inflict, meaning, passion, platoon
08 bulldoze, coercion, division, dynamism, emphasis, exertion, momentum, pressure, railroad, regiment, squadron, strength, violence, vitality
09 battalion, constrain, intensity, pressgang
10 aggression, compulsion, constraint, pressurize
11 arm-twisting, enforcement, functioning, necessitate
13 determination, put pressure on
14 in great numbers, persuasiveness, put the screws on, the third degree

❑**in force**
05 valid
07 binding, current, working
08 in crowds, in droves
09 effective, operative
10 in strength
11 functioning, in operation

**forced**
05 false, stiff
06 wooden
07 feigned, labored, stilted
08 affected, overdone, strained
09 compelled, contrived, insincere, mandatory
10 artificial, obligatory

**forceful**
06 cogent, mighty, potent, strong, urgent
07 dynamic, telling, weighty
08 emphatic, powerful, vehement, vigorous
09 assertive, effective
10 compelling, convincing, impressive, persuasive

**forcible**
06 cogent, forced, mighty, potent, strong
07 by force, violent, weighty
08 coercive, forceful, powerful
09 effective, energetic
10 aggressive, compelling, compulsory, impressive

**forcibly**
07 by force
09 violently
10 vehemently, vigorously
11 under duress
12 compulsorily, emphatically

**ford**
04 wade
05 cross

08 causeway, crossing

**forebear**
06 father
08 ancestor
10 antecedent, forefather, forerunner, progenitor
11 predecessor
12 primogenitor

**foreboding**
04 fear, omen, sign
05 dread, token, worry
07 anxiety, feeling, warning
09 misgiving, suspicion
10 prediction, sixth sense
11 premonition
12 apprehension, presentiment

**forecast**
03 tip
05 augur, guess
06 augury, expect, tip off
07 foresee, outlook, predict
08 estimate, foretell, forewarn, prophecy, prophesy
09 calculate, prognosis
10 anticipate, conjecture, prediction, projection
11 expectation, forewarning, guesstimate, speculation
15 prognostication

**forefather**
06 father
08 ancestor, forebear
10 antecedent, progenitor
11 predecessor
12 primogenitor

**forefront**
03 van
04 fore, lead
05 front
08 vanguard
09 front line, spearhead
10 avant-garde, firing line
11 cutting edge
15 leading position

**forego**
05 forgo
07 precede
10 to go before

**foregoing**
05 above, prior
06 former
07 earlier
08 previous
09 precedent, preceding
10 antecedent
14 aforementioned

**foregone**
05 fixed
08 foreseen
10 inevitable

11 anticipated, cut-and-dried, predictable, preordained
13 predetermined

**foreground**
04 fore
05 front
06 center
09 forefront, limelight
10 prominence
15 leading position

**forehead**
04 brow
05 front
07 frontal, metopic, temples

**foreign**
03 odd
05 alien
06 ethnic, exotic, remote
07 distant, faraway, migrant, outside, strange, unknown
08 borrowed, external, imported, overseas, peculiar
09 immigrant
10 extraneous, inapposite, outlandish, unfamiliar
11 incongruous, unconnected
13 international

**foreigner**
05 alien
07 visitor
08 outsider, stranger
09 immigrant, outlander

**foreknowledge**
09 foresight, prevision
10 prescience
11 forewarning, premonition
12 clairvoyance, precognition
15 prognostication

**foreman**
04 boss
06 ganger, honcho
07 headman, manager, overman, steward
08 overseer
10 supervisor
14 superintendent

**foremost**
03 top
04 main
05 chief, first, front, prime
07 central, highest, leading, premier, primary, supreme
08 advanced, cardinal
09 principal, uppermost
10 preeminent
13 most important

**foreordained**
05 fated
08 destined
09 appointed

11 prearranged, predestined, preordained
13 predetermined

**forerunner**
04 omen, sign
05 envoy, token
06 herald
08 ancestor
09 harbinger, precursor
10 antecedent, forefather
11 predecessor

**foresee**
06 divine, expect
07 predict
08 envisage, forebode, forecast, foretell, prophesy
10 anticipate
13 prognosticate

**foreshadow**
04 bode, mean
05 augur
07 portend, predict, presage, promise, signify, suggest
08 indicate, prophesy
09 prefigure

**foresight**
06 vision
08 planning, prudence
09 provision, readiness
11 discernment, forethought
12 anticipation, perspicacity
14 circumspection, farsightedness
15 forward planning

**forest**
04 wood
05 copse, grove, trees, woods
07 thicket
08 woodland
09 greenwood
10 timberland

**forestall**
04 balk, foil, stop
05 avert, baulk, parry
06 hinder, impede, preemt, thwart
07 head off, obviate, prevent, ward off
08 obstruct, preclude, stave off
09 frustrate, intercept
10 anticipate, get ahead of

**forestry**
09 woodcraft
10 dendrology
11 forestation, woodmanship
12 conservation, silviculture
13 afforestation, arboriculture

**foretaste**
05 whiff
06 sample

07 example, preview, trailer
08 specimen
09 appetizer, foretoken
11 forewarning, premonition

**foretell**
06 divine
07 foresee, predict, presage
08 forecast, forewarn, prophesy
10 foreshadow
13 prognosticate

**forethought**
08 planning, prudence
09 foresight, provision
11 discernment, preparation
12 anticipation, perspicacity
14 circumspection, farsightedness
15 forward planning

**forever**
04 ever
06 always
07 for good
08 evermore
09 endlessly, eternally
10 constantly, for all time
11 continually, incessantly, permanently, perpetually
12 interminably, persistently
15 till kingdom come

**forewarn**
05 alert
06 advise, tip off
07 apprise, caution, previse
08 admonish, dissuade

**foreword**
07 preface
08 prologue
11 front-matter
12 introduction
13 preliminaries

**forfeit**
04 fine, lose, loss
06 forego, give up
07 abandon, damages, penalty
08 hand over, renounce
09 sacrifice, surrender
10 relinquish

**forfeiture**
04 loss
07 escheat
08 giving up
09 attainder, sacrifice, surrender
12 confiscation
13 sequestration
14 relinquishment

**forge**
04 cast, copy, fake, make, mold, work
05 feign, frame, shape
06 create, devise, invent, smithy

07 beat out, falsify, fashion
09 construct, hammer out
11 counterfeit, put together

❏**forge ahead**
07 advance
08 progress
09 go forward
11 make headway, move forward, push forward
12 make progress

**forger**
05 faker, smith
06 framer
09 contriver, falsifier
13 counterfeiter

**forgery**
04 copy, fake, sham
05 fraud, phony
06 faking
07 replica
09 imitation
11 counterfeit
12 reproduction
13 'falsification

**forget**
04 fail, omit
06 ignore
07 dismiss, let slip, neglect
08 overlook, put aside
09 disregard
11 lose sight of
12 slip your mind

❏**forget yourself**
09 misbehave
11 behave badly

**forgetful**
06 dreamy, remiss
08 careless, heedless
09 negligent, oblivious
10 abstracted, distracted
11 inattentive, preoccupied
12 absent-minded
14 scatterbrained

**forgetfulness**
05 lapse
07 amnesia, laxness
10 dreaminess
11 abstraction, inattention
12 carelessness, heedlessness
13 wool-gathering

**forgivable**
05 minor, petty
06 slight, venial
08 innocent, trifling
09 excusable
10 pardonable

**forgive**
05 clear, remit, spare
06 excuse, let off, pardon
07 absolve, condone, let it go

08 overlook, write off
09 exculpate, exonerate
14 bury the hatchet

**forgiveness**
05 mercy
06 pardon
07 amnesty
08 clemency, leniency
09 acquittal, remission
10 absolution
11 exoneration

**forgiving**
04 kind, mild
06 humane
07 clement, lenient
08 merciful, tolerant
09 indulgent
10 forbearing
11 magnanimous, soft-hearted
13 compassionate

**forgo**
05 waive, yield
06 eschew, give up, pass up
07 abandon, forfeit
08 renounce
09 do without, go without, sacrifice, surrender
10 relinquish
11 abstain from, refrain from

**forgotten**
04 gone, lost, past
06 buried, bygone
07 ignored, omitted
09 neglected, out of mind
10 overlooked, unrecalled
11 disregarded, obliterated
13 irrecoverable, irretrievable

**fork**
04 part
05 split
06 branch, divide
07 diverge
08 division, junction, separate
09 bifurcate, branching
10 divergence, separation
11 bifurcation

❏**fork out**
03 pay
04 give
05 pay up, spend
07 cough up
08 shell out

**forked**
05 split, tined
06 furcal
07 divided, furcate, Y-shaped
08 branched, furcular
09 bifurcate, branching, forficate, separated
11 divaricated

## forlorn
03 sad
04 lost
06 bereft, lonely
07 unhappy
08 deserted, desolate, forsaken, helpless, homeless, hopeless, pathetic, pitiable, wretched
09 abandoned, cheerless, desperate, destitute, forgotten, miserable
10 despairing, friendless
12 disconsolate

## form
03 cut
04 cast, grow, kind, make, mold, sort, trim, type, year
05 build, class, forge, found, frame, genre, genus, guise, model, order, paper, set up, shape, sheet, style
06 create, custom, design, devise, fettle, figure, format, make up, manner, nature, show up, stream, system
07 acquire, arrange, compose, develop, fashion, fitness, manners, outline, produce, species, spirits, variety
08 assemble, behavior, comprise, document, organize, planning, protocol
09 be a part of, condition, construct, establish, etiquette, formation, framework, structure, take shape
10 appearance, constitute, convention, silhouette
11 application, arrangement, crystallize, disposition, manufacture, materialize
12 construction, organization
13 configuration, manifestation, questionnaire

## formal
04 prim
05 aloof, exact, fixed, rigid, stiff
06 proper, remote, ritual, solemn, strict
07 correct, ordered, regular, starchy, stately, stilted
08 approved, official, orthodox, reserved
09 organized, unbending
10 ceremonial, controlled, inflexible, prescribed
11 ceremonious, established, punctilious, strait-laced, symmetrical, traditional
13 straight-laced

## formality
04 form, rule
06 custom, ritual
07 decorum, red tape
08 ceremony, protocol
09 etiquette, procedure, propriety, punctilio
10 convention, politeness
11 bureaucracy, correctness

## format
04 form, look, plan, type
05 order, shape, style
06 design, layout, makeup
09 structure
10 appearance, dimensions
11 arrangement
12 construction, presentation
13 configuration

## formation
05 order
06 design, figure, format, layout, makeup, making
07 pattern, phalanx, shaping
08 creation, founding, grouping
09 structure
10 appearance, production
11 arrangement, composition, development, disposition, institution, manufacture
12 construction, organization
13 configuration, establishment

## formative
06 pliant
07 growing, guiding, molding, shaping
08 dominant
09 malleable, teachable
11 controlling, determining, influential, susceptible
13 developmental
14 impressionable

## former
02 ex-
03 old
04 late, past
05 above, first, prior
06 bygone, of yore
07 ancient, earlier, old-time, onetime, quondam
08 departed, long-gone, previous, sometime
09 erstwhile, preceding
10 antecedent, historical
14 first-mentioned

## formerly
04 erst, once
06 before
07 earlier
08 hitherto
09 erstwhile, in the past
10 heretofore, previously

12 historically

## formidable
04 huge
05 great, scary
07 awesome, fearful
08 alarming, colossal, daunting, dreadful, horrific, menacing, powerful, terrific
10 horrifying, impressive, prodigious, staggering, terrifying, tremendous
11 challenging, frightening, redoubtable, threatening
12 intimidating, overwhelming

## formless
05 vague
07 chaotic
08 confused, inchoate, indigest, nebulous
09 amorphous, shapeless
10 incoherent, indefinite
12 disorganized
13 indeterminate

## formula
03 way
04 code, form, rule
06 method, recipe, rubric
08 equation
09 blueprint, principle, procedure, technique
12 prescription
15 fixed expression

## formulate
04 form, plan
05 found, frame, state
06 create, define, design, devise, draw up, evolve, invent
07 compose, develop, express, itemize, prepare, put down, set down, specify, think up
08 conceive
09 originate
10 articulate, give form to

## forsake
04 jilt, quit
05 ditch, forgo, leave
06 desert, disown, forego
07 abandon, cast off, discard
08 jettison, renounce, set aside
09 repudiate, surrender
10 relinquish
15 leave in the lurch

## forsaken
06 dreary, jilted, lonely, remote
07 cast off, forlorn, ignored
08 derelict, deserted, desolate, disowned, rejected
09 abandoned, destitute, discarded, neglected
10 friendless

**forswear**
03 lie
04 deny, drop
05 forgo
06 abjure, cut out, disown, forego, give up, pack in, recant, reject, renege
07 abandon, forsake, perjure, retract
08 disclaim, renounce
09 do without, repudiate

**fort**
04 camp, keep
05 tower
06 castle, donjon, turret
07 citadel, dungeon, redoubt, station
08 fortress, garrison
10 stronghold, watchtower
13 fortification

**forte**
04 bent, gift
06 métier, talent
08 aptitude, strength
09 specialty
11 strong point

**forth**
03 off, out
05 ahead
06 onward, onward
07 forward, outside
08 forwards, into view
13 into existence

**forthcoming**
04 open
05 frank, on tap, ready
06 chatty, coming, future
08 imminent, sociable
09 available, expansive, impending, talkative
10 accessible, loquacious
11 approaching, prospective
13 communicative
14 conversational

**forthright**
04 bold, open
05 blunt, frank, plain
06 candid, direct, honest
09 outspoken
11 plain-spoken
15 straightforward

**forthwith**
06 at once, pronto
07 quickly
08 directly
09 instantly, right away
11 immediately
12 straightaway, without delay

**fortification**
04 fort, keep

06 castle
07 bastion, bulwark, citadel, defense, parapet, rampart
08 fortress, palisade, stockade
09 barricade, earthwork
10 protection, stronghold
11 battlements, buttressing
12 entrenchment
13 reinforcement, strengthening

**fortify**
05 boost, cheer, cover, guard
06 defend, revive, secure
07 hearten, protect, shore up, support, sustain
08 buttress, energize, garrison
09 encourage, reinforce
10 invigorate, strengthen

**fortitude**
04 grit
05 nerve, pluck, spine, valor
06 mettle
07 bravery, courage
08 backbone, firmness, patience, stoicism, tenacity
09 endurance, willpower
10 resolution
11 forbearance·
12 perseverance
13 determination

**fortress**
04 keep
05 tower
06 castle
07 citadel
08 fastness, garrison
10 stronghold
13 fortification

**fortuitous**
05 fluky, lucky
06 casual, chance, random
09 arbitrary, fortunate
10 accidental, unforeseen
12 providential

**fortunate**
05 happy, lucky
06 timely
07 blessed, favored, well-off
08 well-to-do
09 favorable, opportune, promising
10 auspicious, convenient, felicitous, profitable, propitious
11 encouraging, flourishing
12 advantageous, providential

**fortunately**
07 happily, luckily
12 conveniently
14 providentially

**fortune**
03 cup, lot, wad
04 bomb, fate, luck, mint, pile
05 piles
06 assets, bundle, chance, estate, future, income, riches, wealth
07 destiny, history, success
08 accident, big bucks, opulence, property
09 affluence, condition, megabucks, situation
10 prosperity, providence
11 coincidence, serendipity
13 circumstances

**fortuneteller**
04 seer
05 augur, sibyl
06 oracle
07 diviner, palmist, prophet, psychic
09 visionary
10 astrologer, prophetess, soothsayer
12 crystal gazer

**forum**
05 arena, stage
07 meeting, rostrum
08 assembly
09 symposium
10 conference, discussion
12 meetingplace

**forward, forwards**
02 on
03 aid, out
04 back, bold, fore, head, help, mail, post, send, ship
05 ahead, brash, cocky, favor, forth, fresh, front, pushy, speed
06 assist, brazen, cheeky, future, hasten, onward, send on, step up
07 advance, deliver, frontal, further, go-ahead, leading, onwards, promote
08 advanced, dispatch, expedite, familiar, foremost, impudent
09 advancing, audacious, barefaced, confident, premature, presuming, thrusting, transport
10 accelerate, aggressive, facilitate, precocious
11 impertinent, progressive
12 enterprising, overfamiliar, presumptuous
13 overconfident

**forward-looking**
06 modern

## forwardness

07 dynamic, go-ahead, liberal
09 go-getting, reforming
10 avant-garde, far-sighted, innovative
11 enlightened, progressive
12 enterprising

## forwardness

05 cheek
08 audacity, boldness, pertness
09 impudence, pushiness
10 brazenness, cheekiness
11 presumption
12 impertinence
14 over-confidence

## fossil

05 amber, relic
06 dolite
07 old fogy, remains, remnant
08 ammonite, calamite, old fogey
09 coprolite, reliquiae, trilobite
10 fuddy-duddy, graptolite

## fossilized

04 dead
05 passé, stony
07 archaic, extinct
08 hardened, obsolete, ossified, outmoded
09 out of date, petrified
11 prehistoric
12 antediluvian, old-fashioned
13 anachronistic

## foster

03 aid
04 back, feed, help, hold, rear
05 boost, nurse, raise
06 assist, harbor, uphold
07 advance, bring up, care for, cherish, further, nourish, nurture, support
09 cultivate, encourage, look after, stimulate
10 take care of

## foul

03 bad, jam, low, wet
04 base, blue, clog, lewd, mean, rank, soil, vile, wild
05 block, catch, choke, crime, dirty, fetid, gross, muddy, nasty, rainy, rough, snarl, stain, sully, taint, twist
06 coarse, defile, filthy, impure, odious, putrid, ribald, rotten, smelly, smutty, soiled, tangle, vulgar, wicked
07 abusive, blacken, decayed, defiled, ensnare, heinous,

obscene, pollute, profane, rotting, squalid, squally, tainted, unclean, vicious
08 blustery, entangle, horrible, indecent, infected, obstruct, off-color, polluted, shameful, stinking
09 abhorrent, execrable, loathsome, nefarious, offensive, repulsive, revolting, sickening
10 abominable, despicable, disgusting, iniquitous, nauseating, putrescent
11 blasphemous, contaminate
12 contaminated, contemptible, putrefactive

## ❑foul play

05 crime
06 murder
08 homicide
09 deception, dirty work
13 double-dealing, funny business, sharp practice

## foul-mouthed

06 coarse
07 abusive, obscene, profane
09 offensive
11 blasphemous

## found

03 fix, set
04 base, rest, root
05 build, endow, erect, plant, raise, set up, start
06 bottom, locate, settle
08 initiate, organize, position
09 construct, establish, institute, originate
10 constitute, inaugurate

## foundation

03 key
04 base, core, foot
05 basis, heart
06 bottom, ground, reason
07 bedrock, footing, keynote, premise, reasons, support
08 creation, founding
09 endowment, principle, rationale, setting-up
10 groundwork, hypostasis, initiation, substratum
11 fundamental, institution
12 constitution, fundamentals, inauguration, organization, substructure, underpinning
13 establishment
14 understructure
15 first principles

## founder

04 fail, fall, sink
05 abort, maker

06 father, go down
07 builder, capsize, creator, go wrong, misfire, subside
08 collapse, miscarry, submerge
09 architect, developer, initiator, matriarch, organizer, patriarch
10 benefactor, discoverer, originator, prime mover
11 come to grief, fall through

## foundling

04 waif
05 stray
06 orphan, urchin
07 outcast

## fountain

03 jet
04 rise, well
05 fount, spout, spray, spurt
06 origin, source, spring
09 beginning, inception
10 waterworks, wellspring
12 commencement, fountainhead

## foursquare

06 firmly
07 frankly, solidly
08 honestly, squarely
10 resolutely

## fowl

03 hen
04 bird, cock, duck
05 goose, quail
06 bantam, turkey
07 chicken, poultry
08 pheasant, wildfowl

## foxy

03 fly, sly
04 wily
05 canny, sharp
06 artful, crafty, shrewd, tricky
07 cunning, devious, knowing
08 guileful

## foyer

04 hall
05 lobby
09 reception, vestibule
11 antechamber
12 entrance hall

## fracas

03 row
04 riot, rout
05 aggro, brawl, fight, melee
06 affray, barney, ruckus, rumpus, shindy, uproar
07 quarrel, scuffle, trouble
10 donnybrook, free-for-all
11 disturbance

## fraction
03 bit
04 part
05 ratio
06 amount
11 subdivision

## fractious
05 cross, testy
06 crabby, grumpy, touchy
07 awkward, fretful, grouchy
08 captious, choleric, petulant
09 crotchety, irritable
10 refractory
11 bad-tempered, quarrelsome
12 recalcitrant

## fracture
03 gap
04 chip, rent, rift, slit
05 break, cleft, crack, split
06 breach, schism
07 fissure, opening, rupture
08 aperture, breakage, splinter
09 splitting

## fragile
04 fine, weak
05 frail
06 dainty, flimsy, infirm, slight
07 brittle
08 delicate, unstable
09 breakable, frangible
13 insubstantial

## fragility
07 frailty
08 delicacy, weakness
11 brittleness
12 frangibility

## fragment
03 bit
04 chip, part, snip
05 break, crumb, piece, scrap, shard, shred, split
06 divide, morsel, shiver, sliver
07 break up, crumble, portion, remains, remnant, shatter, snippet, split up
08 disunite, particle, splinter
12 come to pieces, disintegrate

## fragmentary
06 broken, uneven
07 partial, scrappy, sketchy
09 piecemeal, scattered
10 disjointed, incomplete
12 disconnected

## fragrance
04 balm, nose, odor, otto
05 aroma, attar, scent, smell
07 bouquet, incense, perfume
09 redolence

## fragrant
05 balmy, sweet
07 odorous, scented
08 aromatic, perfumed, redolent
11 odoriferous
13 sweet-smelling

## frail
04 puny, weak
06 feeble, infirm, slight, unwell
07 brittle, fragile, unsound
09 breakable, frangible
10 vulnerable
11 susceptible
13 insubstantial

## frailty
04 flaw
05 fault
06 defect, foible
07 blemish, failing
08 delicacy, weakness
09 fragility, infirmity, weak point
10 deficiency
11 fallibility, shortcoming
12 imperfection
13 vulnerability

## frame
04 body, case, edge, form, make, mold, plan, plot, size, trap
05 build, fit up, mount, pin on, plant, set up, shell
06 border, casing, cook up, create, devise, encase, figure, map out, sketch
07 carcass, chassis, compose, enclose, setting, support
08 bodywork, conceive, mounting, physique, skeleton, surround
09 construct, formulate, framework, structure
11 incriminate, manufacture, put together
12 construction, substructure

## ❏frame of mind
04 mood
05 humor, state
06 spirit, temper
07 outlook
08 attitude
09 condition
11 disposition, state of mind

## frame-up
03 fix
04 trap
08 put-up job
11 fabrication
15 trumped-up charge

## framework
04 plan, rack
05 frame, shell
06 casing, fabric, scheme
07 lattice, outline, trestle
08 skeleton
09 bare bones, structure
10 foundation, groundwork
12 substructure

## franchise
05 right
07 charter, consent, freedom, liberty, license, warrant
08 immunity, suffrage
09 exemption, privilege
10 concession, permission
13 authorization
15 enfranchisement

## frank
04 free, mark, open
05 bluff, blunt, plain, stamp
06 candid, direct, honest
07 genuine, sincere, upfront
08 explicit, postmark, truthful
09 downright, outspoken
10 forthright
11 plain-spoken
15 straightforward

## frankly
06 freely, openly
07 bluntly, in truth, plainly
08 candidly, directly, honestly
09 to be blunt, to be frank
10 explicitly, truthfully

## frankness
06 candor
08 openness
09 bluntness, sincerity
10 directness
12 truthfulness
13 outspokenness, plain speaking
14 forthrightness

## frantic
03 mad
04 wild
06 hectic, raging, raving
07 berserk, fraught, furious
08 agitated, frenetic, frenzied
09 desperate
10 distracted, distraught
11 overwrought
13 at your wits' end, panic-stricken

## fraternity
04 clan, club
05 guild, order, union
07 company, kinship, society
10 fellowship
11 association, brotherhood, camaraderie, comradeship

**fraternize**
03 mix
05 unite
06 hobnob, mingle
07 consort
09 associate, socialize
11 keep company
12 rub shoulders

**fraud**
03 con, fix
04 fake, hoax, scam, sham
05 cheat, guile, phony, quack, trick
06 deceit, diddle, hoaxer, racket, rip-off
07 bluffer, forgery
08 cheating, impostor, swindler, trickery
09 charlatan, chicanery, deception, pretender, swindling, trickster
10 mountebank
11 counterfeit, fraudulence
12 embezzlement
13 double-dealing, sharp practice

**fraudulent**
04 sham
05 bogus, false, phony, shady
07 crooked
08 cheating, criminal
09 deceitful, deceptive, dishonest, swindling
11 counterfeit, duplicitous
13 double-dealing

**fraught**
04 full
05 laden, tense
06 filled
07 anxious, charged, uptight
08 agitated, attended
09 abounding, bristling
10 distraught, distressed
11 accompanied, overwrought, stressed out

**fray**
03 row, vex
04 riot, wear
05 brawl, clash, fight, set-to
06 battle, combat, dust-up, rumpus, strain, stress
07 frazzle, scuffle, unravel
08 conflict, irritate, wear thin
09 challenge, put on edge
10 excitement, free-for-all
12 become ragged

**frayed**
04 thin, worn
06 ragged
08 tattered, worn thin
09 unraveled

10 threadbare

**freak**
03 fan, nut, odd
04 buff, turn, whim
05 fiend, fluky, quirk, twist
06 addict, chance, mutant, oddity, vagary, weirdo
07 anomaly, bizarre, erratic, monster, oddball, unusual
08 aberrant, abnormal, atypical, mutation, surprise
09 curiosity, deformity
10 aberration, unexpected
11 exceptional, monstrosity
12 irregularity, malformation

**freakish**
03 odd
05 weird
06 fitful, freaky
07 erratic, strange, unusual
08 aberrant, abnormal, fanciful
09 fantastic, grotesque, malformed, monstrous
10 capricious, outlandish
13 unpredictable
14 unconventional

**free**
03 out, rid
04 easy, idle, open, save
05 clear, empty, fluid, let go, loose, spare, untie, vague
06 acquit, casual, exempt, freely, giving, gratis, lavish, let out, ransom, rescue, tied up, unbind, vacant
07 absolve, at large, clear of, deliver, inexact, lacking, liberal, natural, relaxed, release, relieve, unchain, untaken, without
08 at no cost, devoid of, generous, lavishly, liberate, set loose, unburden
09 at liberty, available, copiously, disengage, easygoing, extricate, imprecise, liberally, liberated, sovereign, turn loose
10 abundantly, autonomous, charitable, democratic, emancipate, exempt from, for nothing, generously, munificent, on the house, on the loose, openhanded, unattached, unconfined, unemployed, unhampered, unoccupied, unstinting
11 disentangle, emancipated, free as a bird, independent, spontaneous, uninhibited
12 free of charge, unaffected by, unrestrained

13 at no extra cost, complimentary, self-governing

❑**free and easy**
06 casual
07 relaxed
08 carefree, informal
09 easygoing
11 spontaneous
12 happy-go-lucky

❑**free hand**
05 power, scope
07 freedom, liberty
08 latitude
10 discretion
12 carte blanche

**free will**
07 autarky, freedom, liberty
08 autonomy, volition
11 spontaneity
12 independence
15 self-sufficiency

**freedom**
04 play
05 power, range, right, scope
06 leeway, margin
07 liberty, license, release
08 autonomy, free hand, free rein, home rule, immunity, impunity, latitude
09 democracy, exemption
11 deliverance, flexibility, informality, sovereignty
12 emancipation, independence
14 self-government

**freely**
05 amply
06 easily, openly
07 bluntly, plainly, readily
08 candidly, lavishly
09 liberally, willingly
10 abundantly, generously
11 voluntarily
12 unreservedly
13 spontaneously

**freethinker**
05 deist
07 doubter, infidel, skeptic
08 agnostic
10 unbeliever
11 rationalist

**freeze**
03 fix, ice, set
04 cool, halt, hold, stay, stop
05 chill, frost, ice up
06 harden, quiver, shiver
07 congeal, embargo, get cold, ice over, stiffen, suspend

08 freeze up, glaciate, shut down, shutdown, solidify, stoppage
10 deep freeze, immobilize, moratorium, stand still, standstill, suspension

**freezing**
03 icy, raw
04 cold, numb
05 polar
06 arctic, biting, bitter, chilly, frosty, wintry
07 cutting, glacial, ice-cold, numbing
08 piercing, stinging
12 bitterly cold

**freight**
04 load
05 cargo, goods
06 lading
07 haulage, payload, portage
08 carriage, contents, shipment
09 transport
10 conveyance, freightage
11 consignment, merchandise

**frenetic**
03 mad
04 wild
06 hectic, insane
07 berserk, excited, frantic
08 demented, frenzied
10 distraught, hysterical
11 hyperactive, overwrought

**frenzied**
03 mad
04 amok, wild
06 crazed, hectic, raving
07 berserk, frantic, furious
08 demented, feverish, frenetic
09 desperate, obsessive
10 distracted, distraught
11 overwrought
12 out of control, uncontrolled
13 at your wits' end
14 beside yourself

**frenzy**
03 fit
04 bout, fury, rage
05 burst, fever, mania, spasm
07 madness, seizure, turmoil
08 hysteria, insanity, outburst, paroxysm, wildness
09 agitation, transport
11 derangement, distraction

**frequency**
09 constancy, incidence
10 commonness, prevalence, recurrence, repetition
12 frequentness

**frequent**
05 haunt, usual, visit
06 attend, common, normal
08 everyday, familiar, habitual, numerous, repeated
09 countless, customary, hang out at, patronize, prevalent, recurring
11 commonplace
13 go to regularly
14 go to frequently, happening often

**frequenter**
06 client, patron
07 habitué, haunter, regular
08 customer
14 regular visitor

**frequently**
04 much
05 often
08 commonly
09 many a time, many times
10 oftentimes, repeatedly
11 customarily, over and over

**fresh**
03 new, raw
04 bold, cool, fair, keen, more, pert, pink, pure, rosy
05 alert, brisk, clean, clear, cocky, crisp, crude, extra, novel, other, saucy, vital
06 brazen, bright, cheeky, chilly, latest, recent, rested
07 bracing, forward, glowing, healthy, natural, renewed, revived, unfaded, unusual
08 blooming, bouncing, brand-new, exciting, familiar, impudent, insolent, original, up-to-date, vigorous
09 different, refreshed
10 additional, innovative, raring to go, unpolluted
11 unpreserved, unprocessed
12 overfamiliar, presumptuous, ready for more
13 disrespectful, fresh as a daisy, supplementary
14 unconventional

**freshen**
03 air
05 clean, clear, liven, rouse
06 purify, revive
07 enliven, refresh, restore
09 deodorize, ventilate
10 revitalize
12 reinvigorate

❑**freshen up**
09 get washed
12 wash yourself
14 tidy yourself up

**freshman**
05 frosh, plebe
08 beginner
09 first-year
13 underclassman

**freshness**
04 glow
05 bloom, shine
07 newness, novelty, sparkle
09 cleanness, clearness
10 brightness
11 originality
13 wholesomeness

**fret**
03 vex
04 mope, pine, rile
05 anger, annoy, brood, worry
06 bother, nettle
07 anguish, be upset, trouble
08 irritate
09 be anxious, make a fuss
12 be distressed

**fretful**
04 edgy
05 tense, upset
06 uneasy
07 anxious, fearful, unhappy, uptight, worried
08 restless, troubled
09 disturbed
10 distressed

**friable**
05 crisp
07 brittle, crumbly, powdery

**friar**
03 Fra
04 monk
05 abbot, prior
07 brother
09 mendicant

**friction**
06 strife
07 arguing, chafing, discord, erosion, gnawing, grating, rasping, rivalry, rubbing
08 bad blood, clashing, conflict, scraping, traction
09 animosity, attrition, hostility
10 antagonism, bad feeling, disharmony, dissension, ill feeling, irritation, quarreling, resentment, resistance
11 disputation, excoriation, wearing away
12 disagreement

**friend**
03 pal
04 ally, chum, mate
05 amigo, buddy, crony
06 backer, patron

07 comrade, partner, sponsor
08 familiar, intimate, playmate
09 associate, companion, confidant, supporter
10 benefactor, confidante, subscriber, well-wisher
11 bosom friend, close friend
12 acquaintance

**friendless**
05 alone
06 lonely
07 forlorn, shunned, unloved
08 isolated, lonesome, solitary
09 abandoned, unpopular
10 by yourself, ostracized
12 unbefriended
13 companionless
14 coldshouldered

**friendliness**
06 warmth
08 kindness
09 geniality
10 affability, amiability
11 hospitality, sociability
12 congeniality, conviviality
13 gemütlichkeit
15 approachability

**friendly**
04 fond, kind, warm
05 close, thick, tight
06 chummy, genial, kindly
07 amiable, cordial, helpful
08 amicable, familiar, intimate, outgoing, sociable
09 agreeable, comradely, congenial, convivial, favorable, receptive, welcoming
10 hospitable, neighborly, palsy-walsy
11 good-natured, inseparable, sympathetic
12 affectionate, approachable
13 companionable

**friendship**
04 love
05 amity
06 warmth
07 concord, harmony, rapport
08 affinity, alliance, fondness, goodwill, intimacy
09 affection, closeness
10 amiability, kindliness
11 comradeship, familiarity
12 friendliness
13 companionship, understanding

**fright**
04 fear, funk
05 alarm, panic, scare, shock
06 creeps, dismay, horror, terror

07 jitters, shivers, willies
09 cold sweat
10 blind panic
11 fearfulness, trepidation
12 apprehension, perturbation
13 consternation, heebie-jeebies, knocking knees

**frighten**
05 alarm, daunt, panic, scare, shock, unman
06 appall, dismay, rattle
07 petrify, startle, terrify, unnerve
09 terrorize
10 intimidate, scare silly, scare stiff

**frightened**
05 cowed
06 afraid, frozen, scared
07 alarmed, panicky, trembly
08 startled, unnerved
09 petrified, terrified
10 terrorized
11 in a blue funk, scared silly, scared stiff
13 panic-stricken, scared to death
14 terror-stricken

**frightening**
04 grim
05 hairy, scary
06 creepy, spooky
08 alarming, fearsome
09 traumatic
10 forbidding, formidable, petrifying, terrifying
11 hair-raising
13 bloodcurdling, spine-chilling

**frightful**
04 dire, grim
05 awful, nasty
06 grisly, horrid, odious
07 fearful, ghastly, hideous
08 alarming, dreadful, gruesome, horrible, shocking, terrible
09 abhorrent, appalling, harrowing, loathsome, repulsive, revolting

**frigid**
03 icy
04 cold, cool
05 aloof, chill, polar
06 arctic, bitter, chilly, formal, frosty, frozen, wintry
07 distant, glacial, passive
08 freezing, unloving
09 unfeeling
11 passionless
12 unresponsive

**frigidity**
05 chill
07 iciness
08 coldness
09 aloofness, passivity, stiffness
10 chilliness, frostiness
15 cold-heartedness

**frill**
04 fold, ruff, tuck
05 extra, jabot, ruche
06 finery, fringe, purfle, ruffle
07 flounce, orphrey, valance
08 frippery, furbelow, trimming
09 accessory, fanciness, fandangle, gathering
10 decoration, frilliness
11 ostentation, superfluity
13 embellishment, ornamentation

**frilly**
04 lacy
05 fancy
06 ornate
07 frilled, ruffled, trimmed
08 gathered

**fringe**
03 rim
04 edge, trim
05 frill, limit, skirt, verge
06 border, edging, margin
08 surround, trimming
09 outskirts, perimeter, periphery
10 borderline
13 fringe benefit

**fringed**
05 edged
07 trimmed
08 bordered, tasseled
10 fimbriated

**frippery**
05 froth
06 finery, frills, trivia
07 baubles, gewgaws, trifles
08 glad rags, nonsense, trinkets
09 fussiness, gaudiness, ornaments, showiness
10 adornments, fandangles, flashiness, frilliness, tawdriness, triviality
11 decorations, knickknacks
15 pretentiousness

**frisk**
03 hop
04 leap, play, romp, skip, trip
05 caper, check, dance, sport
06 bounce, cavort, frolic, gambol, prance, search
09 shake down, shakedown
10 body-search

**frisky**
04 high
05 hyper
06 active, bouncy, lively
07 dashing, playful, romping
08 spirited
09 exuberant
10 frolicsome, rollicking
11 full of beans
12 high-spirited
13 in high spirits

**fritter**
04 blow, cake, idle
05 waste
06 misuse
08 misspend, squander
09 dissipate, go through, overspend
10 get through
14 spend like water

**frivolity**
03 fun
04 jest
05 folly
06 gaiety, levity
08 nonsense
09 flippancy, pettiness, silliness
10 triviality
11 foolishness
13 facetiousness, senselessness
14 superficiality

**frivolous**
04 idle, vain, zany
05 inane, light, merry, petty, silly
07 flighty, foolish, jocular, puerile, shallow, trivial
08 flippant, juvenile, trifling
09 facetious, pointless
11 superficial, unimportant
12 lighthearted

**frizzy**
04 wiry
05 crisp, curly
06 curled
07 crimped, frizzed

**frolic**
03 fun, hop
04 game, lark, leap, romp, skip
05 caper, dance, frisk, mirth, prank, revel, sport, spree
06 antics, bounce, cavort, gaiety, gambol, prance
08 escapade
09 amusement, high jinks, make merry, merriment

**frolicsome**
03 gay
05 merry
06 frisky, lively
07 coltish, playful
08 skittish, sportive

**front**
03 air, bow, top
04 face, fore, head, lead, look, mask, meet, show
05 blind, cover, first
06 aspect, before, facade, facing, manner, oppose
07 leading, outside, pretext
08 confront, disguise, exterior, foremost, forepart, frontage, pretense, vanguard
09 forefront, front line
10 appearance, foreground
11 countenance

❏ **in front**
05 ahead, first
06 before
07 leading
09 in advance, preceding, to the fore

**frontier**
04 edge
05 limit, verge
06 border, bounds
07 outpost
08 boundary, confines
09 perimeter
10 borderline, wilderness

**frost**
04 hoar, rime
06 freeze
08 coldness, freeze-up
09 hoarfrost, Jack Frost

**frosty**
03 icy
04 cold, cool, rimy
05 aloof, nippy, polar, stiff
06 arctic, chilly, frozen, wintry
07 glacial, hostile
08 freezing
10 unfriendly
11 standoffish, unwelcoming
12 bitterly cold, discouraging

**froth**
04 fizz, foam, head, scum, suds
05 spume, spumy
06 bubble, lather
07 bubbles, ferment, spumous
13 effervescence

**frothy**
04 vain
05 empty, fizzy, foamy, sudsy
06 bubbly, slight, yeasty
07 foaming, spumous, trivial
08 bubbling, trifling
09 frivolous
10 spumescent
13 insubstantial

**frown**
04 lour, pout

05 glare, scowl
06 glower
07 grimace
09 dirty look
13 look daggers at

❏ **frown on**
07 dislike, grimace
08 object to
10 discourage
12 disapprove of, think badly of
14 take a dim view of

**frowsy**
05 dirty, messy
06 frumpy, sloppy, untidy
07 unkempt
08 frumpish, sluttish, unwashed
09 ungroomed
10 disheveled, slatternly

**frozen**
03 icy, raw
04 hard, iced, numb
05 fixed, polar, rigid, stiff
06 arctic, frigid, frosty
07 chilled, frosted, ice-cold
08 freezing, icebound
10 ice-covered, solidified
12 bitterly cold

**frugal**
06 meager, paltry, scanty
07 careful, sparing, thrifty
09 penny-wise, provident
10 economical, inadequate

**fruit**
04 crop
05 yield
06 effect, profit, result, return
07 benefit, harvest, outcome, produce, product
09 advantage, offspring
11 consequence

► *Types of fruit*:
03 fig
04 date, kaki, kiwi, lime, pear, plum, sloe
05 apple, grape, guava, lemon, mango, melon, olive, papaw, peach
06 banana, casaba, cherry, damson, lychee, orange, papaya, pawpaw, pomelo, quince, tomato
07 apricot, avocado, kumquat, rhubarb, satsuma
08 bilberry, dewberry, honeydew, mandarin
09 blueberry, cantaloup, crab apple, cranberry, greengage, muskmelon, nectarine, persimmon, pineapple, raspberry, star fruit,

tangerine, ugli fruit
10 blackberry, cantaloupe, clementine, elderberry, gooseberry, grapefruit, loganberry, redcurrant, strawberry, watermelon
11 boysenberry, huckleberry, pomegranate
12 blackcurrant, custard-apple, passion fruit
➤ See also FOOD

**fruitful**
04 rich
06 fecund, useful
07 fertile, teeming
08 abundant, prolific
09 effective, rewarding, well-spent
10 beneficial, productive, profitable, worthwhile
11 efficacious
12 advantageous, fruit-bearing

**fruitfulness**
09 fecundity, fertility
10 usefulness
13 profitability

**fruition**
07 success
08 maturity, ripeness
10 attainment, completion, perfection
11 achievement, fulfillment, realization
12 consummation

**fruitless**
04 idle, vain
06 barren, futile
07 sterile, useless
08 abortive, hopeless
09 pointless, worthless
11 ineffectual
12 unproductive, unsuccessful

**fruity**
04 full, nuts, rich
05 crazy, juicy, nutty, spicy
06 mellow
08 resonant
09 fruitlike

**frumpy**
04 drab
05 dated, dingy, dowdy
06 dreary
09 out of date

**frustrate**
04 balk, foil, stop
05 anger, annoy, baulk, block, check, stymy
06 defeat, hamper, hinder, impede, stymie, thwart
07 counter, inhibit, nullify

08 embitter, irritate, obstruct
09 forestall
10 circumvent, disappoint, dissatisfy, neutralize

**frustrated**
05 angry
07 annoyed
08 blighted, thwarted
09 repressed, resentful
10 embittered
12 disappointed, discontented, disheartened, dissatisfied

**frustration**
05 anger
06 defeat
07 balking, failure, foiling
08 baulking, blocking, vexation
09 annoyance, thwarting
10 irritation, resentment
11 obstruction
14 disappointment, nonfulfillment
15 dissatisfaction

**fuddled**
04 hazy
05 drunk, muzzy, tipsy, woozy
06 groggy
07 bemused, muddled, sozzled
08 confused
10 inebriated
11 intoxicated

**fuddy-duddy**
04 prim
05 fussy
06 fossil, square, stuffy
07 old fogy
08 old fogey
11 museum piece, old-fogeyish
12 conservative, old-fashioned, stuffed shirt
13 stick-in-the-mud

**fudge**
04 fake
05 cheat, dodge, evade, hedge, stall
06 fiddle
07 falsify, shuffle
10 equivocate
12 misrepresent

**fuel**
03 fan
04 feed, fire
05 stoke
07 inflame, nourish, stoke up
09 encourage, incentive
10 ammunition, propellant
11 combustible, provocation
13 encouragement

▶ *Types of fuel:*
03 gas, log, oil

04 coal, coke, peat, wood
06 butane, diesel, Sterno
07 briquet, methane, propane
08 charcoal, firewood, gasoline, kerosene, kindling, paraffin
09 briquette, petroleum
10 fossil fuel
11 electricity
12 nuclear power
14 liquid hydrogen

**fugitive**
05 brief, short
06 flying
07 escapee, refugee, runaway
08 deserter, fleeting
09 ephemeral, fugacious, temporary, transient
10 short-lived, transitory

**fulfill**
04 fill, keep, meet, obey
06 answer, effect, finish
07 achieve, execute, satisfy
08 carry out, complete
09 conform to, discharge, implement
10 accomplish, comply with

**fulfilled**
05 happy
07 content, pleased
09 gratified, satisfied

**fulfillment**
07 success
09 discharge, execution
10 completion, observance
11 achievement, realization
12 consummation, satisfaction
14 accomplishment

**full**
03 fat
04 busy, deep, loud, rich, wide
05 ample, buxom, clear, laden, large, plump, round, sated, stout, total, whole
06 active, entire, filled, gorged, jammed, loaded, packed, rotund, strong, utmost
07 bulging, copious, crammed, crowded, highest, maximum, replete, shapely, stuffed
08 abundant, brimming, bursting, complete, detailed, directly, generous, resonant, satiated, squarely, straight, thorough, to the top
09 corpulent, extensive, packed out, satisfied
10 exhaustive, sufficient, unabridged, voluminous
11 overflowing, well-stocked
12 all-inclusive, loose-fitting

13 comprehensive

**❏in full**
05 fully, uncut
06 wholly
07 in total
08 in detail
10 completely
13 in its entirety

**❏to the full**
05 fully
07 utterly
08 entirely
10 thoroughly
11 to the utmost

**full-blooded**
06 hearty
07 devoted
08 thorough, vigorous
09 committed, dedicated
12 enthusiastic, wholehearted

**full-grown**
04 ripe
05 adult, of age
06 mature
07 grown-up
09 developed, full-blown
10 fully grown
12 fullyfledged

**fullness**
04 fill, glut
06 growth, plenty, wideth
07 breadth, satiety, variety
08 dilation, loudness, richness, strength, swelling, totality
09 abundance, ampleness, largeness, repletion, resonance, satedness, satiation, wholeness
10 tumescence
11 enlargement, shapeliness
12 completeness
13 extensiveness

**❏in the fullness of time**
07 finally
08 in the end
10 eventually, ultimately
11 in due course

**full-scale**
05 major
06 all-out
07 in-depth
08 complete, thorough
09 extensive, intensive
10 exhaustive
11 wideranging
13 comprehensive
15 all-encompassing

**fully**
05 quite
06 wholly

07 totally, utterly
08 entirely
09 perfectly
10 altogether, completely, positively, thoroughly
13 in all respects
14 without reserve

**fully-fledged**
06 mature, senior
07 trained
08 graduate
09 full-blown, qualified
14 fully-developed

**fulminate**
04 fume, rage, rail
05 curse, decry
07 condemn, declaim, explode, inveigh
08 denounce, detonate
09 criticize
10 animadvert, vituperate

**fulmination**
06 tirade
07 decrial, obloquy
08 diatribe
09 criticism, explosion, invective, philippic
12 condemnation, denunciation

**fulsome**
05 gross, slimy
07 buttery, cloying, fawning
08 effusive, nauseous, overdone, unctuous
09 excessive, insincere, offensive, sickening
10 inordinate, nauseating, saccharine
11 extravagant, sycophantic
12 ingratiating

**fumble**
04 drop, feel
05 botch, grope, spoil
06 bungle
08 flounder, scrabble
09 mishandle, mismanage

**fume**
03 gas
04 boil, rage, rant, rave
05 smoke, steam, storm, vapor
06 seethe
07 be livid, smolder
09 be furious
11 rant and rave

**fumes**
03 fog, gas
04 haze, reek, smog
05 smell, smoke, stink, vapor
06 stench
07 exhaust

**fumigate**
06 purify
07 cleanse
08 sanitize
09 deodorize, disinfect

**fuming**
05 angry, livid
06 raging
07 boiling, enraged, furious
08 incensed, seething

**fun**
03 joy
04 game, play, romp
05 mirth, sport, witty
06 joking, laughs, lively
07 amusing, jesting, jollity
08 hilarity, laughter, pleasure
09 amusement, diverting, enjoyable, enjoyment
10 recreation, relaxation, skylarking, tomfoolery
11 celebration, distraction, merrymaking, pleasurable
12 entertaining, recreational
13 entertainment

**❏for fun**
08 for kicks
09 for a laugh
12 for enjoyment
14 for the hell of it

**❏in fun**
06 in jest
07 as a joke, to tease
08 jokingly
09 for a laugh, teasingly
13 tongue in cheek

**❏make fun of**
03 rib
04 mock
05 taunt, tease
06 deride, jeer at, send up
07 scoff at, sneer at
08 ridicule
09 humiliate, poke fun at
15 pull someone's leg

**function**
02 do, go
03 act, job, run, use
04 duty, post, role, task, work
05 chore, party, serve
06 affair, behave, dinner
07 operate, perform, purpose
08 capacity, luncheon
09 gathering, reception
11 social event
14 responsibility

**functional**
05 handy
06 useful
07 running, utility, working

09 operative, practical
11 hard-wearing, operational,
serviceable, utilitarian

**functionary**
07 officer
08 employee, official
09 dignitary
10 bureaucrat
12 officeholder

**fund**
04 back, cash, mine, pool, well
05 cache, endow, float, hoard,
kitty, money, stock, store
06 assets, supply, wealth
07 capital, finance, reserve,
savings, sponsor, support
09 endowment, reservoir,
resources, slush fund,
subsidize, trust fund
10 capitalize, collection,
foundation, repository,
storehouse, underwrite
12 accumulation

**fundamental**
03 key
04 main
05 basic, chief, first, prime
07 central, crucial, primary
08 integral, original, profound
09 elemental, essential,
important, principal
10 elementary, underlying
11 rudimentary
13 indispensable

**fundamentally**
07 at heart
08 at bottom, deep down
09 basically, primarily
10 inherently
11 essentially
13 intrinsically

**fundamentals**
04 laws
05 facts, rules
06 basics
09 rudiments
10 brass tacks, essentials
11 necessaries, nitty-gritty
15 first principles

**funeral**
04 wake
06 burial
08 exequies
09 cremation, interment,
obsequies
10 entombment, inhumation

**funereal**
04 dark
05 grave

06 dismal, dreary, gloomy,
solemn, somber, woeful
07 serious
08 exequial, mournful
09 deathlike
10 depressing, sepulchral

**fungus**
07 fungous

▶ *Types of fungus*:
04 rust, scab, smut
05 ergot, yeast
06 blight
08 botrytis, gray mold,
mushroom, puffball
09 black rust, black spot, slime
mold, toadstool
10 myxomycete
11 penicillium, slime fungus
12 brewer's yeast
➤ See also MUSHROOM

**funk**
04 odor
05 dodge, smell
06 balk at, blench, cop out
07 baulk at
08 blue funk
09 duck out of, shirk from
10 flinch from, recoil from
12 chicken out of

**funnel**
04 cone, move, pass, pour
06 convey, direct, filter, siphon
07 channel

**funny**
03 odd
05 a hoot, comic, droll, queer,
shady, wacky, weird, witty
06 absurd, way-out
07 a scream, amusing, bizarre,
comical, curious, dubious,
killing, oddball, offbeat,
risible, strange, unusual
08 farcical, humorous, peculiar
09 hilarious, laughable
10 hysterical, perplexing,
suspicious, uproarious
12 entertaining
13 side-splitting

**fur**
04 coat, down, fell, hair, hide,
pelt, skin, wool
06 fleece, pelage

**furious**
03 mad
04 wild
05 angry, irate, livid
06 fierce, fuming, raging
07 boiling, enraged, in a huff, in
a stew, intense, violent

08 incensed, inflamed,
seething, sizzling, up in arms,
vehement, vigorous
10 hopping mad, infuriated
11 tempestuous

**furnish**
03 rig
04 give
05 endue, equip, grant, offer,
stock
06 afford, bestow, fit out, outfit,
supply
07 appoint, present, provide

**furniture**
07 effects
08 fitments, fittings, movables
10 appliances
11 furnishings, possessions
12 appointments
14 household goods

▶ *Types of furniture*:
03 bed, cot
04 bunk, desk, sofa
05 chair, chest, couch, divan,
stool, suite, table
06 buffet, bureau, cradle,
daybed, fender, lowboy,
rocker, settee
07 armoire, beanbag, cabinet,
camp bed, commode,
highboy, ottoman
08 armchair, bookcase,
cupboard, wardrobe, water
bed
09 camp chair, card table, desk
chair, easy chair, fireplace,
footstool, hall stand,
highchair, side table,
sideboard, washstand
10 chiffonier, dumbwaiter,
escritoire, fire screen,
secretaire
11 chiffonnier, coffee table,
dining chair, dining table,
swivel chair, workstation
12 chaise longue, chesterfield,
china cabinet, gateleg table,
kitchen chair, rocking chair,
Welsh dresser
13 dressing table, four-poster
bed, umbrella stand
14 chest of drawers, refectory
table
15 occasional chair, occasional
table

▶ *Styles of furniture*:
04 Adam, buhl
06 boulle, Empire, Gothic,
rococo, Shaker
07 Art Deco, Baroque, Regency,
Windsor

08 Colonial, Georgian, Sheraton
09 Edwardian, Queen Anne, Shibayama
10 Art Nouveau, provincial
11 Anglo-Indian, Biedermeier, Chippendale, Hepplewhite, Louis-Quinze
12 Gainsborough, Vernis Martin
13 Anglo-Colonial, Arts and Crafts, Dutch Colonial, Louis Philippe, Louis-Quatorze

**furor**
04 fury, fuss, rage, stir, to-do
05 storm
06 outcry, tumult, uproar
08 outburst
09 commotion
10 excitement, hullabaloo
11 disturbance

**furrow**
03 rut
04 knit, line, plow, seam
05 flute, gouge, track
06 crease, groove, trench, trough
07 channel, crinkle, wrinkle
12 draw together

**further**
03 aid, new, too
04 also, ease, help, more, push
05 extra, fresh, speed
06 as well, assist, foster, hasten
07 advance, besides, farther, forward, promote, remoter
08 champion, expedite, moreover
09 encourage, what's more
10 accelerate, additional, facilitate, in addition
11 furthermore
12 additionally
13 supplementary

**furtherance**
04 help
07 backing, pursuit
08 advocacy, boosting
09 advancing, promotion
10 preferment
11 advancement, carrying-out
12 championship, facilitation
13 encouragement

**furthermore**
03 too
04 also
06 as well
07 besides, further
08 moreover
09 what's more
10 in addition
12 additionally

**furthest**
06 utmost
07 extreme, outmost
08 farthest, remotest, ultimate
09 outermost, uttermost

**furtive**
03 sly
06 covert, secret, sneaky
07 cloaked
08 stealthy
09 secretive, underhand
11 clandestine
13 surreptitious

**fury**
03 ire
04 rage
05 anger, force, power, wrath
06 frenzy
07 madness, passion
08 ferocity, violence, wildness
09 intensity, vehemence
10 fierceness, turbulence

**fuse**
04 join, meld, melt, weld
05 blend, merge, smelt, unite
06 solder
08 coalesce, intermix
10 amalgamate, synthesize

**fusillade**
04 fire, hail
05 burst, salvo
06 volley
07 barrage
08 outburst
09 broadside, discharge

**fusion**
05 union
06 merger
07 melting, welding
08 blending, smelting
09 synthesis
12 amalgamation

**fuss**
03 row
04 flap, fret, stir, to-do
05 furor, hoo-ha, panic, tizzy, upset
06 bother, fidget, flurry
07 carry-on, fluster
08 ballyhoo, squabble
09 commotion, confusion, kerfuffle, take pains
10 be in a tizzy, excitement

**fussiness**
08 busyness, niceness, niggling
10 choosiness
11 finickiness
13 particularity, perfectionism
15 persnicketiness

**fussy**
05 fancy, picky
06 choosy, ornate, rococo
07 baroque, finical, finicky
08 pedantic
09 cluttered, difficult, elaborate, quibbling
10 fastidious, nit-picking, particular
11 persnickety
12 hard to please, pettifogging
13 overdecorated

**fusty**
04 damp, dank, rank
05 moldy, musty, passé, stale
06 stuffy
07 airless, archaic
09 moldering
10 malodorous
11 ill-smelling, old-fogeyish
12 old-fashioned, unventilated

**futile**
04 idle, vain
05 empty
06 barren, in vain, wasted
07 forlorn, useless
09 fruitless, pointless, to no avail, worthless
11 ineffective, ineffectual
12 unproductive, unprofitable

**futility**
05 waste
06 vanity
09 emptiness
11 aimlessness, uselessness
13 fruitlessness, pointlessness
15 ineffectiveness

**future**
04 next, to be
05 fated, later
06 coming, to come, unborn
07 outlook, planned
08 destined, eventual
09 designate, hereafter, impending, prospects
11 approaching, forthcoming, in the offing, prospective
12 expectations

**fuzz**
03 nap
04 down, hair, lint, pile
05 fiber, flock, floss, fluff

**fuzzy**
04 hazy
05 downy, faint, foggy, furry, linty, muzzy, vague
06 fleecy, fluffy, frizzy, woolly
07 blurred, fuddled, muffled, shadowy, unclear, velvety
10 ill-defined, indistinct

## gab
03 jaw, yak
04 blab, chat, talk, yack
06 babble, gossip
07 blether, chatter, prattle
08 chitchat
09 loquacity, prattling, small talk
10 blethering, yackety-yak
12 conversation, tittle-tattle

## gabble
04 blab
05 spout
06 babble, cackle, drivel, gaggle, gibber, jabber, waffle
07 blabber, blether, chatter, prattle, sputter, twaddle
08 cackling, nonsense, splutter
09 gibberish
10 blethering

## gad

## ❏ gad about
04 roam, rove
05 range, stray
06 ramble, travel, wander
09 flit about, gallivant

## gadabout
05 rover
07 playboy, rambler
11 gallivanter
14 pleasure-seeker

## gadget
04 tool
05 gismo, gizmo
06 device, widget
07 whatnot, whatsit
09 appliance, implement, invention, thingummy
10 instrument
11 contraption, contrivance, thingamabob, thingamajig, thingumabob, thingumajig

## gaffe
04 goof, slip
06 boo-boo, howler
07 blunder, faux pas, mistake
08 solecism
12 indiscretion

## gaffer
06 old man
09 old geezer
11 electrician
16 chief electrician

## gag
03 pun
04 clog, jest, joke, quip
05 block, choke, heave, retch
06 muffle, muzzle, stifle
07 silence, smother
08 one-liner, suppress, throttle
09 wisecrack, witticism

## gaiety
03 fun, joy
04 glee, show
05 mirth
07 delight, glitter, jollity, sparkle
08 pleasure, vivacity
09 festivity, happiness, joviality, merriment, showiness
10 brightness, brilliance, exuberance, liveliness
11 high spirits, joie de vivre
12 cheerfulness, colorfulness

## gaily
07 happily, merrily
08 blithely, brightly, joyfully
10 cheerfully, colorfully
11 brilliantly
14 lightheartedly

## gain
03 add, get, net, win
04 earn, make, reap, rise
05 clear, gross, reach, yield
06 attain, gather, growth, income, obtain, profit, return, reward, secure
07 achieve, acquire, advance, benefit, collect, headway, improve, procure, produce, realize, revenue, takings
08 addition, dividend, earnings, increase, progress, winnings
09 accretion, advantage, emolument, increment
11 advancement, improvement

## ❏ gain on
07 catch up
08 approach, overtake
09 close with
12 narrow the gap

## ❏ gain time
05 delay, stall
09 temporize
10 dilly-dally
13 procrastinate

## gainful
06 paying, useful
09 fructuous, lucrative, rewarding
10 worthwhile
12 advantageous, remunerative

## gainsay
04 deny
07 dispute
09 challenge, disaffirm
10 contradict, controvert

## gait
04 pace, step, walk
07 bearing
08 carriage

## gala
04 fair, fête
06 fiesta
07 jubilee, pageant
08 carnival, festival, jamboree
09 festivity
10 procession

## galaxy
04 host, mass
05 array, group, stars
06 nebula
08 assembly
09 gathering
10 collection, star system
11 the Milky Way
13 constellation

## gale
04 wind
05 blast, burst, storm
06 squall
08 outburst
09 hurricane, windstorm

## gall
03 irk, nag, vex
04 rile
05 annoy, cheek, nerve, peeve
06 animus, bother, harass, nettle, plague, rancor, rankle
07 provoke
08 acrimony, chutzpah, irritate
09 aggravate, animosity, antipathy, impudence, insolence
10 bitterness, brazenness, effrontery, exasperate
12 impertinence

## gallant
05 brave, manly, noble
06 daring, heroic, plucky, polite
07 courtly, dashing, valiant
08 fearless, gracious, intrepid
09 attentive, audacious,
  courteous, dauntless,
  honorable
10 chivalrous, courageous,
  thoughtful
11 considerate, gentlemanly

## gallantry
05 honor, pluck, valor
06 daring, spirit
07 bravery, courage, heroism
08 audacity, boldness, chivalry,
  courtesy, nobility, valiance
09 manliness
10 politeness
11 courtliness, intrepidity
12 fearlessness, graciousness
13 attentiveness, consideration,
  courteousness,
  dauntlessness
14 thoughtfulness
15 gentlemanliness

## gallery
04 walk
05 porch
06 arcade, circle, museum
07 balcony, passage, veranda
10 art gallery, spectators
➤ See also MUSEUM

## galling
06 bitter, vexing
07 irksome
08 annoying, nettling, plaguing,
  rankling
09 harassing, provoking,
  vexatious
10 bothersome, irritating
11 aggravating, infuriating
12 exasperating

## gallivant
04 roam, rove
05 range, stray
06 ramble, travel, wander
07 traipse
08 gad about
09 flit about, run around

## gallop
03 run
04 dash, race, rush, tear, zoom
05 hurry, shoot, speed
06 scurry, sprint

## gallows
06 gibbet
08 scaffold

## galore
06 lots of, tons of

07 heaps of
08 plenty of, stacks of
10 everywhere, millions of

## galvanize
04 coat, fire, jolt, move, prod,
  spur, stir, urge
05 rouse, shock
06 arouse, awaken, excite
07 animate, enliven, provoke
08 energize, vitalize
09 electrify, stimulate

## gambit
04 move, play, ploy, ruse, wile
06 device, opener, tactic
07 tactics
08 artifice, maneuver
09 stratagem

## gamble
03 bet
04 back, game, play, risk, risk
05 stake, wager
06 chance, hazard
07 lottery, pot luck, venture
09 speculate, take a risk
10 put money on
11 speculation, take a chance,
  try your luck
12 play for money
13 leap in the dark

## gambler
05 dicer, shark, sharp
06 better, bettor
07 sharper
08 gamester
09 daredevil, risk-taker

## gambol
04 jump, leap, romp, skip
05 bound, caper, dance, frisk
06 cavort, frolic, prance

## game
03 fun
04 bold, bout, jest, joke, lame,
  line, meat, meet, play, plot,
  ploy, prey, romp, ruse
05 eager, event, flesh, match,
  prank, ready, sport, trade
06 daring, frolic, gamble,
  quarry, scheme, spoils, tactic
07 contest, pastime, tactics,
  valiant, willing
08 activity, business, fearless,
  inclined, prepared, spirited,
  strategy
09 diversion, intention,
  stratagem
10 courageous, enterprise,
  interested, occupation,
  profession, recreation
11 competition, distraction
12 enthusiastic
13 entertainment

➤ *Types of game animal*:
03 elk, fox
04 bear, boar, deer, deer, duck,
  hare, lion, stag, wolf
05 hyena, moose, quail, snipe
06 grouse, rabbit, turkey
07 caribou, red deer, roe deer
08 antelope, pheasant, wild
  boar, woodcock
09 partridge, waterfowl
10 wild turkey
12 capercaillie
15 white-tailed deer

➤ *Names of games*:
03 nap, tag
04 brag, Clue, crib, dice, faro, I
  spy, pool
05 bingo, bowls, chess, craps,
  darts, jacks, poker, rummy,
  whist
06 bridge, euchre, spades
07 baccara, bowling, canasta,
  hangman, mahjong, marbles,
  old maid, pachisi, pinball,
  snooker, tenpins
08 baccarat, charades,
  checkers, cribbage,
  dominoes, forfeits, gin
  rummy, leapfrog, mahjongg,
  Michigan, Monopoly,
  napoleon, parchesi, Ping-
  Pong, red rover, roulette,
  Scrabble
09 bagatelle, billiards, blackjack,
  hopscotch, Parcheesi,
  parchisi, Simon says, solitaire,
  stud poker, tic-tac-toe,
  twenty-one, vingt-et-un
10 backgammon, post office
11 battleships, chemin de fer,
  hide-and-seek, lawn
  bowling, mumbletypeg,
  table tennis, tick-tack-toe,
  tiddlywinks
13 blindman's buff, hide-and-
  go-seek, musical chairs, spin
  the bottle
14 blindman's bluff, Trivial
  Pursuit
15 Chinese checkers

## gamekeeper
06 keeper, ranger, warden

## gamut
04 area
05 field, range, scope,
  sweep
06 series
07 compass, variety
08 sequence, spectrum

**gang**
03 lot, mob, set
04 band, club, crew, herd, pack, ring, team
05 crowd, group, horde, squad
06 circle, clique, troupe
07 company, coterie

**gangling**
04 bony, tall
05 gaunt, gawky, lanky, rangy
06 gangly, gauche, skinny
07 angular, awkward, spindly
08 raw-boned, ungainly

**gangster**
03 mug
04 goon, thug
05 crook, heavy, rough, tough
06 bandit, robber
07 hoodlum, mobster, ruffian
08 criminal
09 desperado, racketeer

**gap**
04 gulf, hole, lull, rent, rift, void
05 blank, break, chink, cleft, crack, pause, space
06 breach, cavity, cranny, divide, hiatus, lacuna, recess
07 crevice, opening, vacuity
08 aperture, fracture, interval
09 disparity, interlude
10 difference, divergence
12 intermission, interruption
13 discontinuity

**gape**
04 gawk, gawp, gaze, open, part, yawn
05 crack, split, stare
06 goggle, wonder
10 rubberneck

**gaping**
04 open, vast, wide
05 broad
07 yawning
09 cavernous

**garage**
07 carport
14 service station

**garb**
04 gear, robe, togs, wear
05 array, dress, get-up, robes
06 attire, clothe, outfit, rig out
07 apparel, clothes, costume, garment, raiment, uniform
08 clothing
09 vestments
10 appearance, habiliment

**garbage**
03 rot
04 bunk, junk, muck
05 bilge, filth, trash, tripe, waste

06 bunkum, debris, hot air, piffle, refuse, rubble, scraps
07 remains, rubbish, twaddle
08 claptrap, detritus, nonsense, tommyrot
09 gibberish, poppycock

**garble**
05 mix up, slant, twist
06 doctor, jumble, muddle
07 confuse, corrupt, distort
08 mutilate, scramble

**garden**
05 arbor, arena
07 flowers, nursery, orchard
10 garden spot
12 flower garden
14 pleasure garden
15 vegetable garden

**gargantuan**
04 huge, vast
05 giant, large
07 immense, mammoth, massive, titanic
08 colossal, enormous, gigantic, towering
09 leviathan, monstrous
11 elephantine
14 Brobdingnagian

**garish**
04 loud
05 cheap, flash, gaudy, lurid, showy
06 flashy, glitzy, tawdry, vulgar
07 glaring, raffish

**garland**
03 lei
05 adorn, crown
06 honors, laurel, stemma, wreath
07 chaplet, coronal, coronet, festoon, flowers, wreathe
08 decorate, headband

**garment**
04 coat, garb, gear, gown, robe, togs, wear
05 dress, frock, get-up, shirt, skirt
06 attire, blouse, outfit
07 apparel, costume, uniform
08 clothing

**garner**
04 cull, heap, save
05 amass, hoard, store
06 gather
07 collect, deposit, husband, reserve
08 assemble, stow away
10 accumulate

**garnish**
04 deck, trim

05 adorn, grace
07 deck out, enhance, festoon
08 decorate, ornament
09 adornment, embellish
10 decoration
11 enhancement
13 embellishment, ornamentation

**garret**
04 loft
05 attic

**garrison**
03 man
04 base, camp, fort, post, unit
05 guard, mount, place
06 assign, billet, casern, defend, occupy, troops, zareba
07 caserne, command, furnish, outpost, protect, station, zareeba
08 barracks, fortress, position
10 detachment, encampment, stronghold
13 fortification

**garrulous**
04 glib
05 gabby, gassy, windy, wordy
06 chatty, mouthy, prolix
07 prating, verbose, voluble
08 babbling, effusive
09 gossiping, prattling, talkative, yabbering
10 chattering, long-winded, loquacious

**gas**
04 brag
06 hot air
07 bombast
08 gasoline
09 pneumatic

► *Names of gases:*
04 neon
05 CS gas, ether, freon, ozone, radon, xenon
06 butane, helium, oxygen
07 ammonia, krypton, methane, propane, tear gas
08 firedamp, hydrogen, marsh gas, nerve gas, nitrogen
09 acetylene
10 chloroform, mustard gas, natural gas
11 laughing gas
12 nitrous oxide
13 carbon dioxide
14 carbon monoxide

**gash**
03 cut
04 nick, rend, rent, slit, tear
05 gouge, score, slash, wound

**gasoline**
06 incise
08 incision, lacerate
10 laceration

**gasoline**
03 gas
04 fuel
08 gasolene
09 leaded gas
11 unleaded gas
14 leaded gasoline

**gasp**
04 blow, gulp, pant, puff
06 breath, wheeze
07 breathe
11 exclamation

**gastric**
09 abdominal
10 intestinal

**gate**
04 door, exit
06 access, portal
07 barrier, doorway, gateway, opening, passage, takings
08 entrance
09 admission, turnstile

**gather**
04 crop, cull, draw, fold, gain, grow, heap, hear, mass, meet, pick, reap, tuck
05 amass, build, crowd, glean, group, hoard, infer, learn, pleat, pluck, rally, shirr
06 assume, deduce, garner, muster, pick up, pile up, pucker, pull in, ruffle, summon
07 advance, attract, believe, build up, cluster, collect, convene, harvest, hoard up, marshal, round up, surmise
08 assemble, conclude, converge, increase
09 stash away, stockpile
10 accumulate, congregate, understand
12 come together
13 bring together

**gathering**
03 mob
05 crowd, flock, group, horde, party, rally
06 throng
07 company, meeting
08 assembly, conclave, jamboree
10 assemblage, convention
11 convocation, get-together
12 congregation

**gauche**
03 shy

05 gawky, inept
06 clumsy
07 awkward, ill-bred
08 farouche, ignorant, tactless, ungainly
09 graceless, inelegant
10 uncultured, ungraceful, unpolished
15 unsophisticated

**gaudy**
04 loud
05 flash, harsh, showy, stark
06 bright, flashy, garish, glitzy, kitsch, snazzy, tawdry, vulgar
07 glaring, raffish
08 colorful, tinselly
09 brilliant, tasteless
12 meretricious, multicolored, ostentatious

**gauge**
04 area, bore, norm, rate, rule, size, span, test
05 basic, check, count, depth, guess, guide, judge, meter, scope, value, weigh, width
06 assess, degree, extent, height, reckon, sample
07 apprise, caliber, compute, example, measure, pattern
08 estimate, evaluate, exemplar
09 ascertain, benchmark, calculate, criterion, determine, guideline, indicator, yardstick

---

➤ *Types of gauge. We have omitted the word* **gauge** *from names given in the following list but you may need to include this word as part of the solution to some crossword clues.*
04 rain, ring, snap, tide, wind
05 drill, paper, steam, taper, water
06 feeler, radius, strain, vacuum
07 cutting, marking, weather
08 gauge rod, pressure
➤ See also MEASURING INSTRUMENT

**gaunt**
04 bare, bony, grim, lean, thin
05 bleak, harsh, stark
06 skinny, wasted
07 angular, forlorn, haggard
08 desolate, skeletal
09 emaciated
10 cadaverous, hollow-eyed
12 skin and bones

**gauzy**
05 filmy, light, sheer
06 flimsy
08 delicate, gossamer

10 diaphanous, see-through
11 transparent

**gawk**
04 gape, gaze, look, ogle
05 stare
06 goggle

**gawky**
05 inept, lanky
06 clumsy, gauche
07 awkward
08 gangling, ungainly
09 graceless
13 uncoordinated

**gay**
05 gaudy, happy, showy, vivid
06 blithe, bright, flashy, garish, joyful, lively
07 festive
08 animated, carefree, cheerful, colorful, debonair
09 brilliant, fun-loving, sparkling, sprightly, vivacious
10 flamboyant, homosexual
12 lighthearted
15 pleasure-seeking

**gaze**
04 gape, gawk, look, view
05 stare, watch
06 goggle, regard, wonder
11 contemplate

**gazebo**
06 turret
07 balcony
08 pavilion
09 belvedere
11 garden house, summer house

**gazette**
05 daily, paper
06 weekly
07 tabloid
09 newspaper

**gear**
03 cog, fit, kit
05 stuff, tools
06 attire, outfit, tackle
07 baggage, clothes, gearbox, gearing, luggage, prepare
08 clothing, cogwheel, organize, supplies, utensils
09 equipment, gearshift, gearwheel, machinery, mechanism
10 belongings, implements
11 accessories, instruments, possessions
12 contrivances
13 accouterments, accoutrements, paraphernalia

## gel
03 set
07 congeal, gelatin, hair gel, jellify, thicken
08 solidify
09 coagulate

## gelatinous
05 gluey, gooey, gummy
06 sticky, viscid
07 jellied, rubbery, viscous
09 congealed, glutinous
12 mucilaginous

## geld
03 fix
06 neuter, weaken
08 castrate
09 sterilize
10 emasculate

## gem
05 jewel, prize, stone
08 gemstone, treasure
11 masterpiece, pride and joy
13 precious stone

▶ *Types of gemstone:*
03 jet
04 jade, onyx, opal, ruby
05 agate, amber, beryl, coral, pearl, topaz
06 garnet, jasper, zircon
07 cat's eye, citrine, crystal, diamond, emerald, peridot
08 amethyst, fire opal, sapphire
09 cairngorm, carbuncle, carnelian, cornelian, malachite, moonstone, tiger's eye, turquoise
10 aquamarine, bloodstone, chalcedony, chrysolite, rhinestone
11 chrysoberyl, lapis lazuli
13 mother-of-pearl, white sapphire

## genealogy
05 birth
06 family
07 descent, dynasty, lineage
08 ancestry, pedigree
09 parentage
10 family tree
13 family history

## general
05 broad, loose, mixed, rough, total, usual, vague
06 common, global, normal, public, varied
07 blanket, overall, typical
08 accepted, assorted, everyday, habitual, ordinary, standard, sweeping
09 customary, extensive, imprecise, panoramic, prevalent, universal
10 ill-defined, indefinite, prevailing, unspecific, variegated, widespread
11 approximate, wide-ranging
12 all-inclusive
13 comprehensive, heterogeneous
14 across-the-board

▶ *Names of American generals:*
03 **Lee** (Robert E.)
05 **Gates** (Horatio), **Grant** (Ulysses S.), **Scott** (Winfield)
06 **Custer** (George Armstrong), **Patton** (George), **Powell** (Colin), **Taylor** (Maxwell), **Taylor** (Zachary)
07 **Bradley** (Omar), **Forrest** (Nathan Bedford), **Houston** (Samuel), **Jackson** (Andrew), **Jackson** (Thomas "Stonewall"), **Ridgway** (Matthew), **Sherman** (William Tecumseh), **Stewart** (Jeb)
08 **Burnside** (Ambrose), **Marshall** (George), **Mitchell** (Billy), **Pershing** (John)
09 **MacArthur** (Douglas), **McClellan** (George)
10 **Beauregard** (Pierre), **Eisenhower** (Dwight D.), **Washington** (George)
11 **Schwarzkopf** (Norman)

## generality
07 breadth
09 looseness, vagueness
10 commonness, popularity, prevalence
11 catholicity, ecumenicity, inexactness
12 universality
13 impreciseness
14 generalization, indefiniteness
15 approximateness

## generally
06 mainly, mostly
07 as a rule, at large, broadly, chiefly, largely, overall, usually
08 commonly, normally
09 in general
10 by and large, habitually, on the whole, ordinarily
11 customarily, in most cases, universally
14 for the most part
15 taken altogether

## generate
04 form, make
05 breed, cause
06 arouse, create, whip up
07 produce
08 engender, initiate, occasion
09 originate, propagate
10 bring about, give rise to

## generation
05 epoch
07 genesis
08 age group, breeding, creation
09 formation
10 production
11 procreation, propagation
12 reproduction

## generic
06 common
07 blanket, general
09 inclusive, unbranded, universal
10 collective
12 all-inclusive
13 comprehensive

## generosity
06 bounty
07 charity
08 goodness, kindness
10 lavishness, liberality
11 benevolence, magnanimity, munificence
12 philanthropy
14 bigheartedness, openhandedness

## generous
03 big
04 free, full, good, kind, rich
05 ample, lofty, noble
06 lavish
07 copious, liberal
08 abundant, selfless
09 bountiful, plentiful, unselfish, unsparing
10 benevolent, bighearted, charitable, munificent
11 magnanimous, overflowing
13 philanthropic

## genesis
04 dawn, root
05 birth, start
06 origin, outset, source
08 creation, founding
09 beginning, formation, inception
10 generation
11 engendering, propagation

## geneticist

► *Names of geneticists*:
05 **Jones** (Steve)
06 **Beadle** (George Wells),
**Boveri** (Theodor Heinrich),
**Fisher** (Ronald Aylmer),
**Galton** (Francis), **Morgan**
(Thomas Hunt), **Zinder**
(Norton David)
07 **Bateson** (William), **De Vries**
(Hugo Marie), **Lysenko**
(Trofim)
08 **Yanofsky** (Charles)
09 **Lederberg** (Joshua)
10 **Darlington** (Cyril Dean),
**Kettlewell** (Henry Bernard
David), **McClintock**
(Barbara), **Sturtevant**
(Alfred Henry)
➤ See also SCIENTIST

## genial
04 kind, warm
05 happy, jolly
06 hearty, jovial, kindly
07 affable, amiable, cordial
08 cheerful, pleasant, sociable
09 convivial, easygoing
11 good-humored, good-
natured

## geniality
06 warmth
07 jollity
08 gladness, kindness
09 happiness, joviality
10 affability, amiability,
cheeriness, cordiality, good
nature, kindliness
12 cheerfulness, pleasantness

## genie
04 jinn
05 demon, fairy, jinni
06 spirit

## genius
04 bent, gift, nous, sage
05 adept, brain, flair, knack
06 brains
07 ability, egghead, faculty,
maestro, prodigy
08 aptitude, capacity, fine mind,
virtuoso
09 intellect
10 brilliance, cleverness, gray
matter, mastermind
12 intellectual, intelligence
15 little gray cells

## genocide
08 massacre
09 ethnocide, slaughter
15 ethnic cleansing

## genre
04 form, kind, sort, type
05 brand, class, genus, group,
style
06 school, strain
07 fashion, variety
08 category
09 character

## genteel
05 civil
06 formal, polite, urbane
07 courtly, elegant, refined,
stylish
08 cultured, graceful, ladylike,
mannerly, polished, well-
bred
09 courteous
10 cultivated
11 fashionable, gentlemanly,
respectable
12 aristocratic, well-mannered

## gentility
06 gentry, nobles
07 culture, decorum, manners
08 breeding, civility, courtesy,
elegance, nobility, urbanity
09 blue blood, high birth,
propriety
10 good family, politeness,
refinement, upper class
11 aristocracy, courtliness,
gentle birth

## gentle
04 calm, easy, kind, mild, slow,
soft
05 balmy, light, quiet
06 benign, humane, kindly,
placid, serene, slight,
smooth, tender
07 amiable, gradual, lenient
08 merciful, moderate,
peaceful, pleasant, soothing,
tranquil
11 softhearted, sympathetic
13 compassionate,
imperceptible,
tenderhearted

## gentlemanly
05 civil, noble, suave
06 polite, urbane
07 gallant, genteel, refined
08 mannerly, obliging, polished,
well-bred
09 civilized, courteous,
honorable, reputable
10 cultivated

## gentry
08 nobility
09 gentility
10 upper class
11 aristocracy

## genuine
04 open, pure, real, true
05 frank, legal, sound
06 actual, candid, honest, lawful
07 earnest, factual, natural,
sincere
08 bona fide, original, truthful
09 authentic, real McCoy,
veritable
10 legitimate
13 unadulterated, with integrity

## genus
03 set
04 kind, race, sort, type
05 breed, class, genre, group,
order, taxon
07 species
08 category, division
11 subdivision

## geography

► *Terms used in geography*:
03 bay, col, cwm
04 arid, crag, mesa, tail, veld,
wadi, wady
05 butte, delta, taiga, veldt
06 canyon, cirque, tundra, valley
07 caldera, equator, glacial,
isthmus, volcano
08 alluvium, altitude, landmass,
landslip, latitude, meridian
09 accretion, antipodes,
billabong, deviation,
ethnology, landslide,
longitude, relief map
10 coordinate, glaciation,
landlocked, topography
11 archipelago, cartography,
conurbation, hydrography,
vulcanology
13 shield volcano
14 plate tectonics

► *Names of geographers*:
03 **Dee** (John)
04 **Cary** (John)
05 **Barth** (Heinrich), **Cabot**
(Sebastian)
06 **Strabo**
07 **Hakluyt** (Richard),
**Ptolemy**
08 **Humboldt** (Alexander),
**Mercator** (Gerhardus),
**Ortelius**
10 **Huntington** (Ellsworth)
➤ See also SCIENTIST

## geological

► *Names of geological
periods*:
06 Eocene (Epoch)
07 Miocene (Epoch), Permian

(Period)
08 Cambrian (Period), Cenozoic (Era), Devonian (Period), Holocene (Epoch), Jurassic (Period), Mesozoic (Era), Pliocene (Epoch), Silurian (Period), Tertiary (Period), Triassic (Period)
09 Oligocene (Epoch), Paleocene (Epoch), Paleozoic (Era)
10 Cretaceous (Period), Ordovician (Period), Quaternary (Period)
11 Pleistocene (Epoch), Precambrian (Era)
13 Carboniferous (Period)

**germ**
03 bud, bug
04 root, seed
05 cause, spark, start, virus
06 embryo, origin, source, sprout
07 microbe, nucleus
08 bacillus, fountain, rudiment
09 bacterium, beginning, inception
13 microorganism

**germane**
03 apt
04 akin
06 allied, proper
07 apropos, fitting, related
08 apposite, material, relevant, suitable
09 connected, pertinent
10 applicable
11 appropriate

**germinal**
07 seminal
09 embryonic
10 developing, generative
11 rudimentary

**germinate**
03 bud
04 grow
05 shoot, swell
06 sprout
07 burgeon, develop
08 spring up, take root
09 originate

**gestation**
08 drafting, planning, ripening
09 evolution, pregnancy
10 conception, incubation, maturation
11 development

**gesticulate**
04 sign, wave
06 motion, signal
07 gesture

08 indicate

**gesticulation**
04 sign, wave
06 motion, signal
07 gesture
08 movement
10 indication

**gesture**
04 sign, wave
05 point
06 beckon, motion, signal
08 indicate, movement
11 gesticulate

**get**
03 buy, vex, win
04 coax, come, earn, gain, make, take, trap, urge
05 annoy, catch, fetch, get it, grasp, reach, seize, snare
06 arrest, arrive, become, bother, collar, come by, fathom, induce, manage, obtain, secure
07 achieve, acquire, capture, collect, develop, procure, provoke, realize, receive, succeed
08 contract, convince, irritate, organize, persuade, purchase, talk into
09 influence, infuriate
10 comprehend, understand

❏**get about**
06 travel
09 move about
10 move around

❏**get across**
06 convey, impart
07 get over, put over
08 transmit
09 put across
11 communicate

❏**get ahead**
05 get on
06 thrive
07 advance, prosper, succeed
08 flourish, go places, progress
12 make your mark
14 go up in the world

❏**get along**
04 cope, fare
05 agree, get on
06 manage
07 develop, survive
08 hit it off, progress

❏**get around**
04 coax, sway
05 avoid, evade
06 bypass, induce
07 win over

08 persuade
10 circumvent
11 prevail upon

❏**get at**
04 find, hint, mean, slam
05 imply, knock
06 attack, intend, pick on
07 suggest
08 discover
09 criticize, insinuate
11 pick holes in
13 find fault with

❏**get away**
05 leave
06 depart, escape
07 run away

❏**get back**
06 recoup, regain, return
07 recover
08 retrieve
09 repossess, retaliate

❏**get by**
04 cope, fare
06 hang on, manage
07 subsist, survive
12 make ends meet

❏**get down**
06 alight, get off, sadden
07 depress, descend
08 dismount
09 disembark
10 dishearten

❏**get even**
05 repay
07 pay back, requite
11 reciprocate
12 settle a score
14 get your own back

❏**get in**
04 land
05 enter
06 arrive, embark

❏**get off**
04 shed
05 leave
06 alight, detach, remove
07 descend, get down
08 dismount, separate
09 disembark

❏**get on**
04 cope, fare
05 board, mount
06 ascend, embark, manage
07 advance, make out, press on, proceed
08 continue, progress
12 hit it off with

❏**get out**
04 flee, quit
05 leave

**getaway**
06 depart, escape, vacate
07 produce
08 evacuate, withdraw
09 circulate

❑**get out of**
05 avoid, dodge, evade, shirk, skive
06 escape

❑**get over**
06 convey, defeat, impart, master
07 explain, put over, survive
08 complete, deal with, overcome
11 communicate, pull through, recover from

❑**get ready**
07 arrange, prepare
08 rehearse

❑**get rid of**
04 dump, fire
05 eject, expel
06 remove, unload
08 jettison, shake off
09 dispose of, eliminate, get shot of, throw away
10 do away with
12 dispense with

❑**get there**
06 arrive, make it
07 advance, prosper, succeed
08 go places, make good

❑**get together**
04 join, meet
05 rally, unite
06 gather
07 collect
08 assemble, organize
10 congregate
11 collaborate

❑**get up**
04 rise
05 arise, climb, mount, scale, stand
06 ascend
07 stand up

**getaway**
03 lam
05 start
06 escape, flight
08 breakout
10 absconding, decampment

**get-together**
02 do
05 party, rally
06 social, soirée
07 meeting, reunion
08 assembly, function
09 gathering, reception

**get-up**
04 gear, togs
05 vigor
06 energy, outfit
07 clothes
10 get-up-and-go

**ghastly**
03 bad, ill
04 grim
05 awful, grave, nasty
06 horrid
07 hideous, serious
08 critical, dreadful, gruesome, horrible, shocking, terrible
09 appalling, frightful, loathsome, repellent
10 horrendous, terrifying
11 frightening

**ghost**
04 hint, soul
05 shade, spook, trace
06 shadow, spirit, wraith
07 phantom, specter
08 presence, visitant
09 semblance
10 apparition, suggestion

**ghostly**
05 eerie, weird
06 creepy, spooky
07 phantom, shadowy
08 illusory, spectral
09 ghostlike, unearthly
10 wraith-like
12 supernatural

**ghoulish**
06 grisly, morbid
07 macaber, macabre
08 gruesome

**GI**
04 Yank
07 fighter, private, soldier, warrior
10 serviceman
11 fighting man, military man

**giant**
04 huge, ogre, vast
05 jumbo, large, titan
07 Cyclops, Goliath, immense, mammoth, massive, monster, titanic
08 behemoth, colossal, colossus, enormous, gigantic, king-size, whopping
10 gargantuan
14 Brobdingnagian

**gibber**
04 blab, cant
06 babble, cackle, gabble, jabber

07 blabber, chatter, prattle

**gibberish**
06 bunkum, drivel
07 prattle, rubbish, twaddle
08 nonsense, tommyrot
10 balderdash, mumbo jumbo
12 gobbledygook

**gibe, jibe**
03 dig
04 jeer, mock, poke, quip
05 crack, scoff, sneer, taunt, tease
06 deride
07 mockery, teasing
08 derision, ridicule

**giddiness**
06 frenzy, nausea
07 vertigo
09 dizziness, faintness, wooziness
10 wobbliness
15 lightheadedness

**giddy**
04 high, wild
05 dizzy, faint, woozy
06 fickle
07 reeling, stirred
08 frenzied, unsteady
09 impulsive
11 lightheaded, vertiginous

**gift**
03 tip
04 bent, turn
05 bonus, flair, knack, offer, power, skill
06 bestow, bounty, confer, donate, genius, legacy, talent
07 ability, aptness, bequest, faculty, freebie, present
08 aptitude, donation, facility, gratuity, largesse, offering
09 attribute, endowment
10 capability, contribute
11 inheritance, proficiency
12 contribution

**gifted**
05 adept, sharp, smart
06 bright, clever, expert
07 capable, endowed, skilled
08 masterly, skillful, talented
09 brilliant
10 proficient
12 accomplished

**gigantic**
04 huge, vast
05 giant, jumbo
07 immense, mammoth, massive, titanic
08 colossal, enormous, king-size, whopping

**giggle**
10 gargantuan, monumental
14 Brobdingnagian

**giggle**
06 titter
07 snicker, snigger

**gild**
04 coat, deck, trim
05 adorn, array, grace, paint
06 bedeck, enrich
07 enhance, festoon, garnish
08 beautify, brighten, ornament

**gilded**
04 gilt, gold
06 golden
10 gold-plated

**gimcrack**
05 cheap, tacky
06 shoddy, tawdry, trashy
07 chachka, trinket
09 tchotchke
10 knickknack

**gimmick**
04 ploy, ruse
05 dodge, stunt, trick
06 device, gadget, scheme
09 publicity, stratagem
10 attraction

**gingerly**
06 warily
07 charily
09 carefully, prudently
10 cautiously, delicately,
   hesitantly, watchfully
11 tentatively

**Gipsy** see GYPSY

**gird**
04 belt, bind, ring
05 brace, hem in, ready, steel
06 enfold, fasten, girdle
07 enclose, fortify, prepare
08 encircle, get ready, surround
09 encompass

**girdle**
04 band, belt, bind, gird, sash
06 cestus, circle, corset
07 enclose
08 cincture, cingulum, encircle,
   go around, surround
09 waistband
10 cummerbund

**girl**
04 doll, lass, miss
05 chick
06 au pair, maiden, moppet
08 daughter, teenager
09 young lady
10 adolescent, girlfriend,
   schoolgirl, sweetheart,
   young woman

**girlfriend**
04 date, girl
05 lover
06 steady
07 fiancée, partner
08 mistress, old flame
09 young lady
10 sweetheart

**girlish**
08 childish, immature, innocent,
   youthful
09 childlike
11 unmasculine

**girth**
04 band, bulk, size
05 strap
09 perimeter
13 circumference

**gist**
03 nub
04 core, crux, idea, pith
05 drift, point, sense
06 import, marrow, matter
07 essence, keynote, meaning
09 direction, substance
12 quintessence, significance

**give**
03 pay
04 bend, cede, gift, lead, lend,
   move, sink, slip, tell
05 admit, allow, award, endow,
   grant, lay on, leave, put on,
   throw, utter, yield
06 accord, bestow, buckle,
   confer, convey, create,
   devote, direct, donate,
   impart, induce, pay out,
   payout, prompt, reveal,
   supply
07 arrange, concede, declare,
   display, dispose, entrust,
   exhibit, furnish, give way,
   incline, present, produce,
   proffer, provide, publish
08 announce, bequeath,
   collapse, estimate, hand over,
   indicate, make over,
   manifest, occasion, organize,
   set forth, transfer, transmit,
   turn over
09 break down, pronounce
10 contribute, distribute
11 communicate, concentrate

❏**give away**
04 leak
06 betray, expose, reveal
07 concede, divulge, let slip
08 disclose, hand over, inform
   on

❏**give in**
04 quit

05 yield
06 give up, submit
07 concede, give way, succumb
09 chuck it in, surrender
10 call it a day, capitulate
11 admit defeat
15 throw in the towel

❏**give off**
04 emit, vent
05 exude
06 exhale
07 give out, produce, release
08 throw out
09 discharge

❏**give out**
04 deal
05 allot
06 impart, notify
07 conk out, declare, dish out,
   dole out, hand out, mete out,
   publish
08 announce, transmit
09 advertise, broadcast,
   circulate
10 distribute
11 communicate, disseminate

❏**give up**
04 quit, stop
05 cease, waive
06 give in, resign
07 abandon, concede
08 forswear, leave off, renounce
09 sacrifice, surrender
10 capitulate, relinquish
11 discontinue
15 throw in the towel

**give-and-take**
06 banter
08 exchange, repartee
10 compliance, compromise
11 flexibility, negotiation
12 adaptability

**given**
05 prone
06 liable, likely
08 assuming, definite, disposed,
   distinct, inclined
09 specified, in light of
10 individual, particular
11 considering
13 bearing in mind

**giver**
05 angel, donor
06 backer, friend, helper, patron
07 sponsor
08 promoter, provider
09 supporter
10 benefactor, subsidizer
11 contributor
14 philanthropist

**glacial**
03  icy, raw
04  cold
05  chill, gelid, polar, stiff
06  arctic, biting, bitter, chilly, frigid, frosty, frozen, wintry
07  hostile
08  freezing, inimical, piercing

**glad**
04  keen
05  eager, happy, merry, ready
06  bright, cheery, elated, joyful
07  gleeful, pleased, welcome, willing
08  cheerful, disposed, inclined, prepared, thrilled
09  contented, delighted, gratified

**gladden**
05  cheer, elate
06  buck up, please
07  delight, enliven, gratify, hearten, rejoice
08  brighten
09  encourage

**gladly**
04  fain
06  freely
07  happily, readily
09  willingly
10  cheerfully
12  with pleasure

**gladness**
03  joy
05  mirth
06  gaiety
07  delight, jollity
08  felicity, pleasure
09  happiness
10  brightness, joyousness
12  cheerfulness

**glamorous**
05  ritzy, smart
06  flashy, glitzy, glossy, lovely
07  elegant
08  alluring, charming, dazzling, exciting, gorgeous
09  appealing, beautiful
10  attractive, glittering
11  well-dressed

**glamour, glamor**
05  charm, magic
06  allure, appeal, beauty
07  glitter
08  elegance, prestige
10  attraction, excitement
14  attractiveness

**glance**
04  flip, leaf, look, peek, peep, scan, skim, view
05  flash, flick, gleam, glint
06  browse, gander
07  glimpse

**▢glance off**
07  rebound
08  ricochet
09  bounce off

**gland**

► *Types of gland*:
05  lymph, ovary
06  cortex, pineal, thymus
07  adrenal, eccrine, mammary, medulla, parotid, thyroid
08  pancreas, prostate, testicle
09  endocrine, lachrymal, lymph node, pituitary, sebaceous

**glare**
04  beam, glow, look
05  blaze, flame, flare, frown, scowl, shine, stare
06  dazzle, glower
07  reflect
09  black look, dirty look, spotlight
10  brightness, brilliance
11  look daggers

**glaring**
05  gross, lurid, overt
06  patent
07  blatant, obvious
08  flagrant, manifest
10  outrageous
11  conspicuous

**glass**
04  lens, pane
05  specs
06  beaker, goblet, mirror
07  crystal, monocle, tumbler, vitrics
08  pince-nez
09  lorgnette, telescope
10  spectacles

**glassy**
03  icy
04  cold, dull
05  blank, clear, dazed, empty, fixed, shiny
06  glazed, glossy, smooth, vacant
07  deadpan, vacuous
08  lifeless, polished, slippery, unmoving
11  transparent
12  crystal clear
14  expressionless

**glaze**
05  cover, gloss, shine
06  enamel, finish, luster, polish
07  burnish, lacquer, varnish

**gleam**
03  ray
04  beam, glow
05  flare, flash, glint, gloss, shine
06  glance, luster
07  flicker, glimmer, glisten, glitter, radiate, shimmer, sparkle
10  brightness
11  scintillate

**glean**
04  cull, pick, reap
05  amass, learn
06  garner, gather, pick up
07  collect, find out, harvest
10  accumulate

**glee**
07  delight, elation, triumph
08  pleasure
10  exultation
12  exhilaration

**gleeful**
05  happy
06  elated, joyful
07  pleased
08  exultant, jubilant
09  cock-a-hoop, delighted, exuberant, gratified, overjoyed
10  triumphant

**glib**
04  easy
05  slick, suave
06  facile, fluent, smooth
07  voluble
09  insincere, plausible
13  silver-tongued, smooth-talking, smooth-tongued

**glide**
03  fly, run
04  flow, pass, roll, sail, skim, slip
05  coast, drift, float, skate, slide

**glimmer**
03  ray
04  glow, hint, wink
05  blink, flash, gleam, glint, grain, shine, trace
07  glisten, inkling, shimmer, twinkle
10  suggestion

**glimpse**
03  spy
04  espy, look, peek, peep, spot, view
05  sight
06  glance, squint
08  sighting
12  catch sight of

**glint**
05  flash, gleam, shine

**glisten**
07 glimmer, glisten, twinkle
10 glistening
11 scintillate

**glisten**
05 flash, gleam, glint, shine
07 glimmer, glitter, shimmer, sparkle
09 coruscate

**glitter**
05 gleam, glint, glitz, shine
06 dazzle, glamor, luster, tinsel
07 glimmer, glisten, shimmer, sparkle, twinkle
08 splendor
09 coruscate, showiness
10 brightness, brilliance, flashiness, razzmatazz
11 coruscation, scintillate
12 razzle-dazzle

**gloat**
04 crow
05 boast, exult, glory, vaunt
06 relish
07 rejoice, revel in, rub it in, triumph

**global**
05 total
07 general
08 thorough
09 universal, worldwide
10 exhaustive
11 encylopedic, wide-ranging
13 comprehensive, international

**globalization**
10 world trade
14 global business, world influence

**globe**
03 orb
04 ball
05 earth, round, world
06 planet, sphere

**globular**
05 round
07 globate
08 spheroid
09 orbicular, spherical

**globule**
04 ball, bead, drop
05 pearl
06 bubble, pellet
07 droplet, vesicle
08 globulet, particle, vesicula

**gloom**
03 woe
04 dark, dusk
05 cloud, grief, shade
06 misery, shadow, sorrow
07 despair, dimness, sadness
08 darkness, dullness, glumness, the blues, twilight
09 blackness, dejection, murkiness, pessimism
10 depression, desolation, low spirits, melancholy
11 despondency, unhappiness

**gloomy**
03 dim, low, sad
04 dark, down, dull, glum
05 dingy, drear, unlit
06 dismal, dreary, morose, somber
08 dejected, desolate, downcast, overcast
09 depressed, miserable, sorrowful, tenebrous, woebegone
10 depressing, despondent, dispirited, melancholy
11 crepuscular, downhearted, pessimistic
12 disconsolate, in low spirits
14 down in the dumps

**glorify**
04 hail, laud
05 adore, bless, exalt, extol, honor
06 extoll, praise, revere, vilify
07 idolize, lionize, worship
08 eulogize, sanctify, venerate
09 celebrate
10 panegyrize
11 immortalize, romanticize

**glorious**
04 fine
05 famed, grand, great, noble, noted, super
06 bright, famous, superb
07 eminent, honored, perfect, radiant, shining, supreme
08 dazzling, gorgeous, heavenly, majestic, renowned, splendid, terrific
09 beautiful, brilliant, excellent, marvelous, wonderful
10 celebrated, triumphant, victorious
11 illustrious, magnificent

**glory**
04 fame, pomp
05 boast, exult, gloat, honor, kudos
06 praise, renown
07 acclaim, majesty, rejoice, tribute, triumph, worship
08 accolade, blessing, eminence, grandeur, prestige, radiance, splendor
09 adoration, celebrity, gratitude, greatness
10 exaltation, veneration
12 magnificence, resplendence, thanksgiving
15 illustriousness

**gloss**
04 mask, note, show, veil
05 front, gleam, sheen, shine
06 define, façade, luster, polish, veneer
07 comment, explain, shimmer, sparkle, varnish
08 annotate, construe, disguise, footnote, glossary, lip gloss
09 elucidate, interpret, semblance, translate
10 brightness, brilliance, commentary, definition
11 elucidation, explanation, explication, translation
14 interpretation, window dressing

❑**gloss over**
04 hide, mask, veil
05 avoid, evade
06 ignore
07 conceal, cover up
08 disguise
09 whitewash
10 camouflage, smooth over
11 explain away
13 draw a veil over

**glossy**
05 shiny, silky, sleek
06 bright, glassy, glazed, sheeny, smooth
07 shining
08 enameled, gleaming, lustrous, polished
09 brilliant, burnished, sparkling

**glove**
04 mitt
06 mitten
08 gauntlet
11 boxing glove
13 baseball glove

**glow**
04 burn
05 ardor, blush, color, flush, gleam, light, shine
06 fervor, redden, warmth
07 burning, glimmer, passion, radiate, redness, smolder
08 grow pink, look pink, pinkness, radiance, richness, rosiness, splendor
09 intensity, vividness
10 brightness, brilliance, enthusiasm, luminosity
12 satisfaction

**glower**
04 look

**glowing**
05 frown, glare, scowl, stare
09 black look, dirty look
11 look daggers

**glowing**
04 rave, rich, warm
05 ruddy, vivid
06 bright
07 flaming, flushed, vibrant
08 ecstatic, luminous
09 favorable, laudatory, rhapsodic
10 eulogistic, smoldering
11 panegyrical
12 enthusiastic, incandescent
13 complimentary

**glue**
03 fix, gum
04 bond, seal, size
05 affix, epoxy, paste, stick
06 cement, mortar
08 adhesive, fixative, mucilage
09 superglue
11 agglutinate

**gluey**
05 gooey, gummy
06 sticky, viscid
07 viscous
08 adhesive
09 glutinous

**glum**
03 low, sad
04 down, sour
05 gruff, moody, sulky, surly
06 gloomy, morose, sullen
07 crabbed, doleful, unhappy
09 depressed, miserable
10 despondent
14 down in the dumps

**glut**
04 clog, cram, fill, sate
05 choke, flood, gorge, stuff
06 deluge, excess
07 satiate, surfeit, surplus
10 oversupply
11 superfluity
14 superabundance

**glutinous**
05 gluey, gummy
06 mucous, sticky, viscid
07 viscous
08 adhesive, cohesive

**glutton**
03 hog, pig
07 gobbler, guzzler
08 gourmand
09 chow hound
10 greedy-guts

**gluttonous**
05 gutsy
06 greedy

07 hoggish, piggish
10 gluttonish, insatiable, omnivorous
12 gormandizing

**gluttony**
05 greed
08 voracity
10 gormandism, greediness
11 piggishness

**gnarled**
05 bumpy, lumpy, rough
06 gnarly, knotty, rugged
07 knotted, twisted
08 leathery, wrinkled
09 contorted, distorted
13 weather-beaten

**gnash**
04 grit
05 grate, grind

**gnaw**
03 eat, nag
04 bite, chew, fret, prey, wear
05 erode, harry, haunt, munch, worry
06 crunch, devour, harass, nibble, niggle, plague
07 consume, torment, trouble
09 masticate

**go**
03 act, bid, die, fit, get, run, try
04 bash, fare, head, lead, move, pass, quit, scat, shot, span, stab, suit, turn, walk, work
05 begin, drive, end up, fit in, leave, match, occur, reach, scoot, scram, sound, start, vigor
06 accord, be axed, become, depart, effort, energy, extend, manage, pizazz, repair, result, retire, set off, set out, spirit, travel, vanish
07 advance, attempt, give off, journey, operate, perform, pizzazz, proceed, stretch
08 continue, dynamism, endeavor, function, progress, vitality, withdraw
09 animation, disappear, harmonize
10 complement, coordinate, correspond, get-up-and-go, make a sound, make tracks
13 take your leave

❏ **go about**
02 do
06 tackle
07 address, perform
08 approach, attend to, engage in, set about
09 undertake

❏ **go ahead**
05 begin
07 advance, carry on, proceed
08 continue, progress

❏ **go along with**
04 obey
06 accept, follow
07 abide by, support
09 agree with
10 comply with, concur with

❏ **go around**
08 surround
09 circulate

❏ **go at**
05 argue, blame
06 attack, tackle
08 set about
09 criticize

❏ **go away**
05 leave
06 depart, vanish
07 abscond, retreat
08 withdraw
09 disappear

❏ **go back**
06 return, revert
07 retreat

❏ **go back on**
04 deny
08 renege on
09 default on

❏ **go by**
04 flow, heed, obey, pass
05 lapse
06 elapse, follow
07 observe
10 comply with

❏ **go down**
04 drop, fail, fall, fold, lose, sink
07 decline, descend, founder
08 be beaten, collapse, decrease, fall down, submerge
10 degenerate
11 deteriorate
12 come a cropper

❏ **go for**
04 like
05 enjoy
06 aim for, attack, choose, prefer, rush at, select
07 assault, lunge at
08 set about

❏ **go in for**
05 adopt, enter
06 follow, pursue, take up
07 embrace, espouse
08 engage in, practice
09 undertake

## goad

### □ go into
05 probe, study
06 review
07 analyze, dissect, examine
08 check out, consider, look into, research
09 delve into
10 scrutinize
11 investigate

### □ go off
04 quit, turn
05 blast, burst, leave
06 blow up, depart
07 abscond, explode
08 detonate
09 disappear

### □ go on
03 gab, gas
04 last, stay
05 occur
06 endure, happen, natter, remain
07 carry on, chatter, persist, proceed
08 continue, ramble on
09 take place

### □ go out
04 date, exit
05 court, leave
06 depart
08 go steady, withdraw

### □ go over
04 list, read, scan
05 check, study
06 peruse, review, revise, switch
07 discuss, examine, inspect
08 look over, rehearse

### □ go through
04 bear, hunt
05 check, use up
06 endure, suffer
07 consume, examine, undergo
08 squander
09 penetrate
10 experience
11 investigate, look through

### □ go together
03 fit
04 date, suit
05 blend, match
06 accord
08 go steady
09 harmonize
10 complement, coordinate

### □ go under
04 fail, flop, fold, sink
06 go bust
07 founder, succumb
08 collapse, submerge

### □ go with
03 fit
04 date, suit, take
05 blend, match, usher
06 escort
08 go steady
09 accompany, harmonize
10 complement, coordinate

### □ go without
04 lack, want
06 forego
07 abstain
09 do without

### goad
03 nag, vex
04 jolt, prod, push, spur, urge
05 annoy, drive, hound, impel, prick, taunt
06 arouse, harass, incite, induce, prompt
07 inspire, provoke
08 irritate, motivate
09 instigate, stimulate
10 pressurize

### go-ahead
02 OK
04 okay
05 pushy
07 consent, dynamic, forward
08 approval, sanction, thumbs-up, vigorous, warranty
09 ambitious, clearance, energetic, go-getting
10 aggressive, green light, permission, pioneering
11 opportunist, progressive
12 confirmation, enterprising
13 authorization
14 forward-looking

### goal
03 aim, end, net
05 score
06 basket, design, object, target
07 end zone, purpose
08 ambition, crossbar, goal line
09 intention, objective
10 aspiration

### gobble
04 bolt, cram, gulp, wolf
05 gorge, stuff
06 devour, guzzle

### gobbledygook
06 drivel, jargon
07 prattle, rubbish, twaddle
08 nonsense
09 gibberish
10 balderdash
12 psychobabble

### go-between
05 agent
06 broker, medium
08 mediator
09 messenger, middleman
12 intermediary

### goblin
03 elf, imp, nix
05 bogey, bogie, demon, fiend, gnome, kelpy, nixie
06 kelpie, kobold, spirit, sprite
07 brownie, gremlin
08 bogeyman
09 boogeyman, hobgoblin

### God
04 King, Lord, Zeus
05 Allah, Deity, Yahwe
06 Brahma, Father, Yahweh
07 Holy One, Jehovah
08 Almighty
12 Supreme Being

### god, goddess
04 icon, idol
05 deity, power
06 spirit
08 divinity
11 divine being, graven image
➤ See also MYTHOLOGY

▬ *Names of Egyptian gods:*
02 Ra
03 Geb, Nut
04 Apis, Aten, Ptah, Seth
05 Horus, Thoth
06 Amun-Re, Anubis, Osiris

▬ *Names of Egyptian goddesses:*
04 Isis, Maat
06 Hathor
07 Sekhmet
08 Nephthys

▬ *Names of Greek gods:*
03 Pan
04 Ares, Eros, Zeus
05 Atlas, Hades
06 Adonis, Aeolus, Apollo, Boreas, Cronus, Helios, Hermes
07 Nemesis, Oceanus
08 Dionysus, Ganymede, Morpheus, Poseidon, Thanatos
09 Asclepius
10 Hephaestus

▬ *Names of Greek goddesses:*
03 Eos
04 Gaia, Hebe, Hera, Iris, Nike, Rhea
06 Athene, Cybele, Hecate, Selene
07 Artemis, Demeter
08 Arethusa

09 Aphrodite
10 Persephone

▶ *Names of Hindu gods*:
04 Agni, Kama, Rama, Siva
05 Indra, Shiva, Surya
06 Brahma, Ganesa, Varuna, Vishnu
07 Ganesha, Hanuman, Krishna
08 Nataraja
09 Prajapati
10 Jagannatha

▶ *Names of Hindu goddesses*:
04 Kali, Maya, Sita
05 Aditi, Durga, Sakti
06 Shakti
07 Lakshmi, Parvati
09 Sarasvati, Saraswati

▶ *Names of Norse gods*:
03 Bor, Otr, Tyr, Ull
04 Frey, Logi, Loki, Odin, Thor
05 Aegir, Alcis, Mimir, Njord, Vidar, Woden, Wotan
06 Balder, Fafnir, Weland
07 Wayland, Weiland
08 Heimdall

▶ *Names of Norse goddesses*:
03 Hel, Ran, Sif
05 Frigg, Idunn, Nanna, Norns
06 Freyja, Gefion
07 Nerthus
09 Valkyries

▶ *Names of Roman gods*:
04 Mars
05 Cupid, Fides, Janus, Lares, Pluto
06 Apollo, Faunus, Genius, Saturn, Vulcan
07 Bacchus, Jupiter, Mercury, Mithras, Neptune, Penates
08 Silvanus

▶ *Names of Roman goddesses*:
03 Ops
04 Juno, Maia
05 Ceres, Diana, Epona, Fauna, Flora, Venus, Vesta
06 Pomona
07 Bellona, Egreria, Fortuna, Minerva
08 Victoria
10 Prosperina

**Godforsaken**
05 bleak
06 lonely, remote
08 deserted, desolate, isolated
09 miserable
10 depressing

**godless**
05 pagan
06 sinful, unholy, wicked
07 heathen, impious, profane, ungodly
08 agnostic
09 atheistic, faithless
10 irreverent
11 irreligious

**godlike**
04 holy
06 deific, divine, sacred
07 exalted, sublime
08 heavenly
09 celestial
10 superhuman
11 theomorphic
12 transcendent

**godly**
04 good, holy, pure
05 moral, pious
06 devout
07 saintly
09 believing, religious, righteous
10 God-fearing

**godsend**
04 boon
07 bonanza, miracle
08 blessing, windfall

**goggle**
04 gawk, gawp, gaze
05 stare

**going-over**
05 check, study
06 attack, review, survey
07 beating, checkup, chiding, pasting
08 analysis, scolding, scrutiny, whipping
09 criticism, reprimand, thrashing, trouncing
10 inspection
11 castigation, examination
12 chastisement

**goings-on**
08 business, mischief
10 activities, happenings
11 misbehavior, occurrences
13 funny business

**gold**
04 gilt
06 gilded, nugget, riches, wealth
07 bullion

**golden**
04 fair, gilt, gold, rosy
05 blond, happy
06 blonde, flaxen, gilded, yellow

08 glorious, lustrous
09 brilliant, favorable, promising, treasured
10 auspicious, propitious
11 flourishing, resplendent

**golf**

▶ *Types of golf club*:
04 iron, wood
05 spoon
06 driver, mashie, putter
07 brassie, midiron, niblick
09 sand wedge
10 mashie iron
11 driving iron
13 mashie niblick

▶ *Names of golfers*:
04 **Kite** (Tom), **Lyle** (Sandy), **Webb** (Karrie)
05 **Davis** (Laura), **Braid** (James), **Faldo** (Nick), **Hagen** (Walter), **Hogan** (Ben), **Irwin** (Hale), **Jones** (Bobby), **Snead** (Sam Jackson), **Suggs** (Louise), **Woods** (Tiger)
06 **Casper** (Billy), **Garcia** (Sergio), **Nelson** (Byron), **Norman** (Greg), **Palmer** (Arnold), **Player** (Gary), **Vardon** (Harry), **Watson** (Tom), **Wright** (Mickey)
07 **Couples** (Fred), **Jacklin** (Tony), **Sarazen** (Gene), **Stewart** (Payne), **Trevino** (Lee Buck), **Woosnam** (Ian)
08 **Crenshaw** (Ben), **Nicklaus** (Jack), **Olazabal** (Jose Maria), **Torrance** (Sam), **Weiskopf** (Tom), **Zaharias** Babe Didrikson
09 **Sorenstam** (Annika), **Whitworth** (Kathy)
11 **Ballesteros** (Severiano), **Montgomerie** (Colin)
➢ See also SPORT

**gone**
04 away, dead, done, lost, over, past, used
05 spent
06 absent, astray
07 elapsed, missing
08 departed, finished, vanished
11 disappeared
15 over and done with

**goo**
03 mud
04 crud, gunk, mire, muck, ooze, scum, yuck
05 grime, slime, slush
06 grease, matter, sludge

10 stickiness

**good**

04 able, gain, kind, nice, sake

05 adept, honor, large, merit, moral, noble, right, sound, valid

06 behalf, honest, loving, polite, profit, useful, virtue, worthy

07 benefit, capable, fitting, genuine, honesty, purpose, skilled, upright

08 adequate, complete, goodness, gracious, interest, intimate, passable, pleasant, pleasing, reliable, sensible, skillful, suitable, superior, talented, thorough, vigorous, virtuous

09 advantage, agreeable, competent, compliant, efficient, enjoyable, excellent, fantastic, favorable, fortunate, honorable, righteous, tolerable, well-being

10 acceptable, auspicious, beneficial, benevolent, dependable, good as gold, proficient, propitious, reasonable, satisfying, usefulness, worthwhile

11 appropriate, commendable, kindhearted, pleasurable, substantial, uprightness, well-behaved

12 advantageous, considerable, satisfactory

13 philanthropic, righteousness

14 salt of the earth

**□for good**

04 ever

06 always

07 forever

08 evermore

09 eternally

10 for all time

11 permanently

**□make good**

02 do

05 go far

06 effect

07 fulfill, succeed

08 carry out, get ahead, live up to, progress, put right

12 be successful

13 compensate for, make amends for, put into action

15 get on in the world

**goodbye**

03 bye

04 ciao, ta-ta

05 adieu, adios

06 bye-bye, see you, so long

07 cheerio, parting

08 au revoir, farewell, sayonara, swan song, take care

11 arrivederci, be seeing you, leave-taking, see you later, valediction

14 auf Wiedersehen

**good-for-nothing**

03 bum

04 idle, lazy

05 idler

06 loafer, no-good, waster

07 useless, wastrel

08 feckless, indolent, layabout

09 lazybones, reprobate, worthless

10 black sheep, ne'er-do-well, profligate

**good-humored**

05 happy

06 genial, jovial

07 affable, amiable

08 cheerful, friendly, pleasant

09 congenial

12 good-tempered

**good-looking**

04 fair

06 comely, lovely, pretty

08 handsome

09 beautiful

10 attractive

11 presentable

**goodly**

04 good, tidy

05 ample, large

08 sizeable

10 sufficient

11 significant, substantial

12 considerable

**good-natured**

04 kind

06 gentle, kindly

07 helpful, patient

08 friendly, generous, tolerant

10 benevolent

11 kindhearted, sympathetic, warmhearted

12 good-tempered

**goodness**

06 virtue

07 honesty, probity

08 goodwill, kindness

10 compassion, generosity

11 benevolence, helpfulness, uprightness

13 righteousness, wholesomeness

**goods**

04 gear

05 stuff, wares

07 effects, freight

08 chattels, products, property

10 belongings

11 merchandise, possessions

**goodwill**

05 amity, favor

08 kindness

10 compassion, friendship, generosity

11 benevolence

12 friendliness

**goody-goody**

05 pious

08 priggish

13 goody-two-shoes, sanctimonious, self-righteous

**gooey**

04 soft

05 gluey, tacky, thick

06 sloppy, sticky, syrupy, viscid

07 maudlin, mawkish, viscous

09 glutinous

11 sentimental

**gore**

04 stab

05 blood, cruor, grume, spear, stick, wound

06 impale, pierce

09 bloodshed, slaughter

10 bloodiness

**gorge**

03 gap

04 bolt, cram, feed, fill, glut, pass, rift, sate, wolf

05 abyss, chasm, cleft, gully

06 canyon, defile, devour, ravine

07 overeat, surfeit

**gorgeous**

04 rich, sexy

05 grand, showy

06 lovely, pretty, superb

07 opulent

08 dazzling, glorious, splendid, stunning

09 beautiful, glamorous, luxurious, marvelous, ravishing, sumptuous

10 attractive, delightful, impressive

11 good-looking, magnificent, resplendent

**gory**

06 bloody, brutal, grisly, savage

10 sanguinary

12 bloodstained

## gospel
05 credo, creed, truth
06 verity
08 doctrine, good news, teaching
09 certainty
12 New Testament

## gossamer
04 airy, fine, thin
05 gauzy, light, sheer, silky
06 flimsy
08 cobwebby, delicate
10 diaphanous, see-through
11 translucent, transparent

## gossip
03 gas, jaw
04 chat, talk
05 rumor
06 report, tattle
07 blather, blether, chatter, chinwag, hearsay, scandal, tattler, whisper
08 busybody, chitchat, idle talk
09 tell tales, whisperer
10 chew the fat, talebearer
11 mud-slinging
12 tittle-tattle
13 scandalmonger

## gouge
03 cut, dig
04 claw, gash, hack
05 scoop, score, slash
06 chisel, groove, hollow, incise

## gourmand
03 hog, pig
07 epicure, glutton, gourmet, guzzler
08 omnivore
11 gormandizer

## gourmet
06 foodie
07 epicure
08 gourmand
09 bon vivant, epicurean
10 gastronome
11 connoisseur

## govern
03 run
04 curb, head, lead, rule
05 check, quell, reign, steer
06 direct, manage
07 command, conduct, contain, control, preside
08 dominate, regulate, restrain
09 be in power, influence
10 administer, hold office
11 keep in check, superintend

## governess
05 nanny, nurse
06 duenna, mentor
07 teacher, tutress
08 tutoress
09 nursemaid

## governing
06 ruling
07 guiding, leading
08 dominant, reigning
10 commanding, regulatory
11 controlling, predominant

## government
04 rule, sway
05 power, state
06 charge, régime
07 command, control
08 Congress, dominion, ministry
09 authority, restraint
10 domination, leadership, management, parliament
11 authorities, sovereignty
12 powers that be
13 federal agency
14 administration

➤ *Types of government*:
05 junta
06 empire
07 kingdom
08 monarchy, republic
09 autocracy, communism, democracy, despotism, theocracy
10 absolutism, federation, hierocracy, plutocracy
11 triumvirate
12 commonwealth, dictatorship
➤ See also POLITICS

## governor
04 head
05 chief, guide, ruler
06 leader, master
07 viceroy
08 director
09 commander, executive
10 controller
12 commissioner
13 administrator

➤ *Names of U.S. governors*:
04 **Bush** (George W.) of Texas, **Bush** (Jeb) of Florida, **Long** (Huey) of Louisiana
05 **Davis** (Gray) of California, **Ridge** (Thomas) of Pennsylvania
06 **Carter** (James Earl "Jimmy") of Georgia, **Engler** (John) of Michigan, **Faubus** (Orval) or Arkansas, **Minner** (Ruth Ann) of Delaware, **Pataki** (George) of New York,

**Reagan** (Ronald) of California, **Wilder** (L. Douglas) of Virginia, **Wilson** (Pete) of California, **Wilson** (Woodrow) of New Jersey
07 **Clinton** (Bill) of Arkansas, **Ventura** (Jesse) of Minnesota, **Wallace** (George) of Alabama
08 **Coolidge** (Calvin) of Massachusetts, **McKinley** (William) of Ohio, **Richards** (Ann) of Texas
09 **Roosevelt** (Franklin Delano) of New York, **Roosevelt** (Theodore) of New York, **Stevenson** (Adlai) of Illinois
12 **Rockefeller,** (Nelson) of New York

## gown
04 garb, robe
05 dress, frock, habit
07 costume, garment

## grab
03 bag, nab
04 grip, nail, take
05 catch, grasp, pluck, seize
06 clutch, collar, snap up, snatch
07 capture
10 commandeer, take hold of
11 appropriate, catch hold of

## ❑up for grabs
07 to be had
09 available
10 obtainable

## grace
05 adorn, charm, favor, honor, mercy, poise
06 beauty, enrich, pardon, polish, prayer, set off, virtue
07 charity, decency, decorum, dignify, enhance, finesse, fluency
08 blessing, breeding, clemency, courtesy, decorate, elegance, goodness, goodwill, leniency, ornament
09 embellish, etiquette, good taste, propriety
10 compassion, generosity, indulgence, kindliness, loveliness, refinement
11 beneficence, benevolence, cultivation, forgiveness, shapeliness
13 consideration
14 attractiveness

**► *Names of the Three Graces*:**
06 Aglaia, Thalia
10 Euphrosyne
➢ See also MYTHOLOGY

**graceful**
05 agile, fluid
06 nimble, smooth, supple
07 elegant, flowing, slender
08 charming, cultured, polished, tasteful
09 appealing, beautiful
10 attractive, cultivated

**graceless**
04 rude
05 crude, gawky, rough
06 clumsy, coarse, forced, gauche, vulgar
07 awkward, uncouth
08 impolite, improper, ungainly
09 barbarous, inelegant, shameless
10 indecorous
11 ill-mannered
12 unattractive
15 unsophisticated

**gracious**
04 kind, mild
06 kindly, polite
07 elegant, lenient, refined
08 friendly, generous, merciful, obliging, pleasant, tasteful
09 courteous, luxurious, sumptuous
10 beneficent, hospitable
11 considerate, kindhearted
13 accommodating

**gradation**
04 mark, rank, step
05 array, level, stage
06 change, degree, series
07 grading, shading, sorting
08 ordering, sequence
10 succession
11 arrangement, progression

**grade**
04 mark, rank, rate, rung, size, sort, step, type
05 brand, class, order, place, range, stage
06 assess, degree, rating, status
07 arrange, echelon, quality, station
08 category, classify, evaluate, position, standard, standing
10 categorize, pigeonhole
14 classification

**❑ make the grade**
04 pass
07 succeed

**gradient**
04 bank, hill, rise
05 grade, slope
07 incline
09 acclivity, declivity

**gradual**
04 easy, even, slow
06 gentle, steady
07 regular
08 measured, moderate
10 continuous, step by step

**gradually**
06 evenly, gently, slowly
08 bit by bit
09 by degrees, piecemeal
10 cautiously, inch by inch, moderately, step by step
12 continuously, successively
13 imperceptibly, progressively
14 little by little

**graduate**
04 grad, pass, rank, sort
05 grade, group, order, range
06 alumna, move up
07 advance, alumnus, mark off, qualify
08 bachelor, progress
09 calibrate

**graft**
03 bud
04 join, scam
05 affix, scion, shoot, sting
06 growth, insert, rip-off, splice, sprout
07 bribery, engraft, implant
09 con tricks, extortion
10 corruption, dishonesty, transplant
11 dirty tricks
12 implantation
13 sharp practice

**grain**
03 bit, jot, nap, rye
04 corn, iota, meal, oats, rice, seed
05 crumb, scrap, speck, trace, wheat
06 barley, cereal, kernel, morsel
07 granule, modicum, pattern, soupçon, texture
08 fragment, molecule, particle
09 scintilla

**grand**
04 arch, fine, head, main
05 chief, final, great, large, lofty, noble, piano, regal, showy, super
06 lavish, lordly, senior, superb
07 highest, leading, opulent, pompous, stately, supreme
08 glorious, imposing, majestic, palatial, smashing, splendid, striking, terrific
09 ambitious, enjoyable, excellent, fantastic, first-rate, grandiose, luxurious, marvelous, principal, sumptuous, wonderful
10 impressive, monumental, preeminent
11 illustrious, magnificent, outstanding, pretentious
12 ostentatious

**grandeur**
07 dignity, majesty
08 eminence, nobility, opulence, splendor
09 greatness
10 importance, lavishness, prominence
11 stateliness
12 magnificence
13 luxuriousness
14 impressiveness

**grandfather**
06 gramps
07 grandad, grandpa
08 granddad
09 grandaddy

**grandiloquent**
07 flowery, fustian, orotund, pompous
08 inflated
09 bombastic, high-flown
10 euphuistic, rhetorical
11 exaggerated, pretentious
12 high-sounding, magniloquent

**grandiose**
05 grand, lofty, showy
07 pompous, stately
08 imposing, majestic, splendid, striking
09 ambitious, high-flown
10 flamboyant, monumental
11 extravagant, magnificent, pretentious
12 high-sounding, ostentatious

**grandmother**
06 granny
07 grandma, grannie
09 grandmama

**grant**
04 gift, give
05 admit, allow, award
06 accept, bestow, confer, donate, permit, supply
07 agree to, annuity, bequest, bursary, concede, furnish, pension, present, provide, subsidy

## granule

08 accede to, donation
09 allowance, apportion, consent to, endowment, vouchsafe
10 concession, contribute, honorarium
11 acknowledge, scholarship
12 contribution

## granule

03 jot
04 bead, iota, seed
05 crumb, grain, piece, scrap, speck
06 pellet
08 fragment, molecule, particle

## granular

05 lumpy, rough, sandy
06 grainy, gritty
07 crumbly, friable

## graph

04 grid, plot
05 chart, curve, table
07 diagram
08 bar chart, pie chart

## graphic

05 clear, drawn, lucid, vivid
06 cogent, lively, visual
08 detailed, explicit, specific, striking
09 effective, pictorial, realistic
10 blow-by-blow, expressive
11 delineative
12 diagrammatic, illustrative

## grapple

04 grab, grip, hold
05 clasp, fight, grasp, seize
06 clutch, combat, engage
07 address, contend, wrestle
08 confront, cope with, deal with, struggle
09 encounter, lay hold of
14 get to grips with

## grasp

03 get, see
04 grab, grip, hold
05 catch, clasp, seize
06 clutch, master, take in
07 catch on, command, embrace, grapple, mastery, realize
08 clutches, perceive
09 awareness, knowledge, lay hold of
10 comprehend, perception, possession, understand
11 familiarity
13 comprehension, understanding

## grasping

06 greedy

08 covetous
09 mercenary, rapacious
10 avaricious
11 acquisitive

## grass

03 lea, sod
04 lawn, mead, turf
05 field, green
06 common, meadow
07 pasture

---

▶ *Types of grass*:

03 rye
04 bent, cane, corn, oats, reed, rice
05 paddy, wheat
06 bamboo, barley, fescue, millet
07 Bermuda, esparto, papyrus, sorghum, wild oat
08 ryegrass
09 buckwheat, knotgrass, marijuana, sugar cane
10 couch grass
11 marram grass, meadow grass, monkey grass, pampas grass, twitch grass, winter grass

➤ See also PLANT

## grate

03 irk, jar, vex
04 gall, rasp
05 annoy, grind, peeve, shred
06 rankle, scrape
07 scratch
08 irritate
09 aggravate

## grateful

07 obliged
08 beholden, indebted, thankful
09 obligated
12 appreciative

## gratification

05 kicks
06 relish, thrill
07 delight, elation
08 pleasure
09 enjoyment
10 indulgence
12 satisfaction

## gratify

05 favor, humor
06 cosset, pamper, please
07 delight, fulfill, gladden, indulge, placate, satisfy
08 pander to

## grating

04 grid
05 frame, grate, grill, harsh
06 grille
07 irksome, jarring, rasping

08 annoying, grinding, scraping
10 discordant, irritating, scratching

## gratis

04 free
08 at no cost
10 for nothing, on the house
12 free of charge
13 complimentary

## gratitude

06 thanks
10 obligation
12 appreciation, gratefulness, indebtedness, thankfulness

## gratuitous

04 free
06 gratis, unpaid, wanton
08 needless
09 unmerited, voluntary
10 for nothing, unasked-for, undeserved
11 superfluous, uncalled-for, unjustified, unnecessary, unsolicited, unwarranted
12 free of charge
13 complimentary

## gratuity

03 tip
04 gift
06 bounty, reward
07 largess
08 donation, lagnappe, largesse
09 lagniappe, pourboire
10 recompense

## grave

04 grim, tomb
05 acute, cairn, crypt, quiet, sober, staid, vault
06 barrow, gloomy, solemn, somber, urgent
07 crucial, exigent, pensive, serious, subdued, weighty
08 critical, perilous, pressing, reserved
09 dangerous, dignified, hazardous, important, long-faced, mausoleum, sepulcher
10 burial site
11 burial mound, burial place, significant, threatening

## gravel

04 grit, sand
06 stones
07 pebbles, shingle

## gravelly

05 gruff, harsh, rough, thick
06 grainy, gritty, hoarse, pebbly
07 grating, shingly, throaty
08 granular, guttural

**gravestone**
04 slab
06 marker
08 memorial
09 tombstone

**graveyard**
08 boot hill, cemetery, God's acre
10 churchyard, necropolis
12 burial ground, memorial park, potter's field

**gravitate**
04 drop, fall, lean, move, sink, tend
05 drift
06 settle
07 descend, head for, incline
09 be drawn to
11 precipitate

**gravity**
04 pull
06 danger, hazard, weight
07 dignity, reserve, urgency
08 exigency, grimness, severity, sobriety
09 acuteness, heaviness, restraint, solemnity
10 attraction, importance
11 gravitation, seriousness, weightiness
12 significance
13 momentousness

**gray**
03 dim, old, wan
04 dark, dull, pale
05 ashen, bleak, foggy, misty, murky
06 cloudy, dismal, dreary, gloomy, leaden, pallid
07 elderly, neutral, unclear
08 doubtful, overcast
09 ambiguous, cheerless, colorless, debatable, uncertain
10 depressing
13 uninteresting
14 open to question

**graze**
03 rub
04 crop, feed, kiss, skim
05 brush, chafe, shave, touch
06 abrade, browse, scrape
07 pasture, scratch
08 abrasion

**grease**
03 fat, oil
04 lard, suet
05 bribe
06 tallow
07 lanolin
08 dripping

11 lubrication

**greasy**
04 oily, waxy
05 fatty, lardy, oleic, slimy
07 adipose, buttery
08 slippery, unctuous
09 sebaceous
10 oleaginous

**great**
03 ace, big
04 able, cool, huge, mega, vast
05 chief, crack, famed, grand, jumbo, large, major, noted
06 august, expert, famous, superb, wicked
07 crucial, eminent, extreme, immense, leading, mammoth, massive, notable, primary, salient, serious, skilled
08 colossal, critical, dextrous, enormous, fabulous, gigantic, imposing, masterly, renowned, sizeable, skillful, smashing, spacious, splendid, terrific, top-notch, virtuoso, whopping
09 admirable, boundless, brilliant, dexterous, essential, excellent, excessive, extensive, fantastic, first-rate, important, marvelous, momentous, practiced, principal, prominent, wonderful
10 celebrated, impressive, inordinate, proficient, remarkable, tremendous
11 illustrious, magnificent, outstanding, substantial
12 accomplished, considerable
13 distinguished

**greatly**
04 much
06 highly, hugely, vastly
08 markedly, mightily
09 extremely, immensely
10 abundantly, enormously
11 exceedingly
12 considerably
13 significantly, substantially

**greatness**
04 fame, note
05 glory, power
06 genius, renown, weight
08 eminence, grandeur
09 intensity, magnitude
10 excellence, importance
11 distinction, seriousness
12 significance

**greed**
07 avarice, edacity
08 cupidity, gluttony, rapacity, voracity
09 esurience
10 gormandism
11 hoggishness, piggishness
12 covetousness, ravenousness
13 insatiability
15 acquisitiveness

**greedy**
06 grabby, hungry
07 hoggish, piggish, selfish
08 covetous, desirous, edacious, esurient, grabbing, grasping
09 rapacious, voracious
10 avaricious, cupidinous, gluttonous, insatiable
12 gormandizing

**green**
03 lea, new, raw
04 lawn, lush, turf
05 field, fresh, grass, leafy, money, naïve, sward, young
06 common, grassy, meadow, recent, tender, unripe
07 budding, envious, jealous, pasture, verdant
08 covetous, glaucous, ignorant, immature, inexpert, unversed
09 grassland, resentful, untrained
10 ecological, unseasoned
11 eco-friendly, flourishing, putting area, unqualified
13 environmental, inexperienced
15 conservationist, unsophisticated

**greenery**
07 foliage, verdure
08 verdancy
10 vegetation, virescence

**greenhorn**
04 tiro
06 novice, rookie
07 learner
08 beginner, initiate, neophyte, newcomer
09 fledgling
10 apprentice, tenderfoot

**greenhouse**
08 hothouse, solarium
12 conservatory

**greet**
04 hail, kiss, meet
05 nod to
06 accost, salute, wave to
07 address, receive, welcome

10 say hello to
11 acknowledge

**greeting**
03 nod
04 wave
05 hallo, hello
07 address, welcome
09 handshake, reception
10 salutation
14 acknowledgment

**greetings**
04 love
07 regards
08 respects
10 best wishes, good wishes
11 salutations

**gregarious**
06 social
07 affable, cordial
08 friendly, outgoing, sociable
09 convivial, extrovert
13 companionable

**grid**
05 frame, grill
06 grille
07 grating, lattice, network, trellis
08 gridiron

**grief**
03 woe
04 pain
05 agony
06 misery, regret, sorrow
07 anguish, despair, remorse, sadness
08 distress, mourning
09 heartache, suffering
10 affliction, depression, desolation, heartbreak
11 bereavement, despondency, lamentation, tribulation, unhappiness

**grief-stricken**
03 sad
07 unhappy
08 desolate, grieving, mourning, wretched
09 anguished, sorrowful, sorrowing
10 devastated, distressed
11 heartbroken
12 inconsolable
13 brokenhearted

**grievance**
05 gripe, trial, wrong
06 grouse
07 grumble, offense, protest, trouble
09 complaint, objection
10 bone to pick, resentment

**grieve**
04 ache, hurt, pain, weep
05 mourn, shock, upset
06 dismay, lament, offend, sadden, sorrow, suffer
07 afflict, horrify
08 distress

**grievous**
05 grave
06 severe, tragic
08 damaging, dreadful, shocking
09 appalling, atrocious, injurious, monstrous
10 deplorable, outrageous, unbearable
11 devastating, distressing

**grim**
04 dire, dour
05 awful, harsh, stern, surly
06 dogged, fierce, gloomy, grisly, horrid, morose, severe, sullen
07 ghastly
08 dreadful, fearsome, gruesome, horrible, menacing, obdurate, resolute, shocking, sinister, stubborn, terrible
09 appalling, harrowing, tenacious
10 depressing, determined, forbidding, formidable, horrendous, inexorable, persistent, unpleasant, unshakable, unyielding
11 frightening, threatening

**grimace**
03 mug
04 face, pout
05 frown, mouth, scowl, smirk, sneer
09 make a face

**grime**
03 mud
04 crud, dirt, dust, muck, soot, yuck
05 filth
06 grunge

**grimy**
05 dirty, dusty, mucky, muddy, sooty
06 filthy, grubby, smudgy, smutty, soiled

**grind**
03 rub
04 file, mill, rasp, sand, toil, whet
05 crush, grate, grind, labor, pound
06 abrade, kibble, polish, powder

07 crumble
08 drudgery, levigate
09 comminute, granulate, pulverize, triturate

❏**grind down**
05 crush
08 wear down

**grip**
03 bag, hug
04 case, grab, hold
05 catch, clasp, cling, grasp, power, rivet, seize
06 clench, clutch, compel, engage, valise
07 command, control, embrace, engross, involve, mastery
08 clutches, enthrall, entrance, suitcase
09 fascinate, get hold of, hypnotize, influence, latch onto, mesmerize, spellbind
10 domination, grab hold of
11 catch hold of, shoulder bag
12 overnight bag, traveling bag

❏**come to grips with, get to grips with**
05 grasp
06 tackle, take on
08 confront, cope with, deal with, face up to

**gripe**
03 nag
04 beef, carp, moan
05 bitch, groan, whine
06 grouch, grouse
07 griping, grumble, protest
08 complain
09 bellyache, complaint, grievance, objection
15 have a bone to pick

**gripping**
08 exciting, riveting
09 absorbing, thrilling
10 compelling, compulsive, engrossing, entrancing
11 enthralling, fascinating
12 spellbinding
13 unputdownable

**grisly**
04 gory, grim
05 awful
06 horrid
07 ghastly, hideous, macaber, macabre
08 dreadful, gruesome, horrible, shocking, terrible
09 abhorrent, appalling, frightful, loathsome, repulsive, revolting
10 abominable, disgusting, horrifying

**grit**
04 dust, guts, rasp, sand
05 gnash, grate, grind
06 clench, gravel, mettle, scrape
07 bravery, courage, pebbles, resolve, shingle
08 backbone, hardness, strength, tenacity
09 endurance, toughness
10 doggedness, resolution
12 perseverance
13 determination, steadfastness

**gritty**
05 brave, hardy, sandy, tough
06 dogged, grainy, plucky, spunky
08 abrasive, granular, gravelly, resolute, spirited
09 steadfast, tenacious
10 courageous, determined, mettlesome

**grizzle**
04 fret, moan
05 whine, worry
06 snivel
07 grumble, sniffle, snuffle, whimper
08 complain

**grizzled**
04 gray
05 hoary
07 graying
09 canescent
10 gray-headed
13 pepper-and-salt

**groan**
04 moan
05 whine
06 grouch, grouse, lament, object, outcry
07 griping, grumble, protest
08 complain
09 bellyache, complaint, grievance

**grocer**
11 storekeeper, supermarket
12 food merchant

**groggy**
04 dopy
05 dazed, dizzy, dopey, faint, muzzy, shaky, tired, woozy
06 wobbly
07 stunned
08 confused, unsteady
09 befuddled, stupefied
10 bewildered, punch-drunk

**groom**
03 fix
04 tidy

05 brush, coach, curry, drill, preen, prime, train, tutor
06 school, tidy up
07 arrange, husband, prepare, smarten
08 instruct, spruce up
09 stableboy, stableman
10 bridegroom

**groove**
03 cut, rut
04 like, slot
05 canal, ditch, enjoy, gouge, ridge, score, track
06 furrow, gutter, rabbet, rebate, sulcus, trench, trough
07 chamfer, channel
11 indentation

**grooved**
06 fluted, rutted, scored, sulcal
07 sulcate
08 furrowed, rabbeted
09 chamfered, channeled
12 scrobiculate

**grope**
04 feel, fish, hunt, pick
06 fumble, search
08 flounder, scrabble
09 cast about

**gross**
03 big, fat
04 blue, earn, huge, lewd, make, rude, take
05 bawdy, bulky, crude, dirty, heavy, large, obese, plain, sheer, total, utter, whole
06 coarse, earthy, entire, filthy, ribald, risqué, smutty, vulgar
07 blatant, boorish, glaring, hulking, immense, massive, obscene, obvious, serious
08 colossal, complete, flagrant, grievous, improper, indecent, manifest, outright, shameful, shocking
09 aggregate, before tax, corpulent, egregious, offensive, tasteless
10 outrageous, overweight, uncultured
11 insensitive

**grotesque**
03 odd
04 ugly
05 weird
07 bizarre, hideous, macaber, macabre, strange, surreal, twisted
08 deformed, fanciful, freakish
09 distorted, fantastic, ludicrous, malformed, misshapen, monstrous,

unnatural, unsightly, whimsical
10 outlandish, ridiculous
11 extravagant

**grotto**
04 cave
06 cavern, shrine
08 catacomb

**grouch**
04 moan
05 gripe
06 grouse, moaner, whiner
07 grumble
08 grumbler
09 complaint, grievance, objection
10 bellyacher, complainer, crosspatch, malcontent
11 faultfinder

**grouchy**
05 cross, sulky, surly, testy
06 grumpy
08 captious, churlish, petulant
09 crotchety, grumbling, irascible, irritable, querulous, truculent
11 bad-tempered
12 cantankerous

**ground**
04 base, call, clay, dirt, dust, land, lees, loam, park, plot, soil, yard
05 acres, arena, basis, coach, dregs, earth, field, found, train, tutor, wreck
06 bottom, campus, domain, estate, excuse, fields, inform, motive, reason, settle
07 deposit, dry land, educate, gardens, holding, prepare, residue, stadium, surface, terrain
08 initiate, instruct, property, sediment
09 establish, introduce, principle, territory
10 foundation, run aground, terra firma
11 precipitate, vindication
12 acquaint with, surroundings
13 justification
14 conducting body

**groundless**
05 empty, false
08 baseless, illusory
09 imaginary, unfounded
11 unjustified, unsupported
15 unsubstantiated

**groundwork**
04 base
05 basis

**group**
07 footing
08 homework, research
09 spadework
10 essentials, foundation
11 preparation

**group**
03 lot, set
04 band, body, club, crew, gang, knot, link, mass, pack, rank, sort, team, unit
05 batch, bunch, class, crowd, flock, genus, order, party, troop
06 circle, clique, family, gather, huddle
07 arrange, cluster, collect, company, coterie, element, faction, marshal
08 assemble, assembly, caboodle, category, classify, organize
09 associate, formation, gathering
10 categorize, collection, congregate, contingent
11 association, combination
12 congregation, organization

**grouse**
04 beef, carp, moan
05 bitch, gripe, groan, whine
06 grouch
07 grumble, protest
08 complain
09 bellyache, complaint, find fault, grievance, objection

**grove**
04 wood
05 arbor, copse
06 avenue, covert
07 coppice, thicket

**grovel**
04 fawn
05 cower, crawl, creep, defer, kneel, stoop, toady
06 cringe, crouch, kowtow, lie low, suck up
07 bow down, flatter, lie down
08 kiss up to
12 bow and scrape
14 demean yourself

**grow**
03 bud, get, sow, wax
04 farm, rise, stem, turn
05 arise, breed, issue, plant, raise, shoot, swell, widen
06 become, change, expand, extend, mature, spread, spring, sprout, thrive
07 advance, burgeon, develop, enlarge, fill out, improve, produce, stretch, thicken

08 flourish, increase, lengthen, multiply, mushroom, progress
09 cultivate, germinate, originate, propagate
11 proliferate

**growl**
03 yap
04 bark, howl, roar, snap, yelp
05 snarl
06 rumble

**grown-up**
03 man
05 adult, of age, woman
06 mature
09 full-grown
10 fullygrown

**growth**
04 lump, rise
05 tumor
06 spread
07 advance
08 increase, progress, swelling
09 evolution, expansion, extension, flowering, outgrowth, sprouting
10 burgeoning, maturation
11 development, enlargement, excrescence
13 amplification, magnification, proliferation
14 multiplication

**grub**
03 dig
04 eats, food, hunt, meal, nosh, pupa, root, worm
05 delve, larva, snack
06 burrow, ferret, forage, maggot, search
07 rummage
08 excavate
10 sustenance
11 caterpillar
12 refreshments

**grubby**
05 dirty, grimy, messy, mucky, seedy
06 filthy, shabby, soiled
07 scruffy, squalid

**grudge**
04 envy, hate, mind
05 covet, pique, spite, venom
06 animus, enmity, hatred, malice, rancor, resent
07 dislike, ill-will
08 aversion, begrudge, jealousy, object to
09 animosity, antipathy, grievance
10 antagonism, bitterness, resentment

12 hard feelings

**grudging**
07 envious, jealous
09 reluctant, resentful, unwilling
11 halfhearted

**grueling**
04 hard
05 harsh, tough
06 severe, taxing, tiring, trying
07 arduous
08 crushing, draining, grinding
09 demanding, difficult, laborious, punishing, strenuous
10 exhausting
12 backbreaking

**gruesome**
04 grim
05 awful
06 grisly, horrid
07 ghastly, hideous, macaber, macabre
08 dreadful, horrible, horrific, shocking, terrible
09 abhorrent, appalling, frightful, loathsome, monstrous, repellent, repugnant, repulsive, revolting, sickening
10 abominable, disgusting

**gruff**
04 curt, rude, sour
05 blunt, harsh, husky, rough, surly, testy, thick
06 abrupt, grumpy, hoarse, sullen, tetchy
07 brusque, rasping, throaty
08 croaking, impolite
11 bad-tempered
12 discourteous

**grumble**
04 beef, carp, fuss, moan
05 bitch, gripe, growl, whine
06 grouch, grouse, object
07 protest
08 complain
09 bellyache, complaint

**grumpy**
05 cross, sulky, surly
06 crabby, cranky, snappy, sullen, tetchy
07 crabbed, grouchy, in a huff, in a sulk
09 crotchety, irritable
11 bad-tempered, ill-tempered
12 cantankerous, discontented

**guarantee, guaranty**
04 back, bond, oath
06 assure, ensure, insure, pledge, secure, surety

**guarantor**
07 certify, earnest, endorse, promise, protect, warrant
08 contract, covenant, make sure, security, vouch for, warranty
09 assurance, insurance
10 collateral, underwrite
11 make certain, word of honor

**guarantor**
05 angel
06 backer, surety
08 bailsman, bondsman, guaranty
09 guarantee, warranter, warrantor
10 covenantor
11 underwriter

**guard**
02 C.O.
04 mind, save, wall
05 cover, fence, scout, watch
06 beware, buffer, bumper, defend, escort, fender, keeper, patrol, picket, police, screen, secure, sentry, shield
07 barrier, be alert, cushion, defense, look out, lookout, oversee, protect, shelter
08 defender, guardian, preserve, security, sentinel, shepherd, take care, watchdog, watchman
09 bodyguard, custodian, keep watch, protector, safeguard, supervise
10 protection
11 prison guard
18 corrections officer

❑ **off your guard**
06 unwary
07 napping, unaware
08 careless, unawares
10 unprepared
11 inattentive
12 unsuspecting

❑ **on your guard**
04 wary
05 alert, ready
07 careful
08 cautious, vigilant, watchful
09 attentive, wide awake
10 on the alert
11 circumspect
12 on the lookout

**guarded**
04 wary
05 cagey, chary
07 careful
08 cautious, discreet, reserved, reticent, watchful
09 reluctant, secretive

10 restrained
11 circumspect
12 noncommittal

**guardian**
05 guard
06 escort, keeper, warden
07 curator, steward, trustee
08 champion, defender, watchdog
09 attendant, caretaker, custodian, preserver, protector

**guardianship**
04 care
05 aegis, guard, hands, trust
07 custody, defense, keeping
08 guidance, wardship
09 patronage
10 wardenship
11 curatorship, safekeeping, stewardship, trusteeship

**guerrilla**
07 fighter
08 partisan
09 irregular, terrorist
11 bushwhacker, franc-tireur
14 freedom fighter

**guess**
05 fancy, hunch, judge, think
06 assume, reckon, theory
07 predict, suppose, surmise
08 consider, estimate, judgment
09 postulate, reckoning, speculate
10 assumption, conjecture, guestimate, hypothesis, make a guess, prediction
11 extrapolate, guesstimate, hypothesize, speculation, supposition
13 shot in the dark
14 ballpark figure

**guesswork**
06 theory
07 surmise
09 intuition, reckoning
10 assumption, conjecture, estimation, guestimate, hypothesis
11 guesstimate, speculation, supposition
13 extrapolation

**guest**
06 lodger, patron, roomer
07 boarder, company, visitor
08 resident, visitant

**guesthouse**
03 inn
05 hotel
06 hostel

08 hostelry
11 youth hostel
12 rooming house
13 boardinghouse

**guidance**
03 tip
04 help, hint, rule, tips
05 hints
06 advice, charge
07 control, counsel, pointer
08 teaching
09 direction
10 assistance, counseling, directions, guidelines, indication, leadership, management, suggestion
11 indications, information, instruction, suggestions

**guide**
03 key
04 guru, lead, mark, norm, rule, show, sign
05 gauge, model, pilot, point, steer, teach, train, tutor, usher
06 advise, attend, beacon, direct, escort, govern, leader, manage, manual, marker, mentor, ranger, signal
07 adviser, advisor, catalog, command, conduct, control, counsel, courier, educate, example, measure, oversee, pattern, pointer, teacher
08 Baedeker, chaperon, director, exemplar, handbook, instruct, maneuver, navigate, signpost, standard
09 archetype, attendant, benchmark, catalogue, conductor, counselor, criterion, directory, guidebook, guideline, influence, yardstick
10 indication, instructor, show the way
11 preside over, superintend

**guideline**
05 terms
06 advice
07 measure
08 standard
09 benchmark, criterion, direction, framework, parameter, principle, procedure, yardstick
10 constraint, regulation, suggestion, touchstone
11 information, instruction
14 recommendation

## guild
07 company, society
08 alliance
10 fellowship, fraternity
11 association, brotherhood, corporation
12 organization

## guile
04 ruse
05 craft, fraud
06 deceit
07 cunning, knavery, slyness
08 artifice, trickery, wiliness
10 artfulness, cleverness, craftiness, trickiness
11 deviousness
12 gamesmanship
13 double-dealing

## guileless
04 open
05 frank, naïve
06 direct, honest, simple
07 artless, genuine, sincere
08 innocent, straight, trusting, truthful
09 ingenuous, unworldly
11 transparent
15 straightforward, unsophisticated

## guilt
03 rap
05 blame, shame, wrong
06 regret
07 remorse
08 disgrace, dishonor
09 penitence
10 conscience, contrition, misconduct, repentance, wrongdoing
11 compunction, criminality, culpability
12 self-reproach, unlawfulness
14 responsibility, self-accusation
15 blameworthiness

## guiltless
04 pure
05 clean, clear
07 sinless
08 innocent, spotless
09 blameless, faultless, stainless, undefiled, unspotted, unsullied, untainted
10 impeccable, inculpable
11 untarnished
13 above reproach, unimpeachable

## guilty
03 bad
04 evil
05 sorry, wrong

06 sinful, wicked
07 ashamed, at fault, to blame
08 blamable, contrite, criminal, culpable, sheepish
09 convicted, offending
10 shamefaced
11 blameworthy, responsible
12 compunctious

## guise
04 face, form, mask, show
05 front, get-up, shape
06 aspect, custom, façade, manner
08 behavior, demeanor, disguise, likeness, pretense
09 semblance
10 appearance

## gulf
03 bay
04 cove, hole, rift, void
05 abyss, basin, bight, chasm, cleft, gorge, inlet, split
06 canyon, hollow, ravine
07 crevice, fissure, opening
10 separation

► *Names of Gulf states*:
05 Texas
07 Alabama, Florida
09 Louisiana
11 Mississippi

## gullet
03 maw
04 craw, crop
06 throat
09 esophagus

## gullibility
07 naïvety
09 credulity, innocence
10 simplicity
12 trustfulness

## gullible
05 green, naïve
07 foolish
08 innocent, trustful, trusting
09 credulous, ingenuous
12 unsuspecting
13 inexperienced
14 impressionable
15 unsophisticated

## gully
05 ditch, gorge
06 arroyo, canyon, gutter, ravine, valley
07 channel

## gulp
04 bolt, swig, wolf
05 draft, quaff, stuff, swill
06 devour, gobble, guzzle
07 swallow

08 mouthful, tuck into

## gum
03 fix
04 chew, clog, glue, seal
05 affix, paste, resin, stick
06 cement
08 adhesive, fixative
10 chewing gum

## ❏ gum up
04 clog
05 choke
06 hinder, impede
08 obstruct

## gummy
05 gluey, gooey, tacky
06 sticky, viscid
07 viscous

## gumption
03 wit
04 nous
05 savvy
06 acumen
07 ability
08 sagacity
09 acuteness
10 astuteness, cleverness, horse sense, shrewdness
11 common sense, discernment

## gun
03 rod
05 Betsy, fusil, piece, rifle
06 air gun, cannon, heater, mortar, musket, pistol
07 bazooka, carbine, firearm, shooter
08 howitzer, revolver
09 flintlock
10 six-shooter
11 blunderbuss

## gunman
06 hit man, killer, sniper
07 shooter, torpedo
08 assassin, murderer
10 gunslinger

## gurgle
05 plash
06 babble, bubble, burble, murmur, ripple, splash

## guru
04 sage
05 guide, swami, tutor
06 expert, leader, master, mentor, pundit
07 teacher
08 luminary
09 authority, maharishi
10 instructor
12 guiding light

## gush

03 jet, run
04 flow, go on, pour, rush, tide, well
05 burst, flood, issue, spate, spout, spurt, surge
06 babble, effuse, jabber, stream
07 cascade, chatter, enthuse
08 outburst
10 outpouring

## gushing

05 gushy
06 sickly
07 cloying, fulsome, mawkish
08 effusive
09 emotional, excessive
10 saccharine
11 sentimental

## gust

03 fit
04 blow, gale, puff, rush, wind
05 blast, burst, surge
06 breeze, flurry, squall
07 bluster

## gusto

04 élan, zeal, zest
05 verve
06 energy, fervor, relish
07 delight
09 enjoyment
10 enthusiasm, exuberance
12 exhilaration

## gusty

05 blowy, windy
06 breezy
07 squally
08 blustery

## gut

04 draw, loot, sack
05 basic, belly, clean, clear, empty, rifle
06 innate, ravage, strip,
07 enteral, enteric, plunder, ransack, stomach
08 clean out, clear out
09 devastate, heartfelt, intuitive
10 deep-seated, disembowel, eviscerate
11 instinctive

## gutless

04 weak

06 abject, craven, feeble
07 chicken
08 cowardly
09 spineless
11 lily-livered
12 fainthearted
14 chicken-hearted, chicken-livered

## guts

04 grit
05 nerve, pluck, spunk
06 bowels, mettle
07 bravery, courage, innards, insides, viscera
08 audacity, backbone, boldness, entrails
09 fortitude
10 intestines
11 vital organs

## gutsy

04 bold, game
05 brave
06 plucky
07 gallant, staunch
08 resolute, spirited
10 courageous, determined, mettlesome

## gutter

04 duct, pipe, tube
05 ditch, drain, sewer
06 sluice, trench, trough
07 channel, conduit, culvert

## guttersnipe

04 waif
05 gamin
06 urchin
10 ragamuffin
12 street urchin

## guttural

03 low
04 deep
05 gruff, harsh, husky, thick
06 hoarse
07 grating, rasping, throaty
08 croaking, gravelly

## guy

03 boy, joe, lad, man
04 chap
05 youth
06 fellow, person

## guzzle

04 bolt, cram, gulp, swig, wolf
05 quaff, stuff, swill
06 devour, gobble
07 put away, swallow
08 tuck into
09 knock back, polish off

## gymnastics

➤ See also SPORT

▶ *Gymnastic events*:

05 rings, vault
07 high bar
08 tumbling
10 trampoline, uneven bars, uneven bars
11 balance beam, pommel horse
12 parallel bars
13 floor exercise, horizontal bar

▶ *Names of gymnasts*:

03 **Kim** (Nellie), **Ono** (Takashi)
05 **Dawes** (Dominique)
06 **Korbut** (Olga), **Miller** (Shannon), **Retton** (Mary Lou), **Wilson** (Blaine)
07 **Zmeskal** (Kim)
08 **Comaneci** (Nadia), **Latynina** (Larissa)
09 **Andrianov** (Nikolai), **Caslavska** (Vera)
14 **Roethlisberger** (John)

## Gypsy, Gipsy

03 Rom, rye
05 nomad, rover
06 roamer, Romany
07 tzigane, tzigany
08 Bohemian, wanderer

## gyrate

04 spin, turn
05 swirl, twirl, wheel, whirl
06 circle, rotate, spiral, swivel
07 revolve
09 pirouette

## gyration

04 spin, turn
05 swirl, twirl, whirl
06 circle, spiral, swivel
08 rotation, spinning, wheeling, whirling
09 pirouette
10 revolution

**habit**
03 way
04 bent, mode, robe, ways, wont
05 dress, quirk, usage
06 custom, manner, outfit
07 costume, leaning, routine
08 clothing, practice, tendency, vestment
09 addiction, mannerism
10 dependence, proclivity, propensity
11 inclination
12 second nature
14 matter of course

**habitable**
07 livable
08 liveable
11 fit to live in, inhabitable

**habitat**
04 home
06 domain
07 element, terrain
08 dwelling, locality
09 territory
11 environment
12 surroundings

**habitation**
03 pad
04 home
05 abode, house
07 housing, lodging, mansion
08 domicile, dwelling, quarters
09 occupancy, residence, residency
13 accommodation, dwelling place
14 living quarters

**habitual**
03 set
05 fixed, usual
06 common, normal, wonted
07 chronic, regular, routine
08 addicted, constant, hardened
09 confirmed, customary
10 inveterate, persistent
11 established, traditional

**habituate**
05 adapt, inure, train
06 harden, school, season
07 break in

08 accustom
09 acclimate, condition
10 make used to
11 acclimatize, familiarize

**habitué**
06 patron
07 denizen, regular
08 customer
10 frequenter

**hack**
02 ax
03 axe, cut, hew, saw
04 chop, fell, gash, taxi
05 clear, horse, notch, slash, slave
06 mangle, writer
07 taxicab
08 lacerate, mutilate
09 scribbler
10 journalist

**hackle**

❏**get somone's hackles up**
03 bug, irk, vex
04 gall, miff, rile
05 anger, annoy
06 bother, enrage, hassle, heckle, madden, needle, nettle, offend, ruffle
07 affront, incense, outrage, provoke
08 irritate
09 aggravate, infuriate
10 antagonize, exasperate
15 get on your nerves

**hackneyed**
05 banal, corny, stale, stock, tired, trite
06 common
07 clichéd, worn-out
08 overused, timeworn
10 overworked, pedestrian, uninspired, unoriginal
11 commonplace, stereotyped
12 cliché-ridden, run-of-the-mill
13 platitudinous, unimaginative

**hag**
05 harpy, shrew, witch
06 gorgon, virago
08 battle-ax, harridan
09 battle-axe, termagant

**haggard**
03 wan
04 pale, thin
05 drawn, gaunt
06 pallid, wasted
07 drained, ghastly, pinched
08 careworn, shrunken
13 hollow-cheeked

**haggle**
06 barter, bicker, dicker, higgle
07 bargain, dispute, wrangle
08 beat down, squabble
09 negotiate

**hail**
04 come, laud, pelt, rain
05 cheer, exalt, greet, honor, storm
06 batter, praise, salute, shower, volley, wave to
07 acclaim, bombard, welcome
08 flag down, signal to
09 call out to, originate
11 acknowledge, bombardment
14 have been born in, have your home in
15 have your roots in

**hair**
03 fur, mop
04 coat, hide, mane, pelt, wool
05 locks, shock
06 fleece
07 tresses

❏**let your hair down**
05 relax
08 chill out, loosen up
09 hang loose
13 let yourself go
15 let it all hang out

❏**not turn a hair**
08 stay cool
12 keep your cool
14 not bat an eyelid

❏**split hairs**
05 cavil
07 nitpick, quibble
09 find fault

**hairbreadth, hair's-breadth**
04 hair, inch
05 close
07 whisker

10 very narrow

**hairdo**
02 do
03 cut, set
04 perm
05 style
08 coiffure

**hairdresser**
06 barber
07 stylist
08 coiffeur
09 coiffeuse
10 beautician
13 cosmetologist

**hairless**
04 bald
05 shorn
06 shaven
08 tonsured
09 beardless

**hair-raising**
05 eerie, scary
06 creepy
08 alarming, exciting, shocking
09 startling, thrilling
10 horrifying, petrifying, terrifying
11 frightening

**hairstyle**
03 cut, set
08 coiffure

► *Names of hairstyles*:
02 DA
03 bob, bun, wig
04 Afro, crop, perm, pouf
05 bangs, braid, plait
06 curled, mullet, pouffe, toupee
07 beehive, chignon, cowlick, crew cut, crimped, flattop, mohican, pageboy, pigtail, shingle, tonsure, topknot
08 bouffant, ducktail, ponytail, ringlets, skinhead
09 hairpiece, pompadour
10 dreadlocks

**hairy**
05 bushy, furry, fuzzy
06 fleecy, pilose, shaggy, woolly
07 bearded, hirsute
08 unshaven

**halcyon**
04 calm, mild
05 balmy, happy, quiet, still
06 gentle, golden, placid, serene
07 pacific
08 carefree, peaceful, tranquil
10 kingfisher, prosperous
11 flourishing, undisturbed

**hale**
03 fit
04 well
05 sound
06 hearty, robust, strong
07 healthy
09 in the pink
10 able-bodied
12 in fine fettle

**half**
04 part, semi-
05 share
06 barely, halved, partly, period, slight
07 divided, limited, partial, portion, section, segment
08 bisected, fraction, moderate, slightly
09 bisection, equal part, partially
10 equal share, fractional, hemisphere, incomplete, moderately, semicircle
12 divided in two, fifty percent, period of play
13 hemispherical

❑**by half**
03 too
04 very
11 excessively
12 considerably

❑**by halves**
12 inadequately, incompletely
13 halfheartedly

❑**not half**
08 not at all
09 not really

**half-baked**
05 crazy, silly
06 stupid
07 foolish
09 ill-judged, senseless
11 impractical, undeveloped
12 ill-conceived

**halfhearted**
04 weak
06 feeble
08 listless, lukewarm
09 apathetic
10 lackluster
11 indifferent, unconcerned
14 unenthusiastic

**halfway**
03 mid
04 mean
06 median, middle, midway
07 central
09 centrally
11 equidistant, in the middle
12 intermediate

❑**meet someone halfway**
09 make a deal, negotiate
10 compromise
11 give and take
15 make concessions

**half-wit**
03 mug
04 dolt, dope, dork, dupe, fool, geek
05 chump, dumbo, dunce, idiot, moron, ninny, twerp
06 cretin, dimwit, nitwit, stooge
07 buffoon, fathead
08 imbecile
09 birdbrain, blockhead, ignoramus, simpleton
10 nincompoop

**half-witted**
04 dull, dumb
05 batty, crazy, dotty, nutty, silly
06 simple, stupid
07 foolish, idiotic, moronic
08 crackpot
09 dimwitted
12 crackbrained, feebleminded, simple-minded

**hall**
04 dorm
05 foyer, lobby
07 chamber, passage
08 corridor
09 dormitory, vestibule
10 auditorium, passageway
12 assembly room

**hallmark**
04 mark, sign
05 badge, stamp
06 device, emblem, symbol
09 brand name, trademark
10 indication

**hallowed**
04 holy
06 sacred
07 blessed, revered
09 dedicated
10 inviolable, sacrosanct, sanctified
11 consecrated

**hallucinate**
04 trip
05 dream
08 daydream, freak out
09 fantasize, see things
13 imagine things

**hallucination**
04 trip
06 mirage, vision
07 fantasy, figment
08 delirium, delusion, freakout, illusion

10 apparition
14 phantasmagoria

**halo**
04 aura, ring
05 crown, glory
06 corona, gloria, nimbus
07 aureola, aureole
08 gloriole, halation, radiance

**halt**
03 end
04 curb, quit, rest, stem, stop
05 break, cease, check, pause
06 arrest, desist, draw up, finish, impede, pull up
08 deadlock, hold back, stoppage
09 cessation, terminate
10 call it a day, put an end to, standstill
11 come to a stop, discontinue, termination
12 interruption
13 bring to a close

**halting**
06 broken
07 awkward, labored
08 hesitant, unsteady
09 faltering, imperfect, stumbling, uncertain
10 stammering, stuttering

**halve**
05 share, split
06 bisect, divide
07 cut down
10 split in two
11 dichotomize

**halved**
06 shared
07 divided
08 bisected

**hammer**
03 din, hit
04 bang, bash, beat, drum, form, lick, make, mold, plug, rout, slam, slap, slog
05 drive, force, grind, knock, labor, pound, shape
06 attack, batter, beetle, defeat, keep on, mallet, sledge, strike, thrash
07 belabor, clobber, instill, outplay, persist, run down, trounce
08 overcome
09 criticize, denigrate, drive home, overwhelm, persevere, reiterate
10 annihilate
12 sledgehammer

❑ **hammer out**
06 finish, settle
07 resolve, sort out, work out
09 negotiate, thrash out
10 accomplish

**hamper**
03 box
04 curb, foil, stop
05 block, check, cramp
06 basket, bridle, fetter, hinder, hold up, impede, retard, stymie, thwart
07 inhibit, pannier, prevent, shackle
08 encumber, handicap, obstruct, restrain, restrict
09 frustrate, hamstring

**hamstring**
04 foil, stop
05 check, cramp, stymy
06 hinder, hold up, impede, stymie, tendon, thwart
07 cripple, disable
08 encumber, handicap, paralyze, restrain, restrict
09 frustrate
12 incapacitate

**hand**
03 aid, fin, paw
04 care, fist, give, help, mitt, palm, pass
05 arrow, offer, power, yield
06 charge, convey, marker, succor, worker
07 acclaim, command, conduct, control, custody, deliver, laborer, ovation, pointer, present, support, workman, writing
08 applause, cheering, clapping, clutches, employee, farmhand, hand over, handclap, hireling, transmit
09 authority, indicator, influence, operative, ranchhand
10 assistance, management, penmanship, possession
11 calligraphy, handwriting, helping hand, supervision

❑ **at hand**
04 near
05 close, handy, ready
06 to hand
08 imminent
10 accessible

❑ **by hand**
12 precariously
14 on the breadline
15 from hand to mouth

❑ **hand down**
04 give, will
05 grant, leave
06 pass on
08 bequeath, pass down

❑ **hand in glove**
10 hand in hand
14 closely related
15 closely together

❑ **hand out**
07 deal out, dish out, give out, mete out, pass out
08 dispense, share out
10 distribute

❑ **hand over**
04 give, pass
05 yield
06 donate
07 consign, deliver, present
08 transfer, turn over
09 surrender
10 relinquish

❑ **in hand**
05 put by, ready, spare
08 under way
09 available, in reserve
12 under control

❑ **to hand**
04 near
05 close, handy, ready
06 at hand
08 imminent
09 available
10 accessible
13 about to happen

❑ **try your hand**
07 attempt, have a go
09 have a shot, have a stab
10 have a crack

❑ **win hands down**
09 win easily
15 win effortlessly

**handbill**
02 ad
05 flyer
06 letter, notice
07 leaflet
08 circular, pamphlet
13 advertisement

**handbook**
05 guide
06 manual
09 companion, guidebook
10 prospectus
15 instruction book

**handcuff**
06 fasten, fetter, secure
07 manacle, shackle

## handcuffs
07 fetters
08 manacles, shackles

## handful
03 few
04 pain, pest
06 bother, little
08 nuisance
10 smattering
11 small amount, small number
13 pain in the neck
15 thorn in the flesh

## handicap
04 curb, odds
05 block, check, limit
06 defect, hamper, hinder, impair, impede, retard
07 barrier, disable, penalty
08 drawback, encumber, hold back, obstacle, restrict
09 allowance, hindrance
10 constraint, disability, impediment, limitation
11 abnormality, encumbrance, restriction
14 stumbling block

## handicraft
03 art
05 craft, skill
09 craftwork

## handiwork
03 art
05 craft, doing, skill
07 product
08 creation
09 invention
11 achievement
14 responsibility

## handle
03 paw
04 feel, grip, haft, hilt, hold, knob, work
05 drive, grasp, shaft, steer, stock, touch, treat
06 deal in, finger, fondle, manage, market, tackle
07 control, trade in, traffic
08 cope with, deal with
09 supervise
10 take care of

## handling
07 conduct, running
08 approach
09 direction, operation, treatment
10 discussion, management
12 manipulation
14 administration

## handout
04 alms, dole
05 gifts, issue, share
07 charity, freebee, freebie, leaflet
08 brochure, circular, pamphlet
10 free sample, literature
12 press release

## handpicked
05 elect, elite
06 choice, chosen, select
08 screened, selected

## handsome
04 fair, fine
05 hunky, large
06 lavish
07 elegant, liberal, sizable
08 abundant, generous, gorgeous, sizeable
09 plentiful
10 attractive, personable
11 good-looking, magnanimous
12 considerable

## handsomely
06 richly
08 lavishly
09 liberally
10 abundantly, generously
11 plentifully
12 munificently
13 magnanimously

## handwriting
04 hand
06 scrawl, script
07 writing
08 scribble
09 autograph
10 penmanship
11 calligraphy

## handy
04 near
05 adept, ready
06 adroit, at hand, clever, expert, to hand, useful
07 skilled
08 skillful
09 available, dexterous, practical
10 accessible, convenient
11 practicable, within reach

## handyman
09 odd-jobber
15 Jack-of-all-trades

## hang
03 fix, sag
04 flop
05 affix, cling, drape, drift, droop, float, hover, put up, stick, swing
06 append, attach, dangle, fasten, linger, remain
07 flutter, suspend
08 bend over, drop down, hang down, lean over, string up

## ◻ get the hang
05 grasp
06 fathom
10 comprehend, understand
13 get the knack of

## ◻ hang around
05 haunt
06 dawdle, linger, loiter
08 frequent
09 hang about, waste time

## ◻ hang back
06 recoil
07 shy away
08 hesitate, hold back
10 shrink back, stay behind

## ◻ hang fire
04 stop, wait
05 delay, stall, stick
08 hold back
09 vacillate
13 procrastinate

## ◻ hang on
04 grip, wait
05 cling, grasp
06 clutch, endure, hold on, remain, rest on, turn on
07 carry on, hinge on, hold out, persist
08 continue, depend on, hold fast
09 persevere

## ◻ hang over
04 loom
06 impend, menace
08 approach, overhang, threaten

## hangdog
05 cowed
06 abject, guilty
08 cringing, defeated, downcast, sneaking, wretched
09 miserable
10 browbeaten, shamefaced

## hanger-on
05 toady
06 lackey, minion
08 follower, henchman, parasite
09 dependent, sycophant
10 freeloader

## hanging
05 drape, loose
06 floppy
07 drapery, pendent
08 dangling, drooping, flapping, flopping, swinging

**hangout**
09 execution, pendulous, suspended
11 unsupported
12 dropping down

**hangout**
03 den
04 dive
05 haunt, joint, local
12 meetingplace

**hangover**
12 aftereffects, morning after

**hang-up**
05 block, thing
06 phobia
07 problem
08 fixation, idée fixe
09 obsession
10 difficulty, inhibition
11 mental block

**hank**
04 coil, loop, roll
05 piece, skein, twist
06 length

**hanker**

□ **hanker after, hanker for**
05 covet, crave
07 itch for, long for, pine for, wish for
08 yearn for
09 hunger for, thirst for
10 be dying for

**hankering**
04 itch, urge, wish
06 desire, hunger, pining, thirst
07 craving, longing
08 yearning

**hanky-panky**
08 mischief, trickery
09 chicanery, deception
10 dishonesty, subterfuge
11 shenanigans
13 funny business
14 monkey business

**haphazard**
06 casual, chance, random
07 aimless
08 careless, slapdash, slipshod
09 arbitrary, hit-or-miss, irregular
12 disorganized, unmethodical, unsystematic
14 indiscriminate

**hapless**
06 cursed, jinxed
07 unhappy, unlucky
08 ill-fated, luckless, wretched
09 miserable
11 star-crossed, unfortunate

**happen**
04 fall, find, go on
05 arise, ensue, hit on, occur
06 appear, crop up, follow, result, turn up
07 develop, light on, turn out
08 chance on, come true, discover
09 come about, eventuate, stumble on, supervene, take place, transpire
10 come across
11 materialize
13 come into being

**happening**
05 event, scene
06 action, affair, chance
07 episode
08 accident, incident, occasion
10 experience, occurrence, phenomenon
11 eventuality, proceedings
12 circumstance

**happily**
06 gladly
07 luckily, merrily
08 by chance, heartily, joyfully, joyously
09 agreeably, fittingly, gleefully, willingly
10 cheerfully
11 contentedly, delightedly, fortunately, opportunely
12 auspiciously, propitiously
14 providentially

**happiness**
03 joy
05 bliss
06 gaiety
07 delight, ecstasy, elation
08 felicity, gladness, pleasure
09 enjoyment, merriment, merriness
10 blitheness, cheeriness, exuberance, joyfulness
11 contentment, good spirits
12 cheerfulness

**happy**
03 apt, gay
04 glad
05 jolly, lucky, merry
06 blithe, elated, jovial, joyful, joyous, proper
07 content, fitting, gleeful, helpful, pleased, radiant
08 apposite, carefree, cheerful, ecstatic, euphoric, thrilled
09 cock-a-hoop, contented, delighted, favorable, fortunate, gratified, opportune, overjoyed,

rapturous, satisfied, unworried
10 auspicious, beneficial, felicitous, propitious
11 appropriate, in a good mood, on cloud nine, tickled pink
12 advantageous, lighthearted, walking on air
13 floating on air, in good spirits, in high spirits
15 in seventh heaven, on top of the world

**happy-go-lucky**
06 blithe, casual
08 carefree
09 easygoing
10 insouciant, nonchalant
11 improvident
12 devil-may-care, lighthearted

**harangue**
05 spout
06 preach, speech, tirade
07 address, declaim, lecture
08 diatribe
09 hold forth
10 peroration
11 exhortation

**harass**
03 nag, vex
04 fret, tire
05 annoy, harry, hound, worry
06 badger, bother, hassle, pester, plague, stress
07 disturb, dragoon, exhaust, fatigue, provoke, torment, trouble, wear out
08 irritate
09 persecute
10 antagonize, exasperate

**harassed**
05 vexed
07 harried, hassled, hounded, plagued, uptight, worried
08 careworn, pestered, strained, stressed, troubled
09 pressured, tormented
11 pressurized, stressed out
13 under pressure

**harassment**
06 bother, hassle
07 torment, trouble
08 distress, nuisance, vexation
09 annoyance, badgering, pestering
10 irritation, pressuring
11 aggravation, persecution

**harbinger**
04 omen, sign
06 herald
07 portent, warning

09 foretoken, messenger, precursor
10 forerunner, indication

**harbor**
04 dock, hide, hold, port, quay
05 haven, house, nurse, wharf
06 foster, marina, refuge, shield
07 cherish, cling to, mooring, nurture, protect, shelter
09 anchorage, entertain

**hard**
04 busy, cold, firm, grim, keen, real, true
05 cruel, dense, harsh, heavy, rigid, sharp, solid, stern, stiff, tough
06 actual, bitter, knotty, potent, severe, strict, strong, tiring
07 arduous, austere, callous, certain, complex, harmful, heavily, intense, onerous, painful, violent, zealous
08 exacting, forceful, obdurate, pitiless, powerful, puzzling, rigorous, ruthless
09 addictive, assiduous, condensed, difficult, energetic, intricate, laborious, merciless, resistant, strenuous, unfeeling, unsparing
10 compressed, exhausting, implacable, inflexible, oppressive, perplexing, tyrannical, unpleasant, unyielding
11 bewildering, coldhearted, complicated, distressing, industrious, unrelenting
12 backbreaking, disagreeable, enthusiastic, habit-forming, impenetrable, indisputable
13 conscientious, uncomfortable, unsympathetic
14 with difficulty

❑**hard and fast**
03 set
05 fixed, rigid
06 strict
07 binding
08 definite
09 immutable, stringent
10 inflexible, invariable, unchanging
11 unalterable
12 unchangeable
14 uncompromising

❑**hard up**
05 broke, short
06 busted

08 bankrupt, in the red
09 penniless
10 cleaned out, stone broke
11 impecunious
12 impoverished
15 strapped for cash

**hard-bitten**
05 tough
06 dogged, inured, shrewd
07 callous, cynical
08 ruthless
09 practical, realistic, toughened
10 hard-boiled, hardheaded
11 down-to-earth
13 unsentimental

**hard-boiled**
05 tough
07 cynical
10 well-cooked
11 down-to-earth
13 unsentimental

**hard-core**
05 rigid
07 blatant, die-hard, extreme
08 explicit
09 dedicated, steadfast

**harden**
03 set
04 bake, cake, gird
05 inure, nerve, steel
06 anneal, deaden, freeze, season, temper
07 congeal, fortify, petrify, stiffen, toughen
08 accustom, solidify
09 habituate, reinforce, vulcanize
10 strengthen

**hardened**
03 set
06 inured
07 callous, chronic
08 obdurate, seasoned
09 reprobate, toughened
10 accustomed, habituated, inveterate
12 incorrigible, irredeemable

**hardheaded**
05 sharp, tough
06 astute, shrewd
08 rational, sensible
09 hard-nosed, practical, pragmatic, realistic
10 hard-bitten, hard-boiled
11 down-to-earth
13 unsentimental

**hardhearted**
04 cold
05 cruel, stony

06 unkind
07 callous, inhuman
08 pitiless, uncaring
09 heartless, merciless, unfeeling
13 unsympathetic

**hard-hitting**
05 tough
08 critical, directly, forceful, straight, vigorous
12 condemnatory
13 no-holds-barred
14 uncompromising

**hardiness**
09 fortitude, toughness
10 resilience, robustness, ruggedness, sturdiness
11 intrepidity

**hard-line**
05 tough
06 strict
07 extreme
08 militant
10 inflexible, unyielding
12 intransigent

**hardly**
04 just
06 barely
08 not at all, not quite, only just, scarcely

**hardness**
08 coldness, firmness, rigidity, severity
09 harshness, sternness, toughness
10 difficulty, inhumanity
12 pitilessness

**hard pressed**
06 pushed
07 hard put, harried, put upon
08 harassed
09 overtaxed
11 up against it
12 overburdened

**hardship**
04 need, pain, want
05 trial
07 burdens, poverty, trouble
09 adversity, austerity, privation, suffering
10 affliction, misfortune
11 deprivation, destitution, tribulation

**hard-wearing**
05 stout, tough
06 rugged, strong, sturdy
07 durable, lasting
08 well-made
09 resilient
11 built to last

**hard-working**
04 busy
11 industrious

**hardy**
05 stout, tough
06 plucky, robust, strong, sturdy
07 durable, healthy, stoical
08 intrepid, stalwart, vigorous
09 heavy-duty, undaunted
11 indomitable
12 stouthearted

**harebrained**
04 daft, rash, wild
05 giddy, inane, silly
06 stupid
07 foolish
08 careless, crackpot, reckless
14 scatterbrained

**hark**
04 hear, mark, note
06 listen, notice
07 give ear, hearken, pay heed

**❑ hark back**
06 go back, recall, revert
07 regress
08 remember, turn back
09 recollect

**harlequin**
04 fool, zany
05 clown, comic, joker
06 jester
07 buffoon

**harlot**
03 pro
04 tart
05 hussy, tramp, whore
06 hooker
08 call girl, strumpet
10 loose woman, prostitute
11 fallen woman
12 camp follower, streetwalker

**harm**
03 ill, mar
04 hurt, loss, pain, ruin
05 abuse, spoil, wound, wrong
06 damage, impair, injure, injury,
    misuse, molest
07 blemish, destroy
08 ill treat, maltreat
09 adversity, detriment,
    suffering
10 impairment, misfortune
11 destruction, work against

**harmful**
03 bad
05 toxic
07 noxious
08 damaging, wounding

09 dangerous, hazardous,
    injurious, poisonous,
    unhealthy
10 pernicious
11 deleterious, destructive,
    detrimental, unwholesome

**harmless**
04 mild, safe
06 gentle
08 innocent, nontoxic
09 blameless, innocuous
11 inoffensive

**harmonious**
06 mellow
07 cordial, musical, tuneful
08 amicable, balanced, friendly,
    matching, peaceful,
    pleasant, rhythmic
09 congruous, melodious
10 compatible, concordant,
    euphonious, like-minded
11 mellifluous, sympathetic,
    symphonious

**harmonize**
03 mix
04 suit, tone
05 agree, blend, fit in, match
06 accord
07 balance, compose
08 coincide
10 coordinate, correspond, go
    together

**harmony**
04 tune
05 amity, peace, unity
06 accord, melody, unison
07 balance, concord, euphony,
    oneness, rapport
08 goodwill, symmetry
09 agreement, unanimity
10 conformity, consonance
11 concurrence, cooperation,
    tunefulness
12 coordination, friendliness
13 compatibility,
    melodiousness
14 like-mindedness
15 mellifluousness

**harness**
04 gear, tack
05 reins
06 straps, tackle
07 channel, control, exploit,
    utilize
09 equipment, make use of
13 accouterments,
    accoutrements

**❑ in harness**
08 together
11 cooperating
13 collaborating, in cooperation

**harp**

**❑ harp on**
03 nag
05 labor, press, renew
06 repeat
07 dwell on
09 reiterate

**harpoon**
04 barb, dart
05 arrow, spear
07 trident

**harridan**
03 nag
04 fury
05 harpy, scold, shrew, witch
06 dragon, gorgon, tartar, virago
07 hellcat
08 battle-ax
09 battle-axe, termagant,
    Xanthippe

**harried**
05 beset
07 anxious, hassled, plagued,
    ravaged, worried
08 agitated, bothered, harassed,
    troubled
09 pressured, tormented
11 hard-pressed, pressurized

**harrowing**
08 alarming, daunting
09 agonizing, traumatic,
    upsetting
10 disturbing, perturbing,
    terrifying, tormenting
11 distressing, frightening
12 excruciating, heart-rending,
    nerve-racking
13 nerve-wracking

**harry**
03 nag, vex
05 annoy, chivy, worry
06 badger, bother, chivvy,
    harass, hassle, molest, pester,
    plague
07 oppress, torment
09 persecute

**harsh**
04 grim, hard, wild
05 bleak, cruel, gaudy, gruff,
    lurid, rough, sharp, showy,
    stark, stern
06 barren, bitter, bright, brutal,
    coarse, flashy, garish, hoarse,
    savage, severe, strict
07 acerbic, austere, glaring,
    grating, inhuman, jarring,
    rasping, raucous, Spartan
08 abrasive, croaking, dazzling,
    desolate, grinding, guttural,
    pitiless, ruthless, strident

**harshness**
09 dissonant, Draconian, merciless, unfeeling
10 discordant, unpleasant
11 comfortless, ear-piercing
12 inhospitable

**harshness**
05 rigor
08 acerbity, acrimony, asperity, hardness, severity
09 brutality, ill-temper, roughness, starkness, sternness
10 bitterness, coarseness, strictness
12 abrasiveness

**harum-scarum**
04 rash, wild
05 hasty
06 scatty
07 erratic
08 careless, reckless
09 haphazard, impetuous
11 harebrained, precipitate
13 ill-considered, irresponsible
14 scatterbrained

**harvest**
04 crop, gain, pick, reap
05 amass, glean, horde, pluck, stock, store, yield
06 fruits, garner, gather, obtain, return
07 acquire, collect, produce, product, reaping, returns
08 gather in
10 accumulate, collection
11 consequence, ingathering
12 accumulation

**hash**
04 mess, stew
05 botch, mix-up
06 bungle, hotpot, muddle
07 goulash
08 mishmash
09 confusion, lobscouse
10 hodgepodge, hotchpotch

**hashish**
03 pot
04 bang, dope, hash, hemp
05 bhang, ganja, grass
08 cannabis
09 marijuana

**hassle**
03 bug
05 annoy, chivy, harry, hound
06 badger, bother, chivvy, harass, pester
07 dispute, problem, quarrel, trouble, wrangle
08 nuisance, struggle
09 bickering
13 inconvenience

**haste**
04 rush
05 hurry, speed
07 urgency
08 alacrity, celerity, rapidity, rashness, velocity
09 quickness, swiftness
11 impetuosity
15 expeditiousness

**hasten**
03 aid, fly, run
04 bolt, dash, race, rush, tear
05 boost, hurry, press, speed
06 assist, sprint
07 advance, hurry up, quicken, speed up
08 dispatch, expedite, step on it
09 hotfoot it, make haste
10 accelerate, get a move on
11 precipitate, push forward
12 step on the gas

**hastily**
04 fast
05 apace
06 rashly
07 quickly, rapidly
08 chop-chop, speedily
09 hurriedly
10 heedlessly, recklessly
11 double-quick, impetuously, impulsively
13 precipitately

**hasty**
04 fast, rash
05 brief, brisk, quick, rapid, short, swift
06 prompt, rushed, speedy
07 cursory, hurried
08 careless, fleeting, headlong, heedless, reckless
09 hot-headed, impatient, impetuous, impulsive
11 precipitate, thoughtless

**hat**

▶ *Types of hat*:
03 fez, tam
04 hood, kufi
05 beret, busby, derby, miter, snood, toque
06 beanie, boater, bonnet, bowler, cloche, fedora, helmet, mobcap, panama, sun hat, top hat, trilby, turban
07 biretta, Homburg, homburg, pillbox, porkpie, Stetson
08 bearskin, sombrero, straw hat
09 glengarry, sou'wester
10 pokebonnet, porkpie hat
11 baseball cap, deerstalker, mortarboard, southwester, tam-o'-shanter
12 stovepipe hat, ten-gallon hat

**hatch**
04 plan, plot
05 breed, brood, sit on
06 design, devise, invent, scheme
07 concoct, dream up, project, think up
08 conceive, contrive, incubate
09 formulate, originate

**hatchet**
02 ax
03 axe
06 pickax
07 chopper, cleaver, machete, mattock, pickaxe
08 battle-ax, tomahawk
09 battle-axe

**hatchet man**
04 goon
06 critic, killer
07 torpedo
08 assassin, murderer

**hate**
05 abhor
06 detest, enmity, grudge, hatred, loathe, rancor, regret
07 despise, ill will
08 aversion, execrate, loathing
09 abominate, animosity, apologize, hostility
10 abhorrence, antagonism, bitterness, resentment
11 abomination

**hateful**
04 evil, foul, vile
06 horrid, odious
07 heinous
09 abhorrent, execrable, loathsome, obnoxious, offensive, repellent, repugnant, repulsive, revolting
10 abominable, despicable, detestable, disgusting
12 contemptible

**hatred**
04 hate
06 animus, enmity, grudge, rancor
07 ill will
08 aversion, loathing
09 animosity, antipathy, hostility, revulsion
10 abhorrence, antagonism, execration, repugnance
11 abomination, detestation

**haughtiness**
04 airs
05 pride

07 conceit, disdain, hauteur
08 contempt
09 aloofness, arrogance, loftiness
10 snootiness
12 snobbishness

**haughty**
04 vain
05 lofty, proud
06 snooty
07 stuck-up
08 arrogant, snobbish, superior
09 conceited, imperious
10 disdainful
11 overbearing, patronizing, swellheaded
12 supercilious
13 condescending, high and mighty

**haul**
03 lug, tow, tug
04 cart, drag, draw, find, gain, hump, loot, move, pull, push, ship, swag
05 booty, carry, heave, trail, yield
06 convey, convoy, spoils
07 plunder, takings
09 transport

**haunches**
04 hips
05 nates
06 thighs
07 hunkers
08 backside, buttocks

**haunt**
03 den
04 dive
05 beset, curse, harry, recur, spook, visit, worry
06 burden, obsess, plague, prey on
07 hangout, oppress, possess, torment, trouble
08 frequent
09 patronize
11 hang about in, materialize
12 hang around in, meetingplace
14 stamping ground

**haunted**
06 cursed, jinxed, spooky
07 ghostly, plagued, worried
08 obsessed, troubled
09 possessed, tormented

**haunting**
08 poignant
09 evocative, memorable, nostalgic, recurrent
11 atmospheric
13 unforgettable

**have**
03 ask, bid, con, eat, get, own, use
04 bear, down, dupe, feel, find, fool, gain, gulp, hold, keep, make, meet, must, show, take, tell
05 abide, allow, beget, brook, cheat, drink, enjoy, force, order, ought, stand, trick
06 accept, compel, devour, diddle, embody, endure, enjoin, guzzle, oblige, obtain, permit, secure, should, suffer, take in
07 acquire, arrange, command, consume, contain, deceive, embrace, exhibit, express, include, possess, procure, receive, request, require, swallow, swindle, undergo
08 comprise, manifest, organize, persuade, submit to, talk into, tolerate, tuck into
09 consist of, encounter, go through, knock back, partake of, put up with
10 comprehend, experience, take part in
11 demonstrate, give birth to, incorporate, prevail upon
13 participate in

◻**have done with**
04 stop
05 cease
06 desist, give up
09 throw over
10 finish with
13 be through with
15 wash your hands of

◻**have had it**
07 be bored
10 be defeated, have no hope
11 be disgusted, be exhausted, bite the dust
13 be ready to quit

**haven**
04 dock, port
05 oasis
06 asylum, harbor, refuge
07 retreat, shelter
09 anchorage, sanctuary

**haversack**
03 bag
08 backpack, knapsack
09 canvas bag

**havoc**
04 ruin
05 chaos, wreck
06 damage, mayhem
08 shambles, wreckage

11 rack and ruin

**hawk**
04 bark, kite, sell, tout, vend
06 falcon, market, peddle, tercel
07 buzzard, goshawk, haggard, harrier, tiercel
09 marsh hawk, warmonger
10 make a pitch
11 haggard hawk

**hawker**
06 barker, pedlar, vendor
07 peddler
08 falconer, huckster, pitchman

**haywire**
03 mad
04 wild
05 crazy, wrong
07 chaotic, tangled
10 disordered, topsy-turvy
12 disorganized, out of control

**hazard**
04 luck, risk
05 offer, peril, stake
06 chance, danger, gamble, menace, submit, threat
07 pitfall, suggest, venture
08 accident
09 put at risk, speculate
10 jeopardize
13 put in jeopardy
14 expose to danger

**hazardous**
05 hairy, risky
06 chancy, tricky, unsafe
08 insecure, perilous
09 dangerous
10 precarious
11 threatening

**haze**
03 fog
04 blur, film, mist, smog
05 cloud, steam, vapor
06 muddle
09 confusion, fogginess, mistiness, obscurity, smokiness, vagueness
10 cloudiness
12 bewilderment
14 indistinctness

**hazy**
03 dim
05 faint, foggy, fuzzy, milky, misty, muzzy, smoky, vague
06 cloudy, veiled
07 blurred, clouded, obscure
08 overcast
10 ill-defined, indefinite, indistinct

**head**
03 nob, nut, run, tip, top, van, wit

04 apex, bean, boss, conk, fizz, foam, fore, lead, main, mind, peak, rise, rule, wits
05 brain, chair, chief, crest, crown, first, fount, front, froth, guide, prime, ruler, sense, skull
06 brains, charge, climax, crisis, crunch, direct, govern, height, honcho, leader, manage, noddle, noggin, origin, source, spring, summit, toilet, wisdom
07 bubbles, captain, command, control, cranium, dilemma, go first, highest, leading, premier, supreme, topmost
08 calamity, chairman, controls, director, dominant, foremost, governor, vanguard
09 commander, emergency, forefront, intellect, president, principal, reasoning, supervise
10 administer, chairwoman, controller, gray matter, headmaster, leadership, management, preeminent, supervisor, upper story, wellspring
11 catastrophe, chairperson, common sense, superintend, supervision
12 be in charge of, directorship, headmistress, intelligence
13 administrator, be in control of, critical point, understanding
14 be at the front of, superintendent

❑ **go to your head**
06 puff up
08 befuddle
09 inebriate, make dizzy, make drunk, make proud, make woozy
10 intoxicate
12 make arrogant
13 make conceited

❑ **head for**
06 aim for
07 make for, point to, turn for
08 go toward, steer for
10 move toward
12 direct toward

❑ **head off**
05 avert
06 cut off, divert
07 deflect, fend off, prevent, ward off

09 forestall, intercept, interpose, intervene, turn aside

❑ **head over heels**
07 utterly
09 intensely
10 completely, recklessly, thoroughly
14 uncontrollably

❑ **head up**
04 lead
06 direct, manage
12 be in charge of, take charge of

❑ **keep your head**
08 keep calm
12 keep your cool

❑ **lose your head**
05 panic
12 lose your cool

**headache**
04 bane, pest
05 worry
06 bother, hassle
07 problem, trouble
08 migraine, nuisance, vexation

**heading**
04 head, name
05 class, title
06 rubric
07 caption, section, subject
08 category, division, headline

**headland**
04 cape, head, ness
05 point
10 promontory

**headlong**
04 rash
05 hasty
06 rashly, wildly
07 hastily
08 reckless
09 breakneck
10 recklessly
11 precipitate
13 precipitately

**headman**
04 boss
05 chief, ruler
06 leader, sachem
07 captain

**head-on**
06 direct
08 directly, straight
11 full-frontal

**headquarters**
02 HQ
04 base
10 head office, main office
11 nerve center

13 control center

**headstrong**
06 unruly
07 wayward, willful
08 obdurate, stubborn
09 obstinate, pigheaded
10 refractory, self-willed

**headway**
06 ground
07 advance
08 progress

**heady**
07 rousing
08 euphoric, exciting
11 stimulating
12 exhilarating, intoxicating, invigorating, overpowering

**heal**
04 cure, mend
05 salve, treat
06 remedy, settle, soothe
07 assuage, comfort, improve, patch up, restore
08 make good, make well, palliate, put right, set right
09 reconcile
10 make better

**health**
04 form, tone, trim
05 shape, state, vigor
06 fettle
07 fitness, welfare
08 strength
09 condition, good shape, soundness, well-being
10 robustness
12 constitution

**healthy**
03 fit
04 fine, good, well
05 hardy, sound
06 robust, strong, sturdy
07 bracing
08 blooming, sensible, thriving, vigorous
09 in the pink, judicious, wholesome
10 beneficial, nourishing, nutritious, refreshing, salubrious, successful
11 flourishing, in condition, in good shape, stimulating
12 fit as a fiddle, in fine fettle, invigorating
13 hale and hearty

**heap**
03 lot, pot
04 a lot, bank, load, lots, mass, pile, pots, tons

**hear**

05 amass, build, hoard, loads, mound, stack, store
06 bestow, bundle, burden, confer, gather, jalopy, lavish, oodles, plenty, scores, shower, stacks, supply
08 assemble, lashings, millions, mountain
09 abundance, great deal, stockpile
10 quantities

**hear**
03 try
04 heed
05 catch, judge, learn
06 be told, gather, listen, pick up, take in
07 examine, find out, inquire, make out
08 consider, discover, perceive
09 ascertain, eavesdrop
10 adjudicate, be informed, understand
11 investigate
12 pay attention

**hearing**
03 ear
05 range, reach, sound, trial
06 review
07 earshot, inquest, inquiry
08 audience, audition, judgment
09 interview
10 perception
11 examination, inquisition
12 adjudication
13 investigation

**hearsay**
04 buzz, talk
05 rumor
06 gossip, report
11 word of mouth
12 tittle-tattle

**heart**
03 nub
04 core, crux, guts, love, mind, pith, pity
05 pluck
06 center, kernel, marrow, middle, warmth
07 bravery, concern, courage, emotion, essence, feeling, nucleus, passion
08 boldness, keenness, kindness, sympathy
09 affection, character, eagerness, fortitude, sentiment, substance
10 compassion, enthusiasm, resolution, tenderness
12 quintessence
13 determination

► *Parts of the heart:*
10 left atrium, myocardium
11 aortic valve, mitral valve, right atrium
13 bicuspid valve, carotid artery, left ventricle
14 ascending aorta, pulmonary valve, right ventricle, tricuspid valve

❑**at heart**
08 at bottom
09 basically, in essence
11 essentially
13 fundamentally

❑**by heart**
03 pat
06 by rote
07 down pat
08 verbatim
10 parrotlike
11 word for word

❑**change of heart**
07 rethink
14 second thoughts

❑**from the bottom of your heart**
09 earnestly, sincerely
10 profoundly

❑**heart and soul**
08 entirely, heartily
09 devotedly
10 absolutely, completely

❑**set your heart on**
05 crave, yearn
06 desire
07 long for, wish for

❑**take heart**
06 buck up, perk up, revive
07 cheer up
10 brighten up

❑**take to heart**
08 consider
12 be affected by
13 be disturbed by

**heartache**
04 pain
05 agony, grief, worry
06 sorrow
07 anguish, anxiety, despair, remorse, torment, torture
08 distress
09 dejection, suffering
10 affliction, bitterness

**heartbreak**
04 pain
05 agony, grief
06 misery, sorrow
07 anguish, despair, sadness

**heartbreaking**
03 sad
06 tragic
07 painful, pitiful
08 grievous, poignant
09 agonizing, harrowing
12 excruciating
13 disappointing

**heartbroken**
03 sad
09 anguished, miserable, sorrowful, suffering
10 despondent, dispirited
11 crestfallen
12 disappointed, in low spirits

**hearten**
05 boost, cheer, pep up, rouse
06 buck up
07 animate, cheer up, comfort, console, inspire
08 energize, reassure
09 encourage, stimulate

**heartfelt**
04 deep
06 ardent, devout, honest
07 earnest, fervent, genuine, sincere
08 profound

**heartily**
06 deeply, gladly
07 totally
09 cordially, earnestly, genuinely, sincerely
10 absolutely, completely, profoundly, thoroughly

**heartless**
04 cold, hard
05 cruel, harsh
06 brutal, unkind
07 callous, inhuman, unmoved
08 pitiless, ruthless, uncaring
09 merciless, unfeeling
11 coldblooded
13 inconsiderate, unsympathetic

**heart-rending**
03 sad
06 moving, tragic
07 piteous, pitiful
08 pathetic, poignant
09 affecting, agonizing, harrowing
11 distressing

**heartsick**
03 sad
08 dejected, downcast
09 depressed, heartsore
10 despondent, melancholy
12 disappointed

## heartthrob
04 idol, love, star
05 pinup
09 dreamboat, heartbeat
10 sweetheart

## heart-to-heart
06 candid
08 cozy chat
09 tête-à-tête

## heartwarming
06 moving
08 cheering, pleasing, touching
09 affecting, rewarding, uplifting
10 gratifying, satisfying
11 encouraging

## hearty
04 warm
05 ample, large, sound
06 jovial, robust, strong
07 affable, cordial, filling, genuine, healthy, sincere
08 abundant, cheerful, effusive, friendly, generous, sizeable, stalwart, vigorous
09 ebullient, energetic, exuberant, heartfelt, unfeigned
10 boisterous, nourishing
11 substantial
12 enthusiastic, wholehearted

## heat
04 bake, boil, cook, fury, glow, stir, warm, zeal
05 anger, annoy, ardor, broil, fever, flush, roast, rouse, toast
06 calefy, enrage, excite, fervor, pistol, warm up, warmth
07 animate, hotness, inflame, passion, swelter
08 coercion, fervency, pressure
09 fieriness, intensity, microwave, stimulate, vehemence
10 enthusiasm, excitement
12 feverishness
15 high temperature

## heated
05 angry, fiery, fired
06 fierce, raging, roused, stormy
07 enraged, furious, stirred
08 inflamed, vehement, worked-up
10 passionate, stimulated
11 impassioned, tempestuous

## heathen
05 pagan
06 savage
07 foreign, godless, infidel
08 barbaric, idolater
09 barbarian

10 idolatress, idolatrous, philistine, unbeliever
11 irreligious

## heave
03 gag, tug
04 cast, drag, haul, hurl, lift, pull, spew, toss
05 chuck, fling, hitch, hoist, lever, pitch, raise, retch, sling, surge, throw, utter, vomit
07 breathe, express, throw up

## heaven
03 joy, sky
04 Zion
05 bliss, ether, skies
06 Asgard, utopia
07 Asgarth, ecstasy, Elysium, nirvana, Olympus, the blue, up there
08 paradise, Valhalla
09 afterlife, firmament, hereafter, next world
10 abode of God, life to come
13 Elysian Fields, fiddler's green, seventh heaven

## heavenly
04 holy
06 cosmic, divine, lovely
07 angelic, blessed, godlike, perfect, sublime
08 beatific, blissful, cherubic, empyreal, empyrean, glorious, immortal, seraphic
09 beautiful, celestial, enjoyable, exquisite, rapturous, spiritual, unearthly, wonderful
10 enchanting
14 out of this world

## heavily
04 hard
05 sadly, thick
06 slowly
07 closely, densely, solidly, soundly, thickly, utterly
08 clumsily, to excess, woodenly
09 copiously, weightily
10 abundantly, completely, decisively, sluggishly, thoroughly
11 excessively, laboriously

## heaviness
04 bulk
06 weight
07 density, languor
08 deadness, solidity
09 heftiness, lassitude, thickness
10 drowsiness, oppression, sleepiness, somnolence
11 despondency, onerousness, seriousness, weightiness

12 sluggishness
13 ponderousness
14 burdensomeness, oppressiveness

## heavy
03 fat
05 bulky, close, dense, grave, harsh, hefty, humid, laden, large, muggy, solid, thick
06 cloudy, gloomy, leaden, loaded, severe, somber, steamy, sticky, stodgy, strong, sultry, taxing, trying
07 arduous, awkward, crushed, extreme, filling, hulking, intense, irksome, massive, onerous, serious, starchy, tedious, violent, weighty
08 burdened, crushing, exacting, forceful, groaning, overcast, powerful, profound
09 demanding, difficult, laborious, ponderous, strenuous, wearisome
10 burdensome, cumbersome, depressing, despondent, encumbered, immoderate, inordinate, oppressive, overweight, unbearable
11 discouraged, intolerable, substantial, troublesome, weighed down
12 considerable, indigestible
13 uninteresting

## heavy-handed
05 harsh, stern
06 clumsy, severe
07 awkward
08 bungling, despotic, forceful, tactless, unsubtle
09 ham-handed, maladroit
10 autocratic, blundering, oppressive
11 domineering, overbearing

## heavy-hearted
03 sad
04 glum
06 gloomy, morose
08 downcast, mournful
09 depressed, miserable, sorrowful
10 despondent, melancholy

## heckle
04 bait, gibe, jeer
06 hackle, needle, pester
07 catcall, disrupt

## hectic
04 busy, fast, wild
06 heated
07 chaotic, excited, frantic, furious

**hector**

08 bustling, feverish, frenetic, frenzied

**hector**

05 bully, chivy
06 badger, chivvy
08 browbeat, bulldoze, bullyrag, threaten
10 intimidate

**hedge**

04 bush, dike, duck, edge
05 cover, dodge, evade, fence, guard, hem in, limit, stall
06 insure, screen, shield
07 barrier, confine, enclose, fortify, protect, quibble
08 boundary, encircle, restrict, sidestep, surround
09 safeguard, temporize, windbreak
10 equivocate, protection
11 prevaricate

**hedonism**

09 epicurism
10 sensualism, sensuality, sybaritism
11 la dolce vita
13 gratification, luxuriousness
14 self-indulgence, voluptuousness
15 pleasure-seeking

**hedonist**

04 rake
08 sybarite
09 bon vivant, bon viveur
10 sensualist, voluptuary
14 pleasure-seeker

**hedonistic**

09 sybaritic
10 voluptuous
13 self-indulgent
15 pleasure-seeking

**heed**

04 care, mark, mind, note, obey
06 follow, listen, notice, regard
07 caution, observe, respect, thought
08 attend to, consider, take note
09 attention
10 bear in mind, take notice
12 pay attention, watchfulness
13 consideration
15 take into account

**heedful**

07 careful, mindful, prudent
08 cautious, vigilant, watchful
09 attentive, observant, regardful

**heedless**

04 rash
06 unwary

08 careless, reckless
09 foolhardy, negligent, oblivious, unmindful
11 inattentive, precipitate, thoughtless, unconcerned, unobservant

**hefty**

03 big
04 hard, huge
05 ample, beefy, bulky, burly, heavy, large, solid, stout
06 brawny, robust, strong
07 hulking, immense, massive, weighty
08 colossal, forceful, generous, muscular, powerful, sizeable, unwieldy
09 strapping
11 substantial
12 considerable

**height**

03 top
04 apex, peak
05 crest, crown, limit
06 apogee, climax, summit, vertex, zenith
07 hilltop, maximum, stature
08 altitude, highness, pinnacle, tallness, ultimate
09 elevation, extremity, loftiness, uttermost
11 culmination, mountaintop

**heighten**

04 lift
05 add to, boost, exalt, raise
07 amplify, augment, build up, elevate, enhance, improve, magnify, sharpen
08 increase
09 intensify
10 strengthen

**heinous**

04 evil
06 odious, wicked
07 hateful, hideous, vicious
08 flagrant, infamous, shocking
09 abhorrent, atrocious, execrable, loathsome, monstrous, nefarious
10 abominable, despicable, detestable, iniquitous, outrageous, villainous
11 unspeakable
12 contemptible

**heir, heiress**

05 scion
07 legatee
09 inheritor, successor
10 inheritrix
11 beneficiary, inheritress

**helix**

04 coil, curl, loop
05 screw, snail, twist, whorl
06 spiral, volute

**hell**

04 fire
05 abyss, agony, Hades
06 blazes, misery, ordeal, Topheth
07 inferno, Topheth, torment, torture
09 down there, nightmare, perdition, suffering
10 underworld
11 nether world, tribulation
12 lower regions
13 bottomless pit
15 infernal regions

◻**give someone hell**

04 beat, flog
05 annoy, scold
06 harass, pester, punish
07 torment, trouble

◻**hell for leather**

07 quickly, rapidly, swiftly
08 very fast
09 hurriedly, posthaste
13 precipitately

◻**raise hell**

09 be furious
10 hit the roof

**hellbent**

05 fixed
06 dogged, intent
08 obdurate, resolved
09 tenacious
10 determined, inflexible, unwavering
12 intransigent, unhesitating

**hellish**

06 savage, wicked
07 awfully, demonic, satanic
08 accursed, barbaric, damnable, devilish, dreadful, fiendish, infernal
09 atrocious, execrable, extremely, monstrous, nefarious
10 abominable, diabolical, dreadfully

**helm**

05 steer, wheel
06 rudder, tiller

◻**at the helm**

07 leading
08 in charge
09 directing, in command, in control
11 in the saddle
15 holding the reins

## help

- 03 aid, use
- 04 back, balm, ease
- 05 avail, boost, guide, serve
- 06 advice, assist, backup, helper, oblige, remedy, succor
- 07 assuage, backing, be of use, benefit, charity, further, healing, improve, relieve, servant, service, stand by, support, utility
- 08 guidance, mitigate
- 09 advantage, alleviate, cooperate, do your bit, encourage, lend a hand
- 10 ameliorate, assistance, facilitate
- 11 alleviation, cooperation, helping hand, rally around
- 12 amelioration, contribute to, give a boost to, shot in the arm
- 13 encouragement

## helper

- 02 PA
- 04 aide, ally, help, maid, mate
- 06 deputy, second, worker
- 07 partner, servant
- 08 adjutant, coworker, employee, helpmate
- 09 assistant, associate, attendant, auxiliary, colleague, man Friday, supporter
- 10 accomplice, apprentice, girl Friday, subsidiary
- 11 subordinate
- 12 collaborator, right-hand man
- 14 right-hand woman

## helpful

- 04 kind
- 05 of use
- 06 caring, useful
- 08 friendly, obliging, valuable
- 09 of service, practical
- 10 beneficial, benevolent, charitable, neighborly, supportive
- 11 considerate
- 12 advantageous, constructive
- 13 accommodating

## helping

- 05 piece, share
- 06 amount, dollop, ration
- 07 bowlful, portion, serving
- 08 plateful, spoonful
- 09 assisting

## helpless

- 06 feeble, infirm
- 07 forlorn
- 08 disabled, impotent
- 09 dependent, incapable, paralyzed, powerless
- 10 friendless, vulnerable
- 11 debilitated, defenseless, incompetent, unprotected

## helpmate

- 04 wife
- 06 helper, spouse
- 07 consort, husband, partner, support
- 09 assistant, associate, companion, other half
- 10 better half

## helter-skelter

- 08 headlong, pell-mell
- 09 hurriedly
- 10 disorderly, recklessly

## hem

- 04 bind, edge, fold, trim
- 05 frill, skirt
- 06 border, edging, fringe, margin
- 07 fimbria, flounce, valance
- 08 trimming

## ▢ hem in

- 04 trap
- 05 box in, limit, pen in
- 06 shut in
- 07 close in, confine, enclose, hedge in
- 08 restrict, surround
- 09 constrain

## hence

- 04 ergo, thus
- 09 therefore
- 11 accordingly
- 12 consequently

## henceforth

- 05 hence
- 09 from now on, hereafter
- 11 hereinafter, in the future
- 12 henceforward

## henchman

- 04 aide
- 05 crony, heavy
- 06 lackey, minion, yes man
- 08 follower, sidekick
- 09 associate, attendant, bodyguard, supporter, underling
- 11 subordinate

## henpecked

- 04 meek
- 05 timid
- 09 dominated
- 10 browbeaten, subjugated

## herald

- 04 omen, show, sign
- 05 augur, crier, token, usher
- 06 augury, signal
- 07 courier, portend, portent, precede, promise, trumpet, usher in
- 08 announce, proclaim
- 09 announcer, broadcast, harbinger, make known, messenger, precursor
- 10 forerunner, foreshadow, make public, pave the way

## heraldry

➤ *Heraldry terms:*

- 04 arms, lion, orle, pall, pile
- 05 badge, crest, eagle, field, motto
- 06 bezant, blazon, canton, center, charge, dexter, emblem, ensign, helmet, impale, mullet, sejant, shield, volant, wivern
- 07 bordure, chevron, dormant, griffin, lozenge, martlet, passant, phoenix, quarter, rampant, roundel, statant, tierced, unicorn, urinant
- 08 caboched, couchant, insignia, sinister
- 09 displayed
- 10 cinquefoil, coat of arms, cockatrice, escutcheon, fleur-de-lis, quatrefoil

## herbs and spices

➤ *Names of herbs and spices:*

- 03 bay
- 04 dill, mace, mint, sage, wort
- 05 anise, basil, caper, cumin, curry, thyme
- 06 borage, catnip, chilli, chives, cloves, fennel, garlic, ginger, hyssop, lovage, nutmeg, pepper, sesame, sorrel
- 07 cayenne, chervil, comfrey, mustard, oregano, paprika, parsley, saffron, vanilla
- 08 allspice, angelica, bergamot, camomile, cardamom, cardamon, cinnamon, lavender, marjoram, rosemary, tarragon, turmeric
- 09 coriander, fenugreek
- 13 cayenne pepper
➤ See also FOOD

## herculean

- 04 hard, huge
- 05 great, heavy, large, tough
- 06 strong
- 07 arduous, mammoth, massive, onerous

**herd**

08 colossal, enormous, exacting, gigantic, grueling, powerful
09 demanding, difficult, laborious, strenuous
10 formidable, tremendous

**herd**

03 mob
04 goad, host, lead, mass, pack, urge
05 crowd, crush, drive, drove, flock, force, guide, horde, plebs, press, rally, swarm
06 gather, huddle, muster, proles, rabble, throng
07 collect, round up
08 assemble, riffraff
09 multitude, the masses
10 collection, congregate
11 get together

**herdsman**

06 cowboy, cowman, drover, gaucho
07 cowhand, cowherd, vaquero
08 ranchero, stockman, wrangler

**here**

03 now
07 present
10 at this time
11 at this place, at this point, at this stage, in this place, to this place

**here and there**

08 to and fro
12 sporadically

**hereafter**

05 hence, later
09 afterlife, from now on, next world
10 eventually, henceforth, life to come
11 in the future
12 henceforward

**hereditary**

06 family, inborn, inbred, innate
07 genetic, natural
08 inherent
09 ancestral, inherited
10 bequeathed, congenital, handed down
13 transmissible

**heresy**

07 atheism, dissent
08 apostasy, unbelief
09 blasphemy
10 dissidence, heterodoxy, skepticism
11 agnosticism, revisionism

**heretic**

07 atheist, skeptic
08 agnostic, apostate, renegade
09 dissenter, dissident
10 unbeliever
11 free-thinker, revisionist
13 nonconformist

**heretical**

07 impious
08 agnostic, recusant, renegade
09 atheistic, dissident, heterodox, sectarian, skeptical
10 dissenting, irreverent, schismatic, separatist, unorthodox
11 blasphemous, revisionist, unbelieving
12 freethinking, iconoclastic
13 rationalistic

**heritage**

04 past
06 estate, family, legacy
07 bequest, culture, descent, dynasty, history, lineage
08 ancestry, cultural
09 tradition
10 background, birthright, extraction, traditions
11 inheritance

**hermetic**

06 sealed
07 magical, obscure
08 airtight
10 watertight

**hermit**

04 monk
05 loner
07 ascetic, eremite, recluse, stylite
08 anchoret, solitary
09 anchoress, anchorite

**hermitage**

05 haven
06 asylum, refuge
07 hide-out, retreat, shelter
08 cloister, hideaway
09 sanctuary
11 hiding place

**hero**

04 idol, lead, lion, star
05 goody, ideal
06 victor
07 good guy, paragon
08 brave man, cavalier, champion, sandwich
09 conqueror
11 protagonist
12 hero sandwich

**heroic**

04 bold
05 brave, noble
06 daring
07 doughty, gallant, valiant
08 fearless, intrepid, selfless, valorous
09 dauntless, undaunted
10 chivalrous, courageous, determined
11 adventurous, lionhearted
12 stouthearted

**heroine**

04 diva, idol, lead, star
05 ideal
06 victor
07 paragon
08 champion
09 conqueror
10 brave woman
11 leading lady, protagonist

**heroism**

05 valor
06 daring
07 bravery, courage
08 boldness, chivalry
09 fortitude, gallantry
12 fearlessness, selflessness
15 lionheartedness

**hero sandwich**

03 sub
07 poor-boy
09 submarine

**hero worship**

09 adoration, adulation
10 admiration, veneration
11 deification, idolization
12 idealization

**hesitancy**

05 demur, doubt
08 wavering
10 indecision, reluctance
11 reservation, uncertainty
12 doubtfulness, irresolution
13 unwillingness
14 disinclination

**hesitant**

03 shy
04 wary
05 timid
06 unsure
07 dubious, halting
08 doubtful, stalling, wavering
09 demurring, reluctant, tentative, uncertain
10 indecisive, irresolute, stammering, stuttering
11 disinclined, vacillating

**hesitate**

04 halt, wait

**hesitation**
05 delay, demur, pause, stall, waver
06 boggle, dither, falter
07 stammer, stumble, stutter
08 hang back, hold back
09 vacillate
10 dillydally, think twice
12 shilly-shally

**hesitation**
05 delay, doubt, pause
07 waiting
08 stalling, wavering
09 faltering, hesitance, stumbling
10 indecision, reluctance, skepticism, stammering, stuttering, unsureness
11 holding-back, uncertainty, vacillation
12 doubtfulness, irresolution
13 dillydallying, unwillingness
14 second thoughts
15 shilly-shallying

**heterodox**
09 dissident, heretical
10 dissenting, unorthodox
12 freethinking, iconoclastic
13 nonconformist

**heterogeneous**
05 mixed
06 motley, unlike, varied
07 diverse, opposed
08 assorted, catholic, contrary
09 different, disparate, divergent, multiform, unrelated
10 dissimilar
11 diversified, polymorphic
13 miscellaneous

**heterosexual**
06 hetero
08 straight

**hew**
02 ax
03 axe, cut, lop, saw
04 chip, chop, fell, hack, trim
05 carve, model, prune, sever
06 chisel, hammer, sculpt
07 fashion, whittle
09 sculpture

**heyday**
04 peak
05 bloom, flush, prime
06 spring
09 flowering, golden age

**hiatus**
03 gap
04 lull, rest, rift, void
05 break, lapse, pause, space
06 breach, lacuna

08 aperture, interval
10 suspension
12 interruption

**hidden**
04 dark
05 close
06 arcane, covert, latent, masked, occult, secret, unseen, veiled
07 covered, cryptic, obscure
08 abstruse, mystical, shrouded
09 concealed, disguised, recondite
10 indistinct, mysterious, out of sight, under wraps
11 camouflaged

**hide**
03 fur
04 bury, coat, fell, lurk, mask, pelt, skin, stow, veil
05 cloak, cloud, cover, store
06 darken, fleece, hole up, lie low, screen, shadow, shroud
07 conceal, eclipse, leather, obscure, secrete, shelter
08 bottle up, disguise, keep dark, obstruct, suppress, withhold
09 dissemble, stash away, take cover
10 camouflage, go to ground
12 go into hiding
13 draw a veil over
14 keep out of sight, keep under wraps
15 keep a low profile

**hideaway**
03 den
04 hole, lair, nest
07 hideout, retreat, shelter
08 cloister
09 hermitage, sanctuary
11 hiding place

**hidebound**
03 set
05 fixed, rigid
06 narrow
07 bigoted
10 entrenched, intolerant
11 intractable, reactionary

**hideous**
04 grim, ugly
05 awful
06 horrid
07 ghastly, macaber, macabre
08 dreadful, gruesome, horrible, shocking, terrible
09 appalling, frightful, grotesque, monstrous, repellent, repulsive, revolting, unsightly

10 disgusting, horrendous, horrifying, terrifying

**hideout**
03 den
04 hole, lair, nest
05 haven
06 refuge
07 retreat, shelter
08 cloister, hideaway
09 hermitage, sanctuary
11 hiding place

**hiding**
04 veil
05 cover
06 caning, shroud
07 beating, belting, licking, tanning, veiling
08 disguise, drubbing, flogging, spanking, whacking, whipping
09 battering, screening, thrashing, walloping
10 camouflage
11 concealment

**hiding place**
03 den
04 hole, lair, nest
05 cache, cover, haven
07 retreat
08 cloister
09 sanctuary

**hierarchy**
05 scale
06 ladder, series, strata, system
07 grading, ranking
08 echelons
09 structure
12 pecking order

**higgledy-piggledy**
06 anyhow, untidy
07 jumbled, muddled
08 confused, untidily
09 any old how, haphazard
10 confusedly, disorderly, topsy-turvy
11 haphazardly
12 disorganized

**high**
03 bad, top
04 dear, fine, good, peak, tall
05 acute, chief, doped, great, lofty, moral, sharp, steep
06 bombed, choice, classy, costly, de luxe, height, loaded, piping, putrid, rancid, select, shrill, spaced, stoned, strong, summit, tiptop, treble, wasted, worthy, zenith
07 blitzed, decayed, eminent, exalted, extreme, intense,

leading, notable, out of it, perfect, quality, rotting, soaring, upright, violent
08 advanced, elevated, falsetto, forceful, inflated, piercing, powerful, smelling, top-class, towering, turned on, vigorous, virtuous
09 excellent, excessive, exemplary, expensive, first-rate, gilt-edged, honorable, important, principal, prominent, spaced-out, unequaled
10 exorbitant, first-class, noteworthy, surpassing
11 influential, outstanding, penetrating, superlative, ultramodern
12 extortionate, unparalleled
13 distinguished

◻**high and dry**
08 marooned, stranded
09 abandoned, destitute

◻**high and mighty**
05 proud
06 swanky
07 haughty, stuck-up
08 arrogant, snobbish, superior
09 conceited, egotistic, imperious
11 overbearing, overweening, patronizing
13 condescending

**high spirits**
06 bounce, capers, spirit
07 sparkle
08 buoyancy, hilarity, vivacity
09 animation, good cheer
10 ebullience, exuberance, liveliness
11 joie de vivre
12 exhilaration
14 boisterousness

**highborn**
05 noble
08 well-born
09 patrician
11 blue-blooded
12 aristocratic, thoroughbred

**highbrow**
07 bookish, serious
08 academic, cultured, profound
09 scholarly
10 cultivated
12 intellectual
13 sophisticated

**high-class**
04 posh
05 élite, super

06 choice, classy, de luxe, select
07 elegant, quality
08 superior, top-class
09 excellent, exclusive, first-rate, luxurious, top-drawer, top-flight
10 upper-class

**highfalutin, highfaluting**
05 lofty
06 la-di-da, swanky
07 pompous
08 affected
09 bombastic, grandiose
11 pretentious
12 magniloquent, supercilious

**high-flown**
05 lofty
06 florid, la-di-da, ornate
07 pompous
08 affected
09 bombastic, elaborate, grandiose
10 artificial, flamboyant
11 exaggerated, extravagant, pretentious
12 ostentatious
13 grandiloquent

**highhanded**
05 bossy
07 haughty
08 arrogant, despotic
09 arbitrary, imperious
10 autocratic, oppressive, peremptory, tyrannical
11 dictatorial, domineering, overbearing

**highland**
04 hill, rise
05 mound, mount, ridge
06 height, upland
07 plateau
08 mountain
09 elevation

**highlight**
04 best, peak
05 cream, focus
06 accent, climax, play up, set off, show up, stress
07 feature, focus on, point up
09 emphasize, underline
10 accentuate, illuminate
13 put emphasis on

**highly**
04 very, well
06 hugely, vastly, warmly
07 greatly
09 certainly, decidedly, extremely, favorably
12 considerably, tremendously
13 exceptionally
14 appreciatively

**high-minded**
04 fair, good, pure
05 lofty, moral, noble
07 ethical, upright
08 elevated, virtuous
09 honorable, righteous
10 idealistic, principled

**high muck-a-muck**
03 VIP
05 nabob
06 bigwig, fat cat
07 big shot, notable
08 big wheel
09 big cheese
15 high muckety-munk

**high-pitched**
05 acute, sharp, tinny
06 piping, shrill, treble
08 agitated, falsetto, piercing
11 penetrating

**high-powered**
07 driving, dynamic, go-ahead
08 forceful, powerful, vigorous
09 ambitious, assertive, energetic, insistent
10 aggressive
12 enterprising

**high-priced**
04 dear
05 steep, stiff
06 costly
09 excessive, expensive
10 exorbitant
12 extortionate, unreasonable

**high-sounding**
06 florid
07 orotund, pompous, stilted
09 bombastic, grandiose, overblown, ponderous
11 extravagant, pretentious
12 magniloquent, ostentatious
13 grandiloquent

**high-spirited**
06 active, bouncy, daring, lively
07 dashing, dynamic, vibrant
08 animated, spirited, vigorous
09 ebullient, exuberant, vivacious
10 boisterous, frolicsome
11 full of beans

**high-strung**
04 edgy
05 jumpy, tense
06 on edge
07 nervous, uptight, wound up
08 neurotic, restless, stressed
09 excitable, sensitive
13 temperamental

**highwayman**
06 bandit, robber

**hijack**
07 brigand, footpad

**hijack**
05 seize
08 take over
10 commandeer
11 expropriate

**hike**
04 lift, pull, trek, walk, yank
05 hitch, hoist, march, put up, raise, tramp
06 jack up, pull up, push up, ramble, trudge, wander
08 backpack, increase

**hilarious**
05 funny, jolly, merry, noisy
07 a scream, amusing, comical, killing, riotous, risible
08 farcical, humorous
10 boisterous, hysterical, rollicking, uproarious
13 sidesplitting

**hilarity**
03 fun
05 mirth
06 comedy, levity
07 jollity
08 laughter
09 amusement, merriment
10 exuberance
11 high spirits

**hill**
03 tor
04 down, drop, fell, mesa, ramp, rise
05 knoll, mound, mount, slope
06 ascent, height
07 descent, hummock, incline
08 eminence, gradient, mountain
09 acclivity, declivity, elevation
10 prominence
12 rising ground

► *The seven hills of Rome*:
07 Caelian, Viminal
08 Aventine, Palatine, Quirinal
09 Esquiline
10 Capitoline

**hillock**
04 dune, knap, knob
05 knoll, mound
07 hummock

**hilt**
04 grip, haft
05 helve, shaft
06 handle

❏**to the hilt**
05 fully
06 wholly
07 utterly

08 entirely, to the end
10 completely
15 from first to last

**hind**
03 roe
04 deer, rear, tail
08 backside
09 posterior

**hind end**
04 butt, rear
08 backside, buttocks, haunches
09 posterior

**hinder**
04 balk, curb, foil, halt, stop
05 baulk, block, check, delay, stymy
06 arrest, hamper, hold up, impede, oppose, retard, stymie, thwart
07 inhibit, prevent
08 encumber, handicap, hold back, obstruct, slow down
09 forestall, frustrate, hamstring, interrupt

**hindmost**
04 last, tail
07 endmost
08 furthest, rearmost, remotest, terminal, trailing, ultimate
10 concluding

**hindrance**
03 bar
04 curb, drag, foil, snag
05 block, check, delay, hitch
06 holdup
07 barrier
08 handicap, obstacle, stoppage
09 deterrent, restraint
10 difficulty, impediment
11 encumbrance, obstruction, restriction
14 stumbling block

**hinge**
04 hang, rest, turn
05 joint, pivot
06 center, depend
07 revolve

**hint**
03 cue, tip
04 clue, dash, help, sign
05 imply, speck, taste, tinge, touch, trace, whiff
06 advice, allude, nuance, prompt, signal, tip-off
07 inkling, mention, pointer, soupçon, suggest, whisper
08 allusion, indicate, innuendo, intimate, reminder
09 insinuate, suspicion

10 indication, suggestion
11 implication, insinuation

**hinterland**
06 sticks
08 interior
09 backwoods, boondocks
10 hinderland, the boonies
11 backcountry

**hip**
04 coxa, loin, rump
05 aware
06 haunch, pelvis
07 knowing, stylish
11 fashionable

**hippie, hippy**
04 beat
07 beatnik, dropout
08 bohemian
11 flower child

**hire**
03 fee, let, pay
04 book, cost, rent, wage
05 lease, price
06 charge, employ, engage, enlist, rental, retain, salary, sign on, sign up, take on
07 appoint, charter, reserve
10 commission

**hirsute**
05 hairy
06 shaggy
07 bearded, bristly
08 unshaven
11 bewhiskered

**hiss**
03 boo
04 buzz, hoot, jeer, mock, whiz
05 scorn, taunt
06 deride, shrill, sizzle
07 catcall, hissing, scoff at, whistle
08 scoffing, sibilate, taunting
09 raspberry, shout down, sibilance
10 Bronx cheer, sibilation
15 blow raspberries

**historian**
07 diarist
08 annalist, narrator, recorder
09 archivist
10 chronicler
11 chronologer

**historic**
05 famed
06 famous
07 notable
08 renowned
09 memorable, momentous
10 celebrated, remarkable

11 epoch-making, outstanding, significant
13 extraordinary

**historical**
03 old
04 past
05 prior
06 actual, bygone, former, of yore
07 ancient
08 recorded, verified
10 chronicled, documented

**history**
04 life, past, saga, tale
05 story, study
06 annals, record, report
07 account, memoirs, records
08 archives
09 antiquity, biography, chronicle, days of old, olden days, yesterday
10 background, bygone days, chronology, days of yore, experience, the old days, yesteryear
11 credentials, former times
13 autobiography, circumstances

─── *Names of historians*:
04 **Bede** (Saint "The Venerable"), **Livy**
05 **Adams** (Brooks), **Adams** (Henry), **Beard** (Charles Austin), **Beard** (Mary Ritter), **Clark** (Kenneth), **Ensor** (Robert), **Foote** (Shelby), **Nepos** (Cornelius), **Paris** (Matthew), **Ranke** (Leopold von), **Renan** (Ernest)
06 **Arrian**, **Berlin** (Isaiah), **Eliade** (Mircea), **Gibbon** (Edward), **Miller** (Perry), **Nevins** (Allan), **O'Brien** (Conor Cruise), **Sparks** (Jared), **Strabo**, **Taylor** (Alan John Percivale), **Terkel** (Studs), **Turner** (Frederick Jackson), **Vasari** (Giorgio)
07 **Ambrose** (Stephen), **Bullock** (Alan), **Carlyle** (Thomas), **Mommsen** (Theodor), **Pevsner** (Nikolaus Bernhard), **Sallust**, **Tacitus**, **Toynbee** (Arnold), **William** (of Malmesbury), **William** (of Tyre)
08 **Bancroft** (George), **Channing** (Edward), **Foucault** (Michel), **Geoffrey**

(of Monmouth), **Gombrich** (Ernst Hans Josef), **Josephus** (Flavius), **Las Casas** (Emmanuel), **Macaulay** (Thomas Babington, **Michelet** (Jules), **Panofsky** (Erwin), **Plutarch**, **Polybius**, **Xenophon**
09 **Commanger** (Henry Steele), **Dionysius** (of Halicarnassus), **Herodotus**, **Holinshed** (Raphael), **Pausanias**, **Procopius**, **Suetonius**, **Trevelyan** (George Macaulay)
10 **Burckhardt** (Jacob Christopher), **Dio Cassius**, **Thucydides**
11 **Schlesinger** (Arthur Meier), **Trevor-Roper** (Hugh Redwald)
15 **Diodorus Siculus**
➤ See also WRITER

**histrionic**
03 ham
08 affected, dramatic
09 insincere, unnatural
10 artificial, theatrical
11 exaggerated, sensational
12 melodramatic

**histrionics**
05 scene
08 tantrums
09 dramatics, staginess
10 overacting
11 affectation, performance
13 artificiality, theatricality, unnaturalness

**hit**
03 bat, box, tap, zap
04 bang, bash, beat, belt, biff, blow, bump, cuff, harm, move, shot, slap, sock
05 clout, crash, homer, knock, pound, punch, smack, smash, thump, touch, upset, whack
06 affect, batter, buffet, come to, damage, dawn on, double, impact, single, strike, stroke, thrash, triple, wallop, winner
07 beating, clobber, disturb, home run, occur to, perturb, run into, success, triumph, trouble
08 plow into
09 collision, overwhelm, smash into, thrashing
10 clobbering, come to mind, meet head-on
11 collide with

14 have an effect on

❏**hit back**
09 retaliate
10 strike back
13 counterattack

❏**hit it off**
06 warm to
09 get on with
10 grow to like
12 get along with
13 get on well with

❏**hit on**
05 guess
07 light on, realize, think of, uncover
08 arrive at, chance on, discover
09 stumble on

❏**hit out**
04 rail
06 assail, attack, vilify
07 condemn, inveigh, lash out
08 denounce
09 criticize, strike out

**hitch**
03 tie, tug
04 bind, hike, jerk, join, pull, snag, yank, yoke
05 block, catch, check, delay, heave, hoist, unite
06 attach, couple, fasten, hiccup, hike up, holdup, mishap, tether
07 barrier, connect, harness, problem, setback, trouble
08 drawback, obstacle
09 hindrance
10 difficulty, impediment
11 obstruction

**hitherto**
05 so far
07 thus far, till now, up to now
08 until now
10 beforehand, heretofore

**hit-or-miss**
06 casual, random
07 aimless
08 careless
09 haphazard
10 undirected
12 disorganized
13 trial-and-error
14 indiscriminate

**hoard**
04 fund, heap, mass, pile, save
05 amass, buy up, cache, stash, store
06 gather, supply
07 collect, put away, reserve, stack up, stock up

## hoarder

09 reservoir, stash away, stockpile
10 accumulate, collection
11 aggregation
12 accumulation
13 treasure-trove

## hoarder

05 miser, saver
06 magpie
08 gatherer, squirrel
09 collector

## hoary

03 old
04 aged, gray
05 white
07 ancient, antique, archaic, silvery
08 familiar, grizzled
09 venerable
10 antiquated

## hoarse

05 gruff, harsh, husky, raspy, rough
07 grating, rasping, raucous, throaty
08 croaking, gravelly, growling
10 discordant

## hoax

03 con
04 dupe, fake, fool, gull, jest, joke, ruse, scam
05 bluff, cheat, fraud, prank, put-on, spoof, trick
06 delude
07 deceive, fast one, leg-pull, swindle
08 hoodwink, put-up job
09 bamboozle, deception
12 take for a ride
14 pull a fast one on
15 pull someone's leg

## hoaxer

09 mystifier, prankster, trickster
10 bamboozler, hoodwinker

## hobble

04 limp, reel
06 dodder, falter, fetter, hogtie, totter
07 shuffle, stagger, stumble

## hobby

04 game
05 sport
07 leisure, pastime, pursuit
08 activity, interest, sideline
09 amusement, diversion
10 recreation, relaxation
13 entertainment

## hobgoblin

03 elf, imp
04 bogy

---

05 bogey, dwarf, gnome
06 goblin, spirit, sprite
07 bugaboo, bugbear, specter
08 bogeyman
09 boogeyman
10 apparition, evil spirit

## hobnob

03 mix
06 mingle
07 consort
09 associate, socialize
10 fraternize

## hockey

► *Names of hockey teams*:
13 (Dallas) Stars
14 (Boston) Bruins, (St. Louis) Blues
15 (Buffalo) Sabres, (Calgary) Flames, (San Jose) Sharks
16 (Edmonton) Oilers, (New York) Rangers, (Ottawa) Senators, (Phoenix) Coyotes
17 (Detroit) Red Wings, (Florida) Panthers, (Los Angeles) Kings, (New Jersey) Devils
18 (New York) Islanders, (Vancouver) Canucks
19 (Chicago) Blackhawks, (Colorado) Avalanche, (Montreal) Canadiens, (Tampa Bay) Lightning, (Toronto) Maple Leafs
20 (Anaheim) Mighty Ducks, (Carolina) Hurricanes, (Philadelphia) Flyers, (Pittsburgh) Penguins, (Washington) Capitals
21 (Minnesota) North Stars

► *Names of hockey players*:
03 **Orr** (Bobby), **Roy** (Patrick)
04 **Howe** (Gordie), **Hull** (Bobby), **Hull** (Bret), **Jagr** (Jaromir)
05 **Blake** (Rob), **Hasek** (Dominik), **Moore** (Dickie), **Sakic** (Joe)
06 **Clarke** (Bobby), **Dryden** (Ken), **Durnan** (Bill), **Harvey** (Doug), **Leetch** (Brian), **Mikita** (Stan), **Pilote** (Pierre), **Plante** (Jacques), **Potvin** (Denis)
07 **Bourque** (Ray), **Chelios** (Chris), **Gretzky** (Wayne), **Lafleur** (Guy), **Lemieux** (Mario), **Lindros** (Eric), **Messier** (Mark), **Pronger** (Chris)
08 **Esposito** (Phil), **Lidstrom** (Nicklas)

---

## hocus-pocus

04 cant, hoax
06 deceit, humbug, jargon
07 swindle
08 artifice, delusion, nonsense, trickery
09 chicanery, conjuring, deception, imposture
10 mumbo jumbo
11 abracadabra, legerdemain
13 sleight of hand

## hodgepodge

04 mess, stew
06 jumble, medley
07 melange, mixture
08 mishmash
09 confusion
10 collection, hotchpotch, miscellany

## hog

03 pig, sow
04 boar
05 swine
06 corner, porker
07 control, grunter, road hog
08 dominate, wild boar
09 razorback
10 monopolize

## hogwash

03 rot
04 bunk
05 bilge, hooey, trash, tripe
06 bunkum, drivel, hot air, piffle
07 eyewash, rubbish, twaddle
08 claptrap, nonsense, tommyrot
09 poppycock
10 balderdash

## hoi polloi

07 the herd
08 riffraff, the plebs
09 the masses, the proles, the rabble
11 the peasants, the populace
14 the proletariat
15 the common people

## hoist

04 jack, lift, rear
05 crane, erect, heave, raise, winch
06 jack up, pulley, tackle, uplift
07 capstan, elevate, winch up
08 elevator

## hoity-toity

06 snooty, uppity
07 haughty, pompous, stuck-up
08 arrogant, snobbish
10 disdainful
11 overweening
12 supercilious
13 high and mighty

## hold

03 hug, own, run
04 bear, call, curb, deem, fill, grip, have, keep, last, stay, stop, sway, take, view
05 apply, carry, catch, check, clasp, cling, grasp, judge, power, prize, rivet, seize, stick, think, treat, value
06 absorb, adhere, arrest, assume, clutch, detain, enfold, engage, esteem, lock up, occupy, prop up, reckon, regard, remain, retain, summon, take up
07 believe, carry on, cherish, cling to, conduct, confine, contain, control, convene, embrace, engross, fulfill, impound, mastery, possess, support, sustain
08 assemble, buttress, consider, continue, dominion, enthrall, hold dear, hold down, imprison, leverage, maintain, organize, restrain, treasure
09 authority, dominance, fascinate, influence
10 compromise, monopolize
11 accommodate, incarcerate, preside over
13 hold in custody
14 have in your hand
15 have in your hands

### ❏ get hold of

05 reach
06 obtain
07 acquire, contact, speak to

### ❏ hold back

03 bar
04 curb, stop
05 check, delay
06 impede, retain, retard, stifle
07 contain, control, forbear, inhibit, prevent, refrain, repress
08 hesitate, obstruct, restrain, suppress, withhold

### ❏ hold down

04 have, keep
06 occupy
07 oppress
08 dominate, suppress
09 tyrannize

### ❏ hold forth

05 orate, speak, spout
06 preach
07 declaim, lecture
08 harangue

### ❏ hold off

04 wait
05 avoid, defer, delay, repel
06 put off, rebuff
07 fend off, keep off, ward off
08 fight off, postpone, stave off
09 keep at bay

### ❏ hold on

04 grip
05 clasp, grasp, seize
06 endure, hang on, remain
07 carry on, cling to, survive
09 keep going, persevere

### ❏ hold out

04 give, last
05 offer
06 extend, hang on, resist
07 carry on, last out, persist, present, proffer
09 persevere, stand fast, stand firm, withstand

### ❏ hold over

05 defer, delay
06 put off, shelve
08 postpone

### ❏ hold up

03 mug, rob
04 bear, hold, lift, slow
05 brace, carry, delay, raise
06 detain, hinder, impede, prop up, retard
07 put back, set back, shore up, stick up, support, sustain
08 knock off, obstruct
09 knock over, steal from

### ❏ hold water

04 wash, work
07 stand up
08 convince, ring true

### ❏ hold with

07 support
09 agree with, approve of
11 countenance, go along with, subscribe to

### ❏ hold your own

09 stand fast, stand firm, withstand
15 stand your ground

### ❏ put on hold

05 defer, delay
06 put off
08 postpone

## holder

04 case, rest
05 cover, owner, stand
06 casing, keeper, sheath, tenant
07 housing
08 occupant
09 container, custodian, incumbent, possessor
10 proprietor, receptacle

## holdings

04 land
06 assets
08 property
09 resources
10 real estate
11 investments, possessions

## holdup

03 jam
04 raid, snag, wait
05 delay, heist, hitch, theft
07 break-in, mugging, problem, robbery, setback, stickup, trouble
08 burglary, stoppage
10 bottleneck, difficulty, stickup job, traffic jam
11 obstruction

## hole

03 den, fix, gap, jam, pit, set, tip
04 cave, dent, dump, flaw, gash, lair, mess, mine, nest, pore, rent, rift, slit, slot, slum, snag, spot, stab, tear, vent
05 break, chasm, crack, error, fault, hovel, notch, scoop, shack, shaft, space, spike, split
06 breach, burrow, cavern, cavity, covert, crater, defect, dimple, eyelet, hollow, outlet, pickle, pierce, pigpen, pigsty, plight, pocket, recess
07 chamber, fissure, mistake, opening, orifice, pothole
08 aperture, hot water, loophole, puncture, quandary, weakness
09 chuckhole, deep water, perforate
10 depression, difficulty, excavation, pretty pass
11 discrepancy, perforation, predicament
13 inconsistency

### ❏ hole up

06 lie low
09 take cover
10 go to ground
12 go into hiding

### ❏ pick holes in

07 nit-pick, run down
09 criticize
13 find fault with

## hole-and-corner

06 covert, secret, sneaky
07 furtive, humdrum
08 backdoor, hush-hush, stealthy
09 secretive, underhand
11 clandestine, unimportant

**holiday**

13 surreptitious, under-the-table
15 under-the-counter

**holiday**

06 day off
07 holy day
08 feast day, festival
11 anniversary, celebration
12 legal holiday
14 public holiday,
15 national holiday

---

► *Names of U.S. holidays:*

06 Easter
08 Labor Day
09 Christmas
11 Columbus Day, Memorial Day, New Year's Day, Veterans Day
12 Thanksgiving
13 Decoration Day, Presidents' Day
15 Independence Day

**holier-than-thou**

05 pious
08 priggish
10 goody-goody
13 goody-two-shoes, sanctimonious, self-righteous

**holiness**

05 piety
08 divinity, goodness, sanctity
09 godliness
10 devoutness, sacredness
11 blessedness, saintliness
12 spirituality, virtuousness
13 religiousness, righteousness

**holler**

03 cry
04 bawl, howl, roar, yell, yelp, yowl
05 cheer, shout, whoop
06 bellow, clamor, shriek

**hollow**

03 cup, dig, dip, low, pit
04 bowl, cave, dale, deep, dell, dent, dull, flat, glen, hole, nook, sham, vain, void, well
05 empty, false, niche, scoop
06 burrow, cavern, cavity, cirque, cranny, crater, dimple, groove, indent, recess, sunken, trough, vacant, valley
07 channel, concave, deep-set, echoing, muffled, Pyrrhic
08 excavate, indented, rumbling, unfilled
09 concavity, incurvate, insincere, pointless, valueless, worthless
10 artificial, depression, excavation, profitless, unavailing
11 indentation, meaningless
12 hypocritical

**□beat someone hollow**

04 lick, rout
06 hammer, thrash
07 trounce
09 devastate, overwhelm, slaughter
10 annihilate
13 beat all hollow

**holocaust**

06 flames, pogrom
07 carnage, inferno
08 genocide, massacre
09 sacrifice, slaughter
10 extinction, mass murder
11 destruction, devastation
12 annihilation
13 conflagration, extermination

**holy**

05 godly, moral, pious
06 devout, divine, sacred
07 blessed, saintly, sinless
08 faithful, hallowed, virtuous
09 pietistic, religious, righteous, spiritual, venerated
10 sacrosanct, sanctified
11 consecrated

**homage**

05 honor
06 esteem, praise, regard
07 respect, tribute, worship
08 devotion
09 adoration, adulation
10 admiration, veneration

**home**

03 pad
04 digs
05 abode, house, local, roots
06 asylum, cradle, family, hostel, native, refuge, source
07 address, habitat, retreat
08 domestic, domicile, dwelling, interior, internal, national
09 apartment, home plate, household, residence, safe place
10 birthplace, fatherland, habitation, motherland
11 institution, nursing home
13 dwelling place, mother country, native country, place of origin
15 country of origin

**□at home**

06 at ease
07 relaxed, skilled
08 familiar
09 competent
10 conversant
11 comfortable, experienced

**□bring home**

07 impress, instill
09 emphasize, inculcate

**□home in on**

03 aim
05 focus
08 pinpoint, zero in on, zoom in on

**□nothing to write home about**

06 boring
08 inferior, mediocre, ordinary
13 no great shakes

**homeland**

10 fatherland, motherland, native land
13 mother country, native country
15 country of origin

**homeless**

07 nomadic, vagrant
08 forsaken, rootless, vagrants
09 destitute, displaced, itinerant, vagabonds, wandering
10 down-and-out
11 down-and-outs
12 dispossessed, street person
14 of no fixed abode

**homely**

04 cozy, snug, ugly
05 crude, homey, plain
06 folksy, modest, simple
07 natural, relaxed
08 cheerful, domestic, everyday, familiar, friendly, informal, intimate, ordinary, unlovely
09 welcoming
10 hospitable
11 comfortable
12 unattractive
13 unpretentious
15 not much to look at

**homespun**

05 crude, plain, rough
06 coarse, folksy, rustic, simple
07 artless
09 inelegant, unrefined
15 unsophisticated

**homicidal**

07 violent
08 maniacal

**homicide**
09 murderous
10 sanguinary
12 bloodthirsty

**homicide**
06 murder
07 killing, slaying
09 bloodshed, slaughter
12 manslaughter

**homily**
04 talk
06 sermon, speech
07 address, lecture, oration
09 discourse, preaching

**homogeneity**
07 oneness
08 likeness, sameness
09 agreement
10 consonance, similarity, similitude, uniformity

**homogeneous**
05 alike
07 cognate, the same, uniform
08 unvaried
10 all the same
11 all of a piece
13 of the same kind

**homogenize**
04 fuse
05 blend, merge, unite
07 combine
08 coalesce
10 amalgamate

**homologous**
04 like
07 related, similar
08 matching, parallel
09 analogous
10 comparable, equivalent
13 correspondent, corresponding

**homosexual**
03 gay
04 homo
05 queer
06 invert
07 lesbian

**hone**
04 edge, file, whet
05 grind, point
06 polish
07 develop, sharpen

**honest**
04 fair, just, open, real, true
05 blunt, frank, legal, plain
06 candid, direct, lawful, simple
07 ethical, genuine, sincere, up front, upright
08 straight, truthful, virtuous
09 equitable, honorable, impartial, objective, outspoken, reputable
10 aboveboard, forthright, law-abiding, legitimate, on the level, principled, scrupulous, straight-up, upstanding
11 plain-spoken, respectable, trustworthy
13 fair and square, incorruptible, plain-speaking
15 straightforward
17 straight as an arrow

**honestly**
05 truly
06 fairly, justly, openly, really
07 frankly, legally, plainly
08 directly, lawfully, outright
09 honorably
10 on the level, straight up, truthfully
11 in good faith, objectively
12 legitimately

**honesty**
05 honor
06 candor, ethics, virtue
07 balance, probity
08 legality, morality, openness, veracity
09 bluntness, frankness, integrity, rectitude
10 legitimacy
11 genuineness, objectivity, uprightness
12 explicitness, truthfulness
13 plain-speaking, righteousness
14 forthrightness
15 plain-spokenness, trustworthiness

**honorarium**
03 fee, pay, tip
06 reward, salary
09 emolument
12 remuneration

**honorary**
06 formal, unpaid
07 nominal, titular
09 ex officio, honorific
10 in name only, unofficial

**honor**
04 fame, keep
05 award, clear, crown, exalt, favor, glory, pride, prize, title, value
06 accept, credit, esteem, ethics, homage, laurel, morals, praise, renown, repute, revere, reward, trophy, virtue
07 acclaim, applaud, commend, decency, dignity, fulfill, glorify, honesty, probity, respect, tribute, worship
08 accolade, applause, decorate, good name, goodness, morality, remember, venerate
09 adoration, celebrate, discharge, integrity, privilege, recognize, rectitude, reverence
10 compliment, decoration, principles, reputation
11 acclamation, acknowledge, commemorate, distinction, pay homage to, recognition, self-respect, uprightness
12 commendation, pay tribute to, truthfulness
13 righteousness
15 trustworthiness

**honorable**
04 fair, good, just, true
05 great, moral, noble, noted, right
06 decent, famous, honest, trusty, worthy
07 eminent, ethical, notable, sincere, upright
08 reliable, renowned, straight, truthful, virtuous
09 admirable, reputable, respected, righteous
10 dependable, high-minded, principled, upstanding
11 illustrious, prestigious, respectable, trustworthy
13 distinguished

**hood**
04 cowl
05 cover, scarf
07 capouch, capuche, hoodlum, mobster
08 gangster

**hoodlum**
04 hood, lout, thug
05 brute, felon, rowdy, tough
06 gunman, mugger, vandal
07 mobster, ruffian
08 criminal, gangster, hooligan

**hoodwink**
03 con
04 dupe, fool, gull, hoax
05 cheat, trick
06 delude, take in
07 deceive, mislead, swindle
09 bamboozle
12 take for a ride
14 pull a fast one on

**hoof**
04 foot
07 trotter
10 cloven hoof

**hoofed**
06 ungual
08 ungulate
12 cloven-footed, cloven-hoofed

**hook**
03 arc, bag, bow, box, fix, hit, peg, rap
04 barb, bend, blow, clip, cuff, curl, grab, hasp, land, loop, trap
05 angle, catch, clasp, clout, crook, curve, elbow, hitch, knock, punch, snare, thump
06 chorus, enmesh, entrap, fasten, scythe, secure, sickle, stroke, wallop
07 capture, ensnare
08 entangle, fastener

❏ **off the hook**
07 cleared
09 acquitted
10 exonerated, in the clear

**hooked**
04 bent
06 barbed, beaked, curled, curved
07 hamular
08 addicted, aquiline, enamored, hamulate, obsessed, unciform, uncinate
09 dependent

**hooligan**
04 lout, thug
05 rough, rowdy, tough
06 vandal
07 hoodlum, ruffian
10 delinquent

**hoop**
04 band, loop, ring
06 circle, girdle
07 circlet

**hoot**
03 boo, cry
04 call, hiss, howl, jeer, mock
05 shout, sneer, taunt, whoop
06 shriek
07 screech, ululate

**hop**
04 jump, leap, limp, skip, step, trip
05 bound, dance, disco, frisk, jaunt, party, vault
06 bounce, flight, hobble, prance, social, spring

07 journey, shindig
09 excursion

**hope**
04 long, rely, wish
05 await, crave, dream, faith, trust, yearn
06 aspire, assume, belief, desire, expect
07 believe, craving, foresee, longing, promise
08 ambition, optimism, prospect, reckon on, yearning
09 assurance, be hopeful
10 anticipate, aspiration, assumption, confidence, conviction
11 contemplate, expectation
12 anticipation
13 look forward to
14 have confidence
15 hope against hope

**hopeful**
06 bright
07 assured, bullish, buoyant
08 aspirant, aspiring, cheerful, pleasant, positive, sanguine
09 confident, expectant, favorable, promising
10 auspicious, optimistic, propitious
11 encouraging

**hopefully**
05 I hope
08 probably, with hope, with luck
10 expectedly, sanguinely
11 expectantly
14 optimistically

**hopeless**
04 lost, poor, vain, weak
05 awful, grave, lousy
06 futile, gloomy
07 foolish, forlorn, useless
08 dejected, downcast, helpless, pathetic, wretched
09 defeatist, desperate, incurable, pointless, worthless
10 despairing, despondent, impossible
11 downhearted, incompetent, irreparable, pessimistic
12 beyond repair, irremediable, unachievable, unattainable

**horde**
03 mob
04 army, band, crew, gang, herd, host, mass, pack
05 crowd, drove, flock, swarm, troop

06 throng
09 multitude

**horizon**
05 limit, range, scope, vista
07 compass, outlook, skyline
08 prospect
10 perception
11 perspective
13 range of vision

**horizontal**
04 flat
05 level, plane
06 smooth, supine
09 on its side

**hormone**

➤ *Names of hormones*:
05 kinin
07 gastrin, insulin, relaxin
08 androgen, autacoid, estrogen, florigen, glucagon, oxytocin, secretin
09 adrenalin, cortisone, melatonin, prolactin
10 adrenaline
11 epinephrine, vasopressin
12 progesterone, testosterone

**horny**
04 hard, sexy
05 corny
06 ardent
07 callous
08 ceratoid, corneous

**horrendous**
08 dreadful, horrific, shocking, terrible
09 appalling, frightful
10 horrifying, terrifying
11 frightening

**horrible**
04 grim
05 awful, nasty, scary
06 horrid, unkind
07 ghastly, hideous
08 dreadful, gruesome, horrific, shocking, terrible
09 appalling, frightful, harrowing, loathsome, obnoxious, offensive, repulsive, revolting
10 abominable, detestable, disgusting, horrifying, terrifying, unpleasant
11 frightening, hair-raising
12 disagreeable
13 bloodcurdling

**horrid**
04 grim, mean
05 awful, cruel, nasty

**horrific**
07 beastly, ghastly, hateful, hideous
08 dreadful, gruesome, horrific, shocking, terrible
09 appalling, frightful, obnoxious, repulsive, revolting
10 abominable, horrifying, terrifying
11 frightening, hair-raising

**horrific**
05 awful, scary
07 ghastly
08 dreadful, gruesome, shocking, terrible
09 appalling, frightful, harrowing
10 horrifying, terrifying
11 frightening

**horrify**
05 alarm, panic, repel, scare, shock
06 appall, dismay, offend, revolt, sicken
07 disgust, outrage, startle, terrify
08 frighten, nauseate
09 terrorize
10 intimidate, scandalize
12 scare to death

**horror**
04 fear, hate
05 alarm, dread, panic, shock
06 dismay, fright, terror
07 disgust, outrage
08 distaste, loathing
09 awfulness, revulsion
10 abhorrence, repugnance
11 abomination, detestation, ghastliness, hideousness, trepidation
12 apprehension
13 consternation, frightfulness
14 unpleasantness

**horror-struck**
06 aghast
07 shocked, stunned
08 appalled
09 horrified, petrified, terrified
10 frightened
14 horror-stricken

**horse**
03 bay, cob, nag
04 colt, hack, mare, roan
05 filly, mount, steed
06 bronco, dobbin, sorrel
07 broncho, centaur, charger, hackney, mustang
08 stallion

► *Horse and pony breeds*:
04 Arab, barb
05 pinto, shire
06 Morgan
07 Belgian, Hackney, Mustang
08 palomino, Welsh cob
09 appaloosa, Brabancon, Percheron, Welsh pony
10 Clydesdale, Lipizzaner, Lippizaner
12 Shetland pony, Thoroughbred

► *Names of jockeys*:
03 **Day** (Pat)
05 **Baeza** (Braulio), **Smith** (Mike)
06 **Arcaro** (Eddie), **Bailey** (Jerry), **Pincay** (Laffit), **Santos** (Jose)
07 **Cauthen** (Steve), **Cordero** (Angel), **Francis** (Richard Stanley "Dick"), **Stevens** (Gary)
08 **McCarron** (Chris)
09 **Shoemaker** (Willie)
10 **Desormeaux** (Kent)
➤ See also SPORT

► *Famous racehorses*:
05 Cigar, Kelso
06 Forego, Tiznow
08 Affirmed, Citation, Holy Bull, Skip Away
09 John Henry, Kotashaan, Whirlaway
10 Seabiscuit, War Admiral
11 Charismatic, Lady's Secret, Seattle Slew, Secretariat, Sword Dancer
12 Native Dancer
13 Favorite Trick, Sunday Silence
➤ See also SPORT

**horseman, horsewoman**
05 rider
06 cowboy, hussar, jockey, knight
07 dragoon, vaquero
09 caballero
10 cavalryman, equestrian

**horseplay**
06 antics, capers, pranks
08 clowning
09 high jinks
10 buffoonery, skylarking, tomfoolery
11 fun and games
13 fooling around
14 rough-and-tumble

**hortatory**
03 pep
06 urging

08 didactic, edifying
09 homiletic, hortative
10 heartening
11 encouraging, exhortative, exhortatory, inspiriting, instructive, stimulating

**horticulture**
09 gardening
11 cultivation

**hosanna**
05 shout
06 praise, save us
08 alleluia
09 laudation
10 hallelujah

**hose**
04 duct, pipe, sock, tube
06 tubing
07 channel, conduit
08 stocking

**hosiery**
04 hose
05 socks
09 stockings

**hospitable**
04 kind, warm
06 genial
07 cordial, helpful, liberal
08 amicable, friendly, generous, gracious, sociable
09 bountiful, congenial, convivial, receptive, welcoming
10 neighborly, openhanded
11 kindhearted

**hospital**
06 clinic
07 hospice
09 infirmary, institute
10 sanatorium

**hospitality**
05 cheer
06 warmth
07 welcome
08 kindness
10 generosity, liberality
11 helpfulness, sociability
12 congeniality, conviviality, friendliness
13 accommodation, entertainment
14 neighborliness, openhandedness

**host**
02 MC
03 mob
04 army, band, give, herd, mass, pack
05 array, crowd, crush, emcee, horde, swarm, troop

**hostage**
06 myriad, throng
07 compère
08 landlady, landlord
09 innkeeper, introduce, multitude
10 proprietor

**hostage**
07 captive
08 prisoner

**hostel**
03 inn
05 hotel
06 tavern
10 guesthouse
11 youth hostel
13 boardinghouse

**hostile**
07 adverse, opposed, warlike
08 contrary, inimical, opposite
09 bellicose
10 malevolent, unfriendly
11 belligerent, illdisposed, unfavorable
12 antagonistic, inauspicious, inhospitable
13 unsympathetic

**hostilities**
03 war
06 battle, strife
07 warfare
08 conflict, fighting
09 bloodshed

**hostility**
04 hate
06 enmity, hatred, malice
07 cruelty, dislike, ill will
08 aversion
09 animosity, militancy
10 aggression, antagonism, resentment
11 bellicosity, malevolence
12 belligerence, estrangement
14 unfriendliness

**hot**
03 new, red
04 keen, warm
05 angry, eager, fiery, fresh, livid, sharp, spicy
06 baking, fierce, fuming, heated, latest, piping, raging, recent, stolen, strong, sultry, torrid
07 boiling, burning, devoted, earnest, enraged, flushed, furious, intense, peppery, piquant, pungent, searing, violent, zealous
08 diligent, exciting, feverish, incensed, inflamed, parching, pilfered, roasting,

scalding, seething, sizzling, steaming, tropical
09 indignant, scorching
10 blistering, contraband, sweltering

❏ **hot air**
03 gas
04 bosh, bunk
05 bilge, froth, vapor
06 bunkum, piffle
07 blather, blether, bluster, bombast
08 claptrap, nonsense, verbiage
09 empty talk, mere words
10 balderdash

**hotbed**
03 den
04 hive, nest
06 cradle, school
07 nursery, seedbed
14 breeding-ground

**hotblooded**
04 bold, rash, wild
05 fiery, lusty
07 fervent, lustful, sensual
09 impulsive, perfervid
10 passionate
13 temperamental

**hotchpotch**
03 mix
04 mess, stew
06 jumble, medley
07 melange, mixture
08 mishmash
09 confusion
10 collection, hodgepodge, miscellany

**hot dog**
05 frank
06 weenie, weiner, wiener
11 frankforter, frankfurter

**hotel**
03 inn
05 lodge, motel
06 hostel, tavern
08 hostelry

**hotfoot**
07 hastily, in haste, quickly, rapidly, swiftly
08 pell-mell, speedily
09 hurriedly, posthaste
10 at top speed

**hothead**
06 madcap, madman, terror
07 hotspur
09 daredevil, desperado, firebrand

**hotheaded**
04 rash, wild

05 fiery, hasty
08 reckless, volatile, volcanic
09 excitable, explosive, foolhardy, impetuous, impulsive, irascible
10 headstrong

**hothouse**
07 nursery
10 greenhouse
12 conservatory

**hot-tempered**
05 fiery, hasty, testy
07 violent
08 choleric, petulant, volcanic
09 explosive, irascible, irritable

**hound**
03 nag
04 goad, hunt, prod, urge
05 bully, chase, drive, force, harry, stalk, track, trail
06 badger, harass, pursue
07 disturb, provoke
09 persecute

**house**
04 body, clan, firm, hold, home, keep, line
05 guard, lodge, place, put up, store, tribe
06 billet, family, ménage
07 chamber, company, contain, dynasty, kindred, lineage, quarter, sheathe, shelter, theater
08 ancestry, assembly, audience, congress, domestic, domicile, dwelling
09 gathering, household, residence
10 auditorium, enterprise, habitation, parliament, spectators
11 accommodate, corporation, legislature
12 family circle, organization

▶ *Types of house*:
03 hut
05 condo, igloo, lodge, manor, manse, shack, villa
06 chalet, duplex, grange, prefab, shanty, studio
07 cottage, mansion, rectory
08 bungalow, hacienda, log cabin, terraced, vicarage
09 apartment, farmhouse, homestead, parsonage, penthouse, town house
10 maisonette, pied-à-terre, ranch house
11 condominium
➤ See also ACCOMODATION

**◻on the house**
04 free
06 gratis
08 at no cost
10 for nothing
11 without cost
12 free of charge
13 without charge

**housebroken**
05 tamed
07 trained
12 domesticated

**household**
04 home
06 family, ménage
08 domestic
12 family circle

**householder**
05 owner
06 tenant
08 landlady, landlord, occupant, occupier, resident
09 home owner
10 freeholder, proprietor
11 leaseholder

**housekeeping**
10 homemaking
11 housewifery
12 domestic work, running a home
13 home economics, office matters
15 domestic matters, domestic science

**housing**
04 case
05 cover, guard
06 casing, holder, jacket, sheath
07 shelter
08 covering
09 container, dwellings
10 habitation, protection
13 accommodation

**hovel**
04 dump, hole, shed
05 cabin, shack
06 shanty

**hover**
04 flap, hang
05 drift, float, pause, poise, waver
06 linger, seesaw
07 flutter
08 hesitate
09 alternate, fluctuate, hang about, oscillate, vacillate
10 hang around

**however**
03 yet
05 still

06 anyhow, even so, though
10 regardless
11 just the same, nonetheless
12 nevertheless
15 notwithstanding

**howl**
03 bay, cry
04 bawl, hoot, moan, roar, wail, yell, yelp, yowl
05 groan, shout
06 bellow, scream, shriek

**howler**
05 boner, error, gaffe
06 boo-boo
07 blooper, blunder, mistake
08 solecism

**hub**
04 axis, core
05 focus, heart, pivot
06 center, middle
08 linchpin
11 nerve center
13 command center

**hubbub**
03 din
04 riot
05 chaos, noise
06 clamor, racket, tumult, uproar
09 commotion, confusion
10 hullabaloo, hurly-burly
11 disturbance, pandemonium

**huckster**
06 barker, dealer, hawker, pedlar, vendor
07 haggler, packman, peddler

**huddle**
04 cram, knot, mass, pack
05 crowd, flock, hunch, press
06 crouch, gather, nestle
07 cluster, snuggle, squeeze
10 conference, discussion

**hue**
03 dye
04 tint, tone
05 color, light, shade, tinge
06 aspect, nuance
10 complexion

**hue and cry**
03 ado
04 fuss, to-do
05 furor
06 clamor, outcry, rumpus, uproar
07 ruction
08 brouhaha, shouting
10 hullabaloo

**huff**
04 mood, rage, sulk

05 anger, pique
07 bad mood, passion
08 the sulks

**huffy**
05 moody, sulky, surly, testy
06 grumpy, miffed
07 peevish, waspish
08 petulant
09 querulous, resentful

**hug**
04 grip, hold
05 clasp, press
06 clinch, clutch, cuddle, enfold
07 cling to, embrace, enclose
11 stay close to

**huge**
04 vast
05 bulky, giant, great, jumbo
07 immense, mammoth, massive, titanic
08 colossal, enormous, gigantic, unwieldy
09 extensive, monstrous
10 gargantuan, prodigious, stupendous, tremendous

**hulk**
03 oaf
04 clod, hull, loom, lout, lump, ship
05 frame, shell, wreck
06 lubber
09 shipwreck
12 lounge around, slouch around

**hulking**
05 bulky, heavy
06 clumsy
07 awkward, massive, weighty
08 ungainly, unwieldy
09 lumbering

**hull**
03 pod
04 body, husk, pare, peel, rind, skin, trim
05 frame, shell, shuck, strip
06 casing, legume
07 capsule, epicarp, exocarp
08 covering, skeleton
09 framework, structure

**hullabaloo**
03 din
04 fuss, to-do
05 furor, noise
06 hubbub, outcry, racket, tumult, uproar
08 brouhaha
09 commotion, hue and cry
11 disturbance, pandemonium

**hum**
04 buzz, purr, sing

**human**
05 croon, drone, pulse, throb, thrum, whirr
06 mumble, murmur
07 buzzing, purring, vibrate
08 whirring
09 pulsation, throbbing, vibration

**human**
03 man
04 body, soul
05 child, woman
06 humane, mortal, person
07 fleshly
08 fallible
10 anthropoid, individual
11 Homo sapiens, sympathetic
13 flesh and blood

**humane**
04 good, kind, mild
06 benign, gentle, kindly, loving, tender
07 lenient
08 generous, merciful
09 forgiving
10 benevolent, charitable, forbearing
11 considerate, good-natured, kindhearted, sympathetic
12 humanitarian
13 compassionate, understanding

**humanitarian**
04 kind
06 humane
08 altruist, do-gooder
10 altruistic, charitable
13 good Samaritan, philanthropic
14 philanthropist, public-spirited

**humanitarianism**
07 charity
08 goodwill, humanism
10 generosity
11 beneficence, benevolence
12 philanthropy
14 charitableness

**humanity**
03 man
06 people
07 mankind, mortals
08 goodness, sympathy
09 human race, humankind, womankind
10 compassion, humaneness
11 benevolence, Homo sapiens
13 brotherly love, fellow-feeling
15 kindheartedness

**humanize**
04 tame
05 edify

06 better, polish, refine
07 educate, improve
08 civilize
09 cultivate, enlighten
11 domesticate

**humble**
03 low
04 mean, meek, poor
05 abase, crush, lower, lowly, plain
06 common, demean, modest, simple, subdue
07 chasten, deflate, mortify, servile
08 belittle, bring low, disgrace, inferior, ordinary
09 bring down, disparage, humiliate, unrefined
10 low-ranking, obsequious, put to shame, respectful, submissive, unassuming
11 commonplace, deferential, subservient, sycophantic, unassertive, unimportant
12 self-effacing
13 insignificant, unpretentious
14 unostentatious

**humbly**
06 meekly, simply
08 docilely, modestly
09 cap in hand, servilely
12 obsequiously, respectfully, submissively, unassumingly
13 deferentially, subserviently

**humbug**
03 con, rot
04 cant, fake, hoax, sham
05 actor, bluff, cheat, fraud, poser, rogue, swank, trick
06 bunkum, con man, deceit
07 baloney, bluffer, eyewash, rubbish, swindle
08 cheating, claptrap, impostor, nonsense, pretense, swindler, trickery
09 charlatan, con artist, deception, hypocrisy, poppycock, trickster
10 balderdash

**humdrum**
04 dull
05 banal
06 boring, dreary
07 mundane, routine, tedious
08 ordinary, unvaried
10 monotonous, uneventful
11 commonplace, repetitious
12 run-of-the-mill
13 uninteresting

**humid**
03 wet

04 damp, dank
05 close, heavy, moist, muggy
06 clammy, steamy, sticky, sultry
10 oppressive

**humidity**
03 dew
04 damp, mist
07 wetness
08 dampness, dankness, moisture
09 closeness, heaviness, humidness, moistness, mugginess, sogginess
10 clamminess, steaminess, stickiness, sultriness

**humiliate**
05 abase, abash, break, crush, shame
06 demean, humble
07 chasten, deflate, degrade, mortify, put down
08 bring low, confound, disgrace
09 discomfit, discredit, embarrass

**humiliating**
07 shaming
08 humbling
09 degrading
10 disgracing, mortifying
11 disgraceful, ignominious
12 discomfiting, embarrassing

**humiliation**
04 snub
05 shame
06 rebuff
07 affront, put-down
08 crushing, disgrace, dishonor, humbling, ignominy
09 abasement, deflation, discredit, humble pie, indignity
10 chastening, loss of face
11 confounding, degradation
12 discomfiture
13 embarrassment, mortification

**humility**
07 modesty
09 deference, servility
10 diffidence, humbleness
13 self-abasement
14 self-effacement, submissiveness

**hummock**
04 hump
05 knoll, mound
07 hillock
10 prominence

**humorist**
03 wag, wit

**humorous**
05 clown, comic, joker
06 jester
08 comedian, satirist
10 comedienne

**humorous**
04 zany
05 comic, droll, funny, witty
06 absurd
07 amusing, comical, jocular, playful, risible, waggish
08 farcical
09 facetious, hilarious, laughable, ludicrous, satirical, whimsical
10 ridiculous
12 entertaining
13 side-splitting

**humor**
03 fun, wit
04 gags, mood
05 farce, favor, jokes, spoil
06 comedy, pamper, please, satire, temper
07 flatter, gratify, indulge, jesting, mollify, satisfy, spirits
08 drollery, hilarity, pander to
09 amusement, wittiness
10 jocularity, wisecracks
11 disposition, frame of mind, go along with, state of mind, temperament

➤ *The four bodily humors:*
05 blood
06 choler, phlegm
09 black bile
10 melancholy, yellow bile

**humorless**
03 dry
04 dull, glum, grim
05 grave
06 boring, morose, solemn, somber
07 serious, tedious
09 long-faced, unsmiling
10 unlaughing

**hump**
04 arch, bump, knob, lump
05 bulge, crook, curve, hunch, mound
07 hummock
08 swelling
09 outgrowth
10 prominence, protrusion

**humpbacked**
07 crooked, gibbous, hunched, stooped
08 deformed, kyphotic
09 misshapen

**humped**
04 bent

06 arched, curved
07 crooked, gibbous, hunched

**hunch**
04 bend, hump, idea
05 curve, guess, stoop
06 crouch
07 feeling, inkling
09 intuition, suspicion
11 premonition
12 presentiment

**hunger**
03 yen
04 ache, itch, long, pine, wish
05 crave, greed, yearn
06 desire, famine, hanker, pining, starve, thirst
07 craving, longing
08 appetite, voracity, yearning
09 emptiness, esurience, esuriency, hankering
10 greediness, hungriness, starvation
12 malnutrition, ravenousness

**hungry**
04 avid
05 eager, empty
06 aching, greedy, hollow, pining
07 craving, itching, longing, needing, thirsty
08 covetous, desirous, famished, ravenous, starving, underfed, yearning
09 hankering, voracious
12 malnourished
14 could eat a horse, undernourished

**hunk**
04 clod, lump, mass, slab
05 block, chunk, piece, wedge

**hunt**
04 fish, seek
05 chase, hound, quest, scour, stalk, track, trail
06 ferret, forage, pursue, search
07 look for, pursuit, rummage
08 stalking, tracking
09 try to find
11 investigate
13 investigation

**hunter**
07 stalker, trapper
08 huntsman, predator, woodsman

**hurdle**
04 jump, wall
05 fence, hedge
07 barrier, problem, railing
08 handicap, obstacle
09 barricade, hindrance

10 difficulty, impediment
11 obstruction
14 stumbling block

**hurl**
04 cast, fire, send, toss
05 chuck, fling, heave, pitch, sling, throw
06 launch, let fly, propel
07 project
08 catapult

**hurly-burly**
05 chaos
06 bustle, hubbub, hustle, tumult
08 brouhaha, disorder
09 commotion, confusion
11 pandemonium

**hurricane**
04 gale
05 storm
07 tempest, typhoon
13 tropical storm

**hurried**
05 brief, hasty, quick, rapid, swift
06 hectic, rushed, speedy
07 cursory, offhand, shallow
08 careless, fleeting, slapdash
09 breakneck, transient
10 transitory
11 perfunctory, precipitate, superficial

**hurry**
03 fly, run
04 dash, push, rush
05 haste, speed
06 bustle, hasten, hustle
07 quicken, speed up, urgency
08 celerity, dispatch, go all out, rapidity, step on it
09 commotion, confusion, cut and run, make haste, quickness, shake a leg
10 accelerate, get a move on
11 get cracking, run like hell
13 show your heels
15 put your foot down

**hurt**
03 cut, mar, sad
04 ache, harm, pain, sore
05 annoy, grief, smart, spoil, sting, throb, upset, wound
06 aching, blight, bruise, damage, grieve, impair, injure, injury, maimed, misery, offend, sadden, sorrow
07 afflict, annoyed, blemish, bruised, burning, disable, injured, painful, sadness, scarred, scratch, torture, wounded

**hurtful**
08 distress, ill-treat, maltreat, offended, smarting, soreness
09 affronted, aggrieved, be painful, in anguish, lacerated, miserable, sorrowful, suffering, throbbing
10 affliction, debilitate, discomfort, distressed
13 grief-stricken

**hurtful**
06 unkind
07 cutting, harmful, vicious
08 damaging, scathing, wounding
09 injurious, upsetting
11 destructive, distressing

**hurtle**
03 fly
04 dash, dive, race, rush, tear
05 crash, shoot, speed
06 career, charge, plunge, rattle

**husband**
04 mate, save
05 hoard, hubby, store
06 budget, eke out, ration, save up, spouse
07 partner, reserve
08 conserve, put aside
09 economize, other half
12 use carefully, use sparingly

**husbandry**
06 saving, thrift
07 economy, farming, tillage
09 frugality
10 management
11 cultivation, thriftiness
12 conservation

**hush**
04 calm
05 peace, quiet, shush, still
06 repose, settle, shut up, soothe, subdue
07 quieten, silence
08 calmness, pipe down
09 quietness, stillness
11 tranquility
12 peacefulness
14 hold your tongue, not another word

◻**hush up**
03 gag
07 conceal, cover up, silence, smother
08 keep dark, suppress
10 keep secret

**hush-hush**
06 secret
09 top-secret
10 classified, under wraps
12 confidential

**husk**
03 pod
04 bran, case, hull, rind
05 chaff, shell, shuck
07 capsule, epicarp, exocarp
08 covering

**husky**
03 low
04 deep
05 beefy, burly, gruff, harsh
06 brawny, coarse, hoarse
07 rasping, throaty
08 gravelly, muscular
09 strapping, well-built

**hussy**
04 minx, slut, tart, vamp
05 tramp
06 floosy, floozy
07 floosie, floozie, trollop

**hustle**
03 fly
04 dash, fuss, push, rush, stir
05 crowd, elbow, force, hurry, nudge, shove
06 bundle, bustle, hasten, jostle, thrust, tumult
07 swindle
08 activity
09 agitation, commotion
10 hurly-burly, pressurize

**hut**
04 shed
05 cabin, hovel, hutch, shack
06 lean-to, shanty

**hybrid**
05 cross, mixed
07 amalgam, mixture, mongrel
08 combined, compound
09 composite, crossbred, half-blood, half-breed
10 crossbreed
11 combination
13 heterogeneous
14 conglomeration

**hybridize**
05 cross
10 crossbreed, interbreed

**hydrocarbon**
► *Names of hydrocarbons:*
03 wax
06 aldrin, alkane, alkene, alkyne, butane, cetane, decane, ethane, octane, olefin, pyrene, xylene
07 benzene, heptane, methane, olefine, pentane, propane, styrene
08 camphene, diphenyl, menthene, stilbene
09 butadiene
10 mesitylene
11 naphthalene

**hygiene**
06 purity
09 sterility
10 sanitation
11 cleanliness

**hygienic**
04 pure
05 clean
07 aseptic, healthy, sterile
08 germ-free, sanitary
10 salubrious, sterilized
11 disinfected

**hymn**
04 song
05 carol, chant, paean, psalm
06 anthem, choral, chorus
07 cantata, chorale, introit
08 canticle, doxology
09 offertory, spiritual
12 song of praise

**hype**
04 fuss, plug, puff
05 fraud
06 racket
07 build up, buildup, promote, puffing
08 ballyhoo, plugging
09 advertise, deception, promotion, publicity, publicize
10 razzmatazz

**hyperbole**
06 excess
08 overkill
12 exaggeration, extravagance
13 magnification, overstatement

**hypercritical**
05 picky
07 carping, finicky
08 caviling
09 quibbling
10 censorious, nit-picking
11 persnickety
14 over-particular

**hypnotic**
07 numbing
08 magnetic, sedative
09 soporific
10 compelling
11 fascinating, mesmerizing, somniferous
12 irresistible, spellbinding
13 sleep-inducing

**hypnotism**
09 mesmerism

**hypnotize**

10 suggestion
14 autosuggestion

**hypnotize**
07 beguile, bewitch, enchant
08 entrance
09 captivate, fascinate, magnetize, mesmerize, spellbind

**hypochondria**
07 anxiety
08 neurosis
15 hypochondriasis

**hypochondriac**
08 neurotic
14 valetudinarian

**hypocrisy**
04 cant
06 deceit
07 falsity
08 pretense
09 deception, duplicity, phoniness
10 dishonesty, double talk, lip service, pharisaism
11 dissembling, insincerity
12 two-facedness

13 deceitfulness, double-dealing

**hypocrite**
05 fraud, phony, pseud
06 canter, phoney, pseudo
08 Pharisee, Tartuffe
09 pretender
15 whited sepulcher

**hypocritical**
08 two-faced
09 insincere, pharisaic
10 fraudulent, perfidious
11 dissembling, duplicitous, pharisaical
12 Pecksniffian

**hypothesis**
05 axiom
06 theory, thesis
07 premise, theorem
09 postulate
10 assumption, conjecture
11 presumption, proposition, speculation, supposition

**hypothetical**
07 assumed
08 imagined, presumed, proposed, supposed

09 imaginary
11 conjectural, speculative, theoretical

**hysteria**
05 mania, panic
06 frenzy
07 madness
08 delirium, neurosis
09 agitation, hysterics

**hysterical**
03 mad
06 crazed, raving
07 berserk, frantic
08 demented, frenzied, in a panic, neurotic
09 delirious, hilarious, priceless
10 uproarious
11 overwrought
13 sidesplitting
14 beside yourself, uncontrollable

**hysterics**
06 frenzy
07 madness
08 delirium, hysteria, neurosis

**ice**
04 rime
05 chill, frost, glaze
06 freeze, icicle
07 glacier, iciness
10 freeze over, frostiness
11 frozen water, refrigerate

❑**put on ice**
05 defer, delay, table
06 put off, shelve
08 postpone
14 hold in abeyance
15 leave in abeyance

**ice cold**
03 icy, raw
04 iced, numb
05 algid, gelid, polar
06 arctic, frigid, frosty, frozen
07 chilled, frosted, glacial
08 freezing
11 frozen stiff
12 bitterly cold

**icon**
04 idol
05 image
06 figure, symbol
14 representation

**iconoclast**
07 heretic, radical, skeptic
09 dissenter, dissident
10 questioner, unbeliever
11 denunciator
12 image-breaker

**iconoclastic**
08 critical
09 dissident, heretical, skeptical
10 irreverent, subversive
11 dissentient, questioning
12 denunciatory

**icy**
03 raw
04 cold, rimy
05 aloof, chill, gelid, polar
06 arctic, biting, bitter, chilly,
    frigid, frosty, frozen, glassy
07 glacial, hostile, stuck up
08 freezing
10 frostbound
11 indifferent, unemotional

**idea**
03 aim, end
04 clue, goal, plan, view

05 fancy, guess, image, point
06 belief, notion, object, reason,
    theory, vision
07 concept, feeling, inkling,
    opinion, purpose, thought
08 judgment, proposal
09 brainwave, intention,
    objective, suspicion,
    viewpoint
10 conception, conjecture,
    hypothesis, impression,
    perception, suggestion
11 abstraction, proposition
13 understanding
14 interpretation

**ideal**
04 acme, best
05 dream, image, model
06 ethics, morals
07 epitome, optimal, optimum,
    paragon, pattern, perfect,
    supreme, utopian
08 exemplar
09 archetype, nonpareil,
    yardstick
10 archetypal, consummate,
    perfection
11 moral values, theoretical
12 hypothetical
13 ethical values
14 moral standards

**idealism**
10 utopianism
11 romanticism
13 perfectionism

**idealist**
08 optimist, romantic
11 romanticist
13 perfectionist

**idealistic**
07 utopian
08 romantic
10 optimistic, starry-eyed
13 perfectionist

**idealization**
10 apotheosis
11 idolization
13 glamorization, glorification
15 romanticization

**idealize**
07 glorify, idolize, worship
09 glamorize

11 romanticize

**ideally**
06 at best
08 in theory
09 perfectly
13 theoretically
15 in a perfect world

**idée fixe**
06 hangup
08 fixation
09 fixed idea, leitmotif, leitmotiv,
    monomania, obsession

**identical**
04 like, same, twin
05 alike, equal
08 matching, selfsame
09 duplicate
13 one and the same
15 interchangeable

**identifiable**
10 detectable, noticeable
11 discernible, perceptible
12 recognizable, unmistakable
15 distinguishable

**identification**
02 ID
05 badge, brand
06 papers
07 empathy, rapport
08 labeling, sympathy
09 detection, diagnosis,
    documents
11 credentials, recognition
12 identity card
13 fellow feeling

**identify**
03 tag
04 know, name, spot
05 brand, label, place
06 detect, notice, relate
07 catalog, discern, feel for, find
    out, make out, pick out,
    specify
08 classify, diagnose, discover,
    perceive, pinpoint, point out,
    relate to
09 ascertain, catalogue,
    establish, recognize, single
    out
11 distinguish
13 empathize with
14 sympathize with

## identity
03 ego
04 name, self
08 likeness, sameness, selfhood
09 character, existence
10 uniqueness
11 personality, resemblance
13 individuality, particularity
15 distinctiveness

## ideologist
07 teacher, thinker
08 theorist
09 ideologue, visionary
11 doctrinaire, philosopher

## ideology
05 credo, creed, dogma, faith, ideas
06 belief, tenets, theory, thesis
07 beliefs, opinion
08 doctrine, opinions, teaching
09 doctrines, worldview
10 philosophy, principles
11 convictions

## idiocy
08 daftness, insanity
09 absurdity, craziness, silliness, stupidity
11 fatuousness
13 foolhardiness, senselessness

## idiom
05 style, usage
06 jargon, phrase, speech
08 language, locution
10 expression, vernacular
11 phraseology
12 turn of phrase

## idiomatic
09 dialectal
10 vernacular
11 dialectical

## idiosyncrasy
05 freak, habit, quirk, trait
06 oddity
07 feature, quality
09 mannerism
11 peculiarity, singularity
12 eccentricity
13 individuality
14 characteristic

## idiosyncratic
03 odd
06 quirky
08 peculiar, personal, singular
09 eccentric
10 individual
11 distinctive
14 characteristic

## idiot
03 ass
04 clod, dope, dork, fool

05 chump, clown, dumbo, dummy, dunce, ninny, twerp
06 cretin, dimwit, nitwit, shlump, sucker
07 fathead, halfwit
08 dumbbell, imbecile, numskull
09 birdbrain, blockhead, ignoramus, numbskull, simpleton
10 nincompoop

## idiotic
03 mad
04 daft, dumb
05 batty, crazy, dotty, goofy, inane, inept, nutty, silly
06 absurd, simple, stupid
07 fatuous, foolish, moronic, risible
09 half-baked, ludicrous, pointless, senseless
10 half-witted, ridiculous
11 harebrained, nonsensical, thickheaded
12 crackbrained, simple-minded, unreasonable
13 ill-considered, unintelligent

## idle
04 laze, lazy, loaf
05 dally, empty, petty, relax, shirk, slack, waste
06 casual, dawdle, futile, loiter, lounge, putter
07 fritter, jobless, loafish, trivial
08 inactive, indolent, kill time, slothful, sluggish
09 bum around, do nothing, lethargic, pointless
10 take it easy, unemployed, unoccupied
11 ineffectual, inoperative
12 unproductive
13 insignificant, lackadaisical

## idleness
04 ease
05 sloth
06 lazing, torpor
07 inertia, leisure, loafing
08 inaction, laziness
09 indolence
10 inactivity
12 slothfulness, unemployment
13 shiftlessness

## idler
03 bum
05 drone, sloth
06 loafer, waster
07 dawdler, laggard, lounger, shirker, slacker, wastrel
08 layabout, sluggard
09 do-nothing, lazybones

10 malingerer

## idol
03 god
04 hero, icon, star
05 deity, image, pinup
06 effigy, fetish, mammet
07 beloved, darling, heroine
08 favorite
09 superstar
11 graven image
13 fair-haired boy

## idolater
06 adorer, votary
07 admirer, devotee
08 votarist
09 worshiper
10 iconolater

## idolatrous
05 pagan
07 adoring
09 adulatory, heretical, lionizing
10 glorifying, uncritical, worshiping
11 reverential

## idolatry
08 paganism
09 adoration, adulation, fetishism, reverence
10 admiration, exaltation, heathenism, iconolatry
11 deification, hero worship
13 glorification

## idolize
05 adore, deify, exalt
06 admire, dote on, revere
07 adulate, glorify, lionize, worship
08 venerate
09 reverence
11 hero-worship
14 put on a pedestal

## idyllic
05 happy
07 perfect
08 blissful, charming, heavenly, pastoral, peaceful, romantic
09 idealized, unspoiled, wonderful
10 delightful

## if
08 as long as, assuming, in case of, provided, so long as
09 providing, supposing
12 assuming that, in the event of
13 supposing that
15 on condition that

## iffy
05 dodgy
07 dubious
08 doubtful

09 uncertain
**ignite**
04 burn, fire
05 light
06 kindle
07 flare up, inflame
08 spark off, touch off
09 catch fire, set alight, set fire to
11 conflagrate, put a match to
15 burst into flames

**ignoble**
03 low
04 base, mean, vile
06 vulgar
08 shameful, wretched
10 despicable
11 disgraceful
12 contemptible, dishonorable

**ignominious**
04 base
06 abject
08 infamous, shameful
09 degrading
10 despicable, mortifying
11 disgraceful, humiliating
12 contemptible, dishonorable, disreputable, embarrassing
13 discreditable

**ignominy**
05 odium, shame
06 infamy, stigma
07 obloquy
08 contempt, disgrace, dishonor
09 indignity
10 opprobrium
11 degradation, humiliation
13 mortification

**ignoramus**
04 dolt, fool
05 dunce
06 dimwit
07 dullard, half-wit
08 bonehead, imbecile, numskull
09 blockhead, simpleton

**ignorance**
07 naïvety
09 greenness, innocence, stupidity, thickness
12 inexperience

**ignorant**
05 blind, dense, green, naïve, thick
06 stupid
07 unaware
08 backward, innocent
09 in the dark, oblivious, unwitting

10 illiterate, innumerate, uneducated
11 unconscious, uninitiated
12 unacquainted
13 inexperienced

**ignore**
03 cut
04 snub
05 spurn
06 reject, slight
07 cut dead, neglect
08 overlook, pass over
09 disregard
10 brush aside
12 cold-shoulder
14 shut your eyes to, take no notice of, turn a deaf ear to
15 look the other way, turn a blind eye to

**ilk**
04 kind, make, sort, type
05 brand, breed, class
07 variety

**ill**
03 bad
04 evil, harm, hurt, sick, weak
05 amiss, badly, harsh, rough, seedy
06 ailing, barely, groggy, hardly, infirm, injury, laid up, poorly, queasy, sorrow, trials, unkind, unwell
07 adverse, cruelty, disease, harmful, hostile, ominous, problem, ruinous, run down, trouble, unlucky
08 damaging, disaster, diseased, off-color, scantily, scarcely, sinister, unkindly
09 adversely, afflicted, bedridden, by no means, difficult, suffering, unhealthy
10 affliction, indisposed, misfortune, out of sorts, unpleasant
11 deleterious, destruction, destructive, detrimental, tribulation, unfavorable, unfortunate, unpromising
12 inauspicious, unpropitious
14 inauspiciously, insufficiently, unpleasantness, unsuccessfully
15 under the weather

**❏ill at ease**
04 edgy
05 tense
06 on edge, uneasy, unsure
07 anxious, fidgety, nervous
08 hesitant, restless
09 disturbed, unsettled

13 on tenterhooks, self-conscious, uncomfortable

**ill-advised**
04 rash
05 hasty
06 unwise
07 foolish
08 careless, reckless
09 imprudent, misguided
11 injudicious, thoughtless

**ill-bred**
04 rude
05 crass, crude
06 coarse, vulgar
07 boorish, loutish, uncivil, uncouth
08 declasse, impolite, unseemly
11 bad mannered, uncivilized
12 discourteous

**ill-considered**
04 rash
05 hasty
06 unwise
07 foolish
08 careless, heedless
09 imprudent, overhasty
11 improvident, injudicious

**ill-defined**
03 dim
04 hazy
05 fuzzy, vague
06 blurry, woolly
07 blurred, shadowy, unclear
08 nebulous
09 imprecise
10 indefinite, indistinct

**ill-disposed**
06 averse
07 against, hostile, opposed
08 inimical
10 unfriendly
12 antagonistic

**illegal**
06 banned, barred
07 illicit
08 criminal, outlawed, unlawful, wrongful
09 felonious, forbidden
10 prohibited, proscribed
11 black-market, interdicted
13 under-the-table
15 under-the-counter

**illegality**
05 crime
11 criminality, illicitness, lawlessness
12 unlawfulness, wrongfulness

**illegible**
05 faint
07 obscure

10 indistinct, unreadable
12 hieroglyphic
14 indecipherable

**illegitimate**
04 love
07 bastard, illicit, invalid, lawless, natural, unsound
08 improper, spurious, unlawful
09 illogical, incorrect
10 adulterine, adulterous
11 misbegotten
12 unauthorized

**ill-fated**
06 doomed
07 hapless, unhappy, unlucky
08 blighted, luckless
11 unfortunate

**ill-favored**
04 ugly
05 plain
06 homely
08 unlovely
09 offensive, unsightly
10 unpleasant
12 unattractive
15 unprepossessing

**ill feeling**
05 anger, odium, spite, wrath
06 animus, enmity, grudge, malice, rancor
07 dudgeon
08 bad blood, sourness
09 animosity, hostility
10 antagonism, bitterness, resentment
14 disgruntlement

**ill-founded**
08 baseless
10 groundless
11 unjustified, unsupported

**ill-humored**
05 cross, huffy, moody, testy
06 crabby, grumpy, morose, snappy, sullen
07 crabbed, grouchy, peevish, waspish
08 petulant, snappish
09 crotchety, irascible, irritable
11 acrimonious, bad tempered
12 cantankerous, disagreeable
13 quick-tempered

**illiberal**
04 mean
05 petty, tight
06 stingy
07 bigoted, miserly
09 hidebound, niggardly
10 intolerant, prejudiced
11 close-fisted, reactionary, small-minded, tightfisted

12 narrow-minded, parsimonious

**illicit**
06 banned, barred
07 furtive, illegal
08 criminal, unlawful
09 forbidden, ill-gotten
10 contraband, prohibited, unlicensed
11 black market, clandestine
12 illegitimate, unauthorized
13 under-the-table
15 under-the-counter

**illiterate**
08 ignorant, untaught
09 unlearned, untutored
10 uncultured, uneducated, unlettered, unschooled
12 analphabetic

**ill-judged**
04 daft, rash
06 unwise
07 foolish
08 reckless
09 foolhardy, impolitic, imprudent, misguided
10 incautious
11 injudicious, wrongheaded

**ill-mannered**
04 rude
05 crude
06 coarse
07 boorish, loutish, uncivil, uncouth
08 churlish, impolite, insolent
10 unmannerly
11 insensitive
12 badly behaved, discourteous

**ill-natured**
05 cross, nasty, sulky, surly
06 sullen
07 crabbed, vicious
08 churlish, petulant, spiteful
09 malicious, malignant
10 malevolent, unfriendly, unpleasant, vindictive
11 bad tempered

**illness**
06 attack, malady
07 ailment, disease
08 disorder, sickness
09 complaint, condition, infirmity
10 affliction, disability, poor health
13 indisposition

**illogical**
06 absurd, faulty
07 invalid, unsound
08 specious, spurious

09 senseless, untenable
10 fallacious, irrational
11 meaningless, sophistical
12 inconsistent, unscientific

**illogicality**
09 absurdity
10 invalidity
11 unsoundness
12 speciousness
13 irrationality, senselessness
14 fallaciousness

**ill-starred**
06 doomed
07 hapless, unhappy, unlucky
08 blighted
11 star-crossed, unfortunate
12 inauspicious

**ill-tempered**
04 curt
05 cross, sharp, testy
06 grumpy, tetchy, touchy
07 vicious
08 choleric, spiteful
09 impatient, irascible, irritable
11 bad tempered

**ill-timed**
08 untimely
11 inopportune
12 inconvenient, unseasonable
13 inappropriate

**ill-treat**
04 harm
05 abuse, wrong
06 damage, injure, misuse
07 neglect
08 maltreat, mistreat

**ill-treatment**
04 harm
05 abuse
06 damage, injury, misuse
07 neglect
12 maltreatment, mistreatment

**illuminate**
05 light
07 clarify, clear up, explain, light up, shine on
08 brighten, illumine, ornament
09 elucidate, enlighten
10 floodlight, illustrate
12 throw light on

**illuminating**
08 edifying
09 revealing
10 revelatory
11 explanatory, instructive
12 enlightening

**illumination**
03 ray
04 beam

05 light
07 insight
08 lighting, radiance
10 brightness, decoration, perception, revelation
11 irradiation
13 enlightenment, understanding

**illusion**
05 error, fancy
06 mirage
07 chimera, fallacy, fantasy, phantom, specter
08 delusion
09 deception
10 apparition
13 hallucination, misconception
15 false impression, misapprehension

**illusory**
05 false
06 unreal, untrue
07 fancied, seeming
08 apparent, deluding, delusive, delusory, illusive, imagined, mistaken, specious
09 deceptive, erroneous
10 chimerical, fallacious, misleading
11 illusionary
13 unsubstantial

**illustrate**
04 draw, show
06 depict, sketch
07 clarify, explain, picture
08 decorate, ornament
09 elucidate, embellish, exemplify, interpret
10 illuminate
11 demonstrate

**illustrated**
09 decorated, pictorial
11 embellished, illuminated

**illustration**
04 case
05 chart, photo, plate
06 design, sample, sketch
07 analogy, artwork, diagram, drawing, example, picture
08 exemplar, specimen
10 decoration, photograph
11 elucidation, explanation
13 clarification, demonstration
14 representation
15 exemplification

**illustrative**
07 graphic, typical
08 specimen
09 pictorial
11 delineative, descriptive, explanatory, explicatory

12 diagrammatic, exemplifying, illustratory
14 illustrational, representative

**illustrious**
05 famed, great, noble, noted
07 eminent, exalted, honored, notable
08 esteemed, glorious, renowned, splendid
09 acclaimed, prominent, well-known
10 celebrated, preeminent
11 magnificent, outstanding
13 distinguished

**ill will**
05 anger, odium, spite, wrath
06 animus, enmity, grudge, hatred, malice, rancor
07 dislike
08 aversion, bad blood
09 animosity, antipathy, hostility
10 antagonism, resentment
11 indignation, malevolence
12 hard feelings

**image**
04 copy, doll, icon, idol, twin
05 photo
06 double, effigy, figure, notion, ringer, simile, statue, vision
07 imagery, picture, replica
08 figurine, likeness, portrait
09 facsimile, lookalike
10 dead ringer, perception, photograph, reflection
11 resemblance
12 doppelgänger, reproduction
14 representation

**imaginable**
06 likely
08 credible, feasible
09 plausible, thinkable
10 believable, supposable
11 conceivable

**imaginary**
06 dreamy, made-up, unreal
07 fancied, pretend, shadowy
08 fabulous, fanciful, illusory, imagined, invented, mythical, spectral
09 fantastic, fictional, visionary
10 fictitious
11 make-believe, nonexistent
12 hypothetical, mythological
13 hallucinatory

**imagination**
05 dream, fancy
06 vision
07 chimera, insight
08 illusion, mind's eye
09 ingenuity
10 creativity

11 inspiration, originality
12 fancifulness
13 inventiveness
15 resourcefulness

**imaginative**
08 creative, fanciful, inspired, original
09 fantastic, ingenious, inventive, visionary, whimsical
11 full of ideas, resourceful

**imagine**
03 see
04 deem, plan
05 dream, fancy, guess, think
06 assume, create, devise, gather, invent, reckon, scheme, take it
07 believe, dream up, picture, presume, suppose, surmise
08 conceive, envisage
09 conjure up, fantasize, visualize
10 conjecture
11 make believe

**imbalance**
04 bias
09 disparity
10 inequality, unevenness
13 disproportion

**imbecile**
03 ass
04 clod, daft, fool
05 crazy, dopey, dunce, idiot, inane, moron, thick
06 cretin, dimwit, stupid
07 asinine, foolish, half-wit, idiotic, moronic, witless
09 blockhead, simpleton

**imbecility**
06 idiocy
07 amentia, fatuity, inanity
09 asininity, cretinism, stupidity
11 foolishness

**imbibe**
05 drink, lap up, quaff
06 absorb, soak up, take in
07 consume, drink in, receive, swallow

**imbroglio**
04 mess
06 muddle, scrape, tangle
09 confusion
11 embroilment, involvement
12 entanglement

**imbue**
04 fill, tint
05 steep, tinge
06 charge, inject

07 ingrain, instill, pervade, suffuse
08 permeate, saturate
09 inculcate
10 impregnate

**imitate**
03 ape
04 copy, echo, fake, mock
05 forge, mimic, spoof
06 follow, mirror, parody, parrot, repeat, send up
07 emulate, takeoff
08 simulate
09 burlesque, duplicate, replicate, reproduce
10 caricature
11 counterfeit, impersonate

**imitation**
04 copy, fake, faux, mock, sham
05 apery, aping, dummy, phony, spoof
06 ersatz, parody, pseudo
07 forgery, mimicry, replica, takeoff
09 simulated, synthetic
10 artificial, impression, reflection, simulation
11 counterfeit
13 impersonation

**imitative**
04 mock
07 copying, mimetic
09 mimicking, simulated
10 parrotlike

**imitator**
03 ape
04 echo
05 mimic
06 copier, parrot
07 copycat
08 emulator, follower, parodist
12 impersonator
13 impressionist

**immaculate**
04 pure
05 clean
07 perfect, sinless
08 flawless, innocent, spotless, unsoiled
09 blameless, faultless, guiltless, incorrupt, stainless, undefiled, unsullied, untainted
10 impeccable
11 unblemished
12 spick and span

**immaterial**
10 irrelevant
11 of no account, unimportant
15 inconsequential

**immature**
05 green, naïve, young
06 callow, unripe
07 babyish, puerile
08 childish, juvenile
09 infantile
10 adolescent
13 inexperienced

**immaturity**
05 youth
09 greenness, puerility
10 callowness, juvenility, unripeness
11 adolescence, babyishness
12 childishness, inexperience

**immeasurable**
04 vast
07 endless, immense
08 infinite
10 bottomless
11 inestimable, never-ending
12 incalculable, interminable, unfathomable

**immediacy**
07 urgency
08 instancy
09 imminence
10 directness, promptness
11 spontaneity

**immediate**
04 near, next
05 chief, close, swift
06 prompt, speedy, sudden, urgent
07 closest, crucial, instant, nearest, primary
08 abutting, adjacent, critical, next door, pressing
09 important, principal
11 fundamental
12 without delay
13 instantaneous

**immediately**
03 now, PDQ
04 ASAP
06 at once
08 as soon as, directly, promptly, right now, speedily
09 forthwith, instantly, right away, yesterday
10 this minute
11 this instant
12 no sooner than, straight away, without delay
14 unhesitatingly
15 instantaneously

**immemorial**
06 age-old, of yore
07 ancient, archaic
08 timeless
09 ancestral

11 time-honored
12 long-standing

**immense**
04 huge, mega, vast
05 giant, great, jumbo
06 bumper, cosmic
07 mammoth, massive, titanic
08 colossal, enormous, gigantic, whopping
09 extensive, ginormous, Herculean, humongous
10 monumental, tremendous
11 elephantine
14 Brobdingnagian

**immensely**
07 greatly
09 extremely, massively
10 enormously
15 extraordinarily

**immensity**
07 expanse
08 hugeness, vastness
09 greatness, magnitude
11 massiveness
12 enormousness

**immerse**
03 dip
04 bury, duck, dunk, sink, soak
05 bathe, douse, souse
06 absorb, drench, engulf, occupy, plunge
07 baptize, engross, involve
08 saturate, submerge, submerse, wrap up in
09 preoccupy

**immersed**
04 rapt, sunk
06 buried
08 absorbed, consumed, involved, occupied
09 engrossed, wrapped up
11 preoccupied

**immersion**
03 dip
04 bath
07 baptism, dipping, dousing, ducking, dunking, sinking, soaking
08 plunging
10 absorption, engrossing, saturation, submersion
11 involvement
13 preoccupation

**immigrant**
05 alien
07 migrant, settler
08 newcomer
10 new arrival
11 immigrating

## immigrate
06 settle
07 migrate
08 resettle

## imminence
08 approach, instancy, nearness
09 closeness, immediacy
11 propinquity

## imminent
04 near
05 close
06 at hand, coming
08 in the air, on the way
09 impending
11 approaching, forthcoming, in the offing
12 on the horizon
13 about to happen
15 around the corner

## immobile
05 fixed, rigid, stiff, still
06 at rest, frozen, rooted, static
08 unmoving
09 immovable
10 motionless, stationary, stock-still

## immobility
06 fixity
09 fixedness, inertness, stability, stillness
10 steadiness
12 immovability
14 motionlessness

## immobilize
04 halt, stop
06 freeze
07 cripple, disable
08 paralyze, transfix
10 inactivate
14 put out of action

## immoderate
06 lavish, wanton
07 extreme, fulsome
08 enormous, uncurbed
09 egregious, excessive, hubristic, unbridled, unlimited
10 inordinate, outrageous
11 extravagant, intemperate
12 distemperate, uncontrolled, unreasonable, unrestrained, unrestricted
14 unconscionable

## immoderately
08 wantonly
09 extremely
11 excessively
12 inordinately, unreasonably
13 exaggeratedly, extravagantly
14 unrestrainedly

## immoderation
06 excess
10 lavishness
11 prodigality, unrestraint
12 extravagance, intemperance
13 excessiveness
14 overindulgence

## immodest
04 bold, lewd
05 cocky, fresh, saucy
06 brazen, cheeky, coarse, risqué
07 immoral, obscene
08 boastful, improper, impudent, indecent
09 revealing, shameless
10 indecorous

## immodesty
08 audacity, boldness, impurity, lewdness, temerity
09 bawdiness, impudence, indecorum, obscenity
10 coarseness, indelicacy
13 shamelessness
14 indecorousness

## immoral
03 bad
04 base, blue, evil, lewd, vile
05 loose, wrong
06 impure, sinful, wicked
07 corrupt, obscene, raunchy
08 depraved, indecent
09 debauched, dishonest, dissolute, nefarious, reprobate, unethical
10 degenerate, iniquitous, licentious
12 unprincipled, unscrupulous

## immorality
03 sin
04 evil, vice
05 wrong
07 badness
08 impurity, iniquity, lewdness, vileness
09 depravity, indecency, obscenity, turpitude
10 corruption, debauchery, dishonesty, profligacy, sinfulness, wickedness, wrongdoing
13 dissoluteness, transgression
14 licentiousness

## immortal
03 god
05 deity, great
07 abiding, ageless, endless, eternal, goddess, undying
08 divinity, enduring, Olympian, timeless, unfading

09 deathless, memorable, perennial, perpetual
11 everlasting, sempiternal
12 imperishable
13 unforgettable
14 indestructible

## immortality
05 honor
06 renown
08 eternity
09 celebrity, greatness
10 perpetuity
11 distinction, eternal life
12 timelessness
13 deathlessness, glorification
15 everlasting life, imperishability

## immortalize
04 laud
07 glorify
08 enshrine
10 eternalize, perpetuate
11 commemorate, memorialize

## immovable
03 set
04 fast, firm
05 fixed, stuck
06 jammed, rooted, secure
07 adamant, riveted
08 anchored, immobile, resolute, stubborn
09 obstinate, steadfast
10 inflexible, unshakable, unswerving, unwavering, unyielding
12 intransigent
14 uncompromising

## immune
06 exempt, spared
08 absolved, released, relieved
09 protected, resistant
13 unsusceptible

## immunity
07 license, release
09 exception, exemption, indemnity
10 permission, protection, resistance
11 exoneration, inoculation, vaccination
12 immunization

## immunization
04 shot
09 injection
11 inoculation, vaccination

## immunize
06 inject, shield
07 protect
09 inoculate, vaccinate

**immure**
06 shut up, shut-in, wall in
07 confine, enclose
08 cloister, imprison
11 incarcerate

**immutability**
09 constancy, fixedness
10 durability, permanence
14 changelessness
15 unalterableness

**immutable**
05 fixed
08 constant
09 permanent, perpetual, steadfast
10 changeless, inflexible, invariable
11 unalterable
12 unchangeable

**imp**
03 elf
04 brat, minx, Puck
05 demon, devil, gamin, gnome, rogue, scamp
06 goblin, rascal, sprite, urchin
09 hobgoblin, prankster, trickster
12 troublemaker
13 mischief-maker
15 flibbertigibbet

**impact**
03 hit
04 bang, blow, bump
05 brunt, crash, force, knock, shock, smash, whack
06 affect, effect, strike
07 apply to, collide, impinge
09 collision, influence
12 consequences, significance
13 repercussions
14 have an effect on

**impair**
03 mar
04 harm
05 spoil
06 damage, hinder, injure, weaken
07 cripple, disable, vitiate
08 decrease, diminish, enfeeble
10 debilitate
11 deteriorate

**impaired**
04 poor, weak
07 damaged, spoiled, unsound
08 disabled, vitiated
09 defective

**impairment**
04 flaw, harm, hurt, ruin
05 fault
06 damage, injury

08 weakness
09 vitiation
10 disability
11 disablement, dysfunction

**impale**
04 spit, stab
05 lance, prick, spear, spike, stick
06 pierce, skewer
08 transfix
10 run through

**impalpable**
06 subtle
07 elusive, shadowy, tenuous
10 indistinct, intangible
11 incorporeal
13 imperceptible, insubstantial, unsubstantial

**impart**
04 give, lend, tell
06 bestow, confer, convey, pass on, relate, reveal
07 divulge
08 disclose, transmit
10 contribute
11 communicate

**impartial**
04 fair, just
07 neutral
08 detached, unbiased
09 equitable, objective
10 evenhanded, fair-minded
11 nonpartisan
12 unprejudiced

**impartiality**
07 justice
08 equality, fairness
10 detachment, neutrality
11 objectivity
12 unbiasedness
14 evenhandedness
15 nonpartisanship

**impassable**
07 blocked
10 obstructed, unpassable
11 insuperable, unnavigable
12 impenetrable

**impasse**
07 dead end
08 deadlock
09 checkmate, stalemate
10 blind alley, standstill

**impassioned**
05 eager, fiery
06 ardent, fervid, heated
07 blazing, excited, fervent, furious, glowing, intense, rousing, violent

08 animated, forceful, inflamed, inspired, spirited, stirring, vehement, vigorous
09 emotional
10 passionate
12 enthusiastic

**impassive**
04 calm, cool
07 stoical, unmoved
08 composed, laid-back
09 unruffled
10 phlegmatic
11 emotionless, indifferent, unconcerned, unemotional, unexcitable, unflappable
13 dispassionate, imperturbable
14 expressionless

**impatience**
05 haste
08 curtness, keenness, rashness
09 agitation, eagerness, shortness, tenseness
11 brusqueness, impetuosity, intolerance, nervousness
12 irritability, restlessness

**impatient**
04 keen
05 eager, hasty, short, tense, testy
07 brusque, fidgety, fretful, jittery, nervous, restive
08 agitated, restless
09 impetuous, irritable, querulous
10 intolerant
11 precipitate

**impeach**
05 blame
06 accuse, attack, charge, impugn, indict, revile
07 arraign, censure
08 denounce
09 criticize, disparage

**impeachment**
06 charge
10 accusation, indictment
11 arraignment
13 disparagement

**impeccable**
04 pure
07 correct, perfect, precise
08 flawless
09 blameless, exemplary, faultless, stainless
10 immaculate
11 unblemished
14 irreproachable

**impecunious**
04 poor
05 broke, needy

**impede**
08 dirt poor, indigent
09 destitute, insolvent, penniless, penurious
12 impoverished
15 poverty-stricken

**impede**
03 bar
04 clog, curb, slow, stop
05 block, check, delay
06 hamper, hinder, hold up
08 handicap, hold back, obstruct, slow down

**impediment**
03 bar
04 curb, snag
05 block, check
06 burden, defect
07 barrier, setback, stammer, stutter
08 handicap, obstacle
09 hindrance
11 encumbrance, obstruction
14 stumbling block

**impedimenta**
04 gear
07 baggage, effects, luggage
09 equipment
10 belongings
13 accouterments, accoutrements

**impel**
04 goad, move, prod, push, spur, urge
05 drive, force, press
06 compel, excite, incite, oblige, prompt, propel
07 inspire
08 motivate, pressure
09 constrain, instigate, stimulate

**impending**
04 near
05 close
06 at hand, coming
07 brewing, looming
08 imminent, in the air, on the way
11 approaching, forthcoming, in the offing
12 on the horizon
15 around the corner

**impenetrable**
05 dense, solid, thick
07 cryptic, obscure
08 abstruse, baffling, puzzling
09 enigmatic, recondite
10 impassable, mysterious
11 inscrutable
12 unfathomable
14 unintelligible

**impenitence**
08 defiance, obduracy
12 stubbornness
15 incorrigibility

**impenitent**
08 hardened, obdurate
09 unabashed, unashamed
10 uncontrite, unreformed
11 remorseless, unrepentant
12 incorrigible

**imperative**
05 vital
07 crucial
08 critical, pressing
09 essential, necessary
10 compulsory, obligatory

**imperceptible**
04 fine, tiny
05 faint, small, vague
06 minute, slight, subtle
07 obscure, unclear
09 inaudible, minuscule
10 impalpable, indefinite, indistinct, negligible
11 microscopic
12 undetectable
13 indiscernible, infinitesimal

**imperceptibly**
06 slowly, subtly, unseen
08 bit by bit
09 gradually
13 inappreciably, indiscernibly, unobtrusively
14 little by little

**imperfect**
06 faulty, flawed
07 damaged
08 impaired
09 blemished, defective

**imperfection**
04 blot, dent, flaw, spot, tear
05 break, crack, fault, stain, taint
06 blotch, defect, foible
07 blemish, failing, scratch
08 weakness
09 deformity
10 deficiency, impairment, inadequacy
11 shortcoming

**imperial**
05 grand, great, lofty, noble, regal, royal
06 kingly
07 queenly, stately, supreme
08 absolute, glorious, majestic, splendid
09 sovereign
11 magnificent, monarchical

**imperialism**
11 colonialism

12 expansionism
14 empire building

**imperil**
04 risk
06 expose, hazard
08 endanger, threaten
10 compromise, jeopardize
12 expose to risk
13 put in jeopardy

**imperious**
06 lordly
07 haughty
08 arrogant, despotic
09 assertive, masterful
10 autocratic, commanding, highhanded, peremptory, tyrannical
11 dictatorial, domineering, overbearing, overweening

**imperishable**
07 abiding, eternal, undying
08 enduring, immortal, unfading
09 deathless, perennial, permanent, perpetual
11 everlasting
14 indestructible

**impermanent**
06 flying, mortal
07 elusive, passing
08 fleeting, fugitive
09 ephemeral, fugacious, temporary, transient
10 evanescent, fly-by-night, inconstant, transitory

**impermeable**
05 proof
06 sealed
08 hermetic
09 damp proof, nonporous, resistant
10 impassable, impervious, waterproof
12 impenetrable

**impersonal**
04 cold, cool
05 aloof, stiff
06 formal, frigid, remote, stuffy
07 distant, neutral
08 clinical, detached, official, unbiased
09 objective, unfeeling
11 unemotional
13 dispassionate

**impersonate**
03 act, ape
05 mimic
06 parody, pose as
07 imitate, portray

**impersonation**
09 burlesque, pass off as, take off on
10 caricature
12 masquerade as

**impersonation**
05 apery, aping
06 parody
07 mimicry, takeoff
09 burlesque, imitation
10 caricature, impression

**impertinence**
03 lip
04 face, gall
05 brass, cheek, nerve, sauce
08 audacity, boldness, rudeness
09 impudence, insolence
10 brazenness, disrespect, effrontery
11 discourtesy
12 impoliteness
13 shamelessness

**impertinent**
04 bold, pert, rude
05 brash, fresh, sassy, saucy
06 brazen, cheeky
08 impolite, impudent, insolent
09 audacious, shameless
11 ill-mannered
12 discourteous
13 disrespectful

**imperturbability**
08 calmness, coolness
09 composure
10 equanimity
11 tranquility

**imperturbable**
04 calm, cool
07 unmoved
08 composed, tranquil
09 collected, impassive, unruffled
10 untroubled
11 unexcitable, unflappable

**impervious**
05 proof
06 closed, immune, sealed
08 hermetic
09 damp proof, nonporous
10 waterproof, watertight
11 impermeable
12 impenetrable

**impetuosity**
05 haste
08 rashness
09 hastiness
10 impatience
12 recklessness
13 foolhardiness, impetuousness, impulsiveness

15 precipitateness, thoughtlessness

**impetuous**
04 rash
05 hasty
08 headlong, reckless
09 foolhardy, impatient, impulsive, unplanned
11 precipitate, spontaneous, thoughtless
14 unpremeditated
15 spur-of-the-moment

**impetuously**
06 rashly
10 recklessly
11 impulsively
13 precipitately

**impetus**
04 goad, push, spur
05 boost, drive, force, power
06 energy, urging
07 impulse
08 momentum, stimulus
09 incentive, influence
10 motivation
13 encouragement

**impiety**
09 blasphemy, profanity, sacrilege
10 irreligion, unholiness
11 godlessness, irreverence, profaneness, ungodliness

**impinge**
05 touch
06 affect, invade
07 intrude, touch on
08 encroach, infringe, trespass
09 influence

**impious**
06 sinful, unholy
07 godless, profane, ungodly
10 irreverent
11 blasphemous, irreligious
12 sacrilegious

**impish**
05 elfin, gamin
07 naughty, roguish, waggish
10 frolicsome
11 mischievous

**implacability**
12 pitilessness, ruthlessness
13 inexorability, inflexibility, intransigence, mercilessness
14 intractability, relentlessness
15 remorselessness

**implacable**
07 adamant
08 pitiless, ruthless
09 heartless, merciless

10 inexorable, inflexible, relentless, unyielding
11 intractable, remorseless, unforgiving, unrelenting
12 intransigent

**implant**
03 fix, sow
04 root
05 embed, graft
06 insert, instil
07 engraft, instill
09 inculcate

**implausible**
06 flimsy
07 dubious, suspect
08 doubtful, unlikely
10 far-fetched, improbable, incredible
12 questionable, unbelievable, unconvincing
13 hard to believe, inconceivable

**implement**
02 do
04 tool
06 device, effect, gadget
07 execute, fulfill, perform, utensil
08 carry out
09 apparatus, appliance
10 instrument
11 contrivance
13 put into action, put into effect

**implementation**
09 effecting, operation
10 fulfilling, performing
11 carrying out, fulfillment, performance

**implicate**
07 embroil, include, involve
08 entangle
09 associate, be a part of, be party to, inculpate
10 be a party to
11 incriminate

**implicated**
07 party to
08 included, involved
09 embroiled, entangled
10 associated, inculpated
12 incriminated

**implication**
06 effect
07 meaning
08 overtone
09 deduction, inference, undertone
10 suggestion

**implicit**

11 association, consequence, embroilment, inculpation, insinuation, involvement
12 entanglement, ramification, repercussion, significance
13 incrimination

**implicit**
04 full
05 sheer, tacit, total, utter
06 entire, hidden, hinted, latent, unsaid
07 implied, perfect
08 absolute, complete, indirect, inferred, inherent, positive, unspoken, unstated
09 deducible, steadfast, suggested
10 insinuated, understood, unreserved
11 unexpressed, unqualified
12 unhesitating, wholehearted
13 unconditional, unquestioning

**implicitly**
06 firmly
07 totally, utterly
10 absolutely, completely
11 steadfastly
12 unreservedly
14 unhesitatingly, wholeheartedly
15 unconditionally, unquestioningly

**implied**
05 tacit
06 hinted
08 indirect, unspoken, unstated
09 suggested
10 insinuated

**implore**
03 beg
04 pray
05 crave, plead
06 appeal
07 beseech, entreat
09 importune

**imply**
04 hint, mean
06 denote, entail, signal
07 involve, point to, require, signify, suggest
08 indicate, intimate
09 insinuate

**impolite**
04 rude
05 crude, rough
06 cheeky, coarse, vulgar
07 boorish, loutish, uncivil
08 insolent
09 unrefined
10 indecorous, unmannerly

11 bad mannered, ill-mannered, impertinent
12 discourteous
13 disrespectful, inconsiderate

**impoliteness**
08 rudeness
09 insolence, roughness
10 bad manners, coarseness, incivility, indelicacy
11 boorishness, discourtesy
12 churlishness, impertinence

**impolitic**
06 unwise
07 foolish
09 ill-judged, imprudent, maladroit, misguided
10 ill-advised, indiscreet
11 inexpedient, injudicious
12 undiplomatic
13 ill-considered

**import**
04 gist, mean
05 drift, imply, sense
06 thrust, weight
07 bring in, content, essence, meaning, message, signify
08 indicate
09 intention, substance
10 importance
11 consequence, implication
12 significance

**importance**
05 power, value, worth
06 esteem, status, weight
07 concern, urgency
08 eminence, interest, prestige, standing
09 graveness
10 prominence, usefulness
11 consequence, distinction
12 criticalness, significance
13 momentousness
14 noteworthiness

**important**
03 key
04 main
05 chief, grave, major, vital
06 urgent, valued
07 central, crucial, eminent, fateful, leading, notable, pivotal, primary, salient, seminal, serious, weighty
08 critical, esteemed, foremost, historic, material, powerful, priority, relevant, valuable
09 essential, momentous, principal, prominent
10 meaningful, noteworthy, preeminent

11 high ranking, influential, outstanding, prestigious, substantial
13 distinguished

**importunate**
06 dogged, urgent
08 pressing
09 impatient, insistent, tenacious
10 persistent

**importune**
03 beg
04 urge
05 beset, hound, press
06 appeal, badger, cajole, harass, pester, plague
07 request, solicit
09 plead with

**importunity**
06 urging
08 cajolery, hounding, pressing
09 harassing, pestering
10 entreaties, harassment, insistence
11 persistence
12 solicitation

**impose**
03 fix, lay, put, set
04 levy
05 apply, exact, foist, force, lay on, place, put on
06 burden, decree, saddle
07 enforce, exploit, inflict, intrude, obtrude, place on, presume, put upon
08 encroach, encumber, trespass
09 institute, introduce
13 take liberties
15 take advantage of

**imposing**
05 grand, lofty
06 august
07 stately
08 majestic, splendid, striking
09 dignified
10 impressive

**imposition**
03 tax
04 duty, load, task, toll
06 burden, charge, decree, tariff
07 levying
10 constraint, infliction
11 application, encumbrance, enforcement, institution, trespassing
12 encroachment, introduction
13 establishment

**impossibility**
09 absurdity

**impossible**
11 unviability
12 hopelessness, untenability
13 ludicrousness

**impossible**
06 absurd
08 hopeless
09 insoluble, ludicrous
10 incredible, unworkable
11 intolerable, unthinkable
12 preposterous, unattainable,
   unbelievable, unobtainable,
   unreasonable
13 impracticable, inconceivable

**impostor**
04 fake, sham
05 cheat, fraud, phony, quack,
   rogue
06 con man
07 shyster
08 deceiver, swindler
09 charlatan, con artist,
   pretender
10 hoodwinker, mountebank
11 four-flusher
12 impersonator
13 confidence man

**imposture**
03 con, gyp
05 cheat, fraud, trick
07 swindle
08 con trick, quackery
09 deception
13 impersonation

**impotence**
09 inability, infirmity, paralysis
10 disability, enervation,
   inadequacy, incapacity
11 impuissance, uselessness
12 helplessness, incompetence
13 powerlessness
15 ineffectiveness

**impotent**
06 infirm, unable
07 sterile, useless
08 crippled, disabled, helpless
09 enervated, incapable,
   paralyzed, powerless
10 impuissant
11 ineffective
13 incapacitated

**impound**
05 seize
06 lock up, remove, shut up
07 confine
08 take away
10 commandeer, confiscate
11 appropriate, expropriate,
   incarcerate

' **impoverish**
04 ruin

06 beggar
07 deplete
08 bankrupt
09 pauperize

**impoverished**
04 bust, poor
05 empty, needy, skint
06 barren, busted, ruined
07 drained
08 bankrupt, desolate, indigent
09 destitute, penniless,
   penurious
10 down-and-out, stone-broke
11 impecunious
15 poverty-stricken

**impracticability**
11 unviability, uselessness
12 hopelessness
13 impossibility, infeasibility,
   unworkability
14 unsuitableness

**impracticable**
08 unviable
10 impossible, inoperable,
   unfeasible, unworkable
12 unachievable, unattainable

**impractical**
08 romantic
10 idealistic, impossible,
   unworkable
11 unrealistic
13 impracticable, unserviceable

**impracticality**
08 idealism
13 impossibility, infeasibility,
   unworkability

**imprecation**
05 abuse, curse
08 anathema
09 blasphemy, profanity
10 execration
11 malediction

**imprecise**
04 hazy
05 loose, rough, vague
06 sloppy, woolly
07 blurred, inexact
09 ambiguous, equivocal
10 ill-defined, inaccurate,
   indefinite, inexplicit

**impregnable**
06 secure, strong
09 fortified
10 invincible, inviolable,
   unbeatable
11 irrefutable
12 impenetrable, invulnerable,
   unassailable
13 unconquerable

14 indestructible,
   unquestionable

**impregnate**
04 fill, soak
05 imbue, steep
06 drench, infuse
07 pervade, suffuse
08 permeate, saturate
09 fertilize, penetrate
10 inseminate

**impregnation**
10 saturation
11 fertilizing
12 insemination
13 fertilization
14 fructification

**impresario**
08 director, producer, promoter
09 organizer

**impress**
04 mark, move, stir, sway
05 print, stamp, touch
06 affect, indent, instil, strike
07 engrave, imprint, inspire,
   instill
09 bring home, emphasize,
   inculcate, influence,
   underline

**impressed**
05 moved, taken
06 marked, struck
07 excited, grabbed, stamped,
   stirred, touched
08 affected, overawed
10 influenced, knocked out

**impression**
04 dent, idea, mark, sway
05 fancy, hunch, power, print,
   sense, stamp, vibes
06 belief, effect, impact,
   memory, notion, parody
07 control, feeling, imprint,
   mimicry, opinion, outline,
   takeoff, thought
08 illusion, pressure
09 awareness, burlesque,
   imitation, influence,
   sensation, suspicion
10 caricature, conviction
11 indentation
13 impersonation

**impressionability**
07 naïvety
09 greenness
11 gullibility, receptivity
13 receptiveness
14 suggestibility, susceptibility

**impressionable**
05 naïve
07 pliable

08 gullible, moldable
09 receptive
11 persuadable, susceptible

**impressive**
05 grand
07 awesome
08 imposing, powerful
09 inspiring
11 spectacular
12 awe inspiring

**imprint**
03 fix
04 etch, logo, mark, sign
05 badge, brand, print, stamp
06 emblem, emboss
07 engrave, impress
08 colophon
10 impression
11 indentation

**imprison**
03 pen
04 cage, jail
06 detain, intern, lock up
07 confine
11 incarcerate

**imprisoned**
05 caged
06 inside, jailed
07 captive, immured, put away
08 confined, locked up, sent down
09 doing bird, doing time
10 behind bars
12 incarcerated
13 doing porridge

**imprisonment**
09 captivity, detention
10 internment
11 confinement
13 incarceration

**improbability**
05 doubt
07 dubiety
11 dubiousness, uncertainty
12 doubtfulness, unlikelihood, unlikeliness
14 implausibility, ridiculousness

**improbable**
08 doubtful, unlikely
10 far-fetched, incredible
11 implausible
12 questionable, unconvincing

**impromptu**
05 ad-lib
09 extempore
10 improvised, off the cuff, unprepared, unscripted
11 spontaneous, unrehearsed

**improper**
04 rude
05 false, wrong
06 risqué, vulgar
08 indecent, unseemly
09 incorrect, unfitting
10 indecorous, indelicate, unbecoming, unsuitable
11 incongruous
13 inappropriate

**impropriety**
07 blunder, faux pas, mistake
08 bad taste, solecism
09 gaucherie, immodesty, indecency, indecorum, vulgarity
12 unseemliness
13 unsuitability
14 indecorousness

**improve**
04 do up, edit, help, mend
05 amend, fix up
06 better, enrich, look up, perk up, pick up, polish
07 enhance, perfect, recover, rectify, touch up, upgrade
08 progress, put right, set right
09 get better, modernize
10 ameliorate, convalesce, make better, recuperate, streamline

**improvement**
04 gain, rise
07 upswing
08 increase, progress, recovery
09 amendment, upgrading
10 betterment, rectifying
11 enhancement, furtherance, modernizing
12 amelioration

**improvident**
08 careless, prodigal, wasteful
09 imprudent, unthrifty
10 profligate, thriftless
11 extravagant, spendthrift
12 uneconomical

**improvisation**
04 vamp
05 ad-lib, aside
09 ad-libbing, impromptu, invention
11 spontaneity
13 extemporizing

**improvise**
04 vamp
05 ad-lib, rig up, run up
06 devise, invent, make do
07 knock up
08 cobble up, contrive
09 play by ear
11 extemporize

13 throw together
14 cobble together
15 speak off-the-cuff

**improvised**
05 ad-lib
09 extempore, makeshift
10 off-the-cuff, unprepared, unscripted
11 spontaneous, unrehearsed
12 extemporized
14 extemporaneous

**imprudent**
04 rash
06 unwise
07 foolish
08 careless, heedless, reckless
09 foolhardy, impolitic
10 unthinking
11 improvident, injudicious, thoughtless

**impudence**
03 lip
05 cheek, mouth, nerve
08 boldness, pertness, rudeness
09 insolence, sauciness
10 brazenness, effrontery
12 impertinence

**impudent**
04 bold, pert, rude
05 cocky, fresh, saucy
06 brazen, cheeky
07 forward
08 insolent
09 audacious, shameless
11 impertinent
13 disrespectful

**impugn**
06 assail, attack, berate, oppose, resist, revile, vilify
07 censure, dispute, traduce
08 question
09 challenge, criticize
10 vituperate

**impulse**
04 push, urge, whim, wish
05 drive, force, surge
06 desire, motive, notion, thrust
07 caprice, feeling, impetus, passion
08 instinct, momentum, pressure, stimulus
09 impulsion, incentive
10 incitement, inducement, motivation, propulsion
11 inclination, stimulation

**impulsive**
04 rash
05 hasty, quick
06 madcap
08 reckless

09 foolhardy, ill-judged, impetuous, intuitive
10 headstrong, unthinking
11 instinctive, precipitate, spontaneous, thoughtless
13 ill-considered

**impulsiveness**
05 haste
08 rashness
09 hastiness, quickness
10 impatience
11 impetuosity
12 recklessness
13 foolhardiness, impetuousness, intuitiveness, precipitation
15 thoughtlessness

**impunity**
07 amnesty, excusal, freedom, liberty, license
08 immunity, security
09 exemption
10 permission
12 dispensation

**impure**
04 foul, lewd
05 bawdy, crude, dirty
06 amoral, coarse, filthy, smutty, vulgar
07 corrupt, debased, defiled, immoral, sullied, tainted, unclean
08 improper, indecent, polluted, unchaste
09 shameless
11 adulterated
12 contaminated

**impurity**
04 dirt, smut, spot
05 filth, grime, taint
08 foulness, lewdness
09 dirtiness, immodesty, indecency, pollutant, pollution
10 corruption, debasement, immorality
11 contaminant, foreign body, impropriety
12 adulteration
13 contamination, shamelessness

**impute**
05 refer
06 assign, charge, credit
07 ascribe
08 accredit
09 attribute, put down to

**in**
02 at
04 amid, with
05 among

06 amidst, at home, inside, modish, trendy
07 in vogue, popular, stylish
10 all the rage
11 fashionable

**inability**
08 handicap, weakness
09 impotence
10 disability, inadequacy, incapacity, ineptitude
12 incapability, incompetence
13 powerlessness
15 ineffectiveness

**inaccessible**
06 remote
08 isolated
10 out of reach
11 beyond reach, out of the way, unavailable, unreachable
12 impenetrable, unattainable

**inaccuracy**
04 slip
05 boner, error, fault, gaffe
06 boo-boo, defect, howler, slip-up
07 blooper, blunder, erratum, mistake
11 corrigendum, inexactness
12 mistakenness
13 erroneousness

**inaccurate**
03 out
05 false, wrong
06 faulty, flawed, untrue
07 inexact, unsound
08 mistaken
09 defective, erroneous, incorrect

**inaccurately**
07 falsely, wrongly
09 inexactly
10 carelessly
11 defectively, erroneously, incorrectly

**inaction**
06 torpor
07 inertia
08 idleness, lethargy
10 immobility, inactivity, stagnation
14 motionlessness

**inactivate**
04 stop
07 cripple, disable, scupper
10 immobilize

**inactive**
04 idle, lazy, slow
05 inert
06 sleepy, torpid, unused
07 dormant, passive, retired

08 immobile, indolent, lifeless, sluggish, stagnant
09 lethargic, quiescent, sedentary
10 motionless, stationary, unemployed
11 inoperative

**inactivity**
05 sloth
06 stasis, torpor
07 inertia, languor
08 abeyance, dormancy, idleness, inaction, laziness, lethargy
09 indolence, inertness, passivity
10 immobility, quiescence, retirement, stagnation
11 hibernation
12 lifelessness, sluggishness, unemployment

**inadequacy**
04 flaw, lack, want
06 dearth, defect
07 deficit, failing, paucity
08 scarcity, shortage
10 deficiency, inefficacy, meagerness, scantiness
11 shortcoming
12 incapability, incompetence
13 insufficiency

**inadequate**
05 scant, short, unfit
06 meager, scanty, scarce, skimpy, sparse
07 unequal, wanting
09 defective, deficient, incapable, niggardly, too little
11 incompetent, substandard
12 insufficient
13 disappointing, inefficacious, not good enough
14 not up to scratch

**inadequately**
06 poorly, thinly
08 meagerly, scantily, skimpily, sparsely
09 sketchily
14 insufficiently

**inadmissible**
10 disallowed, immaterial, inapposite, irrelevant, prohibited
12 unacceptable
13 inappropriate

**inadvertent**
09 unplanned, unwitting
10 accidental, unintended
11 involuntary, thoughtless, unconscious
13 unintentional

14 unpremeditated

**inadvertently**
09 by mistake
10 by accident, mistakenly
11 unwittingly
12 accidentally, unthinkingly
13 involuntarily, unconsciously
15 unintentionally

**inadvisable**
09 ill-judged, imprudent, misguided
10 ill-advised, indiscreet
11 inexpedient, injudicious
13 ill-considered

**inalienable**
08 absolute, inherent
10 inviolable, sacrosanct
11 unremovable
12 unassailable
13 nonnegotiable

**inane**
05 empty, silly, vapid
06 absurd, stupid
07 fatuous, foolish, idiotic, puerile, vacuous
08 mindless, trifling
09 frivolous, senseless, worthless
10 ridiculous
11 nonsensical

**inanimate**
04 dead
05 inert
06 torpid
07 defunct, dormant, extinct
08 immobile, lifeless, stagnant
09 insensate
10 insentient

**inanity**
05 folly
07 fatuity, vacuity
08 vapidity
09 absurdity, asininity, emptiness, frivolity, puerility, silliness, stupidity
10 imbecility
11 foolishness

**inapplicable**
05 inapt
08 unsuited
09 unrelated
10 immaterial, irrelevant, unsuitable
11 unconnected
12 inconsequent
13 inappropriate

**inapposite**
10 immaterial, irrelevant, out of place, unsuitable
13 inappropriate

**inappropriate**
08 ill-timed, improper, tactless, unseemly, untimely
09 ill suited, tasteless, unfitting
10 ill-fitting, inapposite, indecorous, irrelevant, out of place, unbecoming, unsuitable
11 incongruous, inopportune

**inapt**
08 ill-timed, unsuited
09 ill suited
10 ill-fitting, inapposite, irrelevant, out of place, unsuitable
11 inopportune, unfortunate

**inarticulate**
04 dumb, mute
07 halting, muffled, mumbled, quavery, shaking, unclear
09 faltering, soundless, stumbling, trembling, voiceless
10 disjointed, incoherent, indistinct, stammering, stuttering, tongue-tied
14 unintelligible

**inarticulateness**
08 mumbling
09 hesitancy, stumbling
10 stammering, stuttering
11 incoherence
14 indistinctness

**inattention**
10 dreaminess, negligence
11 daydreaming, distraction
12 heedlessness
13 forgetfulness, preoccupation
15 inattentiveness

**inattentive**
04 deaf
06 dreamy, remiss
08 distrait, heedless
09 forgetful, miles away, negligent, unmindful
10 distracted, regardless
11 daydreaming, in the clouds, preoccupied
12 absent-minded
13 woolgathering

**inaudible**
06 silent
09 noiseless, whispered
10 indistinct
13 imperceptible

**inaugural**
05 first
06 maiden
07 initial, opening
08 exordial, original

09 induction
10 initiation
11 investiture
12 installation, introductory

**inaugurate**
04 open
05 begin, set up, start
06 induct, invest, launch, ordain
07 install, instate, kick off, usher in
08 commence, dedicate, enthrone, get going, initiate
09 institute, introduce, originate
10 commission, consecrate
11 set in motion
14 open officially

**inauguration**
06 launch
07 opening
09 induction, setting up
10 initiation, ordination
11 institution, investiture
12 commencement, consecration, enthronement, installation

**inauspicious**
03 bad
07 ominous, unlucky
08 ill-fated, untimely
10 ill-starred
11 unfavorable, unpromising
12 discouraging, infelicitous, unpropitious

**inborn**
06 inbred, innate
07 connate, natural
08 inherent
09 ingrained, inherited, intuitive
10 congenital, hereditary
11 instinctive

**inbred**
06 innate, native
07 connate, natural
08 inherent
09 ingrained
14 constitutional

**incalculable**
07 endless, immense
08 enormous, infinite
09 boundless, countless, limitless, unlimited
10 numberless
11 inestimable, innumerable
12 immeasurable
13 without number

**incandescent**
05 aglow
06 red-hot
07 glowing
08 dazzling, white-hot

**incantation**
05 chant, spell
06 mantra
07 formula, mantram
10 invocation
11 conjuration

**incapable**
05 inept, unfit
06 feeble, unable
08 helpless, impotent, unfitted, unsuited
10 inadequate
11 incompetent, ineffective, ineffectual, unqualified

**incapacitate**
05 lay up
07 cripple, disable, scupper
08 paralyze
10 debilitate, immobilize
14 put out of action

**incapacitated**
05 drunk, tipsy, unfit
06 laid up, unwell
08 crippled, disabled
09 hamstrung, paralyzed, prostrate, scuppered
10 indisposed
11 immobilized, out of action

**incapacity**
09 impotence, inability, unfitness
10 disability, feebleness, inadequacy, ineptitude
12 incapability, incompetence, incompetency
14 ineffectuality
15 ineffectiveness

**incarcerate**
03 jug
04 cage, jail
06 commit, coop up, detain, intern, lock up, send up
07 confine, impound, put away
08 imprison
09 put in jail
11 put in prison
14 send up the river

**incarceration**
07 bondage, custody, jailing
09 captivity, detention
10 internment
11 confinement
12 imprisonment

**incarnate**
03 red
04 pink, rosy
06 embody
08 embodied, made real, make real, typified

09 corporeal, made flesh, make flesh
10 in the flesh
11 personified

**incarnation**
10 embodiment
13 manifestation
15 personification

**incautious**
04 rash
05 hasty
06 unwary
07 foolish
08 careless, reckless
09 foolhardy, ill-judged, imprudent, impulsive
10 unthinking, unwatchful
11 inattentive, injudicious, precipitate, thoughtless

**incendiary**
04 bomb, mine
06 charge
07 firebug, grenade
08 agitator, arsonist, firebomb, inciting, stirring
09 explosive, firebrand, flammable, insurgent, seditious
10 pyromaniac
11 combustible, dissentious, provocative
12 inflammatory, rabble-rouser
13 rabble-rousing, revolutionary
15 Molotov cocktail

**incense**
03 irk, vex
04 rile
05 anger, aroma, scent
06 enrage, excite, nettle
07 agitate, bouquet, inflame, perfume, provoke
09 aggravate, fragrance, infuriate, joss stick
10 exasperate
14 drive up the wall

**incensed**
03 mad
05 angry, irate
06 fuming, ireful
07 enraged, furious
08 furibund, maddened, up in arms, wrathful
09 indignant, steamed up
10 infuriated
12 on the warpath

**incentive**
04 lure, spur
06 carrot, motive, reward
09 sweetener

10 enticement, incitement, inducement, motivation
13 encouragement

**inception**
04 dawn, rise
05 birth, start
06 origin, outset
07 opening
09 beginning
12 commencement, inauguration

**incessant**
07 nonstop
08 constant, unbroken, unending
09 ceaseless, continual, unceasing
10 continuous, persistent
11 never-ending, unremitting
12 interminable
13 uninterrupted

**incidence**
04 rate
05 range
06 amount, degree, extent
09 frequency
10 occurrence, prevalence

**incident**
05 scene, upset
06 affair, fracas, matter, mishap
07 episode
08 conflict, instance, occasion, skirmish
09 commotion, happening
10 occurrence, proceeding
11 disturbance
12 circumstance
13 confrontation

**incidental**
05 minor, petty, small
06 chance, random
07 related, trivial
08 by chance
09 ancillary, attendant, secondary
10 accidental, fortuitous, peripheral, subsidiary
11 concomitant, subordinate
12 accompanying, contributory, nonessential

**incidentally**
07 apropos, by the by
08 by chance, by the way, casually
09 en passant, in passing
10 by accident
12 accidentally, unexpectedly
14 coincidentally
15 parenthetically

**incinerate**
04 burn
06 burn up
07 cremate
13 reduce to ashes

**incipient**
07 nascent, newborn
08 inchoate, starting
09 beginning, embryonic, inaugural, inceptive
10 commencing, developing
11 originating, rudimentary

**incise**
03 cut
04 etch, gash, nick, slit
05 carve, notch, slash
06 chisel, sculpt
07 cut into, engrave
09 sculpture

**incision**
03 cut
04 gash, nick, slit
05 notch, slash

**incisive**
04 acid, keen
05 acute, sharp
06 astute, biting, shrewd
07 caustic, cutting, mordant
09 sarcastic, trenchant
11 penetrating
13 perspicacious

**incisiveness**
07 sarcasm
08 keenness
09 acuteness, sharpness
10 astuteness, trenchancy
11 penetration
12 perspicacity

**incite**
03 egg
04 goad, prod, spur, urge
05 drive, egg on, impel, rouse
06 arouse, excite, foment, induce, prompt, stir up, whip up, work up
07 agitate, animate, inflame, provoke, trigger
09 encourage, instigate, stimulate

**incitement**
04 goad, prod, spur
05 drive
07 impetus, rousing
08 stimulus
09 agitation, animation, incentive, prompting
10 inducement, motivation
11 instigation, provocation, stimulation
13 encouragement

**inciting**
08 stirring
09 seditious
10 incendiary, subversive
11 provocative
12 inflammatory
13 rabble-rousing

**incivility**
08 rudeness
09 roughness, vulgarity
10 bad manners, coarseness, disrespect
11 boorishness, discourtesy
12 impoliteness

**inclemency**
08 foulness, severity
09 harshness, roughness

**inclement**
05 harsh, nasty, rough
06 severe
11 intemperate, tempestuous

**inclination**
03 bow, nod
04 bank, bend, bias, ramp, tilt
05 angle, pitch, slant, slope, taste, trend
06 ascent, liking
07 incline, leaning
08 affinity, fondness, gradient, penchant, tendency
09 acclivity, affection, declivity, steepness
10 attraction, partiality, preference, proclivity, propensity
11 disposition
12 predilection
14 predisposition

**incline**
03 bow, dip, nod, tip
04 bank, bend, bias, hill, lean, list, ramp, rise, sway, tend, tilt, veer
05 grade, slant, slope, stoop, swing
06 affect, ascent
07 descent, deviate, dispose
08 gradient, persuade
09 acclivity, influence, prejudice

**inclined**
03 apt
04 wont
05 given
06 liable, likely
07 dipping, of a mind, pitched, sloping, tending, tilting, willing
08 disposed

**include**
03 add

04 hold, span
05 admit, cover, enter, put in
06 embody, insert, rope in, take in
07 contain, embrace, enclose, involve, let in on, subsume, throw in
08 allow for, comprise
09 encompass, introduce
10 comprehend
11 incorporate
15 take into account

**including**
04 with
06 adding
08 counting

**inclusion**
08 addition
09 insertion
10 embodiment
11 involvement
12 encompassing
13 comprehension, incorporation

**inclusive**
04 full
06 entire
07 blanket, general, overall
08 catchall, sweeping
12 all-embracing, all-inclusive, encyclopedic
13 comprehensive
14 across-the-board

**incognito**
06 masked, veiled
07 unknown
08 nameless, unmarked
09 disguised
10 in disguise
14 unidentifiable
15 under a false name

**incognizant**
07 unaware
08 ignorant
09 unknowing
11 inattentive, unconscious
12 unacquainted
13 unenlightened

**incoherence**
03 mix
06 jumble, muddle, mumble, mutter
07 stammer, stutter
09 confusion
11 garbledness
13 inconsistency
14 disjointedness

**incoherent**
05 mixed

07 garbled, jumbled, mixed-up, muddled, mumbled, unclear
08 confused, muttered, rambling
09 wandering
10 disjointed, disordered, stammering, stuttering
12 disconnected, inarticulate
14 unintelligible

**incombustible**
09 fireproof
10 flameproof
12 nonflammable
13 fire-resistant
14 flame-resistant

**income**
03 pay
05 gains, means, wages
06 salary
07 profits, returns, revenue
08 earnings, proceeds, receipts
12 remuneration

**incoming**
03 new
06 coming
07 ensuing
08 arriving, entering
09 returning
11 approaching

**incommensurate**
07 unequal
10 inadequate, inordinate
11 inequitable, not adequate
12 insufficient
15 incommensurable

**incommunicable**
08 reserved, taciturn
09 ineffable
11 indefinable, unspeakable, unutterable
13 indescribable, inexpressible

**incomparable**
07 supreme
08 peerless
09 matchless, nonpareil, paramount, unequaled, unmatched, unrivaled
10 inimitable
11 unsurpassed
12 unparalleled, without equal
13 beyond compare
15 without parallel

**incomparably**
08 superbly
09 eminently, supremely
10 far and away, infinitely
12 immeasurably
13 beyond compare, superlatively

**incompatibility**
08 mismatch, variance
09 disparity
10 difference
11 discrepancy, incongruity
12 disagreement
13 contradiction, disparateness, inconsistency

**incompatible**
08 unsuited
09 disparate
10 at variance, discordant, ill-matched, mismatched
11 incongruous, uncongenial
12 antagonistic, inconsistent
13 contradictory
14 irreconcilable

**incompetence**
08 bungling
09 ineptness, unfitness
10 inadequacy, ineptitude
11 uselessness
13 insufficiency, unsuitability
15 ineffectiveness

**incompetent**
05 inept, unfit
06 clumsy, unable
07 awkward, botched, useless
08 bungling, fumbling, inexpert
09 deficient
10 inadequate, unskillful
11 ineffective, unqualified
12 insufficient

**incomplete**
07 lacking, partial, wanting
08 abridged
09 deficient, imperfect, piecemeal, shortened
10 unfinished
11 fragmentary, undeveloped

**incomprehensible**
06 opaque
07 complex, obscure
08 abstruse, baffling, puzzling
09 enigmatic, recondite
10 mysterious, perplexing
11 complicated, inscrutable
12 impenetrable, unfathomable
14 unintelligible

**inconceivable**
09 ludicrous
10 impossible, incredible, staggering
11 implausible, unthinkable
12 mind-boggling, unbelievable, unimaginable

**inconclusive**
05 vague
09 ambiguous, uncertain, undecided, unsettled

10 indecisive, indefinite, up in the air
11 left hanging
13 indeterminate
14 open to question

**incongruity**
05 clash
08 conflict
09 disparity, inaptness
13 contradiction, inconsistency, unsuitability
15 incompatibility

**incongruous**
03 odd
06 absurd, at odds
07 jarring, strange
08 clashing, contrary
10 out of place, unsuitable
11 conflicting
12 incompatible, inconsistent, out of keeping
13 contradictory

**inconsequential**
05 minor, petty
07 trivial
08 trifling
10 immaterial, negligible
11 unimportant
13 insignificant

**inconsiderable**
05 minor, petty, small
06 slight
07 trivial
08 trifling
10 negligible
11 unimportant
13 insignificant

**inconsiderate**
04 rude
06 unkind
07 selfish
08 careless, heedless, tactless, uncaring
10 intolerant, unthinking
11 insensitive, thoughtless, unconcerned
12 self-centered, uncharitable

**inconsiderateness**
08 rudeness
09 unconcern
10 unkindness
11 intolerance, selfishness
12 carelessness, tactlessness
13 insensitivity
15 thoughtlessness
16 self-centeredness

**inconsistency**
07 paradox
08 conflict, variance
09 disparity

**inconsistent**
10 divergence, fickleness
11 contrariety, discrepancy, incongruity
12 disagreement, unsteadiness
13 contradiction, unreliability
14 changeableness

**inconsistent**
05 at odd
06 fickle
07 erratic, varying
08 contrary, variable
09 differing, irregular, mercurial
10 at variance, capricious, changeable, inconstant, out of place
11 conflicting, incongruous
12 in opposition, incompatible, out of keeping
13 contradictory, unpredictable
14 irreconcilable

**inconsolable**
10 despairing, devastated
11 heartbroken
12 disconsolate
13 brokenhearted, grief stricken

**inconspicuous**
06 hidden, low-key, modest
08 discreet, low-keyed, ordinary, retiring
09 concealed
10 indistinct, unassuming
11 camouflaged, unobtrusive
12 unnoticeable, unremarkable
13 insignificant
15 in the background

**inconstant**
06 fickle
07 erratic, mutable, varying, wayward
08 variable, volatile, wavering
09 mercurial, unsettled
10 capricious, changeable, irresolute, unfaithful, unreliable
11 fluctuating, vacillating
12 inconsistent, undependable

**incontestable**
04 sure
07 certain, evident, obvious
10 undeniable
11 indubitable, irrefutable
12 indisputable
14 unquestionable

**incontinent**
06 wanton
09 dissolute, unbridled, unchecked
10 ungoverned
11 promiscuous
12 uncontrolled, ungovernable, unrestrained

14 uncontrollable

**incontrovertible**
10 undeniable
11 beyond doubt, indubitable, irrefutable, self-evident
12 indisputable
14 beyond question, unquestionable

**inconvenience**
04 bind, bore, drag, fuss, pain
06 bother, burden, put out
07 disrupt, disturb
08 nuisance, vexation
09 annoyance, hindrance
10 difficulty, discommode, disruption, impose upon
11 awkwardness, disturbance
12 disadvantage

**inconvenient**
07 awkward
08 ill-timed, untimely, unwieldy
10 cumbersome, unsuitable
11 inopportune
12 unmanageable

**incorporate**
03 mix
04 fuse
05 blend, merge, unify, unite
06 absorb, embody, take in
07 combine, contain, embrace, include, subsume
08 coalesce
09 integrate
10 amalgamate, assimilate
11 consolidate

**incorporation**
05 blend
06 fusion, merger
07 company, society
08 unifying
09 inclusion, subsuming
10 absorption, embodiment, federation
11 association, coalescence, combination, corporation, integration, unification
12 amalgamation, assimilation

**incorporeal**
07 ghostly
08 ethereal, illusory, spectral
10 phantasmal, phantasmic

**incorrect**
05 false, wrong
06 faulty, untrue
07 inexact
08 improper, mistaken
09 erroneous, imprecise
10 fallacious, inaccurate, off the beam

**incorrectness**
05 error
09 falseness, wrongness
10 faultiness, inaccuracy
11 imprecision, inexactness
12 mistakenness, speciousness
13 erroneousness

**incorrigible**
08 hardened, hopeless
09 incurable
10 beyond hope, inveterate
12 irredeemable
13 dyed-in-the-wool

**incorruptibility**
05 honor
06 virtue
07 honesty, probity
08 justness, morality, nobility
09 integrity
11 uprightness
15 trustworthiness

**incorruptible**
04 just
05 moral
06 honest
07 ethical, upright
08 straight, virtuous
09 honorable
10 unbribable
11 trustworthy
14 high principled

**increase**
03 wax
04 bump, gain, go up, grow, hike, rise
05 add to, boost, breed, climb, raise, surge, swell
06 beef up, bump up, expand, growth, hike up, rocket, spiral, step up, step-up, upturn
07 advance, augment, broaden, build up, buildup, develop, enhance, enlarge, magnify, scale up, upsurge
08 addition, escalate, heighten, multiply, mushroom, progress, snowball
09 expansion, extension, increment, propagate
10 accumulate, escalation
11 enlargement, heightening, mushrooming, proliferate, snowballing
12 augmentation
13 proliferation
15 intensification

**increasingly**
11 more and more
12 cumulatively
13 progressively

**incredible**
07 amazing
09 fantastic, marvelous, wonderful
10 astounding, improbable, past belief, remarkable
11 astonishing, implausible
12 beyond belief, preposterous, unbelievable
13 inconceivable

**incredulity**
09 disbelief
10 skepticism

**incredulous**
08 doubtful, doubting
09 skeptical
11 unconvinced
12 disbelieving

**increment**
04 gain
06 growth, step-up
07 accrual
08 addition, increase
09 accretion
10 accruement, supplement
11 advancement
12 augmentation

**incriminate**
06 accuse, charge, indict
07 arraign, impeach
09 implicate, inculpate
13 put the blame on

**inculcate**
05 teach
06 infuse, instil
07 din into, implant, impress, imprint, ingrain, instill
08 drum into
09 drill into
10 hammer into
12 indoctrinate

**inculpate**
05 blame
06 accuse, charge, indict
07 arraign, censure
09 implicate
11 incriminate
13 put the blame on

**incumbent**
07 binding, officer
08 official
09 mandatory, necessary
10 compulsory, obligatory, prescribed
11 functionary
12 office bearer, officeholder

**incur**
04 earn, gain
06 arouse
07 provoke, sustain

10 experience
11 run-up suffer

**incurable**
05 fatal
08 hardened, hopeless, terminal
10 beyond hope, inoperable, inveterate, unhealable
11 untreatable
12 incorrigible
13 dyed-in-the-wool

**incursion**
05 foray, sally
06 sortie
07 inroads
08 invasion
09 irruption
11 penetration
12 infiltration

**indebted**
05 owing
07 obliged
08 beholden, grateful

**indecency**
07 crudity
08 foulness, impurity, lewdness
09 grossness, immodesty, indecorum, obscenity, vulgarity
10 coarseness
13 offensiveness
14 licentiousness

**indecent**
04 foul, lewd
05 bawdy, crude, dirty, gross
06 coarse, filthy, impure, ribald, risqué, smutty, vulgar
07 corrupt, immoral, obscene
08 depraved, immodest, improper, shocking, unseemly
09 offensive, perverted
10 degenerate, indecorous, indelicate, licentious, outrageous, suggestive, unbecoming, unsuitable
12 pornographic
13 inappropriate

**indecipherable**
07 unclear
09 illegible
10 indistinct, unreadable
14 unintelligible

**indecision**
05 doubt
08 wavering
09 hesitancy
10 hesitation
11 ambivalence, fluctuation, uncertainty, vacillation
12 irresolution

14 indecisiveness
15 shilly-shallying

**indecisive**
06 unsure
07 unclear
08 doubtful, hesitant, wavering
09 faltering, tentative, uncertain, undecided, unsettled
10 ambivalent, hesitating, indefinite, irresolute, of two minds, on the fence, wishy-washy
11 fluctuating, vacillating
12 inconclusive, pussyfooting
13 indeterminate
15 shilly-shallying

**indecorous**
04 rude
05 crude, rough
06 coarse, vulgar
07 boorish, uncivil, uncouth
08 churlish, immodest, impolite, improper, indecent, unseemly, untoward
09 tasteless
10 in bad taste, unmannerly
11 ill-mannered, undignified
13 inappropriate

**indecorum**
07 crudity
08 bad taste, rudeness
09 immodesty, indecency, roughness, vulgarity
10 coarseness, uncivility
11 impropriety
12 impoliteness, unseemliness
13 tastelessness

**indeed**
05 truly
06 in fact, really
07 for sure, in truth
08 actually, to be sure
09 certainly
10 absolutely, positively, undeniably
11 doubtlessly, undoubtedly
12 without doubt

**indefatigable**
06 dogged
07 patient, undying
08 diligent, tireless, untiring
09 unfailing, unresting, unwearied
10 unflagging, unwearying
11 persevering, unremitting
13 inexhaustible

**indefensible**
07 exposed
09 unguarded, untenable
10 vulnerable

11 defenseless, inexcusable, unprotected
12 unforgivable, unpardonable
13 insupportable, unjustifiable

**indefinable**
03 dim
04 hazy
05 vague
06 subtle
07 obscure, unclear
10 impalpable, indistinct, unrealized
13 indescribable, inexpressible

**indefinite**
04 hazy
05 fuzzy, loose, vague
07 blurred, general, inexact, obscure, unclear, unfixed, unknown
08 confused, doubtful
09 ambiguous, equivocal, imprecise, uncertain, undecided, undefined, unlimited, unsettled
10 ambivalent, ill-defined, indistinct, unresolved
11 nondescript, unspecified
12 inconclusive, undetermined
13 indeterminate

**indefinitely**
07 forever
09 endlessly, eternally
11 ad infinitum, continually

**indelible**
04 fast
07 lasting
08 enduring, unfading
09 ingrained, permanent
12 imperishable, ineffaceable, ineradicable
14 indestructible

**indelicacy**
07 crudity
08 bad taste, rudeness
09 grossness, immodesty, indecency, obscenity, vulgarity
10 coarseness, smuttiness
11 impropriety
13 offensiveness, tastelessness
14 suggestiveness

**indelicate**
04 blue, rude
05 crude, gross
06 coarse, risqué, vulgar
07 obscene
08 immodest, improper, indecent, off-color, unseemly
09 offensive, tasteless

10 in bad taste, indecorous, suggestive, unbecoming

**indemnify**
03 pay
04 free
05 repay
06 exempt, insure, secure
07 protect, satisfy
09 guarantee, reimburse
10 compensate, underwrite

**indemnity**
07 redress
08 immunity, security
09 assurance, exemption, guarantee, insurance, repayment, safeguard
10 protection, reparation
12 compensation
13 reimbursement

**indent**
03 cut
04 dent, dint, mark, nick, pink
05 notch, order, space
07 request, scallop, serrate
11 requisition

**indentation**
03 cut, dip, pit
04 dent, nick
05 notch, space
06 dimple, furrow, groove, hollow
07 spacing
09 serration
10 depression

**indenture**
04 bond, deal, deed
08 contract, covenant
09 agreement
10 commitment, settlement

**independence**
07 autarky, freedom, liberty
08 autonomy, self-rule
11 sovereignty
12 self-reliance
13 individualism
14 self-government
15 self-sufficiency

**Independence Day**
07 holiday
12 Fourth of July

**independent**
04 free
07 neutral, unaided
08 autarkic, distinct, nonparty, separate
09 autarchic, freelance, impartial, liberated, sovereign, unrelated
10 autonomous, individual, nonaligned, self-ruling

11 self-reliant, unconnected
12 freestanding, freethinking
13 individualist, self-contained, self-governing
14 self-sufficient, self-supporting
15 individualistic

**independently**
04 solo
05 alone
07 unaided
09 on your own
10 by yourself, separately
12 autonomously, individually

**indescribable**
07 amazing
09 ineffable
10 incredible
11 exceptional, indefinable, unspeakable, unutterable
13 extraordinary, inexpressible

**indestructible**
07 durable
11 everlasting, infrangible, unbreakable
12 imperishable

**indeterminate**
05 vague
07 inexact, unclear, unknown
09 ambiguous, equivocal, imprecise, uncertain, undecided, undefined
10 ambivalent, ill-defined, indefinite
11 unspecified

**index**
03 key
04 list, mark, sign
05 guide, table, token
07 catalog, pointer, symptom
09 catalogue, directory

**Indian**
10 aboriginal, Amerindian
14 American Indian, Native American
➤ See also NATIVE AMERICAN

**indicate**
04 mark, mean, read, show, tell
05 imply
06 denote, evince, record
07 display, express, point to, signify, specify, suggest
08 manifest, point out, register
09 designate, represent

**indicated**
06 needed
08 required
09 called for, necessary, suggested
11 recommended

## indication
04 clue, hint, mark, note, omen, sign
06 augury, record, signal
07 inkling, portent, symptom, warning
08 evidence, register
10 intimation, suggestion
11 explanation, requirement
13 manifestation
14 recommendation

## indicative
08 symbolic
10 denotative, suggestive
11 significant, symptomatic
13 demonstrative
14 characteristic

## indicator
04 clue, dial, hand, mark, sign
05 arrow, gauge, index, meter, token
06 needle, signal, symbol
07 display, pointer
08 signpost

## indict
06 accuse, charge, summon
07 arraign, impeach, summons
09 inculpate, prosecute
10 put on trial

## indictment
06 charge
07 summons
10 accusation, allegation
11 arraignment, impeachment, inculpation, prosecution

## indifference
06 apathy
09 disregard, unconcern
10 negligence, neutrality
11 impassivity, nonchalance
13 lack of concern
14 lack of interest

## indifferent
03 bad
04 cold, cool, easy, fair, so-so
05 aloof, blasé
06 medium
07 average, neutral, offhand, unmoved
08 detached, heedless, mediocre, middling, moderate, ordinary, passable, uncaring
09 apathetic, impassive
10 nonchalant, uninvolved
11 unconcerned, unemotional
12 run of the mill, uninterested
13 disinterested

## indigence
04 need, want

06 penury
07 poverty
09 privation
11 deprivation, destitution

## indigenous
06 native
08 original
09 homegrown
10 aboriginal
13 autochthonous

## indigent
04 poor
05 broke, needy
06 in need, in want
08 dirt poor
09 destitute, penniless, penurious
10 down and out, stone-broke
11 impecunious
12 impoverished
13 in dire straits
15 poverty-stricken

## indigestion
07 acidity, pyrosis
08 dyspepsy
09 dyspepsia, heartburn

## indignant
05 angry, irate, livid, riled
06 miffed, peeved
07 annoyed, in a huff
08 up in arms, wrathful
10 infuriated
11 disgruntled

## indignation
03 ire
05 anger, pique, wrath
07 outrage
09 annoyance

## indignity
03 cut
06 injury, insult, slight
07 affront, obloquy, offense
08 disgrace, dishonor, reproach
09 contumely
10 opprobrium
11 humiliation
13 slap in the face
14 kick in the teeth

## indirect
07 curving, devious, oblique, winding
08 rambling, tortuous
09 divergent, wandering
10 circuitous, discursive, meandering, roundabout
12 periphrastic
14 circumlocutory

## indirectly
09 deviously, obliquely
10 secondhand

## indiscernible
06 hidden, minute
07 obscure, unclear
09 invisible, minuscule
10 impalpable, indistinct
11 microscopic
12 undetectable
13 imperceptible, undiscernible

## indiscreet
06 unwary, unwise
08 careless, tactless
09 impolitic, imprudent, shameless
10 unthinking
11 injudicious
12 undiplomatic

## indiscretion
04 boob, slip
05 error, folly, gaffe, lapse
06 slip-up
07 bloomer, blunder, clanger, faux pas, mistake
10 imprudence
12 tactlessness

## indiscriminate
05 mixed
06 motley, random, varied
07 aimless, chaotic, diverse, general
08 careless, confused, sweeping
09 haphazard, hit or miss, wholesale
11 unselective
12 unsystematic
13 miscellaneous

## indiscriminately
08 randomly
09 aimlessly, generally, in the mass, wholesale
10 carelessly
11 haphazardly
13 unselectively

## indispensable
05 basic, vital
06 needed
07 crucial, needful
08 required
09 essential, important, necessary, requisite
10 imperative
11 fundamental

## indisposed
03 ill
04 sick
05 loath
06 ailing, averse, groggy, laid up, poorly, unwell
09 reluctant, unwilling
10 not of a mind, not willing, out of sorts
11 disinclined

12 not of a mind to
13 incapacitated
15 under the weather

**indisposition**
06 malady
07 ailment, disease, illness
08 aversion, disorder, sickness
09 complaint, ill health
10 reluctance
13 unwillingness
14 disinclination

**indisputable**
07 certain
08 absolute, definite, positive
10 undeniable, undisputed
11 indubitable, irrefutable
13 incontestable
14 beyond question,
　　unquestionable

**indissoluble**
05 fixed, solid
10 inviolable
11 inseparable, unbreakable
12 imperishable
13 incorruptible
14 indestructible

**indistinct**
03 dim
04 hazy, pale
05 faded, faint, fuzzy, misty,
　　muted, vague
06 woolly
07 blurred, muffled, obscure,
　　shadowy, unclear
08 confused, muttered
09 ambiguous, undefined
10 ill-defined, indefinite, out of
　　focus
14 indecipherable, unintelligible

**indistinguishable**
04 same
06 cloned
09 identical
10 tantamount
15 interchangeable

**individual**
03 one, own
04 lone, sole, sort, type
05 being, party
06 person, single, unique
07 several, special, typical
08 distinct, original, peculiar,
　　personal, separate, singular
09 character, exclusive
10 human being, particular
11 distinctive
12 personalized
13 idiosyncratic
14 characteristic

**individualism**
06 egoism
11 free thought, originality
12 freethinking, independence,
　　self-interest, self-reliance
13 egocentricity
14 libertarianism

**individualist**
05 loner
06 egoist
08 lone wolf, maverick
10 egocentric, free spirit
11 freethinker, independent

**individualistic**
06 unique
07 special, typical
08 original
09 eccentric
10 particular, unorthodox
11 independent, self-reliant
13 idiosyncratic

**individuality**
09 character
10 uniqueness
11 distinction, originality,
　　peculiarity, personality,
　　singularity
15 distinctiveness

**individually**
06 singly
08 one by one
09 severally
10 separately
13 independently

**indivisible**
10 impartible
11 inseparable, undividable
12 indissoluble
14 indiscerptible

**indoctrinate**
05 drill, teach
07 impress
08 instruct
09 brainwash, inculcate

**indoctrination**
08 drilling, teaching
10 catechesis, instilling
11 catechetics, inculcation,
　　instruction
12 brainwashing

**indolence**
05 sloth
06 apathy, torpor
07 inertia, languor
08 idleness, laziness, lethargy,
　　shirking, slacking
09 inertness, torpidity
10 inactivity, torpidness
11 languidness
12 listlessness, sluggishness

**indolent**
04 idle, lazy, slow
05 inert, slack
06 torpid
07 languid, lumpish
08 fainéant, inactive, listless,
　　slothful, sluggard, sluggish
09 apathetic, do-nothing,
　　lethargic, shiftless
13 lackadaisical

**indomitable**
07 staunch, valiant
08 fearless, intrepid, resolute,
　　stalwart
09 steadfast, undaunted
10 determined, invincible,
　　unbeatable, unyielding
11 lionhearted, unflinching
12 intransigent, unassailable,
　　undefeatable
13 unconquerable

**indubitable**
07 certain, evident, obvious
08 absolute
09 undoubted
10 unarguable, undeniable
11 beyond doubt, irrefutable,
　　undoubtable
12 indisputable, unanswerable
13 beyond dispute,
　　incontestable
14 unquestionable

**induce**
04 coax, draw, move, urge
05 cause, impel, press, tempt
06 effect, incite, lead to, prompt
07 actuate, inspire, produce,
　　provoke
08 generate, motivate,
　　occasion, persuade, talk into
09 encourage, influence,
　　instigate, originate
10 bring about, give rise to
11 prevail upon, set in motion

**inducement**
04 bait, goad, lure, spur
06 carrot, motive, reason,
　　reward
07 impetus
08 stimulus
09 incentive, sweetener
10 enticement, incitement
13 encouragement

**induct**
06 instal, invest, ordain
07 install, swear in
08 enthrone, initiate
09 introduce
10 consecrate, inaugurate

**induction**
09 reasoning

**indulge**

10 conclusion, initiation, ordination
11 institution, investiture
12 consecration, enthronement, inauguration, installation, introduction
14 generalization

**indulge**

03 pet
04 baby
05 favor, humor, spoil, treat
06 coddle, cosset, pamper, regale
07 cater to, gratify, revel in, satisfy, yield to
08 give in to, pander to, wallow in
09 give way to
11 go along with, mollycoddle

**indulgence**

05 favor, treat
06 excess, luxury, pardon
08 lenience
09 remission, tolerance
10 generosity
11 dissipation, fulfillment
12 extravagance, immoderation, intemperance, satisfaction
13 dissoluteness, gratification

**indulgent**

04 fond, kind
06 humane, tender
07 lenient, liberal, patient
08 generous, humoring, spoiling, tolerant
09 cosseting, forgiving, pampering
10 forbearing, permissive
13 mollycoddling, understanding

**industrial**

05 trade
08 business
10 commercial
13 manufacturing

**industrialist**

06 tycoon
07 magnate
08 producer
09 financier
12 manufacturer

**industrious**

04 busy
06 active
08 diligent
09 energetic, laborious
10 busy as a bee, productive
11 hard-working

**industriously**

04 hard
08 actively
13 energetically

**industry**

04 toil
05 labor, trade, vigor
06 effort, energy
08 activity, business, commerce, hard work, sedulity
09 diligence
10 enterprise, production
11 application, persistence
13 laboriousness, manufacturing
14 productiveness

**inebriated**

05 drunk, happy, lit up, merry, tight, tipsy, woozy
06 blotto, bombed, canned, loaded, soused, stewed, stoned, tiddly, wasted
07 drunken, legless, pickled, sloshed, smashed, sozzled, squiffy, wrecked
08 bibulous, tanked up
09 crapulent, dead drunk, paralytic, plastered, well oiled
10 blind drunk, skunk drunk
11 have had a few, intoxicated
12 drunk as a lord, roaring drunk
13 drunk as a skunk, under the table
15 one over the eight

**inedible**

09 uneatable
11 not fit to eat, unpalatable
12 indigestible, unconsumable

**ineducable**

11 unteachable
12 incorrigible

**ineffable**

11 beyond words, unspeakable, unutterable
13 indescribable, inexpressible
14 incommunicable

**ineffective**

04 idle, lame, vain, weak
05 inept
06 feeble, futile
07 useless
08 abortive, impotent
09 fruitless, powerless, to no avail, worthless
10 inadequate, profitless, unavailing
11 incompetent, ineffectual
12 unproductive, unsuccessful

**ineffectual**

04 lame, vain, weak
05 inept
06 feeble, futile
07 useless
08 abortive, impotent
09 fruitless, powerless, worthless
10 inadequate, unavailing
11 incompetent

**inefficacy**

08 futility
10 inadequacy
11 uselessness
15 ineffectiveness, ineffectualness

**inefficiency**

06 laxity, muddle
10 ineptitude, sloppiness
12 incompetence, wastefulness
15 disorganization

**inefficient**

03 lax
05 inept, slack
06 sloppy
08 careless, inexpert, slipshod, wasteful
09 negligent
11 incompetent, ineffective, time wasting, unorganized
12 disorganized

**inelegant**

04 ugly
05 crude, rough
06 clumsy, gauche, vulgar
07 awkward, ill-bred, labored, uncouth
08 ungainly
09 graceless, unrefined

**ineligible**

05 unfit
08 ruled out, unfitted
11 unqualified
12 disqualified, unacceptable

**inept**

06 clumsy
07 awkward, useless
08 bungling, inexpert
09 ham-fisted, ham-handed, incapable, maladroit, unskilful
10 inadequate, unskillful
11 heavy-handed, incompetent
12 unsuccessful

**ineptitude**

08 bungling
09 gaucherie, unfitness
10 clumsiness, gaucheness
11 awkwardness, unhandiness
12 incompetence, inexpertness

13 unskilfulness
14 unskillfulness

**inequality**
04 bias
08 contrast
09 disparity, diversity, imbalance, prejudice, roughness, variation
10 difference, unevenness
11 discrepancy, unequalness
12 irregularity
13 disproportion, nonconformity
14 discrimination

**inequitable**
06 biased, unfair, unjust
07 bigoted, partial, unequal
08 one-sided, partisan
10 intolerant, prejudiced
14 discriminatory

**inequity**
04 bias
09 injustice, prejudice
10 inequality, partiality, unfairness, unjustness
12 one-sidedness, wrongfulness

**inert**
04 dead, idle
05 still
06 sleepy, static, torpid
07 dormant, passive
08 immobile, inactive, indolent, lifeless, listless, sluggish, stagnant, unmoving
09 inanimate, lethargic
10 motionless, stationary, stock-still

**inertia**
05 sloth
06 apathy, torpor
07 languor
08 idleness, inaction, laziness, lethargy
09 indolence, passivity, stillness
10 immobility, inactivity
12 listlessness, slothfulness
14 motionlessness

**inescapable**
04 sure
05 fated
07 assured, certain
10 inevitable, inexorable
11 ineluctable, irrevocable, unalterable, unavoidable

**inessential**
05 extra, spare
08 needless, optional
09 extrinsic, redundant, secondary

10 expendable, extraneous, irrelevant
11 dispensable, superfluity, superfluous, uncalled-for, unessential, unimportant, unnecessary
12 extravagance, nonessential

**inestimable**
04 vast
06 untold
07 immense
08 infinite
09 unlimited
10 invaluable, prodigious
11 uncountable
12 immeasurable, incalculable, unfathomable

**inevitable**
05 fated
07 assured, certain, decreed, settled
08 definite, destined, ordained
09 automatic, necessary
10 inexorable
11 inescapable, predestined, unalterable, unavoidable

**inevitably**
06 surely
09 assuredly, certainly
10 definitely, inexorably
11 inescapably, irrevocably, necessarily, unavoidably
13 automatically

**inexact**
05 fuzzy, loose
06 woolly
07 muddled
09 imprecise
10 fallacious, inaccurate, indefinite, indistinct
11 approximate
13 indeterminate

**inexactitude**
07 blunder, mistake
09 looseness
10 inaccuracy, woolliness
11 imprecision, inexactness
13 approximation, impreciseness
14 indefiniteness

**inexcusable**
10 outrageous
11 blameworthy, intolerable
12 indefensible, unacceptable, unforgivable, unpardonable

**inexhaustible**
07 endless
08 abundant, infinite, tireless, untiring

09 boundless, limitless, unlimited
10 unflagging, unwearying
11 illimitable, measureless, never-ending
13 indefatigable

**inexorable**
06 dogged
08 resolute
09 immovable
10 relentless, unyielding
11 ineluctable, remorseless, unalterable, unrelenting, unstoppable
12 irresistible
13 unpreventable

**inexorably**
10 implacably, inevitably, pitilessly
11 ineluctably, inescapably, irrevocably, mercilessly
12 relentlessly
13 remorselessly

**inexpedient**
05 wrong
06 unwise
07 foolish
09 ill-chosen, ill-judged, impolitic, imprudent, misguided, senseless
10 ill-advised, indiscreet, unsuitable
11 detrimental, impractical, inadvisable, injudicious, unadvisable, undesirable, unfavorable
12 inconvenient, undiplomatic
13 inappropriate
15 disadvantageous

**inexpensive**
05 cheap
06 budget, modest
07 bargain, cut-rate, low cost, reduced
08 low price
09 low priced
10 discounted, economical, reasonable

**inexperience**
07 newness, rawness
09 freshness, ignorance, innocence, naïveness
10 immaturity
12 inexpertness
13 unfamiliarity

**inexperienced**
03 new, raw
05 fresh, green, naïve, young
06 callow
08 ignorant, immature, innocent

10 amateurish, apprentice,
    unseasoned
11 new to the job
12 probationary,
    unaccustomed,
    unacquainted
15 unsophisticated

**inexpert**
03 ham
05 inept
06 clumsy
07 amateur, awkward, unhandy
08 bungling
09 ham-fisted, ham-handed,
    maladroit, untrained
10 amateurish, unskillful
11 incompetent, unpracticed
13 unworkmanlike

**inexplicable**
05 weird
07 strange
08 abstruse, baffling, puzzling
09 enigmatic
10 mysterious, mystifying,
    perplexing
12 unfathomable
13 unaccountable,
    unexplainable

**inexplicably**
09 strangely
10 bafflingly, incredibly,
    puzzlingly
12 mysteriously, mystifyingly
13 unaccountably,
    unexplainably

**inexpressible**
08 nameless
09 ineffable, unsayable
11 unspeakable, unutterable
13 indescribable
14 incommunicable

**inexpressive**
05 blank, empty
06 vacant
07 deadpan
09 impassive
10 pokerfaced
11 emotionless, inscrutable

**inextinguishable**
11 unquellable
12 imperishable, unquenchable
13 irrepressible
14 indestructible

**inextricable**
11 indivisible, inseparable
12 indissoluble, irreversible
13 irretrievable

**inextricably**
11 indivisibly, inseparably
12 indissolubly, irreversibly

13 irretrievably

**infallibility**
09 inerrancy, supremacy
10 perfection
11 omniscience, reliability
12 unerringness
13 faultlessness
14 irrefutability

**infallible**
07 perfect
08 accurate, fail-safe, flawless,
    reliable, sure-fire, unerring
09 faultless, foolproof, unfailing
10 dependable

**infamous**
04 base, evil, vile
06 wicked
08 ill-famed, shameful,
    shocking
09 dastardly, egregious,
    nefarious, notorious
10 iniquitous, outrageous,
    scandalous
11 disgraceful, ignominious
12 dishonorable, disreputable
13 discreditable

**infamy**
04 evil
05 shame
08 baseness, disgrace, dishonor,
    ignominy, vileness, villainy
09 depravity, discredit,
    disrepute, notoriety,
    turpitude
10 wickedness

**infancy**
04 dawn, rise
05 birth, start, youth
07 genesis, origins
08 babyhood
09 beginning, childhood,
    emergence, inception

**infant**
04 babe, baby
05 child, early, minor, young
07 dawning, nascent, newborn,
    toddler
08 emergent, immature,
    juvenile, youthful
09 beginning, little one
10 babe in arms

**infantile**
05 young
07 babyish, puerile
08 childish, immature, juvenile

**infatuated**
03 mad
04 daft, nuts, sold, wild
05 crazy
06 in love

07 far gone, smitten
08 besotted, enamored,
    obsessed
09 bewitched
10 captivated, enraptured,
    fascinated, mesmerized,
    spellbound
11 carried away

**infatuation**
04 love, pash
05 craze, crush, mania, thing
07 passion
08 fixation, fondness
09 obsession
11 fascination
12 besottedness

**infect**
03 mar
05 spoil, taint, touch
06 affect, blight, defile, excite,
    pass on, poison
07 animate, corrupt, inspire,
    pervert, pollute
08 spread to
09 influence, stimulate
11 contaminate

**infection**
03 bug
04 germ
05 virus
06 blight, poison, sepsis
07 disease, illness
08 bacteria, epidemic
09 contagion, influence,
    pollution
10 corruption, defilement,
    pestilence
13 contamination

**infectious**
05 toxic
06 deadly, septic
07 noxious
08 catching, epidemic, virulent
09 infective, polluting,
    spreading
10 compelling, contagious,
    corrupting
12 communicable, irresistible
13 transmissible, transmittable

**infelicitous**
07 unhappy, unlucky
08 untimely, wretched
09 miserable, sorrowful,
    unfitting
10 despairing, unsuitable
11 incongruous, inopportune,
    unfortunate
13 inappropriate

**infer**
06 allude, assume, deduce,
    derive, gather, reason

07 presume, surmise
08 conclude
09 figure out
10 conjecture, understand
11 extrapolate

**inference**
07 reading, surmise
09 corollary, deduction,
reasoning
10 assumption, conclusion,
conjecture
11 consequence, presumption
13 extrapolation
14 interpretation

**inferior**
03 bad, low
04 poor, ropy
05 cheap, lower, lowly, minor
06 humble, junior, menial,
minion, shoddy, vassal
08 mediocre, slipshod
09 secondary, underling
10 low quality, second rate,
subsidiary
11 second class, subordinate,
subservient, substandard

**inferiority**
08 meanness
09 lowliness
10 faultiness, humbleness, low
quality, mediocrity,
shoddiness
12 imperfection, slovenliness,
subservience
13 subordination

**infernal**
04 evil, vile
06 cursed, damned, darned,
Hadean, wicked
07 blasted, demonic, hellish,
satanic
08 accursed, devilish, fiendish,
wretched
09 atrocious, execrable
10 confounded, diabolical,
malevolent

**infertile**
06 barren, effete
07 sterile
08 infecund
09 childless
10 unfruitful
11 unfructuous
12 unproductive

**infertility**
09 sterility
10 barrenness, effeteness
11 infecundity
14 unfruitfulness

**infest**
05 beset, crawl, flood, swarm
06 invade, plague, throng
07 bristle, overrun, pervade
08 permeate, take over
09 penetrate
10 infiltrate

**infested**
05 alive, beset
06 ridden
07 overrun, plagued, ravaged,
teeming
08 crawling, pervaded,
swarming
09 bristling, permeated
11 infiltrated

**infidel**
05 pagan
07 atheist, heathen, heretic,
skeptic
10 unbeliever
11 disbeliever, freethinker
13 irreligionist

**infidelity**
06 affair
07 liaison, perfidy
08 adultery, betrayal, cheating,
intrigue
09 duplicity, falseness,
treachery
10 disloyalty
13 faithlessness, fooling around,
playing around
14 unfaithfulness

**infiltrate**
04 seep, soak
05 enter
06 filter, invade
07 intrude, pervade
08 permeate
09 creep into, insinuate,
penetrate, percolate

**infiltration**
08 invasion
09 intrusion, pervasion
10 permeation
11 insinuation, penetration,
percolation

**infiltrator**
03 spy
04 mole
08 intruder
10 penetrator, subversive
11 double agent, seditionary

**infinite**
04 huge, vast
06 untold
07 endless, immense
08 absolute, enormous

09 boundless, countless,
extensive, limitless,
unbounded, unlimited
10 bottomless, fathomless,
numberless
11 inestimable, innumerable,
never-ending, uncountable
12 immeasurable, incalculable,
interminable, unfathomable
13 inexhaustible, without
number
14 indeterminable

**infinitesimal**
03 wee
04 tiny
05 teeny
06 minute
09 itty-bitty, minuscule
10 negligible
11 microscopic
13 imperceptible
14 inconsiderable

**infinity**
08 eternity, vastness
09 immensity
11 endlessness
12 enormousness

**infirm**
03 ill, old
04 lame, weak
05 frail, shaky
06 ailing, feeble, poorly, sickly,
unwell, wobbly
07 doddery, failing
08 decrepit, disabled, unsteady
09 faltering

**infirmity**
06 clinic
07 ailment, disease, failing,
frailty, illness
08 debility, disorder, hospital,
sickness, weakness
09 complaint, ill health
10 dispensary, feebleness,
sickliness
11 decrepitude, dodderiness,
instability

**inflame**
04 fire, fuel, heat, rile, stir
05 anger, rouse
06 arouse, enrage, excite,
foment, ignite, kindle,
madden, stir up, whip up
07 agitate, incense, provoke
09 aggravate, impassion,
infuriate, stimulate
10 exacerbate, exasperate

**inflamed**
03 hot, red
05 angry
06 heated, septic

07 fevered, flushed
08 festered, infected, poisoned

**inflammable**
08 burnable
09 flammable, ignitable, ignitible
11 combustible

**inflammation**
04 heat, rash, sore
06 sepsis
07 abscess, empyema, redness
08 eruption, erythema, swelling
09 festering, infection, septicity
10 irritation, tenderness

**inflammatory**
05 fiery, rabid
06 septic, tender
07 painful, riotous, swollen
08 allergic, inciting, infected
09 demagogic, explosive, festering, seditious
10 incendiary, incitative
11 instigative, provocative
13 rabble-rousing

**inflate**
05 bloat, boost, raise, swell
06 aerate, blow up, dilate, expand, extend, hike up, pump up, push up, step up
07 enlarge, magnify, puff out
08 escalate, increase, overrate
09 intensify, overstate
10 aggrandize, exaggerate
12 overestimate

**inflated**
05 tumid
07 bloated, blown up, dilated, pompous, swollen
08 extended, tumefied
09 ballooned, bombastic, distended, increased, overblown, puffed out
10 euphuistic
11 exaggerated, intensified
12 magniloquent, ostentatious
13 grandiloquent

**inflation**
04 rise
08 increase
09 expansion

**inflection**
05 pitch
06 rhythm, stress
08 emphasis
10 modulation
12 change of tone

**inflexibility**
08 hardness, obduracy, rigidity
09 obstinacy, stiffness

12 immovability, immutability, inelasticity, stubbornness, unsuppleness
13 immutableness, intransigence
14 intractability

**inflexible**
04 firm, hard, taut
05 fixed, rigid, solid, stiff
06 steely, strict
07 adamant
08 obdurate, resolute, rigorous, stubborn, unsupple
09 immovable, immutable, merciless, obstinate, unbending, unvarying
10 entrenched, implacable, unbendable, unyielding
11 intractable
12 intransigent, unchangeable
13 dyed-in-the-wool
14 uncompromising

**inflict**
05 apply, exact, wreak
06 burden, impose
07 deal out, deliver, enforce, mete out
10 administer, perpetrate

**infliction**
06 burden
07 penalty, trouble
08 exaction, wreaking
10 affliction, imposition, punishment
11 application, castigation, enforcement, retribution
12 chastisement, perpetration

**influence**
04 drag, hold, mold, move, pull, rule, sway
05 alter, clout, color, guide, impel, lobby, power, rouse, shape
06 affect, arouse, change, direct, effect, impact, induce, prompt, weight
07 control, impress, incline
08 guidance, impact on, maneuver, motivate, persuade, pressure, standing, whip hand
09 authority, condition, determine, direction, dominance, instigate, prejudice, supremacy, transform
10 importance, manipulate
11 carry weight, pull strings
14 have an effect on

**influential**
06 moving, potent, strong

07 guiding, leading, telling, weighty
08 dominant, powerful
09 effective, inspiring
10 compelling, convincing, meaningful, persuasive
11 charismatic, controlling, far-reaching, prestigious, significant
12 instrumental
13 authoritative

**influx**
04 flow, rush
05 flood
06 inflow, inrush, stream
07 arrival, ingress
08 invasion
10 inundation

**inform**
03 rat
04 blab, clue, leak, shop, sing, tell
05 brief
06 advise, betray, clue in, fill in, impart, notify, relate, snitch, squeal, tattle, tell on, tip off, wise up
07 apprise, put wise
08 acquaint, announce, denounce, identify, instruct
09 enlighten
10 illuminate, keep posted
11 communicate, incriminate
15 put in the picture

**informal**
04 easy, free
06 casual
07 natural, relaxed
09 easygoing
10 colloquial, unofficial, vernacular

**informality**
04 ease
07 freedom
10 casualness, homeliness, relaxation, simplicity
11 familiarity, naturalness

**informally**
06 easily, freely, simply
08 casually
10 familiarly, on the quiet
12 colloquially, unofficially
14 confidentially

**information**
04 data, dope, file, info, news
05 clues, facts, input
06 advice, record, report
07 details, dossier, message, the word, tidings
08 briefing, bulletin, databank, database, evidence

## informative
09 knowledge
10 communiqué, propaganda, the lowdown
11 instruction, particulars
12 intelligence

## informative
05 newsy
06 chatty, useful
07 gossipy, helpful
08 edifying
09 revealing
11 educational, instructive
12 enlightening, illuminating
13 communicative

## informed
06 au fait, expert, posted, primed, versed
07 abreast, briefed, erudite, learned
08 familiar, up to date
09 in the know
10 acquainted, conversant
11 enlightened
13 knowledgeable

## informer
03 rat, spy
04 mole, nark
05 Judas, sneak
06 snitch
07 stoolie, traitor
08 betrayer, squealer, telltale
09 informant
11 stool pigeon
13 whistleblower

## infraction
06 breach
08 breaking
09 violation
12 infringement
13 contravention, transgression

## infrequent
06 scanty, sparse
08 sporadic, uncommon
09 spasmodic
10 occasional
12 intermittent

## infringe
04 defy
05 break, flout
06 ignore, invade
07 disobey, impinge, intrude, violate
10 contravene, transgress

## infringement
06 breach
07 evasion
08 breaking, defiance, invasion, trespass
09 intrusion, violation
10 infraction

## infuriate
12 disobedience, encroachment
13 contravention, noncompliance, nonobservance, transgression

## infuriate
03 bug, get, vex
04 rile
05 anger, annoy, rouse
06 enrage, madden
07 incense, inflame, provoke
10 antagonize, exasperate

## infuriated
05 angry, irate, livid, vexed
06 heated, roused
07 enraged, flaming, furious, violent
08 agitated, incensed, maddened, provoked
11 exasperated
14 beside yourself

## infuriating
07 galling
08 annoying
09 maddening, provoking, vexatious
11 aggravating, frustrating
12 exasperating

## infuse
04 brew, draw, fill, soak
05 imbue, steep
06 inject, instil
07 instill
08 impart to, saturate
09 inculcate, introduce

## infusion
04 brew
07 soaking
08 steeping
11 inculcation
12 instillation

## ingenious
04 foxy, wily
05 adept, sharp, smart
06 astute, clever, crafty, shrewd
07 cunning, skilful
08 creative, skillful, talented
09 inventive
10 innovative
11 imaginative

## ingenuity
05 flair, knack, skill
06 genius
07 cunning, faculty
08 deftness
09 invention, sharpness
10 astuteness, shrewdness
11 originality, skilfulness
12 creativeness, skillfulness

13 inventiveness
14 innovativeness
15 resourcefulness

## ingenuous
04 open
05 frank, naïve, plain
06 candid, direct, honest, simple
07 artless, genuine, sincere
08 innocent
09 guileless

## ingenuousness
06 candor
07 honesty, naïvety
08 openness
09 frankness, innocence, unreserve
10 directness
11 artlessness, genuineness
13 guilelessness

## inglorious
07 ignoble, obscure, unknown
08 infamous, shameful, unheroic
10 mortifying
11 disgraceful, ignominious
12 dishonorable, disreputable
13 discreditable

## ingrain
05 embed, imbue, infix
06 instil
07 build in, engrain, implant, impress, imprint, instill

## ingrained
06 inborn, inbred
07 built-in
08 embedded, inherent
09 immovable, implanted, permanent
10 deep-rooted, deep-seated

## ingratiate
04 fawn
05 crawl, creep, toady
06 grovel
07 flatter
08 play up to, suck up to
10 curry favor
12 bow and scrape

## ingratiating
07 fawning, servile
08 crawling, toadying, unctuous
10 flattering, obsequious
11 bootlicking, sycophantic, timeserving

## ingratitude
13 thanklessness
14 ungratefulness

## ingredient
04 item, part, unit

06 factor
07 element, feature
09 component
11 constituent

**ingress**
05 entry
06 access
08 entrance
09 admission
10 admittance
12 means of entry, right of entry

**inhabit**
06 live in, occupy, people, settle, stay in
07 dwell in
08 colonize, populate, reside in, settle in

**inhabitant**
06 inmate, lodger, native, tenant
07 citizen, dweller, settler
08 habitant, occupant, occupier, resident

**inhabited**
07 lived in, peopled, settled
08 occupied, tenanted
09 colonized, populated

**inhalation**
06 breath
08 inhaling
09 breathing
11 inspiration, respiration

**inhale**
04 draw
06 draw in, suck in
07 inspire, respire
09 breathe in

**inharmonious**
06 atonal
07 grating, jarring, raucous
08 clashing, jangling, strident
09 dissonant, untuneful
10 discordant, unfriendly
11 cacophonous, inconsonant, unmelodious
12 unharmonious

**inherent**
06 inborn, inbred, innate, native
07 built-in, natural
09 essential, ingrained, inherited, intrinsic
10 hereditary, in the blood

**inherit**
06 be left
07 receive
08 accede to, come into
09 succeed to

**inheritance**
06 legacy
07 bequest

08 heredity, heritage
09 accession, endowment
10 birthright, succession

**inheritor**
04 heir
07 heiress, heritor, legatee
08 heritrix, legatary
09 heritress, recipient, successor
10 inheritrix
11 beneficiary, inheritress

**inhibit**
04 balk, curb, stem, stop
05 baulk, check
06 hamper, hinder, impede, rein in, thwart
07 prevent, repress
08 hold back, obstruct, restrain, restrict, slow down, suppress
09 constrain, frustrate
10 discourage

**inhibited**
07 guarded, subdued, uptight
08 reserved, reticent
09 repressed, withdrawn
10 frustrated, restrained
11 constrained, introverted
13 self-conscious

**inhibition**
04 curb
05 check
06 hang-up
07 reserve
09 hampering, hindrance, restraint, reticence
10 impediment, repression
11 obstruction, restriction

**inhospitable**
04 bare, cold, cool
05 aloof, bleak, empty
06 barren, lonely, unkind
07 hostile, uncivil
08 desolate, inimical
10 forbidding, unfriendly, unsociable, xenophobic
11 uncongenial, unwelcoming
12 unneighborly
13 uninhabitable

**inhuman**
05 cruel
06 animal, brutal, savage
07 bestial, strange, vicious
08 barbaric, sadistic
09 barbarous, merciless
10 diabolical

**inhumane**
05 cruel, harsh
06 unkind
07 callous
08 pitiless, uncaring

09 heartless, unfeeling
11 cold-hearted, hard-hearted, insensitive

**inhumanity**
06 sadism
07 cruelty
08 atrocity
09 barbarism, barbarity, brutality
10 savageness
11 brutishness, callousness, viciousness
12 pitilessness, ruthlessness
13 heartlessness

**inimical**
07 adverse, harmful, hostile, opposed
08 contrary
09 injurious
10 pernicious, unfriendly
11 unfavorable, unwelcoming
12 antagonistic

**inimitable**
08 peerless
09 matchless, nonpareil, unequaled, unmatched, unrivaled
10 unexampled
11 unsurpassed
12 incomparable, unparalleled
13 unsurpassable

**iniquitous**
04 base, evil
06 sinful, unjust, wicked
07 heinous, immoral, vicious
08 accursed, criminal, dreadful, infamous
09 atrocious, nefarious, reprobate
10 abominable
13 reprehensible

**iniquity**
03 sin
04 evil, vice
05 crime, wrong
07 misdeed, offense
08 baseness, enormity
09 evildoing, injustice
10 sinfulness, wickedness, wrongdoing
11 abomination, heinousness, lawlessness, viciousness
13 transgression

**initial**
02 OK
05 basic, early, first, prime
06 letter
07 opening, primary, sign off
08 inchoate, original, starting

**initially**
09  beginning, formative, inaugural, inceptive, incipient
10  commencing, elementary
12  introductory

**initially**
07  at first, firstly
10  at the start, first of all, originally
11  to begin with, to start with
14  at the beginning

**initiate**
04  open
05  admit, begin, drill, let in, set up, start, teach, train
06  enroll, induct, instil, invest, launch, novice, ordain, prompt, rookie, sign up
07  convert, entrant, instill, kick off, learner, pioneer, recruit
08  activate, beginner, commence, instruct, neophyte, newcomer
09  authority, greenhorn, inculcate, instigate, institute, introduce, novitiate, originate, proselyte
10  catechumen, inaugurate, tenderfoot
11  get under way, probationer, set in motion
15  get off the ground

**initiation**
05  debut, entry, start
07  baptism, opening
08  entrance
09  admission, beginning, inception, induction, setting up
10  admittance, enlistment, enrollment, ordination
11  investiture, origination
12  inauguration, installation, introduction
13  rite of passage

**initiative**
02  go
04  lead
05  drive, get-up
08  ambition, dynamism
09  first move, first step
10  enterprise, get-up-and-go
11  opening move, originality
13  inventiveness
14  innovativeness
15  resourcefulness

**inject**
06  infuse, insert, instil
07  instill, shoot up, syringe
08  immunize, mainline

09  inoculate, introduce, vaccinate

**injection**
04  dose, shot
08  addition, infusion
09  insertion
10  instilling
11  inoculation, vaccination
12  immunization, introduction

**injudicious**
04  rash
05  hasty
08  ill-timed
09  ill-judged, impolitic, imprudent, misguided
10  ill-advised, unthinking
11  inadvisable

**injunction**
05  order
06  dictum, ruling
07  command, dictate, mandate
09  directive

**injure**
03  cut, mar
04  harm, hurt, lame, maim, ruin
05  abuse, break, spoil, upset, wound, wrong
06  damage, deface, deform, impair, offend, put out
07  blemish, cripple, disable
08  fracture, ill-treat, maltreat

**injured**
04  hurt, lame
05  upset
06  abused, harmed, pained, put out
07  damaged, grieved, misused, wounded, wronged
08  crippled, disabled, insulted, maligned, offended
09  aggrieved
10  ill-treated, maltreated
13  cut to the quick

**injurious**
03  bad
06  unjust
07  adverse, harmful, hurtful
08  damaging, libelous
09  insulting
10  calumnious, corrupting, iniquitous, pernicious
11  deleterious, destructive, detrimental

**injury**
04  harm, hurt, ruin
05  abuse, wound, wrong
06  damage, insult
07  offense
09  grievance, injustice
10  impairment

12  ill-treatment

**injustice**
05  wrong
08  inequity
09  disparity, prejudice
10  inequality, unfairness, unjustness
12  one-sidedness, partisanship
14  discrimination

**inkling**
04  clue, hint, idea, sign
07  pointer
08  allusion, faintest, foggiest
09  suspicion
10  glimmering, suggestion

**inky**
03  jet
05  black, raven, sooty
08  jet black
09  coal-black
10  pitch-black

**inlaid**
05  inset, lined, tiled
07  studded
08  empestic, enameled, enchased
09  empaistic
11  tessellated

**inland**
05  inner
07  central
08  interior, internal
09  upcountry

**inlay**
05  inset
06  enamel, lining, mosaic, tiling
12  tessellation

**inlet**
03  bay
04  cove
05  bight, creek, fiord, firth, sound
07  opening

**inmate**
07  convict, patient
08  detainee, occupant, prisoner

**inn**
03  bar
05  hotel, local, lodge, motel
06  tavern
08  hostelry
09  roadhouse

**innards**
04  guts
05  works
06  entera, organs, vitals
07  insides, numbles, viscera
08  entrails, interior
09  mechanism

10 intestines
13 inner workings
14 internal organs

**innate**
06 inborn, inbred, native
07 connate, natural
08 inherent
09 inherited, intrinsic, intuitive
10 congenital, hereditary
11 instinctive

**inner**
06 hidden, inside, inward,
   mental, middle, secret
07 central, obscure, private
08 esoteric, interior, internal,
   intimate
09 concealed, emotional,
   innermost
13 psychological

**innermost**
05 basic
06 inmost, secret
07 central, closest, dearest,
   deepest
08 esoteric, intimate
09 essential

**innkeeper**
04 host
07 hostess
08 hotelier, landlady, landlord

**innocence**
06 purity, virtue
07 honesty, naïvety
08 chastity
09 credulity, ignorance,
   naïveness, virginity
10 simplicity
11 artlessness, gullibility
13 ingenuousness,
   unworldliness

**innocent**
04 babe, open, pure
05 child, green, naïve
06 chaste, honest, infant,
   novice, simple
07 artless, ingénue, sinless,
   upright
08 gullible, spotless, trustful,
   trusting, virginal, virtuous
09 childlike, credulous, faultless,
   greenhorn, guileless,
   guiltless, ingenuous,
   righteous, untainted,
   unworldly
10 babe in arms, immaculate,
   tenderfoot
11 inoffensive, unblemished,
   uncorrupted
13 inexperienced
14 above suspicion,
   irreproachable

15 unsophisticated

**innocently**
07 naïvely
09 artlessly
10 trustfully, trustingly
11 credulously, ingenuously

**innocuous**
04 mild, safe
05 bland
08 harmless, innocent
11 inoffensive
15 unobjectionable

**innovation**
06 change
07 newness, novelty
09 neologism, variation
10 alteration, new wrinkle
12 introduction
13 modernization

**innovative**
03 new
05 fresh, novel
07 go-ahead
08 creative, original
09 inventive
11 adventurous, imaginative,
   progressive

**innuendo**
04 hint, slur
08 allusion
09 aspersion
10 intimation, suggestion
11 implication, insinuation

**innumerable**
04 many
06 untold
07 umpteen
08 infinite, numerous
09 countless
10 numberless, unnumbered
11 uncountable

**inoculate**
06 inject
08 immunize
09 safeguard, vaccinate

**inoculation**
04 shot
09 injection
11 vaccination
12 immunization

**inoffensive**
04 mild, safe
05 bland, quiet
08 harmless, retiring
09 innocuous, peaceable
15 unobjectionable

**inoperable**
08 hopeless, terminal
09 incurable

11 intractable, irremovable,
   unremovable, untreatable

**inoperative**
04 idle
05 kaput
06 broken, futile
09 defective, worthless
10 broken-down, not working,
   on the brink, out of order
11 out of action
12 out of service
14 nonfunctioning
15 out of commission

**inopportune**
08 ill-timed, mistimed, untimely
10 unsuitable, wrong timed
11 unfortunate
12 inconvenient, unseasonable
13 inappropriate

**inordinate**
05 great, undue
09 excessive
10 exorbitant, immoderate
11 unwarranted
12 unreasonable, unrestrained,
   unrestricted

**input**
04 code, data
05 facts, key in
06 advice, feed in, insert
07 details, figures, opinion
10 investment
13 two cents worth

**inquest**
07 hearing, inquiry
10 inspection, postmortem
11 examination
13 investigation

**inquietude**
05 worry
06 unease
07 anxiety
08 disquiet
09 agitation, jumpiness
10 solicitude, uneasiness
11 disquietude, nervousness
12 apprehension,
   discomposure, perturbation,
   restlessness

**inquire, enquire**
03 ask
04 quiz
05 probe, query, snoop, study
06 search
07 examine, explore, inspect
08 look into, question, research
10 scrutinize
11 interrogate, investigate

**inquirer, enquirer**
10 questioner, researcher

12 interrogator, investigator

**inquiring, enquiring**
04 nosy
05 eager
06 prying
07 curious, probing
09 searching, skeptical, wondering
10 analytical, interested
11 inquisitive, questioning
13 interrogatory, investigative, investigatory

**inquiry, enquiry**
05 probe, query, study
06 search, survey
07 hearing, inquest
08 question, scrutiny, sounding
10 inspection
11 examination, exploration, inquisition
13 interrogation, investigation

**inquisition**
07 inquest, inquiry, inquiry
08 grilling, quizzing
09 witch hunt
11 examination, questioning, third degree
13 interrogation, investigation

**inquisitive**
04 nosy
06 prying, snoopy, spying
07 curious, probing
08 snooping
09 inquiring, inquiring, intrusive, searching
10 meddlesome
11 interfering, questioning

**inroad**
05 foray, sally
06 attack, charge, sortie
07 advance, assault
08 invasion, progress, trespass
09 incursion, intrusion, onslaught
12 encroachment

**insane**
03 mad
04 daft, loco, nuts
05 batty, crazy, daffy, loony, loopy, nutty, wacky
06 absurd, mental, psycho, screwy, stupid
07 lunatic
08 demented, deranged, unhinged
09 disturbed
11 mentally ill, not all there
13 off your rocker, out of your mind
14 off your trolley
15 non compos mentis

**insanitary**
06 filthy, impure
07 noisome, unclean
08 infected, polluted
09 unhealthy
10 unhygienic, unsanitary
12 contaminated, insalubrious

**insanity**
05 folly, mania
06 frenzy, lunacy
07 madness
08 daftness, delirium, dementia, neurosis
09 craziness, psychosis
11 derangement
13 mental illness

**insatiable**
06 greedy, hungry
08 ravenous
09 rapacious, voracious
10 gluttonous
12 unappeasable, unquenchable
13 unsatisfiable

**inscribe**
03 cut
04 etch, mark, sign
05 carve, stamp, write
06 incise, record
07 address, engrave, impress, imprint
08 dedicate
09 autograph

**inscription**
06 legend
07 caption, epitaph, etching, message, writing
09 autograph, engraving, lettering, signature
10 dedication

**inscrutable**
04 deep
07 cryptic
08 baffling, puzzling
09 enigmatic
10 mysterious, unreadable
12 impenetrable, inexplicable, unfathomable

**insect**

► *Types of insect*:
03 ant, bee, fly, nit
04 flea, gnat, moth, tick, wasp
05 aphid, louse, midge, roach
06 bedbug, cicada, cootie, earwig, hornet, locust, mantis, mayfly, sawfly, sow bug, spider, thrips
07 cricket, firefly, katydid, ladybug, pill bug, termite
08 black fly, bookworm, crane fly, honeybee, horsefly, housefly, lacewing, ladybird, mosquito
09 bumblebee, butterfly, cockroach, damselfly, dragonfly, tsetse fly, wood louse
10 boll weevil, harvestman, silverfish, springtail
11 grasshopper, stick insect
12 lightning bug, water boatman
13 daddy longlegs, leatherjacket, praying mantis
➤ See also ANIMAL

► *Parts of an insect*:
04 head, legs
06 thorax
07 abdomen, antenna, segment
08 forewing, hindwing, mandible
09 mouthpart
10 ovipositor
11 compound eye

**insecure**
04 weak
05 frail, loose, shaky
06 flimsy, unsafe, unsure
07 anxious, nervous, worried
08 hesitant, unstable, unsteady
09 hazardous, uncertain
10 precarious, vulnerable
11 defenseless, unprotected
12 apprehensive

**insecurity**
05 worry
07 anxiety
08 unsafety, weakness
09 frailness, shakiness
10 flimsiness, uneasiness, unsafeness, unsureness
11 instability, nervousness, uncertainty
12 apprehension, unsteadiness
13 vulnerability
14 precariousness

**insensible**
04 cold, deaf, hard, numb
05 aloof, blind, faint, stoic
06 zonked
07 distant, unaware, unmoved
08 comatose, ignorant
09 oblivious, senseless, unfeeling, untouched, zonked out
10 insentient, knocked out, unaffected
11 insensitive, unconscious
12 anesthetized, unresponsive
13 imperceptible, indiscernible

14 dead to the world, out for the count

**insensitive**
05 crass, stoic, tough
07 callous, unmoved
08 hardened, tactless, uncaring
09 heartless, impassive, oblivious, unfeeling
10 impervious, unaffected
11 indifferent, unconcerned
12 thick-skinned, unresponsive
13 unsusceptible

**insensitivity**
08 hardness, immunity
09 toughness, unconcern
10 obtuseness, resistance
12 indifference, tactlessness
14 hardheadedness

**inseparable**
05 close
07 devoted
08 constant, intimate
11 indivisible, undividable

**insert**
02 ad
03 put, set
05 embed, enter, graft, infix, inlay, inset, place, press, put in
06 push in, slip in
07 enclose, engraft, implant, slide in, stick in
08 addition, circular, thrust in
09 enclosure, insertion, interject, interpose, introduce
10 interleave, supplement
11 intercalate, interpolate
13 advertisement

**insertion**
02 ad
05 entry, inlet, inset
07 implant
08 addition
09 inclusion, intrusion
12 introduction, intromission
13 advertisement, interpolation

**inside**
04 core, guts
05 belly, heart, inner
06 center, inward, middle
07 content, indoors, private
08 contents, interior, internal, inwardly, secretly
09 innermost, intrinsic
10 restricted

**insider**
06 member
07 one of us
11 participant, staff member

15 one of the in crowd

**insides**
04 guts
05 belly
06 bowels, organs
07 abdomen, innards, stomach, viscera
08 entrails
10 intestines
14 internal organs

**insidious**
03 sly
04 wily
06 artful, subtle, tricky
07 cunning, devious, furtive
08 sneaking, stealthy
09 deceitful, deceptive
10 perfidious

**insight**
06 acumen, vision
08 judgment
09 intuition, sharpness
10 perception, shrewdness
11 discernment, penetration
12 perspicacity
13 comprehension, understanding

**insightful**
05 acute, sharp
06 astute, shrewd
10 discerning, perceptive, percipient
11 penetrating
13 perspicacious

**insignia**
04 logo, mark, sign
05 badge, brand, crest
06 emblem, ensign, ribbon, symbol
08 hallmark
09 medallion, trademark

**insignificance**
09 pettiness, smallness
10 paltriness, triviality
12 unimportance
13 immateriality, inconsequence, negligibility, worthlessness

**insignificant**
05 minor, petty, small
06 meager, paltry, scanty, slight
07 trivial
08 nugatory, piddling, trifling
10 negligible, peripheral
11 unimportant
13 insubstantial
15 inconsequential

**insincere**
05 false, lying, phony
06 untrue

07 feigned
09 faithless, pretended
10 mendacious, perfidious
11 dissembling, duplicitous, treacherous
12 disingenuous, hypocritical

**insincerity**
04 cant
07 falsity, perfidy
08 pretense
09 duplicity, falseness, hypocrisy, mendacity, phoniness
10 lip service
11 deviousness, dissembling, evasiveness
13 dissimulation, faithlessness

**insinuate**
04 hint
05 get at, imply
06 allude
07 suggest, whisper

◻**insinuate yourself**
04 work, worm
05 sidle
09 get in with
10 curry favor, ingratiate

**insinuation**
04 hint, slur
05 slant
08 allusion, innuendo
09 aspersion
10 intimation, suggestion
11 implication

**insipid**
04 drab, dull, flat, tame, weak
05 banal, bland, trite, vapid
06 anemic, boring, jejune, watery
08 lifeless
09 colorless
10 flavorless, monotonous, spiritless, wishy-washy
13 unimaginative, uninteresting

**insist**
04 aver, hold, urge
05 swear
06 assert, demand, harp on, repeat, stress
07 contend, declare, entreat, persist, require
08 maintain
09 emphasize, stand firm
11 state firmly
15 put your foot down

**insistence**
06 demand, stress, urging
08 emphasis, firmness
09 assertion
10 contention

11 declaration, exhortation, persistence, requirement
13 determination

**insistent**
06 dogged, urgent
07 adamant, exigent
08 emphatic, forceful, pressing
09 incessant, tenacious
10 determined, inexorable, persistent, relentless
11 importunate, persevering, unrelenting, unremitting

**insobriety**
09 inebriety, tipsiness
10 crapulence
11 drunkenness, inebriation
12 intemperance, intoxication

**insolence**
03 lip
04 gall
05 abuse, cheek, mouth, nerve, sauce
06 hubris
07 chutzpa
08 audacity, boldness, chutzpah, defiance, pertness, rudeness
09 impudence, sauciness
10 cheekiness, effrontery
11 forwardness, presumption
12 impertinence

**insolent**
04 bold, rude
05 brash, fresh, saucy
06 brazen, cheeky
07 abusive, defiant, forward
08 impudent
09 audacious
11 ill-mannered, impertinent
12 presumptuous

**insoluble**
07 complex, cryptic, obscure
08 baffling, involved, puzzling
09 enigmatic, intricate
10 mysterious, mystifying, perplexing, unsolvable
11 inscrutable
12 impenetrable, indissoluble, inexplicable, unfathomable
13 unexplainable
14 indecipherable

**insolvency**
04 ruin
07 failure
10 bankruptcy
11 destitution, liquidation

**insolvent**
04 bust
05 broke
06 failed, ruined

08 bankrupt, in the red
09 gone under
10 liquidated, on the rocks
11 gone belly up
13 gone to the wall

**insomnia**
11 wakefulness
12 insomnolence, restlessness
13 sleeplessness

**insouciance**
04 ease
08 airiness
09 flippancy, unconcern
10 breeziness, jauntiness
11 nonchalance
12 carefreeness

**insouciant**
04 airy
06 breezy, casual, jaunty
07 buoyant
08 carefree, flippant, heedless
09 easygoing, unworried
10 nonchalant, untroubled
11 free and easy, unconcerned

**inspect**
03 vet
04 scan, tour, view
05 audit, check, study
06 assess, go over, survey
07 examine, oversee, see over
08 look over, pore over
10 scrutinize
11 investigate, reconnoiter

**inspection**
04 scan, tour
05 audit, check, study
06 review, search, survey
07 checkup, vetting
08 once-over, scrutiny
11 examination
13 investigation

**inspector**
07 auditor, checker
08 assessor, examiner, overseer, reviewer, surveyor
10 scrutineer, supervisor

**inspiration**
04 goad, idea, muse, spur
06 fillip, genius
08 arousing, stimulus, stirring
09 awakening, brainwave
10 bright idea, creativity, motivation
11 imagination, originality, stimulation
12 illumination
13 encouragement, enlightenment, inventiveness

**inspire**
05 imbue, rouse
06 arouse, excite, infuse, kindle, prompt, thrill
07 animate, breathe, enliven, hearten, impress, inflame, quicken, trigger
08 energize, enthrall, motivate, spark off, touch off
09 galvanize, instigate, stimulate
10 bring about, exhilarate

**inspired**
09 brilliant, marvelous, memorable
10 remarkable
11 enthralling, superlative

**inspiring**
07 rousing
08 exciting, stirring
09 affecting, memorable, thrilling, uplifting
10 heartening, impressive
11 enthralling, stimulating
12 exhilarating

**inspirit**
04 move
07 animate, enliven, gladden, hearten, inspire, quicken, refresh
08 embolden
09 encourage, galvanize, stimulate
10 exhilarate, invigorate
12 reinvigorate

**instability**
09 shakiness
10 flimsiness, insecurity, transience, unsafeness, volatility
11 fluctuation, inconstancy, uncertainty, vacillation, variability
12 unsteadiness
14 capriciousness, changeableness, precariousness

**install, instal**
03 fit, fix, lay, put
05 lodge, place, plant, put in, set up
06 induct, insert, locate, ordain, settle
07 instate, situate, station
08 ensconce, position
09 establish, institute, introduce
10 consecrate, inaugurate

**installation**
05 plant
06 siting, system
07 fitting, placing, station
08 location

09  equipment, induction, insertion, machinery
10  ordination, settlement
11  instatement, investiture
12  inauguration
13  establishment

**installment**
04  part
07  chapter, episode, payment, portion, section, segment
08  division
11  part payment

**instance**
04  case, cite, give, name
05  quote
06  adduce, sample
07  example, mention, point to, refer to, request, specify
08  citation, occasion
09  exemplify, prompting
10  incitement, occurrence
11  case in point
12  illustration
15  exemplification

**instant**
04  fast, time
05  flash, jiffy, quick, rapid, shake, swift, trice
06  direct, minute, moment, prompt, second, urgent
08  juncture, occasion
09  immediate, on the spot, twinkling
11  convenience, split second
13  instantaneous

**instantaneous**
04  fast
05  quick, rapid
06  direct, prompt, sudden
07  instant
09  immediate, on the spot

**instantaneously**
06  at once, pronto
07  quickly, rapidly
08  directly, promptly, speedily
09  forthwith, on the spot, right away
11  immediately
12  straight away, there and then, without delay

**instantly**
06  at once, pronto
08  directly
09  forthwith, on the spot, right away
11  immediately
12  straight away, there and then, without delay

**instead**
04  else

06  rather
10  by contrast, in contrast
13  alternatively
15  as an alternative

**instead of**
08  in lieu of
09  in place of
10  rather than

**instigate**
04  goad, move, prod, spur, urge
05  begin, cause, egg on, press, rouse, set on, start
06  excite, foment, incite, induce, kindle, prompt, stir up, whip up
07  inspire, provoke
08  generate, initiate, persuade
09  encourage, stimulate
10  bring about

**instigation**
06  behest, urging
07  bidding
09  incentive, prompting
10  incitement, inducement, initiation, initiative, insistence
13  encouragement

**instigator**
04  goad, spur
06  leader
07  inciter, plotter
08  agitator, fomenter, provoker
09  firebrand, motivator
10  prime mover, ringleader

**instill, instil**
05  drill, imbue, teach
06  infuse
07  din into, implant, impress
09  inculcate, introduce

**instinct**
04  bent, feel, gift, urge
05  drive, flair, hunch, knack
06  talent
07  ability, faculty, feeling, impulse
08  aptitude, tendency
09  intuition
10  gut feeling, sixth sense
11  gut reaction
14  predisposition

**instinctive**
03  gut
06  inborn, innate, native, reflex
07  natural
08  inherent, visceral
09  automatic, impulsive, intuitive
11  involuntary, spontaneous

**instinctively**
09  naturally
11  intuitively

13  automatically, spontaneously

**institute**
03  law
04  rule
05  begin, enact, found, set up, start
06  create, custom, decree, induct, invest, launch, ordain, school
07  academy, appoint, college, develop, install
08  commence, initiate, organize, seminary
09  establish, introduce, originate, principle
10  foundation, inaugurate, university
11  institution
12  conservatory

**institution**
04  club, home, rule
05  guild, usage
06  center, church, custom, league, ritual, school, system
07  college, society
08  creation, founding, hospital, marriage, practice
09  enactment, formation, inception, institute, setting up, tradition
10  convention, foundation, initiation, university
11  association, corporation, nursing home, reformatory
12  commencement, installation, introduction, organization
13  establishment
14  mental hospital

**institutional**
04  cold, drab, dull
06  dreary, formal
07  orderly, routine, uniform
08  accepted, clinical, orthodox
09  cheerless, customary
10  forbidding, impersonal, methodical, monotonous, regimented, systematic
11  established, ritualistic
12  bureaucratic, conventional

**instruct**
03  bid
04  tell
05  coach, drill, guide, order, prime, teach, train, tutor
06  advise, charge, direct, inform, notify, school
07  command, educate, mandate, require

**instruction**
03  key

05 brief, order, rules
06 advice, charge, legend, lesson, manual, orders, ruling
07 classes, command, mandate, priming, tuition
08 briefing, coaching, drilling, guidance, teaching, training, tutelage, tutoring
09 direction, directive, education, schooling
10 directions, guidelines, injunction
11 information, preparation
13 enlightenment
14 recommendation

**instructive**
09 educative, uplifting
11 educational, informative
12 enlightening, illuminating

**instructor**
04 guru
05 coach, guide, tutor
06 master, mentor
07 adviser, pedagog, teacher, trainer
08 educator, exponent, lecturer, mistress
09 pedagogue

**instrument**
04 tool
05 agent, gauge, gismo, means, meter, organ
06 device, gadget, medium
07 channel, utensil
09 apparatus, appliance, implement, indicator, yardstick
11 contraption, contrivance

---

► *Types of musical instruments*:

04 bell, drum, fife, gong, harp, horn, kora, lute, lyre, Moog, oboe, pipe, tuba, viol
05 Amati, banjo, bells, bongo, bugle, cello, chime, flute, hi-hat, kazoo, mbira, organ, piano, pipes, rebec, shawm, sitar, tabla, tabor, vibes, viola
06 cornet, cymbal, fiddle, guitar, rebeck, spinet, tom-tom, violin, zither
07 alphorn, bagpipe, bassoon, celesta, celeste, cowbell, high-hat, kalimba, maracas, marimba, ocarina, panpipe, Pianola, piccolo, sackbut, serpent, sistrum, tambura, theorbo, timpani, trumpet, ukulele, whistle
08 bagpipes, bass drum, bouzouki, cimbalom,

clappers, clarinet, crumhorn, dulcimer, Jew's harp, keyboard, mandolin, melodeon, panpipes, recorder, Steinway, tamboura, theremin, triangle, trombone, virginal
09 accordion, balalaika, bongo drum, castanets, euphonium, flageolet, harmonica, harmonium, Pan's pipes, saxophone, snare drum, Wurlitzer, xylophone
10 bass guitar, clavichord, concertina, cor Anglais, didgeridoo, double bass, flugelhorn, French horn, grand piano, hurdy-gurdy, kettledrum, mouth organ, pianoforte, sousaphone, squeezebox, tambourine, thumb piano, tin whistle, vibraphone
11 Aeolian harp, barrel organ, English horn, fluegelhorn, harpsichord, player piano, synthesizer, violoncello
12 glockenspiel, Stradivarius, viola da gamba
13 slide trombone
14 acoustic guitar, electric guitar
► See also MUSIC

**instrumental**
06 active, useful
07 helpful
08 involved
09 auxiliary, conducive
11 influential, significant
12 contributory

**insubordinate**
04 rude
06 unruly
07 defiant, riotous
09 seditious, turbulent
10 disorderly, rebellious, refractory
11 disobedient, impertinent
12 contumacious, recalcitrant, ungovernable
13 undisciplined

**insubordination**
06 mutiny, revolt
09 rebellion
12 disobedience, insurrection, mutinousness

**insubstantial**
04 poor, puny, thin, weak
06 feeble, flimsy, slight, unreal
07 tenuous
08 fanciful, illusory, vaporous

09 ephemeral
10 chimerical, immaterial
11 incorporeal

**insufferable**
10 unbearable
11 intolerable, unendurable

**insufficiency**
04 lack, need, want
06 dearth
08 scarcity, shortage
10 deficiency, inadequacy

**insufficient**
05 scant, short
06 meager, scanty, scarce, sparse
07 lacking, wanting
09 deficient, not enough
10 inadequate

**insular**
06 closed, cut off, narrow
08 detached, isolated, separate, solitary
09 blinkered, insulated, parochial, withdrawn
10 prejudiced, provincial, xenophobic
12 narrow-minded
13 inward looking

**insularity**
09 isolation, pettiness, prejudice
10 detachment, xenophobia
12 parochiality, solitariness
13 parochialness

**insulate**
03 lag, pad
04 wrap
06 cocoon, cut off, detach, encase, shield
07 cushion, envelop, isolate, protect, shelter

**insulation**
05 cover
06 shield
07 lagging, padding, shelter
08 cladding, stuffing, wrapping
09 cocooning, isolation
10 cushioning, protection

**insult**
04 bait, barb, gibe, hurt, slur, snub
05 abuse, libel, taunt, wound
06 impugn, injure, malign, offend, rebuff, revile, slight
07 affront, mortify, offense, outrage, put-down, slander, traduce
08 ridicule, rudeness
09 aspersion, call names, disparage, indignity
10 calumniate, defamation

12 cold shoulder
13 slap in the face
14 kick in the teeth

**insulting**
04 rude
07 abusive, hurtful
08 insolent, libelous
09 degrading, injurious,
   offensive
10 outrageous, scurrilous,
   slanderous
11 disparaging
12 contemptuous

**insuperable**
10 invincible
12 overwhelming, unassailable
13 unconquerable
14 insurmountable

**insupportable**
09 untenable
11 intolerable, unendurable
12 indefensible, insufferable,
   unacceptable
13 unjustifiable

**insuppressible**
06 lively
09 energetic
11 overzealous, unstoppable,
   unsubduable
12 ungovernable
13 irrepressible

**insurance**
05 cover
06 policy, surety
08 coverage, security, warranty
09 guarantee, indemnity,
   safeguard
10 protection
15 indemnification

**insure**
05 cover
07 protect, warrant
09 guarantee, indemnify
10 underwrite

**insurer**
09 guarantor, warrantor,
   warrenter
11 indemnifier, underwriter

**insurgent**
05 rebel
06 rioter
08 mutineer, partisan, resister
09 seditious
11 seditionist
12 recalcitrant
13 revolutionary, revolutionist
15 insurrectionary,
   insurrectionist

**insurmountable**
10 impossible, invincible
11 insuperable
13 unconquerable

**insurrection**
04 coup, riot
06 mutiny, putsch, revolt, rising
08 sedition, uprising
09 coup d'état, rebellion

**intact**
05 whole
06 entire
07 perfect
08 complete, flawless, integral,
   unbroken, unharmed
09 faultless, undamaged
10 in one piece

**intangible**
04 airy
05 vague
07 elusive, obscure, shadowy,
   unclear
08 abstract, fleeting
09 invisible
10 indefinite
11 undefinable
13 insubstantial

**integral**
04 full
05 basic
08 inherent
09 component, elemental,
   essential, intrinsic, necessary,
   requisite
11 constituent, fundamental

**integrate**
03 mix
04 fuse, join, knit, mesh
05 blend, merge, unite
06 mingle
07 combine
10 amalgamate, assimilate,
   homogenize
11 desegregate, incorporate

**integrated**
05 fused, mixed
06 joined, merged, meshed,
   united
07 blended, mingled, unified
08 cohesive, combined
11 amalgamated, assimilated,
   unseparated
12 desegregated, incorporated
13 part and parcel

**integration**
03 mix
05 blend
06 fusion, merger
07 harmony
11 combination, unification

12 amalgamation, assimilation
13 desegregation,
   incorporation

**integrity**
05 honor, unity
06 purity, virtue
07 decency, honesty, probity
08 cohesion, morality
09 coherence, principle,
   rectitude
11 unification, uprightness
12 completeness

**intellect**
04 mind
05 brain, sense
06 brains, genius, reason,
   wisdom
07 egghead, thinker, thought
08 academic, Einstein,
   highbrow, judgment
10 brainpower, brilliance,
   mastermind
12 intellectual, intelligence
13 comprehension,
   understanding

**intellectual**
06 mental
07 bookish, egghead, erudite,
   learned, logical, thinker
08 academic, cerebral,
   highbrow, studious
09 scholarly

**intelligence**
03 wit
04 data, dope, news, nous, wits
05 brain, facts
06 acumen, advice, brains,
   report, spying, tip-off
07 thought
09 espionage, intellect,
   knowledge, sharpness
10 brainpower, brightness,
   brilliance, cleverness, gray
   matter, perception, the
   lowdown
11 information
12 surveillance
15 little gray cells

**intelligent**
05 acute, alert, quick, sharp,
   smart
06 brainy, bright, clever
08 all there, rational, sensible
09 brilliant, sagacious
10 discerning, perceptive
11 quick-witted
13 using your head
15 using your noggin, using
   your noodle

**intelligentsia**
08 literati

09 academics
11 cognoscenti
13 intellectuals

**intelligibility**
07 clarity
08 lucidity
09 clearness, plainness
10 legibility
11 readability
12 distinctness, explicitness

**intelligible**
05 clear, lucid
07 legible
08 distinct, explicit, readable
14 comprehensible,
   understandable

**intemperance**
06 excess
07 license
10 crapulence, insobriety
11 drunkenness, inebriation,
   unrestraint
12 extravagance,
   immoderation, intoxication
14 overindulgence

**intemperate**
04 wild
07 drunken, extreme, violent
08 prodigal
09 dissolute, excessive
10 immoderate, inebriated,
   licentious, profligate
11 extravagant, incontinent,
   intoxicated, tempestuous
12 uncontrolled, ungovernable,
   unreasonable, unrestrained

**intend**
03 aim
04 mean, plan, plot
06 design, devise, scheme
07 destine, earmark, propose,
   purpose, resolve
09 determine, have a mind
10 have in mind

**intended**
06 fiancé, future
07 fiancée, planned
08 destined, wife-to-be
09 affianced, betrothed
11 husband-to-be, intentional,
   prospective

**intense**
04 deep, keen
05 acute, eager, heavy
06 ardent, fervid, fierce, potent,
   severe, strong
07 burning, earnest, excited,
   fervent, nervous, serious,
   violent, zealous

08 forceful, powerful, profound,
   vigorous
09 consuming, emotional,
   energetic
10 passionate, thoughtful
12 concentrated, enthusiastic

**intensely**
06 deeply
08 ardently, fiercely, strongly
09 fervently
10 profoundly
12 passionately
14 with a vengeance

**intensification**
07 buildup
08 emphasis, increase
09 deepening, worsening
10 escalation, stepping-up
11 heightening
12 acceleration, augmentation
13 concentration,
   magnification,
   reinforcement,
   strengthening

**intensify**
03 fan
04 fire, fuel, whet
05 add to, boost
06 deepen, step-up, worsen
07 augment, build up, enhance,
   magnify, quicken, sharpen
08 escalate, increase
09 aggravate, emphasize,
   reinforce
10 exacerbate, strengthen
11 concentrate
12 bring to a head

**intensity**
04 fire, zeal
05 ardor, depth, force, power,
   vigor
06 energy, fervor, strain
07 emotion, passion, potency
08 fervency, keenness, severity
09 acuteness, eagerness,
   extremity
10 fierceness, profundity
11 earnestness
13 concentration

**intensive**
07 in-depth, intense
08 detailed, thorough
10 exhaustive
12 concentrated
13 thoroughgoing

**intent**
03 aim, end, set
04 bent, firm, goal, hard, idea,
   keen, plan, rapt, view
05 alert, eager, fixed

06 design, enrapt, object,
   steady, target
07 focused, meaning, purpose
08 absorbed, occupied,
   resolved, watchful
09 attentive, committed,
   engrossed, objective,
   wrapped up
10 determined
11 preoccupied
13 concentrating

❑**to all intents and pur-
poses**
08 as good as
09 virtually
10 pretty much, pretty well
11 practically

**intention**
03 aim, end
04 goal, idea, plan
06 design, intent, object, target
07 meaning, purpose
08 ambition
09 objective
10 aspiration

**intentional**
05 meant
07 planned, studied
08 designed, intended
09 conscious, on purpose
10 calculated, considered,
   deliberate, purposeful

**intentionally**
08 by design
09 on purpose
12 deliberately

**intently**
04 hard
06 keenly
07 closely, fixedly
08 steadily

**inter**
04 bury
06 entomb, inhume
09 lay to rest, sepulcher

**interbreed**
05 cross
09 hybridize
10 crossbreed
14 cross-fertilize

**interbreeding**
08 crossing
13 crossbreeding, hybridization

**intercede**
07 mediate
09 interpose, intervene

**intercept**
04 stop
05 block, check, delay, seize

06 ambush, arrest, cut off,
   impede, thwart
07 deflect, head off
08 obstruct
09 frustrate

**intercession**
06 prayer
09 mediation
11 arbitration, interceding
12 intervention
13 interposition

**interchange**
04 swap
05 trade
06 barter, switch
07 replace, reverse, trading
08 crossing, exchange, junction
09 crossroad, transpose
10 cloverleaf, crossroads,
   substitute
11 alternation, reciprocate
12 intersection
13 reciprocation

**interchangeable**
09 identical
10 reciprocal, synonymous
12 exchangeable, transposable

**intercourse**
05 trade, truck
07 contact, traffic
08 commerce, congress,
   converse, dealings
09 communion, relations
12 conversation
13 communication
14 correspondence

**interdict**
03 ban, bar
04 veto
05 debar, taboo
06 forbid, outlaw
07 embargo, prevent, rule out
08 disallow, preclude, prohibit
09 proscribe
10 injunction, preclusion
11 prohibition
12 proscription

**interest**
04 care, gain, grip, heed, note
05 amuse, bonus, charm, hobby,
   share, stake, stock, value
06 absorb, allure, appeal, divert,
   engage, equity, moment,
   notice, occupy, profit, regard,
   return, weight
07 attract, concern, credits,
   engross, involve, pastime,
   portion, premium, pursuit,
   revenue
08 activity, business, dividend,
   priority, proceeds, receipts

09 advantage, amusement,
   attention, captivate, curiosity,
   diversion, fascinate,
   relevance
10 attraction, engagement,
   importance, investment,
   percentage, prominence,
   recreation
11 consequence, fascination,
   involvement, seriousness
12 significance
13 attentiveness, consideration,
   participation

❏ **in the interests of**
10 on behalf of
12 for the sake of
15 for the benefit of

**interested**
04 keen
06 intent
07 curious, gripped, riveted
08 absorbed, affected, involved
09 attentive, concerned,
   engrossed
10 fascinated, implicated
12 enthusiastic

**interesting**
07 amusing, curious, unusual
08 engaging
09 absorbing, appealing
10 attractive, compelling,
   engrossing, intriguing
11 fascinating, stimulating
12 entertaining

**interfere**
03 pry
04 balk
05 abuse, baulk, block, check,
   clash, cramp
06 butt in, impede, meddle,
   molest, tamper
07 assault, intrude
08 conflict, handicap, obstruct
09 interrupt, intervene
10 muscle in on
13 get in the way of
14 poke your nose in
15 stick your nose in

**interference**
06 prying
08 meddling
09 intrusion
11 obstruction
12 interruption, intervention
14 meddlesomeness

**interim**
06 acting, pro tem
07 stand-in, stopgap
08 interval, meantime
09 caretaker, meanwhile
11 interregnum, provisional

**interior**
04 core
05 heart, inner
06 center, depths, inland, inside,
   inward, mental, middle
07 central, nucleus
08 internal, intimate
09 innermost, intrinsic, intuitive,
   spiritual, upcountry
11 instinctive, involuntary,
   spontaneous
13 psychological

**interject**
03 cry
04 call
05 shout, utter
07 exclaim
09 ejaculate, interrupt

**interjection**
03 cry
04 call
05 shout
09 utterance
11 ejaculation, exclamation
12 interruption
13 interpolation

**interlace**
04 knit
05 braid, cross, plait, twine
07 entwine
10 intertwine, interweave,
   reticulate

**interlink**
04 knit, link, mesh
12 interconnect

**interlock**
04 link
12 interconnect
13 clasp together

**interloper**
08 intruder
10 trespasser
11 gatecrasher

**interlude**
04 halt, rest, stop, wait
05 break, letup, pause, spell
06 hiatus, recess
08 breather, interval, stoppage
12 intermission
13 breathing room
14 breathing space

**intermediary**
05 agent
06 broker
08 mediator
09 go-between, middleman
10 arbitrator

**intermediate**
03 mid

04 mean
06 medial, median, middle, midway
07 halfway
09 in-between
12 intermediary

**interment**
06 burial
07 burying, funeral
10 inhumation

**interminable**
04 dull, long
06 boring, prolix
07 endless, eternal, tedious
08 dragging
09 boundless, ceaseless, limitless, perpetual, unlimited, wearisome
10 long-winded, loquacious, monotonous, without end
11 everlasting, never-ending
12 long-drawn-out

**intermingle**
03 mix
04 fuse
05 blend, merge, mix up
06 commix
07 combine
08 intermix
09 commingle, interlace
10 amalgamate, interweave
11 mix together

**intermission**
04 halt, lull, rest, stop
05 break, letup, pause
06 recess
07 respite
08 breather, interval, stoppage
09 cessation, interlude, remission
10 suspension
12 interruption
13 breathing room
14 breathing space

**intermittent**
07 erratic
08 off and on, periodic, sporadic
09 irregular, spasmodic

**intern**
04 hold, jail
06 detain, doctor
07 confine, trainee
08 imprison
10 apprentice

**internal**
05 inner
06 inside, inward, mental
07 in-house, private
08 domestic, interior, intimate, personal

09 emotional, spiritual
10 subjective
13 psychological

**international**
06 global
07 general
09 universal, worldwide
12 cosmopolitan

**internecine**
05 civil, fatal
06 bloody, deadly, family, mortal
08 internal
09 murderous
13 exterminating

**interplay**
08 exchange
11 alternation, give-and-take, interaction, interchange
13 reciprocation, transposition

**interpolate**
03 add
05 put in
06 insert
09 interject, interpose

**interpolation**
06 insert
08 addition
09 insertion
12 interjection

**interpose**
05 put in
06 butt in, insert, step in
07 barge in, intrude, mediate
08 muscle in, thrust in
09 arbitrate, intercede, interject, intervene
11 come between, interpolate
14 poke your nose in

**interpret**
05 solve
06 decode, define, render
07 clarify, explain, expound
08 construe, decipher
09 elucidate, explicate, make clear, translate
10 paraphrase, understand
11 make sense of, shed light on
12 throw light on

**interpretation**
05 sense
07 anagoge, anagogy, meaning, opinion, reading, version
08 analysis, construe, decoding, exegesis
09 rendering
10 exposition, paraphrase
11 deciphering, elucidation, explanation, translation
13 clarification, understanding

**interpretative**
08 exegetic
10 exegetical, expository
11 explanatory, explicatory, hermeneutic
12 interpretive
13 hermeneutical

**interpreter**
07 exegete
08 exponent, linguist
09 annotator, expositor
10 elucidator, translator

**interrogate**
03 ask
04 pump, quiz
05 grill
07 debrief, examine
08 question
12 cross-examine
13 cross-question

**interrogation**
07 inquest, inquiry
08 grilling, quizzing
09 going-over
11 examination, inquisition, questioning, third degree

**interrogative**
07 curious, probing
09 inquiring, quizzical
11 inquisitive, questioning
12 catechetical
13 inquisitional, interrogatory

**interrupt**
05 block, break, cut in, delay
06 butt in, cancel, chip in, cut off, heckle, hold up
07 barge in, barrack, break in, disrupt, disturb, intrude, shout at, suspend
08 cut short, postpone
09 punctuate

**interruption**
04 halt, stop
05 break, delay, pause
06 outage, recess, remark
08 breather, interval
09 cessation, cutting-in, intrusion
10 disruption, suspension
11 disturbance, obstruction
12 interference, interjection, intermission
13 interpolation
14 discontinuance

**intersect**
05 cross
06 bisect, divide
09 cut across
10 crisscross

## intersection
08 crossing, junction
10 cloverleaf, crossroads
11 interchange

## intersperse
03 dot
06 pepper
07 scatter
08 intermix, sprinkle
09 interlard, interpose

## intertwine
05 twine, twirl, twist, weave
07 connect, entwine
10 interweave

## interval
04 lull, rest, time, wait
05 break, delay, pause
06 recess
07 interim
08 breather, meantime
09 interlude, meanwhile
12 intermission

## intervene
04 pass
05 arise, occur
06 befall, elapse, happen, step in
07 intrude, mediate
09 arbitrate, intercede, interfere, interrupt
10 come to pass

## intervening
07 between, mediate
11 interjacent, interposing

## intervention
09 intrusion, mediation
10 stepping-in
11 arbitration, involvement, negotiation
12 intercession, interference, interruption

## interview
03 vet
04 talk
06 assess, dialog, talk to
07 examine, meeting
08 audience, dialogue, evaluate, question, sound out
09 appraisal
10 assessment, conference, discussion, evaluation
11 interrogate
12 consultation, cross-examine
13 cross-question
15 oral examination, press conference

## interviewer
08 assessor, examiner, reporter
09 appraiser, evaluator

10 inquisitor, journalist, questioner
12 interlocutor, interrogator, investigator

## interweave
04 coil, knit
05 blend, braid, cross, twine, twist, weave
07 connect, entwine
10 crisscross, reticulate

## intestinal
05 ileac
06 celiac
07 enteric, gastric
08 duodenal, internal, visceral
09 abdominal, stomachic

## intestines
04 guts
05 colon, offal
06 bowels, vitals
07 innards, insides, viscera
08 entrails

## intimacy
04 love
06 warmth
07 privacy
09 affection, closeness, relations
10 confidence, friendship
11 familiarity
15 confidentiality

## intimate
04 cozy, dear, deep, hint, mate, near, tell, warm
05 bosom, buddy, close, imply, state, thick, tight
06 friend, impart, secret, signal
07 declare, in-depth, private, suggest
08 announce, detailed, familiar, friendly, indicate, informal, internal, personal, profound, thorough
09 associate, cherished, confidant, innermost, insinuate, make known
10 best friend, bosom buddy, confidante, exhaustive
11 close friend, communicate, penetrating
12 affectionate, blood brother, confidential, let it be known
14 thick as thieves

## intimately
05 fully
06 deeply, warmly
07 closely
08 in detail, tenderly
09 inside out, privately
10 familiarly, personally, thoroughly

11 confidingly
12 exhaustively
14 affectionately, confidentially

## intimation
06 notice, signal
07 inkling, warning
08 allusion, reminder
09 reference, statement
10 indication, suggestion
11 declaration
12 announcement
13 communication

## intimidate
03 cow
05 bully, daunt
06 extort, lean on, menace
07 overawe, terrify
08 browbeat, bulldoze, domineer, frighten, pressure, threaten
09 blackmail, terrorize, tyrannize

## intimidation
04 fear
07 threats
08 bullying
10 compulsion
11 arm-twisting, browbeating
13 terrorization, tyrannization

## intolerable
10 impossible, unbearable
11 unendurable
12 insufferable, unacceptable
13 insupportable

## intolerance
07 bigotry
09 dogmatism, prejudice
10 chauvinism, impatience, insularity
12 illiberality
14 discrimination

## intolerant
06 biased, narrow, racist
07 bigoted, insular
08 dogmatic, partisan
09 extremist, fanatical, illiberal, impatient, racialist
10 jingoistic, prejudiced, provincial, xenophobic
12 chauvinistic, narrow-minded, uncharitable

## intonation
04 lilt, tone
05 pitch
06 stress, timbre
07 cadence
08 emphasis
10 inflection, modulation

## intone
03 say

04 sing
05 chant, croon, speak, utter, voice
06 recite
07 declaim
09 enunciate, pronounce

**intoxicate**
06 excite, fuddle, thrill
07 inflame, inspire, stupefy
08 befuddle
09 inebriate, make drunk
10 exhilarate

**intoxicated**
05 drunk, happy, lit up, merry, moved, tight, tipsy, woozy
06 blotto, elated, loaded, soused, stewed, stoned, tiddly
07 bevvied, drunken, excited, legless, pickled, sloshed, smashed, sozzled, squiffy
08 bibulous
09 crapulent, paralytic, plastered, well oiled
10 blind drunk, inebriated, skunk drunk
11 exhilarated, have had a few
12 drunk as a lord, roaring drunk
13 drunk as a skunk, in high spirits, under the table

**intoxicating**
05 heady
07 rousing
08 stirring
09 alcoholic, inebriant, stimulant
11 enthralling
12 exhilarating
15 going to your head

**intoxication**
07 elation, rapture
08 euphoria, pleasure
09 inebriety, tipsiness
10 crapulence, excitement, insobriety
11 drunkenness, inebriation
12 bibulousness, exhilaration, intemperance
15 serious drinking

**intractability**
08 obduracy
09 obstinacy
12 stubbornness
13 pigheadedness

**intractable**
04 wild
06 unruly
07 awkward, wayward, willful
08 contrary, obdurate, perverse, stubborn

09 difficult, fractious, obstinate, pigheaded, unbending
10 headstrong, refractory, self-willed, unamenable, unyielding
11 disobedient
12 cantankerous, intransigent, ungovernable, unmanageable
13 uncooperative, undisciplined
14 uncontrollable

**intransigent**
08 hard-line, obdurate, stubborn
09 immovable, obstinate, tenacious, unbending
10 determined, implacable

**intrepid**
04 bold
05 brave, gutsy
06 daring, gritty, heroic, plucky, spunky
07 doughty, gallant, valiant
08 fearless, spirited, stalwart, valorous
09 audacious, dauntless, undaunted
10 courageous, undismayed
11 lionhearted, unflinching
12 stouthearted

**intrepidness**
04 guts
05 nerve, pluck, valor
06 daring, spirit
07 bravery, courage, heroism, prowess
08 audacity, boldness
09 fortitude, gallantry
11 doughtiness, intrepidity
12 fearlessness
13 dauntlessness, undauntedness
15 lionheartedness

**intricacy**
09 obscurity
10 complexity, knottiness
11 complexness, convolution, involvement
12 complication
13 elaborateness, intricateness

**intricate**
05 fancy
06 knotty, ornate, rococo
07 complex, tangled
08 baffling, involved, puzzling, tortuous
09 elaborate, enigmatic, entangled
10 convoluted, perplexing
11 complicated

**intrigue**
04 draw, plot, pull, ruse, wile
05 amour, cabal, dodge
06 puzzle, scheme
07 attract, connive, liaison, romance
08 artifice, conspire, maneuver, trickery
09 collusion, conniving, fascinate, machinate, stratagem
10 conspiracy, love affair
11 machination
13 double-dealing

**intriguer**
07 plotter, schemer, wangler
08 conniver
09 intrigant
10 intrigante, machinator, wirepuller
11 conspirator
12 collaborator
13 Machiavellian, wheeler-dealer

**intriguing**
08 puzzling, riveting
09 absorbing, appealing, beguiling, diverting
10 attractive, compelling
11 captivating, fascinating, interesting

**intrinsic**
06 inborn, inbred, native
07 built-in, central, genuine, natural
08 inherent, interior
09 elemental, essential
11 fundamental
14 constitutional

**introduce**
05 begin, found, offer, start
06 launch, lead in, submit
07 advance, bring in, develop, precede, preface, present, propose, suggest, usher in
08 acquaint, announce, commence, initiate, lead into, organize
09 establish, institute, originate
10 inaugurate, put forward
11 put in motion, set in motion

**introduction**
05 debut, intro, proem, start
06 launch, lead-in
07 opening, preface, prelude
08 exordium, foreword, overture, preamble, prologue
09 beginning
12 commencement, inauguration

13 establishment, preliminaries
15 first principles

**introductory**
05 basic, early, first
07 initial, opening
08 exordial, isagogic, starting
09 beginning, essential, inaugural, prefatory
10 elementary, initiatory, precursory
11 fundamental, preliminary, preparatory, rudimentary

**introspection**
08 brooding
11 navel-gazing, pensiveness
12 introversion, self-analysis
13 contemplation, soul-searching
14 heart-searching, thoughtfulness
15 self-examination

**introspective**
06 musing
07 pensive
08 brooding, reserved
09 withdrawn
10 meditative, thoughtful
11 introverted
12 self-absorbed
13 contemplative, inward looking

**introverted**
03 shy
05 quiet
08 reserved
09 withdrawn
12 self-absorbed
13 introspective, inward looking

**intrude**
06 butt in, chip in, meddle
07 barge in, obtrude, violate
08 encroach, infringe, trespass
09 gatecrash, interfere, interject, interlope, interrupt

**intruder**
06 raider, robber
07 burglar, prowler
10 interloper, trespasser
11 gate-crasher, infiltrator
12 housebreaker
14 unwelcome guest

**intrusion**
08 meddling, trespass
09 incursion, obtrusion, violation
12 encroachment, gate-crashing, infringement, interference, interruption

**intrusive**
04 nosy

05 pushy
08 invasive, snooping, unwanted
09 obtrusive, officious, uninvited, unwelcome
10 meddlesome
11 impertinent, importunate, interfering, trespassing
12 interrupting, presumptuous

**intuition**
05 hunch
07 feeling, insight
08 instinct
10 gut feeling, perception, sixth sense
12 presentiment

**intuitive**
06 inborn, innate
09 automatic
11 instinctive, intuitional

**inundate**
05 drown, flood, swamp
06 deluge, engulf
07 immerse
08 overflow, saturate, submerge

**inundation**
05 flood, spate, swamp
06 deluge, excess
07 surplus, torrent
08 overflow
09 tidal wave

**inure**
06 harden, temper
07 toughen
08 accustom
09 habituate
11 acclimatize, familiarize

**invade**
05 enter, seize, storm
06 attack, infest, maraud, occupy
07 assault, burst in, intrude, obtrude, overrun, pervade
08 encroach, infringe, take over, trespass
09 descend on, march into, penetrate, swarm over
10 infiltrate
12 enter by force

**invader**
08 attacker, intruder, marauder
09 aggressor, infringer
10 trespasser

**invalid**
03 ill
04 null, sick, void, weak
05 false, frail
06 ailing, feeble, infirm, poorly, sickly, unwell
07 patient, unsound

08 disabled, sufferer
09 bedridden, erroneous, illogical, incorrect, unfounded, untenable
10 fallacious, groundless, ill-founded, irrational
11 debilitated, inoperative, null and void, unjustified, unwarranted
12 convalescent, unacceptable

**invalidate**
04 void
05 annul
06 cancel, negate, revoke
07 nullify, rescind, vitiate

**invalidity**
07 fallacy, falsity, sophism
08 voidness
11 unsoundness
12 illogicality, speciousness
13 inconsistency, incorrectness, irrationality
14 fallaciousness

**invaluable**
08 precious, valuable
13 indispensable

**invariable**
03 set
05 fixed, rigid
06 stable, steady
07 regular, uniform
08 constant, habitual
09 immutable, permanent
10 changeless, consistent, inflexible, unchanging

**invariably**
06 always
09 regularly
10 constantly, habitually, inevitably, repeatedly
11 unfailingly, without fail
12 consistently

**invasion**
06 attack, breach
09 incursion, intrusion, offensive, onslaught, violation
10 occupation
11 penetration
12 encroachment, infiltration, infringement, interference, interruption

**invective**
05 abuse
06 tirade
07 censure, obloquy, sarcasm
08 berating, diatribe, scolding
09 contumely, philippic, reprimand
11 castigation, fulmination

12 denunciation, vilification,
vituperation
13 recrimination, tongue-
lashing

**inveigh**
04 rail
05 blame, scold
06 berate
07 censure, condemn, upbraid
08 denounce, lambaste,
reproach, sound off
09 castigate, criticize, fulminate
10 tongue-lash, vituperate

**inveigle**
03 con
04 coax, lure, wile
06 cajole, entice, lead on,
seduce
07 beguile, wheedle
08 maneuver, persuade
09 sweet-talk
10 manipulate

**invent**
04 coin
06 cook up, create, design,
devise, make up
07 concoct, dream up, hit upon,
imagine, pioneer, think up,
trump up
08 conceive, contrive, discover,
innovate
09 fabricate, formulate,
improvise, originate
10 come up with

**invention**
03 fib, lie
04 fake, myth
06 deceit, design, device,
gadget, genius
07 fantasy, fiction, figment,
forgery, machine, untruth
08 artistry, creation
09 discovery, falsehood,
ingenuity, tall story
10 brainchild, concoction,
contriving, creativity,
innovation
11 contrivance, development,
fabrication, imagination,
inspiration, originality
12 construction
13 falsification, inventiveness

**inventive**
07 fertile, skilful
08 artistic, creative, original,
skillful
09 ingenious
10 innovative
11 imaginative, resourceful

**inventor**
05 maker

07 creator, deviser
08 designer, producer
09 architect, innovator
10 discoverer, originator

---

► *Names of inventors*:
04 **Bell** (Alexander Graham),
**Benz** (Karl), **Biro** (Laszlo),
**Colt** (Samuel), **Land**
(Edwin), **Otis** (Elisha
Graves), **Swan** (Joseph
Wilson), **Watt** (James)
05 **Baird** (John Logie), **Hertz**
(Heinrich), **Mason** (John),
**Maxim** (Hiram Stevens),
**Morse** (Samuel), **Nobel**
(Alfred), **Sousa** (John
Philip), **Tesla** (Nikola), **Volta**
(Alessandro), **Zeiss** (Carl)
06 **Ampère** (André Marie),
**Brunel** (Isambard
Kingdom), **Bunsen** (Robert
Wilhelm), **Diesel** (Rudolf),
**du Pont** (Eleuthere), **Dunlop**
(John), **Eckert** (John
Presper), **Edison** (Thomas
Alva), **Fulton** (Robert),
**McAdam** (John Loudon),
**Newton** (Isaac), **Pascal**
(Blaise), **Pitman** (Isaac),
**Schick** (Jacob), **Sperry**
(Elmer), **Talbot** (William
Henry Fox), **Wright**
(Orville), **Wright** (Wilbur)
07 **Babbage** (Charles),
**Daimler** (Gottlieb),
**Eastman** (George), **Faraday**
(Michael), **Gatling**
(Richard), **Gillett** (King
Camp), **Goddard** (Robert),
**Huygens** (Christiaan),
**Lumière** (Auguste),
**Marconi** (Guglielmo),
**Pasteur** (Louis), **Pullman**
(George), **Whitney** (Eli),
**Whittle** (Frank)
08 **Bessemer** (Henry),
**Birdseye** (Clarence),
**Browning** (John), **Chrysler**
(Walter), **Daguerre** (Louis
Jacques Mandé), **De Forest**
(Lee), **Ericsson** (John),
**Ferranti** (Sebastian Ziani
de), **Franklin** (Benjamin),
**Goodyear** (Charles),
**Sandwich** (John Montagu),
**Sikorsky** (Igor), **Sinclair**
(Clive), **Zamenhof** (Ludwik
Lejzer), **Zeppelin**
(Ferdinand)
09 **Ctesibius**, **Gutenberg**
(Johannes), **Hollerith**
(Herman), **McCormick**

(Cyrus Hall)
10 **Archimedes**, **Fahrenheit**
(Gabriel), **Torricelli**
(Evangelista)
11 **Montgolfier** (Joseph
Michel)
➤ See also SCIENTIST

**inventory**
04 list, roll
05 stock, tally
06 record, roster, supply
07 account, catalog, listing
08 register, schedule
09 catalogue, checklist
11 description

**inverse**
05 other
07 counter
08 contrary, opposite
10 transposed, upside down

**inversion**
08 contrary, opposite
10 antithesis, transposal
13 transposition
14 contraposition

**invert**
06 upturn
07 capsize
08 overturn
09 transpose
10 turn turtle
14 turn upside down

**invertebrate**

► *Types of invertebrate*:
05 coral, fluke, hydra, leech
06 insect, spider, sponge
07 annelid, bivalve, crinoid,
mollusk
08 arachnid, flatworm,
nematode, starfish,
tapeworm
09 arthropod, centipede,
earthworm, gastropod,
jellyfish, millipede,
roundworm, sea urchin,
trematode, trilobite
10 cephalopod, crustacean,
echinoderm, sand dollar, sea
anemone
11 sea cucumber
13 horseshoe crab
➤ See also ANIMAL;
BUTTERFLY; CRUSTACEAN;
INSECT; MOLLUSK; MOTH;
WORM

**invest**
04 fund, give, sink, vest
05 endow, grant, put in, spend
06 bestow, confer, devote, instal,
lay out, ordain

**investigate**
07 empower, entrust, install, provide
10 contribute, inaugurate

**investigate**
05 probe, study
06 go into, search
07 analyze, examine, explore, inspect
08 check out, consider, look into, research
09 delve into
10 scrutinize
11 inquire into
15 give the once-over

**investigation**
05 probe, study
06 review, search, survey
07 hearing, inquest, inquiry
08 analysis, research, scrutiny
10 inspection
11 examination, exploration

**investigative**
10 analytical, inspecting
11 exploratory, fact-finding, researching
13 investigating

**investigator**
06 prober, sleuth
07 analyst
08 analyzer, examiner, explorer, inquirer, reviewer, searcher
09 detective, inspector
10 private eye, questioner, researcher, scrutineer
11 scrutinizer

**investiture**
09 admission, induction
10 coronation, ordination
11 instatement
12 enthronement, inauguration, installation

**investment**
05 stake, stock
06 outlay
07 capital, finance, venture
11 expenditure, speculation
12 contribution

**inveterate**
07 chronic, diehard
08 hard-core, hardened
09 confirmed, incurable
10 entrenched
12 incorrigible, long-standing
13 dyed-in-the-wool

**invidious**
09 difficult, obnoxious, offensive, repugnant
13 objectionable
14 discriminating, discriminatory

**invigorate**
05 brace, pep up, rouse
06 buck up, perk up
07 animate, enliven, fortify, freshen, inspire, liven up, quicken, refresh
08 energize, motivate, vitalize
10 exhilarate, rejuvenate, revitalize, strengthen

**invigorating**
05 fresh, tonic
07 bracing
09 animating, healthful, uplifting, vivifying
10 energizing, refreshing, salubrious
11 restorative, stimulating
12 exhilarating, rejuvenating

**invincible**
10 unbeatable
11 indomitable, insuperable
12 impenetrable, invulnerable, unassailable, undefeatable
13 unconquerable

**inviolability**
08 sanctity
10 sacredness
14 sacrosanctness
15 invulnerability

**inviolable**
04 holy
06 sacred
08 hallowed
10 intemerate, sacrosanct
11 inalienable, unalterable, untouchable

**inviolate**
04 pure
05 whole
06 entire, intact, sacred, unhurt, virgin
08 complete, unbroken, unharmed
09 stainless, undamaged, undefiled, uninjured, unspoiled, unstained, unsullied, untouched
10 intemerate, unpolluted, unprofaned

**invisible**
06 hidden, unseen
09 concealed, imaginary
10 out of sight, unobserved
11 microscopic, nonexistent
12 undetectable
13 indiscernible, infinitesimal

**invitation**
04 bait, call, draw, lure
06 appeal, come-on
07 bidding, request, summons
08 overture, petition
09 challenge
10 allurement, attraction, enticement, incitement, inducement, temptation
11 provocation
12 solicitation
13 encouragement

**invite**
03 ask, bid
04 call, draw, lead, seek
05 tempt
06 allure, appeal, ask for, entice, summon
07 attract, bring on, look for, provoke, request, solicit, welcome
08 petition
09 encourage, entertain

**inviting**
08 alluring, enticing, tempting
09 appealing, beguiling, seductive, welcoming
10 attractive, bewitching, enchanting
11 fascinating

**invocation**
06 appeal, prayer
07 request
08 entreaty, petition
09 epiclesis
10 beseeching
11 conjuration, imploration
12 solicitation, supplication

**invoice**
04 bill
07 account, charges
09 reckoning

**invoke**
03 beg
04 pray
07 beseech, conjure, entreat, implore, request, solicit
08 appeal to, call upon, petition, resort to
09 imprecate
10 supplicate

**involuntary**
06 forced, reflex
07 coerced
09 automatic, compelled, unwilling
10 mechanical, unthinking
11 conditioned, instinctive, spontaneous, unconscious
13 unintentional

**involve**
04 mean
05 cover, imply, mix up

**involved**
06 absorb, affect, denote, draw in, engage, entail, occupy, take in
07 concern, embrace, embroil, engross, include, require
08 entangle, interest
09 associate, encompass, implicate
11 incorporate, necessitate

**involved**
06 knotty
07 complex, jumbled, mixed up, tangled
08 caught up, tortuous
09 concerned, confusing, difficult, elaborate
10 associated, convoluted, implicated, taking part
11 complicated
13 participating

**involvement**
04 part
05 share
07 concern
08 interest
10 connection
11 association, implication
12 entanglement
13 participation

**invulnerability**
13 invincibility, inviolability
14 impregnability
15 impenetrability, unassailability

**invulnerable**
06 secure
10 invincible
12 impenetrable, unassailable
14 indestructible

**inward**
05 inner
06 inmost, inside
08 entering, incoming, interior, internal
09 innermost

**inwardly**
06 inside, within
07 at heart
08 deep down, secretly
09 privately

**iota**
03 bit, jot, tad
04 atom, hint, mite, whit
05 grain, scrap, speck, trace
06 morsel
08 fraction, particle

**irascibility**
09 bad temper, crossness, petulance, shortness, testiness

10 crabbiness, impatience, irritation, touchiness
12 irritability, snappishness

**irascible**
05 cross, testy
06 crabby
07 crabbed, prickly
08 choleric
09 irritable
10 ill-natured
11 bad tempered, ill-tempered
12 cantankerous
13 quick-tempered, short-tempered

**irate**
03 mad
05 angry, livid, vexed
06 fuming, raging
07 annoyed, enraged, furious
08 incensed, up in arms, worked up
09 indignant, irritated
10 infuriated

**ire**
04 fury, rage
05 anger, wrath
06 choler
07 passion
09 annoyance
11 displeasure, indignation

**iridescent**
04 shot
07 rainbow
09 prismatic, sparkling
10 glittering, shimmering, variegated
11 rainbowlike

**irk**
03 bug, get, vex
04 gall, miff, rile
05 anger, annoy, get to, peeve
06 hassle, nettle, put out, ruffle
07 disgust, incense, provoke
08 distress, irritate
09 aggravate, infuriate
10 exasperate

**irksome**
06 boring, trying, vexing
08 annoying, tiresome
09 vexatious
10 bothersome, burdensome, irritating
11 aggravating, infuriating, troublesome
12 disagreeable, exasperating

**iron**
04 firm, hard
05 press, rigid, tough
06 smooth, steely, strong
07 adamant, flatten

10 determined, inflexible

◻**iron out**
06 settle
07 clear up, resolve, sort out
08 deal with, get rid of, put right
09 eliminate, eradicate, harmonize, reconcile
13 straighten out

**ironic**
03 wry
07 mocking
08 derisive, ironical, sardonic, scoffing, scornful, sneering
09 sarcastic, satirical
11 paradoxical

**irons**
05 bonds
06 chains
07 fetters
08 manacles, shackles

**irony**
05 scorn
06 satire
07 mockery, paradox, sarcasm

**irradiate**
06 illume
07 light up, lighten, shine on
08 brighten, illumine
10 illuminate

**irrational**
06 absurd, unwise
07 foolish, invalid, unsound
09 arbitrary, illogical, senseless
10 groundless, ridiculous
11 implausible, nonsensical
12 inconsistent, unreasonable

**irrationality**
08 unreason
09 absurdity
12 illogicality
13 senselessness
14 groundlessness, ridiculousness

**irreconcilable**
06 at odds
08 clashing, contrary, opposite
11 conflicting, incongruous
12 incompatible, inconsistent
13 contradictory

**irrecoverable**
04 lost
09 incurable
11 irreparable
12 irredeemable, irremediable
13 irreclaimable, irretrievable, unsalvageable

**irrefutable**
04 sure
07 certain

## irregular

08 decisive, definite, positive
10 undeniable
11 beyond doubt, indubitable
12 indisputable, unanswerable
13 incontestable
14 beyond question, unquestionable

## irregular

03 odd
05 bumpy, false, lumpy, rough
06 fitful, jagged, pitted, ragged, random, uneven
07 crooked, erratic, lawless, strange, unusual
08 aberrant, abnormal, improper, lopsided, peculiar, sporadic, variable, wavering
09 anomalous, haphazard, spasmodic
10 asymmetric, disorderly, fraudulent, immoderate, occasional, out of order, unofficial, unorthodox
11 exceptional, fluctuating
12 disorganized, inconsistent, intermittent, unmethodical, unprincipled, unsystematic
13 extraordinary
14 unconventional

## irregularity

06 oddity
07 anomaly
08 cheating
09 asymmetry, deviation, roughness
10 aberration, dishonesty, randomness, unevenness
11 abnormality, fluctuation, inconstancy, malpractice, peculiarity, singularity, uncertainty, unorthodoxy, variability
12 eccentricity, lopsidedness
13 haphazardness, inconsistency, unpunctuality
14 disorderliness

## irregularly

08 fitfully, off and on, unevenly
11 erratically, haphazardly, now and again
12 occasionally
13 spasmodically
14 intermittently
15 by fits and starts, in fits and starts

## irrelevance

09 inaptness
10 red herring
12 unimportance
13 inconsequence, unrelatedness

14 inappositeness

## irrelevant

05 inapt
09 unrelated
10 immaterial, inapposite, out of place
12 inapplicable, inconsequent
13 inappropriate
14 beside the point
15 having no bearing

## irreligious

05 pagan
06 sinful, unholy, wicked
07 godless, heathen, impious, profane, ungodly
08 agnostic
09 atheistic, heretical
11 unbelieving, unrighteous

## irremediable

08 hopeless
09 incurable
11 irreparable
12 irreversible
13 irretrievable

## irremovable

03 set
05 fixed, stuck
06 rooted
08 obdurate
09 immovable, ingrained, obstinate, permanent

## irreparable

09 incurable
12 irreversible
13 irretrievable

## irreplaceable

08 peerless, precious
09 essential, matchless, priceless, unmatched
13 indispensable

## irrepressible

06 bubbly
07 buoyant
08 animated
09 ebullient, resilient, vivacious
10 boisterous
11 unstoppable

## irreproachable

07 perfect, sinless
08 flawless, spotless
09 blameless, faultless, guiltless
10 immaculate, impeccable
11 unblemished
13 unimpeachable
14 beyond reproach

## irresistible

06 potent, urgent
08 alluring, charming, enticing, forceful, pressing, tempting

09 ravishing, seductive
10 compelling, enchanting, imperative
11 captivating, fascinating, inescapable, tantalizing, unavoidable
12 overpowering, overwhelming
13 irrepressible, unpreventable
14 uncontrollable

## irresolute

06 fickle, unsure
08 doubtful, hesitant, shifting, unstable, unsteady, variable, wavering
09 dithering, tentative, uncertain, undecided, unsettled
10 ambivalent, hesitating, indecisive, of two minds, on the fence
11 fluctuating, halfhearted, vacillating
12 fainthearted, pussyfooting, undetermined
15 shilly-shallying

## irrespective

◻ **irrespective of**
07 however, whoever
08 ignoring, no matter, whatever
09 never mind, whichever
12 disregarding, not affecting, regardless of
15 notwithstanding

## irresponsible

04 rash, wild
06 unwise
07 erratic, flighty
08 carefree, careless, heedless, reckless
09 negligent
11 injudicious, thoughtless
13 ill-considered, untrustworthy

## irretrievable

04 lost
08 hopeless
11 irreparable, irrevocable
12 irredeemable, unrecallable
13 irrecoverable, unsalvageable

## irreverence

05 cheek, sauce
06 heresy, levity
07 impiety, mockery
08 rudeness
09 blasphemy, flippancy, impudence, insolence, profanity, sacrilege
10 cheekiness, disrespect, irreligion

**irreverent**
11 discourtesy, godlessness, ungodliness
12 impertinence, impoliteness

**irreverent**
04 rude
05 saucy
06 cheeky
07 godless, impious, mocking, profane, ungodly
08 flippant, impolite, impudent, insolent
09 heretical
11 blasphemous, impertinent, irreligious
12 discourteous, sacrilegious
13 disrespectful

**irreversible**
05 final
09 incurable, permanent
11 irreparable, irrevocable, unalterable
12 irremediable
13 irretrievable, unrectifiable

**irrevocable**
05 final, fixed
07 settled
09 immutable
11 unalterable
12 irreversible, unchangeable

**irrigate**
03 wet
04 soak
05 flood, spray, water
07 moisten
08 sprinkle

**irritability**
09 bad temper, crossness, ill-temper, petulance, testiness
10 grumpiness, tetchiness
11 peevishness, prickliness
12 irascibility

**irritable**
05 cross, ratty, short, testy
06 crabby, crusty, grumpy, snappy, touchy
07 peevish, prickly
08 snappish
09 crotchety, irascible
11 bad tempered
12 cantankerous
13 quick-tempered, short-tempered

**irritant**
04 goad, pain
06 bother, menace
07 trouble
08 nuisance, vexation
09 annoyance
11 provocation
15 thorn in the flesh

**irritate**
03 bug, get, irk, jar, rub, vex
04 fret, goad, hurt, itch, rile
05 anger, annoy, chafe, grate, peeve, rouse
06 enrage, harass, nettle
07 incense, inflame, provoke
09 aggravate, drive nuts, infuriate
10 drive crazy, exasperate
13 get your back up
14 drive up the wall
15 get on your nerves

**irritated**
04 edgy
05 angry, cross, irate, irked, riled, vexed
06 miffed, peeved, piqued, put out
07 annoyed, nettled, ruffled
10 displeased
11 discomposed, exasperated

**irritating**
04 sore
05 itchy, pesky
06 thorny, trying, vexing
07 chafing, galling, irksome
08 abrasive, annoying, tiresome
09 maddening, provoking
10 bothersome, disturbing
11 aggravating, displeasing, infuriating, troublesome

**irritation**
04 bind, drag, fury, pain, pest
05 anger, pique
08 nuisance, vexation
09 annoyance, crossness, testiness
10 impatience, snappiness
11 aggravation, displeasure, provocation
12 exasperation, irritability
13 pain in the neck
15 dissatisfaction, thorn in the flesh

**island**
03 cay, key
04 isle
05 atoll, islet
11 archipelago

► *Names of islands and island groups. We have omitted the words* **island** *and* **islands** *from names given in the following list but you may need to include one of these words as part of the solution to some crossword clues.*

03 Cat, Cos, Fyn, Ios, Rab, Rum, Sea
04 Bali, Coll, Cook, Cuba, Eigg,
Elba, Fiji, Ford, Gozo, Guam, Holy, Iona, Java, Jura, Line, Long, Mahe, Maui, Mona, Muck, Mull, Oahu, Sark, Skye, Wake
05 Arran, Barra, Block, Capri, Chios, Cocos, Coney, Corfu, Crete, Ellis, Faroe, Ibiza, Islay, Kauai, Kuril, Lanai, Lundy, Luzon, Malta, Melos, Nauru, Naxos, North, Padre, Palau, Paros, Samoa, Samos, South, Sunda, Timor, Tiree, Tonga
06 Aegean, Andros, Azores, Baffin, Bikini, Borneo, Caicos, Canary, Chagos, Comino, Cyprus, Devil's, Easter, Euboea, Flores, Hainan, Harris, Hawaii, Honshu, Icaria, Ionian, Jersey, Kodiak, Komodo, Kyushu, Lemnos, Lesbos, Midway, Niihau, Orkney, Patmos, Rhodes, Sicily, Skiros, Staffa, Staten, Tahiti, Taiwan, Tobago, Tuvalu, Virgin
07 Bahamas, Bahrain, Bermuda, Celebes, Channel, Comoros, Corsica, Curaçao, Dauphin, Fishers, Frisian, Gilbert, Gotland, Grenada, Iceland, Ireland, Iwo Jima, Jamaica, Key West, Leeward, Madeira, Majorca, Menorca, Mikonos, Mindoro, Minorca, Molokai, Nicobar, Norfolk, Okinawa, Phoenix, Praslin, Rathlin, Réunion, Society, Solomon, St. Kilda, St. Lucia, Stewart, Sumatra, Surtsey, Vanuatu, Zealand
08 Aleutian, Anglesey, Anguilla, Balearic, Coral Sea, Cyclades, Dominica, Falkland, Guernsey, Hawaiian, Hebrides, Hokkaido, Hong Kong, Key Largo, Kiribati, Maldives, Marshall, Mindanao, Moluccas, Pitcairn, Sakhalin, Sandwich, Sardinia, Shetland, Sri Lanka, Sulawesi, Tenerife, Trinidad, Victoria, Windward, Zanzibar
09 Admiralty, Aquidneck, Ascension, Australia, Benbecula, Cape Verde, Christmas, Ellesmere, Galápagos, Greenland, Indonesia, Irian Jaya, Isle of Man, Kahoolawe, Lanzarote, Las Palmas, Manhattan, Marquesas, Mauritius, Melanesia, Nantucket, New

Guinea, North Uist, Santa Cruz, Santa Rosa, Santorini, Singapore, South Seas, South Uist, Stromboli, Vancouver
10 Assateague, Basse-Terre, Cephalonia, Cook Strait, Dodecanese, Heligoland, Hilton Head, Hispaniola, Kalimantan, Madagascar, Martinique, Micronesia, Montserrat, New Britain, New Ireland, Puerto Rico, Samothrace, Seychelles, West Indies
11 Gran Canaria, Grand Bahama, Grand Cayman, Guadalcanal, Isle of Wight, Saint Helena, San Clemente, Scilly Isles, South Orkney
12 Bougainville, Grande Comore, Newfoundland, Prince Edward, Prince Rupert, South Georgia
13 American Samoa, British Virgin, Inner Hebrides, Isles of Scilly, Outer Hebrides, Santa Catalina, South Shetland
14 Papua New Guinea, Tierra del Fuego, Tristan da Cunha, Turks and Caicos
15 French Polynesia, Martha's Vineyard, Wallis and Futuna

**isolate**
06 cut off, detach, maroon, remove, strand
07 exclude, seclude, shut out
08 alienate, cloister, insulate, separate, set apart, shut away
09 keep apart, ostracize, segregate, sequester
10 disconnect, quarantine
12 cold-shoulder

**isolated**
05 alone, apart
06 cut off, lonely, remote, unique
08 abnormal, atypical, deserted, detached, outlying, secluded, solitary, uncommon
09 anomalous, separated, unrelated, untypical

10 cloistered, segregated
11 exceptional, God-forsaken, out-of-the-way

**isolation**
05 exile
08 solitude
09 aloneness, seclusion
10 alienation, detachment, insulation, loneliness, quarantine, remoteness, separation
11 abstraction, segregation
12 dissociation, separateness, solitariness
13 disconnection, sequestration

**issue**
04 copy, emit, flow, gush, ooze, rise, rush, seed, seep, stem
05 arise, exude, heirs, point, spurt, topic, young
06 affair, debate, effect, emerge, family, finale, matter, number, put out, result, scions, spring, supply
07 come out, concern, deal out, deliver, dispute, edition, emanate, give out, outcome, outflow, problem, proceed, produce, progeny, publish, release, subject, version
08 announce, argument, children, delivery, effusion, printing, proclaim
09 broadcast, circulate, discharge, effluence, offspring, originate
10 burst forth, conclusion, distribute, impression, instalment, promulgate, successors
11 circulation, controversy, descendants, disseminate, installment, publication
12 announcement, distribution, promulgation
13 dissemination

☐**at issue**
10 in question
15 under discussion

☐**take issue**
05 argue, fight
06 object

07 contest, dispute, protest, quarrel
09 challenge
13 take exception

**itch**
04 ache, burn, long, pine
05 crave, crawl, yearn
06 desire, hanker, hunger, thirst, tickle, tingle
07 craving, longing, prickle
08 irritate, keenness, pruritis, tingling, yearning
09 eagerness, hankering, prickling
10 irritation

**itching**
05 dying, eager
06 aching, greedy, raring
07 burning, longing
09 hankering, impatient

**item**
05 entry, piece, point, story, thing
06 detail, factor, object
07 account, article, element, feature
09 component, news piece
10 ingredient, particular
13 consideration

**itemize**
04 list
05 count
06 detail, number, record
08 instance, tabulate
09 enumerate
13 particularize
15 make an inventory

**itinerant**
06 roving
07 nomadic, roaming, vagrant
08 drifting, rambling, vagabond
09 traveling, wandering, wayfaring
10 journeying
11 peripatetic

**itinerary**
04 plan, tour
05 route
06 course
07 circuit, journey

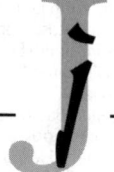

**jab**
04 poke, prod, push, stab
05 elbow, lunge, nudge, punch

**jabber**
03 gab, jaw, yap
06 babble, gabble, mumble,
   ramble, rattle
07 blather, blether, chatter,
   prattle

**jack**

❑ **jack up**
04 hike, lift
05 hoist, raise
07 elevate, inflate
08 increase

**jacket**
04 case, coat, skin, wrap
05 cover, shell
06 casing, folder, jerkin, sheath
07 wrapper
08 covering, wrapping

**jackpot**
07 bonanza
08 top prize, windfall
09 pot of gold
10 first prize

**jaded**
05 bored, fed up, spent, tired,
   weary
06 bushed, done in, dulled
07 wearied, worn out
08 fatigued, tired out
09 exhausted, played out

**jag**
04 barb, snag, spur
05 notch, point, tooth
10 projection, protrusion

**jagged**
06 barbed, broken, ragged,
   snaggy, spiked, uneven
07 notched, toothed
08 indented, saw edged,
   serrated
09 irregular

**jail**
03 can, jug, pen
04 poky, stir
05 clink, pokey
06 cooler, lock up, prison, send
   up
07 confine, put away, slammer
08 big house, imprison
09 calaboose
11 incarcerate, reformatory
12 penitentiary, send to prison
14 send up the river

**jailer**
05 guard, screw
06 keeper, warden
13 prison officer

**jam**
03 fix, mob, ram
04 bind, clog, cram, herd, hole,
   pack, push, spot
05 block, close, crowd, crush,
   force, horde, jelly, press,
   stick, stuff, wedge
06 holdup, pickle, plight,
   scrape, spread, squash,
   throng, thrust
07 confine, congest, squeeze,
   straits, the soup, trouble
08 conserve, gridlock, obstruct,
   preserve, quandary
09 confiture, marmalade,
   multitude, tight spot
10 bottleneck, congestion
11 obstruction, predicament

**jamboree**
04 fête
05 party, rally, spree
06 frolic
07 revelry, shindig
08 carnival, festival, field day
09 festivity, gathering
10 convention
11 celebration, get-together

**jangle**
03 din, jar
05 clang, clank, clash, clink
06 bother, jingle, racket, rattle
07 clangor, clatter, discord,
   jarring
08 irritate
09 cacophony
10 dissonance
13 reverberation

**janitor**
05 super
06 porter
07 doorman
09 caretaker, concierge,
   custodian
14 superintendent

**jar**
03 irk, jug
04 jerk, jolt
05 annoy, clash, grate, shake,
   upset
06 bicker, jangle, nettle, offend,
   rattle
07 agitate, disturb, quarrel,
   trouble, vibrate
08 be at odds, disagree, irritate
09 container
12 be at variance, be in conflict

**jargon**
04 cant
05 argot, idiom, slang, usage
08 legalese, parlance
09 buzzwords, gibberish
10 journalese, mumbo jumbo
11 computerese
12 gobbledygook,
   psychobabble
13 computerspeak

**jarring**
05 harsh
07 grating, jolting, rasping
08 jangling, strident
10 discordant, irritating
11 cacophonous

**jaundiced**
05 jaded
06 biased, bitter
07 bigoted, cynical, hostile,
   icterus
09 resentful, skeptical
10 prejudiced, suspicious
11 distrustful, pessimistic
12 misanthropic
14 unenthusiastic

**jaunt**
04 ride, spin, tour, trip
05 drive
06 junket, outing, ramble, stroll
09 excursion

**jaunty**
04 airy, trim
05 perky, showy, smart
06 bouncy, breezy, dapper,
   lively
07 buoyant, stylish
08 carefree, debonair
09 energetic, sprightly

13 self-confident

**jaw**
03 yak
04 chat, talk, trap
05 chops, mouth
06 babble, confab, gabble, gossip, jabber, muzzle
07 chatter, chin-wag, jawbone, maxilla
08 mandible
10 discussion
12 conversation

**jazz**

➤ *Types of jazz*:
03 bop, hot, rag
04 jive
05 bebop, swing
06 boogie, modern
07 big band, Chicago, ragtime
08 free jazz
09 Dixieland, West Coast
10 avant-garde, Kansas City, mainstream, New Orleans
11 traditional
12 boogie-woogie, Memphis blues
13 straight-ahead
➢ See also MUSIC

❏**jazz up**
07 enliven, liven up
09 smarten up

**jazzy**
05 fancy, gaudy, smart
06 flashy, lively, snazzy
08 spirited, swinging

**jealous**
05 green
07 careful, envious, mindful
08 covetous, desirous, grudging, vigilant, watchful
09 green-eyed, resentful
10 begrudging, possessive, protective, suspicious

**jealousy**
04 envy
05 spite
06 grudge
09 suspicion, vigilance
10 bitterness, resentment
11 carefulness, mindfulness
12 covetousness
14 possessiveness, protectiveness

**jeer**
03 boo
04 gibe, hiss, hoot, mock, razz
05 abuse, chaff, knock, scoff, scorn, sneer, taunt, tease
06 banter, deride, heckle

07 barrack, catcall, mockery
08 derision, ridicule
09 make fun of, shout down

**jejune**
04 arid, dull
05 banal, naïve, silly, vapid
06 barren, callow, meager
07 insipid, prosaic, puerile
08 childish, immature, juvenile
09 colorless
10 spiritless
15 unsophisticated

**jell**
03 set
04 form
07 congeal, thicken
08 take form
11 crystallize

**jeopardize**
04 risk
05 stake
06 gamble, hazard
07 imperil
08 endanger, threaten
09 put at risk
11 take a chance
14 expose to danger

**jeopardy**
04 risk
05 peril
06 danger, hazard, threat
09 liability
12 endangerment
13 vulnerability
14 precariousness

**jerk**
03 jar, jog, tug
04 clod, dope, fool, geek, jolt, nerd, pull, yank
05 idiot, lurch, ninny, twerp
06 twitch, wrench

**jerky**
05 bumpy, jumpy, rough, shaky
06 bouncy, fitful
07 jolting, shaking, twitchy
08 lurching
09 spasmodic
10 convulsive, incoherent
12 disconnected, uncontrolled
13 uncoordinated

**jerry-built**
06 faulty, flimsy, shoddy
07 rickety
08 slipshod, unstable
09 cheapjack, defective
10 ramshackle
11 jerry-rigged, poorly built
14 thrown together

**jersey**
03 cow, top

05 cloth, shirt
06 jumper, woolly
07 sweater
08 pullover

**jest**
03 gag, kid
04 fool, hoax, joke, mock, quip
05 crack, prank, tease, trick
06 banter
07 fooling, kidding, leg-pull
09 tell jokes, wisecrack, witticism

❏**in jest**
05 in fun
07 as a joke, to tease
08 jokingly

**jester**
03 wag, wit
04 fool
05 clown, comic, droll, joker
06 mummer
07 buffoon, juggler
08 comedian, humorist, quipster
09 prankster
10 comedienne
11 merry-andrew

**jet**
03 fly
04 flow, gush, inky, rush, zoom
05 black, ebony, raven, sable, shoot, spout, spray, spurt
06 spring, squirt, stream
08 airplane, fountain
09 sprinkler
10 pitch-black

**jettison**
04 dump
05 chuck, ditch, eject, expel, heave, scrap
06 unload
07 abandon, discard, offload
08 get rid of
09 throw away

**jetty**
04 dock, mole, pier, quay
05 wharf
06 harbor

**jewel**
03 gem
04 rock
05 pearl, prize
07 jewelry
08 gemstone, ornament, sparkler, treasure
09 showpiece
11 masterpiece, pride and joy
13 precious stone

**jewelry**
03 ice

04 gems
06 bijoux, jewels
07 regalia
08 treasure, trinkets
09 ornaments
10 bijouterie

► *Types of jewelry*:
04 ring, stud
05 beads, cameo, chain, tiara
06 amulet, anklet, bangle, brooch, choker, diadem, hatpin, locket, tiepin
07 coronet, earring, pendant
08 bracelet, cuff link, necklace, stickpin
10 signet ring
13 charm bracelet

**Jewish calendar**

► *Months in the Jewish calendar*:
02 Av
04 Adar, Elul, Iyar
05 Iyyar, Nisan, Sivan, Tevet
06 Kislev, Shevat, Tammuz, Tishri
07 Heshvan
09 Adar Sheni

**Jezebel**
04 jade, tart, vamp
05 hussy, whore, witch
06 harlot, wanton
10 loose woman, seductress
11 femme fatale
12 scarlet woman

**jib**
04 balk, sail
05 baulk, stall
06 recoil, refuse, shrink
09 stop short

**jiffy**
03 sec
05 flash, trice
06 minute, moment, second
07 instant
09 twinkling
11 split second

**jig**
03 bob, hop
04 jerk, jump, leap, skip
05 caper, dance, shake
06 bounce, prance, twitch, wiggle, wobble

**jigger**
05 glass
06 gadget
07 chigger
12 whiskey glass

**jiggle**
03 jog
04 jerk, jump

05 shake
06 bounce, fidget, twitch, waggle, wiggle, wobble
07 agitate

**jilt**
05 chuck, ditch, leave, spurn
06 betray, desert, pack in, reject
07 abandon, discard
09 cast aside, throw over

**jingle**
04 ding, poem, ring, song, tune
05 chime, chink, clang, clink, ditty, rhyme, verse
06 chorus, jangle, melody, rattle, tinkle
07 clatter, refrain, ringing
14 tintinnabulate

**jingoism**
10 chauvinism, flag-waving, insularity, militarism, patriotism
11 imperialism, nationalism

**jinx**
03 hex
05 charm, curse, spell
06 hoodoo, voodoo
07 bad luck, bedevil, bewitch, evil eye, gremlin
10 affliction, black magic
12 cast a spell on

**jitters**
06 nerves
07 anxiety, fidgets, jim-jams
09 agitation, the creeps, the shakes, trembling
10 the shivers, the willies
11 nervousness
13 heebie-jeebies

**jittery**
04 edgy
05 jumpy, shaky
07 anxious, fidgety, nervous, panicky, quaking, shivery
08 agitated
09 flustered, perturbed, quivering, trembling

**job**
04 duty, part, post, role, task, work
05 chore, crime, share, stint, trade
06 affair, career, charge, errand, métier, office
07 calling, mission, problem, project, pursuit, venture
08 activity, business, capacity, function, position, province, vocation

10 assignment, employment, line of work, livelihood, occupation, profession
11 consignment, piece of work, undertaking
14 line of business, responsibility

**jobless**
04 free, idle
08 inactive, workless
09 available, out of work
10 unemployed

**jockey**
04 coax, ease, ride
05 rider
06 cajole, induce
07 wheedle
08 horseman, maneuver
09 negotiate
10 equestrian, horsewoman, manipulate

**jocose**
05 droll, funny, merry, witty
06 jovial, joyous
07 comical, jesting, playful, teasing, waggish
08 humorous, mirthful

**jocular**
05 comic, droll, funny, witty
06 jocose, joking, jovial
07 amusing, comical, jesting, playful, waggish
08 humorous

**jocularity**
03 wit
05 humor
06 gaiety
07 fooling, jesting, teasing
08 jocosity, laughter
09 amusement, funniness, jolliness, joviality, merriment
10 jocoseness
11 playfulness, waggishness
12 sportiveness, whimsicality
13 facetiousness

**jog**
03 jar, run
04 bump, jerk, jolt, push, trot
05 elbow, nudge, shove
06 arouse, bounce, canter, joggle, jostle, prompt, remind
09 stimulate

**joie de vivre**
03 joy
04 zest
05 gusto, mirth
06 bounce, gaiety, relish
08 buoyancy
09 enjoyment, merriment

**join**
10 ebullience, enthusiasm, joyfulness

**join**
03 add, tie
04 abut, ally, bind, fuse, glue, knit, link, meet, weld, yoke
05 annex, enter, marry, merge, touch, unify, unite
06 adhere, adjoin, attach, border, cement, couple, enlist, enroll, fasten, sign up, splice
07 combine, connect, verge on
08 border on, converge
09 accompany, affiliate, associate, cooperate
10 amalgamate, team up with
11 collaborate

❑**join in**
06 chip in
07 partake, pitch in
09 cooperate
10 contribute, take part in
11 participate

❑**join up**
04 link
05 enter
06 enlist, enroll, sign up

**joint**
03 bar, fit, hip
04 club, dive, join, knee, knot, seam
05 carve, cut up, elbow, haunt, hinge, nexus, place, roach, sever, stick, union, unite
06 common, couple, divide, fasten, joined, mutual, reefer, shared, spliff, united
07 connect, dissect
08 combined, communal, coupling, junction, juncture
09 dismember, nightclub
10 articulate, collective
11 amalgamated
12 articulation, intersection

**joke**
03 fun, gag, kid, pun
04 fool, hoax, hoot, jape, jest, lark, mock, play, quip, yarn
05 clown, crack, laugh, prank, spoof, sport, tease, trick
06 banter, whimsy
08 one-liner, repartee
09 wisecrack, witticism
10 fool around, funny story
12 take for a ride
15 pull someone's leg

**joker**
03 wag, wit
04 card

05 clown, comic, cutup, droll, sport
06 gagman, jester, kidder
08 comedian, humorist, quipster
09 prankster, trickster
10 comedienne
11 wisecracker
14 practical joker

**jolly**
03 gay
04 glad
05 happy, merry
06 cheery, hearty, jovial, joyful, lively
07 festive, gleeful
08 cheerful, mirthful
09 enjoyable
10 delightful
11 pleasurable

**jolt**
03 hit, jar, jog
04 bang, blow, bump, jerk, push, stun
05 amaze, knock, lurch, nudge, shake, shock, shove, start
06 bounce, jostle, jounce
07 astound, disturb, perturb, shake up, startle
08 astonish, reversal, surprise

**jostle**
03 jog, vie
04 bang, bump, jolt, push
05 crowd, elbow, shove
06 hustle, joggle
07 collide, compete
08 shoulder, struggle

**jot**
03 ace, bit, dot
04 hint, iota, mite, whit
05 grain, scrap, speck, trace
06 detail, morsel, tittle, trifle
07 glimmer, smidgen
08 fraction, particle
09 scintilla

❑**jot down**
04 list, note
06 record
08 scribble

**journal**
03 log
05 diary, paper
06 record, review, weekly
07 account, daybook, gazette, monthly
08 magazine, register
09 chronicle, newspaper
10 periodical
11 publication

**journalism**
04 news
05 media
07 writing
08 the press
09 mass media, reportage, reporting
12 broadcasting, fourth estate, news coverage
14 correspondence, feature writing

**journalist**
04 hack
06 anchor, editor, scribe
07 newsman
08 coanchor, news hawk, reporter, reviewer
09 columnist, newshound, newswoman, paparazzo, stringer,
10 copy editor, newsperson, newswriter
11 broadcaster, commentator
12 newspaperman
13 correspondent, feature writer
14 newspaperwoman

▶ *Names of journalists, editors and newspaper owners:*
03 **Bly** (Nellie), **Day** (Benjamin)
04 **Dana** (Charles), **Eddy** (Mary Baker), **Luce** (Clare Booth), **Luce** (Henry), **Pyle** (Ernie), **Will** (George)
05 **Cooke** (Alistair), **Evans** (Harold), **Evans** (Rowland), **Frost** (David), **Novak** (Robert), **Rowan** (Carl), **Royko** (Mike), **White** (William Allen)
06 **Thomas** (Lowell), **Bierce** (Ambrose), **Broder** (David), **Brokaw** (Tom), **Gallup** (George), **Graham** (Katherine), **Harris** (Benjamin), **Hearst** (William Randolph), **Koppel** (Ted), **Kuralt** (Charles), **Lehrer** (Jim), **Moyers** (Bill), **Murrow** (Edward R.), **Rather** (Dan), **Reston** (James), **Runyon** (Damon), **Safire** (William), **Sawyer** (Diane), **Swayze** (John Cameron), **Thomas** (Helen), **Zenger** (John Peter),
07 **Bennett** (James Gordon), **Bradlee** (Ben), **Breslin** (Jimmy), **Buckley** (William Frank), **Greeley** (Horace),

Higgins (Marguerite), **Huntley** (Chet), **Maxwell** (Robert), **Mencken** (Henry Louis), **Murdoch** (Rupert), **Pearson** (Drew), **Scripps** (Edward), **Stanley** (Henry Morton), **Tarbell** (Ida), **Wallace** (Mike), **Walters** (Barbara)
08 **Anderson** (Jack), **Brinkley** (David), **Cronkite** (Walter), **Garrison** (William Lloyd), **Jennings** (Peter), **Lippmann** (Walter), **Pulitzer** (Joseph), **Reasoner** (Harry), **Sevareid** (Eric), **Thompson** (Dorothy), **Winchell** (Walter), **Woodward** (Bob)
09 **Bernstein** (Carl), **Donaldson** (Sam), **Frederick** (Pauline)
10 **Chancellor** (John)
➤ See also WRITER

## journey
02 go
03 fly
04 hike, ride, roam, rove, sail, tour, trek, trip
05 drive, jaunt, range, tramp
06 cruise, flight, ramble, roving, safari, travel, voyage
07 odyssey, passage, proceed
08 crossing, progress
09 excursion
10 expedition, wanderings
11 peregrinate
13 peregrination

## journeyer
07 pilgrim, rambler, tourist, trekker, voyager
08 traveler, wanderer, wayfarer
12 peregrinator

## joust
03 vie
04 spar, tilt
05 fight, trial
07 compete, contest, quarrel, tourney, wrangle
08 skirmish
10 engagement, tournament

## jovial
05 happy, jolly, merry
06 cheery, genial
07 affable, buoyant, gleeful
08 animated, cheerful, mirthful
13 in good spirits

## joviality
03 fun
04 glee
05 mirth
07 jollity

08 buoyancy, hilarity
09 happiness, merriment
10 affability, ebullience
12 cheerfulness

## joy
04 glee
05 bliss
06 thrill
07 delight, ecstasy, elation, rapture, success, victory
08 felicity, gladness, pleasure, treasure
09 cloud nine, happiness, rejoicing
10 exultation
13 gratification, seventh heaven

## joyful
04 glad
05 happy, merry
06 elated
07 gleeful, pleased
08 cheerful, ecstatic, euphoric
09 delighted, gratified, overjoyed
11 on cloud nine, tickled pink
15 in seventh heaven, on top of the world

## joyless
03 sad
04 dour, glum, grim
05 bleak
06 dismal, dreary, gloomy, somber
07 doleful, forlorn, unhappy
09 cheerless, miserable

## joyous
04 glad
05 happy, merry
06 festal, joyful
07 festive, gleeful
08 cheerful, ecstatic, gladsome, jubilant
09 rapturous

## jubilant
06 elated, joyful
07 excited
08 ecstatic, euphoric, exultant, thrilled
09 exuberant, overjoyed, rejoicing, rhapsodic
10 triumphant

## jubilation
07 ecstasy, elation, jubilee, triumph
08 euphoria, jamboree
10 excitement, exultation
11 celebration

## jubilee
04 fête, gala
08 carnival, feast day, festival

09 festivity
11 anniversary, celebration
13 commemoration

## Judas
07 traitor
08 betrayer, quisling, turncoat
13 tergiversator

## judge
03 ref, try, ump
04 damn, doom, rate
05 gauge, think, value, weigh
06 assess, critic, decide, decree, expert, reckon, review, umpire
07 adjudge, arbiter, condemn, convict, discern, examine, justice, mediate, referee, weigh up
08 appraise, assessor, conclude, consider, estimate, evaluate, mediator
09 arbitrate, ascertain, criticize, determine, evaluator, moderator, ombudsman
10 adjudicate, arbitrator, magistrate
11 adjudicator, connoisseur, distinguish
13 form an opinion, sit in judgment

➤ *Names of judges:*
04 **Bean** (Roy), **Taft** (William)
05 **Black** (Hugo), **Draco**, **Solon**
06 **Breyer** (Stephen), **Burger** (Warren), **Gideon**, **Holmes** (Oliver Wendell), **Scalia** (Antonin), **Souter** (David), **Thomas** (Clarence), **Warren** (Earl)
07 **Brennan** (William Joseph), **Douglas** (William), **Kennedy** (Anthony), **O'Connor** (Sandra Day), **Stevens** (John Paul)
08 **Ginsburg** (Ruth Bader), **Marshall** (John), **Marshall** Thurgood
09 **Rehnquist** (William), **Vyshinsky** (Andrei)
11 **Frankfurter** (Felix)

## judgment
04 doom, fate, view
05 taste
06 acumen, decree, ruling, wisdom
07 finding, opinion, verdict
08 decision, estimate, prudence, sagacity, sentence
09 appraisal, damnation, diagnosis, good sense, mediation

10 assessment, conclusion, conviction, evaluation, perception, punishment, shrewdness
11 arbitration, common sense, discernment, penetration, retribution
12 adjudication, perspicacity
14 discrimination

**judicial**
04 fair
05 legal
08 critical, forensic, unbiased
09 impartial, judiciary, magistral
14 discriminating

**judicious**
04 wise
05 smart, sound
06 astute, clever, shrewd
07 careful, prudent
08 cautious, informed, sensible
09 sagacious
10 considered, discerning, reasonable, thoughtful
11 circumspect, common sense
14 discriminating

**jug**
03 jar, urn
04 ewer, jail, Toby
05 crock
06 carafe, flagon, vessel
07 pitcher, Toby jug
08 decanter

**juggle**
06 adjust, change, doctor
07 balance, falsify, massage
08 disguise, equalize
09 rearrange
10 manipulate, tamper with

**juice**
03 gas, sap
04 fuel
05 fluid, serum
06 liquid, liquor, nectar
07 essence, extract
11 electricity

**juicy**
04 lush, racy
05 lurid, spicy, vivid
06 risqué, watery
08 colorful
09 succulent, thrilling
10 scandalous, suggestive
11 interesting, sensational

**jumble**
03 mix
04 mess
05 chaos, mix-up
06 medley, muddle, tangle
07 clutter, mixture, shuffle

08 disarray, disorder, shambles
09 confusion, potpourri
10 disarrange, hodgepodge, hotchpotch
11 disorganize

**jumbled**
06 untidy
07 chaotic, mixed-up, muddled, tangled
08 confused, shuffled, unsorted
10 disarrayed, disordered
12 disorganized

**jumbo**
04 huge, vast
05 giant
07 immense, mammoth
08 colossal, enormous, gigantic, whopping

**jump**
03 gap, hop, jar, mug
04 gate, go up, hike, jolt, leap, miss, omit, rail, rise, romp, skip
05 avoid, boost, bound, break, caper, clear, fence, frisk, hedge, lapse, leave, lurch, mount, quail, shake, shock, space, spasm, sport, start, surge, vault, wince
06 ascend, attack, beat up, bounce, breach, bypass, cavort, cut out, flinch, frolic, gambol, go over, hiatus, hurdle, ignore, lacuna, pounce, prance, spiral, spring, switch, twitch, upturn
07 advance, assault, barrier, set upon, swoop on, upsurge
08 escalate, increase, interval, leave out, obstacle, omission, overlook, pass over, pounce on
09 barricade, elevation, increment
10 appreciate, escalation

❏**jump at**
04 grab
05 seize
08 pounce on

❏**jump on**
05 blame, chide, fly at, scold
06 berate, rebuke, revile
07 censure, reprove, upbraid
08 reproach
09 castigate, criticize, reprimand

**jumper**
05 smock
06 blouse, jacket, romper
08 jump shot

**jumpy**
04 edgy
05 bumpy, jerky, rough, shaky, tense
06 bouncy, fitful, on edge, uneasy
07 anxious, fidgety, jittery, jolting, nervous, panicky, restive, shaking, twitchy
08 agitated, lurching
09 spasmodic
10 convulsive, incoherent
12 apprehensive, disconnected, uncontrolled
13 uncoordinated

**junction**
04 bond, join, link, seam
05 joint, union
07 joining, linking, welding
08 coupling, crossing, juncture
10 cloverleaf, confluence, crossroads
11 interchange
12 intersection

**juncture**
04 crux, time
05 point, stage
06 minute, moment, period
08 occasion
12 turning point

**jungle**
04 bush, maze
05 chaos, snarl
06 medley, tangle
08 disarray, disorder, mishmash
09 confusion, labyrinth
10 hodgepodge, hotchpotch, miscellany, rain forest

**junior**
05 lower, minor
06 lesser
07 student, younger
08 inferior

**junk**
04 dump
05 chuck, ditch, dregs, scrap, trash, waste
06 debris, litter, refuse
07 clutter, discard, garbage, rubbish, rummage
08 get rid of, jettison, oddments, throw out
09 bric-a-brac, dispose of

**junta**
04 gang, ring
05 cabal, group
06 cartel, clique, league
07 coterie, council, faction
09 camarilla

## jurisdiction
04 area, rule, sway, zone
05 field, orbit, power, range, reach, right, scope
06 bounds, sphere
07 command, control, mastery
08 dominion, province
09 authority, influence
10 domination, leadership
11 prerogative, sovereignty
14 administration

## jury
05 panel
06 jurors

## just
03 apt, due
04 fair, good, only
05 legal, moral, quite, valid
06 barely, hardly, honest, lawful, proper, purely, simply, spot on
07 ethical, exactly, fitting, merited
08 deserved, recently, rightful, scarcely, suitable, unbiased
09 equitable, honorable, impartial, objective, perfectly, precisely, righteous
10 a moment ago, absolutely, completely, evenhanded, fair-minded, legitimate, principled, reasonable, upstanding
11 appropriate, well-founded
12 unprejudiced
13 a short time ago, disinterested

## ◻just about
06 all but, almost, nearly
08 as good as, well-nigh

10 more or less
11 practically

## justice
02 JP
03 law
05 honor, judge, right
06 equity, morals
07 penalty, redress, sheriff
08 fair play, fairness
09 integrity, propriety, rectitude, rightness
10 lawfulness, legitimacy, magistrate, punishment, recompense, reparation
11 objectivity, uprightness
12 compensation, impartiality
13 equitableness, righteousness

## justifiable
05 legal, right, sound, valid
06 lawful, proper
09 excusable, warranted
10 acceptable, defensible, forgivable, legitimate, pardonable, reasonable
11 sustainable, well-founded
12 within reason
14 understandable

## justification
04 plea
05 basis
06 excuse, reason
07 apology, defense, grounds, warrant
10 mitigation
11 explanation, vindication
15 rationalization

## justify
05 clear, prove

06 acquit, defend, excuse, pardon, uphold, verify
07 absolve, bear out, confirm, deserve, explain, forgive, support, sustain, warrant
09 exculpate, vindicate
10 stand up for
11 rationalize
12 substantiate

## justly
06 fairly
07 equally, rightly
08 honestly, lawfully, properly
10 rightfully, with reason
11 impartially, objectively
12 evenhandedly, legitimately

## jut, jut out
06 beetle, extend
07 extrude, project
08 protrude, stick out

## juvenile
03 boy, kid
04 girl
05 child, minor, young, youth
06 callow, infant, junior
07 babyish, puerile
08 childish, immature, teenager, youthful
09 infantile, youngster
10 adolescent
11 young person

## juxtapose
11 put together
15 place side by side

## juxtaposition
08 nearness
09 closeness, proximity

## kaleidoscopic
06 motley
10 changeable, polychrome, variegated
11 many colored
12 ever changing, multicolored, multifarious
13 polychromatic

## kaput
06 broken, ruined
07 defunct, extinct, wrecked
09 conked out, destroyed

## keel

### ❑ keel over
04 drop, fall
05 faint, swoon, upset
07 capsize, founder, pass out
08 black out, collapse, overturn
10 topple over, turn turtle

## keen
04 avid, wild
05 acute, eager, sharp
06 astute, biting, clever, fierce, fond of, liking, shrewd, strong
07 devoted, earnest, fervent, mordant, pointed, pungent
08 incisive, piercing, ruthless
09 assiduous, cutthroat, devoted to, sensitive, trenchant
10 attached to, discerning, perceptive
11 industrious, penetrating, quick-witted, sharp-witted
12 enthusiastic
13 conscientious, perspicacious
14 discriminating

## keenness
06 wisdom
08 industry, sagacity, sapience, sedulity
09 diligence, eagerness, sharpness
10 astuteness, cleverness, enthusiasm, shrewdness, trenchancy
11 discernment, earnestness, penetration, sensitivity
12 incisiveness, perspicacity
17 perspicaciousness

## keep
04 feed, food, fort, hold, mind, save, tend
05 board, deter, guard, hoard, honor, stock, store, tower, watch
06 castle, deal in, detain, foster, hold up, living, remain, shield
07 abide by, care for, carry on, citadel, collect, confine, deposit, dungeon, fulfill, furnish, inhibit, nurture, observe, perform, persist, possess, protect, respect, shelter, store up, support, sustain
08 adhere to, carry out, conserve, continue, fortress, hang on to, hold on to, maintain, obstruct, preserve
09 celebrate, look after, persevere, safeguard, subsidize, watch over
10 accumulate, comply with, effectuate, livelihood, perpetuate, provide for, stronghold, sustenance
11 commemorate, maintenance, subsistence

### ❑ for keeps
06 always
07 for good, forever
10 for all time

### ❑ keep at
04 last, stay, toil
05 grind, labor
06 drudge, endure, finish, remain, slog at
07 carry on, persist, stick at
08 continue, maintain
09 persevere
11 be steadfast

### ❑ keep back
04 curb, hide, stop
05 check, delay, limit
06 hush up, impede, retard
07 conceal, control, reserve
08 restrain, restrict, withhold
09 constrain

### ❑ keep from
04 halt, stop
06 desist, resist
07 forbear, prevent

### ❑ keep in
04 hide
05 quell
06 coop up, detain, shut in, stifle, stop up
07 conceal, confine, repress
08 bottle up, restrain, suppress

### ❑ keep off
05 avoid
07 stay off
09 not go near
12 stay away from, steer clear of

### ❑ keep on
04 last, stay
06 endure, hold on, retain
07 carry on, persist
08 continue, maintain
09 persevere, stick at it
13 stay the course

### ❑ keep on at
03 nag
05 chivy, harry
06 badger, chivvy, harass, pester, plague, pursue

### ❑ keep secret
04 hide
05 sit on
07 conceal
14 keep under wraps

### ❑ keep to
04 obey
07 fulfill, observe, respect, stick to
08 adhere to
10 comply with

### ❑ keep track of
05 trace, watch
06 follow, record
07 monitor, oversee

### ❑ keep up
03 vie
05 equal, match, rival
07 compete, contend, emulate, support, sustain
08 continue, keep pace, maintain, preserve
09 persevere
11 go along with

## keeper
05 guard
06 jailer, warden
07 curator, steward

## keeping

08 defender, governor, guardian, overseer, surveyor
09 attendant, caretaker, custodian
10 supervisor
11 conservator
14 superintendent

## keeping

04 care, cure, ward
05 aegis, trust
06 accord, charge
07 custody, harmony
08 auspices, tutelage
09 agreement, retention
10 conformity, protection
11 maintenance, supervision
12 guardianship, surveillance

## keepsake

05 relic, token
06 emblem, pledge
07 memento
08 reminder, souvenir
11 remembrance

## keg

03 tun, vat
04 butt, cask, drum
06 barrel, firkin
08 hogshead

## ken

05 grasp, range, reach
06 notice
07 compass
09 awareness, knowledge
10 cognizance, perception
13 comprehension, understanding

## kernel

03 nub, nut
04 core, crux, germ, gist, seed
05 grain, heart, stone
06 center, marrow
07 essence, innards, nucleus

## key

03 cay
04 clue, code, main, reef, sign
05 chief, gloss, guide, index, major, pitch, table, vital
06 answer, island, legend, secret
07 central, crucial, leading, pointer
08 decisive, glossary, solution
09 essential, important, indicator, necessary, principal
11 explanation, explication, fundamental, translation
14 interpretation

## keynote

04 core, gist, pith
05 heart, theme

06 accent, center, marrow, stress
07 essence
09 substance

## keystone

04 base, core, crux, root
05 basis
06 ground, motive, source, spring
08 linchpin
10 foundation, mainspring
11 cornerstone

## kick

03 fun, hit, pep, zip
04 bite, blow, boot, buzz, high, jolt, knee, punt, quit, stop, zing
05 break, power, punch
06 effect, give up, recoil, strike, thrill
07 abandon, potency
08 complain, leave off, pleasure, stimulus, strength, striking
10 desist from, excitement
11 stimulation

## ❏ kick around, kick about

07 discuss, toy with
08 play with
09 talk about

## ❏ kick off

04 open
05 begin, start
08 commence, initiate
09 introduce
10 inaugurate
11 get under way

## ❏ kick out

04 fire, oust, sack
05 eject, evict, expel
06 reject, remove
07 boot out, dismiss
08 chuck out, get rid of, throw out
09 discharge

## kickoff

05 start
06 outset, word go
07 opening
09 beginning, inception
12 commencement, introduction

## kid

03 boy, con, lad, tot
04 dupe, fool, girl, gull, hoax, jest, joke
05 child, tease, trick, youth
06 delude, have on, humbug, infant, nipper
07 deceive, pretend, toddler
08 hoodwink, juvenile, teenager, young one

09 little one, youngster
10 adolescent
15 pull someone's leg

## kidnap

05 seize, steal
06 abduct, hijack, snatch
12 hold to ransom

## kill

03 end, sap, use, zap
04 ache, do in, fill, hang, hurt, pass, ruin, slay, veto
05 death, pound, quash, quell, shoot, smart, smite, spend, throb, use up, waste
06 be sore, behead, climax, deaden, finish, murder, occupy, rub out, suffer
07 abolish, bump off, butcher, destroy, execute, put down, smother, take out, wipe out
08 blow away, decimate, dispatch, knock off, massacre, suppress, vote down
09 deathblow, devastate, do to death, eliminate, eradicate, finish off, liquidate, polish off, slaughter, while away
10 annihilate, decapitate, dénouement, do away with, guillotine, put to death, put to sleep
11 assassinate, coup de grâce, electrocute, exterminate

## killer

06 gunman, hit man, slayer
07 butcher, torpedo
08 assassin, homicide, murderer
09 cutthroat
10 hatchet man, liquidator
11 executioner, slaughterer
12 exterminator

## killing

03 hit
04 coup, gain, hard
05 booty
06 absurd, big hit, murder, profit, taxing
07 amusing, arduous, bonanza, carnage, fortune, slaying, success
08 butchery, draining, fatality, genocide, homicide, massacre, windfall
09 bloodshed, execution, fatiguing, hilarious, matricide, patricide, slaughter, uxoricide
10 enervating, exhausting, fratricide, sororicide

11 destruction, elimination, infanticide, liquidation
12 debilitating, manslaughter
13 assassination, extermination

**killjoy**
06 damper, grouch, misery, moaner, whiner
08 dampener
10 complainer, spoilsport, wet blanket
11 party pooper

**kin**
04 clan
05 blood, stock, tribe
06 family, people
07 cousins, kindred, kinfolk, lineage
08 kinfolks
09 relations, relatives
13 consanguinity, flesh and blood

**kind**
03 set
04 good, mild, nice, race, sort, type, warm
05 brand, breed, class, genre, genus, stamp, style
06 benign, family, genial, gentle, giving, humane, kindly, loving, manner, nature, strain
07 amiable, cordial, helpful, patient, species, variety
08 amicable, category, friendly, generous, gracious, obliging
09 character, congenial, indulgent, unselfish
10 altruistic, benevolent, bighearted, charitable, neighborly, persuasion
11 considerate, description, good-hearted, good-natured, magnanimous, softhearted, sympathetic, warmhearted
12 affectionate, humanitarian
13 compassionate, philanthropic, tenderhearted, understanding

**◻in kind**
09 similarly, tit for tat
10 in exchange
12 in like manner

**kindhearted**
04 warm
06 benign, humane
07 helpful
08 generous, obliging
10 altruistic
11 considerate, good-natured, sympathetic, warmhearted

12 humanitarian
13 compassionate, philanthropic, tenderhearted

**kindle**
04 fire, stir
05 light, rouse
06 arouse, awaken, excite, ignite, incite, induce, thrill
07 inflame, inspire, provoke
09 set alight, set fire to, set on fire, stimulate

**kindliness**
06 warmth
07 charity
08 sympathy
09 benignity
10 compassion, generosity
11 beneficence, benevolence

**kindly**
04 good, warm
06 giving, humane
07 cordial, helpful, patient
08 amicable, friendly, generous, pleasant
09 indulgent
10 benevolent, bighearted, charitable, thoughtful
11 considerate, good-natured
13 compassionate

**kindness**
04 help, love
05 favor, grace
06 warmth
07 charity, service
08 altruism, good turn, goodness, goodwill, humanity
09 affection, tolerance
10 assistance, compassion, generosity, humaneness, indulgence
11 benevolence, helpfulness, hospitality
12 friendliness, philanthropy
13 consideration, fellow feeling
14 thoughtfulness
15 considerateness, humanitarianism, warmheartedness

**kindred**
04 akin, clan, folk, like
06 alike, common, family
07 cognate, kinfolk, lineage, related
08 kinfolks
09 connected, relations, relatives
10 affiliated
11 connections
12 relationship

13 consanguinity, corresponding, flesh and blood

**king**
04 lord, star
05 chief, ruler
06 leader, master, prince, top dog
07 big shot, emperor, kingpin, majesty, monarch, supremo
08 big noise
09 big cheese, chieftain, muckamuck, sovereign
11 muckety-muck
13 high muckamuck
15 high muckety-muck

---

➤ *Names of kings. We have omitted the word* **king** *from names given in the following list but you may need to include this word as part of the solution to some crossword clues. The regnal numerals of individual kings have also been omitted.*
03 Zog
04 Fahd, Ivan, Ivan (the Terrible), John, Knut, Offa, Olav, Otto, Paul
05 Boris, Brian, Capet (Hugo), Carol, Creon, David, Edgar, Edred, Edwin (Saint), Henry, Herod (the Great), James, Louis, Murat (Joachim), Penda, Pepin (the Short)
06 Alaric, Albert, Alfred, Attila, Canute (the Great), Clovis, Darius, Duncan, Edmund, Edward, Edward (the Confessor), Edward (the Elder), Edward (the Martyr), Egbert, Faisal, Farouk, Faysal, George, Harald, Harold, Khalid, Philip, Philip (Augustus), Robert, Robert (the Bruce), Rudolf, Sargon, Xerxes
07 Alfonso, Charles (the Great), Croesus, Emanuel, Francis, Hussein, Leopold, Macbeth, Malcolm, Ptolemy, Rameses, Richard, Romulus, Stephen, Tarquin, William, William (the Silent)
08 Ethelred, Ethelred (the Unready), Leonidas, Ramesses, Thutmose
09 Akhenaton, Alexander, Amenhotep, Antiochus, Atahualpa, Athelstan, Cymbeline, Ethelbert, Ethelwulf, Ferdinand, Frederick, Hammurabi,

Hardaknut, Hugo Capet,
Sigismund, Stanislaw,
Theodoric (the Great),
Vortigern, Wenceslas
10 Artaxerxes, Esarhaddon, Juan
Carlos, Tarquinius
11 Charlemagne, Constantine,
Cunobelinus, Hardicanute,
Mithridates, Sennacherib,
Shalmaneser, Tutankhamen
12 Assurbanipal, Boris
Godunov, Herod Agrippa
13 Francis Joseph, Louis-
Philippe
14 Edmund Ironside, Harold
Harefoot, Nebuchadnezzar,
Victor Emmanuel

**kingdom**
04 land
05 realm, reign, state
06 domain, empire, nation
07 country, dynasty
08 dominion, monarchy,
province
09 territory
11 sovereignty

**kingly**
05 regal, royal
06 august
08 imperial, majestic, splendid
09 imperious, sovereign
11 monarchical

**kink**
04 bend, curl, dent, loop, whim
05 crimp, curve, quirk, twist
06 fetish, foible
07 caprice, crinkle, wrinkle
09 deviation
10 perversion

**kinky**
03 odd
04 wavy
05 curly, weird
06 curled, frizzy, quirky, warped
07 crimped, deviant, twisted
08 depraved, freakish
09 perverted, unnatural,
whimsical
10 degenerate, outlandish

**kinship**
05 blood
06 family
07 lineage
08 affinity, alliance, ancestry,
likeness, relation
09 community
10 conformity, connection
11 association, equivalence
12 relationship
13 consanguinity

**kiosk**
05 booth, cabin, stall, stand
08 pavilion
09 bandstand, bookstall,
newsstand
11 summerhouse

**kismet**
03 lot
04 doom, fate
05 karma
07 destiny, fortune

**kiss**
04 buss, lick, neck, peck
05 brush, graze, smack, touch
06 caress, scrape, smooch
07 smacker
08 canoodle, osculate
09 glance off
10 bill and coo, osculation

**kit**
03 set
04 gear, togs
05 get up, stuff, tools
06 outfit, tackle, things
07 baggage, clothes, effects,
luggage
08 clothing, supplies, utensils
09 apparatus, equipment
10 implements, provisions
11 instruments
13 accouterments,
accoutrements,
paraphernalia

❏ **kit out**
03 arm
05 dress, equip, fix up
06 fit out, outfit, rig out, supply

**kittenish**
07 playful
10 coquettish, frolicsome
11 flirtatious

**knack**
04 bent, gift, hang, turn
05 flair, forte, skill, trick
06 genius, talent
07 ability, faculty
08 aptitude, capacity, facility
09 dexterity, expertise,
handiness, quickness
10 adroitness, capability,
competence, propensity
11 proficiency
12 skillfulness

**knapsack**
03 bag
04 pack
06 kit bag
08 backpack, rucksack
09 duffel bag, haversack
11 shoulder bag

**knave**
04 heel
05 cheat, rogue, scamp, swine
06 rascal
07 dastard, villain
08 scalawag, swindler
09 reprobate, scallywag,
scoundrel

**knavery**
05 fraud
06 deceit
07 devilry, roguery
08 mischief, trickery, villainy
09 chicanery, deception,
duplicity, imposture
10 corruption, dishonesty,
hanky-panky
13 double-dealing

**knavish**
06 wicked
07 corrupt, roguish
08 devilish, fiendish, rascally
09 dastardly, deceitful,
dishonest, reprobate
10 fraudulent, villainous
11 mischievous, scoundrelly
12 contemptible, dishonorable,
unscrupulous

**knead**
03 ply, rub
04 form, mold, work
05 press, shape
07 knuckle, massage, squeeze
10 manipulate

**kneel**
03 bow
04 bend
05 stoop
06 curtsy, kowtow, revere
07 bow down, defer to
09 genuflect
13 make obeisance

**knell**
04 peal, ring, toll
05 chime, knoll, sound
07 ringing

**knickknack**
06 bauble, gewgaw, trifle
07 chachka, trinket, whatnot
08 gimcrack, ornament
09 bagatelle, bric-a-brac,
tchotchke

**knife**
03 cut, rip
04 dirk, stab
05 blade, slash, wound
06 carver, cutter, dagger, pierce
07 bayonet, machete, scalpel
08 lacerate, penknife
09 jackknife

10 bowie knife, craft knife
11 pocketknife, switchblade
14 Swiss Army knife

**knight**
07 gallant, soldier, warrior
08 banneret, cavalier,
     champion, horseman
09 chevalier, freelance, man-at-
     arms
10 bannerette, cavalryman,
     equestrian

**knightly**
05 noble
06 heroic
07 courtly, gallant, valiant
08 gracious, intrepid, valorous
09 dauntless, soldierly
10 chivalrous, courageous

**knit**
04 ally, bind, join, knot, link,
     loop, mend, purl
05 unite, weave
06 fasten, gather, secure
08 crotchet
12 draw together

**knob**
03 nub
04 ball, boss, knot, lump
05 gnarl, knurl, swell, tuber,
     tumor
06 handle, switch
07 hillock
08 doorknob, swelling, tubercle
09 capitulum
10 protrusion
12 protuberance

**knock**
03 box, hit, pan, rap, tap
04 bang, bash, belt, blow, bump,
     clip, cuff, dash, jolt, slam, slap
05 clout, crash, pound, punch,
     smack, stamp, swipe, thump,
     whack
06 attack, batter, defeat, rebuff,
     strike, wallop
07 bad luck, banging, censure,
     collide, condemn, failure, run
     down, setback
08 pounding, reversal
09 criticize, deprecate,
     disparage, hammering,
     rejection
10 misfortune
11 pick holes in
12 pull to pieces, tear to pieces
13 find fault with

❑ **knock about, knock
around**
03 gad, hit
04 bash, hurt, roam, rove
05 abuse, punch, range, wound

06 batter, beat up, bruise, buffet,
     damage, injure, ramble,
     strike, travel, wander
07 consort, saunter, traipse
08 go around, maltreat, mistreat
09 associate, manhandle
10 hang around

❑ **knock down**
04 earn, fell, raze
05 clout, floor, level, lower,
     pound, smash, wreck
06 batter, reduce, wallop
07 destroy, run down, run over
08 bowl over, decrease,
     demolish

❑ **knock off**
03 rob
04 do in, fake, kill, lift, slay, stop
05 cease, filch, pinch, steal,
     swipe, waste
06 deduct, finish, murder, pack
     in, pilfer, rip off, snitch
07 bump off, imitate
08 clock out, get rid of, pack it in,
     stop work, take away
09 imitation, terminate
10 do away with, finish work
11 assassinate

❑ **knock out**
02 KO
04 beat, fell, kayo, rout, stun
05 amaze, crush, floor
06 defeat, hammer, thrash
07 astound, impress, startle
08 astonish, bowl over
09 eliminate, prostrate

**knockout**
02 KO
04 kayo
07 stunner, success, triumph
08 jim-dandy, smash hit
09 humdinger, sensation
11 crackerjack

**knoll**
04 hill, knob
05 mound
06 barrow
07 hillock, hummock

**knot**
03 tie
04 band, bind, bond, knit, knob,
     lash, loop, lump, ring
05 bunch, clump, crowd, gnarl,
     group, joint, knurl, leash,
     ravel, twist, weave
06 circle, fasten, secure, splice,
     tangle, tether
07 cluster, entwine
08 entangle, ligature, swelling
09 fastening, gathering

► *Types of knot.* We have
omitted the word **knot** from
names given in the following list
but you may need to include this
word as part of the solution to
some crossword clues.
03 bow, tie
04 bend, flat, loop, reef
05 hitch, slide
06 granny, square
07 bowline, weaver's, Windsor
08 overhand, slipknot, surgeon's
09 half hitch, sheet bend, Turk's
     head
10 clove hitch, sheepshank
11 carrick bend, figure eight,
     timber hitch
12 rolling hitch, weaver's hitch
14 fisherman's bend, running
     bowline

**knotty**
05 bumpy, rough
06 nodose, thorny, tricky
07 complex, gnarled, nodular
08 baffling, puzzling
09 Byzantine, difficult, intricate
10 mystifying, perplexing
11 complicated, troublesome

**know**
05 sense
06 fathom, notice
07 be aware, discern, make out,
     realize, undergo
08 identify, perceive
09 apprehend, be clued in, go
     through, recognize
10 comprehend, experience,
     understand
11 distinguish
12 discriminate
13 associate with, differentiate

**know-how**
05 knack, savvy, skill
07 ability, faculty
09 expertise, knowledge
10 capability, competence
11 savoir-faire

**knowing**
05 aware
06 astute, shrewd
07 cunning
09 conscious
10 discerning, perceptive
11 significant

**knowingly**
08 by design
09 on purpose, purposely,
     willfully
10 designedly
11 consciously

12 calculatedly, deliberately
13 intentionally

**know-it-all**
06 smarty
07 wise guy
08 wiseacre
10 smart aleck
11 smarty-pants

**knowledge**
04 data
05 facts, grasp, skill
06 wisdom
07 ability, know-how
08 intimacy, learning
09 awareness, cognition,
   education, erudition,
   expertise, schooling
10 cognizance
11 conversance, discernment,
   familiarity, information,
   proficiency, scholarship
12 acquaintance, apprehension,
   intelligence

13 consciousness,
   enlightenment

**knowledgeable**
06 au fait, expert
07 erudite, learned
08 educated, familiar, informed,
   lettered, well-read
09 scholarly
10 conversant, well-versed
12 well-informed

**known**
05 noted, plain
06 avowed, famous, patent
07 obvious
08 admitted, familiar, revealed
09 confessed, published
10 celebrated, proclaimed,
   recognized
12 acknowledged

**knuckle**
❏**knuckle down**
10 buckle down

15 start to work hard
❏**knuckle under**
05 defer, yield
06 accede, give in, submit
07 give way, succumb
09 acquiesce, surrender

**kowtow**
04 fawn
05 defer, kneel, toady
06 cringe, grovel, pander, suck
   up
10 curry favor
12 bow and scrape

**kudos**
04 fame
05 glory, honor
06 esteem, praise, regard,
   renown, repute
07 acclaim, laurels
08 plaudits, prestige

**label**
03 dub, tab, tag
04 call, mark, name, term
05 badge, brand, stamp, title
06 define, docket, marker, ticket
07 epithet, sticker
08 classify, identify, nickname
09 brand name, trademark
10 categorize
11 description, designation
12 characterize
14 categorization, classification, identification
15 proprietary name

**laborious**
04 hard
05 heavy, tough
06 tiring, uphill
07 arduous, careful, onerous, tedious
08 diligent, tiresome, toilsome, wearying
09 assiduous, difficult, fatiguing, strenuous, wearisome
11 hard working, industrious, painstaking
12 backbreaking

**labor**
03 job
04 plod, roll, slog, task, toil, toss, turn, work
05 birth, chore, grind, hands, pangs, pitch, slave, sweat
06 drudge, effort, overdo, strain, strive, suffer, throes
07 travail, workers, workmen
08 delivery, drudgery, endeavor, exertion, go all out, hard work, laborers, struggle, work hard
09 diligence, elaborate, employees, workforce
10 childbirth, employment, overstress
11 parturition
12 contractions
13 exert yourself, overemphasize
15 industriousness

**labored**
06 forced
07 awkward, stilted, studied
08 affected, overdone, strained

09 contrived, ponderous, unnatural
11 complicated, overwrought

**laborer**
04 hand
06 menial
07 workman
08 farmhand
10 workingman
12 manual worker
15 ranch hand worker

**labyrinth**
04 maze
06 enigma, jungle, puzzle, riddle, tangle, warren
09 confusion, intricacy
12 complication, entanglement

**labyrinthine**
07 complex, tangled, winding
08 confused, involved, mazelike, puzzling, tortuous
09 Byzantine, intricate
10 convoluted, perplexing

**lace**
04 cord, do up
05 mix in, spike, thong, twine
06 fasten, lacing, string, thread
07 fortify, tatting
08 bootlace, shoelace
10 intertwine, interweave

► *Types of lace*:
04 gold
05 filet, jabot
07 galloon, guipure, macramé, Maltese, Mechlin, pearlin, tatting, torchon
08 Argentan, Brussels, dentelle, Venetian
09 Chantilly, point lace, reticella
10 bobbin lace, mignonette, pillow lace, thread lace
15 needlepoint lace

**lacerate**
03 cut, rip
04 claw, gash, rend, tear
05 slash, wound
06 harrow, injure, mangle
07 afflict, cut open, torture
08 distress, mutilate

**laceration**
03 cut, rip

04 gash, maim, rent, tear
05 slash, wound
10 mutilation

**lachrymose**
05 teary, weepy
06 crying, woeful
07 sobbing, tearful, weeping

**lack**
04 miss, need, void, want
06 dearth
07 absence, not have, paucity, require, vacancy
08 scarcity, shortage
09 emptiness, privation
10 deficiency, have need of, scantiness
11 deprivation, destitution
13 be deficient in, insufficiency
15 not have enough of

**lackadaisical**
04 dull, idle, lazy, limp
08 indolent, listless
09 enervated, lethargic
10 languorous

**lackey**
05 toady, valet
06 flunky, menial, minion, yes man
07 flunkey, servant, steward
10 instrument, manservant

**lacking**
05 minus
07 missing, needing, short of, wanting, without
09 defective, deficient

**lackluster**
04 drab, dull, flat
05 vapid
06 boring, leaden
07 insipid, tedious
08 lifeless
10 spiritless, uninspired
13 unimaginative, uninteresting

**laconic**
05 blunt, brief, crisp, pithy, short, terse
06 abrupt
07 concise
08 incisive, succinct, taciturn
10 economical, to the point

## lacuna
03 gap
04 void
05 blank, break, space
06 cavity, hiatus
08 omission

## lad
03 boy, guy, kid, son
04 chap
05 youth
06 fellow
09 schoolboy, youngster

## laden
04 full
05 taxed
06 jammed, loaded, packed
07 charged, fraught, stuffed
08 burdened, hampered, weighted
09 oppressed
10 encumbered
11 weighed down

## la-di-da
04 posh
06 snooty
07 foppish
08 affected, mannered, snobbish, stuck-up,
11 highfalutin, highfalutin, overrefined, pretentious

## ladle
03 dip
04 bail, dish, lade
05 scoop, spoon
06 shovel

## ❑ladle out
07 dish out, dole out, hand out
10 distribute

## lady
04 dame
05 woman
06 damsel, female, matron
10 noblewoman
11 gentlewoman

## ladylike
06 modest, polite, proper
07 genteel, refined
08 polished, well-bred
11 respectable
12 well-mannered

## lag
05 dally, delay, tarry, trail
06 dawdle, linger, loiter
08 hang back, straggle
10 fall behind
12 drag your feet, shilly-shally
14 bring up the rear

## laggard
05 snail
07 dawdler
08 lingerer, loiterer, slowpoke
09 straggler

## lagoon
04 lake, pond, pool

## laid up
03 ill
04 sick
07 injured
08 disabled
09 bedridden
11 immobilized, out of action
12 hors de combat
13 incapacitated, on the sick list

## laid-back
06 at ease, casual
07 relaxed
09 easygoing, leisurely, unhurried, unworried
10 untroubled
11 free and easy, unflappable
13 imperturbable

## lair

► *Lairs and homes of animals*:
03 den, pen, sty
04 barn, coop, eyry, form, hive, hole, nest
05 aerie, earth, eyrie, lodge
06 burrow, warren
07 dovecot
08 dovecote, vespiary

## laissez faire
09 free trade
10 free market
14 free enterprise

## lake
04 loch, mere, pond, pool, tarn
05 basin, bayou
06 lagoon

► *Names of lakes. We have omitted the word* **lake** *from names given in the following list but you may need to include this word as part of the solution to some crossword clues.*
03 Van
04 Abbé, Biwa, Bled, Chad, Como, Erie, Eyre, Kivu, Mead, Taho, Tana
05 Garda, Great, Huron, Nyasa, Ohrid, Onega, Patos, Poopó
06 Albert, Baikal, Crater, Finger, Geneva, Ladoga, Malawi, Nasser, Saimaa, Taimyr, Taymyr, Vänern
07 Balaton, Chapala, Lucerne, Ontario, Rannoch, Scutari, Torrens, Turkana
08 Balkhash, Bodensee, Lac Léman, Loch Ness, Maggiore, Manitoba, Michigan, Reindeer, Superior, Tiberias, Titicaca, Victoria, Winnipeg
09 Athabasca, Champlain, Constance, Great Bear, Great Salt, Maracaibo, Neuchâtel, Nicaragua, Ullswater, Zeller See
10 Great Slave, Loch Lomond, Okeechobee, Tanganyika, Windermere
11 Great Bitter
12 Kielder Water
13 Coniston Water, Pontchartrain

## lam
03 hit
04 beat, flee, pelt
05 clout, knock, pound, thump, whack
06 batter, escape, flight, pummel, strike, thrash, wallop
07 getaway, leather, vamoose

## lambaste
03 tan
04 beat, drub, flay, flog, whip
05 scold, toast
06 batter, berate, strike, thrash
07 censure, upbraid
09 castigate, criticize

## lame
04 hurt, poor, thin, weak
06 feeble, maimed, poorly
07 halting, injured, limping
08 crippled, disabled, hobbling
12 unconvincing
14 unsatisfactory

## lament
03 cry, sob
04 howl, keen, moan, wail
05 dirge, elegy, mourn, tears
06 bemoan, bewail, grieve, regret, sorrow
07 requiem, ululate, weeping
08 grieving, threnody
09 complaint

## lamentable
04 mean, poor
06 meager, tragic, woeful
07 pitiful
08 grievous, mournful, terrible, wretched
09 miserable, niggardly, sorrowful
10 deplorable, inadequate
11 regrettable

## lamentation
04 keen, moan
05 dirge, elegy, grief
06 plaint, sorrow
07 keening, sobbing, wailing, weeping
08 grieving, jeremiad, mourning, threnody
09 ululation

## laminate
04 coat, face
05 cover, flake, layer, plate
06 veneer

## lamp
04 bulb
05 light
07 lantern
09 light bulb

## lampoon
04 mock, skit
05 spoof
06 parody, satire
07 take off
08 ridicule, satirize, travesty
09 burlesque, make fun of
10 caricature, pasquinade

## lampooner
08 parodist, satirist
11 pasquinader
12 caricaturist

## lance
03 cut
04 pike, slit
05 prick, spear
06 incise, lancet, pierce
07 bayonet, harpoon, javelin
08 puncture

## land
03 get, hit, net, win
04 area, deal, dirt, dock, drop, gain, give, loam, mesa, soil
05 acres, berth, catch, earth, end up, fetch, manor, range, reach, realm, state, tract
06 alight, arrive, direct, domain, estate, fields, ground, nation, obtain, region, saddle, secure, settle, unload
07 achieve, acquire, acreage, capture, country, deliver, deposit, grounds, inflict, procure, terrain
08 dismount, district, encumber, farmland, go ashore, property, province, take down
09 disembark, territory, touch down
10 come to rest, real estate, terra firma
11 countryside

13 native country

## landlady, landlord
04 host
05 owner
07 hostess
08 hotelier
09 innkeeper
10 freeholder, proprietor

## landmark
05 cairn
06 beacon
07 feature
08 boundary, monument
09 milestone
12 turning point

## landscape
04 view
05 scene, vista
06 aspect
07 outlook, scenery
08 panorama, prospect
11 countryside, perspective

## landslide
08 decisive, emphatic, rock fall
09 avalanche
12 overwhelming

## lane
03 way
04 path
05 alley, byway, track
06 avenue, byroad, street
07 footway, pathway, towpath
08 alleyway, driveway, footpath

## language
04 talk
05 style
06 speech
07 diction, wording
08 parlance, phrasing, rhetoric
09 discourse, utterance
10 expression, vocabulary, vocalizing
11 phraseology, terminology, verbalizing
12 conversation
13 communication

---

► *Language terms*:
04 cant
05 argot, idiom, lingo, slang, usage
06 brogue, Creole, jargon, patois, patter, pidgin, syntax, tongue
07 dialect, grammar
08 buzz word, localism
09 etymology, phonetics, semantics
10 journalese, vernacular
11 doublespeak, linguistics, orthography, regionalism
12 lexicography, lingua franca
13 colloquialism

---

► *Languages of the world*:
04 Cree, Lapp, Manx, Thai, Urdu, Zulu
05 Bantu, Croat, Czech, Dutch, Farsi, Greek, Hindi, Iraqi, Irish, Latin, Malay, Maori, Swiss, Tamil, Welsh
06 Afghan, Arabic, Basque, Celtic, Creole, Danish, Eskimo, French, Gaelic, German, Hebrew, Lakota, Magyar, Mohawk, Navaho, Oneida, Polish, Romany, Slovak, Somali
07 Bengali, Burmese, Catalan, Chinese, Cornish, English, Finnish, Flemish, Iranian, Italian, Kurdish, Latvian, Maltese, Mexican, Mohican, Persian, Punjabi, Quechua, Russian, Serbian, Spanish, Swahili, Swedish, Tibetan, Turkish, Volapük, Yiddish
08 Cherokee, Estonian, Hawaiian, Japanese, Mandarin, Romanian, Sanskrit, Scottish
09 Aborigine, Afrikaans, Blackfoot, Cantonese, Esperanto, Ethiopian, Hottentot, Hungarian, Icelandic, Norwegian, Sinhalese, Slovenian, Ukrainian
10 Hindustani, Indonesian, Lithuanian, Patowatomi, Portuguese, Vietnamese
13 Haitian Creole

## languid
04 dull, lazy, limp, slow, weak
05 faint, heavy, inert, weary
06 feeble, pining, sickly, torpid
08 drooping, inactive, listless, sluggish
09 enervated, lethargic
10 languorous, spiritless
11 debilitated, indifferent
13 lackadaisical
14 unenthusiastic

## languish
04 fade, fail, flag, long, mope, pine, sigh, sink, want, wilt
05 brood, droop, faint, waste, yearn
06 desire, grieve, hanker, hunger, sicken, sorrow, weaken, wither

## languor
05 ennui, sloth

06 torpor
07 fatigue, inertia
08 debility, laziness, lethargy
09 heaviness, indolence, lassitude, weariness
10 drowsiness, enervation, relaxation, sleepiness
12 listlessness

**lank**
04 lean, limp, slim, thin
05 gaunt, lanky
06 skinny
07 scraggy, scrawny, slender
08 drooping, lifeless, rawboned
10 lusterless, straggling

**lanky**
04 lank, lean, slim, thin
05 gaunt
07 scraggy, scrawny, slender
08 gangling

**lap**
03 leg, sip, sup
04 fold, lick, wind, wrap
05 cover, drink, round, stage
06 circle, course, encase, enfold, swathe
07 circuit, compass, envelop, overlap, section, swaddle
08 distance, overtake, surround

❏ **lap up**
05 drink
06 absorb, accept

**lapse**
03 end, gap
04 drop, fail, fall, go by, go on, lull, pass, sink, slip, stop
05 break, cease, drift, error, fault, pause, slide
06 elapse, expire, hiatus, run out, slip by, worsen
07 decline, descent, failing, go to pot, mistake, relapse
08 downturn, interval, omission, slip away, slipping
09 backslide, oversight, terminate, worsening
10 aberration, degenerate, negligence
11 backsliding, dereliction, deteriorate, go to the dogs
12 degeneration, indiscretion, intermission, interruption

**lapsed**
06 run out
07 expired, invalid
08 finished, obsolete, outdated
09 out of date, unrenewed

**larceny**
05 theft
06 piracy

07 robbery
08 burglary, stealing, thievery, thieving

**larder**
06 pantry
09 storeroom
11 storage room

**large**
03 big
04 full, high, huge, tall, vast
05 ample, broad, bulky, giant, grand, great, heavy, jumbo, roomy
06 bumper
07 immense, liberal, mammoth, massive, sizable
08 colossal, enormous, generous, gigantic, king-size, spacious, sweeping, whopping
09 extensive, ginormous, grandiose, humongous, king-sized, plentiful
10 commodious, dirty great, exhaustive, monumental, prodigious, stupendous, voluminous
11 far-reaching, substantial
12 considerable
13 comprehensive

❏ **at large**
04 free
08 on the lam, on the run
09 at liberty, generally, in general
10 on the loose, on the whole
11 independent

❏ **by and large**
06 mostly
07 as a rule
09 generally
10 on the whole
14 for the most part

**largely**
06 mainly, mostly
07 chiefly, greatly
09 generally, in the main, primarily
10 by and large
11 principally
13 predominantly
14 for the most part

**large-scale**
04 epic, vast, wide
05 broad
08 sweeping
09 expansive, extensive, wholesale
11 far-reaching, wide-ranging

**largesse**
04 alms, gift

06 bounty
07 charity, handout, present
08 donation, kindness
10 generosity, liberality
11 benefaction, munificence
12 philanthropy
14 openhandedness

**lariat**
04 rope
05 lasso, reata, riata

**lark**
03 job
04 game, play, romp, task
05 antic, caper, chore, fling, prank, revel, sport
06 cavort, frolic, gambol
07 fooling, have fun, skylark
08 activity, escapade, mischief
09 cavorting, fool about, horseplay, mess about

**lascivious**
04 blue, lewd
05 bawdy
06 ribald, smutty, vulgar, wanton
07 lustful, obscene, sensual
08 indecent, prurient, unchaste
09 lecherous, salacious
10 libidinous, licentious, scurrilous, suggestive

**lash**
03 hit, tie, wag
04 beat, bind, blow, dash, flog, join, rope, whip
05 affix, break, flail, flick, pound, scold, strap, swipe
06 attack, batter, berate, buffet, fasten, rebuke, secure, strike, stroke, switch, tether, thrash
07 bawl out, censure, lay into, reprove, scourge, tell off
08 make fast
09 criticize, fulminate

❏ **lash out**
06 strike
08 hit out at
09 criticize
15 speak out against

**lass**
04 girl, miss
05 chick
06 damsel, lassie, maiden
10 schoolgirl, young woman

**lassitude**
06 apathy, torpor
07 fatigue, languor
09 heaviness, tiredness
10 drowsiness
12 listlessness, sluggishness

**last**
03 end

04 go on, keep, stay, take, wear
05 abide, after, close, exist, final
06 behind, ending, endure, finish, hold on, keep on, latest, remain, utmost
07 carry on, closing, extreme, finally, hold out, persist, stand up, subsist, survive
08 continue, furthest, hindmost, previous, rearmost, terminal, ultimate
10 completion, concluding, conclusion, most recent, ultimately

❑**at last**
07 finally
08 at length, in the end
10 eventually, ultimately
11 in due course
12 in conclusion

❑**last word**
04 best, pick, rage
05 cream, vogue
08 final say, ultimate
10 dernier cri, perfection
11 ne plus ultra
12 quintessence
13 final decision
14 crème de la crème

**last-ditch**
05 final
06 all-out
07 frantic
08 frenzied, last-gasp
09 desperate, straining
12 eleventh hour

**lasting**
07 abiding, durable, undying
08 enduring, long-term, unending
09 ceaseless, long-lived, permanent, perpetual, surviving, unceasing
10 persisting, unchanging
11 everlasting, never-ending
12 interminable, long-standing

**lastly**
07 finally, to sum up
08 in the end
12 in conclusion

**latch**
03 bar
04 bolt, hasp, hook, lock
05 catch
06 fasten
09 fastening

❑**latch onto**
03 get
05 grasp, learn
06 follow, obtain

07 realize
08 attach to
10 comprehend, understand

**late**
03 new, old
04 dead, past, slow
05 fresh, tardy
06 behind, former, latest, recent, slowly
07 current, delayed, overdue
08 deceased, departed, formerly, previous, recently, up-to-date
09 belatedly, in arrears, preceding
10 behindhand, dilatorily, last minute, unpunctual
12 unpunctually
14 behind schedule

❑**of late**
06 lately
08 latterly, recently
10 not long ago

**lately**
05 newly
06 of late
08 latterly, recently
10 not long ago

**lateness**
09 tardiness
11 belatedness
12 dilatoriness

**latent**
06 hidden, unseen, veiled
07 dormant, lurking, passive
08 inactive, possible
09 concealed, invisible, potential, quiescent
10 underlying, unrevealed
11 undeveloped, unexpressed

**later**
05 after
07 by and by
08 in a while
09 afterward, following
10 afterwards, subsequent, succeeding
11 in due course, in the future
12 subsequently, successively
13 at a future date, at a future time, some other time

**lateral**
04 side
07 oblique
08 edgeways, edgewise, flanking, indirect, sideward, sideways

**latest**
02 in
03 now

06 modern, newest, with it
08 ultimate, up-to-date
10 most recent
13 up-to-the-minute

**lather**
04 flap, foam, fuss, soap, stew, suds
05 fever, froth, sweat, tizzy
06 dither, whip up
07 anxiety, bubbles, fluster, flutter, shampoo
08 soapsuds

**latitude**
04 play, room, span
05 field, range, reach, scope, space, sweep, width
06 extent, laxity, leeway
07 freedom, liberty, license
12 carte blanche

**latter**
03 end
04 last
05 final, later
06 ending
07 closing, ensuing
10 concluding, succeeding, successive
13 last mentioned

**latter-day**
06 modern
10 present-day
12 contemporary

**latterly**
06 lately, of late
08 hitherto

**lattice**
03 web
04 grid, mesh
07 network, tracery, trellis
08 fretwork, openwork
12 reticulation

**laud**
04 hail
05 extol, honor
06 admire, extoll, praise
07 acclaim, applaud, approve, glorify, magnify

**laudable**
09 admirable, estimable, excellent, exemplary
11 commendable, meritorious
12 praiseworthy

**laudation**
05 glory, kudos, paean
06 eulogy, homage, praise
07 acclaim, tribute
08 accolade, encomium
09 adulation, extolment, panegyric

**laudatory**
10 extollment, veneration
11 acclamation

**laudatory**
09 adulatory, approving
10 eulogistic
11 acclamatory, approbatory, panegyrical

**laugh**
03 fun, yuk
04 hoot, jest, joke, lark, roar
05 prank, sport, trick
06 cackle, giggle, guffaw, scream, titter
07 chortle, chuckle, snigger
09 fall about
12 be in stitches
14 split your sides

❑**laugh at**
04 jeer, mock
05 scorn, taunt
06 deride
07 scoff at
08 ridicule

❑**laugh off**
06 ignore
07 dismiss
08 pooh-pooh, shrug off
10 brush aside
12 make little of

**laughable**
05 comic, droll, funny
06 absurd
07 amusing, comical
08 derisive, derisory, farcical, humorous
09 hilarious, ludicrous
10 ridiculous, uproarious
11 nonsensical
12 entertaining, preposterous
13 sidesplitting

**laughingstock**
04 butt, dupe, fool, mark
06 stooge, target, victim

**laughter**
04 glee
05 mirth
08 giggling, hilarity, laughing
09 amusement, chortling, chuckling, guffawing, merriment, tittering
10 sniggering
11 convulsions

**launch**
04 fire, open
05 begin, float, found, set up, start
06 propel
07 project, send off
08 commence, dispatch, embark on, initiate, organize

09 discharge, instigate, introduce, set afloat
10 inaugurate
11 set in motion

**laundry**
04 wash
07 clothes, washing
10 laundermat, Laundromat
11 launderette
12 dirty clothes

**lavatory**
04 head, john
05 privy
06 toilet
07 latrine
08 bathroom, men's room, outhouse, restroom, wash room
09 cloakroom
10 ladies' room, powder room, women's room

**lavish**
04 free, heap, pour, rich
05 grand, spend, waste
06 bestow, deluge, shower
07 copious, liberal, profuse
08 abundant, generous, prolific, splendid, squander
09 bountiful, dissipate, excessive, luxuriant, plentiful, unlimited, unsparing
10 immoderate, openhanded, profligate, thriftless, unstinting
11 extravagant, intemperate

**law**
03 act
04 code, rule
05 axiom, canon, edict, maxim, order, tenet
06 decree
07 charter, command, formula, lawsuit, precept, statute
09 criterion, directive, enactment, ordinance, principle
10 litigation, regulation
11 commandment, legislation
12 constitution
13 jurisprudence

**law-abiding**
06 decent, honest
07 dutiful, upright
09 honorable
10 upstanding

**lawbreaker**
05 crook, felon
06 outlaw, sinner
07 convict
08 criminal, offender
09 infractor, miscreant

10 delinquent, trespasser
12 transgressor

**lawful**
05 legal, licit, valid
09 legalized, warranted
10 authorized, legitimate, sanctioned

**lawless**
06 unruly
07 illegal
08 anarchic, criminal, mutinous
09 insurgent, seditious
10 anarchical, rebellious
11 lawbreaking
13 revolutionary
15 insurrectionary

**lawlessness**
06 piracy
07 anarchy, mob rule
08 disorder, sedition
09 mobocracy, rebellion
10 insurgency, ochlocracy, revolution
12 insurrection, racketeering

**lawman**
07 marshal, officer, sheriff
09 policeman

**lawsuit**
04 case
05 cause, trial
06 action
10 indictment, litigation
11 legal action, proceedings, prosecution

**lawyer**
07 counsel
08 advocate, attorney
09 counselor, solicitor
10 counsellor, mouthpiece

☛ *Names of lawyers:*
03 **Lie** (Trygve)
04 **John** (Otto)
05 **Nader** (Ralph), **Vance** (Cyrus Roberts)
06 **Bailey** (F. Lee), **Darrow** (Clarence)
07 **Acheson** (Dean), **Cochran** (Johnnie), **Mondale** (Walter Frederick), **O'Connor** (Sandra Day)
08 **Marshall** (Thurgood)
09 **La Guardia** (Fiorello Henry)
10 **Dershowitz** (Alan)

**lax**
05 loose, slack, vague
06 casual, remiss, sloppy
07 inexact, lenient
08 careless, heedless, slipshod

09 easygoing, imprecise, indulgent, negligent
10 neglectful, permissive

**laxative**
05 purge, salts, senna
08 aperient, evacuant, magnesia
09 cathartic, purgative
14 milk of magnesia

**laxity**
08 latitude, leniency, softness
09 looseness, slackness
10 indulgence, negligence, sloppiness
11 imprecision, inexactness, nonchalance
12 carelessness, heedlessness, laissez faire, slovenliness
14 permissiveness

**lay**
03 bet, ode, put, set
04 bear, make, plan, poem, risk, song
05 allot, apply, beget, breed, leave, lodge, lyric, offer, place, plant, posit, wager
06 assign, ballad, burden, chance, charge, design, devise, gamble, hazard, impose, impute, locate, set out, settle
07 amateur, arrange, ascribe, deposit, dispose, inflict, oppress, prepare, present, produce, recline, secular, set down, work out
08 encumber, engender, madrigal, oviposit, position
09 attribute, establish, weigh down
10 put forward
11 give birth to
13 nonspecialist
15 nonprofessional

❏**lay aside**
04 keep, save
05 store
06 put off, reject, shelve
07 abandon, discard, dismiss
08 postpone

❏**lay bare**
04 show
06 expose, reveal, unveil
07 exhibit, uncover
08 disclose

❏**lay down**
04 drop, give
05 state, yield
06 affirm, assert, give up, ordain
07 discard

09 establish, formulate, postulate, prescribe, stipulate, surrender
10 relinquish

❏**lay down the law**
07 dictate
11 pontificate
14 read the riot act

❏**lay hands on**
03 get
04 find, grab, grip
05 bless, clasp, grasp, seize
06 clutch, locate, ordain
07 acquire, confirm, unearth
08 discover
09 get hold of
10 consecrate
12 bring to light

❏**lay in**
05 amass, hoard, store
07 build up, collect, stock up, store up
09 stockpile

❏**lay into**
06 assail, attack
08 let fly at, set about, tear into
09 pitch into

❏**lay it on**
07 flatter
08 butter up, overdo it, soft-soap
09 sweet-talk

❏**lay off**
04 drop, fire, quit, sack, stop
05 cease, let go, let up
06 desist, give up, pay off
07 dismiss, refrain
08 leave off
11 discontinue

❏**lay on**
04 give
05 cater, set up
06 supply
07 furnish, provide
08 organize

❏**lay out**
03 pay
04 fell, give, plan
05 floor, scold, spend
06 design, invest
07 arrange, display, exhibit, flatten
08 demolish, disburse
10 contribute

❏**lay up**
04 keep, save
05 amass, hoard
07 put away, store up
10 accumulate

❏**lay waste**
04 rape, raze, ruin, sack
06 ravage
07 despoil, destroy, pillage
09 devastate, vandalize

**layer**
03 bed, hen, ply, row
04 band, coat, film, seam, tier, vein
05 cover, plate, sheet
06 lamina, mantle
07 blanket, coating, deposit, stratum
08 covering
09 thickness

**layman, laywoman, lay-person**
07 amateur
11 parishioner
15 nonprofessional

**lay off**
04 boot, sack, stop
05 cease
07 dismiss
09 discharge

**layout**
03 map
04 plan
05 draft
06 design, format, sketch
07 outline
09 geography
11 arrangement

**laze**
04 idle, loaf, loll
05 relax
06 lounge

**laziness**
05 sloth
08 idleness, lethargy, slowness
09 fainéance, indolence
12 slothfulness, sluggishness

**lazy**
04 idle, slow
05 inert, slack, tardy
06 torpid
07 languid, work shy
08 bone idle, fainéant, inactive, indolent, slothful, sluggish
09 lethargic, shiftless
10 languorous, slow moving

**lazybones**
03 bum
05 idler
06 loafer, slouch
07 laggard, lounger, shirker, slacker
08 sluggard

## leach
04 seep
06 filter, osmose
08 filtrate
09 lixiviate, percolate

## lead
03 gap, tip, top, van
04 clue, edge, have, head, hint, live, main, move, pass, rule, shot, star, sway
05 balls, cause, chief, excel, first, guide, model, outdo, pilot, plumb, prime, slugs, spend, start, steer, usher
06 direct, escort, exceed, govern, induce, manage, margin, outrun, prompt, sinker, tip-off, weight
07 bring on, bullets, command, conduct, dispose, eclipse, example, incline, leading, pattern, pellets, premier, primary, produce, provoke, surpass, undergo
08 foremost, guidance, interval, outstrip, persuade, priority, regulate, result in, vanguard
09 advantage, be in front, call forth, come first, direction, forefront, indicator, influence, principal, supervise, supremacy, title role, transcend
10 ammunition, bring about, experience, first place, indication, leadership, precedence, suggestion, tend toward
11 heavy weight, leading role, outdistance, preeminence, preside over
12 be in charge of, call the shots

## ❏ lead off
04 open
05 begin, start
08 bat first, commence, initiate
10 inaugurate

## ❏ lead on
04 lure
05 tempt, trick
06 entice, seduce
07 beguile, deceive, mislead
11 string along

## ❏ lead the way
04 show
05 guide
07 go first
09 go in front

## ❏ lead up to
08 approach
09 introduce

10 pave the way, prepare for

## leaden
04 dull, gray, lead
05 dingy, heavy, inert, stiff
06 cloudy, dismal, dreary, gloomy, somber, wooden
07 grayish, labored, onerous, stilted
08 lifeless, listless, overcast, plodding, sluggish
10 lackluster, oppressive, spiritless

## leader
03 CEO
04 boss, head
05 chief, guide, ruler
06 bigwig
07 captain, general, pioneer, skipper
08 chairman, director, governor
09 chieftain, commander, conductor, executive, president, principal
10 chairwoman, figurehead, pathfinder, ringleader
11 chairperson, front-runner, trailblazer
12 guiding light, leading light
13 groundbreaker, prime minister

## leadership
04 rule
07 command
08 guidance, headship
09 authority, captaincy
11 generalship, preeminence, premiership
12 directorship, governorship

## leading
04 main
05 chief, first, front
07 primary, supreme, top rank
08 foremost, greatest
09 number one, paramount, principal
10 preeminent

## leaf
03 pad
04 flip, page, skim
05 blade, bract, calyx, folio, frond, sepal, sheet, thumb
06 browse, glance, needle
07 leaflet
09 cotyledon
12 thumb through
➤ See also PLANT

▶ *Parts of a leaf*:
03 tip
04 vein
05 blade

06 margin, midrib
07 petiole, stipule
08 leaf axil
09 epidermis, leaf cells
12 auxiliary bud

▶ *Leaf shapes*:
04 oval
05 lobed, ovate
06 entire, linear, lyrate, oblong
07 ciliate, cordate, crenate, cuneate, deltoid, dentate, hastate, obovate, palmate, peltate, pinnate, ternate
08 ciliated, digitate, elliptic, reniform, subulate
09 orbicular, runcinate, sagittate, spatulate
10 lanceolate, trifoliate
13 doubly dentate

## leaflet
04 bill
05 flyer, sheet, tract
06 folder
07 handout
08 circular, handbill, pamphlet

## leafy
05 bosky, green, shady, woody
06 shaded, wooded
07 foliose, verdant

## league
04 ally, band, link
05 class, guild, union, unite
06 cartel
07 combine, compact, consort
08 alliance, category, conspire
09 associate, coalition, cooperate, syndicate
10 conference, consortium, federation, fellowship
11 affiliation, association, collaborate, combination, confederacy, confederate, cooperative, corporation, partnership
12 conglomerate
13 collaboration, confederation

## ❏ in league
06 allied, linked
09 in cahoots
10 conspiring, in alliance
11 cooperating, hand in glove, in collusion
13 collaborating

## leak
03 cut
04 drip, ooze, seep, tell
05 break, crack, exude
06 escape, exposé, impart, oozing, reveal, squeal

07 divulge, leakage, leaking, let slip, seepage, seeping, trickle
08 disclose, exposure, give away, puncture
09 discharge, make known
10 disclosure, divulgence, make public, revelation, uncovering
11 percolation
13 spill the beans

**leaky**
05 holey, split
06 porous
07 cracked, leaking
09 permeable, punctured
10 perforated

**lean**
04 arid, bank, bare, bend, bony, lank, list, poor, prop, rest, slim, tend, thin, tilt
05 favor, gaunt, slant, slope
06 barren, prefer, repose, scanty, skinny, sparse
07 angular, incline, recline, scraggy, scrawny, slender
10 inadequate, unfruitful
12 insufficient, unproductive

❏**lean on**
06 rely on
08 depend on, persuade
10 pressurize
13 put pressure on

**leaning**
04 bent, bias
06 liking
08 aptitude, fondness, penchant, tendency
10 attraction, partiality, proclivity, propensity
11 disposition, inclination
12 predilection

**leap**
03 hop
04 jump, rise, romp, skip, soar
05 bound, caper, clear, dance, frisk, mount, surge, vault
06 bounce, cavort, frolic, gambol, rocket, spring
07 soaring, upsurge, upswing
08 escalate, increase, jump over
09 entrechat, skyrocket
10 escalation

❏**by leaps and bounds, in leaps and bounds**
07 quickly, rapidly, swiftly
08 in no time
13 in no time at all

❏**leap at**
04 grab
05 seize

06 jump at, snatch
07 agree to, fall for, swallow
08 pounce on

**learn**
04 hear
05 grasp, study, train
06 absorb, digest, gather, master, pick up, take in
07 acquire, discern, find out, realize
08 discover, memorize
09 ascertain, determine, get wind of
10 assimilate, comprehend, understand
11 have down pat
14 commit to memory

**learned**
06 versed
07 erudite
08 academic, cultured, lettered, literary, studious, well read
09 scholarly
10 widely read
12 intellectual, well informed
13 knowledgeable

**learner**
04 tiro, tyro
05 pupil
06 novice, rookie
07 scholar, student, trainee
08 beginner, neophyte
09 greenhorn
10 apprentice

**learning**
05 study
06 wisdom
07 culture, letters, tuition
09 education, erudition, knowledge, schooling
11 edification, scholarship

**lease**
03 let
04 hire, loan, rent
06 sublet
07 charter
08 sublease

**leash**
04 curb, hold, lead, rein
05 check
06 tether
09 restraint
10 discipline

**least**
06 fewest, lowest
08 smallest
09 slightest

**leathery**
05 rough, tough
07 wizened

08 hardened, wrinkled

**leave**
02 go
04 damp, drop, exit, jilt, move, quit, will
05 allot, break, cease, chuck, ditch, endow, say-so, scoot, scram
06 assign, day off, decamp, depart, desert, go away, retire, set out, vacate
07 abandon, consent, consign, deliver, entrust, forsake, freedom, holiday, liberty, pull out, push off, retreat, take off, time off, vamoose, warrant
08 bequeath, emigrate, furlough, hand down, hand over, run out on, sanction, transmit, up stakes, vacation, withdraw
09 disappear
10 green light, indulgence, make tracks, permission, sabbatical
11 leave behind
12 dispensation
13 authorization

❏**leave off**
03 end
04 halt, quit, stop
05 cease
06 desist, lay off
07 abstain, refrain
08 break off, knock off
09 terminate
11 discontinue

❏**leave out**
03 bar, cut
04 omit
06 except, ignore, reject
07 exclude, neglect
08 overlook, pass over
09 disregard

**leaven**
05 raise, swell
06 expand, puff up
07 ferment, inspire, lighten
09 stimulate

**leavings**
05 dregs, dross, spoil, waste
06 debris, refuse, scraps
07 remains, residue, rubbish
08 detritus
09 leftovers, remainder

**lecher**
04 goat, rake, roué, wolf
07 Don Juan, seducer
08 Casanova

09 adulterer, debauchee, debaucher, libertine, womanizer
11 dirty old man

**lecherous**
04 lewd
06 carnal, wanton
07 lustful, raunchy
08 prurient
09 salacious
10 lascivious, libidinous, licentious, womanizing
12 concupiscent

**lechery**
09 carnality, prurience
10 debauchery, rakishness, sensuality, wantonness
13 concupiscence, salaciousness
14 lasciviousness, libidinousness, licentiousness

**lecture**
04 talk
05 chide, scold, speak, teach
06 berate, homily, lesson, rebuke, sermon, speech
07 address, censure, chiding, expound, reproof, reprove, tell off
08 admonish, berating, harangue, instruct, reproach, scolding
09 discourse, give a talk, hold forth, reprimand, talking-to
10 telling off, upbraiding
11 instruction, make a speech
12 disquisition, dressing-down, tear to pieces

**lecturer**
05 tutor
06 orator, reader, talker
07 pedagog, speaker, teacher
08 academic, preacher
09 declaimer, expounder, haranguer, pedagogue, professor
10 instructor
11 speechifier, speechmaker

**ledge**
04 sill, step
05 ridge, shelf
06 mantel
08 overhang
10 projection
11 mantelpiece, mantelshelf
12 chimney piece

**lee**
06 refuge
07 shelter
09 sanctuary

10 protection

**leech**
07 sponger
08 hanger-on, parasite
09 scrounger
10 freeloader
11 bloodsucker, extortioner
12 extortionist

**leer**
03 eye
04 grin, ogle, wink
05 gloat, smirk, sneer, stare
06 goggle, squint

**leery**
04 wary
05 chary
07 careful, dubious, guarded
08 cautious, doubting
11 distrustful, on your guard

**lees**
05 draff, dregs
07 deposit, grounds, residue
08 sediment

**leeway**
04 play, room
06 margin
08 latitude

**left**
03 red
04 pink, port
07 leftist, liberal, radical
08 left wing, left-hand
09 communist, sinistral, socialist

**left-handed**
08 southpaw
09 sinistral

**leftover**
06 unused
07 uneaten

**leftovers**
05 dregs
06 excess, refuse, scraps
07 remains, residue, surplus
08 leavings, remnants
09 remainder, sweepings

**leg**
03 lap, peg, pin
04 crus, limb, part, prop
05 brace, shank, stage, stump
06 member
07 portion, section, segment, stretch, support, upright
12 underpinning

❏**leg it**
03 run
04 walk
05 hurry

❏**not have a leg to stand on**
11 lack support

❏**on its last legs**
04 weak
06 ailing
07 failing
12 at death's door

❏**pull someone's leg**
03 kid, rib
04 fool, joke
05 tease, trick
11 play a joke on

**legacy**
04 gift
06 estate
08 heirloom, heritage
09 patrimony
11 inheritance

**legal**
05 licit, right, sound, valid
06 lawful, proper
07 allowed
08 forensic, judicial, licensed, rightful
09 allowable, judiciary, legalized, permitted, statutory, warranted
10 aboveboard, acceptable, admissible, authorized, legitimate, sanctioned
11 permissible
12 within the law
14 constitutional

► *Legal terms*:
02 JP
03 bar, res, sue
04 bail, deed, dock, fine, jury, oath, will, writ
05 alibi, asset, bench, brief, claim, felon, judge, lease, party, proof, proxy, title, trial
06 appeal, arrest, bigamy, charge, equity, estate, guilty, lawyer, legacy, pardon, parole, patent, remand, repeal, suitor, waiver
07 accused, alimony, amnesty, caution, charter, codicil, convict, coroner, custody, damages, defense, divorce, examine, hearing, inquest, inquiry, lawsuit, mandate, probate, sheriff, statute, summons, verdict, warrant, witness
08 act of God, advocate, attorney, civil law, contract, covenant, criminal, easement, eviction, evidence, executor, freehold,

hung jury, innocent, judgment, juvenile, litigant, offender, prisoner, receiver, reprieve, sanction, sentence, subpoena, tribunal
09 accessory, acquittal, affidavit, annulment, common law, court case, defendant, endowment, fee simple, indemnity, intestacy, judiciary, leasehold, liability, plaintiff, precedent, probation, solicitor, testimony
10 accomplice, allegation, confession, conveyance, indictment, injunction, magistrate, settlement
11 adjournment, extradition, foreclosure, inheritance, maintenance, plead guilty, proceedings, ward of court
12 Bill of Rights, court-martial, cross-examine, notary public
13 attorney at law, plead innocent, public inquiry
14 plead not guilty, ward of the state
15 clerk of the court, contempt of court, power of attorney
➤ See also COURT; CRIME

**legality**
08 validity
09 rightness, soundness
10 lawfulness, legitimacy

**legalize**
06 permit, ratify
07 license, warrant
08 sanction, validate
10 legitimize
13 decriminalize

**legate**
05 agent, envoy
06 deputy, nuncio
08 delegate, emissary
10 ambassador
12 commissioner

**legatee**
04 heir
06 coheir
07 heiress
09 coheiress, inheritor
10 inheritrix
11 beneficiary

**legation**
07 embassy, mission
09 consulate
10 delegation, deputation

**legend**
03 key

04 myth, saga, tale
05 fable, motto, story
06 cipher
07 caption, fiction, romance
08 folk tale
09 narrative
11 explanation, inscription

➤ *Names from the Arthurian legend*:
03 Kay
04 Bors
06 Arthur, Avalon, Elaine, Gareth (of Orkney), Gawain, Merlin, Modred
07 Camelot, Galahad, Igraine, Tristan
08 Bedivere, Lancelot, Parsifal, Perceval, Tristram
09 Excalibur, Guinevere
11 Morgan le Fay
14 Launcelot du Lac, Uther Pendragon
➤ See also MYTHOLOGY

**legendary**
06 fabled, famous
07 honored
08 fabulous, fanciful, glorious, immortal, mythical, renowned
09 acclaimed, fictional, storybook, well-known
10 celebrated, fictitious, remembered
11 illustrious, traditional

**legerdemain**
08 artifice, trickery
09 chicanery, deception, sophistry
10 hocus-pocus
11 contrivance, maneuvering
12 manipulation
13 sleight of hand

**legible**
04 neat
05 clear, plain
08 distinct, readable
12 decipherable, intelligible

**legion**
04 army, host, mass
05 horde, swarm, troop
06 cohort, myriad, throng
07 brigade, company
08 division, numerous, regiment
09 battalion, countless, multitude
10 numberless

**legislate**
05 enact, order
06 codify, decree, ordain
09 authorize, prescribe

**legislation**
03 act, law
04 bill, code
07 charter, measure, statute
09 enactment, lawmaking, ordinance
11 formulation
12 codification, prescription
13 authorization

**legislative**
09 lawgiving, lawmaking
10 senatorial
13 congressional, parliamentary

**legislator**
05 solon
07 senator
08 lawgiver, lawmaker
10 politician
11 congressman
13 congresswoman
14 representative
15 parliamentarian

**legislature**
05 house
06 senate
07 chamber
08 assembly, congress
10 parliament

**legitimate**
04 fair, real, true
05 legal, licit, sound, valid
06 lawful, proper
07 correct, genuine, logical
08 credible, rightful
09 justified, plausible, statutory, warranted
10 acceptable, admissible, authorized, sanctioned
11 justifiable, well-founded

**legitimize**
07 charter, entitle, license, warrant
08 legalize, sanction, validate
09 authorize

**leisure**
04 ease, rest
05 break
07 freedom, holiday, liberty, time off, time out
08 free time, vacation
09 spare time
10 recreation, relaxation, retirement

❏**at your leisure**
11 unhurriedly
13 in your own time

**leisurely**
04 easy, slow
07 relaxed, restful, unhasty
08 carefree, laid-back, tranquil

09 easygoing, unhurried

**lend**
04 give, loan
05 grant
06 bestow, confer, impart
07 advance, furnish, provide
10 contribute

❑**lend an ear**
04 heed
06 listen
07 hearken

❑**lend a hand**
03 aid
04 help
06 assist

❑**lend itself to**
13 be suitable for

**length**
04 span, term
05 piece, reach, space
06 extent, period
07 measure, portion, section, segment, stretch
08 distance, duration

❑**at length**
06 at last
10 eventually
11 in due course
12 exhaustively
13 in great detail

❑**go to any lengths**
10 do anything
12 go to extremes

**lengthen**
03 eke
06 expand, extend
07 draw out, prolong, spin out, stretch
08 continue, elongate, increase, protract

**lengthwise**
07 endlong, endways, endwise
10 lengthways, vertically
12 horizontally

**lengthy**
04 long
05 wordy
06 prolix
07 diffuse, tedious, verbose
08 drawn out, extended, overlong, rambling
09 prolonged
10 long-winded, protracted
12 long-drawn-out

**leniency**
05 mercy
08 clemency, lenience
09 tolerance

10 compassion, gentleness, humaneness
11 forbearance, forgiveness
14 permissiveness

**lenient**
06 gentle, humane
07 liberal, sparing
08 merciful, moderate
09 forgiving, indulgent
10 forbearing
11 magnanimous, softhearted

**lenitive**
06 easing
08 soothing
10 mitigating, palliative

**leper**
05 lazar
06 pariah
07 outcast
11 undesirable, untouchable
13 social outcast

**lesbian**
03 gay
07 Sapphic, tribade
08 Sapphist, tribadic
10 homosexual

**lesion**
03 cut
04 gash, hurt, sore
05 wound
06 bruise, injury, scrape, trauma
07 scratch
08 abrasion
09 contusion
10 impairment, laceration

**less**
05 fewer
09 not as many, not as much, not so many, not so much
13 smaller amount

**lessen**
03 ebb
04 dull, ease, fail, flag, wane
05 abate, let up, lower, slack
06 deaden, go down, impair, narrow, plunge, reduce, shrink, weaken
07 abridge, curtail, decline, die down, dwindle, ease off, lighten, plummet, relieve, slacken, subside
08 come down, decrease, diminish, moderate, slow down

**lessening**
05 letup
06 easing, ebbing, waning
07 decline, erosion, failure
08 decrease, flagging

09 abatement, dwindling, reduction, weakening
10 diminution, moderation, slackening
11 contraction, curtailment, petering out
12 de-escalation, minimization

**lesser**
05 lower, minor
07 smaller
08 inferior, slighter
09 secondary
11 subordinate

**lesson**
05 class, model, moral
06 course, period, sermon
07 example, lecture, seminar, warning
08 coaching, exercise, teaching, tutorial
09 deterrent
11 instruction

**let**
04 hire, make, rent
05 allow, cause, check, grant, lease
06 enable, permit
07 agree to
08 assent to, obstacle, sanction, tolerate
09 authorize, consent to, hindrance, restraint
10 constraint, give the nod, impediment
11 obstruction, restriction
12 interference

❑**let alone**
04 also
08 as well as
09 apart from, never mind
12 not to mention
13 not forgetting

❑**let down**
04 fail
06 betray, desert
07 abandon
09 fall short
10 disappoint, disenchant, dissatisfy
11 disillusion
15 leave in the lurch

❑**let go**
04 free
06 unhand
07 manumit, release, set free
08 liberate

❑**let in**
05 admit, greet
06 accept, take in
07 include, receive, welcome

11 incorporate
12 allow to enter
❏**let off**
04 emit, fire
06 acquit, excuse, exempt, ignore, pardon
07 explode, give off, release
08 detonate, reprieve
09 discharge, exonerate
❏**let on**
04 blab, tell
06 reveal, squeal
07 divulge, let slip
08 disclose, give away
13 spill the beans
❏**let out**
04 blab, free, leak
06 betray, reveal, squeal
07 let slip, release
08 disclose
09 discharge, make known
13 spill the beans
❏**let up**
03 end
04 ease, halt, stop
05 abate, cease
06 lessen
07 die down, ease off, subside
08 decrease, diminish
❏**let down**
05 slump
07 decline, failure, washout
10 anticlimax
14 disappointment
**lethal**
05 fatal, toxic
06 deadly, mortal
07 deathly, noxious, ruinous
09 dangerous, murderous
**lethargic**
04 dull, idle, lazy, slow
05 heavy, inert, weary
06 drowsy, sleepy, torpid
07 languid
08 listless, slothful, sluggish
09 enervated
**lethargy**
05 sloth
06 torpor
07 inertia, languor
08 dullness, idleness, laziness, slowness
09 lassitude
12 listlessness, sluggishness
**letter**
04 line, mail, sign
05 reply, vowel
06 symbol
07 culture, epistle, message, missive, writing

08 dispatch, grapheme, learning
09 character, consonant, education, erudition
10 literature
13 belles-lettres, communication
14 correspondence
❏**to the letter**
07 exactly
08 strictly
09 by the book, literally
11 religiously, word for word
13 in every detail, punctiliously
**lettered**
06 versed
07 erudite, learned
08 cultured, educated, highbrow, literary, literate, well-read
09 scholarly
10 cultivated, widely read
**letup**
04 lull
05 break, pause
06 recess
07 respite
08 breather, interval
09 abatement, cessation, lessening, remission
10 slackening
**level**
03 aim, tie
04 avow, calm, even, flat, mark, rank, raze, size, tell, tied, zone
05 admit, class, equal, flush, focus, grade, layer, plane, point, stage, story, train
06 amount, degree, direct, even up, extent, height, stable, status, steady, volume
07 aligned, confess, destroy, divulge, echelon, even out, flatten, measure, station, stratum, tell all, uniform
08 altitude, balanced, bulldoze, constant, demolish, equalize, lay waste, matching, position, pull down, quantity, standard, standing, tear down
09 come clean, devastate, elevation, knock down, magnitude, stabilize
10 horizontal, unchanging
11 concentrate, neck and neck, unemotional, unflappable
12 speak plainly
13 self-possessed
14 tell it like it is
15 raze to the ground

❏**on the level**
04 fair, open
06 candid, honest
07 up-front
08 straight
10 above board
13 fair and square
**levelheaded**
04 calm, cool, sane
06 steady
07 prudent
08 balanced, composed, rational, sensible
10 cool-headed, dependable, reasonable
11 circumspect, unflappable
12 even-tempered
13 imperturbable
**lever**
03 bar, pry
04 lift, move, pull
05 force, heave, hoist, jimmy, raise, shift
06 handle, switch
07 crowbar
08 dislodge, joystick
09 handspike
**leverage**
04 pull, rank
05 clout, force, power
06 weight
08 purchase, strength
09 advantage, influence
**leviathan**
04 hulk
05 giant, Titan, whale
07 mammoth, monster
08 behemoth, colossus
10 sea monster
**levitate**
03 fly
04 hang, waft
05 drift, float, glide, hover
**levity**
03 fun
08 hilarity
09 flippancy, frivolity, silliness
10 triviality
11 irreverence
12 carefreeness
13 facetiousness
**levy**
03 due, fee, tax
04 duty, toll
05 exact, raise, tithe
06 assess, charge, demand, duties, excise, gather, impose, impost, tariff
07 collect, customs
10 assessment, collection

12 contribution, subscription

**lewd**
05 bawdy
06 carnal, impure, smutty, vulgar
07 lustful, obscene, raunchy
08 indecent, unchaste
09 lecherous, salacious
10 lascivious, licentious

**lewdness**
04 smut
07 crudity, lechery
09 bawdiness, carnality,
   depravity, indecency,
   obscenity, vulgarity
10 smuttiness
11 lustfulness
13 salaciousness
14 lasciviousness,
   licentiousness

**lexicographer**

➤ *Names of lexicographers
and philologists*:
04 **Bopp** (Franz)
05 **Roget** (Peter Mark), **Sapir**
   (Edward), **Skeat** (Walter
   William)
06 **Brewer** (Ebenezer
   Cobham), **Fowler** (Henry
   Watson), **Freund** (Wilhelm),
   **Hornby** (Albert Sidney),
   **Murray** (James Augustus
   Henry), **Onions** (Charles
   Talbut), **Porter** (Noah)
07 **Chomsky** (Noam), **Craigie**
   (William Alexander),
   **Diderot** (Denis), **Johnson**
   (Samuel), **Mencken** (Henry
   Louis), **Ventris** (Michael
   George Francis), **Webster**
   (Noah)
08 **Chambers** (Ephraim),
   **Larousse** (Pierre Athanase),
   **Saussure** (Ferdinand de)
09 **Furnivall** (Frederick James),
   **Jespersen** (Otto), **Partridge**
   (Eric Honeywood),
   **Worcester** (Joseph)
10 **Amarasimha**, **Burchfield**
   (Robert William)
➤ See also WRITER

**lexicon**
08 word list, wordbook
09 thesaurus
10 dictionary, phrase book,
   vocabulary

**liability**
05 debit
06 burden
07 arrears
08 drawback, nuisance

09 hindrance
10 impediment
11 culpability, encumbrance
12 disadvantage, indebtedness
14 accountability, responsibility

**liable**
03 apt
04 open
05 prone
06 likely
07 subject, tending
08 disposed, inclined
10 answerable
11 accountable, predisposed,
   responsible, susceptible

**liaison**
06 affair
07 contact, romance
08 intrigue
09 go-between
10 connection, love affair
11 cooperation, interchange
12 entanglement, relationship
13 collaboration
15 working together

**liar**
06 fibber
08 deceiver, perjurer
09 falsifier
12 false witness, prevaricator

**libation**
05 drink
08 drinking, oblation
09 sacrifice
13 drink offering
14 alcoholic drink

**libel**
04 slur
05 smear
06 defame, malign, revile, vilify
07 calumny, traduce
08 badmouth
09 aspersion
10 calumniate, defamation,
   muckraking, throw mud at
11 mudslinging
12 vilification

**libelous**
05 false
06 untrue
09 injurious, maligning,
   traducing, vilifying
10 calumnious, defamatory,
   scurrilous
12 calumniatory

**liberal**
06 lavish
07 copious, lenient, profuse,
   radical

08 abundant, catholic,
   generous, handsome,
   tolerant, unbiased
09 bountiful, plentiful,
   unsparing
10 broad based, munificent,
   open-minded, openhanded,
   politician
11 broad-minded, enlightened,
   libertarian, progressive
14 forward-looking

**liberalism**
10 radicalism
12 freethinking
13 progressivism
14 libertarianism
15 humanitarianism

**liberality**
06 bounty
07 breadth, charity
08 altruism, kindness, largesse
09 tolerance
10 generosity, toleration
11 beneficence, benevolence,
   catholicity, magnanimity,
   munificence
12 impartiality, philanthropy
13 progressivism
14 open-mindedness,
   openhandedness,
   permissiveness
15 broad-mindedness

**liberate**
04 free
05 let go
06 let out, redeem, rescue
07 deliver, manumit, release, set
   free, unchain
08 let loose, set loose, unfetter
09 discharge, unshackle
10 emancipate

**liberation**
07 freedom, freeing, release
10 redemption
11 deliverance, manumission
12 emancipation
15 enfranchisement

**liberator**
06 savior
07 rescuer
08 ransomer, redeemer
09 deliverer
10 manumitter
11 emancipator

**libertine**
04 rake, roué
06 lecher
07 Don Juan, lustful, seducer
08 Casanova
09 debauched, debauchee,
   debaucher, dissolute,

lecherous, reprobate,
10 licentious, profligate,
sensualist, voluptuary,
womanizing

**liberty**
05 right
07 freedom, license, release
08 autonomy, sanction
09 franchise, impudence,
insolence
10 disrespect, permission
11 deliverance, entitlement,
familiarity, manumission,
prerogative, presumption
12 emancipation, impertinence,
independence
15 overfamiliarity

◻ **at liberty**
04 free
07 allowed
09 permitted

**libidinous**
04 lewd
06 carnal, wanton
07 lustful, sensual
08 prurient
09 debauched, lecherous,
salacious
10 cupidinous, lascivious
12 concupiscent

**libido**
04 lust
05 ardor
07 passion
08 sex drive
09 eroticism
10 sexual urge
12 erotic desire, sexual desire
14 sexual appetite

**libretto**
04 book, text
05 lines, words
06 lyrics, script

► *Names of librettists*:
04 **Jouy** (Victor Joseph Étienne
de)
05 **Rolli** (Paolo Antonio),
**Smith** (Harry Bache)
06 **Lerner** (Alan Jay)
07 **Da Ponte** (Lorenzo),
**Gilbert** (William
Schwenck), **Sedaine**
(Michel-Jean)
08 **Gershwin** (Ira), **Kirkwood**
(James), **Meredith** (William
Morris)
11 **Hammerstein** (Oscar)
➤ See also MUSIC

**license**
03 tag
04 pass
05 grant, leave, right
06 excess, permit
07 abandon, anarchy, charter,
consent, freedom, liberty
08 approval, document,
sanction, warranty
09 authority, decadence,
exemption, privilege
10 debauchery, immorality,
imprimatur, indulgence,
permission
11 certificate, dissipation,
entitlement, prerogative
12 carte blanche, dispensation,
immoderation,
independence
13 accreditation, authorization,
certification, dissoluteness
14 licentiousness

**license**
05 allow
06 permit
07 certify, warrant
08 accredit, sanction
09 authorize, franchise
14 give permission

**licentious**
04 lewd
06 impure, wanton
07 immoral, lustful
08 depraved
09 abandoned, debauched,
dissolute, lecherous,
libertine
10 lascivious
11 promiscuous

**licentiousness**
04 lust
07 abandon, lechery
08 impurity, lewdness, salacity
10 debauchery, immorality,
wantonness
11 dissipation, promiscuity
13 dissoluteness, salaciousness

**lichen** see ALGAE

**lick**
03 bit, dab, lap, wet
04 beat, dart, hint, spot, wash
05 brush, clean, flick, speck,
taste, touch
06 defeat, hammer, little, ripple,
sample, stroke, thrash,
tongue
07 conquer, flicker, moisten,
smidgen, smidgin, trounce
08 play over, smidgeon,
vanquish

◻ **lick your lips**
05 enjoy, savor
06 relish
09 drool over

**licking**
06 defeat, hiding
07 beating, tanning
08 drubbing
09 thrashing

**lid**
03 cap, hat, top
05 cover
07 stopper
08 covering

**lie**
03 fib
04 keep, laze, rest, stay, trap
05 couch, dwell, exist, reach,
rebut, stand
06 belong, deceit, extend,
invent, lounge, remain,
repose
07 falsify, falsity, fiction, perjure,
perjury, recline, stretch,
untruth, whopper
08 continue, disprove
09 dissemble, fabricate,
falsehood, half-truth,
invention, sprawl out, tall
story
10 equivocate, stretch out
11 dissimulate, fabrication,
prevaricate
12 make up a story,
misrepresent
13 falsification

◻ **give the lie to**
05 rebut
08 disprove
10 contradict, prove false

◻ **lie in wait for**
06 ambush, attack, waylay
08 surprise
09 ambuscade

◻ **lie low**
04 hide, lurk
05 skulk
06 hole up
07 hide out
08 hide away
09 go to earth, take cover
12 go into hiding
15 keep a low profile

**lieutenant**
06 deputy
09 assistant
12 right-hand man
14 right-hand woman
15 second in command

## life

- 04 élan, soul, span, time, zest
- 05 being, fauna, flora, verve, vigor
- 06 breath, career, course, energy, entity, person, pizazz, spirit
- 07 pizzazz, sparkle
- 08 activity, duration, life span, lifetime, vitality, vivacity
- 09 aliveness, animation, biography, existence, human life, life story, viability
- 10 enthusiasm, experience, exuberance, human being, liveliness
- 11 continuance, high spirits
- 12 cheerfulness, living things
- 13 autobiography, fauna and flora

### ❏ come to life
- 06 wake up
- 09 come alive
- 12 become active, become lively
- 14 become exciting

### ❏ give your life
- 06 die for

## life-and-death
- 05 vital
- 07 crucial, serious
- 08 critical

## lifeblood
- 04 core, soul
- 05 heart
- 06 center, spirit
- 09 life force
- 11 inspiration

## lifeless
- 04 dead, dull, gone
- 05 stiff
- 06 barren, boring, wooden
- 07 defunct, sterile
- 08 deceased, desolate
- 09 colorless, inanimate, lethargic
- 10 insensible, lackluster, uninspired
- 11 unconscious, uninhabited, uninspiring

## lifelike
- 04 real, true
- 05 exact, vivid
- 07 natural
- 09 authentic, realistic
- 10 true to life

## lifelong
- 07 abiding, lasting
- 08 constant, enduring, lifetime
- 09 permanent
- 10 persistent

## lifestyle
- 04 life
- 09 way of life
- 11 way of living

## lifetime
- 04 life, span, time
- 06 career, course, period
- 08 duration, life span
- 09 existence

## lift
- 03 end, fly, run
- 04 copy, crib, move, pick, ride, spur, stop
- 05 annul, boost, clear, dig up, drive, exalt, hitch, hoist, raise, relax, shift, steal
- 06 borrow, buoy up, cancel, fillip, hold up, pick up, pull up, remove, revoke, uplift
- 07 airlift, elevate, rescind, root out, scatter, thin out, unearth, upraise
- 08 disperse, dissolve, elevator, hold high, pick-me-up
- 09 disappear, escalator, terminate, transport
- 10 plagiarize
- 11 reassurance
- 12 shot in the arm

## ligature
- 03 tie
- 04 band, bond, cord, link, rope
- 05 strap, thong
- 06 string
- 07 bandage, binding
- 08 ligament
- 10 connection, tourniquet

## light
- 03 day, gay, ray
- 04 airy, beam, bulb, dawn, easy, fair, fine, fire, glow, lamp, mild, pale, thin, weak
- 05 agile, angle, blaze, blond, cheer, faded, faint, flash, funny, glare, gleam, glint, happy, loose, match, merry, petty, put on, quick, shaft, shine, small, style, sunny, taper, torch, witty
- 06 aspect, beacon, blithe, blonde, bright, candle, cheery, flimsy, gentle, ignite, kindle, lively, luster, modest, nimble, pastel, porous, slight, turn on
- 07 amusing, animate, buoyant, cheer up, crumbly, daytime, glowing, insight, lantern, lenient, light up, lighten,

lighter, shining, sunrise, trivial, well lit, whitish
- 08 bleached, brighten, carefree, cheerful, cockcrow, daybreak, daylight, delicate, feathery, floating, graceful, humorous, lambency, luminous, moderate, pleasing, portable, radiance, switch on, trifling, untaxing
- 09 brilliant, dimension, diverting, easily dug, irradiate, knowledge, set alight, set fire to
- 10 brightness, brilliance, digestible, effortless, effulgence, illuminate, luminosity
- 11 crack of dawn, easily moved, elucidation, explanation, illuminated, lightweight, point of view, superficial, undemanding, unimportant
- 12 entertaining, illumination, lighthearted, luminescence
- 13 comprehension, enlightenment, incandescence, insubstantial, understanding
- 14 inconsiderable
- 15 inconsequential

### ❏ bring to light
- 06 expose, notice, reveal
- 07 uncover
- 08 discover

### ❏ come to light
- 09 be exposed, be noticed
- 11 be uncovered
- 12 be discovered

### ❏ in the light of
- 08 in view of
- 09 because of
- 11 considering, remembering
- 13 bearing in mind, keeping in mind

### ❏ light on, light upon
- 04 find, spot
- 05 hit on
- 06 land on
- 08 chance on, discover
- 09 encounter, stumble on
- 10 come across, happen upon

### ❏ shed light on, throw light on, cast light on
- 07 clarify, explain
- 09 elucidate, make clear
- 10 illuminate

## lighten
- 04 calm, ease, glow, lift
- 05 allay, cheer, elate, shine

**light-fingered**
06 buoy up, lessen, reduce, revive, unload, uplift
07 assuage, cheer up, gladden, hearten, inspire, relieve
08 brighten, illumine
09 alleviate, encourage
10 illuminate
11 make lighter
12 make brighter

**light-fingered**
03 sly
06 crafty, shifty
07 crooked, furtive
08 filching, stealing, thieving, thievish
09 dishonest, pilfering
11 shoplifting

**light-footed**
04 spry
05 agile, lithe, swift
06 active, nimble
08 graceful
09 sprightly

**light-headed**
04 airy
05 dizzy, faint, giddy, silly, woozy
07 flighty, foolish, shallow, vacuous
08 flippant, trifling, unsteady
09 delirious, frivolous
11 empty-headed, superficial, vertiginous
14 featherbrained, scatterbrained

**lighthearted**
03 gay
04 glad, high
05 happy, jolly, merry, sunny
06 blithe, bouncy, bright, chirpy, elated, jovial, joyful
07 amusing, playful
08 carefree, cheerful
10 frolicsome, untroubled
12 entertaining, happy-go-lucky
13 in good spirits, in high spirits

**lighthouse**
06 beacon, Pharos

**lightly**
05 gaily
06 airily, easily, gently, mildly, softly, thinly
07 faintly, readily
08 breezily, slightly, sparsely
09 leniently, sparingly
10 carelessly, delicately
12 effortlessly

**lightness**
06 levity

07 agility
08 airiness, buoyancy, delicacy, mildness, thinness
09 litheness
10 blitheness, flimsiness, gentleness, nimbleness, triviality
12 delicateness, gracefulness
14 weightlessness

**lightning**
07 hastily, quickly, rapidly
08 speedily, wildfire
11 immediately, thunderbolt
13 electric storm
14 sheet lightning
15 forked lightning

**lightning bug**
07 firefly
08 glowworm

**lightweight**
05 light, petty
06 flimsy, paltry, slight
08 delicate, feathery
10 negligible, weightless
13 insignificant, insubstantial

**like**
03 dig
04 akin, peer, twin, want, wish
05 adore, alike, enjoy, equal, fancy, go for, match
06 admire, desire, esteem, prefer, select, take to
07 approve, care for, of a kind, similar, welcome
08 be fond of, be keen on, decide on, hold dear
09 analogous, similar to
10 appreciate, comparable, equivalent, resembling
11 counterpart, much the same
12 feel inclined, on the lines of, take kindly to
13 approximating, corresponding
14 in the same way as, take pleasure in
15 along the lines of

**likeable**
06 genial
07 amiable, winning, winsome
08 pleasant, pleasing
09 agreeable, congenial

**likelihood**
06 chance
08 prospect
10 likeliness
11 possibility, probability

**likely**
03 fit
05 prone, right

06 liable, odds-on, proper
07 fitting, hopeful, no doubt, tending
08 credible, expected, feasible, inclined, pleasing, possible, probable, probably
09 in the wind, like as not, plausible, promising
10 acceptable, believable, on the cards, presumably
11 anticipated, appropriate, as like as not, doubtlessly, foreseeable, predictable
12 to be expected

**like-minded**
08 agreeing, in accord
09 in harmony
10 compatible, harmonious

**liken**
05 match
06 equate, relate
07 compare
09 analogize, associate, correlate, juxtapose

**likeness**
04 bust, copy, form, icon
05 guise, image, shape, study
06 effigy, sketch, statue
07 drawing, picture, replica
08 affinity, painting, portrait
09 facsimile, semblance
10 appearance, comparison, photograph, similarity, similitude
11 counterpart, parallelism, resemblance
12 reproduction
14 correspondence, representation

**likewise**
03 too
04 also
07 besides
08 moreover
09 similarly
12 in like manner, in the same way
14 by the same token

**liking**
04 bent, bias, love
05 fancy, taste, thing
06 desire
07 leaning
08 affinity, fondness, penchant, soft spot, tendency, weakness
09 affection
10 attraction, partiality, preference, proclivity, propensity
11 inclination

12 appreciation, predilection

**lilt**
03 air
04 beat, song, sway
06 rhythm
07 cadence, measure
11 rise and fall

**lily**

> ► *Types of lily*:
03 day, may
04 aloe, arum, bell, Lent, pond,
     sego, wood
05 calla, camas, Croft, lotus,
     regal, tiger, torch, water,
     yucca
06 camass, crinum, Easter,
     meadow, smilax
07 African, candock, Madonna,
     quamash
08 asphodel, hyacinth,
     martagon, Solomon's,
     trillium, Turk's cap, victoria
09 amaryllis, herb Paris
10 agapanthus, aspidistra,
     belladonna, black calla,
     fritillary
12 Annunciation
13 butcher's-broom, lily of the
     nile
15 lily of the valley
> ➤ See also PLANT

**lily-white**
04 pure
06 chaste, virgin
08 innocent, spotless, virtuous
09 blameless, faultless,
     untainted
14 irreproachable

**limb**
03 arm, leg
04 fork, part, spur, wing
05 bough
06 branch, member
07 section
08 offshoot
09 appendage, extension,
     extremity
10 projection

❑ **out on a limb**
07 exposed
08 isolated
10 vulnerable

**limber**
05 agile, lithe
06 lissom, pliant, supple
07 elastic, lissome, plastic,
     pliable
08 flexible, graceful

❑ **limber up**
06 warm up

08 exercise, loosen up

**limbo**

❑ **in limbo**
10 in abeyance
11 left hanging
12 left in the air
15 on the back burner

**limelight**
04 fame
06 notice, renown
07 stardom
09 attention, celebrity, public
     eye, publicity, spotlight

**limit**
03 end, lid, rim
04 brim, curb, edge
05 bound, brink, check, verge
06 border, bounds, hinder,
     impede, ration, reduce,
     utmost
07 ceiling, compass, confine,
     control, extreme, maximum,
     Rubicon
08 boundary, confines,
     deadline, frontier, restrain,
     restrict, terminus, ultimate
09 constrain, extremity,
     perimeter, restraint
10 constraint, limitation,
     parameters
11 cutoff point, restriction,
     termination
12 circumscribe
15 point of no return

❑ **the limit**
06 enough, the end
07 too much
11 intolerable
12 the last straw

**limitation**
04 curb, snag
05 block, check
07 control
08 drawback, weakness
09 hindrance, restraint, weak
     point
10 constraint, impediment
11 restriction, shortcoming
12 disadvantage, incapability

**limited**
05 basic, fixed, small
06 finite, narrow, scanty
07 checked, defined, minimal
08 confined
10 controlled, restricted
11 constrained
13 circumscribed

**limitless**
04 vast
07 endless

08 infinite, unending
09 boundless, countless,
     unbounded, undefined
11 measureless, never-ending
12 interminable

**limp**
03 hop, lax
04 gimp, soft, weak
05 frail, hitch, loose, slack,
     spent, tired, weary
06 falter, feeble, flabby, floppy,
     hobble, limber, totter
07 flaccid, pliable, relaxed,
     shamble, shuffle, stagger,
     stumble
08 drooping, fatigued, flexible,
     lameness
09 lethargic
11 debilitated
12 claudication

**limpid**
04 pure
05 clear, lucid, still
06 bright, glassy
07 flowing
11 translucent, transparent
12 crystal clear, intelligible

**line**
03 bar, job, pad, rim, row, way
04 area, axis, back, band, bank,
     belt, book, card, cord, dash,
     draw, edge, face, file, fill, firm,
     kind, make, mark, memo,
     note, part, path, race, rank,
     rope, rule, seam, sort, talk,
     text, tier, type, wire, word,
     work
05 bound, brand, breed, cable,
     chain, cover, field, forte,
     front, hatch, inlay, limit, pitch,
     route, score, shape, slash,
     spiel, stock, strip, stuff, style,
     track, trade, twine, verge,
     words
06 avenue, belief, border,
     career, column, course,
     crease, encase, family, figure,
     fringe, furrow, groove, letter,
     margin, method, parade,
     patter, policy, report,
     scheme, script, series, strain,
     strand, streak, string, stripe,
     stroke, system, thread
07 calling, channel, company,
     conform, contour, descent,
     lineage, message, outline,
     pattern, profile, pursuit,
     scratch, variety, wrinkle
08 activity, ancestry, approach,
     attitude, boundary, business,
     defenses, frontier, heritage,
     ideology, inscribe, interest,

libretto, pedigree, position, postcard, practice, province, sequence, vocation
09 crow's-foot, direction, formation, front line, parentage, perimeter, periphery, procedure, reinforce, sales talk, specialty, specialty, underline
10 appearance, battle zone, employment, extraction, firing line, line of work, occupation, procession, profession, silhouette, specialism, trajectory
11 battlefield, delineation, demarcation
13 configuration
14 course of action, specialization

❏**draw the line**
07 rule out
09 stand firm
11 stop short of
15 put your foot down

❏**in line**
03 due
06 in a row, in step, likely
08 in accord
09 in harmony
10 on the cards
11 in agreement
12 in the running

❏**lay it on the line, put it on the line**
04 risk
07 imperil
08 endanger
10 jeopardize
12 speak frankly

❏**line up**
05 align, array, group, lay on, order, range
06 fall in, obtain, secure
07 arrange, marshal, prepare, procure, produce
08 assemble, organize
09 form ranks
10 straighten

❏**toe the line**
07 conform
12 keep the rules
14 be conventional, follow the rules

**lineage**
04 line, race
05 birth, breed, house, stock
06 family
07 descent
08 ancestry, heredity, pedigree

09 ancestors, forebears, genealogy, offspring
11 descendants

**lineaments**
05 lines
06 aspect, traits, visage
07 outline, profile
08 features, outlines

**lined**
05 feint, ruled
07 creased
08 furrowed, wrinkled

**linen**
06 sheets, shirts
07 lingery
10 white goods
11 pillowcases, tablecloths

**lineup**
03 row
04 bill, cast, line, list, team
05 array
10 order at bat
11 arrangement

**linger**
03 lag
04 idle, last, stay, stop, wait
05 dally, delay, tarry
06 dawdle, endure, hang on, loiter, remain
07 hold out, persist, survive
10 dillydally, hang around
12 take your time
13 procrastinate

**lingerie**
03 bra
04 slip
05 teddy
06 undies
07 panties
08 camisole, frillies
09 brassiere, underwear
11 panty girdle
12 body stocking, underclothes
13 underclothing, undergarments
14 unmentionables

**lingering**
08 dragging
09 prolonged
10 protracted
12 long-drawn-out

**lingo**
04 cant, talk
05 argot, idiom
06 jargon, patois, patter, speech, tongue
07 dialect
08 language, parlance
10 vernacular, vocabulary
11 terminology

**liniment**
03 oil
05 cream, salve
06 balsam, lotion
07 unguent
08 ointment
09 emollient

**lining**
07 backing, padding
11 interfacing
13 reinforcement

**link**
03 tie
04 ally, bind, bond, join, knot, loop, part, ring, yoke
05 joint, merge, piece, tie up, union, unite
06 attach, couple, fasten, hook up, team up
07 bracket, connect, liaison, section
08 cuff link
10 amalgamate, attachment, connection, join forces
11 association, constituent, partnership
12 relationship
13 communication

❏**link up**
04 ally, dock, join
05 merge, unify
06 hook up, team up
07 connect
10 amalgamate, join forces

**linkup**
05 tie-in, union
06 merger
10 connection
11 association, partnership

**lionhearted**
04 bold
05 brave
06 daring, heroic
07 gallant, valiant
08 fearless, intrepid, resolute, stalwart, valorous
10 courageous

**lionize**
05 exalt, honor
06 praise
07 acclaim, adulate, glorify, idolize
10 aggrandize
11 hero-worship
14 put on a pedestal

**lip**
03 rim
04 brim, edge
05 brink, cheek, sauce, verge
06 border, margin

08 back talk, rudeness
09 impudence, insolence
12 impertinence

**liquefaction**
07 melting, thawing
10 dissolving
13 deliquescence

**liquefy**
04 flux, melt, thaw
05 smelt
08 dissolve, fluidize
10 deliquesce

**liqueur**

➤ *Types of liqueur (mostly trademarks)*:
06 kirsch, kümmel
07 absinth, curaçao, ratafia
08 absinthe, advocaat, amaretto, Drambuie, Tia Maria
09 Cointreau
10 chartreuse, maraschino
11 Benedictine
12 cherry brandy, kirschwasser
13 crème de menthe
➤ See also DRINK

**liquid**
03 wet
05 clear, drink, fluid, juice, runny
06 liquor, lotion, melted, molten, sloppy, thawed, watery
07 aqueous, flowing, running
08 solution
09 liquefied

**liquidate**
04 kill, sell
06 cash in, murder, remove, rub out, wind up
07 abolish, break up, destroy, disband, sell off, wipe out
08 dispatch, dissolve, massacre
09 close down, eliminate, terminate
10 annihilate, do away with, put an end to
11 assassinate, exterminate

**liquidize**
05 blend, crush, purée
07 process

**liquor**
04 grog, vino
05 booze, drink, hooch, juice, sauce
06 hootch, liquid, poison, rotgut
07 alcohol, essence, spirits
08 infusion
09 hard stuff, moonshine
10 hard liquor, intoxicant

11 mountain dew, strong drink
14 white lightning

**lissom**
05 agile, light, lithe
06 limber, nimble, pliant, supple
07 pliable, willowy
08 flexible, graceful

**list**
03 tip
04 bill, book, cant, file, heel, lean, note, roll, Root, tilt
05 enter, index, slant, slope, table, tally
06 agenda, enroll, record, roster
07 catalog, compile, incline, invoice, itemize, listing, program, set down
08 calendar, classify, contents, heel over, lean over, register, schedule, syllabus, tabulate
09 catalogue, checklist, directory, enumerate, inventory
10 tabulation
11 enumeration

**listen**
04 hark, hear, heed, mind
07 hearken
08 give ears
09 lend an ear
15 prick up your ears

❏**listen in**
03 bug, tap
07 monitor, wiretap
09 eavesdrop
15 prick up your ears

**listless**
04 dull, limp
05 inert
06 torpid
07 languid, passive
08 inactive, indolent, sluggish
09 apathetic, impassive, lethargic
10 spiritless
11 indifferent

**listlessness**
05 ennui, sloth
06 apathy, torpor
07 languor
08 lethargy
09 indolence, torpidity
11 inattention, languidness

**litany**
04 list
06 prayer
07 account, catalog, recital
09 catalogue
10 invocation, recitation, repetition

11 enumeration

**literacy**
08 learning
09 education, erudition, knowledge
10 articulacy
11 cultivation, learnedness, proficiency, scholarship

**literal**
04 dull, true
05 close, exact
06 actual, boring, strict
07 factual, genuine, humdrum, precise, prosaic, tedious
08 accurate, faithful, verbatim
09 colorless
10 uninspired
11 unvarnished, word for word
12 matter-of-fact

**literally**
05 truly
06 really
07 closely, exactly, plainly
08 actually, strictly, verbatim
09 certainly, precisely
10 faithfully
11 to the letter, word for word

**literary**
06 formal, poetic
07 bookish, erudite, learned, refined
08 cultured, educated, lettered, literate, well-read
09 scholarly
10 colloquial, cultivated, widely read
12 old-fashioned

➤ *Names of literary characters*:
03 Eva (Little), **Fox** (Brer), **Jim** (Lord), **Kaa**, **Kim**, **Lee** (Lorelei), **Pan** (Peter), **Pip**, **Roo**, **Tom** (Uncle), **Una**
04 **Ahab** (Captain), **Bede** (Adam), **Bond** (James), **Budd** (Billy), **Eyre** (Jane), **Finn** (Huckleberry), **Fogg** (Phileas), **Gale** (Dorothy), **Gamp** (Sarah), **Garp** (T.S.), **Gray** (Dorian), **Gump** (Forrest), **Gunn** (Ben), **Heep** (Uriah), **Hood** (Robin), **Hook** (Captain), **Hyde** (Mister), **Jack**, **Joad** )(Tom), **Mole**, **Pooh**, **Pope** (Giant), **Ryan** (Jack), **Slop** (Doctor), **Tigg** (Montague), **Toad** (Mister), **Trim** (Corporal), **Troy** (Sergeant Francis), **Tuck** (Friar)
05 **Akela**, **Aslan**, **Athos**, **Baloo**,

Bates (Miss), **Bloom** (Leopold), **Bloom** (Molly), **Boxer, Brown** (Father), **Chips** (Mister), **Darcy** (Fitzwilliam), **Diver** (Dick), **Doone** (Lorna), **Drood** (Edwin), **Finch** (Atticus), **Flint** (Captain), **Geste** (Beau), **Hardy** (Frank), **Hardy** (Joe), **Henry** (Frederic), **Jones** (Tom), **Kanga, Kipps** (Arthur), **Loman** (Willy), **Lucky, March** (Amy), **March** (Augie), **Maria** (Mad), **Mitty** (Walter), **Moore** (Mrs), **Mosca, Nancy, O'Hara** (Kimball), **O'Hara** (Scarlett), **Piggy, Polly** (Alfred), **Porgy, Pozzo, Price** (Fanny), **Quilp** (Daniel), **Ralph, Ratty, Remus** (Uncle), **Rudge** (Barnaby), **Satan, Sharp** (Becky), **Sikes** (Bill), **Slope** (Reverend Obadiah), **Sloth, Small** (Lennie), **Smike, Smith** (Winston), **Spade** (Sam), **Stubb, Tarka** (the Otter), **Titus, Topsy, Trent** (Little Nell), **Twist** (Oliver)

06 **Aramis, Archer** (Isabelle), **Arthur** (King), **Badger, Barkis, Belial, Ben-Hur** (Judah), **Bennet** (Elizabeth), **Bourgh** (Lady Catherine de), **Bovary** (Emma), **Brodie** (Miss Jean), **Brooke** (Dorothea), **Bumble** (Mister), **Bumppo** (Natty), **Bunter** (Billy), **Butler** (Rhett), **Crusoe** (Robinson), **Dombey** (Paul), **Dorrit** (Amy), **Dorrit** (William), **Du Bois** (Blanche), **Eeyore, Friday** (Man), **Gantry** (Elmer), **Gatsby** (Jay), **Gawain, Hammer** (Mike), **Hannay** (Richard), **Herzog** (Moses), **Holmes** (Sherlock), **Jeeves** (Reginald), **Jekyll** (Doctor Henry), **Legree** (Simon), **Marley** (Jacob), **Marner** (Silas), **Marple** (Jane), **Moreau** (Doctor), **Mowgli, Omnium** (Duke of), **Pickle** (Gamaliel), **Piglet, Pinkie, Pliant** (Dame), **Poirot** (Hercule), **Prynne** (Hester), **Rabbit, Rabbit** (Brer), **Random** (Roderick), **Rob Roy, Sawyer** (Bob), **Sawyer**

(Tom), **Shandy** (Tristram), **Silver** (Long John), **Subtle, Tarzan, Tigger, Tybalt, Tyrone** (James), **Varden** (Dolly), **Wadman** (Widow), **Watson** (Doctor John), **Weller** (Samuel), **Wilkes** (Ashley), **Wilkes** (Melanie), **Wimsey** (Lord Peter), **Wopsle** (Mister), **Yahoos**

07 **Andrews** (Pamela), **Ayeesha, Babbitt** (George), **Baggins** (Bilbo), **Baggins** (Frodo), **Barkley** (Catherine), **Beowulf, Biggles, Bramble** (Matthew), **Brer Fox, Charles** (Nick), **Charles** (Nora), **Clinker** (Humphry), **Crackit** (Toby), **Danvers** (Mrs), **Dawkins** (Jack), **Dedalus** (Stephen), **Deronda** (Daniel), **Despair** (Giant), **Don Juan, Dorigen, Dorothy, Dracula** (Count), **Estella, Fairfax** (Jane), **Gandalf** (the Grey), **Gargery** (Joe), **Grendel, Harding** (Reverend Septimus), **Harlowe** (Clarissa), **Hawkins** (Jim), **Higgins** (Professor Henry), **Hopeful, Humbert** (Humbert), **Ishmael, Jaggers** (Mister), **Jellyby** (Mrs), **Le Fever** (Lieutenant), **Maigret** (Jules), **Marlowe** (Philip), **Newsome** (Chad), **Obadiah, Peachum** (Thomas), **Pierrot, Porthos, Proudie** (Doctor), **Raffles, Rebecca, Scarlet** (Will), **Scrooge** (Ebenezer), **Shipton** (Mother), **Slumkey** (Samuel), **Squeers** (Wackford), **Surface** (Charles), **Surface** (Joseph), **Tiny Tim, Wemmick** (Mister), **Wickham** (George), **William, Witches** (The Three), **Wooster** (Bertie), **Would-be** (Sir Politic)

08 **Absolute** (Captain), **Anderson** (Pastor Anthony), **Backbite** (Sir Benjamin), **Bagheera, Bedivere** (Sir), **Black Dog, Casaubon** (Reverend Edward), **Corleone** (Vito), **Cratchit** (Bob), **Criseyde, Faithful, Flanders** (Moll),

**Flashman, Gloriana, Griselda** (Patient), **Gulliver** (Lemuel), **Havisham** (Miss), **Hrothgar, Jarndyce** (John), **Knightly** (George), **Kowalski** (Stanley), **Ladislaw** (Will), **Lancelot** (Sir), **Lestrade** (Inspector), **MacHeath** (Captain), **Magwitch** (Abel), **Malaprop** (Mrs), **Micawber** (Wilkins), **Moriarty** (Professor James), **Napoleon, Nickleby** (Nicholas), **Paradise** (Sal), **Peggotty** (Clara), **Peterkin, Pickwick** (Samuel), **Queequeg, Santiago, Snowball, Starbuck, Svengali, Tashtego, Thatcher** (Becky), **The Clerk, The Friar, The Reeve, Trotwood** (Betsey), **Tulliver** (Maggie), **Twitcher** (Jemmy), **Vladimir**

09 **Archimago, Bounderby** (Josiah), **Britomart, Bulstrode** (Nicholas), **Caulfield** (Holden), **Cheeryble** (Charles), **Christian, Churchill** (Frank), **Constance, D'Artagnan, Doolittle** (Eliza), **Fezziwig** (Mister), **Gradgrind** (Thomas), **Grandison** (Sir Charles), **Greenwood** (Esther), **harlequin, Lismahago** (Obadiah), **Lochinvar, MacKenzie** (Allison), **Minnehaha, Pecksniff** (Seth), **Pendennis** (Arthur), **Pollyanna, Rochester** (Edward Fairfax), **Scudamour** (Sir), **Shere Khan, The Knight, The Miller, The Squire, The Walrus, Tiger Lily, Trelawney** (Squire), **Van Winkle** (Rip), **Woodhouse** (Emma), **Yossarian** (Captain John), **Zenocrate**

10 **Allan-a-Dale, Big Brother, Brer Rabbit, Challenger** (Professor), **Chuzzlewit** (Martin), **Evangelist, Fauntleroy** (Little Lord), **Great-heart** (Mister), **Heathcliff, Hornblower** (Horatio), **Houyhnhnms, Little John, Little Nell, Maid Marian, Quatermain** (Allan), **The Red King, The**

Tar Baby, Tinkerbell, Tweedledee, Tweedledum
11 **Copperfield** (David), **D'Urberville** (Alec), **Durbeyfield** (Tess), **Mickey Mouse, Mutabilitie, Pumblechook** (Mister), **Ready-to-Halt** (Mister), **The Dormouse, The Franklin, The Man of Law, The Merchant, The Pardoner, The Prioress, The Red Queen, The Summoner, Tiggy-Winkle** (Mrs), **Zawistowska** (Sophie)
12 **Blatant Beast, Chaunticleer, Frankenstein** (Victor), **Humpty-Dumpty, Lilliputians, Rip Van Winkle, The Carpenter, The Mad Hatter, The March Hare, The Pied Piper** (of Hamelin), **The Red Knight, The Scarecrow**
13 **The Jabberwock, The Mock Turtle, The Tin Woodman, The Wife of Bath, Winnie-the-Pooh**
14 **Mephistopheles, Rikki-Tikki-Tavi, The White Rabbit, Worldly Wiseman** (Mister)
15 **The Artful Dodger, The Cowardly Lion, The Three Witches, Valiant-for-Truth**
➤ See also SHAKESPEARE

► *Names of literary critics:*
04 **Bell** (Clive Howard), **Blum** (Léon)
05 **Hicks** (Granville), **Lodge** (David), **Stead** (Christian Karlson)
06 **Arnold** (Matthew), **Calder** (Angus), **Empson** (Sir William), **Leavis** (Frank Raymond), **Leavis** (Queenie Dorothy), **Lukacs** (György Szegedy von), **Sontag** (Susan), **Wilson** (Edmund)
07 **Alvarez** (Alfred), **Barthes** (Roland), **Derrida** (Jacques), **Hoggart** (Richard), **Kermode** (Frank)
08 **Bradbury** (Malcolm Stanley), **Longinus, Nicolson** (Sir Harold George), **Richards** (Ivor Armstrong), **Trilling** (Lionel), **Williams** (Raymond)

**literate**
07 learned
08 cultured, educated
10 able to read, proficient
11 able to write, intelligent
12 intellectual, well educated
13 knowledgeable

**literature**
04 data, pulp
05 facts, paper, prose, verse
06 papers
07 fiction, handout, leaflet, letters
08 brochure, circular, handouts, leaflets, pamphlet, writings
09 brochures, circulars, pamphlets
11 information
12 press release, printed works
13 printed matter
14 published works

► *Types of literature:*
04 epic, saga
05 drama, essay, novel, prose, verse
06 parody, poetry, satire, thesis
07 epistle, fiction, lampoon, novella, polemic, tragedy, trilogy
08 allegory, libretto, pastiche, treatise
09 antinovel, biography, criticism
10 magnum opus, nonfiction, roman à clef
11 Gothic novel
13 autobiography, belles-lettres
15 historical novel, picaresque novel
16 sentimental novel

**lithe**
05 agile
06 limber, lissom, pliant, supple
07 lissome, pliable
08 flexible

**litigant**
04 suer
05 party
08 claimant
09 contender, defendant, disputant, litigator, plaintiff
11 complainant

**litigation**
04 case, suit
06 action
07 dispute, lawsuit, process
11 prosecution

**litigious**
11 belligerent, contentious, quarrelsome
12 disputatious
13 argumentative

**litter**
04 grot, junk, mess, muck
05 brood, strew, trash, young
06 debris, family, refuse
07 garbage, rubbish, scatter
08 detritus
09 confusion, offspring, stretcher

**little**
03 bit, dab, wee
04 baby, cute, dash, drop, hint, mini-, nice, spot, tiny
05 brief, dwarf, minor, petty, pinch, scant, short, small, taste, teeny, touch, trace
06 barely, hardly, meager, midget, minute, paltry, petite, rarely, seldom, skimpy, slight, sparse, trifle
07 modicum, nominal, peanuts, slender, soupçon, trickle, trivial, younger
08 fragment, nugatory, particle, pintsize, trifling
09 ephemeral, miniature, momentary, pintsized, transient
10 attractive, diminutive, negligible, short-lived, smattering, transitory
11 Lilliputian, microscopic, small amount, unimportant
12 infrequently, insufficient
13 infinitesimal, insignificant, next to nothing
14 inconsiderable
15 a drop in the ocean

❑**little by little**
06 slowly
08 bit by bit
09 by degrees, gradually, piecemeal
10 step by step
13 imperceptibly, progressively

**liturgical**
06 formal, ritual, solemn
08 hieratic
10 ceremonial, sacerdotal
11 eucharistic, sacramental

**liturgy**
04 form, rite
06 office, ritual
07 service, worship
09 ordinance, sacrament
10 observance

**live**
02 be
03 hot
04 last, lead, pass, stay

**liveable**

05 abide, alive, dwell, exist, lodge, revel, spend, vital
06 active, alight, behave, endure, lively, reside, urgent
07 animate, be alive, breathe, burning, current, dynamic, flaming, glowing, ignited, inhabit, persist, survive, topical
08 continue, existent, relevant, vigorous, volatile
09 breathing, connected, enjoy life, explosive, pertinent
10 draw breath, unexploded
12 have your home
13 controversial
14 earn your living
15 support yourself

❑**live it up**
05 revel
09 have a ball, make merry
11 make whoopee
15 paint the town red

❑**live on**
04 feed
05 exist
06 rely on
07 live off, subsist

❑**live wire**
06 dynamo
07 hustler, whiz kid
08 go-getter

**liveable**
09 habitable
11 inhabitable

❑**liveable with**
08 bearable, passable, sociable
09 congenial, tolerable
10 compatible, harmonious
13 companionable

**livelihood**
05 means
06 income, living, upkeep
07 support
11 maintenance, subsistence
14 means of support, source of income

**liveliness**
04 brio, zest
05 oomph
06 energy, spirit
08 dynamism, vitality, vivacity
09 animation, quickness
13 sprightliness

**livelong**
05 whole
06 entire

**lively**
04 busy, keen, racy, spry

05 agile, alert, alive, brisk, merry, perky, quick, rapid, vivid
06 active, blithe, bouncy, breezy, bright, chirpy, frisky, gung ho, heated, hectic, jaunty, nimble, strong
07 buoyant, buzzing, crowded, dynamic, graphic, playful, teeming
08 animated, bustling, cheerful, colorful, eventful, exciting, spirited, stirring, striking, vigorous
09 energetic, sprightly, vivacious
10 frolicsome, refreshing
11 imaginative, interesting, stimulating
12 enthusiastic, high-spirited, invigorating

**liven**
05 hot up, pep up, rouse, spice
06 buck up, perk up, stir up
07 animate, enliven, spice up
08 brighten, energize, vitalize
10 invigorate

**liverish**
05 testy
06 crabby, crusty, grumpy, snappy, tetchy
07 crabbed, peevish
09 crotchety, irascible, irritable, splenetic
12 disagreeable
13 quick-tempered

**livery**
04 garb, gear, suit, togs
05 dress, get up, habit
06 attire
07 apparel, clothes, costume, regalia, uniform
08 clothing, garments
09 vestments
11 habiliments

**livid**
03 mad, wan
04 pale, waxy
05 angry, ashen, irate, pasty
06 fuming, leaden, pallid, purple, raging
07 bruised, enraged, furious, ghastly, grayish
08 blanched, incensed, outraged, purplish, seething
09 bloodless, indignant
10 discolored, infuriated
11 deathly pale, exasperated
12 black-and-blue

**living**
04 life, live
05 alive, being, exact, vital

06 active, extant, income, lively
07 animate, current, precise, support
08 animated, existing, vigorous
09 animation, breathing, existence, lifestyle, surviving
10 continuing, livelihood, sustenance
11 going strong, subsistence
14 means of support, source of income

**living room**
06 lounge, parlor
11 drawing room, sitting room

**lizard**

➤ *Types of lizard*:
05 gecko, skink
06 agamid, iguana
08 basilisk, slowworm
09 blindworm, chameleon, salamanda
10 sand lizard
11 gila monster
12 flying lizard, Komodo dragon
13 monitor lizard
➤ See also ANIMAL

**load**
03 tax
04 heap, lade, lots, pile, tons
05 cargo, goods, heaps
06 burden, dozens, hordes, lading, scores, strain, weight
07 freight, oppress, trouble
08 encumber, hundreds, millions, shipment
09 millstone, thousands, weigh down
10 overburden, saddle with
11 consignment, encumbrance

**loaded**
04 full, rich
05 drunk, flush, laden, piled, tight, tipsy
06 biased, filled, heaped, packed, stoned, tiddly
07 charged, drunken, legless, pickled, sloshed, smashed, sozzled, squiffy, stacked, wealthy, well-off
08 affluent, burdened, tanked up, weighted
09 plastered, well oiled
10 blind drunk, in the money, inebriated, well-heeled
11 rolling in it, snowed under
12 drunk as a lord, roaring drunk
13 drunk as a skunk

**loaf**
03 bum

04 cake, idle, laze, lump, mass,
    slab
05 bread, mooch
06 loiter
08 meatloaf
09 bum around, goldbrick
10 hang around, take it easy
12 lounge around

**loafer**
03 bum
05 idler
07 lounger, shirker, wastrel
08 deadbeat, layabout, sluggard
09 goldbrick, lazybones
10 ne'er-do-well
11 goldbricker

**loan**
03 IOU
04 lend
06 credit
07 advance, lending
08 mortgage

**loath**
06 averse
08 grudging, hesitant
09 reluctant, resisting, unwilling
10 indisposed
11 disinclined

**loathe**
04 hate
05 abhor
06 detest
07 despise, dislike
08 execrate, not stand
09 abominate
10 recoil from
15 feel revulsion at

**loathing**
04 hate
05 odium
06 hatred, horror
07 disgust, dislike, ill will
08 aversion
09 antipathy, repulsion,
    revulsion
10 abhorrence, execration,
    repugnance
11 abomination, detestation

**loathsome**
04 vile
06 odious
07 hateful
09 execrable, obnoxious,
    offensive, repellent,
    repugnant, revolting
10 abominable, despicable,
    detestable, disgusting,
    nauseating
12 contemptible, disagreeable

**lob**
04 hurl, lift, loft, toss
05 chuck, fling, heave, pitch,
    throw

**lobby**
04 hall
05 foyer, porch
07 call for, hallway, passage,
    promote, push for, solicit
08 anteroom, campaign,
    corridor, entrance, press for,
    pressure
09 influence, vestibule
10 passageway
11 campaign for, waiting room
12 entrance hall
13 pressure group

**local**
06 narrow, native, parish
07 limited
08 resident
09 community, parochial
10 inhabitant, restricted,
    vernacular
12 neighborhood

**locale**
04 area, site, spot, zone
05 locus, place, scene, venue
08 locality, location, position
11 environment
12 neighborhood

**locality**
04 area, site, spot
05 place, scene
06 locale, region
08 district, position, vicinity
11 environment
12 neighborhood

**localize**
05 limit
07 confine, contain, delimit,
    specify
08 pinpoint, zero in on
10 delimitate, narrow down
11 concentrate

**locate**
03 fix, put, set
04 find, seat, site
05 build, place
06 detect, settle
07 hit upon, situate, station,
    uncover, unearth
08 discover, pinpoint, position
09 establish, track down
10 come across, run to earth

**location**
04 site, spot
05 locus, place, scene, venue
06 locale
07 setting

08 bearings, position
09 situation
11 whereabouts

**lock**
03 bar, hug, jam
04 bolt, curl, join, link, mesh,
    seal, shut, tuft
05 catch, clasp, grasp, latch,
    plait, tress, unite
06 clench, clutch, engage,
    fasten, secure, strand
07 embrace, enclose, entwine,
    grapple, padlock, ringlet
08 encircle, entangle
09 fastening, interlock

▶ *Parts of a lock*:
03 key, pin
04 bolt, hasp, knob, rose, sash
05 latch
06 barrel, keyway, spring, staple
07 key card, keyhole, spindle
08 cylinder, dead bolt, sash bolt
09 face plate, latch bolt
10 escutcheon, latch lever
11 mortise bolt, spindle hole,
    strike plate

❑ **lock out**
03 bar
05 debar
07 exclude

❑ **lock up**
03 pen
04 cage, jail
06 detain, secure, shut in, shut
    up, wall in
07 close up, confine
08 imprison
11 incarcerate
13 put behind bars

**locker**
07 cabinet
08 cupboard
10 footlocker

**lockup**
03 can, jug
04 cell, jail
05 clink
06 cooler, garage, prison
09 locking up
12 penitentiary

**locomotion**
06 action, motion, travel
07 headway, walking
08 movement, progress
09 traveling
10 ambulation

**locution**
05 idiom
06 accent, phrase
07 diction, wording

10 expression, inflection, intonation
12 articulation, turn of phrase

**lodge**
03 den, fix, hut, put
04 bank, club, file, lair, live, make, nest, room, stay
05 board, cabin, dwell, house, imbed, put up
06 billet, branch, reside, submit
07 chapter, deposit, implant, quarter, section, shelter, society, sojourn
08 register
09 gatehouse
11 accommodate, association
12 meeting place

**lodger**
06 inmate, renter, roomer, tenant
07 boarder
11 paying guest

**lodgings**
04 digs
05 abode, board, place, rooms
06 billet
08 quarters
13 accommodation, boarding house

**lofty**
04 high, tall
05 grand, noble, proud
06 lordly, raised, snooty
07 exalted, haughty, sky-high, soaring, stately, sublime
08 arrogant, elevated, imperial, imposing, majestic, superior, towering
09 dignified
10 disdainful
11 illustrious, patronizing
12 supercilious
13 condescending, high and mighty

**log**
04 book, file, note
05 chart, diary, tally, trunk
06 record, timber
07 account, daybook, journal, logbook, set down, write up
08 register

**loggerheads**
▫**at loggerheads**
06 at odds
10 quarreling
11 disagreeing
14 at daggers drawn

**logic**
05 sense
06 reason

08 argument
09 deduction, rationale, reasoning
10 dialectics

**logical**
05 clear, sound, valid
06 cogent
08 coherent, rational, reasoned, sensible
09 deducible, judicious
10 methodical, reasonable
14 well thought out

**logistics**
08 planning, strategy
10 management
12 coordination, organization
13 masterminding, orchestration

**logo**
04 mark, sign
05 badge, image
06 device, emblem, symbol
08 insignia
09 trademark

**loiter**
03 lag
04 idle, loaf
05 dally, delay, mooch, tarry
06 dawdle, linger, lounge
09 hang about, waste time
10 dilly-dally

**loll**
04 flap, flop, hang
05 droop, relax, slump
06 dangle, lounge, slouch, sprawl
07 recline

**lone**
03 one
04 only, sole
05 alone
06 single
08 divorced, forsaken, isolated, separate, solitary
09 abandoned, on your own, separated, unmarried
10 by yourself, unattached

**loneliness**
08 solitude
09 aloneness, isolation, seclusion
12 lonesomeness, solitariness

**lonely**
04 lone
05 alone
06 barren, remote
07 outcast
08 deserted, desolate, isolated, lonesome, secluded, solitary, wretched

09 abandoned, destitute, miserable, reclusive
10 friendless
11 godforsaken, out of the way, uninhabited
12 unfrequented

**loner**
06 hermit
07 mugwump, recluse
08 lone wolf, outsider, solitary
11 independent
13 individualist

**lonesome**
04 lone
05 alone
06 barren, lonely, remote
07 outcast, unhappy
08 deserted, desolate, forsaken, isolated, lonesome, rejected, secluded, solitary, wretched
09 abandoned, destitute, miserable, reclusive
10 friendless
11 out of the way, uninhabited
12 unfrequented

**long**
04 hope, itch, pine, want, wish
05 covet, crave, yearn
06 desire, hanker, hunger, thirst
07 lengthy, spun out, verbose
08 extended, marathon
09 elongated, extensive, prolonged, spread out, stretched
10 protracted
12 interminable, long-drawn-out, stretched out

▫**before long**
04 soon
07 shortly
15 in the near future

**long-drawn-out**
06 prolix
07 lengthy, spun out, tedious
08 marathon, overlong
09 prolonged
10 long-winded, protracted
12 interminable, overextended

**longing**
03 yen
04 avid, hope, itch, urge, wish
05 dream, eager
06 ardent, desire, hunger, hungry, pining, thirst
07 anxious, craving, wanting, wishful, wistful
08 ambition, coveting, desirous, yearning
09 hankering, hungering
10 aspiration

**long lasting**
07 abiding, chronic
08 enduring, unfading
09 lingering, prolonged
10 continuing, protracted

**long-lived**
03 old
07 durable, lasting
08 enduring
09 longevous
11 macrobiotic

**long-standing**
03 old
07 abiding
08 enduring
09 long-lived
11 established, long lasting,
   time-honored, traditional
15 long established

**long-suffering**
07 patient, stoical
08 resigned, tolerant
10 forbearing
13 uncomplaining

**long-winded**
05 wordy
06 prolix
07 diffuse, lengthy, tedious,
   verbose, voluble
10 discursive, protracted
12 long-drawn-out

**long-windedness**
08 longueur
09 garrulity, prolixity, verbosity,
   wordiness
11 lengthiness, tediousness
14 discursiveness

**look**
04 face, gape, gawk, gawp,
   gaze, leer, mien, ogle, peek,
   peep, seem, show, view
05 front, glare, guise, sight,
   stare, study, watch
06 appear, aspect, effect,
   eyeful, façade, gander,
   glance, manner, review,
   squint, survey
07 bearing, display, exhibit,
   eyeball, front on, glimpse
08 features, once-over
09 semblance
10 appearance, complexion,
   expression, impression,
   inspection
11 examination, observation
13 get an eyeful of, take a gander
   at, take a squint at

❑ **look after**
04 mind, tend
05 guard, nurse

07 baby-sit, care for, protect
08 attend to, maintain
09 watch over

❑ **look back**
06 recall
08 remember
09 reminisce, think back

❑ **look down on**
05 scorn, spurn
07 despise, disdain, sneer at
09 disparage, patronize
14 hold in contempt

❑ **look for**
04 seek
05 quest
07 hunt for, hunt out
09 forage for, search for, try to
   find

❑ **look forward to**
05 await
06 expect
07 hope for, long for, wait for
08 envisage, envision
10 anticipate

❑ **look into**
03 dig
05 delve, plumb, probe, study
06 fathom, go into
07 examine, explore, inspect
08 ask about, check out, look
   over, research
10 scrutinize, search into
11 investigate
12 inquire about

❑ **look like**
08 resemble
09 take after

❑ **look on, look upon**
05 count, judge, think
06 regard
08 consider

❑ **look out**
06 beware
07 be alert
08 watch out
09 be careful
12 keep an eye out, pay
   attention
13 be on your guard
14 be on the qui vive

❑ **look over**
04 scan, view
05 check
07 examine, inspect, monitor
08 check out
09 go through
11 read through
13 cast an eye over

❑ **look to**
05 await

06 expect, rely on, turn to
07 count on
10 anticipate, think about

❑ **look up**
04 find, seek
05 visit
06 call on, drop by, perk up, pick
   up, stop by
07 advance, consult, develop,
   hunt for, improve
08 drop in on, look in on,
   progress, research
09 come along, get better,
   search for, track down
10 ameliorate
11 make headway, pay a visit to
12 make progress

❑ **look up to**
05 honor
06 admire, esteem, revere
07 respect
13 think highly of

**look-alike**
04 spit, twin
05 clone, image
06 double, ringer
10 dead ringer
12 doppelgänger
13 spitting image

**lookout**
05 vista, watch
06 affair, pigeon, sentry
07 concern, problem
08 sentinel, watchman
09 crow's nest, fire tower
10 watchtower, widow's walk
15 observation post

❑ **keep a lookout**
05 watch
10 be vigilant
11 remain alert
14 be on the qui vive

**loom**
06 appear, emerge, impend,
   menace
08 overhang, threaten
09 take shape
10 be imminent, overshadow

**loop**
03 tie
04 bend, coil, curl, hoop, knot,
   ring, turn, wind
05 braid, noose
06 circle, eyelet, spiral
08 encircle, loophole, surround
11 convolution

**loophole**
06 escape, excuse, outlet
07 evasion, mistake, pretext
08 omission, pretense

## loose
03 lax, off
04 ease, fast, free, undo
05 baggy, broad, let go, relax,
slack, unpen, untie, vague
06 detach, loosen, unbind,
undone, unhook, unlock,
untied, wanton, weaken
07 at large, escaped, flowing,
general, hanging, immoral,
inexact, movable, release,
sagging, set free, slacken,
unclasp, unleash
08 rambling, released,
unchaste, uncouple,
unfasten, unsteady
09 abandoned, debauched,
disengage, dissolute,
imprecise, shapeless,
uncoupled
10 degenerate, disconnect, ill-
defined, inaccurate,
indefinite, indistinct,
unattached, unconfined,
unfastened, untethered
11 promiscuous
12 disreputable, loose fitting

❏**at loose ends**
04 idle
05 bored, fed up
14 with time to kill

## loosen
04 ease, free, undo
05 let go, loose, relax, untie
06 let out, unbind, weaken
07 deliver, release, set free,
slacken
08 diminish, moderate, set
loose, unfasten

❏**loosen up**
05 let up, relax
06 cool it, ease up, go easy,
lessen, unwind, warm up
07 prepare, slacken, work out
08 chill out, exercise, limber up
09 hang loose

## loot
03 rob
04 haul, raid, sack, swag
05 booty, prize, rifle, steal
06 burgle, maraud, ravage,
riches, spoils
07 despoil, pillage, plunder,
ransack
11 stolen goods, stolen money

## lop
03 cut
04 chop, clip, crop, dock, trim
05 prune, sever
06 cut off, detach, reduce,
remove

07 curtail, shorten, take off
08 truncate

## lope
03 run
05 bound
06 canter, spring, stride

## lopsided
05 askew
06 uneven
07 crooked, tilting, unequal
08 one-sided
10 catawampus, off balance,
unbalanced
11 cattywampus
12 asymmetrical

## loquacious
05 gabby, gassy, wordy
06 chatty
07 gossipy, voluble
09 garrulous, talkative
10 blathering, chattering

## loquacity
09 garrulity
10 chattiness, volubility
12 effusiveness
13 talkativeness

## lord
03 God
04 duke, earl, king, peer
05 baron, chief, count, noble,
ruler
06 Christ, Father, leader, master,
prince, Yahweh
07 captain, emperor, Eternal,
monarch
08 governor, nobleman,
overlord, superior, viscount
09 sovereign
10 aristocrat
11 Jesus Christ

❏**lord it over**
07 oppress, repress, swagger
08 domineer, pull rank
09 put on airs, tyrannize
10 boss around
11 order around, queen it over

## lordly
05 grand, lofty, noble, proud
07 haughty, stately, stuck-up
08 arrogant, imperial, majestic
09 dignified, grandiose,
hubristic, imperious
10 disdainful, high handed,
hoity-toity
11 domineering, magnificent,
overbearing, patronizing
12 aristocratic, supercilious
13 condescending, high and
mighty

## lore
06 wisdom
07 legends, sayings, stories
08 folklore, learning, teaching
09 erudition, knowledge
10 traditions
13 superstitions

## lose
04 drop, fail, miss
05 drain, elude, evade, spend,
use up, waste
06 expend, forget, go down,
ignore, mislay, outrun
07 consume, deplete, exhaust,
forfeit, fritter, get lost,
neglect, not find
08 be beaten, go astray,
misplace, shake off,
squander, throw off
09 disregard, dissipate
10 be defeated, depart from,
stop having, wander from
11 be conquered, be taken
away, come to grief, fail to
grasp, leave behind
12 suffer defeat
14 be unsuccessful
15 throw in the towel

❏**lose out**
06 suffer
07 miss out
14 be unsuccessful
15 be disadvantaged

❏**lose yourself in some-
thing**
12 be absorbed in
13 be engrossed in, be taken up
with
14 be captivated by, be
enthralled by

## loser
04 flop
05 lemon
07 also-ran, failure, has-been,
washout
08 dead loss, runner-up, write-
off
10 nonstarter

## loss
04 dead, debt
05 waste
07 deficit, missing
09 death toll, mislaying,
privation
10 casualties, deficiency,
fatalities, forfeiture
11 bereavement, deprivation
12 disadvantage, misplacement
13 disappearance

❏**at a loss**
07 puzzled

**lost**

09 mystified, perplexed
10 bewildered

**lost**
04 dead, past
06 astray, bygone, damned, doomed, dreamy, fallen, missed
07 at a loss, baffled, defunct, extinct, mislaid, missing, puzzled, strayed, wrecked
08 absorbed, vanished
09 destroyed, engrossed, misplaced, off course, perplexed
10 bewildered, captivated, enthralled, fascinated, spellbound, squandered
11 disappeared, disoriented, preoccupied, untraceable
12 absent-minded, irredeemable
13 disorientated, unrecoverable

**lot**
03 cut, set
04 fate, many, part, plot, tons
05 batch, bunch, crowd, group, heaps, loads, miles, piece, piles, quota, share
06 bundle, dozens, masses, oodles, parcel, ration, stacks
07 destiny, fortune, portion
08 hundreds, millions, quantity
09 a good deal, a quantity, allotment, allowance, situation, thousands
10 assortment, collection
11 consignment, great number, large amount
13 circumstances

❏**a lot**
04 much
05 often
10 frequently
14 to a great degree, to a great extent

❏**throw your lot in with**
10 join forces, team up with
11 combine with

**lotion**
04 balm
05 cream, salve
06 balsam
08 liniment, ointment
09 emollient
11 embrocation

**lottery**
04 draw, risk
05 bingo
06 gamble, hazard, raffle
07 venture
09 Powerball

10 sweepstake
11 speculation

**loud**
04 bold
05 brash, flash, gaudy, noisy, rowdy, showy
06 brazen, flashy, garish, shrill, vulgar
07 blaring, booming, glaring, raucous, roaring
08 emphatic, piercing, resonant, strident, vehement
09 clamorous, deafening, insistent, obtrusive, tasteless
10 aggressive, flamboyant, resounding, stentorian, thundering, vociferous
11 loudmouthed
12 ostentatious

**loudly**
07 lustily, noisily, shrilly
10 fortissimo, stridently, vehemently, vigorously
11 clamorously, deafeningly
12 resoundingly, uproariously, vociferously

**loudmouth**
07 boaster, windbag
08 big mouth, braggart
09 blusterer, swaggerer
11 braggadocio

**loudmouthed**
05 noisy
08 boasting, bragging

**lounge**
03 den
04 idle, laze, loll, sofa
05 couch, relax, slump
06 parlor, repose, sprawl
07 dayroom, lie back, recline
09 lie around, loll about, waste time
10 living room, take it easy
11 drawing room, sitting room
14 cocktail lounge

**lower, lour**
04 loom
05 frown, glare, scowl
06 darken, glower, menace
07 blacken
08 threaten
09 be brewing, cloud over

**lowing, louring**
04 dark, gray, grim
05 black, heavy
06 cloudy, gloomy
07 ominous
08 menacing, overcast
09 darkening
11 threatening

**lousy**
03 bad, ill, low
04 poor, sick
05 awful, seedy
06 poorly, rotten, unwell
08 inferior, terrible
09 miserable
10 out of sorts, second-rate
12 contemptible
15 under the weather

**lout**
03 oaf
04 boor, dolt
05 yahoo
09 barbarian

**loutish**
04 rude
05 crude, rough
06 coarse, oafish, vulgar
07 boorish, uncouth
11 ill-mannered, uncivilized

**lovable**
04 dear
07 winsome
08 adorable, charming
09 appealing, endearing

**love**
03 pet
04 care, dear, lust, zero
05 adore, angel, ardor, enjoy, fancy, honey, lover, prize, savor, taste
06 desire, dote on, liking, regard, relish, warmth
07 be mad on, beloved, care for, cherish, concern, darling, dear one, dearest, delight, idolize, long for, passion, rapture, worship
08 be daft on, be fond of, be nuts on, be sold on, devotion, favorite, fondness, hold dear, intimacy, kindness, pleasure, soft spot, sympathy, treasure, weakness
09 adoration, adulation, affection, be sweet on, delight in, enjoyment, puppy love, scoreless
10 appreciate, attachment, friendship, partiality, sweetheart, tenderness
11 amorousness, be devoted to, be partial to, brotherhood, inclination, infatuation
12 appreciation, have a crush on, like very much
13 be attracted to
14 have a liking for, take pleasure in

15 think the world of
◻**fall in love with**
05 fancy
07 fall for
12 be crazy about, have a crush on, take a shine to
13 have a thing for
15 lose your heart to
◻**in love with**
06 doting, hooked, soft on
07 charmed, smitten, stuck on, sweet on
08 besotted, enamored, mad about
09 nuts about, wild about
10 crazy about, infatuated
12 have a crush on
13 head over heels
◻**love affair**
05 amour
06 affair
07 liaison, passion, romance
◻**make love**
03 pet, woo
10 be intimate
**loveless**
04 cold, hard
06 frigid
08 forsaken, unloving
09 unfeeling
11 insensitive, passionless
**lovelorn**
06 pining
07 longing
08 desiring, lovesick, yearning
**lovely**
04 fair
06 pretty
08 adorable, charming, handsome, pleasant
09 beautiful, enjoyable, exquisite, marvelous, wonderful
10 attractive, delightful, enchanting
11 good-looking
**lover**
03 fan
04 beau, buff, date, vamp, wolf
05 fella, fiend, flame, freak
06 fellow, fiancé, suitor
07 admirer, beloved, devotee, fanatic, fiancée, partner
08 follower, mistress
09 affianced, boyfriend
10 enthusiast, girlfriend, heartthrob, sweetheart
**lovesick**
06 pining
07 longing

08 desiring, lovelorn, yearning
**loving**
04 fond, kind, warm
06 ardent, caring, doting, tender
07 adoring, amorous, devoted
10 passionate
11 sympathetic, warmhearted
12 affectionate
**low**
03 bad, moo, sad
04 base, bass, blue, deep, down, dull, evil, flat, glum, mean, meek, mild, poor, rich, sale, slow, soft
05 cheap, fed up, lowly, muted, nadir, nasty, plain, quiet, scant, short, small, squat
06 bellow, bottom, coarse, common, gentle, gloomy, humble, hushed, junior, little, meager, modest, paltry, scanty, simple, smutty, sparse, sunken, vulgar, wicked
07 adverse, foolish, heinous, hostile, immoral, muffled, obscene, obscure, peasant, reduced, shallow, slashed, stunted, subdued, unhappy
08 depraved, downcast, indecent, inferior, mediocre, moderate, negative, opposing, ordinary, plebeian, resonant, sea level, sonorous, trifling
09 dastardly, deficient, depressed, miserable, quietened, whispered
10 despicable, despondent, inadequate, rock bottom, submissive
11 downhearted, ground level, inexpensive, subordinate, unfavorable, unimportant
12 contemptible, disconsolate, disheartened, dishonorable, insufficient
13 insignificant
14 down in the dumps
**lowborn**
05 lowly
06 humble
07 obscure, peasant
08 mean born, plebeian
10 low ranking
**lowbrow**
05 crude
09 unlearned, unrefined
10 uncultured
12 uncultivated

**lowdown**
04 blue, data, dope, info, news
05 facts
09 depressed
11 information, inside story
12 intelligence
**lower**
04 drop, hush, sink
05 abase, lowly, minor, under
06 debase, demean, junior, lessen, lesser, nether, reduce, weaken
07 cheapen, curtail, degrade, depress, descend, let down, let fall, quieten, set down
08 belittle, decrease, diminish, disgrace, dishonor, inferior, take down
09 bring down, disparage, secondary, undermost
11 second-class, subordinate
**lower** see LOUR
**lowering** see LOURING
**low-grade**
04 poor
08 inferior
09 cheapjack, third-rate
11 poor quality, substandard
14 not up to scratch
**low-key**
04 soft
05 muted, quiet
07 relaxed, subdued
10 restrained
11 understated
**lowly**
04 mean, meek, mild, poor
06 common, humble, junior, modest, simple
07 low born, obscure, peasant
08 inferior, ordinary, plebeian
10 low ranking, submissive
11 subordinate, unimportant
**low-pitched**
03 low
04 bass, deep, rich
07 subdued
08 resonant, sonorous
**low-spirited**
03 low, sad
04 down, glum
05 fed up, moody
06 gloomy
07 unhappy
08 dejected
09 depressed, miserable
10 despondent
11 downhearted
14 down in the dumps

**loyal**
04 firm, true
06 trusty
07 devoted, sincere, staunch
08 constant, faithful, reliable
09 patriotic, steadfast
10 dependable, unchanging

**loyalty**
06 fealty
08 devotion, fidelity
09 constancy
10 allegiance, patriotism
11 reliability, staunchness
12 faithfulness
13 dependability, steadfastness

**lozenge**
05 candy
06 jujube, tablet
07 diamond, gumdrop
08 pastille
09 cough drop

**lubber**
04 clod, dolt, hick, lout, slob
06 sailor
07 bumpkin
10 clodhopper, landlubber

**lubberly**
06 clumsy, coarse, oafish
07 awkward, doltish, loutish, lumpish, uncouth
08 ungainly
09 lumbering
11 clodhopping

**lubricant**
03 fat, oil
04 lard
06 grease
11 lubricating, lubrication

**lubricate**
03 oil, wax
04 lard
05 smear
06 grease, polish
07 moisten
10 moisturize

**lucid**
04 pure, sane
05 clear, plain, sober, sound
06 bright, glassy, limpid
07 beaming, radiant, shining
08 distinct, explicit, gleaming, luminous, pellucid, rational, sensible
09 brilliant, effulgent
10 diaphanous, reasonable
11 clearheaded, crystalline, of sound mind, resplendent, translucent, transparent
12 compos mentis, intelligible
14 comprehensible

**luck**
04 fate
06 chance, hazard
07 destiny, fortune, godsend, success
08 accident, fortuity
10 prosperity
11 good fortune
14 predestination

**❑in luck**
05 lucky
07 favored
09 fortunate
10 auspicious, successful

**❑out of luck**
07 hapless, unlucky
08 luckless
11 unfortunate
12 inauspicious, unsuccessful
13 disadvantaged

**luckily**
08 by chance
10 by accident, by good luck
11 fortunately
12 fortuitously

**luckless**
06 cursed, doomed, jinxed
07 hapless, unhappy, unlucky
08 hopeless, ill-fated
10 calamitous, disastrous, ill-starred
11 star-crossed, unfortunate
12 unpropitious, unsuccessful

**lucky**
06 in luck, timely
07 charmed
09 expedient, fortunate, opportune, promising
10 auspicious, fortuitous, propitious
12 providential

**lucrative**
07 gainful
08 well paid
10 high paying, productive, profitable, worthwhile
11 moneymaking
12 advantageous, profit making, remunerative

**lucre**
04 cash
05 bread, dough, money
06 mammon, riches, wealth

**ludicrous**
04 zany
05 crazy, droll
06 absurd
07 comical, risible
08 farcical, humorous
09 eccentric, hilarious

10 outlandish, ridiculous
12 preposterous

**lug**
03 tow, tug
04 drag, haul, hump, lout, pull, tote
05 carry, heave

**luggage**
04 gear
05 stuff
06 things
07 baggage
10 belongings
11 impedimenta
13 paraphernalia

**lugubrious**
03 sad
04 glum
06 dismal, dreary, gloomy, morose, somber, woeful
07 doleful, serious
08 funereal, mournful
09 sorrowful, woebegone
10 melancholy, sepulchral

**lukewarm**
05 tepid
07 warmish
09 apathetic, Laodicean
11 halfhearted, indifferent
14 unenthusiastic

**lull**
04 calm, ease, hush
05 allay, letup, pause, peace, quell, quiet, still
06 pacify, soothe, subdue
07 assuage, compose, silence
08 calmness
09 stillness
11 tranquility

**lullaby**
04 song
08 berceuse
10 cradlesong

**lumber**
04 junk, plod, wood
05 clump, stamp, stump, trash
06 jumble, refuse, timber, trudge
07 clutter, rubbish, shamble, shuffle, stumble, trundle

**lumbering**
05 heavy
06 bovine, clumsy
07 awkward, hulking, lumpish, massive
08 ungainly, unwieldy
09 ponderous
11 elephantine, heavy-footed

## luminary
03 VIP
04 star
06 bigwig, expert, leader
07 big name, notable
09 authority, celebrity, dignitary, superstar
12 leading light

## luminescent
06 bright
07 glowing, radiant, shining
08 luminous
09 effulgent
10 luciferous
11 fluorescent
14 phosphorescent

## luminous
03 lit
06 bright
07 glowing, radiant, shining
08 dazzling, lustrous
09 brilliant, effulgent
11 fluorescent, illuminated, luminescent

## lump
03 dab, gob, wad
04 ball, bear, bump, cake, clod, fuse, hunk, mass, pool, take
05 blend, brook, bulge, bunch, chunk, clump, group, piece, stand, tumor, unite, wedge
06 endure, gather, growth, nugget, suffer
07 cluster, collect, combine, stomach, swallow
08 bear with, coalesce, swelling, tolerate
09 carbuncle, put up with
10 protrusion, tumescence
11 consolidate, mix together, put together
12 conglomerate, protuberance

## lumpish
05 gawky, heavy
06 clumsy, oafish, obtuse, stolid, stupid
07 awkward, boorish, doltish, hulking
08 bungling, ungainly
09 lethargic, lumbering
10 dull witted
11 elephantine

## lumpy
05 bumpy
06 knobby, nodose, nodous
07 bunched, clotted, curdled
08 granular

## lunacy
05 folly, mania
06 idiocy
07 inanity, madness

08 dementia, insanity
09 absurdity, craziness, stupidity
10 aberration, imbecility
11 derangement, foolishness
12 dementedness, illogicality
13 irrationality, senselessness

## lunatic
03 mad
04 daft, kook, nuts
05 crazy, inane, loony, loopy, nutty, silly, wacky
06 absurd, cuckoo, insane, madman, maniac, psycho
07 foolish, idiotic, nutcase, oddball
08 crackpot, demented, deranged, dipstick, head case, imbecile, madwoman, neurotic
09 disturbed, fruitcake, psychotic, senseless
10 psychopath, unbalanced
11 harebrained
13 off your rocker
15 manic-depressive

## lunch
06 brunch
08 luncheon
10 midday meal

## ❑ out to lunch
04 nuts
05 crazy
06 insane

## lunge
03 cut, hit, jab
04 dart, dash, dive, grab, leap, pass, poke, stab
05 bound, hit at
06 charge, grab at, plunge, pounce, spring, strike, thrust
08 fall upon, strike at
09 pitch into

## lurch
04 reel, rock, roll, sway, veer
05 pitch
06 swerve, totter
07 stagger, stumble

## lure
04 bait, draw
05 decoy, tempt
06 allure, carrot, entice, induce, lead on, seduce
07 attract, beguile, ensnare
08 inveigle
09 seduction
10 allurement, attraction, enticement, inducement, temptation

## lurid
04 gory, loud

05 showy, vivid
06 garish, grisly
07 ghastly, graphic, macabre
08 dazzling, explicit, gruesome, horrific, shocking
09 brilliant, revolting, startling
11 exaggerated, sensational
12 melodramatic

## lurk
05 prowl, skulk, slink, sneak, snoop
06 crouch, lie low
09 lie in wait

## luscious
04 sexy
05 juicy, sweet, tasty, yummy
08 sensuous
09 delicious, desirable, succulent
10 appetizing, delectable
11 scrumptious
13 mouthwatering

## lush
03 sot
04 alky, rich, soak, wino
05 alchy, alkie, dense, dipso, green
06 boozer, lavish, ornate
07 opulent, profuse, teeming, verdant
08 abundant, drunkard, palatial, prolific
09 alcoholic, luxuriant, sumptuous
11 dipsomaniac, extravagant, flourishing, hard drinker

## lust
05 greed
06 desire, hunger, libido
07 avidity, craving, lechery, longing, passion
08 appetite, cupidity, yearning
09 horniness, prurience
10 greediness, sensuality
11 sexual drive
12 covetousness, sexual desire
13 concupiscence
14 lasciviousness, licentiousness

## ❑ lust after
04 need, want
05 covet, crave
06 desire
07 long for
08 yearn for
09 hunger for, thirst for

## lustful
04 lewd
06 carnal, wanton
07 craving, raunchy, sensual
08 prurient, unchaste

**lustily**
09 hankering, lecherous, lickerish, salacious
10 cupidinous, lascivious, libidinous, licentious, passionate
12 concupiscent

**lustily**
08 robustly, strongly
10 forcefully, powerfully, vigorously

**lustiness**
05 vigor
06 energy, health
08 haleness, strength, virility
10 robustness, sturdiness
11 healthiness

**luster**
04 fame, glow
05 gleam, glint, glory, gloss, honor, merit, sheen, shine
06 credit, renown
07 burnish, glitter, shimmer, sparkle
08 lambency, prestige, radiance
10 brightness, brilliance, refulgence

**lustrous**
05 shiny
06 bright, glossy
07 glowing, lambent, radiant
08 dazzling, gleaming, luminous
09 burnished, sparkling, twinkling
10 glistening, glittering, shimmering

**lusty**
04 hale
05 gutsy
06 hearty, robust, sturdy, virile
07 healthy
08 powerful, vigorous
09 energetic, strapping

13 hale and hearty

**luxuriance**
08 lushness, rankness, richness
09 abundance, denseness, fecundity, fertility, profusion
10 exuberance, lavishness, luxuriancy

**luxuriant**
04 lush, rank, rich
05 ample, dense
06 fecund, florid, lavish, ornate
07 fertile, flowery, profuse, riotous, teeming
08 abundant, prolific, thriving
09 elaborate, plentiful
10 flamboyant, productive
11 extravagant, overflowing
13 superabundant

**luxuriate**
04 bask
05 bloom, enjoy, revel
06 abound, relish, wallow
07 burgeon, indulge, prosper
08 flourish

**luxurious**
04 posh, rich
05 cushy, grand, plush
06 de luxe, glitzy, lavish
07 opulent
08 affluent, splendid
09 sumptuous
11 comfortable, magnificent
13 well-appointed

**luxury**
05 extra, treat
07 comfort
08 grandeur, hedonism, opulence, richness, splendor
09 affluence, grandness
10 costliness, indulgence
12 extravagance, magnificence, satisfaction

13 expensiveness, gratification, sumptuousness

**lying**
05 false
06 deceit
07 crooked, falsity, fibbing, perjury
08 two-faced
09 deceitful, dishonest, duplicity, invention
10 dishonesty, mendacious, untruthful
11 crookedness, dissembling, fabrication
13 dissimulating, double-dealing, falsification
14 untruthfulness

**lynch**
04 hang, kill
06 murder
07 execute
10 put to death

**lyric**
06 direct, poetic, strong
07 lyrical, musical
09 emotional
10 passionate, subjective

**lyrical**
05 lyric
06 poetic
07 musical
08 ecstatic, romantic
09 emotional, rapturous, rhapsodic
10 expressive, passionate
11 carried away, impassioned
12 enthusiastic

**lyricist** see SONGWRITER

**lyrics**
04 book, text
05 words
08 libretto

# M m

**macabre, macaber**
04 gory, grim
05 eerie
06 grisly, morbid
07 ghastly, ghostly, hideous
08 chilling, dreadful, ghoulish, gruesome

**mace**
03 gas, rod
04 club
05 spice, staff, stick
06 cudgel

**macerate**
04 mash, pulp, soak
05 blend, steep
06 soften
07 liquefy

**Machiavellian**
04 foxy, wily
06 artful, astute, crafty, shrewd
07 cunning, devious
08 guileful, scheming
09 underhand
10 intriguing, perfidious
11 calculating, opportunist
13 double-dealing

**machination**
04 plot, ploy, ruse, wile
06 design, device, scheme, tactic
08 artifice, intrigue, maneuver
09 stratagem

**machine**
04 tool
05 motor, organ, robot
06 agency, device, engine, gadget, system
07 android, vehicle
08 catalyst, hardware
09 apparatus, appliance, automaton, mechanism
10 instrument
11 contraption, contrivance
12 organization

**machinery**
04 gear
05 tools
06 system, tackle
08 gadgetry, workings
09 apparatus, equipment, mechanism
11 instruments

12 organization

**machinist**
08 mechanic, operator
09 operative

**machismo**
08 maleness, virility
09 manliness, toughness
11 masculinity

**macrocosm**
05 world
06 system
07 culture, society
08 totality, universe
09 community
11 solar system

**mad**
04 avid, daft, fond, loco, nuts, wild
05 angry, batty, crazy, irate, livid, loony, loopy, manic, nutty, rapid
06 absurd, crazed, fuming, insane, raging
07 bananas, blazing, enraged, frantic, furious, hurried, idiotic, lunatic, zealous
08 demented, deranged, frenzied, incensed, maniacal, outraged, reckless, unhinged
09 energetic, fanatical, foolhardy, ludicrous, psychotic, seeing red
10 infatuated, infuriated, off the wall, off your nut, out to lunch, passionate, unbalanced
11 nonsensical
12 preposterous, uncontrolled
13 of unsound mind, off your rocker, out of your mind
14 off your trolley
15 non compos mentis

❑**like mad**
06 avidly, wildly
09 furiously, hurriedly, zealously
11 fanatically, frantically

**madcap**
04 fury, rash, wild
05 crazy, silly
07 flighty, hothead
08 heedless, reckless

09 daredevil, desperado, firebrand, foolhardy, hotheaded, impulsive
11 birdbrained, thoughtless

**madden**
03 bug, irk, vex
05 anger, annoy, upset
06 enrage, hassle
07 agitate, incense, inflame, provoke
09 aggravate, drive nuts, infuriate
10 drive crazy, exasperate
14 drive up the wall
15 get your dander up

**maddening**
07 galling
08 annoying
09 upsetting, vexatious
10 disturbing, irritating
11 infuriating, troublesome
12 exasperating

**made-up**
05 false
06 done up, unreal, untrue
07 painted
08 invented, powdered
09 fairy-tale, fictional, imaginary, trumped-up
10 fabricated
11 make-believe

**madhouse**
05 Babel, chaos
06 asylum, bedlam
08 loony bin, nut house
09 funny farm
11 pandemonium
13 lunatic asylum
14 mental hospital

**madly**
06 wildly
07 crazily, hastily, rapidly, utterly
08 insanely
09 devotedly, excitedly, extremely, fervently, furiously, hurriedly, intensely, violently
10 dementedly, frenziedly, recklessly
11 deliriously, exceedingly, frantically
12 distractedly, hysterically, unreasonably

13 energetically, exceptionally

**madman, madwoman**
03 nut
05 crank, loony
06 maniac
07 lunatic, nut case, oddball
08 crackpot, head case
09 fruitcake, psychotic,
   screwball
10 basket case, psychopath

**madness**
03 ire
04 fury, rage, riot, zeal
05 anger, mania, wrath
06 frenzy, lunacy, raving
07 abandon, passion
08 dementia, hysteria, insanity,
   wildness
09 craziness, psychosis
10 enthusiasm
11 derangement, infatuation

**maelstrom**
05 chaos
06 bedlam, vortex
07 turmoil
09 Charybdis, whirlpool
11 pandemonium

**maestro**
03 ace
06 expert, genius, master,
   wizard
08 composer, virtuoso
09 conductor
12 music teacher

**magazine**
05 depot, paper
06 weekly
07 arsenal, journal, monthly
09 quarterly
10 periodical, storehouse,
   supplement
11 publication
14 ammunition dump
➤ See also NEWSPAPER

➤ *Names of American
magazines*:
02 GQ
03 Inc., Jet
04 Life, Time
05 Ebony, Money, Sport, Vogue,
   Wired
06 Forbes, Health, People
07 Esquire, Gourmet, Harper's,
   McCall's, Playboy, Redbook,
   TV Guide
08 Discover, Newsweek,
   Victoria
09 Family Fun, Seventeen,
   Woman's Day
10 Bon Appetit, Vanity Fair

11 Smithsonian
12 Business Week, Car and
   Driver, Cosmopolitan, Family
   Circle, Mademoiselle, Rolling
   Stone, The New Yorker
13 Home and Garden, Reader's
   Digest
14 Southern Living
16 Good Housekeeping
17 Sports Illustrated
18 National Geographic
23 Christian Science Monitor

**magic**
05 charm, curse, great, spell
06 allure, glamor, hoodoo,
   occult, voodoo
07 demonic, glamour, sorcery
08 black art, charming, illusion,
   magnetic, terrific, trickery,
   wizardry
09 conjuring, deception,
   excellent, magnetism,
   marvelous, occultism,
   wonderful
10 bewitching, black magic,
   enchanting, entrancing,
   mysterious, necromancy,
   witchcraft
11 captivating, enchantment,
   fascinating, fascination,
   legerdemain, thaumaturgy
12 spellbinding, supernatural
13 magical powers, sleight of
   hand, wonderworking

**magician**
05 witch
06 expert, wizard
07 warlock
08 conjurer, sorcerer
09 enchanter
11 illusionist, necromancer,
   spell worker, thaumaturge
12 wonderworker
13 miracle worker,
   thaumaturgist

**magisterial**
06 lordly
08 arrogant, despotic
09 assertive, imperious,
   masterful
10 commanding, highhanded,
   peremptory
11 dictatorial, domineering,
   overbearing
13 authoritarian, authoritative

**magistrate**
02 JP
05 judge
07 bailiff, justice, tribune
12 civil officer

**magnanimity**
05 mercy
07 charity
08 altruism, kindness, largesse,
   nobility
10 generosity, liberality
11 beneficence, benevolence,
   forgiveness, munificence
12 philanthropy, selflessness
13 bountifulness, unselfishness
14 bigheartedness,
   charitableness

**magnanimous**
04 kind
05 noble
07 liberal
08 generous, merciful, selfless
09 bountiful, forgiving, unselfish
10 altruistic, beneficent,
   benevolent, bighearted,
   charitable, munificent,
   ungrudging
13 philanthropic

**magnate**
05 baron, mogul
06 bigwig, fat cat, leader, poo-
   bah, tycoon
07 big shot, notable
09 executive, financier,
   plutocrat
13 industrialist

**magnet**
04 bait, draw, lure
05 charm, focus
06 appeal
10 allurement, attraction,
   enticement, focal point

**magnetic**
08 alluring, charming, hypnotic,
   tempting
09 seductive
10 attractive, bewitching,
   enchanting
11 captivating, charismatic,
   fascinating, mesmerizing,
   tantalizing
12 irresistible

**magnetism**
04 draw, grip, lure, pull
05 charm, magic, power, spell
06 allure
08 charisma
09 hypnotism, mesmerism
10 attraction, temptation
11 captivation, enchantment,
   fascination
12 drawing power
13 seductiveness

**magnification**
08 dilation, increase
09 expansion, inflation

**magnificence**
11 enhancement, enlargement
12 augmentation, exaggeration, overemphasis
13 amplification
15 intensification

**magnificence**
04 pomp
05 glory
06 luxury
07 majesty
08 grandeur, opulence, splendor
10 brilliance, lavishness
13 luxuriousness, sumptuousness

**magnificent**
05 grand, royal
06 august, lavish, superb
07 elegant, exalted, opulent, sublime
08 dazzling, glorious, imposing, majestic, splendid, striking
09 brilliant, grandiose, luxurious, marvelous, sumptuous, wonderful
10 impressive
11 resplendent

**magnify**
06 blow up, deepen, dilate, expand, extend, overdo
07 amplify, broaden, build up, enhance, enlarge, greaten
08 increase, overplay
09 intensify, overstate
10 exaggerate
13 overemphasize

**magniloquence**
07 bombast, fustian
08 euphuism, rhetoric
09 loftiness, pomposity
10 orotundity
14 grandiloquence
15 pretentiousness

**magniloquent**
05 lofty
07 exalted, fustian, orotund, pompous, stilted
08 elevated, sonorous
09 bombastic, high-flown
10 euphuistic, rhetorical
11 declamatory, pretentious
13 grandiloquent

**magnitude**
04 bulk, mass, note, size
06 amount, extent, moment
07 expanse, measure
08 eminence, quantity, strength
09 amplitude, greatness, intensity
10 dimensions, importance
11 consequence, proportions

12 significance

**magnum opus**
10 masterwork
11 chef d'oeuvre, masterpiece

**maid**
04 girl
06 au pair
07 barmaid, servant
08 domestic
09 housemaid, soubrette

**maiden**
03 new
04 girl, lass, miss, pure
05 first, nymph, unwed
06 chaste, damsel, female, lassie, vestal, virgin
07 girlish, initial
08 virginal, virtuous
09 inaugural, unmarried, young girl, young lady
10 young woman
12 introductory

**maidenly**
04 pure
05 unwed
06 chaste, decent, demure, female, gentle, modest, proper, seemly, vestal, virgin
07 girlish
08 virginal, virtuous
09 unmarried

**mail**
04 post, send
05 armor, e-mail
07 airmail, forward, letters, packets, panoply, parcels
08 delivery, dispatch, packages
10 parcel post, post office
12 postal system
13 postal service
14 correspondence, electronic mail

**maim**
04 hurt, lame
05 wound
06 impair, injure
07 cripple, disable
08 mutilate
12 incapacitate
14 put out of action

**main**
03 key, sea
04 head, pipe
05 cable, chief, first, major, ocean, prime, vital
07 central, channel, conduit, crucial, leading, pivotal, premier, primary, supreme
08 cardinal, foremost

09 essential, paramount, principal
10 preeminent
11 outstanding, predominant
13 most important

**◻in the main**
06 mainly, mostly
07 as a rule, chiefly, largely, usually
09 generally, in general
10 by and large, especially, on the whole
14 for the most part

**mainly**
06 mostly
07 as a rule, chiefly, largely, overall, usually
09 generally, in general, in the main
10 by and large, especially, on the whole
11 principally
14 for the most part

**mainspring**
05 cause
06 motive, origin, reason, source
07 impulse
09 generator, incentive
10 motivation, prime mover
11 inspiration
12 driving force, fountainhead

**mainstay**
04 base, prop
05 basis
06 anchor, pillar
07 bulwark, support
08 backbone, buttress, linchpin
10 foundation

**mainstream**
07 average, central, general, regular, typical
08 accepted, mainline, orthodox, standard
11 established
12 conventional

**maintain**
04 aver, avow, feed, hold, keep
05 claim, state
06 affirm, assert, insist, keep up, retain, supply
07 believe, care for, carry on, contend, declare, profess, stand by, support, sustain
08 announce, conserve, continue, fight for, preserve
09 keep going, look after
10 asseverate, perpetuate, provide for, take care of

## maintenance
04 care, keep
06 living, upkeep
07 aliment, alimony, nurture, repairs, support
09 allowance, financing
10 livelihood, sustenance
11 continuance, subsistence
12 alimentation, conservation, continuation, perpetuation, preservation

## majestic
05 grand, noble, regal, royal
06 august, kingly, lordly, superb
07 queenly, stately, sublime
08 glorious, imperial, imposing, princely, splendid
09 dignified
10 impressive, monumental

## majesty
04 pomp
05 glory
07 dignity, royalty
08 grandeur, nobility, regality, splendor
09 sublimity
11 exaltedness

## major
04 main
05 chief, great, older, prime, vital
06 senior
07 crucial, leading, notable, officer, serious, supreme, weighty
08 superior
09 important, paramount
10 preeminent
11 outstanding, significant
15 military officer

## majority
04 bulk, many, mass, most
08 legal age, maturity
09 adulthood
10 lion's share
11 greater part
12 age of consent

## make
03 net, win
04 cook, earn, form, gain, kind, mark, mold, name, sort, type, urge, vote
05 act as, brand, build, cause, clear, drive, elect, erect, force, frame, gross, impel, model, press, put up, score, shape, style, total, write
06 become, coerce, come to, compel, create, devise, draw up, effect, ordain, reckon, render, secure, seduce
07 achieve, acquire, add up to, appoint, arrange, bring in, chalk up, compose, compute, deliver, dragoon, execute, fashion, install, notch up, perform, prepare, produce, realize, require, turn out, variety, work out
08 amount to, assemble, bulldoze, carry out, comprise, engender, estimate, generate, occasion, pressure, reckon up, take home
09 calculate, constrain, construct, designate, discharge, fabricate, get down to, originate, strong-arm, structure, undertake
10 accomplish, bring about, give rise to, pressurize
11 manufacture, mass-produce, prevail upon, put together

## ❑ make away with
04 do in, kill
05 pinch, seize, steal, swipe
06 kidnap, murder, snatch
07 bump off
10 do away with, run off with
11 assassinate, walk off with

## ❑ make believe
04 play
05 dream, enact, feign
07 imagine, play-act, pretend
09 fantasize

## ❑ make do
04 cope
05 get by
06 manage
07 make out, survive
08 get along, scrape by
09 improvise

## ❑ make for
06 aim for, attack, lead to
07 head for, lunge at, produce, promote
10 facilitate, help effect
12 contribute to
13 be conducive to

## ❑ make it
05 reach
06 arrive
07 prosper, succeed, survive
11 come through, pull through

## ❑ make off
05 leave
06 decamp, depart, run off
07 run away
08 clear off
09 cut and run, skedaddle
12 make a getaway
15 take to your heels

## ❑ make off with
05 filch, pinch, steal, swipe
06 abduct, kidnap, pilfer
07 purloin
10 run off with
11 appropriate, walk off with

## ❑ make out
03 see
04 aver, cope, espy, fare, kiss
05 claim, get by, get on, imply, prove
06 affirm, assert, detect, draw up, fathom, fill in, manage
07 declare, discern, fill out, succeed, work out
08 decipher, describe, get along, maintain, make love, perceive, progress, write out
10 comprehend, understand
11 distinguish

## ❑ make over
05 leave
06 assign, change, convey
08 bequeath, renovate, sign over, transfer

## ❑ make up
05 paint, rouge
06 create, devise, doll up, invent
07 compose, concoct, dream up, think up
08 complete
09 construct, fabricate, formulate, make peace
10 constitute, shake hands, supplement
12 be reconciled
14 bury the hatchet

## ❑ make up for
06 offset
08 atone for
13 compensate for, make amends for

## ❑ make up to
06 chat up, fawn on
07 flatter, toady to
08 butter up, suck up to
14 curry favor with
15 make overtures to

## ❑ make up your mind
06 decide
07 resolve
09 determine

## ❑ make way
11 allow to pass, make room for

## make-believe
05 dream
06 made-up, unreal
07 charade, fantasy, pretend

08 dreaming, pretense, role-play
09 imaginary, pretended
10 masquerade, play-acting
11 daydreaming, imagination

**maker**
06 author
07 builder, creator
08 director, producer
09 architect
10 fabricator
11 constructor
12 manufacturer

**makeshift**
06 make-do
07 standby, stopgap
09 expedient, temporary
10 improvised, substitute
13 rough and ready
14 thrown together
15 cobbled together

**makeup**
04 form
05 paint, style
06 format, nature, powder
08 assembly, war paint
09 character, cosmetics, formation, structure
10 maquillage
11 arrangement, composition, disposition, greasepaint, personality, temperament
12 construction, organization

**making**
06 income
07 forging, molding, profits, promise, returns, revenue, takings
08 building, capacity, creating, creation, earnings, modeling, proceeds
09 materials, potential, qualities
10 beginnings, capability, production
11 composition, fabrication, ingredients, manufacture
12 construction, potentiality
13 possibilities

❏**in the making**
06 coming
07 budding, nascent
08 emergent
09 incipient, potential
10 burgeoning, developing
11 up and coming

**maladjusted**
08 neurotic, unstable
09 disturbed, screwed up

**maladministration**
07 misrule

08 bungling
10 corruption, misconduct
11 malfeasance, malpractice, misfeasance, mishandling
12 incompetence, inefficiency
13 mismanagement

**maladroit**
05 inept
06 clumsy, gauche
07 awkward, unhandy
08 bungling, ill-timed, inexpert, tactless, untoward
09 graceless, ham-handed, inelegant
10 unskillful
11 insensitive, thoughtless
12 undiplomatic

**malady**
07 ailment, disease, illness, malaise
08 disorder, sickness
09 breakdown, complaint, infirmity
10 affliction
13 indisposition

**malaise**
05 angst
07 disease, illness
08 sickness, weakness

**malapropism**
06 misuse
09 wrong word
14 misapplication

**malapropos**
05 inapt
08 ill-timed, tactless, untimely
10 inapposite, misapplied, unsuitable
11 inopportune, uncalled-for
13 inappropriate

**malcontent**
05 rebel
06 grouch, moaner, morose, whiner
07 unhappy
08 agitator, grumbler
09 nitpicker, resentful
10 complainer, rebellious
11 bellyaching, disaffected, disgruntled
12 discontented, troublemaker
13 mischief-maker

**male**
03 boy, man
05 he-man, manly
06 boyish, virile
07 manlike
09 masculine

**malediction**
05 curse

07 damning, malison
08 anathema
09 damnation
10 execration
11 imprecation

**malefactor**
05 crook, felon
06 outlaw
07 convict, culprit, villain
08 criminal, evildoer, offender
09 miscreant, misfeasor, wrongdoer
10 delinquent, lawbreaker
12 transgressor

**malevolence**
04 hate
05 spite, venom
06 hatred, malice, rancor
07 ill will
09 hostility, malignity
10 malignancy
11 viciousness
12 spitefulness, vengefulness
13 maliciousness
14 evil-mindedness, vindictiveness

**malevolent**
06 malign
07 baleful, hostile, vicious
08 spiteful, vengeful, venomous
09 malicious, rancorous, resentful
10 evil-minded, maleficent, vindictive

**malformation**
09 deformity
10 distortion
13 disfigurement, misshapenness

**malformed**
04 bent
06 warped
07 crooked, twisted
08 deformed
09 distorted

**malfunction**
04 fail, flaw
05 fault
06 defect
07 conk out, go kaput, go wrong
09 break down, breakdown

**malice**
04 hate
05 spite, venom
06 animus, hatred, rancor
09 animosity, hostility
10 bitchiness
11 malevolence
13 maliciousness
14 vindictiveness

**malicious**
04 evil
06 bitter, malign
07 vicious
08 spiteful, vengeful, venomous
10 evil-minded, malevolent

**malign**
03 bad
04 evil, harm, slur
05 abuse, libel, smear
06 defame, injure, insult, vilify
07 harmful, hostile, hurtful, run down, slander, traduce
08 bad-mouth
09 disparage, injurious, malignant
10 calumniate, malevolent
11 destructive

**malignant**
04 evil
05 fatal
06 deadly, lethal
07 harmful, hostile, vicious
08 spiteful, venomous, virulent
09 cancerous, incurable, malicious
10 malevolent, pernicious
11 destructive
15 life threatening

**malignity**
04 gall, hate
05 spite, venom
06 animus, hatred, malice
08 bad blood
09 animosity, hostility
10 deadliness, wickedness
11 hurtfulness, malevolence, viciousness
13 maliciousness

**malinger**
05 dodge, shirk, skulk, slack

**malingerer**
06 dodger
07 shirker, skulker, slacker

**mall**
04 walk
05 plaza
06 median, street
08 galleria
14 shopping center

**malleable**
06 pliant, supple
07 ductile, plastic, pliable
08 biddable, flexible, tractile, workable
09 compliant, tractable
11 persuadable, susceptible
14 impressionable

**malnutrition**
06 hunger

08 anorexia
09 inanition
10 starvation
12 underfeeding
15 anorexia nervosa

**malodorous**
04 rank
05 fetid, niffy
06 putrid, smelly
07 miasmal, miasmal, miasmic, reeking
08 stinking
09 miasmatic, offensive
12 evil smelling, foul smelling

**malpractice**
10 misconduct, negligence, wrongdoing
11 impropriety
12 carelessness
13 mismanagement

**maltreat**
04 harm, hurt
05 abuse, bully
06 injure, misuse
07 torture
08 ill-treat, mistreat

**maltreatment**
04 harm, hurt
05 abuse
06 damage, ill-use, injury, misuse
07 torture
08 bullying, ill-usage
12 mistreatment

**mammals**

► *Types of mammal*:
02 ox
03 ape, ass, bat, cat, cow, dog, elk, fox, gnu, pig, rat, yak
04 bear, boar, cavy, deer, goat, hare, ibex, kudu, lion, lynx, mink, mole, paca, puma, seal, vole, wolf, zebu
05 aguti, bison, camel, civet, coney, coypu, dingo, eland, genet, horse, human, hyena, hyrax, koala, lemur, llama, loris, moose, mouse, okapi, otter, ounce, panda, potto, rhino, sheep, shrew, skunk, sloth, stoat, tapir, tiger, whale, zebra
06 aye-aye, baboon, badger, beaver, beluga, bobcat, colugo, coypu, coyote, cuscus, dugong, duiker, ermine, ferret, galago, gerbil, gibbon, gopher, impala, jackal, jaguar, jerboa, langur, marmot, marten, monkey,

ocelot, possum, rabbit, rhebok, sea cow, serval, tenrec, vicuna, walrus, wapiti, weasel, wombat
07 ant bear, buffalo, caracal, caribou, chamois, cheetah, dolphin, echidna, fur seal, gazelle, giraffe, gorilla, grampus, grizzly, guanaco, guereza, gymnura, hamster, lemming, leopard, macaque, manatee, meerkat, mole rat, muntjac, muntjak, muskrat, narwhal, opossum, pack rat, panther, peccary, polecat, primate, raccoon, red deer, roe deer, sea lion, tamarin, tarsier, wallaby, warthog, wild ass, wildcat
08 aardvark, aardwolf, anteater, antelope, bush baby, bushbuck, capybara, chipmunk, dormouse, elephant, fruit bat, gray wolf, harp seal, hedgehog, house bat, kangaroo, mandrill, marmoset, mongoose, musk deer, pacarana, pangolin, platypus, porpoise, reedbuck, reindeer, sea otter, sewer rat, squirrel
09 Arctic fox, armadillo, bandicoot, black bear, blue whale, brown bear, dromedary, flying fox, gray whale, guinea pig, mouse deer, orangutan, phalanger, polar bear, porcupine, springbok, waterbuck, wolverine
10 Barbary ape, chevrotain, chimpanzee, chinchilla, coatimundi, common seal, fallow deer, field mouse, giant panda, house mouse, human being, jackrabbit, Kodiak bear, pilot whale, pine marten, prairie dog, rhinoceros, sperm whale, springbuck, vampire bat, white whale, wildebeest
11 grizzly bear, honey badger, killer whale, muntjac deer, muntjak deer, pipistrelle, red squirrel, snow leopard
12 elephant seal, gray squirrel, harvest mouse, hippopotamus, mountain goat, mountain lion, rhesus monkey, spider monkey, two-toed sloth, vervet monkey, water buffalo
13 colobus monkey, elephant

shrew, howling monkey, humpback whale, spiny anteater, Tasmanian wolf, thylacine wolf
14 capuchin monkey, edible dormouse, flying squirrel, Indian elephant, squirrel monkey, Tasmanian devil, three-toed sloth
15 African elephant, black rhinoceros, humpbacked whale, proboscis monkey, ring-tailed lemur, Thomson's gazelle, white rhinoceros
➤ See also ANIMAL; APE; CAT; CATTLE; DOG; MARSUPIAL; MONKEY; PIG; RODENT; SHEEP; WHALE

**mammoth**
04 huge, vast
05 giant, jumbo
06 mighty
07 immense, massive
08 colossal, enormous, gigantic, whopping
09 ginormous, Herculean, leviathan
10 gargantuan, prodigious

**man**
03 boy, guy, lad
04 chap, crew, dude, hand, male
05 adult, human, lover, staff, valet
06 fellow, mister, mortal, people, person, spouse, worker
07 husband, laborer, mankind, partner, servant, soldier, workman
08 employee, factotum, handyman, houseboy, humanity
09 attendant, boyfriend, gentleman, human race, humankind
10 human being, individual, manservant
11 Homo sapiens

**❑to a man**
05 as one
07 bar none
09 one and all
11 unanimously
12 with one voice

**manacle**
04 bind, curb
05 chain, check
06 fetter, hamper
07 inhibit, shackle
08 handcuff, restrain
11 put in chains

**manacles**
05 bonds, cuffs, irons
06 chains
07 fetters
08 shackles
09 bracelets, handcuffs

**manage**
03 run, use
04 cope, fare, head, lead, rule, work
05 get by, get on, guide
06 direct, effect, govern, handle, head up, make do, master
07 achieve, command, conduct, control, make out, operate, oversee, succeed, survive
08 be head of, bring off, deal with, engineer, get along, organize
09 influence, supervise
10 accomplish, administer, bring about, manipulate
11 preside over, superintend
12 be in charge of

**manageable**
06 doable, docile, pliant, viable
07 pliable
08 amenable, feasible
09 tolerable, tractable
10 attainable, reasonable
11 practicable
13 accommodating

**management**
04 care
05 board
06 bosses, charge, owners
07 command, control, running
08 handling, managers
09 direction, directors, executive, governors
10 executives, government, leadership, overseeing
11 directorate, supervision, supervisors
12 organization
14 administration

**manager**
04 boss, head
05 chief
06 honcho
08 director, overseer
09 executive, organizer
10 controller, supervisor
11 comptroller
12 commissioner
13 administrator
14 chief executive

**mandate**
03 law
05 edict, order
06 decree, ruling

07 command, statute, warrant
08 sanction
09 authority, direction, directive, ordinance
10 commission, injunction
11 instruction
13 authorization

**mandatory**
09 essential
10 compulsory, imperative, obligatory

**manful**
04 bold
05 brave, hardy, manly, noble
06 daring, heroic, strong
07 gallant, valiant
08 stalwart, vigorous
10 courageous, determined
11 indomitable, lionhearted, unflinching
12 stouthearted

**manfully**
04 hard
07 bravely, stoutly
09 gallantly, valiantly
10 heroically, stalwartly, vigorously
12 courageously, determinedly

**manger**
04 crib, rack
06 trough

**mangle**
04 hack, maim, maul, rend, ruin
05 botch, crush, spoil, twist, wreck
06 bungle, deform, mess up
07 destroy, distort
08 mutilate
09 disfigure
11 make a mess of

**mangy**
05 dirty, seedy
06 filthy, scabby, shabby, shoddy
07 scruffy
08 tattered
09 moth-eaten

**manhandle**
04 haul, maul, pull, push
05 abuse, heave
06 misuse
07 rough up
10 knock about
11 knock around
13 handle roughly

**manhood**
08 maleness, virility
09 adulthood, manliness
11 masculinity

## mania
04 rage
05 craze
06 desire, fetish, frenzy, lunacy
07 craving, madness, passion
08 dementia, fixation, insanity
09 obsession, psychosis
10 compulsion, enthusiasm
11 fascination, infatuation
13 preoccupation

➤ *Types of mania*:
08 egomania
09 monomania, pyromania, theomania
10 dipsomania, hippomania, narcomania, necromania
11 ablutomania, bibliomania, hedonomania, kleptomania, megalomania, nymphomania
12 thanatomania

## maniac
05 crank, loony
06 psycho
07 fanatic, lunatic, nutcase
08 crackpot, head case
09 fruitcake, psychotic, screwball
10 enthusiast, psychopath

## manifest
04 open, show
05 clear, plain, prove
06 evince, expose, patent, reveal
07 blatant, display, evident, exhibit, express, obvious, visible
08 apparent, distinct, indicate
09 establish, make clear, make plain
10 illustrate
11 conspicuous, demonstrate

## manifestation
04 mark, show, sign
05 token
07 display
08 evidence, exposure
10 appearance, exhibition, exposition, expression, indication
12 illustration
13 demonstration
15 exemplification

## manifesto
08 platform, policies
09 statement
11 declaration, publication
12 announcement, proclamation

## manifold
04 many
06 varied
07 diverse, several, various
08 multiple, numerous
12 multifarious

## manipulate
05 guide, knead, steer, wield
06 direct, doctor, fiddle, handle, wangle
07 control, exploit, falsify, massage, operate, process, utilize
08 engineer
09 influence
10 juggle with, tamper with
11 pull strings

## manipulator
07 handler, schemer, wielder
08 director, engineer, operator
09 exploiter
10 controller, maneuverer, negotiator
13 wheeler-dealer

## mankind
03 man
06 people
08 humanity
09 human race, humankind
11 Homo sapiens, human beings

## manliness
07 bravery, courage
08 boldness, machismo, maleness, strength, virility
10 manfulness, resolution
11 masculinity
12 fearlessness, stalwartness

## manly
04 bold
05 brave, macho, tough
06 rugged, strong, virile
08 powerful, vigorous
09 masculine
10 courageous, determined

## man-made
06 ersatz
09 imitation, simulated, synthetic
10 artificial
12 manufactured

## manner
03 air, way
04 form, look, mien, mode
05 means, style
06 aspect, method, stance
07 bearing, conduct, decorum, fashion, p's and q's, posture, process, routine, variety

## maneuver
08 approach, attitude, behavior, courtesy, demeanor, practice, protocol
09 character, etiquette, procedure, propriety, technique
10 appearance, deportment, politeness
11 formalities
12 social graces, the done thing
13 way of behaving

## mannered
05 posed, put-on
06 pseudo
07 stilted
08 affected, precious
10 artificial, euphuistic
11 pretentious

## mannerism
05 habit, quirk, trait
06 foible
11 peculiarity
12 idiosyncrasy
14 characteristic

## mannerly
05 civil
06 polite
07 genteel, refined
08 decorous, gracious, polished, well-bred
09 civilized, courteous
10 respectful
11 deferential
12 well-mannered

## mannish
05 butch
07 laddish
09 Amazonian, masculine, tomboyish
10 unfeminine, unladylike

## mannishness
08 virilism, virility
09 butchness
11 masculinity

## maneuver
04 move, plan, plot, ploy, ruse
05 dodge, drive, guide, pilot, steer, trick
06 action, device, devise, direct, gambit, handle, jockey, manage, scheme, tactic, wangle
08 contrive, engineer, intrigue, movement, navigate
09 negotiate, stratagem
10 deployment, manipulate, subterfuge
11 machination, pull strings
12 manipulation

**manor**
05 house, villa
06 estate
07 mansion
12 country house, landed estate

**manse**
07 deanery, rectory
08 vicarage
09 parsonage

**manservant**
05 valet
06 butler
08 retainer

**mansion**
05 house, manor, villa
10 manor house
12 country house

**manslaughter**
06 murder
07 killing, slaying
08 homicide
09 matricide, patricide, uxoricide
10 fratricide, sororicide
11 infanticide

**mantle**
04 cape, hide, hood, mask, veil
05 cloak, cover, layer, shawl
06 screen, shroud
07 blanket, conceal, envelop
08 covering, disguise, envelope

**manual**
05 bible, guide
06 by hand
08 Baedeker, handbook, physical, textbook
09 companion, guidebook, vade mecum
10 directions, prospectus
12 hand operated, instructions
15 instruction book

**manufacture**
04 form, make
05 build, forge, frame, model
06 create, devise, invent
07 concoct, dream up, fashion, produce, think up
08 assemble, assembly, building, creation
09 construct, fabricate
10 production
11 fabrication, mass-produce
12 construction
14 mass production

**manufacturer**
05 maker
07 builder, creator
08 producer
11 constructor
13 industrialist

**manure**
04 dung, muck
06 ordure
09 droppings
10 fertilizer

**manuscript**
04 text
05 paper
06 script, scroll, vellum
08 document
09 parchment

**many**
04 tons, wads
05 heaps, piles, scads
06 lots of, masses, oodles, scores, stacks
07 copious, diverse, umpteen
08 billions, hundreds, manifold, millions, multiple, numerous, zillions
09 countless, thousands
11 innumerable
13 multitudinous

**map**
04 plan, plot
05 atlas, chart, graph
06 lay out, sketch
08 town plan
09 delineate, gazetteer
10 street plan

❏**map out**
05 draft
06 draw up, lay out, sketch
07 outline, work out
09 sketch out

**mar**
04 harm, hurt, maim, ruin, scar
05 spoil, stain, taint, wreck
06 damage, deface, impair
07 blemish, tarnish
08 mutilate
09 disfigure
11 detract from

**maraud**
04 loot, raid, sack
07 despoil, pillage, plunder, ransack
08 spoliate
09 depredate

**marauder**
06 bandit, looter, pirate, raider
07 brigand, rustler
08 pillager, predator
09 buccaneer, plunderer
10 freebooter, highwayman

**march**
04 demo, file, gait, hike, pace, step, trek, walk
05 stalk, strut, tramp, tread
06 parade, stride

07 headway, passage
08 footslog, progress
10 procession
11 development, make headway
13 demonstration

**margin**
03 rim
04 brim, edge, play, room, side
05 brink, limit, scope, skirt, space, verge
06 border, leeway, limits
07 confine, surplus
08 boundary, confines, latitude
09 allowance, perimeter, periphery
10 difference
12 differential

**marginal**
05 minor, small
06 minute, slight
07 minimal
09 on the edge
10 borderline, negligible, peripheral
13 insignificant

**marijuana**
03 kef, pot
04 bang, dope, hash, hemp, leaf, weed
05 bhang, ganja, grass
06 ganjah
07 hashish
08 cannabis

**marina**
04 dock, port
06 harbor
07 mooring

**marinade**
04 soak
05 imbue, souse, steep
07 immerse
08 marinate, permeate, saturate

**marine**
03 sea
05 naval
07 aquatic, oceanic, pelagic
08 maritime, nautical, sea water, seagoing
09 salt water, seafaring, thalassic
10 oceangoing, serviceman, thalassian

**mariner**
03 gob, tar
04 salt
06 sailor, sea dog, seaman
07 Jack Tar, jack-tar
08 deckhand, seafarer
09 navigator

## marital
06 wedded
07 married, nuptial, wedding
08 conjugal, marriage
09 connubial
11 matrimonial

## maritime
03 sea
05 naval
06 marine
07 coastal, oceanic, pelagic
08 littoral, nautical, seagoing
09 seafaring

## mark
03 aim, cut, end, see, tag
04 blot, chip, clue, dent, dupe, flag, fool, goal, heed, hint, keep, line, logo, mind, name, nick, note, scar, seal, sign, spot, tick
05 badge, brand, grade, label, level, motto, notch, patch, point, print, proof, score, smear, speck, stage, stain, stamp, token, trace, track
06 assess, blotch, bruise, device, emblem, notice, number, object, pimple, regard, smudge, stigma, symbol, target, tracks, typify
07 blemish, correct, discern, feature, freckle, imprint, observe, purpose, quality, scratch, specify, symptom
08 appraise, bull's-eye, discolor, evaluate, evidence, identify, indicate, monogram
09 attribute, celebrate, character, designate, objective, recognize, trademark, write down
10 assessment, evaluation, impression, indication, percentage, take heed of
11 commemorate, distinguish
12 characterize, fingerprints
14 characteristic, pay attention to

## ᐤmake one's mark
05 get on
06 make it
07 prosper, succeed
12 be successful

## ᐤmark down
03 cut
05 lower, slash
06 reduce

## ᐤmark out
03 fix
07 delimit
08 set apart

09 demarcate, draw lines, single out, tell apart
11 distinguish
13 differentiate

## ᐤmark up
05 put up, raise
06 hike up, jack up

## ᐤwide of the mark
09 incorrect, off target
10 inaccurate, irrelevant
14 beside the point

## marked
05 clear
06 doomed, signal, spotty
07 blotchy, bruised, decided, evident, obvious, scarred, spotted, stained
08 apparent, blotched, distinct, emphatic, striking
09 blemished, condemned, prominent, scratched, suspected
10 noticeable, pronounced
11 conspicuous

## markedly
07 clearly
08 signally
09 blatantly, decidedly, evidently, glaringly, obviously
10 noticeably, strikingly
11 prominently
12 unmistakably
13 conspicuously

## market
04 call, fair, hawk, mall, mart, sell
05 agora, trade
06 bazaar, buying, demand, desire, outlet, peddle, retail
08 business, dealings, exchange, industry
11 stock market
12 offer for sale

## ᐤon the market
06 on sale
07 for sale
09 available, up for sale

## marketable
07 salable
08 in demand, saleable, vendible
10 commercial

## marksman, markswoman
06 sniper
07 deadeye
09 crack shot
12 sharpshooter

## maroon
06 desert, strand
07 abandon, forsake, isolate

08 cast away
09 put ashore

## marriage
04 link
05 union
06 fusion, merger
07 wedding, wedlock
08 alliance, coupling, nuptials
09 matrimony
10 connection
11 affiliation, association, combination, partnership, unification
12 amalgamation, married state
13 confederation

## married
03 wed
05 wived, yoked
06 joined, united, wedded
07 hitched, marital, nuptial, spliced, spousal
08 conjugal
09 connubial
11 matrimonial

## marrow
03 nub
04 core, gist, pith, soul
05 heart, quick, stuff
06 center, kernel, spirit
07 essence, nucleus
09 substance
12 nuts and bolts, quintessence

## marry
03 wed
04 ally, fuse, join, knit, link, weld
05 elope, match, merge, unite
06 couple
07 combine, connect
10 get hitched, get married, get spliced, tie the knot
13 take the plunge
14 lead to the altar
15 join in matrimony

## marsh
03 bog, fen
04 mire
05 bayou, swamp
06 morass, slough
08 quagmire
09 swampland

## marshal
04 lead, rank, take
05 align, array, group, guide, order, usher
06 deploy, draw up, escort, gather, lawman, line up, muster
07 arrange, collect, conduct, officer
08 assemble, organize, shepherd

**marshy**
03 wet
04 miry
05 boggy, fenny, muddy
06 quaggy, spongy, swampy
11 waterlogged

**marsupial**
━━━━━━━━━━━━━━━━━━
► *Types of marsupial*:
05 koala
06 cuscus, wombat
07 opossum, wallaby
08 kangaroo, wallaroo
09 bandicoot, pademelon,
   phalanger
11 rat kangaroo, rock wallaby
12 tree kangaroo
13 Tasmanian wolf
14 Tasmanian devil
➤ See also ANIMAL; MAMMAL

**martial**
04 army
07 warlike
08 militant, military
09 bellicose, soldierly
10 aggressive, pugnacious
11 belligerent

**martinet**
06 tyrant
08 stickler
10 taskmaster
11 slave driver
12 taskmistress
14 disciplinarian

**martyr**
07 crucify, torment, torture
08 sufferer
09 persecute
10 put to death
14 burn at the stake
15 throw to the lions

**martyrdom**
05 agony, death
07 anguish, torment, torture
09 suffering
11 persecution
12 excruciation

**marvel**
04 gape, gawk, gawp, gaze
05 stare
06 genius, wonder
07 miracle, prodigy
09 sensation, spectacle
10 be amazed at, phenomenon

**marvelous**
05 great, magic, super
06 superb
07 amazing, awesome
08 glorious, splendid, terrific

09 excellent, fantastic,
   wonderful
10 astounding, incredible,
   miraculous, stupendous
11 magnificent, sensational,
   spectacular
13 extraordinary

**masculine**
04 male
05 butch, macho, manly
06 strong, virile
07 mannish

**masculinity**
07 manhood
08 machismo, maleness, virility
09 manliness

**mash**
03 pap
04 beat, mush, pulp
05 crush, grind, pound, purée
06 pummel, squash
09 pulverize

**mask**
04 hide, veil
05 blind, cloak, cover, front,
   guise, visor
06 façade, screen, shield,
   veneer
07 conceal, cover up, obscure
08 disguise, pretense

**masquerade**
04 play, pose
06 masque
07 coverup, pretend
08 disguise, pretense
09 deception
10 masked ball
11 costume ball, counterfeit,
   dissimulate, impersonate
15 fancy-dress party, pass
   yourself off

**mass**
03 lot, mob, sum
04 bags, band, body, bulk, heap,
   herd, hunk, load, lots, lump,
   most, pile, size, tons
05 amass, batch, block, bunch,
   chunk, crowd, group, heaps,
   horde, loads, piece, piles,
   rally, swarm, troop
06 gather, muster, rabble,
   scores, throng
07 cluster, collect, general,
   popular
08 assemble, majority, quantity
09 abundance, aggregate,
   Communion, dimension,
   Eucharist, extensive, hoi
   polloi, immensity,
   magnitude, multitude,
   wholesale

10 accumulate, assemblage,
   collection, congregate,
   large-scale
11 greater part, Lord's Supper,
   proletariat
12 accumulation, come
   together, common people,
   working class
13 bring together, Holy
   Communion
14 conglomeration, the rank
   and file, working classes

**massacre**
04 kill, slay
06 murder, pogrom
07 butcher, carnage, wipe out
08 butchery, decimate,
   genocide, homicide
09 bloodbath, holocaust,
   liquidate, slaughter
10 decimation
11 exterminate, liquidation
15 ethnic cleansing

**massage**
03 rub
05 knead
06 pummel
07 rub down, rubdown, shiatsu
09 pummeling
10 Jacuzzi, manipulate,
   osteopathy
11 acupressure, reflexology
13 physiotherapy

**massive**
03 big
04 huge, vast
05 bulky, great, heavy, hefty,
   jumbo, large, solid
06 mighty
07 hulking, immense,
   mammoth, weighty
08 colossal, enormous, gigantic,
   whopping
09 extensive, ginormous
10 monumental
11 substantial

**mast**
03 bar, rod
04 boom, heel, pole, post, spar,
   yard
05 shaft, staff, stick
07 support, upright

**master**
03 pro
04 buff, curb, guru, head, lord,
   main, rule, tame
05 adept, chief, grand, grasp,
   great, learn, owner, prime,
   quell, ruler, tutor

06 bridle, defeat, expert, genius, govern, manage, mentor, pundit, subdue
07 acquire, captain, conquer, control, leading, maestro, pedagog, skilled, skipper, teacher
08 foremost, overcome, overlord, overseer, vanquish, virtuoso
09 commander, overpower, pedagogue, preceptor, principal, subjugate
10 controller, proficient
11 controlling, predominant, triumph over
12 get the hang of, professional, schoolmaster
13 schoolteacher
14 schoolmistress, superintendent

**masterful**
08 arrogant, powerful
10 autocratic, dominating, highhanded, tyrannical
11 controlling, dictatorial, domineering, overbearing
13 authoritative

**masterly**
03 ace
05 adept, crack
06 adroit, expert
07 skilled
08 polished, skillful, superior
09 dexterous, excellent
10 consummate
12 accomplished, professional

**mastermind**
04 plan
05 forge, frame, hatch
06 brains, direct, genius
07 creator, dream up
08 be behind, conceive
09 architect, intellect, organizer
10 prime mover

**masterpiece**
09 work of art
10 magnum opus, masterwork
11 chef d'oeuvre

**mastery**
05 grasp, skill
07 ability, command, control, know-how, prowess
08 dominion
09 authority, dexterity, expertise, knowledge, upper hand
10 domination, virtuosity
11 proficiency, sovereignty
13 comprehension, understanding

**masticate**
03 eat
04 chew
05 champ, chomp, knead, munch
06 crunch

**mat**
03 rug
04 dull, felt, knot, mass
05 doily
06 carpet, tangle
07 cluster, coaster, drugget
13 floor covering

**match**
03 fit, vie
04 ally, bout, copy, fuse, game, join, link, mate, meet, pair, peer, suit, team, test, twin, yoke
05 adapt, agree, blend, equal, event, light, marry, rival, spill, tally, taper, trial, union, unite, vesta
06 accord, couple, double, fellow, go with, merger, oppose, pair up, relate, ringer
07 combine, compare, compete, connect, contest, pairing, replica
08 alliance, coupling, marriage, parallel, tone with
09 accompany, companion, duplicate, harmonize
10 competitor, complement, coordinate, correspond, dead ringer, equivalent, go together, keep up with, one of a pair, pit against, tournament
11 affiliation, combination, competition, counterpart, measure up to, partnership

**matching**
04 like, same, twin
06 double, paired
07 coupled, similar
08 blending, parallel
09 analogous, identical
10 comparable, equivalent
11 harmonizing
12 coordinating
13 complementary, corresponding

**matchless**
06 unique
07 perfect
08 peerless
10 inimitable
12 incomparable, without equal
13 beyond compare

**mate**
03 pal, wed
04 chum, join, pair, twin, wife
05 breed, buddy, china, crony, marry, match
06 couple, fellow, friend, helper, spouse
07 compeer, comrade, husband, partner
08 coworker, make love, work mate
09 assistant, checkmate, classmate, colleague, companion, other half
10 accomplice, apprentice, better half, equivalent
11 counterpart
12 fellow worker

**material**
03 apt
05 cloth, stuff, vital
06 bodily, fabric, matter
07 earthly, germane, serious, textile, weighty, worldly
08 apposite, concrete, palpable, physical, relevant, tangible
09 corporeal, essential, important, momentous, pertinent, substance
11 significant, substantial
13 consequential, indispensable

**materialistic**
09 mercenary
11 mammonistic
13 moneygrubbing

**materialize**
06 appear, happen, turn up
09 take place, take shape
13 become visible, come into being

**materially**
07 greatly
09 basically
11 essentially
12 considerably
13 fundamentally, substantially

**maternal**
06 caring, doting, loving
08 motherly
09 nurturing
10 motherlike, nourishing, protective

**mathematics**
► *Terms used in mathematics:*
02 pi
03 arc, set
04 apex, area, axes, axis, base, cone, cube, edge, face, line, mean, mode, plus, root, side,

sine, skew, unit, zero
05 angle, chaos, chord, curve,
depth, equal, graph, helix,
locus, minus, point, radix,
ratio, solid, speed, total,
width
06 binary, chance, convex,
cosine, degree, factor,
height, length, linear, matrix,
median, number, origin,
radius, sample, sector, spiral,
square, subset, vector,
vertex, volume
07 algebra, average, bearing,
bounded, breadth, chaotic,
concave, decimal, divisor,
formula, fractal, integer,
maximum, measure,
minimum, oblique, product,
segment, tangent
08 addition, analysis, bar chart,
bar graph, binomial, calculus,
constant, converse, cube
root, diameter, discrete,
dividend, division, equation,
exponent, fraction, function,
geometry, gradient, identity,
infinity, multiple, parabola,
pie chart, quadrant, quartile,
quotient, rotation, symmetry,
variable, variance, vertical
09 algorithm, Cartesian,
congruent, factorial,
histogram, hyperbola,
logarithm, numerator, odd
number, operation,
parameter, perimeter,
remainder
10 acute angle, arithmetic,
coordinate, covariance,
derivative, even number,
horizontal, hypotenuse,
percentage, percentile, place
value, proportion, protractor,
reciprocal, reflection, right
angle, square root, statistics,
subtractor
11 coefficient, coordinates,
correlation, denominator,
determinant, equidistant,
exponential, magic square,
mirror image, Möbius strip,
obtuse angle, permutation,
plane figure, prime number,
probability, Pythagorean,
Venn diagram, whole
number
12 asymmetrical, cross section,
random sample,
trigonometry
13 circumference, complex
number, Mandelbrot set,
natural number, ordinal

number, perpendicular,
quadrilateral, triangulation
14 axis of symmetry, cardinal
number, mirror symmetry,
multiplication, negative
number, positive number,
rational number, vulgar
fraction
15 imaginary number, scalene
triangle

---

► *Names of mathematicians:*
03 **Dee** (John), **Lie** (Sophus)
04 **Hero** (of Alexandria), **Venn**
(John)
05 **Boole** (George), **Euler**
(Leonhard), **Gauss** (Carl
Friedrich), **Gödel** (Kurt),
**Klein** (Felix), **Peano**
(Giuseppe), **Wiles** (Andrew)
06 **Euclid**, **Fermat** (Pierre de),
**Fisher** (Ronald Aylmer),
**Galois** (Évariste), **Möbius**
(August Ferdinand), **Napier**
(John), **Newton** (Isaac),
**Pappus** (of Alexandria),
**Pascal** (Blaise), **Peirce**
(Charles), **Turing** (Alan
Mathison), **Veblen** (Oswald),
**Wiener** (Norbert)
07 **Alhazen**, **Babbage**
(Charles), **Cardano**
(Girolamo), **Eudoxus** (of
Cnidus), **Fourier** (Jean
Baptiste Joseph), **Hilbert**
(David), **Laplace** (Pierre
Simon), **Leibniz** (Gottfried
Wilhelm), **Poisson** (Siméon
Denis), **Riemann**
(Bernhard), **Russell**
(Bertrand)
08 **Dedekind** (Julius Wilhelm
Richard), **Lagrange** (Joseph
Louis de), **Lovelace** (Ada),
**Poincaré** (Jules Henri)
09 **Bernoulli** (Daniel),
**Bronowski** (Jacob),
**Descartes** (René),
**Fibonacci** (Leonardo),
**Minkowski** (Hermann),
**Whitehead** (Alfred North)
10 **Apollonius** (of Perga),
**Archimedes**, **Diophantus**,
**Pythagoras**, **Torricelli**
(Evangelista)
12 **Eratosthenes**
➤ See also SCIENTIST

**mating**
06 fusing
07 joining, pairing, uniting
08 breeding, coupling,
matching

**matrimonial**
06 wedded
07 marital, nuptial, wedding
08 conjugal, marriage

**matrimony**
07 wedlock
08 marriage, nuptials
09 espousals
12 married state

**matted**
06 tangly
07 knotted, tangled, tousled
08 uncombed

**matter**
03 pus
04 body, case, note
05 count, event, issue, stuff,
topic, upset, value
06 affair, bother, import,
medium, weight
07 concern, content, episode,
problem, subject, trouble
08 business, incident, interest,
material, nuisance, question
09 discharge, happening,
purulence, secretion,
situation, substance
10 be relevant, importance,
occurrence, proceeding
11 be important, carry weight,
consequence, suppuration
12 circumstance, significance
13 have influence,
inconvenience, mean
something
15 make a difference

❑ **as a matter of fact**
06 in fact, really
08 actually
11 as it happens
12 in actual fact

❑ **no matter**
09 never mind
15 it does not matter, it is
unimportant

**matter-of-fact**
04 dull, flat
05 sober
07 deadpan, prosaic
08 lifeless
10 pedestrian
11 down-to-earth, emotionless,
unemotional
13 unimaginative,
unsentimental
15 straightforward

**mature**
03 age
04 ripe, wise

05 adult, bloom, grown, of age, ready, ripen
06 evolve, grow up, mellow
07 develop, fall due, grownup, perfect, ripened
08 balanced, complete, finished, seasoned, sensible
09 come of age, finalized, full grown, perfected
11 experienced, responsible
13 well developed
14 well thought out

**maturity**
06 wisdom
07 manhood
08 majority, ripeness
09 adulthood, womanhood
10 experience, mellowness
11 coming of age
14 responsibility

**maudlin**
05 drunk, gushy, mushy, soppy, tipsy, weepy
06 sickly, slushy
07 fuddled, mawkish, tearful
09 emotional, half drunk, schmaltzy
10 lachrymose
11 sentimental

**maul**
03 mug, paw
04 beat, belt, claw
05 abuse
06 attack, batter, mangle, molest, thrash, wallop
07 assault
08 lacerate, maltreat, mutilate
09 manhandle

**maunder**
06 babble, gabble, jabber, mutter
07 blather, chatter, meander, prattle, ramble,

**mausoleum**
04 tomb
05 crypt, vault
08 catacomb
09 sepulcher
13 burial chamber

**maverick**
05 rebel, stray
08 agitator, outsider
09 unbranded
13 individualist, nonconformist

**maw**
02 ma
04 jaws, mama
05 abyss, chasm, mouth
06 gullet, throat

**mawkish**
05 gushy, mushy, soppy
06 feeble, sickly, slushy
07 maudlin
09 emotional, schmaltzy
11 sentimental

**maxim**
03 saw
04 rule
05 adage, axiom, gnome, motto
06 byword, saying
07 epigram, precept, proverb
08 aphorism

**maximum**
04 acme, most, peak
06 apogee, height, summit, utmost, zenith
07 biggest, ceiling, highest, largest, supreme, topmost
08 greatest, pinnacle
09 extremity, uppermost
10 upper limit

**maybe**
07 perhaps
08 possibly
09 perchance
12 peradventure

**mayhem**
05 chaos
06 bedlam, tumult, uproar
07 anarchy
08 disorder, madhouse

**mayor**

► *Names of New York mayors*:
04 **Koch** (Edward), **Wood** (Fernando)
05 **Beame** (Abraham)
06 **O'Dwyer** (William), **Wagner** (Robert), **Walker** (James "Gentleman Jim")
07 **Clinton** (De Witt), **Dinkins** (David), **Lindsay** (John)
08 **Giuliani** (Rudolph "Rudy")
09 **Bloomberg** (Michael), **La Guardia** (Fiorello), **McClellan** (George)
12 **Impellitteri** (Vincent)

**maze**
06 jungle, puzzle, tangle
07 complex, network
09 confusion, intricacy, labyrinth

**meadow**
03 lea
04 mead
05 field, grass, green
07 paddock, pasture

09 grassland
11 pastureland

**meager**
04 poor, puny, thin
05 small
06 measly, paltry, scanty, skimpy, slight, sparse, stingy
08 exiguous
09 niggardly
10 negligible

**meagerness**
08 puniness
09 smallness
10 measliness, scantiness, sparseness, stinginess
13 insufficiency

**meal**

► *Meals include*:
04 bite
05 feast, lunch, snack
06 brunch, buffet, dinner, picnic, repast, spread, supper
07 banquet, blowout, cookout, potluck, takeout
08 barbecue, clambake, luncheon, tea party, TV dinner
09 breakfast, leftovers
10 midday meal, tailgating, weeny roast
11 dinner party, evening meal, smorgasbord, weenie roast, wiener roast
14 tailgate picnic

**mealy-mouthed**
04 glib, prim
07 mincing
08 indirect, reticent
09 equivocal, plausible
10 flattering
11 euphemistic
13 smooth-tongued

**mean**
03 aim
04 fate, mode, norm, plan, show, wish, wont
05 cause, cross, cruel, dirty, imply, lowly, mingy, nasty, tight
06 aspire, convey, denote, design, dismal, entail, humble, intend, lead to, median, medium, middle, ordain, shabby, stingy, unkind
07 appoint, average, betoken, connote, destine, express, halfway, involve, miserly, obscure, produce, propose, purport, purpose, selfish, signify, squalid, suggest

08 grasping, indicate, intimate, middling, midpoint, ordinary, result in, stand for, wretched
09 designate, miserable, niggardly, represent, symbolize
10 bring about, compromise, give rise to, have in mind, unpleasant
11 happy medium, tightfisted
12 intermediate, parsimonious
13 penny-pinching
17 close-fisted common

**meander**
04 bend, roam, wind
05 amble, mosey, snake
06 ramble, stroll, wander, zigzag

**meandering**
07 sinuous, snaking, winding
08 indirect, tortuous, twisting
10 serpentine

**meaning**
03 aim
04 gist, goal, idea, plan, wish
05 drift, point, sense, trend, value, worth
06 import, object, thrust
07 essence, message, purpose
09 intention, objective, substance
10 aspiration, definition, expression
11 connotation, elucidation, explanation, explication, implication
12 significance
13 signification
14 interpretation

**meaningful**
07 pointed, warning
08 eloquent, material, pregnant, relevant
10 purposeful, worthwhile
11 significant

**meaningless**
05 empty
06 absurd, futile, hollow
07 aimless, useless, vacuous
09 pointless, senseless, worthless
10 motiveless
14 unintelligible

**meanness**
09 parsimony
10 stinginess
11 miserliness
15 close-fistedness, tightfistedness

**means**
03 way

05 funds, money
06 agency, assets, avenue, course, income, manner, medium, method, riches, wealth
07 capital, channel, fortune, process, vehicle
09 affluence, resources, substance
11 wherewithal

❏**by all means**
08 of course
09 certainly, naturally

❏**by means of**
03 via
05 using
08 by dint of
12 with the aid of
13 with the help of

❏**by no means**
05 never, no way
08 not at all
12 certainly not

**meantime, meanwhile**
06 for now
12 for the moment, in the interim
15 for the time being

**measly**
04 mean, poor, puny
05 mingy, petty
06 meager, paltry, scanty, skimpy, stingy
07 miserly, pitiful
08 beggarly, pathetic, piddling
09 miserable, niggardly
12 contemptible

**measurable**
10 assessable, computable, fathomable
11 appreciable, perceptible
12 quantifiable, quantitative

**measure**
04 area, bulk, deed, mass, norm, part, rate, read, rule, size, step, time, unit
05 depth, gauge, judge, level, meter, piece, plumb, quota, range, ruler, scale, scope, share, sound, units, value, weigh, width
06 action, amount, assess, course, degree, extent, fathom, height, length, ration, record, size up, survey, system, volume, weight
07 compute, expanse, portion, rake-off, statute

08 appraise, capacity, division, estimate, evaluate, quantify, quantity, standard
09 allotment, benchmark, calculate, criterion, determine, magnitude, procedure, yardstick
10 allocation, dimensions, proceeding, touchstone
11 proportions

❏**beyond measure**
09 endlessly, immensely
10 infinitely
12 incalculably

❏**for good measure**
06 as well
08 as a bonus
10 in addition
11 furthermore
12 over and above

❏**measure off**
07 mark out, measure, pace out
10 measure out

❏**measure out**
05 allot, issue
07 deal out, dole out, hand out
08 dispense, share out
09 apportion, parcel out
10 distribute, measure off

❏**measure up**
07 shape up
10 fit the bill, pass muster
12 make the grade
15 come up to scratch

❏**measure up to**
05 equal, match, touch
08 come up to, live up to
09 match up to
11 compare with

**measured**
04 slow
06 steady
07 careful, planned, precise
09 unhurried
10 considered, deliberate
14 well thought out

**measureless**
07 endless, immense
08 infinite
10 bottomless

**measurement**
04 area, bulk, mass, size, unit
05 depth, range, width
06 amount, extent, height, length, sizing, volume, weight
07 expanse, reading
08 capacity, judgment, quantity
09 appraisal, dimension

10 estimation, evaluation,
   proportion
11 calculation, calibration,
   computation, proportions
14 quantification

▬ *Measurements include*:
02 em, en
03 bar, day, erg, ohm, rod, ton
04 acre, foot, gill, gram, hand,
   hour, inch, knot, mile, mole,
   peck, pint, span, volt, watt,
   week, yard, year
05 cable, chain, farad, hertz,
   joule, liter, lumen, meter,
   month, ounce, pound, stone,
   therm, tonne
06 ampere, bushel, decade,
   degree, fathom, gallon,
   jigger, kelvin, league, minute,
   newton, pascal, radian,
   second
07 calorie, candela, century,
   coulomb, decibel, furlong,
   hectare
08 angstrom, kilogram, millibar
09 becquerel, cubic foot, cubic
   inch, cubic yard, foot-pound,
   kilometer, metric ton
10 atmosphere, centimeter,
   cubic meter, fluid ounce,
   horsepower, micrometer,
   millennium, milliliter, square
   foot, square inch, square
   mile, square yard
11 square meter
12 nautical mile
13 hundredweight
15 cubic centimeter, square
   kilometer

## measuring instruments

▬ *Types of measuring
instrument*:
04 rule
05 gauge, meter
06 octant
07 ammeter, balance, burette,
   pipette, sextant
08 calipers, quadrant
09 altimeter, barometer,
   hourglass, optometer,
   pedometer, plumb line,
   pyrometer, steelyard,
   stopwatch, voltmeter, wind
   gauge
10 anemometer, audiometer,
   bathometer, gravimeter,
   hydrometer, micrometer,
   photometer, protractor,
   tachometer, tachymeter,
   theodolite
11 seismograph, speedometer,

tape measure, tensiometer,
thermometer, weighbridge
12 Breathalyzer, galvanometer
13 Geiger counter
➤ See also GAUGE

## meat
03 nub
04 core, crux, gist, grub, pith
05 flesh, heart, point
06 kernel, marrow, viands
07 essence, nucleus
09 substance
➤ See also FOOD

▬ *Cuts of meat*:
03 leg, rib
04 chop, hock, loin, neck, rump,
   shin
05 chine, chuck, flank, scrag,
   shank, T-bone
06 breast, cutlet, fillet, saddle
07 brisket, sirloin
08 escalope, shoulder
09 spareribs

▬ *Some types of meat*:
03 ham
04 beef, duck, hare, lamb, paté,
   pork, veal
05 bacon, brawn, goose, heart,
   jerky, liver, offal, steak, tripe
06 brains, gammon, kidney,
   mutton, oxtail, pigeon,
   rabbit, tongue, turkey
07 chicken, chorizo, rissole,
   sausage, venison
08 trotters
09 hamburger
10 beefburger, ground beef,
   prosciutto, sweetbread
11 pig's knuckle

## meaty
05 beefy, burly, heavy, hunky,
   pithy, solid
06 brawny, fleshy, hearty, sturdy
08 profound
10 meaningful
11 substantial

## mechanic
08 engineer, operator
09 repairman
10 technician

## mechanical
07 routine
08 habitual
09 automated, automatic
11 emotionless, instinctive,
   involuntary, machinelike,
   power driven, unconscious
14 machine powered

## mechanism
05 gears, means, motor, works
06 device, engine, gadget
07 channel, machine, process
08 movement, workings
09 apparatus, appliance,
   machinery, procedure,
   structure, technique
11 contraption, contrivance

## medal
05 award, prize
09 medallion
10 decoration
➤ See also MILITARY

## meddle
03 pry
06 butt in, horn in, tamper
07 intrude
09 interfere, intervene
14 poke your nose in
15 stick your nose in

## meddlesome
04 nosy
09 intruding, intrusive
11 interfering, mischievous

## mediate
06 umpire
07 referee
08 moderate
09 arbitrate, intercede,
   interpose, intervene
10 conciliate

## mediation
11 arbitration, good offices,
   peacemaking
12 conciliation, intercession,
   intervention

## mediator
06 umpire
07 arbiter, referee
09 go-between, middleman,
   moderator, ombudsman
10 arbitrator, interceder,
   peacemaker
11 conciliator, intercessor
12 intermediary

## medical

▬ *Types of medical
equipment*:
03 ECG, MRI
05 clamp, curet, swabs
06 scales
07 cannula, curette, forceps,
   inhaler, scalpel, scanner,
   syringe
08 catheter, iron lung,
   speculum, tweezers, X-ray
   unit
09 aspirator, auriscope,

autoclave, CT scanner,
endoscope, incubator,
nebulizer, retractor
10 audiometer, CAT scanner, ear
syringe, hypodermic, kidney
dish, microscope, oxygen
mask, respirator, sterilizer,
ultrasound
11 body scanner, first-aid kit,
stethoscope, stomach pump,
thermometer
12 resuscitator, surgical mask
13 defibrillator
14 operating table,
ophthalmoscope, oxygen
cylinder

➤ *Types of medical specialist*:
06 doctor
07 dentist
08 optician
09 dietician, homeopath,
internist
10 geriatrist, oncologist,
pediatrist, pharmacist
11 anesthetist, chiropodist,
neurologist, optometrist,
orthopedist, pathologist
12 cardiologist, chiropractor,
embryologist, geriatrician,
gynecologist, hematologist,
homeopathist, obstetrician,
orthodontist, pediatrician,
psychiatrist, psychologist,
toxicologist
13 dermatologist
14 bacteriologist,
pharmacologist
15 endocrinologist,
ophthalmologist,
physiotherapist
➤ See also DOCTOR; NURSE

**medicinal**
07 healing, medical
08 curative, remedial
11 restorative, therapeutic

**medicine**
04 cure, drug
06 remedy
07 panacea
09 analeptic
10 medicament, medication
12 prescription
14 pharmaceutical
➤ See also THERAPY

➤ *Types of medicine*:
04 pill
05 patch, tonic
06 arnica, emetic, gargle, tablet
07 antacid, capsule, inhaler,
linctus, lozenge
08 ear drops, eye drops,

laxative, ointment, pastille
09 paregoric
10 antibiotic, nasal spray,
painkiller, penicillin
11 suppository
➤ See also DRUG

**medieval**
07 antique, archaic
08 historic, obsolete, old-world,
outmoded
09 primitive
10 antiquated
12 antediluvian, old-fashioned
13 unenlightened

**mediocre**
03 bad
04 poor, so-so
07 average
08 adequate, inferior, middling,
ordinary, passable
10 pedestrian, uninspired
11 commonplace, indifferent
12 run-of-the-mill
13 insignificant, no great shakes,
unexceptional
15 undistinguished

**mediocrity**
08 dead loss, poorness
09 nonentity
11 inferiority
12 indifference, ordinariness,
unimportance

**meditate**
04 muse, plan
05 brood, study, think
06 devise, ponder
07 reflect
08 cogitate, consider, mull over,
ruminate
09 think over
10 deliberate
11 contemplate

**meditation**
05 study
06 musing
07 reverie, thought
08 brooding
09 pondering
10 brown study, cogitation,
reflection, rumination
11 cerebration, mulling over,
speculation
12 deliberation, excogitation
13 concentration,
contemplation

**meditative**
07 museful, pensive
08 ruminant, studious
10 cogitative, reflective,
ruminative, thoughtful
12 deliberative

13 contemplative

**medium**
03 way
04 mean, mode, norm
05 means, organ
06 agency, avenue, center,
median, middle, midway
07 average, channel, habitat,
psychic, vehicle
08 ambience, middling,
midpoint, standard
09 channeler, spiritist
10 atmosphere, compromise,
golden mean, instrument
11 clairvoyant, environment,
necromancer
12 intermediate, middle ground,
spiritualist

**medley**
03 mix
06 jumble
07 farrago, melange, mixture,
variety
08 mixed bag
09 potpourri
10 assortment, hodgepodge,
hotchpotch, miscellany
14 conglomeration, omnium-
gatherum

**meek**
04 mild, tame, weak
05 lowly, quiet, timid
06 docile, gentle, humble,
modest
07 patient
08 peaceful, resigned, yielding
09 compliant, spineless
10 forbearing, spiritless,
submissive, unassuming
11 deferential
13 long-suffering, unpretentious

**meekness**
08 docility, humility, mildness,
softness, timidity, weakness
09 deference
10 gentleness, humbleness,
submission
12 acquiescence, peacefulness
14 submissiveness

**meet**
04 abut, bear, face, join, link
05 cross, equal, match, rally,
touch, unite
06 adjoin, answer, gather,
handle, link up, manage,
muster, pay for, suffer, tackle
07 collect, connect, convene,
execute, fulfill, perform, run
into, satisfy

08 assemble, bump into, come up to, converge, cope with, deal with
09 discharge, encounter, forgather, intersect, look after, run across
10 come across, comply with, congregate, experience, happen upon, join up with, rendezvous
11 get together, measure up to
12 come together

**meeting**
04 date
05 tryst, union, venue
07 contact, session
08 abutment, junction
09 concourse, encounter, gathering, interface
10 conference, confluence, discussion, rendezvous
11 appointment, assignation, conjunction, convergence
12 intersection, introduction
13 confrontation
14 point of contact

**megalomania**
13 conceitedness
14 self-importance

**melancholy**
03 low, sad
04 blue, down, glum
05 blues, dumps, gloom, moody
06 dismal, gloomy, sorrow, woeful
07 sadness, unhappy
08 dejected, doldrums, downcast, mournful
09 pessimism, woebegone
10 depression, despondent, dispirited, low spirits, lugubrious
11 downhearted, unhappiness
12 disconsolate, heavy-hearted
14 down in the dumps

**melange**
06 jumble
07 farrago, mixture, variety
08 mixed bag
10 assortment, collection, hodgepodge, hotchpotch, miscellany, salmagundi
14 conglomeration

**melee**
04 fray, mess
05 brawl, broil, chaos, fight, mix-up, scrum, set-to
06 affray, fracas, jumble, ruckus, rumpus, tussle
07 clutter, ruction, scuffle

08 disorder
09 confusion
10 free-for-all

**mellifluous**
05 sweet
06 dulcet, mellow, smooth
07 honeyed, silvery, tuneful
10 euphonious, harmonious
13 sweet sounding

**mellow**
05 juicy, ripen, sweet
06 dulcet, genial, mature, placid, serene, smooth, soften, temper
07 affable, amiable, improve, relaxed, rounded, sweeten, tuneful
08 luscious, pleasant, tranquil
09 easygoing, melodious
10 harmonious
12 full flavored

**melodious**
05 sweet
06 dulcet
07 melodic, musical, tuneful
10 euphonious, harmonious
13 sweet sounding

**melodramatic**
05 hammy, stagy
10 histrionic, theatrical
11 exaggerated, sensational
12 overdramatic
13 overemotional

**melody**
03 air
04 song, tune
05 music, theme
06 rhythm, strain
07 euphony, harmony, refrain
11 musicalness, tunefulness
14 harmoniousness

**melt**
04 fuse, thaw
06 soften
07 defrost, liquefy
08 dissolve, unfreeze
10 deliquesce

❏**melt away**
08 disperse, dissolve, evanesce, fade away
09 disappear, evaporate

**member**
03 arm, leg
04 limb
05 organ
09 appendage, associate, extremity
14 representative

**membership**
09 adherents
10 associates, enrollment, fellowship
11 affiliation, subscribers
15 representatives

**membrane**
04 film, skin
05 hymen, velum
06 septum, tissue
09 diaphragm

**memento**
05 relic, token
06 record, trophy
08 keepsake, memorial, reminder, souvenir
11 remembrance

**memoir**
07 account, journal
09 biography, chronicle

**memoirs**
06 annals
07 diaries, records
08 journals, memories
09 life story
10 chronicles
11 confessions, experiences
13 autobiography, recollections, reminiscences

**memorable**
10 impressive, noteworthy, remarkable
11 distinctive, outstanding, significant
13 consequential, distinguished, extraordinary, unforgettable

**memorandum**
04 memo, note
07 message
08 reminder

**memorial**
06 plaque, shrine
07 memento
08 cenotaph, monument, souvenir
09 mausoleum
11 remembrance
13 commemorative

**memorize**
05 learn
08 remember
11 learn by rote
12 learn by heart
14 commit to memory

**memory**
05 honor
06 recall
07 tribute

11 recognition, remembrance
12 recollection, reminiscence
13 commemoration
14 powers of recall

**menace**
04 loom, lour, pain, pest, risk
05 alarm, bully, daunt, peril, press, scare
06 appall, bother, coerce, danger, dismay, hazard, threat
07 terrify, warning
08 browbeat, bullying, coercion, jeopardy, nuisance, pressure, threaten
09 terrorize
10 intimidate, pressurize
11 ominousness, terrorizing
15 thorn in your side

**menacing**
07 looming, louring, ominous
08 alarming, minatory, sinister
09 Damoclean, impending
10 portentous
11 threatening
12 intimidating, intimidatory

**mend**
03 fix, sew
04 cure, darn, heal
05 amend, emend, patch, refit, renew, stick
06 cobble, reform, remedy, repair, revise
07 correct, improve, patch up, recover, rectify, restore
08 put right, renovate
09 get better, make whole
10 ameliorate, recuperate

**❑on the mend**
07 healing
09 improving
10 recovering
12 convalescent, convalescing, recuperating

**mendacious**
05 false, lying
06 untrue
09 deceitful, deceptive, dishonest, insincere
10 fictitious, perfidious, untruthful
11 duplicitous

**mendacity**
05 lying
06 deceit
07 perfidy, perjury, untruth
09 duplicity, falsehood
10 dishonesty, distortion
13 deceitfulness, falsification
14 untruthfulness

**mendicant**
06 beggar, cadger
07 begging, cadging, moocher
09 scrounger
10 scrounging, supplicant
11 petitionary

**menial**
05 grunt, lowly, slave
06 drudge, minion
07 humdrum, servant, servile, slavish
09 attendant, degrading, demeaning, underling, unskilled

**mensuration**
09 measuring, surveying, valuation
10 assessment, estimation, evaluation
11 calculation, calibration, computation, measurement

**mental**
03 mad
04 loco, nuts
05 crazy, loony
06 insane
07 lunatic
08 abstract, cerebral
09 cognitive, disturbed, psychotic
10 conceptual, off your nut, unbalanced
11 theoretical
12 intellectual
13 off your rocker
14 off your trolley

**mentality**
04 mind
06 brains, makeup
07 faculty, mindset, outlook
08 attitude
09 character, intellect
10 gray matter, psychology
11 disposition, frame of mind
12 intelligence
13 comprehension, understanding, way of thinking

**mentally**
08 inwardly
09 in the mind
14 intellectually, telepathically
15 psychologically, temperamentally

**mention**
03 say
04 cite, name
05 quote, state
06 broach, impart, remark, report

07 bring up, declare, divulge, refer to, speak of, touch on
08 allude to, allusion, citation, disclose, intimate, point out
09 reference, statement
11 acknowledge, communicate, observation
12 announcement, notification
14 acknowledgment

**❑don't mention it**
08 forget it, not at all
09 don't worry
12 it was nothing, it's a pleasure

**❑not to mention**
07 besides
08 as well as, let alone
12 not including
13 not forgetting
14 to say nothing of

**mentioned**
05 cited
06 quoted, stated
08 foresaid, reported
09 aforesaid, forenamed
13 forementioned
14 abovementioned

**mentor**
04 guru
05 coach, guide, swami, tutor
07 adviser, pedagog, teacher
09 counselor, pedagogue, therapist
10 instructor

**menu**
04 card, list
06 tariff
10 bill of fare
11 carte du jour

**mercantile**
07 salable, trading
08 saleable
10 commercial, marketable

**mercenary**
05 hired, venal
06 greedy, sordid
08 covetous, grasping, hireling
09 freelance, on the make
10 avaricious, galloglass
11 acquisitive, condottiere
12 hired soldier
13 materialistic, moneygrubbing
15 money orientated

**merchandise**
04 hype, plug, push, sell, vend
05 cargo, carry, goods, stock, trade, wares
06 deal in, market, peddle, retail, supply
07 freight, produce, promote

**merchant**
08 products, shipment
09 advertise, publicize, traffic in, vendibles
10 buy and sell

**merchant**
06 broker, dealer, seller, trader, vendor
08 retailer, salesman
10 saleswoman, trafficker, wholesaler
11 distributor, salesperson, storekeeper
14 sales executive

**merciful**
04 kind
06 humane
07 lenient, liberal
08 generous, gracious, tolerant
09 forgiving
10 forbearing
13 compassionate, tenderhearted

**merciless**
05 cruel, harsh, rigid, stern
06 severe
07 callous, inhuman
08 inhumane, pitiless, ruthless
09 heartless, unpitying, unsparing
10 implacable, inexorable, intolerant, relentless
11 hardhearted, remorseless, unforgiving

**mercurial**
07 erratic, flighty
08 spirited, unstable, volatile
10 capricious, inconstant
13 temperamental, unpredictable

**mercy**
04 boon, pity
05 favor, grace
06 relief
07 godsend
08 blessing, clemency, leniency, mildness
10 compassion, humaneness
11 forbearance, forgiveness

❑**at the mercy of**
09 exposed to
11 at the whim of
12 in the power of, vulnerable to

**mere**
04 bare, pure
05 petty, plain, sheer, utter
06 common, paltry, simple
08 absolute, complete
10 no more than
13 pure and simple

**merely**
04 just, only
06 barely, hardly, purely, simply
08 scarcely
10 nothing but

**merge**
03 mix
04 fuse, join, meet, meld
05 blend, unite
06 mingle, team up
07 combine, run into
08 coalesce, converge, intermix
10 amalgamate, join forces
11 consolidate, incorporate

**merger**
05 blend, union
06 fusion
08 alliance
09 coalition
11 combination, convergence
12 amalgamation, assimilation
13 confederation, consolidation, incorporation

**merit**
05 asset, claim, value, worth
06 credit, reward, talent, virtue
07 deserts, deserve, justify, quality, warrant
08 goodness
09 advantage
10 excellence, worthiness
11 high quality, strong point
13 justification

**merited**
03 due
04 just
06 earned, worthy
07 condign, fitting
08 deserved, entitled, rightful
09 justified, warranted
11 appropriate

**meritorious**
08 laudable, virtuous
09 deserving, estimable, honorable
10 creditable
11 commendable
12 praiseworthy

**merriment**
03 fun
05 mirth
06 frolic, gaiety
07 jollity, revelry
08 hilarity, laughter
09 festivity, jocundity
11 high spirits

**merry**
04 glad
05 happy, jolly, tipsy
06 blithe, cheery, jovial, joyful

07 amusing, festive
08 carefree, cheerful, mirthful
09 convivial
12 lighthearted

❑**make merry**
04 sing
05 dance, drink
07 carouse, have fun
09 celebrate
10 have a party
13 enjoy yourself

**merry-go-round**
08 carousel
09 whirligig

**merrymaking**
03 fun
05 party, revel
06 gaiety
07 revelry
08 carousal
09 festivity, merriment
11 celebration
13 jollification

**mesh**
03 net, web
04 trap
05 match, snare
06 engage, tangle
07 combine, connect, lattice, netting, network, tracery, trellis
09 harmonize, interlock
10 coordinate, go together
11 fit together, latticework

**mesmerize**
07 stupefy
08 enthrall, entrance, transfix
09 captivate, fascinate, hypnotize, magnetize, spellbind

**mess**
03 fix, jam
04 hash, hole, spot, stew
05 botch, chaos, farce, filth, mix-up
06 bungle, hiccup, jumble, litter, muddle, pickle, plight
07 clutter, dilemma, failure, squalor, trouble, turmoil
08 disarray, disorder, hot water, quandary, shambles
09 confusion, deep water, dirtiness, tight spot
10 difficulty, filthiness, pretty pass, untidiness
11 predicament

❑**mess around, mess about**
07 goof off
08 act silly

09 play about
10 fool around, goof around,
play around
11 putter about
12 putter around

◻ **mess around with, mess about with**
05 upset
06 bother
07 trouble
08 play with
10 meddle with, tamper with
13 fool about with,
inconvenience, interfere
with, play about with
14 fool around with, play around
with

◻ **mess up**
04 foul, muff, ruin
05 botch, dirty, fluff, spoil
06 bungle, foul up, fumble,
jumble, muddle, tangle,
untidy
07 confuse, disrupt, louse up,
screw up
08 dishevel
10 disarrange
11 make a hash of

**message**
02 IM
03 fax
04 gist, idea, memo, note, word
05 cable, drift, e-mail, moral,
point, sense, theme
06 errand, notice, thrust
07 epistle, essence, meaning,
missive, purport
08 bulletin, dispatch
09 voice mail
10 commercial, communiqué,
memorandum
11 implication
12 significance
13 communication

◻ **get the message**
06 follow, take in
07 catch on
08 cotton on
10 comprehend, get the idea,
understand
11 get the point
13 catch the drift

**messenger**
05 agent, envoy
06 bearer, herald, Hermes,
runner
07 carrier, courier
08 emissary
09 errand boy, go-between,
harbinger

**messy**
05 dirty
06 filthy, grubby, sloppy, untidy
07 chaotic, muddled, unkempt
08 confused, littered, slobbish,
slovenly
09 cluttered, shambolic
10 disheveled, disordered, in
disarray

**metal**

► *Names of metal alloys. We have omitted the word* **metal** *from names given in the following list but you may need to include this word as part of the solution to some crossword clues.*

05 brass, Invar, Muntz, steel,
terne
06 bronze, latten, ormolu,
oroide, pewter, solder,
tambac, tombac, tombak, Y-
alloy
07 amalgam, chromel, shakudo,
tutenag
08 cast iron, gunmetal,
Nichrome, orichalc,
speculum, Zircaloy, zircoloy
09 britannia, duralumin, Dutch
foil, Dutch gold, Dutch leaf,
magnalium, pinchbeck,
shibuichi, white gold
10 chromemoly, constantan,
ferroalloy, misch metal,
orichalcum, white brass
11 chrome steel, cupronickel,
white copper
12 gunmetal gray
14 stainless steel

**metallic**
03 tin
04 gold, iron, lead
05 harsh, rough, shiny, steel
06 copper, nickel, silver
07 grating, jarring
08 gleaming, jangling, polished

► *Names of metallic elements and their symbols:*

03 tin (Sn)
04 gold (Au), iron (Fe), lead (Pb),
zinc (Zn)
06 barium (Ba), cerium (Ce),
cesium (Cs), cobalt (Co),
copper (Cu), curium (Cm),
erbium (Er), indium (In),
nickel (Ni), osmium (Os),
radium (Ra), silver (Ag),
sodium (Na)
07 bismuth (Bi), cadmium (Cd),
calcium (Ca), fermium (Fm),
gallium (Ga), hafnium (Hf),

holmium (Ho), iridium (Ir),
lithium (Li), mercury (Hg),
niobium (Nb), rhenium (Re),
rhodium (Rh), terbium (Tb),
thorium (Th), thulium (Tm),
uranium (U), wolfram (W),
yttrium (Y)
08 actinium (Ac), aluminum
(Al), antimony (Sb),
chromium (Cr), europium
(Eu), francium (Fr), lutetium
(Lu), nobelium (No),
platinum (Pt), polonium (Po),
rubidium (Rb), samarium
(Sm), scandium (Sc),
tantalum (Ta), thallium (Tl),
titanium (Ti), tungsten (W),
vanadium (V)
09 americium (Am), berkelium
(Bk), beryllium (Be),
germanium (Ge), lanthanum
(La), magnesium (Mg),
manganese (Mn),
neodymium (Nd),
neptunium (Np), palladium
(Pd), plutonium (Pu),
potassium (K), ruthenium
(Ru), strontium (Sr),
ytterbium (Yb), zirconium
(Zr)
10 dysprosium (Dy), gadolinium
(Gd), lawrencium (Lr) (Lw),
molybdenum (Mo),
promethium (Pm),
technetium (Tc)
11 californium (Cf), einsteinium
(Es)
12 mendeleevium (Md),
praseodymium (Pr),
protactinium (Pa)

**metamorphose**
05 alter
06 change, mutate
09 transform, transmute
12 transmogrify

**metamorphosis**
06 change
07 rebirth
08 mutation
10 alteration
14 transformation
15 transfiguration

**metaphor**
05 image, trope
06 emblem, symbol, visual
07 analogy, picture
08 allegory
10 emblematic
14 figure of speech,
representation

## metaphorical
08 symbolic
10 analogical, emblematic, figurative
11 allegorical

## metaphysical
07 eternal
08 abstract, abstruse, esoteric, profound
09 recondite, spiritual, universal
10 immaterial, impalpable, intangible, subjective
11 incorporeal, theoretical
12 supernatural
13 insubstantial, philosophical
14 transcendental

## mete

## ❑mete out
05 allot
06 assign
07 deal out, dole out, hand out, portion
08 dispense, share out
09 apportion, divide out
10 administer, distribute, measure out

## meteor
05 comet
06 bolide
08 aerolite, aerolith, fireball
12 shooting star

## meteoric
05 brief, quick, rapid, swift
06 speedy, sudden
09 brilliant, momentary, overnight
11 spectacular

## meteorologist
10 weatherman
11 weather girl
13 climatologist

## method
03 way
04 form, mode, plan, rule
05 means, order, route, style
06 course, design, manner, scheme, system
07 fashion, pattern, process, program
08 approach, practice
09 procedure, structure, technique
11 arrangement
13 modus operandi

## methodical
04 neat, tidy
07 logical, ordered, orderly, planned, precise, regular
09 efficient, organized

10 deliberate, meticulous, scrupulous, systematic
11 disciplined, painstaking, well ordered

## meticulous
05 exact, fussy
06 strict
07 careful, precise
08 accurate, detailed, rigorous, thorough
10 fastidious, particular, scrupulous
11 painstaking, punctilious
13 conscientious

## métier
04 line
05 craft, field, forte, trade
06 sphere
07 calling, pursuit
08 business, vocation
09 specialty, specialty
10 occupation, profession
14 line of business

## metropolis
04 city
07 capital
11 megalopolis
12 municipality

## mettle
05 nerve, pluck, spunk, valor, vigor
06 daring, makeup, nature, spirit
07 bravery, caliber, courage, resolve
08 backbone, boldness
09 character, fortitude
11 personality, temperament
13 determination

## mew
04 meow, mewl
05 miaow, whine
09 caterwaul

## mewl
05 whine
06 snivel
07 blubber, grizzle, whimper

## miasma
04 odor, reek
05 fetor, smell, stink
06 stench
08 mephitis
09 effluvium, pollution

## miasmal
04 foul
05 fetid
06 putrid, smelly
07 noisome, noxious, reeking
08 mephitic
10 malodorous
11 unwholesome

## microbe
03 bug
04 germ
05 virus
08 bacillus, pathogen
09 bacterium
13 microorganism

## microscopic
04 tiny
06 minute
09 minuscule
10 negligible
13 infinitesimal
14 extremely small

## midday
04 noon
06 twelve
07 noonday
08 noontide
09 lunchtime
10 twelve noon
12 twelve o'clock

## middle
03 mid
04 core, mean
05 heart, inner, midst
06 center, inside, medial, median, medium, midway
07 central, halfway
08 bull's eye, midpoint
11 equidistant, intervening
12 halfway point, intermediate

## ❑in the middle of
05 among, while
06 during
08 busy with
09 engaged in
12 in the midst of, surrounded by
14 in the process of

## middle class
08 suburban
09 bourgeois
10 gentrified
11 white-collar
12 conventional, professional

## middleman
05 agent
06 broker
09 go-between
10 negotiator
11 distributor
12 entrepreneur, intermediary

## middling
02 OK
04 fair, okay, so-so
06 medium, modest
07 average
08 adequate, mediocre, moderate, passable

09 tolerable
11 indifferent
12 run-of-the-mill, unremarkable
13 unexceptional

**midget**
04 baby, tiny
05 dwarf, gnome, pygmy, small, teeny
06 little, minute, pocket
07 manikin
08 Tom Thumb
09 itsy-bitsy, itty-bitty, miniature
10 diminutive, homunculus, teeny-weeny
11 Lilliputian, pocket-sized
12 teensy-weensy

**midst**
03 hub
04 core
05 bosom, heart, thick
06 center, depths, middle
07 nucleus
08 interior, midpoint

◻**in the midst**
05 among
06 during
12 in the thick of
13 in the middle of

**midway**
07 halfway
11 in the center, in the middle
13 at the midpoint

**mien**
03 air
04 aura, look
06 aspect, manner
07 bearing
08 carriage, demeanor, presence
10 appearance, complexion, deportment, expression
11 countenance

**miffed**
05 irked, upset, vexed
06 peeved, piqued, put out
07 annoyed, in a huff, nettled
08 offended
09 aggrieved, irritated, resentful
10 displeased

**might**
04 sway
05 clout, force, power, valor, vigor
06 energy, muscle
07 ability, potency, prowess, stamina
08 capacity, efficacy, strength
09 heftiness, puissance
10 capability

11 muscularity
12 forcefulness, powerfulness

**mightily**
04 much, very
06 highly, hugely
07 greatly, lustily
08 strongly, very much
09 extremely, intensely
10 forcefully, powerfully
11 exceedingly, strenuously

**mighty**
04 huge, vast
05 bulky, grand, great, hardy, hefty, large, lusty, stout, tough
06 potent, robust, strong
07 immense, massive, titanic
08 colossal, dominant, enormous, forceful, gigantic, powerful, puissant, towering, vigorous
10 monumental, prodigious

**migrant**
05 Gypsy, nomad, rover
06 roving, tinker
07 drifter, nomadic, vagrant
08 drifting, emigrant, traveler, wanderer
09 immigrant, itinerant, traveling, wandering
11 peripatetic

**migrate**
04 hike, move, roam, rove, trek
05 drift
06 travel, voyage, wander
07 journey
08 emigrate, relocate, resettle

**migration**
04 trek
06 roving, travel, voyage
08 diaspora, movement
09 wandering
10 emigration
12 transhumance

**migratory**
05 Gypsy
06 exodus, roving
07 migrant, nomadic, vagrant
08 drifting, shifting
09 immigrant, itinerant, transient, traveling, wandering
11 peripatetic

**mild**
04 calm, fair, kind, meek, soft, warm
05 balmy, bland
06 gentle, humane, mellow, placid, smooth, subtle
07 amiable, clement, insipid, lenient

08 merciful, moderate, pleasant, soothing
09 easygoing, peaceable, sensitive
10 forbearing
11 good-natured

**mildewy**
05 fetid, fusty, moldy, mucid, musty
06 rotten
10 mucedinous

**mildness**
05 mercy
06 lenity, warmth
08 calmness, clemency, docility, kindness, leniency, meekness, softness, sympathy
09 blandness, passivity, placidity
10 gentleness, indulgence, mellowness, moderation, smoothness
11 forbearance, insipidness, tranquility

**milieu**
05 arena, scene
06 locale, medium, sphere
07 element, setting
08 location
10 background
11 environment
12 surroundings

**militant**
07 fighter, soldier, warring, warrior
08 activist, fighting, partisan
09 aggressor, assertive, combatant, combative
10 aggressive, pugnacious
11 belligerent

**military**
04 army, navy
05 armed
06 forces, troops
07 marines, martial, militia, service, warlike
08 air force, services, soldiers
09 soldierly
11 armed forces, disciplined
➤ See also AVIATOR; RANK; SAILOR; SOLDIER

► *Names of U.S. military decorations:*
02 LM, MH, PH
03 DFC, DSC, DSM
10 Bronze Star, Silver Star
11 Purple Heart
12 Medal of Honor
13 Legion of Merit
14 oak-leaf cluster

► *Types of military unit*:
04 file, post
05 cadre, corps, flank, squad, troop
06 cohort, legion, patrol
07 company, militia, phalanx, platoon
08 division, regiment, squadron
09 battalion, effective
10 rifle corps
11 battle group
12 flying column, guard of honor

**militate**

◻ **militate against**
06 damage, oppose, resist
07 contend, counter
09 go against, prejudice
10 act against, counteract
11 be harmful to, tell against
15 be detrimental to

◻ **militate for**
03 aid
04 back, help
07 advance, further, promote

**militia**
09 fencibles, minutemen
10 reservists
12 Army Reserves, Navy Reserves
13 National Guard

**milk**
03 tap, use
04 draw, pump
05 bleed, drain, press, wring
06 rip off, siphon
07 draw off, exploit, express, extract, oppress, squeeze
10 manipulate
15 take advantage of

**milksop**
04 baby, wimp
05 sissy
06 coward
08 weakling
09 mommy's boy
10 namby-pamby
11 Milquetoast

**milky**
05 white
06 chalky, cloudy, opaque
07 clouded

**mill**
04 roll
05 crush, grate, grind, pound, press, quern
06 crunch, powder, roller, thrash
07 crusher, foundry, grinder
09 comminute, pulverize

15 processing plant

◻ **mill around**
05 swarm
06 stream, throng
11 crowd around, press around

**millstone**
04 duty, load, onus
06 burden, weight
09 albatross
10 affliction, grindstone, obligation, quernstone
11 cross to bear, encumbrance

**mime**
05 mimic
06 act out, signal
07 charade, gesture, imitate, mimicry, mummery
08 dumb show, indicate, simulate
09 pantomime, represent
11 impersonate

**mimic**
03 ape
04 copy, echo
06 parody, parrot
07 copycat, copyist, emulate, imitate, take off
08 imitator, resemble, simulate
10 caricature
11 impersonate
12 caricaturist, impersonator
13 impressionist

**mimicry**
05 aping
06 parody
07 copying, takeoff
09 burlesque, imitating, imitation
10 caricature, impression
13 impersonation

**mince**
04 chop, dice, hash, pose
05 grind, spare
06 simper, soften
08 diminish, hold back, moderate, tone down
11 strike a pose
12 attitudinize

**mincing**
05 sissy
06 dainty, la-di-da
07 foppish
08 affected, precious
10 effeminate

**mind**
04 head, heed, mark, note, obey, urge, view, will, wish, wits
05 brain, guard, sense, watch

06 belief, brains, desire, expert, follow, genius, insure, memory, notion, object, psyche, reason, recall, regard, resent, spirit
07 dislike, egghead, opinion, scholar, thinker
08 attend to, attitude, judgment, listen to, make sure, object to, remember, take care, tendency, thinking, thoughts
09 attention, be careful, care about, intellect, intention, look after, mentality, not forget, pay heed to, sentiment, viewpoint, watch over
10 disapprove, gray matter, take care of
11 be annoyed by, inclination, keep an eye on, make certain, point of view, remembrance, take offense
12 be bothered by, be offended by, have charge of, intellectual, intelligence, pay attention, subconscious
13 comprehension, concentrate on, concentration, ratiocination, understanding, way of thinking
15 little gray cells

◻ **be of two minds**
05 waver
06 dither
08 be unsure, hesitate
09 vacillate
12 shilly-shally

◻ **bear in mind, keep in mind**
08 remember
15 take into account

◻ **cross your mind**
06 come to, strike
07 occur to, think of

◻ **make up your mind**
06 choose, decide, settle
07 resolve
09 determine
13 make a decision

◻ **mind's eye**
04 head, mind
11 imagination

◻ **never mind**
08 as well as, forget it, let alone
09 apart from, don't worry
12 not to mention

**mindful**
04 wary
05 alert, alive, aware, chary

07 alive to, careful, heedful
08 sensible, watchful
09 cognizant, conscious

**mindless**
06 stupid
07 foolish, tedious
09 senseless
10 gratuitous, mechanical
11 birdbrained, thoughtless
13 unintelligent

**mine**
03 pit
04 bomb, fund, lode, seam, vein, well
05 delve, dig up, hoard, shaft, stock, store
06 dig for, quarry, trench, tunnel, wealth
07 deposit, extract, reserve, unearth
08 colliery, excavate, treasury
09 coal field, explosive, reservoir, undermine
10 excavation, repository
11 depth charge

**miner**
06 pitman
07 collier
09 coal miner

**mineral**

► *Types of mineral*:
04 alum, mica, ruby, salt, talc
05 beryl, topaz, umber
06 blende, galena, garnet, gypsum, halite, jasper, natron, pyrite, quartz, rutile, spinel, zircon
07 apatite, calcite, crystal, cuprite, diamond, jadeite, olivine
08 chromite, cinnabar, corundum, dolomite, feldspar, fluorite, graphite, ilmenite, nephrite, pyroxene, rock salt, sapphire, siderite, sodalite, steatite
09 aragonite, cairngorm, fluor spar, lodestone, magnetite, malachite, marcasite, muscovite, soapstone, turquoise
10 aquamarine, bloodstone, chalcedony, glauconite, hornblende, meerschaum, orthoclase, pyrolusite, serpentine, sphalerite, tourmaline
11 chrysoberyl, lapis lazuli, pitchblende, salammoniac
13 precious stone
14 sodium chloride

**mingle**
03 mix
04 fuse, join
05 alloy, blend, merge, unite
07 combine
08 coalesce, compound, intermix
09 associate, circulate, commingle, socialize
10 amalgamate

**miniature**
03 toy, wee
04 baby, mini-, tiny
05 dwarf, small, teeny
06 little, midget, minute, teensy
08 pintsize
09 itty-bitty, pintsized
10 diminutive, scaled down, teeny-weeny
12 teensy-weensy

**minimal**
05 least, token
06 minute
07 minimum, nominal
08 littlest, smallest
09 slightest
10 negligible

**minimize**
03 cut
06 reduce, shrink
07 curtail
08 belittle, discount, play down
09 deprecate, disparage
10 trivialize
11 make light of
12 make little of
13 underestimate

**minimum**
05 least, nadir
06 bottom, lowest
07 minimal, tiniest
08 littlest, smallest
09 slightest

**minion**
06 drudge, lackey, menial
07 flunkey, servant
08 follower, hanger-on, hireling
09 attendant, dependent, underling

**minister**
04 dean, tend
05 agent, elder, envoy, nurse, padre, serve, vicar
06 attend, cleric, consul, curate, deacon, divine, legate, parson, pastor, priest, rector, verger, wait on
07 cater to
08 chaplain, delegate, diplomat, emissary, official, preacher, reverend
09 churchman, clergyman, dignitary, executive, look after
10 administer, ambassador, politician, take care of
11 accommodate
12 ecclesiastic, officeholder
14 representative

► *Names of prime ministers*:
02 **Nu** (U)
03 **Kok** (Wim), **Rao** (Pamulaparti Venkata Narasimha)
04 **Bute** (John Stuart), **Dini** (Lamberto), **Eden** (Anthony), **Grey** (Charles), **Home** (Alec Douglas-Home), **Meir** (Golda), **Moro** (Aldo), **Peel** (Robert), **Pitt** (William), **Tojo** (Hideki)
05 **Ahern** (Bertie), **Assad** (Hafez al-), **Banda** (Hastings Kamuzu), **Barak** (Ehud), **Begin** (Menachem), **Blair** (Anthony "Tony"), **Botha** (Louis), **Botha** (Pieter Willem), **Cecil** (Robert), **Derby** (Edward), **Hawke** (Robert), **Heath** (Edward), **Hoxha** (Enver), **Nehru** (Jawaharlal), **North** (Frederick), **Obote** (Milton), **Peres** (Shimon), **Prodi** (Romano), **Putin** (Vladimir), **Rabin** (Yitzhak), **Sadat** (Anwar al-), **Smith** (Ian), **Smuts** (Jan)
06 **Attlee** (Clement), **Bhutto** (Benazir), **Bhutto** (Zulfikar Ali), **Bruton** (John), **Castro** (Fidel), **Chirac** (Jacques), **Fabius** (Laurent), **Gaidar** (Yegor), **Gandhi** (Indira), **Gandhi** (Rajiv), **Gaulle** (Charles de), **Howard** (John), **Hun Sen**, **Jospin** (Lionel), **Manley** (Michael), **Mugabe** (Robert), **Pelham** (Henry), **Pétain** (Philippe), **Pol Pot**, **Shamir** (Yitzhak), **Sharif** (Muhammad Nawaz), **Wilson** (Harold)
07 **Asquith** (Herbert), **Baldwin** (Stanley), **Balfour** (Arthur), **Canning** (George), **Cresson** (Édith), **Dehaene** (Jean-Luc), **Grafton** (Augustus), **Halifax** (Charles Montagu), **Haughey** (Charles), **Keating** (Paul), **Kosygin** (Alexei), **Lubbers** (Ruud), **Molotov**

(Vyacheslav), **Muldoon**
(Robert David), **Nkrumah**
(Kwame), **Nyerere** (Julius),
**Russell** (John), **Trudeau**
(Pierre Elliott), **Vorster**
(John), **Walpole** (Robert),
**Whitlam** (Gough), **Yeltsin**
(Boris)
08 **Aberdeen** (George),
**Bentinck** (William),
**Bismarck** (Otto), **Bonar
Law** (Andrew), **Bulganin**
(Nikolai), **Daladier**
(Édouard), **de Valera**
(Éamon), **Disraeli**
(Benjamin), **Goderich**
(Frederick), **González**
(Felipe), **Kenyatta** (Jomo),
**Mahathir** (bin Mohamad),
**Mulroney** (Brian),
**Nakasone** (Yasuhiro),
**Perceval** (Spencer),
**Poincaré** (Raymond),
**Pompidou** (Georges),
**Portland** (William Henry
Cavendish), **Quisling**
(Vidkun), **Reynolds**
(Albert), **Rosebery**
(Archibald Philip),
**Sidmouth** (Henry),
**Thatcher** (Margaret),
**Verwoerd** (Hendrik)
09 **Andreotti** (Giulio), **Ben-
Gurion** (David), **Callaghan**
(James), **Churchill**
(Winston), **Gladstone**
(William Ewart), **Grenville**
(George), **Grenville**
(William Wyndham), **Kim
Il-sung**, **Kim Jong-Il**,
**Liverpool** (Robert),
**MacDonald** (Ramsay),
**Macmillan** (Sir Harold),
**Melbourne** (William
Lamb), **Mussolini** (Benito),
**Netanyahu** (Binyamin),
**Newcastle** (Thomas),
**Salisbury** (Robert),
**Shelburne** (William)
10 **Berlusconi** (Silvio),
**Clemenceau** (Georges),
**Devonshire** (William
Cavendish), **Fitzgerald**
(Doctor Garrett),
**Jaruzelski** (General
Wojciech), **Lee Kuan Yew**,
**Palmerston** (Henry),
**Rockingham** (Charles),
**Wilmington** (Spencer
Compton)
11 **Chamberlain** (Neville),
**Douglas-Home** (Alec),
**Lloyd-George** (David)

13 **Brookeborough** (Basil)
➢ See also POLITICS

**ministration**
03 aid
04 care, help
05 favor
06 relief, succor
07 service, support
09 patronage
10 assistance

**ministry**
06 bureau, office
07 cabinet
09 the church
10 department, government,
holy orders
13 the priesthood
14 administration

**minor**
05 light, petty, small
06 junior, lesser, slight
07 smaller, trivial, unknown,
younger
08 inferior, trifling
09 secondary
11 subordinate, unimportant
13 insignificant
14 inconsiderable

**minstrel**
04 bard
06 rhymer, singer
08 jongleur, musician
09 joculator
10 troubadour

**mint**
03 new
04 bomb, cast, coin, pile
05 as new, forge, stack, stamp
06 bundle, packet, riches, strike,
unused, wealth
07 fashion, fortune, million,
perfect, produce
08 brand-new
09 construct, undamaged
10 first class, immaculate,
peppermint
11 manufacture, spanking-new,
unblemished

**minuscule**
03 wee
04 fine, tiny
05 teeny
06 little, minute, teensy
09 itsy-bitsy, itty-bitty, miniature
10 diminutive, teeny-weeny
11 Lilliputian, microscopic
12 teensy-weensy
13 infinitesimal

**minute**
04 tiny

05 close, exact, flash, jiffy
06 moment, second, slight
07 instant, precise
08 accurate, critical, detailed,
directly
09 miniature, minuscule, short
time, the moment
10 diminutive, meticulous,
negligible, the instant
11 immediately, Lilliputian,
microscopic, painstaking
13 infinitesimal, insignificant

**◻in a minute**
04 soon
06 pronto
07 shortly
08 in a flash, in a jiffy, very soon
09 in a moment
15 in the near future

**◻up to the minute**
02 in
06 latest, newest, with it
10 all the rage
11 fashionable

**minutely**
07 closely, exactly
08 in detail
09 precisely
10 critically
12 meticulously
13 painstakingly

**minutes**
05 notes
07 details, records
10 memorandum, transcript

**minutiae**
07 details, trifles
08 niceties
10 small print, subtleties
11 finer points, particulars

**miracle**
06 marvel, wonder
07 prodigy
10 phenomenon

**miraculous**
07 amazing
09 marvelous, wonderful
10 astounding, incredible,
phenomenal, remarkable
11 astonishing
12 unbelievable
13 extraordinary

**mirage**
08 illusion, phantasm
13 hallucination
14 phantasmagoria
15 optical illusion

**mire**
03 bog, fen, fix, jam, mud

04 dirt, hole, mess, muck, ooze,
quag, sink, spot, stew
05 marsh, slime, swamp
06 morass, pickle, slough
07 bog down, trouble
08 quagmire
09 marshland

**mirror**
03 ape
04 copy, echo, show, twin
05 clone, glass, image, mimic
06 depict, follow, ringer
07 emulate, imitate, reflect
08 likeness
09 reflector, represent
10 dead ringer, reflection
12 looking glass
13 spitting image

**mirth**
03 fun
04 glee
06 gaiety
07 frolics, jollity, revelry
08 hilarity, laughter, pleasure
09 amusement, enjoyment,
merriment

**mirthful**
05 funny, happy, jolly, merry
06 jocund, jovial
07 amusing
09 hilarious, laughable
10 uproarious

**miry**
04 oozy
05 boggy, mucky, muddy, slimy
06 marshy, swampy

**misadventure**
06 mishap
07 bad luck, debacle, failure, ill
luck, reverse, setback,
tragedy
08 accident, calamity, disaster,
hard luck
09 cataclysm, mischance
10 ill fortune, misfortune
11 catastrophe

**misanthropic**
05 surly
10 antisocial, malevolent,
unfriendly, unsociable
13 unsympathetic

**misanthropy**
11 malevolence
13 antisociality
14 unsociableness

**misapply**
06 misuse
09 misemploy
14 misappropriate

**misapprehend**
11 misconstrue
12 misinterpret
13 misunderstand
15 get the wrong idea

**misapprehension**
05 error
07 fallacy, mistake
08 delusion
09 wrong idea
13 misconception
15 false impression

**misappropriate**
03 nab, rob
05 abuse, filch, pinch, steal
06 pilfer, pocket, thieve
07 swindle
08 embezzle, peculate
09 defalcate

**misappropriation**
05 theft
07 robbing
08 stealing
09 pilfering, pocketing
10 peculation
11 defalcation
12 embezzlement

**misbegotten**
05 shady
06 stolen
07 bastard
09 ill-gotten, purloined
10 ill-advised
12 disreputable, ill-conceived,
illegitimate

**misbehave**
05 act up
06 play up
07 carry on, disobey
10 transgress
15 get up to mischief

**misbehavior**
08 mischief
10 bad manners, misconduct
11 impropriety, misdemeanor,
naughtiness
12 disobedience

**misbelief**
05 error
07 fallacy, mistake
08 delusion, illusion
13 misconception
15 misapprehension

**miscalculate**
03 err
06 slip up
07 blunder
08 miscount, misjudge
12 make a mistake, overestimate
13 underestimate

**miscarriage**
05 error
07 failure
08 aborting, abortion
09 breakdown
10 perversion
13 mismanagement

**miscarry**
04 fail, flop, fold
05 abort
07 founder, go amiss, go wrong,
misfire
10 not come off
11 come to grief
13 come to nothing

**miscellaneous**
05 mixed
06 motley, sundry, varied
07 diverse, jumbled, various
08 assorted
10 variegated
11 diversified
12 multifarious
13 heterogeneous

**miscellany**
03 mix
06 jumble, medley
07 farrago, mixture, variety
08 mishmash, mixed bag,
pastiche
09 patchwork, potpourri
10 assortment, collection,
hodgepodge, hotchpotch
11 gallimaufry, salmagundi,
smorgasbord

**mischance**
04 blow
06 mishap
07 ill luck, tragedy
08 accident, bad break,
calamity, disaster
10 ill fortune, infelicity,
misfortune
12 misadventure

**mischief**
04 evil, harm, hurt
06 damage, injury, pranks, tricks
07 trouble
08 escapade, nuisance
09 devilment
10 carrying-on, hanky-panky,
impishness
11 bad behavior, carryings-on,
misbehavior, naughtiness,
roguishness, shenanigans
13 funny business
14 monkey business

**mischievous**
03 bad
04 evil
06 impish, wicked

07 harmful, hurtful, naughty, playful, roguish, teasing, vicious
08 rascally, spiteful
09 injurious, malicious, malignant
11 destructive, detrimental, disobedient, misbehaving, troublesome
12 badly behaved

**misconceive**
12 misapprehend, misinterpret
13 misunderstand

**misconception**
05 error
07 fallacy, mistake
08 delusion
09 wrong idea
15 false impression, misapprehension

**misconduct**
10 wrongdoing
11 bad behavior, impropriety, malpractice

**misconstrue**
07 misread, mistake
08 misjudge
12 misinterpret
15 take the wrong way

**miscreant**
04 heel
05 knave, rogue, scamp
06 rascal, sinner, wretch
07 dastard, villain
08 criminal, evildoer, vagabond
09 reprobate, scallywag, scoundrel, wrongdoer
10 malefactor, profligate

**misdeed**
03 sin
05 crime, error, fault, wrong
06 felony
07 offense
10 misconduct, wrongdoing
13 transgression

**misdemeanor**
07 misdeed, offense
10 misconduct, wrongdoing
11 malfeasance
13 transgression

**miser**
06 meanie
07 niggard, Scrooge
08 tightwad
09 skinflint
10 cheapskate
11 cheeseparer
12 moneygrubber, penny pincher

**miserable**
03 low, sad
04 base, blue, down, glum, mean, poor
06 dismal, dreary, gloomy, grumpy, meager, measly, paltry, scanty, shabby, sullen
07 forlorn, grouchy, joyless, pitiful, squalid, unhappy
08 dejected, desolate, downcast, pathetic, shameful, wretched
09 cheerless, depressed, niggardly, sorrowful, worthless
10 depressing, despondent
11 downhearted, low-spirited, melancholic
12 disconsolate, impoverished
14 down in the dumps

**miserliness**
08 meanness
09 minginess, parsimony, tightness
10 stinginess
12 cheeseparing
13 niggardliness, penny-pinching, penuriousness
15 tightfistedness
24 close-fistedness frugality

**miserly**
04 mean
05 mingy, tight
06 stingy
09 niggardly, penurious
11 close-fisted, tightfisted
12 cheeseparing, parsimonious
13 moneygrubbing, penny-pinching

**misery**
03 woe
04 pain, want
05 agony, gloom, grief
06 penury, sorrow
07 anguish, despair, poverty, sadness
08 distress, hardship
09 indigence, suffering
10 affliction, depression, melancholy
11 deprivation, destitution, unhappiness
12 wretchedness

**misfire**
04 fail, flop
05 abort
06 go awry
07 founder, go amiss, go wrong
08 miscarry
11 come to grief, fall through
12 come a cropper

**misfit**
05 freak, loner
06 weirdo
07 dropout, oddball
08 lone wolf, maverick
09 eccentric, odd one out

**misfortune**
03 woe
04 blow
05 trial
06 mishap, sorrow
07 bad luck, ill luck, reverse, setback, tragedy
08 accident, calamity, disaster, hard luck, hardship
09 adversity, mischance
11 tribulation

**misgiving**
05 doubt, qualm, worry
06 unease
07 anxiety, scruple
08 distrust
10 hesitation
11 reservation, uncertainty
12 apprehension

**misguided**
04 rash
05 wrong
06 misled
07 deluded, foolish
09 ill judged, imprudent
10 fallacious, ill-advised
13 ill-considered

**mishandle**
04 muff
05 abuse, botch
06 bungle, fumble, mess up
07 screw up
08 maltreat
09 mismanage
10 slap around
11 make a hash of

**mishap**
07 reverse, setback, trouble
08 accident, calamity, disaster, incident
09 adversity
10 ill fortune, misfortune
11 catastrophe, tribulation
12 misadventure

**mishmash**
04 hash, mess, olio
06 jumble, medley, muddle
07 farrago
08 pastiche
09 potpourri
10 hodgepodge, hotchpotch, salmagundi

**misinform**
07 deceive, mislead

**misinformation**
08 hoodwink, misguide
13 give a bum steer

**misinformation**
04 dope, guff, hype, lies
07 baloney, eyewash
08 bum steer, nonsense
14 disinformation

**misinterpret**
07 distort, mistake
11 misconstrue
12 misapprehend
13 misunderstand
15 take the wrong way

**misjudge**
12 miscalculate
13 misunderstand

**mislay**
04 lose, miss
08 misplace

**mislead**
04 fool
05 bluff
06 delude
07 deceive
08 hoodwink
09 misinform
10 lead astray
12 misrepresent, take for a ride
14 pull a fast one on

**misleading**
09 ambiguous, confusing, deceiving, deceptive, equivocal
10 fallacious, unreliable

**mismanage**
06 bungle, foul up, fumble, mess up
09 mishandle
11 make a hash of, make a mess of

**mismatched**
08 clashing, unsuited
10 discordant, unmatching
11 ill assorted, incongruous
12 antipathetic, incompatible

**misogynist**
03 MCP
10 misogamist, woman hater
12 antifeminist
15 male supremacist

**misplace**
04 lose, miss
06 mislay

**misprint**
04 typo
05 error
07 erratum, literal, mistake
11 corrigendum
13 printing error

**misquote**
06 garble, muddle
07 distort, falsify, pervert
09 misreport
12 misrepresent

**misrepresent**
05 slant, twist
07 distort, falsify, pervert
08 misquote, misstate
09 misreport
10 exaggerate
11 misconstrue
12 misinterpret

**misrule**
05 chaos
07 anarchy, turmoil
08 disorder
11 lawlessness
12 indiscipline
13 misgovernment, mismanagement
15 disorganization

**miss**
02 Ms.
03 err, gal
04 blow, fail, flop, girl, lass, lose, maid, muff, omit, skip
05 avoid, dodge, evade, fault, let go, mourn
06 damsel, forego, lament, maiden, not see, regret, strike
07 ache for, failure, let slip, long for, mistake, neglect, not go to, not spot, pine for
08 leave out, omission, overlook, pass over, sidestep, yearn for
09 disregard, fail to get, fail to hit, not notice, oversight, young lady
10 schoolgirl, young woman
11 fail to catch
12 be absent from, fail to notice, mademoiselle
13 feel the loss of, misunderstand, not take part in

❏ **miss out on**
13 not experience
14 lose your chance

**missal**
08 breviary
09 formulary
10 prayer book
11 euchologion, service book

**misshapen**
04 bent, ugly
06 warped
07 crooked, twisted
08 crippled, deformed

09 contorted, distorted, grotesque, malformed

**missile**
04 bomb, dart, shot
05 arrow, shaft, shell
06 bullet, rocket, weapon
07 grenade, missile, torpedo
09 ballistic
10 flying bomb, projectile

**missing**
04 AWOL, gone, lost
06 absent, astray
07 lacking, mislaid, strayed, wanting
09 misplaced
11 disappeared
14 unaccounted for

**mission**
03 aim, job
04 duty, goal, task, work
05 chore, quest
06 charge, errand, office
07 calling, crusade, embassy, purpose, pursuit
08 business, campaign, legation, ministry, vocation
09 operation, task force
10 assignment, commission, delegation, deputation
11 raison d'être, undertaking

**missionary**
05 envoy
07 apostle
08 champion, crusader, emissary, minister, preacher
10 ambassador, evangelist

➤ *Names of missionaries:*
03 **Fox** (George)
05 **Bliss** (Edward), **Carey** (William), **David** (Père Armand), **Jones** (E. Stanley), **Moody** (Dwight Lyman), **Ricci** (Matteo), **Smith** (Eli)
06 **Damien** (Father Joseph), **Judson** (Adoniram), **Judson** (Ann), **Wesley** (John)
07 **Aylward** (Gladys), **Liddell** (Eric Henry), **Theresa** (Mother)
10 **Schweitzer** (Albert)
11 **Livingstone** (David)
➢ See also RELIGION

**missive**
04 note
06 letter, report
07 epistle, message
08 dispatch
10 communiqué
13 communication

**misspent**
06 wasted
07 misused
08 prodigal
10 dissipated, squandered, thrown away

**misstate**
07 distort, falsify
08 misquote
09 misrelate, misreport
12 misrepresent

**mist**
03 dew, fog
04 film, haze, smog, veil
05 cloud, spray, steam, vapor
06 mizzle
07 dimness, drizzle
12 condensation

◻ **mist over, mist up**
03 dim, fog
04 blur, veil
05 fog up, glaze
07 obscure, steam up
09 cloud over

**mistake**
03 err
04 goof, muff, slip
05 boner, botch, error, fault, fluff, gaffe, lapse, mix up
06 boo-boo, howler, slip up
07 blooper, blunder, confuse, erratum, faux pas, misread
08 confound, get wrong, misjudge, misprint, muddle up, solecism
09 oversight
10 aberration, inaccuracy, misreading
11 corrigendum, malapropism, misconstrue, misjudgment, misspelling
12 indiscretion, miscalculate
13 misunderstand
14 miscalculation
15 misapprehension, put your foot in it, slip of the tongue

**mistaken**
05 false, wrong
06 faulty, misled, untrue
07 at fault, deluded, in error
08 deceived
09 erroneous, ill judged, incorrect, misguided, unfounded
10 fallacious, inaccurate
11 inauthentic, misinformed
15 get the wrong idea

**mistakenly**
07 falsely, wrongly
08 unfairly, unjustly

11 erroneously, incorrectly, misguidedly
12 fallaciously, inaccurately

**mistimed**
08 ill-timed, tactless, untimely
10 malapropos
11 inopportune
12 inconvenient, unseasonable
14 unsynchronized

**mistreat**
04 harm, hurt, maul
05 abuse, bully
06 batter, beat up, ill-use, injure, misuse, molest
08 ill-treat, maltreat
09 mishandle
10 knock about, treat badly
11 knock around

**mistreatment**
04 harm, hurt
05 abuse
06 ill-use, injury, misuse
07 cruelty, mauling
08 bullying, ill-usage
09 battering
11 mishandling, molestation
12 ill-treatment, maltreatment

**mistress**
05 lover, woman
07 hetaera, partner
08 ladylove, paramour
09 concubine, courtesan, governess, inamorata, kept woman
10 girlfriend

**mistrust**
05 doubt, qualm
07 caution, suspect
08 be wary of, distrust, wariness
09 chariness, hesitancy, misgiving, suspicion
12 apprehension, reservations
13 have no faith in
14 be suspicious of, have misgivings
15 have doubts about

**mistrustful**
04 wary
05 chary, leery
07 cynical, dubious, fearful
08 cautious, doubtful, hesitant
10 suspicious
11 distrustful

**misty**
03 dim
04 hazy
05 foggy, fuzzy, murky, smoky, vague
06 cloudy, opaque, veiled
07 blurred, obscure, unclear

08 nebulous
10 indistinct

**misunderstand**
08 get wrong
12 misapprehend, misinterpret
15 get the wrong idea

**misunderstanding**
04 rift, tiff
05 clash, error, mix-up
07 discord, dispute, mistake, quarrel
08 argument, conflict
09 wrong idea
10 difference, misreading
11 misjudgment
12 crossed wires
13 misconception
15 false impression, misapprehension

**misunderstood**
07 misread
09 ill judged, misjudged
12 misconstrued
13 unappreciated
14 misinterpreted

**misuse**
04 harm, hurt
05 abuse, waste, wrong
06 ill-use, injure, injury
07 corrupt, pervert
08 ill-treat, misapply, mistreat, squander
10 corruption
11 mishandling
12 exploitation, ill-treatment, maltreatment, mistreatment

**mite**
03 bit, jot, tad
04 atom, iota, whit
05 grain, ounce, scrap, spark, touch, trace
06 morsel
07 modicum, smidgen

**mitigate**
04 ease
05 abate, allay, blunt, remit
06 lessen, modify, pacify, reduce, soften, soothe, temper
07 appease, assuage, lighten, mollify, placate
08 decrease, diminish, moderate, palliate, tone down
09 alleviate, extenuate

**mitigating**
09 modifying, tempering
10 justifying, palliative
11 extenuating

## mitigation
08 allaying, decrease, easement
09 abatement, lessening, reduction, remission, tempering
10 diminution, moderation, palliation
11 alleviation, assuagement

## mix
04 fuse, join, mash, stir, suit
05 agree, alloy, blend, get on, merge, union, unite
06 fold in, fusion, hobnob, medley, merger, mingle
07 amalgam, combine
08 coalesce, compound, emulsify, get along
09 associate, coalition, composite, harmonize, introduce, socialize, synthesis
10 amalgamate, assortment, complement, fraternize, homogenize, synthesize
11 combination, incorporate, intermingle

## ◻ mix in
05 add in, blend, merge
09 introduce
11 incorporate, interpolate

## ◻ mix up
04 code
06 garble, jumble, muddle, puzzle
07 confuse, disturb, involve, mistake, perplex, snarl up
08 bewilder, confound, muddle up
09 implicate
10 complicate

## mixed
05 fused
06 hybrid, motley, varied
07 alloyed, blended, diverse, mingled, mongrel
08 assorted, combined, compound
09 composite, crossbred, equivocal, interbred, uncertain
10 ambivalent
11 amalgamated, diversified
13 miscellaneous

## ◻ mixed up
04 in on
05 upset
07 chaotic, muddled, puzzled
08 caught up, confused, involved

09 disturbed, embroiled, entangled, perplexed, screwed up
10 bewildered, disordered, distracted, implicated, inculpated
11 disoriented, maladjusted

## mixer
05 whisk
06 beater, joiner, shaker
07 blender, meddler, stirrer
08 busybody
10 interferer, liquidizer
12 troublemaker
13 food processor, mischief-maker
15 social gathering

## mixing
05 union
06 fusion
08 blending, mingling
09 interflow, synthesis
11 association, coalescence, combination, socializing
12 amalgamation
13 hybridization

## mixture
05 alloy, blend, cross, union
06 fusion, medley
07 amalgam, melange, variety
08 compound
09 composite, potpourri, synthesis
10 assortment, concoction
11 combination
12 amalgamation
14 conglomeration

## mix-up
04 mess
05 botch, chaos, snafu, snarl
06 foul-up, jumble, muddle, tangle
07 mistake
08 disorder, nonsense
09 confusion

## moan
03 sob
04 beef, carp, howl, sigh, wail, weep
05 bleat, gripe, groan, mourn, whine
06 charge, grieve, grouse, lament
07 censure, grumble, whimper
08 complain
09 bellyache, complaint, criticism
12 faultfinding

## mob
03 set

04 body, crew, fill, gang, herd, host, mass, pack
05 brood, crowd, drove, flock, group, horde, plebs, press, swarm, tribe, troop
06 attack, charge, jostle, masses, pester, rabble, throng
07 besiege, overrun, set upon
08 canaille, populace, riffraff
09 descend on, gathering, hoi polloi, multitude
10 assemblage, collection
11 crowd around, swarm around
13 great unwashed

## mobile
05 agile
06 active, lively, motile, moving, nimble, roving, supple
07 migrant, movable, roaming
08 changing, flexible, portable
09 itinerant, traveling, wandering
10 able to move, ambulatory, expressive, locomotive
11 peripatetic
13 transportable

## mobility
06 motion
07 agility
08 motility, motivity, vivacity
10 locomotion, movability, suppleness
11 flexibility, portability
12 locomobility, locomotivity
14 expressiveness

## mobilize
05 rally, ready
06 summon
07 animate, marshal
08 activate, assemble, get ready, organize
09 galvanize, make ready
14 call into action

## mob rule
08 lynch law
09 mobocracy
10 ochlocracy

## mock
03 ape, kid, rag, rib
04 fake, gibe, jeer, sham
05 bogus, chaff, dummy, faked, false, knock, mimic, phony, scoff, scorn, sneer, taunt, tease
06 deride, ersatz, forged, insult, parody, pseudo
07 emulate, feigned, imitate, lampoon, laugh at, pretend, take off
08 ridicule, satirize, simulate

**mocker**

09 burlesque, imitation, make
   fun of, poke fun at,
   pretended, simulated
10 artificial, caricature,
   fraudulent, substitute
11 counterfeit

**mocker**

05 tease
06 critic, jeerer
07 derider, scoffer, sneerer
08 satirist
09 lampooner, ridiculer
10 lampoonist
11 pasquinader

**mockery**

05 farce, scorn, sneer, spoof
06 parody, satire, send-up
07 apology, disdain, jeering,
   lampoon, ragging, ribbing,
   sarcasm, take-off, teasing
08 ridicule, scoffing, sneering,
   taunting
09 burlesque, contumely
10 caricature

**mocking**

05 snide
07 cynical
08 derisive, derisory, sardonic,
   scoffing, scornful, sneering
09 sarcastic, satirical
10 disdainful, irreverent
12 contemptuous
13 disrespectful

**mode**

03 fad, way
04 form, look, plan, rage
05 craze, style, trend, vogue
06 custom, manner, method,
   system
07 fashion, process
08 approach, practice
09 condition, procedure,
   technique
11 latest thing

**model**

04 base, cast, copy, form, kind,
   make, mark, mode, mold,
   plan, pose, sort, type, wear,
   work
05 carve, dummy, ideal, image,
   poser, shape, sport, style
06 create, design, mockup,
   sample, sculpt, sitter
07 display, epitome, example,
   fashion, paragon, pattern,
   perfect, show off, subject,
   version
08 exemplar, original, paradigm,
   standard, template

09 archetype, exemplary,
   facsimile, imitation,
   mannequin, prototype
10 archetypal, embodiment
12 prototypical
14 perfect example,
   representation

**moderate**

04 calm, cool, curb, ease, fair,
   just, mild, so-so, tame
05 abate, allay, check, sober
06 lessen, medium, modest,
   pacify, soften, steady, subdue
07 average, control, fairish,
   liberal, slacken, subside
08 adequate, centrist, decrease,
   diminish, middling, mitigate,
   modulate, palliate, play
   down, regulate, restrain,
   sensible, tone down
09 alleviate, attenuate, soft-
   pedal, temperate, tolerable
10 controlled, reasonable
11 keep in check
12 nonextremist
13 no great shakes
14 fair to middling
15 middle-of-the-road

**moderately**

05 quite
06 fairly, rather
08 passably, slightly, somewhat
10 reasonably
12 to some extent, within
   reason

**moderation**

07 caution, control, curbing
08 decrease, sobriety
09 abatement, composure,
   lessening, reduction,
   restraint
10 mitigation, temperance
11 alleviation, attenuation, self-
   control
13 self-restraint, temperateness
14 abstemiousness,
   reasonableness

**◻in moderation**

10 moderately
12 within bounds, within limits,
   within reason
15 with self-control

**modern**

02 in
03 new
05 fresh, novel
06 latest, modish, recent, trendy,
   with it
07 current, present
08 advanced, up-to-date
09 in fashion, the latest

10 innovative, present-day
11 progressive
12 contemporary
13 state of the art, up-to-the-
   minute

**modernity**

07 newness, novelty
09 freshness
10 innovation, recentness

**modernize**

05 renew
06 reform, revamp, update
07 refresh, remodel
08 progress, renovate
09 get with it, refurbish
10 regenerate, rejuvenate
13 bring up-to-date

**modest**

03 shy
05 plain, quiet, small, timid
06 chaste, demure, humble,
   simple
07 bashful
08 decorous, discreet,
   moderate, reserved, retiring,
   virtuous
10 reasonable, unassuming
11 inexpensive
12 self-effacing
13 unpretentious
15 self-deprecating

**modesty**

07 coyness, decency, decorum,
   reserve, shyness
08 humility, timidity
09 plainness, reticence
10 chasteness, demureness,
   seemliness, simplicity
11 bashfulness
14 self-effacement
15 self-deprecation

**modicum**

03 bit, tad
04 atom, dash, drop, hint, inch,
   iota, mite
05 crumb, grain, ounce, pinch,
   scrap, shred, speck, tinge,
   touch, trace
06 degree, little
08 fragment, molecule, particle
09 little bit
10 suggestion
11 small amount

**modification**

06 change
07 editing
08 mutation, revision
09 recasting, remolding,
   reworking, tempering,
   variation

10 adaptation, adjustment, alteration, limitation, moderation, modulation, refinement
11 improvement, reformation, restriction
13 qualification

**modify**
04 dull, edit, vary
05· abate, adapt, alter, limit
06 adjust, change, lessen, recast, reduce, reform, revise, rework, soften, temper
07 convert, improve, qualify, remould, reshape
08 decrease, diminish, mitigate, moderate, redesign, tone down

**modish**
02 in
03 hip, mod, now
06 modern, trendy, with it
07 à la mode, stylish, voguish
10 all the rage, avant-garde
11 fashionable, modernistic
13 up-to-the-minute

**modulate**
04 tune, vary
05 alter, lower
06 adjust, change, modify, soften, temper
07 balance, inflect
08 moderate, regulate
09 harmonize

**modulation**
04 tone
05 shade, shift
06 accent, change, tuning
08 lowering
09 inflexion, softening
10 adjustment, alteration, inflection, intonation
13 harmonization

**modus operandi**
06 manner, method, praxis, system
08 practice
09 procedure, technique
11 rule of thumb

**mogul**
03 VIP
05 baron, Mr. Big
06 big gun, bigwig, poo-bah, top dog, tycoon
07 big shot, magnate, supremo
08 big noise, big wheel
09 big cheese, potentate

**moist**
03 wet

04 damp, dank, dewy
05 humid, muggy, rainy, soggy
06 clammy, marshy, watery
07 drizzly, wettish
08 dripping
09 drizzling

**moisten**
03 wet
04 damp, lick, soak
05 water
06 dampen, humify
07 make wet
08 humidify, irrigate
10 moisturize

**moisture**
03 dew, wet
04 damp, rain
05 spray, steam, sweat, vapor, water
06 liquid
07 drizzle, soaking, wetness
08 dampness, humidity
12 condensation, perspiration

**mole**
03 spy
04 dike, pier, spot
05 agent, groin, jetty
06 blotch, groyne
07 barrier, blemish, freckle
08 causeway
10 breakwater, embankment
11 double agent, infiltrator, secret agent

**molest**
04 harm, hurt
05 abuse, harry, hound, tease
06 accost, assail, attack, injure, plague
07 assault, disturb, torment, trouble
08 ill-treat, maltreat, mistreat
13 interfere with

**mollify**
04 calm, ease, lull
05 abate, allay, blunt, quell, quiet, relax
06 lessen, mellow, modify, pacify, soften, soothe, temper
07 appease, assuage, compose, cushion, placate, relieve, sweeten
08 mitigate, moderate
10 conciliate, propitiate

**mollusk**

► *Types of mollusk:*
04 clam, slug
05 conch, cowry, snail, squid, whelk
06 cockle, cowrie, limpet,

mussel, oyster
07 abalone, octopus, scallop, sea slug
08 nautilus, shipworm
09 land snail
10 cuttlefish, nudibranch, periwinkle
➤ See also ANIMAL; CRUSTACEAN

**mollycoddle**
03 pet
04 baby, ruin
05 spoil
06 coddle, cosset, pamper
07 milksop
08 pander to, weakling
09 spoon-feed
11 overprotect

**moment**
02 mo
03 sec
04 jiff, note
05 flash, jiffy, trice, value, worth
06 import, minute, second, weight
07 concern, gravity, instant
08 directly, interest, no sooner
09 short time, substance, the minute
10 importance, the instant
11 consequence, immediately, point in time, seriousness, split second, weightiness
12 significance
13 very short time
14 less than no time

**momentarily**
07 briefly
10 fleetingly, for a moment, for a second
11 temporarily
12 for an instant
13 for a short time

**momentary**
05 brief, hasty, quick, short
08 fleeting
09 ephemeral, transient
10 evanescent, short-lived, transitory

**momentous**
05 grave
07 crucial, fateful, pivotal, serious, weighty
08 critical, decisive, historic
11 epoch-making, significant
12 earthshaking, world-shaking
15 earthshattering, world-shattering

**momentum**
04 push, urge
05 drive, force, power, speed

## monarch

06 energy, impact, thrust
07 impetus, impulse
08 stimulus, strength, velocity
09 incentive
10 propulsion

## monarch

04 czar, king
05 queen, ruler
06 prince
07 emperor, empress
08 princess
09 potentate, sovereign
11 crowned head

## monarchy

05 realm
06 domain, empire
07 kingdom, tyranny
08 dominion, kingship, royalism
09 despotism, monocracy
10 absolutism
11 sovereignty
12 principality
14 sovereign state

## monastery

05 abbey
06 friary, priory
07 convent, nunnery
08 cenobium, cloister

## monastic

07 ascetic, austere
08 celibate, eremitic, secluded
09 cenobitic, reclusive,
   withdrawn
10 anchoritic, cloistered,
   meditative
11 sequestered
13 contemplative

► *Names of monastic orders*:
04 Sufi
05 Taizé
06 Culdee, Essene, Jesuit
08 Buddhist, Capuchin, Grey
   nuns, Minorite, Trappist,
   Ursuline
09 Carmelite, Dominican,
   mendicant
10 Bernardine, Carthusian,
   Cistercian, Conventual,
   Franciscan, Grey friars,
   Norbertine, Poor Clares
11 Augustinian, Benedictine,
   Black friars, Camaldolite,
   Ignorantine, White friars
12 Austin friars
14 Knights Templar, Society of
   Jesus
► See also RELIGION

## monasticism

09 austerity, eremitism
10 asceticism, cenobitism

## monetary

04 cash
05 money
06 fiscal
07 capital
08 economic
09 budgetary, financial,
   pecuniary

## money

04 cash, coin, gelt, loot
05 brass, bread, clams, dough,
   funds, gravy, green, means,
   moola
06 assets, moolah, riches,
   wampum, wealth
07 capital, lettuce, savings,
   shekels
08 big bucks, currency, finances
09 affluence, bank notes,
   megabucks, resources
10 green stuff, prosperity
11 legal tender
12 the necessary
► See also COIN; CURRENCY

❑**in the money**
04 rich
05 flush
06 loaded
07 wealthy, well-off
08 affluent, well-to-do
10 prosperous, well-heeled
11 rolling in it

## money box

04 safe
05 chest
06 coffer
07 cash box
09 piggy bank

## moneyed

04 rich
07 opulent, wealthy, well-off
08 affluent, well-to-do
10 prosperous, well-heeled

## moneygrubbing

07 miserly
08 grasping
09 mercenary
11 acquisitive, mammonistic

## moneymaking

09 lucrative
10 commercial, profitable
12 profit making, remunerative

## mongrel

03 cur
05 cross, mixed
06 hybrid
08 half-bred
09 crossbred, half-breed
10 crossbreed, ill-defined,
   mixed breed

## monitor

03 VDT, VDU
04 CCTV, note, plot, scan
05 check, track, watch
06 record, survey
07 observe, oversee, prefect,
   scanner
08 observer, overseer,
   watchdog
09 supervise
10 supervisor
11 invigilator, keep an eye on,
   keep track of
14 security camera

## monk

05 abbot, friar, prior
06 hermit
07 brother, recluse
08 cenobite
09 anchorite, gyrovague,
   mendicant
10 cloisterer, conventual
13 contemplative

## monkey

03 imp
04 brat, fool, mess, play
05 rogue, scamp
06 fiddle, meddle, putter, rascal,
   simian, tamper, tinker
07 primate
09 interfere, scallywag
13 mischief-maker

► *Types of monkey*:
04 douc, mona, saki, titi
05 diana, drill
06 baboon, grivet, guenon,
   howler, langur, rhesus, spider,
   uakari, vervet, woolly
07 colobus, guereza, hanuman,
   macaque, sapajou, tamarin,
   tarsier
08 capuchin, entellus,
   mangabey, marmoset,
   squirrel, talapoin, wanderoo
09 proboscis
10 Barbary ape
11 douroucouli
► See also ANIMAL

❑**monkey business**
06 pranks
07 foolery
08 clowning, mischief, trickery
09 chicanery
10 hanky-panky, tomfoolery
11 carryings-on, legerdemain,
   shenanigans, skulduggery
12 monkeyshines
13 funny business

## monochrome

08 monotone, unicolor
10 unicolored

**monocle**
08 eyeglass

**monogamous**
10 monandrous, monogynous

**monogamy**
08 monandry, monogyny

**monolingual**
08 monoglot
10 unilingual

**monolith**
06 menhir, sarsen
08 megalith
13 standing stone

**monolithic**
04 huge, vast
05 giant, rigid, solid
07 massive
08 colossal, faceless, gigantic, immobile, unmoving, unvaried
09 immovable
10 fossilized, monumental, unchanging

**monologue, monolog**
05 spiel
09 soliloquy

**monomania**
06 fetish
08 fixation, idée fixe
09 obsession
10 hobbyhorse

**monopolize**
03 hog
05 tie up
06 corner
08 dominate, take over
14 keep to yourself

**monopoly**
06 corner
09 monopsony, sole right
10 domination, sole rights
14 exclusive right

**monotonous**
06 boring, deadly
07 humdrum, routine, tedious, uniform
08 tiresome, unvaried
09 unvarying, wearisome
10 all the same, repetitive
11 repetitious
12 run-of-the-mill
13 uninteresting

**monotony**
06 tedium
07 boredom, routine
08 dullness, sameness
10 repetition, uniformity

13 wearisomeness
14 repetitiveness

**monster**
04 huge, mega, ogre, vast
05 beast, brute, devil, fiend, freak, giant, jumbo, troll
06 dragon, Gorgon, kraken, Medusa, mutant, ogress, savage, Sphinx, wivern, wyvern
07 Cyclops, immense, mammoth, massive, villain
08 behemoth, colossal, colossus, Cyclopes, enormous, gigantic, Minotaur, teratism, whopping
09 barbarian, ginormous, leviathan, monstrous
10 tremendous
11 hippocampus, miscreation, monstrosity
12 Frankenstein, malformation
13 freak of nature
14 Brobdingnagian

**monstrosity**
05 freak, teras
06 horror, mutant
07 eyesore, monster
08 atrocity, enormity
11 hideousness

**monstrous**
04 evil, foul, huge, vast, vile
07 heinous, hideous, immense, inhuman, mammoth, massive
08 abnormal, colossal, deformed, dreadful, enormous, freakish, gigantic, horrible, shocking, teratoid, terrible
09 frightful, grotesque, malformed, misshapen
10 abominable, tremendous

**monument**
05 cairn, cross, relic, token
06 barrow, column, marker, pillar, record, shrine, statue
07 memento, obelisk, witness
08 cenotaph, evidence, memorial, reminder
09 headstone, mausoleum, testament, tombstone
10 gravestone

► *Names of monuments:*
06 Sphinx
08 Cenotaph, Taj Mahal
09 Tsar's Bell
10 Berlin Wall, Ishtar Gate, Marble Arch, Stonehenge
11 Eiffel Tower, Gateway Arch,

Grande Arche, Great Sphinx, Liberty Bell, Machu Picchu
12 Antonine Wall, Hadrian's Wall, Spanish Steps, Statue of Zeus, Tower of Babel
13 Arc de Triomphe, Iwo Jima Statue, Mount Rushmore, Nelson's Column, Trajan's Column, Trevi Fountain
14 Albert Memorial, Stone of Destiny, Tomb of Mausolus
15 Brandenburg Gate, Lincoln Memorial, Statue of Liberty

**monumental**
04 huge, vast
05 great
07 abiding, awesome, immense, lasting, massive
08 colossal, enduring, enormous, historic, immortal, imposing, majestic, memorial, striking
09 important, memorable
10 impressive, tremendous
11 celebratory, epoch-making, exceptional, magnificent, outstanding, significant
12 awe inspiring, overwhelming
13 commemorative, extraordinary, unforgettable

**mood**
04 feel, sulk, tone, vein, whim
05 blues, dumps, humor, pique, tenor
06 spirit, temper
07 climate, feeling
08 ambience, doldrums, the sulks
09 bad temper
10 atmosphere, depression, low spirits, melancholy
11 disposition, frame of mind, state of mind

❏ **in the mood for**
07 eager to
09 willing to
10 disposed to, inclined to
11 feeling like

**moody**
04 glum
05 angry, mopey, sulky, testy
06 broody, crabby, crusty, fickle, gloomy, grumpy, morose, sullen, touchy
07 doleful, in a huff, in a mood
08 downcast, petulant, unstable, volatile
09 crotchety, impulsive, irascible, irritable, miserable
10 capricious, changeable, in a bad mood, melancholy

## moon

13 temperamental, unpredictable

## moon

05 brood, dream, mooch
08 daydream, languish
09 satellite

❑once in a blue moon
06 seldom
08 not often
10 hardly ever, very rarely

## moonlike

05 lunar
06 lunate
07 lunular, selenic
08 crescent
10 crescentic, moon shaped

## moonshine

03 rot
04 bosh, bunk, guff
05 hooch, stuff, tripe
06 bunkum, hootch, hot air, liquor, piffle
07 baloney, blather, blether, bootleg, eyewash, fantasy, hogwash, rubbish
08 claptrap, nonsense, tommyrot
09 moonlight

## moor

04 bind, dock, lash
05 berth, heath, hitch, tie up
06 anchor, fasten, secure, upland
08 make fast, moorland
10 drop anchor

## moot

04 open, pose
05 argue, vexed
06 broach, debate, knotty, submit
07 advance, bring up, propose, suggest
08 academic, arguable, disputed, doubtful
09 debatable, introduce
10 disputable, put forward
12 open to debate, questionable
13 controversial

## mop

04 mane, mass, soak, swab
06 absorb, sponge
10 head of hair

❑mop up
06 absorb, soak up, wipe up
07 clean up, round up
09 finish off

## mope

04 fret, pine, sulk
05 brood, droop, grump

06 grieve, grouch, misery, moaner
07 despair, killjoy
08 languish
09 introvert, pessimist

❑mope around, mope about
04 idle, loll, moon
05 mooch
06 lounge, wander
08 languish

## moral

04 good, just, pure
05 adage, maxim, right
06 chaste, decent, dictum, honest, lesson, proper, saying
07 epigram, ethical, meaning, message, precept, proverb, upright
08 aphorism, virtuous
09 honorable, righteous
10 high-minded, principled, upstanding
11 clean living

## morale

05 heart
06 spirit
07 spirits
10 confidence, self-esteem
11 hopefulness, state of mind
13 esprit de corps
14 self-confidence

## morality

06 ethics, ideals, morals, virtue
07 decency, honesty
08 chastity, goodness
09 integrity, propriety, rectitude, standards
10 principles
13 righteousness

## moralize

06 preach
07 lecture
09 sermonize
11 pontificate

## morals

06 ethics, habits, ideals
07 conduct
08 morality, scruples
09 integrity, moral code, standards
10 principles
11 moral values

## morass

03 bog, fen
04 mess, mire, moss, quag
05 chaos, marsh, swamp
06 slough
08 quagmire

09 confusion, marshland, quicksand

## moratorium

03 ban
04 halt, stay
05 delay
06 freeze
07 embargo, respite
08 stoppage
10 standstill, suspension
12 postponement

## morbid

06 ailing, gloomy, grisly, horrid, morose, somber
07 ghastly, hideous, macaber, macabre
08 diseased, ghoulish, gruesome, horrible
09 unhealthy
10 lugubrious
11 unwholesome
12 insalubrious

## mordant

04 acid
05 edged, harsh, sharp
06 biting, bitter
07 acerbic, caustic, cutting, pungent, vicious, waspish
08 critical, incisive, scathing, stinging, venomous, wounding
09 sarcastic, trenchant
10 astringent

## more

03 new
05 added, again, extra, fresh, other, spare
06 better, longer
07 another, besides, further
09 increased
10 additional
13 supplementary

## moreover

04 also
06 as well
07 besides, further
10 in addition, what is more
11 furthermore
12 additionally

## morgue

07 library
08 mortuary
11 funeral home
12 charnel house
13 funeral parlor

## moribund

05 dying
06 doomed, ebbing, fading, feeble, senile, waning
07 failing

**morning**
08 comatose, expiring, lifeless, stagnant
10 in extremis, stagnating
11 obsolescent, on the way out, wasting away
14 on your last legs

**morning**
02 a.m.
04 dawn
07 sunrise
08 daybreak, daylight
10 before noon, break of day

**moron**
04 clod, dolt, dope, fool
05 dumbo, dunce, idiot
06 cretin, dimwit
07 buffoon, halfwit
08 imbecile
09 simpleton

**moronic**
04 dumb
06 stupid, unwise
08 ignorant
09 ludicrous, pointless, senseless
10 half-witted
12 simple-minded
13 unintelligent

**morose**
04 glum, grim, sour
06 gloomy
08 mournful, taciturn
09 depressed, saturnine
10 lugubrious
11 bad tempered, ill-tempered, melancholic

**morsel**
03 bit
04 bite, part
05 crumb, grain, piece, scrap, slice, taste
06 nibble, tidbit
07 modicum, segment, soupçon
08 fraction, fragment, mouthful, particle

**mortal**
03 man
04 body, dire
05 awful, being, cruel, fatal, grave, great, human, woman
06 bitter, bodily, deadly, lethal, person, severe
07 earthly, extreme, fleshly, intense, killing, worldly
08 creature, temporal, terrible, vengeful
09 corporeal, earthling, ephemeral, transient

10 human being, implacable, individual, perishable, relentless, unbearable

**mortality**
05 death
07 carnage, killing
08 casualty, fatality, humanity
09 death rate, slaughter
10 loss of life, transience
11 earthliness, worldliness
13 perishability

**mortgage**
04 bond, lien, loan
06 pledge
08 security
09 debenture

**mortification**
05 shame
07 chagrin, control
08 disgrace, dishonor, ignominy, vexation
09 abasement, annoyance
10 asceticism, chastening, conquering, discipline, loss of face, punishment, self-denial
11 confounding, humiliation, self-control, subjugation
12 discomfiture
13 embarrassment

**mortified**
06 shamed
07 ashamed, crushed, humbled
09 disgraced, horrified
10 confounded, dishonored, humiliated
11 embarrassed

**mortify**
03 die
04 deny
05 abash, annoy, crush, shame
06 humble, offend, subdue
07 affront, chagrin, chasten, conquer, control, deflate, horrify
08 bring low, chastise, confound, disgrace, dishonor, restrain, suppress
09 discomfit, embarrass, humiliate
10 disappoint, discipline, put to shame

**mortifying**
07 shaming
11 humiliating, ignominious
12 embarrassing

**mortuary**
06 morgue
11 funeral home
12 charnel house

13 funeral parlor

**most**
04 bulk, mass
08 majority
09 almost all, nearly all
10 lion's share
13 preponderance

**mostly**
06 mainly
07 as a rule, chiefly, largely, overall, usually
08 above all
09 generally, in general, in the main
10 especially, on the whole
11 principally
13 predominantly
14 for the most part

**moth**

➤ Types of moth:
03 wax
04 luna, puss
05 gypsy
06 burnet, carpet, lackey, lappet, magpie, turnip, winter
07 buff-tip, clothes, codling, emperor, tussock
08 cecropia, cinnabar, peppered, silkworm
09 browntail
11 garden tiger, pale tussock, swallowtail
12 peach blossom, red underwing
➤ See also ANIMAL

**moth-eaten**
03 old
04 worn
05 dated, mangy, moldy, musty, seedy, stale
06 ragged, shabby
07 ancient, archaic, decayed, worn-out
08 decrepit, tattered
10 threadbare

**mother**
02 ma
03 dam, mam, mom
04 baby, base, bear, mama, rear, tend
05 cause, fount, mamma, mammy, mater, mommy, nurse, raise, roots, spoil
06 matron, origin, pamper, parent, source, spring
07 care for, cherish, indulge, nurture, produce
08 ancestor, fuss over, old woman

09 look after, matriarch
10 bring forth, derivation, foundation, procreator, take care of, wellspring
11 overprotect
12 progenitress
13 materfamilias

**motherly**
04 fond, kind, warm
06 caring, gentle, loving, tender
08 maternal
10 comforting, protective
12 affectionate

**motif**
04 form, idea, logo
05 shape, theme, topic
06 design, device, emblem
08 ornament

**motion**
03 bid, nod
04 sign, wave
05 usher
06 action, beckon, direct, signal
07 gesture, project
08 activity, mobility, motility, movement, progress, proposal
10 indication, suggestion
11 gesticulate, proposition

◻**in motion**
05 going
06 moving
07 on the go, running
08 under way
09 on the move, traveling
10 in progress
11 functioning, operational

**motionless**
05 fixed, inert, rigid, still
06 at rest, frozen, halted, static
07 resting
08 immobile, lifeless, stagnant, standing, unmoving
09 inanimate, paralyzed, unmovable
10 stationary, stock-still, transfixed
13 at a standstill

**motivate**
04 draw, goad, lead, move, push, spur, stir, urge
05 bring, cause, drive, impel
06 arouse, excite, incite, induce, kindle, prompt, propel
07 actuate, inspire, provoke, trigger
08 activate, initiate, persuade
09 encourage, stimulate

**motivation**
04 push, spur, urge

05 drive
06 desire, motive, reason
07 impulse
08 momentum, stimulus
09 incentive, prompting
10 incitement, inducement
11 inspiration, instigation

**motive**
04 goad, lure, spur, urge
05 basis, cause
06 design, desire, ground, object, reason
07 grounds, impulse, purpose
08 occasion, stimulus, thinking
09 incentive, influence, intention, rationale
10 attraction, incitement, inducement, motivation
11 inspiration
13 consideration, encouragement

**motley**
07 dappled, diverse, mottled, piebald, spotted, striped
08 assorted, colorful, many-hued
10 variegated
11 diversified
12 multicolored, multifarious, particolored
13 heterogeneous

**motor**
03 car
04 auto, ride
05 drive
06 engine, travel
07 machine, turbine, vehicle
09 motorbike
10 automobile, motorcycle
12 motor scooter, motor vehicle
➤ See also CAR; VEHICLE

**mottled**
07 blotchy, dappled, flecked
08 blotched, speckled, splotchy, stippled
10 variegated

**motto**
05 adage, axiom, gnome, maxim
06 byword, dictum, slogan
09 catchword, watchword
10 golden rule

**mold**
03 cut, die, rot
04 cast, form, kind, line, make, must, sort, type, work
05 brand, forge, model, shape, stamp, style
06 create, design, format, fungus, mildew, sculpt
07 caliber, fashion, pattern

08 template
09 character, formation, mustiness, structure
12 construction
13 configuration

**molder**
03 rot
05 decay, waste
06 humify, perish
07 corrupt, crumble
09 decompose
10 turn to dust
12 disintegrate

**moldy**
03 bad
05 fusty, musty, stale
06 putrid, rotten
08 blighted, mildewed

**mound**
03 lot
04 bank, dune, heap, hill, pile, rise
05 hoard, knoll, ridge, stack, store
06 barrow, bundle, supply
07 hillock, hummock, tumulus
08 mountain
09 abundance, earthwork, elevation, stockpile
10 collection, embankment
12 accumulation

**mount**
04 base, go up, grow, rise, soar
05 build, climb, frame, get on, get up, horse, put on, scale, set up, stage, stand, steed, swell
06 accrue, ascend, jump on, launch, pile up
07 arrange, backing, build up, climb on, climb up, display, exhibit, fixture, install, prepare, produce, support
08 escalate, increase, jump onto, mounting, multiply, organize
09 clamber up, climb on to, intensify
10 accumulate, get astride

**mountain**
03 alp, lot, tor
04 heap, hill, mass, peak, pile
05 mound, mount, stack
06 height, massif
07 backlog
08 pinnacle
09 abundance, elevation
12 accumulation

▶ *Names of mountaineers:*
04 **Blum** (Arlene), **Hunt** (John),

Lowe (Alex)
05 **Munro** (Hugh Thomas),
**Scott** (Doug)
06 **Bishop** (Barry), **Bishop**
(Brent), **Irvine** (Andrew),
**Necker** (Louis Albert),
**Tilman** (Harold William),
**Uemura** (Naomi)
07 **Bridges** (Dave), **Hillary**
(Edmund), **Houston**
(Charles), **Mallory**
(George), **Shipton** (Eric
Earle), **Simpson** (Myrtle
Lillias), **Tenzing** (Sherpa),
**Whymper** (Edward)
08 **Coolidge** (William
Augustus Brevoort),
**MacInnes** (Hamish),
**Petzoldt** (Paul), **Viesturs**
(Ed), **Whillans** (Don)
09 **Bonington** (Chris)
13 **Tenzing Norgay**
➢ See also SPORT

▶ *Names of mountains and*
*mountain ranges. We have*
*omitted the words* **mount**,
**mountain** *and* **mountains** *from*
*names given in the following list*
*but you may need to include one*
*of these words as part of the*
*solution to some crossword*
*clues.*
02 K2
03 Dom
04 Alps, Blue, Cook, Etna, Fuji,
Hood, Jura, Ossa, Rila, Sion,
Ural
05 Altai, Andes, Atlas, Cloud,
Downs, Eiger, Ghats, Kenya,
Kings, Logan, Matra, Ozark,
Rocky, Table, Tatra
06 Ararat, Deccan, Denali,
Egmont, Elbert, Elbrus,
Hoggar, Lhotse, Makalu,
Mourne, Musala, Pindus,
Taurus, Vosges, Wilson,
Zagros
07 Beskids, Everest, Lebanon,
Olympus, Rainier, Rhodope,
Roraima, Scafell, Skiddaw,
Snowdon, St. Elias, Stanley,
Troödos, Wheeler, Whitney
08 Ben Nevis, Cameroon,
Catskill, Caucasus, Cévennes,
Five Holy, Jungfrau, Kinabalu,
Mauna Kea, Mauna Loa,
McKinley, Mitchell, Pennines,
Pyrenees, Rushmore,
Sawtooth, Snowmass, St.
Helens
09 Allegheny, Annapurna,
Apennines, Blue Ridge,

Dolomites, Grampians,
Guadalupe, Helvellyn,
Himalayas, Hindu Kush,
Humphreys, Lenin Peak,
Longs Peak, Mont Blanc,
Pikes Peak, Tirol Alps,
Zugspitze
10 Adirondack, Bitterroot,
Cader Idris, Cairngorms,
Cantabrian, Carpathian,
Chimborazo, Grand Teton,
Great Smoky, Matterhorn,
Pobedy Peak
11 Appalachian, Arthur's Pass,
Black Forest, Coeur d'Alene,
Gannett Peak, Kilimanjaro,
Mendip Hills
12 Bavarian Alps, Cascade
Range, Cheviot Hills, Darling
Range, Popocatepetl, Sierra
Nevada, Southern Alps, Tibet
Plateau, Victoria Peak
13 Chiltern Hills, Communism
Peak, Kangchenjunga,
Stirling Range
14 Australian Alps, Bavarian
Forest, Bohemian Forest,
Fichtelgebirge, Flinders
Ranges, Grand St. Bernard,
Hamersley Range,
Mackenzie Range, Musgrave
Ranges
15 Guiana Highlands

**mountainous**
04 high, huge, vast
05 hilly, lofty, rocky, steep
06 alpine, craggy, upland
07 immense, massive, soaring
08 colossal, enormous, gigantic,
highland, towering

**mountebank**
04 fake
05 cheat, fraud, phony, pseud,
quack
06 con man
08 impostor, swindler
09 charlatan, con artist, trickster
13 confidence man

**mourn**
04 keen, miss, wail, weep
06 bemoan, bewail, grieve,
lament, regret, sorrow

**mourner**
04 mute
06 keener
08 bereaved

**mournful**
03 sad
06 tragic, woeful
07 elegiac, unhappy

08 dejected, desolate,
downcast, funereal
09 depressed, sorrowful
10 lugubrious, melancholy
11 heartbroken
12 disconsolate, heavy-hearted
13 brokenhearted, grief stricken

**mourning**
05 grief
06 sorrow
07 keening, wailing, weeping
08 grieving
09 sorrowing
11 bereavement, lamentation

**mousy**
03 shy
04 drab, dull
05 plain, quiet, timid
07 grayish
08 brownish, timorous
09 colorless, diffident,
withdrawn

**mouth**
03 gas, lip, say
04 door, form, gall, jaws, lips,
trap, vent
05 chops, delta, inlet, utter
06 babble, hot air, kisser, outlet
07 estuary, opening, orifice,
whisper
08 aperture, boasting, bragging,
idle talk, rudeness
09 empty talk, enunciate,
insolence, pronounce
10 articulate, embouchure

▶ *Parts of the mouth:*
03 gum
05 uvula
06 tongue, tonsil
08 lower lip, upper lip
10 hard palate, soft palate
11 cleft palate
➢ See also TEETH

**mouthful**
03 bit, sip, sup
04 bite, drop, gulp, slug
05 taste
06 morsel, nibble, sample, tidbit

**mouthpiece**
05 agent, organ
06 lawyer
07 journal
08 delegate
09 spokesman
10 periodical
11 publication, spokeswoman
12 propagandist, spokesperson
14 representative

**movable**
06 mobile

**movables**
08 flexible, portable
09 alterable, portative
10 adjustable, changeable
12 transferable
13 transportable

**movables**
04 gear
05 goods, stuff
06 things
07 effects
08 chattels, property
09 furniture
10 belongings
11 impedimenta, possessions

**move**
02 go
03 act
04 lead, pass, push, roll, stir, tack, take, urge, walk
05 bring, budge, carry, cause, drive, fetch, impel, leave, rouse, shift, shunt, sidle, swing, touch, upset
06 action, affect, arouse, change, decamp, depart, device, excite, go away, incite, induce, motion, prompt, propel, remove, switch, travel
07 actuate, advance, agitate, disturb, gesture, impress, incline, inspire, measure, migrate, proceed, propose, provoke, removal, request, step out, suggest
08 activity, advocate, maneuver, motivate, move away, movement, persuade, progress, relocate, transfer
09 influence, migration, move house, recommend, stimulate, stratagem, transport, transpose
10 put forward, relocation, take action
11 make strides
13 gesticulation, repositioning
15 change of address

❏**get a move on**
07 hurry up, speed up
09 make haste, shake a leg
11 get cracking
12 get a hustle on
13 get the lead out
15 put your foot down

❏**on the move**
06 active, moving
07 on the go
08 under way
09 advancing
11 progressing

**movement**
03 act, bit
04 fall, flow, move, part, rise, wing
05 drift, drive, group, party, piece, shift, swing, tempo, trend, works
06 action, change, moving, rhythm, system
07 advance, crusade, current, faction, gesture, passage, portion, section
08 activity, campaign, division, progress, shifting, stirring, tendency, transfer, workings
09 agitation, coalition, evolution, mechanism, variation
10 relocation
11 development, improvement, progression
12 breakthrough, organization
13 gesticulation, repositioning
14 transportation

**movie**
04 film
05 flick, video
06 silent, talkie
07 picture
11 feature film, picture show
13 motion picture, moving picture

**moving**
05 astir
06 active, mobile, motile, urging
07 driving, dynamic, emotive, kinetic, leading
08 arousing, exciting, in motion, pathetic, poignant, stirring, touching, worrying
09 affecting, emotional, inspiring, thrilling, upsetting
10 disturbing, impressive, motivating, persuasive
11 influential, stimulating
12 maneuverable
13 inspirational

**mow**
03 cut
04 clip, crop, trim
05 shear
06 scythe

❏**mow down**
07 butcher, cut down
08 decimate, massacre
09 overwhelm, shoot down, slaughter
11 cut to pieces

**much**
04 a lot, lots

05 ample, great, heaps, loads, often
06 plenty
07 copious, greatly
08 abundant, lashings
09 extensive, plentiful
10 a great deal, frequently, widespread
11 substantial
12 considerable, considerably
14 to a great extent

**muck**
03 goo, mud
04 crud, dirt, dung, gook, mire, scum, yuck
05 filth, grime, guano, gunge, slime
06 manure, ordure, sewage, sludge

❏**muck up**
04 ruin
05 botch, spoil, wreck
06 bungle, mess up
07 louse up, screw up

**mucky**
05 dirty, grimy, messy, muddy, slimy
06 filthy, soiled

**mucous**
05 slimy
06 rheumy, viscid
07 viscous
12 mucilaginous

**mud**
04 mire, ooze, silt
06 sludge

**muddle**
04 daze, mess
05 chaos, mix up, mix-up
06 bemuse, jumble
07 clutter, confuse, perplex
08 befuddle, bewilder, confound, disarray, disorder, jumble up, scramble
09 confusion
11 disorganize

**muddled**
06 woolly
07 chaotic, mixed-up, unclear
08 confused
09 befuddled, perplexed
10 bewildered, disarrayed, disordered, incoherent
13 disorientated

**muddy**
04 dull, foul, hazy, miry, oozy, soil
05 boggy, cloud, dingy, dirty, fuzzy, grimy, mucky, murky

**muff**
06 cloudy, filthy, grubby, jumble, marshy, opaque, quaggy, slushy, swampy, tangle, turbid
07 begrime, blurred, obscure
10 indistinct
11 disorganize, make unclear

**muff**
05 botch, fluff, spoil
06 bungle, fumble, goof up, mess up
07 louse up

**muffle**
03 gag
06 dampen, deaden, muzzle, soften, stifle, wrap up
07 envelop, quieten, smother
08 suppress

**mug**
03 cup, pot, rob
04 bash, face, fool, gull, puss, thug
05 chump
06 attack, batter, beaker, beat up, hold up, jump on, kisser, sucker, visage, waylay
07 assault, grimace, hoodlum, tankard
08 features
09 simpleton, soft touch
10 knock about
11 countenance, knock around

**muggy**
04 damp
05 close, humid, moist
06 clammy, sticky, stuffy, sultry
07 airless
10 oppressive, sweltering

**mulish**
07 defiant
08 perverse, stubborn
09 difficult, obstinate, pigheaded
10 headstrong, inflexible, refractory, self-willed
11 intractable
12 intransigent

**mull**
❑**mull over**
06 muse on, ponder
08 chew over, consider, meditate, ruminate
09 reflect on, think over
10 deliberate, think about
11 contemplate

**multicolored**
06 motley
10 variegated

**multifarious**
04 many

06 legion, varied
07 diverse
08 manifold, multiple, numerous
09 different, multiform

**multiple**
04 many
07 several, various
08 manifold, numerous

**multiplicity**
03 lot
04 host, lots, mass, tons
05 heaps, loads, piles
06 myriad, oodles, scores
09 great deal, profusion

**multiply**
04 grow
05 boost, breed
06 expand, extend, spread
07 augment, build up
08 increase
09 propagate, reproduce
11 proliferate

**multitude**
03 lot, mob
04 herd, host, lots, mass
05 crowd, horde, plebs, swarm
06 legion, people, public, rabble, throng
08 assembly, populace, riffraff
09 hoi polloi
10 common herd

**multitudinous**
04 many
06 legion, myriad
07 teeming, umpteen
08 manifold, numerous, swarming
09 abounding, countless
11 innumerable

**mum**
04 dumb, mute
05 quiet
06 silent
11 close lipped, tightlipped
12 close-mouthed

**mumble**
06 murmur, rumble
11 speak softly
14 speak unclearly, talk to yourself

**mumbo jumbo**
04 cant, rite
05 chant, charm, magic, spell
06 humbug, jargon, ritual
08 claptrap, nonsense
09 gibberish, rigmarole
10 hocus-pocus
12 gobbledygook, superstition

**munch**
03 eat
04 chew
05 champ, chomp
06 crunch
09 masticate

**mundane**
05 banal
06 boring
07 earthly, humdrum, prosaic, routine
08 everyday, ordinary, temporal, workaday
11 commonplace, terrestrial

**municipal**
04 city, town
05 civic, civil, urban

**municipality**
04 city, town
05 burgh
07 borough

**munificence**
08 largesse
10 generosity, liberality
12 generousness, philanthropy
13 bounteousness
14 openhandedness

**munificent**
06 lavish
07 liberal
08 generous, princely
09 bounteous, bountiful
10 freehanded, openhanded
11 magnanimous
13 philanthropic
15 philanthropical

**murder**
04 beat, do in, kill, slay
05 agony, lynch, spoil, waste, wreck
06 misery, ordeal, rub out
07 anguish, bump off, butcher, clobber, destroy, execute, killing, slaying, take out, torment, torture, wipe out
08 blow away, butchery, homicide, knock off, massacre, regicide
09 bloodshed, difficult, eliminate, execution, liquidate, matricide, parricide, patricide, slaughter, uxoricide
10 annihilate, fratricide, put to death, sororicide
11 infanticide, liquidation
12 manslaughter
13 assassination

**murderer**
06 killer, slayer

**murderous**
07 butcher, torpedo
08 assassin, homicide
09 cutthroat
11 slaughterer

**murderous**
06 bloody, deadly, lethal, mortal
07 arduous, killing
09 cutthroat, ferocious, homicidal
12 bloodthirsty

**murky**
03 dim
05 dingy, dirty, foggy, misty, shady
06 cloudy, dismal, dreary, gloomy, turbid
07 obscure
08 overcast
10 mysterious, suspicious

**murmur**
03 hum
04 buzz, carp, purl, purr
05 gripe, whine
06 grouse, intone, mumble, mutter, object, rumble
07 carping, grumble, humming, protest, whining, whisper
08 complain
09 bellyache, complaint, criticize, find fault, grievance, muttering, objection, undertone
15 dissatisfaction

**murmuring**
04 buzz, purr
06 mumble, rumble
07 buzzing, purring, whisper
08 mumbling, rumbling, susurrus
09 muttering
10 whispering
11 murmuration

**muscle**
04 beef
05 brawn, clout, force, might, power, sinew
06 tendon, weight
08 ligament, strength

► *Names of muscles*:
05 psoas
06 biceps, rectus, soleus
07 deltoid, gluteus, triceps
08 scalenus
09 abdominal, sartorius, trapezius
10 quadriceps
13 gastrocnemius
15 pectoralis major, pectoralis minor, peroneal muscles

❑**muscle in**
05 shove
06 butt in, jostle, push in
09 strong-arm

**muscular**
05 beefy, burly, hefty, husky
06 brawny, rugged, sinewy, strong, sturdy
07 fibrous
08 athletic, powerful, stalwart, vigorous
09 strapping

**muse**
05 brood, dream, think, weigh
06 ponder, review
07 reflect
08 cogitate, consider, meditate, mull over, ruminate
09 speculate, think over
10 deliberate
11 contemplate

► *Names of the Muses*:
04 Clio
05 Aoede, Erato, Mneme
06 Melete, Thalia, Urania
07 Euterpe
08 Calliope
09 Melpomene
10 Polyhymnia
11 Terpsichore
➤ See also MYTHOLOGY

**museum**

► *Names of galleries and museums. We have omitted the words* **gallery** *and* **museum** *from names given in the following list but you may need to include these words as part of the solution to some crossword clues.*
04 MOMA, Tate
05 Prado, Terme
06 Correr, Jewish, London, Louvre, Uffizi
07 British, Fogg Art, Hofburg, Pushkin, Science, Vatican, Whitney
08 Bargello, Borghese, Carnegie, Fine Arts, National, Pergamum
09 Accademia, Albertina, Arnolfini, Ashmolean, Belvedere, Cloisters, Deutsches, Hermitage, Holocaust, Modern Art, Sans Souci, Tretyakov
10 Guggenheim, Pinakothek
11 Fitzwilliam, Musée d'Orsay, Pitti Palace, Rijksmuseum
12 Art Institute, Metropolitan

13 Exploratorium, Jean Paul Getty
14 Natural History, State Hermitage
15 Frick Collection
22 Smithsonian Institution

**mush**
03 pap
04 corn, mash, pulp
05 paste, purée, slush, swill
08 schmaltz
11 mawkishness
14 sentimentality

**mushroom**
04 boom, grow
06 expand, fungus, spread, sprout
07 burgeon, shoot up
08 flourish, increase, spring up
11 proliferate

► *Types of mushrooms and toadstools*:
03 cep
05 morel
06 blewit
07 amanita, blewits, boletus, inky cap, parasol
08 puffball, shiitake, truffle,
09 earthstar, fairy ring, fly agaric, stinkhorn
10 champignon, false morel, panther cap, shaggy mane
11 chanterelle, common morel, honey fungus
12 common ink cap, horn of plenty, jack-o'-lantern
13 field mushroom, honey mushroom, horse mushroom
14 button mushroom, meadow mushroom, oyster mushroom
15 beefsteak fungus, destroying angel, parasol mushroom, stinking parasol
16 shiitake mushroom
➤ See also FOOD; FUNGUS

**mushy**
05 pappy, pulpy, weepy
06 doughy, sloppy, slushy, sugary, syrupy
07 mawkish, squashy
09 schmaltzy
10 saccharine
11 sentimental

**music**

► *Types of music*:
03 pop, rap, ska
04 folk, funk, jazz, jive, rock, soul

05 blues, dance, disco, house, R and B, swing
06 ballet, choral, doo-wop, garage, gospel, grunge, hip-hop, new age, reggae, sacred, techno, zydeco
07 chamber, karaoke, ragtime, skiffle
08 ballroom, folk-rock, hard rock, jazz funk, operatic, oratorio, punk rock
09 acid house, bluegrass, classical, Dixieland, honky-tonk, rock n' roll
10 electronic, heavy metal, incidental, jazz fusion, orchestral
11 rock and roll
12 boogie-woogie, instrumental
14 rhythm and blues
➢ See also COMPOSER; CONDUCTOR; INSTRUMENT; JAZZ; LIBRETTO; MUSICAL; MUSICIAN; OPERA; ORATORIO; SINGER; SONG; SONGWRITER

**musical**
06 dulcet, mellow
07 lyrical, melodic, tuneful
09 melodious
10 euphonious, harmonious
11 mellifluous
➢ See also INSTRUMENT; MUSIC

► *Names of musicals:*
04 Cats, Hair, Mame, Rent
05 Annie, Chess, Evita, Gypsy, Zorba
06 Grease, Kismet, The Wiz
07 Cabaret, Camelot, Chicago, Follies, Oliver!, Ragtime
08 Carnival, Carousel, Godspell, Mama Mia!, Peter Pan, Show Boat
09 Brigadoon, Funny Girl, Girl Crazy, Oklahoma!, On the Town
10 Kiss Me Kate, Miss Saigon, My Fair Lady
11 A Chorus Line, Babes in Arms, Carmen Jones, Damn Yankees, Hello Dolly!, Me and My Girl, Sweeney Todd, The King and I, The Music Man
12 Anything Goes, Bye Bye Birdie, Guys and Dolls, Porgy and Bess, South Pacific, The Boy Friend, The Producers, The Producers
13 Aspects of Love, Les Miserables, Man of La

Mancha, The Pajama Game, West Side Story
15 Annie Get Your Gun, La Cage aux Folles, Sunset Boulevard, The Sound of Music
19 Little Shop of Horrors

► *Types of musical composition:*
03 jig, lay, rag
04 aria, hymn, lied, opus, raga, song, tune
05 canon, carol, étude, fugue, gigue, march, opera, piece, rondo, round, suite, tango, track, waltz
06 aubade, ballad, bolero, lieder, masque, minuet, number, shanty, sonata
07 ballade, bourrée, cantata, fanfare, gavotte, mazurka, partita, prelude, requiem, scherzo, toccata
08 concerto, fandango, fantasia, galliard, hornpipe, madrigal, nocturne, operetta, overture, rhapsody, serenade, sonatina, symphony
09 allemande, arabesque, bagatelle, capriccio, écossaise, impromptu, invention, pastorale, polonaise, sarabande, spiritual, voluntary
10 barcarolle, humoresque, intermezzo, opera buffa, tarantella
11 composition, sinfonietta
12 divertimento
14 chorale prelude, concerto grosso

► *Names of musical compositions:*
04 Saul
05 Rodeo
06 Bolero, Elijah, Études, Façade
07 Mazeppa, Messiah
08 Ballades, Caprices, Creation, Drum Mass, Ode to Joy, Peer Gynt
09 Capriccio, Fantaisie, Finlandia, Jerusalem, Nocturnes
10 Arabesques, Bacchanale, Bagatelles, Concertino, The Planets, The Seasons, Water Music
11 Curlew River, Minute Waltz, Requiem Mass, Stabat Mater, Winterreise
12 A Sea Symphony, Danse Macabre, Schéhérézade,

Trout Quintet
13 Carmina Burana, Choral Fantasy, Faust Symphony, Fêtes Galantes, Missa Solemnis, On Wenlock Edge, The Art of Fugue
14 Choral Symphony, Eroica Symphony, Glagolitic Mass, Prague Symphony, Rhapsody in Blue, Slavonic Dances, The Four Seasons
15 A Child of our Time, Children's Corner, Emperor Concerto, Jupiter Symphony, Manfred Symphony, Peter and the Wolf

► *Musical terms:*
03 bar, bis, cue, key, tie
04 a due, alto, bass, beat, clef, coda, fine, flat, fret, hold, mode, mute, note, part, rest, root, slur, solo, tone, tune, turn
05 ad lib, breve, buffo, chord, dolce, drone, forte, grave, largo, lento, lyric, major, meter, minim, minor, pause, piano, piece, pitch, scale, score, shake, sharp, staff, stave, swell, tacet, tempo, tenor, theme, triad, trill, tutti
06 a tempo, adagio, al fine, da capo, encore, finale, legato, medley, melody, octave, phrase, presto, quaver, rhythm, sempre, subito, tenuto, timbre, treble, tuning, unison, upbeat, vivace
07 al segno, allegro, amoroso, andante, animato, attacca, cadence, con brio, con moto, concert, descant, harmony, marcato, mordent, natural, recital, refrain, soprano, tremolo, triplet, vibrato
08 acoustic, alto clef, arpeggio, baritone, bass clef, con fuoco, crotchet, diatonic, doloroso, dominant, downbeat, ensemble, interval, maestoso, moderato, movement, ostinato, ritenuto, semitone, semplice, sequence, staccato, vigoroso, virtuoso
09 alla breve, cantabile, chromatic, contralto, crescendo, glissando, harmonics, imitation, larghetto, orchestra, pizzicato, sextuplet, sostenuto, sotto voce,

spiritoso, tenor clef
10 accidental, affettuoso, allegretto, diminuendo, dissonance, double flat, fortissimo, intonation, mezzo forte, modulation, pentatonic, pianissimo, resolution, simple time, supertonic, tonic sol-fa, treble clef, two-two time
11 accelerando, arrangement, decrescendo, double sharp, fingerboard, leading note, quarter tone, rallentando, subdominant, syncopation
12 acciaccatura, alla cappella, appoggiatura, compound time, counterpoint, four-four time, key signature, six-eight time
13 accompaniment, improvisation, major interval, minor interval, orchestration, three-four time, time signature, transposition
14 demisemiquaver
15 perfect interval

## musician

► *Types of musician*:
03 duo
04 band, bard, diva, duet, trio
05 choir, group, octet, piper
06 bugler, oboist, player, sextet, singer
07 bassist, cellist, drummer, fiddler, flutist, harpist, maestro, pianist, quartet, quintet, soloist
08 composer, ensemble, flautist, organist, virtuoso, vocalist
09 balladeer, conductor, guitarist, orchestra, performer, trumpeter, violinist
10 lead singer, prima donna, trombonist
11 accompanist, mandolinist, saxophonist
12 backing group, clarinettist
15 instrumentalist

► *Names of classical musicians*:
02 **Ma** (Yo-Yo)
03 **Pré** (Jacqueline du)
04 **Hess** (Myra)
05 **Bream** (Julian), **Bülow** (Hans von), **Grove** (George), **Ogdon** (John), **Sharp** (Cecil), **Stern** (Isaac)
06 **Casals** (Pablo), **Galway**

(James), **Köchel** (Ludwig Ritter von), **Rizzio** (David)
07 **Blondel**, **Glennie** (Evelyn), **Heifetz** (Jascha), **Kennedy** (Nigel), **Menuhin** (Yehudi), **Perlman** (Itzhak), **Segovia** (Andrés), **Shankar** (Ravi)
08 **Paganini** (Niccolò), **Sarasate** (Martin Meliton), **Steinway** (Heinrich Engelhard), **Williams** (John)
09 **Ashkenazy** (Vladimir), **Barenboim** (Daniel), **Boulanger** (Nadia), **Guarnieri, Tortelier** (Paul)
10 **Cristofori**, **Paderewski** (Ignacy Jan), **Rubinstein** (Anton), **Rubinstein** (Artur), **Stradivari** (Antonio), **Villa-Lobos** (Heitor)
11 **Theodorakis** (Mikis)
12 **Rostropovich** (Mstislav)
➤ See also MUSIC

## musing
07 reverie
08 dreaming, thinking
10 brown study, cogitation, meditation, rumination
11 cerebration, daydreaming
13 contemplation, introspection, woolgathering

## muss
06 ruffle, tousle
08 dishevel
10 disarrange
11 make a mess of

## must
09 essential, necessity, requisite
10 imperative, sine qua non
11 requirement

## mustache, moustache
06 walrus
08 whiskers
09 handlebar, mustachio
10 face fungus

## muster
04 mass, meet
05 group, rally
06 enroll, gather, parade, summon
07 collect, marshal, meeting, round up
08 assemble, summon up
09 gathering
10 assemblage, congregate
12 call together, come together
13 bring together
14 gather together

❑**pass muster**
07 shape up
09 measure up
12 be acceptable, make the grade
15 come up to scratch

## musty
05 fusty, moldy, stale
06 smelly, stuffy
07 airless, decayed
08 mildewed

## mutability
12 alterability
13 permutability
14 changeableness

## mutable
08 changing, variable, volatile
09 alterable
10 changeable, permutable
15 interchangeable

## mutation
06 change
07 anomaly
09 deviation, variation
10 adaptation
12 modification
14 transformation

## mute
03 mum
04 dumb
05 lower
06 dampen, deaden, muffle, silent, stifle
07 aphasic, quieten, silence
08 suppress, tone down, wordless
09 noiseless, voiceless
10 speechless
11 unexpressed

## muted
06 low-key, subtle
07 muffled, stifled, subdued
08 dampened, low-keyed, softened
10 restrained, suppressed

## mutilate
03 cut, mar
04 hack, lame, maim, ruin
05 cut up, spoil
06 damage, impair, injure
07 butcher, disable
08 lacerate
09 disfigure, dismember
11 cut to pieces

## mutilation
06 damage
07 maiming
10 amputation
12 detruncation, dismembering
13 disfigurement

## mutinous
07 riotous
09 insurgent, seditious
10 rebellious, subversive
11 anarchistic, disobedient
13 insubordinate, revolutionary

## mutiny
04 defy, riot
05 rebel
06 resist, revolt, rise up, strike
08 defiance, uprising
09 rebellion
10 revolution
12 disobedience, insurrection

## mutt
03 cur, dog
04 dope
05 dunce, hound, pooch
07 mongrel
09 blockhead

## mutter
04 beef, carp, fuss
05 gripe, whine
06 grouse, mumble, murmur, object, rumble
07 grumble, protest, stutter
08 complain
09 bellyache
14 talk to yourself

## mutual
05 joint
06 common, shared
09 exchanged

## muzzle
03 gag
05 check, choke
06 censor, fetter, stifle
07 inhibit, silence
08 restrain, suppress

## muzzy
04 hazy
05 dazed, faint, fuzzy, tipsy
06 addled, groggy
07 blurred, muddled, unclear
08 confused
09 befuddled, unfocused
10 bewildered, indistinct

## myopic
06 narrow
08 purblind
11 nearsighted, thoughtless
12 narrow-minded, shortsighted

## myriad
04 army, host
05 flood, horde, swarm
06 scores, throng
09 countless, multitude, thousands
11 innumerable

13 multitudinous

## mysterious
04 dark
05 weird
06 arcane, secret, veiled
07 cryptic, obscure, strange
08 abstruse, baffling, mystical, puzzling
09 enigmatic, recondite, secretive
10 mystifying, perplexing
11 inscrutable
12 inexplicable, unfathomable

## mystery
06 enigma, puzzle, riddle, secret
07 problem, secrecy
08 mystique, question
09 ambiguity, conundrum, curiosity, obscurity, reticence, weirdness
11 furtiveness, strangeness
12 question mark
14 inscrutability
15 inexplicability, unfathomability

## mystical
06 arcane, mystic, occult
08 abstruse, baffling, esoteric
09 recondite, spiritual
10 mysterious, paranormal
12 metaphysical, otherworldly, supernatural
13 preternatural
14 transcendental

## mystify
06 baffle, puzzle
07 confuse, perplex
08 bewilder, confound

## mystique
05 charm, magic, spell
06 glamor
07 glamour, mystery, secrecy
08 charisma
11 fascination

## myth
03 lie
04 saga, tale
05 fable, story
06 legend
07 fantasy, fiction, untruth
08 folk tale
09 fairy tale, invention, tall story
10 fairy story

## mythical
06 fabled, made-up
07 fantasy, pretend
08 fabulous, fanciful, invented
09 fairy-tale, fantastic, imaginary, legendary
10 fictitious

11 make-believe, nonexistent

➤ *Mythical places include*:
03 Dis, Hel
04 Hell, Styx (River)
05 Argos, Babel, Hades, Lethe (River), Pluto, Thule
06 Albion, Asgard, Avalon, Heaven, Narnia, Utgard
07 Alfheim, Arcadia, Camelot, Elysium, Lemuria, Nirvana
08 Amazonia, Atlantis, El Dorado, Niflheim, Paradise, Valhalla, Vanaheim
09 Cockaigne, Fairyland, Purgatory, River Styx
10 River Lethe
11 Ultima Thule
13 Jewel Mountain, The Underworld
15 The Garden of Eden, The Isle of Avalon, The Tower of Babel
➤ See also MYTHOLOGY

## mythological
06 fabled, mythic
08 fabulous
09 fairytale, folkloric, legendary
10 fictitious

➤ *Names of mythological creatures and spirits*:
03 elf, imp, jin, orc, roc
04 djin, faun, fury, jinn, ogre, yeti
05 demon, devil, djinn, dryad, fairy, genie, ghost, ghoul, gnome, golem, harpy, lamia, naiad, nymph, pixie, satyr, shade, Siren, sylph, troll
06 bunyip, dibbuk, djinni, djinny, dragon, dybbuk, Furies, goblin, Gorgon, kraken, Lilith, Medusa, merman, nereid, ogress, Sphinx, sprite, wivern, wyvern
07 banshee, Bigfoot, brownie, centaur, Chimera, Cyclops, gremlin, griffin, lorelei, mermaid, Pegasus, phoenix, unicorn, vampire, windigo
08 basilisk, Cerberus, Minotaur, succubus, werewolf
09 hobgoblin, sasquatch
10 cockatrice, hippogriff, leprechaun, sea serpent
11 hippocampus
15 Loch Ness monster
17 abominable snowman
➤ See also MYTHOLOGY

## mythology
04 lore
05 tales
06 legend
08 folklore

09 folk tales, tradition
10 traditions
➤ See also GOD, GODDESS;
   GRACE; LEGEND; MUSE;
   MYTHICAL; MYTHOLOGICAL;
   SAGE

---

▶ *Celtic mythology*:
03 Anu, Lug
04 Bran, Danu, Lugh, Ogma
05 Balor, Boann, Dagda, Macha,
   Maeve, Neman, Nuada,
   Oisin, Pwyll
06 Brigit, Danaan, Deidre,
   Imbolc, Isolde, Ogmios,
   Ossian
07 Beltane, Branwen, Brighid,
   Samhain, Tristan
08 Manannan, Morrigan,
   Rhiannon, Tir nan-Og
09 Cernunnos, Conchobar
10 Cú Chulainn
11 Finn mac Cool
14 Bran the Blessed, Finn mac
   Cumhail

---

▶ *Characters from Greek
mythology*:
02 Io
04 Ajax, Dido, Echo, Leda, Leto
05 Atlas, Chloe, Circe, Creon,
   Danae, Helen, Hydra, Irene,
   Jason, Kreon, Laius, Lamia,
   Medea, Midas, Minos,
   Niobe, Orion, Priam
06 Aeneas, Aeolus, Amazon,
   Atreus, Cadmus, Castor,

Charon, Chiron, Cronus,
Daphne, Dryads, Europa,
Europe, Furies, Hector,
Hecuba, Icarus, Kronos,
Medusa, Megara, Memnon,
Naiads, Nestor, Nymphs,
Oreads, Phoebe, Pollux,
Satyrs, Scylla, Semele, Sileni,
Sirens, Syrinx, Titans, Triton,
Typhon
07 Actaeon, Arachne, Ariadne,
   Calypso, Chimera, Cyclops,
   Daphnis, Diomede, Electra,
   Galatea, Gorgons, Griffin,
   Gryphon, Harpies, Jocasta,
   Laocoon, Lapiths, Maenads,
   Nereids, Oceanus, Oedipus,
   Orestes, Orpheus, Pandora,
   Pegasus, Perseus, Phaedra,
   Silenus, Theseus, Titania,
   Troilus, Ulysses
08 Achilles, Alcestis, Alcmaeon,
   Antigone, Arethusa,
   Atalanta, Basilisk, Centaurs,
   Cerberus, Chimaera,
   Cressida, Cyclopes,
   Daedalus, Diomedes,
   Endymion, Eurydice,
   Ganymede, Gigantes,
   Heracles, Hercules,
   Hyperion, Lycurgus,
   Meleager, Menelaus,
   Minotaur, Nausicaa,
   Odysseus, Pasiphae,
   Penelope, Phaethon,
   Pleiades, Sisyphus, Tantalus,

Tiresias
09 Agamemnon, Andromeda,
   Argonauts, Autolycus,
   Cassandra, Charybdis,
   Deucalion, Lotophagi,
   Myrmidons, Narcissus,
   Patroclus, Pygmalion,
   Semiramis
10 Amphitryon, Andromache,
   Cassiopeia, Cockatrice,
   Erechtheus, Hamadryads,
   Hesperides, Hippolytus,
   Iphigeneia, Polyphemus,
   Procrustes, Prometheus,
   Telemachus
11 Bellerophon, Lotus-eaters
12 Clytemnestra, Hyperboreans
14 Hero and Leander

---

▶ *Characters from Roman
mythology*:
04 Juno, Luna, Mars
05 Ceres, Diana, Janus, Lamia,
   Lares, Manes, Remus, Sibyl,
   Venus
06 Apollo, Daphne, Saturn,
   Vulcan
07 Bacchus, Fortuna, Jupiter,
   Latinus, Lemures, Lucrece,
   Mercury, Minerva, Neptune,
   Penates, Romulus, Salacia,
   Sibylla, Tarpeia
08 Lucretia
10 Rhea Silvia, Rhea Sylvia

**nab**
04 grab, nail
05 catch, seize
06 arrest, collar, snatch
07 capture
09 apprehend

**nabob**
03 VIP
06 bigwig, tycoon
08 luminary
09 celebrity, personage
11 billionaire, millionaire

**nadir**
06 bottom, depths
08 low point
10 all-time low, rock bottom
11 lowest point

**nag**
03 bug, rip, vex
04 hack, jade, moan, plug
05 harry, horse, scold, worry
06 badger, berate, bother, harass, hassle, niggle, pester, pick on, plague
07 henpeck, torment, upbraid
08 complain, irritate, keep on at
09 racehorse

**nagging**
06 aching
07 moaning, painful
08 critical, niggling, scolding, shrewish, worrying
10 continuous, irritating, nitpicking, persistent

**nail**
03 fix, nab, pin
04 brad, grab, tack
05 catch, clout, rivet, seize, spike, sprig, talon
06 arrest, attach, collar, corner, fasten, hammer, secure, skewer
07 capture, pin down, toenail
08 fastener, identify, sparable
09 apprehend
10 fingernail

**naïve**
04 open
05 frank, green
06 candid, jejune, simple
07 artless, natural

08 gullible, innocent, wide-eyed
09 childlike, credulous, guileless, ingenuous, unworldly
10 unaffected
12 unsuspecting, unsuspicious
13 born yesterday, inexperienced
15 unsophisticated

**naïvety**
09 credulity, greenness, innocence
10 immaturity, simplicity
11 artlessness, gullibility
12 inexperience

**naked**
04 bald, bare, nude, open
05 overt, plain, stark
06 barren, patent, simple
07 blatant, denuded, glaring
08 disrobed, flagrant, in the raw, stripped, treeless
09 au naturel, grassless, in the buff, unadorned, unclothed, uncovered, undressed
10 stark-naked, vulnerable
11 undisguised, unprotected
12 not a stitch on
13 with nothing on
15 in the altogether

**nakedness**
06 nudity
07 the buff, undress
08 baldness, bareness
09 plainness, starkness
10 barrenness, simplicity

**namby-pamby**
04 prim, weak
05 sissy, vapid, weedy
06 anemic, feeble, prissy
07 insipid, mawkish
09 spineless
10 wishy-washy
11 sentimental

**name**
03 dub, tag, VIP
04 call, cite, fame, hero, note, pick, star, term
05 brand, honor, label, style, title

06 bigwig, choose, esteem, expert, handle, renown, repute, select
07 appoint, baptize, entitle, epithet, mention, moniker, specify
08 big noise, christen, classify, cognomen, eminence, identify, luminary, monicker, nickname, nominate
09 a somebody, celebrity, character, designate, dignitary, trademark
10 commission, popularity, prominence, reputation
11 appellation, designation, distinction

► *Boys' names:*
02 Al, Cy, Ed
03 Abe, Alf, Ali, Ben, Bob, Dan, Den, Don, Gil, Gus, Guy, Hew, Huw, Ian, Ike, Ira, Jay, Jem, Jim, Joe, Jon, Ken, Kit, Lee, Len, Leo, Lew, Mat, Max, Nat, Ned, Pat, Rab, Rae, Ray, Reg, Rex, Rob, Rod, Roy, Sam, Sol, Ted, Tim, Tom, Vic
04 Adam, Alan, Alec, Aled, Alex, Algy, Alun, Andy, Bart, Bert, Bill, Bram, Carl, Chad, Clem, Dave, Davy, Dean, Dick, Dirk, Doug, Drew, Eric, Evan, Ezra, Fred, Gabe, Gary, Gene, Glen, Glyn, Hank, Huey, Hugh, Hugo, Iain, Ivan, Jack, Jake, Jeff, Jock, Joel, Joey, John, Jose, Josh, Joss, Jude, Karl, Kirk, Kurt, Kyle, Luis, Luke, Mark, Matt, Mick, Mike, Neal, Neil, Nick, Noel, Owen, Paul, Pete, Phil, Rick, Rolf, Rory, Ross, Ryan, Saul, Sean, Seth, Theo, Toby, Tony, Walt, Will, Zach, Zack
05 Aaron, Abram, Adnan, Alfie, Allan, Allen, Angus, Archy, Barry, Basil, Benny, Billy, Bobby, Boris, Brent, Brett, Brian, Bruce, Bruno, Bryan, Caleb, Cecil, Chaim, Chris, Chuck, Claud, Clint, Clive, Clyde, Colin, Craig, Cyril, Cyrus, Damon, Danny, David, Davie, Denis, Denny, Derek,

Dicky, Dilip, Donal, Duane, Dylan, Eddie, Edgar, Edwin, Elroy, Elton, Elvis, Enoch, Ernie, Errol, Ethan, Felix, Floyd, Frank, Garry, Gavin, Geoff, Gerry, Giles, Glenn, Harry, Henry, Homer, Isaac, Jacob, James, Jamie, Jason, Jerry, Jesse, Jimmy, Keith, Kenny, Kevin, Lance, Larry, Leigh, Lenny, Leroy, Lewis, Lloyd, Logan, Louie, Louis, Lucas, Manny, Micky, Miles, Moses, Myles, Neale, Neddy, Nicky, Nigel, Ollie, Orson, Oscar, Ozzie, Paddy, Percy, Perry, Peter, Piers, Ralph, Randy, Ricky, Robin, Roddy, Roger, Rowan, Rufus, Sammy, Sandy, Scott, Shaun, Shawn, Silas, Simon, Solly, Steve, Teddy, Terry, Tommy, Tyler, Waldo, Wally, Wayne, Willy

06 Adrian, Albert, Alexei, Alexis, Alfred, Andrew, Antony, Archie, Arnold, Arthur, Ashley, Aubrey, Austin, Barney, Bernie, Bertie, Calvin, Caspar, Cedric, Clancy, Claude, Connor, Conrad, Damian, Damien, Daniel, Darren, Dennis, Dermot, Dicken, Dickie, Dickon, Donald, Donnie, Dougal, Dudley, Dugald, Duggie, Duncan, Dustin, Edmund, Edward, Elijah, Ernest, Eugene, Fergus, Freddy, Gareth, George, Gerald, Gerard, Gideon, Gordon, Graham, Gussie, Harold, Harvey, Hayden, Hector, Herbie, Horace, Howard, Hubert, Hughie, Hunter, Isaiah, Israel, Jarvis, Jasper, Jeremy, Jerome, Jervis, Jethro, Jordan, Joseph, Joshua, Julian, Julius, Justin, Kelvin, Laurie, Leslie, Lester, Lionel, Lucius, Luther, Marcel, Marcus, Marlon, Martin, Martyn, Marvin, Melvin, Melvyn, Mervyn, Milton, Morgan, Morris, Murray, Nathan, Nichol, Norman, Oliver, Oswald, Pearce, Philip, Pierce, Randal, Reggie, Reuben, Richie, Robert, Rodney, Roland, Ronald, Rudolf, Rupert, Samuel, Sidney, Steven, Stevie, Stuart, Sydney, Thomas, Timmie, Tobias, Trevor, Tyrone, Vernon,

Victor, Virgil, Walter, Willie
07 Abraham, Ambrose, Anthony, Auberon, Barnaby, Bernard, Bertram, Brandon, Brendan, Cameron, Chandra, Charles, Charley, Charlie, Christy, Clement, Derrick, Desmond, Dominic, Douglas, Eustace, Francis, Frankie, Freddie, Gabriel, Gilbert, Grahame, Herbert, Humphry, Jeffrey, Johnnie, Kenneth, Leonard, Leopold, Lindsay, Lindsey, Malcolm, Matthew, Maurice, Michael, Neville, Nicolas, Orlando, Patrick, Phillip, Quentin, Quintin, Quinton, Randall, Randolf, Raymond, Reynold, Richard, Rudolph, Russell, Shelley, Solomon, Stanley, Stephen, Stewart, Terence, Timothy, Tristan, Vaughan, Vincent, Wilfred, Wilfrid, William, Winston, Zachary
08 Alasdair, Alastair, Algernon, Alistair, Augustus, Barnabas, Benedick, Benjamin, Beverley, Christie, Clarence, Clifford, Emmanuel, Frederic, Geoffrey, Humphrey, Jonathan, Jonathon, Lancelot, Laurence, Lawrence, Matthias, Meredith, Nicholas, Perceval, Percival, Randolph, Reginald, Roderick, Terrance, Theodore, Tristram
09 Alexander, Archibald, Augustine, Christian, Ferdinand, Frederick, Launcelot, Nathaniel, Sebastian, Siegfried, Sylvester
10 Maximilian
11 Bartholomew, Christopher

► *Girls' names*:
02 Di, Jo, Mo
03 Ada, Ali, Amy, Ann, Bea, Bee, Bel, Bet, Cis, Deb, Dee, Dot, Emm, Eva, Eve, Fay, Flo, Gay, Ida, Ivy, Jan, Jay, Jen, Joy, Kay, Kim, Kit, Lea, Lee, Liz, Lou, Mae, May, Meg, Mia, Nan, Pat, Peg, Ria, Ros, Roz, Sal, Sue, Val, Viv, Zoe
04 Abby, Addy, Aggy, Alex, Ally, Alma, Anna, Anne, Babs, Bess, Beth, Cara, Caro, Cass, Cher, Cleo, Cora, Dana, Dawn, Dian, Dora, Edie, Edna, Ella, Emma, Emmy, Erin,

Evie, Faye, Gail, Gale, Gaye, Gert, Gina, Gwen, Hope, Ines, Inez, Inga, Inge, Iris, Irma, Jade, Jane, Jean, Jill, Joan, Jodi, Jody, Joey, Joni, Judy, June, Kate, Katy, Kaye, Lara, Leah, Lena, Lily, Lisa, Lise, Liza, Lois, Lola, Lucy, Lynn, Mary, Maud, Moll, Mona, Myra, Nell, Nina, Nita, Noel, Nora, Olga, Page, Prue, Rita, Rona, Rosa, Rose, Ruby, Ruth, Sara, Sian, Susy, Suzy, Tess, Thea, Tina, Toni, Trix, Vera, Vita, Zara, Zena
05 Adela, Aggie, Agnes, Alice, Allie, Amber, Angel, Angie, Anita, Annie, April, Avril, Becky, Bella, Belle, Beryl, Bessy, Betsy, Betty, Biddy, Bunty, Candy, Carla, Carly, Carol, Cathy, Celia, Chloe, Chris, Cindy, Cissy, Clara, Clare, Coral, Daisy, Debby, Debra, Della, Diana, Diane, Dinah, Dolly, Donna, Doris, Edith, Effie, Eliza, Ellen, Ellie, Elsie, Emily, Emmie, Erica, Ethel, Faith, Fanny, Farah, Fleur, Flora, Freda, Gayle, Gemma, Ginny, Golda, Grace, Greta, Haley, Hatty, Hazel, Heidi, Helen, Helga, Hetty, Hilda, Holly, Honor, Irena, Irene, Ivana, Jamie, Janet, Janis, Jemma, Jenna, Jenny, Jessy, Jinny, Jodie, Joely, Josie, Joyce, Julia, Julie, Karen, Karin, Karla, Kathy, Katie, Kayla, Kelly, Kerry, Kitty, Kylie, Laura, Leigh, Leila, Leona, Letty, Libby, Linda, Lindy, Lorna, Louie, Lucia, Lydia, Lynda, Lynne, Mabel, Madge, Mamie, Mandy, Margo, Maria, Marie, Maude, Mavis, Megan, Mercy, Meryl, Moira, Molly, Morna, Myrna, Nadia, Nancy, Nelly, Nesta, Netty, Nicky, Norah, Norma, Olive, Oprah, Paige, Pansy, Patsy, Patty, Paula, Pearl, Peggy, Penny, Polly, Renée, Rhoda, Rhona, Robin, Robyn, Rosie, Sadie, Sally, Sarah, Sasha, Sibyl, Sindy, Sonia, Sonya, Sophy, Stacy, Susan, Susie, Sybil, Tammy, Tania, Tanya, Tessa, Thora, Tilly, Tracy, Trina, Trish, Trixy, Trudy, Unity, Viola, Wanda, Wendy, Wilma, Zelda
06 Adella, Agatha, Aileen, Alexia, Alexis, Alicia, Alison,

Althea, Alyssa, Amanda, Amelia, Andrea, Angela, Anneka, Annika, Anthea, Aretha, Ashley, Astrid, Audrey, Auriel, Auriol, Aurora, Aurore, Averil, Barbie, Bertha, Bessie, Bianca, Blanch, Bonnie, Brenda, Bridie, Brigid, Brigit, Briony, Carina, Carmel, Carmen, Carola, Carole, Carrie, Cassie, Cathie, Cecily, Celina, Cherie, Cherry, Cicely, Cissie, Claire, Connie, Daphne, Davina, Deanna, Deanne, Debbie, Denise, Dianne, Dionne, Doreen, Dottie, Eartha, Edwina, Eileen, Elaine, Elinor, Eloisa, Eloise, Elvira, Esther, Eunice, Evelyn, Evonne, Frieda, Gertie, Gladys, Glenda, Gloria, Goldie, Gracie, Gwenda, Hailey, Hannah, Hattie, Hayley, Helena, Hermia, Hester, Hilary, Imelda, Imogen, Ingrid, Isabel, Isobel, Janice, Jeanie, Jemima, Jennie, Jessie, Joanie, Joanna, Joanne, Joelle, Joleen, Jolene, Jordon, Judith, Juliet, Karina, Laurel, Lauren, Laurie, Leanne, Leonie, Lesley, Lettie, Lilian, Lisbet, Lizzie, Lolita, Lottie, Louisa, Louise, Lynsey, Maggie, Maisie, Marcia, Marian, Marina, Marion, Marsha, Martha, Mattie, Maxine, Melody, Meriel, Millie, Minnie, Miriam, Monica, Morgan, Muriel, Myriam, Myrtle, Nadine, Nellie, Nicola, Nicole, Noelle, Noreen, Odette, Olivia, Pamela, Petula, Phoebe, Rachel, Raquel, Regina, Rhonda, Rosina, Roxana, Roxane, Sabina, Sabine, Sandra, Selina, Serena, Sharon, Sheela, Sheena, Sheila, Sherry, Sheryl, Silvia, Simone, Sophia, Sophie, Stacey, Stella, Sylvia, Tamara, Taylor, Teresa, Thelma, Tracey, Tricia, Trisha, Trixie, Ulrica, Ursula, Violet, Vivian, Vivien, Winnie, Winona, Yasmin, Yvette, Yvonne

07 Abigail, Annabel, Annette, Antonia, Augusta, Barbara, Beatrix, Belinda, Bernice, Bethany, Bettina, Blanche,

Brianna, Brianne, Bridget, Camilla, Candace, Candice, Candida, Carolyn, Cecilia, Chandra, Charity, Charley, Chelsea, Chelsey, Christy, Clarice, Claudia, Colette, Colleen, Corinna, Corinne, Crystal, Cynthia, Daniela, Deborah, Deirdre, Dolores, Dorothy, Eleanor, Emerald, Estella, Estelle, Eugenia, Eugénie, Felicia, Floella, Frances, Frankie, Georgia, Georgie, Giselle, Gwenyth, Gwyneth, Harriet, Heather, Heloise, Hillary, Isadora, Janetta, Janette, Jasmine, Jeannie, Jessica, Jillian, Jocelin, Jocelyn, Josette, Juliana, Justina, Justine, Kaitlyn, Kathryn, Katrina, Lavinia, Leonora, Letitia, Lettice, Lillian, Lillias, Lindsay, Lindsey, Linette, Lisbeth, Lizbeth, Loretta, Lucilla, Lucille, Lucinda, Lynette, Madison, Madonna, Margery, Marilyn, Marjory, Marlene, Martina, Martine, Matilda, Maureen, Melanie, Melissa, Mildred, Miranda, Nanette, Natalia, Natalie, Natasha, Nichola, Nigella, Ninette, Ophelia, Pandora, Paulina, Pauline, Phyllis, Queenie, Rachael, Rebecca, Roberta, Rosabel, Rosalie, Rosanna, Roxanne, Sabrina, Saffron, Shelagh, Shelley, Shirley, Silvana, Susanna, Tabitha, Theresa, Tiffany, Valerie, Vanessa, Venetia, Yolanda

08 Adelaide, Adrianne, Adrienne, Angelica, Angelina, Arabella, Beatrice, Berenice, Beverley, Caroline, Charlene, Charmian, Chrissie, Christie, Clarinda, Clarissa, Claudine, Cordelia, Courtney, Cressida, Daniella, Danielle, Dorothea, Eleanore, Emmeline, Felicity, Florence, Francine, Georgina, Germaine, Gertrude, Griselda, Isabella, Jeanette, Jennifer, Joceline, Joscelin, Katerina, Kathleen, Kimberly, Lauretta, Lorraine, Madeline, Margaret, Marjorie, Mathilda, Meredith, Michaela, Michelle, Patience, Patricia, Paulette, Penelope,

Primrose, Prudence, Prunella, Rosalind, Rosamond, Rosamund, Roseanna, Roseanne, Rosemary, Samantha, Scarlett, Susannah, Theodora, Veronica, Victoria, Virginia, Winifred

09 Alexandra, Anastasia, Annabella, Annabelle, Cassandra, Catharine, Catherina, Catherine, Charlotte, Charmaine, Christina, Christine, Claudette, Constance, Elisabeth, Elizabeth, Frederica, Gabrielle, Genevieve, Georgette, Georgiana, Geraldine, Guinevere, Gwendolen, Henrietta, Jaqueline, Jeannette, Josephine, Katharine, Katherine, Kimberley, Mackenzie, Madeleine, Millicent, Nicolette, Priscilla, Sigourney, Stephanie, Thomasina

10 Antoinette, Bernadette, Christabel, Clementina, Clementine, Jacqueline, Wilhelmina

**named**
05 cited
06 called, chosen, dubbed, picked, styled, termed, titled
07 branded, labeled
08 baptized, entitled
09 appointed, mentioned, nominated, specified
10 christened, classified, designated, identified, singled out
11 by the name of, trademarked
12 commissioned

**nameless**
07 unknown, unnamed
08 untitled
09 anonymous, unheard-of, unlabeled
10 innominate
11 unspecified, unutterable
12 undesignated, unidentified
13 indescribable, inexpressible, unmentionable

**namely**
02 i.e.
03 viz.
05 to wit
06 that is
11 that is to say
12 in other words, specifically

**nap**
03 nod
04 doze, fuzz, pile, rest, shag
05 fiber, grain, sleep, weave
06 catnap, siesta, snooze
07 drop off, lie down, texture
10 forty winks, light sleep
12 sleep lightly
14 get some shuteye, have forty winks

**narcissism**
06 vanity
07 conceit, egotism
08 egomania, self-love
10 self-regard
13 egocentricity
16 self-centeredness

**narcissistic**
04 vain
09 conceited, egotistic
10 egocentric, self-loving
11 egomaniacal
12 self-centered

**narcotic**
04 drug
06 downer, opiate
07 anodyne, calming, numbing
08 hypnotic, sedative
09 analgesic, somnolent, soporific
10 anesthetic, painkiller, palliative, stupefying
11 painkilling
12 sleeping pill, stupefacient, tranquilizer
13 sleep inducing

**narrate**
04 read, tell
06 recite, relate, report, set out
07 explain, portray, recount
08 describe, rehearse, set forth

**narration**
04 tale
05 story
06 detail, report, sketch
07 account, history, telling
09 chronicle, portrayal, recountal, rehearsal, statement, voice-over
11 description, explanation
12 storytelling

**narrative**
04 tale
05 story
06 detail, report, sketch
07 account, history, reading
09 portrayal, statement
11 description

**narrator**
06 author, writer

08 annalist, reporter
09 describer, raconteur
10 anecdotist, chronicler
11 commentator, storyteller

**narrow**
04 fine, slim, thin, true
05 close, limit, petty, rigid, small, spare, taper, tight
06 biased, lessen, reduce, strict
07 bigoted, cramped, insular, limited, precise, tighten
08 confined, diminish, dogmatic, exiguous, restrict, simplify, tapering
09 constrict, hidebound
10 attenuated, intolerant, prejudiced, restricted
11 constricted, reactionary, small-minded, strait-laced
12 circumscribe, conservative, narrow-minded
13 dyed-in-the-wool

**narrowing**
08 stenosis, tapering, thinning
11 attenuation, contraction
12 constipation, constriction

**narrowly**
04 just
06 barely
07 closely, exactly
08 only just, scarcely, strictly
09 carefully, precisely
10 by a whisker
15 by a hair's breadth

**narrow-minded**
05 petty, rigid
07 bigoted, die-hard, insular
09 exclusive, hidebound, jaundiced, parochial
10 entrenched, inflexible, intolerant, prejudiced
11 opinionated, petty minded, reactionary, small-minded
12 conservative, unreasonable
13 dyed-in-the-wool

**narrowness**
07 bigotry
08 nearness, rigidity, thinness
09 prejudice, tightness
10 insularity, limitation
11 attenuation, slenderness
12 conservatism, constriction
13 exclusiveness
15 small-mindedness

**narrows**
05 sound
07 channel, passage, straits

**nascent**
05 young
06 rising

07 budding, growing
08 evolving, naissant
09 advancing, beginning, embryonic, incipient
10 burgeoning, developing

**nastiness**
05 filth, spite
06 malice
08 foulness, impurity
09 dirtiness, pollution
10 filthiness, smuttiness
11 malevolence, viciousness
12 horribleness, spitefulness, unsavoriness
13 offensiveness
14 unpleasantness

**nasty**
04 blue, foul, mean, rank, vile
05 awful, cruel, dirty, foggy, grave, rainy, yucky
06 filthy, grotty, odious, ribald, smutty, stormy, tricky, unkind
07 hateful, noisome, obscene, serious, squalid, vicious
08 alarming, horrible, indecent, polluted, spiteful, worrying
09 dangerous, difficult, malicious, obnoxious, offensive, repellent, repugnant, repulsive, revolting, sickening
10 disgusting, malevolent, malodorous, unpleasant
11 bad tempered, distasteful
12 disagreeable, pornographic
13 objectionable

**nation**
04 land, race
05 realm, state, tribe
06 people
07 country, kingdom, society
10 population

**national**
05 civic, civil, state
06 native, public, social
07 citizen, federal, subject
08 domestic, internal, resident
10 inhabitant, nationwide
11 countrywide
12 governmental

▶ *Names of National Monuments*:
05 Tonto
06 Navajo
07 El Morro, Wupatki
08 Cabrillo, Colorado, Dinosaur, Lava Beds, Ocmulgee, Tuzigoot
09 Aniakchak, Bandelier, El Malpais, Fort Union, Homestead, Hovenweep,

Jewel Cave, Muir Woods, Pinnacles, Pipestone
10 Aztec Ruins, Chiricahua, Fort Sumter, Petroglyph, Pipe Spring, White Sands, Yucca House
11 Cedar Breaks, Devils Tower, Fort McHenry, Fort Pulaski, Fort Stanwix, Fossil Butte, Hohokam Pima, Oregon Caves, Russell Cave, Scotts Bluff
12 Effigy Mounds, Fort Matanzas, Grand Portage, Poverty Point, Walnut Canyon
13 Castle Clinton, Congaree Swamp, Fort Frederica, Little Big Horn, Rainbow Bridge
14 Buck Island Reef, Canyon de Chelly, Capulin Volcano, Devils Postpile, Great Sand Dunes, Natural Bridges, Timpanogos Cave
15 Agate Fossil Beds, Cape Krusenstern, Casa Grande Ruins, Montezuma Castle, Organ Pipe Cactus, Statue of Liberty
16 Craters of the Moon

➤ *Names of National Parks*:
04 Zion
06 Acadia, Arches, Denali, Katmal
07 Big Bend, Glacier, Olympic, Redwood, Saquaro, Sequola
08 Badlands, Biscayne, Wind cave
09 Haleakala, Lake Clark, Mesa Verde, Voyageurs
10 Crater Lake, Everglades, Glacier Bay, Grand Teton, Great Basin, Hot Springs, Isle Royale, Joshua Tree, Shenandoah
11 Black Canyon, Bryce Canyon, Canyonlands, Capitol Reef, Death Valley, Dry Tortugas, Grand Canyon, Kenai Fjords, Kings Canyon, Kobuk Valley, Mammoth Cave, Yellowstone
12 Mount Rainier
13 American Samoa, North Cascades, Rocky Mountain, Virgin Islands
14 Channel Islands, Lassen Volcanic
15 Carlsbad Caverns, Hawaii Volcanoes, Petrified Forest, Wrangell-St. Elias
16 Gates of the Arctic

**nationalism**
08 jingoism
10 allegiance, chauvinism, patriotism, xenophobia

**nationalistic**
05 loyal
09 patriotic
10 jingoistic, xenophobic
12 chauvinistic, ethnocentric

**nationality**
04 clan, race
05 birth, tribe
06 nation

**nationwide**
05 state
08 national
10 widespread
11 countrywide
12 coast-to-coast

**native**
04 home
05 local, natal
06 inborn, inbred, mother
07 citizen, connate, natural
08 domestic, inherent, original
09 aborigine, homegrown, inherited, intuitive
10 aboriginal, autochthon, congenital, hereditary, indigenous, vernacular
11 instinctive
13 autochthonous

**Native American**
06 Indian
14 American Indian
➤ See also AMERICAN

**nativity**
05 birth
08 delivery
10 childbirth
11 parturition

**natty**
04 chic, neat, trim
05 ritzy, smart
06 dapper, snazzy, spruce
07 elegant, stylish

**natural**
03 raw
04 open, pure, real
05 frank, plain, usual, whole
06 candid, common, inborn, inbred, innate, native, normal, simple, virgin
07 artless, built-in, connate, genuine, organic, routine, sincere, typical, unmixed
08 everyday, inherent, ordinary
09 authentic, guileless, ingenuous, inherited, intuitive, unrefined

10 congenital, indigenous, unaffected
11 instinctive, spontaneous, unprocessed
12 additive free, chemical free, run-of-the-mill
13 unpretentious
15 unsophisticated

**naturalist**
08 botanist
09 biologist, Darwinist, ecologist, zoologist
12 evolutionist
13 life scientist
15 conservationist

**naturalistic**
07 factual, graphic, natural
08 lifelike, real-life
09 realistic
10 true-to-life
12 photographic

**naturalize**
05 adapt, adopt
06 accept
08 accustom
09 acclimate, habituate, introduce
10 assimilate
11 acclimatize, domesticate, familiarize, incorporate
14 make a citizen of

**naturally**
05 natch
06 simply
08 candidly, normally, of course
09 artlessly, certainly, genuinely, obviously, sincerely, typically
10 absolutely
11 ingenuously
13 instinctively, spontaneously

**naturalness**
06 purity
07 realism
08 openness, pureness
09 frankness, plainness, sincerity, wholeness
10 candidness, simplicity
11 artlessness, spontaneity
13 ingenuousness
14 unaffectedness
15 spontaneousness

**nature**
04 kind, mood, sort, type
05 earth, humor, stamp, style, world
06 makeup, temper
07 country, essence, scenery
08 creation, identity, universe
09 character, chemistry
11 countryside, description, disposition, environment,

mother earth, personality, temperament
12 constitution, mother nature
14 natural history

**naught**
03 nil
04 zero
05 zilch
06 nought
07 nothing
11 nothingness

**naughty**
03 bad
04 blue, lewd
05 bawdy
06 risqué, smutty, unruly
07 defiant, obscene, playful, roguish, wayward
08 indecent, perverse
10 refractory
11 disobedient, misbehaving, mischievous
12 badly behaved, exasperating, incorrigible
13 undisciplined

**nausea**
06 hatred, puking
07 disgust, gagging
08 retching, sickness, vomiting
09 revulsion
10 abhorrence, queasiness, repugnance, throwing up
11 airsickness, biliousness, carsickness, seasickness
14 motion sickness, travel sickness
15 morning sickness

**nauseate**
05 repel
06 offend, revolt, sicken
07 disgust, turn off
08 gross out, make sick
15 turn your stomach

**nauseating**
06 odious
09 offensive, repellent, repugnant, repulsive, revolting, sickening
10 detestable, disgusting

**nauseous**
03 ill
04 sick
06 queasy
07 airsick, carsick, seasick
09 nauseated
10 travel sick

**nautical**
05 naval
07 boating, oceanic, sailing
08 maritime, seagoing, yachting

**naval**
03 sea
06 marine
08 maritime, nautical, seagoing
09 seafaring

**navel**
03 hub
06 center, middle
08 omphalos
09 umbilical, umbilicus
11 bellybutton

**navigable**
04 open
05 clear
08 passable
09 crossable, unblocked
10 negotiable

**navigate**
04 helm, plan, plot, sail
05 drive, guide, pilot, steer
06 cruise, direct, voyage
07 journey, skipper
08 maneuver
09 negotiate

**navigation**
07 guiding, sailing
08 cruising, guidance, nautical, piloting, steering, voyaging
10 seamanship
12 helmsmanship

▶ *Navigational aids:*
03 GPS, log
05 chart, Loran, pilot, radar
07 compass, sextant
08 bell buoy, dividers, VHF radio
09 lightship
10 depth gauge, echo ranger, lighthouse, marker buoy
11 chronometer, echo sounder, gyrocompass
13 nautical table
15 astronavigation, magnetic compass

**navigator**
05 pilot
06 seaman
07 mariner
08 helmsman

**navy**
04 blue
05 fleet, ships
06 armada
08 dark blue, flotilla, warships

**nay**
02 no
04 nope
06 in fact, indeed, really
08 actually, to be sure

**near**
04 akin, dear, like
05 alike, close, handy, local
06 at hand, coming, nearby
07 close by, close to, looming
08 approach, imminent, intimate
09 alongside, close in on, immediate, impending
10 accessible, come closer, come toward, comparable, contiguous, draw near to, move toward, not far away
11 approaching, bordering on, forthcoming, get closer to, in the offing, neighboring, within reach
12 contiguous to
13 advance toward
15 at close quarters

❑**near thing**
08 near miss
09 close call
10 close shave
11 nasty moment
12 narrow escape

**nearby**
04 near
05 close, handy
10 accessible, not far away
11 close at hand, neighboring, within reach
13 in the vicinity
14 on your doorstep
15 at close quarters

**nearly**
06 all but, almost
07 close to, closely, roughly
08 as good as, well-nigh
09 just about, virtually
10 more or less
11 practically
13 approximately

**nearness**
08 dearness, intimacy, vicinity
09 closeness, immediacy, imminence, proximity
11 familiarity, propinquity
13 accessibility

**nearsighted**
06 myopic
08 purblind
09 half-blind
12 shortsighted

**neat**
03 apt
04 deft, nice, pure, tidy, trim
05 handy, natty, nifty, smart
06 adroit, clever, dainty, dapper, nimble, simple, spruce, superb, wicked

**07** compact, elegant, ordered, orderly, unmixed
**08** skillful, straight, terrific, well made
**09** admirable, dexterous, efficient, ingenious, marvelous, organized, shipshape, undiluted, wonderful
**10** convenient
**11** well ordered
**12** spick-and-span, user-friendly, well designed
**13** unadulterated
**15** in apple-pie order

**neaten**
**04** edge, tidy, trim
**05** clean, groom
**06** tidy up
**07** arrange, clean up, smarten
**08** round off, spruce up
**09** smarten up
**10** straighten
**12** straighten up

**neatly**
**05** aptly
**06** deftly, nicely, nimbly, tidily
**07** adeptly, agilely, smartly
**08** adroitly, cleverly, daintily
**09** elegantly, precisely, stylishly
**10** accurately, gracefully
**11** dexterously, efficiently
**12** conveniently, methodically
**14** systematically

**neatness**
**05** grace, skill, style
**07** agility, aptness
**08** accuracy, deftness, elegance, niceness, tidiness
**09** adeptness, dexterity, precision, smartness
**10** adroitness, cleverness, daintiness, efficiency, nimbleness, spruceness
**11** orderliness, stylishness
**14** methodicalness

**nebulous**
**03** dim
**04** hazy
**05** fuzzy, misty, vague
**06** cloudy
**07** obscure, shadowy, unclear
**08** abstract, confused, unformed
**09** amorphous, imprecise, shapeless, uncertain
**10** indefinite, indistinct

**necessarily**
**08** of course, perforce
**09** certainly, naturally, therefore
**10** inevitably, willy-nilly

**11** ineluctably, inescapably
**12** by definition, consequently
**13** automatically, axiomatically

**necessary**
**04** sure
**05** vital
**06** needed
**07** certain, crucial, needful
**08** required
**09** de rigueur, essential, mandatory, requisite
**10** compulsory, imperative, inevitable, obligatory
**11** ineluctable, inescapable, unavoidable
**13** indispensable

**necessitate**
**04** need, take
**05** exact, force
**06** compel, demand, entail
**07** call for, involve, require

**necessity**
**04** must, need, want
**06** demand, penury
**09** certainty, essential, indigence, requisite
**10** obligation, sine qua non
**11** desideratum, fundamental, needfulness, requirement
**12** prerequisite

**neck**
**03** pet
**04** kiss, nape
**05** scrag
**06** cervix, scruff, smooch
**07** make out
**08** canoodle

**necklace**
**04** band, torc
**05** beads, chain
**06** choker, gorget, jewels, locket, pearls, string, torque
**07** pendant, rivière

**necromancer**
**05** witch
**06** wizard
**07** diviner, warlock
**08** conjurer, magician, sorcerer
**09** sorceress, spiritist
**12** spiritualist

**necromancy**
**05** magic
**06** hoodoo, voodoo
**07** sorcery
**08** black art, witchery, wizardry
**09** spiritism
**10** black magic, demonology, divination, witchcraft
**12** spiritualism
**13** magical powers

**necropolis**
**07** charnel
**08** boot hill, cemetery, God's acre
**09** graveyard
**10** burial site, churchyard
**11** burial place
**12** burial ground, charnel house

**need**
**04** call, lack, miss, must, want
**06** demand, have to, rely on
**07** call for, pine for, require
**08** depend on, exigency, shortage, yearn for
**09** cry out for, essential, necessity, neediness, requisite
**10** have need of, inadequacy, obligation
**11** be reliant on, desideratum, necessitate, requirement
**12** prerequisite
**13** be compelled to, be dependent on, insufficiency
**14** be desperate for

**◻in need**
**04** poor
**06** hard up
**07** wanting
**08** deprived, indigent
**09** destitute, penniless, penurious
**11** impecunious
**12** impoverished
**13** disadvantaged
**14** on the breadline
**15** poverty-stricken, underprivileged

**needed**
**06** wanted
**07** desired, lacking
**08** required
**09** called for, essential, necessary, requisite
**10** compulsory, obligatory

**needful**
**05** needy, vital
**08** required
**09** necessary, requisite
**10** stipulated

**needle**
**03** irk, nag, nib, pin
**04** bait, barb, goad, hand, rile
**05** annoy, arrow, prick, quill, spike, spine, sting, taunt
**06** bodkin, harass, heckle, marker, nettle, niggle, stylus
**07** bristle, pointer, prickle, provoke, spicula, spicule, torment
**08** irritate, splinter

**needless**
09 aggravate, indicator

**needless**
07 useless
09 pointless, redundant
10 expendable, gratuitous
11 purposeless, superfluous,
    uncalled-for, unnecessary

**needlework**
06 sewing
08 knitting, tapestry
09 fancywork, stitching
10 crocheting, embroidery
11 needlepoint

**needy**
04 poor
06 hard up, in need
07 wanting
08 deprived, indigent
09 destitute, penurious
12 impoverished
15 underprivileged

**ne'er-do-well**
03 bum
05 idler
06 loafer, waster
07 drifter, shirker, wastrel
10 black sheep
14 good-for-nothing

**nefarious**
04 base, evil, foul, vile
06 odious, sinful, wicked
07 heinous, satanic, vicious
08 criminal, depraved,
    infamous, infernal, shameful
09 execrable, monstrous
10 abominable, iniquitous,
    outrageous, villainous
11 opprobrious

**negate**
04 deny, undo, void
05 annul, quash
06 cancel, refute, reject, repeal,
    revoke, squash
07 explode, gainsay, nullify,
    rescind, retract, reverse
08 abrogate, disprove
09 discredit, repudiate
10 contradict, invalidate
11 countermand

**negation**
04 veto
06 denial, repeal
07 inverse, reverse
08 contrary, converse, opposite
09 disavowal, rejection
10 abrogation, disclaimer
12 cancellation, renunciation
13 contradiction, nullification
14 countermanding

**negative**
02 no
03 nay, nix
06 denial, gloomy
07 cynical, denying, refusal
08 contrary, critical, refusing
09 annulling, defeatist,
    rejection, unhelpful
10 dissension, dissenting,
    gainsaying, nullifying
11 pessimistic
12 invalidating, uninterested
13 contradiction, contradictory,
    uncooperative

**neglect**
04 fail, omit
05 scorn, shirk, skimp, spurn
06 fail in, forget, ignore, laxity
07 abandon, default, failure
08 ignoring, let slide, overlook
09 disrepair, oversight
10 be lax about, disrespect,
    negligence, remissness
12 carelessness, heedlessness,
    indifference
13 forgetfulness

**neglected**
08 derelict, untended, untilled
09 abandoned, overgrown
10 uncared-for
11 disregarded, undervalued
12 uncultivated, unmaintained
13 unappreciated
14 underestimated

**neglectful**
03 lax
06 remiss, sloppy
08 careless, heedless, uncaring
09 forgetful, negligent,
    oblivious, unmindful
11 indifferent, thoughtless

**negligence**
07 default, failure, neglect
09 oversight, slackness
10 remissness, sloppiness
11 inattention, shortcoming
12 carelessness, heedlessness,
    indifference
13 forgetfulness
15 thoughtlessness

**negligent**
03 lax
05 slack
06 casual, remiss, sloppy
08 careless, dilatory, heedless
09 forgetful, unmindful
11 indifferent, thoughtless

**negligible**
04 tiny
05 minor, petty, small
06 minute, paltry

07 trivial
08 trifling
11 unimportant
13 imperceptible, insignificant

**negotiable**
04 open
08 arguable, passable
09 debatable, navigable,
    undecided, unsettled
11 contestable, traversable
12 surmountable

**negotiate**
04 deal, pass, talk
05 agree, clear, cross
06 confer, debate, haggle,
    manage, parley, settle
07 arrange, bargain, discuss,
    fulfill, mediate, resolve, work
    out
08 conclude, contract, pass
    over, surmount, transact,
    traverse
09 arbitrate, get around,
    hammer out, intercede,
    thrash out
12 wheel and deal

**negotiation**
05 talks
06 debate, parley
08 haggling
09 diplomacy, mediation
10 bargaining, discussion
11 arbitration, transaction
12 thrashing-out

**negotiator**
06 broker
07 haggler
08 diplomat, mediator, parleyer
09 go-between, moderator
10 ambassador, arbitrator
11 adjudicator, intercessor
12 intermediary
13 wheeler-dealer

**neigh**
06 nicker, whinny

**neighborhood**
04 area, part
06 locale, region
07 quarter
08 district, environs, locality,
    precinct, purlieus, vicinity
09 community, proximity

❏**in the neighborhood of**
04 near
05 about
06 almost, nearby, next to
07 close to, roughly
13 approximately

**neighboring**
04 near, next

**neighborly**
05 local
06 nearby
07 nearest
08 abutting, adjacent
09 adjoining, bordering
10 connecting, contiguous

**neighborly**
04 kind, warm
06 genial
07 amiable, cordial, helpful
08 friendly, obliging, sociable
11 considerate

**nemesis**
04 fate, ruin
08 downfall
09 vengeance
10 punishment
11 destruction, retribution

**neologism**
07 coinage, new word, novelty
09 new phrase, vogue word
10 innovation

**neophyte**
04 tiro, tyro
06 intern, newbie, novice, rookie
07 learner, recruit, trainee
08 beginner, newcomer
09 greenhorn, new member, noviciate, novitiate
10 apprentice, raw recruit
11 probationer

**nepotism**
04 bias
10 family jobs, favoritism, partiality

**nerve**
03 lip
04 gall, grit, guts, will
05 brace, cheek, force, mouth, moxie, pluck, sauce, spunk, steel, valor, vigor
06 daring, mettle, spirit
07 bolster, bravery, courage, fortify, hearten
08 audacity, backbone, boldness, chutzpah, temerity
09 encourage, endurance, fortitude, impudence, insolence
10 brazenness, effrontery
11 intrepidity, presumption
12 fearlessness, impertinence
13 determination
14 cool-headedness

**nerveless**
04 calm, cool, weak
05 inert, slack, timid
06 afraid, feeble, flabby
08 cowardly, unnerved

09 enervated, spineless
10 controlled

**nerve-racking, nerve-wracking**
05 tense
06 trying
08 worrying
09 difficult, harrowing, maddening, stressful
10 nail-biting
11 distressing, frightening

**nerves**
05 worry
06 neural, strain, stress
07 anxiety, jitters, tension
11 butterflies, nervousness
12 collywobbles
13 heebie-jeebies

**nervous**
04 edgy
05 het up, jumpy, tense, timid
06 on edge, uneasy
07 anxious, fearful, fidgety, fretful, in a stew, jittery, keyed up, quaking, twitchy, uptight, worried, wound up
08 agitated, in a sweat, in a tizzy, neurotic, timorous
09 excitable, screwed up
10 high-strung
12 apprehensive
13 on tenterhooks

**nervous breakdown**
06 crisis
07 crackup
08 neurosis
10 depression
11 melancholia
15 mental breakdown

**nervousness**
05 worry
06 strain, stress
07 anxiety, fluster, tension
08 disquiet, edginess, timidity
09 agitation
10 touchiness, uneasiness
12 excitability, perturbation, restlessness, timorousness
13 heebie-jeebies

**nervy**
04 edgy
05 het up, jumpy, shaky, tense
06 on edge, uneasy
07 anxious, fearful, fidgety, jittery, keyed up, twitchy, uptight, worried, wound up
08 agitated, neurotic, strained
09 excitable, flustered
10 high-strung
12 apprehensive

**nescient**
06 stupid, unread
07 unaware
08 agnostic, backward, clueless, ignorant, untaught
09 unlearned, unwitting
10 illiterate, innumerate, uneducated, unschooled

**nest**
03 den, mew
04 aery, cote, eyry, lair
05 aerie, eyrie, haunt, roost
06 nidify
07 hideout, retreat, shelter
08 dovecote, vespiary
10 nesting box, nidificate
12 nidification
14 breeding ground

**nest egg**
04 fund
05 cache, funds, store
07 deposit, reserve, savings
08 reserves
09 hope chest, stockpile

**nestle**
06 cuddle, curl up, nuzzle
07 snuggle
08 cuddle up
09 snuggle up

**nestling**
04 baby
05 chick, owlet, squab
06 eaglet
09 fledgling

**net**
03 bag, get, nab, net, web
04 drag, earn, gain, lace, make, mesh, take, trap
05 broad, catch, clear, drift, final, raise, score, seine, snare, total
06 enmesh, lowest, obtain, pocket, pull in, rake in
07 bring in, capture, dragnet, ensnare, fishnet, lattice, netting, network, overall, receive, retiary
08 after tax, drift net, meshwork, openwork, seine net, take home, ultimate
09 inclusive, reticular, reticulum, safety net
10 accumulate
11 take-home pay
15 after deductions, computer network

**nether**
05 basal, below, lower, under
06 bottom
07 beneath, hellish, Stygian
08 inferior, infernal

**nettle**
10   lower level, underworld
11   underground

**nettle**
03   bug, vex
04   fret, goad
05   annoy, chafe, pique, plant, sting
06   harass, hassle, needle, ruffle
07   incense, provoke, torment
08   irritate

**nettled**
05   angry, cross, huffy, riled, stung, vexed
06   galled, goaded, miffed, peeved, piqued
07   annoyed, needled, ruffled
08   harassed, offended
09   aggrieved, irritable, irritated

**network**
03   net, web
04   grid, lace, maze, mesh
06   matrix, system, the Net, tracks
07   complex, lattice, netting, tracery, webbing
08   channels, filigree, meshwork, openwork
09   circuitry, grapevine, labyrinth, structure
11   arrangement, latticework, the Internet
12   organization
13   bush telegraph, old boy network

**neurosis**
06   phobia
08   disorder, fixation
09   deviation, obsession
11   abnormality, derangement, disturbance, instability
14   mental disorder

**neurotic**
06   phobic
07   anxious, deviant, nervous
08   deranged, paranoid
09   disturbed, obsessive
10   compulsive, irrational

**neuter**
03   fix
04   geld, spay
06   doctor
07   neutral
08   caponize, castrate, unbiased
09   sterilize
10   emasculate, nonaligned, uninvolved
11   nonpartisan, uncommitted
12   unprejudiced

**neutral**
04   drab, dull, fawn, gray, pale
05   beige, bland
07   anodyne, insipid
08   detached, unbiased
09   colorless, impartial, objective
10   evenhanded, indefinite, nonaligned, open-minded, uninvolved
11   indifferent, inoffensive, nonpartisan, uncommitted
12   noncommittal, unprejudiced, unremarkable
13   disinterested, dispassionate
14   expressionless

**neutrality**
10   detachment
11   disinterest
12   impartiality, nonalignment
14   noninvolvement
15   nonintervention

**neutralize**
04   undo
05   annul
06   cancel, negate, offset
07   balance, nullify
09   cancel out, make up for
10   counteract, invalidate
12   incapacitate
14   counterbalance

**never**
05   no way
07   not ever
08   at no time, not at all
11   on no account
13   not for a moment, not on your life
14   not for the world

**never-ending**
07   endless, eternal, nonstop
08   constant, infinite, unending
09   boundless, ceaseless, incessant, limitless, permanent, perpetual, unceasing
10   continuous, persistent, relentless, without end
11   everlasting, unremitting
12   interminable

**nevertheless**
03   but, yet
05   still
06   anyhow, anyway, even so
07   however
09   in any case
10   all the same, for all that, in any event, regardless
11   just the same, nonetheless
15   notwithstanding

**new**
04   mint, more
05   added, extra, fresh, novel
06   latest, modern, recent, trendy, unused, virgin
07   altered, another, changed, current, further, newborn, renewed, strange, unknown
08   advanced, brand-new, original, up-to-date
09   born-again, different, ingenious, refreshed, remodeled
10   additional, avant-garde, futuristic, innovative, modernized, newfangled, pioneering, redesigned, unfamiliar
11   imaginative, ultramodern
12   contemporary, experimental
13   revolutionary, state of the art, up-to-the-minute
14   groundbreaking

**newcomer**
06   intern, newbie, novice, rookie
07   arrival, learner, recruit, settler, trainee
08   beginner, colonist, intruder, neophyte, outsider, stranger
09   foreigner, immigrant
10   apprentice, new arrival, tenderfoot
11   probationer

**newfangled**
03   new
05   novel
06   modern, recent, trendy
08   gimmicky
11   modernistic, ultramodern
12   contemporary
13   state of the art

**newly**
04   anew, just
06   afresh, lately, of late
07   freshly
08   latterly, recently

**newness**
06   oddity
07   novelty, recency
09   freshness
10   innovation, uniqueness
11   originality, strangeness
13   unfamiliarity

**news**
04   data, dope, info, word
05   facts, rumor, story
06   advice, exposé, gossip, latest, report
07   account, scandal, tidings
08   bulletin, dispatch, news item, newscast
09   news flash, statement

10 communiqué, disclosure, revelation
11 information
12 announcement, developments, intelligence, press release
13 communication

**newspaper**
03 rag
05 daily, organ, press, sheet
06 weekly
07 gazette, journal, tabloid
09 newspaper
10 periodical
11 publication

---

► *Names of U.S. newspapers:*
07 Newsday
08 USA Today
09 Fresno Bee
10 Denver Post
11 Boston Globe, Buffalo News, Detroit News, Miami Herald, New York Post
12 Baltimore Sun, Boston Herald, New York Times, Seattle Times, Tampa Tribune
14 Birmingham News, Chicago Tribune, Daily Oklahoman, Kansas City Star, Washington Post
15 Chicago Sun-Times, Hartford Courant, Orlando Sentinel, Washington Times

**newsworthy**
07 notable, unusual
09 arresting, important
10 noteworthy, remarkable
11 interesting, significant

**next**
04 then
05 along, later
06 beside
07 closest, ensuing, nearest
08 adjacent
09 adjoining, afterward, alongside, bordering, following
10 contiguous, subsequent, succeeding, successive, thereafter
11 neighboring
12 subsequently

**nibble**
03 bit, eat
04 bite, gnaw, nosh, peck
05 piece, snack, taste
06 morsel, pick at, tidbit

**nice**
04 fine, good, kind, neat
05 civil, close, exact, sweet

06 genial, kindly, lovely, minute, polite, strict, subtle
07 amiable, amusing, welcome
08 becoming, charming, delicate, friendly, likeable, pleasant
09 agreeable, appealing, courteous, enjoyable
10 acceptable, attractive, delightful, satisfying
11 good-humored, good-natured, pleasurable, respectable, sympathetic
12 entertaining, well-mannered
13 understanding

**nicely**
04 well
08 properly
09 agreeably
10 pleasantly, pleasingly
12 delightfully
14 satisfactorily

**niceness**
05 charm
08 kindness
10 amiability, politeness
12 friendliness, pleasantness
13 agreeableness
14 attractiveness, respectability

**nicety**
06 nuance
07 finesse
08 accuracy, delicacy, subtlety
09 fine point, precision
10 minuteness, refinement

**niche**
04 nook, slot
05 place
06 alcove, corner, cranny, hollow, métier, recess
08 position, vocation
09 cubbyhole

**nickname**
07 epithet, pet name
09 sobriquet
10 diminutive, soubriquet
12 familiar name

**nifty**
04 chic, cool, deft, neat
05 agile, handy, quick, sharp
06 adroit, clever, groovy, spruce
07 stylish
08 skillful

**niggardliness**
08 meanness
09 closeness, parsimony, smallness
10 inadequacy, meagerness, paltriness, scantiness, skimpiness, stinginess

11 miserliness
12 cheese-paring
13 insufficiency
14 hard-fistedness
15 close-fistedness, tightfistedness

**niggardly**
04 mean
05 close, small
06 meager, measly, paltry, scanty, skimpy, stingy
07 miserly, sparing
09 miserable
10 hard-fisted, inadequate
11 close-fisted, tightfisted
12 cheese-paring, insufficient, parsimonious

**niggle**
03 bug, nag
04 carp, moan
05 annoy, upset, worry
06 bother, hassle, pick on, trifle
07 nitpick, quibble, trouble
08 complain, irritate, keep on at
09 be finicky

**night**
04 dark
08 darkness
09 nighttime, nocturnal
15 hours of darkness

**nightclub**
04 club
05 disco
07 cabaret
09 nightspot
11 discotheque

**nightfall**
04 dark, dusk
06 sunset
07 evening, sundown
08 gloaming, twilight
09 crepuscle
10 crepuscule

**nightmare**
05 agony, trial
06 horror, ordeal
07 anguish, incubus, torture
08 bad dream, calamity
12 apprehension

**nightmarish**
06 creepy, unreal
08 alarming, horrible, horrific
10 disturbing, terrifying
11 frightening

**nihilism**
06 denial
07 anarchy, atheism, nullity
08 cynicism, negation, oblivion
09 disbelief, emptiness, pessimism, rejection

**nihilist**
10 abnegation, negativism
11 agnosticism, lawlessness, nothingness, repudiation

**nihilist**
05 cynic
07 atheist, skeptic
08 agitator, agnostic
09 anarchist, pessimist
10 antinomian, negativist
11 disbeliever, negationist
13 revolutionary

**nil**
04 love, none, zero
05 zilch
06 naught, nought
07 nothing
08 goose egg

**nimble**
04 deft, spry
05 agile, alert, brisk, lithe, quick, ready, smart, swift
06 active, clever, lively, prompt
08 vigilant
09 sharp-eyed, sprightly
11 light-footed, quick moving

**nimbleness**
05 grace, skill
07 agility, finesse
08 alacrity, deftness, spryness
09 dexterity, niftiness, smartness
10 adroitness
13 sprightliness

**nimbly**
04 fast
06 deftly, easily, spryly
07 agilely, alertly, briskly, quickly, readily, sharply, smartly, swiftly
08 snappily, speedily
11 dexterously

**nincompoop**
04 clod, dolt, dork, fool, jerk, nerd
05 chump, dunce, idiot, ninny, twerp
06 dimwit, doofus, nitwit
07 half-wit
08 numskull
09 blockhead, simpleton

**nip**
02 go
03 fly, hop, lop, run, sip
04 bite, clip, dash, dock, dram, drop, grip, rush, shot, snip
05 catch, draft, hurry, pinch, tweak
07 portion, squeeze

❑**nip in the bud**
04 halt, stem, stop
05 block, check

06 arrest, impede
08 obstruct
09 frustrate

**nipple**
03 dug, pap, tit
04 teat
05 udder
06 breast
07 mamilla, papilla

**nippy**
03 raw
04 cold
05 brisk, sharp
06 biting, chilly
07 nipping
08 piercing, pinching, stinging

**nirvana**
03 joy
05 bliss, peace
07 ecstasy
08 paradise, serenity
11 tranquility
13 enlightenment

**nitpicking**
05 fussy
07 carping, finicky
08 captious, caviling, pedantic
09 quibbling
12 pettifogging
13 hairsplitting, hypercritical

**nitty-gritty**
06 basics
10 bottom line, brass tacks, essentials, main points
12 fundamentals, nuts and bolts

**nitwit**
04 dork, fool, goof
05 dummy, idiot, ninny
06 dimwit, doofus
07 half-wit
09 numbskull, simpleton
10 nincompoop

**no**
03 naw, nay
04 nope
05 no way
08 no thanks, not at all
11 of course not
13 absolutely not, not on your life
14 over my dead body

**Nobel Prize**

► *Names of Nobel Prize winners:*
02 **Fo** (Dario), **Oë** (Kenzaburo)
03 **Paz** (Octavio)
04 **Belo** (Carlos), **Bohr** (Niels Henrik David), **Born** (Max), **Böll** (Heinrich), **Buck** (Pearl

Sydenstricker), **Cela** (Camilo José), **Duve** (Christian René de), **Fenn**(John), **Gide** (André), **Hull** (Cordell), **Hume** (John), **Katz** (Bernard), **King** (Martin Luther), **Mann** (Thomas), **Mott** (Nevill Francis), **Shaw** (George Bernard), **Tutu** (Desmond), **Urey** (Harold Clayton)
05 **Annan** (Kofi), **Bloch** (Felix), **Bragg** (Lawrence), **Bragg** (William Henry), **Bunin** (Ivan), **Camus** (Albert), **Crick** (Francis Harry Compton), **Curie** (Marie), **Curie** (Pierre), **Davis**(Raymond), **Debye** (Peter Joseph Wilhelm), **Dirac** (Paul Adrien Maurice), **Eliot** (Thomas Stearns), **Euler** (Ulf Svante von), **Fermi** (Enrico), **Golgi** (Camillo), **Grass** (Günter), **Haber** (Fritz), **Hesse** (Hermann), **Klerk** (Frederik Willem de), **Krebs** (Hans Adolf), **Lewis** (Sinclair), **Libby** (Willard Frank), **Monod** (Jacques Lucien), **Pauli** (Wolfgang), **Peres** (Shimon), **Rabin** (Yitzhak), **Sachs** (Nelly), **Salam** (Abdus), **Simon** (Claude), **Soddy** (Frederick), **Stern** (Otto), **Yeats** (William Butler)
06 **Arafat** (Yasser), **Bellow** (Saul), **Bordet** (Jules), **Bunche** (Ralph), **Carrel** (Alexis), **Carter** (Jimmy), **Debreu** (Gerard), **France** (Anatole), **Frisch** (Ragnar), **Glaser** (Donald Arthur), **Hamsun** (Knut), **Heaney** (Seamus), **Hevesy** (George Charles von), **Hewish** (Antony), **Koichi** (Tanaka), **Lorenz** (Konrad Zacharias), **Myrdal** (Gunnar), **Nernst** (Walther Hermann), **Neruda** (Pablo), **O'Neill** (Eugene), **Pavlov** (Ivan), **Perutz** (Max Ferdinand), **Planck** (Max Karl Ernst), **Porter** (George), **Sanger** (Frederick), **Sartre** (Jean-Paul), **Singer** (Isaac Bashevis), **Tagore** (Rabindranath), **Walesa** (Lech), **Watson** (James

Dewey), **Wiesel** (Elie), **Wilson** (Woodrow)
07 **Alvarez** (Luis Walter), **Axelrod** (Julius), **Banting** (Frederick Grant), **Beckett** (Samuel), **Brenner**(Sydney), **Brodsky** (Joseph), **Canetti** (Elias), **Ehrlich** (Paul), **Feynman** (Richard Phillips), **Fleming** (Alexander), **Glashow** (Sheldon Lee), **Golding** (William), **Hodgkin** (Alan Lloyd), **Hodgkin** (Dorothy Mary), **Horvitz** (H. Robert), **Jiménez** (Juan Ramón), **Kertész** (Imre), **Khorana** (Har Gobind), **Kipling** (Rudyard), **Laxness** (Halldór), **Mahfouz** (Naguib), **Mandela** (Nelson), **Marconi** (Guglielmo, **Mauriac** (François), **Medawar** (Peter Brian), **Mistral** (Frédéric), **Mommsen** (Theodor), **Pauling** (Linus Carl), **Penzias** (Arno Allan), **Rotblat** (Joseph), **Röntgen** (Wilhelm Konrad von), **Russell** (Bertrand), **Seaborg** (Glen Theodore), **Seifert** (Jaroslav), **Soyinka** (Wole), **Sulston** (John), **Trimble** (David), **Waksman** (Selman Abraham), **Walcott** (Derek)
08 **Appleton** (Edward Victor), **Asturias** (Miguel Angel), **Chadwick** (James), **Delbrück** (Max), **Einstein** (Albert), **Faulkner** (William), **Friedman** (Milton), **Gajdusek** (Daniel Carleton), **Gell-Mann** (Murray), **Gordimer** (Nadine), **Langmuir** (Irving), **Leontief** (Wassily), **Marshall** (George), **Meyerhof** (Otto Fritz), **Millikan** (Robert Andrews), **Milstein** (Cesar), **Morrison** (Toni), **Mulliken** (Robert Sanderson), **Northrop** (John Howard), **Saramago** (José), **Shockley** (William Bradford), **Tiselius** (Arne Wilhelm Kaurin), **Weinberg** (Steven), **Williams** (Jody), **Wüthrich** (Kurt)
09 **Arrhenius** (Svante August), **Becquerel** (Antoine Henri),

**Cherenkov** (Pavel), **Churchill** (Winston), **Dalai Lama**, **Gorbachev** (Mikhail), **Hemingway** (Ernest), **Kissinger** (Henry), **Masatoshi**(Koshiba), **Michelson** (Albert Abraham), **Sholokhov** (Mikhail), **Steinbeck** (John), **Tinbergen** (Jan), **Tinbergen** (Nikolaas)
10 **Bethe** (Hans Albrecht), **Galsworthy** (John), **Heisenberg** (Werner Karl), **Hofstadter** (Robert), **Lagerkvist** (Pär), **Pirandello** (Luigi), **Ramos-Horta** (José), **Rutherford** (Ernest), **Szymborska** (Wislawa)
11 **Joliot-Curie** (Frédéric), **Joliot-Curie** (Irène), **Maeterlinck** (Count Maurice), **Ramón y Cajal** (Santiago), **Schrödinger** (Erwin)
12 **Solzhenitsyn** (Aleksandr)
13 **Aung San Suu Kyi** (Daw), **Chandrasekhar** (Subrahmanyan), **García Márquez** (Gabriel)

**nobility**
04 nobs
05 elite, honor, lords, peers
06 gentry, nobles
07 dignity, majesty, peerage
09 grandness, integrity
10 excellence, generosity, worthiness
11 aristocracy, high society
15 illustriousness

▶ *Titles of the nobility*:
04 dame, duke, earl, lady, lord, peer
05 baron, count, laird, liege, noble, ruler, thane
06 knight, squire
07 baronet, dowager, duchess, marquis, peeress
08 baroness, countess, life peer, marquess, nobleman, seigneur, viscount
09 grand duke, liege lord
10 aristocrat, noblewoman
11 marchioness, viscountess

**noble**
04 fine, lady, lord, peer
05 grand, great, lofty
06 landed, titled, worthy
07 eminent, exalted, stately

08 elevated, generous, high born, imposing, majestic, virtuous
09 dignified, excellent, honorable, patrician, unselfish
10 aristocrat
11 blue-blooded, high ranking, magnificent
12 aristocratic
15 self-sacrificing

**nobody**
04 none
05 no one
06 cipher, menial
07 nothing
09 nonentity
10 mediocrity, not anybody
14 no one important

**nod**
03 bow, dip, nap
04 beck, doze, sign
05 agree, sleep
06 accept, assent, drowse, salute, signal
07 approve, doze off, drop off, gesture, incline, slumber
08 greeting, indicate, say yes to
10 fall asleep, indication
14 acknowledgment

**node**
03 bud
04 bump, knob, knot, lump
06 growth, nodule
08 swelling
09 carbuncle
12 protuberance

**noise**
03 cry, din, row
05 blare, clash, rumor, sound
06 babble, clamor, hubbub, outcry, racket, report, ruckus, tumult, uproar
07 clatter
11 pandemonium

**noiseless**
04 mute
05 quiet, still
06 hushed, silent
09 inaudible, soundless

**noisome**
03 bad
04 foul
05 fetid
06 putrid, smelly
07 hurtful, noxious, reeking
08 mephitic, stinking
09 obnoxious, offensive, poisonous, repulsive .
10 disgusting, malodorous, nauseating, pernicious

11 deleterious, pestiferous
12 disagreeable, pestilential

**noisy**
04 loud
05 rowdy, vocal
07 blaring, booming, roaring
08 blasting, piercing
09 clamorous, deafening
10 boisterous, thundering, tumultuous, vociferous
12 earsplitting, obstreperous

**nomad**
05 Gypsy, rover, tramp
06 Beduin, roamer
07 Bedouin, migrant, rambler, vagrant
08 traveler, vagabond, wanderer
09 itinerant, transient

**nomadic**
05 Gypsy
06 roving
07 migrant, roaming, vagrant
08 drifting
09 itinerant, migratory, traveling, unsettled, wandering
11 peripatetic
13 peregrinating

**nom de plume**
05 alias
07 pen name
09 pseudonym
11 assumed name

**nomenclature**
06 naming
08 locution, taxonomy
10 vocabulary
11 phraseology, terminology
12 codification
14 classification

**nominal**
05 small, token
06 formal, puppet
07 minimal, titular, trivial
08 so-called, supposed, symbolic, trifling
09 professed, purported
10 in name only, ostensible
11 theoretical
13 insignificant

**nominate**
04 call, name, term
05 elect, put up
06 assign, choose, select
07 appoint, propose, suggest
09 designate, recommend
10 commission

**nomination**
06 choice, naming
08 election, proposal
09 selection

10 submission, suggestion
11 appointment, designation
14 recommendation

**nominee**
06 runner
07 entrant
08 assignee
09 appointee, candidate

**nonaligned**
07 neutral
09 impartial, undecided
10 uninvolved
11 independent, nonpartisan

**nonchalance**
04 calm, cool
06 aplomb
09 sang-froid, unconcern
10 detachment, equanimity
11 insouciance
12 indifference
13 pococurantism
14 self-possession

**nonchalant**
04 calm, cool
05 blasé
06 casual
07 offhand, relaxed
08 detached, laid-back
10 insouciant
11 indifferent, unconcerned
13 dispassionate, imperturbable
15 cool as a cucumber

**noncommittal**
04 wary
05 vague
07 careful, evasive, guarded, neutral, prudent, tactful
08 cautious, discreet, reserved
09 equivocal, tentative
10 diplomatic, indefinite
11 circumspect, unrevealing

**non compos mentis**
04 loco
05 crazy
06 insane
08 deranged, unhinged
10 unbalanced
11 mentally ill
13 of unsound mind

**nonconformist**
05 rebel
07 heretic, radical, seceder
08 maverick
09 dissenter, dissident, eccentric, heretical
10 iconoclast
11 dissentient
12 secessionist
13 individualist
14 fish out of water

**nonconformity**
06 heresy
07 dissent
09 deviation, secession
10 heterodoxy
11 originality
12 eccentricity

**nondescript**
04 drab, dull
05 bland, plain, vague
06 anemic
07 insipid
11 featureless, uninspiring
12 run-of-the-mill, unremarkable
13 indeterminate, undistinctive, unexceptional, uninteresting
15 undistinguished

**none**
03 nil
04 zero
05 no one
06 nobody, not any, not one
07 nothing
08 not a soul
09 not any one

**nonentity**
06 cipher, menial, nobody
07 nothing
10 mediocrity

**nonessential**
09 excessive, redundant
10 expendable, extraneous, peripheral
11 dispensable, inessential, superfluous, unimportant, unnecessary
13 supplementary

**nonetheless**
03 but, yet
05 still
06 anyhow, anyway, even so
07 however
10 regardless
12 nevertheless
15 notwithstanding

**nonexistence**
05 fancy
06 mirage
07 chimera
08 illusion, nonbeing
09 unreality

**nonexistent**
06 unreal
07 fancied, fantasy, missing
08 fanciful, illusory, imagined, mythical
09 fictional, imaginary
10 chimerical, fictitious
11 incorporeal

**nonflammable**
12 hypothetical
13 hallucinatory, insubstantial

**nonflammable**
09 fireproof
13 fire resistant, incombustible
14 flame resistant, flame-retardant

**nonintervention**
08 inaction
09 passivity
12 laissez faire, nonalignment
14 hands-off policy, noninvolvement
15 noninterference

**nonpareil**
06 unique
09 matchless, unequaled, unrivaled
10 inimitable
12 incomparable, unparalleled, without equal
13 beyond compare

**nonpartisan**
04 just
07 neutral
08 detached, unbiased
09 impartial, objective
10 evenhanded
11 independent
12 unprejudiced
13 dispassionate

**nonplus**
04 faze, stun
05 stump
06 baffle, dismay, puzzle
07 astound, confuse, flummox, mystify, perplex
08 astonish, bewilder, confound
09 discomfit, dumbfound, embarrass, take aback
10 disconcert
11 flabbergast
14 discountenance

**nonplussed**
05 fazed
07 at a loss, baffled, floored, puzzled, stumped, stunned
09 astounded, flummoxed, perplexed
10 astonished, bewildered, confounded, taken aback
11 dumbfounded
12 disconcerted
13 flabbergasted
14 out of your depth

**nonsense**
03 rot
04 bosh, bosh, bull, bunk, crap
05 hooey, trash, tripe
06 bunkum, drivel, humbug

07 baloney, blather, hogwash, rubbish, twaddle
08 claptrap, malarkey, tommyrot
09 gibberish, moonshine, poppycock, silliness, stupidity
10 balderdash, mumbo-jumbo
11 foolishness, jabberwocky
12 gobbledegook, gobbledygook
13 senselessness

**nonsensical**
05 crazy, dotty, inane, nutty, silly, wacky
06 absurd, stupid
07 foolish
09 ludicrous, nitwitted, senseless
10 irrational, ridiculous
11 harebrained, meaningless
12 preposterous
14 unintelligible

**nonstop**
07 endless, ongoing
08 constant, steadily, unbroken
09 ceaseless, endlessly, incessant, unceasing
10 constantly, continuous, persistent, relentless
11 ceaselessly, incessantly, never-ending, unceasingly
12 continuously, interminable, interminably, relentlessly
13 round-the-clock, unfalteringly, uninterrupted, unrelentingly, unremittingly
14 around-the-clock
15 uninterruptedly

**nonviolent**
06 dovish, irenic
07 passive
08 pacifist, peaceful
09 peaceable

**nook**
05 niche
06 alcove, cavity, corner, cranny, recess, refuge
07 hideout, opening, shelter
09 cubbyhole

**noon**
06 midday
09 lunchtime
10 twelve noon
12 twelve o'clock

**norm**
04 mean, rule, type
07 average, measure, pattern
08 standard
09 benchmark, criterion
10 touchstone

**normal**
05 usual
06 common
07 average, general, natural, regular, routine, typical
08 accepted, everyday, habitual, ordinary, rational, standard, straight
10 accustomed, mainstream
11 commonplace
12 conventional, well-adjusted

**normality**
06 reason
07 balance, routine
11 averageness, naturalness
12 ordinariness
15 conventionality

**normally**
07 as a rule, as usual, usually
08 commonly
09 generally, naturally, regularly, routinely, typically
10 ordinarily
14 conventionally

**northern**
05 north, polar
06 Arctic, boreal
09 northerly
11 hyperborean

**nose**
03 neb
04 beak, bill, push
05 flair, nasal, snoot, snout
06 hooter, rhinal, schnoz
08 instinct
09 proboscis, schnozzle
10 schnozzola

❑**nose around**
03 pry
05 snoop
06 search
10 poke around, rubberneck

❑**nose out**
06 detect, reveal
07 find out, inquire, uncover
08 discover, sniff out
12 barely defeat

**nosedive**
04 dive, drop
05 swoop
06 header, plunge
07 decline, plummet
08 get worse, submerge

**nosegay**
04 posy
05 bunch, spray
07 bouquet

**nosh**
04 chow, diet, dish, eats, fare, feed, food, grub, meal, menu

## nostalgia

05 board, snack, table
06 fodder, nibble, repast, stores, viands
07 cooking, cuisine, rations
08 delicacy, eatables, victuals
09 nutriment, nutrition
10 provisions, sustenance
11 nourishment, subsistence
12 refreshments

## nostalgia

06 pining, regret
07 longing, regrets
11 remembrance, wistfulness
12 recollection, reminiscence

## nostalgic

06 pining
07 longing, wistful
08 homesick, yearning
09 emotional, regretful
11 reminiscent, sentimental

## nostrum

04 cure, drug, pill
06 elixir, potion, remedy
07 cure-all, panacea
08 medicine
13 universal cure
14 cure for all ills

## nosy

06 prying
07 curious, probing
08 snooping
10 meddlesome
11 inquisitive, interfering
13 eavesdropping

## notability

03 VIP
04 fame
06 esteem, renown, worthy
08 eminence, luminary
09 celebrity, personage
10 importance
11 distinction, heavyweight
12 significance

## notable

03 VIP
04 rare, star
05 great
06 famous, marked, worthy
07 eminent, special, unusual
08 luminary, renowned, somebody, striking
09 celebrity, dignitary, important, memorable, momentous, notorious, personage, well-known
10 celebrated, impressive, notability, noteworthy, noticeable, particular, preeminent, remarkable
11 illustrious, outstanding, significant

13 distinguished, extraordinary, unforgettable

## notably

08 markedly, signally
09 eminently
10 distinctly, especially, noticeably, remarkably, strikingly, uncommonly
12 impressively, particularly
13 outstandingly, significantly
15 extraordinarily

## notation

04 code, note
05 entry, signs
06 cipher, script, system
07 symbols
08 alphabet
09 shorthand
10 characters
13 hieroglyphics

## notch

03 cut
04 gash, mark, nick, snip, step
05 gouge, grade, level, stage
06 degree, groove, indent
07 scratch
08 incision

## □notch up

04 gain, make
05 score
06 attain, record
07 achieve, chalk up
08 register

## notched

05 erose, jaggy
06 eroded, jagged, pinked
08 serrated
10 crenelated, emarginate, serrulated

## note

03 log, see
04 care, fame, mark, memo, tone
05 enter, entry, gloss, token
06 detect, letter, notice, record, regard, remark, renown
07 comment, element, jot down, jotting, mention, message, missive, observe, put down, refer to, touch on
08 eminence, footnote, notation, perceive, prestige, register
09 greatness, write down
10 annotation, commentary, indication, inflection, marginalia, memorandum
11 consequence, distinction
13 communication
15 illustriousness

## noted

05 great
06 famous, of note
07 eminent, notable
08 renowned
09 prominent, respected, well-known
10 celebrated, recognized
11 illustrious
13 distinguished

## notes

05 draft
06 record, report, sketch
07 entries, minutes, outline
08 jottings, synopsis
09 commentary
10 commentary, transcript
11 impressions

## noteworthy

07 notable, unusual
08 striking
09 important, memorable
10 impressive, remarkable
11 exceptional, significant
13 extraordinary

## nothing

03 nix
04 void, zero
05 zilch
06 cipher, menial, naught, nobody, nought
08 goose egg, oblivion
09 emptiness, nonentity, not a thing
11 lightweight, nothingness

## □for nothing

04 free
06 gratis, in vain
08 at no cost, futilely
09 to no avail
10 needlessly, on the house
12 free of charge, with no result

## nothingness

04 void
06 vacuum
07 nullity
08 nihilism, nihility, oblivion
09 emptiness
12 nonexistence

## notice

02 ad
03 see
04 bill, espy, heed, mark, mind, news, note, post, sign, spot
05 order
06 advice, behold, detect, poster, remark, review
07 comment, discern, observe, placard, posting, warning, write-up

08 bulletin, critique, handbill,
   interest, pamphlet, perceive
09 attention, awareness
10 cognizance, intimation
11 declaration, information
12 announcement, notification
13 advertisement, become
   aware of
14 pay attention to

**noticeable**
05 clear, plain
06 patent
07 evident, obvious, visible
08 distinct, manifest, striking
10 detectable, observable
11 appreciable, conspicuous,
   discernible, perceptible
15 distinguishable

**notification**
06 advice, notice
07 message, telling, warning
09 informing, statement
11 declaration, publication
12 announcement, intelligence
13 communication

**notify**
04 tell, warn
05 alert
06 advise, inform, reveal
07 apprise, caution, declare,
   divulge, publish
08 acquaint, announce
09 broadcast, make known
11 communicate

**notion**
04 idea, view, whim, wish
05 curio, fancy
06 belief, desire, theory
07 caprice, concept, thought,
   trinket
10 assumption, conception,
   hypothesis, impression,
   knickknack
11 inclination
12 apprehension
13 understanding

**notional**
06 unreal
07 fancied
08 abstract, fanciful, thematic
09 imaginary, unfounded
10 conceptual, ideational
11 speculative, theoretical
12 hypothetical

**notoriety**
04 fame
06 infamy, repute
07 obloquy, scandal
08 disgrace, dishonor, ignominy
09 disrepute, publicity
10 opprobrium

**notorious**
07 blatant, glaring
08 flagrant, ill famed, infamous
09 egregious, well-known
10 scandalous
11 disgraceful, ignominious, of
   ill repute, opprobrious
12 disreputable
13 talk of the town

**notoriously**
06 openly
07 notably, overtly
08 arrantly, patently
09 blatantly, glaringly, obviously
10 flagrantly, infamously
12 disreputably, scandalously
13 disgracefully, ignominiously

**notwithstanding**
03 yet
06 even so, though
07 despite, however
08 although
09 in spite of
11 nonetheless
12 nevertheless, regardless of

**nought**
03 nil, nix
04 zero
05 zilch
06 naught
07 nothing
08 goose egg
11 nothingness

**nourish**
03 aid
04 feed, have, help, rear,
   tend
05 boost, nurse
06 assist, foster
07 cherish, forward, further,
   nurture, promote, support
08 attend to, maintain
09 cultivate, encourage,
   stimulate
10 provide for, strengthen

**nourishing**
04 good
09 wholesome
10 beneficial, nutritious
11 substantial
12 health giving, invigorating
13 strengthening

**nourishment**
04 diet, food, grub, nosh
07 pabulum
09 nutriment, nutrition
10 sustenance
11 subsistence

**novel**
03 new

04 book, rare, tale
05 fresh, story
06 modern, unique
07 fiction, strange, unusual
08 creative, original
09 different, ingenious,
   inventive, narrative
10 innovative, unorthodox
11 imaginative, resourceful
14 groundbreaking

➤ *Names of novelists and
short-story writers:*
03 Eco (Umberto), Lee
   (Harper), Lee (Laurie), Poe
   (Edgar Allan), Roy
   (Arundhati)
04 Amis (Kingsley), Amis
   (Martin), Baum (L. Frank),
   Behn (Aphra), Böll
   (Heinrich), Buck (Pearl
   Sydenstricker), Dahl
   (Roald), Ford (Ford
   Madox), Grey (Zane), Hogg
   (James), Hugo (Victor),
   Jong (Erica), King
   (Stephen), Levi (Primo),
   Mann (Thomas), Okri
   (Ben), Puzo (Mario), Rhys
   (Jean), Rice (Ann), Roth
   (Philip), Sade (Marquis de),
   Sand (George), Seth
   (Vikram), Snow (Charles
   Percy), Uris (Leon), Wain
   (John), West (Rebecca),
   Wouk (Herman), Zola
   (Emile)
05 Adams (Douglas), Adams
   (Richard), Alger (Horatio),
   Banks (Iain), Bates
   (Herbert Ernest), Brink
   (André), Bunin (Ivan), Byatt
   (Antonia Susan), Camus
   (Albert), Chase (James
   Hadley), Crane (Stephen),
   Defoe (Daniel), Desai
   (Anita), Doyle (Arthur
   Conan), Doyle (Roddy),
   Dumas (Alexandre), Eliot
   (George), Genet (Jean),
   Gogòl (Nikolai), Gorky
   (Maxim), Grass (Günter),
   Haley (Alex), Hardy
   (Thomas), Henry (O.),
   Hesse (Hermann), James
   (Henry), James (Phyllis
   Dorothy), Jones (James),
   Joyce (James), Kafka
   (Franz), Keane (Molly),
   Kesey (Ken), Keyes
   (Frances Parkinson), Lewis
   (Clive Staples), Lewis
   (Sinclair), Lewis

(Wyndham), **Lowry**
(Malcolm), **Marsh** (Ngaio),
**Milne** (Alan Alexander),
**Moore** (Brian), **O'Hara**
(John), **Peake** (Mervyn),
**Percy** (Walker), **Plath**
(Sylvia), **Queen** (Ellery),
**Sagan** (Françoise), **Scott**
(Paul), **Scott** (Sir Walter),
**Shute** (Nevil), **Simon**
(Claude), **Smith** (Martin
Cruz), **Smith** (Wilbur),
**Spark** (Muriel), **Staël**
(Madame de), **Stein**
(Gertrude), **Stowe** (Harriet
Beecher), **Swift** (Graham),
**Swift** (Jonathan), **Turow**
(Scott), **Twain** (Mark), **Tyler**
(Anne), **Verne** (Jules), **Vidal**
(Gore), **Waugh** (Evelyn),
**Wells** (Herbert George),
**White** (Patrick), **White**
(Terence Hanbury), **Wilde**
(Oscar), **Wolfe** (Thomas
Clayton), **Wolfe** (Tom),
**Woolf** (Virginia)

06 **Achebe** (Chinua), **Alcott**
(Louisa May), **Aldiss**
(Brian), **Aragon** (Louis),
**Archer** (Jeffrey), **Asimov**
(Isaac), **Atwood** (Margaret),
**Austen** (Jane), **Balzac**
(Honoré de), **Barrie** (James
Matthew), **Bellow** (Saul),
**Binchy** (Maeve), **Blixen**
(Karen), **Blyton** (Enid),
**Borges** (Jorge Luis), **Braine**
(John), **Brontë** (Anne),
**Brontë** (Charlotte), **Brontë**
(Emily), **Bryson** (Bill),
**Buchan** (John), **Bunyan**
(John), **Butler** (Samuel),
**Capote** (Truman), **Carter**
(Angela), **Cather** (Willa),
**Clancy** (Tom), **Clarke**
(Arthur Charles), **Conrad**
(Joseph), **Cooper** (James
Fenimore), **Cooper** (Jilly),
**Cronin** (Archibald Joseph),
**Didion** (Joan), **Ferber**
(Edna), **Fowles** (John),
**France** (Anatole), **Godden**
(Rumer), **Godwin**
(William), **Goethe** (Johann
Wolfgang von), **Graves**
(Robert), **Greene** (Graham),
**Hamsun** (Knut), **Harris**
(Joel Chandler), **Heller**
(Joseph), **Hornby** (Nick),
**Hughes** (Thomas), **Huxley**
(Aldous), **Irving**
(Washington), **Jerome**
(Jerome Klapka), **Kelman**

(James), **Koontz** (Dean),
**L'Amour** (Louis), **Laclos**
(Pierre Choderlos de),
**Larkin** (Philip), **Lively**
(Penelope), **London** (Jack),
**Mailer** (Norman), **McEwan**
(Ian), **Miller** (Henry),
**Nesbit** (Edith), **O'Brien**
(Edna), **Orwell** (George),
**Powell** (Anthony), **Proust**
(Marcel), **Sapper**, **Sartre**
(Jean-Paul), **Sayers**
(Dorothy Leigh), **Sewell**
(Anna), **Sharpe** (Tom),
**Singer** (Isaac Bashevis),
**Sontag** (Susan), **Steele**
(Danielle), **Sterne**
(Laurence), **Stoker** (Bram),
**Styron** (William), **Tagore**
(Rabindranath), **Thomas**
(Dylan), **Updike** (John),
**Walker** (Alice), **Warren**
(Robert Penn), **Weldon**
(Fay), **Wesley** (Mary),
**Wilder** (Thornton), **Wilson**
(Angus)

07 **Ackroyd** (Peter), **Angelou**
(Maya), **Baldwin** (James),
**Ballard** (James Graham),
**Beckett** (Samuel), **Bennett**
(Arnold), **Burgess**
(Anthony), **Burnett**
(Frances Hodgson), **Calvino**
(Italo), **Canetti** (Elias),
**Carroll** (Lewis), **Chatwin**
(Bruce), **Cheever** (John),
**Chekhov** (Anton), **Clavell**
(James), **Cleland** (John),
**Cocteau** (Jean), **Coetzee**
(John Michael), **Colette**
(Catherine), **Dickens**
(Charles), **Diderot** (Denis),
**Drabble** (Margaret),
**Dreiser** (Theodore),
**Durrell** (Lawrence), **Ellison**
(Ralph), **Fleming** (Ian),
**Follett** (Ken), **Forster**
(Edward Morgan), **Forsyth**
(Frederick), **Francis** (Dick),
**Gaskell** (Mrs. Elizabeth),
**Gautier** (Théophile),
**Gibbons** (Stella), **Gissing**
(George), **Golding**
(William), **Grahame**
(Kenneth), **Grisham** (John),
**Haggard** (Henry Rider),
**Hammett** (Dashiell),
**Hartley** (Leslie Poles),
**Keillor** (Garrison), **Kerouac**
(Jack), **Kipling** (Rudyard),
**Kundera** (Milan), **Lardner**
(Ring), **Laxness** (Halldór),

**Le Carré** (John), **Leonard**
(Elmore), **Lessing** (Doris),
**Maclean** (Alistair),
**Mahfouz** (Naguib),
**Malamud** (Bernard),
**Malraux** (André), **Marryat**
(Captain Frederick),
**Maugham** (William
Somerset), **Mauriac**
(François), **Mishima**
(Yukio), **Mitford** (Nancy),
**Moravia** (Alberto),
**Murdoch** (Iris), **Nabokov**
(Vladimir), **Naipaul**
(Vidiadhar Surajprasad),
**O'Connor** (Flannery),
**Peacock** (Thomas Love),
**Prévost** (l'Abbé), **Pushkin**
(Alexander), **Pynchon**
(Thomas), **Rendell** (Ruth),
**Richler** (Mordecai),
**Robbins** (Harold), **Rowling**
(J. K.), **Rushdie** (Salman),
**Sassoon** (Siegfried),
**Sheldon** (Sidney), **Shelley**
(Mary), **Simenon** (Georges),
**Soyinka** (Wole), **Theroux**
(Paul), **Thurber** (James),
**Tolkien** (John Ronald
Reuel), **Tolstoy** (Leo),
**Walpole** (Hugh), **Wharton**
(Edith), **Wyndham** (John)

08 **Andersen** (Hans Christian),
**Apuleius** (Lucius),
**Barbusse** (Henri),
**Bradbury** (Ray), **Bradford**
(Barbara Taylor), **Brittain**
(Vera), **Brookner** (Anita),
**Bulgakov** (Mikhail),
**Caldwell** (Erskine),
**Cartland** (Barbara),
**Chandler** (Raymond),
**Christie** (Agatha), **Cornwell**
(Patricia), **Crichton**
(Michael), **Day-Lewis**
(Cecil), **Deighton** (Len),
**Disraeli** (Benjamin),
**Donleavy** (James Patrick),
**Faulkner** (William),
**Fielding** (Henry), **Flaubert**
(Gustave), **Forester** (Cecil
Scott), **Goncourt** (Edmond
de), **Gordimer** (Nadine),
**Huysmans** (Joris Karl),
**Ishiguro** (Kazuo), **Jhabvala**
(Ruth Prawer), **Keneally**
(Thomas), **Kingsley**
(Charles), **Koestler**
(Arthur), **Lawrence** (David
Herbert), **McCarthy**
(Cormac), **Melville**
(Herman), **Meredith**
(George), **Michener** (James

Albert), **Mitchell**
(Margaret), **Morrison**
(Toni), **Mortimer** (John),
**Ondaatje** (Michael),
**Remarque** (Erich Maria),
**Rousseau** (Jean Jacques),
**Salinger** (Jerome David),
**Sillitoe** (Alan), **Sinclair**
(Upton), **Smollett** (Tobias),
**Spillane** (Mickey),
**Stendhal, Trollope**
(Anthony), **Turgenev** (Ivan),
**Voltaire** (François-Marie
Arouet de), **Vonnegut** (Kurt)
09 **Allingham** (Margery),
**Bernières** (Louis de),
**Burroughs** (Edgar Rice),
**Burroughs** (William
Seward), **Cervantes** (Miguel
de), **Charteris** (Leslie),
**D'Annunzio** (Gabriele), **De
Quincey** (Thomas), **Dos
Passos** (John), **Du Maurier**
(Daphne), **Du Maurier**
(George), **Edgeworth**
(Maria), **Goldsmith**
(Oliver), **Grossmith**
(George), **Hawthorne**
(Nathaniel), **Hemingway**
(Ernest), **Highsmith**
(Patricia), **Hölderlin**
(Friedrich), **Isherwood**
(Christopher), **Lampedusa**
(Giuseppe Tomasi de),
**Lermontov** (Mikhail),
**Linklater** (Eric),
**Mackenzie** (Compton),
**Mankowitz** (Wolf),
**Mansfield** (Katherine),
**Masefield** (John),
**McCullers** (Carson),
**Monsarrat** (Nicholas),
**Pasternak** (Boris),
**Pratchett** (Terry), **Priestley**
(John Boynton), **Radcliffe**
(Ann), **Santayana** (George),
**Sholokhov** (Mikhail),
**Steinbeck** (John),
**Stevenson** (Robert Louis),
**Thackeray** (William
Makepeace), **Wodehouse**
(Pelham Grenville)
10 **Bainbridge** (Beryl),
**Ballantyne** (Robert
Michael), **Chesterton**
(Gilbert Keith), **De
Beauvoir** (Simone),
**Dostoevsky** (Fyodor),
**Fitzgerald** (Francis Scott),
**Galsworthy** (John),
**Lagerkvist** (Pär),
**Maupassant** (Guy de),
**Pirandello** (Luigi),

**Richardson** (Samuel),
**Strindberg** (August), **Van
der Post** (Laurens),
**Waterhouse** (Keith)
11 **Vargas Llosa** (Mario)
12 **Robbe-Grillet** (Alain),
**Saint-Exupéry** (Antoine
de), **Solzhenitsyn**
(Aleksandr)
13 **Alain-Fournier** (Henri),
**García Márquez** (Gabriel),
**Sackville-West** (Vita)
14 **Compton-Burnett** (Ivy)
➣ See also WRITER

► *Names of novels and
fictional works:*
03 Kim, She
04 Emma, Nana, Omoo, Voss
05 Kipps, Money, Scoop, Sybil,
Typee
06 Herzog, Lolita, Nausea,
Pamela, Rob Roy, The Sea,
Trilby, Utopia, Walden
07 Babbitt, Beloved, Candide,
Catch-22, Dracula, Erewhon,
Ivanhoe, Justine, Lord Jim,
Orlando, Ragtime, Rebecca,
The Bell, The Fall, Ulysses
08 Adam Bede, Clarissa,
Germinal, Jane Eyre,
Lavengro, Lucky Jim,
McTeague, Moby Dick,
Nostromo, Oroonoko, Peter
Pan, Rasselas, The Idiot, The
Trial, The Waves, Tom Jones,
Tom Thumb, Villette, Waverley
09 Beau Geste, Billy Budd, Billy
Liar, Dead Souls, Dubliners,
Hard Times, Kidnapped, O
Pioneers, On the Road,
Rabbit Run, Rogue Male, The
Devils, The Hobbit, Tom
Sawyer
10 Animal Farm, Bleak House,
Cancer Ward, Cannery Row,
Don Quixote, East of Eden,
Edwin Drood, Ethan Frome,
Goldfinger, Howards End,
Lorna Doone, Main Street,
Naked Lunch, Persuasion,
Ragged Dick, Rural Rides,
The Octopus, The Rainbow,
The Tin Drum, Titus Alone,
Titus Groan, Uncle Remus,
Vanity Fair
11 A Tale of a Tub, As I Lay Dying,
Black Beauty, Burmese Days,
Cakes and Ale, Daisy Miller,
Gormenghast, In Cold
Blood, Little Women,
Middlemarch, Mrs. Dalloway,
Oliver Twist, Silas Marner,

Steppenwolf, The Big Sleep,
The Outsider, The Pioneers,
The Third Man, Tobacco
Road, War and Peace,
Westward Ho!, Women in
Love
12 A Suitable Boy, Anna
Karenina, Barnaby Rudge,
Brighton Rock, Casino
Royale, Dombey and Son,
Fear of Flying, Frankenstein,
Invisible Man, Little Dorrit,
Lonesome Dove, Madame
Bovary, Moll Flanders, Of
Mice and Men, Rip Van
Winkle, Room at the Top,
Sister Carrie, The Awakening,
The Ginger Man, The Go-
Between, The Golden Ass,
The Lost World
13 A Kind of Loving, Arabian
Nights, Brave New World,
Call of the Wild, Daniel
Deronda, Doctor Zhivago,
Finnegans Wake, Just So
Stories, Les Misérables, Light
in August, Mansfield Park,
Metamorphosis, North and
South, Schindler's Ark,
Sketches By Boz, Smiley's
People, Sons and Lovers,
Sophie's Choice, Tarka the
Otter, The Awkward Age, The
Bostonians, The Golden
Bowl, The Jungle Book, The
Last Tycoon, The
Mabinogion, The Odessa
File, The Virginians, The
Women's Room, Under Milk
Wood, Watership Down,
Winnie-the-Pooh, Zuleika
Dobson
14 A Handful of Dust, A Room
with a View, A Separate
Peace, A Town Like Alice, All
the King's Men, Cider with
Rosie, Death on the Nile,
Decline and Fall, Fathers and
Sons, Jude the Obscure, Lord
of the Flies, Robinson
Crusoe, The Ambassadors,
The Color Purple, The Coral
Island, The Forsyte Saga, The
Great Gatsby, The Kraken
Wakes, The Long Goodbye,
The Secret Agent, The Time
Machine, The Water-Babies,
The Woodlanders, Treasure
Island, Tristram Shandy, Tropic
of Cancer, Uncle Tom's
Cabin, What Maisie Knew
15 A Christmas Carol, A
Farewell to Arms, A Passage

to India, Cold Comfort Farm, Daphnis and Chloe, Gone with the Wind, Gravity's Rainbow, Huckleberry Finn, Northanger Abbey, Our Mutual Friend, Peregrine Pickle, Portrait of a Lady, Tarzan of the Apes, The African Queen, The House of Mirth, The Invisible Man, The Little Prince, The Secret Garden, The Sun Also Rises, The Woman in White, Three Men in a Boat, To the Lighthouse, Under the Volcano, Where Eagles Dare

16 The Call of the Wild, Valley of the Dolls
17 The Age of Innocence, The Scarlett Letter, The Turn of the Screw
18 All the Pretty Horses, Slaughterhouse Five, The Catcher in the Rye, The Day of the Locusts, The Old Man and the Sea, The Sound and the Fury, To Kill a Mockingbird
19 Looking for Mr. Goodbar
20 A Hazard of New Fortunes, The Last of the Mohicans, The Red Badge of Courage, The Rise of Silas Lapham
21 Go Tell It on the Mountain, Sometimes a Great Notion, The Prince and the Pauper
23 The Bonfire of the Vanities
➤ See also FICTION

**novelty**
06 bauble, gadget, trifle
07 newness, trinket
08 gimcrack, nicknack, rareness, souvenir
09 curiosity, freshness
10 difference, innovation, knickknack, uniqueness
11 originality, strangeness

**novice**
04 tiro, tyro
05 pupil
06 intern, newbie, rookie
07 amateur, learner, recruit
08 beginner, neophyte, newcomer
09 greenhorn, noviciate, novitiate
10 apprentice, raw recruit
11 probationer

**novitiate**
08 training
10 initiation, internship
11 trial period

13 trainee period
14 apprenticeship

**now**
04 next
05 today
06 at once
08 directly, nowadays
09 at present, currently, instantly, presently, right away, these days
10 at this time
11 at the moment, immediately
12 straight away, without delay
15 for the time being

❑**now and then**
07 at times
08 on and off
09 sometimes
10 on occasion
11 desultorily, now and again
12 infrequently, occasionally, once in a while, periodically, sporadically
13 spasmodically
14 from time to time, intermittently

**nowadays**
05 today
09 at present, currently, presently, these days
11 at the moment
15 in this day and age

**noxious**
04 foul
05 toxic
06 deadly
07 harmful, noisome, ruinous
09 poisonous, unhealthy
10 disgusting, pernicious
11 destructive, detrimental

**nuance**
04 hint
05 shade, tinge, touch, trace
07 shading
08 overtone, subtlety
10 refinement, suggestion

**nub**
04 core, crux, gist, meat, pith
05 focus, heart, pivot, point
06 center, kernel, marrow
07 essence, nucleus

**nubile**
04 sexy
05 adult
06 mature
09 desirable
10 attractive, voluptuous
12 marriageable

**nucleus**
03 nub

04 core, crux, meat
05 basis, focus, heart, pivot
06 center, kernel, marrow

**nude**
04 bare
05 naked
07 exposed
08 in the raw, stripped
09 in the buff, unclothed, uncovered, undressed
10 stark-naked
12 not a stitch on
13 with nothing on
15 in the altogether

**nudge**
03 dig, jab, jog
04 bump, poke, prod, push
05 elbow, shove
06 prompt

**nudity**
06 nudism
07 undress
08 bareness
09 nakedness
10 déshabillé, dishabille
15 in the altogether

**nugatory**
04 vain
06 futile
07 invalid, trivial, useless
08 trifling
09 valueless, worthless
10 inadequate, unavailing
11 inoperative, null and void
13 insignificant

**nugget**
04 hunk, lump, mass
05 chunk, clump, piece

**nuisance**
04 bore, drag, pain, pest
06 bother, plague, weight
07 problem, trouble
08 drawback, irritant, vexation
09 annoyance
10 affliction, difficulty, irritation
13 inconvenience

**null**
04 vain, void
07 invalid, revoked, useless
08 annulled, canceled
09 abrogated, nullified, worthless
11 inoperative, invalidated

**nullify**
04 void
05 annul, quash
06 cancel, negate, repeal
07 abolish, rescind, reverse
08 abrogate, renounce
10 counteract, invalidate

11 countermand, discontinue

**nullity**
08 voidness
10 invalidity
12 nonexistence
13 worthlessness

**numb**
04 dead, drug, dull, stun
05 dazed
06 deaden, freeze, frozen
07 drugged, in shock, stunned
09 insensate, paralyzed
10 immobilize, insensible
11 anesthetize
12 anesthetized
14 without feeling

**number**
03 add, sum
04 copy, data, many, unit
05 count, digit, group, horde,
   issue, score, tally, total
06 amount, cipher, figure
07 add up to, company,
   compute, decimal, delimit,
   edition, imprint, include,
   integer, numeral, several
08 fraction, quantity, restrict
09 aggregate, calculate,
   character, enumerate,
   statistic
10 impression

**numberless**
04 many
06 myriad, untold
07 endless
08 infinite, unsummed
09 countless, uncounted
10 unnumbered
11 innumerable
12 immeasurable

**numbness**
06 stupor, torpor
08 deadness, dullness
09 paralysis
12 stupefaction
13 insensateness, insensibility

**numeral**
04 unit
05 digit
06 cipher, figure, number
07 integer
09 character

► *Roman numerals include*:
01 **C** (hundred), **D** (five
   hundred), **I** (one), **L** (fifty),
   **M** (thousand), **V** (five), **X**
   (ten)
02 **II** (two), **IV** (four), **IX** (nine),
   **VI** (six), **XI** (eleven), **XV**
   (fifteen), **XX** (twenty)

03 **III** (three), **VII** (seven), **XII**
   (twelve), **XIV** (fourteen),
   **XIX** (nineteen), **XVI**
   (sixteen)
04 **VIII** (eight), **XIII** (thirteen),
   **XVII** (seventeen)
05 **XVIII** (eighteen)

**numerous**
04 many
06 legion, sundry
07 copious, endless, profuse
08 abundant, manifold
09 countless, plentiful
11 innumerable
13 multitudinous

**numerousness**
09 abundance, profusion
11 copiousness
12 manifoldness, multiplicity
13 countlessness, plentifulness

**numskull**
04 clod, fool, head
05 dummy, dunce, ninny, twerp
06 dimwit, nitwit
07 fathead, half-wit
08 bonehead
09 birdbrain, blockhead,
   simpleton
11 knucklehead

**nun**
06 abbess, sister, vestal, vowess
08 canoness, prioress
14 mother superior

**nuncio**
05 envoy
06 legate
10 ambassador
14 representative

**nunnery**
05 abbey
06 priory
07 convent
08 cloister

**nuptial**
06 bridal, wedded
07 marital, wedding
08 conjugal, hymeneal
09 connubial
11 matrimonial

**nuptials**
06 bridal
07 wedding
08 espousal, marriage, spousals
09 matrimony

**nurse**
03 aid
04 feed, help, keep, tend
05 boost, treat
06 assist, foster, harbor, suckle

07 advance, care for, cherish,
   further, nourish, nurture,
   support, sustain
08 attend to, wet nurse
09 encourage, look after
10 breastfeed, take care of
➤ See also MEDICAL

► *Types of nurse. We have
omitted the word* **nurse** *from
names in this list but you may
need to include this word as part
of the solution to some
crossword clues.*
02 RN
03 LPN, wet
04 home
05 nanny, night, staff
06 school
07 midwife
09 children's, nursemaid,
   practical
10 Registered
11 psychiatric

► *Names of nurses*:
03 **Dix** (Dorothea)
04 **Wald** (Lillian)
05 **Kenny** (Elizabeth)
06 **Alcott** (Louisa May),
   **Barton** (Clara), **Cavell**
   (Edith), **Delano** (Jane)
08 **Schuyler** (Louisa Lee)
11 **Nightingale** (Florence)

**nurture**
04 care, feed, help, rear, tend
05 boost, coach, train, tutor
06 assist, foster, school
07 advance, bring up, care for,
   develop, educate, feeding,
   further, nourish, rearing,
   support, sustain, tending
09 cultivate, education,
   fostering, nutrition
10 sustenance, upbringing
11 cultivation, development,
   furtherance, nourishment

**nut**
03 fan, pip
04 buff, kook, seed
05 fiend, freak, loony, stone
06 kernel, madman, maniac,
   psycho, zealot
07 admirer, devotee, fanatic,
   lunatic, nutcase, oddball
08 head case, madwoman
09 fruitcake, supporter
10 enthusiast, psychopath

► *Types of nut*:
04 pine, tung
05 acorn, pecan, piñon
06 almond, cashew, cobnut,

grugru, litchi, peanut, walnut
07 babusso, coconut, filbert
08 beechnut, chestnut, hazelnut
09 brazil nut, candlenut, macadamia, pistachio
10 hickory nut
➤ See also FOOD

**nutriment**
04 diet, food, grub, nosh
09 nutrition
10 sustenance
11 nourishment, subsistence

**nutrition**
04 diet, food, grub, nosh
07 trophic
09 nutriment
10 sustenance
11 nourishment, subsistence

**nutritious**
04 good

08 balanced
09 nutritive, wholesome
10 beneficial, nourishing, salubrious
12 health giving, invigorating
13 strengthening

**nuts**
03 mad
04 avid, daft, fond, keen, loco, wild
05 crazy, loony, loopy, nutty
06 ardent, crazed, insane
07 berserk, devoted, lunatic, smitten, zealous
08 demented, deranged, unhinged
09 disturbed, fanatical
10 infatuated, out to lunch, passionate, unbalanced
12 enthusiastic

13 off your rocker, out of your mind

**nuts and bolts**
06 basics
07 details
10 components, essentials
11 nitty-gritty
12 fundamentals
14 practicalities

**nuzzle**
03 pet
05 nudge
06 burrow, cuddle, nestle
07 snuggle

**nymph**
04 girl, lass, maid
05 dryad, naiad, oread, sylph
06 damsel, sprite, undine
09 hamadryad

## oaf
04 clod, dolt, gawk, goon, hick, lout
05 chump, dunce, yahoo
06 lubber
07 bumpkin
08 lunkhead
11 hobbledehoy

## oafish
05 gawky, gross, rough
06 coarse, lumpen, stolid
07 doltish, ill-bred, uncouth
08 bungling, churlish, lubberly
10 unmannerly
11 clodhopping, ill-mannered

## oasis
05 haven
06 island, refuge, spring
07 hideout, retreat, sanctum
09 water hole
12 watering hole
13 watering place

## oath
03 vow
04 cuss
05 curse, swear
06 avowal, pledge
07 promise
08 cussword
09 assurance, blasphemy, expletive, obscenity, profanity, swearword
11 attestation, bad language, imprecation, malediction

## obdurate
04 firm, iron, sure
05 stony
06 dogged
07 adamant, willful
08 stubborn
09 immovable, obstinate, pigheaded, steadfast, unbending, unfeeling
10 determined, headstrong, implacable, inflexible, self-willed, unwavering, unyielding
11 hardhearted, intractable, stiff-necked, unrelenting
12 intransigent, strong-minded

## obedience
04 duty
07 respect
08 docility
09 deference, passivity
10 allegiance, compliance, observance, submission
11 amenability, dutifulness
12 acquiescence, subservience, tractability
14 submissiveness

## obedient
06 docile
07 dutiful, pliable
08 amenable, biddable
09 compliant, tractable
10 law-abiding
11 acquiescent, disciplined, subservient, well trained

## obeisance
03 bow
06 curtsy, homage, kowtow, salaam, salute
07 respect
09 deference, reverence
10 salutation, submission
12 genuflection

## obelisk
06 column, dagger, needle, obelus, pillar
08 memorial, monument

## obese
03 big, fat
05 bulky, gross, heavy, large, plump, round, stout
06 flabby, fleshy, portly, rotund
07 outsize, paunchy
09 corpulent, ponderous
10 overweight

## obesity
07 fatness
09 grossness, stoutness
10 chubbiness, corpulence, flabbiness, overweight, portliness, rotundness

## obey
04 heed, keep, mind
05 bow to, defer, yield
06 comply, follow, keep to
07 abide by, act upon, conform, defer to, execute, fulfill, give way, observe
08 adhere to, carry out
09 consent to, surrender
10 toe the line
11 acquiesce in, go by the book
14 do as you are told
15 stick to the rules

## obfuscate
04 blur, hide, mask, veil
05 cloak, cloud, cover, shade
06 muddle, shadow, shroud
07 conceal, confuse, obscure
10 complicate, overshadow

## object
03 aim, end
04 body, butt, goal, idea, item
05 argue, demur, point, thing
06 design, device, gadget, intent, motive, oppose, resist, target, victim
07 article, censure, protest, purpose
08 ambition, complain
09 intention, something, take issue
11 beg to differ, expostulate, remonstrate
13 take exception

## objection
05 demur
07 dissent, protest, scruple
09 challenge, complaint, grievance
10 opposition
11 disapproval
13 remonstration

## objectionable
09 loathsome, obnoxious, offensive, repellent, repugnant, repulsive, revolting, sickening
10 deplorable, detestable, nauseating, unpleasant
12 disagreeable, unacceptable
13 reprehensible

## objective
03 aim, end
04 fair, goal, idea, real, true
06 intent, object, target
07 factual, neutral, purpose
08 detached, unbiased
09 equitable, impartial
10 evenhanded, open-minded, uninvolved
12 unprejudiced

13 disinterested, dispassionate

**objectively**
06 fairly, justly
09 equitably, neutrally
11 impartially
12 evenhandedly
14 with an open mind
15 disinterestedly, dispassionately

**objectivity**
08 fairness, justness, open mind
10 detachment
11 disinterest
12 impartiality
13 equitableness
14 evenhandedness, open-mindedness

**obligate**
04 bind, make
05 force, impel, press
06 coerce, compel
08 pressure
09 constrain, essential
10 pressurize

**obligation**
04 date, debt, duty, onus, plan, task
06 burden, charge, demand
07 promise
08 contract, covenant
09 agreement, liability
10 commitment, compulsion
11 requirement
12 indebtedness
14 accountability, responsibility

**obligatory**
07 binding
08 enforced, required
09 mandatory, necessary, requisite, statutory
10 compulsory, imperative
11 unavoidable

**oblige**
04 bind, help, make
05 force, impel, press, serve
06 assist, compel, please
07 gratify, require
10 pressurize
11 accommodate, necessitate

**obliged**
05 bound
06 forced, in debt
08 beholden, grateful, in debt to, indebted, thankful
09 compelled, duty bound, gratified, obligated
10 honor bound
11 constrained

**obliging**
04 kind

05 civil
06 polite
07 helpful, willing
08 friendly, generous, pleasant
09 agreeable, courteous
11 complaisant, considerate, cooperative, good-natured
13 accommodating

**oblique**
05 slant, slash
06 angled, stroke, tilted, zigzag
07 devious, sloping, virgule
08 diagonal, inclined, slanting
09 divergent
10 circuitous, discursive, meandering, roundabout
12 periphrastic
14 circumlocutory

**obliquely**
06 askant, aslant, aslope
07 askance
09 at an angle, evasively
10 diagonally, indirectly
12 circuitously

**obliterate**
05 erase
06 delete, efface, rub out
07 blot out, destroy, expunge, wipe out
09 eliminate, eradicate, extirpate, strike out
10 annihilate

**obliteration**
07 erasure
10 effacement, expunction
11 blotting out, destruction, elimination, eradication, extirpation
12 annihilation

**oblivion**
07 lethean
08 darkness, deafness
09 blindness, obscurity
11 nothingness, unawareness
12 carelessness, nonexistence
15 unconsciousness

**oblivious**
04 deaf
05 blind
07 unaware
08 careless, heedless, ignorant
09 unheeding, unmindful
10 insensible
11 inattentive, preoccupied, unconcerned, unconscious

**obloquy**
05 abuse, blame, odium, shame
06 attack, infamy, stigma
07 calumny, censure, ill fame, slander

08 disgrace, dishonor, ignominy
09 aspersion, contumely, criticism, disrepute, invective
10 defamation, opprobrium
11 humiliation
12 vilification

**obnoxious**
04 vile
05 nasty
06 horrid, odious
08 annoying, horrible
09 abhorrent, loathsome, offensive, repellent, repugnant, repulsive, revolting, sickening
10 deplorable, detestable, disgusting, nauseating
12 contemptible, disagreeable
13 objectionable

**obscene**
04 blue, foul, lewd, rude, vile
05 bawdy, dirty, gross
06 carnal, coarse, filthy, risqué, sleazy, smutty, vulgar
07 immoral, raunchy
08 improper, indecent, prurient, shocking
09 offensive, shameless
10 disgusting, licentious, lubricious, outrageous, scurrilous, suggestive
12 pornographic

**obscenity**
05 curse, swear
06 sleaze
07 offense, outrage
08 atrocity, impurity, lewdness
09 bawdiness, curseword, dirtiness, eroticism, expletive, indecency, lubricity, profanity, prurience, swearword, vulgarity
10 coarseness, filthiness, immorality, wickedness
11 bad language, heinousness, imprecation, impropriety, malediction, pornography
13 salaciousness
14 four-letter word, lasciviousness, licentiousness

**obscure**
03 dim
04 blur, dark, hazy, hide, mask
05 cloak, cloud, cover, dusky, faint, fuzzy, minor, misty, murky, shade, shady, vague
06 arcane, gloomy, hidden, opaque, remote, screen, shadow, shroud, unsung

**obscurity**
07 blurred, complex, conceal, confuse, cryptic, eclipse, shadowy, unclear, unknown
08 abstruse, esoteric, nameless
09 confusing, enigmatic, obfuscate, recondite, uncertain, unheard-of
10 complicate, indefinite, indistinct, mysterious, overshadow, perplexing
11 Godforsaken, little known, out-of-the-way
12 impenetrable, inexplicable
13 inconspicuous, insignificant
15 undistinguished

**obscurity**
07 mystery
09 ambiguity, confusion
11 unclearness
12 abstruseness
13 reconditeness
14 insignificance
15 impenetrability

**obsequious**
04 oily
06 abject, creepy
07 fawning, servile, slavish
08 cringing, toadying, unctuous
09 groveling
10 flattering
11 bootlicking, deferential, subservient, sycophantic
12 ingratiating

**observable**
05 clear
06 patent
07 evident, obvious, visible
08 apparent, veiwable
10 detectable, noticeable
11 appreciable, discernible, perceivable, perceptible
12 recognizable

**observance**
04 rite
06 custom, notice, ritual
07 heeding, keeping, service
08 ceremony, festival, honoring, practice
09 adherence, attention, following, formality, tradition
10 compliance
11 celebration, fulfillment, performance

**observant**
05 alert, sharp
07 heedful, mindful, on guard
08 hawk-eyed, obedient, orthodox, vigilant, watchful
09 attentive, eagle-eyed, sharp-eyed, wide-awake

**observation**
04 data, note
05 study
06 remark, result, seeing
07 comment, finding, thought
08 noticing, scrutiny, watching
09 attention, statement
10 annotation, monitoring, perception, reflection
11 description, discernment, examination, information
13 consideration

**observe**
03 say, see
04 espy, keep, mark, note, obey, view
05 honor, state, study, utter, watch
06 behold, detect, follow, fulfil, notice, remark
07 comment, declare, discern, examine, execute, fulfill, mention, monitor, perform, respect
08 perceive, remember
09 celebrate, conform to
10 comply with, keep tabs on
11 commemorate, investigate, keep an eye on, keep watch on, miss nothing
12 catch sight of

**observer**
06 viewer
07 watcher, witness
08 beholder, looker-on, onlooker, reporter
09 bystander, spectator
10 eyewitness
11 commentator

**obsess**
04 grip, rule
05 haunt, hound
06 plague, prey on
07 bedevil, consume, control, engross, possess, torment
09 preoccupy
10 monopolize

**obsessed**
05 beset
07 gripped, haunted, plagued
08 hung up on
10 immersed in, infatuated
11 in the grip of, preoccupied

**obsession**
05 mania, thing
06 fetish, hang-up, phobia
07 complex, passion
08 fixation, idée fixe
11 fascination, infatuation
12 one-track mind
13 preoccupation

**obsessive**
08 gripping, haunting
09 consuming, maddening
10 compulsive, tormenting

**obsolescent**
05 aging, dated
06 fading, waning
08 dying out, outdated
09 declining, on the wane
11 on the way out
12 disappearing, old-fashioned, on the decline, past its prime

**obsolete**
03 old
04 dead
05 dated, passé
06 bygone, old hat
07 ancient, disused, extinct
08 in disuse, outmoded
09 discarded, out-of-date
10 antiquated, on the shelf
12 antediluvian, discontinued, old-fashioned
13 superannuated

**obstacle**
03 bar
04 curb, kink, snag, stop
05 catch, check, hitch
06 glitch, hurdle
07 barrier
08 blockade, blockage, drawback, handicap
09 barricade, deterrent
10 difficulty, impediment
11 obstruction
14 stumbling block

**obstinacy**
08 firmness, obduracy, tenacity
10 doggedness, mulishness, perversity
11 frowardness, persistence, willfulness
12 resoluteness, stubbornness
13 inflexibility, intransigence, pigheadedness

**obstinate**
04 firm
06 dogged
07 adamant, willful
08 stubborn
09 immovable, pigheaded, steadfast, unbending
10 determined, headstrong, inflexible, refractory, self-willed, unyielding
11 intractable, persevering
12 intransigent, recalcitrant, strong-minded

**obstreperous**
04 loud, wild
05 noisy, rough, rowdy

**obstruct**
06 unruly
07 raucous, restive, riotous
09 clamorous, out of hand
10 boisterous, disorderly, refractory, tumultuous, uproarious, vociferous
11 intractable, tempestuous
12 uncontrolled, unmanageable
13 undisciplined

**obstruct**
03 bar
04 clog, curb, halt, stop
05 block, check, choke, stall
06 hamper, hinder, hold up, impede, retard, thwart
07 inhibit, obscure, prevent
08 restrict, slow down
09 frustrate, hamstring

**obstruction**
03 bar
04 stop
05 check
07 barrier, embargo
08 blockage, obstacle, sanction, stoppage
09 barricade, deterrent
10 difficulty, impediment
14 stumbling block

**obstructive**
07 awkward
08 blocking, delaying, stalling
09 difficult, hindering
11 restrictive
13 uncooperative

**obtain**
03 get
04 earn, gain, hold, rule
05 exist, reign, seize, stand
06 attain, come by, secure
07 achieve, acquire, procure
09 be in force, be the case
11 be effective, be prevalent
14 get your hands on

**obtainable**
05 on tap, ready
06 at hand, on call
07 to be had
09 available
10 attainable, realizable

**obtrusive**
04 bold, nosy
05 brash, pushy
07 blatant, forward, obvious
08 flagrant, meddling
09 intrusive, officious, prominent
10 meddlesome, noticeable, projecting
11 conspicuous, interfering

**obtuse**
03 dim
04 dull, dumb, slow
05 crass, dense, thick
06 stolid, stupid
09 dimwitted
10 dull witted, slow-witted
12 thick-skinned
13 unintelligent

**obviate**
05 avert
06 divert, remove
07 counter, prevent
08 preclude
09 forestall
10 anticipate, counteract

**obvious**
04 open
05 clear, plain
06 patent
07 evident, glaring, visible
08 apparent, distinct, manifest
10 noticeable, pronounced, undeniable
11 conspicuous
12 crystal clear, unmistakable
15 self-explanatory, straightforward

**obviously**
07 clearly, plainly
08 of course, patently
09 certainly, evidently
10 manifestly, noticeably
11 undoubtedly
12 unmistakably, without doubt

**occasion**
02 do
04 call, case, fete, gala, make, time
05 cause, event, evoke, party
06 affair, create, effect, elicit, lead to, prompt, reason
07 bring on, episode, grounds, inspire, produce, provoke
08 engender, function, generate, instance
09 happening, influence
10 bring about, experience, give rise to, occurrence
11 celebration, get-together, opportunity

**occasional**
03 odd
04 rare
06 casual
08 periodic, sporadic
09 irregular, sometimes
10 incidental, infrequent
12 intermittent
13 once and a while

**occasionally**
07 at times
08 off and on, on and off
09 sometimes
10 now and then, on occasion
11 irregularly, now and again
12 every so often, infrequently, once in a while, periodically, sporadically
14 from time to time, intermittently

**occult**
05 magic
06 arcane, hidden, secret, veiled
07 magical, obscure
08 abstruse, esoteric, mystical
09 black arts, mysticism
10 mysterious
12 supernatural
13 preternatural
14 transcendental

**occupancy**
03 use
06 tenure
07 holding, tenancy
09 ownership, residence
10 habitation, occupation, possession
11 inhabitancy
13 domiciliation

**occupant**
04 user
06 holder, inmate, lessee, renter, tenant
08 occupier, resident, squatter
10 inhabitant
11 householder, leaseholder

**occupation**
03 job, use
04 line, post, work
05 craft, field, trade
06 career, employ, métier
07 calling, capture, control, pursuit, seizure, tenancy
08 activity, business, conquest, invasion, province, takeover
09 occupancy, residence
10 employment, habitation, line of work, possession, profession
11 foreign rule, subjugation

**occupational**
04 work
05 trade
06 career
08 business
10 employment, job related, vocational
12 professional

**occupied**
04 busy, full

**occupy**
05 in use, taken
06 tied up
07 engaged, taken up, working
08 employed, tenanted

**occupy**
03 own, use
04 busy, fill, have, hold
05 amuse, seize, use up
06 divert, employ, invade, live in, people, settle, stay in, take up, tenant
07 capture, dwell in, inhabit, involve, overrun, possess
08 interest, reside in, take over
09 entertain, preoccupy

**occur**
05 arise, exist
06 appear, befall, chance, crop up, dawn on, happen, result, strike, turn up
07 be found, develop, turn out
09 be present, come about, take place, transpire
10 come to mind, come to pass
12 spring to mind
13 cross your mind, enter your head, suggest itself

**occurrence**
04 case
05 event
06 action, affair
07 arising, episode
08 incident, instance
09 happening, incidence
10 appearance
11 development, proceedings
12 circumstance
13 manifestation

**ocean**
03 sea
04 blue, main
05 brine, briny
07 expanse, pelagic, the deep
08 profound, the drink

▶ *Names of oceans. We have omitted the word* **ocean** *from names given in the following list but you may need to include this word as part of the solution to some crossword clues.*
06 Arctic, Indian
07 Pacific
08 Atlantic
09 Antarctic
➢ See also SEA

**odd**
04 lone, only, rare, wild, zany
05 fluky, funny, kinky, queer, spare, wacky, weird

06 chance, far-out, freaky, random, single, sundry, way-out
07 bizarre, curious, deviant, erratic, oddball, strange, surplus, uncanny, unusual, various
08 abnormal, atypical, leftover, peculiar, periodic, singular, uncommon, unpaired
09 different, eccentric, haphazard, irregular, remaining, unmatched
10 incidental, occasional, off the wall, outlandish
11 exceptional, superfluous
13 extraordinary, idiosyncratic, miscellaneous
14 unconventional

❑**odd one out**
05 freak
06 odd-bod, weirdo
07 oddball
09 eccentric
13 nonconformist
14 fish out of water

**oddity**
05 freak, quirk, twist
06 misfit, rarity
07 anomaly
09 character, curiosity
10 phenomenon
11 abnormality, peculiarity
12 eccentricity, idiosyncrasy

**oddment**
03 bit, end
05 patch, piece, scrap, shred
07 remnant, snippet
08 fragment, leftover

**odds**
04 edge, lead
07 chances
09 advantage, supremacy
10 ascendancy, likelihood
11 probability, superiority

❑**at odds**
07 arguing
09 differing
10 in conflict, quarreling
11 disagreeing
13 at loggerheads
14 in disagreement

❑**odds and ends**
04 bits, junk
06 debris, litter, scraps
07 rubbish
08 oddments, remnants, snippets, sundries
10 miscellany
11 this and that
13 bits and pieces

**odious**
04 foul, vile
06 horrid
07 hateful, heinous
08 horrible
09 abhorrent, execrable, loathsome, obnoxious, offensive, repugnant, repulsive, revolting
10 abominable, despicable, detestable, disgusting
12 contemptible, disagreeable
13 objectionable

**odium**
06 hatred, infamy
07 censure, dislike, obloquy
08 contempt, disfavor, disgrace, dishonor
09 animosity, antipathy, discredit, disrepute
10 abhorrence, execration, opprobrium
11 detestation, disapproval
12 condemnation

**odorous**
05 balmy
07 pungent, scented
08 aromatic, fragrant, perfumed, redolent
11 odoriferous
13 sweet smelling

**odor**
05 aroma, scent, smell, stink
06 stench
07 bouquet, perfume
09 fragrance, redolence

**odyssey**
04 trek
06 voyage
07 journey, travels
09 adventure, wandering
13 peregrination

**off**
03 bad, ill, out
04 away, do in, gone, high, sick, slay
05 apart, aside, not on, slack, wrong
06 absent, murder, poorly, rub out, turned
07 bump off
08 away from, below par, canceled, knock off, scrapped
09 abandoned, called off, elsewhere, not at work
11 assassinate, unavailable
14 unsatisfactory
15 under the weather

**offbeat**
05 kooky, wacky, weird

**off-color**
06 far-out, freaky, way-out
07 bizarre, oddball, strange
10 unorthodox
14 unconventional

**off-color**
03 ill
04 rude, sexy, sick
05 dirty
06 coarse, filthy, poorly, risqué, smutty, unwell, vulgar
07 immoral, off form, run down
08 improper, indecent
10 indisposed, out of sorts, suggestive
12 pornographic
15 under the weather

**off duty**
03 off
04 free
07 off work
09 not at work
10 on vacation
14 taking a holiday

**offend**
03 err, sin
04 hurt, miff, snub
05 anger, annoy, repel, upset, wound, wrong
06 injure, insult, revolt, sicken
07 affront, disgust, do wrong, incense, outrage, provoke
08 go astray, nauseate
09 displease
10 exasperate, transgress
11 break the law

**offended**
04 hurt
05 huffy, stung, upset
06 miffed, piqued, put out
07 angered, annoyed, in a huff, wounded
08 incensed, outraged
09 affronted, disgusted

**offender**
07 culprit
08 criminal
09 miscreant, wrongdoer
10 delinquent, lawbreaker
11 guilty party
12 transgressor

**offense**
03 ire, sin
05 anger, crime, pique, wrong
06 injury, insult, slight
07 affront, outrage, umbrage
08 atrocity, trespass
09 annoyance, antipathy, indignity, violation
10 illegal act, infraction, resentment, wrongdoing

11 disapproval, indignation, misdemeanor
12 hard feelings, infringement
13 transgression

◻**take offense**
06 be hurt, resent
07 be angry, be upset
08 be miffed, be put out
09 be annoyed
10 be insulted, be offended
11 be indignant, take umbrage
13 take exception
14 take personally

**offensive**
04 foul, push, raid, rude, vile
05 drive, nasty
06 attack, charge, odious
07 abusive, assault, hurtful
08 annoying, impolite, insolent, invasion, wounding
09 abhorrent, incursion, insulting, loathsome, obnoxious, onslaught, repellent, repugnant, revolting, sickening
10 abominable, affronting, detestable, disgusting, nauseating, unpleasant
11 displeasing, impertinent
12 disagreeable
13 disrespectful, objectionable

**offer**
03 bid, try
04 give, sell, show
06 extend, submit, tender
07 advance, attempt, express, hold out, present, proffer, propose, suggest
08 approach, dedicate, proposal, propound
09 put in a bid, sacrifice, volunteer
10 consecrate, put forward, submission, suggestion
11 come forward, proposition
14 put on the market

**offering**
04 gift
05 tithe
07 handout, present
08 donation, oblation
09 sacrifice
10 dedication
12 consecration, contribution

**offhand**
04 curt, rude
05 ad lib, blasé, terse
06 abrupt, casual
07 brusque, cursory
08 careless, cavalier, laid-back
09 extempore, impromptu
10 off the cuff

11 free and easy, indifferent, perfunctory, unconcerned
12 discourteous, happy-go-lucky, uninterested
13 unceremonious
14 extemporaneous
15 couldn't care less, take it or leave it

**office**
04 base, duty, help, post, role
05 aegis, favor, place
06 bureau, charge
07 backing, service, support
08 advocacy, auspices, business, function, position
09 mediation, workplace
10 commission, employment, obligation, occupation
11 appointment
12 intercession, intervention
14 responsibility
15 place of business

**officer**
04 exec
05 agent, envoy
06 deputy
08 official
09 executive, messenger, policeman
10 bureaucrat
11 board member, functionary, policewoman
12 officeholder
13 administrator, public servant
14 representative

**official**
05 legal
06 formal, kosher, lawful, proper, ritual, solemn, umpire
07 officer, referee, stately
08 accepted, approved, bona fide, endorsed, licensed
09 authentic, certified, dignified, validated
10 accredited, authorized, ceremonial, legitimate, recognized, sanctioned
11 functionary
12 officeholder
13 authenticated, authoritative

**officiate**
05 chair
06 manage, umpire
07 conduct, oversee, preside, referee
10 be in charge, take charge
11 superintend
12 take the chair

**officious**
05 bossy, pushy

**offing**
08 bustling, meddling
09 intrusive, obtrusive
11 dictatorial, domineering, opinionated, overzealous
13 self-important

**offing**
◻**in the offing**
04 near
06 at hand, near by
07 in sight
08 imminent, on the way
10 coming soon, in the cards
11 close at hand
12 on the horizon

**offish**
04 cool
05 aloof
07 haughty, stuck-up
10 unsociable
11 standoffish

**off-key**
04 flat
05 sharp
07 jarring
09 dissonant, out of tune
10 discordant, unsuitable
13 inappropriate

**offload**
04 drop, dump
05 chuck, shift
06 unload
07 deposit
08 get rid of, jettison, unburden
09 disburden, discharge

**offset**
07 balance
09 cancel out, make up for
10 balance out, counteract
12 counterpoise
13 compensate for
14 counterbalance

**offshoot**
03 arm
04 limb
06 branch, result
07 outcome, product, spinoff
09 appendage, byproduct
11 consequence, development

**offspring**
03 kid
04 heir, kids
05 brood, child, heirs, issue, young
06 nipper
07 nippers, progeny
08 children, young one
09 successor, young ones
10 successors
11 descendants

**often**
04 much
09 generally, many a time, many times, regularly
10 frequently, repeatedly
12 time and again

**ogle**
03 eye
04 leer, look
05 eye up, stare
10 make eyes at

**ogre**
04 bogy
05 beast, bogey, brute, demon, devil, fiend, giant, troll
06 savage
07 monster, villain
09 barbarian

**oil**
04 balm
05 cream, salve
06 anoint, grease, lotion
07 unguent
08 liniment, ointment
09 lubricant, lubricate

**oily**
04 glib
05 fatty, suave
06 greasy
07 buttery, servile
08 unctuous
10 obsequious, oleaginous
11 subservient
12 ingratiating
13 smooth talking

**ointment**
03 gel
04 balm
05 cream, salve
06 lotion
08 liniment
09 emollient
11 embrocation

**OK, okay**
03 A-OK, yes
04 fair, fine, good, pass, so-so
05 A-Okay, right
06 agreed, not bad
07 approve, consent, correct, go-ahead, in order, initial, up to par
08 accurate, adequate, all right, approval, passable, sanction, thumbs-up
09 agreement, authorize, consent to, permitted, sign off on, tolerable
10 acceptable, green light, permission, reasonable
11 approbation, endorsement, rubberstamp, up to scratch

12 satisfactory
13 authorization

**old**
02 ex-
04 aged, gray, torn, wise
05 aging, dated, early, passé
06 age-old, bygone, former, mature, past it, primal, senile, shabby
07 ancient, antique, archaic, castoff, classic, decayed, earlier, elderly, lasting, one-time, quondam, veteran, vintage, worn-out
08 decaying, decrepit, earliest, obsolete, original, outdated, outmoded, previous, primeval, pristine, sensible, sometime
09 crumbling, erstwhile, getting on, long-lived, out-of-date, primitive, senescent
10 antiquated, broken down, primordial
11 over the hill, prehistoric, time-honored, traditional
12 antediluvian, long-standing
13 old as the hills, past your prime, unfashionable
14 long in the tooth
15 advanced in years, long established, no spring chicken

**old age**
03 age
06 dotage
07 oldness
08 agedness, senility
09 geriatric
10 senescence
11 elderliness
14 advancing years
15 second childhood

**old-fashioned**
04 dead, past
05 dated, passé
06 old hat, past it, square
07 ancient, archaic, old-time
08 obsolete, old-timey, outdated, outmoded
09 moth-eaten, out-of-date
10 antiquated, fuddy-duddy
11 obsolescent, on the way out
12 antediluvian, out-of-fashion
13 unfashionable
14 behind the times

**old man**
04 boss
05 elder
06 father, gaffer, geezer, grouch

**old-time**

07 husband, old fogy, old goat, oldster
08 employer, grumbler, old fogey, old-timer
09 graybeard, old codger
10 fuddy-duddy, whitebeard
11 grandfather
13 senior citizen
14 elder statesman
➤ See also OLD WOMAN

**old-time**

03 old
04 past
05 dated, passé
06 bygone
07 archaic
08 outdated, outmoded
09 out-of-date
10 antiquated
12 old-fashioned, out-of-fashion
13 unfashionable

**old woman**

03 bag, hag
04 wife
06 gammer, granny, grouch, mother
07 fusspot, old dear, old lady, oldster
08 grumbler
10 complainer
11 grandmother
13 senior citizen
➤ See also OLD MAN

**old-world**

04 past
06 bygone, quaint
07 archaic
08 European
10 antiquated
11 picturesque, traditional
12 old-fashioned

**omen**

04 sign
05 token
06 augury
07 auspice, portent, warning
08 prodrome
09 harbinger
10 foreboding, prediction
11 premonition
15 prognostication

**ominous**

07 fateful, unlucky
08 menacing, minatory, sinister
10 foreboding, portentous
11 threatening, unpromising
12 inauspicious, unpropitious

**omission**

03 gap
04 lack

06 lacuna
07 default, failure, neglect
08 ellipsis
09 avoidance, exception, exclusion, oversight
10 leaving-out, negligence
11 dereliction

**omit**

03 cut
04 drop, fail, miss, skip
05 erase
06 delete, forget, rub out
07 edit out, exclude, expunge, neglect
08 cross out, leave out, overlook, pass over
09 disregard, eliminate
13 fail to mention

**omnibus**

09 anthology, inclusive
10 collection, compendium
11 compendious, compilation
12 encyclopedia
13 comprehensive

**omnipotence**

07 mastery
09 supremacy
10 total power
11 divine right, sovereignty
12 almightiness, plenipotence
13 absolute power, invincibility

**omnipotent**

07 supreme
08 almighty
10 invincible
11 all-powerful, plenipotent

**omnipresent**

07 all-over
08 infinite
09 pervasive, universal
10 all-present, ubiquitous
12 all-pervasive

**omniscient**

07 all-wise
09 all-seeing
10 all-knowing

**omnivorous**

09 voracious
10 gluttonous
14 indiscriminate

**on**

❏**on and off**

08 fitfully, off and on
09 sometimes
10 now and then, on occasion
11 at intervals, irregularly, now and again
12 every so often, occasionally, periodically, sporadically

13 spasmodically
14 from time to time, intermittently

**once**

04 when
05 after
07 long ago, one time
08 as soon as, formerly
09 at one time, in the past
10 at one point
11 in times past
12 in the old days
13 in times gone by, on one occasion, once upon a time

❏**at once**

03 now
06 pronto
08 directly, promptly, right now
09 forthwith, instantly, like a shot, right away, yesterday
11 immediately
12 straightaway, without delay
13 at the same time
14 simultaneously
15 at the same moment

❏**once and for all**

07 finally, for good
10 decisively, positively
11 permanently
12 conclusively, definitively
14 for the last time

❏**once in a while**

07 at times
08 off and on, on and off
09 sometimes
10 now and then, on occasion
11 now and again
12 occasionally, periodically
14 from time to time

**oncoming**

07 looming, nearing
08 upcoming
09 advancing, gathering
11 approaching

**one**

03 ace, wed
04 lone, only, sole
05 alike, equal, fused, whole
06 entire, joined, single, united
08 complete, solitary
10 individual, like-minded

**oneness**

05 unity
08 identity, sameness
09 wholeness
10 singleness
12 completeness

**onerous**

04 hard
05 heavy

06 taxing, tiring
07 arduous, exigent, weighty
08 exacting, wearying
09 demanding, difficult, fatiguing, laborious
10 burdensome, exhausting
12 backbreaking

**oneself**

**❏ by oneself**
04 solo
05 alone
06 lonely, singly
07 forlorn, unaided
08 deserted, forsaken, isolated, lonesome
09 abandoned, on your own
10 by yourself, unassisted
11 independent, without help
12 single-handed
13 independently, unaccompanied

**one-sided**
06 biased, unfair, unjust
07 bigoted, partial, slanted, unequal
08 lopsided, partisan, separate
10 prejudiced, unbalanced
11 independent, inequitable
12 narrow-minded

**one-time**
02 ex-
04 late
06 former
07 quondam
08 previous, sometime
09 erstwhile

**ongoing**
07 current, growing, nonstop
08 constant, evolving
09 incessant, unfolding
10 continuing, developing, in progress, unfinished
11 progressing

**onlooker**
06 gawper, viewer
07 watcher, witness
08 looker-on, observer
09 bystander, spectator
10 eyewitness, rubberneck

**only**
04 just, lone, sole
06 at most, barely, merely, purely, simply, single, solely
10 individual, no more than, nothing but, one and only
11 exclusively, not more than

**onrush**
04 flow, push, rush
05 flood, onset, surge
06 career, charge, stream

08 stampede
09 onslaught

**onset**
05 start
06 attack, charge, outset
08 outbreak
09 beginning, inception
12 commencement

**onslaught**
04 push, raid
05 blitz, drive, foray
06 attack, charge, thrust
07 assault
08 storming
09 offensive
11 bombardment

**onus**
04 duty, load, task
06 burden, charge, weight
09 albatross, liability, millstone
10 obligation
14 responsibility

**onward, onwards**
02 on
05 ahead, forth
06 beyond
07 forward, in front
08 forwards
09 advancing

**oodles**
04 bags, gobs, lots, slew, tons
05 heaps, loads
06 masses
08 lashings

**oomph**
03 pep, vim
04 elan, zing
05 verve, vigor
06 bounce, energy, esprit, pizazz
07 pizzazz, sparkle
08 sexiness, vitality, vivacity
09 animation
10 get-up-and-go

**ooze**
04 drip, drop, emit, leak, seep
05 bleed, drain, exude, slime
06 escape, filter, sludge
07 deposit, dribble, excrete, secrete, trickle
08 alluvium, filtrate, sediment
09 discharge, percolate

**oozy**
04 dewy, miry
05 moist, mucky, muddy, slimy
06 sloppy, sludgy, sweaty
07 weeping
08 dripping
09 uliginous

**opacity**
07 density
09 filminess, milkiness, murkiness, obscurity
10 cloudiness, opaqueness
11 obfuscation, unclearness
15 impenetrability

**opalescent**
04 shot
06 pearly
07 rainbow
10 iridescent, shimmering
11 rainbowlike
12 multicolored
13 polychromatic

**opaque**
03 dim
05 dense, misty, muddy, murky
07 blurred, clouded, cryptic, muddied, obscure, unclear
08 abstruse, baffling, esoteric
09 enigmatic, recondite
12 as clear as mud, impenetrable, unfathomable
14 unintelligible

**open**
04 airy, ajar, free, moot, undo
05 begin, blunt, clear, crack, frank, holey, overt, plain, split, start, uncap, untie
06 broach, candid, direct, flower, gaping, honest, launch, liable, patent, porous, public, simple, spread, unbolt, uncork, unfold, unfurl, unlock, unroll, unseal, vacant
07 blatant, divulge, evident, exposed, general, kick off, lay bare, natural, obvious, outdoor, pour out, unblock, uncover, unlatch, visible, yawning
08 alfresco, apparent, arguable, cellular, commence, disclose, disposed, flagrant, manifest, outdoors, separate, unbarred, unbolted, unfasten, unfenced, unlocked, unsealed, wide open
09 available, come apart, debatable, guileless, ingenuous, navigable, receptive, spread out, unblocked, uncovered, undecided, unlatched, unsettled, well known
10 forthright, inaugurate, out-of-doors, unfastened, unreserved, unresolved, vulnerable

11 honeycombed, set in motion, susceptible, unconcealed, undisguised, unprotected, widely known
12 loosely woven, unobstructed, unrestricted

◻**open onto**
04 face
06 lead to
08 give onto, overlook

**open-air**
06 afield
07 outdoor, outside
08 alfresco, outdoors
10 out-of-doors

**open-and-shut**
05 clear
06 simple
07 obvious
12 easily solved
13 easily decided
15 straightforward

**openhanded**
04 free
06 lavish
07 liberal
08 generous
09 bounteous, bountiful
10 munificent, unstinting
12 eleemosynary, large-hearted

**opening**
03 gap, job
04 cave, dawn, hole, slot, vent
05 break, chasm, chink, cleft, crack, early, first, inlet, onset, place, space, split, start
06 breach, chance, launch, outlet
07 crevice, fissure, initial, kickoff, orifice, preface, rupture, vacancy
08 aperture, foreword, occasion, overture, position, preamble, prologue, starting
09 beginning, inaugural, inception, the word go
10 commencing, interstice
11 opportunity
12 commencement, inauguration, introduction, introductory

**openly**
07 frankly, overtly, plainly
08 brazenly, candidly, directly, honestly, in public
09 blatantly, glaringly
10 flagrantly, in full view
11 shamelessly, unashamedly
12 forthrightly, unreservedly

**open-minded**
07 liberal
08 catholic, tolerant, unbiased
09 impartial, objective
11 broad-minded, enlightened
12 unprejudiced
13 dispassionate
14 latitudinarian

**open-mouthed**
06 amazed
07 shocked
09 astounded, expectant
10 boisterous, vociferous
11 dumbfounded
13 flabbergasted, thunderstruck

**opera**
➤ *Names of operas and operettas:*
04 Aida
05 Faust, Norma, Tosca
06 Carmen, Otello, Salome
07 Fidelio, Macbeth, Nabucco, The Ring, Werther, Wozzeck
08 Falstaff, Idomeneo, Iolanthe, La Bohème, Parsifal, Patience, Turandot
09 Billy Budd, Capriccio, Lohengrin, Rigoletto, Ruddigore, Siegfried, The Mikado, Véronique
10 Cinderella, I Pagliacci, La Traviata, Oedipus Rex, Tannhäuser
11 Don Giovanni, Don Pasquale, HMS Pinafore, Il Trovatore, Peter Grimes, Princess Ida, The Sorceror, Trial by Jury, William Tell
12 Boris Godunov, Così Fan Tutte, Das Rheingold, Eugene Onegin, Manon Lescaut, Nixon in China, Porgy and Bess, The Grand Duke, The Valkyries
13 Albert Herring, Dido and Aeneas, Die Fledermaus, La Belle Hélène, The Desert Song, The Fairy Queen, The Gondoliers, The Magic Flute
14 Ariadne on Naxos, Le Grand Macabre
15 Götterdämmerung, Hansel and Gretel, Madame Butterfly, Naughty Marietta, The Beggar's Opera, The Pearl Fishers
16 The Student Prince
➤ See also MUSIC

**operate**
03 act, run, use
04 work

06 employ, handle, manage
07 control, perform, utilize
08 function

**operation**
03 job, use
04 deal, raid, task
06 action, attack, charge, motion
07 control, process, running, surgery
08 activity, business, campaign, exercise, handling, maneuver
09 procedure
10 enterprise, management
11 functioning, performance, undertaking, utilization
12 manipulation

◻**in operation**
05 going, valid
06 active, viable
07 in force, working
08 in action, workable
09 effective, efficient, in service
10 functional
11 functioning, serviceable

**operational**
05 going, in use, ready
06 usable, viable
07 working
08 in action, workable
09 in service
10 functional
11 functioning
14 in working order

**operative**
03 key, spy
04 dick, hand, mole
05 agent, valid, vital
06 shamus, sleuth, worker
07 artisan, crucial, gumshoe, in force, laborer, working, workman
08 employee, in action, mechanic, operator, relevant, workable
09 detective, machinist
10 functional, private eye
11 double agent, functioning, in operation, operational, secret agent, significant
12 investigator

**operator**
05 agent, mover
06 dealer, driver, trader, worker
07 handler, manager, shyster, surgeon
08 director, mechanic
09 machinist, operative
10 contractor, maneuverer, speculator, technician
13 wheeler-dealer

**operetta** see OPERA

**opiate**
04 drug
06 downer
07 anodyne, bromide
08 narcotic, nepenthe, pacifier, sedative
09 soporific
10 depressant
12 stupefacient, tranquilizer
13 tranquillizer

**opine**
05 guess, judge, think
07 believe, declare, presume, suggest, suppose, surmise, suspect, venture
08 conceive, conclude
09 volunteer
10 conjecture

**opinion**
04 idea, mind, view
06 belief, notion, stance, theory
07 feeling, thought
08 attitude, feelings, judgment, thoughts
09 viewpoint, worldview
10 assessment, assumption, conviction, estimation, persuasion, standpoint
11 point of view
13 way of thinking
15 school of thought

**opinionated**
07 adamant, bigoted, pompous
08 arrogant, cocksure, dogmatic, stubborn
09 obstinate, pigheaded
10 inflexible, pontifical
11 dictatorial, doctrinaire
12 single-minded
13 self-important
14 uncompromising

**opponent**
03 foe
05 enemy, rival
09 adversary, contender, other team
10 antagonist, challenger, competitor, contestant, opposition
11 dissentient

**opportune**
03 apt, fit
04 good
05 happy, lucky
06 proper, timely
07 fitting
08 suitable
09 favorable, fortunate, pertinent, well-timed

10 auspicious, convenient, felicitous, propitious, seasonable
11 appropriate
12 advantageous, providential

**opportunism**
07 realism
10 expediency, pragmatism
12 exploitation
15 taking advantage

**opportunity**
04 shot
05 break
06 chance, look-in, moment
07 opening

**oppose**
04 defy, face
05 check, fight, match
06 attack, combat, hinder, offset, resist, thwart
07 contest, counter, play off
08 confront, contrast, obstruct
09 be against, challenge, juxtapose, stand up to
10 be opposite, contradict, set against
12 argue against, disapprove of
13 take issue with
14 compete against, counterbalance, fly in the face of

**opposed**
04 anti
06 averse
07 against, hostile
08 clashing, contrary, inimical, opposing, opposite
11 conflicting, disagreeing
12 antagonistic, in opposition

**opposing**
05 enemy, rival
06 at odds
07 hostile, opposed, warring
08 clashing, contrary, opposite
09 combatant, differing, oppugnant
10 at variance, contending
11 conflicting, contentious
12 antagonistic, antipathetic, disputatious, incompatible
14 irreconcilable

**opposite**
06 at odds, facing, unlike
07 adverse, hostile, inverse, opposed, reverse
08 clashing, contrary, converse, flip side, fronting
09 different, differing, dissident
10 antithesis, contrasted, face to face, poles apart
12 antithetical, inconsistent

13 contradiction, contradictory, corresponding
14 irreconcilable

**opposition**
03 foe
05 enemy, rival
08 opponent
09 adversary, other side, other team
10 antagonism, resistance
11 competition, disapproval
15 obstructiveness

**oppress**
05 abuse, crush, quash, quell
06 burden, deject, harass, sadden, subdue
07 afflict, depress, enslave, repress, torment, trample
08 dispirit, maltreat, suppress
09 overpower, overwhelm, persecute, subjugate, tyrannize, weigh down
10 discourage, lie heavy on

**oppressed**
06 abused
07 crushed, misused, subject
08 burdened, enslaved, harassed, troubled
09 repressed
10 maltreated, persecuted, subjugated, tyrannized
11 downtrodden
13 disadvantaged
15 underprivileged

**oppression**
05 abuse
07 cruelty, tyranny
08 hardship
09 brutality, despotism, harshness, injustice
10 repression, subjection
11 persecution, subjugation
12 maltreatment

**oppressive**
05 close, cruel, heavy, muggy
06 brutal, stuffy, sultry, unjust
07 airless, inhuman, onerous
08 crushing, despotic, pitiless, ruthless, stifling
09 Draconian, merciless
10 burdensome, ironfisted, ironhanded, repressive, tyrannical
11 domineering, intolerable, iron hearted, overbearing, suffocating

**oppressor**
05 bully
06 despot, tyrant
08 autocrat, dictator, torturer
10 persecutor, subjugator

11 intimidator, slave driver

**opprobrious**
07 abusive
08 insolent, venomous
09 insulting, invective, offensive, vitriolic
10 calumnious, defamatory, derogatory, scurrilous
12 calumniatory, contemptuous, contumelious, vituperative

**opprobrium**
04 slur
05 odium, shame
06 infamy, stigma
07 calumny, censure, obloquy
08 disgrace, dishonor, ignominy, reproach
09 contumely, discredit, disrepute
10 debasement, scurrility
11 degradation

**opt**
04 pick
05 elect, go for
06 choose, decide, select
08 plump for, settle on

**optical instrument**

► *Types of optical instrument*:
05 laser
06 camera
07 sextant
08 spyglass
09 endoscope, periscope, telescope
10 binoculars, theodolite
12 field glasses, opera glasses
13 film projector
14 slide projector
15 magnifying glass, telescopic sight

**optimistic**
06 bright, upbeat
07 bullish, buoyant, hopeful
08 cheerful, positive, sanguine
09 confident, expectant
11 Panglossian, pollyannish

**optimum**
03 top
04 best
05 ideal, model
07 highest, optimal, perfect
11 superlative
13 most favorable

**option**
06 choice
09 selection
10 preference

11 alternative, possibility

**optional**
04 free
05 add-on
08 elective, unforced
09 voluntary
13 discretionary

**opulence**
06 luxury, plenty, riches, wealth
07 fortune
08 fullness, richness
09 abundance, affluence
10 cornucopia, prosperity
11 copiousness
13 sumptuousness
14 superabundance

**opulent**
04 posh, rich
05 plush
06 lavish
07 copious, moneyed, profuse, wealthy, well-off
08 abundant, affluent, prolific, well-to-do
09 luxuriant, luxurious, plentiful, sumptuous
10 prosperous, well-heeled
11 rolling in it
13 superabundant

**opus**
04 work
05 piece
06 oeuvre
08 creation
11 composition

**oracle**
04 guru, sage, seer
05 augur, sibyl
06 augury, expert, mentor, pundit, vision, wizard
07 adviser, prophet
08 prophecy
09 authority
10 divination, high priest, prediction, revelation, soothsayer, specialist
15 prognostication

**oracular**
04 sage, wise
05 grave
06 arcane
07 cryptic, Delphic, obscure
08 abstruse, dogmatic, positive, two-edged
09 ambiguous, equivocal, prescient, prophetic
10 auspicious, haruspical, mysterious, portentous
11 dictatorial, significant
13 authoritative

**oral**
04 said
05 aloud, vocal
06 spoken, verbal
07 audible, out loud, uttered
09 unwritten

**orate**
04 rant, talk
05 speak
07 declaim
08 harangue
09 discourse, hold forth, sermonize, speechify

**oration**
05 spiel
06 homily, sermon, speech
07 address, lecture
09 discourse
11 declamation

**orator**
07 demagog, speaker, spieler
08 lecturer
09 declaimer, demagogue
11 rhetorician, spellbinder
13 public speaker

**oratorical**
08 eloquent, sonorous
09 bombastic, high-flown
10 Ciceronian, rhetorical
11 declamatory
12 elocutionary, magniloquent
13 grandiloquent

**oratorio**

► *Names of oratorios*:
04 Saul
06 Elijah, Esther, Joshua, Samson, Semele
07 Athalia, Deborah, Jephtha, Messiah, Solomon, Susanna
08 Christus, Hercules, Theodora
10 Belshazzar, Oedipus Rex, The Seasons
11 The Creation
13 Israel in Egypt
15 A Child of Our Time, Judas Maccabaeus
➤ See also MUSIC

**oratory**
06 speech
07 diction
08 rhetoric
09 elocution, eloquence
11 declamation
12 speechifying
14 grandiloquence, public speaking

**orb**
03 eye
04 ball, ring

**orbit**
05 globe, mound, round
06 circle, sphere

**orbit**
04 path
05 ambit, range, scope, track
06 circle, course, domain
07 circuit, compass, revolve
10 revolution, trajectory
14 circumnavigate

**orchestrate**
03 fix
05 score
07 arrange, compose, prepare
08 organize
10 coordinate, mastermind
11 put together, stage-manage

**ordain**
03 fix, set
04 call, fate, rule, will
05 elect, frock, order
06 anoint, decree, invest
07 appoint, destine, dictate
09 prescribe, pronounce
10 consecrate, predestine
12 predetermine

**ordeal**
04 pain, test
05 agony, trial
07 anguish, torment, torture
09 nightmare, suffering
11 persecution, tribulation

**order**
03 bid, law
04 book, call, calm, form, kind,
   rank, rule, sect, sort, writ
05 array, class, edict, genus,
   grade, quiet, set up, setup,
   union
06 codify, decree, demand,
   direct, lay out, line up, lineup,
   manage, method, roster,
   system
07 arrange, call for, catalog,
   command, control, dictate,
   dispose, harmony, mandate,
   marshal, pattern, precept,
   request, require, reserve,
   society, sort out, species,
   summons, variety, warrant
08 classify, instruct, neatness,
   organize, regulate,
   sequence, sorority,
   symmetry, tidiness
09 catalogue, directive,
   hierarchy, legislate,
   ordinance, prescribe,
   structure
10 discipline, fraternity,
   injunction, lawfulness,
   regularity, regulation,
   sisterhood, uniformity

11 application, arrangement,
   brotherhood, disposition,
   instruction, law and order,
   requisition, reservation, send
   away for, stipulation,
   systematize, write off for
12 codification, denomination,
   organization, pecking order
13 secret society
14 categorization, classification

□**in order**
02 OK
04 done, neat, okay, tidy
05 right
06 lawful, mended, proper
07 allowed, correct, fitting,
   ordered, orderly, regular
08 all right, arranged, suitable
09 permitted, shipshape
10 acceptable, classified, in
   sequence, systematic
11 appropriate, categorized
13 well organized

□**in order to**
06 so that
11 intending to, with a view to
13 with the result
14 with the purpose

□**order around**
05 bully
08 browbeat, bulldoze,
   dominate, domineer
09 tyrannize
10 boss around, order about,
   push around

□**out of order**
05 kaput
06 broken, untidy
07 haywire, muddled
08 confused, gone phut,
   improper, unseemly
10 broken down, disordered,
   not working, on the blink, on
   the fritz
11 inoperative, uncalled-for
12 disorganized, unacceptable
13 out of sequence
14 not functioning
15 out of commission

**orderly**
04 neat, ruly, tidy, trim
07 in order, ordered, regular
10 controlled, law-abiding,
   methodical, restrained,
   systematic
11 disciplined, well behaved
13 well organized, well
   regulated
15 in apple-pie order

**ordinance**
03 law

04 fiat, rite, rule
05 bylaw, edict, order
06 decree, dictum, ritual, ruling
07 command, statute
08 ceremony, practice
09 directive, sacrament
10 injunction, observance,
   regulation
11 institution

**ordinarily**
07 as a rule, usually
08 commonly, normally
09 generally, in general
11 customarily

**ordinary**
04 dull, fair
05 banal, bland, plain, usual
06 common, normal, simple
07 average, mundane, prosaic,
   regular, routine, typical
08 everyday, familiar, habitual,
   standard, workaday
09 customary, quotidian
10 mainstream, pedestrian
11 commonplace, indifferent,
   nondescript, unmemorable
12 conventional, run-of-the-
   mill, unremarkable
13 unexceptional
15 undistinguished

□**out of the ordinary**
04 rare
06 unique
07 unusual
09 different, memorable
10 noteworthy, remarkable,
   surprising, unexpected
11 exceptional, outstanding
13 extraordinary

**ordnance**
04 arms, guns
06 cannon
07 big guns, weapons
09 artillery, munitions

**ordure**
04 dirt, dung, poop
05 feces, filth, guano
06 egesta, manure
09 droppings, excrement,
   excretion
11 waste matter

**ore**

► *Types of ores:*
03 wad
04 gold
06 galena, rutile, silver
07 bauxite, bornite, cuprite, iron
   ore, uranite
08 goethite, hematite, hematite,
   limonite, siderite, tenorite

**organ**

09  argentite, ironstone, magnetite, malachite, manganite, proustite, tantalite
10  peacock ore, pyrolusite, ruby silver, sphalerite, stephanite
11  cassiterite, pyrargyrite
12  chalcopyrite, pyromorphite, tetrahedrite
13  copper pyrites

**organ**

04  part, tool, unit
05  forum, paper, voice
06  agency, medium, member
07  journal, process, vehicle
08  magazine
09  component, implement, newspaper
10  instrument, mouthpiece
11  constituent, publication

**organic**

06  biotic, inborn, living
07  animate, natural, ordered
08  inherent
09  organized
10  biological, harmonious, structured
11  nonchemical
12  additive free
13  not artificial, pesticide free

**organism**

04  body, cell
05  being, plant, setup, unity
06  animal, entity, system
08  creature
09  bacterium, structure

**organization**

04  body, club, firm, plan
05  group, order, setup, union
06  design, outfit, system
07  company, concern, society
08  grouping
09  authority, formation, operation, structure
10  consortium, management
11  arrangement, association, composition, corporation, development, institution
12  coordination
13  configuration
14  administration, classification

**organize**

03  run
05  begin, found, group, order, see to, set up, shape, start
06  create, manage
07  arrange, catalog, develop, dispose, marshal, prepare, sort out
08  assemble, classify, tabulate

09  catalogue, establish, structure
10  administer, coordinate
11  standardize, systematize

**organized**

04  neat, tidy
07  ordered, orderly, planned
08  arranged
09  efficient
10  structured, systematic
11  well ordered
12  businesslike
13  well regulated

**orgy**

04  bash, bout
05  binge, party, revel, spree
06  excess, frenzy, revels
07  debauch, revelry, splurge
08  bachanal, carousal
09  wild party
10  saturnalia
11  bacchanalia

**orient**

05  adapt, align
06  adjust
08  accustom
09  acclimate, habituate, orientate
11  acclimatize, familiarize
15  get your bearings

**orientation**

07  guiding, leading
08  bearings, location, position
09  alignment, direction, induction, placement
10  adaptation, adjustment, initiation, settling-in
11  acclimation, inclination
15  acclimatization, familiarization

**orifice**

04  hole, pore, rift, slit, slot, vent
05  cleft, crack, inlet, mouth
07  crevice, fissure, opening
08  aperture
11  perforation

**origin**

04  base, dawn, root
05  basis, birth, cause, fount, roots, start, stock
06  family, launch, source, spring
07  dawning, descent, genesis
08  ancestry, creation, pedigree
09  beginning, emergence, etymology, inception, parentage, paternity
10  conception, derivation, extraction, foundation, provenance, wellspring
12  commencement, fountainhead

**original**

03  new
04  real, true, type
05  early, first, model, novel
06  master, primal, unique
07  genuine, initial, opening, pattern, primary, unusual
08  creative, paradigm, standard
09  archetype, authentic, ingenious, inventive, primitive, prototype, real thing
10  archetypal, innovative, pioneering, unorthodox
11  imaginative, resourceful
13  autochthonous
14  groundbreaking

**originality**

07  newness, novelty
09  freshness, ingenuity
10  creativity, innovation
11  imagination, singularity
12  creativeness, eccentricity
13  individuality, inventiveness
14  creative spirit
15  resourcefulness

**originally**

05  first
07  at first, by birth
09  initially
10  at the start
11  at the outset, to begin with
14  in the beginning

**originate**

04  come, flow, form, rise, stem
05  arise, begin, issue, start
06  be born, create, derive, emerge, evolve, invent
07  develop, emanate, pioneer
09  establish, introduce
11  give birth to, set in motion
13  be the father of, be the mother of

**originator**

06  artist, author, father, mother
07  creator, founder, pioneer
08  designer, inventor
09  architect, developer, initiator, innovator

**ornament**

04  deck, gild, trim
05  adorn, frill, jewel
06  bauble, fallal, gewgaw
07  dress up, garnish, trinket
08  decorate, furbelow, trimming
09  accessory, adornment, embellish
10  decoration
13  embellishment

**ornamental**

05  fancy, showy

**ornamentation**
10 attractive, decorative
12 embellishing, embroidering

**ornamentation**
09 adornment, fallalery, garniture
10 decoration, embroidery
11 elaboration
13 embellishment

**ornate**
04 busy
05 fancy, fussy, showy
06 florid, rococo
07 baroque, flowery
09 decorated, elaborate
10 flamboyant, ornamented
11 embellished

**orotund**
04 deep, full, loud, rich
06 ornate, strong
07 booming, pompous
08 imposing, powerful, sonorous
09 bombastic, dignified
10 resonating
11 pretentious
12 magniloquent

**orthodox**
05 sound, usual
06 devout, strict
07 correct, regular
08 accepted, faithful, official, received
10 conformist, recognized
11 established, traditional
12 conservative, conventional
15 well established

**orthodoxy**
08 devotion, trueness
10 conformism, conformity, devoutness, strictness
11 correctness
12 conservatism, faithfulness
13 inflexibility
14 received wisdom, traditionalism
15 conventionality

**oscillate**
04 sway, vary, yo-yo
05 swing, waver
06 seesaw, wigwag
09 fluctuate, vacillate

**oscillation**
08 swinging, wavering
09 seesawing, variation
11 fluctuation, vacillation
15 shilly-shallying

**ossify**
06 harden
07 petrify
08 indurate, rigidify, solidify

09 fossilize

**ostensible**
07 alleged, claimed, feigned, outward, seeming
08 apparent, presumed, so-called, specious, supposed
09 pretended, professed, purported
11 superficial

**ostensibly**
09 allegedly, outwardly, reputedly, seemingly
10 apparently, supposedly
11 professedly, purportedly
13 superficially

**ostentation**
04 pomp, show
05 swank
07 display
08 boasting, flourish, vaunting
09 flaunting, pageantry, showiness, trappings
10 flashiness, pretension, showing off
11 affectation, flamboyance
13 exhibitionism
15 pretentiousness

**ostentatious**
04 loud
05 gaudy, showy
06 flashy, glitzy, kitsch, vulgar
08 affected
10 flamboyant
11 conspicuous, extravagant, pretentious

**ostracism**
05 exile
09 exclusion, expulsion, isolation, rejection
10 banishment
11 deportation
12 cold shoulder, proscription
15 excommunication

**ostracize**
03 bar, cut
04 shun, snub
05 avoid, exile, expel
06 banish, outlaw, reject
07 boycott, exclude, isolate
12 cold-shoulder
13 excommunicate

**other**
04 more
05 extra, spare
07 further, variant
08 distinct, separate
09 different, disparate
10 additional, dissimilar
11 alternative, contrasting

**otherwise**
02 or
05 if not
06 or else, unless

**otherworldly**
03 fey
06 dreamy
07 bemused
08 ethereal
11 preoccupied

**ounce**
03 jot
04 atom, drop, iota, mite, spot, whit
05 crumb, scrap, shred, speck, trace
06 morsel
07 smidgen, smidgin
08 particle, smidgeon

**oust**
04 fire, sack
05 eject, evict, expel
06 depose, put out, topple, unseat
07 boot out, dismiss, turn out
08 displace, drive out, force out, get rid of, throw out
09 overthrow, thrust out
10 disinherit, dispossess

**out**
03 KO'd, set
04 away, bent, dead, gone
05 dated, known, passé, ready
06 asleep, démodé, old hat, public
07 evident, exposed, in bloom, in print, out cold, outside, retired
08 blooming, comatose, divulged, excluded, flied out, in flower
09 available, disclosed, in the open, insistent, not at home, out-of-date, published, struck out, thrown out
10 antiquated, blossoming, determined, disallowed, impossible, insensible, knocked out, obtainable, unsuitable
11 grounded out, in full bloom, unconscious
12 extinguished, inadmissible, old-fashioned
13 unfashionable

**out-and-out**
05 total, utter
06 arrant
07 perfect
08 absolute, complete, outright, thorough

**outbreak**
09 downright
10 consummate, inveterate
11 unmitigated, unqualified
13 dyed-in-the-wool

**outbreak**
04 rash
05 burst, flash, onset
07 flare-up, upsurge
08 epidemic, eruption
09 explosion
13 recrudescence

**outburst**
03 fit
04 gale, gush
05 burst, spasm, storm, surge
06 attack
07 flare-up, seizure
08 eruption, paroxysm
09 explosion
10 outpouring
11 fit of temper

**outcast**
05 exile, leper
06 pariah, reject
07 evacuee, refugee
08 castaway, outsider
11 untouchable
15 persona non grata

**outclass**
03 top
04 beat
05 outdo
07 eclipse, outrank, surpass
08 outrival, outshine, outstrip
10 overshadow
13 leave standing, put in the
   shade

**outcome**
05 issue
06 effect, result, sequel, upshot
07 product
09 end result
10 conclusion
11 aftereffect, consequence

**outcry**
03 cry, row
04 fuss
05 noise
06 clamor, racket, tumult,
   uproar
07 dissent, protest
08 outburst
09 commotion, complaint, hue
   and cry, objection
10 hullabaloo
11 exclamation, hullaballoo,
   indignation

**outdated**
05 dated, passé
06 démodé, old hat, square

08 obsolete, outmoded
09 out-of-date
10 antiquated, superseded
12 old-fashioned, out of fashion
13 unfashionable
14 behind the times

**outdistance**
04 pass
06 outrun
07 outpace, surpass
08 outstrip, overtake
11 leave behind, pull ahead of
13 leave standing

**outdo**
03 cap, top
04 beat
05 excel
06 defeat, exceed
07 eclipse, surpass
08 outclass, outshine, outstrip
11 outdistance
14 get the better of, run rings
   around
16 run circles around

**outdoors**
03 out
07 outdoor, outside
08 alfresco
10 out-of-doors
12 in the open air

**outer**
06 fringe, remote
07 outside, outward, surface
08 exterior, external, outlying,
   outwards
09 outermost
10 peripheral
11 superficial

**outface**
04 defy
05 beard, brave
06 resist
08 confront, outstare
09 brazen out, stare down

**outfit**
03 rig, set
04 crew, firm, gang, garb, gear,
   suit, team, togs, unit
05 dress, equip, fit up, getup,
   group, guise, setup, stock,
   tools, troop
06 attire, fit out, supply, troupe
07 apparel, appoint, clothes,
   company, costume, coterie,
   furnish, provide, turn out
08 accouter, accoutre, business,
   ensemble
09 equipment, trappings
12 organization
13 establishment

**outfitter**
06 sartor, tailor
08 clothier, costumer
09 costumier, couturier
10 couturière, dressmaker
11 haberdasher

**outflow**
04 gush, rush
06 efflux
07 out rush, outfall
08 drainage, effluent, effusion
09 discharge, effluence,
   effluvium, emanation
10 outpouring

**outflowing**
07 gushing, leaking, rushing
08 effluent, spurting
10 debouching
11 discharging

**outgoing**
02 ex-
04 last, open, past, warm
06 former, genial
07 affable, amiable, cordial
08 friendly, retiring, sociable
09 departing, easygoing,
   extrovert, talkative
10 gregarious, unreserved
13 communicative,
   demonstrative

**outgrowth**
05 shoot
06 effect, sprout
07 product, spinoff
08 offshoot, swelling
10 protrusion
12 protuberance

**outhouse**
05 privy
06 toilet
07 latrine
10 porta-potty, porto-potty

**outing**
04 spin, tour, trip
05 jaunt
06 picnic
07 day trip
08 road trip
09 excursion
12 pleasure trip

**outlandish**
03 odd
05 alien, wacky, weird
06 exotic, far-out, way-out
07 bizarre, curious, foreign,
   strange, unknown, unusual
08 peculiar
09 eccentric, unheard-of
10 unfamiliar
13 extraordinary

14 unconventional

**outlandishness**
07 oddness
09 queerness, weirdness
10 exoticness, quaintness
11 bizarreness, strangeness
12 eccentricity

**outlast**
06 defeat
07 outlive, ride out, survive, weather
09 withstand
11 come through

**outlaw**
03 ban, bar
05 debar, exile
06 badman, bandit, forbid, gunman, pirate, robber
07 brigand, condemn, embargo, exclude, outcast
08 criminal, fugitive, prohibit, renegade
09 desperado, proscribe
10 highwayman
13 excommunicate

**outlay**
04 cost
05 price
07 payment
08 expenses, spending
11 expenditure
12 disbursement

**outlet**
04 duct, exit, shop, vent
05 store, valve
06 agency, egress, escape, market, way out
07 conduit, culvert, opening
08 retailer, supplier
11 safety valve

**outline**
04 form, plan
05 draft, shape, trace
06 layout, précis, résumé
07 profile, summary, tracing
08 abstract, rough out, synopsis
09 bare bones, bare facts, delineate, lineament, rough idea, sketch out, summarize
10 main points, silhouette

**outlive**
07 outlast, survive, weather
11 come through, live through

**outlook**
04 view
05 angle, slant
06 aspect, future
07 opinion
08 forecast, prospect

09 prognosis, viewpoint, worldview
11 frame of mind, perspective, point of view
12 expectations

**outlying**
05 outer
06 far-off, remote
07 distant, far away
08 far-flung, isolated, suburban
10 provincial
11 out-of-the-way
12 inaccessible

**outmaneuver**
04 beat
05 outdo
06 outfox, outwit
08 outflank, outsmart, outthink
14 get the better of

**outmoded**
05 dated, passé
06 démodé, old hat, square
07 archaic
08 obsolete
10 antiquated, old-fogyish, superseded
11 obsolescent, old-fogeyish
12 antediluvian, old-fashioned, out of fashion
13 unfashionable
14 behind the times

**out-of-date**
05 dated, passé
06 démodé, old hat, square
07 archaic
08 obsolete, outdated
10 antiquated, old-fogyish, superseded
11 obsolescent, old-fogeyish
12 antediluvian, old-fashioned
13 unfashionable
14 behind the times

**out-of-the-way**
06 far-off, lonely, remote
07 distant, far away, obscure
08 far-flung, isolated, outlying
11 little known
12 inaccessible, unfrequented

**out of work**
04 idle
07 jobless, laid off, unwaged
08 workless
09 on the dole, out of a job
10 unemployed

**outpace**
04 beat, pass
05 outdo
06 outrun
08 outstrip, overhaul, overtake

**outpouring**
04 flow, flux
05 flood, spate, spurt
06 deluge, efflux, stream
07 cascade, outflow, torrent
08 effusion
09 effluence, emanation
11 debouchment
14 disemboguement

**output**
04 gain
05 yield
06 fruits, return
07 harvest, product
10 production
11 achievement, performance
12 productivity

**outrage**
04 evil, fury, rage
05 abuse, anger, shock, wrath
06 enrage, horror, injury, madden, offend, ravage
07 affront, assault, disgust, horrify, incense, scandal
08 atrocity, enormity
09 barbarism, brutality, infuriate, violation
10 scandalize
11 indignation

**outrageous**
04 foul, vile
07 ghastly, heinous, obscene
08 horrible, shocking, terrible
09 excessive, monstrous
10 exorbitant, inordinate, scandalous, unbearable
11 intolerable, unspeakable
12 extortionate, insufferable, preposterous

**outré**
03 odd
05 weird
06 far-out, freaky, way-out
07 bizarre, strange, unusual
09 eccentric
10 outrageous
13 extraordinary
14 unconventional

**outrider**
05 guard
06 escort
09 attendant, bodyguard
10 forerunner
11 trailblazer

**outright**
04 pure
05 clear, total, utter
06 at once, direct, openly
07 perfect, totally, utterly
08 absolute, complete, entirely
09 downright, out-and-out

**outrun**
10 positively, thoroughly
11 categorical, unequivocal, unmitigated, unqualified
12 straight away
13 categorically, unconditional

**outrun**
04 beat, lose, pass
05 excel, outdo
07 outpace, surpass
08 outstrip, overtake, shake off
11 leave behind, outdistance

**outset**
05 start
07 kickoff, opening
09 beginning, inception
12 commencement

**outshine**
04 beat, best
05 dwarf, excel, outdo
07 eclipse, outrank, upstage
08 outclass, outstrip
10 overshadow, put to shame
13 put in the shade

**outside**
05 cover, faint, front, outer, small, vague
06 façade, remote, slight
07 distant, outdoor, outward
08 exterior, external, outdoors, unlikely
09 outermost
10 appearance, extraneous, improbable, negligible
11 superficial

**outsider**
05 alien
06 émigré, misfit
08 emigrant, intruder, newcomer, stranger
09 auslander, foreigner, immigrant, nonmember, odd one out
10 interloper
11 gatecrasher, nonresident

**outskirts**
04 edge
06 margin
07 borders, fringes, suburbs
08 boundary, suburbia
09 perimeter, periphery

**outsmart**
03 con, kid
04 beat, best, dupe
05 trick
06 have on, outfox, outwit
07 deceive
08 outthink
12 take for a ride
14 get the better of, pull a fast one on

**outspoken**
04 free, rude
05 blunt, frank, plain
06 candid, direct
08 explicit
10 forthright, unreserved
11 plainspoken, unequivocal
15 straightforward

**outspread**
04 open, wide
06 expand, extend, flared, opened
08 extended, unfolded
09 expansion, fanned out, spread out
12 outstretched

**outstanding**
03 due
05 famed, great, owing
06 famous, superb, unpaid
07 eminent, notable, ongoing, payable, pending, special
08 leftover, superior
09 excellent, important, memorable, prominent, remaining, unsettled
10 celebrated, impressive, noteworthy, preeminent, remarkable, unfinished
11 exceptional, superlative
13 distinguished, extraordinary

**outstandingly**
07 greatly, notably
09 amazingly, extremely
10 especially, remarkably
13 exceptionally
15 extraordinarily

**outstrip**
03 top
04 beat, pass
05 outdo
06 better, exceed, outrun
07 eclipse, surpass
08 outshine, overtake
09 transcend
11 leave behind, outdistance
13 leave standing

**outward**
05 outer
06 public
07 evident, outside, visible
08 apparent, exterior, external
10 noticeable, ostensible
11 discernible, perceptible, superficial

**outwardly**
07 visibly
09 seemingly
10 apparently, externally, supposedly
12 at first sight, on the surface

13 on the face of it, superficially

**outweigh**
06 exceed
07 surpass
08 overcome, override
11 predominate, prevail over
12 preponderate
13 be greater than, compensate for

**outwit**
03 con, kid
04 beat, dupe
05 cheat, trick
07 deceive, defraud, swindle
08 outsmart, outthink
11 outmaneuver
12 take for a ride
14 be cleverer than, get the better of, pull a fast one on

**outworn**
07 defunct, disused
08 outmoded, rejected
09 hackneyed, moth-eaten
11 discredited, obsolescent
12 old-fashioned

**oval**
05 ovate, ovoid
07 obovate, oviform
09 egg shaped
10 elliptical

**ovation**
06 bravos, cheers, praise
07 acclaim, praises, tribute
08 accolade, applause, cheering, clapping, plaudits
09 laudation
11 acclamation

**oven**
04 kiln
05 range, stove
09 microwave

**over**
02 on, up
04 done, gone, left, past, upon
05 above, aloft, ended, extra, kaput
06 beyond, no more, unused
07 at an end, settled, surplus
08 done with, finished, in excess, more than, overhead
09 completed, concluded, exceeding, forgotten, in the past, remaining, unclaimed
10 higher than, in addition, in charge of, in excess of
11 in command of, superfluous
14 ancient history
15 over and done with

❏ **over and above**
04 plus

07 added to, besides, on top of
08 as well as, let alone
09 along with
12 in addition to, not to mention, together with
❑ **over and over (again)**
05 often
09 ad nauseam, endlessly
10 frequently, repeatedly
11 ad infinitum, continually
12 time and again
13 again and again

**overabundance**
04 glut
06 excess
07 surfeit, surplus
08 plethora
09 profusion
11 superfluity
14 superabundance

**overact**
03 ham
06 overdo
07 lay it on
08 overplay, pile it on
10 exaggerate
12 lay it on thick

**overall**
05 broad, total
06 global
07 all-over, blanket, general
08 complete, umbrella
09 in general, inclusive
10 by and large, on the whole
13 comprehensive

**overalls**
05 pants
06 jumper
08 trousers, work wear
09 coveralls, dungarees

**overawe**
03 awe, cow
05 abash, alarm, daunt, scare
07 petrify, terrify, unnerve
10 disconcert, intimidate

**overbalance**
04 slip, trip
05 upset
07 capsize, tip over
08 fall over, keel over, overturn
10 somersault, topple over
15 lose your balance

**overbearing**
05 bossy, proud
06 snobby, snooty, snotty
08 arrogant, cavalier, despotic, dogmatic, snobbish
09 imperious, officious
10 autocratic, disdainful, highhanded, oppressive

11 dictatorial, domineering
12 contemptuous
13 high-and-mighty

**overblown**
08 inflated, overdone
09 amplified, bombastic, excessive
10 overcharge, overstated
11 extravagant, pretentious
13 self-important

**overcast**
04 dark, dull, gray, hazy
05 foggy, misty
06 cloudy, dismal, dreary, gloomy, leaden, somber
08 darkened

**overcharge**
02 do
03 gyp
04 rook, scam
05 cheat, sting
06 diddle, extort, fleece, rip off
07 swindle
11 shortchange

**overcome**
04 beat, best, lick, rout
05 moved, worst
06 broken, defeat, hammer, master, subdue, thrash
07 conquer, prevail, trounce
08 affected, vanquish
09 overpower, overthrow, overwhelm, rise above
10 bowled over, speechless
11 overpowered, overwhelmed, triumph over
12 lost for words

**overconfident**
04 rash
05 brash, cocky
08 arrogant, cocksure
09 foolhardy, hubristic
10 blustering, swaggering
11 overweening, self-assured
14 overoptimistic

**overcritical**
07 carping, Zoilean
08 captious, caviling, pedantic
10 nit-picking, pernickety
11 persnickety
12 faultfinding, hard to please
13 hairsplitting, hypercritical

**overcrowded**
06 jammed, packed
07 overrun, replete, teeming
08 brimming, swarming
09 chock-full, congested, jam-packed
10 overloaded
11 chockablock, crammed full

13 overpopulated

**overdo**
07 ham it up, lay it on, overact
08 go too far, pile it on
09 overstate
10 exaggerate
11 go overboard, overindulge
12 lay it on thick

❑ **overdo it**
07 crack up
08 overwork
09 do too much
10 sweat blood
11 work too hard
14 strain yourself
15 burn yourself out

**overdone**
05 undue
06 burned
07 charred, dried up, spoiled
08 effusive
09 excessive, overbaked
10 histrionic, inordinate, overcooked, overplayed, overstated
11 exaggerated, unnecessary
14 burned to a crisp
15 burned to a cinder
16 burned to a frazzle

**overdraft**
04 debt
07 arrears, deficit

**overdue**
03 due
04 late, slow
05 owing, tardy
06 unpaid
07 belated, delayed, pending
09 unsettled
10 behindhand, unpunctual
14 behind schedule

**overeat**
04 chow
05 binge, gorge, scarf
06 guzzle, pig out
10 go on a binge, gormandize
11 overindulge
13 stuff yourself

**overeating**
07 bulimia
08 bingeing, gluttony, guzzling
11 gourmandism, hyperphagia
12 gormandizing
14 overindulgence

**overemphasize**
05 labor
07 belabor
10 exaggerate, overstress
13 overdramatize

**overexert**

❑ **overexert yourself**
08 overdo it, overwork
11 work too hard
14 strain yourself
15 overtax yourself, wear yourself out

**overflow**
05 cover, flood, spill, swamp
06 deluge, shower
07 overrun, run over, surplus
08 brim over, flow over, inundate, spillage, well over
09 overspill, spill over
10 bubble over, inundation

**overflowing**
04 full, rife
07 brimful, profuse, teeming
08 inundant, thronged
09 abounding, bountiful
13 superabundant

**overgrowth**
05 uncut
10 escalation
11 hypertrophy
13 overabundance
14 superabundance
15 overdevelopment

**overhang**
03 jut
05 bulge
06 beetle, extend, jut out
07 project
08 bulge out, protrude, stand out, stick out

**overhanging**
07 bulging, jutting, pensile
08 beetling
10 bulging out, jutting out, projecting, protruding
11 standing out, sticking out

**overhaul**
03 fix
04 do up, mend, pass
05 check
06 doctor, repair, revamp, survey
07 check up, examine, inspect, outpace, rebuild, service
09 check over, going-over
10 inspection, renovation
11 examination, recondition, reconstruct
14 reconditioning

**overhead**
05 above, aloft
06 aerial, on high, raised, upward
07 up above, upwards
08 expenses

09 projector
11 overhanging
12 expenditures, regular costs, running costs
14 operating costs

**overheated**
05 angry, fiery
06 too hot
07 excited, flaming
08 agitated, inflamed
11 overexcited, overwrought

**overindulge**
05 binge, booze, gorge, spoil
06 guzzle, pamper, pander, pig out
07 debauch, satiate
09 spoon-feed
10 gluttonize, gormandize
11 mollycoddle

**overindulgence**
05 binge
06 excess
07 debauch, surfeit
10 overeating
12 intemperance

**overjoyed**
06 elated, joyful
08 ecstatic, euphoric, jubilant, thrilled
09 delighted, rapturous
10 enraptured, in raptures
11 high as a kite, on cloud nine, over the moon, tickled pink
12 happy as a clam
14 pleased as Punch
15 in seventh heaven, on top of the world

**overkill**
06 excess
07 surplus
08 overdone
11 superfluity

**overlap**
07 overlay, overlie, shingle
08 coincide, flap over
09 imbricate

**overlay**
04 wrap
05 adorn, cover, inlay
06 veneer
07 blanket, envelop, varnish
08 decorate, laminate

**overload**
03 tax
06 burden, strain
07 oppress, overtax
10 overburden, overcharge

**overlook**
04 face, miss, omit

06 excuse, forget, ignore, pardon, slight, wink at
07 condone, forgive, let pass
08 look onto, look over
09 disregard, front onto
14 take no notice of
15 turn a blind eye to

**overlooked**
08 unheeded, unvalued
10 unregarded, unremarked

**overly**
03 too
06 unduly
11 exceedingly, excessively
12 inordinately, unreasonably

**overnice**
10 nit-picking
11 overprecise, persnickety
13 oversensitive
14 overparticular, overscrupulous

**overplay**
05 color
06 overdo, stress
07 amplify, enhance, enlarge, lay it on, magnify
08 oversell, pile it on
09 dramatize, embroider, emphasize, overstate
10 aggrandize, exaggerate
12 lay it on thick
13 overdramatize, overemphasize
15 stretch the truth

**overpopulated**
06 jammed
07 overrun, teeming
08 swarming
09 chock-full, congested, jam-packed
11 crammed full, overcrowded

**overpower**
04 beat, daze, move, rout
05 crush, floor, quash, quell
06 defeat, master, subdue
07 conquer, stagger, trounce
08 bowl over, overcome, vanquish
09 dumbfound, overwhelm, subjugate
10 immobilize
11 flabbergast
15 gain mastery over

**overpowering**
06 strong
07 extreme
08 forceful, powerful, stifling
09 sickening
10 compelling, nauseating, oppressive, unbearable

11 irrefutable, suffocating
12 irresistible, overwhelming
14 uncontrollable

**overrate**
06 blow up
07 magnify
09 overprize, overvalue
10 overpraise
11 hyperbolize
12 overestimate

**overreach**

▢ **overreach yourself**
06 outwit
08 go too far, overdo it
14 strain yourself
15 burn yourself out

**override**
05 annul, quash
06 cancel, exceed, ignore
07 nullify, rescind, surpass
08 abrogate, outweigh, overcome, overrule
09 disregard, supersede
11 countermand, prevail over, trample over

**overriding**
05 final, first, major, prime, prior
06 ruling
07 pivotal, primary, supreme
08 cardinal, dominant, ultimate
09 essential, number one, paramount, principal
10 compelling, prevailing
11 determining, predominant
13 most important
15 most significant

**overrule**
05 annul
06 cancel, reject, revoke
07 nullify, rescind, reverse
08 abrogate, disallow, override, overturn, vote down
10 invalidate
11 countermand

**overrun**
05 storm, swamp
06 attack, exceed, go over, infest, invade, occupy
07 besiege, run riot
08 inundate, overgrow
09 overshoot, overwhelm, surge over, swarm over
10 spread over

**overseas**
06 abroad, exotic, remote
07 distant, faraway, foreign
08 external
10 far and wide
12 foreign parts
13 international

15 out of the country

**overseer**
04 boss
05 chief
07 foreman, manager
09 forewoman
10 manageress, supervisor
14 superintendent

**overshadow**
03 dim, mar
05 cloud, dwarf, excel, spoil
06 blight, darken
07 eclipse, obscure, surpass
08 dominate, outshine
10 tower above
12 put a damper on
13 put in the shade
14 take the edge off

**oversight**
04 boob, care, gaff
05 error, fault, gaffe, lapse
06 charge, howler, slip-up
07 blunder, control, mistake
08 handling, omission
10 management
11 dereliction, supervision
12 carelessness, surveillance

**overstate**
05 color
06 overdo, stress
07 amplify, enhance, enlarge, lay it on, magnify
08 oversell, pile it on
09 dramatize, emphasize
10 aggrandize, exaggerate
12 lay it on thick
13 overdramatize, overemphasize
15 stretch the truth

**overstatement**
06 excess, parody
09 burlesque, hyperbole
10 caricature
11 enlargement
12 exaggeration, extravagance, overemphasis
13 amplification, embellishment
14 overestimation
15 pretentiousness

**overt**
04 open
05 plain
06 patent, public
07 evident, obvious, visible
08 apparent, manifest, unveiled
10 noticeable, observable
11 unconcealed, undisguised

**overtake**
04 pass

06 befall, engulf, go past, strike
08 happen to, outstrip
09 drive past, overwhelm
11 leave behind, pull ahead of
13 catch unawares
14 take by surprise

**overthrow**
03 end
04 beat, fall, oust, rout, ruin
05 crush, quash, quell, upset
06 defeat, depose, invert, master, subdue, topple, unseat, upturn
07 abolish, conquer, ousting
08 dethrone, displace, downfall, overcome, turn over, vanquish
09 bring down, overpower, overwhelm, unseating
10 deposition
11 destruction, humiliation, suppression, vanquishing
12 dethronement

**overtone**
04 hint
05 sense
06 flavor, nuance
07 feeling
08 innuendo
10 intimation, suggestion
11 implication, insinuation
12 undercurrent
13 hidden meaning

**overture**
05 moves, music, offer
06 gambit, motion, signal
07 prelude
08 advances, approach, proposal
10 invitation, suggestion
11 opening move, proposition
12 introduction
13 opening gambit

**overturn**
04 beat, oust, veto
05 annul, crush, quash, upset
06 cancel, defeat, depose, invert, repeal, revoke, topple, unseat, upturn
07 abolish, capsize, destroy, nullify, rescind, tip over
08 abrogate, dethrone, displace, keel over, override, overrule, set aside, turn over, vanquish
09 bring down, overpower, overthrow, overwhelm
11 overbalance

**overused**
04 worn
05 stale, tired, trite
07 clichéd

**overweening**
08 bromidic
09 hackneyed, played out
10 overworked, threadbare
11 commonplace, stereotyped
13 platitudinous

**overweening**
04 vain
05 cocky, proud
07 haughty, pompous, swollen
08 arrogant, cavalier, cocksure, inflated, insolent
09 conceited, excessive, hubristic, overblown
10 highhanded, immoderate
11 egotistical, extravagant, opinionated
12 presumptuous, supercilious
13 self-confident

**overweight**
03 fat
04 huge
05 bulky, buxom, gross, heavy, hefty, obese, plump, podgy, pudgy, stout
06 chubby, chunky, flabby, portly
07 massive, outsize
09 corpulent
10 potbellied, well padded

**overwhelm**
04 beat, best, daze, lick, rout
05 crush, quash, quell, swamp
06 defeat, deluge, engulf, outwit, subdue, thrash
07 clobber, confuse, destroy, outplay, overrun, prevail, stagger, trounce
08 bowl over, inundate, outsmart, overcome, submerge, vanquish
09 devastate, overpower, overthrow, slaughter, snow under, subjugate
10 overburden
14 get the better of

**overwhelming**
04 huge, vast
05 great, large
07 extreme, immense

08 forceful, powerful, stifling
10 compelling, nauseating, oppressive, unbearable, undeniable
11 irrefutable, suffocating
12 irresistible, overpowering
14 uncontrollable

**overwork**
05 weary
06 burden, strain
07 exhaust, exploit, oppress, overtax, overuse, wear out
08 overdo it, overload
09 do too much
10 overstrain, sweat blood
11 work too hard
15 burn yourself out

**overworked**
04 worn
05 stale, tired, trite
07 clichéd, worn out
08 bromidic
09 exhausted, hackneyed, overtaxed, played out
10 threadbare, unoriginal
11 commonplace, stereotyped, stressed out
13 platitudinous

**overwrought**
04 edgy
05 tense
06 highly, on edge, strung
07 excited, frantic, keyed up, nervous, uptight, wound up
08 agitated, worked up
10 distraught
11 overcharged, overexcited
14 beside yourself

**owe**
10 be in debt to, be in the red
11 be overdrawn, get into debt
12 be indebted to
13 be in arrears to

**owing**
03 due
04 owed
06 unpaid
07 overdue, payable

09 in arrears, unsettled
11 outstanding

❏**owing to**
08 thanks to
09 because of
11 as a result of, on account of

**own**
03 use
04 have, hold, keep
05 enjoy
07 have got, possess, private
08 personal
10 individual, monopolize
13 idiosyncratic

❏**on your own**
04 solo
05 alone
06 single, singly
07 unaided
10 by yourself, unassisted
13 independently, unaccompanied

❏**own up**
05 admit
07 confess
09 come clean
11 acknowledge
12 tell the truth

**owner**
06 holder, keeper, master
08 landlady, landlord, mistress
09 homeowner, possessor
10 freeholder, proprietor
11 householder
12 proprietress

**ownership**
05 title
06 rights
08 dominion, freehold
10 possession
14 proprietorship

**ox**
03 yak
04 bull
05 bison, steer
06 bovine
07 buffalo, bullock

**pace**
04 gait, rate, step, time, walk
05 march, speed, tempo
06 patrol, stride
07 mark off, mark out, measure
08 celerity, rapidity, velocity
09 quickness, swiftness

**pacific**
04 calm, mild
05 quiet, still
06 dovish, irenic, placid, serene
07 equable, halcyon
08 dovelike, peaceful, tranquil
09 peaceable, placatory,
   unruffled
10 nonviolent
11 peace loving, peacemaking
12 conciliatory, pacificatory
14 nonbelligerent

**pacifism**
10 pacificism, Satyagraha
11 nonviolence

**pacifist**
04 bolo, dove
06 conchy
07 conchie
10 pacificist, peace lover

**pacify**
04 calm, lull, tame
05 quiet, still
06 defuse, soothe
07 appease, assuage, compose,
   mollify, placate, put down,
   quieten, silence
08 calm down, moderate
10 conciliate

**pack**
03 bag, jam, mob, ram, set
04 bale, band, cram, fill, load,
   stow, wrap
05 bunch, cover, crate, crowd,
   drove, flock, group, press,
   store, stuff, tie up, wedge
06 bundle, burden, carton, kit
   bag, packet, parcel, wrap up
07 compact, package, squeeze
08 backpack, compress, ditty
   bag, knapsack, rucksack
09 container, fanny pack,
   haversack, saddlebag

❑**pack in**
03 end, jam, mob, ram

04 stop
05 chuck, crowd, stuff, wedge
06 cram in, give up, resign,
   throng
07 squeeze, throw in

❑**pack off**
04 send
07 dismiss
08 dispatch

**package**
03 box, set
04 bale, pack, unit, wrap
05 batch, group, whole
06 carton, entity, packet, parcel
08 gift-wrap
09 container
11 consignment, package tour

**packaging**
06 packet
07 packing, wrapper
08 wrapping
09 container
10 cellophane

**packed**
04 full
06 filled, jammed
07 brimful, crammed, crowded,
   stuffed
09 chock-full, congested, jam-
   packed
11 chockablock

**packet**
04 pack
06 bundle, carton
07 package, package, packing,
   parcel,
09 container
10 packet boat

**pact**
04 bond, deal
06 cartel, treaty
07 compact, entente
08 alliance, contract, covenant
09 agreement, concordat

**pad**
03 paw, run, wad
04 digs, fill, flat, foot, home,
   pack, sole, step, walk
05 stuff, tramp, tread
06 jotter, pallet, studio, tablet,
   tiptoe, trudge

07 cushion, hangout, padding,
   protect, wadding
08 lengthen, notebook,
   quarters, stamp pad
09 apartment, footprint, launch
   pad
10 overcharge, protection

❑**pad out**
06 expand
07 augment, fill out, spin out,
   stretch
08 flesh out, lengthen, protract
09 elaborate

**padding**
06 hot air, lining
07 filling, packing, wadding
08 stuffing, verbiage
09 wordiness
10 cushioning, protection

**paddle**
03 oar, row
04 pull, punt, slop, wade
05 scull, steer, sweep
06 dabble, propel, splash,
   toddle
09 dog paddle

**paddock**
03 pen
04 fold, yard
05 field, pound
06 corral, stable
08 compound, stockade
09 enclosure

**padlock**
04 bolt, lock
05 catch, clasp
09 fastening

**padre**
05 vicar
06 cleric, curate, deacon, father,
   parson, pastor, priest, rector
08 chaplain, minister, reverend
09 clergyman

**paean, pean**
04 hymn
05 psalm
06 anthem, eulogy
08 doxology, encomium, ode to
   joy
09 dithyramb, panegyric
12 song of praise

**pagan**
07 atheist, godless, heathen
10 unbeliever
11 pantheistic

**page**
04 call, leaf, side
05 epoch, event, folio, phase, recto, sheet, stage, verso
06 ask for, period, summon
07 bellboy, bellhop, chapter, episode, pageboy, send for
08 announce, incident
09 attendant, messenger

**pageant**
04 play, show
06 parade
07 display, tableau
09 cavalcade, spectacle
10 procession
14 representation

**pageantry**
04 pomp, show
06 glamor, parade
07 display, glamour, glitter
08 ceremony, flourish, grandeur, splendor
09 spectacle
12 extravagance, magnificence
13 theatricality

**pail**
03 can, tub
04 bail
05 churn
06 bucket, piggin

**pain**
03 ail, woe
04 ache, bore, drag, hurt, pang, pest, rack, stab
05 agony, cramp, grief, smart, spasm, sting, throb, worry
06 aching, be sore, bother, burden, grieve, misery, sadden, sorrow, twinge
07 afflict, agonize, anguish, torment, torture
08 distress, headache, nuisance, vexation
09 annoyance, heartache
10 discomfort, heartbreak, tenderness
13 make miserable

**pained**
04 hurt
05 stung, upset, vexed
07 grieved, injured, wounded
08 offended, saddened
09 aggrieved
10 distressed
11 reproachful

**painful**
04 hard, sore
05 tough
06 aching, tender, touchy
07 arduous, hurting, tedious
08 inflamed, rigorous, shameful, smarting, stabbing
09 agonizing, difficult, harrowing, laborious, miserable, sensitive, strenuous, throbbing, upsetting
10 mortifying, unpleasant
11 distressing
12 disagreeable, excruciating
13 uncomfortable

**painfully**
05 sadly
08 pitiably, terribly, woefully
09 pitifully
10 alarmingly, deplorably, dreadfully
11 agonizingly, excessively
13 distressingly, unfortunately
14 excruciatingly

**painkiller**
07 anodyne
08 lenitive, sedative
09 analgesic
10 anesthetic, palliative

**painless**
04 easy
05 cushy
08 pain-free
09 easy as pie
10 child's play, effortless
11 trouble-free, undemanding
12 a piece of cake, plain sailing

**pains**
05 labor
06 effort
07 trouble
09 diligence

❑**be at pains**
06 bother
07 try hard
08 take care
15 make every effort

**painstaking**
07 careful, devoted
08 diligent, sedulous, thorough
09 assiduous, attentive
10 meticulous, scrupulous
11 hardworking, industrious, persevering, punctilious
13 conscientious

**paint**
04 coat, daub, tell, tint, wash
05 color, evoke, glaze, spray, stain

06 depict, sketch
07 lacquer, narrate, pigment, plaster, portray, recount
08 colorant, coloring, decorate, describe
09 represent, whitewash
10 redecorate

➤ *Types of paint*:
03 oil
05 glaze, gloss, matte
06 enamel, pastel, poster, primer
07 acrylic, gouache, lacquer, scumble, varnish
08 eggshell, emulsion
09 distemper, undercoat, whitewash
10 watercolor
➤ See also ART

❑**paint the town red**
04 rave
05 binge, go out
07 have fun, rejoice
08 live it up
09 celebrate, have a ball, whoop it up
11 go on the town

**painter**
06 artist, dauber, limner
08 colorist
10 oil painter
11 miniaturist, portraitist
13 watercolorist

➤ *Some names of painters, printmakers, illustrators and graphic artists*:
03 **Arp** (Jean), **Dix** (Otto), **Ray** (Man)
04 **Bell** (Vanessa), **Cole** (Thomas), **Dali** (Salvador), **Doré** (Gustave), **Dufy** (Raoul), **Eyck** (Jan van), **Goya** (Francisco de), **Gris** (Juan), **Hals** (Frans), **Hunt** (Holman), **John** (Augustus), **John** (Gwen), **Klee** (Paul), **Long** (Richard), **Marc** (Franz), **Miró** (Joan), **Nash** (Paul), **Wood** (Grant)
05 **Bacon** (Francis), **Blake** (Peter), **Blake** (William), **Bosch** (Hieronymus), **Brown** (Ford Madox), **Burra** (Edward), **Corot** (Camille), **David** (Jacques Louis), **Degas** (Edgar), **Dürer** (Albrecht), **Ernst** (Max), **Freud** (Lucien), **Gorky** (Arshile), **Greco** (El), **Grosz** (George), **Hicks** (Edward), **Hirst** (Damien),

Johns (Jasper), **Kahlo** (Frida), **Kitaj** (Ronald Brooks), **Klimt** (Gustav), **Kline** (Franz), **Lewis** (Wyndham), **Léger** (Fernand), **Lippi** (Filippino), **Lippi** (Fra Filippo), **Lowry** (Laurence Stephen), **Manet** (Edouard), **Monet** (Claude), **Mucha** (Alphonse), **Munch** (Edvard), **Peale** (Rembrandt), **Piper** (John), **Riley** (Bridget), **Sarto** (Andrea del)
06 **Braque** (Georges), **Bratby** (John), **Catlin** (George), **Church** (Frederick), **Claude**, **Derain** (André Louis), **Durand** (Asher Brown), **Escher** (Maurits Cornelis), **Fuseli** (Henri), **Giotto**, **Hopper** (Edward), **Ingres** (Jean Auguste Dominique), **Jarman** (Derek), **Leutze** (Emanuel), **Mabuse**, **Massys** (Quentin), **Millet** (Jean François), **Morris** (William), **Newman** (Barnett), **Palmer** (Samuel), **Pisano** (Nicola), **Renoir** (Pierre Auguste), **Rivera** (Diego), **Rothko** (Mark), **Rubens** (Peter Paul), **Scarfe** (Gerald), **Searle** (Ronald), **Seurat** (Georges), **Sisley** (Alfred), **Stuart** (Gilbert), **Stubbs** (George), **Tanguy** (Yves), **Titian**, **Toledo** (Jose Rey), **Turner** (Joseph Mallord William), **Warhol** (Andy), **Wright** (Joseph)
07 **Attwell** (Mabel Lucie), **Audubon** (John James), **Bellini** (Giovanni), **Bonnard** (Pierre), **Boucher** (François), **Cassatt** (Mary), **Cézanne** (Paul), **Chagall** (Marc), **Chirico** (Giorgio de), **Christo**, **Cimabué**, **Courbet** (Gustave), **Cranach** (Lucas), **Daumier** (Honoré), **Delvaux** (Paul), **Duchamp** (Marcel), **El Greco**, **Gauguin** (Paul), **Hobbema** (Meindert), **Hockney** (David), **Hodgkin** (Howard), **Hofmann** (Hans), **Hogarth** (William), **Holbein** (Hans), **Keating** (Tom), **Matisse** (Henri), **Millais** (John Everett), **Morisot** (Berthe), **O'Keeffe**

(Georgia), **Picabia** (Francis), **Picasso** (Pablo), **Pollock** (Jackson), **Poussin** (Nicolas), **Rackham** (Arthur), **Raeburn** (Henry), **Raphael**, **Russell** (Charles), **Sargent** (John Singer), **Schiele** (Egon), **Sickert** (Walter), **Spencer** (Stanley), **Tenniel** (John), **Tiepolo** (Giovanni Battista), **Uccello** (Paolo), **Utrillo** (Maurice), **Van Eyck** (Jan), **Van Gogh** (Vincent), **Vermeer** (Jan), **Watteau** (Antoine), **Wearing** (Gillian), **Willard** (Archibald)
08 **Angelico** (Fra), **Auerbach** (Frank), **Breughel** (Pieter), **Brueghel** (Pieter), **Delaunay** (Robert), **Dubuffet** (Jean), **Goncourt** (Edmond de), **Hamilton** (Richard), **Hilliard** (Nicholas), **Landseer** (Edwin), **Leonardo**, **Magritte** (René), **Mantegna** (Andrea), **Masaccio**, **Mondrian** (Piet), **Perugino**, **Piranesi** (Giovanni Battista), **Pissarro** (Camille), **Reynolds** (Joshua), **Rockwell** (Norman), **Rossetti** (Dante Gabriel), **Rousseau** (Henri, **Ruisdael** (Jacob van), **Ruysdael** (Jacob van), **Trumbull** (John), **Veronese** (Paolo), **Vlaminck** (Maurice de), **Whistler** (James McNeill)
09 **Beardsley** (Aubrey), **Canaletto**, **Constable** (John), **Correggio**, **De Kooning** (Willem), **Delacroix** (Eugène), **Fragonard** (Jean Honoré), **Friedrich** (Caspar David), **Géricault** (Théodore), **Giorgione**, **Greenaway** (Kate), **Grünewald** (Matthias), **Kandinsky** (Wasily), **Kokoschka** (Oskar), **Lancaster** (Osbert), **Nicholson** (Ben), **Pisanello**, **Rembrandt**, **Remington** (Frederic), **Velázquez** (Diego)
10 **Alma-Tadema** (Lawrence), **Botticelli** (Sandro), **Burne-Jones** (Edward), **Caravaggio** (Michelangelo), **Giacometti** (Alberto), **Modigliani** (Amedeo),

**Motherwell** (Robert), **Sutherland** (Graham), **Tintoretto**
12 **Gainsborough** (Thomas), **Grandma Moses**, **Lichtenstein** (Roy), **Michelangelo**
14 **Andrea del Sarto**, **Claude Lorraine**, **Lucas van Leyden**
15 **Leonardo da Vinci**, **Toulouse-Lautrec** (Henri de)
➤ See also ART

**painting**
03 oil
05 mural
06 fresco
08 likeness, portrait
09 landscape, miniature, portrayal, still life
10 watercolor
➤ See also ART

➤ *Painting terms*:
04 icon, tint, tone, wash
05 bloom, brush, easel, gesso, mural, paint, pieta, tondo
06 canvas, fresco, frieze, primer, sketch
07 cartoon, collage, diptych, drawing, gallery, gouache, impasto, montage, palette, pastels, picture, pigment, scumble, sfumato, stipple, tempera
08 abstract, aquatint, bleeding, charcoal, frottage, hard edge, pastoral, portrait, seascape, thinners, triptych, vignette
09 aquarelle, capriccio, encaustic, flat brush, grisaille, grotesque, landscape, mahlstick, miniature, sgraffito, still life
10 art gallery, craquelure, figurative, monochrome, pentimento, sable brush, silhouette, turpentine, watercolor
11 chiaroscuro, composition, oil painting, perspective, pointillism, trompe l'oeil
12 brush strokes, illustration, palette knife
13 genre painting, underpainting
14 foreshortening

➤ *Some well known paintings, drawings, etchings and engravings*:
04 Flag

05 Manga, Pietà
06 Spring, Wham!
07 Bubbles, Erasmus, Gin Lane, Niagara, Olympia, Targets
08 Guernica, Maja Nude, Mona Lisa, The Ox-Bow
09 Bacchanal, Black Iris, Haystacks, Jerusalem, Night Café, Primavera, The Scream
10 Adam and Eve, Assumption, Beer Street, Blue Horses, Excavation, Las Meninas, Sunflowers, The Angelus, The Hay Wain
11 A Shrimp Girl, Crucifixion, Limp Watches, Maja Clothed, Starry Night, The Gleaners, Water Lilies
12 Buffalo Dance, Peasant Dance, The Nightmare, The Scapegoat, The Umbrellas, Woman Bathing
13 A Bigger Splash, Christ in Glory, Sleeping Gypsy, The Last Supper, The Night Watch
14 A Rake's Progress, American Gothic, Disasters of War, Peasant Wedding, Sistine Madonna, The Ambassadors, The Card Players, The Four Seasons, The Rokeby Venus
15 Flight into Egypt, Madonna and Child, Madonna del Prato, Marriage à la Mode, The Annunciation, The Birth of Venus, The Dance of Death, The Death of Marat, The Flagellation, The Potato Eaters, The Raft of Medusa, The Rape of Europa

**pair**
03 duo, set, two, wed
04 join, link, mate, team, twin
05 brace, marry, match, twins
06 couple, splice
07 bracket, match up, twosome
10 two of a kind
11 put together

**paired**
05 mated, yoked
06 double, in twos, joined
07 coupled, matched, twinned
09 bracketed

**pal**
04 chum, mate
05 buddy, crony
06 friend
07 comrade
08 sidekick
09 companion

**palace**
05 manse
06 castle
07 chateau, mansion

**paleontologists**

► *Names of paleontologists and paleoanthropologists*:
04 **Cope** (Edward Drinker)
05 **Gould** (Stephen Jay), **Marsh** (Othniel Charles)
06 **Forbes** (Edward), **Leakey** (Louis Seymour Bazett), **Leakey** (Mary Douglas), **Leakey** (Richard), **Osborn** (Henry Fairfield)
07 **Andrews** (Roy Chapman), **Granger** (Walter), **Mantell** (Gideon Algernon)
08 **Anderson** (Elaine), **Johanson** (Donald Carl)
09 **Tattersal** (Ian)
➤ See also SCIENTIST

**palatable**
05 tasty, yummy
06 edible, savory
07 eatable, flavory
09 agreeable, enjoyable, flavorous, succulent
10 appetizing, delectable, flavorsome
11 scrumptious
13 mouthwatering

**palate**
05 taste
06 liking
08 appetite

**palatial**
04 posh
05 grand, plush, regal, ritzy
06 deluxe
07 opulent, stately
08 imposing, splendid
09 grandiose, luxurious, sumptuous

**palaver**
04 chat
07 flatter
08 business
09 flattery,
10 conference, discussion

**pale**
03 dim, wan
04 ashy, fade, waxy, weak
05 ashen, faded, faint, fence, light, muted, pasty, peaky, stake, waxen, white
06 anemic, blanch, bleach, chalky, feeble, lessen, pallid, pastel, sallow, whiten
07 drained, insipid

08 bleached, diminish, district
09 colorless, etiolated, territory, washed-out
10 pasty faced

☐**beyond the pale**
08 improper, unseemly
11 intolerable
12 inadmissible, unacceptable
13 inappropriate

**palisade**
05 fence
06 paling
08 stockade
09 barricade, enclosure

**pall**
04 bore, cloy, jade, sate, tire, veil
05 cloak, cloud, gloom, weary
06 damper, mantle, shadow, shroud, sicken
07 disgust, satiate, wear off
08 covering

☐**cast a pall over**
03 mar
05 spoil, upset
06 impair

**palliate**
04 ease
05 abate, allay, cloak, cover
06 soothe, temper
07 assuage, mollify, relieve
08 mitigate, moderate
09 alleviate, extenuate

**palliative**
07 anodyne, calming
08 lenitive, sedative, soothing
09 analgesic, calmative, demulcent
10 painkiller
11 alleviative
12 tranquilizer
13 tranquillizer

**pallid**
03 wan
04 ashy, pale, waxy, weak
05 ashen, bland, pasty, waxen
06 anemic, sallow
07 insipid
09 bloodless, colorless, etiolated, whey-faced
10 pasty-faced, spiritless

**pallor**
07 wanness
09 whiteness
10 chalkiness, etiolation, pallidness, sallowness
13 bloodlessness

**palm**
03 paw
04 grab, hand, hide, mitt, take, tree

**palmist**

06 snatch
11 appropriate

---

▶ *Types of palm*:
03 ita
04 atap, coco, nipa
05 areca, assai, bussu, nikau, Sabal
06 buriti, cohune, corozo, Elaeis, gomuti, gru-gru, jupati, kentia, kittul, raffia, Raphia, rattan
07 babassu, calamus, coquito, Corypha, Euterpe, moriche, oil-palm, palmyra, paxiuba, pupunha, talipat, talipot, wax palm
08 carnauba, coco palm, date palm, palmetto, sago palm
09 macaw palm, sugar palm, toddy palm
10 Chamaerops, Washington
11 coconut palm, coconut tree
12 chiquichiqui, Washingtonia
➤ See also PLANT

❏**palm off**
05 foist
06 fob off, thrust, unload
07 offload, pass off
08 get rid of

**palmist**
11 chiromancer, clairvoyant
13 fortuneteller

**palmistry**
10 chiromancy
12 clairvoyance, clairvoyancy
14 fortunetelling

**palmy**
06 golden, joyous
07 halcyon
08 carefree, glorious, thriving
10 prosperous, successful

**palpable**
05 clear, plain, solid
08 concrete, material, tangible
09 touchable
11 substantial

**palpitate**
04 beat, thud
05 pound, pulse, throb, thump
07 flutter, pulsate

**paltry**
04 mean, poor, puny
05 minor, petty, small, sorry
06 meager, measly, slight
07 trivial
08 derisory, piddling, trifling
09 miserable, worthless
10 negligible
12 contemptible

13 insignificant

**pamper**
03 pet
04 baby
05 spoil
06 coddle, cosset, pander
07 indulge
09 spoon-feed
11 mollycoddle, overindulge

**pampered**
06 petted
07 coddled, spoiled
08 cosseted, indulged
12 mollycoddled

**pamphlet**
05 tract
06 folder, notice
07 booklet, handout, leaflet
08 brochure, chapbook, circular, fly sheet

**pan**
03 pot, wok
04 face, flay, scan, slam
05 fryer, knock, roast, sweep, swing, track
06 hammer, vessel
07 censure, skillet
08 traverse
09 casserole, container, criticize
10 springform
12 pull to pieces
13 find fault with

❏**pan out**
06 happen, result
07 turn out, work out

**panacea**
06 elixir
07 cure-all, nostrum
15 universal remedy

**panache**
04 brio, dash, élan, zest
05 flair, style, verve, vigor
06 energy, spirit
08 flourish
11 flamboyance, ostentation

**pancake**
05 blini, crêpe
06 blintz, makeup
07 hotcake
08 flapjack, slapjack
10 battercake
11 griddlecake

**pandemic**
06 common, global
07 general
09 extensive, universal
10 widespread
11 far-reaching

**pandemonium**
03 din
04 to-do
05 chaos
06 bedlam, hubbub, rumpus, tumult, uproar
09 commotion, confusion, hue and cry
10 hullabaloo, turbulence
11 hullaballoo

**pander**

❏**pander to**
05 humor
06 pamper
07 gratify, indulge

**panegyric**
04 pean
05 paean
06 eulogy, homage, praise
07 glowing, tribute
08 accolade, citation, encomium, eulogium
09 laudatory
10 eulogistic
11 encomiastic
12 commendation
13 complimentary

**panel**
04 beam, jury, slab, team
05 board, dials, drape, knobs, sheet
06 levers
07 buttons, console, council, curtain
08 cartouch, controls, switches
09 cartouche, committee, dashboard
10 commission
11 directorate, instruments

**paneling**
04 dado
08 wainscot
11 wainscoting
12 wainscotting

**pang**
04 ache, pain, stab
05 agony, gripe, prick, qualm, spasm, sting, throe
07 anguish, scruple
08 distress
10 discomfort, uneasiness

**panic**
04 flap
05 alarm
06 frenzy, fright, terror
08 hysteria
09 agitation, overreact
10 go to pieces
11 have kittens

12 lose your cool, lose your
   head
13 lose your nerve

**panic-stricken**
07 frantic, panicky
08 frenzied
09 petrified, terrified
10 frightened, hysterical
11 scared stiff
12 in a cold sweat

**panoply**
05 armor, array, get up, range
06 attire
07 raiment, regalia, turnout
09 equipment, trappings

**panorama**
04 view
05 scene, vista
06 survey
07 scenery
08 overview, prospect
09 landscape
11 perspective

**panoramic**
04 wide
05 broad
06 scenic
07 general, overall
08 sweeping
09 extensive, universal
11 far-reaching, wide-ranging

**pant**
04 ache, blow, gasp, huff, long,
   pine, puff, sigh, want
05 covet, crave, heave, yearn
06 desire, hanker, thirst
11 huff and puff

**panting**
05 eager
06 puffed, winded
07 anxious, craving, gasping,
   longing, puffing
09 hankering, puffed out
10 breathless
11 out of breath, short-winded

**pantomime**
06 masque
07 charade
09 harlequin
12 harlequinade

**pants**
05 jeans
06 briefs, capris, shorts, slacks,
   trunks, undies
07 drawers, panties
08 bloomers, britches, trousers
10 underpants
11 boxer shorts
12 pedal pushers

**pap**
03 goo, rot
04 mash, mush, pulp
05 paste, purée, trash
06 drivel
07 rubbish
08 claptrap, nonsense
09 gibberish

**paper**
03 rag
04 deed, exam
05 daily, essay, organ, study
06 record, report, thesis, weekly
07 article, journal, tabloid
08 document, magazine,
   treatise
09 broadside, monograph,
   newspaper, newsprint,
   wallpaper
10 broadsheet, credential,
   periodical, stationery
11 certificate, composition,
   examination, publication
12 dissertation
14 identification

▶ *Paper sizes*:
04 demy, post, pott
05 atlas, crown, folio, legal, royal
06 medium, octavo, quarto
07 emperor
08 elephant, foolscap, imperial
09 antiquary
10 super royal, typewriter

❏**on paper**
08 in theory, recorded
09 in writing
10 officially
11 on the record, written down
13 theoretically
14 hypothetically
15 in black and white

❏**paper over**
04 hide
07 conceal, cover up, obscure
08 disguise
10 camouflage

**papery**
04 thin
05 frail, light
06 flimsy
07 fragile
08 delicate
09 paper-thin
13 insubstantial

**par**
04 mean, norm
05 level, usual
06 median, parity
07 average, balance
08 equality, standard

11 equilibrium, equivalence
12 equal footing

❏**below par**
05 tired
06 unwell
10 out of sorts
12 below average
14 not up to scratch,
   unsatisfactory
15 under the weather

❏**on a par with**
07 equal to
08 as good as

❏**par for the course**
05 usual
06 normal
07 typical
08 standard

**parable**
05 fable, story
06 lesson
08 allegory
09 moral tale

**parade**
04 file, show
05 array, march, train, vaunt
06 column, flaunt, review
07 display, exhibit, show off
08 brandish, ceremony, file past
09 cavalcade, motorcade,
   spectacle
10 exhibition, procession

**paradigm**
05 ideal, model
07 example, pattern
08 exemplar, original
09 archetype, framework,
   prototype

**paradise**
04 Eden
05 bliss, bliss
06 Heaven, utopia
07 arcadia, Elysium, Elysium,
   nirvana, rapture
09 afterlife, hereafter, next
   world, Shangri-La
12 Garden of Eden
13 Elysian Fields, seventh
   heaven

**paradox**
06 enigma, puzzle, riddle
07 anomaly
11 incongruity
13 contradiction, inconsistency

**paradoxical**
08 baffling, puzzling
09 anomalous, enigmatic,
   illogical
11 incongruous
12 inconsistent

13 contradictory

**paragon**
05 ideal, model
07 epitome, pattern
08 exemplar, last word, standard
09 archetype, criterion, nonpareil, prototype
12 quintessence, the bee's knees

**paragraph**
04 item, part
07 passage, portion, section, segment
10 subsection
11 subdivision

**parallel**
05 agree, equal, liken, match
06 analog
07 aligned, analogy, compare, conform, similar, uniform
08 analogue, likeness, matching, resemble
09 alongside, analogous, correlate, duplicate
10 collateral, comparable, comparison, correspond, equivalent, homologous, resembling, similarity
11 coextensive, correlation, equidistant
13 corresponding

**paralyze**
04 halt, lame, numb, stop
06 deaden, freeze
07 cripple, disable
08 transfix
10 immobilize

**paralyzed**
04 numb
08 crippled, disabled
09 paralytic
10 paraplegic
12 quadriplegic

**paralysis**
04 halt
05 palsy
07 paresis
08 deadness, numbness, shutdown, stoppage
10 immobility, paraplegia, standstill
12 debilitation, quadriplegia
13 powerlessness

**paralytic**
05 drunk
07 legless, palsied
08 crippled, disabled
09 paralyzed
10 hemiplegic, monoplegic
12 quadriplegic

**parameter**
08 boundary, variable
09 criterion, framework, guideline
10 limitation
11 restriction
14 limiting factor

**paramount**
04 main
05 chief, first, prime
07 highest, supreme, topmost
08 cardinal
11 outstanding, predominant

**paramour**
04 beau
05 lover
07 beloved, hetaera
08 mistress
09 courtesan, inamorata, inamorato

**paranoia**
09 delusions, obsession, psychosis

**paranoid**
10 bewildered, suspicious
11 distrustful

**parapet**
04 rail, wall
05 fence, guard
06 paling
07 barrier, bastion, bulwark, defense, railing, rampart
08 barbican
10 battlement, embankment

**paraphernalia**
04 gear
05 stuff, tools
06 tackle, things
07 baggage, effects
09 apparatus, equipment, materials, trappings
10 belongings, implements
11 accessories, odds and ends, possessions
13 accouterments, accoutrements, bits and pieces

**paraphrase**
05 gloss
06 rehash, render, reword
07 restate, version
09 interpret, rendering, rewording, translate
11 restatement, translation
14 interpretation

**parasite**
05 leech
07 entozoa, epizoon, sponger
08 deadbeat, epiphyte
09 endophyte, passenger

10 freeloader
11 bloodsucker

**parasitic**
07 epizoic
08 sponging
09 biogenous, leechlike
11 freeloading, parasitical
12 bloodsucking

**parcel**
03 box, lot, mob
04 area, band, deal, gang, herd, pack, plot, wrap
05 bunch, crowd, flock, group, patch, piece, tie up, tract, troop
06 bundle, carton, pack up, packet, wrap up
07 company, package, portion
08 bundle up, gift-wrap
09 allotment
10 collection

❑**parcel out**
05 allot
06 divide
07 carve up, deal out, dole out, hand out, mete out
08 allocate, dispense, share out
09 apportion, divide out
10 distribute

**parch**
04 bake, burn, sear
05 dry up
06 scorch, wither
07 blister, shrivel
09 dehydrate, desiccate

**parched**
03 dry
04 arid, sear, sere
05 baked
06 burned, seared
07 dried up, gasping, thirsty
08 scorched, withered
09 shriveled, waterless
10 dehydrated, desiccated, dry as a bone

**parchment**
06 scroll, vellum
07 charter, diploma
08 document
10 palimpsest
11 certificate

**pardon**
05 mercy, remit, spare
06 acquit, excuse, let off
07 absolve, amnesty, condone, forgive, release
08 clemency, lenience, liberate, overlook, reprieve

**pardonable**
09 acquittal, discharge, exculpate, exonerate, vindicate
10 absolution, indulgence
11 forbearance, forgiveness
13 let off the hook

**pardonable**
06 venial
09 excusable
10 condonable, forgivable
11 justifiable

**pare**
04 peel, skin, trim
06 reduce
07 cut back, whittle
08 decrease

**parent**
03 dam
04 root, sire
05 beget, raise
06 author, create, father, foster, mother, origin, source
07 bring up, creator, nurture
08 begetter, guardian
09 look after, procreate
10 originator, procreator, progenitor, take care of
15 umbrella company

**parentage**
04 line, race
05 birth, stock
06 family, origin, source, stirps
07 descent, lineage, stirpes
08 ancestry, pedigree
09 filiation, paternity
10 derivation, extraction

**parenthetical**
05 aside
08 inserted
09 bracketed
10 incidental, interposed
11 intervening
13 in parenthesis

**pariah**
05 exile, leper
06 outlaw
07 outcast
08 castaway, unperson
10 Ishmaelite
11 undesirable, untouchable

**paring**
04 peel, rind, skin
05 flake, shred, slice
06 sliver
07 cutting, peeling, shaving, snippet
08 clipping, trimming

**parish**
04 fold, town
05 flock
06 church
07 village
08 district
09 community
11 churchgoers
12 congregation, parishioners

**parity**
03 par
07 analogy
08 affinity, equality
09 agreement, congruity
10 congruence, consonance
11 consistency, parallelism

**park**
03 put, set
04 stop
05 leave, place, plonk
07 commons, deposit, diamond, grounds
08 ballpark, position, woodland
09 grassland
10 open square
13 amusement park

**parlance**
04 cant, talk
05 argot, idiom, lingo
06 jargon, speech, tongue
11 phraseology

**parley**
04 talk
05 speak, talks
06 confab, confer, dialog, powwow
07 consult, council, discuss
08 colloquy, dialogue
09 negotiate, tête-à-tête
10 conference, discussion
11 negotiation

**parliament**
04 diet
05 house
06 senate
07 council
08 assembly, congress
10 lower house, upper house
11 convocation, legislature

► *Names of parliaments and political assemblies:*
04 Dáil, Diet, Duma
05 Forum, Lords
06 Cortes, Majlis, Senate, Soviet
07 Commons, Knesset, Riksdag, Tynwald
08 Assembly, Congress, Lok Sabha, Storting
09 Bundesrat, Bundestag, Directory, Eduskunta, Reichstag, State Duma
10 Convention
11 House of Keys, Star Chamber
12 House of Lords
13 Supreme Soviet
14 Council of State, Estates General, House of Commons, Long Parliament, Rump Parliament
15 People's Assembly, People's Congress
➤ See also POLITICS

**parliamentary**
09 law giving, lawmaking
10 democratic, republican, senatorial
11 legislative
12 governmental
13 congressional, legislatorial

**parlor**
03 den
06 lounge
09 front room
10 living room
11 drawing room, sitting room

**parochial**
04 hick
06 narrow
07 insular, limited
09 blinkered, small-town
10 provincial
12 narrow-minded
13 inward looking

**parochialism**
10 insularity, narrowness
13 provincialism

**parody**
04 skit
05 spoof
06 satire
07 imitate, lampoon, take off
08 satirize, travesty
09 burlesque
10 caricature, distortion, pasquinade

**paroxysm**
05 spasm
07 seizure
10 convulsion

**parrot**
03 ape
04 copy, echo
05 macaw, mimic
06 Amazon, repeat
07 copycat, imitate
08 cockatoo, imitator, parakeet
09 cockatiel
11 learn by rote

**parry**
05 avert, avoid, block, evade, field
07 deflect, fend off, ward off
08 stave off

09 turn aside

**parsimonious**
04 mean
05 close, mingy, tight
06 frugal, stingy
07 miserly
09 niggardly, penurious
11 close-fisted, tightfisted
12 cheese-paring
13 penny-pinching

**parsimony**
08 meanness
09 frugality, minginess, tightness
10 stinginess
11 miserliness
13 niggardliness, penny-pinching
15 tightfistedness

**parson**
05 vicar
06 cleric, pastor, priest, rector
08 minister, preacher, reverend
09 churchman, clergyman

**part**
03 bit, cut, job
04 area, book, duty, gift, half, role, side, tear, wing, work
05 break, chore, facet, piece, quota, scrap, sever, share, skill, slice, split
06 aspect, branch, clause, cleave, detach, divide, factor, module, office, parcel, region, volume
07 article, break up, chapter, disband, disjoin, diverge, element, excerpt, extract, faculty, limited, measure, partial, portion, quarter, scatter, section, segment, split up
08 capacity, disperse, district, division, fraction, fragment, function, get going, particle, separate
09 allotment, character, come apart, component, dimension, dismantle, imperfect, take apart, territory
10 depart from, department, disconnect, go away from, ingredient, percentage, proportion, say goodbye
11 constituent, installment, involvement, not complete
12 separate from
13 take your leave
14 accomplishment, responsibility

□**for the most part**
06 mainly, mostly
09 in the main
10 by and large, on the whole

□**in part**
06 partly
10 up to a point
12 to some degree, to some extent

□**part with**
05 yield
06 forego, give up
07 discard, let go of
10 relinquish

□**take part in**
06 join in
07 partake, share in
08 assist in, engage in, help with
12 be involved in, contribute to
13 participate in

**partake**
05 share
08 take part
10 be involved
11 participate

□**partake of**
03 eat
05 drink, evoke, share
06 evince
07 consume, possess, receive, suggest
11 demonstrate

**partial**
04 part
06 biased, in part, unfair, unjust
07 colored, limited
08 one-sided, partisan
10 incomplete, prejudiced
11 inequitable, predisposed
14 discriminatory

□**partial to**
06 fond of
09 keen about, taken with

**partiality**
04 bias
08 fondness, inequity
09 prejudice
10 preference, proclivity
11 inclination
12 partisanship, predilection
14 predisposition

**partially**
06 in part, partly
08 not fully, somewhat
12 incompletely

**participant**
05 party
06 helper, member, worker
07 entrant, partner

09 associate
10 competitor, contestant
11 contributor, shareholder, stockholder

**participate**
04 join
05 enter, share
06 assist, engage, join in
07 partake
08 take part
09 cooperate, play a part
10 be involved, contribute

**participation**
09 partaking
11 cooperation, involvement, partnership
12 contribution

**particle**
03 bit, jot
04 atom, drop, iota, mite, whit
05 crumb, grain, shred, speck
06 morsel, tittle
07 smidgen
08 molecule

**parti-colored**
06 motley
07 piebald
10 variegated
11 diversified
12 versicolored

**particular**
04 fact, item
05 exact, fussy, picky, point
06 choosy, detail
07 certain, feature, finicky, precise, special
08 detailed, distinct, especial, exacting, peculiar, specific, thorough
10 fastidious, individual, meticulous
11 painstaking, persnickety
12 circumstance
14 discriminating

□**in particular**
07 exactly
08 in detail
09 precisely
10 especially
12 particularly, specifically

**particularity**
04 fact, item
05 point, quirk, trait
06 detail
07 feature
08 instance, property
10 uniqueness
11 peculiarity, singularity
12 circumstance, idiosyncrasy
13 individuality

14 characteristic
15 distinctiveness

**particularize**
06 detail
07 itemize, specify
09 enumerate, stipulate
13 individualize

**particularly**
08 markedly
09 expressly, unusually
10 distinctly, especially, remarkably
12 specifically
13 exceptionally
15 extraordinarily

**parting**
05 adieu, dying, final, split
07 breakup, closing, goodbye, leaving, rupture
08 breaking, division, farewell
09 departing, departure
10 breaking up, concluding, divergence, separation
11 leave-taking, valediction, valedictory

**partisan**
03 fan
06 backer, biased, unfair, votary
07 devotee, partial
08 adherent, one-sided, stalwart
09 factional, guerrilla, sectarian, supporter
10 prejudiced
14 freedom fighter

**partisanship**
04 bias
09 prejudice
10 partiality
12 factionalism, sectarianism

**partition**
04 wall
05 panel, share
06 divide, screen
07 barrier, break up, divider, parting, split up, wall off
08 divide up, division, separate
09 diaphragm, screen off, separator, subdivide
11 room divider, separate off
12 dividing wall

**partly**
06 in part
07 a little
08 slightly, somewhat
09 partially
10 moderately, relatively, up to a point
12 incompletely, to some degree, to some extent

13 in some measure

**partner**
04 ally, mate, wife
06 cohort, friend, helper, spouse
07 comrade, consort, husband
08 coworker, sidekick, teammate
09 associate, boyfriend, colleague, companion, other half
10 accomplice, girlfriend
11 confederate

**partnership**
04 firm
05 union
07 company, society
08 alliance
09 syndicate
10 fellowship, fraternity
11 affiliation, association, brotherhood, corporation
13 confederation

**party**
04 band, body, camp, crew, gang, side, team, unit
05 group, squad
06 league, person
07 company, faction
08 alliance, grouping, litigant
09 defendant, gathering, plaintiff
10 contingent, detachment, individual
11 celebration, get-together, social event
14 political party

► *Types of party*:
03 hen, tea
04 bash, stag
06 dinner, garden, pajama, shower, soiree
07 costume
08 bachelor, barbecue, birthday, cocktail
09 Halloween
10 baby shower, homecoming, retirement
12 bachelorette, bridal shower, housewarming

**parvenu**
07 climber, new-rich, upstart
09 arriviste, newly rich, pretender
12 nouveau riche

**pass**
03 col, gap, lap, run
04 emit, fill, flow, hand, move, play, visa, walk

05 enact, expel, gorge, occur, outdo, spend, throw
06 accept, become, befall, canyon, defile, elapse, exceed, go past, happen, let out, occupy, permit, ratify, ravine, slip by, take up, ticket, travel
07 agree to, approve, excrete, lateral, license, passage, proceed, qualify, release, run past, succeed, surpass, vote for
08 advances, go beyond, graduate, hail Mary, outstrip, overhaul, overtake, passport, progress, sanction, transfer, transmit, traverse
09 authorize, come about, discharge, drive past, get across, go through, take place, transpire, while away
10 get through, permission, suggestion
11 base on balls, leave behind, make your way, outdistance, proposition, pull ahead of, sail through
13 authorization, breeze through, draw level with
14 be successful in, identification

❑ **pass as, pass for**
10 be taken for
12 be regarded as
13 be mistaken for

❑ **pass away**
03 die
06 expire, pass on, peg out, pop off
07 decease
13 kick the bucket
14 give up the ghost

❑ **pass for** see PASS AS

❑ **pass off**
05 cease, feign, go off, occur
06 happen, vanish
07 die down, palm off, wear off
08 fade away
09 disappear, disregard, take place
11 counterfeit

❑ **pass out**
05 faint, swoon
07 deal out, give out, hand out
08 allocate, black out, collapse, flake out, keel over
10 distribute

❑ **pass over**
04 miss
06 forget, ignore

**passable**

08 overlook
09 disregard

**❏pass up**
04 miss
06 ignore, refuse, reject
07 let slip, neglect

**passable**
02 OK
04 fair, okay, so-so
05 clear
08 adequate, all right
09 navigable, tolerable
10 acceptable
11 traversable

**passably**
06 fairly
09 tolerably
10 moderately, reasonably

**passage**
03 way
04 duct, exit, flow, ford, hall, lane, neck, path, road, text, trip
05 aisle, alley, flume, gully, lobby, route, track, verse
06 access, avenue, course, furrow, groove, gutter, strait, trough, voyage
07 channel, conduit, excerpt, extract, hallway, journey
08 citation, corridor, entrance, movement, progress, waterway
09 enactment, paragraph, vestibule
10 transition
11 safe conduct, watercourse
12 thoroughfare

**passageway**
04 hall, lane, path
05 aisle, alley, lobby
07 hallway, passage
08 corridor

**passé**
03 old
05 dated
06 démodé, old hat
07 outworn
08 obsolete, outdated, outmoded
09 out-of-date
11 past its best
12 old-fashioned

**passenger**
04 fare
05 rider
07 voyager
08 commuter, hanger-on, stowaway, traveler
09 fare payer

10 hitchhiker

**passerby**
07 witness
08 looker-on, observer, onlooker
09 bystander, spectator
10 eyewitness, rubberneck

**passing**
03 end
05 brief, death, hasty, quick, short
06 casual, demise, slight
07 cursory, decease, quietus
09 departure, ephemeral, temporary, transient
10 incidental, short-lived
11 superficial, termination
12 transitional

**❏in passing**
07 by the by
08 by the bye, by the way
09 en passant
12 incidentally
15 parenthetically

**passion**
03 fit
04 fire, fury, heat, love, lust, rage, zeal, zest
05 anger, ardor, craze, mania, wrath
06 desire, fervor, spirit, temper
07 avidity, craving, emotion, feeling, tantrum
09 adoration, eagerness, intensity, obsession, vehemence
10 enthusiasm, fanaticism
11 infatuation
12 sexual desire

**passionate**
03 hot
04 avid, keen, sexy, wild
05 eager, fiery
06 erotic, fierce, stormy, sultry
07 aroused, fervent, lustful, sensual, violent, zealous
08 frenzied, inflamed, turned on, vehement
09 emotional, excitable, fanatical, hotheaded, impetuous, impulsive
11 impassioned, tempestuous
12 enthusiastic
13 quick-tempered

**passionless**
04 calm, cold
06 frigid, frosty
07 callous
08 detached
09 apathetic, impassive, unfeeling

11 cold-blooded, cold-hearted, emotionless
13 dispassionate

**passive**
06 docile
07 patient, unmoved
08 inactive, lifeless, resigned
09 apathetic, compliant
10 nonviolent, submissive
11 indifferent, unassertive

**passport**
02 ID
03 key, way
04 door, visa
05 entry, route
06 avenue, papers, permit
07 doorway
09 admission
12 identity card
13 authorization, laissez-passer, means of access
15 travel documents

**password**
03 key
04 word
06 parole, signal
09 watchword
10 open sesame, shibboleth

**past**
04 done, gone, last, late, life, over
05 early, ended, olden
06 bygone, former, gone by, latter, no more, recent
07 ancient, defunct, elapsed, extinct, history, long ago
08 finished, foregone, previous, sometime
09 antiquity, completed, erstwhile, foregoing, forgotten, olden days, preceding
10 background, bygone days, days gone by, days of yore, experience, olden times
11 bygone times, former times, good old days, track record
15 over and done with

**pasta**

► *Types of pasta*:
04 ziti
06 noodle, rotini
07 fusilli, lasagna, lasagne, ravioli, rotelle
08 farfalle, fedelini, linguine, linguini, macaroni, rigatoni
09 fettucine, fettucini, manicotti, spaghetti
10 angel's hair, cannelloni, conchiglie, fettuccine,

tagliarini, tortellini, vermicelli
11 tagliatelle
➤ See also FOOD

**paste**
03 fix, gum, pap
04 beat, drub, glue, mush, pulp
05 blend, purée, putty, stick
06 cement, mastic, wallop
08 adhesive

**pastel**
04 pale, soft
05 chalk, faint, light, muted
06 crayon, low-key, subtle
07 subdued
08 delicate, low-keyed, pastille,
   soft hued

**pastiche**
03 mix
06 jumble, medley
07 farrago, melange, mixture
08 mishmash, mixed bag
09 potpourri
10 assortment, collection,
   hodgepodge, hotchpotch,
   miscellany, salmagundi
11 gallimaufry, smorgasbord
14 conglomeration

**pastille, pastil**
05 sweet
06 jujube, pastel, tablet, troche
07 lozenge
09 cough drop
10 cough sweet

**pastime**
04 game, play
05 hobby, sport
08 activity
09 amusement, diversion
10 recreation, relaxation
13 entertainment
15 leisure activity

**past master**
03 ace
05 adept
06 artist, expert, wizard
07 old hand
08 virtuoso

**pastor**
05 canon, vicar
06 cleric, divine, parson, priest,
   rector
08 minister, preacher
09 churchman, clergyman
12 ecclesiastic

**pastoral**
05 rural
06 rustic, simple
07 bucolic, country, idyllic
08 agrarian, clerical, priestly
12 agricultural

14 ecclesiastical

**pastry**

► *Types of pastry*:
04 filo, puff
05 choux, flaky, short
06 Danish, phyllo
09 rough-puff, suetcrust
10 shortcrust
13 hot-water crust
➤ See also FOOD

**pasture**
05 field, grass
06 meadow
07 grazing, paddock
09 grassland, pasturage
11 grazing land

**pasty**
03 wan
04 pale
06 anemic, pallid, sallow, sickly
09 unhealthy

**pat**
03 dab, pet, tap
04 clap, easy, glib, slap
05 ready, slick, touch
06 caress, facile, fluent, smooth
07 exactly
09 perfectly, precisely
10 flawlessly, simplistic
11 faultlessly

❑**pat someone on the
back**
06 praise
10 compliment
12 congratulate

**patch**
03 bed, bit, fix, lot, pad, sew
04 area, mend, plot, spot, term,
   time
05 cloth, cover, phase, piece,
   scrap, spell, tract
06 parcel, period, repair, stitch
08 covering, material

**patchwork**
05 quilt
06 jumble, medley
07 farrago, mixture
08 mishmash, pastiche
10 hotchpotch

**patchy**
06 fitful, random, spotty, uneven
07 blotchy, erratic, sketchy
09 irregular
12 inconsistent

**patent**
04 open
05 clear, overt, plain, right
07 blatant, evident, glaring,
   license, obvious

08 apparent, flagrant
09 copyright, invention,
   privilege
11 certificate, conspicuous,
   transparent, unequivocal

**paternal**
08 fatherly
10 benevolent, protective

**path**
03 way
04 lane, road, walk
05 route, track, trail
06 avenue, course
07 circuit, passage
08 approach, footpath
09 bridle way, direction

**pathetic**
03 sad
04 poor
05 sorry
06 dismal, feeble, meager,
   moving, woeful
07 pitiful, useless
08 derisory, pitiable, poignant,
   touching, wretched
09 affecting, miserable,
   plaintive, worthless
10 deplorable, inadequate,
   lamentable
12 heart-rending
13 heartbreaking

**pathological**
07 chronic
08 addicted, habitual, hardened
09 confirmed, obsessive
10 compulsive, inveterate

**pathos**
06 misery
07 sadness
09 poignancy
11 pitifulness

**patience**
04 cool
08 calmness, serenity, stoicism
09 composure, diligence,
   endurance, tolerance
10 doggedness, equanimity
11 forbearance, self-control,
   tranquility
12 perseverance
13 long-suffering

**patient**
04 calm, case, cool, mild
06 serene
07 invalid, lenient, stoical
08 composed, sufferer, tolerant
09 forgiving
10 forbearing
11 persevering
12 even-tempered

13 imperturbable, long-
suffering, philosophical,
uncomplaining
14 hanging in there

**patois**
04 cant
05 argot, lingo, slang
06 jargon, patter
07 dialect
10 vernacular
12 lingua franca
13 local parlance

**patriarch**
04 sire
05 elder
06 father
07 founder
09 graybeard
11 grand old man, grandfather
13 paterfamilias

**patrician**
04 peer
05 noble
06 lordly
07 grandee
08 highborn, nobleman
09 gentleman, high-class
10 aristocrat
11 blue-blooded
12 aristocratic, thoroughbred

**patrimony**
06 estate, legacy
07 bequest, portion
08 heritage, property
10 birthright
11 inheritance, possessions

**patriot**
08 jingoist, loyalist
09 flag-waver
10 chauvinist
11 nationalist

**patriotic**
05 loyal
08 loyalist
10 flag-waving, jingoistic
11 nationalist
12 chauvinistic
13 nationalistic

**patriotism**
07 loyalty
08 jingoism
10 chauvinism, flag-waving
11 nationalism

**patrol**
04 beat, tour
05 guard, round, scout, vigil,
watch
06 police, sentry
07 inspect, monitor
08 policing, sentinel, watchman

11 be on the beat, do the
rounds, go the rounds, keep
guard on, keep watch on
12 military unit
13 keep watch over, make the
rounds, night watchman,
police officer, security guard

**patron**
05 angel, buyer
06 backer, client, helper
07 regular, shopper, sponsor
08 advocate, champion,
customer, guardian,
promoter
09 purchaser, supporter
10 benefactor
11 patron saint
13 guardian angel
14 fairy godmother

**patronage**
05 trade
06 buying, custom
07 backing, funding, support
08 business
09 clientele
11 sponsorship
12 subscription

**patronize**
03 aid
04 back, fund, help
06 assist, foster, shop at
07 buy from, finance, promote,
sponsor, support
08 deal with, frequent
10 look down on, talk down to
12 be a regular at

**patronizing**
05 lofty
06 snooty
07 haughty, stuck up
08 superior
10 highhanded
12 supercilious
13 condescending, high-and-
mighty

**patter**
03 pat, tap, yak
04 beat, cant, drum, line, pelt,
trip
05 lingo, pitch, spiel
06 jargon, scurry
07 chatter, monolog, scuttle,
tapping
09 monologue
10 yackety-yak

**pattern**
04 copy, form, mold, norm, plan,
trim
05 guide, ideal, match, model,
motif, order, shape, style

06 design, device, figure, follow,
method, sample, swatch,
system
07 emulate, example, imitate
08 decorate, markings, original,
standard, template
09 blueprint, prototype
10 decoration
11 arrangement, instruction
13 ornamentation

**patterned**
05 moiré
07 figured, printed, watered
09 decorated
10 ornamented

**paucity**
04 lack, want
06 dearth
07 fewness, poverty
08 scarcity, shortage, sparsity
09 smallness
10 meagerness, paltriness,
scantiness, sparseness

**paunch**
05 belly
07 abdomen
08 potbelly
09 bay window, beer belly

**paunchy**
03 fat
05 pudgy, tubby
06 portly, rotund
09 corpulent
10 potbellied

**pauper**
06 beggar
07 have-not
08 bankrupt, indigent
09 insolvent, mendicant
10 down-and-out

**pause**
03 gap
04 halt, lull, rest, stay, stop, wait
05 break, cease, delay, let up
06 desist
07 adjourn, respite, time out
08 break off, breather, hesitate,
hold back, interval,
stoppage, take five
09 cessation, interlude, interrupt
10 hesitation
11 discontinue
12 intermission, interruption
14 breathing space

**pave**
03 tar
04 flag, tile
05 cover, floor
06 Tarmac
07 asphalt, surface

**pavement**
08 blacktop, concrete
10 macadamize

**pave the way for**
08 lead up to
09 introduce, take steps
10 prepare for
11 get ready for
12 make ready for
14 clear the ground, clear the way for

**pavement**
04 road
06 street, Tarmac
07 asphalt, macadam
08 blacktop, concrete

**paw**
03 pad
04 foot, hand, maul
05 touch
06 molest, stroke
07 touch up
09 manhandle, mishandle

**pawn**
04 dupe, hock, risk, tool
06 pledge, puppet, stooge
07 cat's paw, deposit, hostage
08 chessman, guaranty, mortgage
09 plaything
10 chess piece, instrument
11 impignorate

**pawnbroker**
05 uncle
06 lender, usurer
08 pawnshop

**pay**
03 fee
05 atone, remit, spend, wages
06 expend, income, invest, lay out, outlay, profit, refund, return, reward, salary, settle
07 benefit, bring in, cough up, fork out, produce, stipend
08 disburse, earnings, hand over, settle up, shell out
09 discharge, reimburse
10 commission, compensate, emoluments, honorarium, make amends, remunerate
11 foot the bill
12 compensation, pick up the tab, remuneration
13 meet the cost of, reimbursement

**pay back**
05 repay
06 pay off, punish, refund, settle, square
09 reimburse, retaliate
11 get even with, take revenge

13 counterattack

**pay for**
05 atone
09 answer for
10 compensate, cost dearly, make amends
12 face the music
13 be punished for
14 count the cost of, get your deserts

**pay off**
04 fire, sack
05 bribe, clear, repay
06 buy off, grease, lay off, settle, square
07 dismiss
09 discharge, pay in full
10 get results
12 be successful

**pay out**
05 remit, spend
06 lay out
07 fork out
08 disburse, hand over, part with, shell out

**payable**
03 due
04 owed
05 owing
06 unpaid
11 outstanding

**payment**
03 fee, pay
04 fare, hire, toll
06 outlay, reward
07 advance, deposit, premium
08 donation
10 remittance, settlement
11 installment
12 compensation, contribution, remuneration

**payoff**
05 bribe
06 result, reward
07 benefit, outcome
09 hush money, slush fund, sweetener
10 inducement
11 consequence
13 moment of truth
15 protection money

**payola**
05 bribe, graft
10 inducement

**peace**
04 calm, hush, rest
05 amity, quiet, still, truce
06 accord, repose
07 concord, harmony, silence
08 calmness, serenity

09 agreement, armistice, cease-fire, quietness, stillness
10 relaxation
11 nonviolence, restfulness, tranquility
12 amicableness
13 nonaggression

**peaceable**
04 mild
06 gentle, irenic, placid
07 pacific
08 amicable, friendly
09 unwarlike
10 nonviolent
11 inoffensive, peace loving
12 conciliatory
13 nonaggressive

**peaceful**
04 calm
05 quiet, still
06 gentle, placid, serene, sleepy
07 pacific, restful
08 in repose, tranquil
09 peaceable, unruffled
11 undisturbed

**peacemaker**
08 appeaser, pacifier, pacifist, peacenik
11 conciliator, peace monger
12 peace officer

**peacemaking**
06 irenic
07 pacific
08 irenical
09 appeasing
12 conciliatory

**peak**
03 tip, top
04 apex, hill
05 crest, crown, mount, point
06 apogee, climax, summit, zenith
07 maximum
08 mountain, pinnacle
09 culminate, elevation, high point
11 come to a head

**peaky**
03 ill, wan
04 pale, sick
06 pallid, poorly, sickly, unwell
08 off-color
09 washed-out
15 under the weather

**peal**
04 boom, clap, ring, roll, toll
05 chime, clang, knell
06 rumble
07 resound, ring out, ringing
08 carillon, resonate

11 reverberate

**peasant**
03 oaf
04 boor, clod, lout
05 churl, yokel
06 rustic
07 bumpkin, hayseed, redneck
09 hillbilly
10 provincial
14 country bumpkin

**pebble**
04 chip
05 agate, stone
06 gallet, quartz

**peccadillo**
05 error, fault, lapse
07 misdeed
10 infraction
11 delinquency, misdemeanor
12 indiscretion, minor offense

**peck**
03 hit, jab, nag, nip, rap, tap
04 bite, kiss
07 henpeck

**peculiar**
03 odd
05 droll, funny, queer, weird
06 quaint, way-out
07 bizarre, curious, offbeat,
    strange, unusual
08 abnormal, distinct, freakish,
    singular, specific
09 eccentric
10 individual, outlandish,
    particular
11 distinctive
13 idiosyncratic
14 characteristic,
    unconventional
15 individualistic

❑**peculiar to**
08 unique to
09 typical of

**peculiarity**
04 mark
05 quirk, trait
06 foible, oddity
08 hallmark
09 mannerism, weirdness
11 abnormality, bizarreness
12 eccentricity, idiosyncrasy
14 characteristic

**pecuniary**
06 fiscal
08 monetary
09 financial

**pedagogic**
08 academic, didactic, teaching
09 tuitional

10 tuitionary
11 educational
13 instructional

**pedagogue, pedagogue**
06 pedant
07 teacher
08 educator
09 dogmatist, preceptor
10 instructor
12 educationist, schoolmaster
14 educationalist,
    schoolmistress

**pedagogy**
07 tuition
08 teaching, training, tutelage
09 didactics
10 pedagogics

**pedant**
06 purist
07 casuist
08 quibbler
09 dogmatist, nitpicker
10 literalist, scholastic
11 pettifogger
12 hairsplitter, precisionist

**pedantic**
05 exact, fussy
06 purist, stuffy
07 bookish, erudite, finical,
    pompous, precise, stilted
09 quibbling
10 literalist, meticulous,
    nitpicking, particular,
    scrupulous
13 hairsplitting, perfectionist

**pedantry**
08 caviling
09 exactness, quibbling
10 finicality, nitpicking
13 hairsplitting
14 meticulousness
15 punctiliousness

**peddle**
04 hawk, push, sell, tout, vend
05 trade
06 market
07 traffic
12 offer for sale

**pedestal**
04 base, foot
05 stand
06 column, pillar, plinth,
    podium
07 support
08 mounting, platform
10 foundation

❑**put on a pedestal**
05 exalt
06 admire, revere
07 adulate, idolize

11 hero-worship

**pedestrian**
04 dull, flat
05 banal
06 boring, turgid, walker
07 humdrum, mundane,
    prosaic, walking
08 mediocre, plodding, stroller
11 commonplace
12 foot traveler

**pedigree**
04 line, race
05 blood, breed, stock
06 family, stirps, strain
07 descent, lineage, stirpes
08 ancestry, pedigree, purebred
09 full blood, genealogy,
    parentage
10 derivation, extraction, family
    tree
11 full-blooded
12 aristocratic, thoroughbred

**peddler**
06 hawker, seller, trader, vendor
07 chapman, packman
08 huckster
09 cheapjack
10 colporteur
12 street trader

**peek**
03 spy
04 look, peep, peer
05 blink
06 gander, glance
07 glimpse, look-see

**peel**
04 pare, rind, skin, zest
05 flake, scale, strip
06 remove
07 epicarp, exocarp, take off
08 flake off
10 desquamate, integument
11 decorticate

❑**keep your eyes peeled**
07 be alert
12 watch closely
15 keep a lookout for

**peep**
04 look, peek, peer, pipe, word
05 cheep, chirp, sound, tweet
06 gander, glance, squeak,
    squint
07 chirrup, look-see, twitter

**peephole**
05 chink, cleft, crack
07 keyhole, pinhole, spy hole
09 Judas hole

**peer**
04 gaze, look, lord, peep, scan

**peerage** (continued)
05 count, equal, noble
06 fellow, squint
07 examine, inspect
08 confrère, nobleman
10 aristocrat, scrutinize
11 counterpart

► *Names of British peers:*
04 duke, earl
05 baron
07 marquis
08 marquess, viscount

**peerage**
08 nobility
09 top drawer
10 upper crust
11 aristocracy

**peeress**
04 dame, lady
05 noble
10 aristocrat, noblewoman

► *Names of British peeresses:*
07 duchess
08 baroness, countess
11 marchioness, viscountess

**peerless**
06 unique
09 matchless, nonpareil,
unequaled, unmatched,
unrivaled
11 unsurpassed
12 incomparable, second to
none, unparalleled, without
equal
13 beyond compare

**peeve**
03 irk, vex
04 gall
05 annoy, pique
06 nettle
07 provoke
08 irritate
09 aggravate
10 exasperate
14 drive up the wall

**peeved**
05 irked, riled, upset, vexed
06 galled, miffed, piqued, put
out
07 annoyed, in a huff, nettled

**peevish**
05 cross, moody, ratty, sulky,
surly, testy
06 crusty, grumpy, snappy,
sullen, tetchy, touchy
07 crabbed, fretful
08 churlish, petulant
09 crotchety, fractious,
querulous
10 in a bad mood

11 complaining, ill-tempered
12 cantankerous

**peevishness**
05 pique
09 petulance, testiness
12 captiousness
13 querulousness

**peg**
03 fix, hob, nob, pin, set
04 brad, hook, join, knob, mark,
nail, post
05 dowel, limit, prong, screw,
spike, stake
06 attach, fasten, freeze, marker,
secure
07 control, support
09 stabilize

❑**peg away**
07 persist
08 keep at it, plug away
09 persevere, stick at it
10 beaver away

❑**take down a peg or two,
bring down a peg or two**
09 humiliate
13 cut down to size
15 bring down to size

**pejorative**
08 negative
09 slighting
10 belittling, derogatory
11 deprecatory, disparaging
12 unflattering
15 uncomplimentary

**pellet**
04 ball, drop, pill, shot, slug
06 bullet
07 capsule, lozenge

**pell-mell**
07 hastily
08 headlong
09 hurriedly, posthaste
10 at full tilt, feverishly,
heedlessly, recklessly
11 hurry-scurry, hurry-skurry,
impetuously
13 helter-skelter, precipitously

**pellucid**
04 pure
05 clear
06 bright, glassy, limpid
11 translucent, transparent

**pelt**
03 fur, hit, run
04 beat, belt, coat, dash, fell,
hide, hurl, pour, race, rush,
skin, tear, teem
05 hurry, speed, throw

06 assail, attack, batter, career,
charge, fleece, shower,
sprint, strike
07 bombard
11 rain buckets
15 rain cats and dogs

**pen**
03 mew, pin, sty
04 bolt, cage, coop, fold, shut
05 cubby, draft, fence, hedge,
hem in, hutch, pound, quill,
stall, style, write
06 corral, shut up, stylus
07 Biro, compose, confine,
enclose, felt tip, jot down
08 compound, scribble
09 ballpoint, enclosure
10 felt-tip pen
12 ballpoint pen
13 felt-tipped pen

**penal**
08 punitive
10 corrective
11 retributive
12 disciplinary

**penalize**
04 fine
06 punish
07 correct
08 chastise, handicap
09 castigate
10 discipline
12 disadvantage

**penal servitude**
04 life, time
07 stretch
08 sentence
09 doing time, hard labor

**penalty**
04 fine
05 mulct
07 forfeit
08 handicap, sentence
10 punishment
12 disadvantage

**penance**
09 atonement
10 punishment, reparation
13 mortification

**penchant**
04 bent, bias
05 taste
06 liking
07 leaning
08 affinity, fondness, soft spot,
tendency, weakness
10 partiality, preference,
proclivity, propensity
11 disposition, inclination
12 predilection

## pendant
06 locket
08 necklace
09 medallion

## pendent
06 nutant
07 hanging, pensile
08 dangling, drooping, swinging
09 pendulous, suspended

## pending
04 near, till
05 until, while
06 before, coming, during
08 imminent
09 impending
10 on the table, throughout, up in the air
11 approaching, forthcoming, in the offing
12 in the balance

## pendulous
07 hanging, pendent, sagging, swaying
08 dangling, drooping, swinging

## penetrable
06 porous
08 passable, pervious
09 permeable
10 accessible, fathomable
14 comprehensible, understandable

## penetrate
03 see
04 bore, seep, sink, stab
05 crack, enter, grasp, imbue, prick, probe, spike
06 fathom, invade, pierce, sink in
07 get into, make out, pervade, suffuse, work out
08 permeate, puncture, register, saturate
09 perforate
10 comprehend, infiltrate, understand

## penetrating
04 deep, keen, loud, wise
05 acute, clear, sharp
06 biting, shrewd, shrill
07 probing
08 carrying, incisive, piercing, profound, stinging, strident
09 observant, searching
10 discerning, perceptive

## penetration
03 wit
05 entry
06 acumen, inroad

07 insight
08 entrance, incision, invasion, keenness, piercing, pricking, stabbing
09 acuteness, pervasion, sharpness
10 astuteness, perception, permeation, puncturing
11 discernment, perforation
12 infiltration, perspicacity

## peninsula
04 cape, mull, neck
05 point
06 tongue
10 chersonese

## penitence
05 shame
06 regret, sorrow
07 remorse
10 contrition, repentance
11 compunction
12 self-reproach

## penitent
05 sorry
07 ashamed
08 contrite
09 regretful, repentant
10 apologetic, remorseful

## pen name
06 anonym
07 allonym
09 false name, pseudonym
10 nom de plume
11 assumed name

## pennant
04 flag, jack
06 banner, colors, ensign
08 banderol, gonfalon, standard, streamer

## penniless
04 bust, poor
05 broke
08 indigent
09 destitute, flat broke
10 cleaned out, down and out, stone-broke
11 impecunious
12 impoverished
14 on the breadline
15 poverty-stricken, strapped for cash

## penny pincher
05 meany, miser
06 meanie
07 niggard, Scrooge
09 skinflint
10 cheapskate
11 cheeseparer
12 moneygrubber

## penny-pinching
04 mean
05 close, mingy
06 frugal, stingy
07 miserly
09 niggardly, scrimping
11 closefisted, tightfisted
12 cheeseparing, parsimonious

## pension
06 income
07 annuity, benefit, support, welfare
09 allowance
14 superannuation

## pensioner
10 pensionary
13 retired person, senior citizen

## pensive
06 dreamy, musing, solemn
07 serious, wistful
08 absorbed, thinking
09 pondering
10 cogitative, meditative, ruminative, thoughtful
11 preoccupied
13 contemplative

## pent-up
05 caged
06 curbed, held in, jailed
08 confined
09 bottled up, inhibited, repressed
10 restrained, suppressed

## penurious
04 bust, mean, poor
05 close, tight
06 hard up, stingy
07 miserly
08 beggarly, grudging, indigent
09 destitute, flat broke, niggardly, penniless
11 close-fisted, impecunious, tightfisted
12 cheeseparing, impoverished, parsimonious
15 poverty-stricken

## penury
07 beggary, poverty, straits
09 indigence, pauperism
11 destitution
14 impoverishment

## people
04 clan, folk, race
05 folks, tribe
06 family, humans, nation, occupy, public, settle
07 inhabit, mankind, mortals, parents, persons, society
08 citizens, colonize, humanity, populace, populate

**pep**
09 community, humankind, relations, relatives
10 electorate, kith and kin, population
11 human beings, individuals
12 the human race
13 general public

**pep**
05 get-up, verve, vigor
06 energy, spirit
07 sparkle
08 vitality
10 ebullience, exuberance, get-up-and-go, liveliness
11 high spirits
13 effervescence

**❑pep up**
07 inspire, liven up
08 energize, vitalize
09 stimulate
10 exhilarate, invigorate

**pepper**
03 dot
04 bell, pelt
05 blitz, chili, strew
06 shower
07 bombard, cayenne, paprika, poblano, scatter, serrano, spatter
08 habenero, jalapeno, pimiento, sprinkle
09 bespatter

**peppery**
03 hot
05 fiery, sharp, spicy, testy
06 biting, grumpy, lively, touchy
07 caustic, piquant, pungent
08 seasoned, stinging
09 irascible, sarcastic, trenchant
11 hot tempered

**perceive**
03 see
04 espy, feel, know, note, spot, view
05 grasp, learn, sense
06 detect, notice, remark
07 discern, glimpse, make out, observe, realize
09 apprehend, be aware of, recognize
10 appreciate, comprehend, understand
11 distinguish
12 catch sight of
13 be cognizant of

**perceptible**
05 clear, plain
06 patent
07 evident, obvious, visible
08 apparent, distinct, tangible

10 detectable, noticeable, observable
11 appreciable, conspicuous, discernible

**perception**
04 idea, view
05 grasp, sense
07 feeling, insight
09 awareness, knowledge
10 cognizance, conception, impression
11 discernment, observation
13 consciousness, understanding

**perceptive**
04 keen
05 alert, aware, quick, sharp
06 astute, shrewd
09 observant, sharp-eyed
10 discerning
13 perspicacious

**perch**
03 bar
04 land, rest
05 roost
06 alight, settle
07 balance

**perchance**
05 maybe
07 perhaps
08 feasibly, possibly

**percipience**
07 insight
08 judgment
09 awareness, intuition
10 astuteness, perception
11 discernment, penetration
12 perspicacity

**percipient**
05 alert, alive, aware, sharp
06 astute
09 observant, wide-awake
10 discerning, perceptive
11 penetrating
13 perspicacious
14 discriminating

**percolate**
04 drip, leak, ooze, seep
05 drain, leach, sieve
06 filter, strain
14 trickle through

**perdition**
04 doom, hell, loss, ruin
05 Hades
08 downfall, hellfire
09 damnation, ruination
10 underworld
12 annihilation

**peregrination**
04 tour, trek, trip
06 roving, travel, voyage
07 journey, odyssey, roaming
09 traveling, wandering, wayfaring
10 expedition

**peremptory**
04 curt
06 abrupt, lordly
07 summary
08 absolute, dogmatic
09 arbitrary, imperious
10 autocratic, commanding, highhanded, tyrannical
11 dictatorial, domineering, irrefutable, overbearing

**perennial**
07 lasting, undying
08 enduring, immortal
09 perpetual, unceasing
11 everlasting, never-ending

**perfect**
04 pure, true
05 exact, ideal, model, right, sheer, total, utter
06 better, entire, expert, finish, fulfil, polish, refine, superb
07 correct, fulfill, improve, precise, sinless
08 absolute, accurate, complete, faithful, flawless, peerless, skillful, spotless, textbook, thorough, ultimate, unmarred
09 downright, excellent, exemplary, faultless, matchless, out and out, wonderful
10 consummate, immaculate, impeccable, just the job
11 superlative, unblemished

**perfection**
04 acme
05 crown, ideal, model
07 paragon
08 pinnacle, ultimate
10 excellence, refinement
11 improvement, ne plus ultra
12 consummation, flawlessness
13 faultlessness, impeccability, one in a million
14 immaculateness

**perfectionist**
06 pedant, purist
08 idealist, stickler

**perfectly**
05 fully, quite
06 wholly
07 exactly, ideally, totally, utterly
08 entirely, superbly

10 absolutely, altogether,
   completely, flawlessly,
   impeccably, thoroughly
11 faultlessly, wonderfully
12 immaculately, to perfection
14 without blemish

**perfidious**
05 false, Punic
08 disloyal, two-faced
09 deceitful, dishonest, faithless
10 traitorous, treasonous,
   unfaithful
11 double-faced, duplicitous,
   treacherous
13 double-dealing,
   Machiavellian,
   untrustworthy

**perfidy**
06 deceit
07 falsity, treason
08 betrayal
09 duplicity, treachery
10 disloyalty, infidelity
13 double-dealing,
   faithlessness
14 perfidiousness,
   traitorousness

**perforate**
04 bore, gore, hole, stab, tear
05 burst, drill, prick, punch,
   spike, split
06 pierce
07 rupture
08 puncture
11 make holes in

**perforated**
06 porous
07 drilled, pierced
09 punctured

**perforation**
04 hole
05 prick
07 foramen
08 puncture
10 dotted line

**perforce**
10 inevitably, willy-nilly
11 necessarily, of necessity,
   unavoidably

**perform**
02 do, go
03 act, run
04 play, work
05 enact, put on, stage
06 behave, effect, fulfil
07 conduct, execute, fulfill,
   produce, pull off
08 bring off, carry out,
   complete, function
09 discharge, represent

10 accomplish, bring about

**performance**
04 show
06 acting, action
07 conduct
08 behavior
09 discharge, execution,
   portrayal
10 appearance, conducting,
   fulfilment, production
11 carrying out, fulfillment,
   functioning
12 presentation
14 interpretation,
   representation

**performer**
04 doer, mime
05 actor, clown, comic
06 author, dancer, player, singer
07 acrobat, actress, artiste,
   trouper
08 comedian, executor,
   magician, musician, Thespian
10 comedienne
11 entertainer

**perfume**
04 balm, odor
05 aroma, scent, smell
07 bouquet, cologne, essence,
   incense
09 fragrance
11 toilet water
12 eau de Cologne

**perfunctory**
05 brief
07 cursory, hurried, offhand,
   quickly
08 slipshod, slovenly
10 mechanical

**perhaps**
05 maybe
08 feasibly, possibly
09 perchance
11 conceivably

**peril**
04 risk
06 danger, hazard, menace,
   threat
08 jeopardy

**perilous**
04 dire
05 risky
06 chancy, unsafe, unsure
09 dangerous, hazardous
10 precarious, vulnerable

**perimeter**
04 edge
05 limit
06 border, bounds, fringe, limits,
   margin

08 boundary, confines, frontier
09 periphery
11 outer limits

**period**
03 age, dot, end, eon, era
04 date, days, span, stop, term,
   time, turn
05 class, cycle, epoch, phase,
   point, shift, space, spell,
   stage, stint, while, years
06 decade, finish, lesson,
   season
07 session, stretch
08 duration, full stop, interval

**periodic**
06 cyclic
08 cyclical, seasonal
09 recurrent, recurring
10 infrequent, occasional
12 intermittent, once in a while

**periodical**
06 review, weekly
07 journal, monthly
08 magazine
09 quarterly

**peripatetic**
06 mobile, roving
07 migrant, nomadic, roaming
09 itinerant, migratory, traveling,
   wandering
10 ambulatory, journeying

**peripheral**
05 minor, outer
06 lesser
08 marginal, outlying
09 ancillary, outermost
10 borderline, incidental,
   irrelevant, subsidiary
11 surrounding
14 beside the point

**periphery**
03 hem, rim
04 brim, edge
05 ambit, brink, skirt, verge
06 border, fringe, margin
07 circuit
08 boundary
09 outskirts, perimeter

**periphrastic**
07 oblique
08 indirect, rambling, tortuous
10 circuitous, discursive,
   roundabout
14 circumlocutory

**perish**
03 die, rot
04 fail, fall
05 decay, go off
06 depart, expire, peg out, pop
   off, vanish

07　crumble, die away
08　collapse, pass away
09　decompose, disappear, have had it
11　bite the dust, come to an end
12　disintegrate, lose your life
13　kick the bucket
15　breathe your last

**perishable**
10　short-lived
13　biodegradable

**perjure**

❑ **perjure yourself**
03　lie
13　commit perjury

**perjury**
12　false witness
13　false evidence
14　false testimony

**perk**
03　tip
05　bonus, extra
07　benefit, freebie
08　gratuity
09　percolate
10　perquisite
13　fringe benefit
15　golden handshake, golden parachute

❑ **perk up**
05　pep up, rally
06　buck up, look up, revive
07　cheer up, liven up, recover
08　brighten
09　take heart
10　brighten up

**perky**
05　peppy, sunny
06　bouncy, bright, bubbly, cheery, jaunty, lively
08　spirited
09　ebullient, sprightly, vivacious

**permanence**
09　endurance, stability
10　durability, perpetuity
11　persistence
15　imperishability

**permanent**
05　fixed
06　stable
07　durable, eternal, lasting
08　constant, enduring
09　indelible, perennial, perpetual
10　invariable, unchanging
11　established, everlasting, long-lasting
12　imperishable, unchangeable
14　indestructible

**permanently**
06　always
07　forever
08　ever more, for keeps
09　endlessly, eternally, for always, indelibly
10　for all time, unendingly
11　continually, for eternity, forevermore, perpetually
12　in perpetuity, till doomsday
14　forever and ever
15　till kingdom come

**permeable**
06　porous, spongy
09　absorbent
10　absorptive, penetrable

**permeate**
04　fill
05　imbue
07　diffuse, pervade
08　saturate
09　penetrate, percolate
10　impregnate, infiltrate
11　seep through, soak through
13　spread through

**permissible**
02　OK
04　okay
06　kosher, lawful, proper
07　allowed
08　all right
09　allowable, permitted, tolerable
10　acceptable, admissible, legitimate, sanctioned

**permission**
05　leave
06　assent, permit
07　consent, go-ahead, license, warrant
08　approval, sanction, thumbs up
09　agreement, clearance
10　green light
11　approbation
12　dispensation
13　authorization

**permissive**
03　lax
07　lenient, liberal
08　tolerant
09　easygoing, indulgent
10　forbearing
11　broad-minded
14　latitudinarian

**permit**
03　let
04　pass, visa
05　admit, agree, allow, grant
07　consent, license, warrant
08　passport, sanction

09　authorize
12　give the nod to
13　authorization

**permutation**
06　change
09　variation
10　alteration
11　commutation
13　transmutation
14　transformation

**pernicious**
03　bad
04　evil
05　fatal, toxic
06　deadly, wicked
07　harmful, noxious
08　damaging
09　injurious, malignant, pestilent, poisonous
10　maleficent
11　deleterious, destructive, detrimental, unwholesome

**persnickety**
04　nice
05　fussy, picky
06　choosy, fiddly, tricky
07　carping, finical, finicky
08　detailed, exacting
10　fastidious, nitpicking
11　overprecise, punctilious
13　hairsplitting
14　overparticular

**peroration**
04　talk
06　speech
07　address, lecture, summary
08　diatribe
09　recapping, summing-up
10　conclusion
11　declamation, reiteration
14　closing remarks, recapitulation

**perpendicular**
05　erect, plumb, sheer, steep
07　upright
08　straight, vertical
13　at right angles

**perpetrate**
02　do
05　wreak
06　commit, effect
07　execute, inflict, perform
08　carry out

**perpetual**
07　abiding, endless, eternal, lasting, undying
08　constant, enduring, infinite, unending
09　ceaseless, continual, incessant, perennial,

recurrent, unceasing, unfailing
**10** continuous, persistent
**11** everlasting, never-ending

**perpetually**
**09** endlessly, eternally
**10** constantly
**11** ceaselessly, continually, incessantly, unceasingly
**12** persistently

**perpetuate**
**06** keep up
**07** sustain
**08** continue, maintain
**09** keep alive, keep going
**11** immortalize, memorialize

**perpetuity**
**◻in perpetuity**
**06** always
**07** forever
**08** evermore
**09** endlessly, eternally
**10** for all time
**11** perpetually
**14** forever and ever

**perplex**
**06** baffle, muddle, puzzle
**07** confuse, mystify, nonplus
**08** bewilder, confound
**09** bamboozle, dumbfound

**perplexed**
**07** at a loss, baffled, muddled, puzzled
**08** confused
**09** mystified
**10** bamboozled, bewildered, confounded, nonplussed

**perplexing**
**06** knotty, taxing, thorny
**07** amazing, complex, strange
**08** baffling, involved, puzzling
**09** enigmatic, intricate
**10** mysterious, mystifying
**11** bewildering, complicated, paradoxical

**perplexity**
**06** puzzle
**07** dilemma, mystery, paradox
**09** intricacy, labyrinth
**10** complexity, puzzlement
**12** bewilderment, complication
**13** mystification
**15** incomprehension

**perquisite**
**03** tip
**04** perk, plus
**05** bonus, extra
**07** benefit, freebie
**08** dividend, gratuity

**13** fringe benefit

**persecute**
**05** abuse, annoy, bully, hound, worry
**06** badger, harass, hassle, martyr, pester, pursue
**07** oppress, torment, torture
**09** tyrannize, victimize

**persecution**
**05** abuse
**07** torture, tyranny
**09** martyrdom
**10** harassment, oppression
**11** subjugation, suppression
**13** victimization
**14** discrimination

**perseverance**
**07** resolve, stamina
**08** tenacity
**09** constancy, diligence, endurance
**10** doggedness, resolution
**11** persistence
**12** stickability
**13** determination

**persevere**
**04** go on
**06** hang on, hold on, remain
**07** carry on, persist
**08** continue, plug away
**09** keep going, soldier on
**11** hang in there
**12** be persistent
**15** stick to your guns

**persist**
**04** go on, hold, last
**05** abide
**06** endure, hang on, hold on, insist, keep on, linger, remain
**07** carry on
**08** continue, keep at it
**09** keep going, persevere, stand fast, stand firm
**12** be determined, be persistent

**persistence**
**04** grit
**07** stamina
**08** sedulity, tenacity
**09** constancy, endurance
**10** doggedness, resolution
**11** pertinacity
**12** perseverance, stickability
**13** determination, steadfastness

**persistent**
**06** dogged, steady
**07** endless, lasting, zealous
**08** constant, enduring, obdurate, resolute, tireless
**09** assiduous, continual, incessant, obstinate,

perpetual, steadfast, tenacious
**10** determined, relentless, unflagging
**11** never-ending, persevering, unrelenting, unremitting
**12** interminable, pertinacious

**person**
**03** guy, man
**04** body, soul, type
**05** being, human, woman
**06** fellow, mortal
**07** someone
**08** somebody
**09** character
**10** human being, individual

**◻in person**
**10** face to face, in the flesh
**13** as large as life

**persona**
**04** face, mask, part, role
**05** front, image
**06** façade
**09** character
**10** public face
**11** personality

**personable**
**06** pretty
**07** affable, amiable, winning
**08** charming, handsome, likeable, pleasant
**10** attractive
**11** good-looking, presentable

**personage**
**03** VIP
**04** name
**06** bigwig, worthy
**07** big shot, notable
**08** big noise, luminary
**09** celebrity, dignitary
**11** personality
**12** public figure

**personal**
**03** own
**06** secret, unique
**07** abusive, hurtful, private
**08** critical, in person, intimate, peculiar, wounding
**09** exclusive, offensive
**10** individual, particular, subjective
**12** confidential
**14** characteristic

**personality**
**03** VIP
**04** star
**05** charm
**06** makeup, temper, worthy
**08** charisma

09 celebrity, character, dignitary, magnetism
11 disposition, temperament

**personally**
05 alone
06 solely
08 in person
09 privately
11 exclusively
12 individually, particularly, subjectively
14 confidentially

**personification**
05 image
07 essence
08 likeness
09 portrayal, semblance
10 embodiment
11 incarnation
13 manifestation

**personify**
06 embody, mirror, typify
09 epitomize, exemplify, represent, symbolize

**personnel**
04 crew
05 staff
06 people
07 members, workers
08 liveware, manpower
09 employees, work force
10 labor force
14 human resources

**perspective**
04 view
05 angle, scene, slant, vista
06 aspect
07 outlook
08 attitude, prospect, relation
09 viewpoint
10 proportion, standpoint
11 frame of mind, point of view
12 vantage point

**perspicacious**
04 keen
05 alert, aware, quick, sharp
06 astute, shrewd
09 observant, sagacious, sharp-eyed
10 discerning, percipient
11 penetrating
14 discriminating

**perspicacity**
06 acumen, brains
07 insight
08 keenness
09 acuteness, sharpness
10 astuteness, shrewdness
11 discernment, penetration
14 discrimination

**perspicuity**
07 clarity
08 lucidity
09 clearness, plainness
12 distinctness, transparency
13 penetrability

**perspicuous**
05 clear, lucid, plain
07 obvious
08 apparent, distinct
11 self-evident, transparent, unambiguous
12 crystal clear
14 comprehensible
15 straightforward

**perspiration**
05 sweat
08 hidrosis
09 exudation, secretion
11 diaphoresis

**perspire**
04 drip
05 sweat
07 secrete, swelter

**persuadable**
07 pliable
08 amenable, flexible
09 malleable, receptive
10 susceptive

**persuade**
03 con
04 coax, lure, sway, urge
05 argue, lobby, suade, swade, tempt
06 cajole, coerce, entice, induce, lead on, lean on
07 convert, entreat, impress, satisfy, wheedle, win over
08 convince, inveigle, soft-soap, talk into
09 influence, sweet talk
11 bring around, prevail upon

**persuasion**
04 kind, pull, sect, side, sort, sway, view
05 clout, faith, party, power
06 belief, school, urging
07 coaxing, faction, opinion
08 cajolery, coercion, entreaty
09 influence, prompting, viewpoint, wheedling
10 conviction, enticement, inducement, philosophy
11 affiliation, arm-twisting, point of view, winning over
12 denomination
15 school of thought

**persuasive**
05 pushy, slick
06 cogent

07 weighty
08 forceful
09 effective, effectual, plausible
10 compelling, convincing
12 smooth spoken
13 smooth talking

**pert**
04 bold
05 brash, brisk, cocky, fresh, perky, saucy
06 cheeky, daring, jaunty, lively
07 forward
08 impudent, spirited
11 impertinent
12 presumptuous

**pertain**
05 apply, befit, refer
06 bear on, belong, relate
07 concern
09 appertain
10 be relevant
14 have a bearing on

**pertinacious**
06 dogged, mulish, wilful
07 willful
08 obdurate, perverse, resolute, stubborn
09 obstinate, pigheaded, tenacious
10 determined, headstrong, persistent, relentless, self-willed, unyielding
11 intractable, persevering
12 strong willed
14 uncompromising

**pertinent**
03 apt
05 ad rem
07 apropos, fitting, germane
08 apposite, material, relevant
10 applicable, to the point
11 appropriate

**pertness**
05 brass, cheek
08 audacity, boldness, chutzpah
09 brashness, cockiness, impudence, sauciness
10 cheekiness, effrontery
11 forwardness, presumption
12 impertinence

**perturb**
05 alarm, upset, worry
06 bother, ruffle
07 agitate, disturb, fluster
08 disquiet, unsettle
10 discompose, disconcert

**perturbed**
05 upset
07 anxious, nervous, worried
08 agitated, flurried

**perusal**
09 flustered, unsettled

**perusal**
04 look, read, skim
05 check, study
06 browse, glance
10 glance over, inspection
11 examination

**peruse**
04 read, scan, skim
05 check, study
06 browse
07 examine, inspect
11 look through

**pervade**
04 fill
05 imbue
06 affect, charge, infuse
07 diffuse, suffuse
08 permeate, saturate
09 penetrate, percolate
11 pass through
13 spread through

**pervasive**
09 extensive, prevalent, universal
10 ubiquitous, widespread
11 inescapable, omnipresent

**perverse**
06 cussed, unruly, wilful
07 awkward, willful
08 contrary, obdurate, stubborn
09 difficult, obstinate, pigheaded
10 headstrong, rebellious, refractory, unyielding
11 disobedient, intractable, troublesome, wrong headed
12 cantankerous, intransigent

**perversion**
04 vice
08 deviance, travesty, twisting
09 depravity, deviation, kinkiness
10 aberration, corruption, debauchery, immorality
11 abnormality

**perversity**
08 obduracy
09 contumacy, obstinacy
10 cussedness, wilfulness
11 awkwardness, waywardness, willfulness
12 contrariness, disobedience, stubbornness
13 intransigence
14 rebelliousness

**pervert**
04 perv, warp
05 abuse, avert, pervo, twist
06 debase, misuse, weirdo

07 corrupt, debauch, degrade, deprave, deviant, distort
09 debauchee, misdirect
10 degenerate, lead astray
12 misrepresent

**perverted**
05 kinky
06 warped, wicked
07 corrupt, debased, deviant, immoral, twisted
08 abnormal, depraved
09 corrupted, debauched, distorted, unnatural

**pessimism**
05 gloom
07 despair
08 cynicism, distrust, fatalism, glumness
10 gloominess
12 hopelessness

**pessimist**
05 cynic
07 killjoy
08 alarmist, fatalist
09 doomsayer
10 wet blanket
13 prophet of doom
14 doubting Thomas

**pessimistic**
05 bleak
06 gloomy
08 alarmist, doubting, hopeless, negative, resigned
10 despairing, fatalistic, suspicious
11 distrustful
12 discouraging

**pest**
03 bug
04 bane, pain, tick
05 curse, trial
06 blight, bother, pester, plague, vermin
07 scourge
08 irritant, nuisance
09 annoyance, tormentor
13 pain in the neck
14 thorn in the side
15 thorn in the flesh

**pester**
03 irk, nag
05 annoy, get at, hound, worry
06 badger, hassle, plague
07 torment
08 irritate
14 drive up the wall

**pestilence**
06 plague
07 cholera, disease

08 epidemic, pandemic, sickness
09 contagion, infection

**pestilent**
07 harmful, irksome, ruinous
08 annoying, diseased, infected
09 poisonous
10 contagious, infectious, pernicious
11 destructive, infuriating
12 plague-ridden
13 disease-ridden

**pestilential**
07 irksome
08 annoying
10 bothersome, irritating, pernicious
11 infuriating, troublesome

**pet**
03 toy
04 dear, huff, idol, kiss, neck, stew, sulk
05 jewel, spoil, sulks
06 animal, caress, cuddle, fondle, pamper, smooch, stroke, temper
07 bad mood, darling, dearest, favored, indulge, special, tantrum
08 canoodle, favorite, personal, treasure
09 cherished
10 particular
11 teacher's pet
13 fair-haired boy
14 apple of your eye

**peter**
❏**peter out**
04 fade, fail, stop, wane
05 cease
07 die away, dwindle
08 diminish, taper off
09 evaporate, fizzle out

**petite**
04 trim
05 small
06 dainty, little, slight
08 delicate

**petition**
03 ask, beg, bid, sue
04 plea, pray, urge
05 crave, plead, press
06 adjure, appeal, prayer
07 beseech, entreat, implore, protest, request, solicit
08 call upon, entreaty
10 round robin, supplicate
12 solicitation, supplication

**pet name**
08 nickname

**petrified**
10 diminutive, endearment, hypocorism

**petrified**
04 numb
06 aghast, frozen
07 shocked, stunned
08 appalled, benumbed
09 horrified, stupefied, terrified
10 speechless, transfixed
11 dumbfounded, scared stiff
14 horror-stricken, terror-stricken

**petrify**
04 numb, stun
05 alarm, appal, panic
06 appall, ossify
07 horrify, stupefy, terrify
08 frighten, paralyze
09 dumbfound, fossilize
11 turn to stone

**petticoat**
04 girl, slip
05 skirt, woman
08 half slip
10 underskirt
06 lawyer
07 cheater, shyster
09 trickster
15 unethical lawyer

**pettifogging**
05 petty
06 paltry
08 captious, caviling, niggling
09 quibbling
10 nitpicking
11 overrefined, sophistical
13 hairsplitting

**pettish**
05 cross, huffy, sulky
06 grumpy, tetchy, touchy
07 fretful, peevish, waspish
08 petulant, snappish
09 irritable, querulous
11 bad tempered

**petty**
04 mean
05 minor, small
06 little, measly, paltry, slight
07 trivial
08 grudging, piddling, trifling
10 negligible, ungenerous
11 small-minded, unimportant
13 insignificant, no great shakes
15 inconsequential

**petulance**
05 pique
09 sulkiness
10 sullenness
11 peevishness, waspishness
13 querulousness

**petulant**
05 cross, moody, sulky
06 sullen
07 fretful, peevish
09 crotchety, irritable, querulous
11 complaining

**phantom**
05 ghost, spook
06 spirit, vision, wraith
07 specter
10 apparition
13 hallucination

**pharisaical**
12 hypocritical
13 sanctimonious, self-righteous
14 holier-than-thou

**pharisee**
09 hypocrite
10 dissembler

**phase**
04 form, part, step, time
05 point, shape, spell, stage, state
06 aspect, period, season
08 juncture, position

❑**phase in**
05 start
06 ease in
09 introduce

❑**phase out**
04 stop
06 wind up
07 run down
08 taper off, wind down
09 eliminate

**phenomenal**
07 amazing, unusual
08 singular
09 fantastic, marvelous, wonderful
10 astounding, incredible, remarkable, stupendous
11 astonishing, exceptional
12 breathtaking, mind-boggling, unbelievable
13 extraordinary

**phenomenon**
04 fact
05 event, sight
06 marvel, rarity, wonder
07 miracle, prodigy
09 sensation, spectacle
10 appearance, experience, occurrence
12 circumstance

**philander**
05 dally, flirt
08 womanize
10 fool around, mess around

**philanderer**
04 wolf
07 Don Juan, playboy
08 Casanova, lady's man
09 ladies' man, libertine, womanizer
10 lady-killer

**philanthropic**
06 humane
08 generous
09 bounteous, bountiful
10 alms giving, altruistic, benevolent, charitable
12 humanitarian
14 public-spirited
20 munificent openhanded

**philanthropist**
05 donor, giver
06 helper, patron
09 alms giver
10 benefactor
12 humanitarian

**philanthropy**
04 help
06 giving
07 charity
08 altruism
09 patronage
10 alms giving, generosity
11 beneficence, benevolence, munificence
13 bounteousness, bountifulness
14 openhandedness
15 humanitarianism

**philippic**
05 abuse
06 attack, insult, rebuke, tirade
08 diatribe, harangue
09 criticism, onslaught
10 upbraiding
12 denunciation, vituperation

**philistine**
04 boor, lout
05 crass, yahoo
07 boorish, lowbrow
09 barbarian, tasteless, unrefined, vulgarian
10 uncultured
12 uncultivated

**philosopher**
04 guru, sage
07 scholar, thinker
08 analyzer, logician, theorist
12 dialectician
13 metaphysicist
14 epistemologist

▶ *Names of philosophers*:
04 **Ayer** (Alfred Jules), **Hume** (David), **Joad** (Cyril Edwin

Mitchinson), **Kant**
(Immanuel), **Mach** (Ernst),
**Marx** (Karl), **Mill** (John
Stuart), **Otto** (Rudolf), **Ryle**
(Gilbert),**Weil** (Simone)
05 **Adler** (Mortimer), **Bacon**
(Francis), **Bacon** (Roger),
**Bayle** (Pierre), **Bruno**
(Giordano), **Buber**
(Martin), **Burke** (Edmund),
**Comte** (Auguste), **Croce**
(Benedetto), **Dewey** (John),
**Frege** (Gottlob), **Gödel**
(Kurt), **Hegel** (Georg
Wilhelm Friedrich), **James**
(William), **Locke** (John),
**Moore** (George Edward),
**Plato**, **Quine** (Willard),
**Royce** (Josiah)
06 **Anselm** (Saint), **Berlin**
(Isaiah), **Carnap** (Rudolf),
**Engels** (Friedrich), **Fichte**
(Johann Gottlieb), **Herder**
(Johann Gottfried von),
**Hobbes** (Thomas), **Langer**
(Susanne), **Lukács** (Georg),
**Peirce** (Charles), **Popper**
(Karl), **Pyrrho**, **Sartre**
(Jean-Paul), **Strato**,**Thales**
07 **Aquinas** (St. Thomas),
**Bentham** (Jeremy), **Derrida**
(Jacques), **Diderot** (Denis),
**Erasmus** (Desiderius),
**Gorgias**, **Husserl**
(Edmund), **Hypatia**,
**Jaspers** (Karl), **Leibniz**
(Gottfried Wilhelm),
**Marcuse** (Herbert),
**Mencius**, **Proclus**, **Russell**
(Bertrand), **Sankara**,
**Spencer** (Herbert), **Spinoza**
(Baruch), **Steiner** (Rudolf),
**Tillich** (Paul)
08 **Alcmaeon**, **Averroës**,
**Avicenna**, **Berkeley** (Bishop
George), **Boethius** (Anicius
Manlius Severinus),
**Epicurus**, **Foucault**
(Michel), **Hobhouse**
(Leonard), **Longinus**
(Dionysius), **Plotinus**,
**Porphyry**, **Ram Singh**,
**Rousseau** (Jean Jacques),
**Sidgwick** (Henry),
**Socrates**, **Spengler**
(Oswald)
09 **Althusser** (Louis),
**Aristotle**, **Bronowski**
(Jacob), **Confucius**,
**Descartes** (René),
**Feuerbach** (Ludwig),
**Heidegger** (Martin),
**Nietzsche** (Friedrich),

**Santayana** (George),
**Schelling** (Friedrich),
**Whitehead** (Alfred North)
10 **Anaxagoras**, **Aristippus**,
**De Beauvoir** (Simone),
**Democritus**, **Duns Scotus**
(John), **Empedocles**,
**Heraclitus**, **Maimonides**
(Moses), **Parmenides**,
**Posidonius**, **Protagoras**,
**Pythagoras**, **Schweitzer**
(Albert), **Xenocrates**,
**Xenophanes**, **Zeno of Elea**
11 **Anaximander**, **Kierkegaard**
(Sören), **Montesquieu**
(Charles-Louis),
**Reichenbach** (Hans)
12 **Philo Judaeus**,
**Schopenhauer** (Arthur),
**Theophrastus**,**Wittgenstein**
(Ludwig), **Zeno of Citium**
14 **Schleiermacher** (Friedrich)
15 **William of Ockham**

**philosophical**
04 wise
05 stoic
07 logical, patient, stoical
08 abstract, composed
09 collected, realistic, unruffled
10 analytical, meditative,
phlegmatic, thoughtful
12 metaphysical
13 contemplative,
dispassionate, imperturbable

**philosophy**
04 view
06 tenets, values, wisdom
07 beliefs, thought
08 attitude, doctrine, ideology,
thinking
09 viewpoint, worldview
10 principles
11 convictions, point of view

► *Terms used in philosophy*
*include*:
05 deism, logic
06 egoism, ethics, monism,
theism
07 a priori, atheism, atomism,
dualism, realism
08 altruism, ascetism, fatalism,
hedonism, humanism,
idealism, identity, nihilism,
ontology, stoicism
09 deduction, dogmatism,
induction, intuition,
pantheism, sense data,
solipsism, substance,
syllogism, teleology
10 absolutism, aesthetics,
empiricism, entailment,

positivism, pragmatism,
relativism, skepticism
11 a posteriori, agnosticism,
behaviorism, determinism,
historicism, materialism,
metaphysics, rationalism
12 Epicureanism, epistemology,
reductionism
13 antinomianism,
phenomenology,
scholasticism, structuralism
14 existentialism, libertarianism,
utilitarianism

**phlegmatic**
04 calm
06 placid, stolid
07 stoical
09 impassive
11 unemotional
13 dispassionate

**phobia**
04 fear
05 dread
06 hang-up, horror, terror
07 anxiety, dislike
08 aversion, loathing, neurosis
09 antipathy, obsession,
repulsion, revulsion
14 irrational fear

► *Types of phobia*:
09 apiphobia, neophobia,
panphobia, zoophobia
10 acrophobia, autophobia,
cynophobia, demophobia,
pyrophobia, toxiphobia,
xenophobia
11 agoraphobia, astraphobia,
hippophobia, hydrophobia,
necrophobia, tachophobia
12 ailurophobia, entomophobia
13 arachnophobia
14 claustrophobia

**phone**
04 buzz, call, dial, ring
06 call up, ring up
07 contact, handset, hotline
08 land line, receiver
09 cell phone, telephone
11 mobile phone
13 cellular phone

**phony**
04 fake, mock, sham
05 bogus, false, pseud, quack
06 ersatz, forged, pseudo
07 assumed, feigned, forgery
08 affected, impostor, spurious
09 imitation, simulated
10 fraudulent, mountebank
11 counterfeit

**phosphorescent**
08 luminous
11 luminescent, noctilucent

**photocopy**
04 copy
05 print, Xerox
06 run off
09 duplicate, facsimile,
    Photostat

**photograph**
04 film, shot, snap, take
05 image, photo, print, shoot,
    slide, still, video
06 glossy
07 mug shot, picture, tintype
08 likeness, snapshot
09 ferrotype
12 transparency
13 dageurreotype

> *Names of photographers:*
03 **Ray** (Man)
04 **Capa** (Robert), **Hill** (David
    Octavius), **Hine** (Lewis
    Wickes)
05 **Arbus** (Diane), **Brady**
    (Matthew), **Hardy** (Bert),
    **Lange** (Dorothea), **Tames**
    (George)
06 **Abbott** (Berenice), **Arnold**
    (Eve), **Bailey** (David),
    **Beaton** (Cecil), **Cooley**
    (Sam), **Hansen** (Austin),
    **McBean** (Angus), **Miller**
    (Lee), **Niepce** (Joseph
    Nicéphore), **Strand** (Paul),
    **Talbot** (William Henry
    Fox), **Warhol** (Andy),
    **Weston** (Edward)
07 **Brassai**, **Cameron** (Julia
    Margaret), **Carroll** (Lewis),
    **Dodgson** (Charles
    Lutwidge), **Eastman**
    (George), **Gardner**
    (Alexander), **Jackson**
    (William Henry), **Lumière**
    (Auguste), **Snowdon** (Earl
    of)
08 **Daguerre** (Louis),
    **McCullin** (Don), **Steichen**
    (Edward)
09 **Leibovitz** (Annie),
    **Lichfield** (Patrick),
    **Muybridge** (Eadweard
    James), **O'Sullivan**
    (Timothy), **Rodchenko**
    (Alexander), **Stieglitz**
    (Alfred), **Winogrand**
    (Garry)
10 **Cunningham** (Imogen)
11 **Bourke-White** (Margaret),
    **Eisenstaedt** (Alfred)

14 **Armstrong-Jones**
    (Anthony), **Cartier-Bresson**
    (Henri)
   > See also ART

**photographic**
05 exact, vivid
06 filmic
07 graphic, natural, precise
08 accurate, detailed, faithful,
    lifelike
09 cinematic, pictorial, realistic,
    retentive
12 naturalistic

**phrase**
03 put, say
04 term, word
05 couch, frame, idiom, usage,
    utter
06 clause, remark, saying
07 comment, express, present
09 formulate, pronounce
10 expression
11 phraseology
12 construction

**phraseology**
04 cant
05 argot, idiom, style
06 patois, phrase, speech,
    syntax
07 diction, wording, writing
08 language, parlance, phrasing
10 expression
11 terminology

**physical**
04 real
05 solid
06 actual, bodily, carnal, mortal
07 earthly, fleshly, somatic,
    visible
08 concrete, material, palpable,
    tangible
09 corporeal, incarnate
11 examination, medical exam,
    substantial
12 physical exam

**physician**
02 GP, MD
03 doc
05 medic, quack
06 doctor, healer, intern,
    medico
07 surgeon
08 sawbones
10 consultant, specialist
12 practitioner

**physics**

> *Terms used in physics*
*include:*
03 gas, ion, law
04 atom, heat, lens, mass, wave,

work, X-ray
05 field, force, laser, lever, light,
    power, quark, ratio, sound,
    speed
06 charge, couple, energy,
    moment, optics, photon,
    proton, SI unit, volume,
    weight
07 circuit, density, digital,
    entropy, formula, gravity,
    inertia, neutron, nuclear,
    nucleus, statics, tension
08 dynamics, electron,
    equation, friction, gamma
    ray, half-life, infrared,
    molecule, momentum,
    particle, polarity, pressure,
    spectrum, velocity
09 acoustics, frequency,
    magnetism, mechanics,
    radiation, radio wave,
    resonance, sound wave,
    viscosity, white heat
10 elasticity, flash point, heavy
    water, hydraulics, latent heat,
    Mach number, microwaves,
    reflection, refraction,
    relativity, resistance,
    ultrasound
11 diffraction, electricity,
    equilibrium, evaporation,
    light source, oscillation,
    periodic law, sensitivity,
    temperature, ultraviolet
12 absolute zero, acceleration,
    analog signal, boiling point,
    critical mass, hydrostatics,
    interference, laws of motion,
    luminescence, radioisotope,
    spectroscopy
13 beta particles, Big Bang
    theory, bubble chamber,
    chain reaction, freezing
    point, hydrodynamics,
    incandescence, kinetic
    energy, magnetic field,
    nuclear fusion, quantum
    theory, radioactivity,
    semiconductor,
    supersymmetry
14 alpha particles, applied
    physics, circuit breaker,
    nuclear fission, nuclear
    physics, surface tension,
    thermodynamics, transverse
    wave
15 capillary action, center of
    gravity, charged particle,
    electric current,
    electrodynamics, perpetual
    motion, potential energy,
    visible spectrum

► *Names of physicists:*
02 **Wu** (Chien-Shiung)
03 **Lee** (Tsung-Dao), **Ohm**
(Georg Simon)
04 **Abbe** (Ernst), **Bohr** (Niels
Henrik David), **Born** (Max),
**Bose** (Satyendra Nath),
**Hess** (Victor Francis), **Katz**
(Bernard), **Land** (Edwin
Herbert), **Laue** (Max
Theodor Felix von), **Lenz**
(Heinrich Friedrich Emil),
**Mach** (Ernst), **Mott** (Nevill
Francis), **Rabi** (Isidor Isaac),
**Saha** (Meghnad), **Ting**
(Samuel), **Wien** (Wilhelm)
05 **Bethe** (Hans Albrecht),
**Bloch** (Felix), **Bondi**
(Hermann), **Boyle** (Robert),
**Bragg** (Lawrence), **Bragg**
(William Henry), **Curie**
(Marie), **Curie** (Pierre),
**Dewar** (James), **Dirac** (Paul
Adrien Maurice), **Fermi**
(Enrico), **Fuchs** (Klaus),
**Gamow** (George), **Hertz**
(Heinrich Rudolf), **Hooke**
(Robert), **Jeans** (James
Hopwood), **Joule** (James
Prescott), **Kusch** (Polykarp),
**Mayer** (Maria-Goeppert),
**Milne** (Edward Arthur),
**Pauli** (Wolfgang), **Pupin**
(Michael), **Raman**
(Chandrasekhara Venkata),
**Salam** (Abdus), **Segrè**
(Emilio), **Smyth** (Henry
Dewolf), **Stern** (Otto), **Tesla**
(Nikola), **Volta** (Alessandro
Giuseppe Anastasio)
06 **Ampère** (André Marie),
**Bunsen** (Robert Wilhelm),
**Dalton** (John), **Edison**
(Thomas Alva), **Fowler**
(William), **Frisch** (Otto
Robert), **Geiger** (Hans
Wilhelm), **Glaser** (Donald
Arthur), **Huxley** (Hugh
Esmor), **Kelvin** (William
Thomson), **Newton** (Isaac),
**Pascal** (Blaise), **Planck**
(Max), **Rohrer** (Heinrich),
**Stokes** (George Gabriel),
**Taylor** (Geoffrey Ingram),
**Teller** (Edward), **Townes**
(Charles), **Wigner** (Eugene),
**Wilson** (Robert Woodrow)
07 **Alvarez** (Luis Walter),
**Broglie** (Louis-Victor Pierre
Raymond de), **Compton**
(Arthur Holly), **Coulomb**
(Charles Augustin de),

**Doppler** (Christian
Johann), **Eastman** (George),
**Faraday** (Michael),
**Feynman** (Richard Phillips),
**Fresnel** (Augustin Jean),
**Galilei** (Galileo), **Glashow**
(Sheldon Lee), **Goddard**
(Robert Hutchings),
**Hawking** (Stephen
William), **Huygens**
(Christiaan), **Langley**
(Samuel Pierpont), **Lorentz**
(Hendrik Antoon),
**Marconi** (Guglielmo),
**Maxwell** (James Clerk),
**Meitner** (Lise), **Peierls**
(Rudolf Ernst), **Penzias**
(Arno Allan), **Poisson**
(Siméon Denis), **Purcell**
(Edward), **Réaumur** (René
Antoine Ferchault de),
**Richter** (Burton), **Röntgen**
(Wilhelm Konrad von),
**Seaborg** (Glen Theodore),
**Szilard** (Leo), **Vernier**
(Pierre)
08 **Appleton** (Edward Victor),
**Avogadro** (Amedeo),
**Angström** (Anders Jonas),
**Beaufort** (Francis),
**Chadwick** (James), **De
Forest** (Lee), **Delbrück**
(Max), **Einstein** (Albert),
**Gell-Mann** (Murray),
**Langevin** (Paul), **Lemaître**
(Georges Henri), **McMillan**
(Edwin), **Millikan** (Clark),
**Millikan** (Robert
Andrews), **Mulliken**
(Robert Sanderson),
**Regnault** (Henri Victor),
**Sakharov** (Andrei),
**Shockley** (William
Bradford), **Tomonaga** (Sin-
Itiro), **Van Allen** (James
Alfred), **Weinberg** (Steven)
09 **Aristotle**, **Bartholin**
(Erasmus), **Becquerel**
(Antoine Henri), **Birkeland**
(Kristian Olaf Bernhard),
**Boltzmann** (Ludwig),
**Cavendish** (Henry),
**Cherenkov** (Pavel),
**Heaviside** (Oliver),
**Helmholtz** (Hermann von),
**Michelson** (Albert
Abraham), **Rainwater**
(James), **Schwinger** (Julian)
10 **Anaximenes**, **Fahrenheit**
(Daniel), **Heisenberg**
(Werner Karl), **Rutherford**
(Ernest), **Torricelli**
(Evangelista), **Xenocrates**

11 **Chamberlain** (Owen),
**Joliot-Curie** (Frédéric),
**Joliot-Curie** (Irène),
**Leeuwenhoek** (Antoni van),
**Oppenheimer** (Robert),
**Schrödinger** (Erwin),
**Tsiolkovsky** (Konstantin),
**Van de Graaff** (Robert
Jemison)
13 **Chandrasekhar**
(Subrahmanyan)
➤ See also SCIENTIST

**physiognomy**
03 mug
04 face, look, phiz
06 kisser, visage
08 features
11 countenance, physiognomy

**physiologist**

► *Names of physiologists:*
04 **Hyde** (Ida Henrietta), **Levi**
(Rita)
05 **Hubel** (David Hunter),
**Keyes** (Ancel), **Marey**
(Etienne-Jules), **Poole**
(Judith), **Prout** (William),
**Rhode** (William), **Yalow**
(Rosalyn)
06 **Adrian** (Edgar Douglas),
**Bordet** (Jules), **Cannon**
(Walter Bradford), **Gasser**
(Herbert Spencer), **Haller**
(Albrecht von), **Howell**
(William Henry), **Pavlov**
(Ivan), **Pincus** (Gregory
Goodwin)
07 **Banting** (Frederick Grant),
**Beddoes** (Thomas Lovell),
**Diamond** (Jared Mason),
**Galvani** (Luigi), **Haldane**
(John Scott), **Hodgkin**
(Alan Lloyd), **Schwann**
(Theodor)
08 **Beaumont** (William),
**Hartline** (Haldan Keffer),
**Mariotte** (Edmé),
**Meyerhof** (Otto Fritz),
**Richards** (Dickinson
Woodruff)
09 **Blakemore** (Colin),
**Einthoven** (Willem),
**Helmholtz** (Hermann von)
➤ See also SCIENTIST

**physique**
04 body, form
05 build, frame, shape
06 figure, makeup
09 structure
12 constitution

**pick**
03 dig

**picket**
04 best, cull, peck, play, tool
05 cause, cream, elect, elite, favor, fix on, go for, pluck
06 choice, choose, flower, gather, lead to, opt for, option, prefer, prompt, select, take in
07 collect, harvest, produce
08 choicest, decide on, decision, plump for, settle on
09 selection, single out, toothpick
10 preference
14 crème de la crème

❑**pick at**
04 peck
06 nibble
07 toy with
08 play with

❑**pick off**
04 kill
05 shoot
06 detach, fire at, remove
07 take out

❑**pick on**
04 bait
05 blame, bully, get at
06 needle
07 torment
09 persecute

❑**pick out**
06 choose, notice, select
07 discern, make out
08 handpick, perceive
09 recognize, single out

❑**pick up**
03 buy, get
04 find, gain, go on, hear, lift
05 fetch, hoist, learn, rally
06 arrest, collar, detect, gather, obtain, perk up, resume
07 acquire, carry on, collect, improve, receive
08 contract, purchase
09 get better, give a lift
10 begin again, go down with, start again
15 take into custody

**picket**
04 pale, pike, post
05 guard, rebel, spike, stake, watch
06 paling, patrol, sentry
07 boycott, enclose, lookout, outpost, protest, striker, upright
08 blockade, objector, picketer, surround
09 dissident, protester, stanchion
11 demonstrate

12 demonstrator

**pickings**
04 loot, take
05 booty, gravy, yield
06 spoils
07 plunder, profits, returns, rewards
08 earnings, proceeds

**pickle**
03 fix, jam
04 bind, cure, mess, salt
05 sauce, souse, steep
06 relish, scrape
07 chutney, dilemma, straits, vinegar
08 conserve, hot water, marinade, preserve, quandary
09 condiment, tight spot
11 predicament

**pick-me-up**
05 boost, drink, tonic
06 fillip
07 cordial
11 restorative
12 shot in the arm

**pickpocket**
03 dip
05 thief
08 cutpurse, snatcher

**picnic**
05 cinch
06 breeze, outing
08 clambake, pushover, walkover
09 easy as pie, excursion
10 child's play
11 outdoor meal, piece of cake

**pictorial**
05 vivid
06 scenic
07 graphic
09 schematic
11 illustrated, picturesque
12 diagrammatic

**picture**
03 see
04 draw, film, show, tale
05 flick, movie, paint, story
06 appear, depict, flicks, report, sketch
07 account, epitome, essence, imagine, portray
08 conceive, envisage
09 delineate, depiction, portrayal, represent, reproduce, visualize
10 call to mind, illustrate, impression, photograph
11 delineation, description

12 quintessence
13 motion picture
15 personification

➤ *Types of picture*:
03 oil
04 icon, snap
05 cameo, image, mural, pinup, plate, print, slide, still
06 canvas, design, doodle, fresco, mosaic, sketch
07 cartoon, collage, drawing, etching, montage, mug shot, tableau, tintype
08 abstract, graffiti, graphics, likeness, negative, painting, Photofit, portrait, snapshot, tapestry, triptych, vignette
09 engraving, ferrotype, Identikit, landscape, miniature, old master, still life
10 caricature, cheesecake, photograph, silhouette, watercolor
11 oil painting, trompe l'oeil
12 illustration, self-portrait, transparency
13 daguerreotype, passport photo
➤ See also ART

❑**get the picture**
03 see
05 get it, grasp
08 cotton on
10 comprehend, get the idea, understand
11 get the point
13 get the message

❑**put someone in the picture**
06 clue up, fill in, inform, notify, update
10 keep posted

**picturesque**
06 pretty, quaint, scenic
08 charming, colorful, pleasant, pleasing, striking
09 beautiful
10 attractive, delightful, impressive
11 descriptive

**piddling**
04 mean, poor, puny
05 minor, petty, small, sorry
06 meager, measly, paltry, slight
07 trivial
08 derisory, piffling, trifling
09 miserable, worthless
12 contemptible

**pie**
03 pie

04 tart
06 pastry

❑ **pie in the sky**
05 dream
06 hot air, mirage, notion
07 fantasy, reverie, romance
08 daydream, delusion
09 pipe dream
13 castle in Spain
14 castle in the air

**piebald**
04 pied
07 dappled, mottled, spotted
10 variegated
13 black and white

**piece**
03 bit, cut
04 bite, chip, coin, hunk, item, lump, opus, part, slab, unit, work
05 block, chunk, crumb, flake, fleck, quota, scrap, shard, share, sherd, shred, slice, speck, story, study, wedge
06 dollop, length, morsel, pistol, report, review, sample, sliver, tidbit
07 article, element, example, opinion, portion, section, segment, snippet
08 division, fraction, fragment, mouthful, quantity, specimen, splinter
09 allotment, component
10 allocation, percentage, smithereen
11 composition, constituent
12 illustration

❑ **all in one piece**
05 whole
06 entire, intact, unhurt
08 complete, integral, unbroken, unharmed
09 undamaged, uninjured

❑ **go to pieces**
07 crack up
08 collapse
09 break down
11 lose control

❑ **in pieces**
05 kaput
06 broken, in bits, ruined
07 damaged, smashed
09 shattered
13 disintegrated, in smithereens

❑ **piece together**
03 fit, fix
04 join, mend
05 patch, unite
06 attach, repair

07 compose, restore
08 assemble
11 fit together
12 join together

**pièce de résistance**
05 jewel, prize
09 showpiece
10 magnum opus, masterwork
11 chef-d'oeuvre, masterpiece

**piecemeal**
06 patchy, slowly
07 partial
08 bit by bit, discrete, fitfully, sporadic
09 by degrees, partially, scattered
11 at intervals, fragmentary
12 intermittent, unsystematic
14 intermittently, little by little
15 in dribs and drabs

**pied**
06 motley
07 brindle, dappled, flecked, mottled, piebald, spotted
08 brindled, skewbald, streaked
10 variegated
11 varicolored
12 multicolored

**pier**
04 dock, pile, post, quay, slip
05 jetty, wharf
06 column, pillar
07 landing, support, upright
10 breakwater
12 landing place, landing stage

**pierce**
04 bore, fill, hurt, move, pain, stab
05 drill, enter, lance, prick, probe, punch, spear, spike, sting
06 impale, skewer
07 bayonet
08 puncture, transfix
09 penetrate, perforate
13 cut to the quick

**pierced**
06 spiked
07 impaled, speared
09 punctured
10 penetrated, perforated

**piercing**
03 raw
04 cold, keen, loud
05 alert, sharp
06 astute, biting, bitter, fierce, frosty, severe, shrewd, shrill, wintry
07 intense, painful, probing
08 freezing

09 searching
10 discerning, lacerating
11 high-pitched, penetrating
12 earsplitting, excruciating

**piety**
05 faith
07 respect
08 devotion, holiness, sanctity
09 godliness, piousness
10 devoutness
11 saintliness

**piffle**
03 rot
04 bunk, guff
05 hooey, trash, tripe
06 bunkum, drivel
07 rubbish, twaddle
08 nonsense, tommyrot
09 poppycock
10 balderdash, codswallop

**pig**
03 hog, sow
04 boar, pork
05 beast, brute, piggy, swine
06 animal, guzzle, piglet, porker
07 glutton, grunter, guzzler, peccary, warthog
08 gourmand, javelina
10 greedy guts

▶ *Pigs include*:
05 Duroc
07 Montana, Old Spot
08 Hereford, Landrace, Tamworth, wild boar
09 Berkshire, Hampshire, Minnesota, Yorkshire
10 Beltsville, Large White, potbellied, saddleback
11 Middle White, Poland China
12 Chester White, Spotted Swine
➤ See also ANIMAL

**pigeonhole**
03 box, tag
04 file, slot, sort
05 label, niche
06 locker
07 catalog, cubicle, section
08 category, classify
09 catalogue, cubbyhole
10 categorize
11 compartment
14 classification

**pigheaded**
06 mulish, stupid, wilful
07 froward, willful
08 contrary, perverse, stubborn
09 obstinate
10 bullheaded, headstrong, inflexible

11 intractable, wrong-headed
12 intransigent

**pigment**
03 dye, hue
04 tint
05 color, paint, stain
08 coloring, tincture

▶ *Pigments include*:
03 hem
04 haem, heme
05 henna, ocher, ochre, sepia, umber
06 bister, bistre, cobalt, cyanin, flavin, madder, sienna, zaffer, zaffre
07 carmine, crimson, etiolin, flavine, gamboge, melanin, realgar, sinopia
08 carotene, cinnabar, orpiment, rose-pink, verditer, viridian
09 anthocyan, bilirubin, Indian red, lampblack, lithopone, quercetin, zinc white
10 Berlin blue, biliverdin, Chinese red, chlorophyl, green earth, Paris green, pearl white, terre verte, vermillion
11 anthochlore, anthocyanin, chlorophyll, King's yellow, ultramarine, Venetian red
12 Cappagh brown, Chinese white, chrome yellow, Naples yellow, phycoxanthin, Prussian blue, xanthopterin
13 cadmium yellow, Scheele's green, titanium white
➤ See also COLOR; DYE

**pile**
03 bar, fur, jam, nap
04 a lot, down, fuzz, heap, load, lots, mass, mint, pack, post, rush, shag, tons, wool
05 amass, crowd, crush, flock, flood, fluff, heaps, hoard, loads, mound, plush, stack, store
06 bundle, column, gather, packet, piling, riches, stacks, wealth
07 build up, collect, edifice, fortune, squeeze, support, surface, texture, upright
08 assemble, lashings, mountain
10 a great deal, accumulate, assemblage, assortment, collection, foundation, quantities
12 accumulation

❑**pile it on**
06 overdo, stress
07 lay it on, magnify
08 overdo it
09 dramatize, overstate
10 exaggerate
12 lay it on thick

❑**pile up**
07 mount up
08 escalate, increase, multiply
10 accumulate

**pileup**
05 crash, smash, wreck
07 smashup
09 collision

**pilfer**
03 rob
04 lift
05 filch, pinch, steal, swipe
06 snitch, thieve
07 purloin
08 knock off, peculate, shoplift

**pilgrim**
04 haji
05 hadji, hajji
06 palmer
07 devotee
08 crusader, traveler, wanderer, wayfarer
09 worshiper

**pilgrimage**
03 haj
04 hadj, hajj, tour, trip
07 crusade, journey, mission

**pill**
04 ball
06 pellet, tablet
07 capsule, lozenge

**pillage**
03 rob
04 loot, raid, raze, sack
05 booty, rifle, spoil, strip
06 maraud, rapine, ravage, spoils
07 despoil, plunder, ransack, robbery, seizure
08 freeboot, harrying, spoliate
09 depredate, marauding
10 spoliation
11 depredation, devastation

**pillar**
04 mast, pier, pile, pole, post, prop, rock
05 shaft, stele
06 cippus, column
07 bastion, support, upright
08 mainstay
09 stanchion
15 tower of strength

**pillory**
04 lash, mock
05 brand
06 show up
07 laugh at
08 denounce, ridicule
10 stigmatize
11 cast a slur on, pour scorn on
13 hold up to shame

**pillow**
07 bolster, cushion
08 headrest

**pilot**
05 flyer, guide, steer, trial
06 airman, direct, leader
07 aircrew, aviator, captain, conduct, control, operate
08 airwoman, coxswain, helmsman, maneuver, navigate
09 commander, navigator, steersman

**pimp**
08 panderer
09 procurer,

**pimple**
03 dot, zit
04 boil, spot
06 papule
07 pustule
08 swelling

**pin**
03 fix, lay, peg, put
04 bolt, clip, join, nail, tack
05 affix, dowel, place, press, rivet, screw, spike, stick
06 attach, brooch, fasten, impute, secure, staple
07 ascribe
08 fastener, hold down, hold fast, restrain
09 attribute, constrain
10 immobilize

❑**pin down**
05 force, press
06 compel, define
08 hold down, identify, nail down, pinpoint, restrain
09 constrain, determine
10 pressurize
15 put your finger on

**pincers**
05 tongs
07 forceps
08 tweezers

**pinch**
03 bit, jot, nab, nip, tad
04 book, bust, dash, grip, hurt, lift, mite, nail, save

05 catch, cramp, crush, filch, grasp, press, run in, seize, speck, steal, taste, touch, trace, tweak
06 arrest, budget, collar, crisis, detain, pick up, pilfer, snatch, stress
07 capture, confine, cut back, purloin, smidgen, soupçon, squeeze
08 compress, hardship, peculate, pressure
09 economize, emergency
10 difficulty
11 appropriate, predicament, walk off with
13 keep costs down, scrape a living, scrimp and save

❑**in a pinch**
11 if necessary
13 in an emergency

**pinched**
04 pale, thin, worn
05 drawn, gaunt, peaky
07 haggard, starved
08 careworn, narrowed
12 straightened

**pine**
04 ache, fade, fret, long, sigh, wish
05 crave, mourn, yearn
06 desire, grieve, hanker, hunger, thirst, weaken
08 languish
09 waste away

**pinion**
04 bind
05 chain, truss
06 fetter, hobble
07 confine, manacle, pin down, shackle
10 immobilize

**pink**
04 acme, best, peak, rose, rosy
06 flower, height, incise, salmon, summit, tiptop
07 extreme, flushed, reddish, roseate, scallop, serrate

❑**in the pink**
03 fit
04 well
07 healthy
11 in good shape, right as rain
12 in fine fettle
15 in perfect health

**pinnacle**
03 cap, top
04 acme, apex, cone, peak
05 crest, crown, spire

06 apogee, height, needle, summit, turret, vertex, zenith
07 obelisk, pyramid, steeple

**pinpoint**
06 define, locate
07 pin down, specify
08 discover, home in on, identify, nail down, zero in on
11 distinguish
15 put your finger on

**pintpintsize, pintsized**
03 wee
04 tiny
05 dwarf, small
06 little, midget, pocket
09 miniature
10 diminutive, pocketsize
11 pocket-sized

**pioneer**
05 begin, found, set up, start
06 create, invent, launch, leader, open up
07 develop, founder, settler
08 colonist, discover, explorer, initiate, inventor
09 developer, innovator, instigate, introduce, originate, spearhead
10 discoverer, lead the way, pathfinder, pave the way
11 blaze a trail, trailblazer
12 frontiersman
13 groundbreaker
14 break new ground, founding father, frontierswoman

**pious**
04 good, holy
05 godly, moral
06 devout
07 devoted, saintly
08 faithful, reverent, virtuous
09 dedicated, insincere, religious, righteous, spiritual
12 hypocritical
13 sanctimonious, self-righteous
14 holier-than-thou

**pipe**
04 clay, duct, flue, hose, main, peep, play, sing, tube
05 brier, cheep, chirp, hooka, sound, trill, tweet
06 convey, dudeen, funnel, hookah, kalian, siphon, supply, tubing, warble
07 calumet, channel, chirrup, conduct, conduit, deliver, passage, twitter, whistle
08 claypipe, conveyor, cylinder, narghile, overflow, transmit
09 peace pipe

10 meerschaum
12 hubble-bubble

❑**pipe down**
06 shut up
07 be quiet
11 stop talking

**pipe dream**
06 mirage, notion
07 fantasy, romance
08 daydream, delusion
11 pie in the sky
13 castle in Spain
14 castle in the air, castle in the sky

**pipeline**
04 duct, line, pipe, tube
07 channel, conduit, passage
08 conveyor

❑**in the pipeline**
07 planned
08 under way
13 in preparation

**pipsqueak**
05 creep, twerp
06 nobody, squirt
07 nothing, upstart
09 nonentity
11 hobbledehoy
14 whippersnapper

**piquancy**
03 pep, zip
04 bite, edge, kick, tang, zest
05 punch, spice, vigor
06 flavor, ginger, pizazz, relish
07 pizzazz
08 interest, pungency, raciness, vitality
09 sharpness, spiciness
10 excitement, liveliness
11 pepperiness

**piquant**
04 racy, tart
05 juicy, salty, sharp, spicy, tangy, zesty
06 biting, lively, savory
07 peppery, pungent
08 colorful, seasoned, spirited, stinging
09 sparkling
10 intriguing
11 provocative, stimulating
14 highly seasoned

**pique**
03 get, irk, vex
04 gall, goad, huff, miff, rile, spur, stir, whet
05 anger, annoy, peeve, rouse, sting, wound
06 arouse, excite, grudge, kindle, nettle, offend, put out

**piqued**
07 affront, incense, mortify, offense, provoke, umbrage
08 vexation
09 annoyance, galvanize, stimulate
11 displeasure

**piqued**
05 angry, riled, vexed
06 miffed, peeved, put out
07 annoyed
08 offended

**piracy**
05 theft
06 rapine
09 hijacking
10 plagiarism
11 bootlegging, freebooting
12 buccaneering, infringement

**pirate**
04 copy, crib, lift
05 pinch, poach, rover, steal
06 raider
07 brigand, corsair, sea wolf
08 marauder, picaroon, sea rover
09 buccaneer, infringer, sea robber
10 filibuster, freebooter, plagiarist, plagiarize
11 appropriate, plagiarizer

*Names of pirates:*
03 **Tew** (Thomas)
04 **Gunn** (Ben), **Hook** (Captain), **Kidd** (William), **Read** (Mary), **Smee**
05 **Bones** (Billy), **Bonny** (Anne), **Drake** (Francis), **Every** (Henry), **Teach** (Edward)
06 **Morgan** (Henry), **Silver** (Long John)
07 **Dampier** (William), **Lafitte** (Jean)
08 **Black Dog, Blind Pew, Redbeard**
09 **Black Bart**
10 **Barbarossa** (Khair-ed-din), **Blackbeard, Calico Jack**

**pirouette**
04 spin, turn
05 pivot, twirl, whirl

**pistol**
03 gun, rod
04 iron
05 piece
06 zip gun
07 firearm, handgun, sidearm
08 Luger, revolver
09 derringer
10 six-shooter

**pit**
04 dent, gulf, hole, mine, scar
05 abyss, chasm, ditch, notch
06 cavity, crater, dimple, hollow, indent, quarry, trench
07 depress, pothole
08 coal mine, diggings, pockmark, workings
10 depression
11 excavations, indentation
13 orchestra area

❏**pit against**
06 oppose
10 set against

**pitch**
03 aim, fix, key, lob, tar, yak
04 bowl, cant, cast, dive, drop, fall, fire, hurl, keel, line, list, mark, reel, roll, sway, talk, tilt, tone, toss
05 angle, chuck, erect, fling, grade, heave, level, lurch, place, point, put up, set up, slant, sling, slope, sound, spiel, throw
06 degree, direct, extend, gabble, ground, height, jargon, launch, patter, plunge, settle, timbre, topple, tumble, wallow
07 asphalt, bitumen, chatter, incline, plummet
08 flounder, gradient, position, tonality
09 frequency, intensity, steepness
10 modulation
11 inclination
12 fall headlong

❏**pitch in**
04 help
06 join in
09 do your bit, lend a hand
10 be involved
11 participate

**pitch-black**
04 dark, inky
05 black, unlit
08 jet-black
09 coal black, pitch-dark

**pitcher**
03 can, jar, jug, urn
04 ewer
05 crock
06 bottle, hurler, vessel
07 thrower
09 container
14 baseball player

**piteous**
06 moving, woeful
07 pitiful

08 pathetic, pitiable, poignant, wretched
11 distressing
12 heart-rending
13 heartbreaking

**pitfall**
04 snag, trap
05 catch, peril, snare
06 danger, hazard
08 drawback
14 stumbling block

**pith**
03 nub
04 core, crux, gist, meat
05 heart, point, vigor
06 import, kernel, marrow, matter, moment, weight
07 essence
09 substance
11 consequence
12 quintessence, salient point, significance

**pithy**
05 brief, short, terse
06 cogent
07 compact, concise, pointed, summary, telling
08 forceful, incisive, succinct
09 condensed, trenchant
10 expressive, meaningful
13 short and sweet

**pitiable**
03 sad
05 sorry
07 doleful, piteous
08 pathetic, wretched
09 miserable
10 lamentable
11 distressing

**pitiful**
03 low, sad
04 base, mean, poor, vile
06 meager, moving, paltry, shabby, woeful
07 doleful, piteous
08 hopeless, mournful, pathetic, pitiable, wretched
09 miserable, worthless
10 deplorable, despicable, inadequate, lamentable
12 contemptible, heart-rending
13 heartbreaking, insignificant

**pitiless**
05 cruel, harsh
06 brutal, severe
07 callous, inhuman
08 inhumane, ruthless
09 heartless, merciless
10 inexorable, relentless
11 cold-blooded, cold-hearted, hardhearted, unremitting

**pittance**
06 trifle
07 modicum, peanuts
11 chicken feed
14 drop in the ocean

**pitted**
05 holey, rough
06 dented, marked, stoned
07 notched, scarred
08 indented, potholed
09 blemished, depressed
10 pockmarked

**pity**
05 mercy, shame
06 regret, sorrow
07 sadness, weep for
08 distress, sympathy
10 compassion, condolence
11 crying shame
13 commiseration,
   understanding

❏**take pity on**
05 spare
06 pardon
07 feel for
09 show mercy
11 have mercy on
12 feel sorry for

**pivot**
03 hub, lie
04 axis, axle, hang, rely, turn
05 focus, heart, hinge, swing
06 center, rotate, swivel
07 fulcrum, kingpin, spindle
08 linchpin
10 focal point

**pivotal**
05 axial, focal, vital
07 central, crucial
08 cardinal, critical, decisive
09 climactic, important
11 determining

**pixie, pixy**
03 elf
05 fairy
06 goblin, sprite
07 brownie
10 leprechaun

**placard**
02 ad
04 bill, sign
06 notice, poster
07 sticker
13 advertisement

**placate**
04 calm, lull
06 pacify, soothe
07 appease, mollify, win over
08 calm down
10 conciliate, propitiate

**placatory**
07 calming
08 soothing
09 appeasing
10 mollifying
11 peacemaking
12 conciliatory, pacificatory,
   propitiative, propitiatory

**place**
03 fix, job, lay, pad, put, set
04 area, city, digs, duty, home,
   know, part, rank, rest, role,
   room, seat, site, sort, spot,
   task, town, zone
05 abode, class, grade, group,
   hotel, house, leave, lodge,
   niche, plant, point, scene,
   space, stand, state, venue
06 assign, billet, hamlet, instal,
   locale, locate, region, settle,
   status
07 arrange, concern, country,
   deposit, install, lay down, put
   down, set down, setting,
   situate, station, village
08 allocate, building, business,
   classify, district, domicile,
   dwelling, identify, locality,
   location, pinpoint, position,
   property, standing
09 apartment, recognize,
   residence, situation
11 appointment, whereabouts
12 finish second
13 accommodation,
   establishment
14 responsibility

❏**in place**
05 set up
07 in order, working
08 arranged

❏**in place of**
08 in lieu of
09 instead of
13 in exchange for

❏**out of place**
08 tactless, unseemly
09 unfitting
10 inapposite, unsuitable
13 inappropriate

❏**put someone in their
place**
05 crush, shame
06 humble
07 deflate
09 humiliate

❏**take place**
05 occur
06 be held, befall, betide,
   happen
09 come about, transpire

10 come to pass

❏**take the place of**
07 replace
09 supersede
10 stand in for
13 substitute for

**placement**
03 job
07 ranking
08 locating, location, ordering
09 place kick
10 deployment, employment,
   engagement, stationing
11 appointment, arrangement,
   disposition, positioning
12 distribution, installation

**placid**
04 calm, cool, mild
05 quiet, still
06 gentle, serene
07 equable, pacific, restful
08 composed, peaceful,
   tranquil
09 easygoing, peaceable,
   unruffled
10 untroubled
11 unemotional, unflappable
12 even-tempered
13 imperturbable

**plagiarism**
05 theft
06 piracy
07 copying, lifting
08 cribbing

**plagiarist**
05 thief
06 copier, pirate, robber
07 cribber

**plagiarize**
04 copy, crib, lift
05 poach, steal
06 borrow, pirate
07 imitate
09 reproduce
11 appropriate, counterfeit

**plague**
03 bug, dog, vex
05 annoy, curse, haunt, hound,
   swarm, trial, upset, worry
06 bother, hamper, harass,
   hassle, hinder, influx, pester
07 afflict, cholera, disease,
   scourge, torment, torture
08 epidemic, invasion, irritate,
   nuisance, pandemic
09 aggravate, annoyance,
   contagion, infection,
   persecute
10 Black Death, pestilence
11 infestation

**plain**
13 pain in the neck
15 thorn in the flesh

**plain**
04 flat, open, ugly
05 basic, blunt, clear, frank, lucid, overt, stark, usual
06 candid, direct, homely, honest, modest, pampas, patent, simple, simply
07 austere, evident, lowland, obvious, prairie, sincere, visible
08 apparent, flatland, manifest, ordinary, savannah, unlovely
09 grassland, unadorned
10 accessible, forthright, noticeable, restrained
11 discernible, perceptible, self-colored, transparent, unambiguous, undecorated
12 intelligible, unattractive
13 uncomplicated, unembellished
15 straightforward, unprepossessing, unsophisticated

**plainclothes man**
04 dick
06 sleuth
07 gumshoe
09 detective
12 investigator
13 police officer

**plainspoken**
05 blunt, frank
06 candid, direct, honest
08 explicit, outright, truthful
09 downright, outspoken
10 forthright
11 unequivocal
15 straightforward

**plaintive**
03 sad
06 woeful
07 doleful, piteous, pitiful, unhappy, wistful
08 mournful, wretched
09 sorrowful
10 melancholy
11 heartbroken
12 disconsolate, heart-rending

**plan**
03 aim, map, way
04 idea, mean, plot, seek, want, wish
05 chart, draft, frame, means, shape
06 design, devise, intend, invent, layout, map out, method, policy, scheme, sketch, system
07 arrange, develop, diagram, drawing, foresee, formula, outline, prepare, program, project, propose, purpose, resolve, think of, work out
08 contrive, envisage, organize, proposal, scenario, schedule, strategy
09 blueprint, calculate, formulate, intention, procedure
10 mastermind, suggestion
11 arrangement, contemplate, delineation, proposition
12 illustration, scale drawing
14 representation

**plane**
03 fly, jet
04 even, flat, rank, rung, sail, skim, soar, tree, VTOL, wing
05 class, flush, glide, jumbo, level, plain, skate, stage
06 bomber, degree, glider, planar, smooth
07 echelon, fighter, footing, regular, stratum, uniform
08 aircraft, airliner, airplane, jumbo jet
11 flat surface
12 level surface

**planet**

▶ *Names of planets*:
04 Mars
05 Earth, Pluto, Venus
06 Saturn, Uranus
07 Jupiter, Mercury, Neptune

**plant**
03 fix, put, set, sow
04 bury, gear, hide, mill, root, seed, shop, yard
05 found, imbed, lodge, place, works
06 insert, settle
07 conceal, factory, foundry, implant, scatter, secrete, situate
08 disguise, position, workshop
09 apparatus, equipment, establish, machinery

▶ *Types of plant*:
04 bulb, bush, corm, fern, herb, moss, tree, vine, weed
05 algae, grass, shrub
06 annual, cactus, cereal, flower, fungus, hybrid, lichen
07 climber, sapling
08 biennial, cultivar, pot plant, seedling
09 evergreen, perennial, succulent, vegetable
10 house plant, water plant, wildflower
▶ See also ALGAE; BULB; FLOWER; GRASS; LEAF; LILY; PALM; POISONOUS; SEAWEED; SHRUB; TREE; WEED

**plaque**
04 sign
05 badge, brass, medal, plate
06 shield, tablet
09 cartouche, medallion

**plastic**
04 soft
05 false, phony
06 pliant, supple
07 ductile, man-made, pliable
08 flexible, moldable
09 compliant, malleable, receptive, shapeable, synthetic, tractable, unnatural
10 artificial, manageable
14 impressionable

▶ *Types of plastic*:
03 PVC
04 PTFE, uPVC
05 vinyl
06 Teflon
07 Perspex, styrene
08 Bakelite, neoprene, silicone
09 celluloid, Plexiglas, polyester
10 epoxy resin
11 polystyrene
12 polyethylene, polyurethane
13 polypropylene

**plasticity**
07 pliancy
10 pliability, suppleness
11 flexibility, pliableness
12 malleability, tractability

**plate**
03 tin
04 base, coat, dish, gild, pane, sign, slab
05 cover, panel, photo, print, prize
06 lamina, plaque, salver, silver, tablet, veneer
07 anodize, helping, overlay, picture, platter, portion, serving
08 home base, laminate
09 galvanize, platinize
10 bridgework, false teeth, lithograph, photograph
12 electroplate, illustration

**plateau**
04 mesa
05 table
06 upland

**platform**
08 highland
09 tableland

**platform**
04 dais, deck
05 stage, stand
06 podium, policy
07 program, rostrum, soapbox
08 strategy
09 manifesto, party line

**platitude**
06 cliché, truism
07 bromide, inanity
08 banality, chestnut
11 commonplace

**platitudinous**
05 banal, corny, inane, stale, stock, tired, trite, vapid
07 clichéd
08 truistic, well-worn
09 hackneyed
10 overworked
11 commonplace, stereotyped

**platonic**
09 nonsexual, spiritual
10 idealistic
11 incorporeal, nonphysical
12 intellectual, transcendent

**platoon**
04 team
05 group, squad
06 outfit, patrol
07 battery
08 squadron
09 formation
12 military unit
13 football squad

**platter**
04 disc, dish, tray
05 plate
06 record, salver
08 trencher
09 home plate

**plaudits**
06 praise
07 acclaim, hurrays, ovation
08 accolade, applause
09 good press
10 rave review
11 acclamation, approbation
12 pat on the back
15 congratulations, standing ovation

**plausible**
04 glib
07 logical
08 credible, possible, probable
10 believable, convincing, persuasive
11 conceivable
12 smooth spoken

13 smooth talking, smooth-tongued

**play**
03 act, fun
04 game, give, jest, plot, romp, room, show
05 caper, dance, drama, farce, flash, frisk, hobby, kicks, laugh, range, revel, rival, scope, slack, space, sport
06 action, cavort, comedy, fiddle, frolic, gambol, join in, joking, leeway, margin, oppose, take on
07 compete, flicker, freedom, have fun, leisure, liberty, license, pastime, perform, portray, teasing, tragedy, twinkle, vie with
08 exercise, free rein, latitude, movement, take part
09 amusement, challenge, diversion, enjoyment, interplay, looseness, melodrama, operation, play games, represent
10 recreation
11 flexibility, impersonate, interaction, move lightly, participate, performance
13 amuse yourself, enjoy yourself, entertainment, play the part of
14 compete against

▶ *Names of plays:*
03 Art
04 Loot
05 Equus, Faust, Le Cid, Medea, Médée, Roots, Yerma
06 Becket, Harvey, Luther, Phèdre
07 Amadeus, Can't Pay, Electra, Endgame, Galileo, Oleanna, Side Man, Won't Pay
08 Antigone, Betrayal, Everyman, Huis Clos, Oresteia, Peer Gynt, Tartuffe, The Birds, The Flies, The Frogs, The Miser, The Wasps
09 All My Sons, Miss Julie, Pygmalion, Saint Joan, The Clouds, The Rivals
10 Andromaque, Copenhagen, Lysistrata, No Man's Land, Oedipus Rex, Plaza Suite, The Bacchae, The Seagull, Uncle Vanya
11 A Doll's House, Biloxi Blues, Hedda Gabler, Master Class, The Crucible, The Wild Duck, Tobacco Road, Trojan Women

12 Blithe Spirit, Blood Wedding, Hellazpoppin, Major Barbara, Private Lives, Punch and Judy, The Alchemist, The Caretaker, The Mousetrap, The Rainmaker, The Rose Tatoo
13 Arms and the Man, Born Yesterday, Doctor Faustus, Le Misanthrope, Lost in Yonkers, Mister Roberts, The Homecoming, The Jew of Malta, The White Devil, The Winslow Boy
14 Krapp's Last Tape, Life With Father, Man and Superman, Orlando Furioso, The Bald Saprano, The Country Wife
15 A Raisin in the Sun, American Buffalo, Bartholomew Fair, Look Back in Anger, Prometheus Bound, The Beggar's Opera, The Iceman Cometh, The Three Sisters, Waiting For Godot
16 Death of a Salesman
17 Glengarry Glen Ross
19 Tamberlaine the Great
21 A Streetcar Named Desire
➤ See also SHAKESPEARE

❏ **play around with**
07 toy with
08 fool with
09 dally with, flirt with
10 fiddle with, fidget with, meddle with, tamper with, trifle with
13 interfere with
14 mess around with

❏ **play at**
06 affect
07 make out, pretend
10 put on an act, take part in

❏ **play down**
08 downplay, minimize
09 gloss over, underplay
10 understate, undervalue
11 make light of
13 underestimate

❏ **play on**
07 exploit, trade on
08 profit by
12 capitalize on

❏ **play out**
03 act
04 go on
05 enact
06 unfold

❏ **play up**
07 point up
09 highlight, publicize, spotlight

**playboy**
10 exaggerate
19 accentuate emphasize

❑**play up to**
05 toady
07 flatter
08 blandish, bootlick, butter up,
　　soft-soap, suck up to
14 curry favor with

**playboy**
04 rake, roué
08 lady's man
09 ladies' man, libertine,
　　socialite, womanizer
10 lady-killer
11 philanderer
12 man about town

**player**
05 actor
06 artist
07 actress, artiste, athlete,
　　trouper
08 comedian, musician
09 performer, sportsman
10 comedienne, competitor,
　　contestant
11 accompanist, entertainer,
　　participant, sportswoman
15 instrumentalist

**playful**
06 frisky, impish, joking, lively
07 jesting, puckish, roguish,
　　teasing, waggish
08 humorous, spirited, sportive
09 facetious, fun loving,
　　kittenish
10 frolicsome
11 mischievous

**playground**
04 park
08 play area
10 resort area, schoolyard
12 playing field ˋ
13 amusement park

**playmate**
03 pal
04 chum
05 buddy, lover
06 cohort
09 companion
12 child's friend

**plaything**
03 toy
06 bauble, gewgaw, trifle
07 pastime, trinket
08 gimcrack
09 amusement

**playwright**
06 writer
09 dramatist, tragedian
10 dramaturge

12 dramaturgist

---

➤ *Names of playwrights and
screenwriters:*
02 Fo (Dario)
03 Fry (Christopher), **Gay**
　　(John), **Kyd** (Thomas)
04 Bolt (Robert), **Bond**
　　(Edward), **Dane**
　　(Clemence), **Ford** (John),
　　**Hare** (David), **Inge**
　　(William), **Shaw** (George
　　Bernard), **Uhry** (Alfred),
　　**Vega** (Lope de)
05 Albee (Edward), **Allen**
　　(Woody), **Arden** (John),
　　**Behan** (Brendan), **Dumas**
　　(Alexandre), **Eliot** (Thomas
　　Stearns), **Genet** (Jean),
　　**Gogol** (Nikolai), **Havel**
　　(Vaclav), **Ibsen** (Henrik),
　　**Lorca** (Federico García),
　　**Mamet** (David), **Nashe**
　　(Thomas), **Odets** (Clifford),
　　**Orton** (Joe), **Sachs** (Hans),
　　**Sachs** (Nelly), **Simon** (Neil),
　　**Smith** (Dodie), **Synge** (John
　　Millington), **Wilde** (Oscar),
　　**Yeats** (William Butler)
06 Auburn (David), **Barrie**
　　(James Matthew), **Brecht**
　　(Bertolt), **Coward** (Noël),
　　**Dekker** (Thomas), **Dryden**
　　(John), **Galdós** (Benito
　　Pérez), **Goethe** (Johann
　　Wolfgang von), **Greene**
　　(Robert), **Herzog** (Werner),
　　**Huston** (John), **Irving**
　　(John), **Jerome** (Jerome
　　Klapka), **Jonson** (Ben),
　　**Lerner** (Alan Jay), **Mercer**
　　(David), **Miller** (Arthur),
　　**O'Casey** (Sean), **O'Neill**
　　(Eugene), **Pinero** (Arthur
　　Wing), **Pinter** (Harold),
　　**Powell** (Michael), **Sartre**
　　(Jean-Paul), **Schary** (Dore),
　　**Steele** (Richard), **Wesker**
　　(Arnold), **Wilder** (Billy),
　　**Wilder** (Thornton)
07 Anouilh (Jean), **Beckett**
　　(Samuel), **Chapman**
　　(George), **Chekhov** (Anton),
　　**Cocteau** (Jean), **Coppola**
　　(Francis Ford), **Goldman**
　　(William), **Ionesco**
　　(Eugène), **Kubrick**
　　(Stanley), **Lardner** (Ring),
　　**Marlowe** (Christopher),
　　**Marston** (John), **Mishima**
　　(Yukio), **Molière**, **Novello**
　　(Ivor), **Osborne** (John),
　　**Plautus** (Titus Maccius),

Richler (Mordecai),
**Rostand** (Edmond), **Russell**
(Willy), **Saroyan** (William),
**Shaffer** (Peter), **Sheldon**
(Sidney), **Shepard** (Sam),
**Ustinov** (Peter), **Webster**
(John)
08 Anderson (Maxwell),
　　**Beaumont** (Francis),
　　**Congreve** (William),
　　**Davenant** (William),
　　**Fielding** (Henry), **Fletcher**
　　(John), **MacLeish**
　　(Archibald), **Menander**,
　　**Mortimer** (John), **Polanski**
　　(Roman), **Rattigan**
　　(Terence), **Schiller**
　　(Friedrich), **Sheridan**
　　(Richard Brinsley),
　　**Sherwood** (Robert),
　　**Stoppard** (Tom), **Suckling**
　　(John), **Tourneur** (Cyril),
　　**Vanbrugh** (John), **Wedekind**
　　(Frank), **Williams** (Emlyn),
　　**Williams** (Tennessee)
09 Aeschylus, **Ayckbourn**
　　(Alan), **Chayefsky** (Paddy),
　　**Corneille** (Pierre),
　　**D'Annunzio** (Gabriele),
　　**Euripides**, **Goldsmith**
　　(Oliver), **Hansberry**
　　(Lorraine), **Isherwood**
　　(Christopher), **Mankowitz**
　　(Joseph), **Mankowitz**
　　(Wolf), **Margulies**
　　(Donald), **Marinetti**
　　(Filippo Tommaso),
　　**Middleton** (Thomas),
　　**Priestley** (John Boynton),
　　**Sophocles**, **Wycherley**
　　(William)
10 Galsworthy (John),
　　**Pirandello** (Luigi),
　　**Strindberg** (August)
11 Shakespeare (William)
12 Aristophanes,
　　**Beaumarchais** (Pierre-
　　Augustin Caron de)
➤ See also WRITER

**plea**
06 appeal, excuse, prayer
07 defense, request
08 entreaty, petition
10 invocation
11 imploration
13 justification

**plead**
03 ask, beg
05 argue, claim, state
06 adduce, allege, appeal,
　　assert

07 beseech, entreat, implore, request, solicit
08 maintain, petition

**pleasant**
04 fine, nice
07 affable, amiable, amusing
08 charming, friendly, likeable
09 agreeable, congenial, enjoyable
10 delightful, satisfying
11 good-humored

**pleasantry**
04 jest, joke, quip
06 banter, bon mot
08 badinage

**please**
04 like, suit, want, will, wish
05 amuse, charm, cheer, humor
06 choose, desire, divert, fulfil, prefer, see fit
07 delight, fulfill, gladden, gratify, indulge, satisfy
08 appeal to, think fit
09 captivate, entertain
14 give pleasure to

**pleased**
04 glad
05 happy
09 contented, delighted, gratified, satisfied
11 tickled pink

**pleasing**
07 amusing, winning
08 charming, engaging
09 agreeable, enjoyable
10 attractive, delightful, gratifying, satisfying

**pleasurable**
03 fun
07 amusing
09 congenial, diverting, enjoyable
10 delightful, gratifying
12 entertaining

**pleasure**
03 fun, joy
04 will, wish
06 choice, desire
07 delight, leisure
09 amusement, enjoyment
10 preference, recreation
12 satisfaction
13 entertainment, gratification

**pleat**
04 fold, tuck
05 crimp, flute
06 crease, gather, pucker

**plebeian**
03 low

04 base, mean
05 prole
06 coarse, common, worker
07 ignoble, lowborn, peasant
08 commoner
10 lower-class, uncultured
11 proletarian
12 uncultivated, working-class

**plebiscite**
04 poll, vote
06 ballot
09 straw poll, straw vote
10 referendum

**pledge**
03 vow
04 bail, bond, gage, oath, pawn, word
05 swear, vouch
06 surety
07 deposit, promise, warrant
08 covenant, security
09 assurance, guarantee, undertake
10 collateral, take an oath
11 undertaking, word of honor
12 give your word

**plenary**
04 full, open
05 whole
06 entire
07 general
08 absolute, complete, integral, sweeping, thorough
09 unlimited
12 unrestricted
13 unconditional

**plenipotentiary**
05 envoy
06 legate, nuncio
08 emissary, minister
09 dignitary
10 ambassador

**plenitude**
06 bounty, plenty, wealth
08 fullness, plethora
09 abundance, amplitude, profusion, repletion
10 cornucopia, entireness
11 copiousness
13 plenteousness, plentifulness

**plenteous**
06 bumper, lavish
07 copious, fertile, liberal, profuse
08 abundant, fruitful, generous
09 abounding, bounteous, bountiful, luxuriant, plentiful
10 productive

**plentiful**
05 ample

06 bumper, lavish
07 copious, liberal, profuse
08 abundant, fruitful, generous, infinite
09 bounteous, bountiful
10 production, productive
11 overflowing
13 inexhaustible

**plenty**
04 fund, mass, mine
06 riches, volume, wealth
07 fortune
08 fullness, plethora, quantity
09 abundance, affluence, profusion
10 prosperity
11 sufficiency, wealthiness

◻**plenty of**
04 lots, many, tons
05 heaps, loads, piles
06 enough, masses, stacks
09 great deal
11 large amount, large number
14 more than enough

**plethora**
04 glut
06 excess
07 surfeit, surplus
09 profusion
11 superfluity
13 overabundance
14 superabundance

**pliability**
08 docility
10 compliance, elasticity, plasticity
11 amenability, flexibility
12 adaptability, malleability
13 tractableness

**pliable**
05 bendy, lithe
06 docile, pliant, supple
07 elastic, plastic
08 bendable, biddable, flexible, yielding
09 adaptable, compliant, malleable, receptive, tractable
10 manageable, responsive
11 persuadable
14 impressionable

**pliant**
05 bendy, lithe
06 docile, supple
07 elastic, plastic, pliable
08 bendable, flexible, yielding
09 compliant, malleable, tractable
11 persuadable, susceptible

## plight
03 jam, vow
05 state, swear, vouch
06 pickle, pledge, scrape
07 dilemma, promise, propose, straits, trouble
08 contract, covenant, quandary
09 condition, extremity, guarantee, tight spot
10 difficulty
11 dire straits, predicament
13 circumstances

## plod
04 slog, toil
05 clump, grind, stomp, stump, tramp
06 drudge, lumber, trudge
07 peg away
08 plug away
09 persevere, soldier on

## plodder
03 mug, sap
06 drudge, toiler
07 dullard, slogger

## plot
03 lay, lot, map
04 area, draw, mark, plan, ruse
05 cabal, chart, draft, frame, hatch, patch, story, theme, tract
06 action, cook up, design, devise, locate, map out, parcel, scheme, sketch
07 collude, concoct, connive, outline, project, subject
08 conspire, contrive, intrigue, scenario
09 allotment, calculate, machinate, narrative, story line, stratagem
10 conspiracy
11 machination

## plotter
07 planner, schemer
09 intriguer
10 machinator
11 conspirator

## plow
04 till, work
05 break
06 furrow, turn up
09 cultivate

## ❑plow into
07 collide, run into
08 bump into
09 crash into, smash into

## ❑plow through
11 plod through, wade through
13 trudge through

## ploy
04 game, move, ruse, wile
05 dodge, trick
06 device, scheme, tactic
08 artifice, maneuver
09 stratagem
10 subterfuge
11 contrivance

## pluck
04 draw, grit, guts, pick, pull, yank
05 nerve, strum, valor
06 daring, gather, mettle, remove, snatch
07 bravery, courage, harvest
08 backbone, boldness
09 fortitude
11 intrepidity
12 fearlessness

## plucky
04 bold
05 brave, gutsy
06 daring, gritty, heroic, spunky
07 valiant
08 fearless, intrepid, spirited
10 courageous, determined

## plug
02 ad
03 wad
04 bung, cake, chew, cork, fill, hype, pack, puff, push, seal, stop, tout
05 block, blurb, choke, close, stuff, twist
06 market, spigot, stop up
07 mention, promote, stopper
08 good word
09 advertise, promotion, publicity, publicize
10 commercial
13 advertisement

## ❑plug away
06 plod on
07 peg away
08 slog away
09 soldier on

## plum
04 best
05 fruit, prize
06 choice
10 first class

## plumb
05 gauge, probe, sheer, sound
06 fathom, search
07 exactly, explore, measure
08 sound out
09 delve into, penetrate, up and down
10 straight up, vertically
12 straight down
15 perpendicularly

## ❑plumb the depths of
15 reach rock bottom

## plume
04 tuft
05 crest, preen, quill
06 pappus, pinion
07 feather
08 aigrette

## ❑plume yourself on
07 exult in
10 boast about

## plummet
04 dive, drop, fall
06 hurtle, plunge, tumble
08 nose-dive

## plump
03 fat
04 drop, dump, flop, full, sink
05 ample, blunt, buxom, dumpy, podgy, pudgy, round, stout, tubby
06 chubby, portly, rotund
07 bluntly, deposit, put down, set down
09 corpulent
11 well-rounded
15 well upholstered

## plumpness
07 fatness
09 pudginess, rotundity, stoutness, tubbiness
10 chubbiness, corpulence, portliness

## plunder
03 rob
04 loot, raid, sack, swag
05 booty, prize, rifle, steal, strip
06 fleece, maraud, ravage, spoils
07 despoil, pillage, ransack
08 lay waste, pickings
09 depredate, devastate
14 ill-gotten gains

## plunge
03 dip, jab, ram
04 dash, dive, drop, fall, jump, push, rush, sink, stab, tear
05 drive, pitch, shove, stick, swoop, throw
06 career, charge, go down, hurtle, thrust, tumble
07 descend, descent, immerse, plummet
08 dive bomb, nose-dive, submerge
11 drop rapidly, fall rapidly

## plurality
04 bulk, mass, most
06 galaxy, number
07 variety
08 majority

09 diversity, profusion
12 multiplicity, numerousness
13 preponderance

**plus**
03 and
04 gain, perk, with
05 asset, bonus, extra
07 benefit, surplus
08 as well as
09 advantage, good point
12 in addition to, not to mention, over and above, together with

**plush**
04 posh, rich
05 ritzy
06 costly, deluxe, glitzy, lavish, luxury, swanky
07 opulent, stylish
08 affluent, palatial
09 luxurious, sumptuous

**plutocrat**
05 Dives
06 fat cat, tycoon
07 Croesus, magnate, rich man
09 moneybags
10 capitalist

**ply**
04 feed, fold, leaf
05 ferry, layer, sheet
06 assail, employ, follow, handle, harass, lavish, pursue, strand, supply, travel, work at
07 bombard, carry on, utilize
08 exercise, practice
09 importune, thickness

**poach**
04 copy, lift, take
05 steal
06 borrow, pilfer
08 encroach, infringe, trespass
11 appropriate

**pocket**
03 bag
04 gain, lift, mini, take
05 filch, funds, means, money, patch, pinch, pouch, small, steal
06 assets, budget, cavity, hollow, little, pilfer, potted
07 capital, compact, concise, purloin
08 abridged, envelope, finances, pintsize, portable
09 miniature, resources
10 receptacle, small group
11 appropriate, compartment

**pocketbook**
03 bag
05 purse

06 wallet
07 handbag
08 billfold, finances

**pockmark**
03 pit
04 pock, scar
07 blemish

**pod**
04 case, hull, husk
05 shell
06 legume

**podium**
04 dais
05 stage, stand
07 rostrum
08 platform

**poem**

▶ *Types of poem:*
03 lay, ode
04 epic, idyl, song
05 ditty, elegy, epode, haiku, idyll, lyric, rhyme, tanka, verse
06 ballad, epopee, monody, rondel, sonnet
07 couplet, eclogue, epigram, georgic, rondeau, sestina, triolet
08 clerihew, limerick, madrigal, pastoral, versicle
09 free verse, roundelay
11 epithalmium
12 nursery rhyme, prothalamion
➤ See also SONG

▶ *Poems and poetry collections include:*
02 If
04 A Red, Crow, Days, Edda, Home, Hope, Howl, Maud, Odes
05 Comus, Grass, Lamia, Trees
06 Façade, Hellas, Marina, The Fly, Villon
07 Beowulf, Don Juan, Lycidas, Mariana, Marmion, Red Rose, Requiem, The Duel, Ulysses
08 Bermudas, Endymion, Georgics, Gunga Din, Hudibras, Kalevala, Lupercal, Queen Mab, Ramayana, The Bells, The Iliad, The Pearl, The Raven, The Tyger, Tithonus, To Autumn
09 Decameron, Jerusalem, Kubla Khan, Not in Vain, The Aeneid, The Cantos
10 Annabel Lee, Cherry Ripe, Christabel, Dream Songs,

Each and All, Evangeline, In Memoriam, Lalla Rookh, Renascence, The Dunciad, The Odyssey, The Poetics, The Prelude, The Village, View of a Pig
11 Ars Amatoria, High Windows, Holy Sonnets, Humming-Bird, Jabberwocky, Mahabharata, Mending Wall, Ode to Autumn, Remembrance, Song of my Cid, Tam O'Shanter, Thanatopsis, The Eclogues, The Extasie, The Sick Rose, The Sluggard, The Woodlark
12 A Song to Celia, A Witness Tree, Ash Wednesday, Auld Lang Syne, Bhagavad Gita, Eugene Onegin, Faith Healing, Four Quartets, Goblin Market, Hawk Roosting, Homage to Clio, Jubilate Agno, Mercian Hymns, Morte d'Arthur, Ode to Evening, Paradise Lost, Piers Plowman, The Day is Done, The Lucy Poems, The Snowstorm, The Waste Land, The Windhover, To a Waterfowl
13 Arms and the Boy, Gilgamesh Epic, Leaves of Grass, Little Boy Blue, Metamorphoses, Missing the Sea, Naming of Parts, Roman de la Rose, September Song, The Book of Thel
14 A Shropshire Lad, Divina Commedia, Leda and the Swan, Les Fleurs du Mal, Love Songs in Age, Lyrical Ballads, Orlando Furioso, Song of Hiawatha, Strange Meeting, The Barefoot Boy, The Lotus-Eaters
15 Canterbury Tales, Cautionary Tales, Idylls of the King, Ode on Melancholy, Paul Revere's Ride, Summoned by Bells, The Age of Anxiety, The Divine Comedy, The Eve of St. Agnes, The Faerie Queene, The Second Coming

**poet, poetess**
04 bard
06 rhymer
07 elegist, rhymist
08 idyllist, lyricist, minstrel

09 balladeer, poetaster,
poeticule, rhymester,
sonneteer, versifier
➤ See also WRITER

▶ *Names of poets:*
03 **Gay** (John), **Lee** (Laurie),
**Paz** (Octavio), **Poe** (Edgar
Allan)
04 **Amis** (Kingsley), **Blok**
(Alexander), **Dunn**
(Douglas), **Gray** (Thomas),
**Gunn** (Thom), **Hass**
(Robert), **Hill** (Geoffrey),
**Hogg** (James), **Hood**
(Thomas), **Hunt** (Leigh),
**Lear** (Edward), **Muir**
(Edwin), **Nash** (Ogden),
**Ovid**, **Owen** (Wilfred), **Pope**
(Alexander), **Read**
(Thomas), **Rich** (Adrienne),
**Seth** (Vikram), **Tabb** (John
Bannister), **Vega** (Lope de)
05 **Auden** (Wystan Hugh),
**Basho** (Matsuo), **Benét**
(Stephen Vincent), **Blake**
(William), **Burns** (Robert),
**Byron** (George), **Clare**
(John), **Crane** (Hart), **Dante**,
**Donne** (John), **Duffy** (Carol
Ann), **Eliot** (Thomas
Stearns), **Field** (Eugene),
**Frost** (Robert), **Guest**
(Edgar), **Hardy** (Thomas),
**Harte** (Brett), **Heine**
(Heinrich), **Henri** (Adrian),
**Hesse** (Hermann), **Homer**,
**Ibsen** (Henrik), **Keats**
(John), **Lorca** (Federico
García), **Moore** (Marianne),
**O'Hara** (Frank), **Opitz**
(Martin), **Plath** (Sylvia),
**Pound** (Ezra), **Raine**
(Craig), **Riley** (James
Whitcomb), **Rilke** (Rainer
Maria), **Sachs** (Hans),
**Sachs** (Nelly), **Scott** (Sir
Walter), **Smart**
(Christopher), **Smith**
(Stevie), **Spark** (Muriel),
**Tasso** (Torquato), **Wylie**
(Elinor), **Yeats** (William
Butler)
06 **Adcock** (Fleur), **Aragon**
(Louis), **Arnold** (Matthew),
**Artaud** (Antoni), **Barnes**
(William), **Belloc** (Hilaire),
**Benoît**, **Binyon** (Laurence),
**Bishop** (Elizabeth), **Brecht**
(Bertolt), **Brontë** (Anne),
**Brontë** (Emily), **Brooke**
(Rupert), **Bryant** (William
Cullen), **Carver** (Raymond),

**Cowper** (William), **Crabbe**
(George), **Dunbar**
(William), **Eluard** (Paul),
**Empson** (William), **Ennius**
(Quintus), **Fuller** (Roy),
**Goethe** (Johann Wolfgang
von), **Graves** (Robert),
**Gurney** (Ivor), **Heaney**
(Seamus), **Hesiod**, **Horace**,
**Kilmer** (Joyce), **Lanier**
(Sidney), **Larkin** (Philip),
**Lowell** (Amy), **Lowell**
(James Russell), **Lowell**
(Robert), **Millay** (Edna
Saint Vincent), **Milosz**
(Czeslaw), **Milton** (John),
**Morris** (William), **Neruda**
(Pablo), **Ossian**, **Patten**
(Brian), **Pindar**, **Porter**
(Peter), **Racine** (Jean),
**Riding** (Laura), **Sappho**,
**Sidney** (Philip), **Tagore**
(Rabindranath), **Thomas**
(Dylan), **Thomas** (Edward),
**Thomas** (Ronald Stuart),
**Valéry** (Paul), **Villon**
(François), **Virgil**, **Waller**
(Edmund), **Warren** (Robert
Penn)
07 **Addison** (Joseph), **Aneurin**,
**Angelou** (Maya), **Aretino**
(Pietro), **Ariosto**
(Ludovico), **Ashbery** (John),
**Beckett** (Samuel), **Blunden**
(Edmund Charles),
**Brodsky** (Joseph), **Büchner**
(Georg), **Caedmon**,
**Campion** (Thomas),
**Causley** (Charles),
**Chapman** (George),
**Chaucer** (Geoffrey),
**Cocteau** (Jean), **Durrell**
(Lawrence), **Emerson**
(Ralph Waldo), **Gautier**
(Théophile), **Herbert**
(George), **Herrick** (Robert),
**Hopkins** (Gerard Manley),
**Housman** (Alfred Edward),
**Jiménez** (Juan Ramón),
**Johnson** (Samuel), **Kipling**
(Rudyard), **Layamon**,
**Macbeth** (George),
**MacCaig** (Norman),
**MacLean** (Sorley),
**Manzoni** (Alessandro),
**Martial**, **Marvell** (Andrew),
**McGough** (Roger), **Merrill**
(James), **Mishima** (Yukio),
**Novalis**, **Pushkin**
(Alexander), **Rimbaud**
(Arthur), **Roethke**
(Theodore), **Ronsard**
(Pierre de), **Rostand**

(Edmond), **Sassoon**
(Siegfried), **Seferis**, **Seifert**
(Jaroslav), **Shelley** (Percy
Bysshe), **Sitwell** (Edith),
**Sitwell** (Sacheverell),
**Skelton** (John), **Spender**
(Stephen), **Spenser**
(Edmund), **Stevens**
(Wallace), **Terence**, **Thoreau**
(Henry David), **Vaughan**
(Henry), **Vicente** (Gil),
**Walcott** (Derek), **Whitman**
(Walt)
08 **Anacreon**, **Ausonius**
(Decimus Magnus),
**Banville** (Théodore de),
**Berryman** (John), **Brentano**
(Clemens), **Brittain** (Vera),
**Browning** (Elizabeth
Barrett), **Browning**
(Robert), **Catullus** (Gaius
Valerius), **Claudian**,
**Congreve** (William),
**Cummings** (E.E.),
**Cynewulf**, **De La Mare**
(Walter), **Ginsberg** (Allen),
**Laforgue** (Jules), **Langland**
(William), **Lawrence**
(David Herbert), **Leopardi**
(Giacomo), **Lovelace**
(Richard), **Macaulay**
(Dame Rose), **Macaulay**
(Thomas), **MacLeish**
(Archibald), **MacNeice**
(Louis), **Mallarmé**
(Stéphane), **Menander**,
**Palgrave** (Francis Turner),
**Petrarch**, **Robinson** (Edwin
Arlington), **Rossetti**
(Christina), **Rossetti** (Dante
Gabriel), **Sandburg** (Carl),
**Schiller** (Friedrich),
**Schlegel** (August Wilhelm
von), **Suckling** (John),
**Taliesin**, **Tibullus**, **Verlaine**
(Paul), **Whittier** (John
Greenleaf)
09 **Aeschylus**, **Akhmatova**
(Anna), **Bronowski** (Jacob),
**Coleridge** (Samuel Taylor),
**D'Annunzio** (Gabriele),
**Dickinson** (Emily),
**Froissart** (Jean), **Goldsmith**
(Oliver), **Hölderlin**
(Friedrich), **Lamartine**
(Alphonse de), **Lucretius**,
**Marinetti** (Filippo
Tommaso), **Pasternak**
(Boris), **Rochester** (John
Wilmot), **Rosenberg** (Isaac),
**Santayana** (George),
**Southwell** (Robert),
**Swinburne** (Algernon

Charles), **Ungaretti**
(Giuseppe), **Zephaniah**
(Benjamin)
10 **Baudelaire** (Charles),
**Bradstreet** (Anne),
**Chatterton** (Thomas),
**Chesterton** (Gilbert Keith),
**Empedocles, FitzGerald**
(Edward), **La Fontaine**
(Jean de), **Lagerkvist** (Pär),
**Longfellow** (Henry
Wadsworth), **MacDiarmid**
(Hugh), **Mayakovsky**
(Vladimir), **McGonagall**
(William), **Propertius**
(Sextus), **Theocritus**
11 **Apollinaire** (Guillaume),
**Omar Khayyám,**
**Shakespeare** (William),
**Yevtushenko** (Yevegeny)
13 **Sackville-West** (Vita)
14 **Dante Alighieri, Saint-**
**John Perse**

➤ *Names of American poets*
*laureate:*
04 **Dove** (Rita), **Hass** (Robert)
06 **Kunitz** (Stanley), **Pinsky**
(Robert), **Strand** (Mark),
**Warren** (Robert Penn),
**Wilbur** (Richard)
07 **Brodsky** (Joseph), **Collins**
(Billy), **Nemerov** (Howard),
**Van Duyn** (Mona)

➤ *Names of English poets*
*laureate:*
03 **Pye** (Henry James)
04 **Rowe** (Nicholas), **Tate**
(Nahum)
05 **Lewis** (C. Day)
06 **Austin** (Alfred), **Cibber**
(Colley), **Dryden** (John),
**Eusden** (Laurence), **Hughes**
(Ted), **Jonson** (Ben), **Motion**
(Andrew), **Warton**
(Thomas)
07 **Bridges** (Robert), **Southey**
(Robert)
08 **Betjeman** (John), **Davenant**
(William), **Day-Lewis**
(Cecil), **Shadwell** (Thomas),
**Tennyson** (Alfred
09 **Masefield** (John),
**Whitehead** (William)
10 **Wordsworth** (William)

**poetic**
07 flowing, lyrical, prosaic,
rhyming
08 creative, metrical, symbolic
09 sensitive
10 expressive, figurative

**poetry**
04 muse
05 poems, poesy, rhyme, verse
06 lyrics
07 iambics, rhyming, versing
09 free verse, Parnassus, vers
libre
13 versification

**pogrom**
08 genocide, homicide
09 holocaust, slaughter
11 liquidation
12 annihilation
13 extermination
15 ethnic cleansing

**poignancy**
04 pain
06 misery, pathos
07 emotion, feeling, sadness
08 distress, keenness, piquancy
09 intensity, sentiment
10 bitterness, tenderness
11 painfulness, piteousness
12 wretchedness

**poignant**
03 sad
06 moving, tender, tragic
07 painful, piteous, tearful
08 pathetic, touching
09 affecting, upsetting
12 heart-rending
13 heartbreaking

**point**
03 aim, dot, end, nib, nub, run,
tip, top, use
04 area, cape, core, crux, gist,
goal, head, item, mark, meat,
ness, pith, show, site, spot,
time, tine, vein
05 drift, facet, goals, heart,
issue, level, place, score,
sense, speck, spike, stage,
taper, tenor, theme, topic,
total, trait
06 burden, denote, detail,
direct, marrow, matter,
moment, motive, object,
period, reason, signal, thrust
07 essence, feature, instant,
keynote, meaning, outlook,
purpose, quality, signify,
subject, suggest
08 evidence, foreland,
headland, indicate, juncture,
locality, location, property,
question, sharp end
09 attribute, designate,
extremity, gesture at,
intention, main point,
objective, situation
10 particular, promontory

12 significance
14 characteristic

❏**beside the point**
09 pointless, unrelated
10 extraneous, immaterial,
incidental, irrelevant
12 not pertinent

❏**in point of fact**
06 in fact
08 actually
15 as a matter of fact

❏**on the point of**
07 about to, going to, ready to
12 on the verge of

❏**point of view**
05 angle, slant
06 aspect, belief
07 feeling, opinion, outlook
08 approach, attitude,
judgment, position
09 viewpoint
10 standpoint
11 perspective

❏**point out**
04 show
06 remind, reveal
07 mention, point to, specify
08 allude to, identify, indicate
15 draw attention to

❏**point up**
06 stress
09 emphasize, highlight,
underline
15 call attention to

❏**to the point**
03 apt
07 germane
08 apposite, relevant
09 pertinent
11 appropriate

❏**up to a point**
06 partly
08 slightly, somewhat
12 to some degree, to some
extent

**point-blank**
06 direct, openly
07 bluntly, close to, closely,
frankly, plainly
08 abruptly, candidly, directly,
outright, straight
10 explicitly, forthright,
unreserved
12 at close range
15 straightforward

**pointed**
04 keen
05 clear, edged, sharp
06 barbed, biting

## pointer

07 cutting, obvious, telling
08 aculeate, incisive, tapering
09 trenchant
10 fastigiate, lanceolate
11 penetrating

## pointer

03 rod, tip
04 cane, clue, hand, hint, pole, sign
05 arrow, guide, stick
06 advice, needle
07 caution, warning
09 guideline, indicator
10 indication, suggestion
14 recommendation

## pointless

04 vain
06 absurd, futile
07 aimless, foolish, useless
09 fruitless, senseless, to no avail, valueless, worthless
11 meaningless, nonsensical
12 a waste of time, unproductive, unprofitable
14 a waste of effort

## poise

04 cool, hang
05 grace, hover
06 aplomb, steady
07 balance, dignity, support, suspend
08 calmness, coolness, elegance, position, serenity
09 assurance, composure
10 equanimity
11 equilibrium, self-control
13 self-assurance
14 self-possession

## poised

04 calm, cool
05 ready, suave
06 all set, serene, urbane
07 assured, waiting
08 composed, graceful, prepared
09 collected, dignified, expectant, unruffled
11 unflappable
13 self-confident, self-possessed
14 self-controlled

## poison

04 bane, warp
05 spoil, taint, toxin, venom
06 blight, cancer, defile, infect
07 corrupt, deprave, pervert, pollute
09 contagion, pollution
10 adulterate, corruption, malignancy

## poisonous

05 fatal, toxic
06 deadly, lethal, mortal
07 harmful, noxious, vicious
08 spiteful, venomous, virulent
09 cancerous, malignant
10 corrupting, pernicious

➤ *Names of poisonous plants:*

04 arum
05 dwale
07 aconite, amanita, anemone, cowbane, hemlock
08 banewort, foxglove, laburnum, oleander
09 colchicum, digitalis, monkshood, poison ivy, stinkweed, wolfsbane
10 belladonna, cuckoopint, thorn apple, windflower
12 autumn crocus
13 meadow saffron
14 castor oil plant, lords-and-ladies
15 black nightshade
➤ See also PLANT

## poke

03 dig, hit, jab
04 butt, prod, push, stab
05 elbow, money, nudge, punch, purse, shove, stick
06 thrust, wallet
07 cowpoke
08 pokeweed, slowpoke

## poke around

07 look for
09 search for
11 grope around, rake through
13 rummage around

## poke fun at

03 rag, rib
04 jeer, mock
05 spoof, tease
06 parody
08 ridicule

## poke out

06 beetle, extend
07 project
08 protrude, stick out

## poke your nose into

03 pry
06 be nosy
08 meddle in
11 interfere in

## poky, pokey

04 dull, slow, tiny
05 dowdy, small, tight
06 narrow
07 cramped, crowded
08 confined
12 incommodious

## polar

03 icy
04 cold
06 arctic, frigid, frozen
07 central, glacial, guiding
08 freezing, opposite
10 ambivalent
11 conflicting, dichotomous
12 antithetical
13 contradictory

## polarity

07 duality, paradox
09 dichotomy
10 antithesis, opposition
11 ambivalence, contrariety
12 oppositeness
13 contradiction

## pole

03 bar, rod
04 mast, post, spar
05 limit, shaft, staff, stake, stick
06 pillar
07 extreme, support, upright
09 extremity

## poles apart

11 worlds apart
12 incompatible
14 irreconcilable

## polecat

03 rat
05 creep, fitch, skunk
06 ferret, rascal
07 fitchet, stinker

## polemic

06 debate
07 dispute, eristic
08 argument
09 eristical, polemical
11 contentious, controversy
12 disputatious
13 argumentative, controversial

## polemicist

06 arguer
07 debater
08 disputer
09 disputant
11 logomachist

## polemics

06 debate
07 dispute
08 argument
09 logomachy
11 controversy, disputation

## police

02 MP, SP
04 cops, fuzz, heat, pigs
05 check, guard, posse, watch
06 defend, Mounty, patrol, the Law

## police officer

07 control, monitor, Mountie, observe, oversee, protect, the fuzz
08 the Force
09 keep watch, supervise
11 police force, shore patrol
12 constabulary, keep the peace
14 military police

**police officer**
03 cop, pig
04 bull
05 bobby
06 copper, shamus, Smokey, the Law
07 John Law, officer, the fuzz
08 flatfoot
09 constable, detective, men in blue, patrolman, policeman
10 boys in blue, Smokey Bear, traffic cop
11 policewoman
12 peace officer
13 Smokey the Bear

**policy**
04 line, plan
05 rules
06 course, custom, method, scheme, stance, system
07 program
08 approach, position, practice, protocol, schedule
09 procedure
10 guidelines
14 code of practice

**polish**
03 rub, wax
04 buff
05 class, clean, glaze, gloss, grace, poise, rub up, sheen, shine, style
06 finish, luster, refine, veneer
07 brush up, burnish, enhance, finesse, furbish, improve, perfect, sparkle, touch up, varnish
08 breeding, elegance
09 cultivate
10 brightness, brilliance, refinement, smoothness
11 cultivation
14 sophistication

❏**polish off**
04 bolt, down, kill, wolf
06 devour, finish, gobble, murder, rub out
07 bump off, consume
08 complete
09 dispose of, eliminate, liquidate

**polished**
05 adept, shiny, suave, waxed

06 expert, glassy, glossy, polite, smooth, urbane
07 elegant, genteel, perfect, refined, shining, skilful
08 flawless, gleaming, lustrous, masterly, skillful, slippery, well-bred
09 burnished, civilized, excellent, faultless, perfected
10 cultivated, impeccable, proficient
11 outstanding, superlative
12 accomplished, professional, well-mannered
13 sophisticated

**polite**
05 civil, suave
06 polite, urbane
07 elegant, gallant, genteel, refined, tactful
08 cultured, gracious, ladylike, obliging, well-bred
09 civilized, courteous
10 chivalrous, diplomatic, respectful, thoughtful
11 considerate, deferential, gentlemanly, well behaved
12 well-mannered
13 sophisticated

**politeness**
04 tact
05 grace
06 polish
07 culture, manners, respect
08 civility, courtesy, elegance
09 diplomacy, gentility
10 cordiality, discretion, refinement
11 courtliness, cultivation, good manners
12 graciousness, mannerliness
14 respectfulness, thoughtfulness
15 considerateness, gentlemanliness

**politic**
04 sage, wise
06 shrewd
07 prudent, tactful
08 sensible
09 advisable, expedient, opportune
10 diplomatic
12 advantageous

**political**
05 civil
06 public
08 judicial
09 executive
11 legislative, ministerial
12 bureaucratic, governmental

13 congressional, parliamentary
14 administrative, constitutional

**politician**
07 liberal
08 Democrat, diplomat, lame duck, politico
09 statesman
10 Republican
11 independent
12 conservative

**politics**
06 civics
09 diplomacy, power game
10 government, statecraft
13 power struggle, public affairs, statesmanship
14 affairs of state
➤ See also GOVERNMENT; MINISTER; PARLIAMENT; PRESIDENT

**poll**
03 cut, get, net
04 clip, gain, trim, vote
05 count, shear, tally
06 ballot, census, dehorn, sample, survey, voting
07 canvass, pollard
08 question, sampling
09 ballot box, head count
10 plebiscite, referendum
11 electioneer, show of hands
14 market research

**pollute**
03 mar
04 foul, soil, warp
05 dirty, spoil, stain, sully, taint
06 befoul, debase, defile, infect, poison
07 blacken, corrupt, deprave, tarnish, vitiate
10 adulterate
11 contaminate

**pollution**
05 taint
07 fouling
08 foulness, impurity, staining, sullying
09 depravity, dirtiness, infection, muckiness
10 blackening, corruption, debasement, defilement, filthiness, tarnishing
12 adulteration
13 contamination

**polychromatic**
06 motley
07 rainbow
08 many hued
11 many colored, varicolored
12 multicolored
13 kaleidoscopic

## polyglot
08 linguist
12 cosmopolitan, multilingual
13 international, multilinguist

## polymath
06 oracle
09 know-it-all
10 pansophist, polyhistor
13 polyhistorian
15 jack-of-all-trades

## pomp
04 show
05 glory, state
06 parade, ritual
07 display, glitter, majesty
08 ceremony, flourish, grandeur, splendor
09 formality, pageantry, solemnity, spectacle
10 brilliance, ceremonial
11 ostentation
12 magnificence
15 ceremoniousness

## pomposity
07 bombast, fustian
08 euphuism, rhetoric
09 arrogance, turgidity
10 pretension, stuffiness
11 affectation, haughtiness, preachiness
14 self-importance

## pompous
05 proud, windy
06 stuffy, turgid
07 haughty, preachy
08 affected, arrogant
09 bombastic, conceited, grandiose
10 euphuistic
11 overbearing, patronizing, pretentious
12 ostentatious, supercilious
13 self-important

## pond
04 lake, mere, pool, tarn
06 puddle
09 water hole

## ponder
04 muse
05 brood, study, think, weigh
06 reason
07 analyze, examine, reflect
08 cogitate, consider, meditate, mull over
09 cerebrate
10 deliberate, excogitate, puzzle over
11 contemplate, ratiocinate
12 ruminate over
13 give thought to

## ponderous
04 dull, huge
05 bulky, heavy, hefty
06 clumsy, dreary, prolix, stodgy, stolid
07 awkward, labored, massive, serious, stilted, tedious, verbose, weighty
08 lifeless, pedantic, plodding, unwieldy
09 graceless, laborious, lumbering
10 cumbersome, long-winded, pedestrian, slow moving
11 elephantine, heavy-footed, heavy-handed

## ponderousness
06 tedium
09 heaviness, stolidity
11 seriousness, weightiness
13 laboriousness

## pontifical
05 papal
07 pompous, preachy
08 didactic, dogmatic, prelatic
09 apostolic, imperious
10 portentous
11 magisterial, overbearing, pretentious, sermonizing
13 condescending

## pontificate
06 preach
07 declaim, expound, lecture
08 harangue, moralize, perorate, sound off
09 dogmatize, hold forth, pronounce, sermonize
13 lay down the law

## pooh-pooh
05 scoff, scorn, sneer, spurn
06 deride, reject, slight
07 disdain, dismiss, sniff at
08 belittle, minimize, play down, ridicule
09 disparage, disregard

## pool
03 pot
04 ante, bank, fund, lake, mere, pond, ring, tarn, team
05 group, kitty, merge, purse, share
06 cartel, chip in, muck in, puddle, supply
07 combine, jackpot, reserve
09 billiards, syndicate, water hole
10 amalgamate, collective, consortium, contribute
12 swimming pool
15 pocket billiards

## poor
03 bad, low, sad
04 mean, weak
05 broke, lowly, needy
06 barren, faulty, feeble, hard up, humble, in need, meager, measly, paltry, scanty, shoddy, sparse
07 hapless, lacking, reduced, unlucky
08 badly off, below par, exiguous, indigent, inferior, low-grade, mediocre, pathetic, wretched
09 deficient, destitute, imperfect, miserable, penniless, penurious, third-rate, worthless
10 inadequate, low quality, stone-broke, straitened
11 impecunious, substandard, unfortunate
12 impoverished, insufficient, without means
13 below standard
14 on the breadline, unsatisfactory
15 poverty-stricken

## poorly
03 ill
04 sick
05 badly, seedy
06 ailing, feebly, meanly, sickly, unwell
08 below par, off-color
10 indisposed, out of sorts
12 inadequately
13 incompetently
15 under the weather

## pop
02 pa
03 dad, nip, put
04 bang, boom, dash, drop, papa, push, rush, slip, snap, soda
05 burst, crack, daddy, go off, hurry, shoot, shove, slide
06 father, insert, report, thrust
07 explode
08 backfire, top forty
09 bubblegum, explosion

## ❑pop off
03 die
06 pass on, peg out
07 snuff it
08 pass away
09 have had it
13 kick the bucket

## ❑pop up
05 occur

## pope

06 appear, crop up, show up, turn up
11 materialize

**pope**

07 pontiff
10 Holy Father
11 His Holiness
12 Bishop of Rome
13 Vicar of Christ

► *Names of popes. We have omitted the word* **pope** *from names given in the following list but you may need to include this word as part of the solution to some crossword clues. The regnal numerals of individual popes have also been omitted.*

03 Leo
04 Cono, Joan, John, Mark, Paul, Pius
05 Felix, Lando, Linus, Peter, Soter, Urban
06 Adrian, Agatho, Albert, Fabian, Julius, Lucius, Martin, Philip, Sixtus, Victor
07 Clement, Damasus, Gregory, Hadrian, Hilarus, Marinus, Paschal, Pontian, Romanus, Sergius, Stephen, Ursinus, Zosimus
08 Agapetus, Benedict, Boniface, Calixtus, Eugenius, Eusebius, Formosus, Gelasius, Honorius, Innocent, John Paul, Liberius, Nicholas, Novatian, Pelagius, Theodore, Vigilius
09 Alexander, Anacletus, Callistus, Celestine, Cornelius, Deusdedit, Dionysius, Dioscorus, Marcellus, Severinus, Silverius, Sylvester, Symmachus, Theodoric, Valentine, Zacharias
10 Anastasius, Hippolytus, Laurentius, Militiades, Simplicius, Zephyrinus
11 Christopher, Constantine
➤ See also RELIGION

**popinjay**

03 fop
04 beau, dude
05 dandy, pansy, swell
06 parrot
07 coxcomb, peacock

**poppycock**

03 rot
04 bosh, bull, bunk, crap
05 bilge, folly, hooey, trash, tripe
06 drivel, humbug, piffle

07 baloney, blather, rubbish, twaddle
08 claptrap, nonsense, tommyrot
09 gibberish, silliness, stupidity
10 balderdash, codswallop
12 gobbledygook

**populace**

03 mob
04 folk
05 crowd, plebs
06 masses, people, public, rabble
07 natives, society
08 canaille, citizens
09 hoi polloi, multitude, residents
10 common herd
11 inhabitants, proletariat, rank and file
13 general public

**popular**

02 in
03 big, hip, pop
04 cool
05 liked, noted, stock, usual
06 common, famous, modish, simple, trendy, wanted
07 admired, current, desired, favored, general, in favor
08 accepted, approved, favorite, idolized, in demand, ordinary, renowned, standard
09 acclaimed, customary, household, prevalent, universal, well-known, well-liked
10 accessible, all the rage, celebrated, mass-market, prevailing, simplified, widespread
11 fashionable, sought after
12 conventional, nontechnical
13 nonspecialist
14 understandable

**popularity**

04 fame
05 favor, glory, kudos, vogue
06 esteem, regard, renown, repute
07 acclaim, worship
09 adoration, adulation
10 acceptance, mass appeal
11 approbation, idolization, lionization

**popularize**

06 spread
10 generalize
11 democratize, familiarize

**popularly**

06 widely
08 commonly
09 generally, regularly
10 ordinarily
11 customarily, universally
13 traditionally
14 conventionally

**populate**

05 dwell
06 live in, occupy, people, settle
07 inhabit, overrun
08 colonize

**population**

04 folk
06 people
07 natives, society
08 citizens, populace
09 community, occupants, residents
11 inhabitants

**populous**

06 packed
07 crowded, teeming
08 crawling, swarming

**porcelain**

► *Types of porcelain:*

05 Imari, Kraak
06 bisque, Canton, Parian
07 biscuit, faience, nankeen
08 eggshell, Kakiemon
09 bone china, copper red, hard paste, soft paste
11 Capodimonte, chinoiserie, famille-rose
12 blue and white, famille-verte
14 soapstone paste

► *Famous makes of porcelain:*

03 Bow
04 Ming
05 Arita, Derby, Lenox
06 Minton, Sèvres, Vienna
07 Belleek, Bristol, Chelsea, Dresden, Limoges, Meissen, Nanking, Satsuma
08 Caughley, Coalport, Wedgwood
09 Chantilly, Worcester
10 Rockingham
12 Royal Doulton
14 Royal Worcester

**porch**

07 portico, veranda
08 sun porch, verandah
09 vestibule

**pore**

04 hole, vent
06 outlet

07 foramen, opening, orifice
08 aperture
11 perforation

❏**pore over**
04 read, scan
05 brood, study
06 go over, peruse, ponder
07 examine
10 scrutinize

**pornographic**
04 blue, lewd, porn
05 bawdy, dirty, gross
06 coarse, erotic, filthy, risqué, smutty
07 obscene
08 indecent, prurient
11 titillating

**pornography**
04 dirt, porn, smut
05 filth, porno
07 erotica
08 facetiae
09 indecency, obscenity

**porous**
04 airy, open
05 holey
06 spongy
07 foveate
08 cellular, pervious
09 absorbent, permeable
10 foraminous, spongelike

**port**
04 dock
05 haven, jetty, roads
06 harbor
07 seaport
09 anchorage, harborage, roadstead

━ *Names of ports*:
03 Gao, Lae, Vac
04 Aden, Apia, Baku, Bari, Caen, Cebu, Ciba, Cork, Doha, Elat, Faro, Hull, Kiel, Kobe, Linz, Lomé, Lüda, Nice, Oban, Omsk, Oran, Oslo, Oulu, Pula, Riga, Safi, Sfax, Suez, Suva, Tyre, Vigo, Wick
05 Accra, Agana, Aqaba, Arica, Basle, Basra, Beira, Belém, Blyth, Brest, Busan, Colón, Dakar, Davao, Dover, Dubai, Emden, Gavle, Genoa, Ghent, Haifa, Ibiza, Izmir, Kazan, Lagos, Larne, Leith, Liège, Macao, Malmo, Masan, Miami, Nampo, Natal, Omaha, Osaka, Ostia, Palma, Paris, Poole, Praia, Pusan, Rouen, Sakai, Salem, Sitra, Split, Tampa, Tanga,

Tokyo, Tomsk, Tulsa, Tunis, Turku, Ulsan, Vaasa, Varna, Worms, Wuhan
06 Aarhus, Abadan, Agadir, Ancona, Annaba, Ashdod, Avarua, Aveira, Aviles, Balboa, Bamako, Banjul, Batumi, Beirut, Bergen, Bissau, Bombay, Boston, Bremen, Bruges, Calais, Callao, Cannes, Cochin, Dalian, Dammam, Darwin, Denver, Dieppe, Douala, Dublin, Duluth, Dundee, Durban, Durres, El Paso, Galway, Gdansk, Gdynia, Havana, Hobart, Inchon, Jarrow, Jeddah, Juneau, Kandla, Kaunas, Khulna, Lisbon, Lobito, London, Luanda, Lübeck, Madras, Malabo, Malaga, Manama, Manaus, Manila, Maputo, Mersin, Mobile, Muscat, Nacala, Nagoya, Nantes, Napier, Naples, Narvik, Nassau, Nelson, Newark, Niamey, Ningbo, Nouméa, Nyborg, Odense, Odessa, Oporto, Ostend, Penang, Phuket, Quebec, Recife, Rijeka, Rimini, Samara, Samsun, Santos, Sasebo, Sittwe, Sousse, St-Malo, St. John, Sydney, Szeged, Tacoma, Thurso, Timaru, Toledo, Toulon, Toyama, Treves, Velsen, Venice, Warsaw, Whitby, Xiamen, Yangon
07 Aalborg, Abidjan, Ajaccio, Algiers, Almeria, Antibes, Antwerp, Bangkok, Belfast, Bizerta, Bristol, Buffalo, Cabinda, Calabar, Caldera, Calicut, Cardiff, Catania, Cayenne, Chicago, Cologne, Colombo, Conakry, Corinth, Corinto, Dampier, Detroit, Douglas, Dunedin, Dunkirk, Esbjerg, Funchal, Geelong, Glasgow, Grimsby, Halifax, Hamburg, Harstad, Harwich, Hodeida, Honiari, Houston, Ipswich, Iquique, Jakarta, Karachi, Kowloon, Kuching, Kushiro, La Plata, Larnaca, Le Havre, Livorno, Marsala, Memphis, Messina, Mindelo, Mombasa, Newport, Oakland, Okayama, Palermo, Papeete, Paradip, Piraeus, Rangoon, Ravenna, Rosaria,

Rostock, Salerno, San José, San Juan, San Remo, Santa Fe, Sao Tomé, Seattle, Seville, Shimizu, St. John's, St. Louis, Stanley, Swansea, Tallinn, Tampico, Tangier, Taranto, Tel Aviv, Tianjin, Tilbury, Toronto, Trieste, Tripoli, Vitebsk, Vitoria, Wroclaw, Zhdanov
08 Aberdeen, Abu Dhabi, Acapulco, Adelaide, Alicante, Arbroath, Asunción, Auckland, Benghazi, Bordeaux, Boulogne, Brindisi, Brisbane, Cagliari, Calcutta, Cape Town, Castries, Djibouti, Dortmund, Duisburg, Dunleary, Falmouth, Flushing, Freeport, Freetown, Godthaab, Greenock, Guyaquil, Halmstad, Hamilton, Hay Point, Helsinki, Holyhead, Honolulu, Istanbul, Kawasaki, Kingston, Kinshasa, Kirkaldy, Kirkwall, Kismaayo, La Coruna, Lattakia, Limassol, Limerick, Mandalay, Mannheim, Marbella, Monrovia, Montreal, Montrose, Moulmein, Mulhouse, Murmansk, Nagasaki, New Haven, Newhaven, Pago Pago, Plymouth, Port Said, Port-Vila, Portland, Ramsgate, Richmond, Roskilde, Rosslare, Salonica, Salvador, San Diego, San Pedro, Savannah, Shanghai, Simbirsk, Smolensk, St-Tropez, St. Helier, St. Thomas, Stockton, Surabaya, Syracuse, Tauranga, Torshavn, Ullapool, Valencia, Valletta, Veracruz, Voronezh, Weymouth, Yokohama, Zanzibar
09 Algeciras, Amsterdam, Anchorage, Archangel, Astrakhan, Baltimore, Barcelona, Brunswick, Bujumbura, Cartagena, Cherbourg, Cleveland, Constance, Constanta, Dordrecht, Dubrovnik, Europoort, Fall River, Famagusta, Fleetwood, Flensburg, Fortaleza, Frankfurt, Fremantle, Galveston, Gateshead, Gibraltar, Gravesend,

Heraklion, Hiroshima, Immingham, Kagoshima, Karlsruhe, King's Lynn, Kingstown, Langesund, Las Palmas, Launceton, Liverpool, Long Beach, Lowestoft, Magdeburg, Maracaibo, Melbourne, Milwaukee, Mogadishu, Nashville, Newcastle, Nuku'alofa, Palembang, Palm Beach, Pansacola, Paranagua, Peterhead, Phnom Penh, Port Limon, Port Louis, Port Sudan, Reykjavík, Rio Grande, Rochester, Rotterdam, Santander, Sassandra, Sheerness, Singapore, St-Nazaire, Stavanger, Stockholm, Stornoway, Stralsund, Stranraer, Sundsvall, Tarragona, Toamasina, Trebizond, Trondheim, Vancouver, Volgograd, Walvis Bay, Yaroslavl, Zeebrugge

10 Alexandria, Basseterre, Baton Rouge, Belize City, Bratislava, Bridgeport, Bridgetown, Cap Haitian, Casablanca, Charleston, Chittagong, Cienfuegos, Copenhagen, Felixstowe, Folkestone, Fray Bentos, Fredericia, George Town, Georgetown, Gothenburg, Hartlepool, Hildesheim, Iskenderun, Kansas City, Kompong Som, Kuwait City, Libreville, Los Angeles, Manchester, Manzanillo, Marseilles, Montego Bay, Montevideo, New Orleans, Nouakchott, Oranjestad, Paramaribo, Pittsburgh, Port Talbot, Portishead, Portsmouth, Providence, Sacramento, San Lorenzo, Sebastopol, Sevastopol, Strasbourg, Sunderland, Thunder Bay, Townsville, Valparaiso, Wellington, Willemstad, Wilmington, Workington

11 Antofagasta, Bahia Blanca, Bandar Abbas, Brazzaville, Bridlington, Buenos Aires, Charlestown, Chattanooga, Dar es Salaam, Grangemouth, Helsingborg, Livingstone, Lossiemouth, Mar del Plata, New Plymouth, New York City,

Novosibirsk, Panama Canal, Point-a-Pitre, Pointe-Noire, Pondicherry, Port Cartier, Port Moresby, Port of Spain, Punta Arenas, Richards Bay, Rostov-on-Don, Southampton, Three Rivers, Vladivostok

12 Apalachicola, Barranquilla, Buenaventura, Fort de France, Frederikstad, Jacksonville, Kota Kinabalu, Kristiansand, New Amsterdam, New Mangalore, Philadelphia, Ponta Delgada, Port Adelaide, Port Harcourt, Port Victoria, Port-au-Prince, Puerto Cortes, Rio de Janeiro, Saint George's, San Francisco, San Sebastian, Santo Domingo, St. Petersburg, Tel Aviv-Jaffa, Villahermosa

13 Ellesmere Port, Frederikshavn, Great Yarmouth, Ho Chi Minh City, Hook of Holland, Middlesbrough, Port Elizabeth

14 Port Georgetown, Santiago de Cuba

15 Barrow-in-Furness, Frankfurt am Main

**portable**
07 movable
10 conveyable
12 carriageable
13 transportable

**portend**
04 bode
05 augur
06 herald, warn of
07 point to, predict, presage, promise
08 announce, forecast, foretell, forewarn, indicate, threaten
09 adumbrate, be a sign of, foretoken, harbinger
10 foreshadow

**portent**
04 omen, sign
06 augury, threat
07 presage, warning
08 forecast, prodrome
09 harbinger
10 indication
11 forewarning, premonition
15 prognostication

**portentous**
06 solemn

07 fateful, ominous, pompous, weighty
08 menacing, sinister
09 important, momentous
10 foreboding, pontifical, remarkable
11 significant, threatening
13 self-important

**porter**
03 ale
04 beer
06 bearer, redcap, skycap
07 carrier, doorman, janitor
09 caretaker, concierge
10 doorkeeper, gatekeeper
13 door attendant
14 baggage carrier, baggage handler

**portion**
03 bit, cut, lot
04 deal, fate, luck, part
05 allot, piece, quota, share, slice, wedge, whack
06 divide, morsel, parcel, ration
07 carve up, destiny, dole out, fortune, helping, measure, section, segment, serving, slice up, tranche
08 allocate, division, fragment, quantity, share out
09 allowance, partition
10 allocation, distribute
11 installment

**portliness**
07 fatness, obesity
09 plumpness, rotundity, roundness, stoutness, tubbiness
10 chubbiness, corpulence

**portly**
05 ample, plump, round, stout
06 rotund, stocky
09 corpulent
10 overweight

**portrait**
04 icon
06 sketch
07 account, profile
08 likeness, vignette
09 depiction, miniature, portrayal
10 caricature
11 description
14 representation
15 thumbnail sketch

**portray**
03 act
04 draw, play
05 evoke, paint
06 depict, sketch
07 perform, picture

**portrayal** *(continued)*
08 describe
09 personify, represent
10 illustrate
11 impersonate
12 act the part of, characterize
13 play the part of

**portrayal**
05 study
07 drawing, picture
08 painting
09 depiction, evocation, rendering
11 delineation, description, performance
14 representation

**pose**
03 act, air, ask, put, set, sit
04 airs, role, sham
05 feign, front, model, posit
06 affect, create, façade, lead to, stance, submit
07 advance, arrange, bearing, posture, present, pretend, produce, propose, suggest
08 attitude, carriage, position, pretense, propound
09 postulate, put on airs
10 deportment, give rise to, masquerade, put forward, put on an act
11 affectation, impersonate
12 attitudinize

**poser**
04 sham
05 phony, pseud
06 enigma, poseur, puzzle, riddle
07 dilemma, mystery, poseuse, problem, showoff
08 impostor, posturer
09 conundrum
11 brainteaser
12 brain twister
13 exhibitionist, vexed question

**poseur**
04 sham
05 phony, poser, pseud
07 showoff
08 impostor, posturer
13 exhibitionist

**posh**
05 grand, plush, smart, swish
06 classy, deluxe, la-de-da, la-di-da, lavish, luxury, select, swanky
07 elegant, opulent, stylish
08 up-market
09 exclusive, high-class, luxurious, sumptuous
10 upper-class

**posit**
04 pose
06 assert, assume, submit
07 advance, presume
08 propound
09 postulate, predicate
10 put forward

**position**
03 fix, job, put, set
04 area, case, duty, pose, post, rank, role, site, spot, view
05 array, grade, level, place, point, scene, stand, state
06 belief, deploy, factor, instal, lay out, locate, office, plight, settle, stance, status
07 arrange, bearing, dispose, factors, install, opinion, outlook, posture, ranking, setting, situate, station
08 attitude, capacity, locality, location, standing
09 condition, establish, influence, situation, viewpoint
10 background, employment, occupation, standpoint
11 appointment, arrangement, disposition, point of view, predicament, whereabouts
13 circumstances
14 state of affairs

**positive**
04 firm, rank, real, sure
05 clear, sheer, utter
06 actual, direct, upbeat, useful
07 assured, certain, express, helpful, hopeful, precise
08 absolute, cheerful, clear-cut, complete, concrete, decisive, definite, emphatic, explicit, outright, thorough
09 confident, convinced, out-and-out, veritable
10 conclusive, consummate, encouraged, optimistic, productive, undeniable
11 categorical, encouraging, irrefutable, unequivocal, unmitigated
12 constructive, indisputable
13 incontestable

**positively**
06 firmly, surely
09 assuredly, certainly, expressly
10 absolutely, decisively, definitely, undeniably
12 conclusively, emphatically, indisputably
13 categorically, incontestably, unequivocally
14 unquestionably

**possess**
03 get, own
04 gain, have, hold, take
05 enjoy, haunt, seize
06 obsess, obtain, occupy
07 bewitch, control, enchant
08 dominate, take over
09 infatuate, influence
13 be endowed with

**possessed**
06 crazed, cursed, raving
07 berserk, haunted
08 besotted, demented, frenzied, obsessed
09 bedeviled, bewitched, dominated, enchanted, hagridden
10 controlled, infatuated, mesmerized

**possession**
04 grip, hold
05 title
06 tenure
07 control, custody, holding, tenancy
09 ownership
10 occupation
11 ball control
14 proprietorship

**possessions**
04 gear
05 goods, stuff
06 assets, estate, things
07 baggage, effects, luggage
08 chattels, movables, property
10 belongings
13 worldly wealth

**possessive**
06 greedy
07 jealous, selfish
08 clinging, covetous, grasping
10 dominating

**possibility**
04 hope, odds, risk
06 chance, choice, danger, hazard, option, talent
07 promise
08 prospect, recourse
09 potential, prospects
10 advantages, likelihood, preference
11 alternative, feasibility, probability
12 capabilities, expectations, potentiality
13 attainability
14 conceivability, practicability

**possible**
06 doable, likely, odds-on
07 tenable
08 credible, feasible, probable

09 potential, promising
10 achievable, attainable, on the cards
11 conceivable, practicable
14 accomplishable

**possibly**
05 at all, maybe
07 perhaps
09 hopefully
10 by any means
11 by any chance, conceivably
12 peradventure

**post**
03 job, leg, pin, put
04 beat, mail, move, pale, pole, prop, send
05 affix, e-mail, newel, pin up, place, put up, shaft, stake, strut
06 assign, column, locate, office, picket, pillar, report, second
07 airmail, appoint, display, forward, letters, packets, parcels, publish, situate, station, upright, vacancy
08 aerogram, announce, delivery, dispatch, junk mail, packages, position, transfer, transmit
09 publicize, situation, snail mail, stanchion
10 aerogramme, direct mail, employment, parcel post
11 appointment, express mail, surface mail
12 priority mail, standard mail
14 correspondence, electronic mail, first-class mail, registered mail
15 special delivery

**□keep someone posted**
06 fill in, inform
12 keep up to date

**poster**
02 ad
04 bill, sign
06 notice
07 placard, sticker
08 bulletin
12 announcement
13 advertisement

**posterior**
04 back, hind, rear, rump, seat, tail
06 behind, bottom, dorsal, hinder, latter
08 backside, buttocks, haunches, rearward
09 hinder end
12 hindquarters

**posterity**
10 successors
11 descendants

**posthaste**
06 at once, pronto
07 hastily, quickly, swiftly
08 directly, full tilt, promptly, speedily
11 double-quick, immediately
12 straightaway, with all speed

**postman, postwoman**
07 mailman
11 mail carrier
12 postal worker
13 letter carrier

**postmortem**
07 autopsy
08 analysis, necropsy
10 dissection
11 examination

**postpone**
05 defer, delay
06 freeze, put off, shelve
07 adjourn, put back, suspend
08 hold over, prorogue, put on ice
10 pigeonhole, reschedule
13 procrastinate

**postponed**
05 on ice
06 frozen, put off
07 shelved
08 deferred
09 adjourned, suspended
10 in abeyance
15 on the back burner

**postponement**
04 stay
05 delay
06 freeze
08 deferral
09 deferment
10 moratorium, suspension
11 adjournment, prorogation

**postscript**
02 PS
07 codicil
08 appendix, epilogue
09 afterword
12 afterthought

**postulate**
05 posit
07 advance, lay down, presume, propose, suppose
08 theorize
10 presuppose
11 hypothesize

**posture**
04 pose, view

05 stand, strut
06 affect, belief, stance
07 bearing, opinion, show off
08 attitude, carriage, position
10 deportment, standpoint
11 disposition, point of view
12 attitudinize
15 strike attitudes

**posy**
05 spray
06 flower
07 bouquet, corsage, nosegay

**pot**
03 jar, pan, urn
04 bowl, fund, vase
05 basin, kitty, purse
06 teapot, vessel
08 cauldron, crucible
09 coffeepot
10 receptacle

**potbellied**
06 portly
07 bloated, paunchy
09 corpulent, distended

**potbelly**
03 gut, pot
06 paunch
09 beer belly

**potency**
04 kick, sway
05 force, might, power, punch, vigor
06 energy, muscle
08 capacity, efficacy, strength
09 potential, puissance
13 effectiveness
15 efficaciousness

**potent**
06 mighty, strong
07 dynamic, pungent
08 eloquent, forceful, powerful, puissant, vigorous
10 commanding, compelling, convincing, impressive
11 efficacious, influential
12 intoxicating, overpowering

**potentate**
04 king
05 chief, mogul, queen, ruler
06 despot, prince, tyrant
07 emperor, empress, monarch
08 autocrat, dictator, overlord
11 head of state

**potential**
06 hidden, latent, talent
07 ability, promise, would-be
08 capacity, inherent, possible, probable
09 embryonic, promising
10 capability, developing

11 possibility, prospective

**potentiality**
07 ability, promise
08 aptitude, capacity, prospect
10 capability, likelihood
13 possibilities

**potion**
04 brew, dose
05 draft, drink, tonic
06 elixir
07 mixture, philter
08 medicine, potation
10 concoction

**potpourri**
06 jumble, medley
07 melange, mixture
08 mishmash, pastiche
09 confusion, patchwork
10 assortment, collection,
   hodgepodge, hotchpotch,
   miscellany
11 gallimaufry, smorgasbord

**pottery**
05 china
08 ceramics, crockery

━ *Pottery terms:*
04 kiln, slip
05 delft, glaze
06 basalt, enamel, firing,
   flambé, galena, ground,
   jasper, luster, reflet, sagger
07 celadon, ceramic, crazing,
   faience, fairing
08 armorial, bronzing, flatback,
   gombroon, maiolica,
   majolica, monogram,
   slipcast
09 china clay, creamware,
   delftware, ironstone,
   overglaze, porcelain,
   sgraffito, stoneware
10 maker's mark, spongeware,
   terracotta, underglaze
11 crackleware, earthenware,
   graniteware
12 blanc-de-chine
13 Staffordshire, Willow pattern
➢ See also PORCELAIN

**pouch**
03 bag, sac
04 poke, sack
05 purse
06 pocket, wallet
07 sporran
08 reticule
09 container, marsupium
10 receptacle

**pounce**
04 dive, drop, grab, jump, leap
05 bound, lunge, swoop

06 snatch, spring, strike
12 take unawares
13 catch off guard, catch
   unawares
14 take by surprise

**pound**
03 pen
04 bang, beat, drum, fold, jail,
   mash, pelt, thud, yard
05 crush, grind, money, smash,
   stomp, throb, thump, tread
06 batter, corral, hammer,
   pestle, pummel, strike
09 comminute, enclosure,
   palpitate, pulverize, triturate
13 pound sterling

**pour**
03 jet, run, tip
04 emit, flow, gush, leak, ooze,
   rain, rush, spew
05 crowd, flood, issue, serve,
   spill, spout, spurt, swarm
06 decant, stream, throng
07 cascade, come out
08 disgorge, pelt down, piss
   down, team down
09 discharge
10 disembogue
11 rain buckets
15 rain cats and dogs

**pout**
04 moue, sulk
07 grimace
08 long face
09 pull a face

**poverty**
04 lack, need, want
06 dearth, penury
07 paucity
08 poorness, scarcity, shortage
09 indigence, privation
10 bankruptcy, deficiency,
   insolvency, meagerness
11 deprivation, destitution
13 impecuniosity, pennilessness
14 impoverishment

**poverty-stricken**
04 poor
05 broke, needy
08 indigent, strapped
09 destitute, penurious
10 stone-broke
11 impecunious
12 impoverished

**powder**
04 bran, bray, dust, mash, talc
05 crush, grind
06 pestle, pounce, powder
08 levigate, sprinkle
09 comminute, pulverize,
   triturate

**powdery**
03 dry
04 fine
05 dusty, loose
06 chalky, floury, ground
08 levigate
10 pulverized

**power**
04 pull, rule, sway
05 clout, force, juice, might,
   right, teeth, vigor
06 energy, muscle
07 ability, command, control,
   faculty, potency, warrant
08 capacity, clutches, dominion,
   strength
09 authority, intensity, potential,
   supremacy
10 ascendancy, capability,
   competence, domination
11 electricity, prerogative,
   sovereignty
12 forcefulness, potentiality,
   powerfulness
13 authorization

**powerful**
05 burly, tough
06 brawny, mighty, potent,
   robust, strong
08 dominant, forceful, muscular,
   puissant
09 effective, energetic,
   strapping
10 commanding, compelling,
   convincing, persuasive
11 influential
13 authoritative

**powerfully**
08 cogently, forcibly, mightily,
   potently, strongly
10 forcefully, vigorously
12 convincingly, impressively,
   persuasively

**powerless**
04 weak
05 frail, unfit
06 feeble, infirm, unable
07 unarmed
08 disabled, helpless, impotent
09 incapable, paralyzed
11 defenseless, ineffectual

**practicability**
03 use
05 value
07 utility
09 handiness
10 usefulness
11 operability, workability

**practicable**
06 doable, viable
08 workable

**practical**
10 achievable, attainable

**practical**
05 handy
06 actual, strong, useful
07 applied, hands on, skilled, trained, working
08 feasible, suitable, workable, workaday
09 effective, efficient, hard-nosed, pragmatic, realistic
10 functional, hardheaded
11 common sense, down-to-earth, serviceable, utilitarian
12 matter-of-fact

**practicality**
06 basics
07 realism, utility
08 practice
10 usefulness
11 common sense, feasibility, nitty-gritty, workability
12 nuts and bolts
14 serviceability

**practically**
06 all but, almost, nearly
08 in effect, sensibly, well-nigh
09 just about, virtually
10 pretty much, pretty well
11 essentially, in principle
13 pragmatically, realistically
14 matter-of-factly

**practice**
05 apply, drill, habit, study, train, usage
06 career, custom, dry run, follow, method, policy, polish, pursue, refine, warm-up, work at, work on
07 execute, observe, prepare, pursuit, reality, routine, workout
08 business, carry out, dummy run, engage in, exercise, rehearse, training
09 actuality, implement, procedure, rehearsal, tradition, undertake
10 occupation, profession, run-through
11 application, performance, preparation

**practiced**
05 adept
06 expert, versed
07 skilful, skilled, trained
08 finished, masterly, seasoned, skillful
10 consummate, proficient
11 experienced
12 accomplished

**pragmatic**
08 sensible
09 efficient, hard-nosed, practical, realistic
10 hardheaded
12 businesslike, matter-of-fact

**pragmatism**
07 realism
08 humanism
12 practicalism, practicality
14 hardheadedness

**pragmatist**
07 realist
11 opportunist, utilitarian
12 practicalist

**praise**
04 hail, laud
05 cheer, exalt, extol, glory, honor
06 eulogy, extoll, homage
07 acclaim, applaud, commend, flatter, glorify, ovation, tribute, worship
08 accolade, applause, approval, encomium, eulogize, flattery, plaudits, rave over
09 laudation, panegyric
10 admiration, compliment, halleluiah, hallelujah, wax lyrical
11 approbation, speak well of, testimonial
12 commendation, congratulate, pay tribute to
13 speak highly of

**praiseworthy**
08 laudable
09 admirable, deserving, estimable, excellent, exemplary, honorable
11 commendable
12 meritorious,

**praising**
09 adulatory, laudative, laudatory, panegyric
10 eulogistic, flattering, plauditory, worshipful
11 approbatory, encomiastic
12 commendatory
13 complimentary
14 congratulatory

**prance**
04 jump, leap, romp, skip
05 bound, caper, dance, frisk, stalk, strut, swank, vault
06 cavort, curvet, frolic, gambol, parade, spring

**prank**
04 joke, lark

**prat**
05 antic, caper, stunt, trick
08 escapade
13 practical joke

**prattle**
03 gab, jaw
04 chat, talk
06 babble, drivel, gabble, gossip, hot air, jabber, rattle, tattle
07 blather, blether, chatter, prating, twaddle, twitter
08 nonsense
09 gibberish
11 foolishness

**prattler**
06 gossip, magpie, prater, talker
07 babbler, blether, gabbler, tattler, windbag
09 chatterer
10 chatterbox
12 blabbermouth

**pray**
03 ask, beg
05 adore, crave, plead, thank
06 call on, invoke, praise, talk to
07 beseech, entreat, implore, request, solicit, worship
08 petition
10 say a prayer, supplicate
14 say your prayers

**prayer**
04 plea
05 adore, salat, shema, thank
06 abodah, appeal, litany, mantra
07 collect, gayatri, kaddish, request
08 Ave Maria, devotion, entreaty, Hail Mary, petition
09 communion, Our Father
10 invocation
11 Paternoster
12 intercession, supplication
14 the Lord's Prayer

**prayer book**
06 mahzor, missal, siddur
07 ordinal
08 breviary, Triodion
09 euchology, formulary
11 euchologion, service book

**preach**
04 urge
05 teach
06 advise, exhort
07 address, lecture
08 admonish, advocate, harangue, moralize
09 sermonize
10 evangelize
11 give a sermon, pontificate

## preacher
06 parson, ranter, rector
08 homilist, minister, pulpiter
09 clergyman, moralizer,
   pulpiteer
10 evangelist, sermonizer
12 pontificator
13 televangelist

## preaching
05 dogma
06 gospel
07 evangel, kerygma, sermons
08 doctrine, homilies, precepts,
   teaching
10 evangelism, homiletics
11 exhortation, sermonizing
13 pontificating

## preachy
08 didactic, dogmatic, edifying
09 homiletic, hortatory,
   pharisaic, pietistic, religiose
10 moralizing, pontifical
11 exhortatory, sermonizing
13 pontificating

## preamble
05 proem
06 lead-in
07 preface, prelude
08 exordium, foreword,
   overture, prologue
11 preparation
12 introduction
13 preliminaries

## precarious
05 hairy, risky, shaky
06 chancy, unsafe, wobbly
08 insecure, unstable, unsteady
09 dangerous, hazardous,
   uncertain, unsettled
10 unreliable, vulnerable
11 treacherous

## precaution
08 prudence
09 foresight, insurance,
   provision, safeguard
10 protection, providence
11 forethought

## precautionary
07 prudent
08 cautious
09 judicious, provident
10 protective
12 preventative

## precede
04 head, lead
07 preface
08 antecede, antedate, go
   before
09 come first, go ahead of,
   introduce

10 come before
14 take precedence

## precedence
04 lead, rank
08 eminence, priority
09 seniority, supremacy
10 ascendancy, preference
11 preeminence, superiority
12 pride of place

## ❏take precedence over
10 come before

## precedent
05 model
07 example, pattern
08 exemplar, paradigm,
   standard
09 criterion, yardstick

## preceding
05 above, prior, supra
06 former
07 earlier
08 anterior, previous
09 aforesaid, foregoing
10 antecedent, precursive
14 aforementioned

## precept
03 law
04 rule
05 axiom, canon, maxim, motto,
   order
06 charge, decree, dictum,
   rubric, saying
07 command, mandate, statute
09 guideline, ordinance,
   principle
10 injunction, regulation
11 commandment, instruction

## precinct
04 area, zone
05 bound, limit
06 milieu, sector
07 confine, quarter, section
08 boundary, district, division,
   locality, purlieus, vicinity
09 surrounds
13 police station
14 police district, voting district

## precincts
08 environs
09 enclosure
12 neighborhood

## preciosity
06 chichi
11 affectation, floweriness
15 pretentiousness

## precious
04 dear, fine, rare, very
05 loved

06 adored, chichi, choice, costly,
   prized, valued
07 beloved, darling, dearest,
   flowery, revered
08 affected, favorite, idolized,
   mannered, valuable
09 cherished, contrived,
   expensive, priceless,
   simulated, treasured
10 high priced
11 overrefined, pretentious

## precipice
04 crag, drop
05 bluff, brink, cliff, scarp, steep
06 escarp, height
09 cliff face
10 escarpment

## precipitate
04 hurl, rash
05 brief, cause, fling, hasty,
   hurry, quick, rapid, speed,
   swift, throw
06 abrupt, hasten, plunge,
   speedy, sudden, thrust
07 advance, bring on, frantic,
   further, hurried, quicken,
   speed up, trigger, violent
08 expedite, headlong,
   heedless, occasion, reckless
09 breakneck, hotheaded,
   impatient, impetuous,
   impulsive
10 accelerate, bring about,
   indiscreet, unexpected

## precipitous
04 high
05 sharp, sheer, steep
06 abrupt, sudden
08 vertical
13 perpendicular

## précis
05 sum up, table
06 digest, résumé, sketch
07 abridge, epitome, outline,
   shorten, summary
08 abstract, condense, contract,
   synopsis
09 epitomize, summarize,
   synopsize
10 abbreviate, abridgment

## precise
04 nice
05 exact, fixed, right, rigid
06 actual, minute, prissy, strict
07 express, factual, literal
08 accurate, clear-cut, definite,
   faithful, rigorous, specific
10 fastidious, meticulous,
   particular, scrupulous
11 punctilious, unequivocal,
   word for word

13 conscientious

**precisely**
04 to a T
05 plumb, smack
06 spot on
07 exactly
08 on the dot, verbatim
09 correctly, literally
10 accurately, distinctly
11 word for word

**precision**
05 rigor
06 detail
08 accuracy
09 exactness
10 exactitude
11 correctness
12 distinctness, explicitness
14 fastidiousness,
   meticulousness

**preclude**
04 stop
05 check, debar
06 hinder
07 obviate, prevent, rule out
08 prohibit
09 forestall

**precocious**
05 ahead, early, quick, smart
06 bright, clever, gifted, mature
07 forward
08 advanced, far ahead
09 brilliant, premature

**preconceive**
07 presume, project
10 anticipate, presuppose

**preconception**
10 assumption, conjecture
11 expectation, presumption
12 anticipation

**precondition**
09 necessity
10 sine qua non
11 requirement, stipulation
12 prerequisite

**precursor**
06 herald
07 prelude
09 harbinger, messenger
10 antecedent, forerunner
11 trailblazer
13 curtain raiser

**precursory**
05 prior
07 warning
08 anterior, previous
09 preceding
10 antecedent, prevenient
12 introductory

**predatory**
06 greedy, lupine
07 hunting, preying, wolfish
08 covetous, ravaging, thieving
09 rapacious, raptorial,
   voracious
10 avaricious, predacious
11 acquisitive, carnivorous

**predecessor**
08 ancestor, forebear
10 antecedent, forefather,
   forerunner, progenitor

**predestination**
03 lot
04 doom, fate
07 destiny

**predestine**
04 doom, fate
07 destine
09 preordain
10 foreordain

**predetermined**
03 set
05 fated, fixed
06 agreed, doomed
07 settled
08 destined, ordained
11 prearranged, predestined
12 foreordained

**predicament**
03 fix, jam
04 hole, mess, spot, stew
06 crisis, pickle, plight, scrape
07 dilemma, impasse, trouble
08 hot water, quandary
09 deep water, emergency,
   situation, tight spot

**predicate**
04 base, rest
05 build, found, posit
06 ground
07 premise
09 establish
11 be dependent

**predict**
05 augur
06 divine
07 foresee, portend, presage,
   project
08 forecast, foretell, prophesy
11 second-guess
13 prognosticate

**predictable**
04 sure
06 likely, odds-on
07 certain
08 expected, foregone,
   foreseen, probable, reliable
10 dependable, on the cards
11 anticipated, foreseeable

**prediction**
06 augury
08 forecast, prophecy
09 prognosis
10 divination
11 auspication, soothsaying
14 fortunetelling
15 prognostication

**predictive**
07 augural
09 prophetic
10 divinatory, prognostic
11 foretelling

**predilection**
04 bent, bias, love
05 fancy, taste
07 leaning
08 fondness, penchant, soft
   spot, tendency, weakness
10 partiality, preference,
   proclivity, propensity
11 inclination
14 predisposition

**predispose**
04 bias, make, move, sway
06 affect, induce, prompt
07 dispose, incline
09 influence, prejudice

**predisposed**
05 prone, ready
06 biased, minded
07 subject
08 amenable, inclined
09 agreeable, favorable
10 prejudiced
11 susceptible

**predisposition**
04 bent, bias
07 leaning
08 penchant, tendency
09 prejudice, proneness
10 likelihood, preference,
   proclivity, propensity
11 inclination
12 potentiality, predilection
14 susceptibility

**predominance**
04 edge, hold, sway
05 power
06 weight
07 control, mastery, numbers
08 dominion, hegemony
09 dominance, influence,
   supremacy, upper hand
10 ascendancy, prevalence
11 paramountcy, superiority

**predominant**
04 main
05 chief, prime
06 potent, ruling, strong

07 capital, leading, primary, supreme
08 forceful, powerful
09 ascendant, important, in control, paramount, principal, sovereign
10 prevailing
11 controlling, influential
12 preponderant
15 in the ascendancy

**predominate**
04 rule, tell
05 reign
06 obtain
07 prevail
08 dominate, outweigh, override, overrule
09 outnumber, transcend
12 preponderate

**preeminence**
04 fame
06 renown, repute
08 prestige
09 supremacy
10 excellence, prominence
11 paramountcy, superiority

**preeminent**
05 chief, first
07 leading, supreme
08 foremost, superior
09 excellent, matchless, unequaled, unrivaled
10 inimitable
11 exceptional, outstanding, superlative, unsurpassed
12 incomparable, transcendent
13 most important

**preeminently**
08 signally
09 supremely
10 especially
13 par excellence

**preempt**
05 seize, usurp
06 assume, secure
07 acquire, prevent
08 arrogate
09 forestall
10 anticipate
11 appropriate

**preen**
04 bask, deck, do up, trim
05 adorn, array, clean, exult, gloat, groom, pique, plume, pride, primp, prink, slick
06 doll up, smooth
07 dress up, trick up
08 beautify, prettify, trick out
12 congratulate

**preface**
04 open
05 begin, proem, start
06 launch, prefix
07 precede, prelims, prelude
08 exordium, foreword, lead up to, preamble, prologue
09 introduce
11 front matter
12 introduction

**prefatory**
07 opening
08 exordial, proemial
09 preludial, prelusive, prelusory
10 antecedent, precursory
11 explanatory, prefatorial, preliminary, preparatory
12 introductory, prolegomenal
13 perambulatory

**prefect**
04 dean
07 monitor
08 praefect
10 supervisor
13 administrator

**prefer**
03 opt
04 back, file, pick, want, wish
05 adopt, bring, elect, exalt, fancy, favor, go for, honor, lodge, place, press, raise
06 choose, desire, move up, opt for, select
07 advance, elevate, pick out, present, promote, support
08 advocate, plump for
09 recommend, single out
10 aggrandize, like better
11 be partial to, would rather, would sooner

**preferable**
05 nicer
06 better, chosen
07 favored
08 superior
09 advisable, desirable

**preferably**
06 rather, sooner
09 for choice
10 from choice

**preference**
04 bent, bias, pick, wish
05 fancy
06 choice, desire, liking, option
07 leaning
08 cup of tea, favorite, priority
09 selection
10 favoritism, partiality, precedence
11 first choice, inclination

12 predilection
14 discrimination

**preferential**
07 favored, partial, special
08 partisan, superior
09 favorable
10 privileged

**preferment**
04 rise
06 step up
07 dignity
09 elevation, promotion, upgrading
10 betterment, exaltation
11 advancement, furtherance

**preferred**
06 choice, chosen
07 desired, favored
08 approved, selected
09 predilect
10 authorized, sanctioned
11 predilected, recommended

**pregnancy**
09 family way, gestation, gravidity
10 conception
11 parturition
12 childbearing, impregnation
13 fertilization

**pregnant**
04 full, rich
05 heavy
06 loaded
08 eloquent, enceinte
09 expectant, expecting, in the club, with child
10 parturient, suggestive
11 significant
14 in the family way
16 has a bun in the oven

**prehistoric**
07 ancient, archaic
08 earliest, primeval
09 primitive
10 antiquated, primordial
12 antediluvian
14 before the flood

**prejudge**
07 presume
10 anticipate, presuppose
12 predetermine

**prejudice**
04 bias, harm, hurt, ruin, sway
05 color, slant, spoil, wreck
06 damage, hinder, impair, injure, injury
07 bigotry, distort
09 detriment, influence
10 chauvinism, partiality, predispose, preference

11 intolerance, misanthropy
12 disadvantage, one-sidedness, partisanship
14 discrimination
15 be detrimental to

**prejudiced**
06 biased, unfair, unjust
07 bigoted, partial
08 one-sided, partisan
09 distorted, jaundiced
10 chauvinist, influenced
11 predisposed
12 chauvinistic
14 discriminatory

**prejudicial**
07 harmful, hurtful, noxious
08 damaging, inimical
09 injurious
11 deleterious, detrimental
15 disadvantageous

**preliminary**
05 early, first, pilot, proem
07 opening, prelude
08 exordial, exordium, preamble
09 inaugural, prefatory
10 groundwork, precursory
11 formalities, foundations, preparation, preparatory
12 introduction, introductory

**prelude**
05 proem, start
06 herald, opener
07 opening, preface
08 exordium, foreword, overture, preamble, prologue
09 beginning, harbinger, precursor
10 forerunner
11 preliminary, preparation
12 introduction
13 curtain raiser

**premature**
04 rash, soon
05 early, green, hasty
06 unripe
07 too soon
08 abortive, ill-timed, too early, untimely
09 embryonic, impetuous, impulsive
10 half-formed, incomplete
11 inopportune, precipitate, undeveloped
13 ill-considered, jumping the gun

**premeditated**
07 planned
08 intended
10 calculated, deliberate

11 intentional

**premeditation**
06 design
07 purpose
08 planning, plotting, scheming
09 intention
11 forethought
12 deliberation

**premier**
03 top
04 head, main
05 chief, first, prime
07 highest, initial, leading, primary, supreme
08 cardinal, foremost
09 paramount, principal
10 preeminent
13 prime minister

**première**
05 début
07 opening
10 first night
12 first showing, opening night

**premise**
05 basis, posit, state
06 assert, assume, thesis
07 lay down
08 argument
09 assertion, postulate, predicate, statement, stipulate
10 assumption, hypothesis, presuppose, take as true
11 hypothesize, proposition, supposition
14 presupposition

**premises**
04 site
05 place
06 estate, office
07 grounds
08 building, property
13 establishment

**premium**
05 bonus, prize
06 reward
07 payment
08 superior
09 surcharge
10 instalment
11 extra charge, installment
12 overcharging

☐**at a premium**
06 scarce
12 hard to come by, like gold dust
13 in short supply

☐**put a premium on**
05 favor
08 hold dear, treasure

12 regard highly, value greatly
15 set great store by

**premonition**
04 fear, idea, omen, sign
05 hunch, worry
07 anxiety, feeling, portent, presage, warning
09 intuition, misgiving, suspicion
10 foreboding, gut feeling, sixth sense
12 apprehension, funny feeling, presentiment

**preoccupation**
05 thing
07 concern, reverie
08 fixation, interest, oblivion
10 absorption, hobbyhorse
11 abstraction, daydreaming, distraction
15 bee in your bonnet, inattentiveness

**preoccupied**
07 engaged, faraway, pensive, taken up
08 absorbed, distrait
10 abstracted, distracted
11 daydreaming
12 absent-minded
13 deep in thought

**preoccupy**
06 absorb, engage, obsess, occupy, take up
07 involve

**preordain**
04 doom, fate
07 destine
10 foreordain, predestine

**preparation**
04 plan
05 study
06 basics, lotion, potion, supply
07 fitness, mixture
08 assembly, coaching, compound, cosmetic, homework, medicine, planning, practice, revision, training
09 provision, readiness, spadework
10 concoction, groundwork
11 application, arrangement, composition, development
13 preliminaries

**preparatory**
05 basic
07 initial, opening, primary
09 prefatory
10 elementary, precursory

## prepare

11 fundamental, preliminary, rudimentary
12 introductory

### ❑preparatory to
06 before
07 prior to
10 previous to
11 in advance of
15 in expectation of

## prepare
03 fix
04 make, plan
05 coach, draft, equip, prime, set up, study, tee up, train
06 adjust, devise, draw up, fit out, gear up, rig out, supply, warm up
07 arrange, compose, concoct, fashion, produce, provide, psych up
08 assemble, contrive, exercise, get ready, limber up, organize, practice, rehearse
09 construct, make ready
10 pave the way
12 get into shape
14 set the scene for

### ❑prepare yourself
12 gird yourself
13 brace yourself, steel yourself
15 fortify yourself, gird up your loins

## prepared
03 fit, set
05 fixed, ready
07 in order, planned, waiting, willing
08 arranged, disposed, inclined
09 organized

## preparedness
07 fitness
09 alertness, readiness
12 anticipation

## preponderance
04 bulk, mass, sway
05 force, power
06 weight
08 majority
09 dominance, supremacy
10 lion's share, prevalence
12 predominance

## preponderant
06 larger
07 greater
08 foremost, superior
09 important
10 overriding, overruling
11 controlling, predominant

## preponderate
04 rule, tell

07 prevail
08 dominate, override, overrule
09 outnumber
11 predominate, weigh in with
13 turn the scales
14 turn the balance

## prepossessing
04 fair
06 taking
07 winning, winsome
08 alluring, charming, engaging, fetching, handsome, pleasing, striking
09 appealing, beautiful
10 attractive, enchanting
11 captivating, good-looking

## preposterous
05 crazy
06 absurd
08 farcical, shocking
09 ludicrous, senseless
10 impossible, incredible, irrational, ridiculous
11 nonsensical, unthinkable
12 unbelievable, unreasonable

## prerequisite
04 must
05 basic, vital
07 needful, proviso
09 essential, necessary, necessity, requisite
10 imperative, sine qua non
11 requirement
12 precondition

## prerogative
03 due
05 claim, droit, right
07 liberty, license
08 sanction
09 authority, privilege
10 birthright

## presage
04 bode, omen, sign
05 augur
06 augury, herald, warn of
07 point to, portend, portent, predict, promise, warning
08 forecast, foretell, forewarn, indicate
09 adumbrate, be a sign of, harbinger
10 foreshadow
11 forewarning, premonition

## prescience
08 prophecy
09 foresight, prevision
11 second sight
12 precognition
14 farsightedness

## prescient
07 psychic
08 divining
09 farseeing, prophetic
10 discerning, divinatory, farsighted, perceptive
11 foresighted

## prescribe
04 rule
05 limit, order
06 advise, decree, ordain
07 dictate, lay down, specify
09 stipulate

## prescribed
07 decreed
08 assigned, laid down, ordained
09 specified
10 stipulated

## prescription
04 drug
06 advice, recipe, remedy
07 formula, mixture
08 medicine
11 instruction, preparation

## prescriptive
05 rigid
08 didactic, dogmatic
09 customary
10 preceptive
11 dictatorial, legislating, prescribing
13 authoritarian

## presence
03 air
04 aura
05 being, ghost
06 appeal, shadow, spirit
07 bearing, phantom, specter
08 carriage, charisma, demeanor, nearness, vicinity, visitant
09 closeness, existence, magnetism, occupancy, proximity, residence
10 apparition, appearance, attendance

### ❑presence of mind
04 cool
05 poise
06 aplomb
08 calmness, coolness
09 composure, sang-froid
14 unflappability

## present
03 tip
04 gift, give, here, host, near, perk, show

05 award, favor, grant, mount, offer, put on, ready, stage, there
06 at hand, bestow, bounty, confer, depict, donate, extend, nearby, submit, tender, to hand
07 compère, current, display, entrust, exhibit, hold out, perform, picture, portray, proffer
08 announce, describe, donation, existent, existing, gratuity, hand over, largesse, offering, organize, up-to-date
09 attending, available, delineate, endowment, immediate, introduce, make known, represent, sweetener
11 benefaction, demonstrate
12 characterize, contemporary, contribution, put on display

❑**at present**
03 now
09 currently
10 at this time
11 at the moment

❑**for the present**
06 for now, pro tem
12 for the moment
13 in the meantime
15 for the time being

❑**present oneself**
06 appear, emerge, happen, show up, turn up
11 come to light, materialize

❑**the present day**
03 now
05 today
08 nowadays
09 currently

**presentable**
04 neat, tidy
05 clean, smart
06 decent, proper, spruce
12 satisfactory
14 smartly dressed

**presentation**
04 show, talk
05 award
06 layout
07 display, showing, staging
08 bestowal, donating, granting
09 rendition
10 exhibition, production
11 performance
12 disquisition, introduction
13 demonstration

**present-day**
06 living, modern
07 current, present
08 existing, up-to-date
11 fashionable
12 contemporary

**presentiment**
05 hunch
07 feeling, presage
09 intuition, misgiving
10 foreboding
11 premonition

**presently**
03 now
04 soon
07 by and by, shortly
09 at present, currently, in a minute, these days
10 before long
11 at the moment
13 in a short while

**preservation**
06 safety, saving
08 guarding, security
09 upholding
10 conserving, protection
11 maintenance, safekeeping
12 conservation, safeguarding

**preserve**
03 can, dry, jam
04 area, cure, keep, salt, save
05 field, guard, jelly, realm, smoke, store
06 bottle, defend, domain, pickle, retain, shield, sphere
07 protect, reserve, shelter
08 conserve, maintain
09 look after, marmalade, safeguard, sanctuary
10 take care of

**preside**
04 head, lead, rule
05 chair
06 direct, govern, head up
07 conduct, control
09 officiate
12 be in charge of, be in the chair, call the shots

**president**
04 boss, head
05 chief, ruler
06 leader
08 director, governor
11 head of state

► *Names of U.S. presidents. We have omitted the word* **president** *from names given in the following list but you may need to include this word as part of the solution to some crossword clues.*

04 **Bush** (George W.), **Bush** (George), **Ford** (Gerald Rudolph), **Polk** (James Knox), **Taft** (William Howard)
05 **Adams** (John Quincy), **Adams** (John), **Grant** (Ulysses Simpson), **Hayes** (Rutherford Birchard), **Nixon** (Richard Milhous), **Tyler** (John)
06 **Arthur** (Chester Alan), **Carter** (James Earl "Jimmy"), **Hoover** (Herbert), **Monroe** (James), **Pierce** (Franklin), **Reagan** (Ronald), **Taylor** (Zachary), **Truman** (Harry S.), **Wilson** (Woodrow)
07 **Clinton** (William Jefferson "Bill"), **Harding** (Warren Gamaliel), **Jackson** (Andrew), **Johnson** (Andrew), **Johnson** (Lyndon Baines), **Kennedy** (John Fitzgerald), **Lincoln** (Abraham), **Madison** (James)
08 **Buchanan** (James), **Coolidge** (Calvin), **Fillmore** (Millard), **Garfield** (James Abram), **Harrison** (Benjamin), **Harrison** (William Henry), **McKinley** (William), **Van Buren** (Martin)
09 **Cleveland** (Grover), **Jefferson** (Thomas), **Roosevelt** (Franklin Delano), **Roosevelt** (Theodore "Teddy")
10 **Eisenhower** (Dwight David), **Washington** (George)
➤ See also POLITICS

**press**
03 hug, jam, mob
04 cram, iron, mash, pack, push, roll, urge
05 clasp, crowd, crush, flock, force, grasp, horde, knead, pinch, plead, stuff, surge, swarm, troop, worry
06 caress, coerce, compel, cuddle, demand, enfold,

exhort, harass, papers, praise, smooth, squash, throng
07 afflict, besiege, call for, depress, embrace, entreat, flatten, push for, reviews, squeeze, trample, trouble
08 articles, campaign, compress, coverage, insist on, petition, pressmen, pressure, push down, the media
09 constrain, criticism, mass media, multitude, news media, paparazzi, reporters, smooth out, treatment
10 journalism, newspapers, pressurize, presswomen, supplicate
11 journalists
12 fourth estate, newspapermen
13 photographers, printing press, put pressure on
14 correspondents, newspaperwomen
15 printing machine

❏**press on**
04 go on
07 carry on, go ahead, proceed
08 continue

**pressed**
06 forced, pushed, rushed
07 bullied, coerced, hurried, lacking, short of
08 harassed, squashed
10 browbeaten
11 constrained, deficient in, pressurized

**pressing**
06 urgent
07 burning, serious
08 critical
09 demanding, essential, important
12 high priority

**pressure**
04 load
05 force, power
06 burden, demand, duress, hassle, strain, stress, weight
07 tension
08 bullying, coercion, crushing
09 heaviness, squeezing
10 compulsion, constraint
11 compression

**pressurize**
05 bully, drive, force, press
06 coerce, compel, lean on, oblige
07 dragoon

08 browbeat, bulldoze
09 constrain
14 put the screws on

**prestige**
04 fame
05 honor, kudos
06 credit, esteem, regard, renown, status
07 stature
08 eminence, standing
10 importance

**prestigious**
05 great
06 famous
07 eminent, exalted
08 blue chip, esteemed, renowned, up-market
09 important, prominent, reputable, respected, well-known
10 celebrated, impressive
11 high ranking, illustrious, influential
13 distinguished

**presumably**
08 probably
09 doubtless, seemingly
10 apparently, very likely
11 as like as not, doubtlessly

**presume**
04 dare
06 assume, deduce, take it
07 believe, go so far, imagine, suppose, surmise, venture
10 make so bold, presuppose
11 hypothesize
14 take for granted, take the liberty
15 have the audacity

❏**presume on**
05 trust
06 bank on, rely on
07 count on, exploit
08 depend on
15 take advantage of

**presumption**
05 cheek, guess, nerve
07 opinion, surmise
08 audacity, boldness, temerity
09 arrogance, assurance, impudence, inference, insolence
10 assumption, conjecture, effrontery, hypothesis
11 probability, supposition
12 impertinence

**presumptive**
06 likely
07 assumed

08 believed, expected, inferred, probable, supposed
09 designate
10 understood
11 conceivable, prospective

**presumptuous**
04 bold
05 cocky, pushy
06 cheeky
07 forward
08 arrogant, cocksure, impudent, insolent
09 audacious
11 impertinent
12 overfamiliar
13 overconfident

**presuppose**
06 assume
07 presume
14 take for granted

**presupposition**
10 assumption
11 presumption

**pretense**
03 lie
04 mask, ruse, sham, show, veil, wile
05 bluff, cloak, cover, front, guise
06 acting, deceit, façade, faking
07 charade, display, pretext
08 feigning, trickery
09 deception, false show, falsehood, hypocrisy, invention, posturing, semblance, showiness
10 appearance, masquerade, play-acting, simulation
11 affectation, dissembling, fabrication, make believe
13 dissimulation

**pretend**
03 act
04 fake, mime, sham
05 bluff, claim, feign, put on
06 affect, allege, assume
07 imagine, play-act, profess, purport, suppose
08 simulate
09 dissemble, fabricate
10 put on an act
11 counterfeit, impersonate, make believe
15 pass yourself off

**pretended**
04 fake, sham
05 bogus, false, phony, puton
06 avowed, pseudo
07 alleged, feigned, pretend
08 so-called
09 imaginary

**pretender** *(continued)*
10 artificial, fictitious
11 counterfeit

**pretender**
07 claimer
08 aspirant, claimant

**pretension**
04 airs, show
05 claim
06 demand, vanity
07 conceit
08 ambition, pretense
09 showiness
10 aspiration
11 affectation, floweriness, ostentation
13 magniloquence
14 self-importance
15 pretentiousness

**pretentious**
05 showy
06 la-de-da, la-di-da
08 affected, immodest, inflated, mannered
09 ambitious, bombastic, conceited, elaborate, flaunting, grandiose
10 artificial, flamboyant
11 exaggerated, extravagant
12 high-sounding, magniloquent, ostentatious, vainglorious
13 overambitious, self-important

**pretentiousness**
04 show
10 floridness, pretension
11 floweriness, ostentation
13 theatricality
14 attitudinizing

**preternatural**
07 unusual
08 abnormal
11 exceptional
13 extraordinary

**pretext**
04 mask, ploy, ruse, sham, show, veil
05 cloak, cover, guise
06 excuse
08 pretense
09 semblance
10 appearance, red herring

**prettify**
04 deck, do up, gild, trim
05 adorn
06 bedeck, doll up
07 deck out, garnish
08 beautify, decorate, ornament, trick out
09 embellish, smarten up

**pretty**
04 cute, fair, fine, nice
05 bonny, quite
06 comely, dainty, fairly, lovely
07 elegant, winsome
08 charming, delicate, engaging, graceful, handsome, pleasant, pleasing, somewhat
09 appealing, beautiful, tolerably
10 attractive, moderately, personable, reasonably

**prevail**
03 win
04 rule
05 occur, reign
06 abound, obtain
07 conquer, outlast, succeed, triumph
08 hold sway, overcome, overrule
11 carry the day, predominate
12 preponderate

❑ **prevail upon**
04 sway, urge
06 induce, lean on, prompt
07 flatter, incline, win over
08 convince, persuade, pressure, soft-soap, talk into
09 influence, sweet talk
10 pressurize
11 bring around, pull strings

**prevailing**
04 main
05 chief, usual
06 common, ruling
07 current, general, in style, in vogue, popular, supreme
08 dominant, reigning
09 ascendant, most usual, prevalent
10 most common, widespread
11 established, predominant
12 preponderant

**prevalence**
04 hold, rule, sway
07 mastery, primacy
08 currency, ubiquity
09 frequency, profusion
10 acceptance, commonness, regularity
12 omnipresence, predominance, universality
13 pervasiveness, preponderance

**prevalent**
04 rife
06 common
07 current, general, rampant

08 accepted, dominant, everyday, frequent
09 customary, extensive, pervasive, universal
10 prevailing, ubiquitous, widespread
11 established

**prevaricate**
03 lie
05 cavil, dodge, evade, hedge, shift
06 waffle
07 deceive, quibble, shuffle
09 pussyfoot
10 equivocate
12 shilly-shally, tergiversate
13 sit on the fence

**prevarication**
03 fib, lie
04 fibs
06 deceit
07 evasion, fibbing, untruth
08 caviling
09 deception, falsehood, half-truth, quibbling

**prevaricator**
04 liar
06 dodger, evader, fibber
07 casuist, caviler, sophist
08 quibbler
09 hypocrite
10 dissembler
11 pettifogger

**prevent**
03 bar
04 balk, foil, halt, stop
05 avert, avoid, baulk, block, check, deter
06 arrest, hamper, hinder, impede, thwart
07 fend off, head off, inhibit, obviate, ward off
08 hold back, keep from, obstruct, preclude, restrain, stave off
09 forestall, frustrate, intercept
10 anticipate

**prevention**
03 bar
05 check
07 balking, foiling, halting
08 baulking, obstacle
09 arresting, avoidance, hampering, hindrance, obviation, safeguard
10 deterrence, impediment, precaution, preclusion
11 elimination, prophylaxis

**preventive**
06 remedy, shield
08 obstacle

09 deterrent, hindrance, safeguard
10 impediment, inhibitory, preemptive, prevention, protection, protective
11 neutralizer, obstruction, obstructive
12 anticipatory, preventative, prophylactic
13 counteractive, precautionary

**previous**
05 prior
06 former
07 earlier, one-time, quondam
09 erstwhile, foregoing, preceding

**previously**
04 once
06 before
07 earlier
08 formerly, hitherto, until now
09 at one time, in the past
10 beforehand, heretofore

**prey**
04 game, kill
06 quarry, target, victim
07 fall guy

❏**prey on**
04 hunt, kill
05 catch, haunt, seize
06 devour, feed on, plague
07 exploit, oppress, trouble
15 take advantage of

**price**
03 fee, sum, tab
04 bill, cost, levy, rate, toll
05 value, worth
06 amount, assess, charge, damage, figure, outlay, result, reward, tariff
07 expense, forfeit, payment, penalty
08 appraise, estimate, evaluate, expenses, valorize
09 quotation, sacrifice, valuation
10 assessment
11 expenditure
12 consequences

❏**at a price**
09 expensive
11 at a high cost
12 at a high price

❏**at any price**
09 at any cost
15 whatever it takes, whatever the cost

**priceless**
04 dear, rare, rich
05 comic, funny

06 costly, prized
07 a scream, amusing, killing
08 precious, valuable
09 cherished, expensive, hilarious, treasured
10 invaluable
20 riotoussidesplitting

**prick**
03 jab, jag
04 bite, bore, gash, goad, hole, itch, nick, pain, pang, slit, stab
05 harry, punch, smart, spike, sting, worry, wound
06 gnaw at, harass, pierce, plague, prey on, tingle, twinge
07 pinhole, prickle, torment, trouble
08 distress, puncture, smarting
09 perforate
11 perforation

**prickle**
04 barb, itch, pang, spur, tine
05 point, spike, spine, sting, thorn
06 needle, tingle, twinge
07 itching
08 smarting, stinging
14 pins and needles

**prickly**
04 edgy
05 spiky, spiny, spiny
06 spiked, thorny, touchy, tricky
07 bristly, pronged
08 scratchy, smarting, stinging, tingling
09 crotchety, difficult, irritable
11 complicated, troublesome

**pride**
03 ego
05 honor
06 vanity
07 bighead, conceit, dignity, egotism
08 snobbery
09 arrogance, self-image, self-worth
10 self-esteem
11 haughtiness, presumption, self-conceit, self-respect
12 boastfulness, satisfaction
13 gratification
14 self-importance

❏**pride yourself on**
05 vaunt
07 exult in, glory in, revel in
09 brag about, crow about
10 boast about
15 flatter yourself

**priest**
05 padre, vicar
06 deacon, father, parson, pastor
08 man of God, minister
09 churchman, clergyman, deaconess
10 woman of God
11 churchwoman, clergywoman
13 man of the cloth
15 woman of the cloth

**priestess**
03 nun
06 abbess, sister, vestal
08 canoness, prioress
09 deaconess
11 clergywoman

**priestly**
07 Aaronic
08 clerical, hieratic, pastoral
09 Aaronical, canonical
10 priestlike, sacerdotal
14 ecclesiastical

**prig**
05 prude
07 killjoy, puritan
09 Mrs. Grundy, nice Nelly, precisian, Victorian
10 goody-goody, nice Nellie

**priggish**
04 prim, smug
06 stuffy
07 prudish, starchy
10 goody-goody
11 puritanical, strait-laced
12 narrow-minded
13 sanctimonious, self-righteous, straight-laced
14 holier-than-thou

**prim**
05 fussy
06 demure, formal, prissy, proper, stuffy
07 precise, prudish, starchy
08 priggish
10 fastidious, fuddy-duddy, old-maidish, particular
11 puritanical, strait-laced
13 schoolmarmish, straight-laced

**primacy**
07 command
08 dominion
09 dominance, supremacy
10 ascendancy, paramouncy
11 preeminence, superiority

**primal**
04 main

05 basic, chief, first, major, prime
07 central, highest, initial, primary
08 earliest, original, primeval
09 paramount, primitive
10 primordial

**primarily**
05 first
06 mainly, mostly
07 chiefly, firstly
09 basically, in essence, in the main
10 especially
11 essentially, principally
12 particularly
13 fundamentally, predominantly
15 in the first place

**primary**
04 main
05 basic, chief, first, prime
06 simple
07 capital, highest, initial, leading, radical, supreme
08 cardinal, dominant, earliest, foremost, greatest, original, primeval, ultimate
09 beginning, elemental, essential, paramount, principal
10 elementary, primordial
11 fundamental, predominant, rudimentary
12 introductory

**prime**
03 top
04 acme, best, clue, fill, main, peak
05 bloom, brief, chief, coach, equip, train
06 choice, clue in, fill in, flower, height, heyday, inform, notify, select, zenith
07 highest, leading, prepare, quality, supreme
08 best part, foremost, get ready, maturity, pinnacle, standard, top grade
09 excellent, first-rate, principal
10 first-class, preeminent

**primer**
06 manual, reader
08 hornbook, textbook
12 introduction

**primeval**
05 early, first
07 ancient
08 earliest, original
10 primordial
11 instinctive, prehistoric

12 autochthonal

**primitive**
05 crude, early, first, rough
06 savage, simple
07 ancient, natural
08 earliest, original, primeval
10 primordial, uncultured
11 rudimentary, uncivilized, undeveloped

**primordial**
05 early, first
07 ancient
08 earliest, original, primeval
09 primitive
11 instinctive, prehistoric
12 autochthonal

**primp**
05 groom, preen
06 doll up
07 dress up, smarten
08 beautify, spruce up, titivate

**prince, princess**
04 lord
05 ruler
07 monarch
09 potentate, sovereign

► *Names of princes. We have omitted the word* **prince** *from names given in the following list but you may need to include this word as part of the solution to some crossword clues.*
04 Ivan, John (of Gaunt)
05 Edgar (the Atheling), Harry, Henry (the Navigator), James
06 Albert, Andrew, Arthur, Edward, Edward (the Black Prince), Philip
07 Charles, Michael (of Kent), Rainier, Richard, William
08 Vladimir
15 Alexander Nevski

► *Names of princesses. We have omitted the word* **princess** *from names given in the following list but you may need to include this word as part of the solution to some crossword clues.*
04 Anne
05 Alice, Diana, Grace
06 Salome
07 Eugenie, Jezebel, Matilda
08 Beatrice, Caroline, Margaret
09 Alexandra, Charlotte, Elizabeth, Stephanie
10 Pocahontas

**princely**
05 grand, noble, regal, royal

07 liberal, stately
08 generous, handsome, imperial, imposing, majestic, splendid
09 bounteous, sovereign
11 magnanimous, magnificent

**principal**
03 key
04 arch, boss, head, lead, main, star
05 chief, first, major, money, prime, ruler
06 assets, leader, rector, staple
07 capital, highest, leading, primary, supreme
08 cardinal, dominant, foremost, in charge
09 essential, paramount
10 capital sum, headmaster, preeminent
11 controlling
12 capital funds, headmistress
13 most important

**principally**
06 mainly, mostly
07 chiefly
08 above all
09 in the main, primarily
10 especially
14 for the most part

**principle**
03 law
04 code, idea, rule
05 axiom, basis, canon, creed, dogma, honor, maxim, tenet, truth
06 dictum, ethics, morals, theory, virtue
07 decency, formula, precept
08 doctrine, morality, scruples, standard
09 criterion, essential, integrity, rectitude, standards
10 conscience
11 uprightness

❑ **in principle**
07 ideally
08 in theory
09 in essence
13 theoretically

**principled**
05 moral
06 decent
07 ethical, upright
09 honorable, righteous
10 high-minded, scrupulous
11 right-minded
13 conscientious

**print**
04 copy, etch, mark, snap, type
05 fount, issue, photo, stamp

06 design, run off
07 compose, engrave, impress, imprint, letters, picture, publish, replica, typeset
08 snapshot, typeface
09 footprint, lettering
10 characters, impression, lithograph, photograph, typescript
11 fingerprint
12 reproduction

▶ *Printing methods*:
05 litho
07 etching, gravure
08 intaglio
09 collotype, engraving
10 silk-screen, stenciling, stereotypy, xerography
11 die-stamping, duplicating, letterpress, lithography, rotary press
12 linoblocking
13 laser printing
14 inkjet printing, offset printing, photoengraving, screen printing
15 copper engraving

▶ *Printing terms*:
02 em, en
04 copy, font, form, kern, quad, stet, text, tint, type, typo
05 flong, proof, roman, widow
06 galley, gutter, indent, italic, margin, matrix, orphan, Ozalid
07 bromide, carding, castoff, compose, end even, leaders, leading, reprint, strip in, woodcut
08 bad break, boldface, Linotype, logotype, misprint, Monotype, offprint, take over, type spec, typeface
09 catchword, condensed, Intertype, letterset, lowercase, makeready, newsprint, overprint, sans-serif, signature, trim marks, type scale, uppercase, web offset
10 collograph, compositor, first proof, impression, large print, manuscript, ragged left, see-through, stereotype, typescript, typesetter
11 electrotype, initial caps, line printer, ragged right, running head, running text, typesetting, typographer
12 author's proof, expanded type, flatbed press, inking

roller, specimen page
13 composing room, cylinder press, justification, printing press, small capitals, wood engraving
14 relief printing, thermal printer
15 camera-ready copy

❏**in print**
09 available, published
10 obtainable
13 in circulation

**prior**
06 former
07 earlier
08 previous
09 foregoing

❏**prior to**
05 until
06 before
09 preceding
11 earlier than

**priority**
04 rank
05 order
07 the lead
09 essential, main thing, seniority, supremacy
10 first place, paramouncy, precedence, right of way
11 preeminence, requirement, superiority
12 first concern, highest place, pole position, primary issue
13 supreme matter

**priory**
05 abbey
06 friary
07 convent, nunnery
08 cloister
09 monastery

**prison**
03 can, jug, pen
04 brig, cage, cell, jail, stir
05 clink
06 cooler, inside, lockup
07 custody, dungeon, hoosgow, slammer
08 hoosegow
09 detention
10 guardhouse
11 confinement, reformatory
12 imprisonment, penitentiary

**prisoner**
03 con, POW
05 lifer
06 inmate
07 captive, convict, hostage
08 detainee, internee, jailbird, yardbird

13 prisoner of war

**prissy**
04 prim
05 fussy
06 demure, formal, proper, stuffy
07 finicky, precise, prudish, starchy
08 priggish
10 fastidious, old-maidish, particular
11 puritanical, strait-laced
13 schoolmarmish, straight-laced

**pristine**
05 first
06 former, primal, virgin
07 initial, primary
08 earliest, original, primeval
09 primitive, undefiled, unspoiled, unsullied, untouched
10 immaculate, primordial
11 primigenial, uncorrupted

**privacy**
07 retreat, secrecy
08 solitude
09 isolation, quietness, seclusion
10 retirement
11 concealment, privateness
12 independence
13 sequestration
15 confidentiality

**private**
03 PFC
05 quiet
06 hidden, remote, secret
07 soldier, special
08 in secret, intimate, isolated, personal, reserved, retiring, secluded, solitary
09 concealed, exclusive, innermost
10 classified, individual, privatized
11 enlisted man, independent, out-of-the-way, sequestered, undisturbed
12 confidential, off the record
14 denationalized, free enterprise

❏**in private**
07 sub rosa
08 in camera, secretly
12 in confidence

**private detective**
04 dick
06 shamus
07 gumshoe
10 private eye

> See also DETECTIVE

**privateer**
06 marque, pirate
07 brigand, corsair, sea wolf
09 buccaneer, sea robber
10 filibuster, freebooter
> See also PIRATE

**privation**
04 lack, loss, need, want
06 misery, penury
07 poverty
08 distress, hardship
09 indigence, suffering
11 deprivation, destitution

**privilege**
03 due
05 right, title
07 benefit, license
08 immunity, sanction
09 advantage, authority, exemption, franchise
10 birthright, concession
11 entitlement, prerogative

**privileged**
05 elite
06 exempt, immune, ruling
07 favored, private, special
08 powerful
10 advantaged, classified, restricted, sanctioned
12 confidential, off the record

**privy**
06 toilet
07 latrine
08 lavatory, outhouse

❑**privy to**
04 in on
10 apprised of
11 cognizant of
13 informed about
14 in the know about

**prize**
03 aim, pry, top
04 best, gain, goal, loot, love
05 award, booty, honor, medal, purse, stake, value
06 desire, esteem, revere, reward, spoils, stakes, trophy
07 capture, cherish, jackpot, laurels, pennant, pillage, plunder, premium, winning
08 accolade, champion, hold dear, pickings, terrific, top-notch, treasure, winnings
09 excellent, first-rate
10 appreciate
11 outstanding
12 award winning
13 think highly of
14 out of this world

15 set great store by

**prizewinner**
05 champ
06 victor
08 champion, medalist
13 lottery winner

**probability**
04 odds
07 chances
08 prospect
10 likelihood, likeliness
11 expectation, possibility

**probable**
06 likely, odds-on
08 a fair bet, feasible, possible
10 on the cards
11 anticipated, foreseeable, predictable
12 to be expected

**probably**
05 maybe
06 likely
07 perhaps
08 a fair bet, possibly
09 doubtless, like as not
10 apparently, most likely, presumably
11 as like as not, it looks like
13 as likely as not, the chances are
15 in all likelihood

**probation**
04 test
05 trial
07 testing
10 test period
11 supervision, trial period
14 apprenticeship

**probe**
04 bore, poke, prod, sift, test
05 check, drill, plumb, sound, study
06 go into, pierce, search
07 analyze, examine, explore, inquest, inquire, inquiry
08 analysis, look into, research, scrutiny
09 penetrate
10 scrutinize
11 examination, exploration, investigate
13 investigation
14 scrutinization

**probity**
05 honor, worth
06 equity, virtue
07 honesty, justice
08 fairness, fidelity, goodness, morality
09 integrity, rectitude, sincerity

11 uprightness
12 truthfulness
13 honorableness, righteousness
15 trustworthiness

**problem**
03 fix
04 hole, mess, snag
05 poser, worry
06 enigma, pickle, plight, puzzle, riddle
07 dilemma, mystery, trouble
08 quandary, question
09 conundrum, difficult, tight spot
10 delinquent, difficulty
11 brain-teaser, dire straits, predicament, troublesome
12 brain twister, complication, unmanageable
14 no-win situation

**problematic**
04 hard, moot
06 thorny, tricky
07 awkward, dubious
08 doubtful, involved, puzzling
09 debatable, difficult, enigmatic, intricate, uncertain
10 a minefield, perplexing
11 a can of worms, troublesome
12 questionable
13 problematical

**procedure**
03 way
04 move, step
05 means
06 course, custom, method, policy, scheme, system
07 conduct, formula, measure, process, routine
08 practice, strategy
09 operation, technique
11 methodology, performance
12 plan of action
13 modus operandi
14 course of action

**proceed**
04 come, flow, go on, stem
05 begin, ensue, start
06 derive, follow, move on, result, spring
07 advance, carry on, go ahead
08 continue, progress
09 go forward, take steps
11 get underway, make your way, set in motion

**proceedings**
04 case
05 deeds, moves, steps, trial

**proceeds**
06 action, annals, doings, events, report
07 account, affairs, lawsuit, matters, minutes, process, records
08 archives, business, dealings, measures
09 maneuvers
10 activities, happenings, litigation, operations, procedures
12 transactions

**proceeds**
04 gate
05 yield
06 income, profit
07 profits, returns, revenue, takings
08 earnings

**process**
03 way
04 mode, step
05 alter, means, stage, treat
06 action, change, course, growth, handle, manner, method, refine, system
07 advance, changes, convert, prepare
08 deal with, movement, practice, progress
09 evolution, formation, operation, procedure, technique, transform
10 proceeding
11 development, progression

◻**in the process of**
05 being
13 in preparation, in the course of, in the middle of

**procession**
04 file
05 march, train
06 column, parade, series
07 cortège
08 sequence
09 cavalcade, motorcade

**proclaim**
06 affirm, blazon, notify
07 declare, give out, profess, publish, testify, trumpet
08 announce, indicate
09 advertise, broadcast, circulate, make known, pronounce, publicize

**proclamation**
05 edict, order
06 decree, notice
07 command
09 broadcast, manifesto
11 declaration, publication
12 announcement

13 advertisement, pronouncement

**proclivity**
04 bent, bias
07 leaning
08 penchant, tendency, weakness
10 propensity
11 disposition, inclination
12 predilection
14 predisposition

**procrastinate**
05 dally, defer, delay, stall
06 put off, retard
08 postpone, protract
09 temporize
10 dilly-dally, filibuster
11 play for time
12 drag your feet

**procrastination**
08 deferral, delaying, stalling
11 temporizing
13 dilly-dallying
15 delaying tactics

**procreate**
04 sire
05 beget, breed, spawn
06 father, mother
07 produce
08 conceive, engender, generate, multiply
09 propagate, reproduce

**procure**
03 buy, get, win
04 earn, find, gain
06 come by, hustle, obtain, pick up, secure
07 acquire, solicit
08 purchase
09 get hold of, importune
10 lay hands on
11 appropriate, requisition

**procurer**
04 bawd, pimp
05 madam
06 pander
08 panderer

**prod**
03 dig, jab
04 butt, goad, move, poke, push, spur, stir, urge
05 egg on, elbow, nudge, shove
06 incite, prompt, thrust
08 motivate, reminder, stimulus
09 encourage, prompting, stimulate

**prodigal**
06 lavish, wanton, waster
07 copious, profuse, wastrel
08 generous, reckless, wasteful

09 bounteous, bountiful, excessive, exuberant, luxuriant, sumptuous, unsparing, unthrifty
10 big spender, immoderate, profligate, squanderer
11 extravagant, improvident, spendthrift

**prodigality**
06 excess, plenty
09 abundance, profusion
10 exuberance, lavishness, luxuriance, profligacy, wantonness
11 copiousness, dissipation, squandering
12 extravagance, immoderation, intemperance, recklessness, wastefulness

**prodigious**
04 huge, vast
05 giant
07 amazing, immense, mammoth, massive
08 colossal, enormous, gigantic, striking
09 wonderful
10 astounding, inordinate, phenomenal, remarkable, stupendous, tremendous
11 exceptional, spectacular
13 extraordinary

**prodigy**
06 genius, marvel, rarity, wonder
07 whiz kid
08 virtuoso
09 curiosity, sensation
10 mastermind, phenomenon, Wunderkind
11 wonder child
12 child prodigy

**produce**
04 bear, crop, eggs, food, give, grow, make, show
05 breed, cause, evoke, mount, offer, put on, stage, yield
06 create, direct, effect, invent, manage, output, supply
07 advance, develop, exhibit, fashion, furnish, harvest, perform, prepare, present, proffer, provide, provoke
08 assemble, bring out, generate, occasion, organize, products, result in
09 construct, fabricate, originate

**producer**
10 bring about, bring forth, come up with, foodstuffs, give rise to, put forward
11 demonstrate, manufacture, put together
12 bring forward

**producer**
06 farmer, grower
10 impresario
12 manufacturer

**product**
05 goods, wares, yield
06 effect, output, result, upshot
07 article, outcome, spinoff
08 artefact, creation, offshoot
09 commodity, invention
11 consequence, merchandise

**production**
04 film, play, show
05 movie, opera, yield
06 ballet, fruits, making, output
07 harvest, musical, returns
08 building, creation
09 formation
11 fabrication, manufacture, performance
12 presentation, productivity
13 manufacturing

**productive**
06 fecund
07 fertile
08 creative, fruitful, prolific
09 inventive
12 fructiferous, high yielding

**productivity**
05 yield
06 output
08 capacity, work rate
10 efficiency, production
14 productiveness

**profane**
04 foul
05 abuse, crude
06 debase, defile, unholy, vulgar
07 godless, impious, secular, ungodly, worldly
08 temporal
09 desecrate
10 idolatrous, irreverent
11 blasphemous, irreligious
12 sacrilegious, unsanctified
13 unconsecrated

**profanity**
05 abuse, curse
07 cursing, impiety
08 swearing
09 blasphemy, expletive, obscenity, sacrilege, swearword
11 imprecation, irreverence

14 four-letter word

**profess**
03 own
04 aver, avow
05 admit, claim, state
06 affirm, allege, assert
07 declare, make out, pretend
08 announce, maintain, proclaim
09 dissemble
10 lay claim to
11 acknowledge

**professed**
06 avowed
08 declared, so-called
09 pretended, purported, soi-disant
10 ostensible, self-styled

**profession**
03 job
04 line, post
05 claim, craft, trade
06 avowal, career, métier, office
07 calling
08 business, position
09 situation, statement, testimony
10 employment, line of work, occupation, walk of life

**professional**
03 ace, pro
06 expert, master, wizard
07 trained
08 educated, licensed
09 practiced, qualified
10 specialist

**proffer**
04 hand
05 offer
06 extend, submit, tender
07 hold out, present, propose

**proficiency**
05 knack, skill
06 talent
07 ability, mastery
08 aptitude
09 adeptness, dexterity, expertise
10 capability, competence
11 skilfulness
12 skillfulness

**proficient**
04 able
05 adept
06 clever, expert, gifted
07 capable, skilful, skilled, trained
08 masterly, skillful, talented
09 competent, effective, efficient, qualified

11 experienced
12 accomplished

**profile**
02 CV
07 contour, outline
08 portrait, side view, vignette
09 biography
10 silhouette
15 curriculum vitae, thumbnail sketch

**profit**
04 gain
05 avail, value, worth, yield
06 return
07 rake-off, revenue
08 dividend, earnings, proceeds, winnings
09 advantage, make money
10 bottom line
15 line your pockets

❑**profit by, profit from**
07 exploit
08 cash in on
12 capitalize on
15 take advantage of, turn to advantage

**profitable**
07 gainful
08 economic, fruitful, valuable
09 lucrative, rewarding
10 beneficial, in the black, productive
11 moneymaking

**profiteer**
06 extort, fleece
07 exploit, scalper
09 exploiter, racketeer
10 overcharge
12 extortionist
13 make a fast buck

**profiteering**
08 scalping
09 extortion
12 exploitation, racketeering

**profitless**
06 futile
08 gainless
09 fruitless, thankless
12 unproductive, unprofitable

**profligacy**
05 waste
06 excess
10 debauchery, lavishness, wantonness
11 dissipation, prodigality, promiscuity, squandering
12 extravagance, improvidence, recklessness, wastefulness
13 dissoluteness

## profligate
04 rake, roué
06 wanton, waster
07 wastrel
08 prodigal, reckless, wasteful
09 debauched, debauchee, dissolute, excessive
10 dissipated, immoderate, squanderer
11 extravagant, improvident, promiscuous, spendthrift

## profound
04 deep, wise
07 extreme, intense, learned, serious, weighty
08 abstruse, esoteric, thorough
09 heartfelt
10 discerning, thoughtful
11 far-reaching, penetrating
13 philosophical, thoroughgoing

## profoundly
06 deeply, keenly
07 acutely, greatly
08 heartily
09 extremely, intensely
10 thoroughly

## profundity
05 depth
06 acumen, wisdom
08 learning, severity
09 extremity, intensity
11 penetration
12 abstruseness

## profuse
06 lavish
07 copious, fulsome, liberal
08 abundant, generous
09 excessive, luxuriant, plentiful
11 extravagant, overflowing
12 overabundant
13 superabundant

## profusion
04 glut, lots, riot, tons
05 heaps, loads
06 excess, plenty, wealth
08 plethora
09 abundance, plenitude
11 copiousness, superfluity
14 superabundance

## progenitor
06 father, mother, parent, source
08 ancestor, begetter, forebear
10 forefather, forerunner, originator, procreator
12 primogenitor

## progeny
04 race, seed
05 breed, issue, stock, young
06 family, scions
08 children
09 offspring, posterity
11 descendants

## prognosis
07 outlook
08 forecast, prospect
10 prediction, projection
11 expectation
15 prognostication

## prognosticate
05 augur
06 divine, herald
07 betoken, portend, predict, presage
08 forecast, foretell, indicate, prophesy, soothsay
09 harbinger
10 foreshadow

## prognostication
07 surmise
08 forecast, prophecy
09 horoscope, prognosis
10 prediction, projection

## program
04 book, list, plan, show
05 lay on
06 agenda, design, line up, lineup, map out, scheme
07 arrange, episode, itemize, listing, project, work out
08 calendar, playbill, schedule, syllabus
09 broadcast, formulate, simulcast, timetable
10 curriculum, prearrange, production, prospectus
11 performance
12 plan of action

## progress
03 way
04 go on, grow
05 going
06 better, come on, growth, mature
07 advance, blossom, develop, headway, improve, journey, passage, proceed, prosper, recover, shape up
08 continue, flourish, increase, movement
09 evolution, go forward, promotion, upgrading
10 betterment, forge ahead
11 advancement, development, improvement, make headway, make strides, make your way, move forward, progression
12 breakthrough, make progress

## ❏in progress
07 going on
08 underway
09 happening, occurring
10 continuing, proceeding
11 not finished, on the stocks
12 not completed
13 in the pipeline

## progression
05 chain, cycle, order, train
06 course, series, stream, string
07 advance, headway, passage
08 progress, sequence
09 promotion
10 succession
11 advancement, development

## progressive
06 modern
07 dynamic, go-ahead, growing, liberal, radical
08 advanced
09 advancing, reformist
10 avant-garde, continuing, developing, escalating, increasing, innovative
11 enlightened, up-and-coming
12 accelerating, enterprising, intensifying
13 revolutionary
14 forward-looking
15 forward-thinking

## prohibit
03 ban, bar
04 stop, veto
06 forbid, hamper, hinder, impede, outlaw
07 exclude, prevent, rule out
08 obstruct, preclude, restrict
09 interdict, proscribe

## prohibited
05 taboo
06 banned, barred, vetoed
08 verboten
09 embargoed, forbidden
10 disallowed, proscribed
11 interdicted

## prohibition
03 ban, bar
04 veto
07 embargo
08 negation
09 exclusion, forbiddal, interdict
10 alcohol ban, constraint, forbidding, injunction, prevention
11 forbiddance, obstruction
12 interdiction, proscription

## prohibitionist
03 dry
10 teetotaler

**prohibitive**
09 excessive
10 exorbitant
12 extortionate, preposterous, proscriptive

**project**
03 job
04 cast, hurl, idea, plan, task, work
05 bulge, fling, gauge, throw
06 design, expect, extend, jut out, launch, map out, propel, reckon, scheme
07 obtrude, predict, program, propose, venture
08 activity, campaign, contract, estimate, forecast, overhang, proposal, protrude, stand out, stick out
09 calculate, discharge
10 assignment, conception, enterprise, occupation
11 extrapolate, undertaking
12 predetermine

**projectile**
04 ball, shot
05 shell
06 bullet, rocket
07 grenade, missile
10 mortar bomb

**projecting**
08 beetling
09 exsertile, extrusive
10 protrudent, protruding, protrusive
11 overhanging

**projection**
04 plan, sill
05 bulge, ledge, ridge, shelf
07 jutting
08 estimate, forecast, overhang
10 estimation, prediction
11 expectation
12 protuberance

**proletariat**
04 herd
05 plebs
06 masses, proles, rabble
08 canaille, riffraff
09 commoners, hoi polloi
10 commonalty
12 common people, lower classes, working class
13 great unwashed

**proliferate**
05 breed
06 expand, extend, spread, thrive
07 build up, burgeon
08 escalate, increase, multiply, mushroom

**proliferation**
06 spread
07 buildup
08 increase
09 expansion, extension
11 mushrooming
14 multiplication

**prolific**
06 fecund
07 copious, fertile, profuse
08 abundant, fruitful
09 luxuriant
10 productive

**prolix**
05 prosy, wordy
07 lengthy, verbose
08 rambling, tiresome
10 digressive, discursive, long-winded, pleonastic

**prolixity**
08 pleonasm, rambling, verbiage
09 verbosity, wordiness
11 verboseness
14 discursiveness, long-windedness

**prologue**
05 proem
07 preface, prelude
08 exordium, foreword, preamble
11 preliminary, prolegomena
12 introduction

**prolong**
06 extend
07 drag out, draw out, spin out, stretch
08 continue, elongate, lengthen, protract

**promenade**
04 prom, turn, walk
06 airing, parade, stroll
07 saunter, swagger, walkway
09 boulevard, esplanade
11 perambulate
14 constitutional

**prominence**
04 fame, lump, note, rank
05 bulge, mound
06 height, renown
08 eminence, headland, prestige, standing, swelling
09 celebrity
10 importance, projection, promontory, reputation
11 distinction, preeminence
12 protuberance
15 illustriousness

**prominent**
06 famous

07 bulging, eminent, jutting, leading, notable, obvious, popular
08 foremost, renowned, striking
09 acclaimed, important, obtrusive, respected, well-known
10 celebrated, jutting out, noticeable, preeminent, projecting, protruding, protrusive
11 conspicuous, eye-catching, illustrious, outstanding, protuberant, standing out, sticking out
12 unmistakable
13 distinguished

**promiscuity**
09 depravity, looseness
10 debauchery, immorality, profligacy, wantonness
14 licentiousness

**promiscuous**
04 fast
05 loose
06 casual, random, wanton
07 immoral
09 debauched, dissolute
10 licentious, profligate
12 of easy virtue
14 indiscriminate

**promise**
03 vow
04 bond, hint, oath, sign, word
05 augur, flair, swear, vouch
06 assure, denote, hint at, pledge, talent
07 ability, betoken, compact, presage, signify, suggest, warrant
08 aptitude, contract, covenant, evidence, indicate
09 assurance, be a sign of, guarantee, potential, undertake
10 capability, commitment, engagement, indication, suggestion, take an oath
11 undertaking, word of honor
12 give your word

**promised land**
04 Sion, Zion
06 Canaan
07 America
08 paradise
09 Shangri-la
➤ See also HEAVEN

**promising**
04 able, rosy
06 bright, gifted
07 budding, hopeful

**promontory**

09 favorable
10 auspicious, optimistic, propitious

**promontory**

04 cape, head, ness, spur
05 bluff, cliff, point, ridge
08 foreland, headland
09 peninsula, precipice
10 projection, prominence

**promote**

03 aid
04 back, help, hype, plug, push, sell, urge
05 boost, exalt, honor, raise
06 assist, foster, market, move up, prefer, puff up
07 advance, elevate, endorse, espouse, forward, further, nurture, sponsor, support, upgrade
08 advocate, champion
09 advertise, encourage, publicize, recommend, stimulate
10 aggrandize, popularize
12 contribute to

**promotion**

02 PR
04 hype, rise
06 move-up, urging
07 backing, pushing, support
08 advocacy, boosting, campaign, espousal, plugging
09 elevation, fostering, marketing, publicity, upgrading
10 exaltation, preferment, propaganda
11 advancement, advertising, development, furtherance
12 contribution
13 encouragement
14 aggrandizement, recommendation
15 public relations

**prompt**

03 cue
04 lead, prod, spur, urge
05 cause, quick, rapid, sharp, swift
06 elicit, incite, induce, on time, remind, speedy, timely
07 inspire, produce, provoke
08 motivate, on the dot, punctual, reminder, result in, stimulus
09 call forth, encourage, instigate, stimulate
10 give rise to, punctually
11 expeditious, to the minute

13 encouragement

**prompting**

04 hint
06 advice, urging
07 jogging, pushing
08 prodding, reminder
10 incitement, persuasion

**promptly**

03 pdq
04 ASAP
05 sharp
06 on time, pronto
07 quickly, swiftly
08 speedily
09 forthwith, posthaste
10 punctually
15 pretty damn quick

**promptness**

05 haste, speed
08 alacrity, dispatch
09 alertness, briskness, eagerness, quickness, readiness, swiftness
10 expedition
11 promptitude, punctuality, willingness

**promulgate**

05 issue
06 decree, notify, spread
07 declare, promote, publish, release
08 announce, proclaim
09 advertise, broadcast, circulate, publicize
11 communicate, disseminate

**promulgation**

11 news release, publication, publicizing
12 announcement, proclamation, promulgating
13 dissemination

**prone**

03 apt
04 bent, flat
05 given
06 liable, likely
07 subject
08 disposed, inclined
09 prostrate, recumbent
10 full-length, horizontal, procumbent, vulnerable
11 predisposed, susceptible

**proneness**

07 aptness, leaning
08 penchant, tendency
09 liability
10 proclivity, propensity
11 disposition, inclination
14 susceptibility

**prong**

04 fork, spur, tine
05 point, spike
10 projection

**pronounce**

03 say
05 judge, speak, utter, voice
06 affirm, assert, decree, stress
07 declare, express
08 announce, proclaim, vocalize
09 enunciate
10 articulate

**pronounceable**

07 sayable
09 speakable, utterable
10 enunciable

**pronounced**

05 broad, clear, thick
06 marked, strong
07 decided, evident, obvious
08 definite, distinct, positive, striking
10 noticeable
11 conspicuous

**pronouncement**

05 edict
06 decree, dictum
08 judgment
09 assertion, ipse dixit, statement
11 declaration
12 announcement, proclamation

**pronunciation**

06 accent, speech, stress
07 diction, voicing
08 delivery, uttering
09 elocution
10 inflection, intonation, modulation
11 enunciation
12 articulation, vocalization

**proof**

08 evidence
09 repellent, resistant
10 impervious, validation
11 attestation
12 confirmation, verification
13 certification, corroboration, demonstration, documentation
14 authentication, substantiation

**prop**

03 set
04 lean, post, rest, stay
05 brace, shaft, shore, stand, stick, strut, truss

06 anchor, column, hold up, pillar, steady, uphold
07 balance, bolster, shore up, support, sustain, upright
08 buttress, mainstay, maintain, underpin
09 bolster up, propeller, stanchion, supporter
13 stage property

**propaganda**
04 hype, spin
09 promotion, publicity
11 advertising, information
14 disinformation, indoctrination

**propagandist**
07 plugger
08 advocate, promoter
09 proponent, publicist
10 spin doctor
11 pamphleteer
12 proselytizer

**propagate**
04 grow
05 beget, breed, spawn
06 spread
07 diffuse, produce, promote, publish
08 generate, increase, multiply, proclaim, transmit
09 broadcast, circulate, procreate, publicize, reproduce
10 distribute, promulgate
11 communicate, disseminate, proliferate

**propagation**
06 spread
08 breeding, increase, spawning
09 diffusion, promotion, spreading
10 generation
11 circulation, procreation
12 distribution, promulgation, reproduction, transmission
13 dissemination, proliferation
14 multiplication

**propel**
04 move, push, send
05 drive, force, impel, shoot, shove
06 launch, thrust
11 push forward

**propensity**
04 bent, bias
06 foible
07 aptness, leaning
08 penchant, tendency, weakness
09 liability, proneness, readiness

10 proclivity
11 disposition, inclination
14 predisposition, susceptibility

**proper**
04 prim, real, true
05 exact, right
06 actual, decent, formal, polite, strict
07 correct, fitting, genteel, genuine, precise, prudish, refined
08 accepted, accurate, ladylike, orthodox, suitable
10 acceptable
11 appropriate, established, gentlemanly, respectable
12 conventional

**property**
04 gear, land, mark
05 acres, goods, house, means, quirk, trait
06 assets, estate, houses, riches, wealth
07 capital, effects, feature, holding, quality
08 chattels, holdings, premises
09 attribute, buildings, resources
10 belongings, real estate
11 peculiarity, possessions
12 idiosyncrasy
13 paraphernalia
14 characteristic, stage furniture

**prophecy**
06 augury
08 forecast
09 prognosis
10 divination, prediction
11 second sight, soothsaying
14 fortunetelling
15 prognostication

**prophesy**
05 augur
07 foresee, predict
08 forecast, foretell, forewarn
13 prognosticate

**prophet**
04 seer
06 oracle
10 forecaster, foreteller, soothsayer
11 clairvoyant
13 fortuneteller
14 prognosticator

❑**prophet of doom**
08 alarmist, Jeremiah
09 Cassandra, pessimist

**prophetic**
05 vatic
06 mantic

07 augural
08 oracular
09 fatidical, presaging, prescient, sibylline, vaticidal
10 divinatory, predictive, prognostic
11 forecasting
13 foreshadowing

**prophylactic**
10 preventive, protective
12 preventative

**propinquity**
03 tie
08 nearness
09 closeness, proximity
10 connection, contiguity
11 affiliation

**propitiate**
07 appease, mollify, placate, satisfy

**propitiation**
09 placation
11 appeasement
13 mollification

**propitiatory**
09 appeasing, assuaging, pacifying, placatory
10 mollifying

**propitious**
05 happy, lucky
06 benign, bright, kindly, timely
08 friendly, gracious
09 favorable, fortunate, opportune, promising
10 auspicious, beneficial, benevolent, prosperous, reassuring
11 encouraging
12 advantageous, well-disposed

**proponent**
06 backer, friend, patron
08 advocate, champion, defender, exponent, partisan, proposer, upholder
09 apologist, supporter
10 enthusiast, propounder, subscriber, vindicator

**proportion**
03 cut
04 bulk, mass, part, size
05 depth, quota, ratio, scale, share, split, whack, width
06 amount, extent, height, length, volume
07 balance, breadth, measure, portion, segment
08 capacity, division, fraction, quotient, symmetry
09 magnitude

**proportional**

10 dimensions, percentage
12 distribution, measurements, relationship
14 correspondence, slice of the cake

**proportional**

04 even
08 relative
09 analogous, equitable
10 comparable, consistent, equivalent
12 commensurate
13 corresponding, proportionate

**proportionally**

06 evenly
07 pro rata
10 comparably, relatively
14 commensurately
15 correspondingly, proportionately

**proposal**

03 bid
04 plan
05 offer, terms
06 design, motion, scheme, tender
07 program, project
09 manifesto
10 suggestion
11 proposition
12 presentation
14 recommendation

**propose**

03 aim
04 mean, move, name, plan
05 offer, put up
06 design, intend, submit, tender
07 advance, bring up, present, proffer, purpose, suggest
08 advocate, nominate, propound
09 introduce, recommend
10 have in mind, put forward
14 pop the question
15 plight your troth

**proposition**

04 pass, plan, task
06 accost, motion, scheme, tender, theory
07 advance, program, project, solicit, theorem, venture
08 activity, approach, overture, proposal
09 manifesto
10 suggestion
11 make a pass at, undertaking
14 recommendation

**propound**

07 advance, contend, lay down, present, propose, suggest
08 advocate, set forth
09 postulate
10 put forward

**proprietor, proprietress**

05 owner
08 landlady, landlord
09 landowner, possessor
10 deed holder, freeholder
11 leaseholder, titleholder

**propriety**

06 nicety
07 decency, decorum, fitness, manners, modesty, p's and q's
08 breeding, civility, courtesy, delicacy, protocol, standard
09 etiquette, punctilio, rectitude, rightness
10 convention, politeness, refinement, seemliness
11 correctness, good manners
12 becomingness, ladylikeness, suitableness, the done thing
14 respectability
15 appropriateness, gentlemanliness

**propulsion**

04 push
06 thrust
07 impetus, impulse
09 impulsion

**prosaic**

04 dull, flat, tame
05 banal, bland, stale, trite
06 boring
07 humdrum, mundane
08 everyday, ordinary
10 monotonous, pedestrian, uninspired
11 commonplace
12 matter-of-fact
13 unimaginative

**proscribe**

03 ban, bar
04 damn, doom
05 black, exile, expel
06 banish, deport, forbid, outlaw, reject
07 boycott, censure, condemn, embargo, exclude
08 denounce, disallow, prohibit
09 blackball, interdict, ostracize
10 expatriate
13 excommunicate

**proscription**

03 ban, bar
05 exile

07 barring, boycott, censure, damning, embargo
08 ejection, eviction, outlawry
09 exclusion, expulsion, interdict, ostracism, rejection
10 banishment
11 deportation, prohibition
12 condemnation, denunciation, expatriation
15 excommunication

**prosecute**

03 sue, try
06 accuse, charge, indict, summon
07 arraign
08 litigate
10 put on trial
11 take to court
12 bring charges
13 prefer charges

**proselytize**

07 convert, win over
08 persuade
10 bring to God, evangelize
12 make converts

**prosody**

► *Forms of prosody:*

04 foot, iamb
05 canto, envoy, epode, Ionic, meter, paeon
06 cesura, dactyl, rondel, sonnet
07 anapest, ballade, caesura, couplet, elision, pyrrhic, rondeau, Sapphic, spondee, strophe, triolet, trochee, virelay
08 anapaest, choriamb, cinquain, eye rhyme, Pindaric, quatrain, tribrach, trimeter
09 anacrusis, assonance, catalexis, dispondee, ditrochee, free verse, hexameter, macaronic, monometer, monorhyme
10 amphibrach, amphimacer, blank verse, enjambment, galliambic, heptameter, pentameter, rhyme royal, tetrameter, villanelle
11 Alcaic verse, alexandrine, broken rhyme, linked verse, long-measure
12 alliteration, Leonine rhyme, Pythian verse, sprung rhythm
13 abstract verse, heroic couplet, hypermetrical
15 poulters' measure

**prospect**

04 hope, nose, odds, seek, view

05 quest, scene, vista
06 aspect, chance, future, search, survey
07 chances, examine, explore, fossick, inspect, look for, opening, outlook, promise
08 likeness, panorama
09 landscape, spectacle
10 likelihood
11 expectation, perspective, possibility, probability
12 anticipation

**prospective**
04 to-be
06 coming, future, likely
07 awaited, would-be
08 aspiring, destined, expected, hoped-for, imminent, intended, possible, probable
09 designate, potential
11 anticipated, approaching, forthcoming

**prospectus**
04 list, plan
06 scheme
07 catalog, leaflet, outline, program
08 brochure, pamphlet, syllabus, synopsis
09 catalogue, manifesto
10 conspectus, literature

**prosper**
06 do well, flower, thrive
07 advance, burgeon
08 flourish, get ahead, grow rich
09 get on well
14 go up in the world
15 get on in the world

**prosperity**
06 plenty, riches, wealth
07 fortune, success
09 affluence, well-being
11 good fortune, lap of luxury, the good life

**prosperous**
04 rich
07 opulent, wealthy, well-off
08 affluent, thriving, well-to-do
09 well-fixed
10 burgeoning, well-heeled
11 flourishing, rolling in it

**prostitute**
03 pro
04 bawd, drab, moll, tart
05 whore
06 debase, floosy, floozy, harlot, hooker
07 degrade, floosie, floozie, hustler, trollop
08 call girl, strumpet
09 courtesan

10 loose woman
11 fallen woman, fille de joie
12 camp follower, streetwalker

**prostitution**
07 the game, whoring
08 harlotry, whoredom
10 debasement
12 white slavery
13 streetwalking

**prostrate**
04 flat, ruin, tire
05 prone
06 fallen, lay low
07 exhaust, laid low, wear out
09 knock down, lying down, lying flat, paralyzed
10 devastated, horizontal

◻**prostrate yourself**
05 kneel
06 cringe, grovel, kowtow, submit
07 bow down
13 abase yourself

**prostration**
03 bow
05 grief
06 kowtow
07 despair
08 collapse, kneeling, weakness
09 abasement, dejection, obeisance, paralysis, weariness
10 depression, desolation, exhaustion, submission
11 despondency
12 genuflection, helplessness

**protagonist**
04 hero, lead
06 banker, leader
07 heroine
08 adherent, advocate, champion, exponent, mainstay
09 principal, proponent, spokesman, supporter, title role
10 prime mover
11 spokeswoman
12 moving spirit, spokesperson
13 main character
14 chief character, standard-bearer

**protean**
06 amebic
07 amoebic, mutable
08 variable, volatile
09 many-sided, mercurial, multiform, versatile
10 changeable, inconstant
11 polymorphic

12 ever-changing, polymorphous

**protect**
04 keep, save
05 cover, guard
06 defend, escort, harbor, screen, secure, shield
07 care for, shelter
08 conserve, keep safe, preserve
09 look after, safeguard, watch over
10 take care of

**protection**
04 care
05 armor, cover, guard
06 buffer, charge, refuge, safety, screen, shield
07 barrier, bulwark, custody, defense, shelter
08 security
09 insurance, safeguard
11 safekeeping
12 conservation, guardianship, preservation

**protective**
04 wary
08 covering, vigilant, watchful
09 defensive, fireproof, shielding
10 insulating, waterproof

**protector**
06 minder, patron
08 defender, guardian
09 bodyguard, safeguard

**protégé, protégée**
04 ward
05 pupil
06 charge
07 student
09 dependent, discovery
13 fair-haired boy

**protein**

► *Types of protein*:
04 zein
05 abrin, actin, opsin, renin
06 avidin, casein, enzyme, fibrin, globin, myosin
07 albumen, albumin, elastin, fibroin, gliadin, histone, hordein, keratin, legumin, sericin, tubulin
08 aleurone, amandine, collagen, creatine, cytokine, globulin, glutelin, prolamin, proteose, vitellin
09 fibrillin, prolamine, protamine, sclerotin
10 conchiolin, dystrophin, interferon

11 interleukin, lipoprotein, transferrin
12 immunoglobin

**protest**
04 avow, demo, fuss, riot
05 argue, demur, gripe, march, whine
06 affirm, appeal, assert, attest, avowal, insist, object, oppose, outcry, reject
07 boycott, contend, declare, dissent, profess
08 announce, complain, demurral, disagree, proclaim, speak out
09 assertion, complaint, exception, objection, take issue
10 contention, disapprove, opposition
11 affirmation, declaration, demonstrate, kick up a fuss, remonstrate
12 proclamation, protestation
13 demonstration, remonstration, take exception

**protestation**
03 vow
04 oath
06 avowal, outcry, pledge
07 dissent, protest
09 assurance, complaint, objection, statement
10 profession
11 affirmation, declaration
12 asseveration, remonstrance
13 expostulation, remonstration

**protester**
05 rebel
07 opposer, striker
08 agitator, objector, opponent
09 dissenter, dissident
10 complainer
12 demonstrator

**protocol**
06 custom
07 manners, p's and q's
09 etiquette, propriety
10 civilities, convention
11 formalities
14 code of behavior

**prototype**
04 type
05 model
06 mockup
07 example, pattern
08 exemplar, original, paradigm, standard
09 archetype, precedent

**protract**
06 extend
07 drag out, draw out, prolong, spin out, sustain
08 continue, lengthen
09 keep going
10 make longer, stretch out

**protracted**
04 long
07 lengthy
08 drawn out, extended
09 prolonged
12 long-drawn-out

**protrude**
05 bulge
06 beetle, extend, jut out
07 obtrude, poke out, project
08 stand out, stick out

**protruding**
05 proud
07 jutting
09 extrusive, prominent
11 protuberant

**protrusion**
03 jut
04 bump, knob, lump
05 bulge
08 swelling
09 obtrusion, outgrowth
10 projection
12 protuberance

**protuberance**
04 bulb, bump, knob, lump, wart, welt
05 bulge, tuber, tumor
08 swelling, tubercle
09 apophysis, outgrowth
10 protrusion
11 excrescence

**protuberant**
05 proud
07 bulbous, bulging, jutting, popping
08 beetling, swelling
09 prominent
10 protrudent, protruding, protrusive

**proud**
04 glad, smug, vain
05 cocky, grand
07 haughty, pompous, stuck-up
08 arrogant, boastful, jumped-up, puffed up, snobbish, splendid, thrilled
09 big headed, conceited, dignified, gratified, hubristic, imperious, red-letter, wonderful
10 highhanded

11 egotistical, outstanding, overbearing, overweening
12 presumptuous, supercilious
13 high and mighty, self-important
14 full of yourself

**provable**
10 attestable, verifiable
11 confirmable
12 demonstrable

**prove**
04 show, test
06 attest, pan out, try out, verify
07 bear out, confirm, justify, turn out
08 validate
09 ascertain, determine, establish, transpire
11 demonstrate
12 authenticate, substantiate
13 bear witness to

**proven**
08 accepted, attested, verified
09 confirmed, undoubted
11 established

**provenance**
04 root
06 origin, source
10 birthplace, derivation

**provender**
04 fare, food
06 fodder, forage
07 edibles, rations
08 eatables, supplies, victuals
10 foodstuffs, provisions
11 comestibles

**proverb**
03 saw
05 adage, gnome, maxim
06 byword, dictum, saying
07 precept
08 aphorism, apothegm
10 apophthegm

**proverbial**
06 famous
07 typical
08 accepted, renowned
09 axiomatic, customary, legendary
10 archetypal

**provide**
04 give, lend
05 bring, cater, serve, yield
06 afford, impart, supply
07 furnish, present
09 take steps
10 arrange for, contribute, prepare for
11 accommodate

**provided**

12 make plans for, take measures
13 make provision

❏**provide for**
04 fend, keep
05 endow
07 support, sustain
08 maintain

**provided**
05 given
08 as long as, so long as
11 on condition
14 with the proviso

**providence**
04 fate, luck
06 thrift, wisdom
07 destiny, economy, fortune
08 God's will, judgment, prudence
09 foresight
11 forethought

**provident**
07 careful, prudent, thrifty
10 economical, farsighted

**providential**
05 happy, lucky
06 timely
07 welcome
09 fortunate, opportune
10 fortuitous, heaven-sent

**provider**
05 angel, donor, giver
06 earner, funder, source
08 supplier
10 benefactor, wage earner
11 breadwinner

**providing**
05 given
08 as long as, provided
11 on condition
14 with the proviso

**province**
04 area, duty, line, role, zone
05 field, state
06 charge, colony, county, domain, office, pigeon, region, sphere
07 concern
08 business, district, dominion, function
09 territory
10 department, dependency
14 responsibility

► *Names of Canadian provinces and territories*:
05 Yukon
06 Quebec
07 Alberta, Nunavut, Ontario
08 Labrador, Manitoba

10 Nova Scotia
12 New Brunswick, Newfoundland, Saskatchewan
14 Yukon Territory
15 British Columbia
18 Prince Edward Island
20 Northwest Territories
23 Newfoundland and Labrador
➤ See also BOROUGH; COUNTY; STATE

**provincial**
04 hick
06 narrow, rustic
07 country, insular, limited
08 outlying, regional
09 homegrown, parochial, small-town
10 intolerant
12 narrow-minded
15 unsophisticated

**provincialism**
12 parochialism
13 provinciality

**provision**
04 food, plan, step, term
06 stocks, stores, supply
07 measure, proviso, rations
08 eatables, services, supplies
09 allowance, condition, foodstuff, groceries
10 facilities, precaution, sustenance
11 arrangement, preparation, requirement, stipulation
13 qualification, specification

**provisional**
06 pro tem
07 interim, stopgap
09 makeshift, temporary, tentative
11 conditional
12 transitional

**provisionally**
06 pro tem
07 interim
09 meanwhile
15 for the time being

**proviso**
06 clause
07 strings
09 condition, provision
10 limitation
11 requirement, stipulation
13 qualification

**provocation**
04 dare
05 cause, taunt
06 injury, insult, motive, reason
07 affront, grounds, offense

08 stimulus
10 generation, incitement, inducement, motivation
11 aggravation, inspiration, instigation, stimulation

**provocative**
04 sexy
06 erotic
07 galling, teasing
08 alluring, annoying, arousing, exciting, inviting, tempting
09 insulting, offensive, seductive
10 irritating, suggestive
11 aggravating, stimulating, tantalizing, titillating

**provoke**
04 goad, move, prod, rile, spur, stir
05 anger, annoy, cause, egg on, evoke, pique, rouse, taunt, tease
06 elicit, excite, harass, hassle, incite, induce, insult, madden, needle, nettle, prompt, wind up
07 incense, inflame, inspire, produce, promote
08 engender, generate, motivate
09 aggravate, call forth, instigate, stimulate
10 exasperate, give rise to

**provoking**
06 irking, vexing
07 galling, irksome
11 aggravating

**prow**
03 bow
04 fore, head, nose, stem
05 front

**prowess**
05 skill
06 genius, talent
07 ability, command, mastery
08 aptitude, facility
09 adeptness, dexterity, expertise
11 proficiency
12 skillfulness

**prowl**
04 hunt, lurk, nose, roam, rove
05 creep, skulk, slink, sneak
06 cruise, patrol, search
14 move stealthily

**proximity**
08 nearness, vicinity
09 adjacency, closeness
10 contiguity
11 propinquity

**proxy**
05 agent
06 deputy, factor
07 stand-in
08 attorney, delegate
09 surrogate
10 substitute
14 representative

**prude**
04 prig
07 old maid, puritan
09 Mrs. Grundy, Victorian
10 schoolmarm

**prudence**
06 thrift, wisdom
07 caution, economy
09 canniness, foresight, frugality, good sense, husbandry
11 common sense, forethought
13 judiciousness

**prudent**
04 wise
06 frugal
07 careful, politic, thrifty
08 cautious, discreet, sensible
10 economical

**prudery**
08 primness
09 Grundyism
10 prissiness, puritanism
11 overmodesty
12 priggishness, Victorianism

**prudish**
04 prim
06 prissy
08 overnice, priggish
09 Victorian
10 old-maidish, overmodest
11 puritanical, strait-laced
13 schoolmarmish, straight-laced

**prune**
03 cut, lop
04 clip, dock, pare, snip, trim
05 shape
07 shorten

**prurient**
04 lewd
06 erotic, smutty
07 obscene
08 desirous, indecent
09 salacious
12 concupiscent, pornographic

**pry**
03 dig
04 lift, move, nose, peep, peer
05 delve, force, hoist, jimmy, lever, prize, snoop
06 ferret, meddle
07 intrude
08 dislodge
09 interfere
14 poke your nose in
15 stick your nose in

**prying**
04 nosy
08 meddling, snooping
09 intrusive
10 meddlesome
11 inquisitive, interfering

**psalm**
04 hymn, pean, poem, song
05 chant, paean
06 prayer
08 canticle

**pseud**
05 fraud, phony, poser
06 poseur

**pseudo**
04 fake, mock, sham
05 bogus, false, phony, pseud, quasi-
06 ersatz
08 spurious
09 imitation, pretended
10 artificial

**pseudonym**
05 alias
06 anonym
07 allonym, pen name
09 false name, incognito, stage name
10 nom de plume
11 assumed name

**psyche**
04 mind, self, soul
05 anima
06 pneuma, spirit
09 awareness, intellect
12 subconscious
13 consciousness, heart of hearts

**psychiatrist**
06 shrink
07 analyst
09 therapist
10 head doctor
12 headshrinker, psychologist
13 psychoanalyst
15 psychotherapist

**psychic**
06 mental, mystic, occult
08 mystical
09 cognitive, spiritual
10 telepathic
11 clairvoyant, telekinetic
12 extrasensory, supernatural
13 psychological

**psychological**
06 mental
08 cerebral
09 cognitive, imaginary
10 irrational, subjective
11 unconscious
12 subconscious
13 psychosomatic

**psychology**
04 mind
06 habits, makeup
07 mind-set, motives
09 attitudes

──────────

► *Names of psychologists:*
04 **Beck** (Aaron Temkin), **Jung** (Carl)
05 **Adler** (Alfred), **Binet** (Alfred), **Freud** (Anna), **Freud** (Sigmund), **James** (William), **Klein** (Melanie), **Laing** (Ronald David), **Meyer** (Adolf), **Rhine** (Joseph Banks)
06 **Bowlby** (John), **De Bono** (Edward), **Kinsey** (Alfred Charles), **Piaget** (Jean)
07 **Eysenck** (Hans Jürgen), **Persaud** (Raj), **Skinner** (Burrhus Frederic)
08 **Brothers** (Joyce), **Wernicke** (Carl)
09 **Alexander** (Franz Gabriel), **Alzheimer** (Alois), **Rorschach** (Hermann)
➤ See also SCIENTIST

**psychopath**
06 maniac, psycho
07 lunatic
09 psychotic, sociopath

**psychopathic**
03 mad
06 insane
07 lunatic
08 demented, maniacal
09 psychotic

**puberty**
05 teens
10 pubescence
11 adolescence
12 teenage years

**public**
04 fans, open
05 civic, civil, overt, plain
06 masses, nation, people, voters
07 country, exposed, patrons, popular
08 audience, citizens, national, populace

**09** clientèle, community, consumers, customers, followers, multitude, published, universal
**10** celebrated, electorate, population, spectators, supporters
**11** illustrious, influential
**12** nationalized

❑**in public**
**06** openly
**08** publicly
**09** in the open
**11** for all to see

**publican**
**06** taxman
**09** barkeeper, innkeeper
**12** tax collector

**publication**
**04** book
**05** daily, issue
**06** weekly
**07** booklet, journal, leaflet, monthly, release
**08** brochure, handbill, magazine, pamphlet
**09** newspaper, quarterly
**10** disclosure, periodical, production, publishing
**12** announcement, notification, proclamation

**public house**
**03** bar, inn, pub
**05** hotel, lodge
**06** hostel, tavern
**09** roadhouse

**publicity**
**02** PR
**04** hype, plug, puff
**06** splash
**07** buildup, puffery
**09** limelight, promotion
**10** propaganda
**11** advertising
**15** public relations

**publicize**
**04** hype, plug, puff, push
**07** promote
**08** announce
**09** advertise, broadcast, make known, spotlight
**10** make public

**public-spirited**
**10** altruistic, charitable
**12** humanitarian
**13** philanthropic

**publish**
**05** issue, print
**06** report, reveal
**07** declare, release

**08** announce, bring out, disclose, proclaim
**09** advertise, circulate, make known, publicize
**10** distribute, make public
**11** communicate, disseminate

**pucker**
**04** fold, ruck
**05** pleat, purse, shirr
**06** crease, gather, ruffle
**07** crinkle, crumple, screw up, shrivel, wrinkle
**08** compress, contract

**puckered**
**05** pursy
**06** rucked
**07** creased, ruckled
**08** gathered, wrinkled

**puckish**
**03** sly
**06** impish
**07** naughty, playful
**09** whimsical
**10** frolicsome
**11** mischievous

**pudding**
**04** duff
**06** junket
**07** custard, tapioca
**10** brown betty

**puddle**
**04** pool, slop
**05** plash

**pudgy**
**05** plump, podgy, tubby
**06** chubby, chunky, rotund
**08** roly-poly

**puerile**
**07** babyish, foolish, trivial
**08** childish, immature, juvenile
**09** infantile
**10** adolescent

**puff**
**04** blow, drag, draw, gasp, gulp, gust, pant, plug, pull, push, suck, waft
**05** blast, smoke, swell, whiff
**06** breath, expand, flurry, market, praise, wheeze
**07** breathe, promote, puffery
**09** promotion, publicity, publicize

**puffed**
**05** baggy
**07** swollen

❑**puffed up**
**05** proud
**08** arrogant
**09** bigheaded

**11** swell-headed
**14** full of yourself

**puffy**
**07** bloated, dilated, swollen
**08** enlarged, inflated, puffed up
**09** distended

**pugilism**
**06** boxing
**07** the ring
**08** fighting
**13** prizefighting

**pugilist**
**03** pug
**05** boxer
**07** bruiser, fighter, puncher
**12** prizefighter

**pugnacious**
**09** bellicose
**10** aggressive
**11** belligerent, contentious, quarrelsome
**13** argumentative

**puke**
**04** spew
**05** heave, retch, vomit
**07** throw up
**11** regurgitate

**pull**
**03** rip, tow, tug
**04** drag, draw, haul, jerk, lure, tear, yank
**05** heave, pluck, power, tempt
**06** allure, entice, pull in, pull up, remove, sprain, strain, uproot, weight
**07** attract, bring in, draw out, extract, pull out, take out
**09** dislocate, influence, magnetism, magnetize
**10** allurement, attraction
**12** drawing power, forcefulness

❑**pull apart**
**08** separate
**09** criticize, dismantle, dismember
**12** pull to pieces, take to pieces

❑**pull back**
**07** back out, retreat
**08** withdraw
**09** disengage

❑**pull down**
**07** destroy
**08** bulldoze, demolish
**09** dismantle, knock down
**15** raze to the ground

❑**pull in**
**04** book, draw, earn, lure, make, stop
**05** clear, run in, seize

06 arrest, arrive, be paid, detain, entice, rake in
07 attract, bring in, receive
15 take into custody

❑ **pull off**
06 detach, remove, rip off
07 achieve, succeed
08 bring off, carry off, carry out
10 accomplish

❑ **pull out**
04 quit
05 leave
06 depart, desert
07 abandon, back out, move out, retreat
08 evacuate, withdraw

❑ **pull through**
07 recover, survive, weather
10 recuperate

❑ **pull together**
09 cooperate
11 collaborate
12 work together

❑ **pull yourself together**
15 control yourself

❑ **pull up**
04 halt, park, stop
06 draw up, rebuke, uproot
07 tell off
10 take to task

**pulp**
03 pap
04 mash, mush
05 crush, flesh, paste, purée
06 marrow, squash
08 magazine
09 liquidize, pulverize, triturate

**pulpit**
04 dais
07 lectern, rostrum, soapbox
08 platform

**pulpy**
04 soft
05 mushy
06 fleshy
07 paplike, squashy

**pulsate**
04 beat, drum, thud
05 pound, pulse, throb, thump
06 hammer, quiver
07 vibrate
09 oscillate

**pulsating**
09 vibratile, vibrating, vibrative
11 oscillating, palpitating

**pulsation**
05 ictus, pulse
07 beating
09 vibration

11 oscillation, palpitation
12 vibratiuncle

**pulse**
04 beat, drum, seed, thud, tick
05 pound, throb, thump
06 legume, rhythm, stroke
07 vibrate
09 pulsation
11 oscillation
➤ See also BEAN

**pulverize**
05 crush, grind, pound, smash
06 powder, squash, thrash
09 triturate

**pummel**
05 knock, pound, punch, thump
06 batter, hammer, strike

**pump**
04 draw, push, quiz, send, shoe
05 drain, drive, force, grill, heart
06 inject
08 question
11 interrogate

❑ **pump out**
05 drain, empty
07 draw off
08 force out

❑ **pump up**
06 blow up, puff up
07 inflate

**pun**
04 quip
09 witticism
11 paronomasia, play on words
14 double entendre

**punch**
03 bop, box, cut, hit, jab
04 bash, biff, bite, blow, bore, cuff, hole, slug, sock
05 clout, drink, knock, power, stamp, thump, verve, vigor
06 impact, pizazz, pummel, strike, wallop
07 panache, pizzazz
08 puncture, strength
09 perforate
12 forcefulness

**punch-drunk**
05 dazed, dizzy, woozy
06 groggy
07 reeling
08 confused, unsteady
09 befuddled, stupefied

**punchy**
05 zappy
08 forceful, incisive, powerful, spirited, vigorous

**punctilio**
06 nicety

09 exactness
11 finickiness
14 scrupulousness
15 punctiliousness

**punctilious**
05 exact, fussy, picky
06 choosy, formal, proper, strict
07 careful, finicky, precise
10 meticulous, nitpicking, particular, scrupulous
11 persnickety
13 conscientious

**punctual**
05 early, exact, on cue
06 on time, prompt
07 precise
08 on the dot
09 well-timed
10 dead on time, in good time
11 right on time

**punctuality**
10 promptness, regularity
11 promptitude

**punctually**
06 dead on, on time, prompt
08 on the dot, promptly
09 precisely
11 to the minute

**punctuate**
05 break, point
06 pepper
08 sprinkle
09 emphasize, interject, interrupt
10 accentuate
11 intersperse

**puncture**
04 flat, hole, slit
05 burst, prick, spike
06 pierce
07 blowout, deflate, flatten, let down, rupture
08 flat tire
09 penetrate, perforate
11 perforation

**pundit**
04 buff, guru, sage
06 expert, master, savant
07 maestro, teacher
09 authority

**pungent**
03 hot
04 acid, keen, sour, tart
05 acrid, acute, fiery, sharp, spicy, tangy
06 biting, bitter, strong
07 burning, caustic, cutting, peppery, piquant, pointed
08 piercing, scathing, stinging

**punish**
04 beat, cane, fine, flog, hang,
   harm, lash, slap, whip
05 abuse, expel, scold, smack,
   spank
06 batter, damage, defeat,
   demote, disbar, hammer,
   misuse, thrash
07 correct, crucify, kneecap,
   rough up, scourge, trounce
08 chastise, imprison, maltreat,
   penalize
09 castigate
10 discipline
11 bring to book
14 make someone pay, throw
   the book at
15 give someone hell, make an
   example of

**punishable**
08 criminal, culpable, unlawful
10 chargeable, indictable
11 blameworthy, convictable

**punishing**
04 hard
05 cruel, harsh
06 severe, taxing, tiring
07 arduous
08 grueling
09 crippling, demanding,
   fatiguing, strenuous
12 backbreaking

**punishment**
07 deserts, penalty, revenge
08 sentence
10 correction, discipline
11 retribution
12 chastisement

**punitive**
04 hard
05 cruel, harsh, penal
06 severe
09 crippling, punishing
10 burdensome
11 retributive
12 disciplinary

**puny**
04 tiny, weak
05 frail, minor, petty, small
06 feeble, little, measly, sickly
07 stunted, trivial
08 piddling, trifling
10 diminutive, teeny-weeny,
   undersized
12 teensy-weensy
13 insignificant
14 underdeveloped
15 inconsequential

**pupil**
07 learner, protégé, scholar,
   student

08 disciple, protégée
09 schoolboy
10 apprentice, schoolgirl

**puppet**
04 doll, dupe, gull, Judy, pawn,
   tool
05 dummy, Punch
06 stooge
07 cat's-paw
08 creature, quisling
10 figurehead, instrument,
   marionette, mouthpiece

**purchase**
03 buy, get
04 gain, grip, hold
05 grasp
06 assets, pay for, pick up,
   secure, snap up
07 acquire, procure, shop for
08 foothold, leverage
09 advantage
10 go shopping
11 acquisition, splash out on

**purchaser**
05 buyer
06 client, emptor, vendee
07 shopper
08 consumer, customer

**pure**
04 good, neat, real, true
05 clean, clear, fresh, moral,
   sheer, total, utter
06 chaste, decent, honest,
   simple, virgin
07 aseptic, natural, sterile,
   unmixed
08 absolute, abstract,
   academic, flawless, germ-
   free, hygienic, innocent,
   sanitary, spotless, thorough,
   virginal, virtuous
09 downright, unalloyed,
   undefiled, undiluted,
   unsullied
10 antiseptic, immaculate,
   sterilized, uninfected,
   unpolluted
11 theoretical, unblemished,
   unmitigated
13 unadulterated
14 uncontaminated

**purebred**
07 blooded
08 pedigree
09 pedigreed, pureblood
11 full-blooded, pureblooded
12 thoroughbred

**purely**
06 simply, solely, wholly
11 exclusively

**purgative**
05 enema, purge
06 emetic
08 aperient, evacuant, laxative
09 cathartic, cleansing
10 abstersive, depurative,
   · eccoprotic

**purge**
03 rid
04 kill, oust
05 clear, eject, expel, scour
06 purify
07 absolve, cleanse, dismiss,
   wipe out
08 clean out, clear out, get rid of
09 cleansing, eradicate,
   expulsion
11 eradication, exterminate
13 extermination

**purification**
05 purge
08 cleaning
09 cleansing, epuration,
   purgation
10 absolution, depuration,
   filtration, redemption
12 disinfection, sanitization
14 sanctification

**purify**
05 clean, purge
06 distil, filter, redeem
07 absolve, cleanse, distill
08 depurate, filtrate, fumigate,
   sanctify, sanitize
09 disinfect, sterilize

**purifying**
07 purging
09 cathartic, cleansing,
   purgative
10 depurative
12 purificatory

**purism**
08 pedantry
14 fastidiousness

**purist**
06 pedant
07 finicky
08 pedantic, puristic, stickler
09 nitpicker, overexact
10 fastidious, nitpicking
11 overprecise
14 overfastidious,
   overmeticulous,
   overparticular

**puritan**
04 prig
05 prude
06 zealot
07 fanatic, killjoy, pietist
08 moralist, rigorist

**puritanical**
09 Mrs. Grundy, Victorian
14 disciplinarian

**puritanical**
04 prim
05 rigid, stern, stiff
06 proper, severe, strict, stuffy
07 ascetic, austere, bigoted, prudish, puritan, zealous
09 fanatical
10 abstemious, moralistic
11 strait-laced
12 narrow-minded
13 straight-laced

**puritanism**
08 primness, rigidity, severity, zealotry
09 austerity, stiffness
10 abstinence, asceticism, self-denial, strictness
11 prudishness
14 abstemiousness

**purity**
05 honor
06 virtue
07 clarity, decency
08 chastity, goodness, morality
09 cleanness, freshness, innocence, virginity
11 cleanliness, uprightness
12 virtuousness

**purlieus**
06 bounds, limits
07 borders, fringes, suburbs
08 confines, environs, vicinity
09 outskirts, perimeter, periphery, precincts
12 neighborhood, surroundings

**purloin**
03 rob
04 lift, take
05 filch, pinch, steal, swipe
06 finger, pilfer, pocket, remove, snitch, thieve
11 appropriate

**purport**
04 gist, idea, mean, seem, show
05 claim, drift, imply, point, tenor, theme
06 allege, assert, convey, denote, import, intend, pose as, spirit, thrust
07 bearing, betoken, declare, express, meaning, portend, pretend, profess, signify, suggest
08 indicate, maintain, proclaim, tendency
09 direction, substance
11 implication
12 significance

**purpose**
03 aim, end, use
04 gain, goal, good, hope, idea, mean, plan, wish, zeal
05 basis, drive, point, value
06 aspire, decide, design, desire, effect, intend, motive, object, reason, result, settle, target, vision
07 outcome, propose, resolve
08 ambition, firmness, function, tenacity
09 advantage, determine, intention, objective, principle, rationale
10 aspiration, dedication, doggedness, motivation, resolution, usefulness
11 application, contemplate, persistence
12 perseverance
13 determination, justification, steadfastness

❏**on purpose**
08 by design, wilfully
09 knowingly, purposely, willfully
12 deliberately
13 intentionally

**purposeful**
04 firm
06 dogged
07 decided
08 constant, resolute, resolved
09 steadfast, tenacious
10 deliberate, determined, persistent, unwavering
11 persevering, unfaltering
12 single-minded, strong willed

**purposefully**
10 resolutely
11 steadfastly, tenaciously
12 persistently, unwaveringly
13 perseveringly, unfalteringly
14 single-mindedly

**purposeless**
04 vain
07 aimless, useless, vacuous
09 pointless, senseless
10 gratuitous, motiveless

**purposely**
08 by design, wilfully
09 expressly, on purpose, willfully
10 designedly
12 calculatedly, deliberately
13 intentionally

**purse**
05 award, funds, money, pouch, prize
06 pucker, reward, wallet

07 coffers, handbag
08 compress, contract, finances, moneybag, treasury
09 exchequer, resources
10 pocketbook

**pursuance**
09 discharge, execution, following
10 fulfilment
11 fulfillment, performance, prosecution

**pursue**
03 dog
04 hunt, seek, tail
05 chase, harry, hound, stalk, track, trail
06 follow, harass, shadow
07 carry on, conduct, go after, perform
08 aspire to, engage in, maintain, practice, run after
09 persist in, strive for
10 work toward
11 investigate, persevere in

**pursuit**
04 goal, hunt, line
05 chase, craft, hobby, quest, trade, trail
07 pastime, tailing
08 activity, interest, stalking, tracking
09 following, hue and cry, shadowing, specialty
10 occupation
13 investigation

**purvey**
04 sell
05 cater, stock
06 deal in, retail, supply
07 furnish, provide, trade in
08 put about, transmit
09 provision, publicize

**purveyor**
06 dealer, trader
08 provider, provisor, retailer, supplier
09 victualer
11 transmitter
12 communicator

**push**
02 go
03 ram
04 butt, cram, goad, hype, jolt, plug, poke, prod, raid, spur, urge
05 boost, bully, drive, egg on, elbow, foray, force, get-up, impel, knock, nudge, press, shove, vigor
06 charge, coerce, effort, energy, hustle, incite, jostle,

market, plunge, propel, squash, thrust
07 advance, assault, depress, promote, squeeze
08 ambition, dynamism, invasion, persuade, press for, vitality
09 advertise, constrain, encourage, incursion, influence, manhandle, offensive, publicize
10 enterprise, get-up-and-go, initiative, pressurize
12 forcefulness
13 determination
14 put the screws on

**❑push around**
05 bully
07 torment
09 terrorize, victimize
10 intimidate

**❑push off**
04 move
05 leave
06 beat it, depart, go away, set out
07 buzz off
08 clear off, clear out, shove off
09 make a move, push along
10 make tracks

**pushed**
06 hard up, rushed
07 harried, hurried, pinched, pressed, short of
08 harassed, strapped
11 hard pressed
13 under pressure

**pushover**
03 mug
04 dupe, gull
05 cinch
06 picnic, sucker
08 walkover
09 soft touch
10 child's play
11 piece of cake, sitting duck

**pushy**
04 bold
05 bossy, brash
07 forward
08 arrogant, assuming, forceful
09 ambitious, assertive
10 aggressive
11 impertinent
12 presumptuous
13 overconfident

**pusillanimity**
08 timidity, weakness
10 cravenness, feebleness
11 fearfulness, gutlessness
12 cowardliness, timorousness

13 spinelessness

**pusillanimous**
04 weak
05 timid
06 craven, feeble, scared, yellow
07 chicken, fearful, gutless, wimpish
08 cowardly, timorous
09 spineless, weak-kneed
11 lily-livered
12 faint-hearted

**pussyfoot**
03 pad
05 creep, hedge, prowl, slink, steal
06 tiptoe
09 mess about
10 equivocate

**pustule**
04 boil, pock
05 felon, ulcer
06 fester, papule, pimple
07 abscess, blister, whitlow
08 eruption
09 carbuncle

**put**
03 bet, fix, lay, pin, say, set
04 dump, give, levy, post, rank, rest, risk, sink, sort, turn, word
05 apply, class, couch, exact, frame, grade, group, offer, place, plonk, speak, spend, stand, state, utter, voice, wager
06 assign, attach, chance, charge, demand, devote, gamble, impose, impute, invest, locate, phrase, render, settle, submit, tender
07 arrange, ascribe, convert, deposit, dispose, express, inflict, lay down, present, proffer, propose, require, set down, situate, station, subject, suggest
08 classify, dedicate, position, set forth
09 attribute, establish, formulate, lay before, pronounce, set before, translate
10 categorize, contribute, transcribe
12 bring forward

**❑put about**
04 tell
06 spread
09 circulate, make known
11 disseminate

**❑put across**
06 convey
07 explain, get over, put over
09 get across, make clear
11 communicate
12 get through to
14 make understood

**❑put aside**
04 keep, save, stow
05 hoard, lay by, put by, stash, store
06 retain
07 reserve
08 lay aside, salt away, set aside
09 stockpile
13 keep in reserve

**❑put away**
03 eat
04 jail, save, stow, wolf
05 drink, lay by, put by, store
06 commit, devour, guzzle, lock up
07 certify, confine, consume, reserve, swallow
08 imprison, put aside, send down
09 polish off, stockpile

**❑put back**
05 defer, delay
06 freeze, return, shelve
07 replace, restore
08 postpone, put on ice
09 reinstate

**❑put down**
03 fix, lay, log
04 list, snub, stop
05 blame, crush, enter, quash, quell, shame
06 attach, charge, defeat, humble, record
07 ascribe, deflate, destroy, jot down, set down
08 note down, register, stamp out, suppress
09 attribute, deprecate, disparage
10 transcribe

**❑put forward**
05 offer, table
06 submit, tender
07 advance, present, proffer, propose, suggest
08 nominate
09 recommend

**❑put in**
05 enter, input
06 insert, instal, submit
07 install

**❑put off**
05 daunt, defer, delay, deter

06 dismay, divert, shelve, sicken
07 adjourn, confuse, deflect
08 dissuade, distract, postpone, put on ice
09 turn aside
10 discourage, dishearten, reschedule
13 procrastinate

## put on
03 add, don
04 fake, sham, wear
05 affix, apply, feign, mount, place, stage
06 affect, assume, attach
07 dress in, perform, present, pretend, produce
08 simulate

## put out
04 faze
05 annoy, douse, issue, upset
06 bother, quench
07 disturb, perturb, publish, smother
08 announce, disclose, impose on, irritate, unsettle
09 broadcast, circulate, make known
10 extinguish
13 inconvenience

## put through
06 manage
07 achieve, execute
08 bring off, complete, conclude, finalize
10 accomplish

## put together
04 join
05 build
08 assemble
09 construct
11 fit together
13 piece together

## put up
05 build, erect, float, house, lodge, offer, raise
06 bump up, choose, hike up, invest, pledge, supply
07 advance, propose, provide, shelter, suggest
08 increase, nominate
09 construct, recommend
11 accommodate

## put up to
04 goad, urge
05 egg on
06 incite, prompt
08 persuade
09 encourage

## put upon
07 exploit
08 impose on

13 inconvenience, take liberties
14 take for granted
15 take advantage of

## put up with
04 bear, take
05 abide, allow, brook, stand
06 accept, endure, suffer
07 stomach, swallow
08 stand for, tolerate
13 take lying down

## putative
07 alleged, assumed, reputed
08 presumed, reported, supposed
10 reputative
11 conjectural, theoretical
12 hypothetical

## putdown
03 dig
04 gibe, snub
05 sneer
06 insult, rebuff, slight
07 affront, sarcasm
11 humiliation
13 disparagement, slap in the face

## putoff
06 damper
09 deterrent, hindrance
12 disincentive, evasive reply
14 discouragement

## putrefy
03 rot
04 mold
05 addle, decay, go bad, spoil, stink, taint
06 fester, perish
07 corrupt
08 gangrene
09 decompose
11 deteriorate

## putrescent
07 rotting
08 decaying, mephitic, stinking
09 festering, perishing
10 putrefying
11 decomposing

## putrid
03 bad, off
04 foul, rank
05 fetid, moldy
06 addled, rancid, rotten
07 corrupt, decayed, tainted
08 polluted, stinking
10 decomposed
12 contaminated

## putter
05 amble
06 dawdle, loiter, toddle
10 dilly-dally

## putter about
11 fiddle about, tinker about
12 fiddle around, tinker around

## put upon
06 abused
09 exploited, imposed on
10 maltreated, persecuted
14 inconvenienced

## puzzle
04 beat
05 brood, floor, poser, rebus, stump, think
06 baffle, enigma, figure, ponder, riddle
07 anagram, confuse, dilemma, flummox, mystery, mystify, nonplus, paradox, perplex, stagger
08 acrostic, bewilder, confound, consider, meditate, mull over, muse over, question
09 conundrum, crossword
10 deliberate, mind-bender
11 brain-teaser
12 brain twister, jigsaw puzzle
14 rack your brains

## puzzle out
05 crack, solve
06 decode
07 unravel, work out
08 decipher
09 figure out

## puzzled
05 at sea
07 at a loss, baffled, stumped
09 flummoxed, mystified, perplexed
10 bewildered, confounded, nonplussed

## puzzlement
05 doubt
09 confusion
10 bafflement, perplexity
11 incertitude, uncertainty
12 bewilderment
13 mystification

## puzzling
06 knotty
07 bizarre, cryptic, curious, strange, unclear
08 abstruse, baffling, peculiar, tortuous
09 confusing, enigmatic, intricate
10 mysterious, mystifying, perplexing, Sphynx-like
11 bewildering, mind-bending
12 impenetrable, inexplicable, labyrinthine, mind-boggling, unfathomable

**pygmy**
03 toy, wee
04 baby, tiny
05 dwarf, elfin, small
06 midget, minute, pocket
07 manikin, stunted

08 dwarfish, half pint, pintsize
09 miniature, minuscule, pint-
    sized, undersize
10 diminutive, fingerling,
    homunculus, pocketsize,
    undersized

11 Lilliputian, pocket-sized

**pyromaniac**
07 firebug
08 arsonist
10 incendiary

**quack**
04 fake, sham
05 bogus, false, fraud, phony, pseud
06 humbug
08 impostor, so-called
09 charlatan, trickster

**quackery**
04 sham
05 fraud
06 humbug
09 imposture, phoniness
12 charlatanism
13 mountebankery

**quaff**
04 down, gulp, swig
05 booze, drain, drink, swill
06 guzzle, imbibe, tipple
07 carouse, swallow, toss off
09 knock back

**quagmire**
03 bog, fen, fix
04 hole, mess, mire, quag
05 marsh, swamp
06 morass, pickle, slough
09 deep water, tight spot

**quail**
05 cower, quake, shake
06 blench, cringe, falter, flinch, recoil, shiver, shrink
07 shudder, shy away, tremble
08 back away, bobwhite, draw back
09 partridge

**quaint**
03 odd
04 cute
05 droll, sweet
07 bizarre, curious, strange
08 charming, old-world
09 whimsical
10 antiquated
11 picturesque
12 old-fashioned

**quake**
04 move, rock, sway
05 heave, quail, shake, throb
06 quiver, shiver, wobble
07 shudder, tremble, vibrate
08 convulse
10 earthquake

**qualification**
05 rider, skill
06 caveat, degree
07 diploma, fitness, proviso
09 condition, exception, exemption, provision
10 competence, limitation
11 certificate, eligibility, proficiency, reservation, restriction, stipulation
13 certification

**qualified**
03 fit
04 able
06 expert
07 capable, guarded, limited, skilful, skilled, trained
08 eligible, licensed, prepared, reserved, skillful, talented
09 certified, chartered, competent, efficient
10 proficient, restricted
11 conditional, experienced
12 accomplished, professional

**qualify**
04 ease, pass
05 allow, equip, limit, train
06 adjust, lessen, modify, reduce, soften, weaken
07 certify, delimit, empower, entitle, license, warrant
08 graduate, moderate, restrain, restrict, sanction
09 alleviate, authorize

**quality**
04 kind, make, rank, sort, type
05 class, grade, level, merit, trait, value, worth
06 makeup, nature, status
07 caliber, feature, variety
08 eminence, standard
09 attribute, character
10 excellence, refinement
11 distinction, peculiarity, preeminence, superiority
14 characteristic

**qualm**
04 fear
05 doubt, worry
07 anxiety, concern, scruple
08 disquiet
09 hesitancy, misgiving

10 hesitation, reluctance, uneasiness
11 compunction, uncertainty
12 apprehension

**quandary**
03 fix, jam
04 hole, mess
06 muddle, pickle
07 dilemma, impasse, problem
10 difficulty, perplexity
11 predicament

**quantity**
03 lot, sum
04 area, bulk, dose, lots, many, mass, much, part, size
05 heaps, loads, quota, total
06 amount, extent, length, number, volume, weight
07 breadth, expanse, measure
08 capacity
09 aggregate, magnitude
10 proportion

**quarantine**
06 detain
07 isolate
09 detention, isolation

**quarrel**
03 row
04 feud, slam, tiff
05 argue, brawl, clash, set-to
06 bicker, differ, fracas, schism
07 censure, dispute, dissent, fall out, wrangle
08 argument, conflict, disagree, squabble, vendetta
10 contention, difference
11 altercation, controversy
12 disagreement, pull to pieces
15 be at loggerheads

**quarreling**
06 at odds, rowing, strife
07 discord, feuding, warring
09 bickering, scrapping, wrangling
10 at variance, contention, discordant, disharmony, dissension, squabbling
11 altercation, disputation
13 at loggerheads
14 vitilitigation

**quarrelsome**
09 bellicose, irascible, irritable

11 belligerent, contentious
12 disputatious
13 argumentative
14 ready for a fight

**quarry**
03 pit
04 game, goal, kill, mine, prey
05 prize
06 object, target, victim

**quarter**
04 area, coin, digs, part, pity, post, side, spot, zone
05 board, grace, house, mercy, money, point, put up
06 billet, pardon, sector
07 section, shelter, station, two bits
08 clemency, district, division, dwelling, leniency, locality, vicinity
09 one-fourth, residence, territory
10 compassion, habitation
11 accommodate, forgiveness
12 neighborhood, period of play
13 accommodation
14 fifteen minutes

**quarters**
05 rooms
08 barracks, lodgings

**quash**
04 void
05 annul, crush, quell
06 cancel, defeat, revoke
07 nullify, rescind, reverse
08 abrogate, override, overrule, overturn, set aside, suppress
09 overthrow
10 invalidate
11 countermand

**quaver**
05 break, quake, shake, waver
06 quiver, tremor, warble
07 flutter, shudder, tremble, tremolo, vibrate
09 oscillate, vibration

**quay**
04 dock, pier
05 jetty, wharf
06 harbor

**queasy**
03 ill
04 sick
05 faint, green, queer, rough
06 groggy, unwell
07 bilious
08 sickened
09 nauseated, squeamish
10 out of sorts

15 under the weather

**queen**
04 idol
05 belle, charm, ruler, Venus
06 beauty, regina
07 consort, empress, majesty, monarch
08 princess
09 sovereign
10 chess piece

▶ *Names of queens. We have omitted the word* **queen** *from names given in the following list but you may need to include this word as part of the solution to some crossword clues. The regnal numerals of individual queens have also been omitted.*
04 Anne (of Cleves), Grey (Lady Jane), Mary (of Teck), Mary (Queen of Scots), Parr (Catherine)
05 Maria, Marie (de Médici)
06 Boleyn (Anne), Howard (Catherine)
07 Beatrix, Eleanor (of Aquitaine), Eleanor (of Castile), Juliana, Seymour (Jane), Zenobia
08 Adelaide, Boadicea, Boudicca, Caroline (of Ansbach), Caroline (of Brunswick), Isabella (of Castile), Margaret (of Anjou), Victoria
09 Alexandra, Brunhilde, Catherine (de' Medici), Catherine (of Aragon), Catherine (of Braganza), Cleopatra, Elizabeth, Fredegond, Nefertiti, Semiramis
10 Anne Boleyn, Hatshepsut
11 Jane Seymour
13 Catherine Parr, Margaret Tudor
14 Henrietta Maria
15 Catherine Howard, Marie Antoinette

**queenly**
05 grand, noble, regal, royal
06 august
07 stately, sublime
08 gracious, imperial, majestic
09 imperious, sovereign
11 monarchical

**queer**
03 gay, ill, mar, odd
04 foil, harm, iffy, ruin, sick
05 botch, dizzy, faint, fishy, funny, giddy, rough, shady,

spoil, stymy, upset, weird, wreck
06 queasy, shifty, stymie, unwell
07 curious, deviant, strange, suspect, unusual
08 abnormal, peculiar, puzzling, singular
09 eccentric, frustrate, unnatural
10 homosexual, mysterious, out of sorts, outlandish, remarkable, suspicious
11 counterfeit, lightheaded
15 under the weather

**queerness**
11 abnormality, bizarreness, curiousness, peculiarity, singularity, strangeness
12 eccentricity, irregularity
13 anomalousness

**quell**
04 calm, hush, rout
05 allay, crush, quash, quiet
06 defeat, pacify, soothe, squash, stifle, subdue
07 appease, conquer, put down, silence
08 moderate, overcome, suppress, vanquish
10 extinguish

**quench**
04 cool, sate
05 douse, slake
06 put out, stifle
07 satiate, satisfy, smother
08 snuff out, stamp out
10 extinguish

**querulous**
05 cross, fussy, testy
07 carping, fretful, grouchy, peevish
08 captious, critical, petulant
09 fractious, grumbling, irascible, irritable
11 complaining
12 cantankerous, discontented, dissatisfied, faultfinding

**query**
03 ask
07 dispute, inquire, inquiry, problem, quibble, suspect
08 distrust, mistrust, question
09 challenge, suspicion
10 disbelieve, skepticism
11 reservation, uncertainty

**quest**
03 aim
04 goal, hunt
06 search, voyage
07 crusade, inquiry, journey, mission, purpose, pursuit
09 adventure

10 expedition, pilgrimage
11 exploration, undertaking
13 investigation

**question**
04 pump, quiz
05 doubt, grill, issue, point, poser, probe, query, theme, topic
06 debate, matter, motion
07 debrief, dispute, examine, inquire, inquiry, problem
08 argument, proposal
09 catechize, challenge, interview
10 difficulty, disbelieve
11 controversy, interrogate, investigate, uncertainty
12 cross-examine
13 cross-question

❑**out of the question**
06 absurd
10 impossible, ridiculous
11 unthinkable
12 unacceptable, unbelievable

❑**without question**
11 immediately
14 unhesitatingly, unquestionably

**questionable**
04 iffy
05 fishy, shady, vexed
07 dubious, suspect
08 arguable, doubtful, unproven
09 debatable, uncertain
10 disputable, suspicious

**questioner**
07 doubter, skeptic
08 agnostic, examiner, inquirer
09 catechist
10 catechizer, inquisitor, quizmaster
11 disbeliever, interviewer
12 interlocutor, interrogator

**questionnaire**
04 form, quiz, test
06 survey
11 opinion poll
14 market research

**quibble**
04 carp
05 cavil, query
06 niggle
07 nitpick, protest
08 pettifog
09 complaint, criticism, objection
10 equivocate, split hairs

**quibbler**
07 casuist, caviler, niggler, sophist

09 nitpicker
12 hairsplitter

**quibbling**
07 carping, evasive
08 captious, caviling, critical, niggling
09 casuistic
10 nitpicking
13 hairsplitting

**quick**
04 fast, keen
05 agile, alive, brief, brisk, rapid, ready, sharp, smart, swift
06 astute, clever, nimble, prompt, speedy, sudden
07 cursory, express, flat-out, instant
08 fleeting
09 immediate, sprightly
10 discerning, perceptive
11 expeditious, intelligent, perfunctory, sharp-witted
12 without delay
13 instantaneous

**quicken**
04 stir, whet
05 hurry, rouse, speed
06 arouse, excite, hasten, incite, kindle, revive, stir up
07 advance, animate, enliven, hurry up, inspire, speed up
08 energize, expedite, revivify
09 galvanize, stimulate
10 accelerate, invigorate, revitalize, strengthen

**quickly**
04 fast, soon
05 apace, quick
06 presto, pronto
07 briskly, express, hastily, rapidly, readily, swiftly
08 abruptly, promptly, speedily
09 cursorily, hurriedly, instantly, posthaste
11 immediately, on the double
12 lickety-split
14 hell for leather, unhesitatingly
15 instantaneously

**quickness**
05 speed
07 agility
08 keenness, rapidity
09 acuteness, briskness, hastiness, readiness, sharpness, swiftness
10 astuteness, expedition, promptness, speediness, suddenness
12 intelligence
13 precipitation

**quick-tempered**
05 fiery, testy
06 snappy, touchy
07 waspish
08 choleric, petulant, shrewish
09 excitable, explosive, impatient, impulsive, irascible, irritable, splenetic
11 hot tempered, quarrelsome
13 temperamental

**quick-witted**
04 keen
05 acute, alert, sharp, smart
06 astute, bright, clever, crafty
11 intelligent, penetrating

**quiescent**
04 calm
05 inert, quiet, still
06 asleep, at rest, latent, placid, serene, silent
07 dormant, passive, resting
08 inactive, peaceful, tranquil
10 in abeyance, motionless

**quiet**
03 low, shy
04 calm, hush, lull, rest, soft
05 faint, muted, peace, still
06 gentle, hushed, lonely, low-key, placid, repose, serene, silent, sleepy, subtle
07 muffled, silence, subdued
08 discreet, low-keyed, peaceful, reserved, reticent, retiring, secluded, taciturn, tranquil
09 inaudible, introvert, noiseless, soundless, stillness, withdrawn
10 restrained, thoughtful
11 sequestered, tranquility, undisturbed
12 unfrequented
13 unforthcoming, without a sound
15 uncommunicative

**quieten**
04 calm, dull, hush, mute
05 quell, quiet, shush, still
06 deaden, muffle, pacify, reduce, shut up, smooth, soften, soothe, stifle, subdue
07 compose, silence
08 calm down, diminish
11 tranquilize

**quietly**
06 calmly, gently, meekly, mildly, mutely, softly
08 placidly, secretly, silently
09 inaudibly, privately
10 peacefully, tranquilly
11 noiselessly, soundlessly

13 unobtrusively
15 surreptitiously

**quietness**
04 calm, hush, lull
05 peace, quiet, still
06 repose
07 inertia, silence
08 calmness, serenity
09 composure, placidity, stillness
10 inactivity, quiescence
11 tranquility

**quietus**
03 end
05 death
06 demise
07 decease, release
08 dispatch
09 deathblow, discharge
10 extinction
11 acquittance, coup de grâce, death stroke

**quilt**
05 duvet, throw
08 bedcover, coverlet
09 bedspread, comforter, eiderdown
11 counterpane

**quintessence**
04 core, gist, pith, soul
05 heart
06 kernel, marrow, spirit
07 essence, extract, pattern
08 exemplar, quiddity
12 distillation

**quintessential**
05 ideal
07 perfect
08 complete, ultimate
10 consummate, definitive
12 archetypical, prototypical

**quip**
04 gibe, jest, joke
05 crack, quirk
07 epigram, riposte
08 one-liner
09 wisecrack, witticism

**quirk**
04 kink, turn, whim
05 freak, habit, thing, trait, twist
06 foible, hang-up, oddity
07 caprice, feature
09 curiosity, mannerism
11 peculiarity
12 eccentricity, idiosyncrasy

**quisling**
05 Judas
07 traitor
08 betrayer, renegade, turncoat
12 collaborator

14 fifth columnist

**quit**
03 end
04 drop, exit, stop
05 cease, leave
06 depart, desert, give up, go away, resign
07 abandon, abstain, forsake
08 leave off, pack it in, withdraw
11 discontinue

**quite**
05 fully
06 fairly, rather, wholly
07 exactly, totally, utterly
08 entirely, somewhat
09 perfectly, precisely
10 absolutely, completely, moderately, relatively
12 to some extent
13 comparatively

**quits**
04 even
05 equal, level
06 square

❑**call it quits**
04 stop
05 cease
08 break off
09 make peace
11 discontinue
12 stop fighting
14 bury the hatchet

**quitter**
03 rat
06 coward
07 shirker
08 apostate, defector, deserter, recreant, renegade
10 delinquent

**quiver**
05 quake, shake, throb
06 arrows, quaver, shiver, tingle, tremor
07 flicker, flutter, pulsate, shudder, tremble, vibrate
09 arrow case, oscillate, palpitate, pulsation, vibration

**quixotic**
07 Utopian
08 fanciful, romantic
09 impetuous, impulsive, unworldly, visionary
10 chivalrous, idealistic
11 fantastical, unrealistic
13 impracticable

**quiz**
04 pump, test
05 grill
08 game show

11 competition, examination, interrogate, questioning
12 cross-examine
13 cross-question
14 the third degree

▶ *Names of quiz shows:*
06 Gambit
08 Jeopardy!, Password
09 Twenty-One
10 Family Feud
11 College Bowl, What's My Line?
12 Queen for a Day, Stop the Music
13 I've Got a Secret, Who Do You Trust?
14 To Tell the Truth, Wheel of Fortune, You Bet Your Life
15 The Price is Right

**quizzical**
06 amused
07 baffled, curious, mocking, puzzled, teasing
08 humorous, sardonic
09 inquiring, perplexed, satirical, skeptical

**quota**
04 part
05 share, slice, whack
06 ration
07 portion
09 allowance
10 allocation, proportion

**quotation**
04 cost, line, rate
05 piece, price, quote
06 charge, figure, tender
07 cutting, excerpt, extract, passage
08 allusion, citation, estimate

**quote**
04 cite, echo, name
06 recall, recite, repeat
08 allude to
09 recollect, reproduce

**quoted**
05 cited
06 stated
08 reported
10 referred to, reproduced

**quotidian**
05 daily
06 common, normal
07 diurnal, regular, routine
08 day-to-day, everyday, habitual, ordinary, repeated, workaday
09 customary, recurrent
11 commonplace

## rabbit
03 doe
04 cony
05 bunny, coney, daman, hyrax, lapin
06 angora, dassie
08 lop-eared
09 pacemaker
10 cottontail, pacesetter

## rabble
03 mob
05 crowd, horde, plebs
06 masses, throng
08 populace, riffraff
09 hoi polloi
11 proletariat

## rabble-rouser
07 demagog
08 agitator
09 demagogue, firebrand
10 incendiary, ringleader
12 troublemaker

## Rabelaisian
04 lewd, racy
05 bawdy, gross
06 coarse, ribald, risqué, vulgar
08 indecent
09 exuberant, satirical
11 extravagant, uninhibited

## rabid
03 mad
06 ardent, crazed, raging
07 berserk, bigoted, burning, extreme, fervent, frantic, furious, violent, zealous
08 frenzied, maniacal
09 fanatical, obsessive
10 hysterical, irrational
11 hydrophobic, unreasoning
12 narrow-minded

## rabies
11 hydrophobia

## race
03 fly, run
04 bolt, clan, dart, dash, line, rush, tear, zoom
05 blood, chase, color, house, hurry, quest, speed, stock, tribe
06 ethnic, family, gallop, hasten, people, stirps

07 contest, dynasty, kindred, lineage, pursuit, species
09 ethnicity
10 accelerate, contention, extraction, get a move on
11 competition, ethnic group, racial group
➤ See also SPORT

▶ *Types of race:*
03 ski
04 CART, dash, drag, road, sack
05 cycle, horse, relay, yacht
06 hot rod, NASCAR, rowing, slalom, sprint
07 hurdles, Indy car, pancake, pursuit, regatta, sled dog, walking
08 downhill, marathon, scramble, speedway, stock car, swimming
09 Grand Prix, greyhound, motocross, motorboat, SportsCar, time trial
10 cyclocross, Formula One, motorcycle, track event
11 egg-and-spoon
12 cross-country, speed skating, steeplechase

▶ *Names of famous races:*
04 Oaks
05 Derby
06 Le Mans
07 Belmont, St. Leger
08 Boat Race, Milk Race
09 Preakness
11 Admiral's Cup, America's Cup
12 Melbourne Cup, Tour de France
13 Grand National, Kentucky Derby
14 Boston Marathon, London Marathon
15 Monte Carlo Rally, New York Marathon, The Hambletonian

## racecourse
04 oval, turf
05 track
07 circuit
08 speedway
09 racetrack

## racial
04 folk
06 ethnic, tribal
07 genetic
09 ancestral, inherited
12 ethnological, genealogical

## raciness
04 zest
06 energy
08 dynamism, ribaldry
09 animation, bawdiness, freshness, indecency
10 coarseness, ebullience, liveliness, smuttiness
11 naughtiness, zestfulness
12 exhilaration
14 suggestiveness

## racism
04 bias
07 bigotry
08 jingoism
09 apartheid, prejudice, racialism
10 chauvinism, xenophobia
11 segregation
14 discrimination

## racist
05 bigot
07 bigoted
09 racialist
10 chauvinist, intolerant
13 discriminator
14 discriminatory

## rack
04 crib, pain, tear
05 agony, frame, pangs, shake, shelf, stand, wrest, wring
06 harass, harrow, holder, misery, strain, stress, wrench
07 afflict, anguish, crucify, oppress, stretch, support, torment, torture, trestle
08 convulse, distress, lacerate
09 framework, suffering
11 persecution

## racket
03 con, din, row
04 fuss, game
05 dodge, fraud, noise, trick
06 clamor, fiddle, paddle, scheme, uproar
07 swindle, yelling

09 commotion, deception
11 disturbance, pandemonium

**raconteur**
07 relater
08 narrator, reporter
10 anecdotist, chronicler
11 commentator, storyteller

**racy**
04 blue, rude
05 bawdy, crude, dirty, zippy
06 coarse, lively, ribald, risqué, smutty, vulgar
07 buoyant, dynamic, naughty
08 animated, indecent, spirited
09 sparkling, vivacious
10 boisterous, fast moving, indelicate, suggestive

**raddled**
05 drawn, gaunt
06 wasted
07 haggard, unkempt
10 disheveled
15 the worse for wear

**radiance**
03 joy
04 glow
05 bliss, gleam, light, shine
07 delight, ecstasy, elation, glitter, rapture
08 splendor
09 happiness
10 brightness, brilliance, effulgence, luminosity
13 incandescence

**radiant**
06 bright, elated, joyful
07 beaming, glowing, shining
08 blissful, ecstatic, gleaming, glorious, luminous, splendid
09 brilliant, delighted, effulgent, sparkling
11 illuminated, over the moon

**radiate**
04 emit, glow, pour, shed
05 gleam, issue, shine
06 branch, spread
07 diffuse, diverge, emanate, give off, scatter, send out
09 send forth, spread out
10 divaricate
11 disseminate

**radiation**
04 rays
05 waves
08 emission
09 emanation
10 insolation
12 transmission

**radical**
05 basic, rebel, total, utter

06 entire, innate, native
07 drastic, extreme, primary
08 militant, profound, reformer, sweeping, thorough
09 elemental, essential, extremist, fanatical, intrinsic
10 deep-rooted, deep-seated, elementary
11 far-reaching, fundamental
13 comprehensive, revolutionary

**raffish**
04 loud
05 cheap, gaudy, gross, showy
06 casual, coarse, flashy, garish, jaunty, rakish, sporty, trashy, vulgar
07 dashing, uncouth
08 bohemian, improper
09 dissolute, tasteless
10 dissipated, flamboyant
12 devil-may-care, disreputable, meretricious

**raffle**
04 draw
05 sweep
07 lottery
10 sweepstake

**rag**
03 kid, rib
04 bait, duds, jeer, mock
05 cloth, clout, scold, taunt, tease, towel
06 duster, shreds
07 tatters, washrag
08 remnants, ridicule
09 newspaper, washcloth

**ragamuffin**
03 bum
04 waif
05 gamin, tramp
06 urchin
08 vagabond
11 guttersnipe

**ragbag**
06 jumble, medley
07 mixture
08 pastiche
09 confusion, potpourri
10 assemblage, assortment, hodgepodge, hotchpotch, miscellany
14 omnium-gatherum

**rage**
04 fume, fury, rant, rave
05 anger, go mad, storm, wrath
06 frenzy, raving, see red, seethe, temper, tumult
07 explode, madness, rampage, tantrum, thunder
09 blow a fuse

11 blow your top, flip your lid, go up the wall
12 lose your cool
14 foam at the mouth
15 fly off the handle, go off the deep end

❏**all the rage**
06 trendy
07 in vogue, popular, stylish
10 the in thing
11 fashionable

**ragged**
04 poor, rent, torn
05 holey, rough
06 frayed, ripped, rugged, shabby, uneven, untidy
07 erratic, in holes, notched, scruffy, unkempt, worn-out
08 indigent, serrated, tattered
09 destitute, in tatters, irregular
10 down and out, down-at-heel, fragmented, straggling
12 disorganized
13 down-at-the-heel

**raging**
03 mad
04 wild
05 angry, irate
06 fuming, ireful, raving, stormy
07 enraged, furious, violent
08 furibund, incensed, seething
09 turbulent
10 infuriated, tumultuous
11 fulminating

**raid**
04 bust, loot, rush, sack
05 blitz, foray, onset, rifle, swoop
06 assail, attack, charge, forage, holdup, inroad, invade, maraud, sortie, strike
07 assault, break in, pillage, plunder, ransack
09 break into, descend on, incursion, onslaught

**raider**
05 crook, shark, thief
06 looter, pirate, robber
07 brigand, invader, villain
08 attacker, marauder, pillager
09 plunderer, ransacker

**rail**
04 jeer, mock
05 abuse, decry, fence, scoff
06 attack, revile
07 censure, inveigh, protest, railway, upbraid
08 railroad
09 castigate, criticize, fulminate
10 vituperate, vociferate

**railing**
05 fence, rails
06 paling
07 barrier, fencing, parapet
10 balustrade

**raillery**
04 joke
05 chaff, irony, sport
06 banter, joking, satire
07 jesting, kidding, mockery, ragging, ribbing, teasing
08 badinage, diatribe, repartee, ridicule
09 invective
10 persiflage, pleasantry

**railroad**
04 line, rail
05 rails, track
06 tracks
07 railway
13 streetcar line

**rain**
04 pelt, pour, spit, teem
06 deluge, hyetal, mizzle, shower, squall
07 buckets, drizzle, pluvial, torrent
08 downpour, pour down, rainfall, sprinkle
10 cloudburst
12 thunderstorm
13 precipitation
15 rain cats and dogs

**rainbow**
03 arc, bow
04 arch, iris
08 irisated, spectral, spectrum
09 prismatic
10 iridescent, opalescent
11 many-colored
13 kaleidoscopic

► *Colors of the rainbow*:
03 red
04 blue
05 green
06 indigo, orange, violet, yellow
➤ See also COLOR

**rainy**
03 wet
04 damp
07 drizzly, pluvial, showery

**raise**
04 grow, jack, lift, moot, rear, stir
05 amass, boost, breed, build, cause, erect, hoist, put up, rally, rouse, set up, weigh
06 arouse, broach, create, excite, gather, jack up, lift up, muster, step up, uplift

07 amplify, collect, develop, educate, elevate, enhance, nurture, produce, provoke, recruit, suggest, upgrade
08 assemble, heighten, increase
09 construct, cultivate, intensify, introduce
10 accumulate, put forward
11 get together

**raised**
05 cameo
06 relief
07 applied, relievo
08 appliqué, elevated, embossed

**rake**
04 comb, hunt, roué, tool
05 amass, graze, rifle, scour
06 scrape, search, smooth
07 collect, playboy, ransack, rummage, scratch, swinger
08 hedonist, prodigal
09 debauchee, libertine
10 degenerate, profligate
14 pleasure seeker

❏**rake in**
04 earn, make
07 bring in, get paid, receive

❏**rake up**
05 raise
06 drag up, remind, revive
07 bring up, mention
09 introduce

**rake-off**
03 cut
04 part
05 share, slice
07 portion
10 commission

**rakish**
05 loose, natty, sharp, smart
06 breezy, casual, dapper, flashy, jaunty, sinful, snazzy
07 dashing, immoral, raffish
08 debonair, depraved
09 debauched, dissolute, lecherous, libertine
10 degenerate, flamboyant, nonchalant, profligate
12 devil-may-care

**rally**
05 group, march, unite
06 gather, muster, perk up, pick up, reform, revive, summon
07 collect, convene, get well, improve, marshal, meeting, recover, regroup, renewal, reunion, revival, round up

08 assemble, assembly, comeback, jamboree, mobilize, organize, recovery
10 bounce back, conference, congregate, convention, recuperate, resurgence
11 convocation, get together, improvement, mass meeting, pull through
13 bring together, demonstration

**ram**
03 hit, jam
04 beat, bump, butt, cram, dash, drum, pack, slam
05 crash, crowd, drive, force, pound, smash, stuff, wedge

**ramble**
04 hike, roam, rove, tour, trek, trip, walk, wind
05 amble, range, stray, tramp
06 babble, stroll, waffle, wander, zigzag
07 blether, digress, diverge, meander, saunter, traipse
09 excursion, expatiate
15 go off on a tangent

**rambler**
04 rose
05 hiker, rover, tramp
06 roamer, walker
08 wanderer, wayfarer
10 ranch house

**rambling**
05 wordy
06 errant
07 verbose
09 sprawling, spreading
10 circuitous, disjointed, incoherent, long-winded, roundabout, straggling
12 disconnected, long-drawn-out, periphrastic

**ramification**
06 branch, effect, result, sequel, upshot
07 outcome
11 consequence, development, implication
12 complication, divarication

**ramp**
04 rise
05 grade, slope
07 incline
08 gradient
09 acclivity

**rampage**
04 fury, rage, rant, rave, rush
05 furor, storm

**rampant**
06 charge, frenzy, mayhem, uproar
07 run amok, run riot, run wild
09 go berserk
◻ **on the rampage**
04 amok, wild
07 berserk, violent
08 frenzied
09 in a frenzy, violently
12 out of control
**rampant**
04 rank, rife, wild
06 fierce, raging, wanton
07 profuse, riotous, violent
08 epidemic, pandemic
09 excessive, out of hand, unbridled, unchecked
10 widespread
12 out of control, uncontrolled
**rampart**
04 bank, fort, wall
05 fence, guard
07 bulwark, defense, parapet
09 barricade, earthwork
10 embankment, stronghold
13 fortification
**ramshackle**
06 flimsy, ruined, unsafe
07 rickety, rundown
08 decrepit, derelict, unsteady
09 crumbling, neglected
10 broken-down, tumbledown
11 dilapidated
**ranch**
04 farm
06 estate
07 station
08 estancia, hacienda
10 plantation, ranch house
**rancher**
06 cowboy
08 ranch man, ranchero
09 ranch hand
10 ranch owner
11 ranch worker
**rancid**
03 bad
04 foul, high, rank, sour
05 fetid, musty, stale
06 putrid, rotten, turned
07 noisome, noxious
10 malodorous, unpleasant
**rancorous**
06 bitter
07 acerbic, hostile
08 spiteful, vengeful, venomous, virulent
09 resentful, splenetic
10 malevolent, vindictive
11 acrimonious

**rancor**
05 spite, venom
06 animus, enmity, grudge, hatred, malice, spleen
08 acrimony
09 animosity, antipathy, hostility, malignity
10 bitterness, ill feeling, resentment
11 malevolence
13 resentfulness
14 vindictiveness
**random**
06 casual, chance
09 arbitrary, haphazard, hit-or-miss, irregular, unplanned
10 accidental, incidental
12 unmethodical, unsystematic
13 serendipitous
14 indiscriminate
◻ **at random**
09 aimlessly
11 arbitrarily, haphazardly
12 fortuitously, incidentally
14 unmethodically
**randy**
07 amorous, aroused, goatish, lustful, raunchy, satyric
08 turned-on
09 lecherous
10 lascivious
12 concupiscent
**range**
04 area, file, kind, line, oven, rank, roam, sort, span, type
05 align, amble, array, class, cover, field, gamut, genus, group, order, reach, scale, scope, stove, stray, sweep
06 bounds, domain, extend, extent, limits, line up, radius, ramble, series, spread, string, stroll, wander
07 arrange, catalog, compass, species
08 classify, distance, spectrum
09 catalogue, diversity, fluctuate, selection
10 assortment, parameters
**rangy**
05 lanky, leggy, weedy
06 skinny
08 gangling, rawboned
10 long-legged
**rank**
03 row
04 file, foul, line, lush, mark, rate, sort, tier, type, vile
05 acrid, align, caste, class, dense, fetid, grade, gross,

level, order, place, range, sheer, stale, total, utter
06 arrant, coarse, column, degree, line up, putrid, rancid, series, status, string
07 arrange, blatant, echelon, glaring, marshal, profuse, pungent, station, stratum
08 absolute, classify, complete, division, flagrant, mephitic, organize, position, standing, stinking, thorough, vigorous
09 downright, formation, offensive, out-and-out, repulsive, revolting
10 disgusting, malodorous, outrageous
11 unmitigated, unqualified
12 disagreeable, evil smelling
14 classification
➤ See also MILITARY

▶ *Ranks in the U.S. Air Force:*
05 major
06 airman
07 captain, colonel, general
08 sergeant
11 airman basic
12 major general, senior airman
13 staff sergeant
14 master sergeant
15 first lieutenant

▶ *Ranks in the U.S. Army:*
05 major
07 captain, colonel, general, private
08 corporal
10 specialist
12 major general
13 first sergeant, sergeant major, staff sergeant
14 master sergeant
15 first lieutenant

▶ *Ranks in the U.S. Marines:*
05 major
07 captain, colonel, general, private
08 corporal, sergeant
12 major general
13 first sergeant, lance corporal, sergeant major, staff sergeant
14 master sergeant
15 first lieutenant, gunnery sergeant

▶ *Ranks in the U.S. Navy:*
06 ensign, seaman
07 admiral, captain
09 commander, commodore
10 lieutenant
11 rear admiral, vice admiral

12 lieutenant jg, petty officer
13 seaman recruit

▢ **rank and file**
03 mob
05 crowd, plebs
06 masses, rabble
08 populace, riffraff, soldiers
09 hoi polloi
11 ordinary men, proletariat
15 private soldiers

**rankle**
03 bug, irk, vex
04 gall, rile
05 anger, annoy, peeve
08 embitter, irritate

**ransack**
04 comb, loot, raid, sack
05 harry, rifle, scour, strip
06 maraud, ravage, search
07 despoil, pillage, plunder
09 depredate, devastate
13 turn inside out
14 turn upside down

**ransom**
04 free
05 money, price
06 payoff, redeem, rescue
07 deliver, payment, release
08 liberate
10 redemption
11 deliverance, restoration

**rant**
04 rave, roar, yell
05 shout, storm
06 bellow, crying, tirade
07 bluster, bombast, declaim
08 diatribe, harangue, rhetoric, shouting, tub-thump
09 philippic
10 vociferate

**rap**
03 hit, tap
04 bang, blow, chat, clip, cuff, slam, song
05 blame, clout, knock, music, scold, stick, thump, whack
06 punish, rebuke, strike
07 censure, reprove
09 castigate, reprimand
10 punishment
11 castigation

**rapacious**
06 greedy
07 preying, wolfish, wolvish
08 esurient, grasping, ravenous, usurious
09 marauding, predatory, voracious, vulturous
10 avaricious, insatiable, plundering

**rapacity**
05 greed, usury
07 avarice, avidity
08 voracity
09 esurience, esuriency
10 greediness
13 voraciousness

**rape**
03 rob
04 loot, raid, sack
05 abuse, plant, strip
06 defile, rapine, ravage, ravish
07 assault, despoil, looting, pillage, plunder, ransack
08 maltreat, ravaging, spoliate
09 depredate, stripping
10 plundering, spoliation
12 despoliation, maltreatment
13 sexual assault

**rapid**
04 fast
05 brisk, hasty, quick, swift
06 lively, prompt, speedy
07 express, hurried
11 expeditious, precipitate

**rapidity**
04 rush
05 haste, hurry, speed
08 alacrity, celerity, dispatch, velocity
09 briskness, fleetness, quickness, swiftness
10 promptness, speediness
15 expeditiousness

**rapidly**
07 briskly, hastily, swiftly
08 promptly, speedily
09 hurriedly
12 lickety-split
13 expeditiously, precipitately

**rapine**
04 rage, raid
07 looting, pillage, plunder, sacking
08 ravaging
09 stripping, violation
10 defilement, plundering, ransacking, spoliation
11 depredation, devastation
12 despoliation

**rapport**
04 bond, link
07 empathy, harmony
08 affinity, sympathy
12 relationship
13 understanding

**rapprochement**
07 détente, reunion
09 agreement, softening
13 harmonization

14 reconciliation

**rapt**
06 intent
07 charmed, gripped
08 absorbed, thrilled
09 delighted, enchanted, engrossed, entranced
10 captivated, enthralled, fascinated, spellbound

**rapture**
03 joy
05 bliss
07 delight, ecstasy, elation
08 euphoria, felicity
09 cloud nine, transport
11 delectation, enchantment
13 seventh heaven, top of the world

**rapturous**
06 joyful, joyous
07 exalted
08 blissful, ecstatic, euphoric
09 delighted, entranced, overjoyed, rhapsodic
11 on cloud nine, over the moon, tickled pink, transported

**rare**
04 pink
06 scarce, sparse, superb
07 unusual
08 sporadic, uncommon
09 exquisite, matchless
10 half-cooked, infrequent, remarkable
11 exceptional, outstanding
12 like gold dust
15 rare as hen's teeth

**rarefied**
04 high
05 noble
06 select
07 private, refined, special
08 esoteric
09 exclusive

**rarely**
06 hardly, little, seldom
08 scarcely
10 hardly ever
12 infrequently, occasionally
15 once in a blue moon

**raring**
04 keen
05 eager, ready
07 itching, longing, willing
09 desperate, impatient
12 enthusiastic

**rarity**
04 find
05 curio, pearl

06 marvel, wonder
08 scarcity, shortage, treasure
09 curiosity, nonpareil
11 strangeness, unusualness

**rascal**
03 imp
05 devil, rogue, scamp
07 villain, wastrel
08 scalawag
09 scallywag, scoundrel
10 ne'er-do-well
13 mischief-maker
14 good-for-nothing

**rascally**
03 bad, low
07 crooked, knavish, vicious
11 furciferous, mischievous
12 disreputable, unscrupulous
14 good-for-nothing

**rash**
03 run
04 rush, wave
05 flood, hasty, hives, spate
06 deluge, madcap, plague
08 careless, epidemic, eruption,
   outbreak, reckless
09 foolhardy, hotheaded,
   impetuous, imprudent,
   impulsive, unguarded,
   urticaria
10 headstrong, ill-advised,
   indiscreet, nettle rash
11 adventurous, harebrained,
   precipitate, temerarious
13 ill-considered

**rashness**
08 audacity, temerity
09 hastiness, incaution
12 carelessness, heedlessness,
   precipitance, recklessness
13 foolhardiness, impulsiveness,
   precipitation
15 thoughtlessness

**rasp**
03 bug, jar, rub
04 file, sand
05 croak, grate, grind, peeve
06 abrade, cackle, scrape
07 grating, scratch, screech
08 grinding, irritate
09 excoriate, harshness
10 hoarseness
15 get on your nerves

**rasping**
05 gruff, harsh, husky, rough
06 croaky, hoarse
07 grating, jarring, raucous
08 creaking, croaking, scratchy
10 stridulant

**rate**
03 fee, pay
04 cost, deem, rank, toll
05 basis, chide, class, count,
   grade, judge, merit, price,
   ratio, scale, scold, speed,
   tempo, value, weigh, worth
06 admire, amount, assess,
   charge, degree, figure, rating,
   reckon, regard, tariff
07 adjudge, deserve, measure,
   payment, warrant, weigh up
08 appraise, classify, consider,
   estimate, evaluate, relation,
   standard, velocity
10 be worthy of, categorize,
   percentage, proportion
12 be entitled to, have a right to

❏**at any rate**
06 anyway
09 in any case
10 in any event, regardless
12 nevertheless

**rather**
04 a bit, very
05 quite
06 fairly, pretty, sooner
07 a little, instead
08 slightly, somewhat
10 moderately, much sooner,
   preferably, relatively
13 for preference, significantly

**ratify**
06 affirm, uphold
07 agree to, approve, certify,
   confirm, endorse, warrant
08 legalize, sanction, validate
11 corroborate, countersign

**rating**
04 mark, rank
05 class, grade, order, score
06 degree, status
07 grading, placing
08 category, position, standing
10 assessment, evaluation

**ratio**
07 balance
08 fraction, relation, symmetry
10 percentage, proportion
12 relationship

**ration**
03 lot
04 food, part, save
05 allot, issue, limit, share
06 amount, budget, viands
07 control, dole out, hand out,
   helping, measure, portion
08 allocate, conserve, dispense,
   restrict, victuals
09 allowance, apportion

10 allocation, distribute,
   foodstuffs, percentage,
   proportion, provisions

**rational**
04 sane, wise
05 lucid, sound
07 logical, prudent
08 cerebral, sensible, thinking
09 cognitive, judicious, realistic,
   reasoning, sagacious
10 reasonable
11 circumspect, clearheaded,
   intelligent, well-founded
13 ratiocinative

**rationale**
05 basis, logic
06 motive, reason, theory
07 grounds, purpose, reasons
09 principle, reasoning
10 motivation, philosophy
11 explanation, raison d'être

**rationalize**
07 explain, justify
10 account for

**rattle**
04 bang, bump, faze, jolt
05 alarm, clang, clank, clink,
   knock, shake, upset
06 babble, jangle, jingle, put off
07 clatter, confuse, disturb,
   unnerve, vibrate
08 unsettle
10 disconcert
15 throw off balance

❏**rattle off**
04 list
06 recite, repeat
07 reel off

❏**rattle on**
03 gab
04 yack
05 prate
06 gabble, jabber
07 blather, blether, chatter,
   prattle

**raucous**
04 loud
05 harsh, noisy, rough, sharp
06 hoarse, shrill
07 grating, jarring, rasping
08 piercing, strident
10 scratching, screeching
11 ear piercing

**ravage**
04 loot, raze, ruin, sack
05 havoc, level, spoil, wreck
06 damage, maraud
07 despoil, destroy, looting,
   pillage, plunder
08 lay waste, wreckage

09 depredate, devastate
10 desolation, ransacking, spoliation
11 depredation, destruction, devastation

**ravaged**
07 war torn, war worn, wrecked
08 desolate
09 destroyed, ransacked
10 battle torn, devastated

**rave**
04 bash, fume, hail, rage, rant, roar, yell
05 extol, storm
06 extoll, ramble, seethe
07 acclaim, enthuse, explode, thunder
08 boil over, praising
09 excellent, favorable, laudatory, rapturous, wonderful
10 be mad about, wax lyrical
11 flip your lid
12 enthusiastic, lose your cool
14 lose your temper

**ravenous**
06 greedy, hungry
07 starved, wolfish
08 famished, starving
10 insatiable

**ravine**
04 pass
05 abyss, gorge, gully
06 canyon

**raving**
03 mad
04 wild
05 barmy, batty, crazy, loony
06 insane
07 berserk, furious
08 demented, deranged
09 delirious
10 hysterical, unbalanced
13 out of your mind

**ravish**
04 rape
05 abuse, charm
06 defile
07 assault, delight, enchant, enthral, overjoy, violate
08 enthrall, entrance, maltreat
09 captivate, enrapture, fascinate, spellbind

**ravishing**
06 lovely
08 gorgeous, stunning
09 beautiful, seductive
10 bewitching, enchanting

**raw**
03 new, wet

04 bare, cold, damp, open, sore
05 bleak, chill, crude, green, harsh, naïve, naked, plain
06 biting, bitter, bloody, callow, chafed, grazed
07 abraded, exposed, natural
08 immature, uncooked
09 unrefined, unskilled, untrained, untreated
10 excoriated, unprepared
11 unpracticed, unprocessed
13 inexperienced

**ray**
04 beam, hint
05 flash, gleam, glint, shaft
06 streak, stream
10 indication, suggestion

**raze**
04 fell, ruin
05 level, wreck
07 destroy, flatten
08 bulldoze, demolish, pull down, tear down
09 knock down

**re**
04 in re
05 about
09 regarding
10 concerning
12 with regard to
14 on the subject of
15 with reference to

**reach**
04 call, hold, make, ring, span
05 ambit, get to, grasp, phone, power, range, scope, touch
06 attain, extend, extent, ring up
07 achieve, command, compass, contact, stretch
08 amount to, arrive at, distance, latitude
09 authority, extension, get hold of, go as far as
12 get through to, jurisdiction
14 get in touch with

**react**
05 rebel, reply
06 answer, oppose, rise up
07 dissent, respond
09 retaliate
11 acknowledge, reciprocate

**reaction**
05 reply
06 answer, recoil, reflex
08 backlash, feedback, kickback, response, reversal
11 retaliation
12 repercussion
13 counteraction, reciprocation
14 acknowledgment

**reactionary**
07 diehard
09 right-wing
11 right-winger, traditional
12 conservative
14 traditionalist

**read**
04 look, scan, show, skim
05 speak, study, utter
06 browse, decode, peruse, recite
07 declaim, deliver, display, examine, measure, perusal
08 construe, decipher, indicate, pore over, register
09 interpret
10 comprehend, scrutinize, understand
11 leaf through
12 flick through, thumb through
13 browse through

❑**read into**
05 infer
06 deduce, reason
08 construe
09 interpret
12 misinterpret

**readable**
05 clear
07 legible
08 gripping
11 captivating, enthralling, interesting, stimulating
12 decipherable, entertaining, intelligible, worth reading
13 unputdownable
14 comprehensible

**readily**
06 easily, freely, gladly
07 eagerly, happily, quickly, rapidly, swiftly
08 promptly, smoothly, speedily, with ease
09 willingly
14 unhesitatingly

**readiness**
08 aptitude, facility, keenness
09 eagerness, handiness
10 promptness
11 preparation, willingness
12 preparedness

❑**in readiness**
06 on call
08 prepared
09 available, on standby
10 standing by
11 on full alert
13 in preparation

**reading**
04 scan

05 study
06 figure, lesson, record
07 display, edition, passage, perusal, recital, version
08 browsing, decoding
09 rendering, rendition
10 indication, inspection
11 deciphering, examination, measurement
13 understanding
14 interpretation

**ready**
03 fit, set
04 easy, game, keen, near
05 alert, eager, equip, handy, happy, prime, rapid, swift
06 all set, astute, on hand, prompt, speedy, to hand
07 arrange, prepare, willing
08 arranged, disposed, equipped, geared up, organize, prepared
09 available, completed, organized, psyched up
10 accessible, convenient, discerning, perceptive
11 predisposed, resourceful
12 enthusiastic, on the point of

**real**
04 sure, true
05 right, utter, valid
06 actual, honest
07 certain, factual, fervent, genuine, sincere
08 absolute, bona fide, complete, concrete, existing, material, official, physical, positive, rightful, tangible, thorough, truthful
09 authentic, heartfelt, unfeigned, veritable
10 legitimate, unaffected
11 substantial

**real estate**
03 lot
04 land
05 house
06 realty
08 building
11 development

**real estate agent**
07 realtor
13 property agent
14 property broker

**realism**
09 actuality
10 pragmatism
11 genuineness, naturalness
12 authenticity, faithfulness, lifelikeness, truthfulness

**realistic**
04 real, true
05 close, vivid
07 genuine, logical, natural
08 faithful, lifelike, rational, real-life, sensible, truthful
09 hard-nosed, objective, practical, pragmatic
10 hard-boiled, hardheaded, true-to-life, unromantic
11 commonsense, down-to-earth, levelheaded
12 businesslike, clearsighted, matter-of-fact
13 unsentimental

**reality**
04 fact
05 truth
08 real life, validity
09 actuality, certainty, existence, real world
11 genuineness, tangibility
12 authenticity, corporeality

**realization**
04 gain
05 grasp
06 making
07 earning, selling
09 awareness
10 acceptance, cognizance, completion, fulfilment, perception
11 achievement, discernment, fulfillment, performance, recognition
12 appreciation, apprehension
13 comprehension, understanding
14 accomplishment

**realize**
03 net
04 earn, gain, make, sell
05 clear, fetch, grasp, learn
06 accept, effect, fulfil, take in
07 achieve, bring in, catch on, discern, fulfill, produce, sell for
08 complete, cotton on, discover, perceive, tumble to
09 apprehend, ascertain, implement, recognize
10 accomplish, appreciate, bring about, comprehend, effectuate, understand
13 become aware of

**really**
04 very
05 truly
06 highly, in fact, indeed, surely
08 actually, honestly, severely

09 certainly, extremely, genuinely, sincerely
10 absolutely, remarkably
13 categorically, exceptionally

**realm**
04 area, land
05 field, orbit, state, world
06 domain, empire, sphere
07 country, kingdom
08 monarchy, province
12 principality

**reap**
03 cut, get, mow, win
04 crop, gain
06 derive, garner, gather, obtain, secure
07 collect, harvest, realize

**rear**
03 end
04 back, grow, hind, last, lift, loom, rise, rump, soar, tail
05 breed, hoist, nurse, raise, stern, tower, train
06 behind, bottom, foster
07 bring up, care for, educate, elevate, nurture, tail end
08 backside, buttocks, hindmost, instruct, rearmost
09 cultivate, posterior

**rearrange**
04 vary
05 alter, shift
06 adjust, change
07 reorder
08 readjust, rejigger
10 reposition, reschedule

**reason**
03 aim, end, wit
04 case, goal, mind, nous
05 basis, brain, cause, infer, logic, sense, solve, think
06 deduce, excuse, motive, object, reckon, sanity
07 defense, grounds, impetus, purpose, thought, work out
08 argument, cogitate, conclude, gumption, judgment
09 cerebrate, incentive, intellect, intention, rationale, reasoning, syllogize
10 inducement, motivation
11 common sense, explanation, raison d'être
12 intelligence, use your brain
13 comprehension, justification, ratiocination, understanding

❏ **reason with**
04 coax, move, urge
08 persuade
09 argue with, plead with

**reasonable**

10 debate with
11 discuss with
15 remonstrate with

❏ **within reason**

10 moderately
12 in moderation, within bounds, within limits

**reasonable**

03 low
04 fair, just, sane, wise
05 sound
06 modest, viable
07 average, logical
08 credible, moderate, possible, rational, sensible
09 judicious, plausible, practical, sagacious
10 acceptable
11 inexpensive, intelligent
13 no great shakes

**reasoned**

05 clear, sound
07 logical
08 rational, sensible
09 judicious, organized
10 methodical, systematic
14 well-thought-out

**reasoning**

05 logic, proof
08 analysis, argument, thinking
09 deduction, rationale
10 hypothesis, logistical
11 cerebration, supposition
13 ratiocination
14 interpretation
15 rationalization

**reassure**

05 brace, cheer, nerve, rally
06 buoy up
07 cheer up, comfort, hearten
09 encourage

**rebate**

06 refund
09 allowance, deduction, reduction, repayment

**rebel**

03 reb
04 defy, riot
06 flinch, mutiny, oppose, recoil, resist, revolt, rise up
07 defiant, disobey, dissent, heretic, run riot, shy away
08 agitator, apostate, mutineer, mutinous, recusant
09 dissenter, guerrilla, insurgent, Johnny Reb
10 malcontent, schismatic
11 Confederate

13 insubordinate, nonconformist, revolutionary
14 freedom fighter
15 insurrectionary

**rebellion**

04 coup, riot
06 heresy, mutiny, revolt, rising
07 dissent
08 defiance, uprising
09 coup d'état
10 insurgence, opposition, resistance, revolution
12 disobedience, insurrection
15 insubordination

**rebellious**

06 unruly
07 defiant, rioting
08 mutinous
09 insurgent, obstinate, rebelling, resistant, seditious
11 disobedient, intractable
12 contumacious, recalcitrant, unmanageable
13 insubordinate, revolutionary
15 insurrectionary

**rebirth**

07 renewal, revival
11 renaissance, restoration
12 regeneration, rejuvenation, resurrection
13 reincarnation
14 revitalization

**rebound**

06 bounce, recoil, return, spring
08 backfire, ricochet, snap back
09 boomerang
10 backfiring, bounce back
15 come home to roost

**rebuff**

03 cut
04 snub
05 check, spurn
06 refuse, reject, slight
07 decline, put down, putdown, refusal, repulse
08 brushoff, spurning
09 rejection, repudiate
11 repudiation
12 cold shoulder
13 slap in the face
14 discouragement, kick in the teeth

**rebuild**

06 remake
07 reedify, remodel, restore
08 renovate
10 reassemble
11 reconstruct

**rebuke**

04 rate
05 blame, chide, scold
07 censure, reproof, reprove, tell off, upbraid
08 admonish, reproach, scolding
09 castigate, dress down, reprimand
10 admonition
11 castigation, remonstrate
12 give an earful
13 remonstration, tongue-lashing
15 call on the carpet

**rebut**

05 quash
06 defeat, negate, refute
07 confute, explode
08 disprove, overturn
09 discredit
12 give the lie to

**rebuttal**

06 defeat
08 disproof, negation
10 refutation
11 confutation
12 invalidation

**recalcitrant**

06 unruly, wilful
07 defiant, wayward, willful
08 contrary, renitent, stubborn
09 obstinate, unwilling
10 refractory
11 disobedient, intractable
12 contumacious, unmanageable
13 insubordinate, uncooperative
14 uncontrollable

**recall**

05 annul, evoke
06 call up, cancel, memory, repeal, revoke, summon
07 nullify, rescind, retract
08 abrogate, call back, recision, remember, withdraw
09 annulment, order back, recollect, reminisce
10 abrogation, call to mind, revocation, withdrawal
11 remembrance, think back to
12 cancellation, recollection

**recant**

04 deny
06 abjure, disown, revoke
07 disavow, rescind, retract
08 abrogate, disclaim, forswear, renounce, withdraw
09 repudiate
10 apostatize

## recantation
06 denial, revoke
08 apostasy
09 disavowal
10 abjuration, disclaimer, disownment, revocation, withdrawal
11 repudiation
12 renunciation, retractation

## recapitulate
05 recap, sum up
06 repeat, review
07 recount, restate
09 reiterate, summarize
11 go over again
12 run over again

## recede
03 ebb
04 drop, fade, sink, wane
06 go back, lessen, shrink
07 decline, dwindle, fall off, retreat, slacken, subside
08 decrease, diminish, move away, withdraw

## receipt
04 slip, stub
06 ticket
08 delivery
09 receiving, reception
10 acceptance
11 counterfoil
13 being received
14 acknowledgment
15 acknowledgement, proof of purchase

## receipts
06 income, return
07 profits, returns, takings
08 earnings, proceeds

## receive
03 get
04 bear, gain, hear, hold, take
05 admit, greet, let in
06 accept, derive, gather, obtain, pick up, suffer
07 acquire, collect, inherit, sustain, undergo, welcome
08 meet with, perceive
09 apprehend, encounter, entertain, respond to
10 experience, learn about
11 accommodate

## receiver
05 donee, fence, radio, tuner, TV set
07 catcher, grantee, handset, legatee
08 assignee
09 collector, recipient
11 beneficiary
13 television set

14 football player
15 baseball catcher

## recent
03 new
04 late
05 fresh, novel, young
06 latest, modern
08 up-to-date
10 present-day
13 up-to-the-minute

## recently
05 newly
06 lately, of late
10 not long ago

## receptacle
06 holder, vessel
09 container
10 repository

## reception
04 bash
05 party
06 at-home, social
07 receipt, shindig, welcome
08 function, greeting, reaction
09 admission, gathering, receiving
11 get-together, recognition
13 entertainment
15 social gathering

## receptive
04 open
07 willing
08 amenable, flexible, friendly
09 sensitive, welcoming
10 hospitable, interested, open-minded, responsive
11 susceptible, sympathetic
12 approachable
13 accommodating

## recess
03 bay
04 nook, rest
05 break, heart, niche, oriel
06 alcove, bowels, cavity, corner, depths, hollow
07 holiday, innards, reaches, respite, time off, time out
08 interior, interval, vacation
09 bay window
10 depression, penetralia
11 indentation, school break
12 intermission

## recession
05 crash, slide, slump
06 trough
07 decline, failure
08 collapse, downturn
10 depression

## recherché
04 rare

06 arcane, choice, select
07 refined
08 abstruse, esoteric

## recipe
05 guide, means
06 method, system
07 formula, process
09 procedure, technique
10 directions
11 ingredients
12 instructions, prescription

## recipient
05 donee
07 grantee, legatee
08 assignee, receiver
11 beneficiary

## reciprocal
05 joint
06 mutual, shared
08 requited, returned
09 exchanged
11 alternating, correlative
13 complementary, corresponding
14 interdependent

## reciprocate
04 swap
05 match, repay, reply, trade
06 return
07 requite, respond
08 exchange
10 correspond

## recital
04 show
07 account, concert, reading
09 narration, rendering, rendition
10 recitation, repetition
11 declamation, performance
14 interpretation

## recitation
04 poem, tale
05 piece, story, verse
07 monolog, passage, reading, recital, telling
09 monologue, narration

## recite
04 tell
06 relate, repeat
07 declaim, deliver, itemize, narrate, recount, reel off
08 say aloud
09 enumerate, rattle off
10 articulate

## reckless
04 rash, wild
05 hasty
06 madcap
08 careless, heedless

09 daredevil, foolhardy, imprudent, negligent
10 ill-advised, incautious
11 precipitate, thoughtless
12 devil-may-care
13 irresponsible

**recklessness**
07 madness
08 rashness
10 imprudence, negligence
12 carelessness, heedlessness
13 foolhardiness

**reckon**
04 deem, rate
05 add up, count, gauge, guess, judge, tally, think, total
06 assess, assume, esteem, number, regard
07 compute, imagine, suppose, surmise, think of, work out
08 consider, estimate, evaluate
09 calculate, figure out
10 conjecture

▢ **reckon on**
06 bank on, expect, rely on
07 count on, plan for, trust in
08 depend on, figure on
10 anticipate, bargain for
14 take for granted
15 take into account

▢ **reckon with**
04 cope, deal, face
06 expect, handle
07 foresee, plan for
08 consider
10 anticipate, bargain for, settle with
15 take into account

**reckoning**
04 bill, doom
05 score, tally, total
06 charge, number, paying
07 account, opinion, payment
08 addition, estimate, judgment
09 appraisal
10 assessment, estimation, evaluation, punishment, settlement, working-out
11 calculation, computation, enumeration, retribution

**reclaim**
06 redeem, regain, rescue
07 get back, recover, salvage
08 retrieve, take back
09 recapture, reinstate

**recline**
04 loll, rest
06 lounge, repose, sprawl
07 lie down
08 lean back

10 stretch out

**recluse**
03 nun
04 monk
05 loner
06 hermit
07 ascetic, eremite, stylite
08 anchoret, solitary
09 anchoress, anchorite
10 solitarian

**reclusive**
07 ascetic, recluse
08 eremitic, isolated, retiring, secluded, solitary
09 withdrawn
10 anchoritic, cloistered, hermitical
11 sequestered

**recognition**
05 honor
06 reward, salute
07 knowing, placing, respect
08 allowing, approval
09 admission, awareness, detection, discovery, gratitude, knowledge
10 acceptance, admittance, cognizance, confession, perception, validation
11 endorsement, realization
12 appreciation, thankfulness
13 understanding
14 acknowledgment

**recognize**
03 own, see
04 know, spot, tell
05 admit, adopt, allow, grant, honor
06 accept, notice, recall, salute
07 approve, concede, confess, discern, endorse, not miss, pick out, realize, respect
08 identify, perceive, remember, validate
09 apprehend, be aware of
10 appreciate, understand
11 acknowledge
13 be conscious of, be thankful for

**recoil**
04 kick
05 quail, react
06 falter, flinch, shrink
07 misfire, rebound, shy away
08 backfire, backlash, reaction
10 spring back
12 repercussion

**recollect**
06 recall
08 remember
09 reminisce

10 call to mind

**recollection**
06 memory, recall
11 remembrance
12 reminiscence

**recommend**
04 plug, urge
06 advise, exhort, praise
07 advance, approve, commend, counsel, endorse, propose, suggest
08 advocate, vouch for
10 put forward

**recommendation**
03 tip
04 plug
06 advice, praise, urging
07 counsel
08 advocacy, approval, blessing, good word, guidance, proposal
09 reference
10 suggestion
11 endorsement, testimonial

**recompense**
03 pay
05 repay, wages
06 amends, reward
07 damages, guerdon, payment, redress, requite
08 requital
09 indemnify, reimburse, repayment
10 compensate, remunerate, reparation
11 restitution
12 compensation, remuneration, satisfaction

**reconcile**
04 mend
06 accept, adjust, make up, pacify, remedy, settle, square
07 appease, mollify, patch up, placate, resolve, reunite
08 face up to, put right
09 harmonize, make peace
10 conciliate, shake hands
13 make your peace
14 bury the hatchet

**reconciliation**
05 peace
06 accord
07 détente, harmony, reunion
10 adjustment, compromise, resolution, settlement
11 appeasement, harmonizing
13 accommodation, mollification, rapprochement

## recondite
04 dark, deep
06 arcane, hidden, secret
07 obscure
08 abstruse, esoteric, mystical
09 concealed, difficult, intricate
10 mysterious

## recondition
05 renew
06 repair, revamp
07 remodel, restore
08 overhaul, renovate
09 refurbish

## reconnaissance
05 probe, recce
06 patrol, search, survey
08 scouting, scrutiny
10 expedition, inspection
11 exploration, observation
13 investigation
14 reconnoitering

## reconnoiter
04 scan
05 probe
06 patrol, spy out, survey
07 explore, inspect, observe
08 check out
11 investigate

## reconsider
06 modify, review, revise
07 rethink
08 reassess
09 reexamine, think over
10 think twice
13 think better of

## reconstruct
04 redo
06 reform, remake, revamp
07 rebuild, remodel, restore
08 recreate, renovate

## record
02 CD, LP
03 cut, log
04 data, disc, disk, edit, file, keep, list, note, read, show, tape
05 album, chart, diary, entry, notes, trace, video
06 annals, career, memoir, minute, report, single
07 account, blotter, catalog, display, history, journal, logbook, minutes, put down, release
08 archives, cassette, document, evidence, indicate, inscribe, memorial, preserve, register
09 catalogue, chronicle, documents, testimony, videotape, write down

10 background, memorandum, tape record, transcribe
11 compact disc, compact disk, fastest time, photography, put on record
12 personal best
13 police blotter

## ❏ off the record
07 private, sub rosa
09 privately
10 privileged, unofficial
12 confidential, unofficially
14 confidentially

## ❏ on record
05 noted
10 documented
11 written down
13 publicly known

## recorder
05 clerk, steno, video
06 camera, notary, scorer, scribe
07 diarist
08 annalist
09 archivist, historian, registrar, secretary
10 chronicler
11 chronologer, scorekeeper
12 notary public, stenographer, tape recorder

## recount
04 tell
06 depict, detail, impart, recite, relate, repeat, report, unfold
07 narrate, portray
08 describe, rehearse
11 communicate

## recoup
05 repay
06 refund, regain
07 get back, recover, win back
08 make good, retrieve
09 reimburse, repossess

## recourse
06 access, appeal, choice, option, refuge, remedy, resort, way out
09 turning to
11 alternative, possibility

## recover
04 heal, mend
05 rally
06 pick up, recoup, regain, retake, revive
07 get back, get over, get well, improve, reclaim, win back
08 retrieve
09 get better, recapture, repossess

10 ameliorate, bounce back, come around, convalesce, recuperate
11 be on the mend

## recovery
05 rally
06 upturn
07 healing, mending, salvage
08 rallying
09 recapture, recouping, recycling, retrieval
11 improvement, reclamation
12 amelioration, recuperation, repossession
13 convalescence

## recreation
03 fun
04 game, play
05 hobby, sport
07 leisure, pastime
08 pleasure
09 diversion, enjoyment
10 relaxation
11 distraction, refreshment
13 entertainment

## recrimination
08 reprisal
11 retaliation
13 counterattack, countercharge

## recruit
05 draft, raise
06 engage, enlist, enroll, novice, rookie, sign up, take on
07 acquire, convert, draftee, learner, procure, trainee
08 beginner, initiate, newcomer
09 conscript, greenhorn
10 apprentice, new entrant

## rectify
03 fix
04 cure, mend
05 amend, emend, right
06 adjust, better, reform, remedy, repair
07 correct, improve, redress
08 make good, put right

## rectitude
05 honor
06 virtue
07 honesty, justice, probity
09 exactness, integrity
11 correctness, uprightness
13 righteousness
14 scrupulousness

## recumbent
04 flat
05 lying, prone
06 supine
07 leaning, resting

**recuperate**

08 lounging
09 lying down, prostrate, reclining, sprawling
10 horizontal

**recuperate**
04 mend
06 pick up, revive
07 get well, improve, recover
09 get better
10 bounce back, convalesce
11 be on the mend

**recur**
06 return
08 reappear
11 happen again

**recurrent**
07 chronic, regular
08 cyclical, frequent, periodic
10 persistent, repetitive
12 intermittent

**recycle**
04 save
05 reuse
07 reclaim, recover, salvage
09 reprocess

**red**
04 pink, rose, rosy, ruby
05 ruddy
06 auburn, cherry, florid, ginger, maroon, russet, Titian
07 carroty, crimson, flushed, glowing, leftist, scarlet
08 blushing, chestnut, inflamed, rubicund
09 bloodshot, Bolshevik, communist, rufescent, socialist, vermilion
10 shamefaced
11 embarrassed

❑**in the red**
05 broke
06 in debt
08 bankrupt
09 in arrears, insolvent, overdrawn, penniless
10 on the rocks, owing money
13 gone to the wall

❑**see red**
05 go mad
07 explode
08 boil over
11 become angry, blow your top
12 blow your cool, fly into a rage, lose your cool
14 lose your temper
15 fly off the handle

**red-blooded**
05 lusty, manly
06 hearty, robust, strong, virile

08 vigorous

**redden**
05 blush, color, flush, go red
07 crimson, suffuse

**reddish**
04 pink, rosy
05 ruddy, sandy
06 ginger, rufous, russet
08 rubicund
09 bloodshot, rufescent

**redeem**
04 cash, free, save
06 cash in, offset, ransom, recoup, regain, rescue
07 absolve, buy back, convert, deliver, expiate, get back, reclaim, recover, release, salvage, set free, trade in
08 atone for, exchange, liberate, outweigh, retrieve
09 make up for, repossess
10 emancipate, repurchase
13 compensate for

**redemption**
06 ransom, rescue
07 freedom, release, trade-in
08 exchange, recovery
09 atonement, expiation, retrieval, salvation
10 liberation, reparation
11 deliverance, reclamation
12 emancipation, repossession

**redneck**
04 clod, hick
05 aggie, yokel
06 rustic
07 bumpkin, hayseed
09 hillbilly

**redolent**
07 odorous, scented
08 fragrant, perfumed
09 evocative, remindful
10 suggestive
11 reminiscent

**redoubtable**
06 mighty, strong
08 dreadful, fearsome, powerful, resolute, terrible
10 formidable

**redound**
04 tend
05 ensue
06 effect, result
07 conduce, reflect
10 contribute

**redress**
05 amend, right
06 adjust, relief, remedy

07 balance, correct, justice, payment, rectify, requite
08 put right, regulate, requital
10 assistance, correction, recompense, reparation
12 compensation, satisfaction

**reduce**
04 diet, slim, trim
05 halve, lower, slash
06 demote, humble, lessen, shrink, subdue, weaken
07 curtail, deplete, shorten
08 contract, decrease, diminish, discount, downsize, make less, minimize, mitigate
09 bring down, downgrade, go on a diet, humiliate, knock down, overpower
10 abbreviate, lose weight

**reduction**
03 cut
04 drop, fall, loss
07 cutback, decline
08 decrease, discount
09 allowance, deduction, lessening, narrowing, shrinkage, weakening
10 concession, diminution, downsizing, limitation
11 compression, contraction, discounting, subtraction

**redundancy**
06 excess
07 surplus
08 pleonasm, verbiage
09 prolixity, tautology, verbosity, wordiness
10 redundance
11 superfluity, uselessness

**redundant**
05 extra, wordy
06 excess, padded
07 surplus
08 unneeded, unwanted
10 pleonastic
11 superfluous, unnecessary
12 periphrastic, tautological
13 supernumerary

**reef**
03 cay, key
05 ridge
07 sandbar
08 sandbank

**reek**
03 hum
04 fume, odor
05 fetor, smell, stink, vapor
06 exhale, stench
07 malodor
08 mephitis
09 effluvium

**reel**
04 rock, roll, spin, sway, swim
05 dance, fling, lurch, music, pitch, spool, swirl, twirl, waver, wheel, whirl
06 falter, gyrate, totter, wobble
07 revolve, stagger, stumble

**refer**
04 cite, send
05 apply, guide, point, quote
06 allude, belong, direct, hand on, hint at, look at, look up, pass on, relate, turn to
07 bring up, concern, consult, deliver, mention, pertain, speak of, touch on
09 recommend

**referee**
03 ref, ump
05 judge
06 umpire
07 mediate
08 mediator, official
09 arbitrate, intercede
10 adjudicate, arbitrator
11 adjudicator

**reference**
04 hint, note
06 regard, remark, source
07 bearing, mention, respect
08 allusion, citation, footnote
09 character, quotation
10 connection, pertinence
11 credentials, testimonial
13 applicability
14 recommendation

**referendum**
04 poll, vote
06 survey, voting
10 plebiscite

**refine**
04 hone, sift
05 clear, exalt, treat
06 filter, polish, purify
07 clarify, cleanse, distill, elevate, improve, perfect, process
08 civilize

**refined**
04 fine
05 civil, clear, exact
06 polite, subtle, urbane
07 courtly, elegant, genteel, precise, stylish, treated
08 cultured, delicate, filtered, gracious, ladylike, polished, purified, well-bred
09 civilized, distilled, processed, sensitive
10 cultivated
11 gentlemanly
12 well-mannered
13 sophisticated

**refinement**
05 grace, style, taste
06 polish
07 culture, finesse
08 addition, breeding, civility, elegance, subtlety, urbanity
09 amendment, gentility
10 alteration
11 cultivation, good manners, improvement
12 amelioration, modification
14 sophistication

**reflect**
04 echo, mull, muse, show
05 brood, dwell, image, think
06 mirror, ponder, reveal
07 bespeak, display, exhibit, express, imitate, portray
08 cogitate, consider, indicate, manifest, meditate, mull over, ruminate, send back
09 bounce off, cerebrate, reproduce, throw back
10 deliberate
11 contemplate, demonstrate

**reflection**
04 echo, idea, slur, view
05 blame, image, shame, study
07 feeling, opinion, thought
08 likeness, reproach, thinking
09 aspersion, criticism, discredit, disrepute
10 cogitation, expression, meditation, rumination
11 cerebration, mirror image, observation
12 deliberation
13 consideration, contemplation

**reflective**
06 dreamy
07 pensive
08 absorbed
09 pondering, reasoning
10 cogitating, meditative, ruminative, thoughtful
12 deliberative
13 contemplative

**reflex**
08 knee-jerk, unwilled
09 automatic
11 involuntary, spontaneous
14 uncontrollable

**reform**
05 amend, purge
06 change, revamp, revise
07 improve, rebuild, rectify, remodel, shake up
08 renovate, revision

09 amendment, refashion
10 ameliorate, reorganize
11 improvement, reconstruct
12 reconstitute, rehabilitate
14 rehabilitation, reorganization

**reformer**
08 crusader, do-gooder, moralist
13 revolutionary, whistleblower

**refractory**
06 mulish, unruly
07 defiant, naughty, restive, willful
08 perverse, stubborn
09 difficult, obstinate, pigheaded, resistant
10 headstrong
11 disobedient, intractable
12 cantankerous, contumacious, disputatious, recalcitrant, unmanageable
13 uncooperative
14 uncontrollable

**refrain**
04 quit, song, stop, tune
05 avoid, cease
06 burden, chorus, desist, eschew, give up, melody
07 abstain, forbear
08 renounce, response

**refresh**
04 cool, prod, rest, stir
05 brace, renew
06 prompt, remind, revive
07 enliven, freshen, restore
08 activate, energize, revivify
09 reanimate, stimulate
10 invigorate, rejuvenate, revitalize

**refreshing**
03 new
04 cool
05 fresh, novel
07 bracing
08 original, reviving
09 different, inspiring
10 energizing, freshening
11 stimulating
12 exhilarating, invigorating

**refreshment**
04 food
05 drink, snack
07 renewal, revival
10 freshening, sustenance
11 restoration, stimulation
12 invigoration
14 reinvigoration, revitalization

**refreshments**
04 eats, food, grub, nosh
06 drinks, snacks

10 provisions, sustenance

**refrigerate**
04 cool
05 chill
06 freeze

**refuge**
05 haven
06 asylum, island, resort
07 hideout, retreat, shelter
08 hideaway
09 safe house, sanctuary
10 protection
13 place of safety

**refugee**
05 exile
06 émigré
07 escapee, runaway
08 fugitive
15 displaced person

**refulgent**
06 bright
07 beaming, lambent, radiant, shining
08 gleaming, lustrous
09 brilliant, irradiant
10 glistening, glittering
11 resplendent

**refund**
05 repay
06 rebate, return
07 pay back, restore
09 reimburse, repayment

**refurbish**
04 do up, mend
05 refit
06 repair, revamp
07 reequip, remodel, restore
08 overhaul, renovate
10 redecorate
11 recondition

**refusal**
02 no
06 denial, rebuff
08 negation, spurning
09 rejection
11 repudiation, turning-down

**refuse**
04 deny, junk, scum
05 draff, dregs, dross, repel, say no, spurn, trash, waste
06 debris, litter, pass up, rebuff, reject, scoria
07 decline, garbage, rubbish
08 turn down, withhold
13 draw the line at

**refutation**
08 disproof, elenchus, negation, rebuttal
11 confutation

**refute**
05 rebut
06 negate
07 confute, counter, silence
08 disprove
09 discredit, overthrow
12 deny strongly, give the lie to

**regain**
06 recoup, retake
07 get back, reclaim, recover
08 retrieve, return to, take back
09 recapture, repossess

**regal**
05 noble, royal
06 kingly, lordly
07 queenly, stately
08 imperial, majestic, princely
09 sovereign

**regale**
03 ply
05 amuse, feast, serve
06 divert
07 delight, gratify, refresh
09 captivate, entertain

**regard**
03 eye, see
04 care, heed, note, view
05 honor, judge, think, value, watch
06 aspect, behold, esteem, follow, gaze at, look at, matter, notice
07 observe, respect, suppose
08 appraise, approval, consider, estimate, listen to, look upon, respects, sympathy
09 affection, attention, deference, greetings
10 admiration, best wishes, good wishes, scrutinize
11 approbation, compliments, contemplate, salutations
13 consideration

❑ **with regard to, in regard to**
02 re
04 as to, in re
05 about
07 apropos
09 as regards
10 concerning
12 in relation to
13 with respect to
14 on the subject of
15 with reference to

**regardful**
07 careful, dutiful, mindful
08 noticing, watchful
09 attentive, observant
10 respectful, thoughtful
11 circumspect, considerate

**regarding**
02 re
04 as to, in re
05 about
07 apropos
09 as regards
10 concerning, in regard to
12 in relation to, with regard to
13 with respect to
14 on the subject of
15 with reference to

**regardless**
06 anyhow, anyway
09 at any cost, unmindful
10 at any price, neglectful
11 come what may, inattentive, indifferent
12 no matter what

**regenerate**
05 renew
06 change, regrow, revive, uplift
07 refresh, restore
08 reawaken, rekindle, renovate
09 reproduce
10 invigorate, rejuvenate
11 reconstruct, reestablish
12 reconstitute, reinvigorate

**regeneration**
07 renewal
10 renovation
11 restoration
12 rejuvenation, reproduction
14 reconstitution, reconstruction, reinvigoration

**regime**
06 system
07 command, control
10 government, leadership, management
13 establishment
14 administration

**regiment**
04 army, band, body, crew, gang, unit
06 cohort
08 organize
12 military unit

**regimented**
06 strict
07 ordered
09 organized, regulated
11 disciplined

**region**
04 land, part
05 place, range, scope
06 sector, sphere
07 expanse, section, terrain
12 neighborhood

## ◻in the region of
04 some
05 about, circa
06 around, nearly
07 close to, loosely, roughly
09 just about, not far off
10 give or take, more or less
11 approaching
13 approximately, or thereabouts, something like
14 in round numbers

## regional
05 local, zoned
08 district
09 localized, parochial
10 provincial
11 territorial

## register
03 log, say
04 file, list, note, roll, show
05 diary, enter, files, index
06 annals, betray, enlist, enroll, ledger, record, reveal, roster, sign on
07 almanac, catalog, check in, display, exhibit, express, listing, logbook
08 indicate, manifest
09 catalogue, chronicle, directory

## registrar
05 clerk
08 annalist, official, recorder
09 archivist, cataloger, secretary
10 cataloguer, chronicler
15 college official

## regress
03 ebb
05 lapse
06 recede, return, revert
07 relapse, retreat
09 backslide, retrocede
10 degenerate, retrogress
11 deteriorate

## regret
03 rue
06 bemoan, grieve, lament, repent, sorrow
07 deplore, remorse
09 feel sorry, penitence
10 contrition, repentance
12 be distressed, self-reproach
14 disappointment

## regretful
03 sad
05 sorry
06 rueful
07 ashamed
08 contrite, penitent
09 repentant, sorrowful

10 apologetic, remorseful
12 disappointed

## regrettable
03 sad
05 sorry, wrong
07 unhappy, unlucky
10 ill-advised, lamentable
11 distressing, unfortunate
13 disappointing, reprehensible

## regular
04 even, flat
05 daily, fixed, level, usual
06 hourly, normal, smooth, steady, weekly, yearly
07 monthly, orderly, routine, typical, uniform
08 approved, balanced, · constant, frequent, habitual, official, periodic, rhythmic, standard
09 recurring, unvarying
10 consistent, methodical, systematic, unchanging
11 established, symmetrical
12 conventional, evenly spread

## regulate
03 run, set
04 rule, tune
05 guide, order
06 adjust, direct, govern, handle, manage, settle
07 arrange, balance, conduct, control, monitor, oversee
08 moderate, organize
09 supervise
11 superintend, synchronize

## regulation
03 act, law, set
04 rule
05 bylaw, edict, order, usual
06 decree, dictum, ruling
07 command, control, dictate, precept, statute
08 guidance, official, orthodox, required, standard
09 direction, directive, mandatory, statutory
10 management, obligatory, prescribed
11 commandment, legislation, requirement, supervision
14 administration
15 superintendence

## regurgitate
04 puke, spew
05 vomit
06 repeat
07 bring up, restate, throw up
08 disgorge, say again
09 reiterate, tell again

## rehabilitate
04 mend, save
06 adjust, redeem, reform
07 convert, rebuild, restore
08 renovate
09 normalize, reinstate
11 recondition, reconstruct, reestablish, reintegrate

## rehash
05 alter
06 change, review, rework
08 rejigger
09 rearrange, refashion, reshuffle, reworking
13 rearrangement

## rehearsal
05 drill
06 dry run
07 reading, recital
08 dummy run, exercise, practice, trial run
10 run-through

## rehearse
05 drill, train
06 go over, recite, repeat
07 narrate, prepare, recount
08 practice
10 run through

## reign
04 rule, sway
05 exist, occur, power
06 empire, govern, obtain
07 control, prevail
08 dominion, hold sway
10 ascendancy
11 predominate, sovereignty
14 sit on the throne

## reimburse
05 repay
06 refund, return
07 pay back, restore
08 give back
10 compensate, recompense

## rein
04 curb, halt, hold, stop
05 brake, check, limit
06 arrest, bridle
07 control, harness
08 hold back, restrain, restrict
09 restraint

## reindeer
► *Santa Claus' reindeer*:
05 Comet, Cupid, Vixen
06 Dancer, Dasher, Donner
07 Blitzen, Prancer, Rudolph

## reinforce
04 prop, stay
05 brace, shore, steel

07 augment, fortify, stiffen,
   support, toughen
08 buttress, increase
09 emphasize, underline
10 strengthen, supplement

**reinforcement**
04 help, prop, stay
05 brace, shore
06 backup
07 support
08 buttress, emphasis, reserves
11 auxiliaries, enlargement
12 augmentation
13 fortification, strengthening

**reinstate**
06 recall, return
07 replace, restore
09 reappoint, reinstall
11 reestablish

**reinstatement**
06 recall, return
11 replacement, restoration
15 reestablishment

**reiterate**
05 recap, resay
06 repeat, retell, stress
07 iterate, restate
09 emphasize
12 recapitulate

**reject**
04 deny, jilt, veto
05 repel, scrap, spurn
06 rebuff, refuse, second
07 cast off, decline, discard,
   exclude, forsake, outcast
08 brush off, disallow, jettison,
   set aside, turn down
09 eliminate, throw away
14 turn your back on
15 wash your hands of

**rejection**
04 veto
06 denial, rebuff
07 refusal
08 brushoff
09 dismissal, exclusion
11 elimination, jettisoning
12 cold shoulder, renunciation
14 Dear John letter

**rejoice**
05 exult, glory, revel
07 be happy, delight, triumph
08 be joyful
09 be pleased, celebrate
10 jump for joy
11 be delighted

**rejoicing**
03 joy
07 delight, elation, triumph
08 euphoria, gladness, pleasure

09 festivity, happiness
10 exultation, jubilation
11 celebration, merrymaking

**rejoin**
04 quip
05 reply
06 answer, retort, return
07 respond, reunite, riposte

**rejoinder**
04 quip
05 reply
06 answer, retort
07 riposte
08 repartee, response

**rejuvenate**
05 renew
06 revive
07 refresh, restore
08 recharge, rekindle, revivify
09 freshen up, reanimate
10 regenerate, revitalize
12 reinvigorate

**relapse**
04 fail, sink
06 revert, weaken, worsen
07 regress, setback
09 backslide, reversion,
   weakening, worsening
10 degenerate, recurrence,
   regression, retrogress
11 backsliding, deteriorate
13 deterioration, retrogression

**relate**
04 ally, join, link, tell
05 apply, refer
06 couple, detail, recite, report
07 concern, connect, narrate,
   pertain, present, recount
08 describe, hit it off, identify
09 appertain, associate,
   correlate, empathize
10 be relevant, sympathize
14 have a bearing on

**related**
04 akin
05 joint
06 agnate, allied, linked, mutual
07 cognate, kindred
08 relevant
09 connected
10 affiliated, associated
11 concomitant
12 accompanying, interrelated
14 consanguineous,
   interconnected

**relation**
03 kin
04 bond, link
06 family, regard
07 bearing, kindred, kinsman

08 alliance, kinsfolk, relative
09 kinswoman, relevance
10 comparison, connection
11 affiliation, correlation

**relations**
03 kin, sex
05 folks, terms
06 coitus, family
07 coition, contact, kindred
08 dealings, intimacy, kinsfolk
09 relatives
10 lovemaking
11 connections, interaction,
   intercourse
12 associations, relationship
15 carnal knowledge

**relationship**
03 tie
04 bond, link, ties
05 fling, ratio, tie-up
06 affair
07 liaison, rapport, romance
08 affinity, alliance, intimacy,
   parallel
09 chemistry, closeness
10 connection, friendship, love
   affair, proportion, similarity
11 association, correlation,
   involvement

**relative**
03 kin
06 family
07 germane, kindred, kinsman
08 kinsfolk, parallel, relation
09 kinswoman, pertinent
10 reciprocal, respective
11 comparative, correlative
12 commensurate, proportional
13 corresponding,
   proportionate

**relatively**
05 quite
06 fairly, rather
08 somewhat
12 by comparison, in
   comparison
13 comparatively

**relax**
04 calm, cool, ease, rest
05 abate, lower, remit
06 lessen, loosen, reduce,
   sedate, unwind, weaken
07 ease off, slacken
08 calm down, chill out,
   diminish, wind down
09 hang loose
10 take it easy
13 put your feet up
14 take things easy
15 let your hair down

## relaxation
03 fun
04 rest
05 letup
06 easing, repose
07 détente, leisure
09 abatement, amusement, enjoyment, lessening, loosening, unwinding
10 moderation, recreation
11 loosening up, refreshment

## relaxed
04 calm, cool
06 at ease, casual
08 carefree, composed, informal, laid-back
09 collected, easygoing, leisurely, unhurried

## relay
04 race, send, time, turn
05 carry, shift, spell, stint
06 hand on, pass on, period
07 forward, message, program
08 dispatch, transmit
09 broadcast
11 communicate
12 transmission

## release
04 free, undo
05 issue, let go, loose, untie
06 acquit, excuse, exempt, launch, let off, loosen, parole, reveal, unbind, unlock
07 absolve, deliver, divulge, publish, set free, unchain, unleash, unloose
08 announce, bulletin, disclose, liberate, unfasten
09 acquittal, discharge, make known, unshackle
10 absolution, disclosure, emancipate, liberation, publishing, revelation
11 deliverance, exoneration, manumission, publication
12 announcement, emancipation, proclamation

## relegate
05 eject, exile, expel, refer
06 assign, banish, demote, deport, reduce
07 consign, degrade, entrust
08 delegate, dispatch, transfer
09 downgrade
10 expatriate

## relent
05 abate, let up, relax, yield
06 give in, soften, weaken
07 die down, give way, slacken
10 capitulate, come around

## relentless
04 grim, hard
05 cruel, harsh
08 pitiless, ruthless
09 incessant, merciless, punishing, unceasing
10 implacable, inexorable, inflexible, persistent
11 coldhearted, hardhearted, remorseless, unforgiving, unrelenting, unremitting
14 uncompromising

## relevant
03 apt
07 apropos, fitting, germane
08 apposite, material, suitable
09 congruous, pertinent
10 applicable, to the point
11 appropriate, significant

## reliable
04 safe, sure, true
05 solid, sound
06 honest, stable, tested, trusty
07 certain, regular, staunch
08 constant, faithful
09 unfailing
10 dependable
11 predictable, trustworthy

## reliance
05 faith, trust
06 belief, credit
09 assurance
10 confidence, dependence

## relic
05 scrap, token, trace
07 antique, memento, remains, remnant, vestige
08 artefact, fragment, keepsake, survival
11 remembrance

## relief
03 aid
04 cure, help, rest
05 break, letup, proxy
06 backup, easing, remedy, rescue, saving, succor, supply
07 comfort, respite, stand-in, standby, support
08 allaying, breather, soothing
09 abatement, assuaging, diversion, lessening, reduction, remission
10 assistance, palliation, relaxation, substitute
11 alleviation, deliverance, refreshment, replacement
12 interruption

## relieve
03 aid
04 cure, free, heal, help, save

05 abate, allay, break, pause
06 assist, excuse, exempt, lessen, reduce, remove, rescue, soften, soothe, succor
07 assuage, break up, comfort, console, deliver, dismiss, release, replace, set free, slacken, support
08 liberate, palliate, unburden
09 alleviate, interrupt
10 stand in for, substitute
12 take over from

## religion
▶ Names of religions:
03 Zen
04 Shi'a
05 Amish, Baha'i, Druze, Islam, Sunni
06 Sufism, Taoism, voodoo
07 animism, Baha'ism, Essenes, Jainism, Jesuits, Judaism, Lamaism, Moonies, Quakers, Sikhism
08 Baptists, Buddhism, Druidism, Hasidism, Hinduism, paganism, Tantrism
09 Cabbalism, Calvinism, Episcopal, Methodism, Mithraism, Mormonism, occultism, Parseeism, shamanism, Shintoism, Vedantism
10 Adventists, Brahmanism, Evangelism, Gnosticism, Iconoclasm, Puritanism
11 Anabaptists, Anglicanism, Catholicism, Creationism, Hare Krishna, Lutheranism, Manichaeism, Scientology, Zen Buddhism
12 Christianity, Confucianism, Unitarianism
13 Church in Wales, Protestantism, Reform Judaism
14 Church of Christ, Fundamentalism, Pentecostalism, Rastafarianism, Society of Jesus, Zoroastrianism
15 ancestor worship, Church of England, Latter-Day Saints, Presbyterianism
➤ See also ANGEL;
ARCHBISHOP; BIBLE;
BUILDING; CARDINAL;
CELEBRATION; CHURCH;
FESTIVAL; MISSIONARY;
MONASTIC; POPE; RELIGIOUS;
SCRIPTURE; THEOLOGIAN;

VESTMENT; WORSHIP

**religious**
04 holy
05 godly, pious
06 devout, divine, sacred, strict
09 believing, committed, doctrinal, righteous, spiritual
10 devotional, God-fearing, meticulous, scriptural
11 churchgoing, theological
13 conscientious
➤ See also RELIGION

► *Names of religious figures*:
03 **Fry** (Elizabeth), **Hus** (Jan), **Roy** (Ram Mohan)
04 **Eddy** (Mary Baker), **Huss** (John), **John** (of Leyden), **King** (Martin Luther), **Knox** (John), **Penn** (William), **Shaw** (Anna Howard), **Weil** (Simone)
05 **Booth** (William), **Jesus**, **Lao Zi**, **Lewis** (Clive Staples), **Mahdi** (El), **Paris** (Matthew), **Sheen** (Bishop Fulton), **Smith** (Joseph), **Young** (Brigham)
06 **Bakker** (Jim), **Besant** (Annie), **Borgia**, **Browne** (Robert), **Browne** (Thomas), **Buddha**, **Bunyan** (John), **Calvin** (John), **Christ**, **Gandhi** (Mohandas), **Garvey** (Marcus), **Graham** (Billy), **Hillel**, **Hutter** (Leonhard), **Julian** (of Norwich), **Kempis** (Thomas à), **Laotzu**, **Luther** (Martin), **Mather** (Cotton), **Mesmer** (Franz Anton), **Olcott** (Colonel Henry Steel), **Pilate** (Pontius), **Ridley** (Nicholas), **Sunday** (Billy), **Wesley** (John)
07 **Aga Khan**, **Ayeshah**, **Cranmer** (Thomas), **Crowley** (Aleister), **Erasmus** (Desiderius), **Falwell** (Jerry), **Fénelon** (François), **Hubbard** (L. Ron), **Jackson** (Jesse), **Latimer** (Hugh), **Mahatma**, **Mahomet**, **Paisley** (Reverend Ian), **Photius**, **Roberts** (Oral), **Russell** (Charles Taze), **Sithole** (Reverend Ndabaningi), **Spooner** (William Archibald), **Steiner** (Rudolf), **Tyndale** (William), **William** (of Malmesbury), **William** (of Ockham), **William** (of Tyre), **Zwingli** (Huldreich)
08 **Andrewes** (Lancelot), **Barabbas**, **Caiaphas**, **Khomeini** (Ayatollah Ruhollah), **Mahavira** (Vardhamana), **Mohammed**, **Muhammad**, **Pelagius**, **Rasputin** (Grigoriy), **Selassie** (Emperor Haile), **Swaggert** (Jimmy), **Wycliffe** (John)
09 **Akhenaten**, **Bar Kokhba** (Simon), **Blavatsky** (Madame Helena), **Confucius**, **Dalai Lama**, **Guru Nanak**, **McPherson** (Aimee Semple), **Niemöller** (Martin), **Robertson** (Pat), **Zoroaster**
10 **Belshazzar**, **Manichaeus**, **Savonarola** (Girolamo), **Swedenborg** (Emmanuel), **Torquemada** (Tomás de)
11 **Bodhidharma**, **Jesus Christ**, **Prester John**, **Ramakrishna**
12 **Krishnamurti** (Jiddu)
13 **Judas Iscariot**

► *Types of religious officer*:
03 nun
04 dean, guru, imam, monk, pope
05 abbot, canon, elder, friar, padre, prior, rabbi, vicar
06 abbess, bishop, curate, deacon, father, mullah, parson, pastor, priest, rector
07 muezzin, prelate, proctor
08 cardinal, chaplain, minister
09 ayatollah, clergyman, Dalai Lama, deaconess, Monsignor
10 archbishop, archdeacon, chancellor
11 clergywoman
14 mother superior

**relinquish**
04 cede, drop, quit
05 cease, let go, waive, yield
06 desist, forego, give up
07 abandon, forsake, release
08 abdicate, hand over
09 repudiate, surrender

**relish**
04 like, love, tang, zest
05 enjoy, gusto, sauce, savor, spice, vigor
06 pickle
07 chutney, delight, revel in

08 piquancy, pleasure, vivacity
09 enjoyment, flavoring, seasoning
10 appreciate
12 appreciation, satisfaction

**reluctance**
07 dislike
08 aversion, distaste, loathing
10 hesitation, repugnance
13 recalcitrance, unwillingness
14 disinclination

**reluctant**
04 slow
05 loath
06 averse
08 grudging, hesitant
09 unwilling
11 disinclined
14 unenthusiastic

**rely**
04 bank, lean
05 count, trust
06 be sure, depend, reckon
07 swear by

**remain**
04 bide, last, rest, stay, wait
05 abide, dwell, stand, tarry
06 endure, linger
07 persist, prevail, survive
10 be left over, stay behind

**remainder**
04 rest
06 excess
07 balance, remains, remnant, residue, surplus
08 residuum, vestiges
09 leftovers

**remaining**
04 last, left
05 spare
06 unused
07 abiding, lasting, unspent
08 left over, residual
09 lingering, surviving
10 persisting, unfinished

**remains**
04 body, rest
05 ashes, dregs
06 corpse, crumbs, debris, relics, scraps, traces
07 cadaver, carcass, residue
08 dead body, detritus, remnants, vestiges
09 fragments, leftovers, reliquiae, remainder

**remark**
03 say
04 note
05 state
06 assert, notice

07 comment, mention, observe
09 reference, utterance
10 reflection
11 declaration, observation

**remarkable**
03 odd
04 rare
06 signal
07 notable, strange, unusual
08 singular, striking
09 memorable, momentous
10 impressive, noteworthy, phenomenal, surprising
11 conspicuous, exceptional, outstanding, significant
13 distinguished, extraordinary

**remedy**
03 fix
04 cure, ease, heal, help, mend
06 physic, relief, repair, soothe
07 control, correct, nostrum, panacea, rectify, redress, relieve, restore, sort out
08 antidote, medicine, mitigate
09 treatment
10 corrective, counteract, medicament, medication
11 restorative

**remember**
04 keep, mark
05 honor, learn, place
06 recall, retain
08 hark back, memorize
09 celebrate, recognize, recollect, reminisce
10 call to mind
11 commemorate

**remembrance**
05 relic, token
06 memory, recall
07 memento, thought
08 keepsake, memorial, reminder, souvenir
09 nostalgia
11 recognition, testimonial
12 recollection, reminiscence
13 commemoration

**remind**
06 call up, prompt
10 call to mind
11 bring to mind
13 jog your memory

**reminder**
04 hint, memo, note
06 prompt
07 memento
08 souvenir
10 memorandum, suggestion
11 aide-mémoire

**reminisce**
06 recall, review
08 look back, remember
09 recollect, think back
10 retrospect

**reminiscence**
06 memoir, memory, recall
08 anecdote
11 remembrance
12 recollection
13 retrospection

**reminiscent**
08 redolent
09 evocative, nostalgic
10 suggestive

**remiss**
03 lax
04 slow
05 slack, tardy
06 casual, sloppy
07 wayward
08 careless, culpable, dilatory, slipshod
09 forgetful, negligent
11 inattentive, thoughtless
13 lackadaisical

**remission**
04 lull
05 annul, letup
06 excuse, pardon, repeal
07 amnesty, release, respite
08 decrease, reprieve
09 abatement, acquittal, discharge, exemption, lessening, weakening
10 abrogation, absolution, indulgence, moderation, relaxation, rescinding, revocation, slackening
11 alleviation, exoneration
12 cancellation

**remit**
03 pay
04 mail, post, send
05 refer
06 cancel, direct, orders, pass on, remand, repeal, revoke, settle
07 forward, rescind, suspend
08 abrogate, decrease, dispatch, hold over, set aside, transfer

**remittance**
03 fee
07 payment, sending
08 dispatch
09 allowance
13 consideration

**remnant**
03 bit, end

05 piece, scrap, shred, trace
07 oddment, remains, vestige
08 fragment, leftover
09 remainder

**remonstrance**
07 protest, reproof
08 petition
09 complaint, exception, grievance, objection
10 opposition
12 protestation
13 expostulation

**remonstrate**
05 argue, gripe
06 object, oppose
07 dispute, dissent, protest
08 complain
09 challenge
11 expostulate

**remorse**
05 grief, guilt, shame
06 regret, sorrow
10 contrition, repentance
12 self-reproach
13 bad conscience

**remorseful**
03 sad
05 sorry
06 guilty, rueful
07 ashamed
08 contrite, penitent
09 regretful, repentant
10 apologetic
11 guilt-ridden

**remorseless**
05 cruel, harsh, stern
07 callous
08 inhumane, pitiless, ruthless
09 merciless
10 implacable, inexorable, relentless, unmerciful
11 hardhearted, unforgiving, unrelenting, unremitting

**remote**
03 far
04 poor, slim
05 aloof, faint, small
06 far-off, lonely, meager, slight
07 distant, outside, slender
08 detached, doubtful, far-flung, isolated, outlying, secluded
10 improbable, uninvolved
11 God-forsaken, out-of-the-way, standoffish
12 inaccessible
14 unapproachable

**removal**
04 boot, move, push, sack
05 elbow, shift

07 editing, ousting, purging, sacking
08 ejection, eviction, riddance
09 abolition, dismissal, expulsion, uprooting
10 conveyance, detachment, extraction, relegation, relocation, withdrawal
11 dislodgment
12 transporting
13 assassination

**remove**
04 doff, edit, fire, oust, sack, shed
05 carry, eject, erase, evict, expel, purge, shift, strip
06 convey, cut off, cut out, delete, depose, detach, efface, excise, lop off
07 abolish, expurge, extract
08 amputate, condense, get rid of, take away, withdraw
09 discharge, eliminate, strike out, transport
10 blue-pencil, obliterate

**remunerate**
03 pay
05 repay
06 reward
07 redress
09 indemnify, reimburse
10 compensate, recompense

**remuneration**
03 fee, pay
05 wages
06 income, profit, salary
07 payment, stipend
08 earnings, retainer
09 emolument, indemnity
10 honorarium, remittance
12 compensation
13 reimbursement

**remunerative**
04 rich
06 paying
07 gainful
09 lucrative, rewarding
10 profitable, worthwhile
11 moneymaking

**renaissance**
07 new dawn, rebirth, renewal
08 new birth
09 awakening
10 renascence, resurgence
11 reawakening, restoration
12 reappearance, regeneration, rejuvenation, resurrection
13 recrudescence

**renascent**
06 reborn
07 renewed, revived

09 born-again, redivivus, resurgent
10 reanimated, reawakened, reemergent
11 resurrected

**rend**
03 rip
04 stab, tear
05 break, burst, sever, split
06 cleave, divide, pierce
07 rupture, shatter
08 fracture, separate, splinter

**render**
04 give, make, play, show, sing
05 leave
06 change, depict, supply
07 deliver, display, exhibit, perform, present, proffer
08 describe, manifest
09 cause to be, represent

**rendezvous**
04 date, meet
05 haunt, rally, tryst, venue
06 gather, muster, resort
07 collect, convene, meeting
08 assemble, converge
10 engagement
11 appointment, assignation
12 meeting place

**rendition**
07 reading, version
08 delivery
09 depiction, execution, portrayal, rendering
11 arrangement, explanation, performance, translation
12 construction, presentation
14 interpretation

**renegade**
05 rebel
06 outlaw
07 runaway, traitor
08 apostate, betrayer, defector, deserter, disloyal, mutineer, mutinous, recreant, turncoat
09 dissident
10 perfidious, rebellious, traitorous, unfaithful
13 tergiversator

**renege**
05 welsh
07 back off, default
09 backslide, repudiate
10 apostatize

**renew**
06 extend, reform, repair, repeat, resume, revive
07 prolong, refresh, replace, restart, restock, restore
08 overhaul, reaffirm, renovate

09 modernize, refurbish, replenish, transform
10 recommence, regenerate, rejuvenate, revitalize
11 recondition, reestablish, resubscribe
12 reconstitute, reinvigorate

**renewal**
06 repair
10 re-creation, renovation, repetition, resumption
11 reiteration, restatement
12 rejuvenation, resurrection
13 refurbishment, replenishment, resuscitation
14 recommencement, reconstruction, reinvigoration, revitalization

**renounce**
04 deny, shun
05 spurn, waive
06 abjure, disown, eschew, forego, give up, recant
07 abandon, abstain, forsake
08 abdicate, disclaim
09 repudiate, surrender
10 disinherit, relinquish

**renovate**
04 do up
05 refit, renew
06 reform, repair, revamp
07 improve, remodel, restore
08 overhaul
09 modernize, refurbish
10 redecorate
11 recondition
13 give a facelift

**renovation**
05 refit
06 repair
07 renewal
08 facelift
11 improvement, restoration
13 modernization, refurbishment
14 reconditioning

**renown**
04 fame, mark, note
05 honor
06 esteem, repute
07 acclaim, stardom
08 eminence, prestige
09 celebrity
10 prominence, reputation
11 distinction, preeminence

**renowned**
05 famed, noted
06 famous
07 eminent, notable
09 acclaimed, well-known
10 celebrated, preeminent

13 distinguished

**rent**
03 cut, fee, let, rip
04 hire, hole, rift, slit, tear, torn
05 cleft, crack, lease, split
06 breach, let out, sublet
07 charter, hire out, severed
08 cleavage, disunion, division
10 dissension
11 perforation

**renunciation**
06 denial
07 waiving
08 giving up, shunning, spurning
09 disowning, forsaking, rejection, surrender
10 abdication, abnegation, abstinence, desistance, discarding
11 abandonment, disclaiming, repudiation
13 disinheriting
14 relinquishment

**repair**
03 fix, sew
04 darn, form, heal, mend, move, turn
05 patch, refit, renew, state
06 kilter, remedy, remove, resort, retire, revive
07 improve, patch up, rectify, redress, restore, service
08 make good, overhaul, put right, renovate, withdraw
09 condition
11 improvement, restoration

**reparable**
07 curable, savable
08 saveable
10 corrigible, restorable
11 recoverable, rectifiable, retrievable, salvageable

**reparation**
06 amends
07 damages, redress, renewal
08 requital, solatium
09 atonement, indemnity
10 recompense
11 restitution
12 compensation, propitiation

**repartee**
03 wit
06 banter, retort
07 jesting, riposte
08 badinage

**repast**
04 feed, food, meal
06 spread
08 victuals
09 collation, refection

11 nourishment

**repay**
06 avenge, refund, reward, settle, square
09 reimburse, retaliate
10 compensate, recompense, remunerate
11 get even with, reciprocate
12 settle up with

**repayment**
06 rebate, refund, reward
07 payment, redress, revenge
09 tit for tat, vengeance
10 recompense, reparation
11 eye for an eye, retaliation, retribution
12 compensation, remuneration
13 reciprocation, reimbursement

**repeal**
04 void
05 annul, quash
06 abjure, cancel, recall, revoke
07 abolish, nullify, rescind, retract, reverse
08 abrogate, withdraw
09 abolition, annulment
10 abrogation, invalidate, rescinding, rescission, revocation, withdrawal
11 countermand, rescindment
12 cancellation, invalidation
13 nullification

**repeat**
04 copy, echo, redo
05 ditto, quote, recap, rerun
06 go over, parrot, recite, relate, replay, reshow, retell
08 rehearse, say again
09 duplicate, reiterate, reproduce, reshowing
10 repetition
12 recapitulate, reproduction
14 recapitulation

**repeated**
07 regular
08 constant, frequent, periodic
09 recurrent, recurring
10 persistent, rhythmical

**repeatedly**
10 frequently
11 over and over
12 time and again
13 again and again, time after time

**repel**
05 check, fight, parry, spurn
06 oppose, rebuff, refuse, reject, resist, revolt, sicken

07 disgust, hold off, repulse
08 beat back, nauseate
09 drive back, keep at bay

**repellent**
04 foul, vile
07 hateful
08 shocking
09 abhorrent, loathsome, obnoxious, offensive, repugnant, repulsive, revolting, sickening
10 abominable, despicable, disgusting, nauseating
11 distasteful
12 contemptible, disagreeable

**repent**
03 rue
06 lament, recant, regret
07 be sorry, confess, deplore
09 be ashamed
10 be contrite
11 feel remorse, see the light
14 beat your breast

**repentance**
05 grief, guilt, shame, U-turn
06 regret, sorrow
07 penance, remorse
10 contrition, conversion
11 compunction, recantation

**repentant**
05 sorry
06 guilty, rueful
07 ashamed
08 contrite, penitent
09 chastened, regretful
10 apologetic, remorseful

**repercussion**
06 effect, recoil, result, ripple
07 rebound
08 backlash
09 shock wave
11 consequence
13 reverberation

**repertoire**
05 range, stock, store
06 supply
07 reserve
08 routines
09 repertory, reservoir
10 collection, repository

**repetition**
04 echo
07 copying, echoing, reprise
08 sameness
09 echolalia, iteration, rehearsal, tautology
10 recurrence, redundancy
11 duplication, reiteration
14 recapitulation

## repetitious
06 boring, prolix
07 tedious, verbose
09 recurrent
10 long-winded, monotonous, pleonastic, unchanging
12 pleonastical, tautological

## repetitive
08 unvaried
09 automatic, recurrent
10 mechanical, monotonous

## rephrase
06 recast, reword
07 rewrite
10 paraphrase

## repine
04 beef, fret, moan, mope, sulk
05 brood
06 grieve, grouse, lament
07 grumble
08 complain, languish

## replace
04 oust
06 act for, follow, return
07 put back, relieve, restore
08 deputize, pinch-hit, supplant
09 reinstate, supersede
10 stand in for, substitute

## replacement
05 proxy
06 fill-in, supply
07 reserve, stand-in
09 successor, surrogate
10 substitute, understudy
11 pinch hitter

## replenish
05 renew, stock
06 fill up, make up, refill, reload
07 replace, restock, restore
08 recharge

## replete
04 full
05 sated
06 filled, full up, jammed
07 brimful, charged, crammed, glutted, stuffed, teeming
08 brimming, satiated
09 abounding, chock-full
11 well-stocked

## repletion
04 glut
07 satiety
08 fullness, plethora
09 satiation
12 completeness, overfullness
14 superabundance

## replica
04 copy
05 clone, model

09 duplicate, facsimile
12 reproduction

## replicate
03 ape
04 copy
05 clone, mimic
06 follow, repeat
08 re-create
09 duplicate, reproduce

## reply
04 echo
05 react
06 answer, rejoin, retort, return
07 counter, respond, riposte
08 comeback, repartee, response
09 rejoinder, retaliate
11 acknowledge, reciprocate
14 acknowledgment

## report
04 bang, boom, fame, file, item, name, news, note, shot, tale, talk, tell, word
05 brief, cover, crack, crash, honor, noise, piece, relay, rumor, split, state, story
06 credit, detail, esteem, gossip, notify, pass on, record, relate, renown, repute, squeal
07 account, article, declare, divulge, dossier, hearsay, message, minutes, narrate, recount, stature, write-up
08 bulletin, describe, disclose, document, register, set forth
09 broadcast, chronicle, explosion, narrative
10 communiqué, reputation
11 communicate, declaration, description, information, news release
12 announcement
13 communication, reverberation

## reporter
03 cub
04 hack
06 scribe
08 newshawk, stringer
09 anchorman, announcer, columnist, newshound
10 journalist, newscaster
11 anchorwoman, commentator
12 anchorperson, newspaperman
13 correspondent
14 newspaperwoman

## repose
03 lay, lie, put, set
04 calm, ease, laze, lean, rest

05 lodge, peace, place, poise, quiet, relax, sleep, store
06 aplomb, invest
07 deposit, dignity, entrust, recline, respite, slumber
08 calmness, quietude, serenity
09 composure, quietness
10 inactivity, relaxation
11 restfulness, tranquility

## repository
04 bank, safe
05 depot, store, vault
07 archive
08 magazine, treasury
09 container, warehouse
10 depository, receptacle

## reprehensible
03 bad
06 errant, erring, remiss
07 ignoble
08 shameful, unworthy
10 censurable, delinquent
11 blameworthy, disgraceful, opprobrious

## represent
02 be
04 draw, mean, show
05 act as, enact, evoke
06 act for, denote, depict, embody, sketch, typify
07 perform, picture, portray
08 describe, speak for, stand for
09 epitomize, exemplify, personify, symbolize
10 constitute, illustrate
12 characterize, correspond to
13 act on behalf of

## representation
04 bust, icon, play, show
05 envoy, image, model, proxy
06 deputy, sketch, statue
07 account, picture, stand-in
08 delegate, likeness, portrait
09 complaint, depiction, portrayal, spectacle
10 allegation, delegation, deputation, production
11 delineation, description, explanation, performance
12 illustration, presentation

## representative
03 rep
05 agent, envoy, proxy, usual
06 chosen, deputy, normal
07 elected, elector, stand-in, typical
08 delegate, elective, symbolic
09 councilor, exemplary, spokesman
10 ambassador, archetypal, authorized, delegation,

deputation, indicative,
legislator, politician,
saleswoman
11 congressman, spokeswoman
12 commissioner, illustrative,
spokesperson
14 characteristic

**repress**
04 curb
05 check, crush, quash, quell
06 master, muffle, stifle, subdue
07 control, inhibit, oppress, put
down, silence, smother
08 bottle up, dominate,
overcome, restrain, suppress,
vanquish
09 overpower, subjugate

**repressed**
07 uptight
09 inhibited, withdrawn
10 frustrated

**repression**
07 control, gagging, tyranny
08 coercion, muffling,
quashing, quelling, stifling
09 despotism, restraint
10 censorship, constraint,
domination, inhibition,
oppression, smothering
11 holding back, subjugation,
suffocation, suppression
12 dictatorship

**repressive**
05 cruel, harsh, tough
06 severe, strict
08 absolute, coercive, despotic
10 autocratic, dominating,
oppressive, tyrannical
11 dictatorial
12 totalitarian
13 authoritarian

**reprieve**
05 let up, letup, spare
06 acquit, let off, pardon,
redeem, relief, rescue
07 amnesty, relieve, respite
09 remission, show mercy
13 let off the hook

**reprimand**
05 blame, chide, scold, slate
06 berate, rebuke
07 censure, lecture, reproof,
reprove, tell off
08 admonish, reproach
09 castigate, criticize
10 admonition, telling-off,
upbraiding
11 castigation
12 dressing-down

**reprisal**
07 redress, revenge
09 tit for tat, vengeance
11 eye for an eye, retaliation,
retribution
13 recrimination

**reproach**
04 blot, slur
05 blame, chide, scold, scorn,
shame, smear, stain
06 defame, rebuke, stigma
07 censure, condemn, obloquy,
reproof, reprove, upbraid
08 admonish, contempt,
disgrace, dishonor, ignominy,
scolding
09 criticism, criticize, discredit,
disparage, reprehend,
reprimand
10 admonition, opprobrium
11 degradation, disapproval
12 condemnation

**reproachful**
08 critical, scolding, scornful
09 reproving
10 censorious, upbraiding
11 castigating, disparaging,
opprobrious
12 disappointed, faultfinding

**reprobate**
03 bad
04 base, rake, roué, vile
05 knave, rogue, scamp
06 damned, rascal, sinful, sinner,
wicked, wretch
07 corrupt, immoral, villain
08 criminal, depraved, evildoer,
scalawag
09 dissolute, miscreant,
scallywag, scoundrel
10 degenerate, ne'er-do-well,
profligate
12 incorrigible, troublemaker

**reproduce**
03 ape
04 copy, echo, redo, scan
05 breed, spawn, Xerox
06 mirror, remake, repeat
07 emulate, imitate
08 multiply, recreate, simulate
09 bear young, duplicate, give
birth, photocopy, procreate,
propagate, replicate
10 mimeograph, transcribe
11 proliferate, reconstruct
12 Photostat

**reproduction**
04 copy
05 clone, print, Xerox
07 genital, picture, replica
08 breeding

09 duplicate, facsimile,
imitation, photocopy,
Photostat
11 procreation, propagation

**reproductive**
06 sexual
07 genital
10 generative
11 procreative, progenitive,
propagative

**reproof**
06 rebuke
08 berating, reproach, scolding
09 criticism, reprimand
10 admonition, telling-off,
upbraiding
12 dressing-down

**reprove**
05 chide, scold
06 berate, rebuke
07 tell off, upbraid
08 admonish, reproach
09 criticize, reprimand

**reptile**

➤ *Types of reptile*:
04 croc
05 gator, snake
06 caiman, cayman, lizard, turtle
07 serpent, tuatara
08 terrapin, tortoise
09 alligator, crocodile
11 green turtle
13 giant tortoise
14 snapping turtle
➤ See also ANIMAL; DINOSAUR;
LIZARD; SNAKE

**repudiate**
04 deny
06 abjure, desert, disown,
reject, revoke
07 abandon, cast off, disavow,
divorce, forsake, rescind
08 disclaim, renounce
09 disaffirm

**repudiation**
06 denial
09 disavowal, disowning,
rejection
10 abjuration, retraction
11 recantation
12 renunciation
14 disaffirmation

**repugnance**
05 odium
06 hatred, horror, nausea
07 disgust, dislike
08 aversion, distaste, loathing
09 repulsion, revulsion
10 abhorrence, reluctance

**repugnant**
04 foul, vile
06 averse, horrid, odious
07 adverse, hateful, opposed
09 abhorrent, loathsome, obnoxious, offensive, repellent, revolting, sickening
10 abominable, disgusting, nauseating
12 antagonistic, antipathetic, incompatible, inconsistent

**repulse**
04 snub
05 check, repel, spurn
06 defeat, rebuff, refuse, reject
07 beat off, refusal, reverse
08 spurning
09 drive back, rejection
11 repudiation

**repulsion**
06 hatred
07 disgust
08 aversion, distaste, loathing
09 disrelish, revulsion
10 abhorrence, repellence, repellency, repugnance
11 detestation

**repulsive**
04 foul, ugly, vile
05 nasty
06 horrid
07 hateful, heinous, hideous
08 shocking
09 abhorrent, loathsome, obnoxious, offensive, repellent, repugnant, revolting, sickening
10 abominable, despicable, disgusting, nauseating, unpleasant
11 distasteful
12 contemptible, disagreeable

**reputable**
04 good
06 honest, worthy
07 upright
08 esteemed, reliable, virtuous
09 admirable, estimable, excellent, honorable, respected
10 dependable
11 respectable, trustworthy
13 well-thought-of

**reputation**
04 fame, name, rank
05 honor, image
06 credit, esteem, infamy, renown, repute
07 opinion, respect, stature

08 good name, position, prestige, standing
09 character, notoriety
11 distinction
14 respectability

**repute**
04 fame, name
06 esteem, renown
07 stature
08 good name, standing
09 celebrity
10 estimation, reputation
11 distinction

**reputed**
04 held, said
07 alleged, rumored, seeming, thought
08 apparent, believed, presumed, reckoned, regarded, supposed
10 considered, ostensible

**reputedly**
09 allegedly, seemingly
10 apparently, ostensibly, supposedly

**request**
03 beg
04 call, plea, seek, suit
06 appeal, ask for, behest, demand, desire, prayer
07 beseech, entreat, solicit
08 apply for, entreaty, petition
10 supplicate
11 application, petitioning
12 solicitation, supplication

**require**
04 lack, miss, need, want
05 crave, force, order
06 demand, enjoin, entail
07 command, involve, request
08 insist on, instruct
09 be short of, constrain

**required**
03 set
05 vital
06 needed
08 demanded
09 essential, mandatory, necessary, requisite
10 compulsory, obligatory, prescribed, stipulated

**requirement**
04 lack, must, need, term, want
06 demand
07 proviso
09 condition, essential, necessity, provision
10 sine qua non
11 stipulation
12 precondition, prerequisite

13 qualification, specification

**requisite**
03 due, set
06 needed
08 required
09 condition, essential, mandatory, necessary, necessity
10 compulsory, obligatory, prescribed, sine qua non
11 desideratum, requirement
12 precondition, prerequisite
13 qualification, specification

**requisition**
03 use
04 call, take
05 order, seize
06 demand, occupy
07 request, seizure, summons
08 put in for, take over, takeover
10 commandeer, confiscate
11 application, appropriate
12 confiscation
13 appropriation, commandeering

**requital**
06 amends, payoff
07 payment, redress
09 indemnity, quittance, repayment
10 recompense, reparation
11 restitution
12 compensation, satisfaction
15 indemnification

**requite**
05 repay
06 avenge, return, reward
07 redress, respond, satisfy
09 reimburse, retaliate
11 reciprocate

**rescind**
04 void
05 annul, quash
06 cancel, negate, recall, repeal, revoke
07 abolish, nullify, retract, reverse
08 abrogate, overturn, set aside
11 countermand

**rescission**
06 recall, repeal
08 negation, reversal, voidance
09 annulment
10 abrogation, revocation
11 rescindment
12 cancellation, invalidation
13 nullification

**rescue**
04 free, save
06 ransom, redeem

07 deliver, relieve, set free
08 liberate, recovery
09 extricate, salvation
10 emancipate, liberation, redemption
11 deliverance

**research**
05 probe, study, tests
06 assess, review, search
07 analyze, examine, explore, inquiry, inspect, testing
08 analysis, look into, scrutiny
10 experiment, scrutinize
11 examination, exploration, fact-finding, investigate
13 investigation
15 experimentation

**researcher**
07 analyst, student
08 pollster
09 professor, scientist
11 fieldworker
12 experimenter, investigator

**resemblance**
06 parity
07 analogy
08 affinity, likeness, parallel
09 agreement, facsimile
10 comparison, similarity, similitude, uniformity
13 comparability, spitting image
14 correspondence

**resemble**
05 favor
06 be like, mirror
08 approach, look like, parallel
09 duplicate, take after

**resent**
04 envy
06 grudge
07 dislike
08 begrudge, object to
13 take offense at, take umbrage at
15 take exception to

**resentful**
04 hurt
05 angry, irked
06 bitter, miffed, peeved, piqued, put out
07 envious, jealous, wounded
08 grudging, offended
09 aggrieved, indignant
10 embittered, vindictive

**resentment**
03 ire
04 envy, hurt
05 anger, pique, spite
06 grudge, malice

07 dudgeon, ill will, offense, umbrage
08 jealousy, vexation
09 animosity, annoyance
10 bitterness, ill feeling
11 high dudgeon, indignation

**reservation**
04 park
05 demur, doubt, order, qualm
07 booking, enclave, proviso, reserve, scruple
08 homeland, preserve
09 hesitancy, misgiving
10 hesitation, skepticism
11 arrangement, stipulation
13 qualification
14 prearrangement

**reserve**
04 area, bank, book, fund, keep, park, pool, save
05 cache, extra, hoard, spare, stock, store, tract
06 fill-in, retain, shelve, supply
07 earmark, modesty, shyness
08 coldness, coolness, distance, hold back, keep back, lay aside, postpone, set aside
09 aloofness, auxiliary, reservoir, reticence, sanctuary, stockpile
10 accumulate, additional, detachment, remoteness, second-team, substitute, understudy
11 alternative, replacement
13 secretiveness, self-restraint

**❏in reserve**
05 spare
06 in hand, stored, unused
08 set aside

**reserved**
03 shy
04 cold, cool, held, kept
05 aloof, meant, saved, taken
06 booked, modest, remote
07 distant, engaged, ordered
08 arranged, destined, intended, retained, reticent, retiring, set aside
09 diffident, earmarked, secretive, spoken for
10 designated, restrained, unsociable
11 prearranged, standoffish
12 unresponsive
13 unforthcoming
15 uncommunicative

**reservoir**
03 vat
04 bank, fund, lake, pond, pool, tank

05 basin, stock, store
06 holder, source, supply
07 cistern
08 reserves
09 container, stockpile
10 receptacle, repository
11 reservatory

**reshuffle**
05 shift
06 change, revise
07 realign, regroup, shake up
09 rearrange
10 regrouping, reorganize
11 realignment, restructure
13 rearrangement, restructuring
14 redistribution, reorganization

**reside**
03 lie
04 live, rest, stay
05 abide, board, dwell, lodge
06 occupy, remain, settle
07 inhabit, sojourn

**residence**
03 pad
04 digs, home, seat
05 abode, house, manor, place, villa
06 palace
07 lodging, mansion, sojourn
08 domicile, dwelling, lodgings, quarters
09 apartment, dormitory
10 habitation

**resident**
05 guest, local
06 inmate, intern, live-in, lodger, tenant
07 citizen, denizen, dweller, resider
08 occupant, occupier
10 inhabitant, inhabiting
11 householder

**residential**
07 exurban
08 commuter, suburban
12 neighborhood

**residual**
03 net
05 extra
06 excess, unused
07 surplus
08 leftover
09 remaining
10 unconsumed

**residue**
04 lees, rest
05 dregs, extra
06 excess
07 balance, remains, surplus

**resign**
08 overflow, residuum
09 leftovers, remainder

**resign**
04 quit
05 leave, waive
06 forego, give up, retire, vacate
07 abandon, forsake
08 abdicate, step down
09 surrender
10 relinquish

❑**resign yourself**
03 bow
05 yield
06 accept, comply, submit
09 acquiesce
11 come to terms

**resignation**
06 notice
07 waiving
08 patience, stoicism
09 defeatism, departure, passivity, surrender
10 abdication, acceptance, compliance, retirement, submission
12 acquiescence, stepping-down

**resigned**
07 passive, patient, stoical
08 yielding
09 defeatist
10 reconciled, submissive
11 acquiescent, unresisting
12 unprotesting
13 philosophical

**resilience**
04 give
06 bounce, recoil, spring
08 buoyancy, strength
09 hardiness, toughness
10 elasticity, plasticity
11 flexibility, springiness
12 adaptability
14 unshockability

**resilient**
05 hardy, tough
06 bouncy, strong, supple
07 buoyant, elastic, plastic, pliable, rubbery, springy
08 flexible
09 adaptable
13 irrepressible

**resist**
04 buck, curb, defy, halt, stem, stop
05 avoid, check, fight, repel
06 impede, oppose, thwart
07 contend, counter, prevent
08 confront, obstruct, restrain
09 stand up to, withstand

14 hold out against

**resistance**
05 fight
06 battle, combat
07 refusal
08 defiance, fighting, struggle
09 repulsion, restraint
10 contention, impediment, opposition, prevention
11 obstruction
12 withstanding
13 confrontation

**resistant**
05 proof, tough
06 immune, strong
07 defiant, opposed
09 unwilling
10 impervious, unaffected
12 antagonistic, intransigent

**resolute**
03 set
04 bold, firm
05 fixed
06 dogged, intent
07 adamant, decided, earnest
08 constant, obdurate, resolved, stalwart, stubborn
09 dedicated, obstinate, steadfast, tenacious, undaunted
10 determined, relentless, unswerving, unwavering
11 persevering, unflinching
12 single-minded, strong-willed

**resolution**
06 answer, decree, mettle, motion
07 clarity, courage, finding, resolve, solving, verdict
08 boldness, decision, devotion, firmness, solution, tenacity
09 constancy, statement, willpower
10 dedication, doggedness, intentness, working out
11 persistence, proposition
12 perseverance
13 determination, steadfastness

**resolve**
03 fix
04 zeal
05 solve
06 answer, decide, settle
07 courage, sort out, work out
08 boldness, conclude, firmness, settle on, tenacity
09 break down, constancy, determine, willpower
10 dedication, doggedness
11 disentangle, earnestness, persistence, seriousness

12 disintegrate, perseverance
13 determination, steadfastness

**resonant**
04 deep, full, rich
06 plummy, strong
07 booming, ringing, vibrant
08 canorous, sonorous
10 resounding
11 reverberant

**resort**
02 go
03 spa
04 spot
05 haunt, hotel, visit
06 center, chance, course, turn to
08 frequent, recourse, resource
09 expedient, patronize
11 possibility
12 vacation spot
14 course of action

❑**resort to**
03 use
06 employ, turn to
07 utilize
08 exercise
09 make use of
10 fall back on
14 have recourse to

**resound**
04 boom, echo, ring
05 sound
06 reecho
07 thunder
08 resonate
11 reverberate

**resounding**
04 full, loud, rich
07 booming, echoing, notable, ringing, vibrant
08 decisive, emphatic, resonant, sonorous, striking
10 conclusive, impressive, resonating, thunderous
13 reverberating

**resource**
06 action, course
08 strategy
09 expedient, ingenuity
10 enterprise, initiative
11 imagination
12 provide money
13 inventiveness
15 resourcefulness
16 provide materials

**resourceful**
04 able
05 sharp, witty
06 adroit, bright, clever
07 capable

08 creative, original, talented
09 ingenious, inventive, versatile
10 innovative
11 imaginative, quick-witted
12 enterprising

**resourceless**
07 useless
08 feckless, helpless, hopeless
10 inadequate

**resources**
03 wit
04 fund, pool
05 funds, means, money, power, store
06 assets, riches, supply, talent, wealth
07 ability, capital, reserve
08 holdings, property, reserves
09 materials, stockpile
11 wherewithal

**respect**
03 way
04 heed, obey
05 facet, honor, point, sense, value
06 admire, aspect, detail, esteem, follow, fulfil, homage, matter, notice, praise, regard, revere
07 devoirs, feature, fulfill, observe
08 courtesy, relation, venerate
09 approve of, deference, obeisance, reference, reverence
10 admiration, connection, high regard, politeness, veneration
11 approbation, high opinion, salutations
13 consideration, show regard for, think highly of
14 thoughtfulness
15 set great store by

**respectable**
02 OK
04 fair, good, neat, okay, tidy
05 clean
06 decent, honest, worthy
07 upright
08 adequate, all right, decorous, passable
09 dignified, honorable, reputable, respected, tolerable
10 aboveboard, acceptable, reasonable
11 appreciable, clean-living, presentable, trustworthy
12 considerable

**respected**
06 valued
07 admired
08 esteemed
14 highly regarded
15 thought highly of

**respectful**
05 civil
06 humble, polite
07 courtly, dutiful
08 reverent
09 courteous
11 deferential, reverential, subservient

**respecting**
05 about
09 regarding
10 concerning
11 considering
12 with regard to

**respective**
03 own
07 several, special, various
08 personal, relevant, specific
10 individual, particular
13 corresponding

**respects**
07 regards
09 greetings
10 best wishes
11 compliments

**respite**
03 gap
04 halt, lull, rest, stay
05 break, delay, letup, pause
06 hiatus, recess, relief
07 timeout
08 breather, interval, reprieve
09 abatement, remission
10 moratorium, relaxation
11 adjournment
12 intermission, interruption

**resplendent**
06 bright
07 fulgent, radiant, shining
08 glorious, luminous, lustrous, splendid
09 brilliant, effulgent, irradiant, refulgent
13 splendiferous

**respond**
05 react, reply
06 answer, rejoin, retort, return
07 counter
10 answer back
11 acknowledge, reciprocate

**response**
05 reply
06 answer, retort, return
07 riposte

08 comeback, feedback, reaction
09 rejoinder
14 acknowledgment

**responsibility**
04 care, duty, onus, role, task
05 blame, fault, guilt
06 affair, burden, charge
07 concern, honesty
08 business, maturity
09 adulthood, authority
10 obligation
11 culpability, reliability
13 answerability, dependability
14 accountability

**responsible**
04 sane
05 adult, sober, sound
06 guilty, liable, stable, steady
07 at fault, leading, to blame
08 culpable, powerful, rational, reliable, sensible
09 executive, high-level
10 answerable, dependable, in charge of, reasonable
11 accountable, blameworthy, controlling, levelheaded
13 authoritative, conscientious
14 decision making

**responsive**
04 open
05 alert, awake, aware, sharp
06 with it
08 amenable, reactive
09 on the ball, receptive, sensitive
11 forthcoming, susceptible, sympathetic
14 impressionable

**rest**
03 lie, nap, sit
04 base, calm, doze, ease, halt, hang, last, laze, lean, lull, prop, rely, stay, stop
05 break, cease, hinge, pause, relax, sleep, stand
06 depend, endure, excess, holder, lounge, others, recess, remain, repose, siesta, snooze, steady
07 balance, holiday, leisure, lie down, persist, recline, remains, remnant, residue, respite, support, surplus
08 breather, continue, idleness, interval, quietude, remnants, residuum, vacation
09 cessation, interlude, leftovers, remainder, stillness
10 inactivity, relaxation, standstill, take it easy

**restful**

11 tranquility
12 intermission
13 breathing room, put your feet up
14 breathing space

**restful**
04 calm
05 quiet, still
06 placid, serene
07 calming, languid, relaxed
08 peaceful, relaxing, soothing, tranquil

**restitution**
06 amends, refund, return
07 damages, redress
08 requital
09 indemnity, repayment
10 recompense, reparation
11 restoration
12 compensation, remuneration, satisfaction
13 reimbursement

**restive**
04 edgy
05 jumpy, tense
06 uneasy, unruly, wilful
07 anxious, fidgety, fretful, nervous, uptight, wayward, willful
08 agitated, restless
09 impatient, unsettled
10 refractory
12 recalcitrant, unmanageable
13 undisciplined

**restless**
04 edgy
05 jumpy
06 broken, uneasy, unruly
07 anxious, fidgety, fretful, jittery, nervous, restive, uptight, worried
08 agitated, troubled
09 disturbed, impatient, sleepless, unsettled

**restlessness**
06 bustle, unrest
07 anxiety, jitters, turmoil
08 activity, disquiet, edginess, insomnia, movement
09 agitation, jumpiness
10 fitfulness, inquietude
11 disturbance, fretfulness, inconstancy, instability, nervousness, restiveness
13 heebie-jeebies

**restoration**
06 repair, return
07 renewal, revival
08 recovery
10 rebuilding, renovation
11 refreshment, restitution

12 refurbishing, rejuvenation
13 reinstatement
14 reconstruction
15 reestablishment

**restore**
03 fix
04 do up, mend
05 renew
06 repair, return, revamp, revive
07 build up, rebuild, recover, refresh, replace, retouch
08 give back, hand back, renovate, revivify
09 refurbish, reinstate
10 redecorate, rejuvenate
11 recondition, reconstruct, reestablish, reintroduce

**restrain**
03 tie
04 bind, curb, jail, stop    •
05 chain, check
06 arrest, bridle, detain, fetter, hinder, impede, muzzle, subdue
07 confine, control, inhibit, manacle, prevent, repress
08 bottle up, imprison, restrict, suppress
11 hold in check

**restrained**
04 calm, cold, mild, soft
05 aloof, muted, quiet
06 formal, low-key, subtle
07 subdued
08 discreet, low-keyed, moderate, tasteful
09 temperate
10 controlled
11 unemotional, unobtrusive
14 self-controlled
15 uncommunicative

**restraint**
03 tie
04 curb, grip, hold, rein
05 block, bonds, check, limit
06 bridle, chains, duress, limits, muzzle
07 bondage, control, fetters
09 captivity, hindrance
10 constraint, inhibition, limitation, moderation
11 confinement, restriction, self-control, suppression
12 restrictions, straitjacket
14 self-discipline, straightjacket

**restrict**
03 tie
05 bound, cramp, hem in, limit
06 hamper, hinder, impede
07 confine, control, curtail
08 handicap, regulate, restrain

09 constrain, demarcate

**restricted**
05 small, tight
06 narrow, secret
07 cramped, limited, private
08 confined
09 exclusive, regulated
10 controlled

**restriction**
03 ban
04 curb, rule
05 bound, check, limit, stint
07 boundry, confine, embargo, proviso
08 handicap
09 condition, restraint
10 constraint, limitation
13 qualification

**result**
03 end
04 flow, mark, stem
05 arise, ensue, fruit, grade, issue, occur, score
06 effect, emerge, evolve, finish, follow, payoff, sequel, spring, upshot
07 develop, emanate, outcome, proceed, spinoff, verdict
08 decision, judgment, reaction
09 byproduct, culminate, terminate
10 conclusion, end product
11 consequence, culmination, implication

**resume**
04 go on
06 reopen, take up
07 carry on, proceed, restart
08 continue, reoccupy
09 reconvene
10 recommence

**résumé**
02 CV
06 digest, précis, review, sketch
07 outline, summary
08 abstract, overview, synopsis
09 breakdown
14 recapitulation
15 curriculum vitae

**resumption**
07 renewal, restart
09 reopening
12 continuation
14 recommencement
15 reestablishment

**resurgence**
06 return
07 rebirth, revival
10 renascence, resumption
11 reemergence, renaissance

## resurrect

12 reappearance, resurrection
14 revivification

**resurrect**
05 renew
06 revive
07 restore
10 reactivate, revitalize
11 reestablish, reintroduce, resuscitate

**resurrection**
07 rebirth, renewal, revival
08 comeback
10 resurgence
11 renaissance, restoration
12 reappearance
13 resuscitation
14 revitalization
15 reestablishment

**resuscitate**
04 save
05 renew
06 rescue, revive
07 quicken, restore
08 revivify
09 reanimate, resurrect
10 revitalize
11 bring around
12 reinvigorate

**resuscitated**
05 saved
06 reborn
07 revived
08 restored
09 redivivus
11 resurrected

**retain**
03 pay
04 grip, hire, hold, keep, save
06 employ, engage, recall
07 reserve
08 continue, hang on to, hold back, memorize, remember
10 keep hold of, keep in mind

**retainer**
03 fee
05 valet
06 lackey, menial, vassal
07 advance, deposit, servant
08 domestic
09 attendant, dependent, supporter

**retaliate**
06 avenge
07 hit back
09 fight back, get back at
10 strike back
11 reciprocate, take revenge
13 counterattack
14 get your own back

**retaliation**
07 revenge
08 reprisal
09 tit for tat, vengeance
11 eye for an eye, like for like, retribution
13 counterattack, reciprocation

**retard**
04 curb
05 brake, check, delay
06 hinder, hold up, impede
08 handicap, obstruct, restrict

**retardation**
03 lag
05 delay
07 slowing
09 hindering, hindrance
10 deficiency, incapacity
11 obstruction

**retch**
03 gag
04 puke, spew
05 heave, reach, vomit
07 throw up
08 disgorge
11 regurgitate

**retching**
06 nausea, puking
07 gagging
08 reaching, vomiting
12 vomiturition

**reticence**
07 reserve, silence
09 quietness, restraint
10 diffidence
11 taciturnity
13 secretiveness

**reticent**
03 shy
05 quiet
06 silent
08 reserved, taciturn
09 diffident, secretive
10 restrained
11 tightlipped
13 unforthcoming
15 uncommunicative

**retinue**
05 aides, staff, suite, train
06 escort
07 cortège
08 servants
09 entourage, followers, following, personnel
10 attendants

**retire**
05 leave
06 bow out, decamp, depart
07 retreat
08 stop work, withdraw

**retired**
02 ex-
04 past
06 former
07 emerita
08 emeritus

**retirement**
04 exit
07 privacy, retreat
08 solitude
09 departure, obscurity, seclusion
10 loneliness, withdrawal

**retiring**
03 coy, shy
05 quiet, timid
06 humble, modest
07 bashful
08 reserved, reticent
09 diffident, shrinking
10 unassuming
12 self-effacing

**retort**
04 quip
05 reply
06 answer, rejoin, return
07 counter, respond, riposte
08 repartee, response
09 rejoinder, retaliate

**retract**
04 deny
06 abjure, cancel, recant, renege, repeal, revoke
07 disavow, rescind, reverse
08 abrogate, renounce, take back, withdraw

**retreat**
03 den
04 flee, quit
05 haven, leave
06 asylum, decamp, depart, flight, refuge, retire, shrink
07 hideout, privacy, shelter
08 draw back, fall back, hideaway, pull back, solitude, turn tail, withdraw
09 climb down, departure, sanctuary
10 evacuation, give ground, retirement, withdrawal

**retrench**
03 cut
04 pare, save, trim
05 limit, prune
06 lessen, reduce
07 curtail, cut back, husband
08 decrease, slim down
09 economize
15 tighten your belt

## retrenchment
07 cutback, economy, pruning
09 reduction, shrinkage
11 cutting back
12 crosscutting

## retribution
06 reward, talion
07 justice, Nemesis, payment, redress, revenge
08 reprisal, requital
09 repayment, vengeance
10 punishment, recompense
11 just deserts, retaliation
12 compensation, satisfaction

## retrieve
04 mend, save
05 fetch
06 recoup, redeem, regain, repair, rescue, return
07 reclaim, recover, salvage
09 bring back, recapture, repossess

## retrograde
07 reverse
08 backward, downward, negative
09 declining, worsening
13 deteriorating, retrogressive

## retrogress
04 drop, fall, sink, wane
06 recede, revert, worsen
07 decline, regress, relapse
09 backslide
10 degenerate, retrograde
11 deteriorate

## retrogression
03 ebb
04 drop, fall
06 return
07 decline, regress, relapse
09 worsening
10 recidivism, regression
13 deterioration

## retrospect
06 review, survey
09 hindsight
10 reflection
12 recollection, thinking back
13 reexamination

## ❑ in retrospect
11 looking back
12 on reflection, thinking back
13 with hindsight

## retrospective
06 review
10 exhibition
11 retroactive
15 backward-looking

## return
04 gain
05 equal, match, recur, remit, repay, reply, yield
06 answer, go back, income, profit, refund, rejoin, retort, revert, reward
07 benefit, counter, deliver, put back, regress, replace, requite, respond, restore, revenue, riposte, takings, tax form
08 come home, comeback, delivery, exchange, give back, hand back, interest, proceeds, reappear, send back, take back
09 come again, pronounce, reimburse, reinstate, repayment
10 homecoming, recompense
11 handing back, reciprocate, replacement, restoration
12 reappearance
13 reciprocation, reinstatement

## reuse
07 recycle
12 reconstitute

## revamp
04 do up
05 refit
06 recast, repair, revise
07 rebuild, restore
08 overhaul, renovate
09 refurbish
11 recondition, reconstruct

## reveal
04 leak, show, tell
06 betray, expose, let out
07 display, divulge, exhibit, lay bare, let slip, publish, uncover, unearth
08 announce, disclose, give away, manifest, proclaim
09 broadcast, make aware, make known, publicize
10 make public
12 bring to light, expose to view

## revealing
05 sheer
06 daring, low-cut
08 giveaway
10 diaphanous, indicative, revelatory, see-through

## revel
04 bask, crow, gala, rave
05 enjoy, glory, lap up, party, savor
06 relish, wallow
07 carouse, debauch, delight, indulge, rejoice, roister

09 bacchanal, celebrate, festivity, luxuriate
10 have a party, saturnalia
11 celebration, merrymaking
13 jollification
15 paint the town red

## revelation
04 fact, leak, news, show
07 display
08 exposure, giveaway
09 admission, unmasking
10 confession, disclosure, divulgence, exhibition, uncovering, unearthing
11 information, publication
12 announcement, bring to light, broadcasting

## reveler
08 carouser
09 bacchanal, partygoer, roisterer, wassailer
10 celebrator, merrymaker
14 pleasure seeker

## revelry
03 fun
05 party
07 jollity
08 carousal
09 festivity
10 debauchery
11 celebration, merrymaking
13 jollification

## revenge
06 avenge
07 hit back, redress
08 reprisal, requital, vendetta
09 fight back, retaliate, tit for tat, vengeance
11 eye for an eye, get even with, retaliation, retribution
12 satisfaction, settle a score
14 get your own back

## revengeful
06 bitter
08 pitiless, spiteful, vengeful
09 merciless, resentful
10 malevolent, vindictive
11 unforgiving

## revenue
04 gain
05 yield
06 income, profit, return
07 profits, rewards, takings
08 interest, proceeds, receipts

## reverberate
04 boom, echo, ring
06 reecho
07 resound, vibrate
08 resonate

## reverberation
04 echo, wave
06 effect, recoil, result, ripple
07 rebound, ringing
09 reechoing, resonance, shock wave, vibration
10 reflection, resounding
11 consequence
12 repercussion

## revere
05 adore, exalt, honor
06 admire, esteem
07 respect, worship
08 look up to, venerate
09 reverence
11 pay homage to

## reverence
03 awe
05 honor
06 admire, esteem, homage, revere
07 respect, worship
08 devotion, venerate
09 adoration, deference
10 admiration, veneration

## reverent
04 awed
05 pious
06 devout, humble, solemn
10 respectful, worshiping
11 deferential, reverential

## reverie
06 musing, trance
08 daydream
09 pipe dream
11 abstraction, daydreaming
13 preoccupation, woolgathering

## reversal
04 blow
05 check, delay, trial, U-turn
06 defeat, mishap, repeal
07 failure, problem, setback
08 hardship, negation
09 about-face, adversity, annulment, turnabout, volte-face
10 misfortune, rescinding, revocation, turnaround
13 nullification
14 countermanding

## reverse
04 back, blow, flip, rear, swap, undo
05 annul, B-side, check, delay, quash, upend, upset, verso
06 cancel, change, defeat, invert, mishap, negate, repeal, revoke
07 counter, failure, inverse, rescind, retract, setback
08 backward, contrary, converse, flip over, inverted, opposite, reversal, withdraw
09 adversity, backtrack, other side, underside
10 antithesis, difficulty, invalidate, misfortune, turn around
11 countermand, vicissitude
12 change around, misadventure, opposite side
14 turn upside down

## revert
05 lapse
06 go back, resume, return
07 regress, relapse

## review
05 judge, study, weigh
06 assess, report, revise, survey
07 analyze, discuss, examine, inspect, rethink, weigh up
08 analysis, appraise, critique, evaluate, judgment, magazine, reassess, revision, scrutiny
09 appraisal, criticism, criticize, reexamine
10 assessment, commentary, evaluation, periodical, reconsider, reevaluate, scrutinize
11 examination, take stock of
12 reassessment, recapitulate, reevaluation
13 reexamination

## reviewer
05 judge
06 critic
07 arbiter
08 essayist, observer
11 commentator, connoisseur

## revile
05 abuse, libel, scorn, smear
06 defame, malign, vilify
07 despise, slander, traduce
09 denigrate
10 blackguard, calumniate, vituperate

## revise
04 edit
05 alter, amend, emend, mug up
06 change, modify, revamp, reword, update
07 correct, redraft, rewrite
10 reconsider

## revision
06 change, recast
07 editing
08 updating
09 amendment, recasting, rewriting

10 alteration, correction
12 modification

## revitalize
05 renew
06 revive
07 refresh, restore
08 revivify
09 reanimate, resurrect
10 reactivate, rejuvenate

## revival
06 upturn
07 rebirth, renewal, upsurge
08 comeback
09 preaching
10 resurgence
11 camp meeting, reawakening, renaissance
12 resurrection
13 resuscitation, the kiss of life
14 reintroduction, revitalization
16 religious meeting

## revive
05 rally, renew, rouse
07 animate, cheer up, quicken, recover, refresh, restore
08 reawaken, rekindle
09 reanimate
10 invigorate, reactivate, revitalize
11 bring around, reestablish, reintroduce

## revivify
05 renew
06 revive
07 refresh, restore
08 inspirit
09 reanimate
10 invigorate, reactivate, revitalize
11 resuscitate

## reviving
05 tonic
07 bracing
11 reanimating, revivescent, reviviscent, stimulating
12 enheartening, exhilarating, invigorating, refreshening
14 reinvigorating

## revocation
06 repeal
08 quashing, reversal, revoking
09 abolition, annulment, repealing
10 rescinding, rescission, retraction, withdrawal
11 repudiation
12 cancellation, invalidation
13 nullification

## revoke
05 annul, quash

**revolt**
06 cancel, negate, repeal
07 abolish, nullify, rescind,
   retract, reverse
08 abrogate, withdraw
10 invalidate
11 countermand

**revolt**
04 coup, riot, rise
05 rebel, repel, shock
06 defect, mutiny, putsch, resist,
   rise up, rising, sicken
07 disgust, dissent, outrage
08 nauseate, uprising
09 coup d'état, rebellion
10 revolution, take up arms
12 insurrection
15 turn your stomach

**revolting**
04 foul, vile
05 nasty
07 hateful, heinous
08 horrible, shocking
09 abhorrent, appalling,
   loathsome, obnoxious,
   offensive, repellent,
   repugnant, repulsive,
   sickening
10 disgusting, nauseating
11 distasteful

**revolution**
04 coup, spin, turn
05 cycle, orbit, round, wheel
06 change, circle, mutiny,
   putsch, revolt, rising
07 circuit
08 gyration, rotation, uprising
09 coup d'état, rebellion
10 innovation, insurgence
12 insurrection

**revolutionary**
03 new
05 rebel
07 drastic, radical
08 mutineer, mutinous
09 anarchist, extremist,
   insurgent, seditious
10 avant-garde, innovative,
   rebellious, subversive
11 anarchistic, progressive
14 freedom fighter
15 insurrectionary,
   insurrectionist

---

► *Names of revolutionaries:*
03 **Lee** (Robert E.)
04 **Biko** (Steve), **Cade** (Jack),
   **Kett** (Robert), **Marx** (Karl)
05 **Adams** (John), **Adams**
   (Samuel), **Allen** (Ethan),
   **Davis** (Jefferson), **Fanon**
   (Frantz), **Henry** (Patrick),
   **Jones** (John Paul), **Kirov**

(Sergey), **Lenin** (Vladimir
   Ilyich), **Marat** (Jean Paul),
   **Paine** (Thomas), **Sands**
   (Bobby), **Sucre** (Antonio
   José de), **Tyler** (Wat), **Villa**
   (Pancho)
06 **Arafat** (Yasser), **Baader**
   (Andreas), **Castro** (Fidel),
   **Corday** (Charlotte), **Danton**
   (Georges), **Fawkes** (Guy),
   **Fuller** (Margaret), **Revere**
   (Paul), **Stalin** (Joseph),
   **Zapata** (Emiliano)
07 **Bakunin** (Mikhail), **Bolívar**
   (Simón), **Catesby** (Robert),
   **Goldman** (Emma), **Guevara**
   (Che), **Madison** (James),
   **Mandela** (Nelson), **Meinhof**
   (Ulrike Marie), **Princip**
   (Gavrilo), **Sandino**
   (Augusto César), **Savimbi**
   (Jonas), **Trotsky** (Leon),
   **Wallace** (William)
08 **Abu Nidal**, **Bukharin**
   (Nikolay), **Franklin**
   (Benjamin), **Hamilton**
   (Alexander), **Hereward** (the
   Wake), **Kerensky**
   (Alexander), **Lilburne**
   (John), **Mirabeau** (Honoré
   Gabriel Riqueti Comte de),
   **Proudhon** (Pierre Joseph),
   **Zinoviev** (Grigoriy)
09 **Christian** (Fletcher),
   **Garibaldi** (Giuseppe),
   **Guillotin** (Joseph),
   **Jefferson** (Thomas),
   **Kropotkin** (Knyaz Peter),
   **Luxemburg** (Rosa), **Mao**
   **Zedong**, **Spartacus**, **Sun**
   **Yat-Sen**
10 **Washington** (George)
11 **Robespierre** (Maximilien
   de)
13 **Chiang Kai-Shek**

**revolutionize**
06 reform
09 transform
10 reorganize
11 restructure, transfigure
14 turn upside down

**revolve**
04 move, spin, turn
05 orbit, pivot, wheel, whirl
06 circle, gyrate, hang on, rotate,
   swivel, turn on
07 reflect
08 center on

**revolver**
03 gun, rod
06 pistol, six-gun, zip gun
07 firearm, handgun, shooter

10 six-shooter

**revolving**
07 turning
08 gyrating, gyratory, rotating,
   spinning, whirling

**revulsion**
04 hate
06 hatred, nausea, recoil
07 disgust, dislike
08 aversion, distaste, loathing
09 repulsion
10 abhorrence, repugnance
11 abomination, detestation

**reward**
03 pay
04 gain
05 award, bonus, honor, medal,
   merit, prize
06 desert, payoff, profit, return
07 benefit, payment, premium
08 decorate, requital
10 decoration, punishment,
   recompense, remunerate
11 just deserts, retribution
12 compensation,
   remuneration

**rewarding**
08 edifying, fruitful, pleasing
09 enriching, lucrative
10 beneficial, fulfilling,
   gratifying, profitable,
   satisfying, worthwhile
12 advantageous, remunerative

**rewording**
07 editing
08 revision
10 metaphrase, paraphrase,
   rephrasing
11 translation

**rewrite**
04 edit
05 emend
06 revise, reword, rework
07 correct, redraft

**rhetoric**
07 bombast, fustian, oratory
09 eloquence, hyperbole,
   pomposity, prolixity,
   verbosity, wordiness
13 magniloquence
14 grandiloquence

**rhetorical**
05 grand, showy, wordy
06 florid, prolix
07 flowery, pompous, verbose
09 bombastic, high-flown
10 flamboyant, long-winded
11 declamatory, pretentious
12 high-sounding,
   magniloquent

13 grandiloquent

▶ *Types of rhetorical device*:
03 pun
05 irony, trope
06 bathos, climax, simile, zeugma
07 epigram, litotes, meiosis, paradox
08 anaphora, chiasmus, diegesis, ellipsis, innuendo, metaphor, metonymy, oxymoron, parabole
09 dissimile, euphemism, hyperbole, prolepsis, syllepsis, tautology
10 anastrophe, anticlimax, antithesis, apostrophe, dysphemism, epistrophe, metalepsis, synchrysis, synecdoche
11 anacoluthon, antiphrasis, catachresis, enumeration, hypostrophe, parenthesis
12 alliteration, onomatopoeia
13 amplification, dramatic irony, mixed metaphor
14 double entendre, figure of speech
15 pathetic fallacy, personification

**rhyme**
04 poem, song
05 ditty, poesy, verse
06 jingle, poetry
08 limerick

**rhythm**
04 beat, flow, lilt, time
05 meter, pulse, swing, throb
07 measure, pattern
08 movement

**rhythmic**
06 metric, steady
07 flowing, lilting, regular
08 metrical, periodic, repeated
09 pulsating, throbbing
10 rhythmical

**rib**
03 bar
04 band, bone, vein, wale
05 costa, ridge, shaft, tease
07 ribbing, support

**ribald**
03 low
04 base, blue, lewd, racy, rude
05 bawdy, gross
06 coarse, earthy, filthy, risqué, smutty, vulgar
07 jeering, mocking, naughty
08 derisive, indecent, off-color
09 satirical

10 irreverent, licentious
11 foulmouthed, Rabelaisian

**ribaldry**
04 smut
05 filth
07 jeering, lowness, mockery
08 baseness, raciness, rudeness
09 bawdiness, grossness, indecency, vulgarity
10 coarseness, earthiness, scurrility, smuttiness
11 naughtiness
14 licentiousness

**ribbon**
04 band, cord, line, sash
05 braid, cloth, shred, strip
10 decoration

**rich**
04 deep, fine, full, lush, oily
05 fatty, flush, grand, heavy, spicy, sweet, vivid
06 costly, creamy, fecund, ironic, lavish, loaded, mellow, ornate, strong
07 fertile, intense, moneyed, opulent, profuse, steeped, vibrant, wealthy, well-off
08 abundant, affluent, fruitful, gorgeous, luscious, palatial, prolific, resonant, sonorous, splendid
09 abounding, elaborate, laughable, luxurious, plenteous, plentiful, sumptuous, well-fixed
10 full-bodied, outrageous, productive, prosperous, ridiculous, well-heeled
11 made of money, magnificent, mellifluous, overflowing, rolling in it
12 full flavored

**riches**
04 gold
05 lucre, means, money
06 assets, wealth
08 opulence, property, treasure
09 affluence, resources
10 prosperity
11 filthy lucre

**richly**
04 well
05 fully
08 lavishly, strongly, suitably
09 elegantly, opulently
10 completely, gorgeously, palatially, splendidly
11 elaborately, expensively, exquisitely, luxuriously, sumptuously

**rickety**
05 shaky
06 flimsy, wobbly
08 decrepit, derelict, insecure, unstable, unsteady
10 broken-down, jerry-built, ramshackle
11 dilapidated

**rid**
04 free
05 clear, purge
06 purify
07 cleanse, deliver, relieve
08 unburden

❑ **get rid of**
04 dump, junk
05 chuck, ditch, scrap
07 abolish, discard
08 chuck out, jettison
09 dispose of, eliminate
10 do away with, put an end to

**riddance**
06 relief
07 freedom, release, removal
08 disposal, ejection
09 clearance, expulsion
11 deliverance, elimination

**riddle**
03 mar
04 fill, koan, sift
05 poser, sieve
06 enigma, filter, infest, pepper, puzzle, strain, winnow
07 mystery, pervade, problem
08 permeate, puncture
09 conundrum, perforate
11 brainteaser

**ride**
03 sit
04 lift, move, spin, trip, trot
05 drive, jaunt, pedal, steer
06 gallop, handle, harass, manage
08 bestride, dominate, progress

**ridge**
04 band, hill, reef, wale
05 arête, costa, esker, knurl
06 ripple, saddle
07 crinkle, drumlin, hummock, yardang
08 backbone, hog's back, sastrugi
10 escarpment

**ridicule**
03 kid, rag, rib
04 gibe, jeer, mock
05 chaff, irony, scoff, scorn, sneer, taunt, tease
06 banter, deride, parody, satire, send up

07 jeering, lampoon, laugh at,
mockery, sarcasm, teasing
08 badinage, derision, laughter,
pooh-pooh, satirize
09 burlesque, humiliate, make
fun of
10 caricature

**ridiculous**
05 droll, funny, silly
06 absurd, stupid
07 comical, foolish, risible
08 derisory, farcical, humorous
09 laughable, ludicrous
11 nonsensical
12 contemptible, preposterous,
unbelievable

**rife**
06 common, raging
07 general, rampant, teeming
08 abundant, epidemic,
frequent, swarming
09 abounding, prevalent
10 ubiquitous, widespread

**riffraff**
03 mob
04 scum
05 dregs
06 rabble
08 canaille, rent-a-mob
09 hoi polloi
12 undesirables

**rifle**
03 gun, gut, rob
04 loot, sack
05 fusil, piece, strip
06 maraud, musket, search,
weapon
07 carbine, despoil, firearm,
pillage, plunder, ransack,
rummage, shotgun
08 firelock
09 flintlock

**rift**
03 gap, row
04 feud, hole, slit
05 break, chink, cleft, crack,
fault, fight, space, split
06 breach, cranny, schism
07 crevice, fissure, opening
08 conflict, division, fracture
10 alienation, separation
11 altercation
12 disagreement, estrangement

**rig**
03 kit
04 fake, gear
05 forge, twist
06 doctor, fiddle, outfit, tackle
07 distort, falsify, pervert,
vehicle
08 carriage, fittings, fixtures

09 apparatus, equipment
10 manipulate, tamper with
12 misrepresent
13 accouterments,
accoutrements

❑ **rig out**
03 fit
04 garb, robe, trim, wear
05 array, dress, equip, get up
06 attire, clothe, outfit, supply
07 dress up, furnish, provide

❑ **rig up**
05 build, erect, fit up, fix up
07 arrange, knock up
08 assemble, cobble up
09 construct, improvise
11 put together
14 cobble together

**right**
02 OK
03 due, fit, fix
04 good, just, lien, okay, real,
true
05 claim, droit, exact, honor,
legal, moral, power, sound,
valid
06 actual, avenge, ethics, fairly,
honest, lawful, proper, repair,
seemly, settle, unfair, virtue,
wholly
07 correct, ethical, exactly,
factual, fitting, genuine,
honesty, justice, precise,
rectify, redress, warrant
08 accurate, complete, entirely,
fairness, goodness, legality,
morality, properly, rightist,
smack-dab, straight, suitable,
thorough, true-blue, virtuous
09 authentic, authority,
correctly, equitable, factually,
favorable, favorably,
honorable, opportune,
precisely, privilege, propriety,
rectitude, right wing
10 absolutely, accurately,
auspicious, birthright,
completely, lawfulness,
permission, principled,
propitious, reasonable,
straighten
11 appropriate, entitlement,
prerogative, reactionary,
uprightness
12 conservative, satisfactory,
the done thing, truthfulness

❑ **by rights**
06 de jure, justly
07 legally, rightly
08 lawfully, properly
10 rightfully

11 justifiably
12 legitimately

❑ **in the right**
05 right
09 justified, warranted
10 vindicated

❑ **put to rights, set to
rights**
03 fix
06 settle
07 correct, rectify
10 put in order, straighten
13 straighten out

❑ **right away**
03 now
06 at once
08 directly, promptly
09 forthwith, instantly
11 immediately
12 straight away, without delay
13 from the word go

❑ **within your rights**
05 right
07 allowed
08 entitled
09 justified, permitted

**righteous**
04 fair, good, just, pure
05 legal, moral, valid
06 honest, lawful, proper
07 ethical, sinless, upright
08 virtuous
09 blameless, equitable,
guiltless, honorable,
incorrupt, justified,
warranted
10 acceptable, defensible, God-
fearing, law-abiding,
legitimate
11 justifiable, supportable
14 irreproachable

**righteousness**
05 honor
06 dharma, equity, purity, virtue
07 honesty, justice, probity
08 goodness, holiness, morality
09 integrity, rectitude
11 ethicalness, uprightness

**rightful**
03 due
04 just, real, true
05 legal, valid
06 lawful, proper
07 correct, genuine
08 authenic, bona fide, suitable
10 authorized, legitimate

**rightfully**
06 de jure, justly
07 legally, rightly
08 by rights, lawfully, properly

11 justifiably
12 legitimately
**rigid**
03 set
04 firm, hard
05 fixed, harsh, stern, stiff
08 cast-iron, rigorous
09 draconian, inelastic, stringent
10 inflexible, invariable
11 unalterable, unrelenting
12 intransigent
14 uncompromising
**rigmarole**
04 fuss, to-do
06 bother, hassle, jargon
07 palaver, process
08 nonsense
09 commotion
11 performance
**rigorous**
04 firm, hard
05 exact, harsh, rigid, tough
06 severe, strict
07 austere, precise, Spartan
08 exacting, thorough
09 draconian, laborious,
   stringent
10 meticulous, scrupulous
11 painstaking, punctilious
14 uncompromising
**rigor**
05 trial
06 ordeal
08 accuracy, firmness, hardness,
   hardship, rigidity
09 austerity, exactness,
   harshness, precision,
   suffering, toughness
10 strictness, stringency
12 thoroughness
14 meticulousness
15 punctiliousness
**rile**
03 bug, irk, vex
05 anger, annoy, pique, upset
06 nettle, put out
08 irritate
09 aggravate
**rim**
03 lip
04 brim, edge
05 brink, verge
06 border, margin
13 circumference
**rind**
04 husk, peel, skin
05 crust
07 epicarp
10 integument

**ring**
03 mob
04 band, bell, belt, buzz, call,
   ding, disc, disk, dong, echo,
   gang, gird, halo, hoop, loop,
   peal, toll
05 arena, atoll, chime, clang,
   clink, knell, phone
06 call up, cartel, circle, clique,
   collar, girdle, league, tinkle
07 circlet, circuit, combine,
   coterie, enclose, resound
08 ding-dong, encircle,
   resonate, surround
09 enclosure, encompass,
   phone call, syndicate,
   telephone
11 reverberate
**ringleader**
04 boss
05 chief
06 brains, honcho, leader
09 spokesman
10 bellwether, mastermind,
   mouthpiece
11 spokeswoman
12 spokesperson
**rinse**
05 bathe, clean, flush, swill
06 gargle
07 cleanse
09 flush away, wash clean
**riot**
03 row
04 fray, hoot, rage, rant, rave
05 brawl, fight, laugh, rebel
06 affray, fracas, mutiny, revolt,
   rise up, rising, scream,
   tumult, uproar
07 anarchy, rampage, revelry,
   run wild, turmoil
08 disorder, feasting, uprising
09 commotion, confusion, go
   berserk, rebellion
10 debauchery, insurgence,
   turbulence
11 disturbance, lawlessness
12 extravaganza, insurrection
14 go on the rampage
❏ **run riot**
04 rage, rant, rave, tear
05 storm
06 charge
07 rampage, run amok, run wild
09 go berserk
**riotous**
04 loud, wild
05 noisy, rowdy
06 unruly, wanton
07 lawless, violent
08 mutinous

10 boisterous, disorderly,
   rebellious, tumultuous,
   uproarious
12 ungovernable, unrestrained
13 insubordinate
14 uncontrollable
15 insurrectionary
**rip**
03 cut
04 hole, rend, rent, slit, tear
05 burst, shred, slash, split
07 rupture
08 cleavage, lacerate, separate
❏ **rip off**
02 do
03 con
04 dupe
05 cheat, sting, trick
06 diddle, fleece
07 defraud, exploit, swindle
10 overcharge
**ripe**
03 fit
05 grown, ready, right
06 mature, mellow, timely
07 perfect, ripened
09 developed, favorable, full-
   grown, opportune
10 auspicious, fully grown,
   propitious
11 full-fledged
14 fully developed
**ripen**
03 age
06 mature, mellow, season
07 develop
14 come to maturity
**rip-off**
03 con
05 cheat, fraud, sting, theft
06 diddle
07 robbery, swindle
08 con trick
12 exploitation
15 daylight robbery
**riposte**
04 quip
05 reply, sally
06 answer, rejoin, retort, return
07 respond
08 comeback, response
09 rejoinder
11 reciprocate
**ripple**
04 eddy, flow, purl, wave
06 burble, crease, gurgle, result,
   ruffle, wimple
07 lapping, ripplet, wrinkle
08 undulate
09 shock wave

10 undulation
11 consequence, disturbance
12 repercussion
13 reverberation

**rise**
04 flow, go up, grow, hill, leap, loom, riot, soar
05 arise, begin, climb, get up, issue, mount, raise, rebel, slope, start, swell, tower
06 appear, ascend, ascent, emerge, mutiny, resist, revolt, rocket, spring, upturn
07 advance, emanate, improve, incline, react to, respond, slope up, stand up, upsurge
08 escalate, increase, progress, spring up, towering
09 acclivity, elevation, get higher, increment, intensify, originate, promotion
10 escalation, take up arms
11 advancement, get out of bed, improvement
12 amelioration, make progress
13 get to your feet

**risible**
05 comic, droll, funny
06 absurd
07 amusing, comical
08 farcical, humorous
09 hilarious, laughable, ludicrous
10 ridiculous
11 rib-tickling

**rising**
04 riot
06 revolt
08 emerging, mounting, swelling, uprising
09 advancing, ascending
10 increasing, revolution
12 insurrection, intensifying

**risk**
04 dare
06 chance, danger, gamble
07 imperil, venture
08 endanger, jeopardy
10 go for broke, jeopardize
11 possibility, speculation
12 play with fire, put on the line

**risky**
04 iffy
06 chancy, tricky, unsafe
08 high-risk, perilous
09 dangerous, hazardous
10 precarious, touch-and-go

**risqué**
04 blue, racy, rude
05 adult, bawdy, crude, dirty
06 coarse, earthy, ribald, smutty

07 naughty
08 immodest, indecent, off-color
10 indelicate, suggestive

**rite**
04 form
06 custom, office, ritual
07 liturgy, service, worship
08 ceremony, practice
09 formality, ordinance, procedure, sacrament
10 ceremonial, observance

**ritual**
03 act, set
04 form, rite, wont
05 habit, usage
06 custom, formal
07 liturgy, routine, service
08 ceremony, habitual, practice
09 customary, formality, ordinance, sacrament, solemnity, tradition
10 ceremonial, observance, prescribed, procedural
11 celebration, traditional

**rival**
03 foe
04 vier
06 oppose
07 emulate, opposed, vie with
08 opponent, opposing
09 adversary, contender
10 antagonist, challenger, competitor, contestant, in conflict, opposition
11 compete with, competitive, conflicting

**rivalry**
05 vying
07 contest
10 contention, opposition
11 competition
15 competitiveness

**river** 🐟
07 fluvial, potamic
08 waterway
11 watercourse

▶ *Types of river*:
03 cut
04 rill
05 bourn, brook, canal, creek, delta, firth, inlet, mouth
06 runnel, source, stream
07 channel, estuary, rivulet
08 waterway
09 tributary
10 confluence

▶ *Names of rivers*:
02 Ob, Po

03 Don, Ems, Red, San, Tay, Wye
04 Aare, Amur, Avon, Bann, East, Ebro, Eden, Elbe, Kemi, Lena, Nile, Oder, Ohio, Ouse, Oxus, Ravi, Ruhr, Saar, Spey, Styx, Swan, Tees, Towy, Tyne, Vaal, Yalu
05 Adige, Argun, Boyne, Clyde, Congo, Donau, Douro, Fleet, Forth, Indus, James, Jumna, Loire, Marne, Meuse, Mosel, Negro, Niger, Peace, Pearl, Pecos, Plata, Plate, Rhine, Rhône, Seine, Snake, Somme, Tagus, Tiber, Trent, Tweed, Volga, Volta, Weser, Yukon, Zaire
06 Amazon, Brazos, Danube, Dnestr, Gambia, Ganges, Grande, Hudson, Humber, Irtysh, Jordan, Kolyma, Liffey, Mekong, Mersey, Murray, Orange, Ottawa, Pahang, Paraná, Ribble, Severn, Thames, Tigris, Ubangi, Vltava, Wabash, Yellow
07 Alabama, Darling, Dnieper, Garonne, Huang Ho, Lachlan, Limpopo, Lualaba, Madeira, Orinoco, Pechora, Potomac, Salween, Selenga, Sénégal, Shannon, Ucayali, Uruguay, Vistula, Yangtze, Yenisei, Zambezi
08 Achelous, Arkansas, Blue Nile, Canadian, Colorado, Columbia, Delaware, Dniester, Dordogne, Missouri, Okavango, Paraguay, Savannah, Tunguska, Wanganui
09 Euphrates, Irrawaddy, Mackenzie, Rio Grande, Saint John, Tennessee, Tombigbee, White Nile
10 Albert Nile, Bass Strait, Cumberland, Sacramento, San Joaquin, Shenandoah
11 Mississippi, Shatt al-Arab, Susquehanna, Yellowstone
12 Murrumbidgee, Saskatchewan
13 Saint Lawrence

**riveting**
08 exciting, gripping, hypnotic
09 absorbing, arresting
10 engrossing
11 captivating, enthralling, fascinating, interesting
12 spellbinding

**roam**
04 rove, trek, walk

**roar**
05 drift, prowl, range, tramp
06 ramble, stroll, travel, wander
08 ambulate, traverse
11 perambulate, peregrinate

**roar**
03 cry
04 bawl, hoot, howl, yell
05 blare, crash, laugh, shout
06 bellow, guffaw, rumble
07 break up, thunder

**rob**
02 do
03 mug
04 loot, raid, roll, sack
05 cheat, heist, rifle, sting
06 burgle, hold up, rip off
07 defraud, deprive, pillage,
   plunder, ransack, stick up,
   swindle
10 burglarize

**robber**
05 cheat, fraud, thief
06 bandit, con man, looter,
   mugger, pirate, raider
07 brigand, burglar, stealer
08 swindler
09 con artist
10 cat burglar, highwayman
11 safecracker
12 housebreaker

**robbery**
03 con
04 raid
05 fraud, heist, theft
06 holdup, rip-off
07 break-in, larceny, looting,
   mugging, pillage, plunder,
   stickup, swindle
08 burglary, stealing
09 pilferage
12 embezzlement, safecracking
13 housebreaking

**robe**
04 garb, gown, vest, wrap
05 drape, dress, habit
07 apparel, costume, wrapper
08 bathrobe, peignoir
09 housecoat
12 dressing gown

**robot**
06 zombie
07 android, machine
09 automaton

**robust**
03 fit, raw
04 rude, well
05 crude, hardy, tough
06 coarse, earthy, strong, sturdy
07 healthy

08 athletic, forceful, muscular,
   powerful, stalwart, vigorous
09 energetic, strapping
10 no-nonsense

**rock**
04 crag, roll, sway, tilt, toss
05 lurch, pitch, shake, stone
06 pebble, totter, wobble
07 astound, boulder, outcrop
08 undulate
09 dumbfound, oscillate
12 move to and fro

___

► *Types of rock:*
03 ore
04 coal, lava, marl
05 chalk, flint, shale, slate
06 basalt, gabbro, gneiss, gravel,
   marble, schist
07 granite
08 obsidian, porphyry
09 limestone, sandstone
11 pumice stone
12 conglomerate

**rocket**
03 fly
04 soar
07 missile, shoot up
08 escalate, increase
10 projectile

**rocky**
04 hard, weak
05 rough, shaky, stony
06 craggy, rugged, wobbly
08 unstable, unsteady

**rod**
03 bar, gun
04 cane, mace, pole, wand
05 baton, shaft, staff, stick, strut
06 pistol
07 scepter
08 revolver, rhabdoid

**rodent**

___

► *Types of rodent:*
03 rat
04 cavy, cony, hare, pika, vole
05 aguti, coypu, mouse
06 agouti, beaver, ferret, gerbil,
   gopher, jerboa, marmot,
   nutria, rabbit
07 hamster, lemming, meerkat,
   muskrat, ondatra, pack rat,
   potoroo
08 black rat, brown rat,
   capybara, chipmunk,
   dormouse, hedgehog,
   musquash, sewer rat,
   squirrel, water rat
09 bandicoot, groundhog,
   guinea pig, porcupine, water

vole, woodchuck
10 chinchilla, fieldmouse,
   prairie dog
11 kangaroo rat, red squirrel
12 gray squirrel, harvest mouse
➤ See also ANIMAL

**rogue**
05 cheat, crook, fraud, scamp
06 con man, rascal
07 villain, wastrel
08 deceiver, swindler
09 con artist, fraudster,
   miscreant, reprobate,
   scoundrel
10 ne'er-do-well
14 good-for-nothing

**roguish**
05 shady
06 cheeky, impish
07 crooked, knavish, playful
08 criminal, rascally
09 deceitful, dishonest
10 coquettish, frolicsome
11 mischievous

**roister**
04 brag, romp
05 boast, revel, strut
06 frolic
07 bluster, carouse, rollick
09 celebrate, make merry
15 paint the town red

**roisterer**
06 ranter
07 boaster, reveler
08 braggart, carouser
09 blusterer, swaggerer

**roisterous**
04 loud, wild
05 noisy, rowdy
09 clamorous, exuberant
10 boisterous, disorderly
12 obstreperous

**role**
03 job
04 duty, part, post, task
05 cameo
06 walk-on
08 capacity, function, position
09 character, situation
13 impersonation
14 representation

**roll**
03 bun, rob, run, wad
04 bolt, boom, coil, curl, drum,
   file, furl, list, reel, roar, rock,
   spin, sway, toss, turn, wind,
   wrap
05 index, lurch, pitch, spool,
   swell, twirl, twist, wheel

06 billow, bobbin, census, gyrate, muffin, record, roller, roster, rotate, rumble, scroll, tumble
07 biscuit, catalog, envelop, flatten, reeling, resound, revolve, rocking, stagger, thunder, tossing
08 cylinder, gyration, pitching, register, rotation, undulate
09 billowing, catalogue, chronicle, directory, inventory, press down
10 revolution, undulation

❑**roll up**
04 furl
06 arrive, gather
07 convene
08 assemble
10 congregate

**rollicking**
05 merry, noisy
06 hearty, jovial, joyous, lively
07 playful, romping
08 roisting, spirited, sportive
09 cavorting, exuberant
10 boisterous, frolicsome, rip-roaring, roisterous
12 devil-may-care
13 swashbuckling

**rolling**
06 waving
07 heaving, surging
10 undulating

**roly-poly**
03 fat
05 buxom, plump, podgy, pudgy, tubby
06 chubby, rotund
10 overweight

**romance**
03 lie, see, woo
04 date, tale
05 amour, court, novel, story
06 affair, glamor, legend, whimsy
07 fantasy, fiction, liaison, passion
08 intrigue
09 adventure, fairy tale, fantasize, love story, melodrama, sentiment
10 attachment, exaggerate, excitement, love affair

**romantic**
04 fond, wild
05 mushy, soppy
06 loving, sloppy, tender
07 amorous, dreamer, idyllic
08 exciting, fanciful, idealist

09 fairy-tale, fantastic, imaginary, legendary
10 fictitious, idealistic, improbable, lovey-dovey, mysterious, optimistic, passionate, starry-eyed
11 extravagant, fascinating, impractical, sentimental
14 sentimentalist

**Romeo**
05 lover
06 gigolo
07 Don Juan
08 Casanova, lady's man
09 ladies' man
10 lady-killer

**romp**
04 lark, skip
05 caper, frisk, revel, sport
06 cavort, frolic, gambol
07 roister, rollick

**roof**
09 tectiform

▶ *Types of roof*:
03 hip
04 bell, dome, flat, ogee, span
05 gable
06 cupola, lean-to, saddle
07 gambrel, mansard, pitched
08 imperial, pavilion, sawtooth, thatched
09 onion dome
10 imbricated, saucer dome
12 geodesic dome

**rook**
02 do
03 con
04 bilk, bird, crow
05 cheat, sting
06 diddle, fleece, rip off
07 defraud, swindle
10 overcharge

**room**
05 range, scope, space
06 extent, leeway, margin
07 chamber, expanse, legroom
08 capacity, headroom, latitude
09 allowance, elbowroom

**roomy**
04 wide
05 ample, broad, large
08 generous, sizeable, spacious
09 capacious, extensive
10 commodious, voluminous

**root**
03 dig, fix, nub, set
04 base, core, germ, hail, home, pull, seat, seed, stem

05 basis, cause, cheer, embed, fount, heart, radix, tuber
06 anchor, bottom, fasten, kernel, origin, source
07 applaud, cheer on, essence, nucleus, origins, radical, radicle, rhizome, support
09 beginning, establish
10 background, beginnings, derivation, foundation
11 fundamental
12 fountainhead
13 starting point

❑**root and branch**
06 wholly
07 finally, totally, utterly
08 entirely
09 radically
10 completely, thoroughly

❑**root around**
03 dig, pry
04 hunt, nose, poke
05 delve
06 burrow, ferret, forage
07 rummage

❑**root out**
06 dig out, remove, uproot
07 destroy, uncover, unearth
08 discover, get rid of
09 clear away, extirpate
10 put an end to
11 exterminate

**rooted**
04 deep, felt, firm
05 fixed, rigid
06 deeply
07 radical
09 confirmed, ingrained
10 deep-seated, entrenched
11 established

**rope**
03 tie
04 bind, lash, moor
05 hitch
06 fasten, tether
09 funicular

▶ *Types of rope*:
03 guy
04 cord, line, stay, tack, vang, warp
05 brace, cable, lasso, noose
06 halter, hawser, lariat, strand, string, tether
07 bobstay, bowline, cordage, cringle, halyard, lanyard, lashing, marline, painter, towrope
08 buntline, clew line, dragline, dragrope, gantline
09 hackamore

❏**rope in**
06 engage, enlist
07 involve
08 inveigle, persuade, talk into

**roster**
04 list, roll
05 index
06 muster
07 listing
08 register, schedule
09 directory

**rostrum**
04 dais
05 stage
06 podium
08 platform

**rosy**
03 red
04 pink, rose
05 fresh, ruddy, sunny
06 bright, florid
07 flushed, glowing, hopeful, reddish, rose red, roseate
08 blooming, blushing, roselike, rubicund
09 favorable
10 auspicious
14 healthy looking

**rot**
04 bosh, bunk, mold, rust
05 decay, go bad
06 bunkum, drivel, fester, go sour, humbug, perish, piffle
07 baloney, putrefy, rubbish
08 claptrap, nonsense
09 decompose, poppycock
10 degenerate
12 disintegrate, putrefaction
13 decomposition

**rotary**
07 turning
08 gyrating, gyratory, rotating, spinning, whirling
09 revolving

**rotate**
04 reel, roll, spin, turn
05 pivot, whirl
06 gyrate, swivel
07 revolve
08 go around
09 alternate
10 move around
13 take it in turns

**rotation**
04 spin, turn
05 cycle, orbit, whirl
06 swivel
07 turning
08 gyration, sequence, spinning, whirling

09 swiveling
10 revolution, succession

**rotten**
03 bad, ill
04 evil, foul, rank, sick, sour
05 awful, dirty, fetid, lousy, moldy
06 addled, crummy, poorly, putrid, unwell, wicked
07 beastly, corrupt, decayed, immoral, rotting, spoiled, tainted
08 decaying, horrible, inferior, low-grade, stinking
09 moldering
10 decomposed, despicable, putrescent
14 disintegrating

**rotund**
03 fat
04 full, rich
05 heavy, obese, plump, podgy, pudgy, round, stout, tubby
06 chubby, fleshy, portly
07 bulbous, rounded, spheric
08 globular, roly-poly, sonorous
09 corpulent, full-toned, orbicular, rotundate, spherular

**roué**
04 rake
06 lecher, wanton
08 rakehell
09 debauchee, libertine
10 profligate, sensualist

**rough**
03 ill
04 hard, hazy, sick, thug, wild
05 bully, bumpy, crude, draft, gruff, harsh, hasty, husky, noisy, quick, scaly, stony, tough, vague
06 brutal, choppy, coarse, craggy, hoarse, jagged, mockup, poorly, rotten, rugged, severe, shaggy, sketch, stormy
07 bristly, brusque, brutish, cursory, general, gnarled, inexact, outline, prickly, rasping, raucous, sketchy, throaty, violent
08 below par, croaking, forceful, guttural, off-color, scratchy, strident
09 estimated, imprecise, irregular, turbulent, unhealthy, unrefined
10 boisterous, incomplete, unfinished, unpolished

11 approximate, insensitive, rudimentary, tempestuous

❏**rough out**
05 draft
06 mock up, sketch
07 outline
14 give a summary of

❏**rough up**
03 mug
04 bash
06 beat up
08 maltreat, mistreat
09 manhandle
10 knock about

**rough-and-ready**
05 crude
06 make-do, simple
07 hurried, sketchy, stop-gap
09 makeshift, unrefined
10 unpolished
11 provisional

**rough-and-tumble**
05 brawl, fight, melee, scrap
06 affray, dust-up, fracas
07 scuffle
08 struggle

**roughen**
04 chap, rasp
05 chafe, graze, rough, scuff
06 abrade, ruffle
07 coarsen, harshen
08 asperate
09 granulate

**roughneck**
04 goon, lout, thug
05 bully, rowdy, tough
07 bruiser, ruffian
08 bully boy, hooligan
09 oil worker

**round**
03 lap, orb
04 ball, band, beat, bout, disk, game, hoop, path, ring, rung
05 cycle, globe, plump, rough, route, stage, stout
06 bypass, circle, course, curved, period, portly, rotund, series, sphere
07 circlet, circuit, discoid, globate, rounded, routine, session
08 circular, cylinder, globular, golf game, sequence, spheroid
09 corpulent, discoidal, estimated, imprecise, orbicular, spherical
10 ammunition, pass around, ring shaped, succession
11 approximate, cylindrical

**◻round off**
03 cap, end
05 close, crown
06 finish, top off
08 complete, conclude
09 finish off

**◻round up**
04 herd
05 group, rally
06 gather, muster
07 collect, marshal
08 assemble
13 bring together

**roundabout**
07 evasive, oblique, winding
08 indirect, tortuous, twisting
10 circuitous, meandering
14 circumlocutory

**roundly**
06 openly
08 fiercely, severely
09 intensely, violently
10 completely, forcefully,
   thoroughly, vehemently
11 outspokenly

**roundup**
05 rally
06 muster, précis, survey
07 herding, summary
08 assembly, overview
09 collation, gathering
10 collection

**rouse**
04 call, move, stir, wake
05 anger, evoke, get up, start
06 arouse, awaken, excite,
   incite, induce, wake up, whip
   up
07 agitate, disturb, provoke
09 galvanize, stimulate

**rousing**
08 exciting, spirited, stirring
09 inspiring
11 stimulating

**rout**
04 beat, lick
05 chase, crush
06 defeat, dispel, flight,
   hammer, thrash
07 conquer, retreat, trounce
08 conquest, drubbing
09 overthrow, slaughter,
   thrashing, trouncing
11 put to flight, subjugation

**route**
03 run, way
04 beat, path, road, send
06 avenue, course, direct
07 circuit, journey, passage
09 direction, itinerary

10 flight path

**routine**
03 act, rut, way
05 banal, habit, piece, spiel
06 boring, common, custom,
   method, normal, system
07 formula, humdrum, pattern,
   program
08 everyday, familiar, habitual,
   ordinary, practice, schedule
09 customary, hackneyed,
   procedure
11 performance, predictable
12 conventional

**rove**
04 roam
05 drift, range, stray
06 cruise, ramble, stroll, wander
09 gallivant

**rover**
05 Gypsy, nomad
06 ranger
07 drifter, rambler, vagrant
08 gadabout, traveler, wanderer
09 itinerant, transient

**row**
03 din
04 bank, file, line, rank, tier, tiff
05 argue, chain, fight, noise,
   range, scrap, set-to
06 bicker, column, fracas,
   hubbub, racket, rumpus,
   series, string, uproar
07 dispute, quarrel, wrangle
08 argument, conflict,
   sequence, squabble
09 commotion
10 falling-out
11 altercation, arrangement,
   controversy, disturbance
12 disagreement

**rowdy**
04 loud, lout, wild
05 noisy, rough, tough, yahoo
06 unruly
07 brawler, hoodlum, riotous
08 hooligan
10 boisterous, disorderly
12 obstreperous, unrestrained

**royal**
05 grand, regal
06 august, kingly, superb
07 queenly, stately
08 imperial, majestic, princely
09 sovereign
11 magnificent, monarchical

**rub**
04 buff, snag, wipe
05 catch, chafe, clean, grate, put
   on, scour, scrub, smear

06 abrade, buff up, fondle,
   polish, scrape, smooth,
   spread, stroke, work in
07 burnish, massage, scratch
08 drawback, kneading
09 embrocate, hindrance
10 difficulty, impediment

**◻rub in**
06 harp on, stress
09 emphasize, underline
10 make much of

**◻rub off on**
06 affect, change
09 influence, transform
14 have an effect on

**◻rub out**
04 do in, kill
05 erase
06 delete, efface, murder
09 eliminate, finish off, liquidate
10 obliterate, put to death
11 assassinate

**◻rub up the wrong way**
03 bug, get, irk, vex
05 anger, annoy, get to, peeve
06 needle, niggle
08 irritate
11 get one's goat

**rubbish**
03 rot
04 bull, bunk, crap, junk
05 dross, scrap, trash, waste
06 bunkum, debris, drivel, litter,
   piffle, refuse, rubble
07 garbage, twaddle
08 claptrap, detritus, nonsense
09 gibberish, poppycock
10 balderdash
12 gobbledegook,
   gobblydegook

**rubbishy**
05 cheap, petty
06 paltry, shoddy, tawdry, trashy
08 gimcrack
09 third-rate, throw-away

**ruction**
03 row
04 fuss, rout, to-do
05 brawl, scrap, storm
06 fracas, ruckus, rumpus,
   uproar
07 dispute, protest, quarrel
09 commotion
11 altercation, disturbance

**ruddy**
03 red
04 rosy
05 fresh
06 florid

**rude**
07 crimson, flushed, glowing, healthy, reddish, scarlet
08 blooming, blushing

**rude**
04 curt, lewd
05 bawdy, crude, dirty, gross, nasty, rough, sharp, short
06 cheeky, coarse, filthy, ribald, risqué, simple, vulgar
07 abusive, brusque, ill-bred, obscene, uncivil, uncouth
08 ignorant, impolite, improper, impudent, indecent, insolent
09 insulting, primitive, unrefined, untutored
10 indelicate, uneducated, unpleasant, unpolished
11 bad tempered, ill-mannered, impertinent, uncivilized
12 disagreeable, discourteous
13 rough-and-ready

**rudimentary**
05 basic, crude, rough
06 simple
09 embryonic, primitive
10 elementary
11 fundamental, undeveloped
12 introductory

**rudiments**
03 ABC
06 basics
08 elements
10 essentials, principles
12 fundamentals

**rue**
05 mourn
06 bemoan, bewail, grieve, lament, regret, repent
07 be sorry, deplore
11 be regretful

**rueful**
03 sad
05 sorry
06 dismal, woeful
07 doleful, pitiful
08 contrite, grievous, mournful, penitent, pitiable
09 plaintive, repentant, sorrowful, woebegone
10 apologetic, lugubrious, melancholy, remorseful
15 self-reproachful

**ruffian**
04 lout, thug
05 bully, rowdy, tough
07 bruiser, hoodlum, villain
08 bullyboy, hooligan
09 cutthroat, miscreant, roughneck, scoundrel

**ruffle**
03 bug, irk, vex
04 rile
05 anger, annoy, upset
06 crease, hassle, nettle, rattle, rumple, tousle
07 confuse, crumple, fluster, perturb, trouble, wrinkle
08 dishevel, irritate
10 disarrange, discompose

**rugged**
05 rocky, stark, stony, tough
06 craggy, jagged, robust, sinewy, strong, uneven
08 furrowed, muscular
09 irregular, well-built
13 weather-beaten

**ruin**
03 mar
04 fall, harm, loss, raze
05 havoc, smash, spoil, wreck
06 debris, mess up, penury, relics, rubble, traces
07 cripple, destroy, failure, remains, shatter, undoing
08 bankrupt, collapse, demolish, detritus, disaster, downfall, lay waste, vestiges, wreckage
09 indigence, overwhelm, ruination
10 bankruptcy, impoverish, insolvency, wreak havoc
11 destruction, devastation

**ruinous**
07 damaged, in ruins, wrecked
08 decrepit
09 crippling, excessive
10 broken-down, calamitous, devastated, ramshackle
11 cataclysmic, devastating
12 catastrophic, extortionate

**rule**
03 law
04 find, form, lead, sway, wont
05 axiom, canon, guide, maxim, order, power, reign, ruler, tenet
06 decree, govern, manage, regime, ruling, settle, truism
07 control, formula, lay down, precept, prevail, statute
08 dominate, dominion, kingship, practice, protocol, regulate, standard
09 authority, criterion, determine, guideline, officiate, ordinance, principle, pronounce, queenship, supremacy
10 adjudicate, administer, convention, government, leadership, regulation
11 commandment, preside over, restriction, sovereignty
12 call the shots, jurisdiction, straightedge
14 administration

❏**as a rule**
06 mainly
07 usually
08 normally
09 generally, in general
10 by and large, on the whole, ordinarily
14 for the most part

❏**rule out**
03 ban
06 forbid, reject
07 dismiss, exclude, prevent
08 disallow, preclude, prohibit
09 eliminate

**ruler**
▶ *Types of ruler:*
03 aga
04 czar, duce, emir, head, khan, king, lord, raja, rani, shah
05 nabob, nawab, nizam, queen, rajah, ranee, sheik
06 caesar, caliph, consul, Führer, kaiser, leader, mikado, prince, regent, sheikh, shogun, sultan
07 emperor, empress, monarch, pharaoh, premier, sultana, viceroy
08 governor, maharaja, maharani, overlord, princess, suzerain
09 commander, maharajah, maharanee, potentate, president, sovereign
11 head of state
13 prime minister
15 governor-general

**ruling**
06 decree
07 finding, supreme, verdict
08 decision, dominant, in charge, judgment, reigning
09 governing, in control, sovereign
10 commanding, resolution
11 controlling, on the throne
12 adjudication
13 pronouncement

**rumbustious**
04 loud, wild
05 noisy, rough, rowdy
06 robust, unruly, wilful

07 willful
09 clamorous, exuberant
10 boisterous, disorderly,
    refractory, roisterous,
    uproarious
12 unmanageable

**ruminate**
04 muse
05 brood, think
06 ponder
07 reflect
08 chew over, cogitate,
    consider, mull over
10 deliberate
11 contemplate

**rummage**
04 hunt, junk, root
05 delve, rifle
06 forage, jumble, search
07 clutter
10 poke around, root around

**rumor**
04 buzz, news, talk, tell, word
05 bruit, story
06 gossip, report
07 hearsay, scandal, whisper
09 circulate, grapevine
11 information, speculation
13 bush telegraph

**rump**
04 butt, dock, rear, seat
05 croup, trace
06 bottom, haunch
07 remains, remnant, residue,
    vestige
08 backside, buttocks
09 posterior, remainder
12 hindquarters

**rumple**
05 crush
06 crease, pucker, ruffle, tousle
07 crumple, derange, wrinkle
08 dishevel, disorder

**rumpus**
03 row
04 fuss, rout
05 brawl, furor, noise
06 fracas, tumult, uproar
07 ruction
08 brouhaha
09 commotion, confusion,
    kerfuffle
10 disruption
11 disturbance

**run**
03 jog, rip, set, use, way
04 bolt, coop, dart, dash, drip,
    flow, gash, go on, gush, lead,
    line, pass, pour, race, ride,

    road, rush, snag, spin, tear,
    trip, trot, work
05 carry, cross, cycle, drive,
    enter, hurry, jaunt, print,
    range, reach, round, route,
    scoot, score, slide, speed,
    spurt, track
06 career, convey, course,
    direct, extend, gallop,
    manage, outing, period,
    scurry, series, sprint, stream,
    string, travel
07 carry on, cascade, compete,
    conduct, contend, control,
    operate, oversee, perform,
    publish, scamper, scuttle,
    stretch, trickle
08 be played, be staged,
    campaign, carry out,
    continue, organize, progress,
    regulate, sequence, step on it
09 broadcast, challenge,
    enclosure, excursion,
    supervise, transport
10 administer, coordinate,
    succession, take part in
12 be a candidate, be in charge
    of
13 be in operation

❏**in the long run**
06 at last
08 in the end
10 eventually, ultimately

❏**run across**
04 meet
07 run into
08 bump into
09 encounter
10 chance upon, come across

❏**run after**
04 tail
05 chase
06 follow, pursue

❏**run away**
04 bolt, flee, lift
05 elope, leave
06 beat it, decamp, escape
07 abscond
08 clear off, make off,
13 make a run for it

❏**run down**
03 cut, hit
05 knock, weary
06 attack, reduce, weaken
07 curtail, exhaust, run over
08 belittle, decrease, denounce
09 criticize, denigrate,
    disparage, knock down

❏**run for it**
04 bolt, flee
05 scram

06 escape
07 make off, retreat
09 skedaddle

❏**run in**
03 nab
04 book, bust, jail, lift
05 pinch
06 arrest, collar, drop by, pick up,
    stop by
09 apprehend

❏**run into**
03 hit, ram
04 meet
05 crash
08 bump into
09 encounter, run across
10 chance upon
11 collide with

❏**run off**
04 bolt
05 elope, print, xerox
06 decamp, escape
07 abscond, make off, produce,
    run away
09 duplicate, photostat,
    skedaddle

❏**run off with**
09 elope with
11 make off with, run away with

❏**run on**
04 go on, last
06 extend
07 carry on
08 continue
11 keep talking

❏**run out**
03 end
05 cease, close, dry up, expel
06 expire, finish
07 exhaust, give out
08 drive out
09 terminate

❏**run out on**
04 dump, jilt
05 chuck, ditch, leave
07 abandon, forsake
09 walk out on
15 leave in the lurch

❏**run over**
03 hit
06 go over, repeat, review
07 run down
08 overflow, practice, rehearse
09 knock down, reiterate
10 run through

❏**run through**
04 read
05 spend, waste
06 review, survey
07 examine, exhaust, run over

08 practice, rehearse, squander
09 dissipate, go through
11 fritter away

❏**run to**
05 reach
06 afford, come to
07 add up to
08 amount to
12 have enough of

❏**run together**
03 mix
04 fuse, join
05 blend, merge, unite
06 mingle
07 combine
10 amalgamate

**runaway**
05 loose
07 escaped, escapee, refugee
08 decisive, deserter, fugitive
09 absconder
12 out of control, uncontrolled

**rundown**
06 review
07 outline, summary
08 analysis, briefing

**run-down**
04 weak
05 seedy, tired, weary
06 peaked
07 worn-out
08 fatigued
09 exhausted, neglected
10 ramshackle
11 debilitated, dilapidated

**run-in**
05 brush, fight, set-to
06 dust-up, tussle
07 dispute, quarrel, wrangle
08 argument, skirmish
11 altercation, contretemps
13 confrontation

**runner**
03 rug, run
05 go-fer, gofer, racer, shoot,
   sprig
06 bearer, jogger, sprout, stolon
07 athlete, courier, tendril
08 offshoot, smuggler, sprinter
09 flagellum, messenger,
   sarmentum
13 dispatch rider

**running**
06 charge, in a row, racing
07 contest, control, flowing,
   jogging, rushing, working
08 constant, unbroken
09 ceaseless, incessant,
   perpetual, sprinting,
   unceasing

10 continuous, leadership,
   management, successive
11 consecutive, controlling,
   functioning, supervision
12 coordination, in succession
13 uninterrupted
14 administration

**runny**
05 fluid
06 liquid, melted, molten
07 diluted, flowing
09 liquefied

**run-of-the-mill**
06 common, normal
07 average
08 everyday, mediocre,
   middling, ordinary
12 unimpressive, unremarkable
13 no great shakes,
   unexceptional
15 undistinguished

**rupture**
04 rend, rent, rift, tear
05 break, burst, crack, split
06 breach, divide, hernia,
   schism
08 breaking, puncture, separate
12 disagreement

**rural**
06 rustic, sylvan
07 bucolic, country
08 agrarian, pastoral
12 agricultural

**ruse**
04 hoax, plan, ploy, sham, wile
05 blind, dodge, trick
06 device, scheme, tactic
08 artifice, maneuver
09 deception, imposture,
   stratagem
10 subterfuge

**rush**
03 fly, run
04 bolt, dart, dash, flow, gush,
   push, race, raid, stir, tear
05 flood, haste, hurry, press,
   shoot, speed, storm, surge
06 attack, charge, clamor, flurry,
   hasten, sprint, stream
07 assault, urgency
08 activity, dispatch, pressure,
   rapidity, stampede
09 commotion, make haste,
   onslaught, swiftness
10 get a move on, hurly-burly
14 hive of activity
15 hustle and bustle

**rushed**
04 busy, fast
05 hasty, quick, rapid, swift

06 prompt, urgent
07 cursory, hurried
08 careless
09 emergency
11 expeditious, superficial

**rust**
05 decay, stain
07 corrode, oxidize, tarnish
09 corrosion, oxidation,
   verdigris

**rust-colored**
03 red
05 brown, rusty, sandy, tawny
06 auburn, copper, ginger,
   russet, Titian
07 coppery, gingery, reddish
08 chestnut
12 reddish-brown

**rustic**
04 boor, clod, hick, rude
05 churl, rough, rural, yokel
06 coarse, simple, sylvan
07 artless, awkward, bucolic,
   bumpkin, country, peasant
08 homespun, pastoral
09 hillbilly, unrefined
10 provincial, uncultured
11 countrified, countryside
13 country cousin
15 unsophisticated

**rustle**
07 crackle, whisper
08 rustling, susurrus
09 crepitate, crinkling, susurrate
10 whispering
11 crepitation, susurration

**rusty**
03 red
04 dull, poor, weak
05 brown, dated, sandy, stale,
   stiff, tawny
06 auburn, copper, ginger,
   russet, rusted, Titian
07 coppery, gingery, reddish
08 chestnut, corroded,
   outmoded, oxidized
09 deficient, tarnished
10 antiquated, discolored
11 rust-colored, unpracticed
12 old-fashioned, reddish-
   brown
13 out of practice

**rut**
05 ditch, grind, habit, track
06 furrow, groove, gutter,
   system, trough
07 channel, humdrum, pattern,
   pothole, routine
09 chuckhole, treadmill, wheel
   mark
10 daily grind

11 indentation
12 same old story
**ruthless**
04 grim, hard
05 cruel, harsh, stern
06 brutal, fierce, savage, severe

07 callous, inhuman, vicious
08 pitiless
09 barbarous, cutthroat, dog-eat-dog, Draconian, ferocious, heartless,

merciless, unfeeling, unsparing
10 implacable, inexorable, relentless, unmerciful
11 hardhearted, remorseless, unforgiving, unrelenting

**sable**
03 jet
04 dark, inky
05 black, dusky, ebony
06 pitchy, somber
09 coal black, pitch-dark
10 pitch-black

**sabotage**
04 ruin
05 spoil, wreck
06 damage, thwart, weaken
07 destroy, disable, scupper
09 undermine, vandalism, vandalize
11 destruction

**sac**
03 bag
04 cyst
05 bursa, pouch, theca
06 pocket, vesica
07 bladder, saccule, vesicle
08 follicle

**saccharine**
05 mushy, soppy, sweet
06 sugary, syrupy
07 cloying, honeyed, mawkish
09 schmaltzy
11 sentimental, sickly sweet

**sack**
02 ax
03 axe, bag, can, rob
04 fire, loot, poke, raid, raze
05 gunny, rifle, the ax
06 maraud, papers, rapine, ravage, the axe
07 despoil, destroy, dismiss, pillage, plunder, the boot
08 gunnybag, lay waste
09 dismissal, gunnysack, marauding
11 destruction, send packing, the pink slip
12 despoliation
13 walking papers

**sacred**
04 holy
05 godly
06 divine
07 blessed, revered, saintly
08 hallowed, heavenly
09 religious, respected, spiritual, venerable
10 devotional, inviolable, sacrosanct, sanctified
11 consecrated, untouchable
14 ecclesiastical

**sacredness**
08 divinity, holiness, sanctity
09 godliness, solemnity
11 saintliness
13 inviolability, sacrosanctity

**sacrifice**
04 loss
05 let go
06 forego, give up
07 abandon, forfeit, offer up
08 immolate, oblation, offering
09 surrender
10 immolation, relinquish
11 abandonment, destruction

**sacrificial**
06 votive
08 oblatory, piacular
09 expiatory
12 propitiatory

**sacrilege**
06 heresy
07 impiety, mockery, outrage
09 blasphemy, profanity, violation
10 disrespect
11 desecration, irreverence, profanation

**sacrilegious**
07 impious, profane
09 heretical
10 irreverent
11 blasphemous, desecrating, profanatory
13 disrespectful

**sacrosanct**
06 sacred, secure
08 hallowed
09 protected
10 inviolable
11 impregnable, untouchable

**sad**
03 low
04 blue, down, glum
05 fed up, grave, sorry, upset
06 dismal, gloomy, tragic
07 doleful, joyless, pitiful, serious, unhappy, wistful
08 downcast, grievous, mournful, pathetic, pitiable, poignant, touching, wretched
09 depressed, long faced, miserable, sorrowful, upsetting, woebegone
10 depressing, despondent, distressed, lamentable, melancholy, rock bottom
11 distressing, downhearted, regrettable, unfortunate
12 disconsolate, heavy-hearted, in low spirits
13 grief-stricken
14 down in the dumps

**sadden**
06 dismay, grieve
08 cast down, dispirit, distress
10 discourage, dishearten
14 break your heart, drive to despair, get someone down

**saddle**
04 land, load, seat
06 burden, impose, lumber
07 harness
08 encumber

**sadism**
07 cruelty
09 barbarity, brutality
10 bestiality, inhumanity
11 callousness, viciousness
13 heartlessness, sadomasochism, unnaturalness

**sadistic**
05 cruel
06 brutal
07 bestial, inhuman, vicious
09 barbarous, merciless, perverted, unnatural

**sadness**
03 woe
05 grief
06 misery, pathos, regret, sorrow
08 distress, glumness
09 heartache, poignancy
10 dismalness, gloominess, low spirits, melancholy, somberness

**safe**

11 despondency, dolefulness, joylessness, unhappiness
12 mournfulness, wretchedness
13 sorrowfulness
14 lugubriousness

**safe**
04 sure
05 chest, tried, vault
06 coffer, honest, immune, intact, proven, secure, tested, unhurt
07 cashbox, guarded, prudent
08 defended, harmless, nontoxic, unharmed
09 protected, sheltered, strongbox, undamaged, uninjured, unscathed
10 dependable, deposit box, depository, repository
11 impregnable, in good hands, out of danger, trustworthy
12 invulnerable, nonpoisonous, safe as houses, unassailable
13 out of harm's way
14 uncontaminated

**safe-conduct**
04 pass
06 convoy, escort, permit
07 license, warrant
08 passport
13 authorization, laissez-passer

**safeguard**
06 defend, screen, secure, shield, surety
07 defense, protect, shelter
08 preserve, security
09 assurance, guarantee, insurance
10 precaution, protection

**safe house**
06 refuge
11 hiding place

**safekeeping**
04 care, ward
06 charge
07 custody, keeping
08 wardship
10 protection
12 guardianship

**safety**
05 cover
06 refuge
07 shelter, welfare
08 fail-safe, immunity, security
09 safeguard, sanctuary
10 protection, protective
13 football score, precautionary
14 impregnability

**sag**
03 bag, dip, low

04 bend, drop, fail, fall, flag, flop, hang, sink, slip
05 droop, slide, slump
06 falter, weaken
07 decline, subside

**saga**
04 epic, epos, tale, yarn
05 story
06 epopee
07 history, romance
08 epopoeia
09 adventure, chronicle, narrative, soap opera
11 roman-fleuve

**sagacious**
04 sage, wise
05 acute, canny, quick, sharp
06 astute, shrewd
07 knowing
10 farsighted, insightful, perceptive, percipient
11 penetrating
13 perspicacious

**sagacity**
06 acumen, wisdom
07 insight
08 sapience
09 acuteness, canniness, foresight, sharpness
10 astuteness, shrewdness
11 knowingness, penetration, percipience
12 perspicacity
13 understanding

**sage**
04 guru, wise
05 canny, elder, hakam
06 expert, master, savant
07 knowing, learned, mahatma, prudent, sapient, wise man
08 sensible
09 judicious, maharishi, sagacious, wise woman
11 intelligent, philosopher
13 knowledgeable, perspicacious

▶ *The seven sages*:
04 **Bias** (of Priene in Caria)
05 **Solon** (of Athens)
06 **Chilon** (of Sparta), **Thales** (of Miletus)
08 **Pittacus** (of Mitylene)
09 **Cleobulus** (tyrant of Lindus in Rhodes), **Periander** (tyrant of Corinth)
➤ See also MYTHOLOGY.

**sail**
03 fly
04 boat, scud, ship, skim, wing

05 coast, drift, float, glide, pilot, plane, steer, sweep, yacht
06 cruise, embark, voyage
07 captain, skipper
08 navigate, put to sea
09 leave port
11 weigh anchor

▶ *Types of sail*:
03 jib, lug, rig
04 kite
05 genoa, mizen, royal
06 canvas, course, jigger, mizzen
07 foretop, jury rig, lugsail, skysail, spanker, topsail, trysail
08 foresail, gaff sail, headsail, mainsail, staysail
09 foreroyal, moonraker, spinnaker, spritsail
10 Bermuda rig, lateen sail, main course, square sail, topgallant
11 fore-topsail, gaff-topsail, main-topsail
12 forestaysail, studdingsail
13 fore-and-aft rig
14 fore-topgallant

❏**sail into**
06 attack, let fly, turn on
07 assault, lay into
08 set about, tear into

❏**sail through**
10 pass easily
11 romp through

**sailor**
06 seaman
07 mariner
08 seafarer
➤ See also MILITARY; PIRATE

▶ *Types of sailor*:
02 AB
03 cox, gob
04 Jack, mate, salt, swab, WAVE
05 bosun, limey, pilot, rower
06 lascar, marine, master, pirate, purser, rating, sea dog, swabby
07 boatman, captain, crewman, Jack-tar, oarsman, skipper, swabbie
08 bargeman, cabin boy, coxswain, deckhand, helmsman
09 boatswain, buccaneer, fisherman, navigator
10 able seaman, bluejacket
11 yachtswoman
12 tar yachtsman

► *Names of sailors:*
04 **Byng** (George), **Byng** (John), **Cook** (James), **Diaz** (Bartolomeu), **Gama** (Vasco da), **Hood** (Samuel), **Kidd** (William), **Ross** (James Clark), **Ross** (John), **Spee** (Count Maximilian von)
05 **Bligh** (William), **Cabot** (John), **Cabot** (Sebastian), **Doria** (Andrea), **Drake** (Sir Francis), **Henry** (the Navigator), **Jones** (John Paul), **Peary** (Robert Edwin), **Perry** (Matthew)
06 **Baffin** (William), **Beatty** (David), **Benbow** (John), **Bering** (Vitus), **Conner** (Dennis), **Dönitz** (Karl), **Hudson** (Henry), **Nelson** (Horatio), **Nimitz** (Chester), **Semmes** (Raphael), **Tasman** (Abel Janszoon), **Vernon** (Edward)
07 **Barentz** (William), **Hawkins** (John), **Hawkyns** (John), **Laffite** (Jean), **Lafitte** (Jean), **Marryat** (Captain Frederick), **Pytheas**, **Raleigh** (Sir Walter), **Selkirk** (Alexander), **Tirpitz** (Alfred von), **Weddell** (James)
08 **Beaufort** (Francis), **Columbus** (Christopher), **Cousteau** (Jacques Yves), **Farragut** (David), **Jellicoe** (John Rushworth), **Magellan** (Ferdinand), **Pitcairn** (Robert), **Vespucci** (Amerigo)
09 **Christian** (Fletcher), **Frobisher** (Martin), **Grenville** (Richard), **Vancouver** (George)
10 **Chichester** (Francis), **Erik the Red**
11 **Mountbatten** (Louis)
12 **Themistocles**

**saint**

► *Names of saints. We have omitted the word* **saint** *from names given in the following list but you may need to include this word as part of the solution to some crossword clues.*
03 Leo
04 Anne, Bede, Gall, Joan (of Arc), John, John (Chrysostom), John (Neumann), John (of the Cross), John (the Baptist), Jude, Lucy, Luke, Mark, Mary, Mary (Magdalene), Paul
05 Agnes, Aidan, Alban, Basil (the Great), Clare, David, Denis, Giles, James, Peter, Titus, Vitus
06 Andrew, Anselm, Antony, Antony (of Padua), Aquila, Cosmas, Damian, George, Helena, Hilary (of Poitiers), Jerome, Joseph, Joseph (of Arimathea), Justin, Martha, Martin, Monica, Oswald, Philip, Prisca, Simeon, Teresa (of Avila), Thomas, Thomas (Aquinas), Thomas (à Becket), Thomas (Becket), Thomas (More), Ursula
07 Ambrose, Anthony, Anthony (of Padua), Bernard (of Clairvaux), Bridget, Cecilia, Clement, Columba, Crispin, Cyprian, Dominic, Dunstan, Francis (of Assisi), Francis (Xavier), Gregory (of Nazianzus), Gregory (of Tours), Isidore (of Seville), Matthew, Michael, Patrick, Stephen, Swithin, Theresa (of Lisieux), Timothy, Vincent (de Paul), Wilfrid
08 Barnabas, Benedict (of Nursia), Boniface, Cuthbert, Ignatius (of Loyola), Lawrence, Margaret, Nicholas, Polycarp, Veronica, Walpurga
09 Alexander (Nevsky), Augustine (of Canterbury), Augustine (of Hippo), Catherine, Genevieve, Katherine (Drexel), Kentigern, Ladislaus, Methodius, Sebastian, Valentine
10 Bernadette, Stanislaus, Wenceslaus
11 Bonaventure, Christopher
12 Elizabeth Ann (Seton), Justin Martyr
13 Frances Xavier (Cabrini)
15 Aquila and Prisca, Cosmas and Damian

**saintliness**
05 faith, piety
06 purity, virtue
08 chastity, goodness, holiness, morality, sanctity
10 asceticism, devoutness
11 blessedness
12 spirituality

13 righteousness, self-sacrifice

**saintly**
04 good, holy, pure
05 godly, moral, pious
06 devout, worthy
07 angelic, blessed, sinless
08 spotless, virtuous
09 religious, righteous, saintlike, spiritual

**sake**
04 gain, goal, good
05 cause
06 behalf, reason
07 account, benefit, welfare
08 interest
09 advantage, well-being

**salacious**
04 blue, lewd
05 bawdy
06 coarse, ribald, smutty
07 lustful, obscene, raunchy
09 lecherous
10 lascivious, libidinous, lubricious

**salaried**
04 paid
05 waged
11 remunerated, stipendiary

**salary**
03 fee, pay
05 wages
06 income
07 stipend
08 earnings
09 emolument
10 honorarium
12 remuneration

**sale**
04 deal
05 trade
07 bargain, selling, traffic, vending
09 marketing
11 transaction

❑**for sale**
06 on sale
09 available, up for sale
10 obtainable
11 in the stores, on the market

**salable**
08 vendible
09 desirable
10 marketable
12 merchantable

**salesperson**
03 rep
08 salesman
09 salesgirl, saleslady

**salient**
10 salesclerk, saleswoman, shopkeeper
11 salesperson, storekeeper
14 representative, retail merchant

**salient**
04 main
05 chief
08 striking
09 principal, prominent
10 noticeable, pronounced
11 conspicuous, significant

**sallow**
05 pasty, waxen
06 pallid, sickly
09 colorless, jaundiced, yellowish

**sally**
04 dash, jest, joke, quip, raid
05 erupt, foray, issue
06 attack, charge, retort, sortie, thrust
07 assault, riposte, venture
09 promenade, wisecrack, witticism

**salt**
03 wit, zip
04 zest
05 briny, punch, savor, smack, taste, vigor
06 flavor, marine, rating, relish, sailor, saline, seaman
07 mariner
08 brackish, piquancy, pungency, seafarer
09 seasoning
10 liveliness, trenchancy

□ **salt away**
04 bank, hide, save
05 amass, cache, hoard, stash

**salty**
05 briny, spicy, tangy, witty
06 saline, savory
07 piquant
08 brackish
09 trenchant

**salubrious**
07 healthy
08 hygienic, pleasant, sanitary
09 healthful, wholesome
10 beneficial, refreshing
12 health-giving, invigorating

**salutary**
06 timely, useful
08 valuable
10 beneficial, profitable
12 advantageous

**salutation**
06 homage, salute

07 address, welcome
08 greeting, respects

**salute**
03 bow, nod
04 hail, mark, wave
05 greet, honor
06 homage
07 address, tribute
08 greeting
09 celebrate, handshake, recognize
11 acknowledge, celebration, present arms, recognition
14 acknowledgment

**salvage**
04 save
06 redeem, rescue
07 reclaim, recover, restore
08 conserve, preserve, retrieve

**salvation**
06 rescue, saving
08 lifeline
10 liberation, redemption
11 deliverance, reclamation, soteriology
12 preservation

**salve**
04 balm, calm, ease
05 cream
06 lotion, soothe
07 comfort, lighten, relieve
08 liniment, ointment
11 embrocation

**same**
04 like, twin, very
05 alike, ditto, equal
06 mutual
07 similar, uniform
08 matching, selfsame
09 duplicate, identical, unchanged, unvarying
10 carbon copy, changeless, comparable, consistent, equivalent, reciprocal, synonymous, unchanging, unvariable
12 the aforesaid
13 corresponding
15 interchangeable

□ **all the same**
03 but, yet
05 still
06 anyhow, anyway, even so
07 however
09 in any case
10 by any means, for all that, in any event, regardless
11 nonetheless
12 nevertheless
15 notwithstanding

**sameness**
07 oneness
08 identity, likeness, monotony
10 repetition, uniformity
11 consistency, duplication
14 changelessness, predictability
15 standardization

**sample**
03 try
04 test
05 dummy, model, piece, taste, trial
06 swatch
07 example, preview
08 specimen
09 foretaste
12 illustration, illustrative
13 demonstration, demonstrative
14 representative

**sanctify**
05 bless, exalt
06 anoint, hallow, purify, ratify
07 absolve, cleanse
08 canonize, dedicate, make holy, sanction, set apart
10 consecrate, make sacred

**sanctimonious**
05 pious
09 pharisaic, pietistic
10 goody-goody, moralizing
11 pharisaical
12 hypocritical
13 goody-two-shoes, self-righteous
14 holier-than-thou

**sanctimoniousness**
04 cant
06 humbug
09 hypocrisy
10 moralizing, pharisaism
11 complacency, preachiness
12 priggishness, unctuousness

**sanction**
02 OK
03 ban
04 back, okay
05 allow
06 permit, ratify
07 approve, boycott, embargo, endorse, go-ahead, license, license, penalty, warrant
08 accredit, approval, sentence, thumbs up
09 agreement, authority, authorize, deterrent
10 green light, legitimize, permission
11 approbation, endorsement, prohibition, restriction

12  confirmation, ratification

**sanctity**
05  grace, piety
06  purity, virtue
08  devotion, goodness, holiness
10  sacredness
12  spirituality
13  inviolability

**sanctuary**
04  area, park
05  altar, haven, tract
06  asylum, church, mosque, refuge, safety, shrine, temple
07  enclave, hideout, reserve, retreat, sanctum, shelter
08  hideaway, immunity
09  holy place, safeguard
10  protection, tabernacle
12  holy of holies
13  protected area
14  place of worship

**sanctum**
03  den
06  refuge, shrine
07  hideout, retreat
08  hideaway
09  holy place, sanctuary
12  holy of holies

**sand**
04  grit, rock
05  beach, sands, shore
06  desert, strand
07  courage

**sandbank**
03  bar, key
04  dune, reef
07  sandbar, yardang

**sandy**
03  red
05  rusty, tawny
06  ginger, gritty, yellow
07  coppery, gingery, reddish, yellowy
09  psammitic, yellowish
10  arenaceous
13  reddish-yellow

**sane**
04  wise
05  lucid, sober, sound
08  all there, moderate, rational, sensible
09  judicious
11  levelheaded, of sound mind
15  in your right mind

**sang-froid**
04  cool
05  nerve, poise
06  aplomb, phlegm
08  calmness, coolness
09  assurance, composure

10  dispassion, equanimity
11  nonchalance, self-control
12  indifference

**sanguinary**
04  gory, grim
06  bloody, brutal, savage
09  merciless, murderous
12  bloodthirsty

**sanguine**
03  red
04  pink, rosy
05  fresh, ruddy
06  ardent, florid, lively
07  assured, buoyant, flushed, hopeful, unbowed
08  animated, cheerful
09  confident, expectant, unabashed
10  optimistic

**sanitary**
05  clean
07  aseptic, healthy, sterile
08  germfree, hygienic
09  wholesome
10  antiseptic, salubrious
11  disinfected

**sanity**
06  reason, wisdom
08  lucidity, prudence
09  good sense, normality, soundness, stability
11  common sense, rationality
15  levelheadedness, right-mindedness

**sap**
04  clod, fink, fool, jerk, prat
05  bleed, drain, erode, juice, vigor
06  energy, impair, nitwit, reduce, weaken
07  deplete, essence, exhaust
08  diminish, enervate, enfeeble, imbecile
09  lifeblood, undermine
10  debilitate, vital fluid

**sarcasm**
05  irony, scorn
06  gibing, satire
07  acidity, mockery
08  derision, ridicule, scoffing, sneering
10  bitterness, trenchancy
12  spitefulness

**sarcastic**
05  snide
06  biting
07  acerbic, caustic, cynical, jeering, mocking, mordant
08  ironical, sardonic, scathing, scoffing, scornful, sneering

09  satirical

**sardonic**
03  dry
06  biting, bitter
07  cynical, mocking, mordant
08  derisive
09  sarcastic

**sash**
04  band, belt
06  girdle, ribbon
08  cincture
09  waistband
10  cummerbund

**Satan**
06  Belial
07  Abaddon, Lucifer, Old Nick
08  Apollyon, Mephisto, the Devil
09  Beelzebub
10  Old Scratch, the Evil One, the Tempter
14  Mephistopheles

**satanic**
04  dark, evil
05  black
06  damned, sinful, wicked
07  demonic, hellish, inhuman
08  accursed, devilish, fiendish, infernal
10  diabolical, malevolent

**sate**
04  cloy, fill, glut
05  gorge, slake
06  sicken
07  gratify, satiate, satisfy, surfeit
08  overfill, saturate

**satellite**
04  aide, moon
06  lackey, minion, planet, puppet, vassal
07  sputnik
08  adherent, disciple, follower, hanger-on, sidekick
09  attendant, dependent, spaceship, sycophant
10  spacecraft
12  space station

**satiate**
04  cloy, fill, glut, jade, sate
05  gorge, slake, stuff
07  engorge, satisfy, surfeit
08  overfeed, overfill, saturate

**satiety**
07  surfeit
08  fullness
09  repletion
10  saturation
11  repleteness
12  overfullness, satisfaction

## satire
03 wit
04 skit
05 irony, spoof
06 parody
07 lampoon, sarcasm, takeoff
10 caricature

## satirical
06 biting, bitter
07 acerbic, caustic, cutting, cynical, mocking, mordant
08 derisive, incisive, ironical, sardonic, taunting
10 irreverent, ridiculing
11 acrimonious

## satirist
06 mocker
08 parodist
09 lampooner
10 cartoonist, lampoonist
11 pasquinader
12 caricaturist

► *Names of satirists*:
03 **Loy** (Mina)
04 **Isla** (José Francisco de), **Pope** (Alexander)
05 **Brown** (Thomas), **Cooke** (Ebenezer), **Ellis** (George), **Swift** (Jonathan)
06 **Butler** (Samuel), **Giusti** (Giuseppe), **Horace**, **Lucian**, **Murner** (Thomas), **Pindar** (Peter)
07 **Barclay** (John), **Juvenal**, **Marston** (John), **Mencken** (Henry Louis), **Persius**, **Thurber** (James), **Trudeau** (Gary)
08 **Apuleius** (Lucius), **Beerbohm** (Max), **Lucilius** (Gaius), **Rabelais** (François)
09 **Petronius** (Arbiter)
10 **Mandeville** (Bernard)
➤ See also WRITER

## satirize
04 mock
06 deride, parody
07 lampoon, take off
08 ridicule
09 burlesque, criticize
10 caricature

## satisfaction
07 comfort, damages, redress
08 pleasure, requital
09 enjoyment, happiness, indemnity, well-being
10 fulfilment, recompense, reparation, settlement
11 contentment, fulfillment, restitution
12 compensation

13 gratification, reimbursement

## satisfactory
02 OK
04 okay
07 average
08 adequate, all right, passable, suitable
09 competent
10 acceptable, sufficient

## satisfied
04 full, smug, sure
05 happy, sated
07 certain, content, replete
08 pacified, positive, satiated
09 contented, convinced, persuaded, reassured

## satisfy
04 fill, meet, sate
06 answer, assure, fulfil, please, quench, settle
07 appease, assuage, content, delight, fulfill, gratify, indulge, placate, qualify, requite, satiate, suffice, surfeit
08 convince, persuade
09 discharge, indemnify
10 comply with
13 compensate for

## satisfying
08 cheering, pleasing
10 fulfilling, gratifying, persuasive, refreshing
11 pleasurable

## saturate
03 wet
04 fill, glut, sate, soak
05 flood, imbue, souse, steep
06 drench, imbibe
07 pervade, satiate, suffuse, surfeit
08 overfill, permeate, waterlog
10 impregnate

## saturated
06 imbued, soaked, sodden, soused
07 flooded, imbibed, soaking, sopping, steeped
08 drenched, satiated, wringing
09 permeated
11 impregnated, waterlogged

## saturnine
04 dour, dull, glum
05 grave, heavy, moody, stern
06 dismal, gloomy, morose, severe, somber
08 taciturn
10 melancholy, phlegmatic, unfriendly
15 uncommunicative

## sauce
03 dip, lip
05 brass, cheek, mouth, nerve
08 audacity, back talk, dressing, pertness, rudeness
09 condiment, flavoring, flippancy, impudence, insolence
10 brazenness, cheekiness, disrespect
11 presumption
12 impertinence

► *Types of sauce*:
03 jus, soy
04 mint, soja
05 bread, brown, gravy, pesto, salsa, satay, shoyu, white
06 Mornay, panada, tamari, tartar, tomato
07 catchup, custard, ketchup, sabayon, soubise, supreme, Tabasco, tartare
09 béarnaise, chantilly, cranberry, espagnole, remoulade, Worcester
10 chaudfroid, mayonnaise, mousseline, zabaglione
11 hollandaise, horseradish, vinaigrette
12 sweet-and-sour
14 Worcestershire
➤ See also FOOD

## saucy
04 pert, rude
05 fresh, lippy, sassy
06 brazen, cheeky
08 flippant, impudent, insolent
11 impertinent
12 presumptuous
13 disrespectful

## saunter
04 walk
05 amble, mooch, mosey
06 ramble, stroll, wander
09 promenade
14 constitutional

## sausage

► *Types of sausage*:
05 wurst
06 salami, Vienna, weenie, wiener, wienie
07 baloney, bologna, chorizo
08 cervelas, cervelat
09 andouille, bierwurst, bratwurst, pepperoni
10 knackwurst, knockwurst, liverwurst, mortadella
11 frankfurter, wienerwurst
➤ See also FOOD

## savage
04 bite, boor, claw, fell, grim, maul, slam, tear, wild
05 beast, brute, churl, cruel, feral, harsh
06 attack, bloody, brutal, mangle
07 beastly, inhuman, monster, run down, untamed, vicious
08 barbaric, denounce, lacerate, pitiless, ruthless, sadistic, terrible
09 barbarian, barbarous, cutthroat, dog-eat-dog, ferocious, merciless, murderous, primitive
11 uncivilized
12 bloodthirsty

## savagery
06 ferity, sadism
07 cruelty
08 ferocity, wildness
09 barbarity, brutality
10 bestiality, inhumanity
11 viciousness

## savant
04 guru, sage
06 master, pundit
09 authority
10 mastermind
12 intellectual

## save
04 bank, free, hold, keep
05 guard, hoard, lay up, put by, spare, stash, store
06 budget, gather, hinder, redeem, rescue, retain, screen, scrimp, shield
07 bail out, collect, cut back, deliver, obviate, prevent, protect, reclaim, recover, release, reserve, salvage
08 conserve, cut costs, keep safe, liberate, preserve, put aside, set aside
09 economize, safeguard, stockpile
14 live on the cheap
15 tighten your belt

## saving
06 frugal, thrift
07 bargain, capital, careful, nest egg, thrifty
08 discount, reserves
09 reduction, resources
10 economical, mitigating, qualifying
11 investments
12 compensatory, conservation, preservation

## savior
03 God
05 Jesus
06 Christ
07 Messiah, rescuer
08 champion, Emmanuel, redeemer
09 deliverer, Lamb of God, liberator
11 emancipator, Jesus Christ

## savoir-faire
04 tact
05 poise
07 ability, finesse, know-how
08 urbanity
09 assurance, diplomacy, expertise
10 capability, confidence, discretion

## savor
04 hint, like, salt, tang, zest
05 aroma, enjoy, smack, smell, spice, taste, touch, trace
06 flavor, relish
07 bouquet, perfume, revel in, suggest
08 piquancy, seem like
09 delight in, fragrance
10 appreciate, smattering, suggestion

## savory
05 salty, snack, spicy, tangy, tasty, yummy
06 canapé
07 piquant
08 aromatic, luscious
09 appetizer, delicious
10 appetizing, flavorsome
11 bonne bouche, hors d'oeuvre
13 mouthwatering

## saw
03 mot
05 adage, axiom, maxim
06 byword, dictum, saying
07 epigram, proverb
08 aphorism

──────────

► *Types of saw*:
06 jigsaw, ripsaw
07 band saw, bucksaw, fretsaw, hacksaw, handsaw
08 chain saw, panel saw, power saw
09 coping-saw, scroll saw
10 compass saw, keyhole saw
11 circular saw, crosscut saw
➤ See also TOOL

## say
04 aver, call, tell
05 reply, speak, state, utter, voice
06 affirm, allege, answer, assert, convey, inform, insist, recite, rejoin, relate, remark, render, repeat, report, retort, reveal
07 comment, declare, divulge, exclaim, express, mention, observe, suggest, suppose, venture
08 announce, disclose, indicate, intimate, maintain
09 make known, pronounce, volunteer
10 articulate
11 acknowledge, come out with, communicate
12 put into words

## ❏ that is to say
02 i.e.
06 that is
12 in other words

## saying
05 adage, axiom, maxim, motto
06 cliché, dictum, phrase, remark, slogan
07 epigram, precept, proverb
08 aphorism
09 platitude, quotation, statement
10 apophthegm, expression
11 catch phrase

## say-so
02 OK
04 okay, word
06 dictum
07 backing, consent, opinion
08 approval, sanction
09 agreement, assurance, authority
10 permission
13 authorization

## scaffold
05 stage
06 gantry, gibbet
07 gallows
08 platform
09 framework
11 scaffolding

## scald
04 burn, sear
06 scorch
09 cauterize

## scale
04 coat, film, go up
05 climb, crust, flake, gamut, layer, level, mount, order, plate, range, ratio, reach, scope, scurf
06 ascend, degree, extent, furfur, ladder, lamina, plaque,

series, shin up, spread, squama, tartar
07 clamber, compass, conquer, deposit, measure
08 dandruff, scramble, sequence, spectrum, surmount
09 hierarchy, limescale
10 graduation, proportion
11 calibration, progression
12 encrustation

❏**scale down**
04 drop
06 lessen, reduce, shrink
07 cut back, cut down
08 contract, decrease, make less

**scaliness**
06 furfur
08 dandruff
09 flakiness
10 scurfiness, squamation
12 scabrousness

**scaly**
05 flaky, rough
06 scabby, scurfy
08 lepidote, scabrous
09 furfurous

**scamp**
03 imp
06 monkey, rascal, wretch
08 scalawag
09 scallywag
12 troublemaker
13 mischief-maker
14 whippersnapper

**scamper**
04 dart, dash, race, romp, rush
06 frolic, gambol, scurry
07 scuttle

**scan**
05 check, probe, study, sweep
06 go over, search, survey
07 examine, inspect
08 glance at, scrutiny
09 screening
10 inspection, scrutinize
11 examination, investigate
14 run your eye over

**scandal**
04 blot, dirt, pity, slur
05 furor, libel, shame, smear, stain
06 gossip, outcry, rumors, uproar
07 calumny, obloquy, offense, outrage, slander
08 disgrace, dishonor, ignominy, reproach
09 discredit

10 defamation, opprobrium
11 crying shame

**scandalize**
05 appal, repel, shock
06 appall, dismay, insult, offend, revolt
07 affront, disgust, horrify, outrage

**scandalmonger**
07 defamer
08 quidnunc, traducer
09 muckraker
11 calumniator
12 gossipmonger

**scandalous**
08 infamous, shameful, shocking, unseemly
09 appalling, atrocious, malicious
10 defamatory, outrageous, slanderous
11 disgraceful
12 disreputable

**scant**
04 bare
06 little, measly, sparse
07 limited, minimal
08 exiguous
09 deficient, hardly any
10 inadequate, little or no
12 insufficient

**scanty**
04 bare, poor, thin
05 scant, short
06 little, meager, narrow, skimpy, sparse
07 limited
09 deficient
10 inadequate, restricted
12 insufficient

**scapegoat**
05 patsy
06 sucker, victim
07 fall guy
11 whipping boy

**scar**
04 mark
05 brand, shock, spoil, wound
06 damage, deface, injure, injury, lesion, stigma, trauma
07 blemish
09 disfigure
10 defacement, stigmatize, traumatize
13 disfigurement

**scarce**
03 few
04 rare
06 meager, scanty, sparse
07 lacking, unusual

08 uncommon
09 deficient
10 inadequate, infrequent
12 insufficient, like gold dust
13 in short supply
15 rare as hen's teeth

**scarcely**
06 barely, hardly
08 not at all, only just
12 certainly not
13 definitely not

**scarcity**
04 lack, want
06 dearth, rarity
07 paucity
08 exiguity, rareness, shortage
10 deficiency

**scare**
05 alarm, panic, spook, start
06 fright, menace, terror
07 perturb, petrify, startle, terrify, unnerve
08 frighten, threaten
10 intimidate, make afraid

**scared**
06 afraid, shaken
07 alarmed, anxious, fearful, jittery, nervous, panicky, quivery, spooked, worried
08 startled, unnerved
09 petrified, terrified
10 frightened, terrorized
11 in a blue funk
13 having kittens, panic-stricken
14 terror-stricken

**scaremonger**
08 alarmist
09 Cassandra, pessimist
13 prophet of doom

**scarf**
03 boa, eat
05 eat up, shawl, stole
06 cravat
07 muffler
08 babushka, kerchief
11 neckerchief

**scary**
05 eerie, hairy
06 creepy, spooky
08 alarming, chilling, daunting, fearsome, shocking
10 disturbing, formidable, petrifying, terrifying
11 frightening, hair-raising
13 bloodcurdling, spine-chilling

**scathing**
04 acid
05 harsh

06 biting, bitter, brutal, fierce, savage, severe
07 caustic, cutting, mordant
08 critical, scornful, stinging
09 ferocious, trenchant, vitriolic

**scatter**
03 sow
05 fling, strew
06 dispel, divide, spread
07 break up, diffuse, disband
08 disperse, separate, sprinkle
09 broadcast, dissipate
11 disseminate

**scatterbrained**
08 carefree, careless
09 forgetful, frivolous, impulsive, slaphappy
11 empty-headed, harebrained, thoughtless
12 absent-minded
13 woolgathering
14 featherbrained

**scattering**
03 few
07 breakup, handful
10 smattering, sprinkling

**scavenge**
04 hunt, rake
06 forage, search

**scavenger**
05 hyena, raker
07 forager, vulture

**scenario**
04 plan, plot
05 scene, state
06 résumé, scheme, script
07 outline, summary
08 sequence, synopsis
09 situation, story line
10 projection, screenplay

**scene**
03 act, set
04 area, clip, fuss, part, show, site, spot, to-do, view
05 arena, drama, field, furor, place, sight, stage, vista
06 locale, milieu
07 context, display, episode, outlook, pageant, picture, scenery, setting, tableau
08 backdrop, division, incident, locality, location, outburst, panorama, position, prospect
09 commotion, kerfuffle, landscape, situation, specialty, spectacle
10 background, exhibition, proceeding
11 environment, performance

14 area of activity, area of interest

**scenery**
03 set
04 view
05 scene, vista
08 backdrop, panorama, prospect
09 landscape
10 background
11 mise en scène

**scenic**
05 grand
09 beautiful, panoramic
10 attractive, impressive
11 picturesque, spectacular

**scent**
04 nose, odor
05 aroma, smell, sniff
06 detect
07 cologne, discern, essence, perfume
08 perceive, sniff out
09 fragrance
11 toilet water
12 eau de cologne

**scented**
08 aromatic, fragrant, perfumed
13 sweet-smelling

**skeptic**
05 cynic
07 atheist, doubter, scoffer
08 agnostic
11 disbeliever, rationalist
14 doubting Thomas

**skeptical**
07 cynical, dubious
08 doubtful, doubting
11 distrustful, incredulous, questioning, unbelieving, unconvinced
12 disbelieving

**skepticism**
05 doubt
07 atheism, dubiety
08 cynicism, distrust, unbelief
09 disbelief
11 agnosticism, incredulity

**schedule**
04 book, list, plan
05 diary
06 agenda, scheme
07 catalog, program
08 calendar, organize, syllabus
09 catalogue, inventory, itinerary, timetable

**schematic**
07 graphic
08 symbolic

12 diagrammatic, illustrative

**scheme**
03 map
04 idea, plan, plot, ploy, ruse
05 chart, draft, frame
06 design, device, devise, layout, method, schema, sketch, system, tactic
07 connive, diagram, program, project, tactics, work out
08 conspire, contrive, intrigue, maneuver, proposal, schedule, strategy
09 blueprint, procedure, stratagem
10 conspiracy, manipulate, mastermind, suggestion
11 arrangement, proposition
14 course of action

**schemer**
03 fox
07 plotter, wangler
08 conniver, deceiver
09 intriguer
10 machinator, mastermind, politician, wirepuller
11 Machiavelli
13 éminence grise

**scheming**
03 sly
04 foxy, wily
06 artful, crafty, tricky
07 cunning, devious
08 slippery
09 conniving, underhand
11 calculating, duplicitous
13 Machiavellian

**schism**
04 rift, sect
05 break, group, split
06 breach
07 discord, faction, rupture
08 disunion, division, splinter
09 secession
10 detachment, separation

**scholar**
05 pupil
06 expert, pundit
07 egghead, learner, student
08 academic, bookworm
09 authority, schoolboy
10 mastermind, schoolgirl
11 philosopher, schoolchild
12 intellectual

**scholarly**
06 school
07 bookish, erudite, learned
08 academic, highbrow, lettered, studious, well-read
10 scholastic, scientific
12 intellectual

**scholarship**
13 knowledgeable

**scholarship**
05 award, grant
06 wisdom
07 bursary
09 education, erudition, knowledge
10 exhibition, fellowship

**scholastic**
07 bookish, learned, precise
08 academic
09 pedagogic, scholarly
11 educational

**school**
05 class, coach, drill, guild, teach, train, tutor, verse
06 circle, clique, league, pupils
07 academy, college, company, coterie, educate, faction, faculty, prepare, society
08 instruct, seminary, students
09 institute
10 high school, university
12 kindergarten
13 grammar school, nursery school

**schooling**
05 drill
07 tuition
08 coaching, guidance, learning, teaching, training
09 education, grounding
11 instruction, preparation
12 book learning

**schoolteacher**
07 pedagog, teacher
08 educator
09 pedagogue, professor
10 instructor, schoolmarm
12 schoolmaster
14 schoolmistress

**science**
03 art
05 skill
09 expertise, technique
10 discipline, technology

► *Sciences include*:
06 botany
07 anatomy, biology, ecology, geology, physics, zoology
08 agronomy, genetics, oncology, robotics
09 acoustics, astronomy, chemistry, dietetics, economics, geography, mechanics, pathology, sociology
10 biophysics, entomology, geophysics, hydraulics, metallurgy, mineralogy,

morphology, physiology, psychology, toxicology
11 aeronautics, archaeology, climatology, cybernetics, electronics, engineering, life science, linguistics, mathematics, meteorology, ornithology
12 aerodynamics, anthropology, astrophysics, bacteriology, biochemistry, earth science, geochemistry, macrobiotics, microbiology, paleontology, pharmacology
14 medical science, natural science, nuclear physics, thermodynamics
15 computer science, domestic science, electrodynamics, space technology

**scientific**
05 exact
07 orderly, precise
08 accurate, thorough
09 regulated, scholarly
10 methodical, systematic
12 mathematical

► *Names of scientific instruments*:
06 strobe
07 coherer, vernier
08 cryostat, rheostat
09 baroscope, heliostat, hydrostat, hygrostat, image tube, microtome, rheometer, slide rule, telemeter, Tesla coil
10 centrifuge, collimator, eudiometer, heliograph, humidistat, hydrophone, hydroscope, hygrograph, pantograph, radarscope, radiosonde, tachograph, thermostat
11 chronograph, fluoroscope, stroboscope, transformer, transponder, tunnel diode
12 oscillograph, oscilloscope, spectroscope
14 image converter, interferometer

**scientist** see ANATOMY; ANTHROPOLOGIST; ARCHAEOLOGY; ASTRONOMER; BACTERIOLOGIST; BIOCHEMIST; BIOLOGY; BOTANIST; CHEMISTRY; COMPUTER; ECONOMIST; ENGINEER; GENETICIST; GEOGRAPHY; INVENTOR; MATHEMATICS; PALEONTOLOGIST; PHYSICS; PHYSIOLOGIST; PSYCHOLOGY; ZOOLOGIST

**scintillate**
05 blaze, flash, gleam, glint, shine, spark
07 glisten, glitter, sparkle, twinkle
09 coruscate

**scintillating**
05 witty
06 bright, lively
07 shining
08 animated, dazzling
09 brilliant, sparkling, vivacious
10 glittering
12 exhilarating, invigorating

**scion**
04 heir, twig
05 child, graft, shoot
06 branch, sprout
08 offshoot
09 offspring, successor
10 descendant

**scoff**
03 rib
04 gibe, jeer, mock
05 scorn, sneer
06 deride
07 laugh at, poke fun
08 ridicule
09 disparage

**scoffing**
07 cynical, mocking
08 derisive, scathing, sneering
11 disparaging

**scold**
03 nag
05 blame, chide
06 berate, rebuke
07 censure, lecture, reprove, tell off, upbraid
08 lambaste, reproach
09 castigate, reprimand
10 take to task

**scolding**
06 rebuke
07 lecture, reproof
09 reprimand, talking-to
10 telling-off
12 dressing-down

**scoop**
03 dig, dip

**scoot**

04 bail, coup
05 empty, gouge, ladle, spoon
06 bailer, bucket, dipper, exposé, hollow, latest, remove, scrape, shovel
08 excavate
09 exclusive, sensation
10 revelation
11 inside story

**scoot**

03 run, zip
04 bolt, dart, dash, rush, scud
05 hurry, shoot
06 beat it, career, scurry, sprint, tootle
07 scuttle, vamoose
09 skedaddle

**scope**

04 area, room, span
05 ambit, field, orbit, range, reach, realm, space, sweep
06 extent, leeway, limits, sphere
07 breadth, compass, freedom, liberty
08 capacity, confines, coverage, latitude
09 elbowroom, telescope
10 microscope
11 opportunity

**scorch**

04 burn, char, sear
05 dry up, parch, roast, scald, singe
06 wither
07 blacken, shrivel
08 discolor

**scorching**

06 baking, red-hot, torrid
07 boiling, burning, searing
08 roasting, sizzling, tropical
10 blistering, sweltering

**score**

03 cut, get, run, set, sum, win
04 case, earn, gain, gash, goal, hits, line, lots, make, mark, nick, runs, slit
05 adapt, basis, count, goals, gouge, graze, hosts, issue, marks, notch, slash, tally, total, write
06 aspect, attain, basket, crowds, droves, groove, grudge, incise, indent, masses, matter, points, reason, record, result, scrape, twenty
07 achieve, arrange, be one up, chalk up, concern, dispute, engrave, grounds, notch up, outcome, quarrel, scratch, subject

08 argument, hundreds, incision, millions, question, register
09 complaint, grievance, thousands
10 instrument, keep a tally, make it with, multitudes
11 explanation, have sex with, have the edge, orchestrate
13 hit the jackpot

❏ **know the score**

08 be with it
10 understand
12 know the facts

❏ **settle a score**

07 revenge
09 retaliate
10 get revenge
12 pay off a score

❏ **score out**

05 erase
06 cancel, delete, efface, remove
07 expunge
08 cross out
09 strike out
10 obliterate

**scorn**

04 mock, shun
05 spurn
06 deride, rebuff
07 disdain, disgust, dismiss, mockery, sarcasm, scoff at, sneer at, sniff at
08 contempt, derision, ridicule
09 contumely, disparage
10 look down on
11 haughtiness

**scornful**

07 haughty, jeering, mocking
08 arrogant, derisive, scathing, scoffing, sneering
09 insulting, sarcastic, slighting
10 disdainful, dismissive
11 disparaging
12 contemptuous, supercilious

**scornfully**

09 haughtily
10 arrogantly, scathingly
12 disdainfully, dismissively
13 disparagingly
14 contemptuously

**scot-free**

04 safe
06 unhurt
08 unharmed
09 uninjured, unscathed
11 unpunished
15 without a scratch

**scoundrel**

03 cad, rat
04 scab
05 cheat, louse, rogue, scamp, swine
06 rascal
07 dastard, ruffian, stinker, villain
08 vagabond
09 miscreant, reprobate, scallywag
10 ne'er-do-well
14 good-for-nothing
15 snake in the grass

**scour**

03 rub
04 comb, drag, hunt, rake, wash, wipe
05 clean, flush, purge, scrub
06 abrade, forage, polish, scrape, search
07 burnish, cleanse, rummage
10 scrutinize

**scourge**

04 bane, beat, cane, evil, flog, lash, whip
05 birch, curse, flail, strap, trial
06 burden, menace, plague, punish, switch, terror, thrash
07 afflict, torment, torture
08 chastise, nuisance
09 devastate
10 affliction, discipline, misfortune, punishment
13 cat-o'-nine-tails

**scout**

03 spy
04 case, hunt, look, seek
05 probe, snoop, watch
06 escort, search, spy out, survey
07 explore, inspect, look for, lookout, observe, spotter
08 check out, vanguard
11 investigate, reconnoiter
13 talent spotter

**scowl**

04 lour, pout
05 frown, glare
06 glower
07 grimace

**scrabble**

03 dig, paw
04 claw, grub, root
05 grope
06 scrape
07 clamber, scratch

**scraggy**

04 bony, lean, thin
06 skinny, wasted
07 angular, scrawny
09 emaciated

## scram
04 bolt, flee, quit
06 beat it, depart, go away
07 skiddoo
08 clear off, clear out, shove off
09 disappear, skedaddle
15 take to your heels

## scramble
03 mix, run, vie
04 dash, push, race, rush
05 climb, crawl, grope, hurry, mêlée, mix up, scale, vying
06 battle, bustle, hasten, hustle, infuse, jockey, jostle, jumble, muddle, scurry, strive, tussle
07 clamber, compete, contend, disturb, scaling, shuffle
10 free-for-all

## scrap
02 ax
03 axe, bit, row
04 atom, bite, bits, drop, dump, iota, junk, mite, shed, tiff
05 argue, brawl, crumb, ditch, fight, grain, piece, set-to, shred, trace, waste
06 bicker, cancel, dustup, fracas, morsel, sliver, tatter
07 abandon, discard, dispute, quarrel, remains, remnant, scuffle, snippet, vestige, wrangle
08 argument, chuck out, disagree, fraction, fragment, jettison, leavings, mouthful, particle, squabble, write off
09 leftovers
11 odds and ends
13 bits and pieces

## ❑ on the scrapheap
07 totaled
09 discarded, forgotten, redundant
10 jettisoned

## scrape
03 cut, fix, rub
04 bark, file, rasp, skin
05 clean, erase, grate, graze, grind, scour, scuff, shave
06 abrade, pickle, plight
07 dilemma, scratch, trouble
08 abrasion, distress, scrabble
09 tight spot
10 difficulty
11 predicament

## ❑ scrape by, scrape through
05 get by, skimp
06 scrimp

## ❑ scrape through
08 just pass

09 barely win

## ❑ scrape together
07 round up
11 get together
12 pool together

## scrappy
04 game
06 untidy
07 sketchy
08 slapdash, slipshod
09 piecemeal
10 aggressive, disjointed, incomplete
11 fragmentary

## scratch
03 cut, rub
04 claw, etch, gash, line, mark, nick, skin, tear
05 gouge, graze, rough, score, scuff, wound
06 abrade, incise, scrape
07 engrave
08 abrasion, lacerate
09 haphazard, impromptu
10 improvised, laceration
13 rough-and-ready

## ❑ up to scratch
02 OK
04 okay
08 adequate
09 competent, tolerable
10 acceptable, good enough
12 satisfactory

## scrawl
03 jot, pen
06 doodle
07 dash off, jot down, scratch, writing
08 scrabble, scribble, squiggle
10 cacography
11 handwriting

## scrawny
04 bony, lean, thin
05 lanky
06 skinny
07 angular, scraggy
08 rawboned
09 emaciated

## scream
03 cry, wit
04 bawl, hoot, howl, riot, roar, wail, yawp, yell, yelp
05 comic, joker, laugh, shout
06 holler, shriek, squeal
07 screech
08 comedian
10 comedienne

## screech
03 cry
04 howl, yell, yelp

06 shriek, squeal

## screen
03 net, vet
04 hide, mask, mesh, scan, show, sift, sort, test, veil
05 blind, check, cloak, cover, front, gauge, grade, guard, shade, sieve
06 awning, canopy, defend, façade, filter, riddle, shield, shroud
07 conceal, curtain, divider, netting, project, protect, shelter
08 disguise, evaluate
09 partition, safeguard
10 camouflage, protection

## ❑ screen off
04 hide
06 divide
07 conceal
08 fence off, separate
09 divide off
12 partition off

**screenwriter** see PLAY-WRIGHT

## screw
03 fix
04 bolt, brad, milk, turn, wind
05 bleed, cheat, force, rivet, twist
06 adjust, extort, fasten
07 distort, extract, squeeze, swindle, tighten, wrinkle
08 compress, contract, fastener

## ❑ put the screws on
05 force
06 coerce, compel, lean on
07 dragoon

## ❑ screw up
05 botch, spoil
06 bungle, mess up
07 contort, crumple, distort, louse up, tighten, wrinkle
09 mishandle, mismanage
11 make a hash of

## screwy
03 mad, odd
04 daft, nuts
05 batty, crazy, dotty, loopy, nutty, queer, weird
09 eccentric

## scribble
03 jot, pen
05 write
06 doodle, scrawl
07 dash off, jot down, writing
08 scrabble, squiggle
10 cacography
11 handwriting

**scribbler**
04 hack
06 writer
09 pen pusher, potboiler
12 pencil pusher

**scribe**
04 hack
05 clerk
06 author, writer
07 copyist
08 recorder, reporter
09 pen pusher, secretary
10 amanuensis
12 pencil pusher

**scrimmage**
03 row
04 fray, riot
05 brawl, fight, melee, scrap, set-to
07 scuffle
08 practice, skirmish, squabble, struggle
10 free-for-all
11 disturbance
15 line of scrimmage

**scrimp**
04 save
05 limit, pinch, skimp, stint
06 reduce, scrape
07 curtail
08 restrict
09 cut back on, economize
15 tighten your belt

**script**
06 dialog
07 letters, writing
08 dialogue, libretto, longhand, teleplay
10 manuscript, screenplay
11 calligraphy, handwriting

**scripture**

► *Sacred writings of religions*:
02 NT, OT
03 ASV
05 Bayan, Bible, Koran, Qur'an, sutra, sutta, Torah, Vedas, Zohar
06 Gemara, gospel, Granth, Hadith, I Ching, Mishna, Talmud, Tantra
07 epistle, Puranas, Shari'ah
08 Haft Wadi, Halakhah, Ramayana
09 Adi Granth, Apocrypha, Decalogue, Digambara, Hexateuch, scripture, Tripitaka
10 Heptateuch, Lotus Sutra, Pentateuch, Svetambara,

Tao-Te Ching, Upanishads, Zend-Avesta
11 Bardo Thodol, Mahabharata
12 Bhagavad Gita, New Testament, Old Testament
14 Dead Sea Scrolls, Mahayana Sutras, Revised Version
15 Ten Commandments, The Book of Mormon
➤ See also RELIGION

**scroll**
04 list, roll
05 paper
06 roster, volume
08 memorial
09 inventory, parchment

**Scrooge**
05 miser
06 meanie
07 niggard
08 tightwad
09 skinflint
10 cheapskate
12 moneygrubber, penny pincher

**scrounge**
03 beg, bum
05 cadge, mooch
06 borrow, sponge
09 panhandle

**scrounger**
03 bum
06 beggar, cadger
07 moocher, sponger
10 freeloader

**scrub**
02 ax
03 axe, rub
04 bush, drop, wash, wipe
05 brush, clean, scour
06 cancel, delete, forget
07 abandon, abolish, cleanse
09 backwoods, scrubland
10 undersized
13 secondary team
15 secondary player

**scruffy**
06 ragged, shabby
07 run-down, unkempt
09 ungroomed
10 bedraggled, disheveled, down-at-heel
11 down-at-heels
13 down-at-the-heel
14 down-at-the-heels

**scrumptious**
05 tasty, yummy
09 delicious
10 delectable, delightful
13 mouthwatering

**scrunch**
04 chew, mash
05 champ, crush
06 crunch, squash
07 crumple, screw up

**scruple**
04 balk
05 doubt, qualm
06 ethics, morals, shrink
08 hesitate, hold back
09 misgiving, standards
10 principles, reluctance, think twice, uneasiness
11 compunction, reservation
14 second thoughts

**scrupulous**
04 nice
05 exact, moral
06 honest, minute, strict
07 careful, ethical, precise
08 rigorous, thorough
10 fastidious, meticulous
11 painstaking, punctilious
13 conscientious

**scrutinize**
04 scan, sift
05 probe, scour, study
06 go over, peruse, search
07 analyze, examine, explore, inspect, run over
08 look over

**scrutiny**
05 probe, study
06 search
07 inquiry, perusal
08 analysis
10 inspection
11 examination, exploration

**scud**
03 fly
04 blow, dart, race, sail, skim
05 shoot, speed

**scuff**
04 drag
05 brush, graze
06 abrade, scrape
07 scratch

**scuffle**
03 row
04 fray
05 brawl, clash, fight, scrap, set-to
06 affray, dustup, rumpus, tussle
08 struggle
09 commotion
11 disturbance

**sculpt**
03 cut, hew
04 cast, form, mold
05 carve, model, shape

06 chisel
07 fashion
09 sculpture

**sculpture**
➤ See also ART
___

► *Names of sculptors*:
03 **Arp** (Hans)
04 **Caro** (Anthony), **Gabo**
(Naum), **Mach** (David),
**Rude** (François)
05 **Andre** (Carl), **Beuys**
(Joseph), **Frink** (Elizabeth),
**Manzú** (Giacomo), **Moore**
(Henry), **Myron**, **Rodin**
(Auguste), **Segal** (George),
**Smith** (David)
06 **Calder** (Alexander), **Canova**
(Antonio), **Deacon**
(Richard), **Kapoor** (Anish),
**Marini** (Marino), **Pisano**
(Andrea), **Pisano**
(Giovanni), **Scopas**
07 **Bernini** (Gianlorenzo),
**Borglum** (Gutzon), **Cellini**
(Benvenuto), **Christo**,
**Duchamp** (Marcel), **Epstein**
(Jacob), **Gormley** (Antony),
**Noguchi** (Isamu), **Phidias**
08 **Brancusi** (Constantin),
**Chadwick** (Lynn), **Ghiberti**
(Lorenzo), **Hepworth**
(Barbara), **Lachaise**
(Gaston), **Landseer**
(Edwin), **Paolozzi** (Eduardo
Luigi), **Pheidias**, **Tinguely**
(Jean)
09 **Borromini** (Francesco),
**Bourgeois** (Louise),
**Donatello**, **Greenough**
(Horatio), **Remington**
(Frederic), **Roubiliac** (Louis
François), **Whiteread**
(Rachel)
10 **Giacometti** (Alberto),
**Polyclitus**, **Praxiteles**,
**Schwitters** (Kurt),
**Verrocchio** (Andrea del)
11 **Goldsworthy** (Andy)
12 **Michelangelo**
15 **Leonardo da Vinci**
___

► *Names of sculptures*:
04 Adam
05 Angel, Cupid, David, House,
Medea, Pieta, Torso
07 Bacchus, Genesis, Mercury,
Merzbau, Spiders, The Kiss,
The Wall
08 Ecce Homo, Have Pity!,
Piscator
09 A Universe, Seated Man,
Slate Cone

10 Double Talk, Ledge Piece,
Mt. Rushmore, Running Man,
Single Form, The Thinker
11 Kiss and Tell
12 Bronco Buster, Feast of
Herod
13 Fallen Warrior, Standing
Woman
14 Cosimo de' Medici, Fontana
Magiore, Japanese War God,
Sailing Tonight, The Age of
Bronze, The Gates of Hell
15 Athena Promachos, Christ in
Majesty, Figure and Clouds,
Recumbent Figure

**scum**
04 film, foam
05 dregs, dross, froth, trash
06 rabble
07 rubbish
08 riffraff
10 impurities
14 dregs of society, lowest of the
low

**scupper**
04 foil, ruin
05 scrap, wreck
07 scuttle
09 overthrow

**scurf**
05 scale
06 furfur
08 dandruff
09 flakiness, scaliness
12 scabrousness

**scurfy**
05 flaky, scaly
06 scabby
12 furfuraceous

**scurrility**
05 abuse
07 obloquy
08 foulness, rudeness
09 nastiness, vulgarity
10 coarseness
11 abusiveness
12 vituperation
13 offensiveness

**scurrilous**
04 foul, rude
06 coarse, vulgar
07 abusive, obscene
08 libelous
09 insulting, offensive
10 defamatory, scandalous,
slanderous
11 disparaging
12 vituperative

**scurry**
04 dart, dash, race, rush, scud,
skim, trot
05 hurry, scoot, whirl
06 bustle, flurry, hasten, sprint
07 scamper, scuttle

**scurvy**
04 base, mean, vile
05 dirty, sorry
06 abject, rotten, scummy,
shabby
07 disease, low-down
10 despicable
12 contemptible

**scuttle**
05 hurry
06 bucket, bustle, hasten, scurry
07 scamper, scutter
08 scramble
11 coal scuttle

**sea**
04 deep, host, main, mass, salt
05 briny, ocean
06 afloat
07 aquatic, expanse, oceanic
09 abundance, multitude,
profusion, saltwater,
seafaring
___

► *Names of seas. We have
omitted the word* **sea** *from
names given in the following list
but you may need to include this
word as part of the solution to
some crossword clues.*
03 Red
04 Aral, Azov, Dead, Java, Kara,
Ross
05 Black, Coral, Irish, Japan,
North, South, Timor, White
06 Aegean, Baltic, Bering,
Ionian, Tasman, Yellow
07 Andaman, Arabian, Barents,
Caspian, Celebes, Galilee,
Marmara, Okhotsk, Weddell
08 Adriatic, Beaufort, Bismarck,
Labrador, Ligurian, Sargasso
09 Caribbean, East China,
Greenland, Norwegian
10 South China, Tyrrhenian
13 Mediterranean
➤ See also OCEAN

❑**at sea**
06 adrift
07 baffled, puzzled
08 confused
09 mystified, perplexed
10 bewildered

**seafaring**
05 naval
06 marine

07 oceanic, sailing
08 maritime, nautical
10 oceangoing

**seal**
04 cork, plug, shut, stop
05 close, stamp
06 animal, clinch, fasten, ratify, secure, settle, signet, stop up
07 close up, stopper, tighten
08 conclude, finalize, insignia
09 assurance
10 imprimatur, waterproof
11 attestation
12 ratification
14 authentication

❑**seal off**
06 cut off
07 block up, isolate, shut off
08 close off, fence off
09 cordon off, segregate
10 quarantine

**sealed**
04 shut
06 closed, corked
08 hermetic

**seam**
04 join, line, lode, vein, weld
05 joint, layer
07 closure, stratum
08 junction

**seaman**
02 AB
03 tar
04 Jack, swab
06 rating, sailor, sea dog, swabby
07 Jack-tar, mariner, swabbie
08 deck hand, seafarer
10 bluejacket
➤ See also SAILOR

**seamy**
05 nasty, rough
06 sleazy, sordid
07 squalid
08 unsavory
12 disreputable

**sear**
03 fry
04 burn, char, seal, wilt
05 brand, brown, singe
06 scorch, sizzle, wither
09 cauterize

**search**
03 pry
04 comb, hunt, look, seek, sift
05 check, frisk, probe, quest, rifle, scour
06 forage, survey

07 examine, explore, inquire, inquiry, inspect, pursuit, ransack, rifling, rummage
08 research, scrutiny
10 inspection, ransacking, scrutinize
11 examination, exploration, investigate, look through
13 investigation

**searching**
06 intent, minute
07 probing
08 piercing, thorough
11 penetrating

**seaside**
05 beach, coast, sands, shore
08 littoral, seashore

**season**
03 age
04 fall, salt, span, term, time
05 pep up, phase, ripen, spell, spice, treat
06 autumn, flavor, harden, mature, mellow, period, spring, summer, temper, winter
07 add zest, prepare, toughen

❑**in season**
09 available
10 obtainable
11 on the market

**seasonable**
06 timely
07 fitting, welcome
09 opportune, well-timed
12 providential

**seasoned**
06 mature
07 veteran
08 hardened
09 practiced, weathered
10 habituated
11 conditioned, established, experienced, long-serving
12 acclimatized

**seasoning**
04 salt
05 herbs, sauce, spice
06 pepper, relish
09 condiment, flavoring

**seat**
03 fit, fix, hub, pew, put, set, sit
04 axis, base, form, hold, site
05 bench, cause, chair, heart, house, place, stall, stool
06 bottom, center, ground, instal, locate, origin, reason, settle, source, throne
07 contain, deposit, footing, install, mansion

08 location, position
09 residence, situation
10 foundation
11 accommodate, stately home

**seating**
05 seats
06 chairs, places
13 accommodation

**seaweed**
04 alga
05 varec, vraic
06 varech
07 seaware
13 marine seaweed

➤ *Types of seaweed*:
05 laver, wrack
06 tangle
07 oarweed
08 gulfweed, rockweed, sargasso
09 carrageen, Irish moss
12 bladder wrack
➤ See also PLANT

**secede**
04 quit
05 break, leave
06 resign, retire
08 separate, split off, withdraw
09 break away

**secession**
05 break, split
06 schism
09 breakaway, defection
10 withdrawal

**secluded**
06 hidden, lonely, remote
07 private
08 isolated, shut away, solitary
09 concealed, sheltered
10 cloistered
11 out-of-the-way, sequestered
12 unfrequented

**seclusion**
06 hiding
07 privacy, retreat, secrecy, shelter
08 solitude
09 isolation
10 remoteness, retirement
13 sequestration

**second**
03 aid
04 back, help, move, next, send, twin
05 extra, flash, jiffy, lower, other, shift, trice
06 assign, assist, back up, backer, backup, change,

double, helper, lesser,
minute, moment
07 advance, approve, endorse,
forward, further, instant,
promote, support
08 inferior, relocate, repeated,
transfer
09 agree with, alternate,
assistant, attendant, auxiliary,
duplicate, encourage,
following, secondary,
supporter, twinkling
10 additional, subsequent,
succeeding, supporting
11 alternative, split second,
subordinate
13 supplementary

**secondary**
05 extra, lower, minor, spare
06 backup, lesser, relief, second
07 derived, reserve
08 indirect, inferior
09 ancillary, auxiliary, resulting
10 derivative, subsidiary,
supporting
11 alternative, subordinate,
unimportant

**second-class**
04 mail
08 inferior, mediocre
11 indifferent, unimportant
15 undistinguished

**second-hand**
03 old
04 used, worn
08 borrowed, indirect
09 nearly new, vicarious
10 hand-me-down
13 formerly owned

**second-in-command**
06 backer, helper
09 assistant, attendant,
supporter

**second-rate**
04 poor
05 cheap, lousy, tacky
06 lesser, shoddy, tawdry, tinpot
07 tinhorn
08 inferior, low-grade,
mediocre
11 substandard

**secrecy**
07 mystery, privacy, stealth
09 seclusion
10 confidence, covertness
11 concealment, furtiveness
15 confidentiality

**secret**
03 key, sly
04 code, deep

05 close
06 answer, arcane, closet,
covert, cut off, enigma,
hidden, lonely, occult,
remote, unseen
07 cryptic, furtive, mystery,
private, unknown
08 abstruse, discreet, hush-
hush, isolated, secluded,
shrouded, shut away, stealthy
09 concealed, disguised,
recondite, sensitive,
sheltered, underhand
10 backstairs, classified,
cloistered, confidence,
mysterious, restricted,
undercover, unrevealed
11 camouflaged, clandestine,
inside story, underground,
undisclosed, unpublished
12 confidential, unfrequented
13 hole-and-corner, private
matter, surreptitious, under-
the-table
14 cloak-and-dagger
15 between you and me, under-
the-counter

❏**in secret**
07 on the q.t., privily, quietly
08 covertly, in camera
10 on the quiet, under cover,
unobserved
12 huggermugger

**secretary**
04 desk
05 clerk
06 scribe, typist
10 amanuensis, escritoire, girl
Friday

## Secretary of State

► *Names of U.S. Secretaries
of State*:
03 **Hay** (John)
04 **Clay** (Henry), **Fish**
(Hamilton), **Haig**
(Alexander), **Hull** (Cordell),
**Rusk** (Dean)
05 **Adams** (John Quincy),
**Baker** (James), **Bryan**
(William Jennings), **Vance**
(Cyrus)
06 **Dulles** (John Foster),
**Monroe** (James), **Powell**
(Colin), **Rogers** (William),
**Seward** (William), **Shultz**
(George)
07 **Acheson** (Dean), **Calhoun**
(John C.), **Madison** (James),
**Webster** (Daniel)
08 **Albright** (Madeleine),
**Buchanan** (James),

**Marshall** (George), **Van
Buren** (Martin)
09 **Jefferson** (Thomas),
**Kissinger** (Henry)
11 **Christopher** (Warren)

**secrete**
04 bury, emit, hide, leak, ooze,
take
05 cache, cover, exude, leach
06 screen, shroud
07 conceal, cover up, emanate,
excrete, give off, produce,
release, send out
09 discharge, stash away

**secretion**
07 leakage, osmosis, release
08 emission
09 discharge, emanation,
exudation

**secretive**
04 cagy, deep
05 cagey, close, quiet
07 cryptic
08 reserved, reticent, taciturn
09 enigmatic, withdrawn
11 tightlipped
15 uncommunicative

**secretly**
07 on the q.t., privily, quietly
08 covertly, in camera
09 furtively, in private, privately
10 on the quiet, stealthily,
undercover, unobserved
12 in confidence
13 clandestinely
14 confidentially
15 surreptitiously

**sect**
04 camp, cult, wing
05 group, order, party
06 school
07 faction
12 denomination
13 splinter group

**sectarian**
06 narrow, zealot
07 fanatic, insular
08 cliquish, partisan
09 exclusive, factional, fanatical,
parochial
10 sect member
12 narrow-minded
13 fractionalist

**section**
03 bit
04 area, part, wing, zone
05 piece, slice
06 branch, region, sector
07 chapter, passage, portion,
segment

**sectional**
08 district, division, fraction, fragment
09 component, paragraph
10 department, instalment
11 installment

**sectional**
05 class, local
07 divided, partial
08 regional, separate
09 exclusive, factional, localized, sectarian
10 separatist

**sector**
04 area, part, zone
05 field
06 branch, region
07 quarter, section
08 category, district, division
11 subdivision

**secular**
03 lay
05 civil, state
07 earthly, profane, worldly
08 temporal
12 nonreligious, nonspiritual

**secure**
03 fix, get, tie
04 bolt, fast, firm, gain, land, lash, lock, moor, nail, safe, shut, sure
05 chain, close, fixed, guard, rivet, solid, tight
06 assure, attach, closed, come by, defend, fasten, insure, locked, screen, sealed, steady, sturdy
07 acquire, assured, certain, confirm, padlock, procure, relaxed, settled, sponsor
08 definite, fastened, make fast, make safe, unharmed
09 confident, contented, establish, get hold of, guarantee, protected, reassured, safeguard, steadfast
10 batten down, conclusive, underwrite
11 impregnable, well-founded

**security**
04 care, ease, gage
05 cover
06 asylum, pledge, refuge, safety, surety
07 custody, defense
08 immunity, warranty
09 assurance, guarantee, insurance, safeguard
10 collateral, protection, safeguards

**sedate**
11 peace of mind, precautions, safekeeping
12 preservation, surveillance
15 invulnerability

**sedate**
04 calm
05 quiet, sober, staid, stiff
06 demure, pacify, seemly, serene, soothe
08 composed, tranquil
09 collected, dignified
11 unflappable
12 tranquillize

**sedative**
06 downer, opiate
07 anodyne, calming
08 lenitive, narcotic, relaxing, soothing
09 calmative, soporific
11 barbiturate
12 sleeping pill, tranquilizer
13 tranquillizer

**sedentary**
05 still
06 seated
07 sitting
08 immobile, inactive
09 deskbound
10 stationary

**sediment**
04 lees, silt
05 dregs
07 deposit, grounds, residue
08 residuum
11 precipitate

**sedition**
06 mutiny, revolt
07 treason
09 agitation, rebellion
10 disloyalty, subversion
11 fomentation
13 rabble-rousing

**seditious**
08 disloyal, inciting, mutinous
09 agitating, dissident, fomenting
10 rebellious, subversive
13 revolutionary
15 insurrectionist

**seduce**
04 lure, ruin
05 charm, tempt
06 allure, entice
07 attract, beguile, corrupt, deceive, deprave, ensnare, mislead
08 inveigle

**seducer**
04 goat, wolf
05 flirt

07 charmer, Don Juan
08 Casanova, Lothario
09 libertine, womanizer
11 philanderer

**seduction**
04 lure
06 allure, appeal, come-on
10 allurement, corruption, enticement, temptation
11 beguilement

**seductive**
04 sexy
06 sultry
08 alluring, enticing, inviting
09 beguiling
10 attractive, bewitching, come-hither
11 flirtatious, provocative

**seductress**
04 vamp
05 Circe, siren
07 Lorelei
09 temptress
11 femme fatale

**sedulous**
08 diligent, tireless, untiring
09 assiduous, laborious
10 determined, persistent
11 industrious, persevering
13 conscientious

**see**
04 espy, know, lead, meet, note, show, spot, view
05 grasp, sight, visit, watch
06 behold, decide, fathom, follow, look at, notice, regard, take in
07 discern, find out, glimpse, make out, observe, picture, realize, witness
08 consider, envisage, forecast, perceive
09 ascertain, interview, recognize, set eyes on, visualize
10 appreciate, comprehend, get a look at, understand
11 distinguish, investigate
12 catch sight of

❏**see about**
06 manage, repair
07 arrange, sort out
08 attend to, deal with, organize
09 look after
10 take care of

❏**see through**
07 persist, realize
08 stick out
09 get wise to, not give up, persevere

**seed**

14 not be taken in by
15 not be deceived by

□ **see to**

03 fix
06 insure, manage, repair
07 arrange, sort out
08 attend to, deal with, make sure, organize
09 look after
10 take care of
11 make certain

**seed**

03 egg, pip
04 germ, ovum, root
05 cause, child, grain, heirs, ovule, semen, spawn, sperm, start, stone, young
06 embryo, family, kernel, origin, reason, source
07 nucleus, reasons
08 children, young one
09 beginning, offspring, young ones
10 successors
11 descendants
12 spermatozoon

□ **go to seed, run to seed**

05 decay
07 decline
08 get worse
10 degenerate, go downhill

**seedy**

03 ill
04 sick
05 dirty, mangy, rough
06 ailing, poorly, shabby, unwell
07 rundown, scruffy, squalid
08 off-color
10 out of sorts
11 dilapidated

**seek**

03 aim, ask, beg, try
04 want
06 aspire, desire, follow, invite, pursue, strive
07 attempt, entreat, hunt for, inquire, look for, request, solicit
08 endeavor
09 search for

**seeker**

05 chela
06 novice
07 student
08 disciple, inquirer, searcher

**seem**

04 feel, look
05 sound
06 appear
08 look like

11 pretend to be

**seeming**

05 quasi-
06 pseudo
07 assumed, outward, surface
08 apparent, external, specious, supposed
09 pretended
10 ostensible
11 superficial

**seemingly**

10 apparently, ostensibly
12 on the surface
13 on the face of it, superficially

**seemly**

03 fit
04 meet, nice
06 decent, proper
07 fitting
08 becoming, decorous, suitable
09 befitting
11 appropriate

**seep**

04 drip, leak, ooze, soak, well
08 permeate
09 percolate

**seepage**

04 leak
06 oozing
07 leakage, osmosis
08 dripping
11 percolation

**seer, seeress**

05 augur, sibyl
06 oracle
07 prophet
08 foreseer
11 soothsayer,

**seesaw**

04 yo-yo
05 pitch, swing, teter
09 alternate, fluctuate, oscillate
12 teeter-totter

**seethe**

04 boil, fizz, foam, fume, rage, rise, teem
05 froth, storm, surge, swarm, swell
06 bubble, see red, simmer
07 be livid, explode, ferment, smolder
08 boil over
10 effervesce

**see-through**

05 filmy, gauzy, sheer
06 flimsy
08 gossamer
11 translucent, transparent

**segment**

04 part
05 slice, wedge
06 divide
07 portion, section
08 division, separate
11 compartment

**segregate**

06 cut off
07 exclude, isolate
08 separate, set apart
09 keep apart
10 dissociate, quarantine

**segregation**

09 apartheid, isolation
10 jim crowism, quarantine, separation
12 dissociation, setting apart
13 sequestration
14 discrimination

**seize**

03 nab
04 grab, grip, hold, nail, take
05 annex, catch, grasp, usurp
06 abduct, arrest, clutch, collar, hijack, kidnap, snatch
07 capture, impound
09 apprehend, get hold of
10 commandeer, confiscate
11 appropriate, sequestrate

**seizure**

03 fit
05 spasm
06 arrest, attack, hijack, taking
07 capture
08 paroxysm
10 convulsion

**seldom**

06 rarely
10 hardly ever
12 infrequently
15 once in a blue moon

**select**

03 top
04 best, pick, posh
05 draft, elect, élite, favor, prime
06 choice, choose, finest, invite, opt for, prefer
07 appoint, limited, special
08 decide on, selected, settle on, superior
09 excellent, exclusive, first-rate, single out
10 first-class, handpicked, privileged
11 high-quality

**selection**

04 pick
05 draft

**selective**
06 choice, lineup, medley, option
09 anthology, potpourri
10 assortment, collection, miscellany, preference

**selective**
05 fussy, picky
06 choosy
07 careful, finicky
10 fastidious, particular
14 discriminating

**self**
01 I
03 ego
04 soul
08 identity
11 personality

**self-assertive**
05 bossy, pushy
07 pushing
08 forceful
10 aggressive, commanding, highhanded, peremptory
11 overbearing, overweening

**self-assurance**
06 aplomb
09 assurance, cockiness
10 confidence
12 cocksureness
14 self-confidence

**self-assured**
05 cocky
09 confident
13 sure of oneself

**self-centered**
07 selfish
09 egotistic
10 egocentric
11 egotistical
12 narcissistic

**self-confident**
04 bold, cool
07 assured
08 composed, fearless, positive
09 confident, unabashed

**self-conscious**
03 coy, shy
05 timid
07 awkward, bashful, nervous
08 blushing, insecure, retiring, sheepish, timorous
09 diffident, ill at ease, shrinking
11 embarrassed
13 uncomfortable

**self-control**
04 cool
08 calmness, patience
09 composure, restraint, willpower

10 temperance
14 self-discipline

**self-denial**
10 asceticism, moderation, temperance
12 selflessness
13 self-sacrifice, unselfishness
14 abstemiousness, self-abnegation

**self-esteem**
03 ego
05 pride
07 dignity
11 amour-propre, self-respect

**self-evident**
08 manifest
09 axiomatic
10 undeniable

**self-glorification**
06 egoism
07 egotism, narcism
08 egomania, self-love
10 narcissism
11 egocentrism

**self-government**
08 autarchy, autonomy, home rule
09 democracy
12 independence

**self-importance**
06 vanity
07 conceit, donnism
09 arrogance, cockiness, pomposity, pushiness
10 the bighead
13 bumptiousness, conceitedness

**self-important**
04 vain
05 cocky, proud, pushy
07 pompous
08 arrogant, egoistic
09 conceited, strutting
10 swaggering
11 swellheaded

**self-indulgence**
08 hedonism
10 profligacy, sensualism
11 dissipation
12 extravagance, intemperance
13 dissoluteness

**self-indulgent**
10 dissipated, hedonistic, immoderate, profligate
11 extravagant, intemperate

**self-interest**
11 self-serving, selfishness

**selfish**
04 mean

06 greedy
08 covetous
09 egotistic, mercenary
10 egocentric
11 egotistical, self-seeking, self-serving
12 self-centered
13 inconsiderate

**selfishness**
05 greed
07 egotism
08 meanness

**selfless**
08 generous
09 unselfish
10 altruistic
13 philanthropic
15 self-sacrificing

**self-possessed**
04 calm, cool
06 poised
08 composed, together
09 collected, confident
11 unflappable

**self-possession**
04 cool
05 poise
06 aplomb
08 calmness, coolness
09 composure, sang-froid
10 confidence
14 unflappability

**self-reliance**
07 autarky
11 self-support
12 independence
15 self-sufficiency

**self-reliant**
08 autarkic
10 autarkical
11 independent
14 self-sufficient

**self-respect**
05 pride
07 dignity
11 amour-propre

**self-restraint**
08 patience
09 willpower
10 moderation, temperance
11 forbearance
14 abstemiousness

**self-righteous**
04 smug
05 pious
08 priggish, superior
10 complacent, goody-goody
12 hypocritical

13 goody two-shoes, sanctimonious
14 holier-than-thou

**self-righteousness**
09 piousness
12 priggishness
15 pharisaicalness

**self-sacrifice**
08 altruism
10 generosity
12 selflessness
13 unselfishness

**self-satisfaction**
05 pride
08 smugness
11 complacency, contentment

**self-satisfied**
04 smug
05 proud
08 puffed up
10 complacent

**self-seeking**
07 selfish
09 careerist, mercenary, on the make
11 acquisitive, calculating, gold-digging
13 opportunistic
14 fortune-hunting

**self-styled**
07 would-be
08 so-called
09 pretended, professed, soi-disant

**self-supporting**
11 independent
14 self-sufficient

**self-willed**
06 cussed, wilful
07 willful
08 stubborn
09 obstinate, pigheaded
10 headstrong, refractory
11 intractable, stiff-necked
12 ungovernable

**sell**
04 hawk, hype, push, tout, vend
05 carry, stock, trade
06 barter, deal in, export, handle, import, market, peddle, retail
07 auction, promote, trade in, win over
08 exchange, persuade
09 advertise, dispose of, traffic in
11 merchandise

❏**sell out**
04 fail

05 rat on
06 betray, fink on
08 run out of
11 double-cross
12 be out of stock
13 stab in the back

**seller**
06 dealer, trader, vendor
08 merchant, retailer, supplier
14 retail merchant

**selling**
07 dealing, trading, traffic
09 marketing, promotion
11 trafficking
13 merchandising

**semblance**
03 air
04 look, mask, show
05 front, guise, image
06 aspect, façade, veneer
08 likeness, pretense
10 apparition, appearance, similarity
11 resemblance

**seminal**
05 major
08 creative, original
09 formative, important
10 innovative, productive
11 imaginative, influential

**seminary**
06 school
07 academy, college
09 institute
15 religious school, training college

**Senate**
08 Congress
10 upper house
11 legislature

▶ *Names of U.S. Senators*:
04 **Byrd** (Robert), **Clay** (Henry), **Dodd** (Christopher), **Long** (Huey), **Lott** (Trent), **Reid** (Harry), **Taft** (Robert)
05 **Biden** (Joseph), **Hatch** (Orrin), **Helms** (Jesse), **Kerry** (John), **Leahy** (Patrick), **Levin** (Carl), **Lodge** (Henry Cabot), **Lugar** (Richard), **Smith** (Margaret Chase)
06 **Baucus** (Max), **Conrad** (Kent), **Graham** (Bob), **Harkin** (Tom), **Inouye** (Daniel), **McCain** (John), **Shelby** (Richard), **Warner** (John)
07 **Calhoun** (John C.), **Clinton**

(Hillary Rodham), **Daschle** (Tom), **Dirksen** (Everett), **Douglas** (Stephen), **Kennedy** (Edward), **Kennedy** (John F.), **Kennedy** (Robert)
08 **Bingaman** (Jeff), **Hollings** (Ernest), **Humphrey** (Hubert), **Jeffords** (James), **McCarthy** (Joseph), **Sarbanes** (Paul), **Thurmond** (Strom)
09 **Feinstein** (Dianne), **Fulbright** (J. William), **Goldwater** (Barry), **Lieberman** (Joe)
11 **Rockefeller** (John D., IV)

**send**
04 beam, cast, emit, fire, hurl, mail, move
05 drive, fling, radio, relay, remit, shoot, throw
06 arouse, convey, direct, excite, get off, launch, propel, thrill, turn on
07 address, consign, deliver, forward, project
08 dispatch, transmit
09 broadcast, discharge
11 communicate
12 put in the mail

❏**send for**
05 order
06 summon
07 call for, command, request

**send off**
05 start
07 goodbye
08 farewell
09 departure
11 leave-taking

**senile**
03 old
04 aged
07 doddery
08 confused, decrepit
09 doddering, senescent

**senility**
06 dotage, old age
09 infirmity
10 senescence
11 decrepitude
14 senile dementia

**senior**
02 Sr.
05 chief, doyen, elder, first, major, older
07 doyenne
08 superior
11 high-ranking
13 last-year pupil

## senior citizen
05 elder
07 oldster, retiree
08 retirant
09 pensioner
10 golden ager
13 retired person

## seniority
03 age
04 rank
06 status
08 priority, standing
10 importance, precedence
11 superiority

## sensation
05 furor, sense, vibes
06 thrill
07 feeling, success, triumph
09 commotion
10 impression, perception
13 consciousness

## sensational
05 lurid
07 amazing
08 dramatic, exciting, stirring
09 startling, thrilling
10 astounding, impressive, scandalous
12 breathtaking, electrifying, melodramatic

## sense
03 wit
04 feel, mind, nous, wits
05 brain, drift, grasp, logic, point, savvy, tenor
06 brains, detect, divine, import, intuit, notice, nuance, pick up, reason, wisdom
07 discern, faculty, feeling, meaning, observe, purport, purpose, realize, suspect
08 gumption, judgment, perceive, prudence
09 awareness, be aware of, intuition, sensation, substance
10 appreciate, comprehend, impression, perception
11 common sense
12 appreciation, apprehension, intelligence, significance
13 understanding
14 interpretation

## ❑ make sense of
05 grasp
06 fathom
07 make out
09 figure out
10 comprehend

## senseless
03 mad, out
04 daft, numb
05 batty, crazy, dotty, silly
06 absurd, futile, stupid, unwise
07 fatuous, foolish, idiotic, moronic, out cold, stunned
08 deadened, mindless
09 illogical, insensate, ludicrous, pointless
10 insensible, irrational, ridiculous
11 nonsensical, unconscious
12 anesthetized, unreasonable

## sensibility
05 taste
07 insight
08 delicacy, emotions, feelings
09 awareness, intuition
10 sentiments
11 discernment
12 appreciation
14 susceptibility

## sensible
04 sane, wise
05 aware, sharp, sober, sound, tough
06 clever, mature, shrewd, strong
07 logical, prudent, working
08 everyday, ordinary, rational
09 judicious, practical, realistic, sagacious, sensitive
10 discerning, farsighted, functional, perceptive, reasonable, responsive, vulnerable
11 commonsense, down-to-earth, levelheaded, susceptible, well-advised
14 commonsensical

## ❑ sensible of
07 alive to, aware of
09 mindful of
11 cognizant of, conscious of, sensitive to

## sensitive
04 fine, soft
05 aware, exact
06 tender, touchy, tricky
07 awkward, careful, fragile, precise, tactful
08 delicate, discreet, reactive, sentient
09 difficult, emotional, irritable
10 diplomatic, perceptive, responsive, vulnerable
11 considerate, problematic, susceptible, sympathetic, thin-skinned

## sensitivity
08 delicacy, fineness, softness, sympathy
09 awareness, fragility
11 discernment
12 appreciation
14 responsiveness, susceptibility

## sensual
04 lewd, sexy
06 animal, bodily, carnal, erotic, sexual, sultry
07 fleshly, lustful, worldly
08 physical
13 self-indulgent

## sensuality
08 sexiness
09 animalism, carnality
10 debauchery, profligacy
11 gourmandize, libertinism

## sensuous
04 lush, rich
08 pleasant, pleasing
09 aesthetic, luxurious
10 gratifying, voluptuous

## sentence
03 rap
04 doom
05 judge, order
06 decree, punish, ruling
07 condemn, verdict
08 decision, penalize
10 punishment
13 pronouncement
14 pass judgment on

## sententious
05 brief, pithy, short, terse
06 gnomic
07 canting, compact, concise, laconic, pointed, pompous, preachy
08 succinct
09 axiomatic
10 aphoristic, judgmental, moralistic, moralizing
12 epigrammatic
13 sanctimonious

## sentient
04 live
05 aware
09 conscious, sensitive
10 responsive

## sentiment
04 idea, view
07 emotion, feeling, opinion, romance, thought
08 attitude, judgment, softness
10 persuasion, tenderness
11 mawkishness, point of view, romanticism, sensibility

## sentimental
05 corny, gushy, mushy, sappy, soppy, weepy
06 loving, sickly, sloppy, slushy, sugary, tender
07 gushing, maudlin, mawkish
08 pathetic, romantic, touching
09 emotional, schmaltzy
10 lovey-dovey
11 softhearted, tear-jerking

## sentimentality
05 slush
06 bathos
08 schmaltz
10 sloppiness, tenderness
11 mawkishness, romanticism

## sentry
05 guard, watch
06 picket
07 lookout
08 sentinel, watchman

## separable
09 divisible
10 detachable, particular
11 independent
15 distinguishable

## separate
04 part
05 alone, apart, sever, split
06 cut off, detach, divide, remove, single, sunder
07 diverge, divorce, isolate, several, split up
08 abstract, break off, discrete, distinct, disunite, solitary, uncouple, withdraw
09 come apart, disparate, disunited, partition, segregate, take apart, unrelated
10 autonomous, disconnect, disjointed, individual, particular, segregated, unattached
11 disentangle, independent, part company, unconnected
15 become estranged

## separated
05 apart
06 parted
07 divided, split up
08 isolated, sundered
09 disunited
10 segregated
12 disconnected

## separately
05 alone, apart
06 singly
09 severally
10 discretely, personally
12 individually

## separating
08 dividing, divisive
09 isolating
11 intervening, segregating
12 partitioning

## separation
03 gap
04 rift
05 split
06 schism
07 breakup, divorce, parting, split-up
09 apartheid, severance
10 detachment, divergence, uncoupling
11 leave-taking, segregation
12 dissociation, estrangement
13 disconnection, disengagement

## septic
06 putrid
08 infected, poisoned
09 festering
10 putrefying
11 suppurating
12 putrefactive

## sepulchral
05 grave
06 dismal, gloomy, morbid, solemn, somber, woeful
08 funereal, mournful
10 lugubrious, melancholy

## sepulcher
04 tomb
05 grave, vault
09 mausoleum
11 burial place

## sequel
06 payoff, result, upshot
07 outcome
08 follow-up
11 consequence, development
12 continuation

## sequence
05 chain, cycle, order, train
06 course, series, string
10 procession, succession
11 consequence, progression

## sequester
06 detach, remove
07 impound, isolate, seclude, shut off
08 insulate, set apart
10 commandeer, confiscate

## sequestered
06 lonely, remote
07 outback, private, retired
08 isolated, secluded
10 cloistered
11 out-of-the-way

## sequestrate
05 seize
07 impound
09 sequester
10 commandeer, confiscate

## seraphic
07 angelic, saintly, sublime
08 beatific, blissful, heavenly
09 celestial

## serendipity
04 luck
06 chance
07 fortune
08 accident, fortuity
11 coincidence, good fortune

## serene
04 calm, cool
05 quiet
06 placid
08 peaceful, tranquil
09 unclouded, unruffled
11 undisturbed, unflappable
13 imperturbable

## serenity
04 calm, cool
05 peace
08 calmness, quietude
09 placidity
11 tranquility
12 peacefulness
14 unflappability

## serf
05 helot, slave
06 thrall
07 bondman, servant, villein
08 bondmaid, bondsman
09 bond-slave, bondwoman
10 bondswoman
11 bondservant

## series
03 row, run, set
04 line
05 chain, cycle, order, train
06 course, stream, string
07 playoff
08 sequence
10 succession
11 arrangement, progression
13 concatenation

## serious
04 deep, dour, grim
05 grave, heavy, sober, stern
06 no joke, severe, solemn, somber
07 crucial, earnest, genuine, pensive, sincere, weighty
08 critical, pressing, worrying
09 difficult, humorless, long-faced, momentous, unsmiling

10 precarious
11 preoccupied, significant
12 life-and-death
13 consequential, of
   consequence

**seriously**
05 badly
06 sorely
07 acutely, gravely
08 severely, solemnly
09 earnestly, sincerely
10 critically, grievously
11 dangerously, joking apart
12 thoughtfully
13 distressingly

**seriousness**
06 moment, weight
07 gravity, urgency
08 gravitas, sobriety
09 solemnity, staidness,
   sternness
10 importance, sedateness
11 earnestness
13 humorlessness

**sermon**
06 homily
07 address, lecture, message,
   oration
08 harangue
09 discourse, talking-to
11 declamation, exhortation

**serpentine**
05 snaky
07 coiling, crooked, sinuous,
   snaking, winding
08 tortuous, twisting
09 snakelike
10 meandering

**serrated**
06 jagged
07 notched, sawlike, toothed
08 indented, saw-edged
10 saw-toothed, serrulated

**serried**
05 close, dense
06 massed
07 compact, crowded

**servant**
04 help
06 helper, menial
08 hireling, retainer
09 ancillary, assistant, attendant

**serve**
03 act, aid
04 help, wait
06 answer, assist, attend, dish
   up, fulfil, succor, supply, wait
   on
07 benefit, deliver, dole out,
   fulfill, further, give out,

perform, present, provide,
satisfy, suffice, support, work
for
08 carry out, complete, function
09 discharge, go through
10 distribute, minister to, take
   care of

**service**
03 job, use
04 army, duty, help, mass, navy,
   rite, tune, turn, work
06 duties, forces, ritual
07 benefit, marines, repairs,
   worship
08 air force, ceremony, function,
   maintain, overhaul
09 advantage, amenities,
   ordinance, resources,
   sacrament, servicing, utilities
10 assistance, coast guard,
   employment, facilities,
   usefulness
11 armed forces

**serviceable**
06 usable, useful
09 practical
10 functional
11 utilitarian

**servile**
03 low
04 base, mean
05 lowly
06 abject, humble, menial
07 fawning, slavish, subject
08 cringing, toadying
09 groveling
10 obsequious, submissive
11 bootlicking, brownnosing,
   subservient, sycophantic

**servility**
08 baseness, meanness,
   toadyism
09 abjection
10 sycophancy
12 subservience
13 self-abasement

**serving**
05 share
06 amount, ration
07 bowlful, helping, portion
08 plateful, spoonful

**servitude**
06 chains, thrall
07 bondage, serfdom, slavery
08 thraldom
09 obedience, vassalage
10 villeinage
11 enslavement, subjugation

**session**
04 time, year

05 spell
06 period
07 hearing, meeting, sitting
08 assembly, semester
10 conference, discussion,
   school term
➤ See also TERM

**set**
03 fix, gel, kit, lay, put
04 band, firm, gang, give, look,
   plan, sink, turn
05 batch, begin, class, crowd,
   fixed, grant, group, place,
   plonk, ready, rigid, scene,
   score, start, stock, usual,
   write
06 adjust, agreed, all set, assign,
   circle, clique, create, decide,
   devise, go down, harden,
   impose, insert, instal, locate,
   ordain, outfit, prompt, select,
   series, settle, strict, vanish
07 agree on, appoint, arrange,
   confirm, congeal, decided,
   deposit, faction, install, lay
   down, prepare, produce,
   provide, put down, regular,
   resolve, scenery, settled,
   situate, specify, stiffen,
   thicken
08 allocate, arranged, backdrop,
   everyday, finished, get ready,
   habitual, ordained, organize,
   position, prepared, regulate,
   sequence, solidify, standard
09 appointed, coagulate,
   customary, designate,
   determine, disappear,
   establish, ingrained, make
   ready, prescribe, scheduled,
   specified, stipulate
10 assemblage, assortment,
   background, collection,
   compendium, entrenched,
   give rise to, inflexible,
   prescribed
11 crystallize, established, mise
   en scène, prearranged,
   stereotyped, traditional
12 conventional
13 predetermined

❑**set about**
05 begin, start
06 attack, tackle
08 commence, embark on
09 get down to, undertake

❑**set against**
05 weigh
06 divide, oppose
07 balance, compare
08 contrast, disunite
09 juxtapose

**set apart**
07 mark off
08 put aside, separate
11 distinguish
13 differentiate

**set aside**
04 keep, save
06 cancel, reject, revoke
07 discard, reserve, reverse
08 abrogate, discount, keep back, lay aside, overrule, overturn, put aside, separate
09 stash away
13 keep in reserve

**set back**
04 slow
05 check, delay
06 hinder, hold up, impede, retard, thwart

**set down**
04 note
06 affirm, assert, record
07 lay down
08 note down
09 establish, formulate, prescribe, stipulate
12 put in writing

**set forth**
05 leave
06 depart
07 expound, present
08 start out
09 delineate, elucidate

**set in**
05 begin, start
06 arrive
08 commence

**set off**
05 begin, leave, start
06 depart, ignite, prompt
07 display, enhance, explode, show off, trigger
08 activate, contrast, detonate, initiate, start out, touch off
10 trigger off
11 set in motion
15 throw into relief

**set on**
06 attack, beat up, turn on
07 assault, lay into, set upon

**set out**
05 begin, leave, start
06 depart, lay out
07 arrange, display, exhibit, explain, present
08 describe, start out

**set up**
05 array, begin, build, erect, fit up, found, frame, raise, start
07 arrange, elevate, prepare

08 assemble, initiate, organize
09 construct, establish
10 inaugurate
11 incriminate

**setback**
04 blow, snag
05 delay, hitch, upset
06 hiccup, holdup
07 reverse
08 reversal
10 impediment

**setting**
04 site
05 frame, scene
06 locale, milieu
07 context, scenery
08 location, position
10 background
11 environment, mise en scène, perspective
12 surroundings

**setting-up**
08 creation, founding
10 foundation, initiation
12 inauguration, introduction
13 establishment

**settle**
03 fix, pay
04 drop, fall, foot, land, live, sink
05 agree, clear, order, solve
06 adjust, alight, choose, clinch, decide, occupy, reside, square
07 agree on, appoint, arrange, confirm, cough up, descend, fork out, inhabit, patch up, resolve, subside
08 colonize, complete, conclude, decide on, organize, populate, square up
09 determine, discharge, establish, light upon, reconcile
10 compromise, put in order
12 put down roots

**settle down**
05 still
06 soothe
07 compose, quieten
08 calm down

**settlement**
04 camp
06 colony, hamlet
07 kibbutz, payment, village
08 contract, decision, defrayal
09 agreement, discharge
10 completion, encampment, resolution
11 arrangement, termination
12 colonization

13 establishment
14 reconciliation

**settler**
06 sooner
07 pioneer
08 colonist, newcomer, squatter
09 colonizer, immigrant
11 homesteader

**set-to**
03 row
04 spat
05 brush, fight, run-in, scrap
06 dustup, fracas
07 contest, quarrel, wrangle
08 argument, squabble
10 falling-out
11 altercation

**setup**
04 dupe
05 cinch
06 format, sucker, system
08 business
09 framework, structure
11 arrangement, disposition
12 organization

**sever**
03 cut, end
04 chop, hack, part, rend
05 cease, split
06 cleave, cut off, detach, divide, lop off, secede
07 chop off, disjoin, tear off
08 amputate, break off, dissolve, separate
09 terminate
10 disconnect

**several**
04 a few, many, some
06 sundry
07 diverse, various
08 assorted, distinct, multiple, separate
09 a number of, different, disparate, quite a few

**severally**
06 apiece, singly
08 seriatim
10 discretely, separately
12 individually, particularly, respectively, specifically

**severe**
04 grim, hard
05 acute, grave, harsh, plain, rigid, stern, tough
06 fierce, strict, strong, taxing
07 arduous, ascetic, austere, drastic, extreme, intense, serious, Spartan, violent
08 exacting, forceful, pitiless, powerful, rigorous

**severely**
09 dangerous, demanding, difficult, draconian, merciless, stringent, unbending, unsmiling
10 burdensome, inexorable, relentless, tyrannical
11 strait-laced
13 straight-laced

**severely**
04 hard
05 badly
06 grimly, sorely
07 acutely, gravely, harshly, sharply, sternly
08 bitterly, strictly
09 extremely, intensely
10 critically, rigorously
11 dangerously

**severity**
05 rigor
07 gravity
08 grimness, hardness, strength
09 extremity, harshness, intensity, plainness, sharpness
10 fierceness, Spartanism, strictness, stringency
11 seriousness
12 forcefulness

**sew**
03 hem
04 darn, mend, seam, tack
05 baste
06 stitch
09 embroider

**sex**
02 it
05 union
06 gender, libido
08 intimacy, nubility, sexiness
09 sexuality
10 lovemaking
12 reproduction
15 sexual relations

**sexless**
06 neuter
07 asexual, unsexed
08 unsexual
15 parthenogenetic

**sexton**
06 verger
09 caretaker, sacristan
11 gravedigger

**sexual**
06 carnal, erotic
07 sensual
08 venereal
12 reproductive

**sexuality**
06 desire

08 sexiness, virility
09 carnality, eroticism
10 sensuality
12 sexual desire

**sexy**
06 erotic, nubile, slinky
07 raunchy, sensual
08 alluring, arousing
09 desirable, provoking, salacious, seductive
10 suggestive, voluptuous
11 provocative, titillating
12 pornographic

**shabby**
04 worn
05 dowdy, faded
06 frayed, ragged, shoddy, unfair
07 scruffy, worn-out
08 shameful, tattered
10 despicable, threadbare
12 contemptible, dishonorable, disreputable

**shack**
03 hut
04 dump, hole, shed
05 cabin, hovel, hutch
06 lean-to, shanty

**shackle**
03 tie
04 bind, bond, iron, rope
05 chain, limit
06 fetter, hamper, impede, secure, tether, thwart
07 manacle, trammel
08 encumber, handcuff, handicap, restrain, restrict
09 bracelets, constrain

**shade**
03 dim, hue, tad
04 dash, dusk, hide, hint, tint, tone, veil
05 blind, color, cover, ghost, gloom, tinge, touch, trace, visor
06 awning, canopy, darken, degree, memory, nuance, screen, shadow, shroud, spirit
07 conceal, curtain, dimness, parasol, phantom, protect, shadows, shelter, specter
08 covering, darkness, gloaming, twilight
09 gradation, obscurity, suspicion
10 apparition, gloominess, overshadow, suggestion
12 semidarkness

❑**a shade**
06 a touch
07 a little, a trifle

08 slightly

❑**put in the shade**
05 dwarf, excel
07 eclipse, outrank, surpass
08 outclass, outshine

**shadow**
03 dog
04 dusk, hint, tail
05 cloud, gloom, shade, shape, trace, trail
06 darken, follow
07 dimness, remnant, vestige
08 darkness, follower, gloaming, twilight
09 companion, obscurity
10 foreboding, silhouette, suggestion
13 tenebrousness

❑**a shadow of your former self**
07 remnant, vestige
13 poor imitation

**shadowy**
03 dim
04 dark, hazy
05 faint, murky, vague
06 gloomy, unreal
07 ghostly, obscure, phantom
08 ethereal, nebulous, spectral
09 tenebrose, tenebrous
10 ill-defined, indistinct, mysterious, tenebrious
11 crepuscular

**shady**
03 dim
04 cool, dark, iffy
05 fishy, leafy
06 veiled
07 covered, dubious, obscure, shadowy, suspect, umbrose
08 screened, shielded, shrouded
09 tenebrous, underhand
10 caliginous, suspicious, tenebrious, umbrageous
11 underhanded
12 disreputable, questionable
13 untrustworthy

**shaft**
03 bar, ray, rod
04 beam, dart, duct, flue, pole, stem, well
05 arrow, shank, stick, winze
06 handle, pencil, pillar, tunnel

**shaggy**
05 bushy, hairy
06 woolly
07 crinose, hirsute, unshorn
10 long-haired

## shake

03 wag
04 bump, faze, jerk, jolt, rock, roll, stir, sway, wave
05 alarm, heave, lower, quake, rouse, shock, swing, throb, upset, wield
06 bounce, lessen, quiver, rattle, reduce, shiver, totter, weaken, wobble
07 agitate, disturb, perturb, quaking, shudder, tremble, unnerve, vibrate
08 brandish, convulse, diminish, distress, flourish, frighten, unsettle
09 oscillate, undermine, vibration
10 convulsion, discompose, intimidate
11 disturbance, oscillation

◻ **shake a leg**
08 step on it
10 get a move on, look lively
11 get cracking

◻ **shake off**
04 lose
05 elude
06 escape
08 dislodge, get rid of, outstrip
11 give the slip, leave behind

◻ **shake up**
05 alarm, shock, upset
06 rattle
07 unnerve
08 distress, unsettle
10 reorganize

## Shakespeare

► *Characters in Shakespeare's plays:*
03 Hal (Prince), Nym, Sly (Christopher)
04 Dull, Fool (The), Ford (Mistress), Hero, Iago, John (Don), John (King), Kate, Kent (Earl of), Lear (King), Moth, Page (Mistress), Puck, Snug
05 Ariel, Belch (Sir Toby), Celia, Diana, Edgar, Feste, Flute, Gobbo (Launcelot), Julia, Maria, Nurse, Paris (Count), Pedro (Don), Regan, Romeo, Snout, Timon, Titus, Viola
06 Alonso, Angelo, Antony (Mark), Armado (Don Adriano de), Audrey, Banquo, Bianca, Bottom (Nick), Brutus, Cassio, Cloten, Cobweb, Dromio, Duncan (King), Edmund, Emilia, Fabian, Hamlet, Hecate,

Hector, Helena, Hermia, Imogen, Jaques, Juliet, Oberon, Oliver (de Bois), Olivia, Orsino, Oswald, Pistol, Porter, Portia, Quince, Silvia, Thisbe, Yorick
07 Adriana, Antonio, Caliban, Capulet, Claudio, Costard, Fleance, Goneril, Gonzalo, Horatio, Hotspur, Iachimo, Jessica, Laertes, Leontes, Lorenzo, Macbeth, Macbeth (Lady), Macduff, Malcolm, Mariana, Martext (Sir Oliver), Miranda, Octavia, Ophelia, Orlando, Othello, Paulina, Perdita, Proteus, Pyramus, Quickly (Mistress), Shylock, Sycorax, Theseus, Titania, Troilus
08 Bardolph, Bassanio, Beatrice, Benedick, Benvolio, Claudius, Cordelia, Cressida, Dogberry, Falstaff (Sir John), Florizel, Fluellen, Gertrude, Hermione, Isabella, Laurence (Friar), Lucretia, Lysander, Malvolio, Mercutio, Montague, Pericles, Polonius, Prospero, Rosalind, Rosaline, Stephano, Trinculo
09 Aguecheek (Sir Andrew), Antigonus, Cleopatra, Cornelius, Cymbeline, Demetrius, Desdemona, Enobarbus, Frederick (Duke), Hippolyta, Hortensio, Katharina, Katharine (Princess of France), Petruchio, Polixenes, Sebastian, Valentine, Vincentio (Duke)
10 Coriolanus, Fortinbras, Gloucester (Earl of), Holofernes, Jaquenetta, Starveling, Touchstone
11 Mustard-seed, Peasblossom, Rosencrantz
12 Guildenstern, Julius Caesar, Three Witches
15 Robin Goodfellow, Titus Andronicus

─────────────

► *Names of Shakespeare's plays:*
06 Hamlet (Prince of Denmark), Henry V
07 Henry IV (Parts 1 and 2), Henry VI (Parts 1, 2 and 3), Macbeth, Othello (The Moor of Venice)
08 King John, King Lear, Pericles
09 Cymbeline, Henry VIII,

Richard II
10 Coriolanus, Richard III, The Tempest
11 As You Like It
12 Julius Caesar, Twelfth Night (or What You Will)
13 Timon of Athens
14 Romeo and Juliet, The Winter's Tale
15 Titus Andronicus
16 Love's Labours Lost
17 Measure for Measure, The Comedy of Errors
18 Antony and Cleopatra, Troilus and Cressida
19 Much Ado About Nothing, The Merchant of Venice, The Taming of the Shrew
20 All's Well That Ends Well
21 A Midsummer Night's Dream
22 The Merry Wives of Windsor
23 The Two Gentlemen of Verona

## shake up

08 upheaval
11 disturbance
13 rearrangement
14 reorganization

## shaky

04 iffy, weak
05 rocky
06 flimsy, wobbly
07 rickety, tottery, unsound
08 insecure, unstable, unsteady
09 doddering, faltering, quivering, tentative, tottering, tremulous, uncertain
10 precarious, unreliable
12 questionable

## shallow

04 idle
05 empty, petty, shoal
06 flimsy, simple, slight
07 foolish, not deep, surface, trivial
08 ignorant, skin-deep, trifling
09 frivolous, insincere
11 meaningless, superficial
12 lacking depth

## sham

04 copy, fake, hoax, mock
05 bogus, cheat, false, feign, fraud, phony, put on, put-on
06 humbug
07 forgery, imitate, pretend
08 deceiver, imposter, pretense
09 charlatan, dissemble, imposture, simulated, synthetic

10 artificial, simulation
11 counterfeit, make-believe

**shaman**
06 powwow
07 angakok, angekok
08 magician, sorcerer
11 medicine man, witch doctor
13 medicine woman

**shamble**
04 drag, limp
06 hobble, scrape, toddle
07 shuffle

**shambles**
04 mess
05 chaos, havoc, wreck
06 bedlam, muddle, pigpen, pigsty
08 abattoir, butchery, disarray, disorder, madhouse
14 slaughterhouse
15 disorganization

**shambling**
06 clumsy
08 lurching, ungainly, unsteady
09 lumbering, shuffling

**shame**
04 pity
05 abash, guilt, stain, sully, taint
06 debase, humble, infamy, show up, stigma
07 degrade, mortify, remorse
08 confound, disgrace, dishonor, ignominy, ridicule
09 discredit, embarrass, humiliate
10 misfortune, opprobrium
11 degradation, humiliation
13 embarrassment, mortification
14 disappointment

❏**put to shame**
06 humble, show up
07 eclipse, mortify, surpass
08 disgrace, outclass, outshine
09 embarrass, humiliate

**shamefaced**
07 abashed, ashamed
08 blushing, contrite, penitent, red-faced, sheepish

**shameful**
04 base, mean, vile
07 heinous, ignoble, shaming
08 shocking, unworthy
09 atrocious
10 mortifying, outrageous, scandalous
11 disgraceful, ignominious
12 contemptible, embarrassing
13 discreditable, reprehensible

**shameless**
06 brazen, wanton
07 blatant, defiant
08 flagrant, hardened, immodest
09 audacious, barefaced, unabashed, unashamed
10 impenitent, indecorous, unbecoming
12 incorrigible, unprincipled

**shanty**
03 hut
04 shed
05 cabin, hovel, hutch, shack
06 lean-to

**shape**
03 cut
04 cast, form, make, mold, plan, trim
05 adapt, alter, block, build, carve, forge, frame, guise, model, state
06 create, design, devise, fettle, figure, format, kilter, sculpt
07 fashion, outline, pattern, profile, remodel, whittle
08 contours, likeness, physique
09 character, condition, construct, influence, sculpture, structure
10 appearance, silhouette
13 configuration

▶ *Names of shapes*:
04 cone, cube, oval
06 circle, cuboid, oblong, sphere, square
07 diamond, ellipse, hexagon, nonagon, octagon, polygon, pyramid, rhombus
08 crescent, cylinder, heptagon, pentagon, quadrant, triangle
09 rectangle, trapezium, trapezoid
10 hemisphere, octahedron, polyhedron, semicircle
11 tetrahedron
13 parallelogram, quadrilateral
15 scalene triangle

❏**shape up**
07 develop
08 flourish, progress
09 become fit, take shape
11 make headway, move forward
12 make progress

**shapeless**
08 formless, nebulous, unformed
09 amorphous, irregular
12 unstructured

**shapely**
04 neat, trim
07 elegant
10 attractive, curvaceous, voluptuous, well-turned

**shard**
04 chip, part
05 piece
06 shiver
08 fragment, particle, splinter

**share**
03 cut, due, lot
04 part
05 allot, quota, split, whack
06 assign, divide, ration
07 carve up, deal out, dole out, give out, go Dutch, partake, portion
08 allocate, dividend, division, go halves
09 allotment, allowance, apportion
10 allocation, distribute, go halvsies, percentage, proportion
12 contribution, go fifty-fifty
14 bit of the action, slice of the cake

❏**share out**
05 allot
06 assign
07 divvy up, give out, hand out, mete out
08 divide up
09 apportion, parcel out
10 distribute

**shark**
04 fish
05 crook
08 swindler
11 extortioner
13 wheeler-dealer

▶ *Types of shark*:
03 fox
04 blue, mako
05 ghost, nurse, tiger, whale
07 basking, dogfish, leopard, requiem
08 mackerel, thresher
09 man-eating, porbeagle
10 great white, hammerhead, shovelhead
➤ See also ANIMAL

**sharp**
03 hep, sly
04 acid, keen, sour, tart, wily
05 acrid, acute, alert, clear, edged, harsh, natty, quick, rapid, smart, spiky, tight

**sharpen**

06 abrupt, acidic, artful, astute, barbed, biting, clever, crafty, fierce, jagged, severe, shrewd, snappy, sudden
07 acerbic, cunning, exactly, extreme, intense, piquant, pointed, pungent, stylish
08 clear-cut, distinct, incisive, on the dot, piercing, promptly, scathing, serrated, stabbing, suddenly, venomous, vinegary
09 dishonest, observant, precisely, trenchant, vitriolic
10 discerning, knife-edged, needlelike, perceptive, punctually, razor edged, razor sharp, unexpected
11 intelligent, penetrating, quick-witted, well-defined
12 unexpectedly

**sharpen**
04 edge, file, hone, keen, whet
05 grind, strop
09 acuminate

**sharp-eyed**
08 hawk-eyed
09 eagle-eyed, observant
11 keen-sighted
12 sharp-sighted

**sharpness**
05 venom
07 clarity, cruelty, sarcasm, vitriol
08 keenness, severity
09 acuteness, harshness, intensity
10 astuteness, definition, fierceness, shrewdness
11 penetration
12 incisiveness
14 perceptiveness

**shatter**
04 dash, ruin
05 burst, crack, smash, split, upset, wreck
06 shiver
07 destroy, explode
08 demolish, overturn, splinter
09 devastate, overwhelm, pulverize

**shattered**
06 broken
07 cracked, crushed, rattled, smashed
09 destroyed
10 devastated, splintered

**shattering**
06 severe
08 crushing, damaging
10 paralyzing

11 devastating

**shave**
03 cut
04 crop, pare, trim
05 graze, plane, shear
06 barber, fleece, scrape
07 cut back, whittle

**sheaf**
05 bunch, truss
06 armful, bundle

**sheath**
04 case
05 shell
06 casing, sleeve
08 envelope, scabbard

**shed**
03 hut
04 cast, drop, emit, molt
05 shack, spill
06 lean-to, shanty, slough
07 cast off, discard, scatter
08 building, get rid of, outhouse

**sheen**
05 gleam, gloss, shine
06 luster, patina, polish
07 burnish

**sheep**
03 ewe, ram, tup
04 lamb
06 wether
10 bellwether

▸ *Sheep include*:
05 urial
06 aoudad, argali, bharal, merino, Navajo
07 bighorn, caracul, Cheviot, karakul, Lincoln, mouflon, Suffolk
08 Columbia, Cotswold, moufflon
09 blackface, broadtail, Leicester, Southdown
11 Rambouillet, Wensleydale
➤ See also ANIMAL

**sheepish**
07 abashed, ashamed, foolish
09 chastened, mortified
10 shamefaced
11 embarrassed

**sheer**
04 fine, mere, pure, thin, veer
05 gauzy, sharp, steep, utter
06 abrupt, flimsy, swerve
07 deviate
08 absolute, gossamer, thorough, vertical
09 downright, out-and-out, veritable
10 diaphanous, see-through

11 precipitous, transparent, unmitigated
13 perpendicular, thoroughgoing

**sheet**
04 coat, film, leaf, page, pane, skin, slab
05 cover, folio, layer, panel, piece, plate, reach, sweep
06 lamina, veneer
07 blanket, expanse, overlay, stratum, surface
08 bed linen
09 newspaper

**shelf**
03 bar
04 bank, reef, sill, step
05 bench, ledge, shoal
07 counter, sandbar, terrace
08 sandbank
09 bookshelf
11 mantelpiece, mantelshelf

**shell**
03 pod
04 boat, bomb, case, hull, husk, rind
05 blitz, crust, frame, shuck
06 bullet, casing, fire on
07 chassis, grenade, missile
08 carapace, skeleton
10 integument

❑**shell out**
04 ante, give
05 spend
06 donate, expend, lay out, pay out
07 cough up, fork out
10 contribute

**shellfish** see CRUSTACEAN; MOLLUSK

**shelter**
04 hide, roof
05 cover, guard, haven, put up
06 asylum, harbor, refuge, safety, shield
07 lodging, protect
08 security
09 safeguard, sanctuary
10 protection

**sheltered**
04 cozy, snug, warm
05 quiet, shady
07 covered
08 shielded
09 protected, unworldly
10 cloistered

**shelve**
05 defer, table
06 put off
07 suspend

08 lay aside, mothball, postpone, put on ice
10 pigeonhole

**shepherd**
04 herd, lead
05 guide, steer, usher
06 convoy, escort
07 conduct, marshal
08 guardian, herdsman
09 protector
11 shepherdess

**shield**
05 cover, guard, shade, targe
06 defend, screen, shadow
07 buckler, bulwark, defense, protect, rampart, shelter, support
09 protector, safeguard
10 escutcheon, protection

**shift**
04 move, span, time, vary, veer
05 alter, budge, carry, spell, stint, U-turn
06 adjust, change, modify, period, remove, swerve, switch
07 removal, stretch
08 dislodge, displace, get rid of, movement, relocate, transfer
09 fluctuate, rearrange, transpose, variation
10 alteration, relocation, reposition
11 fluctuation
12 displacement, modification

**shiftless**
04 idle, lazy
05 inept
07 aimless
08 feckless, goalless, indolent
11 incompetent, ineffectual, inefficient, unambitious
13 directionless, irresponsible, lackadaisical
14 good-for-nothing

**shifty**
04 iffy, wily
05 shady
06 crafty, tricky
07 cunning, devious, dubious, evasive, furtive
08 scheming, slippery
09 deceitful, dishonest, underhand
11 duplicitous
13 untrustworthy

**shilly-shally**
05 waver
06 dither, falter, seesaw, teeter
08 hesitate

09 fluctuate, hem and haw, mess about, vacillate
10 dilly-dally, mess around
11 prevaricate

**shimmer**
04 glow
05 gleam, glint
06 luster
07 flicker, glimmer, glisten, glitter, sparkle, twinkle
11 iridescence, scintillate

**shimmering**
05 shiny
07 glowing, shining
08 gleaming, luminous, lustrous
10 aventurine, glistening, glittering, iridescent
12 incandescent

**shin**
03 leg
05 climb, mount, scale, shoot, tibia
06 ascend
07 clamber
08 scramble

**shine**
03 rub, wax
04 beam, buff, glow
05 excel, flash, gleam, glint, gloss, light, rub up, sheen
06 dazzle, luster, patina, polish
07 burnish, flicker, glimmer, glisten, glitter, radiate, shimmer, sparkle, twinkle
08 lambency, radiance
10 brightness, effulgence, incandesce
12 luminescence
13 incandescence

**shininess**
05 gleam, sheen, shine
06 luster, polish
07 burnish, glitter

**shining**
06 bright
07 beaming, eminent, glowing, leading, radiant
08 flashing, gleaming, glinting, glorious, luminous, splendid
09 brilliant, effulgent, sparkling, twinkling
10 glistening, glittering, preeminent, shimmering
11 illustrious, outstanding, resplendent
12 incandescent
13 distinguished

**shiny**
05 silky, sleek
06 bright, glossy

08 gleaming, lustrous, polished
09 burnished
10 glistening, shimmering

**ship**
03 tug
04 boat, mail, send
05 craft, ferry, liner, yacht
06 export, tanker, vessel
07 steamer, trawler
08 dispatch
➢ See also BOAT; SAIL; VEHICLE

▶ *Parts of a ship*:
03 bow, oar
04 brig, bunk, deck, head, helm, hold, keel, mast, port, prow, sail
05 berth, bilge, cabin, cleat, davit, hatch, stack, stern, wheel, winch
06 anchor, bridge, fo'c'sle, funnel, galley, gunnel, hawser, rigger, rudder, tiller
07 capstan, gangway, gun deck, gunwale, hammock, oarlock, top deck, transom
08 boat deck, bulkhead, bulwarks, hatchway, main deck, poop deck, porthole, wardroom
09 afterdeck, crow's nest, gangplank, lower deck, periscope, stanchion, starboard, stateroom, waterline
10 boiler room, engine room, figurehead, flight deck, forecastle, pilot house
11 paddle wheel, quarter deck, torpedo tube
12 Plimsoll line
13 promenade deck

▶ *Names of famous ships*:
04 Ajax, Argo, Hood, Nina
05 Argus, Maine, Pinta
06 Beagle, Bounty, France, Hunley, Oriana, Pequod, Renown
07 Amistad, Arizona, Belfast, Blücher, Monitor, Pelican, Potomac, Repulse, Tirpitz, Titanic, Victory
08 Ark Royal, Bismarck, Canberra, Graf Spee, Mary Rose, Missouri, Nautilus
09 Aquitania, Brittania, Brittanic, Cutty Sark, Discovery, Endeavour, Gneisenau, Lusitania, Mayflower, Merrimack, Queen Mary, Sheffield, Terranova, Téméraire

**shipshape**
10 Enterprise, Golden Hind, Hispaniola, Mauretania, Prinz Eugen, Santa Maria
11 Dawn Treader, Dreadnought, Scharnhorst
12 Constitution, Great Britain, Great Eastern, Great Western, Marie Celeste, Old Ironsides
14 Admiral Alabama, Flying Dutchman, Queen Elizabeth
15 Bon Homme Richard, General Belgrano

**shipshape**
04 neat, tidy, trim
07 orderly
12 businesslike, spick-and-span
13 well-organized

**shirk**
04 duck, shun
05 avoid, dodge, evade, slack
08 be truant, get out of
09 play hooky
10 play truant, shrink from

**shirker**
05 idler
06 dodger, loafer, truant
07 quitter, slacker
10 malingerer

**shiver**
05 break, crack, quake, shake, shard, shred, smash, split
06 quiver, sliver, tremor, twitch
07 flutter, shatter, shaving, shudder, tremble, vibrate
08 fragment, splinter
09 palpitate, vibration
11 smithereens

**shivery**
06 chilly
07 chilled, nervous, quaking, quivery, shaking, trembly
08 fluttery, shuddery

**shoal**
04 mass
05 flock, group, horde, swarm
07 sandbar, shallow

**shock**
03 jar
04 blow, daze, jerk, jolt, numb, stun
05 amaze, appal, crash, repel, shake, start, upset
06 appall, dismay, fright, horror, impact, offend, revolt, sicken, trauma
07 agitate, astound, disgust, jarring, outrage, perturb, startle, unnerve
08 bewilder, bowl over, paralyze, surprise

09 bombshell, collision, dumbfound, take aback
10 scandalize, traumatize
13 rude awakening
15 bolt from the blue

**shocking**
07 ghastly, hideous
08 dreadful, horrific
09 appalling, atrocious, frightful, loathsome, monstrous
10 abominable, horrifying, outrageous, scandalous
11 unspeakable

**shoddy**
04 poor
05 cheap, tacky
06 tawdry, trashy
08 inferior, slapdash, slipshod

**shoemaker**
07 cobbler
09 bootmaker

**shoemaking**
08 cobblery, cobbling
10 bootmaking

**shoot**
03 aim, bud, fly, hit, lob, zap
04 bolt, dart, dash, film, fire, grow, hurl, kick, kill, race, rush, slip, snap, tear, twig
05 blast, fling, graft, hurry, scion, shell, speed, sprig, throw, video, whisk, wound
06 branch, charge, direct, hurtle, injure, launch, let off, propel, sprint, sprout, streak
07 bombard, burgeon, cutting, gun down, pick off, project, snipe at, stretch, tendron
08 offshoot, open fire
09 discharge, germinate
10 photograph

**shop**
03 buy, get
05 store
06 market, outlet
07 consume
08 boutique, emporium, purchase
09 buy things, stock up on
10 go shopping
12 retail outlet

**shore**
04 bank, hold, prop, sand, stay
05 beach, brace, coast, front, sands
06 hold up, prop up, strand
07 seaside, shingle, support
08 buttress, lakeside, littoral, seaboard, seashore, underpin

09 foreshore, promenade, reinforce
10 strengthen, waterfront

**shorn**
03 cut
04 bald
06 shaved, shaven
07 crewcut, cropped
08 deprived, stripped

**short**
03 low, shy
04 curt, poor, rude
05 blunt, brief, crisp, gruff, pithy, scant, sharp, small, squat, teeny, terse, tight
06 abrupt, direct, little, meager, petite, scanty, scarce, slight, snappy, sparse, stubby
07 brusque, compact, concise, cursory, summary, uncivil
08 abridged, abruptly, fleeting, pint-size, succinct, suddenly
09 condensed, curtailed, deficient, ephemeral, minuscule, momentary, pint-sized, temporary, truncated
10 diminutive, evanescent, inadequate, summarized, to the point, transitory
11 abbreviated
12 discourteous, insufficient

❑**fall short**
09 be lacking
12 be inadequate
14 be insufficient

❑**in short**
07 in a word, in brief
09 concisely
11 in a few words, in a nutshell

❑**short of**
05 low on, shy of
07 lacking, missing, short on, wanting
08 less than
09 other than, pushed for

**shortage**
04 lack, need, want
06 dearth
07 absence, deficit, paucity, poverty
08 scarcity
10 deficiency, inadequacy
13 insufficiency

**shortcoming**
04 flaw
05 fault
06 defect, foible
07 failing, frailty
08 drawback, weakness
12 imperfection

## shorten

03 cut
04 crop, dock, pare, trim
05 prune
06 lessen, reduce, take up
07 abridge, curtail, cut down
08 condense, contract, decrease, pare down, truncate
10 abbreviate

## shortened

08 abridged
09 condensed
11 abbreviated

## short-lived

05 brief, short
08 caducous, fleeting
09 ephemeral, fugacious, momentary
10 evanescent

## shortly

04 soon
06 curtly
07 by and by, tersely
08 abruptly, directly, in a while
09 presently
10 before long
14 in a little while

## shortsighted

04 rash
05 hasty
06 myopic, unwise
08 careless, heedless
09 impolitic, imprudent
10 ill-advised, unthinking
11 improvident, injudicious, nearsighted, thoughtless

## short-staffed

11 shorthanded
12 understaffed
13 below strength

## short-tempered

05 fiery, testy
06 crusty, touchy
08 choleric
09 impatient, irascible, irritable

## short-winded

07 gasping, panting, puffing
10 breathless

## shot

02 go
03 fix, hit, jab, lob, try
04 ammo, ball, bang, bash, dose, kick, slug, snap, stab, turn
05 blast, crack, fling, image, moiré, photo, print, snort, throw
06 bullet, effort, jigger, pellet

07 attempt, gunfire, missile, mottled, picture
08 endeavor
09 discharge, explosion, injection
10 ammunition, iridescent, photograph, projectile
11 inoculation, vaccination
12 immunization

## ❏call the shots

04 head, lead
06 direct, head up, manage
07 command
09 give a lead, supervise
10 be in charge

## ❏like a shot

06 at once
07 eagerly
09 instantly, willingly
11 immediately

## ❏shot in the arm

05 boost
06 fillip, uplift
08 stimulus

## ❏shot in the dark

05 guess
09 guesswork, wild guess
10 blind guess, conjecture
11 speculation

## shoulder

04 bear, push
05 carry, elbow, force, press, shove
06 accept, assume, jostle, take on, thrust
07 support, sustain

## ❏rub shoulders with

07 mix with
10 hobnob with
13 associate with, socialize with
14 fraternize with

## ❏shoulder to shoulder

07 closely
10 hand in hand, side by side
13 cooperatively

## shout

03 bay, cry
04 bawl, call, howl, roar, yell
05 cheer
06 bellow, cry out, holler, scream, shriek, squawk
07 call out
11 rant and rave
14 raise your voice

## shove

04 jolt, push
05 barge, crowd, drive, elbow, force, press
06 jostle, propel, thrust

## ❏shove off

05 leave, scram
06 beat it, depart
07 get lost, push off, vamoose
08 clear off, clear out
09 skedaddle

## shovel

03 dig
04 heap, move
05 clear, scoop, shift, spade
06 bucket, dredge

## show

03 air
04 expo, fair, lead, mean, sign
05 array, front, guide, movie, prove, steer, teach, usher
06 affair, appear, arrive, attend, depict, direct, escort, expose, façade, parade, set out, turn up
07 clarify, conduct, display, divulge, exhibit, explain, expound, express, panache, pizzazz, portray, present, produce, program, showing, signify, staging, suggest, uncover
08 disclose, indicate, instruct, manifest, point out, register
09 elucidate, exemplify, make clear, make known, operation, spectacle
10 appearance, exhibition, exposition, illustrate, production, profession
11 affectation, demonstrate, flamboyance, ostentation, performance, undertaking
12 extravaganza, presentation
13 entertainment, manifestation
14 representation, window dressing

## ❏show off

04 brag
05 boast, strut, swank
06 flaunt, parade, set off
07 display, enhance, exhibit, swagger
11 demonstrate

## ❏show up

04 come, show
05 shame
06 appear, arrive, expose, reveal, turn up, unmask
07 lay bare, let down, mortify
08 disgrace, pinpoint
09 embarrass, highlight, humiliate
10 put to shame
11 make visible

**showdown**
07 face-off
10 dénouement
13 confrontation, moment of
truth

**shower**
04 fall, hail, heap, load, pour, rain
05 party, spray
06 deluge, lavish, stream, volley
07 barrage, torrent
08 inundate, sprinkle
09 drizzling, overwhelm
10 baby shower, sprinkling
12 bridal shower

**showiness**
05 glitz, swank
06 pizazz
07 glitter, pizzazz
10 flashiness, razzmatazz
11 flamboyance, ostentation
12 razzle-dazzle

**showing**
06 record
07 account, display, staging
08 evidence
10 appearance, exhibition
11 performance, track record
12 presentation
14 representation

**showing-off**
05 swank
07 egotism, swagger
08 boasting, bragging
09 vainglory
10 peacockery
11 braggadocio
13 exhibitionism

**showman**
09 performer, publicist
10 impresario, ringmaster
11 entertainer

**showoff**
05 poser
06 poseur
07 boaster, egotist, know-all,
peacock
08 braggart
09 know-it-all, swaggerer
13 exhibitionist

**showy**
04 loud
05 fancy, flash, gaudy
06 flashy, garish, ornate, swanky,
tawdry
10 flamboyant, glittering
12 ostentatious

**shred**
03 bit, jot, rag
04 atom, chop, iota, mite, tear,
whit

05 cut up, grain, piece, rip up,
scrap, slice, speck, trace,
whisp
06 ribbon, sliver, tatter, tear up
07 modicum, remnant, snippet
08 fragment, particle

**shrew**
03 nag
04 Fury
05 bitch, scold, vixen
06 dragon, virago
08 battle-ax, harridan, spitfire
09 battle-axe, termagant,
Xanthippe

**shrewd**
03 sly
04 keen, wily
05 acute, alert, canny, sharp
06 artful, astute, crafty
07 cunning
10 calculated, discerning
11 calculating, intelligent
14 discriminating

**shrewdly**
05 slyly
06 wisely
07 cannily
08 artfully, astutely, craftily

**shrewdness**
06 acumen, wisdom
08 astucity
09 acuteness, canniness,
sharpness
10 astuteness
11 penetration

**shrewish**
07 nagging
08 captious, scolding, vixenish
10 henpecking
12 faultfinding, sharp-tongued

**shriek**
04 howl, wail, yell
06 cry out, scream, squawk,
squeal
07 screech

**shrill**
04 high
05 acute, sharp
06 treble
08 piercing, strident
11 high-pitched, penetrating
12 earsplitting

**shrine**
04 dome, fane, tope
05 stupa
06 chapel, church, dagoba,
grotto, temple, vimana
09 holy place, sanctuary
10 tabernacle

**shrink**
04 balk, shun
05 baulk, cower, quail, wince
06 cringe, flinch, lessen, narrow,
recoil, reduce, retire, wither
07 atrophy, dwindle, shorten,
shrivel, shy away
08 back away, contract,
decrease, withdraw

**shrivel**
03 dry
04 burn, sear, wilt
05 dry up, parch
06 pucker, scorch, shrink, wither
07 dwindle, frizzle, wrinkle
08 pucker up
09 dehydrate, desiccate

**shriveled**
03 dry
04 sere
07 dried up, wizened
08 puckered, shrunken,
withered, wrinkled
09 emaciated
10 desiccated

**shroud**
04 hide, pall, veil, wrap
05 cloak, cloth, cloud, cover
06 mantle, screen, swathe
07 blanket, conceal, envelop
08 cerement
09 cerecloth
12 grave clothes, winding sheet

**shrouded**
06 hidden, veiled
07 cloaked, clouded, covered,
swathed, wrapped
09 concealed, enveloped

**shrug**
□**shrug off**
06 ignore
07 dismiss, neglect
09 disregard
14 take no notice of

**shrub**

► *Names of shrubs:*
03 ivy
04 hebe, rose
05 broom, holly, lilac, peony
06 azalea, daphne, laurel,
mallow, mimosa, privet
07 boxwood, dogwood,
fuchsia, heather, jasmine
08 buddleia, camellia, clematis,
gardenia, hawthorn,
japonica, laburnum,
lavender, magnolia,
mesquite, musk rose,
viburnum, wistaria

**shrunken**
09 forsythia, hydrangea
10 witch hazel
11 honeysuckle
12 rhododendron
➤ See also PLANT

**shrunken**
05 gaunt
09 emaciated, shriveled
10 cadaverous

**shudder**
05 heave, quake, shake, spasm
06 quiver, shiver, tremor
07 tremble
08 convulse
10 convulsion

**shuffle**
03 mix
04 drag, limp
05 mix up
06 doddle, falter, hobble, jumble, scrape, switch, toddle
07 confuse, scuffle, shamble
08 intermix, jumble up
09 rearrange
10 move around, reorganize

**shun**
05 avoid, elude, evade, spurn
06 eschew, ignore
09 ostracize
11 shy away from
12 coldshoulder, keep away from, steer clear of

**shut**
03 bar
04 bolt, lock, seal, slam
05 close, latch
06 fasten, secure
11 put the lid on

❑**shut down**
04 halt, stop
05 cease, close
07 suspend
09 close down, switch off, terminate
10 inactivate
11 discontinue

❑**shut in**
04 cage
05 box in, hem in
06 cage in, entomb, immure, keep in
07 confine, enclose, fence in
08 imprison, restrain

❑**shut off**
06 cut off
07 isolate, seclude
08 separate
09 segregate

❑**shut out**
03 bar
04 hide, mask, veil
05 blank, cover, debar, exile
06 banish, outlaw, screen
07 conceal, exclude
09 ostracize
13 hold scoreless

❑**shut up**
03 gag
04 hush, jail
05 quiet
06 clam up, coop up, hush up, immure, intern, lock up
07 confine, keep mum, quieten, silence
08 imprison, pipe down
11 incarcerate
14 hold your tongue

**shutter**
05 blind, shade
06 louver, screen
08 jalousie

**shuttle**
03 ply
05 shunt
06 seesaw, travel
09 alternate
10 spacecraft
11 shuttlecock

**shy**
03 coy
05 chary, mousy, timid
06 demure, modest
07 bashful, nervous
08 reserved, reticent, retiring, timorous
09 diffident, inhibited, shrinking, withdrawn
11 embarrassed, introverted
13 self-conscious

❑**fight shy of**
04 shun
05 avoid, spurn
06 eschew
12 steer clear of

❑**shy away**
04 balk, buck, rear
05 avoid, baulk, quail, start, wince
06 flinch, recoil, shrink, swerve
08 back away

**shyness**
07 coyness, modesty
08 timidity
09 mousiness, timidness
10 diffidence

**sibling**
03 sis
04 twin

06 sister
07 brother
12 sister-german
13 brother-german

**sibyl**
04 seer
06 oracle, Pythia
07 seeress
09 pythoness, sorceress, wise woman
10 prophetess

**sick**
03 ill
04 weak
05 angry, black, bored, cruel, fed up, gross, tired, weary
06 ailing, groggy, laid up, poorly, puking, queasy, unwell
07 annoyed, bilious, enraged
08 nauseous, off color, retching, vomiting
09 hacked off, nauseated, tasteless
10 browned off, cheesed off, indisposed, out of sorts
12 sick and tired
15 under the weather

**sicken**
03 get
05 appal, catch, repel
06 appall, pick up, put off, revolt
07 develop, disgust, turn off
08 contract, nauseate
09 succumb to
15 turn your stomach

**sickening**
04 foul, vile
08 nauseous, shocking
09 appalling, loathsome, offensive, repellent, repulsive, revolting
10 disgusting, nauseating, off-putting
11 distasteful
14 stomach-turning

**sickly**
03 wan
04 pale, sick, weak
05 faint, frail, gushy, mushy, soppy, sweet
06 ailing, feeble, infirm, pallid, slushy, syrupy
08 delicate

**sickness**
03 bug
06 malady, nausea, puking
07 ailment, disease, illness
08 disorder, retching, vomiting
09 complaint, ill health
10 affliction, queasiness, throwing up

## side

11 biliousness
13 indisposition

## side

03 end, rim
04 area, bank, camp, edge, face, hand, jamb, sect, team, view, wing
05 angle, brink, cause, facet, flank, limit, minor, party, shore, slant, verge
06 aspect, border, fringe, lesser, margin, region, sector
07 faction, lateral, oblique, profile, section
08 boundary, district, flanking, interest, marginal, sidelong
09 secondary, viewpoint
10 standpoint, subsidiary
11 point of view, subordinate

## ❑ side by side

15 next to each other

## ❑ side with

04 back
05 favor
06 prefer
07 support, vote for
08 join with
09 agree with
10 team up with
13 be on the side of

## sidelong

06 covert
07 oblique
08 indirect, sideward, sideways

## sidestep

05 avoid, dodge, elude, evade, shirk, skirt
06 bypass
10 circumvent

## sidetrack

06 divert
07 deflect, head off
08 distract

## sideways

07 askance, athwart, lateral, oblique, slanted
08 edgeways, edgewise, indirect, sidelong, sideward
09 laterally, obliquely

## sidle

04 edge, inch
05 creep, slink, sneak

## siege

04 bout
07 seizure
08 blockade
11 besiegement
12 encirclement
13 beleaguerment

## siesta

03 nap
04 doze, rest
05 sleep
06 catnap, repose, snooze
10 forty winks, relaxation

## sieve

04 sift, sort
06 filter, remove, riddle, screen, sifter, strain, winnow
08 colander, separate, strainer

## sift

04 sort
06 filter, riddle, strain, winnow
08 pore over, separate

## sigh

04 moan
05 swish
06 exhale, grieve, lament, rustle
07 breathe, suspire, whisper
08 complain
09 susurrate

## ❑ sigh for

04 long, pine, weep
05 mourn, yearn
06 grieve, lament

## sight

03 see
04 espy, look, show, spot, view
05 range, scene
06 behold, fright, glance, seeing, vision
07 eyesore, glimpse, make out, wonders
08 beauties, features, perceive
09 spectacle
10 appearance, exhibition, perception
11 curiosities, distinguish, monstrosity, observation
13 field of vision, range of vision

➤ *Ways of describing sight impairment*:
06 myopic
08 purblind
09 amaurotic, half-blind, sand-blind, snow-blind
10 astigmatic, colorblind, farsighted, night-blind, stone-blind
11 blind as a bat, hemeralopic, longsighted, nearsighted
12 shortsighted

## ❑ catch sight of

03 see
04 mark, note, spot, view
06 look at, notice
07 glimpse, make out
08 identify, perceive

## ❑ lose sight of

04 omit
06 forget, ignore
07 neglect
08 overlook, put aside
09 disregard

## ❑ set your sights on

05 aim at
09 strive for
10 work toward
12 aspire toward

## sightseer

07 tourist, visitor
10 rubberneck, vacationer
12 excursionist
15 visiting fireman

## sign

03 act, nod
04 clue, code, hint, logo, mark, omen, show, wave, wink
05 arrow, badge, board, proof, token, trace, write
06 action, augury, beckon, cipher, emblem, figure, marker, motion, notice, poster, signal, symbol
07 earmark, endorse, express, gesture, initial, placard, pointer, portent, presage, symptom
08 evidence, indicate, inscribe, insignia, movement
09 autograph, character, harbinger, indicator
10 foreboding, indication, suggestion
11 communicate, forewarning, gesticulate
13 gesticulation, manifestation
14 representation
15 prognostication

## ❑ sign over

06 convey
07 consign, deliver, entrust
08 make over, transfer, turn over

## ❑ sign up

04 hire, join
05 enrol
06 employ, engage, enlist, enroll, join up, sign on, take on
07 recruit
08 register
09 volunteer
15 join the services

## signal

03 nod
04 clue, hint, mark, show, sign, wave, wink
05 alert, light, token

06 beacon, beckon, motion, tip-off
07 eminent, express, gesture, message, notable, pointer, signify, symptom, warning
08 evidence, indicate, striking
09 important, momentous
10 impressive, indication, noteworthy, remarkable
11 communicate, conspicuous, gesticulate, outstanding, significant
13 distinguished, extraordinary

**signature**
04 mark, name
05 theme
08 initials
09 autograph, theme song
11 endorsement, inscription, John Hancock

**significance**
04 gist
05 force, point, sense
06 import, matter, weight
07 essence, meaning, message, purport
08 interest
09 magnitude, relevance, solemnity
10 importance
11 consequence, implication, seriousness
12 implications, significance
13 consideration

**significant**
03 key
05 vital
06 marked
07 crucial, fateful, ominous, serious, weighty
08 critical, eloquent, material, pregnant, relevant, symbolic
09 important, memorable, momentous
10 expressive, indicative, meaningful, noteworthy, suggestive

**significantly**
10 noticeably
11 appreciably, perceptibly
12 considerably

**signify**
04 mean, show
05 count, imply
06 convey, denote, matter, signal
07 betoken, declare, exhibit, express, portend, suggest
08 indicate, intimate, proclaim, stand for, transmit
09 represent, symbolize
10 be relevant

11 be important, carry weight, communicate

**signpost**
04 clue, sign
06 marker
07 placard, pointer, symptom
09 guidepost, indicator

**silence**
03 gag
04 calm, hush, lull, mute
05 abate, peace, quell, quiet, still
06 deaden, muffle, muzzle, stifle, subdue
07 quieten, reserve
08 calmness, dumbness, muteness, suppress
09 dumbfound, quietness, reticence, stillness
10 strike dumb
11 tranquility
12 peacefulness

**silent**
03 mum
04 calm, dumb, mute
05 muted, quiet, still, tacit
08 implicit, peaceful, reserved, reticent, taciturn, unspoken, unvoiced, wordless
09 inaudible, noiseless, soundless, voiceless
10 speechless, tongue-tied, understood
11 tightlipped

**silently**
06 calmly, dumbly, mutely
07 quietly, tacitly, unheard
11 noiselessly, soundlessly

**silhouette**
04 form
05 shape
06 shadow
07 contour, outline, profile
08 stand out
09 delineate
11 delineation

**silky**
05 sleek
06 glossy, satiny, silken, smooth
07 velvety

**silly**
04 daft, dope, dopy, fool, rash, soft
05 barmy, dopey, dotty, dumbo, goose, idiot, inane, loony, loopy, ninny, nutty
06 absurd, duffer, stupid, unwise
07 fatuous, foolish, half-wit, idiotic, puerile
08 childish, immature, reckless

09 foolhardy, illogical, imprudent, ludicrous, pointless, senseless, simpleton
10 irrational, ridiculous
11 injudicious, meaningless, thoughtless
12 preposterous, unreasonable
13 irresponsible, unintelligent
14 scatterbrained

**silt**
03 mud
04 ooze
06 sludge
07 deposit, residue
08 alluvium, sediment

❑**silt up**
04 clog
05 block, choke

**silvan**
05 leafy
06 wooded
08 forestal, forested, woodland
09 arboreous, forestine
11 tree-covered

**similar**
04 akin, like
05 alike, close
07 related, uniform
09 analogous
10 comparable, homologous
11 homogeneous, much the same
13 corresponding

**similarity**
07 analogy, kinship
08 likeness, sameness
09 agreement, closeness
10 congruence
11 concordance, homogeneity, resemblance
13 comparability, compatibility
14 correspondence

**similarly**
08 likewise
09 by analogy, uniformly
12 in the same way
14 by the same token
15 correspondingly

**similitude**
07 analogy
08 affinity, likeness, relation, sameness
09 agreement, closeness
10 congruence
11 resemblance
14 correspondence

**simmer**
04 burn, fume, rage, stew
06 bubble, seethe

07 smolder
10 boil gently, cook gently
◻ **simmer down**
06 lessen
07 subside
08 calm down, cool down
**simpering**
03 coy
05 silly
08 affected, giggling, smirking
13 self-conscious
**simple**
04 bald, easy
05 basic, clear, crude, cushy, naïve, plain, silly, stark
06 a cinch, honest, stupid
07 artless, classic, foolish, idiotic, natural, sincere, unfussy
08 backward, innocent, no-frills, ordinary, retarded
09 a pushover, ingenuous, unadorned
10 effortless, elementary, half-witted
11 rudimentary, undecorated
12 a piece of cake, feebleminded
13 uncomplicated, unembellished, unpretentious
14 comprehensible
15 straightforward, unsophisticated
**simple-minded**
05 idiot
07 foolish, moronic, natural
08 imbecile
09 dimwitted
11 addleheaded
12 addlebrained, feebleminded
**simpleton**
04 dolt, dope, fool
05 booby, dunce, idiot, ninny
06 nitwit
07 dullard
08 imbecile, numskull
09 blockhead
**simplicity**
04 ease
06 candor, purity
07 clarity, honesty, naïvety
08 easiness, facility, lucidity, openness
09 frankness, innocence, plainness, restraint, sincerity, starkness
10 clean lines, directness, simpleness
11 artlessness, naturalness
13 guilelessness

14 elementariness
15 intelligibility
**simplify**
07 clarify, explain, unravel
08 make easy, untangle
10 make easier
11 disentangle
**simplistic**
03 pat
05 naïve
06 facile, simple
07 shallow
08 sweeping
14 oversimplified
**simply**
04 just, only
05 quite
06 merely, purely, solely
07 clearly, lucidly, plainly
10 altogether, completely
**simulate**
03 act
04 copy, echo, fake, sham
05 feign, mimic, put on
06 affect, assume, parrot
07 imitate, pretend, reflect
08 parallel
09 duplicate, reproduce
11 counterfeit, make believe
**simulated**
04 fake, mock, sham
05 bogus, phony, put-on
06 pseudo
07 man-made
09 imitation, insincere, pretended, synthetic
10 artificial, substitute
11 inauthentic, make-believe
**simultaneous**
10 concurrent, synchronic
15 contemporaneous
**sin**
04 evil, fall
05 crime, error, fault, guilt, lapse, stray, wrong
07 impiety, misdeed, offense
08 go astray, iniquity, trespass
10 immorality, sinfulness, transgress, wickedness
13 fall from grace, transgression

▶ *The seven deadly sins*:
04 envy, lust
05 anger, greed, pride, sloth
08 gluttony
**sincere**
04 open, pure, real, true
05 frank
06 candid, direct, honest, simple

07 artless, earnest, fervent, genuine, natural, serious, unmixed, up front
08 bona fide, truthful
09 guileless, heartfelt, ingenuous, unfeigned
10 above board, no-nonsense, unaffected
11 plainspoken, trustworthy
12 wholehearted
13 unadulterated
15 straightforward
**sincerely**
05 truly
08 honestly
09 earnestly, genuinely, in earnest
10 truthfully
**sincerity**
05 honor, truth
06 candor
07 honesty, probity
08 openness
09 frankness, integrity
10 directness
11 artlessness, earnestness, genuineness, seriousness, uprightness
12 truthfulness
13 guilelessness, ingenuousness
15 trustworthiness
**sinecure**
04 snap
05 cinch
07 plum job
08 cushy job
10 gravy train, soft option
**sinewy**
04 wiry
06 strong
07 stringy
08 athletic, muscular
**sinful**
03 bad
04 evil
05 wrong
06 erring, fallen, guilty, unholy, wicked
07 corrupt, immoral, impious, ungodly
08 criminal, depraved, wrongful
10 iniquitous
11 irreligious, unrighteous
**sinfulness**
03 sin
05 guilt
07 impiety
08 iniquity, peccancy
09 depravity
10 corruption, immorality, wickedness

**sing**

11 peccability, ungodliness
13 transgression
15 unrighteousness

**sing**
03 hum
04 pipe
05 chant, chirp, croon, trill, yodel
06 inform, intone, quaver, squeel, warble
07 confess
08 serenade, vocalize
14 blow the whistle

◘**sing out**
04 bawl, call, yell
05 shout
06 bellow, cry out, holler

**singe**
04 burn, char, sear
06 scorch
07 blacken

**singer**
➤ See also MUSIC

► *Types of singer*:
04 alto, bass, diva
05 mezzo, tenor
06 cantor, chorus, treble
07 crooner, pop star, soloist, soprano, warbler
08 baritone, castrato, choirboy, falsetto, minstrel, songster, vocalist
09 balladeer, chanteuse, choirgirl, chorister, contralto, pop singer, precentor
10 folk singer, prima donna, songstress, troubadour
11 carol singer, opera singer
12 countertenor, mezzo-soprano
13 basso profundo, country singer

► *Names of classical singers*:
04 **Butt** (Clara), **Lind** (Jenny), **Popp** (Lucia)
05 **Baker** (Janet), **Eames** (Emma), **Evans** (Geraint), **Gigli** (Beniamino), **Lanza** (Mario), **Lenya** (Lotte), **Melba** (Nellie), **Patti** (Adelina), **Pears** (Peter)
06 **Callas** (Maria), **Caruso** (Enrico), **Crooks** (Richard), **Duncan** (Todd), **Farrar** (Geraldine), **Peerce** (Jan), **Steber** (Eleanor), **Tucker** (Richard), **Turner** (Eva), **Warren** (Leonard)
07 **Caballé** (Montserrat), **Domingo** (Plácido), **Ferrier**

(Kathleen), **Hammond** (Joan), **Lehmann** (Lotte), **Nilsson** (Birgit), **Nordica** (Lillian), **Tibbett** (Lawrence), **Traubel** (Helen)
08 **Althouse** (Paul), **Anderson** (Marian), **Carreras** (José), **Ponselle** (Rosa), **Te Kanawa** (Kiri)
09 **Chaliapin** (Fyodor), **Pavarotti** (Luciano)
10 **Söderström** (Elisabeth), **Sutherland** (Joan)
11 **Schwarzkopf** (Elisabeth)

► *Names of folk musicians and singers*:
03 **Gow** (Niel)
04 **Baez** (Joan), **Bain** (Aly)
05 **Dylan** (Bob), **Sharp** (Cecil James)
06 **Denver** (John), **Fisher** (Archie), **Foster** (Stephen Collins), **Fraser** (Marjory Kennedy), **Mackay** (Charles), **Nairne** (Carolina), **Pogues, Runrig, Seeger** (Pete)
07 **Clannad, Gaughan** (Dick), **Guthrie** (Arlo), **Guthrie** (Woody), **MacColl** (Ewan), **Robeson** (Paul), **Skinner** (James Scott), **Thomson** (George)
08 **Rafferty** (Gerry)
09 **Dubliners, Henderson** (Hamish), **Leadbelly, Robertson** (Jeannie)
12 **Kingston Trio**

► *Names of jazz musicians and singers*:
03 **Guy** (Buddy), **Lee** (Peggy), **Ory** (Kid)
04 **Cole** (Nat "King"), **Getz** (Stan), **King** (B. B.), **Monk** (Thelonius), **Pine** (Courtney), **Shaw** (Artie)
05 **Basie** (Count), **Corea** (Chick), **Davis** (Miles), **Evans** (Gil), **Hines** (Earl), **Jones** (Quincy), **Roach** (Max), **Smith** (Bessie), **Sun Ra, Tatum** (Art)
06 **Barber** (Chris), **Bechet** (Sidney), **Blakey** (Art), **Dorsey** (Tommy), **Garner** (Errol), **Gordon** (Dexter), **Herman** (Woody), **Hooker** (John Lee), **Joplin** (Scott), **Kenton** (Stan), **Miller** (Glenn), **Mingus** (Charles), **Morton** (Jelly Roll), **Oliver**

(King), **Parker** (Charlie), **Powell** (Bud), **Simone** (Nina), **Tracey** (Stan), **Walker** (T-Bone), **Waller** (Thomas "Fats"), **Waters** (Muddy)
07 **Bennett** (Tony), **Brubeck** (Dave), **Charles** (Ray), **Coleman** (Ornette), **Goodman** (Benny), **Hampton** (Lionel "Hamp"), **Hancock** (Herbie), **Hawkins** (Coleman), **Holiday** (Billie "Lady Day"), **Hot Five, Ibrahim** (Abdullah), **Jackson** (Milt), **Jarrett** (Keith), **Metheny** (Pat), **Mezzrow** (Mezz), **Rollins** (Sonny), **Shorter** (Wayne), **Vaughan** (Sarah)
08 **Adderley** (Cannonball), **All Stars, Calloway** (Cab), **Coltrane** (John), **Gershwin** (George), **Hot Seven, Marsalis** (Wynton), **Mulligan** (Gerry), **Peterson** (Oscar)
09 **Armstrong** (Louis "Satchmo"), **Dankworth** (John), **Ellington** (Duke), **Gillespie** (Dizzy), **Grappelli** (Stephane), **Leadbelly, Lyttelton** (Humphrey), **Reinhardt** (Django), **Teagarden** (Jack)
10 **Fitzgerald** (Ella), **McLaughlin** (John)
11 **Beiderbecke** (Bix), **Howling Wolf**
12 **Jazz Warriors**

► *Names of pop musicians*:
03 **Eno** (Brian), **Jam, Lee** (Peggy), **Pop** (Iggy), **R.E.M., Yes**
04 **Abba, Baez** (Joan), **Blur, Bush** (Kate), **Cash** (Johnny), **Cher, Cole** (Nat "King"), **Cole** (Natalie), **Como** (Perry), **Cray** (Robert), **Crow** (Sheryl), **Cure, Devo, Dury** (Ian), **Gaye** (Marvin), **Joel** (Billy), **John** (Elton), **Kiss, Lulu, Piaf** (Edith), **Pulp, Reed** (Lou), **Ross** (Diana), **Sade, Seal, Vega** (Suzanne), **Wham!**
05 **Adams** (Bryan), **Berry** (Chuck), **Black** (Cilla), **Bolan** (Marc), **Bowie** (David), **Brown** (James), **Byrds, Carey** (Mariah), **Clash, Cohen** (Leonard),

Darin (Bobby), **Davis** (Sammy, **Doors, Dylan** (Bob), **Ferry** (Bryan), **Flack** (Roberta), **Haley** (Bill, **Horne** (Lena), **James** (Etta), **Jones** (Grace), **Jones** (Tom), **Kinks, Lewis** (Jerry Lee), **Oasis, Queen, Simon** (Paul), **Starr** (Ringo), **Waits** (Tom), **White** (Barry), **Wings, Young** (Neil), **Zappa** (Frank), **ZZ Top,** and the Comets), Jr.)

06 **Bassey** (Shirley), **Buffet** (Jimmy), **Cooper** (Alice), **Crosby** (Bing), **Damned, Denver** (John), **Domino** (Fats), **Jolson** (Al), **Joplin** (Janis), **Knight** (Gladys, **Lennon** (John), **Marley** (Bob), **Midler** (Bette), **Newman** (Randy), **Parton** (Dolly), **Pitney** (Gene), **Pogues, Police, Prince, Richie** (Lionel), **Sedaka** (Neil), **Simone** (Nina), **Smiths, Spears** (Britney), **Summer** (Donna), **The Who, Turner** (Tina), **Wonder** (Stevie), and the Pips)

07 **Beatles, Bee Gees, Bennett** (Tony), **Blondie, Bon Jovi, Charles** (Ray), **Clapton** (Eric), **Cochran** (Eddie), **Collins** (Phil), **Diamond** (Neil), **Diddley** (Bo), **Gabriel** (Peter), **Garland** (Judy), **Genesis, Guthrie** (Woody), **Hendrix** (Jimi), **Hollies, Houston** (Whitney), **Jackson** (Janet), **Jackson** (Michael), **Madonna, Mercury** (Freddie), **Michael** (George), **Minogue** (Kylie), **Monkees, Orbison** (Roy), **Osmonds, Perkins** (Carl), **Pickett** (Wilson), **Presley** (Elvis), **Redding** (Otis), **Richard** (Cliff), **Santana, Shadows, Sinatra** (Frank), **Stevens** (Cat), **Stewart** (Rod), **Vincent** (Gene), **Warwick** (Dionne)

08 **Costello** (Elvis), **Franklin** (Aretha), **Harrison** (George), **Liberace, McEntire** (Reba), **Mitchell** (Joni), **Morrison** (Van), **Oldfield** (Mike), **Van Halen, Vandross** (Luther), **Williams** (Andy), **Williams** (Hank), **Williams** (Robbie)

09 **Aerosmith, Garfunkel** (Art), **Kraftwerk, McCartney** (Paul), **Motorhead, Pink Floyd, Puff Daddy** (and the Family), **Radiohead, Roxy Music, Simply Red, Status Quo, Steely Dan, Streisand** (Barbra), **The Eagles, Thin Lizzy**

10 **Carpenters, Deep Purple, Duran Duran, Eurythmics, Guns N' Roses, Iron Maiden, Moody Blues, Portishead, Pretenders, Sex Pistols, Spice Girls, Stranglers, The Animals**

11 **Armatrading** (Joan), **Culture Club, Dire Straits, Human League, Judas Priest, Led Zeppelin, Public Enemy, Simple Minds, Springfield** (Dusty), **Springsteen** (Bruce), **Temptations, The Drifters**

12 **Black Sabbath, Fleetwood Mac, Grateful Dead, Talking Heads, The Beach Boys, The Big Bopper**

13 **Chubby Checker, Little Richard, Rolling Stones, Spandau Ballet**

14 **Everly Brothers, Pointer Sisters, Public Image Ltd**

15 **Neville Brothers**

**single**
03 one
04 free, lone, only, sole
06 unique
08 distinct, isolated, separate, singular, solitary, unbroken
09 on your own, unmarried
10 individual, one and only, particular, unattached

❏**single out**
06 choose, select
07 isolate
08 identify, pinpoint, separate, set apart
09 highlight
11 distinguish, separate out

**single-handed**
04 solo
05 alone
07 unaided
09 on your own
10 by yourself, unassisted

**single-minded**
03 set
05 fixed
06 dogged

08 resolute, tireless
09 dedicated, obsessive
10 unswerving, unwavering
12 monomaniacal
13 single-hearted

**singly**
06 solely
08 one by one
10 on their own, one at a time, separately
12 individually

**singular**
03 odd
06 unique
07 curious, strange, unusual
08 atypical, peculiar, uncommon
09 eccentric
10 remarkable
11 exceptional, outstanding
13 extraordinary

**singularity**
06 oddity
07 oddness
10 uniqueness
11 peculiarity, strangeness
12 eccentricity, idiosyncrasy
13 particularity
15 black-hole center

**singularly**
08 signally
09 unusually
10 especially, remarkably, uncommonly
12 particularly
13 exceptionally, outstandingly
15 extraordinarily

**sinister**
04 left
06 malign
07 baleful, harmful, ominous
08 menacing
10 malevolent, portentous
11 disquieting, threatening
12 inauspicious

**sink**
03 dig, dip, ebb, lay, sag, set
04 bore, dive, drop, fail, fall, flag, plow, risk, ruin, slip
05 drill, droop, drown, embed, lapse, lower, put in, slump, stoop, wreck
06 engulf, go down, invest, lessen, plunge, weaken, worsen
07 decline, degrade, descend, dwindle, founder, immerse, plummet, scupper, scuttle, subside, succumb
08 collapse, decrease, diminish, submerge

09 disappear, penetrate
10 degenerate, go downhill

**sinless**
04 pure
08 innocent, virtuous
09 faultless, guiltless
11 uncorrupted

**sinner**
08 criminal, evildoer, offender
09 miscreant, reprobate, wrongdoer
10 malefactor
12 transgressor

**sinuous**
06 curved, slinky
07 bending, coiling, curling, curving, turning, winding
08 tortuous, twisting
10 meandering, serpentine, undulating

**sip**
03 sup
05 drink, taste
06 sample
08 mouthful, spoonful

**siren**
04 vamp
05 alarm, Circe
06 tocsin
07 charmer, Lorelei
08 car alarm
09 fire alarm, temptress
10 seductress, smoke alarm
11 femme fatale
12 burglar alarm

**sissy**
04 baby, soft, weak, wimp
05 pansy, softy
06 coward, feeble
07 milksop, unmanly, wimpish
08 cowardly, weakling
09 mommy's boy
10 effeminate, namby-pamby

**sister**
03 nun
04 girl
05 woman
06 abbess, fellow, friend
07 comrade, partner, sibling
08 prioress, relation, relative
09 associate, colleague, companion

**sit**
03 lie
04 hang, hold, meet, pose, rest, seat
05 brood, perch, place, roost, squat, stand
06 gather, locate, settle

07 consult, contain, convene, deposit, situate
08 assemble, position
10 deliberate
11 accommodate, be in session

**sitcom**

► *Names of sitcoms:*
04 MASH, Soap, Taxi
05 Coach, Ellen, Maude
06 Benson, Cheers, Cybill
07 Dream On, Frazier, Friends
08 Get Smart, Roseanne, Seinfeld, Spin City
09 Bewitched, Empty Nest, Gomer Pyle, I Love Lucy
10 Ally McBeal, Family Ties, Green Acres, Night Court
11 Mad About You, Murphy Brown, The Lucy Show
12 Evening Shade, The Cosby Show, The Odd Couple, Will and Grace
13 The Jeffersons, Three's Company
14 All in the Family, Chico and the Man, The Golden Girls, The Wonder Years
15 Father Knows Best, Gilligan's Island, I Dream of Jeannie

**site**
03 lot, put, set
04 area, plot, spot
05 place, scene
06 ground, instal, locate
07 install, setting, situate, station
08 locality, location, position
09 situation

**sitting**
05 spell
06 period
07 hearing, meeting, session
08 assembly
12 consultation

**situate**
05 place
06 instal, locate
07 install, station
08 position

**situation**
03 job
04 case, post, rank, seat, site, spot
05 place, score, setup, state
06 affair, locale, milieu, office, status
07 affairs, climate, picture, setting, station
08 locality, location, position, scenario
09 condition

10 conditions, employment
11 environment, predicament, state of play
12 lie of the land, what's going on
13 circumstances
14 state of affairs

**size**
04 area, bulk, mass
05 range, scale
06 amount, extent, height, length, volume
07 expanse
08 vastness
09 immensity, magnitude
10 dimensions
11 measurement, proportions
12 measurements

❏**size up**
03 eye
04 rate
05 gauge, judge
06 assess
07 measure, weigh up
08 appraise, estimate, evaluate

**sizeable**
11 substantial
12 considerable

**sizzle**
03 fry
04 hiss, spit
07 crackle, frizzle, sputter

**skeletal**
05 drawn, gaunt
06 wasted
07 haggard
08 shrunken
09 emaciated, fleshless
10 cadaverous
11 skin-and-bone
13 hollow-cheeked

**skeleton**
04 plan
05 basic, bones, draft, frame
06 lowest, sketch
07 minimum, outline, support
08 smallest
09 bare bones, framework, structure

**sketch**
04 draw, plan
05 draft, paint
06 depict, design, pencil
07 croquis, diagram, drawing, outline, portray
08 abstract, block out, rough out, skeleton, vignette
09 delineate, represent
11 delineation, description
14 representation

**sketchily**
07 hastily, roughly, vaguely
08 patchily
09 cursorily
11 imperfectly
12 inadequately, incompletely
13 perfunctorily

**sketchy**
05 crude, hasty, rough, vague
06 meager, patchy, slight
07 cursory, scrappy
09 defective, deficient, imperfect
10 inadequate, incomplete, unfinished, unpolished
11 perfunctory, provisional, superficial
12 insufficient

**skier**

───────────────

► *Names of skiers*:
03 **Moe** (Tommy)
04 **Hess** (Erica)
05 **Killy** (Jean Claude), **Lindh** (Hilary), **Mahre** (Phil), **Roffe** (Diann), **Tomba** (Alberto)
06 **Figini** (Michela), **Sailer** (Toni), **Street** (Picabo)
07 **Johnson** (Bill), **Klammer** (Franz), **Nykanen** (Matti)
08 **McKinney** (Tamara), **Stenmark** (Ingemark), **Walliser** (Maria)
09 **Armstrong** (Debbie), **Schneider** (Vreni)
10 **Girardelli** (Marc), **Moser-Proll** (Annemarie), **Zurbriggen** (Pirmin)
► See also SPORT

**skillful, skilful**
04 able, deft, good
05 adept, handy, smart
06 adroit, clever, expert, gifted, versed
07 capable, cunning, skilled, trained
08 masterly, tactical, talented
09 competent, dexterous, efficient, practiced
10 proficient, well-versed
11 experienced
12 accomplished, professional

**skill**
03 art
05 knack
07 ability, finesse, mastery
08 deftness, facility
09 adeptness, expertise, handiness, technique

10 adroitness, cleverness, competence, efficiency, experience, expertness
11 proficiency
14 accomplishment
15 professionalism

**skilled**
04 able, good
05 adept
06 expert, gifted
07 capable, trained
08 masterly, schooled, skillful, talented
09 competent, efficient, practiced, qualified
10 proficient
11 experienced
12 accomplished, professional

**skim**
03 fly
04 sail, scan, skip
05 brush, cream, float, glide, graze, plane, skate, touch
06 bounce
07 run over
08 glance at, separate
09 despumate
10 run through

**skimp**
06 scrimp
09 cut back on, economize
10 cut corners
12 be economical
15 tighten your belt

**skimpy**
04 thin
05 short, small, tight
06 meager, measly, scanty, sparse
09 niggardly
10 inadequate

**skin**
03 pod
04 fell, film, flay, hide, hull, husk, peel, pelt, rind
05 cover, crust, cutis, derma, graze, layer, strip
06 casing, corium, dermis, fleece, scrape
07 coating, cuticle, outside, surface
08 covering, membrane, tegument
09 epidermis
10 integument

❏ **by the skin of your teeth**
06 barely
08 narrowly, only just
10 a near thing
11 a close thing

**skin-deep**
07 outward, shallow, surface
08 external
10 artificial
11 superficial

**skinflint**
05 miser
06 meanie
07 niggard, Scrooge
08 tightwad
11 cheeseparer
12 penny pincher

**skinny**
04 info, lean, thin
05 facts
06 gossip
07 scraggy, scrawny
08 skeletal, underfed
09 emaciated
11 information, skin-and-bone
14 undernourished

**skip**
03 bob, cut, hop
04 dart, jump, leap, miss, omit, pass, race, rush, tear
05 bound, caper, dance, dodge, frisk
06 bounce, cavort, gambol, prance, spring
08 leave out

**skirmish**
05 argue, brawl, brush, clash, fight, mêlée, scrap, set-to
06 affray, battle, combat, dustup, fracas, tussle
07 scuffle
08 argument, conflict
11 altercation
13 confrontation

**skirt**
04 edge
05 avoid, evade, flank
06 border, bypass, circle
07 garment
08 go around
10 circumvent

**skit**
05 spoof
06 parody, satire, sketch
07 takeoff
09 burlesque
10 caricature

**skittish**
07 fidgety, flighty, nervous, playful, restive
09 excitable, frivolous
12 highly strung

**skulduggery**
08 foul play, trickery
09 chicanery, duplicity

13 double-dealing
15 underhandedness

**skulk**
04 hide, lurk
05 prowl, slink, sneak, steal
09 lie in wait, pussyfoot

**sky**
03 air
05 space
06 welkin
07 heavens, the blue
08 empyreal, empyrean, supernal
09 celestial, firmament
10 atmosphere
13 vault of heaven

**slab**
04 hunk, lump
05 block, brick, chunk, piece, slice, wedge

**slack**
03 lax
04 give, idle, lazy, limp, play, slow
05 loose, quiet, shirk
06 excess, leeway, sloppy
07 flaccid, relaxed, sagging
08 inactive, malinger, sluggish
09 negligent
10 neglectful, permissive

**slacken**
❑**slacken off**
04 ease, slow
05 abate, relax
06 lessen, loosen, reduce
07 get less, release
08 decrease, diminish, moderate, slow down
10 take it easy

**slacker**
05 idler
06 loafer
07 dawdler, shirker
08 layabout
10 malingerer
12 clock-watcher

**slake**
04 sate
06 quench, reduce
07 assuage, gratify, satiate, satisfy
10 extinguish

**slam**
03 pan
04 bang, dash, hurl, slap
05 crash, fling, smash, throw, thump
06 attack
07 rubbish, run down

08 denounce
09 criticize
12 pull to pieces, tear to shreds

**slander**
05 smear
06 defame, malign, vilify
07 calumny, obloquy, scandal, traduce
08 badmouth, vilipend
09 aspersion
10 calumniate, defamation, sling mud at
11 mudslinging, traducement
12 vilification
13 smear campaign

**slanderous**
06 untrue
07 abusive
09 aspersive, aspersory, insulting, malicious
10 calumnious, defamatory
12 calumniatory

**slang**
04 cant
05 argot, lingo
06 jargon, patois, patter
09 vulgarism
11 doublespeak
13 colloquialism

**slant**
04 bend, bias, lean, list, ramp, skew, tilt, view, warp
05 angle, pitch, slope, twist
06 camber, shelve
07 distort, incline, leaning
08 attitude, diagonal, gradient
09 prejudice, viewpoint
10 distortion
11 inclination, point of view

**slanting**
05 askew
06 tilted
07 oblique
08 diagonal
11 on an incline

**slap**
03 hit
04 bang, biff, clap, cuff, daub, dead, slam, sock
05 apply, clout, plonk, plumb, plump, punch, right, smack, spank, stick, thump, whack
06 spread, strike, wallop
07 clobber, exactly, plaster, put down, set down
08 directly, straight
09 precisely

❑**slap in the face**
04 blow, snub
06 insult, rebuff, rebuke

07 affront, putdown, repulse
11 humiliation

**slapdash**
04 rash
05 hasty, messy
06 clumsy, sloppy, untidy
07 hurried, offhand
08 careless, slipshod, slovenly
11 perfunctory, thoughtless
14 thrown-together

**slaphappy**
06 casual
08 reckless, slapdash
09 haphazard, hit-or-miss
10 nonchalant
13 irresponsible

**slapstick**
05 farce
09 horseplay
10 buffoonery, knockabout

**slash**
02 ax
03 axe, cut, rip
04 curb, gash, hack, rend, rent, slit, tear
05 knife, prune, score
08 decrease, incision, lacerate

**slatternly**
05 dirty, dowdy
06 frowzy, frumpy, untidy
07 unclean, unkempt
08 slipshod, slovenly, sluttish
10 bedraggled

**slaughter**
04 kill, slay
06 murder
07 butcher, carnage, killing
08 butchery, massacre
09 bloodbath, bloodshed, liquidate
10 annihilate, put to death
11 exterminate

**slave**
04 serf, slog, toil
05 grind, labor, sweat
06 drudge, lackey, menial, thrall, vassal
07 bondman, servant, villein
08 bondsman
09 bondwoman
10 bondswoman
11 bondservant

**slaver**
05 drool
06 drivel, trader
07 dribble, slobber
08 salivate
11 slave trader

**slavery**
04 yoke
06 thrall
07 bondage, serfdom
08 thraldom
09 captivity, servitude, vassalage
11 enslavement, subjugation

**slavish**
03 low
04 mean
06 abject, menial, strict
07 fawning, literal, servile
08 cringing
09 groveling
10 obsequious, submissive
11 deferential, sycophantic

**slay**
04 kill
05 amuse
06 murder, rub out
07 butcher, delight, destroy, execute
08 dispatch, massacre
09 eliminate, slaughter

**slaying**
06 murder
07 killing
08 butchery, dispatch, massacre
09 slaughter
11 destruction, elimination

**sleazy**
05 seedy, tacky
06 crummy, sordid
07 rundown, squalid
12 disreputable

**sleek**
05 shiny, silky
06 glossy, silken, smooth
11 well-groomed

**sleep**
03 nap
04 doze, rest
06 catnap, nod off, repose, siesta, snooze
07 drop off, shuteye, slumber
08 be asleep, crash out, drift off, flake out
09 hibernate
10 fall asleep, forty winks
11 have a snooze, hibernation
14 have forty winks
15 go out like a light

**sleepiness**
06 torpor
07 languor
09 heaviness, oscitancy
10 drowsiness, somnolence

**sleeping**
04 idle

06 asleep
07 dormant, passive, unaware
08 comatose, inactive, off guard
10 slumbering
11 daydreaming, hibernating, inattentive

**sleepless**
05 alert, awake
07 wakeful
08 restless, vigilant, watchful
09 disturbed, insomniac, wide-awake

**sleeplessness**
08 insomnia
11 wakefulness
12 insomnolence

**sleepwalker**
12 noctambulist, somnambulist

**sleepwalking**
12 noctambulism, somnambulism

**sleepy**
04 dull, slow
05 heavy, quiet, still, tired, weary
06 drowsy, torpid
07 languid
08 comatose, hypnotic, peaceful, sluggish
09 lethargic, somnolent, soporific
10 languorous

**sleight of hand**
05 magic, skill
08 artifice, trickery
09 deception, dexterity
10 adroitness
11 legerdemain

**slender**
04 lean, slim, thin, trim
05 faint, scant, small
06 feeble, flimsy, little, meager, remote, scanty, slight, svelte
07 tenuous, willowy
08 graceful
09 sylphlike, willowish
10 inadequate
12 insufficient
14 inconsiderable

**sleuth**
04 dick, tail
06 shadow
07 gumshoe, tracker
09 detective
10 bloodhound, private eye

**slice**
03 cut
04 chop, hunk, part, slab

05 carve, chunk, cut up, piece, sever, share, wafer, wedge, whack
06 divide, rasher, sliver
07 helping, portion, section, segment, tranche
09 allotment

**slick**
04 deft, easy, glib
05 quick, sharp, shiny, silky, sleek, suave
06 adroit, satiny, smarmy, smooth
07 skilful
08 masterly, polished, skillful, unctuous
09 dexterous, efficient, plausible, well-oiled
11 streamlined
12 smooth-spoken
13 smooth-talking, sophisticated, well-organized

**slide**
03 ski
04 drop, fall, skid, skim, slip
05 chute, coast, glide, plane, skate
06 lessen, plunge, worsen
07 decline, plummet, slither
08 decrease
10 depreciate
11 deteriorate
12 transparency
15 playground slide

**slight**
03 cut
04 slim, slur, snub
05 elfin, frail, minor, petty, scant, scorn, small, spurn
06 dainty, ignore, insult, little, minute, modest, offend, paltry, petite, rebuff, subtle
07 affront, despise, disdain, fragile, slender, trivial
08 delicate, rudeness
09 disparage
10 diminutive, negligible
11 discourtesy, unimportant
13 insubstantial, slap in the face
14 kick in the teeth

**slighting**
07 abusive
08 scornful
09 insulting, offensive
10 belittling, disdainful, slanderous
11 disparaging
15 uncomplimentary

**slightly**
04 a bit

**slim**
06 rather
07 a little

**slim**
04 diet, lean, poor, thin, trim
05 faint, scant, small
06 flimsy, little, meager, reduce, remote, scanty, slight, svelte
07 slender, tenuous, willowy
09 go on a diet, sylphlike, willowish
10 inadequate, lose weight

**slime**
03 goo, mud
04 gunk, mess, muck, ooze, yuck

**slimy**
04 miry, oily, oozy
05 muddy
06 greasy, mucous, sludgy, sticky
07 servile, viscous
08 creeping, slippery, toadying, unctuous

**sling**
03 lob, shy
04 band, hang, hurl, loop, toss
05 chuck, fling, heave, pitch, strap, swing, throw
07 bandage, support, suspend
08 catapult
14 alcoholic drink

**slink**
04 lurk, slip
05 creep, prowl, sidle, skulk, sneak, steal

**slinky**
05 sleek
07 sinuous
08 clinging
09 skintight
12 close-fitting
13 figure-hugging

**slip**
04 fall, flub, note, sink, skid, slim, trip, wear
05 boner, error, fault, glide, jupon, lapse, mix-up, paper, skate, slide, slink, slump, snafu, steal, strip
06 boo-boo, coupon, goof up, howler, kirtle, plunge, slight, worsen
07 blooper, blunder, decline, failure, get into, go to pot, mistake, slender, slither, take off, voucher
08 decrease, omission
09 oversight, petticoat
10 change into, underskirt
11 certificate, deteriorate

12 indiscretion
15 lose your balance, lose your footing

❏**give someone the slip**
04 duck
05 dodge
08 shake off
10 escape from

❏**let slip**
04 leak, tell
06 betray, let out, reveal
07 divulge

❏**slip up**
03 err
04 goof
05 botch, fluff
06 bungle, cock up, goof up, mess up
07 blunder, stumble
08 get wrong
10 pull a boner
11 make a boo-boo, miss the boat
12 miscalculate

**slipper**
04 mule, pump
05 thong
06 loafer, sandal
08 flip-flop, moccasin, pantofle
09 pantoffle

**slippery**
03 icy, wet
04 foxy, oily
05 slimy
06 clever, crafty, greasy, shifty, smooth
07 cunning, devious, evasive
09 deceitful, dishonest
10 perfidious, unreliable
11 duplicitous, treacherous
13 untrustworthy

**slipshod**
03 lax
06 casual, sloppy, untidy
08 careless, slapdash, slovenly
09 negligent

**slip-up**
04 flub, slip
05 error, fault, mix-up, snafu
06 boo-boo, goof-up, howler, mishap
07 blooper, blunder, mistake
09 oversight

**slit**
03 cut, rip
04 gash, rend, rent, tear, vent
05 knife, lance, slash, slice, split
06 pierce
07 fissure, opening
08 aperture, incision

**slither**
04 skid, slip, worm
05 creep, slide, snake

**sliver**
04 chip
05 flake, piece, scrap, shard, shred, slice, wafer
06 paring, shiver
07 shaving
08 fragment, splinter

**slob**
03 oaf, pig
04 boor, clod, lout
06 sloven

**slobber**
05 drool
06 drivel, slaver
07 dribble
08 salivate

**slog**
04 bash, belt, hike, plod, slug, sock, toil, trek, work
05 grind, labor, slave, slosh, thump
06 effort, trudge
08 exertion, struggle
11 plow through

**slogan**
05 motto
06 jingle, war cry
09 battle cry, catchword, watchword
11 catch phrase, rallying cry

**slop**
05 slosh, spill
08 overflow, splatter

**slope**
03 dip, tip
04 drop, fall, lean, rise, tilt
05 pitch, slant
07 incline

❏**slope off**
08 slip away, sneak off

**sloping**
05 askew
06 angled
07 beveled, canting, leaning, oblique, tilting
08 inclined, slanting
09 inclining
11 acclivitous, declivitous

**sloppy**
03 wet
05 corny, gushy, hasty, messy, mushy, runny, soggy, soppy
06 clumsy, sickly, slushy, watery
07 hurried, splashy
08 careless, slapdash, slipshod, slovenly

09 hit-or-miss, schmaltzy
11 sentimental

**slosh**
04 pour, slap, slog, slop, wade
05 plash, slush
06 splash
08 splatter

**slot**
03 fit, gap, put
04 hole, slit, spot, time, vent
05 crack, niche, notch, place, space
06 assign, groove, insert, instal, window
07 channel, install, opening, vacancy
08 aperture, position
10 pigeonhole
11 slot machine

**sloth**
06 torpor
07 inertia
08 idleness, laziness
09 fainéance, indolence

**slothful**
04 idle, lazy
06 torpid
07 work-shy
08 fainéant, inactive, indolent

**slouch**
04 bend, loll
05 droop, hunch, slump, stoop
06 lounge
07 shamble, shuffle

**slovenly**
05 dirty, messy
06 sloppy, untidy
07 scruffy, unclean, unkempt
08 careless, slipshod, sluttish
10 slatternly
12 disorganized

**slow**
04 curb, dull, dumb, late, lazy
05 brake, check, delay, quiet, slack, tardy, thick
06 averse, ease up, hold up, retard, stupid
07 gradual, tedious
08 creeping, dilatory, handicap, keep back, measured, plodding, retarded, sluggish, stagnant
09 ponderous, prolonged, unhurried, unwilling
10 decelerate, dull-witted, protracted, slow-witted, uneventful
11 reduce speed
12 long-drawn-out

13 at a snail's pace, time-consuming
14 put the brakes on

**slowly**
05 largo, lento
06 adagio, lazily
09 by degrees, larghetto
10 ploddingly, sluggishly
11 ponderously, unhurriedly
13 at a snail's pace
14 little by little

**sludge**
03 mud
04 gunk, mire, muck, ooze, silt, slag, slop
05 dregs, slime, slush, swill
07 residue
08 sediment

**sluggish**
04 dull, idle, lazy, slow
06 torpid
07 languid
08 inactive, indolent, lifeless, listless, slothful
09 apathetic, lethargic
10 languorous, slow-moving

**sluggishness**
06 apathy, phlegm, torpor
07 inertia, languor
08 dullness, lethargy, slowness
09 indolence, lassitude
10 drowsiness, stagnation
12 listlessness, slothfulness

**sluice**
04 gate, wash
05 canal, drain, flush, slosh, swill
06 drench
07 channel
08 irrigate
09 floodgate

**slum**
06 ghetto
07 skid row

**slumber**
03 nap
04 doze, rest
05 sleep
06 drowse, repose, snooze
10 forty winks

**slummy**
07 decayed, rundown, squalid
08 wretched
10 ramshackle

**slump**
03 low, sag
04 bend, fail, fall, flop, loll, sink
05 crash, droop, slide
06 plunge, slouch, trough
07 decline, plummet, subside

08 collapse, downturn, nose dive
09 recession
10 depression

**slur**
05 libel, smear, stain
06 insult, slight, stigma
07 affront, calumny, slander
08 disgrace, innuendo
09 aspersion, discredit
11 insinuation

**slush**
04 gush, mush, pulp, snow
06 drivel
08 schmaltz
10 sloppiness
11 mawkishness
14 sentimentality

**slut**
04 drab, tart
05 bitch
06 hooker, sloven
07 floosie, trollop
08 slattern
10 loose woman, prostitute

**sly**
04 foxy, wily
05 canny, smart
06 artful, astute, covert, crafty, shifty, shrewd, sneaky, subtle, tricky
07 devious, furtive
08 guileful, scheming, stealthy
09 conniving, underhand

❑**on the sly**
07 on the q.t.
08 covertly, in secret
09 furtively, in private

**smack**
03 box, hit
04 bang, belt, blow, clap, cuff, dash, hint, slap, tang, thud, zest
05 crash, evoke, punch, savor, spank, speck, taste, tinge, touch, trace, whack, whiff
06 flavor, hint at, nuance, relish, strike, thwack
07 exactly, savor of, suggest
08 directly, piquancy, straight
09 precisely
11 bring to mind, remind you of

❑**smack your lips**
05 savor
06 relish
09 delight in, drool over

**small**
03 wee
04 mean, mini-, poky, puny, tiny
05 minor, petty, short, teeny

**06** little, meager, minute, paltry, petite, pocket, slight
**07** ashamed, compact, trivial
**08** degraded, pintsize, trifling
**09** miniature, minuscule, pintsized
**10** diminutive, humiliated, inadequate, negligible
**11** microscopic, unimportant
**13** insignificant

**small-minded**
**04** mean
**05** petty, rigid
**06** biased
**07** bigoted, insular
**09** parochial
**12** narrow-minded

**smalltime**
**05** minor, petty
**08** piddling

**smart**
**03** nip
**04** ache, burn, chic, cool, hurt, neat, posh, tidy, trim
**05** acute, sharp, sting, throb
**06** astute, bright, clever, dapper, glitzy, modish, shrewd, snazzy, spruce, tingle, twinge
**07** elegant, stylish
**11** fashionable, intelligent, presentable, well-dressed, well-groomed

**smart aleck, smart alec**
**07** know-all, wise guy
**08** wiseacre
**09** know-it-all
**11** smarty-pants

**smarten**
**05** clean, groom
**06** neaten, polish
**08** spruce up

**smash**
**03** hit, run
**04** bang, bash, bump, dash, ruin
**05** break, crack, crash, crush, drive, knock, prang, thump, wreck
**06** defeat, pileup, strike
**07** collide, destroy, shatter
**08** accident, demolish
**09** collision, pulverize
**12** disintegrate

**smashing**
**05** great, super
**08** fabulous, terrific
**09** excellent, fantastic, first-rate, wonderful
**10** first-class, tremendous

**smattering**
**04** dash

**07** handful, modicum
**09** rudiments
**10** sprinkling

**smear**
**03** rub
**04** blot, coat, daub, slap, slur, spot
**05** cover, libel, patch, stain, sully, taint
**06** blotch, defame, malign, smudge, spread, streak, vilify
**07** blacken, obloquy, slander, tarnish
**08** badmouth
**09** aspersion
**10** calumniate, defamation
**11** mudslinging

**smell**
**04** nose, odor, reek
**05** aroma, savor, scent, sniff, snuff, stink, trace, whiff
**06** stench
**07** perfume
**08** mephitis

**smelly**
**03** bad
**04** foul, high
**05** fetid
**06** putrid
**07** noisome, reeking
**08** mephitic, stinking
**10** malodorous

**smile**
**04** beam, grin, leer
**05** smirk, sneer
**06** simper

**smirk**
**04** grin, leer
**05** sneer

**smitten**
**07** charmed, plagued
**08** enamored
**09** afflicted
**10** bowled over, captivated, infatuated

**smog**
**03** fog
**04** haze, mist
**05** fumes, smaze, smoke
**07** pea soup
**09** pollution
**11** fog and smoke

**smoke**
**03** dry, fog, gas
**04** cure, pipe, puff, smog
**05** cigar, fumes
**07** cigaret, light up, smolder
**08** fumigate, preserve
**09** cigarette

**smoky**
**04** dark, gray, hazy
**05** black, foggy
**06** cloudy, smoggy

**smolder**
**04** boil, burn, rage
**06** fester, seethe, simmer
**12** be suppressed

**smooth**
**04** calm, ease, easy, even, flat, glib, help, iron, roll, sand
**05** allay, flush, level, plane, press, sleek, slick, suave
**06** assist, glassy, pacify, polish, silken, soothe, steady, urbane
**07** appease, assuage, even out, flatten, mollify, plaster, rub down, velvety
**08** calm down, mitigate, palliate, polished, tranquil
**09** alleviate, burnished, encourage, plausible
**10** effortless, facilitate, make easier, persuasive
**11** like a mirror, trouble-free, undisturbed
**12** ingratiating, plain sailing
**13** overconfident, sophisticated, uninterrupted

**smoothly**
**06** calmly, easily, evenly, mildly
**07** equably
**08** fluently
**10** peacefully, tranquilly
**12** effortlessly

**smoothness**
**04** ease, flow
**07** fluency
**08** calmness, evenness, facility
**10** efficiency, regularity

**smooth-talking**
**04** glib
**05** bland, slick, suave
**06** facile, smooth
**09** plausible
**10** persuasive
**12** smooth-spoken
**13** silver-tongued

**smother**
**04** damp
**05** choke, cover, snuff
**06** dampen, muffle, put out, stifle
**07** repress
**08** suppress
**09** overwhelm, suffocate
**10** asphyxiate, extinguish

**smudge**
**04** blot, blur, daub, mark, soil, spot

**smug**
05 dirty, smear, stain
06 blotch, smutch, streak
07 blacken, blemish
08 besmirch

**smug**
08 priggish, superior
10 complacent
13 self-righteous, self-satisfied
14 holier-than-thou

**smuggler**
04 mule
06 runner
09 gunrunner, rumrunner
10 bootlegger, moonshiner
13 contrabandist

**smutty**
04 blue, lewd, racy
05 bawdy, crude, dirty
06 ribald, risqué, vulgar
07 obscene, raunchy
08 improper, indecent, off-color, prurient
09 salacious
10 indelicate, suggestive

**snack**
04 bite
06 tidbit
07 nibbles
08 sandwich
09 bite to eat, light meal
12 refreshments

**snag**
04 hole, tear
05 catch, hitch
07 problem
08 drawback, obstacle
10 difficulty
12 complication
14 stumbling block

**snake**

► *Types of snake*:
03 asp, boa
05 adder, cobra, mamba, racer, viper
06 python, taipan
07 rattler
08 anaconda, moccasin, pit viper
09 bullsnake, king cobra, puff adder, tree snake
10 copperhead, coral snake, fer-de-lance, grass snake, green snake, sidewinder, water snake
11 cottonmouth, diamondback, garter snake, gopher snake, indigo snake, rattlesnake, smooth snake
13 water moccasin
14 boa constrictor

➤ See also ANIMAL

**snap**
03 nip
04 bark, bite, film, grip, shot, span, take, time
05 break, catch, crack, flick, grasp, growl, photo, print, seize, shoot, snarl, spell, split, still, stint
06 abrupt, bark at, fillip, period, record, retort, snatch, sudden
07 crackle, growl at, instant, picture, snarl at, stretch
08 fracture, separate, snapshot, splinter
09 immediate, lash out at, on-the-spot
10 photograph
14 speak sharply to

❑**snap up**
03 nab
04 grab
05 grasp, pluck, seize
06 pick up, snatch
08 pounce on

**snappy**
04 chic, edgy
05 brisk, cross, natty, quick, smart, testy
06 lively, snazzy, touchy, trendy
07 brusque, stylish
09 crotchety, energetic, irascible, irritable
11 bad-tempered, fashionable
13 quick-tempered

**snare**
03 gin, net
04 drum, trap, wire
05 catch, noose, seize
06 entrap
07 capture, ensnare, springe

**snarl**
04 bark, howl, knot, snap, yelp
05 growl, ravel, twist
06 enmesh, tangle
07 confuse, embroil, entwine
08 complain, entangle
10 complicate

**snatch**
03 bag, nab
04 gain, grab, grip, pull
05 grasp, pluck, seize, steal, swipe, wrest
06 abduct, kidnap, wrench
07 section, segment, snippet
08 fragment
11 make off with

**snazzy**
05 jazzy, ritzy, showy, smart

**sneak**
03 pad, rat
04 lurk, mole, sing, slip
05 creep, prowl, rat on, slink, split, steal
06 covert, fink on, secret, snitch, squeal
07 furtive, smuggle, stool on
08 inform on, informer, squealer, telltale
09 tell tales
13 whistleblower

**sneaking**
06 hidden, secret
07 furtive, lurking, nagging
08 grudging, unvoiced
09 intuitive
11 unexpressed
13 surreptitious, uncomfortable

**sneaky**
03 low, sly
04 base, mean
05 nasty, shady, snide
07 devious, furtive, lowdown
08 cowardly, guileful, slippery
09 deceitful, malicious
12 unscrupulous
13 double-dealing, untrustworthy

**sneer**
04 gibe, jeer, mock
05 laugh, scoff, scorn, taunt
06 deride, insult, slight
07 disdain, mockery
08 derision, ridicule
10 look down on

**snicker**
05 laugh, sneer
06 giggle, titter
07 chortle, chuckle, snigger

**snide**
04 mean
05 nasty
06 biting, unkind
07 jeering, mocking
08 derisive, scathing, scoffing, spiteful, taunting
09 malicious, sarcastic

**sniff**
04 hint, nose
05 aroma, scent, smell, snuff, trace, whiff
06 inhale
07 breathe, snuffle
10 suggestion
11 get a whiff of

❑**sniff at**
04 mock, shun

**sniffy**
05 spurn
06 deride, refuse, reject, slight
07 disdain, dismiss, laugh at, scoff at, sneer at

**sniffy**
06 snobby
07 haughty
08 scoffing, scornful, sneering, snobbish, superior
10 disdainful
12 supercilious

**snigger**
05 laugh, smirk, sneer
06 giggle, titter
07 chortle, chuckle, snicker

**snip**
03 bit, cut
04 clip, crop, trim
05 piece, prune
07 snippet
08 clipping, fragment

**snippet**
03 bit
04 part
05 piece, scrap, shred
06 snatch
07 cutting, portion, section, segment
08 clipping, fragment, particle

**snivel**
03 cry, sob
04 bawl, blub
05 sniff, whine
07 sniffle, snuffle

**sniveling**
06 crying
07 whining
09 sniffling, snuffling

**snobbery**
04 airs, side
09 arrogance, loftiness
10 pretension, snootiness, uppishness
11 haughtiness, superiority
13 airs and graces

**snobbish**
05 lofty, proud
06 snooty, uppity
07 haughty, stuck-up
08 affected, superior
10 hoity-toity
11 pretentious
12 supercilious
13 high and mighty

**snoop**
03 pry, spy
04 poke
05 prowl
07 meddler, Paul Pry, snooper

08 busybody, meddling
09 interfere
10 nose around
12 interference
15 stick your nose in

**snooper**
03 pry, spy
05 snoop
07 meddler, Paul Pry

**snooze**
03 nap
04 doze
05 sleep
06 catnap, nod off, siesta
07 drop off, shut-eye, slumber
14 have forty winks

**snout**
04 beak, nose
05 snoot, trunk
06 hooter, muzzle
07 schnozz
09 proboscis, schnozzle
10 schnozzola

**snow**
05 drift, sleet, slush
08 blizzard

**snub**
03 cut
04 shun
06 ignore, insult, slight
07 affront, mortify
12 coldshoulder
13 slap in the face

**snug**
04 cozy, warm
05 comfy, tight
06 homely, secure
08 friendly, intimate
09 sheltered, skintight
11 comfortable
12 closefitting

**snuggle**
06 cozy up, cuddle, curl up, nestle, nuzzle

**soak**
03 wet
05 bathe, imbue, souse, steep
06 drench, infuse
07 immerse
08 marinate, permeate, saturate, submerge
09 penetrate

**soaking**
06 soaked, sodden
07 sopping
08 drenched, dripping, wringing
09 saturated, streaming
10 sopping wet, wet through

11 waterlogged

**soap opera**

➤ *Names of soap operas:*
08 Passions, Somerset
09 Ryan's Hope
10 Love of Life, The Doctors
11 Dark Shadows
12 Another World, Guiding Light, Santa Barbara
13 All My Children, Bright Promise, One Life to Live
14 Days of Our Lives, The Edge of Night
15 As the World Turns, General Hospital

**soar**
03 fly
04 rise, wing
05 climb, glide, tower
06 ascend, rocket, spiral
07 take off
08 escalate
09 skyrocket

**sob**
03 cry
06 boohoo, snivel
07 blubber

**sober**
03 dry
04 calm, dark, drab
05 grave, plain, quiet, staid
06 sedate, serene, solemn, somber, steady
07 serious, subdued
08 composed, rational
09 abstinent, dignified, practical, realistic, temperate
10 abstemious, on the wagon, restrained, thoughtful
14 self-controlled

**sobriety**
07 gravity
08 calmness
09 composure, restraint, solemnity, staidness
10 abstinence, temperance
14 abstemiousness

**so-called**
07 alleged, nominal, would-be
08 supposed
09 professed, soi-disant
10 self-styled

**sociability**
10 affability, chumminess
12 congeniality, conviviality, friendliness
14 gregariousness

**sociable**
06 chummy, genial

07 affable
08 familiar, friendly, outgoing
09 convivial
10 gregarious
13 companionable

**social**
03 bee
04 ball
05 civic, dance, group, party
06 common, public, soiree
07 cordial, general
09 community, gathering, reception
11 get-together
13 entertainment

**socialism**
07 leftism, Marxism
08 Leninism
09 communism, Stalinism, welfarism
10 Trotskyism

**socialist**
03 red
06 commie, leftie
07 leftist
08 left-wing
09 communist
10 left-winger, Trotskyist, Trotskyite

**socialize**
03 mix
05 party
06 hobnob, mingle
09 entertain
10 be sociable, meet people
11 get together

**society**
04 band, body, club
05 elite, group, guild, union
06 circle, gentry, league, nation, people, public, swells
07 company, culture, mankind
08 alliance, humanity, sorority
09 community, human race, humankind
10 federation, fellowship, fraternity, friendship, population, sisterhood
11 aristocracy, association, brotherhood, camaraderie, corporation, high society, the smart set
12 civilization
13 companionship, the upper class, the upper crust

**sodden**
03 wet
05 boggy, soggy
06 marshy, soaked
09 saturated
11 waterlogged

**soft**
03 dim, lax, low
04 easy, kind, mild, pale, weak
05 bland, cushy, downy, faint, furry, light, mushy, muted, pulpy, quiet, silky, sweet
06 dulcet, fleecy, gentle, hushed, low-key, mellow, pastel, pliant, silken, smooth, spongy, tender
07 diffuse, ductile, elastic, flowing, lenient, liberal, plastic, pliable, squashy, squishy, subdued, velvety
08 delicate, low-keyed, merciful, soothing, squelchy, tolerant, yielding
09 easygoing, forgiving, indulgent, malleable, sensitive, spineless
10 forbearing, restrained
11 comfortable, softhearted, sympathetic
12 affectionate

**soft drink**
03 pop
04 cola, soda
08 beverage
15 carbonated drink

**soften**
03 pad
04 calm, ease, melt
05 abate, lower, quell, relax, still
06 lessen, muffle, reduce, soothe, subdue, temper
07 appease, assuage, cushion, lighten, liquefy, mollify
08 diminish, mitigate, moderate, palliate
09 alleviate

❑**soften up**
04 melt
06 disarm, weaken
07 win over
08 butter up, soft-soap
10 conciliate

**softhearted**
06 gentle, tender
11 sentimental, sympathetic, warmhearted
12 affectionate
13 compassionate

**soft-pedal**
06 go easy, subdue
08 moderate, play down, tone down

**soft spot**
08 penchant, weakness
10 partiality

**soggy**
03 wet
04 damp
05 boggy, heavy, moist, pulpy
06 soaked, sodden, spongy
11 waterlogged

**soil**
04 clay, dirt, dust, foul, land, loam, spot
05 dirty, earth, humus, muddy, smear, stain, sully
06 defile, ground, region, smudge
07 begrime, country, pollute, tarnish
08 besmirch
09 territory
10 terra firma

**soiled**
05 dirty, grimy
07 spotted, stained, sullied
08 maculate, polluted

**sojourn**
04 rest, stay, stop
05 abide, lodge, tarry, visit
06 reside
08 stopover
13 peregrination

**solace**
05 allay, cheer
06 relief, soften, soothe
07 comfort, console
10 condolence
11 alleviation, consolation

**soldier**
➤ See also MILITARY

▶ *Types of soldier*:
02 GI
03 NCO
05 cadet, grunt
06 gunner, hussar, lancer, marine, sapper, sentry
07 dogface, draftee, dragoon, fighter, officer, orderly, private, recruit, regular, trooper, warrior
08 commando, doughboy, fusilier, partisan, rifleman
09 centurion, conscript, guardsman, guerrilla, mercenary, reservist
10 cavalryman, Green Beret, serviceman
11 enlisted man, infantryman, legionnaire, paratrooper, Territorial

▶ *Names of soldiers*:
03 **Cid** (El), **Lee** (Robert Edward), **Ney** (Michel), **Wet**

(Christian de), **Zia**
(Muhammad)
04 Cade (Jack), **Foch**
(Ferdinand), **Haig**
(Alexander), **Haig**
(Douglas), **Jodl** (Alfred),
**John** (Don), **Khan** (Ayub),
**Röhm** (Ernst),**Tojo** (Hideki)
05 **Allen** (Ethan), **Bader**
(Douglas), **Botha** (Louis),
**Bowie** (James), **Bruce**
(Robert), **Cimon**, **Clive**
(Robert), **Dayan** (Moshe),
**Essex** (Robert Devereux),
**Gates** (Horatio), **Grant**
(Ulysses Simpson), **Inönü**
(Ismet), **Monck** (George),
**Murat** (Joachim), **Perón**
(Juan), **Pride** (Thomas),
**Smuts** (Jan), **Sucre**
(Antonio José de), **Sully**
(Maximilien de Béthune
Duc de),**Timur**, **Zhu De**
06 **Antony** (Mark), **Arnold**
(Benedict), **Brutus** (Marcus
Junius), **Caesar** (Julius),
**Cortés** (Hernán), **Custer**
(George Armstrong),
**Edward** (the Black Prince),
**Egmont** (Graaf van Gavre),
**Eugene** (of Savoy), **Franco**
(Francisco), **Gaulle**
(Charles de), **Gordon**
(Charles George), **Granby**
(John Manners), **Greene**
(Nathanael), **Marius**
(Gaius), **Moltke** (Helmuth),
**Napier** (Robert), **Nasser**
(Gamal Abd al-), **Patton**
(George), **Pétain** (Philippe),
**Pompey**, **Raglan** (Fitzroy
James Henry Somerset),
**Revere** (Paul), **Rommel**
(Erwin), **Rupert** (Prince),
**Scipio** (Publius Cornelius),
**Zhukov** (Giorgiy)
07 **Agrippa** (Marcus
Vipsanius), **Allenby**
(Edmund), **Atatürk**
(Mustapha Kemal),
**Baldwin**, **Blücher** (Gebbard
Leberecht von Fürst von),
**Bourbon** (Charles), **Boycott**
(Charles Cunningham),
**Bradley** (Omar Nelson),
**Cassius**, **Coligny** (Gaspard
de), **Dreyfus** (Alfred),
**Farnese** (Alessandro),
**Gaddafi** (Muammar),
**Gemayel** (Bashir), **Jackson**
(Thomas Jonathan),
**Kutuzov** (Mikhail),
**Lambert** (John), **Maurice**

(Prince), **Metaxas**
(Ioannis), **Pizarro**
(Francisco), **Ptolemy**,
**Sherman** (William
Tecumseh),**Tancred**,
**Warwick** (Richard Neville),
**William** (Prince of Orange)
08 **Agricola** (Gnaeus Julius),
**Antonius** (Marcus),
**Arminius**, **Badoglio**
(Pietro), **Bentinck**
(William), **Boadicea**,
**Burnside** (Ambrose
Everett), **Campbell** (Colin),
**Cardigan** (James Thomas
Brudenell), **Cromwell**
(Oliver), **Eichmann** (Adolf),
**Harrison** (William Henry),
**Hereward** (the Wake),
**Horrocks** (Brian), **Ironside**
(William), **Itúrbide**
(Agustín de), **Lawrence**
(Thomas Edward),
**Lucullus** (Lucius Licinius),
**Marshall** (George Catlett),
**Mengistu** (Haile Mariam),
**Montfort** (Simon de),
**Montrose** (James Graham),
**Napoleon**, **Pershing** (John
Joseph), **Potemkin**
(Grigoriy), **Seleucus**,
**Sheridan** (Philip Henry),
**Sikorski** (Wladyslaw),
**Stanhope** (James),
**Tokugawa** (Ieyasu),
**Wolseley** (Garnet),
**Xenophon**,**Yamagata**
(Prince Aritomo)
09 **Alexander** (Harold),
**Antonescu** (Ion),
**Bonaparte** (Jérôme),
**Carausius** (Marcus
Aurelius Mausaeus),
**Cavendish** (William),
**Gneisenau** (August),
**Hasdrubal**, **Hideyoshi**
(Toyotomi), **Kim Il-sung**,
**Kitchener** (Herbert),
**Lafayette** (Marie Joseph),
**MacArthur** (Douglas),
**Miltiades**, **Spartacus**
10 **Abercromby** (Ralph),
**Alanbrooke** (Alan Francis
Brooke), **Alcibiades**,
**Auchinleck** (Claude),
**Belisarius**, **Clausewitz**
(Karl von), **Cumberland**
(William Augustus),
**Eisenhower** (Dwight
David), **Germanicus**,
**Hindenburg** (Paul von),
**Karageorge**, **Montgomery**

(Bernard), **Schlieffen**
(Alfred), **Stroessner**
(Alfredo),**Washington**
(George),**Wellington**
(Arthur Wellesley)
11 **Baden-Powell** (Robert),
**Black Prince**, **Genghis
Khan**, **Marlborough** (John
Churchill), **Mohammed Ali**,
**Münchhausen** (Baron von)
12 **Ptolemy Soter**,
**Stauffenburg** (Claus, Graf
Neithardt von)
13 **Fabius Maximus** (Quintus)
15 **Scipio Africanus** (Publius
Cornelius), **Seleucus
Nicator**

◻**soldier on**
06 hold on, keep on
08 continue, keep at it, plug
away
09 keep going, persevere, stick
at it

**sole**
03 one
04 fish, lone, only
06 single, unique
08 singular, solitary
10 individual

**solecism**
05 boner, error, gaffe, lapse
06 boo-boo, howler
07 blooper, blunder, faux pas,
mistake
08 cacology
09 gaucherie
11 anacoluthon, incongruity

**solely**
04 only
05 alone
06 merely, singly
08 entirely, uniquely
11 exclusively

**solemn**
04 glum
05 grave, sober
06 formal, somber
07 earnest, genuine, pompous,
serious, sincere, stately
08 imposing, majestic
09 dignified, venerable
10 ceremonial, thoughtful
11 ceremonious, reverential
12 awe-inspiring

**solemnity**
04 rite
06 ritual
07 dignity, gravity
08 ceremony, grandeur, sanctity
10 ceremonial, observance

**solemnize**
11 celebration, formalities, proceedings

**solemnize**
05 honor
07 dignify, observe
09 celebrate

**solicit**
03 ask, beg, sue
04 pray, seek, tout
05 apply, crave, plead
06 ask for, hustle
07 canvass, request
08 apply for, petition
09 importune

**solicitor**
06 lawyer
07 counsel
08 advocate, attorney
10 petitioner

**solicitous**
05 eager
06 caring, uneasy
07 anxious, worried, zealous
08 troubled
09 attentive, concerned
12 apprehensive

**solicitude**
04 care
07 concern
13 attentiveness, consideration

**solid**
04 firm, hard, pure, real
05 dense, sound, thick, valid
06 cogent, decent, stable, strong, sturdy, trusty, worthy
07 compact, durable, genuine, unmixed, upright, weighty
08 concrete, reliable, sensible, tangible, unbroken
09 steadfast, well-built
10 continuous, dependable, unshakable
11 levelheaded, long-lasting, respectable, substantial, trustworthy, well-founded
12 well-grounded
13 authoritative

**solidarity**
05 unity
06 accord
07 concord, harmony
08 cohesion
09 soundness, stability, unanimity
14 like-mindedness

**solidify**
03 gel, set
04 cake, clot, jell
06 go hard, harden
07 congeal

09 coagulate
10 become hard
11 crystallize

**solitary**
03 nun
04 lone, monk, sole
05 alone, loner
06 hermit, lonely, single
07 ascetic, eremite, recluse, retired
08 desolate, lone wolf, lonesome, separate
09 anchoress, anchorite, reclusive, withdrawn
10 by yourself, cloistered, friendless, hermitical, unsociable
13 companionless, individualist

**solitude**
07 privacy
09 aloneness
10 loneliness
12 introversion, lonesomeness
13 reclusiveness, unsociability

**solution**
03 key
06 answer, remedy, way out
07 cure-all, panacea, solvent
08 quick fix
10 resolution, suspension, unraveling
11 elucidation, explanation
13 clarification

**solve**
05 crack
06 answer, fathom, settle
07 clear up, explain, rectify, resolve, unravel, work out
08 decipher, put right
09 figure out, interpret, puzzle out

**solvent**
10 in the black

**somber**
04 dark, drab, dull
05 dingy, grave, shady, sober
06 dismal, gloomy, solemn
07 joyless, serious
08 funereal
10 lugubrious, melancholy

**somebody**
03 VIP
04 name, star
05 mogul, nabob
06 bigwig
07 big shot, magnate, notable, someone
08 luminary

09 celebrity, dignitary, key figure, personage, superstar, top banana
10 panjandrum
13 household name

**someday**
05 later
06 one day
07 by and by
08 sometime
10 eventually, ultimately
11 in due course
13 sooner or later
14 one of these days

**somehow**
10 by any means
11 by some means, come what may
15 by hook or by crook, one way or another

**sometime**
02 ex-
04 late, then
06 former, one day
07 earlier, one-time, quondam, retired, someday
08 emeritus, previous
09 erstwhile, in the past

**sometimes**
07 at times
08 off and on, on and off
10 now and then, on occasion
11 now and again
12 every so often, occasionally, once in a while
14 from time to time

**somnolent**
04 dozy
06 drowsy, sleepy, torpid
08 comatose, oscitant
09 half-awake, heavy-eyed, soporific

**son**
03 boy, lad
05 child, scion
06 native
08 disciple
09 offspring
10 descendant, inhabitant

**song**

► _Types of song_:
03 air, lay, ode
04 aria, hymn, lied, lilt, soul, tune
05 blues, carol, chant, dirge, ditty, elegy, lyric, psalm, yodel
06 anthem, ballad, chorus, jingle, lyrics, melody,

number, shanty
07 calypso, cantata, canzone, chanson, chantey, descant, lullaby, pop song, refrain, requiem, war song, wassail
08 birdcall, birdsong, canticle, folk song, love song, madrigal, serenade, threnody
09 barcarole, cantilena, plainsong, roundelay, spiritual
10 gospel song, plainchant, recitative
11 rock and roll
12 nursery rhyme
➤ See also POEM

▶ *Titles of pop songs include*:
02 Oh
05 Fever, Layla, Money, No Cry, Relax, Think
06 Apache, Exodus
07 Hey Jude, Imagine, No Woman
08 Candy Man, Hound Dog, Parklife, Peggy Sue, Spaceman, The Twist, Too Young, Waterloo
09 Billy Jean, China Girl, Jean Genie, Never Ever, Penny Lane, Release Me, Stand By Me, Two Tribes
10 All Shook Up, Blue Velvet, Bright Eyes, Bye Bye Love, Jealous Guy, Moving On Up, Perfect Day, Purple Haze, Purple Rain, Secret Love, Sex Machine, Wonderwall
11 American Pie, Don't Be Cruel, From Me To You, Light My Fire, Like a Virgin, Mrs. Robinson, Pretty Woman, Set Them Free, She Loves You, Space Oddity, Tutti Frutti, Vaya con Dios, Voodoo Child
12 Ashes To Ashes, Baby Come Back, Born in the U.S.A., Born to be Wild, Come On Eileen, Common People, Dancing Queen, Eleanor Rigby, Johnny B. Goode, Mack The Knife, Magic Moments, Ode to Billy Jo, Paint It Black, Pretty Vacant, The Passenger, The Way We Were, The Young Ones
13 Blueberry Hill, Can't Buy Me Love, Ebony and Ivory, Get Off My Cloud, Hard Day's Night, Jailhouse Rock, Mull of Kintyre, Only the Lonely
14 Ain't That a Shame, Bette

Davis Eyes, Good Vibrations, Karma Chameleon, Love on the Rocks, That'll Be The Day, The Power of Love, Wonderful World
15 Blowin' in the Wind, Candle in the Wind, Heartbreak Hotel, I Shot the Sheriff, In the Name of Love, Jumpin' Jack Flash, Killing Me Softly, Love is All Around, Money for Nothing, Mr. Tambourine Man, Paperback Writer, Puppet on a String, Rivers of Babylon, Smoke on the Water, Too Much Too Young, Unchained Melody, Wish You Were Here, Yellow Submarine
16 You're Still the One
20 Try a Little Tenderness
25 (Sittin On the) Dock of the Bay
➤ See also MUSIC

## song and dance
05 pitch, spiel
08 flimflam
10 double talk
11 performance

## songster
06 singer
07 crooner, warbler
08 minstrel, vocalist
09 balladeer, chanteuse, chorister
10 troubadour

## songwriter

▶ *Names of songwriters and lyricists*:
04 **Anka** (Paul), **Bart** (Lionel), **Cahn** (Sammy), **Cash** (Johnny), **John** (Elton), **Kern** (Jerome), **King** (Carole), **Reed** (Lou), **Rice** (Tim)
05 **Berry** (Chuck), **Blake** (Eubie), **Brown** (James), **Cohan** (George Michael), **David** (Hal), **Dylan** (Bob), **Holly** (Buddy), **Loewe** (Frederick), **Simon** (Paul), **Sousa** (John Philip), **Weill** (Kurt)
06 **Berlin** (Irving), **Coward** (Noël), **Foster** (Stephen), **Joplin** (Scott), **Leiber** (Jerry), **Lennon** (John), **Lerner** (Alan Jay), **Marley** (Bob), **Mercer** (Johnny), **Oliver** (King), **Porter** (Cole), **Sedaka** (Neil),

**Seeger** (Pete), **Waller** (Thomas "Fats")
07 **Diamond** (Neil), **Gilbert** (William), **Guthrie** (Woody), **Herbert** (Victor), **Loesser** (Frank), **MacColl** (Ewan), **Mancini** (Henry), **Novello** (Ivor), **Rodgers** (Richard), **Romberg** (Sigmund), **Stoller** (Mike)
08 **Coltrane** (John), **Gershwin** (George), **Hamlisch** (Marvin), **Mitchell** (Joni), **Sondheim** (Stephen)
09 **Bacharach** (Burt), **Bernstein** (Leonard), **McCartney** (Paul)
10 **Carmichael** (Hoagy)
11 **Hammerstein** (Oscar), **Lloyd Webber** (Andrew)
➤ See also MUSIC

## sonorous
04 full, loud, rich
07 orotund, ringing, rounded
08 plangent, resonant
10 resounding

## soon
06 pronto
07 in a jiff, shortly
08 in a jiffy, in no time
09 any minute, in a minute, in a moment, presently
10 before long
12 any minute now, in a short time
13 in no time at all
14 in a little while, in a moment or two
15 in the near future

## soothe
04 calm, ease, hush, lull
05 allay, quiet, salve, still
06 pacify, settle, soften, temper
07 appease, assuage, comfort, mollify, quieten, relieve
08 calm down, mitigate, palliate
09 alleviate
12 tranquillize

## soothing
05 balmy
07 calming, easeful, restful
08 balsamic, lenitive, relaxing
09 demulcent, emollient
10 palliative

## soothsayer
04 seer
05 augur, sibyl
07 diviner, prophet
08 haruspex

## sophisticated
05 suave

06 subtle, urbane
07 complex, elegant, refined, stylish, worldly
08 advanced, cultured
09 elaborate, intricate
10 cultivated
11 complicated, experienced, worldly-wise
12 cosmopolitan

**sophistication**
05 poise
07 culture, finesse
08 elegance, urbanity
10 experience
11 savoir-faire, savoir-vivre, worldliness

**sophistry**
07 fallacy, quibble, sophism
08 elenchus
09 casuistry

**soporific**
06 opiate, sleepy
08 hypnotic, narcotic, sedative
09 somnolent
12 sleeping pill, tranquilizer
13 sleep-inducing, tranquilizing, tranquillizer
14 tranquillizing

**soppy**
03 wet
04 daft, soft, wild
05 corny, mushy, rainy, silly, weepy
06 sloppy, slushy
07 cloying, sopping, wimpish
09 schmaltzy
10 lovey-dovey
11 sentimental

**sorcerer**
04 Magi
05 Magus, witch
06 voodoo, wizard
07 angakok, angekok, warlock
08 magician
09 enchanter, sorceress
11 necromancer, thaumaturge
13 thaumaturgist

**sorcery**
05 charm, magic, spell
06 voodoo
08 wizardry
10 black magic, necromancy, witchcraft
11 thaumaturgy

**sordid**
03 low
04 base, foul, mean, vile
05 dirty, mucky, seamy, seedy
06 filthy, shabby, sleazy

07 corrupt, debased, immoral, miserly, squalid, unclean
08 degraded, shameful
09 debauched, mercenary
11 ignominious, self-seeking

**sore**
03 cut, raw, red
04 boil, hurt
05 angry, chafe, graze, ulcer, upset, vexed, wound
06 aching, bitter, chafed, lesion, scrape, tender
07 abscess, annoyed, bruised, burning, injured, painful
08 inflamed, offended, smarting, stinging, swelling
09 aggrieved, resentful

**sorrow**
03 woe
05 dolor, grief, mourn, trial
06 bewail, grieve, lament, misery
07 agonize, anguish, feel sad, remorse, sadness, trouble
08 distress, hardship, mourning
09 heartache, suffering
10 affliction, heartbreak
11 tribulation, unhappiness
12 wretchedness
13 feel miserable

**sorrowful**
03 sad, wae
06 rueful, woeful
07 doleful, painful, piteous, tearful, unhappy
08 dejected, grievous, mournful, wretched
09 afflicted, depressed, miserable, woebegone
10 lamentable, lugubrious, melancholy
12 disconsolate, heart-rending, heavy-hearted

**sorry**
03 sad
04 down, poor
05 moved, upset
06 dismal
07 ashamed, pitiful, pitying, unhappy
08 contrite, grievous, pathetic, penitent, shameful, wretched
09 concerned, miserable, regretful, repentant
10 apologetic, distressed, remorseful, shamefaced
11 guilt-ridden, sympathetic
12 heart-rending

**sort**
03 set

04 kind, make, race, rank, sift, type
05 brand, breed, class, genre, genus, grade, group, order, stamp, style
06 divide, family, nature, screen
07 arrange, catalog, quality, species, variety
08 category, classify, organize, separate
09 catalogue, character, segregate
10 categorize, distribute, put in order
11 description, systematize
12 denomination

❑**out of sorts**
03 ill
04 sick, weak
05 cross
06 ailing, crabby, groggy, grumpy, poorly, queasy, snappy, unwell
07 grouchy, in a mood, run down
08 below par, off-color
09 irritable
10 in a bad mood
14 down in the dumps, down in the mouth
15 under the weather

❑**sort out**
04 rank
05 class, grade, group, order, solve
06 choose, divide, select
07 arrange, resolve
08 classify, put right, separate
10 categorize, put in order

**sortie**
04 raid, rush
05 foray, sally
06 attack, charge
09 offensive

**so-so**
02 OK
04 fair, okay
06 not bad
07 average, neutral
08 adequate, middling, passable
09 tolerable
11 indifferent, respectable
12 run-of-the-mill
13 unexceptional
14 fair to middling
15 undistinguished

**soul**
03 man
04 life, mind
05 model, woman

06 person, psyche, spirit
07 epitome, essence, example
08 creature, humanity
09 character, inner self, intellect
10 compassion, embodiment, human being, individual, inner being
11 inspiration, sensitivity
13 heart of hearts, understanding
15 personification

**soul food**

▶ *Types of soul food*:
04 ribs, yams
08 chitlins, ham hocks
09 corn bread
12 chitterlings
13 black-eyed peas, collard greens
17 macaroni and cheese

**soulful**
06 moving
08 eloquent, mournful, profound
09 emotional, heartfelt, sensitive
10 expressive, meaningful

**soulless**
04 cold, dead, mean
07 callous, ignoble, inhuman
09 unfeeling
10 mechanical, spiritless
12 mean-spirited
13 unsympathetic
14 soul-destroying

**sound**
03 din, fit, say, voe
04 echo, firm, good, peal, ring, sane, test, toll, tone, true, well
05 chime, fiord, firth, go off, inlet, noise, plumb, probe, right, solid, tenor, utter, valid, voice, whole
06 cogent, fathom, intact, report, robust, secure, stable, strait, sturdy, timbre, unhurt
07 channel, estuary, examine, express, healthy, inspect, logical, measure, passage, perfect, resound, weighty
08 complete, orthodox, rational, reliable, resonate, thorough, unbroken, vigorous
09 enunciate, judicious, pronounce, resonance, undamaged, uninjured
10 articulate, dependable, reasonable, unimpaired
11 description, disease-free, in good shape, investigate,

reverberate, substantial, trustworthy, well-founded
12 in fine fettle, in good health, sound as a bell, well-grounded
13 authoritative, reverberation
14 sound as a dollar
15 in good condition

▶ *Types of sound*:
03 cry, hum, pip, pop, sob, tap
04 bang, beep, boom, buzz, clap, echo, fizz, hiss, honk, hoot, moan, peal, ping, plop, ring, roar, sigh, slam, snap, thud, tick, toot, wail, yell
05 blare, blast, bleep, chime, chink, clack, clang, clank, clash, click, clink, crack, crash, creak, drone, grate, groan, knock, smack, sniff, snore, snort, swish, throb, thump, twang, whine, whirr, whoop
06 bubble, crunch, gurgle, hiccup, jangle, jingle, murmur, patter, rattle, report, rumble, rustle, scrape, scream, sizzle, splash, squeak, squeal, tinkle
07 clatter, crackle, grizzle, screech, squelch, thunder, whimper, whistle
08 splutter
11 reverberate

▶ *Sounds animals make*:
03 bay, caw, coo, low, mew, moo, yap
04 bark, bray, crow, hiss, hoot, howl, meow, purr, roar, woof, yelp
05 bleat, chirp, cluck, croak, growl, grunt, neigh, quack, snarl, tweet
06 bellow, cackle, gobble, squawk, squeak, warble, whinny
07 chirrup, twitter

❑**sound out**
03 ask
04 pump
05 probe
06 survey
07 canvass, examine
08 question, research

**soup**
05 broth, gumbo, stock
06 bisque, borsch, potage, potato
07 chowder
08 consommé, gazpacho
10 minestrone

11 French onion, vichyssoise
12 mulligatawny

**sour**
03 bad, off
04 acid, tart
05 acidy, nasty, ratty, sharp, spoil, surly, tangy
06 acetic, bitter, rancid, turned
07 crabbed, curdled, pungent
08 aciduous, alienate, embitter, vinegary
09 resentful
10 embittered, unpleasant
11 acrimonious
12 disagreeable

**source**
04 mine, rise, root, ylem
05 cause, start
06 author, origin, spring, supply
08 wellhead
09 beginning, informant
10 originator, primordium, provenance, wellspring
12 fountainhead

**sourpuss**
05 grump, shrew
06 grouse, kvetch, misery, whiner
07 killjoy
10 crosspatch

**souse**
04 dunk, sink, soak
05 douse, steep
06 drench, pickle, plunge
07 immerse
08 marinade, marinate, saturate, submerge

**souvenir**
05 relic, token
06 trophy
07 memento
08 keepsake, reminder
11 remembrance

**sovereign**
04 coin, czar, king
05 chief, queen, royal, ruler
06 kingly, ruling, utmost
07 emperor, empress, monarch
08 gold coin, imperial, majestic, princely
09 paramount, potentate, principal, unequaled, unrivaled
10 autonomous, self-ruling
11 British coin, independent
13 self-governing

**sovereignty**
03 raj
07 primacy

**sow**

08 autonomy, dominion, imperium, kingship, regality
09 queenship, supremacy
10 ascendancy, domination, suzerainty
12 independence

**sow**
03 pig
04 seed
05 lodge, plant, strew
06 spread
07 bestrew, implant, scatter
08 disperse
09 broadcast, female pig
10 distribute
11 disseminate

**space**
03 gap
04 area, play, room, seat, span, time
05 array, blank, break, chasm, range, scope, shift, spell
06 cosmos, extent, galaxy, lacuna, margin, volume
07 arrange, be apart, dispose, expanse, opening, stretch
08 capacity, interval, latitude, omission, set apart, universe
09 clearance, elbowroom, expansion, string out
10 interstice, stretch out
11 solar system, the Milky Way
12 intermission
13 accommodation

**spacious**
03 big
04 huge, open, vast, wide
05 ample, broad, large, roomy
07 immense, sizable
09 capacious, extensive
10 commodious

**spadework**
05 labor
08 drudgery, homework
10 foundation, groundwork
11 preparation

**span**
04 arch, last, link, term, time
05 cover, cross, range, reach, scope
06 bridge, extend, extent, length, period, spread
07 compass, include, stretch
08 bestride, duration, traverse

**spank**
03 tan
04 cane, slap
05 smack, whack
06 paddle, thrash, thwack, wallop

**spanking**
04 fast, fine
05 brisk, quick, smart, swift
06 lively, snappy, speedy
07 exactly, totally, utterly
08 gleaming, paddling, vigorous
10 absolutely, completely, strikingly
12 invigorating

**spar**
03 box
04 pole, spat, tiff
05 argue, scrap
06 bicker
07 contend, contest, dispute
08 skirmish, squabble

**spare**
04 bony, free, give, lank, lean, over, save, slim, thin
05 allow, scant
06 afford, defend, frugal, let off, meager, pardon, scanty, unused
07 forgive, leisure, protect, release, reserve, scraggy, scrawny, sparing, surplus
08 leftover, reprieve, unwanted
09 auxiliary, emergency, safeguard
10 additional, unoccupied
11 show mercy to, superfluous
12 dispense with
13 supernumerary, supplementary
15 all skin and bones

□**to spare**
05 extra
06 unused
07 surplus
08 left over

**sparing**
05 mingy
06 frugal, meager, stingy
07 careful, prudent, thrifty
10 economical

**spark**
03 bit, jot
04 atom, hint, iota
05 flash, gleam, glint, trace
07 flicker, glimmer, vestige
10 suggestion

□**spark off**
04 stir
05 cause, start
06 excite, incite, prompt
07 inspire, provoke, trigger
08 occasion, start off, touch off
10 trigger off
11 precipitate

**sparkle**
03 vim
04 beam, dash, fizz, glow, life
05 get-up, gleam, glint, shine, spark
06 bubble, dazzle, energy, pizazz, spirit
07 be witty, flicker, glimmer, glisten, glitter, pizzazz, shimmer, twinkle
08 radiance, vitality, vivacity
09 animation, coruscate
10 brilliance, ebullience, effervesce, enthusiasm, get-up-and-go, liveliness
11 coruscation, scintillate

**sparkling**
05 fizzy, witty
06 bubbly, lively
08 flashing, gleaming
10 carbonated, glittering
11 coruscating
12 effervescent
13 scintillating

**sparse**
06 meager, scanty, scarce
08 sporadic
09 scattered
10 infrequent

**Spartan**
05 bleak, harsh, plain
06 frugal, severe, simple, strict
07 ascetic, austere
11 disciplined, self-denying

**spasm**
03 fit, tic
04 bout, jerk
05 burst, cramp
06 access, attack, frenzy, twitch
07 seizure
08 eruption, paroxysm
10 convulsion
11 contraction

**spasmodic**
05 jerky
06 fitful
07 erratic
08 periodic, sporadic
12 intermittent

**spate**
04 flow, rush
05 flood
06 deluge
07 torrent
10 outpouring

**spatter**
04 daub, soil
05 dirty, spray
06 bedaub, shower, splash
07 bestrew, scatter, speckle

08 splatter, sprinkle

**spay**
04 geld
06 neuter
08 castrate
09 sterilize

**speak**
03 gab, say, yak
04 chat, talk, tell
05 state, utter, voice
07 address, declaim, declare, express
08 converse
09 enunciate, hold forth, pronounce
10 articulate
11 communicate

❑**speak for**
06 act for
08 stand for
09 represent
15 speak on behalf of

❑**speak of**
07 discuss, mention, refer to
13 make mention of
15 make reference to

❑**speak out, speak up**
06 defend
07 protest, support

❑**speak to**
04 warn
05 scold
06 accost, rebuke
07 address, lecture, tell off, upbraid
08 admonish
09 dress down, reprimand

❑**speak up**
10 talk loudly
14 raise your voice, talk more loudly
➤ See also SPEAK OUT

**speaker**
06 orator, talker
08 lecturer
10 mouthpiece, prolocutor

**spearhead**
03 van
04 head, lead
05 front, guide
08 initiate, overseer, vanguard
11 cutting edge, trailblazer

**special**
06 choice, select, unique
07 notable, precise, unusual
08 detailed, peculiar, singular
09 different, exclusive, important, memorable, momentous, red-letter

10 noteworthy, particular, remarkable
11 distinctive, exceptional, outstanding, significant
13 distinguished, extraordinary
14 characteristic

**specialist**
06 brains, expert, master
11 connoisseur
12 professional

**specialty**
05 field, forte
06 talent
08 strength
09 specialty

**specially**
08 uniquely
09 expressly
10 distinctly, explicitly
11 exclusively
12 particularly, specifically

**species**
04 kind, sort, type
05 breed, class, genus, group
07 variety
08 category

**specific**
03 set
05 exact, fixed
07 limited, precise, special
08 clear-cut, definite, detailed
10 particular
11 unambiguous, unequivocal

**specification**
06 detail
10 particular
11 delineation, description, instruction, stipulation

**specify**
04 cite, list, name
06 define, detail, set out
07 itemize
08 describe, spell out
09 designate, stipulate
13 particularize

**specimen**
04 copy, type
06 sample
07 example, exhibit, pattern
08 exemplar, paradigm

**specious**
05 false
06 untrue
07 unsound
09 deceptive, plausible
10 fallacious, misleading
11 sophistical

**speck**
03 bit, dot, jot

04 atom, blot, mark, spot, whit
05 fleck, shred, stain, trace
07 blemish, speckle
08 particle

**speckled**
06 dotted, spotty
07 dappled, flecked, spotted
08 freckled, stippled

**spectacle**
04 show
05 scene, sight
06 marvel, parade, wonder
07 display, pageant, picture
09 curiosity
10 exhibition, phenomenon
12 extravaganza

**spectacular**
04 show
05 grand
06 daring
07 amazing, opulent, pageant
08 colorful, dazzling, dramatic, glorious, splendid, striking, stunning
09 spectacle
10 exhibition, impressive, remarkable, staggering
11 astonishing, eye-catching, magnificent, outstanding, resplendent, sensational
12 breathtaking, extravaganza, ostentatious
13 extraordinary

**spectator**
06 viewer
07 watcher, witness
08 beholder, looker-on, observer, onlooker
09 bystander
10 eyewitness, rubberneck

**spectral**
05 eerie, weird
06 spooky
07 ghostly, phantom
09 unearthly
11 disembodied, incorporeal
12 supernatural

**specter**
04 fear
05 ghost, shade, spook
06 menace, shadow, spirit, threat, vision, wraith
07 phantom
08 presence, revenant, visitant
10 apparition

**speculate**
04 muse, risk
05 guess
06 gamble, hazard, wonder

**speculation**
07 reflect, suppose, surmise, venture
08 cogitate, consider, theorize
10 conjecture, deliberate
11 contemplate, hypothesize

**speculation**
04 risk
05 guess
06 gamble, hazard, theory
07 surmise
09 guesswork
10 conjecture, hypothesis
11 supposition
13 flight of fancy

**speculative**
04 iffy
05 risky, vague
06 chancy
08 notional, unproven
09 hazardous, tentative, uncertain
10 indefinite
11 conjectural, theoretical
12 hypothetical
13 suppositional

**speech**
04 talk
05 lingo, spiel, voice, words
06 dialog, jargon, patter, tirade, tongue
07 address, dialect, diction, lecture, monolog, oration
08 delivery, dialogue, diatribe, language
09 discourse, monologue, philippic, soliloquy
11 enunciation
12 articulation, conversation
13 communication, pronunciation

**speechless**
03 mum
04 dumb, mute
06 silent
10 dumbstruck, tongue-tied
11 dumbfounded, obmutescent
12 inarticulate
13 thunderstruck

**speed**
04 belt, dash, pace, pelt, race, rate, rush, tear, zoom
05 haste, hurry, tempo
06 career, gallop, hurtle, sprint
07 quicken
08 alacrity, celerity, dispatch, momentum, rapidity, step on it, velocity
09 bowl along, go flat out, quickness, swiftness
10 accelerate, burn rubber, promptness

12 acceleration, step on the gas
14 go full throttle
15 put your foot down

❑**speed up**
05 hurry
06 hasten, spur on, step up
07 advance, forward, quicken
08 expedite, go faster, step on it
09 stimulate
10 accelerate, facilitate
11 precipitate, put on a spurt
12 gain momentum, step on the gas
13 floor the pedal
15 put your foot down

**speedily**
04 fast
07 hastily, quickly, rapidly, swiftly
08 promptly
09 hurriedly, posthaste

**speedy**
04 fast
05 hasty, quick, rapid, swift
06 nimble, prompt
07 cursory, express, hurried
09 immediate
11 expeditious, precipitate

**spell**
03 hex
04 bout, span, term, time, turn
05 augur, charm, magic, patch
06 allure, course, extent, herald, period, trance, voodoo
07 portend, presage, session, signify, sorcery, stretch
08 indicate, interval, witchery
09 magnetism
10 attraction
11 abracadabra, bewitchment, enchantment, fascination, incantation

❑**spell out**
06 detail
07 clarify, explain, specify
09 elucidate, emphasize, make clear, stipulate

**spellbinding**
08 gripping, riveting
10 bewitching, entrancing
11 captivating, enthralling, mesmerizing

**spellbound**
04 rapt
07 charmed, gripped, riveted
09 bewitched, entranced
10 captivated, enraptured, enthralled, hypnotized, mesmerized, transfixed

**spend**
02 do

03 use
04 blow, fill, kill, pass
05 apply, put in, use up, waste
06 devote, expend, finish, invest, lay out, occupy, pay out
07 consume, exhaust, fork out, fritter
08 disburse, shell out, squander
09 splash out, while away

**spendthrift**
07 wastrel
08 prodigal, wasteful
10 profligate, squanderer
11 extravagant, improvident

**spent**
05 all in, weary
06 bushed, done in, effete, pooped, used up
07 drained, worn out
08 consumed, dead beat, expended, finished, tired out
09 burned out, exhausted, pooped out

**spew**
04 gush, puke
05 issue, retch, spurt, vomit
07 spit out, throw up
08 disgorge
11 regurgitate

**sphere**
03 orb, set
04 area, ball, band, rank
05 class, crowd, field, globe, group, realm, round, scope
06 circle, clique, domain, extent
07 compass, globule
08 capacity, function, province
09 specialty, territory
10 department

**spherical**
05 round
06 rotund
07 globate, globoid, globose
08 globular
09 orbicular

**spice**
03 pep, zap, zip
04 kick, life, stir, tang, zest
05 color, gusto, hot up, liven, pep up, rouse, savor
06 buck up, perk up, relish, stir up
07 animate, enliven, liven up
08 brighten, energize, piquancy, vitalize
09 flavoring, seasoning
10 excitement, invigorate
11 put life into
➤ See also HERBS AND SPICES

**spick and span**
04 neat, tidy, trim
05 clean
06 spruce
08 polished, scrubbed, spotless, well-kept
10 immaculate

**spicy**
03 hot
04 racy, tart
05 juicy, sharp, tangy
06 ribald, risqué
07 peppery, piquant, pungent
08 aromatic, seasoned
10 flavorsome, scandalous, suggestive
11 sensational

**spider**

► *Types of arachnid and spider*:
04 mite, tick
07 araneid, skillet
08 scorpion
09 frying pan, tarantula
10 black widow, harvestman, wolf spider
12 book scorpion, brown recluse, whip scorpion
13 daddy longlegs
14 trapdoor spider
15 funnel-web spider
➤ See also ANIMAL

**spiel**
05 pitch
06 patter, speech
07 oration, recital

**spike**
03 add
04 barb, drug, lace, load, nail, spit, tine
05 block, mix in, point, prick, prong, rowel, spear, spine, stake, stick
06 impale, skewer
09 frustrate
13 make alcoholic

**spill**
04 fall, flow, pour, shed, slop, well
05 upset
06 run out, tumble
07 run over, scatter
08 accident, disgorge, overflow, overturn
09 discharge

❑**spill the beans**
03 rat
04 blab, tell
06 inform, squeal, tell on
07 stool on

15 give the game away

**spin**
03 run
04 flap, reel, ride, tell, tizz, trip, turn
05 drive, jaunt, panic, state, swirl, tizzy, twirl, twist, wheel, whirl, whirr
06 circle, dither, gyrate, invent, make up, outing, relate, rotate, swivel
07 dream up, fluster, revolve
08 gyration, rotation
09 fabricate, pirouette
10 revolution, turn around

❑**spin out**
06 extend, pad out
07 amplify, draw out, prolong
08 lengthen, protract

**spindle**
03 pin, rod
04 axis, axle
05 arbor, fusee, pivot

**spindly**
04 long, thin
05 lanky, weedy
06 gangly, skinny
07 spidery
08 gangling, skeletal
10 attenuated

**spine**
04 barb, grit, guts
05 pluck, quill, spike, thorn
06 dorsum, needle, rachis
07 bristle, courage, prickle
08 backbone
09 fortitude, vertebrae
12 spinal column
15 vertebral column

**spine-chilling**
05 eerie, scary
10 horrifying, terrifying
11 frightening, hair-raising
13 bloodcurdling

**spineless**
04 soft, weak
05 timid
06 feeble, yellow
07 chicken, wimpish
08 cowardly, timorous
11 lily-livered
12 fainthearted

**spiny**
06 briery, thorny
07 prickly, spinous, thistly
09 acanthous, spiculate
12 acanthaceous

**spiral**
04 coil, go up, gyre, rise, soar, wind
05 climb, helix, screw, twist, whorl
06 circle, coiled, gyrate, rocket, volute, wreath
07 cochlea, helical, voluted, whorled, winding, wreathe
08 circular, cochlear, curlicue, escalate, increase, scrolled, twisting, volution
09 cochleate, corkscrew
11 convolution

**spire**
03 tip, top
04 peak
05 crest, point, spike, tower
06 belfry, summit, turret
07 steeple
08 pinnacle

**spirit**
03 air, zip
04 fire, gist, grit, guts, kick, life, mind, mood, soul, zeal, zest
05 angel, ardor, demon, devil, fairy, fiend, force, ghost, humor, pluck, shade, spook, spunk, tenor, vigor
06 energy, makeup, mettle, morale, pizazz, psyche, shadow, sprite, temper, wraith
07 bravery, courage, essence, feeling, meaning, outlook, phantom, pizzazz, purport, quality, sparkle, specter
08 attitude, backbone, feelings, tendency, visitant, vivacity
09 animation, character, principle, substance, willpower
10 apparition, atmosphere, complexion, enterprise, enthusiasm, liveliness, motivation, resolution
11 disposition, implication, temperament
13 determination
14 characteristic

❑**spirit away**
05 carry, seize, steal, whisk
06 abduct, convey, kidnap, remove, snitch
07 capture, purloin

**spirited**
05 fiery
06 feisty, lively, plucky
07 valiant
08 animated, vigorous
09 energetic, vivacious

10   courageous, determined

**spiritless**
06   anemic
07   languid
08   lifeless, listless
09   apathetic
10   despondent, lackluster,
     wishy-washy

**spirits**
04   mood
05   humor
06   liquor, temper
07   alcohol
08   attitude, emotions, feelings
09   firewater, moonshine
11   strong drink, temperament
12   strong liquor, the hard stuff

▶   *Types of liquid spirit*:
03   gin, rum
05   vodka
06   brandy, cognac, grappa,
     Scotch, whisky
07   aquavit, bourbon, tequila,
     whiskey
08   Armagnac, Calvados,
     schnapps
09   aqua vitae, moonshine,
     slivovitz
10   rye whiskey
11   malt whiskey
➤   See also DRINK

**spiritual**
04   holy
06   divine, sacred
08   ethereal, heavenly
09   religious, unworldly
10   devotional, intangible
11   incorporeal
12   otherworldly

**spit**
04   hawk, hiss, rasp
05   drool, eject, issue
06   phlegm, saliva, slaver,
     sputum
07   dribble, spittle
08   splutter
11   expectorate

**spite**
03   irk, vex
04   evil, gall, hate, hurt
05   annoy, upset, venom, wound
06   grudge, hatred, injure,
     malice, offend, put out,
     rancor
07   ill will, provoke
09   animosity, vengeance
10   bitterness, ill feeling,
     resentment
11   malevolence

❏**in spite of**
07   against, defying, despite
12   regardless of, undeterred by
15   notwithstanding

**spiteful**
05   catty, cruel, nasty, snide
06   barbed, bitchy, bitter
08   vengeful, venomous
09   malicious, resentful
10   vindictive

**spitting image**
04   twin
05   clone
06   double, ringer
07   picture, replica
08   likeness
09   lookalike
10   dead ringer
13   exact likeness

**splash**
03   wet
04   beat, dash, daub, plop, slop,
     spot, stir, wade, wash
05   bathe, break, burst, patch,
     slosh, smack, spray, stain,
     surge, touch
06   blazon, buffet, dabble,
     effect, impact, paddle,
     plunge, shower, spread,
     squirt, streak, strike, wallow
07   display, exhibit, scatter,
     spatter, splotch, trumpet
08   splatter, sprinkle
09   publicity, publicize,
     sensation

**spleen**
04   bile, gall
05   spite, venom
06   animus, hatred, malice,
     rancor
07   ill will
08   acrimony
09   animosity, bad temper,
     hostility, malignity
10   bitterness, resentment
11   biliousness, malevolence
12   spitefulness
14   vindictiveness

**splendid**
04   fine, rich
05   grand, great, super
06   bright, lavish, superb
07   glowing, opulent, radiant,
     stately, sublime, supreme
08   dazzling, fabulous, glorious,
     imposing, renowned
09   brilliant, luxurious,
     marvelous, refulgent,
     sumptuous, wonderful
10   glittering, impressive

11   magnificent, outstanding,
     resplendent

**splendor**
04   glow, pomp, show
05   gleam, glory
06   dazzle, luster, luxury
07   display, majesty
08   ceremony, grandeur,
     opulence, radiance, richness
09   spectacle
10   brightness, brilliance
12   magnificence, resplendence
13   sumptuousness

**splenetic**
04   acid, sour
05   angry, cross, testy
06   crabby, morose, touchy
07   bilious, crabbed, peevish
08   choleric, churlish, spiteful
09   irascible, irritable, rancorous

**splice**
03   tie
04   bind, join, knit, mesh
05   braid, graft, marry, plait
06   fasten
07   connect

❏**get spliced**
03   wed
10   get hitched, get married, tie
     the knot
13   take the plunge

**splinter**
04   chip
05   break, flake, piece, shard,
     shred, smash, split
06   cleave, paring, shiver, sliver
07   crumble, shatter, shaving
08   fracture, fragment
11   smithereens
12   disintegrate

**split**
03   cut, gap, rip
04   chop, dual, open, part, rend,
     rent, rift, shop, slit, tear
05   allot, break, burst, cleft,
     crack, halve, share, slash
06   betray, bisect, breach,
     broken, cleave, cloven,
     divide, schism, shiver
07   break up, breakup, carve up,
     cracked, crevice, disband,
     discord, divided, divorce,
     dole out, fissure, hand out,
     rupture, twofold
08   allocate, bisected, disunion,
     disunite, division, ruptured,
     separate, set apart, splinter
09   apportion, fractured, parcel
     out, partition

10 alienation, difference, dissension, distribute, divergence, separation
11 incriminate, part company
12 estrangement

❑**split hairs**
05 cavil
07 nit-pick, quibble
08 pettifog
09 find fault
10 overrefine

❑**split up**
04 part
07 break up, disband, divorce
08 separate
11 get divorced, part company

**split-up**
07 breakup, divorce, parting
10 alienation, separation
12 estrangement

**spoil**
03 mar, rot
04 foul, harm, hurt, sour, turn
05 go bad, taint, upset
06 coddle, cosset, damage, deface, deform, go sour, impair, injure, mess up, pamper
07 blemish, destroy, indulge, pollute, tarnish
08 go rotten
09 decompose, disfigure
11 contaminate, deteriorate, overindulge
12 put a damper on

❑**spoil for**
10 be eager for, be intent on

**spoils**
04 gain, haul, loot, swag
05 booty
06 prizes, profit
07 benefit, plunder
08 pickings, winnings
10 spoliation

**spoilsport**
07 killjoy, meddler
10 wet blanket
11 party pooper
14 dog in the manger

**spoken**
04 oral, said, told
06 stated, verbal, voiced
07 uttered
08 phonetic
09 expressed

**spokesman, spokeswoman**
05 voice
08 delegate
10 mouthpiece

12 spokesperson

**sponge**
03 beg, bum, mop
04 swab, wash, wipe
05 cadge, clean
08 freeload, scrounge

**sponger**
03 bum
06 beggar, cadger
08 hanger-on, parasite
09 scrounger
10 freeloader

**spongy**
04 soft
05 light
06 porous
07 elastic, springy, squashy
09 absorbent, cushioned, resilient

**sponsor**
04 back, fund
05 angel
06 backer, friend, patron, surety
07 finance, promote, support
08 bankroll, promoter
09 godfather, godmother, guarantee, guarantor, supporter
10 underwrite
11 be a patron of, underwriter

**spontaneous**
07 natural, willing
08 unforced
09 extempore, impromptu, impulsive, unplanned, voluntary
10 unprompted
11 instinctive, unrehearsed
14 unpremeditated
15 spur of the moment

**spontaneously**
09 extempore, impromptu, on impulse, unplanned
10 off the cuff, unprompted
11 impulsively, voluntarily
13 instinctively
15 of your own accord

**spoof**
04 fake, game, hoax, joke
05 bluff, prank, trick
06 parody, satire
07 lampoon, leg-pull, mockery, takeoff
09 burlesque, deception

**spooky**
05 eerie, scary, weird
06 creepy
07 ghostly, uncanny
09 unearthly
11 frightening, hair-raising

13 spine-chilling

**spoon-feed**
04 baby
05 spoil
06 coddle, cosset, pamper
07 indulge
11 mollycoddle, overindulge

**sporadic**
06 random
07 erratic
09 irregular, spasmodic
10 infrequent, occasional
12 intermittent

**sport**
03 fun
04 game, play, wear
05 humor
06 banter, joking
07 display, exhibit, jesting, mockery, pastime, show off
08 activity, exercise, pleasure, ridicule, sneering
09 amusement, diversion
10 recreation
13 entertainment

► *Names of sports:*
04 golf, judo, polo, pool
05 bowls, darts, rodeo, rugby
06 boules, boxing, diving, hockey, karate, kung fu, quoits, racing, rowing, skiing, soccer, squash, tennis
07 angling, archery, bobsled, bowling, cricket, croquet, curling, fencing, fishing, gliding, hunting, jogging, jujitsu, netball, sailing, snooker, surfing, tenpins, walking
08 aerobics, baseball, canoeing, climbing, football, handball, lacrosse, pétanque, Ping Pong, shooting, softball, swimming, yachting
09 badminton, billiards, bobsleigh, ice hockey, potholing, sky diving, tae kwon do, water polo, wrestling
10 auto racing, basketball, drag racing, gymnastics, ice skating, volleyball
11 field hockey, horse racing, motor racing, show jumping, table tennis, water-skiing, windsurfing
12 orienteering, pitch and putt, rock climbing, trampolining, trapshooting
13 roller skating, skeet shooting, track and field, weightlifting

14 mountaineering, stock-car racing
15 greyhound racing
➤ See also ATHLETIC;
GYMNASTIC; RACE; STADIUM

► *Names of miscellaneous sportspeople:*
03 **Ali** (Muhammad)
04 **Bird** (Larry), **Dean** (Christopher), **Khan** (Jahangir), **Kwan** (Michelle), **Ruth** (George Herman "Babe"), **Witt** (Katerina)
05 **Bonds** (Barry), **Curry** (John), **Elway** (John), **Ender** (Kornelia), **Hogan** (Ben), **Spitz** (Mark), **Woods** ("Tiger")
06 **Fraser** (Dawn), **Hamill** (Dorothy), **Jenner** (Bruce), **Jordan** (Michael), **Namath** (Joe), **O'Neill** (Shaquille), **Palmer** (Arnold)
07 **Cousins** (Robin), **Gretzky** (Wayne), **Hinault** (Bernard), **Johnson** (Earvin "Magic"), **McEnroe** (John), **Rodnina** (Irina), **Sampras** (Pete), **Stewart** (Payne), **Torvill** (Jayne)
08 **Andretti** (Mario), **Boardman** (Chris), **DiMaggio** (Joe), **Indurain** (Miguel), **Kerrigan** (Nancy), **Redgrave** (Stephen), **Williams** (Ted), **Williams** (Venus)
09 **Armstrong** (Lance)
11 **Chamberlain** (Wilt "the Stilt"), **Weissmuller** (Johnny)
➤ See also ATHLETE;
BASEBALL; BOXER; CHESS;
CRICKET; FOOTBALL; GOLF;
GYMNASTICS; HORSE;
MOTOR; MOUNTAINEER;
RUGBY; SKIER; TENNIS

**sporting**
04 fair, just
09 honorable
10 reasonable
11 considerate, gentlemanly, respectable
13 sportsmanlike

**sportive**
06 frisky, jaunty, lively
07 coltish, playful
08 skittish
10 frolicsome, rollicking

**sporty**
05 natty, showy

06 casual, jaunty, snazzy, trendy
07 outdoor, stylish
08 athletic, informal

**spot**
03 bit, dot, fix, jam, pip, see
04 area, bite, blot, boil, daub, espy, flaw, hole, mark, mess, pock, site, slot, soil, some
05 fleck, local, place, point, scene, speck, stain, taint
06 blotch, descry, detect, little, morsel, notice, papula, papule, pimple, plight, scrape, smudge, splash
07 blemish, discern, make out, observe, program, pustule, setting, speckle, splotch, trouble
08 identify, locality, location, position, quandary
09 blackhead, recognize, situation
10 difficulty
11 predicament, small amount
12 catch sight of

**spotless**
04 pure
05 clean, white
07 shining
08 gleaming, innocent, unmarked, virginal
09 unstained, unsullied, untainted
10 immaculate
11 unblemished

**spotlight**
06 stress
07 feature, focus on, point up
08 emphasis
09 attention, emphasize, highlight, limelight, public eye, underline
10 accentuate, illuminate
15 draw attention to

**spotted**
04 pied
06 dotted, spotty
07 dappled, flecked, guttate, macular, mottled, piebald
08 brindled, polka-dot

**spotty**
04 pied
06 dotted, pimply
07 piebald, pimpled
08 speckled
12 inconsistent

**spouse**
04 mate, wife
05 hubby
06 missus
07 consort, husband, partner

09 companion, other half
10 better half
16 significant other

**spout**
03 jet
04 emit, flow, go on, gush, pour, rant, rose, spew
05 orate, shoot, spurt
06 geyser, nozzle, outlet
08 fountain, gargoyle
09 discharge, expatiate, hold forth, sermonize
11 pontificate

**sprawl**
04 flop, loll
05 slump, trail
06 lounge, slouch, spread
07 recline, stretch

**spray**
03 jet, wet
04 foam, gush, mist, posy
05 froth, spout, sprig, spume
06 branch, shower, wreath
07 aerosol, bouquet, corsage, scatter, spatter
08 atomizer, fumigate, sprinkle
09 spindrift, sprinkler, vaporizer

**spread**
03 jam, lay, set
04 coat, grow, land, open, span
05 apply, cover, feast, layer, order, party, put on, ranch, reach, smear, strew, widen
06 butter, dilate, expand, extend, extent, fan out, sprawl, unfold, unfurl, unroll
07 advance, arrange, banquet, broaden, diffuse, enlarge, expanse, open out, radiate, scatter, stretch
08 escalate, transmit
09 advertise, broadcast, circulate, diffusion, expansion, get around, large meal, make known, propagate, publicize, spill over
10 dispersion, distribute, escalation, grow bigger, make public, promulgate
11 communicate, development, dinner party, disseminate, proliferate
12 broadcasting, distribution, transmission
13 communication, dissemination, proliferation

**spree**
04 bout, orgy
05 binge, fling, revel
07 carouse, debauch, splurge

## sprig
04 stem, twig
05 bough, shoot, spray
06 branch

## sprightly
04 airy, spry
06 active, jaunty, lively, nimble
09 energetic, vivacious
10 frolicsome

## spring
03 spa
04 coil, grow, leap, root, well
05 arise, bound, issue, start
06 appear, bounce, derive, emerge, geyser, origin, season, source, spirit
07 develop, emanate, proceed, rebound
08 buoyancy, wellhead
09 briskness, originate
10 elasticity, resilience
11 flexibility
12 fountainhead

## ❏ spring up
04 grow
07 develop, shoot up
08 mushroom, sprout up
13 come into being

## springy
06 bouncy, spongy
07 buoyant, elastic, rubbery, tensile
08 flexible, stretchy
09 resilient

## sprinkle
04 dust
05 spray, strew
06 pepper, powder, shower
07 scatter, spatter, trickle

## sprinkling
04 dash
05 touch, trace
07 dusting, handful
10 scattering, smattering

## sprint
03 fly, run, zip
04 belt, dart, dash, race, tear
05 scoot, shoot

## sprite
03 elf, imp
04 puck
05 dryad, fairy, naiad, nymph, pixie, pouke, sylph
06 goblin, kelpie, spirit
07 brownie
10 apparition, leprechaun

## sprout
03 bud
05 shoot

06 come up
07 develop
08 put forth, spring up
09 germinate

## spruce
04 chic, cool, neat, trim
05 natty, sleek, smart
06 dapper, snazzy
07 elegant
11 well-dressed, well-groomed
13 well-turned-out

## ❏ spruce up
05 groom, preen, primp
06 neaten, tidy up
07 dress up
08 titivate
09 smarten up

## spry
05 agile, brisk
06 active, nimble, supple
09 energetic, sprightly

## spume
04 fizz, foam, head, suds
05 froth
06 lather
07 bubbles
13 effervescence

## spunk
04 grit, guts
05 heart, nerve, pluck
06 bottle, mettle, spirit
07 courage

## spur
04 goad, poke, prod, urge
05 drive, impel, prick
06 fillip, incite, induce, motive, prompt, propel
07 impetus
08 stimulus
09 incentive, stimulant, stimulate
10 incitement, motivation

## ❏ on the spur of the moment
09 impromptu, on impulse
13 spontaneously, thoughtlessly
15 without planning

## spurious
04 fake, mock, sham
05 bogus, false, phony
10 artificial

## spurn
04 snub
05 scorn
06 rebuff, reject
07 repulse, say no to
08 turn away, turn down
09 disregard, repudiate

## spurt
03 jet
04 gush, pour, rush
05 burst, erupt, issue, shoot, spate, spray, surge
06 squirt, stream
08 eruption, increase

## spy
03 see
04 espy, mole, spot
05 spook
06 descry, notice
07 glimpse, gumshoe, observe, snooper
08 discover
10 enemy agent
11 double agent, secret agent
12 catch sight of, foreign agent
14 fifth columnist
15 undercover agent

➤ *Names of spies:*
04 **Hale** (Nathan), **Hiss** (Alger)
05 **Blake** (George), **Blunt** (Anthony Frederick), **Fuchs** (Klaus Emil Julius), **Wynne** (Greville)
06 **Howell** (James), **Philby** (Kim), **Tubman** (Harriet)
07 **Burgess** (Guy Francis de Moncy), **Maclean** (Donald)
08 **Lonsdale** (Gordon Arnold), **Mata Hari**
09 **Carstares** (William), **Rosenberg** (Ethel), **Rosenberg** (Julius)

## ❏ spy on
05 watch
07 observe
10 keep tabs on
11 keep an eye on

## squabble
03 row
04 spat, tiff
05 argue, clash, set to, set-to
06 bicker
07 dispute, quarrel, wrangle
08 argument
09 have words

## squad
04 band, crew, gang, team, unit
05 force, group, troop
06 patrol
07 brigade, company

## squalid
03 low
04 foul, mean, vile
05 dingy, dirty, grimy, mucky, nasty, seedy
06 filthy, grubby, sleazy, sordid, untidy

**squall**
- 07 obscene, run-down, unclean, unkempt
- 08 slovenly, wretched
- 09 offensive, repulsive
- 10 broken-down, ramshackle, uncared-for

**squall**
- 04 blow, gale, gust, howl, moan, wail, wind, yell, yowl
- 05 groan, storm

**squally**
- 05 blowy, gusty, rough, windy
- 06 stormy
- 08 blustery

**squalor**
- 04 dirt
- 05 decay, filth, grime
- 07 neglect

**squander**
- 04 blow
- 05 spend, waste
- 07 consume, scatter, splurge
- 08 misspend
- 09 dissipate, throw away
- 11 fritter away

**square**
- 03 fit
- 04 even, fair, fogy, just, quad, true
- 05 adapt, agree, align, fogey, level, match, plaza, tally
- 06 accord, honest, settle
- 07 balance, conform, diehard, old fogy
- 08 old fogey, put right, regulate, set right, settle up, straight
- 09 conformer, equitable, harmonize, reconcile
- 10 conformist, correspond, fuddy-duddy, on the level, quadrangle, straighten
- 11 rectangular, right-angled, strait-laced
- 12 conservative, old-fashioned
- 13 perpendicular, quadrilateral, straight-laced
- 14 traditionalist

**squash**
- 03 jam
- 04 game, mash, pack, pulp, snub
- 05 crowd, crush, grind, pound, press, quash, quell, smash, stamp
- 07 distort, flatten, put down, silence, squeeze, squelch, trample
- 08 compress, macerate, suppress
- 09 humiliate, pulverize

**squashy**
- 05 mushy, pappy, pulpy
- 06 spongy
- 07 squishy
- 08 squelchy, yielding

**squat**
- 03 sit
- 04 bend
- 05 dumpy, hunch, short
- 06 chunky, crouch, stocky, stubby
- 08 thickset

**squawk**
- 03 cry
- 04 crow, hoot, yelp
- 05 croak
- 06 cackle, scream, shriek
- 07 screech

**squeak**
- 04 peep, pipe
- 05 cheep, creak, whine
- 06 squeal

**squeal**
- 03 cry, rat
- 04 howl, tell, wail, yelp
- 05 shout, sneak, split
- 06 betray, inform, scream, shriek, snitch, squawk
- 07 screech
- 09 tell tales

**squeamish**
- 06 queasy
- 08 delicate, nauseous
- 09 nauseated
- 10 fastidious, particular

**squeeze**
- 03 hug, jam, nip, ram
- 04 cram, grip, hold, mash, milk, pack, pulp, push
- 05 bleed, crowd, crush, force, pinch, press, shove, stuff, wedge, wrest, wring
- 06 clutch, cuddle, extort, lean on, squash
- 07 embrace, extract, tighten
- 08 compress, pressure
- 10 congestion, pressurize
- 14 put the screws on

**squint**
- 04 awry
- 05 askew
- 07 crooked, oblique
- 08 cockeyed, indirect
- 09 off-center
- 10 strabismic, strabismus
- 11 off-centered

**squirm**
- 05 shift, twist
- 06 fidget, wiggle, writhe
- 07 agonize, wriggle

- 08 flounder, squiggle

**squirt**
- 03 jet
- 04 emit, gush, pour, spew, well
- 05 eject, expel, issue, shoot, spout, spray, spurt, surge
- 06 shorty, shrimp, stream
- 07 spew out
- 09 discharge, ejaculate

**stab**
- 03 cut, jab, try
- 04 bash, gash, gore, pain, shot
- 05 crack, knife, prick, slash, spear, stick, whirl, wound
- 06 pierce, skewer, thrust, twinge
- 07 attempt, bayonet, venture
- 08 incision, puncture, transfix

☐ **stab in the back**
- 06 betray
- 07 deceive, sell out, slander
- 08 inform on
- 11 double-cross

**stabbing**
- 08 piercing, shooting, stinging

**stability**
- 08 firmness, solidity
- 09 constancy, soundness
- 10 durability, regularity, uniformity
- 11 reliability

**stable**
- 04 fast, firm, sure
- 05 fixed, solid, sound
- 06 secure, static, steady, strong, sturdy
- 07 abiding, durable, lasting, regular, uniform
- 08 balanced, enduring
- 09 permanent
- 10 dependable, invariable, unchanging
- 11 established, long-lasting, well-founded

**stack**
- 04 heap, load, many, mass, pile, save, tons
- 05 amass, heaps, hoard, loads, mound, piles, stock, store
- 06 gather, masses, oodles
- 09 stockpile
- 10 accumulate, collection
- 12 accumulation

**stadium**
- 04 bowl, ring
- 05 arena, field, track
- 11 sports field
- 12 sports ground

► *Sporting stadiums and venues include*:
05 Ascot, Lords, Monza
06 Le Mans
07 Daytona, San Siro
09 Alamodome, Newmarket, St. Andrews
10 Epsom Downs, Fenway Park, Meadowbank, Monte Carlo
11 Georgia Dome, Sandown Park, Shea Stadium, the Rose Bowl
12 Busch Stadium, Lambeau Field, Soldier Field, Texas Stadium, Wrigley Field
13 Caesar's Palace, Giants Stadium, Phillips Arena, Staples Center, the Albert Hall, the Cotton Bowl, the Orange Bowl, Yankee Stadium
14 Anaheim Stadium
15 Flushing Meadows, Gillette Stadium, Maracana Stadium, Veterans Stadium

**staff**
03 man, rod
04 cane, crew, prop, team, wand
05 baton, crook, equip, stick
06 crutch, occupy, supply
07 crosier, workers
08 officers, teachers
09 employees, personnel, workforce

**stage**
03 lap, leg
04 dais, give, step, time
05 apron, arena, field, floor, lay on, level, mount, phase, point, put on, scene, stand
06 direct, length, period, podium, sphere
07 arrange, perform, produce, rostrum, setting, soapbox
08 backdrop, division, engineer, juncture, platform
10 background
11 orchestrate

❏ **the stage**
03 rep
05 drama
07 the play, theater
09 dramatics, the boards, theatrics
11 Thespian art
13 the footlights

**stagger**
04 reel, rock, roll, stun, sway
05 amaze, lurch, pitch, waver
06 falter, teeter, totter, wobble
07 astound, nonplus, stupefy

08 astonish, bowl over, confound, hesitate, surprise
09 dumbfound, overwhelm
11 flabbergast

**staggering**
07 amazing
10 astounding, stupefying, surprising
11 astonishing
12 mind-boggling

**stagnant**
04 dull, foul, slow
05 dirty, quiet, stale, still
06 filthy, smelly, torpid
08 brackish, inactive, sluggish, standing
10 motionless

**stagnate**
04 idle
05 decay
07 decline, putrefy
08 languish, vegetate
09 do nothing
11 deteriorate

**staid**
04 calm, prim
05 grave, quiet, sober, stiff
06 proper, sedate, solemn, somber, steady
07 serious, starchy
08 composed, decorous

**stain**
03 dye
04 blot, mark, slur, spot, tint
05 color, smear, sully, taint, tinge
06 blotch, damage, injure, injury, smudge
07 blacken, blemish, tarnish
08 besmirch, discolor, disgrace, dishonor
13 discoloration

**stake**
03 bet, peg, rod, tie
04 ante, hold, pale, pole, post, prop, race, risk
05 brace, claim, prize, put in, share, spike, state, stick, tie up, wager
06 chance, demand, fasten, gamble, hazard, hold up, paling, picket, pierce, pledge, secure
07 concern, contest, declare, support, venture
08 interest, standard, winnings
09 establish, grubstake
10 investment, lay claim to
11 competition, involvement, requisition

❏ **stake out**
05 watch
07 mark out, observe, reserve
09 demarcate
11 keep an eye on

**stale**
03 dry, old
04 flat, hard, sour
05 jaded, moldy, stock, tired, trite
07 clichéd, worn-out
09 hackneyed
11 commonplace, stereotyped

**stalemate**
03 tie
04 draw, halt
07 impasse
08 deadlock, standoff

**stalk**
04 hunt, stem, tail, twig, walk
05 haunt, march, track, trail
06 branch, pursue, shadow
07 petiole
08 peduncle

**stall**
03 pen
04 coop
05 booth, defer, delay, hedge, kiosk, place, stand, table
06 hold up, put off
07 counter, cubicle, surface
08 obstruct, platform, postpone, put on ice
09 enclosure, stonewall, temporize
10 equivocate
11 compartment, play for time
12 drag your feet

**stalwart**
05 burly, hardy, loyal, stout
06 brawny, robust, rugged, strong, sturdy, trusty
07 devoted, staunch, valiant
08 faithful, muscular, reliable
09 steadfast, strapping
10 dependable, determined
11 indomitable

**stamina**
04 grit
05 force, power, vigor
06 energy
09 endurance, fortitude
10 resilience, resistance
12 staying power

**stammer**
04 lisp
06 falter
07 stumble, stutter
08 hesitate
12 speech defect

## stamp

03 cut, fix, tag
04 beat, cast, form, kind, mark, mash, mold, pulp, seal, sort, type
05 brand, breed, crush, label, pound, print, tread
06 emboss, squash
07 engrave, impress, imprint, quality, trample, variety
08 hallmark, identify, inscribe
09 character, signature
10 categorize, impression
11 attestation, description
12 characterize
13 authorization

### ◻stamp out
05 crush, quash, quell
06 quench, scotch
07 destroy, put down
08 suppress
09 eliminate, eradicate, extirpate

## stampede
03 fly, run
04 dash, flee, rout, rush
05 shoot
06 charge, flight, gallop, onrush, sprint

## stance
04 line
05 angle, slant, stand
06 policy
07 bearing, opinion, posture
08 attitude, carriage, position
09 viewpoint
10 deportment, standpoint
11 point of view

## stanch
04 halt, plug, stay, stem, stop
05 block, check

## stand
04 base, bear, case, dais, hold, line, rack, rise
05 abide, allow, angle, booth, brook, erect, exist, frame, get up, place, shelf, slant, stage, stall, table, upend
06 endure, locate, obtain, policy, remain, stance, suffer, tripod
07 be erect, be valid, counter, opinion, prevail, soapbox, stand up, station, stomach, support, undergo, weather
08 attitude, cope with, pedestal, platform, position, tolerate
09 put up with, viewpoint, withstand
11 point of view

### ◻stand by
04 back, wait
06 defend, hold to, uphold
07 stick by, support
08 adhere to, side with
10 stand up for, stick up for

### ◻stand for
04 bear, mean
05 allow, brook
06 denote, endure
07 betoken, signify, stomach
08 indicate, tolerate
09 put up with, represent, symbolize

### ◻stand in for
07 replace
08 cover for
10 understudy
11 deputize for, pinch-hit for
13 substitute for

### ◻stand out
06 extend, jut out
07 poke out, project
08 stick out
09 be obvious
11 catch the eye
12 be noticeable
13 be conspicuous, stick out a mile

### ◻stand up
04 rise
05 get up
06 cohere, hold up
09 hold water
13 get to your feet
14 rise to your feet

### ◻stand up for
06 adhere, defend, uphold
07 protect, stand by, support
08 champion, fight for
10 stick up for

### ◻stand up to
04 defy, face
05 brave
06 endure, oppose, resist
08 confront, face up to
09 challenge, withstand

## standard
03 set
04 code, flag, norm, rule, type
05 ethic, gauge, grade, ideal, level, moral, stock, usual
06 banner, colors, normal, staple
07 average, example, pattern, popular, quality, regular, scruple, typical
08 exemplar, gonfalon, ordinary, orthodox, paradigm
09 archetype, benchmark, criterion, customary, guideline, principle, yardstick
10 recognized, touchstone
11 established, requirement
12 conventional
13 authoritative, specification

## standard-bearer
04 head
06 leader
07 soldier
09 candidate
11 color-bearer

## standardize
09 normalize
10 homogenize, regularize
11 systematize

## stand-in
05 locum, proxy
06 deputy, second
08 delegate, stuntman
09 surrogate
10 stuntwoman, substitute, understudy
11 pinch hitter
14 representative

## standing
04 rank
05 erect, fixed
06 repute, status
07 footing, lasting, regular, station, upended, upright
08 duration, eminence, position, vertical
09 existence, permanent, perpetual, seniority
10 on your feet, reputation
13 perpendicular

## standoff
03 tie
07 impasse
08 blockade, deadlock

## standoffish
04 cold, cool
05 aloof
06 remote
07 distant
09 withdrawn
10 unfriendly, unsociable
14 unapproachable

## standpoint
05 angle, slant
06 stance
07 station
08 position
11 perspective, point of view

## standstill
04 halt, lull, rest, stop
06 holdup, log-jam
07 impasse

**staple**
08 dead stop, deadlock, gridlock, stoppage
09 cessation, stalemate

**staple**
03 key
04 main
05 basic, chief, major
08 foremost, standard
09 essential, important, necessary

**star**
03 orb, sun
04 idol, lead
06 famous, planet
07 big name, big shot, leading
08 asterisk, asteroid, luminary
09 brilliant, celebrity, paramount, principal, satellite, superstar
10 celebrated, leading man, preeminent
11 illustrious, leading lady
12 heavenly body, leading light
13 celestial body

━ *Names and types of star and comet*:
04 Mira, nova, Vega
05 comet, Deneb, Merak, Spica
06 meteor, Pollux, pulsar, quasar, Sirius
07 Antares, Canopus, Capella, Dog Star, Polaris
08 Arcturus, Pole Star, red dwarf, red giant
09 Aldebaran, Fomalhaut, North Star, supernova
10 Betelgeuse, brown dwarf, supergiant, white dwarf
11 falling star, neutron star
12 Barnard's star, Halley's comet, shooting star
13 Alpha Centauri
15 Proxima Centauri
➤ See also CONSTELLATION

**starchy**
04 prim
05 stiff
06 formal, stuffy
11 strait-laced
13 straight-laced

**stare**
04 gape, gawk, gawp, gaze, look
05 glare, watch
06 goggle

❏ **be staring you in the face**
13 stick out a mile

**stark**
04 bald, bare, grim, pure
05 bleak, blunt, harsh, plain, quite, sheer, total, utter
06 arrant, barren, dreary, gloomy, severe, wholly
07 austere, totally, utterly
08 absolute, complete, desolate, entirely, flagrant, forsaken, thorough
09 downright, out-and-out, unadorned
10 absolutely, completely, consummate, depressing
11 unmitigated
13 unembellished

**stark-naked**
04 nude
05 naked
08 in the raw, stripped
09 buck naked, in the buff, in the nude
15 in the altogether

**start**
04 dawn, jerk, jump, leap, open
05 arise, begin, birth, break, found, issue, leave, onset, set up, spasm, wince
06 create, flinch, launch, origin, outset, set off, set out, shrink, turn on, twitch
07 kick off, opening, trigger
08 activate, commence, embark on, fire away, get going, initiate
09 beginning, emergence, establish, inception, instigate, institute, introduce, originate
10 embark upon, inaugurate, initiation, trigger off
11 get cracking, get under way, institution, origination
12 commencement, inauguration, introduction
13 come into being
14 bring into being
15 get things moving

**startle**
05 alarm, amaze, scare, upset
07 astound
08 astonish, frighten, surprise

**startling**
08 alarming, dramatic
10 astounding, surprising, unexpected
11 astonishing

**starvation**
05 death
06 famine, hunger
07 fasting
12 malnutrition

**starve**
03 die
04 deny, diet, fast
06 hunger, perish
07 deprive

**starving**
05 dying
06 hungry
08 famished, ravenous, underfed

**stash**
04 fund, heap, hide, pile, stow
05 cache, hoard, lay up, store
07 conceal, reserve, secrete
08 salt away
09 reservoir, stockpile
12 accumulation

**state**
03 put, say
04 aver, flap, land, tell
05 glory, panic, realm, shape, tizzy, utter, voice
06 affirm, assert, bother, formal, nation, plight, public, report, reveal, set out
07 council, country, declare, divulge, express, kingdom, majesty, present, specify
08 announce, disclose, national, official, position, proclaim, republic
09 condition, make known, situation, territory
10 articulate, federation, government, promulgate
11 authorities, communicate, predicament
12 governmental
13 circumstances
➤ See also BOROUGH; COUNTY; PROVINCE

━ *U.S. states*:
04 Iowa, Ohio, Utah
05 Idaho, Maine, Texas
06 Alaska, Hawaii, Kansas, Nevada, Oregon
07 Alabama, Arizona, Florida, Georgia, Indiana, Montana, New York, Vermont, Wyoming
08 Arkansas, Colorado, Delaware, Illinois, Kentucky, Maryland, Michigan, Missouri, Nebraska, Oklahoma, Virginia
09 Louisiana, Minnesota, New Jersey, New Mexico, Tennessee, Wisconsin
10 California, Washington
11 Connecticut, Mississippi, North Dakota, Rhode Island, South Dakota
12 New Hampshire,

Pennsylvania, West Virginia
13  Massachusetts, North
Carolina, South Carolina

► *Postal state abbreviations*:
02  AK, AL, AR, AZ, CA, CO, CT,
DE, FL, GA, HI, IA, ID, IL, IN,
KS, KY, LA, MA, MD, ME, MI,
MN, MO, MS, MT, NC, ND,
NE, NH, NJ, NM, NV, NY, OH,
OK, OR, PA, RI, SC, SD, TN,
TX, UT, VT, VA, WA, WI, WV,
WY

► *Traditional state abbreviations*:
02  Ga., Ky., La., Md., Mo., N.C.,
N.H., N.J., N.Y., Pa., R.I., S.C.,
Va., Vt.
03  Ala., Ark., Del., Fla., Ill., Ind.,
Nev., Tex., Wis., W.Va., Wyo.
04  Ariz., Colo., Conn., Iowa,
Kans., Mass., Mich., Minn.,
Miss., Mont., N.Dak., Nebr.,
N.Mex., Ohio, Okla., Oreg.,
S.Dak., Tenn., Utah, Wash.
05  Calif., Idaho, Maine
06  Alaska, Hawaii

► *State nicknames. We have omitted the word* **State** *from names given in the following list but you may need to include this word as part of the solution to some crossword clues.*
03  Bay (Massachusetts), Gem
(Idaho)
05  Aloha (Hawaii), First
(Delaware), Ocean (Rhode
Island), Peach (Georgia)
06  Badger (Wisconsin), Beaver
(Oregon), Coyote (South
Dakota), Empire (New York),
Garden (New Jersey),
Golden (California), Show
Me (Missouri), Silver
(Nevada), Sooner
(Oklahoma)
07  Beehive (Utah), Buckeye
(Ohio), Granite (New
Hampshire), Hawkeye
(Iowa), Hoosier (Indiana),
Natural (Arkansas), Old Line
(Maryland), Pelican
(Louisiana), Prairie (Illinois),
Tar Heel (North Carolina)
08  Equality (Wyoming),
Keystone (Pennsylvania),
Lone Star (Texas), Magnolia
(Mississippi), Mountain
(West Virginia), Palmetto
(South Carolina), Pine Tree
(Maine), Sunshine (Florida),
Treasure (Montana)

09  Bluegrass (Kentucky),
Evergreen (Washington),
North Star (Minnesota),
Sunflower (Kansas),
Volunteer (Tennessee)
10  Centennial (Colorado),
Cornhusker (Nebraska),
Great Lakes (Michigan)
11  Grand Canyon (Arizona), Old
Dominion (Virginia), Peace
Garden (North Dakota)
12  Constitution (Connecticut),
Heart of Dixie (Alabama)
13  Green Mountain (Vermont)
15  The Last Frontier (Alaska)
17  Land of Enchantment (New
Mexico)

❑ **in a state**
05  het up, upset
07  anxious, in a stew, ruffled
08  agitated, in a tizzy, worked
up
09  flustered
10  distressed
13  panic-stricken

**stately**
05  grand, noble, regal, royal
06  august, solemn
08  imperial, imposing, majestic,
measured, splendid
10  ceremonial, deliberate
11  ceremonious, magnificent

**statement**
06  report
07  account
09  assertion, testimony,
utterance
10  disclosure, revelation
11  affirmation, declaration
12  announcement,
proclamation
13  communication

**state of affairs**
04  case
09  condition, situation
12  lie of the land
13  circumstances

**statesman, stateswoman**
06  leader
08  diplomat
10  politician
11  grand old man

**static**
05  fixed, inert, still
07  resting
08  immobile, unmoving
10  motionless, stationary
13  at a standstill

**station**
03  set

04  base, halt, post, rank, send,
site, stop
05  class, depot, grade, level,
place
06  assign, locate, office, status
08  exchange, garrison, location,
position, standing, terminal
09  establish

**stationary**
05  fixed, inert, still
06  moored, parked, static
08  constant, immobile, standing
10  motionless
13  at a standstill

**statue**
04  bust, head, idol
05  image
06  bronze, effigy, figure
07  carving
08  figurine
09  sculpture, statuette

**statuesque**
07  stately
08  handsome, imposing,
majestic

**stature**
04  fame, rank, size
06  height, renown
08  attitude, eminence, prestige,
standing, tallness

**status**
04  rank
05  class, grade, level, state
06  degree, weight
07  station
08  eminence, position, prestige,
standing
09  condition
10  importance, reputation
11  consequence, distinction

**statute**
03  act, law
05  edict, ukase
09  enactment, ordinance

**staunch**
04  firm, halt, plug, stay, stem,
stop, sure, true
05  block, check, loyal, stout
06  arrest, trusty
08  constant, faithful, reliable
09  steadfast
10  dependable
11  trustworthy

**stave**
❑ **stave off**
04  foil
05  avert, avoid, parry, repel
07  deflect, fend off, repulse,
ward off

09 keep at bay, turn aside

**stay**
04 curb, halt, keep, last, live, prop, rest, stop, wait
05 abide, block, board, brace, check, delay, lodge, pause, tarry, visit
06 arrest, endure, hinder, linger, put off, remain, reside, settle
07 adjourn, control, persist, prevent, sojourn, support, suspend
08 obstruct, postpone, prorogue, reprieve, restrain, stopover
09 deferment, remission, stanchion
10 suspension
12 postponement

**staying power**
04 grit
07 stamina
08 strength
09 endurance, fortitude
10 resilience, resistance

**steadfast**
06 stable, steady
07 staunch
08 constant, faithful, reliable
09 dedicated
11 unfaltering, unflinching

**steady**
04 beau, calm, even, firm
05 brace, check, fixed, sober, still
06 poised, secure, stable
07 balance, compose, control, regular, serious, settled, support, uniform
08 balanced, constant, habitual, reliable, restrain
09 boyfriend, immovable, stabilize, steadfast, unvarying
10 consistent, dependable, girlfriend, motionless, sweetheart, unchanging, unvariable, unwavering
12 well-balanced
13 imperturbable

**steal**
04 lift, slip, snip, take
05 creep, filch, heist, pinch, poach, slide, slink, sneak, swipe
06 abduct, kidnap, pilfer, pocket, rip off, snatch, thieve, tiptoe
07 bargain, good buy, purloin
08 discount, embezzle, giveaway, knock off, peculate, shoplift

09 reduction
10 plagiarize
11 appropriate, make off with
12 make away with, special offer

**stealing**
05 theft
06 piracy
07 larceny, robbery
08 burglary, filching, pinching, poaching, thievery, thieving
09 pilferage, pilfering
10 peculation, plagiarism, purloining
11 shoplifting
12 embezzlement
13 appropriation

**stealth**
07 secrecy, slyness
10 covertness, sneakiness
11 furtiveness

**stealthy**
03 sly
06 covert, secret, sneaky
07 cunning, furtive
09 secretive, underhand
11 unobtrusive

**steam**
04 haze, mist
05 vapor, vigor
06 energy
07 stamina
08 dampness, moisture
10 enthusiasm
12 condensation

❑**get steamed up**
08 get angry, get het up
10 get annoyed, get excited
12 fly into a rage, get flustered

❑**steam up**
05 fog up
06 mist up

❑**under your own steam**
05 alone
10 by yourself
11 without help
13 independently

**steamship**
05 liner
06 packet
09 steamboat, vaporetto
10 packet boat, paddle boat
13 paddle steamer

**steamy**
03 hot
04 blue, damp, hazy, sexy
05 close, humid, misty, muggy
06 erotic, sticky, sultry, sweaty, vapory

07 amorous, gaseous, lustful, raunchy, sensual
08 vaporous
10 passionate, sweltering

**steed**
03 nag
04 hack, jade
05 horse, mount
07 charger

**steel**
05 brace, nerve
06 harden
07 fortify, prepare, toughen

**steely**
04 firm, gray, hard
05 harsh
08 blue-gray, pitiless, resolute
09 merciless, steel-blue
10 determined, inflexible

**steep**
04 damp, dear, fill, high, soak
05 brine, imbue, sharp, sheer, souse, stiff
06 abrupt, costly, drench, imbrue, infuse, pickle, seethe, sudden
07 extreme, immerse, moisten, pervade, suffuse
08 headlong, macerate, marinate, permeate, saturate, submerge, vertical
09 excessive, expensive
10 exorbitant, inordinate, overpriced
11 acclivitous, declivitous, precipitous
12 extortionate, unreasonable

**steeple**
05 spire, tower
06 belfry, turret

**steer**
03 cox
05 guide, pilot, usher
06 direct
07 conduct, control
08 navigate

❑**steer clear of**
04 shun
05 avoid, dodge, evade, skirt
06 bypass, escape, eschew
10 circumvent

**stem**
03 dam
04 come, curb, flow, halt, stop
05 arise, block, check, issue, shoot, stalk, stock, trunk
06 arrest, branch, derive, resist, spring, stanch
07 contain, develop, emanate, staunch

09 originate

**stench**
04 odor, reek
05 smell, stink, whiff
06 miasma

**stentorian**
06 strong
07 booming, ringing, vibrant
08 resonant, sonorous, strident
10 thunderous

**step**
03 act
04 deed, gait, move, pace, rank, rung, walk
05 grade, level, phase, point, print, stage, stair, stamp, trace, track, tramp, tread
06 action, degree, effort, stride
07 advance, measure, process
08 footstep, maneuver, progress
09 expedient, footprint, procedure
14 course of action

❑**in step**
08 in unison, together
11 in agreement

❑**out of step**
06 at odds

❑**step by step**
06 slowly
08 bit by bit, gradatim
09 gradually

❑**step down**
04 quit
05 leave
06 resign, retire
08 abdicate, withdraw

❑**step in**
09 intercede, interfere, intervene

❑**step up**
05 boost, raise
07 augment, build up, speed up
08 escalate, increase
09 intensify

❑**watch your step**
07 look out
08 take care, watch out
09 be careful
12 mind how you go

**stereotype**
03 tag
04 mold
05 label, model
06 cliché
07 formula, pattern
08 typecast
10 categorize, pigeonhole

**stereotyped**
05 banal, corny, stale, stock, tired, trite
07 clichéd
08 overused, standard
09 hackneyed
12 cliché-ridden, standardized

**sterile**
04 arid, bare, pure, vain
05 clean
06 barren, futile
07 aseptic, useless
08 abortive, germ-free, germless, infecund
09 fruitless, infertile, pointless
10 antiseptic, sterilized
11 disinfected, ineffectual
12 unproductive, unprofitable

**sterility**
06 atocia, purity
07 asepsis
08 futility
09 cleanness, impotence
10 barrenness, inefficacy
11 infertility
13 fruitlessness, pointlessness
14 unfruitfulness
15 ineffectiveness

**sterilize**
04 geld, spay
06 neuter, purify
08 castrate, fumigate
09 disinfect

**sterling**
04 pure, real, true
07 genuine
08 standard
09 authentic, excellent
10 first-class

**stern**
04 back, grim, poop, rear, tail
05 cruel, harsh, rigid, stark, tough
06 severe, somber, strict
07 austere, tail end
08 exacting, rigorous
09 demanding, Draconian, stringent, unsparing
10 forbidding, inflexible, relentless, tyrannical, unyielding
11 unrelenting
13 authoritarian

**stew**
04 boil, cook, fret, fuss, hash
05 daube, sweat, tizzy, worry
06 bother, braise, pother, ragout, simmer
07 agonize, chowder, goulash
08 pot-au-feu
09 agitation, casserole

13 Brunswick stew

**steward**
06 butler, factor, waiter
07 manager, marshal
09 attendant
15 flight attendant

**stick**
03 fix, gum, jab, jam, lay, pin, put, set
04 bear, bind, bond, clog, drop, fuse, glue, grip, hold, join, last, poke, push, rest, site, stab, stay, stop, tack, tape, trap, twig, weld
05 abide, affix, cling, dwell, paste, place, prick, spear, stand
06 adhere, attach, branch, cement, endure, fasten, impale, insert, instal, linger, locate, pierce, remain, secure, solder, switch, thrust
07 carry on, deposit, install, persist, stomach
08 continue, position, puncture, tolerate, transfix
09 put up with

► *Types of stick*:
03 lug, rod
04 cane, club, cosh, pike, pole, post, wand, whip
05 baton, billy, birch, crook, staff, stake
06 crutch, cudgel
07 cigaret, scepter
08 bludgeon
09 cigarette, truncheon
10 shillelagh
11 hockey stick
12 walking stick

❑**stick by**
06 defend, hold to, uphold
07 stand by, support
08 adhere to, champion
10 stand up for

❑**stick it out**
07 persist
08 continue, keep at it, plug away
09 persevere
11 hang in there

❑**stick out**
06 extend, jut out
07 poke out, project
08 protrude
13 be conspicuous

❑**stick up for**
06 defend, uphold
07 protect, stand by, support
08 champion, fight for

## stickiness

13 take the side of

**stick with**
06 keep at
07 persist
08 continue, plug away
09 persevere

**the sticks**
04 bush
07 boonies, outback
09 backwoods, boondocks
15 middle of nowhere

**stickiness**
03 goo
09 glueyness, gooeyness,
 viscidity

**stick-in-the-mud**
04 fogy
06 fossil, square
07 old fogy
10 fuddy-duddy
13 unadventurous

**stickler**
06 maniac, pedant, purist
07 fanatic, fusspot
13 perfectionist

**sticky**
05 close, gluey, gooey, gummy,
 humid, muggy, tacky
06 clammy, sultry, tricky
07 awkward, viscoid, viscous
08 adhesive, delicate, ticklish
09 difficult, glutinous, sensitive
10 oppressive, sweltering

**stiff**
04 cold, firm, hard, prim, taut
05 aloof, brisk, fresh, harsh,
 large, rigid, solid, tense, tight,
 tough, windy
06 aching, chilly, formal, severe,
 strict, strong, tiring
07 arduous, austere, awkward,
 drastic, extreme, pompous
08 decorous, exacting, forceful,
 hardened, priggish, reserved,
 rigorous, strigent
09 arthritic, demanding,
 difficult, inelastic, laborious,
 rheumatic, unbending
10 inflexible, unyielding
11 ceremonious, challenging,
 rheumaticky, standoffish
12 intoxicating

**stiffen**
03 set
04 jell
05 brace, steel, tense
06 harden, starch
07 congeal, fortify, tense up,
 thicken, tighten
08 solidify

09 coagulate, reinforce
10 strengthen

**stiff-necked**
05 proud
07 haughty
08 arrogant, stubborn
09 obstinate
11 opinionated
12 contumacious
14 uncompromising

**stifle**
05 choke, crush
06 dampen, muffle
07 repress, silence, smother
08 hold back, restrain, suppress
09 suffocate
10 asphyxiate, extinguish

**stigma**
04 blot, mark, slur, spot
05 brand, shame, stain, taint
07 blemish

**stigmatize**
04 mark
05 brand, label, shame, stain
06 vilify
07 blemish, condemn
08 denounce, disgrace

**still**
03 but, yet
04 calm, hush
05 abate, allay, inert, peace,
 quiet
06 even so, hushed, pacify,
 serene, settle, silent, smooth,
 soothe, static, subdue,
 though
07 appease, assuage, however,
 quieten, restful, silence
08 although, immobile, inactive,
 lifeless, moderate, peaceful,
 restrain, serenity, stagnant,
 tranquil, unmoving, until
 now
09 noiseless, quietness,
 sedentary, unruffled
10 for all that, motionless,
 stationary, stock-still
11 nonetheless, tranquility,
 tranquilize, undisturbed
12 nevertheless, peacefulness,
 tranquillize
15 notwithstanding

**stilted**
05 stiff
06 forced, wooden
07 labored
09 unnatural
10 artificial

**stimulant**
05 tonic

07 pep pill, reviver
08 caffeine, pick-me-up
11 restorative

**stimulate**
03 fan
04 fire, goad, spur, urge
05 impel, rouse
06 arouse, incite, induce, kindle,
 whip up
07 inspire, provoke, trigger
09 encourage, instigate
10 trigger off

**stimulating**
07 rousing
08 galvanic, stirring
09 inspiring, provoking
10 intriguing
11 provocative
12 exhilarating

**stimulus**
04 goad, jolt, prod, push, spur
06 fillip
07 impetus
10 incitement, inducement
11 provocation
12 shot in the arm

**sting**
03 con, nip
04 bite, burn, edge, hurt, pain
05 annoy, cheat, prick, smart,
 spite, trick, upset, wound
06 fiddle, fleece, grieve, injure,
 injury, malice, needle, nettle,
 offend, rip off, tingle
07 defraud, provoke, sarcasm,
 swindle
08 distress, irritate, pungency,
 urticate
12 incisiveness, take for a ride

**stinging**
07 burning, hurtful
08 aculeate, smarting, tingling,
 urticant, wounding
09 aculeated, offensive

**stingy**
04 mean
07 miserly
11 closefisted, tightfisted
12 cheeseparing, parsimonious
13 penny-pinching

**stink**
03 hum, row
04 flap, fuss, odor, reek, stir
05 be bad, furor, smell
06 bother, hassle, stench
07 malodor
08 bad smell
09 commotion, foul smell
12 song and dance

## stinker
03 cad, cur, rat
05 creep, swine
06 horror, plight
07 bounder, dastard, problem, shocker
09 scoundrel
10 difficulty, impediment
11 predicament

## stinking
03 bad
04 foul, vile
05 awful, nasty
06 rotten

## stint
03 bit, job
04 save, task, time, turn
05 limit, pinch, quota, share, shift, spell
06 period, scrimp
07 skimp on, stretch
08 begrudge, withhold
09 economize
10 assignment
11 restriction

## stipulate
06 demand
07 lay down, require, set down, specify
08 insist on

## stipulation
06 demand
07 proviso
11 requirement
12 precondition, prerequisite
13 specification

## stir
04 beat, flap, fuss, jail, move, whip
05 blend, budge, rouse, shake, shift, tizzy, touch
06 affect, bustle, flutter, flurry, prison, quiver, rustle, thrill, tumult, twitch, uproar
07 agitate, disturb, ferment, flutter, inspire, tremble
08 activity, disorder, movement
09 agitation, commotion
10 excitement
11 disturbance

## ❑stir up
04 fire, spur
05 drive, impel, rouse, waken
06 arouse, awaken, excite, incite, kindle, prompt
07 agitate, animate, inflame, inspire, provoke, quicken
08 motivate
09 galvanize, stimulate

## stirring
05 heady
07 emotive, rousing
08 dramatic, exciting, spirited
09 inspiring, thrilling
12 exhilarating, intoxicating

## stitch
03 hem, sew
04 darn, mend, seam, tack
09 embroider

## stock
04 cows, fund, heap, keep, line, pigs, pile, race, sell
05 banal, basic, blood, bonds, breed, cache, carry, equip, funds, goods, herds, hoard, money, range, sheep, store, tired, trite, usual, wares
06 assets, cattle, deal in, flocks, handle, horses, market, shares, strain, supply
07 animals, capital, clichéd, descent, holding, lineage, regular, reserve, routine, species, variety, worn-out
08 ancestry, equities, ordinary, overused, pedigree, quantity, standard
09 essential, genealogy, hackneyed, inventory, livestock, parentage, relatives, reservoir, selection, stockpile
10 background, collection, extraction, investment, repertoire, securities
11 commodities, farm animals, merchandise, stereotyped
12 accumulation, conventional, run-of-the-mill

## ❑in stock
09 available

## ❑stock up
04 fill, heap, load, save
05 amass, buy up, hoard, lay in, store
09 provision, replenish, stockpile
10 accumulate

## ❑take stock
06 assess, review
07 weigh up
08 appraise, evaluate, reassess
09 reexamine
10 reevaluate

## stockpile
04 fund, heap, keep
05 amass, cache, hoard, store
10 accumulate

## stock-still
05 inert, still
06 static
08 immobile
10 motionless, stationary

## stocky
05 broad, dumpy, short, solid, squat
06 chunky, stubby, stumpy, sturdy
08 thickset

## stodgy
04 dull
05 heavy, solid, staid
06 boring, formal, leaden, solemn, stuffy, turgid
07 filling, starchy, tedious
10 fuddy-duddy, spiritless

## stoical
07 patient
08 resigned
09 accepting, impassive
10 forbearing, phlegmatic
13 long-suffering, uncomplaining

## stoicism
07 ataraxy
08 ataraxia, fatalism, patience
11 forbearance, resignation
13 long-suffering

## stolid
04 dull, slow
05 heavy
06 bovine, solemn, wooden
07 lumpish
09 apathetic, impassive
10 phlegmatic
11 unemotional

## stomach
03 gut
04 bear, craw, guts, take, zest
05 abide, belly, brook, stand, taste, tummy
06 desire, endure, hunger, liking, paunch, relish, suffer
07 abdomen, courage, insides, passion
08 appetite, potbelly, submit to, tolerate
09 approve of, put up with
11 breadbasket, corporation, inclination
13 determination

## stone
03 gem, pip, pit, set
04 rock, seed, sett, slab
05 flint, jewel, lapis
06 cobble, kernel, pebble
07 boulder
08 endocarp, gemstone

09 flagstone, headstone, tombstone
10 concretion, gravestone

**stony**
03 icy
04 cold, hard
05 blank, rocky, stern
06 chilly, frigid, frosty, gritty, pebbly, severe, steely
07 adamant, callous, deadpan, hostile, shingly
08 gravelly, pitiless
09 heartless, merciless
10 inexorable, poker-faced
11 indifferent, unforgiving
14 expressionless

**stooge**
04 butt, dupe, foil, pawn
06 lackey, puppet
07 cat's-paw, fall guy

**stoop**
03 bow, sag
04 bend, duck, lean, sink
05 deign, droop, hunch, kneel, lower, porch, slump, squat
06 crouch, resort, slouch
07 bending, descend, ducking, incline
09 go so far as, go so low as, vouchsafe
10 condescend
13 lower yourself

**stop**
03 bar, end
04 bung, cork, halt, kick, live, plug, quit, rest, seal, stay, stem
05 block, board, break, cease, check, close, cover, dwell, lodge, pause, put up, stage, stall, visit
06 arrest, defeat, desist, finish, hinder, impede, pack in, reside, settle, stanch, thwart
07 abandon, bus stop, prevent, refrain, sojourn, station, staunch, suspend
08 conclude, give over, knock off, leave off, obstruct, terminal
09 cessation, frustrate, intercept, interrupt, roadblock, terminate
10 conclusion, standstill
11 come to an end, destination, discontinue, nip in the bud, termination
12 bring to an end
14 discontinuance
15 discontinuation

**stopgap**
06 resort
09 expedient, makeshift, temporary
10 improvised, substitute
12 expediential
13 improvisation

**stopover**
04 rest, stop
05 break, visit
07 sojourn
13 overnight stay

**stoppage**
04 halt, stop
05 check, sit-in
06 arrest, strike
07 closure, removal, walkout
08 blockage, shutdown
09 cessation, deduction, occlusion
10 standstill
11 obstruction, termination

**stopper**
04 bung, cork, plug, seal
06 spigot

**store**
02 PX
04 bank, fund, heap, keep, load, mine, save, shop
05 cache, hoard, lay by, lay in, lay up, stash, stock
06 esteem, gather, grocer, larder, plenty, supply
07 buttery, collect, deposit, grocery, lay down, put down, reserve
08 put aside, quantity, salt away
09 abundance, reservoir, stockpile, warehouse
10 accumulate, chain store, commissary, depository, five-and-ten, repository, storehouse
11 five-and-dime, supermarket
12 accumulation, post exchange, retail outlet

❏ **lay store by, put store by, set store by**
05 value
06 admire
13 think highly of

**storehouse**
04 barn, fund, hold, silo
05 depot, vault
06 armory, cellar, garner, larder, wealth
07 arsenal, granary
08 entrepot, treasury
09 repertory, warehouse
10 depository, repository

**storm**
03 row
04 fume, rage, rant, rave, roar, rush, stir, tear, to-do
05 furor, shout, stamp
06 assail, attack, charge, clamor, seethe, tumult, uproar
07 assault, explode, flounce, thunder, turmoil
08 brouhaha, outburst
09 commotion, kerfuffle, offensive, onslaught

▸ *Types of storm*:
04 gale
05 buran
06 squall
07 cyclone, monsoon, tempest, tornado, typhoon
08 blizzard, downpour
09 dust devil, dust storm, hailstorm, hurricane, rainstorm, sandstorm, snowstorm, whirlwind
10 cloudburst
12 thunderstorm
15 electrical storm
➢ See also WIND

**stormy**
04 foul, wild
05 gusty, rainy, rough, windy
06 choppy, raging
09 turbulent
11 tempestuous

**story**
03 eck, fib, lie, rib
04 item, plot, tale, tier
05 fable, floor, level, novel
06 flight, record, report
07 account, article, episode, feature, fiction, history, recital, untruth
08 anecdote
09 chronicle, falsehood, narrative

**storyteller**
04 bard, liar
06 fibber
08 narrator, novelist, telltale
09 raconteur
10 anecdotist, chronicler, raconteuse

**stout**
04 bold
05 beefy, brave, bulky, burly, gutsy, hardy, heavy, obese, plump, solid, thick, tough, tubby
06 brawny, fleshy, heroic, plucky, portly, robust, stocky, strong, sturdy
07 durable, hulking, valiant

**stove**
08 fearless, forceful, muscular, resolute, valorous, vigorous
09 corpulent, dauntless
10 courageous, determined, overweight
11 substantial

**stove**
04 kiln, oven
05 grill, range
06 cooker, heater
07 furnace
13 potbelly stove

**stow**
04 cram, load, pack
05 place, stash, store, stuff
07 deposit, put away

**straggle**
03 lag
04 roam, rove
05 amble, drift, range, stray, trail
07 scatter
09 string out
10 dilly-dally

**straggly**
06 random, untidy
08 drifting, rambling, straying
09 irregular, strung out

**straight**
04 even, fair, flat, just, neat, pure, tidy, true
05 blunt, frank, level, right
06 candid, decent, direct, honest, unbent
07 aligned, bluntly, clearly, frankly, in order, orderly, plainly, sincere, upright
08 arranged, candidly, directly, faithful, honestly, promptly, reliable, unbroken, vertical
09 honorable, organized, outspoken, shipshape, unbending, undiluted
10 continuous, forthright, horizontal, law-abiding, point-blank, successive, unswerving
11 consecutive, immediately, respectable, trustworthy
12 continuously, conventional, forthrightly, successively
13 consecutively, unadulterated, uninterrupted
14 as the crow flies
15 straightforward

❑**straight away**
03 now
06 at once, pronto
08 directly
09 instantly, right away
11 immediately
12 there and then, without delay

**straighten**
04 tidy
05 align, order
06 adjust, neaten, tidy up
07 arrange
10 put in order

❑**straighten out**
06 reform, settle, tidy up
07 clear up, correct, realign, rectify, resolve, sort out
08 put right
10 put in order, regularize
11 disentangle

❑**straighten up**
06 reform, tidy up
10 stand erect
12 stand upright

**straightforward**
04 easy, open
05 clear, frank
06 candid, direct, honest, simple
07 genuine, sincere
08 truthful
09 outspoken
10 child's play, elementary, forthright, unexacting
11 undemanding
12 a piece of cake
13 plain-speaking, uncomplicated

**strain**
03 air, tax, try, tug, way
04 kind, sift, song, sort, tear, tune, type, vein
05 blood, breed, drain, drive, exert, force, heave, sieve, stock, theme, trace, trait, twist, worry, wring
06 burden, demand, duress, effort, extend, family, filter, injure, injury, melody, screen, sprain, streak, stress, strive, tauten, weaken, wrench
07 descent, express, fatigue, lineage, overtax, quality, squeeze, stretch, tension, tighten, variety
08 ancestry, endeavor, exertion, go all out, pedigree, pressure, separate, tendency
09 weariness
10 exhaustion, suggestion
12 do your utmost
14 characteristic
15 make every effort

**strained**
05 false, stiff, tense
06 forced, uneasy, wooden
07 awkward, labored
09 unnatural

**strainer**
05 sieve
06 filter, riddle, screen, sifter
08 colander

**strait**
04 hole, mess
05 inlet, sound
06 crisis, pickle, plight
07 channel, dilemma, narrows, poverty
08 distress, hardship
09 emergency, extremity
10 difficulty, perplexity
11 predicament

**straitened**
04 poor
07 limited, reduced
09 difficult
10 distressed, restricted
12 impoverished

**strait-laced, straight-laced**
04 prim
06 narrow, proper, strict, stuffy
07 prudish, starchy

**strand**
04 sand, wire
05 beach, fiber, sands, shore
06 factor, length, string, thread
07 element, feature
08 filament, seashore
09 component, foreshore
10 ingredient, waterfront

**stranded**
07 aground, beached, wrecked
08 forsaken, marooned
10 high and dry
11 shipwrecked
14 left in the lurch

**strange**
03 new, odd
05 alien, funny, kinky, novel, queer, wacky, weird
06 exotic, freaky, unreal
07 bizarre, curious, foreign, oddball, offbeat, surreal, uncanny, unknown, unusual
08 abnormal, peculiar, singular, uncommon
09 eccentric, fantastic, irregular, unheard-of
10 unexpected, unfamiliar
11 unexplained
12 inexplicable
13 extraordinary

**strangeness**
06 oddity
07 oddness
09 queerness

**straighten** (column right top)
11 constrained, embarrassed
13 uncomfortable

**stranger**
10 exoticness
11 abnormality, peculiarity, singularity
12 eccentricity, irregularity

**stranger**
05 alien, guest
07 visitor
08 newcomer, outsider
09 foreigner, immigrant, nonmember

❏ **a stranger to**
10 unversed in
14 unaccustomed to, unfamiliar with

**strangle**
03 gag
05 check, choke
06 keep in, stifle
07 inhibit, repress, smother
08 hold back, restrain, suppress, throttle
09 suffocate
10 asphyxiate

**strap**
03 tie
04 band, beat, belt, bind, cord, flog, lash, whip
05 leash, thong, truss
06 fasten, secure
07 bandage, scourge

**strapping**
03 big
05 beefy, burly, hunky, husky
06 brawny, sturdy
07 hulking
09 well-built

**stratagem**
04 plan, plot, ploy, ruse, wile
05 dodge, trick
06 device, scheme, tactic
08 artifice, intrigue, maneuver
09 deception
11 machination

**strategic**
03 key
05 vital
07 crucial, planned, politic
08 critical, decisive, tactical
09 essential, important
10 calculated, deliberate

**strategy**
04 game, plan
06 design, policy, scheme
07 program, tactics
08 approach, game plan, planning, schedule
09 blueprint, procedure
12 plan of action

**stratum**
03 bed
04 lode, rank, seam, tier, vein
05 caste, class, grade, group, layer, level, table
07 bracket, station
14 stratification

**stray**
03 err, odd
04 lost, roam, rove
05 amble, drift, freak, range
06 chance, ramble, random, wander
07 deviate, digress, diverge, get lost, meander, roaming
08 go astray, homeless, straggle
09 abandoned, wander off
10 accidental, occasional
15 go off on a tangent

**streak**
04 band, dart, dash, race, rush, tear, vein, zoom
05 flash, fleck, smear, speed, spell, touch, trace
06 hurtle, period, sprint, strain, stripe, stroke
07 element, stretch, striate
08 run naked

**streaked**
05 lined
06 banded, barred
07 brinded, brindle, flecked, streaky, striate
08 brindled

**stream**
03 fly, jet, run
04 flap, flow, gush, pour, rill, rush, tide
05 brook, burst, creek, crowd, drift, float, flood, issue, river, spill, spout, surge, trail
06 deluge, efflux, rillet
07 cascade, rivulet, torrent
09 tributary
10 outpouring

**streamer**
04 flag
06 banner, ensign, pennon
07 pennant
08 gonfalon, standard, vexillum

**streamlined**
05 sleek, slick
06 smooth
07 well-run
09 efficient, organized
10 modernized, time-saving
11 aerodynamic

**street**
❏ **man in the street**
07 Jane Doe, Joe Blow, John Doe
09 Joe Doakes, Mr. Average
10 Joe Citizen, Joe Six-pack, Mrs. Average
11 John Q. Public
13 average person
14 ordinary person
15 ordinary citizen

**strength**
04 bent, gift, guts
05 ardor, asset, brawn, clout, force, forte, power, sinew, vigor
06 energy, health, métier, muscle, talent, weight
07 bravery, courage, fitness, passion, potency, stamina
08 aptitude, fervency, firmness, pungency, solidity
09 advantage, fortitude, hardiness, intensity, specialty, vehemence
10 durability, resilience, resistance, resolution, robustness
11 persistence, strong point
12 forcefulness
13 determination, effectiveness
14 impregnability, persuasiveness

❏ **on the strength of**
09 because of
10 by virtue of
11 on account of
12 on the basis of

**strengthen**
05 brace, rally, steel
06 back up, beef up, harden, prop up
07 bolster, brace up, build up, confirm, fortify, hearten, nourish, refresh, restore, shore up, stiffen, support, toughen
08 buttress, heighten, increase
09 encourage, intensify, reinforce
10 invigorate
11 consolidate, corroborate
12 substantiate

**strenuous**
04 bold, hard, keen
05 eager, heavy, tough
06 active, taxing, tiring, uphill
07 arduous, earnest, weighty
08 forceful, grueling, resolute, spirited, tireless, vigorous

**stress**
09 demanding, difficult, energetic, laborious, tenacious
10 determined, exhausting
13 indefatigable

**stress**
04 beat
05 force, ictus, value, worry
06 accent, hassle, strain, trauma, weight
07 anxiety, point up, tension, trouble
08 distress, emphasis, pressure
09 emphasize, highlight, spotlight, underline
10 accentuate, exaggerate, importance, underscore
12 accentuation, significance

**stretch**
03 run, tax, try
04 area, last, pull, push, term, test, time
05 offer, range, reach, space, spell, stint, sweep, tract, widen
06 expand, extend, extent, go up to, period, spread, strain, tauten, unfold, unroll
07 broaden, draw out, expanse, project, prolong
08 continue, distance, elongate, lengthen, protract, reach out
09 challenge, go as far as
10 straighten
11 become wider
12 become longer
14 prison sentence

◻ **stretch out**
05 reach, relax
06 extend, put out, sprawl
07 hold out, lie down, recline

◻ **stretch your legs**
06 stroll
08 exercise
09 move about, promenade, take a walk
10 go for a walk, take the air

**strew**
04 toss
06 litter, spread
07 bestrew, scatter
08 bespread, disperse, sprinkle
10 besprinkle

**stricken**
03 hit
06 struck
07 injured, smitten, wounded
08 affected
09 afflicted

**strict**
04 firm, hard, true
05 clear, close, exact, harsh, rigid, stern, total, tough, utter
06 narrow, severe
07 austere, literal, precise
08 absolute, accurate, clear-cut, complete, faithful, orthodox, rigorous
09 religious, stringent
10 inflexible, meticulous, no-nonsense, particular, scrupulous
13 authoritarian, conscientious, thoroughgoing
14 disciplinarian, uncompromising

**strictness**
05 rigor
08 accuracy, rigidity, severity
09 austerity, precision
10 stringency

**stricture**
04 flak
05 blame, bound, limit
06 rebuke
07 censure, confine, control, reproof
09 criticism, restraint, tightness
10 constraint
11 restriction
12 ball and chain
13 animadversion

**stride**
04 pace, step, walk
05 tread
07 advance
08 movement, progress
11 progression

**strident**
04 loud
05 harsh, rough
07 grating, jarring, raucous
08 clashing, jangling
09 clamorous, unmusical
10 discordant, screeching, stridulant, vociferous

**strife**
06 battle, combat
07 discord, dispute, ill-will, quarrel, rivalry, warfare
08 argument, conflict, fighting, friction, struggle
09 animosity, bickering, hostility, wrangling
10 contention, ill-feeling
11 controversy
12 disagreement

**strike**
03 aid, box, hit, rap
04 bang, beat, belt, biff, blow, cuff, feel, find, look, raid, rush, seem, slap, sock, trap
05 adopt, clout, knock, pound, punch, reach, sit-in, smack, sound, storm, swipe, thump, touch, whack
06 affect, ambush, appear, assail, assume, attack, batter, buffet, charge, clinch, come to, dawn on, hammer, mutiny, revolt, stroke, take on, thrash, thwack, wallop
07 achieve, agree on, assault, clobber, embrace, impress, occur to, protest, sit-down, uncover, unearth, walk out, walkout
08 arrive at, come upon, discover, look like, pounce on, register, set about, settle on, stop work, stoppage
09 down tools, encounter, good pitch
10 chance upon, come to mind, happen upon
11 collide with
12 hunger strike
13 demonstration, wildcat strike

◻ **strike back**
07 hit back
09 fight back, retaliate
11 get even with
14 get your own back, pay someone back

◻ **strike down**
04 kill, ruin, slay
05 smite
06 murder
07 afflict, destroy
11 assassinate

◻ **strike out**
03 fan
05 erase
06 delete, remove, rub out
08 cross out

◻ **strike up**
05 begin, start
07 kick off
08 commence, initiate
09 establish, instigate

**striking**
06 pretty
07 evident, obvious, salient, visible
08 dazzling, distinct, gorgeous, stunning
09 arresting, beautiful, glamorous, memorable
10 attractive, impressive, noticeable, remarkable

**string**
11 astonishing, conspicuous, good-looking, outstanding
13 extraordinary

**string**
03 row
04 cord, file, hang, line, link, loop, rope, yarn
05 cable, chain, fiber, sling, tie up, train, twine
06 column, fasten, series, strand, stream, thread
07 catches, connect, festoon
08 provisos, sequence
10 conditions, succession
11 limitations
12 restrictions
13 prerequisites

**□ string along**
04 dupe, fool, hoax
05 bluff
06 humbug
07 deceive
12 take for a ride

**□ string out**
06 extend, fan out, wander
08 disperse, lengthen, protract, space out, straggle
09 spread out
10 stretch out

**□ string up**
03 top
04 hang, kill
05 lynch

**stringent**
04 firm, hard
05 harsh, rigid, tight, tough
06 severe, strict
08 exacting, rigorous
09 demanding
10 inflexible

**stringy**
04 ropy, wiry
05 chewy, tough
06 sinewy
07 fibrous, gristly
08 leathery

**strip**
03 bar, bit, gut
04 band, belt, flay, lath, loot, peel, sash, skin, slat, slip
05 clear, empty, piece, shred, strap, thong
06 denude, divest, expose, ribbon, stripe, swathe
07 deprive, disrobe, lay bare, ransack, uncover, undress
08 clean out, unclothe
09 dismantle, excoriate, pull apart, take apart
10 dispossess

12 take to pieces

**stripe**
03 bar
04 band, belt, line, sort, type
05 flash, fleck, strip
06 streak

**striped**
06 banded, barred, stripy
07 streaky, vittate
08 striated

**stripling**
03 boy, lad
05 youth
08 teenager
09 fledgling, youngster
10 adolescent

**strive**
03 try, vie
04 toil, work
05 fight, labor
06 battle, combat, engage, strain
07 attempt, compete, contend, contest, try hard
08 campaign, endeavor, struggle
12 do your utmost

**stroke**
03 hit, pat, pet, rub
04 belt, biff, blow, coup, line, move, slap
05 knock, shock, smack, spasm, sweep, swipe, thump, touch, whack
06 action, attack, caress, fondle, thwack, wallop
07 clobber, massage, seizure
08 flourish, movement
10 thrombosis
14 accomplishment

**stroll**
04 turn, walk
05 amble
06 dawdle, ramble, wander
07 meander, saunter
10 go for a walk
14 constitutional
15 stretch your legs

**stroller**
04 pram
06 walker
07 dawdler, rambler
08 wanderer
09 baby buggy, saunterer
12 baby carriage

**strong**
03 fit, hot
04 deep, firm, keen, well
05 beefy, brave, burly, clear, eager, great, gutsy, hardy,

heady, husky, lusty, sharp, solid, sound, spicy, stout, tough, valid, vivid
06 active, ardent, biting, brawny, fierce, marked, mighty, potent, robust, rugged, severe, sinewy, sturdy, urgent
07 devoted, durable, fervent, graphic, healthy, intense, obvious, piquant, pungent, telling, violent, weighty
08 athletic, clear-cut, decisive, forceful, muscular, positive, powerful, profound, resolute, stalwart, vehement, vigorous
09 assertive, committed, confident, effective, heavy-duty, resilient, strapping, undiluted, well-built
10 aggressive, compelling, convincing, courageous, determined, formidable, passionate, persistent, persuasive, pronounced, reinforced, remarkable
11 hard-wearing, long-lasting
12 concentrated, enthusiastic, single-minded, strong-minded, strong-willed
13 single-hearted, well-protected
14 highly seasoned

**strong-arm**
08 bullying, coercive, forceful, physical, thuggish
11 threatening
12 intimidatory

**stronghold**
04 fort, keep
07 bastion, citadel
08 fortress

**strong-minded**
04 firm
08 resolute
09 tenacious, unbending
10 determined, iron-willed, unwavering
14 uncompromising

**strong point**
04 bent, gift
05 asset, forte, thing
06 métier, talent
08 strength

**strong-willed**
06 wilful
07 willful
08 obdurate, stubborn
09 obstinate
10 inflexible, self-willed
11 intractable

12 intransigent, recalcitrant

**structural**
08 tectonic
11 formational
14 constructional

**structure**
04 form
05 build, frame, setup, shape
06 design, fabric, makeup
07 arrange, edifice
08 assemble, building, erection, organize
09 construct, formation, framework
11 arrangement, composition
12 conformation, constitution, construction, organization
13 configuration

**struggle**
03 vie
04 toil, work
05 brawl, clash, fight, labor
06 battle, combat, effort, strain, strife, strive
07 contend, contest, grapple, scuffle, wrestle
08 conflict, exertion, skirmish
09 difficult
11 competition, hostilities
13 exert yourself

**strut**
05 swank
06 parade, prance
07 peacock, swagger

**stub**
03 hit
04 butt
05 stump
06 strike
07 receipt
11 cigaret butt, counterfoil
13 cigarette butt

**stubborn**
05 rigid
06 dogged, mulish, wilful
07 willful
08 obdurate
09 obstinate, pigheaded
10 headstrong, inflexible, unyielding
11 intractable, stiff-necked
12 intransigent, recalcitrant

**stubby**
05 dumpy, short, squat
06 chunky, stumpy
08 thickset

**stuck**
04 fast, firm
05 fixed, glued
06 beaten, jammed, rooted

07 at a loss, baffled, stumped
08 cemented, embedded, fastened, immobile
09 perplexed, unmovable
10 bogged down, nonplussed

❑**stuck on**
06 fond of, keen on
08 mad about
09 nuts about, wild about
10 crazy about, dotty about

**stuck-up**
05 proud
06 snooty, uppity
07 haughty
08 arrogant, snobbish
10 hoity-toity
11 patronizing
13 high and mighty

**studded**
06 dotted
07 flecked, spotted
08 spangled

**student**
04 coed
05 cadet, pupil
06 junior, premed, senior
07 learner, scholar, trainee
08 disciple, freshman
09 schoolboy, sophomore
10 apprentice, schoolgirl
12 postgraduate
13 undergraduate
15 graduate student

**studied**
08 affected
09 conscious, contrived, unnatural
10 artificial, calculated, deliberate, purposeful
11 intentional

**studio**
06 school
07 art room, atelier
08 workroom, workshop

**studious**
07 bookish, serious
08 academic, diligent, sedulous, thorough
09 assiduous, scholarly
10 meticulous, thoughtful
12 intellectual

**study**
03 den
04 cram, read, scan
05 learn, weigh
06 bone up, peruse, ponder, read up, revise, thesis
07 analyze, examine, inquiry, library, major in, reading, thought

08 analysis, consider, critique, homework, learning, pore over, research, revision, scrutiny, workroom
09 attention, monograph
10 deliberate, inspection, scrutinize
11 contemplate, examination, investigate, preparation, scholarship
13 contemplation, investigation

**stuff**
03 jam, kit, pad, ram
04 cram, fill, gear, load, pack, push, sate, stow
05 block, crowd, force, goods, gorge, items, press, shove
06 bung up, fabric, gobble, guzzle, matter, pig out, tackle, things, thrust
07 essence, luggage, objects, overeat, satiate, squeeze
08 articles, compress, material, obstruct
09 equipment, materials, substance
10 belongings, gormandize
11 overindulge, possessions
13 paraphernalia

**stuffing**
04 down
05 kapok
07 filling, packing, padding, wadding
08 dressing, quilting
09 forcemeat

**stuffy**
04 dull, prim
05 close, heavy, muggy, musty, staid, stale, stiff
06 stodgy, sultry
07 airless, pompous, starchy
08 stifling
10 fuddy-duddy, oppressive
11 strait-laced, suffocating
12 unventilated
13 straight-laced

**stultify**
04 dull, numb
05 blunt
07 nullify, smother, stupefy

**stumble**
04 fall, reel, slip, trip
05 lurch
06 falter
07 blunder, stagger, stammer, stutter
08 flounder, hesitate
15 lose your balance

❑**stumble on**
04 find

08 discover
09 encounter
10 chance upon, happen upon

**stumbling block**
04 snag
08 obstacle
09 hindrance
10 difficulty, impediment
11 obstruction

**stump**
04 butt, foil, stub
06 baffle, defeat, outwit, puzzle
07 confuse, flummox, mystify, nonplus, perplex
08 bewilder, confound
09 bamboozle, dumbfound
11 electioneer

**stumped**
05 stuck
07 baffled, floored, stymied
09 flummoxed, perplexed
10 bamboozled, nonplussed

**stumpy**
05 dumpy, squat, thick
06 chunky, stocky, stubby
08 thickset

**stun**
04 daze
05 amaze, shock
07 astound, confuse, stagger, stupefy
08 astonish, bewilder, bowl over, confound, knock out
09 dumbfound, overpower
11 flabbergast

**stunned**
04 numb
05 dazed
06 amazed
07 floored, shocked
09 astounded, staggered, stupefied

**stunner**
03 wow
05 peach, siren
06 beauty, looker, lovely
07 charmer, dazzler
08 knockout
09 sensation
10 good-looker

**stunning**
07 amazing
08 dazzling, smashing, striking
09 marvelous, ravishing, wonderful
10 staggering
11 sensational, spectacular

**stunt**
03 act

04 curb, deed, feat, slow, stop, turn
05 check, dwarf, trick
06 action, arrest, hamper, hinder, impede, retard, wheeze
07 exploit
08 restrict

**stunted**
04 tiny
05 small
06 little
07 dwarfed
10 diminutive, undersized

**stupefaction**
04 daze
06 wonder
08 blackout, numbness
09 amazement
10 bafflement
12 bewilderment

**stupefy**
04 daze, dull, numb, stun
05 amaze, shock
07 astound, stagger
08 bowl over, knock out
09 devastate, dumbfound

**stupendous**
06 superb
07 amazing, immense
08 colossal, stunning
09 thrilling
10 prodigious, tremendous
12 breathtaking, overwhelming

**stupid**
03 dim, mad
04 dull, dumb, rash, slow
05 crass, dazed, dense, dopey, inane, silly, thick
06 absurd, futile, groggy
07 fatuous, foolish, idiotic, lunatic, moronic, puerile, stunned
08 mindless, sluggish
09 brainless, foolhardy, imbecilic, ludicrous, senseless, stupefied
10 dull-witted, half-witted
11 meaningless, nonsensical, not all there
12 feebleminded, simpleminded
13 thick as a plank

**stupidity**
05 folly
06 idiocy, lunacy
07 fatuity, inanity, naïvety
08 futility
09 absurdity, asininity, puerility
10 imbecility, ineptitude

**stupor**
04 coma, daze
06 torpor, trance
07 inertia
08 blackout, oblivion
12 state of shock, stupefaction
13 insensibility

**sturdy**
05 hardy, solid, stout
06 hearty, robust, strong
07 durable, staunch
08 muscular, powerful, resolute, stalwart, vigorous
09 steadfast, well-built
10 determined

**stutter**
06 falter, mumble
07 stammer, stumble
08 hesitate, splutter

**style**
03 cut, dub, fad, tag, way
04 call, chic, dash, form, kind, make, mode, name, sort, term, tone, type
05 adapt, flair, genre, label, shape, taste, tenor, title, trend, vogue
06 custom, design, luxury, manner, method, polish, stylus, tailor, wealth
07 fashion, panache, pattern, produce, variety, wording
08 approach, category, elegance, grandeur, language, phrasing, urbanity
09 affluence, designate, technique
10 appearance, denominate, expression, refinement
11 methodology

**stylish**
04 chic
05 natty, ritzy, smart
06 classy, dressy, modish, snappy, snazzy, trendy, urbane
07 à la mode, elegant, in vogue, refined, voguish
08 polished
11 fashionable
13 sophisticated

**stylus**
03 pen
04 hand
05 index, probe, style
06 needle
07 pointer

**stymie, stymy**
04 balk, foil
05 baulk, stump

06 baffle, defeat, hinder, puzzle, thwart
07 flummox, mystify, nonplus
08 confound
09 bamboozle, frustrate

**suave**
04 glib
05 bland, civil
06 polite, smooth, urbane
07 affable, refined, worldly
08 charming, debonair, polished, unctuous
09 agreeable, civilized, courteous
13 sophisticated

**suavity**
05 charm
08 civility, courtesy, urbanity
09 sauveness
10 refinement
14 sophistication

**subaqueous**
08 demersal, undersea
09 submarine, submersed
10 subaquatic, underwater

**subconscious**
02 id
03 ego
04 deep
05 inner
06 hidden, latent, psyche
08 superego
09 innermost, intuitive, repressed
10 subliminal, suppressed, underlying
11 instinctive, unconscious

**subdue**
04 damp, tame
05 check, crush, quash, quell
06 defeat, humble, master, mellow, reduce, soften, stifle
07 conquer, control, overrun, quieten, repress, subject
08 moderate, overcome, restrain, suppress, vanquish
09 overpower, subjugate
10 discipline

**subdued**
03 dim, sad
04 soft
05 grave, muted, quiet, sober, still
06 hushed, low-key, pastel, shaded, silent, solemn, somber, subtle
08 dejected, delicate, downcast, lifeless, low-keyed, softened
09 depressed, toned down
10 restrained

11 crestfallen, unobtrusive
14 down in the dumps

**subject**
03 apt
05 bound, field, issue, point, prone, theme, topic
06 affair, aspect, client, expose, liable, likely, matter, subdue, submit, vassal, victim
07 captive, citizen, exposed, lay open
08 inferior, liegeman, national, question
09 dependent, dependent, subjugate, underling
10 answerable, contingent, discipline, subjugated, submissive, vulnerable
11 conditional, constrained, participant, subordinate, subservient, susceptible

**subjection**
06 chains, defeat
07 bondage, mastery, slavery
08 shackles
09 captivity
10 domination, oppression
11 enslavement, subjugation

**subjective**
06 biased
08 personal
09 emotional, intuitive
10 individual, prejudiced
11 instinctive
13 idiosyncratic

**subjugate**
04 tame
05 crush, quell
06 defeat, master, subdue
07 conquer, enslave, oppress
08 overcome, vanquish
09 overpower, overthrow
14 get the better of
15 gain mastery over

**sublimate**
06 divert, purify, refine
07 channel, elevate
08 heighten, redirect, transfer
09 transmute

**sublime**
04 high
05 grand, lofty, utter
07 exalted, supreme
08 elevated, glorious
09 spiritual
12 transcendent

**submerge**
03 dip
04 bury, duck, dunk, sink
05 drown, flood, swamp

06 deluge, engulf, go down, plunge
07 immerse, plummet
08 inundate, submerse
09 overwhelm
12 go under water
13 put under water

**submerged**
04 sunk
06 hidden, sunken, unseen
07 drowned, swamped
08 immersed
09 concealed, inundated, submersed
10 underwater

**submission**
05 entry
06 assent, tender
08 meekness, offering, proposal
09 assertion, deference, obedience, passivity, statement, surrender
10 compliance, suggestion
11 resignation
12 acquiescence, capitulation, introduction, presentation
14 submissiveness

**submissive**
04 meek, weak
06 docile, humble, supine
07 passive, servile
08 biddable, obedient, yielding
09 compliant, malleable
10 weak-willed
11 acquiescent, deferential, subservient, unresisting
12 ingratiating, self-effacing
13 accommodating, uncomplaining

**submit**
03 bow
04 aver, bend, move
05 argue, claim, offer, state, yield
06 accede, comply, give in, tender
07 give way, present, proffer, propose, succumb, suggest
09 acquiesce, introduce, surrender
10 capitulate, put forward
12 knuckle under
15 lay down your arms

**subordinate**
04 aide
05 gofer, lower, lowly, minor
06 deputy, junior, lesser, menial, second, vassal
08 inferior, sidekick
09 ancillary, assistant, attendant, auxiliary, dependent,

dependent, secondary, underling
10 subsidiary
12 second fiddle

**subordination**
09 servitude
10 dependence, subjection, submission
11 inferiority
12 subservience

**subscribe**
04 back, fork, give
05 agree
06 accede, donate, pledge
07 approve, consent, endorse, support
08 advocate, shell out
10 contribute, underwrite
13 take regularly
15 pay for regularly

**subscription**
04 dues, gift
07 payment
08 donation, offering
12 contribution
13 membership fee

**subsequent**
04 next
05 later
06 future.
07 ensuing
09 following, resulting
10 consequent, succeeding

**subsequently**
05 after, later
09 afterward
12 consequently

**subservient**
05 lower, minor
06 junior, lesser, useful
07 fawning, servile
08 inferior, toadying, unctuous
09 ancillary, auxiliary, secondary
10 obsequious, subsidiary
11 deferential, subordinate
12 ingratiating, instrumental

**subside**
03 ebb
04 drop, ease, fall, sink, wane
05 abate, let up, lower
06 cave in, lessen, recede, settle
07 decline, descend, dwindle, quieten, slacken
08 collapse, decrease, diminish, get lower, moderate

**subsidence**
07 decline, descent, sinking
08 decrease, settling
10 settlement, slackening
12 detumescence

**subsidiary**
05 minor
08 division, offshoot
09 ancillary, assistant, auxiliary
10 additional, supporting
11 subordinate, subservient

**subsidize**
03 aid
04 back, fund
07 endorse, finance, promote, sponsor, support
08 invest in
10 underwrite

**subsidy**
03 aid
04 help
05 grant
07 backing, finance, funding, support
10 subvention
11 endorsement, sponsorship
12 contribution, underwriting

**subsist**
04 live
05 exist
06 endure
07 survive

**subsistence**
06 living
07 aliment, alimony, support
08 survival
10 livelihood, sustenance
11 maintenance

**substance**
04 body, gist, mass, meat, pith, text
05 basis, force, means, money, power, theme, topic
06 assets, burden, fabric, ground, import, matter, riches, wealth, weight
07 essence, meaning, reality, subject
08 material, solidity, validity
09 affluence, resources
10 foundation
11 materiality, tangibility
12 corporeality, significance
13 subject matter
15 meat and potatoes

**substandard**
04 poor
06 shoddy
08 below par, inferior
09 imperfect
10 inadequate, second-rate
14 not up to scratch

**substantial**
04 main, real, rich

05 basic, solid, sound, stout, tough
06 actual, strong, sturdy
07 durable, sizable, wealthy, weighty
08 concrete, inherent, material, powerful, tangible, valuable
09 corporeal, essential, intrinsic, well-built
10 prosperous, successful
11 fundamental, significant
12 considerable

**substantially**
07 largely
10 materially
11 essentially
12 considerably
13 fundamentally, significantly
14 to a great extent

**substantiate**
05 prove
06 back up, uphold, verify
07 bear out, confirm, support
08 validate
11 corroborate

**substitute**
04 swap, temp
05 agent, cover, proxy
06 acting, change, deputy, fill in, relief, supply, switch
07 relieve, replace, reserve, stand-in, standby, stopgap
08 deputize, exchange, stuntman
09 surrogate
10 stuntwoman, understudy
11 pinch hitter, replacement

**substitution**
04 swap
06 change, switch
08 exchange
11 interchange, replacement

**subterfuge**
04 ploy, ruse, wile
05 dodge, trick
06 excuse, scheme
07 evasion, pretext
08 artifice, intrigue, maneuver, pretense
09 deception, duplicity, stratagem
11 deviousness
12 machinations

**subtle**
03 sly
04 deep, fine, mild, nice, wily
06 astute, crafty, low-key, shrewd, slight
07 complex, cunning, devious, elusive, implied, tactful
08 delicate, discreet, indirect

09 intricate, toned down
11 understated
14 discriminating

**subtlety**
05 guile, skill
06 acumen, nicety, nuance
07 cunning, finesse, slyness
08 delicacy, sagacity, wiliness
09 intricacy, mutedness
10 refinement
11 discernment
14 discrimination, sophistication

**subtract**
04 dock
05 debit
06 deduct, remove
08 take away, withdraw

**suburb**
07 fringes
08 purlieus, suburbia
09 outskirts
12 commuter belt
13 bedroom suburb, dormitory town
15 dormitory suburb

**suburban**
04 dull
07 insular
08 commuter
09 bourgeois
11 middle-class, residential
12 conventional

**subversive**
07 riotous, traitor
08 quisling
09 dissident, seditious, terrorist
10 disruptive, incendiary, traitorous, treasonous
11 seditionist, treacherous
12 inflammatory
13 revolutionary
14 fifth columnist, freedom fighter

**subvert**
04 ruin
05 upset, wreck
06 debase
07 corrupt, disrupt
08 sabotage
09 undermine

**subway**
05 metro
06 tunnel
14 underground way

**succeed**
04 work
05 ensue, get on
06 attain, do well, follow, fulfil, manage

07 achieve, fulfill, prosper, pull off, realize, replace, work out
08 flourish, go places, make good
09 come after, win the day
10 accomplish, get results
14 fall on your feet, land on your feet, take the place of

❏ **succeed to**
06 accede, assume
07 inherit, replace
08 come into, take over
09 enter upon, supersede

**succeeding**
04 next
05 later
06 coming, to come
07 ensuing
09 following
10 subsequent, successive

**success**
03 hit, VIP, wow
04 fame, luck, star
05 smash
06 winner
07 fortune, triumph, victory
08 champion, eminence, smash hit, somebody
09 celebrity, sensation
10 attainment, bestseller, fulfilment, prosperity
11 achievement, fulfillment, realization
14 accomplishment

**successful**
07 booming, popular, wealthy
08 affluent, fruitful, thriving
09 fortunate, lucrative, rewarding, well-known
10 prosperous, triumphant, victorious
11 bestselling, flourishing, moneymaking

**successfully**
04 fine, well
05 great
08 famously
10 swimmingly
11 beautifully
12 victoriously

**succession**
03 run
04 flow, line
05 chain, cycle, order, train
06 course, series, string
08 sequence
09 accession
10 assumption, procession
11 inheritance, progression
12 continuation

❏ **in succession**
07 running
12 sequentially
13 consecutively

**successive**
06 serial
07 running
09 following
10 sequential, succeeding
11 consecutive

**successively**
07 running
12 sequentially
13 consecutively

**successor**
04 heir
06 relief
09 inheritor
10 descendant, next in line, substitute
11 beneficiary, replacement

**succinct**
05 brief, crisp, pithy, short, terse
07 compact, concise, in a word
09 condensed
10 to the point

**succor**
03 aid
04 help
06 assist, foster, relief
07 comfort, relieve, support
10 assistance, minister to

**succulent**
04 lush, rich
05 juicy, moist
06 fleshy, mellow
08 luscious
13 mouthwatering

**succumb**
04 fall
05 catch, die of, yield
06 give in, pick up, submit
07 give way
08 collapse, contract
09 surrender
10 capitulate, go down with
12 knuckle under

**suck**
04 draw
05 drain
06 absorb, blot up, draw in, imbibe, soak up
07 extract

❏ **suck up to**
04 fawn
05 toady
07 flatter, truckle
09 brown-nose
10 curry favor, ingratiate

**sucker**
03 mug, sap
04 butt, dupe, fool
06 stooge, victim
07 cat's-paw
08 pushover

**suckle**
04 feed
05 nurse
07 nourish
10 breast-feed

**sudden**
04 fast, rash, snap
05 hasty, quick, rapid, sharp, swift
06 abrupt, prompt, speedy
07 hurried
09 immediate, impetuous, impulsive
13 instantaneous, unanticipated
15 spur-of-the-moment

**suddenly**
07 quickly, sharply
08 abruptly
11 immediately
12 all of a sudden, out of the blue
14 without warning
15 instantaneously

**suddenness**
05 haste
09 hastiness
10 abruptness
13 impulsiveness

**suds**
05 froth
06 lather
07 bubbles

**sue**
03 beg
05 plead
06 appeal, charge, indict, summon
07 beseech, solicit
08 petition
09 prosecute
11 take to court

**suffer**
04 ache, bear, feel, hurt
05 abide, stand
06 endure, grieve, sorrow
07 agonize, support, sustain, undergo
08 tolerate
09 go through, put up with
10 experience

**suffering**
04 hurt, pain
05 agony
06 misery, ordeal, plight

07 anguish, hurting, torment, torture
08 distress, hardship
09 adversity
10 affliction, discomfort
12 wretchedness

**suffice**
02 do
05 serve
06 answer
07 content, satisfy
10 be adequate, fit the bill
11 fill the bill

**sufficiency**
06 enough, plenty
08 adequacy
12 adequateness

**sufficient**
05 ample
06 decent, enough, plenty
08 adequate
09 effective
12 satisfactory

**suffocate**
05 choke
06 stifle
07 smother
08 strangle, throttle
10 asphyxiate

**suffrage**
09 franchise
11 right to vote
15 enfranchisement

**suffuse**
05 bathe, flood, imbue, steep
06 infuse, redden, spread
07 pervade
08 permeate

**sugary**
05 corny, gushy, mushy, soppy, sweet
06 sickly, sloppy, slushy
07 gushing, maudlin, mawkish
09 emotional, schmaltzy
10 lovey-dovey
11 sentimental

**suggest**
04 hint, move
05 evoke, float, imply
06 advise, submit
07 counsel, propose
08 advocate, indicate, intimate
09 insinuate, recommend
10 put forward
11 bring to mind

**suggestion**
04 hint, idea, plan
05 touch, trace
07 pointer

08 innuendo, proposal
09 suspicion
10 indication, intimation
11 implication, insinuation, proposition
14 recommendation

**suggestive**
04 blue, lewd
05 bawdy, dirty
06 ribald, risqué, sexual, smutty
08 immodest, improper, indecent, off-color, redolent
09 evocative
10 expressive, indelicate, indicative
11 provocative, reminiscent, titillating

**suicide**
06 suttee
08 felo-de-se, hara-kiri
10 self-murder
11 ending it all
15 killing yourself, self-destruction

**suit**
03 fit
04 case
05 befit, cause, dress, match, trial
06 action, answer, become, outfit, please
07 contest, costume, dispute, flatter, gratify, lawsuit, process, qualify, satisfy, suffice
08 argument, clothing, ensemble
09 agree with, tally with
10 complement, fit the bill, litigation
11 fill the bill, proceedings, prosecution

**suitability**
07 aptness, fitness
11 convenience, fittingness
12 appositeness
15 appropriateness

**suitable**
03 apt, due, fit
05 right
06 proper, seemly, suited
07 fitting
08 adequate, apposite, becoming, relevant
09 befitting, in keeping, opportune, pertinent
10 acceptable, applicable, compatible, convenient
11 appropriate, well-matched
12 satisfactory

**suitably**
05 fitly, quite
08 properly
09 fittingly
10 acceptably
11 accordingly
13 appropriately

**suitcase**
03 bag
04 case, grip
05 trunk
06 valise
07 carry-on, luggage
09 flight bag, travel bag
10 vanity case
11 attaché case, hand luggage, portmanteau
12 overnight bag
15 hand-held luggage

**suite**
03 set
05 rooms, train
06 escort, series
07 retinue
08 sequence, servants
09 apartment, entourage, followers, furniture, household, retainers
10 attendants, collection

**suitor**
04 beau
05 lover, swain, wooer
07 admirer
08 follower, young man
09 boyfriend

**sulk**
04 huff, miff, mood, mope, pout
05 brood, grump, pique
06 grouse, temper

**sulky**
05 cross, huffy, moody
06 grumpy, miffed, put out, sullen
08 brooding, grudging
09 resentful
10 out of sorts

**sullen**
04 dark, dull, glum, sour
05 heavy, moody, sulky, surly
06 dismal, gloomy, leaden, morose, silent, somber
08 churlish, perverse, stubborn
09 resentful

**sullenness**
08 brooding, glumness
09 glowering, moodiness, sulkiness, surliness

**sully**
03 mar
04 soil, spot

05 dirty, spoil, stain, taint
06 befoul, damage, defile
07 blemish, pollute, tarnish
08 besmirch, disgrace
11 contaminate

**sultry**
04 sexy
05 close, humid, muggy
06 sticky, stuffy
07 airless, sensual
08 alluring, stifling, tempting
09 seductive
10 oppressive, sweltering, voluptuous
11 provocative, suffocating

**sum**
05 score, tally, total, whole
06 amount, number, result
07 summary
08 entirety, quantity, sum total
09 aggregate, reckoning

**❏sum up**
06 embody, review
09 epitomize, exemplify, summarize
11 encapsulate
14 put in a nutshell

**summarily**
07 hastily, swiftly
08 abruptly, promptly, speedily
09 forthwith
11 arbitrarily, immediately
12 peremptorily, without delay

**summarize**
05 recap, sum up
06 précis, review, sketch
07 abridge, outline, shorten
08 condense
09 epitomize
10 abbreviate
11 encapsulate

**summary**
05 brief, hasty, short, swift
06 digest, précis, prompt, review, résumé, speedy
07 cursory, instant, outline, rundown
08 abstract, succinct, synopsis
09 arbitrary, immediate
10 abridgment, main points, peremptory
12 without delay

**summer house**
06 gazebo
08 pavilion
09 belvedere

**summit**
03 top
04 acme, apex, head, peak
05 crest, crown, point

06 apogee, climax, height, vertex, zenith
08 pinnacle
11 culmination
14 leaders' meeting

**summon**
05 order, rally, rouse
06 arouse, beckon, demand, gather, invite, muster
07 convene, convoke, send for
08 assemble, mobilize

**❏summon up**
05 evoke, rally, rouse
06 arouse, gather, muster
10 call to mind

**summons**
04 call, writ
05 order
08 citation, subpoena
10 injunction

**sumptuous**
05 grand, plush
06 costly, deluxe, lavish, superb
07 opulent
08 gorgeous, splendid
09 expensive, luxurious
11 extravagant, magnificent

**sun**
03 Sol, tan
04 bask, bask, star
05 brown, light
06 suntan
08 daylight, insolate, sunbathe, sunlight, sunshine

**sunbathe**
03 sun, tan
04 bake, bask
08 insolate

**sunburned, sunburnt**
03 red
05 brown
06 burned, tanned
07 bronzed, peeling
09 blistered, suntanned

**sunder**
04 chop, part
05 sever, split
06 cleave, divide
08 dissever, separate

**sundry**
04 a few, some
07 diverse, several, various
08 assorted
09 different
13 miscellaneous

**sunk**
06 doomed, failed, in a fix, in a jam, ruined
07 done for

**sunken**
08 finished
09 submerged
10 up the creek

**sunken**
05 drawn, lower
06 buried, hollow
07 concave, haggard, lowered
08 recessed
09 depressed, submerged

**sunless**
04 dark, gray, hazy
06 cloudy, dismal, dreary, gloomy, somber
08 overcast
10 depressing

**sunny**
05 clear, happy, merry
06 blithe, bright, joyful, sunlit
07 beaming, radiant, smiling, summery
09 brilliant, cloudless
10 optimistic
12 lighthearted

**sunrise**
04 dawn
05 sunup
06 aurora
08 cockcrow, daybreak, daylight
10 break of day, first light
11 crack of dawn

**sunset**
03 eve
04 dusk
07 evening, sundown
08 gloaming, twilight
09 nightfall
10 close of day

**super**
03 ace
04 cool, neat
05 great
06 superb, wicked
08 glorious, peerless, smashing, terrific, top-notch
09 excellent, marvelous, matchless, wonderful
11 magnificent, outstanding, sensational
12 incomparable

**superannuated**
04 aged
07 elderly, retired
08 decrepit, obsolete
10 antiquated
12 pensioned off

**superb**
06 choice, lavish
08 fabulous, smashing, splendid, terrific

09 brilliant, excellent, exquisite, first-rate, wonderful
10 first-class
11 outstanding, superlative

**supercilious**
05 lofty, proud
06 lordly, snooty, snotty, uppity
07 haughty, stuck-up
08 arrogant, scornful
09 imperious
10 disdainful
11 overbearing, patronizing
13 condescending

**superficial**
05 outer
06 casual, facile, slight
07 cursory, hurried, seeming, shallow, surface
08 cosmetic, external, skin-deep, slapdash
11 lightweight, perfunctory

**superficially**
08 casually
09 hurriedly, seemingly
10 externally, ostensibly
12 on the surface

**superfluity**
04 glut
06 excess
07 surfeit, surplus
08 pleonasm, plethora
10 exuberance, redundancy
14 superabundance

**superfluous**
05 extra, spare
06 excess
07 surplus
08 unneeded
09 excessive, redundant, remaining
10 gratuitous
11 uncalled-for, unnecessary, unwarranted
13 supernumerary

**superhuman**
06 divine, heroic
09 herculean
10 phenomenal, prodigious
12 supernatural
13 preternatural

**superintend**
06 direct, handle, manage
07 control, inspect, oversee
09 supervise
10 administer
12 be in charge of
13 be in control of

**superintendence**
06 charge
07 control, running

09 direction
10 management
11 supervision
12 surveillance

**superintendent**
04 boss
07 curator, foreman, manager
08 director, governor, overseer
09 conductor, custodian, inspector, straw boss
10 controller, supervisor

**superior**
04 boss, fine
05 chief, lofty, prime, prize
06 better, choice, deluxe, higher, lordly, select, senior, snooty, uppity
07 foreman, greater, haughty, manager, quality, stuck-up
08 director, snobbish, top-notch
09 admirable, excellent, exclusive, first-rate, high-class, preferred, principal, top-flight, unrivaled
10 disdainful, first-class, supervisor
11 exceptional, high-quality, patronizing, pretentious
12 higher in rank, supercilious
13 condescending

**superiority**
08 eminence
09 supremacy
10 ascendancy
11 preeminence
12 predominance

**superlative**
07 highest, supreme
08 greatest, peerless
09 excellent, first-rate, matchless, unrivaled
10 first-class
11 outstanding, unsurpassed
12 transcendent, unparalleled

**supernatural**
05 eerie, magic, weird
06 hidden, mystic, occult
07 ghostly, magical, phantom, psychic
08 mystical
09 spiritual, unnatural
10 paranormal
12 metaphysical, otherworldly
13 preternatural

**supernumerary**
05 extra, spare
06 excess
07 surplus
09 excessive, redundant
11 superfluous

## supersede
05 usurp
07 replace, succeed
08 displace, supplant

## superstition
04 myth
05 magic
12 old wives' tale

## superstitious
08 mythical
10 groundless, irrational

## supervise
05 watch
06 direct
07 conduct, control, inspect, oversee
09 look after, watch over
11 keep an eye on, preside over, superintend

## supervision
06 charge
07 control
09 direction, oversight
10 inspection
12 surveillance
15 superintendence

## supervisor
07 foreman, manager, steward
08 director, overseer
09 forewoman, inspector
14 superintendent

## supervisory
10 overseeing
11 directorial
14 superintendent

## supine
04 flat, idle
07 languid, passive
08 inactive
09 prostrate, recumbent
10 horizontal

## supper
04 meal
06 dinner
11 evening meal

## supplant
04 oust
05 usurp
06 remove, topple, unseat
07 replace
08 displace
09 overthrow, supersede

## supple
05 lithe
06 limber, pliant, supple
07 bending, elastic, plastic, pliable
08 flexible
11 loose-limbed

13 double-jointed

## supplement
05 add to, add-on, boost, extra, rider
06 eke out, extend, fill up, insert, sequel
07 augment, codicil
08 addendum, addition, additive, appendix, increase
10 complement, postscript
15 newspaper insert

## supplementary
05 added, extra
09 auxiliary, secondary
10 additional
13 complementary

## suppliant
07 begging, craving
09 imploring
10 beseeching, entreating
11 importunate
12 supplicating

## supplicant
06 suitor
07 pleader
09 applicant, postulant, suppliant
10 petitioner

## supplicate
04 pray
05 plead
06 appeal, invoke
07 beseech, entreat, request, solicit
08 petition

## supplication
04 plea, suit
06 appeal, orison, prayer
07 request
08 entreaty, petition, pleading, rogation
10 invocation
11 imploration
12 solicitation

## supplicatory
07 begging
09 imploring, precative
10 beseeching
11 imprecatory, petitioning
12 supplicating

## supplier
06 dealer, seller, vendor
08 provider, retailer
10 wholesaler

## supply
04 fill, food, fund, give, heap, mass, pile, sell

05 cache, endow, endue, equip, grant, hoard, stock, store, yield
06 amount, donate, fit out, outfit, source, stores
07 furnish, produce, proffer, provide, rations, reserve
08 quantity
09 equipment, grubstake, materials, reservoir, stockpile
10 contribute, provisions

## support
03 aid
04 back, base, bear, care, feed, food, fund, help, keep, post, prop, stay
05 brace, carry, grant
06 assist, back up, be with, crutch, defend, foster, hold up, pillar, prop up, ratify, relief, second, verify
07 backing, bear out, bolster, care for, comfort, confirm, endorse, finance, funding, loyalty, nourish, promote, run with, shore up, sponsor, subsidy, sustain, trestle
08 advocate, approval, be behind, buttress, champion, donation, maintain, skeleton, strength, sympathy, underpin, validate
09 bolster up, encourage, grubstake, look after, patronage, provision, reinforce, subsidize
10 allegiance, foundation, protection, provide for, strengthen, sustenance, take care of, underwrite
11 be in favor of, corroborate, foundations, maintenance, rally around, sponsorship, subsistence
12 contribute to, contribution, substantiate, substructure, underpinning
15 take the weight of

## supporter
03 fan
04 ally
05 angel, donor, voter
06 friend, helper, patron
07 partner, sponsor
08 adherent, advocate, champion, co-worker, defender, follower, promoter, seconder
09 apologist

## supportive
06 caring
07 helpful

**suppose**
10 comforting, reassuring
11 encouraging, sympathetic

**suppose**
05 fancy, guess, imply, infer, judge, posit, think
06 assume, expect, reckon
07 believe, imagine, presume, require, surmise
08 conclude, consider
09 postulate
10 conjecture, presuppose
11 hypothesize
14 take for granted

**supposed**
07 alleged, assumed, reputed, rumored
08 believed, imagined, presumed, putative, reported, so-called
12 hypothetical

◻**supposed to**
07 meant to
09 obliged to
10 intended to, required to

**supposition**
04 idea
05 guess
06 notion, theory
07 surmise
10 assumption, conjecture, hypothesis
11 postulation, presumption, speculation
14 presupposition

**suppress**
05 check, crush, quash, quell
06 censor, squash, stifle, subdue
07 inhibit, repress, silence, smother
08 restrain, strangle, vanquish, withhold
10 put an end to
11 clamp down on, crack down on

**suppression**
07 coverup
08 crushing, quashing, quelling
09 clampdown, crackdown
10 censorship, smothering

**suppurate**
04 ooze, weep
06 fester, gather
08 maturate
09 discharge

**suppuration**
03 pus
09 diapyesis, festering

**supremacy**
04 rule, sway

05 power
07 control, mastery, primacy
08 dominion, hegemony
10 ascendancy, domination
11 paramountcy, preeminence, sovereignty
12 predominance

**supreme**
03 top
04 best, head
05 chief, first, prime
06 utmost
07 extreme, highest, leading
08 crowning, foremost, greatest, peerless, ultimate
09 first-rate, matchless, principal, sovereign
10 first-class, preeminent
11 predominant, superlative
12 second-to-none, world-beating

**sure**
04 fast, firm, safe
05 bound, clear, loyal, solid
06 secure, stable, steady, tested
07 assured, certain, decided, precise
08 accurate, faithful, home free, positive, reliable, sure-fire, unerring
09 confident, convinced, effective, foolproof, steadfast, undoubted, unfailing
10 dependable, guaranteed, inevitable, infallible, sure-footed, undeniable, unwavering
11 trustworthy, unfaltering
12 indisputable, never-failing, unmistakable
14 sound as a dollar, unquestionable

**surely**
06 firmly
09 assuredly, certainly
10 definitely, inevitably
11 confidently, doubtlessly, indubitably, undoubtedly
12 without doubt
14 unquestionably

**surety**
04 bail, bond
06 pledge, safety
07 deposit, hostage, warrant
08 bondsman, security, warranty
09 certainty, guarantee, guarantor, indemnity, insurance, mortgager, mortgagor

**surface**
03 top
04 face, rise, side, skin
05 arise, outer, plane
06 appear, come up, emerge, façade, veneer
07 outside, outward
08 covering, exterior, external
11 come to light, materialize, superficial

◻**on the surface**
13 superficially

**surfeit**
04 cram, fill, glut
05 gorge, stuff
06 excess
07 satiate, satiety, surplus
08 bellyful, overfeed, overfill, plethora
14 superabundance

**surge**
04 eddy, flow, gush, pour, rise, roll, rush, wave
05 sweep, swell, swirl, waves
06 efflux, seethe, stream
07 pouring, upsurge, upswing

**surgeon**
───────────────────
► *Names of surgeons:*
04 **Bell** (Charles), **Mayo** (Charles Horace), **Mayo** (William James), **Reed** (Walter)
05 **Broca** (Paul Pierre), **Paget** (James)
06 **Carrel** (Alexis), **Cooper** (Astley), **Gorgas** (William Crawford), **Hunter** (John), **Lister** (Joseph), **Thorek** (Max), **Treves** (Frederick)
07 **Barnard** (Christian Neethling), **Burkitt** (Denis Parsons), **Cushing** (Harvey Williams), **DeBakey** (Michael Ellis)
08 **Beaumont** (William), **Billroth** (Theodor), **Charnley** (John), **McDowell** (Ephraim)
➤ See also DOCTOR

**surly**
05 gruff
06 crusty, sullen
07 brusque, uncivil
08 churlish
10 ill-natured, ungracious

**surmise**
04 idea
05 fancy, guess, infer, opine
06 assume, deduce, notion

07 imagine, opinion, presume, suppose, suspect, thought
08 conclude, consider
09 deduction, inference, speculate, suspicion
10 assumption, conclusion, conjecture, hypothesis
11 possibility, presumption, speculation, supposition

**surmount**
06 exceed, master
07 conquer, get over, surpass
08 overcome, vanquish

**surpass**
04 beat
05 excel, outdo
06 better, exceed
07 eclipse
08 outclass, outshine, outstrip
09 transcend
10 overshadow, tower above

**surpassing**
09 matchless, unrivaled
10 inimitable
11 outstanding, unsurpassed
12 incomparable, transcendent

**surplus**
04 glut
05 extra, spare
06 excess, unused
07 balance, residue, surfeit
08 left over
09 leftovers, redundant, remainder, remaining

**surprise**
03 wow
04 stun
05 amaze
06 wonder
07 astound, startle
08 astonish, bewilder, bowl over
09 amazement, bombshell, burst in on, take aback
11 flabbergast, incredulity
12 astonishment, bewilderment
13 catch in the act, catch unawares
14 catch red-handed
15 bolt from the blue

**surprised**
06 amazed
08 startled
10 astonished
11 open-mouthed

**surprising**
07 amazing
09 wonderful
10 astounding, incredible, remarkable, unexpected, unforeseen

11 astonishing, unlooked-for

**surrender**
04 cede
05 waive, yield
06 give up, resign, submit
07 abandon, cession, concede, let go of, succumb, waiving
08 abdicate, renounce, yielding
10 abdication, relinquish
11 abandonment, leave behind, resignation
12 renunciation
14 relinquishment

**surreptitious**
03 sly
06 covert, sneaky
07 furtive
08 stealthy
09 underhand
11 clandestine

**surrogate**
05 proxy
07 stand-in
10 substitute
11 replacement

**surround**
04 gird, ring
05 beset, hem in
06 encase, girdle
07 confine, enclose, envelop, environ, fence in
08 encircle
09 encompass

**surrounding**
06 nearby
08 adjacent, suburban
09 adjoining, bordering
10 encircling
11 neighboring

**surroundings**
05 scene
06 milieu
07 element, habitat, setting
08 ambience, environs, locality, vicinity
10 background
11 environment
12 neighborhood

**surveillance**
05 watch
08 scrutiny
10 inspection, monitoring
11 observation, supervision
15 superintendence

**survey**
03 map
04 plan, plot, poll, scan, view
05 audit, chart, probe, study
06 assess, look at, review
07 examine, inspect, measure

08 appraise, consider, estimate, evaluate, look over, overview, research, scrutiny
09 appraisal, check over, valuation
10 assessment, inspection
11 examination, opinion poll, reconnoiter
13 consideration, questionnaire
14 market research

**surveyor**
08 assessor, examiner
09 geodesist, inspector

**survive**
04 cope, last, live, stay
05 exist, rally
06 endure, live on, make it, manage, remain
07 hold out, outlast, outlive, persist, recover, weather
08 be extant, continue
09 withstand
11 pull through

**susceptibility**
08 tendency, weakness
09 liability, proneness
10 proclivity, propensity
11 gullibility, sensitivity
13 vulnerability
14 predisposition, suggestibility

**susceptible**
05 given, prone
06 liable, tender
07 subject
08 disposed, gullible, inclined
09 credulous, easily led, receptive, sensitive
10 responsive, vulnerable
11 defenseless, suggestible
14 impressionable

**suspect**
04 feel, iffy
05 doubt, fancy, fishy, guess, infer
07 believe, dubious, suppose, surmise
08 be wary of, conclude, consider, distrust, doubtful, misdoubt, mistrust
09 debatable, smell a rat, speculate
10 conjecture, have a hunch, suspicious, unreliable
12 questionable
13 be uneasy about
15 have doubts about, have qualms about

**suspend**
04 hang
05 cease, defer, delay, swing, table

**suspended**
06 arrest, dangle, shelve
07 adjourn, exclude, keep out, shut out, unfrock
08 postpone, prorogue, put on ice
09 interrupt
11 discontinue
13 put in abeyance

**suspended**
06 tabled
07 hanging, pendent, pending
08 deferred, put on ice
09 postponed

**suspense**
07 anxiety, mystery, tension
10 expectancy
11 expectation, nervousness, uncertainty
12 anticipation, apprehension

**suspension**
04 stay
05 break, delay
07 respite
08 abeyance, deferral
09 cessation, deferment, exclusion, remission
10 moratorium, unfrocking
12 intermission, interruption, postponement

**suspicion**
04 hint, idea
05 hunch, shade, tinge, touch
06 notion, shadow
07 glimmer, soupçon
08 distrust, mistrust, wariness
09 chariness, misgiving, scintilla
10 skepticism, suggestion
12 apprehension, funny feeling

**suspicious**
03 odd
04 iffy, wary
05 chary, fishy, shady
06 shifty, uneasy, unsure
07 dubious, strange, suspect
08 doubtful, peculiar
09 dishonest, skeptical
10 suspecting
11 distrustful, mistrustful
12 disbelieving, questionable
13 looking guilty

**sustain**
04 bear, feed, help, hold
06 assist, endure, foster, keep up, suffer, uphold
07 comfort, nourish, nurture, prolong, support, undergo
08 continue, happen to, maintain, protract
09 encourage, go through, keep going
10 experience, provide for

14 give strength to

**sustained**
06 steady
08 constant
09 perpetual, prolonged
10 continuous, protracted
11 unremitting
12 long-drawn-out

**sustenance**
04 fare, food, grub, nosh
06 viands
07 aliment, support
08 victuals
09 provender, refection
10 livelihood, provisions
11 comestibles, nourishment

**svelte**
04 slim
05 lithe
06 lissom, urbane
07 elegant, shapely, slender, willowy
08 graceful, polished
09 sylphlike
13 sophisticated

**swagger**
04 brag, crow, show
05 boast, strut, swank
06 parade, prance
07 bluster, show off
08 parading, prancing
09 arrogance
11 ostentation

**swallow**
03 buy, eat
04 bear, bird, down, gulp, swig, take
05 abide, drink, quaff, scoff, stand, trust
06 accept, devour, endure, guzzle, ingest, stifle
07 believe, consume, contain, fall for, repress, smother, stomach
08 gobble up, hold back, suppress, tolerate
09 knock back, polish off, put up with

❏**swallow up**
06 absorb, enfold, engulf
07 envelop, overrun
09 overwhelm

**swamp**
03 bog, fen, mud
04 mire, quag, sink
05 beset, flood, marsh
06 deluge, drench, engulf, morass, slough
07 besiege, wash out

08 inundate, overload, quagmire, saturate, submerge, waterlog
09 overwhelm, weigh down

**swampy**
04 miry
05 boggy, fenny, soggy
06 marshy, quaggy
07 paludal
08 squelchy
11 waterlogged

**swank**
04 brag, show
05 boast, strut
07 conceit, show off, swagger
09 vainglory
10 showing-off
11 ostentation
15 pretentiousness

**swanky**
04 posh, rich
05 fancy, flash, grand, plush, ritzy, showy, smart
06 deluxe, flashy, lavish, plushy
12 ostentatious

**swap, swop**
05 bandy, trade
06 barter, switch
08 exchange
09 transpose
10 substitute

**swarm**
03 mob
04 army, herd, host, mass, pack
05 crowd, drove, flock, flood, horde, shoal, surge
06 myriad, stream, throng
10 congregate

❏**be swarming with**
08 abound in
13 be crowded with, be overrun with, be teeming with
14 be crawling with

**swarthy**
05 black, brown, dusky
06 tanned
11 dark-skinned

**swashbuckling**
07 dashing, gallant
09 daredevil
10 flamboyant

**swathe**
03 lap
04 bind, fold, furl, wind, wrap
05 cloak, drape
06 enwrap, shroud
07 bandage, envelop, sheathe, swaddle
08 enshroud

**sway**
04 bend, lean, reel, rock, roll, rule, veer, wave
05 clout, lurch, power, swing
06 affect, direct, divert, govern, induce, swerve, wobble
07 command, control, convert, incline, stagger, win over
08 convince, dominate, dominion, hegemony, overrule, persuade
09 authority, influence
10 ascendancy, government, leadership
11 bring around, prevail upon, sovereignty
12 jurisdiction, predominance

**swear**
03 vow
04 aver, avow, cuss
05 blind, curse
06 abjure, affirm, assert, attest, insist, pledge
07 declare, promise, testify
08 maledict
09 blaspheme, imprecate
10 asseverate, take an oath
11 take the oath
14 pledge yourself, turn the air blue, use bad language

□**swear by**
07 trust in
08 depend on
09 believe in
11 have faith in

**swearing**
07 cursing, cussing
09 blasphemy, profanity
10 coprolalia, expletives
12 imprecations, maledictions

**swearword**
04 oath
05 curse
09 blasphemy, expletive, obscenity, profanity
11 bad language, imprecation
12 foul language
14 four-letter word

**sweat**
04 drip, flap, fuss, toil
05 chore, exude, labor, panic, sudor, tizzy, worry
06 dither, effort
07 anxiety, fluster, secrete, swelter
08 drudgery, hidrosis, moisture, perspire
09 agitation
10 stickiness
11 diaphoresis
12 perspiration

**sweaty**
04 damp
05 moist
06 clammy, sticky
10 perspiring

**sweep**
03 arc, fly
04 bend, drag, dust, move, pass, poke, push, race, sail, scud, skim, span, tear, whip
05 brush, clean, clear, curve, drive, elbow, force, glide, range, scope, shove, swing, vista, whisk
06 action, extent, remove, stroke, thrust
07 clean up, clear up, compass, expanse, gesture, stretch
08 movement, vastness
09 curvature, immensity

**sweeping**
04 wide
05 broad
06 global
07 blanket, general, radical
09 extensive, wholesale
11 far-reaching, wide-ranging
12 all-embracing, all-inclusive
13 comprehensive
14 across-the-board, indiscriminate

**sweepstake**
04 draw
06 raffle, sweeps
07 lottery
08 gambling

**sweet**
04 cute, dear, kind, pure, ripe, soft
05 balmy, candy, clean, clear, fresh, glacé
06 bonbon, dulcet, kindly, lovely, mellow, pretty, sickly, sugary, syrupy, tender
07 amiable, brownie, candied, darling, dessert, honeyed, lovable, musical, odorous, tuneful, winning, winsome
08 adorable, aromatic, charming, engaging, fragrant, likeable, luscious, perfumed, pleasant, pleasing, precious, redolent
09 agreeable, ambrosial, appealing, beautiful, cherished, delicious, melodious, treasured, wholesome
10 attractive, confection, delightful, euphonious, harmonious, saccharine

11 mellifluous, odoriferous
12 affectionate
13 confectionery

► *Names of sweet treats:*
04 soda
05 fudge, halva, jello, taffy
06 bonbon, halvah, nougat
07 caramel, fondant, gumdrop, praline, truffle
08 bull's-eye, ice cream, lollipop, marzipan
09 jelly bean, liquorice, milkshake
10 candy apple, peppermint
11 barley sugar, cotton candy, marshmallow
12 butterscotch, chocolate bar
14 Turkish delight
➤ See also FOOD

□**sweet on**
06 fond of, keen on
08 mad about
10 crazy about
14 infatuated with

**sweeten**
05 honey, sugar
06 mellow, soften, soothe, temper
07 appease, mollify, relieve
08 mitigate
09 alleviate

**sweetheart**
04 dear, love
05 flame, honey, lover, Romeo, swain
06 steady, suitor
07 admirer, beloved, darling
09 betrothed, boyfriend, inamorata, inamorato, valentine
10 girlfriend

**sweetness**
07 euphony, harmony
09 dulcitude, fragrance
10 succulence, sugariness

**sweet-smelling**
07 odorous
08 aromatic, fragrant, perfumed, redolent
11 odoriferous

**swell**
04 beau, grow, posh, rise, wave
05 bloat, bulge, dandy, grand, great, mount, ritzy, smart, surge
06 bigwig, billow, blow up, deluxe, dilate, expand, extend, fatten, flashy, puff up, swanky

07 augment, balloon, distend, enlarge, inflate, stylish
08 escalate, heighten, increase, mushroom, snowball
09 cockscomb, exclusive, intensify, skyrocket
10 accelerate, undulation

**swelling**
04 boil, bump, lump
05 bulge
07 blister
09 puffiness
10 distension, tumescence
12 protuberance

**sweltering**
03 hot
05 humid, muggy
06 baking, clammy, steamy, sticky, sultry, torrid
07 airless, boiling
08 roasting, sizzling, stifling
10 oppressive
11 suffocating

**swerve**
04 bend, skew, turn, veer
05 sheer, shift, swing, twist
07 deflect, deviate, diverge

**swift**
04 fast
05 agile, brief, brisk, fleet, hasty, quick, rapid
06 abrupt, flying, lively, nimble, prompt, speedy, sudden
07 express, hurried
11 expeditious

**swiftly**
07 express
09 instantly, posthaste
10 double time
11 double-quick
12 hotfooting it

**swiftness**
05 speed
08 alacrity, celerity, dispatch, velocity

**swill**
04 gulp, swig
05 drain, drink, quaff, slops, waste
06 guzzle, imbibe, refuse
07 consume, hogwash, swallow, toss off
08 pigswill, scorings
09 knock back

❏ **swill out**
05 clean, flush, rinse
06 drench, sluice
07 cleanse, wash out

**swim**
03 bob
05 bathe, float
07 snorkel
08 take a dip

► *Swimming strokes*:
05 crawl
09 butterfly, dog paddle, freestyle
10 backstroke, sidestroke
12 breaststroke

**swimming pool**
04 lido, pond, tank
10 natatorium
11 leisure pool
12 swimming hole

**swimsuit**
06 bikini, trunks
11 bathing suit

**swindle**
03 con
04 dupe, rook, scam
05 cheat, fraud, sting, trick
06 diddle, fiddle, fleece, racket, rip off, rip-off
07 deceive, defraud, exploit
10 overcharge
12 put one over on
13 double-dealing, sharp practice

**swindler**
04 hood, rook
05 cheat, fraud, rogue, shark
06 con man
07 fiddler, hoodlum, hustler
08 chiseler
09 con artist

**swine**
03 hog, pig
04 boar, boor
05 beast, brute, rogue

**swing**
04 bend, hang, jazz, lean, make, move, rock, spin, sway, turn, vary, veer, wave, wind
05 curve, fix up, music, pivot, set up, shift, twist
06 change, dangle, rhythm, rotate, stroke, swerve
07 achieve, arrange, incline
08 movement, organize
09 fluctuate, oscillate, pendulate
10 dance music
11 fluctuation, oscillation

**swinging**
03 hip
06 lively, modern, trendy, with it
07 dynamic, stylish
10 jet-setting

11 fashionable

**swipe**
03 hit
04 biff, blow, lift, slap, sock, whip
05 clout, filch, lunge, pinch, smack, steal, whack
06 pilfer, strike, stroke, wallop

**swirl**
04 curl, eddy, spin
05 twirl, twist, wheel, whirl
07 agitate, revolve
09 circulate

**swish**
04 flog, lash, wave, whip
05 swing, swirl, twirl, whirl, whisk
06 rustle, swoosh, thrash, whoosh
07 whistle

**switch**
03 rod
04 cane, swap, twig, veer, whip
05 birch, shift, trade, whisk
06 branch, divert, twitch
07 deflect, deviate, replace
08 exchange, reversal
09 about-face, transpose
10 substitute
12 substitution

**swivel**
04 spin, turn
05 pivot, twirl, wheel
06 gyrate, rotate
07 revolve

**swollen**
05 puffy, tumid
07 bloated, bulbous, bulging
08 inflated, puffed up
09 distended, tumescent

**swoop**
04 dive, drop, fall, rush
05 lunge, stoop
06 attack, plunge, pounce

**swop** see SWAP

**sword**
04 épée, foil
05 blade, saber, steel
06 katana, rapier
08 scimitar

❏ **cross swords**
05 argue, fight
07 contend, contest, dispute, quarrel, wrangle

**sworn**
07 devoted, eternal
08 attested
09 confirmed
10 implacable

**sybarite**
07 epicure, playboy
08 hedonist, parasite
09 bon vivant, epicurean
10 sensualist, voluptuary
14 pleasure-seeker

**sybaritic**
07 sensual
09 epicurean, luxurious
10 hedonistic, voluptuous
14 pleasure-loving
15 pleasure-seeking

**sycophancy**
07 fawning
08 cringing, flattery, toadyism
09 adulation, groveling, kowtowing, servility, truckling
11 bootlicking, brown-nosing, slavishness
14 obsequiousness

**sycophant**
05 slave, toady
06 fawner, yes man
07 cringer, sponger
08 groveler, hanger-on, parasite, truckler
09 flatterer, toadeater
10 bootlicker, brown-noser

**sycophantic**
05 slimy
07 fawning, servile, slavish
08 cringing, toadying, unctuous
09 groveling, truckling
10 flattering, obsequious, toadeating
11 bootlicking, brown-nosing, timeserving
12 ingratiating

**syllabus**
04 plan
07 outline, program
08 schedule
10 curriculum
13 course outline

**syllogism**
08 argument
09 deduction
11 epicheirema, proposition

**sylphlike**
04 slim
05 lithe
06 slight, svelte
07 elegant, slender, willowy

**symbiotic**
07 epizoan, epizoic
09 commensal, epizootic
10 endophytic, synergetic
11 cooperative, interactive
14 interdependent

**symbol**
04 logo, mark, sign, type
05 badge, image, token
06 device, emblem, figure
09 character, ideograph
14 representation

**symbolic**
05 token
07 typical
10 emblematic, figurative, meaningful, symbolical
11 allegorical, significant
12 illustrative, metaphorical
14 representative

**symbolize**
06 denote, typify
07 betoken, signify
08 stand for
09 epitomize, exemplify, personify, represent

**symmetrical**
04 even
07 regular, uniform
08 balanced, parallel
10 consistent, harmonious
12 proportional
13 corresponding

**symmetry**
07 balance, harmony
08 evenness
09 agreement, congruity
10 regularity, uniformity
11 consistency, parallelism, proportions
14 correspondence

**sympathetic**
04 kind, warm
06 caring, kindly, tender
07 pitying
08 likeable, pleasant, sociable
09 agreeable, concerned, congenial, consoling
10 comforting, compatible, interested, like-minded, solicitous, supportive
11 considerate, kindhearted
12 appreciative, well-disposed
13 compassionate, understanding

**sympathetically**
09 feelingly
11 sensitively
12 responsively
14 appreciatively
15 understandingly

**sympathize**
04 pity
07 care for, console, feel for
09 empathize, respond to
10 appreciate, understand

11 commiserate
12 feel sorry for, identify with

**sympathizer**
03 fan
06 backer
08 adherent, condoler, partisan
09 supporter

**sympathy**
04 pity
06 accord, solace, warmth
07 comfort, empathy, harmony, rapport, support
08 affinity, approval, kindness
10 compassion, tenderness
11 condolences, consolation
13 commiseration, consideration, fellow feeling, understanding
14 correspondence, thoughtfulness
15 warmheartedness

**symptom**
04 mark, note, sign
05 token
06 signal
07 feature
08 evidence, prodrome
10 expression, indication
13 demonstration, manifestation
14 characteristic

**symptomatic**
07 typical
10 indicative, suggestive
14 characteristic

**syndicate**
04 bloc, ring
05 group
06 cartel
08 alliance
11 association

**synonymous**
07 similar, the same
09 identical
10 comparable, equivalent, tantamount
13 substitutable
15 interchangeable

**synopsis**
06 digest, précis, review, résumé
07 outline, summary
08 abstract
10 abridgment

**synthesis**
05 alloy, blend
07 amalgam
08 compound
09 composite
11 coalescence, combination, integration

12 amalgamation

**synthesize**
05 alloy, blend, merge
07 combine
08 coalesce, compound
09 integrate
10 amalgamate

**synthetic**
04 fake, mock, sham
06 ersatz, pseudo-
07 man-made
09 imitation, simulated
10 artificial
12 manufactured

**syrupy**
05 mushy, soppy, sweet
06 sickly, slushy, sugary

07 honeyed, maudlin, mawkish
09 schmaltzy
10 lovey-dovey, saccharine
11 sentimental, sickly sweet

**system**
03 way
04 mode, plan, rule
05 logic, means, setup
06 method, scheme
07 network, process, routine
08 approach, practice
09 mechanism, procedure,
   structure, technique
11 arrangement, methodology
12 coordination, organization
13 modus operandi
14 classification

**systematic**
07 logical, orderly, planned
09 efficient, organized
10 methodical, scientific,
   structured
11 well-ordered, well-planned
12 standardized
13 well-organized

**systematize**
04 plan
05 order
08 classify, organize, regiment,
   regulate, tabulate
09 structure
10 schematize
11 rationalize, standardize

## tab
03 tag
04 flap
05 label
06 marker, ticket
07 sticker

## ❏ keep tabs on
07 observe
11 keep an eye on
12 watch closely

## tabby
03 cat
04 wavy
06 banded, gossip, stripy
07 mottled, striped
08 brindled, gossiper, streaked

## table
03 bar
04 desk, fare, food, grub, list, menu, plan, slab
05 board, chart, graph, index
06 figure, record
07 program
08 postpone, register, schedule
09 timetable, worktable
10 tabulation

## tableau
05 scene
08 vignette
09 portrayal, spectacle
13 tableau vivant

## tablet
04 ball, pill
05 bolus
06 pellet
07 capsule, lozenge

## taboo
05 curse
06 banned, vetoed
08 anathema, ruled out
09 forbidden
10 prohibited, proscribed
11 prohibition, restriction
12 interdiction, proscription
13 unmentionable

## tabulate
04 list, sort
05 chart, index, order, range
06 codify
07 catalog
08 classify
09 catalogue
10 categorize

## tacit
06 silent
07 implied
08 implicit, inferred, unspoken, unvoiced, wordless
10 understood

## taciturn
05 aloof, quiet
06 silent
08 detached, reserved, reticent
09 withdrawn
11 tight-lipped
12 closemouthed
13 unforthcoming
15 uncommunicative

## tack
03 add, fix, pin, sew, way
04 line, nail, path, plan, turn, veer
05 affix, annex, baste
06 append, attach, course, policy, staple, stitch
07 bearing, deviate, heading, process
08 approach, strategy
09 direction, thumbtack
12 line of action

## tackle
03 rig, try
04 gear, grab, halt, stop, take
05 begin, block, catch, grasp, seize, stuff, tools
06 attack, handle, things
07 attempt, go about, harness, lineman
08 confront, deal with, face up to, obstruct, set about
09 apparatus, bring down, equipment, intercept, trappings
12 interception, intervention
13 accouterments, accoutrements, paraphernalia
14 football player
15 apply yourself to

## tacky
05 gaudy, gluey, gooey, messy
06 flashy, shoddy, sticky, tawdry
07 kitschy, scruffy
09 tasteless

## tact
08 delicacy, judgment, prudence, subtlety
09 diplomacy
10 adroitness, discretion
11 discernment, savoir-faire, sensitivity, tactfulness
13 consideration, understanding
14 thoughtfulness

## tactful
06 adroit, polite, subtle
07 careful, politic, prudent
08 delicate, discreet
09 judicious, sensitive
10 diplomatic, thoughtful
11 considerate

## tactic
04 move, plan, ploy, ruse
05 means, moves, shift, trick
06 device, method, scheme
08 approach, maneuver, strategy
09 expedient, procedure, stratagem
12 line of attack
14 course of action

## tactical
05 smart
06 adroit, artful, clever, shrewd
07 planned, politic, prudent
09 judicious, strategic
10 calculated

## tactician
05 brain
07 planner
10 mastermind, strategist

## tactless
04 rude
05 rough
06 clumsy, gauche, unkind
07 awkward, hurtful
08 careless, impolite, unsubtle
09 impolitic, maladroit
10 blundering, indiscreet
11 insensitive, thoughtless
12 discourteous, undiplomatic

## tactlessness
08 rudeness
09 bad timing, gaucherie
10 clumsiness, indelicacy
11 boorishness, discourtesy

12 impoliteness, indiscretion
13 insensitivity, maladroitness
15 thoughtlessness

**tag**
03 add, cue, dub, tab
04 call, mark, name, tack, term
05 affix, annex, badge, label, motto, quote, style, title
06 append, attach, fasten, phrase, saying, ticket
07 epithet, proverb, sticker
08 allusion, christen, identify
11 description, stock phrase
12 license plate
14 identification

❏**tag along**
05 trail
06 follow, shadow
09 accompany

**tail**
03 dog, end
04 back, rear, rump
05 stalk, track, trail
06 behind, bottom, caudal, cercal, follow, pursue, shadow, shamus, sleuth
08 backside
09 appendage, posterior
10 conclusion, private eye
12 investigator

❏**tail off**
03 die
04 drop, fade, wane
07 decline, drop off, dwindle
08 decrease, peter out

❏ **turn tail**
04 bolt, flee
06 beat it, decamp, escape
07 abscond, retreat, run away
09 skedaddle

**tailor**
03 cut, fit
04 suit, trim
05 adapt, alter, shape, style
06 adjust, modify
07 convert, fashion, modiste
08 clothier, costumer, seamster
09 costumier, couturier, outfitter
10 dressmaker, seamstress
11 accommodate

**tailor-made**
05 ideal, right
06 fitted, suited
07 perfect
11 custom-built
13 made-to-measure

**taint**
04 blot, flaw, harm, ruin, soil
05 dirty, fault, muddy, shame, smear, spoil, stain, sully

06 befoul, blight, damage, defile, infect, injure, stigma
07 blacken, blemish, corrupt, deprave, pollute, tarnish
08 dishonor
09 contagion, infection, pollution
10 adulterate, corruption
11 contaminate
13 contamination

**take**
03 bag, buy, eat, get, use, win
04 bear, deem, draw, gain, gate, grab, haul, hire, hold, last, lead, lift, rent, view
05 adopt, bring, carry, catch, drink, drive, ferry, fetch, filch, grasp, guide, learn, lease, pinch, seize, steal, study, think, use up, usher
06 abduct, accept, assume, choose, clutch, convey, deduct, demand, derive, devour, endure, escort, fathom, follow, gather, guzzle, imbibe, income, kidnap, obtain, occupy, pay for, profit, pursue, reckon, remove, return, select, snatch, suffer
07 achieve, acquire, believe, call for, capture, conduct, conquer, consume, contain, deliver, examine, major in, measure, presume, procure, profits, purloin, receive, require, returns, revenue, stomach, suppose, swallow
08 carry off, consider, cotton on, deal with, proceeds, purchase, receipts, settle on, shepherd, subtract, tolerate, vanquish
09 accompany, apprehend, eliminate, fathom out, get hold of, put up with, respond to, transport, undertake, withstand
10 comprehend, confiscate, experience, understand
11 accommodate, appropriate, have room for, necessitate
12 have space for
15 have a capacity of

❏**take aback**
04 stun
05 shock, upset
06 dismay
07 astound, stagger, startle
08 astonish, bewilder, surprise
10 disconcert

❏**take after**
04 echo
05 favor
06 be like, mirror
08 look like

❏**take apart**
07 analyze
08 separate
09 dismantle
11 disassemble

❏**take back**
04 deny
06 recant, regain, return
07 reclaim, restore, retract
08 disclaim, renounce, withdraw
09 repossess, repudiate
12 eat one's words

❏**take down**
04 note, raze
05 level, lower
06 record
08 demolish
10 put on paper, transcribe
11 disassemble, make a note of

❏**take in**
03 con
04 dupe, fool
05 cheat, cover, grasp, trick
06 absorb, digest
07 deceive, embrace, include, mislead, realize, receive, shelter, swindle, welcome
08 comprise, hoodwink
09 bamboozle, encompass
10 appreciate, assimilate, comprehend, understand
11 accommodate, incorporate

❏**take off**
04 doff, drop, flee, rise
05 climb, leave, strip
06 decamp, deduct, depart, detach, divest, do well, remove
07 abscond, catch on, discard, lift off, prosper, pull off, run away, succeed, tear off
08 discount, flourish, go places, subtract, throw off
09 skedaddle
13 become popular
14 become airborne

❏**take on**
04 face, hire
05 fight
06 accept, assume, employ, engage, enlist, enroll, oppose, retain, tackle
07 acquire, recruit, vie with
09 undertake
11 compete with, contend with

## ❑take out
05 set up
06 borrow, cut out, detach, escort, excise, remove
07 arrange, extract, pull out
08 organize, settle on
09 accompany, go out with

## ❑take over
06 buy out
12 take charge of
13 gain control of

## ❑take to
04 like
05 begin, start
08 commence, cotton to, set about
12 become fond of

## ❑take up
04 fill, lift
05 adopt, begin, raise, start
06 absorb, accept, assume, engage, occupy, pick up, pursue, resume
07 agree to, carry on, engross
08 commence, continue, embark on

## takeoff
05 spoof
06 ascent, flight, parody
07 liftoff, mimicry
08 climbing, travesty
09 departure, imitation
10 caricature
13 impersonation

## takeover
04 coup
06 buyout, merger
09 coalition
12 amalgamation
13 incorporation

## taking
08 charming, engaging, fetching
09 appealing, beguiling
10 attractive, compelling, delightful, enchanting
11 captivating, fascinating
14 prepossessing,

## takings
04 gain, gate
05 yield
06 income
07 profits, returns, revenue
08 earnings, pickings, proceeds, receipts

## tale
03 fib, lie
04 epic, myth, saga, yarn
05 fable, rumor, spiel, story
06 legend, report
07 account, parable, untruth

08 allegory, anecdote
09 narrative, tall story
11 fabrication

## talent
04 bent, feel, gift
05 flair, forte, knack, skill
06 genius
07 ability, aptness, faculty
08 aptitude, capacity, facility, strength

## talented
04 able, deft
05 adept
06 adroit, clever, gifted
07 capable, skilful
08 skillful
09 brilliant, versatile
12 accomplished

## talisman
04 idol, juju
05 charm, totem
06 amulet, fetish, grigri, mascot
07 abraxas, periapt
08 gris-gris
10 phylactery
11 rabbit's foot

## talk
03 gab, jaw, rap, say
04 blab, cant, chat, tell
05 grass, lingo, orate, rumor, slang, speak, spiel, voice, words
06 babble, confab, confer, debate, dialog, gossip, jargon, sermon, speech, squeal
07 address, chatter, chinwag, confess, dialect, discuss, express, lecture, meeting, oration, prattle, seminar
08 converse, dialogue, idiolect, inform on, language
09 discourse, interview, negotiate, symposium, tell tales, tête-à-tête, utterance
10 articulate, bargaining, conference, discussion
11 communicate, negotiation
12 consultation, conversation, disquisition, spread rumors, tittle-tattle
13 spill the beans
15 give the game away

## ❑talk back
06 retort
07 riposte
09 retaliate
10 answer back, be cheeky to

## ❑talk big
04 brag, crow
05 boast, swank, vaunt

07 bluster, show off
10 exaggerate

## ❑talk down to
09 patronize
10 look down on

## ❑talk into
04 coax, sway
07 win over
08 convince, persuade
11 bring around

## ❑talk out of
04 stop
05 deter
06 put off
07 prevent
08 dissuade
10 discourage

## talkative
05 gabby, gassy, vocal, wordy
06 chatty, mouthy
07 gossipy, verbose, voluble
09 expansive, garrulous
10 long-winded, loquacious
11 forthcoming
13 communicative

## talker
06 orator
07 speaker
08 lecturer
10 chatterbox
11 speechmaker

## talking-to
06 rebuke
07 lecture, reproof
08 reproach, scolding
09 reprimand
10 telling-off
12 dressing-down

## tall
03 big
04 hard, high
05 giant, great, lanky, lofty
07 dubious, sky-high, soaring
08 elevated, exacting, gigantic, towering, unlikely
09 demanding, difficult
10 far-fetched, improbable
11 challenging, implausible
12 preposterous, unbelievable

## tallness
06 height
07 stature
08 altitude
09 loftiness

## tally
03 add, fit, sum, tab, tag
05 add up, agree, count, match, score, tie in, total
06 accord, concur, reckon, record, square, ticket

09 duplicate, harmonize, reckoning
10 correspond
11 enumeration

**tame**
04 calm, curb, dull, flat, meek
05 bland, quell, train, vapid
06 boring, bridle, docile, feeble, gentle, master, pacify, soften, subdue
07 break in, insipid, subdued, tedious, trained
08 broken in, lifeless
09 subjugate, tractable
10 discipline, housebreak, spiritless, unexciting
11 bring to heel, disciplined, domesticate
12 domesticated
13 unadventurous, uninteresting
14 unenterprising

**tamper**
03 fix, rig
06 meddle, tinker
07 corrupt
09 interfere, mess about
10 manipulate, monkey with
14 poke your nose in
15 stick your nose in

**tan**
04 beat, belt, cane, flog, lash
05 brown, clout, spank, strap
06 bronze, thrash, wallop
07 go brown, sunburn

**tang**
03 pep
04 bite, edge, hint, kick
05 punch, savor, smack, smell, spice, taste, tinge, touch, trace
06 flavor
08 piquancy, pungency
09 sharpness

**tangible**
04 hard, real
05 solid
06 actual
07 evident, tactile, visible
08 concrete, definite, material, palpable, physical, positive
09 touchable
11 discernible, perceptible, substantial, well-defined
12 unmistakable

**tangle**
03 mat, web
04 coil, knot, maze, mesh, mess
05 catch, mix-up, snarl, twist
06 enmesh, entrap, muddle
07 embroil, ensnare, involve

08 convolve, entangle
09 confusion, imbroglio, implicate, interlace
10 intertwine, intertwist
11 convolution, embroilment
12 complication, entanglement

**tangled**
05 messy
06 knotty, matted
07 complex, knotted, mixed up, muddled, snarled, twisted
08 confused, involved, tortuous
10 convoluted, disheveled
11 complicated

**tangy**
04 acid, tart
05 fresh, sharp, spicy
06 biting, strong
07 piquant, pungent

**tank**
03 vat
04 jail
05 basin
06 panzer
07 cistern
08 aquarium
09 container, reservoir
14 armored vehicle

**tantalize**
04 bait, balk
05 taunt, tease, tempt
06 allure, entice, lead on, thwart
07 provoke, torment, torture
09 frustrate, titillate

**tantamount**
05 equal
08 as good as
09 the same as
10 equivalent, synonymous
12 commensurate

**tantrum**
03 fit, pet
04 fury, rage
05 scene, storm
07 flare-up
08 outburst, paroxysm
11 fit of temper

**tap**
03 bug, hit, pat, rap, use
04 beat, drum, milk, mine
05 bleed, dance, drain, knock, spout, touch, valve
06 faucet, quarry, siphon, spigot, strike
07 exploit, stopper, utilize
08 receiver, stopcock
15 listening device

**❏on tap**
05 handy, ready
06 at hand, on hand

09 available
10 accessible

**tape**
03 tie
04 band, bind, seal
05 stick, strip, video
06 fasten, record, ribbon
07 binding
08 cassette
09 audiotape, recording, videotape
10 tape-record
11 masking tape
12 adhesive tape, magnetic tape
13 Scotch tape, tape-recording, videocassette
14 video recording

**taper**
04 fade, slim, thin, wane, wick
06 candle, die off, narrow
07 die away, dwindle, tail off
08 decrease, diminish
09 attenuate

**tardily**
04 late
06 slowly
09 belatedly
10 sluggishly
12 late in the day, unpunctually
15 at the last minute

**tardiness**
08 dawdling, lateness, slowness
11 belatedness
12 dilatoriness, sluggishness
13 unpunctuality

**tardy**
04 late, slow
05 slack
07 belated, delayed, overdue
08 dawdling, dilatory, sluggish
10 last-minute, unpunctual

**target**
03 aim, end
04 butt, game, goal, mark, prey
06 object, quarry, victim
07 purpose
08 ambition, bull's-eye
09 intention, objective
11 sitting duck

**tariff**
03 tab, tax
04 duty, fare, levy, menu, rate, toll
06 excise
07 charges, customs
09 price list
10 bill of fare

**tarnish**
03 dim, mar

**tarry**
04 blot, dull, film, rust, spot
05 spoil, stain, sully, taint
07 blacken, blemish, corrode
08 besmirch, discolor
13 discoloration

**tarry**
03 lag
04 bide, rest, stay, stop, wait
05 abide, dally, delay, pause
06 dawdle, linger, loiter, remain

**tart**
03 pie
04 acid, drab, flan, slut, sour
05 sharp, tangy, tramp, whore
06 biting, bitter, hooker, pastry
07 acerbic, caustic, cutting, piquant, pungent, trollop
08 call girl, incisive, sardonic, scathing
09 sarcastic, trenchant
10 astringent, prostitute
11 fallen woman, fille de joie
12 streetwalker

**task**
03 job
04 duty, toil, work
05 chore
06 burden, charge, errand
07 mission
08 activity, business, exercise
10 assignment, commission, employment, engagement, enterprise, occupation
11 piece of work, undertaking

❏**take to task**
05 blame, scold
06 rebuke
07 censure, lecture, reprove, tell off, upbraid
08 reproach
09 criticize, reprimand

**taste**
03 bit, sip, try
04 dash, drop, feel, tang, test
05 grace, piece, savor, smack, style
06 flavor, liking, morsel, nibble, relish, sample, tidbit
07 culture, finesse, leaning, soupçon, undergo
08 appetite, breeding, elegance, fondness, judgment, mouthful, penchant
09 encounter, etiquette, gustative, gustatory, propriety
10 preference, refinement
11 cultivation, discernment, inclination, stylishness
12 predilection, tastefulness

14 discrimination

**tasteful**
05 smart
07 elegant, refined, stylish
08 artistic, charming, cultured, delicate, graceful, pleasing
09 aesthetic, judicious
10 cultivated, harmonious, restrained, well-judged
14 discriminating

**tasteless**
04 dull, flat, loud, mild, rude, thin, weak
05 bland, cheap, crass, crude, gaudy, showy, stale, tacky
06 flashy, kitsch, tawdry, vulgar
07 insipid, uncouth
08 improper, tactless, unseemly
09 inelegant, unfitting
10 flavorless
11 watered-down
13 uninteresting

**tasting**
05 assay, trial
07 testing
08 sampling
09 gustation

**tasty**
05 spicy, sweet, tangy, yummy
06 savory
07 piquant
08 luscious
09 delicious, palatable
10 appetizing, delectable, flavorsome
11 scrumptious
13 mouth-watering

**tatter**

❏**in tatters**
06 broken, in rags, ruined
07 wrecked
08 in pieces, in shreds
09 destroyed, in ribbons

**tattered**
04 torn
06 frayed, ragged, ripped
07 scruffy

**tattler**
06 gossip
08 busybody, informer, snitcher, telltale
10 newsmonger, talebearer, taleteller, tattletale
13 scandalmonger

**taunt**
03 dig, rib
04 bait, barb, gibe, jeer, mock
05 sneer, tease
06 deride, insult, revile

07 catcall, mockery, provoke, sarcasm, teasing, torment
08 derision, ridicule, taunting
09 make fun of, poke fun at

**taut**
05 rigid, stiff, tense, tight
06 tensed
08 strained
09 stretched, tightened
10 contracted

**tautological**
07 verbose
09 redundant
10 pleonastic, repetitive
11 superfluous

**tautology**
08 pleonasm
10 redundancy, repetition
11 duplication, perissology, superfluity
14 repetitiveness

**tavern**
03 bar, inn, pub
05 joint
06 saloon
08 alehouse, hostelry, taphouse
09 roadhouse
12 watering hole

**tawdry**
05 fancy, gaudy, showy, tacky
06 flashy, garish, vulgar
09 tasteless

**tawny**
03 tan
05 khaki, sandy
06 fulvid, golden, yellow
07 fulvous
08 xanthous

**tax**
03 sap, try
04 duty, levy, load, test, tire
05 drain, exact, weary, weigh
06 charge, fiscal, strain, stress, surtax, tariff, weaken
07 exhaust, stretch
08 encumber, enervate, overload, pressure
09 weigh down
13 make demands on

**taxi**
03 cab
04 hack
06 fiacre, hansom
07 hackney, taxicab
09 hansom cab
12 hackney coach

**taxing**
04 hard
05 heavy, tough

06 tiring, trying
07 onerous, wearing
08 draining, exacting, wearying
09 demanding, punishing, stressful, wearisome
10 enervating, exhausting

**teach**
04 show
05 coach, drill, train, tutor
06 advise, direct, ground, impart, inform, school
07 counsel, educate, lecture
08 instruct
09 condition, enlighten, inculcate
10 discipline
11 demonstrate, give lessons
12 indoctrinate

**teacher**
04 dean, guru
05 coach, guide, tutor
06 doctor, fellow, master, mentor, pundit
07 adviser, crammer, pedagog, trainer
08 educator, lecturer, mistress
09 governess, maharishi, pedagogue, preceptor, principal, professor
10 headmaster, instructor, schoolmarm
11 preceptress
12 demonstrator, headmistress, private tutor, schoolmaster
13 supply teacher
14 schoolmistress

**teaching**
05 dogma, tenet
07 precept, tuition
08 doctrine, pedagogy
09 doctrinal, education
11 instruction

**team**
03 set
04 band, crew, five, gang, nine, side
05 bunch, group, shift, squad
06 eleven, lineup, stable, troupe
07 company, defense, offense, quintet

❑**team up**
04 join, yoke
05 match, unite
07 combine
09 cooperate
11 collaborate
12 work together

**teamwork**
10 fellowship, team spirit
11 cooperation, joint effort
12 coordination

13 collaboration, esprit de corps

**tear**
03 fly, nip, rip, run, zap, zip
04 belt, bolt, claw, dart, dash, gash, grab, hole, pull, race, rend, rent, rush, whiz, zoom
05 hurry, pluck, seize, sever, shoot, shred, slash, speed, split, wound, wrest
06 career, charge, divide, gallop, mangle, snatch, sprint, sunder
07 rupture, scratch
09 pull apart
10 break apart, laceration

❑**in tears**
05 upset, weepy
06 crying
07 sobbing, wailing, weeping
09 emotional, sorrowful
10 blubbering

**tearful**
03 sad
05 upset, weepy
06 crying
07 doleful, sobbing, weeping
08 mournful
09 emotional, sorrowful
10 blubbering, distressed, lachrymose, whimpering

**tease**
03 kid, rag, rib, vex
04 bait, gibe, goad, mock
05 annoy, taunt, worry
06 badger, banter, needle
07 provoke, torment
08 irritate, ridicule
09 aggravate, tantalize

**technical**
06 expert
07 applied
09 practical
10 electronic, mechanical, scientific, specialist
11 specialized
13 technological

**technique**
03 art, way
05 craft, knack, means, style
06 manner, method, system
07 ability, fashion, know-how
08 approach, artistry, facility
09 dexterity, execution, expertise, procedure
11 proficiency, skilfulness
12 skillfulness
13 craftsmanship, modus operandi

**tedious**
04 drab, dull, flat

05 banal
06 boring, dreary, tiring
07 humdrum, prosaic, routine
08 lifeless, tiresome, unvaried
09 laborious, wearisome
10 long-winded, monotonous

**tedium**
05 ennui
07 boredom, routine
08 banality, drabness, dullness, monotony, sameness
10 dreariness

**teem**
04 bear, brim
05 burst, crawl, swarm
06 abound
07 bristle, produce
08 increase, multiply, overflow
09 pullulate
11 proliferate

**teeming**
04 full
05 alive, thick
06 packed
08 abundant, brimming, bursting, crawling, fruitful, numerous, swarming
09 bristling, chock-full
11 chockablock, overflowing, pullulating

**teenage**
08 immature, juvenile, teenaged, youthful
10 adolescent

**teenager**
03 boy
04 girl
05 minor, youth
08 juvenile
10 adolescent, young adult
11 young person

**teeny**
03 wee
04 tiny
05 small
06 little, minute, teensy, weensy
09 itsy-bitsy, itty-bitty, miniature, minuscule
10 diminutive, teeny-weeny
11 Lilliputian, microscopic
12 teensy-weensy

**teeter**
04 reel, rock, roll, sway
05 pitch, pivot, shake, waver
06 seesaw, totter, wobble
07 balance, stagger, tremble

**teetotal**
06 entire
08 complete
09 abstinent, temperate

**teetotaler**
10 abstemious, on the wagon

**teetotaler**
03 dry
09 abstainer
10 nondrinker

**telegram**
04 wire
05 cable
07 message

**telegraph**
04 send, wire
05 cable, telex
06 signal
08 transmit
11 teleprinter
14 radiotelegraph
15 radiotelegraphy

**telepathy**
03 ESP
10 sixth sense
11 mind reading
12 clairvoyance

**telephone**
04 buzz, call, dial, ring
06 call up, ring up
08 receiver
09 give a buzz

**telescope**
06 reduce, shrink, squash
07 abridge, compact, curtail, shorten, squeeze
08 compress, condense, contract, spyglass, truncate
10 abbreviate, concertina, instrument

**televise**
03 air
04 beam, show
05 cable, put on, relay
06 screen
08 transmit
09 broadcast

**television**
02 TV
03 set
07 the tube
08 boob tube, idiot box
11 small screen

► *Names of television stars:*
03 **Fox** (Michael J.)
04 **Alda** (Alan), **Ball** (Lucille), **Burr** (Raymond), **Coca** (Imogene), **Daly** (Tyne), **Falk** (Peter), **Hawn** (Goldie), **Leno** (Jay), **Swit** (Loretta), **Wyle** (Noah)
05 **Baker** (Kathy), **Benny** (Jack), **Berle** (Milton), **Carey** (Drew), **Clark**

(Dick), **Cosby** (Bill), **Ebert** (Roger), **Franz** (Dennis), **Gless** (Sharon), **Moore** (Garry), **Moore** (Mary Tyler), **Murry** (Bill), **Nimoy** (Leonard), **Perry** (Matthew), **Sheen** (Charles), **Shore** (Dinah), **White** (Betty), **Young** (Robert)
06 **Arthur** (Bea), **Barker** (Bob), **Caesar** (Sid), **Carson** (Johnny), **Carter** (Lynda), **Cavett** (Dick), **Conrad** (William), **Danson** (Ted), **Garner** (James), **Gellar** (Sarah Michelle), **Hagman** (Larry), **Howard** (Ron), **Kudrow** (Lisa), **Malden** (Karl), **Martin** (Steve), **O'Brien** (Conan), **Parker** (Sarah Jessica), **Pierce** (David Hyde), **Rivera** (Geraldo), **Rivers** (Joan), **Rogers** (Fred), **Thomas** (Danny), **Thomas** (Marlo), **Thomas** (Richard)
07 **Aniston** (Jennifer), **Burnett** (Carol), **Clooney** (George), **Donahue** (Phil), **Gifford** (Kathie Lee), **Godfrey** (Arthur), **Goodman** (John), **Grammer** (Kelsey), **Griffin** (Merv), **Klugman** (Jack), **Lithgow** (John), **Newhart** (Bob), **O'Connor** (Carroll), **Philbin** (Regis), **Randall** (Tony), **Savalas** (Telly), **Shatner** (William), **Silvers** (Phil), **Skelton** (Red), **Van Dyke** (Dick), **Winfrey** (Oprah)
08 **Anderson** (Gillian), **Duchovny** (David), **O'Donnell** (Rosie), **Osbourne** (Ozzy), **Roseanne**, **Springer** (Jerry), **Williams** (Montel)
09 **Degeneres** (Ellen), **Flockhart** (Calista), **Letterman** (David), **Principal** (Victoria), **Schwimmer** (David), **Shandling** (Garry)
10 **Gandolfini** (James), **Hasselhoff** (David)

**tell**
03 bid, rat, say, see
04 blab, show, talk
05 alter, brief, drain, order, speak, state, utter
06 advise, betray, charge, decree, direct, impart,

inform, notify, recite, relate, report, reveal, sketch, snitch, squeal
07 apprise, command, confess, declare, dictate, discern, divulge, exhaust, let know, make out, mention, narrate, portray, recount, require
08 acquaint, announce, denounce, disclose, identify, inform on, instruct
09 broadcast, delineate, make known, recognize
10 comprehend, understand
11 communicate, distinguish
12 discriminate
13 differentiate, spill the beans, take its toll of
14 give the lowdown, have an effect on
15 give the game away

❑**tell off**
05 chide, scold
06 berate, rebuke
07 censure, lecture, reprove, upbraid
08 reproach
09 dress down, reprimand
14 give a talking-to

**teller**
05 clerk
06 banker
07 cashier
08 informer, narrator
09 bank clerk, treasurer

**telling**
06 cogent, marked
09 effective, revealing
10 impressive, persuasive
11 significant

**telling-off**
06 rebuke
07 chiding, lecture, reproof
08 reproach, scolding
09 reprimand
10 upbraiding
12 dressing-down

**telltale**
03 spy
05 sneak
06 snitch
07 tattler
08 giveaway, informer, snitcher, squealer
09 indicator, revealing
10 meaningful, noticeable
11 perceptible, secret agent
15 snake in the grass

**temerity**
04 gall
05 cheek, nerve

**temper**
- 06 daring
- 08 audacity, boldness, rashness
- 09 impudence
- 12 impertinence, recklessness

**temper**
- 04 calm, cool, fury, mood, rage
- 05 allay, anger, humor, storm
- 06 anneal, harden, lessen, modify, nature, reduce, soften, weaken
- 07 assuage, flare-up, fortify, passion, tantrum, toughen
- 08 calmness, ill humor, mitigate, moderate, palliate, tone down
- 09 alleviate, character, composure
- 10 conniption, resentment, strengthen
- 11 disposition, fit of temper, frame of mind, temperament
- 12 constitution, irritability

**lose your temper**
- 05 go mad
- 06 lose it, see red
- 07 explode
- 08 boil over, get angry
- 09 blow a fuse, go up a wall
- 10 hit the roof
- 11 blow a gasket, blow your top, flip your lid
- 12 fly into a rage, lose your cool
- 13 get aggravated, hit the ceiling, throw a tantrum
- 14 foam at the mouth
- 15 fly off the handle, go off the deep end

**temperament**
- 04 bent, mood, soul
- 05 humor
- 06 makeup, nature
- 09 character
- 10 complexion, volatility
- 11 disposition, frame of mind, personality, state of mind
- 12 constitution, excitability

**temperamental**
- 05 fiery, moody
- 06 inborn, innate, touchy
- 08 inherent, neurotic, volatile
- 09 emotional, excitable, explosive, hotheaded, impatient, ingrained, irritable, mercurial, sensitive
- 10 capricious, congenital, hotblooded, passionate
- 12 highly strung
- 13 overemotional, unpredictable

**temperance**
- 08 sobriety

- 09 austerity, restraint
- 10 abstinence, continence, moderation, self-denial
- 11 prohibition, self-control, teetotalism
- 13 self-restraint
- 14 abstemiousness, self-discipline

**temperate**
- 04 calm, fair, mild
- 05 balmy, sober
- 06 gentle, stable
- 07 clement, equable
- 08 balanced, composed, moderate, pleasant, sensible, teetotal
- 09 abstinent, agreeable, easygoing
- 10 abstemious, controlled, reasonable, restrained
- 12 even-tempered
- 14 self-controlled, self-restrained

**tempest**
- 04 gale
- 05 furor, storm
- 06 squall, tumult, uproar
- 07 cyclone, tornado, typhoon
- 09 commotion, hurricane

**tempestuous**
- 04 wild
- 05 gusty, rough, windy
- 06 fierce, raging, stormy
- 07 furious, squally, violent
- 09 turbulent
- 10 passionate, tumultuous
- 11 impassioned
- 12 uncontrolled

**temple**
- 06 church, mosque, pagoda
- 09 sanctuary, synagogue
- 10 tabernacle
- 14 place of worship

**tempo**
- 04 beat, pace, rate, time
- 05 meter, pulse, speed, throb
- 07 cadence, measure
- 08 velocity

**temporal**
- 06 carnal, mortal
- 07 earthly, fleshly, profane, secular, worldly
- 08 material
- 11 terrestrial

**temporarily**
- 06 pro tem
- 07 briefly
- 10 fleetingly
- 11 momentarily, transiently
- 12 in the interim, transitorily

- 15 for the time being

**temporary**
- 05 brief
- 06 fill-in, pro tem
- 07 interim, passing, stopgap
- 08 fleeting, temporal
- 09 ephemeral, fugacious, makeshift, momentary, short-term, transient
- 10 evanescent, short-lived
- 11 impermanent, provisional

**temporize**
- 05 delay, pause, stall
- 09 hem and haw
- 10 equivocate
- 11 play for time
- 12 tergiversate

**tempt**
- 04 bait, coax, draw, lure
- 06 allure, cajole, entice, incite
- 07 attract, provoke
- 08 inveigle, persuade
- 09 tantalize

**temptation**
- 04 bait, draw, lure, pull
- 06 allure, appeal, urging
- 08 cajolery
- 09 influence, seduction
- 10 attraction, enticement, invitation, persuasion

**tempting**
- 08 alluring, enticing, inviting
- 09 seductive
- 10 appetizing, attractive
- 11 tantalizing
- 13 mouthwatering

**temptress**
- 04 vamp
- 05 flirt, siren
- 07 Delilah
- 08 coquette
- 10 seductress
- 11 enchantress, femme fatale

**tenable**
- 06 viable
- 08 credible, feasible, rational
- 09 plausible, reachable
- 10 believable, defendable
- 11 justifiable, supportable

**tenacious**
- 04 fast, firm
- 06 dogged, secure, sticky
- 07 adamant
- 08 adhesive, clinging, stubborn
- 09 obstinate, steadfast
- 10 determined, persistent, relentless, unswerving
- 11 unshakeable
- 12 intransigent, single-minded

## tenacity
05 force, power
07 resolve
08 firmness, obduracy, strength
09 obstinacy, toughness
10 doggedness, resolution
11 application, persistence
12 perseverance, stubbornness
13 determination, steadfastness
14 indomitability

## tenancy
05 lease
06 tenure
09 leasehold, occupancy
10 occupation, possession

## tenant
08 occupant, occupier, resident
10 inhabitant, landholder
11 leaseholder

## tend
04 bear, bend, keep, lead, lean
05 nurse, point, see to, watch
06 attend, manage, wait on
07 care for, incline, nurture
08 attend to, maintain
09 cultivate, look after
10 minister to, take care of

## tendency
04 bent, bias
05 drift, trend
07 bearing, heading, leaning
09 direction, proneness
10 partiality, proclivity
11 disposition, inclination
14 predisposition

## tender
03 bid, new, raw, red
04 fond, give, kind, soft, sore
05 early, frail, green, juicy,
   money, offer, price, young
06 aching, callow, caring,
   dainty, extend, fleshy, gentle,
   kindly, loving, submit
07 advance, amorous, bruised,
   proffer, propose, suggest
08 currency, delicate, estimate,
   immature, proposal,
   romantic, youthful
09 evocative, sensitive,
   succulent, volunteer
10 submission, suggestion
11 considerate, sentimental,
   softhearted, sympathetic
12 affectionate
13 compassionate,
   inexperienced

## tenderhearted
04 fond, kind, mild, warm
06 benign, caring, gentle,
   humane, kindly, loving
09 sensitive

10 benevolent, responsive
11 considerate, kindhearted,
   sentimental, softhearted,
   sympathetic, warmhearted
12 affectionate
13 compassionate

## tenderness
04 ache, care, love, pain, pity
06 aching, liking, warmth
08 bruising, devotion, fondness,
   humanity, kindness, softness,
   soreness, sympathy,
   weakness
09 affection, greenness
10 attachment, callowness,
   compassion, gentleness,
   humaneness, immaturity
11 amorousness, benevolence,
   painfulness, sensitivity
12 inexperience, inflammation
13 consideration, sensitiveness,
   vulnerability
15 softheartedness,
   warmheartedness

## tenet
04 rule, view
05 canon, credo, creed, dogma,
   maxim
06 belief, thesis
07 opinion, precept
08 doctrine, teaching
09 principle
10 conviction
11 presumption
14 article of faith

## tennis
► *Names of tennis players*:
04 Ashe (Arthur), Borg
   (Bjorn), Cash (Pat), Graf
   (Steffi), Hoad (Lewis Alan),
   King (Billie Jean), Ryan
   (Elizabeth), Wade (Virginia)
05 Budge (Donald), Bueno
   (Maria), Court (Margaret),
   Evert (Chris), Laver (Rod),
   Lendl (Ivan), Lloyd (Chris),
   Perry (Fred), Seles
   (Monica), Wills (Helen)
06 Agassi (Andre), Barker
   (Sue), Becker (Boris),
   Cawley (Yvonne), Edberg
   (Stefan), Gibson (Althea),
   Henman (Tim), Hingis
   (Martina)
07 Brookes (Norman Everard),
   Connors (Jimmy), Godfree
   (Kitty), LaCoste (Rene),
   Lenglen (Suzanne),
   Maskell (Dan), McEnroe
   (John), Nastase (Ilie),
   Novotna (Jana), Renshaw

(Willie), Sampras (Pete)
08 Connolly (Maureen
   Catherine), Gonzales
   (Pancho), Rusedski (Greg),
   Sabatini (Gabriela),
   Williams (Serena),
   Williams (Venus)
09 Davenport (Lindsay),
   Goolagong (Yvonne)
11 Navratilova (Martina)
► See also SPORT

## tenor
04 gist, path
05 drift, point, sense, theme
06 burden, course, intent, spirit
07 essence, meaning, purpose
09 direction, substance

## tense
04 edgy, taut, work
05 brace, jumpy, rigid, stiff, tight
06 strain, uneasy
07 anxious, charged, fidgety,
   fraught, jittery, keyed up,
   nervous, stiffen, stretch,
   tighten, uptight, worried
08 contract, exciting, strained
09 screwed up, stressful
10 distraught, nail-biting
11 overwrought, stressed out
12 apprehensive, nerve-racking
13 nerve-wracking

## tension
05 clash, worry
06 nerves, strain, stress, unrest
07 anxiety, discord, dispute
08 conflict, disquiet, distress,
   edginess, friction, pressure,
   rigidity, suspense, tautness
09 agitation, antipathy, hostility,
   stiffness, straining, tightness
10 antagonism, contention,
   dissension, opposition
11 nervousness
12 apprehension

## tent
► *Types of tent. We have
omitted the word tent from
names given in the following list
but you may need to include this
word as part of the solution to
some crossword clues.*
03 box, pup
04 bell, dome, tipi
05 frame, tepee
06 big top, canopy, canvas,
   circus, oxygen, teepee,
   wigwam
08 umbrella
10 tabernacle

## tentative
04 test
05 pilot, timid, trial
06 unsure
08 cautious, doubtful, hesitant
09 faltering, uncertain
11 conjectural, exploratory, provisional, speculative
12 experimental

## tenterhooks

### ❏ on tenterhooks
07 anxious, excited, nervous, waiting
09 impatient
10 in suspense
15 with bated breath

## tenuous
04 fine, hazy, slim, thin, weak
05 shaky, vague
06 flimsy, slight
07 dubious, fragile, slender
08 delicate, doubtful
12 questionable
13 insubstantial

## tenure
04 term, time
07 holding, tenancy
08 duration
09 occupancy, residence
10 habitation, incumbency, occupation, possession

## tepid
04 cool
07 warmish
08 lukewarm
09 apathetic
11 halfhearted, indifferent
14 unenthusiastic

## term
03 dub, end, tag
04 call, name, span, time, word
05 costs, label, limit, rates, space, spell, style, title
06 course, finish, period, phrase, points, prices, season, tariff
07 charges, clauses, details, entitle, epithet, footing, quarter, session, stretch
08 duration, fruition, interval, locution, position, provisos, semester, standing, terminus
09 condition
10 conclusion, expression, provisions
11 appellation, culmination, designation, particulars
12 relationship, stipulations
14 qualifications, specifications

### ❏ come to terms
06 accept, submit
14 resign yourself

### ❏ in terms of
09 as regards
10 in regard to
12 in relation to, with regard to
13 with respect to

## terminal
03 end, VDT
04 last
05 depot, dying, fatal, final
06 deadly, lethal, mortal
07 console, extreme, monitor, station
08 keyboard, terminus
09 extremity, incurable
10 concluding
11 termination

## terminate
03 end
04 stop
05 abort, cease, close, lapse
06 cut off, expire, finish, result, run out, wind up
08 complete, conclude
10 put an end to
11 come to an end, discontinue
12 bring to an end

## termination
03 end
05 close, finis, issue
06 demise, effect, ending, expiry, finale, finish, result
08 abortion
09 cessation
10 completion, conclusion
15 discontinuation

## terminology
05 terms, words
06 jargon
08 language
10 vocabulary
11 expressions, phraseology
12 nomenclature

## terminus
03 end
04 goal
05 close, limit
06 target
08 boundary
11 destination, termination

## terrain
04 land
06 ground
07 country
09 landscape, territory
10 topography
11 countryside

## terrestrial
06 global
07 earthly, mundane, worldly

## terrible
03 bad
04 foul, grim, poor, vile
05 awful, grave, great, nasty
06 horrid, severe
07 extreme, hateful, hideous, intense, serious
08 dreadful, gruesome, horrible, horrific, shocking
09 abhorrent, appalling, desperate, frightful, harrowing, obnoxious, offensive, repulsive, revolting
10 disgusting, outrageous
11 exceptional, unspeakable
12 incorrigible

## terribly
04 much, very
07 awfully, greatly
09 decidedly, extremely, seriously
10 thoroughly
11 desperately, exceedingly, frightfully

## terrific
03 ace
04 cool, huge, neat
05 crack, great, super
06 superb, wicked
07 amazing, awesome, intense
08 enormous, fabulous, gigantic
09 brilliant, excellent, fantastic, marvelous, wonderful
10 remarkable, stupendous, tremendous
11 magnificent, outstanding, sensational
12 breathtaking
13 extraordinary

## terrified
04 awed
06 scared
07 alarmed
08 appalled, dismayed
09 horrified, petrified
10 frightened
11 intimidated, panic-struck, scared stiff
12 horror-struck
13 panic-stricken, scared to death
14 horror-stricken

## terrify
05 appal, panic, scare, shock
06 appall
07 horrify, petrify
08 frighten, paralyze
09 terrorize

10 intimidate, scare stiff

**territorial**
04 area
05 zonal
08 district, domainal, regional
09 localized, sectional
11 topographic
12 geographical

**territory**
04 area, land, zone
05 field, tract
06 domain, region, sector
07 terrain
08 district, preserve, province
10 dependency
12 jurisdiction

**terror**
04 fear
05 alarm, demon, devil, dread, fiend, panic, rogue, shock
06 dismay, fright, horror, rascal
07 monster
09 terrorism
12 intimidation

**terrorize**
05 alarm, bully, scare, shock
06 coerce, menace
07 horrify, oppress, terrify
08 browbeat, frighten, threaten
09 strong-arm
10 intimidate

**terse**
04 curt
05 blunt, brief, crisp, pithy, short
06 abrupt, gnomic, snappy
07 brusque, concise, laconic
08 incisive, succinct
09 condensed
10 elliptical, to the point
12 epigrammatic

**test**
03 sap, SAT, try
04 exam
05 assay, check, final, probe, proof, prove, study, trial, weary
06 assess, ordeal, sample, screen, try out, verify
07 analyze, checkup, examine, exhaust, inspect, midterm, stretch, wear out
08 analysis, appraise, audition, enervate, evaluate
09 probation, questions
10 assessment, evaluation, experiment, inspection, pilot study, scrutinize
11 examination
13 questionnaire
14 scrutinization

**testament**
04 will
05 proof
07 earnest, tribute, witness
08 evidence
09 testimony
11 attestation
15 exemplification

**testify**
04 avow, show
05 state, swear, vouch
06 affirm, assert, attest, verify
07 certify, confirm, declare, endorse, support
11 bear witness, corroborate
12 give evidence, substantiate

**testimonial**
07 tribute
09 character, reference
10 credential
11 certificate, endorsement
12 commendation

**testimony**
05 proof
07 support, witness
08 evidence
09 affidavit, statement
10 profession, submission
11 affirmation, attestation, declaration
12 confirmation, verification
13 corroboration

**testy**
05 cross
06 crusty, grumpy, snappy, sullen, tetchy, touchy
07 crabbed, peevish, waspish
08 captious, petulant, snappish
09 crotchety, impatient, irascible, irritable, splenetic
11 bad-tempered, quarrelsome
12 cantankerous
13 quick-tempered

**tetchy**
06 crusty, grumpy, touchy
07 peevish
09 crotchety, irascible, irritable
11 bad-tempered

**tête-à-tête**
04 chat, talk
06 confab
12 conversation, heart-to-heart

**tether**
03 tie
04 bind, bond, lead, line, rope
05 chain, leash
06 fasten, fetter, secure
09 fastening, restraint

**text**
04 book

05 theme, topic, verse, words
06 matter, source
07 chapter, content, passage, subject, wording
08 sentence, textbook

**texture**
04 feel
05 grain, touch, weave
06 fabric, finish, tissue
07 quality, surface
10 appearance
11 composition, consistency

**thank**
06 credit
09 recognize
10 appreciate, be grateful
11 acknowledge, say thank you

**thankful**
07 obliged, pleased
08 beholden, grateful, indebted, relieved
12 appreciative

**thankless**
10 unrequited, unrewarded
11 unrewarding
12 unprofitable, unrecognized
13 unappreciated
14 unacknowledged

**thanks**
06 credit
08 bless you
09 gratitude
11 much obliged, recognition
12 appreciation, gratefulness, thanksgiving
14 acknowledgment

❑**thanks to**
05 due to
07 owing to, through
09 because of
11 as a result of, on account of

**thaw**
04 melt, warm
05 de-ice, relax
07 defrost, liquefy
08 defreeze, loosen up

**theater**
03 rep
05 drama, odeum
06 cinema, lyceum
08 the stage
09 dramatics, multiplex, playhouse, the boards, theatrics
10 auditorium, opera house
11 picture show, Thespian art
12 amphitheater, movie theater
13 the footlights
➤ See also DIRECTOR

► *Parts of a theater*:
03 box, pit, set
04 flat, grid, loge
05 apron, flies, spots, stage, wings
06 border, bridge, circle, floats, floods, lights, loggia
07 balcony, catwalk, gallery, rostrum, the gods, upstage
08 coulisse, trapdoor
09 backstage, cyclorama, downstage, forestage, green room, mezzanine, tormentor
10 auditorium, footlights, fourth wall, prompt side, proscenium
11 dress circle
12 orchestra pit
13 orchestra seat, safety curtain
14 opposite prompt, proscenium arch, revolving stage

► *Names of New York theaters. We have omitted the word **theater** from names given in the following list but you may need to include this word as part of the solution to some crossword clues.*

04 Cort
05 Booth, Lyric
06 Golden, Lyceum, Palace
07 Belasco, St. James
08 Broadway, Gershwin, Imperial, Majestic, Minskoff, Music Box, Plymouth, Schubert
09 Neil Simon
10 Helen Hayes
12 Carnegie Hall, Eugene O'Neill, Lunt-Fontanne, Winter Garden
13 Mark Hellinger
14 Brooks Atkinson, Ethel Barrymore, Richard Rodgers, Vivian Beaumont
18 Radio City Music Hall

**theatrical**
05 showy
08 affected, dramatic, mannered, thespian
09 emotional
10 artificial, histrionic
11 exaggerated, extravagant
12 melodramatic, ostentatious

► *Theatrical forms include*:
04 mime, play
05 farce, opera, revue
06 ballet, circus, comedy, kabuki, masque

07 cabaret, concert, monolog, mummery, musical, pageant, tableau, tragedy, variety
08 operetta
09 burlesque, melodrama, monologue, pantomime
10 marionette, vaudeville
11 black comedy, miracle play, mystery play
12 Grand Guignol, morality play, Punch and Judy
13 fringe theater, musical comedy, puppet theater, street theater
15 comedy of manners

**theft**
05 fraud
07 larceny, lifting, mugging, robbery, swiping
08 burglary, pinching, stealing, thieving
09 pilfering, swindling
10 purloining
11 kleptomania, shoplifting
12 embezzlement, plagiarizing

**thematic**
08 notional
10 conceptual

**theme**
04 gist, idea, text, tune
05 essay, motif, paper, topic
06 melody, thesis, thread
07 essence, keynote, subject
09 leitmotif
13 subject matter

**then**
04 also, next, soon, thus
05 after
07 besides, further, so and so
08 moreover
09 as a result, therefore
10 at that time, in addition
11 accordingly, at that point, furthermore, in those days
12 additionally, at a later date, consequently, subsequently

**theologian**

► *Names of theologians*:
03 Eck (Johann Mayer von)
04 Bede (St.), Otto (Rudolf), Paul (St.), Cardinal)
05 Arius, Barth (Karl), Buber (Martin), Cyril (of Alexandria), Paley (William), Pusey (Edward Bouverie), Young (Thomas), St.)
06 Alcuin, Anselm (St.), Calvin (John), Hooker (Richard), Jansen (Cornelius), Jerome

(St.), Mather (Increase), Newman (John Henry, Origen, Pascal (Blaise), Cardinal)
07 Abelard (Peter), Aquinas (St. Thomas), Bernard (of Clairvaux, Clement (of Alexandria), Cyprian (St.), Eckhart (Johannes), Gregory (of Nazianzus, Gregory (of Nyssa), Grotius (Hugo), Lombard (Peter), Sankara, Spinoza (Baruch), Tillich (Paul Johannes), William (of Ockham), St.), St.)
08 Berengar (of Tours), Bultmann (Rudolf Karl), Eusebius, Ignatius (of Loyola, Irenaeus (St.), Sprenger (Jacob), St.)
09 Augustine (St.), Nagarjuna
10 Bellarmine (St. Robert), Bonhoeffer (Dietrich), Duns Scotus (John), Schweitzer (Albert), Swedenborg (Emanuel), Tertullian
12 Justin Martyr (St.)
➤ See also RELIGION

**theological**
06 divine
09 doctrinal, religious
10 scriptural
12 hierological
14 ecclesiastical

**theorem**
04 rule
06 dictum
07 formula
09 postulate, principle
10 hypothesis
11 proposition

**theoretical**
04 pure
05 ideal
07 on paper
08 abstract, academic, notional
10 conceptual
11 conjectural, speculative
12 hypothetical

**theorize**
05 guess
08 propound
09 formulate, postulate
10 conjecture
11 hypothesize

**theory**
06 notion, scheme, thesis
07 opinion, surmise
08 proposal

10 conjecture, hypothesis
11 postulation, presumption, speculation, supposition

**therapeutic**
04 good
05 tonic
06 curing
07 healing
08 curative, remedial, salutary
10 beneficial, corrective
11 restorative
12 advantageous, ameliorative

**therapy**
04 cure
05 tonic
06 remedy
07 healing
09 treatment

---

► *Types of therapy. The word* **therapy** *has been omitted from items in this list but you may need to include this word as part of the solution to some crossword clues.*

03 art, sex
04 play
05 drama, group, music
06 beauty, family, speech
07 Gestalt, Rolfing, shiatsu
08 aversion
09 herbalism
10 homeopathy, osteopathy, regression, ultrasound
11 acupressure, acupuncture, biofeedback, moxibustion, naturopathy, reflexology
12 aromatherapy, chemotherapy, chiropractic, faith healing, hydrotherapy, hypnotherapy, occupational, radiotherapy
13 physiotherapy, psychotherapy

**thereabouts**
05 about
07 roughly
13 approximately

**thereafter**
04 next
09 after that, afterward
12 subsequently

**therefore**
04 ergo, then, thus
09 as a result
11 accordingly

**thesaurus**
07 lexicon
08 treasury, wordbook
10 dictionary, repository, storehouse, vocabulary

12 encyclopedia

**thesis**
04 idea, view
05 essay, paper, theme, topic
06 theory
07 opinion, premise, subject
08 argument, proposal, treatise
10 contention, hypothesis
11 composition, proposition
12 disquisition, dissertation

**thick**
03 big, fat, hub
04 deep, dull, dumb, full, slow
05 broad, bulky, close, dense, dopey, husky, midst, murky, solid, stiff, stout
06 center, chunky, croaky, filled, middle, packed, simple, strong, stupid
07 clotted, compact, crowded, foolish, rasping, teeming, throaty, unclear, viscous
08 abundant, brimming, bursting, crawling, croaking, gravelly, guttural, numerous, swarming
09 abounding, brainless, condensed, dim-witted
10 coagulated, indistinct, noticeable, pronounced
11 overflowing, substantial
12 concentrated, impenetrable

**thicken**
03 gel, set
04 cake, clot, jell
07 congeal, stiffen
08 condense, solidify
09 coagulate

**thicket**
04 wood
05 brush, copse, grove
06 maquis
07 coppice
10 underbrush

**thickhead**
04 clod, dolt, dope, fool
05 chump, dummy, dunce, idiot, moron
06 dimwit, nitwit
07 fathead, pinhead
08 imbecile, numskull
09 blockhead

**thickheaded**
04 slow
05 dense, dopey, thick
06 obtuse, stupid
07 asinine, doltish, moronic
09 dimwitted, imbecilic
10 dull-witted, slow-witted
11 blockheaded

**thickness**
03 bed, ply
04 body, bulk, film
05 girth, layer, sheet, width
07 breadth, density, stratum
08 diameter
09 bulkiness, closeness, solidness, viscosity
11 consistency

**thickset**
05 beefy, bulky, burly, solid
06 brawny, stocky, sturdy
08 muscular, powerful
09 well-built

**thick-skinned**
07 callous
08 hardened
09 hard-nosed, unfeeling
10 hard-boiled
11 insensitive
15 tough as old boots

**thief**
06 bandit, mugger, pirate, robber
07 brigand, burglar, filcher, poacher, stealer
08 pilferer, swindler
09 embezzler, plunderer
10 pickpocket, shoplifter
12 housebreaker, kleptomaniac

**thieve**
03 rob
04 lift
05 cheat, filch, heist, pinch, poach, steal, swipe
06 pilfer, rip off, snatch
07 plunder, purloin, snaffle
08 embezzle, knock off
14 misappropriate

**thieving**
05 theft
06 piracy
07 larceny, lifting, mugging, robbery
08 banditry, burglary, filching, stealing, thievery
09 pilferage, pilfering
10 peculation, ripping off
11 knocking off, shoplifting
12 embezzlement

**thievish**
09 dishonest, furacious, larcenous, rapacious
10 fraudulent
13 light-fingered
14 sticky-fingered

**thin**
04 bony, fine, lame, lean, poor, rare, slim, soft, trim, weak

05 faint, filmy, gaunt, gauzy, lanky, light, quiet, runny, scant, sheer, spare, wispy
06 dilute, feeble, flimsy, lessen, meager, narrow, paltry, rarefy, reduce, refine, scarce, skimpy, skinny, slight, sparse, wasted, watery
07 diluted, scraggy, scrawny, slender, spindly, weed out
08 anorexic, decrease, delicate, diminish, gossamer, hairline, shrunken, skeletal, straggly
09 attenuate, defective, deficient, emaciated, paper-thin, scattered, untenable
10 attenuated, diaphonous, see-through, wishy-washy
11 high-pitched, implausible, transparent, underweight
14 undernourished

❑**on thin ice**
06 at risk, unsafe
10 in jeopardy, precarious, vulnerable

**thing**
04 body, deed, fact, feat, idea, item, love, task, togs, tool
05 chore, fancy, gismo, gizmo, goods, point, stuff, tools, trait
06 action, affair, aspect, attire, desire, detail, device, doodad, entity, factor, fetish, gadget, hang-up, horror, liking, matter, notion, object, phobia, tackle
07 apparel, article, baggage, clothes, concept, dislike, effects, exploit, feature, leaning, luggage, problem, thought, whatsis, whatsit, whatzit
08 affinity, aversion, clothing, creature, fixation, fondness, garments, idée fixe, incident, penchant, property, soft spot, weakness
09 affection, apparatus, attribute, condition, equipment, happening, implement, mechanism, obsession, proneness, substance
10 belongings, instrument, partiality, particular, phenomenon, preference, proceeding, propensity
11 contrivance, eventuality, inclination, possessions, thingamabob, thingamajig, thingumabob, thingumajig
12 predilection

13 paraphernalia, preoccupation
14 characteristic, responsibility
15 whatchamacallit

❑**the thing**
03 hip
04 cool
06 latest, modish
07 current, in vogue, popular
09 the latest
10 all the rage
11 fashionable

**think**
04 deem, hold, muse, plan
05 brood, guess, judge, opine
06 expect, figure, ponder, reason, reckon, regard
07 believe, imagine, presume, reflect, suppose, surmise
08 chew over, cogitate, conceive, conclude, consider, estimate, meditate, mull over, ruminate
09 calculate, cerebrate, determine, visualize
10 cogitation, conjecture, deliberate, evaluation, meditation, reflection
11 concentrate, contemplate
12 deliberation
13 consideration, contemplation

❑**think better of**
06 revise
07 rethink
10 reconsider, think again, think twice
11 get cold feet

❑**think much of**
04 rate
05 prize, value
06 admire, esteem
07 respect
10 set store by
13 think highly of

❑**think nothing of**
13 consider usual
14 consider normal

❑**think over**
06 ponder
07 weigh up
08 consider, meditate, mull over, ruminate
11 contemplate, reflect upon

❑**think up**
06 create, design, devise, invent
07 concoct, dream up, imagine
08 conceive, contrive
09 visualize

**thinkable**
06 likely
08 feasible, possible
10 imaginable, reasonable
11 conceivable

**thinker**
04 sage
05 brain
07 scholar
08 theorist
09 intellect
10 ideologist, mastermind
11 philosopher

**thinking**
04 idea, view
07 logical, outlook, thought
08 rational, sensible, thoughts
09 appraisal, reasoning
10 analytical, assessment, conclusion, evaluation, meditative, philosophy, reflective, thoughtful
11 conclusions, intelligent
12 intellectual
13 contemplative, philosophical, sophisticated

**thin-skinned**
06 snappy, tender, touchy
09 irritable, sensitive
11 easily upset, susceptible
14 hypersensitive

**third-rate**
03 bad
04 poor
06 shoddy
08 inferior, low-grade, mediocre, slipshod
10 low-quality

**thirst**
03 yen
04 long, lust
05 crave, yearn
06 desire, hanker, hunger
07 aridity, craving, drought, dryness, longing, passion
09 eagerness, hankering
11 drouthiness, parchedness
12 droughtiness

**thirsty**
03 dry
04 arid, avid, keen
07 burning, craving, gasping, itching, longing, parched
08 desirous, yearning
10 dehydrated

**thong**
04 band, belt, cord, lash
05 strap, strip
06 sandal
08 flip-flop, swimsuit, whiplash

10 underpants
11 bathing suit
**thorn**
04 barb
05 point, spike, spine
06 needle
07 bristle, prickle
**thorny**
05 sharp, spiky, spiny, vexed
06 barbed, knotty, tricky, trying
07 awkward, bristly, complex, irksome, pointed, prickly, spinose, spinous
09 acanthous, difficult
10 convoluted
11 problematic, troublesome
**thorough**
04 deep, full, pure
05 sheer, total, utter
06 entire
07 careful, in-depth, perfect
08 absolute, complete
09 efficient, extensive, intensive, out-and-out
10 exhaustive, meticulous, scrupulous, widespread
11 painstaking, unqualified
12 all-embracing, all-inclusive
13 comprehensive
**thoroughbred**
08 pedigree, purebred
09 full-blood, pedigreed
11 full-blooded
**thoroughfare**
03 way
04 road
06 access, artery, avenue, street
07 highway, passage, roadway
08 turnpike
09 boulevard
10 passageway
**thoroughly**
05 fully, quite
07 totally, utterly
08 entirely
09 carefully, downright, every inch, inside out, perfectly
10 absolutely, completely
12 exhaustively, scrupulously
13 root and branch
15 comprehensively
**though**
03 but, yet
05 still, while
06 even if, even so
07 granted, however
08 allowing, although
10 all the same, for all that
11 nonetheless
12 nevertheless

15 notwithstanding
**thought**
04 care, heed, hope, idea, plan
05 dream, study, touch
06 belief, musing, notion, reason, regard, theory
07 concept, concern, feeling, gesture, opinion, purpose
08 prospect, sympathy, thinking
09 attention, intention, pondering, reasoning
10 cogitation, conception, conclusion, conviction, estimation, meditation, reflection, rumination
11 cerebration, expectation
12 anticipation, deliberation
13 consideration, contemplation, introspection
**thoughtful**
04 deep, kind, wary
05 quiet
06 caring, dreamy
07 careful, heedful, helpful, mindful, pensive, serious
08 profound, studious, thinking
09 attentive, unselfish
10 reflective, solicitous
11 considerate, sympathetic
13 contemplative, in a brown study, lost in thought
**thoughtless**
05 hasty, silly
06 remiss, stupid, unwise
07 foolish, selfish
08 careless, heedless, impolite, mindless, reckless, tactless
09 imprudent, negligent
10 ill-advised, indiscreet
11 insensitive, precipitate
12 absent-minded
13 ill-considered, inconsiderate
**thrall**
05 power
07 bondage, serfdom, slavery
08 thraldom
09 servitude, vassalage
10 subjection
11 enslavement, subjugation
**thrash**
03 hit, tan
04 beat, belt, cane, drub, flog, lash, lick, rout, whip
05 crush, flail, spank, whack, whale
06 defeat, hammer, punish
07 clobber, scourge, trounce
08 vanquish
09 overwhelm, slaughter

◻**thrash out**
07 discuss, resolve
09 hammer out, negotiate
**thrashing**
04 rout
06 caning, defeat, hiding
07 beating, belting, lamming, lashing, licking, pasting
08 crushing, drubbing, whipping
09 hammering, trouncing
10 clobbering, punishment
**thread**
04 ease, inch, line, move, pass, plot, push, wind, yarn
05 fiber, strip, theme, weave
06 course, strand, streak, string
08 filament
09 direction, storyline
14 train of thought
**threadbare**
03 old
04 worn
05 stale, tired
06 frayed, ragged, shabby
07 scruffy, worn-out
08 overused, well-worn
09 hackneyed, moth-eaten
12 cliché-ridden
**threat**
04 omen, risk
05 peril
06 danger, hazard, menace
07 portent, presage, warning
09 ultimatum
11 commination
**threaten**
04 loom, warn
05 augur, bully
06 extort, lean on, menace
07 imperil, portend, presage
08 endanger, forebode
09 blackmail, comminate, terrorize
10 be imminent, foreshadow, intimidate, jeopardize, pressurize, push around
14 put the screws on
**threatening**
07 looming, ominous, warning
08 menacing, minatory, sinister
09 impending, minacious
10 cautionary, foreboding
12 inauspicious, intimidatory
**threesome**
04 trio
05 triad
06 triple, triune, troika
07 trilogy, trinity, triplet
08 triptych

11  triumvirate

**threshold**
04  dawn, door, sill
05  brink, entry, start, verge
07  doorway, opening
08  doorstep, entrance
09  beginning, inception

**thrift**
06  saving
07  economy
09  frugality, husbandry,
    parsimony
11  carefulness
12  conservation

**thriftless**
08  prodigal, wasteful
09  imprudent, unthrifty
10  profligate
11  dissipative, extravagant,
    improvident, spendthrift

**thrifty**
06  frugal, saving
07  careful, prudent, sparing
10  conserving, economical
12  parsimonious

**thrill**
04  buzz, glow, kick, move, stir
05  flush, rouse, shake, throb
06  arouse, charge, excite,
    quiver, shiver, tingle, tremor
07  delight, feeling, flutter,
    frisson, shudder, tremble
08  pleasure
09  adventure, sensation,
    stimulate, vibration
10  excitement, exhilarate
11  give a buzz to, give a kick to

**thrilling**
07  quaking, rousing, shaking
08  exciting, gripping, stirring
09  shivering, trembling
11  hair-raising, sensational
12  electrifying, soul-stirring

**thrive**
04  boom, gain, grow
05  bloom
06  do well, profit
07  advance, blossom, burgeon,
    develop, prosper, succeed
08  flourish, increase

**thriving**
07  booming, healthy, wealthy
08  affluent, blooming
10  blossoming, burgeoning,
    prosperous, successful
11  comfortable, flourishing

**throat**
04  craw
05  gorge

06  fauces, gullet
07  jugular, weasand
08  guttural, throttle, windpipe
09  esophagus

**throaty**
03  low
04  deep
05  gruff, husky, thick
06  hoarse
07  rasping, raucous
08  guttural

**throb**
04  beat, drum
05  pound, pulse, thump
07  pulsate, vibrate
08  pounding, thumping
09  palpitate, vibration
11  palpitation

**throe**
03  fit
04  pain, pang, stab
05  agony, spasm
07  anguish, seizure, travail
08  distress, paroxysm
10  convulsion

**throng**
03  jam, mob
04  bevy, cram, fill, host, mass
05  bunch, crowd, crush, horde
09  multitude
10  congregate, mill around
12  congregation

**throttle**
05  check, choke
06  keep in, stifle
07  inhibit, silence, smother
08  restrain, strangle, suppress
09  suffocate
10  asphyxiate
11  strangulate

**through**
02  by, in
03  via
04  done
05  due to, ended, using
06  across, direct, during
07  between, by way of, express,
    nonstop, owing to
08  finished, thanks to
09  because of, by means of,
    completed
10  by virtue of, terminated,
    throughout, to the end of
11  as a result of, on account of

❏**through and through**
05  fully
06  wholly
07  totally, utterly
08  entirely
09  to the core

10  altogether, completely
12  unreservedly
15  from top to bottom

**throughout**
06  during, widely
07  all over
09  all around
10  all through, completely,
    everywhere, in all parts
11  extensively, in every part

**throw**
03  lob, pin, put
04  cast, emit, fell, give, hurl,
    send, shed, toss, turn
05  chuck, fling, floor, heave,
    pitch, sling, upset
06  baffle, propel, put out,
    spread, tackle, unseat
07  confuse, disturb, perplex,
    project, radiate, unhorse
08  astonish, catapult, confound,
    coverlet, dislodge, organize,
    overturn, surprise, switch on,
    unsaddle
09  bring down, discomfit,
    dumbfound, prostrate
10  disconcert
13  lose on purpose

❏**throw away**
04  blow, dump, lose
05  ditch, pitch, scrap, waste
07  discard
08  chuck out, get rid of, jettison
09  chuck away, dispose of
11  fritter away

❏**throw off**
04  drop, shed
05  elude
07  abandon, cast off, discard
08  get rid of, jettison, shake off

❏**throw out**
05  ditch, eject, evict, expel
07  diffuse, discard, dismiss,
    emanate, give off, produce,
    radiate, turn out
08  jettison, point out
12  dispense with
13  retire a runner

❏**throw over**
04  drop, jilt, quit
05  chuck, leave
06  desert, reject
07  abandon, discard, forsake
10  finish with

❏**throw up**
03  gag
04  barf, puke, quit, spew
05  heave, leave, retch, vomit
06  pack in, resign
07  abandon, chuck in

**throwaway**
08 disgorge, renounce
11 regurgitate

**throwaway**
05 cheap
06 casual
07 offhand, passing
08 careless
10 disposable, expendable
13 biodegradable

**thrust**
03 jab, jam, ram
04 butt, gist, push, stab, urge
05 drift, drive, foist, force, impel, lunge, point, power, shove, tenor, theme, wedge
06 burden, impose, pierce, plunge, propel, saddle
07 essence, impetus, inflict
08 encumber, momentum
09 substance

**thud**
04 bang, bash, wham
05 clonk, clump, clunk, crash, knock, smack, thump
06 wallop

**thug**
05 tough
06 killer, mugger, robber
07 hoodlum, ruffian, villain
08 assassin, gangster, hooligan
09 cutthroat, roughneck

**thumb**

□**thumb through**
08 glance at
11 flip through, leaf through
12 flick through
13 browse through

**thumbnail**
05 brief, pithy, quick, short
07 compact, concise
08 succinct
09 miniature

**thumbs down**
02 no
06 rebuff
07 refusal
08 negation, turndown
09 rejection
11 disapproval

**thumbs up**
02 OK
03 yes
04 okay
07 go-ahead
08 approval, sanction
10 acceptance, green light
11 affirmation

**thump**
03 box, hit, rap

04 bang, beat, blow, slap, thud
05 clout, crash, knock, pound, punch, smack, throb, whack
06 batter, hammer, strike, thrash, thwack, wallop
09 palpitate

**thumping**
04 huge, very
06 really, severe
07 extreme, greatly, immense, mammoth, massive, titanic
08 colossal, enormous, gigantic, severely, terrific
09 excessive, extremely
10 impressive, monumental, thundering, tremendous

**thunder**
04 bang, clap, peal, roar, roll
05 blast, crack, crash
06 bellow, rumble
07 resound
11 reverberate
13 reverberation

**thundering**
04 very
05 great
06 really
08 enormous, severely
09 excessive, extremely, intensely, unusually
10 monumental, remarkable, tremendous

**thunderous**
04 loud
07 booming, roaring
08 rumbling
09 deafening
10 resounding, tumultuous
12 earsplitting

**thunderstruck**
05 agape, dazed
06 aghast, amazed
07 floored, shocked, stunned
09 astounded, flummoxed, paralyzed, staggered
10 bowled over, nonplussed
11 dumbfounded, open-mouthed
13 flabbergasted

**thus**
02 so
04 ergo, then
05 hence
08 like this
09 as follows, in this way, therefore
11 accordingly
12 consequently

**thwack**
03 hit

04 bash, beat, blow, flog, slap
05 clout, smack, thump, whack
06 buffet, wallop

**thwart**
04 balk, foil, stop
05 baulk, block, check, cross, stymy
06 defeat, hamper, hinder, impede, oppose, stymie
07 prevent
08 obstruct
09 frustrate

**tic**
05 spasm
06 twitch
13 tic douloureux

**tick**
03 tap
04 beat, line, mark, mite
05 check, click
06 insect
08 indicate, ticktock
09 check mark

□**tick off**
05 anger
08 irritate
09 make angry

**ticker**
04 bomb
05 clock, heart, watch
06 tapper

**ticket**
03 tag
04 card, pass, slip, stub
05 label, token
06 coupon, docket
07 sticker, voucher

**tickle**
05 amuse, touch
06 divert, please, stroke, thrill
07 delight, gratify
08 delicacy

**ticklish**
05 risky
06 knotty, thorny, touchy, tricky
07 awkward
09 difficult, sensitive
11 problematic

**tidbit**
05 scrap, snack, treat
06 dainty, morsel
11 bonne bouche

**tide**
03 ebb, run
04 flow, flux
05 drift, tenor, trend
06 course, stream
07 current
08 movement, tendency

## ❏ **tide over**
03 aid
06 assist
07 help out
09 keep going
11 help through

## **tidings**
04 dope, news, word
06 advice, report
07 message
09 greetings
11 information

## **tidy**
04 fair, good, neat, trim
05 ample, clean, groom, order, smart
06 neaten, spruce
07 arrange, clean up, clear up, ordered, orderly, smarten
08 sizeable, spruce up
09 efficient, organized, shipshape
10 immaculate, methodical, straighten, systematic
11 uncluttered, well-ordered
12 considerable, spick-and-span

## **tie**
03 fix
04 band, bind, bond, clip, curb, draw, duty, join, knot, lash, link, moor, rope, tape
05 ascot, chain, limit, strap, unite
06 attach, be even, bow tie, couple, cravat, fasten, hamper, hinder, ribbon, secure, tether
07 be equal, confine, connect, kinship, liaison, necktie, shackle
08 dead heat, restrain, standoff
09 constrain, fastening, hindrance, restraint
10 allegiance, commitment, connection, constraint, friendship, limitation, obligation
11 be all square, restriction
12 relationship

## ❏ **tie down**
06 hamper, hinder
07 confine
08 restrain, restrict
09 constrain

## ❏ **tie-up**
03 jam
04 bind, do up, lash, moor, rope
05 chain, truss

06 attach, engage, fasten, occupy, secure, settle, tether, wind up, wrap up
08 finalize, keep busy
10 traffic jam

## **tie-in**
04 link
05 tie-up
06 hookup
07 liaison
08 relation
10 connection
11 affiliation, association
12 coordination, relationship

## **tier**
03 row
04 band, bank, belt, line, rank
05 floor, layer, level, stage
07 echelon, stratum

## **tiff**
03 pet, row
04 huff, spat, sulk
05 fight, scrap, set-to, words
07 dispute, quarrel, tantrum
08 squabble
10 difference, falling-out
12 disagreement

## **tight**
04 fast, firm, mean, snug, taut
05 close, drunk, fixed, merry, rigid, tense, tipsy, tough
06 pissed, scarce, sealed, secure, severe, stingy, stoned, strict, tricky
07 compact, cramped, legless, limited, miserly, sloshed, smashed, sozzled
08 airtight, clenched, hermetic, rigorous, strained, tanked up
09 niggardly, plastered, skintight, stretched, stringent, well-oiled
10 compressed, inadequate, inflexible, restricted, soundproof, watertight
11 constricted, intoxicated, neck and neck, tightfisted
12 closefitting, parsimonious, tight as a tick
13 figure-hugging, penny-pinching

## **tighten**
05 close, cramp, crush, tense
06 fasten, narrow, secure
07 squeeze, stiffen, stretch
09 constrict, pull tight
10 constringe

## **tightfisted**
04 mean
05 mingy, tight
06 stingy

07 miserly, sparing
08 grasping
09 niggardly
12 parsimonious
13 penny-pinching

## **tight-lipped**
03 mum
04 mute
05 quiet
06 silent
09 secretive
11 closelipped
12 closemouthed
13 unforthcoming
15 uncommunicative

## **tightwad**
05 miser
07 scrooge
09 skinflint
10 cheapskate
11 cheeseparer
12 penny-pincher

## **till**
02 to
03 dig
04 farm, plow, up to, work
05 until
09 cultivate
10 cash drawer

## **tilt**
03 tip
04 cant, duel, lean, list, spar
05 angle, clash, fight, joust, pitch, slant, slope
06 attack, charge, combat
07 contend, contest, incline
10 tournament
11 inclination

## ❏ **at full tilt**
06 all out
07 flat out
08 very fast
10 at full pelt, at top speed
11 at full speed, very quickly

## **timber**
03 log
04 beam, lath, pole, spar, wood
05 board, plank, trees
06 forest
09 character

## **timbre**
04 ring, tone
05 color
07 quality
09 resonance
12 voice quality

## **time**
03 age, era, fix, set
04 date, life, peak, span, term

05 clock, count, epoch, meter, point, space, spell, stage, tempo, while
06 adjust, heyday, moment, period, rhythm, season
07 arrange, control, instant, measure, program, session, stretch, timeout
08 duration, instance, interval, juncture, lifespan, lifetime, occasion, temporal
09 calculate

❏**all the time**
06 always
07 forever
10 constantly
11 continually, incessantly, perpetually

❏**at one time**
04 once
07 long ago
08 formerly
09 right then
10 at one point, previously
11 in times past
12 then and there

❏**at the same time**
06 anyway, even so
07 however
10 altogether
11 nonetheless
12 concurrently, nevertheless
14 simultaneously

❏**at times**
09 sometimes
10 now and then
11 now and again, on occasions
12 every so often
14 from time to time

❏**behind the times**
05 dated
06 old hat
09 out of date
10 fuddy-duddy
12 old-fashioned, out of fashion
13 unfashionable

❏**behind time**
04 late
07 delayed, overdue
14 behind schedule

❏**for the time being**
06 for now, pro tem
08 meantime, right now
09 at present, meanwhile
11 at the moment, temporarily
12 for the moment
13 for the present

❏**from time to time**
07 at times
09 sometimes

10 now and then, on occasion
11 now and again
12 occasionally, once in a while, periodically, sporadically
13 spasmodically
14 intermittently

❏**in good time**
05 early
06 on time
07 quickly
11 ahead of time
15 ahead of schedule, at the proper time

❏**in time**
06 on time
10 not too late, punctually

❏**on time**
05 sharp
06 dead on
07 exactly
08 on the dot, promptly
09 precisely
10 punctually

❏**play for time**
05 delay, stall
08 hang fire, hesitate
10 filibuster
13 procrastinate

❏**time after time**
05 often
09 many times
10 frequently, repeatedly
12 time and again
13 again and again

**time-honored**
03 old
05 fixed, usual
06 age-old
07 ancient
08 historic
09 customary, venerable
10 accustomed
11 established, traditional
12 conventional

**timeless**
07 abiding, eternal, lasting
08 immortal, unending
09 immutable, permanent
10 changeless, unchanging

**timely**
06 prompt
08 punctual, suitable
09 opportune, well-timed
10 convenient, felicitous
11 appropriate

**timetable**
04 list
06 agenda, roster
07 listing, program
08 calendar, schedule

09 itinerary

**timeworn**
03 old
04 aged, worn
05 dated, hoary, lined, passé, stale, stock, tired, trite
06 ragged, ruined, shabby
07 clichéd, run-down
08 bromidic, decrepit, dogeared, shopworn, well-worn, wrinkled
09 hackneyed, weathered

**timid**
03 shy
06 afraid, scared, yellow
07 bashful, chicken, fearful, gutless, nervous, wimpish
08 cowardly, retiring, timorous
09 shrinking, spineless
10 frightened, irresolute
11 lily-livered
12 apprehensive, fainthearted
13 yellow-bellied
14 chicken-hearted

**timorous**
03 coy, shy
05 mousy, timid
06 afraid, modest, scared
07 bashful, fearful, nervous
08 cowardly, retiring
09 diffident, shrinking, tentative, trembling
10 frightened, irresolute
12 apprehensive, fainthearted
13 pusillanimous

**tincture**
03 dye, hue
04 dash, hint, tint
05 color, imbue, scent, shade, smack, stain, tinge, touch, trace
06 flavor, infuse, season
07 suffuse
10 suggestion

**tinge**
03 bit, dye
04 dash, drop, hint, tint, wash
05 color, imbue, shade, touch, trace
08 tincture
10 smattering, suggestion

**tingle**
06 shiver, thrill, tickle, tremor
07 prickle, tremble, vibrate
08 stinging, tickling
09 prickling
10 goose bumps, goose flesh
12 goose pimples
14 pins and needles

**tinker**
03 toy
04 play
05 fixer
06 dabble, fiddle, meddle, mender, putter, tamper, trifle
07 Mr. Fixit
09 itinerant, mess about
10 fool around, mess around
15 jack-of-all-trades

**tinkle**
04 ding, peal, ring
05 chime, chink, clink
06 jangle, jingle

**tinsel**
05 gaudy
07 display, glitter, spangle
08 frippery, gimcrack, specious
09 gaudiness
10 garishness, triviality
11 flamboyance, ostentation
13 artificiality, worthlessness

**tint**
03 dye, hue
04 cast, tone, wash
05 color, rinse, shade, taint, tinge
06 affect, streak
08 tincture

**tiny**
03 wee
04 mini-
05 small, teeny
06 little, midget, minute, petite, pocket, slight
09 itsy-bitsy, itty-bitty, miniature, minuscule, pint-sized
10 diminutive, negligible
11 Lilliputian, microscopic
13 infinitesimal, insignificant

**tip**
03 cap, end, nib, top
04 acme, apex, cant, clue, doff, gift, head, hint, info, lean, list, peak, perk, pour, tell, tilt
05 bonus, point, slant, spill
06 advice, reward, summit, topple, unload
07 incline, pointer, pour out, present, suggest, warning
08 forecast, forewarn, gratuity, pinnacle
09 baksheesh, extremity, pourboire
10 perquisite, suggestion, topple over
11 information
14 recommendation

**tip-off**
04 clue, hint
07 pointer, warning

11 information

**tipple**
04 swig
05 booze, drink, quaff
06 imbibe, liquor, poison
07 alcohol, indulge

**tippler**
03 sot
04 lush, soak, wino
05 dipso, drunk, toper
06 bibber, boozer, sponge
07 drinker
08 drunkard
09 inebriate
11 dipsomaniac, hard drinker

**tipsy**
05 drunk, happy, merry, tight, tipsy
06 mellow
07 squiffy
08 squiffed

**tirade**
05 abuse
08 diatribe, harangue, outburst
09 invective, philippic
11 fulmination

**tire**
04 bore, drop, flag
05 drain, weary
07 exhaust, fatigue, tire out
08 enervate

**tired**
04 beat
05 all in, bored, corny, fed up, jaded, stale, trite, weary
06 bushed, drowsy, sleepy
07 clichéd, worn out
08 dead beat, dog-tired, fatigued, flagging
09 enervated, exhausted, hackneyed, shattered
11 ready to drop

**tireless**
06 dogged
08 diligent, resolute, untiring
09 energetic, unwearied
10 determined, unflagging
13 indefatigable

**tiresome**
04 dull
06 boring, tiring, trying
07 humdrum, irksome, tedious
08 annoying
09 fatiguing, laborious, vexatious, wearisome
10 irritating, monotonous
12 exasperating

**tiring**
04 hard

05 tough
06 taxing
07 arduous
08 draining, exacting, wearying
09 fatiguing, laborious, strenuous, wearisome
10 enervating, exhausting

**tiro** see TYRO

**tissue**
03 web
04 mesh
05 flesh, gauze, stuff
07 network, texture
08 gossamer, material
10 Kleenex
11 toilet paper

**tit for tat**
07 revenge
08 requital
10 quid pro quo
11 blow for blow, eye for an eye, lex talionis, like for like, retaliation
13 countercharge

**titan**
04 Rhea, Thea
05 Atlas, Coeus, Crius, giant
06 Cronus, Phoebe, Tethys, Themis
07 Iapetus, Oceanus
08 colossus, Hercules, Hyperion, superman
09 leviathan, Mnemosyne

**titanic**
04 huge, vast
05 giant, jumbo
06 mighty
07 immense, massive
08 colossal, enormous, gigantic, towering
09 cyclopean, herculean
10 monumental, prodigious
11 mountainous

**titbit** see TIDBIT

**tithe**
03 pay, tax
04 duty, give, levy, rent, toll
05 tenth
06 charge, impost, tariff

**titillate**
05 tease
06 arouse, excite, thrill, tickle
08 interest, intrigue
09 stimulate, tantalize

**titillating**
04 lewd, sexy
06 erotic
07 teasing
08 arousing, exciting

**titivate**
09 seductive, thrilling
10 intriguing, suggestive
11 provocative, stimulating

**titivate**
05 preen, primp, prink
06 doll up, make up
08 spruce up

**title**
03 dub, tag
04 call, game, name, rank, term
05 claim, crown, deeds, label, match, prize, right, style
06 credit, handle, legend, office, stakes, status, trophy
07 contest, credits, heading, moniker, titular
08 headline, position
09 designate, sobriquet
11 appellation, designation
12 championship
13 form of address

**titter**
04 mock
05 laugh
06 cackle, giggle
07 chuckle, snicker, snigger

**tittle-tattle**
03 jaw, yak
04 chat, yack
05 rumor
06 gossip, yak-yak
07 blather, blether, chatter, hearsay, prattle, twaddle
08 chitchat, yack-yack
09 tell tales, yakety-yak
10 yackety-yak

**titular**
05 token
07 nominal
08 official, so-called

**toadstool** see MUSHROOM

**toady**
04 fawn
05 crawl, creep
06 cringe, fawner, grovel, jackal, kowtow, lackey, minion, suck up, yes man
07 crawler, flatter, flunkey
08 bootlick, butter up, groveler, hanger-on, parasite, truckler
09 brownnose, flatterer, sycophant
10 bootlicker, brownnoser, curry favor
11 kiss the feet

**toast**
04 bake, heat, warm
05 bread, brown, crisp, drink, grill, honor

06 heat up, pledge, salute, warm up
07 drink to, tribute
10 salutation
11 compliments

**today**
03 now
07 just now, this day
08 nowadays, right now
09 these days
11 this evening, this morning, this very day
12 at this moment
13 this afternoon
14 the present time

**toddle**
04 reel, rock, sway
05 lurch, shake, waver
06 falter, teeter, totter, waddle
07 stagger, stumble
14 walk unsteadily

**to-do**
04 flap, fuss, stew, stir
05 furor, hoo-ha
06 bother, bustle, flurry, rumpus, tumult, uproar
07 quarrel, ruction, turmoil
08 brouhaha
09 agitation, commotion
10 excitement
11 disturbance, performance

**together**
04 calm, cool
06 in a row, stable, united
07 as a team, jointly
08 composed, in unison
09 all at once, at one time, in concert, organized
10 hand in hand, side by side
11 down-to-earth, levelheaded
12 collectively, concurrently, continuously, in succession, successively, well-adjusted, well-balanced
13 at the same time, consecutively, in conjunction
14 simultaneously
15 in collaboration

**toil**
04 slog, work
05 grind, labor, slave, sweat
06 drudge, effort, strive
08 drudgery, exertion, hard work, industry, struggle
10 donkeywork
11 application, elbow grease
15 work like a Trojan

**toiler**
05 slave
06 drudge, menial, worker
07 laborer, slogger

10 workaholic

**toilet**
03 can, pot
04 head, john
05 privy
07 latrine, the mens'
08 bathroom, lavatory, outhouse, restroom, washroom
09 cloakroom, the ladies', the women's
10 powder room
11 convenience, the mens' room
13 the ladies' room, the women's room

**toilsome**
04 hard
05 tough
06 severe, taxing, uphill
07 arduous, painful, tedious
09 difficult, fatiguing, herculean, laborious, strenuous, wearisome
12 backbreaking

**token**
04 clue, disk, mark, sign
06 coupon, emblem, symbol
07 counter, memento, minimal, nominal, voucher, warning
08 evidence, keepsake, memorial, reminder, souvenir, symbolic
10 emblematic, indication
11 perfunctory, recognition
13 demonstration
14 representation

**tolerable**
02 OK
04 fair, okay, so-so
06 not bad
07 average
08 adequate, all right, bearable, mediocre, middling, ordinary, passable
10 acceptable, reasonable
13 no great shakes, unexceptional

**tolerance**
06 lenity
07 laxness, stamina
08 leniency, patience
09 allowance, clearance, endurance, fortitude, toughness, variation
10 indulgence, liberalism, toleration
11 forbearance
13 understanding
14 open-mindedness, permissiveness

15 broad-mindedness

**tolerant**
03 lax
04 fair, soft
07 lenient, liberal, patient
08 catholic
09 compliant, easygoing, forgiving, indulgent
10 charitable, forbearing, open-minded, permissive
11 broad-minded, kindhearted, magnanimous, sympathetic
12 unprejudiced
13 understanding

**tolerate**
04 bear, take
05 abide, admit, allow, stand
06 accept, endure, permit
07 condone, indulge, receive
08 sanction
09 put up with
11 countenance

**toleration**
06 lenity
07 laxness, stamina
08 leniency, sympathy
09 allowance, endurance, fortitude, toughness
10 acceptance, indulgence, liberalism, resilience, resistance, sufferance
11 forbearance, magnanimity
14 open-mindedness, permissiveness
15 broad-mindedness

**toll**
03 fee, tax
04 call, cost, duty, levy, loss, peal, ring, warn
05 chime, clang, knell, sound
06 charge, damage, herald, injury, signal, strike, tariff
07 payment, penalty
08 announce

**tomb**
05 crypt, grave, vault
08 catacomb, cenotaph
09 mausoleum, sepulcher
11 burial place

**tombstone**
05 stone
06 marker
08 memorial, monument
09 headstone
10 gravestone

**tome**
04 book, opus, work
06 volume

**tomfoolery**
04 lark

05 hooey
06 idiocy
07 inanity
08 clowning, mischief
09 horseplay, silliness
10 buffoonery, skylarking
11 foolishness, shenanigans
12 childishness, larking about

**tone**
03 air, hue
04 feel, mood, note, tint, vein
05 color, humor, pitch, shade, sound, style, tenor, tinge, tonal
06 accent, effect, go with, manner, timbre
07 quality
08 attitude, tincture, tonality
10 coordinate, expression, go well with, inflection, intonation, modulation

◻**tone down**
06 dampen, soften, temper
08 mitigate, moderate, play down, restrain
09 alleviate, soft-pedal

◻**tone up**
04 trim
07 freshen, shape up, touch up
10 invigorate

**tongue**
04 cant, talk
05 argot, idiom, lingo, organ, slang
06 jargon, patois, speech
07 dialect, glottic, lingual
08 language, parlance
10 vernacular

**tongue-tied**
04 dumb, mute
06 silent
10 dumbstruck, speechless
12 inarticulate, lost for words

**tonic**
06 bracer, fillip
08 pick-me-up
09 analeptic, refresher, stimulant
11 restorative
12 shot in the arm

**too**
04 also, over, very
06 as well, overly, unduly
07 besides
08 likewise, moreover
09 extremely
10 in addition
11 excessively, furthermore
12 inordinately

**tool**
04 dupe, pawn, work
05 agent, chase, gismo, means
06 agency, device, flunky, gadget, medium, puppet, stooge
07 cat's-paw, fashion, flunkey, machine, utensil, vehicle
08 artefact, artifact, decorate, hireling
09 apparatus, implement
10 instrument
11 contraption, contrivance

---

► *Types of tool*:
02 ax
03 adz, awl, axe, die, hod, hoe, saw
04 file, fork, jack, pick, plow, rake, rasp, rule, vice
05 auger, bevel, clamp, dolly, drill, level, plane, punch, ruler, snips, spade, tongs
06 bodkin, buffer, chisel, dibble, gimlet, hammer, jigsaw, mallet, mortar, needle, pestle, pickax, pliers, reamer, sander, scribe, scythe, shears, shovel, sickle, trowel, weeder, wrench
07 bradawl, chopper, cleaver, crowbar, forceps, fret saw, hacksaw, handsaw, hayfork, mattock, pickaxe, pincers, scalpel, scriber, spatula, stapler, T square
08 billhook, chain saw, dividers, penknife, scissors, spray gun, thresher, tweezers
09 pitchfork, plumb line, set square, staple gun
10 jackhammer, keyhole saw, paper knife, protractor
11 brace and bit, crochet hook, crosscut saw, pocketknife, pruning hook, screwdriver, spirit level
12 sledgehammer, socket wrench, straightedge
13 pinking shears, pruning shears, soldering iron
➤ See also SAW

**tooth**
04 fang, tush, tusk
05 molar, prong
06 dentil
07 incisor
08 denticle
10 masticator

► *Types of teeth. We have omitted the word* **tooth** *from names given in the following list but you may need to include this word as part of the solution to some crossword clues.*

03 cap
04 baby, back, fang, gold, milk, tush, tusk
05 crown, false, first, molar, plate
06 bridge, canine, cuspid, wisdom
07 denture, grinder, incisor
08 bicuspid, dentures, dogtooth, eyetooth, premolar
09 bucktooth
10 carnassial
12 snaggletooth
14 central incisor, lateral incisor

**toothsome**
04 nice
05 sweet, tasty, yummy
08 luscious, tempting
09 delicious, palatable
10 appetizing, delectable, flavorsome
11 scrumptious
13 mouthwatering

**top**
03 cap, lid, tip
04 acme, apex, beat, best, head, lead, main, peak, rule
05 chief, crest, crown, first, outdo, prime, shirt, upper
06 apogee, better, blouse, climax, exceed, finest, jersey, jumper, summit, T-shirt, vertex, zenith
07 garnish, highest, leading, maximum, stopper, supreme, surpass, sweater, topmost
08 decorate, dominant, foremost, greatest, outstrip, pinnacle, pullover, surmount, tee shirt
09 finish off, paramount, principal, uppermost
10 preeminent, sweatshirt
11 culminating, culmination

❏ **on top of the world**
05 happy
06 elated
08 ecstatic, exultant, thrilled
09 overjoyed
11 exhilarated, on cloud nine, over the moon

❏ **over the top**
07 extreme, too much

09 excessive
10 exorbitant, immoderate
11 extravagant, uncalled-for
12 unreasonable

**topic**
05 issue, point, theme
06 matter, thesis
07 subject
08 argument, question

**topical**
06 recent
07 current, popular
08 familiar, relevant, up-to-date
12 contemporary

**topmost**
03 top
05 first, upper
06 apical
07 highest, leading, supreme
08 dominant, foremost, loftiest
09 principal, uppermost

**top-notch**
03 ace, top
04 cool, fine, mega
05 crack, prime, super
06 superb
07 leading, premier, supreme
08 peerless, splendid, superior
09 admirable, excellent, first-rate, matchless, top-flight
10 first-class
11 exceptional, outstanding
12 second-to-none

**topple**
04 fall, oust
05 upset
06 totter, tumble, unseat
08 collapse, dethrone, displace
09 bring down, overthrow
11 overbalance

**topsy-turvy**
07 chaotic, jumbled, mixed-up
08 confused
09 inside out
10 disorderly, upside down
11 disarranged, in confusion

**torch**
05 brand, light
07 cresset
08 flambeau

**torment**
03 vex
04 bane, pain, pest
05 agony, annoy, tease, worry
06 badger, harass, harrow, misery, ordeal, pester, plague
07 afflict, agitate, anguish, bedevil, scourge, torture, trouble
08 distress, vexation

09 persecute, suffering
10 affliction, harassment
11 persecution, provocation
15 thorn in the flesh

**torn**
03 cut
04 rent, slit
05 split
06 ragged, ripped, unsure
07 divided
08 wavering
09 dithering, lacerated, uncertain, undecided
10 irresolute
11 vacillating

**tornado**
07 cyclone, twister
09 whirlwind

**torpid**
04 dead, dull, lazy, numb, slow
05 inert
06 drowsy, sleepy, supine
07 passive
08 inactive, indolent, lifeless, listless, sluggish
09 apathetic, lethargic, nerveless, somnolent

**torpor**
05 sloth
06 apathy
07 inertia, languor
08 dullness, hebetude, laziness, lethargy, numbness
09 indolence, inertness, passivity, torpidity
10 drowsiness, inactivity, sleepiness, somnolence
12 listlessness, sluggishness

**torrent**
04 gush, rush
05 flood, spate, storm
06 deluge, stream, volley
07 barrage, cascade
08 downpour, outburst
10 inundation

**torrid**
03 hot
04 arid, sexy
06 desert, erotic, steamy
07 amorous, blazing, parched
08 scorched, sizzling, stifling
09 scorching, waterless
10 passionate, sweltering

**tortuous**
06 zigzag
07 curving, sinuous, winding
08 indirect, involved, twisting
10 circuitous, convoluted, roundabout, serpentine
11 complicated

## torture
04 pain, rack
05 abuse, agony, worry
06 harrow, plague, punish
07 afflict, crucify, torment
09 persecute, suffering
10 affliction, excruciate
11 persecution

## toss
03 lob
04 cast, flip, jolt, rock, roll
05 chuck, fling, heave, lurch, pitch, shake, sling, throw

## tot
04 baby
05 child
06 infant
07 toddler

## total
03 add, all, lot, sum
04 full, make, mass, rank
05 add up, count, reach, sheer, sum up, utter, whole
06 come to, entire
07 count up, perfect
08 absolute, amount to, complete, entirety, outright, thorough, totality
09 aggregate, downright
11 unmitigated, unqualified
13 comprehensive

## totalitarian
08 despotic, one-party
09 tyrannous
10 monolithic, oppressive
11 dictatorial
12 undemocratic
13 authoritarian

## totality
03 all, sum
05 total, whole
06 cosmos
08 entirety, fullness, universe
09 aggregate, wholeness
12 completeness

## totally
05 fully, quite
06 wholly
07 utterly
08 entirely
10 absolutely, completely
12 consummately
14 wholeheartedly
15 unconditionally

## totter
04 reel, rock, roll, sway
05 lurch, shake, waver
06 falter, teeter, wobble
07 be shaky, stagger, stumble
10 be unstable, be unsteady

## touch
03 bit, eat, hit, jot, pat, pet, tap
04 abut, dash, feel, hint, hold, meet, move, skim, stir
05 brush, cover, drink, equal, flair, knack, match, pinch, reach, rival, skill, speck, style, taste, tinge, trace, upset, weave, whiff
06 adjoin, affect, aspect, attain, better, border, broach, caress, come to, detail, devour, finger, finish, fondle, handle, haptic, manner, method, nicety, sadden, strike, stroke, tickle
07 concern, contact, disturb, impinge, impress, inspire, involve, mention, refer to, soupçon, speak of, surface, tactile, texture
08 addition, allude to, approach, come near
09 dexterity, direction, tactility, technique
10 connection, suggestion
12 request money
13 hold a candle to
14 be contiguous to, have an effect on, have an impact on
15 come into contact

## ❑touch off
04 fire
05 begin, cause, light
06 foment, ignite, set off
07 actuate, provoke, trigger
08 initiate, spark off
10 trigger off

## ❑touch up
06 revamp
07 brush up, enhance, improve, patch up, perfect, retouch
08 polish up, renovate
12 request money

## touch-and-go
04 dire, near
05 close, hairy, risky
06 sticky, tricky
08 critical, delicate, perilous
09 dangerous, uncertain
10 precarious

## touched
03 mad
04 daft
05 batty, crazy, dotty, loopy, moved, nutty, upset
06 insane
07 stirred
08 affected, deranged, inspired
09 disturbed, impressed
10 influenced, unbalanced

## touchiness
09 bad temper, testiness
10 grumpiness, tetchiness
11 crabbedness, grouchiness
12 captiousness, irascibility, irritability

## touching
06 moving, tender
07 piteous, pitiful
08 pathetic, pitiable, poignant
09 affecting, emotional

## touchstone
04 norm, test
05 gauge, guide, model, proof
07 measure, pattern
08 standard, template
09 benchmark, yardstick

## touchy
04 edgy
05 cross
06 grumpy
07 crabbed, grouchy, prickly
08 captious
09 irascible, irritable
11 bad-tempered, thin-skinned
13 oversensitive

## tough
03 fit
04 firm, grim, hard, lout, thug
05 brute, bully, burly, chewy, hardy, harsh, rigid, rough, rowdy, solid, stern, stiff
06 knotty, robust, severe, strict, strong, sturdy, uphill
07 adamant, arduous, callous, durable, fibrous, gristly, rubbery, unlucky, violent
08 baffling, exacting, hardened, hooligan, leathery, muscular
09 difficult, laborious, obstinate, resilient, resistant, strenuous, well-built
10 determined, perplexing
11 distressing, unfortunate
14 tough as leather, uncompromising

## toughen
05 brace
06 harden
07 fortify, stiffen
09 reinforce
10 strengthen

## toughness
04 grit
08 firmness, obduracy, strength, tenacity
09 hardiness
10 resilience, resistance
13 determination, inflexibility

## tour
04 ride, trip
05 drive, jaunt, round, visit
06 course, outing
07 circuit
08 go around, sightsee
09 excursion
10 expedition, inspection
13 peregrination

## tourist
07 visitor, voyager
08 traveler
09 sightseer, sojourner
10 rubberneck, vacationer

## tournament
04 meet
05 event, joust, match
06 series
07 contest, meeting, tourney
11 competition
12 championship

## tousled
07 ruffled, rumpled, tangled
10 disheveled
11 disarranged

## tout
03 ask
04 hawk, plug, push, sell
05 trade
06 appeal, market, peddle
07 promote, solicit
09 advertise

## tow
03 lug, tug
04 drag, draw, haul, pull
05 trail

## ❑ in tow
10 being towed
11 under escort
12 accompanying
15 being controlled

## toward
02 to
03 for
06 almost, nearly
07 close to, nearing
10 concerning, on the way to

## tower
03 cap, top
04 loom, rear, rise, soar
05 excel, mount
06 ascend, exceed
08 dominate, overlook
10 overshadow
13 high structure

➤ *Types of tower. We have omitted the word* **tower** *from names given in the following list but you may need to include this word as part of the solution to some crossword clues.*
04 bell, fort, keep, silo
05 minah, spire, water
06 belfry, castle, church, column, donjon, Eiffel, pagoda, turret
07 bastion, citadel, lookout, minaret, mirador, steeple
08 barbican, bastille, fortress, hill fort, Martello
09 belvedere, campanile, gate tower
10 lighthouse, skyscraper, stronghold, watchtower
13 fortification, Tower of London

## towering
04 high, tall
05 great, lofty
07 extreme, soaring
08 gigantic, imposing
10 impressive, monumental
11 magnificent, outstanding
12 overpowering

## town
04 burg, city
05 exurb, urban
06 podunk, pueblo, suburb
07 borough, village
08 township
10 metropolis, settlement
11 conurbation
12 municipality, one-horse town
13 jerkwater town
➤ See also CITY

## town resident
06 towner, townie
07 burgher, citizen, oppidan
08 townsman, urbanite
10 townswoman

## toxic
06 deadly, lethal
07 baneful, harmful, noxious
09 dangerous, poisonous

## toy
04 play
05 dally, flirt, sport
06 bauble, fiddle, tinker, trifle
07 trinket
09 mess about, plaything
10 mess around

## trace
03 bit, dog, jot, map
04 copy, dash, draw, find, hint, hunt, mark, seek, sign, spot

05 chart, draft, pinch, scent, smack, spoor, stalk, tinge, touch, track, trail
06 depict, detect, follow, pursue, shadow, sketch
07 mark out, outline, remains, remnant, soupçon, uncover, unearth, vestige
08 discover, evidence
09 suspicion, track down
10 indication, suggestion

## track
03 dog, way
04 hunt, path, rail, tail, wake
05 chase, orbit, route, scent, spoor, stalk, trace, trail
06 course, groove, pursue
08 footmark, footstep
09 footprint
10 trajectory

## ❑ keep track of
05 check, watch
06 follow, record
07 monitor, observe
11 keep an eye on

## ❑ make tracks
02 go
04 dash
05 leave, scram
06 beat it, depart
10 hit the road

## ❑ track down
04 find
05 catch, dig up, trace
06 expose, turn up
07 capture, nose out, run down, uncover, unearth
08 hunt down, sniff out
09 ferret out
10 run to earth

## track and field
➤ *Names of track-and-field athletes:*
03 **Coe** (Sebastian)
04 **Budd** (Zola), **Cram** (Steve), **Koch** (Marita)
05 **Bubka** (Sergei), **Hayes** (Bob), **Jones** (Marion), **Lewis** (Carl), **Marsh** (Mike), **Moses** (Edwin), **Nurmi** (Paavo), **Ovett** (Steve), **Owens** (Jesse), **Watts** (Quincy), **Young** (Kevin)
06 **Adkins** (Derrick), **Aouita** (Said), **Austin** (Charles), **Barnes** (Randy), **Batten** (Kim), **Beamon** (Bob), **Conley** (Mike), **Devers** (Gail), **Greene** (Maurice), **Hysong** (Nick), **Jenner**

(Bruce), **Joyner** (Florence Griffith), **O'Brien** (Dan), **Oerter** (Al), **Powell** (Mike), **Ritter** (Louise), **Stulce** (Michael), **Thorpe** (Jim)
07 **DeLoach** (Joe), **Dragila** Stacy), **Edwards** (Jonathan), **Fosbury** (Dick), **Gunnell** (Sally), **Johnson** (Allen), **Johnson** (Ben), **Johnson** (Cornelius), **Johnson** (Michael), **Kingdom** (Roger), **Mathias** (Bob), **Rudolph** (Wilma), **Wilkins** (Mac)
08 **Christie** (Linford), **Harrison** (Kenny), **Phillips** (Andre), **Thompson** (Daley)
09 **Bannister** (Roger), **Sanderson** (Tessa)
12 **Joyner-Kersee** (Jackie)

──────────

▶ *Track-and-field events include*:
03 run
04 race, walk
05 relay
06 discus, hammer, sprint
07 hurdles, javelin, shot put
08 high jump, long jump, marathon
09 decathlon, pole vault
10 heptathlon, pentathlon, triple jump
11 discus throw, hammer throw
12 javelin throw, steeplechase

**tract**
03 lot
04 area, plot, zone
05 essay
06 homily, region
07 booklet, expanse, leaflet, stretch
08 pamphlet, treatise
09 discourse, monograph
12 disquisition, dissertation

**tractable**
04 tame
06 docile, pliant
07 pliable, willing
08 amenable, biddable, obedient, yielding
09 compliant, malleable
10 governable, manageable
12 controllable

**traction**
04 drag, grip, pull
05 draft
07 haulage, pulling
08 adhesion, friction

**trade**
03 buy, job, run
04 deal, line, sell, swap, work
05 craft, skill
06 barter, buying, custom, market, peddle, switch
07 dealing, selling, traffic
08 business, commerce, exchange, transact
09 marketing
10 do business, line of work, occupation, profession
11 merchandise, trafficking
12 transactions

**trademark**
04 logo, mark, name, sign
05 badge, brand, label, stamp
06 emblem, symbol
08 hallmark, insignia
09 brand name, specialty, trade name
11 peculiarity
12 idiosyncrasy
14 characteristic

**trader**
05 buyer
06 broker, dealer, seller, vendor
07 peddler
08 merchant, retailer, supplier
09 marketeer, tradesman
10 shopkeeper, trafficker
11 storekeeper, tradeswoman
14 retail merchant

**tradesman, tradeswoman**
05 buyer
06 dealer, seller, vendor, worker
08 merchant, retailer
09 craftsman
10 journeyman, shopkeeper
11 craftswoman, storekeeper

**tradition**
03 way
04 rite
05 habit, usage
06 belief, custom, praxis, ritual
08 ceremony, folklore, practice
10 convention, observance
11 institution

**traditional**
03 old, set
04 folk, oral
05 fixed, usual
06 age-old
08 habitual, historic
09 customary, unwritten
11 established, time-honored
12 conventional

**traduce**
04 slag
05 abuse, decry, knock, smear
06 defame, insult, malign, revile, vilify
07 blacken, run down, slander

09 denigrate, deprecate, disparage
10 calumniate, depreciate
12 misrepresent

**traducer**
06 abuser
07 defamer, knocker, smearer
08 asperser, vilifier
09 detractor, slanderer
10 denigrator, deprecator, disparager, mudslinger

**traffic**
03 buy
04 cars, deal, sell
05 trade
06 barter, peddle
07 dealing, freight, trading
08 business, commerce, peddling, shipping, vehicles
09 relations
10 do business, passengers
11 automobiles
12 illegal trade
14 transportation

**trafficker**
06 broker, dealer, trader
07 peddler
08 merchant
10 drug dealer

**tragedy**
04 blow
08 calamity, disaster
10 affliction, misfortune
11 catastrophe, unhappiness

**tragic**
03 sad
04 dire
05 awful, fatal
07 unhappy, unlucky
08 dreadful, ill-fated, pitiable, shocking, terrible, wretched
09 appalling, miserable
10 deplorable, disastrous
11 unfortunate
12 catastrophic

**trail**
03 dog, lag, tow, way
04 drag, draw, hang, haul, hunt, path, pull, road, tail, wake
05 chase, route, scent, spoor, stalk, sweep, trace, track
06 dangle, dawdle, follow, pursue, shadow, stream
08 be behind, footpath, straggle
09 footmarks, lag behind
10 footprints

❑**trail away**
04 fade, sink
06 lessen, shrink, weaken
07 die away, dwindle, tail off

**train**

08 decrease, diminish, fade away, fall away, melt away, peter out, taper off, trail off
09 disappear

**train**

03 aim, set
04 cars, file, line, path
05 coach, drill, focus, groom, learn, point, study, suite, teach, trail, tutor
06 Amtrak, column, convoy, ground, series, stream, string
07 caravan, cortège, educate, prepare, retinue, work out
08 exercise, instruct, practice, rehearse, sequence
09 entourage, followers, household, inculcate
10 attendants, discipline, procession, succession
12 railroad cars
13 concatenation, Orient Express

**trainer**

05 coach, tutor
07 handler, teacher
08 educator
10 instructor
15 flight simulator

**training**

05 drill
07 lessons, tuition, workout
08 coaching, exercise, learning, practice, teaching, tutoring
09 education, grounding, schooling
10 discipline, working out
11 instruction, preparation
14 apprenticeship

**traipse**

03 gad
04 plod, slog, trek, wall
05 trail, tramp
06 slouch, trudge, wander

**trait**

07 feature, quality
09 attribute
11 peculiarity
12 idiosyncrasy
14 characteristic

**traitor**

05 Judas
08 betrayer, deceiver, defector, deserter, informer, quisling, renegade, turncoat
12 collaborator, double-dealer
13 double-crosser
14 Benedict Arnold, fifth columnist

**traitorous**

05 false
06 untrue
08 apostate, disloyal, renegade
09 faithless, seditious
10 perfidious, unfaithful
11 treacherous, treasonable
13 double-dealing
14 double-crossing

**trajectory**

04 line, path
05 orbit, route, track, trail
06 course, flight
10 flight path

**trammel**

03 bar, net, tie
04 bond, clog, curb, rein
05 block, catch, chain, check
06 enmesh, entrap, fetter, hamper, hinder, impede
07 ensnare, inhibit, shackle
08 handicap, restrain, restrict
09 hindrance
10 impediment

**tramp**

03 bum
04 hike, hobo, plod, roam, rove, slut, tart, trek, walk
05 march, stamp, stomp, stump, trail, tread, wench, whore
06 ramble, trudge
07 drifter, traipse, trollop, vagrant
08 vagabond
10 down-and-out, loose woman, prostitute
12 down-and-outer

**trample**

05 crush, stamp, tread
06 squash
07 flatten

**trance**

05 dream, spell
06 stupor
07 ecstasy, rapture, reverie
08 hypnosis
09 catalepsy

**tranquil**

04 calm, cool
05 quiet, still
06 hushed, placid, serene
07 relaxed, restful
08 laid-back, peaceful
12 even-tempered
13 imperturbable

**tranquility**

04 calm, hush, rest
05 peace, quiet
06 repose

08 ataraxia, calmness, coolness, quietude, serenity
09 quietness, stillness
10 equanimity, sedateness
11 restfulness
12 peacefulness

**tranquilize, tranquillize**

04 calm, lull
05 quell, quiet, relax
06 pacify, sedate
09 narcotize

**tranquilizer, tranquillizer**

06 downer, opiate
08 narcotic, sedative
09 calmative
11 barbiturate
12 sleeping pill

**transact**

06 handle, manage, settle
07 conduct, execute, perform
08 carry out, conclude
09 discharge, negotiate
10 accomplish

**transaction**

04 deal, deed
06 action, affair, doings
07 affairs, bargain, minutes
08 business, handling
09 agreement, enactment
10 enterprise, proceeding
11 negotiation, proceedings

**transcend**

04 beat
05 excel, outdo
06 exceed
07 eclipse, surpass
08 go beyond, outshine
09 rise above

**transcendence**

09 sublimity, supremacy
10 ascendancy, excellence
11 preeminence, superiority
12 predominance
13 transcendency
15 incomparability

**transcendent**

07 sublime, supreme
08 numinous, peerless
09 excellent, excelling, ineffable, matchless, spiritual
10 superhuman, surpassing
11 magnificent, superlative
12 unparalleled
13 unsurpassable

**transcendental**

08 mystical
09 spiritual
10 mysterious
12 metaphysical, otherworldly, supernatural

13 preternatural

**transcribe**
04 copy, note
06 copy up, record, render
07 copy out, rewrite, write up
08 take down, write out
09 reproduce, translate
13 transliterate

**transcript**
04 copy, note
06 record
10 manuscript
11 translation
13 student record, transcription
15 transliteration

**transfer**
04 move, take
05 carry, grant, shift
06 change, convey, remove, ticket
07 consign, removal
08 document, relocate, transmit
09 transport, transpose
10 assignment, conveyance, relocation, transplant
12 displacement, transference, transmission
13 transposition

**transfigure**
05 alter, exalt
06 change
07 convert, glorify
09 transform, transmute
11 apotheosize
12 metamorphose

**transfix**
04 hold, stun
05 rivet, spear, spike, stick
06 impale, pierce, skewer
07 engross, petrify
08 paralyze
09 mesmerize, spellbind

**transform**
05 adapt, alter, renew
06 change
07 convert, rebuilt, remodel
11 reconstruct, transfigure
12 metamorphose, transmogrify

**transformation**
06 change
08 mutation
09 sea change
10 alteration, metastasis
13 metamorphosis
15 transfiguration

**transfuse**
06 instil
07 instill, pervade, suffuse
08 permeate, transfer

**transgress**
03 err, sin
05 break, lapse
06 breach, exceed, offend
07 disobey, violate
08 infringe, overstep, trespass
09 misbehave

**transgression**
03 sin
04 debt
05 crime, fault, lapse, wrong
06 breach
07 misdeed, offense
08 iniquity, trespass
09 violation
10 infraction, peccadillo
11 misbehavior, misdemeanor
12 infringement

**transgressor**
05 felon
06 debtor, sinner
07 culprit, villain
08 criminal, evildoer, offender
09 miscreant, wrongdoer
10 lawbreaker, trespasser

**transience**
07 brevity
08 caducity, fugacity
09 briefness, shortness
11 evanescence
12 ephemerality, fleetingness
14 transitoriness

**transient**
05 brief, short
06 flying
07 passing
08 fleeting
09 ephemeral, fugacious, momentary, temporary
10 short-lived, transitory

**transit**
06 travel
07 haulage, journey, passage
08 carriage, crossing, shipment, transfer
10 conveyance, journeying
14 transportation

◻**in transit**
05 by air, by sea
06 by rail, by road
07 en route
08 on the way
09 traveling

**transition**
04 flux, move
06 change, switch
07 passage, passing
08 movement, progress
10 changeover, conversion
11 development, progression

13 metamorphosis, transmutation
14 transformation

**transitional**
07 passing
08 changing
09 temporary, unsettled
11 provisional
12 evolutionary, intermediate
13 developmental

**transitory**
05 brief, short
07 passing
08 fleeting
09 ephemeral, fugacious, temporary, transient

**translate**
04 move
05 alter, shift
06 change, decode, render
08 construe, decipher, transfer
09 interpret, transmute
10 paraphrase, transcribe
12 transmogrify

**translation**
04 crib, move
05 gloss, shift
06 change
09 rendering, rendition
10 alteration, conversion
11 explanation, metaphrasis
13 metamorphosis, transcription, transmutation
14 interpretation, transformation

**translator**
07 exegete, glosser
08 dragoman, linguist, polyglot
09 glossator
10 metaphrast, paraphrast
11 interpreter, paraphraser

**translucent**
05 clear
06 limpid
08 pellucid
10 diaphanous, see-through
11 transparent

**transmigration**
13 reincarnation
14 metempsychosis, Pythagoreanism, transformation

**transmission**
04 show
06 signal, spread
07 episode, gearbox, program, sending
08 relaying, shipment, transfer
09 broadcast, diffusion
10 conveyance, production

**transmit**
12 broadcasting, transference, transporting
13 communication, dissemination

**transmit**
04 bear, send
05 carry, radio, relay, remit
06 convey, pass on, spread
07 diffuse, forward, network
08 dispatch, transfer
09 broadcast, transport
11 communicate, disseminate

**transmute**
05 alter
06 change, remake
07 convert
09 transform, translate
11 transfigure
12 metamorphose, transmogrify

**transparency**
05 photo, slide
07 clarity, picture
09 filminess, frankness, gauziness, limpidity
10 candidness, directness, limpidness, photograph
12 apparentness, explicitness, pellucidness, translucence
13 translucidity

**transparent**
04 open
05 clear, filmy, gauzy, sheer
06 candid, direct, patent
07 evident, obvious, visible
08 distinct, explicit, pellucid
10 diaphanous, see-through
11 discernible, perceptible, translucent, undisguised
12 unmistakable

**transpire**
05 arise, ensue, occur, prove
06 appear, befall, happen
07 come out, turn out
09 come about, take place
10 come to pass
11 be disclosed, become known, come to light

**transplant**
04 move
05 graft, repot, shift
06 remove, uproot
07 replant
08 displace, relocate, resettle

**transport**
04 bear, haul, move, ship, take
05 bliss, bring, carry, exile, plane
06 banish, convey, deport, remove

07 delight, ecstasy, elation, rapture, removal
08 airplane, euphoria, transfer
09 captivate, carry away, electrify, spellbind
13 seventh heaven

**transportation**
07 freight, haulage, transit, vehicle
08 carriage, shipment, shipping, transfer
10 conveyance

**transpose**
04 move, swap
05 alter, shift
06 change, invert, switch
07 convert, reorder
08 exchange, transfer
10 substitute

**transverse**
05 cross
07 oblique
08 diagonal
09 crossways, crosswise

**trap**
03 gin, net
04 dupe, lure, mesh, wile
05 catch, mouth, noose, snare, trick
06 ambush, corner, device, enmesh, entrap
07 beguile, confine, deceive, ensnare, pitfall, springe
08 artifice, inveigle, trickery
09 booby trap, stratagem
10 subterfuge

**trapped**
05 duped, stuck
06 caught, netted, snared
08 ambushed, cornered, deceived, ensnared
09 inveigled
10 surrounded

**trapper**
06 hunter
08 huntsman, voyageur
09 fur trader
12 backwoodsman, frontiersman

**trappings**
04 gear
05 dress
06 finery, livery, things
07 clothes, panoply, raiment
08 fittings, fixtures, housings
09 equipment, trimmings
10 adornments, fripperies
11 decorations, furnishings

13 accouterments, accoutrements, paraphernalia

**trash**
03 rot
04 bull, bunk, junk, scum
05 dregs, tripe, waste
06 drivel, litter, rabble, refuse
07 garbage, rubbish
10 balderdash
12 gobbledegook, gobbledygook

**trash can**
06 ashcan
08 dumpster
10 garbage can
11 wastebasket
16 wastepaper basket

**trashy**
05 cheap
06 flimsy, shabby, shoddy, tawdry, tinsel
08 inferior, rubbishy
09 third-rate, worthless

**trauma**
04 hurt, jolt, pain
05 agony, shock, upset, wound
06 damage, injury, lesion
07 anguish, torture
09 suffering

**traumatic**
07 harmful, hurtful, painful
08 shocking, wounding
09 stressful, upsetting
11 distressing, frightening

**travail**
04 slog, toil
05 grind, labor, sweat, tears
06 effort, strain, stress
08 distress, exertion, hardship
09 suffering
10 birth pangs, childbirth, labor pains
11 tribulation

**travel**
04 move, roam, rove, tour
05 cover, cross
06 ramble, voyage, wander
07 explore, journey, passage, proceed, touring, tourism
08 progress, traverse
09 excursion, make a trip
10 expedition, go overseas, journeying, wanderings
11 see the world, sightseeing
13 globe-trotting

**traveler**
03 rep
04 hobo
05 Gypsy, hiker, nomad, tramp

**traveling**
06 driver, tinker, tourer
07 drifter, migrant, pilgrim, tourist, vagrant, voyager
08 commuter, explorer, salesman, vagabond, wanderer, wayfarer
09 itinerant, passenger
12 globe-trotter
14 representative

**traveling**
06 mobile, moving, roving
07 migrant, nomadic, vagrant
09 itinerant, migrating, migratory, wayfaring
11 peripatetic

**traverse**
03 ply
04 ford, roam, span
05 cross, range
06 bridge, wander
08 go across, pass over
09 go through, negotiate
12 travel across

**travesty**
04 sham
05 farce, spoof
06 parody
07 mockery, takeoff
09 burlesque, tall story
10 caricature, perversion

**treacherous**
03 icy
05 false, risky
06 unsafe, untrue
08 disloyal, perilous, slippery
09 dangerous, deceitful, hazardous, two-timing
10 perfidious, traitorous, unfaithful, unreliable
11 duplicitous
12 backstabbing
14 double-crossing

**treacherously**
07 falsely
10 disloyally
11 deceitfully, faithlessly
12 perfidiously

**treachery**
07 treason
08 betrayal, sabotage
09 duplicity, falseness, perfidy
10 disloyalty, infidelity
13 deceitfulness, double-dealing, faithlessness
14 double-crossing

**tread**
04 gait, pace, plod, step, trek
05 crush, march, press, stamp
06 squash, stride, trudge
07 flatten, trample

08 footfall, footmark, footstep
09 footprint, press down, tire layer
12 stairway step

▫ **tread on someone's toes**
03 irk, vex
05 annoy, upset
06 bruise, injure, offend
07 affront
08 infringe

**treason**
06 mutiny
07 perfidy
08 sedition
09 duplicity, rebellion, treachery
10 disloyalty, subversion
11 lese majesty

**treasonable**
08 disloyal, mutinous
09 faithless, seditious
10 perfidious, rebellious, subversive, traitorous

**treasure**
04 cash, gems, gold, love
05 adore, cache, guard, hoard, money, prize, value
06 jewels, riches, wealth
07 cherish, fortune, worship

**treasurer**
06 bursar, purser
07 cashier

**treasury**
04 bank
05 cache, hoard, store, vault
06 assets, corpus
07 capital, coffers
09 exchequer, thesaurus
10 repository, storehouse

**treat**
03 buy, fun, rub, use
04 cure, give, heal, tend, view
05 amuse, apply, goody, lay on, nurse, put on, smear, stand
06 handle, manage, pay for, regale, regard, review, thrill
07 discuss, present, take out
08 attend to, consider, deal with, medicate, surprise
09 excursion, look after
10 indulgence, minister to
12 behave toward

**treatise**
05 essay, paper, study, tract
06 thesis
08 pamphlet
09 discourse, monograph
10 exposition
12 disquisition, dissertation

**treatment**
04 care, cure
05 usage
06 action, remedy
07 conduct, dealing, healing, nursing, surgery, therapy
08 behavior, coverage, dealings, handling
10 medicament, medication
12 manipulation, therapeutics

**treaty**
04 bond, deal, pact
07 bargain, compact
08 alliance, contract, covenant
09 agreement, concordat

► *Names of treaties and agreements*:
04 Rome (Treaty of)
05 Dover (Treaty of), Ghent (Treaty of), Paris (Treaties of)
06 Amiens (Treaty of), Poland (Partitions of), Tilsit (Treaties of)
07 Utrecht (Peace of)
09 Bucharest (Treaties of), Pressburg (Treaty of)
10 Magna Carta, Paris Pacts, Versailles (Treaty of), Warsaw Pact, Westphalia (Peace of)
11 Locarno Pact, Westminster (Treaty of)
12 Brest-Litovsk (Treaty of)
13 Social Chapter, Triple Entente
14 Hague Agreement, Hoare-Laval Pact
15 Entente Cordiale, Munich Agreement

**treble**
04 high
06 piping, shrill, triple
09 threefold
11 high-pitched

**tree**
04 bush
05 shrub
08 arboreal

► *Types of tree*:
03 ash, bay, box, elm, fig, fir, gum, oak, yew
04 lime, palm, pear, pine, plum, teak
05 alder, apple, aspen, balsa, beech, birch, cedar, elder, fruit, hazel, larch, lemon, maple, pecan, plane, rowan
06 acacia, almond, bonsai, cashew, cherry, citrus, laurel, linden, mimosa, orange, poplar, spruce, tupelo, walnut, willow

## trek

07 buckeye, conifer, cypress, dogwood, hickory, palmeto, redwood, sequoia
08 basswood, chestnut, date palm, Dutch elm, hardwood, hawthorn, hornbeam, magnolia, mahogany, softwood, sycamore, tamarisk
09 deciduous, evergreen, jacaranda, whitebeam
10 cottonwood, eucalyptus, paper birch, rubber tree, witch hazel
11 coconut palm, mountain ash, pussy willow, silver birch
12 monkey puzzle, rhododendron
13 horse chestnut, weeping willow
➤ See also PLANT

## trek
04 hike, plod, slog, trip, walk
05 march, tramp
06 ramble, safari, trudge
07 journey, odyssey, traipse
10 expedition

## trellis
03 net
04 grid, mesh
05 grate
06 grille
07 grating, lattice, network
09 framework
12 reticulation

## tremble
04 rock
05 quake, shake
06 quiver, shiver, tremor
07 shudder, vibrate

## trembling
06 shakes
07 quaking, rocking, shaking
09 quavering, quivering, shivering, vibration
11 oscillation

## tremendous
04 huge, vast
05 great
06 wicked
07 amazing, immense, massive
08 colossal, enormous, gigantic, smashing, terrific
09 marvelous, wonderful
10 impressive, incredible, remarkable
11 exceptional, sensational
13 extraordinary

## tremor
05 quake, shake, shock
06 quaver, quiver, wobble

07 tremble
09 trembling, vibration
10 earthquake

## tremulous
05 jumpy, timid
06 afraid, scared
07 anxious, excited, fearful, jittery, nervous, shaking
08 agitated, unsteady, wavering
09 shivering, trembling
10 frightened

## trench
03 cut, pit, sap
04 foss, rill
05 ditch, drain, fosse
06 furrow, gutter, trough
07 channel
08 waterway
09 earthwork
10 excavation
12 entrenchment

## trenchant
05 acute, blunt, sharp, terse
06 astute, biting
07 acerbic, caustic, mordant
08 clear-cut, emphatic, forceful, incisive, scathing
09 effective
10 forthright, perceptive
11 penetrating, unequivocal
13 perspicacious

## trend
03 fad
05 craze, drift, style, vogue
06 course, latest
07 current, fashion, leaning
08 tendency
09 direction

## trendy
02 in
03 hip
04 cool, tony
05 funky, natty
06 groovy, modish, with it
07 faddish, stylish, voguish
10 all the rage
11 fashionable
13 up to the minute

## trepidation
04 fear
05 alarm, dread, worry
06 dismay, fright, nerves, qualms, tremor, unease
07 anxiety, emotion, jitters
09 cold sweat, trembling
10 misgivings, uneasiness
11 butterflies, nervousness
12 apprehension, perturbation

## trespass
03 sin

06 invade, offend
07 impinge, intrude, violate
08 encroach, infringe, invasion
09 intrusion, violation
10 transgress, wrongdoing
12 encroachment, infringement
13 contravention, transgression

## trespasser
06 sinner
07 poacher
08 criminal, intruder, offender
11 gatecrasher
12 transgressor

## tress
04 curl, hair, lock, tail
05 braid, bunch, plait
07 pigtail, ringlet

## trial
04 bane, case, pest, test
05 assay, dummy, grief, pilot
06 burden, dry run, hassle, misery, ordeal, tryout
07 hearing, inquiry, lawsuit, retrial, testing, trouble
08 audition, distress, dummy run, hardship, nuisance, practice, tribunal, vexation
09 adversity, probation, rehearsal, suffering
10 affliction, experiment
11 cross to bear, exploratory, provisional, tribulation
12 experimental, probationary

## triangle
➤ Types of triangle:
05 acute, right
06 obtuse, reflex
07 scalene
08 straight
09 congruent, isosceles
11 acute-angled, equilateral, right-angled
12 obtuse-angled

## triangular
08 trigonal
09 trigonous
10 three-sided, trilateral
13 three-cornered
14 triangle-shaped

## tribal
05 class, group
06 ethnic, family, native
10 indigenous

## tribe
04 clan, race, sept
05 blood, caste, house, stock
06 family, nation, people
07 dynasty
11 ethnic group

**tribulation**
03 woe
04 blow, care, pain
05 curse, grief, trial, worry
06 misery, ordeal, sorrow
07 reverse, travail, trouble
08 distress, hardship, vexation
09 adversity, suffering
10 affliction, misfortune
11 unhappiness

**tribunal**
03 bar
05 bench, court, trial
07 hearing

**tribute**
03 tax
04 duty, gift, levy
05 honor, paean, proof
06 charge, credit, eulogy, homage, praise
07 payment, present, respect
08 accolade, applause, enconium, offering
09 gratitude, panegyric
10 compliment
11 recognition, testimonial
12 commendation

**trice**
03 sec
04 wink
05 flash, jiffy, shake
06 minute, moment, second
07 instant

**trick**
03 art, con, gag, kid
04 dupe, fake, fool, gift, hoax, jape, joke, mock, ploy, ruse, scam, trap
05 antic, bluff, bogus, cheat, dodge, false, flair, fraud, knack, prank, skill, stunt
06 deceit, delude, diddle, ersatz, forged, have on, mirage, outwit, take in
07 ability, beguile, deceive, defraud, fast one, feigned, frame-up, know-how, mislead, swindle
08 artifice, capacity, facility, hoodwink, illusion
09 deception, imitation
10 apparition, artificial, capability, subterfuge
11 counterfeit, legerdemain
12 take for a ride, trick of light
13 practical joke
14 pull a fast one on

❏**trick out**
04 do up
05 adorn, array
06 attire, bedeck
07 dress up
08 decorate, ornament

**trickery**
05 fraud, guile
06 deceit
07 cunning
08 artifice, cheating, illusion, pretense, wiliness
09 chicanery, deception, duplicity, swindling
10 dishonesty, hanky-panky, subterfuge
11 shenanigans, skulduggery
12 monkeyshines, skullduggery
13 double-dealing, funny business, sleight of hand
14 monkey business

**trickle**
04 drip, drop, leak, ooze, seep
06 filter
07 dribble, seepage
09 percolate

**trickster**
05 cheat, fraud, joker
06 con man, hoaxer
07 cozener, diddler, tricker
08 deceiver, impostor, swindler
09 con artist, pretender

**tricky**
03 sly
04 foxy, wily
06 artful, crafty, subtle, thorny
07 awkward, cunning, devious
08 delicate, scheming, slippery
09 deceitful, difficult, sensitive

**tried**
06 proved, tested
08 reliable
10 dependable
11 established, trustworthy

**trifle**
03 bit, toy
04 dash, drop, fool, play, spot
05 dally, flirt, sport, touch, trace
06 bauble, dabble, trivia
07 nothing, trinket
09 mess about, plaything
10 knickknack, mess around, triviality

**trifling**
05 minor, petty, silly, small
06 paltry, slight
07 foolish, shallow, trivial
09 frivolous, worthless
10 negligible
11 superficial, unimportant
13 insignificant
15 inconsequential

**trigger**
04 spur

05 catch, cause, lever, start
06 elicit, prompt, set off, switch
07 produce, provoke
08 activate, generate, initiate, spark off, stimulus
11 set in motion

**trim**
03 cut, fit
04 chop, clip, crop, dock, edge, neat, pare, slim, snip, tidy
05 adorn, array, braid, dress, frill, natty, order, prune, shape, shave, shear, smart, state
06 adjust, border, dapper, edging, fettle, fringe, health, neaten, reduce, snazzy, spruce, svelte, tidy up
07 arrange, compact, curtail, cut down, festoon, fitness, garnish, orderly, slender
08 contract, decorate, decrease, diminish, ornament, trimming
09 condition, cut back on, embellish, shipshape
11 in good order, presentable
12 spick-and-span
13 well-turned-out

**trimming**
05 braid, extra, frill
06 border, edging, fringe, paring, piping
07 cutting, falbala, garnish
08 clipping, frou-frou, furbelow
09 accessory, adornment
10 decoration
11 fimbriation
13 embellishment, ornamentation

**trinket**
05 jewel
06 bauble, gewgaw, trifle
08 gimcrack, ornament
09 bagatelle
10 knickknack

**trio**
05 triad
06 triune, troika
07 trilogy, trinity, triplet
08 triunity
09 threesome
10 triplicity
11 triumvirate

**trip**
03 hop, run
04 fall, ride, skip, slip, tour
05 caper, dance, dream, drive, error, foray, gaffe, jaunt, slide
06 gambol, outing, spring, tiptoe, tumble, voyage

**tripe**
07 fantasy, faux pas, journey, mistake, stagger, stumble
09 excursion, false step
10 apparition, expedition
13 hallucination
15 lose your footing

□**trip up**
04 trap
05 catch, snare, trick
06 ambush, outwit, waylay
07 ensnare
08 catch out, outsmart, surprise

**tripe**
03 rot
04 blah, bosh, guff
05 trash
06 bunkum, drivel
07 garbage, hogwash, inanity, rubbish, twaddle
08 claptrap, nonsense
09 poppycock
10 balderdash

**triple**
04 trio
05 triad
06 treble, triune, troika
07 trilogy, trinity, triplet
08 three-ply, three-way, triunity
09 threefold, threesome
10 three times, tripartite, triplicate, triplicity
11 three-bagger, triumvirate
12 three-base hit

**trite**
04 dull, worn
05 banal, corny, stale, stock
06 common
07 clichéd, routine, worn-out
08 clichéed, ordinary
09 hackneyed
10 threadbare, unoriginal
11 commonplace, stereotyped
12 run-of-the-mill
13 platitudinous

**triumph**
03 hit, joy, win
04 beat, coup, crow, feat
05 exult, gloat, glory, revel
06 defeat
07 conquer, elation, mastery, prevail, prosper, rejoice, succeed, success, victory
08 conquest, overcome, vanquish, walkover
09 overwhelm, win the day
10 exultation, jubilation
11 achievement, celebration

**triumphant**
05 proud
06 elated, joyful
07 winning

08 exultant, glorious, jubilant
09 cock-a-hoop, rejoicing
10 conquering, successful, swaggering, victorious
12 prizewinning

**trivia**
03 pap
07 details, trifles
08 minutiae
12 trivialities
13 irrelevancies

**trivial**
05 banal, minor, petty, small
06 flimsy, little, measly, paltry
08 everyday, piddling, trifling
09 frivolous, worthless
11 meaningless, unimportant
13 insignificant, no great shakes
15 inconsequential

**triviality**
06 detail, trifle
09 frivolity, pettiness, smallness
11 foolishness
13 worthlessness
14 insignificance

**trivialize**
07 devalue, scoff at
08 belittle, minimize, play down
09 underplay

**troop**
03 mob
04 army, band, body, crew, gang, herd, pack, team, unit
05 crowd, group, horde, march
06 parade, stream, troupe, trudge
07 company, traipse
08 division, military, soldiers
09 Boy Scouts
10 contingent, Girl Scouts, servicemen
11 armed forces
12 servicewomen

**trophy**
03 cup
05 award, plate, prize
06 spoils
07 laurels, memento
08 souvenir

**tropical**
03 hot
05 humid
06 steamy, sultry, torrid
07 boiling
08 stifling
10 sweltering

**trot**
03 jog, run
06 bustle, canter, scurry

□**trot out**
06 adduce, recite, repeat
07 bring up, exhibit
08 bring out, rehearse
09 reiterate

**troubadour**
04 bard, poet
06 singer
08 jongleur, minstrel, trouveur, trouvère
09 balladeer, cantabank
11 minnesinger

**trouble**
03 ado, fix, jam, vex, woe
04 care, fuss, mess, pain
05 annoy, pains, upset, worry
06 bother, burden, effort, harass, hassle, pickle, put out, sadden, scrape, unease, unrest
07 afflict, ailment, concern, disturb, illness, perplex, perturb, problem
08 disorder, disquiet, distress, exertion, fighting, hardship, hot water, irritate, nuisance, problems, struggle, upheaval, vexation
09 adversity, annoyance, breakdown, commotion, complaint, heartache, suffering, tight spot, weigh down
10 affliction, difficulty, disability, disconcert, irritation, misfortune
11 malfunction, tribulation
13 inconvenience, make the effort
14 thoughtfulness

**troublemaker**
07 hellion, inciter, stirrer
08 agitator
10 incendiary, instigator, ringleader
12 rabble-rouser
13 mischief-maker

**troublesome**
05 rowdy
06 taxing, thorny, tricky, trying
07 awkward, irksome
08 annoying, tiresome
09 demanding, difficult, laborious, worrisome
10 bothersome, disturbing, irritating, rebellious

**trough**
04 crib, duct
05 ditch, drain, flame, gully
06 feeder, furrow, gutter, hollow, manger, trench

**trounce**

07 channel, conduit
10 depression

**trounce**

04 beat, best, drub, lick, rout
05 crush, paste
06 defeat, hammer, punish,
   thrash, wallop
07 clobber
09 overwhelm, slaughter

**troupe**

03 set
04 band, cast
05 group, troop
06 actors
07 company

**trouper**

05 actor
06 player
07 artiste, old hand, veteran
08 thespian
09 performer
11 entertainer
13 police officer

**trousers**

05 jeans, pants
06 denims, slacks
08 breeches, britches, flannels,
   Levis
09 dungarees

**truancy**

07 absence
08 shirking
11 absenteeism, French leave,
   malingering
12 playing hooky

**truant**

05 idler, shirk
06 absent, dodger
07 missing, runaway, shirker
08 absentee, deserter, malinger
09 play hooky
10 malingerer, play truant

**truce**

04 lull, rest, stay
05 break, letup, peace
09 armistice, cease-fire,
   cessation
10 moratorium, suspension

**truck**

03 van
05 float, trade, wagon
06 pickup
07 contact, traffic, vehicle
08 business, commerce,
   dealings, exchange
09 dump truck, relations
11 intercourse
13 communication

**truculent**

04 rude
05 cross
06 fierce, savage, sullen
07 defiant, hostile, violent
09 bellicose, combative
10 aggressive, pugnacious
11 bad-tempered, belligerent,
   ill-tempered, quarrelsome
12 antagonistic, discourteous,
   obstreperous
13 argumentative, disrespectful

**trudge**

04 haul, hike, plod, slog, toil,
   trek, walk
05 clump, march, stump, tramp
07 shuffle, traipse

**true**

04 fast, firm, real
05 close, exact, loyal, right
06 actual, honest, proper, trusty
07 correct, devoted, exactly,
   factual, genuine, precise,
   rightly, sincere, staunch
08 accurate, constant, faithful,
   honestly, properly, reliable,
   rightful, truthful, unerring
09 authentic, correctly,
   honorable, precisely,
   steadfast, veracious,
   veritable
10 accurately, dependable,
   faithfully, legitimate,
   truthfully
11 trustworthy, veraciously

**true-blue**

05 loyal
06 trusty
07 devoted, staunch
08 constant, faithful, orthodox
09 committed, dedicated
10 unwavering
12 card-carrying
13 dyed-in-the-wool
14 uncompromising

**truism**

05 axiom, truth
06 cliché

**truly**

04 very
06 in fact, indeed, really, surely
07 exactly, greatly, rightly
08 actually, honestly, properly
09 certainly, correctly,
   extremely, genuinely, in
   reality, precisely, sincerely
10 constantly, definitely,
   truthfully, undeniably
11 indubitably, undoubtedly

**trump**

◻**trump up**
04 fake
06 cook up, create, devise,
   invent, make up
07 concoct
08 contrive
09 fabricate

**trumped-up**

04 fake
05 faked, false, phony
06 made-up, untrue
08 cooked-up, invented,
   spurious
09 concocted, contrived,
   falsified
10 fabricated

**trumpery**

05 cheap, nasty, showy
06 flashy, shabby, shoddy,
   tawdry, trashy
07 useless
08 rubbishy, trifling
09 valueless, worthless
12 meretricious

**trumpet**

03 bay, cry
04 call, horn, roar
05 blare, blast, bugle, shout
06 bellow, herald
07 clarion
08 announce, proclaim

**truncate**

03 cut, lop
04 clip, crop, dock, pare, trim
05 prune
07 curtail, shorten
10 abbreviate

**truncheon**

04 club, cosh
05 baton, billy, staff, stick
06 cudgel
09 billy club, shillalah
10 knobkerrie, shillelagh

**trunk**

04 body, case, nose, stem
05 chest, crate, snout, torso
06 coffer
07 luggage
08 suitcase
09 proboscis
11 portmanteau

**truss**

03 pad, tie
04 bind, pack, prop, stay, wrap
05 brace, joist, strap, strut
06 bundle, fasten, pinion,
   secure, tether
07 bandage, binding, support
08 buttress

**trust**
04 care, duty, give, hope
05 faith
06 bank on, belief, charge, credit, expect, rely on
07 believe, confide, count on, custody, entrust, imagine
08 be sure of, credence, depend on, reliance
09 assurance, certainty
10 confidence, conviction
11 safekeeping, trusteeship
12 guardianship
14 responsibility

**trustee**
05 agent
06 keeper
08 executor, guardian
09 custodian, executrix, fiduciary
13 administrator

**trusting**
05 naïve
06 unwary
08 gullible, innocent, trustful
09 credulous, ingenuous
12 unsuspecting

**trustworthy**
04 true
05 loyal
06 honest, stable
07 devoted, ethical, upright
08 faithful, reliable, sensible
09 committed, honorable, steadfast
10 dependable
11 level headed, responsible

**trusty**
04 firm, true
05 loyal, solid
06 honest, steady, strong
07 convict, staunch, upright
08 faithful, prisoner, reliable
10 dependable, supportive
11 responsible, trustworthy

**truth**
04 fact
05 axiom, facts, honor, maxim
06 candor, truism
07 honesty, loyalty, realism, reality
08 accuracy, fidelity, veracity
09 actuality, exactness, frankness, home truth, integrity, precision
11 correctness, genuineness
12 authenticity, faithfulness, truthfulness
14 the gospel truth

**truthful**
04 open, true

05 exact, frank, right, valid
06 candid, honest
07 correct, factual, sincere
08 accurate, faithful, straight
09 realistic, veracious, veritable
11 trustworthy

**truthfulness**
06 candor
07 honesty
08 openness, veracity
09 frankness, sincerity
12 straightness
13 righteousness

**try**
02 go
03 aim, sap, tax
04 bash, shot, stab, test, tire
05 assay, crack, drain, judge, taste, trial, whirl
06 effort, sample, strain, stress, strive, try out, weaken
07 attempt, examine, exhaust, have a go, stretch, venture
08 appraise, endeavor, evaluate
09 have a bash, have a shot, have a stab
10 experiment, have a crack
11 investigate

❑**try out**
04 test
05 taste, try on
06 sample
07 inspect
08 check out, evaluate

**trying**
04 hard
05 tough
06 taxing
07 arduous, testing
08 annoying, tiresome
09 demanding, difficult, vexatious, wearisome
10 bothersome, irritating
11 aggravating, troublesome
12 exasperating

**tub**
03 keg, tun, vat
04 bath, butt, cask
05 basin
06 barrel
07 bathtub
08 hogshead

**tubby**
03 fat
05 obese, plump, porky, pudgy, stout
06 chubby, padded, portly, rotund
08 roly-poly
09 corpulent
10 overweight

15 well-upholstered

**tube**
02 TV
04 duct, hose, pipe
05 inlet, shaft, spout
06 outlet
07 channel, conduit
08 boob tube, cylinder
10 television

**tubular**
06 tubate
08 pipelike, tubelike, tubiform, tubulate, tubulous

**tuck**
04 cram, ease, fold, push
05 pleat, stuff
06 crease, gather, insert, pucker, ruffle, thrust

❑**tuck away**
04 hide, save
05 hoard, store
06 save up
07 conceal
09 stash away

❑**tuck in, tuck into**
03 eat
05 eat up, feast, gorge
06 devour, gobble
08 wolf down

❑**tuck in, tuck up**
06 fold in, wrap up
07 cover up
08 make snug, put to bed

**tuft**
04 knot, wisp
05 beard, clump, crest, truss
06 tassel
09 flocculus

**tug**
03 lug, tow
04 boat, drag, draw, haul, jerk, pull, yank
05 heave, pluck
06 wrench

**tuition**
07 lessons
08 coaching, guidance, teaching, training
09 education, school fee, schooling
11 instruction

**tumble**
04 dive, drop, fall, flop, roll, trip
05 heave, lurch, pitch, slide
06 plunge, topple, trip up
07 decline, plummet, stumble
08 collapse, decrease
09 knock down, overthrow
12 fall headlong

**❏tumble to**
05 grasp
07 realize
08 perceive
10 cotton on to, understand

**tumbledown**
05 shaky
06 ruined, unsafe
07 crumbly, rickety, ruinous
08 decrepit, unstable, unsteady
09 crumbling, tottering
10 broken-down, ramshackle
11 dilapidated

**tumbler**
03 cup, mug
05 glass
06 beaker, goblet
07 acrobat, gymnast

**tumid**
07 bloated, bulbous, bulging, flowery, fulsome, pompous, stilted, swollen
08 affected, enlarged, inflated, puffed up
09 bombastic, distended, grandiose, high-flown, overblown, tumescent
10 euphuistic
11 pretentious, protuberant

**tumor**
04 lump
06 cancer, growth
07 myeloma, sarcoma
08 lymphoma, melanoma, neoplasm, swelling
09 carcinoma

**tumult**
03 din, row
04 riot, stir
05 babel, brawl, chaos, noise
06 bedlam, clamor, fracas, hubbub, racket, rumpus, uproar
07 turmoil
08 disarray, disorder, shouting
09 agitation, commotion, confusion
10 hullabaloo
11 disturbance, pandemonium

**tumultuous**
04 loud, wild
05 noisy, rowdy
06 fierce, hectic, raging, stormy
07 fervent, riotous, violent
08 frenzied, troubled
09 clamorous, deafening, disturbed, turbulent
12 uncontrolled

**tune**
03 air, set

04 song
05 adapt, motif, pitch, theme
06 adjust, attune, melody, strain, temper
08 regulate
09 harmonize

**❏change your tune**
14 change your mind

**❏in tune with**
12 agreeing with, in accord with
13 in harmony with
14 in sympathy with
15 in agreement with

**tuneful**
06 catchy, mellow
07 melodic, musical
08 pleasant, sonorous
09 agreeable, melodious
10 euphonious, harmonious
11 mellifluous

**tuneless**
05 harsh
06 atonal
08 clashing
09 dissonant, unmelodic, unmusical
10 discordant, unpleasant
11 cacophonous, unmelodious

**tunnel**
03 dig
04 bore, hole, mine
05 shaft
06 burrow, subway
07 chimney, gallery, passage
08 excavate, mole hole
09 undermine, underpass
10 rabbit hole

**turbid**
03 dim
04 foul, hazy
05 dense, foggy, fuzzy, muddy, murky, thick
06 cloudy, impure, opaque
07 clouded, muddled, unclear
08 confused, feculent
09 turbulent, unsettled
10 disordered, incoherent

**turbulence**
05 chaos, storm
06 tumult, unrest
07 boiling, turmoil
09 agitation, commotion, confusion, roughness
11 instability, pandemonium

**turbulent**
04 wild
05 rough, rowdy
06 choppy, raging, stormy
07 furious, riotous, violent
08 agitated, blustery, mutinous

09 in turmoil, unsettled
10 boisterous, disorderly, rebellious, tumultuous
11 tempestuous

**turf**
03 sod
04 lawn
05 grass, sward
09 racetrack, territory

**turgid**
07 bulging, flowery, fulsome, pompous, swollen
08 affected, inflated
09 bombastic, grandiose, high-flown, overblown
11 extravagant, pretentious
12 magniloquent, ostentatious

**turmoil**
03 din, row
05 chaos, noise
06 bedlam, bustle, flurry, hubbub, tumult, uproar
07 ferment, trouble
08 disarray, disquiet, upheaval
09 agitation, commotion
10 turbulence
11 disturbance, pandemonium

**turn**
02 go
03 aim, fit
04 bend, cast, form, grow, make, mold, move, pass, reel, roll, sour, spin, veer, walk, wind
05 adapt, alter, apply, go bad, hinge, pivot, point, shape, shift, spoil, swing, twirl, twist, whirl
06 adjust, appeal, become, change, circle, curdle, direct, divert, gyrate, invert, modify, mutate, resort, rotate, spiral, swerve, swivel
07 convert, fashion, remodel, reverse, revolve
08 go around
09 transform, transmute
12 metamorphose

**❏to a turn**
07 exactly
09 correctly, perfectly, precisely
12 to prefection

**❏turn against**
08 distrust
12 disapprove of

**❏turn aside**
05 avert, parry
06 depart
07 deflect, deviate, diverge

**❏turn away**
05 avert

06 depart, reject
07 deflect, deviate
08 move away
12 cold shoulder

**❏turn down**
04 mute, veto
05 lower, spurn
06 lessen, muffle, rebuff, reduce, refuse, reject, soften
07 decline, quieten
08 decrease

**❏turn in**
06 give in, give up, hand in, retire, return, submit, tender
07 deliver, go to bed
08 give back, hand over
09 hit the hay, surrender
10 hit the sack

**❏turn of events**
06 affair, result
07 outcome
08 incident
09 happening

**❏turn off**
04 bore, quit, stop
06 divert, offend, put off, sicken
07 deviate, disgust, turn out
08 nauseate, shut down
09 branch off, switch off
10 depart from, disconnect, discourage, disenchant

**❏turn of phrase**
05 idiom, style
06 saying
07 diction
08 locution, metaphor
10 expression
11 phraseology

**❏turn on**
05 start
06 arouse, attack, excite, fall on, please, plug in, rest on, thrill
07 attract, connect, hinge on, lay into, round on, set upon
08 activate, switch on
09 stimulate

**❏turn out**
02 go
04 come, fire, make, sack
05 clear, dress, empty, end up, ensue, evict, expel
06 appear, arrive, attend, banish, become, clothe, deport, emerge, happen, pan out, result, show up, turn up, unplug
07 develop, dismiss, drum out, kick out, present, turn off
08 assemble, chuck out, churn out, clean out, clear out

09 be present, come about, discharge, fabricate, switch off, transpire
10 disconnect
11 manufacture

**❏turn over**
04 flip
05 upend, upset
06 assign, invert, ponder
07 capsize, consign, deliver, examine, reverse
08 consider, hand over, keel over, mull over, overturn, ruminate, transfer
09 reflect on, surrender
10 deliberate, turn turtle
11 contemplate

**❏turn over a new leaf**
05 amend, begin
06 change, reform
07 improve, shape up
10 begin again
12 mend your ways
14 change your ways, clean up your act

**❏turn up**
03 hem
04 bend, bias, come, find, loop, show, time
05 alter, crack, curve, dig up, raise, shift, stint
06 appear, arrive, attend, change, expose, reveal
07 amplify, deviate, diverge, drift in, scare up, turn out, uncover
08 disclose, discover, increase, turn into, unearth,
09 be present, intensify
10 make louder
12 bring to light

**turncoat**
03 rat
04 fink, scab
07 seceder, traitor
08 apostate, defector, deserter, renegate
10 backslider
13 tergiversator

**turning**
04 bend, fork, turn
05 curve
07 turnoff
08 junction

**turning point**
04 crux
06 crisis
09 watershed
10 crossroads
13 moment of truth

**turnout**
04 gate, gear, togs
05 array, crowd, dress, getup
06 attire, number, outfit
07 clothes
08 assembly, audience
09 gathering
10 assemblage, attendance
12 congregation

**turnover**
04 flow
05 yield
06 change, income, output
07 outturn, profits
08 business, movement
10 production
12 productivity

**turpitude**
04 evil
07 badness
08 baseness, foulness, iniquity, vileness, villainy
09 depravity
10 corruption, degeneracy, immorality, sinfulness, wickedness
11 corruptness, viciousness
13 nefariousness
14 flagitiousness

**tussle**
03 row, vie
04 bout, fray
05 brawl, fight, melee, scrap, set-to
06 battle, dustup, fracas
07 contest, dispute, grapple, scuffle, wrestle
08 conflict, scramble, struggle
09 scrimmage

**tutelage**
03 eye
04 care
05 aegis
06 charge
07 custody, tuition
08 guidance, teaching
09 education, patronage, schooling, vigilance
11 instruction, preparation
12 guardianship

**tutor**
04 guru
05 coach, drill, teach, train
06 direct, mentor, school
07 educate, lecture, teacher
08 guardian, instruct, lecturer
09 supervise
10 instructor, supervisor

**tutorial**
05 class
06 lesson

**TV**
07 guiding, seminar, teach-in
08 coaching, didactic, teaching
09 educative, educatory
13 instructional

**TV**
03 set
07 the tube
08 boob tube, idiot box, receiver
10 television
11 small screen
13 television set

**twaddle**
03 rot
04 bunk, guff
05 stuff, trash
06 bunkum, drivel, gabble, hot air, piffle
07 blather, blether, garbage, hogwash, inanity, rubbish
08 claptrap, nonsense
09 poppycock
10 balderdash
12 gobbledygook

**tweak**
03 nip, tug
04 jerk, pull
05 pinch, twist
06 twitch

**twiddle**
04 turn
05 twirl, twist
06 adjust, fiddle, finger, swivel

**twig**
05 shoot, sprig, stick, withe, withy
06 branch

**twilight**
03 dim, ebb
04 dusk, last
05 dying, final, gloom
06 ebbing, sunset
07 decline, dimness, evening
08 gloaming
09 crepuscle, darkening, declining, half-light
10 crepuscule
11 crepuscular

**twin**
04 dual, join, mate, pair, yoke
05 clone, match
06 couple, double, ringer
07 matched, twofold
08 likeness, matching, parallel
09 corollary, duplicate, identical, look-alike
10 complement, equivalent
11 counterpart, symmetrical
13 corresponding

**twine**
04 bend, coil, cord, curl, knit, knot, loop, rope, wind, wrap, yarn
05 braid, plait, twist, weave
06 spiral, string, tangle, thread
07 entwine, wreathe

**twinge**
04 ache, pain, pang, stab
05 cramp, pinch, prick, spasm, throb, throe
06 stitch

**twinkle**
04 wink
05 flash, gleam, glint, light, shine
07 flicker, glimmer, glisten, glitter, shining, sparkle
09 coruscate
11 coruscation, scintillate

**twinkling**
02 mo
03 sec
04 jiff, tick
05 flash, jiffy, nitid, shake, trice
06 bright, moment, second
07 instant, shining, winking
08 flashing, gleaming
09 sparkling
10 flickering, glimmering, glistening, glittering
11 coruscating

**twirl**
04 coil, curl, spin, turn, wind
05 pivot, twist, wheel, whirl
06 gyrate, rotate, spiral, swivel
07 revolve
08 gyration, rotation
09 pirouette

**twirling**
05 gyral
07 pivotal
08 gyratory, pivoting, rotating, rotatory, spinning, whirling
09 revolving
11 pirouetting

**twist**
04 bend, coil, curl, flaw, kink, loop, rick, roll, skew, spin, turn, warp, whim, wind
05 alter, braid, break, curve, freak, plait, quirk, screw, twine, twirl, weave, wring
06 change, defect, deform, foible, garble, oddity, rotate, spiral, sprain, squirm, strain, swivel, tangle, wrench, wrench, writhe, zigzag
07 contort, distort, entwine, falsify, pervert, revolve, wreathe, wriggle

08 entangle, misquote, misshape, squiggle, surprise
09 misreport, turnabout
10 aberration, contortion, distortion, intertwine, perversion
11 convolution, peculiarity
12 idiosyncrasy, misrepresent

◻**twist someone's arm**
05 bully, force
06 coerce, lean on
07 dragoon
08 bulldoze, persuade
10 intimidate, pressurize
14 put the screws on

**twisted**
03 odd
06 warped
07 deviant, sinuous, winding
09 perverted, unnatural

**twister**
05 cheat, crook, fraud, phony, rogue
06 con man
07 cyclone, tornado
08 deceiver, swindler
09 con artist, scoundrel, trickster
10 blackguard

**twitch**
03 tic, tug
04 jerk, jump, pull
05 blink, pluck, shake, spasm
06 quiver, shiver, snatch, tremor

**twitter**
03 cry
04 sing, song
05 cheep, chirp, tweet
06 gabble, gossip, warble
07 blather, blether, chatter, chirrup, prattle, whistle
08 chirping, tweeting
10 chirruping

**two-faced**
05 false, lying
07 devious
09 deceitful, insincere
10 Janus-faced, perfidious
11 dissembling, duplicitous, treacherous
12 hypocritical
13 double-dealing, untrustworthy

**tycoon**
05 baron, mogul
06 fat cat
07 big shot, magnate
08 big noise
09 big cheese, financier
10 capitalist

**type**
12 entrepreneur
13 industrialist

**type**
04 face, font, form, kind, make, mark, sort
05 brand, breed, class, fount, genre, genus, group, model, order, print, stamp, style
06 letter, number, strain, symbol
07 letters, numbers, pattern, species, symbols, variety
08 category, exemplar, keyboard, original, printing, specimen, standard
09 archetype, character, lettering, prototype, typewrite
11 description, designation
14 classification

**typhoon**
04 wind
05 storm
06 .squall
07 cyclone, tornado, twister
09 hurricane, whirlwind
13 tropical storm

**typical**
05 model, stock, usual
06 normal
07 average, classic

08 ordinary, standard
10 archetypal, stereotype
12 conventional, illustrative
14 characteristic, quintessential

**typically**
07 as a rule, usually
08 normally
09 routinely
10 habitually, ordinarily

**typify**
06 embody
09 epitomize, exemplify, represent, symbolize
11 encapsulate
12 characterize

**tyrannical**
05 cruel, harsh
06 severe, strict, unjust
08 despotic, ruthless
09 arbitrary, imperious
10 autocratic, highhanded, oppressive, repressive
11 dictatorial, domineering, magisterial, overbearing
12 overpowering, totalitarian
13 authoritarian

**tyrannize**
05 bully, crush
07 enslave, oppress, repress

08 browbeat, domineer, suppress
09 subjugate, terrorize
10 intimidate, lord it over

**tyranny**
07 cruelty
08 severity
09 autocracy, despotism, harshness, injustice
10 absolutism, oppression
12 dictatorship, ruthlessness
13 imperiousness

**tyrant**
05 bully
06 despot
08 autocrat, dictator, martinet
09 oppressor
11 slave driver
13 authoritarian

**tyro, tiro**
05 pupil
06 novice, rookie
07 learner, student, trainee
08 beginner, freshman, initiate, neophyte
09 greenhorn, novitiate
10 apprentice, catechumen, tenderfoot

**ubiquitous**
06 common, global
09 pervasive, universal
10 everywhere
11 ever-present, omnipresent

**ubiquity**
09 frequency
10 popularity, prevalence
12 omnipresence, universality

**ugliness**
04 evil
06 danger, horror, menace
08 enormity, vileness
09 deformity
11 monstrosity

**ugly**
04 evil, foul, vile
05 grave, nasty, plain
06 homely, horrid
07 hideous, hostile
08 deformed, shocking, sinister, terrible, unlovely
09 dangerous, grotesque, loathsome, misshapen, monstrous, obnoxious, offensive, repulsive, revolting, unsightly
10 disgusting, ill-favored, unpleasant
11 threatening
12 disagreeable, unattractive
13 objectionable
15 unprepossessing

**ulcer**
04 boil, noma, sore
06 canker, fester
07 abscess
08 open sore
09 impostume

**ulterior**
06 covert, hidden, secret
07 private, selfish
09 concealed, secondary

**ultimate**
03 end
04 best, last, peak
05 basic, final
06 height, summit, utmost
07 epitome, highest, maximum, primary, supreme, topmost
08 eventual, furthest, greatest, last word, remotest, terminal

09 elemental
10 daddy of all, perfection
11 culmination, fundamental, mother of all, superlative

**ultimately**
06 at last
07 finally
08 after all, in the end
09 basically, primarily
10 eventually
13 fundamentally, sooner or later

**ultra-**
05 extra
09 extremely, unusually
10 especially, remarkably
11 excessively
13 exceptionally
15 extraordinarily

**ululate**
04 howl, keen, wail
05 mourn
06 holler, lament, scream

**umbrage**
□ **take umbrage**
11 take offense
13 take exception
14 take personally

**umbrella**
05 aegis, cover
06 agency
07 overall, parasol
08 sunshade
10 protection
11 bumbershoot
15 protective force

**umpire**
03 ref, ump
05 judge
07 arbiter, mediate, referee
08 mediator, moderate
09 arbitrate, moderator
10 arbitrator

**umpteen**
08 millions, numerous, very many
09 a good many, countless, thousands
11 innumerable

**unabashed**
04 bold

06 brazen
07 blatant
09 unashamed, undaunted

**unable**
05 unfit
08 impotent
09 incapable, powerless
10 unequipped
11 ineffectual, unqualified

**unabridged**
05 uncut, whole
06 entire
08 complete
10 full-length
11 uncondensed, unshortened

**unacceptable**
09 obnoxious, offensive
10 unpleasant, unsuitable
11 intolerable, undesirable
12 inadmissible
14 unsatisfactory

**unaccommodating**
05 rigid
09 unbending
10 inflexible, unyielding
11 disobliging
12 intransigent
13 uncooperative

**unaccompanied**
04 lone, solo
05 alone
06 single
08 solitary
09 on your own
10 by yourself, unattended, unescorted
12 single-handed

**unaccountable**
07 bizarre, curious
08 baffling, peculiar, puzzling
10 mysterious
11 astonishing
12 impenetrable, inexplicable, unfathomable
13 not answerable, unexplainable

**unaccustomed**
06 unused
07 strange, unusual
08 uncommon, unwonted
10 unexpected, unfamiliar
11 unpracticed

**unacquainted**

12 unacquainted
13 unprecedented

**unacquainted**

06 unused
07 strange
08 ignorant
10 unfamiliar
12 unaccustomed
13 inexperienced

**unadorned**

05 plain, stark
06 severe, simple
11 undecorated, unvarnished
12 unornamented
13 unembellished
15 straightforward

**unaffected**

04 pure
05 naïve, plain
06 candid, honest, simple
07 artless, genuine, natural,
   sincere, unmoved
09 guileless, ingenuous,
   unaltered, unchanged,
   unspoiled
10 unassuming
11 indifferent, unconcerned
13 unpretentious
15 straightforward

**unafraid**

04 bold
05 brave
06 daring
08 fearless, intrepid
09 audacious, dauntless
10 courageous
13 imperturbable

**unalterable**

05 final, fixed, rigid
09 immutable, permanent
10 inflexible, invariable,
   unchanging, unyielding
12 unchangeable

**unanimity**

05 unity
06 accord, unison
07 concert, concord, harmony
09 agreement, consensus
10 congruence
11 concurrence, consistency
14 like-mindedness

**unanimous**

05 as one, joint
06 common, united
08 in accord
09 concerted
10 concordant, consistent,
   harmonious, like-minded
11 in agreement

**unanimously**

05 as one
06 nem. Con.
09 in concert, of one mind,
   unopposed
10 conjointly
12 with one voice
15 by common consent, with all
   agreeing

**unanswerable**

10 unarguable, undeniable
11 irrefutable
12 indisputable, irrefragable
13 incontestable

**unappetizing**

08 unsavory
09 tasteless
10 uninviting, unpleasant
11 unappealing, unpalatable
12 disagreeable, unattractive

**unapproachable**

04 cold, cool
05 aloof
06 remote
07 distant
08 reserved
09 withdrawn
10 forbidding, unfriendly
11 standoffish
12 inaccessible, unresponsive

**unapt**

05 inapt, inept, unfit
08 unfitted, unsuited
10 inapposite, malapropos,
   unsuitable
13 inappropriate

**unarmed**

07 exposed
08 helpless
10 vulnerable
11 defenseless, unprotected

**unashamed**

04 open
07 blatant
09 shameless, unabashed
10 impenitent
11 undisguised, unrepentant

**unasked**

08 unbidden, unsought
09 uninvited, voluntary
11 spontaneous, unannounced,
   unsolicited

**unassailable**

06 proven, secure
08 absolute, positive
10 conclusive, invincible,
   inviolable, undeniable
11 impregnable, irrefutable
12 indisputable, invulnerable
13 incontestable

**unassertive**

03 shy
04 meek
05 mousy, quiet, timid
08 backward, retiring, timorous
09 diffident
10 unassuming

**unassuming**

04 meek
05 quiet
06 demure, humble, modest,
   simple
07 natural
08 reticent, retiring
10 restrained
13 unpretentious

**unattached**

04 free
05 loose
06 single
09 available, fancy-free,
   footloose, unmarried
10 by yourself
11 independent, uncommitted
12 unaffiliated

**unattended**

05 alone
08 forsaken
09 neglected, unguarded
12 unsupervised
13 unaccompanied

**unattractive**

04 ugly
05 plain
06 homely
08 unsavory
09 offensive, repellent, unsightly
10 ill-favored, uninviting,
   unpleasant
11 distasteful, unappealing,
   undesirable, unpalatable
12 disagreeable, unappetizing
15 unprepossessing

**unauthorized**

07 illegal, illicit
09 forbidden, irregular
10 prohibited, unofficial
12 illegitimate, unsanctioned

**unavailing**

04 vain
06 beaten, failed, futile, losing
07 unlucky, useless
08 abortive, defeated, luckless
09 fruitless
10 frustrated
11 ineffective, unfortunate
12 unprofitable, unsuccessful

**unavoidable**

05 fated
08 destined, required

**09** mandatory, necessary
**10** compulsory, inevitable, inexorable, obligatory
**11** ineluctable, inescapable, predestined
**13** predetermined

**unaware**
**08** heedless, ignorant
**09** in the dark, oblivious, unknowing, unmindful
**10** insentient
**11** unconscious
**12** unsuspecting

**unawares**
**08** off guard
**10** by surprise, mistakenly, unprepared
**12** accidentally, unthinkingly
**13** inadvertently
**15** unintentionally

**unbalanced**
**03** mad
**05** crazy, loopy
**06** biased, insane, uneven, unfair, unjust
**07** lunatic, unequal, unsound
**08** demented, deranged, lopsided, one-sided, partisan, unstable, unsteady
**09** disturbed
**10** irrational, prejudiced
**11** inequitable, mentally ill
**12** asymmetrical, crackbrained

**unbearable**
**08** the limit
**11** intolerable, unendurable
**12** excruciating, insufferable, the last straw, unacceptable
**13** insupportable

**unbeatable**
**04** best
**07** supreme
**09** excellent, matchless
**10** invincible
**11** indomitable, unstoppable
**13** unconquerable

**unbeaten**
**07** supreme, unbowed
**10** triumphant, undefeated, victorious
**11** unconquered, unsurpassed

**unbecoming**
**08** unseemly
**09** unsightly
**10** indecorous, indelicate, unladylike, unsuitable
**11** unbefitting
**12** unattractive
**13** ungentlemanly

**unbelief**
**05** doubt
**07** atheism
**10** skepticism
**11** agnosticism, incredulity

**unbelievable**
**07** amazing
**10** far-fetched, impossible, improbable, incredible, outlandish, staggering
**11** implausible, unthinkable
**12** unconvincing, unimaginable
**13** extraordinary, inconceivable

**unbeliever**
**07** atheist, infidel, skeptic
**08** agnostic
**11** nullifidian

**unbelieving**
**07** dubious
**08** doubtful, doubting
**09** skeptical
**11** incredulous, nullifidian, unconvinced, unpersuaded

**unbend**
**04** thaw
**05** relax, untie
**06** uncoil, uncurl
**08** loosen up, unbutton
**10** straighten

**unbending**
**04** firm
**05** aloof, rigid, stern, stiff, tough
**06** formal, severe, strict
**08** hard-line, resolute, stubborn
**10** inflexible, unyielding
**12** intransigent

**unbiased**
**04** fair, just
**07** neutral
**08** tolerant
**09** impartial, objective, uncolored
**10** evenhanded, fair-minded, open-minded
**12** unprejudiced
**13** disinterested, dispassionate

**unbidden**
**07** unasked
**08** unforced, unwanted
**09** uninvited, unwelcome, voluntary
**10** unprompted
**11** spontaneous, unsolicited

**unbind**
**04** free, undo
**05** loose, untie
**06** loosen
**07** release, unchain, unloose
**08** unfasten, unfetter

**unblemished**
**04** pure
**05** clear
**07** perfect
**08** flawless, spotless, unflawed
**09** unspotted, unstained
**11** untarnished

**unblinking**
**04** calm, cool
**06** steady
**07** assured
**08** composed, fearless, unafraid
**09** impassive
**11** emotionless, unemotional, unflinching
**13** imperturbable

**unblushing**
**06** brazen
**07** blatant
**08** immodest
**09** shameless

**unborn**
**06** coming, future, to come
**07** awaited, in utero
**08** expected
**09** embryonic
**10** subsequent, succeeding

**unbosom**
**04** bare, tell
**05** admit
**06** let out, reveal
**07** confess, confide, divulge, lay bare, pour out, tell all
**08** disclose, unburden

**unbounded**
**04** vast
**07** endless
**08** infinite
**09** boundless, limitless, unchecked, unlimited
**12** unrestrained, unrestricted

**unbreakable**
**09** resistant, toughened
**11** infrangible
**12** shatterproof
**14** indestructible

**unbridled**
**07** rampant, riotous
**08** uncurbed
**09** excessive, unchecked
**10** licentious, profligate
**11** intemperate
**12** uncontrolled, unrestrained
**13** unconstrained

**unbroken**
**05** solid, whole
**06** entire, intact
**07** endless, nonstop
**08** complete, constant
**09** perpetual, unceasing

**unburden**
10 continuous, successive
13 uninterrupted

**unburden**
04 bare, tell
05 empty
06 let out, reveal, unload
07 confess, confide, divulge, lay bare, offload, pour out, tell all, uncover
08 disclose

**uncalled-for**
07 unasked
08 needless, unsought
09 unwelcome
10 gratuitous, undeserved
11 unjustified, unwarranted

**uncanny**
03 odd
05 eerie, queer, weird
06 creepy, spooky
07 bizarre, strange
08 eldritch
09 unearthly
10 incredible, mysterious
12 supernatural
13 preternatural, unaccountable

**uncaring**
04 cold
07 callous, unmoved
09 unfeeling
11 indifferent, unconcerned
13 unsympathetic

**unceasing**
07 endless, eternal, nonstop, undying
08 constant, unending
09 ceaseless, continual, incessant, perpetual
10 continuous, relentless
11 everlasting, never-ending, never-ending, unrelenting, unremitting
12 interminable

**unceremonious**
04 rude
06 abrupt, casual, sudden
08 impolite, informal, laid-back
09 easygoing
11 undignified
12 discourteous
13 disrespectful

**uncertain**
04 iffy, open
05 risky, shaky, vague
06 unsure
07 dubious, erratic
08 doubtful, hesitant, insecure, wavering
09 undecided, unsettled

10 ambivalent, changeable, inconstant, indefinite, of two minds, touch and go, unresolved, up in the air
11 speculative, unconfirmed, unconvinced, vacillating
12 equivocating, in the balance, undetermined
13 unforeseeable, unpredictable

**uncertainty**
05 doubt, qualm
06 qualms
07 dilemma
09 ambiguity, confusion
10 hesitation, insecurity, perplexity, puzzlement, skepticism, uneasiness
11 ambivalence
12 bewilderment, irresolution

**unchallengeable**
10 conclusive
11 irrefutable
12 indisputable
13 incontestable

**unchangeable**
09 immutable, permanent
10 changeless, invariable
12 irreversible

**unchanging**
07 abiding, eternal, lasting
08 constant, enduring
09 permanent, perpetual, steadfast, unvarying
10 changeless, invariable

**uncharitable**
04 hard, mean
05 cruel, harsh, stern
06 severe, unkind
07 callous
09 unfeeling
10 ungenerous
11 hardhearted, insensitive, unforgiving

**uncharted**
06 virgin
07 foreign, strange, unknown
10 unexplored, unfamiliar

**unchaste**
04 lewd
05 loose
06 fallen, impure, wanton
08 depraved, immodest
10 licentious
11 promiscuous

**uncivil**
04 curt, rude
05 gruff, surly
06 abrupt

07 bearish, boorish, brusque, ill-bred, uncouth
08 churlish, impolite
10 ungracious, unmannerly
11 bad-mannered, ill-mannered
12 discourteous

**uncivilized**
04 wild
05 rough
06 savage
07 boorish, brutish, untamed
08 barbaric
09 barbarian, primitive
10 antisocial, uncultured

**unclassifiable**
07 elusive
10 ill-defined, indefinite, indistinct
11 indefinable, undefinable
13 indescribable, indeterminate
14 unidentifiable

**unclean**
03 bad ·
04 evil, foul
05 dirty, grimy
06 filthy, grubby, impure, soiled
07 defiled, sullied, tainted
08 polluted
10 unhygienic
11 adulterated, unwholesome
12 contaminated

**unclear**
03 dim
04 hazy, iffy
05 foggy, vague
06 unsure
07 dubious, obscure
08 doubtful
09 uncertain, unsettled
10 indefinite, indistinct

**unclothed**
04 bare, nude
05 naked
06 unclad
08 disrobed, stripped
09 in the buff, undressed
10 stark naked
15 in the altogether

**uncomfortable**
04 cold, hard
05 tense
06 on edge, uneasy
07 anxious, awkward, nervous, painful, worried
08 troubled
09 disturbed
10 ill-fitting, irritating
11 discomfited, embarrassed
13 self-conscious

## uncommitted
07 neutral
08 floating
09 fancy-free, undecided
10 nonaligned, uninvolved
11 independent, nonpartisan

## uncommon
03 odd
04 rare
05 queer
06 scarce
07 strange, unusual
08 abnormal, atypical, peculiar, singular, striking
10 infrequent, unfamiliar
11 distinctive, outstanding
15 rare as hen's teeth

## uncommonly
09 extremely, strangely, unusually
10 abnormally, peculiarly, remarkably, singularly
12 particularly
13 exceptionally, outstandingly

## uncommunicative
08 reserved, reticent, retiring, taciturn
09 diffident, withdrawn
11 tight-lipped
12 unresponsive
13 unforthcoming

## uncomplicated
06 direct, simple
10 uninvolved
11 undemanding
15 straightforward

## uncompromising
05 rigid
07 die-hard
08 obdurate, stubborn
09 immovable, obstinate, unbending
10 inexorable, inflexible, unyielding
12 intransigent

## unconcealable
05 clear, plain
07 obvious
08 manifest
13 irrepressible

## unconcealed
04 open
05 frank, overt
06 patent
07 blatant, evident, obvious, visible
08 apparent, manifest
10 noticeable
11 conspicuous

## unconcern
06 apathy
10 detachment, remoteness
11 callousness, insouciance, nonchalance
12 indifference

## unconcerned
04 cool
05 aloof
06 casual, remote
07 distant, unmoved
08 detached, uncaring
09 apathetic, oblivious
10 complacent, insouciant, nonchalant, uninvolved
11 indifferent, unperturbed
12 uninterested
13 dispassionate

## unconditional
04 full
05 total, utter
08 absolute, complete, outright, positive
09 downright, out-and-out, unlimited
10 conclusive, unreserved
11 unequivocal, unqualified
12 unrestricted, wholehearted
13 thoroughgoing

## unconfirmed
08 unproved, unproven
10 unratified, unverified
14 uncorroborated
15 unauthenticated, unsubstantiated

## unconformity
12 irregularity
13 disconformity, discontinuity

## uncongenial
08 unsuited
10 discordant, unfriendly, uninviting, unpleasant
12 antipathetic, incompatible, unattractive

## unconnected
08 detached, separate
09 illogical, unrelated
10 disjointed, incoherent, irrational, unattached
11 independent, off the point

## unconquerable
10 inveterate, invincible, unbeatable, unyielding
11 indomitable, insuperable
12 overpowering, undefeatable
13 irrepressible
14 insurmountable

## unconscionable
06 amoral
08 criminal
09 excessive, unethical
10 immoderate, outrageous
12 preposterous, unprincipled, unreasonable, unscrupulous

## unconscious
03 out
05 blind, dazed
06 asleep, innate, latent, reflex, zonked
07 drugged, fainted, in a coma, out cold, stunned, unaware
08 comatose, heedless, ignorant
09 automatic, impulsive, oblivious, senseless, unmindful, unwitting, zonked out
10 blacked out, insensible, knocked out, subliminal, suppressed, unthinking
11 inadvertent, incognizant, instinctive, involuntary
13 unintentional
14 dead to the world, out for the count

## unconstraint
07 abandon, freedom
10 liberality
12 laissez-faire

## uncontrollable
03 mad
04 wild
06 strong, unruly
07 furious, violent
11 intractable
12 out of control, ungovernable, unmanageable

## uncontrolled
04 wild
06 unruly
07 rampant, riotous, violent
09 unbridled, unchecked
10 boisterous, unhindered
12 unrestrained
13 undisciplined

## unconventional
03 odd
04 rare, zany
05 wacky
06 freaky, fringe, way-out
07 bizarre, oddball, offbeat
08 abnormal, bohemian, original, uncommon
09 different, eccentric, irregular
10 individual, unorthodox
11 alternative, uncustomary
13 idiosyncratic

## unconvincing
04 lame, weak
06 feeble, flimsy
07 dubious, suspect
08 doubtful, unlikely

10 improbable
11 implausible
12 questionable

**uncoordinated**
05 inept
06 clumsy
07 awkward
08 bumbling, bungling, ungainly
09 maladroit

**uncouth**
04 rude
05 crude, rough
06 clumsy, coarse, vulgar
07 awkward, boorish, loutish
08 impolite, unseemly
09 graceless, unrefined
10 uncultured
11 bad-mannered, ill-mannered, uncivilized
15 unsophisticated

**uncover**
04 bare, leak, open, peel, show
05 dig up, strip
06 detect, exhume, expose, reveal, unmask, unveil
07 divulge, lay bare, unearth
08 disclose, discover
09 make known
12 bring to light

**uncritical**
12 undiscerning
13 nonjudgmental, unquestioning

**unctuous**
04 glib, oily
05 slick, suave
06 creamy, greasy, smooth
07 fawning, gushing, servile
09 insincere, pietistic, plausible
10 obsequious
11 sycophantic
12 ingratiating

**uncultivated**
04 wild
06 fallow
07 natural

**uncultured**
09 unrefined
12 uncultivated
15 unsophisticated

**undaunted**
07 unbowed
08 fearless, intrepid, resolute
09 dauntless, steadfast
10 undeterred, undismayed
11 indomitable

**undecided**
04 moot, open

07 dubious, unknown
08 doubtful, hesitant, wavering
09 debatable, dithering, uncertain, unsettled
10 ambivalent, irresolute, of two minds, unresolved, up in the air
12 equivocating

**undecorated**
05 plain, stark
06 severe, simple
07 austere
08 inornate
09 classical, unadorned
10 functional
13 unembellished

**undefeated**
07 supreme, winning
08 unbeaten
10 triumphant, victorious
11 unconquered, unsurpassed
12 unvanquished

**undefended**
07 exposed, unarmed
09 pregnable, unguarded
10 vulnerable
11 defenseless, unfortified, unprotected

**undefiled**
04 pure
05 clean, clear
06 chaste, intact
08 spotless, unsoiled, virginal
09 inviolate, unsullied
10 immaculate

**undefined**
04 hazy
05 vague
06 woolly
07 inexact, tenuous, unclear
08 formless, nebulous
09 imprecise
10 indefinite, indistinct
11 unexplained, unspecified
13 indeterminate

**undemonstrative**
04 cold, cool
05 aloof, stiff
06 formal, remote
07 distant
08 reserved, reticent
10 phlegmatic, restrained
11 unemotional

**undeniable**
04 sure
06 patent, proven
07 certain, evident, obvious
08 definite, manifest, positive
11 beyond doubt, indubitable, irrefutable

12 indisputable, unmistakable
14 beyond question, unquestionable

**undependable**
07 erratic
08 unstable, variable
09 mercurial, uncertain
10 inconstant, unreliable
11 fair-weather, treacherous
12 inconsistent
13 irresponsible, unpredictable

**under**
04 down, less
05 below, lower
07 beneath
08 junior to, less than
09 lower than
10 inferior to, underneath
11 secondary to
13 subordinate to, subservient to

**underclothes**
06 undies
08 lingerie
09 underwear
13 underclothing, undergarments
14 unmentionables

**undercover**
06 covert, hidden, secret
07 furtive, private
08 hush-hush, stealthy
11 clandestine, underground
12 confidential, intelligence
13 surreptitious

**undercurrent**
04 aura, hint
05 drift, sense, tinge, trend
06 flavor
07 feeling
08 tendency, undertow
09 underflow, undertone
10 atmosphere, suggestion

**undercut**
08 excavate, gouge out, scoop out, underbid
09 hollow out, undermine
10 underprice

**underestimate**
08 misjudge, play down
09 underrate
10 look down on, trivialize, undervalue

**undergo**
04 bear
05 stand
06 endure, suffer
07 sustain, weather
08 submit to, tolerate

## underground

09 go through, put up with, withstand
10 experience

## underground

06 covert, secret
07 furtive, illegal
10 subversive, undercover, unofficial
11 alternative, below ground, clandestine
12 subterranean
13 revolutionary
15 below the surface

## undergrowth

05 brush, scrub
06 bushes
07 thicket
09 brushwood
10 underbrush, vegetation
11 ground cover

## underhand

03 sly
05 shady
06 crafty, secret, sneaky
07 devious, furtive, immoral
08 improper, stealthy
09 deceitful, deceptive, dishonest, unethical
11 clandestine
12 unscrupulous

## underline

06 stress
07 point up
09 emphasize, highlight
10 accentuate, underscore
15 draw attention to

## underling

05 gofer
06 lackey, menial, minion
07 flunkey, servant
08 hireling, inferior
11 subordinate

## underlying

04 root
05 basal, basic
06 hidden, latent, veiled
09 essential, intrinsic
10 elementary
11 fundamental

## undermine

05 erode
06 damage, impair, injure, tunnel, weaken
07 destroy, subvert, vitiate
08 excavate, sabotage, wear away

## underprivileged

04 poor
05 needy
06 in need, in want

---

08 deprived
09 destitute, oppressed
13 disadvantaged

## underrate

08 belittle
09 sell short
10 depreciate, look down on, undervalue
13 underestimate

## undersell

06 reduce
08 play down, undercut
09 disparage, sell short
10 depreciate, understate

## undersized

04 puny, tiny
05 dwarf, pygmy, small
06 little, minute
07 runtish, stunted
08 pint-size
09 miniature, pint-sized
11 underweight
14 underdeveloped

## understand

03 get, see
04 hear, know
05 click, grasp, learn, savvy, think
06 accept, assume, fathom, gather, take in
07 believe, discern, make out, presume, realize, suppose
08 conclude, cotton on, perceive, tumble to
09 apprehend, empathize, figure out, recognize
10 appreciate, comprehend, sympathize
11 commiserate
12 get the hang of, identify with
13 get the message, get the picture

## understanding

04 idea, kind, pact, view
05 grasp, sense, trust
06 accord, belief, loving, notion, tender, wisdom
07 bargain, comfort, compact, empathy, entente, feeling, harmony, insight, lenient, opinion, patient, support
08 judgment, sympathy, tolerant
09 agreement, awareness, intellect, knowledge, sensitive
10 compassion, forbearing, impression, perception, supportive, thoughtful
11 considerate, consolation, discernment, realization, sympathetic

---

12 appreciation, apprehension, intelligence
13 compassionate, comprehension
14 interpretation

## understate

08 belittle, minimize, play down
09 soft-pedal, underplay
11 make light of

## understatement

07 litotes, meiosis
09 restraint
12 minimization, underplaying

## understood

05 tacit
07 assumed, implied
08 accepted, implicit, inferred, presumed, unspoken, unstated
09 unwritten

## understudy

06 deputy, double, fill in, relief
07 reserve, stand-in
10 substitute
11 replacement

## undertake

05 agree, begin
06 accept, assume, pledge, tackle, take on
07 attempt, promise
08 commence, contract, embark on, endeavor, set about
09 guarantee

## undertaker

08 embalmer
09 mortician
15 funeral director

## undertaking

03 job, vow
04 task, word
06 affair, effort, pledge, scheme
07 promise, venture, warrant
08 business
09 assurance, guarantee
10 commitment, enterprise

## undertone

04 aura, hint
05 tinge, touch, trace
06 flavor, murmur
07 feeling, whisper
10 intimation, suggestion
12 undercurrent

## undervalue

09 disparage, sell short, underrate
10 depreciate, look down on
13 underestimate

## underwater
06 sunken
08 immersed, undersea
09 submarine, submerged
10 subaquatic, subaqueous

## underwear
06 undies
08 lingerie
12 underclothes
13 undergarments
14 unmentionables

## underweight
04 thin
08 underfed
10 undersized
11 half-starved
14 undernourished

## underworld
04 hell
05 Hades
06 the mob
08 gangland
10 the inferno
13 criminal world
14 organized crime

## underwrite
04 back, fund, sign
06 insure
07 approve, confirm, endorse, finance, support
09 authorize, guarantee

## undesirable
04 foul
05 nasty
09 obnoxious, offensive, repugnant, unwelcome
13 objectionable

## undeveloped
07 dwarfed, stunted
08 immature, inchoate, unformed
09 embryonic, potential
10 developing, Third-World

## undignified
08 improper, ungainly, unseemly
09 inelegant
10 indecorous

## undisciplined
04 wild
06 unruly, wilful
07 wayward, willful
11 disobedient
12 disorganized, obstreperous, uncontrolled, unrestrained

## undisguised
04 open
05 frank, naked, overt, stark
06 patent

07 blatant, evident, obvious
08 explicit, manifest, outright
09 unadorned
11 transparent, unconcealed

## undisguisedly
06 openly
07 frankly, overtly
08 outright, patently
09 blatantly, obviously
13 transparently

## undisputed
04 sure
07 certain
08 accepted
09 undoubted
10 conclusive, recognized, undeniable
11 irrefutable, uncontested
12 indisputable, unchallenged, unquestioned

## undistinguished
05 banal
06 common
08 inferior, mediocre, ordinary
10 pedestrian
11 indifferent, not up to much
12 unremarkable
13 no great shakes, unexceptional

## undisturbed
04 calm, even
05 quiet
06 placid, serene
07 equable
08 composed, tranquil
09 unruffled, untouched
10 unaffected, untroubled
11 unconcerned, unperturbed
13 uninterrupted

## undivided
04 full
05 solid, total, whole
06 entire, intact, united
08 complete, unbroken
09 dedicated, exclusive, unanimous
12 concentrated, wholehearted

## undo
05 loose, quash, spoil, untie, unzip, wreck
06 defeat, loosen, repeal, revoke, unhook, unlock
07 nullify, release, reverse
08 overturn, unbuckle, unbutton, unfasten

## undoing
04 ruin
05 shame
06 defeat
08 collapse, disgrace, downfall

09 overthrow, ruination
11 destruction

## undomesticated
04 wild
05 feral
06 savage
07 natural, untamed

## undone
05 loose
06 ruined, untied
07 ignored, omitted, unlaced
08 betrayed, unlocked
09 destroyed
10 passed over, unbuttoned, unfastened, unfinished
11 outstanding, uncompleted, unfulfilled

## undoubted
04 sure
07 certain
08 definite
10 undisputed
11 indubitable, irrefutable, uncontested
12 indisputable, unchallenged
14 unquestionable

## undoubtedly
06 surely
07 no doubt
08 of course
09 assuredly, certainly
10 definitely, undeniably
11 beyond doubt, indubitably
12 unmistakably, without doubt
14 unquestionably

## undreamed-of
08 undreamt
09 undreamed, unheard-of
10 incredible, miraculous, unexpected, unforeseen, unhoped-for, unimagined
11 astonishing, unsuspected

## undress
05 strip
06 divest, nudity, remove
07 disrobe, peel off, take off
08 unclothe
10 déshabillé, dishabille

## undressed
04 bare, nude
05 naked
08 disrobed, stripped
09 unclothed
10 stark naked

## undue
07 extreme
08 improper, needless
09 excessive
10 inordinate, undeserved

11 uncalled-for, unjustified, unnecessary, unwarranted
13 inappropriate

**undulate**
04 roll, wave
05 heave, surge, swell
06 billow, ripple
11 rise and fall

**undulating**
04 wavy
07 rolling, sinuous
08 flexuose, flexuous, rippling
09 billowing

**unduly**
03 too
04 over
11 excessively
12 immoderately, inordinately
13 unjustifiably, unnecessarily

**undutiful**
05 slack
06 remiss
08 careless, disloyal, unfilial
09 negligent
10 neglectful

**undying**
07 abiding, eternal, lasting
08 constant, immortal, infinite, unending, unfading
09 deathless, perpetual
11 everlasting, sempiternal
12 imperishable
14 indestructible

**unearth**
05 dig up
06 exhume, expose, reveal
07 uncover
08 discover, disinter, excavate
12 bring to light

**unearthly**
04 eery
05 eerie, weird
06 creepy
07 ghostly, phantom, strange, uncanny, ungodly
08 eldritch
12 otherworldly, supernatural
13 preternatural, spine-chilling

**uneasiness**
05 alarm, doubt, worry
06 qualms, unease
07 anxiety
08 disquiet
09 misgiving
10 inquietude
11 nervousness
12 apprehension, perturbation

**uneasy**
04 edgy

05 nervy, shaky, tense, upset
06 on edge, unsure
07 alarmed, anxious, jittery, keyed up, nervous, twitchy, worried, wound up
08 agitated, insecure, restless, strained, troubled, worrying
09 disturbed, perturbed, unnerving, unsettled
10 disturbing, perturbing
12 apprehensive
13 uncomfortable

**uneconomic**
10 loss-making
12 uncommercial, unprofitable

**uneducated**
06 unread
08 ignorant, untaught
09 benighted
10 illiterate, philistine, uncultured, unschooled

**unemotional**
04 cold, cool
08 detached, reserved
09 apathetic, impassive, objective, unfeeling
10 phlegmatic
11 indifferent
13 dispassionate

**unemphatic**
10 played-down
11 underplayed, understated

**unemployed**
04 idle
07 jobless, laid off, unwaged
09 on the dole, out of work, redundant

**unending**
07 endless, eternal, nonstop, undying
08 constant
09 ceaseless, continual, incessant, perpetual, unceasing
10 continuous, relentless
11 everlasting, never-ending, unrelenting, unremitting
12 interminable

**unendurable**
10 unbearable
11 intolerable
12 insufferable, overwhelming
13 insupportable

**unenthusiastic**
04 cool
05 blasé, bored
07 neutral, unmoved
08 lukewarm
09 apathetic, Laodicean
10 nonchalant

11 halfhearted, unimpressed
12 uninterested, unresponsive

**unenviable**
09 difficult, thankless
11 uncongenial, undesirable
12 disagreeable

**unequal**
06 biased, uneven, unfair, unjust, unlike
07 not up to, varying
08 lopsided, unfitted, unsuited
09 incapable, unmatched
10 unbalanced
11 incompetent, inequitable, unqualified
12 asymmetrical, not cut out for
14 discriminatory

**unequaled**
08 peerless
09 matchless, nonpareil, paramount, unmatched, unrivaled
10 inimitable
11 unsurpassed
12 incomparable, unparalleled

**unequivocal**
05 clear, plain
06 direct
07 evident, express
08 absolute, definite, explicit, positive, straight
11 categorical, unambiguous
12 unmistakable
15 straightforward

**unerring**
04 dead, sure
05 exact
07 certain, perfect, uncanny
08 accurate
09 faultless, unfailing
10 impeccable, infallible

**unerringly**
04 dead
10 accurately, infallibly
11 unfailingly

**unethical**
05 shady, wrong
07 illegal, illicit, immoral
08 improper
12 dishonorable, disreputable, unprincipled, unscrupulous

**uneven**
03 odd
05 bumpy, lumpy, rough
06 coarse, fitful, patchy, unfair
07 crooked, erratic, unequal
08 lopsided, one-sided, unsteady, variable
09 irregular, spasmodic
10 ill-matched, unbalanced

11 fluctuating, inequitable
12 asymmetrical, inconsistent, intermittent

**uneventful**
04 dull
05 quiet
06 boring
07 humdrum, routine, tedious
10 monotonous, unexciting

**unexampled**
05 novel
06 unique
09 unequaled, unheard-of, unmatched
12 incomparable, unparalleled
13 unprecedented

**unexceptional**
06 common, normal
07 average, typical
08 mediocre, ordinary
11 indifferent
12 run-of-the-mill, unimpressive, unremarkable
15 undistinguished

**unexcitable**
04 calm, cool
06 serene
08 composed, laid-back
09 easygoing
10 phlegmatic
13 imperturbable, self-possessed

**unexpected**
06 chance
10 accidental, fortuitous, unforeseen
11 unlooked-for
13 unanticipated, unpredictable

**unexpectedly**
08 by chance
12 fortuitously, out of the blue
13 unpredictably
14 without warning

**unexpressive**
06 vacant
07 deadpan
09 impassive
11 emotionless, inscrutable
14 expressionless

**unfading**
07 abiding, durable, lasting
08 enduring
09 evergreen

**unfailing**
04 sure, true
06 steady
07 certain, staunch, undying
08 constant, faithful, reliable
09 steadfast

10 dependable, infallible

**unfair**
06 biased, unjust
07 bigoted, crooked, partial, slanted
08 one-sided, partisan
09 arbitrary, unmerited
10 prejudiced, unbalanced, undeserved
11 inequitable, uncalled-for, unwarranted
12 below the belt

**unfairness**
04 bias
07 bigotry
08 inequity
09 injustice, prejudice
10 partiality
12 one-sidedness, partisanship
14 discrimination

**unfaithful**
05 false
06 fickle, untrue
08 cheating, disloyal
09 deceitful, dishonest, faithless, two-timing
10 adulterous, inconstant, perfidious, unreliable
11 duplicitous, treacherous
13 untrustworthy

**unfaltering**
04 firm
06 steady
08 constant, resolute, tireless, untiring
09 steadfast, unfailing
10 unflagging, unswerving, unwavering, unyielding
11 unflinching
12 pertinacious
13 indefatigable

**unfamiliar**
05 alien
07 foreign, strange, unknown
09 uncharted
10 unexplored
12 unaccustomed

**unfashionable**
03 out
05 dated, passé
06 démodé, old hat, square
08 obsolete, outmoded
09 out-of-date, unpopular
12 old-fashioned

**unfasten**
04 open, undo
05 untie
06 detach, loosen, unlock
08 separate, uncouple
10 disconnect

**unfathomable**
04 deep
06 hidden
08 abstruse, baffling, esoteric, profound
09 unplumbed, unsounded
10 bottomless, fathomless, mysterious, unknowable
11 inscrutable, unthinkable
12 immeasurable, impenetrable, inexplicable, unbelievable
14 indecipherable

**unfavorable**
03 bad
04 poor
07 adverse, hostile, ominous
08 critical, inimical, negative
11 inopportune, threatening
12 discouraging, inauspicious
15 disadvantageous, uncomplimentary

**unfeeling**
04 cold, hard
05 cruel, harsh, stony
07 callous, inhuman
08 pitiless, uncaring
09 apathetic, heartless
11 hardhearted, insensitive
13 unsympathetic

**unfeigned**
04 pure, real
07 genuine, natural, sincere
08 unforced
09 authentic, heartfelt
10 unaffected
12 wholehearted

**unfettered**
04 free
09 unbridled, unchecked
10 unhindered
11 uninhibited, untrammeled
12 unrestrained
13 unconstrained

**unfinished**
05 crude, rough
07 sketchy
10 incomplete
11 uncompleted, unfulfilled
14 unaccomplished

**unfit**
05 inapt, inept
06 feeble, flabby, unable
07 unequal, useless
08 decrepit, unsuited
09 incapable, unhealthy, untrained
10 inadequate, unsuitable
11 debilitated, incompetent, ineffective, unqualified
13 inappropriate

14 out of condition

**unflagging**
06 steady
07 staunch
08 constant, tireless, untiring
09 unceasing, unfailing
10 persistent, unswerving
11 persevering, unfaltering
12 never-failing
13 indefatigable

**unflappable**
04 calm, cool
07 equable
08 composed
09 collected, unruffled
10 phlegmatic
11 levelheaded
13 imperturbable, self-possessed

**unflattering**
06 candid, honest
08 critical
09 outspoken
10 unbecoming
11 unfavorable
15 uncomplimentary

**unflinching**
06 steady
07 staunch
08 resolute, stalwart, unshaken
09 steadfast
10 unblinking, unswerving
11 unfaltering

**unfold**
04 grow, open, show, tell
06 emerge, evolve, relate, result, reveal, spread
07 develop, explain, open out, present, work out
08 disclose
09 elaborate, spread out
10 straighten, stretch out

**unforeseen**
10 unexpected
11 unlooked-for, unpredicted
13 unanticipated, unpredictable

**unforgettable**
07 notable, special
08 historic, striking
09 memorable, momentous
10 noteworthy, remarkable
11 distinctive, exceptional, significant

**unforgivable**
08 shameful
10 deplorable, outrageous
11 disgraceful, inexcusable, intolerable
12 indefensible, unpardonable
13 reprehensible, unjustifiable

**unforgiven**
10 unabsolved, unredeemed

**unfortunate**
07 adverse, hapless, ruinous, unhappy, unlucky
08 hopeless, ill-fated, ill-timed, luckless, untimely, untoward
10 calamitous, deplorable, disastrous, ill-advised, lamentable, unsuitable
11 injudicious, inopportune, regrettable, unfavorable
12 unsuccessful
13 inappropriate
15 disadvantageous

**unfortunately**
04 alas
05 sadly
09 unhappily, unluckily, worse luck
11 regrettably

**unfounded**
08 baseless, spurious, unproven
10 groundless
11 conjectural, unjustified, unsupported
14 uncorroborated
15 unsubstantiated

**unfrequented**
06 remote
08 desolate, isolated, secluded
09 unvisited

**unfriendly**
04 cold, cool, sour
05 aloof, surly
06 chilly, frosty, unkind
07 distant, hostile
08 inimical, strained
10 aggressive, unsociable
11 ill-disposed, quarrelsome, standoffish, unwelcoming
12 antagonistic, inhospitable

**unfrock**
06 demote, depose
07 degrade, dismiss, suspend

**unfruitful**
06 barren
07 sterile
08 infecund
09 fruitless, infertile
11 infructuous, unrewarding
12 unproductive, unprofitable

**ungainly**
05 gawky
06 clumsy, gauche
07 awkward, loutish, uncouth
08 gangling, unwieldy
09 inelegant, lumbering, maladroit

**ungodly**
06 sinful, wicked
07 corrupt, godless, immoral, impious, profane
09 unearthly
10 iniquitous, outrageous
11 blasphemous, irreligious
12 preposterous, unreasonable

**ungovernable**
04 wild
06 unruly
10 rebellious, refractory
12 unmanageable
14 uncontrollable

**ungracious**
04 rude
07 boorish, ill-bred, uncivil
08 churlish, impolite
09 graceless
10 unmannerly
11 bad-mannered
12 discourteous
13 disrespectful

**ungrateful**
07 selfish, uncivil
08 heedless, impolite
09 thankless
10 ungracious, unthankful
14 unappreciative

**unguarded**
04 rash
06 unwary
08 careless, heedless, off-guard
09 foolhardy, imprudent
10 incautious, indiscreet, undefended, unthinking
11 defenseless, inattentive, thoughtless, unprotected
13 ill-considered

**unhappily**
04 alas
05 sadly
08 sad to say
09 unluckily, worse luck
11 regrettably, sad to relate
13 unfortunately

**unhappy**
03 low, sad
04 blue, down, glum
05 fed up, inapt
06 clumsy, gloomy
07 awkward, hapless, unlucky
08 dejected, downcast, ill-fated, mournful, tactless
09 depressed, long-faced, miserable, sorrowful, woebegone
10 despondent, dispirited, ill-advised, ill-starred, melancholy, unsuitable

**unharmed**
11 crestfallen, injudicious, unfortunate
12 disconsolate
13 inappropriate
14 down in the dumps

**unharmed**
04 safe
05 sound, whole
06 intact, unhurt
09 undamaged, uninjured, unscathed, untouched

**unhealthy**
03 ill
04 sick, weak
06 ailing, feeble, infirm, poorly, sickly, unwell
07 invalid, noxious, unsound
09 injurious, unnatural
10 insanitary, unhygienic
11 unwholesome
12 insalubrious

**unheard-of**
06 unsung
07 obscure, unknown, unusual
10 outrageous, unfamiliar
11 undreamed-of
12 unacceptable, unbelievable, undiscovered, unimaginable
13 inconceivable

**unheeded**
07 ignored, unnoted
09 disobeyed, unnoticed
10 overlooked, unobserved
11 disregarded

**unheralded**
10 unexpected, unforeseen
11 unannounced
12 unpublicized

**unhesitating**
06 prompt
07 instant
09 automatic, immediate
10 unwavering
11 spontaneous, unfaltering
12 wholehearted
13 instantaneous, unquestioning

**unhinge**
05 craze, upset
06 madden
07 confuse, derange, unnerve
08 disorder, distract, drive mad
09 unbalance

**unholy**
06 sinful, wicked
07 corrupt, godless, immoral, impious, ungodly
09 unearthly
10 iniquitous
11 blasphemous, irreligious

**unhoped-for**
10 unexpected, unforeseen
11 undreamed-of, unlooked-for
13 unanticipated

**unhurried**
04 calm, easy, slow
06 sedate
07 relaxed
08 laid-back
09 easygoing, leisurely
10 deliberate

**unhurt**
04 safe
05 sound, whole
06 intact
08 unharmed
09 uninjured, unscathed, untouched

**unhygienic**
04 foul
05 dirty
06 filthy, impure
07 noisome, noxious, unclean
08 feculent, infected, polluted
09 unhealthy
10 insanitary
12 contaminated, insalubrious

**unidentified**
07 strange, unknown, unnamed
08 nameless, unmarked
09 anonymous, incognito
10 mysterious, unfamiliar

**unification**
05 union
06 enosis, fusion, merger
07 uniting
11 coalescence, combination

**uniform**
04 even, flat, garb, same, suit
05 alike, dress, equal, robes
06 livery, outfit, smooth, stable, steady
07 costume, regalia, regular
08 constant, unbroken
09 identical, unvarying
10 consistent, unchanging
11 homogeneous, regimentals

**uniformity**
08 evenness, monotony, sameness
09 constancy
10 regularity
11 homogeneity
12 homomorphism

**unify**
03 mix
04 bind, fuse, join, weld
05 blend, merge, unite
07 combine
08 coalesce

09 integrate
10 amalgamate
11 consolidate
12 come together
13 bring together

**unifying**
07 uniting
11 combinative, combinatory, esemplastic, integrating
13 consolidative

**unimaginable**
07 amazing
09 fantastic, unheard-of
10 far-fetched, incredible, outlandish
11 implausible, unthinkable
12 mind-boggling, preposterous, unbelievable
13 extraordinary, inconceivable

**unimaginative**
05 banal, stale
06 barren, boring
07 mundane, routine
09 hackneyed
10 pedestrian, uninspired
12 matter-of-fact

**unimpeachable**
07 perfect
09 faultless
10 immaculate, impeccable
11 unblemished
12 unassailable
14 irreproachable

**unimpeded**
04 free, open
05 clear
08 all-round
09 all-around, unblocked, unchecked
10 unhampered, unhindered
11 untrammeled
12 unrestrained

**unimportant**
05 minor, petty
06 slight
07 trivial
08 marginal, nugatory, trifling
09 no big deal, secondary
10 immaterial, incidental, irrelevant, negligible, peripheral
13 insignificant
15 inconsequential

**unimpressive**
08 mediocre, ordinary
11 commonplace, indifferent
12 unremarkable
13 unexceptional, uninteresting, unspectacular
15 undistinguished

**uninhabited**
05 empty
06 vacant
08 deserted, desolate
09 abandoned, unpeopled
10 unoccupied
11 unpopulated .

**uninhibited**
04 free, open
09 abandoned, liberated,
   outspoken
10 unreserved
11 spontaneous
12 unrestrained
13 unconstrained
15 unselfconscious

**uninspired**
04 dull
05 stale, stock, trite
06 boring
07 humdrum, prosaic
08 ordinary
10 pedestrian, unexciting
11 uninspiring
13 unimaginative, uninteresting

**unintelligent**
04 dull, dumb, slow
05 dense, silly, thick
06 obtuse, stupid
09 brainless
10 half-witted, unthinking
11 empty-headed

**unintelligible**
07 complex, garbled, jumbled,
   muddled, obscure
08 involved, puzzling
09 illegible, scrambled
10 incoherent, mysterious,
   unreadable
11 complicated
12 impenetrable, inarticulate,
   unfathomable
14 indecipherable

**unintentional**
09 unplanned, unwitting
10 accidental, fortuitous,
   unintended
11 inadvertent, involuntary
14 unpremeditated

**uninterested**
05 blasé, bored
09 apathetic, impassive
11 indifferent, unconcerned
14 unenthusiastic

**uninteresting**
03 dry
04 drab, dull, flat, tame
05 stale
06 boring, dreary
07 humdrum, prosaic, tedious

10 pedestrian, unexciting
11 uninspiring

**uninterrupted**
07 endless, nonstop
08 constant, unbroken
09 ceaseless, unceasing
10 continuous
11 undisturbed, unremitting

**uninvited**
07 unasked
08 unsought, unwanted
09 unwelcome
11 unsolicited .

**uninviting**
08 unsavory
09 offensive, repellent, repulsive
10 unpleasant
11 distasteful, unappealing
12 unappetizing, unattractive

**uninvolved**
04 free
09 fancy-free, footloose
10 unattached, unhampered,
   unhindered
11 independent, uncommitted,
   untrammeled

**union**
04 club
05 blend, unity
06 fusion, merger
07 harmony, joining, mixture,
   wedding, wedlock
08 alliance, juncture, marriage,
   nuptials
09 agreement, coalition,
   matrimony, synthesis,
   unanimity
10 consortium, federation,
   labor union, trade union
11 combination, confederacy,
   unification

**unique**
04 lone, only, sole
06 single
08 peerless, solitary
09 matchless, nonpareil,
   unequaled, unrivaled
10 inimitable, one and only, one
   of a kind, sui generis
12 incomparable, unparalleled

**unison**
05 unity
06 accord
07 concert, concord
09 unanimity

**unit**
03 one
04 item, part
05 piece, whole
06 entity, module, system

07 element, section, segment
09 component

**unite**
04 ally, band, fuse, join, link,
   pool, weld
05 blend, marry, merge, unify
06 couple
07 combine, connect
08 coalesce, federate
09 associate, cooperate
10 amalgamate, join forces
11 confederate, consolidate
12 pull together

**united**
03 one
06 agreed, allied, pooled
07 unified
08 combined, in accord
09 concerted, unanimous
10 collective
11 in agreement

**unity**
05 peace, union
06 accord
07 concert, harmony, oneness
09 agreement, consensus,
   unanimity, wholeness
10 solidarity
11 unification

**universal**
05 total, whole
06 common, cosmic, global
07 general
08 all-round
09 all-around, worldwide
10 ubiquitous
11 omnipresent
12 all-embracing, all-inclusive
13 comprehensive
14 across-the-board

**universality**
08 entirety, totality, ubiquity
10 commonness, generality,
   prevalence

**universally**
06 always
09 uniformly
10 everywhere, invariably
12 ubiquitously

**universe**
05 world
06 cosmos, nature
08 creation
09 firmament, macrocosm

**university**
06 school
07 academy, college, varsity
08 academia
09 institute
15 higher education

► *Names of Ivy League schools:*
04 Yale
05 Brown
07 Cornell, Harvard
08 Columbia
09 Dartmouth, Princeton
12 Pennsylvania
➢ See also COLLEGE

**unjust**
06 biased, unfair
07 partial
08 one-sided, partisan
10 prejudiced, undeserved
11 inequitable, unjustified
12 unreasonable

**unjustifiable**
09 excessive
10 immoderate, outrageous
11 inexcusable, unwarranted
12 indefensible, unacceptable, unreasonable

**unkempt**
05 messy
06 shabby, sloppy, untidy
07 rumpled, scruffy, tousled
08 slobbish, slovenly, uncombed
09 ungroomed
10 disheveled, disordered

**unkind**
04 mean
05 cruel, harsh, nasty, snide
07 callous, inhuman, vicious
08 inhumane, pitiless, uncaring
09 heartless, malicious
10 malevolent, unfriendly
11 coldhearted, hardhearted
12 uncharitable

**unkindness**
05 spite
07 cruelty
08 meanness
09 harshness
15 hardheartedness

**unknowable**
08 infinite
12 incalculable, unfathomable, unimaginable

**unknown**
05 alien
06 hidden, secret, untold
07 foreign, strange, unnamed
08 nameless
09 anonymous, uncharted
10 mysterious, unexplored, unfamiliar
12 unidentified

**unlawful**
06 banned
07 illegal, illicit
08 criminal, outlawed
09 forbidden
10 prohibited, unlicensed
12 illegitimate
13 against the law

**unleash**
04 free
05 loose, untie
07 release, unloose
08 let loose, untether

**unlettered**
08 ignorant, untaught
09 unlearned, untutored
10 illiterate, uneducated

**unlike**
07 diverse, opposed, unequal
08 distinct, opposite
09 different, disparate, divergent, unrelated
10 contrasted, dissimilar
11 as opposed to
12 in contrast to, incompatible

**unlikely**
06 remote, slight
07 distant, dubious, suspect
08 doubtful
10 far-fetched, improbable, unexpected
11 implausible
12 unbelievable, unimaginable
13 inconceivable

**unlimited**
07 endless, immense
08 complete, infinite
09 boundless, countless, extensive, unbounded
10 indefinite, unhampered
12 immeasurable, unrestricted
13 unconditional, unconstrained
15 all-encompassing

**unload**
04 dump
05 empty
07 offload, relieve
08 unburden
09 discharge

**unlock**
04 free, open, undo
05 unbar
06 unbolt
07 release, unlatch
08 unfasten

**unlooked-for**
06 chance
08 surprise

10 fortuitous, unexpected, unforeseen
11 unthought-of
13 unanticipated

**unloved**
08 loveless, unwanted
09 neglected
10 uncared-for

**unlucky**
04 poor
06 cursed, doomed, jinxed
07 adverse, hapless, ominous
08 ill-fated, luckless, untoward, wretched
09 miserable
10 calamitous, disastrous, ill-starred, unpleasant
11 star-crossed, unfavorable, unfortunate, unpromising
12 catastrophic, inauspicious, unpropitious, unsuccessful
14 down on your luck
15 disadvantageous

**unmanageable**
06 unruly
07 awkward
08 unwieldy
10 cumbersome, disorderly, refractory
12 incommodious, inconvenient, ungovernable
14 uncontrollable

**unmanly**
04 soft, weak
05 sissy, timid, weedy
06 craven, feeble, prissy, yellow
07 chicken, gutless, wimpish
08 cowardly
09 weak-kneed
10 effeminate, namby-pamby
11 milquetoast
14 chicken-hearted

**unmannerly**
04 rude
07 boorish, ill-bred, low-bred, uncivil, uncouth
08 impolite
09 graceless
10 ungracious
12 discourteous
13 disrespectful

**unmarried**
05 unwed
06 single
08 celibate
09 available
10 unattached

**unmask**
04 bare, show
06 expose, reveal, unveil

**unmatched**

07 uncover
08 disclose, discover

**unmatched**
06 unique
07 supreme
08 peerless
09 matchless, nonpareil, paramount, unequaled, unrivaled
10 consummate, unexampled
11 unsurpassed
12 incomparable, unparalleled
13 beyond compare

**unmentionable**
05 taboo
08 immodest, indecent, shameful, shocking
10 abominable, scandalous, unpleasant
11 disgraceful, unspeakable, unutterable
12 embarrassing

**unmerciful**
05 cruel
07 callous
08 pitiless
09 heartless, merciless
10 implacable, relentless
11 remorseless, unrelenting

**unmethodical**
07 muddled
09 haphazard, illogical
11 unorganized
12 unsystematic

**unmindful**
07 unaware
08 careless, heedless
09 forgetful, negligent, oblivious, unheeding
10 neglectful, regardless
11 inattentive, indifferent, unconscious

**unmistakable**
05 clear, plain
06 patent
07 blatant, certain, evident, glaring, obvious
08 clear-cut, definite, distinct, explicit, manifest, striking
10 pronounced, undeniable
11 conspicuous, indubitable
12 indisputable
14 beyond question, unquestionable

**unmitigated**
04 grim, pure, rank
05 harsh, sheer, utter
06 arrant
07 intense, perfect

08 absolute, complete, outright, thorough
09 downright, out-and-out
10 consummate, unmodified, unrelieved
11 unrelenting, unremitting
12 unalleviated, undiminished
13 thoroughgoing

**unmoved**
04 cold, firm
06 steady
07 adamant, dry-eyed
08 resolute, resolved, unshaken
09 impassive, unbending, untouched
10 inflexible, unaffected
11 indifferent, unimpressed

**unnatural**
05 false, queer, stiff
06 forced, staged
07 labored, stilted, strange, uncanny, unusual
08 abnormal, affected, freakish, peculiar, strained
09 contrived, insincere, perverted
10 artificial
13 unspontaneous

**unnecessary**
06 wasted
08 needless, unneeded, unwanted
09 redundant
10 expendable, gratuitous, unrequired
11 dispensable, inessential, superfluous, uncalled-for
12 nonessential, tautological

**unnerve**
05 alarm, daunt, scare, shake, unman, upset, worry
06 deject, dismay, put out, rattle
07 fluster, perturb
08 confound, disquiet, frighten, unsettle
10 disconcert, intimidate

**unnoticed**
06 unseen
08 unheeded
10 overlooked, unobserved, unremarked
12 unrecognized

**unobtrusive**
05 quiet
06 low-key, modest
07 subdued
08 retiring
10 restrained, unassuming
12 unnoticeable
13 inconspicuous

**unobtrusively**
07 quietly
08 modestly
10 on the quiet
15 inconspicuously, surreptitiously

**unoccupied**
04 free, idle
05 empty
06 vacant
08 deserted, inactive
10 unemployed
11 uninhabited

**unofficial**
07 illegal, private
08 informal, personal
10 undeclared
12 confidential, off-the-record, unauthorized

**unoriginal**
05 stale, trite
06 copied
07 cribbed, derived
09 hackneyed
10 derivative, uninspired

**unorthodox**
06 fringe
07 unusual
08 abnormal
09 eccentric, heterodox
11 alternative
13 nonconformist
14 unconventional

**unpaid**
03 due
05 owing
07 overdue, payable, pending, unwaged
09 unsettled, voluntary
10 unsalaried
11 outstanding, uncollected

**unpalatable**
08 inedible, unsavory
09 repugnant, uneatable
11 distasteful
12 disagreeable, unappetizing

**unparalleled**
04 rare
07 supreme
08 peerless
09 matchless, unequaled, unmatched, unrivaled
11 unsurpassed
12 incomparable, without equal
13 beyond compare, unprecedented

**unpardonable**
08 shameful
10 deplorable, outrageous, scandalous

11 disgraceful, inexcusable
12 indefensible, unforgivable
14 unconscionable

**unperturbed**
04 calm, cool
06 placid, poised, serene
08 composed, tranquil
09 unexcited, unruffled, unworried
10 untroubled
11 unflustered

**unpleasant**
03 bad
04 foul, mean, rude
05 nasty, surly
08 impolite
09 offensive
10 ill-natured, unfriendly
11 distasteful, undesirable, unpalatable
12 disagreeable, unattractive

**unpleasantness**
05 furor, upset
06 bother
07 scandal, trouble
10 ill-feeling

**unpolished**
04 rude
05 crude, rough
06 coarse, vulgar
07 uncouth
09 unrefined
13 rough and ready
15 unsophisticated

**unpopular**
07 ignored, shunned, unloved
08 disliked, rejected, unwanted
10 friendless
13 unfashionable

**unprecedented**
03 new
05 novel
07 unknown, unusual
08 abnormal, freakish, original, uncommon
09 unequaled, unheard-of, unrivaled
10 remarkable
11 exceptional
12 unparalleled
13 extraordinary, revolutionary

**unpredictable**
06 chance, fickle, random
07 erratic
08 unstable, variable, volatile
09 mercurial
10 capricious, changeable, inconstant, unreliable
13 unforeseeable

**unprejudiced**
04 fair, just
08 balanced, unbiased
09 impartial, objective, uncolored
10 evenhanded
11 enlightened, nonpartisan

**unpremeditated**
09 extempore, impromptu, impulsive, unplanned
10 off-the-cuff, unprepared
11 spontaneous, unrehearsed
15 spur-of-the-moment

**unprepared**
05 ad-lib
07 unready
09 unplanned, unwilling
10 improvised, off-the-cuff
11 ill-equipped, spontaneous, unrehearsed
12 unsuspecting

**unpretentious**
05 plain
06 honest, humble, modest, simple
07 natural
08 ordinary
10 unaffected, unassuming
11 unobtrusive
14 unostentatious
15 straightforward

**unprincipled**
07 corrupt, crooked, devious, immoral
09 deceitful, dishonest, underhand, unethical
12 unscrupulous

**unproductive**
04 arid, idle, vain
06 barren, futile, otiose
07 sterile, useless
09 fruitless, infertile, worthless
10 unfruitful
11 ineffective, unrewarding
12 unprofitable

**unprofessional**
09 negligent, unethical
10 amateurish
11 incompetent, inefficient
13 inexperienced

**unpromising**
08 doubtful
11 unfavorable
12 discouraging, inauspicious, unpropitious

**unprotected**
05 naked
06 unsafe
07 exposed, unarmed
08 helpless

09 uncovered, unguarded
10 unattended, undefended, unshielded, vulnerable
11 defenseless, unfortified, unsheltered

**unprovable**
12 unverifiable
14 indemonstrable, undemonstrable

**unqualified**
05 total, unfit, utter
07 amateur, perfect
08 absolute, complete, outright, positive, thorough
09 downright, incapable, out-and-out, untrained
10 ineligible, unlicensed, unprepared, unreserved
11 categorical, ill-equipped, unequivocal, unmitigated
12 unrestricted, wholehearted
13 unconditional

**unquestionable**
04 sure
06 patent
07 certain, obvious
08 absolute, definite, manifest
09 faultless
10 conclusive, undeniable
11 indubitable, irrefutable, self-evident, unequivocal
12 indisputable, unmistakable
13 incontestable
14 beyond question

**unquestioning**
11 unqualified
12 unhesitating, wholehearted
13 unconditional

**unravel**
04 free, undo
05 solve
06 unknot, unwind
07 clear up, explain, resolve, sort out, work out
08 separate, untangle
09 extricate, figure out, penetrate
11 disentangle
13 straighten out

**unreadable**
07 complex, garbled, jumbled, muddled, obscure
09 illegible, scrambled
10 incoherent, mysterious
11 complicated
12 impenetrable, inarticulate, unfathomable
14 indecipherable, unintelligible

**unreal**
04 fake, mock, sham

## unrealistic

05 false
06 made-up
07 bizarre, pretend
08 fanciful, illusory, mythical, nebulous
09 fairy-tale, fantastic, imaginary, pretended, synthetic
10 artificial, chimerical, fabricated, fictitious, immaterial
11 make-believe, nonexistent
13 insubstantial

## unrealistic

08 quixotic, romantic
10 idealistic, impossible, unworkable
11 impractical, theoretical
13 impracticable
14 over-optimistic

## unreasonable

05 silly, steep, undue
06 absurd, biased, stupid, unfair, unjust
08 perverse
09 arbitrary, excessive, expensive, illogical, ludicrous, senseless
10 far-fetched, immoderate, irrational, outrageous
11 nonsensical, uncalled-for, unjustified, unwarranted
12 extortionate, inconsistent, preposterous, unacceptable

## unrecognizable

07 altered, changed
09 disguised, incognito
10 unknowable

## unrecognized

06 unseen
07 ignored
08 unheeded
10 overlooked, unobserved, unremarked
11 disregarded

## unrefined

03 raw
05 crude
06 coarse, vulgar
10 uncultured, unfinished, unpolished
11 unprocessed
12 uncultivated
15 unsophisticated

## unregenerate

06 sinful, wicked
08 obdurate, stubborn
09 obstinate, shameless
10 impenitent, unreformed
11 intractable, unrepentant
12 incorrigible, recalcitrant

## unrelated

09 different, disparate
10 dissimilar, extraneous, irrelevant
11 independent, off the point, unconnected
12 unassociated
14 beside the point

## unrelenting

05 cruel
06 steady
08 constant, pitiless, ruthless, unabated, unbroken
09 ceaseless, continual, incessant, merciless, unceasing, unsparing
10 continuous, inexorable, relentless, unmerciful
11 remorseless, unforgiving, unremitting
12 intransigent

## unreliable

04 iffy
06 fickle
07 unsound
08 doubtful, slippery
09 deceptive
10 inaccurate
12 unconvincing, undependable
13 irresponsible, untrustworthy

## unremitting

08 constant, unabated
09 ceaseless, continual, incessant, perpetual, unceasing
10 continuous, relentless
11 remorseless, unrelenting

## unrepentant

08 hardened, obdurate
09 shameless, unashamed
10 impenitent
12 incorrigible, unapologetic

## unreserved

04 free, full, open
05 frank, total
06 candid, direct, entire
08 absolute, complete, outgoing
09 outspoken
10 forthright
11 uninhibited, unqualified
12 unrestrained, wholehearted
13 demonstrative, unconditional

## unreservedly

07 utterly
08 entirely, outright
10 completely
14 wholeheartedly

## unresisting

04 meek
06 docile
07 passive
08 obedient
10 submissive

## unresolved

04 moot
05 vague, vexed
08 doubtful, unsolved
09 undecided, unsettled
10 indefinite, up in the air
12 undetermined

## unresponsive

04 dead
06 silent
07 unmoved
09 apathetic
11 indifferent
13 unsympathetic

## unrest

06 unease
07 discord, protest, turmoil
08 disorder, disquiet
09 agitation, rebellion
10 dissension, uneasiness
12 perturbation, restlessness

## unrestrained

04 free
09 abandoned, unbounded, unbridled, unchecked
10 boisterous, immoderate, unhindered, unreserved
11 intemperate, uninhibited
12 uncontrolled
13 unconstrained

## unrestricted

04 free, open
05 clear
09 unbounded, unimpeded, unlimited, unopposed
10 free-for-all, unhindered
12 unobstructed

## unripe

05 green
07 unready
08 immature
09 unripened

## unrivaled

07 supreme
08 peerless
09 matchless, nonpareil, unequaled
10 inimitable
12 incomparable, unparalleled, without equal
13 beyond compare

## unruffled

04 calm, cool, even
06 serene, smooth

08 composed, tranquil
10 untroubled
11 undisturbed, unperturbed

**unruly**
04 wild
05 rowdy
07 lawless, riotous, wayward
10 disorderly, headstrong,
   rebellious, refractory
11 disobedient, intractable
12 obstreperous, ungovernable
14 uncontrollable

**unsafe**
05 hairy, risky
06 chancy
07 unsound
08 insecure, perilous, unstable
09 dangerous, hazardous
10 precarious

**unsaid**
05 tacit
08 implicit, unspoken, unstated,
   unvoiced
09 unuttered
10 undeclared, understood
11 unexpressed, unmentioned
12 unpronounced

**unsatisfactory**
04 poor
08 inferior, mediocre
09 defective, deficient
10 inadequate, unsuitable
11 displeasing, frustrating
12 unsatisfying
13 disappointing, dissatisfying

**unsavory**
06 sordid
07 squalid
09 obnoxious, offensive,
   repellent, repugnant,
   repulsive, revolting
10 unpleasant
11 distasteful, unpalatable
12 disagreeable, unappetizing

**unscathed**
04 safe
05 sound, whole
06 intact, unhurt
08 unharmed
09 undamaged, uninjured

**unscrupulous**
07 corrupt, crooked, immoral
08 improper, ruthless
09 dishonest, unethical
12 unprincipled

**unseasonable**
08 ill-timed, untimely
10 malapropos, unsuitable
11 inopportune

**unseasoned**
05 green
08 unprimed
09 unmatured, untreated
10 unprepared, untempered

**unseat**
04 oust
05 throw
06 depose, remove, topple
07 dismiss, unhorse
08 displace, unsaddle

**unseemly**
08 improper, indecent
10 indecorous, indelicate,
   unbecoming, unsuitable
11 unbefitting, undignified
13 inappropriate

**unseen**
06 hidden, veiled
09 concealed, invisible,
   unnoticed
10 undetected, unobserved

**unselfish**
04 kind
08 generous, selfless
10 altruistic, charitable,
   openhanded
11 magnanimous, self-denying
13 disinterested, philanthropic
15 self-sacrificing

**unsentimental**
05 tough
09 practical, pragmatic, realistic,
   unfeeling
10 hardheaded, unromantic
11 levelheaded, unemotional

**unsettle**
05 shake, throw, upset
06 bother, rattle, ruffle
07 agitate, confuse, disturb,
   fluster, perturb, trouble
09 discomfit, unbalance
10 discompose, disconcert
11 destabilize

**unsettled**
04 edgy, open
05 owing, shaky, tense, upset
06 on edge, shaken, uneasy,
   unpaid
07 anxious, fidgety, nervous,
   payable
08 agitated, confused, deserted,
   desolate, doubtful, insecure,
   troubled, unnerved,
   unstable, unsteady, variable
09 abandoned, disturbed,
   flustered, in arrears,
   uncertain, undecided

10 changeable, inconstant,
   unoccupied, unresolved, up
   in the air
11 outstanding, uninhabited,
   unpopulated
12 undetermined
13 unpredictable

**unshakable**
04 firm, sure
05 fixed
06 stable
07 staunch
08 constant, resolute
09 immovable, steadfast
10 determined, unswerving,
   unwavering
12 unassailable

**unsightly**
04 ugly
07 hideous
12 disagreeable, unattractive
15 unprepossessing

**unskillful, unskilful**
05 inept
06 clumsy, gauche
07 awkward
08 bungling, fumbling, inexpert,
   untaught
09 maladroit, unskilled
10 amateurish, untalented
11 incompetent, unpracticed,
   unqualified
14 unprofessional

**unskilled**
08 inexpert
09 unskilful, untrained
10 unskillful
11 incompetent, unpracticed,
   unqualified
13 inexperienced
14 unprofessional

**unsociable**
04 cold, cool
05 aloof
07 distant, hostile
08 reserved, retiring, taciturn
09 reclusive, withdrawn
10 unfriendly
11 introverted, standoffish,
   uncongenial

**unsolicited**
07 unasked
08 unsought, unwanted
09 uninvited, unwelcome,
   voluntary
10 gratuitous, unasked-for
11 uncalled-for, unrequested

**unsophisticated**
05 basic, crude, naïve, plain
06 simple

07 artless, natural
08 innocent
09 guileless, ingenuous, unworldly
13 inexperienced, uncomplicated
15 straightforward

**unsound**
04 iffy, weak
05 false, frail, shaky
06 ailing, broken, faulty, flawed, unsafe, unwell, wobbly
07 invalid, rickety
08 delicate, deranged, insecure, unhinged, unstable
09 defective, erroneous, illogical, unfounded
10 fallacious, ill-founded, unbalanced, unreliable

**unsparing**
05 harsh, stern
06 lavish, severe
07 liberal, profuse
08 abundant, generous
09 bountiful, plenteous, plentiful
10 implacable, munificent, openhanded, relentless, unstinting

**unspeakable**
08 dreadful, horrible, shocking, terrible
09 appalling, execrable, frightful, monstrous
11 unthinkable, unutterable
13 indescribable, inexpressible

**unspectacular**
04 dull
06 boring, common
07 average
08 ordinary, plodding
12 unimpressive, unremarkable

**unspoiled, unspoilt**
07 natural, perfect
08 unharmed
09 preserved, unchanged, undamaged, untouched
10 unaffected, unimpaired
11 unblemished
15 unsophisticated

**unspoken**
05 tacit
06 silent, unsaid
07 assumed, implied
08 implicit, inferred, unstated, wordless
09 unuttered, voiceless
10 undeclared, understood
11 unexpressed

**unstable**
03 mad
04 daft
05 crazy, loopy, moody, risky, shaky
06 fitful, insane, unsafe, wobbly
07 erratic, rickety, unsound
08 deranged, insecure, unhinged, unsteady, variable, volatile, wavering
09 disturbed, mercurial, tottering
10 capricious, changeable, inconstant, precarious, unbalanced, unreliable
11 fluctuating, vacillating
12 inconsistent
13 unpredictable, untrustworthy

**unsteady**
05 shaky
06 unsafe, wobbly
07 doddery, rickety
08 insecure, unstable
09 irregular, tottering
10 flickering, inconstant, precarious, unreliable
11 treacherous

**unstinting**
06 lavish
07 liberal, profuse
08 abundant, generous, prodigal
09 abounding, bountiful, plentiful, unsparing
10 munificent, ungrudging

**unsubstantiated**
07 dubious
08 unproved, unproven
09 debatable
10 disputable, unattested, unverified
11 unconfirmed, unsupported
12 questionable
14 uncorroborated

**unsuccessful**
04 vain
06 beaten, failed, futile, licked, losing
07 failing, sterile, unlucky, useless
08 abortive, defeated, luckless, thwarted
09 fruitless
10 frustrated, unavailing
11 ineffective, ineffectual

**unsuitable**
05 inapt, inept, unfit
08 improper, unseemly
10 inapposite, malapropos, out of place

11 incongruous
12 incompatible, infelicitous
13 inappropriate

**unsullied**
04 pure
05 clean
06 intact
07 perfect
08 pristine, spotless, unsoiled
09 stainless
10 immaculate

**unsung**
07 obscure, unknown
08 unhailed
09 anonymous
12 uncelebrated, unrecognized
14 unacknowledged

**unsure**
07 dubious, unknown
08 doubtful, hesitant, insecure, wavering
09 dithering, skeptical, tentative, uncertain, undecided
10 ambivalent, indefinite, irresolute, of two minds, suspicious
11 uncommitted, unconvinced
12 equivocating

**unsurpassed**
08 unbeaten
09 matchless
10 unexcelled
11 exceptional, superlative
12 incomparable

**unsurprising**
08 expected, forecast, foreseen
09 looked-for, predicted
10 forseeable
11 anticipated

**unsuspecting**
06 unwary
07 unaware
08 innocent, trustful, trusting
09 credulous, ingenuous
11 unconscious
12 unsuspicious

**unswerving**
04 firm, sure, true
05 fixed
06 direct, steady
07 devoted, staunch
08 constant, resolute, untiring
09 dedicated, steadfast
10 unwavering
11 undeviating, unfaltering

**unsympathetic**
04 cold, hard
05 cruel, harsh, stony
07 callous, hostile, unmoved

08 pitiless, soulless, uncaring
11 indifferent, insensitive
12 antagonistic, unresponsive

**unsystematic**
07 chaotic, jumbled, muddled
08 confused, slapdash
09 haphazard, unplanned
10 disorderly
11 unorganized
12 disorganized, unmethodical
14 indiscriminate

**untamed**
04 wild
05 feral
06 fierce, savage
09 barbarous
14 undomesticated

**untangle**
04 undo
05 solve
07 resolve, unravel, work out
09 extricate
11 disentangle
13 straighten out

**untarnished**
04 pure
05 clean
06 bright, intact
07 glowing, shining
08 polished, pristine, spotless, unsoiled, unspoilt
09 stainless, unspoiled, unspotted, unstained, unsullied
10 immaculate, impeccable
11 unblemished
13 unimpeachable

**untenable**
05 rocky, shaky
06 flawed
07 unsound
09 illogical
10 fallacious
13 insupportable, unsustainable

**unthinkable**
08 unlikely
09 illogical, unheard-of
10 impossible, outrageous
11 implausible
12 preposterous, unbelievable, unimaginable, unreasonable
13 inconceivable

**unthinking**
04 rash, rude
06 unkind
08 careless, heedless, impolite, tactless
09 automatic, impulsive, negligent
10 indiscreet, mechanical

11 insensitive, instinctive, involuntary, thoughtless, unconscious
12 undiplomatic
13 inconsiderate

**untidy**
05 messy
06 sloppy
07 chaotic, haywire, jumbled, muddled, rumpled, scruffy, unkempt
08 slipshod, slovenly
09 cluttered
10 disheveled, disorderly, topsy-turvy
12 disorganized, unsystematic

**untie**
04 free, undo
05 loose
06 loosen, unbind, unknot, unwrap
07 release, unhitch, unleash
08 unfasten

**untimely**
08 ill-timed
09 premature
10 malapropos, unsuitable
11 inopportune, unfortunate
12 inauspicious, inconvenient, infelicitous, unseasonable
13 inappropriate

**untiring**
06 dogged, steady
07 devoted, staunch
08 constant, resolute, tireless
09 tenacious, unfailing
10 determined, persistent, unflagging
11 persevering, unfaltering
13 indefatigable

**untold**
08 infinite
09 boundless, countless, uncounted
10 unnumbered, unreckoned
11 innumerable, uncountable, undreamed-of
12 immeasurable, incalculable, unimaginable
13 inconceivable, inexpressible

**untouched**
06 intact, unhurt
09 unaltered, unchanged, undamaged, unscathed
10 unaffected, unimpaired
11 unimpressed

**untoward**
07 adverse, awkward, ominous, unlucky

08 annoying, contrary, ill-timed, improper, unseemly, untimely, worrying
10 indecorous, unbecoming, unexpected, unsuitable
11 inopportune, unfavorable, unfortunate
12 inauspicious, inconvenient, unpropitious
13 inappropriate

**untrained**
07 amateur
08 inexpert, untaught
09 unskilled
10 uneducated, unschooled
11 incompetent, unqualified
13 inexperienced
14 unprofessional

**untried**
03 new
05 novel
08 unproved, untested
10 innovative, innovatory
11 exploratory
12 experimental
13 unestablished

**untroubled**
04 calm, cool
06 placid, serene, steady
08 composed, peaceful, tranquil
09 impassive, unexcited, unruffled, unworried
11 unconcerned, undisturbed, unflustered, unperturbed

**untrue**
05 false, wrong
06 made-up
07 inexact
08 disloyal, mistaken, two-faced
09 deceitful, deceptive, dishonest, erroneous, incorrect, trumped-up
10 fabricated, fallacious, fraudulent, inaccurate, misleading, perfidious, unfaithful, untruthful
13 untrustworthy

**untrustworthy**
05 false
06 fickle, untrue
08 disloyal, two-faced, untrusty
09 deceitful, dishonest, faithless
10 capricious, fly-by-night, unreliable
11 duplicitous, treacherous

**untruth**
03 fib, lie
04 tale
05 lying, story
06 deceit

07 fiction, perjury, whopper
09 falsehood, invention, tall
story
11 fabrication, made-up story

**untruthful**
05 false, lying
06 untrue
08 invented, two-faced
09 deceitful, dishonest,
fictional, insincere
10 fabricated, fallacious,
mendacious

**untwine**
06 uncoil, unwind
07 unravel, untwist
10 disentwine

**untwist**
06 uncoil, unwind
07 unravel, untwine

**untutored**
06 simple
07 artless
08 ignorant, inexpert, unversed
09 unlearned, untrained
10 illiterate, uneducated
13 inexperienced

**unused**
03 new
04 idle
05 blank, clean, extra, fresh,
spare
07 surplus
08 leftover, untapped
09 available, remaining,
untouched
10 unemployed, unfamiliar
12 unaccustomed

**unusual**
03 odd
04 rare
05 queer, weird
07 bizarre, curious, offbeat,
special, strange
08 abnormal, atypical, singular,
uncommon
09 anomalous, different
10 phenomenal, remarkable,
surprising, unexpected,
unfamiliar, unorthodox
11 exceptional
13 extraordinary
14 unconventional

**unutterable**
09 egregious, ineffable
11 unspeakable
13 indescribable

**unvarnished**
04 bare, pure
05 frank, naked, plain, sheer,
stark

06 candid, honest, simple
09 unadorned
11 undisguised
15 straightforward

**unveil**
04 bare
06 betray, expose, reveal,
unmask
07 divulge, lay bare, lay open,
uncover
08 disclose, discover
09 make known
12 bring to light
13 take the lid off

**unwanted**
06 otiose
07 outcast, surplus, useless
08 rejected, unneeded
09 redundant, undesired,
uninvited, unwelcome
11 superfluous, unnecessary,
unsolicited

**unwarranted**
06 unjust
10 gratuitous, groundless,
undeserved, unprovoked
11 inexcusable, uncalled-for,
unjustified, unnecessary
12 indefensible, unreasonable
13 unjustifiable

**unwary**
08 heedless, off guard
09 imprudent, unguarded
10 incautious, unthinking
11 thoughtless

**unwavering**
06 steady, sturdy
07 staunch
08 constant, resolute, unshaken,
untiring
09 dedicated, steadfast,
tenacious
10 consistent, determined,
unflagging, unswerving,
unyielding
11 undeviating, unfaltering
12 single-minded, unhesitating

**unwelcome**
08 excluded, rejected,
unwanted, worrying
09 uninvited, unpopular
11 undesirable, unpalatable
12 disagreeable, unacceptable

**unwell**
03 ill
04 sick
06 ailing, groggy, poorly, sickly
08 off-color
09 unhealthy
10 indisposed, out of sorts

11 debilitated
15 under the weather

**unwholesome**
03 bad, wan
04 evil, junk, pale
05 pasty
06 anemic, pallid, sickly, wicked
07 harmful, immoral, noxious,
tainted
09 degrading, depraving,
poisonous, unhealthy
10 corrupting, insalutary,
insanitary, perverting,
unhygienic
12 insalubrious

**unwieldy**
05 bulky, hefty
06 clumsy
07 awkward, hulking, weighty
08 ungainly
09 ponderous
10 cumbersome
12 unmanageable

**unwilling**
05 loath
08 grudging, hesitant, loathful
09 reluctant, resistant
10 indisposed
11 disinclined

**unwillingness**
08 nolition, slowness
09 hesitancy
10 reluctance
12 backwardness, loathfulness
13 indisposition
14 disinclination

**unwind**
04 undo
05 relax
06 cool it, loosen, uncoil, unreel,
unroll, unwrap
07 unravel, untwist
08 chill out, wind down
10 take it easy
11 disentangle
13 put your feet up
14 take things easy
15 let your hair down

**unwise**
04 rash
05 silly
06 stupid
07 foolish
09 foolhardy, ill-judged,
impolitic, imprudent,
senseless
10 ill-advised, indiscreet
11 injudicious, thoughtless
12 shortsighted
13 ill-considered, irresponsible

## unwitting
07 unaware
09 unknowing, unplanned
10 accidental, unintended, unthinking
11 inadvertent, unconscious
12 unsuspecting
13 unintentional

## unwonted
04 rare
07 strange, unusual
08 atypical, peculiar, singular, uncommon
09 unheard-of
10 unexpected, unfamiliar
11 exceptional
12 unaccustomed

## unworldly
05 green, naïve
08 gullible, innocent
09 ingenuous, spiritual, visionary
10 idealistic, provincial
11 impractical
12 metaphysical, otherworldly
14 transcendental

## unworried
09 unruffled
10 undismayed, untroubled
11 unperturbed

## unworthy
04 base
07 ignoble
08 improper, inferior, shameful
09 unfitting
10 despicable, ineligible, unbecoming, unsuitable
11 disgraceful, incongruous, unbefitting, undeserving
12 contemptible, dishonorable, disreputable
13 discreditable, inappropriate
14 unprofessional

## unwritten
04 oral
05 tacit
08 accepted, implicit
10 recognized, understood
11 traditional, word-of-mouth

## unyielding
04 firm
05 rigid, solid, tough
07 adamant, staunch
08 hard-line, obdurate, resolute, stubborn
09 immovable, obstinate, steadfast, unbending
10 determined, implacable, inexorable, inflexible, relentless, unwavering
11 intractable, unrelenting

12 intransigent
14 uncompromising

## up-and-coming
09 go-getting, promising

## upbeat
06 bright, cheery
07 bullish, buoyant, hopeful
08 cheerful, positive
10 optimistic
11 encouraging

## upbraid
05 chide, scold
06 berate, rebuke
07 censure, reprove
08 admonish, reproach
09 castigate, criticize, reprimand

## upbringing
07 nurture, raising, rearing
08 breeding, teaching, training
09 education, parenting
11 cultivation, instruction

## update
05 amend, renew
06 revamp, revise
07 correct, upgrade
09 modernize

## upgrade
05 raise
06 better, update
07 advance, elevate, enhance, improve, promote
09 modernize
10 ameliorate, make better

## upheaval
05 chaos, upset
07 shake-up, turmoil
10 disruption, revolution

## uphill
04 hard
05 tough
06 taxing, tiring
07 arduous, onerous
08 grueling
09 difficult, laborious, strenuous, wearisome
10 burdensome, exhausting

## uphold
04 back, keep
06 defend, hold to
07 confirm, endorse, fortify, justify, promote, stand by, support, sustain
08 advocate, champion, maintain
09 vindicate
10 strengthen

## upkeep
07 running, support

08 expenses, overhead
10 sustenance
11 expenditure, maintenance, subsistence
12 conservation, preservation, running costs
14 operating costs

## uplift
04 lift
05 boost, edify, elate, exalt, heave, hoist, raise
06 better, refine
07 advance, elevate, improve, inspire, upgrade
08 civilize
09 cultivate, enlighten
10 ameliorate, betterment, enrichment, refinement
11 advancement, cultivation, edification, enhancement, improvement
13 enlightenment

## upper
03 top
04 drug, high
06 higher, senior
07 eminent, exalted, greater, loftier, topmost
08 elevated, superior
09 important, uppermost
10 upper berth
12 farther north

## ▫upper hand
04 edge, sway
07 control, mastery
08 dominion
09 advantage, dominance, supremacy
10 ascendancy, domination

## upper-class
05 elite, noble
06 swanky
08 high-born, well-born, well-bred
09 exclusive, high-class, patrician, top-drawer
11 blue-blooded
12 aristocratic

## uppermost
03 top
05 chief, first, major
07 highest, leading, primary, supreme, topmost
08 dominant, foremost, greatest, loftiest
09 paramount, principal
10 preeminent
11 predominant

## uppity
07 stuck-up
08 arrogant, snobbish

**upright**
09 bigheaded, bumptious, conceited
10 hoity-toity
11 impertinent, overweening
12 presumptuous, supercilious
13 self-important

**upright**
04 good
05 erect, moral, noble, sheer, steep
06 decent, honest, worthy
07 ethical
08 straight, vertical, virtuous
09 honorable, reputable, righteous
10 high-minded, principled, upstanding
11 respectable, trustworthy
13 incorruptible, perpendicular

**uprising**
06 mutiny, putsch, revolt, rising
09 coup d'état, rebellion
10 insurgence, revolution
12 insurrection

**uproar**
03 din
04 riot
05 furor, noise
06 bedlam, clamor, fracas, hubbub, mayhem, outcry, racket, rumpus, tumult
07 ruction, turmoil
08 brouhaha, disorder
09 commotion, confusion
10 hullabaloo, turbulence
11 pandemonium

**uproarious**
04 loud, wild
05 noisy, rowdy
07 riotous
09 clamorous, deafening, hilarious
10 boisterous, rip-roaring, rollicking
11 ripsnorting

**uproot**
04 move
05 rip up
06 pull up, remove
07 destroy, weed out, wipe out
08 displace

**upset**
03 bug, tip
05 het up, shake, shock, spill
06 dismay, grieve, put out, ruffle, shaken, topple
07 agitate, annoyed, capsize, fluster, illness, perturb, reverse, shake-up, trouble, unnerve, uptight

08 agitated, bothered, confused, dismayed, disorder, distress, in a state, overturn, sickness, surprise, troubled, unsteady, upheaval, worked up
09 agitation, complaint, disturbed, flustered, knock over, overthrow, perturbed, unsettled
10 discompose, disconcert, disruption, distressed
11 destabilize, discomposed, disorganize, disturbance
12 disconcerted, perturbation

**upshot**
06 finish, payoff, result
07 outcome
10 conclusion, dénouement
11 consequence, culmination

**upside down**
05 upset
07 chaotic, jumbled, muddled, upended
08 confused, inverted, messed up, upturned
10 disordered, overturned, topsy-turvy, wrong way up
11 wrong side up

**upstanding**
04 firm, good, true
05 erect, moral
07 ethical, upright
08 virtuous
09 honorable
10 principled

**upstart**
07 parvenu
09 arriviste
12 nouveau riche
13 social climber
14 whippersnapper

**uptight**
04 edgy
05 tense
06 hung up, on edge, uneasy
07 anxious, nervous

**up-to-date**
02 in
03 new
04 cool
06 latest, modern, recent, trendy
07 current
09 in fashion, prevalent
10 all the rage, present-day
11 fashionable
12 contemporary
13 state-of-the-art

**upturn**
04 rise
05 boost
07 revival, upsurge, upswing
08 increase, recovery
11 improvement
12 amelioration

**urban**
04 city, town
05 civic
07 built-up, oppidan
08 downtown
09 inner-city, municipal
12 metropolitan

**urbane**
05 civil, suave
06 smooth
07 elegant, refined
08 cultured, debonair, mannerly, polished
09 civilized, courteous
10 cultivated
12 well-mannered
13 sophisticated

**urbanity**
06 polish
07 culture, suavity
08 civility, courtesy, elegance
10 refinement, smoothness
11 cultivation, worldliness
14 sophistication

**urchin**
04 brat, waif
05 gamin
10 ragamuffin
11 guttersnipe

**urge**
03 beg, yen
04 goad, itch, need, prod, push, spur, wish
05 drive, egg on, fancy, force, impel, plead, press
06 advise, appeal, compel, desire, exhort, hasten, incite, induce
07 beseech, counsel, entreat, impetus, implore, impulse, longing
08 advocate, persuade
09 constrain, eagerness, encourage, instigate, recommend, stimulate
10 compulsion
11 inclination

**urgency**
05 haste, hurry
08 exigency, pressure, priority
09 extremity, necessity
10 importance
11 importunity, seriousness
14 imperativeness

## urgent

- 05 eager, grave, vital
- 07 crucial, earnest, exigent, instant, serious
- 08 critical, pressing
- 09 essential, immediate, important, insistent
- 10 compelling, imperative, persistent, persuasive
- 11 top priority

## usable

- 05 valid
- 07 current, working
- 09 available, practical
- 10 functional
- 11 exploitable, operational, serviceable

## usage

- 03 use, way
- 04 form, mode, rule
- 05 habit
- 06 custom, method
- 07 control, routine, running
- 08 handling, practice
- 09 etiquette, operation, procedure, tradition, treatment
- 10 convention, employment, management, regulation
- 11 application

## use

- 03 end, ply
- 04 call, good, help, milk, need, work
- 05 abuse, apply, avail, bleed, cause, enjoy, point, right, spend, treat, usage, value, waste, wield, worth
- 06 demand, draw on, employ, expend, handle, misuse, object, profit
- 07 ability, benefit, consume, exhaust, exploit, operate, purpose, service, utilize
- 08 deal with, exercise, impose on, maneuver, occasion, practice, resort to
- 09 advantage, go through, make use of, necessity, operation, privilege
- 10 employment, get through, manipulate, usefulness
- 11 application, utilization
- 12 exploitation, manipulation
- 13 bring into play
- 15 take advantage of

## ❏ used to

- 08 inured to
- 10 adjusted to, at home with
- 12 acclimated to, accustomed to, familiar with, in the habit of, no stranger to
- 14 acclimatized to

## ❏ use up

- 05 drain, waste
- 06 absorb, devour, finish
- 07 consume, deplete, exhaust

## used

- 07 castoff
- 08 shopworn
- 09 nearly new
- 10 hand-me-down, secondhand
- 13 formerly owned

## useful

- 04 able
- 05 handy, nifty
- 06 expert
- 07 helpful, skilful, skilled
- 08 fruitful, skillful, valuable
- 09 effective, practical, practiced, rewarding
- 10 all-purpose, beneficial, convenient, functional, productive, proficient, profitable, worthwhile
- 11 experienced
- 12 advantageous

## usefulness

- 05 avail, value, worth
- 07 benefit, service, utility
- 08 efficacy
- 10 efficiency
- 11 convenience
- 12 practicality
- 15 serviceableness

## useless

- 04 idle, vain, weak
- 06 futile
- 08 hopeless, unusable
- 09 fruitless, incapable, pointless, to no avail, unhelpful, worthless
- 10 broken-down, unavailing, unworkable
- 11 impractical, incompetent, ineffective, ineffectual
- 12 unproductive, unprofitable
- 13 inefficacious

## uselessness

- 08 futility, idleness
- 10 ineptitude
- 12 hopelessness, incompetence
- 14 impracticality, ineffectuality
- 15 ineffectiveness

## usher

- 04 lead, show
- 05 guide, pilot, steer
- 06 direct, escort

- 07 conduct, doorman
- 09 accompany, attendant, usherette
- 10 doorkeeper

## ❏ usher in

- 06 herald, launch, ring in
- 07 precede
- 08 announce, initiate
- 09 introduce
- 10 inaugurate
- 13 pave the way for

## usual

- 05 stock
- 06 common, normal, wonted
- 07 average, general, regular, routine, typical
- 08 everyday, familiar, habitual, ordinary, standard
- 09 customary
- 10 accustomed, recognized
- 11 established, traditional
- 12 conventional
- 13 unexceptional

## usually

- 06 mainly, mostly
- 07 as a rule, chiefly
- 08 commonly, normally
- 09 generally, in the main, routinely, typically
- 10 by and large, on the whole, ordinarily

## usurer

- 07 shylock
- 09 loan shark
- 11 moneylender
- 12 extortionist

## usurp

- 05 annex, seize, steal
- 08 arrogate, take over
- 10 commandeer
- 11 appropriate

## usury

- 09 extortion
- 12 moneylending

## utensil

- 04 tool
- 06 device, gadget
- 09 apparatus, appliance, implement
- 10 instrument
- 11 contrivance

▶ *Kitchen utensils:*
- 03 wok
- 04 fork
- 05 corer, grill, knife, ladle, sieve, spoon, tongs, whisk
- 06 frypan, grater, mincer, peeler, sifter, skewer, tureen
- 07 blender, cleaver, cocotte, ice

pick, ramekin, skillet, spatula, steamer, terrine
08 breadbox, colander, cruet set, dish rack, egg timer, grill pan, Mason jar, oven mitt, ramequin, saucepan, stockpot, teaspoon, wine rack
09 bain-marie, baking pan, brochette, can opener, casserole, cookie jar, corkscrew, egg slicer, fondue set, frying pan, jello mold, liquefier, punch bowl, spice rack, toast rack
10 breadboard, butter dish, egg coddler, egg poacher, knife block, mixing bowl, nutcracker, pepper mill, rolling pin, tablespoon, wine cooler
11 baking sheet, cheeseboard, cookie sheet, garlic press, pastry board, pastry brush, roasting pan, wooden spoon
12 bottle opener, butter curler, cheese slicer, deep-fat fryer, dessertspoon, flour dredger, measuring cup, nutmeg grater, pastry cutter, potato masher, potato peeler, salad spinner
13 chopping block, food processor, kitchen scales, lemon squeezer
14 pressure cooker

**utilitarian**
05 lowly
06 useful
08 sensible
09 effective, efficient, practical, pragmatic

10 convenient, functional
11 down-to-earth, serviceable
13 unpretentious

**utility**
03 use
04 good, help
05 avail, value, worth
07 benefit, fitness, service
10 efficiency, usefulness
12 practicality
15 serviceableness

**utilize**
03 use
06 employ
07 exploit
08 put to use, resort to
09 make use of
13 turn to account

**utmost**
03 top
04 best, last, most, peak
05 final
07 extreme, hardest, highest, maximum, supreme
08 farthest, furthest, greatest, remotest, ultimate
09 outermost, paramount
11 furthermost

**Utopia**
04 Eden
05 bliss
06 heaven
07 Elysium
08 paradise
09 Shangri-La
12 Garden of Eden
13 heaven on earth

**Utopian**
05 dream, ideal
07 Elysian, perfect, wishful

08 fanciful, illusory, romantic
09 fantastic, visionary
10 chimerical, idealistic, unworkable
11 impractical

**utter**
03 say
04 tell
05 sheer, sound, speak, stark, state, total, voice
06 arrant, entire, reveal
07 declare, deliver, divulge, express, perfect
08 absolute, announce, complete, positive, proclaim, vocalize
09 downright, enunciate, out-and-out, pronounce, verbalize
10 articulate, consummate
11 unqualified
13 thoroughgoing

**utterance**
04 word
06 remark, speech
09 statement
10 expression
11 declaration, enunciation
12 announcement, articulation
13 pronouncement

**utterly**
06 wholly
07 totally
08 entirely
09 downright, perfectly
10 absolutely, completely

**U-turn**
08 reversal
09 about-face, volte-face

**vacancy**
03 job
04 post, room
05 place
07 opening
08 position
09 situation

**vacant**
04 free, void
05 blank, empty, inane
06 absent, dreamy, unused
07 deadpan, vacuous
08 deserted, not in use, unfilled
09 abandoned, available
10 unoccupied, unthinking
11 inattentive, uninhabited
12 absent-minded
14 expressionless

**vacate**
04 quit
05 leave
08 evacuate, withdraw

**vacation**
04 rest
05 break, leave
06 recess
07 holiday, time off
08 furlough

**vacillate**
04 sway
05 waver
08 hesitate
09 fluctuate, oscillate, temporize
12 shilly-shally, tergiversate

**vacillating**
08 hesitant, wavering
09 uncertain
10 irresolute

**vacillation**
08 wavering
09 hesitancy
10 hesitation, indecision
11 fluctuation, inconstancy
12 irresolution
13 temporization
14 tergiversation

**vacuity**
04 void
05 space
06 apathy, vacuum
07 inanity
09 blankness, emptiness

**vacuous**
04 idle, void
05 blank, empty, inane
06 stupid, vacant
08 unfilled
09 apathetic, incurious

**vacuum**
04 void
05 chasm, space
06 lacuna
09 emptiness
11 nothingness

**vagabond**
03 bum
04 hobo
05 nomad, rover, tramp
06 beggar, rascal
07 migrant, outcast, vagrant
08 wanderer, wayfarer
09 itinerant
10 down-and-out

**vagary**
04 whim
05 fancy, humor, quirk
06 notion, whimsy
07 caprice

**vagrancy**
08 nomadism
09 traveling, wandering
10 itinerancy
12 homelessness, rootlessness

**vagrant**
04 hobo
05 tramp
06 beggar, roving
07 drifter, gangrel, nomadic
08 homeless, rootless, vagabond
09 itinerant, shiftless, wandering
12 rolling stone

**vague**
03 dim, lax
04 hazy
05 faint, foggy, fuzzy, loose, misty, rough
06 unsure, woolly
07 blurred, evasive, inexact, obscure, shadowy, unclear
08 nebulous
09 ambiguous, amorphous, imprecise, uncertain, undefined, unfocused
10 ill-defined, indefinite, indistinct, out of focus
13 indeterminate

**vaguely**
05 dimly
07 faintly
08 slightly, vacantly
09 inexactly, obscurely
11 imprecisely
14 absent-mindedly

**vagueness**
07 dimness
08 haziness
09 ambiguity, faintness, fuzziness, obscurity
10 woolliness
11 imprecision, uncertainty

**vain**
04 idle
05 empty, proud
06 futile, hollow
07 haughty, stuck-up, useless
08 abortive, arrogant
09 bigheaded, conceited, fruitless, pointless, worthless
10 groundless, swaggering
11 egotistical, pretentious, swellheaded
12 narcissistic, unproductive
13 high and mighty, self-important

❏ **in vain**
09 to no avail, uselessly
11 fruitlessly
14 unsuccessfully

**valediction**
07 goodbye, sendoff
08 farewell
11 leave-taking

**valedictory**
04 last
05 final
07 parting
08 farewell
14 farewell speech

**valet**
03 man
10 manservant
14 valet de chambre

**valetudinarian**
05 frail
06 feeble, infirm, sickly, weakly
07 invalid
08 delicate, neurotic

**valiant**
04 bold
05 brave
06 heroic, plucky
07 gallant, staunch
08 fearless, intrepid, valorous
10 courageous

**valid**
04 good, just
05 legal, sound
06 cogent, lawful, proper
07 logical, weighty
08 bona fide, credible
09 authentic
10 legitimate, reasonable
11 justifiable, well-founded

**validate**
06 attest, ratify
07 certify, confirm, endorse
08 legalize
10 underwrite
12 authenticate, substantiate

**validity**
05 force, logic, point
07 cogency, grounds
08 legality
09 soundness, substance
10 lawfulness, legitimacy

**valley**
03 cwm
04 dale, dell, glen, vale
05 basin, gorge, gulch, gully
06 canyon, cirque, hollow, strath

**valorous**
04 bold
05 brave
06 heroic, plucky
07 doughty, gallant, valiant
08 fearless, intrepid, stalwart
10 courageous, mettlesome

**valor**
06 mettle, spirit
07 bravery, courage, heroism
09 fortitude, gallantry
11 intrepidity

**valuable**
06 costly, prized, useful, worthy
07 helpful
08 fruitful, precious
09 expensive, important, priceless, treasured
10 beneficial, profitable, worthwhile
12 advantageous, constructive

**valuation**
06 survey
08 estimate
10 assessment, evaluation
12 appraisement

**value**
03 use
04 cost, gain, good, rate
05 merit, price, prize, worth
06 admire, assess, esteem, ethics, morals, profit, survey
07 benefit, cherish, utility
08 appraise, estimate, evaluate, hold dear, treasure
09 advantage, standards
10 appreciate, importance, principles, usefulness
12 desirability, significance
15 set great store by

**valued**
04 dear
05 loved
06 prized
07 beloved
08 esteemed
09 cherished, treasured
14 highly regarded

**van**
04 lead
05 truck, wagon
06 leader
07 trailer
08 carriage, vanguard

**vanguard**
03 van
04 fore, lead
05 front
06 leader
09 forefront, front line, spearhead

**vanish**
04 exit, fade
06 depart, die out
07 fade out
08 dissolve, evanesce, fade away, melt away
09 disappear, fizzle out

**vanity**
04 airs
05 pride
07 conceit, egotism
08 futility, idleness, self-love
09 arrogance
10 narcissism, pretension, triviality
11 affectation, ostentation, self-conceit

**vanquish**
04 beat, rout
05 crush, quell

06 defeat, master, subdue
07 conquer, repress
08 confound, overcome
09 overwhelm, subjugate

**vapid**
04 dull, flat, limp, weak
05 banal, bland, stale, trite
06 boring, jejune, watery
07 insipid, tedious, vacuous
08 lifeless
09 colorless
10 wishy-washy

**vaporous**
04 fumy, vain
05 foggy, misty
06 steamy
07 gaseous
10 chimerical
13 insubstantial

**vapor**
03 fog
04 damp, haze, mist
05 fumes, smoke, steam
06 breath
07 exhaust

**variable**
06 factor, fickle, fitful, uneven
07 mutable, protean
08 flexible, shifting, wavering
09 parameter
10 changeable, inconstant
11 chameleonic, fluctuating
13 unpredictable

**variance**
04 odds
06 strife
07 discord, dissent
08 conflict, division
10 difference, disharmony, dissension, divergence
12 disagreement

**variant**
07 derived, deviant
08 modified
09 different, divergent
11 alternative

**variation**
06 change
07 novelty, variety
09 departure, deviation
10 alteration, difference, inflection, modulation
11 discrepancy, fluctuation

**varied**
05 mixed
06 motley, sundry
07 diverse, various
08 assorted
09 different
12 multifarious

**variegated**
13 heterogeneous, miscellaneous

**variegated**
06 motley
07 dappled, marbled, mottled
08 speckled, streaked

**variety**
04 kind, make, sort, type
05 brand, breed, class, range
06 medley, strain
07 mixture, species
08 category
09 diversity, potpourri, variation
10 assortment, collection, difference, miscellany
12 multiplicity
13 dissimilarity

**various**
04 many
05 mixed
06 motley, unlike, varied
07 diverse, several, varying
08 assorted, distinct
09 different, differing, disparate
10 dissimilar, variegated
11 diversified
13 heterogeneous, miscellaneous

**varnish**
03 lac
05 glaze, gloss, japan, resin
06 enamel, polish, veneer
07 coating, lacquer, shellac

**vary**
05 alter, clash
06 change, depart, differ, modify
07 diverge, inflect, reorder
08 be at odds, disagree, modulate
09 alternate, diversify, fluctuate, permutate, transform
12 metamorphose

**vase**
03 jar, jug, urn
04 ewer
06 hydria, vessel
07 amphora, pitcher

**vassal**
04 serf
05 liege, slave
06 thrall
07 bondman, subject, villein
08 bondsman
11 bondservant

**vassalage**
07 bondage, serfdom, slavery
08 thraldom
09 servitude
10 dependence, villeinage

11 subjugation

**vast**
04 huge
07 immense, massive
08 colossal, enormous, far-flung, gigantic
09 boundless, extensive, limitless, monstrous
10 monumental
12 immeasurable

**vat**
03 tub
04 kier, tank
06 barrel, vessel

**vault**
04 arch, jump, roof, span, tomb
05 bound, clear, crypt
06 cavern, cellar, hurdle
08 leapfrog
09 mausoleum
10 depository, repository, strong room, wine cellar

**vaunt**
04 brag, crow
05 boast, swank
06 flaunt, parade
07 exult in, show off, trumpet
15 blow your own horn

**veer**
04 tack, turn
05 sheer, shift, swing, wheel
06 change, swerve
07 deviate, diverge

**vegetable**

➤ *Names of vegetables*:
03 pea, yam
04 bean, beet, corn, kale, leek, okra, spud
05 chard, cress, onion, savoy
06 carrot, celery, cowpea, endive, fennel, garlic, lentil, pepper, potato, radish, squash, turnip
07 cabbage, chicory, lettuce, parsnip, pumpkin, salsify, shallot, soybean, spinach, wax bean
08 broccoli, celeriac, cucumber, eggplant, kohlrabi, mushroom, pole bean, rutabaga, scallion, zucchini
09 artichoke, asparagus, broad bean, pinto bean, red pepper, sweet corn
10 butter bean, kidney bean, red cabbage, watercress
11 cauliflower, green pepper, sweet potato
12 black-eyed pea, savoy cabbage

14 Brussels sprout, globe artichoke
15 vegetable marrow
➤ See also FOOD

**vegetate**
07 moulder
08 go to seed, languish, stagnate
10 degenerate
11 deteriorate

**vegetation**
05 flora, trees
06 plants
07 flowers, herbage, verdure
08 greenery

**vehemence**
04 fire, heat, zeal
05 ardor, force, power, verve
06 energy, fervor, warmth
07 passion, urgency
08 emphasis, fervency, strength, violence
09 animation, intensity
10 enthusiasm

**vehement**
06 ardent, fervid, fierce, heated, strong, urgent
07 earnest, fervent, intense, violent, zealous
08 animated, forceful, forcible, powerful, spirited
10 passionate
11 impassioned
12 enthusiastic

**vehicle**
05 means, organ
06 agency, medium
07 channel
09 mechanism
10 conveyance, instrument
14 transportation

➤ *Types of vehicle*:
02 RV
03 bus, cab, car, gig, jet, SUV, van
04 bike, boat, dray, hack, pram, ship, sled, tank, taxi, tram, trap
05 blimp, coach, cycle, moped, plane, sulky, train, truck, wagon
06 camper, hansom, landau, litter, sledge, sleigh, surrey, tandem, troika
07 balloon, bicycle, bobsled, chariot, dogcart, hackney, minibus, omnibus, phaeton, Pullman, scooter, shuttle, sleeper, tractor, trailer
08 airplane, barouche, brougham, cable car, forklift,

jumbo jet, rickshaw, snowplow, toboggan, tricycle, wagon-lit
09 ambulance, bobsleigh, dirigible, motorbike, streetcar
10 motorcycle, post chaise, sedan chair, spacecraft, stagecoach, wheelchair
11 sleeping car, steamroller
12 space shuttle
➢ See also AIRCRAFT; BICYCLE; BOAT; CAR; MOTOR; SHIP

---

► *International Vehicle Registrations*:
01 **A** (Austria), **B** (Belgium), **C** (Cuba), **D** (Germany), **E** (Spain), **F** (France), **H** (Hungary), **I** (Italy), **J** (Japan), **K** (Cambodia), **L** (Luxembourg), **M** (Malta), **N** (Norway), **P** (Portugal), **S** (Sweden), **T** (Thailand), **V** (Vatican City), **Z** (Zambia)
02 **AL** (Albania), **BD** (Bangladesh), **BG** (Bulgaria), **BH** (Belize), **BR** (Brazil), **BS** (The Bahamas), **CH** (Switzerland), **CI** (Côte d'Ivoire), **CL** (Sri Lanka), **CO** (Colombia), **CR** (Costa Rica), **CY** (Cyprus), **CZ** (Czech Republic), **DK** (Denmark), **DY** (Benin), **DZ** (Algeria), **EC** (Ecuador), **ES** (El Salvador), **ET** (Egypt), **FL** (Liechtenstein), **FR** (Faroe Islands), **GB** (Great Britain), **GE** (Georgia), **GH** (Ghana), **GR** (Greece), **HK** (Hong Kong), **HR** (Croatia), **IL** (Israel), **IR** (Iran), **IS** (Iceland), **JA** (Jamaica), **KS** (Kyrgyzstan), **KZ** (Kazakhzstan), **LB** (Liberia), **LS** (Lesotho), **LT** (Lithuania), **LV** (Latvia), **MA** (Morocco), **MC** (Monaco), **MK** (Macedonia), **MS** (Mauritius), **MW** (Malawi), **NA** (Netherlands Antilles), **NL** (Netherlands), **NZ** (New Zealand), **PA** (Panama), **PE** (Peru), **PK** (Pakistan), **PL** (Poland), **PY** (Paraguay), **RA** (Argentina), **RB** (Botswana), **RC** (Taiwan), **RH** (Haiti), **RI** (Indonesia), **RL** (Lebanon), **RM** (Madagascar), **RN** (Niger), **RO** (Romania), **RP** (Philippines), **RU** (Burundi), **SD** (Swaziland), **SK** (Slovakia), **SN** (Senegal), **SU** (Belarus), **SY** (Seychelles), **TG** (Togo), **TJ** (Tajikistan), **TM** (Turkmenistan), **TN** (Tunisia), **TR** (Turkey), **TT** (Trinidad and Tobago), **UA** (Ukraine), **VN** (Vietnam), **WD** (Dominica), **WG** (Grenada), **WL** (St Lucia), **WS** (Samoa), **WV** (St Vincent and the Grenadines), **YU** (Yugoslavia), **YV** (Venezuela), **ZA** (South Africa), **ZW** (Zimbabwe)
03 **ADN** (Yemen), **AFG** (Afghanistan), **AND** (Andorra), **AUS** (Australia), **BDS** (Barbados), **BIH** (Bosnia-Herzegovina), **BRN** (Bahrain), **BRU** (Brunei), **BUR** (Myanmar), **CDN** (Canada), **DOM** (Dominican Republic), **EAK** (Kenya), **EAT** (Tanzania), **EAU** (Uganda), **EST** (Estonia), **ETH** (Ethiopia), **FIN** (Finland), **FJI** (Fiji), **GBA** (Alderney), **GBG** (Guernsey), **GBJ** (Jersey), **GBM** (Isle of Man), **GBZ** (Gibraltar), **GCA** (Guatemala), **GUY** (Guyana), **HKJ** (Jordan), **IND** (India), **IRL** (Ireland), **IRQ** (Iraq), **KWT** (Kuwait), **LAO** (Laos), **LAR** (Libya), **MAL** (Malaysia), **MEX** (Mexico), **NAM** (Namibia), **NIC** (Nicaragua), **PNG** (Papua New Guinea), **RCA** (Central African Republic), **RCB** (Congo), **RCH** (Chile), **RIM** (Mauritania), **RMM** (Mali), **ROK** (Korea), **ROU** (Uruguay), **RSM** (San Marino), **RUS** (Russia), **RWA** (Rwanda), **SGP** (Singapore), **SLO** (Slovenia), **SME** (Suriname), **SYR** (Syria), **USA** (United States of America), **WAG** (The Gambia), **WAL** (Sierra Leone), **WAN** (Nigeria), **ZRE** (Democratic Republic of Congo)

**veil**
04 film, hide, mask
05 blind, cloak, cover, shade
06 canopy, mantle, purdah, screen, shadow, shroud
07 conceal, curtain, obscure
08 covering, disguise
10 camouflage

**vein**
04 lode, mode, mood, seam
05 humor, style, tenor
06 strain, streak
07 stratum
11 blood vessel, disposition, inclination

---

► *Veins and arteries*:
05 aorta, iliac, renal
06 portal, radial, tibial
07 carotid, femoral, gastric, hepatic, jugular, saphena
08 axillary, brachial, temporal
09 pulmonary

**veined**
05 jaspe
07 marbled
08 streaked

**velocity**
04 pace, rate
05 speed

**venal**
07 buyable, corrupt
08 bribable, grafting
10 simoniacal
11 corruptible

**vendetta**
04 feud
06 enmity
07 quarrel, rivalry
08 bad blood
09 blood feud

**vendor**
06 hawker, seller, trader
07 peddler
08 merchant, salesman, supplier

**veneer**
04 mask, show
05 front, gloss, guise, layer
06 façade, finish
07 coating, display, surface
08 covering, pretense

**venerable**
04 aged, wise
06 august
07 honored, revered
08 esteemed
09 dignified, respected

**venerate**
05 adore, honor
06 esteem, revere

07 respect, worship

**veneration**
03 awe
06 esteem
07 respect, worship
08 devotion
09 adoration, reverence

**vengeance**
07 revenge
08 reprisal, requital
11 retaliation, retribution

❏**with a vengeance**
09 furiously, like crazy, violently
10 forcefully, powerfully,
    vigorously
11 to the utmost
13 energetically

**vengeful**
08 avenging, punitive, spiteful
09 rancorous
10 revengeful, vindictive
11 retaliatory, retributive

**venial**
05 minor
06 slight
09 excusable
10 forgivable, pardonable

**venom**
04 hate
05 spite, toxin
06 enmity, malice, poison,
    rancor
07 ill will
08 acrimony
09 animosity, hostility, virulence
11 malevolence

**venomous**
05 fatal, toxic
06 bitter, deadly, lethal
07 noxious, vicious
08 spiteful, virulent
09 malicious, malignant,
    poisonous, rancorous
10 malevolent, vindictive

**vent**
03 air, gap
04 duct, emit, hole
05 utter, voice
06 let out, outlet
07 express, passage, release
08 aperture

**ventilate**
03 air
04 cool
06 aerate, debate
07 discuss, express, freshen

**venture**
04 dare, risk
05 fling, stake, wager

06 chance, gamble, hazard
07 advance, exploit, imperil,
    presume, project, suggest
08 endanger, endeavor, make
    bold
09 adventure, speculate,
    volunteer
10 enterprise, put forward
11 speculation, undertaking

**venturesome**
04 bold
06 daring, plucky
08 fearless, intrepid
09 audacious, daredevil,
    dauntless
11 adventurous
12 enterprising

**veracious**
04 true
06 honest
07 factual, genuine, precise
08 accurate, credible, truthful
15 straightforward

**veracity**
05 truth
06 candor
07 honesty, probity
08 accuracy
09 frankness, precision,
    rectitude
10 exactitude
12 truthfulness

**verbal**
04 oral, said
05 vocal
06 spoken
10 linguistic

**verbatim**
07 closely, exactly
09 literally, precisely
11 to the letter, word for word

**verbiage**
08 pleonasm
09 prolixity, verbosity,
    wordiness
11 periphrasis
14 circumlocution

**verbose**
05 windy, wordy
06 prolix
07 diffuse
09 garrulous
10 long-winded, loquacious,
    pleonastic
12 periphrastic
14 circumlocutory

**verbosity**
08 verbiage

09 garrulity, logorrhea,
    loquacity, prolixity,
    windiness, wordiness
11 diffuseness
14 long-windedness

**verdant**
04 lush
05 fresh, green, leafy, virid
11 viridescent

**verdict**
06 ruling
07 finding, opinion
08 decision, judgment,
    sentence
10 assessment, conclusion
12 adjudication

**verdure**
05 grass
07 foliage, herbage, pasture
08 greenery, verdancy, viridity
09 greenness
12 viridescence

**verge**
03 rim
04 brim, edge
05 brink, limit
06 border, edging, margin
08 boundary
09 threshold

❏**verge on**
08 approach, border on
10 tend toward
11 come close to

**verification**
05 proof
10 validation
11 attestation
12 confirmation
13 corroboration
14 authentication,
    substantiation

**verify**
05 prove
06 attest
07 bear out, confirm
08 accredit, validate
11 corroborate
12 authenticate, substantiate

**verisimilitude**
09 semblance
10 likeliness
11 credibility, ring of truth
12 authenticity, plausibility

**verity**
05 truth
08 validity, veracity
09 actuality, soundness
12 authenticity, truthfulness

**vernacular**
05 idiom, lingo, local
06 common, jargon, native, speech, tongue, vulgar
07 dialect, popular
08 informal, language, parlance
10 colloquial, indigenous

**versatile**
08 all-round, flexible, variable
09 adaptable, all-around, many-sided
10 adjustable, all-purpose
12 multifaceted, multipurpose

**verse**
05 meter, rhyme
06 jingle, poetry, stanza
07 strophe
08 doggerel

**versed**
04 read
07 learned, skilled
08 familiar, seasoned
09 competent, practiced
10 conversant, proficient
11 experienced
13 knowledgeable

**versifier**
04 poet
06 rhymer, verser
07 poetess, rhymist
09 poetaster, rhymester

**version**
04 form, kind, type
05 model, style
06 design, report
07 account, reading, variant
09 rendering
10 adaptation, paraphrase
14 interpretation

**vertex**
04 acme, apex, peak
06 apogee, height, summit, zenith
08 pinnacle
12 highest point

**vertical**
05 erect, on end, sheer
07 upright
10 straight up, upstanding
13 perpendicular

**vertigo**
09 dizziness, giddiness
15 lightheadedness

**verve**
03 zip
04 brio, dash, élan, life
05 force, gusto, vigor
06 energy, fervor, pizazz, relish, spirit

07 pizazz, sparkle
08 vitality, vivacity
09 animation
10 enthusiasm, liveliness

**very**
04 bare, mere, pure, true
05 exact, sheer, truly, utter
06 actual, really, simple
07 acutely, genuine, perfect
08 selfsame, suitable
09 exceeding, extremely, identical
10 remarkably, uncommonly
11 appropriate, exceedingly
12 particularly
13 exceptionally

**vessel**
03 jar, jug, pot
04 bark, boat, bowl, ship
05 craft
06 barque, holder
09 container
10 receptacle

**vest**
05 endow, grant
06 bestow, bodice, confer, supply, weskit
07 empower
08 sanction

**vestibule**
04 hall
05 foyer, lobby, porch
07 portico
08 anteroom, entrance
12 entrance hall

**vestige**
04 hint, mark, sign
05 print, scrap, token, touch, trace, track, whiff
06 relics
07 glimmer, inkling, remains, remnant, residue
09 remainder, suspicion
10 impression, indication

**vestigial**
07 reduced
09 remaining, surviving
10 incomplete
11 rudimentary, undeveloped

**vestment**

► *Types of clerical vestment:*
03 alb
04 cope, cowl, hood
05 cotta, ephod, frock, habit, miter, scarf, stole
06 mantle, rochet, tippet, wimple
07 biretta, cassock, pallium, soutane, tunicle

08 chasuble, dalmatic, scapular, skullcap, surplice, yarmulka
09 dog collar
10 Geneva gown
11 Geneva bands
14 clerical collar
➤ See also RELIGION

**vet**
05 audit, check
06 review, survey
07 examine, inspect, veteran
08 appraise, check out
10 scrutinize
11 investigate
12 veterinarian

**veteran**
03 old, pro
06 stager
07 old hand
08 old-timer, seasoned, war horse
09 ex-soldier, old stager
10 past master
11 experienced, long-serving
13 battle-scarred

**veto**
03 ban
05 block
06 forbid, reject
07 embargo, rule out
08 disallow, prohibit, turn down
09 interdict, proscribe
11 prohibition
12 proscription

**vex**
04 fret
05 annoy, upset, worry
06 bother, harass, hassle, needle, pester, put out
07 agitate, disturb, perturb, provoke, torment, trouble
08 distress, irritate
09 aggravate
10 exasperate

**vexation**
04 bind, bore, pain
05 anger, pique, upset, worry
07 chagrin
08 headache, irritant, nuisance
09 annoyance
11 aggravation, frustration
12 exasperation
15 thorn in the flesh

**vexatious**
05 pesky
06 trying
07 irksome, nagging, teasing
08 annoying, worrying
09 provoking, worrisome
10 bothersome, irritating, tormenting

**vexed**
11 aggravating, infuriating, troublesome
12 exasperating

**vexed**
04 moot
05 irate, riled, upset
06 miffed, peeved, put out
07 annoyed, debated, hassled, nettled, ruffled, worried
08 agitated, bothered, disputed, harassed, provoked, troubled
09 contested, difficult, disturbed, flustered, in dispute, irritated, perplexed
10 aggravated, distressed
11 exasperated

**viable**
08 feasible, operable, possible, workable
10 achievable
11 practicable, sustainable

**vibes**
04 aura, feel
08 ambience, feelings
10 atmosphere, vibrations

**vibrant**
05 vivid
06 bright, lively
07 dynamic
08 animated, electric, spirited, striking, vigorous
09 brilliant, energetic, sparkling, vivacious
12 electrifying

**vibrate**
05 shake, swing, throb
06 quiver, shiver
07 pulsate, resound, tremble
08 resonate
11 reverberate

**vibration**
05 pulse, throb
06 quiver, tremor
07 frisson, shaking, shudder
09 pulsation, resonance, throbbing, trembling
10 resounding
13 reverberation

**vicar**
06 cleric, parson, pastor, priest, rector
08 chaplain, minister
09 clergyman
11 clergywoman

**vicarious**
06 acting
08 indirect
09 surrogate
10 empathetic, secondhand
11 substituted

**vice**
03 sin
04 evil, flaw
05 fault
06 defect, foible
07 blemish, failing
08 bad habit, iniquity, weakness
09 depravity, evildoing
10 degeneracy, immorality, wickedness, wrongdoing
12 besetting sin, imperfection
13 transgression

**vice president**

► *Names of U.S. Vice Presidents:*
04 **Burr** (Aaron), **Bush** (George), **Ford** (Gerald), **Gore** (Albert), **King** (William)
05 **Adams** (John), **Agnew** (Spiro), **Dawes** (Charles), **Gerry** (Elbridge), **Nixon** (Richard), **Tyler** (John)
06 **Arthur** (Chester), **Cheney** (Richard), **Colfax** (Schuyler), **Curtis** (Charles), **Dallas** (George), **Garner** (John Nance), **Hamlin** (Hannibal), **Hobart** (Garret), **Morton** (Levi), **Quayle** (Dan), **Wilson** (Henry)
07 **Barkley** (Alben), **Calhoun** (John Caldwell), **Clinton** (George), **Johnson** (Andrew), **Johnson** (Lyndon), **Johnson** (Richard), **Mondale** (Walter), **Sherman** (James), **Wallace** (Henry), **Wheeler** (William), **Woodrow** (Wilson)
08 **Coolidge** (Calvin), **Fillmore** (Millard), **Humphrey** (Hubert), **Marshall** (Thomas), **Tompkins** (Daniel), **Van Buren** (Martin)
09 **Fairbanks** (Charles), **Hendricks** (Thomas), **Jefferson** (Thomas), **Roosevelt** (Theodore), **Stevenson** (Adlai)
11 **Rockefeller** (Nelson)
12 **Breckinridge** (John)

**vice versa**
09 inversely
10 oppositely
12 contrariwise

**vicinity**
08 district, environs, locality

12 neighborhood, surroundings

**vicious**
04 mean, vile
05 catty, cruel, nasty
06 bitchy, brutal, fierce, savage
07 heinous, violent
08 depraved, spiteful, venomous, virulent
09 barbarous, ferocious, malicious
10 malevolent, vindictive

**viciousness**
05 spite, venom
06 malice, rancor
07 cruelty
08 ferocity, savagery
09 brutality, depravity, virulence
10 bitchiness
12 spitefulness

**vicissitude**
05 shift, twist
08 mutation
09 deviation, variation
10 alteration, revolution
11 alternation, fluctuation

**victim**
04 dupe, prey
06 martyr, quarry, sucker
07 fall guy
08 casualty, fatality, sufferer
09 sacrifice, scapegoat

**victimize**
05 bully, cheat, trick
06 pick on, prey on
09 persecute
15 take advantage of

**victor**
05 champ, first
06 top dog, winner
08 champion
09 conqueror
11 prize winner
12 gold medalist
15 gold-medal winner

**victorious**
05 first
07 winning
08 champion, unbeaten
10 conquering, successful
12 prize-winning

**victory**
03 win
07 mastery, success, triumph
08 conquest
11 subjugation, superiority

**victuals**
04 chow, eats, food, grub, nosh
05 bread
06 stores, viands

**vie**
07 aliment, edibles, rations
08 eatables, supplies
10 provisions, sustenance
11 comestibles

**vie**
05 fight, rival
06 strive
07 compete, contend, contest

**view**
03 see
04 idea, look, scan
05 angle, judge, scene, sight, study, vista, watch
06 belief, gaze at, look at, notion, regard, review, sketch, survey, vision
07 account, examine, feeling, glimpse, inspect, observe, opinion, outlook, picture, thought, witness
08 attitude, consider, judgment, panorama, perceive, portrait, prospect, scrutiny
09 landscape, portrayal, sentiment, spectacle
10 assessment, conviction, impression, inspection, perception, scrutinize
11 contemplate, examination, observation, perspective
13 contemplation, range of vision

**❏in view of**
11 considering
13 bearing in mind

**viewer**
07 watcher
08 observer, onlooker
09 spectator

**viewpoint**
05 angle, slant
06 stance
08 attitude, position
10 standpoint
11 perspective

**vigil**
05 watch
07 lookout
08 stakeout

**vigilance**
07 caution
09 alertness
11 observation, wakefulness
12 watchfulness
13 attentiveness

**vigilant**
05 alert, aware
08 cautious, watchful
09 observant, wide-awake
11 on your guard

12 on the lookout

**vigorous**
05 brisk, lusty, sound, stout, tough, vital
06 active, lively, robust, strong
07 dynamic, healthy, intense
08 animated, athletic, forceful, forcible, powerful, spirited
09 effective, energetic, strenuous
11 flourishing, full-blooded

**vigorously**
07 briskly, eagerly, lustily
08 heartily, strongly
10 forcefully, powerfully
11 strenuously
13 energetically

**vigor**
03 pep, zip
04 brio, dash
05 force, gusto, might, oomph, power, verve
06 energy, health, spirit
07 potency, stamina
08 activity, dynamism, strength, vitality, vivacity

**vile**
03 bad, low
04 base, evil, foul, mean
05 nasty
06 impure, putrid, rotten, sinful, wicked
07 corrupt, debased, noxious, vicious
08 depraved, horrible, wretched
09 appalling, degrading, loathsome, miserable, obnoxious, offensive, repugnant, repulsive, revolting, sickening
10 degenerate, despicable, disgusting, iniquitous, nauseating, unpleasant
11 disgraceful, distasteful
12 contemptible, disagreeable

**vileness**
04 evil
07 outrage
08 baseness, foulness, meanness, ugliness
09 depravity, profanity
10 corruption, degeneracy

**vilification**
05 abuse
07 calumny
09 aspersion, contumely, criticism, invective
10 defamation, scurrility
11 denigration, mudslinging
12 calumniation, vituperation
13 disparagement

**vilify**
04 slam
05 abuse, decry, smear
06 berate, debase, defame, malign, revile
07 asperse, slander, traduce
08 bad-mouth, denounce
09 denigrate, disparage
10 calumniate, stigmatize, vituperate

**village**
04 burg
06 hamlet
09 community
10 settlement

**villain**
05 baddy, devil, knave, rogue
06 rascal, wretch
08 criminal, evildoer
09 miscreant, reprobate, scoundrel, wrongdoer
10 malefactor

**villainous**
03 bad
04 evil, vile
06 sinful, wicked
07 debased, heinous, vicious
08 criminal, fiendish
09 nefarious, notorious
10 degenerate, iniquitous
11 disgraceful, opprobrious

**villainy**
03 sin
04 vice
05 crime
07 badness, knavery, roguery
08 atrocity, baseness, iniquity
09 depravity, rascality, turpitude
10 wickedness
11 criminality, delinquency

**vindicate**
06 acquit, uphold, verify
07 absolve, justify, warrant
08 advocate, champion
09 exonerate
11 corroborate

**vindication**
07 apology, defense
11 exoneration, extenuation
13 justification
14 substantiation

**vindictive**
08 spiteful, vengeful, venomous
09 malicious, rancorous
10 revengeful
11 unforgiving

**vintage**
03 era, old
04 best, crop, fine, rare, ripe, time, type, wine, year

**violate**
05 epoch, model, prime
06 choice, mature, origin, period, select
07 classic, harvest, quality, supreme, veteran
08 enduring, superior
09 gathering, venerable
11 high-quality

**violate**
04 rape
05 break, flout, wreck
06 breach, defile, invade, molest, ravish
07 debauch, disobey, disrupt, infract, outrage, profane
08 infringe
09 desecrate
10 contravene, transgress
13 interfere with

**violation**
05 abuse
06 breach
07 offense, outrage
08 trespass
09 sacrilege
10 defilement, spoliation
11 desecration, profanation
12 infringement
13 contravention, transgression

**violence**
04 fury
05 force, might, power
06 frenzy, tumult
07 cruelty, passion
08 ferocity, fighting, savagery, severity, strength, wildness
09 bloodshed, brutality, roughness, vehemence
10 aggression, fierceness, turbulence
11 hostilities

**violent**
04 wild
05 acute, cruel, fiery, great, harsh, rough, sharp
06 brutal, fierce, savage, strong
07 extreme, furious, intense, riotous, vicious
08 forceful, forcible, maddened, powerful, vehement
09 ferocious, hotheaded, impetuous, murderous, turbulent
10 aggressive, passionate, tumultuous
11 destructive, devastating
12 bloodthirsty, excruciating

**VIP**
04 star
06 bigwig
07 big shot, magnate, notable

08 luminary
09 big cheese, celebrity, dignitary, personage

**virago**
04 fury
05 scold, shrew, vixen
06 dragon, gorgon, tartar
07 hellcat
08 battle-ax, harridan
09 battle-axe, termagant, Xanthippe

**virgin**
03 new
04 girl, pure
05 fresh
06 chaste, intact, maiden, modest, vestal
08 celibate, maidenly, spotless, unspoilt, virginal
09 stainless, undefiled, unspoiled, untouched
10 immaculate

**virginal**
04 pure
05 fresh, snowy, white
06 chaste, vestal, virgin
08 maidenly, pristine, spotless
09 undefiled, untouched
10 immaculate
11 uncorrupted, undisturbed

**virginity**
06 purity, virtue
08 chastity
10 chasteness, maidenhood

**virile**
05 lusty, macho, manly
06 potent, strong
08 forceful, muscular, vigorous
09 masculine, strapping
10 red-blooded

**virility**
05 vigor
07 manhood, potency
08 machismo
09 manliness
11 masculinity

**virtual**
07 implied
08 implicit, in effect
09 effective, essential, potential, practical
11 prospective
12 in all but name

**virtually**
06 almost, nearly
08 as good as, in effect
09 in essence
10 more or less
11 effectively

**virtue**
04 plus
05 asset, honor, merit, worth
06 credit
07 benefit, honesty, justice, probity, quality
08 goodness, morality, strength
09 advantage, rectitude
10 excellence, worthiness
14 high-mindedness

➤ *The seven principal virtues*:
04 hope
05 faith
07 charity, justice
08 prudence
09 fortitude
10 temperance

❏**by virtue of**
07 by way of, owing to
08 by dint of, thanks to
09 because of, by means of
11 on account of

**virtuosity**
05 éclat, flair, skill
06 finish, polish
07 bravura, finesse, mastery
08 artistry, wizardry
09 expertise
10 brilliance

**virtuoso**
06 expert, genius, master
07 maestro, prodigy, skilful
08 dazzling, masterly, skillful
09 brilliant, excellent

**virtuous**
05 moral
06 decent, honest, worthy
07 angelic, ethical, upright
08 innocent
09 exemplary, honorable, righteous
10 upstanding
11 clean-living, respectable

**virulence**
05 spite, venom
06 hatred, malice, poison, rancor, spleen
07 vitriol
08 acrimony, toxicity
10 antagonism, malignancy, resentment
11 malevolence

**virulent**
05 fatal, toxic
06 bitter, deadly, lethal, severe
07 extreme, intense, vicious
08 spiteful, venomous
09 malicious, malignant, poisonous, vitriolic

**viscera**
10  malevolent, pernicious, vindictive

**viscera**
04  guts
06  bowels, vitals
07  innards, insides
08  entrails
10  intestines

**viscous**
05  gluey, gooey, gummy, tacky
06  mucous, sticky, viscid
09  glutinous
10  gelatinous
12  mucilaginous

**visible**
04  open
05  clear, overt, plain
06  patent
07  evident, exposed, obvious
08  apparent, manifest, palpable
10  noticeable, observable
11  conspicuous, discernible, perceivable, perceptible
15  distinguishable

**vision**
04  idea, view
05  dream, ghost, image, sight
06  mirage, seeing, wraith
07  chimera, fantasy, insight, phantom, picture, specter
08  daydream, eyesight
09  foresight, intuition
10  apparition, conception, perception
11  imagination, mental image
13  hallucination, mental picture
14  farsightedness
15  optical illusion

**visionary**
04  seer
06  dreamy, mystic, unreal
07  dreamer, prophet, Utopian
08  fanciful, idealist, illusory, quixotic, romantic, theorist
09  fantasist, prophetic
10  daydreamer, Don Quixote, farsighted, idealistic, ivory-tower, perceptive
11  impractical, unrealistic

**visit**
04  call, stay, stop
05  curse, pop in, smite
06  call in, call on, drop by, look in, plague, punish, stop by
07  afflict, sojourn, trouble
08  drop in on, go and see, go over to, stay with
09  excursion
10  go around to
13  spend time with

**visitation**
05  trial, visit
06  blight, ordeal
10  affliction, appearance, inspection, punishment
11  catastrophe, examination
13  manifestation

**visitor**
05  guest
06  caller
07  company, tourist
08  traveler
10  vacationer

**vista**
04  view
05  scene
07  outlook
08  panorama, prospect
11  perspective

**visual**
05  optic
06  ocular
07  optical, visible
10  observable
11  discernible, perceptible

**visualize**
03  see
07  imagine, picture
08  conceive, envisage

**vital**
03  key
05  alive, basic
06  lively, living, urgent
07  crucial, dynamic, vibrant
08  animated, critical, decisive, forceful, spirited, vigorous
09  energetic, essential, necessary, vivacious
10  imperative, life-giving, quickening
11  fundamental, significant
12  invigorating, life-and-death
13  indispensable

**vitality**
04  life, zest
05  get-up, oomph, vigor
06  energy, pizazz, spirit
07  pizzazz, sparkle, stamina
08  strength, vivacity
09  animation
10  exuberance, get-up-and-go, liveliness

**vitamin**
━━━━━━━━━━━━━━━━━━━━━
▶  *Types of vitamins:*
01  A, B, C, D, E, G, H, K, P
06  biotin, citrin, niacin
07  retinol, thiamin
08  carotene, thiamine
09  folic acid, menadione

10  calciferol, pyridoxine, riboflavin, tocopherol
11  menaquinone
12  ascorbic acid
13  nicotinic acid

**vitiate**
03  mar
04  harm, ruin
05  spoil, sully, taint
06  blight, debase, defile, impair, injure, weaken
07  blemish, devalue, nullify
09  undermine
10  invalidate
11  contaminate

**vitriolic**
06  biting, bitter
07  abusive, acerbic, caustic, mordant, vicious
08  sardonic, scathing, venomous, virulent
09  malicious, trenchant
11  acrimonious, destructive
12  vituperative

**vituperate**
05  abuse, blame
06  berate, revile, vilify
07  censure, upbraid
09  castigate

**vituperation**
05  abuse, blame, stick
07  censure, obloquy
08  diatribe
09  contumely, invective, philippic, reprimand
11  castigation, objurgation

**vituperative**
07  abusive
09  insulting, withering
10  censorious, derogatory
11  fulminatory, opprobrious
12  calumniatory, denunciatory

**vivacious**
06  bubbly, lively
08  animated, cheerful, spirited
09  ebullient, sparkling
12  effervescent, high-spirited, lighthearted

**vivacity**
04  brio, élan
06  energy, spirit
08  activity, dynamism, vitality
09  animation
10  ebullience, liveliness
13  effervescence

**vivid**
05  clear, lurid, sharp
06  bright, lively, strong
07  dynamic, glaring, glowing, graphic, intense, vibrant

**vividness**
08 animated, colorful, dazzling, distinct, dramatic, lifelike, powerful, spirited, striking, vigorous
09 brilliant, memorable, realistic

**vividness**
04 glow, life
07 clarity, realism
08 lucidity, radiance, strength
09 intensity
10 brilliancy, refulgence

**vocabulary**
05 idiom, lexis, words
07 lexicon
08 glossary, language, wordbook
09 thesaurus
10 dictionary

**vocal**
04 loud, oral, said
05 blunt, frank, noisy
06 shrill, spoken, voiced
07 uttered
08 eloquent, strident
09 expressed, outspoken
10 articulate, vociferous

**vocation**
03 job
04 line, post, role, work
05 craft, trade
06 career, métier, office
07 calling, mission, pursuit
08 business
10 employment, occupation, profession

**vociferous**
04 loud
05 noisy, vocal
08 strident, vehement
09 clamorous, outspoken
10 forthright, thundering

**vogue**
03 fad
04 mode
05 craze, style, taste, trend
07 fashion, the rage
08 the thing
09 the latest
10 popularity

❑**in vogue**
02 in
03 hip
06 modish, trendy, with it
07 popular, stylish
11 fashionable
13 up-to-the-minute

**voice**
03 air, say
04 tone, view, vote, will, wish
05 organ, sound, utter, words

06 airing, assert, convey, medium, speech, talk of
07 declare, divulge, express, mention, opinion, speak of
08 decision, disclose, language
09 enunciate, utterance, verbalize
10 articulate, inflection, intonation, mouthpiece
12 articulation

**void**
03 gap
04 emit, lack, vain, want
05 annul, blank, clear, empty, space
06 cancel, devoid, hollow, lacuna, vacant, vacuum
07 invalid, nullify, opening, useless, vacuity
08 defecate, evacuate
09 discharge, emptiness, nullified
10 invalidate, unoccupied

**volatile**
06 fickle, fitful, lively
07 erratic, flighty
08 unstable, unsteady, volcanic
09 explosive, mercurial, unsettled, up-and-down
10 capricious, changeable
13 temperamental, unpredictable

**volcano**

▶ *Names of volcanoes. We have omitted the word* mount *from names given in the following list but you may need to include this word as part of the solution to some crossword clues.*
03 Apo, Usu
04 Etna, Fuji, Hood, Taal
05 Hekla, Kenya, Mayon, Pelée, Thera, Thira
06 Hudson, Sangay, Shasta
07 Kilauea, Rainier, Redoubt, Ruapehu, Vulcano
08 Cotopaxi, Krakatoa, Mauna Kea, Mauna Loa, Pinatubo, Vesuvius, Wrangell
09 Paricutín, Pichincha, Santorini, Stromboli, Tongariro
10 Chimborazo, Tungurahua
12 Citlaltépetl, Popocatepetl
13 Mount St. Helens
15 Haleakala Crater
➤ See also MOUNTAIN

**volition**
04 will
06 choice, option

08 choosing, election, free will
10 preference, resolution
13 determination

**volley**
04 hail
05 blast, burst, salvo
06 return, shower
07 barrage
09 cannonade, discharge, fusillade

**volte-face**
05 U-turn
08 reversal
09 about-face, turnabout

**voluble**
06 chatty, fluent
09 garrulous, talkative
10 articulate, loquacious

**volume**
04 book, bulk, mass, size
05 sound, space
06 amount
07 omnibus
08 capacity, loudness, quantity
09 aggregate, amplitude
10 dimensions

**voluminous**
04 full
05 ample, bulky, large, roomy
08 spacious
09 billowing, capacious

**voluntarily**
06 freely
08 by choice
09 purposely, willingly
15 of your own accord

**voluntary**
04 free
06 unpaid
08 honorary, optional
10 deliberate, purposeful
11 intentional

**volunteer**
05 offer
06 enlist, tender
07 proffer, propose, suggest
10 put forward
11 step forward
12 candy striper
13 charity worker

**voluptuary**
07 playboy
08 hedonist, sybarite
09 bon vivant, debauchee, epicurean, libertine
10 profligate, sensualist
14 pleasure-seeker

**voluptuous**
05 buxom

07 opulent, sensual, shapely
09 luxurious, seductive
10 hedonistic
11 full-figured
13 self-indulgent

**vomit**
04 barf, puke, spew
05 fetch, heave, retch
06 be sick
07 bring up, throw up
11 regurgitate

**vomiting**
06 emesis, puking
07 barfing, spewing
08 ejection, retching, sickness
13 regurgitation

**voracious**
04 avid
06 greedy, hungry
08 edacious, ravening
09 devouring, rapacious
10 gluttonous, prodigious

**voracity**
05 greed
06 hunger
07 avidity, edacity
08 rapacity
12 ravenousness

**vortex**
04 eddy
05 whirl
09 maelstrom, whirlpool, whirlwind

**votary**
06 addict
07 devotee
08 adherent, disciple, follower

**vote**
03 opt
04 poll
05 elect, put in
06 ballot, choose, return
07 declare, reelect, suggest
08 election, plump for, suffrage
09 franchise
10 plebiscite, referendum
12 go to the polls
15 enfranchisement

**vouch**
❑ **vouch for**
06 affirm, assert, verify
07 certify, confirm, endorse, support, swear to, warrant
08 attest to, speak for
09 answer for, guarantee
10 asseverate

**voucher**
04 chit
05 paper, token
06 coupon, ticket
07 receipt
08 document

**vouchsafe**
04 cede, give
05 deign, grant, yield
06 bestow, confer, impart

**vow**
04 oath
05 swear
06 affirm, devote, pledge
07 profess, promise
08 dedicate
09 undertake
12 give your word

**voyage**
04 sail, tour, trip
06 cruise, travel
07 journey, odyssey, passage, travels
08 crossing
10 expedition

**vulgar**
03 low
04 lewd, loud, rude
05 bawdy, crude, dirty, gaudy, rough, showy, tacky
06 coarse, common, filthy, flashy, garish, glitzy, kitsch, ribald, risqué, tawdry
07 boorish, general, ill-bred, obscene, popular, uncouth
08 impolite, improper, indecent, off-color, ordinary
09 offensive, tasteless, unrefined
10 indelicate, suggestive, vernacular
11 distasteful
12 ostentatious
13 cheap and nasty
15 unsophisticated

**vulgarity**
07 crudity
08 ribaldry
09 indecency
11 ostentation

**vulnerable**
07 exposed
08 helpless, wide open
09 powerless, sensitive
11 defenseless, susceptible, unprotected
12 open to attack

**wacky**
03 odd
04 daft, wild, zany
05 crazy, goofy, loony, loopy, nutty, silly
06 screwy
07 offbeat
09 eccentric

**wad**
03 gob
04 lump, mass, plug, roll
05 block, chunk
06 bundle

**wadding**
06 filler, lining
07 filling, packing, padding
08 stuffing
10 cotton wool
13 cotton batting

**waddle**
04 rock, sway
06 toddle, totter, wobble

**wade**
04 ford, loll, roll
05 cross, lurch
06 splash, wallow, welter
08 flounder, traverse

❏**wade in, wade into**
05 set to
06 attack
07 pitch in
08 tear into
10 launch into
11 plow through
12 trawl through

**waffle**
04 cake
06 babble, jabber
07 blather, prattle
10 battercake

**waft**
04 blow, puff
05 carry, draft, drift, float, glide, scent, whiff
06 breath, breeze
07 current

**wag**
03 bob, nod, wit
04 fool, rock, wave
05 clown, comic, droll, joker, shake, swing

06 jester, quiver, waggle, wiggle, wobble
08 banterer, comedian, humorist
10 comedienne

**wage**
03 fee, pay
06 reward, salary
07 carry on, conduct, payment
08 earnings, engage in
09 allowance, emolument
12 remuneration

**wager**
03 bet
04 ante, risk
05 stake
06 gamble, hazard, pledge
07 lay odds, venture
09 speculate

**waggish**
05 droll, funny, merry, witty
07 comical, jesting, jocular, playful, puckish, roguish
09 bantering, facetious

**waggle**
05 shake
06 jiggle, wiggle, wobble
09 oscillate

**wagon**
03 van
04 cart, dray
05 buggy, truck
07 vehicle
08 carriage
10 paddy wagon
11 patrol wagon
12 station wagon

**waif**
05 stray
06 orphan
09 foundling

**wail**
03 cry, sob
04 howl, keen, moan, yowl
06 lament
07 ululate, weeping
09 complaint, ululation

**wait**
04 halt, rest, stay
05 abide, delay, pause, tarry
06 hang on, linger, remain

08 hang fire, interval
10 hang around, hesitation
12 bide your time, intermission

❏**wait on**
04 tend
05 serve
08 attend to
09 look after

**waiter, waitress**
04 host, tray
06 butler, carhop, salver, server
07 hostess, steward
09 attendant
10 stewardess

**waive**
05 defer, yield
06 forego, give up, resign
08 renounce, set aside
09 do without, surrender
10 relinquish

**waiver**
08 deferral
09 remission, surrender
10 abdication, disclaimer

**wake**
04 fire, goad, path, prod, rear, rise, stir, warn, wash, whet
05 alert, arise, awake, egg on, evoke, get up, rouse, track, trail, train, vigil, waken, watch
06 arouse, awaken, excite
07 animate, funeral
08 activate, backwash
09 aftermath, stimulate
10 deathwatch

**wakeful**
04 wary
05 alert
08 vigilant, watchful
09 observant, sleepless
10 unsleeping

**waken**
04 fire, rise, stir, wake, whet
05 awake, get up, rouse
06 arouse, awaken, ignite, kindle
07 animate, enliven, quicken
08 activate
09 galvanize, stimulate

**walk**
03 pad, way

04 gait, hike, lane, pace, path, plod, roam, step, trek, trip
05 alley, amble, guide, march, mince, mosey, route, stalk, steal, stomp, strut, track, trail, tramp, tread
06 avenue, escort, hoof it, parade, patrol, patter, ramble, stride, stroll, toddle, totter, trudge, wander
07 conduct, jaywalk, pathway, saunter, trample, walkway
08 carriage, footpath, shepherd, sidewalk
09 accompany, esplanade, promenade
10 shank's mare, shank's pony
11 base on balls, perambulate, putter along
14 constitutional, go by shank's pony, go on shank's mare
15 stretch your legs
16 ride on shank's mare, ride on shank's pony

❑**walk away with, walk off with**
03 win
04 lift
05 pinch, steal
09 go off with
11 make off with
12 take the prize

❑**walk of life**
04 area, line
05 arena, field, trade
06 career, métier, sphere
07 calling, pursuit
08 activity, vocation
10 background, occupation

❑**walk out**
05 leave
06 mutiny, revolt, strike
10 go on strike

❑**walk out on**
05 leave
06 desert
07 abandon, forsake

**walker**
05 hiker
07 rambler, trekker
08 stroller
10 pedestrian

**walkout**
06 revolt, strike
07 leaving, protest
08 stoppage

**walkover**
05 cinch
08 pushover
10 child's play

11 piece of cake
12 one-horse race

**walkway**
04 lane, path
07 catwalk, passage, pathway
08 footpath, sidewalk
09 esplanade, promenade

**wall**
03 dam
04 dike
05 block, fence, gable, hedge, levee
06 bailey, corral, immure
07 barrier, bulwark, parapet, rampart
08 bulkhead
09 barricade, revetment, roadblock
10 battlement, breakwater, embankment
13 retaining wall

**wallet**
05 pouch, purse
06 folder, holder
08 billfold
10 pocketbook

**wallop**
03 hit
04 bash, beat, belt, blow, drub, kick, lick, rout, swat
05 clout, crush, paste, pound, punch, thump, whack
06 batter, buffet, defeat, strike, thrash, thwack
07 clobber, trounce

**wallow**
04 bask, loll, roll, wade
05 enjoy, glory, lurch, revel
06 relish, splash, welter
07 delight, indulge
08 flounder
09 luxuriate

**wan**
04 pale, weak
05 ashen, bleak, faint, pasty, waxen, weary, white
06 anemic, feeble, pallid, sickly
07 ghastly
09 colorless, washed out, whey-faced

**wand**
03 rod
04 mace, twig
05 baton, sprig, staff, stick
07 scepter

**wander**
04 rave, roam, rove, veer
05 amble, drift, range, stray
06 babble, depart, gibber, ramble, stroll

07 deviate, digress, diverge, meander, saunter
08 go astray, straggle
11 lose your way, peregrinate
12 talk nonsense

**wanderer**
03 bum
05 Gypsy, nomad, rover, stray
07 drifter, rambler, vagrant
08 stroller, traveler, vagabond, wayfarer
09 itinerant, straggler
12 rolling stone

**wandering**
06 roving
07 journey, meander, nomadic, odyssey, travels, vagrant
08 drifting, homeless, rambling, rootless, vagabond
09 itinerant, migratory, strolling, traveling, walkabout, wayfaring
10 meandering
11 peripatetic
13 peregrination

**wane**
03 dim, ebb
04 drop, fade, fail, fall, sink
05 abate, decay, droop
06 lessen, shrink, weaken
07 decline, dwindle, subside
08 decrease, diminish, fade away, peter out

❑**on the wane**
06 ebbing, fading
08 dropping, moribund
09 declining, dwindling, lessening, subsiding, weakening
11 on the way out
12 on the decline

**wangle**
03 fix
06 fiddle, manage, scheme
07 arrange, pull off
08 contrive, engineer

**want**
04 lack, like, lust, miss, need, wish
05 covet, crave, fancy
06 dearth, demand, desire, hunger, penury, pining, thirst
07 absence, call for, craving, hope for, long for, paucity, pine for, poverty, require
08 appetite, coveting, feel like, scarcity, shortage, yearn for, yearning
09 be without, hunger for, indigence, privation, thirst for

**wanting**
10 deficiency, inadequacy, scantiness
11 destitution, requirement
13 be deficient in, insufficiency

**wanting**
05 short
06 absent, faulty
07 lacking, missing
09 defective, deficient, imperfect
10 inadequate
11 substandard
12 insufficient, unacceptable
13 disappointing

**wanton**
04 lewd, rake, rash, roué, slut, tart, wild
05 whore
06 harlot, impure, lecher
07 Don Juan, immoral, trollop
08 Casanova, reckless
09 abandoned, debauchee, dissolute, pointless, shameless
10 dissipated, gratuitous, groundless, prostitute, unprovoked, voluptuary
11 extravagant, promiscuous
12 unrestrained
13 unjustifiable

**war**
05 clash, fight
06 battle, combat, enmity, strife, strive
08 campaign, conflict, fighting, skirmish, struggle
09 bloodshed
10 antagonism, take up arms
11 cross swords, hostilities

► *Types of war*:
05 blitz, jihad
06 ambush, attack, battle, hot war
07 assault, cold war, holy war
08 civil war, invasion, skirmish, struggle, total war, trade war, world war
09 guerrilla, maneuvers
10 blitzkrieg, engagement, nuclear war, resistance
11 bombardment, germ warfare, war of nerves
12 state of siege
13 armed conflict, counterattack, jungle warfare
14 war of attrition
15 chemical warfare

► *Names of wars*:
05 Roses (Wars of the)

07 Gulf War, Pacific (War of the), Zulu War
08 Boer Wars, Chaco War, Civil War, Crusades, Religion (Wars of), Sikh Wars
09 Dutch Wars, Korean War, Maori Wars, Opium Wars, Punic Wars, Six-Day War, Trojan War, World War I
10 Afghan Wars, Balkan Wars, Crimean War, Gallic Wars, Indian Wars, Jenkins' Ear (War of), Mexican War, Vietnam War, World War II
11 Bishops' Wars, Football War, Iran-Iraq War, Peasants' War, Persian Wars
12 Black Hawk War, Falklands War, Independence (War of), Yom Kippur War
13 First World War, Peninsular War, Seven Years' War
14 Boxer Rebellion, Eighty Years' War, Indian Civil War, Indian Uprising, July Revolution, Napoleonic Wars, Persian Gulf War, Second World War, Thirty Years' War
15 Easter Rebellion, Hundred Years' War, Russian Civil War, Spanish Civil War

➤ See also BATTLE

**warble**
04 call, sing, song
05 chirp, trill, yodel
06 quaver
07 chirrup, twitter

**war cry**
05 motto
06 slogan
09 battle cry, watchword
11 rallying cry

**ward**
04 area, room, unit, zone
05 minor, pupil
06 charge
07 cubicle, protégé, quarter
08 district, division, precinct, protégée
09 apartment, dependent
11 compartment
12 hospital area

❑**ward off**
05 avert, avoid, block, dodge, evade, parry, repel
07 beat off, deflect, fend off
08 stave off, turn away
09 drive back, turn aside

**warden**
06 jailer, keeper, ranger, warder

07 curator, janitor, steward
08 guardian, overseer, watchman
09 caretaker, custodian
10 supervisor
12 churchwarden
13 prison officer
14 prison official, superintendent

**warder**
05 guard
06 keeper
09 custodian

**wardrobe**
05 trunk
06 attire, closet
07 apparel, armoire, cabinet, clothes, outfits
08 cupboard
11 costume room
12 clothespress

**warehouse**
04 stow
05 depot, store
08 entrepot
09 stockroom
10 depository, repository, storehouse

**wares**
05 goods, stock, stuff
07 produce
08 products
11 commodities, merchandise

**warfare**
04 arms
05 blows
06 battle, combat, strife
07 contest, discord
08 campaign, conflict, fighting
11 hostilities
13 passage of arms

**warily**
06 cagily
07 charily
08 gingerly, uneasily
09 carefully, guardedly
10 cautiously, hesitantly
12 suspiciously

**wariness**
04 care
06 unease
07 caution
08 caginess, distrust, prudence
09 alertness, attention, foresight, hesitancy, suspicion, vigilance
10 discretion
12 apprehension
14 circumspection

**warlike**
07 hawkish, hostile, martial
08 militant
09 bellicose, combative
10 aggressive, pugnacious
11 belligerent
12 antagonistic, bloodthirsty, militaristic, warmongering

**warlock**
05 demon
06 wizard
08 conjurer, magician, sorcerer
09 enchanter
11 necromancer

**warm**
04 fine, heat, melt, stir, thaw
05 balmy, eager, sunny, tepid
06 ardent, excite, hearty, heat up, heated, mellow, reheat
07 animate, cordial, enliven, fervent, intense, liven up, sincere
08 cheerful, friendly, lukewarm
09 heartfelt, temperate
15 put some life into

❑**warm up**
06 heat up, reheat
07 enliven
08 exercise, limber up, loosen up

**warm-blooded**
06 ardent, lively
07 earnest, fervent
08 spirited
09 excitable, vivacious
10 hot-blooded, passionate
12 enthusiastic

**warm-hearted**
04 kind
06 kindly, loving, tender
07 cordial
11 kindhearted, sympathetic
12 affectionate
13 compassionate, tenderhearted

**warmth**
04 care, fire, heat, love, zeal
05 ardor
06 fervor
07 hotness, passion
08 sympathy
09 affection, intensity, vehemence
10 enthusiasm, kindliness, tenderness

**warn**
04 tell, urge
05 alert
06 advise, tip off
07 caution, counsel, reprove

08 admonish, forewarn
09 reprimand
10 give notice

**warning**
04 hint, omen, sign
05 alarm, alert
06 advice, augury, caveat, lesson, notice, signal, threat, tip-off
07 caution, counsel, ominous, portent, presage
08 monition
10 admonition, admonitory, cautionary
11 information, premonition, premonitory, threatening
12 notification
13 advance notice

**warp**
04 bend, bent, bias, kink, turn
05 quirk, twist
06 defect, deform
07 contort, corrupt, pervert
08 misshape
10 contortion, distortion, perversion

**warrant**
04 back, writ
05 allow, order, swear
06 affirm, avouch, permit, pledge, uphold
07 approve, call for, certify, consent, declare, empower, endorse, entitle, justify, license, support, voucher
08 sanction, security, vouch for
09 answer for, authority, authorize, consent to, guarantee
10 commission, permission, underwrite, validation
11 necessitate
13 authorization, justification

**warrantable**
05 legal, right
06 lawful, proper
09 allowable
10 defensible, reasonable
11 justifiable, permissible

**warranty**
04 bond
06 pledge
07 promise
08 contract, covenant, security
09 assurance, guarantee

**warring**
07 hostile, opposed
08 fighting, opposing
09 combatant, embattled
11 belligerent, conflicting, doing battle

**warrior**
02 GI
07 fighter, soldier
08 champion, warhorse
09 combatant
10 serviceman
11 fighting man

**wart**
04 lump
06 growth
07 verruca
12 protuberance

**wary**
04 cagy
05 alert, cagey, chary
07 careful, guarded
08 cautious, vigilant, watchful
09 attentive, wide-awake
10 on the alert, suspicious
11 circumspect, distrustful, on your guard
12 on the lookout

**wash**
03 mop
04 flow, hose, soak, wave, wipe
05 bathe, clean, rinse, scrub, surge, sweep, swill
06 douche, shower, splash, sponge, stream
07 cleanse, coating, launder, laundry, shampoo, stand up
08 cleaning, hose down, swab down
09 cleansing, freshen up
10 laundering, pass muster
11 carry weight
12 bear scrutiny
15 bear examination

❑**wash your hands of**
07 abandon
08 give up on

**washed-out**
03 wan
04 flat, pale
05 drawn, faded
06 pallid
07 drained, haggard
08 blanched, bleached
09 colorless, exhausted, knackered
10 lackluster

**washed-up**
04 done
05 tired
07 done for, through
08 finished
09 cleaned up, exhausted

**washout**
04 flop
06 fiasco

07  debacle, failure
08  disaster
11  lead balloon

**waspish**
05  cross, testy
06  bitchy, touchy
07  prickly
08  snappish
11  bad-tempered, ill-tempered

**waste**
04  bare, blow, loss, rape, raze, ruin, sack, wild
05  abuse, bleak, drain, dregs, dross, empty, erode, extra, scrap, slops, trash
06  barren, debris, litter, misuse, refuse, unused, wither
07  atrophy, consume, despoil, destroy, exhaust, garbage, neglect, pillage, rubbish, shrivel, splurge, useless
08  effluent, leftover, misspend, squander, unwanted
09  depredate, devastate, dissipate, leftovers
10  debilitate, devastated
11  dissipation, fritter away, offscouring, prodigality, squandering
12  extravagance, unproductive
13  supernumerary

**wasted**
04  dead, high, weak
05  drunk, gaunt
06  killed, ruined
07  smashed
08  shrunken, withered
09  atrophied, emaciated, shriveled
11  intoxicated

**wasteful**
08  prodigal
10  profligate
11  extravagant, improvident, spendthrift
12  uneconomical

**wasteland**
04  void, wild
05  waste, wilds
06  desert
08  dust bowl
09  emptiness
10  barrenness, wilderness

**wasting**
08  marasmic
10  destroying, emaciating, enfeebling
11  devastating

**wastrel**
05  idler

06  loafer
07  lounger, shirker
10  ne'er-do-well, profligate
11  spendthrift

**watch**
04  heed, keep, mark, mind, note, scan, view
05  clock, guard, vigil
06  look on, regard, survey
07  eyeball, inspect, look out, lookout, monitor, observe, protect, stare at
08  take care, take heed
09  alertness, attention, be careful, look after, timepiece, vigilance
10  keep tabs on, wristwatch
11  chronometer, contemplate, keep an eye on, observation, pocket watch, superintend, supervision
12  pay attention, surveillance

❑**watch out**
06  notice
07  look out
10  be vigilant
12  keep a lookout

❑**watch over**
04  mind
05  guard
07  protect
09  look after
11  keep an eye on
14  stand guard over

**watchdog**
07  monitor
08  guard dog, guardian
09  custodian, ombudsman, protector
10  scrutineer

**watcher**
03  spy
06  sentry, viewer
07  lookout, witness
08  audience, looker-on, observer, onlooker
09  bystander, spectator
10  eyewitness

**watchful**
04  wary
05  alert, chary
08  cautious, vigilant
09  attentive, observant, wide awake
11  on your guard
12  on the lookout, on the qui vive

**watchfulness**
07  caution
08  wariness

09  alertness, attention, suspicion, vigilance

**watchman**
05  guard
06  sentry
07  lookout
08  sentinel
09  caretaker, custodian
13  security guard

**watchword**
05  maxim, motto
06  byword, signal, slogan
08  buzz word, password
09  battle cry, catchword
10  shibboleth
11  catch phrase, countersign, rallying-cry

**water**
03  sea, wet
04  aqua-, hose, lake, rain, soak
05  douse, flood, fluid, ocean, river, spray
06  dampen, drench, liquid, stream
07  current, moisten, torrent
08  flooding, hose down, irrigate, moisture, saturate, sprinkle

❑**water down**
04  thin
06  dilute, soften, weaken
08  play down, tone down
10  adulterate

**watercourse**
04  wadi, wady
05  brook, canal, creek, crick, ditch, river
06  stream
07  channel
09  stream bed
12  water channel

**waterfall**
04  fall
05  chute, falls
07  cascade, torrent
08  cataract

► *Names of waterfalls. We have omitted the word* **falls** *from names given in the following list but you may need to include this word as part of the solution to some crossword clues.*
05  Akaka, Angel, Pilao, Seven, Tysse
06  Ormeli, Ribbon
07  Feather, Niagara
08  Cascades, Itatinga, Kaieteur, Shoshone, Victoria
09  Churchill, Fall Creek, Horseshoe, Multnomah

10 Cleve-Garth
11 Taughannock, Yellowstone
13 Lower Yosemite, Upper
   Yosemite

**waterproof**
07 proofed
09 damp-proof
10 impervious
14 water-repellent, water-
   resistant

**watertight**
05 sound
08 airtight, hermetic
09 foolproof
12 indisputable, unassailable

**watery**
04 damp, thin, weak
05 fluid, moist, runny, soggy
07 aqueous, diluted, hydrous,
   insipid
10 flavorless, wishy-washy

**wave**
03 wag
04 curl, flap, flow, foam, rash,
   rush, sign, stir, surf, sway, waft
05 drift, flood, froth, surge,
   sweep, swell, swing, trend
06 billow, comber, ripple, roller,
   signal, stream
07 breaker, current, flutter,
   gesture, upsurge, wavelet
08 brandish, flourish, undulate,
   whitecap
10 undulation
11 gesticulate, ground swell,
   white horses

❏**make waves**
11 rock the boat, upset things
12 cause trouble

**waver**
04 rock, sway, vary
06 dither, falter, seesaw, teeter,
   totter, wobble
07 stagger, tremble
08 hesitate
09 fluctuate, hum and haw,
   oscillate, vacillate
10 equivocate

**waverer**
08 ditherer, falterer
09 hesitater, hesitator
14 shilly-shallier

**wavering**
08 doubtful, doubting, havering,
   hesitant, hovering
09 dithering
10 in two minds
15 shilly-shallying

**wavy**
05 curly, curvy
06 ridged, zigzag
07 curling, curving, rippled,
   sinuous, winding
10 undulating

**wax**
04 grow, rise
05 mount, swell, widen
06 become, expand, polish
07 broaden, develop, enlarge,
   fill out, magnify
08 increase

**waxen**
03 wan
04 pale
05 ashen, livid, white
06 anemic, pallid
07 ghastly, whitish
09 bloodless, colorless

**waxy**
04 soft
05 pasty, waxen
06 pallid
07 cereous
09 ceraceous

**way**
04 lane, mode, path, plan, road,
   tool, wont
05 habit, lines, means, route,
   style, track, trail, trait, usage
06 access, avenue, course,
   custom, manner, method,
   street, system, temper
07 channel, conduct, fashion,
   highway, passage, pathway,
   process, roadway
08 approach, behavior, practice,
   strategy
09 direction, mannerism,
   procedure, technique
11 disposition, peculiarity,
   personality, temperament
12 idiosyncrasy, thoroughfare
14 characteristic, course of
   action
15 instrumentality

❏**by the way**
09 en passant, in passing
12 incidentally
15 parenthetically

❏**give way**
05 break, yield
06 cave in, fall in, give in, submit
07 concede, retreat
08 collapse, withdraw
10 capitulate

❏**underway**
05 afoot, begun, going
07 started

08 in motion
10 in progress
11 in operation

❏**way of life**
05 world
09 lifestyle, situation
12 how things are

❏**ways and means**
03 way
04 cash
05 funds, tools
07 capital, methods
08 capacity, reserves
09 procedure, resources
10 capability
11 wherewithal

**wayfarer**
05 Gypsy, nomad, rover
06 walker
07 trekker, voyager
08 traveler, wanderer
09 itinerant, journeyer

**wayfaring**
06 roving
07 nomadic, walking
08 drifting, rambling, voyaging
09 itinerant, traveling,
   wandering
10 journeying
11 peripatetic

**waylay**
05 catch, seize
06 accost, ambush, hold up
09 intercept

**way-out**
04 wild
05 crazy, weird
06 far-out, freaky
07 bizarre, offbeat, unusual
09 eccentric, fantastic
10 avant-garde, outlandish
11 progressive
12 experimental
14 unconventional

**wayward**
06 fickle, unruly, wilful
07 peevish, willful
08 contrary, obdurate, perverse,
   stubborn
09 obstinate
10 capricious, rebellious,
   refractory, self-willed
11 disobedient, intractable

**weak**
03 dim, low
04 lame, poor, puny, soft
05 faint, frail, shaky, weedy
06 feeble, infirm, sickly, slight

07 diluted, exposed, fragile, insipid, lacking, stifled, unsound, worn out
08 cowardly, delicate, fatigued
09 defective, deficient, enervated, exhausted, imperfect, powerless, spineless, tasteless, unhealthy, untenable
10 inadequate, indecisive, irresolute, vulnerable
11 adulterated, debilitated, defenseless, ineffectual
12 inconclusive, unconvincing
13 imperceptible

**weaken**
03 sap
04 fade, fail, flag, thin, tire
05 abate, droop, lower
06 dilute, ease up, lessen, reduce, soften, temper
07 cripple, disable, exhaust
08 diminish, enervate, enfeeble, mitigate, moderate, soften up
09 undermine, water down
10 debilitate
12 incapacitate

**weakening**
06 easing, fading, waning
08 dilution, flagging, lowering
09 abatement, dwindling, lessening, reduction
10 moderation
12 diminishment

**weakling**
04 drip, wimp
05 mouse, sissy
06 coward

**weak-minded**
07 pliable
09 compliant, spineless
10 indecisive, irresolute, submissive
11 complaisant, persuadable, persuasible
12 faint-hearted, feeble-minded
13 pusillanimous

**weakness**
04 flaw
05 fault
06 defect, foible, liking
07 failing, frailty, passion
08 debility, soft spot
09 impotence, infirmity
10 deficiency, enervation, feebleness, proclivity
11 inclination, shortcoming
12 Achilles' heel, predilection
13 powerlessness, vulnerability

**weal**
04 mark, scar, welt
05 ridge, wound
06 streak, stripe
07 welfare
08 cicatrix
09 cicatrice, contusion, well-bring

**wealth**
04 cash, mass
05 funds, goods, means, money, store
06 assets, bounty, mammon, plenty, riches
07 capital, finance, fortune
08 opulence, property, treasure
09 abundance, affluence, plenitude, profusion, resources, substance
10 cornucopia, prosperity
11 copiousness, possessions

**wealthy**
04 rich
06 loaded
07 moneyed, opulent, well-off
08 affluent, well-to-do
10 prosperous, well-heeled
11 comfortable, made of money
12 stinking rich

**weapon**

▶ *Weapons include*:
03 gas, gun, gun
04 bomb, Colt, cosh, dirk, épée, foil, mine, pike, Scud
05 CS gas, H-bomb, knife, lance, Luger, rifle, saber, sling, spear, sword
06 air gun, cannon, cudgel, dagger, Exocet, magnum, Mauser, mortar, musket, pistol, poleax, rapier, rocket, six-gun
07 assegai, bayonet, bazooka, Bren gun, carbine, halberd, harpoon, longbow, machete, poleaxe, poniard, shotgun, Sten gun, stun gun, torpedo
08 air rifle, atom bomb, battleax, blowpipe, catapult, claymore, crossbow, field gun, howitzer, land mine, revolver, scimitar, stiletto, time bomb, tomahawk, tommy gun
09 battleaxe, boomerang, Mills bomb, truncheon
10 atomic bomb, bowie knife, broadsword, machine gun, shillelagh, six-shooter
11 Agent Orange, blunderbuss,

bow and arrow, cluster bomb, depth charge, elephant gun, hand grenade, Kalashnikov, switchblade
12 flamethrower
13 brass knuckles, Cruise missile, knuckle-duster, submachine gun
14 Gatling grenade, incendiary bomb
15 Winchester rifle

**wear**
03 don, rub, use
04 bear, fray, have, show
05 carry, dress, erode, sport
06 abrade, attire
07 clothes, corrode, costume, display, dress in, erosion, exhibit
08 abrasion, clothing, friction
09 corrosion
10 durability, employment
11 be clothed in, deteriorate

❑**wear down**
05 erode
06 abrade, lessen, reduce
07 consume, corrode, rub away
08 diminish, macerate
09 grind down, undermine
10 chip away at

❑**wear off**
03 ebb
04 fade, wane
05 abate
06 lessen, weaken
07 dwindle, subside
08 decrease, diminish

❑**wear on**
04 go by, go on, pass
06 elapse

❑**wear out**
03 sap
04 fray, tire
05 drain, erode
06 impair, strain, stress
07 consume, exhaust, fatigue
08 enervate
11 deteriorate, wear through

**weariness**
05 ennui
07 fatigue, languor
09 lassitude, tiredness
10 enervation, exhaustion

**wearing**
06 taxing, tiring, trying
07 erosive, irksome
08 tiresome
09 fatiguing, wearisome
10 exhausting, oppressive

**wearisome**
04 dull
06 boring, dreary, trying
07 humdrum, irksome, tedious
08 annoying, tiresome
09 fatiguing, vexatious
10 bothersome, burdensome,
   exhausting, monotonous
11 troublesome
12 exasperating

**weary**
03 bug, fag, irk, sap, tax
04 beat, bore, fade, fail, jade,
   tire
05 all in, drain, fed up, jaded,
   tired
06 burden, bushed, done in,
   drowsy, sicken, sleepy
07 drained, fatigue, tire out,
   worn-out
08 dead beat, dog-tired,
   enervate, fatigued, irritate
09 exhausted
10 debilitate, exasperate
12 bored to tears, sick and tired

**wearying**
06 taxing, tiring, trying
07 wearing
08 draining
10 exhausting

**weather**
03 air, dry
05 brave, stand
06 endure, expose, harden,
   resist, season, suffer
07 climate, outlook, ride out,
   survive, toughen
08 humidity, overcome, stick
   out, surmount
09 rise above, withstand
10 cloudiness, conditions, get
   through
11 come through, pull through
➤ See also STORM; WIND

❑**under the weather**
03 ill
04 sick
05 queer, seedy
06 ailing, groggy, poorly
08 below par, hung over, off-
   color
09 squeamish
10 indisposed, out of sorts
15 the worse for wear

**weave**
04 fuse, knit, lace, spin, wind
05 braid, merge, plait, twist
06 create, make up, zigzag
07 compose, entwine
08 contrive
09 construct, fabricate

10 crisscross, intertwine
11 put together

**web**
03 net
04 knot, mesh, trap, weft
06 tangle
07 complex, lattice, netting
08 lacework

**wed**
04 ally, fuse, join, link, yoke
05 marry, merge, unite
06 splice
07 combine, espouse
10 get hitched, tie the knot

**wedded**
06 joined
07 marital, married, nuptial
08 conjugal
09 connubial
11 matrimonial

**wedding**
05 union
06 bridal
07 nuptial, wedlock
08 hymeneal, hymenean,
   marriage, nuptials
09 matrimony
11 epithalamic, matrimonial

**wedge**
03 fit, jam, ram
04 cram, lump, pack, push
05 block, chock, chunk, crowd,
   force, lodge, piece
06 thrust
08 triangle

**wedlock**
05 union
08 marriage
09 matrimony

**wee**
04 tiny
05 small, teeny, weeny
06 little, midget, minute, teensy,
   weensy
09 itsy-bitsy, itty-bitty, miniature
10 diminutive, negligible, teeny-
   weeny
11 Lilliputian
12 teensy-weensy

**weed**

► *Types of weed*:
04 dock, moss
05 daisy, vetch
06 oxalis, spurge, yarrow
07 bracken, burdock, pigweed,
   ragweed, ribwort
08 bindweed, duckweed,
   knapweed, self-heal,
   toadflax, woodrush

09 chickweed, cocklebur,
   coltsfoot, dandelion,
   goldenrod, ground ivy,
   groundsel, horsetail,
   knotgrass, liverwort,
   marijuana, pearlwort, poison
   ivy, poison oak, snakeweed,
   speedwell
10 cinquefoil, couch grass, dead
   nettle, sow thistle, thale cress
11 ground elder, meadow grass,
   sheep sorrel, white clover
12 lamb's quarter
13 butter-and-eggs, pineapple
   weed
14 shepherd's purse, sleeping
   beauty
15 lesser celandine
➤ See also PLANT

❑**weed out**
06 remove
07 root out
08 get rid of
09 eliminate, eradicate

**weedy**
04 lean, puny, thin, weak
05 lanky
06 feeble, skinny
07 insipid, scrawny, wimpish
08 gangling, ungainly
10 undersized

**weekly**
05 paper
08 magazine
09 every week, newspaper,
   once a week
10 hebdomadal, periodical
12 hebdomadally

**weep**
03 cry, sob
04 bawl, blub, moan, wail
05 mourn, whine
06 grieve, lament, snivel
07 blubber, whimper
09 be in tears, shed tears

**weepy**
05 teary
06 crying, labile
07 sobbing, tearful, weeping
09 melodrama
10 lachrymose, tear-jerker

**weigh**
06 burden, ponder
07 afflict, balance, examine,
   trouble
08 consider, evaluate
09 reflect on, think over
10 deliberate, meditate on
11 contemplate, hoist anchor

**❏weigh down**
04 load
06 burden
07 depress, get down, oppress
08 bear down, overload
09 press down

**❏weigh up**
06 assess, ponder, size up
07 balance, compare, examine
08 chew over, consider, evaluate, mull over
09 think over
10 deliberate
11 contemplate

**weight**
04 duty, load, mass, onus, sway
05 angle, clout, force, power, slant, twist, value, worry
06 burden, impact, strain
07 ballast, gravity, oppress, tonnage, trouble
08 dumbbell, handicap, poundage, pressure, quantity
09 authority, influence, prejudice, substance, unbalance, weigh down
10 importance
11 avoirdupois, encumbrance
12 significance
14 responsibility

**weightless**
04 airy
05 light

**weighty**
05 bulky, grave, heavy, hefty
06 solemn, taxing
07 massive, serious
09 important, momentous
10 burdensome
11 significant, substantial
13 authoritative, consequential

**weird**
03 odd
04 eery
05 eerie, queer
06 creepy, spooky, way-out
07 bizarre, ghostly, strange, uncanny
08 freakish, peculiar
12 supernatural
13 preternatural

**weirdo**
03 nut
05 crank, freak, loony
07 nutcase, oddball
08 crackpot
09 eccentric, fruitcake, queer fish

**welcome**
04 hail, meet

05 greet
06 accept, salute
07 embrace, popular, receive
08 greeting, pleasant, pleasing
09 agreeable, approve of, desirable, reception, red carpet
10 acceptable, gratifying, refreshing, salutation
11 appreciated, hospitality

**weld**
04 bind, bond, fuse, join, link, seal, seam
05 joint, unite
06 cement, solder
07 connect

**welfare**
04 good
06 health, income, profit
07 benefit, comfort, payment, pension, sick pay, success
08 interest, security
09 advantage, allowance, happiness, well-being
10 prosperity
15 unemployment pay

**well**
02 OK
03 far, fit, jet, run
04 ably, fine, flow, good, gush, okay, ooze, pool, rise, rush, seep
05 flood, fount, fully, issue, lucky, right, sound, spout, spurt, surge, swell
06 proper, robust, source, spring, stream, strong
07 adeptly, happily, healthy, luckily, rightly, trickle
08 all right, brim over, expertly, fountain, genially, moreover, pleasing, probably, properly, suitably, thriving, wellhead
09 agreeable, agreeably, carefully, correctly, fittingly, fortunate, reservoir, skilfully
10 able-bodied, completely, skillfully, wellspring
11 approvingly, comfortably, competently, effectively, excellently, flourishing
12 considerably, in good health, proficiently, prosperously, satisfactory, successfully
13 elevator shaft, hale and hearty, industriously, substantially
14 satisfactorily

**❏as well**
03 too
04 also

07 besides
08 moreover
10 in addition
11 furthermore
14 into the bargain

**❏as well as**
09 along with
12 in addition to, over and above, together with
14 to say nothing of

**well-advised**
04 wise
05 sound
06 shrewd
07 politic, prudent
09 judicious, sagacious

**well-balanced**
04 even, sane
05 sober, sound
06 stable
08 rational, sensible, together
10 harmonious, reasonable
11 levelheaded, symmetrical
12 well-adjusted

**well-behaved**
04 good
08 obedient
10 good as gold, respectful
11 considerate, cooperative

**well-being**
04 good
07 comfort, welfare
09 happiness
10 good health

**well-bred**
05 civil
06 polite, urbane
07 gallant, genteel, refined
08 cultured, ladylike, mannerly
09 courteous
10 cultivated, upper-crust
11 blue-blooded, gentlemanly
12 aristocratic, well-mannered
13 well-brought-up

**well-built**
04 buff
05 beefy, burly, stout
06 brawny, strong
08 muscular
09 strapping

**well-deserved**
04 just, meet
06 earned
07 condign, merited
09 justified

**well-disposed**
08 amicable, friendly
09 agreeable, favorable, well-aimed

11 sympathetic

## ❏well-done
07 skilful
08 skillful
10 successful, well cooked
12 satisfactory

## well-dressed
04 chic, neat, tidy, trim
05 natty, smart
06 dapper, spruce
07 elegant, stylish

## well-founded
05 right, sound, valid
06 proper
08 sensible
09 plausible, warranted
10 reasonable
11 justifiable, sustainable

## well-groomed
04 neat, tidy, trim
05 smart
06 dapper, spruce
11 well-dressed
13 well-turned-out

## well-known
05 famed, noted, usual
06 common, famous
07 eminent, notable
08 renowned
10 celebrated
11 illustrious

## well-nigh
06 all but, almost, nearly
09 just about, virtually
11 practically

## well-off
04 rich
05 flush, lucky
07 moneyed, wealthy
08 affluent, thriving, well-to-do
10 prosperous
11 comfortable, rolling in it
12 stinking rich

## well-read
08 cultured, educated, literate
12 well-informed
13 knowledgeable

## well-spoken
05 clear
06 fluent
08 coherent, eloquent
10 articulate
13 well-expressed

## well-thought-of
07 admired, honored, revered
08 esteemed
09 respected, venerated
10 looked up to
14 highly regarded

## well-to-do
04 rich
07 moneyed, wealthy, well-off
08 affluent
10 prosperous, well-heeled
11 comfortable, rolling in it

## well-versed
06 au fait
10 conversant

## well-wisher
03 fan
09 supporter
11 sympathizer

## well-worn
05 corny, stale, tired, trite
06 frayed, ragged, shabby
07 scruffy, worn out
08 overused, timeworn
09 hackneyed
10 threadbare, unoriginal
11 commonplace, stereotyped

## welsh
05 cheat
06 diddle
07 defraud, swindle

## welt
04 mark, scar, weal
05 ridge, wound
06 streak, stripe
08 cicatrix
09 cicatrice, contusion

## welter
03 web
04 mess, roll, toss, wade
05 heave, lurch, pitch
06 jumble, muddle, soaked, tumble, wallow
07 stained, turmoil
08 flounder, mish-mash
09 confusion
10 hodgepodge, hotchpotch

## wend

## ❏wend your way
02 go
04 hike, move, plod, walk
06 travel, trudge, wander
07 meander, proceed
08 progress

## wet
03 dip
04 damp, dank, drip, rain, soak, soft
05 douse, flood, humid, imbue, moist, rainy, soggy, spray, steep, swamp, water
06 clammy, dampen, drench, liquid, soaked, sodden, splash, spongy

07 drizzle, moisten, pouring, raining, showery, soaking, sopping
08 dampness, drenched, dripping, humidity, irrigate, moisture, saturate, sprinkle
09 moistness
11 waterlogged

## ❏wet behind the ears
03 new, raw
05 green, naïve
06 callow
08 immature, innocent
13 inexperienced

## wetness
03 wet
04 damp
05 water
06 liquid
08 humidity, moisture
09 sogginess
12 condensation

## whack
03 box, cut, hit, rap
04 bang, bash, beat, belt, blow, cuff, slap, sock
05 clout, thump
06 murder, strike, stroke, thrash, wallop
07 clobber

## whale

▶ *Types of whale. We have omitted the word* **whale** *from names given in the following list but you may need to include this word as part of the solution to some crossword clues.*

03 fin
04 blue, gray
05 black, minke, pigmy, piked, pilot, right, sperm, white
06 baleen, beaked, beluga, finner, killer
07 bowhead, dolphin, finback, grampus, Layard's, narwhal, rorqual, toothed
08 cachalot, humpback, porpoise
09 Greenland, grindhval, razorback, whalebone
10 bottlenose, humpbacked
11 bottle-nosed
12 river dolphin
14 harbor porpoise
➤ See also ANIMAL

## wharf
04 dock, pier, quay, slip
05 jetty, stage
08 dockyard, quayside
12 landing levee, landing place

## whatchamacallit

06 doodad
07 whatnot, whatsis, whatsit, whatzit
09 thingummy
10 thingumbob
11 thingamabob, thingamajig, thingumabob, thingumajig
12 thingummybob, thingummyjig

## wheedle

04 coax, draw
05 charm, court
06 cajole, entice, induce
07 beguile, flatter, win over
08 inveigle, persuade, talk into

## wheel

04 roll, spin, turn
05 orbit, pivot, swing, whirl
06 circle, gyrate, rotate, swivel
07 revolve
08 go around, gyration, rotation
10 revolution

► *Types of wheel. We have omitted the word* **wheel** *from names given in the following list but you may need to include this word as part of the solution to some crossword clues.*

03 big
04 idle, mill, worm
05 wagon, water
06 caster, castor, charka, escape, Ferris, paddle, prayer
07 charka, driving, potter's, ratchet
08 cogwheel, flywheel, roulette, spinning, sprocket, steering
09 cartwheel, Catherine, gearwheel
13 spinning jenny
14 wheel of fortune

## ❑at the wheel

07 driving, turning
08 in charge, steering
09 at the helm, directing, in command, in control
11 responsible

## wheeze

03 gag
04 gasp, hiss, idea, joke, pant, plan, ploy, rasp, ruse
05 cough, prank, stunt, trick
06 scheme
08 anecdote, chestnut
13 practical joke

## whereabouts

08 location, position, vicinity

## wherewithal

04 cash
05 funds, means, money
07 capital
09 resources
11 necessaries

## whet

04 edge, file, hone, stir
05 grind, rouse
06 arouse, awaken, excite, incite, kindle
07 provoke, quicken, sharpen
09 stimulate, titillate

## whiff

04 gust, hint, miss, odor, puff, reek
05 aroma, scent, smell, sniff, stink, trace
06 breath, stench
09 strikeout
10 suggestion

## while

04 span, time
05 spell
06 period, season
08 interval

## ❑while away

04 pass
05 spend, use up
06 devote, occupy

## whim

03 fad
04 idea, urge
05 craze, fancy, freak, humor, quirk
06 notion, vagary
07 caprice, conceit, impulse

## whimper

03 cry, sob
04 mewl, moan, weep
05 groan, whine
06 snivel
07 grizzle, sniffle

## whimsical

03 odd
05 droll, funny, queer, weird
06 quaint, quirky
07 curious, playful, unusual
08 fanciful, peculiar
09 eccentric, impulsive
10 capricious

## whine

03 cry, sob
04 beef, carp, moan, wail
05 gripe, groan
06 grouch, grouse
07 grizzle, grumble, whimper
08 complain
09 bellyache, complaint

## whip

03 fly, mix, tan
04 beat, belt, cane, crop, dart, dash, flit, flog, goad, jerk, lash, lick, prod, pull, push, rout, rush, spur, stir, tear, urge, yank
05 birch, clout, drive, flash, rouse, strap, whack, whisk
06 defeat, punish, snatch, switch, thrash, wallop
07 agitate, scourge, sjambok
09 castigate, horsewhip
10 discipline, flagellate, riding-crop
13 cat-o'-nine-tails

## ❑whip up

06 arouse, excite, foment, incite, kindle, stir up
07 inflame, provoke, psych up
09 instigate

## whippersnapper

05 scamp
06 nipper, rascal, squirt
07 upstart
08 scalawag
09 scallawag, scallywag
11 hobbledehoy

## whipping

06 caning, hiding
07 beating, lashing, tanning
08 birching, flogging, spanking
09 thrashing, walloping
11 castigation
12 flagellation

## whirl

04 daze, reel, roll, spin, turn
05 pivot, round, swirl, twirl, twist, wheel
06 bustle, circle, flurry, gyrate, hubbub, muddle, rotate, strive, swivel, tumult, uproar
07 revolve
08 gyration, rotation
09 agitation, commotion, confusion, giddiness, pirouette
10 hurly-burly, revolution, turn around
12 merry-go-round

## ❑give something a whirl

07 attempt, have a go, venture
08 endeavor
09 have a bash, have a shot, have a stab
10 have a crack

## whirlpool

04 eddy
06 vortex
09 maelstrom

**whirlwind**
05 hasty, quick, rapid, swift
06 speedy, vortex
07 cyclone, tornado, twister
09 impetuous, impulsive, lightning

**whisk**
03 fly, mix
04 beat, bolt, dart, dash, dive, race, rush, stir, whip, whiz, wipe
05 broom, brush, flick, froth, hurry, shoot, speed, sweep
06 beater, hasten

**whiskey, whisky**
03 rye
06 Scotch
07 bourbon
09 firewater, moonshine
12 the hard stuff

**whisper**
04 buzz, hint, hiss, sigh
05 rumor, sough, tinge, trace, whiff
06 breath, gossip, mumble, murmur, mutter
07 breathe, divulge, soupçon
08 innuendo, low voice
09 insinuate, suspicion, susurrate, undertone
10 suggestion
11 insinuation

**whistle**
04 call, pipe, toot
05 cheep, chirp, flute, siren
06 signal, warble

□**blow the whistle**
06 inform, report
09 call a halt
11 cause to stop

**whit**
03 bit, jot
04 atom, dash, hoot, iota, mite
05 crumb, grain, speck, trace
06 little
07 modicum
08 fragment, particle

**white**
03 wan
04 gray, pale, pure
05 ashen, hoary, ivory, light, milky, pasty, snowy, waxen
06 creamy, pallid, silver
09 Caucasian, Caucasoid, colorless, stainless, undefiled
10 immaculate
12 light-skinned

**white-collar**
08 clerical, salaried
09 executive, nonmanual

12 professional

**whiten**
04 fade, pale
06 blanch, bleach
08 etiolate

**whitewash**
04 beat, best, drub, hide, lick
05 crush, paste
06 hammer, thrash
07 conceal, cover up, trounce
08 suppress
09 deception, gloss over
10 camouflage
11 concealment, make light of

**whittle**
03 cut, hew, use
04 pare, trim
05 carve, shape, shave
06 reduce, scrape
07 consume, eat away
08 diminish, wear away
09 undermine

**whole**
03 all, fit, lot
04 full, mint, unit, well
05 piece, sound, total, uncut
06 entire, entity, intact, unhurt
07 healthy, perfect
08 complete, ensemble, entirety, totality
09 aggregate
10 everything, in one piece

□**on the whole**
06 mostly
07 as a rule
09 generally, in general, in the main
10 by and large
13 predominantly
14 for the most part

**wholehearted**
04 real, true, warm
07 devoted, earnest, genuine, sincere, zealous
08 complete, emphatic
09 committed, heartfelt
10 unreserved, unstinting
11 unqualified

**wholesale**
04 mass
05 broad, total
06 en bloc
07 massive, totally
08 outright, sweeping
09 extensive, massively
11 wide-ranging
12 all-inclusive
13 comprehensive
14 indiscriminate

**wholesome**
04 good, pure
05 clean, moral
06 decent, proper
07 bracing, ethical, healthy
08 edifying, salutary, virtuous
09 healthful, honorable, improving, righteous, uplifting
10 beneficial, nourishing, salubrious
11 respectable
12 invigorating

**wholly**
03 all
05 fully
06 purely
07 totally, utterly
08 entirely
09 perfectly
10 completely, thoroughly
11 exclusively
14 in every respect

**whoop**
04 hoop, hoot, roar, yell
05 cheer, shout
06 holler, hurray, scream, shriek

**whopper**
03 lie
05 giant, jumbo
09 falsehood, tall story
11 fabrication

**whopping**
04 huge, vast
05 giant, great, large
07 immense, massive
08 enormous, gigantic
10 monumental, tremendous

**whore**
04 bawd, tart
06 harlot, hooker
07 hustler, trollop
08 call girl, strumpet
09 courtesan
10 prostitute
11 fallen woman, fille de joie
12 scarlet woman, streetwalker

**whorehouse**
07 brothel
08 bordello, cathouse
10 bawdyhouse

**whorl**
04 coil, turn
05 helix, twist
06 spiral, vortex
09 corkscrew
11 convolution

**wicked**
03 bad
04 cool, evil, foul, vile

05 awful, nasty
06 fierce, impish, severe, sinful
07 corrupt, debased, harmful,
heinous, immoral, intense,
ungodly, vicious
08 depraved, devilish, dreadful,
rascally, shameful, terrible
09 admirable, atrocious,
dissolute, egregious,
excellent, nefarious,
offensive, worthless
10 abominable, iniquitous,
scandalous, villainous
11 troublesome, unrighteous
12 blackhearted, unprincipled

**wickedness**
03 sin
04 evil
08 atrocity, iniquity, vileness
09 amorality, depravity,
reprobacy
10 corruption, immorality,
sinfulness
11 abomination

**wickerwork**
06 wattle, wicker
10 basketwork, wattlework

**wide**
04 full, vast
05 ample, baggy, broad, fully,
great, loose, roomy
06 astray, remote
07 dilated, general, immense,
outside
08 expanded, spacious
09 all the way, extensive, off-
course, off-target
10 completely, off the mark
11 far-reaching
13 comprehensive

**wide-awake**
04 keen, wary
05 alert, aware, sharp
06 astute, roused
07 heedful, wakened
08 vigilant, watchful
09 conscious, observant, on the
ball
10 on your toes
11 quick-witted
12 on the qui vive

**widely**
07 broadly
11 extensively

**widen**
06 dilate, expand, spread
07 broaden, distend, enlarge

**wide-open**
06 gaping, spread
07 exposed

10 vulnerable
11 defenseless, unprotected
12 outstretched

**wide-ranging**
05 broad
08 sweeping, thorough
09 extensive, important
10 widespread
11 far-reaching, significant
13 comprehensive

**widespread**
04 rife
05 broad
06 common
07 general
08 far-flung, sweeping
09 extensive, pervasive,
prevalent, universal
11 far-reaching

**width**
04 beam, span
05 girth, range, reach, scope
06 extent
07 breadth, compass, measure
08 diameter, wideness
09 amplitude

**wield**
03 ply, use
04 have, hold, wave
05 exert, shake, swing
06 employ, handle, manage
07 command, control, possess
08 brandish, exercise, flourish
10 manipulate

**wife**
03 Mrs.
04 mate
05 bride
06 missus, spouse
07 partner
08 helpmate
09 companion, other half
10 better half

**wiggle**
03 wag
05 shake, twist
06 jiggle, squirm, twitch,
waggle, writhe
07 wriggle

**wild**
03 mad
04 daft, keen, nuts, rash
05 angry, crazy, feral
06 fierce, fuming, raging,
savage, stormy, unruly
07 bananas, berserk, enraged,
fervent, frantic, furious,
lawless, natural, rampant,
riotous, untamed, violent,
wayward

08 demented, desolate,
frenzied, incensed, reckless,
unbroken, vehement
09 barbarous, ferocious,
primitive, turbulent
10 boisterous, hopping mad,
infuriated, passionate
11 extravagant, tempestuous,
uncivilized
12 uncultivated, ungovernable,
unmanageable
13 impracticable, undisciplined
14 undomesticated

**wilderness**
05 waste, wilds
06 desert, jungle
09 wasteland

**wildlife**
05 fauna
07 animals

**wilds**
07 outback
09 the sticks, wasteland
10 wilderness
12 the boondocks

**wiles**
04 ploy, ruse
05 dodge, fraud, guile, trick
06 deceit, device
07 cunning
08 cheating, maneuver, trickery
09 chicanery, deception,
stratagem
10 artfulness, craftiness,
subterfuge
11 contrivance

**willful, wilful**
06 dogged, mulish
07 planned, wayward
08 contrary, obdurate, perverse,
stubborn
09 obstinate, pigheaded
10 calculated, deliberate,
determined, headstrong,
inflexible, refractory, self-
willed, unyielding
11 intentional, intractable
12 intransigent, premeditated
14 uncompromising

**will**
03 aim
04 mind, want, wish
05 fancy, leave, order
06 choice, compel, confer,
decree, desire, intend,
option, ordain, pass on
07 command, purpose, resolve
08 bequeath, decision, pass
down, transfer, volition
09 dispose of, intention,
willpower

**willing**
10 discretion, resolution
11 disposition, inclination
13 determination

**willing**
04 game, glad, keen
05 eager, happy, ready
07 content, pleased
08 amenable, biddable, disposed, inclined, prepared, so-minded
09 agreeable, compliant, favorable
10 consenting
11 cooperative
12 enthusiastic, well-disposed

**willingly**
06 freely, gladly
07 eagerly, happily, readily
08 by choice
11 voluntarily

**willingness**
04 will, wish
05 favor
06 desire
08 volition
09 readiness
11 disposition, inclination

**willowy**
04 slim
06 lissom, supple
07 slender
08 graceful
09 lithesome, sylphlike

**willpower**
04 grit, will
07 resolve
10 doggedness, resolution
11 self-command, self-mastery
13 determination
14 self-discipline

**willy-nilly**
08 perforce
10 irresolute
11 necessarily, of necessity
12 whether or not
13 helter-skelter

**wilt**
03 ebb, sag
04 fade, flag, sink, wane
05 droop, faint
06 lessen, weaken, wither
07 dwindle, shrivel

**wily**
03 fly, sly
04 foxy
06 artful, astute, crafty, shifty, shrewd, tricky
07 cunning
08 guileful, scheming
09 designing, underhand

10 intriguing

**wimp**
04 drip, fool, jerk, nerd
05 clown, softy
07 milksop
08 weakling

**win**
03 get, net
04 earn, gain
06 attain, obtain, secure
07 achieve, acquire, collect, conquer, mastery, prevail, procure, receive, succeed, success, triumph, victory
08 conquest
10 accomplish, strike gold
12 come out on top, turn up trumps

❏**win over**
04 sway
05 charm
07 attract, convert
08 convince, persuade
09 influence
10 talk around
11 bring around

**wince**
04 jerk, jump
05 cower, quail, start
06 cringe, flinch, recoil, shrink

**wind**
03 air
04 bend, coil, curl, furl, gale, gust, loop, puff, reel, roll, turn, wrap
05 curve, draft, snake, twine, twist
06 breath, breeze, spiral
07 bluster, current, meander, wreathe
08 encircle

▶ *Types of wind. We have omitted the word* **wind** *from names given in the following list but you may need to include this word as part of the solution to some crossword clues.*

04 berg, bise, bora, east, föhn, helm
05 north, trade, zonda
06 levant, samiel, simoom, zephyr
07 austral, chinook, cyclone, El Niño, etesian, gregale, khamsin, meltemi, mistral, monsoon, pampero, sirocco, tornado
08 favonian, libeccio, westerly, williwaw
09 harmattan, hurricane,

nor'wester, southerly
10 prevailing, tramontana, willy-willy
11 anticyclone, northeaster, southwester
➤ See also STORM

❏**in the wind**
06 likely
08 expected, probable
10 on the cards

❏**wind down**
05 relax
06 ease up, lessen, reduce
07 decline, dwindle, subside
08 calm down, slow down
11 come to an end, quieten down
12 bring to an end

❏**wind up**
03 end
04 stop
05 close, end up
06 finish, settle
08 conclude, finish up
09 liquidate
12 bring to an end
13 bring to a close

**windbag**
06 gasbag, gossip
07 boaster
08 bigmouth, braggart
09 blatherer

**winded**
10 breathless
11 out of breath

**windfall**
07 bonanza, godsend, jackpot
13 treasure-trove

**winding**
06 spiral
07 bending, crooked, curving, sinuate, sinuous, turning
08 flexuose, flexuous, sinuated, tortuous, twisting
10 convoluted, meandering, serpentine
11 anfractuous

**window**
04 pane
05 light

▶ *Types of window. We have omitted the word* **window** *from names given in the following list but you may need to include this word as part of the solution to some crossword clues.*

03 bay, bow
04 rose, sash, shop
05 oriel, store, wheel

**06** dormer, French, lancet, louver, ticket
**07** compass, lucarne, transom
**08** bull's-eye, casement, fanlight, marigold, porthole, skylight
**09** decorated, mullioned
**10** windowpane, windshield
**11** oeil-de-boeuf
**12** double-glazed, stained-glass
**13** double-glazing
**14** Catherine wheel

**windpipe**
**06** throat
**07** trachea

**windy**
**05** blowy, empty, gusty, wordy
**06** breezy, flimsy, prolix, stormy, turgid
**07** squally, verbose
**08** blustery, rambling
**09** bombastic, garrulous
**10** long-winded
**11** tempestuous

**wine**

► *Types of wine*:
**03** Dao, dry, sec
**04** Asti, brut, Cava, fino, hock, port, rosé, Sekt
**05** Douro, Fitou, Gamay, Mâcon, Médoc, Rioja, Soave, sweet, Syrah
**06** Alsace, Barolo, Beaune, claret, grappa, Graves, Malaga, Merlot, Muscat, sherry, Shiraz
**07** Auslese, Chablis, Chianti, demi-sec, Madeira, Margaux, Marsala, moselle, oloroso, Orvieto, red wine, retsina, sangria, Vouvray
**08** Bordeaux, Burgundy, Frascati, Grenache, house red, Malvasia, Muscadet, muscatel, New World, Pauillac, Pinotage, Riesling, ruby port, Sancerre, Sauterne, Sémillon, Spätlese, Spumante, vermouth
**09** Bardolino, blush wine, champagne, dry sherry, Frizzante, Hermitage, house wine, Lambrusco, Pinot Noir, Sauternes, sparkling, St-Émilion, table wine, tawny port, tonic wine, white port, white wine, Zinfandel
**10** Beaujolais, Chambertin, Chardonnay, Constantia, house white, Manzanilla, Mateus Rosé, mulled wine,

Pinot Blanc, vinho verde
**11** alcohol-free, amontillado, Chenin Blanc, Niersteiner, sweet sherry, vintage port, vintage wine
**12** Blanc de Noirs, Côtes du Rhône, medium sherry, Valpolicella
**13** Blanc de Blancs, Château Lafite, fortified wine, Liebfraumilch
**14** Lacrima Christi, Sauvignon Blanc
**15** Gewürtztraminer
► See also DRINK

► *Wine-bottle sizes include*:
**06** flagon, magnum
**08** jeroboam, Rehoboam
**09** Balthazar
**10** Methuselah, Salmanazar
**14** Nebuchadnezzar
► See also BOTTLE

**wine glass**
**05** flute
**06** goblet, rummer

**wing**
**04** flit, race, soar, zoom
**05** annex, glide, group, hurry, speed
**06** branch, hasten
**07** faction, section, segment
**09** extension

**wink**
**05** blink, flash, gleam, glint
**06** moment, second
**07** flicker, flutter, glimmer, glitter, instant, nictate, sparkle, twinkle
**10** glimmering
**11** nictitation, split second

❑**wink at**
**06** ignore
**07** condone, neglect
**08** overlook, pass over
**09** disregard
**15** turn a blind eye to

**winkle**
**07** draw out, extract, mollusk, pry worm
**10** periwinkle

**winner**
**06** victor

**winning**
**08** alluring, charming, engaging, fetching
**09** beguiling, endearing
**10** bewitching, conquering, successful, undefeated, victorious

**11** captivating

**winnings**
**05** booty, gains, prize
**06** prizes, spoils
**07** jackpot, profits

**winnow**
**03** fan
**04** sift, sort
**06** divide
**08** separate

**winsome**
**05** sweet
**06** comely, lovely, pretty
**08** charming, fetching
**09** beguiling, endearing
**10** enchanting
**11** captivating

**wintry**
**03** icy, raw
**04** cold, cool
**05** bleak, harsh, snowy
**06** arctic, biting, chilly, frosty, frozen, hiemal
**07** glacial, hostile
**08** freezing, hibernal
**10** unfriendly

**wipe**
**03** dry, mop, rub
**04** dust, swab
**05** brush, clean, clear, erase
**06** remove, sponge
**08** get rid of, take away

❑**wipe out**
**05** erase
**06** efface
**07** blot out, destroy, expunge
**08** demolish, massacre
**09** eradicate, extirpate
**10** annihilate, obliterate
**11** exterminate

**wirepulling**
**05** clout
**08** intrigue, plotting, scheming
**09** influence
**12** manipulation

**wiry**
**04** lean, wavy
**05** rough, tough
**06** coarse, strong
**08** muscular

**wisdom**
**05** sense
**06** reason
**07** insight
**08** judgment, learning, prudence, sagacity, sapience
**09** erudition, foresight, knowledge

**wise**
11 common sense, discernment, penetration
12 intelligence
13 enlightenment, understanding
14 circumspection

**wise**
05 aware, sound
06 clever, shrewd
07 erudite, knowing, politic, prudent, sapient
08 rational, sensible
09 judicious, sagacious
10 discerning, farsighted, perceptive, reasonable
11 circumspect, enlightened, experienced, well-advised
13 knowledgeable

**❑ put wise**
04 tell, warn
06 clue in, fill in, inform, notify, tip off, wise up
07 apprise
15 put in the picture

**wisecrack**
03 gag, pun
04 barb, gibe, jest, joke, quip
09 witticism

**wise guy**
06 smarty
08 wiseacre
09 smart alec
10 smart aleck
11 smarty-pants

**wish**
03 ask, bid, yen
04 hope, long, lust, need, pine, urge, want, whim, will
05 crave, fancy, order, yearn
06 aspire, desire, direct, hanker, hunger, liking, prefer, thirst
07 bidding, command, craving, longing, request, require
08 fondness, instruct, yearning
09 hankering
10 aspiration, preference
11 inclination, instruction

**wishy-washy**
04 flat, thin, weak
05 bland, vapid
06 feeble, watery
07 insipid
09 tasteless
10 indecisive
11 watered-down

**wisp**
04 lock
05 piece, shred, twist
06 strand, thread

**wispy**
04 fine, thin
05 faint, frail, light
06 flimsy
08 delicate, ethereal, gossamer
13 insubstantial

**wistful**
03 sad
06 dreamy, musing
07 forlorn, longing, pensive
08 dreaming, yearning
10 meditative, melancholy, reflective, thoughtful
13 contemplative

**wit**
03 wag
04 nous
05 comic, humor, joker, sense
06 banter, brains, levity, reason, wisdom
07 insight, marbles
08 badinage, comedian, gumption, humorist, judgment, repartee, sagacity, satirist
09 intellect
10 comedienne, jocularity
11 common sense
12 intelligence
13 understanding

**witch**
03 hag, hex
08 magician
09 occultist, sorceress
11 enchantress, necromancer

**witchcraft**
05 magic, spell
06 voodoo
07 sorcery
08 wizardry
09 occultism, the occult
10 black magic, divination, necromancy
11 the black art

**witch doctor**
06 shaman
07 angekok
08 magician
11 medicine man
13 medicine woman

**witch hunt**
08 hounding
09 hue and cry
11 McCarthyism

**with it**
03 hip
04 cool
06 groovy, modish, trendy
08 up-to-date
13 up-to-the-minute

**withdraw**
06 recall, recant, recede, recoil, remove, retire, revoke
07 back out, drop out, extract, nullify, rescind, retract, retreat, scratch
08 disclaim, fall back, take away
14 absent yourself

**withdrawal**
04 exit
06 exodus, recall
07 removal, retreat
09 departure, secession
10 evacuation, extraction, retirement, revocation
11 falling back, recantation, repudiation

**withdrawn**
03 shy
05 aloof, quiet
06 hidden, remote, silent
07 distant, private
08 detached, isolated, reserved, retiring, secluded, solitary, taciturn
09 introvert, shrinking
10 unsociable
11 introverted, out-of-the-way
15 uncommunicative

**wither**
03 die, dry
04 fade, wane, wilt
05 decay, droop, dry up, waste
06 die off, shrink, weaken
07 decline, dwindle, shrivel
08 fade away, languish

**withering**
08 scathing, wounding
10 mortifying
11 humiliating
12 contemptuous

**withhold**
04 curb, hide
06 deduct, refuse, retain
07 conceal, control, decline, repress, reserve
08 hold back, keep back, restrain, suppress
11 keep in check

**withstand**
04 bear, defy, face
05 brave, fight, stand
06 endure, oppose, resist, take on, thwart
07 hold off, hold out, last out, survive, weather
08 confront, cope with, tolerate
09 put up with, stand fast, stand firm, stand up to

## witless
04 daft, dull
05 crazy, inane, silly
06 stupid
07 foolish, idiotic, moronic
08 mindless
09 cretinous, imbecilic, senseless
11 empty-headed

## witness
03 see
04 mark, note, sign, view
05 prove, watch
06 affirm, attest, depose, look on, notice, verify, viewer
07 bear out, confirm, endorse, observe, support, testify, watcher
08 deponent, looker-on, observer, onlooker, perceive
09 attestant, bystander, spectator, testifier
10 eyewitness
11 bear witness, corroborate, countersign

## witticism
03 pun
04 quip
06 bon mot
07 epigram, riposte
08 one-liner, repartee
09 wisecrack
10 pleasantry

## witty
05 comic, droll, funny
06 clever, lively
07 amusing, jocular, waggish
08 fanciful, humorous, original
09 whimsical

## wizard
04 star, whiz
05 witch
06 expert, genius, master
07 hotshot, maestro, warlock
08 conjurer, magician, sorcerer, virtuoso
09 enchanter, occultist
11 necromancer, thaumaturge
13 thaumaturgist

## wizened
07 dried up, gnarled
08 shrunken, withered, wrinkled
09 shriveled

## wobble
05 quake, shake, waver
06 teeter, totter
07 quaking, stagger, vibrate
09 fluctuate, oscillate, vibration
12 shilly-shally, unsteadiness

## wobbly
05 shaky
07 doddery, rickety
08 unstable, unsteady
09 doddering, quavering, teetering, tottering
10 unbalanced

## woe
04 pain
05 gloom, grief, tears, trial
06 burden, misery, sorrow
07 anguish, sadness, trouble
08 calamity, distress, hardship
09 adversity, dejection, heartache, suffering
10 affliction, heartbreak, melancholy, misfortune
11 tribulation

## woebegone
03 sad
04 blue
06 gloomy
07 doleful, forlorn, tearful
08 dejected, downcast, mournful, wretched
09 miserable, sorrowful
10 dispirited, lugubrious
11 downhearted
12 disconsolate
14 down in the mouth

## woeful
03 bad, sad
04 mean, poor
05 awful, cruel, lousy, sorry
06 feeble, gloomy, paltry, rotten, tragic
07 doleful, unhappy
08 dreadful, grieving, grievous, hopeless, mournful, pathetic, pitiable, shocking, terrible, wretched
09 miserable, sorrowful
10 calamitous, deplorable, disastrous, lamentable
11 disgraceful, distressing
12 catastrophic, disconsolate, heart-rending
13 heartbreaking

## wolf
05 Romeo
06 lecher
07 Don Juan, seducer
08 Casanova, lady's man
09 ladies' man, womanizer
10 lady-killer
11 philanderer

## ❑ wolf down
04 bolt, cram, gulp
05 gorge, stuff
06 devour, gobble

## woman
04 dame, girl, lady, maid
05 broad
06 female, maiden, matron

## womanhood
05 woman
08 maturity
09 adulthood, womankind, womenfolk, womenkind

## womanizer
04 wolf
05 Romeo
06 lecher
07 Don Juan, seducer
08 Casanova
09 ladies' man
10 lady-killer
11 philanderer

## womanly
06 female
08 feminine, ladylike, motherly, womanish
10 effeminate

## wonder
03 awe
05 doubt, query, sight, think
06 marvel, puzzle
07 miracle, prodigy, reflect
08 be amazed, question
09 amazement, curiosity, nonpareil, spectacle
10 admiration, conjecture, phenomenon, stand in awe
11 ask yourself, fascination
12 astonishment, be astonished, bewilderment

► *The seven wonders of the world:*
06 Pharos (of Alexandria)
08 Colossus (of Rhodes), Pyramids (of Egypt)
09 Mausoleum (of Halicarnassus)
12 Statue of Zeus (at Olympia)
14 Hanging Gardens (of Babylon)
15 Temple of Artemis (at Ephesus)

## wonderful
06 superb
07 amazing, awesome, strange
08 fabulous, smashing, terrific
09 admirable, brilliant, excellent, fantastic, marvelous, startling
10 astounding, incredible, phenomenal, stupendous, tremendous
11 astonishing, sensational
13 extraordinary

**wont**
14 out of this world

**wont**
03 use, way
04 rule, used
06 custom
07 routine
08 inclined, practice
10 accustomed, habituated

**wonted**
05 usual
06 normal
08 habitual
09 customary

**woo**
04 seek
05 chase, court
06 pursue
07 attract, look for
09 cultivate, encourage
10 pay court to

**wood**
05 copse, grove, trees, woods
06 forest, lumber, planks, timber
07 coppice, spinney
08 woodland
10 plantation, timberland

▸ *Types of wood*:
03 ash, elm, oak, yew
04 deal, lime, pine, sasa, teak
05 alder, aspen, balsa, beech,
 birch, cedar, ebony, maple,
 plane, ramin, utile
06 cherry, linden, obeche,
 padauk, poplar, sapele,
 veneer, walnut, willow
07 barwood, boxwood,
 bubinga, camwood, hickory,
 plywood, redwood,
 sapwood
08 amaranth, basswood,
 chestnut, cocobolo,
 cordwood, firewood,
 hardwood, kindling,
 kingwood, mahogany,
 pulpwood, red lauan,
 rosewood, silky oak,
 softwood, sycamore
09 blackwood, brushwood,
 chipboard, green wood,
 hardboard, heartwood,
 matchwood, satinwood,
 tigerwood, tulipwood,
 whitewood, zebrawood
10 afrormosia, bitterwood,
 brazilwood, cottonwood,
 paper birch, sandalwood
11 black cherry, lignum vitae,
 purpleheart, tulip poplar,
 white walnut, yellow birch
12 seasoned wood
13 sweet chestnut

❏ **out of the woods**
10 home and dry, in the clear
11 out of danger
12 safe and sound

**wooded**
05 woody
06 sylvan
08 forested, timbered

**wooden**
05 blank, empty, rigid, stiff
06 leaden, stodgy, timber
07 deadpan, stilted
08 lifeless
10 spiritless
12 unresponsive
14 expressionless

**woodland**
04 wood
05 copse, grove, trees, woods
06 forest
07 boscage, coppice, spinney,
 thicket

**woody**
05 bosky
06 sylvan, xyloid
08 forested, ligneous
11 tree-covered

**wool**
04 down, hair, yarn
06 fleece
07 floccus

❏ **pull the wool over
someone's eyes**
03 con
04 dupe, fool
06 delude, take in
07 deceive
08 hoodwink
09 bamboozle
12 put one over on
14 pull a fast one on

**woolgathering**
11 daydreaming, distraction,
 inattention
13 preoccupation

**woolly**
04 hazy
05 downy, foggy, fuzzy, hairy,
 vague
06 cloudy, fleecy, fluffy, frizzy,
 jersey, shaggy
07 muddled, sweater, unclear
08 cardigan, confused,
 nebulous, pullover
10 flocculent, ill-defined,
 indefinite, indistinct

**woozy**
05 dazed, dizzy, rocky, tipsy
06 wobbly

07 bemused, blurred, fuddled
08 confused, unsteady
09 befuddled, nauseated

**word**
03 put, say, vow
04 book, buzz, chat, dope, info,
 name, news, oath, talk, term,
 text, will
05 couch, honor, order, rumor,
 state, write
06 advice, decree, gossip, lyrics,
 notice, phrase, pledge,
 remark, report, script, signal
07 account, coinage, comment,
 explain, express, go-ahead,
 hearsay, lowdown, message,
 promise, synonym, tidings,
 vocable, warning, whisper
08 bulletin, dispatch, libretto,
 thumbs-up
09 assurance, guarantee,
 statement, utterance
10 expression, green light
11 commandment, declaration,
 information, undertaking
12 conversation, intelligence
13 communication

❏ **have words**
03 row
05 argue
06 bicker
07 dispute, quarrel
08 disagree, squabble

❏ **in a word**
07 briefly, in brief, in short
09 concisely, to be brief
10 succinctly
11 in a nutshell

❏ **word for word**
07 closely, exactly
08 verbatim
09 literally, precisely
10 accurately

**wordiness**
08 verbiage
09 logorrhea, prolixity, verbosity

**wording**
05 style, words
07 diction, wordage
08 language, phrasing, verbiage
10 expression
11 phraseology, terminology
13 choice of words

**word-perfect**
05 exact
08 accurate, faithful
13 letter-perfect

**wordplay**
03 pun, wit
07 punning

08 repartee
10 witticisms

**wordy**
06 prolix
07 diffuse, verbose
08 rambling
10 discursive, long-winded, loquacious

**work**
03 art, dig, fix, job, run, use
04 acts, book, deed, duty, form, line, make, mold, move, opus, play, poem, shop, slog, task, till, toil
05 cause, chore, craft, drive, graft, guide, knead, labor, model, piece, shape, shift, skill, slave, trade
06 action, career, charge, create, doings, drudge, effect, effort, fiddle, go well, handle, manage, métier, oeuvre, wangle
07 achieve, actions, arrange, calling, control, execute, fashion, mission, operate, peg away, perform, process, prosper, pull off, pursuit, succeed, travail, trouble, writing
08 business, contrive, creation, drudgery, engineer, exertion, function, have a job, industry, movement, painting, plug away, vocation
09 cultivate
10 accomplish, assignment, be employed, bring about, commission, employment, livelihood, manipulate, occupation, production, profession
11 achievement, be effective, composition, elbow grease, undertaking, workmanship
12 be successful
13 exert yourself
14 be satisfactory, earn your living, line of business

❑**work out**
04 plan
05 drill, solve, total, train
06 come to, devise, evolve, go well, invent, pan out
07 add up to, arrange, clear up, come out, develop, keep fit, prosper, resolve, sort out, succeed, turn out
08 amount to, contrive, exercise, organize, practice
09 calculate, construct, figure out, formulate, puzzle out

10 understand
11 be effective, put together

❑**work up**
05 rouse
06 arouse, incite, kindle, stir up
07 agitate, build up, inflame
08 generate
09 instigate, stimulate

**workable**
06 doable, viable
08 feasible, possible
09 practical, realistic
11 practicable

**workaday**
04 dull
06 common
07 humdrum, mundane, routine
08 everyday, familiar, laboring, ordinary
09 practical
11 commonplace
12 run-of-the-mill

**worker**
04 hand
07 artisan, laborer, workman
08 employee, farmhand
09 craftsman, operative, ranchhand, tradesman, workhorse
10 wage earner
11 craftswoman, proletarian, staff member
13 member of staff

**workforce**
05 labor, staff
08 manpower
09 employees, personnel
10 labor force

**working**
05 going
06 action, active, manner, method
07 process, routine, running
08 employed, movement
09 operating, operative
11 functioning, operational
12 up and running

**workings**
04 guts, mine
05 parts, shaft, works
06 quarry, system
07 innards
08 diggings
09 machinery, mechanism
11 excavations

**workman, workwoman**
04 hand
06 worker
07 laborer
08 farmhand

09 ranchhand

**workmanlike**
05 adept
06 expert
07 careful, skilful, skilled
08 skillful
10 proficient
12 professional, satisfactory

**workmanship**
03 art
05 craft, skill
06 finish
08 artistry
09 execution, handiwork
10 handicraft
13 craftsmanship

**workout**
05 drill
08 exercise, practice, training
10 gymnastics, isometrics

**works**
04 guts, mill
05 parts, plant
07 factory, foundry, innards
08 good acts, workings, writings
09 good deeds, mechanism
11 good actions
12 working parts
13 installations

**workshop**
04 mill, shop
05 class, plant, works
06 garage, studio
07 atelier, factory, seminar
09 symposium
10 study group
15 discussion group

**world**
03 age, era, man
04 area, days, life, star
05 earth, epoch, field, globe, group, realm, times
06 cosmos, domain, nature, people, period, planet, sphere, system
07 kingdom, mankind, reality, section, society
08 creation, division, everyone, humanity, universe
09 everybody, existence, human race, humankind, situation, way of life
10 department, experience
12 heavenly body

▶ *World heritage sites*:
03 Omo, Taï
04 Agra, San'a, Tyre
05 Aksum, Awash, Bosra, Copán, Delos, Galle, Hatra,

Ohrid, Petra, Quito, Uluru
06 Abomey, Aleppo, Bassae,
Byblos, Cyrene, Darién,
Göreme, Paphos, Potosí,
Sangay, Sousse, Thebes,
Treves
07 Abu Mena, Avebury,
Baalbek, Djemila, Garamba,
San Juan, Segovia, Virunga
08 Agra Fort, Alhambra,
Altamira, Carthage, Chartres,
Hattusas, Mount Tai,
Palenque, Pyramids,
Sabratha, Salvador, Shark
Bay, Sigiriya, Stari Ras, Taj
Mahal, Valletta
09 Abu Simbel, Auschwitz,
Epidaurus, Gros Morne,
Mesa Verde, Nemrut Dag,
Parthenon, Serengeti
10 El Escorial, Everglades,
Generalife, Hierapolis,
Hildesheim, Ironbridge,
Monte Albán, Monticello,
Persepolis, Pont du Gard,
Stonehenge, Versailles
11 Ajanta caves, Ellora caves,
Gorée Island, Hagia Sophia,
Leptis Magna, Machu
Picchu, Madara Rider,
Mohenjo-daro, Teotihuacán,
Vatican City, Western Wall
12 Hadrian's Wall
13 Fontainebleau, Fontenay
Abbey, Great Zimbabwe, Rila
Monastery
14 Aldabra Islands, Blenheim
Palace, Elephanta caves,
Fountains Abbey, Giant's
Causeway, Heraion of
Samos, Imperial Palace
15 Aachen Cathedral, Mont-
Saint-Michel, Speyer
Cathedral, Statue of Liberty

◻ **out of this world**
08 fabulous
09 fantastic, marvelous
10 incredible, phenomenal,
remarkable
13 indescribable

**worldly**
06 carnal, greedy, urbane
07 earthly, knowing, mundane,
profane, secular
08 covetous, grasping, material,
physical, temporal
09 ambitious, corporeal
10 avaricious, streetwise
11 experienced, terrestrial
12 cosmopolitan
13 materialistic, sophisticated

**worldwide**
06 global
07 general
08 catholic
09 universal

**worm**
──────────
► *Types of worm*:
05 fluke, leech
07 annelid, eelworm, lugworm,
pinworm
08 flatworm, hookworm,
nematode, sea mouse,
tapeworm
09 earthworm, roundworm
10 blood fluke, liver fluke,
ribbon worm, threadworm
➤ See also ANIMAL

**worn**
05 all in, drawn, jaded, spent,
tired, weary
06 bushed, done in, frayed,
ragged, shabby
07 haggard
08 careworn, dog-tired
09 exhausted
10 threadbare

◻ **worn out**
05 all in, tatty, weary
06 bushed, done in, shabby
08 decrepit, dog-tired, tired out
09 exhausted
10 threadbare
13 on its last legs

**worried**
05 tense, upset, wired
06 afraid, on edge, uneasy
07 anxious, nervous, uptight
08 agonized, bothered,
dismayed, strained, troubled
09 concerned, disturbed, ill at
ease, perturbed
10 disquieted, distracted,
distraught, distressed,
frightened
11 overwrought
12 apprehensive
14 hot and bothered

**worrisome**
06 uneasy, vexing
07 anxious, fretful, irksome,
jittery
08 insecure, worrying
09 agonizing, upsetting
10 bothersome, disturbing, nail-
biting, perturbing
11 disquieting, distressing,
frightening, troublesome
12 apprehensive

**worry**
03 bug, nag, vex

04 bite, care, fear, fret, pest,
stew, tizz
05 annoy, go for, harry, tease,
tizzy, trial, upset
06 attack, bother, burden, hang-
up, harass, hassle, misery,
pester, plague, savage, strain,
stress, unease
07 agitate, agonize, anguish,
anxiety, concern, disturb,
perturb, problem, tension,
torment, trouble
08 disquiet, distress, irritate,
nuisance, unsettle, vexation
09 aggravate, agitation,
annoyance, misgiving
10 irritation, perplexity
11 disturbance, fearfulness
12 apprehension, perturbation
14 responsibility

**worrying**
06 trying, uneasy
07 anxious
08 niggling
09 harassing, upsetting
10 disturbing, nail-biting,
perturbing, unsettling
11 disquieting, distressing,
troublesome

**worsen**
04 sink, slip
06 weaken
07 decline, go to pot
08 heighten, increase
09 aggravate, intensify
10 degenerate, exacerbate, go
downhill
11 deteriorate

**worsening**
05 decay
07 decline
10 pejoration
12 degeneration, exacerbation
13 deterioration, retrogression

**worship**
04 laud, love
05 adore, deify, exalt, glory
06 homage, praise, revere
07 adulate, glorify, idolize
08 devotion, idolatry, venerate
09 adoration, adulation,
devotions
10 exaltation, veneration
11 deification
13 glorification

────────────────
► *Places of worship*:
03 wat
04 shul
05 abbey
06 bethel, chapel, church,
mosque, pagoda, shrine,

temple
07 chantry, minster, synagog
08 gurdwara
09 cathedral, synagogue
10 tabernacle
12 meetinghouse
➢ See also RELIGION

**worst**
04 beat, best, drub, last
05 crush, least
06 defeat, lowest, master,
subdue
07 conquer
08 overcome, vanquish
09 overpower, overthrow,
subjugate, whitewash
14 get the better of

**worth**
03 use
04 cost, gain, good, help, rate
05 avail, merit, price, value
06 credit, desert, profit, virtue
07 benefit, deserts, quality,
service, utility
08 eminence
09 advantage, valuation
10 excellence, importance,
usefulness, worthiness
12 significance

**worthless**
03 low
04 poor, vile
05 cheap
06 futile, paltry, trashy
07 corrupt, trivial, useless
08 nugatory, rubbishy, trifling,
unusable
09 pointless, valueless
10 despicable, unavailing
11 ineffectual, meaningless,
unimportant
12 contemptible
13 insignificant
14 good-for-nothing

**worthwhile**
04 good
06 useful, worthy
07 gainful, helpful
08 valuable
10 beneficial, productive,
profitable
11 justifiable
12 advantageous, constructive

**worthy**
03 fit
06 decent, honest
07 big shot, notable, upright
08 laudable, luminary, reliable,
valuable, virtuous
09 admirable, big cheese,
deserving, dignitary,

excellent, honorable,
personage, reputable,
righteous
10 creditable, worthwhile
11 appropriate, commendable,
meritorious, respectable

**would-be**
07 budding, hopeful
08 aspiring, striving

**wound**
03 cut, hit
04 ache, blow, gash, harm, hurt,
pain, scar, stab, tear
05 graze, grief, shock, slash,
upset
06 damage, grieve, injure, injury,
insult, lesion, offend, pierce,
slight, trauma
07 anguish, mortify, scratch,
torment
08 distress, lacerate, puncture
10 heartbreak, laceration,
traumatize

**wraith**
05 ghost, shade, spook
06 spirit
07 phantom, specter
08 revenant
10 apparition

**wrangle**
03 row
04 spar, tiff
05 clash, fight, scrap, set-to
06 barney, bicker, tussle
07 contend, contest, dispute, fall
out, quarrel
08 argument, squabble
09 altercate
11 altercation, controversy

**wrap**
04 bind, cape, pack, robe, wind
05 cloak, cover, shawl, stole
06 cocoon, encase, enfold,
mantle, muffle, parcel, roll
up, shroud, swathe
07 enclose, envelop, immerse,
package
08 bundle up, parcel up,
surround

❏**wrap up**
03 end
06 pack up, parcel, wind up
07 package
08 complete, conclude, parcel
up, round off
09 finish off, summarize,
terminate
13 bring to a close

**wrapper**
04 case

05 cover, paper
06 casing, jacket, sheath, sleeve
08 covering, envelope,
wrapping
09 packaging
10 dust jacket
11 dust wrapper

**wrapping**
04 case, foil
05 paper
06 carton
07 tinfoil, wrapper
08 envelope
09 packaging
10 bubble wrap, cellophane
11 blister pack

**wrath**
03 ire
04 fury, rage
05 anger
06 choler, spleen, temper

**wrathful**
05 angry, irate
06 bitter, ireful, raging
07 enraged, furious
08 furibund, incensed
12 on the warpath

**wreak**
04 vent
05 cause
06 bestow, create
07 execute, express, inflict,
unleash
08 carry out, exercise
10 bring about, perpetrate

**wreath**
03 lei
04 band, loop, ring
06 circle
07 chaplet, circlet, garland

**wreathe**
04 coil, wind, wrap
05 adorn, crown, twine, twist
06 enfold, enwrap, shroud
07 entwine, envelop, festoon
08 encircle, surround
10 intertwine, interweave

**wreck**
03 mar
04 loss, mess, raze, ruin, sink
05 break, crash, smash, spoil,
total
06 debris, jalopy, pieces, ravage,
rubble
07 destroy, flotsam, remains,
shatter, smashup, torpedo,
undoing
08 accident, bankrupt,
breaking, demolish, derelict,
disaster, smashing

09 devastate, fragments, ruination, shipwreck
10 demolition, disruption, shattering
11 destruction, devastation
13 play havoc with

**wreckage**
06 debris, pieces, rubble
07 flotsam
08 detritus

**wrench**
03 rip, tug
04 ache, blow, jerk, pain, pang, pull, tear, yank
05 force, twist, wrest, wring
06 sorrow, sprain, strain
07 distort, sadness
08 upheaval
12 monkey wrench
14 crescent wrench

**wrest**
03 win
04 pull, take
05 force, seize, twist, wring
06 strain, wrench
07 extract

**wrestle**
03 vie
05 fight
06 battle, combat, strive, tussle
07 contend, grapple, scuffle
08 struggle

**wretch**
03 rat
04 worm
05 devil, rogue, swine
06 rascal
07 outcast, ruffian, villain
08 vagabond
09 miscreant, scoundrel
14 good-for-nothing

**wretched**
03 bad, low, sad
04 base, mean, poor, vile
05 awful, sorry
06 gloomy, paltry
07 forlorn, hapless, piteous, pitiful, unhappy
08 dejected, downcast, dreadful, hopeless, horrible, inferior, pathetic, pitiable, shameful, shocking, terrible
09 appalling, atrocious, depressed, miserable, worthless
10 deplorable, despicable, distressed, melancholy, outrageous
11 crestfallen, unfortunate
12 contemptible, disconsolate
13 brokenhearted

**wriggle**
04 edge, jerk, turn, worm
05 crawl, dodge, sidle, slink, snake, twist
06 jiggle, squirm, waggle, wiggle, writhe
08 maneuver, squiggle
09 extricate

**wring**
04 hurt, rack, rend, tear
05 exact, force, screw, twist, wound, wrest
06 coerce, extort, mangle, pierce, wrench
07 extract, squeeze, torture

**wrinkle**
06 crease, furrow, gather, pucker, rumple, wimple
07 crinkle, crumple, shrivel
09 corrugate, crow's-foot, novel idea
11 corrugation

**wrinkled**
06 ridged, rugate, rugose
07 creased, crinkly, rumpled
08 crinkled, crumpled, furrowed, puckered, rivelled

**writ**
06 decree
07 summons
08 subpoena
10 court order

**write**
03 pen
04 copy, note
05 draft, print
06 author, create, draw up, record, scrawl
07 compose, dash off, jot down, put down, set down
08 inscribe, note down, register, scribble, take down
09 autograph, freelance
10 correspond, transcribe
11 communicate

❏**write off**
05 annul
06 cancel, delete
07 nullify
08 amortize, cross out
09 disregard

**writer**

► *Types of writers:*
04 bard, hack, poet
05 clerk
06 author, critic, editor, pen pal, penman, rhymer, scribe, typist
07 copyist, diarist

08 annalist, essayist, lyricist, novelist, reporter, satirist, stringer
09 columnist, dramatist, historian, pen pusher, scribbler, sonneteer
10 biographer, chronicler, copywriter, freelancer, journalist, keyboarder, librettist, playwright
11 contributor, ghostwriter, storyteller, transcriber
12 pencil pusher, poet laureate, scriptwriter, speech writer
13 calligraphist, correspondent, court reporter, fiction writer, lexicographer
14 autobiographer
15 editorial writer
➤ See also BIOGRAPHY; DIARY; ESSAY; FABLE; HISTORY; JOURNALIST; LEXICOGRAPHER; NOVEL; PLAYWRIGHT; POET; SATIRIST

**writhe**
04 coil, jerk, toss
05 twist
06 squirm, thrash, wiggle
07 contort, wriggle
12 twist and turn

**writing**
04 hand, opus, text, work
05 print, prose, words
06 poetry, scrawl, script, volume
08 document, scribble
10 manuscript, penmanship
11 calligraphy, composition, handwriting, publication

**written**
07 drawn up, set down
08 recorded
09 in writing
10 documental, documented
11 documentary, transcribed

**wrong**
03 bad, sin
04 awry, back, evil, harm, hurt
05 amiss, crime, error, false
06 astray, faulty, injure, injury, malign, sinful, unfair, unjust, wicked
07 crooked, illegal, illicit, immoral, in error, misdeed, offense, oppress, reverse, to blame, wrongly
08 contrary, criminal, dishonor, faultily, ill-treat, improper, inequity, iniquity, inverted,

maltreat, mistaken, trespass, unlawful

09 defective, discredit, dishonest, erroneous, felonious, grievance, imprecise, incorrect, injustice, inside out, unethical, unfitting

10 fallacious, immorality, inaccurate, inapposite, malapropos, out of order, unsuitable, wickedness

11 blameworthy, unjustified

12 dishonorable, infringement, unlawfulness

13 inappropriate, transgression, wide of the mark

**❑go wrong**

04 fail

05 stray

08 collapse, go astray

09 break down

11 come to grief, malfunction

12 become undone, come a cropper

13 become unstuck

**❑in the wrong**

06 guilty

07 at fault, in error, to blame

08 mistaken

**wrongdoer**

05 felon

06 sinner

08 criminal

09 miscreant

10 lawbreaker, trespasser

12 transgressor

**wrongdoing**

03 sin

04 evil

05 crime, error, fault

06 felony

07 misdeed, offense

08 iniquity, mischief

13 transgression

**wrongful**

04 evil

06 sinful, unfair, unjust, wicked

07 illegal, illicit, immoral

08 criminal, improper, unlawful

09 dishonest, unethical

11 unjustified, unwarranted

12 illegitimate

13 reprehensible

**wrongly**

05 badly

07 in error

10 mistakenly

11 erroneously, incorrectly

12 inaccurately

**wrought**

04 made

06 beaten, ornate, shaped

07 created

09 fashioned

10 ornamented

**wry**

03 dry

05 askew, droll, witty

06 ironic, uneven, warped

07 crooked, mocking, twisted

08 deformed, sardonic

09 contorted, distorted

**xenophobia**
06 racism
09 racialism
13 ethnocentrism

**xenophobic**
06 racist

09 parochial, racialist
13 ethnocentrist

**xerox**
04 copy
05 print
06 run off

09 duplicate, photocopy,
   reproduce
12 Photostat

**Xerox**
09 duplicate, facsimile,
   photocopy

# Y y

**yack**
03 gab, jaw, yak, yap
04 chat
06 confab, gossip, harp on, hot air, jabber, tattle, yak-yak
07 chatter, chinwag, prattle
08 yack-yack
09 yakety-yak
11 yackety-yack

**yank**
03 tug
04 haul, jerk, pull
05 heave
06 snatch, wrench

**Yank**
02 GI
06 Yankee
08 American

**Yankee**
02 GI
04 Yank
08 American
10 Northerner
12 New Englander, Union soldier

**yap**
03 gab, jaw
04 bark, yelp
06 babble, jabber, yatter
07 chatter, prattle

**yard**
04 lawn, quad
05 court
07 grounds, measure
08 farmyard
09 courtyard
10 churchyard, playground, quadrangle
11 measurement

**yardstick**
05 gauge, scale
07 measure
08 standard
09 benchmark, criterion, guideline

**yarn**
04 tale
05 fable, fiber, story
06 strand, thread
08 anecdote
09 tall story

**yawning**
04 huge, vast, wide
06 gaping
09 cavernous

**yearly**
08 annually, per annum
09 every year, once a year
11 perennially

**yearn**
04 ache, itch, long, pine, want
05 covet, crave, fancy
06 desire, hanker, hunger, thirst

**yearning**
03 yen
05 fancy
06 desire, hunger, pining, thirst
07 craving, longing
09 hankering

**yell**
04 bawl, howl, roar, yelp, yowl
05 shout, whoop
06 bellow, cry out, holler, scream, shriek, squeal
07 screech

**yellow**
04 buff, gold
05 lemon, tawny
06 canary, coward, flaxen, golden
07 chicken, saffron
08 cowardly, primrose

**yelp**
03 bay, cry, yap, yip
04 bark, yell, yowl

**yen**
04 itch, lust
06 desire, hunger
07 craving, longing, passion
08 yearning
09 hankering

**yes**
02 OK
03 aye, yep
04 okay, yeah
05 quite, right
06 agreed
08 all right
11 affirmative

**yes man**
05 toady
07 crawler

08 groveler
09 sycophant, toadeater
10 bootlicker

**yet**
03 but, too
04 also, even
05 still
06 even so
07 already, besides, however
08 hitherto, moreover
10 all the same, for all that, heretofore, in addition
11 just the same, nonetheless
12 nevertheless
15 notwithstanding

**yield**
03 bow, net, pay
04 bear, cede, crop, earn
05 allow
06 accede, cave in, comply, give in, income, profit, return, supply
07 bring in, concede, consent, furnish, give way, harvest, produce, product, provide, revenue, succumb
08 earnings, generate, proceeds, renounce
09 acquiesce, surrender
10 capitulate, relinquish
15 throw in the towel

**yielding**
04 easy, soft
06 pliant, spongy, supple
07 elastic, pliable, springy
08 biddable, flexible
09 compliant, tractable
11 acquiescent, unresisting

**yoke**
04 bond, join, link
05 hitch, unite
06 burden, couple
07 bondage, harness
08 coupling
10 oppression

**yokel**
04 boor, clod, hick
06 rustic
07 bucolic, peasant
09 hillbilly
10 clodhopper
13 country cousin

14   country bumpkin

**young**
03   kid, new
04   baby
05   brood, early, green, issue, small
06   babies, family, infant, junior, litter, little, recent
07   growing, progeny, teenage
08   childish, children, immature, juvenile, youthful
09   fledgling, offspring
10   adolescent, little ones

**youngster**
03   boy, kid, lad
04   girl, lass, tike
05   child, youth
06   shaver
07   toddler

08   teenager
10   adolescent

**youth**
03   boy, kid, lad
04   kids
05   teens
07   boyhood
08   girlhood, juvenile, teenager
09   childhood
10   adolescent, immaturity
11   adolescence
12   inexperience

**youthful**
05   fresh, young
06   active, boyish, lively
07   girlish
08   childish, immature, juvenile
09   sprightly
13   inexperienced

**youthfulness**
08   vivacity
09   freshness
10   juvenility, liveliness
13   sprightliness, vivaciousness

**yowl**
03   bay, cry
04   howl, wail, yell, yelp
09   caterwaul

**yucky**
05   dirty, messy, mucky
06   filthy, sickly
08   horrible
09   revolting
10   disgusting
11   sentimental

# Zz

**zany**
05 crazy, kooky, loony, wacky
07 amusing, comical
09 eccentric
10 ridiculous

**zap**
03 hit
05 shoot
07 destroy, wipe out

**zeal**
04 fire, zest
05 ardor, gusto, verve, vigor
06 energy, fervor, spirit
07 passion
09 eagerness, intensity, vehemence
10 dedication, fanaticism

**zealot**
05 bigot
07 fanatic, radical
08 militant, partisan
09 extremist

**zealous**
05 eager, fiery
06 ardent, fervid
07 devoted, fervent, intense
09 dedicated, fanatical
10 passionate
11 impassioned

**zenith**
03 top
04 acme, apex, peak
06 apogee, height, summit
08 meridian, pinnacle
09 high point

**zero**
03 nil
04 love
05 aught, zilch
06 naught, nought
07 nothing
08 goose egg

**zero in on**
05 fix on
07 focus on, level at, train on
08 home in on, pinpoint
13 concentrate on

**zest**
04 tang, zeal, zing
05 gusto, savor, spice, taste, vigor
06 flavor, relish
08 appetite, keenness, piquancy
09 eagerness, enjoyment
10 exuberance, liveliness
11 joie de vivre

**zigzag**
05 curve, snake
07 crooked, sinuous, winding
10 meandering, serpentine

**zing**
02 go
03 zip
04 brio, dash, élan, life, zest
05 oomph, vigor
06 energy, pizazz, spirit
07 pizzazz, sparkle
08 vitality
09 animation
10 liveliness
11 joie de vivre

**zip**
02 go
03 fly, pep
04 dash, élan, life, race, rush, tear, whiz, zest, zing, zoom
05 drive, get-up, gusto, oomph, scoot, shoot, speed, verve, vigor
06 energy, pizazz, spirit
07 pizzazz, sparkle
08 vitality
10 get-up-and-go, liveliness

**zodiac**

► *Signs of the Zodiac*:
03 Leo, Ram
04 Bull, Crab, Fish, Goat, Lion
05 Aries, Libra, Twins, Virgo
06 Archer, Cancer, Gemini, Pisces, Scales, Taurus, Virgin
07 Scorpio
08 Aquarius, Scorpion
09 Capricorn
11 Sagittarius, Water Bearer

**zone**
04 area, belt
06 region, sector, sphere
07 section, stratum
08 district, province
09 territory

**zoo**
06 aviary
09 menagerie
10 animal park, petting zoo, safari park
12 wildlife park
16 zoological garden

**zoologist**

► *Names of zoologists*:
04 **Beer** (Gavin Rylands de), **Mayr** (Ernst Walter)
05 **Clark** (Eugenie), **Fabre** (Jean Henri), **Hubel** (David Hunter), **Hyatt** (Alpheus), **Kühne** (Wilhelm)
06 **Carson** (Rachael), **Fossey** (Dian), **Frisch** (Karl von), **Kinsey** (Alfred), **Lorenz** (Konrad Zacharias), **Morris** (Desmond John), **Müller** (Johannes Peter), **Osborn** (Henry Fairfield), **Pavlov** (Ivan), **Yerkes** (Robert)
07 **Agassiz** (Louis), **Audubon** (John James), **Ditmars** (Raymond), **Durrell** (Gerald), **Galvani** (Luigi), **Hodgkin** (Alan Lloyd), **Mantell** (Gideon Algernon), **Medawar** (Peter Brian), **Merriam** (Clinton), **Perkins** (Marlin)
09 **Aristotle**, **Tinbergen** (Nikolaas)
11 **Sherrington** (Charles Scott)
► See also SCIENTIST

**zoom**
03 fly, zap, zip
04 buzz, dash, lens, race, tear, whiz
05 flash, shoot, speed, vroom
06 hurtle, streak
11 rise quickly